THE SPORT AMERICANA ®

PRICE GUIDE

NO. 11

By

DR. JAMES BECKETT

 Printed in the U.S.A., 1989. Published by Edgewater Book Company Inc., Box 40238, Cleveland, OH 44140, in conjunction with Den's Collectors Den.

ISBN 0-937424-43-9

About the Author

Jim Beckett, the leading authority on sport card values in the United States, maintains a wide range of activities in the world of sports. He possesses one of the finest collections of sports cards and autographs in the world, has made numerous appearances on radio and television, and has been frequently cited in many national publications. He was awarded the first "Special Achievement Award" for Contributions to the Hobby by the National Sports Collectors Convention in 1980 and the "Jock-Jasperson Award" for Hobby Dedication in 1983.

Dr. Beckett is the author of *The Sport Americana Football, Hockey, Basketball and Boxing Price Guide*, *The Official Price Guide to Football Cards*, *The Sport Americana Baseball Card Price Guide*, *The Official Price Guide to Baseball Cards*, *The Sport Americana Price Guide to Baseball Collectibles*, *The Sport Americana Baseball Memorabilia and Autograph Price Guide*, and *The Sport Americana Alphabetical Baseball Card Checklist*. In addition, he is the founder, author, and editor of *Beckett Baseball Card Monthly*, a magazine dedicated to advancing the card collecting hobby.

Jim Beckett received his Ph.D. in Statistics from Southern Methodist University in 1975. He resides in Dallas with his wife Patti and their daughters, Christina, Rebecca, and Melissa, while actively pursuing his writing and consultancy careers.

1st Full Time Dealer - Starting May 1, 1970

3 CARD SETS FOR 1989

TOPPS
792 Cards
$27.00 ppd

SCORE
660 Cards
Plus 56 Trivia
$24.00 ppd

WADE BOGGS 26 THIRD BASE

SPORTFLICS
225 Cards
Plus 153 Trivia
$40.50 ppd.

1988 BASEBALL SETS

Topps (792 Cards)	$28.50 ppd
Fleer (660 Cards)	50.00 ppd
Sportflics (225 & Trivia)	43.00 ppd
Score	33.50 ppd

GLOSSY SETS

Fleer (660 cards, collectors tin, Plus World Series Set)	$67.50 ppd
Topps (792 cards)	140.00 ppd
Score (660)	150.00 ppd.

EXTENDED SETS

Topps (132 Cards)	$17.00 ppd
Fleer (132 Cards)	15.00 ppd
Fleer Glossy (132 Cards plus Collectors Tin)	25.00 ppd
Donruss Best (336)	36.95 ppd
Donruss "Rookies" (56 cards)	13.50 ppd
Score Glossy (110 cards & Trivia)	15.75 ppd

"88 PAGE CATALOG"

Subscribe today to "the" catalog of cards. This 88 page catalog is loaded with cards from the 1900's to present. It contains Baseball, Football, Basketball and Hockey cards. Sets and singles. Also Magazines and More!! 23 pages loaded with One-of-a-Kind Specials. Printed in three colors.

Issued 3 times yearly.

Send $1.00 for the next 3 BIG Issues
Canada residents $1.00 per issue (shipped 1st Class)

PARTIAL LIST OF SETS AVAILABLE

(All sets are in Nr MT-Mint Condition)
All sets are shipped in numerical order, postpaid via UPS, in damage-free boxes.
NOTE: All prices subject to change without notice.

BASEBALL SETS

Negro League Stars (119)	$10.50
1987 Topps (792)	36.00
1987 Fleer (660)	66.00
1987 Sportflics (200 plus trivia)	41.00
1987 Sportflics Rookies (50 plus trivia)	18.00
1987 Fleer Glossy (660 in collectors tin, plus World Series)	63.50
1987 Topps Glossy (792)	125.00
1987 Topps Traded (132)	17.00
1987 Fleer Update (132)	17.50
1987 Fleer Glossy Update (132 plus tin)	18.75
1987 Donruss Opening Day (272)	27.00
1987 Donruss Rookies (56)	22.00
1986 Topps (792)	46.00
1986 Topps Traded (132)	20.00
1986 Fleer (660)	68.50
1986 Fleer Update (132)	24.00
1986 Donruss (660)	136.00
1986 Donruss Highlights (56)	8.00
1986 Sportflics (200)	49.00
1986 SF Decade Greats (75)	20.75
1986 SF Rookies (50)	19.50
1985 Topps (792)	116.00
1985 Topps Traded (132)	26.00
1985 Fleer (660)	106.00
1985 Fleer Update (132)	21.00
1985 Donruss (660)	151.00
1985 Donruss-Leaf (264)	47.50
1984 Topps (792)	106.00
1984 Topps Traded (132)	111.00
1984 Fleer (660)	121.00
1984 Fleer Update (132)	286.00
1984 Donruss (658)	286.00
1983 Topps (792)	98.50
1983 Topps Traded (132)	71.00
1983 Fleer (660)	53.50
1983 Donruss (660)	56.00
1982 Topps (792)	86.00
1982 Topps Traded (132)	31.00
1982 Fleer (660)	33.50
1982 Donruss (660)	36.00
1981 Topps (726)	91.00
1981 Topps Traded (132)	33.50
1981 Fleer (660)	26.00
1981 Donruss (605)	33.50
1980 Topps (726)	150.00
1979 Topps (726) (Wills-Rangers)	152.50
1979 Topps (726) Wills-Blue Jays	147.50
1978 Topps (726)	225.00
1977 Topps (660)	275.00
1976 Topps (660)	250.00
1975 Topps (660)	525.00
1974 Topps (660)	365.00
1973 Topps (660)	675.00
1987 Topps AS Glossy (22)	5.50
1986 Topps AS Glossy (22)	6.00
1986 Topps Super (60)	12.50
1986 Topps 3D (30)	18.50
1986 Topps Mini (66)	10.75
1986 Fleer Mini (120)	14.25
1986 Fleer AS Stick (132)	22.75
1985 Topps 3D (30)	32.50
1983 Topps Glossy (40)	11.50
1977 Topps Cloth Patches & CL (73)	76.00
1983 Kelloggs (60)	21.00
1982 Kelloggs (64)	16.50
1981 Kelloggs (66)	17.00
1980 Kelloggs (60)	26.00
1972 Kell BB Greats (15)	31.00
1981 Fleer AS Stickers (128)	40.00
1959 Fleer Ted Williams (79) w/o #68	250.00

FOOTBALL SETS

1988 Topps (396)	$13.95
1988 1000 Yards Club (28)	8.00
1987 Topps (396)	14.50
1987 1000 Yards Club (24)	7.75
1986 Topps (396)	16.00
1986 1000 Yds.	8.00
1985 Topps (396)	17.00
1985 Topps Glossy (11)	4.75
1985 Topps USFL (132)	32.50
1984 Topps (396)	23.50
1984 Topps USFL (132)	126.00
1984 Topps Glossy (30)	10.00
1983 Topps (396)	21.00
1983 Topps Stickers (33)	5.00
1982 Topps (428)	24.00
1981 Topps (528)	26.00
1981 Topps Stickers (28)	10.50
1980 Topps (528)	$33.50
1979 Topps (528)	43.50
1978 Topps (528)	46.00
1977 Topps (528)	73.50
1976 Topps (528)	151.00
1975 Topps (528)	96.00
1974 Topps (528)	106.00
1973 Topps (528)	116.00
1972 Topps (351)	390.00
1971 Topps (263)	170.00
1970 Topps (263)	175.00
1970 Topps Super (35)	110.00
1974 Fleer H of F (50)	12.50
1972 Canadian Leag. (132)	45.00
1971 Canadian League (132)	80.00
1970 Kelloggs 3D (60)	35.00

BASKETBALL SETS

1988-89 Fleer (132)	$12.00
1987-88 Fleer (132)	21.00
1986-87 Fleer (132)	42.00
1981-82 Topps (198)	18.50
1980-81 Topps (88)	16.00
1979-80 Topps (132)	18.00
1978-79 Topps (132)	19.00
1977-78 Topps (132)	22.00
1976-77 Topps (144) Large	$43.50
1975-76 Topps (330)	101.00
1974-75 Topps (264)	61.00
1973-74 Topps (264)	66.00
1972-73 Topps (264)	86.00
1971-72 Topps (233)	140.00
1970-71 Topps (175)	175.00

HOCKEY SETS

1988-89 O-Pee-Chee (264)	$15.00
1987-88 Topps (198)	36.00
1987-88 O-Pee-Chee (264)	23.50
1984-85 Topps (165)	17.50
1983-84 O-Pee-Chee (396)	25.00
1982-83 O-Pee-Chee (396)	26.00
1981-82 Topps (198)	18.50
1980-81 Topps (264)	23.50
1979-80 Topps (264)	$91.00
1978-79 Topps (264)	31.00
1977-78 Topps (264)	36.00
1976-77 Topps (264)	41.00
1976-76 Topps (330)	85.00
1974-75 Topps (264)	70.00
1973-74 Topps (198)	100.00
1972-73 Topps (176)	95.00
1971-72 Topps (132)	92.50
1968-69 Topps (132)	125.00

All above prices are postpaid in U.S. Funds. CANADA CUSTOMERS: Please send postal money order in US funds only and an additional $6.00 per set for sets over 250 cards. $3.00 per set for sets under 250 cards for shipping your sets. ALASKA, HAWAII, PUERTO RICO, APO, FPO & P.O. BOX CUSTOMERS: Add an additional $4.00 per set for sets over 250 cards and $2.50 per set for sets under 250 cards for shipping your sets.

BASEBALL CARDS BY SERIES SALE

We have series of baseball cards available from 1968-1974. All series in Near-Mint to Mint condition. The numbers in parenthesis indicate the card numbers in the particular series. We have also included a partial listing of the stars in each series. All prices postpaid.

1968	Series #4 (284-370)	includes 10 Sporting News All Stars, Banks, Maris, McCovey, Staub	$130.00
	Series #6 (458-533)	includes Bird Belters (F. Robby, B. Robby), Brock, F. Robinson, Super Stars Card	POR
	Series #6 (458-533)	same as above except lacking 7 commons	140.00
	Series #7 (534-598)	includes Wood, Hisle, Palmer, Bouton (scarce)	130.00
1969	Series #1 (1-109)	includes League Leaders, Banks, Brock, Clemente, Bench, Aaron, Morgan, M. Wills	190.00
	Series #4 (328-425)	includes 10 Sporting News All Stars, Kaline, Drysdale, Killebrew, Marichal	130.00
	Series #5 (426-512)	includes 10 Sporting News All Stars, Mantle, Carew, McCovey, Seaver, G. Perry	330.00
	Series #5 (426-512)	same as above except lacking #500 Mantle	220.00
1970	Series #2 (133-263)	includes McCovey, Munson Rookie, R. Jackson, Killebrew, Carlton, B. Robinson	155.00
	Series #3 (264-372)	includes Clemente, Seaver, Carew, Brock, World Series cards, Hisle	140.00
	Series #4 (373-459)	includes 10 Sporting News All Stars, Powell, Hodges, McLain, Bonds	125.00
	Series #5 (460-546)	includes 10 Sporting News All Stars, Aaron, Morgan, Stargell, Gibson, Oliva	130.00
	Series #6 (547-633)	includes Mays, Rose, Hunter, Banks, M. Wills, Staub, G. Perry	205.00
	Series #7 (634-720)	includes Bench, Kaline, F. Robinson, Ryan, Lolich, Santo (scarce)	315.00
1971	Series #1 (1-132)	includes League Leaders, Munson, R. Jackson, Rose, McCovey, Carlton, Hunter	165.00
	Series #2 (133-263)	includes Bench, Carew, Seaver, Kaline, Stargell, Martin, Hodges, G. Perry	120.00
	Series #3 (264-393)	includes Garvey, B. Robinson, Foster Rookie, Morgan, World Series cards	185.00
	Series #3 (264-393)	same as above except lacking #341 Garvey	130.00
	Series #4 (394-523)	includes Aaron, Gibson, Ryan, John, Luzinski Rookie	120.00
1972	Series #1 (1-132)	includes Mays, Yaz, B. Robinson, Morgan, Gibson, League Leaders, Killebrew	125.00
	Series #2 (133-263)	includes Brock, Blue, Powell, Foster, World Series cards, McGraw	100.00
	Series #3 (264-394)	includes Aaron, Clemente, McCovey, Hunter, G. Perry, Palmer, John, Kid Pictures	115.00
	Series #6 (657-787)	includes Garvey, Carew, (Carlton, F. Robinson, Morgan-traded) (scarce)	435.00
1973	Series #1 (1-132)	includes Aaron, Rose, Clemente, B. Robinson, League Leaders	130.00
	Series #2 (133-264)	includes Yaz, Jackson, Garvey, Fisk, Palmer, Gossage, Munson	115.00
	Series #3 (265-396)	includes Kaline, Carlton, Mays, Carew, Seaver, Stargell, Bench, Brock	125.00
	Series #5 (529-660)	includes Schmidt Rookie, 15 other Rookie Star cards (scarce)	365.00
	Series #5 (529-660)	same as above except lacking #615 Schmidt	215.00
1974	Series #4 (397-528)	includes Winfield Rookie, Killebrew, Cooper, W.S. cards, Powell	65.00
	Series #5 (529-660)	includes Madlock & Griffey Rookies, 11 other Rookie Star cards, Garvey, Gossage	60.00

ALWAYS BUYING!! TOP PRICES PAID

Colgan Chips cards, Tobacco cards (1885-1915) Coupon. Kotton Cigarettes, T205 Gold Border. T206 White Border, T207 Brown background, 1933-38 Goudey, 1939-41 Play Ball.
Any or all Milwaukee Braves, Green Bay Packers items.
We are buying cards (gum, tobacco, meats, bread, cereal, wieners, etc) issued prior to 1973
Anything unusual that may be of interest
Will pay premium prices for desirable items
Send description or list for immediate quote

OUR 42nd YEAR IN CARDS

735 Old Wausau Road
P.O. Box 863, Dept. 587
Stevens Point, WI 54481
(715) 344-8687

WITH OVER 35 MILLION CARDS IN STOCK...WE HAVE AMERICA'S MOST COMPLETE STOCK OF SPORTS TRADING CARDS. Full money back guarantee if you are not completely satisfied with our service and products. YOU, the customers are always NO 1 to us!

To receive Super Service it is necessary to send a POSTAL MONEY ORDER with your order.
(All personal checks are held 15 days for clearance)
(Charge orders add 5% to total)
Minimum charge order $10.00.

35,000,000 cards in stock!

TOBACCO AND CARAMEL REPRINT SETS

All Sets To Be Delivered In February.

We are now offering the 1911 T205 Gold Border, 1912 T207 Brown Background, 1909 E95 Philadelphia Caramel and the 1922 E120 American Caramel. Each of these sets will be reprinted in their original size. The world's most modern technology has been used to make these sets some of the most stunning ever reprinted.

1911 T205 Gold Border includes:	1912 T207 Brown Background includes:	1909 E95 Philadelphia Caramels includes:	1922 E120 American Caramel includes:
Cobb	Bender	Bender	Alexander
Speaker	Bresnahan	Chance	Cobb
Young	Chance	Cobb	Frisch
Mathewson	Johnson	Collins	Hornsby
Johnson	Lewis	Crawford	Johnson
Bender	Loudermilk	Plank	Ruth
Chance	McGraw	Mathewson	Traynor
Joss	Miller	Cicotte	Speaker
McGraw	Speaker	Evers	Maranville
Wallace	Tinker	Wagner	Heilmann
Complete set (209 cards) $21.95 ppd.	**Complete set (205 cards) $21.95 ppd.**	**Complete set (25 cards) $6.95 ppd.**	**Complete set (240 cards) $23.95 ppd.**

Special: All 4 Sets .... $62.50 ppd.

Acknowledgments

A great deal of hard work went into this volume, and it could not have been done without help from many people. Our thanks are extended to each and every one of you.

Those who have worked closely with us on this and many other books, have again proven themselves invaluable -- Frank and Vivian Barning (*Baseball Hobby News*), Chris Benjamin, Sy Berger (Topps), Card Collectors Co., Cartophilium (Andrew Pywowarczuk), Ira Cetron, Mike Cramer (Pacific Trading Cards), Bill and Diane Dodge, Richard Duglin (Baseball Cards-n-More), Gervise Ford, Larry and Jeff Fritsch, Tony Galovich (American Card Exchange), Georgia Music and Sports (Dick DeCourcy and Floyd Parr), Bill Goodwin (St. Louis Baseball Cards), Mike and Howard Gordon, John Greenwald, Wayne Grove, Bill Haber, Bill Henderson, Danny Hitt, Tom Imboden, Allan Kaye (*Baseball Card News*), Rick Keplinger, David Kohler (SportsCards Plus), Paul Lewicki, Neil Lewis (Leaf), Lew Lipset, Norman Liss (Topps), Major League Marketing (Dan Shedrick, Tom Day, Jack Kling), Mid-Atlantic Coin Exchange (Bill Bossert), David "Otis" Miller, Dick Millerd, Brian Morris, Vincent Murray (Fleer), B.A. Murry, Ralph Nozaki, Jack Pollard, Gavin Riley, Alan Rosen (Mr. Mint), John Rumierz, San Diego Sport Collectibles (Bill Goepner and Nacho Arredondo), Mike Schechter, Barry Sloate, John Spalding, Sports Collectors Store, Frank Steele, Murvin Sterling, Lee Temanson, Ed Twombly (New England Bullpen), Gary Walter, and Kit Young. Finally we owe a special acknowledgment to Dennis W. Eckes, "Mr. Sport Americana." The success of the *Beckett Price Guides* has always been the result of a team effort.

Special mention goes to two people this year. These two long-time collectors are recognized for repeated contributions to the hobby as well as to this *Price Guide*. In fact if you look closely through some very old hobby publications from the early 1960s, you may see their names occasionally on articles and ads. Looking back after eleven years I just wanted to thank them for their part in the growth of the hobby and of this *Price Guide*. They are both friends and outstanding collectors. Thank you, Wayne Grove and B.A. Murry. Over the years I have gotten most of Wayne's input over the phone or in person. Wayne and I agree on most things, but when we do disagree, I pay special attention to his opinion. B.A. did a fine job marking up revised prices in last year's *Beckett #10* as well as last month's *Beckett Monthly*. B.A. also should be recognized for his early pioneering work on Topps series breakdowns. Discussions with him (as well as with others) over the years have been most helpful in establishing the proper series breakdowns and scarcity for early Topps cards. You both have my thanks as well as a lifetime subscription to *Beckett Monthly*.

Many other people have provided price input, illustrative material, checklist verifications, errata, and/or background information. We should like to individually thank Abco Card Galleries, Ab D Cards (Dale Wesolewski), Michael Abromavage, Jerry Adamic, Lee Adams, Ron Adelson, Tony Adkins, A.J.'s Sport Stop, Bob Alexander, All Star Sports Collectibles, Tom Allen, Bob Almeida, Read Andersen, Dennis Anderson, Bob Andrus, Rick Anthony, Rick Apter, Mark Argo (Olde South Cards), Mike Armstrong, Neil Armstrong (World Series Cards), David Aubry, B and C Collectable Cards, Ball Four Cards, Seth Banks, Joe Barney, Ed Barry (Ed's Collectibles), Jim Bartlett, Bob Bartosz (Baseball Card Shop), Bay State Cards (Lenny DeAngelico), Tom Beers, Carl Berg, Darrell Berger, Bernie's Bullpen, Beulah Sports, Joseph Binkowski, Levi Bleam, Bob Blount, Bob Boffa, Tim Bond (Tim's Cards & Comics), Sam

Boxberger, Peter Brennan, John Brigandi, Charles A. Brooks, Jake Bubelis, Mike Buckley, Mike Bundschuh, Frank Burns, Jay Burton, Chris Cadwallader, California Card Co., David Call (9th Inning Baseball Card Shop), Christopher Campbell, Eric Cann, Michael Carey, Chris Caruso, Frank Caruso, Anthony Caton, Sandy Chan, Dwight Chapin, Shannon Chavez, Ray Cherry, Dick Cianciotto, Ronn Citrenbaum, CJ's Cubbie Hole, Richard Clement, Tim Cline (Home Plate Cards), Dennis Cobb, Gary Coburn, Jeff Cockrum, Andrew Cohen, Brian Cohen, G. Colatosti, Rob Cole, Jason Coleman, Barry Colla, Collectibles Unlimited (John Alward and Deb Ingram), Collection de Sport AZ (Ronald Villaneuve), Ryan Collins, Comics Plus, Alvin Conner, Curt Cooter, Kevin Corcoran, David Costantino, Wade Council, Don Covello, Nathan Crabbe, Taylor Crane, James Critzer, Brian Cummings, John Curtis, Allen Custer, Dave Dame, Dale Dannhaus, Donna R. Davis, Jason DeBrower, Joe Denning, Albert DeSantis, Mike Diacin, Gilbert Dickason, James Dickson, Greg Diehl, Ken Diemer, Ken Dinerman (California Cruizers), George Doherty, George Dolence, Richard Dolloff (Dolloff Coin Center), John Dorsey, George C. Dougherty, Kevin and Ryan Eagan, David Ebner, Ed's Card Shop, Josh Egli, Jacob Ellerbrock, Bob Elliot, Jason Ehrlich, Mike Epstein, Doak Ewing, Damon Fain, Bryan Falatovich, David and Mark Federman, Chuck Ferrero, David Festberg, Eli Fillmore, Jay Finglass, Howard Fleischman, Michael Folk, Perry Fong, Frank Fox (The Card Shop), Justin Fox, Robert Foye, Steve Freeburne, Steve Freedman, Brian French, Jeff Freyer, Brian Frost, Tom Galik (Fielders Choice), Scott Gallagher, Mike Gallela, David Garrett, Billy Gauthier, Jeffrey Gentes, Scotty Gennusa, Willie George, Bob Gilbert (Brewer Sports Collectibles), Dick Goddard, Steve Gold (AU Sports), Greg Goldstein (Dragon's Den), Jeff Goldstein, Brett Goodman, Jim Goodman, Jim Goodreid, Jan Gould, Scott Grady, Gary Graham, Stephen Grauf, Grauer's Collectables, Victor Guzman, Charlie Hall, Hall's Nostalgia, Michael Hamel, Hershell Hanks, Bill Hannan, Eric Hatch, Herbert Hatchel, Don Hartman, Mark Hausner, Brian Heathman, Leonard Hellicher, Joel Hellman, James Hilgert, P.J. Hill, Ron Hill, David Hilshorst, Joseph John and Becky Hilton, Lee Hintze, John Hodson, Cliff Holmes, Home Plate of Utah (Ken Edick), Darcy Howe, Michael and Roger Huang, Robert Huber, Donald Hughes, Wayne Hurley, Doug Ingram, JJ's Budget Baseball Cards, J.R. Sports Collectibles, Karl Jacob, Paul Jastrzembski, Matt Jenks, Jay Johnson, Matthew Jones, Stewart W. Jones, Dave Jurgensmeier, Richard Kaiman, Jason Kaiser, Jason Karam, Brian Karimead, Jay and Mary Kasper, Frank Katen, Dr. Neil Katz, Kevin Kearns, Donald Kerstetter, Leroy King, John Kish, Russell Kitrick, Richard Klein, Ernie Kohlstruk, Aaron Kramer, Kipp Krukowski, John Kubat, Thomas Kunnecke, John Kyranos, Jason Lassic, Charles Laurent, Dan Lavin, Phil Lee, Morley Leeking, Charles Leinberry, Irv Lerner, Tony Light, Steve Limbert, Michael Livreri, Chris Lockwood, Dale Loebs, Mike London, Casey Lowe, Jeff Lupke, Scott Lyons, Jim Macie, Mark Macrae, Adam Magary, Steve Mamanella, Dave Marabella, Paul Marchant, Pete Marcia, Nicholas Marino, Bill Mastro, Kyle Matschke, Dr. William McAvoy, Michael McDonald (The Sports Page), Gail McEldowney, Brian McEvoy, Tony McLaughlin, Steve McLemore, Mendal Mearkle (Chariots, Inc.), Ken Melanson, Kelly Melone, Wayne Menicucci, Blake Meyer (Lone Star Sportscards), Toby Meyer, Joe Michalowicz, Cary Miller, George J. Miller, John Miller, Lee Miller, Wayne Miller, Mitchell's Baseball Cards, Ida Montgomery, Mark Moore, John Moseley, Mark Muir, Bradley Nathan, Edward Nazzaro (The Collector), Tim Nepjuk, Dustin Newhouse, Tony Niemann, Ninth Inning Baseball Card Shop, Nostalgia World, Mike O'Brien, Keith Olbermann, Oldies and Goodies, Ron Oser, Michael Palazzo, Andy Paloukas, Bruce Parker (All-American

Cards & Comics), Eric Passetti, Clay Pasternack, Mickey Payne, Bill Pekarik (Pastime Hobbies), Lucy Pelletier, Thomas Perozini, Michael Perrotta, Gerald Perry, Tom Pfirrmann, Jeffrey Phillips, Aaron Pierce, Bob Poet, Allen Powell, J.P. Plunkett (P.S.N. Sportscards), Paul Pollard, Michael Poynter, Mahes Prasad, Jeff Prillaman (Southern Cards), Carson Ralston, Rick Rapa and Barry Sanders (Atlanta Sports Cards), Rick Rateike (Extra Innings, Inc.), Eric Ratliff, R.W. Ray, Tom Reale, Tom Reid, Dr. Joseph Revella, Derek Reynolds, James Ricci, Dave Ring, Rich Rinker, Chad Roberts, Gene Roberts, Jeff Rockholt, Harold Rogers, Donald Rooks, Clifton Rouse, George Rusnak, Henry M. Rutland, Rick Ryan, Greg Ryer, Terry Sack, Joe Sak, Jennifer Salems, Sam's Baseball Cards (Sam Jackson), San Francisco Card Exchange, Keith Saroka, Gary Sawatzki, Robert Scagnelli, Matthew Schlesinger, Kenneth Schmitt, Shawn Schuetz, Brad Schurter, Scott and Craig's Sportsworld, David Seidman, Tom Shaughnessy, Tom Shanyfelt, Ricky Sharma, Bill Shaw, Marty Shaw, Gerry Shebib, Val Shikman, Joel Slaughter, Michael Small, Robert Smathers, Barry Smith, Daren Smith, Shawn Smith, Michael Soroky, Phil Spector (Scoreboard, Inc.), Bill Spetrino, James Stahl, Jim Starbuck, Rick Stineman, Tim Strandberg, Richard Strobino, Richard Stroud, Ron Stumpf, Barrie Sullivan, Superior Sport Card, Bill Susoev, Brian Swanson, Ian Taylor, Lyle Telfer, Kevin Terplak, Richard Thurman, Joshua Tjiong, Bud Tompkins, Ronald Tousignant, Kevin Trexler, Dr. Ralph Triplette, Matthew Turner, Howard Unger, James Vargas, Joe Verhaeghe, Ralph Villagomez, Dimitry Vladimirov, Jonathan Waler, Robert Wardell, Chris Waters, George Weaver, Mark Weber, Stephen Weber, Philip Wegeng, Lewis Weinerman, Larry Weinstein, Bill Wesslund, Richard West, Rick Wilcoxon, Casey Willett, Jeff Williams, Mark Willis, Eric Wilson, Todd Wilson, Opry Winston, Bill Wise, Jay Wolt (Cavalcade of Sports), Allan Wong, Stephen Wood, Pete Wooten, Kevin Wynn, Craig Wyzik, Steve Yanowsky, Sandy Yelnick, Yesterday's Heroes, Henry Yu, Ted Zanidakis, Robert Zanze, William Zeller, and Karl Zinke.

Every year we make active solicitations for input to that year's edition and we are particularly appreciative of help (large and small) provided for this volume. While we receive many inquiries, comments, and questions regarding material within this book -- and, in fact, each and every one is read and digested -- time constraints prevent us from personally replying. We hope that the letters will continue, and that even though no reply is received, you will feel that you are making significant contributions to the hobby through your interest and comments.

Special thanks go the staff of *Beckett Publications* for their help. Editorial Director Fred Reed was very helpful with the editing of the introductory section, the production of the advertising pages, and the supervision of the extensive production support team. He was ably assisted by Jeff Amano, Therese Bellar, Lou Cather, Theo Chen, Pepper Hastings, Sara Jenks, Jay Johnson, Tricia Jones, and Rudy Klancnick. The overall operations of *Beckett Monthly* were skillfully directed by Claire Backus. Working with her were Jan Dickerson, Joe Galindo, Mary Gregory, Julie Grove, Beth Hartke, Debbie Kingsbury, Ruth Price, Cindy Struble, and Jay Yarid. James and Sandi Beane performed several major system programming jobs for us this year in order to help us accomplish our work faster and more accurately. The whole *Beckett Publications* team has my thanks for jobs well done. Thank you, everyone.

I also thank my family, especially my wife, Patti, and daughters, Christina, Rebecca, and Melissa, for putting up with me again.

The Sport Americana Price Guide Table of Contents

Index to Advertisers

Preface

Isn't it great? Every year this book gets bigger and bigger with all the new sets coming out. But even more exciting is that every year there are more collectors, more shows, more stores, and ... more interest in the cards we love so much. This edition has been enhanced and expanded from the previous edition. The cards you collect -- who they are, what they look like, where they are from, and (most important to many of you) what their current values are -- are enumerated within. Many of the features contained in the other *Beckett Price Guides* have been incorporated into this volume since condition grading, nomenclature, and many other aspects of collecting are common to the card hobby in general. We hope you find the book both interesting and useful in your collecting pursuits.

The Beckett Guide has been successful where other attempts have failed because it is complete, current, and valid. This *Price Guide* contains not just one, but three, prices by condition for all the baseball cards in the issues listed. These account for almost all the baseball cards in existence. The prices were added to the card lists just prior to printing and reflect not the author's opinions or desires but the going retail prices for each card, based on the marketplace (sports memorabilia conventions and shows, hobby papers, current mail order catalogs, local club meetings, auction results, and other firsthand reportings of actually realized prices).

What is the BEST Price Guide available (on the market) today? Of course card sellers will prefer the Price Guide with the highest prices as the best -- while card buyers will naturally prefer the one with the lowest prices. Accuracy, however, is the true test. Use the Price Guide used by more collectors and dealers than all the others combined. Look for the Beckett name. I won't put my name on anything I won't stake my reputation on. Not the lowest and not the highest -- but the most accurate, with integrity.

To facilitate your use of this book, read the complete introductory section in the pages following before going to the pricing pages. Every collectible field has its own terminology; we've tried to capture most of these terms and definitions in our glossary. Please read carefully the section on grading and the condition of your cards as you will not be able to determine which price column is appropriate for a given card without first knowing its condition.

Welcome to the world of baseball cards.

Sincerely, Dr. James Beckett

Jim Beckett

DEALERS WE CARRY IT ALL!

Protecto® Plastic Pages

QTY (Pages)	EACH	PRICE	Shipping & Handling
25		$ 5.95	Postpaid
50		9.50	Postpaid
100		15.95	Postpaid
250		31.95	Postpaid
500	12¢	60.00	
1,000	11.5¢	115.00	SHIPPED
2,000	11¢	220.00	FREIGHT
3,000	10.5¢	315.00	COLLECT
5,000	10¢	500.00	

SIZES AVAILABLE:
9 pocket 1957 to 1983
8 pocket 52-56 Topps
9 pocket Top Load
6 pocket Police Sets
4 pocket Postcards — '64 Giants
2 pocket 5x7 Photos
1 pocket 8x10 Photos
1 pocket 9x11 Photos/Yearbooks
12 pocket Stickers

Baseball Card Boxes

WHOLESALE TO THE PUBLIC

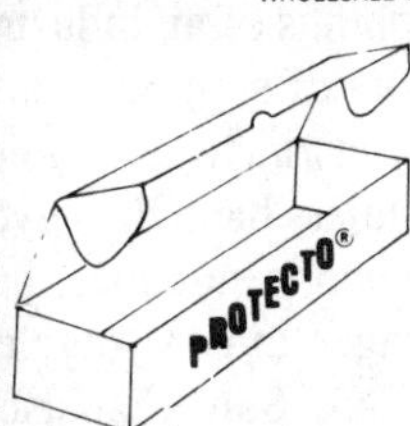

CAL-CARDS INTRODUCES
The Finest Boxes In The World At The Lowest Prices Now At Wholesale Prices

Protecto® Indestructo
White Corrugated Boxes • Front Wing Locks • Boxes Secure On Outside • Cannot Damage Cards
(No. of box is amount of cards box holds)
Sizes: ALL SIZES (postpaid) 100 minimum
CC-660 $32⁰⁰, CC-726 $33⁰⁰, CC-800 $33⁰⁰

Protecto® CARD-GARDS

INDIVIDUAL CARD PROTECTION

Unconditionally Guaranteed!

WHY PAY MORE!!

Protecto® CARD-GARDS Special Offer

$10⁹⁵ — 1000 CARD-GARDS
$29⁰⁰ — 3000 CARD-GARDS
$39⁰⁰ — 5000 CARD-GARDS

Each **Protecto® CARD-GARDS** Holds 1 Card
Standard size 2⅝x3⅝. Will fit all Topps — 1957 to present. Fleer and Donruss — 1981 to present and most sports & non-sports cards. Slip cards in and out with ease • **Protecto® CARD-GARDS** will protect, preserve your cards from finger marks, dust, scratches, prevent corners from becoming "dog eared" • Use heavy-duty **Protecto® CARD-GARDS** to view, file and store • **Protecto® CARD-GARDS** are made of crystal clear polyethylene • Contains no PVC, and guaranteed not to crack • Packed in quantities of 100 for your convenience • *Dealer inquiries invited.*

Dealers & Stores Write or Call For Pricing

Super Sale Protecto® Plastic Pages

1000 $109
POSTPAID
The very best! Guaranteed Safe! 9-Pocket Top or Side Load! 5 to 6 Gauge Heavy!

Poly-Flex Plastic Pages

1000 $99
POSTPAID
Slightly Thinner Page! Safe & Durable! Crystal Clear!

Econoline Plastic Pages

1000 $89
POSTPAID
Best Buy! High Quality! Slightly Clouded! Safe & Durable! Not As Clear!

Protecto® Albums

Deluxe Card Albums

These padded albums have a vinyl pocket on the spine for labeling • Heavy duty design • Durable over-printing and glossed to produce a rich, realistic leather appearance • 2 sizes regular and jumbo • Completely covers sheet • Imprint *"Baseball Card Album"*

Both sizes of **Protecto Albums** are available in Midnight Blue with silver lettering, Burgundy with gold, Black with gold and Brown with silver.
Dealers Call or Write for Special Pricing!

Look

DEALERS-STORES

• All NFL, MLB, NBA Caps, Wool, Wool Blend, Mesh, Twill, Cords • Sized "Pro Caps" • 102 Colleges — Arizona to Yale • All Teams including NHL Pennants and Bumper Strips • Sports Illustrated Posters • Nike Posters • Costacos Posters • Ball Holders • Batting Helmets • All-Pro Wrist Bands • Rawlings Baseballs — National & American Leagues • All Peter David Pins For NFL, MLB, NBA • Topps • Donruss • Fleer • Baseball Cards • Non-Sports Cards • Sports Photos 8x10 • And Much More
Cal-Cards is the largest distributor of sports products at wholesale prices in the United States!

One of the Largest Wholesalers In The Nation!

CAL-CARDS
SUBSIDIARY OF SPORTSWORLD
P.O. BOX 107, GARDENA, CA 90248
213-679-5000

Introduction

Welcome to the exciting world of baseball card collecting, America's fastest-growing avocation. You have made a good choice in buying this book, since it will open up to you the entire panorama of this field in the simplest, most concise way.

It is estimated that nearly a quarter of a million different baseball cards have been issued during the past century. And the number of total cards put out by all manufacturers last year has been estimated at several billion with a retail value of more than $150 million. Sales of older cards by dealers may account for a like amount. With all that cardboard available in the marketplace, it should be no surprise that several million sports fans like you collect baseball cards today, and that number is growing by hundreds of thousands each year.

The growth of *Beckett Baseball Card Monthly* is another indication of this rising crescendo of popularity for baseball cards. Founded less than four years ago by Dr. James Beckett, the author of this price guide, *Beckett Monthly* has grown to the pinnacle of the baseball card hobby with nearly a half million readers anxiously awaiting each enjoyable issue.

So collecting baseball cards -- while still pursued as a hobby with youthful exuberance by kids in the neighborhood -- has also taken on the trappings of an industry, with thousands of full- and part-time card dealers, as well as vendors of supplies, clubs and conventions. In fact, each year since 1980 thousands of hobbyists have assembled for a National Sports Collectors Convention, at which hundreds of dealers have displayed their wares, seminars have been conducted, autographs penned by sports notables, and millions of cards changed hands. These colossal affairs have been staged in Los Angeles, Detroit, St. Louis, Chicago, New York, Anaheim, Arlington (TX), San Francisco, Atlantic City, and this year back in Chicago at the Hyatt Regency downtown. So baseball card collecting is really national in scope!

This increasing interest has been reflected in card values. As more collectors compete for available supplies, card prices (especially for premium-grade cards) rise. A national publication indicated a "very strong advance" in baseball card prices during the past decade, and a quick perusal of prices in this book compared to the figures in earlier editions of this price guide will quickly confirm this. Which brings us back around again to the book you have in your hands. Many prices have literally doubled! It is the best annual guide available to this exciting world of baseball cards. Read it and use it. May your enjoyment and your card collection increase in the coming months and years.

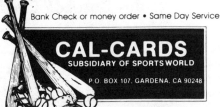

How to Collect

Each collection is personal and reflects the individuality of its owner. There are no set rules on how to collect cards. Since card collecting is a hobby or leisure pastime, what you collect, how much you collect, and how much time and money you spend collecting are entirely up to you. The funds you have available for collecting and your own personal taste should determine how you collect. Information and ideas presented here are intended to help you get the most enjoyment from this hobby.

It is impossible to collect every card ever produced. Therefore, beginners as well as intermediate and advanced collectors usually specialize in some way. One of the reasons this hobby is popular is that individual collectors can define and tailor their collecting methods to match their own tastes. To give you some ideas of the various approaches to collecting, we will list some of the more popular areas of specialization.

Many collectors select complete sets from particular years. For example, they may concentrate on assembling complete sets from all the years since their birth or since they became avid sports fans. They may try to collect a card for every player during that specified period of time.

Many others wish to acquire only certain players. Usually such players are the superstars of the sport, but occasionally collectors will specialize in all the cards of players who attended certain colleges or came from certain towns. Some collectors are only interested in the first cards or rookie cards of certain players. A handy guide for collectors interested in pursuing the hobby this way is the recently updated *Sport Americana Alphabetical Checklist No. 3.*

Another fun way to collect cards is by team. Most fans have a favorite team, and it is natural for that loyalty to be translated into a desire for cards of the players on that favorite team. For most of the recent years, team sets (all the cards from a given team for that year) are readily available at a reasonable price. *The Sport Americana Team Baseball Card Checklist* will open up this field to the collector.

Obtaining Cards

Several avenues are open to card collectors. Cards can be purchased in the traditional way at the local candy, grocery, or drug stores, with the bubble gum or other products included. In recent years, it has also become possible to purchase complete sets of baseball cards through mail order advertisers found in traditional sports media publications, such as *The Sporting News*, *Baseball Digest*, *Street & Smith* yearbooks, and others. These sets are also advertised in the card collecting periodicals. Many collectors will begin by subscribing to at least one of the monthly hobby publications, all with good up-to-date information. In fact, subscription offers can be found in the advertising section of this book.

Most serious card collectors obtain old (and new) cards from one or more of several main sources: (1) trading or buying from other collectors or dealers; (2) responding to sale or auction ads in the monthly hobby publications; and/or (3) attending sports collectibles shows or conventions. We advise that you try all three methods since each has its own distinct advantages: (1) trading is a great way to make new friends; (2)

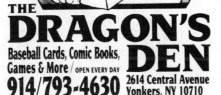

monthly hobby periodicals help you keep up with what's going on in the hobby (including when and where the conventions are happening); and (3) shows provide enjoyment and the opportunity to view millions of collectibles under one roof, in addition to meeting some of the hundreds or even thousands of other collectors with similar interests who also attend the shows.

Preserving Your Cards

Cards are fragile. They must be handled properly in order to retain their value. Careless handling can easily result in creased or bent cards. It is, however, not recommended that tweezers or tongs be used to pick up your cards since such utensils might mar or indent card surfaces and thus reduce those cards' conditions and values. In general, your cards should be handled directly as little as possible. This is sometimes easier to say than to do. Although there are still many who use custom boxes, storage trays, or even shoe boxes, plastic sheets are the preferred method of storing cards. A collection stored in plastic pages in a three-ring album allows you to view your collection at any time without the need to touch the card itself. For a large collection, some collectors may use a combination of the above methods.

When purchasing plastic sheets for your cards, be sure that you find the pocket size that fits the cards snugly. Don't put your 1951 Bowmans in a sheet designed to fit 1981 Topps. Most hobby and collectibles shops and virtually all collectors' conventions will have these plastic pages available in quantity for the various sizes offered or you can purchase them directly from the advertisers in this book.

Damp, sunny and/or hot conditions -- no, this is not a weather forecast -- are three elements to avoid in extremes if you are interested in preserving your collection. Too much (or too little) humidity can cause gradual deterioration of a card. Direct, bright sun (or fluorescent light) over time will bleach out the color of a card. Extreme heat accelerates the decomposition of the card. On the other hand, many cards have lasted more than 50 years without much scientific intervention. So be cautious, even if the above factors typically present a problem only when present in the extreme. It never hurts to be prudent.

Collecting/Investing

Collecting individual players and collecting complete sets are both popular vehicles for investment and speculation. Most investors and speculators stock up on complete sets or on quantities of players they think have good investment potential. There is obviously no guarantee in this book, or anywhere else for that matter, that cards will outperform the stock market or other investment alternatives in the future. After all, baseball cards do not pay quarterly dividends. Nevertheless, investors have noticed a favorable trend in the past performance of baseball and other sports collectibles, and certain cards and sets have outperformed just about any other investment in some years.

Some of the obvious questions are: Which cards? When to buy? When to sell? The best investment you can make is in your own education. The more you know about your collection and the hobby, the more informed the decisions you will be able to make. We're not selling investment tips. We're selling information about the current value of baseball cards. It's up to you to use that information to your best advantage.

Nomenclature

Each hobby has its own language to describe its area of interest. The nomenclature traditionally used for trading cards is derived from the *American Card Catalog*, published in 1960 by Nostalgia Press. That catalog, written by Jefferson Burdick (who is called the "Father of Card Collecting" for his pioneering work), uses letter and number designations for each separate set of cards.

The letter used in the ACC designation refers to the generic type of card. While both sport and non-sport issues are classified in the ACC, we shall confine ourselves to the sport issues. The following list defines the letters and their meanings as used by the American Card Catalog.

(none) or N - 19th Century U.S. Tobacco
B - Blankets
D - Bakery Inserts Including Bread
E - Early Candy and Gum
F - Food Inserts
H - Advertising
M - Periodicals
PC - Postcards
R - Candy and Gum Cards 1930 to Present
T - 20th Century U.S. Tobacco
UO - Gas and Oil Inserts
V - Canadian Candy
W - Exhibits, Strip Cards, Team Issues

Following the letter prefix and an optional hyphen are one-, two-, or three-digit numbers, 1-999. These typically represent the company or entity issuing the cards. In several cases, the ACC number is extended by an additional hyphen and another one- or two-digit numerical suffix. For example, the 1957 Topps regular series baseball card issue carries an ACC designation of R414-11. The "R" indicates a Candy or Gum Card produced since 1930. The "414" is the ACC designation for Topps Chewing Gum baseball card issues, and the "11" is the ACC designation for the 1957 regular issue (Topps' eleventh baseball set).

Like other traditional methods of identification, this system provides order to the process of cataloging cards; however, most serious collectors learn the ACC designation of the popular sets by repetition and familiarity, rather than by attempting to "figure out" what they might or should be.

From 1948 forward, collectors and dealers commonly refer to all sets by their year, maker, type of issue, and any other distinguishing characteristic. For example, such a characteristic could be an unusual issue or one of several regular issues put out by a specific maker in a single year. Regional issues are usually referred to by year, maker, and sometimes by title or theme of the set.

BASEBALL CARD CENTER

90 TOLEDO BLADE BLVD.
RT CHARLOTTE, FL 33948
-624-4020

TWO LOCATIONS

2245-B WINKLER AVE.
FORT MYERS, FL 33901
813-278-3232

LICENSED PRO SPORT & COLLEGIATE MERCHANDISE

MERCHANDISE LINES

Come to the
FUN STORE!!

HOURS:
MON.-THURS. 10-9
FRI.-SAT. 10-10
SUN. 1-5

VISIT OUR STORES
WHEN IN FLORIDA.

WE BUY CARDS

. . . . MORE THAN JUST A CARD SHOP!

Glossary/Legend

Our glossary defines terms frequently used in the card collecting hobby. Many of these terms are also common to other types of sports memorabilia collecting. Some terms may have several meanings depending on use.

AAS - Action All Stars, a postcard-size set issued by the Donruss Company.

ACC - Acronym for *American Card Catalog.*

ALL STAR CARD - A card portraying an All Star Player of the previous year that says "All Star" on its face.

ALPH - Alphabetical.

AS - Abbreviation for All Star (card).

ATG - All Time Great card.

BLANKET - A felt square (normally 5" to 6") portraying a baseball player.

BOX - Card issued on a box or a card depicting a Boxer.

BRICK - A group of cards, usually 50 or more having common characteristics, that is intended to be bought, sold, or traded as a unit.

CABINETS - Very popular and highly valuable photographs on thick card stock produced in the 19th and early 20th century.

CHECKLIST - A list of the cards contained in a particular set. The list is always in numerical order if the cards are numbered. Some unnumbered sets are artificially numbered in alphabetical order, or by team and alphabetically within the team for convenience.

CHECKLIST CARD - A card that lists in order the cards and players in the set or series. Older checklist cards in mint condition that have not been checked off are very desirable.

CL - Abbreviation for Checklist.

COA - Abbreviation for Coach.

COIN - A small disc of metal or plastic portraying a player in its center.

COLLECTOR - A person who engages in the hobby of collecting cards primarily for his own enjoyment, with any profit motive being secondary.

COLLECTOR ISSUE - A set produced for the sake of the card itself with no product or service sponsor. It derives its name from the fact that most of these sets are produced for sale directly to the hobby market.

COMBINATION CARD - A single card depicting two or more players (but not a team card).

COMMON CARD - The typical card of any set; it has no premium value accruing from subject matter, numerical scarcity, popular demand, or anomaly.

COM - Card issued by the Post Cereal Company through their mail-in offer.

CONVENTION - A large weekend gathering of dealers and collectors at a single location for the purpose of buying, selling, and sometimes trading sports memorabilia items. Conventions are open to the public and sometimes feature celebrities, door prizes, films, contests, etc.

CONVENTION ISSUE - A set produced in conjunction with a sports collectibles convention to commemorate or promote the show.

COR - Correct or corrected card.

COUPON - See Tab.

IN THE BEGINNING,
THERE WAS...
30's HORRORS OF WAR
UH-OH
MARS ATTACKS 60's
G.P.K. 80's
Then there was...
what's next?
and NOW...
Be In The Know!
NONSPORTS

CREASE - A wrinkle on the card, usually caused by bending the card. Creases are a common defect from careless handling.

CY - Cy Young Award.

DEALER - A person who engages in buying, selling, and trading sports collectibles or supplies. A dealer may also be a collector, but as a dealer, he anticipates a profit.

DIE-CUT - A card with part of its stock partially cut, allowing one or more parts to be folded or removed. After removal or appropriate folding, the remaining part of the card can frequently be made to stand up.

DISC - A circular-shaped card.

DISPLAY CARD - A sheet, usually containing three to nine cards, that is printed and used by the manufacturer to advertise and/or display the packages containing his products and cards. The backs of display cards are blank or contain advertisements.

DK - Diamond King (artwork produced by Perez-Steele for Donruss).

DP - Double Print (a card that was printed in double the quantity compared to the other cards in the same series).

ERA - Earned Run Average.

ERR - Error card (see also COR).

ERROR CARD - A card with erroneous information, spelling, or depiction on either side of the card. Not all errors are corrected by the producing card company.

EXHIBIT - The generic name given to thick stock, postcard-size cards with single color obverse pictures. The name is derived from the Exhibit Supply Co. of Chicago, the principal manufacturer of this type of card. These are also known as Arcade cards since they were found in many arcades.

FDP - First Draft Pick (see 1985 Topps Baseball).

FULL SHEET - A complete sheet of cards that has not been cut up into individual cards by the manufacturer. Also called an uncut sheet.

HALL OF FAMER - (HOF'er) A card that portrays a player who has been inducted into the Hall of Fame.

HIGH NUMBER - The cards in the last series of numbers in a year in which such higher-numbered cards were printed or distributed in significantly lesser amounts than the lower-numbered cards. The high-number designation refers to a scarcity of the high-numbered cards. Not all years have high numbers in terms of this definition.

HOC - House of Collectibles.

HOF - Acronym for Hall of Fame.

HOR - Horizontal pose on card as opposed to the standard vertical orientation found on most cards.

HR - Abbreviation for Home Run.

IA - In Action (type of card).

INSERT - A card of a different type, e.g., a poster, or any other sports collectible contained and sold in the same package along with a card or cards of a major set.

ISSUE - Synonymous with set, but usually used in conjunction with a manufacturer, e.g., a Topps issue.

KP - Kid Picture (a sub-series issued in the Topps Baseball sets of 1972 and 1973).

LAYERING - The separation or peeling of one or more layers of the card stock, usually at the corner of the card.

LEGITIMATE ISSUE - A set produced to promote or boost sales of a product or service, e.g., bubble gum, cereal, cigarettes, etc. Most collector issues are not legitimate issues in this sense.

LHP - Left Handed Pitcher.

LID - A circular-shaped card (possibly with tab) that forms the top of the container for the product being promoted.

LL - Living Legends (Donruss 1984) or large letters.

MAJOR SET - A set produced by a national manufacturer of cards containing a large number of cards. Usually 100 or more different cards comprise the set.

MG - Abbreviation for Manager.

MINI - A small card; specifically, a Topps baseball card of identical design but smaller dimensions than the regular Topps issue of 1975.

ML - Major League.

MVP - Most Valuable Player.

NNOF - No Name on Front (see 1949 Bowman).

NOF - Name on Front (see 1949 Bowman).

NON-SPORT CARD - A card from a set whose major theme is a subject other than a sports subject. A card of a sports figure or event that is part of a non-sport set is still a non-sport card, e.g., while the "Look 'N' See" non-sport card set contains a card of Babe Ruth, a sports figure, that card is a non-sport card.

NOTCHING - The grooving of the card, usually caused by fingernails, rubber bands, or bumping card edges against other objects.

NY - New York.

OBVERSE - The front, face, or pictured side of the card.

OLY - Olympics (see 1985 Topps Baseball; the members of the 1984 U.S. Olympic Baseball team were a featured sub-series).

OPT - Option.

P - Pitcher or Pitching pose.

P1 - First Printing.

P2 - Second Printing.

P3 - Third Printing.

PANEL - An extended card that is composed of two or more individual cards. Often the panel forms the back part of the container for the product being promoted, e.g., a Hostess panel, a Bazooka panel, an Esskay Meat panel.

PCL - Pacific Coast League.

PG - Price Guide.

PLASTIC SHEET - A clear, plastic page that is punched for insertion into a binder (with standard three-ring spacing) containing pockets for displaying cards. Many different styles of sheets exist with pockets of varying sizes to hold the many differing card formats.

PREMIUM - A card, sometimes on photographic stock, that is purchased or obtained in conjunction with/or redemption for another card or product. The premium is not packaged in the same unit as the primary item.

PUZZLE CARD - A card whose back contains a part of a picture which, when joined correctly with other puzzle cards, forms the completed picture.

PUZZLE PIECE - An die-cut piece designed to interlock with similar pieces.

RARE - A card or series of cards of very limited availability. Unfortunately, "rare" is a subjective term sometimes used indiscriminately. Rare cards are harder to obtain than scarce cards.

RB - Record Breaker card.

REGIONAL - A card issued and distributed only in a limited geographical area of the country. The producer is not a major, national producer of trading cards.

REVERSE - The back or narrative side of the card.

RHP - Right-Handed Pitcher.

ROY - Acronym for Rookie of the Year.

RR - Rated Rookies (a subset featured in the Donruss Baseball sets).

SA - Super Action or Sport Americana.

SASE - Self-Addressed, Stamped Envelope.

SB - Stolen Bases.

SCARCE - A card or series of cards of limited availability. This subjective term is sometimes used indiscriminately to promote or hype value. Scarce cards are not as difficult to obtain as rare cards.

SCR - Script name on back (see 1949 Bowman Baseball).

SEMI-HIGH - A card from the next to last series of a sequentially issued set. It has more value than an average card and generally less value than a high number. A card is not called a semi-high unless the next to last series in which it exists has an additional premium attached to it.

SERIES - The entire set of cards issued by a particular producer in a particular year, e.g., the 1971 Topps series. Also, within a particular set, series can refer to a group of (consecutively numbered) cards printed at the same time, e.g., the first series of the 1957 Topps issue (numbers 1 through 88).

SET - One each of the entire run of cards of the same type produced by a particular manufacturer during a single year. In other words, if you have a (complete) set of 1976 Topps then you have every card from number 1 up through and including number 660, i.e., all the different cards that were produced.

SKIP-NUMBERED - A set that has many unissued card numbers between the lowest number in the set and the highest number in the set, e.g., the 1948 Leaf baseball set contains 98 cards skip-numbered from number 1 to number 168. A major set in which a few numbers were not printed is not considered to be skip-numbered.

SO - Strikeouts.

SP - Single or Short Print (a card which was printed in lesser quantity compared to the other cards in the same series; see also DP and TP).

SPECIAL CARD - A card that portrays something other than a single player or team, for example, a card that portrays the previous year's statistical leaders or the results from the previous year's post-season action.

SS - Abbreviation for Shortstop.

STAMP - Adhesive-backed papers depicting a player. The stamp may be individual or in a sheet of many stamps. Moisture must be applied to the adhesive in order for the stamp to be attached to another surface.

STAR CARD - A card that portrays a player of some repute, usually determined by his ability; however, sometimes referring to sheer popularity.

STICKER - A card with a removable layer that can be affixed to (stuck onto) another surface.

STOCK - The cardboard or paper on which the card is printed.

STRIP CARDS - A sheet or strip of cards, particularly popular in the 1920s and 1930s, with the individual cards usually separated by broken or dotted lines.

SUPERSTAR CARD - A card that portrays a superstar, e.g., a Hall of Fame member or a Hall of Fame prospect.

SV - Super Veteran.

TAB - A card portion set off from the rest of the card, usually with perforations, that may be removed without damaging the central character or event depicted by the card.

TBC - Turn Back the Clock cards.

TEAM CARD - A card that depicts an entire team.

TEST SET - A set, usually containing a small number of cards, issued by a national card producer and distributed in a limited section or sections of the country. Presumably, the purpose of a test set is to test market appeal for a particular type of card.

TL - Team Leader card.

TP - Triple Print (a card that was printed in triple the quantity compared to the other cards in the same series).

TR - Trade or Traded.

TRIMMED - A card cut down from its original size. Trimmed cards are undesirable to most collectors.

VARIATION - One of two or more cards from the same series with the same number (or player with identical pose if the series is unnumbered) differing from one another by some aspect, the different feature stemming from the printing or stock of the card. This can be caused when the manufacturer of the cards notices an error in one (or more) of the cards, makes the changes, and then resumes the print run. In this case there will be two versions or variations of the same card. Sometimes one of the variations is relatively scarce.

VERT - Vertical pose on card.

WAS - Washington.

WS - World Series card.

Business of Baseball Card Collecting

Determining Value

Why are some cards more valuable than others? Obviously, the economic law of supply and demand is applicable to card collecting just as it is to any other field where a commodity is bought, sold, or traded.

Supply (the number of cards available on the market) is less than the total number of cards originally produced since attrition diminishes that original quantity. Each year a percentage of cards are typically thrown away, destroyed, or otherwise lost to collectors. This percentage is smaller today than it was in the past because more and more people have become increasingly aware of the value of their cards. For those who collect only "Mint" condition cards, the supply of older cards can be quite small indeed. Until recently, collectors were not so conscious of the need to preserve the condition of their cards. For this reason, it is difficult to know exactly how many 1953 Topps are currently available, Mint or otherwise. It is generally accepted that there are fewer 1953 Topps available than 1963, 1973, or 1983 Topps cards. If demand were equal for each of these sets, the law of supply and demand would increase the price for the least available sets. Demand, however, is not equal for all sets, so price correlations can be complicated.

The demand for a card is influenced by many factors. These include: (1) the age of the card; (2) the number of cards printed; (3) the player(s) portrayed on the card; (4) the attractiveness and popularity of the set; and perhaps most important, (5) the physical condition of the card.

In general, (1) the older the card, (2) the fewer the number of the cards printed, (3) the more famous the player, (4) the more attractive and popular the set, or (5) the better the condition of the card, the higher the value of the card will be. There are exceptions to all but one of these factors: the condition of the card. Given two cards similar in all respects except condition, the one in the best condition will always be valued higher.

While there are certain guidelines that help to establish the value of a card, the exceptions and peculiarities make any simple, direct mathematical formula to determine card values impossible.

Regional Variation

Two types of price variations exist among the sections of the country where a card is bought or sold. The first is the general price variation on all cards bought and sold in one geographical area as compared to another. Card prices are slightly higher on the East and West coasts, and slightly lower in the middle of the country. Although prices may vary from the East to the West, or from the Southwest to the Midwest, the prices listed in this guide are nonetheless presented as a consensus of all sections of this large and diverse country.

Still, prices for a particular player's cards may well be higher in his home team's area than in other regions. This exhibits the second type of regional price variation in which local players are favored over those from distant areas. For example, an Al Kaline card would be valued higher in Detroit than in Cincinnati because Kaline played in Detroit; therefore, the demand there for Al Kaline cards is higher than it is in Cincinnati.

On the other hand, a Johnny Bench card would be priced higher in Cincinnati where he played than in Detroit for similar reasons. Sometimes even common player cards command such a premium from hometown collectors.

Set Prices

A somewhat paradoxical situation exists in the price of a complete set versus the combined cost of the individual cards in the set. In nearly every case, the sum of the prices for the individual cards is higher than the cost for the complete set. This is especially prevalent in the cards of the past few years. The reasons for this apparent anomaly stem from the habits of collectors and from the carrying costs to dealers. Today each card in a set is normally produced in the same quantity as all others in its set. However, many collectors pick up only stars, superstars, and particular teams. As a result, the dealer is left with a shortage of certain player cards and an abundance of others. He therefore incurs an expense in simply "carrying" these less desirable cards in stock. On the other hand, if he sells a complete set, he gets rid of large numbers of cards at one time. For this reason, he is often willing to receive less money for a complete set. By doing this, he recovers all of his costs and also receives some profit.

The disparity between the price of the complete set and that for the sum of the individual cards has also been influenced by the fact that the major manufacturers are now pre-collating card sets. Since "pulling" individual cards from the sets of all three manufacturers involves a specific type of labor (and cost), the singles or star card market is not affected significantly by pre-collation.

Set prices also do not include rare card varieties, unless specifically stated. Of course, the prices for sets do include one example of each type for the given set, but this is the least expensive variety.

Scarce Series

Scarce series occur because cards issued before 1974 were made available to the public each year in several series of finite numbers of cards, rather than all cards of the set being available for purchase at one time. At some point during the year, usually toward the end of the baseball season, interest in current year baseball cards waned. Consequently, the manufacturers produced smaller numbers of these later series of cards. Nearly all nationwide issues from post-World War II manufacturers (1948 to 1973) exhibit these series variations. In the past Topps, for example, has issued series consisting of many different numbers of cards, including 55, 66, 80, 88, and others. Recently Topps has settled on what is now their standard sheet size of 132 cards.

While the number of cards within a given series is usually the same as the number of cards on one printed sheet, this is not always the case. For example, Bowman used 36 cards on its standard printed sheets, but in 1948 substituted 12 cards during later print runs of that year's baseball cards. Twelve of the cards from the initial sheet of 36 cards were removed and replaced by 12 different cards giving, in effect, a first series of 36 cards and a second series of 12 new cards. This replacement produced a scarcity of 24 cards -- the 12 cards removed from the original sheet and the 12 new cards added to the sheet. A full sheet of 1948 Bowman cards (second printing) shows that card numbers 37 through 48 have replaced 12 of the cards on the first printing sheet.

The Topps Gum Company has also created scarcities and/or excesses of certain cards in many of their sets. Topps, however, has most frequently gone the other direction by double printing some of the cards. Double printing causes an abundance of cards of the players who are on the same sheet more than one time. During the years from 1978 to 1981, Topps double printed 66 cards out of their large 726-card set. The Topps practice of double printing cards in earlier years is the most logical explanation for the known scarcities of particular cards in some of these Topps sets.

Grading Your Cards

Each hobby has its own grading terminology -- stamps, coins, comic books, beer cans, right down the line. Collectors of sports cards are no exception. The one invariable criterion for determining the value of a card is its condition: the better the condition of the card, the more valuable it is. However, condition grading is very subjective. Individual card dealers and collectors differ in the strictness of their grading, but the stated condition of a card should be determined without regard to whether it is being bought or sold.

The physical defects which lower the condition of a card are usually quite apparent, but each individual places his own estimation (negative value in this case) on these defects. We present the condition guide for use in determining values listed in this price guide in the hopes that excess subjectivity can be minimized.

The defects listed in the condition guide below are those either placed in the card at the time of printing -- uneven borders, focus -- or those defects that can occur to a card under normal handling -- corner sharpness, gloss, edge wear, light creases -- and finally, environmental conditions -- browning. Other defects to cards are caused by human carelessness and in all cases should be noted separately and in addition to the condition grade. Among the more common alterations are heavy creases, tape, tape stains, rubber band marks, water damage, smoke damage, trimming, paste, tears, writing, pin or tack holes, any back damage, and missing parts (tabs, tops, coupons, backgrounds).

Centering

It is important to define in words and pictures what is meant by certain frequently used hobby terms relating to grading cards. The adjacent pictures portray various stages of centering. Centering can range from well-centered to slightly off-centered to off-centered to badly off-centered to miscut.

Slightly Off-Centered: A slightly off-center card is one which upon close inspection is found to have one border bigger than the opposite border. This degree is only offensive to a purist.

Off-Centered: An off-center card has one border which is noticeably more than twice as wide as the opposite border.

Badly Off-Centered: A badly off-center card has virtually no border on one side of the card.

Miscut: A miscut card actually shows part of the adjacent card in its larger border and consequently a corresponding amount of its card is cut off.

Corner Wear

Degrees of corner wear generate several common terms used and useful to accurate grading. The wear on card corners can be expressed as fuzzy corners, corner wear or slightly rounded corners, rounded corners, badly rounded corners.

Fuzzy Corners: Fuzzy corners still come to a right angle (to a point) but the point has begun to fray slightly.

Corner Wear or Slightly Rounded Corners: The slight fraying of the corners has increased to where there is no longer a point to the corner. Nevertheless the corner is still reasonably sharp. There may be evidence of some slight loss of color in the corner also.

Rounded Corners: The corner is definitely no longer sharp but is not badly rounded.

Badly Rounded Corners: The corner is rounded to an objectionable degree. Excessive wear and rough handling are evident.

Creases

The third, and perhaps most frequent, common defect is the crease; the degree of creasing in a card is very difficult to show in a drawing or picture. On giving the specific condition of an expensive card for sale, the seller should note any creases additionally. Creases can be categorized as to severity according to the following scale.

Light Crease: A light crease is a crease which is barely noticeable on close inspection. In fact when cards are in plastic sheets or holders, a light crease may not be seen (until the card is taken out of the holder). A light crease on the front is much more serious than a light crease on the card back only.

Medium Crease: A medium crease is noticeable when held and studied at arm's length by the naked eye, but does not overly detract from the appearance of the card. It is an obvious crease, but not one that breaks the picture surface of the card.

Heavy Crease: A heavy crease is one which has torn or broken through the card's picture surface, e.g., puts a tear in the photo surface.

Alterations

Deceptive Trimming: Deceptive trimming occurs when someone alters the card in order (1) to shave off edge wear, (2) to improve the sharpness of the corners, or (3) to improve centering -- obviously their objective is to falsely increase the perceived value of the card to an unsuspecting buyer. The shrinkage is usually only evident if the trimmed card is compared to an adjacent full-sized card or if the trimmed card is itself measured.

Obvious Trimming: Obvious trimming is noticeable and unfortunate. It is usually performed by non-collectors who give no thought to the present or future value of their cards.

Deceptively Retouched Borders: This occurs when the borders (especially on those cards with dark borders) are touched up on the edges and corners with magic marker of appropriate color in order to make the card appear to be mint.

CENTERING

WELL-CENTERED

SLIGHTLY OFF-CENTERED

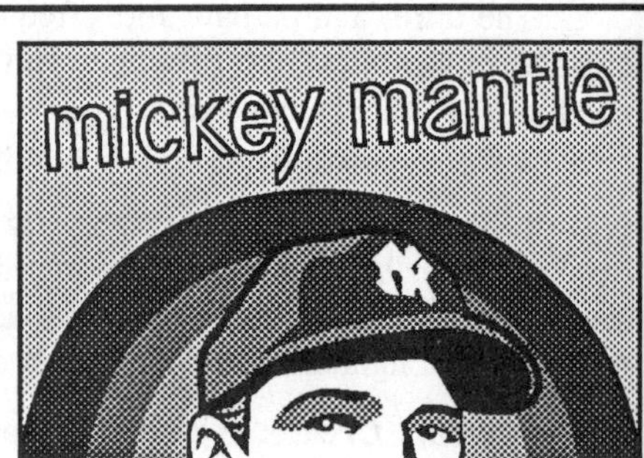

OFF-CENTERED

BADLY OFF-CENTERED

MISCUT

CORNER WEAR

The partial cards shown at the right have been photographed at 300%. This was done in order to magnify each card's corner wear to such a degree that differences could be shown on a printed page.

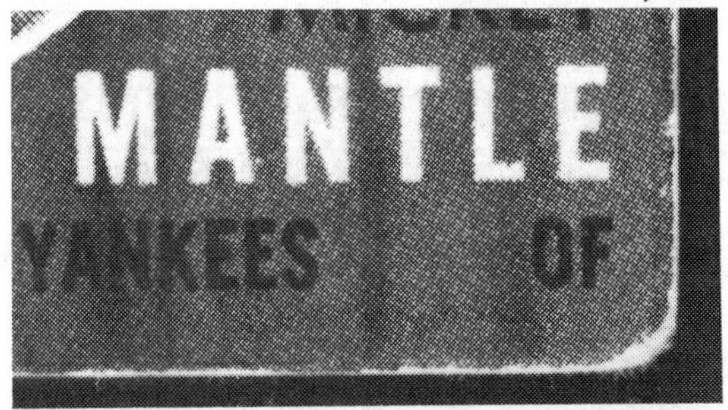

The 1962 Topps Mickey Mantle card definitely has a rounded corner. Some may say that this corner is badly rounded, but that is a judgment call.

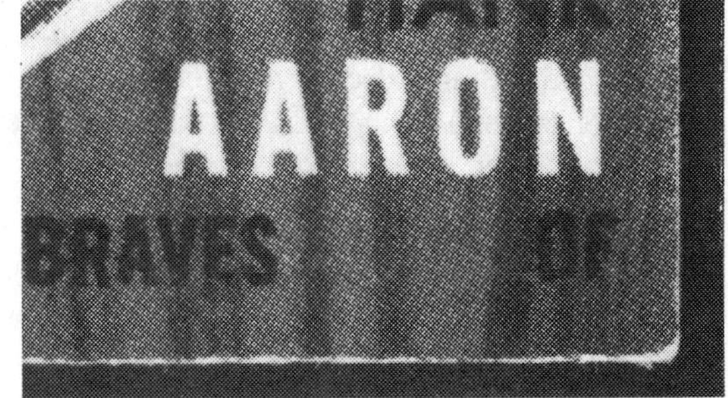

The 1962 Topps Hank Aaron card has a slightly rounded corner. Note that there is definite corner wear evident by the fraying and that there is no longer a sharp point to which the corner converges.

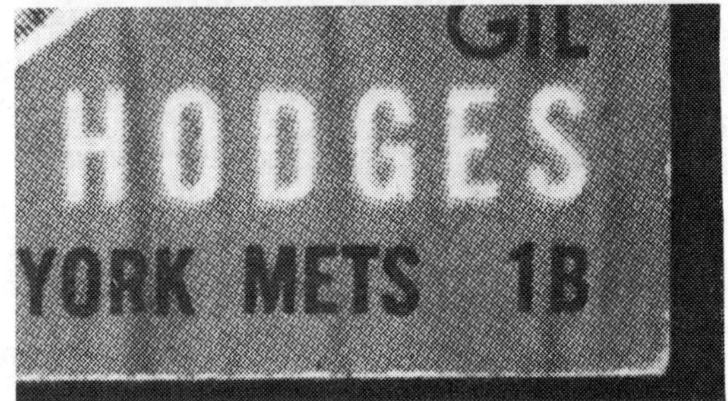

The 1962 Topps Gil Hodges card has corner wear; it is slightly better than the Aaron card above. Nevertheless some collectors might classify this Hodges corner as slightly rounded.

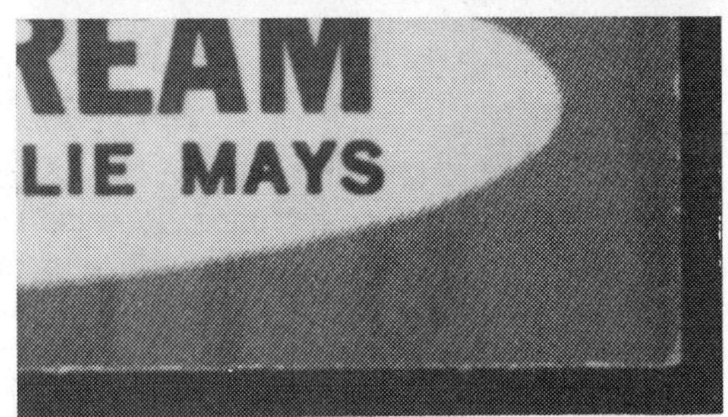

The 1962 Topps Manager's Dream card showing Mantle and Mays has slight corner wear. This is not a fuzzy corner as very slight wear is noticeable on the card's photo surface.

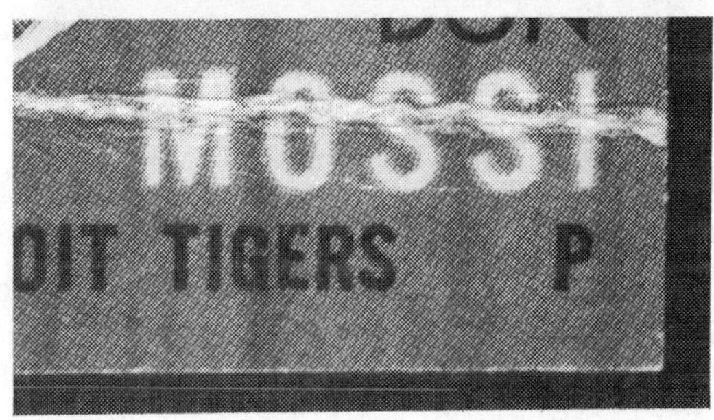

The 1962 Topps Don Mossi card has very slight corner wear such that it might be called a fuzzy corner. A close look at the original card shows that the corner is not perfect, but almost. However, note that corner wear is somewhat academic on this card. As you can plainly see, the heavy crease going across his name breaks through the photo surface.

Categorization of Defects

A "Micro Defect" would be fuzzy corners, slight off-centering, printer's lines, printer's spots, slightly out of focus, or slight loss of original gloss. A NrMT card may have one micro defect. An Ex-MT card may have two or more micro defects.

A "Minor Defect" would be corner wear or slight rounding, off-centering, light crease on back, wax or gum stains on reverse, loss of original gloss, writing or tape marks on back, or rubber band marks. An Excellent card may have minor defects.

A "Major Defect" would be rounded corner(s), badly off-centering, crease(s), deceptive trimming, deceptively retouched borders, pin hole, staple hole, incidental writing or tape marks on front, warping, water stains, or sun fading. A VG card may have one major defect. A Good card may have two or more major defects.

A "Catastrophic Defect" is the worst kind of defect and would include such defects as badly rounded corner(s), miscutting, heavy crease(s), obvious trimming, punch hole, tack hole, tear(s), corner missing or clipped, destructive writing on front. A Fair card may have one catastrophic defect. A Poor card has two or more catastrophic defects.

Condition Guide

MINT (M OR MT) - A card with no defects. The card has sharp corners, even borders, original gloss or shine on the surface, sharp focus of the picture, smooth edges, no signs of wear, and white borders. A Mint card (that is, a card that is worth a "Mint" price) does NOT have printers' lines or other printing defects or other serious quality control problems that should have been discovered by the producing card company before distribution. Note also that there is no allowance made for the age of the card.

NEAR MINT (NrMT) - A card with a micro defect. Any of the following would be sufficient to lower the grade of a card from Mint to the Near Mint category: layering at some of the corners (fuzzy corners), a very small amount of the original gloss lost, very minor wear on the edges, slightly off-center borders, slight wear visible only on close inspection, slight off-whiteness of the borders.

EXCELLENT-MINT (EX-MT) - A card with micro defects, but no minor defects. Two or three of the following would be sufficient to lower the grade of a card from Mint to the Excellent-Mint category: layering at some of the corners (fuzzy corners), a very small amount of the original gloss lost, minor wear on the edges, slightly off-center borders, slight wear visible only on close inspection, slight off-whiteness of the borders.

EXCELLENT (EX OR E) - A card with minor defects. Any of the following would be sufficient to lower the grade of a card from Mint to the Excellent category: slight rounding at some of the corners, a small amount of the original gloss lost, minor wear on the edges, off-center borders, wear visible only on close inspection; off-whiteness of the borders.

VERY GOOD (VG) - A card that has been handled but not abused: Some rounding at all corners, slight layering or scuffing at one or two corners, slight notching on edges, gloss lost from the surface but not scuffed, borders might be somewhat uneven but some white is visible on all borders, noticeable yellowing or browning of borders, pictures may be slightly off focus.

GOOD (G) - A well-handled card, rounding and some layering at the corners, scuffing at the corners and minor scuffing on the face, borders noticeably uneven and browning, loss of gloss on the face, notching on the edges.

FAIR (F) - Round and layering corners, brown and dirty borders, frayed edges, noticeable scuffing on the face, white not visible on one or more borders, cloudy focus.

POOR (P) - An abused card: The lowest grade of card, frequently some major physical alteration has been performed on the card, collectible only as a filler until a better-condition replacement can be obtained.

Categories between these major condition grades are frequently used, such as Very Good to Excellent (VG-E), Fair to Good (F-G), etc. Such grades indicate a card with all qualities at least in the lower of the two categories, but with several qualities in the higher of the two categories. In the case of Ex-Mt, it essentially refers to a card which is halfway between Excellent and Mint.

Unopened "Mint" cards and factory-collated sets are considered Mint in their unknown (and presumed perfect) state. However, once opened or broken out, each of these cards is graded (and valued) in its own right by taking into account any quality control defects (such as off-centering, printer's lines, machine creases, or gum stains) that may be present in spite of the fact that the card has never been handled.

Cards before 1980 which are priced in the Price Guide in a top condition of NrMT, are obviously worth an additional premium when offered in strict Mint condition. This additional premium increases relative to the age and scarcity of the card. For example, Mint cards from the late '70s may bring only a 10% premium for Mint (above NrMT), whereas high demand cards from pre-World War II vintage sets can be sold for as much as double the NrMT price when offered in strict Mint condition.

Selling Your Cards

Just about every collector sells cards or will sell cards eventually. Someday you may be interested in selling your duplicates or maybe even your whole collection. You may sell to other collectors, friends, or dealers. You may even sell cards you purchased from a certain dealer back to that same dealer. In any event, it helps to know some of the mechanics of the typical transaction between buyer and seller.

Dealers will buy cards in order to resell them to other collectors who are interested in the cards. Dealers will always pay a higher percentage for items which (in their opinion) can be resold quickly, and a much lower percentage for those items which are perceived as having low demand and hence are slow moving. In either case, dealers must buy at a price that allows for the expense of doing business and a fair margin for profit.

If you have cards for sale, the best advice we can give is that you get three offers for your cards and take the best offer, all things considered. Note, the "best" offer may not be the one for the highest amount. And remember, if a dealer really wants your cards, he won't let you get away without making his best competitive offer. Another alternative is to take your cards to a nearby convention and either auction them off in the show auction or offer them for sale to some of the dealers present.

Many people think nothing of going into a department store and paying $15 for an item of clothing for which the store paid $5. But, if you were selling your $15 card to a dealer and he offered you only $5 for it, you might think his mark-up unreasonable. To complete the analogy: most department stores (and card dealers) that pay $10 for $15 items eventually go out of business. An exception to this is when the dealer knows that a willing buyer for the merchandise you are attempting to sell is only a phone call away. Then an offer of 2/3 or maybe 70% of the book value will still allow him to make a reasonable profit due to the short time he will need to hold the merchandise. Nevertheless, most cards and collections will bring offers in the range of 25% to 50% of retail price. Material from the past five to ten years or so is very plentiful. Don't be surprised if your best offer is only 20% of the book value for these recent years.

Interesting Notes

The numerically first card of an issue is the single card most likely to obtain excessive wear. Consequently, you will typically find the price on the number one card (in Mint condition) somewhat higher than might otherwise be the case. Similarly, but to a lesser extent (because normally the less important, reverse side of the card is the one exposed), the numerically last card in an issue is also prone to abnormal wear. This extra wear and tear occurs because the first and last cards are exposed to the elements (human element included) more than any other cards. They are generally end cards in any brick formations, rubber bandings, stackings on wet surfaces, and like activities.

Sports cards have no intrinsic value. The value of a card, like the value of other collectibles, can only be determined by you and your enjoyment in viewing and possessing these cardboard swatches.

Remember, the buyer ultimately determines the price of each baseball card. You are the determining price factor because you have the ability to say "No" to the price of any card by not exchanging your hard-earned money for a given card. When the cost of a trading card exceeds the enjoyment you will receive from it, your answer should be "No." We assess and report the prices. You set them!

We are always interested in receiving the price input of collectors and dealers from around the country. We happily credit major contributors. We welcome your opinions, since your contributions assist us in ensuring a better guide each year. If you would like to join our survey list for the next editions of this book and others authored by Dr. Beckett, please send your name and address to Dr. James Beckett, 3410 MidCourt, Suite 110, Carrollton, Texas 75006.

Advertising

Within this price guide you will find advertisements for sports memorabilia material, mail order, and retail sports collectibles establishments. All advertisements were accepted in good faith based on the reputation of the advertiser; however, neither the author, the publisher, the distributors, nor the other advertisers in the price guide accept any responsibility for any particular advertiser not complying with the terms of his or her ad.

Readers should also be aware that prices in advertisements are subject to change over the annual period before a new edition of this volume is issued each spring. When replying to an advertisement late in the baseball year, the reader should take this into account, and contact the dealer by phone or in writing for up-to-date price information. Should you come into contact with any of the advertisers in this guide as a result of their advertisement herein, please mention to them this source as your contact.

Additional Reading

With the increase in popularity of the hobby in recent years, there has been a corresponding increase in available literature. Below is a list of the books and periodicals which receive our highest recommendation and which we hope will further advance your knowledge and enjoyment of our great hobby.

The Sport Americana Price Guide to Baseball Collectibles by Dr. James Beckett (Second Edition, $12.95, released 1988, published by Edgewater Book Company) -- the complete guide/checklist with up to date values for box cards, coins, labels, Canadian cards, stamps, stickers, pins, etc.

The Sport Americana Football, Hockey, Basketball and Boxing Card Price Guide by Dr. James Beckett (Fifth Edition, $12.95, released 1987, published by Edgewater Book Company) -- the most comprehensive price guide/checklist ever issued on football and other non-baseball sports cards. No serious hobbyist should be without it.

The Official Price Guide to Football Cards by Dr. James Beckett (Eighth Edition, $4.95, released 1988, published by The House of Collectibles) -- an abridgement of the *Sport Americana Price Guide* listed above in a convenient and economical pocket-size format providing Dr. Beckett's pricing of the major football sets since 1948.

The Sport Americana Baseball Memorabilia and Autograph Price Guide by Dr. James Beckett and Dennis W. Eckes (First Edition, $8.95, released 1982, co-published by Den's Collectors Den and Edgewater Book Company) -- the most complete book ever produced on baseball memorabilia other than baseball cards. This book presents in an illustrated, logical fashion information on baseball memorabilia and autographs which had been heretofore unavailable to the collector.

The Sport Americana Alphabetical Baseball Card Checklist by Dr. James Beckett (Third Edition, $9.95, released 1988, co-published by Den's Collectors Den and Edgewater Book Company) -- an illustrated, alphabetical listing, by the last name of the player portrayed on the card, of virtually all baseball cards (Major League and Minor League) produced up through 1988.

The Sport Americana Price Guide to the Non-Sports Cards by Christopher Benjamin and Dennis W. Eckes (Third Edition (Part Two), $12.95, released 1988, published by Edgewater Book Company) -- the definitive guide to all popular non-sports American tobacco and bubble gum cards. In addition to cards, illustrations and prices for wrappers are also included. Part Two covers non-sports cards from 1961 through 1987.

The Sport Americana Baseball Address List by Jack Smalling and Dennis W. Eckes (Fifth Edition, $10.95, released 1988, published by Edgewater Book Company) -- the definitive guide for autograph hunters giving addresses and deceased information for virtually all major league baseball players past and present.

The Sport Americana Baseball Card Team Checklist by Jeff Fritsch and Dennis W. Eckes (Third Edition, $9.95, released 1987, co-published by Den's Collectors Den and Edgwater Book Company) -- includes all Topps, Bowman, Fleer, Play Ball, Goudey, and Donruss cards, with the players portrayed on the cards listed with the teams for whom they played. The book is invaluable to the collector who specializes in an individual team because it is the most complete baseball card team checklist available.

Hockey Card Checklist and Price Guide by Andrew Pywowarczuk (Ninth Edition, publisher: Cartophilium) -- contains the most complete list of hockey card checklists ever assembled including a listing of Bee Hive photos.

The Encyclopedia of Baseball Cards, Volume I: 19th Century Cards by Lew Lipset ($11.95, released 1983, published by the author) -- everything you ever wanted to know about 19th century cards.

The Encyclopedia of Baseball Cards, Volume II: Early Gum and Candy Cards by Lew Lipset ($10.95, released 1984, published by the author) -- everything you ever wanted to know about Early Candy and Gum cards.

The Encyclopedia of Baseball Cards, Volume III: 20th Century Tobacco Cards, 1909-1932 by Lew Lipset ($12.95, released 1986, published by the author) -- everything you ever wanted to know about old tobacco cards.

Beckett Baseball Card Monthly authored and edited by Dr. James Beckett -- contains the most extensive and accepted monthly price guide, feature articles, "who's hot and who's not" section, convention calendar, and numerous letters to and responses from the editor. Now published 12 times annually, it is the hobby's largest paid circulation periodical.

Errata

There are thousands of names, more than 100,000 prices, and untold other words in this book. There are going to be a few typographical errors, a few misspellings, and possibly, a number or two out of place. If you catch a blooper, drop me a note directly or in care of the publisher, and we will fix it up in the next year's edition.

Prices in this Guide

Prices found in this guide reflect current retail rates just prior to the printing of this book. They do not reflect the FOR SALE prices of the author, the publisher, the distributors, the advertisers, or any card dealers associated with this guide. No one is obligated in any way to buy, sell, or trade his or her cards based on these prices. The price listings were compiled by the author from actual buy/sell transactions at sports conventions, buy/sell advertisements in the hobby papers, for sale prices from dealer catalogs and price lists, and discussions with leading hobbyists in the U.S. and Canada. All prices are in U.S. dollars.

1962 American Tract Society

I RECOMMEND JESUS CHRIST

As a teenage boy I chose athletics as my god. Although I didn't fall on my knees each day before a carved image of a baseball player, I might just as well have, because baseball occupied the very throne of my life.

Near the end of my junior year in high school, I removed baseball from the throne of my life and replaced it with the only person who is worthy of our worship and trust, Jesus Christ, the Son of God and Saviour of the world. I accepted, by faith, what He accomplished when He died on the cross nearly 2,000 years ago. He paid the penalty for my sin and enabled me to be restored to that perfect relationship with God that had been broken by sin.

It is impossible for us to earn the right to be once again reunited with God as His children. Rather, this right is offered to us as a gift if we believe in Jesus Christ and accept Him as the Saviour and Lord of our life. This is Christianity; not a religion, not a church, but a relationship with Jesus Christ that restores the shine, vitality, and meaning to life.

"As many as received him (Christ), **to them gave he power to become the sons of God, even to them that believe on his name"** (John 1:12).

St. Augustine said: "Thou hast made us for thyself O God, and restless are our hearts until they rest in thee."

May I recommend Jesus Christ to you?

— Jerry Kindall

American Tract Society — a non-profit organization
Publishers of Christian Literature since 1825
Oradell, New Jersey **Tracard No. 51**

These cards are quite attractive and feature the "pure card" concept that is always popular with collectors, i.e., no borders or anything else on the card front to detract from the color photo. The cards are numbered on the back and are actually part of a much larger set with a Christian theme. The set features Christian ballplayers giving first-person testimonies on the card backs telling how Jesus Christ has changed their lives. These cards are sometimes referred to as "Tracards." The cards measure approximately 2 3/4" by 3 1/2". The set price below refers to only one of each player, not including any variations.

	NRMT	VG-E	GOOD
COMPLETE SET (4)	12.00	5.00	1.20
COMMON PLAYER	3.00	1.20	.30
☐ 43A Bobby Richardson (black print on back)	6.00	2.40	.60
☐ 43B Bobby Richardson (blue print on back)	6.00	2.40	.60
☐ 43C Bobby Richardson (black print on back with Play Ball in red)	6.00	2.40	.60
☐ 43D Bobby Richardson (black print on back with exclamation point after Play Ball)	6.00	2.40	.60
☐ 51A Jerry Kindall (portrait from chest up, black print on back)	3.00	1.20	.30
☐ 51B Jerry Kindall (on one knee with bat, blue print on back)	3.00	1.20	.30
☐ 52A Felipe Alou (on one knee looking up, black print on back)	4.00	1.60	.40
☐ 52B Felipe Alou (on one knee looking up, blue print on back)	4.00	1.60	.40
☐ 52C Felipe Alou (batting pose)	4.00	1.60	.40
☐ 66 Al Worthington (black print on back)	3.00	1.20	.30

1948 Babe Ruth Story

The 1948 Babe Ruth Story set of 28 black and white numbered cards (measuring 2" by 2 1/2") was issued by the Philadelphia Chewing Gum Company to commemorate the 1949 movie of the same name starring William Bendix, Claire Trevor, and Charles Bickford. Babe Ruth himself appears on several cards. The last 12 cards (17 to 28) are more difficult to obtain than other cards in the set and are also more desirable in that most picture actual players as well as actors from the movie. Supposedly these last

Photograph from ROY DEL RUTH'S Production "THE BABE RUTH STORY" An Allied Artists Picture

No. 15

Babe Ruth (at bat) William Bendix

Dramatic Home Run!

It was the third game of the 1932 World Series between the Yankees and the Chicago Cubs. The Yanks and Cubs were feuding and Babe Ruth was the target for jeers and insults as he stepped to the plate in Chicago's Wrigley Field. Charley Root was pitching for the Cubs in the fifth inning. Deliberately, the Babe took two strikes, and after each strike, by pantomime, pointed to the distant center field bleachers. Before Root let go his third pitch, the Bambino pointed again—and then made good. The ball sailed deep into the open seats in center field—baseball's most amazing home run.

SWELL BUBBLE GUM

Philadelphia Chewing Gum Corporation
Havertown, Pa.

12 cards were issued much later after the first 16 cards had already been released and distributed. The ACC designation for this set is R421.

	NRMT	VG-E	GOOD
COMPLETE SET	700.00	280.00	70.00
COMMON PLAYER (1-16)	10.00	4.00	1.00
COMMON PLAYER (17-28)	25.00	10.00	2.50
☐ 1 The Babe Ruth Story In the Making (Babe Ruth shown with William Bendix)	60.00	10.00	2.00
☐ 2 Bat Boy Becomes the Babe	10.00	4.00	1.00
☐ 3 Claire Hodgson played by Claire Trevor	10.00	4.00	1.00
☐ 4 Babe Ruth played by William Bendix; Claire Hodgson played by Claire Trevor	10.00	4.00	1.00
☐ 5 Brother Matthias played by Charles Bickford	10.00	4.00	1.00
☐ 6 Phil Conrad played by Sam Levene	10.00	4.00	1.00
☐ 7 Night Club Singer played by Gertrude Niesen	10.00	4.00	1.00
☐ 8 Baseball's Famous Deal	10.00	4.00	1.00
☐ 9 Babe Ruth played by William Bendix; Mrs.Babe Ruth played by Claire Trevor	10.00	4.00	1.00
☐ 10 Actors for Babe Ruth, Mrs. Babe Ruth, and Brother Matthias	10.00	4.00	1.00
☐ 11 Babe Ruth played by William Bendix; Miller Huggins played by Fred Lightner	10.00	4.00	1.00
☐ 12 Babe Ruth played by William Bendix; Johnny Sylvester played by George Marshall	10.00	4.00	1.00
☐ 13 Actors for Mr., Mrs. and Johnny Sylvester	10.00	4.00	1.00
☐ 14 When A Feller Needs A Friend	10.00	4.00	1.00
☐ 15 Dramatic Home Run	10.00	4.00	1.00
☐ 16 The Homer That Set the Record	10.00	4.00	1.00
☐ 17 The Slap That Started Baseball's Most Famous Career	25.00	10.00	2.50
☐ 18 The Babe Plays Santa Claus	25.00	10.00	2.50
☐ 19 Actors for Ed Barrow, Jacob Ruppert, and Miller Huggins	25.00	10.00	2.50
☐ 20 Broken Window Paid Off	25.00	10.00	2.50
☐ 21 Regardless of the Generation/ Babe Ruth	25.00	10.00	2.50
☐ 22 Charley Grimm and William Bendix	25.00	10.00	2.50
☐ 23 Ted Lyons and William Bendix	30.00	12.00	3.00
☐ 24 Lefty Gomez, William Bendix, and Bucky Harris	40.00	16.00	4.00
☐ 25 Babe Ruth and William Bendix	80.00	32.00	8.00
☐ 26 Babe Ruth and William Bendix	80.00	32.00	8.00
☐ 27 Babe Ruth and Claire Trevor	80.00	32.00	8.00

□ 28	William Bendix, Babe Ruth, Claire Trevor	80.00	32.00	8.00

1934-36 Batter-Up

The 1934-36 Batter-Up set issued by National Chicle contains 192 blank-backed die-cut cards. Numbers 1 to 80 are 2 3/8" by 3 1/4" in size while 81 to 192 are 2 3/8" by 3". The latter are more difficult to find than the former. The pictures come in basic black and white or in tints of blue, brown, green, purple, red, or sepia. There are three combination cards (each featuring two players per card) in the high series (98, 111, and 115). The ACC designation for the set is R318. Cards with backs removed are graded fair at best.

		NRMT	VG-E	GOOD
	COMPLETE SET	14000.00	6000.00	2000.00
	COMMON PLAYER (1-80)	30.00	12.00	3.00
	COMMON PLAYER (81-192)	70.00	28.00	7.00
□ 1	Wally Berger	60.00	24.00	6.00
□ 2	Ed Brandt	30.00	12.00	3.00
□ 3	Al Lopez	60.00	24.00	6.00
□ 4	Dick Bartell	30.00	12.00	3.00
□ 5	Carl Hubbell	90.00	36.00	9.00
□ 6	Bill Terry	90.00	36.00	9.00
□ 7	Pepper Martin	40.00	16.00	4.00
□ 8	Jim Bottomley	60.00	24.00	6.00
□ 9	Tom Bridges	35.00	14.00	3.50
□ 10	Rick Ferrell	60.00	24.00	6.00
□ 11	Ray Benge	30.00	12.00	3.00
□ 12	Wes Ferrell	35.00	14.00	3.50
□ 13	Chalmer Cissell	30.00	12.00	3.00
□ 14	Pie Traynor	90.00	36.00	9.00
□ 15	Leroy Mahaffey	30.00	12.00	3.00
□ 16	Chick Hafey	60.00	24.00	6.00
□ 17	Lloyd Waner	60.00	24.00	6.00
□ 18	Jack Burns	30.00	12.00	3.00
□ 19	Buddy Myer	30.00	12.00	3.00
□ 20	Bob Johnson	35.00	14.00	3.50
□ 21	Arky Vaughan	60.00	24.00	6.00
□ 22	Red Rolfe	35.00	14.00	3.50
□ 23	Lefty Gomez	100.00	40.00	10.00
□ 24	Earl Averill	60.00	24.00	6.00
□ 25	Mickey Cochrane	100.00	40.00	10.00
□ 26	Van Lingle Mungo	35.00	14.00	3.50
□ 27	Mel Ott	110.00	45.00	11.00
□ 28	Jimmy Foxx	125.00	50.00	12.50
□ 29	Jimmy Dykes	35.00	14.00	3.50
□ 30	Bill Dickey	100.00	40.00	10.00
□ 31	Lefty Grove	110.00	45.00	11.00
□ 32	Joe Cronin	90.00	36.00	9.00
□ 33	Frank Frisch	90.00	36.00	9.00
□ 34	Al Simmons	75.00	30.00	7.50
□ 35	Rogers Hornsby	125.00	50.00	12.50
□ 36	Ted Lyons	60.00	24.00	6.00
□ 37	Rabbit Maranville	60.00	24.00	6.00
□ 38	Jimmy Wilson	30.00	12.00	3.00
□ 39	Willie Kamm	30.00	12.00	3.00
□ 40	Bill Hallahan	30.00	12.00	3.00
□ 41	Gus Suhr	30.00	12.00	3.00
□ 42	Charlie Gehringer	75.00	30.00	7.50
□ 43	Joe Heving	30.00	12.00	3.00
□ 44	Adam Comorosky	30.00	12.00	3.00
□ 45	Tony Lazzeri	40.00	16.00	4.00
□ 46	Sam Leslie	30.00	12.00	3.00
□ 47	Bob Smith	30.00	12.00	3.00
□ 48	Willis Hudlin	30.00	12.00	3.00
□ 49	Carl Reynolds	30.00	12.00	3.00
□ 50	Fred Schulte	30.00	12.00	3.00
□ 51	Cookie Lavagetto	35.00	14.00	3.50
□ 52	Hal Schumacher	30.00	12.00	3.00
□ 53	Roger Cramer	35.00	14.00	3.50
□ 54	Sylvester Johnson	30.00	12.00	3.00
□ 55	Ollie Bejma	30.00	12.00	3.00
□ 56	Sam Byrd	30.00	12.00	3.00
□ 57	Hank Greenberg	110.00	45.00	11.00
□ 58	Bill Knickerbocker	30.00	12.00	3.00
□ 59	Bill Urbanski	30.00	12.00	3.00
□ 60	Eddie Morgan	30.00	12.00	3.00
□ 61	Rabbit McNair	30.00	12.00	3.00
□ 62	Ben Chapman	35.00	14.00	3.50
□ 63	Roy Johnson	30.00	12.00	3.00
□ 64	Dizzy Dean	250.00	100.00	25.00
□ 65	Zeke Bonura	30.00	12.00	3.00
□ 66	Fred Marberry	30.00	12.00	3.00
□ 67	Gus Mancuso	30.00	12.00	3.00
□ 68	Joe Vosmik	30.00	12.00	3.00
□ 69	Earl Grace	30.00	12.00	3.00
□ 70	Tony Piet	30.00	12.00	3.00
□ 71	Rollie Hemsley	30.00	12.00	3.00
□ 72	Fred Fitzsimmons	30.00	12.00	3.00
□ 73	Hack Wilson	90.00	36.00	9.00
□ 74	Chick Fullis	30.00	12.00	3.00
□ 75	Fred Frankhouse	30.00	12.00	3.00
□ 76	Ethan Allen	30.00	12.00	3.00
□ 77	Heine Manush	60.00	24.00	6.00
□ 78	Rip Collins	30.00	12.00	3.00
□ 79	Tony Cuccinello	30.00	12.00	3.00
□ 80	Joe Kuhel	30.00	12.00	3.00
□ 81	Tom Bridges	80.00	32.00	8.00
□ 82	Clint Brown	70.00	28.00	7.00
□ 83	Albert Blanche	70.00	28.00	7.00
□ 84	Boze Berger	70.00	28.00	7.00
□ 85	Goose Goslin	150.00	60.00	15.00
□ 86	Lefty Gomez	200.00	80.00	20.00
□ 87	Joe Glenn	70.00	28.00	7.00
□ 88	Cy Blanton	70.00	28.00	7.00
□ 89	Tom Carey	70.00	28.00	7.00
□ 90	Ralph Birkofer	70.00	28.00	7.00
□ 91	Fred Gabler	70.00	28.00	7.00
□ 92	Dick Coffman	70.00	28.00	7.00
□ 93	Ollie Bejma	70.00	28.00	7.00
□ 94	Leroy Parmelee	70.00	28.00	7.00
□ 95	Carl Reynolds	70.00	28.00	7.00
□ 96	Ben Cantwell	70.00	28.00	7.00
□ 97	Curtis Davis	70.00	28.00	7.00
□ 98	Webb and Wally Moses	80.00	32.00	8.00
□ 99	Ray Benge	70.00	28.00	7.00
□ 100	Pie Traynor	175.00	70.00	18.00
□ 101	Phil Cavarretta	80.00	32.00	8.00
□ 102	Pep Young	70.00	28.00	7.00
□ 103	Willis Hudlin	70.00	28.00	7.00
□ 104	Mickey Haslin	70.00	28.00	7.00
□ 105	Oswald Bluege	70.00	28.00	7.00
□ 106	Paul Andrews	70.00	28.00	7.00
□ 107	Ed Brandt	70.00	28.00	7.00
□ 108	Don Taylor	70.00	28.00	7.00
□ 109	Thornton Lee	70.00	28.00	7.00
□ 110	Hal Schumacher	70.00	28.00	7.00
□ 111	Hayes and Ted Lyons	110.00	45.00	11.00
□ 112	Odell Hale	70.00	28.00	7.00
□ 113	Earl Averill	150.00	60.00	15.00
□ 114	Italo Chelini	70.00	28.00	7.00
□ 115	Andrews and Bottomley	110.00	45.00	11.00
□ 116	Bill Walker	70.00	28.00	7.00
□ 117	Bill Dickey	250.00	100.00	25.00
□ 118	Gerald Walker	70.00	28.00	7.00
□ 119	Ted Lyons	150.00	60.00	15.00
□ 120	Eldon Auker	70.00	28.00	7.00
□ 121	Bill Hallahan	70.00	28.00	7.00
□ 122	Fred Lindstrom	150.00	60.00	15.00
□ 123	Oral Hildebrand	70.00	28.00	7.00
□ 124	Luke Appling	150.00	60.00	15.00
□ 125	Pepper Martin	90.00	36.00	9.00
□ 126	Rick Ferrell	150.00	60.00	15.00
□ 127	Ival Goodman	70.00	28.00	7.00
□ 128	Joe Kuhel	70.00	28.00	7.00
□ 129	Ernie Lombardi	150.00	60.00	15.00
□ 130	Charlie Gehringer	200.00	80.00	20.00
□ 131	Van Lingle Mungo	80.00	32.00	8.00
□ 132	Larry French	70.00	28.00	7.00
□ 133	Buddy Myer	70.00	28.00	7.00
□ 134	Mel Harder	90.00	36.00	9.00
□ 135	Augie Galan	70.00	28.00	7.00
□ 136	Gabby Hartnett	150.00	60.00	15.00
□ 137	Stan Hack	80.00	32.00	8.00

□ 138	Billy Herman	150.00	60.00	15.00
□ 139	Bill Jurges	70.00	28.00	7.00
□ 140	Bill Lee	70.00	28.00	7.00
□ 141	Zeke Bonura	70.00	28.00	7.00
□ 142	Tony Piet	70.00	28.00	7.00
□ 143	Paul Dean	90.00	36.00	9.00
□ 144	Jimmy Foxx	300.00	120.00	30.00
□ 145	Joe Medwick	175.00	70.00	18.00
□ 146	Rip Collins	70.00	28.00	7.00
□ 147	Mel Almada	70.00	28.00	7.00
□ 148	Allan Cooke	70.00	28.00	7.00
□ 149	Moe Berg	90.00	36.00	9.00
□ 150	Dolph Camilli	70.00	28.00	7.00
□ 151	Oscar Melillo	70.00	28.00	7.00
□ 152	Bruce Campbell	70.00	28.00	7.00
□ 153	Lefty Grove	250.00	100.00	25.00
□ 154	Johnny Murphy	80.00	32.00	8.00
□ 155	Luke Sewell	80.00	32.00	8.00
□ 156	Leo Durocher	175.00	70.00	18.00
□ 157	Lloyd Waner	150.00	60.00	15.00
□ 158	Gus Bush	70.00	28.00	7.00
□ 159	Jimmy Dykes	80.00	32.00	8.00
□ 160	Steve O'Neill	70.00	28.00	7.00
□ 161	General Crowder	70.00	28.00	7.00
□ 162	Joe Cascarella	70.00	28.00	7.00
□ 163	Daniel (Bud) Hafey	70.00	28.00	7.00
□ 164	Gilly Campbell	70.00	28.00	7.00
□ 165	Ray Hayworth	70.00	28.00	7.00
□ 166	Frank Demaree	70.00	28.00	7.00
□ 167	John Babich	70.00	28.00	7.00
□ 168	Marvin Owen	70.00	28.00	7.00
□ 169	Ralph Kress	70.00	28.00	7.00
□ 170	Mule Haas	70.00	28.00	7.00
□ 171	Frank Higgins	70.00	28.00	7.00
□ 172	Wally Berger	80.00	32.00	8.00
□ 173	Frank Frisch	175.00	70.00	18.00
□ 174	Wes Ferrell	80.00	32.00	8.00
□ 175	Pete Fox	70.00	28.00	7.00
□ 176	John Vergez	70.00	28.00	7.00
□ 177	Billy Rogell	70.00	28.00	7.00
□ 178	Don Brennan	70.00	28.00	7.00
□ 179	Jim Bottomley	150.00	60.00	15.00
□ 180	Travis Jackson	150.00	60.00	15.00
□ 181	Red Rolfe	90.00	36.00	9.00
□ 182	Frank Crosetti	100.00	40.00	10.00
□ 183	Joe Cronin	150.00	60.00	15.00
□ 184	Schoolboy Rowe	90.00	36.00	9.00
□ 185	Chuck Klein	175.00	70.00	18.00
□ 186	Lon Warneke	70.00	28.00	7.00
□ 187	Gus Suhr	70.00	28.00	7.00
□ 188	Ben Chapman	80.00	32.00	8.00
□ 189	Clint Brown	70.00	28.00	7.00
□ 190	Paul Derringer	90.00	36.00	9.00
□ 191	John Burns	70.00	28.00	7.00
□ 192	John Broaca	100.00	35.00	7.00

1988 Bazooka

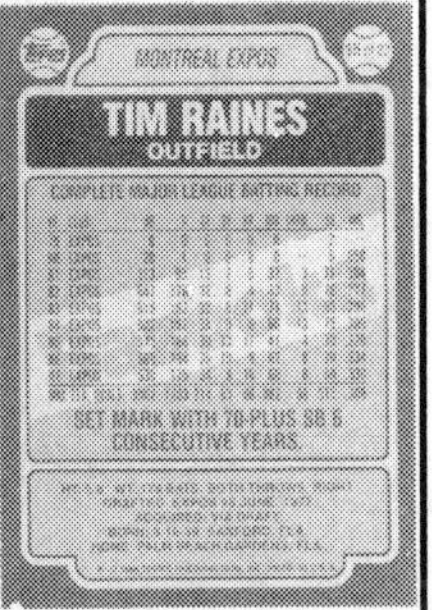

There are 22 cards in the set; cards are standard size, 2 1/2" by 3 1/2". The cards have extra thick white borders. Card backs are printed in blue and red on white card stock. Cards are numbered on the back; they were numbered by Topps alphabetically. The word "Bazooka" only appears faintly as background for the statistics on the back of the card. Cards were available inside specially marked boxes of Bazooka gum retailing for form 59 cents to 99 cents. The emphasis in the player selection for this set is on the emerging young stars of baseball.

		MINT	EXC	G-VG
COMPLETE SET (22)		10.00	4.00	1.00
COMMON PLAYER (1-22)		.30	.12	.03
□ 1	George Bell	.40	.16	.04
□ 2	Wade Boggs	1.00	.40	.10
□ 3	Jose Canseco	2.00	.80	.20
□ 4	Roger Clemens	.90	.36	.09
□ 5	Vince Coleman	.50	.20	.05
□ 6	Eric Davis	.90	.36	.09
□ 7	Tony Fernandez	.30	.12	.03
□ 8	Dwight Gooden	.75	.30	.07
□ 9	Tony Gwynn	.60	.24	.06
□ 10	Wally Joyner	.60	.24	.06
□ 11	Don Mattingly	1.50	.60	.15
□ 12	Willie McGee	.30	.12	.03
□ 13	Mark McGwire	1.00	.40	.10
□ 14	Kirby Puckett	.75	.30	.07
□ 15	Tim Raines	.40	.16	.04
□ 16	Dave Righetti	.30	.12	.03
□ 17	Cal Ripken	.50	.20	.05
□ 18	Juan Samuel	.30	.12	.03
□ 19	Ryne Sandberg	.40	.16	.04
□ 20	Benny Santiago	.40	.16	.04
□ 21	Darryl Strawberry	1.00	.40	.10
□ 22	Todd Worrell	.30	.12	.03

1958 Bell Brand

The 1958 Bell Brand Potato Chips set of 10 unnumbered cards features members of the Los Angeles Dodgers exclusively. Each card has a 1/4" dark green border, and the Gino Cimoli, Johnny Podres, and Duke Snider cards are more difficult to find; they are marked with an SP (short printed) in the checklist below. The cards measure 3" by 4". This set marks the first year for the Dodgers in Los Angeles and includes a Campanella card despite the fact that he never played for the team in California. The ACC designation is F339-1.

		NRMT	VG-E	GOOD
COMPLETE SET (10)		850.00	340.00	85.00
COMMON PLAYER (1-10)		35.00	14.00	3.50
□ 1	Roy Campanella	100.00	40.00	10.00
□ 2	Gino Cimoli SP	125.00	50.00	12.50
□ 3	Don Drysdale	70.00	28.00	7.00
□ 4	Jim Gilliam	40.00	16.00	4.00
□ 5	Gil Hodges	60.00	24.00	6.00
□ 6	Sandy Koufax	90.00	36.00	9.00
□ 7	Johnny Podres SP	135.00	54.00	13.50
□ 8	Pee Wee Reese	70.00	28.00	7.00
□ 9	Duke Snider SP	225.00	90.00	22.00
□ 10	Don Zimmer	35.00	14.00	3.50

1960 Bell Brand

The 1960 Bell Brand Potato Chips set of 20 full color, numbered cards features Los Angeles Dodgers only. Because these cards, measuring 2 1/2" by 3 1/2", were issued in packages of potato chips, many cards suffered from stains. Clem Labine, Johnny Klippstein, and Walter Alston are somewhat more difficult to obtain than other cards in the set; they are marked with SP (short printed) in the checklist below. The ACC designation for this set is F339-2.

		NRMT	VG-E	GOOD
COMPLETE SET (20)		550.00	220.00	65.00
COMMON PLAYER (1-20)		15.00	6.00	1.50
□ 1	Norm Larker	15.00	6.00	1.50
□ 2	Duke Snider	50.00	20.00	5.00
□ 3	Danny McDevitt	15.00	6.00	1.50
□ 4	Jim Gilliam	20.00	8.00	2.00

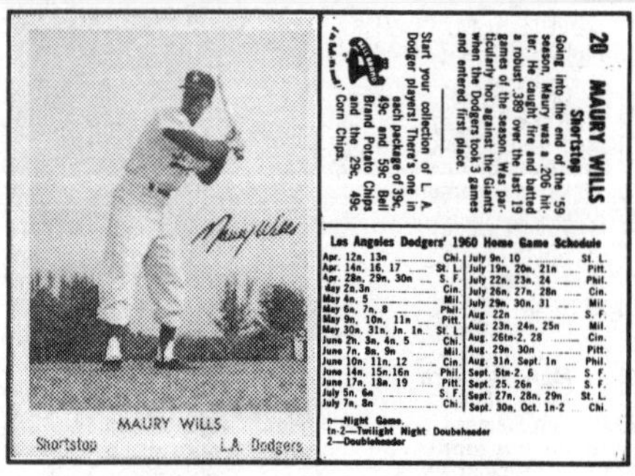

□ 5 Rip Repulski	15.00	6.00	1.50
□ 6 Clem Labine SP	80.00	32.00	8.00
□ 7 John Roseboro	15.00	6.00	1.50
□ 8 Carl Furillo	20.00	8.00	2.00
□ 9 Sandy Koufax	60.00	24.00	6.00
□ 10 Joe Pignatano	15.00	6.00	1.50
□ 11 Chuck Essegian	15.00	6.00	1.50
□ 12 John Klippstein SP	90.00	36.00	9.00
□ 13 Ed Roebuck	15.00	6.00	1.50
□ 14 Don Demeter	15.00	6.00	1.50
□ 15 Roger Craig	20.00	8.00	2.00
□ 16 Stan Williams	15.00	6.00	1.50
□ 17 Don Zimmer	15.00	6.00	1.50
□ 18 Walt Alston SP	100.00	40.00	10.00
□ 19 Johnny Podres	20.00	8.00	2.00
□ 20 Maury Wills	30.00	12.00	3.00

1961 Bell Brand

The 1961 Bell Brand Potato Chips set of 20 full color cards features Los Angeles Dodger players only and is numbered by the uniform numbers of the players. The cards are slightly smaller (2 7/16" by 3 1/2") than the 1960 Bell Brand cards and are on thinner paper stock. The ACC designation is F339-3.

	NRMT	VG-E	GOOD
COMPLETE SET (20)	300.00	130.00	32.00
COMMON PLAYER (1-51)	10.00	4.00	1.00
□ 3 Willie Davis	12.00	5.00	1.20
□ 4 Duke Snider	40.00	16.00	4.00
□ 5 Norm Larker	10.00	4.00	1.00
□ 8 John Roseboro	10.00	4.00	1.00
□ 9 Wally Moon	10.00	4.00	1.00
□ 11 Bob Lillis	10.00	4.00	1.00
□ 12 Tom Davis	12.00	5.00	1.20
□ 14 Gil Hodges	20.00	8.00	2.00
□ 16 Don Demeter	10.00	4.00	1.00
□ 19 Jim Gilliam	12.00	5.00	1.20
□ 22 John Podres	12.00	5.00	1.20
□ 24 Walt Alston MG	20.00	8.00	2.00
□ 30 Maury Wills	20.00	8.00	2.00
□ 32 Sandy Koufax	50.00	20.00	5.00
□ 34 Norm Sherry	10.00	4.00	1.00
□ 37 Ed Roebuck	10.00	4.00	1.00
□ 38 Roger Craig	15.00	6.00	1.50
□ 40 Stan Williams	10.00	4.00	1.00
□ 43 Charlie Neal	10.00	4.00	1.00
□ 51 Larry Sherry	10.00	4.00	1.00

1962 Bell Brand

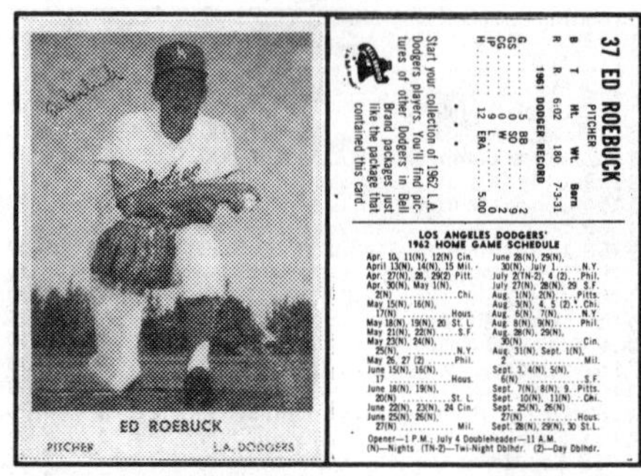

The 1962 Bell Brand Potato Chips set of 20 full color cards features Los Angeles Dodger players only and is numbered by the uniform numbers of the players. These cards were printed on a high quality glossy paper, much better than the previous two years, virtually eliminating the grease stains. This set is distinguished by a 1962 Home schedule on the backs of the cards. The cards measure 2 7/16" by 3 1/2", the same size as the year before. The ACC designation is F339-4.

	NRMT	VG-E	GOOD
COMPLETE SET (20)	250.00	100.00	25.00
COMMON PLAYER (1-56)	10.00	4.00	1.00
□ 3 Willie Davis	12.00	5.00	1.20
□ 4 Duke Snider	40.00	16.00	4.00
□ 6 Ron Fairly	10.00	4.00	1.00
□ 8 John Roseboro	10.00	4.00	1.00
□ 9 Wally Moon	10.00	4.00	1.00
□ 12 Tom Davis	12.00	5.00	1.20
□ 16 Ron Perranoski	10.00	4.00	1.00
□ 19 Jim Gilliam	12.00	5.00	1.20
□ 20 Daryl Spencer	10.00	4.00	1.00
□ 22 John Podres	12.00	5.00	1.20
□ 24 Walt Alston MG	20.00	8.00	2.00
□ 25 Frank Howard	12.00	5.00	1.20
□ 30 Maury Wills	20.00	8.00	2.00
□ 32 Sandy Koufax	50.00	20.00	5.00
□ 34 Norm Sherry	10.00	4.00	1.00
□ 37 Ed Roebuck	10.00	4.00	1.00
□ 40 Stan Williams	10.00	4.00	1.00
□ 51 Larry Sherry	10.00	4.00	1.00
□ 53 Don Drysdale	25.00	10.00	2.50
□ 56 Lee Walls	10.00	4.00	1.00

1951 Berk Ross

The 1951 Berk Ross set consists of 72 cards (each measuring 2 1/16" by 2 1/2") with tinted photographs, divided evenly into four series (designated in the checklist as A, B, C and D). The cards were marketed in boxes containing two card panels, without gum, and the set includes stars of other sports as well as baseball players. Intact panels are worth 20% more than the sum of the individual cards. The ACC designation is W532-1. In every series the first ten cards are baseball players; the set has a heavy emphasis on Yankees and Phillies players as they were in the World Series the year before.

	NRMT	VG-E	GOOD
COMPLETE SET (72)	450.00	180.00	65.00
COMMON BASEBALL	5.00	2.00	.50

HIT PARADE OF CHAMPIONS
1951
Trade Mark Reg. U.S. Pat. Off.
RICHIE ASHBURN
Outfield, Philadelphia Phillies
Member of Philadelphia Phillies
National League Champions
Born March 19, 1927
Tilden, Nebraska
Height 5-11, Weight 170
Throws Right, Bats Left
1950 Hit .303 in 151 Games
No. 1-9 © Berk Ross Inc., New York, N.Y.

COMMON FOOTBALL	5.00	2.00	.50
COMMON OTHERS	3.00	1.20	.30
□ A1 Al Rosen	7.50	3.00	.75
□ A2 Bob Lemon	11.00	4.50	1.10
□ A3 Phil Rizzuto	13.50	6.00	1.50
□ A4 Hank Bauer	7.00	2.80	.70
□ A5 Billy Johnson	5.00	2.00	.50
□ A6 Jerry Coleman	5.00	2.00	.50
□ A7 Johnny Mize	12.00	5.00	1.20
□ A8 Dom DiMaggio	7.50	3.00	.75
□ A9 Richie Ashburn	10.00	4.00	1.00
□ A10 Del Ennis	5.00	2.00	.50
□ A11 Bob Cousy	6.50	2.60	.65
□ A12 Dick Schnittker	3.00	1.20	.30
□ A13 Ezzard Charles	3.50	1.40	.35
□ A14 Leon Hart	5.00	2.00	.50
□ A15 James Martin	5.00	2.00	.50
□ A16 Ben Hogan	4.00	1.60	.40
□ A17 Bill Durnan	4.00	1.60	.40
□ A18 Bill Quackenbush	3.00	1.20	.30
□ B1 Stan Musial	45.00	18.00	4.50
□ B2 Warren Spahn	13.50	6.00	1.50
□ B3 Tom Henrich	6.50	2.60	.65
□ B4 Yogi Berra	25.00	10.00	2.50
□ B5 Joe DiMaggio	75.00	30.00	7.50
□ B6 Bobby Brown	7.00	2.80	.70
□ B7 Granny Hamner	5.00	2.00	.50
□ B8 Willie Jones	5.00	2.00	.50
□ B9 Stan Lopata	5.00	2.00	.50
□ B10 Mike Goliat	5.00	2.00	.50
□ B11 Sherman White	5.00	2.00	.50
□ B12 Joe Maxim	3.00	1.20	.30
□ B13 Ray Robinson	5.00	2.00	.50
□ B14 Doak Walker	7.50	3.00	.75
□ B15 Emil Sitko	3.00	1.20	.30
□ B16 Jack Stewart	3.00	1.20	.30
□ B17 Dick Button	4.00	1.60	.40
□ B18 Melvin Patton	3.00	1.20	.30
□ C1 Ralph Kiner	12.00	5.00	1.20
□ C2 Bill Goodman	5.00	2.00	.50
□ C3 Allie Reynolds	7.50	3.00	.75
□ C4 Vic Raschi	7.00	2.80	.70
□ C5 Joe Page	6.00	2.40	.60
□ C6 Eddie Lopat	7.50	3.00	.75
□ C7 Andy Seminick	5.00	2.00	.50
□ C8 Dick Sisler	5.00	2.00	.50
□ C9 Eddie Waitkus	5.00	2.00	.50
□ C10 Ken Heintzelman	5.00	2.00	.50
□ C11 Paul Unruh	3.00	1.20	.30
□ C12 Jake LaMotta	5.00	2.00	.50
□ C13 Ike Williams	3.00	1.20	.30
□ C14 Wade Walker	3.00	1.20	.30
□ C15 Rodney Franz	3.00	1.20	.30
□ C16 Sid Abel	4.00	1.60	.40
□ C17 Claire Sherman	3.00	1.20	.30
□ C18 Jesse Owens	5.00	2.00	.50
□ D1 Gene Woodling	6.50	2.60	.65
□ D2 Cliff Mapes	5.00	2.00	.50
□ D3 Fred Sontort	5.00	2.00	.50
□ D4 Tommy Byrne	5.00	2.00	.50
□ D5 Whitey Ford	15.00	6.00	1.50
□ D6 Jim Konstanty	5.00	2.00	.50
□ D7 Russ Meyer	5.00	2.00	.50
□ D8 Robin Roberts	11.00	4.50	1.10
□ D9 Curt Simmons	6.00	2.40	.60
□ D10 Sam Jethroe	5.00	2.00	.50
□ D11 Bill Sharman	4.00	1.60	.40
□ D12 Sandy Saddler	3.00	1.20	.30
□ D13 Margaret DuPont	3.00	1.20	.30
□ D14 Arnold Galiffa	5.00	2.00	.50
□ D15 Charlie Justice	6.00	2.40	.60
□ D16 Glen Cunningham	3.00	1.20	.30
□ D17 Gregory Rice	3.00	1.20	.30
□ D18 Harrison Dillard	3.00	1.20	.30

1952 Berk Ross

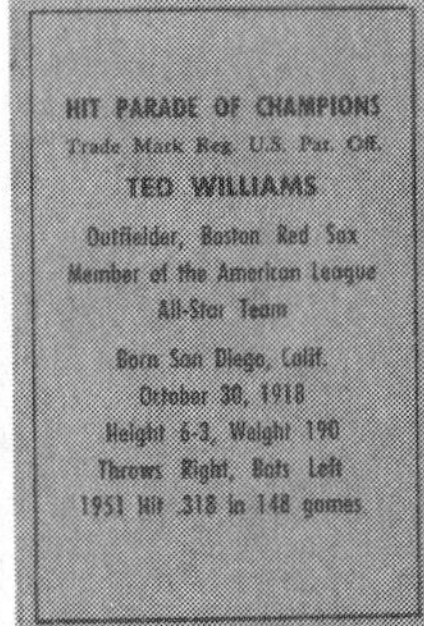

The 1952 Berk Ross set of 72 unnumbered, tinted photocards, each measuring 2" by 3", seems to have been patterned after the highly successful 1951 Bowman set. The reverses of Ewell Blackwell and Nellie Fox are transposed while Phil Rizzuto comes with two different poses. There is a card of Joe DiMaggio even though he retired after the 1951 season. The ACC designation for this set is W532-2, and the cards have been assigned numbers in the alphabetical checklist below.

	NRMT	VG-E	GOOD
COMPLETE SET (72)	2750.00	1250.00	450.00
COMMON PLAYER (1-71)	9.00	3.75	.90
□ 1 Richie Ashburn	20.00	8.00	2.00
□ 2 Hank Bauer	14.00	5.75	1.40
□ 3 Yogi Berra	80.00	32.00	8.00
□ 4 Ewell Blackwell (photo actually Nellie Fox)	14.00	5.75	1.40
□ 5 Bobby Brown	14.00	5.75	1.40
□ 6 Jim Busby	9.00	3.75	.90
□ 7 Roy Campanella	100.00	40.00	10.00
□ 8 Chico Carrasquel	9.00	3.75	.90
□ 9 Jerry Coleman	10.00	4.00	1.00
□ 10 Joe Collins	9.00	3.75	.90
□ 11 Alvin Dark	12.00	5.00	1.20
□ 12 Dom DiMaggio	14.00	5.75	1.40
□ 13 Joe DiMaggio	500.00	200.00	50.00
□ 14 Larry Doby	14.00	5.75	1.40
□ 15 Bobby Doerr	25.00	10.00	2.50
□ 16 Bob Elliott	10.00	4.00	1.00
□ 17 Del Ennis	9.00	3.75	.90
□ 18 Ferris Fain	9.00	3.75	.90
□ 19 Bob Feller	60.00	24.00	6.00
□ 20 Nellie Fox (photo actually Ewell Blackwell)	14.00	5.75	1.40
□ 21 Ned Garver	9.00	3.75	.90
□ 22 Clint Hartung	9.00	3.75	.90
□ 23 Jim Hearn	9.00	3.75	.90
□ 24 Gil Hodges	35.00	14.00	3.50
□ 25 Monte Irvin	25.00	10.00	2.50
□ 26 Larry Jansen	9.00	3.75	.90
□ 27 Sheldon Jones	9.00	3.75	.90
□ 28 George Kell	25.00	10.00	2.50
□ 29 Monte Kennedy	9.00	3.75	.90
□ 30 Ralph Kiner	30.00	12.00	3.00
□ 31 Dave Koslo	9.00	3.75	.90
□ 32 Bob Kuzava	9.00	3.75	.90
□ 33 Bob Lemon	25.00	10.00	2.50
□ 34 Whitey Lockman	9.00	3.75	.90
□ 35 Ed Lopat	15.00	6.00	1.50
□ 36 Sal Maglie	12.00	5.00	1.20
□ 37 Mickey Mantle	800.00	320.00	80.00
□ 38 Billy Martin	25.00	10.00	2.50
□ 39 Willie Mays	250.00	100.00	25.00
□ 40 Gil McDougald	14.00	5.75	1.40
□ 41 Minnie Minoso	14.00	5.75	1.40
□ 42 Johnny Mize	30.00	12.00	3.00
□ 43 Tom Morgan	9.00	3.75	.90
□ 44 Don Mueller	10.00	4.00	1.00
□ 45 Stan Musial	150.00	60.00	15.00

□ 46 Don Newcombe	15.00	6.00	1.50
□ 47 Ray Noble	9.00	3.75	.90
□ 48 Joe Ostrowski	9.00	3.75	.90
□ 49 Mel Parnell	10.00	4.00	1.00
□ 50 Vic Raschi	14.00	5.75	1.40
□ 51 Pee Wee Reese	45.00	18.00	4.50
□ 52 Allie Reynolds	16.00	6.50	1.60
□ 53 Bill Rigney	9.00	3.75	.90
□ 54A Phil Rizzuto (bunting)	40.00	16.00	4.00
□ 54B Phil Rizzuto (swinging)	40.00	16.00	4.00
□ 55 Robin Roberts	25.00	10.00	2.50
□ 56 Eddie Robinson	9.00	3.75	.90
□ 57 Jackie Robinson	150.00	60.00	15.00
□ 58 Preacher Roe	14.00	5.75	1.40
□ 59 Johnny Sain	14.00	5.75	1.40
□ 60 Red Schoendienst	12.00	5.00	1.20
□ 61 Duke Snider	100.00	40.00	10.00
□ 62 George Spencer	9.00	3.75	.90
□ 63 Eddie Stanky	10.00	4.00	1.00
□ 64 Hank Thompson	9.00	3.75	.90
□ 65 Bobby Thomson	14.00	5.75	1.40
□ 66 Vic Wertz	9.00	3.75	.90
□ 67 Wally Westlake	9.00	3.75	.90
□ 68 Wes Westrum	9.00	3.75	.90
□ 69 Ted Williams	250.00	100.00	25.00
□ 70 Gene Woodling	10.00	4.00	1.00
□ 71 Gus Zernial	9.00	3.75	.90

1986 Big League Chew

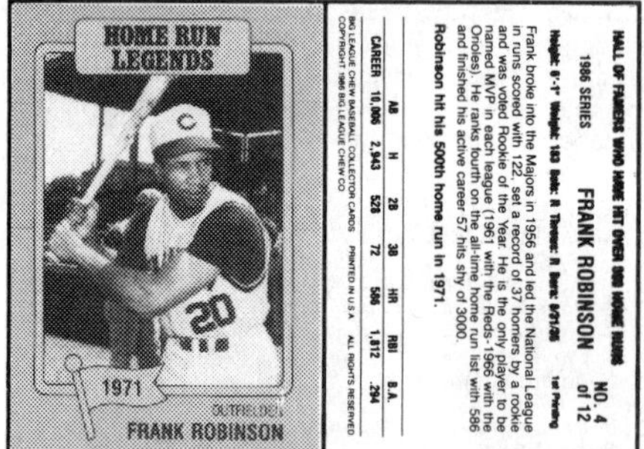

This 12-card set was produced by Big League Chew and was inserted in with their packages of chewing gum, which were shaped and styled after a pouch of chewing tobacco. The cards were found one per pouch of shredded chewing gum or were available through a mail-in offer of two coupons and 2.00 for a complete set. The players featured are members of the 500 career home run club. The backs are printed in blue ink on white card stock. The cards are standard size, 2 1/2" by 3 1/2" and are subtitled "Home Run Legends." The front of each card shows a year inside a small flag; the year is the year that player passed 500 homers.

	MINT	EXC	G-VG
COMPLETE SET (12)	4.50	1.80	.45
COMMON PLAYER (1-12)	.30	.12	.03
□ 1 Hank Aaron	.50	.20	.05
□ 2 Babe Ruth	.90	.36	.09
□ 3 Willie Mays	.50	.20	.05
□ 4 Frank Robinson	.30	.12	.03
□ 5 Harmon Killebrew	.30	.12	.03
□ 6 Mickey Mantle	1.00	.40	.10
□ 7 Jimmie Foxx	.30	.12	.03
□ 8 Ted Williams	.50	.20	.05
□ 9 Ernie Banks	.40	.16	.04
□ 10 Eddie Mathews	.30	.12	.03
□ 11 Mel Ott	.30	.12	.03
□ 12 500 HR Members	.30	.12	.03

1987 Boardwalk and Baseball

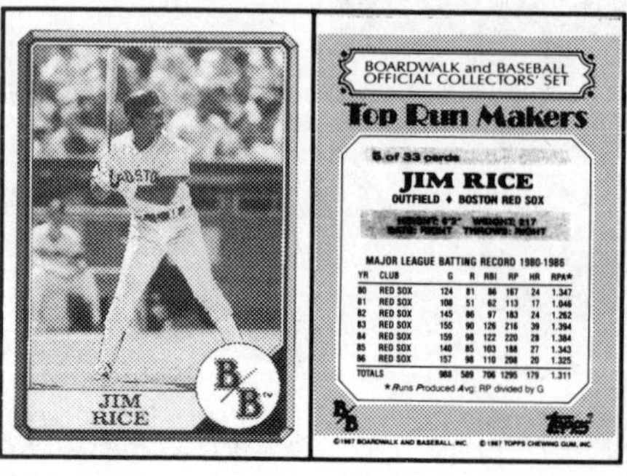

This 33-card set was produced by Topps for distribution by the new "Boardwalk and Baseball" Theme Park located near Orlando, Florida. The cards are standard size, 2 1/2" by 3 1/2", and come in a custom blue collector box. The full-color fronts are surrounded by a pink and black frame border. The card backs are printed in pink and black on white card stock. The set is subtitled "Top Run Makers." Hence no pitchers are included in the set. The checklist for the set is given on the back panel of the box.

	MINT	EXC	G-VG
COMPLETE SET (33)	5.00	2.00	.50
COMMON PLAYER (1-33)	.10	.04	.01
□ 1 Mike Schmidt	.40	.16	.04
□ 2 Eddie Murray	.30	.12	.03
□ 3 Dale Murphy	.35	.14	.03
□ 4 Dave Winfield	.25	.10	.02
□ 5 Jim Rice	.20	.08	.02
□ 6 Cecil Cooper	.10	.04	.01
□ 7 Dwight Evans	.15	.06	.01
□ 8 Rickey Henderson	.30	.12	.03
□ 9 Robin Yount	.25	.10	.02
□ 10 Andre Dawson	.20	.08	.02
□ 11 Gary Carter	.25	.10	.02
□ 12 Keith Hernandez	.20	.08	.02
□ 13 George Brett	.35	.14	.03
□ 14 Bill Buckner	.10	.04	.01
□ 15 Tony Armas	.10	.04	.01
□ 16 Harold Baines	.10	.04	.01
□ 17 Don Baylor	.10	.04	.01
□ 18 Steve Garvey	.25	.10	.02
□ 19 Lance Parrish	.15	.06	.01
□ 20 Dave Parker	.10	.04	.01
□ 21 Buddy Bell	.10	.04	.01
□ 22 Cal Ripken	.30	.12	.03
□ 23 Bob Horner	.10	.04	.01
□ 24 Tim Raines	.25	.10	.02
□ 25 Jack Clark	.20	.08	.02
□ 26 Leon Durham	.10	.04	.01
□ 27 Pedro Guerrero	.15	.06	.01
□ 28 Kent Hrbek	.20	.08	.02
□ 29 Kirk Gibson	.30	.12	.03
□ 30 Ryne Sandberg	.25	.10	.02
□ 31 Wade Boggs	.60	.24	.06
□ 32 Don Mattingly	1.00	.40	.10
□ 33 Darryl Strawberry	.50	.20	.05

1987 Bohemian Padres

The Bohemian Hearth Bread Company issued this 22-card set of San Diego Padres. The cards measure 2 1/2" by 3 1/2" and feature a distinctive yellow border on the front of the cards. Card backs provide career year-by-year statistics.

	MINT	EXC	G-VG
COMPLETE SET (22)	35.00	14.00	3.50
COMMON PLAYER	.60	.24	.06

☐ 1 Garry Templeton	.75	.30	.07
☐ 4 Joe Cora	.75	.30	.07
☐ 5 Randy Ready	.75	.30	.07
☐ 6 Steve Garvey	4.00	1.60	.40
☐ 7 Kevin Mitchell	1.00	.40	.10
☐ 8 John Kruk	2.00	.80	.20
☐ 9 Benito Santiago	5.00	2.00	.50
☐ 10 Larry Bowa MG	1.00	.40	.10
☐ 11 Tim Flannery	.60	.24	.06
☐ 14 Carmelo Martinez	1.00	.40	.10
☐ 16 Marvell Wynne	.60	.24	.06
☐ 19 Tony Gwynn	10.00	4.00	1.00
☐ 21 James Steels	.60	.24	.06
☐ 22 Stan Jefferson	1.00	.40	.10
☐ 30 Eric Show	1.00	.40	.10
☐ 31 Ed Whitson	.75	.30	.07
☐ 34 Storm Davis	1.00	.40	.10
☐ 37 Craig Lefferts	.60	.24	.06
☐ 40 Andy Hawkins	.75	.30	.07
☐ 41 Lance McCullers	1.00	.40	.10
☐ 43 Dave Dravecky	1.00	.40	.10
☐ 54 Rich Gossage	2.00	.80	.20

1947 Bond Bread

The 1947 Bond Bread Jackie Robinson set features 13 unnumbered cards of Jackie in different action or portrait poses; each card measures 2 1/4" by 3 1/2". Card number 7, which is the only card in the set to contain a facsimile autograph, was apparently issued in greater quantity than other cards in the set. Several of the cards have a horizontal format; these are marked in the checklist below by HOR. The ACC designation is D302.

	NRMT	VG-E	GOOD
COMPLETE SET	3600.00	1600.00	400.00
COMMON PLAYER (1-13)	300.00	120.00	30.00

☐ 1 Sliding into base, cap, ump in photo, HOR	300.00	120.00	30.00
☐ 2 Running down 3rd base line	300.00	120.00	30.00
☐ 3 Batting, bat behind head, facing camera	300.00	120.00	30.00
☐ 4 Moving towards second, throw almost to glove, HOR	300.00	120.00	30.00
☐ 5 Taking throw at first, HOR	300.00	120.00	30.00
☐ 6 Jumping high in the air for ball	300.00	120.00	30.00
☐ 7 Profile with glove in front of head; facsimile autograph)	200.00	80.00	20.00
☐ 8 Leaping over second base, ready to throw	300.00	120.00	30.00
☐ 9 Portrait, holding glove over head	300.00	120.00	30.00
☐ 10 Portrait, holding bat perpendicular to body	300.00	120.00	30.00
☐ 11 Reaching for throw, glove near ankle	300.00	120.00	30.00
☐ 12 Leaping for throw, no scoreboard in background	300.00	120.00	30.00
☐ 13 Portrait, holding bat parallel to body	300.00	120.00	30.00

1948 Bowman

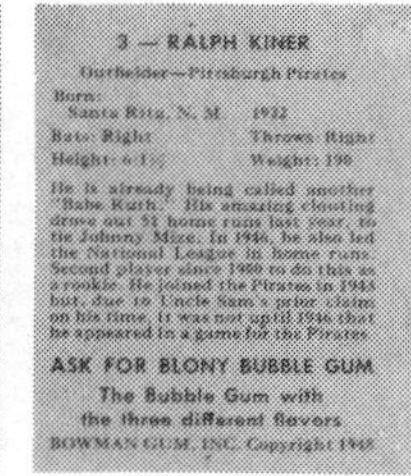

The 48-card Bowman set of 1948 was the first major set of the post-war period. Each 2 1/16" by 2 1/2" card had a black and white photo of a current player, with his biographical information printed in black ink on a gray back. Due to the printing process and the 36-card sheet size upon which Bowman was then printing, the 12 cards marked with an SP in the checklist are scarcer numerically, as they were removed from the printing sheet in order to make room for the 12 high numbers (37-48). Many cards are found with over-printed, transposed, or blank backs.

	NRMT	VG-E	GOOD
COMPLETE SET	1700.00	750.00	275.00
COMMON PLAYER (1-36)	12.00	5.00	1.20
COMMON PLAYER (37-48)	20.00	8.00	2.00
COMMON PLAYER SP	30.00	12.00	3.00

☐ 1 Bob Elliott	60.00	8.00	1.50
☐ 2 Ewell Blackwell	22.00	9.00	2.20
☐ 3 Ralph Kiner	70.00	28.00	7.00
☐ 4 Johnny Mize	50.00	20.00	5.00
☐ 5 Bob Feller	80.00	32.00	8.00
☐ 6 Yogi Berra	325.00	130.00	32.00
☐ 7 Peter Reiser SP	36.00	15.00	3.60
☐ 8 Phil Rizzuto SP	135.00	54.00	13.50
☐ 9 Walker Cooper	12.00	5.00	1.20
☐ 10 Buddy Rosar	12.00	5.00	1.20
☐ 11 Johnny Lindell	12.00	5.00	1.20

□ 12 Johnny Sain	27.00	11.00	2.70
□ 13 Willard Marshall SP	30.00	12.00	3.00
□ 14 Allie Reynolds	32.00	13.00	3.20
□ 15 Eddie Joost	12.00	5.00	1.20
□ 16 Jack Lohrke SP	30.00	12.00	3.00
□ 17 Enos Slaughter	50.00	20.00	5.00
□ 18 Warren Spahn	110.00	45.00	11.00
□ 19 Tommy Henrich	20.00	8.00	2.00
□ 20 Buddy Kerr SP	30.00	12.00	3.00
□ 21 Ferris Fain	15.00	6.00	1.50
□ 22 Floyd Bevens SP	30.00	12.00	3.00
□ 23 Larry Jansen	12.00	5.00	1.20
□ 24 Dutch Leonard SP	30.00	12.00	3.00
□ 25 Barney McCosky	12.00	5.00	1.20
□ 26 Frank Shea SP	30.00	12.00	3.00
□ 27 Sid Gordon	12.00	5.00	1.20
□ 28 Emil Verban SP	30.00	12.00	3.00
□ 29 Joe Page SP	35.00	14.00	3.50
□ 30 Whitey Lockman SP	35.00	14.00	3.50
□ 31 Bill McCahan	12.00	5.00	1.20
□ 32 Bill Rigney	12.00	5.00	1.20
□ 33 Bill Johnson	12.00	5.00	1.20
□ 34 Sheldon Jones SP	30.00	12.00	3.00
□ 35 Snuffy Stirnweiss	15.00	6.00	1.50
□ 36 Stan Musial	425.00	170.00	42.00
□ 37 Clint Hartung	20.00	8.00	2.00
□ 38 Red Schoendienst	45.00	18.00	4.50
□ 39 Augie Galan	20.00	8.00	2.00
□ 40 Marty Marion	45.00	18.00	4.50
□ 41 Rex Barney	20.00	8.00	2.00
□ 42 Ray Poat	20.00	8.00	2.00
□ 43 Bruce Edwards	20.00	8.00	2.00
□ 44 Johnny Wyrostek	20.00	8.00	2.00
□ 45 Hank Sauer	30.00	12.00	3.00
□ 46 Herman Wehmeier	20.00	8.00	2.00
□ 47 Bobby Thomson	45.00	18.00	4.50
□ 48 Dave Koslo	45.00	12.00	2.50

1949 Bowman

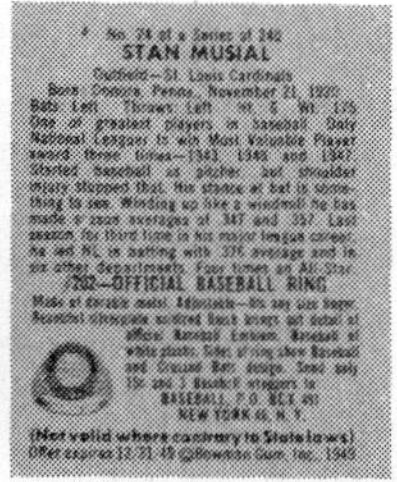

The cards in this 240-card set measure 2 1/16" by 2 1/2". In 1949 Bowman took an intermediate step between black and white and full color with this set of tinted photos on colored backgrounds. Collectors should note the series price variations which reflect some inconsistencies in the printing process. There are four major varieties in name printing which are noted in the checklist below: NOF: name on front; NNOF: no name on front; PR: printed name on back; and SCR: script name on back. These variations resulted when Bowman used twelve of the lower numbers to fill out the last press sheet of 36 cards adding to numbers 217-240. Cards 1-3 and 5-73 can be found with either gray or white backs.

	NRMT	VG-E	GOOD
COMPLETE SET	11500.00	5000.00	2000.00
COMMON CARD 1-3/5-36/73	12.50	5.00	1.25
COMMON CARD (37-72)	13.50	6.00	1.50
COMMON CARD (4/74-108)	11.00	4.50	1.10
COMMON CARD (109-144)	10.00	4.00	1.00
COMMON CARD (145-180)	75.00	30.00	7.50
COMMON CARD (181-216)	70.00	28.00	7.00
COMMON CARD (217-240)	70.00	28.00	7.00
□ 1 Vern Bickford	50.00	9.00	2.00
□ 2 Whitey Lockman	12.50	5.00	1.25
□ 3 Bob Porterfield	12.50	5.00	1.25
□ 4A Jerry Priddy NNOF	11.00	4.50	1.10
□ 4B Jerry Priddy NOF	35.00	14.00	3.50
□ 5 Hank Sauer	15.00	6.00	1.50
□ 6 Phil Cavarretta	15.00	6.00	1.50
□ 7 Joe Dobson	12.50	5.00	1.25
□ 8 Murray Dickson	12.50	5.00	1.25
□ 9 Ferris Fain	15.00	6.00	1.50
□ 10 Ted Gray	12.50	5.00	1.25
□ 11 Lou Boudreau	36.00	15.00	3.60
□ 12 Cass Michaels	12.50	5.00	1.25
□ 13 Bob Chesnes	12.50	5.00	1.25
□ 14 Curt Simmons	20.00	8.00	2.00
□ 15 Ned Garver	12.50	5.00	1.25
□ 16 Al Kozar	12.50	5.00	1.25
□ 17 Earl Torgeson	12.50	5.00	1.25
□ 18 Bobby Thomson	18.00	7.25	1.80
□ 19 Bobby Brown	25.00	10.00	2.50
□ 20 Gene Hermanski	12.50	5.00	1.25
□ 21 Frank Baumholtz	12.50	5.00	1.25
□ 22 Peanuts Lowrey	12.50	5.00	1.25
□ 23 Bobby Doerr	40.00	16.00	4.00
□ 24 Stan Musial	350.00	140.00	35.00
□ 25 Carl Scheib	12.50	5.00	1.25
□ 26 George Kell	40.00	16.00	4.00
□ 27 Bob Feller	85.00	34.00	8.50
□ 28 Don Kolloway	12.50	5.00	1.25
□ 29 Ralph Kiner	45.00	18.00	4.50
□ 30 Andy Seminick	12.50	5.00	1.25
□ 31 Dick Kokos	12.50	5.00	1.25
□ 32 Eddie Yost	12.50	5.00	1.25
□ 33 Warren Spahn	80.00	32.00	8.00
□ 34 Dave Koslo	12.50	5.00	1.25
□ 35 Vic Raschi	25.00	10.00	2.50
□ 36 Pee Wee Reese	100.00	40.00	10.00
□ 37 John Wyrostek	13.50	6.00	1.50
□ 38 Emil Verban	13.50	6.00	1.50
□ 39 Billy Goodman	15.00	6.00	1.50
□ 40 Red Munger	13.50	6.00	1.50
□ 41 Lou Brissie	13.50	6.00	1.50
□ 42 Hoot Evers	13.50	6.00	1.50
□ 43 Dale Mitchell	15.00	6.00	1.50
□ 44 Dave Philley	13.50	6.00	1.50
□ 45 Wally Westlake	13.50	6.00	1.50
□ 46 Robin Roberts	125.00	50.00	12.50
□ 47 Johnny Sain	20.00	8.00	2.00
□ 48 Willard Marshall	13.50	6.00	1.50
□ 49 Frank Shea	13.50	6.00	1.50
□ 50 Jackie Robinson	450.00	180.00	45.00
□ 51 Herman Wehmeier	13.50	6.00	1.50
□ 52 Johnny Schmitz	13.50	6.00	1.50
□ 53 Jack Kramer	13.50	6.00	1.50
□ 54 Marty Marion	18.00	7.25	1.80
□ 55 Eddie Joost	13.50	6.00	1.50
□ 56 Pat Mullin	13.50	6.00	1.50
□ 57 Gene Bearden	13.50	6.00	1.50
□ 58 Bob Elliott	15.00	6.00	1.50
□ 59 Jack Lohrke	13.50	6.00	1.50
□ 60 Yogi Berra	225.00	90.00	22.00
□ 61 Rex Barney	13.50	6.00	1.50
□ 62 Grady Hatton	13.50	6.00	1.50
□ 63 Andy Pafko	15.00	6.00	1.50
□ 64 Dom DiMaggio	20.00	8.00	2.00
□ 65 Enos Slaughter	45.00	18.00	4.50
□ 66 Elmer Valo	13.50	6.00	1.50
□ 67 Alvin Dark	18.00	7.25	1.80
□ 68 Sheldon Jones	13.50	6.00	1.50
□ 69 Tommy Henrich	18.00	7.25	1.80
□ 70 Carl Furillo	40.00	16.00	4.00
□ 71 Vern Stephens	15.00	6.00	1.50
□ 72 Tommy Holmes	15.00	6.00	1.50
□ 73 Billy Cox	18.00	7.25	1.80
□ 74 Tom McBride	11.00	4.50	1.10
□ 75 Eddie Mayo	11.00	4.50	1.10
□ 76 Bill Nicholson	11.00	4.50	1.10
□ 77 Ernie Bonham	11.00	4.50	1.10
□ 78A Sam Zoldak NNOF	11.00	4.50	1.10
□ 78B Sam Zoldak NOF	35.00	14.00	3.50
□ 79 Ron Northey	11.00	4.50	1.10
□ 80 Bill McCahan	11.00	4.50	1.10
□ 81 Virgil Stallcup	11.00	4.50	1.10
□ 82 Joe Page	18.00	7.25	1.80
□ 83A Bob Scheffing NNOF	11.00	4.50	1.10
□ 83B Bob Scheffing NOF	35.00	14.00	3.50
□ 84 Roy Campanella	400.00	160.00	40.00
□ 85A Johnny Mize NNOF	50.00	20.00	5.00
□ 85B Johnny Mize NOF	100.00	40.00	10.00
□ 86 Johnny Pesky	11.00	4.50	1.10
□ 87 Randy Gumpert	11.00	4.50	1.10
□ 88A Bill Salkeld NNOF	11.00	4.50	1.10
□ 88B Bill Salkeld NOF	35.00	14.00	3.50
□ 89 Mizell Platt	11.00	4.50	1.10
□ 90 Gil Coan	11.00	4.50	1.10
□ 91 Dick Wakefield	11.00	4.50	1.10
□ 92 Willie Jones	11.00	4.50	1.10
□ 93 Ed Stevens	11.00	4.50	1.10
□ 94 Mickey Vernon	20.00	8.00	2.00
□ 95 Howie Pollet	11.00	4.50	1.10
□ 96 Taft Wright	11.00	4.50	1.10

□ 97 Danny Litwhiler	11.00	4.50	1.10
□ 98A Phil Rizzuto NNOF	75.00	30.00	7.50
□ 98B Phil Rizzuto NOF	150.00	60.00	15.00
□ 99 Frank Gustine	11.00	4.50	1.10
□ 100 Gil Hodges	125.00	50.00	12.50
□ 101 Sid Gordon	11.00	4.50	1.10
□ 102 Stan Spence	11.00	4.50	1.10
□ 103 Joe Tipton	11.00	4.50	1.10
□ 104 Ed Stanky	16.00	6.50	1.60
□ 105 Bill Kennedy	11.00	4.50	1.10
□ 106 Jake Early	11.00	4.50	1.10
□ 107 Eddie Lake	11.00	4.50	1.10
□ 108 Ken Heintzelman	11.00	4.50	1.10
□ 109A Ed Fitzgerald SCR	10.00	4.00	1.00
□ 109B Ed Fitzgerald PR	30.00	12.00	3.00
□ 110 Early Wynn	80.00	32.00	8.00
□ 111 Red Schoendienst	20.00	8.00	2.00
□ 112 Sam Chapman	10.00	4.00	1.00
□ 113 Ray LaManno	10.00	4.00	1.00
□ 114 Allie Reynolds	24.00	10.00	2.40
□ 115 Dutch Leonard	10.00	4.00	1.00
□ 116 Joe Hatton	10.00	4.00	1.00
□ 117 Walker Cooper	10.00	4.00	1.00
□ 118 Sam Mele	10.00	4.00	1.00
□ 119 Floyd Baker	10.00	4.00	1.00
□ 120 Cliff Fannin	10.00	4.00	1.00
□ 121 Mark Christman	10.00	4.00	1.00
□ 122 George Vico	10.00	4.00	1.00
□ 123 Johnny Blatnick	10.00	4.00	1.00
□ 124A Danny Murtaugh SCR	10.00	4.00	1.00
□ 124B Danny Murtaugh PR	30.00	12.00	3.00
□ 125 Ken Keltner	10.00	4.00	1.00
□ 126A Al Brazle SCR	10.00	4.00	1.00
□ 126B Al Brazle PR	30.00	12.00	3.00
□ 127A Hank Majeski SCR	10.00	4.00	1.00
□ 127B Hank Majeski PR	30.00	12.00	3.00
□ 128 Johnny VanderMeer	16.00	6.50	1.60
□ 129 Bill Johnson	10.00	4.00	1.00
□ 130 Harry Walker	10.00	4.00	1.00
□ 131 Paul Lehner	10.00	4.00	1.00
□ 132A Al Evans SCR	10.00	4.00	1.00
□ 132B Al Evans PR	30.00	12.00	3.00
□ 133 Aaron Robinson	10.00	4.00	1.00
□ 134 Hank Borowy	10.00	4.00	1.00
□ 135 Stan Rojek	10.00	4.00	1.00
□ 136 Hank Edwards	10.00	4.00	1.00
□ 137 Ted Wilks	10.00	4.00	1.00
□ 138 Buddy Rosar	10.00	4.00	1.00
□ 139 Hank Arft	10.00	4.00	1.00
□ 140 Ray Scarborough	10.00	4.00	1.00
□ 141 Ulysses Lupien	10.00	4.00	1.00
□ 142 Eddie Waitkus	10.00	4.00	1.00
□ 143A Bob Dillinger SCR	10.00	4.00	1.00
□ 143B Bob Dillinger PR	30.00	12.00	3.00
□ 144 Mickey Haefner	10.00	4.00	1.00
□ 145 Sylvester Donnelly	75.00	30.00	7.50
□ 146 Mike McCormick	75.00	30.00	7.50
□ 147 Bert Singleton	75.00	30.00	7.50
□ 148 Bob Swift	75.00	30.00	7.50
□ 149 Roy Partee	75.00	30.00	7.50
□ 150 Allie Clark	75.00	30.00	7.50
□ 151 Mickey Harris	75.00	30.00	7.50
□ 152 Clarence Maddern	75.00	30.00	7.50
□ 153 Phil Masi	75.00	30.00	7.50
□ 154 Clint Hartung	75.00	30.00	7.50
□ 155 Mickey Guerra	75.00	30.00	7.50
□ 156 Al Zarilla	75.00	30.00	7.50
□ 157 Walt Masterson	75.00	30.00	7.50
□ 158 Harry Brecheen	75.00	30.00	7.50
□ 159 Glen Moulder	75.00	30.00	7.50
□ 160 Jim Blackburn	75.00	30.00	7.50
□ 161 Jocko Thompson	75.00	30.00	7.50
□ 162 Preacher Roe	75.00	30.00	7.50
□ 163 Clyde McCullough	75.00	30.00	7.50
□ 164 Vic Wertz	90.00	36.00	9.00
□ 165 Snuffy Stirnweiss	90.00	36.00	9.00
□ 166 Mike Tresh	75.00	30.00	7.50
□ 167 Babe Martin	75.00	30.00	7.50
□ 168 Doyle Lade	75.00	30.00	7.50
□ 169 Jeff Heath	75.00	30.00	7.50
□ 170 Bill Rigney	75.00	30.00	7.50
□ 171 Dick Fowler	75.00	30.00	7.50
□ 172 Eddie Pellagrini	75.00	30.00	7.50
□ 173 Eddie Stewart	75.00	30.00	7.50
□ 174 Terry Moore	100.00	40.00	10.00
□ 175 Luke Appling	110.00	45.00	11.00
□ 176 Ken Raffensberger	75.00	30.00	7.50
□ 177 Stan Lopata	75.00	30.00	7.50
□ 178 Tom Brown	75.00	30.00	7.50
□ 179 Hugh Casey	90.00	36.00	9.00
□ 180 Connie Berry	75.00	30.00	7.50
□ 181 Gus Niarhos	70.00	28.00	7.00
□ 182 Hall Peck	70.00	28.00	7.00
□ 183 Lou Stringer	70.00	28.00	7.00
□ 184 Bob Chipman	70.00	28.00	7.00
□ 185 Pete Reiser	90.00	36.00	9.00
□ 186 Buddy Kerr	70.00	28.00	7.00
□ 187 Phil Marchildon	70.00	28.00	7.00
□ 188 Karl Drews	70.00	28.00	7.00
□ 189 Earl Wooten	70.00	28.00	7.00
□ 190 Jim Hearn	70.00	28.00	7.00
□ 191 Joe Haynes	70.00	28.00	7.00
□ 192 Harry Gumbert	70.00	28.00	7.00
□ 193 Ken Trinkle	70.00	28.00	7.00
□ 194 Ralph Branca	100.00	40.00	10.00
□ 195 Eddie Bockman	70.00	28.00	7.00
□ 196 Fred Hutchinson	90.00	36.00	9.00
□ 197 Johnny Lindell	70.00	28.00	7.00
□ 198 Steve Gromek	70.00	28.00	7.00
□ 199 Tex Hughson	70.00	28.00	7.00
□ 200 Jess Dobernic	70.00	28.00	7.00
□ 201 Sibby Sisti	70.00	28.00	7.00
□ 202 Larry Jansen	70.00	28.00	7.00
□ 203 Barney McCosky	70.00	28.00	7.00
□ 204 Bob Savage	70.00	28.00	7.00
□ 205 Dick Sisler	70.00	28.00	7.00
□ 206 Bruce Edwards	70.00	28.00	7.00
□ 207 Johnny Hopp	80.00	32.00	8.00
□ 208 Dizzy Trout	80.00	32.00	8.00
□ 209 Charlie Keller	90.00	36.00	9.00
□ 210 Joe Gordon	90.00	36.00	9.00
□ 211 Boo Ferriss	70.00	28.00	7.00
□ 212 Ralph Hamner	70.00	28.00	7.00
□ 213 Red Barrett	70.00	28.00	7.00
□ 214 Richie Ashburn	375.00	150.00	37.00
□ 215 Kirby Higbe	70.00	28.00	7.00
□ 216 Schoolboy Rowe	80.00	32.00	8.00
□ 217 Marino Pieretti	70.00	28.00	7.00
□ 218 Dick Kryhoski	70.00	28.00	7.00
□ 219 Virgil "Fire" Trucks	80.00	32.00	8.00
□ 220 Johnny McCarthy	70.00	28.00	7.00
□ 221 Bob Muncrief	70.00	28.00	7.00
□ 222 Alex Kellner	70.00	28.00	7.00
□ 223 Bobby Hofman	70.00	28.00	7.00
□ 224 Satchell Paige	1000.00	400.00	100.00
□ 225 Gerry Coleman	90.00	36.00	9.00
□ 226 Duke Snider	800.00	320.00	80.00
□ 227 Fritz Ostermueller	70.00	28.00	7.00
□ 228 Jackie Mayo	70.00	28.00	7.00
□ 229 Ed Lopat	110.00	45.00	11.00
□ 230 Augie Galan	70.00	28.00	7.00
□ 231 Earl Johnson	70.00	28.00	7.00
□ 232 George McQuinn	70.00	28.00	7.00
□ 233 Larry Doby	110.00	45.00	11.00
□ 234 Rip Sewell	70.00	28.00	7.00
□ 235 Jim Russell	70.00	28.00	7.00
□ 236 Fred Sanford	70.00	28.00	7.00
□ 237 Monte Kennedy	70.00	28.00	7.00
□ 238 Bob Lemon	200.00	80.00	20.00
□ 239 Frank McCormick	80.00	32.00	8.00
□ 240 Babe Young (photo actually Bobby Young)	100.00	40.00	8.00

1950 Bowman

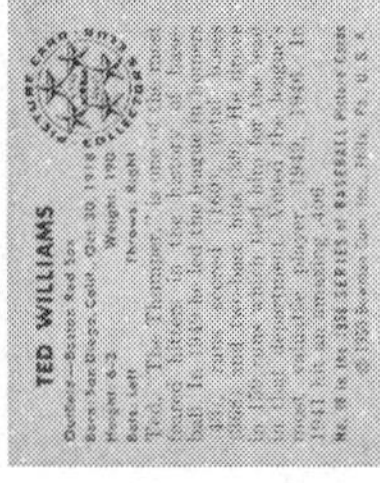

The cards in this 252-card set measure 2 1/16" by 2 1/2". This set, marketed in 1950 by Bowman, represented a major improvement in terms of quality over their previous efforts. Each card was a beautifully colored line drawing developed from a simple photograph. The first 72 cards are the scarcest in the set, while the final 72 cards may be found with or without the copyright line. This was the only Bowman sports set to carry the famous "5-Star" logo.

	NRMT	VG-E	GOOD
COMPLETE SET	6500.00	3000.00	900.00
COMMON PLAYER (1-72)	30.00	12.00	3.00
COMMON PLAYER (73-252)	12.00	5.00	1.20
☐ 1 Mel Parnell	200.00	20.00	4.00
☐ 2 Vern Stephens	32.00	13.00	3.20
☐ 3 Dom DiMaggio	40.00	16.00	4.00
☐ 4 Gus Zernial	35.00	14.00	3.50
☐ 5 Bob Kuzava	30.00	12.00	3.00
☐ 6 Bob Feller	100.00	40.00	10.00
☐ 7 Jim Hegan	32.00	13.00	3.20
☐ 8 George Kell	50.00	20.00	5.00
☐ 9 Vic Wertz	32.00	13.00	3.20
☐ 10 Tommy Henrich	35.00	14.00	3.50
☐ 11 Phil Rizzuto	80.00	32.00	8.00
☐ 12 Joe Page	35.00	14.00	3.50
☐ 13 Ferris Fain	32.00	13.00	3.20
☐ 14 Alex Kellner	30.00	12.00	3.00
☐ 15 Al Kozar	30.00	12.00	3.00
☐ 16 Roy Sievers	35.00	14.00	3.50
☐ 17 Sid Hudson	30.00	12.00	3.00
☐ 18 Eddie Robinson	30.00	12.00	3.00
☐ 19 Warren Spahn	90.00	36.00	9.00
☐ 20 Bob Elliott	32.00	13.00	3.20
☐ 21 Pee Wee Reese	100.00	40.00	10.00
☐ 22 Jackie Robinson	450.00	180.00	45.00
☐ 23 Don Newcombe	55.00	22.00	5.50
☐ 24 Johnny Schmitz	30.00	12.00	3.00
☐ 25 Hank Sauer	32.00	13.00	3.20
☐ 26 Grady Hatton	30.00	12.00	3.00
☐ 27 Herman Wehmeier	30.00	12.00	3.00
☐ 28 Bobby Thomson	35.00	14.00	3.50
☐ 29 Eddie Stanky	32.00	13.00	3.20
☐ 30 Eddie Waitkus	30.00	12.00	3.00
☐ 31 Del Ennis	32.00	13.00	3.20
☐ 32 Robin Roberts	65.00	26.00	6.50
☐ 33 Ralph Kiner	55.00	22.00	5.50
☐ 34 Murry Dickson	30.00	12.00	3.00
☐ 35 Enos Slaughter	50.00	20.00	5.00
☐ 36 Eddie Kazak	30.00	12.00	3.00
☐ 37 Luke Appling	45.00	18.00	4.50
☐ 38 Bill Wight	30.00	12.00	3.00
☐ 39 Larry Doby	40.00	16.00	4.00
☐ 40 Bob Lemon	50.00	20.00	5.00
☐ 41 Hoot Evers	30.00	12.00	3.00
☐ 42 Art Houtteman	30.00	12.00	3.00
☐ 43 Bobby Doerr	50.00	20.00	5.00
☐ 44 Joe Dobson	30.00	12.00	3.00
☐ 45 Al Zarilla	30.00	12.00	3.00
☐ 46 Yogi Berra	300.00	120.00	30.00
☐ 47 Jerry Coleman	35.00	14.00	3.50
☐ 48 Lou Brissie	30.00	12.00	3.00
☐ 49 Elmer Valo	30.00	12.00	3.00
☐ 50 Dick Kokos	30.00	12.00	3.00
☐ 51 Ned Garver	30.00	12.00	3.00
☐ 52 Sam Mele	30.00	12.00	3.00
☐ 53 Clyde Vollmer	30.00	12.00	3.00
☐ 54 Gil Coan	30.00	12.00	3.00
☐ 55 Buddy Kerr	30.00	12.00	3.00
☐ 56 Del Crandall	35.00	14.00	3.50
☐ 57 Vern Bickford	30.00	12.00	3.00
☐ 58 Carl Furillo	40.00	16.00	4.00
☐ 59 Ralph Branca	35.00	14.00	3.50
☐ 60 Andy Pafko	32.00	13.00	3.20
☐ 61 Bob Rush	30.00	12.00	3.00
☐ 62 Ted Kluszewski	40.00	16.00	4.00
☐ 63 Ewell Blackwell	35.00	14.00	3.50
☐ 64 Al Dark	35.00	14.00	3.50
☐ 65 Dave Koslo	30.00	12.00	3.00
☐ 66 Larry Jansen	30.00	12.00	3.00
☐ 67 Willie Jones	30.00	12.00	3.00
☐ 68 Curt Simmons	32.00	13.00	3.20
☐ 69 Wally Westlake	30.00	12.00	3.00
☐ 70 Bob Chesnes	30.00	12.00	3.00
☐ 71 Red Schoendienst	35.00	14.00	3.50
☐ 72 Howie Pollet	30.00	12.00	3.00
☐ 73 Willard Marshall	12.00	5.00	1.20
☐ 74 Johnny Antonelli	16.00	6.50	1.60
☐ 75 Roy Campanella	250.00	100.00	25.00
☐ 76 Rex Barney	12.00	5.00	1.20
☐ 77 Duke Snider	200.00	80.00	20.00
☐ 78 Mickey Owen	14.00	5.75	1.40
☐ 79 Johnny VanderMeer	16.00	6.50	1.60
☐ 80 Howard Fox	12.00	5.00	1.20
☐ 81 Ron Northey	12.00	5.00	1.20
☐ 82 Whitey Lockman	14.00	5.75	1.40
☐ 83 Sheldon Jones	12.00	5.00	1.20
☐ 84 Richie Ashburn	40.00	16.00	4.00
☐ 85 Ken Heintzelman	12.00	5.00	1.20
☐ 86 Stan Rojek	12.00	5.00	1.20
☐ 87 Bill Werle	12.00	5.00	1.20
☐ 88 Marty Marion	16.00	6.50	1.60
☐ 89 Red Munger	12.00	5.00	1.20
☐ 90 Harry Brecheen	12.00	5.00	1.20
☐ 91 Cass Michaels	12.00	5.00	1.20
☐ 92 Hank Majeski	12.00	5.00	1.20
☐ 93 Gene Bearden	12.00	5.00	1.20
☐ 94 Lou Boudreau	35.00	14.00	3.50
☐ 95 Aaron Robinson	12.00	5.00	1.20
☐ 96 Virgil Trucks	14.00	5.75	1.40
☐ 97 Maurice McDermott	12.00	5.00	1.20
☐ 98 Ted Williams	450.00	180.00	45.00
☐ 99 Billy Goodman	14.00	5.75	1.40
☐ 100 Vic Raschi	20.00	8.00	2.00
☐ 101 Bobby Brown	20.00	8.00	2.00
☐ 102 Billy Johnson	12.00	5.00	1.20
☐ 103 Eddie Joost	12.00	5.00	1.20
☐ 104 Sam Chapman	12.00	5.00	1.20
☐ 105 Bob Dillinger	12.00	5.00	1.20
☐ 106 Cliff Fannin	12.00	5.00	1.20
☐ 107 Sam Dente	12.00	5.00	1.20
☐ 108 Ray Scarborough	12.00	5.00	1.20
☐ 109 Sid Gordon	12.00	5.00	1.20
☐ 110 Tommy Holmes	14.00	5.75	1.40
☐ 111 Walker Cooper	12.00	5.00	1.20
☐ 112 Gil Hodges	60.00	24.00	6.00
☐ 113 Gene Hermanski	12.00	5.00	1.20
☐ 114 Wayne Terwilliger	12.00	5.00	1.20
☐ 115 Roy Smalley	12.00	5.00	1.20
☐ 116 Virgil Stallcup	12.00	5.00	1.20
☐ 117 Bill Rigney	12.00	5.00	1.20
☐ 118 Clint Hartung	12.00	5.00	1.20
☐ 119 Dick Sisler	12.00	5.00	1.20
☐ 120 John Thompson	12.00	5.00	1.20
☐ 121 Andy Seminick	12.00	5.00	1.20
☐ 122 Johnny Hopp	12.00	5.00	1.20
☐ 123 Dino Restelli	12.00	5.00	1.20
☐ 124 Clyde McCullough	12.00	5.00	1.20
☐ 125 Del Rice	12.00	5.00	1.20
☐ 126 Al Brazle	12.00	5.00	1.20
☐ 127 Dave Philley	12.00	5.00	1.20
☐ 128 Phil Masi	12.00	5.00	1.20
☐ 129 Joe Gordon	14.00	5.75	1.40
☐ 130 Dale Mitchell	14.00	5.75	1.40
☐ 131 Steve Gromek	12.00	5.00	1.20
☐ 132 James"Mickey" Vernon	14.00	5.75	1.40
☐ 133 Don Kolloway	12.00	5.00	1.20
☐ 134 Paul Trout	12.00	5.00	1.20
☐ 135 Pat Mullin	12.00	5.00	1.20
☐ 136 Warren Rosar	12.00	5.00	1.20
☐ 137 Johnny Pesky	12.00	5.00	1.20
☐ 138 Allie Reynolds	22.00	9.00	2.20
☐ 139 Johnny Mize	45.00	18.00	4.50
☐ 140 Pete Suder	12.00	5.00	1.20
☐ 141 Joe Coleman	12.00	5.00	1.20
☐ 142 Sherman Lollar	12.00	5.00	1.20
☐ 143 Eddie Stewart	12.00	5.00	1.20
☐ 144 Al Evans	12.00	5.00	1.20
☐ 145 Jack Graham	12.00	5.00	1.20
☐ 146 Floyd Baker	12.00	5.00	1.20
☐ 147 Mike Garcia	14.00	5.75	1.40
☐ 148 Early Wynn	40.00	16.00	4.00
☐ 149 Bob Swift	12.00	5.00	1.20
☐ 150 George Vico	12.00	5.00	1.20
☐ 151 Fred Hutchinson	14.00	5.75	1.40
☐ 152 Ellis Kinder	12.00	5.00	1.20
☐ 153 Walt Masterson	12.00	5.00	1.20
☐ 154 Gus Niarhos	12.00	5.00	1.20
☐ 155 Frank Shea	12.00	5.00	1.20
☐ 156 Fred Sanford	12.00	5.00	1.20
☐ 157 Mike Guerra	12.00	5.00	1.20
☐ 158 Paul Lehner	12.00	5.00	1.20
☐ 159 Joe Tipton	12.00	5.00	1.20
☐ 160 Mickey Harris	12.00	5.00	1.20
☐ 161 Sherry Robertson	12.00	5.00	1.20
☐ 162 Eddie Yost	12.00	5.00	1.20
☐ 163 Earl Torgeson	12.00	5.00	1.20
☐ 164 Sibby Sisti	12.00	5.00	1.20
☐ 165 Bruce Edwards	12.00	5.00	1.20
☐ 166 Joe Hatton	12.00	5.00	1.20
☐ 167 Preacher Roe	22.00	9.00	2.20
☐ 168 Bob Scheffing	12.00	5.00	1.20
☐ 169 Hank Edwards	12.00	5.00	1.20
☐ 170 Dutch Leonard	12.00	5.00	1.20
☐ 171 Harry Gumbert	12.00	5.00	1.20
☐ 172 Peanuts Lowrey	12.00	5.00	1.20
☐ 173 Lloyd Merriman	12.00	5.00	1.20
☐ 174 Hank Thompson	14.00	5.75	1.40
☐ 175 Monte Kennedy	12.00	5.00	1.20
☐ 176 Sylvester Donnelly	12.00	5.00	1.20
☐ 177 Hank Borowy	12.00	5.00	1.20
☐ 178 Eddie Fitzgerald	12.00	5.00	1.20
☐ 179 Chuck Diering	12.00	5.00	1.20
☐ 180 Harry Walker	12.00	5.00	1.20
☐ 181 Marino Pieretti	12.00	5.00	1.20
☐ 182 Sam Zoldak	12.00	5.00	1.20
☐ 183 Mickey Haefner	12.00	5.00	1.20

	NRMT	VG-E	GOOD
□ 184 Randy Gumpert	12.00	5.00	1.20
□ 185 Howie Judson	12.00	5.00	1.20
□ 186 Ken Keltner	12.00	5.00	1.20
□ 187 Lou Stringer	12.00	5.00	1.20
□ 188 Earl Johnson	12.00	5.00	1.20
□ 189 Owen Friend	12.00	5.00	1.20
□ 190 Ken Wood	12.00	5.00	1.20
□ 191 Dick Starr	12.00	5.00	1.20
□ 192 Bob Chipman	12.00	5.00	1.20
□ 193 Pete Reiser	14.00	5.75	1.40
□ 194 Billy Cox	14.00	5.75	1.40
□ 195 Phil Cavarretta	14.00	5.75	1.40
□ 196 Doyle Lade	12.00	5.00	1.20
□ 197 Johnny Wyrostek	12.00	5.00	1.20
□ 198 Danny Litwhiler	12.00	5.00	1.20
□ 199 Jack Kramer	12.00	5.00	1.20
□ 200 Kirby Higbe	12.00	5.00	1.20
□ 201 Pete Castiglione	12.00	5.00	1.20
□ 202 Cliff Chambers	12.00	5.00	1.20
□ 203 Danny Murtaugh	12.00	5.00	1.20
□ 204 Granny Hamner	12.00	5.00	1.20
□ 205 Mike Goliat	12.00	5.00	1.20
□ 206 Stan Lopata	12.00	5.00	1.20
□ 207 Max Lanier	12.00	5.00	1.20
□ 208 Jim Hearn	12.00	5.00	1.20
□ 209 Johnny Lindell	12.00	5.00	1.20
□ 210 Ted Gray	12.00	5.00	1.20
□ 211 Charley Keller	14.00	5.75	1.40
□ 212 Gerry Priddy	12.00	5.00	1.20
□ 213 Carl Scheib	12.00	5.00	1.20
□ 214 Dick Fowler	12.00	5.00	1.20
□ 215 Ed Lopat	25.00	10.00	2.50
□ 216 Bob Porterfield	12.00	5.00	1.20
□ 217 Casey Stengel MG	80.00	32.00	8.00
□ 218 Cliff Mapes	12.00	5.00	1.20
□ 219 Hank Bauer	40.00	16.00	4.00
□ 220 Leo Durocher MG	35.00	14.00	3.50
□ 221 Don Mueller	21.00	8.50	2.10
□ 222 Bobby Morgan	12.00	5.00	1.20
□ 223 Jim Russell	12.00	5.00	1.20
□ 224 Jack Banta	12.00	5.00	1.20
□ 225 Eddie Sawyer MG	14.00	5.75	1.40
□ 226 Jim Konstanty	21.00	8.50	2.10
□ 227 Bob Miller	12.00	5.00	1.20
□ 228 Bill Nicholson	12.00	5.00	1.20
□ 229 Frank Frisch	35.00	14.00	3.50
□ 230 Bill Serena	12.00	5.00	1.20
□ 231 Preston Ward	12.00	5.00	1.20
□ 232 Al Rosen	35.00	14.00	3.50
□ 233 Allie Clark	12.00	5.00	1.20
□ 234 Bobby Shantz	18.00	7.25	1.80
□ 235 Harold Gilbert	12.00	5.00	1.20
□ 236 Bob Cain	12.00	5.00	1.20
□ 237 Bill Salkeld	12.00	5.00	1.20
□ 238 Vernal Jones	12.00	5.00	1.20
□ 239 Bill Howerton	12.00	5.00	1.20
□ 240 Eddie Lake	12.00	5.00	1.20
□ 241 Neil Berry	12.00	5.00	1.20
□ 242 Dick Kryhoski	12.00	5.00	1.20
□ 243 Johnny Groth	12.00	5.00	1.20
□ 244 Dale Coogan	12.00	5.00	1.20
□ 245 Al Papai	12.00	5.00	1.20
□ 246 Walt Dropo	18.00	7.25	1.80
□ 247 Irv Noren	12.00	5.00	1.20
□ 248 Sam Jethroe	14.00	5.75	1.40
□ 249 Snuffy Stirnweiss	14.00	5.75	1.40
□ 250 Ray Coleman	12.00	5.00	1.20
□ 251 John Moss	12.00	5.00	1.20
□ 252 Billy DeMars	60.00	8.00	1.50

1951 Bowman

The cards in this 324-card set measure 2 1/16" by 3 1/8". Many of the obverses of the cards appearing in the 1951 Bowman set are enlargements of those appearing in the previous year. The high number series (253-324) is highly valued and contains the true "Rookie" cards of Mickey Mantle and Willie Mays. Card number 195 depicts Paul Richards in caricature. George Kell's card (#46) incorrectly lists him as being in the "1941" Bowman series. Player names are found printed in a panel on the front of the card. These cards were supposedly also sold in sheets in variety stores in the Philadelphia area.

	NRMT	VG-E	GOOD
COMPLETE SET (324)	13000.00	5500.00	1800.00
COMMON PLAYER (1-36)	13.50	6.00	1.50
COMMON PLAYER (37-72)	12.00	5.00	1.20
COMMON PLAYER (73-252)	10.00	4.00	1.00
COMMON PLAYER (253-324)	40.00	16.00	4.00
□ 1 Whitey Ford	750.00	100.00	20.00
□ 2 Yogi Berra	250.00	100.00	25.00
□ 3 Robin Roberts	45.00	18.00	4.50
□ 4 Del Ennis	15.00	6.00	1.50
□ 5 Dale Mitchell	15.00	6.00	1.50
□ 6 Don Newcombe	20.00	8.00	2.00
□ 7 Gil Hodges	45.00	18.00	4.50
□ 8 Paul Lehner	13.50	6.00	1.50
□ 9 Sam Chapman	13.50	6.00	1.50
□ 10 Red Schoendienst	18.00	7.25	1.80
□ 11 Red Munger	13.50	6.00	1.50
□ 12 Hank Majeski	13.50	6.00	1.50
□ 13 Eddie Stanky	15.00	6.00	1.50
□ 14 Al Dark	16.00	6.50	1.60
□ 15 Johnny Pesky	13.50	6.00	1.50
□ 16 Maurice McDermott	13.50	6.00	1.50
□ 17 Pete Castiglione	13.50	6.00	1.50
□ 18 Gil Coan	13.50	6.00	1.50
□ 19 Sid Gordon	13.50	6.00	1.50
□ 20 Del Crandell (sic, Crandall)	15.00	6.00	1.50
□ 21 Snuffy Stirnweiss	15.00	6.00	1.50
□ 22 Hank Sauer	15.00	6.00	1.50
□ 23 Hoot Evers	13.50	6.00	1.50
□ 24 Ewell Blackwell	15.00	6.00	1.50
□ 25 Vic Raschi	20.00	8.00	2.00
□ 26 Phil Rizzuto	50.00	20.00	5.00
□ 27 Jim Konstanty	16.00	6.50	1.60
□ 28 Eddie Waitkus	13.50	6.00	1.50
□ 29 Allie Clark	13.50	6.00	1.50
□ 30 Bob Feller	80.00	32.00	8.00
□ 31 Roy Campanella	175.00	70.00	18.00
□ 32 Duke Snider	135.00	54.00	13.50
□ 33 Bob Hooper	13.50	6.00	1.50
□ 34 Marty Marion	16.00	6.50	1.60
□ 35 Al Zarilla	13.50	6.00	1.50
□ 36 Joe Dobson	13.50	6.00	1.50
□ 37 Whitey Lockman	13.50	6.00	1.50
□ 38 Al Evans	12.00	5.00	1.20
□ 39 Ray Scarborough	12.00	5.00	1.20
□ 40 Gus Bell	16.00	6.50	1.60
□ 41 Eddie Yost	12.00	5.00	1.20
□ 42 Vern Bickford	12.00	5.00	1.20
□ 43 Billy DeMars	12.00	5.00	1.20
□ 44 Roy Smalley	12.00	5.00	1.20
□ 45 Art Houtteman	12.00	5.00	1.20
□ 46 George Kell 1941	40.00	16.00	4.00
□ 47 Grady Hatton	12.00	5.00	1.20
□ 48 Ken Raffensberger	12.00	5.00	1.20
□ 49 Jerry Coleman	14.00	5.75	1.40
□ 50 Johnny Mize	45.00	18.00	4.50
□ 51 Andy Seminick	12.00	5.00	1.20
□ 52 Dick Sisler	12.00	5.00	1.20
□ 53 Bob Lemon	35.00	14.00	3.50
□ 54 Ray Boone	14.00	5.75	1.40
□ 55 Gene Hermanski	12.00	5.00	1.20
□ 56 Ralph Branca	16.00	6.50	1.60
□ 57 Alex Kellner	12.00	5.00	1.20
□ **58 Enos Slaughter**	**40.00**	**18.00**	**4.00**
□ 59 Randy Gumpert	12.00	5.00	1.20
□ 60 Chico Carrasquel	12.00	5.00	1.20
□ 61 Jim Hearn	12.00	5.00	1.20
□ 62 Lou Boudreau	33.00	15.00	4.00
□ 63 Bob Dillinger	12.00	5.00	1.20
□ 64 Bill Werle	12.00	5.00	1.20
□ 65 Mickey Vernon	15.00	6.00	1.50
□ 66 Bob Elliott	14.00	5.75	1.40
□ 67 Roy Sievers	14.00	5.75	1.40
□ 68 Dick Kokos	12.00	5.00	1.20

- ☐ 69 Johnny Schmitz 12.00 5.00 1.20
- ☐ 70 Ron Northey 12.00 5.00 1.20
- ☐ 71 Jerry Priddy 12.00 5.00 1.20
- ☐ 72 Lloyd Merriman 12.00 5.00 1.20
- ☐ 73 Tommy Byrne 12.00 5.00 1.20
- ☐ 74 Billy Johnson 12.00 5.00 1.20
- ☐ 75 Russ Meyer 10.00 4.00 1.00
- ☐ 76 Stan Lopata 10.00 4.00 1.00
- ☐ 77 Mike Goliat 10.00 4.00 1.00
- ☐ 78 Early Wynn 35.00 14.00 3.50
- ☐ 79 Jim Hegan 12.00 5.00 1.20
- ☐ 80 Pee Wee Reese 90.00 36.00 9.00
- ☐ 81 Carl Furillo 21.00 8.50 2.10
- ☐ 82 Joe Tipton 10.00 4.00 1.00
- ☐ 83 Carl Scheib 10.00 4.00 1.00
- ☐ 84 Barney McCosky 10.00 4.00 1.00
- ☐ 85 Eddie Kazak 10.00 4.00 1.00
- ☐ 86 Harry Brecheen 10.00 4.00 1.00
- ☐ 87 Floyd Baker 10.00 4.00 1.00
- ☐ 88 Eddie Robinson 10.00 4.00 1.00
- ☐ 89 Hank Thompson 12.00 5.00 1.20
- ☐ 90 Dave Koslo 10.00 4.00 1.00
- ☐ 91 Clyde Vollmer 10.00 4.00 1.00
- ☐ 92 Vern Stephens 12.00 5.00 1.20
- ☐ 93 Danny O'Connell 10.00 4.00 1.00
- ☐ 94 Clyde McCullough 10.00 4.00 1.00
- ☐ 95 Sherry Robertson 10.00 4.00 1.00
- ☐ 96 Sandy Consuegra 10.00 4.00 1.00
- ☐ 97 Bob Kuzava 10.00 4.00 1.00
- ☐ 98 Willard Marshall 10.00 4.00 1.00
- ☐ 99 Earl Torgeson 10.00 4.00 1.00
- ☐ 100 Sherm Lollar 12.00 5.00 1.20
- ☐ 101 Owen Friend 10.00 4.00 1.00
- ☐ 102 Dutch Leonard 10.00 4.00 1.00
- ☐ 103 Andy Pafko 12.00 5.00 1.20
- ☐ 104 Virgil Trucks 12.00 5.00 1.20
- ☐ 105 Don Kolloway 10.00 4.00 1.00
- ☐ 106 Pat Mullin 10.00 4.00 1.00
- ☐ 107 Johnny Wyrostek 10.00 4.00 1.00
- ☐ 108 Virgil Stallcup 10.00 4.00 1.00
- ☐ 109 Allie Reynolds 21.00 8.50 2.10
- ☐ 110 Bobby Brown 20.00 8.00 2.00
- ☐ 111 Curt Simmons 12.00 5.00 1.20
- ☐ 112 Willie Jones 10.00 4.00 1.00
- ☐ 113 Bill Nicholson 10.00 4.00 1.00
- ☐ 114 Sam Zoldak 10.00 4.00 1.00
- ☐ 115 Steve Gromek 10.00 4.00 1.00
- ☐ 116 Bruce Edwards 10.00 4.00 1.00
- ☐ 117 Eddie Miksis 10.00 4.00 1.00
- ☐ 118 Preacher Roe 18.00 7.25 1.80
- ☐ 119 Eddie Joost 10.00 4.00 1.00
- ☐ 120 Joe Coleman 10.00 4.00 1.00
- ☐ 121 Gerry Staley 10.00 4.00 1.00
- ☐ 122 Joe Garagiola 80.00 32.00 8.00
- ☐ 123 Howie Judson 10.00 4.00 1.00
- ☐ 124 Gus Niarhos 10.00 4.00 1.00
- ☐ 125 Bill Rigney 10.00 4.00 1.00
- ☐ 126 Bobby Thomson 20.00 8.00 2.00
- ☐ 127 Sal Maglie 25.00 10.00 2.50
- ☐ 128 Ellis Kinder 10.00 4.00 1.00
- ☐ 129 Matt Batts 10.00 4.00 1.00
- ☐ 130 Tom Saffell 10.00 4.00 1.00
- ☐ 131 Cliff Chambers 10.00 4.00 1.00
- ☐ 132 Cass Michaels 10.00 4.00 1.00
- ☐ 133 Sam Dente 10.00 4.00 1.00
- ☐ 134 Warren Spahn 60.00 24.00 6.00
- ☐ 135 Walker Cooper 10.00 4.00 1.00
- ☐ 136 Ray Coleman 10.00 4.00 1.00
- ☐ 137 Dick Starr 10.00 4.00 1.00
- ☐ 138 Phil Cavarretta 12.00 5.00 1.20
- ☐ 139 Doyle Lade 10.00 4.00 1.00
- ☐ 140 Eddie Lake 10.00 4.00 1.00
- ☐ 141 Fred Hutchinson 12.00 5.00 1.20
- ☐ 142 Aaron Robinson 10.00 4.00 1.00
- ☐ 143 Ted Kluszewski 20.00 8.00 2.00
- ☐ 144 Herman Wehmeier 10.00 4.00 1.00
- ☐ 145 Fred Sanford 10.00 4.00 1.00
- ☐ 146 Johnny Hopp 12.00 5.00 1.20
- ☐ 147 Ken Heintzelman 10.00 4.00 1.00
- ☐ 148 Granny Hamner 10.00 4.00 1.00
- ☐ 149 Bubba Church 10.00 4.00 1.00
- ☐ 150 Mike Garcia 12.00 5.00 1.20
- ☐ 151 Larry Doby 16.00 6.50 1.60
- ☐ 152 Cal Abrams 10.00 4.00 1.00
- ☐ 153 Rex Barney 10.00 4.00 1.00
- ☐ 154 Pete Suder 10.00 4.00 1.00
- ☐ 155 Lou Brissie 10.00 4.00 1.00
- ☐ 156 Del Rice 10.00 4.00 1.00
- ☐ 157 Al Brazle 10.00 4.00 1.00
- ☐ 158 Chuck Diering 10.00 4.00 1.00
- ☐ 159 Eddie Stewart 10.00 4.00 1.00
- ☐ 160 Phil Masi 10.00 4.00 1.00
- ☐ 161 Wes Westrum 10.00 4.00 1.00
- ☐ 162 Larry Jansen 10.00 4.00 1.00
- ☐ 163 Monte Kennedy 10.00 4.00 1.00
- ☐ 164 Bill Wight 10.00 4.00 1.00
- ☐ 165 Ted Williams 375.00 150.00 37.00
- ☐ 166 Stan Rojek 10.00 4.00 1.00
- ☐ 167 Murry Dickson 10.00 4.00 1.00
- ☐ 168 Sam Mele 10.00 4.00 1.00
- ☐ 169 Sid Hudson 10.00 4.00 1.00
- ☐ 170 Sibby Sisti 10.00 4.00 1.00
- ☐ 171 Buddy Kerr 10.00 4.00 1.00
- ☐ 172 Ned Garver 10.00 4.00 1.00
- ☐ 173 Hank Arft 10.00 4.00 1.00
- ☐ 174 Mickey Owen 12.00 5.00 1.20
- ☐ 175 Wayne Terwilliger 10.00 4.00 1.00
- ☐ 176 Vic Wertz 12.00 5.00 1.20
- ☐ 177 Charlie Keller 12.00 5.00 1.20
- ☐ 178 Ted Gray 10.00 4.00 1.00
- ☐ 179 Danny Litwhiler 10.00 4.00 1.00
- ☐ 180 Howie Fox 10.00 4.00 1.00
- ☐ 181 Casey Stengel MG 70.00 28.00 7.00
- ☐ 182 Tom Ferrick 10.00 4.00 1.00
- ☐ 183 Hank Bauer 21.00 8.50 2.10
- ☐ 184 Eddie Sawyer MG 12.00 5.00 1.20
- ☐ 185 Jimmy Bloodworth 10.00 4.00 1.00
- ☐ 186 Richie Ashburn 30.00 12.00 3.00
- ☐ 187 Al Rosen 17.00 7.00 1.70
- ☐ 188 Bobby Avila 12.00 5.00 1.20
- ☐ 189 Erv Palica 10.00 4.00 1.00
- ☐ 190 Joe Hatton 10.00 4.00 1.00
- ☐ 191 Billy Hitchcock 10.00 4.00 1.00
- ☐ 192 Hank Wyse 10.00 4.00 1.00
- ☐ 193 Ted Wilks 10.00 4.00 1.00
- ☐ 194 Peanuts Lowrey 10.00 4.00 1.00
- ☐ 195 Paul Richards 15.00 6.00 1.50
  (caricature)
- ☐ 196 Billy Pierce 18.00 7.25 1.80
- ☐ 197 Bob Cain 10.00 4.00 1.00
- ☐ 198 Monte Irvin 45.00 18.00 4.50
- ☐ 199 Sheldon Jones 10.00 4.00 1.00
- ☐ 200 Jack Kramer 10.00 4.00 1.00
- ☐ 201 Steve O'Neill 10.00 4.00 1.00
- ☐ 202 Mike Guerra 10.00 4.00 1.00
- ☐ 203 Vernon Law 15.00 6.00 1.50
- ☐ 204 Vic Lombardi 10.00 4.00 1.00
- ☐ 205 Mickey Grasso 10.00 4.00 1.00
- ☐ 206 Conrado Marrero 10.00 4.00 1.00
- ☐ 207 Billy Southworth 10.00 4.00 1.00
- ☐ 208 Blix Donnelly 10.00 4.00 1.00
- ☐ 209 Ken Wood 10.00 4.00 1.00
- ☐ 210 Les Moss 10.00 4.00 1.00
- ☐ 211 Hal Jeffcoat 10.00 4.00 1.00
- ☐ 212 Bob Rush 10.00 4.00 1.00
- ☐ 213 Neil Berry 10.00 4.00 1.00
- ☐ 214 Bob Swift 10.00 4.00 1.00
- ☐ 215 Ken Peterson 10.00 4.00 1.00
- ☐ 216 Connie Ryan 10.00 4.00 1.00
- ☐ 217 Joe Page 15.00 6.00 1.50
- ☐ 218 Ed Lopat 25.00 10.00 2.50
- ☐ 219 Gene Woodling 27.00 11.00 2.70
- ☐ 220 Bob Miller 10.00 4.00 1.00
- ☐ 221 Dick Whitman 10.00 4.00 1.00
- ☐ 222 Thurman Tucker 10.00 4.00 1.00
- ☐ 223 Johnny VanderMeer 15.00 6.00 1.50
- ☐ 224 Billy Cox 12.00 5.00 1.20
- ☐ 225 Dan Bankhead 12.00 5.00 1.20
- ☐ 226 Jimmy Dykes 12.00 5.00 1.20
- ☐ 227 Bobby Schantz 14.00 5.75 1.40
  (sic, Shantz)
- ☐ 228 Cloyd Boyer 12.00 5.00 1.20
- ☐ 229 Bill Howerton 10.00 4.00 1.00
- ☐ 230 Max Lanier 10.00 4.00 1.00
- ☐ 231 Luis Aloma 10.00 4.00 1.00
- ☐ 232 Nelson Fox 50.00 20.00 5.00
- ☐ 233 Leo Durocher MG 35.00 14.00 3.50
- ☐ 234 Clint Hartung 10.00 4.00 1.00
- ☐ 235 Jack Lohrke 10.00 4.00 1.00
- ☐ 236 Warren Rosar 10.00 4.00 1.00
- ☐ 237 Billy Goodman 12.00 5.00 1.20
- ☐ 238 Peter Reiser 14.00 5.75 1.40
- ☐ 239 Bill MacDonald 10.00 4.00 1.00
- ☐ 240 Joe Haynes 10.00 4.00 1.00
- ☐ 241 Irv Noren 10.00 4.00 1.00
- ☐ 242 Sam Jethroe 10.00 4.00 1.00
- ☐ 243 Johnny Antonelli 12.00 5.00 1.20
- ☐ 244 Cliff Fannin 10.00 4.00 1.00
- ☐ 245 John Berardino 12.00 5.00 1.20
- ☐ 246 Bill Serena 10.00 4.00 1.00
- ☐ 247 Bob Ramazotti 10.00 4.00 1.00
- ☐ 248 Johnny Klippstein 10.00 4.00 1.00
- ☐ 249 Johnny Groth 10.00 4.00 1.00
- ☐ 250 Hank Borowy 10.00 4.00 1.00
- ☐ 251 Willard Ramsdell 10.00 4.00 1.00
- ☐ 252 Dixie Howell 10.00 4.00 1.00
- ☐ 253 Mickey Mantle 5500.00 2000.00 400.00
- ☐ 254 Jackie Jensen 90.00 36.00 9.00
- ☐ 255 Milo Candini 40.00 16.00 4.00
- ☐ 256 Ken Sylvestri 40.00 16.00 4.00

□	257 Birdie Tebbetts	45.00	18.00	4.50
□	258 Luke Easter	45.00	18.00	4.50
□	259 Chuck Dressen MG	50.00	20.00	5.00
□	260 Carl Erskine	80.00	32.00	8.00
□	261 Wally Moses	45.00	18.00	4.50
□	262 Gus Zernial	45.00	18.00	4.50
□	263 Howie Pollet	40.00	16.00	4.00
□	264 Don Richmond	40.00	16.00	4.00
□	265 Steve Bilko	40.00	16.00	4.00
□	266 Harry Dorish	40.00	16.00	4.00
□	267 Ken Holcomb	40.00	16.00	4.00
□	268 Don Mueller	45.00	18.00	4.50
□	269 Ray Noble	40.00	16.00	4.00
□	270 Willard Nixon	40.00	16.00	4.00
□	271 Tommy Wright	40.00	16.00	4.00
□	272 Billy Meyer MG	40.00	16.00	4.00
□	273 Danny Murtaugh	45.00	18.00	4.50
□	274 George Metkovich	40.00	16.00	4.00
□	275 Bucky Harris MG	55.00	22.00	5.50
□	276 Frank Quinn	40.00	16.00	4.00
□	277 Roy Hartsfield	40.00	16.00	4.00
□	278 Norman Roy	40.00	16.00	4.00
□	279 Jim Delsing	40.00	16.00	4.00
□	280 Frank Overmire	40.00	16.00	4.00
□	281 Al Widmar	40.00	16.00	4.00
□	282 Frank Frisch	60.00	24.00	6.00
□	283 Walt Dubiel	40.00	16.00	4.00
□	284 Gene Bearden	40.00	16.00	4.00
□	285 Johnny Lipon	40.00	16.00	4.00
□	286 Bob Usher	40.00	16.00	4.00
□	287 Jim Blackburn	40.00	16.00	4.00
□	288 Bobby Adams	40.00	16.00	4.00
□	289 Cliff Mapes	45.00	18.00	4.50
□	290 Bill Dickey	150.00	60.00	15.00
□	291 Tommy Henrich	60.00	24.00	6.00
□	292 Eddie Pellegrini	40.00	16.00	4.00
□	293 Ken Johnson	40.00	16.00	4.00
□	294 Jocko Thompson	40.00	16.00	4.00
□	295 Al Lopez MG	70.00	28.00	7.00
□	296 Bob Kennedy	45.00	18.00	4.50
□	297 Dave Philley	40.00	16.00	4.00
□	298 Joe Astroth	40.00	16.00	4.00
□	299 Clyde King	45.00	18.00	4.50
□	300 Hal Rice	40.00	16.00	4.00
□	301 Tommy Glaviano	40.00	16.00	4.00
□	302 Jim Busby	40.00	16.00	4.00
□	303 Marv Rotblatt	40.00	16.00	4.00
□	304 Al Gettell	40.00	16.00	4.00
□	305 Willie Mays	1600.00	600.00	200.00
□	306 Jim Piersall	80.00	32.00	8.00
□	307 Walt Masterson	40.00	16.00	4.00
□	308 Ted Beard	40.00	16.00	4.00
□	309 Mel Queen	40.00	16.00	4.00
□	310 Erv Dusak	40.00	16.00	4.00
□	311 Mickey Harris	40.00	16.00	4.00
□	312 Gene Mauch	50.00	20.00	5.00
□	313 Ray Mueller	40.00	16.00	4.00
□	314 Johnny Sain	50.00	20.00	5.00
□	315 Zack Taylor	40.00	16.00	4.00
□	316 Duane Pillette	40.00	16.00	4.00
□	317 Smokey Burgess	50.00	20.00	5.00
□	318 Warren Hacker	40.00	16.00	4.00
□	319 Red Rolfe	45.00	18.00	4.50
□	320 Hal White	40.00	16.00	4.00
□	321 Earl Johnson	40.00	16.00	4.00
□	322 Luke Sewell	45.00	18.00	4.50
□	323 Joe Adcock	60.00	24.00	6.00
□	324 Johnny Pramesa	75.00	25.00	5.00

1952 Bowman

The cards in this 252-card set measure 2 1/16" by 3 1/8". While the Bowman set of 1952 retained the card size introduced in 1951, it employed a modification of color tones from the two preceding years. The cards also appeared with a facsimile autograph on the front and, for the first time since 1949, premium advertising on the back. The 1952 set was sold in sheets as well as in gum packs. Artwork for 15 cards that were never issued was recently discovered.

		NRMT	VG-E	GOOD
	COMPLETE SET (252)	7000.00	3000.00	900.00
	COMMON PLAYER (1-36)	15.00	6.00	1.50
	COMMON PLAYER (37-144)	12.00	5.00	1.20
	COMMON PLAYER (145-180)	11.00	4.50	1.10
	COMMON PLAYER (181-216)	10.00	4.00	1.00
	COMMON PLAYER (217-252)	25.00	10.00	2.50
□	1 Yogi Berra	400.00	100.00	20.00
□	2 Bobby Thomson	22.00	9.00	2.20
□	3 Fred Hutchinson	18.00	7.25	1.80
□	4 Robin Roberts	40.00	16.00	4.00
□	5 Minnie Minoso	30.00	12.00	3.00
□	6 Virgil Stallcup	15.00	6.00	1.50
□	7 Mike Garcia	18.00	7.25	1.80
□	8 Pee Wee Reese	80.00	32.00	8.00
□	9 Vern Stephens	18.00	7.25	1.80
□	10 Bob Hooper	15.00	6.00	1.50
□	11 Ralph Kiner	36.00	15.00	3.60
□	12 Max Surkont	15.00	6.00	1.50
□	13 Cliff Mapes	15.00	6.00	1.50
□	14 Cliff Chambers	15.00	6.00	1.50
□	15 Sam Mele	15.00	6.00	1.50
□	16 Turk Lown	15.00	6.00	1.50
□	17 Ed Lopat	24.00	10.00	2.40
□	18 Don Mueller	18.00	7.25	1.80
□	19 Bob Cain	15.00	6.00	1.50
□	20 Willie Jones	15.00	6.00	1.50
□	21 Nelson Fox	27.00	11.00	2.70
□	22 Willard Ramsdell	15.00	6.00	1.50
□	23 Bob Lemon	35.00	14.00	3.50
□	24 Carl Furillo	22.00	9.00	2.20
□	25 Mickey McDermott	15.00	6.00	1.50
□	26 Eddie Joost	15.00	6.00	1.50
□	27 Joe Garagiola	50.00	20.00	5.00
□	28 Ray Hartsfield	15.00	6.00	1.50
□	29 Ned Garver	15.00	6.00	1.50
□	30 Red Schoendienst	21.00	8.50	2.10
□	31 Eddie Yost	15.00	6.00	1.50
□	32 Eddie Miksis	15.00	6.00	1.50
□	33 Gil McDougald	40.00	16.00	4.00
□	34 Alvin Dark	18.00	7.25	1.80
□	35 Granny Hamner	15.00	6.00	1.50
□	36 Cass Michaels	15.00	6.00	1.50
□	37 Vic Raschi	16.00	6.50	1.60
□	38 Whitey Lockman	13.50	6.00	1.50
□	39 Vic Wertz	13.50	6.00	1.50
□	40 Bubba Church	12.00	5.00	1.20
□	41 Chico Carrasquel	12.00	5.00	1.20
□	42 Johnny Wyrostek	12.00	5.00	1.20
□	43 Bob Feller	75.00	30.00	7.50
□	44 Roy Campanella	150.00	60.00	15.00
□	45 Johnny Pesky	12.00	5.00	1.20
□	46 Carl Scheib	12.00	5.00	1.20
□	47 Pete Castiglione	12.00	5.00	1.20
□	48 Vern Bickford	12.00	5.00	1.20
□	49 Jim Hearn	12.00	5.00	1.20
□	50 Gerry Staley	12.00	5.00	1.20
□	51 Gil Coan	12.00	5.00	1.20
□	52 Phil Rizzuto	50.00	20.00	5.00
□	53 Richie Ashburn	27.00	11.00	2.70
□	54 Billy Pierce	15.00	6.00	1.50
□	55 Ken Raffensberger	12.00	5.00	1.20
□	56 Clyde King	13.50	6.00	1.50
□	57 Clyde Vollmer	12.00	5.00	1.20
□	58 Hank Majeski	12.00	5.00	1.20
□	59 Murry Dickson	12.00	5.00	1.20
□	60 Sid Gordon	12.00	5.00	1.20
□	61 Tommy Byrne	12.00	5.00	1.20
□	62 Joe Presko	12.00	5.00	1.20
□	63 Irv Noren	12.00	5.00	1.20
□	64 Roy Smalley	12.00	5.00	1.20
□	65 Hank Bauer	20.00	8.00	2.00
□	66 Sal Maglie	16.00	6.50	1.60
□	67 Johnny Groth	12.00	5.00	1.20
□	68 Jim Busby	12.00	5.00	1.20
□	69 Joe Adcock	13.50	6.00	1.50
□	70 Carl Erskine	18.00	7.25	1.80
□	71 Vernon Law	13.50	6.00	1.50
□	72 Earl Torgeson	12.00	5.00	1.20

□ 73	Gerry Coleman	13.50	6.00	1.50
□ 74	Wes Westrum	12.00	5.00	1.20
□ 75	George Kell	32.00	13.00	3.20
□ 76	Del Ennis	13.50	6.00	1.50
□ 77	Eddie Robinson	12.00	5.00	1.20
□ 78	Lloyd Merriman	12.00	5.00	1.20
□ 79	Lou Brissie	12.00	5.00	1.20
□ 80	Gil Hodges	45.00	18.00	4.50
□ 81	Billy Goodman	13.50	6.00	1.50
□ 82	Gus Zernial	13.50	6.00	1.50
□ 83	Howie Pollet	12.00	5.00	1.20
□ 84	Sam Jethroe	12.00	5.00	1.20
□ 85	Marty Marion	15.00	6.00	1.50
□ 86	Cal Abrams	12.00	5.00	1.20
□ 87	Mickey Vernon	13.50	6.00	1.50
□ 88	Bruce Edwards	12.00	5.00	1.20
□ 89	Billy Hitchcock	12.00	5.00	1.20
□ 90	Larry Jansen	12.00	5.00	1.20
□ 91	Don Kolloway	12.00	5.00	1.20
□ 92	Eddie Waitkus	12.00	5.00	1.20
□ 93	Paul Richards	13.50	6.00	1.50
□ 94	Luke Sewell	13.50	6.00	1.50
□ 95	Luke Easter	13.50	6.00	1.50
□ 96	Ralph Branca	16.00	6.50	1.60
□ 97	Willard Marshall	12.00	5.00	1.20
□ 98	Jimmy Dykes	13.50	6.00	1.50
□ 99	Clyde McCullough	12.00	5.00	1.20
□ 100	Sibby Sisti	12.00	5.00	1.20
□ 101	Mickey Mantle	1500.00	600.00	125.00
□ 102	Peanuts Lowrey	12.00	5.00	1.20
□ 103	Joe Haynes	12.00	5.00	1.20
□ 104	Hal Jeffcoat	12.00	5.00	1.20
□ 105	Bobby Brown	18.00	7.25	1.80
□ 106	Randy Gumpert	12.00	5.00	1.20
□ 107	Del Rice	12.00	5.00	1.20
□ 108	George Metkovich	12.00	5.00	1.20
□ 109	Tom Morgan	12.00	5.00	1.20
□ 110	Max Lanier	12.00	5.00	1.20
□ 111	Hoot Evers	12.00	5.00	1.20
□ 112	Smokey Burgess	13.50	6.00	1.50
□ 113	Al Zarilla	12.00	5.00	1.20
□ 114	Frank Hiller	12.00	5.00	1.20
□ 115	Larry Doby	16.00	6.50	1.60
□ 116	**Duke Snider**	**110.00**	**45.00**	**10.00**
□ 117	Bill Wight	12.00	5.00	1.20
□ 118	Ray Murray	12.00	5.00	1.20
□ 119	Bill Howerton	12.00	5.00	1.20
□ 120	Chet Nichols	12.00	5.00	1.20
□ 121	Al Corwin	12.00	5.00	1.20
□ 122	Billy Johnson	12.00	5.00	1.20
□ 123	Sid Hudson	12.00	5.00	1.20
□ 124	Birdie Tebbetts	13.50	6.00	1.50
□ 125	Howie Fox	12.00	5.00	1.20
□ 126	Phil Cavarretta	13.50	6.00	1.50
□ 127	Dick Sisler	12.00	5.00	1.20
□ 128	Don Newcombe	18.00	7.25	1.80
□ 129	Gus Niarhos	12.00	5.00	1.20
□ 130	Allie Clark	12.00	5.00	1.20
□ 131	Bob Swift	12.00	5.00	1.20
□ 132	Dave Cole	12.00	5.00	1.20
□ 133	Dick Kryhoski	12.00	5.00	1.20
□ 134	Al Brazle	12.00	5.00	1.20
□ 135	Mickey Harris	12.00	5.00	1.20
□ 136	Gene Hermanski	12.00	5.00	1.20
□ 137	Stan Rojek	12.00	5.00	1.20
□ 138	Ted Wilks	12.00	5.00	1.20
□ 139	Jerry Priddy	12.00	5.00	1.20
□ 140	Ray Scarborough	12.00	5.00	1.20
□ 141	Hank Edwards	12.00	5.00	1.20
□ 142	Early Wynn	32.00	13.00	3.20
□ 143	Sandy Consuegra	12.00	5.00	1.20
□ 144	Joe Hatton	12.00	5.00	1.20
□ 145	Johnny Mize	45.00	18.00	4.50
□ 146	Leo Durocher MG	30.00	12.00	3.00
□ 147	Marlin Stuart	11.00	4.50	1.10
□ 148	Ken Heintzelman	11.00	4.50	1.10
□ 149	Howie Judson	11.00	4.50	1.10
□ 150	Herman Wehmeier	11.00	4.50	1.10
□ 151	Al Rosen	17.00	7.00	1.70
□ 152	Billy Cox	13.50	6.00	1.50
□ 153	Fred Hatfield	11.00	4.50	1.10
□ 154	Ferris Fain	13.50	6.00	1.50
□ 155	Billy Meyer	11.00	4.50	1.10
□ 156	Warren Spahn	50.00	20.00	5.00
□ 157	Jim Delsing	11.00	4.50	1.10
□ 158	Bucky Harris MG	25.00	10.00	2.50
□ 159	Dutch Leonard	11.00	4.50	1.10
□ 160	Eddie Stanky	13.50	6.00	1.50
□ 161	Jackie Jensen	21.00	8.50	2.10
□ 162	Monte Irvin	30.00	12.00	3.00
□ 163	Johnny Lipon	11.00	4.50	1.10
□ 164	Connie Ryan	11.00	4.50	1.10
□ 165	Saul Rogovin	11.00	4.50	1.10
□ 166	Bobby Adams	11.00	4.50	1.10
□ 167	Bobby Avila	13.50	6.00	1.50
□ 168	Preacher Roe	18.00	7.25	1.80
□ 169	Walt Dropo	13.50	6.00	1.50
□ 170	Joe Astroth	11.00	4.50	1.10
□ 171	Mel Queen	11.00	4.50	1.10
□ 172	Ebba St.Claire	11.00	4.50	1.10
□ 173	Gene Bearden	11.00	4.50	1.10
□ 174	Mickey Grasso	11.00	4.50	1.10
□ 175	Ransom Jackson	11.00	4.50	1.10
□ 176	Harry Brecheen	11.00	4.50	1.10
□ 177	Gene Woodling	16.00	6.50	1.60
□ 178	Dave Williams	13.50	6.00	1.50
□ 179	Pete Suder	11.00	4.50	1.10
□ 180	Eddie Fitzgerald	11.00	4.50	1.10
□ 181	Joe Collins	13.50	6.00	1.50
□ 182	Dave Koslo	10.00	4.00	1.00
□ 183	Pat Mullin	10.00	4.00	1.00
□ 184	Curt Simmons	13.50	6.00	1.50
□ 185	Eddie Stewart	10.00	4.00	1.00
□ 186	Frank Smith	10.00	4.00	1.00
□ 187	Jim Hegan	12.00	5.00	1.20
□ 188	Charlie Dressen MG	13.50	6.00	1.50
□ 189	Jim Piersall	14.00	5.75	1.40
□ 190	Dick Fowler	10.00	4.00	1.00
□ 191	Bob Friend	14.00	5.75	1.40
□ 192	John Cusick	10.00	4.00	1.00
□ 193	Bobby Young	10.00	4.00	1.00
□ 194	Bob Porterfield	10.00	4.00	1.00
□ 195	Frank Baumholtz	10.00	4.00	1.00
□ 196	Stan Musial	325.00	130.00	32.00
□ 197	Charlie Silvera	10.00	4.00	1.00
□ 198	Chuck Diering	10.00	4.00	1.00
□ 199	Ted Gray	10.00	4.00	1.00
□ 200	Ken Silvestri	10.00	4.00	1.00
□ 201	Ray Coleman	10.00	4.00	1.00
□ 202	Harry Perkowski	10.00	4.00	1.00
□ 203	Steve Gromek	10.00	4.00	1.00
□ 204	Andy Pafko	10.00	4.00	1.00
□ 205	Walt Masterson	10.00	4.00	1.00
□ 206	Elmer Valo	10.00	4.00	1.00
□ 207	George Strickland	10.00	4.00	1.00
□ 208	Walker Cooper	10.00	4.00	1.00
□ 209	Dick Littlefield	10.00	4.00	1.00
□ 210	Archie Wilson	10.00	4.00	1.00
□ 211	Paul Minner	10.00	4.00	1.00
□ 212	Solly Hemus	10.00	4.00	1.00
□ 213	Monte Kennedy	10.00	4.00	1.00
□ 214	Ray Boone	10.00	4.00	1.00
□ 215	Sheldon Jones	10.00	4.00	1.00
□ 216	Matt Batts	10.00	4.00	1.00
□ 217	Casey Stengel	100.00	40.00	10.00
□ 218	**Willie Mays**	**750.00**	**325.00**	**75.00**
□ 219	Neil Berry	25.00	10.00	2.50
□ 220	Russ Meyer	25.00	10.00	2.50
□ 221	Lou Kretlow	25.00	10.00	2.50
□ 222	Dixie Howell	25.00	10.00	2.50
□ 223	Harry Simpson	25.00	10.00	2.50
□ 224	Johnny Schmitz	25.00	10.00	2.50
□ 225	Del Wilber	25.00	10.00	2.50
□ 226	Alex Kellner	25.00	10.00	2.50
□ 227	Clyde Sukeforth	25.00	10.00	2.50
□ 228	Bob Chipman	25.00	10.00	2.50
□ 229	Hank Arft	25.00	10.00	2.50
□ 230	Frank Shea	25.00	10.00	2.50
□ 231	Dee Fondy	25.00	10.00	2.50
□ 232	Enos Slaughter	60.00	24.00	6.00
□ 233	Bob Kuzava	25.00	10.00	2.50
□ 234	Fred Fitzsimmons	25.00	10.00	2.50
□ 235	Steve Souchock	25.00	10.00	2.50
□ 236	Tommy Brown	25.00	10.00	2.50
□ 237	Sherman Lollar	30.00	12.00	3.00
□ 238	Roy McMillan	30.00	12.00	3.00
□ 239	Dale Mitchell	30.00	12.00	3.00
□ 240	Billy Loes	30.00	12.00	3.00
□ 241	Mel Parnell	30.00	12.00	3.00
□ 242	Everett Kell	25.00	10.00	2.50
□ 243	Red Munger	25.00	10.00	2.50
□ 244	Lew Burdette	45.00	18.00	4.50
□ 245	George Schmees	25.00	10.00	2.50
□ 246	Jerry Snyder	25.00	10.00	2.50
□ 247	John Pramesa	25.00	10.00	2.50
□ 248	Bill Werle	25.00	10.00	2.50
□ 249	Hank Thompson	30.00	12.00	3.00
□ 250	Ivan Delock	25.00	10.00	2.50
□ 251	Jack Lohrke	25.00	10.00	2.50
□ 252	Frank Crosetti	100.00	15.00	3.00

1953 Bowman Color

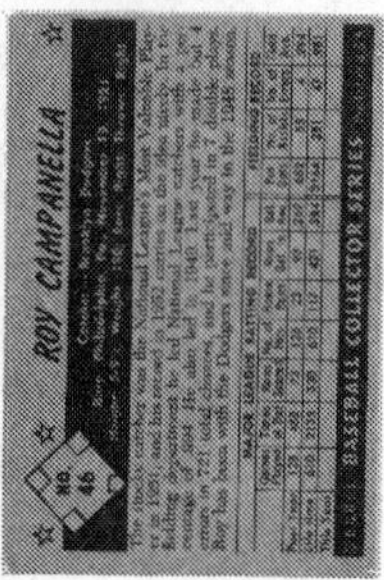

The cards in this 160-card set measure 2 1/2" by 3 3/4". The 1953 Bowman Color set, considered by many to be the best looking set of the modern era, contains Kodachrome photographs with no names or facsimile autographs on the face. Numbers 113 to 160 are somewhat more difficult to obtain. There are two cards of Al Corwin (126 and 149). Card number 159 is actually a picture of Floyd Baker.

	NRMT	VG-E	GOOD
COMPLETE SET (160)	**8000.00**	**3600.00**	**1200.00**
COMMON PLAYER (1-96)	21.00	8.50	2.10
COMMON PLAYER (97-112)	25.00	10.00	2.50
COMMON PLAYER (113-128)	40.00	16.00	4.00
COMMON PLAYER (129-160)	30.00	12.00	3.00

No.	Player	NRMT	VG-E	GOOD
☐ 1	Dave Williams	80.00	12.00	2.50
☐ 2	Vic Wertz	23.00	9.50	2.30
☐ 3	Sam Jethroe	21.00	8.50	2.10
☐ 4	Art Houtteman	21.00	8.50	2.10
☐ 5	Sid Gordon	21.00	8.50	2.10
☐ 6	Joe Ginsberg	21.00	8.50	2.10
☐ 7	Harry Chiti	21.00	8.50	2.10
☐ 8	Al Rosen	30.00	12.00	3.00
☐ 9	Phil Rizzuto	60.00	24.00	6.00
☐ 10	Richie Ashburn	36.00	15.00	3.60
☐ 11	Bobby Shantz	25.00	10.00	2.50
☐ 12	Carl Erskine	28.00	11.50	2.80
☐ 13	Gus Zernial	23.00	9.50	2.30
☐ 14	Billy Loes	23.00	9.50	2.30
☐ 15	Jim Busby	21.00	8.50	2.10
☐ 16	Bob Friend	23.00	9.50	2.30
☐ 17	Jerry Staley	21.00	8.50	2.10
☐ 18	Nelson Fox	33.00	15.00	3.50
☐ 19	Alvin Dark	23.00	9.50	2.30
☐ 20	Don Lenhardt	21.00	8.50	2.10
☐ 21	Joe Garagiola	50.00	20.00	5.00
☐ 22	Bob Porterfield	21.00	8.50	2.10
☐ 23	Herman Wehmeier	21.00	8.50	2.10
☐ 24	Jackie Jensen	28.00	11.50	2.80
☐ 25	Hoot Evers	21.00	8.50	2.10
☐ 26	Roy McMillan	21.00	8.50	2.10
☐ 27	Vic Raschi	28.00	11.50	2.80
☐ 28	Smokey Burgess	23.00	9.50	2.30
☐ 29	Bobby Avila	23.00	9.50	2.30
☐ 30	Phil Cavarretta	23.00	9.50	2.30
☐ 31	Jimmy Dykes	23.00	9.50	2.30
☐ **32**	**Stan Musial**	**350.00**	**140.00**	**32.00**
☐ 33	Pee Wee Reese HOR	175.00	70.00	18.00
☐ 34	Gil Coan	21.00	8.50	2.10
☐ 35	Maurice McDermott	21.00	8.50	2.10
☐ 36	Minnie Minoso	27.00	11.00	2.70
☐ 37	Jim Wilson	21.00	8.50	2.10
☐ 38	Harry Byrd	21.00	8.50	2.10
☐ 39	Paul Richards MG	23.00	9.50	2.30
☐ 40	Larry Doby	25.00	10.00	2.50
☐ 41	Sammy White	21.00	8.50	2.10
☐ 42	Tommy Brown	21.00	8.50	2.10
☐ 43	Mike Garcia	23.00	9.50	2.30
☐ 44	Berra/Bauer/Mantle	325.00	130.00	32.00
☐ 45	Walt Dropo	21.00	8.50	2.10
☐ 46	Roy Campanella	175.00	70.00	18.00
☐ 47	Ned Garver	21.00	8.50	2.10
☐ 48	Hank Sauer	23.00	9.50	2.30
☐ 49	Eddie Stanky	23.00	9.50	2.30
☐ 50	Lou Kretlow	21.00	8.50	2.10
☐ 51	Monte Irvin	45.00	18.00	4.50
☐ 52	Marty Marion	28.00	11.50	2.80
☐ 53	Del Rice	21.00	8.50	2.10
☐ 54	Chico Carrasquel	21.00	8.50	2.10
☐ 55	Leo Durocher MG	45.00	18.00	4.50
☐ 56	Bob Cain	21.00	8.50	2.10
☐ 57	Lou Boudreau MG	45.00	18.00	4.50
☐ 58	Willard Marshall	21.00	8.50	2.10
☐ **59**	**Mickey Mantle**	**1350.00**	**500.00**	**125.00**
☐ 60	Granny Hamner	21.00	8.50	2.10
☐ 61	George Kell	50.00	20.00	5.00
☐ 62	Ted Kluszewski	30.00	12.00	3.00
☐ 63	Gil McDougald	30.00	12.00	3.00
☐ 64	Curt Simmons	25.00	10.00	2.50
☐ 65	Robin Roberts	50.00	20.00	5.00
☐ 66	Mel Parnell	23.00	9.50	2.30
☐ 67	Mel Clark	21.00	8.50	2.10
☐ 68	Allie Reynolds	30.00	12.00	3.00
☐ 69	Charley Grimm MG	23.00	9.50	2.30
☐ 70	Clint Courtney	21.00	8.50	2.10
☐ 71	Paul Minner	21.00	8.50	2.10
☐ 72	Ted Gray	21.00	8.50	2.10
☐ 73	Billy Pierce	25.00	10.00	2.50
☐ 74	Don Mueller	23.00	9.50	2.30
☐ 75	Saul Rogovin	21.00	8.50	2.10
☐ 76	Jim Hearn	21.00	8.50	2.10
☐ 77	Mickey Grasso	21.00	8.50	2.10
☐ 78	Carl Furillo	30.00	12.00	3.00
☐ 79	Ray Boone	23.00	9.50	2.30
☐ 80	Ralph Kiner	50.00	20.00	5.00
☐ 81	Enos Slaughter	50.00	20.00	5.00
☐ 82	Joe Astroth	21.00	8.50	2.10
☐ 83	Jack Daniels	21.00	8.50	2.10
☐ 84	Hank Bauer	28.00	11.50	2.80
☐ 85	Solly Hemus	21.00	8.50	2.10
☐ 86	Harry Simpson	21.00	8.50	2.10
☐ 87	Harry Perkowski	21.00	8.50	2.10
☐ 88	Joe Dobson	21.00	8.50	2.10
☐ 89	Sandy Consuegra	21.00	8.50	2.10
☐ 90	Joe Nuxhall	23.00	9.50	2.30
☐ 91	Steve Souchock	21.00	8.50	2.10
☐ 92	Gil Hodges	80.00	32.00	8.00
☐ 93	Phil Rizzuto and Billy Martin	125.00	50.00	12.50
☐ 94	Bob Addis	21.00	8.50	2.10
☐ 95	Wally Moses	21.00	8.50	2.10
☐ 96	Sal Maglie	25.00	10.00	2.50
☐ 97	Ed Mathews	125.00	50.00	12.50
☐ 98	Hector Rodriguez	25.00	10.00	2.50
☐ 99	Warren Spahn	100.00	40.00	10.00
☐ 100	Bill Wight	25.00	10.00	2.50
☐ 101	Red Schoendienst	30.00	12.00	3.00
☐ 102	Jim Hegan	27.00	11.00	2.70
☐ 103	Del Ennis	27.00	11.00	2.70
☐ 104	Luke Easter	27.00	11.00	2.70
☐ 105	Eddie Joost	25.00	10.00	2.50
☐ 106	Ken Raffensberger	25.00	10.00	2.50
☐ 107	Alex Kellner	25.00	10.00	2.50
☐ 108	Bobby Adams	25.00	10.00	2.50
☐ 109	Ken Wood	25.00	10.00	2.50
☐ 110	Bob Rush	25.00	10.00	2.50
☐ 111	Jim Dyck	25.00	10.00	2.50
☐ 112	Toby Atwell	25.00	10.00	2.50
☐ 113	Karl Drews	40.00	16.00	4.00
☐ 114	Bob Feller	200.00	80.00	20.00
☐ 115	Cloyd Boyer	40.00	16.00	4.00
☐ 116	Eddie Yost	40.00	16.00	4.00
☐ 117	Duke Snider	450.00	180.00	45.00
☐ 118	Billy Martin	175.00	70.00	18.00
☐ 119	Dale Mitchell	45.00	18.00	4.50
☐ 120	Marlin Stuart	40.00	16.00	4.00
☐ 121	Yogi Berra	450.00	180.00	45.00
☐ 122	Bill Serena	40.00	16.00	4.00
☐ 123	Johnny Lipon	40.00	16.00	4.00
☐ 124	Charlie Dressen MG	50.00	20.00	5.00
☐ 125	Fred Hatfield	40.00	16.00	4.00
☐ 126	Al Corwin	40.00	16.00	4.00
☐ 127	Dick Kryhoski	40.00	16.00	4.00
☐ 128	Whitey Lockman	45.00	18.00	4.50
☐ 129	Russ Meyer	30.00	12.00	3.00
☐ 130	Cass Michaels	30.00	12.00	3.00
☐ 131	Connie Ryan	30.00	12.00	3.00
☐ 132	Fred Hutchinson	35.00	14.00	3.50
☐ 133	Willie Jones	30.00	12.00	3.00
☐ 134	Johnny Pesky	30.00	12.00	3.00
☐ 135	Bobby Morgan	30.00	12.00	3.00
☐ 136	Jim Brideweser	30.00	12.00	3.00
☐ 137	Sam Dente	30.00	12.00	3.00
☐ 138	Bubba Church	30.00	12.00	3.00
☐ 139	Pete Runnels	35.00	14.00	3.50
☐ 140	Al Brazle	30.00	12.00	3.00
☐ 141	Frank Shea	30.00	12.00	3.00
☐ 142	Larry Miggins	30.00	12.00	3.00
☐ 143	Al Lopez MG	60.00	24.00	6.00
☐ 144	Warren Hacker	30.00	12.00	3.00
☐ 145	George Shuba	35.00	14.00	3.50
☐ 146	Early Wynn	90.00	36.00	9.00
☐ 147	Clem Koshorek	30.00	12.00	3.00

□ 148 Billy Goodman	35.00	14.00	3.50
□ 149 Al Corwin	30.00	12.00	3.00
□ 150 Carl Scheib	30.00	12.00	3.00
□ 151 Joe Adcock	40.00	16.00	4.00
□ 152 Clyde Vollmer	30.00	12.00	3.00
□ 153 Whitey Ford	350.00	140.00	35.00
□ 154 Turk Lown	30.00	12.00	3.00
□ 155 Allie Clark	30.00	12.00	3.00
□ 156 Max Surkont	30.00	12.00	3.00
□ 157 Sherman Lollar	35.00	14.00	3.50
□ 158 Howard Fox	30.00	12.00	3.00
□ 159 Mickey Vernon (photo actually Floyd Baker)	35.00	14.00	3.50
□ 160 Cal Abrams	50.00	15.00	3.00

1953 Bowman BW

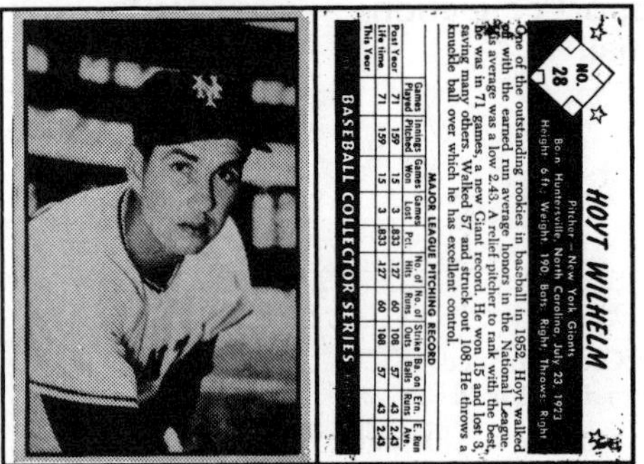

The cards in this 64-card set measure 2 1/2" by 3 3/4". Some collectors believe that the high cost of producing the 1953 color series forced Bowman to issue this set in black and white, since the two sets are identical in design except for the element of color. This set was also produced in fewer numbers than its color counterpart, and is popular among collectors for the challenge involved in completing it.

	NRMT	VG-E	GOOD
COMPLETE SET (64)	1900.00	850.00	250.00
COMMON PLAYER (1-64)	25.00	10.00	2.50
□ 1 Gus Bell	80.00	15.00	3.00
□ 2 Willard Nixon	25.00	10.00	2.50
□ 3 Bill Rigney	25.00	10.00	2.50
□ 4 Pat Mullin	25.00	10.00	2.50
□ 5 Dee Fondy	25.00	10.00	2.50
□ 6 Ray Murray	25.00	10.00	2.50
□ 7 Andy Seminick	25.00	10.00	2.50
□ 8 Pete Suder	25.00	10.00	2.50
□ 9 Walt Masterson	25.00	10.00	2.50
□ 10 Dick Sisler	25.00	10.00	2.50
□ 11 Dick Gernert	25.00	10.00	2.50
□ 12 Randy Jackson	25.00	10.00	2.50
□ 13 Joe Tipton	25.00	10.00	2.50
□ 14 Bill Nicholson	25.00	10.00	2.50
□ 15 Johnny Mize	100.00	40.00	10.00
□ 16 Stu Miller	30.00	12.00	3.00
□ 17 Virgil Trucks	30.00	12.00	3.00
□ 18 Billy Hoeft	30.00	12.00	3.00
□ 19 Paul LaPalme	25.00	10.00	2.50
□ 20 Eddie Robinson	25.00	10.00	2.50
□ 21 Clarence Podbielan	25.00	10.00	2.50
□ 22 Matt Batts	25.00	10.00	2.50
□ 23 Wilmer Mizell	25.00	10.00	2.50
□ 24 Del Wilber	25.00	10.00	2.50
□ 25 Johnny Sain	50.00	20.00	5.00
□ 26 Preacher Roe	50.00	20.00	5.00
□ 27 Bob Lemon	90.00	36.00	9.00
□ 28 Hoyt Wilhelm	90.00	36.00	9.00
□ 29 Sid Hudson	25.00	10.00	2.50
□ 30 Walker Cooper	25.00	10.00	2.50
□ 31 Gene Woodling	40.00	16.00	4.00
□ 32 Rocky Bridges	25.00	10.00	2.50
□ 33 Bob Kuzava	25.00	10.00	2.50
□ 34 Ebba St.Claire	25.00	10.00	2.50
□ 35 Johnny Wyrostek	25.00	10.00	2.50
□ 36 Jim Piersall	40.00	16.00	4.00
□ 37 Hal Jeffcoat	25.00	10.00	2.50
□ 38 Dave Cole	25.00	10.00	2.50
□ 39 Casey Stengel	250.00	100.00	25.00
□ 40 Larry Jansen	25.00	10.00	2.50
□ 41 Bob Ramazotti	25.00	10.00	2.50
□ 42 Howie Judson	25.00	10.00	2.50
□ 43 Hal Bevan	25.00	10.00	2.50
□ 44 Jim Delsing	25.00	10.00	2.50
□ 45 Irv Noren	30.00	12.00	3.00
□ 46 Bucky Harris	50.00	20.00	5.00
□ 47 Jack Lohrke	25.00	10.00	2.50
□ 48 Steve Ridzik	25.00	10.00	2.50
□ 49 Floyd Baker	25.00	10.00	2.50
□ 50 Dutch Leonard	25.00	10.00	2.50
□ 51 Lou Burdette	40.00	16.00	4.00
□ 52 Ralph Branca	35.00	14.00	3.50
□ 53 Morris Martin	25.00	10.00	2.50
□ 54 Bill Miller	25.00	10.00	2.50
□ 55 Don Johnson	25.00	10.00	2.50
□ 56 Roy Smalley	25.00	10.00	2.50
□ 57 Andy Pafko	25.00	10.00	2.50
□ 58 Jim Konstanty	30.00	12.00	3.00
□ 59 Duane Pillette	25.00	10.00	2.50
□ 60 Billy Cox	30.00	12.00	3.00
□ 61 Tom Gorman	25.00	10.00	2.50
□ 62 Keith Thomas	25.00	10.00	2.50
□ 63 Steve Gromek	25.00	10.00	2.50
□ 64 Andy Hansen	40.00	15.00	3.00

1954 Bowman

The cards in this 224-card set measure 2 1/2" by 3 3/4". A contractual problem apparently resulted in the deletion of the number 66 Ted Williams card from this Bowman set, thereby creating a scarcity which is highly valued among collectors. The set price below does NOT include number 66 Williams. Many errors in players' statistics exist (and some were corrected) while a few players' names were printed on the front, instead of appearing as a facsimile autograph.

	NRMT	VG-E	GOOD
COMPLETE SET (224)	3000.00	1250.00	450.00
COMMON PLAYER (1-128)	5.00	2.00	.50
COMMON PLAYER (129-224)	6.00	2.40	.60
□ 1 Phil Rizzuto	125.00	20.00	4.00
□ 2 Jackie Jensen	9.00	3.75	.90
□ 3 Marion Fricano	5.00	2.00	.50
□ 4 Bob Hooper	5.00	2.00	.50
□ 5 Bill Hunter	5.00	2.00	.50
□ 6 Nelson Fox	11.00	4.50	1.10
□ 7 Walt Dropo	5.00	2.00	.50
□ 8 Jim Busby	5.00	2.00	.50
□ 9 Davey Williams	6.00	2.40	.60
□ 10 Carl Erskine	9.00	3.75	.90
□ 11 Sid Gordon	5.00	2.00	.50
□ 12 Roy McMillan	5.00	2.00	.50
□ 13 Paul Minner	5.00	2.00	.50
□ 14 Gerry Staley	5.00	2.00	.50
□ 15 Richie Ashburn	12.00	5.00	1.20
□ 16 Jim Wilson	5.00	2.00	.50
□ 17 Tom Gorman	5.00	2.00	.50
□ 18 Hoot Evers	5.00	2.00	.50
□ 19 Bobby Shantz	7.00	2.80	.70
□ 20 Art Houtteman	5.00	2.00	.50

□ 21 Vic Wertz	6.00	2.40	.60
□ 22 Sam Mele	5.00	2.00	.50
□ 23 Harvey Kuenn	16.00	6.50	1.60
□ 24 Bob Porterfield	5.00	2.00	.50
□ 25 Wes Westrum	5.00	2.00	.50
□ 26 Billy Cox	6.00	2.40	.60
□ 27 Dick Cole	5.00	2.00	.50
□ 28 Jim Greengrass	5.00	2.00	.50
□ 29 Johnny Klippstein	5.00	2.00	.50
□ 30 Del Rice	5.00	2.00	.50
□ 31 Smoky Burgess	6.00	2.40	.60
□ 32 Del Crandall	6.00	2.40	.60
□ 33A Vic Raschi (no mention of trade on back)	9.00	3.75	.90
□ 33B Vic Raschi (traded to St.Louis)	18.00	7.25	1.80
□ 34 Sammy White	5.00	2.00	.50
□ 35 Eddie Joost	5.00	2.00	.50
□ 36 George Strickland	5.00	2.00	.50
□ 37 Dick Kokos	5.00	2.00	.50
□ 38 Minnie Minoso	8.00	3.25	.80
□ 39 Ned Garver	5.00	2.00	.50
□ 40 Gil Coan	5.00	2.00	.50
□ 41 Alvin Dark	7.00	2.80	.70
□ 42 Billy Loes	5.00	2.00	.50
□ 43 Bob Friend	6.00	2.40	.60
□ 44 Harry Perkowski	5.00	2.00	.50
□ 45 Ralph Kiner	25.00	10.00	2.50
□ 46 Rip Repulski	5.00	2.00	.50
□ 47 Granny Hamner	5.00	2.00	.50
□ 48 Jack Dittmer	5.00	2.00	.50
□ 49 Harry Byrd	5.00	2.00	.50
□ 50 George Kell	22.00	9.00	2.20
□ 51 Alex Kellner	5.00	2.00	.50
□ 52 Joe Ginsberg	5.00	2.00	.50
□ 53 Don Lenhardt	5.00	2.00	.50
□ 54 Chico Carrasquel	5.00	2.00	.50
□ 55 Jim Delsing	5.00	2.00	.50
□ 56 Maurice McDermott	5.00	2.00	.50
□ 57 Hoyt Wilhelm	22.00	9.00	2.20
□ 58 Pee Wee Reese	45.00	18.00	4.50
□ 59 Bob Schultz	5.00	2.00	.50
□ 60 Fred Baczewski	5.00	2.00	.50
□ 61 Eddie Miksis	5.00	2.00	.50
□ 62 Enos Slaughter	22.00	9.00	2.20
□ 63 Earl Torgeson	5.00	2.00	.50
□ 64 Eddie Mathews	35.00	14.00	3.50
□ 65 Mickey Mantle	700.00	280.00	70.00
□ 66A Ted Williams	2100.00	800.00	200.00
□ 66B Jim Piersall	100.00	40.00	10.00
□ 67 Carl Scheib	5.00	2.00	.50
□ 68 Bobby Avila	5.00	2.00	.50
□ 69 Clint Courtney	5.00	2.00	.50
□ 70 Willard Marshall	5.00	2.00	.50
□ 71 Ted Gray	5.00	2.00	.50
□ 72 Eddie Yost	5.00	2.00	.50
□ 73 Don Mueller	6.00	2.40	.60
□ 74 Jim Gilliam	9.00	3.75	.90
□ 75 Max Surkont	5.00	2.00	.50
□ 76 Joe Nuxhall	6.00	2.40	.60
□ 77 Bob Rush	5.00	2.00	.50
□ 78 Sal Yvars	5.00	2.00	.50
□ 79 Curt Simmons	6.00	2.40	.60
□ 80 Johnny Logan	6.00	2.40	.60
□ 81 Jerry Coleman	7.00	2.80	.70
□ 82 Billy Goodman	6.00	2.40	.60
□ 83 Ray Murray	5.00	2.00	.50
□ 84 Larry Doby	8.50	3.50	.85
□ 85 Jim Dyck	5.00	2.00	.50
□ 86 Harry Dorish	5.00	2.00	.50
□ 87 Don Lund	5.00	2.00	.50
□ 88 Tom Umphlett	5.00	2.00	.50
□ 89 Willie Mays	250.00	100.00	25.00
□ 90 Roy Campanella	90.00	36.00	9.00
□ 91 Cal Abrams	5.00	2.00	.50
□ 92 Ken Raffensberger	5.00	2.00	.50
□ 93 Bill Serena	5.00	2.00	.50
□ 94 Solly Hemus	5.00	2.00	.50
□ 95 Robin Roberts	22.00	9.00	2.20
□ 96 Joe Adcock	6.00	2.40	.60
□ 97 Gil McDougald	10.00	4.00	1.00
□ 98 Ellis Kinder	5.00	2.00	.50
□ 99 Pete Suder	5.00	2.00	.50
□ 100 Mike Garcia	6.00	2.40	.60
□ 101 Don Larsen	15.00	6.00	1.50
□ 102 Billy Pierce	6.00	2.40	.60
□ 103 Steve Souchock	5.00	2.00	.50
□ 104 Frank Shea	5.00	2.00	.50
□ 105 Sal Maglie	8.50	3.50	.85
□ 106 Clem Labine	6.00	2.40	.60
□ 107 Paul LaPalme	5.00	2.00	.50
□ 108 Bobby Adams	5.00	2.00	.50
□ 109 Roy Smalley	5.00	2.00	.50
□ 110 Red Schoendienst	8.50	3.50	.85
□ 111 Murry Dickson	5.00	2.00	.50
□ 112 Andy Pafko	5.00	2.00	.50
□ 113 Allie Reynolds	12.00	5.00	1.20
□ 114 Willard Nixon	5.00	2.00	.50
□ 115 Don Bollweg	5.00	2.00	.50
□ 116 Luke Easter	5.00	2.00	.50
□ 117 Dick Kryhoski	5.00	2.00	.50
□ 118 Bob Boyd	5.00	2.00	.50
□ 119 Fred Hatfield	5.00	2.00	.50
□ 120 Mel Hoderlein	5.00	2.00	.50
□ 121 Ray Katt	5.00	2.00	.50
□ 122 Carl Furillo	11.00	4.50	1.10
□ 123 Toby Atwell	5.00	2.00	.50
□ 124 Gus Bell	6.00	2.40	.60
□ 125 Warren Hacker	5.00	2.00	.50
□ 126 Cliff Chambers	5.00	2.00	.50
□ 127 Del Ennis	6.00	2.40	.60
□ 128 Ebba St.Claire	5.00	2.00	.50
□ 129 Hank Bauer	11.00	4.50	1.10
□ 130 Milt Bolling	6.00	2.40	.60
□ 131 Joe Astroth	6.00	2.40	.60
□ 132 Bob Feller	50.00	20.00	5.00
□ 133 Duane Pillette	6.00	2.40	.60
□ 134 Luis Aloma	6.00	2.40	.60
□ 135 Johnny Pesky	7.00	2.80	.70
□ 136 Clyde Vollmer	6.00	2.40	.60
□ 137 Al Corwin	6.00	2.40	.60
□ 138 Gil Hodges	35.00	14.00	3.50
□ 139 Preston Ward	6.00	2.40	.60
□ 140 Saul Rogovin	6.00	2.40	.60
□ 141 Joe Garagiola	28.00	11.50	2.80
□ 142 Al Brazle	6.00	2.40	.60
□ 143 Willie Jones	6.00	2.40	.60
□ 144 Ernie Johnson	6.00	2.40	.60
□ 145 Billy Martin	35.00	14.00	3.50
□ 146 Dick Gernert	6.00	2.40	.60
□ 147 Joe DeMaestri	6.00	2.40	.60
□ 148 Dale Mitchell	7.00	2.80	.70
□ 149 Bob Young	6.00	2.40	.60
□ 150 Cass Michaels	6.00	2.40	.60
□ 151 Pat Mullin	6.00	2.40	.60
□ 152 Mickey Vernon	7.00	2.80	.70
□ 153 Whitey Lockman	7.00	2.80	.70
□ 154 Don Newcombe	11.00	4.50	1.10
□ 155 Frank Thomas	7.00	2.80	.70
□ 156 Rocky Bridges	6.00	2.40	.60
□ 157 Turk Lown	6.00	2.40	.60
□ 158 Stu Miller	6.00	2.40	.60
□ 159 Johnny Lindell	6.00	2.40	.60
□ 160 Danny O'Connell	6.00	2.40	.60
□ 161 Yogi Berra	100.00	40.00	10.00
□ 162 Ted Lepcio	6.00	2.40	.60
□ 163A Dave Philley (no mention of trade on back)	7.00	2.80	.70
□ 163B Dave Philley (traded to Cleveland)	17.00	7.00	1.70
□ 164 Early Wynn	22.00	9.00	2.20
□ 165 Johnny Groth	6.00	2.40	.60
□ 166 Sandy Consuegra	6.00	2.40	.60
□ 167 Billy Hoeft	6.00	2.40	.60
□ 168 Ed Fitzgerald	6.00	2.40	.60
□ 169 Larry Jansen	6.00	2.40	.60
□ 170 Duke Snider	80.00	32.00	8.00
□ 171 Carlos Bernier	6.00	2.40	.60
□ 172 Andy Seminick	6.00	2.40	.60
□ 173 Dee Fondy	6.00	2.40	.60
□ 174 Pete Castiglione	6.00	2.40	.60
□ 175 Mel Clark	6.00	2.40	.60
□ 176 Vern Bickford	6.00	2.40	.60
□ 177 Whitey Ford	45.00	18.00	4.50
□ 178 Del Wilber	6.00	2.40	.60
□ 179 Morris Martin	6.00	2.40	.60
□ 180 Joe Tipton	6.00	2.40	.60
□ 181 Les Moss	6.00	2.40	.60
□ 182 Sherman Lollar	7.00	2.80	.70
□ 183 Matt Batts	6.00	2.40	.60
□ 184 Mickey Grasso	6.00	2.40	.60
□ 185 Daryl Spencer	6.00	2.40	.60
□ 186 Russ Meyer	6.00	2.40	.60
□ 187 Vernon Law	7.00	2.80	.70
□ 188 Frank Smith	6.00	2.40	.60
□ 189 Randy Jackson	6.00	2.40	.60
□ 190 Joe Presko	6.00	2.40	.60
□ 191 Karl Drews	6.00	2.40	.60
□ 192 Lou Burdette	8.50	3.50	.85
□ 193 Eddie Robinson	6.00	2.40	.60
□ 194 Sid Hudson	6.00	2.40	.60
□ 195 Bob Cain	6.00	2.40	.60
□ 196 Bob Lemon	22.00	9.00	2.20
□ 197 Lou Kretlow	6.00	2.40	.60
□ 198 Virgil Trucks	7.00	2.80	.70
□ 199 Steve Gromek	6.00	2.40	.60
□ 200 Conrado Marrero	6.00	2.40	.60

□ 201 Bobby Thomson	9.00	3.75	.90
□ 202 George Shuba	7.00	2.80	.70
□ 203 Vic Janowicz	7.00	2.80	.70
□ 204 Jackie Collum	6.00	2.40	.60
□ 205 Hal Jeffcoat	6.00	2.40	.60
□ 206 Steve Bilko	6.00	2.40	.60
□ 207 Stan Lopata	6.00	2.40	.60
□ 208 Johnny Antonelli	7.00	2.80	.70
□ 209 Gene Woodling	9.00	3.75	.90
□ 210 Jim Piersall	9.00	3.75	.90
□ 211 Al Robertson	6.00	2.40	.60
□ 212 Owen Friend	6.00	2.40	.60
□ 213 Dick Littlefield	6.00	2.40	.60
□ 214 Ferris Fain	7.00	2.80	.70
□ 215 Johnny Bucha	6.00	2.40	.60
□ 216 Jerry Snyder	6.00	2.40	.60
□ 217 Henry Thompson	7.00	2.80	.70
□ 218 Preacher Roe	10.00	4.00	1.00
□ 219 Hal Rice	6.00	2.40	.60
□ 220 Hobie Landrith	6.00	2.40	.60
□ 221 Frank Baumholtz	6.00	2.40	.60
□ 222 Memo Luna	6.00	2.40	.60
□ 223 Steve Ridzik	6.00	2.40	.60
□ 224 Bill Bruton	20.00	4.00	.75

1955 Bowman

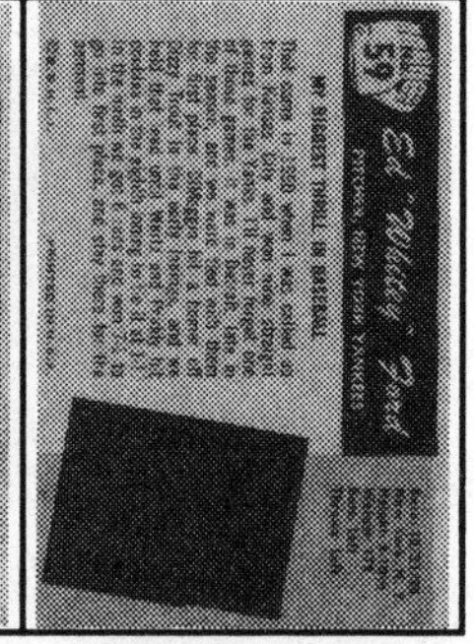

The cards in this 320-card set measure 2 1/2" by 3 3/4". The Bowman set of 1955 is known as the "TV set" because each player photograph is cleverly shown within a television set design. The set contains umpire cards, some transposed pictures (e.g., Johnsons and Bollings), an incorrect spelling for Harvey Kuenn, and a traded line for Palica (all of which are noted in the checklist below). Some three-card advertising strips exist.

	NRMT	VG-E	GOOD
COMPLETE SET (320)	**3750.00**	**1650.00**	**550.00**
COMMON PLAYER (1-96)	**5.00**	**2.00**	**.50**
COMMON PLAYER (97-224)	**4.00**	**1.60**	**.40**
COMMON PLAYER (225-320)	10.00	4.00	1.00
COMMON UMPIRES (225-320)	15.00	6.00	1.50
□ 1 Hoyt Wilhelm	75.00	10.00	2.00
□ 2 Alvin Dark	7.00	2.80	.70
□ 3 Joe Coleman	5.00	2.00	.50
□ 4 Eddie Waitkus	5.00	2.00	.50
□ 5 Jim Robertson	5.00	2.00	.50
□ 6 Pete Suder	5.00	2.00	.50
□ 7 Gene Baker	5.00	2.00	.50
□ 8 Warren Hacker	5.00	2.00	.50
□ 9 Gil McDougald	10.00	4.00	1.00
□ 10 Phil Rizzuto	33.00	13.00	3.00
□ 11 Bill Bruton	6.00	2.40	.60
□ 12 Andy Pafko	6.00	2.40	.60
□ 13 Clyde Vollmer	5.00	2.00	.50
□ 14 Gus Keriazakos	5.00	2.00	.50
□ 15 Frank Sullivan	5.00	2.00	.50
□ 16 Jim Piersall	8.00	3.25	.80
□ 17 Del Ennis	6.00	2.40	.60
□ 18 Stan Lopata	5.00	2.00	.50
□ 19 Bobby Avila	6.00	2.40	.60
□ 20 Al Smith	5.00	2.00	.50
□ 21 Don Hoak	6.00	2.40	.60
□ 22 Roy Campanella	75.00	30.00	7.50
□ 23 Al Kaline	75.00	30.00	7.50
□ 24 Al Aber	5.00	2.00	.50
□ 25 Minnie Minoso	8.00	3.25	.80
□ 26 Virgil Trucks	6.00	2.40	.60
□ 27 Preston Ward	5.00	2.00	.50
□ 28 Dick Cole	5.00	2.00	.50
□ 29 Red Schoendienst	9.00	3.75	.90
□ 30 Bill Sarni	5.00	2.00	.50
□ 31 Johnny Temple	6.00	2.40	.60
□ 32 Wally Post	6.00	2.40	.60
□ 33 Nellie Fox	11.00	4.50	1.10
□ 34 Clint Courtney	5.00	2.00	.50
□ 35 Bill Tuttle	5.00	2.00	.50
□ 36 Wayne Belardi	5.00	2.00	.50
□ 37 Pee Wee Reese	40.00	16.00	4.00
□ 38 Early Wynn	18.00	7.25	1.80
□ 39 Bob Darnell	5.00	2.00	.50
□ 40 Vic Wertz	6.00	2.40	.60
□ 41 Mel Clark	5.00	2.00	.50
□ 42 Bob Greenwood	5.00	2.00	.50
□ 43 Bob Buhl	5.00	2.00	.50
□ 44 Danny O'Connell	5.00	2.00	.50
□ 45 Tom Umphlett	5.00	2.00	.50
□ 46 Mickey Vernon	6.00	2.40	.60
□ 47 Sammy White	5.00	2.00	.50
□ 48A Milt Bolling ERR (name on back is Frank Bolling)	6.00	2.40	.60
□ 48B Milt Bolling COR	20.00	8.00	2.00
□ 49 Jim Greengrass	5.00	2.00	.50
□ 50 Hobie Landrith	5.00	2.00	.50
□ 51 Elvin Tappe	5.00	2.00	.50
□ 52 Hal Rice	5.00	2.00	.50
□ 53 Alex Kellner	5.00	2.00	.50
□ 54 Don Bollweg	5.00	2.00	.50
□ 55 Cal Abrams	6.00	2.40	.60
□ 56 Billy Cox	7.00	2.80	.70
□ 57 Bob Friend	6.00	2.40	.60
□ 58 Frank Thomas	6.00	2.40	.60
□ 59 Whitey Ford	40.00	16.00	4.00
□ 60 Enos Slaughter	20.00	8.00	2.00
□ 61 Paul LaPalme	5.00	2.00	.50
□ 62 Royce Lint	5.00	2.00	.50
□ 63 Irv Noren	6.00	2.40	.60
□ 64 Curt Simmons	6.00	2.40	.60
□ 65 Don Zimmer	10.00	4.00	1.00
□ 66 George Shuba	6.00	2.40	.60
□ 67 Don Larsen	11.00	4.50	1.10
□ 68 Elston Howard	20.00	8.00	2.00
□ 69 Billy Hunter	5.00	2.00	.50
□ 70 Lou Burdette	8.00	3.25	.80
□ 71 Dave Jolly	5.00	2.00	.50
□ 72 Chet Nichols	5.00	2.00	.50
□ 73 Eddie Yost	5.00	2.00	.50
□ 74 Jerry Snyder	5.00	2.00	.50
□ 75 Brooks Lawrence	5.00	2.00	.50
□ 76 Tom Poholsky	5.00	2.00	.50
□ 77 Jim McDonald	5.00	2.00	.50
□ 78 Gil Coan	5.00	2.00	.50
□ 79 Willie Miranda	5.00	2.00	.50
□ 80 Lou Limmer	5.00	2.00	.50
□ 81 Bobby Morgan	5.00	2.00	.50
□ 82 Lee Walls	5.00	2.00	.50
□ 83 Max Surkont	5.00	2.00	.50
□ 84 George Freese	5.00	2.00	.50
□ 85 Cass Michaels	5.00	2.00	.50
□ 86 Ted Gray	5.00	2.00	.50
□ 87 Randy Jackson	5.00	2.00	.50
□ 88 Steve Bilko	5.00	2.00	.50
□ 89 Lou Boudreau MG	18.00	7.25	1.80
□ 90 Art Ditmar	5.00	2.00	.50
□ 91 Dick Marlowe	5.00	2.00	.50
□ 92 George Zuverink	5.00	2.00	.50
□ 93 Andy Seminick	5.00	2.00	.50
□ 94 Hank Thompson	6.00	2.40	.60
□ 95 Sal Maglie	8.00	3.25	.80
□ 96 Ray Narleski	5.00	2.00	.50
□ 97 Johnny Podres	10.00	4.00	1.00
□ 98 Jim Gilliam	9.00	3.75	.90
□ 99 Jerry Coleman	6.00	2.40	.60
□ 100 Tom Morgan	5.00	2.00	.50
□ 101A Don Johnson ERR (photo actually Ernie Johnson)	5.00	2.00	.50
□ 101B Don Johnson COR	15.00	6.00	1.50
□ 102 Bobby Thomson	7.00	2.80	.70
□ 103 Eddie Mathews	30.00	12.00	3.00
□ 104 Bob Porterfield	4.00	1.60	.40
□ 105 Johnny Schmitz	4.00	1.60	.40
□ 106 Del Rice	4.00	1.60	.40
□ 107 Solly Hemus	4.00	1.60	.40
□ 108 Lou Kretlow	4.00	1.60	.40
□ 109 Vern Stephens	5.00	2.00	.50
□ 110 Bob Miller	4.00	1.60	.40
□ 111 Steve Ridzik	4.00	1.60	.40
□ 112 Granny Hamner	4.00	1.60	.40

□ 113	Bob Hall	4.00	1.60	.40
□ 114	Vic Janowicz	5.00	2.00	.50
□ 115	Roger Bowman	4.00	1.60	.40
□ 116	Sandy Consuegra	4.00	1.60	.40
□ 117	Johnny Groth	4.00	1.60	.40
□ 118	Bobby Adams	4.00	1.60	.40
□ 119	Joe Astroth	4.00	1.60	.40
□ 120	Ed Burtschy	4.00	1.60	.40
□ 121	Rufus Crawford	4.00	1.60	.40
□ 122	Al Corwin	4.00	1.60	.40
□ 123	Marv Grissom	4.00	1.60	.40
□ 124	Johnny Antonelli	6.00	2.40	.60
□ 125	Paul Giel	4.00	1.60	.40
□ 126	Billy Goodman	5.00	2.00	.50
□ 127	Hank Majeski	4.00	1.60	.40
□ 128	Mike Garcia	6.00	2.40	.60
□ 129	Hal Naragon	4.00	1.60	.40
□ 130	Richie Ashburn	11.00	4.50	1.10
□ 131	Willard Marshall	4.00	1.60	.40
□ 132A	Harvey Kueen ERR (sic, Kuenn)	7.00	2.80	.70
□ 132B	Harvey Kuenn COR	16.00	6.50	1.60
□ 133	Charles King	4.00	1.60	.40
□ 134	Bob Feller	40.00	16.00	4.00
□ 135	Lloyd Merriman	4.00	1.60	.40
□ 136	Rocky Bridges	4.00	1.60	.40
□ 137	Bob Talbot	4.00	1.60	.40
□ 138	Davey Williams	5.00	2.00	.50
□ 139	Shantz Brothers Wilmer and Bobby	6.00	2.40	.60
□ 140	Bobby Shantz	6.00	2.40	.60
□ 141	Wes Westrum	5.00	2.00	.50
□ 142	Rudy Regalado	4.00	1.60	.40
□ 143	Don Newcombe	8.00	3.25	.80
□ 144	Art Houtteman	4.00	1.60	.40
□ 145	Bob Nieman	4.00	1.60	.40
□ 146	Don Liddle	4.00	1.60	.40
□ 147	Sam Mele	4.00	1.60	.40
□ 148	Bob Chakales	4.00	1.60	.40
□ 149	Cloyd Boyer	4.00	1.60	.40
□ 150	Billy Klaus	4.00	1.60	.40
□ 151	Jim Brideweser	4.00	1.60	.40
□ 152	Johnny Klippstein	4.00	1.60	.40
□ 153	Eddie Robinson	4.00	1.60	.40
□ 154	Frank Lary	6.00	2.40	.60
□ 155	Jerry Staley	4.00	1.60	.40
□ 156	Jim Hughes	4.00	1.60	.40
□ 157A	Ernie Johnson ERR (photo actually Don Johnson)	5.00	2.00	.50
□ 157B	Ernie Johnson COR	15.00	6.00	1.50
□ 158	Gil Hodges	28.00	11.50	2.80
□ 159	Harry Byrd	5.00	2.00	.50
□ 160	Bill Skowron	10.00	4.00	1.00
□ 161	Matt Batts	4.00	1.60	.40
□ 162	Charlie Maxwell	4.00	1.60	.40
□ 163	Sid Gordon	4.00	1.60	.40
□ 164	Toby Atwell	4.00	1.60	.40
□ 165	Maurice McDermott	4.00	1.60	.40
□ 166	Jim Busby	4.00	1.60	.40
□ 167	Bob Grim	6.00	2.40	.60
□ 168	Yogi Berra	75.00	30.00	7.50
□ 169	Carl Furillo	10.00	4.00	1.00
□ 170	Carl Erskine	8.00	3.25	.80
□ 171	Robin Roberts	18.00	7.25	1.80
□ 172	Willie Jones	4.00	1.60	.40
□ 173	Chico Carrasquel	4.00	1.60	.40
□ 174	Sherm Lollar	5.00	2.00	.50
□ 175	Wilmer Shantz	4.00	1.60	.40
□ 176	Joe DeMaestri	4.00	1.60	.40
□ 177	Willard Nixon	4.00	1.60	.40
□ 178	Tom Brewer	4.00	1.60	.40
□ 179	Hank Aaron	160.00	65.00	15.00
□ 180	Johnny Logan	5.00	2.00	.50
□ 181	Eddie Miksis	4.00	1.60	.40
□ 182	Bob Rush	4.00	1.60	.40
□ 183	Ray Katt	4.00	1.60	.40
□ 184	Willie Mays	160.00	65.00	15.00
□ 185	Vic Raschi	7.00	2.80	.70
□ 186	Alex Grammas	4.00	1.60	.40
□ 187	Fred Hatfield	4.00	1.60	.40
□ 188	Ned Garver	4.00	1.60	.40
□ 189	Jack Collum	4.00	1.60	.40
□ 190	Fred Baczewski	4.00	1.60	.40
□ 191	Bob Lemon	18.00	7.25	1.80
□ 192	George Strickland	4.00	1.60	.40
□ 193	Howie Judson	4.00	1.60	.40
□ 194	Joe Nuxhall	5.00	2.00	.50
□ 195A	Erv Palica (without trade)	5.00	2.00	.50
□ 195B	Erv Palica (with trade)	15.00	6.00	1.50
□ 196	Russ Meyer	4.00	1.60	.40
□ 197	Ralph Kiner	22.00	9.00	2.20
□ 198	Dave Pope	4.00	1.60	.40
□ 199	Vernon Law	6.00	2.40	.60
□ 200	Dick Littlefield	4.00	1.60	.40
□ 201	Allie Reynolds	11.00	4.50	1.10
□ 202	Mickey Mantle	375.00	150.00	35.00
□ 203	Steve Gromek	4.00	1.60	.40
□ 204A	Frank Bolling ERR (name on back is Milt Bolling)	5.00	2.00	.50
□ 204B	Frank Bolling COR	15.00	6.00	1.50
□ 205	Rip Repulski	4.00	1.60	.40
□ 206	Ralph Beard	4.00	1.60	.40
□ 207	Frank Shea	4.00	1.60	.40
□ 208	Ed Fitzgerald	4.00	1.60	.40
□ 209	Smokey Burgess	5.00	2.00	.50
□ 210	Earl Torgeson	4.00	1.60	.40
□ 211	Sonny Dixon	4.00	1.60	.40
□ 212	Jack Dittmer	4.00	1.60	.40
□ 213	George Kell	18.00	7.25	1.80
□ 214	Billy Pierce	6.00	2.40	.60
□ 215	Bob Kuzava	4.00	1.60	.40
□ 216	Preacher Roe	7.00	2.80	.70
□ 217	Del Crandall	5.00	2.00	.50
□ 218	Joe Adcock	6.00	2.40	.60
□ 219	Whitey Lockman	5.00	2.00	.50
□ 220	Jim Hearn	4.00	1.60	.40
□ 221	Hector Brown	4.00	1.60	.40
□ 222	Russ Kemmerer	4.00	1.60	.40
□ 223	Hal Jeffcoat	4.00	1.60	.40
□ 224	Dee Fondy	4.00	1.60	.40
□ 225	Paul Richards	12.00	5.00	1.20
□ 226	W. McKinley UMP	15.00	6.00	1.50
□ 227	Frank Baumholtz	10.00	4.00	1.00
□ 228	John Phillips	10.00	4.00	1.00
□ 229	Jim Brosnan	12.00	5.00	1.20
□ 230	Al Brazle	10.00	4.00	1.00
□ 231	Jim Konstanty	12.00	5.00	1.20
□ 232	Birdie Tebbetts	12.00	5.00	1.20
□ 233	Bill Serena	10.00	4.00	1.00
□ 234	Dick Bartell	10.00	4.00	1.00
□ 235	J. Paparella UMP	15.00	6.00	1.50
□ 236	Murry Dickson	10.00	4.00	1.00
□ 237	Johnny Wyrostek	10.00	4.00	1.00
□ 238	Eddie Stanky	12.00	5.00	1.20
□ 239	Edwin Rommel UMP	15.00	6.00	1.50
□ 240	Billy Loes	12.00	5.00	1.20
□ 241	Johnny Pesky	12.00	5.00	1.20
□ 242	Ernie Banks	250.00	100.00	25.00
□ 243	Gus Bell	12.00	5.00	1.20
□ 244	Duane Pillette	10.00	4.00	1.00
□ 245	Bill Miller	10.00	4.00	1.00
□ 246	Hank Bauer	20.00	8.00	2.00
□ 247	Dutch Leonard	10.00	4.00	1.00
□ 248	Harry Dorish	10.00	4.00	1.00
□ 249	Billy Gardner	12.00	5.00	1.20
□ 250	Larry Napp UMP	15.00	6.00	1.50
□ 251	Stan Jok	10.00	4.00	1.00
□ 252	Roy Smalley	10.00	4.00	1.00
□ 253	Jim Wilson	10.00	4.00	1.00
□ 254	Bennett Flowers	10.00	4.00	1.00
□ 255	Pete Runnels	12.00	5.00	1.20
□ 256	Owen Friend	10.00	4.00	1.00
□ 257	Tom Alston	10.00	4.00	1.00
□ 258	John Stevens UMP	15.00	6.00	1.50
□ 259	Don Mossi	12.00	5.00	1.20
□ 260	Edwin Hurley UMP	15.00	6.00	1.50
□ 261	Walt Moryn	10.00	4.00	1.00
□ 262	Jim Lemon	12.00	5.00	1.20
□ 263	Eddie Joost	10.00	4.00	1.00
□ 264	Bill Henry	10.00	4.00	1.00
□ 265	Albert Barlick UMP	15.00	6.00	1.50
□ 266	Mike Fornieles	10.00	4.00	1.00
□ 267	Jim Honochick UMP	40.00	16.00	4.00
□ 268	Roy Lee Hawes	10.00	4.00	1.00
□ 269	Joe Amalfitano	10.00	4.00	1.00
□ 270	Chico Fernandez	10.00	4.00	1.00
□ 271	Bob Hooper	10.00	4.00	1.00
□ 272	John Flaherty UMP	15.00	6.00	1.50
□ 273	Bubba Church	10.00	4.00	1.00
□ 274	Jim Delsing	10.00	4.00	1.00
□ 275	William Grieve UMP	15.00	6.00	1.50
□ 276	Ike Delock	10.00	4.00	1.00
□ 277	Ed Runge UMP	15.00	6.00	1.50
□ 278	Charles Neal	15.00	6.00	1.50
□ 279	Hank Soar UMP	15.00	6.00	1.50
□ 280	Clyde McCullough	10.00	4.00	1.00
□ 281	Charles Berry UMP	15.00	6.00	1.50
□ 282	Phil Cavarretta	12.00	5.00	1.20
□ 283	Nestor Chylak UMP	15.00	6.00	1.50
□ 284	Bill Jackowski UMP	15.00	6.00	1.50
□ 285	Walt Dropo	12.00	5.00	1.20
□ 286	Frank Secory UMP	15.00	6.00	1.50
□ 287	Ron Mrozinski	10.00	4.00	1.00
□ 288	Dick Smith	10.00	4.00	1.00
□ 289	Arthur Gore UMP	15.00	6.00	1.50
□ 290	Hershell Freeman	10.00	4.00	1.00

□ 291 Frank Dascoli UMP	15.00	6.00	1.50
□ 292 Marv Blaylock	10.00	4.00	1.00
□ 293 Thomas Gorman UMP	15.00	6.00	1.50
□ 294 Wally Moses	12.00	5.00	1.20
□ 295 Lee Ballanfant UMP	15.00	6.00	1.50
□ 296 Bill Virdon	30.00	12.00	3.00
□ 297 Dusty Boggess UMP	15.00	6.00	1.50
□ 298 Charlie Grimm	12.00	5.00	1.20
□ 299 Lon Warneke UMP	15.00	6.00	1.50
□ 300 Tommy Byrne	12.00	5.00	1.20
□ 301 William Engeln UMP	15.00	6.00	1.50
□ 302 Frank Malzone	16.00	6.50	1.60
□ 303 Jocko Conlan UMP	45.00	18.00	4.50
□ 304 Harry Chiti	10.00	4.00	1.00
□ 305 Frank Umont UMP	15.00	6.00	1.50
□ 306 Bob Cerv	15.00	6.00	1.50
□ 307 Babe Pinelli UMP	15.00	6.00	1.50
□ 308 Al Lopez MG	35.00	14.00	3.50
□ 309 Hal Dixon UMP	15.00	6.00	1.50
□ 310 Ken Lehman	10.00	4.00	1.00
□ 311 Lawrence Goetz UMP	15.00	6.00	1.50
□ 312 Bill Wight	10.00	4.00	1.00
□ 313 Augie Donatelli UMP	20.00	8.00	2.00
□ 314 Dale Mitchell	12.00	5.00	1.20
□ 315 Cal Hubbard UMP	45.00	18.00	4.50
□ 316 Marion Fricano	10.00	4.00	1.00
□ 317 William Summers UMP	15.00	6.00	1.50
□ 318 Sid Hudson	10.00	4.00	1.00
□ 319 Albert Schroll	10.00	4.00	1.00
□ 320 George Susce Jr.	20.00	5.00	1.00

1977 Burger King Yankees

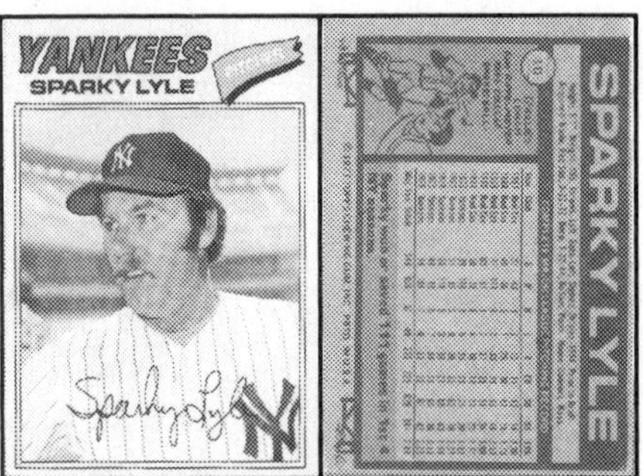

The cards in this 24-card set measure 2 1/2" by 3 1/2". The cards in this set marked with an asterisk have different poses than those cards in the regular 1977 Topps set. The checklist card is unnumbered and the Piniella card was issued subsequent to the original printing.

	NRMT	VG-E	GOOD
COMPLETE SET (24)	35.00	14.00	3.50
COMMON PLAYER (1-23)	.35	.14	.03
□ 1 Yankees Team Billy Martin MG	.75	.30	.07
□ 2 Thurman Munson *	4.00	1.60	.40
□ 3 Fran Healy	.35	.14	.03
□ 4 Jim Hunter	2.00	.80	.20
□ 5 Ed Figueroa	.35	.14	.03
□ 6 Don Gullett *	.50	.20	.05
□ 7 Mike Torrez *	.50	.20	.05
□ 8 Ken Holtzman	.35	.14	.03
□ 9 Dick Tidrow	.35	.14	.03
□ 10 Sparky Lyle	.50	.20	.05
□ 11 Ron Guidry	2.00	.80	.20
□ 12 Chris Chambliss	.50	.20	.05
□ 13 Willie Randolph *	1.00	.40	.10
□ 14 Bucky Dent * (shown as White Sox in 1977 Topps)	.75	.30	.07
□ 15 Graig Nettles * (closer photo than in 1977 Topps)	1.50	.60	.15
□ 16 Fred Stanley	.35	.14	.03
□ 17 Reggie Jackson	4.00	1.60	.40
□ 18 Mickey Rivers	.50	.20	.05
□ 19 Roy White	.35	.14	.03
□ 20 Jim Wynn	.50	.20	.05
□ 21 Paul Blair * (shown as Oriole in 1977 Topps)	.50	.20	.05
□ 22 Carlos May *	.35	.14	.03
□ 23 Lou Piniella	20.00	8.00	2.00
□ xx Checklist card (unnumbered)	.15	.06	.01

1978 Burger King Astros

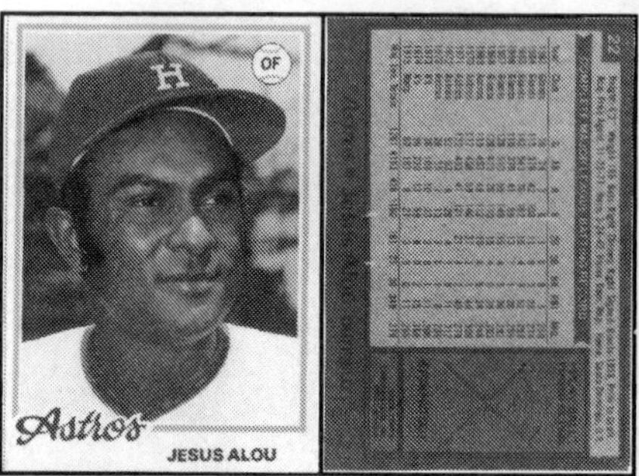

The cards in this 23-card set measure 2 1/2" by 3 1/2". Released in local Houston Burger King outlets during the 1978 season, this Houston Astros series contains the standard 22 numbered player cards and one unnumbered checklist. The player poses found to differ from the regular Topps issue are marked with astericks.

	NRMT	VG-E	GOOD
COMPLETE SET	10.00	4.00	1.00
COMMON PLAYER (1-23)	.30	.12	.03
□ 1 Bill Virdon MG	.75	.30	.07
□ 2 Joe Ferguson	.30	.12	.03
□ 3 Ed Herrmann	.30	.12	.03
□ 4 J.R. Richard	.90	.36	.09
□ 5 Joe Niekro	1.00	.40	.10
□ 6 Floyd Bannister	1.00	.40	.10
□ 7 Joaquin Andujar	.90	.36	.09
□ 8 Ken Forsch	.40	.16	.04
□ 9 Mark Lemongello	.30	.12	.03
□ 10 Joe Sambito	.40	.16	.04
□ 11 Gene Pentz	.30	.12	.03
□ 12 Bob Watson	.60	.24	.06
□ 13 Julio Gonzales	.30	.12	.03
□ 14 Enos Cabell	.30	.12	.03
□ 15 Roger Metzger	.30	.12	.03
□ 16 Art Howe	.75	.30	.07
□ 17 Jose Cruz	.90	.36	.09
□ 18 Cesar Cedeno	.75	.30	.07
□ 19 Terry Puhl	.50	.20	.05
□ 20 Wilbur Howard	.30	.12	.03
□ 21 Dave Bergman *	.40	.16	.04
□ 22 Jesus Alou *	.40	.16	.04
□ 23 Checklist card (unnumbered)	.05	.02	.00

1978 Burger King Rangers

The cards in this 23-card set measure 2 1/2" by 3 1/2". This set of 22 numbered player cards (featuring the Texas Rangers) and one unnumbered checklist was issued regionally by Burger King in 1978. Astericks denote poses different from those found in the regular Topps cards of this year.

	NRMT	VG-E	GOOD
COMPLETE SET	10.00	4.00	1.00
COMMON PLAYER (1-23)	.30	.12	.03
□ 1 Billy Hunter MG	.30	.12	.03
□ 2 Jim Sundberg	.50	.20	.05

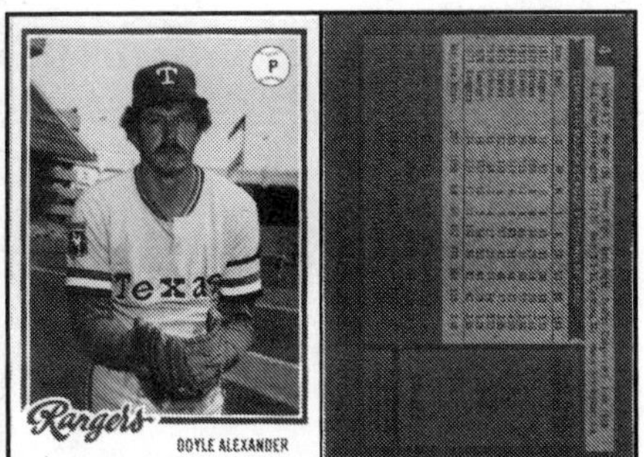

	NRMT	VG-E	GOOD
□ 3 John Ellis	.30	.12	.03
□ 4 Doyle Alexander	.75	.30	.07
□ 5 Jon Matlack *	.60	.24	.06
□ 6 Dock Ellis	.40	.16	.04
□ 7 Doc Medich	.40	.16	.04
□ 8 Fergie Jenkins *	1.50	.60	.15
□ 9 Len Barker	.30	.12	.03
□ 10 Reggie Cleveland *	.30	.12	.03
□ 11 Mike Hargrove	.40	.16	.04
□ 12 Bump Wills	.30	.12	.03
□ 13 Toby Harrah	.75	.30	.07
□ 14 Bert Campaneris	.50	.20	.05
□ 15 Sandy Alomar	.30	.12	.03
□ 16 Kurt Bevacqua	.30	.12	.03
□ 17 Al Oliver *	.90	.36	.09
□ 18 Juan Beniquez	.50	.20	.05
□ 19 Claudell Washington	.75	.30	.07
□ 20 Richie Zisk	.50	.20	.05
□ 21 John Lowenstein *	.30	.12	.03
□ 22 Bobby Thompson *	.30	.12	.03
□ 23 Checklist card (unnumbered)	.05	.02	.00

1978 Burger King Tigers

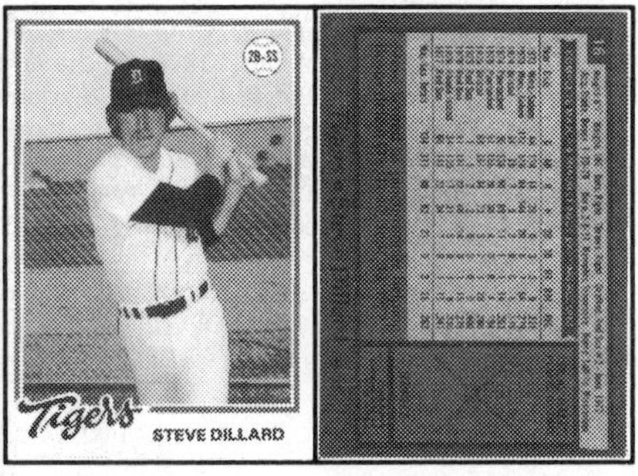

The cards in this 23-card set measure 2 1/2" by 3 1/2". Twenty-three color cards, 22 players and one numbered checklist, comprise the 1978 Burger King Tigers set issued in the Detroit area. The cards marked with an asterisk contain photos different from those appearing on the Topps regular issue cards of that year.

	NRMT	VG-E	GOOD
COMPLETE SET	40.00	16.00	4.00
COMMON PLAYER (1-23)	.30	.12	.03
□ 1 Ralph Houk MG	.50	.20	.05
□ 2 Milt May	.30	.12	.03
□ 3 John Wockenfuss	.30	.12	.03
□ 4 Mark Fidrych	.75	.30	.07
□ 5 Dave Rozema	.30	.12	.03
□ 6 Jack Billingham *	.30	.12	.03
□ 7 Jim Slaton *	.30	.12	.03
□ 8 Jack Morris *	9.00	3.75	.90
□ 9 John Hiller	.50	.20	.05
□ 10 Steve Foucault	.30	.12	.03
□ 11 Milt Wilcox	.30	.12	.03

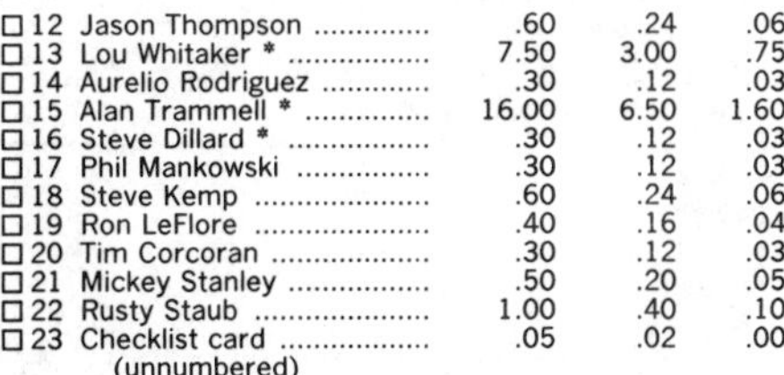

	NRMT	VG-E	GOOD
□ 12 Jason Thompson	.60	.24	.06
□ 13 Lou Whitaker *	7.50	3.00	.75
□ 14 Aurelio Rodriguez	.30	.12	.03
□ 15 Alan Trammell *	16.00	6.50	1.60
□ 16 Steve Dillard *	.30	.12	.03
□ 17 Phil Mankowski	.30	.12	.03
□ 18 Steve Kemp	.60	.24	.06
□ 19 Ron LeFlore	.40	.16	.04
□ 20 Tim Corcoran	.30	.12	.03
□ 21 Mickey Stanley	.50	.20	.05
□ 22 Rusty Staub	1.00	.40	.10
□ 23 Checklist card (unnumbered)	.05	.02	.00

1978 Burger King Yankees

The cards in this 23 card set measure 2 1/2" by 3 1/2". These cards were distributed in packs of three players plus a checklist at Burger King's New York area outlets. Cards with an asterisk have different poses than those in the Topps regular issue.

	NRMT	VG-E	GOOD
COMPLETE SET	9.00	3.75	.90
COMMON PLAYER (1-23)	.20	.08	.02
□ 1 Billy Martin MG	.40	.16	.04
□ 2 Thurman Munson	2.50	1.00	.25
□ 3 Cliff Johnson	.20	.08	.02
□ 4 Ron Guidry	1.25	.50	.12
□ 5 Ed Figueroa	.20	.08	.02
□ 6 Dick Tidrow	.20	.08	.02
□ 7 Jim Hunter	1.50	.60	.15
□ 8 Don Gullett	.25	.10	.02
□ 9 Sparky Lyle	.40	.16	.04
□ 10 Rich Gossage *	.90	.36	.09
□ 11 Rawly Eastwick *	.20	.08	.02
□ 12 Chris Chambliss	.25	.10	.02
□ 13 Willie Randolph	.60	.24	.06
□ 14 Graig Nettles	.75	.30	.07
□ 15 Bucky Dent	.25	.10	.02
□ 16 Jim Spencer *	.20	.08	.02
□ 17 Fred Stanley	.20	.08	.02
□ 18 Lou Piniella	.40	.16	.04
□ 19 Roy White	.25	.10	.02
□ 20 Mickey Rivers	.25	.10	.02
□ 21 Reggie Jackson	2.50	1.00	.25
□ 22 Paul Blair	.20	.08	.02
□ 23 Checklist card (unnumbered)	.05	.02	.00

1979 Burger King Phillies

The cards in this 23-card set measure 2 1/2" by 3 1/2". The 1979 Burger King Phillies set follows the regular format of 22 player cards and one unnumbered checklist card. The asterisk indicates where the pose differs from the Topps card of that year.

	NRMT	VG-E	GOOD
COMPLETE SET	6.00	2.40	.60

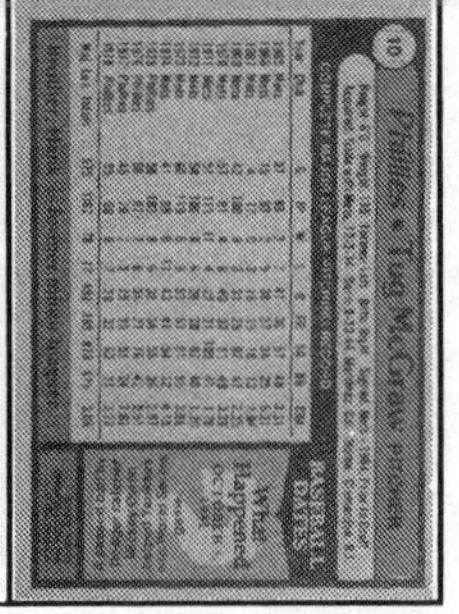

COMMON PLAYER (1-23)	.10	.04	.01
☐ 1 Danny Ozark MG *	.10	.04	.01
☐ 2 Bob Boone	.40	.16	.04
☐ 3 Tim McCarver	.40	.16	.04
☐ 4 Steve Carlton	1.50	.60	.15
☐ 5 Larry Christenson	.10	.04	.01
☐ 6 Dick Ruthven	.10	.04	.01
☐ 7 Ron Reed	.10	.04	.01
☐ 8 Randy Lerch	.10	.04	.01
☐ 9 Warren Brusstar	.10	.04	.01
☐ 10 Tug McGraw	.30	.12	.03
☐ 11 Nino Espinosa *	.10	.04	.01
☐ 12 Doug Bird *	.10	.04	.01
☐ 13 Pete Rose *	2.50	1.00	.25
☐ 14 Manny Trillo *	.15	.06	.01
☐ 15 Larry Bowa	.40	.16	.04
☐ 16 Mike Schmidt	1.75	.70	.17
☐ 17 Pete Mackanin *	.10	.04	.01
☐ 18 Jose Cardenal	.10	.04	.01
☐ 19 Greg Luzinski	.40	.16	.04
☐ 20 Garry Maddox	.15	.06	.01
☐ 21 Bake McBride	.10	.04	.01
☐ 22 Greg Gross *	.10	.04	.01
☐ 23 Checklist card (unnumbered)	.05	.02	.00

1979 Burger King Yankees

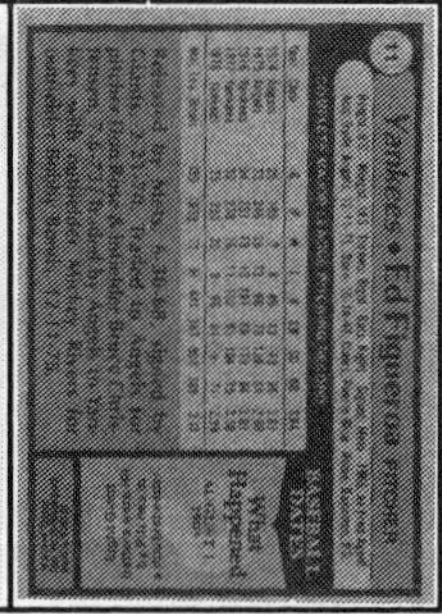

The cards in this 23-card set measure 2 1/2" X 3 1/2". There are 22 numbered cards and one unnumbered checklist in the 1979 Burger King Yankee set. The poses of Guidry, Tiant, John and Beniquez, each marked with an asterisk below, are different from their poses appearing in the regular Topps issue. The team card has a picture of Lemon rather than Martin.

	NRMT	VG-E	GOOD
COMPLETE SET (23)	6.00	2.40	.60
COMMON PLAYER (1-23)	.10	.04	.01
☐ 1 Yankees Team: Bob Lemon MG *	.30	.12	.03
☐ 2 Thurman Munson	1.50	.60	.15
☐ 3 Cliff Johnson	.10	.04	.01
☐ 4 Ron Guidry *	.90	.36	.09
☐ 5 Jay Johnstone	.25	.10	.02
☐ 6 Jim Hunter	1.00	.40	.10
☐ 7 Jim Beattie	.10	.04	.01
☐ 8 Luis Tiant *	.25	.10	.02
☐ 9 Tommy John *	.60	.24	.06
☐ 10 Rich Gossage	.60	.24	.06
☐ 11 Ed Figueroa	.10	.04	.01
☐ 12 Chris Chambliss	.15	.06	.01
☐ 13 Willie Randolph	.40	.16	.04
☐ 14 Bucky Dent	.15	.06	.01
☐ 15 Graig Nettles	.50	.20	.05
☐ 16 Fred Stanley	.10	.04	.01
☐ 17 Jim Spencer	.10	.04	.01
☐ 18 Lou Piniella	.30	.12	.03
☐ 19 Roy White	.15	.06	.01
☐ 20 Mickey Rivers	.15	.06	.01
☐ 21 Reggie Jackson	1.75	.70	.17
☐ 22 Juan Beniquez *	.20	.08	.02
☐ 23 Checklist card (unnumbered)	.05	.02	.00

1980 Burger King Phillies

The cards in this 23-card set measure 2 1/2" by 3 1/2". The 1980 edition of Burger King Phillies follows the established pattern of 22 numbered player cards and one unnumbered checklist. Cards marked with astericks contain poses different from those found in the regular 1980 Topps cards. This was the first Burger King set to carry the Burger King logo and hence does not generate the same confusion that the three previous years do for collectors trying to distinguish Burger King cards from the very similar Topps cards of the same years.

	MINT	EXC	G-VG
COMPLETE SET (23)	5.00	2.00	.50
COMMON PLAYER (1-23)	.10	.04	.01
☐ 1 Dallas Green MG *	.30	.12	.03
☐ 2 Bob Boone	.30	.12	.03
☐ 3 Keith Moreland *	.75	.30	.07
☐ 4 Pete Rose	2.50	1.00	.25
☐ 5 Manny Trillo	.15	.06	.01
☐ 6 Mike Schmidt	1.50	.60	.15
☐ 7 Larry Bowa	.35	.14	.03
☐ 8 John Vukovich *	.10	.04	.01
☐ 9 Bake McBride	.10	.04	.01
☐ 10 Garry Maddox	.15	.06	.01
☐ 11 Greg Luzinski	.25	.10	.02
☐ 12 Greg Gross	.10	.04	.01
☐ 13 Del Unser	.10	.04	.01
☐ 14 Lonnie Smith *	.15	.06	.01
☐ 15 Steve Carlton	1.25	.50	.12
☐ 16 Larry Christenson	.10	.04	.01
☐ 17 Nino Espinosa	.10	.04	.01
☐ 18 Randy Lerch	.10	.04	.01
☐ 19 Dick Ruthven	.10	.04	.01
☐ 20 Tug McGraw	.25	.10	.02
☐ 21 Ron Reed	.10	.04	.01
☐ 22 Kevin Saucier *	.10	.04	.01
☐ 23 Checklist card (unnumbered)	.05	.02	.00

1980 Burger King Pitch/Hit/Run

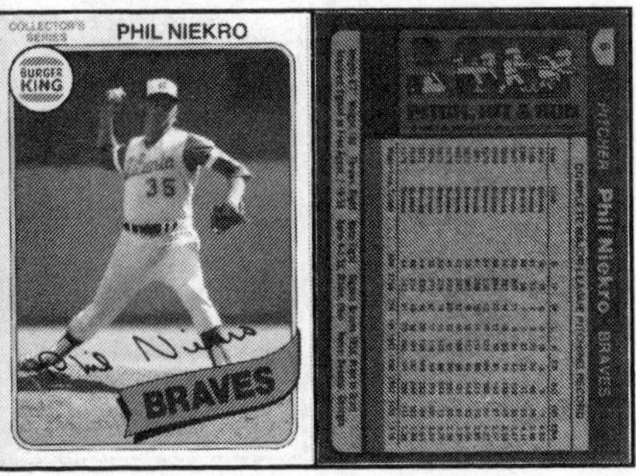

The cards in this 34 card set measure 2 1/2" by 3 1/2". The "Pitch, Hit, and Run" set was a promotion introduced by Burger King in 1980. The cards carry a Burger King logo on the front and those marked by an asterisk in the checklist contain a different photo from that found in the regularly issued Topps series. Cards 1-11 are pitchers, 12-22 are hitters, and 23-33 are speedsters. Within each subgroup, the players are numbered corresponding to the alphabetical order of their names. The unnumbered checklist card was triple printed and is the least valuable card in the set.

	MINT	EXC	G-VG
COMPLETE SET (34)	10.00	4.00	1.00
COMMON PLAYER (1-34)	.10	.04	.01
☐ 1 Vida Blue *	.10	.04	.01
☐ 2 Steve Carlton	1.00	.40	.10
☐ 3 Rollie Fingers	.30	.12	.03
☐ 4 Ron Guidry *	.30	.12	.03
☐ 5 Jerry Koosman *	.15	.06	.01
☐ 6 Phil Niekro	.50	.20	.05
☐ 7 Jim Palmer *	.75	.30	.07
☐ 8 J.R. Richard	.10	.04	.01
☐ 9 Nolan Ryan *	1.00	.40	.10
☐ 10 Tom Seaver *	1.00	.40	.10
☐ 11 Bruce Sutter	.15	.06	.01
☐ 12 Don Baylor	.15	.06	.01
☐ 13 George Brett	1.00	.40	.10
☐ 14 Rod Carew	.75	.30	.07
☐ 15 George Foster	.15	.06	.01
☐ 16 Keith Hernandez *	.75	.30	.07
☐ 17 Reggie Jackson *	1.25	.50	.12
☐ 18 Fred Lynn *	.20	.08	.02
☐ 19 Dave Parker	.25	.10	.02
☐ 20 Jim Rice	.50	.20	.05
☐ 21 Pete Rose	2.00	.80	.20
☐ 22 Dave Winfield *	1.00	.40	.10
☐ 23 Bobby Bonds *	.15	.06	.01
☐ 24 Enos Cabell	.10	.04	.01
☐ 25 Cesar Cedeno	.10	.04	.01
☐ 26 Julio Cruz	.10	.04	.01
☐ 27 Ron LeFlore *	.10	.04	.01
☐ 28 Dave Lopes *	.10	.04	.01
☐ 29 Omar Moreno *	.10	.04	.01
☐ 30 Joe Morgan *	.75	.30	.07
☐ 31 Bill North	.10	.04	.01
☐ 32 Frank Taveras	.10	.04	.01
☐ 33 Willie Wilson	.15	.06	.01
☐ 34 Unnumbered Checklist	.05	.02	.00

1982 Burger King Indians

The cards in this 12-card set measure 3" by 5". Tips From The Dugout is the series title of this set issued on a one card per week basis by the Burger King chain in the Cleveland area. Each card contains a black and white photo of manager Dave Garcia or coaches Goryl, McCraw, Queen and Sommers, under

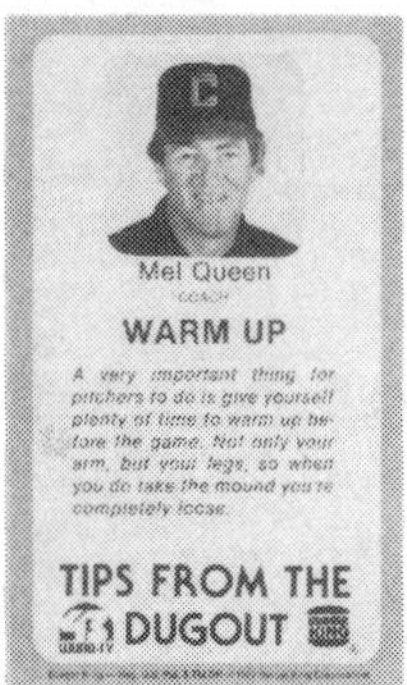

whom appears a paragraph explaining some aspect of inside baseball. The photo and "Tip" are set upon a large yellow area surrounded by green borders. The cards are not numbered and are blank- backed. The logos of Burger King and WUAB-TV appear at the base of the card.

	MINT	EXC	G-VG
COMPLETE SET (12)	5.00	2.00	.50
COMMON PLAYER (1-12)	.50	.20	.05
☐ 1 Dave Garcia: Be in the Game	.50	.20	.05
☐ 2 Dave Garcia: Sportsmanship	.50	.20	.05
☐ 3 Johnny Goryl: Rounding Bases	.50	.20	.05
☐ 4 Johnny Goryl: 3B Running	.50	.20	.05
☐ 5 Tom McCraw: Follow Thru	.50	.20	.05
☐ 6 Tom McCraw: Selecting a Bat	.50	.20	.05
☐ 7 Tom McCraw: Watch the Ball	.50	.20	.05
☐ 8 Mel Queen: Master One Pitch	.50	.20	.05
☐ 9 Mel Queen: Warm Up	.50	.20	.05
☐ 10 Dennis Sommers: Protect Fingers	.50	.20	.05
☐ 11 Dennis Sommers: Tagging 1st Base	.50	.20	.05
☐ 12 Dennis Sommers	.50	.20	.05

1986 Burger King All Pro

This 20-card set was distributed in Burger King restaurants across the country. They were produced as panels of three where the middle card was actually a special discount coupon card. The folded panel was given with the purchase of a Whopper. Each individual card measures 2 1/2" by 3 1/2". The team logos have been airbrushed from the pictures. The cards are numbered on the front at the top.

	MINT	EXC	G-VG
COMPLETE SET (20)	6.00	2.40	.60
COMMON PLAYER (1-20)	.20	.08	.02
☐ 1 Tony Pena	.20	.08	.02
☐ 2 Dave Winfield	.50	.20	.05
☐ 3 Fernando Valenzuela	.30	.12	.03
☐ 4 Pete Rose	.80	.32	.08
☐ 5 Mike Schmidt	.60	.24	.06
☐ 6 Steve Carlton	.40	.16	.04
☐ 7 Glenn Wilson	.20	.08	.02
☐ 8 Jim Rice	.40	.16	.04
☐ 9 Wade Boggs	.80	.32	.08
☐ 10 Juan Samuel	.30	.12	.03
☐ 11 Dale Murphy	.60	.24	.06
☐ 12 Reggie Jackson	.60	.24	.06
☐ 13 Kirk Gibson	.50	.20	.05
☐ 14 Eddie Murray	.50	.20	.05
☐ 15 Cal Ripken	.40	.16	.04
☐ 16 Willie McGee	.30	.12	.03
☐ 17 Dwight Gooden	.60	.24	.06
☐ 18 Steve Garvey	.50	.20	.05
☐ 19 Don Mattingly	1.00	.40	.10
☐ 20 George Brett	.60	.24	.06

1987 Burger King All-Pro

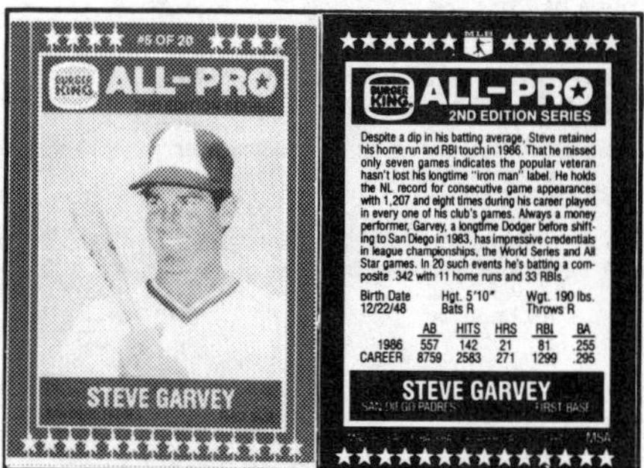

This 20-card set consists of 10 panels of two cards each joined together along with a promotional coupon. Individual cards measure 2 1/2" by 3 1/2" whereas the panels measure 3 1/2" by 7 5/8". MSA (Mike Schechter Associates produced the cards for Burger King; there are no Major League logos on the cards. The cards are numbered on the front.

	MINT	EXC	G-VG
COMPLETE SET (20)	4.50	1.80	.45
COMMON PLAYER (1-20)	.20	.08	.02
☐ 1 Wade Boggs	.80	.32	.08
☐ 2 Gary Carter	.40	.16	.04
☐ 3 Will Clark	.80	.32	.08
☐ 4 Roger Clemens	.70	.28	.07
☐ 5 Steve Garvey	.40	.16	.04
☐ 6 Ron Darling	.30	.12	.03
☐ 7 Pedro Guerrero	.30	.12	.03
☐ 8 Von Hayes	.20	.08	.02
☐ 9 Rickey Henderson	.50	.20	.05
☐ 10 Keith Hernandez	.40	.16	.04
☐ 11 Wally Joyner	.60	.24	.06
☐ 12 Mike Krukow	.20	.08	.02
☐ 13 Don Mattingly	1.00	.40	.10
☐ 14 Ozzie Smith	.30	.12	.03
☐ 15 Tony Pena	.20	.08	.02
☐ 16 Jim Rice	.30	.12	.03
☐ 17 Mike Schmidt	.60	.24	.06
☐ 18 Ryne Sandberg	.40	.16	.04
☐ 19 Darryl Strawberry	.60	.24	.06
☐ 20 Fernando Valenzuela	.30	.12	.03

MAKE FRIENDS: By attending a sports collectibles convention, you'll pick up items for your collection, and likely see your friends there, too.

1988 Chef Boyardee

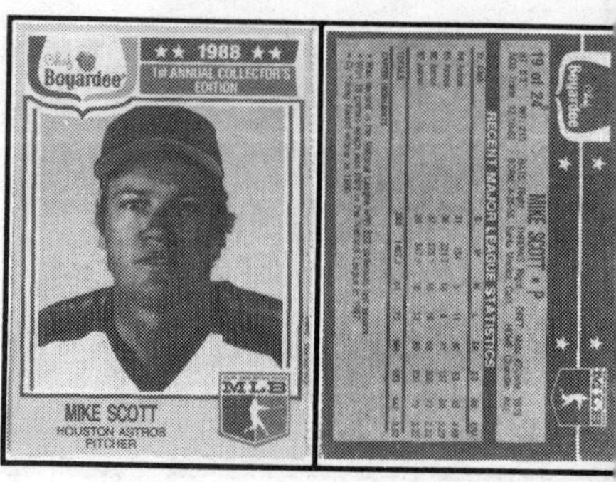

This 24-card set was distributed as a perforate sheet of four rows and six columns of cards in retur for ten proofs of puchase of Chef Boyardee products. The card photos on the fronts are in fu color with a light blue border but are not shown wit team logos. The card backs are numbered an printed in red and blue on gray card stock. Individua cards measure approximately 2 1/2" by 3 1/2" an show the Chef Boyardee logo in the upper righ corner of the obverse. Card backs feature year- by year season statistics since 1984.

	MINT	EXC	G-V
COMPLETE SET (24)	13.50	5.00	1.0
COMMON PLAYER (1-24)	.30	.12	.0
☐ 1 Mark McGwire	1.25	.50	.1
☐ 2 Eric Davis	.90	.30	.0
☐ 3 Jack Morris	.40	.15	.0
☐ 4 George Bell	.40	.15	.0
☐ 5 Ozzie Smith	.50	.20	.0
☐ 6 Tony Gwynn	.60	.25	.0
☐ 7 Cal Ripken	.60	.25	.0
☐ 8 Todd Worrell	.30	.12	.0
☐ 9 Larry Parrish	.30	.12	.0
☐ 10 Gary Carter	.50	.20	.0
☐ 11 Ryne Sandberg	.50	.20	.0
☐ 12 Keith Hernandez	.50	.20	.0
☐ 13 Kirby Puckett	.90	.40	.06
☐ 14 Mike Schmidt	.90	.40	.06
☐ 15 Frank Viola	.50	.20	.04
☐ 16 Don Mattingly	2.00	.90	.15
☐ 17 Dale Murphy	.75	.35	.06
☐ 18 Andre Dawson	.50	.20	.04
☐ 19 Mike Scott	.40	.16	.03
☐ 20 Rickey Henderson	.75	.35	.06
☐ 21 Jim Rice	.40	.18	.04
☐ 22 Wade Boggs	1.25	.50	.10
☐ 23 Roger Clemens	1.00	.40	.07
☐ 24 Fernando Valenzuela	.50	.20	.04

1985 CIGNA Phillies

This colorful 16-card set (measuring 2 5/8" by 4 1/8") features the Philadelphia Phillies and was also sponsored by CIGNA Corporation. Cards are numbered on the back and contain a safety tip as such the set is frequently categorized and referenced as a safety set. Cards are also numbered by uniform number on the front.

	MINT	EXC	G-VG
COMPLETE SET (16)	5.00	2.00	.50
COMMON PLAYER	.20	.08	.02
☐ 1 Juan Samuel	.50	.20	.05
☐ 2 Von Hayes	.50	.20	.05
☐ 3 Ozzie Virgil	.30	.12	.03
☐ 4 Mike Schmidt	1.50	.60	.15
☐ 5 Greg Gross	.20	.08	.02

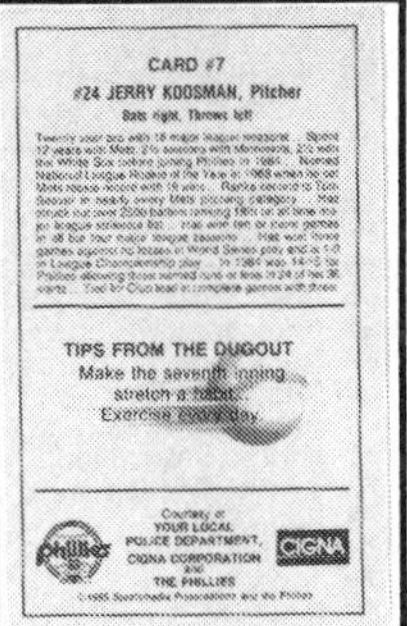

☐ 6 Tim Corcoran	.20	.08	.02
☐ 7 Jerry Koosman	.30	.12	.03
☐ 8 Jeff Stone	.20	.08	.02
☐ 9 Glenn Wilson	.30	.12	.03
☐ 10 Steve Jeltz	.20	.08	.02
☐ 11 Garry Maddox	.20	.08	.02
☐ 12 Steve Carlton	1.00	.40	.10
☐ 13 John Denny	.25	.10	.02
☐ 14 Kevin Gross	.40	.16	.04
☐ 15 Shane Rawley	.40	.16	.04
☐ 16 Charlie Hudson	.30	.12	.03

1986 CIGNA Phillies

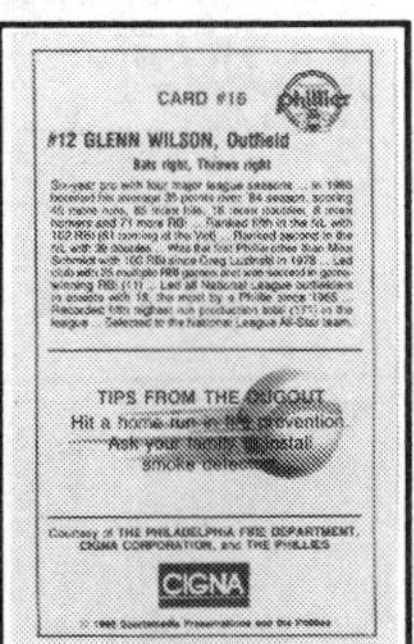

This 16-card set was sponsored by CIGNA Corp. and was given away by the Philadelphia area Fire Departments. Cards measure 2 3/4" by 4 1/8" and feature full color fronts. The card backs are printed in maroon and black on white card stock. Although the uniform numbers are given on the front of the card, the cards are numbered on the back in the order listed below.

	MINT	EXC	G-VG
COMPLETE SET (16)	5.00	2.00	.50
COMMON PLAYER	.20	.08	.02
☐ 1 Juan Samuel	.50	.20	.05
☐ 2 Don Carman	.30	.12	.03
☐ 3 Von Hayes	.50	.20	.05
☐ 4 Kent Tekulve	.30	.12	.03
☐ 5 Greg Gross	.20	.08	.02
☐ 6 Shane Rawley	.40	.16	.04
☐ 7 Darren Daulton	.20	.08	.02
☐ 8 Kevin Gross	.40	.16	.04
☐ 9 Steve Jeltz	.20	.08	.02
☐ 10 Mike Schmidt	1.50	.60	.15
☐ 11 Steve Bedrosian	.60	.24	.06
☐ 12 Gary Redus	.30	.12	.03
☐ 13 Charles Hudson	.30	.12	.03
☐ 14 John Russell	.20	.08	.02
☐ 15 Fred Toliver	.20	.08	.02
☐ 16 Glenn Wilson	.30	.12	.03

1985 Circle K

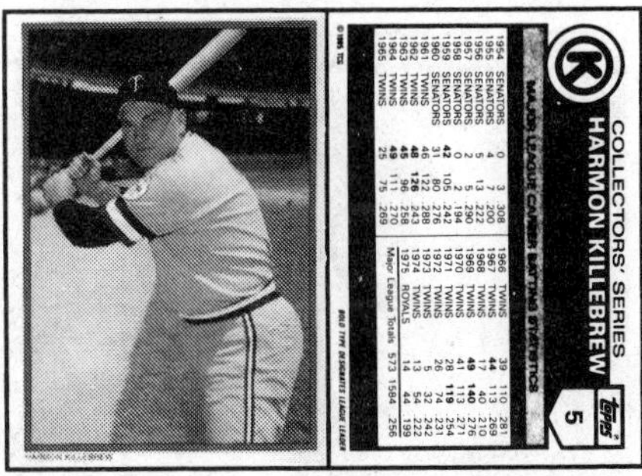

The cards in this 33-card set measure 2 1/2" by 3 1/2" and were issued with accompanying box. In 1985, Topps produced this set for Circle K; cards were printed in Ireland. Cards are numbered on the back according to each player's rank on the all-time career Home Run list. The backs are printed in blue and red on white card stock. The card fronts are glossy and each player is named in the lower left corner. Most of the obverses are in color, although the older vintage players are pictured in black and white. Joe DiMaggio was not included in the set; card #31 does not exist. It was intended to be DiMaggio but he apparently would not consent to be included in the set.

	MINT	EXC	G-VG
COMPLETE SET (33)	4.00	1.60	.40
COMMON PLAYER (1-34)	.10	.04	.01
☐ 1 Hank Aaron	.40	.16	.04
☐ 2 Babe Ruth	.80	.32	.08
☐ 3 Willie Mays	.40	.16	.04
☐ 4 Frank Robinson	.15	.06	.01
☐ 5 Harmon Killebrew	.15	.06	.01
☐ 6 Mickey Mantle	1.00	.40	.10
☐ 7 Jimmie Foxx	.15	.06	.01
☐ 8 Willie McCovey	.20	.08	.02
☐ 9 Ted Williams	.40	.16	.04
☐ 10 Ernie Banks	.20	.08	.02
☐ 11 Eddie Mathews	.15	.06	.01
☐ 12 Mel Ott	.15	.06	.01
☐ 13 Reggie Jackson	.40	.16	.04
☐ 14 Lou Gehrig	.40	.16	.04
☐ 15 Stan Musial	.30	.12	.03
☐ 16 Willie Stargell	.20	.08	.02
☐ 17 Carl Yastrzemski	.40	.16	.04
☐ 18 Billy Williams	.15	.06	.01
☐ 19 Mike Schmidt	.35	.14	.03
☐ 20 Duke Snider	.30	.12	.03
☐ 21 Al Kaline	.20	.08	.02
☐ 22 Johnny Bench	.30	.12	.03
☐ 23 Frank Howard	.10	.04	.01
☐ 24 Orlando Cepeda	.10	.04	.01
☐ 25 Norm Cash	.10	.04	.01
☐ 26 Dave Kingman	.10	.04	.01
☐ 27 Rocky Colavito	.10	.04	.01
☐ 28 Tony Perez	.10	.04	.01
☐ 29 Gil Hodges	.10	.04	.01
☐ 30 Ralph Kiner	.10	.04	.01
☐ 31 Joe DiMaggio (not included in set, card does not exist)	.00	.00	.00
☐ 32 Johnny Mize	.15	.06	.01
☐ 33 Yogi Berra	.25	.10	.02
☐ 34 Lee May	.10	.04	.01

1987 Classic Game

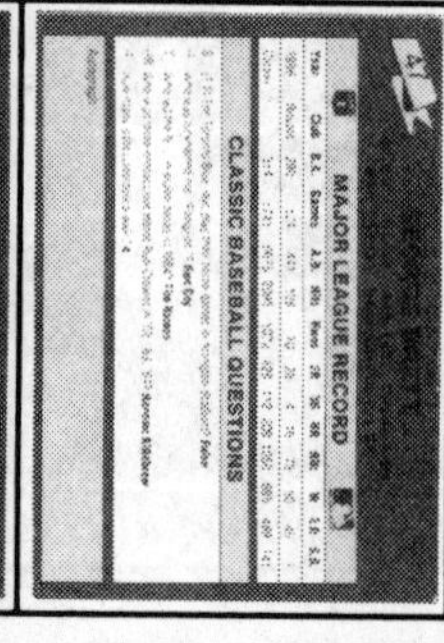

This 100-card set was actually distributed as part of a trivia board game. The card backs contain several trivia questions (and answers) which are used to play the game. A dark green border frames the full color photo. The games were produced by Game Time, Ltd. and were available in toy stores as well as from card dealers.

	MINT	EXC	G-VG
COMPLETE SET (100)	18.00	7.25	1.80
COMMON PLAYER (1-100)	.10	.04	.01

	MINT	EXC	G-VG
☐ 1 Pete Rose	1.00	.40	.10
☐ 2 Len Dykstra	.15	.06	.01
☐ 3 Darryl Strawberry	.75	.30	.07
☐ 4 Keith Hernandez	.25	.10	.02
☐ 5 Gary Carter	.25	.10	.02
☐ 6 Wally Joyner	.90	.36	.09
☐ 7 Andres Thomas	.10	.04	.01
☐ 8 Pat Dodson	.10	.04	.01
☐ 9 Kirk Gibson	.30	.12	.03
☐ 10 Don Mattingly	1.25	.50	.12
☐ 11 Dave Winfield	.30	.12	.03
☐ 12 Rickey Henderson	.30	.12	.03
☐ 13 Dan Pasqua	.10	.04	.01
☐ 14 Don Baylor	.10	.04	.01
☐ 15 Bo Jackson	1.00	.40	.10
☐ 16 Pete Incaviglia	.50	.20	.05
☐ 17 Kevin Bass	.10	.04	.01
☐ 18 Barry Larkin	.20	.08	.02
☐ 19 Dave Magadan	.15	.06	.01
☐ 20 Steve Sax	.20	.08	.02
☐ 21 Eric Davis	1.00	.40	.10
☐ 22 Mike Pagliarulo	.15	.06	.01
☐ 23 Fred Lynn	.15	.06	.01
☐ 24 Reggie Jackson	.50	.20	.05
☐ 25 Larry Parrish	.15	.06	.01
☐ 26 Tony Gwynn	.50	.20	.05
☐ 27 Steve Garvey	.40	.16	.04
☐ 28 Glenn Davis	.20	.08	.02
☐ 29 Tim Raines	.30	.12	.03
☐ 30 Vince Coleman	.30	.12	.03
☐ 31 Willie McGee	.20	.08	.02
☐ 32 Ozzie Smith	.20	.08	.02
☐ 33 Dave Parker	.15	.06	.01
☐ 34 Tony Pena	.10	.04	.01
☐ 35 Ryne Sandberg	.25	.10	.02
☐ 36 Brett Butler	.15	.06	.01
☐ 37 Dale Murphy	.50	.20	.05
☐ 38 Bob Horner	.10	.04	.01
☐ 39 Pedro Guerrero	.15	.06	.01
☐ 40 Brook Jacoby	.10	.04	.01
☐ 41 Carlton Fisk	.15	.06	.01
☐ 42 Harold Baines	.10	.04	.01
☐ 43 Rob Deer	.10	.04	.01
☐ 44 Robin Yount	.25	.10	.02
☐ 45 Paul Molitor	.20	.08	.02
☐ 46 Jose Canseco	1.50	.60	.15
☐ 47 George Brett	.50	.20	.05
☐ 48 Jim Presley	.15	.06	.01
☐ 49 Rich Gedman	.10	.04	.01
☐ 50 Larry Parrish	.10	.04	.01
☐ 51 Eddie Murray	.30	.12	.03
☐ 52 Cal Ripken	.30	.12	.03
☐ 53 Kent Hrbek	.20	.08	.02
☐ 54 Gary Gaetti	.20	.08	.02
☐ 55 Kirby Puckett	.75	.30	.07
☐ 56 George Bell	.25	.10	.02
☐ 57 Tony Fernandez	.20	.08	.0[illegible]
☐ 58 Jesse Barfield	.20	.08	.0[illegible]
☐ 59 Jim Rice	.20	.08	.0[illegible]
☐ 60 Wade Boggs	1.00	.40	.1[illegible]
☐ 61 Marty Barrett	.10	.04	.0[illegible]
☐ 62 Mike Schmidt	.60	.24	.0[illegible]
☐ 63 Von Hayes	.15	.06	.0[illegible]
☐ 64 Jeff Leonard	.10	.04	.0[illegible]
☐ 65 Chris Brown	.10	.04	.0[illegible]
☐ 66 Dave Smith	.10	.04	.0[illegible]
☐ 67 Mike Krukow	.10	.04	.0[illegible]
☐ 68 Ron Guidry	.20	.08	.0[illegible]
☐ 69 Rob Woodward	.10	.04	.01
☐ 70 Rob Murphy	.10	.04	.01
☐ 71 Andres Galarraga	.30	.12	.0[illegible]
☐ 72 Dwight Gooden	.75	.30	.07
☐ 73 Bob Ojeda	.15	.06	.01
☐ 74 Sid Fernandez	.15	.06	.01
☐ 75 Jesse Orosco	.10	.04	.01
☐ 76 Roger McDowell	.15	.06	.01
☐ 77 John Tudor (misspelled Tutor)	.20	.08	.02
☐ 78 Tom Browning	.15	.06	.01
☐ 79 Rick Aguilera	.15	.06	.01
☐ 80 Lance McCullers	.15	.06	.01
☐ 81 Mike Scott	.25	.10	.02
☐ 82 Nolan Ryan	.40	.16	.04
☐ 83 Bruce Hurst	.20	.08	.02
☐ 84 Roger Clemens	.75	.30	.07
☐ 85 Oil Can Boyd	.10	.04	.01
☐ 86 Dave Righetti	.15	.06	.01
☐ 87 Dennis Rasmussen	.15	.06	.01
☐ 88 Bret Saberhagen	.20	.08	.02
☐ 89 Mark Langston	.20	.08	.02
☐ 90 Jack Morris	.20	.08	.02
☐ 91 Fernando Valenzuela	.20	.08	.02
☐ 92 Orel Hershiser	.60	.24	.06
☐ 93 Rick Honeycutt	.10	.04	.01
☐ 94 Jeff Reardon	.15	.06	.01
☐ 95 John Habyan	.10	.04	.01
☐ 96 Goose Gossage	.15	.06	.01
☐ 97 Todd Worrell	.20	.08	.02
☐ 98 Floyd Youmans	.10	.04	.01
☐ 99 Don Aase	.10	.04	.01
☐ 100 John Franco	.15	.06	.01

1987 Classic Update Yellow

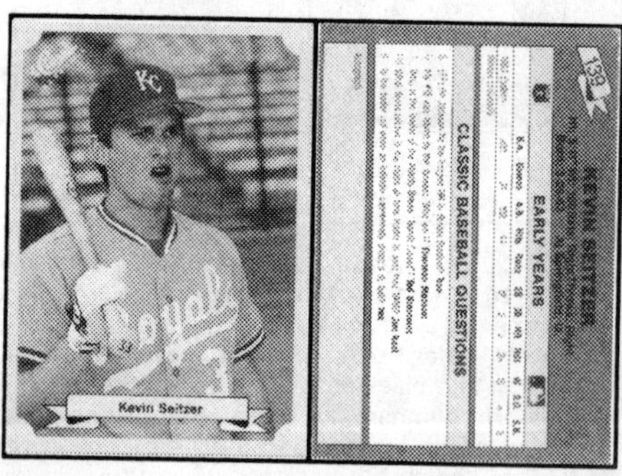

This 50-card set was actually distributed as part of an update to a trivia board game, but (unlike the original Classic game) was sold without the game. The set is sometimes referred to as the "Travel Edition" of the game. The card backs contain several trivia questions (and answers) which are used to play the game. A yellow border frames the full color photo. The games were produced by Game Time, Ltd. and were available in toy stores as well as from card dealers. Cards are numbered beginning with 101, as they are an extension of the original set.

	MINT	EXC	G-VG
COMPLETE SET (50)	7.50	3.00	.75
COMMON PLAYER (101-150)	.10	.04	.01
☐ 101 Mike Schmidt	.40	.16	.04
☐ 102 Eric Davis	1.00	.40	.10
☐ 103 Pete Rose	.60	.24	.06

□ 104	Don Mattingly	1.25	.50	.12
□ 105	Wade Boggs	1.00	.40	.10
□ 106	Dale Murphy	.30	.12	.03
□ 107	Glenn Davis	.20	.08	.02
□ 108	Wally Joyner	.75	.30	.07
□ 109	Bo Jackson	.50	.20	.05
□ 110	Cory Snyder	.25	.10	.02
□ 111	Jim Lindeman	.10	.04	.01
□ 112	Kirby Puckett	.50	.20	.05
□ 113	Barry Bonds	.20	.08	.02
□ 114	Roger Clemens	.60	.24	.06
□ 115	Oddibe McDowell	.10	.04	.01
□ 116	Bret Saberhagen	.15	.06	.01
□ 117	Joe Magrane	.15	.06	.01
□ 118	Scott Fletcher	.10	.04	.01
□ 119	Mark McLemore	.10	.04	.01
□ 120	Who Me (Joe Niekro)	.10	.04	.01
□ 121	Mark McGwire	1.00	.40	.10
□ 122	Darryl Strawberry	.75	.30	.07
□ 123	Mike Scott	.15	.06	.01
□ 124	Andre Dawson	.20	.08	.02
□ 125	Jose Canseco	1.25	.50	.12
□ 126	Kevin McReynolds	.25	.10	.02
□ 127	Joe Carter	.20	.08	.02
□ 128	Casey Candaele	.10	.04	.01
□ 129	Matt Nokes	.40	.16	.04
□ 130	Kal Daniels	.40	.16	.04
□ 131	Pete Incaviglia	.20	.08	.02
□ 132	Benito Santiago	.60	.24	.06
□ 133	Barry Larkin	.20	.08	.02
□ 134	Gary Pettis	.10	.04	.01
□ 135	B.J. Surhoff	.15	.06	.01
□ 136	Juan Nieves	.10	.04	.01
□ 137	Jim Deshaies	.10	.04	.01
□ 138	Pete O'Brien	.15	.06	.01
□ 139	Kevin Seitzer	.90	.36	.09
□ 140	Devon White	.25	.10	.02
□ 141	Rob Deer	.15	.06	.01
□ 142	Kurt Stillwell	.15	.06	.01
□ 143	Edwin Correa	.10	.04	.01
□ 144	Dion James	.10	.04	.01
□ 145	Danny Tartabull	.25	.10	.02
□ 146	Jerry Browne	.10	.04	.01
□ 147	Ted Higuera	.15	.06	.01
□ 148	Jack Clark	.20	.08	.02
□ 149	Ruben Sierra	.40	.16	.04
□ 150	McGwire/Eric Davis	.90	.36	.09
□ 153	Mark McGwire	.75	.30	.07
□ 154	Eric Davis	.75	.30	.07
□ 155	Wade Boggs	1.00	.40	.10
□ 156	Dale Murphy	.50	.20	.05
□ 157	Andre Dawson	.30	.12	.03
□ 158	Roger Clemens	.75	.30	.07
□ 159	Kevin Seitzer	.50	.20	.05
□ 160	Benito Santiago	.50	.20	.05
□ 161	Kal Daniels	.40	.16	.04
□ 162	John Kruk	.20	.08	.02
□ 163	Bill Ripken	.20	.08	.02
□ 164	Kirby Puckett	.50	.20	.05
□ 165	Jose Canseco	2.00	.80	.20
□ 166	Matt Nokes	.40	.16	.04
□ 167	Mike Schmidt	.50	.20	.05
□ 168	Tim Raines	.25	.10	.02
□ 169	Ryne Sandberg	.25	.10	.02
□ 170	Dave Winfield	.25	.10	.02
□ 171	Dwight Gooden	.50	.20	.05
□ 172	Bret Saberhagen	.20	.08	.02
□ 173	Willie McGee	.20	.08	.02
□ 174	Jack Morris	.15	.06	.01
□ 175	Jeff Leonard	.10	.04	.01
□ 176	Cal Ripken	.30	.12	.03
□ 177	Pete Incaviglia	.20	.08	.02
□ 178	Devon White	.20	.08	.02
□ 179	Nolan Ryan	.30	.12	.03
□ 180	Ruben Sierra	.20	.08	.02
□ 181	Todd Worrell	.15	.06	.01
□ 182	Glenn Davis	.20	.08	.02
□ 183	Frank Viola	.20	.08	.02
□ 184	Cory Snyder	.25	.10	.02
□ 185	Tracy Jones	.10	.04	.01
□ 186	Terry Steinbach	.15	.06	.01
□ 187	Julio Franco	.15	.06	.01
□ 188	Larry Sheets	.10	.04	.01
□ 189	John Marzano	.10	.04	.01
□ 190	Kevin Elster	.15	.06	.01
□ 191	Vincente Palacios	.10	.04	.01
□ 192	Kent Hrbek	.15	.06	.01
□ 193	Eric Bell	.10	.04	.01
□ 194	Kelly Downs	.15	.06	.01
□ 195	Jose Lind	.15	.06	.01
□ 196	Dave Stewart	.15	.06	.01
□ 197	Mark McGwire and Jose Canseco	1.00	.40	.10
□ 198	Phil Niekro Cleveland Indians	.20	.08	.02
□ 199	Phil Niekro Toronto Blue Jays	.20	.08	.02
□ 200	Phil Niekro Atlanta Braves	.20	.08	.02

1988 Classic Red

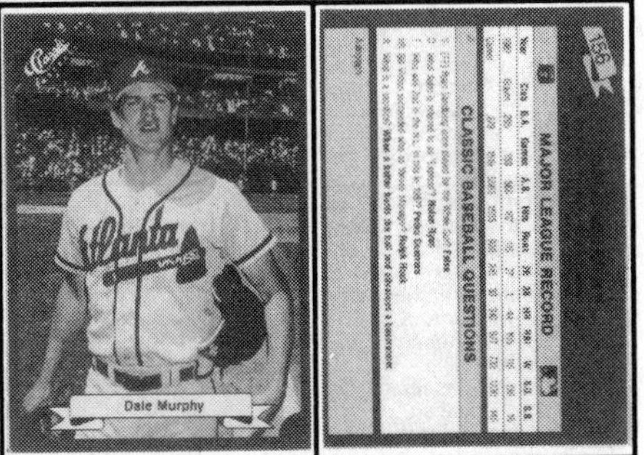

This 50-card red-bordered set was actually distributed as part of an update to a trivia board game, but (unlike the original Classic game) was sold without the game. The card backs contain several trivia questions (and answers) which are used to play the game. A red border frames the full color photo. The games were produced by Game Time, Ltd. and were available in toy stores as well as from card dealers. Cards are numbered beginning with 151 as they are an extension of the original sets.

		MINT	EXC	G-VG
COMPLETE SET (50)		7.50	3.00	.75
COMMON PLAYER (151-200)		.10	.04	.01
□ 151	Mark McGwire and Don Mattingly	1.00	.40	.10
□ 152	Don Mattingly	1.25	.50	.12

1988 Classic Blue

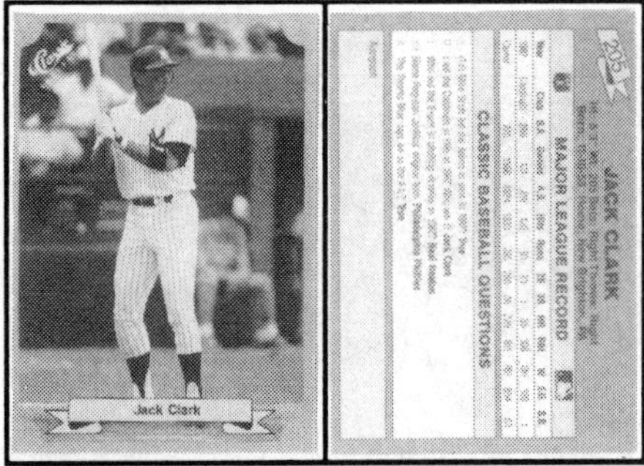

This 50-card blue-bordered set was actually distributed as part of an update to a trivia board game, but (unlike the original Classic game) was sold without the game. The card backs contain several trivia questions (and answers) which are used to play the game. A blue border frames the full color photo. The games were produced by Game Time, Ltd. and were available in toy stores as well as from card dealers. Cards are numbered beginning with 201 as they are an extension of the original sets.

	MINT	EXC	G-VG
COMPLETE SET (50)	7.50	3.00	.75

COMMON PLAYER (201-250)	.10	.04	.01
□ 201 Eric Davis and Dale Murphy	1.00	.40	.10
□ 202 B.J. Surhoff	.20	.08	.02
□ 203 John Kruk	.20	.08	.02
□ 204 Sam Horn	.30	.12	.03
□ 205 Jack Clark	.20	.08	.02
□ 206 Wally Joyner	.50	.20	.05
□ 207 Matt Nokes	.40	.16	.04
□ 208 Bo Jackson	.50	.20	.05
□ 209 Darryl Strawberry	.75	.30	.07
□ 210 Ozzie Smith	.20	.08	.02
□ 211 Don Mattingly	1.25	.50	.12
□ 212 Mark McGwire	1.00	.40	.10
□ 213 Eric Davis	.75	.30	.07
□ 214 Wade Boggs	1.00	.40	.10
□ 215 Dale Murphy	.50	.20	.05
□ 216 Andre Dawson	.30	.12	.03
□ 217 Roger Clemens	.50	.20	.05
□ 218 Kevin Seitzer	.40	.16	.04
□ 219 Benito Santiago	.40	.16	.04
□ 220 Tony Gwynn	.40	.16	.04
□ 221 Mike Scott	.20	.08	.02
□ 222 Steve Bedrosian	.10	.04	.01
□ 223 Vince Coleman	.25	.10	.02
□ 224 Rick Sutcliffe	.10	.04	.01
□ 225 Will Clark	.60	.24	.06
□ 226 Pete Rose	1.00	.40	.10
□ 227 Mike Greenwell	1.25	.50	.12
□ 228 Ken Caminiti	.15	.06	.01
□ 229 Ellis Burks	.75	.30	.07
□ 230 Dave Magadan	.20	.08	.02
□ 231 Alan Trammell	.20	.08	.02
□ 232 Paul Molitor	.20	.08	.02
□ 233 Gary Gaetti	.20	.08	.02
□ 234 Rickey Henderson	.50	.20	.05
□ 235 Danny Tartabull (photo actually Hal McRae)	.30	.12	.03
□ 236 Bobby Bonilla	.20	.08	.02
□ 237 Mike Dunne	.15	.06	.01
□ 238 Al Leiter	.25	.10	.02
□ 239 John Farrell	.15	.06	.01
□ 240 Joe Magrane	.15	.06	.01
□ 241 Mike Henneman	.15	.06	.01
□ 242 George Bell	.25	.10	.02
□ 243 Gregg Jeffries	1.50	.60	.15
□ 244 Jay Buhner	.30	.12	.03
□ 245 Todd Benzinger	.25	.10	.02
□ 246 Matt Williams	.20	.08	.02
□ 247 Mark McGwire and Don Mattingly	1.50	.60	.15
□ 248 George Brett	.50	.20	.05
□ 249 Jimmy Key	.10	.04	.01
□ 250 Mark Langston	.10	.04	.01

1981 Coke

The cards in this 132-card set measure 2 1/2" by 3 1/2". In 1981, Topps produced 11 sets of 12 cards each for the Coca-Cola Company. Each set features 11 star players for a particular team plus an advertising card with the team name on the front. Although the cards are numbered in the upper right corner of the back from 1 to 11, they are renumbered below within team, i.e., Boston Red Sox (1-12), Chicago Cubs (13-24), Chicago White Sox (25-36), Cincinnati Reds (37-48), Detroit Tigers (49-60), Houston Astros (61-72), Kansas City Royals (73-84), New York Mets (85-96), Philadelphia Phillies (97-108), Pittsburgh Pirates (109-120), and St. Louis Cardinals (121-132). Within each team the player actually numbered #1 (on the card back) is the first player below and the player numbered #11 is the last in that team's list. These player cards are quite similar to the 1981 Topps issue but feature a Coca-Cola logo on both the front and the back. The advertising card for each team features, on its back, an offer for obtaining an uncut sheet of 1981 Topps cards. These promotional cards were actually issued by Coke in only a few of the cities, and most of these cards have reached collectors hands through dealers who have purchased the cards through suppliers.

	MINT	EXC	G-VG
COMPLETE SET (132)	21.00	8.50	2.10
COMMON PLAYER	.05	.02	.00
COMMON CHECKLIST	.03	.01	.00
□ 1 Tom Burgmeier	.05	.02	.00
□ 2 Dennis Eckersley	.75	.30	.07
□ 3 Dwight Evans	.50	.20	.05
□ 4 Bob Stanley	.10	.04	.01
□ 5 Glenn Hoffman	.05	.02	.00
□ 6 Carney Lansford	.35	.14	.03
□ 7 Frank Tanana	.15	.06	.01
□ 8 Tony Perez	.35	.14	.03
□ 9 Jim Rice	1.00	.40	.10
□ 10 Dave Stapleton	.05	.02	.00
□ 11 Carl Yastrzemski	2.00	.80	.20
□ 12 Red Sox Checklist (unnumbered)	.03	.01	.00
□ 13 Tim Blackwell	.05	.02	.00
□ 14 Bill Buckner	.20	.08	.02
□ 15 Ivan DeJesus	.05	.02	.00
□ 16 Leon Durham	.25	.10	.02
□ 17 Steve Henderson	.05	.02	.00
□ 18 Mike Krukow	.15	.06	.01
□ 19 Ken Reitz	.05	.02	.00
□ 20 Rick Reuschel	.35	.14	.03
□ 21 Scot Thompson	.05	.02	.00
□ 22 Dick Tidrow	.05	.02	.00
□ 23 Mike Tyson	.05	.02	.00
□ 24 Cubs Checklist (unnumbered)	.03	.01	.00
□ 25 Britt Burns	.15	.06	.01
□ 26 Todd Cruz	.05	.02	.00
□ 27 Rich Dotson	.35	.14	.03
□ 28 Jim Essian	.05	.02	.00
□ 29 Ed Farmer	.05	.02	.00
□ 30 Lamar Johnson	.05	.02	.00
□ 31 Ron LeFlore	.10	.04	.01
□ 32 Chet Lemon	.10	.04	.01
□ 33 Bob Molinaro	.05	.02	.00
□ 34 Jim Morrison	.05	.02	.00
□ 35 Wayne Nordhagen	.05	.02	.00
□ 36 White Sox Checklist (unnumbered)	.03	.01	.00
□ 37 Johnny Bench	1.50	.60	.15
□ 38 Dave Collins	.10	.04	.01
□ 39 Dave Concepcion	.20	.08	.02
□ 40 Dan Driessen	.05	.02	.00
□ 41 George Foster	.25	.10	.02
□ 42 Ken Griffey	.15	.06	.01
□ 43 Tom Hume	.05	.02	.00
□ 44 Ray Knight	.15	.06	.01
□ 45 Ron Oester	.10	.04	.01
□ 46 Tom Seaver	1.50	.60	.15
□ 47 Mario Soto	.15	.06	.01
□ 48 Reds Checklist (unnumbered)	.03	.01	.00
□ 49 Champ Summers	.05	.02	.00
□ 50 Al Cowens	.05	.02	.00
□ 51 Rich Hebner	.05	.02	.00
□ 52 Steve Kemp	.10	.04	.01
□ 53 Aurelio Lopez	.05	.02	.00
□ 54 Jack Morris	.75	.30	.07
□ 55 Lance Parrish	.75	.30	.07
□ 56 Johnny Wockenfuss	.05	.02	.00
□ 57 Alan Trammell	1.25	.50	.12
□ 58 Lou Whitaker	.60	.24	.06
□ 59 Kirk Gibson	2.00	.80	.20
□ 60 Tigers Checklist (unnumbered)	.03	.01	.00
□ 61 Alan Ashby	.05	.02	.00

□ 62 Cesar Cedeno	.10	.04	.01
□ 63 Jose Cruz	.15	.06	.01
□ 64 Art Howe	.15	.06	.01
□ 65 Rafael Landestoy	.05	.02	.00
□ 66 Joe Niekro	.20	.08	.02
□ 67 Terry Puhl	.10	.04	.01
□ 68 J.R. Richard	.15	.06	.01
□ 69 Nolan Ryan	1.50	.60	.15
□ 70 Joe Sambito	.10	.04	.01
□ 71 Don Sutton	.90	.36	.09
□ 72 Astros Checklist (unnumbered)	.03	.01	.00
□ 73 Willie Aikens	.10	.04	.01
□ 74 George Brett	1.50	.60	.15
□ 75 Larry Gura	.10	.04	.01
□ 76 Dennis Leonard	.10	.04	.01
□ 77 Hal McRae	.10	.04	.01
□ 78 Amos Otis	.10	.04	.01
□ 79 Dan Quisenberry	.20	.08	.02
□ 80 U.L. Washington	.05	.02	.00
□ 81 John Wathan	.15	.06	.01
□ 82 Frank White	.20	.08	.02
□ 83 Willie Wilson	.25	.10	.02
□ 84 Royals Checklist (unnumbered)	.03	.01	.00
□ 85 Neil Allen	.10	.04	.01
□ 86 Doug Flynn	.05	.02	.00
□ 87 Dave Kingman	.25	.10	.02
□ 88 Randy Jones	.05	.02	.00
□ 89 Pat Zachry	.05	.02	.00
□ 90 Lee Mazzilli	.10	.04	.01
□ 91 Rusty Staub	.20	.08	.02
□ 92 Craig Swan	.05	.02	.00
□ 93 Frank Taveras	.05	.02	.00
□ 94 Alex Trevino	.05	.02	.00
□ 95 Joel Youngblood	.05	.02	.00
□ 96 Mets Checklist (unnumbered)	.03	.01	.00
□ 97 Bob Boone	.25	.10	.02
□ 98 Larry Bowa	.25	.10	.02
□ 99 Steve Carlton	1.25	.50	.12
□ 100 Greg Luzinski	.20	.08	.02
□ 101 Garry Maddox	.10	.04	.01
□ 102 Bake McBride	.05	.02	.00
□ 103 Tug McGraw	.20	.08	.02
□ 104 Pete Rose	2.00	.80	.20
□ 105 Mike Schmidt	1.50	.60	.15
□ 106 Lonnie Smith	.10	.04	.01
□ 107 Manny Trillo	.05	.02	.00
□ 108 Phillies Checklist (unnumbered)	.03	.01	.00
□ 109 Jim Bibby	.05	.02	.00
□ 110 John Candelaria	.15	.06	.01
□ 111 Mike Easler	.10	.04	.01
□ 112 Tim Foli	.05	.02	.00
□ 113 Phil Garner	.10	.04	.01
□ 114 Bill Madlock	.20	.08	.02
□ 115 Omar Moreno	.05	.02	.00
□ 116 Ed Ott	.05	.02	.00
□ 117 Dave Parker	.50	.20	.05
□ 118 Willie Stargell	1.00	.40	.10
□ 119 Kent Tekulve	.10	.04	.01
□ 120 Pirates Checklist (unnumbered)	.03	.01	.00
□ 121 Bob Forsch	.10	.04	.01
□ 122 George Hendrick	.10	.04	.01
□ 123 Keith Hernandez	.75	.30	.07
□ 124 Tom Herr	.15	.06	.01
□ 125 Sixto Lezcano	.05	.02	.00
□ 126 Ken Oberkfell	.05	.02	.00
□ 127 Darrell Porter	.10	.04	.01
□ 128 Tony Scott	.05	.02	.00
□ 129 Lary Sorensen	.05	.02	.00
□ 130 Bruce Sutter	.20	.08	.02
□ 131 Garry Templeton	.10	.04	.01
□ 132 Cardinals Checklist (unnumbered)	.03	.01	.00

1982 Coke Red Sox

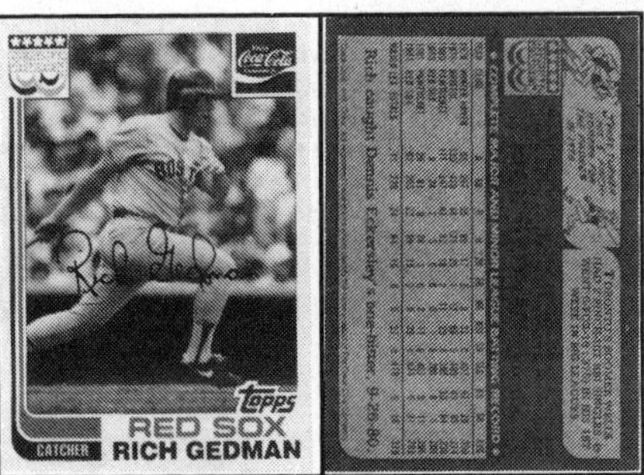

The cards in this 22-card set measure 2 1/2" by 3 1/2". This set of Boston Red Sox ballplayers was issued locally in the Boston area as a joint promotion by Brigham's Ice Cream Stores and Coca-Cola. The pictures are identical to those in the Topps regular 1982 issue, except that the colors are brighter and the Brigham and Coke logos appear inside the frame line. The reverses are done in red, black and gray, in contrast to the Topps set, and the number appears to the right of the position listing. The cards were initally distributed in three-card cello packs with an ice cream or Coca-Cola purchase but later became available as sets within the hobby. The unnumbered title or advertising card carries a premium offer on the reverse.

	MINT	EXC	G-VG
COMPLETE SET (23)	5.00	2.00	.50
COMMON PLAYER (1-23)	.05	.02	.00
□ 1 Gary Allenson	.05	.02	.00
□ 2 Tom Burgmeier	.05	.02	.00
□ 3 Mark Clear	.10	.04	.01
□ 4 Steve Crawford	.05	.02	.00
□ 5 Dennis Eckersley	.60	.24	.06
□ 6 Dwight Evans	.75	.30	.07
□ 7 Rich Gedman	.75	.30	.07
□ 8 Garry Hancock	.05	.02	.00
□ 9 Glen Hoffman	.05	.02	.00
□ 10 Carney Lansford	.25	.10	.02
□ 11 Rick Miller	.05	.02	.00
□ 12 Reid Nichols	.05	.02	.00
□ 13 Bob Ojeda	.25	.10	.02
□ 14 Tony Perez	.35	.14	.03
□ 15 Chuck Rainey	.05	.02	.00
□ 16 Jerry Remy	.05	.02	.00
□ 17 Jim Rice	.90	.36	.09
□ 18 Bob Stanley	.15	.06	.01
□ 19 Dave Stapleton	.05	.02	.00
□ 20 Mike Torrez	.10	.04	.01
□ 21 John Tudor	.35	.14	.03
□ 22 Carl Yastrzemski	2.00	.80	.20
□ 23 Title Card (unnumbered)	.03	.01	.00

1982 Coke Reds

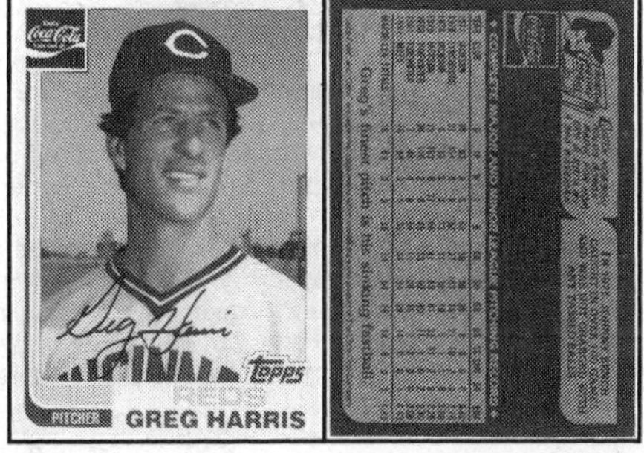

The cards in this 22-card set measure 2 1/2" by 3 1/2". The 1982 Coca-Cola Cincinnati Reds set, issued in conjunction with Topps, contains 22 cards of current Reds players. Although the cards of 15 players feature the exact photo used in the Topps' regular issue, the Coke photos have better coloration and appear sharper than their Topps counterparts. Six players, Cedeno, Harris, Hurdle, Kern, Krenchicki, and Trevino are new to the Redleg uniform via trades, while Joel Householder had formerly appeared on the Reds' 1982 Topps "Future Stars" card. The cards are numbered 1 to 22 on the red and gray reverse, and the Coke logo appears on both sides of the card. There is an unnumbered title card which contains a premium offer on the reverse.

	MINT	EXC	G-VG
COMPLETE SET (23)	5.00	2.00	.50
COMMON PLAYER (1-23)	.05	.02	.00
□ 1 Johnny Bench	1.50	.60	.15
□ 2 Bruce Berenyi	.05	.02	.00
□ 3 Larry Biittner	.05	.02	.00
□ 4 Cesar Cedeno	.10	.04	.01
□ 5 Dave Concepcion	.20	.08	.02
□ 6 Dan Driessen	.10	.04	.01
□ 7 Greg Harris	.15	.06	.01
□ 8 Paul Householder	.05	.02	.00
□ 9 Tom Hume	.05	.02	.00
□ 10 Clint Hurdle	.05	.02	.00
□ 11 Jim Kern	.05	.02	.00
□ 12 Wayne Krenchicki	.05	.02	.00
□ 13 Rafael Landestoy	.05	.02	.00
□ 14 Charlie Leibrandt	.25	.10	.02
□ 15 Mike O'Berry	.05	.02	.00
□ 16 Ron Oester	.10	.04	.01
□ 17 Frank Pastore	.05	.02	.00
□ 18 Joe Price	.05	.02	.00
□ 19 Tom Seaver	1.50	.60	.15
□ 20 Mario Soto	.20	.08	.02
□ 21 Alex Trevino	.05	.02	.00
□ 22 Mike Vail	.05	.02	.00
□ 23 Title Card (unnumbered)	.03	.01	.00

1985 Coke White Sox

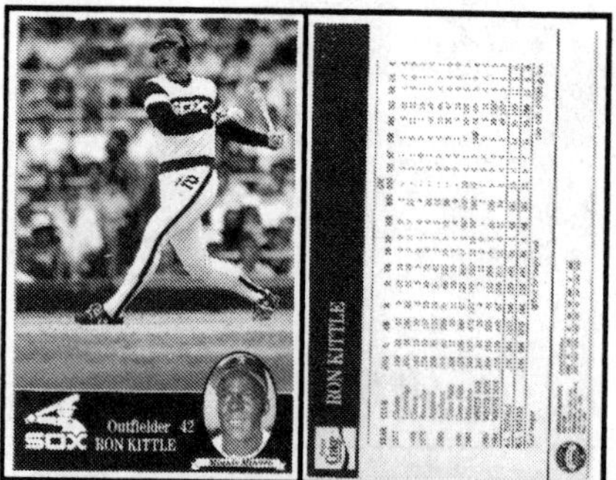

This 30-card set features present and past Chicago White Sox players and personnel. Cards measure 2 5/8" by 4 1/8" and feature a red band at the bottom of the card. Within the red band are the White Sox logo, the player's name, position, uniform number, and a small oval portrait of an all-time White Sox Great at a similar position. the cards were available two at a time at Tuesday night White Sox home games or as a complete set through membership in the Coca-Cola White Sox Fan Club. The cards below are numbered by uniform number; the last three cards are unnumbered.

	MINT	EXC	G-VG
COMPLETE SET (30)	10.00	4.00	1.00
COMMON PLAYER	.25	.10	.02
□ 0 Oscar Gamble Zeke Bonura	.25	.10	.02
□ 1 Scott Fletcher Luke Appling	.50	.20	.05
□ 3 Harold Baines Bill Melton	.75	.30	
□ 5 Luis Salazar Chico Carrasquel	.25	.10	
□ 7 Marc Hill Sherm Lollar	.25	.10	.02
□ 8 Daryl Boston Jim Landis	.25	.10	.02
□ 10 Tony LaRussa Al Lopez	.50	.20	.05
□ 12 Julio Cruz Nellie Fox	.35	.14	.03
□ 13 Ozzie Guillen Luis Aparicio	1.00	.40	.10
□ 17 Jerry Hairston Smoky Burgess	.25	.10	.02
□ 20 Joe DeSa Carlos May	.25	.10	.02
□ 22 Joel Skinner J.C. Martin	.25	.10	.02
□ 23 Rudy Law Bill Skowron	.25	.10	.02
□ 24 Floyd Bannister Red Faber	.50	.20	.05
□ 29 Greg Walker Dick Allen	.75	.30	.07
□ 30 Gene Nelson Early Wynn	.35	.14	.03
□ 32 Tim Hulett Pete Ward	.25	.10	.02
□ 34 Richard Dotson Ed Walsh	.50	.20	.05
□ 37 Dan Spillner Thornton Lee	.25	.10	.02
□ 40 Britt Burns Gary Peters	.35	.14	.03
□ 41 Tom Seaver Ted Lyons	1.50	.60	.15
□ 40 Ron Kittle Minnie Minoso	.50	.20	.05
□ 43 Bob James Hoyt Wilhelm	.35	.14	.03
□ 44 Tom Paciorek Eddie Collins	.35	.14	.03
□ 46 Tim Lollar Billy Pierce	.25	.10	.02
□ 50 Juan Agosto Wilbur Wood	.25	.10	.02
□ 72 Carlton Fisk Ray Schalk	.60	.24	.06
□ xx Comiskey Park (unnumbered)	.25	.10	.02
□ xx Nancy Faust (park organist) (unnumbered)	.25	.10	.02
□ xx Ribbie and Roobarb (unnumbered)	.25	.10	.02

1986 Coke White Sox

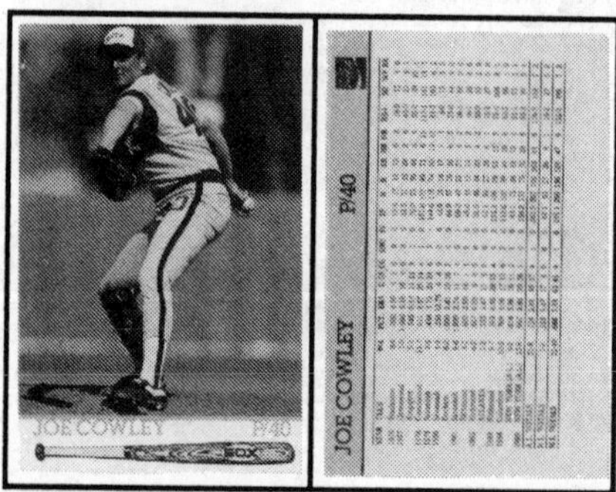

This colorful 30-card set features a borderless photo on top of a blue-on-white name, position, and uniform number. Card backs provide complete major and minor season-by- season career statistical information. Since the cards are unnumbered, they are numbered below according to uniform number. The cards measure approximately 2 5/8" by 4". The five unnumbered non-player cards are listed at the end of the checklist below.

	MINT	EXC	G-VG
COMPLETE SET (30)	9.00	3.75	.90
COMMON PLAYER	.20	.08	.02

☐ 1 Wayne Tolleson	.30	.12	.03
☐ 3 Harold Baines	.90	.36	.09
☐ 7 Marc Hill	.20	.08	.02
☐ 8 Daryl Boston	.20	.08	.02
☐ 12 Julio Cruz	.20	.08	.02
☐ 13 Ozzie Guillen	.60	.24	.06
☐ 17 Jerry Hairston	.20	.08	.02
☐ 19 Floyd Bannister	.40	.16	.04
☐ 20 Reid Nichols	.20	.08	.02
☐ 22 Joel Skinner	.20	.08	.02
☐ 24 Dave Schmidt	.30	.12	.03
☐ 26 Bobby Bonilla	.90	.36	.09
☐ 29 Greg Walker	.60	.24	.06
☐ 30 Gene Nelson	.30	.12	.03
☐ 32 Tim Hulett	.20	.08	.02
☐ 33 Neil Allen	.30	.12	.03
☐ 34 Richard Dotson	.40	.16	.04
☐ 40 Joe Cowley	.20	.08	.02
☐ 41 Tom Seaver	1.00	.40	.10
☐ 42 Ron Kittle	.50	.20	.05
☐ 43 Bob James	.20	.08	.02
☐ 44 John Cangelosi	.30	.12	.03
☐ 50 Juan Agosto	.20	.08	.02
☐ 52 Joel Davis	.30	.12	.03
☐ 72 Carlton Fisk	.60	.24	.06
☐ xx Nancy Faust ORG (unnumbered)	.20	.08	.02
☐ xx Ken "Hawk" Harrelson (unnumbered)	.30	.12	.03
☐ xx Tony LaRussa MG (unnumbered)	.30	.12	.03
☐ xx Minnie Minoso CO (unnumbered)	.30	.12	.03
☐ xx Ribbie and Roobarb (unnumbered)	.20	.08	.02

1987 Coke Tigers

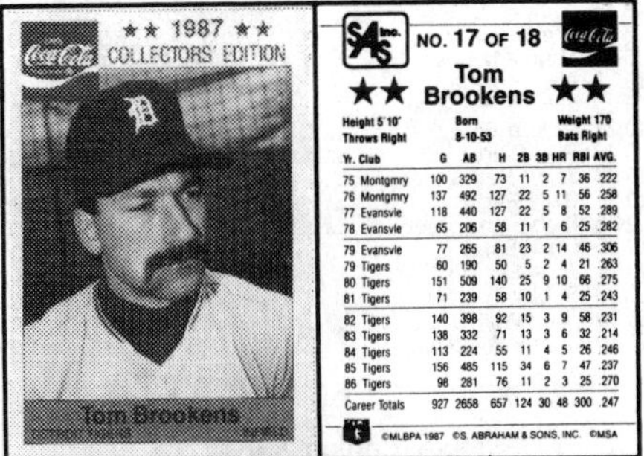

Coca-Cola in collaboration with S. Abraham and Sons issued a set of 18 cards featuring the Detroit Tigers. The cards are numbered on the back. The cards are distinguished by the bright yellow border framing the full-color picture of the player on the front. The cards were issued in panels of four: three player cards and a team logo card. The cards measure the standard 2 1/2" by 3 1/2" and were produced by MSA, Mike Schechter Associates.

	MINT	EXC	G-VG
COMPLETE SET (18)	5.00	2.00	.50
COMMON PLAYER (1-18)	.20	.08	.02
☐ 1 Kirk Gibson	.75	.30	.07
☐ 2 Larry Herndon	.20	.08	.02
☐ 3 Walt Terrell	.30	.12	.03
☐ 4 Alan Trammell	.75	.30	.07
☐ 5 Frank Tanana	.30	.12	.03
☐ 6 Pat Sheridan	.20	.08	.02
☐ 7 Jack Morris	.50	.20	.05
☐ 8 Mike Heath	.20	.08	.02
☐ 9 Dave Bergman	.20	.08	.02
☐ 10 Chet Lemon	.30	.12	.03
☐ 11 Dwight Lowry	.20	.08	.02
☐ 12 Dan Petry	.20	.08	.02
☐ 13 Darrell Evans	.30	.12	.03
☐ 14 Darnell Coles	.20	.08	.02
☐ 15 Willie Hernandez	.30	.12	.03
☐ 16 Lou Whitaker	.40	.16	.04
☐ 17 Tom Brookens	.20	.08	.02
☐ 18 John Grubb	.20	.08	.02

1987 Coke White Sox

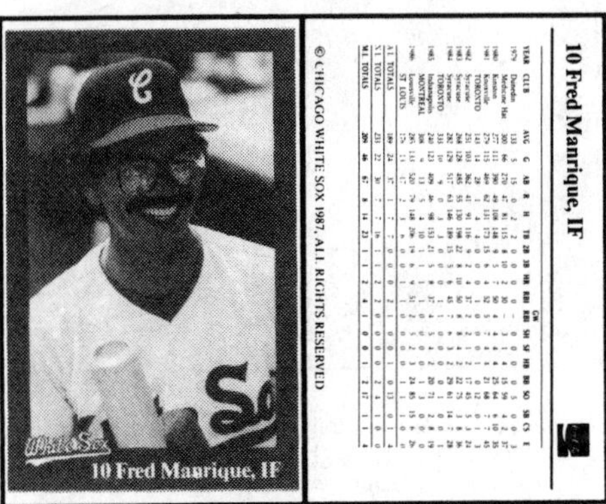

This colorful 30-card set features a card front with a blue-bordered photo and name, position, and uniform number. Card backs provide complete major and minor season-by- season career statistical information. Since the cards are unnumbered, they are numbered below in uniform number order. The cards measure approximately 2 5/8" by 4". The three unnumbered non-player cards are listed at the end. The card set, sponsored by Coca-Cola, is an exclusive for fan club members who join (for 10.00) in 1987.

	MINT	EXC	G-VG
COMPLETE SET (30)	7.00	2.80	.70
COMMON PLAYER (1-30)	.20	.08	.02
☐ 1 Jerry Royster 1	.20	.08	.02
☐ 2 Harold Baines 3	.50	.20	.05
☐ 3 Ron Karkovice 5	.20	.08	.02
☐ 4 Daryl Boston 8	.20	.08	.02
☐ 5 Fred Manrique 10	.20	.08	.02
☐ 6 Steve Lyons 12	.20	.08	.02
☐ 7 Ozzie Guillen 13	.40	.16	.04
☐ 8 Russ Morman 14	.20	.08	.02
☐ 9 Donnie Hill 15	.20	.08	.02
☐ 10 Jim Fregosi MG 16	.30	.12	.03
☐ 11 Jerry Hairston 17	.20	.08	.02
☐ 12 Floyd Bannister 19	.30	.12	.03
☐ 13 Gary Redus 21	.30	.12	.03
☐ 14 Ivan Calderon 22	.50	.20	.05
☐ 15 Ron Hassey 25	.30	.12	.03
☐ 16 Jose DeLeon 26	.30	.12	.03
☐ 17 Greg Walker 29	.50	.20	.05
☐ 18 Tim Hulett 32	.20	.08	.02
☐ 19 Neil Allen 33	.30	.12	.03
☐ 20 Richard Dotson 34	.30	.12	.03
☐ 21 Ray Searage 36	.20	.08	.02
☐ 22 Bobby Thigpen 37	.50	.20	.05
☐ 23 Jim Winn 40	.20	.08	.02
☐ 24 Bob James 43	.20	.08	.02
☐ 25 Joel McKeon 50	.20	.08	.02
☐ 26 Joel Davis 52	.20	.08	.02
☐ 27 Carlton Fisk 72	.50	.20	.05
☐ 28 Nancy Faust ORG (unnumbered)	.20	.08	.02
☐ 29 Minnie Minoso (unnumbered)	.30	.12	.03
☐ 30 Robbie and Roobarb (unnumbered)	.20	.08	.02

1988 Coke Padres

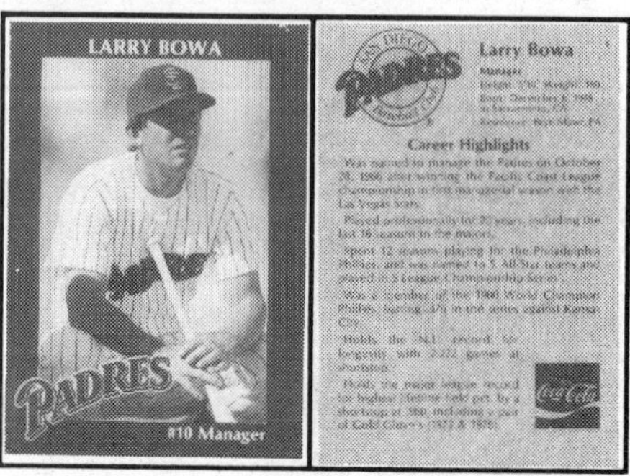

These cards were actually issued as two separate promotions. The first eight cards were issued as a perforated sheet (approximately 7 1/2" by 10 1/2") as a Coca Cola Junior Padres Club promotion. The other 12 cards were issued later on specific game days to members of the Junior Padres Club. All the cards are standard size, 2 1/2" by 3 1/2" and are unnumbered. Cards that were on the perforated panel are indicated by PAN in the checklist below. Since the cards are unnumbered, they are listed below by uniform number, which is featured prominently on the card fronts.

	MINT	EXC	G-VG
COMPLETE SET (21)	25.00	10.00	2.50
COMMON PANEL PLAYER	.50	.20	.05
COMMON NON-PAN PLAYER	1.00	.40	.10
☐ 1 Garry Templeton PAN	.50	.20	.05
☐ 5 Randy Ready PAN	.50	.20	.05
☐ 7 Keith Moreland	1.00	.40	.10
☐ 8 John Kruk	1.50	.60	.15
☐ 9 Benito Santiago	4.00	1.60	.40
☐ 10 Larry Bowa MG PAN	.50	.20	.05
☐ 11 Tim Flannery PAN	.50	.20	.05
☐ 14 Carmelo Martinez	1.00	.40	.10
☐ 15 Jack McKeon MG	1.00	.40	.10
☐ 19 Tony Gwynn	8.00	3.25	.80
☐ 22 Stan Jefferson	1.50	.60	.15
☐ 27 Mark Parent	1.00	.40	.10
☐ 30 Eric Show	1.50	.60	.15
☐ 31 Eddie Whitson	1.50	.60	.15
☐ 35 Chris Brown PAN	.75	.30	.07
☐ 41 Lance McCullers	1.50	.60	.15
☐ 45 Jimmy Jones PAN	.75	.30	.07
☐ 48 Mark Davis PAN	.75	.30	.07
☐ 51 Greg Booker	1.00	.40	.10
☐ 55 Mark Grant PAN	.50	.20	.05
☐ xx Padres Logo PAN (program explanation on reverse)	.50	.20	.05

1988 Coke White Sox

This colorful 30-card set features a card front with a red-bordered photo and name and position. Card backs provide a narrative without any statistical tables. Since the cards are unnumbered, they are numbered below in alphabetical order according to the subject's name or card's title. The cards measure approximately 2 5/8" by 3 1/2". The card set, sponsored by Coca-Cola, was for fan club members who join (for 10.00) in 1988. The cards were also given out at the May 22nd game at Comiskey Park. These cards do not even list the player's uniform number anywhere on the card. Card backs are printed in black and gray on thin white card stock.

	MINT	EXC	G-VG
COMPLETE SET (30)	6.00	2.40	.60
COMMON PLAYER (1-30)	.15	.06	.01
☐ 1 Harold Baines	.35	.14	.03
☐ 2 Daryl Boston	.15	.06	.01
☐ 3 Ivan Calderon	.35	.14	.03
☐ 4 Comiskey Park	.15	.06	.01
☐ 5 John Davis	.25	.10	.02
☐ 6 Nancy Faust (organist)	.15	.06	.01
☐ 7 Jim Fregosi MG	.25	.10	.02
☐ 8 Carlton Fisk	.45	.18	.04
☐ 9 Ozzie Guillen	.35	.14	.03
☐ 10 Donnie Hill	.15	.06	.01
☐ 11 Rick Horton	.25	.10	.02
☐ 12 Lance Johnson	.25	.10	.02
☐ 13 Dave LaPoint	.25	.10	.02
☐ 14 Bill Long	.15	.06	.01
☐ 15 Steve Lyons	.15	.06	.01
☐ 16 Jack McDowell	.35	.14	.03
☐ 17 Fred Manrique	.15	.06	.01
☐ 18 Minnie Minoso	.35	.14	.03
☐ 19 Dan Pasqua	.25	.10	.02
☐ 20 John Pawlowski	.15	.06	.01
☐ 21 Melido Perez	.35	.14	.03
☐ 22 Billy Pierce	.25	.10	.02
☐ 23 Jerry Reuss	.25	.10	.02
☐ 24 Gary Redus	.25	.10	.02
☐ 25 Ribbie and Roobarb	.15	.06	.01
☐ 26 Mark Salas	.15	.06	.01
☐ 27 Jose Segura	.25	.10	.02
☐ 28 Bobby Thigpen	.35	.14	.03
☐ 29 Greg Walker	.35	.14	.03
☐ 30 Kenny Williams	.25	.10	.02

1986 Conlon Series 1

This 60-card set was produced from the black and white photos in the Charles Martin Conlon collection. Each set comes with a special card which contains the number of that set out of the 12,000 sets which were produced. The cards measure 2 1/2" by 3 1/2" and are printed in sepia tones. The cards are individually numbered on the back.

	MINT	EXC	G-VG
COMPLETE SET (60)	12.50	5.00	1.25
COMMON PLAYER (1-60)	.20	.08	.02
☐ 1 Henry Louis Gehrig	.75	.30	.07
☐ 2 Tyrus Raymond Cobb	.75	.30	.07
☐ 3 Grover C. Alexander	.30	.12	.03
☐ 4 Walter Perry Johnson	.50	.20	.05
☐ 5 William Joseph Klem	.20	.08	.02
☐ 6 Tyrus Raymond Cobb	.75	.30	.07
☐ 7 Gordon S. Cochrane	.30	.12	.03
☐ 8 Paul Glee Waner	.20	.08	.02
☐ 9 Joseph Edward Cronin	.20	.08	.02
☐ 10 Jay Hanna Dean	.50	.20	.05
☐ 11 Leo Ernest Durocher	.30	.12	.03
☐ 12 James Emory Foxx	.30	.12	.03
☐ 13 George Herman Ruth	1.00	.40	.10
☐ 14 Miguel Angel Gonzalez Frank Francis Frisch Clyde Ellsworth Wares	.20	.08	.02
☐ 15 Carl Owen Hubbell	.30	.12	.03
☐ 16 Miller James Huggins	.20	.08	.02
☐ 17 Henry Louis Gehrig	.75	.30	.07
☐ 18 Connie McGillicuddy	.30	.12	.03
☐ 19 Henry Emmett Manush	.20	.08	.02
☐ 20 George Herman Ruth	1.00	.40	.10
☐ 22 John L.R. Martin	.20	.08	.02
☐ 23 Christopher Mathewson	.50	.20	.05
☐ 24 Tyrus Raymond Cobb	.75	.30	.07
☐ 25 Stanley R. Harris	.20	.08	.02
☐ 26 Waite Charles Hoyt	.20	.08	.02
☐ 27 Richard W. Marquard	.20	.08	.02
☐ 28 Joseph V. McCarthy	.20	.08	.02
☐ 29 John Joseph McGraw	.20	.08	.02
☐ 30 Tristram Speaker	.30	.12	.03
☐ 31 William Harold Terry	.30	.12	.03
☐ 32 Christopher Mathewson	.50	.20	.05
☐ 33 Charles D. Stengel	.50	.20	.05
☐ 34 Robert William Meusel	.20	.08	.02
☐ 35 George Edward Waddell	.20	.08	.02
☐ 36 Melvin Thomas Ott	.30	.12	.03
☐ 37 Roger T. Peckinpaugh	.20	.08	.02
☐ 38 Harold Joseph Traynor	.20	.08	.02
☐ 39 Charles Albert Bender	.20	.08	.02
☐ 40 John Wesley Coombs	.20	.08	.02
☐ 41 Tyrus Raymond Cobb	.75	.30	.07
☐ 42 Harry Edwin Heilmann	.20	.08	.02
☐ 43 Charles L. Gehringer	.30	.12	.03
☐ 44 Rogers Hornsby	.50	.20	.05
☐ 45 Vernon Gomez	.40	.16	.04
☐ 46 Christopher Mathewson	.50	.20	.05
☐ 47 Robert Moses Grove	.45	.18	.04
☐ 48 George Herman Ruth	1.00	.40	.10
☐ 49 Frederick C. Merkle	.20	.08	.02
☐ 50 George Herman Ruth	1.00	.40	.10
☐ 51 Herbert J. Pennock	.20	.08	.02
☐ 52 Henry Louis Gehrig	.75	.30	.07
☐ 53 Fred Clifford Clarke	.20	.08	.02
☐ 54 George Herman Ruth	1.00	.40	.10
☐ 55 John Peter Wagner	.50	.20	.05
☐ 56 Lewis Robert Wilson	.30	.12	.03
☐ 57 Henry Louis Gehrig	.75	.30	.07
☐ 58 Lloyd James Waner	.20	.08	.02
☐ 59 Charles Martin Conlon	.20	.08	.02
☐ 60 Conlon and Margie	.20	.08	.02
☐ xx Set Number Card (unnumbered)	.20	.08	.02

1987 Conlon Series 2

The second series of 60 Charles Martin Conlon photo cards was produced by World Wide Sports in conjunction with The Sporting News. The cards are standard size, 2 1/2" by 3 1/2" and are in a sepia tone. Supposedly 12,000 sets were produced. The photos were selected and background information written by Paul MacFarlane of The Sporting News. The cards are individually numbered on the back.

	MINT	EXC	G-VG
COMPLETE SET (60)	10.00	4.00	1.00
COMMON PLAYER (1-60)	.20	.08	.02
☐ 1 Henry Gehrig	.75	.30	.07
☐ 2 Vernon Gomez	.40	.16	.04
☐ 3 Christopher Mathewson	.50	.20	.05
☐ 4 Grover Alexander	.30	.12	.03
☐ 5 Tyrus Cobb	.75	.30	.07
☐ 6 Walter Johnson	.50	.20	.05
☐ 7 Charles Adams	.20	.08	.02
☐ 8 Nicholas Altrock	.20	.08	.02
☐ 9 Al Schacht	.20	.08	.02
☐ 10 Hugh Critz	.20	.08	.02
☐ 11 Henry Cullop	.20	.08	.02
☐ 12 Jacob Daubert	.20	.08	.02
☐ 13 William Donovan	.20	.08	.02
☐ 14 Charles Hafey	.20	.08	.02
☐ 15 William Hallahan	.20	.08	.02
☐ 16 Fred Haney	.20	.08	.02
☐ 17 Charles Hartnett	.20	.08	.02
☐ 18 Walter Henline	.20	.08	.02
☐ 19 Edwin Rommel	.20	.08	.02
☐ 20 Ralph Pinelli	.20	.08	.02
☐ 21 Robert Meusel	.20	.08	.02
☐ 22 Emil Meusel	.20	.08	.02
☐ 23 Smead Jolley	.20	.08	.02
☐ 24 Isaac Boone	.20	.08	.02
☐ 25 Earl Webb	.20	.08	.02
☐ 26 Charles Comiskey	.30	.12	.03
☐ 27 Edward Collins	.30	.12	.03
☐ 28 George Weaver	.20	.08	.02
☐ 29 Edward Cicotte	.20	.08	.02
☐ 30 Samuel Crawford	.20	.08	.02
☐ 31 Charles Dressen	.20	.08	.02
☐ 32 Arthur Fletcher	.20	.08	.02
☐ 33 Hugh Duffy	.30	.12	.03
☐ 34 Ira Flagstead	.20	.08	.02
☐ 35 Harry Hooper	.20	.08	.02
☐ 36 George Lewis	.20	.08	.02
☐ 37 James Dykes	.20	.08	.02
☐ 38 Leon Goslin	.20	.08	.02
☐ 39 Henry Gowdy	.20	.08	.02
☐ 40 Charles Grimm	.20	.08	.02
☐ 41 Mark Koenig	.20	.08	.02
☐ 42 James Hogan	.20	.08	.02
☐ 43 William Jacobson	.20	.08	.02
☐ 44 Fielder Jones	.20	.08	.02
☐ 45 George Kelly	.20	.08	.02
☐ 46 Adolpho Luque	.20	.08	.02
☐ 47 Walter Maranville	.20	.08	.02
☐ 48 Carl Mays	.20	.08	.02
☐ 49 Edward Plank	.30	.12	.03
☐ 50 Hubert Pruett	.20	.08	.02
☐ 51 John Quinn	.20	.08	.02
☐ 52 Charles Rhem	.20	.08	.02
☐ 53 Amos Rusie	.30	.12	.03
☐ 54 Edd Roush	.20	.08	.02
☐ 55 Raymond Schalk	.20	.08	.02
☐ 56 Ernest Shore	.20	.08	.02
☐ 57 Joe Wood	.20	.08	.02
☐ 58 George Sisler	.30	.12	.03
☐ 59 James Thorpe	.50	.20	.05
☐ 60 Earl Whitehill	.20	.08	.02

1988 Conlon Series 3

This third series of 30 Charles Martin Conlon photo cards was produced by World Wide Sports in conjunction with The Sporting News. The cards are standard size, 2 1/2" by 3 1/2" and are in a sepia tone. The photos were selected and background information written by Paul MacFarlane of The

Sporting News. These cards are unnumbered and hence are listed below in alphabetical order. Series 3 is indicated in the lower right corner of each card's reverse. A black and white logo for the "Baseball Immortals" and The Conlon Collection is overprinted in the lower left corner of each obverse.

	MINT	EXC	G-VG
COMPLETE SET (30)	5.50	2.20	.55
COMMON PLAYER (1-30)	.20	.08	.02
□ 1 Ace Adams	.20	.08	.02
□ 2 Grover C. Alexander	.25	.10	.02
□ 3 Elden Auker	.20	.08	.02
□ 4 Jack Barry	.20	.08	.02
□ 5 Wally Berger	.20	.08	.02
□ 6 Ben Chapman	.20	.08	.02
□ 7 Mickey Cochrane	.25	.10	.02
□ 8 Frankie Crosetti	.20	.08	.02
□ 9 Paul Dean	.20	.08	.02
□ 10 Leo Durocher	.25	.10	.02
□ 11 Wes Ferrell	.20	.08	.02
□ 12 Hank Gowdy	.20	.08	.02
□ 13 Andy High	.20	.08	.02
□ 14 Rogers Hornsby	.30	.12	.03
□ 15 Carl Hubbell	.25	.10	.02
□ 16 Joe Judge	.20	.08	.02
□ 17 Tony Lazzeri	.20	.08	.02
□ 18 Pepper Martin	.20	.08	.02
□ 19 Lee Meadows	.20	.08	.02
□ 20 Johnny Murphy	.20	.08	.02
□ 21 Steve O'Neil	.20	.08	.02
□ 22 Ed Plank	.25	.10	.02
□ 23 Jack "Picus" Quinn	.20	.08	.02
□ 24 Charley Root	.20	.08	.02
□ 25 Babe Ruth	.75	.30	.07
□ 26 Fred Snodgrass	.20	.08	.02
□ 27 Tris Speaker	.30	.12	.03
□ 28 Bill Terry	.25	.10	.02
□ 29 Jeff Tesreau	.20	.08	.02
□ 30 George Toporcer	.20	.08	.02

1988 Conlon Series 4

This fourth series of 30 Charles Martin Conlon photo cards was produced by World Wide Sports in conjunction with The Sporting News. The cards are standard size, 2 1/2" by 3 1/2" and are in a sepia tone. The photos were selected and background information written by Paul MacFarlane of The Sporting News. These cards are unnumbered and hence are listed below in alphabetical order. Series 4 is indicated in the lower right corner of each card's reverse. A black and white logo for the "Baseball Immortals" and The Conlon Collection is overprinted in the lower left corner of each obverse.

	MINT	EXC	G-VG
COMPLETE SET (30)	5.50	2.20	.55
COMMON PLAYER (1-30)	.20	.08	.02
□ 1 Dale Alexander	.20	.08	.02
□ 2 Morris Badgro	.20	.08	.02
□ 3 Dick Bartell	.20	.08	.02
□ 4 Max Bishop	.20	.08	.02
□ 5 Hal Chase	.20	.08	.02
□ 6 Ty Cobb	.50	.20	.05
□ 7 Nick Cullop	.20	.08	.02
□ 8 Dizzy Dean	.35	.14	.03
□ 9 Charlie Dressen	.20	.08	.02
□ 10 Jimmy Dykes	.20	.08	.02
□ 11 Art Fletcher	.20	.08	.02
□ 12 Charlie Grimm	.20	.08	.02
□ 13 Lefty Grove	.30	.12	.03
□ 14 Baby Doll Jacobson	.20	.08	.02
□ 15 Bill Klem	.25	.10	.02
□ 16 Mark Koenig	.20	.08	.02
□ 17 Duffy Lewis	.20	.08	.02
□ 18 Carl Mays	.20	.08	.02
□ 19 Fred Merkle	.20	.08	.02
□ 20 Greasy Neale	.20	.08	.02
□ 21 Mel Ott	.25	.10	.02
□ 22 Babe Pinelli	.20	.08	.02
□ 23 Flint Rhem	.20	.08	.02
□ 24 Slim Sallee (misspelled Salee on card back)	.20	.08	.02
□ 25 Al Simmons	.20	.08	.02
□ 26 George Sisler	.25	.10	.02
□ 27 Riggs Stephenson	.20	.08	.02
□ 28 Jim Thorpe	.40	.16	.04
□ 29 Bill Wambsganss	.20	.08	.02
□ 30 Cy Young	.30	.12	.03

1988 Conlon Series 5

This fifth series of 30 Charles Martin Conlon photo cards was produced by World Wide Sports in conjunction with The Sporting News. The cards are standard size, 2 1/2" by 3 1/2" and are in a sepia tone. The photos were selected and background information written by Paul MacFarlane of The Sporting News. These cards are unnumbered and hence are listed below in alphabetical order. Series 5 is indicated in the lower right corner of each card's reverse. A black and white logo for the "Baseball Immortals" and The Conlon Collection is overprinted in the lower left corner of each obverse.

	MINT	EXC	G-VG
COMPLETE SET (30)	5.50	2.20	.55
COMMON PLAYER (1-30)	.20	.08	.02

□ 1 Nick Altrock	.20	.08	.02
□ 2 Del Baker	.20	.08	.02
□ 3 Moe Berg	.20	.08	.02
□ 4 Zeke Bonura	.20	.08	.02
□ 5 Eddie Collins	.25	.10	.02
□ 6 Hughie Critz	.20	.08	.02
□ 7 George Dauss	.20	.08	.02
□ 8 Joe Dugan	.20	.08	.02
□ 9 Howard Ehmke	.20	.08	.02
□ 10 James Emory Foxx	.35	.14	.03
□ 11 Frankie Frisch	.25	.10	.02
□ 12 Lou Gehrig	.50	.20	.05
□ 13 Charlie Gehringer	.25	.10	.02
□ 14 Kid Gleason	.20	.08	.02
□ 15 Lefty Gomez	.25	.10	.02
□ 16 Babe Herman	.20	.08	.02
□ 17 Bill James	.20	.08	.02
□ 18 Joe Kuhel	.20	.08	.02
□ 19 Dolf Luque	.20	.08	.02
□ 20 John McGraw	.25	.10	.02
□ 21 Stuffy McInnis	.20	.08	.02
□ 22 Bob Meusel	.20	.08	.02
□ 23 Lefty O'Doul	.20	.08	.02
□ 24 Hub Pruett	.20	.08	.02
□ 25 Paul Richards	.20	.08	.02
□ 26 Bob Shawkey	.20	.08	.02
□ 27 Gabby Street	.20	.08	.02
□ 28 Johnny Tobin	.20	.08	.02
□ 29 Rube Waddell	.25	.10	.02
□ 30 Billy Werber	.20	.08	.02

1988 Conlon American All-Stars

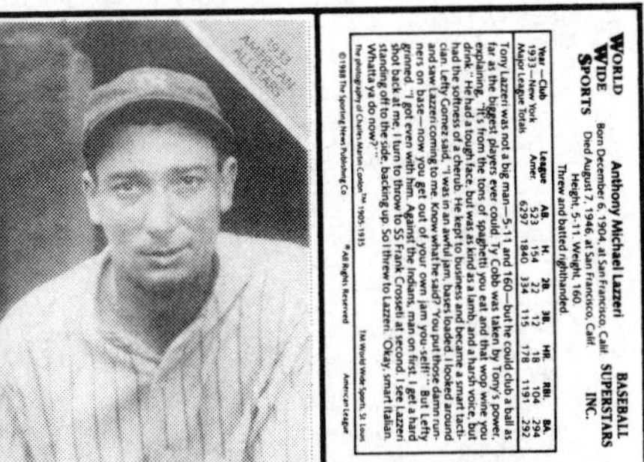

This set of 24 Charles Martin Conlon photo cards was produced by World Wide Sports in conjunction with The Sporting News. The cards are standard size, 2 1/2" by 3 1/2" and are in a sepia tone. The photos (members of the 1933 American League All-Star team) were selected and background information written by Paul MacFarlane of The Sporting News. These cards are unnumbered and hence are listed below in alphabetical order. American League is indicated in the lower right corner of each card's reverse. In the upper right corner of each card's obverse is printed "1933 American All Stars."

	MINT	EXC	G-VG
COMPLETE SET (24)	4.50	1.80	.45
COMMON PLAYER (1-24)	.20	.08	.02
□ 1 Luke Appling	.25	.10	.02
□ 2 Earl Averill	.20	.08	.02
□ 3 Tommy Bridges	.20	.08	.02
□ 4 Ben Chapman	.20	.08	.02
□ 5 Mickey Cochrane	.30	.12	.03
□ 6 Joe Cronin	.25	.10	.02
□ 7 Alvin Crowder	.20	.08	.02
□ 8 Bill Dickey	.30	.12	.03
□ 9 James Emory Foxx	.30	.12	.03
□ 10 Lou Gehrig	.50	.20	.05
□ 11 Charlie Gehringer	.25	.10	.02
□ 12 Lefty Gomez	.25	.10	.02
□ 13 Lefty Grove	.30	.12	.03
□ 14 Mel Harder	.20	.08	.02
□ 15 Pinky Higgins	.20	.08	.02

□ 16 Urban Hodapp	.20	.08	.02
□ 17 Roy Johnson	.20	.08	.02
□ 18 Joe Kuhel	.20	.08	.02
□ 19 Tony Lazzeri	.25	.10	.02
□ 20 Heinie Manush	.20	.08	.02
□ 21 Babe Ruth	.75	.30	.07
□ 22 Al Simmons	.20	.08	.02
□ 23 Evar Swanson	.20	.08	.02
□ 24 Earl Whitehill	.20	.08	.02

1988 Conlon National All-Stars

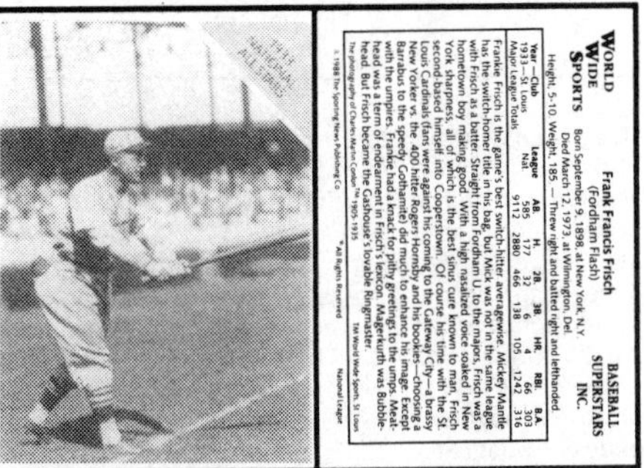

This set of 24 Charles Martin Conlon photo cards was produced by World Wide Sports in conjunction with The Sporting News. The cards are standard size, 2 1/2" by 3 1/2" and are in a sepia tone. The photos (members of the 1933 National League All-Star team) were selected and background information written by Paul MacFarlane of The Sporting News. These cards are unnumbered and hence are listed below in alphabetical order. American League is indicated in the lower right corner of each card's reverse. In the upper right corner of each card's obverse is printed "1933 National All Stars."

	MINT	EXC	G-VG
COMPLETE SET (24)	4.50	1.80	.45
COMMON PLAYER (1-24)	.20	.08	.02
□ 1 Wally Berger	.20	.08	.02
□ 2 Guy Bush	.20	.08	.02
□ 3 Ripper Collins	.20	.08	.02
□ 4 Spud Davis	.20	.08	.02
□ 5 Dizzy Dean	.35	.14	.03
□ 6 Johnny Frederick	.20	.08	.02
□ 7 Larry French	.20	.08	.02
□ 8 Frankie Frisch	.25	.10	.02
□ 9 Chick Fullis	.20	.08	.02
□ 10 Chick Hafey	.20	.08	.02
□ 11 Carl Hubbell	.30	.12	.03
□ 12 Chuck Klein	.25	.10	.02
□ 13 Fred Lindstrom	.20	.08	.02
□ 14 Pepper Martin	.20	.08	.02
□ 15 Joe Medwick	.25	.10	.02
□ 16 Tony Piet	.20	.08	.02
□ 17 Wes Schulmerich	.20	.08	.02
□ 18 Hal Schumacher	.20	.08	.02
□ 19 Riggs Stephenson	.20	.08	.02
□ 20 Bill Terry	.25	.10	.02
□ 21 Pie Traynor	.25	.10	.02
□ 22 Arky Vaughan	.25	.10	.02
□ 23 Paul Waner	.25	.10	.02
□ 24 Lon Warneke	.20	.08	.02

1988 Conlon Negro All-Stars

This set of 12 Charles Martin Conlon photo cards was produced by World Wide Sports in conjunction with The Sporting News. The cards are standard size, 2 1/2" by 3 1/2" and are in a sepia tone. The photos

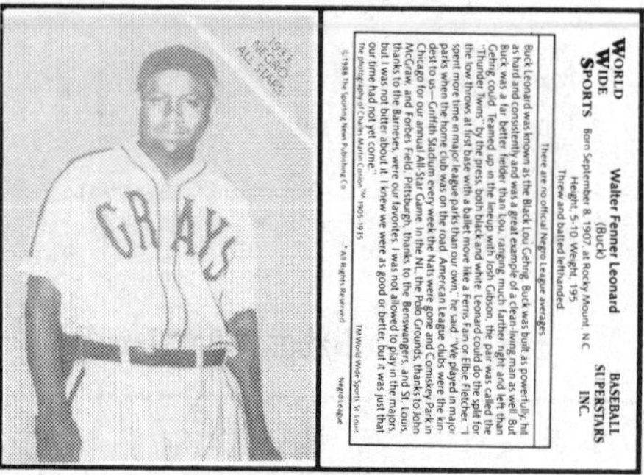

(Negro League All Stars from 1933) were selected and background information written by Paul MacFarlane of The Sporting News. These cards are unnumbered and hence are listed below in alphabetical order. Negro League is indicated in the lower right corner of each card's reverse. In the upper right corner of each card's obverse is printed "1933 Negro All Stars." The photo quality on some of the cards is very poor suggesting that the original photo or negative may have been enlarged to an excessive degree.

	MINT	EXC	G-VG
COMPLETE SET (12)	2.50	1.00	.25
COMMON PLAYER (1-12)	.20	.08	.02
☐ 1 Cool Papa Bell	.25	.10	.02
☐ 2 Oscar Charleston	.25	.10	.02
☐ 3 Martin DiHigo	.25	.10	.02
☐ 4 Rube Foster	.20	.08	.02
☐ 5 Josh Gibson	.30	.12	.03
☐ 6 Judy Johnson	.25	.10	.02
☐ 7 Buck Leonard	.25	.10	.02
☐ 8 John Henry Lloyd	.25	.10	.02
☐ 9 Dave Malarcher	.20	.08	.02
☐ 10 Satch Paige	.30	.12	.03
☐ 11 Willie Wells	.25	.10	.02
☐ 12 Smoky Joe Williams	.25	.10	.02

1914 Cracker Jack

The cards in this 144-card set measure 2 1/4" by 3". This "Series of colored pictures of Famous Ball Players and Managers" was issued in packages of Cracker Jack in 1914. The cards have tinted photos set against red backgrounds and many are found with caramel stains. The set also contains Federal League players. The company claims to have printed 15 million cards. The 1914 series can be distinguished from the 1915 issue by the advertising found on the back of the cards. The ACC catalog number is E145-1.

	NRMT	VG-E	GOOD
COMPLETE SET	17500.00	7500.00	2500.00
COMMON PLAYER (1-144)	65.00	26.00	6.50
☐ 1 Otto Knabe	65.00	26.00	6.50
☐ 2 Frank Baker	150.00	60.00	15.00
☐ 3 Joe Tinker	150.00	60.00	15.00
☐ 4 Larry Doyle	65.00	26.00	6.50
☐ 5 Ward Miller	65.00	26.00	6.50
☐ 6 Eddie Plank (Phila. AL)	200.00	80.00	20.00
☐ 7 Eddie Collins (Phila. AL)	200.00	80.00	20.00
☐ 8 Rube Oldring	65.00	26.00	6.50
☐ 9 Artie Hoffman	65.00	26.00	6.50
☐ 10 John McInnis	90.00	36.00	9.00
☐ 11 George Stovall	65.00	26.00	6.50
☐ 12 Connie Mack	250.00	100.00	25.00
☐ 13 Art Wilson	65.00	26.00	6.50
☐ 14 Sam Crawford	150.00	60.00	15.00
☐ 15 Reb Russell	65.00	26.00	6.50
☐ 16 Howie Camnitz	65.00	26.00	6.50
☐ 17 Roger Bresnahan (Catcher)	150.00	60.00	15.00
☐ 18 Johnny Evers	150.00	60.00	15.00
☐ 19 Chief Bender (Phila. AL)	200.00	80.00	20.00
☐ 20 Cy Falkenberg	65.00	26.00	6.50
☐ 21 Heine Zimmerman	65.00	26.00	6.50
☐ 22 Joe Wood	125.00	50.00	12.50
☐ 23 Charles Comiskey	175.00	70.00	18.00
☐ 24 George Mullen	65.00	26.00	6.50
☐ 25 Michael Simon	65.00	26.00	6.50
☐ 26 James Scott	65.00	26.00	6.50
☐ 27 Bill Carrigan	65.00	26.00	6.50
☐ 28 Jack Barry	65.00	26.00	6.50
☐ 29 Vean Gregg (Cleve)	90.00	36.00	9.00
☐ 30 Ty Cobb	2500.00	1000.00	300.00
☐ 31 Heine Wagner	65.00	26.00	6.50
☐ 32 Mordecai Brown	150.00	60.00	15.00
☐ 33 Amos Strunk	65.00	26.00	6.50
☐ 34 Ira Thomas	65.00	26.00	6.50
☐ 35 Harry Hooper	150.00	60.00	15.00
☐ 36 Ed Walsh	150.00	60.00	15.00
☐ 37 Grover Alexander	300.00	120.00	30.00
☐ 38 Red Dooin (Phila. NL)	65.00	26.00	6.50
☐ 39 Chick Gandil	90.00	36.00	9.00
☐ 40 Jimmy Austin (St.L. AL)	65.00	26.00	6.50
☐ 41 Tommy Leach	65.00	26.00	6.50
☐ 42 Al Bridwell	65.00	26.00	6.50
☐ 43 Rube Marquard (NY NL)	175.00	70.00	18.00
☐ 44 Charles Tesreau	65.00	26.00	6.50
☐ 45 Fred Luderus	65.00	26.00	6.50
☐ 46 Bob Groom	65.00	26.00	6.50
☐ 47 Josh Devore (Phila. NL)	65.00	26.00	6.50
☐ 48 Harry Lord	150.00	60.00	15.00
☐ 49 John Miller	65.00	26.00	6.50
☐ 50 John Hummell	65.00	26.00	6.50
☐ 51 Nap Rucker	65.00	26.00	6.50
☐ 52 Zach Wheat	150.00	60.00	15.00
☐ 53 Otto Miller	65.00	26.00	6.50
☐ 54 Marty O'Toole	65.00	26.00	6.50
☐ 55 Dick Hoblitzel (Cinc.)	65.00	26.00	6.50
☐ 56 Clyde Milan	65.00	26.00	6.50
☐ 57 Walter Johnson	750.00	300.00	75.00
☐ 58 Wally Schang	65.00	26.00	6.50
☐ 59 Harry Gessler	65.00	26.00	6.50
☐ 60 Rollie Zeider	150.00	60.00	15.00
☐ 61 Ray Schalk	150.00	60.00	15.00
☐ 62 Jay Cashion	150.00	60.00	15.00
☐ 63 Babe Adams	65.00	26.00	6.50
☐ 64 Jimmy Archer	65.00	26.00	6.50
☐ 65 Tris Speaker	350.00	140.00	35.00
☐ 66 Napoleon Lajoie (Cleve.)	450.00	180.00	45.00
☐ 67 Otis Crandall	65.00	26.00	6.50
☐ 68 Honus Wagner	600.00	240.00	60.00
☐ 69 John McGraw	225.00	90.00	22.00
☐ 70 Fred Clarke	150.00	60.00	15.00
☐ 71 Chief Meyers	65.00	26.00	6.50
☐ 72 John Boehling	65.00	26.00	6.50
☐ 73 Max Carey	150.00	60.00	15.00
☐ 74 Frank Owens	65.00	26.00	6.50
☐ 75 Miller Huggins	150.00	60.00	15.00
☐ 76 Claude Hendrix	65.00	26.00	6.50
☐ 77 Hugh Jennings	150.00	60.00	15.00
☐ 78 Fred Merkle	90.00	36.00	9.00
☐ 79 Ping Bodie	65.00	26.00	6.50
☐ 80 Ed Ruelbach	65.00	26.00	6.50
☐ 81 J.C. Delehanty	65.00	26.00	6.50
☐ 82 Gavvy Cravath	90.00	36.00	9.00

Player	NRMT	VG-E	GOOD
□ 83 Russ Ford	65.00	26.00	6.50
□ 84 E.E. Knetzer	65.00	26.00	6.50
□ 85 Buck Herzog	65.00	26.00	6.50
□ 86 Burt Shotten	65.00	26.00	6.50
□ 87 Forrest Cady	65.00	26.00	6.50
□ 88 Christy Mathewson	750.00	300.00	75.00
(Pitching)			
□ 89 Lawrence Cheney	65.00	26.00	6.50
□ 90 Frank Smith	65.00	26.00	6.50
□ 91 Roger Peckinpaugh	65.00	26.00	6.50
□ 92 Al Demaree (N.Y. NL)	65.00	26.00	6.50
□ 93 Derrill Pratt	150.00	60.00	15.00
(Throwing)			
□ 94 Eddie Cicotte	90.00	36.00	9.00
□ 95 Ray Keating	65.00	26.00	6.50
□ 96 Beals Becker	65.00	26.00	6.50
□ 97 John (Rube) Benton	65.00	26.00	6.50
□ 98 Frank LaPorte	65.00	26.00	6.50
□ 99 Frank Chance	500.00	200.00	50.00
□ 100 Thomas Seaton	65.00	26.00	6.50
□ 101 Frank Schulte	65.00	26.00	6.50
□ 102 Ray Fisher	65.00	26.00	6.50
□ 103 Joe Jackson	1600.00	700.00	200.00
□ 104 Vic Saier	65.00	26.00	6.50
□ 105 James Lavender	65.00	26.00	6.50
□ 106 Joe Birmingham	65.00	26.00	6.50
□ 107 Tom Downey	65.00	26.00	6.50
□ 108 Sherwood Magee	65.00	26.00	6.50
(Phila. NL)			
□ 109 Fred Blanding	65.00	26.00	6.50
□ 110 Bob Bescher	65.00	26.00	6.50
□ 111 Jim Callahan	150.00	60.00	15.00
□ 112 Ed Sweeney	65.00	26.00	6.50
□ 113 George Suggs	65.00	26.00	6.50
□ 114 Geo. J. Moriarty	65.00	26.00	6.50
□ 115 Addison Brennan	65.00	26.00	6.50
□ 116 Rollie Zeider	65.00	26.00	6.50
□ 117 Ted Easterly	65.00	26.00	6.50
□ 118 Ed Konetchy (Pitts.)	65.00	26.00	6.50
□ 119 George Perring	65.00	26.00	6.50
□ 120 Mike Doolan	65.00	26.00	6.50
□ 121 Perdue (Boston NL)	65.00	26.00	6.50
□ 122 Owen Bush	65.00	26.00	6.50
□ 123 Slim Sallee	65.00	26.00	6.50
□ 124 Earl Moore	65.00	26.00	6.50
□ 125 Bert Niehoff	65.00	26.00	6.50
□ 126 Walter Blair	65.00	26.00	6.50
□ 127 Butch Schmidt	65.00	26.00	6.50
□ 128 Steve Evans	65.00	26.00	6.50
□ 129 Ray Caldwell	65.00	26.00	6.50
□ 130 Ivy Wingo	65.00	26.00	6.50
□ 131 George Baumgardner	65.00	26.00	6.50
□ 132 Les Nunamaker	65.00	26.00	6.50
□ 133 Branch Rickey	200.00	80.00	20.00
□ 134 Armando Marsans	65.00	26.00	6.50
(Cincinnati)			
□ 135 Bill Killefer	65.00	26.00	6.50
□ 136 Rabbit Maranville	150.00	60.00	15.00
□ 137 William Rariden	65.00	26.00	6.50
□ 138 Hank Gowdy	65.00	26.00	6.50
□ 139 Rebel Oakes	65.00	26.00	6.50
□ 140 Danny Murphy	65.00	26.00	6.50
□ 141 Cy Barger	65.00	26.00	6.50
□ 142 Eugene Packard	65.00	26.00	6.50
□ 143 Jake Daubert	90.00	36.00	9.00
□ 144 James C. Walsh	100.00	40.00	10.00

1915 Cracker Jack

The cards in this 176-card set measure 2 1/4" by 3". When turned over in a lateral motion, a 1915 "series of 176" Cracker Jack card shows the back printing upside-down. Cards were available in boxes of Cracker Jack or from the company for "100 Cracker Jack coupons, or one coupon and 25 cents." An album was available for "50 coupons or one coupon and 10 cents." The set essentially duplicates E145-1 (1914 Cracker Jack) except for some additional cards and new poses. Players in the Federal League are indicated by FED in the checklist below. The ACC designation is E145-2.

	NRMT	VG-E	GOOD
COMPLETE SET	16500.00	6500.00	2450.00
COMMON PLAYER (1-144)	55.00	22.00	5.50
COMMON PLAYER (145-176)	65.00	26.00	6.50

Player	NRMT	VG-E	GOOD
□ 1 Otto Knabe	75.00	30.00	7.50
□ 2 Frank Baker	135.00	54.00	13.50
□ 3 Joe Tinker	135.00	54.00	13.50
□ 4 Larry Doyle	55.00	22.00	5.50
□ 5 Ward Miller	55.00	22.00	5.50
□ 6 Eddie Plank	175.00	70.00	18.00
(St.L. FED)			
□ 7 Eddie Collins	175.00	70.00	18.00
(Chicago AL)			
□ 8 Rube Oldring	55.00	22.00	5.50
□ 9 Artie Hoffman	55.00	22.00	5.50
□ 10 John McInnis	75.00	30.00	7.50
□ 11 George Stovall	55.00	22.00	5.50
□ 12 Connie Mack	225.00	90.00	22.00
□ 13 Art Wilson	55.00	22.00	5.50
□ 14 Sam Crawford	135.00	54.00	13.50
□ 15 Reb Russell	55.00	22.00	5.50
□ 16 Howie Camnitz	55.00	22.00	5.50
□ 17 Roger Bresnahan	135.00	54.00	13.50
□ 18 Johnny Evers	135.00	54.00	13.50
□ 19 Chief Bender	150.00	60.00	15.00
(Baltimore FED)			
□ 20 Cy Falkenberg	55.00	22.00	5.50
□ 21 Heine Zimmerman	55.00	22.00	5.50
□ 22 Joe Wood	75.00	30.00	7.50
□ 23 Charles Comiskey	150.00	60.00	15.00
□ 24 George Mullen	55.00	22.00	5.50
□ 25 Michael Simon	55.00	22.00	5.50
□ 26 James Scott	55.00	22.00	5.50
□ 27 Bill Carrigan	55.00	22.00	5.50
□ 28 Jack Barry	55.00	22.00	5.50
□ 29 Vean Gregg	75.00	30.00	7.50
(Boston AL)			
□ 30 Ty Cobb	2000.00	900.00	300.00
□ 31 Heine Wagner	55.00	22.00	5.50
□ 32 Mordecai Brown	135.00	54.00	13.50
□ 33 Amos Strunk	55.00	22.00	5.50
□ 34 Ira Thomas	55.00	22.00	5.50
□ 35 Harry Hooper	135.00	54.00	13.50
□ 36 Ed Walsh	135.00	54.00	13.50
□ 37 Grover C. Alexander	250.00	100.00	25.00
□ 38 Red Dooin (Cinc.)	55.00	22.00	5.50
□ 39 Chick Gandil	75.00	30.00	7.50
□ 40 Jimmy Austin	75.00	30.00	7.50
(Pitts. FED)			
□ 41 Tommy Leach	55.00	22.00	5.50
□ 42 Al Bridwell	55.00	22.00	5.50
□ 43 Rube Marquard	150.00	60.00	15.00
(Brooklyn FED)			
□ 44 Charles Tesreau	55.00	22.00	5.50
□ 45 Fred Luderus	55.00	22.00	5.50
□ 46 Bob Groom	55.00	22.00	5.50
□ 47 Josh Devore	75.00	30.00	7.50
(Boston NL)			
□ 48 Steve O'Neill	55.00	22.00	5.50
□ 49 John Miller	55.00	22.00	5.50
□ 50 John Hummell	55.00	22.00	5.50
□ 51 Nap Rucker	55.00	22.00	5.50
□ 52 Zach Wheat	135.00	54.00	13.50
□ 53 Otto Miller	55.00	22.00	5.50
□ 54 Marty O'Toole	55.00	22.00	5.50
□ 55 Dick Hoblitzel	75.00	30.00	7.50
(Boston AL)			
□ 56 Clyde Milan	55.00	22.00	5.50
□ 57 Walter Johnson	600.00	240.00	60.00
□ 58 Wally Schang	55.00	22.00	5.50
□ 59 Harry Gessler	55.00	22.00	5.50
□ 60 Oscar Dugey	55.00	22.00	5.50
□ 61 Ray Schalk	135.00	54.00	13.50
□ 62 Willie Mitchell	55.00	22.00	5.50
□ 63 Babe Adams	55.00	22.00	5.50
□ 64 Jimmy Archer	55.00	22.00	5.50
□ 65 Tris Speaker	300.00	120.00	30.00
□ 66 Napoleon Lajoie	350.00	140.00	35.00
(Phila. AL)			

☐ 67 Otis Crandall	55.00	22.00	5.50
☐ 68 Honus Wagner	500.00	200.00	50.00
☐ 69 John McGraw	175.00	70.00	18.00
☐ 70 Fred Clarke	135.00	54.00	13.50
☐ 71 Chief Meyers	55.00	22.00	5.50
☐ 72 John Boehling	55.00	22.00	5.50
☐ 73 Max Carey	135.00	54.00	13.50
☐ 74 Frank Owens	55.00	22.00	5.50
☐ 75 Miller Huggins	135.00	54.00	13.50
☐ 76 Claude Hendrix	55.00	22.00	5.50
☐ 77 Hugh Jennings	135.00	54.00	13.50
☐ 78 Fred Merkle	75.00	30.00	7.50
☐ 79 Ping Bodie	55.00	22.00	5.50
☐ 80 Ed Ruelbach	55.00	22.00	5.50
☐ 81 J.C. Delehanty	55.00	22.00	5.50
☐ 82 Gavvy Cravath	75.00	30.00	7.50
☐ 83 Russ Ford	55.00	22.00	5.50
☐ 84 E.E. Knetzer	55.00	22.00	5.50
☐ 85 Buck Herzog	55.00	22.00	5.50
☐ 86 Burt Shotten	55.00	22.00	5.50
☐ 87 Forrest Cady	55.00	22.00	5.50
☐ 88 Christy Mathewson (Portrait)	600.00	240.00	60.00
☐ 89 Lawrence Cheney	55.00	22.00	5.50
☐ 90 Frank Smith	55.00	22.00	5.50
☐ 91 Roger Peckinpaugh	55.00	22.00	5.50
☐ 92 Al Demaree (Phila. NL)	75.00	30.00	7.50
☐ 93 Derrill Pratt (Portrait)	75.00	30.00	7.50
☐ 94 Eddie Cicotte	75.00	30.00	7.50
☐ 95 Ray Keating	55.00	22.00	5.50
☐ 96 Beals Becker	55.00	22.00	5.50
☐ 97 John (Rube) Benton	55.00	22.00	5.50
☐ 98 Frank LaPorte	55.00	22.00	5.50
☐ 99 Hal Chase	175.00	70.00	18.00
☐ 100 Thomas Seaton	55.00	22.00	5.50
☐ 101 Frank Schulte	55.00	22.00	5.50
☐ 102 Ray Fisher	55.00	22.00	5.50
☐ 103 Joe Jackson	1350.00	550.00	125.00
☐ 104 Vic Saier	55.00	22.00	5.50
☐ 105 James Lavender	55.00	22.00	5.50
☐ 106 Joe Birmingham	55.00	22.00	5.50
☐ 107 Thomas Downey	55.00	22.00	5.50
☐ 108 Sherwood Magee (Boston NL)	75.00	30.00	7.50
☐ 109 Fred Blanding	55.00	22.00	5.50
☐ 110 Bob Bescher	55.00	22.00	5.50
☐ 111 Herbie Moran	55.00	22.00	5.50
☐ 112 Ed Sweeney	55.00	22.00	5.50
☐ 113 George Suggs	55.00	22.00	5.50
☐ 114 Geo. J. Moriarty	55.00	22.00	5.50
☐ 115 Addison Brennan	55.00	22.00	5.50
☐ 116 Rollie Zeider	55.00	22.00	5.50
☐ 117 Ted Easterly	55.00	22.00	5.50
☐ 118 Ed Konetchy (Pitts. FED)	75.00	30.00	7.50
☐ 119 George Perring	55.00	22.00	5.50
☐ 120 Mike Doolan	55.00	22.00	5.50
☐ 121 Perdue (St.L. NL)	55.00	22.00	5.50
☐ 122 Owen Bush	55.00	22.00	5.50
☐ 123 Slim Sallee	55.00	22.00	5.50
☐ 124 Earl Moore	55.00	22.00	5.50
☐ 125 Bert Niehoff (Phila. NL)	55.00	22.00	5.50
☐ 126 Walter Blair	55.00	22.00	5.50
☐ 127 Butch Schmidt	55.00	22.00	5.50
☐ 128 Steve Evans	55.00	22.00	5.50
☐ 129 Ray Caldwell	55.00	22.00	5.50
☐ 130 Ivy Wingo	55.00	22.00	5.50
☐ 131 Geo. Baumgardner	55.00	22.00	5.50
☐ 132 Les Nunamaker	55.00	22.00	5.50
☐ 133 Branch Rickey	175.00	70.00	18.00
☐ 134 Armando Marsans (St.L. FED)	75.00	30.00	7.50
☐ 135 William Killefer	55.00	22.00	5.50
☐ 136 Rabbit Maranville	135.00	54.00	13.50
☐ 137 William Rariden	55.00	22.00	5.50
☐ 138 Hank Gowdy	75.00	30.00	7.50
☐ 139 Rebel Oakes	55.00	22.00	5.50
☐ 140 Danny Murphy	55.00	22.00	5.50
☐ 141 Cy Barger	55.00	22.00	5.50
☐ 142 Eugene Packard	55.00	22.00	5.50
☐ 143 Jake Daubert	75.00	30.00	7.50
☐ 144 James C. Walsh	75.00	30.00	7.50
☐ 145 Ted Cather	65.00	26.00	6.50
☐ 146 George Tyler	65.00	26.00	6.50
☐ 147 Lee Magee	65.00	26.00	6.50
☐ 148 Owen Wilson	65.00	26.00	6.50
☐ 149 Hal Janvrin	65.00	26.00	6.50
☐ 150 Doc Johnston	65.00	26.00	6.50
☐ 151 George Whitted	65.00	26.00	6.50
☐ 152 George McQuillen	65.00	26.00	6.50
☐ 153 Bill James	65.00	26.00	6.50
☐ 154 Dick Rudolph	65.00	26.00	6.50
☐ 155 Joe Connolly	65.00	26.00	6.50
☐ 156 Jean Dubuc	65.00	26.00	6.50
☐ 157 George Kaiserling	65.00	26.00	6.50
☐ 158 Fritz Maisel	65.00	26.00	6.50
☐ 159 Heine Groh	90.00	36.00	9.00
☐ 160 Benny Kauff	65.00	26.00	6.50
☐ 161 Ed Rousch	175.00	70.00	18.00
☐ 162 George Stallings	65.00	26.00	6.50
☐ 163 Bert Whaling	65.00	26.00	6.50
☐ 164 Bob Shawkey	90.00	36.00	9.00
☐ 165 Eddie Murphy	65.00	26.00	6.50
☐ 166 Joe Bush	90.00	36.00	9.00
☐ 167 Clark Griffith	175.00	70.00	18.00
☐ 168 Vin Campbell	65.00	26.00	6.50
☐ 169 Raymond Collins	65.00	26.00	6.50
☐ 170 Hans Lobert	65.00	26.00	6.50
☐ 171 Earl Hamilton	65.00	26.00	6.50
☐ 172 Erskine Mayer	65.00	26.00	6.50
☐ 173 Tilly Walker	65.00	26.00	6.50
☐ 174 Robert Veach	65.00	26.00	6.50
☐ 175 Joseph Benz	65.00	26.00	6.50
☐ 176 Jim Vaughn	100.00	40.00	10.00

1982 Cracker Jack

The cards in this 16-card set measure 2 1/2" by 3 1/2"; cards came in two sheets of 8 cards, plus an advertising card with a title in the center, which measured 7 1/2" by 10 1/2". Cracker Jack reentered the baseball card market for the first time since 1915 to promote the first "Old Timers Baseball Classic" held July 19, 1982. The color player photos have a Cracker Jack border and have either green (NL) or red (AL) frame lines and name panels. The Cracker Jack logo appears on both sides of each card, with AL players numbered 1-8 and NL players numbered 9-16. Of the 16 ballplayers pictured, five did not appear at the game. At first, the two sheets were available only through the mail but are now commonly found in hobby circles. The set was prepared for Cracker Jack by Topps. The prices below reflect individual card prices; the price for complete panels would be about 20 more than the sum of the card prices for those players on the panel.

	MINT	EXC	G-VG
COMPLETE SET (16)	6.00	2.40	.60
COMMON PLAYER (1-16)	.15	.06	.01
☐ 1 Larry Doby	.15	.06	.01
☐ 2 Bob Feller	.60	.24	.06
☐ 3 Whitey Ford	.60	.24	.06
☐ 4 Al Kaline	.60	.24	.06
☐ 5 Harmon Killebrew	.35	.14	.03
☐ 6 Mickey Mantle	2.00	.80	.20
☐ 7 Tony Oliva	.15	.06	.01
☐ 8 Brooks Robinson	.60	.24	.06
☐ 9 Hank Aaron	.90	.36	.09
☐ 10 Ernie Banks	.50	.20	.05
☐ 11 Ralph Kiner	.40	.16	.04
☐ 12 Ed Mathews	.30	.12	.03
☐ 13 Willie Mays	.90	.36	.09

□ 14 Robin Roberts	.30	.12	.03
□ 15 Duke Snider	.60	.24	.06
□ 16 Warren Spahn	.50	.20	.05

1980-83 Cramer Legends

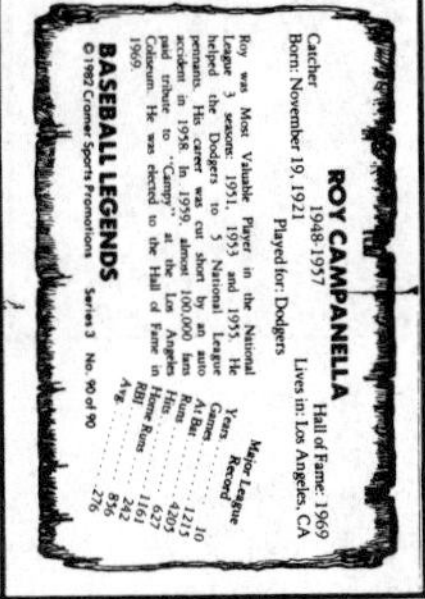

This 124-card set is actually four 30-card subsets plus a four-card wax box bottom panel. The set was distributed by series over several years beginning in 1980 with the first 30 cards. The set was produced by Pacific Trading Cards and is frequently referred to as Cramer Legends for the founder of Pacific Trading cards, Mike Cramer. Cards are standard size, 2 1/2" by 3 1/2" and are golden-toned. Even though the wax box cards are numbered from 121-124 and called "series 5", the set is considered complete without them.

	MINT	EXC	G-VG
COMPLETE SET (120)	12.50	5.00	1.25
COMMON PLAYER (1-120)	.10	.04	.01
COMMON PLAYER (121-124)	.20	.08	.02
□ 1 Babe Ruth	.75	.30	.07
□ 2 Heinie Manush	.10	.04	.01
□ 3 Rabbit Maranville	.10	.04	.01
□ 4 Earl Averill	.10	.04	.01
□ 5 Joe DiMaggio	.50	.20	.05
□ 6 Mickey Mantle	.75	.30	.07
□ 7 Hank Aaron	.25	.10	.02
□ 8 Stan Musial	.20	.08	.02
□ 9 Bill Terry	.10	.04	.01
□ 10 Sandy Koufax	.20	.08	.02
□ 11 Ernie Lombardi	.10	.04	.01
□ 12 Dizzy Dean	.20	.08	.02
□ 13 Lou Gehrig	.40	.16	.04
□ 14 Walter Alston	.10	.04	.01
□ 15 Jackie Robinson	.20	.08	.02
□ 16 Jimmie Foxx	.10	.04	.01
□ 17 Billy Southworth	.10	.04	.01
□ 18 Honus Wagner	.20	.08	.02
□ 19 Duke Snider	.20	.08	.02
□ 20 Rogers Hornsby	.20	.08	.02
□ 21 Paul Waner	.10	.04	.01
□ 22 Luke Appling	.10	.04	.01
□ 23 Billy Herman	.10	.04	.01
□ 24 Lloyd Waner	.10	.04	.01
□ 25 Fred Hutchinson	.10	.04	.01
□ 26 Eddie Collins	.10	.04	.01
□ 27 Lefty Grove	.20	.08	.02
□ 28 Chuck Connors	.20	.08	.02
□ 29 Lefty O'Doul	.10	.04	.01
□ 30 Hank Greenberg	.15	.06	.01
□ 31 Ty Cobb	.40	.16	.04
□ 32 Enos Slaughter	.10	.04	.01
□ 33 Ernie Banks	.15	.06	.01
□ 34 Christy Mathewson	.15	.06	.01
□ 35 Mel Ott	.10	.04	.01
□ 36 Pie Traynor	.10	.04	.01
□ 37 Clark Griffith	.10	.04	.01
□ 38 Mickey Cochrane	.10	.04	.01
□ 39 Joe Cronin	.10	.04	.01
□ 40 Leo Durocher	.10	.04	.01
□ 41 Home Run Baker	.10	.04	.01
□ 42 Joe Tinker	.10	.04	.01
□ 43 John McGraw	.10	.04	.01
□ 44 Bill Dickey	.10	.04	.01
□ 45 Walter Johnson	.20	.08	.02
□ 46 Frankie Frisch	.10	.04	.01
□ 47 Casey Stengel	.20	.08	.02
□ 48 Willie Mays	.30	.12	.03
□ 49 Johnny Mize	.10	.04	.01
□ 50 Roberto Clemente	.20	.08	.02
□ 51 Burleigh Grimes	.10	.04	.01
□ 52 Pee Wee Reese	.15	.06	.01
□ 53 Bob Feller	.20	.08	.02
□ 54 Brooks Robinson	.20	.08	.02
□ 55 Sam Crawford	.10	.04	.01
□ 56 Robin Roberts	.15	.06	.01
□ 57 Warren Spahn	.20	.08	.02
□ 58 Joe McCarthy	.10	.04	.01
□ 59 Jocko Conlan	.10	.04	.01
□ 60 Satchel Paige	.20	.08	.02
□ 61 Ted Williams	.25	.10	.02
□ 62 George Kelly	.10	.04	.01
□ 63 Gil Hodges	.10	.04	.01
□ 64 Jim Bottomley	.10	.04	.01
□ 65 Al Kaline	.20	.08	.02
□ 66 Harvey Kuenn	.10	.04	.01
□ 67 Yogi Berra	.20	.08	.02
□ 68 Nellie Fox	.10	.04	.01
□ 69 Harmon Killebrew	.15	.06	.01
□ 70 Ed Roush	.10	.04	.01
□ 71 Mordecai Brown	.10	.04	.01
□ 72 Gabby Hartnett	.10	.04	.01
□ 73 Early Wynn	.10	.04	.01
□ 74 Nap Lajoie	.10	.04	.01
□ 75 Charlie Grimm	.10	.04	.01
□ 76 Joe Garagiola	.20	.08	.02
□ 77 Ted Lyons	.10	.04	.01
□ 78 Mickey Vernon	.10	.04	.01
□ 79 Lou Boudreau	.10	.04	.01
□ 80 Al Dark	.10	.04	.01
□ 81 Ralph Kiner	.15	.06	.01
□ 82 Phil Rizzuto	.15	.06	.01
□ 83 Stan Hack	.10	.04	.01
□ 84 Frank Chance	.10	.04	.01
□ 85 Ray Schalk	.10	.04	.01
□ 86 Bill McKechnie	.10	.04	.01
□ 87 Travis Jackson	.10	.04	.01
□ 88 Pete Reiser	.10	.04	.01
□ 89 Carl Hubbell	.10	.04	.01
□ 90 Roy Campanella	.20	.08	.02
□ 91 Cy Young	.10	.04	.01
□ 92 Kiki Cuyler	.10	.04	.01
□ 93 Chief Bender	.10	.04	.01
□ 94 Richie Ashburn	.15	.06	.01
□ 95 Riggs Stephenson	.10	.04	.01
□ 96 Minnie Minoso	.10	.04	.01
□ 97 Hack Wilson	.10	.04	.01
□ 98 Al Lopez	.10	.04	.01
□ 99 Willie Keeler	.10	.04	.01
□ 100 Fred Lindstrom	.10	.04	.01
□ 101 Roger Maris	.20	.08	.02
□ 102 Roger Bresnahan	.10	.04	.01
□ 103 Monty Stratton	.10	.04	.01
□ 104 Goose Goslin	.10	.04	.01
□ 105 Earl Combs	.10	.04	.01
□ 106 Pepper Martin	.10	.04	.01
□ 107 Joe Jackson	.25	.10	.02
□ 108 George Sisler	.10	.04	.01
□ 109 Red Ruffing	.10	.04	.01
□ 110 Johnny Vander Meer	.10	.04	.01
□ 111 Herb Pennock	.10	.04	.01
□ 112 Chuck Klein	.10	.04	.01
□ 113 Paul Derringer	.10	.04	.01
□ 114 Addie Joss	.10	.04	.01
□ 115 Bobby Thomson	.10	.04	.01
□ 116 Chick Hafey	.10	.04	.01
□ 117 Lefty Gomez	.10	.04	.01
□ 118 George Kell	.10	.04	.01
□ 119 Al Simmons	.10	.04	.01
□ 120 Bob Lemon	.10	.04	.01
□ 121 Hoyt Wilhelm (wax box card)	.25	.10	.02
□ 122 Arky Vaughan (wax box card)	.20	.08	.02
□ 123 Frank Robinson (wax box card)	.25	.10	.02
□ 124 Grover Alexander (wax box card)	.20	.08	.02

1982 Cubs Red Lobster

The cards in this 28-card set measure 2 1/4" by 3 1/2". This set of Chicago Cubs players was co-produced by the Cubs and Chicago-area Red Lobster restaurants and was introduced as a promotional

giveaway on August 20, 1982, at Wrigley Field. The cards contain borderless color photos of 25 players, manager Lee Elia, the coaching staff, and a team picture. A facsimile autograph appears on the front, and the cards run in sequence by uniform number. While the coaches have a short biographical sketch on back, the player cards simply list the individual's professional record.

	MINT	EXC	G-VG
COMPLETE SET (28)	10.00	4.00	1.00
COMMON PLAYER	.20	.08	.02
☐ 1 Larry Bowa	.50	.20	.05
☐ 4 Lee Elia MG	.20	.08	.02
☐ 6 Keith Moreland	.40	.16	.04
☐ 7 Jody Davis	.50	.20	.05
☐ 10 Leon Durham	.30	.12	.03
☐ 15 Junior Kennedy	.20	.08	.02
☐ 17 Bump Wills	.20	.08	.02
☐ 18 Scot Thompson	.20	.08	.02
☐ 21 Jay Johnstone	.30	.12	.03
☐ 22 Bill Buckner	.50	.20	.05
☐ 23 Ryne Sandberg	4.00	1.60	.40
☐ 24 Jerry Morales	.20	.08	.02
☐ 25 Gary Woods	.20	.08	.02
☐ 28 Steve Henderson	.20	.08	.02
☐ 29 Bob Molinaro	.20	.08	.02
☐ 31 Fergie Jenkins	.80	.32	.08
☐ 33 Al Ripley	.20	.08	.02
☐ 34 Randy Martz	.20	.08	.02
☐ 36 Mike Proly	.20	.08	.02
☐ 37 Ken Kravec	.20	.08	.02
☐ 38 Willie Hernandez	.50	.20	.05
☐ 39 Bill Campbell	.20	.08	.02
☐ 41 Dick Tidrow	.20	.08	.02
☐ 46 Lee Smith	.75	.30	.07
☐ 47 Doug Bird	.20	.08	.02
☐ 48 Dickie Noles	.20	.08	.02
☐ xx Team Picture (unnumbered)	.40	.16	.04
☐ xx Coaches Card (unnumbered)	.30	.12	.03

1983 Cubs Thorn Apple Valley

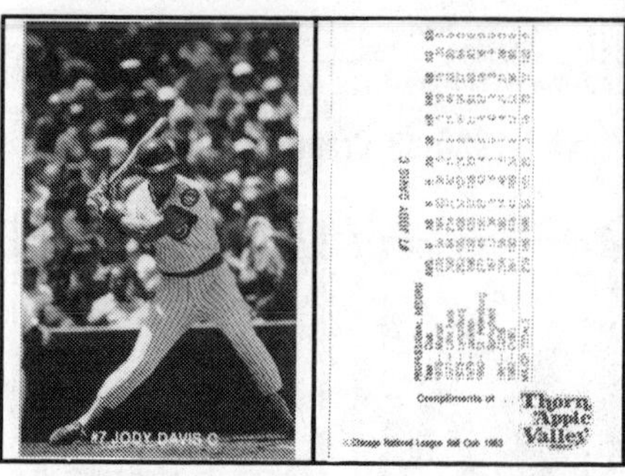

This set of 28 Chicago Cubs features full-color action photos on the front and was sponsored by Thorn Apple Valley. The cards measure 2 1/4" by 3 1/2". The backs provide year-by-year statistics. The cards are unnumbered except for uniform number; they are listed below by uniform with the special cards listed at the end.

	MINT	EXC	G-VG
COMPLETE SET (28)	9.00	3.75	.90
COMMON PLAYER	.25	.10	.02
☐ 1 Larry Bowa	.45	.18	.04
☐ 6 Keith Moreland	.35	.14	.03
☐ 7 Jody Davis	.45	.18	.04
☐ 10 Leon Durham	.35	.14	.03
☐ 11 Ron Cey	.45	.18	.04
☐ 16 Steve Lake	.25	.10	.02
☐ 20 Thad Bosley	.25	.10	.02
☐ 21 Jay Johnstone	.35	.14	.03
☐ 22 Bill Buckner	.45	.18	.04
☐ 23 Ryne Sandberg	2.50	1.00	.25
☐ 24 Jerry Morales	.25	.10	.02
☐ 25 Gary Woods	.25	.10	.02
☐ 27 Mel Hall	.45	.18	.04
☐ 29 Tom Veryzer	.25	.10	.02
☐ 30 Chuck Rainey	.25	.10	.02
☐ 31 Fergie Jenkins	.60	.24	.06
☐ 32 Craig Lefferts	.35	.14	.03
☐ 33 Joe Carter	2.00	.80	.20
☐ 34 Steve Trout	.25	.10	.02
☐ 36 Mike Proly	.25	.10	.02
☐ 39 Bill Campbell	.25	.10	.02
☐ 41 Warren Brusstar	.25	.10	.02
☐ 44 Dick Ruthven	.25	.10	.02
☐ 46 Lee Smith	.45	.18	.04
☐ 48 Dickie Noles	.25	.10	.02
☐ 26 Manager/Coaches Lee Elia MG Ruben Amaro Billy Connors Duffy Dyer Fred Koenig John Vukovich (unnumbered)	.25	.10	.02
☐ 27 Team Photo (unnumbered)	.25	.10	.02

1984 Cubs Seven-Up

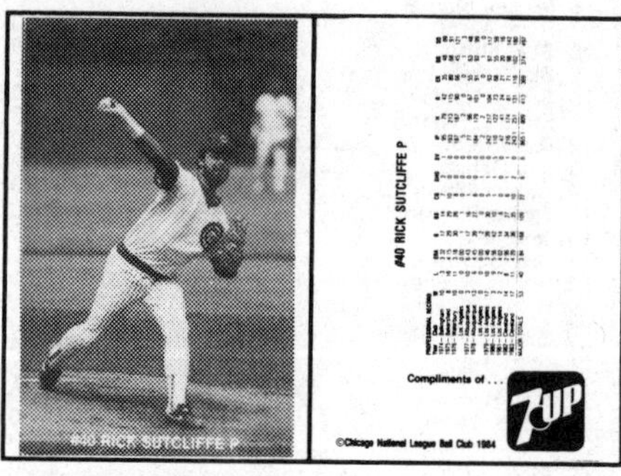

This 28-card set was sponsored by 7-Up. The cards are in full color and measure 2 1/4" by 3 1/2". The card backs are printed in black on white card stock. This set is tougher to find than the other similar Cubs sets since the Cubs were more successful (on the field) in 1984 winning their division, that is, virtually all of the cards printed were distributed during the "Baseball Card Day" promotion (August 12th) which was much better attended that year.

	MINT	EXC	G-VG
COMPLETE SET (28)	12.50	5.00	1.25
COMMON PLAYER	.40	.16	.04
☐ 1 Larry Bowa	.75	.30	.07
☐ 6 Keith Moreland	.50	.20	.05

	MINT	EXC	G-VG
☐ 7 Jody Davis	.60	.24	.06
☐ 10 Leon Durham	.50	.20	.05
☐ 11 Ron Cey	.50	.20	.05
☐ 15 Ron Hassey	.40	.16	.04
☐ 18 Richie Hebner	.40	.16	.04
☐ 19 Dave Owen	.40	.16	.04
☐ 20 Bob Dernier	.50	.20	.05
☐ 21 Jay Johnstone	.60	.24	.06
☐ 23 Ryne Sandberg	2.50	1.00	.25
☐ 24 Scott Sanderson	.50	.20	.05
☐ 25 Gary Woods	.40	.16	.04
☐ 27 Thad Bosley	.40	.16	.04
☐ 28 Henry Cotto	.40	.16	.04
☐ 34 Steve Trout	.50	.20	.05
☐ 36 Gary Matthews	.50	.20	.05
☐ 39 George Frazier	.40	.16	.04
☐ 40 Rick Sutcliffe	.90	.36	.09
☐ 41 Warren Brusstar	.40	.16	.04
☐ 42 Rich Bordi	.40	.16	.04
☐ 43 Dennis Eckersley	.90	.36	.09
☐ 44 Dick Ruthven	.40	.16	.04
☐ 46 Lee Smith	.60	.24	.06
☐ 47 Rick Reuschel	.75	.30	.07
☐ 49 Tim Stoddard	.40	.16	.04
☐ xx Coaches (unnumbered)	.40	.16	.04
☐ xx Jim Frey MG (unnumbered)	.40	.16	.04

1985 Cubs Seven-Up Cubs

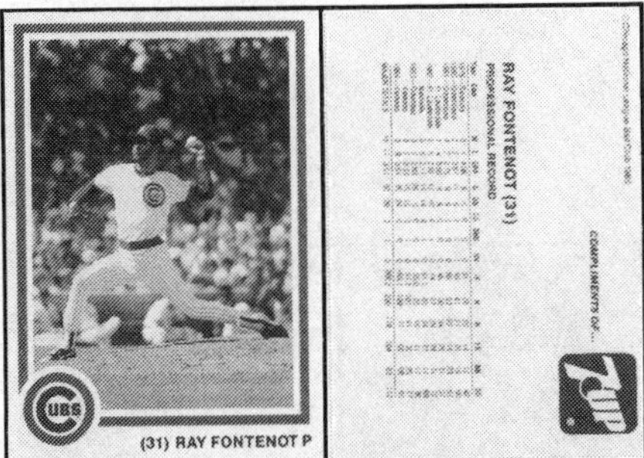

This 28-card set was distributed on August 14th at Wrigley Field for the game against the Expos. The cards measure 2 1/2" by 3 1/2" and were distributed wrapped in cellophane. The cards are unnumbered except for uniform number. The card backs are printed in black on white with a 7-Up logo in the upper right hand corner.

	MINT	EXC	G-VG
COMPLETE SET (28)	6.00	2.40	.60
COMMON PLAYER	.15	.06	.01
☐ 1 Larry Bowa	.35	.14	.03
☐ 6 Keith Moreland	.25	.10	.02
☐ 7 Jody Davis	.35	.14	.03
☐ 10 Leon Durham	.25	.10	.02
☐ 11 Ron Cey	.25	.10	.02
☐ 15 Davey Lopes	.25	.10	.02
☐ 16 Steve Lake	.15	.06	.01
☐ 18 Rich Hebner	.15	.06	.01
☐ 20 Bob Dernier	.25	.10	.02
☐ 21 Scott Sanderson	.15	.06	.01
☐ 22 Billy Hatcher	.35	.14	.03
☐ 23 Ryne Sandberg	1.75	.70	.17
☐ 24 Brian Dayett	.15	.06	.01
☐ 25 Gary Woods	.15	.06	.01
☐ 27 Thad Bosley	.15	.06	.01
☐ 28 Chris Speier	.15	.06	.01
☐ 31 Ray Fontenot	.15	.06	.01
☐ 34 Steve Trout	.25	.10	.02
☐ 36 Gary Matthews	.25	.10	.02
☐ 39 George Frazier	.15	.06	.01
☐ 40 Rick Sutcliffe	.50	.20	.05
☐ 41 Warren Brusstar	.15	.06	.01
☐ 42 Lary Sorensen	.15	.06	.01
☐ 43 Dennis Eckersley	.50	.20	.05
☐ 44 Dick Ruthven	.15	.06	.01
☐ 46 Lee Smith	.35	.14	.03
☐ xx Jim Frey MG (unnumbered)	.15	.06	.01
☐ xx Cubs Coaching Staff: Ruben Amaro, Billy Connors, Johnny Oates, John Vukovich, Don Zimmer (unnumbered)	.15	.06	.01

1986 Cubs Gatorade

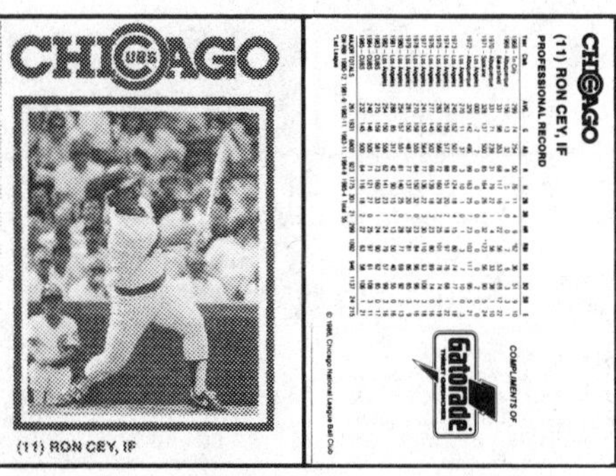

This 28-card set was given out at Wrigley Field on the Cubs' special "baseball card" promotion held July 17th for the game against the Giants. The set was sponsored by Gatorade. The cards are unnumbered except for uniform number. Card backs feature blue print on white card stock. The cards measure 2 7/8" by 4 1/4" and are in full color.

	MINT	EXC	G-VG
COMPLETE SET (28)	6.00	2.40	.60
COMMON PLAYER	.10	.04	.01
☐ 4 Gene Michael MG	.20	.08	.02
☐ 6 Keith Moreland	.25	.10	.02
☐ 7 Jody Davis	.30	.12	.03
☐ 10 Leon Durham	.25	.10	.02
☐ 11 Ron Cey	.25	.10	.02
☐ 12 Shawon Dunston	.60	.24	.06
☐ 15 Davey Lopes	.20	.08	.02
☐ 16 Terry Francona	.10	.04	.01
☐ 18 Steve Christmas	.15	.06	.01
☐ 19 Manny Trillo	.10	.04	.01
☐ 20 Bob Dernier	.10	.04	.01
☐ 21 Scott Sanderson	.10	.04	.01
☐ 22 Jerry Mumphrey	.10	.04	.01
☐ 23 Ryne Sandberg	1.50	.60	.15
☐ 27 Thad Bosley	.10	.04	.01
☐ 28 Chris Speier	.10	.04	.01
☐ 29 Steve Lake	.10	.04	.01
☐ 31 Ray Fontenot	.10	.04	.01
☐ 34 Steve Trout	.10	.04	.01
☐ 36 Gary Matthews	.20	.08	.02
☐ 39 George Frazier	.10	.04	.01
☐ 40 Rick Sutcliffe	.40	.16	.04
☐ 43 Dennis Eckersley	.45	.18	.04
☐ 46 Lee Smith	.25	.10	.02
☐ 48 Jay Baller	.10	.04	.01
☐ 49 Jamie Moyer	.20	.08	.02
☐ 50 Guy Hoffman	.10	.04	.01
☐ xx Coaches Card (unnumbered)	.10	.04	.01

1987 Cubs David Berg

This 28-card set was given out at Wrigley Field on the Cubs' special "baseball card" promotion held July 29th. The set was sponsored by David Berg Pure Beef Hot Dogs. The cards are unnumbered except for uniform number. Card backs feature red and blue

print on white card stock. The cards measure 2 7/8" by 4 1/4" and are in full color.

	MINT	EXC	G-VG
COMPLETE SET (28)	6.00	2.40	.60
COMMON PLAYER	.15	.06	.01
□ 1 Dave Martinez	.25	.10	.02
□ 4 Gene Michael MG	.20	.08	.02
□ 6 Keith Moreland	.25	.10	.02
□ 7 Jody Davis	.30	.12	.03
□ 8 Andre Dawson	1.00	.40	.10
□ 10 Leon Durham	.20	.08	.02
□ 11 Jim Sundberg	.15	.06	.01
□ 12 Shawon Dunston	.30	.12	.03
□ 19 Manny Trillo	.15	.06	.01
□ 20 Bob Dernier	.15	.06	.01
□ 21 Scott Sanderson	.15	.06	.01
□ 22 Jerry Mumphrey	.15	.06	.01
□ 23 Ryne Sandberg	1.00	.40	.10
□ 24 Brian Dayett	.15	.06	.01
□ 29 Chico Walker	.15	.06	.01
□ 31 Greg Maddux	.60	.24	.06
□ 33 Frank DiPino	.15	.06	.01
□ 34 Steve Trout	.15	.06	.01
□ 36 Gary Matthews	.25	.10	.02
□ 37 Ed Lynch	.15	.06	.01
□ 39 Ron Davis	.15	.06	.01
□ 40 Rick Sutcliffe	.35	.14	.03
□ 46 Lee Smith	.25	.10	.02
□ 47 Dickie Noles	.15	.06	.01
□ 49 Jamie Moyer	.25	.10	.02
□ xx Coaching Staff	.15	.06	.01

1988 Cubs David Berg

This 27-card set was given out at Wrigley Field with every paid admission on the Cubs' special "baseball card" promotion held August 24th. The set was sponsored by David Berg Pure Beef Hot Dogs and the Venture store chain. The cards are unnumbered except for uniform number. Card backs feature primarily black print on white card stock. The cards measure approximately 2 7/8" by 4 1/4" and are in full color.

	MINT	EXC	G-VG
COMPLETE SET (27)	6.00	2.40	.60
COMMON PLAYER	.15	.06	.01
□ 2 Vance Law	.25	.10	.02
□ 4 Don Zimmer MG	.25	.10	.02
□ 7 Jody Davis	.25	.10	.02
□ 8 Andre Dawson	.50	.20	.05
□ 9 Damon Berryhill	.50	.20	.05
□ 12 Shawon Dunston	.35	.14	.03
□ 17 Mark Grace	1.00	.40	.10
□ 18 Angel Salazar	.15	.06	.01
□ 19 Manny Trillo	.15	.06	.01
□ 21 Scott Sanderson	.15	.06	.01
□ 22 Jerry Mumphrey	.15	.06	.01
□ 23 Ryne Sandberg	.65	.26	.06
□ 24 Gary Varsho	.35	.14	.03
□ 25 Rafael Palmiero	.50	.20	.05
□ 28 Mitch Webster	.15	.06	.01
□ 30 Darrin Jackson	.25	.10	.02
□ 31 Greg Maddux	.50	.20	.05
□ 32 Calvin Schiraldi	.25	.10	.02
□ 33 Frank DiPino	.15	.06	.01
□ 37 Pat Perry	.15	.06	.01
□ 40 Rick Sutcliffe	.35	.14	.03
□ 41 Jeff Pico	.15	.06	.01
□ 45 Al Nipper	.15	.06	.01
□ 49 Jamie Moyer	.25	.10	.02
□ 50 Les Lancaster	.15	.06	.01
□ 54 Rich Gossage	.25	.10	.02
□ xx Cubs Coaching Staff Joe Altobelli CO Chuck Cottier CO Larry Cox CO Jose Martinez CO Dick Pole CO	.15	.06	.01

1954 Dan Dee

The cards in this 29-card set measure 2 1/2" by 3 5/8". Most of the cards marketed by Dan Dee in bags of potato chips in 1954 depict players from the Indians or Pirates. The Pirate players in the set are much tougher to find than the Cleveland Indians players. The pictures used for Yankee players were also employed in the Briggs and Stahl-Meyer sets. Dan Dee cards have a waxed surface, but are commonly found with product stains. Paul Smith and Walker Cooper are considered the known scarcities. The ACC designation for this set is F342.

	NRMT	VG-E	GOOD
COMPLETE SET	2800.00	1200.00	400.00
COMMON PLAYER (1-29)	40.00	16.00	4.00
COMMON PIRATE PLAYER	60.00	24.00	6.00
□ 1 Bobby Avila	40.00	16.00	4.00
□ 2 Hank Bauer	50.00	20.00	5.00
□ 3 Walker Cooper Pittsburgh Pirates	250.00	100.00	25.00
□ 4 Larry Doby	50.00	20.00	5.00
□ 5 Luke Easter	40.00	16.00	4.00
□ 6 Bob Feller	150.00	60.00	15.00
□ 7 Bob Friend Pittsburgh Pirates	75.00	30.00	7.50

☐ 8 Mike Garcia	40.00	16.00	4.00
☐ 9 Sid Gordon Pittsburgh Pirates	60.00	24.00	6.00
☐ 10 Jim Hegan	40.00	16.00	4.00
☐ 11 Gil Hodges	100.00	40.00	10.00
☐ 12 Art Houtteman	40.00	16.00	4.00
☐ 13 Monte Irvin	80.00	32.00	8.00
☐ 14 Paul LaPalme Pittsburgh Pirates	60.00	24.00	6.00
☐ 15 Bob Lemon	80.00	32.00	8.00
☐ 16 Al Lopez	80.00	32.00	8.00
☐ 17 Mickey Mantle	800.00	320.00	80.00
☐ 18 Dale Mitchell	40.00	16.00	4.00
☐ 19 Phil Rizzuto	100.00	40.00	10.00
☐ 20 Curt Roberts Pittsburgh Pirates	60.00	24.00	6.00
☐ 21 Al Rosen	50.00	20.00	5.00
☐ 22 Red Schoendienst	50.00	20.00	5.00
☐ 23 Paul Smith Pittsburgh Pirates	400.00	160.00	40.00
☐ 24 Duke Snider	150.00	60.00	15.00
☐ 25 George Strickland	40.00	16.00	4.00
☐ 26 Max Surkont Pittsburgh Pirates	60.00	24.00	6.00
☐ 27 Frank Thomas Pittsburgh Pirates	100.00	40.00	10.00
☐ 28 Wally Westlake	40.00	16.00	4.00
☐ 29 Early Wynn	80.00	32.00	8.00

1933 Delong

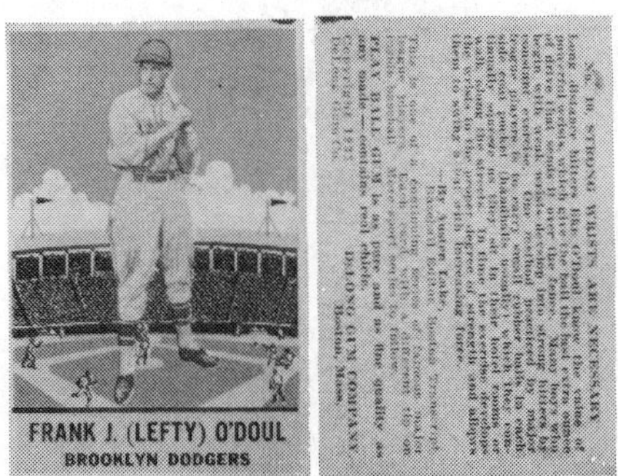

The cards in this 24-card set measures 2" by 3". The 1933 Delong Gum set of 24 multi-colored cards was, along with the 1933 Goudey Big League series, one of the first baseball card sets issued with chewing gum. It was the only card set issued by this company. The reverse text was written by Austen Lake, who also wrote the sports tips found on the Diamond Stars series which began in 1934, leading to speculation that Delong was bought out by National Chicle. The ACC designation for this set is R333.

	NRMT	VG-E	GOOD
COMPLETE SET (24)	7000.00	3000.00	900.00
COMMON PLAYER (1-24)	150.00	60.00	15.00
☐ 1 Marty McManus	150.00	60.00	15.00
☐ 2 Al Simmons	225.00	90.00	22.00
☐ 3 Oscar Melillo	150.00	60.00	15.00
☐ 4 William Terry	275.00	110.00	27.00
☐ 5 Charlie Gehringer	275.00	110.00	27.00
☐ 6 Mickey Cochrane	275.00	110.00	27.00
☐ 7 Lou Gehrig	2250.00	900.00	300.00
☐ 8 Kiki Cuyler	225.00	90.00	22.00
☐ 9 Bill Urbanski	150.00	60.00	15.00
☐ 10 Lefty O'Doul	175.00	70.00	18.00
☐ 11 Fred Lindstrom	225.00	90.00	22.00
☐ 12 Pie Traynor	250.00	100.00	25.00
☐ 13 Rabbit Maranville	225.00	90.00	22.00
☐ 14 Lefty Gomez	250.00	100.00	25.00
☐ 15 Riggs Stephenson	150.00	60.00	15.00
☐ 16 Lon Warneke	150.00	60.00	15.00
☐ 17 Pepper Martin	175.00	70.00	18.00
☐ 18 Jim Dykes	150.00	60.00	15.00
☐ 19 Chick Hafey	225.00	90.00	22.00
☐ 20 Joe Vosmik	150.00	60.00	15.00
☐ 21 Jimmie Foxx	500.00	200.00	50.00
☐ 22 Chuck Klein	250.00	100.00	25.00
☐ 23 Lefty Grove	350.00	140.00	35.00
☐ 24 Goose Goslin	225.00	90.00	22.00

1934-36 Diamond Stars

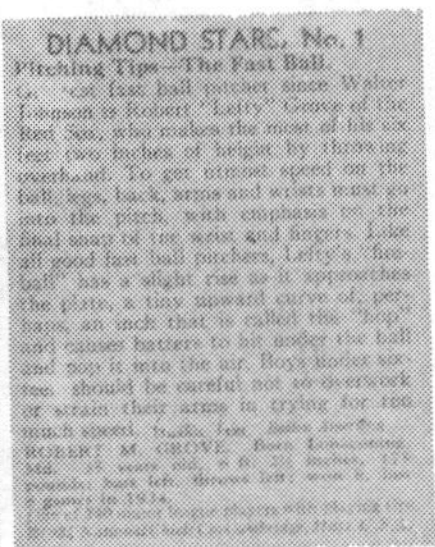

The cards in this 108-card set measure 2 3/8" by 2 7/8". The Diamond Stars set produced by National Chicle from 1934-36 is also commonly known as R327 (ACC). The year of production can be determined by the statistics contained on the back of the card. There are at least 168 possible front/back combinations counting blue (B) and green (G) backs over all three years. The last twelve cards are repeat players and are quite scarce. A blank backed proof sheet of 12 additional cards was recently discovered and has been reproduced from this original artwork and assigned numbers and text by Sport Americana. The checklist below lists the year(s) and back color(s) for the cards. Cards 32 through 72 were issued only in 1935 with green ink on back. Cards 73 through 84 were issued three ways: 35B, 35G, and 36B. Card numbers 85 through 108 were issued only in 1936 with blue ink on back. The complete set price below refers to the set of 108, one of each number.

	NRMT	VG-E	GOOD
COMPLETE SET (108)	8000.00	3300.00	1200.00
COMMON PLAYER (1-31)	30.00	12.00	3.00
COMMON PLAYER (32-72)	35.00	14.00	3.50
COMMON PLAYER (73-84)	40.00	16.00	4.00
COMMON PLAYER (85-96)	60.00	24.00	6.00
COMMON PLAYER (97-108)	200.00	80.00	20.00
☐ 1 Lefty Grove (34G, 35G)	500.00	60.00	10.00
☐ 2A Al Simmons (34G, 35G) (Sox on uniform)	75.00	30.00	7.50
☐ 2B Al Simmons (36B) (No name on uniform)	100.00	40.00	10.00
☐ 3 Rabbit Maranville (34G, 35G)	60.00	24.00	6.00
☐ 4 Buddy Myer (34G, 35G, 36B)	30.00	12.00	3.00
☐ 5 Tommy Bridges (34G, 35G, 36B)	35.00	14.00	3.50
☐ 6 Max Bishop (34G, 35G)	30.00	12.00	3.00
☐ 7 Lew Fonseca (34G, 35G)	30.00	12.00	3.00
☐ 8 Joe Vosmik (34G, 35G, 36B)	30.00	12.00	3.00
☐ 9 Mickey Cochrane (34G, 35G, 36B)	75.00	30.00	7.50
☐ 10A Leroy Mahaffey (34G, 35G) (A's on uniform)	30.00	12.00	3.00
☐ 10B Leroy Mahaffey (36B) (No name on uniform)	50.00	20.00	5.00
☐ 11 Bill Dickey (34G, 35G)	125.00	50.00	12.50
☐ 12 F. Walker 34G, 35G, 36B)	30.00	12.00	3.00

□ 13 George Blaeholder (34G, 35G)	30.00	12.00	3.00
□ 14 Bill Terry (34G, 35G)	75.00	30.00	7.50
□ 15 Dick Bartell (34G, 35G)	30.00	12.00	3.00
□ 16 Lloyd Waner (34G, 35G, 36B)	60.00	24.00	6.00
□ 17 Frank Frisch (34G, 35G)	75.00	30.00	7.50
□ 18 Chick Hafey (34G, 35G)	60.00	24.00	6.00
□ 19 Van Lingle Mungo (34G, 35G)	30.00	12.00	3.00
□ 20 Frank Hogan (34G, 35G)	30.00	12.00	3.00
□ 21 Johnny Vergez (34G, 35G)	30.00	12.00	3.00
□ 22 Jimmy Wilson (34G, 35G, 36B)	30.00	12.00	3.00
□ 23 Bill Hallahan (34G, 35G)	30.00	12.00	3.00
□ 24 Earl Adams (34G, 35G)	30.00	12.00	3.00
□ 25 Wally Berger (35G)	35.00	14.00	3.50
□ 26 Pepper Martin 35G, 36B)	35.00	14.00	3.50
□ 27 Pie Traynor (35G)	90.00	36.00	9.00
□ 28 Al Lopez (35G)	75.00	30.00	7.50
□ 29 Red Rolfe (35G)	35.00	14.00	3.50
□ 30A Heine Manush (35G) (W on sleeve)	75.00	30.00	7.50
□ 30B Heine Manush (36B) (No W on sleeve)	100.00	40.00	10.00
□ 31 Kiki Cuyler (35G, 36B)	60.00	24.00	6.00
□ 32 Sam Rice	70.00	28.00	7.00
□ 33 Schoolboy Rowe	40.00	16.00	4.00
□ 34 Stan Hack	40.00	16.00	4.00
□ 35 Earl Averill	70.00	28.00	7.00
□ 36A "Earnie" Lombardi (sic, Ernie)	100.00	40.00	10.00
□ 36B "Ernie" Lombardi	80.00	32.00	8.00
□ 37 Billy Urbanski	35.00	14.00	3.50
□ 38 Ben Chapman	40.00	16.00	4.00
□ 39 Carl Hubbell	80.00	32.00	8.00
□ 40 Blondy Ryan	35.00	14.00	3.50
□ 41 Harvey Hendrick	35.00	14.00	3.50
□ 42 Jimmy Dykes	40.00	16.00	4.00
□ 43 Ted Lyons	70.00	28.00	7.00
□ 44 Rogers Hornsby	200.00	80.00	20.00
□ 45 Jo Jo White	35.00	14.00	3.50
□ 46 Red Lucas	35.00	14.00	3.50
□ 47 Bob Bolton	35.00	14.00	3.50
□ 48 Rick Ferrell	70.00	28.00	7.00
□ 49 Buck Jordan	35.00	14.00	3.50
□ 50 Mel Ott	125.00	50.00	12.50
□ 51 Burgess Whitehead	35.00	14.00	3.50
□ 52 Tuck Stainback	35.00	14.00	3.50
□ 53 Oscar Melillo	35.00	14.00	3.50
□ 54A "Hank" Greenburg (sic, Greenberg)	150.00	60.00	15.00
□ 54B "Hank" Greenberg	125.00	50.00	12.50
□ 55 Tony Cuccinello	35.00	14.00	3.50
□ 56 Gus Suhr	35.00	14.00	3.50
□ 57 Cy Blanton	35.00	14.00	3.50
□ 58 Glenn Myatt	35.00	14.00	3.50
□ 59 Jim Bottomley	80.00	32.00	8.00
□ 60 Red Ruffing	80.00	32.00	8.00
□ 61 Bill Werber	35.00	14.00	3.50
□ 62 Fred Frankhouse	35.00	14.00	3.50
□ 63 Travis Jackson	70.00	28.00	7.00
□ 64 Jimmy Foxx	200.00	80.00	20.00
□ 65 Zeke Bonura	35.00	14.00	3.50
□ 66 Ducky Medwick	80.00	32.00	8.00
□ 67 Marvin Owen	35.00	14.00	3.50
□ 68 Sam Leslie	35.00	14.00	3.50
□ 69 Earl Grace	35.00	14.00	3.50
□ 70 Hal Trosky	40.00	16.00	4.00
□ 71 Ossie Bluege	35.00	14.00	3.50
□ 72 Tony Piet	35.00	14.00	3.50
□ 73 Fritz Ostermueller	40.00	16.00	4.00
□ 74 Tony Lazzeri	60.00	24.00	6.00
□ 75 Jack Burns	40.00	16.00	4.00
□ 76 Billy Rogell	40.00	16.00	4.00
□ 77 Charlie Gehringer	80.00	32.00	8.00
□ 78 Joe Kuhel	40.00	16.00	4.00
□ 79 Willis Hudlin	40.00	16.00	4.00
□ 80 Lou Chiozza	40.00	16.00	4.00
□ 81 Bill Delancey	40.00	16.00	4.00
□ 82A Johnny Babich (Dodgers on uniform)	50.00	20.00	5.00
□ 82B Johnny Babich (No name on uniform)	50.00	20.00	5.00
□ 83 Paul Waner	80.00	32.00	8.00
□ 84 Sam Byrd	40.00	16.00	4.00
□ 85 Moose Solters	60.00	24.00	6.00
□ 86 Frank Crosetti	90.00	36.00	9.00
□ 87 Steve O'Neill	70.00	28.00	7.00
□ 88 George Selkirk	80.00	32.00	8.00
□ 89 Joe Stripp	60.00	24.00	6.00
□ 90 Ray Hayworth	60.00	24.00	6.00
□ 91 Bucky Harris	100.00	40.00	10.00
□ 92 Ethan Allen	60.00	24.00	6.00
□ 93 General Crowder	60.00	24.00	6.00
□ 94 Wes Ferrell	80.00	32.00	8.00
□ 95 Luke Appling	125.00	50.00	12.50
□ 96 Lew Riggs	60.00	24.00	6.00
□ 97 Al Lopez	300.00	120.00	30.00
□ 98 Schoolboy Rowe	225.00	90.00	22.00
□ 99 Pie Traynor	350.00	140.00	35.00
□ 100 Earl Averill	300.00	120.00	30.00
□ 101 Dick Bartell	200.00	80.00	20.00
□ 102 Van Lingle Mungo	200.00	80.00	20.00
□ 103 Bill Dickey	450.00	180.00	45.00
□ 104 Red Rolfe	200.00	80.00	20.00
□ 105 Ernie Lombardi	300.00	120.00	30.00
□ 106 Red Lucas	200.00	80.00	20.00
□ 107 Stan Hack	200.00	80.00	20.00
□ 108 Wally Berger	225.00	90.00	22.00

1988 Domino's Tigers

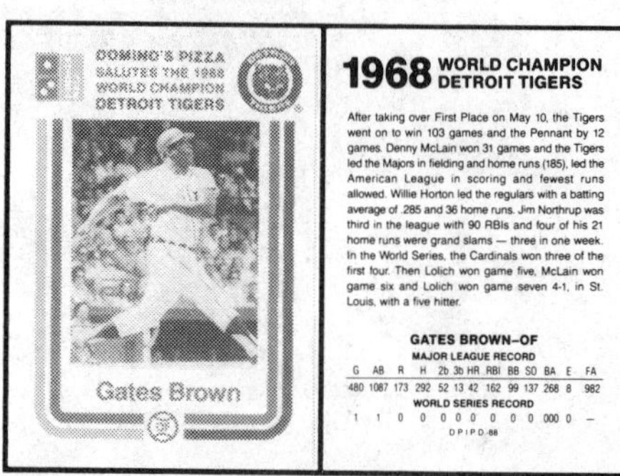

This rather unattractive set commemorates the 20th anniversary of the Detroit Tigers' World Championship season in 1968. The card stock used is rather thin. The cards measure approximately 2 1/2" by 3 1/2". There are a number of errors in the set including biographical errors, misspellings, and photo misidentifications. Players are pictured in black and white inside a red and blue horseshoe. The numerous factual errors in the set detract from the set's collectibility in the eyes of many collectors.

	MINT	EXC	G-VG
COMPLETE SET (28)	6.00	2.40	.60
COMMON PLAYER (1-28)	.10	.04	.01
□ 1 Gates Brown	.15	.06	.01
□ 2 Norm Cash	.20	.08	.02
□ 3 Wayne Comer	.10	.04	.01
□ 4 Pat Dobson	.15	.06	.01
□ 5 Bill Freehan	.20	.08	.02
□ 6 Ernie Harwell	.15	.06	.01
□ 7 John Hiller	.15	.06	.01
□ 8 Willie Horton	.15	.06	.01
□ 9 Al Kaline	.75	.30	.07
□ 10 Fred Lasher	.10	.04	.01
□ 11 Mickey Lolich	.25	.10	.02
□ 12 Tom Matchick	.10	.04	.01
□ 13 Ed Mathews	.50	.20	.05
□ 14 Dick McAuliffe	.10	.04	.01
□ 15 Denny McLain	.30	.12	.03
□ 16 Don McMahon	.15	.06	.01
□ 17 Jim Northrup	.15	.06	.01
□ 18 Ray Oyler	.10	.04	.01
□ 19 Daryl Patterson	.10	.04	.01
□ 20 Jim Price	.10	.04	.01
□ 21 Joe Sparma	.10	.04	.01

Card	MINT	EXC	G-VG
□ 22 Mickey Stanley	.15	.06	.01
□ 23 Dick Tracewski	.10	.04	.01
□ 24 Jon Warden	.10	.04	.01
□ 25 Don Wert	.10	.04	.01
□ 26 Earl Wilson	.15	.06	.01
□ 27 Pizza Buck Coupon	.10	.04	.01
□ 28 Title Card Old Timers Game 1988	.10	.04	.01

1981 Donruss

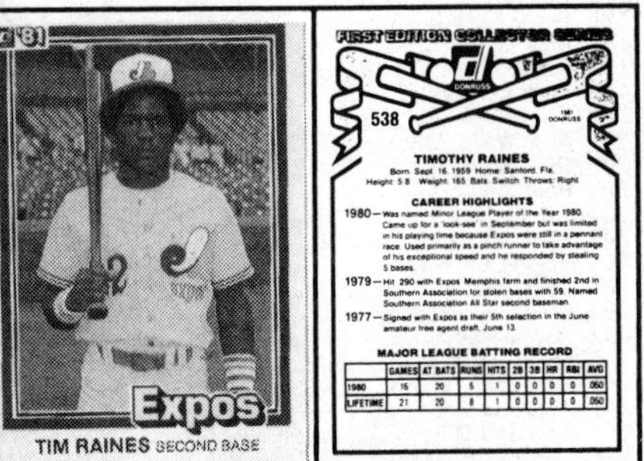

The cards in this 605-card set measure 2 1/2" by 3 1/2". In 1981 Donruss launched itself into the baseball card market with a set containing 600 numbered cards and five unnumbered checklists. Even though the five checklist cards are unnumbered they are numbered below (601-605) for convenience in reference. The cards are printed on thin stock and more than one pose exists for several popular players. The numerous errors of the first print run were later corrected by the company. These are marked P1 and P2 in the checklist below.

	MINT	EXC	G-VG
COMPLETE SET (P1)	28.00	11.50	2.80
COMPLETE SET (P2)	24.00	10.00	2.40
COMMON PLAYER (1-605)	.03	.01	.00
□ 1 Ozzie Smith	.50	.10	.02
□ 2 Rollie Fingers	.30	.12	.03
□ 3 Rick Wise	.03	.01	.00
□ 4 Gene Richards	.03	.01	.00
□ 5 Alan Trammell	.45	.18	.04
□ 6 Tom Brookens	.03	.01	.00
□ 7A Duffy Dyer P1 1980 batting average has decimal point	.10	.04	.01
□ 7B Duffy Dyer P2 1980 batting average has no decimal point	.06	.02	.00
□ 8 Mark Fidrych	.10	.04	.01
□ 9 Dave Rozema	.03	.01	.00
□ 10 Ricky Peters	.03	.01	.00
□ 11 Mike Schmidt	1.00	.40	.10
□ 12 Willie Stargell	.35	.14	.03
□ 13 Tim Foli	.03	.01	.00
□ 14 Manny Sanguillen	.06	.02	.00
□ 15 Grant Jackson	.03	.01	.00
□ 16 Eddie Solomon	.03	.01	.00
□ 17 Omar Moreno	.03	.01	.00
□ 18 Joe Morgan	.30	.12	.03
□ 19 Rafael Landestoy	.03	.01	.00
□ 20 Bruce Bochy	.03	.01	.00
□ 21 Joe Sambito	.03	.01	.00
□ 22 Manny Trillo	.03	.01	.00
□ 23A Dave Smith P1 Line box around stats is not complete	.35	.14	.03
□ 23B Dave Smith P2 Box totally encloses stats at top	.35	.14	.03
□ 24 Terry Puhl	.06	.02	.00
□ 25 Bump Wills	.03	.01	.00
□ 26A John Ellis P1 ERR Photo on front shows Danny Walton	.60	.24	.06
□ 26B John Ellis P2 COR	.10	.04	.01
□ 27 Jim Kern	.03	.01	.00
□ 28 Richie Zisk	.06	.02	.00
□ 29 John Mayberry	.06	.02	.00
□ 30 Bob Davis	.03	.01	.00
□ 31 Jackson Todd	.03	.01	.00
□ 32 Al Woods	.03	.01	.00
□ 33 Steve Carlton	.60	.24	.06
□ 34 Lee Mazzilli	.03	.01	.00
□ 35 John Stearns	.03	.01	.00
□ 36 Roy Lee Jackson	.03	.01	.00
□ 37 Mike Scott	.60	.24	.06
□ 38 Lamar Johnson	.03	.01	.00
□ 39 Kevin Bell	.03	.01	.00
□ 40 Ed Farmer	.03	.01	.00
□ 41 Ross Baumgarten	.03	.01	.00
□ 42 Leo Sutherland	.03	.01	.00
□ 43 Dan Meyer	.03	.01	.00
□ 44 Ron Reed	.03	.01	.00
□ 45 Mario Mendoza	.03	.01	.00
□ 46 Rick Honeycutt	.03	.01	.00
□ 47 Glenn Abbott	.03	.01	.00
□ 48 Leon Roberts	.03	.01	.00
□ 49 Rod Carew	.60	.24	.06
□ 50 Bert Campaneris	.06	.02	.00
□ 51A Tom Donahue P1 ERR Name on front misspelled Donahue	.15	.06	.01
□ 51B Tom Donohue P2 COR	.10	.04	.01
□ 52 Dave Frost	.03	.01	.00
□ 53 Ed Halicki	.03	.01	.00
□ 54 Dan Ford	.03	.01	.00
□ 55 Garry Maddox	.06	.02	.00
□ 56A Steve Garvey P1 "Surpassed 25 HR"	1.25	.50	.12
□ 56B Steve Garvey P2 "Surpassed 21 HR"	.60	.24	.06
□ 57 Bill Russell	.06	.02	.00
□ 58 Don Sutton	.30	.12	.03
□ 59 Reggie Smith	.10	.04	.01
□ 60 Rick Monday	.06	.02	.00
□ 61 Ray Knight	.10	.04	.01
□ 62 Johnny Bench	.65	.26	.06
□ 63 Mario Soto	.10	.04	.01
□ 64 Doug Bair	.03	.01	.00
□ 65 George Foster	.20	.08	.02
□ 66 Jeff Burroughs	.06	.02	.00
□ 67 Keith Hernandez	.35	.14	.03
□ 68 Tom Herr	.15	.06	.01
□ 69 Bob Forsch	.06	.02	.00
□ 70 John Fulgham	.03	.01	.00
□ 71A Bobby Bonds P1 ERR 986 lifetime HR	.30	.12	.03
□ 71B Bobby Bonds P2 COR 326 lifetime HR	.10	.04	.01
□ 72A Rennie Stennett P1 "breaking broke leg"	.10	.04	.01
□ 72B Rennie Stennett P2 Word "broke" deleted	.06	.02	.00
□ 73 Joe Strain	.03	.01	.00
□ 74 Ed Whitson	.06	.02	.00
□ 75 Tom Griffin	.03	.01	.00
□ 76 Billy North	.03	.01	.00
□ 77 Gene Garber	.03	.01	.00
□ 78 Mike Hargrove	.03	.01	.00
□ 79 Dave Rosello	.03	.01	.00
□ 80 Ron Hassey	.06	.02	.00
□ 81 Sid Monge	.03	.01	.00
□ 82A Joe Charboneau P1 '78 highlights, "For some reason"	.15	.06	.01
□ 82B Joe Charboneau P2 phrase "For some reason" deleted	.10	.04	.01
□ 83 Cecil Cooper	.15	.06	.01
□ 84 Sal Bando	.06	.02	.00
□ 85 Moose Haas	.06	.02	.00
□ 86 Mike Caldwell	.03	.01	.00
□ 87A Larry Hisle P1 '77 highlights, line ends with "28 RBI"	.15	.06	.01
□ 87B Larry Hisle P2 correct line "28 HR"	.10	.04	.01
□ 88 Luis Gomez	.03	.01	.00
□ 89 Larry Parrish	.06	.02	.00
□ 90 Gary Carter	.60	.24	.06
□ 91 Bill Gullickson	.25	.10	.02
□ 92 Fred Norman	.03	.01	.00
□ 93 Tommy Hutton	.03	.01	.00
□ 94 Carl Yastrzemski	1.00	.40	.10
□ 95 Glenn Hoffman	.03	.01	.00
□ 96 Dennis Eckersley	.20	.08	.02
□ 97A Tom Burgmeier P1 ERR Throws: Right	.10	.04	.01
□ 97B Tom Burgmeier P2	.06	.02	.00

COR Throws: Left
□ 98 Win Remmerswaal .... .03 .01 .00
□ 99 Bob Horner .... .20 .08 .02
□ 100 George Brett .... .80 .32 .08
□ 101 Dave Chalk .... .03 .01 .00
□ 102 Dennis Leonard .... .06 .02 .00
□ 103 Renie Martin .... .03 .01 .00
□ 104 Amos Otis .... .10 .04 .01
□ 105 Graig Nettles .... .15 .06 .01
□ 106 Eric Soderholm .... .03 .01 .00
□ 107 Tommy John .... .20 .08 .02
□ 108 Tom Underwood .... .03 .01 .00
□ 109 Lou Piniella .... .10 .04 .01
□ 110 Mickey Klutts .... .03 .01 .00
□ 111 Bobby Murcer .... .10 .04 .01
□ 112 Eddie Murray .... .80 .32 .08
□ 113 Rick Dempsey .... .06 .02 .00
□ 114 Scott McGregor .... .06 .02 .00
□ 115 Ken Singleton .... .10 .04 .01
□ 116 Gary Roenicke .... .03 .01 .00
□ 117 Dave Revering .... .03 .01 .00
□ 118 Mike Norris .... .03 .01 .00
□ 119 Rickey Henderson .... 1.75 .70 .17
□ 120 Mike Heath .... .03 .01 .00
□ 121 Dave Cash .... .03 .01 .00
□ 122 Randy Jones .... .03 .01 .00
□ 123 Eric Rasmussen .... .03 .01 .00
□ 124 Jerry Mumphrey .... .03 .01 .00
□ 125 Richie Hebner .... .03 .01 .00
□ 126 Mark Wagner .... .03 .01 .00
□ 127 Jack Morris .... .30 .12 .03
□ 128 Dan Petry .... .10 .04 .01
□ 129 Bruce Robbins .... .03 .01 .00
□ 130 Champ Summers .... .03 .01 .00
□ 131A Pete Rose P1 .... 2.00 .80 .20
last line ends with
"see card 251"
□ 131B Pete Rose P2 .... 1.25 .50 .12
last line corrected
"see card 371"
□ 132 Willie Stargell .... .35 .14 .03
□ 133 Ed Ott .... .03 .01 .00
□ 134 Jim Bibby .... .03 .01 .00
□ 135 Bert Blyleven .... .15 .06 .01
□ 136 Dave Parker .... .30 .12 .03
□ 137 Bill Robinson .... .06 .02 .00
□ 138 Enos Cabell .... .03 .01 .00
□ 139 Dave Bergman .... .03 .01 .00
□ 140 J.R. Richard .... .10 .04 .01
□ 141 Ken Forsch .... .03 .01 .00
□ 142 Larry Bowa .... .15 .06 .01
□ 143 Frank LaCorte .... .03 .01 .00
(photo actually
Randy Niemann)
□ 144 Dennis Walling .... .03 .01 .00
□ 145 Buddy Bell .... .15 .06 .01
□ 146 Ferguson Jenkins .... .18 .08 .01
□ 147 Dannny Darwin .... .03 .01 .00
□ 148 John Grubb .... .03 .01 .00
□ 149 Alfredo Griffin .... .10 .04 .01
□ 150 Jerry Garvin .... .03 .01 .00
□ 151 Paul Mirabella .... .03 .01 .00
□ 152 Rick Bosetti .... .03 .01 .00
□ 153 Dick Ruthven .... .03 .01 .00
□ 154 Frank Taveras .... .03 .01 .00
□ 155 Craig Swan .... .03 .01 .00
□ 156 Jeff Reardon .... .60 .24 .06
□ 157 Steve Henderson .... .03 .01 .00
□ 158 Jim Morrison .... .03 .01 .00
□ 159 Glenn Borgmann .... .03 .01 .00
□ 160 LaMarr Hoyt .... .25 .10 .02
□ 161 Rich Wortham .... .03 .01 .00
□ 162 Thad Bosley .... .03 .01 .00
□ 163 Julio Cruz .... .03 .01 .00
□ 164A Del Unser P1 .... .10 .04 .01
no "3B" heading
□ 164B Del Unser P2 .06 .02 .00
Batting record on back
corrected ("3B")
□ 165 Jim Anderson .... .03 .01 .00
□ 166 Jim Beattie .... .03 .01 .00
□ 167 Shane Rawley .... .10 .04 .01
□ 168 Joe Simpson .... .03 .01 .00
□ 169 Rod Carew .... .60 .24 .06
□ 170 Fred Patek .... .06 .02 .00
□ 171 Frank Tanana .... .10 .04 .01
□ 172 Alfredo Martinez .... .03 .01 .00
□ 173 Chris Knapp .... .03 .01 .00
□ 174 Joe Rudi .... .06 .02 .00
□ 175 Greg Luzinski .... .15 .06 .01
□ 176 Steve Garvey .... .65 .26 .06
□ 177 Joe Ferguson .... .03 .01 .00
□ 178 Bob Welch .... .15 .06 .01
□ 179 Dusty Baker .... .10 .04 .01
□ 180 Rudy Law .... .03 .01 .00
□ 181 Dave Concepcion .... .15 .06 .0
□ 182 Johnny Bench .... .65 .26 .06
□ 183 Mike LaCoss .... .03 .01 .0
□ 184 Ken Griffey .... .10 .04 .0
□ 185 Dave Collins .... .03 .01 .0
□ 186 Brian Asselstine .... .03 .01 .0
□ 187 Garry Templeton .... .10 .04 .0
□ 188 Mike Phillips .... .03 .01 .0
□ 189 Pete Vuckovich .... .06 .02 .0
□ 190 John Urrea .... .03 .01 .0
□ 191 Tony Scott .... .03 .01 .0
□ 192 Darrell Evans .... .15 .06 .0
□ 193 Milt May .... .03 .01 .0
□ 194 Bob Knepper .... .10 .04 .0
□ 195 Randy Moffitt .... .03 .01 .0
□ 196 Larry Herndon .... .03 .01 .0
□ 197 Rick Camp .... .03 .01 .0
□ 198 Andre Thornton .... .06 .02 .0
□ 199 Tom Veryzer .... .03 .01 .0
□ 200 Gary Alexander .... .03 .01 .0
□ 201 Rick Waits .... .03 .01 .0
□ 202 Rick Manning .... .03 .01 .00
□ 203 Paul Molitor .... .25 .10 .02
□ 204 Jim Gantner .... .03 .01 .00
□ 205 Paul Mitchell .... .03 .01 .00
□ 206 Reggie Cleveland .... .03 .01 .00
□ 207 Sixto Lezcano .... .03 .01 .00
□ 208 Bruce Benedict .... .03 .01 .00
□ 209 Rodney Scott .... .03 .01 .00
□ 210 John Tamargo .... .03 .01 .00
□ 211 Bill Lee .... .06 .02 .00
□ 212 Andre Dawson .... .40 .16 .04
□ 213 Rowland Office .... .03 .01 .00
□ 214 Carl Yastrzemski .... 1.00 .40 .10
□ 215 Jerry Remy .... .03 .01 .00
□ 216 Mike Torrez .... .06 .02 .00
□ 217 Skip Lockwood .... .03 .01 .00
□ 218 Fred Lynn .... .20 .08 .02
□ 219 Chris Chambliss .... .10 .04 .01
□ 220 Willie Aikens .... .03 .01 .00
□ 221 John Wathan .... .10 .04 .01
□ 222 Dan Quisenberry .... .15 .06 .01
□ 223 Willie Wilson .... .15 .06 .01
□ 224 Clint Hurdle .... .03 .01 .00
□ 225 Bob Watson .... .06 .02 .00
□ 226 Jim Spencer .... .03 .01 .00
□ 227 Ron Guidry .... .20 .08 .02
□ 228 Reggie Jackson .... .85 .34 .08
□ 229 Oscar Gamble .... .06 .02 .00
□ 230 Jeff Cox .... .03 .01 .00
□ 231 Luis Tiant .... .10 .04 .01
□ 232 Rich Dauer .... .03 .01 .00
□ 233 Dan Graham .... .03 .01 .00
□ 234 Mike Flanagan .... .10 .04 .01
□ 235 John Lowenstein .... .03 .01 .00
□ 236 Benny Ayala .... .03 .01 .00
□ 237 Wayne Gross .... .03 .01 .00
□ 238 Rick Langford .... .03 .01 .00
□ 239 Tony Armas .... .10 .04 .01
□ 240A Bob Lacy P1 ERR .... .30 .12 .03
Name misspelled
Bob "Lacy"
□ 240B Bob Lacey P2 COR .... .10 .04 .01
□ 241 Gene Tenace .... .06 .02 .00
□ 242 Bob Shirley .... .03 .01 .00
□ 243 Gary Lucas .... .06 .02 .00
□ 244 Jerry Turner .... .03 .01 .00
□ 245 John Wockenfuss .... .03 .01 .00
□ 246 Stan Papi .... .03 .01 .00
□ 247 Milt Wilcox .... .03 .01 .00
□ 248 Dan Schatzeder .... .03 .01 .00
□ 249 Steve Kemp .... .10 .04 .01
□ 250 Jim Lentine .... .03 .01 .00
□ 251 Pete Rose .... 1.25 .50 .12
□ 252 Bill Madlock .... .15 .06 .01
□ 253 Dale Berra .... .03 .01 .00
□ 254 Kent Tekulve .... .06 .02 .00
□ 255 Enrique Romo .... .03 .01 .00
□ 256 Mike Easler .... .06 .02 .00
□ 257 Chuck Tanner MG .... .06 .02 .00
□ 258 Art Howe .... .10 .04 .01
□ 259 Alan Ashby .... .06 .02 .00
□ 260 Nolan Ryan .... .60 .24 .06
□ 261A Vern Ruhle P1 ERR .... .60 .24 .06
Photo on front
actually Ken Forsch
□ 261B Vern Ruhle P2 COR .... .10 .04 .01
□ 262 Bob Boone .... .15 .06 .01
□ 263 Cesar Cedeno .... .10 .04 .01
□ 264 Jeff Leonard .... .15 .06 .01
□ 265 Pat Putnam .... .03 .01 .00
□ 266 Jon Matlack .... .03 .01 .00
□ 267 Dave Rajsich .... .03 .01 .00
□ 268 Bill Sample .... .03 .01 .00
□ 269 Damaso Garcia .... .10 .04 .01

□ 270 Tom Buskey .03 .01 .00
□ 271 Joey McLaughlin .03 .01 .00
□ 272 Barry Bonnell .03 .01 .00
□ 273 Tug McGraw .10 .04 .01
□ 274 Mike Jorgensen .03 .01 .00
□ 275 Pat Zachry .03 .01 .00
□ 276 Neil Allen .06 .02 .00
□ 277 Joel Youngblood .03 .01 .00
□ 278 Greg Pryor .03 .01 .00
□ 279 Britt Burns .20 .08 .02
□ 280 Rich Dotson .45 .18 .04
□ 281 Chet Lemon .06 .02 .00
□ 282 Rusty Kuntz .03 .01 .00
□ 283 Ted Cox .03 .01 .00
□ 284 Sparky Lyle .10 .04 .01
□ 285 Larry Cox .03 .01 .00
□ 286 Floyd Bannister .06 .02 .00
□ 287 Byron McLaughlin .03 .01 .00
□ 288 Rodney Craig .03 .01 .00
□ 289 Bobby Grich .10 .04 .01
□ 290 Dickie Thon .10 .04 .01
□ 291 Mark Clear .06 .02 .00
□ 292 Dave Lemanczyk .03 .01 .00
□ 293 Jason Thompson .03 .01 .00
□ 294 Rick Miller .03 .01 .00
□ 295 Lonnie Smith .06 .02 .00
□ 296 Ron Cey .10 .04 .01
□ 297 Steve Yeager .03 .01 .00
□ 298 Bobby Castillo .03 .01 .00
□ 299 Manny Mota .06 .02 .00
□ 300 Jay Johnstone .06 .02 .00
□ 301 Dan Driessen .03 .01 .00
□ 302 Joe Nolan .03 .01 .00
□ 303 Paul Householder .03 .01 .00
□ 304 Harry Spilman .03 .01 .00
□ 305 Cesar Geronimo .03 .01 .00
□ 306A Gary Mathews P1 ERR Name misspelled .30 .12 .03
□ 306B Gary Matthews P2 COR .10 .04 .01
□ 307 Ken Reitz .03 .01 .00
□ 308 Ted Simmons .15 .06 .01
□ 309 John Littlefield .03 .01 .00
□ 310 George Frazier .03 .01 .00
□ 311 Dane Iorg .03 .01 .00
□ 312 Mike Ivie .03 .01 .00
□ 313 Dennis Littlejohn .03 .01 .00
□ 314 Gary Lavelle .03 .01 .00
□ 315 Jack Clark .30 .12 .03
□ 316 Jim Wohlford .03 .01 .00
□ 317 Rick Matula .03 .01 .00
□ 318 Toby Harrah .06 .02 .00
□ 319A Dwane Kuiper P1 ERR Name misspelled .15 .06 .01
□ 319B Duane Kuiper P2 COR .10 .04 .01
□ 320 Len Barker .03 .01 .00
□ 321 Victor Cruz .03 .01 .00
□ 322 Dell Alston .03 .01 .00
□ 323 Robin Yount .40 .16 .04
□ 324 Charlie Moore .03 .01 .00
□ 325 Lary Sorensen .03 .01 .00
□ 326A Gorman Thomas P1 2nd line on back: "30 HR mark 4th" .30 .12 .03
□ 326B Gorman Thomas P2 "30 HR mark 3rd" .10 .04 .01
□ 327 Bob Rodgers MG .06 .02 .00
□ 328 Phil Niekro .30 .12 .03
□ 329 Chris Speier .03 .01 .00
□ 330A Steve Rodgers P1 ERR Name misspelled .30 .12 .03
□ 330B Steve Rogers P2 COR .10 .04 .01
□ 331 Woodie Fryman .03 .01 .00
□ 332 Warren Cromartie .03 .01 .00
□ 333 Jerry White .03 .01 .00
□ 334 Tony Perez .20 .08 .02
□ 335 Carlton Fisk .20 .08 .02
□ 336 Dick Drago .03 .01 .00
□ 337 Steve Renko .03 .01 .00
□ 338 Jim Rice .30 .12 .03
□ 339 Jerry Royster .03 .01 .00
□ 340 Frank White .10 .04 .01
□ 341 Jamie Quirk .03 .01 .00
□ 342A Paul Spittorff P1 ERR Name misspelled .15 .06 .01
□ 342B Paul Splittorff P2 COR .10 .04 .01
□ 343 Marty Pattin .03 .01 .00
□ 344 Pete LaCock .03 .01 .00
□ 345 Willie Randolph .10 .04 .01
□ 346 Rick Cerone .03 .01 .00
□ 347 Rich Gossage .15 .06 .01
□ 348 Reggie Jackson .85 .34 .08
□ 349 Ruppert Jones .03 .01 .00
□ 350 Dave McKay .03 .01 .00
□ 351 Yogi Berra CO .20 .08 .02
□ 352 Doug DeCinces .06 .02 .00
□ 353 Jim Palmer .40 .16 .04
□ 354 Tippy Martinez .03 .01 .00
□ 355 Al Bumbry .03 .01 .00
□ 356 Earl Weaver MG .10 .04 .01
□ 357A Bob Picciolo P1 ERR Name misspelled .15 .06 .01
□ 357B Rob Picciolo P2 COR .06 .02 .00
□ 358 Matt Keough .03 .01 .00
□ 359 Dwayne Murphy .03 .01 .00
□ 360 Brian Kingman .03 .01 .00
□ 361 Bill Fahey .03 .01 .00
□ 362 Steve Mura .03 .01 .00
□ 363 Dennis Kinney .03 .01 .00
□ 364 Dave Winfield .50 .20 .05
□ 365 Lou Whitaker .25 .10 .02
□ 366 Lance Parrish .35 .14 .03
□ 367 Tim Corcoran .03 .01 .00
□ 368 Pat Underwood .03 .01 .00
□ 369 Al Cowens .03 .01 .00
□ 370 Sparky Anderson MG .06 .02 .00
□ 371 Pete Rose 1.25 .50 .12
□ 372 Phil Garner .03 .01 .00
□ 373 Steve Nicosia .03 .01 .00
□ 374 John Candelaria .10 .04 .01
□ 375 Don Robinson .06 .02 .00
□ 376 Lee Lacy .03 .01 .00
□ 377 John Milner .03 .01 .00
□ 378 Craig Reynolds .03 .01 .00
□ 379A Luis Pujois P1 ERR Name misspelled .15 .06 .01
□ 379B Luis Pujols P2 COR .06 .02 .00
□ 380 Joe Niekro .10 .04 .01
□ 381 Joaquin Andujar .10 .04 .01
□ 382 Keith Moreland .35 .14 .03
□ 383 Jose Cruz .10 .04 .01
□ 384 Bill Virdon MG .06 .02 .00
□ 385 Jim Sundberg .06 .02 .00
□ 386 Doc Medich .03 .01 .00
□ 387 Al Oliver .15 .06 .01
□ 388 Jim Norris .03 .01 .00
□ 389 Bob Bailor .03 .01 .00
□ 390 Ernie Whitt .06 .02 .00
□ 391 Otto Velez .03 .01 .00
□ 392 Roy Howell .03 .01 .00
□ 393 Bob Walk .30 .12 .03
□ 394 Doug Flynn .03 .01 .00
□ 395 Pete Falcone .03 .01 .00
□ 396 Tom Hausman .03 .01 .00
□ 397 Elliott Maddox .03 .01 .00
□ 398 Mike Squires .03 .01 .00
□ 399 Marvis Foley .03 .01 .00
□ 400 Steve Trout .06 .02 .00
□ 401 Wayne Nordhagen .03 .01 .00
□ 402 Tony LaRussa MG .06 .02 .00
□ 403 Bruce Bochte .03 .01 .00
□ 404 Bake McBride .03 .01 .00
□ 405 Jerry Narron .03 .01 .00
□ 406 Rob Dressler .03 .01 .00
□ 407 Dave Heaverlo .03 .01 .00
□ 408 Tom Paciorek .03 .01 .00
□ 409 Carney Lansford .15 .06 .01
□ 410 Brian Downing .06 .02 .00
□ 411 Don Aase .03 .01 .00
□ 412 Jim Barr .03 .01 .00
□ 413 Don Baylor .15 .06 .01
□ 414 Jim Fregosi .06 .02 .00
□ 415 Dallas Green MG .10 .04 .01
□ 416 Dave Lopes .10 .04 .01
□ 417 Jerry Reuss .06 .02 .00
□ 418 Rick Sutcliffe .25 .10 .02
□ 419 Derrel Thomas .03 .01 .00
□ 420 Tommy Lasorda MG .10 .04 .01
□ 421 Charles Leibrandt .35 .14 .03
□ 422 Tom Seaver .50 .20 .05
□ 423 Ron Oester .06 .02 .00
□ 424 Junior Kennedy .03 .01 .00
□ 425 Tom Seaver .50 .20 .05
□ 426 Bobby Cox MG .03 .01 .00
□ 427 Leon Durham .35 .14 .03
□ 428 Terry Kennedy .06 .02 .00
□ 429 Silvio Martinez .03 .01 .00
□ 430 George Hendrick .06 .02 .00
□ 431 Red Schoendienst MG .06 .02 .00
□ 432 Johnnie LeMaster .03 .01 .00
□ 433 Vida Blue .10 .04 .01
□ 434 John Montefusco .06 .02 .00
□ 435 Terry Whitfield .03 .01 .00
□ 436 Dave Bristol MG .03 .01 .00
□ 437 Dale Murphy 1.25 .50 .12
□ 438 Jerry Dybzinski .03 .01 .00
□ 439 Jorge Orta .03 .01 .00
□ 440 Wayne Garland .03 .01 .00
□ 441 Miguel Dilone .03 .01 .00

☐ 442	Dave Garcia MG	.03	.01	.00
☐ 443	Don Money	.03	.01	.00
☐ 444A	Buck Martinez P1 ERR (reverse negative)	.15	.06	.01
☐ 444B	Buck Martinez P2 COR	.06	.02	.00
☐ 445	Jerry Augustine	.03	.01	.00
☐ 446	Ben Oglivie	.06	.02	.00
☐ 447	Jim Slaton	.03	.01	.00
☐ 448	Doyle Alexander	.10	.04	.01
☐ 449	Tony Bernazard	.06	.02	.00
☐ 450	Scott Sanderson	.06	.02	.00
☐ 451	Dave Palmer	.06	.02	.00
☐ 452	Stan Bahnsen	.03	.01	.00
☐ 453	Dick Williams MG	.06	.02	.00
☐ 454	Rick Burleson	.06	.02	.00
☐ 455	Gary Allenson	.03	.01	.00
☐ 456	Bob Stanley	.03	.01	.00
☐ 457A	John Tudor P1 ERR lifetime W-L "9.7"	1.25	.50	.12
☐ 457B	John Tudor P2 COR corrected "9-7"	1.00	.40	.10
☐ 458	Dwight Evans	.25	.10	.02
☐ 459	Glenn Hubbard	.03	.01	.00
☐ 460	U.L. Washington	.03	.01	.00
☐ 461	Larry Gura	.03	.01	.00
☐ 462	Rich Gale	.03	.01	.00
☐ 463	Hal McRae	.06	.02	.00
☐ 464	Jim Frey MG	.03	.01	.00
☐ 465	Bucky Dent	.10	.04	.01
☐ 466	Dennis Werth	.03	.01	.00
☐ 467	Ron Davis	.03	.01	.00
☐ 468	Reggie Jackson	.85	.34	.08
☐ 469	Bobby Brown	.03	.01	.00
☐ 470	Mike Davis	.30	.12	.03
☐ 471	Gaylord Perry	.30	.12	.03
☐ 472	Mark Belanger	.06	.02	.00
☐ 473	Jim Palmer	.40	.16	.04
☐ 474	Sammy Stewart	.03	.01	.00
☐ 475	Tim Stoddard	.03	.01	.00
☐ 476	Steve Stone	.06	.02	.00
☐ 477	Jeff Newman	.03	.01	.00
☐ 478	Steve McCatty	.03	.01	.00
☐ 479	Billy Martin MG	.15	.06	.01
☐ 480	Mitchell Page	.03	.01	.00
☐ 481	Cy Young Winner 1980 Steve Carlton	.30	.12	.03
☐ 482	Bill Buckner	.15	.06	.01
☐ 483A	Ivan DeJesus P1 ERR lifetime hits "702"	.10	.04	.01
☐ 483B	Ivan DeJesus P2 COR lifetime hits "642"	.06	.02	.00
☐ 484	Cliff Johnson	.03	.01	.00
☐ 485	Lenny Randle	.03	.01	.00
☐ 486	Larry Milbourne	.03	.01	.00
☐ 487	Roy Smalley	.03	.01	.00
☐ 488	John Castino	.03	.01	.00
☐ 489	Ron Jackson	.03	.01	.00
☐ 490A	Dave Roberts P1 Career Highlights: "Showed pop in"	.10	.04	.01
☐ 490B	Dave Roberts P2 "Declared himself"	.06	.02	.00
☐ 491	MVP: George Brett	.50	.20	.05
☐ 492	Mike Cubbage	.03	.01	.00
☐ 493	Rob Wilfong	.03	.01	.00
☐ 494	Danny Goodwin	.03	.01	.00
☐ 495	Jose Morales	.03	.01	.00
☐ 496	Mickey Rivers	.06	.02	.00
☐ 497	Mike Edwards	.03	.01	.00
☐ 498	Mike Sadek	.03	.01	.00
☐ 499	Lenn Sakata	.03	.01	.00
☐ 500	Gene Michael MG	.03	.01	.00
☐ 501	Dave Roberts	.03	.01	.00
☐ 502	Steve Dillard	.03	.01	.00
☐ 503	Jim Essian	.03	.01	.00
☐ 504	Rance Mulliniks	.03	.01	.00
☐ 505	Darrell Porter	.03	.01	.00
☐ 506	Joe Torre MG	.10	.04	.01
☐ 507	Terry Crowley	.03	.01	.00
☐ 508	Bill Travers	.03	.01	.00
☐ 509	Nelson Norman	.03	.01	.00
☐ 510	Bob McClure	.03	.01	.00
☐ 511	Steve Howe	.10	.04	.01
☐ 512	Dave Rader	.03	.01	.00
☐ 513	Mick Kelleher	.03	.01	.00
☐ 514	Kiko Garcia	.03	.01	.00
☐ 515	Larry Biittner	.03	.01	.00
☐ 516A	Willie Norwood P1 Career Highlights "Spent most of"	.10	.04	.01
☐ 516B	Willie Norwood P2 "Traded to Seattle"	.06	.02	.00
☐ 517	Bo Diaz	.06	.02	.00
☐ 518	Juan Beniquez	.03	.01	.00

☐ 519	Scot Thompson	.03	.01	.0
☐ 520	Jim Tracy	.03	.01	.0
☐ 521	Carlos Lezcano	.03	.01	.0
☐ 522	Joe Amalfitano MG	.03	.01	.0
☐ 523	Preston Hanna	.03	.01	.0
☐ 524A	Ray Burris P1 Career Highlights: "Went on ..."	.10	.04	.0
☐ 524B	Ray Burris P2 "Drafted by ..."	.06	.02	.0
☐ 525	Broderick Perkins	.03	.01	.0
☐ 526	Mickey Hatcher	.10	.04	.0
☐ 527	John Goryl MG	.03	.01	.0
☐ 528	Dick Davis	.03	.01	.0
☐ 529	Butch Wynegar	.03	.01	.0
☐ 530	Sal Butera	.03	.01	.0
☐ 531	Jerry Koosman	.10	.04	.0
☐ 532A	Geoff Zahn P1 Career Highlights: "Was 2nd in"	.10	.04	.0
☐ 532B	Geoff Zahn P2 "Signed a 3 year"	.06	.02	.0
☐ 533	Dennis Martinez	.10	.04	.0
☐ 534	Gary Thomasson	.03	.01	.0
☐ 535	Steve Macko	.03	.01	.0
☐ 536	Jim Kaat	.18	.08	.0
☐ 537	Best Hitters George Brett Rod Carew	1.25	.50	.1
☐ 538	Tim Raines	5.00	2.00	.5
☐ 539	Keith Smith	.03	.01	.0
☐ 540	Ken Macha	.03	.01	.0
☐ 541	Burt Hooton	.03	.01	.0
☐ 542	Butch Hobson	.03	.01	.0
☐ 543	Bill Stein	.03	.01	.0
☐ 544	Dave Stapleton	.03	.01	.0
☐ 545	Bob Pate	.03	.01	.0
☐ 546	Doug Corbett	.06	.02	.0
☐ 547	Darrell Jackson	.03	.01	.0
☐ 548	Pete Redfern	.03	.01	.0
☐ 549	Roger Erickson	.03	.01	.0
☐ 550	Al Hrabosky	.06	.02	.0
☐ 551	Dick Tidrow	.03	.01	.0
☐ 552	Dave Ford	.03	.01	.0
☐ 553	Dave Kingman	.15	.06	.0
☐ 554A	Mike Vail P1 Career Highlights: "After two ..."	.10	.04	.0
☐ 554B	Mike Vail P2 "Traded to ..."	.06	.02	.0
☐ 555A	Jerry Martin P1 Career Highlights: "Overcame a ..."	.10	.04	.0
☐ 555B	Jerry Martin P2 "Traded to ..."	.06	.02	.0
☐ 556A	Jesus Figueroa P1 Career Highlights: "Had an ..."	.10	.04	.0
☐ 556B	Jesus Figueroa P2 "Traded to ..."	.06	.02	.0
☐ 557	Don Stanhouse	.03	.01	.0
☐ 558	Barry Foote	.03	.01	.0
☐ 559	Tim Blackwell	.03	.01	.0
☐ 560	Bruce Sutter	.15	.06	.0
☐ 561	Rick Reuschel	.10	.04	.0
☐ 562	Lynn McGlothen	.03	.01	.0
☐ 563A	Bob Owchinko P1 Career Highlights: "Traded to ..."	.10	.04	.0
☐ 563B	Bob Owchinko P2 "Involved in a ..."	.06	.02	.0
☐ 564	John Verhoeven	.03	.01	.0
☐ 565	Ken Landreaux	.03	.01	.0
☐ 566A	Glen Adams P1 ERR Name misspelled	.15	.06	.0
☐ 566B	Glenn Adams P2 COR	.06	.02	.0
☐ 567	Hosken Powell	.03	.01	.0
☐ 568	Dick Noles	.03	.01	.0
☐ 569	Danny Ainge	.35	.14	.0
☐ 570	Bobby Mattick MG	.03	.01	.0
☐ 571	Joe Lefebvre	.03	.01	.0
☐ 572	Bobby Clark	.03	.01	.0
☐ 573	Dennis Lamp	.03	.01	.0
☐ 574	Randy Lerch	.03	.01	.0
☐ 575	Mookie Wilson	.40	.16	.0
☐ 576	Ron LeFlore	.03	.01	.0
☐ 577	Jim Dwyer	.03	.01	.0
☐ 578	Bill Castro	.03	.01	.0
☐ 579	Greg Minton	.03	.01	.0
☐ 580	Mark Littell	.03	.01	.0
☐ 581	Andy Hassler	.03	.01	.0
☐ 582	Dave Stieb	.30	.12	.0
☐ 583	Ken Oberkfell	.03	.01	.0
☐ 584	Larry Bradford	.03	.01	.0
☐ 585	Fred Stanley	.03	.01	.0

□ 586	Bill Caudill	.03	.01	.00
□ 587	Doug Capilla	.03	.01	.00
□ 588	George Riley	.03	.01	.00
□ 589	Willie Hernandez	.15	.06	.01
□ 590	MVP: Mike Schmidt	.50	.20	.05
□ 591	Cy Young Winner 1980: Steve Stone	.06	.02	.00
□ 592	Rick Sofield	.03	.01	.00
□ 593	Bombo Rivera	.03	.01	.00
□ 594	Gary Ward	.06	.02	.00
□ 595A	Dave Edwards P1 Career Highlights: "Sidelined the"	.10	.04	.01
□ 595B	Dave Edwards P2 "Traded to ..."	.06	.02	.00
□ 596	Mike Proly	.03	.01	.00
□ 597	Tommy Boggs	.03	.01	.00
□ 598	Greg Gross	.03	.01	.00
□ 599	Elias Sosa	.03	.01	.00
□ 600	Pat Kelly	.03	.01	.00
□ 601A	Checklist 1 P1 ERR unnumbered (51 Donahue)	.10	.01	.00
□ 601B	Checklist 1 P2 COR unnumbered (51 Donohue)	.75	.10	.01
□ 602	Checklist 2 unnumbered	.08	.01	.00
□ 603A	Checklist 3 P1 ERR unnumbered (306 Mathews)	.10	.01	.00
□ 603B	Checklist 3 P2 COR unnumbered (306 Matthews)	.10	.01	.00
□ 604A	Checklist 4 P1 ERR unnumbered (379 Pujois)	.10	.01	.00
□ 604B	Checklist 4 P2 COR unnumbered (379 Pujols)	.10	.01	.00
□ 605A	Checklist 5 P1 ERR unnumbered (566 Glen Adams)	.10	.01	.00
□ 605B	Checklist 5 P2 COR unnumbered (566 Glenn Adams)	.10	.01	.00

1982 Donruss

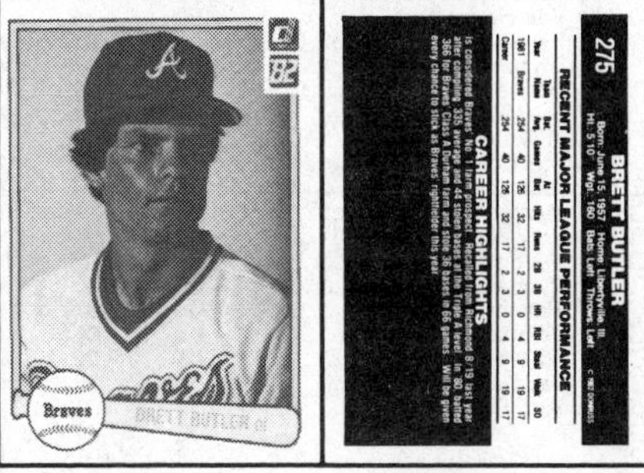

The 1982 Donruss set contains 653 numbered cards and the seven unnumbered checklists; each card measures 2 1/2" by 3 1/2". The first 26 cards of this set are entitled Donruss Diamond Kings (DK) and feature the artwork of Dick Perez of Perez-Steele Galleries. The set was marketed with puzzle pieces rather than with bubble gum. There are 63 pieces to the puzzle, which when put together make a collage of Babe Ruth entitled "Hall of Fame Diamond King." The card stock in this year's Donruss cards is considerably thicker than that of the 1981 cards. The seven unnumbered checklist cards are arbitrarily assigned numbers 654 through 660 and are listed at the end of the list below.

		MINT	EXC	G-VG
	COMPLETE SET (660)	30.00	12.00	3.00
	COMMON PLAYER (1-660)	.03	.01	.00
□ 1	Pete Rose DK	1.50	.60	.15
□ 2	Gary Carter DK	.50	.20	.05
□ 3	Steve Garvey DK	.55	.22	.05
□ 4	Vida Blue DK	.10	.04	.01
□ 5A	Alan Trammel DK ERR (name misspelled)	1.00	.40	.10
□ 5B	Alan Trammell DK COR	.40	.16	.04
□ 6	Len Barker DK	.08	.03	.01
□ 7	Dwight Evans DK	.20	.08	.02
□ 8	Rod Carew DK	.50	.20	.05
□ 9	George Hendrick DK	.08	.03	.01
□ 10	Phil Niekro DK	.30	.12	.03
□ 11	Richie Zisk DK	.08	.03	.01
□ 12	Dave Parker DK	.30	.12	.03
□ 13	Nolan Ryan DK	.55	.22	.05
□ 14	Ivan DeJesus DK	.08	.03	.01
□ 15	George Brett DK	.75	.30	.07
□ 16	Tom Seaver DK	.50	.20	.05
□ 17	Dave Kingman DK	.12	.05	.01
□ 18	Dave Winfield DK	.50	.20	.05
□ 19	Mike Norris DK	.08	.03	.01
□ 20	Carlton Fisk DK	.20	.08	.02
□ 21	Ozzie Smith DK	.25	.10	.02
□ 22	Roy Smalley DK	.08	.03	.01
□ 23	Buddy Bell DK	.10	.04	.01
□ 24	Ken Singleton DK	.10	.04	.01
□ 25	John Mayberry DK	.08	.03	.01
□ 26	Gorman Thomas DK	.10	.04	.01
□ 27	Earl Weaver MG	.06	.02	.00
□ 28	Rollie Fingers	.20	.08	.02
□ 29	Sparky Anderson MG	.06	.02	.00
□ 30	Dennis Eckersley	.20	.08	.02
□ 31	Dave Winfield	.50	.20	.05
□ 32	Burt Hooton	.03	.01	.00
□ 33	Rick Waits	.03	.01	.00
□ 34	George Brett	.65	.26	.06
□ 35	Steve McCatty	.03	.01	.00
□ 36	Steve Rogers	.03	.01	.00
□ 37	Bill Stein	.03	.01	.00
□ 38	Steve Renko	.03	.01	.00
□ 39	Mike Squires	.03	.01	.00
□ 40	George Hendrick	.06	.02	.00
□ 41	Bob Knepper	.10	.04	.01
□ 42	Steve Carlton	.50	.20	.05
□ 43	Larry Biittner	.03	.01	.00
□ 44	Chris Welsh	.03	.01	.00
□ 45	Steve Nicosia	.03	.01	.00
□ 46	Jack Clark	.25	.10	.02
□ 47	Chris Chambliss	.06	.02	.00
□ 48	Ivan DeJesus	.03	.01	.00
□ 49	Lee Mazzilli	.03	.01	.00
□ 50	Julio Cruz	.03	.01	.00
□ 51	Pete Redfern	.03	.01	.00
□ 52	Dave Stieb	.20	.08	.02
□ 53	Doug Corbett	.03	.01	.00
□ 54	Jorge Bell	6.00	2.40	.60
□ 55	Joe Simpson	.03	.01	.00
□ 56	Rusty Staub	.12	.05	.01
□ 57	Hector Cruz	.03	.01	.00
□ 58	Claudell Washington	.08	.03	.01
□ 59	Enrique Romo	.03	.01	.00
□ 60	Gary Lavelle	.03	.01	.00
□ 61	Tim Flannery	.03	.01	.00
□ 62	Joe Nolan	.03	.01	.00
□ 63	Larry Bowa	.15	.06	.01
□ 64	Sixto Lezcano	.03	.01	.00
□ 65	Joe Sambito	.03	.01	.00
□ 66	Bruce Kison	.03	.01	.00
□ 67	Wayne Nordhagen	.03	.01	.00
□ 68	Woodie Fryman	.03	.01	.00
□ 69	Billy Sample	.03	.01	.00
□ 70	Amos Otis	.08	.03	.01
□ 71	Matt Keough	.03	.01	.00
□ 72	Toby Harrah	.06	.02	.00
□ 73	Dave Righetti	1.50	.60	.15
□ 74	Carl Yastrzemski	1.00	.40	.10
□ 75	Bob Welch	.10	.04	.01
□ 76A	Alan Trammel ERR (name misspelled)	1.00	.40	.10
□ 76B	Alan Trammell CORR	.35	.14	.03
□ 77	Rick Dempsey	.03	.01	.00
□ 78	Paul Molitor	.25	.10	.02
□ 79	Dennis Martinez	.06	.02	.00
□ 80	Jim Slaton	.03	.01	.00
□ 81	Champ Summers	.03	.01	.00
□ 82	Carney Lansford	.12	.05	.01
□ 83	Barry Foote	.03	.01	.00
□ 84	Steve Garvey	.50	.20	.05
□ 85	Rick Manning	.03	.01	.00
□ 86	John Wathan	.06	.02	.00
□ 87	Brian Kingman	.03	.01	.00
□ 88	Andre Dawson	.35	.14	.03

☐ 89	Jim Kern	.03	.01	.00
☐ 90	Bobby Grich	.08	.03	.01
☐ 91	Bob Forsch	.03	.01	.00
☐ 92	Art Howe	.08	.03	.01
☐ 93	Marty Bystrom	.03	.01	.00
☐ 94	Ozzie Smith	.30	.12	.03
☐ 95	Dave Parker	.25	.10	.02
☐ 96	Doyle Alexander	.08	.03	.01
☐ 97	Al Hrabosky	.06	.02	.00
☐ 98	Frank Taveras	.03	.01	.00
☐ 99	Tim Blackwell	.03	.01	.00
☐ 100	Floyd Bannister	.06	.02	.00
☐ 101	Alfredo Griffin	.08	.03	.01
☐ 102	Dave Engle	.03	.01	.00
☐ 103	Mario Soto	.06	.02	.00
☐ 104	Ross Baumgarten	.03	.01	.00
☐ 105	Ken Singleton	.08	.03	.01
☐ 106	Ted Simmons	.15	.06	.01
☐ 107	Jack Morris	.20	.08	.02
☐ 108	Bob Watson	.06	.02	.00
☐ 109	Dwight Evans	.18	.08	.01
☐ 110	Tom Lasorda MG	.08	.03	.01
☐ 111	Bert Blyleven	.15	.06	.01
☐ 112	Dan Quisenberry	.12	.05	.01
☐ 113	Rickey Henderson	.75	.30	.07
☐ 114	Gary Carter	.45	.18	.04
☐ 115	Brian Downing	.06	.02	.00
☐ 116	Al Oliver	.10	.04	.01
☐ 117	LaMarr Hoyt	.08	.03	.01
☐ 118	Cesar Cedeno	.08	.03	.01
☐ 119	Keith Moreland	.06	.02	.00
☐ 120	Bob Shirley	.03	.01	.00
☐ 121	Terry Kennedy	.06	.02	.00
☐ 122	Frank Pastore	.03	.01	.00
☐ 123	Gene Garber	.03	.01	.00
☐ 124	Tony Pena	.30	.12	.03
☐ 125	Allen Ripley	.03	.01	.00
☐ 126	Randy Martz	.03	.01	.00
☐ 127	Richie Zisk	.06	.02	.00
☐ 128	Mike Scott	.30	.12	.03
☐ 129	Lloyd Moseby	.25	.10	.02
☐ 130	Rob Wilfong	.03	.01	.00
☐ 131	Tim Stoddard	.03	.01	.00
☐ 132	Gorman Thomas	.12	.05	.01
☐ 133	Dan Petry	.06	.02	.00
☐ 134	Bob Stanley	.03	.01	.00
☐ 135	Lou Piniella	.10	.04	.01
☐ 136	Pedro Guerrero	.40	.16	.04
☐ 137	Len Barker	.03	.01	.00
☐ 138	Rich Gale	.03	.01	.00
☐ 139	Wayne Gross	.03	.01	.00
☐ 140	Tim Wallach	.90	.36	.09
☐ 141	Gene Mauch MG	.03	.01	.00
☐ 142	Doc Medich	.03	.01	.00
☐ 143	Tony Bernazard	.03	.01	.00
☐ 144	Bill Virdon MG	.03	.01	.00
☐ 145	John Littlefield	.03	.01	.00
☐ 146	Dave Bergman	.03	.01	.00
☐ 147	Dick Davis	.03	.01	.00
☐ 148	Tom Seaver	.45	.18	.04
☐ 149	Matt Sinatro	.03	.01	.00
☐ 150	Chuck Tanner MG	.03	.01	.00
☐ 151	Leon Durham	.08	.03	.01
☐ 152	Gene Tenace	.03	.01	.00
☐ 153	Al Bumbry	.03	.01	.00
☐ 154	Mark Brouhard	.03	.01	.00
☐ 155	Rick Peters	.03	.01	.00
☐ 156	Jerry Remy	.03	.01	.00
☐ 157	Rick Reuschel	.10	.04	.01
☐ 158	Steve Howe	.03	.01	.00
☐ 159	Alan Bannister	.03	.01	.00
☐ 160	U.L. Washington	.03	.01	.00
☐ 161	Rick Langford	.03	.01	.00
☐ 162	Bill Gullickson	.06	.02	.00
☐ 163	Mark Wagner	.03	.01	.00
☐ 164	Geoff Zahn	.03	.01	.00
☐ 165	Ron LeFlore	.06	.02	.00
☐ 166	Dane Iorg	.03	.01	.00
☐ 167	Joe Niekro	.10	.04	.01
☐ 168	Pete Rose	1.25	.50	.12
☐ 169	Dave Collins	.03	.01	.00
☐ 170	Rick Wise	.03	.01	.00
☐ 171	Jim Bibby	.03	.01	.00
☐ 172	Larry Herndon	.03	.01	.00
☐ 173	Bob Horner	.18	.08	.01
☐ 174	Steve Dillard	.03	.01	.00
☐ 175	Mookie Wilson	.10	.04	.01
☐ 176	Dan Meyer	.03	.01	.00
☐ 177	Fernando Arroyo	.03	.01	.00
☐ 178	Jackson Todd	.03	.01	.00
☐ 179	Darrell Jackson	.03	.01	.00
☐ 180	Al Woods	.03	.01	.00
☐ 181	Jim Anderson	.03	.01	.00
☐ 182	Dave Kingman	.15	.06	.01
☐ 183	Steve Henderson	.03	.01	.00
☐ 184	Brian Asselstine	.03	.01	.0
☐ 185	Rod Scurry	.03	.01	.0
☐ 186	Fred Breining	.03	.01	.0
☐ 187	Danny Boone	.03	.01	.0
☐ 188	Junior Kennedy	.03	.01	.0
☐ 189	Sparky Lyle	.10	.04	.0
☐ 190	Whitey Herzog MG	.06	.02	.0
☐ 191	Dave Smith	.08	.03	.0
☐ 192	Ed Ott	.03	.01	.0
☐ 193	Greg Luzinski	.12	.05	.0
☐ 194	Bill Lee	.06	.02	.0
☐ 195	Don Zimmer MG	.03	.01	.0
☐ 196	Hal McRae	.06	.02	.0
☐ 197	Mike Norris	.03	.01	.0
☐ 198	Duane Kuiper	.03	.01	.0
☐ 199	Rick Cerone	.03	.01	.0
☐ 200	Jim Rice	.30	.12	.0
☐ 201	Steve Yeager	.03	.01	.0
☐ 202	Tom Brookens	.03	.01	.0
☐ 203	Jose Morales	.03	.01	.0
☐ 204	Roy Howell	.03	.01	.0
☐ 205	Tippy Martinez	.03	.01	.0
☐ 206	Moose Haas	.03	.01	.0
☐ 207	Al Cowens	.03	.01	.0
☐ 208	Dave Stapleton	.03	.01	.0
☐ 209	Bucky Dent	.08	.03	.0
☐ 210	Ron Cey	.10	.04	.0
☐ 211	Jorge Orta	.03	.01	.0
☐ 212	Jamie Quirk	.03	.01	.0
☐ 213	Jeff Jones	.03	.01	.0
☐ 214	Tim Raines	.90	.36	.0
☐ 215	Jon Matlack	.03	.01	.0
☐ 216	Rod Carew	.50	.20	.0
☐ 217	Jim Kaat	.15	.06	.01
☐ 218	Joe Pittman	.03	.01	.0
☐ 219	Larry Christenson	.03	.01	.0
☐ 220	Juan Bonilla	.03	.01	.0
☐ 221	Mike Easler	.03	.01	.0
☐ 222	Vida Blue	.08	.03	.01
☐ 223	Rick Camp	.03	.01	.0
☐ 224	Mike Jorgensen	.03	.01	.0
☐ 225	Jody Davis	.35	.14	.03
☐ 226	Mike Parrott	.03	.01	.00
☐ 227	Jim Clancy	.06	.02	.00
☐ 228	Hosken Powell	.03	.01	.00
☐ 229	Tom Hume	.03	.01	.00
☐ 230	Britt Burns	.06	.02	.00
☐ 231	Jim Palmer	.35	.14	.03
☐ 232	Bob Rodgers MG	.03	.01	.00
☐ 233	Milt Wilcox	.03	.01	.00
☐ 234	Dave Revering	.03	.01	.00
☐ 235	Mike Torrez	.03	.01	.00
☐ 236	Robert Castillo	.03	.01	.00
☐ 237	Von Hayes	.90	.36	.09
☐ 238	Renie Martin	.03	.01	.00
☐ 239	Dwayne Murphy	.03	.01	.00
☐ 240	Rodney Scott	.03	.01	.00
☐ 241	Fred Patek	.03	.01	.00
☐ 242	Mickey Rivers	.06	.02	.00
☐ 243	Steve Trout	.03	.01	.00
☐ 244	Jose Cruz	.10	.04	.01
☐ 245	Manny Trillo	.03	.01	.00
☐ 246	Lary Sorensen	.03	.01	.00
☐ 247	Dave Edwards	.03	.01	.00
☐ 248	Dan Driessen	.03	.01	.00
☐ 249	Tommy Boggs	.03	.01	.00
☐ 250	Dale Berra	.03	.01	.00
☐ 251	Ed Whitson	.06	.02	.00
☐ 252	Lee Smith	.55	.22	.05
☐ 253	Tom Paciorek	.03	.01	.00
☐ 254	Pat Zachry	.03	.01	.00
☐ 255	Luis Leal	.03	.01	.00
☐ 256	John Castino	.03	.01	.00
☐ 257	Rich Dauer	.03	.01	.00
☐ 258	Cecil Cooper	.15	.06	.01
☐ 259	Dave Rozema	.03	.01	.00
☐ 260	John Tudor	.20	.08	.02
☐ 261	Jerry Mumphrey	.03	.01	.00
☐ 262	Jay Johnstone	.06	.02	.00
☐ 263	Bo Diaz	.06	.02	.00
☐ 264	Dennis Leonard	.06	.02	.00
☐ 265	Jim Spencer	.03	.01	.00
☐ 266	John Milner	.03	.01	.00
☐ 267	Don Aase	.03	.01	.00
☐ 268	Jim Sundberg	.06	.02	.00
☐ 269	Lamar Johnson	.03	.01	.00
☐ 270	Frank LaCorte	.03	.01	.00
☐ 271	Barry Evans	.03	.01	.00
☐ 272	Enos Cabell	.03	.01	.00
☐ 273	Del Unser	.03	.01	.00
☐ 274	George Foster	.12	.05	.01
☐ 275	Brett Butler	.60	.24	.06
☐ 276	Lee Lacy	.03	.01	.00
☐ 277	Ken Reitz	.03	.01	.00
☐ 278	Keith Hernandez	.35	.14	.03

□ 279 Doug DeCinces	.08	.03	.01
□ 280 Charlie Moore	.03	.01	.00
□ 281 Lance Parrish	.25	.10	.02
□ 282 Ralph Houk MG	.03	.01	.00
□ 283 Rich Gossage	.18	.08	.01
□ 284 Jerry Reuss	.06	.02	.00
□ 285 Mike Stanton	.03	.01	.00
□ 286 Frank White	.08	.03	.01
□ 287 Bob Owchinko	.03	.01	.00
□ 288 Scott Sanderson	.03	.01	.00
□ 289 Bump Wills	.03	.01	.00
□ 290 Dave Frost	.03	.01	.00
□ 291 Chet Lemon	.06	.02	.00
□ 292 Tito Landrum	.03	.01	.00
□ 293 Vern Ruhle	.03	.01	.00
□ 294 Mike Schmidt	.75	.30	.07
□ 295 Sam Mejias	.03	.01	.00
□ 296 Gary Lucas	.03	.01	.00
□ 297 John Candelaria	.08	.03	.01
□ 298 Jerry Martin	.03	.01	.00
□ 299 Dale Murphy	.90	.36	.09
□ 300 Mike Lum	.03	.01	.00
□ 301 Tom Hausman	.03	.01	.00
□ 302 Glenn Abbott	.03	.01	.00
□ 303 Roger Erickson	.03	.01	.00
□ 304 Otto Velez	.03	.01	.00
□ 305 Danny Goodwin	.03	.01	.00
□ 306 John Mayberry	.06	.02	.00
□ 307 Lenny Randle	.03	.01	.00
□ 308 Bob Bailor	.03	.01	.00
□ 309 Jerry Morales	.03	.01	.00
□ 310 Rufino Linares	.03	.01	.00
□ 311 Kent Tekulve	.06	.02	.00
□ 312 Joe Morgan	.30	.12	.03
□ 313 John Urrea	.03	.01	.00
□ 314 Paul Householder	.03	.01	.00
□ 315 Garry Maddox	.06	.02	.00
□ 316 Mike Ramsey	.03	.01	.00
□ 317 Alan Ashby	.03	.01	.00
□ 318 Bob Clark	.03	.01	.00
□ 319 Tony LaRussa MG	.06	.02	.00
□ 320 Charlie Lea	.03	.01	.00
□ 321 Danny Darwin	.03	.01	.00
□ 322 Cesar Geronimo	.03	.01	.00
□ 323 Tom Underwood	.03	.01	.00
□ 324 Andre Thornton	.06	.02	.00
□ 325 Rudy May	.03	.01	.00
□ 326 Frank Tanana	.08	.03	.01
□ 327 Davey Lopes	.08	.03	.01
□ 328 Richie Hebner	.03	.01	.00
□ 329 Mike Flanagan	.08	.03	.01
□ 330 Mike Caldwell	.03	.01	.00
□ 331 Scott McGregor	.06	.02	.00
□ 332 Jerry Augustine	.03	.01	.00
□ 333 Stan Papi	.03	.01	.00
□ 334 Rick Miller	.03	.01	.00
□ 335 Graig Nettles	.12	.05	.01
□ 336 Dusty Baker	.06	.02	.00
□ 337 Dave Garcia MG	.03	.01	.00
□ 338 Larry Gura	.03	.01	.00
□ 339 Cliff Johnson	.03	.01	.00
□ 340 Warren Cromartie	.03	.01	.00
□ 341 Steve Comer	.03	.01	.00
□ 342 Rick Burleson	.06	.02	.00
□ 343 John Martin	.03	.01	.00
□ 344 Craig Reynolds	.03	.01	.00
□ 345 Mike Proly	.03	.01	.00
□ 346 Ruppert Jones	.03	.01	.00
□ 347 Omar Moreno	.03	.01	.00
□ 348 Greg Minton	.03	.01	.00
□ 349 Rick Mahler	.25	.10	.02
□ 350 Alex Trevino	.03	.01	.00
□ 351 Mike Krukow	.06	.02	.00
□ 352A Shane Rawley ERR (photo actually Jim Anderson)	.75	.30	.07
□ 352B Shane Rawley COR	.10	.04	.01
□ 353 Garth Iorg	.03	.01	.00
□ 354 Pete Mackanin	.03	.01	.00
□ 355 Paul Moskau	.03	.01	.00
□ 356 Richard Dotson	.08	.03	.01
□ 357 Steve Stone	.06	.02	.00
□ 358 Larry Hisle	.03	.01	.00
□ 359 Aurelio Lopez	.03	.01	.00
□ 360 Oscar Gamble	.03	.01	.00
□ 361 Tom Burgmeier	.03	.01	.00
□ 362 Terry Forster	.06	.02	.00
□ 363 Joe Charboneau	.06	.02	.00
□ 364 Ken Brett	.03	.01	.00
□ 365 Tony Armas	.08	.03	.01
□ 366 Chris Speier	.03	.01	.00
□ 367 Fred Lynn	.18	.08	.01
□ 368 Buddy Bell	.12	.05	.01
□ 369 Jim Essian	.03	.01	.00
□ 370 Terry Puhl	.03	.01	.00

□ 371 Greg Gross	.03	.01	.00
□ 372 Bruce Sutter	.15	.06	.01
□ 373 Joe Lefebvre	.03	.01	.00
□ 374 Ray Knight	.08	.03	.01
□ 375 Bruce Benedict	.03	.01	.00
□ 376 Tim Foli	.03	.01	.00
□ 377 Al Holland	.03	.01	.00
□ 378 Ken Kravec	.03	.01	.00
□ 379 Jeff Burroughs	.03	.01	.00
□ 380 Pete Falcone	.03	.01	.00
□ 381 Ernie Whitt	.06	.02	.00
□ 382 Brad Havens	.03	.01	.00
□ 383 Terry Crowley	.03	.01	.00
□ 384 Don Money	.03	.01	.00
□ 385 Dan Schatzeder	.03	.01	.00
□ 386 Gary Allenson	.03	.01	.00
□ 387 Yogi Berra MG	.15	.06	.01
□ 388 Ken Landreaux	.03	.01	.00
□ 389 Mike Hargrove	.03	.01	.00
□ 390 Darryl Motley	.06	.02	.00
□ 391 Dave McKay	.03	.01	.00
□ 392 Stan Bahnsen	.03	.01	.00
□ 393 Ken Forsch	.03	.01	.00
□ 394 Mario Mendoza	.03	.01	.00
□ 395 Jim Morrison	.03	.01	.00
□ 396 Mike Ivie	.03	.01	.00
□ 397 Broderick Perkins	.03	.01	.00
□ 398 Darrell Evans	.12	.05	.01
□ 399 Ron Reed	.03	.01	.00
□ 400 Johnny Bench	.55	.22	.05
□ 401 Steve Bedrosian	.90	.36	.09
□ 402 Bill Robinson	.03	.01	.00
□ 403 Bill Buckner	.12	.05	.01
□ 404 Ken Oberkfell	.03	.01	.00
□ 405 Cal Ripken Jr.	7.50	3.00	.75
□ 406 Jim Gantner	.03	.01	.00
□ 407 Kirk Gibson	1.50	.60	.15
□ 408 Tony Perez	.15	.06	.01
□ 409 Tommy John	.18	.08	.01
□ 410 Dave Stewart	1.00	.40	.10
□ 411 Dan Spillner	.03	.01	.00
□ 412 Willie Aikens	.03	.01	.00
□ 413 Mike Heath	.03	.01	.00
□ 414 Ray Burris	.03	.01	.00
□ 415 Leon Roberts	.03	.01	.00
□ 416 Mike Witt	.85	.34	.08
□ 417 Bob Molinaro	.03	.01	.00
□ 418 Steve Braun	.03	.01	.00
□ 419 Nolan Ryan	.50	.20	.05
□ 420 Tug McGraw	.10	.04	.01
□ 421 Dave Concepcion	.12	.05	.01
□ 422A Juan Eichelberger ERR (photo actually Gary Lucas)	.65	.26	.06
□ 422B Juan Eichelberger COR	.08	.03	.01
□ 423 Rick Rhoden	.10	.04	.01
□ 424 Frank Robinson MG	.12	.05	.01
□ 425 Eddie Miller	.03	.01	.00
□ 426 Bill Caudill	.03	.01	.00
□ 427 Doug Flynn	.03	.01	.00
□ 428 Larry Andersen UER (misspelled Anderson on card front)	.03	.01	.00
□ 429 Al Williams	.03	.01	.00
□ 430 Jerry Garvin	.03	.01	.00
□ 431 Glenn Adams	.03	.01	.00
□ 432 Barry Bonnell	.03	.01	.00
□ 433 Jerry Narron	.03	.01	.00
□ 434 John Stearns	.03	.01	.00
□ 435 Mike Tyson	.03	.01	.00
□ 436 Glenn Hubbard	.03	.01	.00
□ 437 Eddie Solomon	.03	.01	.00
□ 438 Jeff Leonard	.08	.03	.01
□ 439 Randy Bass	.03	.01	.00
□ 440 Mike LaCoss	.03	.01	.00
□ 441 Gary Matthews	.06	.02	.00
□ 442 Mark Littell	.03	.01	.00
□ 443 Don Sutton	.25	.10	.02
□ 444 John Harris	.03	.01	.00
□ 445 Vada Pinson CO	.06	.02	.00
□ 446 Elias Sosa	.03	.01	.00
□ 447 Charlie Hough	.08	.03	.01
□ 448 Willie Wilson	.12	.05	.01
□ 449 Fred Stanley	.03	.01	.00
□ 450 Tom Veryzer	.03	.01	.00
□ 451 Ron Davis	.03	.01	.00
□ 452 Mark Clear	.03	.01	.00
□ 453 Bill Russell	.06	.02	.00
□ 454 Lou Whitaker	.15	.06	.01
□ 455 Dan Graham	.03	.01	.00
□ 456 Reggie Cleveland	.03	.01	.00
□ 457 Sammy Stewart	.03	.01	.00
□ 458 Pete Vuckovich	.08	.03	.01
□ 459 John Wockenfuss	.03	.01	.00

□ 460	Glenn Hoffman	.03	.01	.00
□ 461	Willie Randolph	.10	.04	.01
□ 462	Fernando Valenzuela	.70	.28	.07
□ 463	Ron Hassey	.03	.01	.00
□ 464	Paul Splittorff	.03	.01	.00
□ 465	Rob Picciolo	.03	.01	.00
□ 466	Larry Parrish	.06	.02	.00
□ 467	Johnny Grubb	.03	.01	.00
□ 468	Dan Ford	.03	.01	.00
□ 469	Silvio Martinez	.03	.01	.00
□ 470	Kiko Garcia	.03	.01	.00
□ 471	Bob Boone	.12	.05	.01
□ 472	Luis Salazar	.10	.04	.01
□ 473	Randy Niemann	.03	.01	.00
□ 474	Tom Griffin	.03	.01	.00
□ 475	Phil Niekro	.30	.12	.03
□ 476	Hubie Brooks	.30	.12	.03
□ 477	Dick Tidrow	.03	.01	.00
□ 478	Jim Beattie	.03	.01	.00
□ 479	Damaso Garcia	.06	.02	.00
□ 480	Mickey Hatcher	.08	.03	.01
□ 481	Joe Price	.03	.01	.00
□ 482	Ed Farmer	.03	.01	.00
□ 483	Eddie Murray	.65	.26	.06
□ 484	Ben Oglivie	.06	.02	.00
□ 485	Kevin Saucier	.03	.01	.00
□ 486	Bobby Murcer	.10	.04	.01
□ 487	Bill Campbell	.03	.01	.00
□ 488	Reggie Smith	.10	.04	.01
□ 489	Wayne Garland	.03	.01	.00
□ 490	Jim Wright	.03	.01	.00
□ 491	Billy Martin MG	.15	.06	.01
□ 492	Jim Fanning MG	.03	.01	.00
□ 493	Don Baylor	.15	.06	.01
□ 494	Rick Honeycutt	.03	.01	.00
□ 495	Carlton Fisk	.18	.08	.01
□ 496	Denny Walling	.03	.01	.00
□ 497	Bake McBride	.03	.01	.00
□ 498	Darrell Porter	.03	.01	.00
□ 499	Gene Richards	.03	.01	.00
□ 500	Ron Oester	.03	.01	.00
□ 501	Ken Dayley	.20	.08	.02
□ 502	Jason Thompson	.03	.01	.00
□ 503	Milt May	.03	.01	.00
□ 504	Doug Bird	.03	.01	.00
□ 505	Bruce Bochte	.03	.01	.00
□ 506	Neil Allen	.06	.02	.00
□ 507	Joey McLaughlin	.03	.01	.00
□ 508	Butch Wynegar	.03	.01	.00
□ 509	Gary Roenicke	.03	.01	.00
□ 510	Robin Yount	.50	.20	.05
□ 511	Dave Tobik	.03	.01	.00
□ 512	Rich Gedman	.40	.16	.04
□ 513	Gene Nelson	.08	.03	.01
□ 514	Rick Monday	.06	.02	.00
□ 515	Miguel Dilone	.03	.01	.00
□ 516	Clint Hurdle	.03	.01	.00
□ 517	Jeff Newman	.03	.01	.00
□ 518	Grant Jackson	.03	.01	.00
□ 519	Andy Hassler	.03	.01	.00
□ 520	Pat Putnam	.03	.01	.00
□ 521	Greg Pryor	.03	.01	.00
□ 522	Tony Scott	.03	.01	.00
□ 523	Steve Mura	.03	.01	.00
□ 524	Johnnie LeMaster	.03	.01	.00
□ 525	Dick Ruthven	.03	.01	.00
□ 526	John McNamara MG	.03	.01	.00
□ 527	Larry McWilliams	.03	.01	.00
□ 528	Johnny Ray	.75	.30	.07
□ 529	Pat Tabler	.65	.26	.06
□ 530	Tom Herr	.10	.04	.01
□ 531A	San Diego Chicken	.90	.36	.09
	(with TM)			
□ 531B	San Diego Chicken	.70	.28	.07
	(without TM)			
□ 532	Sal Butera	.03	.01	.00
□ 533	Mike Griffin	.03	.01	.00
□ 534	Kelvin Moore	.03	.01	.00
□ 535	Reggie Jackson	.55	.22	.05
□ 536	Ed Romero	.03	.01	.00
□ 537	Derrel Thomas	.03	.01	.00
□ 538	Mike O'Berry	.03	.01	.00
□ 539	Jack O'Connor	.03	.01	.00
□ 540	Bob Ojeda	.50	.20	.05
□ 541	Roy Lee Jackson	.03	.01	.00
□ 542	Lynn Jones	.03	.01	.00
□ 543	Gaylord Perry	.30	.12	.03
□ 544A	Phil Garner ERR	.75	.30	.07
	(reverse negative)			
□ 544B	Phil Garner COR	.10	.04	.01
□ 545	Garry Templeton	.08	.03	.01
□ 546	Rafael Ramirez	.03	.01	.00
□ 547	Jeff Reardon	.12	.05	.01
□ 548	Ron Guidry	.20	.08	.02
□ 549	Tim Laudner	.30	.12	.03

□ 550	John Henry Johnson	.03	.01	.0
□ 551	Chris Bando	.03	.01	.0
□ 552	Bobby Brown	.03	.01	.0
□ 553	Larry Bradford	.03	.01	.0
□ 554	Scott Fletcher	.60	.24	.0
□ 555	Jerry Royster	.03	.01	.0
□ 556	Shooty Babitt	.03	.01	.0
	(spelled Babbitt			
	on front)			
□ 557	Kent Hrbek	3.00	1.20	.3
□ 558	Yankee Winners	.12	.05	.0
	Ron Guidry			
	Tommy John			
□ 559	Mark Bomback	.03	.01	.0
□ 560	Julio Valdez	.03	.01	.0
□ 561	Buck Martinez	.03	.01	.0
□ 562	Mike Marshall	1.25	.50	.1
	(Dodger hitter)			
□ 563	Rennie Stennett	.03	.01	.0
□ 564	Steve Crawford	.03	.01	.0
□ 565	Bob Babcock	.03	.01	.0
□ 566	Johnny Podres CO	.06	.02	.0
□ 567	Paul Serna	.03	.01	.0
□ 568	Harold Baines	.45	.18	.0
□ 569	Dave LaRoche	.03	.01	.0
□ 570	Lee May	.06	.02	.0
□ 571	Gary Ward	.06	.02	.0
□ 572	John Denny	.06	.02	.0
□ 573	Roy Smalley	.03	.01	.0
□ 574	Bob Brenly	.20	.08	.0
□ 575	Bronx Bombers	.45	.18	.0
	Reggie Jackson			
	Dave Winfield			
□ 576	Luis Pujols	.03	.01	.0
□ 577	Butch Hobson	.03	.01	.0
□ 578	Harvey Kuenn MG	.06	.02	.0
□ 579	Cal Ripken Sr. CO	.08	.03	.0
□ 580	Juan Berenguer	.03	.01	.0
□ 581	Benny Ayala	.03	.01	.0
□ 582	Vance Law	.20	.08	.0
□ 583	Rick Leach	.03	.01	.0
□ 584	George Frazier	.03	.01	.0
□ 585	Phillies Finest	.75	.30	.0
	Pete Rose			
	Mike Schmidt			
□ 586	Joe Rudi	.06	.02	.0
□ 587	Juan Beniquez	.03	.01	.0
□ 588	Luis DeLeon	.08	.03	.0
□ 589	Craig Swan	.03	.01	.0
□ 590	Dave Chalk	.03	.01	.0
□ 591	Billy Gardner	.03	.01	.0
□ 592	Sal Bando	.06	.02	.0
□ 593	Bert Campaneris	.06	.02	.0
□ 594	Steve Kemp	.06	.02	.0
□ 595A	Randy Lerch ERR	.65	.26	.0
	(Braves)			
□ 595B	Randy Lerch COR	.06	.02	.0
	(Brewers)			
□ 596	Bryan Clark	.03	.01	.0
□ 597	David Ford	.03	.01	.0
□ 598	Mike Scioscia	.15	.06	.0
□ 599	John Lowenstein	.03	.01	.0
□ 600	Rene Lachemann MG	.06	.02	.0
□ 601	Mick Kelleher	.03	.01	.0
□ 602	Ron Jackson	.03	.01	.0
□ 603	Jerry Koosman	.08	.03	.0
□ 604	Dave Goltz	.03	.01	.0
□ 605	Ellis Valentine	.03	.01	.0
□ 606	Lonnie Smith	.06	.02	.0
□ 607	Joaquin Andujar	.10	.04	.0
□ 608	Garry Hancock	.03	.01	.0
□ 609	Jerry Turner	.03	.01	.0
□ 610	Bob Bonner	.03	.01	.0
□ 611	Jim Dwyer	.03	.01	.0
□ 612	Terry Bulling	.03	.01	.0
□ 613	Joel Youngblood	.03	.01	.0
□ 614	Larry Milbourne	.03	.01	.0
□ 615	Gene Roof	.06	.02	.0
	(name on front			
	is Phil Roof)			
□ 616	Keith Drumwright	.03	.01	.0
□ 617	Dave Rosello	.03	.01	.0
□ 618	Rickey Keeton	.03	.01	.0
□ 619	Dennis Lamp	.03	.01	.0
□ 620	Sid Monge	.03	.01	.0
□ 621	Jerry White	.03	.01	.0
□ 622	Luis Aguayo	.03	.01	.0
□ 623	Jamie Easterly	.03	.01	.0
□ 624	Steve Sax	2.25	.90	.22
□ 625	Dave Roberts	.03	.01	.0
□ 626	Rick Bosetti	.03	.01	.0
□ 627	Terry Francona	.10	.04	.0
□ 628	Pride of Reds	.35	.14	.03
	Tom Seaver			
	Johnny Bench			

□ 629	Paul Mirabella	.03	.01	.00
□ 630	Rance Mulliniks	.03	.01	.00
□ 631	Kevin Hickey	.03	.01	.00
□ 632	Reid Nichols	.03	.01	.00
□ 633	Dave Geisel	.03	.01	.00
□ 634	Ken Griffey	.06	.02	.00
□ 635	Bob Lemon MG	.10	.04	.01
□ 636	Orlando Sanchez	.03	.01	.00
□ 637	Bill Almon	.03	.01	.00
□ 638	Danny Ainge	.12	.05	.01
□ 639	Willie Stargell	.35	.14	.03
□ 640	Bob Sykes	.03	.01	.00
□ 641	Ed Lynch	.08	.03	.01
□ 642	John Ellis	.03	.01	.00
□ 643	Ferguson Jenkins	.15	.06	.01
□ 644	Lenn Sakata	.03	.01	.00
□ 645	Julio Gonzalez	.03	.01	.00
□ 646	Jesse Orosco	.08	.03	.01
□ 647	Jerry Dybzinski	.03	.01	.00
□ 648	Tommy Davis	.06	.02	.00
□ 649	Ron Gardenhire	.06	.02	.00
□ 650	Felipe Alou CO	.06	.02	.00
□ 651	Harvey Haddix CO	.03	.01	.00
□ 652	Willie Upshaw	.06	.02	.00
□ 653	Bill Madlock	.10	.04	.01
□ 654A	DK Checklist (unnumbered) (with Trammel)	.25	.04	.00
□ 654B	DK Checklist (unnumbered) (with Trammell)	.12	.01	.00
□ 655	Checklist 1 (unnumbered)	.08	.01	.00
□ 656	Checklist 2 (unnumbered)	.08	.01	.00
□ 657	Checklist 3 (unnumbered)	.08	.01	.00
□ 658	Checklist 4 (unnumbered)	.08	.01	.00
□ 659	Checklist 5 (unnumbered)	.08	.01	.00
□ 660	Checklist 6 (unnumbered)	.08	.01	.00

1983 Donruss

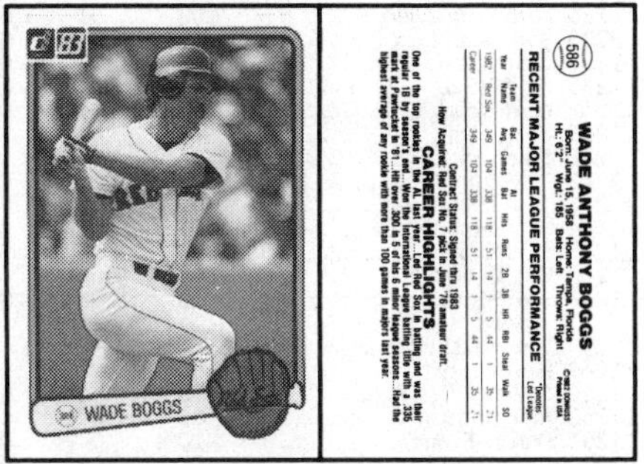

The cards in this 660-card set measure 2 1/2" by 3 1/2". The 1983 Donruss baseball set, issued with a 63-piece Diamond King puzzle, again leads off with a 26-card Diamond Kings (DK) series. Of the remaining 634 cards, two are combination cards, one portrays the San Diego Chicken, one shows the completed Ty Cobb puzzle, and seven are unnumbered checklist cards. The seven unnumbered checklist cards are arbitrarily assigned numbers 654 through 660 and are listed at the end of the list below. The Donruss logo and the year of issue are shown in the upper left corner of the obverse. The card backs have black print on yellow and white and are numbered on a small ball design. The complete set price below includes only the more common of each variation pair.

	MINT	EXC	G-VG
COMPLETE SET (660)	45.00	18.00	4.50
COMMON PLAYER (1-660)	.03	.01	.00

□ 1	Fern.Valenzuela DK	.50	.15	.03
□ 2	Rollie Fingers DK	.20	.08	.02
□ 3	Reggie Jackson DK	.50	.20	.05
□ 4	Jim Palmer DK	.35	.14	.03
□ 5	Jack Morris DK	.25	.10	.02
□ 6	George Foster DK	.12	.05	.01
□ 7	Jim Sundberg DK	.08	.03	.01
□ 8	Willie Stargell DK	.35	.14	.03
□ 9	Dave Stieb DK	.15	.06	.01
□ 10	Joe Niekro DK	.10	.04	.01
□ 11	Rickey Henderson DK	.60	.24	.06
□ 12	Dale Murphy DK	.75	.30	.07
□ 13	Toby Harrah DK	.08	.03	.01
□ 14	Bill Buckner DK	.10	.04	.01
□ 15	Willie Wilson DK	.12	.05	.01
□ 16	Steve Carlton DK	.40	.16	.04
□ 17	Ron Guidry DK	.20	.08	.02
□ 18	Steve Rogers DK	.08	.03	.01
□ 19	Kent Hrbek DK	.40	.16	.04
□ 20	Keith Hernandez DK	.35	.14	.03
□ 21	Floyd Bannister DK	.08	.03	.01
□ 22	Johnny Bench DK	.45	.18	.04
□ 23	Britt Burns DK	.08	.03	.01
□ 24	Joe Morgan DK	.30	.12	.03
□ 25	Carl Yastrzemski DK	.85	.34	.08
□ 26	Terry Kennedy DK	.08	.03	.01
□ 27	Gary Roenicke	.03	.01	.00
□ 28	Dwight Bernard	.03	.01	.00
□ 29	Pat Underwood	.03	.01	.00
□ 30	Gary Allenson	.03	.01	.00
□ 31	Ron Guidry	.18	.08	.01
□ 32	Burt Hooton	.03	.01	.00
□ 33	Chris Bando	.03	.01	.00
□ 34	Vida Blue	.08	.03	.01
□ 35	Rickey Henderson	.55	.22	.05
□ 36	Ray Burris	.03	.01	.00
□ 37	John Butcher	.03	.01	.00
□ 38	Don Aase	.03	.01	.00
□ 39	Jerry Koosman	.08	.03	.01
□ 40	Bruce Sutter	.15	.06	.01
□ 41	Jose Cruz	.08	.03	.01
□ 42	Pete Rose	1.00	.40	.10
□ 43	Cesar Cedeno	.08	.03	.01
□ 44	Floyd Chiffer	.03	.01	.00
□ 45	Larry McWilliams	.03	.01	.00
□ 46	Alan Fowlkes	.03	.01	.00
□ 47	Dale Murphy	.85	.34	.08
□ 48	Doug Bird	.03	.01	.00
□ 49	Hubie Brooks	.08	.03	.01
□ 50	Floyd Bannister	.06	.02	.00
□ 51	Jack O'Connor	.03	.01	.00
□ 52	Steve Senteney	.03	.01	.00
□ 53	Gary Gaetti	3.00	1.20	.30
□ 54	Damaso Garcia	.06	.02	.00
□ 55	Gene Nelson	.03	.01	.00
□ 56	Mookie Wilson	.08	.03	.01
□ 57	Allen Ripley	.03	.01	.00
□ 58	Bob Horner	.18	.08	.01
□ 59	Tony Pena	.15	.06	.01
□ 60	Gary Lavelle	.03	.01	.00
□ 61	Tim Lollar	.03	.01	.00
□ 62	Frank Pastore	.03	.01	.00
□ 63	Garry Maddox	.06	.02	.00
□ 64	Bob Forsch	.03	.01	.00
□ 65	Harry Spilman	.03	.01	.00
□ 66	Geoff Zahn	.03	.01	.00
□ 67	Salome Barojas	.03	.01	.00
□ 68	David Palmer	.03	.01	.00
□ 69	Charlie Hough	.08	.03	.01
□ 70	Dan Quisenberry	.15	.06	.01
□ 71	Tony Armas	.08	.03	.01
□ 72	Rick Sutcliffe	.15	.06	.01
□ 73	Steve Balboni	.08	.03	.01
□ 74	Jerry Remy	.03	.01	.00
□ 75	Mike Scioscia	.06	.02	.00
□ 76	John Wockenfuss	.03	.01	.00
□ 77	Jim Palmer	.35	.14	.03
□ 78	Rollie Fingers	.20	.08	.02
□ 79	Joe Nolan	.03	.01	.00
□ 80	Pete Vuckovich	.06	.02	.00
□ 81	Rick Leach	.03	.01	.00
□ 82	Rick Miller	.03	.01	.00
□ 83	Graig Nettles	.12	.05	.01
□ 84	Ron Cey	.10	.04	.01
□ 85	Miguel Dilone	.03	.01	.00
□ 86	John Wathan	.06	.02	.00
□ 87	Kelvin Moore	.03	.01	.00
□ 88A	Byrn Smith ERR (sic, Bryn)	.15	.06	.01
□ 88B	Bryn Smith COR	.75	.30	.07
□ 89	Dave Hostetler	.06	.02	.00
□ 90	Rod Carew	.45	.18	.04
□ 91	Lonnie Smith	.06	.02	.00
□ 92	Bob Knepper	.08	.03	.01

☐ 93	Marty Bystrom	.03	.01	.00
☐ 94	Chris Welsh	.03	.01	.00
☐ 95	Jason Thompson	.03	.01	.00
☐ 96	Tom O'Malley	.03	.01	.00
☐ 97	Phil Niekro	.25	.10	.02
☐ 98	Neil Allen	.03	.01	.00
☐ 99	Bill Buckner	.10	.04	.01
☐ 100	Ed VandeBerg	.03	.01	.00
☐ 101	Jim Clancy	.03	.01	.00
☐ 102	Robert Castillo	.03	.01	.00
☐ 103	Bruce Berenyi	.03	.01	.00
☐ 104	Carlton Fisk	.15	.06	.01
☐ 105	Mike Flanagan	.08	.03	.01
☐ 106	Cecil Cooper	.15	.06	.01
☐ 107	Jack Morris	.20	.08	.02
☐ 108	Mike Morgan	.03	.01	.00
☐ 109	Luis Aponte	.03	.01	.00
☐ 110	Pedro Guerrero	.30	.12	.03
☐ 111	Len Barker	.03	.01	.00
☐ 112	Willie Wilson	.12	.05	.01
☐ 113	Dave Beard	.03	.01	.00
☐ 114	Mike Gates	.03	.01	.00
☐ 115	Reggie Jackson	.50	.20	.05
☐ 116	George Wright	.03	.01	.00
☐ 117	Vance Law	.03	.01	.00
☐ 118	Nolan Ryan	.40	.16	.04
☐ 119	Mike Krukow	.06	.02	.00
☐ 120	Ozzie Smith	.25	.10	.02
☐ 121	Broderick Perkins	.03	.01	.00
☐ 122	Tom Seaver	.40	.16	.04
☐ 123	Chris Chambliss	.06	.02	.00
☐ 124	Chuck Tanner MG	.03	.01	.00
☐ 125	Johnnie LeMaster	.03	.01	.00
☐ 126	Mel Hall	.55	.22	.05
☐ 127	Bruce Bochte	.03	.01	.00
☐ 128	Charlie Puleo	.03	.01	.00
☐ 129	Luis Leal	.03	.01	.00
☐ 130	John Pacella	.03	.01	.00
☐ 131	Glenn Gulliver	.03	.01	.00
☐ 132	Don Money	.03	.01	.00
☐ 133	Dave Rozema	.03	.01	.00
☐ 134	Bruce Hurst	.30	.12	.03
☐ 135	Rudy May	.03	.01	.00
☐ 136	Tom Lasorda MG	.06	.02	.00
☐ 137	Dan Spillner (photo actually Ed Whitson)	.06	.02	.00
☐ 138	Jerry Martin	.03	.01	.00
☐ 139	Mike Norris	.03	.01	.00
☐ 140	Al Oliver	.10	.04	.01
☐ 141	Daryl Sconiers	.03	.01	.00
☐ 142	Lamar Johnson	.03	.01	.00
☐ 143	Harold Baines	.20	.08	.02
☐ 144	Alan Ashby	.03	.01	.00
☐ 145	Garry Templeton	.06	.02	.00
☐ 146	Al Holland	.03	.01	.00
☐ 147	Bo Diaz	.06	.02	.00
☐ 148	Dave Concepcion	.10	.04	.01
☐ 149	Rick Camp	.03	.01	.00
☐ 150	Jim Morrison	.03	.01	.00
☐ 151	Randy Martz	.03	.01	.00
☐ 152	Keith Hernandez	.35	.14	.03
☐ 153	John Lowenstein	.03	.01	.00
☐ 154	Mike Caldwell	.03	.01	.00
☐ 155	Milt Wilcox	.03	.01	.00
☐ 156	Rich Gedman	.10	.04	.01
☐ 157	Rich Gossage	.15	.06	.01
☐ 158	Jerry Reuss	.06	.02	.00
☐ 159	Ron Hassey	.03	.01	.00
☐ 160	Larry Gura	.03	.01	.00
☐ 161	Dwayne Murphy	.03	.01	.00
☐ 162	Woodie Fryman	.03	.01	.00
☐ 163	Steve Comer	.03	.01	.00
☐ 164	Ken Forsch	.03	.01	.00
☐ 165	Dennis Lamp	.03	.01	.00
☐ 166	David Green	.03	.01	.00
☐ 167	Terry Puhl	.03	.01	.00
☐ 168	Mike Schmidt	.60	.24	.06
☐ 169	Eddie Milner	.10	.04	.01
☐ 170	John Curtis	.03	.01	.00
☐ 171	Don Robinson	.03	.01	.00
☐ 172	Rich Gale	.03	.01	.00
☐ 173	Steve Bedrosian	.25	.10	.02
☐ 174	Willie Hernandez	.12	.05	.01
☐ 175	Ron Gardenhire	.03	.01	.00
☐ 176	Jim Beattie	.03	.01	.00
☐ 177	Tim Laudner	.06	.02	.00
☐ 178	Buck Martinez	.03	.01	.00
☐ 179	Kent Hrbek	.35	.14	.03
☐ 180	Alfredo Griffin	.08	.03	.01
☐ 181	Larry Andersen	.03	.01	.00
☐ 182	Pete Falcone	.03	.01	.00
☐ 183	Jody Davis	.10	.04	.01
☐ 184	Glenn Hubbard	.03	.01	.00
☐ 185	Dale Berra	.03	.01	.00
☐ 186	Greg Minton	.03	.01	.00
☐ 187	Gary Lucas	.03	.01	.00
☐ 188	Dave Van Gorder	.03	.01	.00
☐ 189	Bob Dernier	.03	.01	.00
☐ 190	Willie McGee	1.75	.70	.17
☐ 191	Dickie Thon	.03	.01	.00
☐ 192	Bob Boone	.10	.04	.01
☐ 193	Britt Burns	.03	.01	.00
☐ 194	Jeff Reardon	.10	.04	.01
☐ 195	Jon Matlack	.06	.02	.00
☐ 196	Don Slaught	.30	.12	.03
☐ 197	Fred Stanley	.03	.01	.00
☐ 198	Rick Manning	.03	.01	.00
☐ 199	Dave Righetti	.20	.08	.02
☐ 200	Dave Stapleton	.03	.01	.00
☐ 201	Steve Yeager	.03	.01	.00
☐ 202	Enos Cabell	.03	.01	.00
☐ 203	Sammy Stewart	.03	.01	.00
☐ 204	Moose Haas	.03	.01	.00
☐ 205	Lenn Sakata	.03	.01	.00
☐ 206	Charlie Moore	.03	.01	.00
☐ 207	Alan Trammell	.30	.12	.03
☐ 208	Jim Rice	.25	.10	.02
☐ 209	Roy Smalley	.03	.01	.00
☐ 210	Bill Russell	.06	.02	.00
☐ 211	Andre Thornton	.06	.02	.00
☐ 212	Willie Aikens	.03	.01	.00
☐ 213	Dave McKay	.03	.01	.00
☐ 214	Tim Blackwell	.03	.01	.00
☐ 215	Buddy Bell	.08	.03	.01
☐ 216	Doug DeCinces	.08	.03	.01
☐ 217	Tom Herr	.08	.03	.01
☐ 218	Frank LaCorte	.03	.01	.00
☐ 219	Steve Carlton	.35	.14	.03
☐ 220	Terry Kennedy	.06	.02	.00
☐ 221	Mike Easler	.03	.01	.00
☐ 222	Jack Clark	.25	.10	.02
☐ 223	Gene Garber	.03	.01	.00
☐ 224	Scott Holman	.03	.01	.00
☐ 225	Mike Proly	.03	.01	.00
☐ 226	Terry Bulling	.03	.01	.00
☐ 227	Jerry Garvin	.03	.01	.00
☐ 228	Ron Davis	.03	.01	.00
☐ 229	Tom Hume	.03	.01	.00
☐ 230	Marc Hill	.03	.01	.00
☐ 231	Dennis Martinez	.06	.02	.00
☐ 232	Jim Gantner	.03	.01	.00
☐ 233	Larry Pashnick	.03	.01	.00
☐ 234	Dave Collins	.03	.01	.00
☐ 235	Tom Burgmeier	.03	.01	.00
☐ 236	Ken Landreaux	.03	.01	.00
☐ 237	John Denny	.08	.03	.01
☐ 238	Hal McRae	.06	.02	.00
☐ 239	Matt Keough	.03	.01	.00
☐ 240	Doug Flynn	.03	.01	.00
☐ 241	Fred Lynn	.18	.08	.01
☐ 242	Billy Sample	.03	.01	.00
☐ 243	Tom Paciorek	.03	.01	.00
☐ 244	Joe Sambito	.03	.01	.00
☐ 245	Sid Monge	.03	.01	.00
☐ 246	Ken Oberkfell	.03	.01	.00
☐ 247	Joe Pittman (photo actually Juan Eichelberger)	.08	.03	.01
☐ 248	Mario Soto	.06	.02	.00
☐ 249	Claudell Washington	.08	.03	.01
☐ 250	Rick Rhoden	.08	.03	.01
☐ 251	Darrell Evans	.10	.04	.01
☐ 252	Steve Henderson	.03	.01	.00
☐ 253	Manny Castillo	.03	.01	.00
☐ 254	Craig Swan	.03	.01	.00
☐ 255	Joey McLaughlin	.03	.01	.00
☐ 256	Pete Redfern	.03	.01	.00
☐ 257	Ken Singleton	.08	.03	.01
☐ 258	Robin Yount	.30	.12	.03
☐ 259	Elias Sosa	.03	.01	.00
☐ 260	Bob Ojeda	.10	.04	.01
☐ 261	Bobby Murcer	.08	.03	.01
☐ 262	Candy Maldonado	.60	.24	.06
☐ 263	Rick Waits	.03	.01	.00
☐ 264	Greg Pryor	.03	.01	.00
☐ 265	Bob Owchinko	.03	.01	.00
☐ 266	Chris Speier	.03	.01	.00
☐ 267	Bruce Kison	.03	.01	.00
☐ 268	Mark Wagner	.03	.01	.00
☐ 269	Steve Kemp	.06	.02	.00
☐ 270	Phil Garner	.03	.01	.00
☐ 271	Gene Richards	.03	.01	.00
☐ 272	Renie Martin	.03	.01	.00
☐ 273	Dave Roberts	.03	.01	.00
☐ 274	Dan Driessen	.03	.01	.00
☐ 275	Rufino Linares	.03	.01	.00
☐ 276	Lee Lacy	.03	.01	.00
☐ 277	Ryne Sandberg	4.00	1.60	.40
☐ 278	Darrell Porter	.03	.01	.00

□ 279 Cal Ripken	1.00	.40	.10
□ 280 Jamie Easterly	.03	.01	.00
□ 281 Bill Fahey	.03	.01	.00
□ 282 Glenn Hoffman	.03	.01	.00
□ 283 Willie Randolph	.08	.03	.01
□ 284 Fernando Valenzuela	.25	.10	.02
□ 285 Alan Bannister	.03	.01	.00
□ 286 Paul Splittorff	.03	.01	.00
□ 287 Joe Rudi	.06	.02	.00
□ 288 Bill Gullickson	.03	.01	.00
□ 289 Danny Darwin	.03	.01	.00
□ 290 Andy Hassler	.03	.01	.00
□ 291 Ernesto Escarrega	.03	.01	.00
□ 292 Steve Mura	.03	.01	.00
□ 293 Tony Scott	.03	.01	.00
□ 294 Manny Trillo	.03	.01	.00
□ 295 Greg Harris	.03	.01	.00
□ 296 Luis DeLeon	.03	.01	.00
□ 297 Kent Tekulve	.06	.02	.00
□ 298 Atlee Hammaker	.06	.02	.00
□ 299 Bruce Benedict	.03	.01	.00
□ 300 Fergie Jenkins	.12	.05	.01
□ 301 Dave Kingman	.12	.05	.01
□ 302 Bill Caudill	.03	.01	.00
□ 303 John Castino	.03	.01	.00
□ 304 Ernie Whitt	.06	.02	.00
□ 305 Randy Johnson	.03	.01	.00
□ 306 Garth Iorg	.03	.01	.00
□ 307 Gaylord Perry	.25	.10	.02
□ 308 Ed Lynch	.03	.01	.00
□ 309 Keith Moreland	.06	.02	.00
□ 310 Rafael Ramirez	.03	.01	.00
□ 311 Bill Madlock	.10	.04	.01
□ 312 Milt May	.03	.01	.00
□ 313 John Montefusco	.06	.02	.00
□ 314 Wayne Krenchicki	.03	.01	.00
□ 315 George Vukovich	.03	.01	.00
□ 316 Joaquin Andujar	.10	.04	.01
□ 317 Craig Reynolds	.03	.01	.00
□ 318 Rick Burleson	.06	.02	.00
□ 319 Richard Dotson	.08	.03	.01
□ 320 Steve Rogers	.03	.01	.00
□ 321 Dave Schmidt	.15	.06	.01
□ 322 Bud Black	.20	.08	.02
□ 323 Jeff Burroughs	.06	.02	.00
□ 324 Von Hayes	.20	.08	.02
□ 325 Butch Wynegar	.03	.01	.00
□ 326 Carl Yastrzemski	.75	.30	.07
□ 327 Ron Roenicke	.03	.01	.00
□ 328 Howard Johnson	2.25	.90	.22
□ 329 Rick Dempsey	.03	.01	.00
□ 330A Jim Slaton (bio printed black on white)	.06	.02	.00
□ 330B Jim Slaton (bio printed black on yellow)	.10	.04	.01
□ 331 Benny Ayala	.03	.01	.00
□ 332 Ted Simmons	.12	.05	.01
□ 333 Lou Whitaker	.15	.06	.01
□ 334 Chuck Rainey	.03	.01	.00
□ 335 Lou Piniella	.10	.04	.01
□ 336 Steve Sax	.35	.14	.03
□ 337 Toby Harrah	.06	.02	.00
□ 338 George Brett	.65	.26	.06
□ 339 Davey Lopes	.08	.03	.01
□ 340 Gary Carter	.40	.16	.04
□ 341 John Grubb	.03	.01	.00
□ 342 Tim Foli	.03	.01	.00
□ 343 Jim Kaat	.12	.05	.01
□ 344 Mike LaCoss	.03	.01	.00
□ 345 Larry Christenson	.03	.01	.00
□ 346 Juan Bonilla	.03	.01	.00
□ 347 Omar Moreno	.03	.01	.00
□ 348 Chili Davis	.35	.14	.03
□ 349 Tommy Boggs	.03	.01	.00
□ 350 Rusty Staub	.10	.04	.01
□ 351 Bump Wills	.03	.01	.00
□ 352 Rick Sweet	.03	.01	.00
□ 353 Jim Gott	.30	.12	.03
□ 354 Terry Felton	.03	.01	.00
□ 355 Jim Kern	.03	.01	.00
□ 356 Bill Almon	.03	.01	.00
□ 357 Tippy Martinez	.03	.01	.00
□ 358 Roy Howell	.03	.01	.00
□ 359 Dan Petry	.08	.03	.01
□ 360 Jerry Mumphrey	.03	.01	.00
□ 361 Mark Clear	.03	.01	.00
□ 362 Mike Marshall	.25	.10	.02
□ 363 Lary Sorenson	.03	.01	.00
□ 364 Amos Otis	.08	.03	.01
□ 365 Rick Langford	.03	.01	.00
□ 366 Brad Mills	.03	.01	.00
□ 367 Brian Downing	.06	.02	.00
□ 368 Mike Richardt	.03	.01	.00
□ 369 Aurelio Rodriguez	.03	.01	.00
□ 370 Dave Smith	.06	.02	.00
□ 371 Tug McGraw	.10	.04	.01
□ 372 Doug Bair	.03	.01	.00
□ 373 Ruppert Jones	.03	.01	.00
□ 374 Alex Trevino	.03	.01	.00
□ 375 Ken Dayley	.06	.02	.00
□ 376 Rod Scurry	.03	.01	.00
□ 377 Bob Brenly	.06	.02	.00
□ 378 Scot Thompson	.03	.01	.00
□ 379 Julio Cruz	.03	.01	.00
□ 380 John Stearns	.03	.01	.00
□ 381 Dale Murray	.03	.01	.00
□ 382 Frank Viola	3.75	1.50	.37
□ 383 Al Bumbry	.03	.01	.00
□ 384 Ben Oglivie	.06	.02	.00
□ 385 Dave Tobik	.03	.01	.00
□ 386 Bob Stanley	.03	.01	.00
□ 387 Andre Robertson	.03	.01	.00
□ 388 Jorge Orta	.03	.01	.00
□ 389 Ed Whitson	.06	.02	.00
□ 390 Don Hood	.03	.01	.00
□ 391 Tom Underwood	.03	.01	.00
□ 392 Tim Wallach	.18	.08	.01
□ 393 Steve Renko	.03	.01	.00
□ 394 Mickey Rivers	.06	.02	.00
□ 395 Greg Luzinski	.10	.04	.01
□ 396 Art Howe	.08	.03	.01
□ 397 Alan Wiggins	.15	.06	.01
□ 398 Jim Barr	.03	.01	.00
□ 399 Ivan DeJesus	.03	.01	.00
□ 400 Tom Lawless	.06	.02	.00
□ 401 Bob Walk	.08	.03	.01
□ 402 Jimmy Smith	.03	.01	.00
□ 403 Lee Smith	.12	.05	.01
□ 404 George Hendrick	.06	.02	.00
□ 405 Eddie Murray	.50	.20	.05
□ 406 Marshall Edwards	.03	.01	.00
□ 407 Lance Parrish	.25	.10	.02
□ 408 Carney Lansford	.15	.06	.01
□ 409 Dave Winfield	.40	.16	.04
□ 410 Bob Welch	.10	.04	.01
□ 411 Larry Milbourne	.03	.01	.00
□ 412 Dennis Leonard	.06	.02	.00
□ 413 Dan Meyer	.03	.01	.00
□ 414 Charlie Lea	.03	.01	.00
□ 415 Rick Honeycutt	.03	.01	.00
□ 416 Mike Witt	.20	.08	.02
□ 417 Steve Trout	.03	.01	.00
□ 418 Glenn Brummer	.03	.01	.00
□ 419 Denny Walling	.03	.01	.00
□ 420 Gary Matthews	.06	.02	.00
□ 421 Charlie Leibrandt (Liebrandt on front of card)	.08	.03	.01
□ 422 Juan Eichelberger (photo actually Joe Pittman)	.06	.02	.00
□ 423 Matt Guante	.06	.02	.00
□ 424 Bill Laskey	.03	.01	.00
□ 425 Jerry Royster	.03	.01	.00
□ 426 Dickie Noles	.03	.01	.00
□ 427 George Foster	.12	.05	.01
□ 428 Mike Moore	.35	.14	.03
□ 429 Gary Ward	.06	.02	.00
□ 430 Barry Bonnell	.03	.01	.00
□ 431 Ron Washington	.03	.01	.00
□ 432 Rance Mulliniks	.03	.01	.00
□ 433 Mike Stanton	.03	.01	.00
□ 434 Jesse Orosco	.08	.03	.01
□ 435 Larry Bowa	.12	.05	.01
□ 436 Biff Pocoroba	.03	.01	.00
□ 437 Johnny Ray	.15	.06	.01
□ 438 Joe Morgan	.30	.12	.03
□ 439 Eric Show	.35	.14	.03
□ 440 Larry Biittner	.03	.01	.00
□ 441 Greg Gross	.03	.01	.00
□ 442 Gene Tenace	.06	.02	.00
□ 443 Danny Heep	.03	.01	.00
□ 444 Bobby Clark	.03	.01	.00
□ 445 Kevin Hickey	.03	.01	.00
□ 446 Scott Sanderson	.03	.01	.00
□ 447 Frank Tanana	.08	.03	.01
□ 448 Cesar Geronimo	.03	.01	.00
□ 449 Jimmy Sexton	.03	.01	.00
□ 450 Mike Hargrove	.03	.01	.00
□ 451 Doyle Alexander	.08	.03	.01
□ 452 Dwight Evans	.18	.08	.01
□ 453 Terry Forster	.08	.03	.01
□ 454 Tom Brookens	.03	.01	.00
□ 455 Rich Dauer	.03	.01	.00
□ 456 Rob Picciolo	.03	.01	.00
□ 457 Terry Crowley	.03	.01	.00
□ 458 Ned Yost	.03	.01	.00
□ 459 Kirk Gibson	.40	.16	.04

□ 460	Reid Nichols	.03	.01	.00
□ 461	Oscar Gamble	.03	.01	.00
□ 462	Dusty Baker	.06	.02	.00
□ 463	Jack Perconte	.03	.01	.00
□ 464	Frank White	.08	.03	.01
□ 465	Mickey Klutts	.03	.01	.00
□ 466	Warren Cromartie	.03	.01	.00
□ 467	Larry Parrish	.06	.02	.00
□ 468	Bobby Grich	.08	.03	.01
□ 469	Dane Iorg	.03	.01	.00
□ 470	Joe Niekro	.10	.04	.01
□ 471	Ed Farmer	.03	.01	.00
□ 472	Tim Flannery	.03	.01	.00
□ 473	Dave Parker	.20	.08	.02
□ 474	Jeff Leonard	.08	.03	.01
□ 475	Al Hrabosky	.06	.02	.00
□ 476	Ron Hodges	.03	.01	.00
□ 477	Leon Durham	.06	.02	.00
□ 478	Jim Essian	.03	.01	.00
□ 479	Roy Lee Jackson	.03	.01	.00
□ 480	Brad Havens	.03	.01	.00
□ 481	Joe Price	.03	.01	.00
□ 482	Tony Bernazard	.03	.01	.00
□ 483	Scott McGregor	.06	.02	.00
□ 484	Paul Molitor	.18	.08	.01
□ 485	Mike Ivie	.03	.01	.00
□ 486	Ken Griffey	.06	.02	.00
□ 487	Dennis Eckersley	.15	.06	.01
□ 488	Steve Garvey	.40	.16	.04
□ 489	Mike Fischlin	.03	.01	.00
□ 490	U.L. Washington	.03	.01	.00
□ 491	Steve McCatty	.03	.01	.00
□ 492	Roy Johnson	.03	.01	.00
□ 493	Don Baylor	.12	.05	.01
□ 494	Bobby Johnson	.03	.01	.00
□ 495	Mike Squires	.03	.01	.00
□ 496	Bert Roberge	.03	.01	.00
□ 497	Dick Ruthven	.03	.01	.00
□ 498	Tito Landrum	.03	.01	.00
□ 499	Sixto Lezcano	.03	.01	.00
□ 500	Johnny Bench	.45	.18	.04
□ 501	Larry Whisenton	.03	.01	.00
□ 502	Manny Sarmiento	.03	.01	.00
□ 503	Fred Breining	.03	.01	.00
□ 504	Bill Campbell	.03	.01	.00
□ 505	Todd Cruz	.03	.01	.00
□ 506	Bob Bailor	.03	.01	.00
□ 507	Dave Stieb	.18	.08	.01
□ 508	Al Williams	.03	.01	.00
□ 509	Dan Ford	.03	.01	.00
□ 510	Gorman Thomas	.10	.04	.01
□ 511	Chet Lemon	.06	.02	.00
□ 512	Mike Torrez	.03	.01	.00
□ 513	Shane Rawley	.06	.02	.00
□ 514	Mark Belanger	.06	.02	.00
□ 515	Rodney Craig	.03	.01	.00
□ 516	Onix Concepcion	.03	.01	.00
□ 517	Mike Heath	.03	.01	.00
□ 518	Andre Dawson	.35	.14	.03
□ 519	Luis Sanchez	.03	.01	.00
□ 520	Terry Bogener	.03	.01	.00
□ 521	Rudy Law	.03	.01	.00
□ 522	Ray Knight	.08	.03	.01
□ 523	Joe Lefebvre	.03	.01	.00
□ 524	Jim Wohlford	.03	.01	.00
□ 525	Julio Franco	1.75	.70	.17
□ 526	Ron Oester	.03	.01	.00
□ 527	Rick Mahler	.06	.02	.00
□ 528	Steve Nicosia	.03	.01	.00
□ 529	Junior Kennedy	.03	.01	.00
□ 530A	Whitey Herzog MG (bio printed black on white)	.10	.04	.01
□ 530B	Whitey Herzog MG (bio printed black on yellow)	.10	.04	.01
□ 531A	Don Sutton (blue border on photo)	.40	.16	.04
□ 531B	Don Sutton (green border on photo)	.40	.16	.04
□ 532	Mark Brouhard	.03	.01	.00
□ 533A	Sparky Anderson MG (bio printed black on white)	.10	.04	.01
□ 533B	Sparky Anderson MG (bio printed black on yellow)	.10	.04	.01
□ 534	Roger LaFrancois	.03	.01	.00
□ 535	George Frazier	.03	.01	.00
□ 536	Tom Niedenfuer	.08	.03	.01
□ 537	Ed Glynn	.03	.01	.00
□ 538	Lee May	.06	.02	.00
□ 539	Bob Kearney	.03	.01	.00
□ 540	Tim Raines	.45	.18	.0
□ 541	Paul Mirabella	.03	.01	.0
□ 542	Luis Tiant	.08	.03	.0
□ 543	Ron LeFlore	.06	.02	.0
□ 544	Dave LaPoint	.35	.14	.0
□ 545	Randy Moffitt	.03	.01	.0
□ 546	Luis Aguayo	.03	.01	.0
□ 547	Brad Lesley	.03	.01	.0
□ 548	Luis Salazar	.06	.02	.0
□ 549	John Candelaria	.08	.03	.0
□ 550	Dave Bergman	.03	.01	.0
□ 551	Bob Watson	.06	.02	.0
□ 552	Pat Tabler	.12	.05	.0
□ 553	Brent Gaff	.03	.01	.0
□ 554	Al Cowens	.03	.01	.0
□ 555	Tom Brunansky	.50	.20	.0
□ 556	Lloyd Moseby	.12	.05	.0
□ 557A	Pascual Perez ERR (Twins in glove)	2.00	.80	.2
□ 557B	Pascual Perez COR (Braves in glove)	.10	.04	.0
□ 558	Willie Upshaw	.06	.02	.0
□ 559	Richie Zisk	.06	.02	.0
□ 560	Pat Zachry	.03	.01	.0
□ 561	Jay Johnstone	.08	.03	.0
□ 562	Carlos Diaz	.06	.02	.0
□ 563	John Tudor	.15	.06	.0
□ 564	Frank Robinson MG	.12	.05	.0
□ 565	Dave Edwards	.03	.01	.0
□ 566	Paul Householder	.03	.01	.0
□ 567	Ron Reed	.03	.01	.0
□ 568	Mike Ramsey	.03	.01	.0
□ 569	Kiko Garcia	.03	.01	.0
□ 570	Tommy John	.15	.06	.0
□ 571	Tony LaRussa MG	.06	.02	.0
□ 572	Joel Youngblood	.03	.01	.0
□ 573	Wayne Tolleson	.20	.08	.02
□ 574	Keith Creel	.03	.01	.0
□ 575	Billy Martin MG	.12	.05	.01
□ 576	Jerry Dybzinski	.03	.01	.00
□ 577	Rick Cerone	.03	.01	.00
□ 578	Tony Perez	.15	.06	.01
□ 579	Greg Brock	.35	.14	.03
□ 580	Glen Wilson	.30	.12	.03
□ 581	Tim Stoddard	.03	.01	.00
□ 582	Bob McClure	.03	.01	.00
□ 583	Jim Dwyer	.03	.01	.00
□ 584	Ed Romero	.03	.01	.00
□ 585	Larry Herndon	.03	.01	.00
□ 586	Wade Boggs	17.00	7.00	1.70
□ 587	Jay Howell	.06	.02	.00
□ 588	Dave Stewart	.15	.06	.01
□ 589	Bert Blyleven	.15	.06	.01
□ 590	Dick Howser MG	.08	.03	.01
□ 591	Wayne Gross	.03	.01	.00
□ 592	Terry Francona	.03	.01	.00
□ 593	Don Werner	.03	.01	.00
□ 594	Bill Stein	.03	.01	.00
□ 595	Jesse Barfield	.65	.26	.06
□ 596	Bobby Molinaro	.03	.01	.00
□ 597	Mike Vail	.03	.01	.00
□ 598	Tony Gwynn	9.00	3.75	.90
□ 599	Gary Rajsich	.03	.01	.00
□ 600	Jerry Ujdur	.03	.01	.00
□ 601	Cliff Johnson	.03	.01	.00
□ 602	Jerry White	.03	.01	.00
□ 603	Bryan Clark	.03	.01	.00
□ 604	Joe Ferguson	.03	.01	.00
□ 605	Guy Sularz	.03	.01	.00
□ 606A	Ozzie Virgil (green border on photo)	.10	.04	.01
□ 606B	Ozzie Virgil (orange border on photo)	.10	.04	.01
□ 607	Terry Harper	.03	.01	.00
□ 608	Harvey Kuenn MG	.06	.02	.00
□ 609	Jim Sundberg	.06	.02	.00
□ 610	Willie Stargell	.35	.14	.03
□ 611	Reggie Smith	.08	.03	.01
□ 612	Rob Wilfong	.03	.01	.00
□ 613	The Niekro Brothers Joe Niekro Phil Niekro	.12	.05	.01
□ 614	Lee Elia MG	.03	.01	.00
□ 615	Mickey Hatcher	.08	.03	.01
□ 616	Jerry Hairston	.03	.01	.00
□ 617	John Martin	.03	.01	.00
□ 618	Wally Backman	.20	.08	.02
□ 619	Storm Davis	.45	.18	.04
□ 620	Alan Knicely	.03	.01	.00
□ 621	John Stuper	.03	.01	.00
□ 622	Matt Sinatro	.03	.01	.00
□ 623	Gene Petralli	.06	.02	.00
□ 624	Duane Walker	.03	.01	.00

□ 625	Dick Williams MG	.03	.01	.00
□ 626	Pat Corrales MG	.03	.01	.00
□ 627	Vern Ruhle	.03	.01	.00
□ 628	Joe Torre MG	.08	.03	.01
□ 629	Anthony Johnson	.03	.01	.00
□ 630	Steve Howe	.03	.01	.00
□ 631	Gary Woods	.03	.01	.00
□ 632	LaMarr Hoyt	.08	.03	.01
□ 633	Steve Swisher	.03	.01	.00
□ 634	Terry Leach	.25	.10	.02
□ 635	Jeff Newman	.03	.01	.00
□ 636	Brett Butler	.12	.05	.01
□ 637	Gary Gray	.03	.01	.00
□ 638	Lee Mazzilli	.03	.01	.00
□ 639A	Ron Jackson ERR (A's in glove)	10.00	4.00	1.00
□ 639B	Ron Jackson COR (Angels in glove, red border on photo)	.15	.06	.01
□ 639C	Ron Jackson COR (Angels in glove, green border on photo)	.50	.20	.05
□ 640	Juan Beniquez	.03	.01	.00
□ 641	Dave Rucker	.03	.01	.00
□ 642	Luis Pujols	.03	.01	.00
□ 643	Rick Monday	.06	.02	.00
□ 644	Hosken Powell	.03	.01	.00
□ 645	The Chicken	.20	.08	.02
□ 646	Dave Engle	.03	.01	.00
□ 647	Dick Davis	.03	.01	.00
□ 648	Frank Robinson Vida Blue Joe Morgan	.12	.05	.01
□ 649	Al Chambers	.03	.01	.00
□ 650	Jesus Vega	.03	.01	.00
□ 651	Jeff Jones	.03	.01	.00
□ 652	Marvis Foley	.03	.01	.00
□ 653	Ty Cobb Puzzle Card	.03	.01	.00
□ 654A	Dick Perez/Diamond King Checklist (unnumbered) (word "checklist" omitted from back)	.15	.02	.00
□ 654B	Dick Perez/Diamond King Checklist (unnumbered) (word "checklist" is on back)	.15	.02	.00
□ 655	Checklist 1 (unnumbered)	.07	.01	.00
□ 656	Checklist 2 (unnumbered)	.07	.01	.00
□ 657	Checklist 3 (unnumbered)	.07	.01	.00
□ 658	Checklist 4 (unnumbered)	.07	.01	.00
□ 659	Checklist 5 (unnumbered)	.07	.01	.00
□ 660	Checklist 6 (unnumbered)	.07	.01	.00

1983 Donruss Action All-Stars

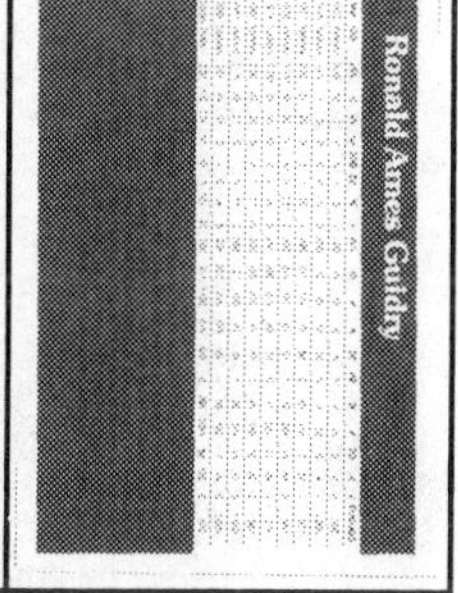

The cards in this 60-card set measure 3 1/2" by 5". The 1983 Action All-Stars series depicts 60 major leagers in a distinctive new style. Each card contains a large close-up on the left and an action photo on the right. Team affiliations appear as part of the background design, and the cards have cranberry color borders. The backs contain the card number, the player's major league line record, and biographical material. A 63-piece Mickey Mantle puzzle (three pieces on one card per pack) was marketed as an insert premium.

	MINT	EXC	G-VG
COMPLETE SET (60)	6.00	2.40	.60
COMMON PLAYER (1-60)	.05	.02	.00

□	1	Eddie Murray	.40	.16	.04
□	2	Dwight Evans	.15	.06	.01
□	3A	Reggie Jackson ERR (red screen on back covers some stats)	.75	.30	.07
□	3B	Reggie Jackson COR	.60	.24	.06
□	4	Greg Luzinski	.10	.04	.01
□	5	Larry Herndon	.05	.02	.00
□	6	Al Oliver	.10	.04	.01
□	7	Bill Buckner	.10	.04	.01
□	8	Jason Thompson	.05	.02	.00
□	9	Andre Dawson	.25	.10	.02
□	10	Greg Minton	.05	.02	.00
□	11	Terry Kennedy	.05	.02	.00
□	12	Phil Niekro	.20	.08	.02
□	13	Willie Wilson	.10	.04	.01
□	14	Johnny Bench	.35	.14	.03
□	15	Ron Guidry	.10	.04	.01
□	16	Hal McRae	.05	.02	.00
□	17	Damaso Garcia	.05	.02	.00
□	18	Gary Ward	.05	.02	.00
□	19	Cecil Cooper	.10	.04	.01
□	20	Keith Hernandez	.25	.10	.02
□	21	Ron Cey	.05	.02	.00
□	22	Rickey Henderson	.40	.16	.04
□	23	Nolan Ryan	.40	.16	.04
□	24	Steve Carlton	.30	.12	.03
□	25	John Stearns	.05	.02	.00
□	26	Jim Sundberg	.05	.02	.00
□	27	Joaquin Andujar	.05	.02	.00
□	28	Gaylord Perry	.20	.08	.02
□	29	Jack Clark	.20	.08	.02
□	30	Bill Madlock	.05	.02	.00
□	31	Pete Rose	.60	.24	.06
□	32	Mookie Wilson	.05	.02	.00
□	33	Rollie Fingers	.15	.06	.01
□	34	Lonnie Smith	.05	.02	.00
□	35	Tony Pena	.05	.02	.00
□	36	Dave Winfield	.25	.10	.02
□	37	Tim Lollar	.05	.02	.00
□	38	Rod Carew	.30	.12	.03
□	39	Toby Harrah	.05	.02	.00
□	40	Buddy Bell	.05	.02	.00
□	41	Bruce Sutter	.10	.04	.01
□	42	George Brett	.45	.18	.04
□	43	Carlton Fisk	.10	.04	.01
□	44	Carl Yastrzemski	.60	.24	.06
□	45	Dale Murphy	.45	.18	.04
□	46	Bob Horner	.10	.04	.01
□	47	Dave Concepcion	.05	.02	.00
□	48	Dave Stieb	.10	.04	.01
□	49	Kent Hrbek	.20	.08	.02
□	50	Lance Parrish	.15	.06	.01
□	51	Joe Niekro	.10	.04	.01
□	52	Cal Ripken	.35	.14	.03
□	53	Fernando Valenzuela	.25	.10	.02
□	54	Richie Zisk	.05	.02	.00
□	55	Leon Durham	.05	.02	.00
□	56	Robin Yount	.30	.12	.03
□	57	Mike Schmidt	.50	.20	.05
□	58	Gary Carter	.40	.16	.04
□	59	Fred Lynn	.10	.04	.01
□	60	Checklist card	.05	.02	.00

1983 Donruss HOF Heroes

The cards in this 44-card set measure 2 1/2" by 3 1/2". Although it was issued with the same Mantle puzzle as the Action All Stars set, the Donruss Hall of Fame Heroes set is completely different in content and design. Of the 44 cards in the set, 42 are Dick Perez artwork portraying Hall of Fame members, while one card depicts the completed Mantle puzzle

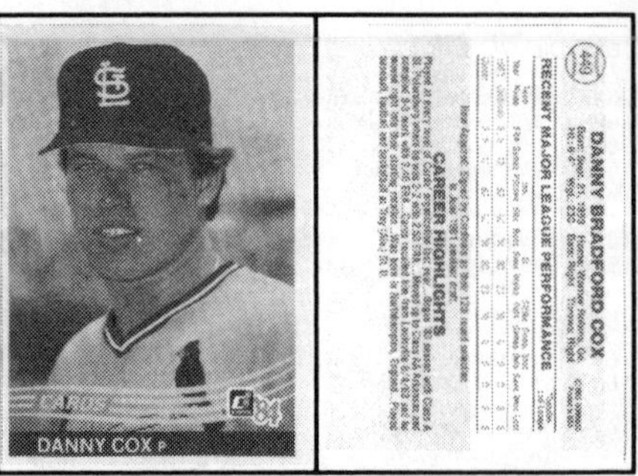

and the last card is a checklist. The red, white, and blue backs contain the card number and a short player biography. The cards were packaged 8 cards plus one puzzle card (3 pieces) for 30 cents in the summer of 1983.

	MINT	EXC	G-VG
COMPLETE SET (44)	4.50	1.80	.45
COMMON PLAYER (1-44)	.05	.02	.00
□ 1 Ty Cobb	.40	.16	.04
□ 2 Walter Johnson	.15	.06	.01
□ 3 Christy Mathewson	.15	.06	.01
□ 4 Josh Gibson	.15	.06	.01
□ 5 Honus Wagner	.15	.06	.01
□ 6 Jackie Robinson	.15	.06	.01
□ 7 Mickey Mantle	.75	.30	.07
□ 8 Luke Appling	.05	.02	.00
□ 9 Ted Williams	.20	.08	.02
□ 10 Johnny Mize	.05	.02	.00
□ 11 Satchel Paige	.05	.02	.00
□ 12 Lou Boudreau	.05	.02	.00
□ 13 Jimmie Foxx	.10	.04	.01
□ 14 Duke Snider	.15	.06	.01
□ 15 Monte Irvin	.05	.02	.00
□ 16 Hank Greenberg	.05	.02	.00
□ 17 Roberto Clemente	.15	.06	.01
□ 18 Al Kaline	.15	.06	.01
□ 19 Frank Robinson	.10	.04	.01
□ 20 Joe Cronin	.05	.02	.00
□ 21 Burleigh Grimes	.05	.02	.00
□ 22 The Waner Brothers Paul Waner Lloyd Waner	.05	.02	.00
□ 23 Grover Alexander	.05	.02	.00
□ 24 Yogi Berra	.15	.06	.01
□ 25 Cool Papa Bell	.05	.02	.00
□ 26 Bill Dickey	.05	.02	.00
□ 27 Cy Young	.10	.04	.01
□ 28 Charlie Gehringer	.05	.02	.00
□ 29 Dizzy Dean	.15	.06	.01
□ 30 Bob Lemon	.05	.02	.00
□ 31 Red Ruffing	.05	.02	.00
□ 32 Stan Musial	.15	.06	.01
□ 33 Carl Hubbell	.10	.04	.01
□ 34 Hank Aaron	.20	.08	.02
□ 35 John McGraw	.05	.02	.00
□ 36 Bob Feller	.15	.06	.01
□ 37 Casey Stengel	.10	.04	.01
□ 38 Ralph Kiner	.10	.04	.01
□ 39 Roy Campanella	.15	.06	.01
□ 40 Mel Ott	.10	.04	.01
□ 41 Robin Roberts	.10	.04	.01
□ 42 Early Wynn	.05	.02	.00
□ 43 Mantle Puzzle card	.05	.02	.00
□ 44 Checklist card	.05	.02	.00

1984 Donruss

The 1984 Donruss set contains a total of 660 cards, each measuring 2 1/2" by 3 1/2"; however, only 658 are numbered. The first 26 cards in the set are again Diamond Kings (DK) although the drawings this year were styled differently and are easily differentiated from other DK issues. A new feature, Rated Rookies (RR), was introduced with this set with Bill Madden's 20 selections comprising numbers 27 through 46. Two "Living Legend" cards designated A (featuring Gaylord Perry and Rollie Fingers) and B (featuring Johnny Bench and Carl Yastrzemski) were issued as bonus cards in wax packs, but were not issued in the vending sets sold to hobby dealers. The seven unnumbered checklist cards are arbitrarily assigned numbers 652 through 658 and are listed at the end of the list below. The designs on the fronts of the Donruss cards changed considerably from the past two years. The backs contain statistics and are printed in green and black ink. The cards were distributed with a 63-piece puzzle of Duke Snider. There are no extra variation cards included in the complete set price below.

	MINT	EXC	G-VG
COMPLETE SET (658)	225.00	90.00	22.00
COMMON PLAYER (1-660)	.10	.04	.01
□ 1A Robin Yount DK ERR (Perez Steel)	.75	.20	.04
□ 1B Robin Yount DK COR	1.50	.60	.15
□ 2A Dave Concepcion DK ERR (Perez Steel)	.15	.06	.01
□ 2B Dave Concepcion DK COR	.30	.12	.03
□ 3A Dwayne Murphy DK ERR (Perez Steel)	.15	.06	.01
□ 3B Dwayne Murphy DK COR	.30	.12	.03
□ 4A John Castino DK ERR (Perez Steel)	.15	.06	.01
□ 4B John Castino DK COR	.30	.12	.03
□ 5A Leon Durham DK ERR (Perez Steel)	.15	.06	.01
□ 5B Leon Durham DK COR	.30	.12	.03
□ 6A Rusty Staub DK ERR (Perez Steel)	.15	.06	.01
□ 6B Rusty Staub DK COR	.30	.12	.03
□ 7A Jack Clark DK ERR (Perez Steel)	.40	.16	.04
□ 7B Jack Clark DK COR	.80	.32	.08
□ 8A Dave Dravecky DK ERR (Perez Steel)	.15	.06	.01
□ 8B Dave Dravecky DK COR	.30	.12	.03
□ 9A Al Oliver DK ERR (Perez Steel)	.15	.06	.01
□ 9B Al Oliver DK COR	.30	.12	.03
□ 10A Dave Righetti DK ERR (Perez Steel)	.25	.10	.02
□ 10B Dave Righetti DK COR	.50	.20	.05
□ 11A Hal McRae DK ERR (Perez Steel)	.15	.06	.01
□ 11B Hal McRae DK COR	.30	.12	.03
□ 12A Ray Knight DK ERR (Perez Steel)	.15	.06	.01
□ 12B Ray Knight DK COR	.30	.12	.03
□ 13A Bruce Sutter DK ERR (Perez Steel)	.15	.06	.01
□ 13B Bruce Sutter DK COR	.30	.12	.03
□ 14A Bob Horner DK ERR (Perez Steel)	.20	.08	.02
□ 14B Bob Horner DK COR	.40	.16	.04
□ 15A Lance Parrish DK ERR (Perez Steel)	.30	.12	.03
□ 15B Lance Parrish DK COR	.60	.24	.06

□ 16A Matt Young DK ERR ..... .15 .06 .01
(Perez Steel)
□ 16B Matt Young DK COR .... .30 .12 .03
□ 17A Fred Lynn DK ERR .... .20 .08 .02
(Perez Steel)
(A's logo on back)
□ 17B Fred Lynn DK COR ...... .40 .16 .04
□ 18A Ron Kittle DK ERR .... .20 .08 .02
(Perez Steel)
□ 18B Ron Kittle DK COR ...... .40 .16 .04
□ 19A Jim Clancy DK ERR ...... .15 .06 .01
(Perez Steel)
□ 19B Jim Clancy DK COR ..... .30 .12 .03
□ 20A Bill Madlock DK ERR .... .15 .06 .01
(Perez Steel)
□ 20B Bill Madlock DK COR ... .30 .12 .03
□ 21A Larry Parrish DK .... .15 .06 .01
ERR (Perez Steel)
□ 21B Larry Parrish DK .... .30 .12 .03
COR
□ 22A Eddie Murray DK ERR .. 1.00 .40 .10
(Perez Steel)
□ 22B Eddie Murray DK COR . 2.00 .80 .20
□ 23A Mike Schmidt DK ERR . 1.25 .50 .12
(Perez Steel)
□ 23B Mike Schmidt DK COR . 2.50 1.00 .25
□ 24A Pedro Guerrero DK ...... .30 .12 .03
ERR (Perez Steel)
□ 24B Pedro Guerrero DK ...... .60 .24 .06
COR
□ 25A Andre Thornton DK ...... .15 .06 .01
ERR (Perez Steel)
□ 25B Andre Thornton DK ...... .30 .12 .03
COR
□ 26A Wade Boggs DK ERR .... 3.50 1.40 .35
(Perez Steel)
□ 26B Wade Boggs DK COR ... 6.00 2.40 .60
□ 27 Joel Skinner RR .... .25 .10 .02
□ 28 Tommy Dunbar RR .... .15 .06 .01
□ 29A Mike Stenhouse RR ...... .25 .10 .02
ERR (no back number)
□ 29B Mike Stenhouse RR ..... 2.50 1.00 .25
COR (number on back)
□ 30A Ron Darling RR ERR ..... 6.00 2.40 .60
(no number on back)
□ 30B Ron Darling RR COR 10.00 4.00 1.00
□ 31 Dion James RR .... .75 .30 .07
□ 32 Tony Fernandez RR .... 7.50 3.00 .75
□ 33 Angel Salazar RR .... .15 .06 .01
□ 34 Kevin McReynolds RR 11.00 4.50 1.10
□ 35 Dick Schofield RR .... .75 .30 .07
□ 36 Brad Komminsk RR .... .20 .08 .02
□ 37 Tim Teufel RR .... .45 .18 .04
□ 38 Doug Frobel RR .... .15 .06 .01
□ 39 Greg Gagne RR .... .45 .18 .04
□ 40 Mike Fuentes RR .... .15 .06 .01
□ 41 Joe Carter RR 11.00 4.50 1.10
□ 42 Mike Brown RR .... .15 .06 .01
(Angels OF)
□ 43 Mike Jeffcoat RR .... .15 .06 .01
□ 44 Sid Fernandez RR .... 5.00 2.00 .50
□ 45 Brian Dayett RR .... .20 .08 .02
□ 46 Chris Smith RR .... .15 .06 .01
□ 47 Eddie Murray .... 1.00 .40 .10
□ 48 Robin Yount .... .65 .26 .06
□ 49 Lance Parrish .... .35 .14 .03
□ 50 Jim Rice .... .45 .18 .04
□ 51 Dave Winfield .... .85 .34 .08
□ 52 Fernando Valenzuela ...... .45 .18 .04
□ 53 George Brett .... 1.25 .50 .12
□ 54 Rickey Henderson .... 1.25 .50 .12
□ 55 Gary Carter .... .65 .26 .06
□ 56 Buddy Bell .... .15 .06 .01
□ 57 Reggie Jackson .... 1.25 .50 .12
□ 58 Harold Baines .... .25 .10 .02
□ 59 Ozzie Smith .... .40 .16 .04
□ 60 Nolan Ryan .... .85 .34 .08
□ 61 Pete Rose .... 2.50 1.00 .25
□ 62 Ron Oester .... .10 .04 .01
□ 63 Steve Garvey .... .80 .32 .08
□ 64 Jason Thompson .... .10 .04 .01
□ 65 Jack Clark .... .35 .14 .03
□ 66 Dale Murphy .... 1.50 .60 .15
□ 67 Leon Durham .... .15 .06 .01
□ 68 Darryl Strawberry 27.00 10.00 2.50
□ 69 Richie Zisk .... .10 .04 .01
□ 70 Kent Hrbek .... .50 .20 .05
□ 71 Dave Stieb .... .25 .10 .02
□ 72 Ken Schrom .... .10 .04 .01
□ 73 George Bell .... 1.50 .60 .15
□ 74 John Moses .... .15 .06 .01
□ 75 Ed Lynch .... .10 .04 .01
□ 76 Chuck Rainey .... .10 .04 .01
□ 77 Biff Pocoroba .... .10 .04 .01
□ 78 Cecilio Guante .... .10 .04 .01
□ 79 Jim Barr .... .10 .04 .01
□ 80 Kurt Bevacqua .... .10 .04 .01
□ 81 Tom Foley .... .10 .04 .01
□ 82 Joe Lefebvre .... .10 .04 .01
□ 83 Andy Van Slyke .... 4.00 1.60 .40
□ 84 Bob Lillis MG .... .10 .04 .01
□ 85 Rick Adams .... .10 .04 .01
□ 86 Jerry Hairston .... .10 .04 .01
□ 87 Bob James .... .20 .08 .02
□ 88 Joe Altobelli MG .... .10 .04 .01
□ 89 Ed Romero .... .10 .04 .01
□ 90 John Grubb .... .10 .04 .01
□ 91 John Henry Johnson ...... .10 .04 .01
□ 92 Juan Espino .... .10 .04 .01
□ 93 Candy Maldonado .... .25 .10 .02
□ 94 Andre Thornton .... .15 .06 .01
□ 95 Onix Concepcion .... .10 .04 .01
□ 96 Donnie Hill .... .15 .06 .01
(listed as P,
should be 2B)
□ 97 Andre Dawson UER .... .65 .26 .06
(wrong middle name,
should be Nolan)
□ 98 Frank Tanana .... .15 .06 .01
□ 99 Curt Wilkerson .... .15 .06 .01
□ 100 Larry Gura .... .10 .04 .01
□ 101 Dwayne Murphy .... .10 .04 .01
□ 102 Tom Brennan .... .10 .04 .01
□ 103 Dave Righetti .... .30 .12 .03
□ 104 Steve Sax .... .40 .16 .04
□ 105 Dan Petry .... .15 .06 .01
□ 106 Cal Ripken .... 1.25 .50 .12
□ 107 Paul Molitor .... .30 .12 .03
□ 108 Fred Lynn .... .25 .10 .02
□ 109 Neil Allen .... .10 .04 .01
□ 110 Joe Niekro .... .15 .06 .01
□ 111 Steve Carlton .... .65 .26 .06
□ 112 Terry Kennedy .... .15 .06 .01
□ 113 Bill Madlock .... .20 .08 .02
□ 114 Chili Davis .... .25 .10 .02
□ 115 Jim Gantner .... .10 .04 .01
□ 116 Tom Seaver .... .75 .30 .07
□ 117 Bill Buckner .... .20 .08 .02
□ 118 Bill Caudill .... .10 .04 .01
□ 119 Jim Clancy .... .10 .04 .01
□ 120 John Castino .... .10 .04 .01
□ 121 Dave Concepcion .... .20 .08 .02
□ 122 Greg Luzinski .... .20 .08 .02
□ 123 Mike Boddicker .... .20 .08 .02
□ 124 Pete Ladd .... .10 .04 .01
□ 125 Juan Berenguer .... .10 .04 .01
□ 126 John Montefusco .... .10 .04 .01
□ 127 Ed Jurak .... .10 .04 .01
□ 128 Tom Niedenfuer .... .15 .06 .01
□ 129 Bert Blyleven .... .20 .08 .02
□ 130 Bud Black .... .10 .04 .01
□ 131 Gorman Heimueller .... .10 .04 .01
□ 132 Dan Schatzeder .... .10 .04 .01
□ 133 Ron Jackson .... .10 .04 .01
□ 134 Tom Henke .... .85 .34 .08
□ 135 Kevin Hickey .... .10 .04 .01
□ 136 Mike Scott .... .35 .14 .03
□ 137 Bo Diaz .... .10 .04 .01
□ 138 Glenn Brummer .... .10 .04 .01
□ 139 Sid Monge .... .10 .04 .01
□ 140 Rich Gale .... .10 .04 .01
□ 141 Brett Butler .... .20 .08 .02
□ 142 Brian Harper .... .15 .06 .01
□ 143 John Rabb .... .10 .04 .01
□ 144 Gary Woods .... .10 .04 .01
□ 145 Pat Putnam .... .10 .04 .01
□ 146 Jim Acker .... .15 .06 .01
□ 147 Mickey Hatcher .... .20 .08 .02
□ 148 Todd Cruz .... .10 .04 .01
□ 149 Tom Tellmann .... .10 .04 .01
□ 150 John Wockenfuss .... .10 .04 .01
□ 151 Wade Boggs 10.00 4.00 1.00
□ 152 Don Baylor .... .20 .08 .02
□ 153 Bob Welch .... .15 .06 .01
□ 154 Alan Bannister .... .10 .04 .01
□ 155 Willie Aikens .... .10 .04 .01
□ 156 Jeff Burroughs .... .10 .04 .01
□ 157 Bryan Little .... .10 .04 .01
□ 158 Bob Boone .... .20 .08 .02
□ 159 Dave Hostetler .... .10 .04 .01
□ 160 Jerry Dybzinski .... .10 .04 .01
□ 161 Mike Madden .... .15 .06 .01
□ 162 Luis DeLeon .... .10 .04 .01
□ 163 Willie Hernandez .... .25 .10 .02
□ 164 Frank Pastore .... .10 .04 .01
□ 165 Rick Camp .... .10 .04 .01
□ 166 Lee Mazzilli .... .10 .04 .01
□ 167 Scot Thompson .... .10 .04 .01
□ 168 Bob Forsch .... .10 .04 .01
□ 169 Mike Flanagan .... .15 .06 .01

□ 170 Rick Manning .10 .04 .01
□ 171 Chet Lemon .15 .06 .01
□ 172 Jerry Remy .10 .04 .01
□ 173 Ron Guidry .25 .10 .02
□ 174 Pedro Guerrero .45 .18 .04
□ 175 Willie Wilson .20 .08 .02
□ 176 Carney Lansford .20 .08 .02
□ 177 Al Oliver .20 .08 .02
□ 178 Jim Sundberg .10 .04 .01
□ 179 Bobby Grich .15 .06 .01
□ 180 Rich Dotson .15 .06 .01
□ 181 Joaquin Andujar .15 .06 .01
□ 182 Jose Cruz .15 .06 .01
□ 183 Mike Schmidt 1.50 .60 .15
□ 184 Gary Redus .40 .16 .04
□ 185 Garry Templeton .15 .06 .01
□ 186 Tony Pena .20 .08 .02
□ 187 Greg Minton .10 .04 .01
□ 188 Phil Niekro .40 .16 .04
□ 189 Ferguson Jenkins .20 .08 .02
□ 190 Mookie Wilson .15 .06 .01
□ 191 Jim Beattie .10 .04 .01
□ 192 Gary Ward .15 .06 .01
□ 193 Jesse Barfield .40 .16 .04
□ 194 Pete Filson .10 .04 .01
□ 195 Roy Lee Jackson .10 .04 .01
□ 196 Rick Sweet .10 .04 .01
□ 197 Jesse Orosco .10 .04 .01
□ 198 Steve Lake .10 .04 .01
□ 199 Ken Dayley .10 .04 .01
□ 200 Manny Sarmiento .10 .04 .01
□ 201 Mark Davis .20 .08 .02
□ 202 Tim Flannery .10 .04 .01
□ 203 Bill Scherrer .10 .04 .01
□ 204 Al Holland .10 .04 .01
□ 205 Dave Von Ohlen .10 .04 .01
□ 206 Mike LaCoss .10 .04 .01
□ 207 Juan Beniquez .10 .04 .01
□ 208 Juan Agosto .10 .04 .01
□ 209 Bobby Ramos .10 .04 .01
□ 210 Al Bumbry .10 .04 .01
□ 211 Mark Brouhard .10 .04 .01
□ 212 Howard Bailey .10 .04 .01
□ 213 Bruce Hurst .30 .12 .03
□ 214 Bob Shirley .10 .04 .01
□ 215 Pat Zachry .10 .04 .01
□ 216 Julio Franco .30 .12 .03
□ 217 Mike Armstrong .10 .04 .01
□ 218 Dave Beard .10 .04 .01
□ 219 Steve Rogers .10 .04 .01
□ 220 John Butcher .10 .04 .01
□ 221 Mike Smithson .15 .06 .01
□ 222 Frank White .15 .06 .01
□ 223 Mike Heath .10 .04 .01
□ 224 Chris Bando .10 .04 .01
□ 225 Roy Smalley .10 .04 .01
□ 226 Dusty Baker .15 .06 .01
□ 227 Lou Whitaker .25 .10 .02
□ 228 John Lowenstein .10 .04 .01
□ 229 Ben Oglivie .15 .06 .01
□ 230 Doug DeCinces .15 .06 .01
□ 231 Lonnie Smith .15 .06 .01
□ 232 Ray Knight .15 .06 .01
□ 233 Gary Matthews .15 .06 .01
□ 234 Juan Bonilla .10 .04 .01
□ 235 Rod Scurry .10 .04 .01
□ 236 Atlee Hammaker .15 .06 .01
□ 237 Mike Caldwell .10 .04 .01
□ 238 Keith Hernandez .45 .18 .04
□ 239 Larry Bowa .15 .06 .01
□ 240 Tony Bernazard .10 .04 .01
□ 241 Damaso Garcia .10 .04 .01
□ 242 Tom Brunansky .30 .12 .03
□ 243 Dan Driessen .10 .04 .01
□ 244 Ron Kittle .30 .12 .03
□ 245 Tim Stoddard .10 .04 .01
□ 246 Bob L. Gibson .15 .06 .01
(Brewers Pitcher)
□ 247 Marty Castillo .10 .04 .01
□ 248 Don Mattingly 65.00 26.00 6.50
("traiing" on back)
□ 249 Jeff Newman .10 .04 .01
□ 250 Alejandro Pena .45 .18 .04
□ 251 Toby Harrah .15 .06 .01
□ 252 Cesar Geronimo .10 .04 .01
□ 253 Tom Underwood .10 .04 .01
□ 254 Doug Flynn .10 .04 .01
□ 255 Andy Hassler .10 .04 .01
□ 256 Odell Jones .10 .04 .01
□ 257 Rudy Law .10 .04 .01
□ 258 Harry Spilman .10 .04 .01
□ 259 Marty Bystrom .10 .04 .01
□ 260 Dave Rucker .10 .04 .01
□ 261 Ruppert Jones .10 .04 .01
□ 262 Jeff R. Jones .10 .04 .01
(Reds OF)
□ 263 Gerald Perry 2.00 .80 .20
□ 264 Gene Tenace .15 .06 .01
□ 265 Brad Wellman .10 .04 .01
□ 266 Dickie Noles .10 .04 .01
□ 267 Jamie Allen .10 .04 .01
□ 268 Jim Gott .15 .06 .01
□ 269 Ron Davis .10 .04 .01
□ 270 Benny Ayala .10 .04 .01
□ 271 Ned Yost .10 .04 .01
□ 272 Dave Rozema .10 .04 .01
□ 273 Dave Stapleton .10 .04 .01
□ 274 Lou Piniella .15 .06 .01
□ 275 Jose Morales .10 .04 .01
□ 276 Brod Perkins .10 .04 .01
□ 277 Butch Davis .15 .06 .01
□ 278 Tony Phillips .15 .06 .01
□ 279 Jeff Reardon .15 .06 .01
□ 280 Ken Forsch .10 .04 .01
□ 281 Pete O'Brien 1.75 .70 .17
□ 282 Tom Paciorek .10 .04 .01
□ 283 Frank LaCorte .10 .04 .01
□ 284 Tim Lollar .10 .04 .01
□ 285 Greg Gross .10 .04 .01
□ 286 Alex Trevino .10 .04 .01
□ 287 Gene Garber .10 .04 .01
□ 288 Dave Parker .30 .12 .03
□ 289 Lee Smith .20 .08 .02
□ 290 Dave LaPoint .15 .06 .01
□ 291 John Shelby .60 .24 .06
□ 292 Charlie Moore .10 .04 .01
□ 293 Alan Trammell .50 .20 .05
□ 294 Tony Armas .15 .06 .01
□ 295 Shane Rawley .15 .06 .01
□ 296 Greg Brock .15 .06 .01
□ 297 Hal McRae .15 .06 .01
□ 298 Mike Davis .15 .06 .01
□ 299 Tim Raines .75 .30 .07
□ 300 Bucky Dent .15 .06 .01
□ 301 Tommy John .25 .10 .02
□ 302 Carlton Fisk .25 .10 .02
□ 303 Darrell Porter .10 .04 .01
□ 304 Dickie Thon .15 .06 .01
□ 305 Garry Maddox .15 .06 .01
□ 306 Cesar Cedeno .15 .06 .01
□ 307 Gary Lucas .10 .04 .01
□ 308 Johnny Ray .25 .10 .02
□ 309 Andy McGaffigan .10 .04 .01
□ 310 Claudell Washington .15 .06 .01
□ 311 Ryne Sandberg 2.00 .80 .20
□ 312 George Foster .25 .10 .02
□ 313 Spike Owen .30 .12 .03
□ 314 Gary Gaetti .90 .36 .09
□ 315 Willie Upshaw .15 .06 .01
□ 316 Al Williams .10 .04 .01
□ 317 Jorge Orta .10 .04 .01
□ 318 Orlando Mercado .10 .04 .01
□ 319 Junior Ortiz .10 .04 .01
□ 320 Mike Proly .10 .04 .01
□ 321 Randy Johnson .10 .04 .01
□ 322 Jim Morrison .10 .04 .01
□ 323 Max Venable .10 .04 .01
□ 324 Tony Gwynn 4.00 1.60 .40
□ 325 Duane Walker .10 .04 .01
□ 326 Ozzie Virgil .10 .04 .01
□ 327 Jeff Lahti .10 .04 .01
□ 328 Bill Dawley .15 .06 .01
□ 329 Rob Wilfong .10 .04 .01
□ 330 Marc Hill .10 .04 .01
□ 331 Ray Burris .10 .04 .01
□ 332 Allan Ramirez .10 .04 .01
□ 333 Chuck Porter .10 .04 .01
□ 334 Wayne Krenchicki .10 .04 .01
□ 335 Gary Allenson .10 .04 .01
□ 336 Bobby Meacham .15 .06 .01
□ 337 Joe Beckwith .10 .04 .01
□ 338 Rick Sutcliffe .25 .10 .02
□ 339 Mark Huismann .15 .06 .01
□ 340 Tim Conroy .15 .06 .01
□ 341 Scott Sanderson .10 .04 .01
□ 342 Larry Biittner .10 .04 .01
□ 343 Dave Stewart .25 .10 .02
□ 344 Darryl Motley .10 .04 .01
□ 345 Chris Codiroli .15 .06 .01
□ 346 Rich Behenna .10 .04 .01
□ 347 Andre Robertson .10 .04 .01
□ 348 Mike Marshall .20 .08 .02
□ 349 Larry Herndon .10 .04 .01
□ 350 Rich Dauer .10 .04 .01
□ 351 Cecil Cooper .15 .06 .01
□ 352 Rod Carew .65 .26 .06
□ 353 Willie McGee .40 .16 .04
□ 354 Phil Garner .10 .04 .01
□ 355 Joe Morgan .40 .16 .04
□ 356 Luis Salazar .15 .06 .01

□ 357 John Candelaria	.15	.06	.01
□ 358 Bill Laskey	.10	.04	.01
□ 359 Bob McClure	.10	.04	.01
□ 360 Dave Kingman	.20	.08	.02
□ 361 Ron Cey	.15	.06	.01
□ 362 Matt Young	.15	.06	.01
□ 363 Lloyd Moseby	.20	.08	.02
□ 364 Frank Viola	1.00	.40	.10
□ 365 Eddie Milner	.10	.04	.01
□ 366 Floyd Bannister	.10	.04	.01
□ 367 Dan Ford	.10	.04	.01
□ 368 Moose Haas	.10	.04	.01
□ 369 Doug Bair	.10	.04	.01
□ 370 Ray Fontenot	.10	.04	.01
□ 371 Luis Aponte	.10	.04	.01
□ 372 Jack Fimple	.10	.04	.01
□ 373 Neal Heaton	.20	.08	.02
□ 374 Greg Pryor	.10	.04	.01
□ 375 Wayne Gross	.10	.04	.01
□ 376 Charlie Lea	.10	.04	.01
□ 377 Steve Lubratich	.10	.04	.01
□ 378 Jon Matlack	.10	.04	.01
□ 379 Julio Cruz	.10	.04	.01
□ 380 John Mizerock	.10	.04	.01
□ 381 Kevin Gross	.40	.16	.04
□ 382 Mike Ramsey	.10	.04	.01
□ 383 Doug Gwosdz	.10	.04	.01
□ 384 Kelly Paris	.15	.06	.01
□ 385 Pete Falcone	.10	.04	.01
□ 386 Milt May	.10	.04	.01
□ 387 Fred Breining	.10	.04	.01
□ 388 Craig Lefferts	.15	.06	.01
□ 389 Steve Henderson	.10	.04	.01
□ 390 Randy Moffitt	.10	.04	.01
□ 391 Ron Washington	.10	.04	.01
□ 392 Gary Roenicke	.10	.04	.01
□ 393 Tom Candiotti	.35	.14	.03
□ 394 Larry Pashnick	.10	.04	.01
□ 395 Dwight Evans	.25	.10	.02
□ 396 Goose Gossage	.20	.08	.02
□ 397 Derrel Thomas	.10	.04	.01
□ 398 Juan Eichelberger	.10	.04	.01
□ 399 Leon Roberts	.10	.04	.01
□ 400 Davey Lopes	.15	.06	.01
□ 401 Bill Gullickson	.10	.04	.01
□ 402 Geoff Zahn	.10	.04	.01
□ 403 Billy Sample	.10	.04	.01
□ 404 Mike Squires	.10	.04	.01
□ 405 Craig Reynolds	.10	.04	.01
□ 406 Eric Show	.15	.06	.01
□ 407 John Denny	.15	.06	.01
□ 408 Dann Bilardello	.10	.04	.01
□ 409 Bruce Benedict	.10	.04	.01
□ 410 Kent Tekulve	.15	.06	.01
□ 411 Mel Hall	.15	.06	.01
□ 412 John Stuper	.10	.04	.01
□ 413 Rick Dempsey	.10	.04	.01
□ 414 Don Sutton	.40	.16	.04
□ 415 Jack Morris	.35	.14	.03
□ 416 John Tudor	.30	.12	.03
□ 417 Willie Randolph	.20	.08	.02
□ 418 Jerry Reuss	.15	.06	.01
□ 419 Don Slaught	.15	.06	.01
□ 420 Steve McCatty	.10	.04	.01
□ 421 Tim Wallach	.25	.10	.02
□ 422 Larry Parrish	.15	.06	.01
□ 423 Brian Downing	.15	.06	.01
□ 424 Britt Burns	.15	.06	.01
□ 425 David Green	.10	.04	.01
□ 426 Jerry Mumphrey	.10	.04	.01
□ 427 Ivan DeJesus	.10	.04	.01
□ 428 Mario Soto	.10	.04	.01
□ 429 Gene Richards	.10	.04	.01
□ 430 Dale Berra	.10	.04	.01
□ 431 Darrell Evans	.20	.08	.02
□ 432 Glenn Hubbard	.10	.04	.01
□ 433 Jody Davis	.15	.06	.01
□ 434 Danny Heep	.10	.04	.01
□ 435 Ed Nunez	.20	.08	.02
□ 436 Bobby Castillo	.10	.04	.01
□ 437 Ernie Whitt	.15	.06	.01
□ 438 Scott Ullger	.10	.04	.01
□ 439 Doyle Alexander	.20	.08	.02
□ 440 Domingo Ramos	.10	.04	.01
□ 441 Craig Swan	.10	.04	.01
□ 442 Warren Brusstar	.10	.04	.01
□ 443 Len Barker	.10	.04	.01
□ 444 Mike Easler	.10	.04	.01
□ 445 Renie Martin	.10	.04	.01
□ 446 Dennis Rasmussen	.90	.36	.09
□ 447 Ted Power	.15	.06	.01
□ 448 Charlie Hudson	.30	.12	.03
□ 449 Danny Cox	.75	.30	.07
□ 450 Kevin Bass	.25	.10	.02
□ 451 Daryl Sconiers	.10	.04	.01
□ 452 Scott Fletcher	.25	.10	.02
□ 453 Bryn Smith	.15	.06	.01
□ 454 Jim Dwyer	.10	.04	.01
□ 455 Rob Picciolo	.10	.04	.01
□ 456 Enos Cabell	.10	.04	.01
□ 457 Dennis Boyd	.85	.34	.08
□ 458 Butch Wynegar	.10	.04	.01
□ 459 Burt Hooton	.10	.04	.01
□ 460 Ron Hassey	.10	.04	.01
□ 461 Danny Jackson	3.50	1.40	.35
□ 462 Bob Kearney	.10	.04	.01
□ 463 Terry Francona	.10	.04	.01
□ 464 Wayne Tolleson	.10	.04	.01
□ 465 Mickey Rivers	.10	.04	.01
□ 466 John Wathan	.10	.04	.01
□ 467 Bill Almon	.10	.04	.01
□ 468 George Vukovich	.10	.04	.01
□ 469 Steve Kemp	.15	.06	.01
□ 470 Ken Landreaux	.10	.04	.01
□ 471 Milt Wilcox	.10	.04	.01
□ 472 Tippy Martinez	.10	.04	.01
□ 473 Ted Simmons	.20	.08	.02
□ 474 Tim Foli	.10	.04	.01
□ 475 George Hendrick	.15	.06	.01
□ 476 Terry Puhl	.10	.04	.01
□ 477 Von Hayes	.20	.08	.02
□ 478 Bobby Brown	.10	.04	.01
□ 479 Lee Lacy	.10	.04	.01
□ 480 Joel Youngblood	.10	.04	.01
□ 481 Jim Slaton	.10	.04	.01
□ 482 Mike Fitzgerald	.10	.04	.01
□ 483 Keith Moreland	.10	.04	.01
□ 484 Ron Roenicke	.10	.04	.01
□ 485 Luis Leal	.10	.04	.01
□ 486 Bryan Oelkers	.10	.04	.01
□ 487 Bruce Berenyi	.10	.04	.01
□ 488 LaMarr Hoyt	.15	.06	.01
□ 489 Joe Nolan	.10	.04	.01
□ 490 Marshall Edwards	.10	.04	.01
□ 491 Mike Laga	.10	.04	.01
□ 492 Rick Cerone	.10	.04	.01
□ 493 Rick Miller (listed as Mike on card front)	.10	.04	.01
□ 494 Rick Honeycutt	.10	.04	.01
□ 495 Mike Hargrove	.10	.04	.01
□ 496 Joe Simpson	.10	.04	.01
□ 497 Keith Atherton	.10	.04	.01
□ 498 Chris Welsh	.10	.04	.01
□ 499 Bruce Kison	.10	.04	.01
□ 500 Bobby Johnson	.10	.04	.01
□ 501 Jerry Koosman	.15	.06	.01
□ 502 Frank DiPino	.10	.04	.01
□ 503 Tony Perez	.20	.08	.02
□ 504 Ken Oberkfell	.10	.04	.01
□ 505 Mark Thurmond	.15	.06	.01
□ 506 Joe Price	.10	.04	.01
□ 507 Pascual Perez	.20	.08	.02
□ 508 Marvell Wynne	.15	.06	.01
□ 509 Mike Krukow	.15	.06	.01
□ 510 Dick Ruthven	.10	.04	.01
□ 511 Al Cowens	.10	.04	.01
□ 512 Cliff Johnson	.10	.04	.01
□ 513 Randy Bush	.30	.12	.03
□ 514 Sammy Stewart	.10	.04	.01
□ 515 Bill Schroeder	.15	.06	.01
□ 516 Aurelio Lopez	.10	.04	.01
□ 517 Mike Brown (Red Sox pitcher)	.15	.06	.01
□ 518 Graig Nettles	.20	.08	.02
□ 519 Dave Sax	.10	.04	.01
□ 520 Gerry Willard	.10	.04	.01
□ 521 Paul Splittorff	.10	.04	.01
□ 522 Tom Burgmeier	.10	.04	.01
□ 523 Chris Speier	.10	.04	.01
□ 524 Bobby Clark	.10	.04	.01
□ 525 George Wright	.10	.04	.01
□ 526 Dennis Lamp	.10	.04	.01
□ 527 Tony Scott	.10	.04	.01
□ 528 Ed Whitson	.10	.04	.01
□ 529 Ron Reed	.10	.04	.01
□ 530 Charlie Puleo	.10	.04	.01
□ 531 Jerry Royster	.10	.04	.01
□ 532 Don Robinson	.10	.04	.01
□ 533 Steve Trout	.10	.04	.01
□ 534 Bruce Sutter	.20	.08	.02
□ 535 Bob Horner	.20	.08	.02
□ 536 Pat Tabler	.20	.08	.02
□ 537 Chris Chambliss	.15	.06	.01
□ 538 Bob Ojeda	.20	.08	.02
□ 539 Alan Ashby	.10	.04	.01
□ 540 Jay Johnstone	.15	.06	.01
□ 541 Bob Dernier	.10	.04	.01
□ 542 Brook Jacoby	1.75	.70	.17
□ 543 U.L. Washington	.10	.04	.01

□ 544	Danny Darwin	.10	.04	.01
□ 545	Kiko Garcia	.10	.04	.01
□ 546	Vance Law	.20	.08	.02
□ 547	Tug McGraw	.20	.08	.02
□ 548	Dave Smith	.15	.06	.01
□ 549	Len Matuszek	.10	.04	.01
□ 550	Tom Hume	.10	.04	.01
□ 551	Dave Dravecky	.15	.06	.01
□ 552	Rick Rhoden	.15	.06	.01
□ 553	Duane Kuiper	.10	.04	.01
□ 554	Rusty Staub	.20	.08	.02
□ 555	Bill Campbell	.10	.04	.01
□ 556	Mike Torrez	.10	.04	.01
□ 557	Dave Henderson	.30	.12	.03
□ 558	Len Whitehouse	.10	.04	.01
□ 559	Barry Bonnell	.10	.04	.01
□ 560	Rick Lysander	.10	.04	.01
□ 561	Garth Iorg	.10	.04	.01
□ 562	Bryan Clark	.10	.04	.01
□ 563	Brian Giles	.10	.04	.01
□ 564	Vern Ruhle	.10	.04	.01
□ 565	Steve Bedrosian	.30	.12	.03
□ 566	Larry McWilliams	.10	.04	.01
□ 567	Jeff Leonard UER (listed as P on card front)	.20	.08	.02
□ 568	Alan Wiggins	.10	.04	.01
□ 569	Jeff Russell	.30	.12	.03
□ 570	Salome Barojas	.10	.04	.01
□ 571	Dane Iorg	.10	.04	.01
□ 572	Bob Knepper	.15	.06	.01
□ 573	Gary Lavelle	.10	.04	.01
□ 574	Gorman Thomas	.15	.06	.01
□ 575	Manny Trillo	.10	.04	.01
□ 576	Jim Palmer	.50	.20	.05
□ 577	Dale Murray	.10	.04	.01
□ 578	Tom Brookens	.10	.04	.01
□ 579	Rich Gedman	.15	.06	.01
□ 580	Bill Doran	1.50	.60	.15
□ 581	Steve Yeager	.10	.04	.01
□ 582	Dan Spillner	.10	.04	.01
□ 583	Dan Quisenberry	.20	.08	.02
□ 584	Rance Mulliniks	.10	.04	.01
□ 585	Storm Davis	.15	.06	.01
□ 586	Dave Schmidt	.15	.06	.01
□ 587	Bill Russell	.15	.06	.01
□ 588	Pat Sheridan	.20	.08	.02
□ 589	Rafael Ramirez ERR (A's on front)	.15	.06	.01
□ 590	Bud Anderson	.10	.04	.01
□ 591	George Frazier	.10	.04	.01
□ 592	Lee Tunnell	.15	.06	.01
□ 593	Kirk Gibson	.60	.24	.06
□ 594	Scott McGregor	.15	.06	.01
□ 595	Bob Bailor	.10	.04	.01
□ 596	Tommy Herr	.15	.06	.01
□ 597	Luis Sanchez	.10	.04	.01
□ 598	Dave Engle	.10	.04	.01
□ 599	Craig McMurtry	.15	.06	.01
□ 600	Carlos Diaz	.10	.04	.01
□ 601	Tom O'Malley	.10	.04	.01
□ 602	Nick Esasky	.40	.16	.04
□ 603	Ron Hodges	.10	.04	.01
□ 604	Ed VandeBerg	.10	.04	.01
□ 605	Alfredo Griffin	.15	.06	.01
□ 606	Glenn Hoffman	.10	.04	.01
□ 607	Hubie Brooks	.20	.08	.02
□ 608	Richard Barnes	.10	.04	.01
□ 609	Greg Walker	.50	.20	.05
□ 610	Ken Singleton	.15	.06	.01
□ 611	Mark Clear	.10	.04	.01
□ 612	Buck Martinez	.10	.04	.01
□ 613	Ken Griffey	.15	.06	.01
□ 614	Reid Nichols	.10	.04	.01
□ 615	Doug Sisk	.10	.04	.01
□ 616	Bob Brenly	.10	.04	.01
□ 617	Joey McLaughlin	.10	.04	.01
□ 618	Glenn Wilson	.15	.06	.01
□ 619	Bob Stoddard	.10	.04	.01
□ 620	Lenn Sakata UER (listed as Len on card front)	.10	.04	.01
□ 621	Mike Young	.45	.18	.04
□ 622	John Stefero	.15	.06	.01
□ 623	Carmelo Martinez	.30	.12	.03
□ 624	Dave Bergman	.10	.04	.01
□ 625	Runnin' Reds (sic, Redbirds) David Green Willie McGee Lonnie Smith Ozzie Smith	.25	.10	.02
□ 626	Rudy May	.10	.04	.01
□ 627	Matt Keough	.10	.04	.01
□ 628	Jose DeLeon	.40	.16	.04
□ 629	Jim Essian	.10	.04	.01
□ 630	Darnell Coles	.40	.16	.04
□ 631	Mike Warren	.15	.06	.01
□ 632	Del Crandall MG	.10	.04	.01
□ 633	Dennis Martinez	.15	.06	.01
□ 634	Mike Moore	.15	.06	.01
□ 635	Lary Sorensen	.10	.04	.01
□ 636	Rick Nelson	.10	.04	.01
□ 637	Omar Moreno	.10	.04	.01
□ 638	Charlie Hough	.15	.06	.01
□ 639	Dennis Eckersley	.30	.12	.03
□ 640	Walt Terrell	.35	.14	.03
□ 641	Denny Walling	.10	.04	.01
□ 642	Dave Anderson	.25	.10	.02
□ 643	Jose Oquendo	.40	.16	.04
□ 644	Bob Stanley	.10	.04	.01
□ 645	Dave Geisel	.10	.04	.01
□ 646	Scott Garrelts	.35	.14	.03
□ 647	Gary Pettis	.45	.18	.04
□ 648	Duke Snider Puzzle Card	.10	.04	.01
□ 649	Johnnie LeMaster	.10	.04	.01
□ 650	Dave Collins	.10	.04	.01
□ 651	The Chicken	.20	.08	.02
□ 652	DK Checklist (unnumbered)	.10	.01	.00
□ 653	Checklist 1-130 (unnumbered)	.08	.01	.00
□ 654	Checklist 131-234 (unnumbered)	.08	.01	.00
□ 655	Checklist 235-338 (unnumbered)	.08	.01	.00
□ 656	Checklist 339-442 (unnumbered)	.08	.01	.00
□ 657	Checklist 443-546 (unnumbered)	.08	.01	.00
□ 658	Checklist 547-651 (unnumbered)	.08	.01	.00
□ A	Living Legends A Gaylord Perry Rollie Fingers	2.00	.80	.20
□ B	Living Legends B Carl Yastrzemski Johnny Bench	5.00	2.00	.50

1984 Donruss Action All-Stars

The cards in this 60-card set measure 3 1/2" by 5". For the second year in a row, Donruss issued a postcard-size card set. The set was distributed with a 63-piece Ted Williams puzzle. Unlike last year, when the fronts of the cards contained both an action and a portrait shot of the player, the fronts of this year's cards contain only an action photo. On the backs, the top section contains the card number and a full-color portrait of the player pictured on the front. The bottom half features the player's career statistics.

		MINT	EXC	G-VG
COMPLETE SET (60)		6.00	2.40	.60
COMMON PLAYER (1-60)		.05	.02	.00
□ 1	Gary Lavelle	.05	.02	.00
□ 2	Willie McGee	.15	.06	.01
□ 3	Tony Pena	.05	.02	.00
□ 4	Lou Whitaker	.10	.04	.01
□ 5	Robin Yount	.25	.10	.02

6	Doug DeCinces	.05	.02	.00
7	John Castino	.05	.02	.00
8	Terry Kennedy	.05	.02	.00
9	Rickey Henderson	.40	.16	.04
10	Bob Horner	.15	.06	.01
11	Harold Baines	.10	.04	.01
12	Buddy Bell	.05	.02	.00
13	Fernando Valenzuela	.20	.08	.02
14	Nolan Ryan	.35	.14	.03
15	Andre Thornton	.05	.02	.00
16	Gary Redus	.05	.02	.00
17	Pedro Guerrero	.20	.08	.02
18	Andre Dawson	.25	.10	.02
19	Dave Stieb	.10	.04	.01
20	Cal Ripken	.35	.14	.03
21	Ken Griffey	.05	.02	.00
22	Wade Boggs	1.00	.40	.10
23	Keith Hernandez	.25	.10	.02
24	Steve Carlton	.35	.14	.03
25	Hal McRae	.05	.02	.00
26	John Lowenstein	.05	.02	.00
27	Fred Lynn	.10	.04	.01
28	Bill Buckner	.10	.04	.01
29	Chris Chambliss	.05	.02	.00
30	Richie Zisk	.05	.02	.00
31	Jack Clark	.20	.08	.02
32	George Hendrick	.05	.02	.00
33	Bill Madlock	.05	.02	.00
34	Lance Parrish	.15	.06	.01
35	Paul Molitor	.20	.08	.02
36	Reggie Jackson	.50	.20	.05
37	Kent Hrbek	.20	.08	.02
38	Steve Garvey	.40	.16	.04
39	Carney Lansford	.10	.04	.01
40	Dale Murphy	.50	.20	.05
41	Greg Luzinski	.10	.04	.01
42	Larry Parrish	.05	.02	.00
43	Ryne Sandberg	.45	.18	.04
44	Dickie Thon	.05	.02	.00
45	Bert Blyleven	.10	.04	.01
46	Ron Oester	.05	.02	.00
47	Dusty Baker	.05	.02	.00
48	Steve Rogers	.05	.02	.00
49	Jim Clancy	.05	.02	.00
50	Eddie Murray	.40	.16	.04
51	Ron Guidry	.20	.08	.02
52	Jim Rice	.25	.10	.02
53	Tom Seaver	.35	.14	.03
54	Pete Rose	.75	.30	.07
55	George Brett	.45	.18	.04
56	Dan Quisenberry	.10	.04	.01
57	Mike Schmidt	.50	.20	.05
58	Ted Simmons	.10	.04	.01
59	Dave Righetti	.15	.06	.01
60	Checklist card	.05	.01	.00

1984 Donruss Champions

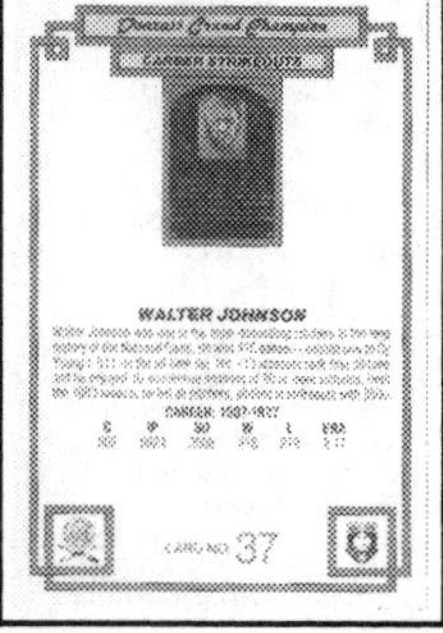

The cards in this 60-card set measure 3 1/2" by 5". The 1984 Donruss Champions set is a hybrid photo/artwork issue. Grand Champions, listed GC in the checklist below, feature the artwork of Dick Perez of Perez-Steele Galleries. Current players in the set feature photographs. The theme of this postcard-size set features a Grand Champion and those current players that are directly behind him in a baseball statistical category, for example, Season Home Runs (1-7), Career Home Runs (8-13), Season Batting Average (14-19), Career Batting Average (20-25), Career Hits (26-30), Career Victories (31-36), Career Strikeouts (37-42), Most Valuable Players (43-49), World Series stars (50-54), and All-Star heroes (55-59). The cards were issued in cello packs with pieces of the Duke Snider puzzle.

		MINT	EXC	G-VG
	COMPLETE SET (60)	5.50	2.20	.55
	COMMON PLAYER (1-60)	.05	.02	.00
1	Babe Ruth GC	.75	.30	.07
2	George Foster	.10	.04	.01
3	Dave Kingman	.10	.04	.01
4	Jim Rice	.20	.08	.02
5	Gorman Thomas	.05	.02	.00
6	Ben Oglivie	.05	.02	.00
7	Jeff Burroughs	.05	.02	.00
8	Hank Aaron GC	.30	.12	.03
9	Reggie Jackson	.40	.16	.04
10	Carl Yastrzemski	.50	.20	.05
11	Mike Schmidt	.40	.16	.04
12	Graig Nettles	.10	.04	.01
13	Greg Luzinski	.05	.02	.00
14	Ted Williams GC	.35	.14	.03
15	George Brett	.40	.16	.04
16	Wade Boggs	.75	.30	.07
17	Hal McRae	.05	.02	.00
18	Bill Buckner	.10	.04	.01
19	Eddie Murray	.30	.12	.03
20	Rogers Hornsby GC	.10	.04	.01
21	Rod Carew	.30	.12	.03
22	Bill Madlock	.05	.02	.00
23	Lonnie Smith	.05	.02	.00
24	Cecil Cooper	.10	.04	.01
25	Ken Griffey	.05	.02	.00
26	Ty Cobb GC	.40	.16	.04
27	Pete Rose	.60	.24	.06
28	Rusty Staub	.05	.02	.00
29	Tony Perez	.15	.06	.01
30	Al Oliver	.10	.04	.01
31	Cy Young GC	.10	.04	.01
32	Gaylord Perry	.15	.06	.01
33	Ferguson Jenkins	.10	.04	.01
34	Phil Niekro	.20	.08	.02
35	Jim Palmer	.25	.10	.02
36	Tommy John	.10	.04	.01
37	Walter Johnson GC	.15	.06	.01
38	Steve Carlton	.30	.12	.03
39	Nolan Ryan	.35	.14	.03
40	Tom Seaver	.35	.14	.03
41	Don Sutton	.15	.06	.01
42	Bert Blyleven	.10	.04	.01
43	Frank Robinson GC	.15	.06	.01
44	Joe Morgan	.15	.06	.01
45	Rollie Fingers	.15	.06	.01
46	Keith Hernandez	.25	.10	.02
47	Robin Yount	.25	.10	.02
48	Cal Ripken	.30	.12	.03
49	Dale Murphy	.45	.18	.04
50	Mickey Mantle GC	.75	.30	.07
51	Johnny Bench	.40	.16	.04
52	Carlton Fisk	.10	.04	.01
53	Tug McGraw	.05	.02	.00
54	Paul Molitor	.15	.06	.01
55	Carl Hubbell GC	.10	.04	.01
56	Steve Garvey	.30	.12	.03
57	Dave Parker	.15	.06	.01
58	Gary Carter	.25	.10	.02
59	Fred Lynn	.10	.04	.01
60	Checklist card	.05	.01	.00

1985 Donruss

The cards in this 660-card set measure 2 1/2" by 3 1/2". The 1985 Donruss regular issue cards have fronts that feature jet black borders on which orange lines have been placed. The fronts contain the standard team logo, player's name, position, and Donruss logo. The cards were distributed with puzzle pieces from a Dick Perez rendition of Lou Gehrig. The first 26 cards of the set feature Diamond Kings (DK), for the fourth year in a row; the artwork on the Diamond Kings was again produced by the Perez-

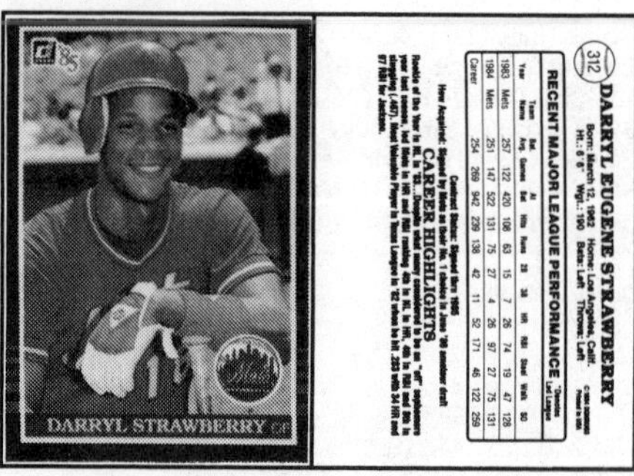

Steele Galleries. Cards 27-46 feature Rated Rookies (RR). The unnumbered checklist cards are arbitrarily numbered below as numbers 654 through 660.

	MINT	EXC	G-VG
COMPLETE SET (660)	135.00	54.00	13.50
COMMON PLAYER (1-660)	.06	.02	.00
☐ 1 Ryne Sandberg DK	.60	.15	.03
☐ 2 Doug DeCinces DK	.10	.04	.01
☐ 3 Richard Dotson DK	.10	.04	.01
☐ 4 Bert Blyleven DK	.15	.06	.01
☐ 5 Lou Whitaker DK	.20	.08	.02
☐ 6 Dan Quisenberry DK	.15	.06	.01
☐ 7 Don Mattingly DK	6.00	2.40	.60
☐ 8 Carney Lansford DK	.15	.06	.01
☐ 9 Frank Tanana DK	.10	.04	.01
☐ 10 Willie Upshaw DK	.10	.04	.01
☐ 11 Claudell Washington DK	.10	.04	.01
☐ 12 Mike Marshall DK	.15	.06	.01
☐ 13 Joaquin Andujar DK	.10	.04	.01
☐ 14 Cal Ripken DK	.50	.20	.05
☐ 15 Jim Rice DK	.35	.14	.03
☐ 16 Don Sutton DK	.25	.10	.02
☐ 17 Frank Viola DK	.45	.18	.04
☐ 18 Alvin Davis DK	.40	.16	.04
☐ 19 Mario Soto DK	.10	.04	.01
☐ 20 Jose Cruz DK	.10	.04	.01
☐ 21 Charlie Lea DK	.10	.04	.01
☐ 22 Jesse Orosco DK	.10	.04	.01
☐ 23 Juan Samuel DK	.30	.12	.03
☐ 24 Tony Pena DK	.15	.06	.01
☐ 25 Tony Gwynn DK	.75	.30	.07
☐ 26 Bob Brenly DK	.10	.04	.01
☐ 27 Danny Tartabull RR	7.00	2.80	.70
☐ 28 Mike Bielecki RR	.15	.06	.01
☐ 29 Steve Lyons RR	.15	.06	.01
☐ 30 Jeff Reed RR	.10	.04	.01
☐ 31 Tony Brewer RR	.10	.04	.01
☐ 32 John Morris RR	.15	.06	.01
☐ 33 Daryl Boston RR	.20	.08	.02
☐ 34 Alfonso Pulido RR	.10	.04	.01
☐ 35 Steve Kiefer RR	.15	.06	.01
☐ 36 Larry Sheets RR	.75	.30	.07
☐ 37 Scott Bradley RR	.30	.12	.03
☐ 38 Calvin Schiraldi RR	.30	.12	.03
☐ 39 Shawon Dunston RR	1.25	.50	.12
☐ 40 Charlie Mitchell RR	.10	.04	.01
☐ 41 Billy Hatcher RR	.90	.36	.09
☐ 42 Russ Stephans RR	.10	.04	.01
☐ 43 Alejandro Sanchez RR	.10	.04	.01
☐ 44 Steve Jeltz RR	.10	.04	.01
☐ 45 Jim Traber RR	.35	.14	.03
☐ 46 Doug Loman RR	.15	.06	.01
☐ 47 Eddie Murray	.50	.20	.05
☐ 48 Robin Yount	.35	.14	.03
☐ 49 Lance Parrish	.25	.10	.02
☐ 50 Jim Rice	.30	.12	.03
☐ 51 Dave Winfield	.40	.16	.04
☐ 52 Fernando Valenzuela	.25	.10	.02
☐ 53 George Brett	.60	.24	.06
☐ 54 Dave Kingman	.15	.06	.01
☐ 55 Gary Carter	.35	.14	.03
☐ 56 Buddy Bell	.12	.05	.01
☐ 57 Reggie Jackson	.50	.20	.05
☐ 58 Harold Baines	.18	.08	.01
☐ 59 Ozzie Smith	.25	.10	.02
☐ 60 Nolan Ryan	.45	.18	.04
☐ 61 Mike Schmidt	.75	.30	.07
☐ 62 Dave Parker	.18	.08	.01
☐ 63 Tony Gwynn	1.00	.40	.10
☐ 64 Tony Pena	.12	.05	.01
☐ 65 Jack Clark	.25	.10	.02
☐ 66 Dale Murphy	.80	.32	.08
☐ 67 Ryne Sandberg	.40	.16	.04
☐ 68 Keith Hernandez	.35	.14	.03
☐ 69 Alvin Davis	2.00	.80	.20
☐ 70 Kent Hrbek	.35	.14	.03
☐ 71 Willie Upshaw	.06	.02	.00
☐ 72 Dave Engle	.06	.02	.00
☐ 73 Alfredo Griffin	.10	.04	.01
☐ 74A Jack Perconte (Career Highlights four lines)	.15	.06	.01
☐ 74B Jack Perconte (Career Highlights three lines)	.15	.06	.01
☐ 75 Jesse Orosco	.06	.02	.00
☐ 76 Jody Davis	.10	.04	.01
☐ 77 Bob Horner	.15	.06	.01
☐ 78 Larry McWilliams	.06	.02	.00
☐ 79 Joel Youngblood	.06	.02	.00
☐ 80 Alan Wiggins	.06	.02	.00
☐ 81 Ron Oester	.06	.02	.00
☐ 82 Ozzie Virgil	.06	.02	.00
☐ 83 Ricky Horton	.20	.08	.02
☐ 84 Bill Doran	.15	.06	.01
☐ 85 Rod Carew	.45	.18	.04
☐ 86 LaMarr Hoyt	.10	.04	.01
☐ 87 Tim Wallach	.15	.06	.01
☐ 88 Mike Flanagan	.10	.04	.01
☐ 89 Jim Sundberg	.06	.02	.00
☐ 90 Chet Lemon	.10	.04	.01
☐ 91 Bob Stanley	.06	.02	.00
☐ 92 Willie Randolph	.10	.04	.01
☐ 93 Bill Russell	.10	.04	.01
☐ 94 Julio Franco	.15	.06	.01
☐ 95 Dan Quisenberry	.15	.06	.01
☐ 96 Bill Caudill	.06	.02	.00
☐ 97 Bill Gullickson	.06	.02	.00
☐ 98 Danny Darwin	.06	.02	.00
☐ 99 Curtis Wilkerson	.06	.02	.00
☐ 100 Bud Black	.06	.02	.00
☐ 101 Tony Phillips	.06	.02	.00
☐ 102 Tony Bernazard	.06	.02	.00
☐ 103 Jay Howell	.10	.04	.01
☐ 104 Burt Hooton	.06	.02	.00
☐ 105 Milt Wilcox	.06	.02	.00
☐ 106 Rich Dauer	.06	.02	.00
☐ 107 Don Sutton	.25	.10	.02
☐ 108 Mike Witt	.12	.05	.01
☐ 109 Bruce Sutter	.12	.05	.01
☐ 110 Enos Cabell	.06	.02	.00
☐ 111 John Denny	.10	.04	.01
☐ 112 Dave Dravecky	.10	.04	.01
☐ 113 Marvell Wynne	.06	.02	.00
☐ 114 Johnnie LeMaster	.06	.02	.00
☐ 115 Chuck Porter	.06	.02	.00
☐ 116 John Gibbons	.10	.04	.01
☐ 117 Keith Moreland	.06	.02	.00
☐ 118 Darnell Coles	.10	.04	.01
☐ 119 Dennis Lamp	.06	.02	.00
☐ 120 Ron Davis	.06	.02	.00
☐ 121 Nick Esasky	.10	.04	.01
☐ 122 Vance Law	.10	.04	.01
☐ 123 Gary Roenicke	.06	.02	.00
☐ 124 Bill Schroeder	.06	.02	.00
☐ 125 Dave Rozema	.06	.02	.00
☐ 126 Bobby Meacham	.06	.02	.00
☐ 127 Marty Barrett	.30	.12	.03
☐ 128 R.J. Reynolds	.25	.10	.02
☐ 129 Ernie Camacho (photo actually Rich Thompson)	.06	.02	.00
☐ 130 Jorge Orta	.06	.02	.00
☐ 131 Lary Sorensen	.06	.02	.00
☐ 132 Terry Francona	.06	.02	.00
☐ 133 Fred Lynn	.15	.06	.01
☐ 134 Bob Jones	.06	.02	.00
☐ 135 Jerry Hairston	.06	.02	.00
☐ 136 Kevin Bass	.12	.05	.01
☐ 137 Garry Maddox	.10	.04	.01
☐ 138 Dave LaPoint	.10	.04	.01
☐ 139 Kevin McReynolds	1.00	.40	.10
☐ 140 Wayne Krenchicki	.06	.02	.00
☐ 141 Rafael Ramirez	.06	.02	.00
☐ 142 Rod Scurry	.06	.02	.00
☐ 143 Greg Minton	.06	.02	.00
☐ 144 Tim Stoddard	.06	.02	.00
☐ 145 Steve Henderson	.06	.02	.00
☐ 146 George Bell	.60	.24	.06
☐ 147 Dave Meier	.10	.04	.01
☐ 148 Sammy Stewart	.06	.02	.00
☐ 149 Mark Brouhard	.06	.02	.00
☐ 150 Larry Herndon	.06	.02	.00
☐ 151 Oil Can Boyd	.10	.04	.01
☐ 152 Brian Dayett	.06	.02	.00
☐ 153 Tom Niedenfuer	.06	.02	.00
☐ 154 Brook Jacoby	.15	.06	.01

□ 155	Onix Concepcion	.06	.02	.00
□ 156	Tim Conroy	.06	.02	.00
□ 157	Joe Hesketh	.15	.06	.01
□ 158	Brian Downing	.10	.04	.01
□ 159	Tommy Dunbar	.06	.02	.00
□ 160	Marc Hill	.06	.02	.00
□ 161	Phil Garner	.06	.02	.00
□ 162	Jerry Davis	.06	.02	.00
□ 163	Bill Campbell	.06	.02	.00
□ 164	John Franco	1.00	.40	.10
□ 165	Len Barker	.06	.02	.00
□ 166	Benny Distefano	.10	.04	.01
□ 167	George Frazier	.06	.02	.00
□ 168	Tito Landrum	.06	.02	.00
□ 169	Cal Ripken	.50	.20	.05
□ 170	Cecil Cooper	.12	.05	.01
□ 171	Alan Trammell	.30	.12	.03
□ 172	Wade Boggs	5.50	2.20	.55
□ 173	Don Baylor	.15	.06	.01
□ 174	Pedro Guerrero	.30	.12	.03
□ 175	Frank White	.10	.04	.01
□ 176	Rickey Henderson	.60	.24	.06
□ 177	Charlie Lea	.06	.02	.00
□ 178	Pete O'Brien	.15	.06	.01
□ 179	Doug DeCinces	.10	.04	.01
□ 180	Ron Kittle	.20	.08	.02
□ 181	George Hendrick	.10	.04	.01
□ 182	Joe Niekro	.10	.04	.01
□ 183	Juan Samuel	1.00	.40	.10
□ 184	Mario Soto	.06	.02	.00
□ 185	Goose Gossage	.15	.06	.01
□ 186	Johnny Ray	.15	.06	.01
□ 187	Bob Brenly	.06	.02	.00
□ 188	Craig McMurtry	.06	.02	.00
□ 189	Leon Durham	.10	.04	.01
□ 190	Dwight Gooden	11.00	4.50	1.10
□ 191	Barry Bonnell	.06	.02	.00
□ 192	Tim Teufel	.10	.04	.01
□ 193	Dave Stieb	.15	.06	.01
□ 194	Mickey Hatcher	.10	.04	.01
□ 195	Jesse Barfield	.25	.10	.02
□ 196	Al Cowens	.06	.02	.00
□ 197	Hubie Brooks	.10	.04	.01
□ 198	Steve Trout	.06	.02	.00
□ 199	Glenn Hubbard	.06	.02	.00
□ 200	Bill Madlock	.10	.04	.01
□ 201	Jeff Robinson (Giants pitcher)	.30	.12	.03
□ 202	Eric Show	.06	.02	.00
□ 203	Dave Concepcion	.10	.04	.01
□ 204	Ivan DeJesus	.06	.02	.00
□ 205	Neil Allen	.06	.02	.00
□ 206	Jerry Mumphrey	.06	.02	.00
□ 207	Mike Brown (Angels OF)	.06	.02	.00
□ 208	Carlton Fisk	.15	.06	.01
□ 209	Bryn Smith	.06	.02	.00
□ 210	Tippy Martinez	.06	.02	.00
□ 211	Dion James	.10	.04	.01
□ 212	Willie Hernandez	.10	.04	.01
□ 213	Mike Easler	.06	.02	.00
□ 214	Ron Guidry	.20	.08	.02
□ 215	Rick Honeycutt	.06	.02	.00
□ 216	Brett Butler	.10	.04	.01
□ 217	Larry Gura	.06	.02	.00
□ 218	Ray Burris	.06	.02	.00
□ 219	Steve Rogers	.06	.02	.00
□ 220	Frank Tanana	.10	.04	.01
□ 221	Ned Yost	.06	.02	.00
□ 222	Bret Saberhagen	4.00	1.60	.40
□ 223	Mike Davis	.10	.04	.01
□ 224	Bert Blyleven	.15	.06	.01
□ 225	Steve Kemp	.10	.04	.01
□ 226	Jerry Reuss	.10	.04	.01
□ 227	Darrell Evans	.15	.06	.01
□ 228	Wayne Gross	.06	.02	.00
□ 229	Jim Gantner	.06	.02	.00
□ 230	Bob Boone	.15	.06	.01
□ 231	Lonnie Smith	.10	.04	.01
□ 232	Frank DiPino	.06	.02	.00
□ 233	Jerry Koosman	.10	.04	.01
□ 234	Graig Nettles	.15	.06	.01
□ 235	John Tudor	.15	.06	.01
□ 236	John Rabb	.06	.02	.00
□ 237	Rick Manning	.06	.02	.00
□ 238	Mike Fitzgerald	.06	.02	.00
□ 239	Gary Matthews	.10	.04	.01
□ 240	Jim Presley	1.00	.40	.10
□ 241	Dave Collins	.06	.02	.00
□ 242	Gary Gaetti	.40	.16	.04
□ 243	Dann Bilardello	.06	.02	.00
□ 244	Rudy Law	.06	.02	.00
□ 245	John Lowenstein	.06	.02	.00
□ 246	Tom Tellman	.06	.02	.00
□ 247	Howard Johnson	.65	.26	.06
□ 248	Ray Fontenot	.06	.02	.00
□ 249	Tony Armas	.10	.04	.01
□ 250	Candy Maldonado	.10	.04	.01
□ 251	Mike Jeffcoat	.06	.02	.00
□ 252	Dane Iorg	.06	.02	.00
□ 253	Bruce Bochte	.06	.02	.00
□ 254	Pete Rose	1.50	.60	.15
□ 255	Don Aase	.06	.02	.00
□ 256	George Wright	.06	.02	.00
□ 257	Britt Burns	.06	.02	.00
□ 258	Mike Scott	.30	.12	.03
□ 259	Len Matuszek	.06	.02	.00
□ 260	Dave Rucker	.06	.02	.00
□ 261	Craig Lefferts	.06	.02	.00
□ 262	Jay Tibbs	.15	.06	.01
□ 263	Bruce Benedict	.06	.02	.00
□ 264	Don Robinson	.06	.02	.00
□ 265	Gary Lavelle	.06	.02	.00
□ 266	Scott Sanderson	.06	.02	.00
□ 267	Matt Young	.06	.02	.00
□ 268	Ernie Whitt	.06	.02	.00
□ 269	Houston Jimenez	.06	.02	.00
□ 270	Ken Dixon	.10	.04	.01
□ 271	Peter Ladd	.06	.02	.00
□ 272	Juan Berenguer	.06	.02	.00
□ 273	Roger Clemens	14.00	5.75	1.40
□ 274	Rick Cerone	.06	.02	.00
□ 275	Dave Anderson	.06	.02	.00
□ 276	George Vukovich	.06	.02	.00
□ 277	Greg Pryor	.06	.02	.00
□ 278	Mike Warren	.06	.02	.00
□ 279	Bob James	.06	.02	.00
□ 280	Bobby Grich	.10	.04	.01
□ 281	Mike Mason	.06	.02	.00
□ 282	Ron Reed	.06	.02	.00
□ 283	Alan Ashby	.06	.02	.00
□ 284	Mark Thurmond	.06	.02	.00
□ 285	Joe Lefebvre	.06	.02	.00
□ 286	Ted Power	.06	.02	.00
□ 287	Chris Chambliss	.10	.04	.01
□ 288	Lee Tunnell	.06	.02	.00
□ 289	Rich Bordi	.06	.02	.00
□ 290	Glenn Brummer	.06	.02	.00
□ 291	Mike Boddicker	.12	.05	.01
□ 292	Rollie Fingers	.18	.08	.01
□ 293	Lou Whitaker	.18	.08	.01
□ 294	Dwight Evans	.18	.08	.01
□ 295	Don Mattingly	14.00	5.75	1.40
□ 296	Mike Marshall	.15	.06	.01
□ 297	Willie Wilson	.12	.05	.01
□ 298	Mike Heath	.06	.02	.00
□ 299	Tim Raines	.45	.18	.04
□ 300	Larry Parrish	.10	.04	.01
□ 301	Geoff Zahn	.06	.02	.00
□ 302	Rich Dotson	.10	.04	.01
□ 303	David Green	.06	.02	.00
□ 304	Jose Cruz	.10	.04	.01
□ 305	Steve Carlton	.40	.16	.04
□ 306	Gary Redus	.06	.02	.00
□ 307	Steve Garvey	.45	.18	.04
□ 308	Jose DeLeon	.06	.02	.00
□ 309	Randy Lerch	.06	.02	.00
□ 310	Claudell Washington	.10	.04	.01
□ 311	Lee Smith	.10	.04	.01
□ 312	Darryl Strawberry	4.00	1.60	.40
□ 313	Jim Beattie	.06	.02	.00
□ 314	John Butcher	.06	.02	.00
□ 315	Damaso Garcia	.06	.02	.00
□ 316	Mike Smithson	.06	.02	.00
□ 317	Luis Leal	.06	.02	.00
□ 318	Ken Phelps	.35	.14	.03
□ 319	Wally Backman	.10	.04	.01
□ 320	Ron Cey	.10	.04	.01
□ 321	Brad Komminsk	.06	.02	.00
□ 322	Jason Thompson	.06	.02	.00
□ 323	Frank Williams	.15	.06	.01
□ 324	Tim Lollar	.06	.02	.00
□ 325	Eric Davis	17.00	7.00	1.70
□ 326	Von Hayes	.15	.06	.01
□ 327	Andy Van Slyke	.50	.20	.05
□ 328	Craig Reynolds	.06	.02	.00
□ 329	Dick Schofield	.10	.04	.01
□ 330	Scott Fletcher	.10	.04	.01
□ 331	Jeff Reardon	.10	.04	.01
□ 332	Rick Dempsey	.06	.02	.00
□ 333	Ben Oglivie	.10	.04	.01
□ 334	Dan Petry	.10	.04	.01
□ 335	Jackie Gutierrez	.06	.02	.00
□ 336	Dave Righetti	.15	.06	.01
□ 337	Alejandro Pena	.10	.04	.01
□ 338	Mel Hall	.10	.04	.01
□ 339	Pat Sheridan	.06	.02	.00
□ 340	Keith Atherton	.06	.02	.00
□ 341	David Palmer	.06	.02	.00
□ 342	Gary Ward	.10	.04	.01

□ 343 Dave Stewart .15 .06 .01
□ 344 Mark Gubicza 1.00 .40 .10
□ 345 Carney Lansford .12 .05 .01
□ 346 Jerry Willard .06 .02 .00
□ 347 Ken Griffey .10 .04 .01
□ 348 Franklin Stubbs .35 .14 .03
□ 349 Aurelio Lopez .06 .02 .00
□ 350 Al Bumbry .06 .02 .00
□ 351 Charlie Moore .06 .02 .00
□ 352 Luis Sanchez .06 .02 .00
□ 353 Darrell Porter .06 .02 .00
□ 354 Bill Dawley .06 .02 .00
□ 355 Charles Hudson .06 .02 .00
□ 356 Garry Templeton .10 .04 .01
□ 357 Cecilio Guante .06 .02 .00
□ 358 Jeff Leonard .10 .04 .01
□ 359 Paul Molitor .20 .08 .02
□ 360 Ron Gardenhire .06 .02 .00
□ 361 Larry Bowa .10 .04 .01
□ 362 Bob Kearney .06 .02 .00
□ 363 Garth Iorg .06 .02 .00
□ 364 Tom Brunansky .20 .08 .02
□ 365 Brad Gulden .06 .02 .00
□ 366 Greg Walker .10 .04 .01
□ 367 Mike Young .10 .04 .01
□ 368 Rick Waits .06 .02 .00
□ 369 Doug Bair .06 .02 .00
□ 370 Bob Shirley .06 .02 .00
□ 371 Bob Ojeda .10 .04 .01
□ 372 Bob Welch .10 .04 .01
□ 373 Neal Heaton .06 .02 .00
□ 374 Danny Jackson UER .30 .12 .03
(photo actually
Frank Wills)
□ 375 Donnie Hill .06 .02 .00
□ 376 Mike Stenhouse .06 .02 .00
□ 377 Bruce Kison .06 .02 .00
□ 378 Wayne Tolleson .06 .02 .00
□ 379 Floyd Bannister .06 .02 .00
□ 380 Vern Ruhle .06 .02 .00
□ 381 Tim Corcoran .06 .02 .00
□ 382 Kurt Kepshire .06 .02 .00
□ 383 Bobby Brown .06 .02 .00
□ 384 Dave Van Gorder .06 .02 .00
□ 385 Rick Mahler .06 .02 .00
□ 386 Lee Mazzilli .06 .02 .00
□ 387 Bill Laskey .06 .02 .00
□ 388 Thad Bosley .06 .02 .00
□ 389 Al Chambers .06 .02 .00
□ 390 Tony Fernandez .45 .18 .04
□ 391 Ron Washington .06 .02 .00
□ 392 Bill Swaggerty .06 .02 .00
□ 393 Bob L. Gibson .06 .02 .00
□ 394 Marty Castillo .06 .02 .00
□ 395 Steve Crawford .06 .02 .00
□ 396 Clay Christiansen .06 .02 .00
□ 397 Bob Bailor .06 .02 .00
□ 398 Mike Hargrove .06 .02 .00
□ 399 Charlie Leibrandt .06 .02 .00
□ 400 Tom Burgmeier .06 .02 .00
□ 401 Razor Shines .10 .04 .01
□ 402 Rob Wilfong .06 .02 .00
□ 403 Tom Henke .15 .06 .01
□ 404 Al Jones .06 .02 .00
□ 405 Mike LaCoss .06 .02 .00
□ 406 Luis DeLeon .06 .02 .00
□ 407 Greg Gross .06 .02 .00
□ 408 Tom Hume .06 .02 .00
□ 409 Rick Camp .06 .02 .00
□ 410 Milt May .06 .02 .00
□ 411 Henry Cotto .10 .04 .01
□ 412 David Von Ohlen .06 .02 .00
□ 413 Scott McGregor .10 .04 .01
□ 414 Ted Simmons .10 .04 .01
□ 415 Jack Morris .20 .08 .02
□ 416 Bill Buckner .10 .04 .01
□ 417 Butch Wynegar .06 .02 .00
□ 418 Steve Sax .20 .08 .02
□ 419 Steve Balboni .06 .02 .00
□ 420 Dwayne Murphy .06 .02 .00
□ 421 Andre Dawson .30 .12 .03
□ 422 Charlie Hough .10 .04 .01
□ 423 Tommy John .15 .06 .01
□ 424A Tom Seaver ERR .90 .36 .09
(photo actually
Floyd Bannister)
□ 424B Tom Seaver COR 4.50 1.80 .45
□ 425 Tommy Herr .10 .04 .01
□ 426 Terry Puhl .06 .02 .00
□ 427 Al Holland .06 .02 .00
□ 428 Eddie Milner .06 .02 .00
□ 429 Terry Kennedy .06 .02 .00
□ 430 John Candelaria .10 .04 .01
□ 431 Manny Trillo .06 .02 .00
□ 432 Ken Oberkfell .06 .02 .00
□ 433 Rick Sutcliffe .20 .08 .02
□ 434 Ron Darling .90 .36 .09
□ 435 Spike Owen .06 .02 .00
□ 436 Frank Viola .45 .18 .04
□ 437 Lloyd Moseby .15 .06 .01
□ 438 Kirby Puckett 11.00 4.50 1.10
□ 439 Jim Clancy .06 .02 .00
□ 440 Mike Moore .06 .02 .00
□ 441 Doug Sisk .06 .02 .00
□ 442 Dennis Eckersley .20 .08 .02
□ 443 Gerald Perry .20 .08 .02
□ 444 Dale Berra .06 .02 .00
□ 445 Dusty Baker .10 .04 .01
□ 446 Ed Whitson .06 .02 .00
□ 447 Cesar Cedeno .10 .04 .01
□ 448 Rick Schu .20 .08 .02
□ 449 Joaquin Andujar .10 .04 .01
□ 450 Mark Bailey .10 .04 .01
□ 451 Ron Romanick .10 .04 .01
□ 452 Julio Cruz .06 .02 .00
□ 453 Miguel Dilone .06 .02 .00
□ 454 Storm Davis .10 .04 .01
□ 455 Jaime Cocanower .10 .04 .01
□ 456 Barbaro Garbey .06 .02 .00
□ 457 Rich Gedman .10 .04 .01
□ 458 Phil Niekro .25 .10 .02
□ 459 Mike Scioscia .10 .04 .01
□ 460 Pat Tabler .10 .04 .01
□ 461 Darryl Motley .06 .02 .00
□ 462 Chris Codiroli .06 .02 .00
□ 463 Doug Flynn .06 .02 .00
□ 464 Billy Sample .06 .02 .00
□ 465 Mickey Rivers .06 .02 .00
□ 466 John Wathan .06 .02 .00
□ 467 Bill Krueger .06 .02 .00
□ 468 Andre Thornton .10 .04 .01
□ 469 Rex Hudler .20 .08 .02
□ 470 Sid Bream .35 .14 .03
□ 471 Kirk Gibson .35 .14 .03
□ 472 John Shelby .06 .02 .00
□ 473 Moose Haas .06 .02 .00
□ 474 Doug Corbett .06 .02 .00
□ 475 Willie McGee .35 .14 .03
□ 476 Bob Knepper .10 .04 .01
□ 477 Kevin Gross .06 .02 .00
□ 478 Carmelo Martinez .06 .02 .00
□ 479 Kent Tekulve .10 .04 .01
□ 480 Chili Davis .10 .04 .01
□ 481 Bobby Clark .06 .02 .00
□ 482 Mookie Wilson .10 .04 .01
□ 483 Dave Owen .06 .02 .00
□ 484 Ed Nunez .06 .02 .00
□ 485 Rance Mulliniks .06 .02 .00
□ 486 Ken Schrom .06 .02 .00
□ 487 Jeff Russell .06 .02 .00
□ 488 Tom Paciorek .06 .02 .00
□ 489 Dan Ford .06 .02 .00
□ 490 Mike Caldwell .06 .02 .00
□ 491 Scottie Earl .06 .02 .00
□ 492 Jose Rijo .40 .16 .04
□ 493 Bruce Hurst .15 .06 .01
□ 494 Ken Landreaux .06 .02 .00
□ 495 Mike Fischlin .06 .02 .00
□ 496 Don Slaught .06 .02 .00
□ 497 Steve McCatty .06 .02 .00
□ 498 Gary Lucas .06 .02 .00
□ 499 Gary Pettis .10 .04 .01
□ 500 Marvis Foley .06 .02 .00
□ 501 Mike Squires .06 .02 .00
□ 502 Jim Pankovitz .06 .02 .00
□ 503 Luis Aguayo .06 .02 .00
□ 504 Ralph Citarella .06 .02 .00
□ 505 Bruce Bochy .06 .02 .00
□ 506 Bob Owchinko .06 .02 .00
□ 507 Pascual Perez .10 .04 .01
□ 508 Lee Lacy .06 .02 .00
□ 509 Atlee Hammaker .06 .02 .00
□ 510 Bob Dernier .06 .02 .00
□ 511 Ed VandeBerg .06 .02 .00
□ 512 Cliff Johnson .06 .02 .00
□ 513 Len Whitehouse .06 .02 .00
□ 514 Dennis Martinez .10 .04 .01
□ 515 Ed Romero .06 .02 .00
□ 516 Rusty Kuntz .06 .02 .00
□ 517 Rick Miller .06 .02 .00
□ 518 Dennis Rasmussen .15 .06 .01
□ 519 Steve Yeager .06 .02 .00
□ 520 Chris Bando .06 .02 .00
□ 521 U.L. Washington .06 .02 .00
□ 522 Curt Young .40 .16 .04
□ 523 Angel Salazar .06 .02 .00
□ 524 Curt Kaufman .06 .02 .00
□ 525 Odell Jones .06 .02 .00
□ 526 Juan Agosto .06 .02 .00
□ 527 Denny Walling .06 .02 .00

☐ 528 Andy Hawkins	.10	.04	.01
☐ 529 Sixto Lezcano	.06	.02	.00
☐ 530 Skeeter Barnes	.06	.02	.00
☐ 531 Randy Johnson	.06	.02	.00
☐ 532 Jim Morrison	.06	.02	.00
☐ 533 Warren Brusstar	.06	.02	.00
☐ 534A Jeff Pendleton ERR (wrong first name)	.80	.32	.08
☐ 534B Terry Pendleton COR	2.50	1.00	.25
☐ 535 Vic Rodriguez	.10	.04	.01
☐ 536 Bob McClure	.06	.02	.00
☐ 537 Dave Bergman	.06	.02	.00
☐ 538 Mark Clear	.06	.02	.00
☐ 539 Mike Pagliarulo	1.75	.70	.17
☐ 540 Terry Whitfield	.06	.02	.00
☐ 541 Joe Beckwith	.06	.02	.00
☐ 542 Jeff Burroughs	.06	.02	.00
☐ 543 Dan Schatzeder	.06	.02	.00
☐ 544 Donnie Scott	.06	.02	.00
☐ 545 Jim Slaton	.06	.02	.00
☐ 546 Greg Luzinski	.12	.05	.01
☐ 547 Mark Salas	.15	.06	.01
☐ 548 Dave Smith	.06	.02	.00
☐ 549 John Wockenfuss	.06	.02	.00
☐ 550 Frank Pastore	.06	.02	.00
☐ 551 Tim Flannery	.06	.02	.00
☐ 552 Rick Rhoden	.10	.04	.01
☐ 553 Mark Davis	.10	.04	.01
☐ 554 Jeff Dedmon	.10	.04	.01
☐ 555 Gary Woods	.06	.02	.00
☐ 556 Danny Heep	.06	.02	.00
☐ 557 Mark Langston	2.00	.80	.20
☐ 558 Darrell Brown	.06	.02	.00
☐ 559 Jimmy Key	2.00	.80	.20
☐ 560 Rick Lysander	.06	.02	.00
☐ 561 Doyle Alexander	.10	.04	.01
☐ 562 Mike Stanton	.06	.02	.00
☐ 563 Sid Fernandez	.65	.26	.06
☐ 564 Richie Hebner	.06	.02	.00
☐ 565 Alex Trevino	.06	.02	.00
☐ 566 Brian Harper	.06	.02	.00
☐ 567 Dan Gladden	.45	.18	.04
☐ 568 Luis Salazar	.10	.04	.01
☐ 569 Tom Foley	.06	.02	.00
☐ 570 Larry Andersen	.06	.02	.00
☐ 571 Danny Cox	.10	.04	.01
☐ 572 Joe Sambito	.06	.02	.00
☐ 573 Juan Beniquez	.06	.02	.00
☐ 574 Joel Skinner	.06	.02	.00
☐ 575 Randy St.Claire	.06	.02	.00
☐ 576 Floyd Rayford	.06	.02	.00
☐ 577 Roy Howell	.06	.02	.00
☐ 578 John Grubb	.06	.02	.00
☐ 579 Ed Jurak	.06	.02	.00
☐ 580 John Montefusco	.06	.02	.00
☐ 581 Orel Hershiser	11.00	4.50	1.10
☐ 582 Tom Waddell	.10	.04	.01
☐ 583 Mark Huismann	.06	.02	.00
☐ 584 Joe Morgan	.25	.10	.02
☐ 585 Jim Wohlford	.06	.02	.00
☐ 586 Dave Schmidt	.10	.04	.01
☐ 587 Jeff Kunkel	.10	.04	.01
☐ 588 Hal McRae	.10	.04	.01
☐ 589 Bill Almon	.06	.02	.00
☐ 590 Carmen Castillo	.06	.02	.00
☐ 591 Omar Moreno	.06	.02	.00
☐ 592 Ken Howell	.15	.06	.01
☐ 593 Tom Brookens	.06	.02	.00
☐ 594 Joe Nolan	.06	.02	.00
☐ 595 Willie Lozado	.10	.04	.01
☐ 596 Tom Nieto	.10	.04	.01
☐ 597 Walt Terrell	.06	.02	.00
☐ 598 Al Oliver	.10	.04	.01
☐ 599 Shane Rawley	.10	.04	.01
☐ 600 Denny Gonzalez	.10	.04	.01
☐ 601 Mark Grant	.10	.04	.01
☐ 602 Mike Armstrong	.06	.02	.00
☐ 603 George Foster	.12	.05	.01
☐ 604 Davey Lopes	.10	.04	.01
☐ 605 Salome Barojas	.06	.02	.00
☐ 606 Roy Lee Jackson	.06	.02	.00
☐ 607 Pete Filson	.06	.02	.00
☐ 608 Duane Walker	.06	.02	.00
☐ 609 Glenn Wilson	.10	.04	.01
☐ 610 Rafael Santana	.30	.12	.03
☐ 611 Roy Smith	.10	.04	.01
☐ 612 Ruppert Jones	.06	.02	.00
☐ 613 Joe Cowley	.06	.02	.00
☐ 614 Al Nipper (photo actually Mike Brown)	.20	.08	.02
☐ 615 Gene Nelson	.06	.02	.00
☐ 616 Joe Carter	1.50	.60	.15
☐ 617 Ray Knight	.10	.04	.01
☐ 618 Chuck Rainey	.06	.02	.00
☐ 619 Dan Driessen	.06	.02	.00
☐ 620 Daryl Sconiers	.06	.02	.00
☐ 621 Bill Stein	.06	.02	.00
☐ 622 Roy Smalley	.06	.02	.00
☐ 623 Ed Lynch	.06	.02	.00
☐ 624 Jeff Stone	.15	.06	.01
☐ 625 Bruce Berenyi	.06	.02	.00
☐ 626 Kelvin Chapman	.10	.04	.01
☐ 627 Joe Price	.06	.02	.00
☐ 628 Steve Bedrosian	.15	.06	.01
☐ 629 Vic Mata	.10	.04	.01
☐ 630 Mike Krukow	.06	.02	.00
☐ 631 Phil Bradley	1.00	.40	.10
☐ 632 Jim Gott	.10	.04	.01
☐ 633 Randy Bush	.10	.04	.01
☐ 634 Tom Browning	1.50	.60	.15
☐ 635 Lou Gehrig Puzzle Card	.06	.02	.00
☐ 636 Reid Nichols	.06	.02	.00
☐ 637 Dan Pasqua	.75	.30	.07
☐ 638 German Rivera	.10	.04	.01
☐ 639 Don Schulze	.06	.02	.00
☐ 640A Mike Jones (Career Highlights, five lines)	.10	.04	.01
☐ 640B Mike Jones (Career Highlights, four lines)	.10	.04	.01
☐ 641 Pete Rose	1.00	.40	.10
☐ 642 Wade Rowdon	.10	.04	.01
☐ 643 Jerry Narron	.06	.02	.00
☐ 644 Darrell Miller	.10	.04	.01
☐ 645 Tim Hulett	.10	.04	.01
☐ 646 Andy McGaffigan	.06	.02	.00
☐ 647 Kurt Bevacqua	.06	.02	.00
☐ 648 John Russell	.10	.04	.01
☐ 649 Ron Robinson	.20	.08	.02
☐ 650 Donnie Moore	.06	.02	.00
☐ 651A Two for the Title Dave Winfield Don Mattingly (yellow letters)	5.00	2.00	.50
☐ 651B Two for the Title Dave Winfield Don Mattingly (white letters)	6.00	2.40	.60
☐ 652 Tim Laudner	.06	.02	.00
☐ 653 Steve Farr	.10	.04	.01
☐ 654 DK Checklist 1-26 (unnumbered)	.09	.01	.00
☐ 655 Checklist 27-130 (unnumbered)	.07	.01	.00
☐ 656 Checklist 131-234 (unnumbered)	.07	.01	.00
☐ 657 Checklist 235-338 (unnumbered)	.07	.01	.00
☐ 658 Checklist 339-442 (unnumbered)	.07	.01	.00
☐ 659 Checklist 443-546 (unnumbered)	.07	.01	.00
☐ 660 Checklist 547-653 (unnumbered)	.07	.01	.00

1985 Donruss Wax Box Cards

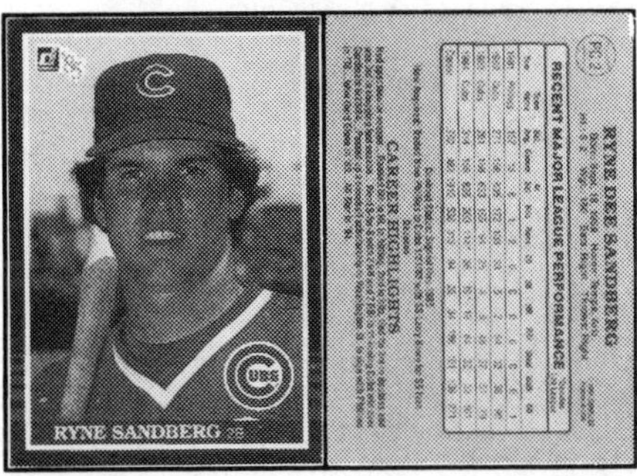

The boxes in which the wax packs (of the 1985 Donruss regular issue baseball cards) were contained feature four baseball cards, with backs. The complete set price of the regular issue set does not include these cards; they are considered a separate set. The cards measure the standard 2 1/2" by 3 1/2" and are styled the same as the regular Donruss cards. The cards are numbered but with the prefix PC before the number. The value of the panel uncut is slightly greater, perhaps by 25% greater, than the value of the individual cards cut up carefully.

	MINT	EXC	G-VG
COMPLETE SET (4)	4.50	1.80	.45
COMMON PLAYER	.05	.02	.00
☐ PC1 Dwight Gooden	4.00	1.60	.40
☐ PC2 Ryne Sandberg	.50	.20	.05
☐ PC3 Ron Kittle	.15	.06	.01
☐ PUZ Lou Gehrig Puzzle Card	.05	.02	.00

1985 Donruss Super DK's

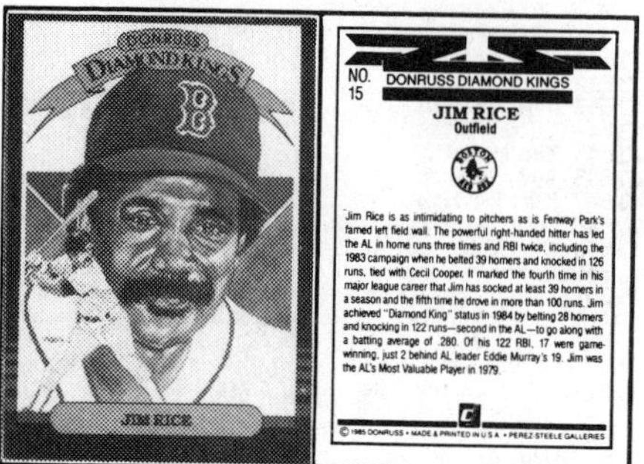

The cards in this 28-card set measure 4 15/16 by 6 3/4". The 1985 Donruss Diamond Kings Supers set contains enlarged cards of the first 26 cards of the Donruss regular set of this year. In addition, the Diamond Kings checklist card, a card of artist Dick Perez, and a Lou Gehrig puzzle card are included in the set. The set was the brain-child of the Perez-Steele Galleries and could be obtained via a write-in offer on the wrappers of the Donruss regular cards of this year. The Gehrig puzzle card is actually a 12-piece jigsaw puzzle. The back of the checklist card is blank; however, the Dick Perez card back gives a short history of Dick Perez and the Perez-Steele Galleries. The offer for obtaining this set was detailed on the wax pack wrappers; three wrappers plus 9.00 was required for this mail-in offer.

	MINT	EXC	G-VG
COMPLETE SET (28)	11.00	4.50	1.10
COMMON PLAYER (1-26)	.20	.08	.02
☐ 1 Ryne Sandberg	.75	.30	.07
☐ 2 Doug DeCinces	.20	.08	.02
☐ 3 Richard Dotson	.20	.08	.02
☐ 4 Bert Blyleven	.30	.12	.03
☐ 5 Lou Whitaker	.30	.12	.03
☐ 6 Dan Quisenberry	.20	.08	.02
☐ 7 Don Mattingly	5.00	2.00	.50
☐ 8 Carney Lansford	.30	.12	.03
☐ 9 Frank Tanana	.20	.08	.02
☐ 10 Willie Upshaw	.20	.08	.02
☐ 11 Claudell Washington	.20	.08	.02
☐ 12 Mike Marshall	.25	.10	.02
☐ 13 Joaquin Andujar	.20	.08	.02
☐ 14 Cal Ripken	1.00	.40	.10
☐ 15 Jim Rice	.50	.20	.05
☐ 16 Don Sutton	.40	.16	.04
☐ 17 Frank Viola	.60	.24	.06
☐ 18 Alvin Davis	.50	.20	.05
☐ 19 Mario Soto	.20	.08	.02
☐ 20 Jose Cruz	.20	.08	.02
☐ 21 Charlie Lea	.20	.08	.02
☐ 22 Jesse Orosco	.20	.08	[illegible]
☐ 23 Juan Samuel	.40	.16	[illegible]
☐ 24 Tony Pena	.20	.08	[illegible]
☐ 25 Tony Gwynn	1.25	.50	[illegible]
☐ 26 Bob Brenly	.20	.08	[illegible]
☐ 27 Checklist card (unnumbered)	.05	.02	[illegible]
☐ 28 Dick Perez (unnumbered) (History of DK's)	.10	.04	.01

1985 Donruss Action All-Stars

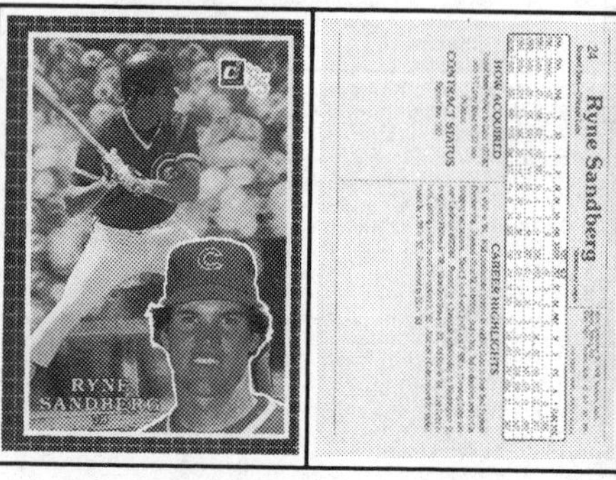

The cards in this 60-card set measure 3 1/2" by 5". For the third year in a row, Donruss issued a set of Action All-Stars. This set features action photos on the obverse which also contains a portrait inset of the player. The backs, unlike the year before, do not contain a full color picture of the player but list, if space is available, full statistical data, biographical data, career highlights, and acquisition and contract status. The cards were issued with a Lou Gehrig puzzle card.

	MINT	EXC	G-VG
COMPLETE SET (60)	6.00	2.40	.60
COMMON PLAYER (1-60)	.05	.02	.00
☐ 1 Tim Raines	.30	.12	.03
☐ 2 Jim Gantner	.05	.02	.00
☐ 3 Mario Soto	.05	.02	.00
☐ 4 Spike Owen	.05	.02	.00
☐ 5 Lloyd Moseby	.10	.04	.01
☐ 6 Damaso Garcia	.05	.02	.00
☐ 7 Cal Ripken	.30	.12	.03
☐ 8 Dan Quisenberry	.10	.04	.01
☐ 9 Eddie Murray	.35	.14	.03
☐ 10 Tony Pena	.05	.02	.00
☐ 11 Buddy Bell	.10	.04	.01
☐ 12 Dave Winfield	.25	.10	.02
☐ 13 Ron Kittle	.15	.06	.01
☐ 14 Rich Gossage	.10	.04	.01
☐ 15 Dwight Evans	.15	.06	.01
☐ 16 Alvin Davis	.15	.06	.01
☐ 17 Mike Schmidt	.50	.20	.05
☐ 18 Pascual Perez	.05	.02	.00
☐ 19 Tony Gwynn	.40	.16	.04
☐ 20 Nolan Ryan	.40	.16	.04
☐ 21 Robin Yount	.25	.10	.02
☐ 22 Mike Marshall	.15	.06	.01
☐ 23 Brett Butler	.10	.04	.01
☐ 24 Ryne Sandberg	.30	.12	.03
☐ 25 Dale Murphy	.60	.24	.06
☐ 26 George Brett	.50	.20	.05
☐ 27 Jim Rice	.25	.10	.02
☐ 28 Ozzie Smith	.20	.08	.02
☐ 29 Larry Parrish	.05	.02	.00
☐ 30 Jack Clark	.20	.08	.02
☐ 31 Manny Trillo	.05	.02	.00
☐ 32 Dave Kingman	.10	.04	.01
☐ 33 Geoff Zahn	.05	.02	.00
☐ 34 Pedro Guerrero	.20	.08	.02
☐ 35 Dave Parker	.15	.06	.01
☐ 36 Rollie Fingers	.15	.06	.01
☐ 37 Fernando Valenzuela	.20	.08	.02
☐ 38 Wade Boggs	.75	.30	.07
☐ 39 Reggie Jackson	.60	.24	.06

□ 40 Kent Hrbek	.25	.10	.02
□ 41 Keith Hernandez	.25	.10	.02
□ 42 Lou Whitaker	.10	.04	.01
□ 43 Tom Herr	.05	.02	.00
□ 44 Alan Trammell	.20	.08	.02
□ 45 Butch Wynegar	.05	.02	.00
□ 46 Leon Durham	.05	.02	.00
□ 47 Dwight Gooden	1.25	.50	.12
□ 48 Don Mattingly	1.50	.60	.15
□ 49 Phil Niekro	.20	.08	.02
□ 50 Johnny Ray	.10	.04	.01
□ 51 Doug DeCinces	.05	.02	.00
□ 52 Willie Upshaw	.05	.02	.00
□ 53 Lance Parrish	.10	.04	.01
□ 54 Jody Davis	.05	.02	.00
□ 55 Steve Carlton	.30	.12	.03
□ 56 Juan Samuel	.15	.06	.01
□ 57 Gary Carter	.25	.10	.02
□ 58 Harold Baines	.10	.04	.01
□ 59 Eric Show	.05	.02	.00
□ 60 Checklist Card	.05	.01	.00

1985 Donruss Highlights

Dale Murphy

National League Player of the Month April

Before the '85 National League season was even one month old, fans were fitting Dale Murphy for a place in the record books alongside Hack Wilson who, in '30 set National League records of 56 homers and 190 RBI. The reason for such lofty comparisons was obvious. Murphy tied a major league record for most RBI in one month with 29 in April of '85. In addition, the Atlanta Braves' perennial All-Star centerfielder and two-time winner of the Most Valuable Player Award, hit nine homers. His batting average for the month was .380, including 8 doubles, 62 total bases and 17 runs scored in just 19 games. Along with his offensive stats, Murphy kept his consecutive games playing streak going through 515 entering May.

NO. 5

© 1985 LEAF-DONRUSS MADE & PRINTED IN U.S.A.

This 56-card set features the players and pitchers of the month for each league as well as a number of highlight cards commemorating the 1985 season. The Donruss Company dedicated the last two cards to their own selections for Rookies of the Year (ROY). This set proved to be more popular than the Donruss Company had predicted, as their first and only print run was exhausted before card dealers' initial orders were filled.

	MINT	EXC	G-VG
COMPLETE SET (56)	21.00	8.50	2.10
COMMON PLAYER (1-56)	.10	.04	.01
□ 1 Tom Seaver: Sets Opening Day Record	.40	.16	.04
□ 2 Rollie Fingers: Sets AL Save Mark	.15	.06	.01
□ 3 Mike Davis: AL Player April	.10	.04	.01
□ 4 Charlie Leibrandt: AL Pitcher April	.10	.04	.01
□ 5 Dale Murphy: NL Player April	.75	.30	.07
□ 6 Fernando Valenzuela: NL Pitcher April	.25	.10	.02
□ 7 Larry Bowa: NL Shortstop Record	.10	.04	.01
□ 8 Dave Concepcion: Joins Reds' 2000 Hit Club	.10	.04	.01
□ 9 Tony Perez: Eldest Grand Slammer	.15	.06	.01
□ 10 Pete Rose: NL Career Run Leader	1.25	.50	.12
□ 11 George Brett: AL Player May	.75	.30	.07
□ 12 Dave Stieb: AL Pitcher May	.15	.06	.01
□ 13 Dave Parker: NL Player May	.15	.06	.01
□ 14 Andy Hawkins: NL Pitcher May	.10	.04	.01
□ 15 Andy Hawkins: Records 11th Straight Win	.10	.04	.01
□ 16 Von Hayes: Two Homers in First Inning	.15	.06	.01
□ 17 Rickey Henderson: AL Player June	.75	.30	.07
□ 18 Jay Howell: AL Pitcher June	.10	.04	.01
□ 19 Pedro Guerrero: NL Player June	.20	.08	.02
□ 20 John Tudor: NL Pitcher June	.15	.06	.01
□ 21 Hernandez/Carter: Marathon Game Iron Men	.30	.12	.03
□ 22 Nolan Ryan: Records 4000th K	.50	.20	.05
□ 23 LaMarr Hoyt: All-Star Game MVP	.10	.04	.01
□ 24 Oddibe McDowell: 1st Ranger to Hit for Cycle	.30	.12	.03
□ 25 George Brett: AL Player July	.75	.30	.07
□ 26 Bret Saberhagen: AL Pitcher July	.50	.20	.05
□ 27 Keith Hernandez: NL Player July	.25	.10	.02
□ 28 Fernando Valenzuela: NL Pitcher July	.25	.10	.02
□ 29 W.McGee/V.Coleman: Record Setting Base Stealers	.75	.30	.07
□ 30 Tom Seaver: Notches 300th Career Win	.35	.14	.03
□ 31 Rod Carew: Strokes 3000th Hit	.35	.14	.03
□ 32 Dwight Gooden: Establishes Met Record	1.25	.50	.12
□ 33 Dwight Gooden: Achieves Strikeout Milestone	1.25	.50	.12
□ 34 Eddie Murray: Explodes for 9 RBI	.50	.20	.05
□ 35 Don Baylor: AL Career HBP Leader	.15	.06	.01
□ 36 Don Mattingly: AL Player August	2.50	1.00	.25
□ 37 Dave Righetti: AL Pitcher August	.15	.06	.01
□ 38 Willie McGee: NL Player August	.25	.10	.02
□ 39 Shane Rawley: NL Pitcher August	.10	.04	.01
□ 40 Pete Rose: Ty-Breaking Hit	1.25	.50	.12
□ 41 Andre Dawson: Hits 3 HR's Drives in 8 Runs	.25	.10	.02
□ 42 Rickey Henderson: Sets Yankee Theft Mark	.75	.30	.07
□ 43 Tom Browning: 20 Wins in Rookie Season	.20	.08	.02
□ 44 Don Mattingly: Yankee Milestone for Hits	2.50	1.00	.25
□ 45 Don Mattingly: AL Player September	2.50	1.00	.25
□ 46 Charlie Leibrandt: AL Pitcher September	.10	.04	.01
□ 47 Gary Carter: NL Player September	.30	.12	.03
□ 48 Dwight Gooden: NL Pitcher September	1.25	.50	.12
□ 49 Wade Boggs: Major League Record Setter	2.00	.80	.20
□ 50 Phil Niekro: Hurls Shutout for 300th Win	.20	.08	.02
□ 51 Darrell Evans: Venerable HR King	.10	.04	.01
□ 52 Willie McGee: NL Switch-Hitting Record	.20	.08	.02
□ 53 Dave Winfield: Equals DiMaggio Feat	.35	.14	.03
□ 54 Vince Coleman: Donruss NL ROY	2.00	.80	.20
□ 55 Ozzie Guillen: Donruss AL ROY	.40	.16	.04
□ 56 Checklist card (unnumbered)	.10	.01	.00

1986 Donruss

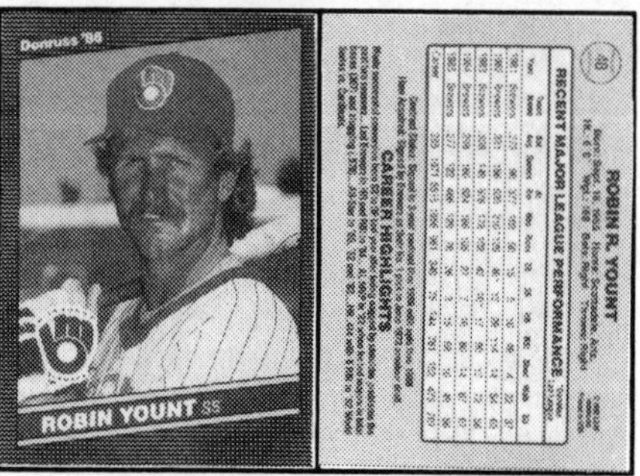

The cards in this 660-card set measure 2 1/2" by 3 1/2". The 1986 Donruss regular issue cards have fronts that feature blue borders. The fronts contain the standard team logo, player's name, position, and Donruss logo. The cards were distributed with puzzle pieces from a Dick Perez rendition of Hank Aaron. The first 26 cards of the set are Diamond Kings (DK), for the fifth year in a row; the artwork on the Diamond Kings was again produced by the Perez-Steele Galleries. Cards 27-46 again feature Rated Rookies (RR); Danny Tartabull is included in this subset for the second year in a row. The unnumbered checklist cards are arbitrarily numbered below as numbers 654 through 660.

	MINT	EXC	G-VG
COMPLETE SET (660)	110.00	45.00	11.00
COMMON PLAYER (1-660)	.05	.02	.00
□ 1 Kirk Gibson DK	.35	.12	.02
□ 2 Goose Gossage DK	.15	.06	.01
□ 3 Willie McGee DK	.25	.10	.02
□ 4 George Bell DK	.25	.10	.02
□ 5 Tony Armas DK	.10	.04	.01
□ 6 Chili Davis DK	.10	.04	.01
□ 7 Cecil Cooper DK	.12	.05	.01
□ 8 Mike Boddicker DK	.10	.04	.01
□ 9 Davey Lopes DK	.10	.04	.01
□ 10 Bill Doran DK	.10	.04	.01
□ 11 Bret Saberhagen DK	.30	.12	.03
□ 12 Brett Butler DK	.10	.04	.01
□ 13 Harold Baines DK	.15	.06	.01
□ 14 Mike Davis DK	.10	.04	.01
□ 15 Tony Perez DK	.15	.06	.01
□ 16 Willie Randolph DK	.12	.05	.01
□ 17 Bob Boone DK	.12	.05	.01
□ 18 Orel Hershiser DK	1.00	.40	.10
□ 19 Johnny Ray DK	.12	.05	.01
□ 20 Gary Ward DK	.10	.04	.01
□ 21 Rick Mahler DK	.10	.04	.01
□ 22 Phil Bradley DK	.20	.08	.02
□ 23 Jerry Koosman DK	.10	.04	.01
□ 24 Tom Brunansky DK	.20	.08	.02
□ 25 Andre Dawson DK	.30	.12	.03
□ 26 Dwight Gooden DK	1.00	.40	.10
□ 27 Kal Daniels RR	4.50	1.80	.45
□ 28 Fred McGriff RR	5.00	2.00	.50
□ 29 Cory Snyder RR	3.50	1.40	.35
□ 30 Jose Guzman RR	.35	.14	.03
□ 31 Ty Gainey RR	.15	.06	.01
□ 32 Johnny Abrego RR	.10	.04	.01
□ 33A Andres Galarraga RR (no accent)	4.50	1.80	.45
□ 33B Andrés Galarraga RR (accent over e)	5.00	2.00	.50
□ 34 Dave Shipanoff RR	.10	.04	.01
□ 35 Mark McLemore RR	.10	.04	.01
□ 36 Marty Clary RR	.10	.04	.01
□ 37 Paul O'Neill RR	.30	.12	.03
□ 38 Danny Tartabull RR	1.50	.60	.15
□ 39 Jose Canseco RR	55.00	22.00	5.50
□ 40 Juan Nieves RR	.30	.12	.03
□ 41 Lance McCullers RR	.45	.18	.04
□ 42 Rick Surhoff RR	.10	.04	.01
□ 43 Todd Worrell RR	.80	.32	.08
□ 44 Bob Kipper RR	.10	.04	.01
□ 45 John Habyan RR	.10	.04	.0
□ 46 Mike Woodard RR	.10	.04	.0
□ 47 Mike Boddicker	.08	.03	.0
□ 48 Robin Yount	.35	.14	.0
□ 49 Lou Whitaker	.12	.05	.0
□ 50 Oil Can Boyd	.08	.03	.0
□ 51 Rickey Henderson	.40	.16	.0
□ 52 Mike Marshall	.12	.05	.0
□ 53 George Brett	.50	.20	.05
□ 54 Dave Kingman	.10	.04	.0
□ 55 Hubie Brooks	.08	.03	.0
□ 56 Oddibe McDowell	.25	.10	.0
□ 57 Doug DeCinces	.08	.03	.0
□ 58 Britt Burns	.05	.02	.00
□ 59 Ozzie Smith	.20	.08	.02
□ 60 Jose Cruz	.08	.03	.01
□ 61 Mike Schmidt	.50	.20	.05
□ 62 Pete Rose	.75	.30	.07
□ 63 Steve Garvey	.40	.16	.04
□ 64 Tony Pena	.08	.03	.01
□ 65 Chili Davis	.10	.04	.01
□ 66 Dale Murphy	.50	.20	.05
□ 67 Ryne Sandberg	.30	.12	.03
□ 68 Gary Carter	.30	.12	.03
□ 69 Alvin Davis	.15	.06	.01
□ 70 Kent Hrbek	.20	.08	.02
□ 71 George Bell	.30	.12	.03
□ 72 Kirby Puckett	2.25	.90	.22
□ 73 Lloyd Moseby	.10	.04	.01
□ 74 Bob Kearney	.05	.02	.00
□ 75 Dwight Gooden	2.25	.90	.22
□ 76 Gary Matthews	.08	.03	.01
□ 77 Rick Mahler	.05	.02	.00
□ 78 Benny Distefano	.05	.02	.00
□ 79 Jeff Leonard	.12	.05	.01
□ 80 Kevin McReynolds	.50	.20	.05
□ 81 Ron Oester	.05	.02	.00
□ 82 John Russell	.05	.02	.00
□ 83 Tommy Herr	.10	.04	.01
□ 84 Jerry Mumphrey	.05	.02	.00
□ 85 Ron Romanick	.05	.02	.00
□ 86 Daryl Boston	.05	.02	.00
□ 87 Andre Dawson	.30	.12	.03
□ 88 Eddie Murray	.35	.14	.03
□ 89 Dion James	.05	.02	.00
□ 90 Chet Lemon	.08	.03	.01
□ 91 Bob Stanley	.05	.02	.00
□ 92 Willie Randolph	.08	.03	.01
□ 93 Mike Scioscia	.08	.03	.01
□ 94 Tom Waddell	.05	.02	.00
□ 95 Danny Jackson	.30	.12	.03
□ 96 Mike Davis	.08	.03	.01
□ 97 Mike Fitzgerald	.05	.02	.00
□ 98 Gary Ward	.08	.03	.01
□ 99 Pete O'Brien	.10	.04	.01
□ 100 Bret Saberhagen	.45	.18	.04
□ 101 Alfredo Griffin	.08	.03	.01
□ 102 Brett Butler	.08	.03	.01
□ 103 Ron Guidry	.15	.06	.01
□ 104 Jerry Reuss	.08	.03	.01
□ 105 Jack Morris	.15	.06	.01
□ 106 Rick Dempsey	.05	.02	.00
□ 107 Ray Burris	.05	.02	.00
□ 108 Brian Downing	.08	.03	.01
□ 109 Willie McGee	.18	.08	.01
□ 110 Bill Doran	.10	.04	.01
□ 111 Kent Tekulve	.08	.03	.01
□ 112 Tony Gwynn	.75	.30	.07
□ 113 Marvell Wynne	.05	.02	.00
□ 114 David Green	.05	.02	.00
□ 115 Jim Gantner	.05	.02	.00
□ 116 George Foster	.12	.05	.01
□ 117 Steve Trout	.05	.02	.00
□ 118 Mark Langston	.15	.06	.01
□ 119 Tony Fernandez	.15	.06	.01
□ 120 John Butcher	.05	.02	.00
□ 121 Ron Robinson	.05	.02	.00
□ 122 Dan Spillner	.05	.02	.00
□ 123 Mike Young	.08	.03	.01
□ 124 Paul Molitor	.15	.06	.01
□ 125 Kirk Gibson	.25	.10	.02
□ 126 Ken Griffey	.08	.03	.01
□ 127 Tony Armas	.08	.03	.01
□ 128 Mariano Duncan	.15	.06	.01
□ 129 Pat Tabler	.08	.03	.01
□ 130 Frank White	.08	.03	.01
□ 131 Carney Lansford	.10	.04	.01
□ 132 Vance Law	.08	.03	.01
□ 133 Dick Schofield	.08	.03	.01
□ 134 Wayne Tolleson	.05	.02	.00
□ 135 Greg Walker	.08	.03	.01
□ 136 Denny Walling	.05	.02	.00
□ 137 Ozzie Virgil	.05	.02	.00
□ 138 Ricky Horton	.05	.02	.00
□ 139 LaMarr Hoyt	.08	.03	.01

□ 140 Wayne Krenchicki	.05	.02	.00
□ 141 Glenn Hubbard	.05	.02	.00
□ 142 Cecilio Guante	.05	.02	.00
□ 143 Mike Krukow	.05	.02	.00
□ 144 Lee Smith	.08	.03	.01
□ 145 Edwin Nunez	.05	.02	.00
□ 146 Dave Stieb	.12	.05	.01
□ 147 Mike Smithson	.05	.02	.00
□ 148 Ken Dixon	.05	.02	.00
□ 149 Danny Darwin	.05	.02	.00
□ 150 Chris Pittaro	.05	.02	.00
□ 151 Bill Buckner	.08	.03	.01
□ 152 Mike Pagliarulo	.15	.06	.01
□ 153 Bill Russell	.08	.03	.01
□ 154 Brook Jacoby	.12	.05	.01
□ 155 Pat Sheridan	.05	.02	.00
□ 156 Mike Gallego	.05	.02	.00
□ 157 Jim Wohlford	.05	.02	.00
□ 158 Gary Pettis	.08	.03	.01
□ 159 Toby Harrah	.08	.03	.01
□ 160 Richard Dotson	.08	.03	.01
□ 161 Bob Knepper	.08	.03	.01
□ 162 Dave Dravecky	.05	.02	.00
□ 163 Greg Gross	.05	.02	.00
□ 164 Eric Davis	3.50	1.40	.35
□ 165 Gerald Perry	.15	.06	.01
□ 166 Rick Rhoden	.08	.03	.01
□ 167 Keith Moreland	.05	.02	.00
□ 168 Jack Clark	.25	.10	.02
□ 169 Storm Davis	.08	.03	.01
□ 170 Cecil Cooper	.10	.04	.01
□ 171 Alan Trammell	.25	.10	.02
□ 172 Roger Clemens	3.50	1.40	.35
□ 173 Don Mattingly	5.50	2.20	.55
□ 174 Pedro Guerrero	.25	.10	.02
□ 175 Willie Wilson	.10	.04	.01
□ 176 Dwayne Murphy	.05	.02	.00
□ 177 Tim Raines	.30	.12	.03
□ 178 Larry Parrish	.05	.02	.00
□ 179 Mike Witt	.10	.04	.01
□ 180 Harold Baines	.15	.06	.01
□ 181 Vince Coleman (BA 2.67 on back)	2.25	.90	.22
□ 182 Jeff Heathcock	.05	.02	.00
□ 183 Steve Carlton	.30	.12	.03
□ 184 Mario Soto	.05	.02	.00
□ 185 Goose Gossage	.12	.05	.01
□ 186 Johnny Ray	.10	.04	.01
□ 187 Dan Gladden	.08	.03	.01
□ 188 Bob Horner	.15	.06	.01
□ 189 Rick Sutcliffe	.12	.05	.01
□ 190 Keith Hernandez	.30	.12	.03
□ 191 Phil Bradley	.12	.05	.01
□ 192 Tom Brunansky	.15	.06	.01
□ 193 Jesse Barfield	.25	.10	.02
□ 194 Frank Viola	.35	.14	.03
□ 195 Willie Upshaw	.05	.02	.00
□ 196 Jim Beattie	.05	.02	.00
□ 197 Darryl Strawberry	1.75	.70	.17
□ 198 Ron Cey	.10	.04	.01
□ 199 Steve Bedrosian	.12	.05	.01
□ 200 Steve Kemp	.08	.03	.01
□ 201 Manny Trillo	.05	.02	.00
□ 202 Garry Templeton	.08	.03	.01
□ 203 Dave Parker	.15	.06	.01
□ 204 John Denny	.08	.03	.01
□ 205 Terry Pendleton	.08	.03	.01
□ 206 Terry Puhl	.05	.02	.00
□ 207 Bobby Grich	.08	.03	.01
□ 208 Ozzie Guillen	.40	.16	.04
□ 209 Jeff Reardon	.10	.04	.01
□ 210 Cal Ripken	.40	.16	.04
□ 211 Bill Schroeder	.05	.02	.00
□ 212 Dan Petry	.08	.03	.01
□ 213 Jim Rice	.20	.08	.02
□ 214 Dave Righetti	.12	.05	.01
□ 215 Fernando Valenzuela	.25	.10	.02
□ 216 Julio Franco	.12	.05	.01
□ 217 Darryl Motley	.05	.02	.00
□ 218 Dave Collins	.05	.02	.00
□ 219 Tim Wallach	.10	.04	.01
□ 220 George Wright	.05	.02	.00
□ 221 Tommy Dunbar	.05	.02	.00
□ 222 Steve Balboni	.05	.02	.00
□ 223 Jay Howell	.08	.03	.01
□ 224 Joe Carter	.35	.14	.03
□ 225 Ed Whitson	.05	.02	.00
□ 226 Orel Hershiser	1.75	.70	.17
□ 227 Willie Hernandez	.10	.04	.01
□ 228 Lee Lacy	.05	.02	.00
□ 229 Rollie Fingers	.15	.06	.01
□ 230 Bob Boone	.10	.04	.01
□ 231 Joaquin Andujar	.10	.04	.01
□ 232 Craig Reynolds	.05	.02	.00
□ 233 Shane Rawley	.08	.03	.01
□ 234 Eric Show	.08	.03	.01
□ 235 Jose DeLeon	.05	.02	.00
□ 236 Jose Uribe	.30	.12	.03
□ 237 Moose Haas	.05	.02	.00
□ 238 Wally Backman	.08	.03	.01
□ 239 Dennis Eckersley	.15	.06	.01
□ 240 Mike Moore	.08	.03	.01
□ 241 Damaso Garcia	.05	.02	.00
□ 242 Tim Teufel	.05	.02	.00
□ 243 Dave Concepcion	.10	.04	.01
□ 244 Floyd Bannister	.05	.02	.00
□ 245 Fred Lynn	.15	.06	.01
□ 246 Charlie Moore	.05	.02	.00
□ 247 Walt Terrell	.05	.02	.00
□ 248 Dave Winfield	.30	.12	.03
□ 249 Dwight Evans	.15	.06	.01
□ 250 Dennis Powell	.10	.04	.01
□ 251 Andre Thornton	.08	.03	.01
□ 252 Onix Concepcion	.05	.02	.00
□ 253 Mike Heath	.05	.02	.00
□ 254A David Palmer ERR (position 2B)	.10	.04	.01
□ 254B David Palmer COR (position P)	.60	.24	.06
□ 255 Donnie Moore	.05	.02	.00
□ 256 Curtis Wilkerson	.05	.02	.00
□ 257 Julio Cruz	.05	.02	.00
□ 258 Nolan Ryan	.35	.14	.03
□ 259 Jeff Stone	.05	.02	.00
□ 260 John Tudor	.12	.05	.01
□ 261 Mark Thurmond	.05	.02	.00
□ 262 Jay Tibbs	.05	.02	.00
□ 263 Rafael Ramirez	.05	.02	.00
□ 264 Larry McWilliams	.05	.02	.00
□ 265 Mark Davis	.08	.03	.01
□ 266 Bob Dernier	.05	.02	.00
□ 267 Matt Young	.05	.02	.00
□ 268 Jim Clancy	.05	.02	.00
□ 269 Mickey Hatcher	.08	.03	.01
□ 270 Sammy Stewart	.05	.02	.00
□ 271 Bob L. Gibson	.05	.02	.00
□ 272 Nelson Simmons	.08	.03	.01
□ 273 Rich Gedman	.08	.03	.01
□ 274 Butch Wynegar	.05	.02	.00
□ 275 Ken Howell	.08	.03	.01
□ 276 Mel Hall	.08	.03	.01
□ 277 Jim Sundberg	.05	.02	.00
□ 278 Chris Codiroli	.05	.02	.00
□ 279 Herman Winningham	.10	.04	.01
□ 280 Rod Carew	.35	.14	.03
□ 281 Don Slaught	.05	.02	.00
□ 282 Scott Fletcher	.08	.03	.01
□ 283 Bill Dawley	.05	.02	.00
□ 284 Andy Hawkins	.08	.03	.01
□ 285 Glenn Wilson	.08	.03	.01
□ 286 Nick Esasky	.08	.03	.01
□ 287 Claudell Washington	.08	.03	.01
□ 288 Lee Mazzilli	.05	.02	.00
□ 289 Jody Davis	.08	.03	.01
□ 290 Darrell Porter	.05	.02	.00
□ 291 Scott McGregor	.08	.03	.01
□ 292 Ted Simmons	.10	.04	.01
□ 293 Aurelio Lopez	.05	.02	.00
□ 294 Marty Barrett	.12	.05	.01
□ 295 Dale Berra	.05	.02	.00
□ 296 Greg Brock	.05	.02	.00
□ 297 Charlie Leibrandt	.05	.02	.00
□ 298 Bill Krueger	.05	.02	.00
□ 299 Bryn Smith	.05	.02	.00
□ 300 Burt Hooton	.05	.02	.00
□ 301 Stu Cliburn	.08	.03	.01
□ 302 Luis Salazar	.05	.02	.00
□ 303 Ken Dayley	.05	.02	.00
□ 304 Frank DiPino	.05	.02	.00
□ 305 Von Hayes	.12	.05	.01
□ 306 Gary Redus	.05	.02	.00
□ 307 Craig Lefferts	.05	.02	.00
□ 308 Sammy Khalifa	.08	.03	.01
□ 309 Scott Garrelts	.08	.03	.01
□ 310 Rick Cerone	.05	.02	.00
□ 311 Shawon Dunston	.10	.04	.01
□ 312 Howard Johnson	.25	.10	.02
□ 313 Jim Presley	.15	.06	.01
□ 314 Gary Gaetti	.25	.10	.02
□ 315 Luis Leal	.05	.02	.00
□ 316 Mark Salas	.05	.02	.00
□ 317 Bill Caudill	.05	.02	.00
□ 318 Dave Henderson	.10	.04	.01
□ 319 Rafael Santana	.05	.02	.00
□ 320 Leon Durham	.08	.03	.01
□ 321 Bruce Sutter	.12	.05	.01
□ 322 Jason Thompson	.05	.02	.00
□ 323 Bob Brenly	.05	.02	.00
□ 324 Carmelo Martinez	.05	.02	.00
□ 325 Eddie Milner	.05	.02	.00

☐ 326	Juan Samuel	.15	.06	.01
☐ 327	Tom Nieto	.05	.02	.00
☐ 328	Dave Smith	.08	.03	.01
☐ 329	Urbano Lugo	.05	.02	.00
☐ 330	Joel Skinner	.05	.02	.00
☐ 331	Bill Gullickson	.05	.02	.00
☐ 332	Floyd Rayford	.05	.02	.00
☐ 333	Ben Oglivie	.08	.03	.01
☐ 334	Lance Parrish	.15	.06	.01
☐ 335	Jackie Gutierrez	.05	.02	.00
☐ 336	Dennis Rasmussen	.10	.04	.01
☐ 337	Terry Whitfield	.05	.02	.00
☐ 338	Neal Heaton	.05	.02	.00
☐ 339	Jorge Orta	.05	.02	.00
☐ 340	Donnie Hill	.05	.02	.00
☐ 341	Joe Hesketh	.05	.02	.00
☐ 342	Charlie Hough	.08	.03	.01
☐ 343	Dave Rozema	.05	.02	.00
☐ 344	Greg Pryor	.05	.02	.00
☐ 345	Mickey Tettleton	.08	.03	.01
☐ 346	George Vukovich	.05	.02	.00
☐ 347	Don Baylor	.10	.04	.01
☐ 348	Carlos Diaz	.05	.02	.00
☐ 349	Barbaro Garbey	.05	.02	.00
☐ 350	Larry Sheets	.12	.05	.01
☐ 351	Ted Higuera	1.50	.60	.15
☐ 352	Juan Beniquez	.05	.02	.00
☐ 353	Bob Forsch	.05	.02	.00
☐ 354	Mark Bailey	.05	.02	.00
☐ 355	Larry Andersen	.05	.02	.00
☐ 356	Terry Kennedy	.05	.02	.00
☐ 357	Don Robinson	.05	.02	.00
☐ 358	Jim Gott	.05	.02	.00
☐ 359	Earnie Riles	.25	.10	.02
☐ 360	John Christensen	.05	.02	.00
☐ 361	Ray Fontenot	.05	.02	.00
☐ 362	Spike Owen	.05	.02	.00
☐ 363	Jim Acker	.05	.02	.00
☐ 364	Ron Davis	.08	.03	.01
☐ 365	Tom Hume	.05	.02	.00
☐ 366	Carlton Fisk	.15	.06	.01
☐ 367	Nate Snell	.05	.02	.00
☐ 368	Rick Manning	.05	.02	.00
☐ 369	Darrell Evans	.10	.04	.01
☐ 370	Ron Hassey	.05	.02	.00
☐ 371	Wade Boggs	3.00	1.20	.30
☐ 372	Rick Honeycutt	.05	.02	.00
☐ 373	Chris Bando	.05	.02	.00
☐ 374	Bud Black	.05	.02	.00
☐ 375	Steve Henderson	.05	.02	.00
☐ 376	Charlie Lea	.05	.02	.00
☐ 377	Reggie Jackson	.45	.18	.04
☐ 378	Dave Schmidt	.08	.03	.01
☐ 379	Bob James	.05	.02	.00
☐ 380	Glenn Davis	2.00	.80	.20
☐ 381	Tim Corcoran	.05	.02	.00
☐ 382	Danny Cox	.10	.04	.01
☐ 383	Tim Flannery	.05	.02	.00
☐ 384	Tom Browning	.20	.08	.02
☐ 385	Rick Camp	.05	.02	.00
☐ 386	Jim Morrison	.05	.02	.00
☐ 387	Dave LaPoint	.08	.03	.01
☐ 388	Davey Lopes	.08	.03	.01
☐ 389	Al Cowens	.05	.02	.00
☐ 390	Doyle Alexander	.08	.03	.01
☐ 391	Tim Laudner	.05	.02	.00
☐ 392	Don Aase	.05	.02	.00
☐ 393	Jaime Cocanower	.05	.02	.00
☐ 394	Randy O'Neal	.05	.02	.00
☐ 395	Mike Easler	.05	.02	.00
☐ 396	Scott Bradley	.05	.02	.00
☐ 397	Tom Niedenfuer	.05	.02	.00
☐ 398	Jerry Willard	.05	.02	.00
☐ 399	Lonnie Smith	.05	.02	.00
☐ 400	Bruce Bochte	.05	.02	.00
☐ 401	Terry Francona	.05	.02	.00
☐ 402	Jim Slaton	.05	.02	.00
☐ 403	Bill Stein	.05	.02	.00
☐ 404	Tim Hulett	.05	.02	.00
☐ 405	Alan Ashby	.05	.02	.00
☐ 406	Tim Stoddard	.05	.02	.00
☐ 407	Garry Maddox	.08	.03	.01
☐ 408	Ted Power	.05	.02	.00
☐ 409	Len Barker	.05	.02	.00
☐ 410	Denny Gonzalez	.05	.02	.00
☐ 411	George Frazier	.05	.02	.00
☐ 412	Andy Van Slyke	.25	.10	.02
☐ 413	Jim Dwyer	.05	.02	.00
☐ 414	Paul Householder	.05	.02	.00
☐ 415	Alejandro Sanchez	.05	.02	.00
☐ 416	Steve Crawford	.05	.02	.00
☐ 417	Dan Pasqua	.10	.04	.01
☐ 418	Enos Cabell	.05	.02	.00
☐ 419	Mike Jones	.05	.02	.00
☐ 420	Steve Kiefer	.05	.02	.00
☐ 421	Tim Burke	.25	.10	.02
☐ 422	Mike Mason	.05	.02	.00
☐ 423	Ruppert Jones	.05	.02	.00
☐ 424	Jerry Hairston	.05	.02	.00
☐ 425	Tito Landrum	.05	.02	.00
☐ 426	Jeff Calhoun	.05	.02	.00
☐ 427	Don Carman	.25	.10	.02
☐ 428	Tony Perez	.12	.05	.01
☐ 429	Jerry Davis	.05	.02	.00
☐ 430	Bob Walk	.08	.03	.01
☐ 431	Brad Wellman	.05	.02	.00
☐ 432	Terry Forster	.08	.03	.01
☐ 433	Billy Hatcher	.12	.05	.01
☐ 434	Clint Hurdle	.05	.02	.00
☐ 435	Ivan Calderon	.85	.34	.08
☐ 436	Pete Filson	.05	.02	.00
☐ 437	Tom Henke	.12	.05	.01
☐ 438	Dave Engle	.05	.02	.00
☐ 439	Tom Filer	.05	.02	.00
☐ 440	Gorman Thomas	.10	.04	.01
☐ 441	Rick Aguilera	.25	.10	.02
☐ 442	Scott Sanderson	.05	.02	.00
☐ 443	Jeff Dedmon	.05	.02	.00
☐ 444	Joe Orsulak	.12	.05	.01
☐ 445	Atlee Hammaker	.05	.02	.00
☐ 446	Jerry Royster	.05	.02	.00
☐ 447	Buddy Bell	.10	.04	.01
☐ 448	Dave Rucker	.05	.02	.00
☐ 449	Ivan DeJesus	.05	.02	.00
☐ 450	Jim Pankovits	.05	.02	.00
☐ 451	Jerry Narron	.05	.02	.00
☐ 452	Bryan Little	.05	.02	.00
☐ 453	Gary Lucas	.05	.02	.00
☐ 454	Dennis Martinez	.08	.03	.01
☐ 455	Ed Romero	.05	.02	.00
☐ 456	Bob Melvin	.10	.04	.01
☐ 457	Glenn Hoffman	.05	.02	.00
☐ 458	Bob Shirley	.05	.02	.00
☐ 459	Bob Welch	.08	.03	.01
☐ 460	Carmen Castillo	.05	.02	.00
☐ 461	Dave Leeper (outfielder)	.08	.03	.01
☐ 462	Tim Birtsas	.12	.05	.01
☐ 463	Randy St.Claire	.05	.02	.00
☐ 464	Chris Welsh	.05	.02	.00
☐ 465	Greg Harris	.05	.02	.00
☐ 466	Lynn Jones	.05	.02	.00
☐ 467	Dusty Baker	.08	.03	.01
☐ 468	Roy Smith	.05	.02	.00
☐ 469	Andre Robertson	.05	.02	.00
☐ 470	Ken Landreaux	.05	.02	.00
☐ 471	Dave Bergman	.05	.02	.00
☐ 472	Gary Roenicke	.05	.02	.00
☐ 473	Pete Vuckovich	.05	.02	.00
☐ 474	Kirk McCaskill	.35	.14	.03
☐ 475	Jeff Lahti	.05	.02	.00
☐ 476	Mike Scott	.35	.14	.03
☐ 477	Darren Daulton	.15	.06	.01
☐ 478	Graig Nettles	.10	.04	.01
☐ 479	Bill Almon	.05	.02	.00
☐ 480	Greg Minton	.05	.02	.00
☐ 481	Randy Ready	.05	.02	.00
☐ 482	Lenny Dykstra	1.00	.40	.10
☐ 483	Thad Bosley	.05	.02	.00
☐ 484	Harold Reynolds	.45	.18	.04
☐ 485	Al Oliver	.10	.04	.01
☐ 486	Roy Smalley	.05	.02	.00
☐ 487	John Franco	.15	.06	.01
☐ 488	Juan Agosto	.05	.02	.00
☐ 489	Al Pardo	.05	.02	.00
☐ 490	Bill Wegman	.12	.05	.01
☐ 491	Frank Tanana	.08	.03	.01
☐ 492	Brian Fisher	.30	.12	.03
☐ 493	Mark Clear	.05	.02	.00
☐ 494	Len Matuszek	.05	.02	.00
☐ 495	Ramon Romero	.05	.02	.00
☐ 496	John Wathan	.05	.02	.00
☐ 497	Rob Picciolo	.05	.02	.00
☐ 498	U.L. Washington	.05	.02	.00
☐ 499	John Candelaria	.08	.03	.01
☐ 500	Duane Walker	.05	.02	.00
☐ 501	Gene Nelson	.05	.02	.00
☐ 502	John Mizerock	.05	.02	.00
☐ 503	Luis Aguayo	.05	.02	.00
☐ 504	Kurt Kepshire	.05	.02	.00
☐ 505	Ed Wojna	.10	.04	.01
☐ 506	Joe Price	.05	.02	.00
☐ 507	Milt Thompson	.30	.12	.03
☐ 508	Junior Ortiz	.05	.02	.00
☐ 509	Vida Blue	.08	.03	.01
☐ 510	Steve Engel	.05	.02	.00
☐ 511	Karl Best	.05	.02	.00
☐ 512	Cecil Fielder	.20	.08	.02
☐ 513	Frank Eufemia	.08	.03	.01
☐ 514	Tippy Martinez	.05	.02	.00

- ☐ 515 Billy Robidoux .10 .04 .01
- ☐ 516 Bill Scherrer .05 .02 .00
- ☐ 517 Bruce Hurst .15 .06 .01
- ☐ 518 Rich Bordi .05 .02 .00
- ☐ 519 Steve Yeager .05 .02 .00
- ☐ 520 Tony Bernazard .05 .02 .00
- ☐ 521 Hal McRae .08 .03 .01
- ☐ 522 Jose Rijo .08 .03 .01
- ☐ 523 Mitch Webster .35 .14 .03
- ☐ 524 Jack Howell .35 .14 .03
- ☐ 525 Alan Bannister .05 .02 .00
- ☐ 526 Ron Kittle .10 .04 .01
- ☐ 527 Phil Garner .05 .02 .00
- ☐ 528 Kurt Bevacqua .05 .02 .00
- ☐ 529 Kevin Gross .05 .02 .00
- ☐ 530 Bo Diaz .05 .02 .00
- ☐ 531 Ken Oberkfell .05 .02 .00
- ☐ 532 Rick Reuschel .10 .04 .01
- ☐ 533 Ron Meridith .08 .03 .01
- ☐ 534 Steve Braun .05 .02 .00
- ☐ 535 Wayne Gross .05 .02 .00
- ☐ 536 Ray Searage .05 .02 .00
- ☐ 537 Tom Brookens .05 .02 .00
- ☐ 538 Al Nipper .05 .02 .00
- ☐ 539 Billy Sample .05 .02 .00
- ☐ 540 Steve Sax .15 .06 .01
- ☐ 541 Dan Quisenberry .10 .04 .01
- ☐ 542 Tony Phillips .05 .02 .00
- ☐ 543 Floyd Youmans .40 .16 .04
- ☐ 544 Steve Buechele .25 .10 .02
- ☐ 545 Craig Gerber .05 .02 .00
- ☐ 546 Joe DeSa .05 .02 .00
- ☐ 547 Brian Harper .05 .02 .00
- ☐ 548 Kevin Bass .08 .03 .01
- ☐ 549 Tom Foley .05 .02 .00
- ☐ 550 Dave Van Gorder .05 .02 .00
- ☐ 551 Bruce Bochy .05 .02 .00
- ☐ 552 R.J. Reynolds .05 .02 .00
- ☐ 553 Chris Brown .45 .18 .04
- ☐ 554 Bruce Benedict .05 .02 .00
- ☐ 555 Warren Brusstar .05 .02 .00
- ☐ 556 Danny Heep .05 .02 .00
- ☐ 557 Darnell Coles .05 .02 .00
- ☐ 558 Greg Gagne .05 .02 .00
- ☐ 559 Ernie Whitt .05 .02 .00
- ☐ 560 Ron Washington .05 .02 .00
- ☐ 561 Jimmy Key .15 .06 .01
- ☐ 562 Billy Swift .10 .04 .01
- ☐ 563 Ron Darling .30 .12 .03
- ☐ 564 Dick Ruthven .05 .02 .00
- ☐ 565 Zane Smith .25 .10 .02
- ☐ 566 Sid Bream .05 .02 .00
- ☐ 567A Joel Youngblood ERR (position P) .10 .04 .01
- ☐ 567B Joel Youngblood COR (position IF) .60 .24 .06
- ☐ 568 Mario Ramirez .05 .02 .00
- ☐ 569 Tom Runnels .05 .02 .00
- ☐ 570 Rick Schu .05 .02 .00
- ☐ 571 Bill Campbell .05 .02 .00
- ☐ 572 Dickie Thon .05 .02 .00
- ☐ 573 Al Holland .05 .02 .00
- ☐ 574 Reid Nichols .05 .02 .00
- ☐ 575 Bert Roberge .05 .02 .00
- ☐ 576 Mike Flanagan .08 .03 .01
- ☐ 577 Tim Leary .35 .14 .03
- ☐ 578 Mike Laga .05 .02 .00
- ☐ 579 Steve Lyons .05 .02 .00
- ☐ 580 Phil Niekro .20 .08 .02
- ☐ 581 Gilberto Reyes .10 .04 .01
- ☐ 582 Jamie Easterly .05 .02 .00
- ☐ 583 Mark Gubicza .12 .05 .01
- ☐ 584 Stan Javier .25 .10 .02
- ☐ 585 Bill Laskey .05 .02 .00
- ☐ 586 Jeff Russell .05 .02 .00
- ☐ 587 Dickie Noles .05 .02 .00
- ☐ 588 Steve Farr .05 .02 .00
- ☐ 589 Steve Ontiveros .12 .05 .01
- ☐ 590 Mike Hargrove .05 .02 .00
- ☐ 591 Marty Bystrom .05 .02 .00
- ☐ 592 Franklin Stubbs .08 .03 .01
- ☐ 593 Larry Herndon .05 .02 .00
- ☐ 594 Bill Swaggerty .05 .02 .00
- ☐ 595 Carlos Ponce .05 .02 .00
- ☐ 596 Pat Perry .10 .04 .01
- ☐ 597 Ray Knight .08 .03 .01
- ☐ 598 Steve Lombardozzi .15 .06 .01
- ☐ 599 Brad Havens .05 .02 .00
- ☐ 600 Pat Clements .12 .05 .01
- ☐ 601 Joe Niekro .08 .03 .01
- ☐ 602 Hank Aaron Puzzle Card .08 .03 .01
- ☐ 603 Dwayne Henry .08 .03 .01
- ☐ 604 Mookie Wilson .08 .03 .01
- ☐ 605 Buddy Biancalana .05 .02 .00
- ☐ 606 Rance Mulliniks .05 .02 .00
- ☐ 607 Alan Wiggins .05 .02 .00
- ☐ 608 Joe Cowley .05 .02 .00
- ☐ 609A Tom Seaver (green borders on name) .40 .16 .04
- ☐ 609B Tom Seaver (yellow borders on name) 1.25 .50 .12
- ☐ 610 Neil Allen .05 .02 .00
- ☐ 611 Don Sutton .25 .10 .02
- ☐ 612 Fred Toliver .10 .04 .01
- ☐ 613 Jay Baller .08 .03 .01
- ☐ 614 Marc Sullivan .08 .03 .01
- ☐ 615 John Grubb .05 .02 .00
- ☐ 616 Bruce Kison .05 .02 .00
- ☐ 617 Bill Madlock .10 .04 .01
- ☐ 618 Chris Chambliss .08 .03 .01
- ☐ 619 Dave Stewart .12 .05 .01
- ☐ 620 Tim Lollar .05 .02 .00
- ☐ 621 Gary Lavelle .05 .02 .00
- ☐ 622 Charlie Hudson .05 .02 .00
- ☐ 623 Joel Davis .12 .05 .01
- ☐ 624 Joe Johnson .12 .05 .01
- ☐ 625 Sid Fernandez .15 .06 .01
- ☐ 626 Dennis Lamp .05 .02 .00
- ☐ 627 Terry Harper .05 .02 .00
- ☐ 628 Jack Lazorko .05 .02 .00
- ☐ 629 Roger McDowell .60 .24 .06
- ☐ 630 Mark Funderburk .10 .04 .01
- ☐ 631 Ed Lynch .05 .02 .00
- ☐ 632 Rudy Law .05 .02 .00
- ☐ 633 Roger Mason .10 .04 .01
- ☐ 634 Mike Felder .12 .05 .01
- ☐ 635 Ken Schrom .05 .02 .00
- ☐ 636 Bob Ojeda .08 .03 .01
- ☐ 637 Ed VandeBerg .05 .02 .00
- ☐ 638 Bobby Meacham .05 .02 .00
- ☐ 639 Cliff Johnson .05 .02 .00
- ☐ 640 Garth Iorg .05 .02 .00
- ☐ 641 Dan Driessen .05 .02 .00
- ☐ 642 Mike Brown OF .05 .02 .00
- ☐ 643 John Shelby .05 .02 .00
- ☐ 644 Pete Rose (Ty-Breaking) .35 .14 .03
- ☐ 645 The Knuckle Brothers (Phil Niekro, Joe Niekro) .10 .04 .01
- ☐ 646 Jesse Orosco .05 .02 .00
- ☐ 647 Billy Beane .15 .06 .01
- ☐ 648 Cesar Cedeno .08 .03 .01
- ☐ 649 Bert Blyleven .10 .04 .01
- ☐ 650 Max Venable .05 .02 .00
- ☐ 651 Fleet Feet (Vince Coleman, Willie McGee) .30 .12 .03
- ☐ 652 Calvin Schiraldi .08 .03 .01
- ☐ 653 King of Kings (Pete Rose) .65 .26 .06
- ☐ 654 CL: Diamond Kings (unnumbered) .08 .01 .00
- ☐ 655A CL 1: 27-130 (unnumbered) (45 Beane ERR) .10 .01 .00
- ☐ 655B CL 1: 27-130 (unnumbered) (45 Habyan COR) .50 .05 .01
- ☐ 656 CL 2: 131-234 (unnumbered) .06 .01 .00
- ☐ 657 CL 3: 235-338 (unnumbered) .06 .01 .00
- ☐ 658 CL 4: 339-442 (unnumbered) .06 .01 .00
- ☐ 659 CL 5: 443-546 (unnumbered) .06 .01 .00
- ☐ 660 CL 6: 547-653 (unnumbered) .06 .01 .00

1986 Donruss Wax Box Cards

The cards in this 4-card set measure the standard 2 1/2" by 3 1/2". Cards have essentially the same design as the 1986 Donruss regular issue set. The cards were printed on the bottoms of the regular issue wax pack boxes. The four cards (PC4 to PC6 plus a Hank Aaron puzzle card) are considered a separate set in their own right and are not typically included in a complete set of the regular issue 1986

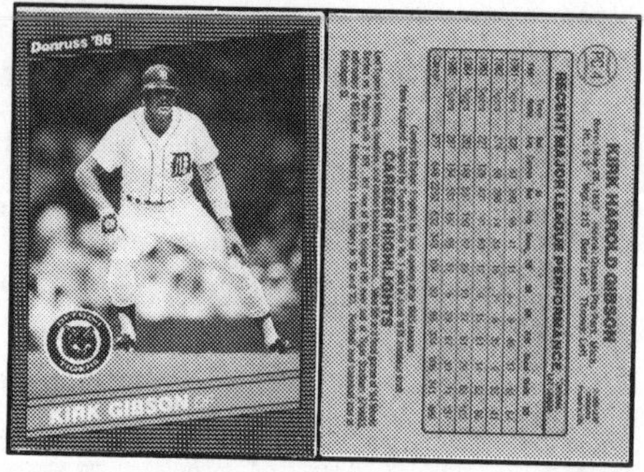

Donruss cards. The value of the panel uncut is slightly greater, perhaps by 25% greater, than the value of the individual cards cut up carefully.

	MINT	EXC	G-VG
COMPLETE SET (4)	.60	.24	.06
COMMON PLAYERS	.05	.02	.00
☐ PC4 Kirk Gibson	.50	.20	.05
☐ PC5 Willie Hernandez	.10	.04	.01
☐ PC6 Doug DeCinces	.10	.04	.01
☐ PUZ Hank Aaron Puzzle Card	.05	.02	.00

1986 Donruss All-Stars

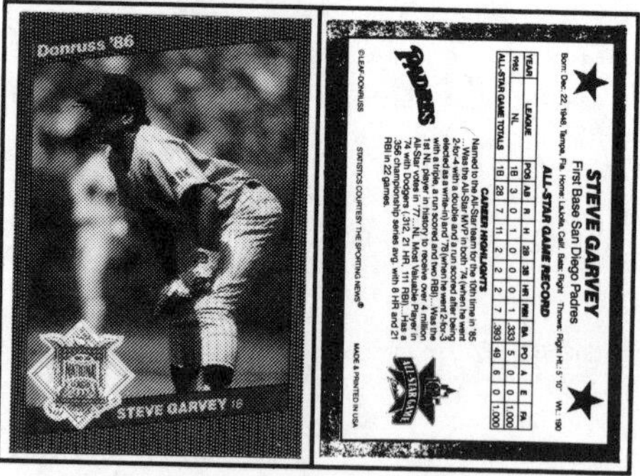

The cards in this 60-card set measure 3 1/2" by 5". Players featured were involved in the 1985 All-Star game played in Minnesota. Cards are very similar in design to the 1986 Donruss regular issue set. The backs give each player's All-Star game statistics and have an orange-yellow border.

	MINT	EXC	G-VG
COMPLETE SET (60)	6.00	2.40	.60
COMMON PLAYERS (1-60)	.05	.02	.00
☐ 1 Tony Gwynn	.35	.14	.03
☐ 2 Tommy Herr	.05	.02	.00
☐ 3 Steve Garvey	.30	.12	.03
☐ 4 Dale Murphy	.50	.20	.05
☐ 5 Darryl Strawberry	.60	.24	.06
☐ 6 Graig Nettles	.10	.04	.01
☐ 7 Terry Kennedy	.05	.02	.00
☐ 8 Ozzie Smith	.20	.08	.02
☐ 9 LaMarr Hoyt	.05	.02	.00
☐ 10 Rickey Henderson	.40	.16	.04
☐ 11 Lou Whitaker	.10	.04	.01
☐ 12 George Brett	.40	.16	.04
☐ 13 Eddie Murray	.35	.14	.03
☐ 14 Cal Ripken	.30	.12	.03
☐ 15 Dave Winfield	.25	.10	.02
☐ 16 Jim Rice	.20	.08	.02
☐ 17 Carlton Fisk	.10	.04	.01
☐ 18 Jack Morris	.10	.04	.01
☐ 19 Jose Cruz	.05	.02	.00
☐ 20 Tim Raines	.20	.08	.02
☐ 21 Nolan Ryan	.35	.14	.0
☐ 22 Tony Pena	.05	.02	.0
☐ 23 Jack Clark	.15	.06	.0
☐ 24 Dave Parker	.10	.04	.0
☐ 25 Tim Wallach	.05	.02	.0
☐ 26 Ozzie Virgil	.05	.02	.0
☐ 27 Fernando Valenzuela	.20	.08	.0
☐ 28 Dwight Gooden	.75	.30	.0
☐ 29 Glenn Wilson	.05	.02	.0
☐ 30 Garry Templeton	.05	.02	.0
☐ 31 Goose Gossage	.10	.04	.0
☐ 32 Ryne Sandberg	.25	.10	.0
☐ 33 Jeff Reardon	.10	.04	.0
☐ 34 Pete Rose	.90	.36	.09
☐ 35 Scott Garrelts	.05	.02	.00
☐ 36 Willie McGee	.15	.06	.01
☐ 37 Ron Darling	.15	.06	.01
☐ 38 Dick Williams MG	.05	.02	.00
☐ 39 Paul Molitor	.20	.08	.02
☐ 40 Damaso Garcia	.05	.02	.00
☐ 41 Phil Bradley	.10	.04	.01
☐ 42 Dan Petry	.05	.02	.00
☐ 43 Willie Hernandez	.10	.04	.01
☐ 44 Tom Brunansky	.10	.04	.01
☐ 45 Alan Trammell	.20	.08	.02
☐ 46 Donnie Moore	.05	.02	.00
☐ 47 Wade Boggs	.90	.36	.09
☐ 48 Ernie Whitt	.05	.02	.00
☐ 49 Harold Baines	.10	.04	.01
☐ 50 Don Mattingly	1.25	.50	.12
☐ 51 Gary Ward	.05	.02	.00
☐ 52 Bert Blyleven	.10	.04	.01
☐ 53 Jimmy Key	.10	.04	.01
☐ 54 Cecil Cooper	.10	.04	.01
☐ 55 Dave Stieb	.10	.04	.01
☐ 56 Rich Gedman	.05	.02	.00
☐ 57 Jay Howell	.05	.02	.00
☐ 58 Sparky Anderson MG	.05	.02	.00
☐ 59 Minneapolis Metrodome	.05	.02	.00
☐ 60 Checklist card (unnumbered)	.05	.01	.00

1986 Donruss All-Star Box

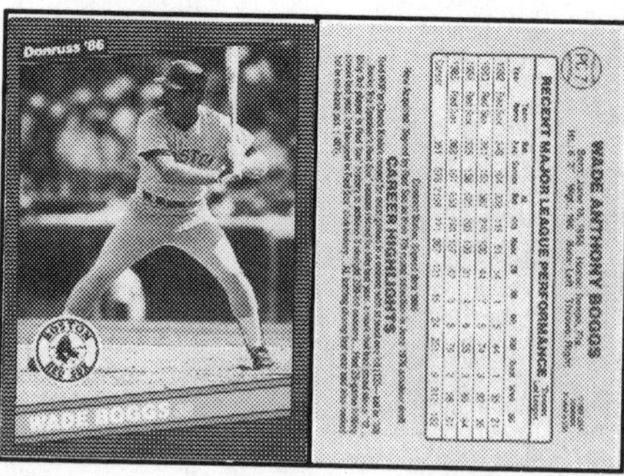

The cards in this 4-card set measure the standard 2 1/2" by 3 1/2" in spite of the fact that they form the bottom of the wax pack box for the larger Donruss All-Star cards. These box cards have essentially the same design as the 1986 Donruss regular issue set. The cards were printed on the bottoms of the Donruss All-Star (3 1/2" by 5") wax pack boxes. The four cards (PC7 to PC9 plus a Hank Aaron puzzle card) are considered a separate set in their own right and are not typically included in a complete set of the regular issue 1986 Donruss All-Star (or regular) cards. The value of the panel uncut is slightly greater, perhaps by 25% greater, than the value of the individual cards cut up carefully.

	MINT	EXC	G-VG
COMPLETE SET (4)	1.25	.50	.12
COMMON PLAYERS	.05	.02	.00
☐ PC7 Wade Boggs	1.25	.50	.12
☐ PC8 Lee Smith	.10	.04	.01
☐ PC9 Cecil Cooper	.10	.04	.01

		MINT	EXC	G-VG
☐ PUZ	Hank Aaron Puzzle Card	.05	.02	.00

1986 Donruss Pop-Ups

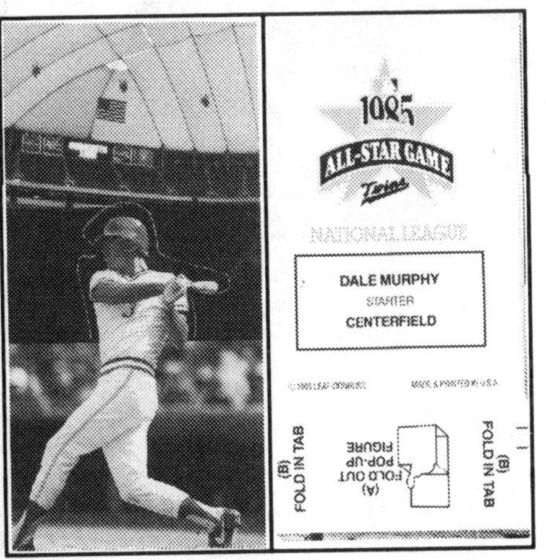

This set is the companion of the 1986 Donruss All-Star (60) set; as such it features the first 18 cards of that set (the All-Star starting line-ups) in a pop-up, die-cut type of card. These cards (measuring (2 1/2" by 5") can be "popped up" to feature a standing card showing the player in action in front of the Metrodome ballpark background. Although this set is unnumbered it is numbered in the same order as its companion set, presumably according to the respective batting orders of the starting line-ups. The first nine numbers below are National Leaguers and the last nine are American Leaguers. See also the Donruss All-Star checklist card which contains a checklist for the Pop-Ups as well.

		MINT	EXC	G-VG
	COMPLETE SET (18)	4.00	1.60	.40
	COMMON PLAYERS (1-18)	.10	.04	.01
☐ 1	Tony Gwynn	.40	.16	.04
☐ 2	Tommy Herr	.10	.04	.01
☐ 3	Steve Garvey	.40	.16	.04
☐ 4	Dale Murphy	.50	.20	.05
☐ 5	Darryl Strawberry	.60	.24	.06
☐ 6	Graig Nettles	.10	.04	.01
☐ 7	Terry Kennedy	.10	.04	.01
☐ 8	Ozzie Smith	.20	.08	.02
☐ 9	LaMarr Hoyt	.10	.04	.01
☐ 10	Rickey Henderson	.50	.20	.05
☐ 11	Lou Whitaker	.15	.06	.01
☐ 12	George Brett	.50	.20	.05
☐ 13	Eddie Murray	.40	.16	.04
☐ 14	Cal Ripken	.40	.16	.04
☐ 15	Dave Winfield	.30	.12	.03
☐ 16	Jim Rice	.25	.10	.02
☐ 17	Carlton Fisk	.15	.06	.01
☐ 18	Jack Morris	.15	.06	.01

1986 Donruss Super DK's

This 29-card set of large Diamond Kings features the full-color artwork of Dick Perez. The set could be obtained from Perez-Steele Galleries by sending three Donruss wrappers and 9.00. The cards measure 4 7/8" by 6 13/16" and are identical in design to the Diamond King cards in the Donruss regular issue.

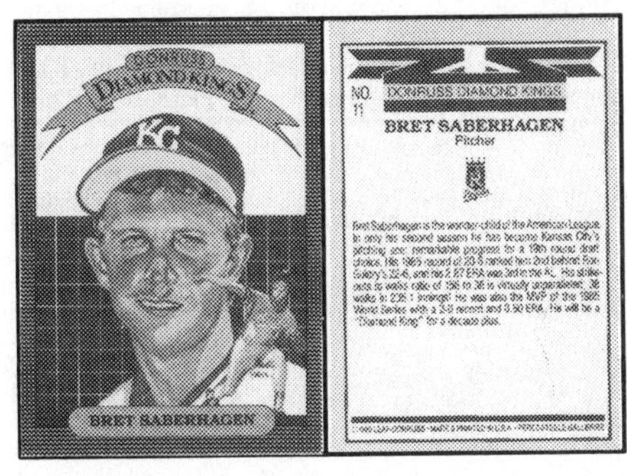

		MINT	EXC	G-VG
	COMPLETE SET (29)	10.00	4.00	1.00
	COMMON PLAYER (1-26)	.20	.08	.02
☐ 1	Kirk Gibson	.50	.20	.05
☐ 2	Goose Gossage	.30	.12	.03
☐ 3	Willie McGee	.30	.12	.03
☐ 4	George Bell	.35	.14	.03
☐ 5	Tony Armas	.20	.08	.02
☐ 6	Chili Davis	.20	.08	.02
☐ 7	Cecil Cooper	.25	.10	.02
☐ 8	Mike Boddicker	.25	.10	.02
☐ 9	Davey Lopes	.20	.08	.02
☐ 10	Bill Doran	.25	.10	.02
☐ 11	Bret Saberhagen	.45	.18	.04
☐ 12	Brett Butler	.25	.10	.02
☐ 13	Harold Baines	.30	.12	.03
☐ 14	Mike Davis	.20	.08	.02
☐ 15	Tony Perez	.30	.12	.03
☐ 16	Willie Randolph	.30	.12	.03
☐ 17	Bob Boone	.30	.12	.03
☐ 18	Orel Hershiser	1.00	.40	.10
☐ 19	Johnny Ray	.30	.12	.03
☐ 20	Gary Ward	.20	.08	.02
☐ 21	Rick Mahler	.20	.08	.02
☐ 22	Phil Bradley	.30	.12	.03
☐ 23	Jerry Koosman	.30	.12	.03
☐ 24	Tom Brunansky	.30	.12	.03
☐ 25	Andre Dawson	.50	.20	.05
☐ 26	Dwight Gooden	1.25	.50	.12
☐ 27	Pete Rose King of Kings	1.25	.50	.12
☐ 28	Checklist card (unnumbered)	.10	.01	.00
☐ 29	Aaron Large Puzzle (unnumbered)	.20	.08	.02

1986 Donruss Rookies

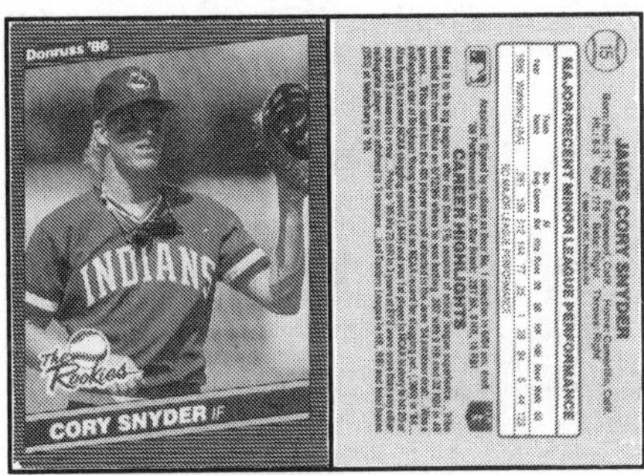

The 1986 Donruss "The Rookies" set features 56 cards plus a 15-piece puzzle of Hank Aaron. Cards are in full color and are standard size, 2 1/2" by 3 1/2". The set was distributed in a small green box with gold lettering. Although the set was wrapped in cellophane, the top card was #1 Joyner resulting in a percentage of (Joyner) cards arriving in less than perfect condition. Card fronts are similar in design to the 1986 Donruss regular issue except for the presence of "The Rookies" logo in the lower left corner and a bluish green border instead of a blue border.

	MINT	EXC	G-VG
COMPLETE SET (56)	21.00	8.50	2.10
COMMON PLAYER (1-56)	.08	.03	.01

		MINT	EXC	G-VG
☐ 1	Wally Joyner	4.00	1.00	.20
☐ 2	Tracy Jones	.55	.22	.05
☐ 3	Allan Anderson	.40	.16	.04
☐ 4	Ed Correa	.20	.08	.02
☐ 5	Reggie Williams	.15	.06	.01
☐ 6	Charlie Kerfeld	.15	.06	.01
☐ 7	Andres Galarraga	.90	.36	.09
☐ 8	Bob Tewksbury	.15	.06	.01
☐ 9	Al Newman	.15	.06	.01
☐ 10	Andres Thomas	.25	.10	.02
☐ 11	Barry Bonds	1.25	.50	.12
☐ 12	Juan Nieves	.15	.06	.01
☐ 13	Mark Eichhorn	.15	.06	.01
☐ 14	Dan Plesac	.35	.14	.03
☐ 15	Cory Snyder	1.25	.50	.12
☐ 16	Kelly Gruber	.08	.03	.01
☐ 17	Kevin Mitchell	.45	.18	.04
☐ 18	Steve Lombardozzi	.08	.03	.01
☐ 19	Mitch Williams	.25	.10	.02
☐ 20	John Cerutti	.20	.08	.02
☐ 21	Todd Worrell	.45	.18	.04
☐ 22	Jose Canseco	7.50	3.00	.75
☐ 23	Pete Incaviglia	.85	.34	.08
☐ 24	Jose Guzman	.15	.06	.01
☐ 25	Scott Bailes	.15	.06	.01
☐ 26	Greg Mathews	.30	.12	.03
☐ 27	Eric King	.20	.08	.02
☐ 28	Paul Assenmacher	.15	.06	.01
☐ 29	Jeff Sellers	.20	.08	.02
☐ 30	Bobby Bonilla	1.25	.50	.12
☐ 31	Doug Drabek	.35	.14	.03
☐ 32	Will Clark	4.00	1.60	.40
☐ 33	Leon "Bip" Roberts	.15	.06	.01
☐ 34	Jim Deshaies	.35	.14	.03
☐ 35	Mike Lavalliere	.25	.10	.02
☐ 36	Scott Bankhead	.20	.08	.02
☐ 37	Dale Sveum	.30	.12	.03
☐ 38	Bo Jackson	2.50	1.00	.25
☐ 39	Rob Thompson	.35	.14	.03
☐ 40	Eric Plunk	.20	.08	.02
☐ 41	Bill Bathe	.15	.06	.01
☐ 42	John Kruk	.50	.20	.05
☐ 43	Andy Allanson	.15	.06	.01
☐ 44	Mark Portugal	.15	.06	.01
☐ 45	Danny Tartabull	.85	.34	.08
☐ 46	Bob Kipper	.08	.03	.01
☐ 47	Gene Walter	.15	.06	.01
☐ 48	Rey Quinones	.25	.10	.02
☐ 49	Bobby Witt	.50	.20	.05
☐ 50	Bill Mooneyham	.15	.06	.01
☐ 51	John Cangelosi	.20	.08	.02
☐ 52	Ruben Sierra	1.75	.70	.17
☐ 53	Rob Woodward	.15	.06	.01
☐ 54	Ed Hearn	.15	.06	.01
☐ 55	Joel McKeon	.15	.06	.01
☐ 56	Checklist card	.08	.01	.00

1986 Donruss Highlights

Donruss' second edition of Highlights was released late in 1986. The cards are standard size, measuring 2 1/2" by 3 1/2" and are glossy in appearance. Cards commemorate events during the 1986 season, as well as players and pitchers of the month from each league. The set was distributed in its own red, white, blue, and gold box along with a small Hank Aaron puzzle. Card fronts are similar to the regular 1986 Donruss issue except that the Highlights logo is positioned in the lower left- hand corner and the borders are in gold instead of blue. The backs are printed in black and gold on white card stock.

	MINT	EXC	G-VG
COMPLETE SET (56)	7.50	3.00	.75
COMMON PLAYER (1-56)	.06	.02	.00

George Brett
Royals' all-time hit man
April 23

A record that was inevitable to be broken was eclipsed the afternoon of April 23, 1986 when George Brett became the Kansas City Royals' all-time leader in hits. Because he has established so many hitting feats since joining the Royals in 1973 (two batting titles, nine .300 seasons, three American League hit titles etc.), most Royal-watchers just assumed Brett already was the team's all-time hit leader. But it was not until he doubled in the first inning off Dennis Rasmussen of the New York Yankees on April 23 for his 1,978th hit that Brett officially became the Royals' all-time leader. He broke the record of Amos Otis, who played for the Royals from 1970-83. Brett's double was the only hit he would get that day and the Yankees went on to win the game, 2-1, with Rasmussen yielding just two other hits.

NO. 3

© 1986 LEAF, INC. MADE & PRINTED IN U.S.A.

		MINT	EXC	G-VG
☐ 1	Will Clark Homers in First At-Bat	.50	.20	.05
☐ 2	Jose Rijo Oakland Milestone for Strikeouts	.06	.02	.00
☐ 3	George Brett Royals' All-Time Hit Man	.25	.10	.02
☐ 4	Mike Schmidt Phillies RBI Leader	.30	.12	.03
☐ 5	Roger Clemens KKKKKKKKKK KKKKKKKKKK	.40	.16	.04
☐ 6	Roger Clemens AL Pitcher April	.40	.16	.04
☐ 7	Kirby Puckett AL Player April	.35	.14	.03
☐ 8	Dwight Gooden NL Pitcher April	.40	.16	.04
☐ 9	Johnny Ray NL Player April	.06	.02	.00
☐ 10	Reggie Jackson Eclipses Mantle HR Record	.35	.14	.03
☐ 11	Wade Boggs First Five Hit Game of Career	.65	.26	.06
☐ 12	Don Aase AL Pitcher May	.06	.02	.00
☐ 13	Wade Boggs AL Player May	.65	.26	.06
☐ 14	Jeff Reardon NL Pitcher May	.06	.02	.00
☐ 15	Hubie Brooks NL Player May	.06	.02	.00
☐ 16	Don Sutton Notches 300th	.10	.04	.01
☐ 17	Roger Clemens Starts 14-0	.40	.16	.04
☐ 18	Roger Clemens AL Pitcher June	.40	.16	.04
☐ 19	Kent Hrbek AL Player June	.15	.06	.01
☐ 20	Rick Rhoden NL Pitcher June	.06	.02	.00
☐ 21	Kevin Bass NL Player June	.06	.02	.00
☐ 22	Bob Horner Blasts four HRs in one Game	.10	.04	.01
☐ 23	Wally Joyner Starting All-Star Rookie	.60	.24	.06
☐ 24	Darryl Strawberry Starts Third Straight All-Star Game	.45	.18	.04
☐ 25	Fernando Valenzuela Ties All-Star Game Record	.15	.06	.01
☐ 26	Roger Clemens All-Star Game MVP	.40	.16	.04
☐ 27	Jack Morris AL Pitcher July	.10	.04	.01
☐ 28	Scott Fletcher AL Player July	.06	.02	.00
☐ 29	Todd Worrell NL Pitcher July	.10	.04	.01
☐ 30	Eric Davis NL Player July	.65	.26	.06
☐ 31	Bert Blyleven Records 3000th Strikeout	.10	.04	.01

	MINT	EXC	G-VG
□ 32 Bobby Doerr .... '86 HOF Inductee	.15	.06	.01
□ 33 Ernie Lombardi .... '86 HOF Inductee	.15	.06	.01
□ 34 Willie McCovey .... '86 HOF Inductee	.20	.08	.02
□ 35 Steve Carlton .... Notches 4000th K	.20	.08	.02
□ 36 Mike Schmidt .... Surpasses DiMaggio Record	.30	.12	.03
□ 37 Juan Samuel .... Records 3rd "Quadruple Double"	.10	.04	.01
□ 38 Mike Witt .... AL Pitcher August	.10	.04	.01
□ 39 Doug DeCinces .... AL Player August	.06	.02	.00
□ 40 Bill Gullickson .... NL Pitcher August	.06	.02	.00
□ 41 Dale Murphy .... NL Player August	.35	.14	.03
□ 42 Joe Carter .... Sets Tribe Offensive Record	.15	.06	.01
□ 43 Bo Jackson .... Longest HR in Royals Stadium	.65	.26	.06
□ 44 Joe Cowley .... Majors 1st No-Hitter in 2 Years	.06	.02	.00
□ 45 Jim Deshaies .... Sets ML Strikeout Record	.06	.02	.00
□ 46 Mike Scott .... No Hitter Clinches Division	.15	.06	.01
□ 47 Bruce Hurst .... AL Pitcher September	.10	.04	.01
□ 48 Don Mattingly .... AL Player September	.90	.36	.09
□ 49 Mike Krukow .... NL Pitcher September	.06	.02	.00
□ 50 Steve Sax .... NL Player September	.15	.06	.01
□ 51 John Cangelosi .... AL Rookie Steals Record	.10	.04	.01
□ 52 Dave Righetti .... ML Save Mark	.10	.04	.01
□ 53 Don Mattingly .... Yankee Record for Hits and Doubles	.90	.36	.09
□ 54 Todd Worrell .... Donruss NL ROY	.15	.06	.01
□ 55 Jose Canseco .... Donruss AL ROY	1.25	.50	.12
□ 56 Checklist card	.06	.01	.00

1987 Donruss

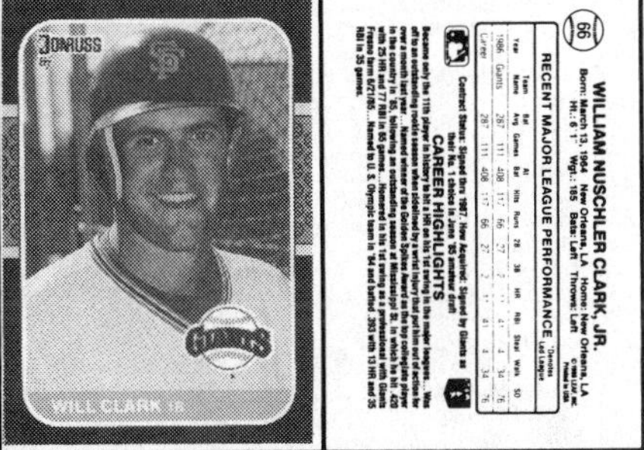

This 660-card set was distributed along with a puzzle of Roberto Clemente. The checklist cards are numbered throughout the set as multiples of 100. The wax pack boxes again contain a separate four cards printed on the bottom of the box. Cards measure 2 1/2" by 3 1/2" and feature a black and gold border on the front; the backs are also done in black and gold on white card stock. The popular Diamond King subset returns for the sixth consecutive year. Some of the Diamond King (1-26) selections are repeats from prior years; Perez-Steele Galleries has indicated that a five-year rotation will be maintained in order to avoid depleting the pool of available worthy "kings" on some of the teams. Three of the Diamond Kings have a variation (on the reverse) where the yellow strip behind the words "Donruss Diamond Kings" is not printed and hence the background is white.

	MINT	EXC	G-VG
COMPLETE SET (660)	40.00	15.00	4.00
COMMON PLAYER (1-660)	.03	.01	.00
□ 1 Wally Joyner DK	1.25	.40	.08
□ 2 Roger Clemens DK	.65	.26	.06
□ 3 Dale Murphy DK	.50	.20	.05
□ 4 Darryl Strawberry DK	.50	.20	.05
□ 5 Ozzie Smith DK	.15	.06	.01
□ 6 Jose Canseco DK	2.00	.80	.20
□ 7 Charlie Hough DK	.08	.03	.01
□ 8 Brook Jacoby DK	.08	.03	.01
□ 9 Fred Lynn DK	.15	.06	.01
□ 10 Rick Rhoden DK	.08	.03	.01
□ 11 Chris Brown DK	.12	.05	.01
□ 12 Von Hayes DK	.10	.04	.01
□ 13 Jack Morris DK	.15	.06	.01
□ 14A Kevin McReynolds DK .. (yellow strip missing on back)	.85	.34	.08
□ 14B Kevin McReynolds DK ..	.35	.14	.03
□ 15 George Brett DK	.40	.16	.04
□ 16 Ted Higuera DK	.20	.08	.02
□ 17 Hubie Brooks DK	.08	.03	.01
□ 18 Mike Scott DK	.25	.10	.02
□ 19 Kirby Puckett DK	.40	.16	.04
□ 20 Dave Winfield DK	.30	.12	.03
□ 21 Lloyd Moseby DK	.10	.04	.01
□ 22A Eric Davis DK .... (yellow strip missing on back)	2.50	1.00	.25
□ 22B Eric Davis DK	1.00	.40	.10
□ 23 Jim Presley DK	.12	.03	.01
□ 24 Keith Moreland DK	.08	.03	.01
□ 25A Greg Walker DK .... (yellow strip missing on back)	.50	.20	.05
□ 25B Greg Walker DK	.12	.05	.01
□ 26 Steve Sax DK	.20	.08	.02
□ 27 DK Checklist 1-26	.09	.01	.00
□ 28 B.J. Surhoff RR	.45	.18	.04
□ 29 Randy Myers RR	.60	.24	.06
□ 30 Ken Gerhart RR	.25	.10	.02
□ 31 Benito Santiago RR	1.50	.60	.15
□ 32 Greg Swindell RR	.80	.32	.08
□ 33 Mike Birkbeck RR	.15	.06	.01
□ 34 Terry Steinbach RR	.50	.20	.05
□ 35 Bo Jackson RR	1.25	.50	.12
□ 36 Greg Maddux RR	1.00	.40	.10
□ 37 Jim Lindeman RR	.20	.08	.02
□ 38 Devon White RR	.90	.36	.09
□ 39 Eric Bell RR	.10	.04	.01
□ 40 Will Fraser RR	.10	.04	.01
□ 41 Jerry Browne RR	.10	.04	.01
□ 42 Chris James RR	.75	.30	.07
□ 43 Rafael Palmeiro RR	1.50	.60	.15
□ 44 Pat Dodson RR	.15	.06	.01
□ 45 Duane Ward RR	.15	.06	.01
□ 46 Mark McGwire RR	7.00	2.80	.70
□ 47 Bruce Fields RR .... (photo actually Darnell Coles)	.10	.04	.01
□ 48 Eddie Murray	.25	.10	.02
□ 49 Ted Higuera	.18	.08	.01
□ 50 Kirk Gibson	.25	.10	.02
□ 51 Oil Can Boyd	.06	.02	.00
□ 52 Don Mattingly	2.25	.90	.22
□ 53 Pedro Guerrero	.15	.06	.01
□ 54 George Brett	.30	.12	.03
□ 55 Jose Rijo	.06	.02	.00
□ 56 Tim Raines	.25	.10	.02
□ 57 Ed Correa	.20	.08	.02
□ 58 Mike Witt	.10	.04	.01
□ 59 Greg Walker	.08	.03	.01
□ 60 Ozzie Smith	.20	.08	.02
□ 61 Glenn Davis	.25	.10	.02
□ 62 Glenn Wilson	.06	.02	.00
□ 63 Tom Browning	.12	.05	.01
□ 64 Tony Gwynn	.45	.18	.04

□ 65	R.J. Reynolds	.03	.01	.00
□ 66	Will Clark	2.50	1.00	.25
□ 67	Ozzie Virgil	.03	.01	.00
□ 68	Rick Sutcliffe	.10	.04	.01
□ 69	Gary Carter	.25	.10	.02
□ 70	Mike Moore	.03	.01	.00
□ 71	Bert Blyleven	.08	.03	.01
□ 72	Tony Fernandez	.15	.06	.01
□ 73	Kent Hrbek	.18	.08	.01
□ 74	Lloyd Moseby	.08	.03	.01
□ 75	Alvin Davis	.12	.05	.01
□ 76	Keith Hernandez	.25	.10	.02
□ 77	Ryne Sandberg	.20	.08	.02
□ 78	Dale Murphy	.45	.18	.04
□ 79	Sid Bream	.03	.01	.00
□ 80	Chris Brown	.08	.03	.01
□ 81	Steve Garvey	.30	.12	.03
□ 82	Mario Soto	.03	.01	.00
□ 83	Shane Rawley	.06	.02	.00
□ 84	Willie McGee	.12	.05	.01
□ 85	Jose Cruz	.08	.03	.01
□ 86	Brian Downing	.06	.02	.00
□ 87	Ozzie Guillen	.08	.03	.01
□ 88	Hubie Brooks	.08	.03	.01
□ 89	Cal Ripken	.30	.12	.03
□ 90	Juan Nieves	.06	.02	.00
□ 91	Lance Parrish	.12	.05	.01
□ 92	Jim Rice	.18	.08	.01
□ 93	Ron Guidry	.12	.05	.01
□ 94	Fernando Valenzuela	.18	.08	.01
□ 95	Andy Allanson	.08	.03	.01
□ 96	Willie Wilson	.10	.04	.01
□ 97	Jose Canseco	6.50	2.60	.65
□ 98	Jeff Reardon	.08	.03	.01
□ 99	Bobby Witt	.30	.12	.03
□ 100	Checklist	.06	.01	.00
□ 101	Jose Guzman	.06	.02	.00
□ 102	Steve Balboni	.03	.01	.00
□ 103	Tony Phillips	.03	.01	.00
□ 104	Brook Jacoby	.08	.03	.01
□ 105	Dave Winfield	.30	.12	.03
□ 106	Orel Hershiser	.35	.14	.03
□ 107	Lou Whitaker	.10	.04	.01
□ 108	Fred Lynn	.12	.05	.01
□ 109	Bill Wegman	.03	.01	.00
□ 110	Donnie Moore	.03	.01	.00
□ 111	Jack Clark	.18	.08	.01
□ 112	Bob Knepper	.06	.02	.00
□ 113	Von Hayes	.08	.03	.01
□ 114	Leon "Bip" Roberts	.08	.03	.01
□ 115	Tony Pena	.08	.03	.01
□ 116	Scott Garrelts	.03	.01	.00
□ 117	Paul Molitor	.12	.05	.01
□ 118	Darryl Strawberry	.75	.30	.07
□ 119	Shawon Dunston	.08	.03	.01
□ 120	Jim Presley	.08	.03	.01
□ 121	Jesse Barfield	.15	.06	.01
□ 122	Gary Gaetti	.15	.06	.01
□ 123	Kurt Stillwell	.25	.10	.02
□ 124	Joel Davis	.03	.01	.00
□ 125	Mike Boddicker	.06	.02	.00
□ 126	Robin Yount	.30	.12	.03
□ 127	Alan Trammell	.20	.08	.02
□ 128	Dave Righetti	.10	.04	.01
□ 129	Dwight Evans	.10	.04	.01
□ 130	Mike Scioscia	.03	.01	.00
□ 131	Julio Franco	.08	.03	.01
□ 132	Bret Saberhagen	.20	.08	.02
□ 133	Mike Davis	.03	.01	.00
□ 134	Joe Hesketh	.03	.01	.00
□ 135	Wally Joyner	1.75	.70	.17
□ 136	Don Slaught	.03	.01	.00
□ 137	Daryl Boston	.03	.01	.00
□ 138	Nolan Ryan	.30	.12	.03
□ 139	Mike Schmidt	.40	.16	.04
□ 140	Tommy Herr	.06	.02	.00
□ 141	Garry Templeton	.06	.02	.00
□ 142	Kal Daniels	.90	.36	.09
□ 143	Billy Sample	.03	.01	.00
□ 144	Johnny Ray	.08	.03	.01
□ 145	Rob Thompson	.25	.10	.02
□ 146	Bob Dernier	.03	.01	.00
□ 147	Danny Tartabull	.30	.12	.03
□ 148	Ernie Whitt	.03	.01	.00
□ 149	Kirby Puckett	.55	.22	.05
□ 150	Mike Young	.03	.01	.00
□ 151	Ernest Riles	.03	.01	.00
□ 152	Frank Tanana	.06	.02	.00
□ 153	Rich Gedman	.06	.02	.00
□ 154	Willie Randolph	.06	.02	.00
□ 155	Bill Madlock	.08	.03	.01
□ 156	Joe Carter	.20	.08	.02
□ 157	Danny Jackson	.15	.06	.01
□ 158	Carney Lansford	.08	.03	.01
□ 159	Bryn Smith	.03	.01	.00

□ 160	Gary Pettis	.03	.01	.00
□ 161	Oddibe McDowell	.10	.04	.01
□ 162	John Cangelosi	.10	.04	.01
□ 163	Mike Scott	.20	.08	.02
□ 164	Eric Show	.06	.02	.00
□ 165	Juan Samuel	.12	.05	.01
□ 166	Nick Esasky	.03	.01	.00
□ 167	Zane Smith	.06	.02	.00
□ 168	Mike Brown (Pirates OF)	.03	.01	.00
□ 169	Keith Moreland	.03	.01	.00
□ 170	John Tudor	.10	.04	.01
□ 171	Ken Dixon	.03	.01	.00
□ 172	Jim Gantner	.03	.01	.00
□ 173	Jack Morris	.12	.05	.01
□ 174	Bruce Hurst	.12	.05	.01
□ 175	Dennis Rasmussen	.06	.02	.00
□ 176	Mike Marshall	.10	.04	.01
□ 177	Dan Quisenberry	.10	.04	.01
□ 178	Eric Plunk	.08	.03	.01
□ 179	Tim Wallach	.08	.03	.01
□ 180	Steve Buechele	.03	.01	.00
□ 181	Don Sutton	.15	.06	.01
□ 182	Dave Schmidt	.06	.02	.00
□ 183	Terry Pendleton	.06	.02	.00
□ 184	Jim Deshaies	.15	.06	.01
□ 185	Steve Bedrosian	.12	.05	.01
□ 186	Pete Rose	.55	.22	.05
□ 187	Dave Dravecky	.03	.01	.00
□ 188	Rick Reuschel	.06	.02	.00
□ 189	Dan Gladden	.06	.02	.00
□ 190	Rick Mahler	.03	.01	.00
□ 191	Thad Bosley	.03	.01	.00
□ 192	Ron Darling	.18	.08	.01
□ 193	Matt Young	.03	.01	.00
□ 194	Tom Brunansky	.12	.05	.01
□ 195	Dave Stieb	.10	.04	.01
□ 196	Frank Viola	.15	.06	.01
□ 197	Tom Henke	.08	.03	.01
□ 198	Karl Best	.03	.01	.00
□ 199	Dwight Gooden	.75	.30	.07
□ 200	Checklist	.06	.01	.00
□ 201	Steve Trout	.03	.01	.00
□ 202	Rafael Ramirez	.03	.01	.00
□ 203	Bob Walk	.06	.02	.00
□ 204	Roger Mason	.03	.01	.00
□ 205	Terry Kennedy	.03	.01	.00
□ 206	Ron Oester	.03	.01	.00
□ 207	John Russell	.03	.01	.00
□ 208	Greg Mathews	.20	.08	.02
□ 209	Charlie Kerfeld	.03	.01	.00
□ 210	Reggie Jackson	.40	.16	.04
□ 211	Floyd Bannister	.03	.01	.00
□ 212	Vance Law	.06	.02	.00
□ 213	Rich Bordi	.03	.01	.00
□ 214	Dan Plesac	.30	.12	.03
□ 215	Dave Collins	.03	.01	.00
□ 216	Bob Stanley	.03	.01	.00
□ 217	Joe Niekro	.08	.03	.01
□ 218	Tom Niedenfuer	.03	.01	.00
□ 219	Brett Butler	.08	.03	.01
□ 220	Charlie Leibrandt	.03	.01	.00
□ 221	Steve Ontiveros	.03	.01	.00
□ 222	Tim Burke	.03	.01	.00
□ 223	Curtis Wilkerson	.03	.01	.00
□ 224	Pete Incaviglia	.75	.30	.07
□ 225	Lonnie Smith	.03	.01	.00
□ 226	Chris Codiroli	.03	.01	.00
□ 227	Scott Bailes	.10	.04	.01
□ 228	Rickey Henderson	.35	.14	.03
□ 229	Ken Howell	.03	.01	.00
□ 230	Darnell Coles	.03	.01	.00
□ 231	Don Aase	.03	.01	.00
□ 232	Tim Leary	.10	.04	.01
□ 233	Bob Boone	.08	.03	.01
□ 234	Ricky Horton	.03	.01	.00
□ 235	Mark Bailey	.03	.01	.00
□ 236	Kevin Gross	.03	.01	.00
□ 237	Lance McCullers	.06	.02	.00
□ 238	Cecilio Guante	.03	.01	.00
□ 239	Bob Melvin	.03	.01	.00
□ 240	Billy Jo Robidoux	.03	.01	.00
□ 241	Roger McDowell	.08	.03	.01
□ 242	Leon Durham	.06	.02	.00
□ 243	Ed Nunez	.03	.01	.00
□ 244	Jimmy Key	.10	.04	.01
□ 245	Mike Smithson	.03	.01	.00
□ 246	Bo Diaz	.03	.01	.00
□ 247	Carlton Fisk	.12	.05	.01
□ 248	Larry Sheets	.08	.03	.01
□ 249	Juan Castillo	.03	.01	.00
□ 250	Eric King	.12	.05	.01
□ 251	Doug Drabek	.25	.10	.02
□ 252	Wade Boggs	1.50	.60	.15
□ 253	Mariano Duncan	.03	.01	.00

□ 254 Pat Tabler	.06	.02	.00
□ 255 Frank White	.06	.02	.00
□ 256 Alfredo Griffin	.06	.02	.00
□ 257 Floyd Youmans	.08	.03	.01
□ 258 Rob Wilfong	.03	.01	.00
□ 259 Pete O'Brien	.08	.03	.01
□ 260 Tim Hulett	.03	.01	.00
□ 261 Dickie Thon	.03	.01	.00
□ 262 Darren Daulton	.03	.01	.00
□ 263 Vince Coleman	.40	.16	.04
□ 264 Andy Hawkins	.06	.02	.00
□ 265 Eric Davis	1.50	.60	.15
□ 266 Andres Thomas	.18	.08	.01
□ 267 Mike Diaz	.10	.04	.01
□ 268 Chili Davis	.08	.03	.01
□ 269 Jody Davis	.06	.02	.00
□ 270 Phil Bradley	.08	.03	.01
□ 271 George Bell	.25	.10	.02
□ 272 Keith Atherton	.03	.01	.00
□ 273 Storm Davis	.06	.02	.00
□ 274 Rob Deer	.15	.06	.01
□ 275 Walt Terrell	.03	.01	.00
□ 276 Roger Clemens	1.50	.60	.15
□ 277 Mike Easler	.03	.01	.00
□ 278 Steve Sax	.15	.06	.01
□ 279 Andre Thornton	.06	.02	.00
□ 280 Jim Sundberg	.03	.01	.00
□ 281 Bill Bathe	.08	.03	.01
□ 282 Jay Tibbs	.03	.01	.00
□ 283 Dick Schofield	.03	.01	.00
□ 284 Mike Mason	.03	.01	.00
□ 285 Jerry Hairston	.03	.01	.00
□ 286 Bill Doran	.08	.03	.01
□ 287 Tim Flannery	.03	.01	.00
□ 288 Gary Redus	.03	.01	.00
□ 289 John Franco	.08	.03	.01
□ 290 Paul Assenmacher	.08	.03	.01
□ 291 Joe Orsulak	.03	.01	.00
□ 292 Lee Smith	.06	.02	.00
□ 293 Mike Laga	.03	.01	.00
□ 294 Rick Dempsey	.03	.01	.00
□ 295 Mike Felder	.06	.02	.00
□ 296 Tom Brookens	.03	.01	.00
□ 297 Al Nipper	.03	.01	.00
□ 298 Mike Pagliarulo	.08	.03	.01
□ 299 Franklin Stubbs	.06	.02	.00
□ 300 Checklist	.06	.01	.00
□ 301 Steve Farr	.03	.01	.00
□ 302 Bill Mooneyham	.06	.02	.00
□ 303 Andres Galarraga	.35	.14	.03
□ 304 Scott Fletcher	.06	.02	.00
□ 305 Jack Howell	.06	.02	.00
□ 306 Russ Morman	.12	.05	.01
□ 307 Todd Worrell	.18	.08	.01
□ 308 Dave Smith	.06	.02	.00
□ 309 Jeff Stone	.03	.01	.00
□ 310 Ron Robinson	.03	.01	.00
□ 311 Bruce Bochy	.03	.01	.00
□ 312 Jim Winn	.03	.01	.00
□ 313 Mark Davis	.06	.02	.00
□ 314 Jeff Dedmon	.03	.01	.00
□ 315 Jamie Moyer	.20	.08	.02
□ 316 Wally Backman	.06	.02	.00
□ 317 Ken Phelps	.08	.03	.01
□ 318 Steve Lombardozzi	.03	.01	.00
□ 319 Rance Mulliniks	.03	.01	.00
□ 320 Tim Laudner	.03	.01	.00
□ 321 Mark Eichhorn	.12	.05	.01
□ 322 Lee Guetterman	.12	.05	.01
□ 323 Sid Fernandez	.12	.05	.01
□ 324 Jerry Mumphrey	.03	.01	.00
□ 325 David Palmer	.03	.01	.00
□ 326 Bill Almon	.03	.01	.00
□ 327 Candy Maldonado	.08	.03	.01
□ 328 John Kruk	.35	.14	.03
□ 329 John Denny	.03	.01	.00
□ 330 Milt Thompson	.06	.02	.00
□ 331 Mike Lavalliere	.20	.08	.02
□ 332 Alan Ashby	.03	.01	.00
□ 333 Doug Corbett	.03	.01	.00
□ 334 Ron Karkovice	.06	.02	.00
□ 335 Mitch Webster	.06	.02	.00
□ 336 Lee Lacy	.03	.01	.00
□ 337 Glenn Braggs	.35	.14	.03
□ 338 Dwight Lowry	.10	.04	.01
□ 339 Don Baylor	.08	.03	.01
□ 340 Brian Fisher	.06	.02	.00
□ 341 Reggie Williams	.10	.04	.01
□ 342 Tom Candiotti	.03	.01	.00
□ 343 Rudy Law	.03	.01	.00
□ 344 Curt Young	.03	.01	.00
□ 345 Mike Fitzgerald	.03	.01	.00
□ 346 Ruben Sierra	1.25	.50	.12
□ 347 Mitch Williams	.20	.08	.02
□ 348 Jorge Orta	.03	.01	.00
□ 349 Mickey Tettleton	.03	.01	.00
□ 350 Ernie Camacho	.03	.01	.00
□ 351 Ron Kittle	.08	.03	.01
□ 352 Ken Landreaux	.03	.01	.00
□ 353 Chet Lemon	.03	.01	.00
□ 354 John Shelby	.03	.01	.00
□ 355 Mark Clear	.03	.01	.00
□ 356 Doug DeCinces	.06	.02	.00
□ 357 Ken Dayley	.03	.01	.00
□ 358 Phil Garner	.03	.01	.00
□ 359 Steve Jeltz	.03	.01	.00
□ 360 Ed Whitson	.03	.01	.00
□ 361 Barry Bonds	.90	.36	.09
□ 362 Vida Blue	.06	.02	.00
□ 363 Cecil Cooper	.08	.03	.01
□ 364 Bob Ojeda	.08	.03	.01
□ 365 Dennis Eckersley	.12	.05	.01
□ 366 Mike Morgan	.03	.01	.00
□ 367 Willie Upshaw	.03	.01	.00
□ 368 Allan Anderson	.35	.14	.03
□ 369 Bill Gullickson	.03	.01	.00
□ 370 Bobby Thigpen	.30	.12	.03
□ 371 Juan Beniquez	.03	.01	.00
□ 372 Charlie Moore	.03	.01	.00
□ 373 Dan Petry	.06	.02	.00
□ 374 Rod Scurry	.03	.01	.00
□ 375 Tom Seaver	.30	.12	.03
□ 376 Ed VandeBerg	.03	.01	.00
□ 377 Tony Bernazard	.03	.01	.00
□ 378 Greg Pryor	.03	.01	.00
□ 379 Dwayne Murphy	.03	.01	.00
□ 380 Andy McGaffigan	.03	.01	.00
□ 381 Kirk McCaskill	.06	.02	.00
□ 382 Greg Harris	.03	.01	.00
□ 383 Rich Dotson	.06	.02	.00
□ 384 Craig Reynolds	.03	.01	.00
□ 385 Greg Gross	.03	.01	.00
□ 386 Tito Landrum	.03	.01	.00
□ 387 Craig Lefferts	.03	.01	.00
□ 388 Dave Parker	.12	.05	.01
□ 389 Bob Horner	.10	.04	.01
□ 390 Pat Clements	.03	.01	.00
□ 391 Jeff Leonard	.08	.03	.01
□ 392 Chris Speier	.03	.01	.00
□ 393 John Moses	.03	.01	.00
□ 394 Garth Iorg	.03	.01	.00
□ 395 Greg Gagne	.06	.02	.00
□ 396 Nate Snell	.03	.01	.00
□ 397 Bryan Clutterbuck	.06	.02	.00
□ 398 Darrell Evans	.08	.03	.01
□ 399 Steve Crawford	.03	.01	.00
□ 400 Checklist	.06	.01	.00
□ 401 Phil Lombardi	.10	.04	.01
□ 402 Rick Honeycutt	.03	.01	.00
□ 403 Ken Schrom	.03	.01	.00
□ 404 Bud Black	.03	.01	.00
□ 405 Donnie Hill	.03	.01	.00
□ 406 Wayne Krenchicki	.03	.01	.00
□ 407 Chuck Finley	.06	.02	.00
□ 408 Toby Harrah	.03	.01	.00
□ 409 Steve Lyons	.03	.01	.00
□ 410 Kevin Bass	.06	.02	.00
□ 411 Marvell Wynne	.03	.01	.00
□ 412 Ron Roenicke	.03	.01	.00
□ 413 Tracy Jones	.30	.12	.03
□ 414 Gene Garber	.03	.01	.00
□ 415 Mike Bielecki	.03	.01	.00
□ 416 Frank DiPino	.03	.01	.00
□ 417 Andy Van Slyke	.20	.08	.02
□ 418 Jim Dwyer	.03	.01	.00
□ 419 Ben Oglivie	.06	.02	.00
□ 420 Dave Bergman	.03	.01	.00
□ 421 Joe Sambito	.03	.01	.00
□ 422 Bob Tewksbury	.10	.04	.01
□ 423 Len Matuszek	.03	.01	.00
□ 424 Mike Kingery	.12	.05	.01
□ 425 Dave Kingman	.08	.03	.01
□ 426 Al Newman	.08	.03	.01
□ 427 Gary Ward	.03	.01	.00
□ 428 Ruppert Jones	.03	.01	.00
□ 429 Harold Baines	.10	.04	.01
□ 430 Pat Perry	.03	.01	.00
□ 431 Terry Puhl	.03	.01	.00
□ 432 Don Carman	.03	.01	.00
□ 433 Eddie Milner	.03	.01	.00
□ 434 LaMarr Hoyt	.03	.01	.00
□ 435 Rick Rhoden	.06	.02	.00
□ 436 Jose Uribe	.03	.01	.00
□ 437 Ken Oberkfell	.03	.01	.00
□ 438 Ron Davis	.03	.01	.00
□ 439 Jesse Orosco	.03	.01	.00
□ 440 Scott Bradley	.03	.01	.00
□ 441 Randy Bush	.03	.01	.00
□ 442 John Cerutti	.12	.05	.01
□ 443 Roy Smalley	.03	.01	.00

□ 444	Kelly Gruber	.03	.01	.00
□ 445	Bob Kearney	.03	.01	.00
□ 446	Ed Hearn	.06	.02	.00
□ 447	Scott Sanderson	.03	.01	.00
□ 448	Bruce Benedict	.03	.01	.00
□ 449	Junior Ortiz	.03	.01	.00
□ 450	Mike Aldrete	.25	.10	.02
□ 451	Kevin McReynolds	.30	.12	.03
□ 452	Rob Murphy	.25	.10	.02
□ 453	Kent Tekulve	.03	.01	.00
□ 454	Curt Ford	.10	.04	.01
□ 455	Davey Lopes	.06	.02	.00
□ 456	Bobby Grich	.06	.02	.00
□ 457	Jose DeLeon	.03	.01	.00
□ 458	Andre Dawson	.25	.10	.02
□ 459	Mike Flanagan	.06	.02	.00
□ 460	Joey Meyer	.65	.26	.06
□ 461	Chuck Cary	.12	.05	.01
□ 462	Bill Buckner	.08	.03	.01
□ 463	Bob Shirley	.03	.01	.00
□ 464	Jeff Hamilton	.25	.10	.02
□ 465	Phil Niekro	.15	.06	.01
□ 466	Mark Gubicza	.08	.03	.01
□ 467	Jerry Willard	.03	.01	.00
□ 468	Bob Sebra	.10	.04	.01
□ 469	Larry Parrish	.03	.01	.00
□ 470	Charlie Hough	.06	.02	.00
□ 471	Hal McRae	.06	.02	.00
□ 472	Dave Leiper	.03	.01	.00
□ 473	Mel Hall	.06	.02	.00
□ 474	Dan Pasqua	.08	.03	.01
□ 475	Bob Welch	.06	.02	.00
□ 476	Johnny Grubb	.03	.01	.00
□ 477	Jim Traber	.06	.02	.00
□ 478	Chris Bosio	.15	.06	.01
□ 479	Mark McLemore	.03	.01	.00
□ 480	John Morris	.03	.01	.00
□ 481	Billy Hatcher	.08	.03	.01
□ 482	Dan Schatzeder	.03	.01	.00
□ 483	Rich Gossage	.10	.04	.01
□ 484	Jim Morrison	.03	.01	.00
□ 485	Bob Brenly	.03	.01	.00
□ 486	Bill Schroeder	.03	.01	.00
□ 487	Mookie Wilson	.06	.02	.00
□ 488	Dave Martinez	.20	.08	.02
□ 489	Harold Reynolds	.06	.02	.00
□ 490	Jeff Hearron	.08	.03	.01
□ 491	Mickey Hatcher	.03	.01	.00
□ 492	Barry Larkin	1.00	.40	.10
□ 493	Bob James	.03	.01	.00
□ 494	John Habyan	.03	.01	.00
□ 495	Jim Adduci	.12	.05	.01
□ 496	Mike Heath	.03	.01	.00
□ 497	Tim Stoddard	.03	.01	.00
□ 498	Tony Armas	.06	.02	.00
□ 499	Dennis Powell	.03	.01	.00
□ 500	Checklist	.06	.01	.00
□ 501	Chris Bando	.03	.01	.00
□ 502	Dave Cone	4.00	1.60	.40
□ 503	Jay Howell	.06	.02	.00
□ 504	Tom Foley	.03	.01	.00
□ 505	Ray Chadwick	.06	.02	.00
□ 506	Mike Loynd	.08	.03	.01
□ 507	Neil Allen	.03	.01	.00
□ 508	Danny Darwin	.03	.01	.00
□ 509	Rick Schu	.03	.01	.00
□ 510	Jose Oquendo	.03	.01	.00
□ 511	Gene Walter	.03	.01	.00
□ 512	Terry McGriff	.12	.05	.01
□ 513	Ken Griffey	.06	.02	.00
□ 514	Benny Distefano	.03	.01	.00
□ 515	Terry Mulholland	.08	.03	.01
□ 516	Ed Lynch	.03	.01	.00
□ 517	Bill Swift	.03	.01	.00
□ 518	Manny Lee	.06	.02	.00
□ 519	Andre David	.03	.01	.00
□ 520	Scott McGregor	.06	.02	.00
□ 521	Rick Manning	.03	.01	.00
□ 522	Willie Hernandez	.08	.03	.01
□ 523	Marty Barrett	.08	.03	.01
□ 524	Wayne Tolleson	.03	.01	.00
□ 525	Jose Gonzalez	.20	.08	.02
□ 526	Cory Snyder	.75	.30	.07
□ 527	Buddy Biancalana	.03	.01	.00
□ 528	Moose Haas	.03	.01	.00
□ 529	Wilfredo Tejada	.06	.02	.00
□ 530	Stu Cliburn	.03	.01	.00
□ 531	Dale Mohorcic	.15	.06	.01
□ 532	Ron Hassey	.03	.01	.00
□ 533	Ty Gainey	.03	.01	.00
□ 534	Jerry Royster	.03	.01	.00
□ 535	Mike Maddux	.15	.06	.01
□ 536	Ted Power	.03	.01	.00
□ 537	Ted Simmons	.10	.04	.01
□ 538	Rafael Belliard	.08	.03	.01
□ 539	Chico Walker	.08	.03	.0
□ 540	Bob Forsch	.03	.01	.0
□ 541	John Stefero	.03	.01	.0
□ 542	Dale Sveum	.20	.08	.0
□ 543	Mark Thurmond	.03	.01	.00
□ 544	Jeff Sellers	.15	.06	.0
□ 545	Joel Skinner	.03	.01	.00
□ 546	Alex Trevino	.03	.01	.00
□ 547	Randy Kutcher	.08	.03	.0
□ 548	Joaquin Andujar	.08	.03	.0
□ 549	Casey Candaele	.12	.05	.0
□ 550	Jeff Russell	.03	.01	.0
□ 551	John Candelaria	.06	.02	.0
□ 552	Joe Cowley	.03	.01	.0
□ 553	Danny Cox	.06	.02	.0
□ 554	Denny Walling	.03	.01	.00
□ 555	Bruce Ruffin	.20	.08	.0
□ 556	Buddy Bell	.08	.03	.0
□ 557	Jimmy Jones	.35	.14	.0
□ 558	Bobby Bonilla	1.00	.40	.1
□ 559	Jeff Robinson (Giants pitcher)	.06	.02	.00
□ 560	Ed Olwine	.06	.02	.00
□ 561	Glenallen Hill	.12	.05	.01
□ 562	Lee Mazzilli	.03	.01	.00
□ 563	Mike Brown (pitcher)	.03	.01	.00
□ 564	George Frazier	.03	.01	.00
□ 565	Mike Sharperson	.08	.03	.01
□ 566	Mark Portugal	.08	.03	.01
□ 567	Rick Leach	.03	.01	.00
□ 568	Mark Langston	.10	.04	.01
□ 569	Rafael Santana	.03	.01	.00
□ 570	Manny Trillo	.03	.01	.00
□ 571	Cliff Speck	.06	.02	.00
□ 572	Bob Kipper	.03	.01	.00
□ 573	Kelly Downs	.30	.12	.03
□ 574	Randy Asadoor	.08	.03	.01
□ 575	Dave Magadan	.45	.18	.04
□ 576	Marvin Freeman	.15	.06	.01
□ 577	Jeff Lahti	.03	.01	.00
□ 578	Jeff Calhoun	.03	.01	.00
□ 579	Gus Polidor	.03	.01	.00
□ 580	Gene Nelson	.03	.01	.00
□ 581	Tim Teufel	.03	.01	.00
□ 582	Odell Jones	.03	.01	.00
□ 583	Mark Ryal	.08	.03	.01
□ 584	Randy O'Neal	.03	.01	.00
□ 585	Mike Greenwell	8.00	3.25	.80
□ 586	Ray Knight	.06	.02	.00
□ 587	Ralph Bryant	.12	.05	.01
□ 588	Carmen Castillo	.03	.01	.00
□ 589	Ed Wojna	.03	.01	.00
□ 590	Stan Javier	.06	.02	.00
□ 591	Jeff Musselman	.15	.06	.01
□ 592	Mike Stanley	.20	.08	.02
□ 593	Darrell Porter	.03	.01	.00
□ 594	Drew Hall	.12	.05	.01
□ 595	Rob Nelson	.20	.08	.02
□ 596	Bryan Oelkers	.03	.01	.00
□ 597	Scott Nielsen	.15	.06	.01
□ 598	Brian Holton	.20	.08	.02
□ 599	Kevin Mitchell	.30	.12	.03
□ 600	Checklist	.06	.01	.00
□ 601	Jackie Gutierrez	.03	.01	.00
□ 602	Barry Jones	.15	.06	.01
□ 603	Jerry Narron	.03	.01	.00
□ 604	Steve Lake	.03	.01	.00
□ 605	Jim Pankovits	.03	.01	.00
□ 606	Ed Romero	.03	.01	.00
□ 607	Dave LaPoint	.06	.02	.00
□ 608	Don Robinson	.03	.01	.00
□ 609	Mike Krukow	.03	.01	.00
□ 610	Dave Valle	.03	.01	.00
□ 611	Len Dykstra	.10	.04	.01
□ 612	Roberto Clemente Puzzle Card	.06	.02	.00
□ 613	Mike Trujillo	.03	.01	.00
□ 614	Damaso Garcia	.03	.01	.00
□ 615	Neal Heaton	.03	.01	.00
□ 616	Juan Berenguer	.03	.01	.00
□ 617	Steve Carlton	.20	.08	.02
□ 618	Gary Lucas	.03	.01	.00
□ 619	Geno Petralli	.03	.01	.00
□ 620	Rick Aguilera	.03	.01	.00
□ 621	Fred McGriff	.75	.30	.07
□ 622	Dave Henderson	.06	.02	.00
□ 623	Dave Clark	.20	.08	.02
□ 624	Angel Salazar	.03	.01	.00
□ 625	Randy Hunt	.03	.01	.00
□ 626	John Gibbons	.03	.01	.00
□ 627	Kevin Brown	.15	.06	.01
□ 628	Bill Dawley	.03	.01	.00
□ 629	Aurelio Lopez	.03	.01	.00
□ 630	Charlie Hudson	.03	.01	.00

□631 Ray Soff	.06	.02	.00
□632 Ray Hayward	.08	.03	.01
□633 Spike Owen	.03	.01	.00
□634 Glenn Hubbard	.03	.01	.00
□635 Kevin Elster	.60	.24	.06
□636 Mike LaCoss	.03	.01	.00
□637 Dwayne Henry	.03	.01	.00
□638 Rey Quinones	.20	.08	.02
□639 Jim Clancy	.03	.01	.00
□640 Larry Andersen	.03	.01	.00
□641 Calvin Schiraldi	.06	.02	.00
□642 Stan Jefferson	.30	.12	.03
□643 Marc Sullivan	.03	.01	.00
□644 Mark Grant	.03	.01	.00
□645 Cliff Johnson	.03	.01	.00
□646 Howard Johnson	.12	.05	.01
□647 Dave Sax	.03	.01	.00
□648 Dave Stewart	.08	.03	.01
□649 Danny Heep	.03	.01	.00
□650 Joe Johnson	.03	.01	.00
□651 Bob Brower	.20	.08	.02
□652 Rob Woodward	.03	.01	.00
□653 John Mizerock	.03	.01	.00
□654 Tim Pyznarski	.12	.05	.01
□655 Luis Aquino	.06	.02	.00
□656 Mickey Brantley	.15	.06	.01
□657 Doyle Alexander	.06	.02	.00
□658 Sammy Stewart	.03	.01	.00
□659 Jim Acker	.03	.01	.00
□660 Pete Ladd	.03	.01	.00

1987 Donruss Wax Box Cards

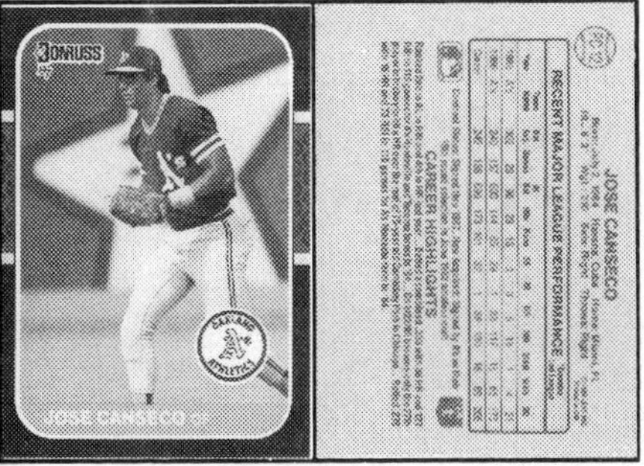

The cards in this 4-card set measure the standard 2 1/2" by 3 1/2". Cards have essentially the same design as the 1987 Donruss regular issue set. The cards were printed on the bottoms of the regular issue wax pack boxes. The four cards (PC10 to PC12 plus a Roberto Clemente puzzle card) are considered a separate set in their own right and are not typically included in a complete set of the regular issue 1987 Donruss cards. The value of the panel uncut is slightly greater, perhaps by 25% greater, than the value of the individual cards cut up carefully.

	MINT	EXC	G-VG
COMPLETE SET (4)	1.50	.60	.15
COMMON PLAYER	.05	.02	.00
□ PC10 Dale Murphy	.30	.12	.03
□ PC11 Jeff Reardon	.10	.04	.01
□ PC12 Jose Canseco	1.25	.50	.12
□ PUZ Roberto Clemente (Puzzle Card)	.05	.02	.00

1987 Donruss Super DK's

This 28-card set was available through a mail-in offer detailed on the wax packs. The set was sent in return for 8.00 and three wrappers plus 1.50 postage and handling. The set features the popular Diamond King

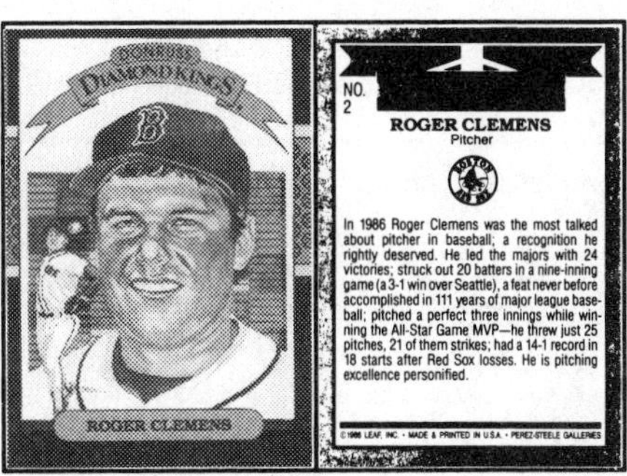

subseries in large (approximately 4 7/8" by 6 13/16") form. Dick Perez of Perez- Steele Galleries did another outstanding job on the artwork. The cards are essentially a large version of the Donruss regular issue Diamond Kings.

	MINT	EXC	G-VG
COMPLETE SET (28)	11.00	4.50	1.10
COMMON PLAYER (1-26)	.15	.06	.01
□ 1 Wally Joyner	1.00	.40	.10
□ 2 Roger Clemens	1.25	.50	.12
□ 3 Dale Murphy	.60	.24	.06
□ 4 Darryl Strawberry	.75	.30	.07
□ 5 Ozzie Smith	.30	.12	.03
□ 6 Jose Canseco	2.50	1.00	.25
□ 7 Charlie Hough	.15	.06	.01
□ 8 Brook Jacoby	.15	.06	.01
□ 9 Fred Lynn	.20	.08	.02
□10 Rick Rhoden	.15	.06	.01
□11 Chris Brown	.20	.08	.02
□12 Von Hayes	.20	.08	.02
□13 Jack Morris	.25	.10	.02
□14 Kevin McReynolds	.40	.16	.04
□15 George Brett	.50	.20	.05
□16 Ted Higuera	.30	.12	.03
□17 Hubie Brooks	.15	.06	.01
□18 Mike Scott	.30	.12	.03
□19 Kirby Puckett	.75	.30	.07
□20 Dave Winfield	.50	.20	.05
□21 Lloyd Moseby	.15	.06	.01
□22 Eric Davis	1.25	.50	.12
□23 Jim Presley	.20	.08	.02
□24 Keith Moreland	.15	.06	.01
□25 Greg Walker	.15	.06	.01
□26 Steve Sax	.25	.10	.02
□27 DK Checklist 1-26	.10	.01	.00
□28 Roberto Clemente Large Puzzle (unnumbered)	.25	.10	.02

1987 Donruss All-Stars

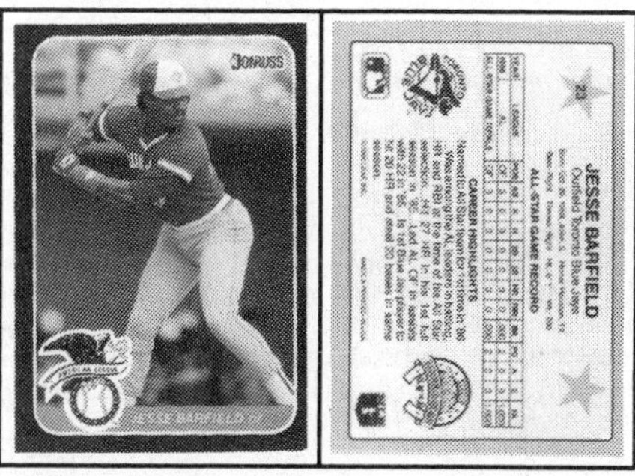

This 60-card set features cards measuring 3 1/2" by 5". Card fronts are in full color with a black border. The card backs are printed in black and blue on white card stock. Cards are numbered on the back. Card backs feature statistical information about the player's performance in past All-Star games. The set was distributed in packs which also contained a Pop-Up.

	MINT	EXC	G-VG
COMPLETE SET (60)	6.00	2.40	.60
COMMON PLAYER (1-60)	.05	.02	.00
□ 1 Wally Joyner	.70	.28	.07
□ 2 Dave Winfield	.25	.10	.02
□ 3 Lou Whitaker	.10	.04	.01
□ 4 Kirby Puckett	.50	.20	.05
□ 5 Cal Ripken	.35	.14	.03
□ 6 Rickey Henderson	.45	.18	.04
□ 7 Wade Boggs	.80	.32	.08
□ 8 Roger Clemens	.70	.28	.07
□ 9 Lance Parrish	.10	.04	.01
□ 10 Dick Howser MG	.05	.02	.00
□ 11 Keith Hernandez	.25	.10	.02
□ 12 Darryl Strawberry	.50	.20	.05
□ 13 Ryne Sandberg	.30	.12	.03
□ 14 Dale Murphy	.40	.16	.04
□ 15 Ozzie Smith	.20	.08	.02
□ 16 Tony Gwynn	.40	.16	.04
□ 17 Mike Schmidt	.40	.16	.04
□ 18 Dwight Gooden	.60	.24	.06
□ 19 Gary Carter	.30	.12	.03
□ 20 Whitey Herzog MG	.05	.02	.00
□ 21 Jose Canseco	1.00	.40	.10
□ 22 John Franco	.10	.04	.01
□ 23 Jesse Barfield	.10	.04	.01
□ 24 Rick Rhoden	.05	.02	.00
□ 25 Harold Baines	.10	.04	.01
□ 26 Sid Fernandez	.10	.04	.01
□ 27 George Brett	.40	.16	.04
□ 28 Steve Sax	.15	.06	.01
□ 29 Jim Presley	.10	.04	.01
□ 30 Dave Smith	.05	.02	.00
□ 31 Eddie Murray	.30	.12	.03
□ 32 Mike Scott	.20	.08	.02
□ 33 Don Mattingly	1.00	.40	.10
□ 34 Dave Parker	.20	.08	.02
□ 35 Tony Fernandez	.15	.06	.01
□ 36 Tim Raines	.30	.12	.03
□ 37 Brook Jacoby	.10	.04	.01
□ 38 Chili Davis	.10	.04	.01
□ 39 Rich Gedman	.05	.02	.00
□ 40 Kevin Bass	.05	.02	.00
□ 41 Frank White	.05	.02	.00
□ 42 Glenn Davis	.20	.08	.02
□ 43 Willie Hernandez	.10	.04	.01
□ 44 Chris Brown	.10	.04	.01
□ 45 Jim Rice	.20	.08	.02
□ 46 Tony Pena	.05	.02	.00
□ 47 Don Aase	.05	.02	.00
□ 48 Hubie Brooks	.05	.02	.00
□ 49 Charlie Hough	.05	.02	.00
□ 50 Jody Davis	.10	.04	.01
□ 51 Mike Witt	.10	.04	.01
□ 52 Jeff Reardon	.10	.04	.01
□ 53 Ken Schrom	.05	.02	.00
□ 54 Fernando Valenzuela	.20	.08	.02
□ 55 Dave Righetti	.15	.06	.01
□ 56 Shane Rawley	.05	.02	.00
□ 57 Ted Higuera	.15	.06	.01
□ 58 Mike Krukow	.05	.02	.00
□ 59 Lloyd Moseby	.10	.04	.01
□ 60 Checklist Card	.05	.01	.00

1987 Donruss All-Star Box

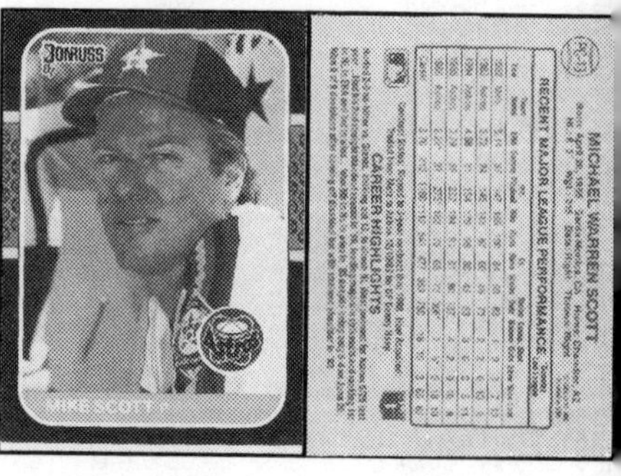

The cards in this 4-card set measure the standard 2 1/2" by 3 1/2" in spite of the fact that they form the bottom of the wax pack box for the larger Donruss All-Star cards. These box cards have essentially the same design as the 1987 Donruss regular issue set. The cards were printed on the bottoms of the Donruss All-Star (3 1/2" by 5") wax pack boxes. The four cards (PC13 to PC15 plus a Roberto Clemente puzzle card) are considered a separate set in their own right and are not typically included in a complete set of the 1987 Donruss All-Star (or regular) cards. The value of the panel uncut is slightly greater, perhaps by 25% greater, than the value of the individual cards cut up carefully.

	MINT	EXC	G-VG
COMPLETE SET (4)	.75	.30	.0[illegible]
COMMON PLAYERS	.05	.02	.0[illegible]
□ PC13 Mike Scott	.20	.08	.0[illegible]
□ PC14 Roger Clemens	.60	.24	.0[illegible]
□ PC15 Mike Krukow	.05	.02	.0[illegible]
□ PUZ Roberto Clemente Puzzle Card	.05	.02	.0[illegible]

1987 Donruss Pop-Ups

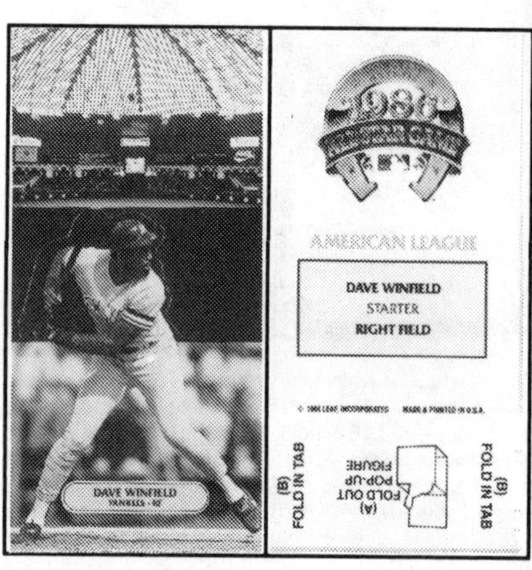

This 20-card set features "fold-out" cards measuring 2 1/2" by 5". Card fronts are in full color. Cards are unnumbered but are listed in the same order as the Donruss All- Stars on the All-Star checklist card. Card backs present essentially no information about the player. The set was distributed in packs which also contained All-Star cards (3 1/2" by 5").

	MINT	EXC	G-VG
COMPLETE SET (20)	4.00	1.60	.40
COMMON PLAYER (1-20)	.10	.04	.01
□ 1 Wally Joyner	.60	.24	.06
□ 2 Dave Winfield	.25	.10	.02
□ 3 Lou Whitaker	.15	.06	.01
□ 4 Kirby Puckett	.50	.20	.05
□ 5 Cal Ripken	.30	.12	.03
□ 6 Rickey Henderson	.40	.16	.04
□ 7 Wade Boggs	.80	.32	.08
□ 8 Roger Clemens	.70	.28	.07
□ 9 Lance Parrish	.15	.06	.01
□ 10 Dick Howser MG	.10	.04	.01
□ 11 Keith Hernandez	.25	.10	.02
□ 12 Darryl Strawberry	.50	.20	.05
□ 13 Ryne Sandberg	.30	.12	.03

☐ 14 Dale Murphy	.40	.16	.04
☐ 15 Ozzie Smith	.20	.08	.02
☐ 16 Tony Gwynn	.40	.16	.04
☐ 17 Mike Schmidt	.40	.16	.04
☐ 18 Dwight Gooden	.60	.24	.06
☐ 19 Gary Carter	.30	.12	.03
☐ 20 Whitey Herzog MG	.10	.04	.01

1987 Donruss Opening Day

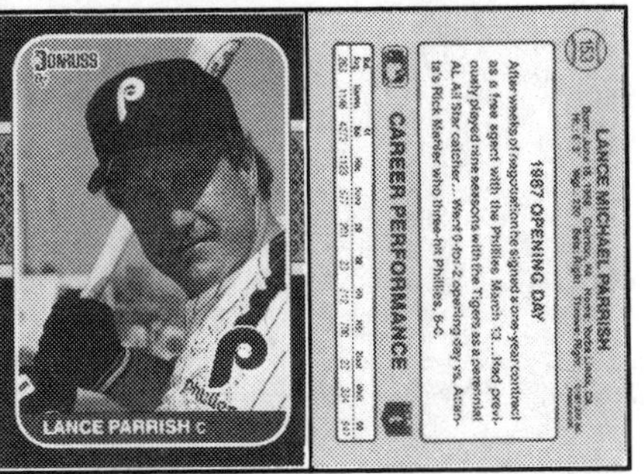

This innovative set of 272 cards features a card for each of the players in the starting line-ups of all the teams on Opening Day 1987. Cards are the standard size, 2 1/2" by 3 1/2" and are packaged as a complete set in a specially designed box. Cards are very similar in design to the 1987 regular Donruss issue except that these "OD" cards have a maroon border instead of a black border. The set features the first card in a Major League uniform of Joey Cora, Mark Davidson, Donnell Nixon, Bob Patterson, and Alonzo Powell. Teams in the same city share a checklist card. A 15-piece puzzle of Roberto Clemente is also included with every complete set. The error on Bobby Bonds was corrected very early in the press run, supposedly less than one percent of the sets have the error.

	MINT	EXC	G-VG
COMPLETE SET (272)	18.00	7.25	1.80
COMMON PLAYER (1-248)	.05	.02	.00
COMMON LOGO (249-272)	.03	.01	.00
☐ 1 Doug DeCinces	.05	.02	.00
☐ 2 Mike Witt	.10	.04	.01
☐ 3 George Hendrick	.05	.02	.00
☐ 4 Dick Schofield	.05	.02	.00
☐ 5 Devon White	.60	.24	.06
☐ 6 Butch Wynegar	.05	.02	.00
☐ 7 Wally Joyner	1.00	.40	.10
☐ 8 Mark McLemore	.05	.02	.00
☐ 9 Brian Downing	.05	.02	.00
☐ 10 Gary Pettis	.05	.02	.00
☐ 11 Bill Doran	.10	.04	.01
☐ 12 Phil Garner	.05	.02	.00
☐ 13 Jose Cruz	.10	.04	.01
☐ 14 Kevin Bass	.10	.04	.01
☐ 15 Mike Scott	.20	.08	.02
☐ 16 Glenn Davis	.15	.06	.01
☐ 17 Alan Ashby	.05	.02	.00
☐ 18 Billy Hatcher	.15	.06	.01
☐ 19 Craig Reynolds	.05	.02	.00
☐ 20 Carney Lansford	.10	.04	.01
☐ 21 Mike Davis	.05	.02	.00
☐ 22 Reggie Jackson	.35	.14	.03
☐ 23 Mickey Tettleton	.05	.02	.00
☐ 24 Jose Canseco	2.50	1.00	.25
☐ 25 Rob Nelson	.05	.02	.00
☐ 26 Tony Phillips	.05	.02	.00
☐ 27 Dwayne Murphy	.05	.02	.00
☐ 28 Alfredo Griffin	.05	.02	.00
☐ 29 Curt Young	.05	.02	.00
☐ 30 Willie Upshaw	.05	.02	.00
☐ 31 Mike Sharperson	.05	.02	.00
☐ 32 Rance Mulliniks	.05	.02	.00
☐ 33 Ernie Whitt	.05	.02	.00
☐ 34 Jesse Barfield	.15	.06	.01
☐ 35 Tony Fernandez	.15	.06	.01
☐ 36 Lloyd Moseby	.10	.04	.01
☐ 37 Jimmy Key	.10	.04	.01
☐ 38 Fred McGriff	.40	.16	.04
☐ 39 George Bell	.25	.10	.02
☐ 40 Dale Murphy	.35	.14	.03
☐ 41 Rick Mahler	.05	.02	.00
☐ 42 Ken Griffey	.10	.04	.01
☐ 43 Andres Thomas	.05	.02	.00
☐ 44 Dion James	.05	.02	.00
☐ 45 Ozzie Virgil	.05	.02	.00
☐ 46 Ken Oberkfell	.05	.02	.00
☐ 47 Gary Roenicke	.05	.02	.00
☐ 48 Glenn Hubbard	.05	.02	.00
☐ 49 Bill Schroeder	.05	.02	.00
☐ 50 Greg Brock	.05	.02	.00
☐ 51 Billy Jo Robidoux	.05	.02	.00
☐ 52 Glenn Braggs	.15	.06	.01
☐ 53 Jim Gantner	.05	.02	.00
☐ 54 Paul Molitor	.15	.06	.01
☐ 55 Dale Sveum	.10	.04	.01
☐ 56 Ted Higuera	.15	.06	.01
☐ 57 Rob Deer	.10	.04	.01
☐ 58 Robin Yount	.25	.10	.02
☐ 59 Jim Lindeman	.10	.04	.01
☐ 60 Vince Coleman	.30	.12	.03
☐ 61 Tommy Herr	.05	.02	.00
☐ 62 Terry Pendleton	.05	.02	.00
☐ 63 John Tudor	.15	.06	.01
☐ 64 Tony Pena	.10	.04	.01
☐ 65 Ozzie Smith	.20	.08	.02
☐ 66 Tito Landrum	.05	.02	.00
☐ 67 Jack Clark	.20	.08	.02
☐ 68 Bob Dernier	.05	.02	.00
☐ 69 Rick Sutcliffe	.10	.04	.01
☐ 70 Andre Dawson	.25	.10	.02
☐ 71 Keith Moreland	.05	.02	.00
☐ 72 Jody Davis	.05	.02	.00
☐ 73 Brian Dayett	.05	.02	.00
☐ 74 Leon Durham	.05	.02	.00
☐ 75 Ryne Sandberg	.20	.08	.02
☐ 76 Shawon Dunston	.10	.04	.01
☐ 77 Mike Marshall	.15	.06	.01
☐ 78 Bill Madlock	.05	.02	.00
☐ 79 Orel Hershiser	.60	.24	.06
☐ 80 Mike Ramsey	.10	.04	.01
☐ 81 Ken Landreaux	.05	.02	.00
☐ 82 Mike Scioscia	.05	.02	.00
☐ 83 Franklin Stubbs	.05	.02	.00
☐ 84 Mariano Duncan	.05	.02	.00
☐ 85 Steve Sax	.15	.06	.01
☐ 86 Mitch Webster	.05	.02	.00
☐ 87 Reid Nichols	.05	.02	.00
☐ 88 Tim Wallach	.10	.04	.01
☐ 89 Floyd Youmans	.10	.04	.01
☐ 90 Andres Galarraga	.35	.14	.03
☐ 91 Hubie Brooks	.05	.02	.00
☐ 92 Jeff Reed	.05	.02	.00
☐ 93 Alonzo Powell	.10	.04	.01
☐ 94 Vance Law	.05	.02	.00
☐ 95 Bob Brenly	.05	.02	.00
☐ 96 Will Clark	1.00	.40	.10
☐ 97 Chili Davis	.10	.04	.01
☐ 98 Mike Krukow	.05	.02	.00
☐ 99 Jose Uribe	.05	.02	.00
☐ 100 Chris Brown	.10	.04	.01
☐ 101 Rob Thompson	.10	.04	.01
☐ 102 Candy Maldonado	.10	.04	.01
☐ 103 Jeff Leonard	.10	.04	.01
☐ 104 Tom Candiotti	.05	.02	.00
☐ 105 Chris Bando	.05	.02	.00
☐ 106 Cory Snyder	.50	.20	.05
☐ 107 Pat Tabler	.05	.02	.00
☐ 108 Andre Thornton	.05	.02	.00
☐ 109 Joe Carter	.15	.06	.01
☐ 110 Tony Bernazard	.05	.02	.00
☐ 111 Julio Franco	.10	.04	.01
☐ 112 Brook Jacoby	.10	.04	.01
☐ 113 Brett Butler	.10	.04	.01
☐ 114 Donnell Nixon	.10	.04	.01
☐ 115 Alvin Davis	.15	.06	.01
☐ 116 Mark Langston	.20	.08	.02
☐ 117 Harold Reynolds	.10	.04	.01
☐ 118 Ken Phelps	.05	.02	.00
☐ 119 Mike Kingery	.05	.02	.00
☐ 120 Dave Valle	.05	.02	.00
☐ 121 Rey Quinones	.05	.02	.00
☐ 122 Phil Bradley	.10	.04	.01
☐ 123 Jim Presley	.10	.04	.01
☐ 124 Keith Hernandez	.25	.10	.02
☐ 125 Kevin McReynolds	.25	.10	.02
☐ 126 Rafael Santana	.05	.02	.00
☐ 127 Bob Ojeda	.10	.04	.01
☐ 128 Darryl Strawberry	.75	.30	.07
☐ 129 Mookie Wilson	.05	.02	.00

□ 130	Gary Carter	.25	.10	.02
□ 131	Tim Teufel	.05	.02	.00
□ 132	Howard Johnson	.15	.06	.01
□ 133	Cal Ripken	.30	.12	.03
□ 134	Rick Burleson	.05	.02	.00
□ 135	Fred Lynn	.10	.04	.01
□ 136	Eddie Murray	.25	.10	.02
□ 137	Ray Knight	.05	.02	.00
□ 138	Alan Wiggins	.05	.02	.00
□ 139	John Shelby	.05	.02	.00
□ 140	Mike Boddicker	.10	.04	.01
□ 141	Ken Gerhart	.10	.04	.01
□ 142	Terry Kennedy	.05	.02	.00
□ 143	Steve Garvey	.30	.12	.03
□ 144	Marvell Wynne	.05	.02	.00
□ 145	Kevin Mitchell	.10	.04	.01
□ 146	Tony Gwynn	.60	.24	.06
□ 147	Joey Cora	.10	.04	.01
□ 148	Benito Santiago	.75	.30	.07
□ 149	Eric Show	.10	.04	.01
□ 150	Garry Templeton	.10	.04	.01
□ 151	Carmelo Martinez	.05	.02	.00
□ 152	Von Hayes	.10	.04	.01
□ 153	Lance Parrish	.10	.04	.01
□ 154	Milt Thompson	.05	.02	.00
□ 155	Mike Easler	.05	.02	.00
□ 156	Juan Samuel	.15	.06	.01
□ 157	Steve Jeltz	.05	.02	.00
□ 158	Glenn Wilson	.05	.02	.00
□ 159	Shane Rawley	.05	.02	.00
□ 160	Mike Schmidt	.30	.12	.03
□ 161	Andy Van Slyke	.20	.08	.02
□ 162	Johnny Ray	.10	.04	.01
□ 163A	Barry Bonds ERR (photo actually Johnny Ray)	100.00	40.00	10.00
□ 163B	Barry Bonds COR	.25	.10	.02
□ 164	Junior Ortiz	.05	.02	.00
□ 165	Rafael Belliard	.05	.02	.00
□ 166	Bob Patterson	.10	.04	.01
□ 167	Bobby Bonilla	.20	.08	.02
□ 168	Sid Bream	.05	.02	.00
□ 169	Jim Morrison	.05	.02	.00
□ 170	Jerry Browne	.05	.02	.00
□ 171	Scott Fletcher	.05	.02	.00
□ 172	Ruben Sierra	.75	.30	.07
□ 173	Larry Parrish	.05	.02	.00
□ 174	Pete O'Brien	.10	.04	.01
□ 175	Pete Incaviglia	.35	.14	.03
□ 176	Don Slaught	.05	.02	.00
□ 177	Oddibe McDowell	.10	.04	.01
□ 178	Charlie Hough	.05	.02	.00
□ 179	Steve Buechele	.05	.02	.00
□ 180	Bob Stanley	.05	.02	.00
□ 181	Wade Boggs	1.00	.40	.10
□ 182	Jim Rice	.20	.08	.02
□ 183	Bill Buckner	.10	.04	.01
□ 184	Dwight Evans	.15	.06	.01
□ 185	Spike Owen	.05	.02	.00
□ 186	Don Baylor	.10	.04	.01
□ 187	Marc Sullivan	.05	.02	.00
□ 188	Marty Barrett	.10	.04	.01
□ 189	Dave Henderson	.05	.02	.00
□ 190	Bo Diaz	.05	.02	.00
□ 191	Barry Larkin	.25	.10	.02
□ 192	Kal Daniels	.50	.20	.05
□ 193	Terry Francona	.05	.02	.00
□ 194	Tom Browning	.15	.06	.01
□ 195	Ron Oester	.05	.02	.00
□ 196	Buddy Bell	.10	.04	.01
□ 197	Eric Davis	1.00	.40	.10
□ 198	Dave Parker	.15	.06	.01
□ 199	Steve Balboni	.05	.02	.00
□ 200	Danny Tartabull	.25	.10	.02
□ 201	Ed Hearn	.05	.02	.00
□ 202	Buddy Biancalana	.05	.02	.00
□ 203	Danny Jackson	.20	.08	.02
□ 204	Frank White	.10	.04	.01
□ 205	Bo Jackson	.60	.24	.06
□ 206	George Brett	.35	.14	.03
□ 207	Kevin Seitzer	1.50	.60	.15
□ 208	Willie Wilson	.10	.04	.01
□ 209	Orlando Mercado	.05	.02	.00
□ 210	Darrell Evans	.10	.04	.01
□ 211	Larry Herndon	.05	.02	.00
□ 212	Jack Morris	.15	.06	.01
□ 213	Chet Lemon	.05	.02	.00
□ 214	Mike Heath	.05	.02	.00
□ 215	Darnell Coles	.05	.02	.00
□ 216	Alan Trammell	.25	.10	.02
□ 217	Terry Harper	.05	.02	.00
□ 218	Lou Whitaker	.10	.04	.01
□ 219	Gary Gaetti	.20	.08	.02
□ 220	Tom Nieto	.05	.02	.00
□ 221	Kirby Puckett	.50	.20	.05
□ 222	Tom Brunansky	.10	.04	.0
□ 223	Greg Gagne	.05	.02	.0
□ 224	Dan Gladden	.05	.02	.0
□ 225	Mark Davidson	.10	.04	.0
□ 226	Bert Blyleven	.10	.04	.0
□ 227	Steve Lombardozzi	.05	.02	.0
□ 228	Kent Hrbek	.25	.10	.0
□ 229	Gary Redus	.05	.02	.0
□ 230	Ivan Calderon	.10	.04	.0
□ 231	Tim Hulett	.05	.02	.0
□ 232	Carlton Fisk	.15	.06	.0
□ 233	Greg Walker	.10	.04	.0
□ 234	Ron Karkovice	.05	.02	.0
□ 235	Ozzie Guillen	.15	.06	.0
□ 236	Harold Baines	.15	.06	.0
□ 237	Donnie Hill	.05	.02	.0
□ 238	Rich Dotson	.10	.04	.0
□ 239	Mike Pagliarulo	.10	.04	.0
□ 240	Joel Skinner	.05	.02	.0
□ 241	Don Mattingly	1.50	.60	.1
□ 242	Gary Ward	.05	.02	.0
□ 243	Dave Winfield	.25	.10	.0
□ 244	Dan Pasqua	.10	.04	.0
□ 245	Wayne Tolleson	.05	.02	.0
□ 246	Willie Randolph	.10	.04	.0
□ 247	Dennis Rasmussen	.10	.04	.0
□ 248	Rickey Henderson	.40	.16	.0
□ 249	Angels Logo	.03	.01	.0
□ 250	Astros Logo	.03	.01	.0
□ 251	A's Logo	.03	.01	.0
□ 252	Blue Jays Logo	.03	.01	.0
□ 253	Braves Logo	.03	.01	.0
□ 254	Brewers Logo	.03	.01	.0
□ 255	Cardinals Logo	.03	.01	.0
□ 256	Dodgers Logo	.03	.01	.0
□ 257	Expos Logo	.03	.01	.0
□ 258	Giants Logo	.03	.01	.0
□ 259	Indians Logo	.03	.01	.0
□ 260	Mariners Logo	.03	.01	.0
□ 261	Orioles Logo	.03	.01	.0
□ 262	Padres Logo	.03	.01	.0
□ 263	Phillies Logo	.03	.01	.0
□ 264	Pirates Logo	.03	.01	.0
□ 265	Rangers Logo	.03	.01	.0
□ 266	Red Sox Logo	.03	.01	.0
□ 267	Reds Logo	.03	.01	.0
□ 268	Royals Logo	.03	.01	.0
□ 269	Tigers Logo	.03	.01	.0
□ 270	Twins Logo	.03	.01	.0
□ 271	Chicago Logos	.03	.01	.0
□ 272	New York Logos	.03	.01	.0

1987 Donruss Rookies

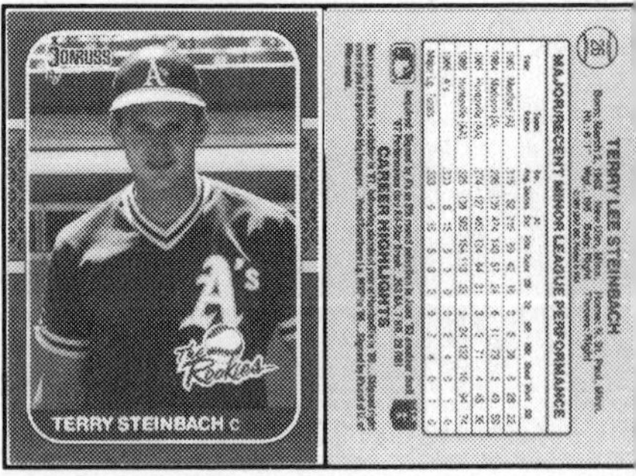

The 1987 Donruss "The Rookies" set features 5 cards plus a 15-piece puzzle of Roberto Clemente Cards are in full color and are standard size, 2 1/2 by 3 1/2". The set was distributed in a small gree and black box with gold lettering. Card fronts ar similar in design to the 1987 Donruss regular issu except for the presence of "The Rookies" logo in th lower left corner and a green border instead of black border.

	MINT	EXC	G-V
COMPLETE SET (56)	12.50	5.00	1.2
COMMON PLAYER (1-56)	.05	.02	.C

☐ 1 Mark McGwire	2.50	1.00	.20
☐ 2 Eric Bell	.05	.02	.00
☐ 3 Mark Williamson	.15	.06	.01
☐ 4 Mike Greenwell	3.00	1.20	.30
☐ 5 Ellis Burks	1.75	.70	.17
☐ 6 DeWayne Buice	.15	.06	.01
☐ 7 Mark McLemore	.05	.02	.00
☐ 8 Devon White	.35	.14	.03
☐ 9 Willie Fraser	.05	.02	.00
☐ 10 Len Lancaster	.10	.04	.01
☐ 11 Ken Williams	.25	.10	.02
☐ 12 Matt Nokes	.65	.26	.06
☐ 13 Jeff Robinson (Tigers pitcher)	.45	.18	.04
☐ 14 Bo Jackson	.60	.24	.06
☐ 15 Kevin Seitzer	1.50	.60	.15
☐ 16 Billy Ripken	.25	.10	.02
☐ 17 B.J. Surhoff	.15	.06	.01
☐ 18 Chuck Crim	.15	.06	.01
☐ 19 Mike Birkbeck	.05	.02	.00
☐ 20 Chris Bosio	.05	.02	.00
☐ 21 Les Straker	.15	.06	.01
☐ 22 Mark Davidson	.15	.06	.01
☐ 23 Gene Larkin	.35	.14	.03
☐ 24 Ken Gerhart	.10	.04	.01
☐ 25 Luis Polonia	.30	.12	.03
☐ 26 Terry Steinbach	.25	.10	.02
☐ 27 Mickey Brantley	.20	.08	.02
☐ 28 Mike Stanley	.15	.06	.01
☐ 29 Jerry Browne	.05	.02	.00
☐ 30 Todd Benzinger	.45	.18	.04
☐ 31 Fred McGriff	.75	.30	.07
☐ 32 Mike Henneman	.35	.14	.03
☐ 33 Casey Candaele	.10	.04	.01
☐ 34 Dave Magadan	.25	.10	.02
☐ 35 David Cone	1.25	.50	.12
☐ 36 Mike Jackson	.20	.08	.02
☐ 37 John Mitchell	.15	.06	.01
☐ 38 Mike Dunne	.25	.10	.02
☐ 39 John Smiley	.35	.14	.03
☐ 40 Joe Magrane	.50	.20	.05
☐ 41 Jim Lindeman	.15	.06	.01
☐ 42 Shane Mack	.30	.12	.03
☐ 43 Stanley Jefferson	.20	.08	.02
☐ 44 Benito Santiago	.65	.26	.06
☐ 45 Matt Williams	.45	.18	.04
☐ 46 Dave Meads	.10	.04	.01
☐ 47 Rafael Palmeiro	.60	.24	.06
☐ 48 Bill Long	.12	.05	.01
☐ 49 Bob Brower	.10	.04	.01
☐ 50 James Steels	.10	.04	.01
☐ 51 Paul Noce	.15	.06	.01
☐ 52 Greg Maddux	.35	.14	.03
☐ 53 Jeff Musselman	.10	.04	.01
☐ 54 Brian Holton	.10	.04	.01
☐ 55 Chuck Jackson	.15	.06	.01
☐ 56 Checklist Card	.05	.01	.00

1987 Donruss Highlights

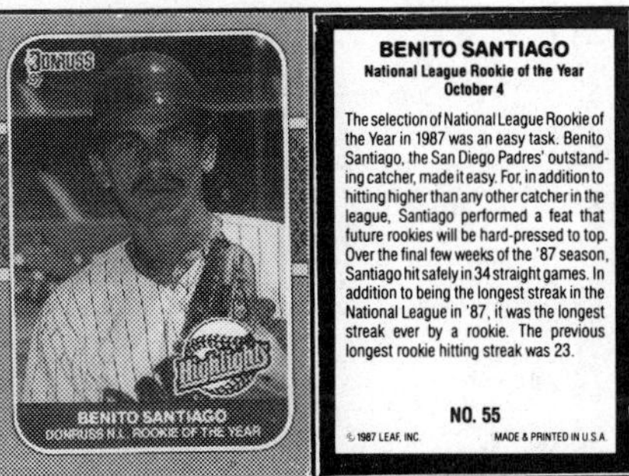

DONRUSS
Highlights
BENITO SANTIAGO
DONRUSS N.L. ROOKIE OF THE YEAR
BENITO SANTIAGO
National League Rookie of the Year
October 4
The selection of National League Rookie of the Year in 1987 was an easy task. Benito Santiago, the San Diego Padres' outstanding catcher, made it easy. For, in addition to hitting higher than any other catcher in the league, Santiago performed a feat that future rookies will be hard-pressed to top. Over the final few weeks of the '87 season, Santiago hit safely in 34 straight games. In addition to being the longest streak in the National League in '87, it was the longest streak ever by a rookie. The previous longest rookie hitting streak was 23.
NO. 55
© 1987 LEAF, INC.
MADE & PRINTED IN U.S.A.

Donruss' third (and last) edition of Highlights was released late in 1987. The cards are standard size, measuring 2 1/2" by 3 1/2" and are glossy in appearance. Cards commemorate events during the 1987 season, as well as players and pitchers of the month from each league. The set was distributed in its own red, black, blue, and gold box along with a small Roberto Clemente puzzle. Card fronts are similar to the regular 1987 Donruss issue except that the Highlights logo is positioned in the lower right-hand corner and the borders are in blue instead of black. The backs are printed in black and gold on white card stock.

	MINT	EXC	G-VG
COMPLETE SET (56)	7.50	3.00	.75
COMMON PLAYER (1-56)	.06	.02	.00
☐ 1 Juan Nieves First No-Hitter	.06	.02	.00
☐ 2 Mike Schmidt Hits 500th Homer	.25	.10	.02
☐ 3 Eric Davis NL Player April	.35	.14	.03
☐ 4 Sid Fernandez NL Pitcher April	.10	.04	.01
☐ 5 Brian Downing AL Player April	.06	.02	.00
☐ 6 Bret Saberhagen AL Pitcher April	.15	.06	.01
☐ 7 Tim Raines Free Agent Returns	.15	.06	.01
☐ 8 Eric Davis NL Player May	.35	.14	.03
☐ 9 Steve Bedrosian NL Pitcher May	.06	.02	.00
☐ 10 Larry Parrish AL Player May	.06	.02	.00
☐ 11 Jim Clancy AL Pitcher May	.06	.02	.00
☐ 12 Tony Gwynn NL Player June ERR (over "20" hits)	.20	.08	.02
☐ 13 Orel Hershiser NL Pitcher June	.35	.14	.03
☐ 14 Wade Boggs AL Player June	.50	.20	.05
☐ 15 Steve Ontiveros AL Pitcher June	.06	.02	.00
☐ 16 Tim Raines All Star Game Hero	.15	.06	.01
☐ 17 Don Mattingly Consecutive Game Homerun Streak	.65	.26	.06
☐ 18 Ray Dandridge 1987 HOF Inductee	.15	.06	.01
☐ 19 Jim "Catfish" Hunter 1987 HOF Inductee	.15	.06	.01
☐ 20 Billy Williams 1987 HOF Inductee	.15	.06	.01
☐ 21 Bo Diaz NL Player July	.06	.02	.00
☐ 22 Floyd Youmans NL Pitcher July	.06	.02	.00
☐ 23 Don Mattingly AL Player July	.65	.26	.06
☐ 24 Frank Viola AL Pitcher July	.15	.06	.01
☐ 25 Bobby Witt Strikes Out Four Batters in One Inning	.15	.06	.01
☐ 26 Kevin Seitzer Ties AL 9-Inning Game Hit Mark	.50	.20	.05
☐ 27 Mark McGwire Sets Rookie HR Record	.75	.30	.07
☐ 28 Andre Dawson Sets Cubs' 1st Year Homer Mark	.20	.08	.02
☐ 29 Paul Molitor Hits in 39 Straight Games	.15	.06	.01
☐ 30 Kirby Puckett Record Weekend	.35	.14	.03
☐ 31 Andre Dawson NL Player August	.20	.08	.02
☐ 32 Doug Drabek NL Pitcher August	.06	.02	.00
☐ 33 Dwight Evans AL Player August	.10	.04	.01
☐ 34 Mark Langston AL Pitcher August	.10	.04	.01
☐ 35 Wally Joyner 100 RBI in 1st Two Major League Seasons	.30	.12	.03
☐ 36 Vince Coleman 100 SB in 1st Three Major League Seasons	.20	.08	.02
☐ 37 Eddie Murray Orioles' All Time Homer King	.20	.08	.02

□ 38 Cal Ripken Ends Consecutive Innings Streak	.20	.08	.02
□ 39 Blue Jays Hit Record 10 Homers In One Game (McGriff/Ducey/Whitt)	.06	.02	.00
□ 40 McGwire/Canseco Equal A's RBI Marks	.90	.36	.09
□ 41 Bob Boone Sets All-Time Catching Record	.06	.02	.00
□ 42 Darryl Strawberry Sets Mets' One-Season Home Run Mark	.35	.14	.03
□ 43 Howard Johnson NL's All-Time Switchhit HR King	.15	.06	.01
□ 44 Wade Boggs Five Straight 200 Hit Seasons	.50	.20	.05
□ 45 Benito Santiago Eclipses Rookie Game Hitting Streak	.35	.14	.03
□ 46 Mark McGwire Eclipses Jackson's A's HR Record	.75	.30	.07
□ 47 Kevin Seitzer 13th Rookie to Collect 200 Hits	.50	.20	.05
□ 48 Don Mattingly Sets Slam Record	.75	.30	.07
□ 49 Darryl Strawberry NL Player September	.35	.14	.03
□ 50 Pascual Perez NL Pitcher September	.06	.02	.00
□ 51 Alan Trammell AL Player September	.15	.06	.01
□ 52 Doyle Alexander AL Pitcher September	.06	.02	.00
□ 53 Nolan Ryan Strikeout King Again	.25	.10	.02
□ 54 Mark McGwire Donruss AL ROY	.75	.30	.07
□ 55 Benito Santiago Donruss NL ROY	.50	.20	.05
□ 56 Checklist Card	.06	.01	.00

1988 Donruss

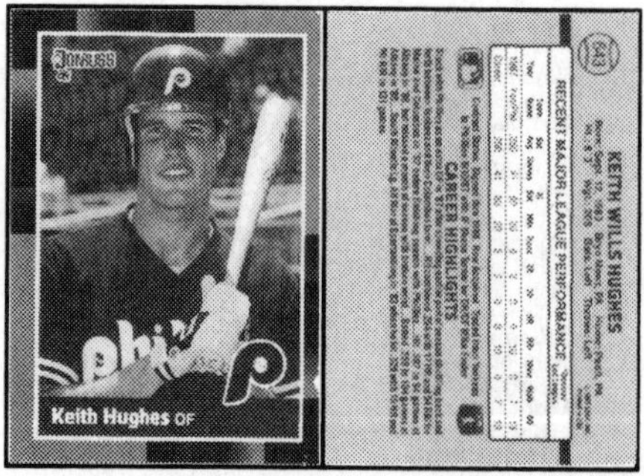

This 660-card set was distributed along with a puzzle of Stan Musial. The six regular checklist cards are numbered throughout the set as multiples of 100. Cards measure 2 1/2" by 3 1/2" and feature a distinctive black and blue border on the front. The popular Diamond King subset returns for the seventh consecutive year. Rated Rookies are featured again as cards 28-47. Cards marked as SP (short printed) from 648-660 are more difficult to find than the other 13 SP's in the lower 600s. These 26 cards listed as SP were apparently pulled from the printing sheet to make room for the 26 Bonus MVP cards. Six of the checklist cards were done two different ways to reflect the inclusion or exclusion of the Bonus MVP cards in the wax packs. In the checklist below the A variations (for the checklist cards) are from the wax packs and the B variations are from the factory collated sets.

	MINT	EXC	G-V
COMPLETE SET (660)	28.00	11.50	2.8
COMMON PLAYER (1-660)	.03	.01	.0

	MINT	EXC	G-V
□ 1 Mark McGwire DK	1.00	.25	.0
□ 2 Tim Raines DK	.20	.08	.0
□ 3 Benito Santiago DK	.35	.14	.0
□ 4 Alan Trammell DK	.20	.08	.0
□ 5 Danny Tartabull DK	.20	.08	.0
□ 6 Ron Darling DK	.15	.06	.0
□ 7 Paul Molitor DK	.18	.08	.0
□ 8 Devon White DK	.20	.08	.0
□ 9 Andre Dawson DK	.25	.10	.0
□ 10 Julio Franco DK	.08	.03	.0
□ 11 Scott Fletcher DK	.08	.03	.0
□ 12 Tony Fernandez DK	.15	.06	.0
□ 13 Shane Rawley DK	.10	.04	.0
□ 14 Kal Daniels DK	.20	.08	.0
□ 15 Jack Clark DK	.20	.08	.0
□ 16 Dwight Evans DK	.15	.06	.0
□ 17 Tommy John DK	.15	.06	.0
□ 18 Andy Van Slyke DK	.20	.08	.0
□ 19 Gary Gaetti DK	.20	.08	.0
□ 20 Mark Langston DK	.12	.05	.0
□ 21 Will Clark DK	.60	.24	.0
□ 22 Glenn Hubbard DK	.08	.03	.0
□ 23 Billy Hatcher DK	.10	.04	.0
□ 24 Bob Welch DK	.08	.03	.0
□ 25 Ivan Calderon DK	.10	.04	.0
□ 26 Cal Ripken Jr. DK	.25	.10	.0
□ 27 DK Checklist 1-26	.06	.01	.0
□ 28 Mackey Sasser	.30	.12	.0
□ 29 Jeff Treadway	.35	.14	.0
□ 30 Mike Campbell	.20	.08	.0
□ 31 Lance Johnson	.20	.08	.0
□ 32 Nelson Liriano	.20	.08	.0
□ 33 Shawn Abner	.30	.12	.0
□ 34 Roberto Alomar	.70	.28	.0
□ 35 Shawn Hillegas	.20	.08	.0
□ 36 Joey Meyer	.20	.08	.0
□ 37 Kevin Elster	.20	.08	.0
□ 38 Jose Lind	.30	.12	.0
□ 39 Kirt Manwaring	.30	.12	.0
□ 40 Mark Grace	3.00	1.20	.3
□ 41 Jody Reed	.50	.20	.0
□ 42 John Farrell	.25	.10	.0
□ 43 Al Leiter	1.00	.40	.1
□ 44 Gary Thurman	.30	.12	.0
□ 45 Vincente Palacios	.15	.06	.0
□ 46 Eddie Williams	.15	.06	.0
□ 47 Jack McDowell	.25	.10	.0
□ 48 Ken Dixon	.03	.01	.0
□ 49 Mike Birkbeck	.03	.01	.0
□ 50 Eric King	.03	.01	.0
□ 51 Roger Clemens	.50	.20	.0
□ 52 Pat Clements	.03	.01	.0
□ 53 Fernando Valenzuela	.15	.06	.0
□ 54 Mark Gubicza	.08	.03	.0
□ 55 Jay Howell	.03	.01	.0
□ 56 Floyd Youmans	.03	.01	.0
□ 57 Ed Correa	.03	.01	.0
□ 58 DeWayne Buice	.10	.04	.0
□ 59 Jose DeLeon	.03	.01	.0
□ 60 Danny Cox	.06	.02	.00
□ 61 Nolan Ryan	.30	.12	.03
□ 62 Steve Bedrosian	.08	.03	.01
□ 63 Tom Browning	.10	.04	.01
□ 64 Mark Davis	.03	.01	.00
□ 65 R.J. Reynolds	.03	.01	.00
□ 66 Kevin Mitchell	.08	.03	.01
□ 67 Ken Oberkfell	.03	.01	.00
□ 68 Rick Sutcliffe	.08	.03	.01
□ 69 Dwight Gooden	.45	.18	.04
□ 70 Scott Bankhead	.08	.03	.01
□ 71 Bert Blyleven	.08	.03	.01
□ 72 Jimmy Key	.08	.03	.01
□ 73 Les Straker	.10	.04	.01
□ 74 Jim Clancy	.03	.01	.00
□ 75 Mike Moore	.06	.02	.00
□ 76 Ron Darling	.12	.05	.01
□ 77 Ed Lynch	.03	.01	.00
□ 78 Dale Murphy	.35	.14	.03
□ 79 Doug Drabek	.06	.02	.00
□ 80 Scott Garrelts	.03	.01	.00
□ 81 Ed Whitson	.03	.01	.00
□ 82 Rob Murphy	.03	.01	.00
□ 83 Shane Rawley	.03	.01	.00
□ 84 Greg Mathews	.06	.02	.00
□ 85 Jim Deshaies	.06	.02	.00
□ 86 Mike Witt	.08	.03	.01
□ 87 Donnie Hill	.03	.01	.00

☐ 88	Jeff Reed	.03	.01	.00
☐ 89	Mike Boddicker	.06	.02	.00
☐ 90	Ted Higuera	.10	.04	.01
☐ 91	Walt Terrell	.03	.01	.00
☐ 92	Bob Stanley	.03	.01	.00
☐ 93	Dave Righetti	.08	.03	.01
☐ 94	Orel Hershiser	.25	.10	.02
☐ 95	Chris Bando	.03	.01	.00
☐ 96	Bret Saberhagen	.12	.05	.01
☐ 97	Curt Young	.03	.01	.00
☐ 98	Tim Burke	.03	.01	.00
☐ 99	Charlie Hough	.03	.01	.00
☐ 100A	Checklist 28-137	.06	.01	.00
☐ 100B	Checklist 28-133	.06	.01	.00
☐ 101	Bobby Witt	.08	.03	.01
☐ 102	George Brett	.30	.12	.03
☐ 103	Mickey Tettleton	.03	.01	.00
☐ 104	Scott Bailes	.03	.01	.00
☐ 105	Mike Pagliarulo	.08	.03	.01
☐ 106	Mike Scioscia	.03	.01	.00
☐ 107	Tom Brookens	.03	.01	.00
☐ 108	Ray Knight	.06	.02	.00
☐ 109	Dan Plesac	.06	.02	.00
☐ 110	Wally Joyner	.45	.18	.04
☐ 111	Bob Forsch	.03	.01	.00
☐ 112	Mike Scott	.15	.06	.01
☐ 113	Kevin Gross	.03	.01	.00
☐ 114	Benito Santiago	.30	.12	.03
☐ 115	Bob Kipper	.03	.01	.00
☐ 116	Mike Krukow	.03	.01	.00
☐ 117	Chris Bosio	.03	.01	.00
☐ 118	Sid Fernandez	.08	.03	.01
☐ 119	Jody Davis	.06	.02	.00
☐ 120	Mike Morgan	.03	.01	.00
☐ 121	Mark Eichhorn	.03	.01	.00
☐ 122	Jeff Reardon	.08	.03	.01
☐ 123	John Franco	.08	.03	.01
☐ 124	Richard Dotson	.06	.02	.00
☐ 125	Eric Bell	.03	.01	.00
☐ 126	Juan Nieves	.03	.01	.00
☐ 127	Jack Morris	.12	.05	.01
☐ 128	Rick Rhoden	.03	.01	.00
☐ 129	Rich Gedman	.03	.01	.00
☐ 130	Ken Howell	.03	.01	.00
☐ 131	Brook Jacoby	.08	.03	.01
☐ 132	Danny Jackson	.15	.06	.01
☐ 133	Gene Nelson	.03	.01	.00
☐ 134	Neal Heaton	.03	.01	.00
☐ 135	Willie Fraser	.03	.01	.00
☐ 136	Jose Guzman	.03	.01	.00
☐ 137	Ozzie Guillen	.06	.02	.00
☐ 138	Bob Knepper	.06	.02	.00
☐ 139	Mike Jackson	.15	.06	.01
☐ 140	Joe Magrane	.30	.12	.03
☐ 141	Jimmy Jones	.06	.02	.00
☐ 142	Ted Power	.03	.01	.00
☐ 143	Ozzie Virgil	.03	.01	.00
☐ 144	Felix Fermin	.10	.04	.01
☐ 145	Kelly Downs	.06	.02	.00
☐ 146	Shawon Dunston	.06	.02	.00
☐ 147	Scott Bradley	.03	.01	.00
☐ 148	Dave Stieb	.08	.03	.01
☐ 149	Frank Viola	.12	.05	.01
☐ 150	Terry Kennedy	.03	.01	.00
☐ 151	Bill Wegman	.03	.01	.00
☐ 152	Matt Nokes	.50	.20	.05
☐ 153	Wade Boggs	.90	.36	.09
☐ 154	Wayne Tolleson	.03	.01	.00
☐ 155	Mariano Duncan	.03	.01	.00
☐ 156	Julio Franco	.08	.03	.01
☐ 157	Charlie Leibrandt	.03	.01	.00
☐ 158	Terry Steinbach	.12	.05	.01
☐ 159	Mike Fitzgerald	.03	.01	.00
☐ 160	Jack Lazorko	.03	.01	.00
☐ 161	Mitch Williams	.03	.01	.00
☐ 162	Greg Walker	.08	.03	.01
☐ 163	Alan Ashby	.03	.01	.00
☐ 164	Tony Gwynn	.30	.12	.03
☐ 165	Bruce Ruffin	.03	.01	.00
☐ 166	Ron Robinson	.03	.01	.00
☐ 167	Zane Smith	.03	.01	.00
☐ 168	Junior Ortiz	.03	.01	.00
☐ 169	Jamie Moyer	.03	.01	.00
☐ 170	Tony Pena	.08	.03	.01
☐ 171	Cal Ripken	.20	.08	.02
☐ 172	B.J. Surhoff	.10	.04	.01
☐ 173	Lou Whitaker	.10	.04	.01
☐ 174	Ellis Burks	1.25	.50	.12
☐ 175	Ron Guidry	.10	.04	.01
☐ 176	Steve Sax	.12	.05	.01
☐ 177	Danny Tartabull	.20	.08	.02
☐ 178	Carney Lansford	.06	.02	.00
☐ 179	Casey Candaele	.03	.01	.00
☐ 180	Scott Fletcher	.03	.01	.00
☐ 181	Mark McLemore	.03	.01	.00
☐ 182	Ivan Calderon	.08	.03	.01
☐ 183	Jack Clark	.15	.06	.01
☐ 184	Glenn Davis	.15	.06	.01
☐ 185	Luis Aguayo	.03	.01	.00
☐ 186	Bo Diaz	.03	.01	.00
☐ 187	Stan Jefferson	.06	.02	.00
☐ 188	Sid Bream	.03	.01	.00
☐ 189	Bob Brenly	.03	.01	.00
☐ 190	Dion James	.03	.01	.00
☐ 191	Leon Durham	.03	.01	.00
☐ 192	Jesse Orosco	.03	.01	.00
☐ 193	Alvin Davis	.08	.03	.01
☐ 194	Gary Gaetti	.12	.05	.01
☐ 195	Fred McGriff	.35	.14	.03
☐ 196	Steve Lombardozzi	.03	.01	.00
☐ 197	Rance Mulliniks	.03	.01	.00
☐ 198	Rey Quinones	.03	.01	.00
☐ 199	Gary Carter	.25	.10	.02
☐ 200A	Checklist 138-247	.06	.01	.00
☐ 200B	Checklist 134-239	.06	.01	.00
☐ 201	Keith Moreland	.03	.01	.00
☐ 202	Ken Griffey	.06	.02	.00
☐ 203	Tommy Gregg	.15	.06	.01
☐ 204	Will Clark	.75	.30	.07
☐ 205	John Kruk	.10	.04	.01
☐ 206	Buddy Bell	.08	.03	.01
☐ 207	Von Hayes	.08	.03	.01
☐ 208	Tommy Herr	.06	.02	.00
☐ 209	Craig Reynolds	.03	.01	.00
☐ 210	Gary Pettis	.03	.01	.00
☐ 211	Harold Baines	.08	.03	.01
☐ 212	Vance Law	.03	.01	.00
☐ 213	Ken Gerhart	.03	.01	.00
☐ 214	Jim Gantner	.03	.01	.00
☐ 215	Chet Lemon	.06	.02	.00
☐ 216	Dwight Evans	.10	.04	.01
☐ 217	Don Mattingly	1.25	.50	.12
☐ 218	Franklin Stubbs	.03	.01	.00
☐ 219	Pat Tabler	.06	.02	.00
☐ 220	Bo Jackson	.40	.16	.04
☐ 221	Tony Phillips	.03	.01	.00
☐ 222	Tim Wallach	.08	.03	.01
☐ 223	Ruben Sierra	.25	.10	.02
☐ 224	Steve Buechele	.03	.01	.00
☐ 225	Frank White	.06	.02	.00
☐ 226	Alfredo Griffin	.06	.02	.00
☐ 227	Greg Swindell	.10	.04	.01
☐ 228	Willie Randolph	.06	.02	.00
☐ 229	Mike Marshall	.10	.04	.01
☐ 230	Alan Trammell	.15	.06	.01
☐ 231	Eddie Murray	.20	.08	.02
☐ 232	Dale Sveum	.03	.01	.00
☐ 233	Dick Schofield	.03	.01	.00
☐ 234	Jose Oquendo	.03	.01	.00
☐ 235	Bill Doran	.06	.02	.00
☐ 236	Milt Thompson	.03	.01	.00
☐ 237	Marvell Wynne	.03	.01	.00
☐ 238	Bobby Bonilla	.18	.08	.01
☐ 239	Chris Speier	.03	.01	.00
☐ 240	Glenn Braggs	.08	.03	.01
☐ 241	Wally Backman	.03	.01	.00
☐ 242	Ryne Sandberg	.20	.08	.02
☐ 243	Phil Bradley	.08	.03	.01
☐ 244	Kelly Gruber	.03	.01	.00
☐ 245	Tom Brunansky	.10	.04	.01
☐ 246	Ron Oester	.03	.01	.00
☐ 247	Bobby Thigpen	.03	.01	.00
☐ 248	Fred Lynn	.12	.05	.01
☐ 249	Paul Molitor	.12	.05	.01
☐ 250	Darrell Evans	.08	.03	.01
☐ 251	Gary Ward	.03	.01	.00
☐ 252	Bruce Hurst	.10	.04	.01
☐ 253	Bob Welch	.06	.02	.00
☐ 254	Joe Carter	.12	.05	.01
☐ 255	Willie Wilson	.08	.03	.01
☐ 256	Mark McGwire	1.25	.50	.12
☐ 257	Mitch Webster	.03	.01	.00
☐ 258	Brian Downing	.03	.01	.00
☐ 259	Mike Stanley	.08	.03	.01
☐ 260	Carlton Fisk	.10	.04	.01
☐ 261	Billy Hatcher	.08	.03	.01
☐ 262	Glenn Wilson	.06	.02	.00
☐ 263	Ozzie Smith	.12	.05	.01
☐ 264	Randy Ready	.03	.01	.00
☐ 265	Kurt Stillwell	.03	.01	.00
☐ 266	David Palmer	.03	.01	.00
☐ 267	Mike Diaz	.03	.01	.00
☐ 268	Rob Thompson	.06	.02	.00
☐ 269	Andre Dawson	.20	.08	.02
☐ 270	Lee Guetterman	.03	.01	.00
☐ 271	Willie Upshaw	.03	.01	.00
☐ 272	Randy Bush	.03	.01	.00
☐ 273	Larry Sheets	.08	.03	.01
☐ 274	Rob Deer	.08	.03	.01
☐ 275	Kirk Gibson	.18	.08	.01

□ 276	Marty Barrett	.08	.03	.01
□ 277	Rickey Henderson	.25	.10	.02
□ 278	Pedro Guerrero	.15	.06	.01
□ 279	Brett Butler	.06	.02	.00
□ 280	Kevin Seitzer	1.00	.40	.10
□ 281	Mike Davis	.03	.01	.00
□ 282	Andres Galarraga	.30	.12	.03
□ 283	Devon White	.18	.08	.01
□ 284	Pete O'Brien	.08	.03	.01
□ 285	Jerry Hairston	.03	.01	.00
□ 286	Kevin Bass	.06	.02	.00
□ 287	Carmelo Martinez	.03	.01	.00
□ 288	Juan Samuel	.08	.03	.01
□ 289	Kal Daniels	.25	.10	.02
□ 290	Albert Hall	.03	.01	.00
□ 291	Andy Van Slyke	.15	.06	.01
□ 292	Lee Smith	.06	.02	.00
□ 293	Vince Coleman	.20	.08	.02
□ 294	Tom Niedenfuer	.03	.01	.00
□ 295	Robin Yount	.20	.08	.02
□ 296	Jeff Robinson (Tigers pitcher)	.30	.12	.03
□ 297	Todd Benzinger	.40	.16	.04
□ 298	Dave Winfield	.20	.08	.02
□ 299	Mickey Hatcher	.06	.02	.00
□ 300A	Checklist 248-357	.06	.01	.00
□ 300B	Checklist 240-345	.06	.01	.00
□ 301	Bud Black	.03	.01	.00
□ 302	Jose Canseco	1.75	.70	.17
□ 303	Tom Foley	.03	.01	.00
□ 304	Pete Incaviglia	.18	.08	.01
□ 305	Bob Boone	.06	.02	.00
□ 306	Bill Long	.10	.04	.01
□ 307	Willie McGee	.10	.04	.01
□ 308	Ken Caminiti	.20	.08	.02
□ 309	Darren Daulton	.03	.01	.00
□ 310	Tracy Jones	.08	.03	.01
□ 311	Greg Booker	.03	.01	.00
□ 312	Mike LaValliere	.03	.01	.00
□ 313	Chili Davis	.08	.03	.01
□ 314	Glenn Hubbard	.03	.01	.00
□ 315	Paul Noce	.10	.04	.01
□ 316	Keith Hernandez	.18	.08	.01
□ 317	Mark Langston	.08	.03	.01
□ 318	Keith Atherton	.03	.01	.00
□ 319	Tony Fernandez	.10	.04	.01
□ 320	Kent Hrbek	.12	.05	.01
□ 321	John Cerutti	.03	.01	.00
□ 322	Mike Kingery	.03	.01	.00
□ 323	Dave Magadan	.10	.04	.01
□ 324	Rafael Palmeiro	.30	.12	.03
□ 325	Jeff Dedmon	.03	.01	.00
□ 326	Barry Bonds	.20	.08	.02
□ 327	Jeffrey Leonard	.06	.02	.00
□ 328	Tim Flannery	.03	.01	.00
□ 329	Dave Concepcion	.08	.03	.01
□ 330	Mike Schmidt	.30	.12	.03
□ 331	Bill Dawley	.03	.01	.00
□ 332	Larry Andersen	.03	.01	.00
□ 333	Jack Howell	.03	.01	.00
□ 334	Ken Williams	.20	.08	.02
□ 335	Bryn Smith	.03	.01	.00
□ 336	Billy Ripken	.15	.06	.01
□ 337	Greg Brock	.03	.01	.00
□ 338	Mike Heath	.03	.01	.00
□ 339	Mike Greenwell	1.25	.50	.12
□ 340	Claudell Washington	.03	.01	.00
□ 341	Jose Gonzalez	.03	.01	.00
□ 342	Mel Hall	.03	.01	.00
□ 343	Jim Eisenreich	.06	.02	.00
□ 344	Tony Bernazard	.03	.01	.00
□ 345	Tim Raines	.20	.08	.02
□ 346	Bob Brower	.03	.01	.00
□ 347	Larry Parrish	.03	.01	.00
□ 348	Thad Bosley	.03	.01	.00
□ 349	Dennis Eckersley	.10	.04	.01
□ 350	Cory Snyder	.20	.08	.02
□ 351	Rick Cerone	.03	.01	.00
□ 352	John Shelby	.03	.01	.00
□ 353	Larry Herndon	.03	.01	.00
□ 354	John Habyan	.03	.01	.00
□ 355	Chuck Crim	.08	.03	.01
□ 356	Gus Polidor	.03	.01	.00
□ 357	Ken Dayley	.03	.01	.00
□ 358	Danny Darwin	.03	.01	.00
□ 359	Lance Parrish	.10	.04	.01
□ 360	James Steels	.10	.04	.01
□ 361	Al Pedrique	.10	.04	.01
□ 362	Mike Aldrete	.06	.02	.00
□ 363	Juan Castillo	.03	.01	.00
□ 364	Len Dykstra	.08	.03	.01
□ 365	Luis Quinones	.06	.02	.00
□ 366	Jim Presley	.08	.03	.01
□ 367	Lloyd Moseby	.08	.03	.01
□ 368	Kirby Puckett	.35	.14	.03
□ 369	Eric Davis	.75	.30	.0
□ 370	Gary Redus	.03	.01	.0
□ 371	Dave Schmidt	.03	.01	.0
□ 372	Mark Clear	.03	.01	.0
□ 373	Dave Bergman	.03	.01	.0
□ 374	Charles Hudson	.03	.01	.0
□ 375	Calvin Schiraldi	.03	.01	.0
□ 376	Alex Trevino	.03	.01	.0
□ 377	Tom Candiotti	.03	.01	.0
□ 378	Steve Farr	.03	.01	.0
□ 379	Mike Gallego	.03	.01	.0
□ 380	Andy McGaffigan	.03	.01	.0
□ 381	Kirk McCaskill	.03	.01	.0
□ 382	Oddibe McDowell	.08	.03	.0
□ 383	Floyd Bannister	.03	.01	.0
□ 384	Denny Walling	.03	.01	.0
□ 385	Don Carman	.03	.01	.0
□ 386	Todd Worrell	.10	.04	.0
□ 387	Eric Show	.03	.01	.0
□ 388	Dave Parker	.10	.04	.0
□ 389	Rick Mahler	.03	.01	.0
□ 390	Mike Dunne	.15	.06	.0
□ 391	Candy Maldonado	.08	.03	.0
□ 392	Bob Dernier	.03	.01	.0
□ 393	Dave Valle	.03	.01	.0
□ 394	Ernie Whitt	.03	.01	.0
□ 395	Juan Berenguer	.03	.01	.0
□ 396	Mike Young	.03	.01	.0
□ 397	Mike Felder	.03	.01	.0
□ 398	Willie Hernandez	.06	.02	.0
□ 399	Jim Rice	.15	.06	.0
□ 400A	Checklist 358-467	.06	.01	.0
□ 400B	Checklist 346-451	.06	.01	.0
□ 401	Tommy John	.10	.04	.0
□ 402	Brian Holton	.03	.01	.0
□ 403	Carmen Castillo	.03	.01	.0
□ 404	Jamie Quirk	.03	.01	.0
□ 405	Dwayne Murphy	.03	.01	.0
□ 406	Jeff Parrett	.15	.06	.0
□ 407	Don Sutton	.12	.05	.0
□ 408	Jerry Browne	.03	.01	.0
□ 409	Jim Winn	.03	.01	.0
□ 410	Dave Smith	.03	.01	.0
□ 411	Shane Mack	.15	.06	.0
□ 412	Greg Gross	.03	.01	.0
□ 413	Nick Esasky	.03	.01	.0
□ 414	Damaso Garcia	.03	.01	.0
□ 415	Brian Fisher	.03	.01	.0
□ 416	Brian Dayett	.03	.01	.0
□ 417	Curt Ford	.03	.01	.0
□ 418	Mark Williamson	.10	.04	.0
□ 419	Bill Schroeder	.03	.01	.0
□ 420	Mike Henneman	.20	.08	.0
□ 421	John Marzano	.10	.04	.0
□ 422	Ron Kittle	.08	.03	.0
□ 423	Matt Young	.03	.01	.0
□ 424	Steve Balboni	.03	.01	.0
□ 425	Luis Polonia	.20	.08	.0
□ 426	Randy St.Claire	.03	.01	.0
□ 427	Greg Harris	.03	.01	.0
□ 428	Johnny Ray	.08	.03	.0
□ 429	Ray Searage	.03	.01	.0
□ 430	Ricky Horton	.03	.01	.0
□ 431	Gerald Young	.35	.14	.0
□ 432	Rick Schu	.03	.01	.0
□ 433	Paul O'Neill	.06	.02	.0
□ 434	Rich Gossage	.08	.03	.01
□ 435	John Cangelosi	.03	.01	.0
□ 436	Mike LaCoss	.03	.01	.0
□ 437	Gerald Perry	.08	.03	.01
□ 438	Dave Martinez	.06	.02	.0
□ 439	Darryl Strawberry	.40	.16	.04
□ 440	John Moses	.03	.01	.0
□ 441	Greg Gagne	.03	.01	.0
□ 442	Jesse Barfield	.12	.05	.01
□ 443	George Frazier	.03	.01	.0
□ 444	Garth Iorg	.03	.01	.0
□ 445	Ed Nunez	.03	.01	.0
□ 446	Rick Aguilera	.03	.01	.0
□ 447	Jerry Mumphrey	.03	.01	.0
□ 448	Rafael Ramirez	.03	.01	.0
□ 449	John Smiley	.20	.08	.02
□ 450	Atlee Hammaker	.03	.01	.0
□ 451	Lance McCullers	.06	.02	.0
□ 452	Guy Hoffman	.03	.01	.0
□ 453	Chris James	.10	.04	.01
□ 454	Terry Pendleton	.06	.02	.0
□ 455	Dave Meads	.10	.04	.01
□ 456	Bill Buckner	.08	.03	.01
□ 457	John Pawlowski	.10	.04	.01
□ 458	Bob Sebra	.03	.01	.0
□ 459	Jim Dwyer	.03	.01	.00
□ 460	Jay Aldrich	.10	.04	.01
□ 461	Frank Tanana	.03	.01	.00
□ 462	Oil Can Boyd	.03	.01	.00

□ 463 Dan Pasqua	.06	.02	.00
□ 464 Tim Crews	.10	.04	.01
□ 465 Andy Allanson	.03	.01	.00
□ 466 Bill Pecota	.10	.04	.01
□ 467 Steve Ontiveros	.03	.01	.00
□ 468 Hubie Brooks	.06	.02	.00
□ 469 Paul Kilgus	.15	.06	.01
□ 470 Dale Mohorcic	.03	.01	.00
□ 471 Dan Quisenberry	.08	.03	.01
□ 472 Dave Stewart	.08	.03	.01
□ 473 Dave Clark	.06	.02	.00
□ 474 Joel Skinner	.03	.01	.00
□ 475 Dave Anderson	.03	.01	.00
□ 476 Dan Petry	.03	.01	.00
□ 477 Carl Nichols	.10	.04	.01
□ 478 Ernest Riles	.03	.01	.00
□ 479 George Hendrick	.06	.02	.00
□ 480 John Morris	.03	.01	.00
□ 481 Manny Hernandez	.10	.04	.01
□ 482 Jeff Stone	.03	.01	.00
□ 483 Chris Brown	.06	.02	.00
□ 484 Mike Bielecki	.03	.01	.00
□ 485 Dave Dravecky	.03	.01	.00
□ 486 Rick Manning	.03	.01	.00
□ 487 Bill Almon	.03	.01	.00
□ 488 Jim Sundberg	.03	.01	.00
□ 489 Ken Phelps	.06	.02	.00
□ 490 Tom Henke	.06	.02	.00
□ 491 Dan Gladden	.06	.02	.00
□ 492 Barry Larkin	.15	.06	.01
□ 493 Fred Manrique	.10	.04	.01
□ 494 Mike Griffin	.03	.01	.00
□ 495 Mark Knudson	.10	.04	.01
□ 496 Bill Madlock	.06	.02	.00
□ 497 Tim Stoddard	.03	.01	.00
□ 498 Sam Horn	.35	.14	.03
□ 499 Tracy Woodson	.20	.08	.02
□ 500A Checklist 468-577	.06	.01	.00
□ 500B Checklist 452-557	.06	.01	.00
□ 501 Ken Schrom	.03	.01	.00
□ 502 Angel Salazar	.03	.01	.00
□ 503 Eric Plunk	.03	.01	.00
□ 504 Joe Hesketh	.03	.01	.00
□ 505 Greg Minton	.03	.01	.00
□ 506 Geno Petralli	.03	.01	.00
□ 507 Bob James	.03	.01	.00
□ 508 Robbie Wine	.10	.04	.01
□ 509 Jeff Calhoun	.03	.01	.00
□ 510 Steve Lake	.03	.01	.00
□ 511 Mark Grant	.03	.01	.00
□ 512 Frank Williams	.03	.01	.00
□ 513 Jeff Blauser	.20	.08	.02
□ 514 Bob Walk	.06	.02	.00
□ 515 Craig Lefferts	.03	.01	.00
□ 516 Manny Trillo	.03	.01	.00
□ 517 Jerry Reed	.03	.01	.00
□ 518 Rick Leach	.03	.01	.00
□ 519 Mark Davidson	.15	.06	.01
□ 520 Jeff Ballard	.15	.06	.01
□ 521 Dave Stapleton	.06	.02	.00
□ 522 Pat Sheridan	.03	.01	.00
□ 523 Al Nipper	.03	.01	.00
□ 524 Steve Trout	.03	.01	.00
□ 525 Jeff Hamilton	.06	.02	.00
□ 526 Tommy Hinzo	.10	.04	.01
□ 527 Lonnie Smith	.03	.01	.00
□ 528 Greg Cadaret	.15	.06	.01
□ 529 Bob McClure	.03	.01	.00
("Rob" on front)			
□ 530 Chuck Finley	.03	.01	.00
□ 531 Jeff Russell	.03	.01	.00
□ 532 Steve Lyons	.03	.01	.00
□ 533 Terry Puhl	.03	.01	.00
□ 534 Eric Nolte	.15	.06	.01
□ 535 Kent Tekulve	.03	.01	.00
□ 536 Pat Pacillo	.08	.03	.01
□ 537 Charlie Puleo	.03	.01	.00
□ 538 Tom Prince	.12	.05	.01
□ 539 Greg Maddux	.20	.08	.02
□ 540 Jim Lindeman	.03	.01	.00
□ 541 Pete Stanicek	.25	.10	.02
□ 542 Steve Kiefer	.06	.02	.00
□ 543A Jim Morrison ERR	.06	.02	.00
(no decimal before lifetime average)			
□ 543B Jim Morrison COR	.06	.02	.00
□ 544 Spike Owen	.03	.01	.00
□ 545 Jay Buhner	.50	.20	.05
□ 546 Mike Devereaux	.30	.12	.03
□ 547 Jerry Don Gleaton	.03	.01	.00
□ 548 Jose Rijo	.03	.01	.00
□ 549 Dennis Martinez	.03	.01	.00
□ 550 Mike Loynd	.03	.01	.00
□ 551 Darrell Miller	.03	.01	.00
□ 552 Dave LaPoint	.03	.01	.00

□ 553 John Tudor	.08	.03	.01
□ 554 Rocky Childress	.10	.04	.01
□ 555 Wally Ritchie	.10	.04	.01
□ 556 Terry McGriff	.06	.02	.00
□ 557 Dave Leiper	.03	.01	.00
□ 558 Jeff Robinson	.06	.02	.00
(Pirates pitcher)			
□ 559 Jose Uribe	.03	.01	.00
□ 560 Ted Simmons	.08	.03	.01
□ 561 Lester Lancaster	.10	.04	.01
□ 562 Keith Miller	.20	.08	.02
(New York Mets)			
□ 563 Harold Reynolds	.03	.01	.00
□ 564 Gene Larkin	.25	.10	.02
□ 565 Cecil Fielder	.03	.01	.00
□ 566 Roy Smalley	.03	.01	.00
□ 567 Duane Ward	.03	.01	.00
□ 568 Bill Wilkinson	.10	.04	.01
□ 569 Howard Johnson	.10	.04	.01
□ 570 Frank DiPino	.03	.01	.00
□ 571 Pete Smith	.15	.06	.01
□ 572 Darnell Coles	.03	.01	.00
□ 573 Don Robinson	.03	.01	.00
□ 574 Rob Nelson	.06	.02	.00
□ 575 Dennis Rasmussen	.06	.02	.00
□ 576 Steve Jeltz	.03	.01	.00
□ 577 Tom Pagnozzi	.15	.06	.01
□ 578 Ty Gainey	.03	.01	.00
□ 579 Gary Lucas	.03	.01	.00
□ 580 Ron Hassey	.03	.01	.00
□ 581 Herm Winningham	.03	.01	.00
□ 582 Rene Gonzales	.12	.05	.01
□ 583 Brad Komminsk	.03	.01	.00
□ 584 Doyle Alexander	.03	.01	.00
□ 585 Jeff Sellers	.03	.01	.00
□ 586 Bill Gullickson	.03	.01	.00
□ 587 Tim Belcher	.20	.08	.02
□ 588 Doug Jones	.35	.14	.03
□ 589 Melido Perez	.30	.12	.03
□ 590 Rick Honeycutt	.03	.01	.00
□ 591 Pascual Perez	.06	.02	.00
□ 592 Curt Wilkerson	.03	.01	.00
□ 593 Steve Howe	.03	.01	.00
□ 594 John Davis	.15	.06	.01
□ 595 Storm Davis	.06	.02	.00
□ 596 Sammy Stewart	.03	.01	.00
□ 597 Neil Allen	.03	.01	.00
□ 598 Alejandro Pena	.03	.01	.00
□ 599 Mark Thurmond	.03	.01	.00
□ 600A Checklist 578-BC26	.06	.01	.00
□ 600B Checklist 558-660	.06	.01	.00
□ 601 Jose Mesa	.20	.08	.02
□ 602 Don August	.25	.10	.02
□ 603 Terry Leach SP	.10	.04	.01
□ 604 Tom Newell	.15	.06	.01
□ 605 Randall Byers SP	.20	.08	.02
□ 606 Jim Gott	.03	.01	.00
□ 607 Harry Spilman	.03	.01	.00
□ 608 John Candelaria	.06	.02	.00
□ 609 Mike Brumley	.15	.06	.01
□ 610 Mickey Brantley	.08	.03	.01
□ 611 Jose Nunez SP	.20	.08	.02
□ 612 Tom Nieto	.03	.01	.00
□ 613 Rick Reuschel	.06	.02	.00
□ 614 Lee Mazzilli SP	.06	.02	.00
□ 615 Scott Lusader	.20	.08	.02
□ 616 Bobby Meacham	.03	.01	.00
□ 617 Kevin McReynolds SP	.15	.06	.01
□ 618 Gene Garber	.03	.01	.00
□ 619 Barry Lyons SP	.20	.08	.02
□ 620 Randy Myers	.10	.04	.01
□ 621 Donnie Moore	.03	.01	.00
□ 622 Domingo Ramos	.03	.01	.00
□ 623 Ed Romero	.03	.01	.00
□ 624 Greg Myers	.15	.06	.01
□ 625 Ripken Family	.08	.03	.01
□ 626 Pat Perry	.03	.01	.00
□ 627 Andres Thomas SP	.06	.02	.00
□ 628 Matt Williams SP	.35	.14	.03
□ 629 Dave Hengel	.20	.08	.02
□ 630 Jeff Musselman SP	.06	.02	.00
□ 631 Tim Laudner	.03	.01	.00
□ 632 Bob Ojeda SP	.08	.03	.01
□ 633 Rafael Santana	.03	.01	.00
□ 634 Wes Gardner	.25	.10	.02
□ 635 Roberto Kelly SP	.50	.20	.05
□ 636 Mike Flanagan SP	.06	.02	.00
□ 637 Jay Bell	.20	.08	.02
□ 638 Bob Melvin	.03	.01	.00
□ 639 Damon Berryhill	.35	.14	.03
□ 640 David Wells SP	.25	.10	.02
□ 641 Puzzle Card	.03	.01	.00
(Stan Musial)			
□ 642 Doug Sisk	.03	.01	.00
□ 643 Keith Hughes	.20	.08	.02

☐ 644	Tom Glavine	.15	.06	.01
☐ 645	Al Newman	.03	.01	.00
☐ 646	Scott Sanderson	.03	.01	.00
☐ 647	Scott Terry	.10	.04	.01
☐ 648	Tim Teufel SP	.08	.03	.01
☐ 649	Garry Templeton SP	.08	.03	.01
☐ 650	Manny Lee SP	.08	.03	.01
☐ 651	Roger McDowell SP	.10	.04	.01
☐ 652	Mookie Wilson SP	.10	.04	.01
☐ 653	David Cone SP	.80	.32	.08
☐ 654	Ron Gant SP	1.00	.40	.10
☐ 655	Joe Price SP	.08	.03	.01
☐ 656	George Bell SP	.25	.10	.02
☐ 657	Gregg Jefferies SP	7.00	2.80	.70
☐ 658	Todd Stottlemyre SP	.40	.16	.04
☐ 659	Geronimo Berroa SP	.45	.18	.04
☐ 660	Jerry Royster SP	.08	.03	.01

1988 Donruss Bonus MVP's

This 26-card set was distributed along with the regular 1988 Donruss issue as random inserts with the rack and wax packs. These bonus cards are numbered with the prefix BC for bonus cards and were supposedly produced in the same quantities as the other 660 regular issue cards. The "most valuable" player was selected from each of the 26 teams. Cards measure 2 1/2" by 3 1/2" and feature the same distinctive black and blue border on the front as the regular issue. The cards are distinguished by the MVP logo in the upper left corner of the obverse. The last 13 cards numerically are considered to be somewhat tougher to find than the first 13 cards.

		MINT	EXC	G-VG
COMPLETE SET (26)		10.00	4.00	1.00
COMMON PLAYER (BC1-BC13)		.07	.03	.01
COMMON PLAYER (BC14-BC26)		.15	.06	.01
☐ BC1	Cal Ripken	.25	.10	.02
☐ BC2	Eric Davis	.70	.28	.07
☐ BC3	Paul Molitor	.15	.06	.01
☐ BC4	Mike Schmidt	.35	.14	.03
☐ BC5	Ivan Calderon	.07	.03	.01
☐ BC6	Tony Gwynn	.40	.16	.04
☐ BC7	Wade Boggs	.85	.34	.08
☐ BC8	Andy Van Slyke	.15	.06	.01
☐ BC9	Joe Carter	.15	.06	.01
☐ BC10	Andre Dawson	.20	.08	.02
☐ BC11	Alan Trammell	.20	.08	.02
☐ BC12	Mike Scott	.15	.06	.01
☐ BC13	Wally Joyner	.50	.20	.05
☐ BC14	Dale Murphy	.40	.16	.04
☐ BC15	Kirby Puckett	.50	.20	.05
☐ BC16	Pedro Guerrero	.20	.08	.02
☐ BC17	Kevin Seitzer	.70	.28	.07
☐ BC18	Tim Raines	.25	.10	.02
☐ BC19	George Bell	.20	.08	.02
☐ BC20	Darryl Strawberry	.75	.30	.07
☐ BC21	Don Mattingly	1.50	.60	.15
☐ BC22	Ozzie Smith	.20	.08	.02
☐ BC23	Mark McGwire	1.00	.40	.10
☐ BC24	Will Clark	.75	.30	.07
☐ BC25	Alvin Davis	.15	.06	.01
☐ BC26	Ruben Sierra	.20	.08	.02

1988 Donruss Super DK's

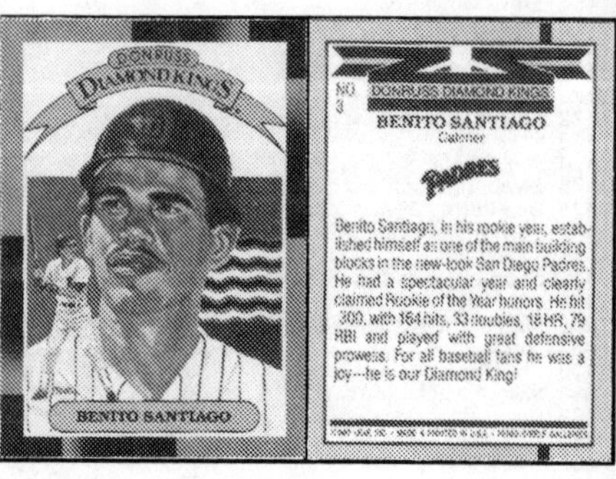

This 26-player card set was available through a mail-in offer detailed on the wax packs. The set was sent in return for 8.00 and three wrappers plus 1.50 postage and handling. The set features the popular Diamond King subseries in large (approximately 4 7/8" by 6 13/16") form. Dick Perez of Perez-Steele Galleries did another outstanding job on the artwork. The cards are essentially a large version of the Donruss regular issue Diamond Kings.

		MINT	EXC	G-VG
COMPLETE SET (26)		10.00	4.00	1.00
COMMON PLAYER (1-26)		.15	.06	.01
☐ 1	Mark McGwire DK	1.50	.60	.15
☐ 2	Tim Raines DK	.50	.20	.05
☐ 3	Benito Santiago DK	.90	.36	.09
☐ 4	Alan Trammell DK	.35	.14	.03
☐ 5	Danny Tartabull DK	.50	.20	.05
☐ 6	Ron Darling DK	.25	.10	.02
☐ 7	Paul Molitor DK	.25	.10	.02
☐ 8	Devon White DK	.35	.14	.03
☐ 9	Andre Dawson DK	.35	.14	.03
☐ 10	Julio Franco DK	.25	.10	.02
☐ 11	Scott Fletcher DK	.15	.06	.01
☐ 12	Tony Fernandez DK	.25	.10	.02
☐ 13	Shane Rawley DK	.15	.06	.01
☐ 14	Kal Daniels DK	.50	.20	.05
☐ 15	Jack Clark DK	.50	.20	.05
☐ 16	Dwight Evans DK	.25	.10	.02
☐ 17	Tommy John DK	.25	.10	.02
☐ 18	Andy Van Slyke DK	.35	.14	.03
☐ 19	Gary Gaetti DK	.35	.14	.03
☐ 20	Mark Langston DK	.25	.10	.02
☐ 21	Will Clark DK	1.00	.40	.10
☐ 22	Glenn Hubbard DK	.15	.06	.01
☐ 23	Billy Hatcher DK	.25	.10	.02
☐ 24	Bob Welch DK	.15	.06	.01
☐ 25	Ivan Calderon DK	.25	.10	.02
☐ 26	Cal Ripken Jr. DK	.60	.24	.06

1988 Donruss All-Stars

This 64-card set features cards measuring standard size, 2 1/2" by 3 1/2". Card fronts are in full color with a solid blue and black border. The card backs are printed in black and blue on white card stock. Cards are numbered on the back inside a blue star in the upper right hand corner. Card backs feature statistical information about the player's performance in past All-Star games. The set was distributed in packs which also contained a Pop-Up. The AL Checklist card #32 has two uncorrected errors on it, Wade Boggs is erroneously listed as the AL Leftfielder and Dan Plesac is erroneously listed as being the Tigers Pitcher.

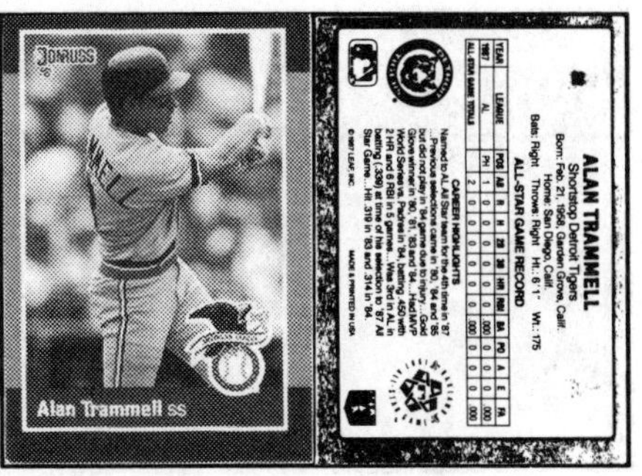

	MINT	EXC	G-VG
COMPLETE SET (64)	7.00	2.80	.70
COMMON PLAYER (1-64)	.10	.04	.01
□ 1 Don Mattingly	.80	.32	.08
□ 2 Dave Winfield	.25	.10	.02
□ 3 Willie Randolph	.15	.06	.01
□ 4 Rickey Henderson	.35	.14	.03
□ 5 Cal Ripken	.25	.10	.02
□ 6 George Bell	.20	.08	.02
□ 7 Wade Boggs	.65	.26	.06
□ 8 Bret Saberhagen	.20	.08	.02
□ 9 Terry Kennedy	.10	.04	.01
□ 10 John McNamara MG	.10	.04	.01
□ 11 Jay Howell	.10	.04	.01
□ 12 Harold Baines	.10	.04	.01
□ 13 Harold Reynolds	.10	.04	.01
□ 14 Bruce Hurst	.15	.06	.01
□ 15 Kirby Puckett	.35	.14	.03
□ 16 Matt Nokes	.25	.10	.02
□ 17 Pat Tabler	.10	.04	.01
□ 18 Dan Plesac	.10	.04	.01
□ 19 Mark McGwire	.65	.26	.06
□ 20 Mike Witt	.10	.04	.01
□ 21 Larry Parrish	.10	.04	.01
□ 22 Alan Trammell	.20	.08	.02
□ 23 Dwight Evans	.10	.04	.01
□ 24 Jack Morris	.15	.06	.01
□ 25 Tony Fernandez	.15	.06	.01
□ 26 Mark Langston	.10	.04	.01
□ 27 Kevin Seitzer	.50	.20	.05
□ 28 Tom Henke	.10	.04	.01
□ 29 Dave Righetti	.15	.06	.01
□ 30 Oakland Stadium	.10	.04	.01
□ 31 Wade Boggs	.65	.26	.06
□ 32 AL Checklist	.10	.01	.00
□ 33 Jack Clark	.25	.10	.02
□ 34 Darryl Strawberry	.40	.16	.04
□ 35 Ryne Sandberg	.25	.10	.02
□ 36 Andre Dawson	.25	.10	.02
□ 37 Ozzie Smith	.20	.08	.02
□ 38 Eric Davis	.50	.20	.05
□ 39 Mike Schmidt	.35	.14	.03
□ 40 Mike Scott	.20	.08	.02
□ 41 Gary Carter	.25	.10	.02
□ 42 Davey Johnson MG	.10	.04	.01
□ 43 Rick Sutcliffe	.10	.04	.01
□ 44 Willie McGee	.15	.06	.01
□ 45 Hubie Brooks	.10	.04	.01
□ 46 Dale Murphy	.35	.14	.03
□ 47 Bo Diaz	.10	.04	.01
□ 48 Pedro Guerrero	.20	.08	.02
□ 49 Keith Hernandez	.20	.08	.02
□ 50 Ozzie Virgil UER (Phillies logo on card back, wrong birth year)	.10	.04	.01
□ 51 Tony Gwynn	.35	.14	.03
□ 52 Rick Reuschel UER (Pirates logo on card back)	.10	.04	.01
□ 53 John Franco	.10	.04	.01
□ 54 Jeffrey Leonard	.10	.04	.01
□ 55 Juan Samuel	.15	.06	.01
□ 56 Orel Hershiser	.50	.20	.05
□ 57 Tim Raines	.25	.10	.02
□ 58 Sid Fernandez	.15	.06	.01
□ 59 Tim Wallach	.10	.04	.01
□ 60 Lee Smith	.10	.04	.01
□ 61 Steve Bedrosian	.10	.04	.01
□ 62 Tim Raines	.25	.10	.02
□ 63 Ozzie Smith	.20	.08	.02
□ 64 NL Checklist	.10	.01	.00

1988 Donruss Pop-Ups

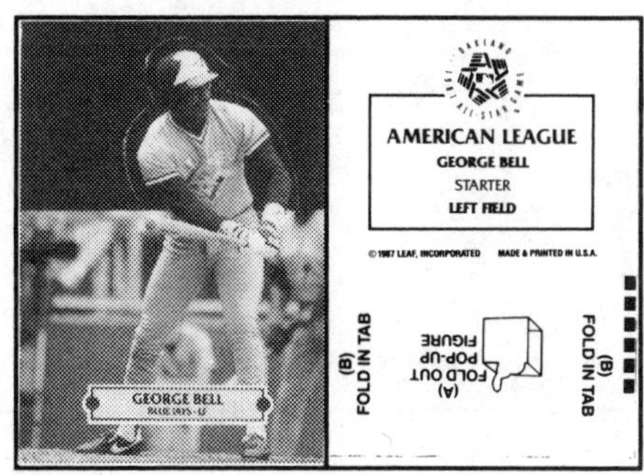

This 20-card set features "fold-out" cards measuring standard size, 2 1/2" by 3 1/2". Card fronts are in full color. Cards are unnumbered but are listed in the same order as the Donruss All-Stars on the All-Star checklist card. Card backs present essentially no information about the player. The set was distributed in packs which also contained All-Star cards. In order to remain in mint condition, the cards should not be popped up.

	MINT	EXC	G-VG
COMPLETE SET (20)	4.00	1.60	.40
COMMON PLAYER (1-20)	.10	.04	.01
□ 1 Don Mattingly	.90	.36	.09
□ 2 Dave Winfield	.25	.10	.02
□ 3 Willie Randolph	.15	.06	.01
□ 4 Rickey Henderson	.35	.14	.03
□ 5 Cal Ripken	.30	.12	.03
□ 6 George Bell	.20	.08	.02
□ 7 Wade Boggs	.75	.30	.07
□ 8 Bret Saberhagen	.20	.08	.02
□ 9 Terry Kennedy	.10	.04	.01
□ 10 John McNamara MG	.10	.04	.01
□ 11 Jack Clark	.20	.08	.02
□ 12 Darryl Strawberry	.40	.16	.04
□ 13 Ryne Sandberg	.20	.08	.02
□ 14 Andre Dawson	.20	.08	.02
□ 15 Ozzie Smith	.20	.08	.02
□ 16 Eric Davis	.75	.30	.07
□ 17 Mike Schmidt	.45	.18	.04
□ 18 Mike Scott	.20	.08	.02
□ 19 Gary Carter	.25	.10	.02
□ 20 Davey Johnson MG	.10	.04	.01

1988 Donruss Rookies

The 1988 Donruss "The Rookies" set features 56 cards plus a 15-piece puzzle of Stan Musial. Cards are in full color and are standard size, 2 1/2" by 3 1/2". The set was distributed in a small green and black box with gold lettering. Card fronts are similar in design to the 1988 Donruss regular issue except for the presence of "The Rookies" logo in the lower right corner and a green and black border instead of a blue and black border on the fronts.

	MINT	EXC	G-VG
COMPLETE SET (56)	11.00	4.50	1.10
COMMON PLAYER (1-56)	.05	.02	.00
□ 1 Mark Grace	1.75	.75	.15
□ 2 Mike Campbell	.10	.04	.01
□ 3 Todd Frohwirth	.10	.04	.01
□ 4 Dave Stapleton	.05	.02	.00
□ 5 Shawn Abner	.15	.06	.01

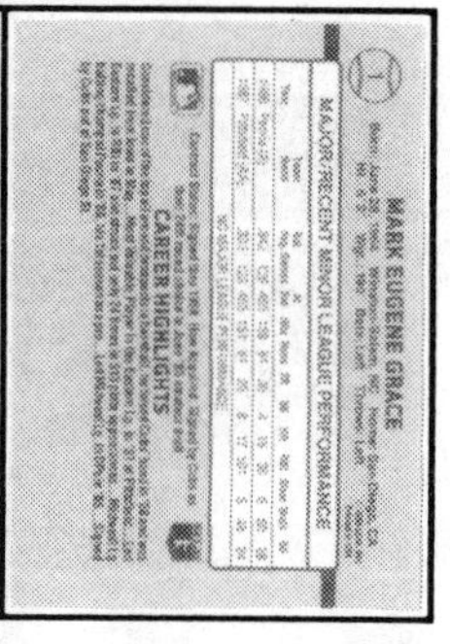

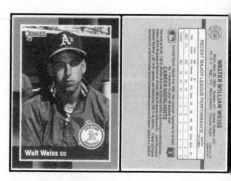

□ 6	Jose Cecena	.12	.05	.01
□ 7	Dave Gallagher	.25	.10	.02
□ 8	Mark Parent	.12	.05	.01
□ 9	Cecil Espy	.15	.06	.01
□ 10	Pete Smith	.08	.03	.01
□ 11	Jay Buhner	.20	.08	.02
□ 12	Pat Borders	.25	.10	.02
□ 13	Doug Jennings	.25	.10	.02
□ 14	Brady Anderson	.35	.14	.03
□ 15	Pete Stanicek	.15	.06	.01
□ 16	Roberto Kelly	.20	.08	.02
□ 17	Jeff Treadway	.15	.06	.01
□ 18	Walt Weiss	1.00	.40	.10
□ 19	Paul Gibson	.15	.06	.01
□ 20	Tim Crews	.05	.02	.00
□ 21	Melido Perez	.15	.06	.01
□ 22	Steve Peters	.15	.06	.01
□ 23	Craig Worthington	.25	.10	.02
□ 24	John Trautwein	.15	.06	.01
□ 25	DeWayne Vaughn	.10	.04	.01
□ 26	David Wells	.08	.03	.01
□ 27	Al Leiter	.25	.10	.02
□ 28	Tim Belcher	.20	.08	.02
□ 29	Johnny Paredes	.15	.06	.01
□ 30	Chris Sabo	1.75	.70	.17
□ 31	Damon Berryhill	.25	.10	.02
□ 32	Randy Milligan	.20	.08	.02
□ 33	Gary Thurman	.15	.06	.01
□ 34	Kevin Elster	.20	.08	.02
□ 35	Roberto Alomar	.30	.12	.03
□ 36	Edgar Martinez UER (photo actually Edwin Nunez)	.30	.12	.03
□ 37	Todd Stottlemyre	.15	.06	.01
□ 38	Joey Meyer	.20	.08	.02
□ 39	Carl Nichols	.05	.02	.00
□ 40	Jack McDowell	.15	.06	.01
□ 41	Jose Bautista	.15	.06	.01
□ 42	Sil Campusano	.25	.10	.02
□ 43	John Dopson	.20	.08	.02
□ 44	Jody Reed	.25	.10	.02
□ 45	Darrin Jackson	.25	.10	.02
□ 46	Mike Capel	.15	.06	.01
□ 47	Ron Gant	.30	.12	.03
□ 48	John Davis	.05	.02	.00
□ 49	Kevin Coffman	.12	.05	.01
□ 50	Cris Carpenter	.30	.12	.03
□ 51	Mackey Sasser	.20	.08	.02
□ 52	Luis Alicea	.15	.06	.01
□ 53	Bryan Harvey	.35	.14	.03
□ 54	Steve Ellsworth	.15	.06	.01
□ 55	Mike Macfarlane	.25	.10	.02
□ 56	Checklist Card	.05	.01	.00

1988 Donruss Athletics Book

The 1988 Donruss Athletics Team Book set features 27 cards (three pages with nine cards on each page) plus a large full-page puzzle of Stan Musial. Cards are in full color and are standard size, 2 1/2" by 3 1/2". The set was distributed as a four-page book; although the puzzle page was perforated, the card pages were not. The cover of the "Team Collection" book is primarily bright red. Card fronts are very similar in design to the 1988 Donruss regular issue. The card numbers on the backs are the same for those players that are the same as in the regular Donruss set; the new players pictured are numbered on the back as "NEW." The book is usually sold intact.

		MINT	EXC	G-VG
COMPLETE SET (27)		6.00	2.40	.60
COMMON PLAYER		.10	.04	.01
□ 97	Curt Young	.10	.04	.01
□ 133	Gene Nelson	.10	.04	.01
□ 158	Terry Steinbach	.20	.08	.02
□ 178	Carney Lansford	.20	.08	.02
□ 221	Tony Phillips	.10	.04	.01
□ 256	Mark McGwire	1.00	.40	.10
□ 302	Jose Canseco	2.00	.80	.20
□ 349	Dennis Eckersley	.35	.14	.03
□ 379	Mike Gallego	.10	.04	.01
□ 425	Luis Polonia	.10	.04	.01
□ 467	Steve Ontiveros	.10	.04	.01
□ 472	Dave Stewart	.25	.10	.02
□ 503	Eric Plunk	.10	.04	.01
□ 528	Greg Cadaret	.10	.04	.01
□ 590	Rick Honeycutt	.10	.04	.01
□ 595	Storm Davis	.20	.08	.02
□ NEW	Don Baylor	.15	.06	.01
□ NEW	Ron Hassey	.10	.04	.01
□ NEW	Dave Henderson	.15	.06	.01
□ NEW	Glenn Hubbard	.10	.04	.01
□ NEW	Stan Javier	.10	.04	.01
□ NEW	Dave Jennings	.25	.10	.02
□ NEW	Edward Jurak	.10	.04	.01
□ NEW	Dave Parker	.20	.08	.02
□ NEW	Walt Weiss	1.00	.40	.10
□ NEW	Bob Welch	.15	.06	.01
□ NEW	Matt Young	.10	.04	.01

1988 Donruss Cubs Team Book

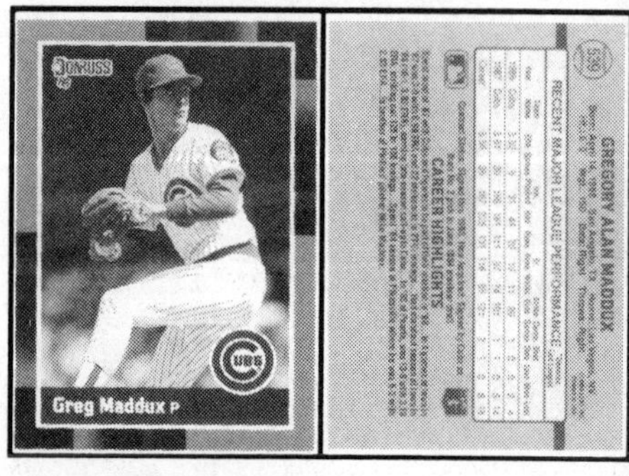

The 1988 Donruss Cubs Team Book set features 27 cards (three pages with nine cards on each page) plus a large full-page puzzle of Stan Musial. Cards are in full color and are standard size, 2 1/2" by 3 1/2". The set was distributed as a four-page book; although the puzzle page was perforated, the card pages were not. The cover of the "Team Collection" book is primarily bright red. Card fronts are very similar in design to the 1988 Donruss regular issue. The card numbers on the backs are the same for those players that are the same as in the regular Donruss set; the new players pictured are numbered on the back as "NEW." The book is usually sold intact.

	MINT	EXC	G-VG
COMPLETE SET (27)	5.00	2.00	.50
COMMON PLAYER	.10	.04	.01
□ 40 Mark Grace	1.25	.50	.12
□ 68 Rick Sutcliffe	.20	.08	.02
□ 119 Jody Davis	.15	.06	.01
□ 146 Shawon Dunston	.20	.08	.02
□ 169 Jamie Moyer	.15	.06	.01
□ 191 Leon Durham	.15	.06	.01
□ 242 Ryne Sandberg	.30	.12	.03
□ 269 Andre Dawson	.30	.12	.03
□ 315 Paul Noce	.15	.06	.01
□ 324 Rafael Palmeiro	.50	.20	.05
□ 438 Dave Martinez	.15	.06	.01
□ 447 Jerry Mumphrey	.10	.04	.01
□ 488 Jim Sundberg	.10	.04	.01
□ 516 Manny Trillo	.10	.04	.01
□ 539 Greg Maddux	.25	.10	.02
□ 561 Les Lancaster	.10	.04	.01
□ 570 Frank DiPino	.10	.04	.01
□ 639 Damon Berryhill	.30	.12	.03
□ 646 Scott Sanderson	.10	.04	.01
□ NEW Mike Bielecki	.10	.04	.01
□ NEW Rich Gossage	.15	.06	.01
□ NEW Drew Hall	.15	.06	.01
□ NEW Darrin Jackson	.25	.10	.02
□ NEW Vance Law	.15	.06	.01
□ NEW Al Nipper	.10	.04	.01
□ NEW Angel Salazar	.10	.04	.01
□ NEW Calvin Schiraldi	.15	.06	.01

1988 Donruss Mets Team Book

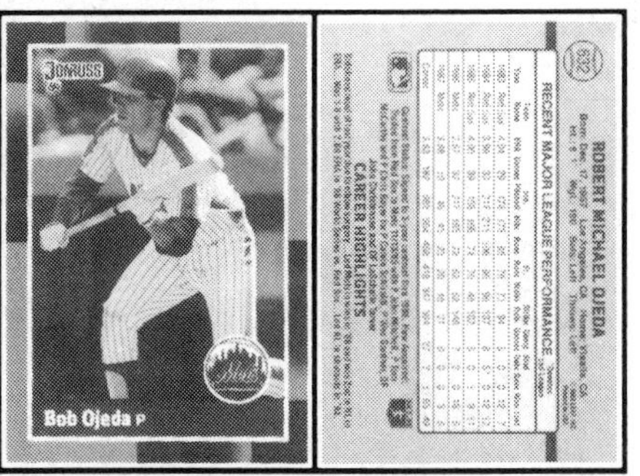

The 1988 Donruss Mets Team Book set features 27 cards (three pages with nine cards on each page) plus a large full-page puzzle of Stan Musial. Cards are in full color and are standard size, 2 1/2" by 3 1/2". The set was distributed as a four-page book; although the puzzle page was perforated, the card pages were not. The cover of the "Team Collection" book is primarily bright red. Card fronts are very similar in design to the 1988 Donruss regular issue. The card numbers on the backs are the same for those players that are the same as in the regular Donruss set; the new players pictured are numbered on the back as "NEW." The book is usually sold intact.

	MINT	EXC	G-VG
COMPLETE SET (27)	6.00	2.40	.60
COMMON PLAYER	.10	.04	.01
□ 37 Kevin Elster	.20	.08	.02
□ 69 Dwight Gooden	.50	.20	.05
□ 76 Ron Darling	.25	.10	.02
□ 118 Sid Fernandez	.20	.08	.02
□ 199 Gary Carter	.25	.10	.02
□ 241 Wally Backman	.10	.04	.01
□ 316 Keith Hernandez	.25	.10	.02
□ 323 Dave Magadan	.20	.08	.02
□ 364 Lee Dykstra	.15	.06	.01
□ 439 Darryl Strawberry	.75	.30	.07
□ 446 Rick Aguilera	.15	.06	.01
□ 562 Keith Miller	.15	.06	.01
□ 569 Howard Johnson	.20	.08	.02
□ 603 Terry Leach	.15	.06	.01
□ 614 Lee Mazzilli	.10	.04	.01
□ 617 Kevin McReynolds	.25	.10	.02
□ 619 Barry Lyons	.10	.04	.01
□ 620 Randy Myers	.20	.08	.02
□ 632 Bob Ojeda	.15	.06	.01
□ 648 Tim Teufel	.10	.04	.01
□ 651 Roger McDowell	.15	.06	.01
□ 652 Mookie Wilson	.15	.06	.01
□ 653 David Cone	.40	.16	.04
□ 657 Greg Jefferies	1.50	.60	.15
□ NEW Jeff Innis	.20	.08	.02
□ NEW Mackey Sasser	.15	.06	.01
□ NEW Gene Walter	.10	.04	.01

1988 Donruss Red Sox Team Book

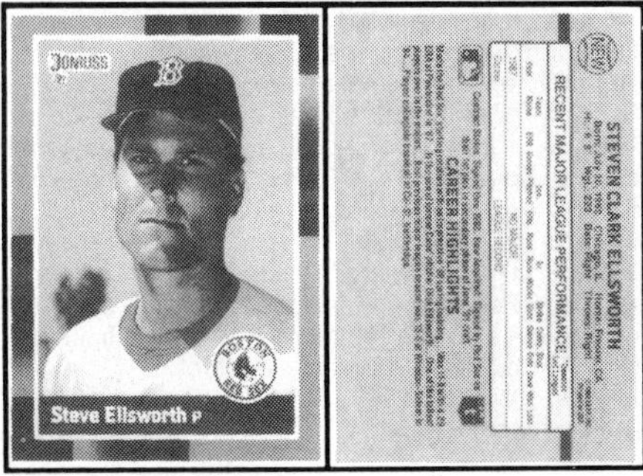

The 1988 Donruss Red Sox Team Book set features 27 cards (three pages with nine cards on each page) plus a large full-page puzzle of Stan Musial. Cards are in full color and are standard size, 2 1/2" by 3 1/2". The set was distributed as a four-page book; although the puzzle page was perforated, the card pages were not. The cover of the "Team Collection" book is primarily bright red. Card fronts are very similar in design to the 1988 Donruss regular issue. The card numbers on the backs are the same for those players that are the same as in the regular Donruss set; the new players pictured are numbered on the back as "NEW." The book is usually sold intact.

	MINT	EXC	G-VG
COMPLETE SET (27)	5.00	2.00	.50
COMMON PLAYER	.10	.04	.01
□ 41 Jody Reed	.30	.12	.03
□ 51 Roger Clemens	.75	.30	.07
□ 92 Bob Stanley	.10	.04	.01
□ 129 Rich Gedman	.15	.06	.01
□ 153 Wade Boggs	1.25	.50	.12
□ 174 Ellis Burks	.75	.30	.07
□ 216 Dwight Evans	.20	.08	.02
□ 252 Bruce Hurst	.25	.10	.02
□ 276 Marty Barrett	.15	.06	.01
□ 297 Todd Benzinger	.25	.10	.02
□ 339 Mike Greenwell	1.25	.50	.12
□ 399 Jim Rice	.25	.10	.02
□ 421 John Marzano	.15	.06	.01
□ 462 Oil Can Boyd	.15	.06	.01
□ 498 Sam Horn	.25	.10	.02
□ 544 Spike Owen	.10	.04	.01
□ 585 Jeff Sellers	.10	.04	.01
□ 623 Ed Romero	.10	.04	.01
□ 634 Wes Gardner	.15	.06	.01
□ NEW Brady Anderson	.25	.10	.02
□ NEW Rick Cerone	.10	.04	.01
□ NEW Steve Ellsworth	.15	.06	.01
□ NEW Dennis Lamp	.10	.04	.01
□ NEW Kevin Romine	.10	.04	.01
□ NEW Lee Smith	.15	.06	.01
□ NEW Mike Smithson	.10	.04	.01
□ NEW John Trautwein	.15	.06	.01

1988 Donruss Yankees Team Book

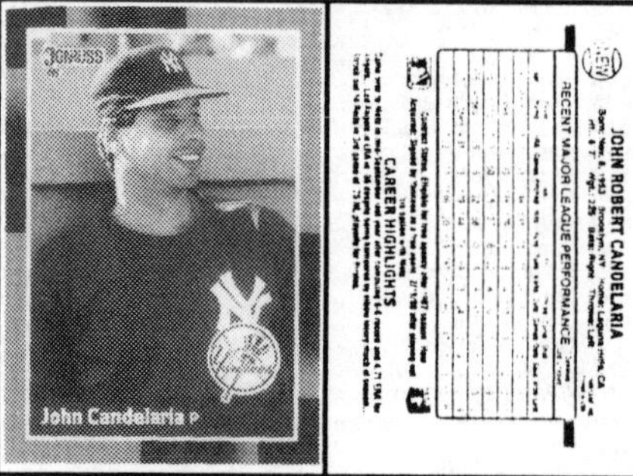

The 1988 Donruss Yankees Team Book set features 27 cards (three pages with nine cards on each page) plus a large full-page puzzle of Stan Musial. Cards are in full color and are standard size, 2 1/2" by 3 1/2". The set was distributed as a four-page book; although the puzzle page was perforated, the card pages were not. The cover of the "Team Collection" book is primarily bright red. Card fronts are very similar in design to the 1988 Donruss regular issue. The card numbers on the backs are the same for those players that are the same as in the regular Donruss set; the new players pictured are numbered on the back as "NEW." The book is usually sold intact.

	MINT	EXC	G-VG
COMPLETE SET (27)	5.00	2.00	.50
COMMON PLAYER	.10	.04	.01
☐ 43 Al Leiter	.35	.14	.03
☐ 93 Dave Righetti	.20	.08	.02
☐ 105 Mike Pagliarulo	.15	.06	.01
☐ 128 Rick Rhoden	.15	.06	.01
☐ 175 Ron Guidry	.20	.08	.02
☐ 217 Don Mattingly	1.50	.60	.15
☐ 228 Willie Randolph	.20	.08	.02
☐ 251 Gary Ward	.10	.04	.01
☐ 277 Rickey Henderson	.60	.24	.06
☐ 278 Dave Winfield	.40	.16	.04
☐ 340 Claudell Washington	.15	.06	.01
☐ 374 Charles Hudson	.15	.06	.01
☐ 401 Tommy John	.20	.08	.02
☐ 474 Joel Skinner	.10	.04	.01
☐ 497 Tim Stoddard	.10	.04	.01
☐ 545 Jay Buhner	.25	.10	.02
☐ 616 Bobby Meacham	.10	.04	.01
☐ 635 Roberto Kelly	.25	.10	.02
☐ NEW John Candelaria	.15	.06	.01
☐ NEW Jack Clark	.25	.10	.02
☐ NEW Jose Cruz	.15	.06	.01
☐ NEW Richard Dotson	.15	.06	.01
☐ NEW Cecilo Guante	.10	.04	.01
☐ NEW Lee Guetterman	.15	.06	.01
☐ NEW Rafael Santana	.10	.04	.01
☐ NEW Steve Shields	.10	.04	.01
☐ NEW Don Slaught	.10	.04	.01

1988 Donruss Baseball's Best

This innovative set of 336 cards was released by Donruss very late in the 1988 season to be sold in large national retail chains as a complete packaged set. Cards are the standard size, 2 1/2" by 3 1/2" and are packaged as a complete set in a specially designed box. Cards are very similar in design to the 1988 regular Donruss issue except that these cards have a orange and black borders instead of a blue and black borders. Six (2 1/2" by 3 1/2") 15-piece puzzles of Stan Musial are also included with every complete set.

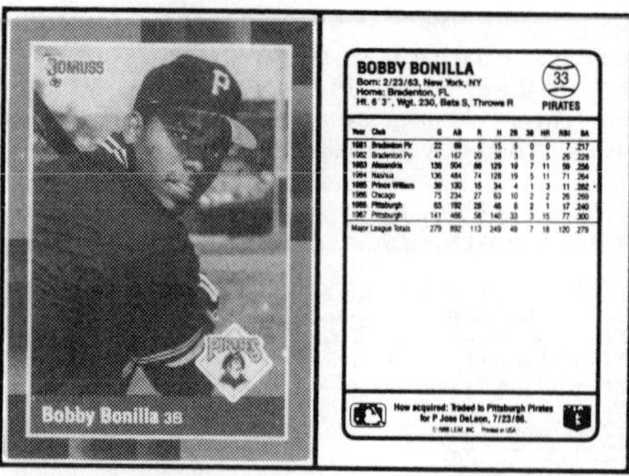

	MINT	EXC	G-VG
COMPLETE SET (336)	24.00	10.00	2.40
COMMON PLAYER (1-336)	.05	.02	.00
☐ 1 Don Mattingly	1.00	.40	.10
☐ 2 Ron Gant	.35	.14	.03
☐ 3 Bob Boone	.10	.04	.01
☐ 4 Mark Grace	.75	.30	.07
☐ 5 Andy Allanson	.05	.02	.00
☐ 6 Kal Daniels	.20	.08	.02
☐ 7 Floyd Bannister	.05	.02	.00
☐ 8 Alan Ashby	.05	.02	.00
☐ 9 Marty Barrett	.10	.04	.01
☐ 10 Tim Belcher	.15	.06	.01
☐ 11 Harold Baines	.10	.04	.01
☐ 12 Hubie Brooks	.05	.02	.00
☐ 13 Doyle Alexander	.05	.02	.00
☐ 14 Gary Carter	.20	.08	.02
☐ 15 Glenn Braggs	.10	.04	.01
☐ 16 Steve Bedrosian	.10	.04	.01
☐ 17 Barry Bonds	.20	.08	.02
☐ 18 Bert Blyleven	.10	.04	.01
☐ 19 Tom Brunansky	.10	.04	.01
☐ 20 John Candelaria	.05	.02	.00
☐ 21 Shawn Abner	.15	.06	.01
☐ 22 Jose Canseco	1.50	.60	.15
☐ 23 Brett Butler	.10	.04	.01
☐ 24 Scott Bradley	.05	.02	.00
☐ 25 Ivan Calderon	.10	.04	.01
☐ 26 Rich Gossage	.10	.04	.01
☐ 27 Brian Downing	.05	.02	.00
☐ 28 Jim Rice	.15	.06	.01
☐ 29 Dion James	.05	.02	.00
☐ 30 Terry Kennedy	.05	.02	.00
☐ 31 George Bell	.15	.06	.01
☐ 32 Scott Fletcher	.05	.02	.00
☐ 33 Bobby Bonilla	.15	.06	.01
☐ 34 Tim Burke	.05	.02	.00
☐ 35 Darrell Evans	.10	.04	.01
☐ 36 Mike Davis	.05	.02	.00
☐ 37 Shawon Dunston	.10	.04	.01
☐ 38 Kevin Bass	.10	.04	.01
☐ 39 George Brett	.25	.10	.02
☐ 40 David Cone	.30	.12	.03
☐ 41 Ron Darling	.15	.06	.01
☐ 42 Roberto Alomar	.25	.10	.02
☐ 43 Dennis Eckersley	.10	.04	.01
☐ 44 Vince Coleman	.20	.08	.02
☐ 45 Sid Bream	.05	.02	.00
☐ 46 Gary Gaetti	.15	.06	.01
☐ 47 Phil Bradley	.10	.04	.01
☐ 48 Jim Clancy	.05	.02	.00
☐ 49 Jack Clark	.15	.06	.01
☐ 50 Mike Krukow	.05	.02	.00
☐ 51 Henry Cotto	.05	.02	.00
☐ 52 Rich Dotson	.05	.02	.00
☐ 53 Jim Gantner	.05	.02	.00
☐ 54 John Franco	.05	.02	.00
☐ 55 Pete Incaviglia	.15	.06	.01
☐ 56 Joe Carter	.15	.06	.01
☐ 57 Roger Clemens	.50	.20	.05
☐ 58 Gerald Perry	.05	.02	.00
☐ 59 Jack Howell	.05	.02	.00
☐ 60 Vance Law	.05	.02	.00
☐ 61 Jay Bell	.05	.02	.00
☐ 62 Eric Davis	.50	.20	.05
☐ 63 Gene Garber	.05	.02	.00
☐ 64 Glenn Davis	.15	.06	.01

☐ 65	Wade Boggs	.75	.30	.07
☐ 66	Kirk Gibson	.25	.10	.02
☐ 67	Carlton Fisk	.10	.04	.01
☐ 68	Casey Candaele	.05	.02	.00
☐ 69	Mike Heath	.05	.02	.00
☐ 70	Kevin Elster	.10	.04	.01
☐ 71	Greg Brock	.05	.02	.00
☐ 72	Don Carman	.05	.02	.00
☐ 73	Doug Drabek	.05	.02	.00
☐ 74	Greg Gagne	.05	.02	.00
☐ 75	Danny Cox	.10	.04	.01
☐ 76	Rickey Henderson	.35	.14	.03
☐ 77	Chris Brown	.05	.02	.00
☐ 78	Terry Steinbach	.10	.04	.01
☐ 79	Will Clark	.50	.20	.05
☐ 80	Mickey Brantley	.10	.04	.01
☐ 81	Ozzie Guillen	.10	.04	.01
☐ 82	Greg Maddux	.15	.06	.01
☐ 83	Kirk McCaskill	.05	.02	.00
☐ 84	Dwight Evans	.15	.06	.01
☐ 85	Ozzie Virgil	.05	.02	.00
☐ 86	Mike Morgan	.05	.02	.00
☐ 87	Tony Fernandez	.10	.04	.01
☐ 88	Jose Guzman	.05	.02	.00
☐ 89	Mike Dunne	.10	.04	.01
☐ 90	Andres Galarraga	.25	.10	.02
☐ 91	Mike Henneman	.10	.04	.01
☐ 92	Alfredo Griffin	.05	.02	.00
☐ 93	Rafael Palmeiro	.25	.10	.02
☐ 94	Jim Deshaies	.05	.02	.00
☐ 95	Mark Gubicza	.10	.04	.01
☐ 96	Dwight Gooden	.50	.20	.05
☐ 97	Howard Johnson	.15	.06	.01
☐ 98	Mark Davis	.05	.02	.00
☐ 99	Dave Stewart	.10	.04	.01
☐ 100	Joe Magrane	.10	.04	.01
☐ 101	Brian Fisher	.05	.02	.00
☐ 102	Kent Hrbek	.05	.02	.00
☐ 103	Kevin Gross	.05	.02	.00
☐ 104	Tom Henke	.05	.02	.00
☐ 105	Mike Pagliarulo	.10	.04	.01
☐ 106	Kelly Downs	.05	.02	.00
☐ 107	Alvin Davis	.10	.04	.01
☐ 108	Willie Randolph	.10	.04	.01
☐ 109	Rob Deer	.10	.04	.01
☐ 110	Bo Diaz	.05	.02	.00
☐ 111	Paul Kilgus	.05	.02	.00
☐ 112	Tom Candiotti	.05	.02	.00
☐ 113	Dale Murphy	.35	.14	.03
☐ 114	Rick Mahler	.05	.02	.00
☐ 115	Wally Joyner	.50	.20	.05
☐ 116	Ryne Sandberg	.25	.10	.02
☐ 117	John Farrell	.10	.04	.01
☐ 118	Nick Esasky	.05	.02	.00
☐ 119	Bo Jackson	.35	.14	.03
☐ 120	Bill Doran	.10	.04	.01
☐ 121	Ellis Burks	.50	.20	.05
☐ 122	Pedro Guerrero	.20	.08	.02
☐ 123	Dave LaPoint	.10	.04	.01
☐ 124	Neal Heaton	.05	.02	.00
☐ 125	Willie Hernandez	.10	.04	.01
☐ 126	Roger McDowell	.10	.04	.01
☐ 127	Ted Higuera	.10	.04	.01
☐ 128	Von Hayes	.10	.04	.01
☐ 129	Mike LaValliere	.05	.02	.00
☐ 130	Dan Gladden	.05	.02	.00
☐ 131	Willie McGee	.15	.06	.01
☐ 132	Al Leiter	.20	.08	.02
☐ 133	Mark Grant	.05	.02	.00
☐ 134	Bob Welch	.05	.02	.00
☐ 135	Dave Dravecky	.05	.02	.00
☐ 136	Mark Langston	.10	.04	.01
☐ 137	Dan Pasqua	.10	.04	.01
☐ 138	Rick Sutcliffe	.10	.04	.01
☐ 139	Dan Petry	.05	.02	.00
☐ 140	Rich Gedman	.10	.04	.01
☐ 141	Ken Griffey Sr.	.10	.04	.01
☐ 142	Eddie Murray	.25	.10	.02
☐ 143	Jimmy Key	.10	.04	.01
☐ 144	Dale Mohorcic	.05	.02	.00
☐ 145	Jose Lind	.10	.04	.01
☐ 146	Dennis Martinez	.05	.02	.00
☐ 147	Chet Lemon	.05	.02	.00
☐ 148	Orel Hershiser	.35	.14	.03
☐ 149	Dave Martinez	.05	.02	.00
☐ 150	Billy Hatcher	.10	.04	.01
☐ 151	Charlie Leibrandt	.05	.02	.00
☐ 152	Keith Hernandez	.20	.08	.02
☐ 153	Kevin McReynolds	.25	.10	.02
☐ 154	Tony Gwynn	.35	.14	.03
☐ 155	Stan Javier	.05	.02	.00
☐ 156	Tony Pena	.05	.02	.00
☐ 157	Andy Van Slyke	.15	.06	.01
☐ 158	Gene Larkin	.10	.04	.01
☐ 159	Chris James	.10	.04	.01
☐ 160	Fred McGriff	.35	.14	.03
☐ 161	Rick Rhoden	.10	.04	.01
☐ 162	Scott Garrelts	.05	.02	.00
☐ 163	Mike Campbell	.10	.04	.01
☐ 164	Dave Righetti	.10	.04	.01
☐ 165	Paul Molitor	.15	.06	.01
☐ 166	Danny Jackson	.15	.06	.01
☐ 167	Pete O'Brien	.10	.04	.01
☐ 168	Julio Franco	.10	.04	.01
☐ 169	Mark McGwire	.75	.30	.07
☐ 170	Zane Smith	.10	.04	.01
☐ 171	Johnny Ray	.10	.04	.01
☐ 172	Lester Lancaster	.05	.02	.00
☐ 173	Mel Hall	.10	.04	.01
☐ 174	Tracy Jones	.10	.04	.01
☐ 175	Kevin Seitzer	.45	.18	.04
☐ 176	Bob Knepper	.05	.02	.00
☐ 177	Mike Greenwell	1.25	.50	.12
☐ 178	Mike Marshall	.10	.04	.01
☐ 179	Melido Perez	.15	.06	.01
☐ 180	Tim Raines	.25	.10	.02
☐ 181	Jack Morris	.10	.04	.01
☐ 182	Darryl Strawberry	.50	.20	.05
☐ 183	Robin Yount	.25	.10	.02
☐ 184	Lance Parrish	.10	.04	.01
☐ 185	Darnell Coles	.05	.02	.00
☐ 186	Kirby Puckett	.50	.20	.05
☐ 187	Terry Pendleton	.05	.02	.00
☐ 188	Don Slaught	.05	.02	.00
☐ 189	Jimmy Jones	.10	.04	.01
☐ 190	Dave Parker	.15	.06	.01
☐ 191	Mike Aldrete	.05	.02	.00
☐ 192	Mike Moore	.05	.02	.00
☐ 193	Greg Walker	.10	.04	.01
☐ 194	Calvin Schiraldi	.05	.02	.00
☐ 195	Dick Schofield	.05	.02	.00
☐ 196	Jody Reed	.15	.06	.01
☐ 197	Pete Smith	.10	.04	.01
☐ 198	Cal Ripken	.25	.10	.02
☐ 199	Lloyd Moseby	.10	.04	.01
☐ 200	Ruben Sierra	.15	.06	.01
☐ 201	R.J. Reynolds	.05	.02	.00
☐ 202	Bryn Smith	.05	.02	.00
☐ 203	Gary Pettis	.05	.02	.00
☐ 204	Steve Sax	.15	.06	.01
☐ 205	Frank DiPino	.05	.02	.00
☐ 206	Mike Scott	.15	.06	.01
☐ 207	Kurt Stillwell	.10	.04	.01
☐ 208	Mookie Wilson	.05	.02	.00
☐ 209	Lee Mazzilli	.05	.02	.00
☐ 210	Lance McCullers	.10	.04	.01
☐ 211	Rick Honeycutt	.05	.02	.00
☐ 212	John Tudor	.15	.06	.01
☐ 213	Jim Gott	.05	.02	.00
☐ 214	Frank Viola	.20	.08	.02
☐ 215	Juan Samuel	.10	.04	.01
☐ 216	Jesse Barfield	.15	.06	.01
☐ 217	Claudell Washington	.05	.02	.00
☐ 218	Rick Reuschel	.10	.04	.01
☐ 219	Jim Presley	.10	.04	.01
☐ 220	Tommy John	.15	.06	.01
☐ 221	Dan Plesac	.05	.02	.00
☐ 222	Barry Larkin	.15	.06	.01
☐ 223	Mike Stanley	.05	.02	.00
☐ 224	Cory Snyder	.20	.08	.02
☐ 225	Andre Dawson	.25	.10	.02
☐ 226	Ken Oberkfell	.05	.02	.00
☐ 227	Devon White	.15	.06	.01
☐ 228	Jamie Moyer	.10	.04	.01
☐ 229	Brook Jacoby	.10	.04	.01
☐ 230	Rob Murphy	.10	.04	.01
☐ 231	Bret Saberhagen	.15	.06	.01
☐ 232	Nolan Ryan	.30	.12	.03
☐ 233	Bruce Hurst	.15	.06	.01
☐ 234	Jesse Orosco	.05	.02	.00
☐ 235	Bobby Thigpen	.10	.04	.01
☐ 236	Pascual Perez	.05	.02	.00
☐ 237	Matt Nokes	.20	.08	.02
☐ 238	Bob Ojeda	.10	.04	.01
☐ 239	Joey Meyer	.10	.04	.01
☐ 240	Shane Rawley	.05	.02	.00
☐ 241	Jeff Robinson	.10	.04	.01
☐ 242	Jeff Reardon	.10	.04	.01
☐ 243	Ozzie Smith	.15	.06	.01
☐ 244	Dave Winfield	.25	.10	.02
☐ 245	John Kruk	.10	.04	.01
☐ 246	Carney Lansford	.10	.04	.01
☐ 247	Candy Maldonado	.10	.04	.01
☐ 248	Ken Phelps	.10	.04	.01
☐ 249	Ken Williams	.10	.04	.01
☐ 250	Al Nipper	.05	.02	.00
☐ 251	Mark McLemore	.05	.02	.00
☐ 252	Lee Smith	.05	.02	.00
☐ 253	Albert Hall	.05	.02	.00
☐ 254	Billy Ripken	.10	.04	.01

☐ 255	Kelly Gruber	.05	.02	.00
☐ 256	Charlie Hough	.05	.02	.00
☐ 257	John Smiley	.10	.04	.01
☐ 258	Tim Wallach	.10	.04	.01
☐ 259	Frank Tanana	.10	.04	.01
☐ 260	Mike Scioscia	.05	.02	.00
☐ 261	Damon Berryhill	.15	.06	.01
☐ 262	Dave Smith	.05	.02	.00
☐ 263	Willie Wilson	.10	.04	.01
☐ 264	Len Dykstra	.10	.04	.01
☐ 265	Randy Myers	.10	.04	.01
☐ 266	Keith Moreland	.05	.02	.00
☐ 267	Eric Plunk	.05	.02	.00
☐ 268	Todd Worrell	.10	.04	.01
☐ 269	Bob Walk	.05	.02	.00
☐ 270	Keith Atherton	.05	.02	.00
☐ 271	Mike Schmidt	.35	.14	.03
☐ 272	Mike Flanagan	.05	.02	.00
☐ 273	Rafael Santana	.05	.02	.00
☐ 274	Rob Thompson	.10	.04	.01
☐ 275	Rey Quinones	.05	.02	.00
☐ 276	Cecilio Guante	.05	.02	.00
☐ 277	B.J. Surhoff	.10	.04	.01
☐ 278	Chris Sabo	.75	.30	.07
☐ 279	Mitch Williams	.05	.02	.00
☐ 280	Greg Swindell	.10	.04	.01
☐ 281	Alan Trammell	.15	.06	.01
☐ 282	Storm Davis	.10	.04	.01
☐ 283	Chuck Finley	.05	.02	.00
☐ 284	Dave Stieb	.10	.04	.01
☐ 285	Scott Bailes	.05	.02	.00
☐ 286	Larry Sheets	.10	.04	.01
☐ 287	Danny Tartabull	.20	.08	.02
☐ 288	Checklist	.05	.02	.00
☐ 289	Todd Benzinger	.15	.06	.01
☐ 290	John Shelby	.05	.02	.00
☐ 291	Steve Lyons	.05	.02	.00
☐ 292	Mitch Webster	.05	.02	.00
☐ 293	Walt Terrell	.05	.02	.00
☐ 294	Pete Stanicek	.05	.02	.00
☐ 295	Chris Bosio	.05	.02	.00
☐ 296	Milt Thompson	.05	.02	.00
☐ 297	Fred Lynn	.10	.04	.01
☐ 298	Juan Berenguer	.05	.02	.00
☐ 299	Ken Dayley	.05	.02	.00
☐ 300	Joel Skinner	.05	.02	.00
☐ 301	Benito Santiago	.35	.14	.03
☐ 302	Ron Hassey	.05	.02	.00
☐ 303	Jose Uribe	.05	.02	.00
☐ 304	Harold Reynolds	.10	.04	.01
☐ 305	Dale Sveum	.05	.02	.00
☐ 306	Glenn Wilson	.05	.02	.00
☐ 307	Mike Witt	.10	.04	.01
☐ 308	Ron Robinson	.05	.02	.00
☐ 309	Denny Walling	.05	.02	.00
☐ 310	Joe Orsulak	.05	.02	.00
☐ 311	David Wells	.05	.02	.00
☐ 312	Steve Buechele	.05	.02	.00
☐ 313	Jose Oquendo	.05	.02	.00
☐ 314	Floyd Youmans	.05	.02	.00
☐ 315	Lou Whitaker	.10	.04	.01
☐ 316	Fernando Valenzuela	.15	.06	.01
☐ 317	Mike Boddicker	.10	.04	.01
☐ 318	Gerald Young	.10	.04	.01
☐ 319	Frank White	.10	.04	.01
☐ 320	Bill Wegman	.05	.02	.00
☐ 321	Tom Niedenfuer	.05	.02	.00
☐ 322	Ed Whitson	.05	.02	.00
☐ 323	Curt Young	.05	.02	.00
☐ 324	Greg Mathews	.05	.02	.00
☐ 325	Doug Jones	.15	.06	.01
☐ 326	Tommy Herr	.10	.04	.01
☐ 327	Kent Tekulve	.05	.02	.00
☐ 328	Rance Mulliniks	.05	.02	.00
☐ 329	Checklist	.05	.02	.00
☐ 330	Craig Lefferts	.05	.02	.00
☐ 331	Franklin Stubbs	.05	.02	.00
☐ 332	Rick Cerone	.05	.02	.00
☐ 333	Dave Schmidt	.05	.02	.00
☐ 334	Larry Parrish	.05	.02	.00
☐ 335	Tom Browning	.10	.04	.01
☐ 336	Checklist	.05	.02	.00

1989 Donruss

This 660-card set was distributed along with a puzzle of Warren Spahn. The six regular checklist cards are numbered throughout the set as multiples of 100. Cards measure 2 1/2" by 3 1/2" and feature a

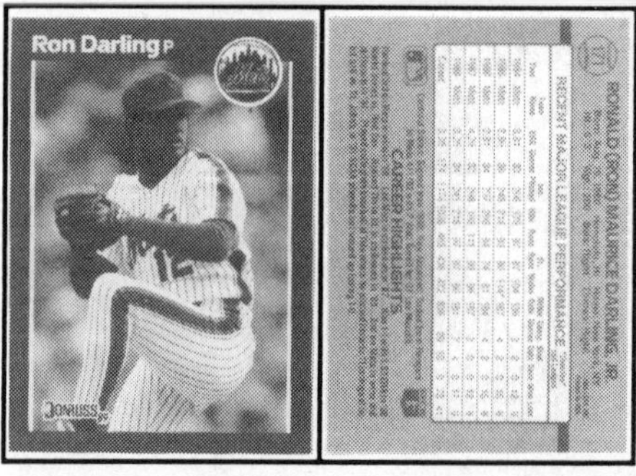

distinctive black side border with an alternating coating. The popular Diamond King subset returns for the eighth consecutive year. Rated Rookies are featured again as cards 28-47. The Donruss '89 logo appears in the lower left corner of every obverse.

		MINT	EXC	G-VG
	COMPLETE SET (660)	24.00	10.00	2.40
	COMMON PLAYER (1-660)	.03	.01	.00
☐ 1	Mike Greenwell DK	.50	.20	.04
☐ 2	Bobby Bonilla DK	.15	.06	.01
☐ 3	Pete Incaviglia DK	.12	.05	.01
☐ 4	Chris Sabo DK	.50	.20	.05
☐ 5	Robin Yount DK	.20	.08	.02
☐ 6	Tony Gwynn DK	.25	.10	.02
☐ 7	Carlton Fisk DK	.12	.05	.01
☐ 8	Cory Snyder DK	.15	.06	.01
☐ 9	David Cone DK	.25	.10	.02
☐ 10	Kevin Seitzer DK	.20	.08	.02
☐ 11	Rick Reuschel DK	.08	.03	.01
☐ 12	Johnny Ray DK	.08	.03	.01
☐ 13	Dave Schmidt DK	.08	.03	.01
☐ 14	Andres Galarraga DK	.15	.06	.01
☐ 15	Kirk Gibson DK	.15	.06	.01
☐ 16	Fred McGriff DK	.20	.08	.02
☐ 17	Mark Grace DK	.50	.20	.05
☐ 18	Jeff Robinson DT DK	.12	.05	.01
☐ 19	Vince Coleman DK	.15	.06	.01
☐ 20	Dave Henderson DK	.08	.03	.01
☐ 21	Harold Reynolds DK	.08	.03	.01
☐ 22	Gerald Perry DK	.10	.04	.01
☐ 23	Frank Viola DK	.15	.06	.01
☐ 24	Steve Bedrosian DK	.10	.04	.01
☐ 25	Glenn Davis DK	.15	.06	.01
☐ 26	Don Mattingly DK	.50	.20	.05
☐ 27	DK Checklist	.06	.01	.00
☐ 28	Sandy Alomar Jr. RR	.90	.36	.09
☐ 29	Steve Searcy RR	.25	.10	.02
☐ 30	Cameron Drew RR	.25	.10	.02
☐ 31	Gary Sheffield RR	1.50	.60	.15
☐ 32	Erik Hanson RR	.20	.08	.02
☐ 33	Ken Griffey Jr. RR	1.25	.50	.12
☐ 34	Greg Harris RR San Diego Padres	.20	.08	.02
☐ 35	Gregg Jefferies RR	2.00	.80	.20
☐ 36	Luis Medina RR	.45	.18	.04
☐ 37	Carlos Quintana RR	.35	.14	.03
☐ 38	Felix Jose RR	.25	.10	.02
☐ 39	Cris Carpenter RR	.20	.08	.02
☐ 40	Ron Jones RR	.30	.12	.03
☐ 41	Dave West RR	.50	.20	.05
☐ 42	Randy Johnson RR	.25	.10	.02
☐ 43	Mike Harkey RR	.50	.20	.05
☐ 44	Pete Harnisch RR	.20	.08	.02
☐ 45	Tom Gordon RR	.30	.12	.03
☐ 46	Gregg Olson RR	.30	.12	.03
☐ 47	Alex Sanchez RR	.30	.12	.03
☐ 48	Ruben Sierra	.12	.05	.01
☐ 49	Rafael Palmeiro	.12	.05	.01
☐ 50	Ron Gant	.15	.06	.01
☐ 51	Cal Ripken	.15	.06	.01
☐ 52	Wally Joyner	.20	.08	.02
☐ 53	Gary Carter	.15	.06	.01
☐ 54	Andy Van Slyke	.12	.05	.01
☐ 55	Robin Yount	.15	.06	.01
☐ 56	Pete Incaviglia	.12	.05	.01
☐ 57	Greg Brock	.03	.01	.00
☐ 58	Melido Perez	.06	.02	.00
☐ 59	Craig Lefferts	.03	.01	.00
☐ 60	Gary Pettis	.03	.01	.00
☐ 61	Danny Tartabull	.15	.06	.01
☐ 62	Guillermo Hernandez	.06	.02	.00

HOUSE OF CARDS

Bill Huggins

Nick Shoff Steve Terman

The Baseball Card Store with All-Star Values

• **Store # 301-933-0355**

2411 UNIVERSITY BLVD. WEST
P.O. BOX 1911
WHEATON, MARYLAND 20902

HOURS: Monday to Friday 11 A.M. to 7:30 P.M., Saturday 11 A.M. to 6 P.M., Sunday 11 A.M. to 4 P.M.

MARYLAND'S LARGEST SELECTION of Baseball and Football Sports Cards. We Specialize in Pre-WW II Cards and items. We Buy, Sell and Trade!!!

We're located just 20 minutes from downtown Washington, D.C.

We are interested in buying collections of all types of cards, and sports memorabilia. Try us!

TERRY SACK

Baseball Cards
Sports Memorabilia, Accessories
Retail/Wholesale

Black Tie Baseball Productions
Show Promotions, Party Planning

Specializing in unopened cases, boxes, and sets.

64 Dorcar Road • Newton Centre, MA 02159 • (617) 964-7477

TAS Enterprises

(Checks payable toTerry Sack)

***1989 Factory Sets**

1989 Topps Factory (in red, white & blue boxes)	22.95 p.pd
1989 Fleer Factory	24.95 p.pd
1989 Donruss Factory	24.95 p.pd
1989 Score Factory	19.95 p.pd
1989 Upper Deck Factory Set, Ltd.	59.95 p.pd

1989 four set special (Topps, Fleer, Donruss & Score) ....89.95 p.pd

***1989 Wax Boxes**

Topps	13.00 + 2.00 p/h
Fleer	25.00 + 2.00 p/h
Donruss	15.00 + 2.00 p/h
Score	13.00 + 2.00 p/h

1989 four Wax Box Special: 69.00 p.pd

•Call for Case Prices•

•Call for Other Year Sets & Wax Prices•

*Prices should be good until 7/1/89, subject to availability. We reserve the right to limit quantities. Prices subject to change without notice.

Mass. Residents add 5% Sales Tax or Resale Number.

Sports Connection

875 Eglington Ave. West #11
Toronto, Ontario M6C 3Z9
CANADA

Specializing in baseball, hockey and other sports memorabilia.
(*Beckett Monthly* available)

HAWAII

We have Honolulu's best selection of rookie cards, star cards, complete sets, 1950s and 1960s cards, unopened packs, and more.

Stop by for a visit when you vacation in paradise.
For hours call 808-395-0117 (days) or 808-395-5913 (evenings)

Aloha!

Jim Mayfield

Buying collections & individual cards . . . call.

□ 63	Ozzie Smith	.12	.05	.01
□ 64	Gary Gaetti	.10	.04	.01
□ 65	Mark Davis	.06	.02	.00
□ 66	Lee Smith	.06	.02	.00
□ 67	Dennis Eckersley	.10	.04	.01
□ 68	Wade Boggs	.50	.20	.05
□ 69	Mike Scott	.10	.04	.01
□ 70	Fred McGriff	.15	.06	.01
□ 71	Tom Browning	.08	.03	.01
□ 72	Claudell Washington	.06	.02	.00
□ 73	Mel Hall	.03	.01	.00
□ 74	Don Mattingly	1.00	.40	.10
□ 75	Steve Bedrosian	.08	.03	.01
□ 76	Juan Samuel	.08	.03	.01
□ 77	Mike Scioscia	.03	.01	.00
□ 78	Dave Righetti	.08	.03	.01
□ 79	Alfredo Griffin	.06	.02	.00
□ 80	Eric Davis	.30	.12	.03
□ 81	Juan Berenguer	.03	.01	.00
□ 82	Todd Worrell	.08	.03	.01
□ 83	Joe Carter	.10	.04	.01
□ 84	Steve Sax	.10	.04	.01
□ 85	Frank White	.06	.02	.00
□ 86	John Kruk	.06	.02	.00
□ 87	Rance Mulliniks	.03	.01	.00
□ 88	Alan Ashby	.03	.01	.00
□ 89	Charlie Leibrandt	.03	.01	.00
□ 90	Frank Tanana	.03	.01	.00
□ 91	Jose Canseco	1.00	.40	.10
□ 92	Barry Bonds	.10	.04	.01
□ 93	Harold Reynolds	.03	.01	.00
□ 94	Mark McLemore	.03	.01	.00
□ 95	Mark McGwire	.50	.20	.05
□ 96	Eddie Murray	.15	.06	.01
□ 97	Tim Raines	.15	.06	.01
□ 98	Rob Thompson	.03	.01	.00
□ 99	Kevin McReynolds	.15	.06	.01
□ 100	Checklist	.06	.01	.00
□ 101	Carlton Fisk	.08	.03	.01
□ 102	Dave Martinez	.03	.01	.00
□ 103	Glenn Braggs	.03	.01	.00
□ 104	Dale Murphy	.25	.10	.02
□ 105	Ryne Sandberg	.15	.06	.01
□ 106	Dennis Martinez	.03	.01	.00
□ 107	Pete O'Brien	.06	.02	.00
□ 108	Dick Schofield	.03	.01	.00
□ 109	Henry Cotto	.03	.01	.00
□ 110	Mike Marshall	.08	.03	.01
□ 111	Keith Moreland	.03	.01	.00
□ 112	Tom Brunansky	.08	.03	.01
□ 113	Kelly Gruber	.03	.01	.00
□ 114	Brook Jacoby	.08	.03	.01
□ 115	Keith Brown	.10	.04	.01
□ 116	Matt Nokes	.10	.04	.01
□ 117	Keith Hernandez	.12	.05	.01
□ 118	Bob Forsch	.03	.01	.00
□ 119	Bert Blyleven	.08	.03	.01
□ 120	Willie Wilson	.08	.03	.01
□ 121	Tommy Gregg	.03	.01	.00
□ 122	Jim Rice	.10	.04	.01
□ 123	Bob Knepper	.03	.01	.00
□ 124	Danny Jackson	.10	.04	.01
□ 125	Eric Plunk	.03	.01	.00
□ 126	Brian Fisher	.03	.01	.00
□ 127	Mike Pagliarulo	.08	.03	.01
□ 128	Tony Gwynn	.20	.08	.02
□ 129	Lance McCullers	.06	.02	.00
□ 130	Andres Galarraga	.12	.05	.01
□ 131	Jose Uribe	.03	.01	.00
□ 132	Kirk Gibson	.15	.06	.01
□ 133	David Palmer	.03	.01	.00
□ 134	R.J. Reynolds	.03	.01	.00
□ 135	Greg Walker	.06	.02	.00
□ 136	Kirk McCaskill	.03	.01	.00
□ 137	Shawon Dunston	.06	.02	.00
□ 138	Andy Allanson	.03	.01	.00
□ 139	Rob Murphy	.03	.01	.00
□ 140	Mike Aldrete	.03	.01	.00
□ 141	Terry Kennedy	.03	.01	.00
□ 142	Scott Fletcher	.03	.01	.00
□ 143	Steve Balboni	.03	.01	.00
□ 144	Bret Saberhagen	.10	.04	.01
□ 145	Ozzie Virgil	.03	.01	.00
□ 146	Dale Sveum	.03	.01	.00
□ 147	Darryl Strawberry	.35	.14	.03
□ 148	Harold Baines	.08	.03	.01
□ 149	George Bell	.12	.05	.01
□ 150	Dave Parker	.08	.03	.01
□ 151	Bobby Bonilla	.12	.05	.01
□ 152	Mookie Wilson	.03	.01	.00
□ 153	Ted Power	.03	.01	.00
□ 154	Nolan Ryan	.20	.08	.02
□ 155	Jeff Reardon	.06	.02	.00
□ 156	Tim Wallach	.06	.02	.00
□ 157	Jamie Moyer	.03	.01	.00
□ 158	Rich Gossage	.08	.03	.01
□ 159	Dave Winfield	.15	.06	.01
□ 160	Von Hayes	.08	.03	.01
□ 161	Willie McGee	.08	.03	.01
□ 162	Rich Gedman	.06	.02	.00
□ 163	Tony Pena	.06	.02	.00
□ 164	Mike Morgan	.03	.01	.00
□ 165	Charlie Hough	.03	.01	.00
□ 166	Mike Stanley	.03	.01	.00
□ 167	Andre Dawson	.12	.05	.01
□ 168	Joe Boever	.08	.03	.01
□ 169	Pete Stanicek	.03	.01	.00
□ 170	Bob Boone	.06	.02	.00
□ 171	Ron Darling	.08	.03	.01
□ 172	Bob Walk	.06	.02	.00
□ 173	Rob Deer	.06	.02	.00
□ 174	Steve Buechele	.03	.01	.00
□ 175	Ted Higuera	.08	.03	.01
□ 176	Ozzie Guillen	.06	.02	.00
□ 177	Candy Maldonado	.06	.02	.00
□ 178	Doyle Alexander	.06	.02	.00
□ 179	Mark Gubicza	.08	.03	.01
□ 180	Alan Trammell	.15	.06	.01
□ 181	Vince Coleman	.15	.06	.01
□ 182	Kirby Puckett	.30	.12	.03
□ 183	Chris Brown	.06	.02	.00
□ 184	Marty Barrett	.06	.02	.00
□ 185	Stan Javier	.03	.01	.00
□ 186	Mike Greenwell	.75	.30	.07
□ 187	Billy Hatcher	.06	.02	.00
□ 188	Jimmy Key	.06	.02	.00
□ 189	Nick Esasky	.03	.01	.00
□ 190	Don Slaught	.03	.01	.00
□ 191	Cory Snyder	.15	.06	.01
□ 192	John Candelaria	.06	.02	.00
□ 193	Mike Schmidt	.20	.08	.02
□ 194	Kevin Gross	.03	.01	.00
□ 195	John Tudor	.08	.03	.01
□ 196	Neil Allen	.03	.01	.00
□ 197	Orel Hershiser	.25	.10	.02
□ 198	Kal Daniels	.12	.05	.01
□ 199	Kent Hrbek	.12	.05	.01
□ 200	Checklist	.06	.01	.00
□ 201	Joe Magrane	.06	.02	.00
□ 202	Scott Bailes	.03	.01	.00
□ 203	Tim Belcher	.08	.03	.01
□ 204	George Brett	.20	.08	.02
□ 205	Benito Santiago	.20	.08	.02
□ 206	Tony Fernandez	.10	.04	.01
□ 207	Gerald Young	.06	.02	.00
□ 208	Bo Jackson	.20	.08	.02
□ 209	Chet Lemon	.06	.02	.00
□ 210	Storm Davis	.06	.02	.00
□ 211	Doug Drabek	.03	.01	.00
□ 212	Mickey Brantley	.06	.02	.00
□ 213	Devon White	.08	.03	.01
□ 214	Dave Stewart	.06	.02	.00
□ 215	Dave Schmidt	.03	.01	.00
□ 216	Bryn Smith	.03	.01	.00
□ 217	Brett Butler	.06	.02	.00
□ 218	Bob Ojeda	.06	.02	.00
□ 219	Steve Rosenberg	.10	.04	.01
□ 220	Hubie Brooks	.06	.02	.00
□ 221	B.J. Surhoff	.06	.02	.00
□ 222	Rick Mahler	.03	.01	.00
□ 223	Rick Sutcliffe	.08	.03	.01
□ 224	Neal Heaton	.03	.01	.00
□ 225	Mitch Williams	.03	.01	.00
□ 226	Chuck Finley	.03	.01	.00
□ 227	Mark Langston	.08	.03	.01
□ 228	Jesse Orosco	.03	.01	.00
□ 229	Ed Whitson	.03	.01	.00
□ 230	Terry Pendleton	.03	.01	.00
□ 231	Lloyd Moseby	.08	.03	.01
□ 232	Greg Swindell	.08	.03	.01
□ 233	John Franco	.08	.03	.01
□ 234	Jack Morris	.10	.04	.01
□ 235	Howard Johnson	.10	.04	.01
□ 236	Glenn Davis	.12	.05	.01
□ 237	Frank Viola	.15	.06	.01
□ 238	Kevin Seitzer	.20	.08	.02
□ 239	Gerald Perry	.08	.03	.01
□ 240	Dwight Evans	.08	.03	.01
□ 241	Jim Deshaies	.03	.01	.00
□ 242	Bo Diaz	.03	.01	.00
□ 243	Carney Lansford	.08	.03	.01
□ 244	Mike LaValliere	.03	.01	.00
□ 245	Rickey Henderson	.20	.08	.02
□ 246	Roberto Alomar	.20	.08	.02
□ 247	Jimmy Jones	.06	.02	.00
□ 248	Pascual Perez	.06	.02	.00
□ 249	Will Clark	.35	.14	.03
□ 250	Fernando Valenzuela	.12	.05	.01
□ 251	Shane Rawley	.03	.01	.00
□ 252	Sid Bream	.03	.01	.00

DEN'S COLLECTORS DEN

PLASTIC CARD PROTECTING PAGES
LARGEST SELECTION IN THE HOBBY

FINEST QUALITY PLASTIC SHEETS

DEN'S COLLECTORS DEN

HOME OF SPORT AMERICANA

DEPT. PG11
P.O. BOX 606, LAUREL, MD 20707

Featuring:

- NON–MIGRATING PLASTIC IN ALL SHEETS
- PLASTIC THAT DOES NOT STICK TOGETHER
- STIFFNESS TO RESIST CARD CURLING
- INTELLIGENT DESIGN
- RESISTANCE TO CRACKING
- FULL COVERAGE OF CARDS, PHOTOS, ENVELOPES

SEND ONLY $ 1.00 for DEN'S BIG CATALOGUE
CATALOGUE sent FREE with each ORDER

NO MIX & MATCH

STYLE	POCKETS / CAPACITY	RECOMMENDED FOR	PRICE EACH (Does not include Post. & Hand.) 1–24	25–99	100–299	300 plus
9	9 / 18	TOPPS (1957 to present), FLEER, DONRUSS SCORE, SPORTFLICS, TCMA, LEAF (1960), All standard 2½" X 3½" cards, SIDE LOAD	.25	.23	.21	.19
9T	9 / 18	SAME AS STYLE 9 ABOVE, TOP LOAD	.25	.23	.21	.19
8	8 / 16	TOPPS (1952–1956, 1988 Big), BOWMAN (1953–1955)	.25	.23	.21	.19
12	12 / 24	BOWMAN (1948–1950), TOPPS (1951), TOPPS (Stickers), FLEER (Minis & Stickers)	.25	.23	.21	.19
1	1 / 2	PHOTOGRAPHS (8" X 10")	.25	.23	.21	.19
2	2 / 4	PHOTOGRAPHS (5" X 7"), TOPPS (1984, 1985 & 1986 Supers)	.25	.23	.21	.19
4	4 / 8	POSTCARDS, EXHIBITS, PEREZ–STEELE (Hall of Fame postcards), DONRUSS (1983–1987 All-Stars), TOPPS (1964,70,71 Supers)	.25	.23	.21	.19
6P	6 / 12	POLICE AND SAFETY CARDS (All sports)	.25	.23	.21	.19
18	18 / 36	T206 and most other T CARDS, BAZOOKA (1963–1967 Individual cards), Many 19th Century cards (N Cards)	.40	.40	35	.35
9G	9 / 18	GOUDEY, DIAMOND STARS, LEAF (1948)	.40	.40	.35	.35
9PB	9 / 18	PLAY BALL, BOWMAN (1951-52), All GUM, INC. Cards, TOPPS (Minis), DOUBLE PLAY	.40	.40	.35	.35
1C	1 / 2	TURKEY RED (T3), PRESS GUIDES, PEREZ–STEELE (Greatest Moments), Many WRAPPERS (Sport & non-sport)	.40	.40	.35	.35
3	3 / 6	3–CARD PANELS (Hostess, Star, Zeller's)	.40	.40	.35	.35
6V	6 / 12	TOPPS (Double Headers, Greatest Moments, 1951 Connie Mack, Current All-Stars, Team, 1965 Football and Hockey, Bucks, 1969–1970 Basketball, T201 (Mecca Double folders), T202 (Hassan Triple folders), DADS (Hockey), DONRUSS (1986–87 Pop–Ups)	.40	.40	.35	.35
6D	6 / 12	RED MAN (With or without tabs), DISCS, KAHN'S (1955–1967)	.40	.40	.35	.35
1Y	1 / 1	YEARBOOKS, PROGRAMS, MAGAZINES, Pocket Size is 9" X 12"	.40	.40	.35	.35
1S	1 / 2	MAGAZINE PAGES and PHOTOS, SMALL PROGRAMS, CRACKER JACK (1982 sheets), Pocket Size is 8½" X 11"	.40	.40	.35	.35
10	10 / 10	MATCHBOOK COVERS (Standard 20 match)	.40	.40	.35	.35
3E	3 / 3	FIRST DAY COVERS, BASEBALL COM–MEMORATIVE ENVELOPES	.40	.40	.35	.35
3L	3 / 6	SQUIRT PANELS, PEPSI (1963), FLEER (Stamps in strips)	.40	.40	.35	.35

POSTAGE & HANDLING SCHEDULE
$ .01 to $ 20.00 add $ 2.00
$ 20.01 to $ 29.99 add $ 2.50
$ 30.00 to $ 49.99 add $ 3.00
$ 50.00 or more add $ 4.00

VISA/MASTER CHARGE ACCEPTED

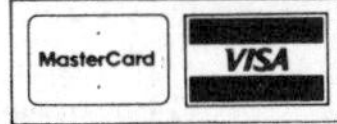

MARYLAND RESIDENTS ADD 5% SALES TAX
CANADIAN ORDERS – BOOKS ONLY
Canadian orders, orders outside the contiguous United States, APO and FPO add 25% additional
U.S. FUNDS ONLY

☐ 253 Steve Lyons .03 .01 .00
☐ 254 Brian Downing .03 .01 .00
☐ 255 Mark Grace .75 .30 .07
☐ 256 Tom Candiotti .03 .01 .00
☐ 257 Barry Larkin .10 .04 .01
☐ 258 Mike Krukow .03 .01 .00
☐ 259 Billy Ripken .03 .01 .00
☐ 260 Cecilio Guante .03 .01 .00
☐ 261 Scott Bradley .03 .01 .00
☐ 262 Floyd Bannister .03 .01 .00
☐ 263 Pete Smith .03 .01 .00
☐ 264 Jim Gantner .03 .01 .00
☐ 265 Roger McDowell .06 .02 .00
☐ 266 Bobby Thigpen .06 .02 .00
☐ 267 Jim Clancy .03 .01 .00
☐ 268 Terry Steinbach .08 .03 .01
☐ 269 Mike Dunne .08 .03 .01
☐ 270 Dwight Gooden .30 .12 .03
☐ 271 Mike Heath .03 .01 .00
☐ 272 Dave Smith .03 .01 .00
☐ 273 Keith Atherton .03 .01 .00
☐ 274 Tim Burke .03 .01 .00
☐ 275 Damon Berryhill .10 .04 .01
☐ 276 Vance Law .03 .01 .00
☐ 277 Rich Dotson .06 .02 .00
☐ 278 Lance Parrish .08 .03 .01
☐ 279 Denny Walling .03 .01 .00
☐ 280 Roger Clemens .35 .14 .03
☐ 281 Greg Mathews .03 .01 .00
☐ 282 Tom Niedenfuer .03 .01 .00
☐ 283 Paul Kilgus .03 .01 .00
☐ 284 Jose Guzman .03 .01 .00
☐ 285 Calvin Schiraldi .03 .01 .00
☐ 286 Charlie Puleo .03 .01 .00
☐ 287 Joe Orsulak .03 .01 .00
☐ 288 Jack Howell .03 .01 .00
☐ 289 Kevin Elster .06 .02 .00
☐ 290 Jose Lind .06 .02 .00
☐ 291 Paul Molitor .10 .04 .01
☐ 292 Cecil Espy .10 .04 .01
☐ 293 Bill Wegman .03 .01 .00
☐ 294 Dan Pasqua .06 .02 .00
☐ 295 Scott Garrelts .03 .01 .00
☐ 296 Walt Terrell .03 .01 .00
☐ 297 Ed Hearn .03 .01 .00
☐ 298 Lou Whitaker .08 .03 .01
☐ 299 Ken Dayley .03 .01 .00
☐ 300 Checklist .06 .01 .00
☐ 301 Tommy Herr .06 .02 .00
☐ 302 Mike Brumley .03 .01 .00
☐ 303 Ellis Burks .30 .12 .03
☐ 304 Curt Young .03 .01 .00
☐ 305 Jody Reed .06 .02 .00
☐ 306 Bill Doran .06 .02 .00
☐ 307 David Wells .03 .01 .00
☐ 308 Ron Robinson .03 .01 .00
☐ 309 Rafael Santana .03 .01 .00
☐ 310 Julio Franco .06 .02 .00
☐ 311 Jack Clark .12 .05 .01
☐ 312 Chris James .06 .02 .00
☐ 313 Milt Thompson .03 .01 .00
☐ 314 John Shelby .03 .01 .00
☐ 315 Al Leiter .15 .06 .01
☐ 316 Mike Davis .03 .01 .00
☐ 317 Chris Sabo 1.00 .40 .10
☐ 318 Greg Gagne .03 .01 .00
☐ 319 Jose Oquendo .03 .01 .00
☐ 320 John Farrell .03 .01 .00
☐ 321 Franklin Stubbs .03 .01 .00
☐ 322 Kurt Stillwell .03 .01 .00
☐ 323 Shawn Abner .06 .02 .00
☐ 324 Mike Flanagan .03 .01 .00
☐ 325 Kevin Bass .06 .02 .00
☐ 326 Pat Tabler .06 .02 .00
☐ 327 Mike Henneman .03 .01 .00
☐ 328 Rick Honeycutt .03 .01 .00
☐ 329 John Smiley .03 .01 .00
☐ 330 Rey Quinones .03 .01 .00
☐ 331 Johnny Ray .06 .02 .00
☐ 332 Bob Welch .06 .02 .00
☐ 333 Larry Sheets .06 .02 .00
☐ 334 Jeff Parrett .03 .01 .00
☐ 335 Rick Reuschel .06 .02 .00
☐ 336 Randy Myers .08 .03 .01
☐ 337 Ken Williams .03 .01 .00
☐ 338 Andy McGaffigan .03 .01 .00
☐ 339 Joey Meyer .08 .03 .01
☐ 340 Dion James .03 .01 .00
☐ 341 Les Lancaster .03 .01 .00
☐ 342 Tom Foley .03 .01 .00
☐ 343 Geno Petralli .03 .01 .00
☐ 344 Dan Petry .03 .01 .00
☐ 345 Alvin Davis .08 .03 .01
☐ 346 Mickey Hatcher .06 .02 .00
☐ 347 Marvell Wynne .03 .01 .00
☐ 348 Danny Cox .06 .02 .00
☐ 349 Dave Stieb .08 .03 .01
☐ 350 Jay Bell .03 .01 .00
☐ 351 Jeff Treadway .06 .02 .00
☐ 352 Luis Salazar .03 .01 .00
☐ 353 Lenny Dykstra .08 .03 .01
☐ 354 Juan Agosto .03 .01 .00
☐ 355 Gene Larkin .08 .03 .01
☐ 356 Steve Farr .03 .01 .00
☐ 357 Paul Assenmacher .03 .01 .00
☐ 358 Todd Benzinger .06 .02 .00
☐ 359 Larry Andersen .03 .01 .00
☐ 360 Paul O'Neill .06 .02 .00
☐ 361 Ron Hassey .03 .01 .00
☐ 362 Jim Gott .03 .01 .00
☐ 363 Ken Phelps .06 .02 .00
☐ 364 Tim Flannery .03 .01 .00
☐ 365 Randy Ready .03 .01 .00
☐ 366 Nelson Santovenia .10 .04 .01
☐ 367 Kelly Downs .06 .02 .00
☐ 368 Danny Heep .03 .01 .00
☐ 369 Phil Bradley .06 .02 .00
☐ 370 Jeff Robinson .03 .01 .00
Pittsburgh Pirates
☐ 371 Ivan Calderon .08 .03 .01
☐ 372 Mike Witt .08 .03 .01
☐ 373 Greg Maddux .12 .05 .01
☐ 374 Carmen Castillo .03 .01 .00
☐ 375 Jose Rijo .06 .02 .00
☐ 376 Joe Price .03 .01 .00
☐ 377 Rene C. Gonzales .03 .01 .00
☐ 378 Oddibe McDowell .06 .02 .00
☐ 379 Jim Presley .06 .02 .00
☐ 380 Brad Wellman .03 .01 .00
☐ 381 Tom Glavine .03 .01 .00
☐ 382 Dan Plesac .06 .02 .00
☐ 383 Wally Backman .03 .01 .00
☐ 384 Dave Gallagher .15 .06 .01
☐ 385 Tom Henke .06 .02 .00
☐ 386 Luis Polonia .03 .01 .00
☐ 387 Junior Ortiz .03 .01 .00
☐ 388 David Cone .30 .12 .03
☐ 389 Dave Bergman .03 .01 .00
☐ 390 Danny Darwin .03 .01 .00
☐ 391 Dan Gladden .06 .02 .00
☐ 392 John Dopson .15 .06 .01
☐ 393 Frank DiPino .03 .01 .00
☐ 394 Al Nipper .03 .01 .00
☐ 395 Willie Randolph .06 .02 .00
☐ 396 Don Carman .03 .01 .00
☐ 397 Scott Terry .03 .01 .00
☐ 398 Rick Cerone .03 .01 .00
☐ 399 Tom Pagnozzi .03 .01 .00
☐ 400 Checklist .06 .01 .00
☐ 401 Mickey Tettleton .03 .01 .00
☐ 402 Curtis Wilkerson .03 .01 .00
☐ 403 Jeff Russell .03 .01 .00
☐ 404 Pat Perry .03 .01 .00
☐ 405 Jose Alvarez .10 .04 .01
☐ 406 Rick Schu .03 .01 .00
☐ 407 Sherman Corbett .10 .04 .01
☐ 408 Dave Magadan .08 .03 .01
☐ 409 Bob Kipper .03 .01 .00
☐ 410 Don August .08 .03 .01
☐ 411 Bob Brower .06 .02 .00
☐ 412 Chris Bosio .03 .01 .00
☐ 413 Jerry Reuss .03 .01 .00
☐ 414 Atlee Hammaker .03 .01 .00
☐ 415 Jim Walewander .10 .04 .01
☐ 416 Mike Macfarlane .12 .05 .01
☐ 417 Pat Sheridan .03 .01 .00
☐ 418 Pedro Guerrero .10 .04 .01
☐ 419 Allan Anderson .06 .02 .00
☐ 420 Mark Parent .12 .05 .01
☐ 421 Bob Stanley .03 .01 .00
☐ 422 Mike Gallego .03 .01 .00
☐ 423 Bruce Hurst .08 .03 .01
☐ 424 Dave Meads .03 .01 .00
☐ 425 Jesse Barfield .10 .04 .01
☐ 426 Rob Dibble .12 .05 .01
☐ 427 Joel Skinner .03 .01 .00
☐ 428 Ron Kittle .08 .03 .01
☐ 429 Rick Rhoden .03 .01 .00
☐ 430 Bob Dernier .03 .01 .00
☐ 431 Steve Jeltz .03 .01 .00
☐ 432 Rick Dempsey .03 .01 .00
☐ 433 Roberto Kelly .12 .05 .01
☐ 434 Dave Anderson .03 .01 .00
☐ 435 Herm Winningham .03 .01 .00
☐ 436 Al Newman .03 .01 .00
☐ 437 Jose DeLeon .03 .01 .00
☐ 438 Doug Jones .06 .02 .00
☐ 439 Brian Holton .03 .01 .00
☐ 440 Jeff Montgomery .08 .03 .01
☐ 441 Dickie Thon .03 .01 .00

☐ 442 Cecil Fielder .03 .01 .00
☐ 443 John Fishel .12 .05 .01
☐ 444 Jerry Don Gleaton .03 .01 .00
☐ 445 Paul Gibson .12 .05 .01
☐ 446 Walt Weiss .50 .20 .05
☐ 447 Glenn Wilson .03 .01 .00
☐ 448 Mike Moore .03 .01 .00
☐ 449 Chili Davis .06 .02 .00
☐ 450 Dave Henderson .06 .02 .00
☐ 451 Jose Bautista .10 .04 .01
☐ 452 Rex Hudler .03 .01 .00
☐ 453 Bob Brenly .03 .01 .00
☐ 454 Mackey Sasser .10 .04 .01
☐ 455 Daryl Boston .03 .01 .00
☐ 456 Mike Fitzgerald .03 .01 .00
Montreal Expos
☐ 457 Jeffrey Leonard .06 .02 .00
☐ 458 Bruce Sutter .08 .03 .01
☐ 459 Mitch Webster .03 .01 .00
☐ 460 Joe Hesketh .03 .01 .00
☐ 461 Bobby Witt .06 .02 .00
☐ 462 Stew Cliburn .03 .01 .00
☐ 463 Scott Bankhead .03 .01 .00
☐ 464 Ramon Martinez .30 .12 .03
☐ 465 Dave Leiper .03 .01 .00
☐ 466 Luis Alicea .12 .05 .01
☐ 467 John Cerutti .03 .01 .00
☐ 468 Ron Washington .03 .01 .00
☐ 469 Jeff Reed .03 .01 .00
☐ 470 Jeff Robinson .06 .02 .00
Detroit Tigers
☐ 471 Sid Fernandez .08 .03 .01
☐ 472 Terry Puhl .03 .01 .00
☐ 473 Charlie Lea .03 .01 .00
☐ 474 Israel Sanchez .08 .03 .01
☐ 475 Bruce Benedict .03 .01 .00
☐ 476 Oil Can Boyd .06 .02 .00
☐ 477 Craig Reynolds .03 .01 .00
☐ 478 Frank Williams .03 .01 .00
☐ 479 Greg Cadaret .03 .01 .00
☐ 480 Randy Kramer .12 .05 .01
☐ 481 Dave Eiland .12 .05 .01
☐ 482 Eric Show .03 .01 .00
☐ 483 Garry Templeton .06 .02 .00
☐ 484 Wallace Johnson .03 .01 .00
☐ 485 Kevin Mitchell .06 .02 .00
☐ 486 Tim Crews .03 .01 .00
☐ 487 Mike Maddux .03 .01 .00
☐ 488 Dave LaPoint .03 .01 .00
☐ 489 Fred Manrique .03 .01 .00
☐ 490 Greg Minton .03 .01 .00
☐ 491 Doug Dascenzo .15 .06 .01
☐ 492 Willie Upshaw .03 .01 .00
☐ 493 Jack Armstrong .20 .08 .02
☐ 494 Kirt Manwaring .03 .01 .00
☐ 495 Jeff Ballard .03 .01 .00
☐ 496 Jeff Kunkel .03 .01 .00
☐ 497 Mike Campbell .03 .01 .00
☐ 498 Gary Thurman .03 .01 .00
☐ 499 Zane Smith .03 .01 .00
☐ 500 Checklist .06 .01 .00
☐ 501 Mike Birkbeck .03 .01 .00
☐ 502 Terry Leach .06 .02 .00
☐ 503 Shawn Hillegas .03 .01 .00
☐ 504 Manny Lee .03 .01 .00
☐ 505 Doug Jennings .20 .08 .02
☐ 506 Ken Oberkfell .03 .01 .00
☐ 507 Tim Teufel .03 .01 .00
☐ 508 Tom Brookens .03 .01 .00
☐ 509 Rafael Ramirez .03 .01 .00
☐ 510 Fred Toliver .03 .01 .00
☐ 511 Brian Holman .10 .04 .01
☐ 512 Mike Bielecki .03 .01 .00
☐ 513 Jeff Pico .10 .04 .01
☐ 514 Charles Hudson .03 .01 .00
☐ 515 Bruce Ruffin .03 .01 .00
☐ 516 Larry McWilliams .03 .01 .00
☐ 517 Jeff Sellers .03 .01 .00
☐ 518 John Costello .10 .04 .01
☐ 519 Brady Anderson .20 .08 .02
☐ 520 Craig McMurtry .03 .01 .00
☐ 521 Ray Hayward .03 .01 .00
☐ 522 Drew Hall .03 .01 .00
☐ 523 Mark Lemke .20 .08 .02
☐ 524 Oswald Peraza .10 .04 .01
☐ 525 Bryan Harvey .25 .10 .02
☐ 526 Rick Aguilera .03 .01 .00
☐ 527 Tom Prince .06 .02 .00
☐ 528 Mark Clear .03 .01 .00
☐ 529 Jerry Browne .03 .01 .00
☐ 530 Juan Castillo .03 .01 .00
☐ 531 Jack McDowell .08 .03 .01
☐ 532 Chris Speier .03 .01 .00
☐ 533 Darrell Evans .06 .02 .00
☐ 534 Luis Aquino .03 .01 .00
☐ 535 Eric King .03 .01 .0
☐ 536 Ken Hill .12 .05 .0
☐ 537 Randy Bush .03 .01 .0
☐ 538 Shane Mack .06 .02 .0
☐ 539 Tom Bolton .08 .03 .0
☐ 540 Gene Nelson .03 .01 .0
☐ 541 Wes Gardner .03 .01 .0
☐ 542 Ken Caminiti .03 .01 .0
☐ 543 Duane Ward .03 .01 .0
☐ 544 Norm Charlton .12 .05 .0
☐ 545 Hal Morris .15 .06 .0
☐ 546 Rich Yett .03 .01 .0
☐ 547 Hensley Meulens .85 .34 .0
☐ 548 Greg Harris .03 .01 .0
Philadelphia Phillies
☐ 549 Darren Daulton .03 .01 .0
☐ 550 Jeff Hamilton .03 .01 .0
☐ 551 Luis Aguayo .03 .01 .0
☐ 552 Tim Leary .06 .02 .0
☐ 553 Ron Oester .03 .01 .0
☐ 554 Steve Lombardozzi .03 .01 .0
☐ 555 Tim Jones .15 .06 .0
☐ 556 Bud Black .03 .01 .0
☐ 557 Alejandro Pena .03 .01 .0
☐ 558 Jose DeJesus .10 .04 .0
☐ 559 Dennis Rasmussen .06 .02 .0
☐ 560 Pat Borders .12 .05 .0
☐ 561 Craig Biggio .12 .05 .0
☐ 562 Luis De Los Santos .25 .10 .0
☐ 563 Fred Lynn .08 .03 .0
☐ 564 Todd Burns .20 .08 .0
☐ 565 Felix Fermin .03 .01 .0
☐ 566 Darnell Coles .03 .01 .0
☐ 567 Willie Fraser .03 .01 .0
☐ 568 Glenn Hubbard .03 .01 .0
☐ 569 Craig Worthington .25 .10 .0
☐ 570 Johnny Paredes .10 .04 .01
☐ 571 Don Robinson .03 .01 .0
☐ 572 Barry Lyons .03 .01 .0
☐ 573 Bill Long .03 .01 .0
☐ 574 Tracy Jones .06 .02 .0
☐ 575 Juan Nieves .03 .01 .0
☐ 576 Andres Thomas .03 .01 .00
☐ 577 Rolando Roomes .15 .06 .01
☐ 578 Luis Rivera .03 .01 .00
☐ 579 Chad Kreuter .15 .06 .01
☐ 580 Tony Armas .06 .02 .00
☐ 581 Jay Buhner .10 .04 .01
☐ 582 Ricky Horton .03 .01 .00
☐ 583 Andy Hawkins .06 .02 .00
☐ 584 Sil Campusano .25 .10 .02
☐ 585 Dave Clark .06 .02 .00
☐ 586 Van Snider .25 .10 .02
☐ 587 Todd Frohwirth .03 .01 .00
☐ 588 Puzzle Card .03 .01 .00
Warren Spahn
☐ 589 William Brennan .12 .05 .01
☐ 590 German Gonzalez .10 .04 .01
☐ 591 Ernie Whitt .03 .01 .00
☐ 592 Jeff Blauser .03 .01 .00
☐ 593 Spike Owen .03 .01 .00
☐ 594 Matt Williams .08 .03 .01
☐ 595 Lloyd McClendon .03 .01 .00
☐ 596 Steve Ontiveros .03 .01 .00
☐ 597 Scott Medvin .12 .05 .01
☐ 598 Hipolito Pena .12 .05 .01
☐ 599 Jerald Clark .20 .08 .02
☐ 600 Checklist .06 .01 .00
☐ 601 Carmelo Martinez .03 .01 .00
☐ 602 Mike LaCoss .03 .01 .00
☐ 603 Mike Devereaux .08 .03 .01
☐ 604 Alex Madrid .15 .06 .01
☐ 605 Gary Redus .03 .01 .00
☐ 606 Lance Johnson .03 .01 .00
☐ 607 Terry Clark .15 .06 .01
☐ 608 Manny Trillo .03 .01 .00
☐ 609 Scott Jordan .12 .05 .01
☐ 610 Jay Howell .03 .01 .00
☐ 611 Francisco Melendez .15 .06 .01
☐ 612 Mike Boddicker .06 .02 .00
☐ 613 Kevin Brown .03 .01 .00
☐ 614 Dave Valle .03 .01 .00
☐ 615 Tim Laudner .03 .01 .00
☐ 616 Andy Nezelek .12 .05 .01
☐ 617 Chuck Crim .03 .01 .00
☐ 618 Jack Savage .08 .03 .01
☐ 619 Adam Peterson .08 .03 .01
☐ 620 Todd Stottlemyre .08 .03 .01
☐ 621 Lance Blankenship .15 .06 .01
☐ 622 Miguel Garcia .10 .04 .01
☐ 623 Keith Miller .03 .01 .00
New York Mets
☐ 624 Ricky Jordan 1.25 .50 .12
☐ 625 Ernest Riles .03 .01 .00
☐ 626 John Moses .03 .01 .00

		MINT	EXC	G-VG
□ 627	Nelson Liriano	.03	.01	.00
□ 628	Mike Smithson	.03	.01	.00
□ 629	Scott Sanderson	.03	.01	.00
□ 630	Dale Mohorcic	.03	.01	.00
□ 631	Marvin Freeman	.03	.01	.00
□ 632	Mike Young	.03	.01	.00
□ 633	Dennis Lamp	.03	.01	.00
□ 634	Dante Bichette	.15	.06	.01
□ 635	Curt Schilling	.12	.05	.01
□ 636	Scott May	.12	.05	.01
□ 637	Mike Schooler	.15	.06	.01
□ 638	Rick Leach	.03	.01	.00
□ 639	Tom Lampkin	.12	.05	.01
□ 640	Brian Meyer	.12	.05	.01
□ 641	Brian Harper	.03	.01	.00
□ 642	John Smoltz	.25	.10	.02
□ 643	Jose: 40/40 Club (Jose Canseco)	.30	.12	.03
□ 644	Bill Schroeder	.03	.01	.00
□ 645	Edgar Martinez	.10	.04	.01
□ 646	Dennis Cook	.12	.05	.01
□ 647	Barry Jones	.03	.01	.00
□ 648	Orel: 59 and Counting (Orel Hershiser)	.15	.06	.01
□ 649	Rod Nichols	.12	.05	.01
□ 650	Jody Davis	.06	.02	.00
□ 651	Bob Milacki	.25	.10	.02
□ 652	Mike Jackson	.03	.01	.00
□ 653	Derek Lilliquist	.15	.06	.01
□ 654	Paul Mirabella	.03	.01	.00
□ 655	Mike Diaz	.03	.01	.00
□ 656	Jeff Musselman	.03	.01	.00
□ 657	Jerry Reed	.03	.01	.00
□ 658	Kevin Blankenship	.15	.06	.01
□ 659	Wayne Tolleson	.03	.01	.00
□ 660	Eric Hetzel	.15	.06	.01

1989 Donruss Bonus MVP's

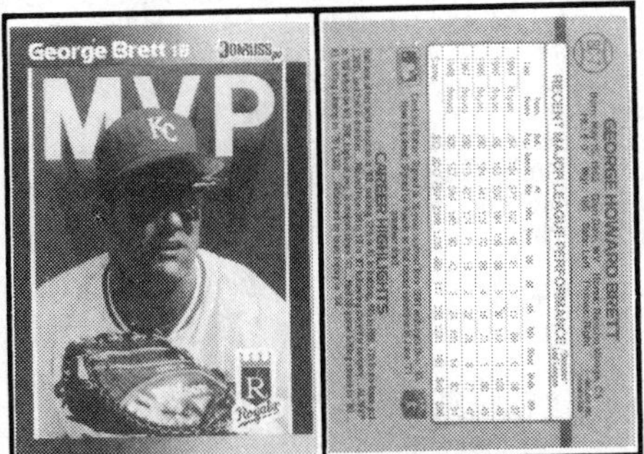

This 26-card set was distributed along with the regular 1989 Donruss issue as random inserts with the rack and wax packs. These bonus cards are numbered with the prefix BC for bonus cards and were supposedly produced in the same quantities as the other 660 regular issue cards. The 'most valuable" player was selected from each of the 26 teams. Cards measure 2 1/2" by 3 1/2" and feature the same distinctive side border as the regular issue. The cards are distinguished by the bold MVP logo in the upper background of the obverse.

		MINT	EXC	G-VG
	COMPLETE SET (26)	10.00	4.00	1.00
	COMMON PLAYER (BC1-BC26)	.10	.04	.01
□ BC1	Kirby Puckett	.35	.14	.03
□ BC2	Mike Scott	.15	.06	.01
□ BC3	Joe Carter	.20	.08	.02
□ BC4	Orel Hershiser	.30	.12	.03
□ BC5	Jose Canseco	1.00	.40	.10
□ BC6	Darryl Strawberry	.50	.20	.05
□ BC7	George Brett	.25	.10	.02
□ BC8	Andre Dawson	.15	.06	.01
□ BC9	Paul Molitor	.15	.06	.01
□ BC10	Andy Van Slyke	.15	.06	.01
□ BC11	Dave Winfield	.25	.10	.02
□ BC12	Kevin Gross	.10	.04	.01
□ BC13	Mike Greenwell	.60	.24	.06
□ BC14	Ozzie Smith	.20	.08	.02
□ BC15	Cal Ripken	.20	.08	.02
□ BC16	Andres Galarraga	.15	.06	.01
□ BC17	Alan Trammell	.15	.06	.01
□ BC18	Kal Daniels	.15	.06	.01
□ BC19	Fred McGriff	.15	.06	.01
□ BC20	Tony Gwynn	.25	.10	.02
□ BC21	Wally Joyner	.25	.10	.02
□ BC22	Will Clark	.40	.16	.04
□ BC23	Ozzie Guillen	.10	.04	.01
□ BC24	Gerald Perry	.10	.04	.01
□ BC25	Alvin Davis	.10	.04	.01
□ BC26	Ruben Sierra	.15	.06	.01

1989 Donruss Super DK's

This 26-player card set was available through a mail-in offer detailed on the wax packs. The set was sent in return for 8.00 and three wrappers plus 2.00 postage and handling. The set features the popula- Diamond King subseries in large (approximately 4 7/8" by 6 13/16") form. Dick Perez of Perez-Steele Galleries did another outstanding job on the artwork. The cards are essentially a large version of the Donruss regular issue Diamond Kings.

		MINT	EXC	G-VG
	COMPLETE SET (26)	10.00	4.00	1.00
	COMMON PLAYER (1-26)	.15	.06	.01
□ 1	Mike Greenwell DK	1.00	.40	.10
□ 2	Bobby Bonilla DK	.30	.12	.03
□ 3	Pete Incaviglia DK	.25	.10	.02
□ 4	Chris Sabo DK	1.00	.40	.10
□ 5	Robin Yount DK	.50	.20	.05
□ 6	Tony Gwynn DK	.65	.26	.06
□ 7	Carlton Fisk DK	.25	.10	.02
□ 8	Cory Snyder DK	.30	.12	.03
□ 9	David Cone DK	.50	.20	.05
□ 10	Kevin Seitzer DK	.45	.18	.04
□ 11	Rick Reuschel DK	.15	.06	.01
□ 12	Johnny Ray DK	.15	.06	.01
□ 13	Dave Schmidt DK	.15	.06	.01
□ 14	Andres Galarraga DK	.30	.12	.03
□ 15	Kirk Gibson DK	.45	.18	.04
□ 16	Fred McGriff DK	.40	.16	.04
□ 17	Mark Grace DK	1.00	.40	.10
□ 18	Jeff Robinson DT DK	.25	.10	.02
□ 19	Vince Coleman DK	.35	.14	.03
□ 20	Dave Henderson DK	.15	.06	.01
□ 21	Harold Reynolds DK	.15	.06	.01
□ 22	Gerald Perry DK	.20	.08	.02
□ 23	Frank Viola DK	.35	.14	.03
□ 24	Steve Bedrosian DK	.20	.08	.02
□ 25	Glenn Davis DK	.40	.16	.04
□ 26	Don Mattingly DK	1.25	.50	.12

1989 Donruss All-Stars

These All-Stars are standard size, 2 1/2" by 3 1/2" and very similar in design to the regular issue of 1989 Donruss. The set is distinguished by the presence of the respective League logos in the lower right corner of each obverse. The cards are numbered on the backs. The players chosen for the set are essentially the participants at the previous year's All-Star Game. Individual wax packs of All Stars (suggested retail price of 35 cents) contained one Pop-Up, five All-Star cards, and a Warren Spahn puzzle card.

	MINT	EXC	G-VG
COMPLETE SET (64)	7.00	2.80	.70
COMMON PLAYER (1-64)	.07	.03	.01
□ 1 Mark McGwire	.65	.26	.06
□ 2 Jose Canseco	1.00	.40	.10
□ 3 Paul Molitor	.15	.06	.01
□ 4 Rickey Henderson	.35	.14	.03
□ 5 Cal Ripken Jr.	.25	.10	.02
□ 6 Dave Winfield	.25	.10	.02
□ 7 Wade Boggs	.75	.30	.07
□ 8 Frank Viola	.15	.06	.01
□ 9 Terry Steinbach	.10	.04	.01
□ 10 Tom Kelly MG	.07	.03	.01
□ 11 George Brett	.35	.14	.03
□ 12 Doyle Alexander	.07	.03	.01
□ 13 Gary Gaetti	.15	.06	.01
□ 14 Roger Clemens	.50	.20	.05
□ 15 Mike Greenwell	1.00	.40	.10
□ 16 Dennis Eckersley	.15	.06	.01
□ 17 Carney Lansford	.10	.04	.01
□ 18 Mark Gubicza	.10	.04	.01
□ 19 Tim Laudner	.07	.03	.01
□ 20 Doug Jones	.15	.06	.01
□ 21 Don Mattingly	1.00	.40	.10
□ 22 Dan Plesac	.10	.04	.01
□ 23 Kirby Puckett	.50	.20	.05
□ 24 Jeff Reardon	.07	.03	.01
□ 25 Johnny Ray	.07	.03	.01
□ 26 Jeff Russell	.07	.03	.01
□ 27 Harold Reynolds	.07	.03	.01
□ 28 Dave Stieb	.10	.04	.01
□ 29 Kurt Stillwell	.07	.03	.01
□ 30 Jose Canseco	1.50	.60	.15
□ 31 Terry Steinbach	.10	.04	.01
□ 32 AL Checklist	.07	.01	.00
□ 33 Will Clark	.75	.30	.07
□ 34 Darryl Strawberry	.65	.26	.06
□ 35 Ryne Sandberg	.25	.10	.02
□ 36 Andre Dawson	.25	.10	.02
□ 37 Ozzie Smith	.20	.08	.02
□ 38 Vince Coleman	.20	.08	.02
□ 39 Bobby Bonilla	.15	.06	.01
□ 40 Dwight Gooden	.50	.20	.05
□ 41 Gary Carter	.25	.10	.02
□ 42 Whitey Herzog MG	.07	.03	.01
□ 43 Shawon Dunston	.10	.04	.01
□ 44 David Cone	.35	.14	.03
□ 45 Andres Galarraga	.25	.10	.02
□ 46 Mark Davis	.07	.03	.01
□ 47 Barry Larkin	.15	.06	.01
□ 48 Kevin Gross	.10	.04	.01
□ 49 Vance Law	.07	.03	.01
□ 50 Orel Hershiser	.50	.20	.05
□ 51 Willie McGee	.15	.06	.01
□ 52 Danny Jackson	.15	.06	.01
□ 53 Rafael Palmeiro	.20	.08	.02
□ 54 Bob Knepper	.07	.03	.01
□ 55 Lance Parrish	.10	.04	.01
□ 56 Greg Maddux	.15	.06	.01
□ 57 Gerald Perry	.10	.04	.01
□ 58 Bob Walk	.07	.03	.01
□ 59 Chris Sabo	.50	.20	.05
□ 60 Todd Worrell	.15	.06	.01
□ 61 Andy Van Slyke	.15	.06	.01
□ 62 Ozzie Smith	.20	.08	.02
□ 63 Riverfront Stadium	.07	.03	.01
□ 64 NL Checklist	.07	.01	.00

1989 Donruss Pop-Ups

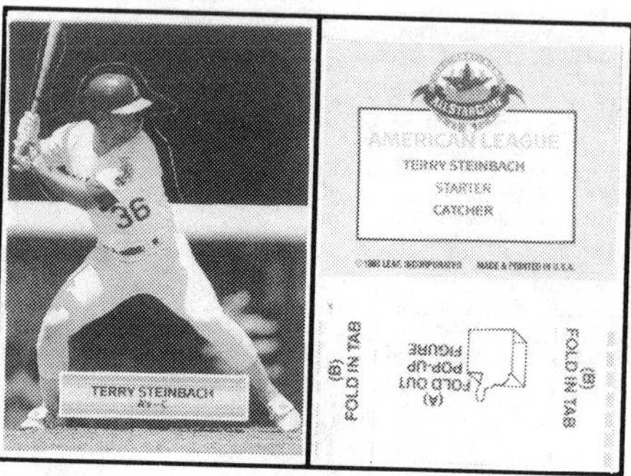

These Pop-Ups are borderless and standard size, 2 1/2" by 3 1/2". The cards are unnumbered; however the All Star checklist card lists the same numbers as the All Star cards. Those numbers are used below for reference. The players chosen for the set are essentially the starting lineups for the previous year's All-Star Game. Individual wax packs of All Stars (suggested retail price of 35 cents) contained one Pop-Up, five All-Star cards, and a puzzle card.

	MINT	EXC	G-VG
COMPLETE SET (20)	4.00	1.60	.40
COMMON PLAYER	.10	.04	.01
□ 1 Mark McGwire	.60	.24	.06
□ 2 Jose Canseco	1.00	.40	.10
□ 3 Paul Molitor	.20	.08	.02
□ 4 Rickey Henderson	.40	.16	.04
□ 5 Cal Ripken Jr.	.30	.12	.03
□ 6 Dave Winfield	.30	.12	.03
□ 7 Wade Boggs	.75	.30	.07
□ 8 Frank Viola	.20	.08	.02
□ 9 Terry Steinbach	.20	.08	.02
□ 10 Tom Kelly MG	.10	.04	.01
□ 33 Will Clark	.60	.24	.06
□ 34 Darryl Strawberry	.60	.24	.06
□ 35 Ryne Sandberg	.30	.12	.03
□ 36 Andre Dawson	.25	.10	.02
□ 37 Ozzie Smith	.20	.08	.02
□ 38 Vince Coleman	.20	.08	.02
□ 39 Bobby Bonilla	.20	.08	.02
□ 40 Dwight Gooden	.50	.20	.05
□ 41 Gary Carter	.30	.12	.03
□ 42 Whitey Herzog MG	.10	.04	.01

1986 Dorman's Cheese

This 20-card set was issued in panels of two cards. The individual cards measure 1 1/2" by 2" whereas the panels measure 3" by 2". Team logos have been removed from the photos as these cards were not licensed by Major League Baseball (team owners). The backs contain a minimum of information.

	MINT	EXC	G-VG
COMPLETE SET (20)	18.00	7.25	1.80
COMMON PLAYER (1-20)	.70	.28	.07
☐ 1 George Brett	1.25	.50	.12
☐ 2 Jack Morris	.70	.28	.07
☐ 3 Gary Carter	.90	.36	.09
☐ 4 Cal Ripken	1.00	.40	.10
☐ 5 Dwight Gooden	1.25	.50	.12
☐ 6 Kent Hrbek	.70	.28	.07
☐ 7 Rickey Henderson	1.25	.50	.12
☐ 8 Mike Schmidt	1.25	.50	.12
☐ 9 Keith Hernandez	.90	.36	.09
☐ 10 Dale Murphy	1.25	.50	.12
☐ 11 Reggie Jackson	1.00	.40	.10
☐ 12 Eddie Murray	1.00	.40	.10
☐ 13 Don Mattingly	3.00	1.20	.30
☐ 14 Ryne Sandberg	.90	.36	.09
☐ 15 Willie McGee	.70	.28	.07
☐ 16 Robin Yount	1.00	.40	.10
☐ 17 Rick Sutcliffe	.70	.28	.07
☐ 18 Wade Boggs	2.00	.80	.20
☐ 19 Dave Winfield	1.00	.40	.10
☐ 20 Jim Rice	.90	.36	.09

1941 Double Play

The cards in this 75-card set measure 2 1/2" by 3 1/8". The 1941 Double Play set, listed as R330 in the American Card Catalog, was a blank-backed issue distributed by Gum Products. It consists of 75 numbered cards (two consecutive numbers per card), each depicting two players in sepia tone photographs. Cards 81-100 contain action poses, and the last 50 numbers of the set are slightly harder to find. Cards that have been cut in half to form "singles" have a greatly reduced value.

	NRMT	VG-E	GOOD
COMPLETE SET (150)	2700.00	1150.00	375.00
COMMON PAIRS (1-100)	18.00	7.25	1.80
COMMON PAIRS (101-150)	22.00	9.00	2.20
☐ 1 Larry French and 2 Vance Page	18.00	7.25	1.80
☐ 3 Billy Herman and 4 Stan Hack	22.00	9.00	2.20
☐ 5 Lonnie Frey and 6 Johnny VanderMeer	22.00	9.00	2.20
☐ 7 Paul Derringer and 8 Bucky Walters	22.00	9.00	2.20
☐ 9 Frank McCormick and 10 Bill Werber	18.00	7.25	1.80
☐ 11 Jimmy Ripple and 12 Ernie Lombardi	22.00	9.00	2.20
☐ 13 Alex Kampouris and 14 Whitlow Wyatt	18.00	7.25	1.80
☐ 15 Mickey Owen and 16 Paul Waner	25.00	10.00	2.50
☐ 17 Cookie Lavagetto and 18 Pete Reiser	22.00	9.00	2.20
☐ 19 James Wasdell and 20 Dolf Camilli	18.00	7.25	1.80
☐ 21 Dixie Walker and 22 Joe Medwick	25.00	10.00	2.50
☐ 23 Pee Wee Reese and 24 Kirby Higbe	75.00	30.00	7.50
☐ 25 Harry Danning and 26 Cliff Melton	18.00	7.25	1.80
☐ 27 Harry Gumbert and 28 Burgess Whitehead	18.00	7.25	1.80
☐ 29 Joe Orengo and 30 Joe Moore	18.00	7.25	1.80
☐ 31 Mel Ott and 32 Norman Young	50.00	20.00	5.00
☐ 33 Lee Handley and 34 Arky Vaughan	25.00	10.00	2.50
☐ 35 Bob Klinger and 36 Stanley Brown	18.00	7.25	1.80
☐ 37 Terry Moore and 38 Gus Mancuso	18.00	7.25	1.80
☐ 39 Johnny Mize and 40 Enos Slaughter	75.00	30.00	7.50
☐ 41 Johnny Cooney and 42 Sibby Sisti	18.00	7.25	1.80
☐ 43 Max West and 44 Carvel Rowell	18.00	7.25	1.80
☐ 45 Danny Litwhiler and 46 Merrill May	18.00	7.25	1.80
☐ 47 Frank Hayes and 48 Al Brancato	18.00	7.25	1.80
☐ 49 Bob Johnson and 50 Bill Nagel	18.00	7.25	1.80
☐ 51 Buck Newsom and 52 Hank Greenberg	35.00	14.00	3.50
☐ 53 Barney McCosky and 54 Charlie Gehringer	35.00	14.00	3.50
☐ 55 Mike Higgins and 56 Dick Bartell	18.00	7.25	1.80
☐ 57 Ted Williams and 58 Jim Tabor	200.00	80.00	20.00
☐ 59 Joe Cronin and 60 Jimmie Foxx	100.00	40.00	10.00
☐ 61 Lefty Gomez and 62 Phil Rizzuto	125.00	50.00	12.50
☐ 63 Joe DiMaggio and 64 Charlie Keller	300.00	120.00	30.00
☐ 65 Red Rolfe and 66 Bill Dickey	60.00	24.00	6.00
☐ 67 Joe Gordon and 68 Red Ruffing	50.00	20.00	5.00
☐ 69 Mike Tresh and 70 Luke Appling	25.00	10.00	2.50
☐ 71 Moose Solters and 72 Johnny Rigney	18.00	7.25	1.80
☐ 73 Buddy Myer and 74 Ben Chapman	18.00	7.25	1.80
☐ 75 Cecil Travis and 76 George Case	18.00	7.25	1.80
☐ 77 Joe Krakauskas and 78 Bob Feller	60.00	24.00	6.00
☐ 79 Ken Keltner and 80 Hal Trosky	18.00	7.25	1.80
☐ 81 Ted Williams and 82 Joe Cronin	250.00	100.00	25.00
☐ 83 Joe Gordon and 84 Charlie Keller	25.00	10.00	2.50
☐ 85 Hank Greenberg and 86 Red Ruffing	100.00	40.00	10.00
☐ 87 Hal Trosky and 88 George Case	18.00	7.25	1.80
☐ 89 Mel Ott and 90 Burgess Whitehead	45.00	18.00	4.50
☐ 91 Harry Danning and 92 Harry Gumbert	18.00	7.25	1.80
☐ 93 Norman Young and 94 Cliff Melton	18.00	7.25	1.80
☐ 95 Jimmy Ripple and 96 Bucky Walters	18.00	7.25	1.80
☐ 97 Stanley Jack and 98 Bob Klinger	18.00	7.25	1.80
☐ 99 Johnny Mize and 100 Dan Litwhiler	30.00	12.00	3.00
☐ 101 Dom Dallesandro and 102 Augie Galan	22.00	9.00	2.20
☐ 103 Bill Lee and 104 Phil Cavarretta	22.00	9.00	2.20
☐ 105 Lefty Grove and 106 Bobby Doerr	100.00	40.00	10.00
☐ 107 Frank Pytlak and 108 Dom DiMaggio	25.00	10.00	2.50
☐ 109 Jerry Priddy and 110 Johnny Murphy	22.00	9.00	2.20
☐ 111 Tommy Henrich and 112 Marius Russo	25.00	10.00	2.50
☐ 113 Frank Crosetti and	25.00	10.00	2.50

	114 John Sturm			
□115	Ival Goodman and 116 Myron McCormick	22.00	9.00	2.20
□117	Eddie Joost and 118 Ernie Koy	22.00	9.00	2.20
□119	Lloyd Waner and 120 Hank Majeski	30.00	12.00	3.00
□121	Buddy Hassett and 122 Eugene Moore	22.00	9.00	2.20
□123	Nick Etten and 124 John Rizzo	22.00	9.00	2.20
□125	Sam Chapman and 126 Wally Moses	22.00	9.00	2.20
□127	Johnny Babich and 128 Dick Siebert	22.00	9.00	2.20
□129	Nelson Potter and 130 Benny McCoy	22.00	9.00	2.20
□131	Clarence Campbell and 132 Lou Boudreau	35.00	14.00	3.50
□133	Rollie Hemsley and 134 Mel Harder	25.00	10.00	2.50
□135	Gerald Walker and 136 Joe Heving	22.00	9.00	2.20
□137	Johnny Rucker and 138 Ace Adams	22.00	9.00	2.20
□139	Morris Arnovich and 140 Carl Hubbell	45.00	18.00	4.50
□141	Lew Riggs and 142 Leo Durocher	35.00	14.00	3.50
□143	Fred Fitzsimmons and 144 Joe Vosmik	22.00	9.00	2.20
□145	Frank Crespi and 146 Jim Brown	22.00	9.00	2.20
□147	Don Heffner and 148 Harland Clift	22.00	9.00	2.20
□149	Debs Garms and 150 Elbert Fletcher	22.00	9.00	2.20

1950 Drake's

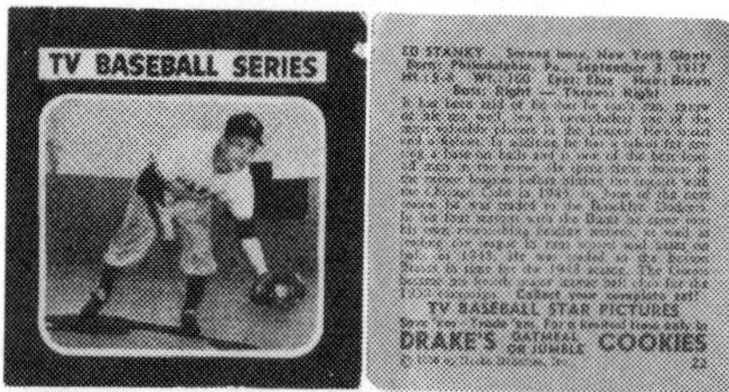

The cards in this 36-card set measure 2 1/2" by 2 1/2". The 1950 Drake's Cookies set contains numbered black and white cards. The players are pictured inside a simulated television screen and the caption "TV Baseball Series" appears on the cards. The players selected for this set show a heavy representation of players from New York teams. The ACC designation for this set is D358.

	NRMT	VG-E	GOOD
COMPLETE SET (36)	2100.00	950.00	325.00
COMMON PLAYER (1-36)	35.00	14.00	3.50
□ 1 Preacher Roe	50.00	20.00	5.00
□ 2 Clint Hartung	35.00	14.00	3.50
□ 3 Earl Torgeson	35.00	14.00	3.50
□ 4 Lou Brissie	35.00	14.00	3.50
□ 5 Duke Snider	200.00	80.00	20.00
□ 6 Roy Campanella	250.00	100.00	25.00
□ 7 Sheldon Jones	35.00	14.00	3.50
□ 8 Whitey Lockman	35.00	14.00	3.50
□ 9 Bobby Thomson	50.00	20.00	5.00
□ 10 Dick Sisler	35.00	14.00	3.50
□ 11 Gil Hodges	110.00	45.00	11.00
□ 12 Eddie Waitkus	35.00	14.00	3.50
□ 13 Bobby Kerr	35.00	14.00	3.50
□ 14 Warren Spahn	135.00	54.00	13.50
□ 15 Buddy Kerr	35.00	14.00	3.50
□ 16 Sid Gordon	35.00	14.00	3.50
□ 17 Willard Marshall	35.00	14.00	3.50
□ 18 Carl Furillo	60.00	24.00	6.00
□ 19 Pee Wee Reese	135.00	54.00	13.50
□ 20 Alvin Dark	50.00	20.00	5.00
□ 21 Del Ennis	35.00	14.00	3.50
□ 22 Ed Stanky	35.00	14.00	3.50
□ 23 Tom Henrich	50.00	20.00	5.00
□ 24 Yogi Berra	200.00	80.00	20.00
□ 25 Phil Rizzuto	135.00	54.00	13.50
□ 26 Jerry Coleman	35.00	14.00	3.50
□ 27 Joe Page	35.00	14.00	3.50
□ 28 Allie Reynolds	60.00	24.00	6.00
□ 29 Ray Scarborough	35.00	14.00	3.50
□ 30 Birdie Tebbetts	35.00	14.00	3.50
□ 31 Maurice McDermott	35.00	14.00	3.50
□ 32 Johnny Pesky	35.00	14.00	3.50
□ 33 Dom DiMaggio	60.00	24.00	6.00
□ 34 Vern Stephens	35.00	14.00	3.50
□ 35 Bob Elliott	35.00	14.00	3.50
□ 36 Enos Slaughter	135.00	54.00	13.50

1981 Drake's

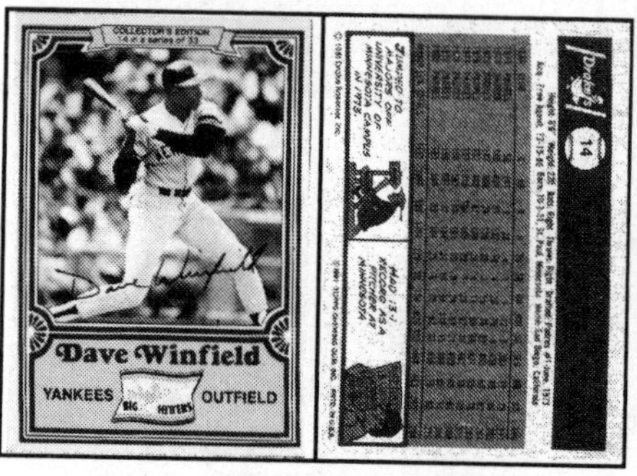

The cards in this 33-card set measure 2 1/2" by 3 1/2". The 1981 Drake's Bakeries set contains National and American League stars. Produced in conjunction with Topps and released to the public in Drake's Cakes, this set features red frames for American League players and blue frames for National League players. A Drake's Cakes logo with the words "Big Hitters" appears on the lower front of each card. The backs are quite similar to the 1981 Topps backs but contain the Drake's logo, a different card number, and a short paragraph entitled "What Makes a Big Hitter?" at the top of the card.

	MINT	EXC	G-VG
COMPLETE SET (33)	6.00	2.40	.60
COMMON PLAYER (1-33)	.05	.02	.00
□ 1 Carl Yastrzemski	.75	.30	.07
□ 2 Rod Carew	.45	.18	.04
□ 3 Pete Rose	1.00	.40	.10
□ 4 Dave Parker	.20	.08	.02
□ 5 George Brett	.60	.24	.06
□ 6 Eddie Murray	.60	.24	.06
□ 7 Mike Schmidt	.60	.24	.06
□ 8 Jim Rice	.25	.10	.02
□ 9 Fred Lynn	.15	.06	.01
□ 10 Reggie Jackson	.75	.30	.07
□ 11 Steve Garvey	.50	.20	.05
□ 12 Ken Singleton	.05	.02	.00
□ 13 Bill Buckner	.05	.02	.00
□ 14 Dave Winfield	.35	.14	.03
□ 15 Jack Clark	.20	.08	.02
□ 16 Cecil Cooper	.10	.04	.01
□ 17 Bob Horner	.15	.06	.01
□ 18 George Foster	.10	.04	.01
□ 19 Dave Kingman	.10	.04	.01
□ 20 Cesar Cedeno	.05	.02	.00
□ 21 Joe Charboneau	.05	.02	.00
□ 22 George Hendrick	.05	.02	.00
□ 23 Gary Carter	.35	.14	.03
□ 24 Al Oliver	.10	.04	.01
□ 25 Bruce Bochte	.05	.02	.00
□ 26 Jerry Mumphrey	.05	.02	.00
□ 27 Steve Kemp	.05	.02	.00
□ 28 Bob Watson	.05	.02	.00
□ 29 John Castino	.05	.02	.00
□ 30 Tony Armas	.05	.02	.00
□ 31 John Mayberry	.05	.02	.00
□ 32 Carlton Fisk	.15	.06	.01
□ 33 Lee Mazzilli	.05	.02	.00

1982 Drake's

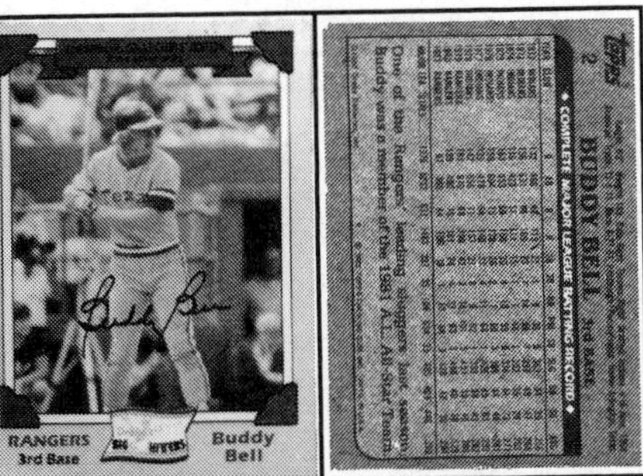

The cards in this 33-card set measure 2 1/2" by 3 1/2". The 1982 Drake's Big Hitters series cards each has the title "2nd Annual Collectors' Edition" in a ribbon design at the top of the picture area. Each color player photo has "photo mount" designs in the corners, red for the AL and green for the NL. The reverses are green and blue, the same as the regular 1982 Topps format, and the photos are larger than those of the previous year. Of the 33 hitters featured, 19 represent the National League. There are 21 returnees from the 1981 set and only one photo, that of Kennedy, is the same as that appearing in the regular Topps issue. The Drake's logo appears centered in the bottom border on the obverse.

	MINT	EXC	G-VG
COMPLETE SET (33)	6.00	2.40	.60
COMMON PLAYER (1-33)	.05	.02	.00
□ 1 Tony Armas	.05	.02	.00
□ 2 Buddy Bell	.10	.04	.01
□ 3 Johnny Bench	.50	.20	.05
□ 4 George Brett	.60	.24	.06
□ 5 Bill Buckner	.05	.02	.00
□ 6 Rod Carew	.40	.16	.04
□ 7 Gary Carter	.40	.16	.04
□ 8 Jack Clark	.20	.08	.02
□ 9 Cecil Cooper	.10	.04	.01
□ 10 Jose Cruz	.05	.02	.00
□ 11 Dwight Evans	.15	.06	.01
□ 12 Carlton Fisk	.15	.06	.01
□ 13 George Foster	.10	.04	.01
□ 14 Steve Garvey	.45	.18	.04
□ 15 Kirk Gibson	.45	.18	.04
□ 16 Mike Hargrove	.05	.02	.00
□ 17 George Hendrick	.05	.02	.00
□ 18 Bob Horner	.15	.06	.01
□ 19 Reggie Jackson	.65	.26	.06
□ 20 Terry Kennedy	.05	.02	.00
□ 21 Dave Kingman	.10	.04	.01
□ 22 Greg Luzinski	.10	.04	.01
□ 23 Bill Madlock	.05	.02	.00
□ 24 John Mayberry	.05	.02	.00
□ 25 Eddie Murray	.50	.20	.05
□ 26 Graig Nettles	.10	.04	.01
□ 27 Jim Rice	.25	.10	.02
□ 28 Pete Rose	.80	.32	.08
□ 29 Mike Schmidt	.65	.26	.06
□ 30 Ken Singleton	.05	.02	.00
□ 31 Dave Winfield	.35	.14	.03
□ 32 Butch Wynegar	.05	.02	.00
□ 33 Richie Zisk	.05	.02	.00

1983 Drake's

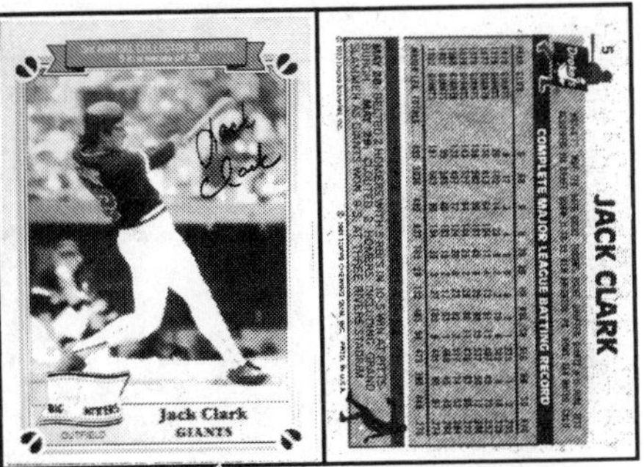

The cards in this 33-card series measure 2 1/2" by 3 1/2". For the third year in a row, Drake's Cakes, in conjunction with Topps, issued a set entitled Big Hitters. The fronts appear very similar to those of the previous two years with slight variations on the framelines and player identification sections. The backs are the same as the Topps backs of this year except for the card number and the Drake's logo.

	MINT	EXC	G-VG
COMPLETE SET (33)	5.00	2.00	.50
COMMON PLAYER (1-33)	.05	.02	.00
□ 1 Don Baylor	.10	.04	.01
□ 2 Bill Buckner	.10	.04	.01
□ 3 Rod Carew	.40	.16	.04
□ 4 Gary Carter	.40	.16	.04
□ 5 Jack Clark	.20	.08	.02
□ 6 Cecil Cooper	.10	.04	.01
□ 7 Dwight Evans	.15	.06	.01
□ 8 George Foster	.10	.04	.01
□ 9 Pedro Guerrero	.25	.10	.02
□ 10 George Hendrick	.05	.02	.00
□ 11 Bob Horner	.15	.06	.01
□ 12 Reggie Jackson	.60	.24	.06
□ 13 Steve Kemp	.05	.02	.00
□ 14 Dave Kingman	.10	.04	.01
□ 15 Bill Madlock	.05	.02	.00
□ 16 Gary Matthews	.05	.02	.00
□ 17 Hal McRae	.05	.02	.00
□ 18 Dale Murphy	.60	.24	.06
□ 19 Eddie Murray	.50	.20	.05
□ 20 Ben Oglivie	.05	.02	.00
□ 21 Al Oliver	.10	.04	.01
□ 22 Jim Rice	.25	.10	.02
□ 23 Cal Ripken	.40	.16	.04
□ 24 Pete Rose	.90	.36	.09
□ 25 Mike Schmidt	.60	.24	.06
□ 26 Ken Singleton	.05	.02	.00
□ 27 Gorman Thomas	.05	.02	.00
□ 28 Jason Thompson	.05	.02	.00
□ 29 Mookie Wilson	.05	.02	.00
□ 30 Willie Wilson	.10	.04	.01
□ 31 Dave Winfield	.35	.14	.03
□ 32 Carl Yastrzemski	.75	.30	.07
□ 33 Robin Yount	.35	.14	.03

1984 Drake's

The cards in this 33-card set measure 2 1/2" by 3 1/2". The Fourth Annual Collectors Edition of baseball cards produced by Drake's Cakes in conjunction with Topps continued this now annual set entitled Big Hitters. As in previous years, the front contains a frameline in which the title of the set, the Drake's logo, and the player's name, his team, and position appear. The cards all feature the player in a batting action pose. While the cards fronts are different from the Topps fronts of this year, the backs differ only in the card number and the use of the Drake's logo instead of the Topps logo.

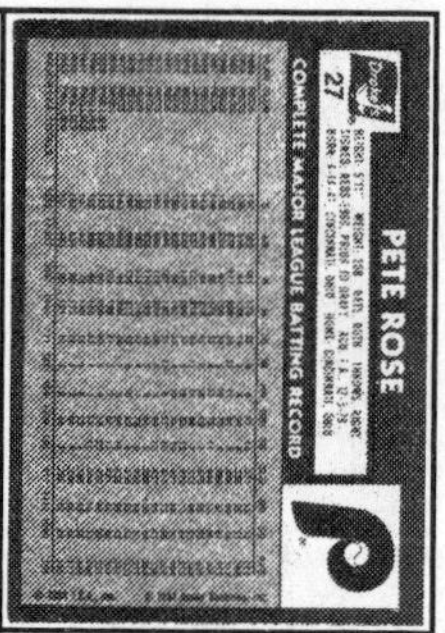

	MINT	EXC	G-VG
COMPLETE SET (33)	5.00	2.00	.50
COMMON PLAYER (1-33)	.05	.02	.00
☐ 1 Don Baylor	.10	.04	.01
☐ 2 Wade Boggs	.90	.36	.09
☐ 3 George Brett	.60	.24	.06
☐ 4 Bill Buckner	.05	.02	.00
☐ 5 Rod Carew	.40	.16	.04
☐ 6 Gary Carter	.40	.16	.04
☐ 7 Ron Cey	.05	.02	.00
☐ 8 Cecil Cooper	.10	.04	.01
☐ 9 Andre Dawson	.25	.10	.02
☐ 10 Steve Garvey	.40	.16	.04
☐ 11 Pedro Guerrero	.20	.08	.02
☐ 12 George Hendrick	.05	.02	.00
☐ 13 Keith Hernandez	.20	.08	.02
☐ 14 Bob Horner	.15	.06	.01
☐ 15 Reggie Jackson	.60	.24	.06
☐ 16 Steve Kemp	.05	.02	.00
☐ 17 Ron Kittle	.10	.04	.01
☐ 18 Greg Luzinski	.10	.04	.01
☐ 19 Fred Lynn	.10	.04	.01
☐ 20 Bill Madlock	.05	.02	.00
☐ 21 Gary Matthews	.05	.02	.00
☐ 22 Dale Murphy	.60	.24	.06
☐ 23 Eddie Murray	.50	.20	.05
☐ 24 Al Oliver	.10	.04	.01
☐ 25 Jim Rice	.25	.10	.02
☐ 26 Cal Ripken	.40	.16	.04
☐ 27 Pete Rose	.90	.36	.09
☐ 28 Mike Schmidt	.65	.26	.06
☐ 29 Darryl Strawberry	1.50	.60	.15
☐ 30 Alan Trammell	.20	.08	.02
☐ 31 Mookie Wilson	.05	.02	.00
☐ 32 Dave Winfield	.35	.14	.03
☐ 33 Robin Yount	.30	.12	.03

1985 Drake's

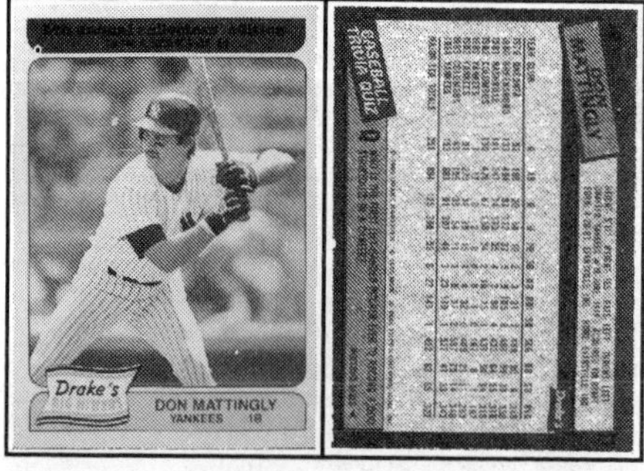

The cards in this 44-card set measure 2 1/2" by 3 1/2". The Fifth Annual Collectors Edition of baseball cards produced by Drake's Cakes in conjunction with Topps continued this apparently annual set with a new twist, for the first time, 11 pitchers were included. The "Big Hitters" are numbered 1-33 and the pitchers are numbered 34-44; each subgroup is ordered alphabetically. The cards are numbered in the upper right corner of the backs of the cards. The complete set could be obtained directly from the company by sending 2.95 with four proofs of purchase.

	MINT	EXC	G-V
COMPLETE SET (44)	10.00	4.00	1.0
COMMON PLAYER (1-33)	.05	.02	.0
COMMON PLAYER (34-44)	.10	.04	.01
☐ 1 Tony Armas	.05	.02	.0
☐ 2 Harold Baines	.10	.04	.01
☐ 3 Don Baylor	.10	.04	.01
☐ 4 George Brett	.60	.24	.06
☐ 5 Gary Carter	.40	.16	.04
☐ 6 Ron Cey	.05	.02	.00
☐ 7 Jose Cruz	.05	.02	.00
☐ 8 Alvin Davis	.15	.06	.01
☐ 9 Chili Davis	.05	.02	.00
☐ 10 Dwight Evans	.15	.06	.01
☐ 11 Steve Garvey	.40	.16	.04
☐ 12 Kirk Gibson	.35	.14	.03
☐ 13 Pedro Guerrero	.20	.08	.02
☐ 14 Tony Gwynn	.40	.16	.04
☐ 15 Keith Hernandez	.25	.10	.02
☐ 16 Kent Hrbek	.20	.08	.02
☐ 17 Reggie Jackson	.65	.26	.06
☐ 18 Gary Matthews	.05	.02	.00
☐ 19 Don Mattingly	1.25	.50	.12
☐ 20 Dale Murphy	.60	.24	.06
☐ 21 Eddie Murray	.50	.20	.05
☐ 22 Dave Parker	.15	.06	.01
☐ 23 Lance Parrish	.15	.06	.01
☐ 24 Tim Raines	.30	.12	.03
☐ 25 Jim Rice	.25	.10	.02
☐ 26 Cal Ripken	.40	.16	.04
☐ 27 Juan Samuel	.20	.08	.02
☐ 28 Ryne Sandberg	.30	.12	.03
☐ 29 Mike Schmidt	.60	.24	.06
☐ 30 Darryl Strawberry	.75	.30	.07
☐ 31 Alan Trammell	.25	.10	.02
☐ 32 Dave Winfield	.30	.12	.03
☐ 33 Robin Yount	.30	.12	.03
☐ 34 Mike Boddicker	.10	.04	.01
☐ 35 Steve Carlton	.30	.12	.03
☐ 36 Dwight Gooden	1.00	.40	.10
☐ 37 Willie Hernandez	.10	.04	.01
☐ 38 Mark Langston	.15	.06	.01
☐ 39 Dan Quisenberry	.10	.04	.01
☐ 40 Dave Righetti	.15	.06	.01
☐ 41 Tom Seaver	.35	.14	.03
☐ 42 Bob Stanley	.10	.04	.01
☐ 43 Rick Sutcliffe	.10	.04	.01
☐ 44 Bruce Sutter	.10	.04	.01

1986 Drake's

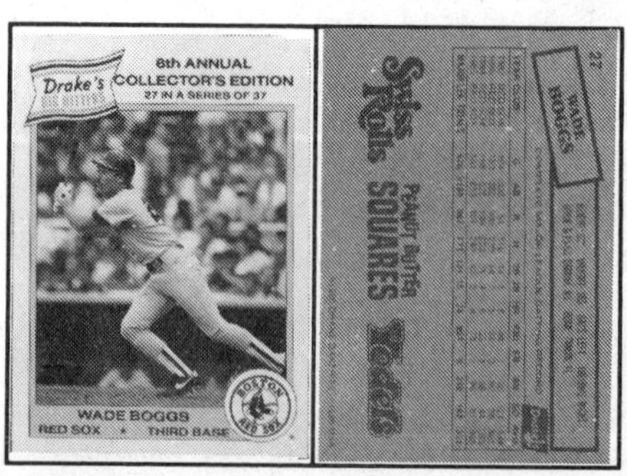

This set of 37 cards was distributed as back panels of various Drake's snack products. Each individual card measures 2 1/2" by 3 1/2". Each specially marked package features two, three, or four cards on the back. The set is easily recognized by the Drake's logo and "6th Annual Collector's Edition" at the top of the obverse. Cards are numbered on the ont and the back. Cards below are coded based on e product upon which they appeared, for example, ople Pies (AP), Cherry Pies (CP), Chocolate Donut elites (CDD), Coffee Cake Jr. (CCJ), Creme nortcakes (CS), Devil Dogs (DD), Fudge Brownies UD), Funny Bones (FB), Peanut Butter Squares BS), Powdered Sugar Donut Delites (PSDD), Ring ng Jr. (RDJ), Sunny Doodles (SD), Swiss Rolls (SR), ankee Doodles (YD), and Yodels (Y). The last nine ards are pitchers. Complete panels would be valued pproximately 25% higher than the individual card ices listed below.

	MINT	EXC	G-VG
OMPLETE SET (37)	27.00	11.00	2.70
OMMON PLAYER (1-37)	.30	.12	.03
1 Gary Carter Y	.75	.30	.07
2 Dwight Evans Y	.40	.16	.04
3 Reggie Jackson SR	1.00	.40	.10
4 Dave Parker SR	.40	.16	.04
5 Rickey Henderson FB	1.00	.40	.10
6 Pedro Guerrero FB	.40	.16	.04
7 Don Mattingly YD	3.00	1.20	.30
8 Mike Marshall YD	.40	.16	.04
9 Keith Moreland YD	.30	.12	.03
10 Keith Hernandez CS	.60	.24	.06
11 Cal Ripken CS	.75	.30	.07
12 Dale Murphy RDJ	1.00	.40	.10
13 Jim Rice RDJ	.50	.20	.05
14 George Brett CCJ	.75	.30	.07
15 Tim Raines CCJ	.60	.24	.06
16 Darryl Strawberry DD	1.25	.50	.12
17 Bill Buckner DD	.30	.12	.03
18 Dave Winfield AP	.50	.20	.05
19 Ryne Sandberg AP	.50	.20	.05
20 Steve Balboni AP	.30	.12	.03
21 Tommy Herr AP	.30	.12	.03
22 Pete Rose CP	1.25	.50	.12
23 Willie McGee CP	.40	.16	.04
24 Harold Baines CP	.40	.16	.04
25 Eddie Murray CP	.75	.30	.07
26 Mike Schmidt SD/FUD	1.25	.50	.12
27 Wade Boggs SD/FUD	2.00	.80	.20
28 Kirk Gibson SD/FUD	.60	.24	.06
29 Bret Saberhagen PBS	.50	.20	.05
30 John Tudor PBS	.40	.16	.04
31 Orel Hershiser PBS	.75	.30	.07
32 Ron Guidry CDD	.40	.16	.04
33 Nolan Ryan CDD	.75	.30	.07
34 Dave Stieb CDD	.40	.16	.04
35 Dwight Gooden SDD	1.00	.40	.10
36 Fern.Valenzuela SDD	.50	.20	.05
37 Tom Browning SDD	.40	.16	.04

1987 Drake's

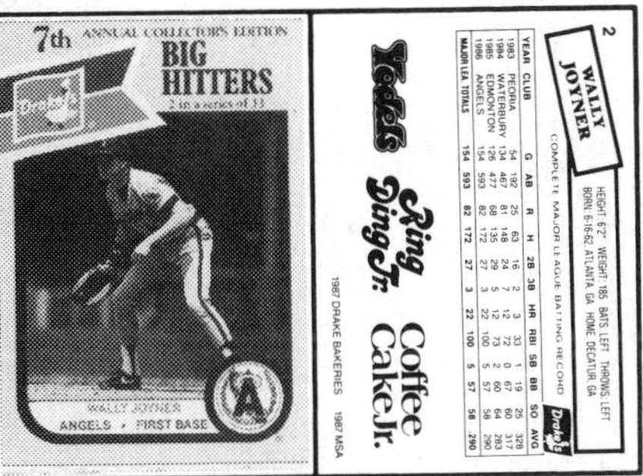

This 33-card set features 25 top hitters and eight top pitchers. Cards were printed in groups of two, three, or four on the backs of Drake's bakery products. Individual cards measure 2 1/2" by 3 1/2" and tout the 7th annual edition. Card backs feature year-by-year season statistics. The cards are numbered such that the pitchers are listed numerically last. Complete panels would be valued approximately 25% higher than the individual card prices listed below.

	MINT	EXC	G-VG
COMPLETE SET (33)	25.00	10.00	2.50
COMMON PLAYER (1-33)	.30	.12	.03
□ 1 Darryl Strawberry	1.25	.50	.12
□ 2 Wally Joyner	1.00	.40	.10
□ 3 Von Hayes	.30	.12	.03
□ 4 Jose Canseco	2.50	1.00	.25
□ 5 Dave Winfield	.60	.24	.06
□ 6 Cal Ripken	.75	.30	.07
□ 7 Keith Moreland	.30	.12	.03
□ 8 Don Mattingly	2.50	1.00	.25
□ 9 Willie McGee	.40	.16	.04
□ 10 Keith Hernandez	.60	.24	.06
□ 11 Tony Gwynn	.90	.36	.09
□ 12 Rickey Henderson	.90	.36	.09
□ 13 Dale Murphy	.90	.36	.09
□ 14 George Brett	.90	.36	.09
□ 15 Jim Rice	.50	.20	.05
□ 16 Wade Boggs	2.00	.80	.20
□ 17 Kevin Bass	.30	.12	.03
□ 18 Dave Parker	.40	.16	.04
□ 19 Kirby Puckett	.90	.36	.09
□ 20 Gary Carter	.60	.24	.06
□ 21 Ryne Sandberg	.60	.24	.06
□ 22 Harold Baines	.40	.16	.04
□ 23 Mike Schmidt	1.00	.40	.10
□ 24 Eddie Murray	.75	.30	.07
□ 25 Steve Sax	.40	.16	.04
□ 26 Dwight Gooden	.75	.30	.07
□ 27 Jack Morris	.40	.16	.04
□ 28 Ron Darling	.40	.16	.04
□ 29 Fernando Valenzuela	.50	.20	.05
□ 30 John Tudor	.40	.16	.04
□ 31 Roger Clemens	.75	.30	.07
□ 32 Nolan Ryan	.75	.30	.07
□ 33 Mike Scott	.50	.20	.05

1988 Drake's Big Hitters

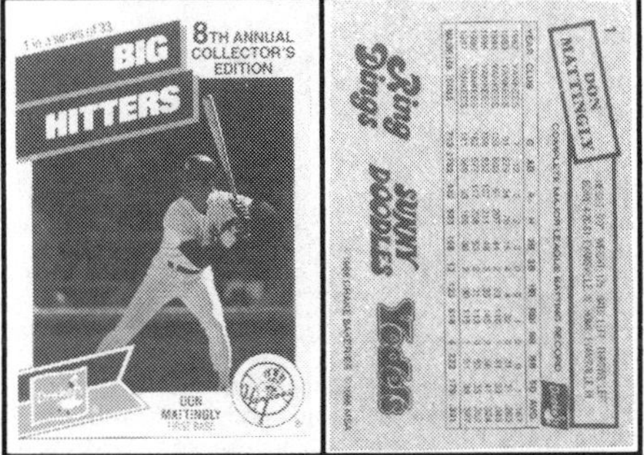

This 33-card set features 27 top hitters and six top pitchers. Cards were printed in groups of two, three, or four on the backs of Drake's bakery products. Individual cards measure approximately 2 1/2" by 3 1/2" and tout the 8th annual edition. Card backs feature year-by-year season statistics. The cards are numbered such that the pitchers are listed numerically last. The product affiliations are as follows, 1-2 Ring Dings, 3-4 Devil Dogs, 5-6 Coffee Cakes, 7-9 Yankee Doodles, 10-11 Funny Bones, 12-14 Fudge Brownies, 15-18 Cherry Pies, 19-21 Sunny Doodles, 22- 24 Powdered Sugar Donuts, 25-27 Chocolate Donuts, 28-29 Yodels, and 30-33 Apple Pies. Complete panels would be valued approximately 25% higher than the individual card prices listed below.

	MINT	EXC	G-VG
COMPLETE SET (33)	25.00	10.00	2.50
COMMON PLAYER (1-33)	.30	.12	.03

□ 1 Don Mattingly	2.50	1.00	.25
□ 2 Tim Raines	.60	.24	.06
□ 3 Darryl Strawberry	1.25	.50	.12
□ 4 Wade Boggs	2.00	.80	.20
□ 5 Keith Hernandez	.60	.24	.06
□ 6 Mark McGwire	1.00	.40	.10
□ 7 Rickey Henderson	.90	.36	.09
□ 8 Mike Schmidt	.90	.36	.09
□ 9 Dwight Evans	.40	.16	.04
□ 10 Gary Carter	.60	.24	.06
□ 11 Paul Molitor	.50	.20	.05
□ 12 Dave Winfield	.60	.24	.06
□ 13 Alan Trammell	.50	.20	.05
□ 14 Tony Gwynn	.75	.30	.07
□ 15 Dale Murphy	.75	.30	.07
□ 16 Andre Dawson	.50	.20	.05
□ 17 Von Hayes	.30	.12	.03
□ 18 Willie Randolph	.30	.12	.03
□ 19 Kirby Puckett	.90	.36	.09
□ 20 Juan Samuel	.30	.12	.03
□ 21 Eddie Murray	.75	.30	.07
□ 22 George Bell	.40	.16	.04
□ 23 Larry Sheets	.30	.12	.03
□ 24 Eric Davis	.90	.36	.09
□ 25 Cal Ripken	.60	.24	.06
□ 26 Pedro Guerrero	.40	.16	.04
□ 27 Will Clark	1.00	.40	.10
□ 28 Dwight Gooden	.90	.36	.09
□ 29 Frank Viola	.50	.20	.05
□ 30 Roger Clemens	.75	.30	.07
□ 31 Rick Sutcliffe	.40	.16	.04
□ 32 Jack Morris	.40	.16	.04
□ 33 John Tudor	.40	.16	.04

1966 East Hills Pirates

The 1966 East Hills Pirates set consists of 25 large (3 1/4" by 4 1/4"), full color photos of Pittsburgh Pirate ballplayers. These blank-backed cards are numbered in the lower right corner according to the uniform number of the individual depicted. The set was distributed by various stores located in the East Hills Shopping Center. The ACC catalog number for this set is F405.

	NRMT	VG-E	GOOD
COMPLETE SET (25)	25.00	10.00	2.50
COMMON PLAYER (1-45)	.40	.16	.04
□ 3 Harry Walker MG	.60	.24	.06
□ 7 Bob Bailey	.40	.16	.04
□ 8 Willie Stargell	6.00	2.40	.60
□ 9 Bill Mazeroski	2.00	.80	.20
□ 10 Jim Pagliaroni	.40	.16	.04
□ 11 Jose Pagan	.40	.16	.04
□ 12 Jerry May	.40	.16	.04
□ 14 Gene Alley	.60	.24	.06
□ 15 Manny Mota	.75	.30	.07
□ 16 Andy Rodgers	.40	.16	.04
□ 17 Donn Clendenon	.60	.24	.06
□ 18 Matty Alou	.75	.30	.07
□ 19 Pete Mikkelsen	.40	.16	.04
□ 20 Jesse Gonder	.40	.16	.04
□ 21 Bob Clemente	10.00	4.00	1.00
□ 22 Woody Fryman	.40	.16	.0
□ 24 Jerry Lynch	.40	.16	.0
□ 25 Tommie Sisk	.40	.16	.0
□ 26 Roy Face	1.00	.40	.1
□ 28 Steve Blass	.60	.24	.0
□ 32 Vernon Law	1.00	.40	.1
□ 34 Al McBean	.40	.16	.0
□ 39 Bob Veale	.60	.24	.0
□ 43 Don Cardwell	.40	.16	.0
□ 45 Gene Michael	.60	.24	.0

1959 Fleer

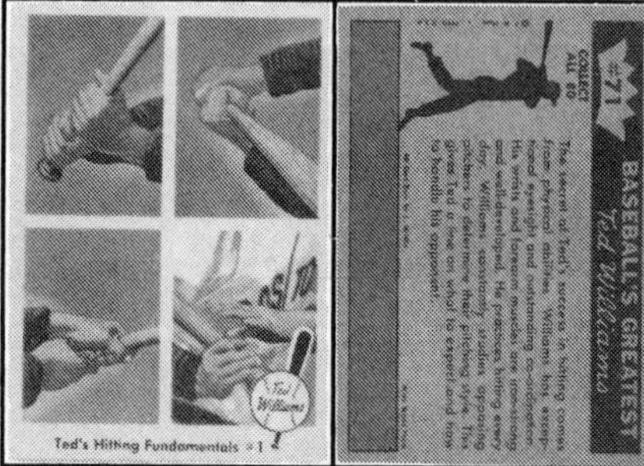

The cards in this 80-card set measure 2 1/2" by 3 1/2". The 1959 Fleer set, designated as R418-1 in the ACC, portrays the life of Ted Williams. The wording of the wrapper, "Baseball's Greatest Series," has led to speculation that Fleer contemplated similar sets honoring other baseball immortals, but chose to develop instead the format of the 1960 and 1961 issues. Card number 68, which was withdrawn early in production, is considered scarce and has even been counterfeited; the fake has a rosy coloration and a cross-hatch pattern visible over the picture area.

	NRMT	VG-E	GOOD
COMPLETE SET (80)	375.00	150.00	37.0
COMMON CARDS (1-80)	1.75	.70	.1
□ 1 The Early Years	9.00	1.00	.2
□ 2 Ted's Idol Babe Ruth	5.00	2.00	.5
□ 3 Practice Makes Perfect	1.75	.70	.1
□ 4 Learns Fine Points	1.75	.70	.1
□ 5 Ted's Fame Spreads	1.75	.70	.1
□ 6 Ted Turns Pro	1.75	.70	.1
□ 7 From Mound to Plate	1.75	.70	.1
□ 8 1937 First Full Season	1.75	.70	.1
□ 9 First Step to Majors	1.75	.70	.1
□ 10 Gunning as Pastime	1.75	.70	.1
□ 11 First Spring Training (with Jimmie Foxx)	3.00	1.20	.3
□ 12 Burning Up Minors	1.75	.70	.1
□ 13 1939 Shows Will Stay	1.75	.70	.1
□ 14 Outstanding Rookie '39	1.75	.70	.1
□ 15 Licks Sophomore Jinx	1.75	.70	.1
□ 16 1941 Greatest Year	1.75	.70	.1
□ 17 How Ted Hit .400	1.75	.70	.1
□ 18 1941 All Star Hero	1.75	.70	.1
□ 19 Ted Wins Triple Crown	1.75	.70	.1
□ 20 On to Naval Training	1.75	.70	.1
□ 21 Honors for Williams	1.75	.70	.1
□ 22 1944 Ted Solos	1.75	.70	.1
□ 23 Williams Wins Wings	1.75	.70	.1
□ 24 1945 Sharpshooter	1.75	.70	.1
□ 25 1945 Ted Discharged	1.75	.70	.1
□ 26 Off to Flying Start	1.75	.70	.1
□ 27 7/9/46 One Man Show	1.75	.70	.1
□ 28 The Williams Shift	1.75	.70	.1
□ 29 Ted Hits for Cycle	1.75	.70	.1
□ 30 Beating Williams Shift	1.75	.70	.1
□ 31 Sox Lose Series	1.75	.70	.1
□ 32 Most Valuable Player	1.75	.70	.1
□ 33 Another Triple Crown	1.75	.70	.1

34 Runs Scored Record	1.75	.70	.17
35 Sox Miss Pennant	1.75	.70	.17
36 Banner Year for Ted	1.75	.70	.17
37 1949 Sox Miss Again	1.75	.70	.17
38 1949 Power Rampage	1.75	.70	.17
39 1950 Great Start	1.75	.70	.17
40 Ted Crashes into Wall	1.75	.70	.17
41 1950 Ted Recovers	1.75	.70	.17
42 Slowed by Injury	1.75	.70	.17
43 Double Play Lead	1.75	.70	.17
44 Back to Marines	1.75	.70	.17
45 Farewell to Baseball	1.75	.70	.17
46 Ready for Combat	1.75	.70	.17
47 Ted Crash Lands Jet	1.75	.70	.17
48 1953 Ted Returns	1.75	.70	.17
49 Smash Return	1.75	.70	.17
50 1954 Spring Injury	1.75	.70	.17
51 Ted is Patched Up	1.75	.70	.17
52 1954 Ted's Comeback	1.75	.70	.17
53 Comeback is Success	1.75	.70	.17
54 Ted Hooks Big One	1.75	.70	.17
55 Retirement "No Go"	1.75	.70	.17
56 2000th Hit	1.75	.70	.17
57 400th Homer	1.75	.70	.17
58 Williams Hits .388	1.75	.70	.17
59 Hot September for Ted	1.75	.70	.17
60 More Records for Ted	1.75	.70	.17
61 1957 Outfielder Ted	1.75	.70	.17
62 1958 Sixth Batting Title	1.75	.70	.17
63 Ted's All-Star Record	1.75	.70	.17
64 Daughter and Daddy	1.75	.70	.17
65 1958 August 30	1.75	.70	.17
66 1958 Powerhouse	1.75	.70	.17
67 Two Famous Fishermen	3.00	1.20	.30
68 Ted Signs for 1959	225.00	90.00	22.00
69 A Future Ted Williams	1.75	.70	.17
70 Williams and Thorpe	3.00	1.20	.30
71 Hitting Fund. 1	1.75	.70	.17
72 Hitting Fund. 2	1.75	.70	.17
73 Hitting Fund. 3	1.75	.70	.17
74 Here's How	1.75	.70	.17
75 Williams' Value to Sox	1.75	.70	.17
76 On Base Record	1.75	.70	.17
77 Ted Relaxes	1.75	.70	.17
78 Honors for Williams	1.75	.70	.17
79 Where Ted Stands	1.75	.70	.17
80 Ted's Goals for 1959	3.00	1.20	.30

1960 Fleer

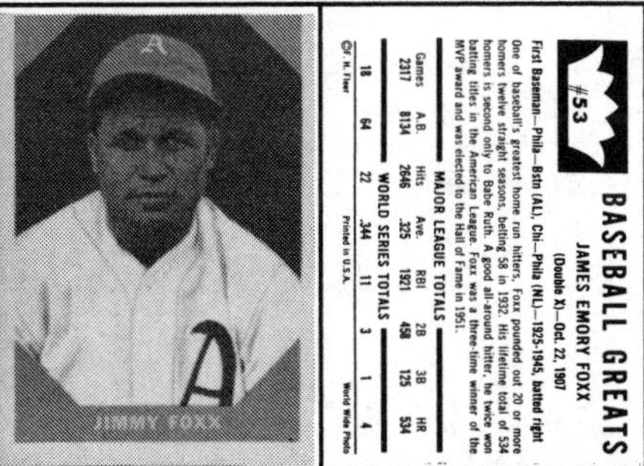

The cards in this 79-card set measure 2 1/2" by 3 1/2". The cards from the 1960 Fleer series of Baseball Greats are sometimes mistaken for 1930s cards by collectors not familiar with this set. The cards each contain a tinted photo of a baseball immortal, and were issued in one series. There are no known scarcities, although a number 80 card (Pepper Martin reverse with either a Tinker, Collins, or Grove obverse) exists (this is not considered part of the set). The catalog designation for 1960 Fleer is R418-2.

	NRMT	VG-E	GOOD
COMPLETE SET (79)	200.00	80.00	20.00
COMMON PLAYER (1-79)	1.25	.50	.12

□ 1 Napoleon Lajoie	9.00	2.00	.40
□ 2 Christy Mathewson	5.00	2.00	.50
□ 3 George H. Ruth	25.00	10.00	2.50
□ 4 Carl Hubbell	2.00	.80	.20
□ 5 Grover Alexander	2.00	.80	.20
□ 6 Walter P. Johnson	5.00	2.00	.50
□ 7 Charles A. Bender	1.25	.50	.12
□ 8 Roger P. Bresnahan	1.25	.50	.12
□ 9 Mordecai P. Brown	1.25	.50	.12
□ 10 Tristram Speaker	2.00	.80	.20
□ 11 Joseph(Arky) Vaughan	1.25	.50	.12
□ 12 Zachariah Wheat	1.25	.50	.12
□ 13 George Sisler	1.25	.50	.12
□ 14 Connie Mack	2.00	.80	.20
□ 15 Clark C. Griffith	1.25	.50	.12
□ 16 Louis Boudreau	2.00	.80	.20
□ 17 Ernest Lombardi	1.25	.50	.12
□ 18 Henry Manush	1.25	.50	.12
□ 19 Martin Marion	1.25	.50	.12
□ 20 Edward Collins	1.25	.50	.12
□ 21 James Maranville	1.25	.50	.12
□ 22 Joseph Medwick	1.25	.50	.12
□ 23 Edward Barrow	1.25	.50	.12
□ 24 Gordon Cochrane	2.00	.80	.20
□ 25 James J. Collins	1.25	.50	.12
□ 26 Robert Feller	5.00	2.00	.50
□ 27 Lucius Appling	2.00	.80	.20
□ 28 Lou Gehrig	12.00	5.00	1.20
□ 29 Charles Hartnett	1.25	.50	.12
□ 30 Charles Klein	1.25	.50	.12
□ 31 Anthony Lazzeri	1.25	.50	.12
□ 32 Aloysius Simmons	1.25	.50	.12
□ 33 Wilbert Robinson	1.25	.50	.12
□ 34 Edgar Rice	1.25	.50	.12
□ 35 Herbert Pennock	1.25	.50	.12
□ 36 Melvin Ott	2.00	.80	.20
□ 37 Frank O'Doul	1.25	.50	.12
□ 38 John Mize	2.00	.80	.20
□ 39 Edmund Miller	1.25	.50	.12
□ 40 Joseph Tinker	1.25	.50	.12
□ 41 John Baker	1.25	.50	.12
□ 42 Tyrus Cobb	12.00	5.00	1.20
□ 43 Paul Derringer	1.25	.50	.12
□ 44 Adrian Anson	1.25	.50	.12
□ 45 James Bottomley	1.25	.50	.12
□ 46 Edward S. Plank	1.25	.50	.12
□ 47 Denton (Cy) Young	3.50	1.40	.35
□ 48 Hack Wilson	2.00	.80	.20
□ 49 Edward Walsh	1.25	.50	.12
□ 50 Frank Chance	1.25	.50	.12
□ 51 Arthur Vance	1.25	.50	.12
□ 52 William Terry	2.00	.80	.20
□ 53 James Foxx	3.00	1.20	.30
□ 54 Vernon Gomez	2.00	.80	.20
□ 55 Branch Rickey	1.25	.50	.12
□ 56 Raymond Schalk	1.25	.50	.12
□ 57 John Evers	1.25	.50	.12
□ 58 Charles Gehringer	2.00	.80	.20
□ 59 Burleigh Grimes	1.25	.50	.12
□ 60 Robert (Lefty) Grove	2.50	1.00	.25
□ 61 George Waddell	1.25	.50	.12
□ 62 John (Honus) Wagner	5.00	2.00	.50
□ 63 Charles(Red) Ruffing	1.25	.50	.12
□ 64 Kenesaw M. Landis	1.25	.50	.12
□ 65 Harry Heilmann	1.25	.50	.12
□ 66 John McGraw	2.00	.80	.20
□ 67 Hugh Jennings	1.25	.50	.12
□ 68 Harold Newhouser	1.25	.50	.12
□ 69 Waite Hoyt	1.25	.50	.12
□ 70 Louis (Bobo) Newsom	1.25	.50	.12
□ 71 Howard(Earl) Averill	1.25	.50	.12
□ 72 Theodore Williams	20.00	8.00	2.00
□ 73 Warren Giles	1.25	.50	.12
□ 74 Ford Frick	1.25	.50	.12
□ 75 Hazen (Kiki) Cuyler	1.25	.50	.12
□ 76 Paul Waner	1.25	.50	.12
□ 77 Harold(Pie) Traynor	1.25	.50	.12
□ 78 Lloyd Waner	1.25	.50	.12
□ 79 Ralph Kiner	2.50	1.00	.25
□ 80 Pepper Martin * (Collins, Tinker, or Grove pictured)	150.00	60.00	15.00

1961 Fleer

The cards in this 154-card set measure 2 1/2" by 3 1/2". In 1961, Fleer continued its Baseball Greats format by issuing this series of cards. The set was

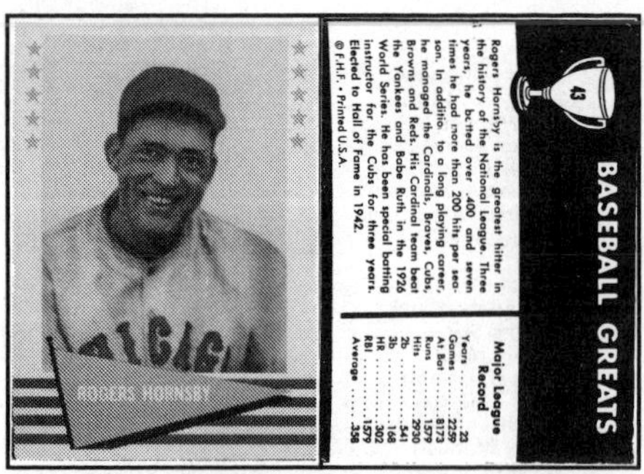

released in two distinct series, 1-88 and 89-154 (of which the last is more difficult to obtain). The players within each series are conveniently numbered in alphabetical order. It appears that this set continued to be issued the following year by Fleer. The catalog number for this set is F418-3.

	NRMT	VG-E	GOOD
COMPLETE SET (154)	400.00	160.00	40.00
COMMON PLAYER (1-88)	1.25	.50	.12
COMMON PLAYER (89-154)	2.50	1.00	.25
☐ 1 Baker/Cobb/Wheat (checklist back)	12.00	2.00	.40
☐ 2 Grover C. Alexander	2.00	.80	.20
☐ 3 Nick Altrock	1.25	.50	.12
☐ 4 Cap Anson	1.25	.50	.12
☐ 5 Earl Averill	1.25	.50	.12
☐ 6 Frank Baker	1.25	.50	.12
☐ 7 Dave Bancroft	1.25	.50	.12
☐ 8 Chief Bender	1.25	.50	.12
☐ 9 Jim Bottomley	1.25	.50	.12
☐ 10 Roger Bresnahan	1.25	.50	.12
☐ 11 Mordecai Brown	1.25	.50	.12
☐ 12 Max Carey	1.25	.50	.12
☐ 13 Jack Chesbro	1.25	.50	.12
☐ 14 Ty Cobb	12.00	5.00	1.20
☐ 15 Mickey Cochrane	2.00	.80	.20
☐ 16 Eddie Collins	1.25	.50	.12
☐ 17 Earle Combs	1.25	.50	.12
☐ 18 Charles Comiskey	1.25	.50	.12
☐ 19 Kiki Cuyler	1.25	.50	.12
☐ 20 Paul Derringer	1.25	.50	.12
☐ 21 Howard Ehmke	1.25	.50	.12
☐ 22 W. Evans	1.25	.50	.12
☐ 23 Johnny Evers	1.25	.50	.12
☐ 24 Urban Faber	1.25	.50	.12
☐ 25 Bob Feller	5.00	2.00	.50
☐ 26 Wes Ferrell	1.25	.50	.12
☐ 27 Lew Fonseca	1.25	.50	.12
☐ 28 Jimmy Foxx	3.00	1.20	.30
☐ 29 Ford Frick	1.25	.50	.12
☐ 30 Frank Frisch	2.00	.80	.20
☐ 31 Lou Gehrig	12.00	5.00	1.20
☐ 32 Charlie Gehringer	2.00	.80	.20
☐ 33 Warren Giles	1.25	.50	.12
☐ 34 Lefty Gomez	2.00	.80	.20
☐ 35 Goose Goslin	1.25	.50	.12
☐ 36 Clark Griffith	1.25	.50	.12
☐ 37 Burleigh Grimes	1.25	.50	.12
☐ 38 Lefty Grove	2.50	1.00	.25
☐ 39 Chick Hafey	1.25	.50	.12
☐ 40 Jesse Haines	1.25	.50	.12
☐ 41 Gabby Hartnett	1.25	.50	.12
☐ 42 Harry Heilmann	1.25	.50	.12
☐ 43 Rogers Hornsby	3.00	1.20	.30
☐ 44 Waite Hoyt	1.25	.50	.12
☐ 45 Carl Hubbell	2.00	.80	.20
☐ 46 Miller Huggins	1.25	.50	.12
☐ 47 Hugh Jennings	1.25	.50	.12
☐ 48 Ban Johnson	1.25	.50	.12
☐ 49 Walter Johnson	5.00	2.00	.50
☐ 50 Ralph Kiner	2.50	1.00	.25
☐ 51 Chuck Klein	1.25	.50	.12
☐ 52 Johnny Kling	1.25	.50	.12
☐ 53 K.M. Landis	1.25	.50	.12
☐ 54 Tony Lazzeri	1.25	.50	.12
☐ 55 Ernie Lombardi	1.25	.50	.12
☐ 56 Dolf Luque	1.25	.50	.12
☐ 57 Heine Manush	1.25	.50	.12
☐ 58 Marty Marion	1.25	.50	.12
☐ 59 Christy Mathewson	5.00	2.00	.50
☐ 60 John McGraw	2.00	.80	.20
☐ 61 Joe Medwick	1.25	.50	
☐ 62 E. (Bing) Miller	1.25	.50	
☐ 63 Johnny Mize	2.00	.80	
☐ 64 John Mostil	1.25	.50	
☐ 65 Art Nehf	1.25	.50	
☐ 66 Hal Newhouser	1.25	.50	
☐ 67 D. (Bobo) Newsom	1.25	.50	
☐ 68 Mel Ott	2.00	.80	
☐ 69 Allie Reynolds	1.25	.50	
☐ 70 Sam Rice	1.25	.50	
☐ 71 Eppa Rixey	1.25	.50	
☐ 72 Edd Roush	1.25	.50	
☐ 73 Schoolboy Rowe	1.25	.50	
☐ 74 Red Ruffing	1.25	.50	
☐ 75 Babe Ruth	25.00	10.00	
☐ 76 Joe Sewell	1.25	.50	
☐ 77 Al Simmons	1.25	.50	
☐ 78 George Sisler	1.25	.50	
☐ 79 Tris Speaker	2.00	.80	
☐ 80 Fred Toney	1.25	.50	
☐ 81 Dazzy Vance	1.25	.50	
☐ 82 Jim Vaughn	1.25	.50	
☐ 83 Ed Walsh	1.25	.50	
☐ 84 Lloyd Waner	1.25	.50	
☐ 85 Paul Waner	1.25	.50	
☐ 86 Zack Wheat	1.25	.50	
☐ 87 Hack Wilson	2.00	.80	
☐ 88 Jimmy Wilson	1.25	.50	
☐ 89 Sisler and Traynor (checklist back)	10.00	2.00	
☐ 90 Babe Adams	2.50	1.00	
☐ 91 Dale Alexander	2.50	1.00	
☐ 92 Jim Bagby	2.50	1.00	
☐ 93 Ossie Bluege	2.50	1.00	
☐ 94 Lou Boudreau	5.00	2.00	
☐ 95 Tom Bridges	2.50	1.00	
☐ 96 Donie Bush	2.50	1.00	
☐ 97 Dolph Camilli	2.50	1.00	
☐ 98 Frank Chance	3.50	1.40	
☐ 99 Jimmy Collins	3.50	1.40	
☐ 100 Stan Coveleskie	3.50	1.40	
☐ 101 Hugh Critz	2.50	1.00	
☐ 102 Alvin Crowder	2.50	1.00	
☐ 103 Joe Dugan	2.50	1.00	
☐ 104 Bibb Falk	2.50	1.00	
☐ 105 Rick Ferrell	3.50	1.40	
☐ 106 Art Fletcher	2.50	1.00	
☐ 107 Dennis Galehouse	2.50	1.00	
☐ 108 Chick Galloway	2.50	1.00	
☐ 109 Mule Haas	2.50	1.00	
☐ 110 Stan Hack	2.50	1.00	
☐ 111 Bump Hadley	2.50	1.00	
☐ 112 Billy B. Hamilton	3.50	1.40	
☐ 113 Joe Hauser	2.50	1.00	
☐ 114 Babe Herman	2.50	1.00	
☐ 115 Travis Jackson	4.50	1.80	
☐ 116 Eddie Joost	2.50	1.00	
☐ 117 Addie Joss	4.50	1.80	
☐ 118 Joe Judge	2.50	1.00	
☐ 119 Joe Kuhel	2.50	1.00	
☐ 120 Napoleon Lajoie	7.50	3.00	
☐ 121 Dutch Leonard	2.50	1.00	
☐ 122 Ted Lyons	3.50	1.40	
☐ 123 Connie Mack	7.50	3.00	
☐ 124 Rabbit Maranville	3.50	1.40	
☐ 125 Fred Marberry	2.50	1.00	
☐ 126 Joe McGinnity	4.50	1.80	
☐ 127 Oscar Melillo	2.50	1.00	
☐ 128 Ray Mueller	2.50	1.00	
☐ 129 Kid Nichols	3.50	1.40	
☐ 130 Lefty O'Doul	2.50	1.00	
☐ 131 Bob O'Farrell	2.50	1.00	
☐ 132 Roger Peckinpaugh	2.50	1.00	
☐ 133 Herb Pennock	3.50	1.40	
☐ 134 George Pipgras	2.50	1.00	
☐ 135 Eddie Plank	4.50	1.80	
☐ 136 Ray Schalk	3.50	1.40	
☐ 137 Hal Schumacher	2.50	1.00	
☐ 138 Luke Sewell	2.50	1.00	
☐ 139 Bob Shawkey	2.50	1.00	
☐ 140 Riggs Stephenson	2.50	1.00	
☐ 141 Billy Sullivan	2.50	1.00	
☐ 142 Bill Terry	6.00	2.40	
☐ 143 Joe Tinker	3.50	1.40	
☐ 144 Pie Traynor	4.50	1.80	
☐ 145 Hal Trosky	2.50	1.00	
☐ 146 George Uhle	2.50	1.00	
☐ 147 Johnny VanderMeer	3.50	1.40	
☐ 148 Arky Vaughan	3.50	1.40	
☐ 149 Rube Waddell	3.50	1.40	
☐ 150 Honus Wagner	12.00	5.00	
☐ 151 Dixie Walker	2.50	1.00	
☐ 152 Ted Williams	30.00	12.00	
☐ 153 Cy Young	9.00	3.75	
☐ 154 Ross Young	6.00	2.40	

1963 Fleer

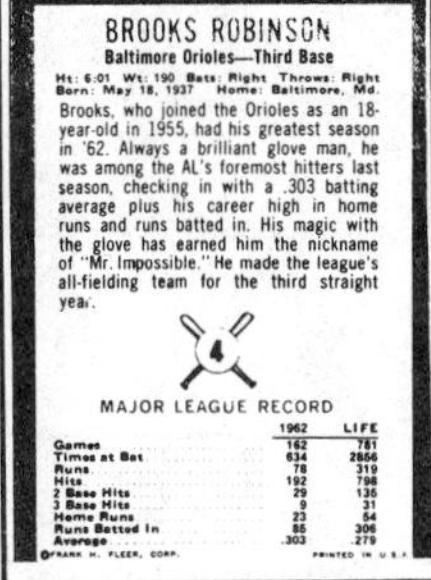

The cards in this 66-card set measure 2 1/2" by 3 1/2". The Fleer set of current baseball players was marketed in 1963 in a gum card-style waxed wrapper package which contained a cherry cookie instead of gum. The cards were printed in sheets of 66 with the scarce card of Adcock apparently being replaced by the unnumbered checklist card for the final press run. The complete set price includes the checklist card. The catalog designation for this set is R418-4.

	NRMT	VG-E	GOOD
COMPLETE SET (67)	500.00	200.00	60.00
COMMON PLAYER (1-66)	1.75	.70	.17
□ 1 Steve Barber	4.00	1.00	.20
□ 2 Ron Hansen	1.75	.70	.17
□ 3 Milt Pappas	2.50	1.00	.25
□ 4 Brooks Robinson	18.00	7.25	1.80
□ 5 Willie Mays	40.00	16.00	4.00
□ 6 Lou Clinton	1.75	.70	.17
□ 7 Bill Monbouquette	1.75	.70	.17
□ 8 Carl Yastrzemski	40.00	16.00	4.00
□ 9 Ray Herbert	1.75	.70	.17
□ 10 Jim Landis	1.75	.70	.17
□ 11 Dick Donovan	1.75	.70	.17
□ 12 Tito Francona	1.75	.70	.17
□ 13 Jerry Kindall	1.75	.70	.17
□ 14 Frank Lary	2.50	1.00	.25
□ 15 Dick Howser	3.00	1.20	.30
□ 16 Jerry Lumpe	1.75	.70	.17
□ 17 Norm Siebern	1.75	.70	.17
□ 18 Don Lee	1.75	.70	.17
□ 19 Albie Pearson	1.75	.70	.17
□ 20 Bob Rodgers	2.50	1.00	.25
□ 21 Leon Wagner	1.75	.70	.17
□ 22 Jim Kaat	4.00	1.60	.40
□ 23 Vic Power	1.75	.70	.17
□ 24 Rich Rollins	1.75	.70	.17
□ 25 Bobby Richardson	4.50	1.80	.45
□ 26 Ralph Terry	2.50	1.00	.25
□ 27 Tom Cheney	1.75	.70	.17
□ 28 Chuck Cottier	1.75	.70	.17
□ 29 Jim Piersall	3.00	1.20	.30
□ 30 Dave Stenhouse	1.75	.70	.17
□ 31 Glen Hobbie	1.75	.70	.17
□ 32 Ron Santo	3.00	1.20	.30
□ 33 Gene Freese	1.75	.70	.17
□ 34 Vada Pinson	3.00	1.20	.30
□ 35 Bob Purkey	1.75	.70	.17
□ 36 Joe Amalfitano	1.75	.70	.17
□ 37 Bob Aspromonte	1.75	.70	.17
□ 38 Dick Farrell	1.75	.70	.17
□ 39 Al Spangler	1.75	.70	.17
□ 40 Tommy Davis	2.50	1.00	.25
□ 41 Don Drysdale	13.50	6.00	1.00
□ 42 Sandy Koufax	35.00	14.00	3.50
□ 43 Maury Wills	21.00	8.50	2.10
□ 44 Frank Bolling	1.75	.70	.17
□ 45 Warren Spahn	15.00	6.00	1.50
□ 46 Joe Adcock SP	75.00	30.00	7.50
□ 47 Roger Craig	3.50	1.40	.35
□ 48 Al Jackson	1.75	.70	.17
□ 49 Rod Kanehl	1.75	.70	.17
□ 50 Ruben Amaro	1.75	.70	.17
□ 51 Johnny Callison	2.50	1.00	.25
□ 52 Clay Dalrymple	1.75	.70	.17
□ 53 Don Demeter	1.75	.70	.17
□ 54 Art Mahaffey	1.75	.70	.17
□ 55 Smokey Burgess	2.50	1.00	.25
□ 56 Roberto Clemente	35.00	14.00	3.50
□ 57 Roy Face	3.00	1.20	.30
□ 58 Vern Law	2.50	1.00	.25
□ 59 Bill Mazeroski	4.00	1.60	.40
□ 60 Ken Boyer	4.00	1.60	.40
□ 61 Bob Gibson	13.50	6.00	1.00
□ 62 Gene Oliver	1.75	.70	.17
□ 63 Bill White	2.50	1.00	.25
□ 64 Orlando Cepeda	4.50	1.80	.45
□ 65 Jim Davenport	2.50	1.00	.25
□ 66 Billy O'Dell	1.75	.70	.17
□ 67 Checklist card (unnumbered)	150.00	25.00	5.00

1970 Fleer World Series

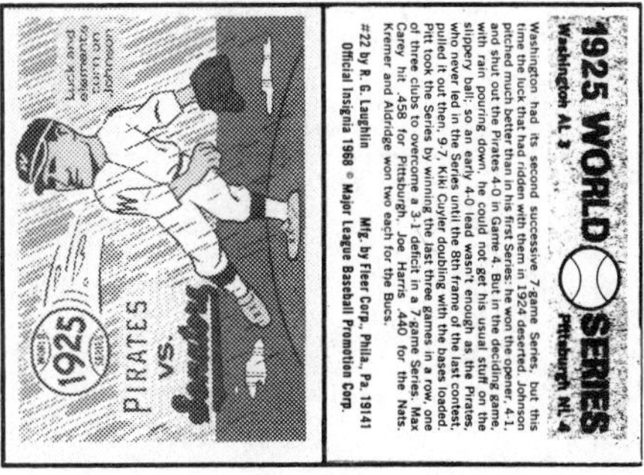

This set of 66 cards was distributed by Fleer. The cards are standard size, 2 1/2" by 3 1/2" and are in crude color on the front with light blue printing on white card stock on the back. All the years are represented except for 1904 when no World Series was played. In the list below, the winning series team is listed first. The year of the Series on the obverse is inside a white baseball.

	NRMT	VG-E	GOOD
COMPLETE SET (66)	17.50	8.00	2.00
COMMON PLAYER (1-66)	.25	.10	.02
□ 1 1903 Red Sox/Pirates	.25	.10	.02
□ 2 1905 Giants/A's (Christy Mathewson)	.35	.14	.03
□ 3 1906 White Sox/Cubs	.25	.10	.02
□ 4 1907 Cubs/Tigers	.25	.10	.02
□ 5 1908 Cubs/Tigers (Tinker/Evers/Chance)	.35	.14	.03
□ 6 1909 Pirates/Tigers (Wagner/Cobb)	.45	.18	.04
□ 7 1910 A's/Cubs (Bender/Coombs)	.25	.10	.02
□ 8 1911 A's/Giants (John McGraw)	.25	.10	.02
□ 9 1912 Red Sox/Giants	.25	.10	.02
□ 10 1913 A's/Giants	.25	.10	.02
□ 11 1914 Braves/A's	.25	.10	.02
□ 12 1915 Red Sox/Phillies (Babe Ruth)	.75	.30	.07
□ 13 1916 Red Sox/Dodgers (Babe Ruth)	.75	.30	.07
□ 14 1917 White Sox/Giants	.25	.10	.02
□ 15 1918 Red Sox/Cubs	.25	.10	.02
□ 16 1919 Reds/White Sox	.25	.10	.02
□ 17 1920 Indians/Dodgers (Stan Coveleski)	.25	.10	.02
□ 18 1921 Giants/Yankees (Commissioner Landis)	.25	.10	.02
□ 19 1922 Giants/Yankees	.25	.10	.02
□ 20 1923 Yankees/Giants (Babe Ruth)	.75	.30	.07
□ 21 1924 Senators/Giants (John McGraw)	.25	.10	.02
□ 22 1925 Pirates/Senators (Walter Johnson)	.35	.14	.03
□ 23 1926 Cardinals/Yankees	.25	.10	.02

		NRMT	VG-E	GOOD
	(Alexander/Lazzeri)			
□ 24	1927 Yankees/Pirates	.25	.10	.02
□ 25	1928 Yankees/Cardinals . (Ruth/Gehrig)	.75	.30	.07
□ 26	1929 A's/Cubs	.25	.10	.02
□ 27	1930 A's/Cardinals	.25	.10	.02
□ 28	1931 Cardinals/A's .... (Pepper Martin)	.25	.10	.02
□ 29	1932 Yankees/Cubs .... (Ruth/Gehrig)	.75	.30	.07
□ 30	1933 Giants/Senators ..... (Mel Ott)	.35	.14	.03
□ 31	1934 Cardinals/Tigers	.25	.10	.02
□ 32	1935 Tigers/Cubs .... (Gehringer/Bridges)	.35	.14	.03
□ 33	1936 Yankees/Giants	.25	.10	.02
□ 34	1937 Yankees/Giants ...... (Carl Hubbell)	.25	.10	.02
□ 35	1938 Yankees/Cubs .... (Lou Gehrig)	.50	.20	.05
□ 36	1939 Yankees/Reds	.25	.10	.02
□ 37	1940 Reds/Tigers	.25	.10	.02
□ 38	1941 Yankees/Dodgers ...	.25	.10	.02
□ 39	1942 Cardinals/Yankees .	.25	.10	.02
□ 40	1943 Yankees/Cardinals .	.25	.10	.02
□ 41	1944 Cardinals/Browns ...	.25	.10	.02
□ 42	1945 Tigers/Cubs .... (Hank Greenberg)	.25	.10	.02
□ 43	1946 Cardinals/Red Sox . (Enos Slaughter)	.25	.10	.02
□ 44	1947 Yankees/Dodgers ... (Al Gionfriddo)	.25	.10	.02
□ 45	1948 Indians/Braves	.25	.10	.02
□ 46	1949 Yankees/Dodgers ... (Reynolds/Roe)	.25	.10	.02
□ 47	1950 Yankees/Phillies	.25	.10	.02
□ 48	1951 Yankees/Giants	.25	.10	.02
□ 49	1952 Yankees/Dodgers ... (Mize/Snider)	.40	.16	.04
□ 50	1953 Yankees/Dodgers ... (Carl Erskine)	.25	.10	.02
□ 51	1954 Giants/Indians .... (Johnny Antonelli)	.25	.10	.02
□ 52	1955 Dodgers/Yankees ... (Johnny Podres)	.25	.10	.02
□ 53	1956 Yankees/Dodgers ...	.25	.10	.02
□ 54	1957 Braves/Yankees ..... (Lew Burdette)	.25	.10	.02
□ 55	1958 Yankees/Braves ..... (Bob Turley)	.25	.10	.02
□ 56	1959 Dodgers/Wh.Sox .... (Chuck Essegian)	.25	.10	.02
□ 57	1960 Pirates/Yankees	.25	.10	.02
□ 58	1961 Yankees/Reds .... (Whitey Ford)	.35	.14	.03
□ 59	1962 Yankees/Giants	.25	.10	.02
□ 60	1963 Dodgers/Yankees ... (Moose Skowron)	.25	.10	.02
□ 61	1964 Cardinals/Yankees . (Bobby Richardson)	.35	.14	.03
□ 62	1965 Dodgers/Twins	.25	.10	.02
□ 63	1966 Orioles/Dodgers	.25	.10	.02
□ 64	1967 Cardinals/Red Sox .	.25	.10	.02
□ 65	1968 Tigers/Cardinals	.25	.10	.02
□ 66	1969 Mets/Orioles	.35	.14	.03

1971 Fleer World Series

This set of 68 cards was distributed by Fleer. The cards are standard size, 2 1/2" by 3 1/2" and are in crude color on the front with brown printing on white card stock on the back. All the years are represented in this set as 1904 when no World Series was played is represented by a card explaining why there was no World Series that year. In the list below, the winning series team is listed first. The year of the Series on the obverse is inside a white square over the official World Series logo.

		NRMT	VG-E	GOOD
COMPLETE SET (68)		17.50	8.00	2.00
COMMON PLAYER (1-68)		.25	.10	.02
□ 1	1903 Red Sox/Pirates ..... (Cy Young)	.35	.14	.03
□ 2	1904 NO Series .... (John McGraw)	.35	.14	.03

		NRMT	VG-E	GOOD
□ 3	1905 Giants/A's .... (Mathewson, Bender, and McGinnity)	.35	.14	.0
□ 4	1906 White Sox/Cubs	.25	.10	.0
□ 5	1907 Cubs/Tigers	.25	.10	.0
□ 6	1908 Cubs/Tigers .... (Ty Cobb)	.50	.20	.0
□ 7	1909 Pirates/Tigers	.25	.10	.0
□ 8	1910 A's/Cubs .... (Eddie Collins)	.25	.10	.0
□ 9	1911 A's/Giants .... (Home Run Baker)	.25	.10	.0
□ 10	1912 Red Sox/Giants	.25	.10	.0
□ 11	1913 A's/Giants .... (Christy Mathewson)	.40	.16	.0
□ 12	1914 Braves/A's	.25	.10	.0
□ 13	1915 Red Sox/Phillies ..... (Grover Alexander)	.25	.10	.0
□ 14	1916 Red Sox/Dodgers ...	.25	.10	.0
□ 15	1917 White Sox/Giants ... (Red Faber)	.25	.10	.0
□ 16	1918 Red Sox/Cubs .... (Babe Ruth)	.75	.30	.07
□ 17	1919 Reds/White Sox	.25	.10	.02
□ 18	1920 Indians/Dodgers	.25	.10	.02
□ 19	1921 Giants/Yankees ...... (Waite Hoyt)	.25	.10	.02
□ 20	1922 Giants/Yankees	.25	.10	.02
□ 21	1923 Yankees/Giants ...... (Herb Pennock)	.25	.10	.02
□ 22	1924 Senators/Giants ..... (Walter Johnson)	.40	.16	.04
□ 23	1925 Pirates/Senators .... (Cuyler/W.Johnson)	.40	.16	.04
□ 24	1926 Cardinals/Yankees . (Rogers Hornsby)	.40	.16	.04
□ 25	1927 Yankees/Pirates	.25	.10	.02
□ 26	1928 Yankees/Cardinals . (Lou Gehrig)	.50	.20	.05
□ 27	1929 A's/Cubs	.25	.10	.02
□ 28	1930 A's/Cardinals .... (Jimmie Foxx)	.40	.16	.04
□ 29	1931 Cardinals/A's .... (Pepper Martin)	.25	.10	.02
□ 30	1932 Yankees/Cubs .... (Babe Ruth)	.75	.30	.07
□ 31	1933 Giants/Senators ..... (Carl Hubbell)	.25	.10	.02
□ 32	1934 Cardinals/Tigers	.25	.10	.02
□ 33	1935 Tigers/Cubs .... (Mickey Cochrane)	.35	.14	.03
□ 34	1936 Yankees/Giants ...... (Red Rolfe)	.25	.10	.02
□ 35	1937 Yankees/Giants ...... (Tony Lazzeri)	.25	.10	.02
□ 36	1938 Yankees/Cubs	.25	.10	.02
□ 37	1939 Yankees/Reds	.25	.10	.02
□ 38	1940 Reds/Tigers	.25	.10	.02
□ 39	1941 Yankees/Dodgers ...	.25	.10	.02
□ 40	1942 Cardinals/Yankees .	.25	.10	.02
□ 41	1943 Yankees/Cardinals .	.25	.10	.02
□ 42	1944 Cardinals/Browns ...	.25	.10	.02
□ 43	1945 Tigers/Cubs .... (Hank Greenberg)	.25	.10	.02
□ 44	1946 Cardinals/Red Sox . (Enos Slaughter)	.25	.10	.02
□ 45	1947 Yankees/Dodgers ...	.25	.10	.02
□ 46	1948 Indians/Braves	.25	.10	.02
□ 47	1949 Yankees/Dodgers ... (Preacher Roe)	.25	.10	.02
□ 48	1950 Yankees/Phillies ..... (Allie Reynolds)	.25	.10	.02
□ 49	1951 Yankees/Giants ...... (Ed Lopat)	.25	.10	.02
□ 50	1952 Yankees/Dodgers ...	.35	.14	.03

		NRMT	VG-E	GOOD
	(Johnny Mize)			
☐ 51	1953 Yankees/Dodgers	.25	.10	.02
☐ 52	1954 Giants/Indians	.25	.10	.02
☐ 53	1955 Dodgers/Yankees (Duke Snider)	.40	.16	.04
☐ 54	1956 Yankees/Dodgers	.25	.10	.02
☐ 55	1957 Braves/Yankees	.25	.10	.02
☐ 56	1958 Yankees/Braves (Hank Bauer)	.25	.10	.02
☐ 57	1959 Dodgers/Wh.Sox (Duke Snider)	.40	.16	.04
☐ 58	1960 Pirates/Yankees	.25	.10	.02
☐ 59	1961 Yankees/Reds (Whitey Ford)	.35	.14	.03
☐ 60	1962 Yankees/Giants	.25	.10	.02
☐ 61	1963 Dodgers/Yankees	.25	.10	.02
☐ 62	1964 Cardinals/Yankees	.25	.10	.02
☐ 63	1965 Dodgers/Twins	.25	.10	.02
☐ 64	1966 Orioles/Dodgers	.25	.10	.02
☐ 65	1967 Cardinals/Red Sox	.25	.10	.02
☐ 66	1968 Tigers/Cardinals	.25	.10	.02
☐ 67	1969 Mets/Orioles	.35	.14	.03
☐ 68	1970 Orioles/Reds	.35	.14	.03

1972 Fleer Famous Feats

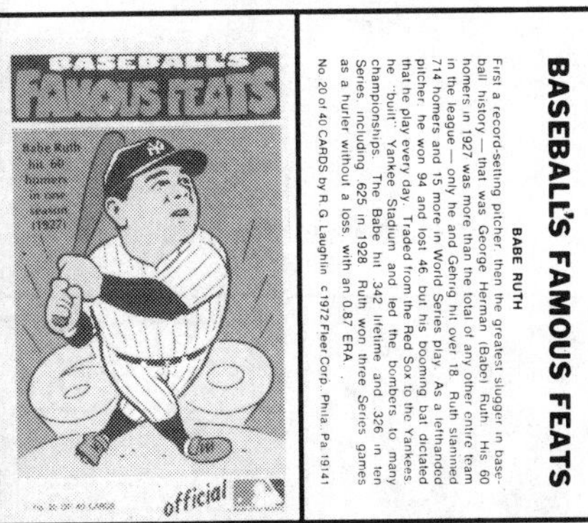

This Fleer set of 40 cards features the artwork of sports artist R.G. Laughlin. The set is titled "Baseball's Famous Feats." The cards are numbered both on the front and back. The backs are printed in light blue on white card stock. The cards measure approximately 2 1/2" by 4". This set was licensed by Major League Baseball.

		NRMT	VG-E	GOOD
	COMPLETE SET (40)	10.00	4.00	1.00
	COMMON PLAYER (1-40)	.30	.12	.03
☐ 1	Joe McGinnity	.30	.12	.03
☐ 2	Rogers Hornsby	.40	.16	.04
☐ 3	Christy Mathewson	.50	.20	.05
☐ 4	Dazzy Vance	.30	.12	.03
☐ 5	Lou Gehrig	.60	.24	.06
☐ 6	Jim Bottomley	.30	.12	.03
☐ 7	Johnny Evers	.30	.12	.03
☐ 8	Walter Johnson	.50	.20	.05
☐ 9	Hack Wilson	.30	.12	.03
☐ 10	Wilbert Robinson	.30	.12	.03
☐ 11	Cy Young	.40	.16	.04
☐ 12	Rudy York	.30	.12	.03
☐ 13	Grover C. Alexander	.30	.12	.03
☐ 14	Fred Toney and Hippo Vaughan	.30	.12	.03
☐ 15	Ty Cobb	.60	.24	.06
☐ 16	Jimmie Foxx	.40	.16	.04
☐ 17	Hub Leonard	.30	.12	.03
☐ 18	Eddie Collins	.30	.12	.03
☐ 19	Joe Oeschger and Leon Cadore	.30	.12	.03
☐ 20	Babe Ruth	.75	.30	.07
☐ 21	Honus Wagner	.50	.20	.05
☐ 22	Red Rolfe	.30	.12	.03
☐ 23	Ed Walsh	.30	.12	.03
☐ 24	Paul Waner	.30	.12	.03
☐ 25	Mel Ott	.40	.16	.04
☐ 26	Eddie Plank	.30	.12	.03
☐ 27	Sam Crawford	.30	.12	.03
☐ 28	Napoleon Lajoie	.40	.16	.04
☐ 29	Ed Reulbach	.30	.12	.03
☐ 30	Pinky Higgins	.30	.12	.03
☐ 31	Bill Klem	.30	.12	.03
☐ 32	Tris Speaker	.40	.16	.04
☐ 33	Hank Gowdy	.30	.12	.03
☐ 34	Lefty O'Doul	.30	.12	.03
☐ 35	Lloyd Waner	.30	.12	.03
☐ 36	Chuck Klein	.30	.12	.03
☐ 37	Deacon Phillippe	.30	.12	.03
☐ 38	Ed Delahanty	.30	.12	.03
☐ 39	Jack Chesbro	.30	.12	.03
☐ 40	Willie Keeler	.30	.12	.03

1973 Fleer Wildest Days

Baseball's WILDEST DAYS AND PLAYS
The star who sat out the World Series!

Baseball's WILDEST DAYS AND PLAYS
The Star Who Sat Out The World Series!
It's often the unhappy lot of a star player to miss the World Series due to an injury—but in 1927 a healthy star sat out the fall classic. Kiki Cuyler, a future Hall-of-Famer, had broken up the '25 Series with a bases-clearing double off Walter Johnson in the final game. While missing much of the '27 season with an injury, he still hit over .300. But he had quarreled with his new manager, Donie Bush, over being moved from third to second in the batting order—where Kiki didn't want to hit. He was fined once for not sliding. Both were stubborn, and Bush traded Cuyler before the next season. Despite Pittsburgh chants of "We want Cuyler!" he never appeared in the '27 Series.
No. 14 of 42 CARDS by R. G. Laughlin
©1973 Fleer Corp., Phila., Pa. 19141

This Fleer set of 42 cards is titled "Baseball's Wildest Days and Plays" and features the artwork of sports artist R.G. Laughlin. The cards are numbered on the back. The backs are printed in dark red on white card stock. The cards measure approximately 2 1/2" by 4". This set was not licensed by Major League Baseball.

		NRMT	VG-E	GOOD
	COMPLETE SET (42)	10.00	4.00	1.00
	COMMON PLAYER (1-42)	.30	.12	.03
☐ 1	Cubs and Phillies Score 49 Runs in Game	.30	.12	.03
☐ 2	Frank Chance Five HBP's in One Day	.30	.12	.03
☐ 3	Jim Thorpe Homered into 3 States	.50	.20	.05
☐ 4	Eddie Gaedel Midget in Majors	.30	.12	.03
☐ 5	Most Tied Game Ever	.30	.12	.03
☐ 6	Seven Errors in One Inning	.30	.12	.03
☐ 7	Four 20-Game Winners But No Pennant	.30	.12	.03
☐ 8	Dummy Hoy Umpires Signal Strikes	.30	.12	.03
☐ 9	Fourteeen Hits in One Inning	.30	.12	.03
☐ 10	Yankees Not Shut Out For Two Years	.30	.12	.03
☐ 11	Buck Weaver 17 Straight Fouls	.30	.12	.03
☐ 12	George Sisler Greatest Thrill Was as a Pitcher	.30	.12	.03
☐ 13	Wrong-Way Baserunner	.30	.12	.03
☐ 14	Kiki Cuyler Sits Out Series	.30	.12	.03
☐ 15	Grounder Climbed Wall	.30	.12	.03
☐ 16	Gabby Street Washington Monument	.30	.12	.03
☐ 17	Mel Ott Ejected Twice	.30	.12	.03
☐ 18	Shortest Pitching Career	.30	.12	.03
☐ 19	Three Homers in One Inning	.30	.12	.03
☐ 20	Bill Byron	.30	.12	.03

Singing Umpire			
☐ 21 Fred Clarke	.30	.12	.03
Walking Steal of Home			
☐ 22 Christy Mathewson	.40	.16	.04
373rd Win Discovered			
☐ 23 Hitting Through the Unglaub Arc	.30	.12	.03
☐ 24 Jim O'Rourke	.30	.12	.03
Catching at 52			
☐ 25 Fired for Striking Out in Series	.30	.12	.03
☐ 26 Eleven Run Inning on One Hit	.30	.12	.03
☐ 27 58 Innings in 3 Days	.30	.12	.03
☐ 28 Homer on Warm-Up Pitch	.30	.12	.03
☐ 29 Giants Win 26 Straight But Finish Fourth	.30	.12	.03
☐ 30 Player Who Stole First Base	.30	.12	.03
☐ 31 Ernie Shore	.30	.12	.03
Perfect Game in Relief			
☐ 32 Greatest Comeback	.30	.12	.03
☐ 33 All-Time Flash-In-The-Pan	.30	.12	.03
☐ 34 Pruett Fanned Ruth 19 out of 31	.50	.20	.05
☐ 35 Fixed Batting Race Cobb/Lajoie	.40	.16	.04
☐ 36 Wild-Pitch Rebound Play	.30	.12	.03
☐ 37 17 Straight Scoring Innings	.30	.12	.03
☐ 38 Wildest Opening Day	.30	.12	.03
☐ 39 Baseball's Strike One	.30	.12	.03
☐ 40 Opening Day No Hitter That Didn't Count	.30	.12	.03
☐ 41 Jimmie Foxx	.40	.16	.04
Six Straight Walks in One Game			
☐ 42 Entire Team Hit and Scored in Inning	.30	.12	.03

1974 Fleer Baseball Firsts

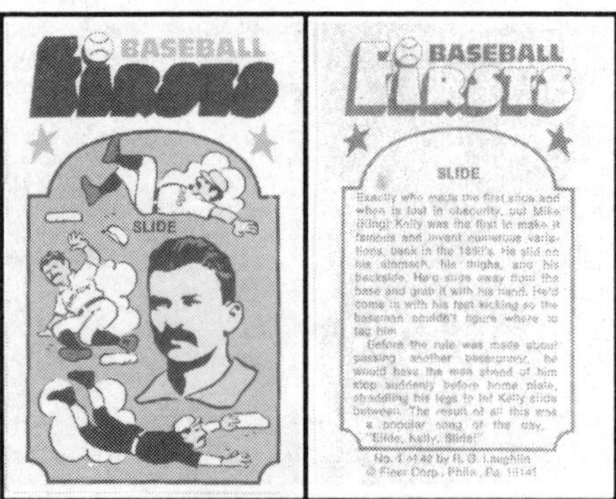

This Fleer set of 42 cards is titled "Baseball Firsts" and features the artwork of sports artist R.G. Laughlin. The cards are numbered on the back. The backs are printed in black on gray card stock. The cards measure approximately 2 1/2" by 4". This set was not licensed by Major League Baseball.

	NRMT	VG-E	GOOD
COMPLETE SET (42)	7.50	3.00	.75
COMMON PLAYER (1-42)	.20	.08	.02
☐ 1 Slide	.20	.08	.02
☐ 2 Spring Training	.20	.08	.02
☐ 3 Bunt	.20	.08	.02
☐ 4 Catcher's Mask	.20	.08	.02
☐ 5 Four Straight Homers (Lou Gehrig)	.40	.16	.04
☐ 6 Radio Broadcast	.20	.08	.02
☐ 7 Numbered Uniforms	.20	.08	.02
☐ 8 Shin Guards	.20	.08	.02
☐ 9 Players Association	.20	.08	.02
☐ 10 Knuckleball	.20	.08	.0
☐ 11 Player With Glasses	.20	.08	.0[illegible]
☐ 12 Baseball Cards	.50	.20	.0[illegible]
☐ 13 Standardized Rules	.20	.08	.0[illegible]
☐ 14 Grand Slam	.20	.08	.0[illegible]
☐ 15 Player Fined	.20	.08	.0[illegible]
☐ 16 Presidential Opener	.20	.08	.0[illegible]
☐ 17 Player Transaction	.20	.08	.0[illegible]
☐ 18 All-Star Game	.20	.08	.0[illegible]
☐ 19 Scoreboard	.20	.08	.0[illegible]
☐ 20 Cork Center Ball	.20	.08	.0[illegible]
☐ 21 Scorekeeping	.20	.08	.0[illegible]
☐ 22 Domed Stadium	.20	.08	.0[illegible]
☐ 23 Batting Helmet	.20	.08	.0[illegible]
☐ 24 Fatality	.20	.08	.0[illegible]
☐ 25 Unassisted Triple Play	.20	.08	.0[illegible]
☐ 26 Home Run At Night	.20	.08	.0[illegible]
☐ 27 Black Major Leaguer	.20	.08	.0[illegible]
☐ 28 Pinch Hitter	.20	.08	.0[illegible]
☐ 29 Million-Dollar World Series	.20	.08	.0[illegible]
☐ 30 Tarpaulin	.20	.08	.0[illegible]
☐ 31 Team Initials	.20	.08	.0[illegible]
☐ 32 Pennant Playoff	.20	.08	.0[illegible]
☐ 33 Glove	.20	.08	.0[illegible]
☐ 34 Curve Ball	.20	.08	.0[illegible]
☐ 35 Night Game	.20	.08	.0[illegible]
☐ 36 Admission Charge	.20	.08	.0[illegible]
☐ 37 Farm System	.20	.08	.0[illegible]
☐ 38 Telecast	.20	.08	.0[illegible]
☐ 39 Commissioner	.20	.08	.0[illegible]
☐ 40 .400 Hitter	.20	.08	.0[illegible]
☐ 41 World Series	.20	.08	.0[illegible]
☐ 42 Player Into Service	.20	.08	.0[illegible]

1975 Fleer Pioneers

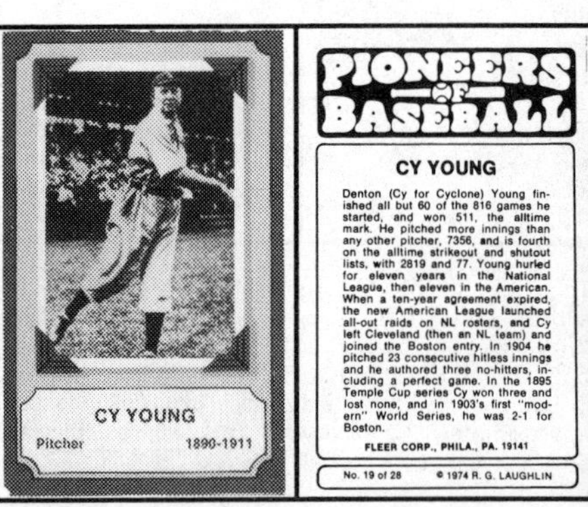

This 28-card set of brown and white sepia-toned photos of old timers is subtitled "Pioneers of Baseball. The graphics artwork was done by R.G. Laughlin. The cards measure 2 1/2" by 4". The card backs are a narrative about the particular player. The cards are numbered on the back at the bottom.

	NRMT	VG-E	GOOD
COMPLETE SET (28)	10.00	4.00	1.00
COMMON PLAYER (1-28)	.35	.14	.03
☐ 1 Cap Anson	.75	.30	.07
☐ 2 Harry Wright	.45	.18	.04
☐ 3 Buck Ewing	.45	.18	.04
☐ 4 A.G. Spalding	.45	.18	.04
☐ 5 Old Hoss Radbourn	.45	.18	.04
☐ 6 Dan Brouthers	.45	.18	.04
☐ 7 Roger Bresnahan	.45	.18	.04
☐ 8 Mike Kelly	.45	.18	.04
☐ 9 Ned Hanlon	.35	.14	.03
☐ 10 Ed Delahanty	.45	.18	.04
☐ 11 Pud Galvin	.45	.18	.04
☐ 12 Amos Rusie	.45	.18	.04
☐ 13 Tommy McCarthy	.45	.18	.04
☐ 14 Ty Cobb	1.00	.40	.10
☐ 15 John McGraw	.45	.18	.04
☐ 16 Home Run Baker	.45	.18	.04
☐ 17 Johnny Evers	.45	.18	.04
☐ 18 Nap Lajoie	.45	.18	.04

☐ 19 Cy Young	.60	.24	.06
☐ 20 Eddie Collins	.45	.18	.04
☐ 21 John Glasscock	.35	.14	.03
☐ 22 Hal Chase	.35	.14	.03
☐ 23 Mordecai Brown	.45	.18	.04
☐ 24 Jake Daubert	.35	.14	.03
☐ 25 Mike Donlin	.35	.14	.03
☐ 26 John Clarkson	.45	.18	.04
☐ 27 Buck Herzog	.35	.14	.03
☐ 28 Art Nehf	.35	.14	.03

1981 Fleer

The cards in this 660-card set measure 2 1/2" by 3 1/2". This issue of cards marks Fleer's first entry into the current player baseball card market since 1963. Players from the same team are conveniently grouped together by number in the set. The teams are ordered (by 1980 standings) as follows: Philadelphia (1-27), Kansas City (28-50), Houston (51-78), New York Yankees (79-109), Los Angeles (110-141), Montreal (142-168), Baltimore (169-195), Cincinnati (196-220), Boston (221-241), Atlanta (242-267), California (268-290), Chicago Cubs (291-315), New York Mets (316-338), Chicago White Sox (339-350 and 352-359), Pittsburgh (360-386), Cleveland (387-408), Toronto (409-431), San Francisco (432-458), Detroit (459-483), San Diego (484-506), Milwaukee (507-527), St. Louis (528-550), Minnesota (551-571), Oakland (351 and 572-594), Seattle (595-616), and Texas (617- 637). Cards 638-660 feature specials and checklists. The cards of pitchers in this set erroneously show a heading (on the card backs) of "Batting Record" over their career pitching statistics. There were three distinct printings: the two following the primary run were designed to correct numerous errors. The variations caused by these multiple printings are noted in the checklist below (P1, P2, or P3).

	MINT	EXC	G-VG
COMPLETE SET (P1)	30.00	12.00	3.00
COMPLETE SET (P2)	24.00	10.00	2.40
COMPLETE SET (P3)	25.00	10.00	2.50
COMMON PLAYER (1-660)	.03	.01	.00
☐ 1 Pete Rose	2.00	.80	.20
☐ 2 Larry Bowa	.15	.06	.01
☐ 3 Manny Trillo	.03	.01	.00
☐ 4 Bob Boone	.15	.06	.01
☐ 5 Mike Schmidt See 640A	1.00	.40	.10
☐ 6A Steve Carlton P1 Pitcher of Year See also 660A Back "1066 Cardinals"	.65	.26	.06
☐ 6B Steve Carlton P2 Pitcher of Year Back "1066 Cardinals"	.65	.26	.06
☐ 6C Steve Carlton P3 "1966 Cardinals"	2.00	.80	.20
☐ 7 Tug McGraw See 657A	.10	.04	.01
☐ 8 Larry Christenson	.03	.01	.00
☐ 9 Bake McBride	.03	.01	.00
☐ 10 Greg Luzinski	.10	.04	.01
☐ 11 Ron Reed	.03	.01	.00
☐ 12 Dickie Noles	.03	.01	.00
☐ 13 Keith Moreland	.35	.14	.03
☐ 14 Bob Walk	.30	.12	.03
☐ 15 Lonnie Smith	.06	.02	.00
☐ 16 Dick Ruthven	.03	.01	.00
☐ 17 Sparky Lyle	.10	.04	.01
☐ 18 Greg Gross	.03	.01	.00
☐ 19 Garry Maddox	.06	.02	.00
☐ 20 Nino Espinosa	.03	.01	.00
☐ 21 George Vukovich	.03	.01	.00
☐ 22 John Vukovich	.03	.01	.00
☐ 23 Ramon Aviles	.03	.01	.00
☐ 24A Ken Saucier P1 Name on front "Ken"	.06	.02	.00
☐ 24B Ken Saucier P2 Name on front "Ken"	.06	.02	.00
☐ 24C Kevin Saucier P3 Name on front "Kevin"	.35	.14	.03
☐ 25 Randy Lerch	.03	.01	.00
☐ 26 Del Unser	.03	.01	.00
☐ 27 Tim McCarver	.15	.06	.01
☐ 28 George Brett See 655A	1.00	.40	.10
☐ 29 Willie Wilson See 653A	.15	.06	.01
☐ 30 Paul Splittorff	.03	.01	.00
☐ 31 Dan Quisenberry	.15	.06	.01
☐ 32A Amos Otis P1 Batting Pose "Outfield" (32 on back)	.10	.04	.01
☐ 32B Amos Otis P2 "Series Starter" (483 on back)	.10	.04	.01
☐ 33 Steve Busby	.03	.01	.00
☐ 34 U.L. Washington	.03	.01	.00
☐ 35 Dave Chalk	.03	.01	.00
☐ 36 Darrell Porter	.03	.01	.00
☐ 37 Marty Pattin	.03	.01	.00
☐ 38 Larry Gura	.03	.01	.00
☐ 39 Renie Martin	.03	.01	.00
☐ 40 Rich Gale	.03	.01	.00
☐ 41A Hal McRae P1 "Royals" on front in black letters	.50	.20	.05
☐ 41B Hal McRae P2 "Royals" on front in blue letters	.10	.04	.01
☐ 42 Dennis Leonard	.03	.01	.00
☐ 43 Willie Aikens	.03	.01	.00
☐ 44 Frank White	.10	.04	.01
☐ 45 Clint Hurdle	.03	.01	.00
☐ 46 John Wathan	.10	.04	.01
☐ 47 Pete LaCock	.03	.01	.00
☐ 48 Rance Mulliniks	.03	.01	.00
☐ 49 Jeff Twitty	.03	.01	.00
☐ 50 Jamie Quirk	.03	.01	.00
☐ 51 Art Howe	.10	.04	.01
☐ 52 Ken Forsch	.03	.01	.00
☐ 53 Vern Ruhle	.03	.01	.00
☐ 54 Joe Niekro	.10	.04	.01
☐ 55 Frank LaCorte	.03	.01	.00
☐ 56 J.R. Richard	.10	.04	.01
☐ 57 Nolan Ryan	.60	.24	.06
☐ 58 Enos Cabell	.03	.01	.00
☐ 59 Cesar Cedeno	.10	.04	.01
☐ 60 Jose Cruz	.10	.04	.01
☐ 61 Bill Virdon MG	.03	.01	.00
☐ 62 Terry Puhl	.06	.02	.00
☐ 63 Joaquin Andujar	.10	.04	.01
☐ 64 Alan Ashby	.03	.01	.00
☐ 65 Joe Sambito	.03	.01	.00
☐ 66 Denny Walling	.03	.01	.00
☐ 67 Jeff Leonard	.15	.06	.01
☐ 68 Luis Pujols	.03	.01	.00
☐ 69 Bruce Bochy	.03	.01	.00
☐ 70 Rafael Landestoy	.03	.01	.00
☐ 71 Dave Smith	.35	.14	.03
☐ 72 Danny Heep	.20	.08	.02
☐ 73 Julio Gonzalez	.03	.01	.00
☐ 74 Craig Reynolds	.03	.01	.00
☐ 75 Gary Woods	.03	.01	.00
☐ 76 Dave Bergman	.03	.01	.00
☐ 77 Randy Niemann	.03	.01	.00
☐ 78 Joe Morgan	.30	.12	.03
☐ 79 Reggie Jackson See 650A	.85	.34	.08
☐ 80 Bucky Dent	.10	.04	.01
☐ 81 Tommy John	.15	.06	.01
☐ 82 Luis Tiant	.10	.04	.01

□ 83 Rick Cerone	.03	.01	.00
□ 84 Dick Howser MG	.10	.04	.01
□ 85 Lou Piniella	.10	.04	.01
□ 86 Ron Davis	.03	.01	.00
□ 87A Craig Nettles P1 ERR (Name on back misspelled "Craig")	12.00	5.00	1.20
□ 87B Graig Nettles P2 COR .. "Graig"	.30	.12	.03
□ 88 Ron Guidry	.20	.08	.02
□ 89 Rich Gossage	.15	.06	.01
□ 90 Rudy May	.03	.01	.00
□ 91 Gaylord Perry	.25	.10	.02
□ 92 Eric Soderholm	.03	.01	.00
□ 93 Bob Watson	.06	.02	.00
□ 94 Bobby Murcer	.10	.04	.01
□ 95 Bobby Brown	.03	.01	.00
□ 96 Jim Spencer	.03	.01	.00
□ 97 Tom Underwood	.03	.01	.00
□ 98 Oscar Gamble	.03	.01	.00
□ 99 Johnny Oates	.03	.01	.00
□ 100 Fred Stanley	.03	.01	.00
□ 101 Ruppert Jones	.03	.01	.00
□ 102 Dennis Werth	.03	.01	.00
□ 103 Joe Lefebvre	.03	.01	.00
□ 104 Brian Doyle	.03	.01	.00
□ 105 Aurelio Rodriguez	.03	.01	.00
□ 106 Doug Bird	.03	.01	.00
□ 107 Mike Griffin	.03	.01	.00
□ 108 Tim Lollar	.03	.01	.00
□ 109 Willie Randolph	.10	.04	.01
□ 110 Steve Garvey	.60	.24	.06
□ 111 Reggie Smith	.10	.04	.01
□ 112 Don Sutton	.30	.12	.03
□ 113 Burt Hooton	.03	.01	.00
□ 114A Dave Lopes P1 small hand on back	.50	.20	.05
□ 114B Dave Lopes P2 no hand	.10	.04	.01
□ 115 Dusty Baker	.06	.02	.00
□ 116 Tom Lasorda MG	.10	.04	.01
□ 117 Bill Russell	.06	.02	.00
□ 118 Jerry Reuss	.06	.02	.00
□ 119 Terry Forster	.06	.02	.00
□ 120A Bob Welch P1 Name on back Bob	.20	.08	.02
□ 120B Bob Welch P2 Name on back Robert	.20	.08	.02
□ 121 Don Stanhouse	.03	.01	.00
□ 122 Rick Monday	.03	.01	.00
□ 123 Derrel Thomas	.03	.01	.00
□ 124 Joe Ferguson	.03	.01	.00
□ 125 Rick Sutcliffe	.25	.10	.02
□ 126A Ron Cey P1 small hand on back	.50	.20	.05
□ 126B Ron Cey P2 no hand	.10	.04	.01
□ 127 Dave Goltz	.03	.01	.00
□ 128 Jay Johnstone	.06	.02	.00
□ 129 Steve Yeager	.03	.01	.00
□ 130 Gary Weiss	.03	.01	.00
□ 131 Mike Scioscia	.50	.20	.05
□ 132 Vic Davalillo	.03	.01	.00
□ 133 Doug Rau	.03	.01	.00
□ 134 Pepe Frias	.03	.01	.00
□ 135 Mickey Hatcher	.10	.04	.01
□ 136 Steve Howe	.10	.04	.01
□ 137 Robert Castillo	.03	.01	.00
□ 138 Gary Thomasson	.03	.01	.00
□ 139 Rudy Law	.03	.01	.00
□ 140 Fernand Valenzuela (sic, Fernando)	4.50	1.80	.45
□ 141 Manny Mota	.06	.02	.00
□ 142 Gary Carter	.50	.20	.05
□ 143 Steve Rogers	.06	.02	.00
□ 144 Warren Cromartie	.03	.01	.00
□ 145 Andre Dawson	.35	.14	.03
□ 146 Larry Parrish	.06	.02	.00
□ 147 Rowland Office	.03	.01	.00
□ 148 Ellis Valentine	.03	.01	.00
□ 149 Dick Williams MG	.03	.01	.00
□ 150 Bill Gullickson	.25	.10	.02
□ 151 Elias Sosa	.03	.01	.00
□ 152 John Tamargo	.03	.01	.00
□ 153 Chris Speier	.03	.01	.00
□ 154 Ron LeFlore	.03	.01	.00
□ 155 Rodney Scott	.03	.01	.00
□ 156 Stan Bahnsen	.03	.01	.00
□ 157 Bill Lee	.06	.02	.00
□ 158 Fred Norman	.03	.01	.00
□ 159 Woodie Fryman	.03	.01	.00
□ 160 Dave Palmer	.06	.02	.00
□ 161 Jerry White	.03	.01	.00
□ 162 Roberto Ramos	.03	.01	.00
□ 163 John D'Acquisto	.03	.01	.00

□ 164 Tommy Hutton	.03	.01	.00
□ 165 Charlie Lea	.15	.06	.01
□ 166 Scott Sanderson	.06	.02	.00
□ 167 Ken Macha	.03	.01	.00
□ 168 Tony Bernazard	.06	.02	.00
□ 169 Jim Palmer	.40	.16	.04
□ 170 Steve Stone	.06	.02	.00
□ 171 Mike Flanagan	.10	.04	.01
□ 172 Al Bumbry	.03	.01	.00
□ 173 Doug DeCinces	.06	.02	.00
□ 174 Scott McGregor	.06	.02	.00
□ 175 Mark Belanger	.06	.02	.00
□ 176 Tim Stoddard	.03	.01	.00
□ 177A Rick Dempsey P1 small hand on front	.50	.20	.05
□ 177B Rick Dempsey P2 no hand	.10	.04	.01
□ 178 Earl Weaver MG	.06	.02	.00
□ 179 Tippy Martinez	.03	.01	.00
□ 180 Dennis Martinez	.06	.02	.00
□ 181 Sammy Stewart	.03	.01	.00
□ 182 Rich Dauer	.03	.01	.00
□ 183 Lee May	.06	.02	.00
□ 184 Eddie Murray	.75	.30	.07
□ 185 Benny Ayala	.03	.01	.00
□ 186 John Lowenstein	.03	.01	.00
□ 187 Gary Roenicke	.03	.01	.00
□ 188 Ken Singleton	.10	.04	.01
□ 189 Dan Graham	.03	.01	.00
□ 190 Terry Crowley	.03	.01	.00
□ 191 Kiko Garcia	.03	.01	.00
□ 192 Dave Ford	.03	.01	.00
□ 193 Mark Corey	.03	.01	.00
□ 194 Lenn Sakata	.03	.01	.00
□ 195 Doug DeCinces	.06	.02	.00
□ 196 Johnny Bench	.65	.26	.06
□ 197 Dave Concepcion	.15	.06	.01
□ 198 Ray Knight	.10	.04	.01
□ 199 Ken Griffey	.06	.02	.00
□ 200 Tom Seaver	.50	.20	.05
□ 201 Dave Collins	.03	.01	.00
□ 202A George Foster P1 Slugger number on back 216	.15	.06	.01
□ 202B George Foster P2 Slugger number on back 202	.15	.06	.01
□ 203 Junior Kennedy	.03	.01	.00
□ 204 Frank Pastore	.03	.01	.00
□ 205 Dan Driessen	.03	.01	.00
□ 206 Hector Cruz	.03	.01	.00
□ 207 Paul Moskau	.03	.01	.00
□ 208 Charlie Leibrandt	.35	.14	.03
□ 209 Harry Spilman	.03	.01	.00
□ 210 Joe Price	.06	.02	.00
□ 211 Tom Hume	.03	.01	.00
□ 212 Joe Nolan	.03	.01	.00
□ 213 Doug Bair	.03	.01	.00
□ 214 Mario Soto	.10	.04	.01
□ 215A Bill Bonham P1 small hand on back	.50	.20	.05
□ 215B Bill Bonham P2 no hand	.06	.02	.00
□ 216 George Foster See 202	.15	.06	.01
□ 217 Paul Householder	.03	.01	.00
□ 218 Ron Oester	.06	.02	.00
□ 219 Sam Mejias	.03	.01	.00
□ 220 Sheldon Burnside	.03	.01	.00
□ 221 Carl Yastrzemski	1.00	.40	.10
□ 222 Jim Rice	.30	.12	.03
□ 223 Fred Lynn	.20	.08	.02
□ 224 Carlton Fisk	.20	.08	.02
□ 225 Rick Burleson	.06	.02	.00
□ 226 Dennis Eckersley	.20	.08	.02
□ 227 Butch Hobson	.03	.01	.00
□ 228 Tom Burgmeier	.03	.01	.00
□ 229 Garry Hancock	.03	.01	.00
□ 230 Don Zimmer MG	.03	.01	.00
□ 231 Steve Renko	.03	.01	.00
□ 232 Dwight Evans	.20	.08	.02
□ 233 Mike Torrez	.03	.01	.00
□ 234 Bob Stanley	.03	.01	.00
□ 235 Jim Dwyer	.03	.01	.00
□ 236 Dave Stapleton	.03	.01	.00
□ 237 Glen Hoffman	.03	.01	.00
□ 238 Jerry Remy	.03	.01	.00
□ 239 Dick Drago	.03	.01	.00
□ 240 Bill Campbell	.03	.01	.00
□ 241 Tony Perez	.20	.08	.02
□ 242 Phil Niekro	.30	.12	.03
□ 243 Dale Murphy	1.25	.50	.12
□ 244 Bob Horner	.20	.08	.02
□ 245 Jeff Burroughs	.03	.01	.00
□ 246 Rick Camp	.03	.01	.00

□ 247 Bob Cox MG	.03	.01	.00
□ 248 Bruce Benedict	.03	.01	.00
□ 249 Gene Garber	.03	.01	.00
□ 250 Jerry Royster	.03	.01	.00
□ 251A Gary Matthews P1 small hand on back	.50	.20	.05
□ 251B Gary Matthews P2 no hand	.10	.04	.01
□ 252 Chris Chambliss	.10	.04	.01
□ 253 Luis Gomez	.03	.01	.00
□ 254 Bill Nahorodny	.03	.01	.00
□ 255 Doyle Alexander	.10	.04	.01
□ 256 Brian Asselstine	.03	.01	.00
□ 257 Biff Pocoroba	.03	.01	.00
□ 258 Mike Lum	.03	.01	.00
□ 259 Charlie Spikes	.03	.01	.00
□ 260 Glenn Hubbard	.03	.01	.00
□ 261 Tommy Boggs	.03	.01	.00
□ 262 Al Hrabosky	.06	.02	.00
□ 263 Rick Matula	.03	.01	.00
□ 264 Preston Hanna	.03	.01	.00
□ 265 Larry Bradford	.03	.01	.00
□ 266 Rafael Ramirez	.25	.10	.02
□ 267 Larry McWilliams	.03	.01	.00
□ 268 Rod Carew	.55	.22	.05
□ 269 Bobby Grich	.10	.04	.01
□ 270 Carney Lansford	.15	.06	.01
□ 271 Don Baylor	.15	.06	.01
□ 272 Joe Rudi	.06	.02	.00
□ 273 Dan Ford	.03	.01	.00
□ 274 Jim Fregosi	.06	.02	.00
□ 275 Dave Frost	.03	.01	.00
□ 276 Frank Tanana	.10	.04	.01
□ 277 Dickie Thon	.10	.04	.01
□ 278 Jason Thompson	.03	.01	.00
□ 279 Rick Miller	.03	.01	.00
□ 280 Bert Campaneris	.06	.02	.00
□ 281 Tom Donohue	.03	.01	.00
□ 282 Brian Downing	.06	.02	.00
□ 283 Fred Patek	.03	.01	.00
□ 284 Bruce Kison	.03	.01	.00
□ 285 Dave LaRoche	.03	.01	.00
□ 286 Don Aase	.03	.01	.00
□ 287 Jim Barr	.03	.01	.00
□ 288 Alfredo Martinez	.03	.01	.00
□ 289 Larry Harlow	.03	.01	.00
□ 290 Andy Hassler	.03	.01	.00
□ 291 Dave Kingman	.15	.06	.01
□ 292 Bill Buckner	.12	.05	.01
□ 293 Rick Reuschel	.10	.04	.01
□ 294 Bruce Sutter	.15	.06	.01
□ 295 Jerry Martin	.03	.01	.00
□ 296 Scot Thompson	.03	.01	.00
□ 297 Ivan DeJesus	.03	.01	.00
□ 298 Steve Dillard	.03	.01	.00
□ 299 Dick Tidrow	.03	.01	.00
□ 300 Randy Martz	.03	.01	.00
□ 301 Lenny Randle	.03	.01	.00
□ 302 Lynn McGlothen	.03	.01	.00
□ 303 Cliff Johnson	.03	.01	.00
□ 304 Tim Blackwell	.03	.01	.00
□ 305 Dennis Lamp	.03	.01	.00
□ 306 Bill Caudill	.03	.01	.00
□ 307 Carlos Lezcano	.03	.01	.00
□ 308 Jim Tracy	.03	.01	.00
□ 309 Doug Capilla	.03	.01	.00
□ 310 Willie Hernandez	.12	.05	.01
□ 311 Mike Vail	.03	.01	.00
□ 312 Mike Krukow	.06	.02	.00
□ 313 Barry Foote	.03	.01	.00
□ 314 Larry Biittner	.03	.01	.00
□ 315 Mike Tyson	.03	.01	.00
□ 316 Lee Mazzilli	.03	.01	.00
□ 317 John Stearns	.03	.01	.00
□ 318 Alex Trevino	.03	.01	.00
□ 319 Craig Swan	.03	.01	.00
□ 320 Frank Taveras	.03	.01	.00
□ 321 Steve Henderson	.03	.01	.00
□ 322 Neil Allen	.06	.02	.00
□ 323 Mark Bomback	.03	.01	.00
□ 324 Mike Jorgensen	.03	.01	.00
□ 325 Joe Torre MG	.10	.04	.01
□ 326 Elliott Maddox	.03	.01	.00
□ 327 Pete Falcone	.03	.01	.00
□ 328 Ray Burris	.03	.01	.00
□ 329 Claudell Washington	.06	.02	.00
□ 330 Doug Flynn	.03	.01	.00
□ 331 Joel Youngblood	.03	.01	.00
□ 332 Bill Almon	.03	.01	.00
□ 333 Tom Hausman	.03	.01	.00
□ 334 Pat Zachry	.03	.01	.00
□ 335 Jeff Reardon	.60	.24	.06
□ 336 Wally Backman	.40	.16	.04
□ 337 Dan Norman	.03	.01	.00
□ 338 Jerry Morales	.03	.01	.00
□ 339 Ed Farmer	.03	.01	.00
□ 340 Bob Molinaro	.03	.01	.00
□ 341 Todd Cruz	.03	.01	.00
□ 342A Britt Burns P1 small hand on front	.40	.16	.04
□ 342B Britt Burns P2 no hand	.20	.08	.02
□ 343 Kevin Bell	.03	.01	.00
□ 344 Tony LaRussa MG	.06	.02	.00
□ 345 Steve Trout	.06	.02	.00
□ 346 Harold Baines	1.75	.70	.17
□ 347 Richard Wortham	.03	.01	.00
□ 348 Wayne Nordhagen	.03	.01	.00
□ 349 Mike Squires	.03	.01	.00
□ 350 Lamar Johnson	.03	.01	.00
□ 351 Rickey Henderson	1.75	.70	.17
□ 352 Francisco Barrios	.03	.01	.00
□ 353 Thad Bosley	.03	.01	.00
□ 354 Chet Lemon	.06	.02	.00
□ 355 Bruce Kimm	.03	.01	.00
□ 356 Richard Dotson	.45	.18	.04
□ 357 Jim Morrison	.03	.01	.00
□ 358 Mike Proly	.03	.01	.00
□ 359 Greg Pryor	.03	.01	.00
□ 360 Dave Parker	.25	.10	.02
□ 361 Omar Moreno	.03	.01	.00
□ 362A Kent Tekulve P1 Back "1071 Waterbury" and "1078 Pirates"	.15	.06	.01
□ 362B Kent Tekulve P2 "1971 Waterbury" and "1978 Pirates"	.10	.04	.01
□ 363 Willie Stargell	.35	.14	.03
□ 364 Phil Garner	.03	.01	.00
□ 365 Ed Ott	.03	.01	.00
□ 366 Don Robinson	.06	.02	.00
□ 367 Chuck Tanner MG	.03	.01	.00
□ 368 Jim Rooker	.03	.01	.00
□ 369 Dale Berra	.03	.01	.00
□ 370 Jim Bibby	.03	.01	.00
□ 371 Steve Nicosia	.03	.01	.00
□ 372 Mike Easler	.06	.02	.00
□ 373 Bill Robinson	.06	.02	.00
□ 374 Lee Lacy	.03	.01	.00
□ 375 John Candelaria	.10	.04	.01
□ 376 Manny Sanguillen	.06	.02	.00
□ 377 Rick Rhoden	.10	.04	.01
□ 378 Grant Jackson	.03	.01	.00
□ 379 Tim Foli	.03	.01	.00
□ 380 Rod Scurry	.06	.02	.00
□ 381 Bill Madlock	.12	.05	.01
□ 382A Kurt Bevacqua P1 ERR (P on cap backwards)	.20	.08	.02
□ 382B Kurt Bevacqua P2 COR	.06	.02	.00
□ 383 Bert Blyleven	.15	.06	.01
□ 384 Eddie Solomon	.03	.01	.00
□ 385 Enrique Romo	.03	.01	.00
□ 386 John Milner	.03	.01	.00
□ 387 Mike Hargrove	.03	.01	.00
□ 388 Jorge Orta	.03	.01	.00
□ 389 Toby Harrah	.06	.02	.00
□ 390 Tom Veryzer	.03	.01	.00
□ 391 Miguel Dilone	.03	.01	.00
□ 392 Dan Spillner	.03	.01	.00
□ 393 Jack Brohamer	.03	.01	.00
□ 394 Wayne Garland	.03	.01	.00
□ 395 Sid Monge	.03	.01	.00
□ 396 Rick Waits	.03	.01	.00
□ 397 Joe Charboneau	.10	.04	.01
□ 398 Gary Alexander	.03	.01	.00
□ 399 Jerry Dybzinski	.03	.01	.00
□ 400 Mike Stanton	.03	.01	.00
□ 401 Mike Paxton	.03	.01	.00
□ 402 Gary Gray	.03	.01	.00
□ 403 Rick Manning	.03	.01	.00
□ 404 Bo Diaz	.06	.02	.00
□ 405 Ron Hassey	.03	.01	.00
□ 406 Ross Grimsley	.03	.01	.00
□ 407 Victor Cruz	.03	.01	.00
□ 408 Len Barker	.03	.01	.00
□ 409 Bob Bailor	.03	.01	.00
□ 410 Otto Velez	.03	.01	.00
□ 411 Ernie Whitt	.06	.02	.00
□ 412 Jim Clancy	.06	.02	.00
□ 413 Barry Bonnell	.03	.01	.00
□ 414 Dave Stieb	.30	.12	.03
□ 415 Damaso Garcia	.10	.04	.01
□ 416 John Mayberry	.06	.02	.00
□ 417 Roy Howell	.03	.01	.00
□ 418 Dan Ainge	.35	.14	.03
□ 419A Jesse Jefferson P1 Back says Pirates	.06	.02	.00
□ 419B Jesse Jefferson P2	.06	.02	.00

Back says Pirates
□ 419C Jesse Jefferson P3 ...... .35 .14 .03
Back says Blue Jays
□ 420 Joey McLaughlin .... .03 .01 .00
□ 421 Lloyd Moseby .... .90 .36 .09
□ 422 Al Woods .... .03 .01 .00
□ 423 Garth Iorg .... .03 .01 .00
□ 424 Doug Ault .... .03 .01 .00
□ 425 Ken Schrom .... .06 .02 .00
□ 426 Mike Willis .... .03 .01 .00
□ 427 Steve Braun .... .03 .01 .00
□ 428 Bob Davis .... .03 .01 .00
□ 429 Jerry Garvin .... .03 .01 .00
□ 430 Alfredo Griffin .... .10 .04 .01
□ 431 Bob Mattick MG .... .03 .01 .00
□ 432 Vida Blue .... .10 .04 .01
□ 433 Jack Clark .... .30 .12 .03
□ 434 Willie McCovey .... .35 .14 .03
□ 435 Mike Ivie .... .03 .01 .00
□ 436A Darrel Evans P1 ERR ... .40 .16 .04
Name on front "Darrel"
□ 436B Darrell Evans P2 .... .15 .06 .01
Name on front
"Darrell"
□ 437 Terry Whitfield .... .03 .01 .00
□ 438 Rennie Stennett .... .03 .01 .00
□ 439 John Montefusco .... .06 .02 .00
□ 440 Jim Wohlford .... .03 .01 .00
□ 441 Bill North .... .03 .01 .00
□ 442 Milt May .... .03 .01 .00
□ 443 Max Venable .... .03 .01 .00
□ 444 Ed Whitson .... .06 .02 .00
□ 445 Al Holland .... .06 .02 .00
□ 446 Randy Moffitt .... .03 .01 .00
□ 447 Bob Knepper .... .10 .04 .01
□ 448 Gary Lavelle .... .03 .01 .00
□ 449 Greg Minton .... .03 .01 .00
□ 450 Johnnie LeMaster .... .03 .01 .00
□ 451 Larry Herndon .... .03 .01 .00
□ 452 Rich Murray .... .03 .01 .00
□ 453 Joe Pettini .... .03 .01 .00
□ 454 Allen Ripley .... .03 .01 .00
□ 455 Dennis Littlejohn .... .03 .01 .00
□ 456 Tom Griffin .... .03 .01 .00
□ 457 Alan Hargesheimer .... .03 .01 .00
□ 458 Joe Strain .... .03 .01 .00
□ 459 Steve Kemp .... .06 .02 .00
□ 460 Sparky Anderson MG ..... .06 .02 .00
□ 461 Alan Trammell .... .35 .14 .03
□ 462 Mark Fidrych .... .10 .04 .01
□ 463 Lou Whitaker .... .20 .08 .02
□ 464 Dave Rozema .... .03 .01 .00
□ 465 Milt Wilcox .... .03 .01 .00
□ 466 Champ Summers .... .03 .01 .00
□ 467 Lance Parrish .... .25 .10 .02
□ 468 Dan Petry .... .10 .04 .01
□ 469 Pat Underwood .... .03 .01 .00
□ 470 Rick Peters .... .03 .01 .00
□ 471 Al Cowens .... .03 .01 .00
□ 472 John Wockenfuss .... .03 .01 .00
□ 473 Tom Brookens .... .03 .01 .00
□ 474 Richie Hebner .... .03 .01 .00
□ 475 Jack Morris .... .30 .12 .03
□ 476 Jim Lentine .... .03 .01 .00
□ 477 Bruce Robbins .... .03 .01 .00
□ 478 Mark Wagner .... .03 .01 .00
□ 479 Tim Corcoran .... .03 .01 .00
□ 480A Stan Papi P1 .... .15 .06 .01
Front as Pitcher
□ 480B Stan Papi P2 .... .10 .04 .01
Front as Shortstop
□ 481 Kirk Gibson .... 3.50 1.40 .35
□ 482 Dan Schatzeder .... .03 .01 .00
□ 483A Amos Otis P1 .... .10 .04 .01
See card 32
□ 483B Amos Otis P2 .... .10 .04 .01
See card 32
□ 484 Dave Winfield .... .50 .20 .05
□ 485 Rollie Fingers .... .30 .12 .03
□ 486 Gene Richards .... .03 .01 .00
□ 487 Randy Jones .... .03 .01 .00
□ 488 Ozzie Smith .... .30 .12 .03
□ 489 Gene Tenace .... .03 .01 .00
□ 490 Bill Fahey .... .03 .01 .00
□ 491 John Curtis .... .03 .01 .00
□ 492 Dave Cash .... .03 .01 .00
□ 493A Tim Flannery P1 .... .15 .06 .01
Batting right
□ 493B Tim Flannery P2 .... .06 .02 .00
Batting left
□ 494 Jerry Mumphrey .... .03 .01 .00
□ 495 Bob Shirley .... .03 .01 .00
□ 496 Steve Mura .... .03 .01 .00
□ 497 Eric Rasmussen .... .03 .01 .00
□ 498 Broderick Perkins .... .03 .01 .00
□ 499 Barry Evans .... .03 .01 .0
□ 500 Chuck Baker .... .03 .01 .0
□ 501 Luis Salazar .... .15 .06 .0
□ 502 Gary Lucas .... .06 .02 .0
□ 503 Mike Armstrong .... .06 .02 .0
□ 504 Jerry Turner .... .03 .01 .0
□ 505 Dennis Kinney .... .03 .01 .0
□ 506 Willie Montanez .... .03 .01 .0
□ 507 Gorman Thomas .... .10 .04 .0
□ 508 Ben Oglivie .... .06 .02 .0
□ 509 Larry Hisle .... .06 .02 .0
□ 510 Sal Bando .... .06 .02 .0
□ 511 Robin Yount .... .40 .16 .0
□ 512 Mike Caldwell .... .03 .01 .0
□ 513 Sixto Lezcano .... .03 .01 .0
□ 514A Bill Travers P1 ERR ...... .20 .08 .0
"Jerry Augustine"
with Augustine back
□ 514B Bill Travers P2 COR ...... .10 .04 .0
□ 515 Paul Molitor .... .25 .10 .0
□ 516 Moose Haas .... .03 .01 .0
□ 517 Bill Castro .... .03 .01 .0
□ 518 Jim Slaton .... .03 .01 .0
□ 519 Lary Sorensen .... .03 .01 .0
□ 520 Bob McClure .... .03 .01 .0
□ 521 Charlie Moore .... .03 .01 .0
□ 522 Jim Gantner .... .03 .01 .0
□ 523 Reggie Cleveland .... .03 .01 .0
□ 524 Don Money .... .03 .01 .0
□ 525 Bill Travers .... .03 .01 .0
□ 526 Buck Martinez .... .03 .01 .0
□ 527 Dick Davis .... .03 .01 .0
□ 528 Ted Simmons .... .15 .06 .0
□ 529 Garry Templeton .... .10 .04 .0
□ 530 Ken Reitz .... .03 .01 .0
□ 531 Tony Scott .... .03 .01 .0
□ 532 Ken Oberkfell .... .03 .01 .0
□ 533 Bob Sykes .... .03 .01 .0
□ 534 Keith Smith .... .03 .01 .0
□ 535 John Littlefield .... .03 .01 .0
□ 536 Jim Kaat .... .15 .06 .0
□ 537 Bob Forsch .... .03 .01 .0
□ 538 Mike Phillips .... .03 .01 .0
□ 539 Terry Landrum .... .06 .02 .0
□ 540 Leon Durham .... .35 .14 .0
□ 541 Terry Kennedy .... .06 .02 .0
□ 542 George Hendrick .... .06 .02 .0
□ 543 Dane Iorg .... .03 .01 .0
□ 544 Mark Littell .... .03 .01 .0
□ 545 Keith Hernandez .... .35 .14 .0
□ 546 Silvio Martinez .... .03 .01 .0
□ 547A Don Hood P1 ERR .... .20 .08 .02
"Pete Vuckovich"
with Vuckovich back
□ 547B Don Hood P2 COR .... .10 .04 .01
□ 548 Bobby Bonds .... .10 .04 .01
□ 549 Mike Ramsey .... .03 .01 .00
□ 550 Tom Herr .... .15 .06 .01
□ 551 Roy Smalley .... .03 .01 .00
□ 552 Jerry Koosman .... .06 .02 .00
□ 553 Ken Landreaux .... .03 .01 .00
□ 554 John Castino .... .03 .01 .00
□ 555 Doug Corbett .... .06 .02 .00
□ 556 Bombo Rivera .... .03 .01 .00
□ 557 Ron Jackson .... .03 .01 .00
□ 558 Butch Wynegar .... .03 .01 .00
□ 559 Hosken Powell .... .03 .01 .00
□ 560 Pete Redfern .... .03 .01 .00
□ 561 Roger Erickson .... .03 .01 .00
□ 562 Glenn Adams .... .03 .01 .00
□ 563 Rick Sofield .... .03 .01 .00
□ 564 Geoff Zahn .... .03 .01 .00
□ 565 Pete Mackanin .... .03 .01 .00
□ 566 Mike Cubbage .... .03 .01 .00
□ 567 Darrell Jackson .... .03 .01 .00
□ 568 Dave Edwards .... .03 .01 .00
□ 569 Rob Wilfong .... .03 .01 .00
□ 570 Sal Butera .... .03 .01 .00
□ 571 Jose Morales .... .03 .01 .00
□ 572 Rick Langford .... .03 .01 .00
□ 573 Mike Norris .... .03 .01 .00
□ 574 Rickey Henderson .... 1.75 .70 .17
□ 575 Tony Armas .... .10 .04 .01
□ 576 Dave Revering .... .03 .01 .00
□ 577 Jeff Newman .... .03 .01 .00
□ 578 Bob Lacey .... .03 .01 .00
□ 579 Brian Kingman .... .03 .01 .00
□ 580 Mitchell Page .... .03 .01 .00
□ 581 Billy Martin MG .... .15 .06 .01
□ 582 Rob Picciolo .... .03 .01 .00
□ 583 Mike Heath .... .03 .01 .00
□ 584 Mickey Klutts .... .03 .01 .00
□ 585 Orlando Gonzalez .... .03 .01 .00
□ 586 Mike Davis .... .30 .12 .03
□ 587 Wayne Gross .... .03 .01 .00

Card	Player	Mint	Exc	G-VG
□ 588	Matt Keough	.03	.01	.00
□ 589	Steve McCatty	.03	.01	.00
□ 590	Dwayne Murphy	.03	.01	.00
□ 591	Mario Guerrero	.03	.01	.00
□ 592	Dave McKay	.03	.01	.00
□ 593	Jim Essian	.03	.01	.00
□ 594	Dave Heaverlo	.03	.01	.00
□ 595	Maury Wills MG	.06	.02	.00
□ 596	Juan Beniquez	.03	.01	.00
□ 597	Rodney Craig	.03	.01	.00
□ 598	Jim Anderson	.03	.01	.00
□ 599	Floyd Bannister	.06	.02	.00
□ 600	Bruce Bochte	.03	.01	.00
□ 601	Julio Cruz	.03	.01	.00
□ 602	Ted Cox	.03	.01	.00
□ 603	Dan Meyer	.03	.01	.00
□ 604	Larry Cox	.03	.01	.00
□ 605	Bill Stein	.03	.01	.00
□ 606	Steve Garvey	.55	.22	.05
□ 607	Dave Roberts	.03	.01	.00
□ 608	Leon Roberts	.03	.01	.00
□ 609	Reggie Walton	.03	.01	.00
□ 610	Dave Edler	.03	.01	.00
□ 611	Larry Milbourne	.03	.01	.00
□ 612	Kim Allen	.03	.01	.00
□ 613	Mario Mendoza	.03	.01	.00
□ 614	Tom Paciorek	.03	.01	.00
□ 615	Glenn Abbott	.03	.01	.00
□ 616	Joe Simpson	.03	.01	.00
□ 617	Mickey Rivers	.06	.02	.00
□ 618	Jim Kern	.03	.01	.00
□ 619	Jim Sundberg	.06	.02	.00
□ 620	Richie Zisk	.06	.02	.00
□ 621	Jon Matlack	.03	.01	.00
□ 622	Ferguson Jenkins	.15	.06	.01
□ 623	Pat Corrales MG	.03	.01	.00
□ 624	Ed Figueroa	.03	.01	.00
□ 625	Buddy Bell	.15	.06	.01
□ 626	Al Oliver	.12	.05	.01
□ 627	Doc Medich	.03	.01	.00
□ 628	Bump Wills	.03	.01	.00
□ 629	Rusty Staub	.10	.04	.01
□ 630	Pat Putnam	.03	.01	.00
□ 631	John Grubb	.03	.01	.00
□ 632	Danny Darwin	.03	.01	.00
□ 633	Ken Clay	.03	.01	.00
□ 634	Jim Norris	.03	.01	.00
□ 635	John Butcher	.06	.02	.00
□ 636	Dave Roberts	.03	.01	.00
□ 637	Billy Sample	.03	.01	.00
□ 638	Carl Yastrzemski	1.00	.40	.10
□ 639	Cecil Cooper	.15	.06	.01
□ 640A	Mike Schmidt P1	1.00	.40	.10
	(Portrait)			
	"Third Base"			
	(number on back 5)			
□ 640B	Mike Schmidt P2	1.00	.40	.10
	"1980 Home Run King"			
	(640 on back)			
□ 641A	CL: Phils/Royals P1	.10	.01	.00
	41 is Hal McRae			
□ 641B	CL: Phils/Royals P2	.10	.01	.00
	41 is Hal McRae,			
	Double Threat			
□ 642	CL: Astros/Yankees	.08	.01	.00
□ 643	CL: Expos/Dodgers	.08	.01	.00
□ 644A	CL: Reds/Orioles P1	.10	.01	.00
	202 is George Foster			
□ 644B	CL: Reds/Orioles P2	.10	.01	.00
	202 is Foster Slugger			
□ 645A	Rose/Bowa/Schmidt	2.00	.80	.20
	Triple Threat P1			
	(No number on back)			
□ 645B	Rose/Bowa/Schmidt	1.00	.40	.10
	Triple Threat P2			
	(Back numbered 645)			
□ 646	CL: Braves/Red Sox	.08	.01	.00
□ 647	CL: Cubs/Angels	.08	.01	.00
□ 648	CL: Mets/White Sox	.08	.01	.00
□ 649	CL: Indians/Pirates	.08	.01	.00
□ 650A	Reggie Jackson	1.25	.50	.12
	Mr. Baseball P1			
	Number on back 79			
□ 650B	Reggie Jackson	.85	.34	.08
	Mr. Baseball P2			
	Number on back 650			
□ 651	CL: Giants/Blue Jays	.08	.01	.00
□ 652A	CL: Tigers/Padres P1	.10	.01	.00
	483 is listed			
□ 652B	CL: Tigers/Padres P2	.10	.01	.00
	483 is deleted			
□ 653A	Willie Wilson P1	.10	.04	.01
	Most Hits Most Runs			
	Number on back 29			
□ 653B	Willie Wilson P2	.10	.04	.01
	Most Hits Most Runs			
	Number on back 653			
□ 654A	CL:Brewers/Cards P1	.10	.01	.00
	514 Jerry Augustine			
	547 Pete Vuckovich			
□ 654B	CL:Brewers/Cards P2	.10	.01	.00
	514 Billy Travers			
	547 Don Hood			
□ 655A	George Brett P1	1.25	.50	.12
	.390 Average			
	Number on back 28			
□ 655B	George Brett P2	.85	.34	.08
	.390 Average			
	Number on back 655			
□ 656	CL: Twins/Oakland A's	.08	.01	.00
□ 657A	Tug McGraw P1	.10	.04	.01
	Game Saver			
	Number on back 7			
□ 657B	Tug McGraw P2	.10	.04	.01
	Game Saver			
	Number on back 657			
□ 658	CL: Rangers/Mariners	.08	.01	.00
□ 659A	Checklist P1	.10	.01	.00
	of Special Cards			
	Last lines on front			
	Wilson Most Hits			
□ 659B	Checklist P2	.10	.01	.00
	of Special Cards			
	Last lines on front			
	Otis Series Starter			
□ 660A	Steve Carlton P1	.65	.26	.06
	Golden Arm			
	Back "1066 Cardinals"			
	Number on back 6			
□ 660B	Steve Carlton P2	.65	.26	.06
	Golden Arm			
	Number on back 660			
	Back "1066 Cardinals"			
□ 660C	Steve Carlton P3	2.00	.80	.20
	Golden Arm			
	"1966 Cardinals"			

1981 Fleer Sticker Cards

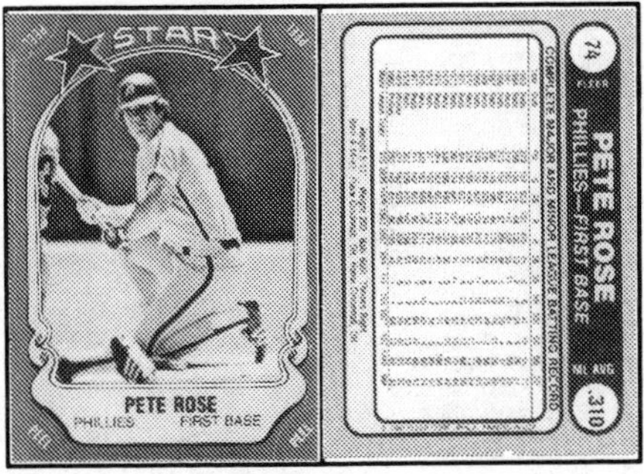

The stickers in this 128-sticker set measure 2 1/2" by 3 1/2". The 1981 Fleer Baseball Star Stickers consist of numbered cards with peelable, full color sticker fronts and three unnumbered checklists. The backs of the numbered player cards are the same as the 1981 Fleer regular issue cards except for the numbers, while the checklist cards (cards 126-128 below) have sticker fronts of Jackson (1-42), Brett (43-83) and Schmidt (84- 125).

	MINT	EXC	G-VG
COMPLETE SET (128)	40.00	16.00	4.00
COMMON PLAYER (1-128)	.15	.06	.01

Card	Player	Mint	Exc	G-VG
□ 1	Steve Garvey	1.75	.70	.17
□ 2	Ron LeFlore	.15	.06	.01
□ 3	Ron Cey	.20	.08	.02
□ 4	Dave Revering	.15	.06	.01
□ 5	Tony Armas	.15	.06	.01
□ 6	Mike Norris	.15	.06	.01
□ 7	Steve Kemp	.20	.08	.02
□ 8	Bruce Bochte	.15	.06	.01
□ 9	Mike Schmidt	2.50	1.00	.25
□ 10	Scott McGregor	.20	.08	.02

□ 11	Buddy Bell	.25	.10	.02
□ 12	Carney Lansford	.20	.08	.02
□ 13	Carl Yastrzemski	3.00	1.20	.30
□ 14	Ben Oglivie	.15	.06	.01
□ 15	Willie Stargell	1.25	.50	.12
□ 16	Cecil Cooper	.25	.10	.02
□ 17	Gene Richards	.15	.06	.01
□ 18	Jim Kern	.15	.06	.01
□ 19	Jerry Koosman	.20	.08	.02
□ 20	Larry Bowa	.25	.10	.02
□ 21	Kent Tekulve	.15	.06	.01
□ 22	Dan Driessen	.15	.06	.01
□ 23	Phil Niekro	.75	.30	.07
□ 24	Dan Quisenberry	.30	.12	.03
□ 25	Dave Winfield	1.75	.70	.17
□ 26	Dave Parker	.60	.24	.06
□ 27	Rick Langford	.15	.06	.01
□ 28	Amos Otis	.20	.08	.02
□ 29	Bill Buckner	.20	.08	.02
□ 30	Al Bumbry	.15	.06	.01
□ 31	Bake McBride	.15	.06	.01
□ 32	Mickey Rivers	.15	.06	.01
□ 33	Rick Burleson	.20	.08	.02
□ 34	Dennis Eckersley	.35	.14	.03
□ 35	Cesar Cedeno	.20	.08	.02
□ 36	Enos Cabell	.15	.06	.01
□ 37	Johnny Bench	2.50	1.00	.25
□ 38	Robin Yount	1.75	.70	.17
□ 39	Mark Belanger	.15	.06	.01
□ 40	Rod Carew	1.75	.70	.17
□ 41	George Foster	.60	.24	.06
□ 42	Lee Mazzilli	.15	.06	.01
□ 43	Triple Threat: Pete Rose Larry Bowa Mike Schmidt	2.00	.80	.20
□ 44	J.R. Richard	.20	.08	.02
□ 45	Lou Piniella	.20	.08	.02
□ 46	Ken Landreaux	.15	.06	.01
□ 47	Rollie Fingers	.50	.20	.05
□ 48	Joaquin Andujar	.20	.08	.02
□ 49	Tom Seaver	2.00	.80	.20
□ 50	Bobby Grich	.20	.08	.02
□ 51	Jon Matlack	.15	.06	.01
□ 52	Jack Clark	.60	.24	.06
□ 53	Jim Rice	1.00	.40	.10
□ 54	Rickey Henderson	2.00	.80	.20
□ 55	Roy Smalley	.15	.06	.01
□ 56	Mike Flanagan	.20	.08	.02
□ 57	Steve Rogers	.15	.06	.01
□ 58	Carlton Fisk	.50	.20	.05
□ 59	Don Sutton	.60	.24	.06
□ 60	Ken Griffey	.20	.08	.02
□ 61	Burt Hooton	.15	.06	.01
□ 62	Dusty Baker	.20	.08	.02
□ 63	Vida Blue	.20	.08	.02
□ 64	Al Oliver	.20	.08	.02
□ 65	Jim Bibby	.15	.06	.01
□ 66	Tony Perez	.40	.16	.04
□ 67	Davy Lopes	.20	.08	.02
□ 68	Bill Russell	.15	.06	.01
□ 69	Larry Parrish	.20	.08	.02
□ 70	Garry Maddox	.15	.06	.01
□ 71	Phil Garner	.15	.06	.01
□ 72	Graig Nettles	.35	.14	.03
□ 73	Gary Carter	1.75	.70	.17
□ 74	Pete Rose	4.50	1.80	.45
□ 75	Greg Luzinski	.30	.12	.03
□ 76	Ron Guidry	.50	.20	.05
□ 77	Gorman Thomas	.25	.10	.02
□ 78	Jose Cruz	.20	.08	.02
□ 79	Bob Boone	.30	.12	.03
□ 80	Bruce Sutter	.30	.12	.03
□ 81	Chris Chambliss	.20	.08	.02
□ 82	Paul Molitor	.60	.24	.06
□ 83	Tug McGraw	.25	.10	.02
□ 84	Ferguson Jenkins	.40	.16	.04
□ 85	Steve Carlton	1.75	.70	.17
□ 86	Miguel Dilone	.15	.06	.01
□ 87	Reggie Smith	.25	.10	.02
□ 88	Rick Cerone	.15	.06	.01
□ 89	Alan Trammell	1.00	.40	.10
□ 90	Doug DeCinces	.25	.10	.02
□ 91	Sparky Lyle	.25	.10	.02
□ 92	Warren Cromartie	.15	.06	.01
□ 93	Rick Reuschel	.30	.12	.03
□ 94	Larry Hisle	.15	.06	.01
□ 95	Paul Splittorff	.20	.08	.02
□ 96	Manny Trillo	.15	.06	.01
□ 97	Frank White	.25	.10	.02
□ 98	Fred Lynn	.50	.20	.05
□ 99	Bob Horner	.50	.20	.05
□ 100	Omar Moreno	.15	.06	.01
□ 101	Dave Concepcion	.20	.08	.02
□ 102	Larry Gura	.20	.08	.02
□ 103	Ken Singleton	.20	.08	.0
□ 104	Steve Stone	.15	.06	.0
□ 105	Richie Zisk	.15	.06	.0
□ 106	Willie Wilson	.30	.12	.0
□ 107	Willie Randolph	.30	.12	.0
□ 108	Nolan Ryan	2.00	.80	.2
□ 109	Joe Morgan	1.00	.40	.1
□ 110	Bucky Dent	.25	.10	.0
□ 111	Dave Kingman	.35	.14	.0
□ 112	John Castino	.15	.06	.0
□ 113	Joe Rudi	.15	.06	.0
□ 114	Ed Farmer	.15	.06	.0
□ 115	Reggie Jackson	2.50	1.00	.2
□ 116	George Brett	2.50	1.00	.2
□ 117	Eddie Murray	2.25	.90	.2
□ 118	Rich Gossage	.50	.20	.0
□ 119	Dale Murphy	2.50	1.00	.2
□ 120	Ted Simmons	.25	.10	.0
□ 121	Tommy John	.50	.20	.0
□ 122	Don Baylor	.40	.16	.0
□ 123	Andre Dawson	1.50	.60	.1
□ 124	Jim Palmer	1.25	.50	.1
□ 125	Garry Templeton	.25	.10	.0
□ 126	CL 1: Reggie Jackson	1.25	.50	.1
□ 127	CL 2: George Brett	1.25	.50	.1
□ 128	CL 3: Mike Schmidt	1.25	.50	.1

1982 Fleer

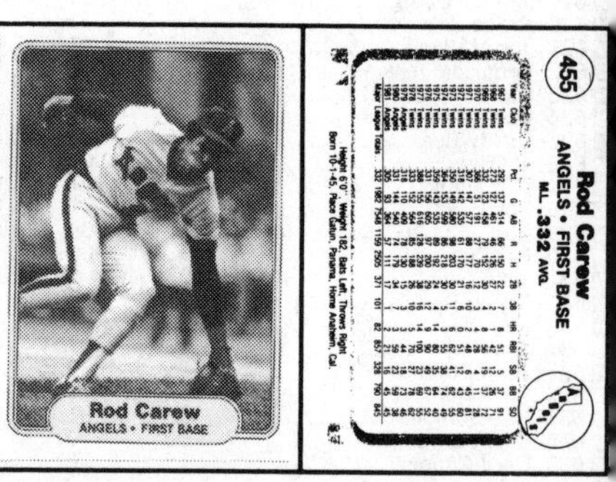

The cards in this 660-card set measure 2 1/2" by 3 1/2". The 1982 Fleer set is again ordered by teams; in fact the players within each team are listed in alphabetical order. The teams are ordered (by 1981 standings) as follows: Los Angeles (1- 29), New York Yankees (30-56), Cincinnati (57-84), Oakland (85-109), St. Louis (110-132), Milwaukee (133-156), Baltimore (157- 182), Montreal (183-211), Houston (212-237), Philadelphia (238- 262), Detroit (263-286), Boston (287-312), Texas (313-334), Chicago White Sox (335-358), Cleveland (359-382), San Francisco (383-403), Kansas City (404-427), Atlanta (428-449), California (450-474), Pittsburgh (475-501), Seattle (502-519), New York Mets (520-544), Minnesota (545-565), San Diego (566-585), Chicago Cubs (586-607), and Toronto (608-627). Cards numbered 628 through 646 are special cards highlighting some of the stars and leaders of the 1981 season. The last 14 cards in the set (647-660) are checklist cards. The backs feature player statistics and a full color team logo in the upper right-hand corner of each card.

		MINT	EXC	G-VG
COMPLETE SET (660)		30.00	12.00	3.0
COMMON PLAYER (1-660)		.03	.01	.0
□ 1	Dusty Baker	.12	.03	.01
□ 2	Robert Castillo	.03	.01	.00
□ 3	Ron Cey	.10	.04	.01
□ 4	Terry Forster	.06	.02	.00
□ 5	Steve Garvey	.50	.20	.05
□ 6	Dave Goltz	.03	.01	.00
□ 7	Pedro Guerrero	.35	.14	.03
□ 8	Burt Hooton	.03	.01	.00

☐	9	Steve Howe	.03	.01	.00
☐	10	Jay Johnstone	.06	.02	.00
☐	11	Ken Landreaux	.03	.01	.00
☐	12	Davey Lopes	.08	.03	.01
☐	13	Mike Marshall	1.25	.50	.12
☐	14	Bobby Mitchell	.03	.01	.00
☐	15	Rick Monday	.03	.01	.00
☐	16	Tom Niedenfuer	.20	.08	.02
☐	17	Ted Power	.20	.08	.02
☐	18	Jerry Reuss	.06	.02	.00
☐	19	Ron Roenicke	.03	.01	.00
☐	20	Bill Russell	.06	.02	.00
☐	21	Steve Sax	2.00	.80	.20
☐	22	Mike Scioscia	.06	.02	.00
☐	23	Reggie Smith	.08	.03	.01
☐	24	Dave Stewart	1.00	.40	.10
☐	25	Rick Sutcliffe	.20	.08	.02
☐	26	Derrel Thomas	.03	.01	.00
☐	27	Fernando Valenzuela	.50	.20	.05
☐	28	Bob Welch	.10	.04	.01
☐	29	Steve Yeager	.03	.01	.00
☐	30	Bobby Brown	.03	.01	.00
☐	31	Rick Cerone	.03	.01	.00
☐	32	Ron Davis	.03	.01	.00
☐	33	Bucky Dent	.08	.03	.01
☐	34	Barry Foote	.03	.01	.00
☐	35	George Frazier	.03	.01	.00
☐	36	Oscar Gamble	.03	.01	.00
☐	37	Rich Gossage	.18	.08	.01
☐	38	Ron Guidry	.18	.08	.01
☐	39	Reggie Jackson	.60	.24	.06
☐	40	Tommy John	.15	.06	.01
☐	41	Rudy May	.03	.01	.00
☐	42	Larry Milbourne	.03	.01	.00
☐	43	Jerry Mumphrey	.03	.01	.00
☐	44	Bobby Murcer	.08	.03	.01
☐	45	Gene Nelson	.20	.08	.02
☐	46	Graig Nettles	.12	.05	.01
☐	47	Johnny Oates	.03	.01	.00
☐	48	Lou Piniella	.10	.04	.01
☐	49	Willie Randolph	.08	.03	.01
☐	50	Rick Reuschel	.10	.04	.01
☐	51	Dave Revering	.03	.01	.00
☐	52	Dave Righetti	1.50	.60	.15
☐	53	Aurelio Rodriguez	.03	.01	.00
☐	54	Bob Watson	.06	.02	.00
☐	55	Dennis Werth	.03	.01	.00
☐	56	Dave Winfield	.50	.20	.05
☐	57	Johnny Bench	.55	.22	.05
☐	58	Bruce Berenyi	.03	.01	.00
☐	59	Larry Biittner	.03	.01	.00
☐	60	Scott Brown	.03	.01	.00
☐	61	Dave Collins	.03	.01	.00
☐	62	Geoff Combe	.03	.01	.00
☐	63	Dave Concepcion	.10	.04	.01
☐	64	Dan Driessen	.03	.01	.00
☐	65	Joe Edelen	.03	.01	.00
☐	66	George Foster	.12	.05	.01
☐	67	Ken Griffey	.06	.02	.00
☐	68	Paul Householder	.03	.01	.00
☐	69	Tom Hume	.03	.01	.00
☐	70	Junior Kennedy	.03	.01	.00
☐	71	Ray Knight	.08	.03	.01
☐	72	Mike LaCoss	.03	.01	.00
☐	73	Rafael Landestoy	.03	.01	.00
☐	74	Charlie Leibrandt	.06	.02	.00
☐	75	Sam Mejias	.03	.01	.00
☐	76	Paul Moskau	.03	.01	.00
☐	77	Joe Nolan	.03	.01	.00
☐	78	Mike O'Berry	.03	.01	.00
☐	79	Ron Oester	.03	.01	.00
☐	80	Frank Pastore	.03	.01	.00
☐	81	Joe Price	.03	.01	.00
☐	82	Tom Seaver	.45	.18	.04
☐	83	Mario Soto	.06	.02	.00
☐	84	Mike Vail	.03	.01	.00
☐	85	Tony Armas	.08	.03	.01
☐	86	Shooty Babitt	.03	.01	.00
☐	87	Dave Beard	.03	.01	.00
☐	88	Rick Bosetti	.03	.01	.00
☐	89	Keith Drumright	.03	.01	.00
☐	90	Wayne Gross	.03	.01	.00
☐	91	Mike Heath	.03	.01	.00
☐	92	Rickey Henderson	.75	.30	.07
☐	93	Cliff Johnson	.03	.01	.00
☐	94	Jeff Jones	.03	.01	.00
☐	95	Matt Keough	.03	.01	.00
☐	96	Brian Kingman	.03	.01	.00
☐	97	Mickey Klutts	.03	.01	.00
☐	98	Rick Langford	.03	.01	.00
☐	99	Steve McCatty	.03	.01	.00
☐	100	Dave McKay	.03	.01	.00
☐	101	Dwayne Murphy	.03	.01	.00
☐	102	Jeff Newman	.03	.01	.00
☐	103	Mike Norris	.03	.01	.00
☐	104	Bob Owchinko	.03	.01	.00
☐	105	Mitchell Page	.03	.01	.00
☐	106	Rob Picciolo	.03	.01	.00
☐	107	Jim Spencer	.03	.01	.00
☐	108	Fred Stanley	.03	.01	.00
☐	109	Tom Underwood	.03	.01	.00
☐	110	Joaquin Andujar	.08	.03	.01
☐	111	Steve Braun	.03	.01	.00
☐	112	Bob Forsch	.03	.01	.00
☐	113	George Hendrick	.06	.02	.00
☐	114	Keith Hernandez	.35	.14	.03
☐	115	Tom Herr	.08	.03	.01
☐	116	Dane Iorg	.03	.01	.00
☐	117	Jim Kaat	.15	.06	.01
☐	118	Tito Landrum	.03	.01	.00
☐	119	Sixto Lezcano	.03	.01	.00
☐	120	Mark Littell	.03	.01	.00
☐	121	John Martin	.03	.01	.00
☐	122	Silvio Martinez	.03	.01	.00
☐	123	Ken Oberkfell	.03	.01	.00
☐	124	Darrell Porter	.03	.01	.00
☐	125	Mike Ramsey	.03	.01	.00
☐	126	Orlando Sanchez	.03	.01	.00
☐	127	Bob Shirley	.03	.01	.00
☐	128	Lary Sorensen	.03	.01	.00
☐	129	Bruce Sutter	.15	.06	.01
☐	130	Bob Sykes	.03	.01	.00
☐	131	Garry Templeton	.08	.03	.01
☐	132	Gene Tenace	.03	.01	.00
☐	133	Jerry Augustine	.03	.01	.00
☐	134	Sal Bando	.06	.02	.00
☐	135	Mark Brouhard	.03	.01	.00
☐	136	Mike Caldwell	.03	.01	.00
☐	137	Reggie Cleveland	.03	.01	.00
☐	138	Cecil Cooper	.15	.06	.01
☐	139	Jamie Easterly	.03	.01	.00
☐	140	Marshall Edwards	.03	.01	.00
☐	141	Rollie Fingers	.20	.08	.02
☐	142	Jim Gantner	.03	.01	.00
☐	143	Moose Haas	.03	.01	.00
☐	144	Larry Hisle	.03	.01	.00
☐	145	Roy Howell	.03	.01	.00
☐	146	Rickey Keeton	.03	.01	.00
☐	147	Randy Lerch	.03	.01	.00
☐	148	Paul Molitor	.20	.08	.02
☐	149	Don Money	.03	.01	.00
☐	150	Charlie Moore	.03	.01	.00
☐	151	Ben Oglivie	.06	.02	.00
☐	152	Ted Simmons	.12	.05	.01
☐	153	Jim Slaton	.03	.01	.00
☐	154	Gorman Thomas	.10	.04	.01
☐	155	Robin Yount	.50	.20	.05
☐	156	Pete Vuckovich	.08	.03	.01
☐	157	Benny Ayala	.03	.01	.00
☐	158	Mark Belanger	.06	.02	.00
☐	159	Al Bumbry	.03	.01	.00
☐	160	Terry Crowley	.03	.01	.00
☐	161	Rich Dauer	.03	.01	.00
☐	162	Doug DeCinces	.06	.02	.00
☐	163	Rick Dempsey	.03	.01	.00
☐	164	Jim Dwyer	.03	.01	.00
☐	165	Mike Flanagan	.08	.03	.01
☐	166	Dave Ford	.03	.01	.00
☐	167	Dan Graham	.03	.01	.00
☐	168	Wayne Krenchicki	.03	.01	.00
☐	169	John Lowenstein	.03	.01	.00
☐	170	Dennis Martinez	.08	.03	.01
☐	171	Tippy Martinez	.03	.01	.00
☐	172	Scott McGregor	.06	.02	.00
☐	173	Jose Morales	.03	.01	.00
☐	174	Eddie Murray	.60	.24	.06
☐	175	Jim Palmer	.35	.14	.03
☐	176	Cal Ripken	7.50	3.00	.75
☐	177	Gary Roenicke	.03	.01	.00
☐	178	Lenn Sakata	.03	.01	.00
☐	179	Ken Singleton	.08	.03	.01
☐	180	Sammy Stewart	.03	.01	.00
☐	181	Tim Stoddard	.03	.01	.00
☐	182	Steve Stone	.06	.02	.00
☐	183	Stan Bahnsen	.03	.01	.00
☐	184	Ray Burris	.03	.01	.00
☐	185	Gary Carter	.45	.18	.04
☐	186	Warren Cromartie	.03	.01	.00
☐	187	Andre Dawson	.35	.14	.03
☐	188	Terry Francona	.10	.04	.01
☐	189	Woodie Fryman	.03	.01	.00
☐	190	Bill Gullickson	.06	.02	.00
☐	191	Grant Jackson	.03	.01	.00
☐	192	Wallace Johnson	.06	.02	.00
☐	193	Charlie Lea	.06	.02	.00
☐	194	Bill Lee	.06	.02	.00
☐	195	Jerry Manuel	.03	.01	.00
☐	196	Brad Mills	.03	.01	.00
☐	197	John Milner	.03	.01	.00
☐	198	Rowland Office	.03	.01	.00

□ 199 David Palmer .03 .01 .00
□ 200 Larry Parrish .06 .02 .00
□ 201 Mike Phillips .03 .01 .00
□ 202 Tim Raines 1.75 .70 .17
□ 203 Bobby Ramos .03 .01 .00
□ 204 Jeff Reardon .15 .06 .01
□ 205 Steve Rogers .06 .02 .00
□ 206 Scott Sanderson .03 .01 .00
□ 207 Rodney Scott (photo actually Tim Raines) .15 .06 .01
□ 208 Elias Sosa .03 .01 .00
□ 209 Chris Speier .03 .01 .00
□ 210 Tim Wallach .80 .32 .08
□ 211 Jerry White .03 .01 .00
□ 212 Alan Ashby .06 .02 .00
□ 213 Cesar Cedeno .08 .03 .01
□ 214 Jose Cruz .10 .04 .01
□ 215 Kiko Garcia .03 .01 .00
□ 216 Phil Garner .03 .01 .00
□ 217 Danny Heep .03 .01 .00
□ 218 Art Howe .08 .03 .01
□ 219 Bob Knepper .10 .04 .01
□ 220 Frank LaCorte .03 .01 .00
□ 221 Joe Niekro .10 .04 .01
□ 222 Joe Pittman .03 .01 .00
□ 223 Terry Puhl .03 .01 .00
□ 224 Luis Pujols .03 .01 .00
□ 225 Craig Reynolds .03 .01 .00
□ 226 J.R. Richard .10 .04 .01
□ 227 Dave Roberts .03 .01 .00
□ 228 Vern Ruhle .03 .01 .00
□ 229 Nolan Ryan .50 .20 .05
□ 230 Joe Sambito .03 .01 .00
□ 231 Tony Scott .03 .01 .00
□ 232 Dave Smith .08 .03 .01
□ 233 Harry Spilman .03 .01 .00
□ 234 Don Sutton .30 .12 .03
□ 235 Dickie Thon .06 .02 .00
□ 236 Denny Walling .03 .01 .00
□ 237 Gary Woods .03 .01 .00
□ 238 Luis Aguayo .03 .01 .00
□ 239 Ramon Aviles .03 .01 .00
□ 240 Bob Boone .12 .05 .01
□ 241 Larry Bowa .15 .06 .01
□ 242 Warren Brusstar .03 .01 .00
□ 243 Steve Carlton .50 .20 .05
□ 244 Larry Christenson .03 .01 .00
□ 245 Dick Davis .03 .01 .00
□ 246 Greg Gross .03 .01 .00
□ 247 Sparky Lyle .10 .04 .01
□ 248 Garry Maddox .06 .02 .00
□ 249 Gary Matthews .06 .02 .00
□ 250 Bake McBride .03 .01 .00
□ 251 Tug McGraw .10 .04 .01
□ 252 Keith Moreland .06 .02 .00
□ 253 Dickie Noles .03 .01 .00
□ 254 Mike Proly .03 .01 .00
□ 255 Ron Reed .03 .01 .00
□ 256 Pete Rose 1.25 .50 .12
□ 257 Dick Ruthven .03 .01 .00
□ 258 Mike Schmidt .75 .30 .07
□ 259 Lonnie Smith .06 .02 .00
□ 260 Manny Trillo .03 .01 .00
□ 261 Del Unser .03 .01 .00
□ 262 George Vukovich .03 .01 .00
□ 263 Tom Brookens .03 .01 .00
□ 264 George Cappuzzello .03 .01 .00
□ 265 Marty Castillo .03 .01 .00
□ 266 Al Cowens .03 .01 .00
□ 267 Kirk Gibson .75 .30 .07
□ 268 Richie Hebner .03 .01 .00
□ 269 Ron Jackson .03 .01 .00
□ 270 Lynn Jones .03 .01 .00
□ 271 Steve Kemp .06 .02 .00
□ 272 Rick Leach .03 .01 .00
□ 273 Aurelio Lopez .03 .01 .00
□ 274 Jack Morris .25 .10 .02
□ 275 Kevin Saucier .03 .01 .00
□ 276 Lance Parrish .20 .08 .02
□ 277 Rick Peters .03 .01 .00
□ 278 Dan Petry .06 .02 .00
□ 279 David Rozema .03 .01 .00
□ 280 Stan Papi .03 .01 .00
□ 281 Dan Schatzeder .03 .01 .00
□ 282 Champ Summers .03 .01 .00
□ 283 Alan Trammell .35 .14 .03
□ 284 Lou Whitaker .15 .06 .01
□ 285 Milt Wilcox .03 .01 .00
□ 286 John Wockenfuss .03 .01 .00
□ 287 Gary Allenson .03 .01 .00
□ 288 Tom Burgmeier .03 .01 .00
□ 289 Bill Campbell .03 .01 .00
□ 290 Mark Clear .03 .01 .00
□ 291 Steve Crawford .03 .01 .00
□ 292 Dennis Eckersley .15 .06 .01
□ 293 Dwight Evans .18 .08 .01
□ 294 Rich Gedman .40 .16 .04
□ 295 Garry Hancock .03 .01 .00
□ 296 Glenn Hoffman .03 .01 .00
□ 297 Bruce Hurst .60 .24 .06
□ 298 Carney Lansford .15 .06 .01
□ 299 Rick Miller .03 .01 .00
□ 300 Reid Nichols .03 .01 .00
□ 301 Bob Ojeda .45 .18 .04
□ 302 Tony Perez .15 .06 .01
□ 303 Chuck Rainey .03 .01 .00
□ 304 Jerry Remy .03 .01 .00
□ 305 Jim Rice .30 .12 .03
□ 306 Joe Rudi .06 .02 .00
□ 307 Bob Stanley .03 .01 .00
□ 308 Dave Stapleton .03 .01 .00
□ 309 Frank Tanana .06 .02 .00
□ 310 Mike Torrez .03 .01 .00
□ 311 John Tudor .20 .08 .02
□ 312 Carl Yastrzemski 1.00 .40 .10
□ 313 Buddy Bell .12 .05 .01
□ 314 Steve Comer .03 .01 .00
□ 315 Danny Darwin .03 .01 .00
□ 316 John Ellis .03 .01 .00
□ 317 John Grubb .03 .01 .00
□ 318 Rick Honeycutt .03 .01 .00
□ 319 Charlie Hough .08 .03 .01
□ 320 Ferguson Jenkins .15 .06 .01
□ 321 John Henry Johnson .03 .01 .00
□ 322 Jim Kern .03 .01 .00
□ 323 Jon Matlack .03 .01 .00
□ 324 Doc Medich .03 .01 .00
□ 325 Mario Mendoza .03 .01 .00
□ 326 Al Oliver .10 .04 .01
□ 327 Pat Putnam .03 .01 .00
□ 328 Mickey Rivers .06 .02 .00
□ 329 Leon Roberts .03 .01 .00
□ 330 Billy Sample .03 .01 .00
□ 331 Bill Stein .03 .01 .00
□ 332 Jim Sundberg .06 .02 .00
□ 333 Mark Wagner .03 .01 .00
□ 334 Bump Wills .03 .01 .00
□ 335 Bill Almon .03 .01 .00
□ 336 Harold Baines .25 .10 .02
□ 337 Ross Baumgarten .03 .01 .00
□ 338 Tony Bernazard .03 .01 .00
□ 339 Britt Burns .06 .02 .00
□ 340 Richard Dotson .10 .04 .01
□ 341 Jim Essian .03 .01 .00
□ 342 Ed Farmer .03 .01 .00
□ 343 Carlton Fisk .15 .06 .01
□ 344 Kevin Hickey .03 .01 .00
□ 345 LaMarr Hoyt .08 .03 .01
□ 346 Lamar Johnson .03 .01 .00
□ 347 Jerry Koosman .08 .03 .01
□ 348 Rusty Kuntz .03 .01 .00
□ 349 Dennis Lamp .03 .01 .00
□ 350 Ron LeFlore .06 .02 .00
□ 351 Chet Lemon .06 .02 .00
□ 352 Greg Luzinski .10 .04 .01
□ 353 Bob Molinaro .03 .01 .00
□ 354 Jim Morrison .03 .01 .00
□ 355 Wayne Nordhagen .03 .01 .00
□ 356 Greg Pryor .03 .01 .00
□ 357 Mike Squires .03 .01 .00
□ 358 Steve Trout .03 .01 .00
□ 359 Alan Bannister .03 .01 .00
□ 360 Len Barker .03 .01 .00
□ 361 Bert Blyleven .12 .05 .01
□ 362 Joe Charboneau .06 .02 .00
□ 363 John Denny .06 .02 .00
□ 364 Bo Diaz .06 .02 .00
□ 365 Miguel Dilone .03 .01 .00
□ 366 Jerry Dybzinski .03 .01 .00
□ 367 Wayne Garland .03 .01 .00
□ 368 Mike Hargrove .03 .01 .00
□ 369 Toby Harrah .06 .02 .00
□ 370 Ron Hassey .06 .02 .00
□ 371 Von Hayes .90 .36 .09
□ 372 Pat Kelly .03 .01 .00
□ 373 Duane Kuiper .03 .01 .00
□ 374 Rick Manning .03 .01 .00
□ 375 Sid Monge .03 .01 .00
□ 376 Jorge Orta .03 .01 .00
□ 377 Dave Rosello .03 .01 .00
□ 378 Dan Spillner .03 .01 .00
□ 379 Mike Stanton .03 .01 .00
□ 380 Andre Thornton .06 .02 .00
□ 381 Tom Veryzer .03 .01 .00
□ 382 Rick Waits .03 .01 .00
□ 383 Doyle Alexander .08 .03 .01
□ 384 Vida Blue .08 .03 .01
□ 385 Fred Breining .03 .01 .00
□ 386 Enos Cabell .03 .01 .00

□ 387 Jack Clark	.30	.12	.03
□ 388 Darrell Evans	.12	.05	.01
□ 389 Tom Griffin	.03	.01	.00
□ 390 Larry Herndon	.03	.01	.00
□ 391 Al Holland	.03	.01	.00
□ 392 Gary Lavelle	.03	.01	.00
□ 393 Johnnie LeMaster	.03	.01	.00
□ 394 Jerry Martin	.03	.01	.00
□ 395 Milt May	.03	.01	.00
□ 396 Greg Minton	.03	.01	.00
□ 397 Joe Morgan	.30	.12	.03
□ 398 Joe Pettini	.03	.01	.00
□ 399 Alan Ripley	.03	.01	.00
□ 400 Billy Smith	.03	.01	.00
□ 401 Rennie Stennett	.03	.01	.00
□ 402 Ed Whitson	.06	.02	.00
□ 403 Jim Wohlford	.03	.01	.00
□ 404 Willie Aikens	.03	.01	.00
□ 405 George Brett	.70	.28	.07
□ 406 Ken Brett	.03	.01	.00
□ 407 Dave Chalk	.03	.01	.00
□ 408 Rich Gale	.03	.01	.00
□ 409 Cesar Geronimo	.03	.01	.00
□ 410 Larry Gura	.03	.01	.00
□ 411 Clint Hurdle	.03	.01	.00
□ 412 Mike Jones	.03	.01	.00
□ 413 Dennis Leonard	.06	.02	.00
□ 414 Renie Martin	.03	.01	.00
□ 415 Lee May	.06	.02	.00
□ 416 Hal McRae	.06	.02	.00
□ 417 Darryl Motley	.06	.02	.00
□ 418 Rance Mulliniks	.03	.01	.00
□ 419 Amos Otis	.08	.03	.01
□ 420 Ken Phelps	.75	.30	.07
□ 421 Jamie Quirk	.03	.01	.00
□ 422 Dan Quisenberry	.15	.06	.01
□ 423 Paul Splittorff	.03	.01	.00
□ 424 U.L. Washington	.03	.01	.00
□ 425 John Wathan	.06	.02	.00
□ 426 Frank White	.08	.03	.01
□ 427 Willie Wilson	.12	.05	.01
□ 428 Brian Asselstine	.03	.01	.00
□ 429 Bruce Benedict	.03	.01	.00
□ 430 Tommy Boggs	.03	.01	.00
□ 431 Larry Bradford	.03	.01	.00
□ 432 Rick Camp	.03	.01	.00
□ 433 Chris Chambliss	.08	.03	.01
□ 434 Gene Garber	.03	.01	.00
□ 435 Preston Hanna	.03	.01	.00
□ 436 Bob Horner	.18	.08	.01
□ 437 Glenn Hubbard	.03	.01	.00
□ 438A All Hrabosky (height 5'1")	20.00	8.00	2.00
□ 438B Al Hrabosky (height 5'1")	1.00	.40	.10
□ 438C Al Hrabosky (height 5'10")	.10	.04	.01
□ 439 Rufino Linares	.05	.02	.00
□ 440 Rick Mahler	.25	.10	.02
□ 441 Ed Miller	.03	.01	.00
□ 442 John Montefusco	.06	.02	.00
□ 443 Dale Murphy	.90	.36	.09
□ 444 Phil Niekro	.30	.12	.03
□ 445 Gaylord Perry	.30	.12	.03
□ 446 Biff Pocoroba	.03	.01	.00
□ 447 Rafael Ramirez	.06	.02	.00
□ 448 Jerry Royster	.03	.01	.00
□ 449 Claudell Washington	.08	.03	.01
□ 450 Don Aase	.03	.01	.00
□ 451 Don Baylor	.15	.06	.01
□ 452 Juan Beniquez	.03	.01	.00
□ 453 Rick Burleson	.06	.02	.00
□ 454 Bert Campaneris	.06	.02	.00
□ 455 Rod Carew	.50	.20	.05
□ 456 Bob Clark	.03	.01	.00
□ 457 Brian Downing	.06	.02	.00
□ 458 Dan Ford	.03	.01	.00
□ 459 Ken Forsch	.03	.01	.00
□ 460A Dave Frost (5 mm space before ERA)	.40	.16	.04
□ 460B Dave Frost (1 mm space)	.06	.02	.00
□ 461 Bobby Grich	.08	.03	.01
□ 462 Larry Harlow	.03	.01	.00
□ 463 John Harris	.03	.01	.00
□ 464 Andy Hassler	.03	.01	.00
□ 465 Butch Hobson	.03	.01	.00
□ 466 Jesse Jefferson	.03	.01	.00
□ 467 Bruce Kison	.03	.01	.00
□ 468 Fred Lynn	.20	.08	.02
□ 469 Angel Moreno	.03	.01	.00
□ 470 Ed Ott	.03	.01	.00
□ 471 Fred Patek	.03	.01	.00
□ 472 Steve Renko	.03	.01	.00
□ 473 Mike Witt	.85	.34	.08
□ 474 Geoff Zahn	.03	.01	.00
□ 475 Gary Alexander	.03	.01	.00
□ 476 Dale Berra	.03	.01	.00
□ 477 Kurt Bevacqua	.03	.01	.00
□ 478 Jim Bibby	.03	.01	.00
□ 479 John Candelaria	.08	.03	.01
□ 480 Victor Cruz	.03	.01	.00
□ 481 Mike Easler	.03	.01	.00
□ 482 Tim Foli	.03	.01	.00
□ 483 Lee Lacy	.03	.01	.00
□ 484 Vance Law	.08	.03	.01
□ 485 Bill Madlock	.20	.08	.02
□ 486 Willie Montanez	.03	.01	.00
□ 487 Omar Moreno	.03	.01	.00
□ 488 Steve Nicosia	.03	.01	.00
□ 489 Dave Parker	.25	.10	.02
□ 490 Tony Pena	.25	.10	.02
□ 491 Pascual Perez	.08	.03	.01
□ 492 Johnny Ray	.85	.34	.08
□ 493 Rick Rhoden	.08	.03	.01
□ 494 Bill Robinson	.06	.02	.00
□ 495 Don Robinson	.06	.02	.00
□ 496 Enrique Romo	.03	.01	.00
□ 497 Rod Scurry	.03	.01	.00
□ 498 Eddie Solomon	.03	.01	.00
□ 499 Willie Stargell	.35	.14	.03
□ 500 Kent Tekulve	.06	.02	.00
□ 501 Jason Thompson	.03	.01	.00
□ 502 Glenn Abbott	.03	.01	.00
□ 503 Jim Anderson	.03	.01	.00
□ 504 Floyd Bannister	.06	.02	.00
□ 505 Bruce Bochte	.03	.01	.00
□ 506 Jeff Burroughs	.06	.02	.00
□ 507 Bryan Clark	.03	.01	.00
□ 508 Ken Clay	.03	.01	.00
□ 509 Julio Cruz	.03	.01	.00
□ 510 Dick Drago	.03	.01	.00
□ 511 Gary Gray	.03	.01	.00
□ 512 Dan Meyer	.03	.01	.00
□ 513 Jerry Narron	.03	.01	.00
□ 514 Tom Paciorek	.03	.01	.00
□ 515 Casey Parsons	.03	.01	.00
□ 516 Lenny Randle	.03	.01	.00
□ 517 Shane Rawley	.08	.03	.01
□ 518 Joe Simpson	.03	.01	.00
□ 519 Richie Zisk	.06	.02	.00
□ 520 Neil Allen	.06	.02	.00
□ 521 Bob Bailor	.03	.01	.00
□ 522 Hubie Brooks	.25	.10	.02
□ 523 Mike Cubbage	.03	.01	.00
□ 524 Pete Falcone	.03	.01	.00
□ 525 Doug Flynn	.03	.01	.00
□ 526 Tom Hausman	.03	.01	.00
□ 527 Ron Hodges	.03	.01	.00
□ 528 Randy Jones	.03	.01	.00
□ 529 Mike Jorgensen	.03	.01	.00
□ 530 Dave Kingman	.12	.05	.01
□ 531 Ed Lynch	.08	.03	.01
□ 532 Mike Marshall (screwball pitcher)	.06	.02	.00
□ 533 Lee Mazzilli	.03	.01	.00
□ 534 Dyar Miller	.03	.01	.00
□ 535 Mike Scott	.30	.12	.03
□ 536 Rusty Staub	.10	.04	.01
□ 537 John Stearns	.03	.01	.00
□ 538 Craig Swan	.03	.01	.00
□ 539 Frank Taveras	.03	.01	.00
□ 540 Alex Trevino	.03	.01	.00
□ 541 Ellis Valentine	.03	.01	.00
□ 542 Mookie Wilson	.08	.03	.01
□ 543 Joel Youngblood	.03	.01	.00
□ 544 Pat Zachry	.03	.01	.00
□ 545 Glenn Adams	.03	.01	.00
□ 546 Fernando Arroyo	.03	.01	.00
□ 547 John Verhoeven	.03	.01	.00
□ 548 Sal Butera	.03	.01	.00
□ 549 John Castino	.03	.01	.00
□ 550 Don Cooper	.03	.01	.00
□ 551 Doug Corbett	.03	.01	.00
□ 552 Dave Engle	.03	.01	.00
□ 553 Roger Erickson	.03	.01	.00
□ 554 Danny Goodwin	.03	.01	.00
□ 555A Darrell Jackson (black cap)	1.00	.40	.10
□ 555B Darrell Jackson (red cap with T)	.10	.04	.01
□ 555C Darrell Jackson (red cap, no emblem)	5.00	2.00	.50
□ 556 Pete Mackanin	.03	.01	.00
□ 557 Jack O'Connor	.03	.01	.00
□ 558 Hosken Powell	.03	.01	.00
□ 559 Pete Redfern	.03	.01	.00
□ 560 Roy Smalley	.03	.01	.00
□ 561 Chuck Baker UER (shortshop on front)	.03	.01	.00

☐ 562 Gary Ward .06 .02 .00
☐ 563 Rob Wilfong .03 .01 .00
☐ 564 Al Williams .03 .01 .00
☐ 565 Butch Wynegar .03 .01 .00
☐ 566 Randy Bass .06 .02 .00
☐ 567 Juan Bonilla .03 .01 .00
☐ 568 Danny Boone .03 .01 .00
☐ 569 John Curtis .03 .01 .00
☐ 570 Juan Eichelberger .03 .01 .00
☐ 571 Barry Evans .03 .01 .00
☐ 572 Tim Flannery .03 .01 .00
☐ 573 Ruppert Jones .03 .01 .00
☐ 574 Terry Kennedy .06 .02 .00
☐ 575 Joe Lefebvre .03 .01 .00
☐ 576A John Littlefield ERR 60.00 24.00 6.00
(left handed)
☐ 576B John Littlefield COR .06 .02 .00
(right handed)
☐ 577 Gary Lucas .03 .01 .00
☐ 578 Steve Mura .03 .01 .00
☐ 579 Broderick Perkins .03 .01 .00
☐ 580 Gene Richards .03 .01 .00
☐ 581 Luis Salazar .06 .02 .00
☐ 582 Ozzie Smith .30 .12 .03
☐ 583 John Urrea .03 .01 .00
☐ 584 Chris Welsh .03 .01 .00
☐ 585 Rick Wise .03 .01 .00
☐ 586 Doug Bird .03 .01 .00
☐ 587 Tim Blackwell .03 .01 .00
☐ 588 Bobby Bonds .08 .03 .01
☐ 589 Bill Buckner .10 .04 .01
☐ 590 Bill Caudill .03 .01 .00
☐ 591 Hector Cruz .03 .01 .00
☐ 592 Jody Davis .35 .14 .03
☐ 593 Ivan DeJesus .03 .01 .00
☐ 594 Steve Dillard .03 .01 .00
☐ 595 Leon Durham .08 .03 .01
☐ 596 Rawly Eastwick .03 .01 .00
☐ 597 Steve Henderson .03 .01 .00
☐ 598 Mike Krukow .06 .02 .00
☐ 599 Mike Lum .03 .01 .00
☐ 600 Randy Martz .03 .01 .00
☐ 601 Jerry Morales .03 .01 .00
☐ 602 Ken Reitz .03 .01 .00
☐ 603A Lee Smith ERR 1.25 .50 .12
(Cubs logo reversed)
☐ 603B Lee Smith COR .65 .26 .06
☐ 604 Dick Tidrow .03 .01 .00
☐ 605 Jim Tracy .03 .01 .00
☐ 606 Mike Tyson .03 .01 .00
☐ 607 Ty Waller .03 .01 .00
☐ 608 Danny Ainge .12 .05 .01
☐ 609 Jorge Bell 6.00 2.40 .60
☐ 610 Mark Bomback .03 .01 .00
☐ 611 Barry Bonnell .03 .01 .00
☐ 612 Jim Clancy .06 .02 .00
☐ 613 Damaso Garcia .06 .02 .00
☐ 614 Jerry Garvin .03 .01 .00
☐ 615 Alfredo Griffin .08 .03 .01
☐ 616 Garth Iorg .03 .01 .00
☐ 617 Luis Leal .03 .01 .00
☐ 618 Ken Macha .03 .01 .00
☐ 619 John Mayberry .06 .02 .00
☐ 620 Joey McLaughlin .03 .01 .00
☐ 621 Lloyd Moseby .15 .06 .01
☐ 622 Dave Stieb .15 .06 .01
☐ 623 Jackson Todd .03 .01 .00
☐ 624 Willie Upshaw .06 .02 .00
☐ 625 Otto Velez .03 .01 .00
☐ 626 Ernie Whitt .06 .02 .00
☐ 627 Al Woods .03 .01 .00
☐ 628 All Star Game .06 .02 .00
Cleveland, Ohio
☐ 629 All Star Infielders .06 .02 .00
Frank White and
Bucky Dent
☐ 630 Big Red Machine .08 .03 .01
Dan Driessen
Dave Concepcion
George Foster
☐ 631 Bruce Sutter .08 .03 .01
Top NL Relief Pitcher
☐ 632 "Steve and Carlton" .20 .08 .02
Steve Carlton and
Carlton Fisk
☐ 633 Carl Yastrzemski .30 .12 .03
3000th Game
☐ 634 Dynamic Duo .30 .12 .03
Johnny Bench and
Tom Seaver
☐ 635 West Meets East .20 .08 .02
Fernando Valenzuela
and Gary Carter
☐ 636A Fernando Valenzuela: .45 .18 .04
NL SO King ("he" NL)
☐ 636B Fernando Valenzuela: .20 .08 .02
NL SO King ("the" NL)
☐ 637 Mike Schmidt .30 .12 .03
Home Run King
☐ 638 NL All Stars .18 .08 .01
Gary Carter and
Dave Parker
☐ 639 Perfect Game .06 .02 .00
Len Barker and
Bo Diaz
(catcher actually
Ron Hassey)
☐ 640 Pete and Re-Pete 1.50 .60 .15
Pete Rose and Son
☐ 641 Phillies Finest .30 .12 .03
Lonnie Smith
Mike Schmidt
Steve Carlton
☐ 642 Red Sox Reunion .08 .03 .01
Fred Lynn and
Dwight Evans
☐ 643 Rickey Henderson .25 .10 .02
Most Hits and Runs
☐ 644 Rollie Fingers .10 .04 .01
Most Saves AL
☐ 645 Tom Seaver .20 .08 .02
Most 1981 Wins
☐ 646A Yankee Powerhouse .75 .30 .07
Reggie Jackson and
Dave Winfield
(comma on back
after outfielder)
☐ 646B Yankee Powerhouse .40 .16 .04
Reggie Jackson and
Dave Winfield
(no comma)
☐ 647 CL: Yankees/Dodgers .08 .01 .00
☐ 648 CL: A's/Reds .07 .01 .00
☐ 649 CL: Cards/Brewers .07 .01 .00
☐ 650 CL: Expos/Orioles .07 .01 .00
☐ 651 CL: Astros/Phillies .07 .01 .00
☐ 652 CL: Tigers/Red Sox .07 .01 .00
☐ 653 CL: Rangers/White Sox .07 .01 .00
☐ 654 CL: Giants/Indians .07 .01 .00
☐ 655 CL: Royals/Braves .07 .01 .00
☐ 656 CL: Angels/Pirates .07 .01 .00
☐ 657 CL: Mariners/Mets .07 .01 .00
☐ 658 CL: Padres/Twins .07 .01 .00
☐ 659 CL: Blue Jays/Cubs .07 .01 .00
☐ 660 Specials Checklist .10 .01 .00

1983 Fleer

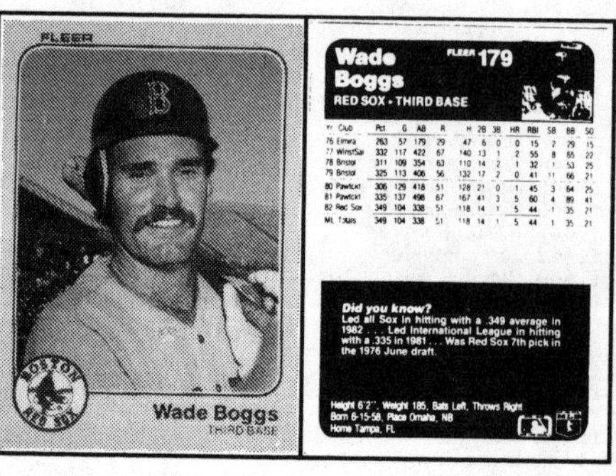

The cards in this 660-card set measure 2 1/2" by 3 1/2". In 1983, for the third straight year, Fleer has produced a baseball series numbering 660 cards. Of these, 1-628 are player cards, 629-646 are special cards, and 647-660 are checklist cards. The player cards are again ordered alphabetically within team. The team order relates back to each team's on-field performance during the previous year, i.e., World Champion Cardinals (1-25), AL Champion Brewers (26-51), Baltimore (52-75), California (76-103), Kansas City (104-128), Atlanta (129-152), Philadelphia (153-176), Boston (177-200), Los Angeles (201-227), Chicago White Sox (228-251),

San Francisco (252-276), Montreal (277-301), Pittsburgh (302-326), Detroit (327-351), San Diego (352-375), New York Yankees (376-399), Cleveland (400-423), Toronto (424-444), Houston (445-469), Seattle (470-489), Chicago Cubs (490-512), Oakland (513-535), New York Mets (536-561), Texas (562-583), Cincinnati (584-606), and Minnesota (607-628). The front of each card has a colorful team logo at bottom left and the player's name and position at lower right. The reverses are done in shades of brown on white. The cards are numbered on the back next to a small black and white photo of the player.

	MINT	EXC	G-VG
COMPLETE SET (660)	45.00	18.00	4.50
COMMON PLAYER (1-660)	.03	.01	.00
☐ 1 Joaquin Andujar	.12	.04	.01
☐ 2 Doug Bair	.03	.01	.00
☐ 3 Steve Braun	.03	.01	.00
☐ 4 Glenn Brummer	.03	.01	.00
☐ 5 Bob Forsch	.03	.01	.00
☐ 6 David Green	.03	.01	.00
☐ 7 George Hendrick	.06	.02	.00
☐ 8 Keith Hernandez	.35	.14	.03
☐ 9 Tom Herr	.08	.03	.01
☐ 10 Dane Iorg	.03	.01	.00
☐ 11 Jim Kaat	.12	.05	.01
☐ 12 Jeff Lahti	.03	.01	.00
☐ 13 Tito Landrum	.03	.01	.00
☐ 14 Dave LaPoint	.35	.14	.03
☐ 15 Willie McGee	1.75	.70	.17
☐ 16 Steve Mura	.03	.01	.00
☐ 17 Ken Oberkfell	.03	.01	.00
☐ 18 Darrell Porter	.03	.01	.00
☐ 19 Mike Ramsey	.03	.01	.00
☐ 20 Gene Roof	.03	.01	.00
☐ 21 Lonnie Smith	.06	.02	.00
☐ 22 Ozzie Smith	.30	.12	.03
☐ 23 John Stuper	.03	.01	.00
☐ 24 Bruce Sutter	.12	.05	.01
☐ 25 Gene Tenace	.06	.02	.00
☐ 26 Jerry Augustine	.03	.01	.00
☐ 27 Dwight Bernard	.03	.01	.00
☐ 28 Mark Brouhard	.03	.01	.00
☐ 29 Mike Caldwell	.03	.01	.00
☐ 30 Cecil Cooper	.12	.05	.01
☐ 31 Jamie Easterly	.03	.01	.00
☐ 32 Marshall Edwards	.03	.01	.00
☐ 33 Rollie Fingers	.18	.08	.01
☐ 34 Jim Gantner	.03	.01	.00
☐ 35 Moose Haas	.03	.01	.00
☐ 36 Roy Howell	.03	.01	.00
☐ 37 Peter Ladd	.03	.01	.00
☐ 38 Bob McClure	.03	.01	.00
☐ 39 Doc Medich	.03	.01	.00
☐ 40 Paul Molitor	.18	.08	.01
☐ 41 Don Money	.03	.01	.00
☐ 42 Charlie Moore	.03	.01	.00
☐ 43 Ben Oglivie	.06	.02	.00
☐ 44 Ed Romero	.03	.01	.00
☐ 45 Ted Simmons	.12	.05	.01
☐ 46 Jim Slaton	.03	.01	.00
☐ 47 Don Sutton	.30	.12	.03
☐ 48 Gorman Thomas	.10	.04	.01
☐ 49 Pete Vuckovich	.06	.02	.00
☐ 50 Ned Yost	.03	.01	.00
☐ 51 Robin Yount	.35	.14	.03
☐ 52 Benny Ayala	.03	.01	.00
☐ 53 Bob Bonner	.03	.01	.00
☐ 54 Al Bumbry	.03	.01	.00
☐ 55 Terry Crowley	.03	.01	.00
☐ 56 Storm Davis	.45	.18	.04
☐ 57 Rich Dauer	.03	.01	.00
☐ 58 Rick Dempsey (posing batting lefty)	.06	.02	.00
☐ 59 Jim Dwyer	.03	.01	.00
☐ 60 Mike Flanagan	.06	.02	.00
☐ 61 Dan Ford	.03	.01	.00
☐ 62 Glenn Gulliver	.03	.01	.00
☐ 63 John Lowenstein	.03	.01	.00
☐ 64 Dennis Martinez	.06	.02	.00
☐ 65 Tippy Martinez	.03	.01	.00
☐ 66 Scott McGregor	.06	.02	.00
☐ 67 Eddie Murray	.55	.22	.05
☐ 68 Joe Nolan	.03	.01	.00
☐ 69 Jim Palmer	.35	.14	.03
☐ 70 Cal Ripken Jr.	1.00	.40	.10
☐ 71 Gary Roenicke	.03	.01	.00
☐ 72 Lenn Sakata	.03	.01	.00
☐ 73 Ken Singleton	.08	.03	.01
☐ 74 Sammy Stewart	.03	.01	.00
☐ 75 Tim Stoddard	.03	.01	.00
☐ 76 Don Aase	.03	.01	.00
☐ 77 Don Baylor	.12	.05	.01
☐ 78 Juan Beniquez	.03	.01	.00
☐ 79 Bob Boone	.10	.04	.01
☐ 80 Rick Burleson	.06	.02	.00
☐ 81 Rod Carew	.40	.16	.04
☐ 82 Bobby Clark	.03	.01	.00
☐ 83 Doug Corbett	.03	.01	.00
☐ 84 John Curtis	.03	.01	.00
☐ 85 Doug DeCinces	.08	.03	.01
☐ 86 Brian Downing	.06	.02	.00
☐ 87 Joe Ferguson	.03	.01	.00
☐ 88 Tim Foli	.03	.01	.00
☐ 89 Ken Forsch	.03	.01	.00
☐ 90 Dave Goltz	.03	.01	.00
☐ 91 Bobby Grich	.08	.03	.01
☐ 92 Andy Hassler	.03	.01	.00
☐ 93 Reggie Jackson	.50	.20	.05
☐ 94 Ron Jackson	.03	.01	.00
☐ 95 Tommy John	.15	.06	.01
☐ 96 Bruce Kison	.03	.01	.00
☐ 97 Fred Lynn	.18	.08	.01
☐ 98 Ed Ott	.03	.01	.00
☐ 99 Steve Renko	.03	.01	.00
☐ 100 Luis Sanchez	.03	.01	.00
☐ 101 Rob Wilfong	.03	.01	.00
☐ 102 Mike Witt	.15	.06	.01
☐ 103 Geoff Zahn	.03	.01	.00
☐ 104 Willie Aikens	.03	.01	.00
☐ 105 Mike Armstrong	.03	.01	.00
☐ 106 Vida Blue	.06	.02	.00
☐ 107 Bud Black	.20	.08	.02
☐ 108 George Brett	.60	.24	.06
☐ 109 Bill Castro	.03	.01	.00
☐ 110 Onix Concepcion	.03	.01	.00
☐ 111 Dave Frost	.03	.01	.00
☐ 112 Cesar Geronimo	.03	.01	.00
☐ 113 Larry Gura	.03	.01	.00
☐ 114 Steve Hammond	.03	.01	.00
☐ 115 Don Hood	.03	.01	.00
☐ 116 Dennis Leonard	.06	.02	.00
☐ 117 Jerry Martin	.03	.01	.00
☐ 118 Lee May	.06	.02	.00
☐ 119 Hal McRae	.06	.02	.00
☐ 120 Amos Otis	.08	.03	.01
☐ 121 Greg Pryor	.03	.01	.00
☐ 122 Dan Quisenberry	.12	.05	.01
☐ 123 Don Slaught	.30	.12	.03
☐ 124 Paul Splittorff	.03	.01	.00
☐ 125 U.L. Washington	.03	.01	.00
☐ 126 John Wathan	.06	.02	.00
☐ 127 Frank White	.08	.03	.01
☐ 128 Willie Wilson	.12	.05	.01
☐ 129 Steve Bedrosian	.35	.14	.03
☐ 130 Bruce Benedict	.03	.01	.00
☐ 131 Tommy Boggs	.03	.01	.00
☐ 132 Brett Butler	.10	.04	.01
☐ 133 Rick Camp	.03	.01	.00
☐ 134 Chris Chambliss	.08	.03	.01
☐ 135 Ken Dayley	.06	.02	.00
☐ 136 Gene Garber	.03	.01	.00
☐ 137 Terry Harper	.03	.01	.00
☐ 138 Bob Horner	.18	.08	.01
☐ 139 Glenn Hubbard	.03	.01	.00
☐ 140 Rufino Linares	.03	.01	.00
☐ 141 Rick Mahler	.06	.02	.00
☐ 142 Dale Murphy	.85	.34	.08
☐ 143 Phil Niekro	.25	.10	.02
☐ 144 Pascual Perez	.08	.03	.01
☐ 145 Biff Pocoroba	.03	.01	.00
☐ 146 Rafael Ramirez	.03	.01	.00
☐ 147 Jerry Royster	.03	.01	.00
☐ 148 Ken Smith	.03	.01	.00
☐ 149 Bob Walk	.06	.02	.00
☐ 150 Claudell Washington	.08	.03	.01
☐ 151 Bob Watson	.06	.02	.00
☐ 152 Larry Whisenton	.03	.01	.00
☐ 153 Porfirio Altamirano	.03	.01	.00
☐ 154 Marty Bystrom	.03	.01	.00
☐ 155 Steve Carlton	.35	.14	.03
☐ 156 Larry Christenson	.03	.01	.00
☐ 157 Ivan DeJesus	.03	.01	.00
☐ 158 John Denny	.08	.03	.01
☐ 159 Bob Dernier	.03	.01	.00
☐ 160 Bo Diaz	.06	.02	.00
☐ 161 Ed Farmer	.03	.01	.00
☐ 162 Greg Gross	.03	.01	.00
☐ 163 Mike Krukow	.06	.02	.00
☐ 164 Garry Maddox	.06	.02	.00
☐ 165 Gary Matthews	.06	.02	.00
☐ 166 Tug McGraw	.10	.04	.01
☐ 167 Bob Molinaro	.03	.01	.00
☐ 168 Sid Monge	.03	.01	.00

□ 169 Ron Reed	.03	.01	.00
□ 170 Bill Robinson	.06	.02	.00
□ 171 Pete Rose	1.00	.40	.10
□ 172 Dick Ruthven	.03	.01	.00
□ 173 Mike Schmidt	.60	.24	.06
□ 174 Manny Trillo	.03	.01	.00
□ 175 Ozzie Virgil	.03	.01	.00
□ 176 George Vuckovich	.03	.01	.00
□ 177 Gary Allenson	.03	.01	.00
□ 178 Luis Aponte	.03	.01	.00
□ 179 Wade Boggs	17.00	7.00	1.70
□ 180 Tom Burgmeier	.03	.01	.00
□ 181 Mark Clear	.03	.01	.00
□ 182 Dennis Eckersley	.15	.06	.01
□ 183 Dwight Evans	.15	.06	.01
□ 184 Rich Gedman	.10	.04	.01
□ 185 Glenn Hoffman	.03	.01	.00
□ 186 Bruce Hurst	.15	.06	.01
□ 187 Carney Lansford	.12	.05	.01
□ 188 Rick Miller	.03	.01	.00
□ 189 Reid Nichols	.03	.01	.00
□ 190 Bob Ojeda	.10	.04	.01
□ 191 Tony Perez	.15	.06	.01
□ 192 Chuck Rainey	.03	.01	.00
□ 193 Jerry Remy	.03	.01	.00
□ 194 Jim Rice	.25	.10	.02
□ 195 Bob Stanley	.03	.01	.00
□ 196 Dave Stapleton	.03	.01	.00
□ 197 Mike Torrez	.03	.01	.00
□ 198 John Tudor	.15	.06	.01
□ 199 Julio Valdez	.03	.01	.00
□ 200 Carl Yastrzemski	.80	.32	.08
□ 201 Dusty Baker	.06	.02	.00
□ 202 Joe Beckwith	.03	.01	.00
□ 203 Greg Brock	.35	.14	.03
□ 204 Ron Cey	.10	.04	.01
□ 205 Terry Forster	.06	.02	.00
□ 206 Steve Garvey	.40	.16	.04
□ 207 Pedro Guerrero	.30	.12	.03
□ 208 Burt Hooton	.03	.01	.00
□ 209 Steve Howe	.03	.01	.00
□ 210 Ken Landreaux	.03	.01	.00
□ 211 Mike Marshall	.20	.08	.02
□ 212 Candy Maldonado	.60	.24	.06
□ 213 Rick Monday	.06	.02	.00
□ 214 Tom Niedenfuer	.06	.02	.00
□ 215 Jorge Orta	.03	.01	.00
□ 216 Jerry Reuss	.06	.02	.00
□ 217 Ron Roenicke	.03	.01	.00
□ 218 Vicente Romo	.03	.01	.00
□ 219 Bill Russell	.06	.02	.00
□ 220 Steve Sax	.30	.12	.03
□ 221 Mike Scioscia	.06	.02	.00
□ 222 Dave Stewart	.15	.06	.01
□ 223 Derrel Thomas	.03	.01	.00
□ 224 Fernando Valenzuela	.25	.10	.02
□ 225 Bob Welch	.10	.04	.01
□ 226 Ricky Wright	.03	.01	.00
□ 227 Steve Yeager	.03	.01	.00
□ 228 Bill Almon	.03	.01	.00
□ 229 Harold Baines	.20	.08	.02
□ 230 Salome Barojas	.03	.01	.00
□ 231 Tony Bernazard	.03	.01	.00
□ 232 Britt Burns	.06	.02	.00
□ 233 Richard Dotson	.08	.03	.01
□ 234 Ernesto Escarrega	.03	.01	.00
□ 235 Carlton Fisk	.15	.06	.01
□ 236 Jerry Hairston	.03	.01	.00
□ 237 Kevin Hickey	.03	.01	.00
□ 238 LaMarr Hoyt	.06	.02	.00
□ 239 Steve Kemp	.06	.02	.00
□ 240 Jim Kern	.03	.01	.00
□ 241 Ron Kittle	.60	.24	.06
□ 242 Jerry Koosman	.08	.03	.01
□ 243 Dennis Lamp	.03	.01	.00
□ 244 Rudy Law	.03	.01	.00
□ 245 Vance Law	.08	.03	.01
□ 246 Ron LeFlore	.06	.02	.00
□ 247 Greg Luzinski	.10	.04	.01
□ 248 Tom Paciorek	.03	.01	.00
□ 249 Aurelio Rodriguez	.03	.01	.00
□ 250 Mike Squires	.03	.01	.00
□ 251 Steve Trout	.03	.01	.00
□ 252 Jim Barr	.03	.01	.00
□ 253 Dave Bergman	.03	.01	.00
□ 254 Fred Breining	.03	.01	.00
□ 255 Bob Brenly	.06	.02	.00
□ 256 Jack Clark	.25	.10	.02
□ 257 Chili Davis	.25	.10	.02
□ 258 Darrell Evans	.10	.04	.01
□ 259 Alan Fowlkes	.03	.01	.00
□ 260 Rich Gale	.03	.01	.00
□ 261 Atlee Hammaker	.03	.01	.00
□ 262 Al Holland	.03	.01	.00
□ 263 Duane Kuiper	.03	.01	.00

□ 264 Bill Laskey	.03	.01	.00
□ 265 Gary Lavelle	.03	.01	.00
□ 266 Johnnie LeMaster	.03	.01	.00
□ 267 Renie Martin	.03	.01	.00
□ 268 Milt May	.03	.01	.00
□ 269 Greg Minton	.03	.01	.00
□ 270 Joe Morgan	.25	.10	.02
□ 271 Tom O'Malley	.06	.02	.00
□ 272 Reggie Smith	.06	.02	.00
□ 273 Guy Sularz	.03	.01	.00
□ 274 Champ Summers	.03	.01	.00
□ 275 Max Venable	.03	.01	.00
□ 276 Jim Wohlford	.03	.01	.00
□ 277 Ray Burris	.03	.01	.00
□ 278 Gary Carter	.35	.14	.03
□ 279 Warren Cromartie	.03	.01	.00
□ 280 Andre Dawson	.35	.14	.03
□ 281 Terry Francona	.03	.01	.00
□ 282 Doug Flynn	.03	.01	.00
□ 283 Woody Fryman	.03	.01	.00
□ 284 Bill Gullickson	.06	.02	.00
□ 285 Wallace Johnson	.06	.02	.00
□ 286 Charlie Lea	.03	.01	.00
□ 287 Randy Lerch	.03	.01	.00
□ 288 Brad Mills	.03	.01	.00
□ 289 Dan Norman	.03	.01	.00
□ 290 Al Oliver	.08	.03	.01
□ 291 David Palmer	.03	.01	.00
□ 292 Tim Raines	.40	.16	.04
□ 293 Jeff Reardon	.10	.04	.01
□ 294 Steve Rogers	.06	.02	.00
□ 295 Scott Sanderson	.03	.01	.00
□ 296 Dan Schatzeder	.03	.01	.00
□ 297 Bryn Smith	.08	.03	.01
□ 298 Chris Speier	.03	.01	.00
□ 299 Tim Wallach	.18	.08	.01
□ 300 Jerry White	.03	.01	.00
□ 301 Joel Youngblood	.03	.01	.00
□ 302 Ross Baumgarten	.03	.01	.00
□ 303 Dale Berra	.03	.01	.00
□ 304 John Candelaria	.08	.03	.01
□ 305 Dick Davis	.03	.01	.00
□ 306 Mike Easler	.03	.01	.00
□ 307 Richie Hebner	.03	.01	.00
□ 308 Lee Lacy	.03	.01	.00
□ 309 Bill Madlock	.10	.04	.01
□ 310 Larry McWilliams	.03	.01	.00
□ 311 John Milner	.03	.01	.00
□ 312 Omar Moreno	.03	.01	.00
□ 313 Jim Morrison	.03	.01	.00
□ 314 Steve Nicosia	.03	.01	.00
□ 315 Dave Parker	.18	.08	.01
□ 316 Tony Pena	.15	.06	.01
□ 317 Johnny Ray	.15	.06	.01
□ 318 Rick Rhoden	.08	.03	.01
□ 319 Don Robinson	.03	.01	.00
□ 320 Enrique Romo	.03	.01	.00
□ 321 Manny Sarmiento	.03	.01	.00
□ 322 Rod Scurry	.03	.01	.00
□ 323 Jim Smith	.03	.01	.00
□ 324 Willie Stargell	.35	.14	.03
□ 325 Jason Thompson	.03	.01	.00
□ 326 Kent Tekulve	.06	.02	.00
□ 327 Tom Brookens	.03	.01	.00
□ 328 Enos Cabell	.03	.01	.00
□ 329 Kirk Gibson	.40	.16	.04
□ 330 Larry Herndon	.03	.01	.00
□ 331 Mike Ivie	.03	.01	.00
□ 332 Howard Johnson	2.25	.90	.22
□ 333 Lynn Jones	.03	.01	.00
□ 334 Rick Leach	.03	.01	.00
□ 335 Chet Lemon	.06	.02	.00
□ 336 Jack Morris	.18	.08	.01
□ 337 Lance Parrish	.25	.10	.02
□ 338 Larry Pashnick	.03	.01	.00
□ 339 Dan Petry	.08	.03	.01
□ 340 Dave Rozema	.03	.01	.00
□ 341 Dave Rucker	.03	.01	.00
□ 342 Elias Sosa	.03	.01	.00
□ 343 Dave Tobik	.03	.01	.00
□ 344 Alan Trammell	.30	.12	.03
□ 345 Jerry Turner	.03	.01	.00
□ 346 Jerry Ujdur	.03	.01	.00
□ 347 Pat Underwood	.03	.01	.00
□ 348 Lou Whitaker	.15	.06	.01
□ 349 Milt Wilcox	.03	.01	.00
□ 350 Glenn Wilson	.30	.12	.03
□ 351 John Wockenfuss	.03	.01	.00
□ 352 Kurt Bevacqua	.03	.01	.00
□ 353 Juan Bonilla	.03	.01	.00
□ 354 Floyd Chiffer	.03	.01	.00
□ 355 Luis DeLeon	.03	.01	.00
□ 356 Dave Dravecky	.35	.14	.03
□ 357 Dave Edwards	.03	.01	.00
□ 358 Juan Eichelberger	.03	.01	.00

☐ 359 Tim Flannery	.03	.01	.00
☐ 360 Tony Gwynn	9.00	3.75	.90
☐ 361 Ruppert Jones	.03	.01	.00
☐ 362 Terry Kennedy	.06	.02	.00
☐ 363 Joe Lefebvre	.03	.01	.00
☐ 364 Sixto Lezcano	.03	.01	.00
☐ 365 Tim Lollar	.03	.01	.00
☐ 366 Gary Lucas	.03	.01	.00
☐ 367 John Montefusco	.03	.01	.00
☐ 368 Broderick Perkins	.03	.01	.00
☐ 369 Joe Pittman	.03	.01	.00
☐ 370 Gene Richards	.03	.01	.00
☐ 371 Luis Salazar	.06	.02	.00
☐ 372 Eric Show	.35	.14	.03
☐ 373 Garry Templeton	.08	.03	.01
☐ 374 Chris Welsh	.03	.01	.00
☐ 375 Alan Wiggins	.10	.04	.01
☐ 376 Rick Cerone	.03	.01	.00
☐ 377 Dave Collins	.03	.01	.00
☐ 378 Roger Erickson	.03	.01	.00
☐ 379 George Frazier	.03	.01	.00
☐ 380 Oscar Gamble	.03	.01	.00
☐ 381 Goose Gossage	.15	.06	.01
☐ 382 Ken Griffey	.06	.02	.00
☐ 383 Ron Guidry	.18	.08	.01
☐ 384 Dave LaRoche	.03	.01	.00
☐ 385 Rudy May	.03	.01	.00
☐ 386 John Mayberry	.06	.02	.00
☐ 387 Lee Mazzilli	.03	.01	.00
☐ 388 Mike Morgan	.03	.01	.00
☐ 389 Jerry Mumphrey	.03	.01	.00
☐ 390 Bobby Murcer	.10	.04	.01
☐ 391 Graig Nettles	.12	.05	.01
☐ 392 Lou Piniella	.08	.03	.01
☐ 393 Willie Randolph	.08	.03	.01
☐ 394 Shane Rawley	.08	.03	.01
☐ 395 Dave Righetti	.20	.08	.02
☐ 396 Andre Robertson	.03	.01	.00
☐ 397 Roy Smalley	.03	.01	.00
☐ 398 Dave Winfield	.40	.16	.04
☐ 399 Butch Wynegar	.03	.01	.00
☐ 400 Chris Bando	.03	.01	.00
☐ 401 Alan Bannister	.03	.01	.00
☐ 402 Len Barker	.03	.01	.00
☐ 403 Tom Brennan	.03	.01	.00
☐ 404 Carmelo Castillo	.06	.02	.00
☐ 405 Miguel Dilone	.03	.01	.00
☐ 406 Jerry Dybzinski	.03	.01	.00
☐ 407 Mike Fischlin	.03	.01	.00
☐ 408 Ed Glynn (photo actually Bud Anderson)	.03	.01	.00
☐ 409 Mike Hargrove	.03	.01	.00
☐ 410 Toby Harrah	.06	.02	.00
☐ 411 Ron Hassey	.03	.01	.00
☐ 412 Von Hayes	.18	.08	.01
☐ 413 Rick Manning	.03	.01	.00
☐ 414 Bake McBride	.03	.01	.00
☐ 415 Larry Milbourne	.03	.01	.00
☐ 416 Bill Nahorodny	.03	.01	.00
☐ 417 Jack Perconte	.03	.01	.00
☐ 418 Lary Sorensen	.03	.01	.00
☐ 419 Dan Spillner	.03	.01	.00
☐ 420 Rick Sutcliffe	.15	.06	.01
☐ 421 Andre Thornton	.06	.02	.00
☐ 422 Rick Waits	.03	.01	.00
☐ 423 Eddie Whitson	.06	.02	.00
☐ 424 Jesse Barfield	.65	.26	.06
☐ 425 Barry Bonnell	.03	.01	.00
☐ 426 Jim Clancy	.06	.02	.00
☐ 427 Damaso Garcia	.03	.01	.00
☐ 428 Jerry Garvin	.03	.01	.00
☐ 429 Alfredo Griffin	.08	.03	.01
☐ 430 Garth Iorg	.03	.01	.00
☐ 431 Roy Lee Jackson	.03	.01	.00
☐ 432 Luis Leal	.03	.01	.00
☐ 433 Buck Martinez	.03	.01	.00
☐ 434 Joey McLaughlin	.03	.01	.00
☐ 435 Lloyd Moseby	.12	.05	.01
☐ 436 Rance Mulliniks	.03	.01	.00
☐ 437 Dale Murray	.03	.01	.00
☐ 438 Wayne Nordhagen	.03	.01	.00
☐ 439 Gene Petralli	.06	.02	.00
☐ 440 Hosken Powell	.03	.01	.00
☐ 441 Dave Stieb	.15	.06	.01
☐ 442 Willie Upshaw	.06	.02	.00
☐ 443 Ernie Whitt	.06	.02	.00
☐ 444 Al Woods	.03	.01	.00
☐ 445 Alan Ashby	.06	.02	.00
☐ 446 Jose Cruz	.08	.03	.01
☐ 447 Kiko Garcia	.03	.01	.00
☐ 448 Phil Garner	.03	.01	.00
☐ 449 Danny Heep	.03	.01	.00
☐ 450 Art Howe	.08	.03	.01
☐ 451 Bob Knepper	.08	.03	.01
☐ 452 Alan Knicely	.03	.01	.00
☐ 453 Ray Knight	.08	.03	.01
☐ 454 Frank LaCorte	.03	.01	.00
☐ 455 Mike LaCoss	.03	.01	.00
☐ 456 Randy Moffitt	.03	.01	.00
☐ 457 Joe Niekro	.10	.04	.01
☐ 458 Terry Puhl	.03	.01	.00
☐ 459 Luis Pujols	.03	.01	.00
☐ 460 Craig Reynolds	.03	.01	.00
☐ 461 Bert Roberge	.03	.01	.00
☐ 462 Vern Ruhle	.03	.01	.00
☐ 463 Nolan Ryan	.40	.16	.04
☐ 464 Joe Sambito	.03	.01	.00
☐ 465 Tony Scott	.03	.01	.00
☐ 466 Dave Smith	.06	.02	.00
☐ 467 Harry Spilman	.03	.01	.00
☐ 468 Dickie Thon	.03	.01	.00
☐ 469 Denny Walling	.03	.01	.00
☐ 470 Larry Andersen	.03	.01	.00
☐ 471 Floyd Bannister	.06	.02	.00
☐ 472 Jim Beattie	.03	.01	.00
☐ 473 Bruce Bochte	.03	.01	.00
☐ 474 Manny Castillo	.03	.01	.00
☐ 475 Bill Caudill	.03	.01	.00
☐ 476 Bryan Clark	.03	.01	.00
☐ 477 Al Cowens	.03	.01	.00
☐ 478 Julio Cruz	.03	.01	.00
☐ 479 Todd Cruz	.03	.01	.00
☐ 480 Gary Gray	.03	.01	.00
☐ 481 Dave Henderson	.35	.14	.03
☐ 482 Mike Moore	.35	.14	.03
☐ 483 Gaylord Perry	.25	.10	.02
☐ 484 Dave Revering	.03	.01	.00
☐ 485 Joe Simpson	.03	.01	.00
☐ 486 Mike Stanton	.03	.01	.00
☐ 487 Rick Sweet	.03	.01	.00
☐ 488 Ed VandeBerg	.03	.01	.00
☐ 489 Richie Zisk	.06	.02	.00
☐ 490 Doug Bird	.03	.01	.00
☐ 491 Larry Bowa	.10	.04	.01
☐ 492 Bill Buckner	.10	.04	.01
☐ 493 Bill Campbell	.03	.01	.00
☐ 494 Jody Davis	.08	.03	.01
☐ 495 Leon Durham	.08	.03	.01
☐ 496 Steve Henderson	.03	.01	.00
☐ 497 Willie Hernandez	.10	.04	.01
☐ 498 Ferguson Jenkins	.15	.06	.01
☐ 499 Jay Johnstone	.08	.03	.01
☐ 500 Junior Kennedy	.03	.01	.00
☐ 501 Randy Martz	.03	.01	.00
☐ 502 Jerry Morales	.03	.01	.00
☐ 503 Keith Moreland	.06	.02	.00
☐ 504 Dickie Noles	.03	.01	.00
☐ 505 Mike Proly	.03	.01	.00
☐ 506 Allen Ripley	.03	.01	.00
☐ 507 Ryne Sandberg	4.00	1.60	.40
☐ 508 Lee Smith	.10	.04	.01
☐ 509 Pat Tabler	.30	.12	.03
☐ 510 Dick Tidrow	.03	.01	.00
☐ 511 Bump Wills	.03	.01	.00
☐ 512 Gary Woods	.03	.01	.00
☐ 513 Tony Armas	.08	.03	.01
☐ 514 Dave Beard	.03	.01	.00
☐ 515 Jeff Burroughs	.06	.02	.00
☐ 516 John D'Acquisto	.03	.01	.00
☐ 517 Wayne Gross	.03	.01	.00
☐ 518 Mike Heath	.03	.01	.00
☐ 519 Rickey Henderson	.60	.24	.06
☐ 520 Cliff Johnson	.03	.01	.00
☐ 521 Matt Keough	.03	.01	.00
☐ 522 Brian Kingman	.03	.01	.00
☐ 523 Rick Langford	.03	.01	.00
☐ 524 Davey Lopes	.08	.03	.01
☐ 525 Steve McCatty	.03	.01	.00
☐ 526 Dave McKay	.03	.01	.00
☐ 527 Dan Meyer	.03	.01	.00
☐ 528 Dwayne Murphy	.03	.01	.00
☐ 529 Jeff Newman	.03	.01	.00
☐ 530 Mike Norris	.03	.01	.00
☐ 531 Bob Owchinko	.03	.01	.00
☐ 532 Joe Rudi	.06	.02	.00
☐ 533 Jimmy Sexton	.03	.01	.00
☐ 534 Fred Stanley	.03	.01	.00
☐ 535 Tom Underwood	.03	.01	.00
☐ 536 Neil Allen	.03	.01	.00
☐ 537 Wally Backman	.10	.04	.01
☐ 538 Bob Bailor	.03	.01	.00
☐ 539 Hubie Brooks	.10	.04	.01
☐ 540 Carlos Diaz	.06	.02	.00
☐ 541 Pete Falcone	.03	.01	.00
☐ 542 George Foster	.12	.05	.01
☐ 543 Ron Gardenhire	.03	.01	.00
☐ 544 Brian Giles	.03	.01	.00
☐ 545 Ron Hodges	.03	.01	.00
☐ 546 Randy Jones	.03	.01	.00

□ 547	Mike Jorgensen	.03	.01	.00
□ 548	Dave Kingman	.12	.05	.01
□ 549	Ed Lynch	.03	.01	.00
□ 550	Jesse Orosco	.06	.02	.00
□ 551	Rick Ownbey	.03	.01	.00
□ 552	Charlie Puleo	.03	.01	.00
□ 553	Gary Rajsich	.03	.01	.00
□ 554	Mike Scott	.30	.12	.03
□ 555	Rusty Staub	.10	.04	.01
□ 556	John Stearns	.03	.01	.00
□ 557	Craig Swan	.03	.01	.00
□ 558	Ellis Valentine	.03	.01	.00
□ 559	Tom Veryzer	.03	.01	.00
□ 560	Mookie Wilson	.08	.03	.01
□ 561	Pat Zachry	.03	.01	.00
□ 562	Buddy Bell	.10	.04	.01
□ 563	John Butcher	.03	.01	.00
□ 564	Steve Comer	.03	.01	.00
□ 565	Danny Darwin	.03	.01	.00
□ 566	Bucky Dent	.08	.03	.01
□ 567	John Grubb	.03	.01	.00
□ 568	Rick Honeycutt	.03	.01	.00
□ 569	Dave Hostetler	.06	.02	.00
□ 570	Charlie Hough	.08	.03	.01
□ 571	Lamar Johnson	.03	.01	.00
□ 572	Jon Matlack	.03	.01	.00
□ 573	Paul Mirabella	.03	.01	.00
□ 574	Larry Parrish	.06	.02	.00
□ 575	Mike Richardt	.03	.01	.00
□ 576	Mickey Rivers	.06	.02	.00
□ 577	Billy Sample	.03	.01	.00
□ 578	Dave Schmidt	.15	.06	.01
□ 579	Bill Stein	.03	.01	.00
□ 580	Jim Sundberg	.06	.02	.00
□ 581	Frank Tanana	.08	.03	.01
□ 582	Mark Wagner	.03	.01	.00
□ 583	George Wright	.03	.01	.00
□ 584	Johnny Bench	.45	.18	.04
□ 585	Bruce Berenyi	.03	.01	.00
□ 586	Larry Biittner	.03	.01	.00
□ 587	Cesar Cedeno	.08	.03	.01
□ 588	Dave Concepcion	.10	.04	.01
□ 589	Dan Driessen	.03	.01	.00
□ 590	Greg Harris	.03	.01	.00
□ 591	Ben Hayes	.03	.01	.00
□ 592	Paul Householder	.03	.01	.00
□ 593	Tom Hume	.03	.01	.00
□ 594	Wayne Krenchicki	.03	.01	.00
□ 595	Rafael Landestoy	.03	.01	.00
□ 596	Charlie Leibrandt	.06	.02	.00
□ 597	Eddie Milner	.10	.04	.01
□ 598	Ron Oester	.03	.01	.00
□ 599	Frank Pastore	.03	.01	.00
□ 600	Joe Price	.03	.01	.00
□ 601	Tom Seaver	.40	.16	.04
□ 602	Bob Shirley	.03	.01	.00
□ 603	Mario Soto	.06	.02	.00
□ 604	Alex Trevino	.03	.01	.00
□ 605	Mike Vail	.03	.01	.00
□ 606	Duane Walker	.03	.01	.00
□ 607	Tom Brunansky	.55	.22	.05
□ 608	Bobby Castillo	.03	.01	.00
□ 609	John Castino	.03	.01	.00
□ 610	Ron Davis	.03	.01	.00
□ 611	Lenny Faedo	.03	.01	.00
□ 612	Terry Felton	.03	.01	.00
□ 613	Gary Gaetti	3.00	1.20	.30
□ 614	Mickey Hatcher	.03	.01	.00
□ 615	Brad Havens	.03	.01	.00
□ 616	Kent Hrbek	1.25	.50	.12
□ 617	Randy Johnson	.03	.01	.00
□ 618	Tim Laudner	.08	.03	.01
□ 619	Jeff Little	.03	.01	.00
□ 620	Bobby Mitchell	.03	.01	.00
□ 621	Jack O'Connor	.03	.01	.00
□ 622	John Pacella	.03	.01	.00
□ 623	Pete Redfern	.03	.01	.00
□ 624	Jesus Vega	.03	.01	.00
□ 625	Frank Viola	3.75	1.50	.37
□ 626	Ron Washington	.03	.01	.00
□ 627	Gary Ward	.06	.02	.00
□ 628	Al Williams	.03	.01	.00
□ 629	Red Sox All-Stars Carl Yastrzemski Dennis Eckersley Mark Clear	.25	.10	.02
□ 630	"300 Career Wins" Gaylord Perry and Terry Bulling 5/6/82	.10	.04	.01
□ 631	Pride of Venezuela Dave Concepcion and Manny Trillo	.06	.02	.00
□ 632	All-Star Infielders Robin Yount and Buddy Bell	.15	.06	.01

□ 633	Mr.Vet and Mr.Rookie Dave Winfield and Kent Hrbek	.20	.08	.02
□ 634	Fountain of Youth Willie Stargell and Pete Rose	.65	.26	.06
□ 635	Big Chiefs Toby Harrah and Andre Thornton	.06	.02	.00
□ 636	Smith Brothers Ozzie and Lonnie	.08	.03	.01
□ 637	Base Stealers' Threat Bo Diaz and Gary Carter	.10	.04	.01
□ 638	All-Star Catchers Carlton Fisk and Gary Carter	.12	.05	.01
□ 639	The Silver Shoe Rickey Henderson	.25	.10	.02
□ 640	Home Run Threats Ben Oglivie and Reggie Jackson	.18	.08	.01
□ 641	Two Teams Same Day Joel Youngblood August 4, 1982	.06	.02	.00
□ 642	Last Perfect Game Ron Hassey and Len Barker	.06	.02	.00
□ 643	Black and Blue Bud Black	.06	.02	.00
□ 644	Black and Blue Vida Blue	.06	.02	.00
□ 645	Speed and Power Reggie Jackson	.25	.10	.02
□ 646	Speed and Power Rickey Henderson	.25	.10	.02
□ 647	CL: Cards/Brewers	.07	.01	.00
□ 648	CL: Orioles/Angels	.07	.01	.00
□ 649	CL: Royals/Braves	.07	.01	.00
□ 650	CL: Phillies/Red Sox	.07	.01	.00
□ 651	CL: Dodgers/White Sox	.07	.01	.00
□ 652	CL: Giants/Expos	.07	.01	.00
□ 653	CL: Pirates/Tigers	.07	.01	.00
□ 654	CL: Padres/Yankees	.07	.01	.00
□ 655	CL: Indians/Blue Jays	.07	.01	.00
□ 656	CL: Astros/Mariners	.07	.01	.00
□ 657	CL: Cubs/A's	.07	.01	.00
□ 658	CL: Mets/Rangers	.07	.01	.00
□ 659	CL: Reds/Twins	.07	.01	.00
□ 660	CL: Specials/Teams	.09	.01	.00

1984 Fleer

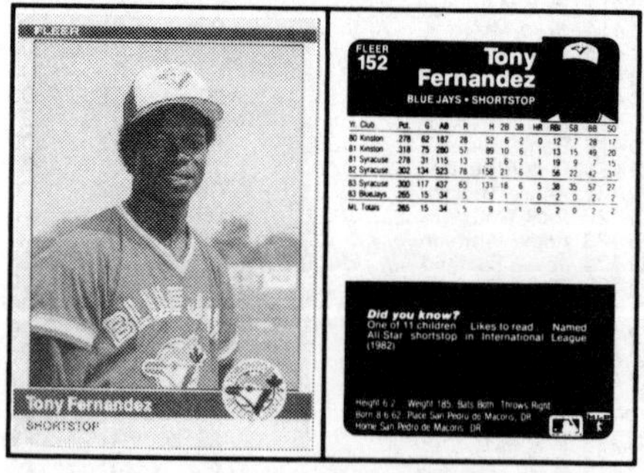

The cards in this 660-card set measure 2 1/2" by 3 1/2". The 1984 Fleer card set featured fronts with full-color team logos along with the player's name and position and the Fleer identification. The set features many imaginative photos, several multi-player cards, and many more action shots than the 1983 card set. The backs are quite similar to the 1983 backs except that blue rather than brown ink is used. The player cards are alphabetized within team and the teams are ordered by their 1983 season finish and won-lost record, e.g., Baltimore (1-23), Philadelphia (24-49), Chicago White Sox (50-73), Detroit (74-95), Los Angeles (96-118), New York

Yankees (119-144), Toronto (145- 169), Atlanta (170-193), Milwaukee (194-219), Houston (220-244), Pittsburgh (245-269), Montreal (270-293), San Diego (294-317), St. Louis (318-340), Kansas City (341-364), San Francisco (365- 387), Boston (388-412), Texas (413-435), Oakland (436-461), Cincinnati (462-485), Chicago (486-507), California (508-532), Cleveland (533-555), Minnesota (556-579), New York Mets (580- 603), and Seattle (604-625). Specials (626-646) and checklist cards (647-660) make up the end of the set.

	MINT	EXC	G-VG
COMPLETE SET (660)	100.00	40.00	10.00
COMMON PLAYER (1-660)	.05	.02	.00
□ 1 Mike Boddicker	.20	.05	.01
□ 2 Al Bumbry	.05	.02	.00
□ 3 Todd Cruz	.05	.02	.00
□ 4 Rich Dauer	.05	.02	.00
□ 5 Storm Davis	.10	.04	.01
□ 6 Rick Dempsey	.05	.02	.00
□ 7 Jim Dwyer	.05	.02	.00
□ 8 Mike Flanagan	.10	.04	.01
□ 9 Dan Ford	.05	.02	.00
□ 10 John Lowenstein	.05	.02	.00
□ 11 Dennis Martinez	.10	.04	.01
□ 12 Tippy Martinez	.05	.02	.00
□ 13 Scott McGregor	.10	.04	.01
□ 14 Eddie Murray	.60	.24	.06
□ 15 Joe Nolan	.05	.02	.00
□ 16 Jim Palmer	.35	.14	.03
□ 17 Cal Ripken	.75	.30	.07
□ 18 Gary Roenicke	.05	.02	.00
□ 19 Lenn Sakata	.05	.02	.00
□ 20 John Shelby	.40	.16	.04
□ 21 Ken Singleton	.10	.04	.01
□ 22 Sammy Stewart	.05	.02	.00
□ 23 Tim Stoddard	.05	.02	.00
□ 24 Marty Bystrom	.05	.02	.00
□ 25 Steve Carlton	.40	.16	.04
□ 26 Ivan DeJesus	.05	.02	.00
□ 27 John Denny	.10	.04	.01
□ 28 Bob Dernier	.05	.02	.00
□ 29 Bo Diaz	.05	.02	.00
□ 30 Kiko Garcia	.05	.02	.00
□ 31 Greg Gross	.05	.02	.00
□ 32 Kevin Gross	.35	.14	.03
□ 33 Von Hayes	.15	.06	.01
□ 34 Willie Hernandez	.15	.06	.01
□ 35 Al Holland	.05	.02	.00
□ 36 Charles Hudson	.25	.10	.02
□ 37 Joe Lefebvre	.05	.02	.00
□ 38 Sixto Lezcano	.05	.02	.00
□ 39 Garry Maddox	.10	.04	.01
□ 40 Gary Matthews	.10	.04	.01
□ 41 Len Matuszek	.05	.02	.00
□ 42 Tug McGraw	.10	.04	.01
□ 43 Joe Morgan	.25	.10	.02
□ 44 Tony Perez	.20	.08	.02
□ 45 Ron Reed	.05	.02	.00
□ 46 Pete Rose	1.00	.40	.10
□ 47 Juan Samuel	3.50	1.40	.35
□ 48 Mike Schmidt	.65	.26	.06
□ 49 Ozzie Virgil	.05	.02	.00
□ 50 Juan Agosto	.15	.06	.01
□ 51 Harold Baines	.20	.08	.02
□ 52 Floyd Bannister	.05	.02	.00
□ 53 Salome Barojas	.05	.02	.00
□ 54 Britt Burns	.05	.02	.00
□ 55 Julio Cruz	.05	.02	.00
□ 56 Richard Dotson	.10	.04	.01
□ 57 Jerry Dybzinski	.05	.02	.00
□ 58 Carlton Fisk	.20	.08	.02
□ 59 Scott Fletcher	.25	.10	.02
□ 60 Jerry Hairston	.05	.02	.00
□ 61 Kevin Hickey	.05	.02	.00
□ 62 Marc Hill	.05	.02	.00
□ 63 LaMarr Hoyt	.10	.04	.01
□ 64 Ron Kittle	.20	.08	.02
□ 65 Jerry Koosman	.10	.04	.01
□ 66 Dennis Lamp	.05	.02	.00
□ 67 Rudy Law	.05	.02	.00
□ 68 Vance Law	.10	.04	.01
□ 69 Greg Luzinski	.10	.04	.01
□ 70 Tom Paciorek	.05	.02	.00
□ 71 Mike Squires	.05	.02	.00
□ 72 Dick Tidrow	.05	.02	.00
□ 73 Greg Walker	.45	.18	.04
□ 74 Glenn Abbott	.05	.02	.00
□ 75 Howard Bailey	.05	.02	.00
□ 76 Doug Bair	.05	.02	.00
□ 77 Juan Berenguer	.05	.02	.00
□ 78 Tom Brookens	.05	.02	.00
□ 79 Enos Cabell	.05	.02	.00
□ 80 Kirk Gibson	.40	.16	.04
□ 81 John Grubb	.05	.02	.00
□ 82 Larry Herndon	.05	.02	.00
□ 83 Wayne Krenchicki	.05	.02	.00
□ 84 Rick Leach	.05	.02	.00
□ 85 Chet Lemon	.10	.04	.01
□ 86 Aurelio Lopez	.05	.02	.00
□ 87 Jack Morris	.20	.08	.02
□ 88 Lance Parrish	.25	.10	.02
□ 89 Dan Petry	.10	.04	.01
□ 90 Dave Rozema	.05	.02	.00
□ 91 Alan Trammell	.35	.14	.03
□ 92 Lou Whitaker	.15	.06	.01
□ 93 Milt Wilcox	.05	.02	.00
□ 94 Glenn Wilson	.10	.04	.01
□ 95 John Wockenfuss	.05	.02	.00
□ 96 Dusty Baker	.10	.04	.01
□ 97 Joe Beckwith	.05	.02	.00
□ 98 Greg Brock	.10	.04	.01
□ 99 Jack Fimple	.05	.02	.00
□ 100 Pedro Guerrero	.30	.12	.03
□ 101 Rick Honeycutt	.05	.02	.00
□ 102 Burt Hooton	.05	.02	.00
□ 103 Steve Howe	.05	.02	.00
□ 104 Ken Landreaux	.05	.02	.00
□ 105 Mike Marshall	.20	.08	.02
□ 106 Rick Monday	.10	.04	.01
□ 107 Jose Morales	.05	.02	.00
□ 108 Tom Niedenfuer	.10	.04	.01
□ 109 Alejandro Pena	.30	.12	.03
□ 110 Jerry Reuss	.10	.04	.01
□ 111 Bill Russell	.10	.04	.01
□ 112 Steve Sax	.25	.10	.02
□ 113 Mike Scioscia	.10	.04	.01
□ 114 Derrel Thomas	.05	.02	.00
□ 115 Fernando Valenzuela	.25	.10	.02
□ 116 Bob Welch	.10	.04	.01
□ 117 Steve Yeager	.05	.02	.00
□ 118 Pat Zachry	.05	.02	.00
□ 119 Don Baylor	.15	.06	.01
□ 120 Bert Campaneris	.10	.04	.01
□ 121 Rick Cerone	.05	.02	.00
□ 122 Ray Fontenot	.05	.02	.00
□ 123 George Frazier	.05	.02	.00
□ 124 Oscar Gamble	.05	.02	.00
□ 125 Goose Gossage	.15	.06	.01
□ 126 Ken Griffey	.10	.04	.01
□ 127 Ron Guidry	.20	.08	.02
□ 128 Jay Howell	.15	.06	.01
□ 129 Steve Kemp	.10	.04	.01
□ 130 Matt Keough	.05	.02	.00
□ 131 Don Mattingly	33.00	12.00	2.50
□ 132 John Montefusco	.05	.02	.00
□ 133 Omar Moreno	.05	.02	.00
□ 134 Dale Murray	.05	.02	.00
□ 135 Graig Nettles	.15	.06	.01
□ 136 Lou Piniella	.10	.04	.01
□ 137 Willie Randolph	.15	.06	.01
□ 138 Shane Rawley	.10	.04	.01
□ 139 Dave Righetti	.20	.08	.02
□ 140 Andre Robertson	.05	.02	.00
□ 141 Bob Shirley	.05	.02	.00
□ 142 Roy Smalley	.05	.02	.00
□ 143 Dave Winfield	.40	.16	.04
□ 144 Butch Wynegar	.05	.02	.00
□ 145 Jim Acker	.10	.04	.01
□ 146 Doyle Alexander	.10	.04	.01
□ 147 Jesse Barfield	.30	.12	.03
□ 148 Jorge Bell	.85	.34	.08
□ 149 Barry Bonnell	.05	.02	.00
□ 150 Jim Clancy	.05	.02	.00
□ 151 Dave Collins	.05	.02	.00
□ 152 Tony Fernandez	4.50	1.80	.45
□ 153 Damaso Garcia	.05	.02	.00
□ 154 Dave Geisel	.05	.02	.00
□ 155 Jim Gott	.10	.04	.01
□ 156 Alfredo Griffin	.10	.04	.01
□ 157 Garth Iorg	.05	.02	.00
□ 158 Roy Lee Jackson	.05	.02	.00
□ 159 Cliff Johnson	.05	.02	.00
□ 160 Luis Leal	.05	.02	.00
□ 161 Buck Martinez	.05	.02	.00
□ 162 Joey McLaughlin	.05	.02	.00
□ 163 Randy Moffitt	.05	.02	.00
□ 164 Lloyd Moseby	.15	.06	.01
□ 165 Rance Mulliniks	.05	.02	.00
□ 166 Jorge Orta	.05	.02	.00
□ 167 Dave Stieb	.20	.08	.02
□ 168 Willie Upshaw	.10	.04	.01
□ 169 Ernie Whitt	.05	.02	.00
□ 170 Len Barker	.05	.02	.00

☐ 171	Steve Bedrosian	.20	.08	.02
☐ 172	Bruce Benedict	.05	.02	.00
☐ 173	Brett Butler	.15	.06	.01
☐ 174	Rick Camp	.05	.02	.00
☐ 175	Chris Chambliss	.10	.04	.01
☐ 176	Ken Dayley	.05	.02	.00
☐ 177	Pete Falcone	.05	.02	.00
☐ 178	Terry Forster	.10	.04	.01
☐ 179	Gene Garber	.05	.02	.00
☐ 180	Terry Harper	.05	.02	.00
☐ 181	Bob Horner	.20	.08	.02
☐ 182	Glenn Hubbard	.05	.02	.00
☐ 183	Randy Johnson	.05	.02	.00
☐ 184	Craig McMurtry	.10	.04	.01
☐ 185	Donnie Moore	.05	.02	.00
☐ 186	Dale Murphy	.80	.32	.08
☐ 187	Phil Niekro	.25	.10	.02
☐ 188	Pascual Perez	.20	.08	.02
☐ 189	Biff Pocoroba	.05	.02	.00
☐ 190	Rafael Ramirez	.05	.02	.00
☐ 191	Jerry Royster	.05	.02	.00
☐ 192	Claudell Washington	.10	.04	.01
☐ 193	Bob Watson	.10	.04	.01
☐ 194	Jerry Augustine	.05	.02	.00
☐ 195	Mark Brouhard	.05	.02	.00
☐ 196	Mike Caldwell	.05	.02	.00
☐ 197	Tom Candiotti	.25	.10	.02
☐ 198	Cecil Cooper	.15	.06	.01
☐ 199	Rollie Fingers	.20	.08	.02
☐ 200	Jim Gantner	.05	.02	.00
☐ 201	Bob L. Gibson	.10	.04	.01
☐ 202	Moose Haas	.05	.02	.00
☐ 203	Roy Howell	.05	.02	.00
☐ 204	Pete Ladd	.05	.02	.00
☐ 205	Rick Manning	.05	.02	.00
☐ 206	Bob McClure	.05	.02	.00
☐ 207	Paul Molitor	.20	.08	.02
☐ 208	Don Money	.05	.02	.00
☐ 209	Charlie Moore	.05	.02	.00
☐ 210	Ben Oglivie	.10	.04	.01
☐ 211	Chuck Porter	.05	.02	.00
☐ 212	Ed Romero	.05	.02	.00
☐ 213	Ted Simmons	.15	.06	.01
☐ 214	Jim Slaton	.05	.02	.00
☐ 215	Don Sutton	.25	.10	.02
☐ 216	Tom Tellmann	.05	.02	.00
☐ 217	Pete Vuckovich	.10	.04	.01
☐ 218	Ned Yost	.05	.02	.00
☐ 219	Robin Yount	.35	.14	.03
☐ 220	Alan Ashby	.05	.02	.00
☐ 221	Kevin Bass	.20	.08	.02
☐ 222	Jose Cruz	.10	.04	.01
☐ 223	Bill Dawley	.10	.04	.01
☐ 224	Frank DiPino	.05	.02	.00
☐ 225	Bill Doran	.75	.30	.07
☐ 226	Phil Garner	.05	.02	.00
☐ 227	Art Howe	.10	.04	.01
☐ 228	Bob Knepper	.10	.04	.01
☐ 229	Ray Knight	.10	.04	.01
☐ 230	Frank LaCorte	.05	.02	.00
☐ 231	Mike LaCoss	.05	.02	.00
☐ 232	Mike Madden	.05	.02	.00
☐ 233	Jerry Mumphrey	.05	.02	.00
☐ 234	Joe Niekro	.10	.04	.01
☐ 235	Terry Puhl	.05	.02	.00
☐ 236	Luis Pujols	.05	.02	.00
☐ 237	Craig Reynolds	.05	.02	.00
☐ 238	Vern Ruhle	.05	.02	.00
☐ 239	Nolan Ryan	.40	.16	.04
☐ 240	Mike Scott	.30	.12	.03
☐ 241	Tony Scott	.05	.02	.00
☐ 242	Dave Smith	.10	.04	.01
☐ 243	Dickie Thon	.05	.02	.00
☐ 244	Denny Walling	.05	.02	.00
☐ 245	Dale Berra	.05	.02	.00
☐ 246	Jim Bibby	.05	.02	.00
☐ 247	John Candelaria	.10	.04	.01
☐ 248	Jose DeLeon	.30	.12	.03
☐ 249	Mike Easler	.05	.02	.00
☐ 250	Cecilio Guante	.05	.02	.00
☐ 251	Richie Hebner	.05	.02	.00
☐ 252	Lee Lacy	.05	.02	.00
☐ 253	Bill Madlock	.15	.06	.01
☐ 254	Milt May	.05	.02	.00
☐ 255	Lee Mazzilli	.05	.02	.00
☐ 256	Larry McWilliams	.05	.02	.00
☐ 257	Jim Morrison	.05	.02	.00
☐ 258	Dave Parker	.18	.08	.01
☐ 259	Tony Pena	.15	.06	.01
☐ 260	Johnny Ray	.15	.06	.01
☐ 261	Rick Rhoden	.10	.04	.01
☐ 262	Don Robinson	.05	.02	.00
☐ 263	Manny Sarmiento	.05	.02	.00
☐ 264	Rod Scurry	.05	.02	.00
☐ 265	Kent Tekulve	.10	.04	.01
☐ 266	Gene Tenace	.05	.02	.0
☐ 267	Jason Thompson	.05	.02	.0
☐ 268	Lee Tunnell	.10	.04	.01
☐ 269	Marvell Wynne	.10	.04	.01
☐ 270	Ray Burris	.05	.02	.0
☐ 271	Gary Carter	.40	.16	.04
☐ 272	Warren Cromartie	.05	.02	.0
☐ 273	Andre Dawson	.35	.14	.03
☐ 274	Doug Flynn	.05	.02	.0
☐ 275	Terry Francona	.05	.02	.0
☐ 276	Bill Gullickson	.05	.02	.0
☐ 277	Bob James	.15	.06	.01
☐ 278	Charlie Lea	.05	.02	.0
☐ 279	Bryan Little	.05	.02	.0
☐ 280	Al Oliver	.10	.04	.01
☐ 281	Tim Raines	.40	.16	.04
☐ 282	Bobby Ramos	.05	.02	.0
☐ 283	Jeff Reardon	.10	.04	.01
☐ 284	Steve Rogers	.05	.02	.00
☐ 285	Scott Sanderson	.05	.02	.00
☐ 286	Dan Schatzeder	.05	.02	.00
☐ 287	Bryn Smith	.10	.04	.01
☐ 288	Chris Speier	.05	.02	.00
☐ 289	Manny Trillo	.05	.02	.00
☐ 290	Mike Vail	.05	.02	.00
☐ 291	Tim Wallach	.15	.06	.01
☐ 292	Chris Welsh	.05	.02	.00
☐ 293	Jim Wohlford	.05	.02	.00
☐ 294	Kurt Bevacqua	.05	.02	.00
☐ 295	Juan Bonilla	.05	.02	.00
☐ 296	Bobby Brown	.05	.02	.00
☐ 297	Luis DeLeon	.05	.02	.00
☐ 298	Dave Dravecky	.10	.04	.01
☐ 299	Tim Flannery	.05	.02	.00
☐ 300	Steve Garvey	.50	.20	.05
☐ 301	Tony Gwynn	2.50	1.00	.25
☐ 302	Andy Hawkins	.45	.18	.04
☐ 303	Ruppert Jones	.05	.02	.00
☐ 304	Terry Kennedy	.10	.04	.01
☐ 305	Tim Lollar	.05	.02	.00
☐ 306	Gary Lucas	.05	.02	.00
☐ 307	Kevin McReynolds	6.50	2.60	.65
☐ 308	Sid Monge	.05	.02	.00
☐ 309	Mario Ramirez	.05	.02	.00
☐ 310	Gene Richards	.05	.02	.00
☐ 311	Luis Salazar	.05	.02	.00
☐ 312	Eric Show	.10	.04	.01
☐ 313	Elias Sosa	.05	.02	.00
☐ 314	Garry Templeton	.10	.04	.01
☐ 315	Mark Thurmond	.10	.04	.01
☐ 316	Ed Whitson	.05	.02	.00
☐ 317	Alan Wiggins	.05	.02	.00
☐ 318	Neil Allen	.05	.02	.00
☐ 319	Joaquin Andujar	.10	.04	.01
☐ 320	Steve Braun	.05	.02	.00
☐ 321	Glenn Brummer	.05	.02	.00
☐ 322	Bob Forsch	.05	.02	.00
☐ 323	David Green	.05	.02	.00
☐ 324	George Hendrick	.10	.04	.01
☐ 325	Tom Herr	.10	.04	.01
☐ 326	Dane Iorg	.05	.02	.00
☐ 327	Jeff Lahti	.05	.02	.00
☐ 328	Dave LaPoint	.10	.04	.01
☐ 329	Willie McGee	.35	.14	.03
☐ 330	Ken Oberkfell	.05	.02	.00
☐ 331	Darrell Porter	.05	.02	.00
☐ 332	Jamie Quirk	.05	.02	.00
☐ 333	Mike Ramsey	.05	.02	.00
☐ 334	Floyd Rayford	.05	.02	.00
☐ 335	Lonnie Smith	.10	.04	.01
☐ 336	Ozzie Smith	.25	.10	.02
☐ 337	John Stuper	.05	.02	.00
☐ 338	Bruce Sutter	.15	.06	.01
☐ 339	Andy Van Slyke	2.50	1.00	.25
☐ 340	Dave Von Ohlen	.05	.02	.00
☐ 341	Willie Aikens	.05	.02	.00
☐ 342	Mike Armstrong	.05	.02	.00
☐ 343	Bud Black	.05	.02	.00
☐ 344	George Brett	.70	.28	.07
☐ 345	Onix Concepcion	.05	.02	.00
☐ 346	Keith Creel	.05	.02	.00
☐ 347	Larry Gura	.05	.02	.00
☐ 348	Don Hood	.05	.02	.00
☐ 349	Dennis Leonard	.10	.04	.01
☐ 350	Hal McRae	.10	.04	.01
☐ 351	Amos Otis	.10	.04	.01
☐ 352	Gaylord Perry	.25	.10	.02
☐ 353	Greg Pryor	.05	.02	.00
☐ 354	Dan Quisenberry	.15	.06	.01
☐ 355	Steve Renko	.05	.02	.00
☐ 356	Leon Roberts	.05	.02	.00
☐ 357	Pat Sheridan	.20	.08	.02
☐ 358	Joe Simpson	.05	.02	.00
☐ 359	Don Slaught	.05	.02	.00
☐ 360	Paul Splittorff	.05	.02	.00

□ 361 U.L. Washington	.05	.02	.00
□ 362 John Wathan	.05	.02	.00
□ 363 Frank White	.10	.04	.01
□ 364 Willie Wilson	.15	.06	.01
□ 365 Jim Barr	.05	.02	.00
□ 366 Dave Bergman	.05	.02	.00
□ 367 Fred Breining	.05	.02	.00
□ 368 Bob Brenly	.05	.02	.00
□ 369 Jack Clark	.30	.12	.03
□ 370 Chili Davis	.15	.06	.01
□ 371 Mark Davis	.10	.04	.01
□ 372 Darrell Evans	.15	.06	.01
□ 373 Atlee Hammaker	.10	.04	.01
□ 374 Mike Krukow	.10	.04	.01
□ 375 Duane Kuiper	.05	.02	.00
□ 376 Bill Laskey	.05	.02	.00
□ 377 Gary Lavelle	.05	.02	.00
□ 378 Johnnie LeMaster	.05	.02	.00
□ 379 Jeff Leonard	.10	.04	.01
□ 380 Randy Lerch	.05	.02	.00
□ 381 Renie Martin	.05	.02	.00
□ 382 Andy McGaffigan	.05	.02	.00
□ 383 Greg Minton	.05	.02	.00
□ 384 Tom O'Malley	.05	.02	.00
□ 385 Max Venable	.05	.02	.00
□ 386 Brad Wellman	.05	.02	.00
□ 387 Joel Youngblood	.05	.02	.00
□ 388 Gary Allenson	.05	.02	.00
□ 389 Luis Aponte	.05	.02	.00
□ 390 Tony Armas	.10	.04	.01
□ 391 Doug Bird	.05	.02	.00
□ 392 Wade Boggs	7.00	2.80	.70
□ 393 Dennis Boyd	.40	.16	.04
□ 394 Mike Brown (Red Sox pitcher)	.10	.04	.01
□ 395 Mark Clear	.05	.02	.00
□ 396 Dennis Eckersley	.20	.08	.02
□ 397 Dwight Evans	.20	.08	.02
□ 398 Rich Gedman	.10	.04	.01
□ 399 Glenn Hoffman	.05	.02	.00
□ 400 Bruce Hurst	.20	.08	.02
□ 401 John Henry Johnson	.05	.02	.00
□ 402 Ed Jurak	.05	.02	.00
□ 403 Rick Miller	.05	.02	.00
□ 404 Jeff Newman	.05	.02	.00
□ 405 Reid Nichols	.05	.02	.00
□ 406 Bob Ojeda	.10	.04	.01
□ 407 Jerry Remy	.05	.02	.00
□ 408 Jim Rice	.25	.10	.02
□ 409 Bob Stanley	.05	.02	.00
□ 410 Dave Stapleton	.05	.02	.00
□ 411 John Tudor	.15	.06	.01
□ 412 Carl Yastrzemski	.70	.28	.07
□ 413 Buddy Bell	.15	.06	.01
□ 414 Larry Biittner	.05	.02	.00
□ 415 John Butcher	.05	.02	.00
□ 416 Danny Darwin	.05	.02	.00
□ 417 Bucky Dent	.10	.04	.01
□ 418 Dave Hostetler	.05	.02	.00
□ 419 Charlie Hough	.10	.04	.01
□ 420 Bobby Johnson	.05	.02	.00
□ 421 Odell Jones	.05	.02	.00
□ 422 Jon Matlack	.05	.02	.00
□ 423 Pete O'Brien	1.00	.40	.10
□ 424 Larry Parrish	.10	.04	.01
□ 425 Mickey Rivers	.10	.04	.01
□ 426 Billy Sample	.05	.02	.00
□ 427 Dave Schmidt	.10	.04	.01
□ 428 Mike Smithson	.10	.04	.01
□ 429 Bill Stein	.05	.02	.00
□ 430 Dave Stewart	.20	.08	.02
□ 431 Jim Sundberg	.10	.04	.01
□ 432 Frank Tanana	.10	.04	.01
□ 433 Dave Tobik	.05	.02	.00
□ 434 Wayne Tolleson	.10	.04	.01
□ 435 George Wright	.05	.02	.00
□ 436 Bill Almon	.05	.02	.00
□ 437 Keith Atherton	.05	.02	.00
□ 438 Dave Beard	.05	.02	.00
□ 439 Tom Burgmeier	.05	.02	.00
□ 440 Jeff Burroughs	.10	.04	.01
□ 441 Chris Codiroli	.10	.04	.01
□ 442 Tim Conroy	.10	.04	.01
□ 443 Mike Davis	.10	.04	.01
□ 444 Wayne Gross	.05	.02	.00
□ 445 Garry Hancock	.05	.02	.00
□ 446 Mike Heath	.05	.02	.00
□ 447 Rickey Henderson	.60	.24	.06
□ 448 Donnie Hill	.10	.04	.01
□ 449 Bob Kearney	.05	.02	.00
□ 450 Bill Krueger	.10	.04	.01
□ 451 Rick Langford	.05	.02	.00
□ 452 Carney Lansford	.10	.04	.01
□ 453 Davey Lopes	.10	.04	.01
□ 454 Steve McCatty	.05	.02	.00
□ 455 Dan Meyer	.05	.02	.00
□ 456 Dwayne Murphy	.05	.02	.00
□ 457 Mike Norris	.05	.02	.00
□ 458 Ricky Peters	.05	.02	.00
□ 459 Tony Phillips	.10	.04	.01
□ 460 Tom Underwood	.05	.02	.00
□ 461 Mike Warren	.10	.04	.01
□ 462 Johnny Bench	.50	.20	.05
□ 463 Bruce Berenyi	.05	.02	.00
□ 464 Dann Bilardello	.05	.02	.00
□ 465 Cesar Cedeno	.10	.04	.01
□ 466 Dave Concepcion	.15	.06	.01
□ 467 Dan Driessen	.05	.02	.00
□ 468 Nick Esasky	.35	.14	.03
□ 469 Rich Gale	.05	.02	.00
□ 470 Ben Hayes	.05	.02	.00
□ 471 Paul Householder	.05	.02	.00
□ 472 Tom Hume	.05	.02	.00
□ 473 Alan Knicely	.05	.02	.00
□ 474 Eddie Milner	.05	.02	.00
□ 475 Ron Oester	.05	.02	.00
□ 476 Kelly Paris	.10	.04	.01
□ 477 Frank Pastore	.05	.02	.00
□ 478 Ted Power	.05	.02	.00
□ 479 Joe Price	.05	.02	.00
□ 480 Charlie Puleo	.05	.02	.00
□ 481 Gary Redus	.25	.10	.02
□ 482 Bill Scherrer	.05	.02	.00
□ 483 Mario Soto	.05	.02	.00
□ 484 Alex Trevino	.05	.02	.00
□ 485 Duane Walker	.05	.02	.00
□ 486 Larry Bowa	.10	.04	.01
□ 487 Warren Brusstar	.05	.02	.00
□ 488 Bill Buckner	.10	.04	.01
□ 489 Bill Campbell	.05	.02	.00
□ 490 Ron Cey	.10	.04	.01
□ 491 Jody Davis	.10	.04	.01
□ 492 Leon Durham	.10	.04	.01
□ 493 Mel Hall	.20	.08	.02
□ 494 Ferguson Jenkins	.15	.06	.01
□ 495 Jay Johnstone	.10	.04	.01
□ 496 Craig Lefferts	.15	.06	.01
□ 497 Carmelo Martinez	.25	.10	.02
□ 498 Jerry Morales	.05	.02	.00
□ 499 Keith Moreland	.05	.02	.00
□ 500 Dickie Noles	.05	.02	.00
□ 501 Mike Proly	.05	.02	.00
□ 502 Chuck Rainey	.05	.02	.00
□ 503 Dick Ruthven	.05	.02	.00
□ 504 Ryne Sandberg	1.25	.50	.12
□ 505 Lee Smith	.15	.06	.01
□ 506 Steve Trout	.05	.02	.00
□ 507 Gary Woods	.05	.02	.00
□ 508 Juan Beniquez	.05	.02	.00
□ 509 Bob Boone	.15	.06	.01
□ 510 Rick Burleson	.10	.04	.01
□ 511 Rod Carew	.50	.20	.05
□ 512 Bobby Clark	.05	.02	.00
□ 513 John Curtis	.05	.02	.00
□ 514 Doug DeCinces	.10	.04	.01
□ 515 Brian Downing	.10	.04	.01
□ 516 Tim Foli	.05	.02	.00
□ 517 Ken Forsch	.05	.02	.00
□ 518 Bobby Grich	.10	.04	.01
□ 519 Andy Hassler	.05	.02	.00
□ 520 Reggie Jackson	.60	.24	.06
□ 521 Ron Jackson	.05	.02	.00
□ 522 Tommy John	.15	.06	.01
□ 523 Bruce Kison	.05	.02	.00
□ 524 Steve Lubratich	.05	.02	.00
□ 525 Fred Lynn	.15	.06	.01
□ 526 Gary Pettis	.30	.12	.03
□ 527 Luis Sanchez	.05	.02	.00
□ 528 Daryl Sconiers	.05	.02	.00
□ 529 Ellis Valentine	.05	.02	.00
□ 530 Rob Wilfong	.05	.02	.00
□ 531 Mike Witt	.15	.06	.01
□ 532 Geoff Zahn	.05	.02	.00
□ 533 Bud Anderson	.05	.02	.00
□ 534 Chris Bando	.05	.02	.00
□ 535 Alan Bannister	.05	.02	.00
□ 536 Bert Blyleven	.15	.06	.01
□ 537 Tom Brennan	.05	.02	.00
□ 538 Jamie Easterly	.05	.02	.00
□ 539 Juan Eichelberger	.05	.02	.00
□ 540 Jim Essian	.05	.02	.00
□ 541 Mike Fischlin	.05	.02	.00
□ 542 Julio Franco	.40	.16	.04
□ 543 Mike Hargrove	.05	.02	.00
□ 544 Toby Harrah	.05	.02	.00
□ 545 Ron Hassey	.05	.02	.00
□ 546 Neal Heaton	.20	.08	.02
□ 547 Bake McBride	.05	.02	.00
□ 548 Broderick Perkins	.05	.02	.00
□ 549 Lary Sorensen	.05	.02	.00

□ 550 Dan Spillner .05 .02 .00
□ 551 Rick Sutcliffe .20 .08 .02
□ 552 Pat Tabler .15 .06 .01
□ 553 Gorman Thomas .10 .04 .01
□ 554 Andre Thornton .10 .04 .01
□ 555 George Vukovich .05 .02 .00
□ 556 Darrell Brown .05 .02 .00
□ 557 Tom Brunansky .25 .10 .02
□ 558 Randy Bush .20 .06 .01
□ 559 Bobby Castillo .05 .02 .00
□ 560 John Castino .05 .02 .00
□ 561 Ron Davis .05 .02 .00
□ 562 Dave Engle .05 .02 .00
□ 563 Lenny Faedo .05 .02 .00
□ 564 Pete Filson .05 .02 .00
□ 565 Gary Gaetti .75 .30 .07
□ 566 Mickey Hatcher .10 .04 .01
□ 567 Kent Hrbek .40 .16 .04
□ 568 Rusty Kuntz .05 .02 .00
□ 569 Tim Laudner .10 .04 .01
□ 570 Rick Lysander .05 .02 .00
□ 571 Bobby Mitchell .05 .02 .00
□ 572 Ken Schrom .05 .02 .00
□ 573 Ray Smith .05 .02 .00
□ 574 Tim Teufel .25 .10 .02
□ 575 Frank Viola 1.00 .40 .10
□ 576 Gary Ward .10 .04 .01
□ 577 Ron Washington .05 .02 .00
□ 578 Len Whitehouse .05 .02 .00
□ 579 Al Williams .05 .02 .00
□ 580 Bob Bailor .05 .02 .00
□ 581 Mark Bradley .10 .04 .01
□ 582 Hubie Brooks .15 .06 .01
□ 583 Carlos Diaz .05 .02 .00
□ 584 George Foster .15 .06 .01
□ 585 Brian Giles .05 .02 .00
□ 586 Danny Heep .05 .02 .00
□ 587 Keith Hernandez .30 .12 .03
□ 588 Ron Hodges .05 .02 .00
□ 589 Scott Holman .05 .02 .00
□ 590 Dave Kingman .15 .06 .01
□ 591 Ed Lynch .05 .02 .00
□ 592 Jose Oquendo .35 .14 .03
□ 593 Jesse Orosco .05 .02 .00
□ 594 Junior Ortiz .05 .02 .00
□ 595 Tom Seaver .40 .16 .04
□ 596 Doug Sisk .05 .02 .00
□ 597 Rusty Staub .10 .04 .01
□ 598 John Stearns .05 .02 .00
□ 599 Darryl Strawberry 18.00 7.25 1.80
□ 600 Craig Swan .05 .02 .00
□ 601 Walt Terrell .30 .12 .03
□ 602 Mike Torrez .05 .02 .00
□ 603 Mookie Wilson .10 .04 .01
□ 604 Jamie Allen .05 .02 .00
□ 605 Jim Beattie .05 .02 .00
□ 606 Tony Bernazard .05 .02 .00
□ 607 Manny Castillo .05 .02 .00
□ 608 Bill Caudill .05 .02 .00
□ 609 Bryan Clark .05 .02 .00
□ 610 Al Cowens .05 .02 .00
□ 611 Dave Henderson .20 .08 .02
□ 612 Steve Henderson .05 .02 .00
□ 613 Orlando Mercado .05 .02 .00
□ 614 Mike Moore .10 .04 .01
□ 615 Ricky Nelson .15 .06 .01
(Jamie Nelson's stats on back)
□ 616 Spike Owen .20 .08 .02
□ 617 Pat Putnam .05 .02 .00
□ 618 Ron Roenicke .05 .02 .00
□ 619 Mike Stanton .05 .02 .00
□ 620 Bob Stoddard .05 .02 .00
□ 621 Rick Sweet .05 .02 .00
□ 622 Roy Thomas .05 .02 .00
□ 623 Ed VandeBerg .05 .02 .00
□ 624 Matt Young .10 .04 .01
□ 625 Richie Zisk .05 .02 .00
□ 626 Fred Lynn .10 .04 .01
1982 AS Game RB
□ 627 Manny Trillo .10 .04 .01
1983 AS Game RB
□ 628 Steve Garvey .20 .08 .02
NL Iron Man
□ 629 Rod Carew .20 .08 .02
AL Batting Runner-Up
□ 630 Wade Boggs .60 .24 .06
AL Batting Champion
□ 631 Tim Raines: Letting .20 .08 .02
Go of the Raines
□ 632 Al Oliver .10 .04 .01
Double Trouble
□ 633 Steve Sax .15 .06 .01
AS Second Base
□ 634 Dickie Thon .10 .04 .01
AS Shortstop
□ 635 Ace Firemen .10 .04 .01
Dan Quisenberry
and Tippy Martinez
□ 636 Reds Reunited .40 .16 .04
Joe Morgan
Pete Rose
Tony Perez
□ 637 Backstop Stars .10 .04 .01
Lance Parrish
Bob Boone
□ 638 Geo.Brett and G.Perry .15 .06 .01
Pine Tar 7/24/83
□ 639 1983 No Hitters .10 .04 .01
Dave Righetti
Mike Warren
Bob Forsch
□ 640 Bench and Yaz .35 .14 .03
Retiring Superstars
□ 641 Gaylord Perry .10 .04 .01
Going Out In Style
□ 642 Steve Carlton .15 .06 .01
300 Club and
Strikeout Record
□ 643 Altobelli and Owens .10 .04 .01
WS Managers
□ 644 Rick Dempsey .10 .04 .01
World Series MVP
□ 645 Mike Boddicker .10 .04 .01
WS Rookie Winner
□ 646 Scott McGregor .10 .04 .01
WS Clincher
□ 647 CL: Orioles/Royals .08 .01 .00
□ 648 CL: Phillies/Giants .07 .01 .00
□ 649 CL: White Sox/Red Sox .07 .01 .00
□ 650 CL: Tigers/Rangers .07 .01 .00
□ 651 CL: Dodgers/A's .07 .01 .00
□ 652 CL: Yankees/Reds .07 .01 .00
□ 653 CL: Blue Jays/Cubs .07 .01 .00
□ 654 CL: Braves/Angels .07 .01 .00
□ 655 CL: Brewers/Indians .07 .01 .00
□ 656 CL: Astros/Twins .07 .01 .00
□ 657 CL: Pirates/Mets .07 .01 .00
□ 658 CL: Expos/Mariners .07 .01 .00
□ 659 CL: Padres/Specials .07 .01 .00
□ 660 CL: Cardinals/Teams .08 .01 .00

1984 Fleer Update

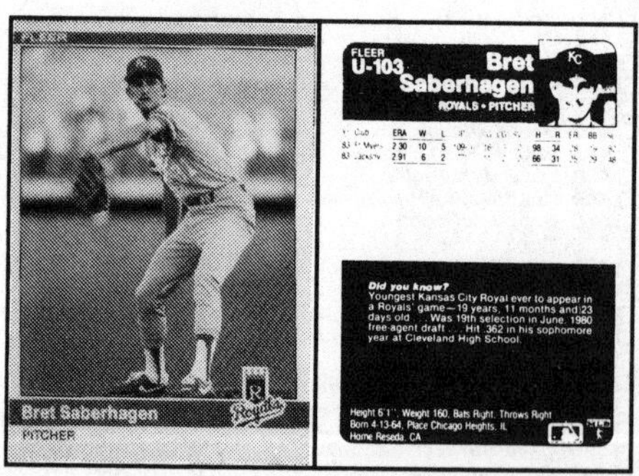

The cards in this 132-card set measure 2 1/2" by 3 1/2". For the first time, the Fleer Gum Company issued a traded, extended, or update set. The purpose of the set was the same as the traded sets issued by Topps over the past four years, i.e., to portray players with their proper team for the current year and to portray rookies who were not in their regular issue. Like the Topps Traded sets of the past four years, the Fleer Update sets were distributed through hobby channels only. The set was quite popular with collectors, and apparently, the print run was relatively short, as the set was quickly in short supply and exhibited a rapid and dramatic price increase. The cards are numbered on the back with a U prefix; the order corresponds to the alphabetical order of the subjects' names.

	MINT	EXC	G-VG
COMPLETE SET (132)	250.00	100.00	25.00
COMMON PLAYER (1-132)	.20	.08	.02

	Card	Player	MINT	EXC	G-VG
□	1U	Willie Aikens	.20	.08	.02
□	2U	Luis Aponte	.20	.08	.02
□	3U	Mark Bailey	.30	.12	.03
□	4U	Bob Bailor	.20	.08	.02
□	5U	Dusty Baker	.30	.12	.03
□	6U	Steve Balboni	.30	.12	.03
□	7U	Alan Bannister	.20	.08	.02
□	8U	Marty Barrett	3.50	1.40	.35
□	9U	Dave Beard	.20	.08	.02
□	10U	Joe Beckwith	.20	.08	.02
□	11U	Dave Bergman	.20	.08	.02
□	12U	Tony Bernazard	.20	.08	.02
□	13U	Bruce Bochte	.20	.08	.02
□	14U	Barry Bonnell	.20	.08	.02
□	15U	Phil Bradley	3.50	1.40	.35
□	16U	Fred Breining	.20	.08	.02
□	17U	Mike Brown (Angels OF)	.20	.08	.02
□	18U	Bill Buckner	.40	.16	.04
□	19U	Ray Burris	.20	.08	.02
□	20U	John Butcher	.20	.08	.02
□	21U	Brett Butler	.40	.16	.04
□	22U	Enos Cabell	.20	.08	.02
□	23U	Bill Campbell	.20	.08	.02
□	24U	Bill Caudill	.20	.08	.02
□	25U	Bobby Clark	.20	.08	.02
□	26U	Bryan Clark	.20	.08	.02
□	27U	Roger Clemens	85.00	34.00	8.50
□	28U	Jaime Cocanower	.30	.12	.03
□	29U	Ron Darling	10.00	4.00	1.00
□	30U	Alvin Davis	7.00	2.80	.70
□	31U	Bob Dernier	.20	.08	.02
□	32U	Carlos Diaz	.20	.08	.02
□	33U	Mike Easler	.20	.08	.02
□	34U	Dennis Eckersley	1.00	.40	.10
□	35U	Jim Essian	.20	.08	.02
□	36U	Darrell Evans	.40	.16	.04
□	37U	Mike Fitzgerald	.30	.12	.03
□	38U	Tim Foli	.20	.08	.02
□	39U	John Franco	6.00	2.40	.60
□	40U	George Frazier	.20	.08	.02
□	41U	Rich Gale	.20	.08	.02
□	42U	Barbaro Garbey	.30	.12	.03
□	43U	Dwight Gooden	70.00	28.00	7.00
□	44U	Goose Gossage	.75	.30	.07
□	45U	Wayne Gross	.20	.08	.02
□	46U	Mark Gubicza	3.50	1.40	.35
□	47U	Jackie Gutierrez	.30	.12	.03
□	48U	Toby Harrah	.30	.12	.03
□	49U	Ron Hassey	.30	.12	.03
□	50U	Richie Hebner	.20	.08	.02
□	51U	Willie Hernandez	.60	.24	.06
□	52U	Ed Hodge	.20	.08	.02
□	53U	Ricky Horton	.60	.24	.06
□	54U	Art Howe	.30	.12	.03
□	55U	Dane Iorg	.20	.08	.02
□	56U	Brook Jacoby	3.00	1.20	.30
□	57U	Dion James	.75	.30	.07
□	58U	Mike Jeffcoat	.30	.12	.03
□	59U	Ruppert Jones	.20	.08	.02
□	60U	Bob Kearney	.20	.08	.02
□	61U	Jimmy Key	6.00	2.40	.60
□	62U	Dave Kingman	.40	.16	.04
□	63U	Brad Komminsk	.30	.12	.03
□	64U	Jerry Koosman	.30	.12	.03
□	65U	Wayne Krenchicki	.20	.08	.02
□	66U	Rusty Kuntz	.20	.08	.02
□	67U	Frank LaCorte	.20	.08	.02
□	68U	Dennis Lamp	.20	.08	.02
□	69U	Tito Landrum	.30	.12	.03
□	70U	Mark Langston	7.00	2.80	.70
□	71U	Rick Leach	.20	.08	.02
□	72U	Craig Lefferts	.20	.08	.02
□	73U	Gary Lucas	.20	.08	.02
□	74U	Jerry Martin	.20	.08	.02
□	75U	Carmelo Martinez	.30	.12	.03
□	76U	Mike Mason	.30	.12	.03
□	77U	Gary Matthews	.30	.12	.03
□	78U	Andy McGaffigan	.20	.08	.02
□	79U	Joey McLaughlin	.20	.08	.02
□	80U	Joe Morgan	2.00	.80	.20
□	81U	Darryl Motley	.30	.12	.03
□	82U	Graig Nettles	.90	.36	.09
□	83U	Phil Niekro	2.00	.80	.20
□	84U	Ken Oberkfell	.20	.08	.02
□	85U	Al Oliver	.40	.16	.04
□	86U	Jorge Orta	.20	.08	.02
□	87U	Amos Otis	.30	.12	.03
□	88U	Bob Owchinko	.20	.08	.02
□	89U	Dave Parker	1.00	.40	.10
□	90U	Jack Perconte	.20	.08	.02
□	91U	Tony Perez	1.25	.50	.12
□	92U	Gerald Perry	2.50	1.00	.25
□	93U	Kirby Puckett	75.00	30.00	7.50
□	94U	Shane Rawley	.40	.16	.04
□	95U	Floyd Rayford	.20	.08	.02
□	96U	Ron Reed	.20	.08	.02
□	97U	R.J. Reynolds	1.00	.40	.10
□	98U	Gene Richards	.20	.08	.02
□	99U	Jose Rijo	1.50	.60	.15
□	100U	Jeff Robinson (Giants pitcher)	.75	.30	.07
□	101U	Ron Romanick	.30	.12	.03
□	102U	Pete Rose	15.00	6.00	1.50
□	103U	Bret Saberhagen	17.00	7.00	1.70
□	104U	Scott Sanderson	.30	.12	.03
□	105U	Dick Schofield	.75	.30	.07
□	106U	Tom Seaver	7.00	2.80	.70
□	107U	Jim Slaton	.20	.08	.02
□	108U	Mike Smithson	.20	.08	.02
□	109U	Lary Sorensen	.20	.08	.02
□	110U	Tim Stoddard	.20	.08	.02
□	111U	Jeff Stone	.40	.16	.04
□	112U	Champ Summers	.20	.08	.02
□	113U	Jim Sundberg	.30	.12	.03
□	114U	Rick Sutcliffe	.60	.24	.06
□	115U	Craig Swan	.20	.08	.02
□	116U	Derrel Thomas	.20	.08	.02
□	117U	Gorman Thomas	.40	.16	.04
□	118U	Alex Trevino	.20	.08	.02
□	119U	Manny Trillo	.20	.08	.02
□	120U	John Tudor	.50	.20	.05
□	121U	Tom Underwood	.20	.08	.02
□	122U	Mike Vail	.20	.08	.02
□	123U	Tom Waddell	.30	.12	.03
□	124U	Gary Ward	.30	.12	.03
□	125U	Terry Whitfield	.20	.08	.02
□	126U	Curtis Wilkerson	.30	.12	.03
□	127U	Frank Williams	.50	.20	.05
□	128U	Glenn Wilson	.30	.12	.03
□	129U	John Wockenfuss	.20	.08	.02
□	130U	Ned Yost	.20	.08	.02
□	131U	Mike Young	.60	.24	.06
□	132U	Checklist: 1-132	.20	.02	.00

1985 Fleer

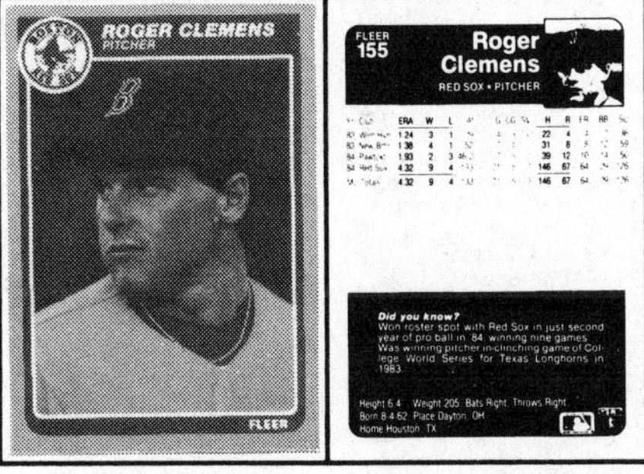

The cards in this 660-card set measure 2 1/2" by 3 1/2". The 1985 Fleer set features fronts which contain the team logo along with the player's name and position. The borders enclosing the photo are color-coded to correspond to the player's team. In each case, the color is one of the standard colors of that team, e.g., orange for Baltimore, red for St. Louis, etc. The backs feature the same name, number, and statistics format that Fleer has been using over the past few years. The cards are ordered alphabetically within team. The teams are ordered based on their respective performance during the prior year, e.g., World Champion Detroit Tigers (1-25), NL Champion San Diego (26- 48), Chicago Cubs (49-71), New York Mets (72-95), Toronto (96- 119), New York Yankees (120-147), Boston (148-169), Baltimore (170-195), Kansas City (196-218), St.

Louis (219-243), Philadelphia (244-269), Minnesota (270-292), California (293- 317), Atlanta (318-342), Houston (343-365), Los Angeles (366- 391), Montreal (392-413), Oakland (414-436), Cleveland (437-460), Pittsburgh (461-481), Seattle (482-505), Chicago White Sox (506- 530), Cincinnati (531-554), Texas (555-575), Milwaukee (576-601), and San Francisco (602-625). Specials (626-643), Rookie pairs (644-653), and checklist cards (654-660) complete the set. The black and white photo on the reverse is included for the third straight year.

	MINT	EXC	G-VG
COMPLETE SET (660)	100.00	40.00	10.00
COMMON PLAYER (1-660)	.05	.02	.00
☐ 1 Doug Bair	.10	.02	.00
☐ 2 Juan Berenguer	.05	.02	.00
☐ 3 Dave Bergman	.05	.02	.00
☐ 4 Tom Brookens	.05	.02	.00
☐ 5 Marty Castillo	.05	.02	.00
☐ 6 Darrell Evans	.12	.05	.01
☐ 7 Barbaro Garbey	.05	.02	.00
☐ 8 Kirk Gibson	.30	.12	.03
☐ 9 John Grubb	.05	.02	.00
☐ 10 Willie Hernandez	.12	.05	.01
☐ 11 Larry Herndon	.05	.02	.00
☐ 12 Howard Johnson	.50	.20	.05
☐ 13 Ruppert Jones	.05	.02	.00
☐ 14 Rusty Kuntz	.05	.02	.00
☐ 15 Chet Lemon	.08	.03	.01
☐ 16 Aurelio Lopez	.05	.02	.00
☐ 17 Sid Monge	.05	.02	.00
☐ 18 Jack Morris	.20	.08	.02
☐ 19 Lance Parrish	.20	.08	.02
☐ 20 Dan Petry	.08	.03	.01
☐ 21 Dave Rozema	.05	.02	.00
☐ 22 Bill Scherrer	.05	.02	.00
☐ 23 Alan Trammell	.30	.12	.03
☐ 24 Lou Whitaker	.15	.06	.01
☐ 25 Milt Wilcox	.05	.02	.00
☐ 26 Kurt Bevacqua	.05	.02	.00
☐ 27 Greg Booker	.05	.02	.00
☐ 28 Bobby Brown	.05	.02	.00
☐ 29 Luis DeLeon	.05	.02	.00
☐ 30 Dave Dravecky	.08	.03	.01
☐ 31 Tim Flannery	.05	.02	.00
☐ 32 Steve Garvey	.40	.16	.04
☐ 33 Goose Gossage	.15	.06	.01
☐ 34 Tony Gwynn	1.00	.40	.10
☐ 35 Greg Harris	.05	.02	.00
☐ 36 Andy Hawkins	.08	.03	.01
☐ 37 Terry Kennedy	.08	.03	.01
☐ 38 Craig Lefferts	.05	.02	.00
☐ 39 Tim Lollar	.05	.02	.00
☐ 40 Carmelo Martinez	.08	.03	.01
☐ 41 Kevin McReynolds	1.00	.40	.10
☐ 42 Graig Nettles	.12	.05	.01
☐ 43 Luis Salazar	.08	.03	.01
☐ 44 Eric Show	.08	.03	.01
☐ 45 Garry Templeton	.08	.03	.01
☐ 46 Mark Thurmond	.05	.02	.00
☐ 47 Ed Whitson	.05	.02	.00
☐ 48 Alan Wiggins	.05	.02	.00
☐ 49 Rich Bordi	.05	.02	.00
☐ 50 Larry Bowa	.10	.04	.01
☐ 51 Warren Brusstar	.05	.02	.00
☐ 52 Ron Cey	.10	.04	.01
☐ 53 Henry Cotto	.08	.03	.01
☐ 54 Jody Davis	.08	.03	.01
☐ 55 Bob Dernier	.05	.02	.00
☐ 56 Leon Durham	.08	.03	.01
☐ 57 Dennis Eckersley	.15	.06	.01
☐ 58 George Frazier	.05	.02	.00
☐ 59 Richie Hebner	.05	.02	.00
☐ 60 Dave Lopes	.08	.03	.01
☐ 61 Gary Matthews	.08	.03	.01
☐ 62 Keith Moreland	.08	.03	.01
☐ 63 Rick Reuschel	.10	.04	.01
☐ 64 Dick Ruthven	.05	.02	.00
☐ 65 Ryne Sandberg	.40	.16	.04
☐ 66 Scott Sanderson	.05	.02	.00
☐ 67 Lee Smith	.10	.04	.01
☐ 68 Tim Stoddard	.05	.02	.00
☐ 69 Rick Sutcliffe	.15	.06	.01
☐ 70 Steve Trout	.05	.02	.00
☐ 71 Gary Woods	.05	.02	.00
☐ 72 Wally Backman	.10	.04	.01
☐ 73 Bruce Berenyi	.05	.02	.00
☐ 74 Hubie Brooks	.08	.03	.01
☐ 75 Kelvin Chapman	.08	.03	.01
☐ 76 Ron Darling	1.00	.40	.1
☐ 77 Sid Fernandez	.85	.34	.0
☐ 78 Mike Fitzgerald	.05	.02	.0
☐ 79 George Foster	.12	.05	.0
☐ 80 Brent Gaff	.05	.02	.0
☐ 81 Ron Gardenhire	.05	.02	.0
☐ 82 Dwight Gooden	9.00	3.75	.9
☐ 83 Tom Gorman	.05	.02	.0
☐ 84 Danny Heep	.05	.02	.0
☐ 85 Keith Hernandez	.30	.12	.0
☐ 86 Ray Knight	.10	.04	.01
☐ 87 Ed Lynch	.05	.02	.00
☐ 88 Jose Oquendo	.08	.03	.01
☐ 89 Jesse Orosco	.05	.02	.00
☐ 90 Rafael Santana	.30	.12	.03
☐ 91 Doug Sisk	.05	.02	.00
☐ 92 Rusty Staub	.10	.04	.01
☐ 93 Darryl Strawberry	3.50	1.40	.35
☐ 94 Walt Terrell	.08	.03	.01
☐ 95 Mookie Wilson	.08	.03	.01
☐ 96 Jim Acker	.05	.02	.00
☐ 97 Willie Aikens	.05	.02	.00
☐ 98 Doyle Alexander	.08	.03	.01
☐ 99 Jesse Barfield	.30	.12	.03
☐ 100 George Bell	.40	.16	.04
☐ 101 Jim Clancy	.05	.02	.00
☐ 102 Dave Collins	.05	.02	.00
☐ 103 Tony Fernandez	.25	.10	.02
☐ 104 Damaso Garcia	.05	.02	.00
☐ 105 Jim Gott	.05	.02	.00
☐ 106 Alfredo Griffin	.08	.03	.01
☐ 107 Garth Iorg	.05	.02	.00
☐ 108 Roy Lee Jackson	.05	.02	.00
☐ 109 Cliff Johnson	.05	.02	.00
☐ 110 Jimmy Key	1.25	.50	.12
☐ 111 Dennis Lamp	.05	.02	.00
☐ 112 Rick Leach	.05	.02	.00
☐ 113 Luis Leal	.05	.02	.00
☐ 114 Buck Martinez	.05	.02	.00
☐ 115 Lloyd Moseby	.12	.05	.01
☐ 116 Rance Mulliniks	.05	.02	.00
☐ 117 Dave Stieb	.15	.06	.01
☐ 118 Willie Upshaw	.05	.02	.00
☐ 119 Ernie Whitt	.05	.02	.00
☐ 120 Mike Armstrong	.05	.02	.00
☐ 121 Don Baylor	.12	.05	.01
☐ 122 Marty Bystrom	.05	.02	.00
☐ 123 Rick Cerone	.05	.02	.00
☐ 124 Joe Cowley	.05	.02	.00
☐ 125 Brian Dayett	.05	.02	.00
☐ 126 Tim Foli	.05	.02	.00
☐ 127 Ray Fontenot	.05	.02	.00
☐ 128 Ken Griffey	.08	.03	.01
☐ 129 Ron Guidry	.15	.06	.01
☐ 130 Toby Harrah	.08	.03	.01
☐ 131 Jay Howell	.08	.03	.01
☐ 132 Steve Kemp	.08	.03	.01
☐ 133 Don Mattingly	10.00	4.00	1.00
☐ 134 Bobby Meacham	.05	.02	.00
☐ 135 John Montefusco	.05	.02	.00
☐ 136 Omar Moreno	.05	.02	.00
☐ 137 Dale Murray	.05	.02	.00
☐ 138 Phil Niekro	.25	.10	.02
☐ 139 Mike Pagliarulo	1.50	.60	.15
☐ 140 Willie Randolph	.10	.04	.01
☐ 141 Dennis Rasmussen	.25	.10	.02
☐ 142 Dave Righetti	.18	.08	.01
☐ 143 Jose Rijo	.40	.16	.04
☐ 144 Andre Robertson	.05	.02	.00
☐ 145 Bob Shirley	.05	.02	.00
☐ 146 Dave Winfield	.35	.14	.03
☐ 147 Butch Wynegar	.05	.02	.00
☐ 148 Gary Allenson	.05	.02	.00
☐ 149 Tony Armas	.08	.03	.01
☐ 150 Marty Barrett	.30	.12	.03
☐ 151 Wade Boggs	4.00	1.60	.40
☐ 152 Dennis Boyd	.10	.04	.01
☐ 153 Bill Buckner	.10	.04	.01
☐ 154 Mark Clear	.05	.02	.00
☐ 155 Roger Clemens	11.00	4.50	1.10
☐ 156 Steve Crawford	.05	.02	.00
☐ 157 Mike Easler	.05	.02	.00
☐ 158 Dwight Evans	.15	.06	.01
☐ 159 Rich Gedman	.10	.04	.01
☐ 160 Jackie Gutierrez (W.Boggs on deck)	.15	.06	.01
☐ 161 Bruce Hurst	.15	.06	.01
☐ 162 John Henry Johnson	.05	.02	.00
☐ 163 Rick Miller	.05	.02	.00
☐ 164 Reid Nichols	.05	.02	.00
☐ 165 Al Nipper	.15	.06	.01
☐ 166 Bob Ojeda	.10	.04	.01
☐ 167 Jerry Remy	.05	.02	.00
☐ 168 Jim Rice	.25	.10	.02
☐ 169 Bob Stanley	.05	.02	.00

☐ 170	Mike Boddicker	.10	.04	.01
☐ 171	Al Bumbry	.05	.02	.00
☐ 172	Todd Cruz	.05	.02	.00
☐ 173	Rich Dauer	.05	.02	.00
☐ 174	Storm Davis	.10	.04	.01
☐ 175	Rick Dempsey	.05	.02	.00
☐ 176	Jim Dwyer	.05	.02	.00
☐ 177	Mike Flanagan	.08	.03	.01
☐ 178	Dan Ford	.05	.02	.00
☐ 179	Wayne Gross	.05	.02	.00
☐ 180	John Lowenstein	.05	.02	.00
☐ 181	Dennis Martinez	.08	.03	.01
☐ 182	Tippy Martinez	.05	.02	.00
☐ 183	Scott McGregor	.08	.03	.01
☐ 184	Eddie Murray	.45	.18	.04
☐ 185	Joe Nolan	.05	.02	.00
☐ 186	Floyd Rayford	.05	.02	.00
☐ 187	Cal Ripken	.50	.20	.05
☐ 188	Gary Roenicke	.05	.02	.00
☐ 189	Lenn Sakata	.05	.02	.00
☐ 190	John Shelby	.05	.02	.00
☐ 191	Ken Singleton	.08	.03	.01
☐ 192	Sammy Stewart	.05	.02	.00
☐ 193	Bill Swaggerty	.08	.03	.01
☐ 194	Tom Underwood	.05	.02	.00
☐ 195	Mike Young	.15	.06	.01
☐ 196	Steve Balboni	.05	.02	.00
☐ 197	Joe Beckwith	.05	.02	.00
☐ 198	Bud Black	.05	.02	.00
☐ 199	George Brett	.50	.20	.05
☐ 200	Onix Concepcion	.05	.02	.00
☐ 201	Mark Gubicza	.85	.34	.08
☐ 202	Larry Gura	.05	.02	.00
☐ 203	Mark Huismann	.05	.02	.00
☐ 204	Dane Iorg	.05	.02	.00
☐ 205	Danny Jackson	1.25	.50	.12
☐ 206	Charlie Leibrandt	.08	.03	.01
☐ 207	Hal McRae	.08	.03	.01
☐ 208	Darryl Motley	.05	.02	.00
☐ 209	Jorge Orta	.05	.02	.00
☐ 210	Greg Pryor	.05	.02	.00
☐ 211	Dan Quisenberry	.12	.05	.01
☐ 212	Bret Saberhagen	3.00	1.20	.30
☐ 213	Pat Sheridan	.05	.02	.00
☐ 214	Don Slaught	.05	.02	.00
☐ 215	U.L. Washington	.05	.02	.00
☐ 216	John Wathan	.05	.02	.00
☐ 217	Frank White	.08	.03	.01
☐ 218	Willie Wilson	.12	.05	.01
☐ 219	Neil Allen	.05	.02	.00
☐ 220	Joaquin Andujar	.08	.03	.01
☐ 221	Steve Braun	.05	.02	.00
☐ 222	Danny Cox	.10	.04	.01
☐ 223	Bob Forsch	.05	.02	.00
☐ 224	David Green	.05	.02	.00
☐ 225	George Hendrick	.08	.03	.01
☐ 226	Tom Herr	.08	.03	.01
☐ 227	Ricky Horton	.20	.08	.02
☐ 228	Art Howe	.08	.03	.01
☐ 229	Mike Jorgensen	.05	.02	.00
☐ 230	Kurt Kepshire	.08	.03	.01
☐ 231	Jeff Lahti	.05	.02	.00
☐ 232	Tito Landrum	.05	.02	.00
☐ 233	Dave LaPoint	.08	.03	.01
☐ 234	Willie McGee	.30	.12	.03
☐ 235	Tom Nieto	.05	.02	.00
☐ 236	Terry Pendleton	.45	.18	.04
☐ 237	Darrell Porter	.05	.02	.00
☐ 238	Dave Rucker	.05	.02	.00
☐ 239	Lonnie Smith	.08	.03	.01
☐ 240	Ozzie Smith	.25	.10	.02
☐ 241	Bruce Sutter	.12	.05	.01
☐ 242	Andy Van Slyke	.50	.20	.05
☐ 243	Dave Von Ohlen	.05	.02	.00
☐ 244	Larry Andersen	.05	.02	.00
☐ 245	Bill Campbell	.05	.02	.00
☐ 246	Steve Carlton	.40	.16	.04
☐ 247	Tim Corcoran	.05	.02	.00
☐ 248	Ivan DeJesus	.05	.02	.00
☐ 249	John Denny	.08	.03	.01
☐ 250	Bo Diaz	.05	.02	.00
☐ 251	Greg Gross	.05	.02	.00
☐ 252	Kevin Gross	.08	.03	.01
☐ 253	Von Hayes	.15	.06	.01
☐ 254	Al Holland	.05	.02	.00
☐ 255	Charles Hudson	.05	.02	.00
☐ 256	Jerry Koosman	.08	.03	.01
☐ 257	Joe Lefebvre	.05	.02	.00
☐ 258	Sixto Lezcano	.05	.02	.00
☐ 259	Garry Maddox	.08	.03	.01
☐ 260	Len Matuszek	.05	.02	.00
☐ 261	Tug McGraw	.10	.04	.01
☐ 262	Al Oliver	.10	.04	.01
☐ 263	Shane Rawley	.10	.04	.01
☐ 264	Juan Samuel	.35	.14	.03
☐ 265	Mike Schmidt	.50	.20	.05
☐ 266	Jeff Stone	.15	.06	.01
☐ 267	Ozzie Virgil	.05	.02	.00
☐ 268	Glenn Wilson	.08	.03	.01
☐ 269	John Wockenfuss	.05	.02	.00
☐ 270	Darrell Brown	.05	.02	.00
☐ 271	Tom Brunansky	.20	.08	.02
☐ 272	Randy Bush	.08	.03	.01
☐ 273	John Butcher	.05	.02	.00
☐ 274	Bobby Castillo	.05	.02	.00
☐ 275	Ron Davis	.05	.02	.00
☐ 276	Dave Engle	.05	.02	.00
☐ 277	Pete Filson	.05	.02	.00
☐ 278	Gary Gaetti	.35	.14	.03
☐ 279	Mickey Hatcher	.10	.04	.01
☐ 280	Ed Hodge	.05	.02	.00
☐ 281	Kent Hrbek	.35	.14	.03
☐ 282	Houston Jimenez	.05	.02	.00
☐ 283	Tim Laudner	.08	.03	.01
☐ 284	Rick Lysander	.05	.02	.00
☐ 285	Dave Meier	.08	.03	.01
☐ 286	Kirby Puckett	10.00	4.00	1.00
☐ 287	Pat Putnam	.05	.02	.00
☐ 288	Ken Schrom	.05	.02	.00
☐ 289	Mike Smithson	.05	.02	.00
☐ 290	Tim Teufel	.05	.02	.00
☐ 291	Frank Viola	.40	.16	.04
☐ 292	Ron Washington	.05	.02	.00
☐ 293	Don Aase	.05	.02	.00
☐ 294	Juan Beniquez	.05	.02	.00
☐ 295	Bob Boone	.10	.04	.01
☐ 296	Mike Brown (Angels OF)	.05	.02	.00
☐ 297	Rod Carew	.40	.16	.04
☐ 298	Doug Corbett	.05	.02	.00
☐ 299	Doug DeCinces	.08	.03	.01
☐ 300	Brian Downing	.08	.03	.01
☐ 301	Ken Forsch	.05	.02	.00
☐ 302	Bobby Grich	.10	.04	.01
☐ 303	Reggie Jackson	.45	.18	.04
☐ 304	Tommy John	.15	.06	.01
☐ 305	Curt Kaufman	.08	.03	.01
☐ 306	Bruce Kison	.05	.02	.00
☐ 307	Fred Lynn	.15	.06	.01
☐ 308	Gary Pettis	.08	.03	.01
☐ 309	Ron Romanick	.05	.02	.00
☐ 310	Luis Sanchez	.05	.02	.00
☐ 311	Dick Schofield	.10	.04	.01
☐ 312	Daryl Sconiers	.05	.02	.00
☐ 313	Jim Slaton	.05	.02	.00
☐ 314	Derrel Thomas	.05	.02	.00
☐ 315	Rob Wilfong	.05	.02	.00
☐ 316	Mike Witt	.12	.05	.01
☐ 317	Geoff Zahn	.05	.02	.00
☐ 318	Len Barker	.05	.02	.00
☐ 319	Steve Bedrosian	.15	.06	.01
☐ 320	Bruce Benedict	.05	.02	.00
☐ 321	Rick Camp	.05	.02	.00
☐ 322	Chris Chambliss	.08	.03	.01
☐ 323	Jeff Dedmon	.08	.03	.01
☐ 324	Terry Forster	.08	.03	.01
☐ 325	Gene Garber	.05	.02	.00
☐ 326	Albert Hall	.10	.04	.01
☐ 327	Terry Harper	.05	.02	.00
☐ 328	Bob Horner	.18	.08	.01
☐ 329	Glenn Hubbard	.05	.02	.00
☐ 330	Randy Johnson	.05	.02	.00
☐ 331	Brad Komminsk	.08	.03	.01
☐ 332	Rick Mahler	.05	.02	.00
☐ 333	Craig McMurtry	.05	.02	.00
☐ 334	Donnie Moore	.05	.02	.00
☐ 335	Dale Murphy	.65	.26	.06
☐ 336	Ken Oberkfell	.05	.02	.00
☐ 337	Pascual Perez	.08	.03	.01
☐ 338	Gerald Perry	.40	.16	.04
☐ 339	Rafael Ramirez	.05	.02	.00
☐ 340	Jerry Royster	.05	.02	.00
☐ 341	Alex Trevino	.05	.02	.00
☐ 342	Claudell Washington	.08	.03	.01
☐ 343	Alan Ashby	.05	.02	.00
☐ 344	Mark Bailey	.08	.03	.01
☐ 345	Kevin Bass	.10	.04	.01
☐ 346	Enos Cabell	.05	.02	.00
☐ 347	Jose Cruz	.10	.04	.01
☐ 348	Bill Dawley	.05	.02	.00
☐ 349	Frank DiPino	.05	.02	.00
☐ 350	Bill Doran	.15	.06	.01
☐ 351	Phil Garner	.05	.02	.00
☐ 352	Bob Knepper	.10	.04	.01
☐ 353	Mike LaCoss	.05	.02	.00
☐ 354	Jerry Mumphrey	.05	.02	.00
☐ 355	Joe Niekro	.10	.04	.01
☐ 356	Terry Puhl	.05	.02	.00
☐ 357	Craig Reynolds	.05	.02	.00
☐ 358	Vern Ruhle	.05	.02	.00

☐ 359 Nolan Ryan	.40	.16	.04
☐ 360 Joe Sambito	.05	.02	.00
☐ 361 Mike Scott	.30	.12	.03
☐ 362 Dave Smith	.08	.03	.01
☐ 363 Julio Solano	.08	.03	.01
☐ 364 Dickie Thon	.05	.02	.00
☐ 365 Denny Walling	.05	.02	.00
☐ 366 Dave Anderson	.05	.02	.00
☐ 367 Bob Bailor	.05	.02	.00
☐ 368 Greg Brock	.08	.03	.01
☐ 369 Carlos Diaz	.05	.02	.00
☐ 370 Pedro Guerrero	.25	.10	.02
☐ 371 Orel Hershiser	9.00	3.75	.90
☐ 372 Rick Honeycutt	.05	.02	.00
☐ 373 Burt Hooton	.05	.02	.00
☐ 374 Ken Howell	.15	.06	.01
☐ 375 Ken Landreaux	.05	.02	.00
☐ 376 Candy Maldonado	.10	.04	.01
☐ 377 Mike Marshall	.15	.06	.01
☐ 378 Tom Niedenfuer	.08	.03	.01
☐ 379 Alejandro Pena	.08	.03	.01
☐ 380 Jerry Reuss	.08	.03	.01
☐ 381 R.J. Reynolds	.25	.10	.02
☐ 382 German Rivera	.08	.03	.01
☐ 383 Bill Russell	.08	.03	.01
☐ 384 Steve Sax	.20	.08	.02
☐ 385 Mike Scioscia	.08	.03	.01
☐ 386 Franklin Stubbs	.35	.14	.03
☐ 387 Fernando Valenzuela	.25	.10	.02
☐ 388 Bob Welch	.10	.04	.01
☐ 389 Terry Whitfield	.05	.02	.00
☐ 390 Steve Yeager	.05	.02	.00
☐ 391 Pat Zachry	.05	.02	.00
☐ 392 Fred Breining	.05	.02	.00
☐ 393 Gary Carter	.30	.12	.03
☐ 394 Andre Dawson	.30	.12	.03
☐ 395 Miguel Dilone	.05	.02	.00
☐ 396 Dan Driessen	.05	.02	.00
☐ 397 Doug Flynn	.05	.02	.00
☐ 398 Terry Francona	.05	.02	.00
☐ 399 Bill Gullickson	.05	.02	.00
☐ 400 Bob James	.05	.02	.00
☐ 401 Charlie Lea	.05	.02	.00
☐ 402 Bryan Little	.05	.02	.00
☐ 403 Gary Lucas	.05	.02	.00
☐ 404 David Palmer	.05	.02	.00
☐ 405 Tim Raines	.35	.14	.03
☐ 406 Mike Ramsey	.05	.02	.00
☐ 407 Jeff Reardon	.10	.04	.01
☐ 408 Steve Rogers	.05	.02	.00
☐ 409 Dan Schatzeder	.05	.02	.00
☐ 410 Bryn Smith	.05	.02	.00
☐ 411 Mike Stenhouse	.05	.02	.00
☐ 412 Tim Wallach	.12	.05	.01
☐ 413 Jim Wohlford	.05	.02	.00
☐ 414 Bill Almon	.05	.02	.00
☐ 415 Keith Atherton	.05	.02	.00
☐ 416 Bruce Bochte	.05	.02	.00
☐ 417 Tom Burgmeier	.05	.02	.00
☐ 418 Ray Burris	.05	.02	.00
☐ 419 Bill Caudill	.05	.02	.00
☐ 420 Chris Codiroli	.05	.02	.00
☐ 421 Tim Conroy	.05	.02	.00
☐ 422 Mike Davis	.08	.03	.01
☐ 423 Jim Essian	.05	.02	.00
☐ 424 Mike Heath	.05	.02	.00
☐ 425 Rickey Henderson	.45	.18	.04
☐ 426 Donnie Hill	.05	.02	.00
☐ 427 Dave Kingman	.10	.04	.01
☐ 428 Bill Krueger	.05	.02	.00
☐ 429 Carney Lansford	.10	.04	.01
☐ 430 Steve McCatty	.05	.02	.00
☐ 431 Joe Morgan	.18	.08	.01
☐ 432 Dwayne Murphy	.05	.02	.00
☐ 433 Tony Phillips	.05	.02	.00
☐ 434 Lary Sorensen	.05	.02	.00
☐ 435 Mike Warren	.05	.02	.00
☐ 436 Curt Young	.35	.14	.03
☐ 437 Luis Aponte	.05	.02	.00
☐ 438 Chris Bando	.05	.02	.00
☐ 439 Tony Bernazard	.05	.02	.00
☐ 440 Bert Blyleven	.10	.04	.01
☐ 441 Brett Butler	.10	.04	.01
☐ 442 Ernie Camacho	.05	.02	.00
☐ 443 Joe Carter	1.75	.70	.17
☐ 444 Carmelo Castillo	.05	.02	.00
☐ 445 Jamie Easterly	.05	.02	.00
☐ 446 Steve Farr	.20	.08	.02
☐ 447 Mike Fischlin	.05	.02	.00
☐ 448 Julio Franco	.15	.06	.01
☐ 449 Mel Hall	.10	.04	.01
☐ 450 Mike Hargrove	.05	.02	.00
☐ 451 Neal Heaton	.05	.02	.00
☐ 452 Brook Jacoby	.25	.10	.02
☐ 453 Mike Jeffcoat	.05	.02	.00
☐ 454 Don Schulze	.08	.03	.01
☐ 455 Roy Smith	.08	.03	.01
☐ 456 Pat Tabler	.10	.04	.01
☐ 457 Andre Thornton	.08	.03	.01
☐ 458 George Vukovich	.05	.02	.00
☐ 459 Tom Waddell	.08	.03	.01
☐ 460 Jerry Willard	.05	.02	.00
☐ 461 Dale Berra	.05	.02	.00
☐ 462 John Candelaria	.08	.03	.01
☐ 463 Jose DeLeon	.05	.02	.00
☐ 464 Doug Frobel	.05	.02	.00
☐ 465 Cecilio Guante	.05	.02	.00
☐ 466 Brian Harper	.05	.02	.00
☐ 467 Lee Lacy	.05	.02	.00
☐ 468 Bill Madlock	.10	.04	.01
☐ 469 Lee Mazzilli	.05	.02	.00
☐ 470 Larry McWilliams	.05	.02	.00
☐ 471 Jim Morrison	.05	.02	.00
☐ 472 Tony Pena	.12	.05	.01
☐ 473 Johnny Ray	.10	.04	.01
☐ 474 Rick Rhoden	.10	.04	.01
☐ 475 Don Robinson	.05	.02	.00
☐ 476 Rod Scurry	.05	.02	.00
☐ 477 Kent Tekulve	.08	.03	.01
☐ 478 Jason Thompson	.05	.02	.00
☐ 479 John Tudor	.15	.06	.01
☐ 480 Lee Tunnell	.05	.02	.00
☐ 481 Marvell Wynne	.05	.02	.00
☐ 482 Salome Barojas	.05	.02	.00
☐ 483 Dave Beard	.05	.02	.00
☐ 484 Jim Beattie	.05	.02	.00
☐ 485 Barry Bonnell	.05	.02	.00
☐ 486 Phil Bradley	1.00	.40	.10
☐ 487 Al Cowens	.05	.02	.00
☐ 488 Alvin Davis	1.75	.70	.17
☐ 489 Dave Henderson	.15	.06	.01
☐ 490 Steve Henderson	.05	.02	.00
☐ 491 Bob Kearney	.05	.02	.00
☐ 492 Mark Langston	1.50	.60	.15
☐ 493 Larry Milbourne	.05	.02	.00
☐ 494 Paul Mirabella	.05	.02	.00
☐ 495 Mike Moore	.10	.04	.01
☐ 496 Edwin Nunez	.05	.02	.00
☐ 497 Spike Owen	.05	.02	.00
☐ 498 Jack Perconte	.05	.02	.00
☐ 499 Ken Phelps	.10	.04	.01
☐ 500 Jim Presley	.80	.32	.08
☐ 501 Mike Stanton	.05	.02	.00
☐ 502 Bob Stoddard	.05	.02	.00
☐ 503 Gorman Thomas	.10	.04	.01
☐ 504 Ed VandeBerg	.05	.02	.00
☐ 505 Matt Young	.05	.02	.00
☐ 506 Juan Agosto	.05	.02	.00
☐ 507 Harold Baines	.15	.06	.01
☐ 508 Floyd Bannister	.05	.02	.00
☐ 509 Britt Burns	.05	.02	.00
☐ 510 Julio Cruz	.05	.02	.00
☐ 511 Richard Dotson	.10	.04	.01
☐ 512 Jerry Dybzinski	.05	.02	.00
☐ 513 Carlton Fisk	.15	.06	.01
☐ 514 Scott Fletcher	.10	.04	.01
☐ 515 Jerry Hairston	.05	.02	.00
☐ 516 Marc Hill	.05	.02	.00
☐ 517 LaMarr Hoyt	.08	.03	.01
☐ 518 Ron Kittle	.15	.06	.01
☐ 519 Rudy Law	.05	.02	.00
☐ 520 Vance Law	.08	.03	.01
☐ 521 Greg Luzinski	.10	.04	.01
☐ 522 Gene Nelson	.05	.02	.00
☐ 523 Tom Paciorek	.05	.02	.00
☐ 524 Ron Reed	.05	.02	.00
☐ 525 Bert Roberge	.05	.02	.00
☐ 526 Tom Seaver	.30	.12	.03
☐ 527 Roy Smalley	.05	.02	.00
☐ 528 Dan Spillner	.05	.02	.00
☐ 529 Mike Squires	.05	.02	.00
☐ 530 Greg Walker	.10	.04	.01
☐ 531 Cesar Cedeno	.10	.04	.01
☐ 532 Dave Concepcion	.10	.04	.01
☐ 533 Eric Davis	16.00	6.50	1.60
☐ 534 Nick Esasky	.08	.03	.01
☐ 535 Tom Foley	.05	.02	.00
☐ 536 John Franco	1.00	.40	.10
☐ 537 Brad Gulden	.05	.02	.00
☐ 538 Tom Hume	.05	.02	.00
☐ 539 Wayne Krenchicki	.05	.02	.00
☐ 540 Andy McGaffigan	.05	.02	.00
☐ 541 Eddie Milner	.05	.02	.00
☐ 542 Ron Oester	.05	.02	.00
☐ 543 Bob Owchinko	.05	.02	.00
☐ 544 Dave Parker	.15	.06	.01
☐ 545 Frank Pastore	.05	.02	.00
☐ 546 Tony Perez	.15	.06	.01
☐ 547 Ted Power	.05	.02	.00
☐ 548 Joe Price	.05	.02	.00

549	Gary Redus	.08	.03	.01
550	Pete Rose	1.00	.40	.10
551	Jeff Russell	.15	.06	.01
552	Mario Soto	.05	.02	.00
553	Jay Tibbs	.15	.06	.01
554	Duane Walker	.05	.02	.00
555	Alan Bannister	.05	.02	.00
556	Buddy Bell	.10	.04	.01
557	Danny Darwin	.05	.02	.00
558	Charlie Hough	.08	.03	.01
559	Bobby Jones	.05	.02	.00
560	Odell Jones	.05	.02	.00
561	Jeff Kunkel	.08	.03	.01
562	Mike Mason	.08	.03	.01
563	Pete O'Brien	.10	.04	.01
564	Larry Parrish	.08	.03	.01
565	Mickey Rivers	.08	.03	.01
566	Billy Sample	.05	.02	.00
567	Dave Schmidt	.08	.03	.01
568	Donnie Scott	.05	.02	.00
569	Dave Stewart	.15	.06	.01
570	Frank Tanana	.08	.03	.01
571	Wayne Tolleson	.05	.02	.00
572	Gary Ward	.08	.03	.01
573	Curtis Wilkerson	.05	.02	.00
574	George Wright	.05	.02	.00
575	Ned Yost	.05	.02	.00
576	Mark Brouhard	.05	.02	.00
577	Mike Caldwell	.05	.02	.00
578	Bobby Clark	.05	.02	.00
579	Jaime Cocanower	.05	.02	.00
580	Cecil Cooper	.12	.05	.01
581	Rollie Fingers	.15	.06	.01
582	Jim Gantner	.05	.02	.00
583	Moose Haas	.05	.02	.00
584	Dion James	.10	.04	.01
585	Pete Ladd	.05	.02	.00
586	Rick Manning	.05	.02	.00
587	Bob McClure	.05	.02	.00
588	Paul Molitor	.20	.08	.02
589	Charlie Moore	.05	.02	.00
590	Ben Oglivie	.08	.03	.01
591	Chuck Porter	.05	.02	.00
592	Randy Ready	.25	.10	.02
593	Ed Romero	.05	.02	.00
594	Bill Schroeder	.05	.02	.00
595	Ray Searage	.05	.02	.00
596	Ted Simmons	.12	.05	.01
597	Jim Sundberg	.05	.02	.00
598	Don Sutton	.25	.10	.02
599	Tom Tellmann	.05	.02	.00
600	Rick Waits	.05	.02	.00
601	Robin Yount	.35	.14	.03
602	Dusty Baker	.08	.03	.01
603	Bob Brenly	.05	.02	.00
604	Jack Clark	.20	.08	.02
605	Chili Davis	.10	.04	.01
606	Mark Davis	.08	.03	.01
607	Dan Gladden	.45	.18	.04
608	Atlee Hammaker	.05	.02	.00
609	Mike Krukow	.08	.03	.01
610	Duane Kuiper	.05	.02	.00
611	Bob Lacey	.05	.02	.00
612	Bill Laskey	.05	.02	.00
613	Gary Lavelle	.05	.02	.00
614	Johnnie LeMaster	.05	.02	.00
615	Jeff Leonard	.10	.04	.01
616	Randy Lerch	.05	.02	.00
617	Greg Minton	.05	.02	.00
618	Steve Nicosia	.05	.02	.00
619	Gene Richards	.05	.02	.00
620	Jeff Robinson (Giants pitcher)	.30	.12	.03
621	Scot Thompson	.05	.02	.00
622	Manny Trillo	.05	.02	.00
623	Brad Wellman	.05	.02	.00
624	Frank Williams	.20	.08	.02
625	Joel Youngblood	.05	.02	.00
626	Cal Ripken IA	.20	.08	.02
627	Mike Schmidt IA	.30	.12	.03
628	Giving The Signs Sparky Anderson	.05	.02	.00
629	AL Pitcher's Nightmare Dave Winfield Rickey Henderson	.20	.08	.02
630	NL Pitcher's Nightmare Mike Schmidt Ryne Sandberg	.20	.08	.02
631	NL All-Stars Darryl Strawberry Gary Carter Steve Garvey Ozzie Smith	.25	.10	.02
632	A-S Winning Battery Gary Carter Charlie Lea	.10	.04	.01
633	NL Pennant Clinchers Steve Garvey Goose Gossage	.12	.05	.01
634	NL Rookie Phenoms Dwight Gooden Juan Samuel	.75	.30	.07
635	Toronto's Big Guns Willie Upshaw	.08	.03	.01
636	Toronto's Big Guns Lloyd Moseby	.08	.03	.01
637	HOLLAND: Al Holland	.05	.02	.00
638	TUNNELL: Lee Tunnell	.05	.02	.00
639	500th Homer Reggie Jackson	.30	.12	.03
640	4000th Hit Pete Rose	.45	.18	.04
641	Father and Son Cal Ripken Jr. and Sr.	.15	.06	.01
642	Cubs: Division Champs	.05	.02	.00
643	Two Perfect Games and One No-Hitter: Mike Witt David Palmer Jack Morris	.08	.03	.01
644	Willie Lozado and Vic Mata	.10	.04	.01
645	Kelly Gruber and Randy O'Neal	.30	.12	.03
646	Jose Roman and Joel Skinner	.10	.04	.01
647	Steve Kiefer and Danny Tartabull	5.00	2.00	.50
648	Rob Deer and Alejandro Sanchez	.90	.36	.09
649	Bill Hatcher and Shawon Dunston	1.25	.50	.12
650	Ron Robinson and Mike Bielecki	.20	.08	.02
651	Zane Smith and Paul Zuvella	.40	.16	.04
652	Joe Hesketh and Glenn Davis	6.00	2.40	.60
653	John Russell and Steve Jeltz	.15	.06	.01
654	CL: Tigers/Padres and Cubs/Mets	.07	.01	.00
655	CL: Blue Jays/Yankees and Red Sox/Orioles	.07	.01	.00
656	CL: Royals/Cardinals and Phillies/Twins	.07	.01	.00
657	CL: Angels/Braves and Astros/Dodgers	.07	.01	.00
658	CL: Expos/A's and Indians/Pirates	.07	.01	.00
659	CL: Mariners/Wh.Sox and Reds/Rangers	.07	.01	.00
660	CL: Brewers/Giants and Special Cards	.10	.01	.00

1985 Fleer Limited Edition

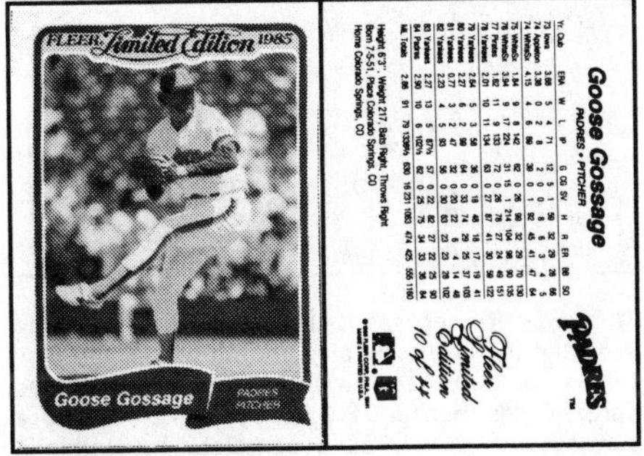

This 44-card set features standard size cards (2 1/2" by 3 1/2") which were distributed in a colorful box as a complete set. The back of the box gives a complete checklist of the cards in the set. The cards are ordered alphabetically by the player's name. Backs of the cards are yellow and white whereas the fronts show a picture of the player inside a red banner-type border.

	MINT	EXC	G-VG
COMPLETE SET (44)	5.00	2.00	.50
COMMON PLAYER (1-44)	.05	.02	.00

	MINT	EXC	G-VG
☐ 1 Buddy Bell	.05	.02	.00
☐ 2 Bert Blyleven	.05	.02	.00
☐ 3 Wade Boggs	1.00	.40	.10
☐ 4 George Brett	.50	.20	.05
☐ 5 Rod Carew	.35	.14	.03
☐ 6 Steve Carlton	.30	.12	.03
☐ 7 Alvin Davis	.15	.06	.01
☐ 8 Andre Dawson	.25	.10	.02
☐ 9 Steve Garvey	.30	.12	.03
☐ 10 Goose Gossage	.10	.04	.01
☐ 11 Tony Gwynn	.40	.16	.04
☐ 12 Keith Hernandez	.25	.10	.02
☐ 13 Kent Hrbek	.20	.08	.02
☐ 14 Reggie Jackson	.50	.20	.05
☐ 15 Dave Kingman	.10	.04	.01
☐ 16 Ron Kittle	.10	.04	.01
☐ 17 Mark Langston	.10	.04	.01
☐ 18 Jeff Leonard	.05	.02	.00
☐ 19 Bill Madlock	.05	.02	.00
☐ 20 Don Mattingly	1.25	.50	.12
☐ 21 Jack Morris	.15	.06	.01
☐ 22 Dale Murphy	.50	.20	.05
☐ 23 Eddie Murray	.35	.14	.03
☐ 24 Tony Pena	.05	.02	.00
☐ 25 Dan Quisenberry	.10	.04	.01
☐ 26 Tim Raines	.25	.10	.02
☐ 27 Jim Rice	.20	.08	.02
☐ 28 Cal Ripken	.35	.14	.03
☐ 29 Pete Rose	.75	.30	.07
☐ 30 Nolan Ryan	.35	.14	.03
☐ 31 Ryne Sandberg	.25	.10	.02
☐ 32 Steve Sax	.15	.06	.01
☐ 33 Mike Schmidt	.50	.20	.05
☐ 34 Tom Seaver	.35	.14	.03
☐ 35 Ozzie Smith	.20	.08	.02
☐ 36 Mario Soto	.05	.02	.00
☐ 37 Dave Stieb	.10	.04	.01
☐ 38 Darryl Strawberry	.60	.24	.06
☐ 39 Rick Sutcliffe	.10	.04	.01
☐ 40 Alan Trammell	.20	.08	.02
☐ 41 Willie Upshaw	.05	.02	.00
☐ 42 Fernando Valenzuela	.20	.08	.02
☐ 43 Dave Winfield	.25	.10	.02
☐ 44 Robin Yount	.25	.10	.02

1985 Fleer Update

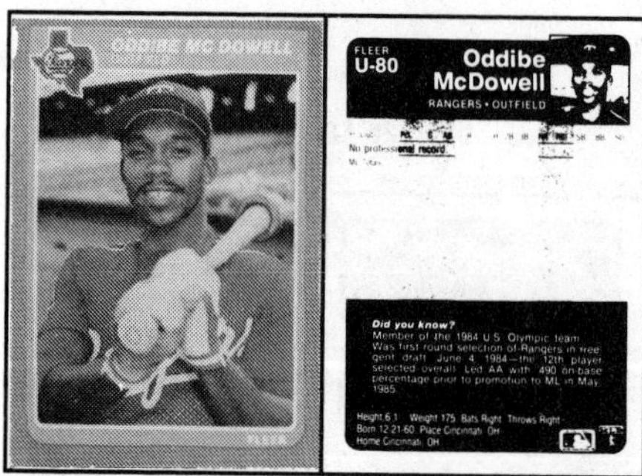

This 132-card set was issued late in the collecting year and features new players and players on new teams compared to the 1985 Fleer regular issue cards. Cards measure 2 1/2" by 3 1/2" and were distributed together as a complete set within a special box. The cards are numbered with a U prefix and are ordered alphabetically by the player's name.

	MINT	EXC	G-VG
COMPLETE SET (132)	16.00	6.50	1.60
COMMON PLAYER (1-132)	.06	.02	.00

	MINT	EXC	G-VG
☐ U1 Don Aase	.10	.04	.01
☐ U2 Bill Almon	.06	.02	.00
☐ U3 Dusty Baker	.10	.04	.01
☐ U4 Dale Berra	.06	.02	.0
☐ U5 Karl Best	.10	.04	.0
☐ U6 Tim Birtsas	.15	.06	.0
☐ U7 Vida Blue	.10	.04	.0
☐ U8 Rich Bordi	.06	.02	.0
☐ U9 Daryl Boston	.10	.04	.0
☐ U10 Hubie Brooks	.20	.08	.0
☐ U11 Chris Brown	.50	.20	.0
☐ U12 Tom Browning	1.25	.50	.1
☐ U13 Al Bumbry	.06	.02	.0
☐ U14 Tim Burke	.35	.14	.0
☐ U15 Ray Burris	.06	.02	.0
☐ U16 Jeff Burroughs	.06	.02	.0
☐ U17 Ivan Calderon	.85	.34	.0
☐ U18 Jeff Calhoun	.15	.06	.0
☐ U19 Bill Campbell	.06	.02	.0
☐ U20 Don Carman	.30	.12	.0
☐ U21 Gary Carter	.75	.30	.0
☐ U22 Bobby Castillo	.06	.02	.0
☐ U23 Bill Caudill	.06	.02	.0
☐ U24 Rick Cerone	.06	.02	.0
☐ U25 Jack Clark	.40	.16	.0
☐ U26 Pat Clements	.15	.06	.0
☐ U27 Stewart Cliburn	.10	.04	.01
☐ U28 Vince Coleman	5.00	2.00	.5
☐ U29 Dave Collins	.06	.02	.0
☐ U30 Fritz Connally	.10	.04	.01
☐ U31 Henry Cotto	.06	.02	.0
☐ U32 Danny Darwin	.06	.02	.0
☐ U33 Darren Daulton	.15	.06	.01
☐ U34 Jerry Davis	.10	.04	.01
☐ U35 Brian Dayett	.10	.04	.01
☐ U36 Ken Dixon	.15	.06	.01
☐ U37 Tommy Dunbar	.06	.02	.00
☐ U38 Mariano Duncan	.25	.10	.02
☐ U39 Bob Fallon	.10	.04	.01
☐ U40 Brian Fisher	.30	.12	.03
☐ U41 Mike Fitzgerald	.06	.02	.00
☐ U42 Ray Fontenot	.06	.02	.00
☐ U43 Greg Gagne	.35	.14	.03
☐ U44 Oscar Gamble	.06	.02	.00
☐ U45 Jim Gott	.10	.04	.01
☐ U46 David Green	.06	.02	.00
☐ U47 Alfredo Griffin	.10	.04	.01
☐ U48 Ozzie Guillen	.70	.28	.07
☐ U49 Toby Harrah	.10	.04	.01
☐ U50 Ron Hassey	.06	.02	.00
☐ U51 Rickey Henderson	1.00	.40	.10
☐ U52 Steve Henderson	.06	.02	.00
☐ U53 George Hendrick	.10	.04	.01
☐ U54 Teddy Higuera	2.50	1.00	.25
☐ U55 Al Holland	.06	.02	.00
☐ U56 Burt Hooton	.06	.02	.00
☐ U57 Jay Howell	.10	.04	.01
☐ U58 LaMarr Hoyt	.10	.04	.01
☐ U59 Tim Hulett	.15	.06	.01
☐ U60 Bob James	.10	.04	.01
☐ U61 Cliff Johnson	.06	.02	.00
☐ U62 Howard Johnson	1.00	.40	.10
☐ U63 Ruppert Jones	.06	.02	.00
☐ U64 Steve Kemp	.10	.04	.01
☐ U65 Bruce Kison	.06	.02	.00
☐ U66 Mike LaCoss	.06	.02	.00
☐ U67 Lee Lacy	.06	.02	.00
☐ U68 Dave LaPoint	.10	.04	.01
☐ U69 Gary Lavelle	.06	.02	.00
☐ U70 Vance Law	.10	.04	.01
☐ U71 Manny Lee	.15	.06	.01
☐ U72 Sixto Lezcano	.06	.02	.00
☐ U73 Tim Lollar	.06	.02	.00
☐ U74 Urbano Lugo	.10	.04	.01
☐ U75 Fred Lynn	.25	.10	.02
☐ U76 Steve Lyons	.10	.04	.01
☐ U77 Mickey Mahler	.06	.02	.00
☐ U78 Ron Mathis	.10	.04	.01
☐ U79 Len Matuszek	.06	.02	.00
☐ U80 Oddibe McDowell (part of bio actually Roger's)	.65	.26	.06
☐ U81 Roger McDowell (part of bio actually Oddibe's)	1.00	.40	.10
☐ U82 Donnie Moore	.06	.02	.00
☐ U83 Ron Musselman	.10	.04	.01
☐ U84 Al Oliver	.15	.06	.01
☐ U85 Joe Orsulak	.20	.08	.02
☐ U86 Dan Pasqua	.55	.22	.05
☐ U87 Chris Pittaro	.10	.04	.01
☐ U88 Rick Reuschel	.15	.06	.01
☐ U89 Earnie Riles	.25	.10	.02
☐ U90 Jerry Royster	.06	.02	.00
☐ U91 Dave Rozema	.06	.02	.00
☐ U92 Dave Rucker	.06	.02	.00
☐ U93 Vern Ruhle	.06	.02	.00
☐ U94 Mark Salas	.15	.06	.01

☐ U95	Luis Salazar	.10	.04	.01
☐ U96	Joe Sambito	.06	.02	.00
☐ U97	Billy Sample	.06	.02	.00
☐ U98	Alejandro Sanchez	.10	.04	.01
☐ U99	Calvin Schiraldi	.20	.08	.02
☐ U100	Rick Schu	.20	.08	.02
☐ U101	Larry Sheets	.50	.20	.05
☐ U102	Ron Shephard	.10	.04	.01
☐ U103	Nelson Simmons	.10	.04	.01
☐ U104	Don Slaught	.06	.02	.00
☐ U105	Roy Smalley	.06	.02	.00
☐ U106	Lonnie Smith	.10	.04	.01
☐ U107	Nate Snell	.10	.04	.01
☐ U108	Lary Sorensen	.06	.02	.00
☐ U109	Chris Speier	.06	.02	.00
☐ U110	Mike Stenhouse	.10	.04	.01
☐ U111	Tim Stoddard	.06	.02	.00
☐ U112	John Stuper	.06	.02	.00
☐ U113	Jim Sundberg	.10	.04	.01
☐ U114	Bruce Sutter	.25	.10	.02
☐ U115	Don Sutton	.60	.24	.06
☐ U116	Bruce Tanner	.10	.04	.01
☐ U117	Kent Tekulve	.10	.04	.01
☐ U118	Walt Terrell	.10	.04	.01
☐ U119	Mickey Tettleton	.10	.04	.01
☐ U120	Rich Thompson	.10	.04	.01
☐ U121	Louis Thornton	.10	.04	.01
☐ U122	Alex Trevino	.06	.02	.00
☐ U123	John Tudor	.20	.08	.02
☐ U124	Jose Uribe	.30	.12	.03
☐ U125	Dave Valle	.10	.04	.01
☐ U126	Dave Von Ohlen	.06	.02	.00
☐ U127	Curt Wardle	.10	.04	.01
☐ U128	U.L. Washington	.06	.02	.00
☐ U129	Ed Whitson	.10	.04	.01
☐ U130	Herm Winningham	.15	.06	.01
☐ U131	Rich Yett	.10	.04	.01
☐ U132	Checklist U1-U132	.06	.01	.00

1986 Fleer

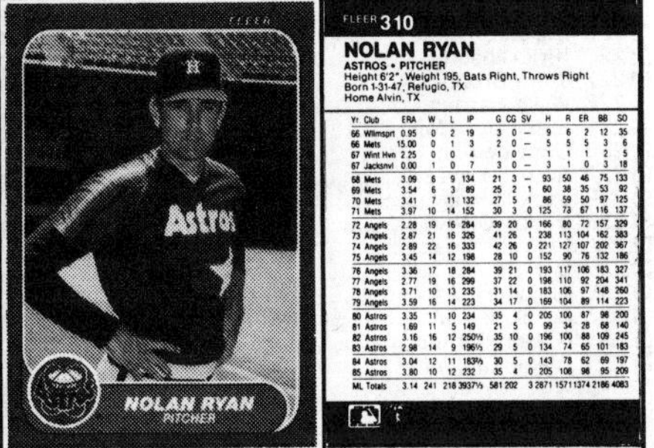

The cards in this 660-card set measure 2 1/2" by 3 1/2". The 1986 Fleer set features fronts which contain the team logo along with the player's name and position. The player cards are alphabetized within team and the teams are ordered by their 1985 season finish and won-lost record, e.g., Kansas City (1-25), St. Louis (26-49), Toronto (50-73), New York Mets (74-97), New York Yankees (98-122), Los Angeles (123-147), California (148- 171), Cincinnati (172-196), Chicago White Sox (197-220), Detroit (221-243), Montreal (244-267), Baltimore (268-291), Houston (292- 314), San Diego (315-338), Boston (339-360), Chicago Cubs (361- 385), Minnesota (386-409), Oakland (410-432), Philadelphia (433- 457), Seattle (458-481), Milwaukee (482-506), Atlanta (507-532), San Francisco (533-555), Texas (556-578), Cleveland (579-601), and Pittsburgh (602-625). Specials (626-643), Rookie pairs (644- 653), and checklist cards (654-660) complete the set. The border enclosing the photo is dark blue. The backs feature the same name, number, and statistics format that Fleer has been using over the past few years. The Dennis and Tippy Martinez cards were apparently switched in the set numbering, as their adjacent numbers (279 and 280) were reversed on the Orioles checklist card.

		MINT	EXC	G-VG
COMPLETE SET (660)		90.00	36.00	9.00
COMMON PLAYER (1-660)		.05	.02	.00
☐ 1	Steve Balboni	.10	.02	.00
☐ 2	Joe Beckwith	.05	.02	.00
☐ 3	Buddy Biancalana	.05	.02	.00
☐ 4	Bud Black	.05	.02	.00
☐ 5	George Brett	.45	.18	.04
☐ 6	Onix Concepcion	.05	.02	.00
☐ 7	Steve Farr	.05	.02	.00
☐ 8	Mark Gubicza	.12	.05	.01
☐ 9	Dane Iorg	.05	.02	.00
☐ 10	Danny Jackson	.30	.12	.03
☐ 11	Lynn Jones	.05	.02	.00
☐ 12	Mike Jones	.05	.02	.00
☐ 13	Charlie Leibrandt	.05	.02	.00
☐ 14	Hal McRae	.08	.03	.01
☐ 15	Omar Moreno	.05	.02	.00
☐ 16	Darryl Motley	.05	.02	.00
☐ 17	Jorge Orta	.05	.02	.00
☐ 18	Dan Quisenberry	.12	.05	.01
☐ 19	Bret Saberhagen	.40	.16	.04
☐ 20	Pat Sheridan	.05	.02	.00
☐ 21	Lonnie Smith	.05	.02	.00
☐ 22	Jim Sundberg	.05	.02	.00
☐ 23	John Wathan	.05	.02	.00
☐ 24	Frank White	.08	.03	.01
☐ 25	Willie Wilson	.10	.04	.01
☐ 26	Joaquin Andujar	.08	.03	.01
☐ 27	Steve Braun	.05	.02	.00
☐ 28	Bill Campbell	.05	.02	.00
☐ 29	Cesar Cedeno	.08	.03	.01
☐ 30	Jack Clark	.25	.10	.02
☐ 31	Vince Coleman	2.25	.90	.22
☐ 32	Danny Cox	.10	.04	.01
☐ 33	Ken Dayley	.05	.02	.00
☐ 34	Ivan DeJesus	.05	.02	.00
☐ 35	Bob Forsch	.05	.02	.00
☐ 36	Brian Harper	.05	.02	.00
☐ 37	Tom Herr	.08	.03	.01
☐ 38	Ricky Horton	.05	.02	.00
☐ 39	Kurt Kepshire	.05	.02	.00
☐ 40	Jeff Lahti	.05	.02	.00
☐ 41	Tito Landrum	.05	.02	.00
☐ 42	Willie McGee	.15	.06	.01
☐ 43	Tom Nieto	.05	.02	.00
☐ 44	Terry Pendleton	.08	.03	.01
☐ 45	Darrell Porter	.05	.02	.00
☐ 46	Ozzie Smith	.20	.08	.02
☐ 47	John Tudor	.15	.06	.01
☐ 48	Andy Van Slyke	.25	.10	.02
☐ 49	Todd Worrell	.90	.36	.09
☐ 50	Jim Acker	.05	.02	.00
☐ 51	Doyle Alexander	.08	.03	.01
☐ 52	Jesse Barfield	.20	.08	.02
☐ 53	George Bell	.30	.12	.03
☐ 54	Jeff Burroughs	.05	.02	.00
☐ 55	Bill Caudill	.05	.02	.00
☐ 56	Jim Clancy	.05	.02	.00
☐ 57	Tony Fernandez	.15	.06	.01
☐ 58	Tom Filer	.05	.02	.00
☐ 59	Damaso Garcia	.05	.02	.00
☐ 60	Tom Henke	.15	.06	.01
☐ 61	Garth Iorg	.05	.02	.00
☐ 62	Cliff Johnson	.05	.02	.00
☐ 63	Jimmy Key	.12	.05	.01
☐ 64	Dennis Lamp	.05	.02	.00
☐ 65	Gary Lavelle	.05	.02	.00
☐ 66	Buck Martinez	.05	.02	.00
☐ 67	Lloyd Moseby	.10	.04	.01
☐ 68	Rance Mulliniks	.05	.02	.00
☐ 69	Al Oliver	.10	.04	.01
☐ 70	Dave Stieb	.12	.05	.01
☐ 71	Louis Thornton	.10	.04	.01
☐ 72	Willie Upshaw	.05	.02	.00
☐ 73	Ernie Whitt	.05	.02	.00
☐ 74	Rick Aguilera	.25	.10	.02
☐ 75	Wally Backman	.08	.03	.01
☐ 76	Gary Carter	.30	.12	.03
☐ 77	Ron Darling	.25	.10	.02
☐ 78	Len Dykstra	1.00	.40	.10
☐ 79	Sid Fernandez	.15	.06	.01
☐ 80	George Foster	.12	.05	.01
☐ 81	Dwight Gooden	2.00	.80	.20
☐ 82	Tom Gorman	.05	.02	.00
☐ 83	Danny Heep	.05	.02	.00

☐ 84	Keith Hernandez	.30	.12	.03
☐ 85	Howard Johnson	.20	.08	.02
☐ 86	Ray Knight	.08	.03	.01
☐ 87	Terry Leach	.15	.06	.01
☐ 88	Ed Lynch	.05	.02	.00
☐ 89	Roger McDowell	.45	.18	.04
☐ 90	Jesse Orosco	.05	.02	.00
☐ 91	Tom Paciorek	.05	.02	.00
☐ 92	Ronn Reynolds	.05	.02	.00
☐ 93	Rafael Santana	.05	.02	.00
☐ 94	Doug Sisk	.05	.02	.00
☐ 95	Rusty Staub	.10	.04	.01
☐ 96	Darryl Strawberry	1.25	.50	.12
☐ 97	Mookie Wilson	.08	.03	.01
☐ 98	Neil Allen	.05	.02	.00
☐ 99	Don Baylor	.10	.04	.01
☐ 100	Dale Berra	.05	.02	.00
☐ 101	Rich Bordi	.05	.02	.00
☐ 102	Marty Bystrom	.05	.02	.00
☐ 103	Joe Cowley	.05	.02	.00
☐ 104	Brian Fisher	.25	.10	.02
☐ 105	Ken Griffey	.08	.03	.01
☐ 106	Ron Guidry	.15	.06	.01
☐ 107	Ron Hassey	.05	.02	.00
☐ 108	Rickey Henderson	.40	.16	.04
☐ 109	Don Mattingly	3.50	1.40	.35
☐ 110	Bobby Meacham	.05	.02	.00
☐ 111	John Montefusco	.05	.02	.00
☐ 112	Phil Niekro	.18	.08	.01
☐ 113	Mike Pagliarulo	.15	.06	.01
☐ 114	Dan Pasqua	.15	.06	.01
☐ 115	Willie Randolph	.10	.04	.01
☐ 116	Dave Righetti	.12	.05	.01
☐ 117	Andre Robertson	.05	.02	.00
☐ 118	Billy Sample	.05	.02	.00
☐ 119	Bob Shirley	.05	.02	.00
☐ 120	Ed Whitson	.05	.02	.00
☐ 121	Dave Winfield	.30	.12	.03
☐ 122	Butch Wynegar	.05	.02	.00
☐ 123	Dave Anderson	.05	.02	.00
☐ 124	Bob Bailor	.05	.02	.00
☐ 125	Greg Brock	.05	.02	.00
☐ 126	Enos Cabell	.05	.02	.00
☐ 127	Bobby Castillo	.05	.02	.00
☐ 128	Carlos Diaz	.05	.02	.00
☐ 129	Mariano Duncan	.20	.08	.02
☐ 130	Pedro Guerrero	.25	.10	.02
☐ 131	Orel Hershiser	1.75	.70	.17
☐ 132	Rick Honeycutt	.05	.02	.00
☐ 133	Ken Howell	.05	.02	.00
☐ 134	Ken Landreaux	.05	.02	.00
☐ 135	Bill Madlock	.10	.04	.01
☐ 136	Candy Maldonado	.10	.04	.01
☐ 137	Mike Marshall	.12	.05	.01
☐ 138	Len Matuszek	.05	.02	.00
☐ 139	Tom Niedenfuer	.05	.02	.00
☐ 140	Alejandro Pena	.05	.02	.00
☐ 141	Jerry Reuss	.08	.03	.01
☐ 142	Bill Russell	.08	.03	.01
☐ 143	Steve Sax	.18	.08	.01
☐ 144	Mike Scioscia	.08	.03	.01
☐ 145	Fernando Valenzuela	.25	.10	.02
☐ 146	Bob Welch	.08	.03	.01
☐ 147	Terry Whitfield	.05	.02	.00
☐ 148	Juan Beniquez	.05	.02	.00
☐ 149	Bob Boone	.10	.04	.01
☐ 150	John Candelaria	.08	.03	.01
☐ 151	Rod Carew	.30	.12	.03
☐ 152	Stewart Cliburn	.08	.03	.01
☐ 153	Doug DeCinces	.08	.03	.01
☐ 154	Brian Downing	.08	.03	.01
☐ 155	Ken Forsch	.05	.02	.00
☐ 156	Craig Gerber	.05	.02	.00
☐ 157	Bobby Grich	.08	.03	.01
☐ 158	George Hendrick	.08	.03	.01
☐ 159	Al Holland	.05	.02	.00
☐ 160	Reggie Jackson	.35	.14	.03
☐ 161	Ruppert Jones	.05	.02	.00
☐ 162	Urbano Lugo	.05	.02	.00
☐ 163	Kirk McCaskill	.35	.14	.03
☐ 164	Donnie Moore	.05	.02	.00
☐ 165	Gary Pettis	.05	.02	.00
☐ 166	Ron Romanick	.05	.02	.00
☐ 167	Dick Schofield	.05	.02	.00
☐ 168	Daryl Sconiers	.05	.02	.00
☐ 169	Jim Slaton	.05	.02	.00
☐ 170	Don Sutton	.18	.08	.01
☐ 171	Mike Witt	.10	.04	.01
☐ 172	Buddy Bell	.10	.04	.01
☐ 173	Tom Browning	.25	.10	.02
☐ 174	Dave Concepcion	.10	.04	.01
☐ 175	Eric Davis	3.00	1.20	.30
☐ 176	Bo Diaz	.05	.02	.00
☐ 177	Nick Esasky	.05	.02	.00
☐ 178	John Franco	.10	.04	.01
☐ 179	Tom Hume	.05	.02	.0
☐ 180	Wayne Krenchicki	.05	.02	.0
☐ 181	Andy McGaffigan	.05	.02	.0
☐ 182	Eddie Milner	.05	.02	.0
☐ 183	Ron Oester	.05	.02	.0
☐ 184	Dave Parker	.15	.06	.01
☐ 185	Frank Pastore	.05	.02	.00
☐ 186	Tony Perez	.12	.05	.01
☐ 187	Ted Power	.05	.02	.00
☐ 188	Joe Price	.05	.02	.00
☐ 189	Gary Redus	.05	.02	.00
☐ 190	Ron Robinson	.05	.02	.00
☐ 191	Pete Rose	.65	.26	.06
☐ 192	Mario Soto	.05	.02	.00
☐ 193	John Stuper	.05	.02	.00
☐ 194	Jay Tibbs	.05	.02	.00
☐ 195	Dave Van Gorder	.05	.02	.00
☐ 196	Max Venable	.05	.02	.00
☐ 197	Juan Agosto	.05	.02	.00
☐ 198	Harold Baines	.12	.05	.01
☐ 199	Floyd Bannister	.05	.02	.00
☐ 200	Britt Burns	.05	.02	.00
☐ 201	Julio Cruz	.05	.02	.00
☐ 202	Joel Davis	.15	.06	.01
☐ 203	Richard Dotson	.08	.03	.01
☐ 204	Carlton Fisk	.15	.06	.01
☐ 205	Scott Fletcher	.10	.04	.01
☐ 206	Ozzie Guillen	.35	.14	.03
☐ 207	Jerry Hairston	.05	.02	.00
☐ 208	Tim Hulett	.05	.02	.00
☐ 209	Bob James	.05	.02	.00
☐ 210	Ron Kittle	.12	.05	.01
☐ 211	Rudy Law	.05	.02	.00
☐ 212	Bryan Little	.05	.02	.00
☐ 213	Gene Nelson	.05	.02	.00
☐ 214	Reid Nichols	.05	.02	.00
☐ 215	Luis Salazar	.08	.03	.01
☐ 216	Tom Seaver	.30	.12	.03
☐ 217	Dan Spillner	.05	.02	.00
☐ 218	Bruce Tanner	.08	.03	.01
☐ 219	Greg Walker	.08	.03	.01
☐ 220	Dave Wehrmeister	.05	.02	.00
☐ 221	Juan Berenguer	.05	.02	.00
☐ 222	Dave Bergman	.05	.02	.00
☐ 223	Tom Brookens	.05	.02	.00
☐ 224	Darrell Evans	.10	.04	.01
☐ 225	Barbaro Garbey	.05	.02	.00
☐ 226	Kirk Gibson	.25	.10	.02
☐ 227	John Grubb	.05	.02	.00
☐ 228	Willie Hernandez	.10	.04	.01
☐ 229	Larry Herndon	.05	.02	.00
☐ 230	Chet Lemon	.08	.03	.01
☐ 231	Aurelio Lopez	.05	.02	.00
☐ 232	Jack Morris	.18	.08	.01
☐ 233	Randy O'Neal	.05	.02	.00
☐ 234	Lance Parrish	.18	.08	.01
☐ 235	Dan Petry	.08	.03	.01
☐ 236	Alejandro Sanchez	.05	.02	.00
☐ 237	Bill Scherrer	.05	.02	.00
☐ 238	Nelson Simmons	.08	.03	.01
☐ 239	Frank Tanana	.08	.03	.01
☐ 240	Walt Terrell	.05	.02	.00
☐ 241	Alan Trammell	.25	.10	.02
☐ 242	Lou Whitaker	.12	.05	.01
☐ 243	Milt Wilcox	.05	.02	.00
☐ 244	Hubie Brooks	.10	.04	.01
☐ 245	Tim Burke	.25	.10	.02
☐ 246	Andre Dawson	.30	.12	.03
☐ 247	Mike Fitzgerald	.05	.02	.00
☐ 248	Terry Francona	.05	.02	.00
☐ 249	Bill Gullickson	.05	.02	.00
☐ 250	Joe Hesketh	.05	.02	.00
☐ 251	Bill Laskey	.05	.02	.00
☐ 252	Vance Law	.08	.03	.01
☐ 253	Charlie Lea	.05	.02	.00
☐ 254	Gary Lucas	.05	.02	.00
☐ 255	David Palmer	.05	.02	.00
☐ 256	Tim Raines	.30	.12	.03
☐ 257	Jeff Reardon	.10	.04	.01
☐ 258	Bert Roberge	.05	.02	.00
☐ 259	Dan Schatzeder	.05	.02	.00
☐ 260	Bryn Smith	.05	.02	.00
☐ 261	Randy St.Claire	.05	.02	.00
☐ 262	Scot Thompson	.05	.02	.00
☐ 263	Tim Wallach	.10	.04	.01
☐ 264	U.L. Washington	.05	.02	.00
☐ 265	Mitch Webster	.35	.14	.03
☐ 266	Herm Winningham	.10	.04	.01
☐ 267	Floyd Youmans	.35	.14	.03
☐ 268	Don Aase	.05	.02	.00
☐ 269	Mike Boddicker	.08	.03	.01
☐ 270	Rich Dauer	.05	.02	.00
☐ 271	Storm Davis	.08	.03	.01
☐ 272	Rick Dempsey	.05	.02	.00
☐ 273	Ken Dixon	.05	.02	.00

□ 274	Jim Dwyer	.05	.02	.00
□ 275	Mike Flanagan	.08	.03	.01
□ 276	Wayne Gross	.05	.02	.00
□ 277	Lee Lacy	.05	.02	.00
□ 278	Fred Lynn	.15	.06	.01
□ 279	Tippy Martinez	.05	.02	.00
□ 280	Dennis Martinez	.08	.03	.01
□ 281	Scott McGregor	.08	.03	.01
□ 282	Eddie Murray	.30	.12	.03
□ 283	Floyd Rayford	.05	.02	.00
□ 284	Cal Ripken	.35	.14	.03
□ 285	Gary Roenicke	.05	.02	.00
□ 286	Larry Sheets	.20	.08	.02
□ 287	John Shelby	.05	.02	.00
□ 288	Nate Snell	.08	.03	.01
□ 289	Sammy Stewart	.05	.02	.00
□ 290	Alan Wiggins	.05	.02	.00
□ 291	Mike Young	.08	.03	.01
□ 292	Alan Ashby	.05	.02	.00
□ 293	Mark Bailey	.05	.02	.00
□ 294	Kevin Bass	.08	.03	.01
□ 295	Jeff Calhoun	.08	.03	.01
□ 296	Jose Cruz	.08	.03	.01
□ 297	Glenn Davis	.75	.30	.07
□ 298	Bill Dawley	.05	.02	.00
□ 299	Frank DiPino	.05	.02	.00
□ 300	Bill Doran	.10	.04	.01
□ 301	Phil Garner	.05	.02	.00
□ 302	Jeff Heathcock	.05	.02	.00
□ 303	Charlie Kerfeld	.10	.04	.01
□ 304	Bob Knepper	.08	.03	.01
□ 305	Ron Mathis	.08	.03	.01
□ 306	Jerry Mumphrey	.05	.02	.00
□ 307	Jim Pankovits	.05	.02	.00
□ 308	Terry Puhl	.05	.02	.00
□ 309	Craig Reynolds	.05	.02	.00
□ 310	Nolan Ryan	.30	.12	.03
□ 311	Mike Scott	.30	.12	.03
□ 312	Dave Smith	.08	.03	.01
□ 313	Dickie Thon	.05	.02	.00
□ 314	Denny Walling	.05	.02	.00
□ 315	Kurt Bevacqua	.05	.02	.00
□ 316	Al Bumbry	.05	.02	.00
□ 317	Jerry Davis	.05	.02	.00
□ 318	Luis DeLeon	.05	.02	.00
□ 319	Dave Dravecky	.05	.02	.00
□ 320	Tim Flannery	.05	.02	.00
□ 321	Steve Garvey	.35	.14	.03
□ 322	Goose Gossage	.12	.05	.01
□ 323	Tony Gwynn	.65	.26	.06
□ 324	Andy Hawkins	.05	.02	.00
□ 325	LaMarr Hoyt	.08	.03	.01
□ 326	Roy Lee Jackson	.05	.02	.00
□ 327	Terry Kennedy	.05	.02	.00
□ 328	Craig Lefferts	.05	.02	.00
□ 329	Carmelo Martinez	.05	.02	.00
□ 330	Lance McCullers	.40	.16	.04
□ 331	Kevin McReynolds	.40	.16	.04
□ 332	Graig Nettles	.10	.04	.01
□ 333	Jerry Royster	.05	.02	.00
□ 334	Eric Show	.08	.03	.01
□ 335	Tim Stoddard	.05	.02	.00
□ 336	Garry Templeton	.08	.03	.01
□ 337	Mark Thurmond	.05	.02	.00
□ 338	Ed Wojna	.10	.04	.01
□ 339	Tony Armas	.08	.03	.01
□ 340	Marty Barrett	.10	.04	.01
□ 341	Wade Boggs	2.50	1.00	.25
□ 342	Dennis Boyd	.08	.03	.01
□ 343	Bill Buckner	.10	.04	.01
□ 344	Mark Clear	.05	.02	.00
□ 345	Roger Clemens	3.00	1.20	.30
□ 346	Steve Crawford	.05	.02	.00
□ 347	Mike Easler	.05	.02	.00
□ 348	Dwight Evans	.15	.06	.01
□ 349	Rich Gedman	.08	.03	.01
□ 350	Jackie Gutierrez	.05	.02	.00
□ 351	Glenn Hoffman	.05	.02	.00
□ 352	Bruce Hurst	.15	.06	.01
□ 353	Bruce Kison	.05	.02	.00
□ 354	Tim Lollar	.05	.02	.00
□ 355	Steve Lyons	.05	.02	.00
□ 356	Al Nipper	.05	.02	.00
□ 357	Bob Ojeda	.08	.03	.01
□ 358	Jim Rice	.20	.08	.02
□ 359	Bob Stanley	.05	.02	.00
□ 360	Mike Trujillo	.05	.02	.00
□ 361	Thad Bosley	.05	.02	.00
□ 362	Warren Brusstar	.05	.02	.00
□ 363	Ron Cey	.08	.03	.01
□ 364	Jody Davis	.08	.03	.01
□ 365	Bob Dernier	.05	.02	.00
□ 366	Shawon Dunston	.10	.04	.01
□ 367	Leon Durham	.08	.03	.01
□ 368	Dennis Eckersley	.15	.06	.01
□ 369	Ray Fontenot	.05	.02	.00
□ 370	George Frazier	.05	.02	.00
□ 371	Bill Hatcher	.15	.06	.01
□ 372	Dave Lopes	.08	.03	.01
□ 373	Gary Matthews	.08	.03	.01
□ 374	Ron Meredith	.05	.02	.00
□ 375	Keith Moreland	.05	.02	.00
□ 376	Reggie Patterson	.05	.02	.00
□ 377	Dick Ruthven	.05	.02	.00
□ 378	Ryne Sandberg	.20	.08	.02
□ 379	Scott Sanderson	.05	.02	.00
□ 380	Lee Smith	.08	.03	.01
□ 381	Lary Sorensen	.05	.02	.00
□ 382	Chris Speier	.05	.02	.00
□ 383	Rick Sutcliffe	.12	.05	.01
□ 384	Steve Trout	.05	.02	.00
□ 385	Gary Woods	.05	.02	.00
□ 386	Bert Blyleven	.10	.04	.01
□ 387	Tom Brunansky	.15	.06	.01
□ 388	Randy Bush	.08	.03	.01
□ 389	John Butcher	.05	.02	.00
□ 390	Ron Davis	.05	.02	.00
□ 391	Dave Engle	.05	.02	.00
□ 392	Frank Eufemia	.05	.02	.00
□ 393	Pete Filson	.05	.02	.00
□ 394	Gary Gaetti	.20	.08	.02
□ 395	Greg Gagne	.08	.03	.01
□ 396	Mickey Hatcher	.08	.03	.01
□ 397	Kent Hrbek	.18	.08	.01
□ 398	Tim Laudner	.05	.02	.00
□ 399	Rick Lysander	.05	.02	.00
□ 400	Dave Meier	.05	.02	.00
□ 401	Kirby Puckett	2.00	.80	.20
□ 402	Mark Salas	.05	.02	.00
□ 403	Ken Schrom	.05	.02	.00
□ 404	Roy Smalley	.05	.02	.00
□ 405	Mike Smithson	.05	.02	.00
□ 406	Mike Stenhouse	.05	.02	.00
□ 407	Tim Teufel	.05	.02	.00
□ 408	Frank Viola	.30	.12	.03
□ 409	Ron Washington	.05	.02	.00
□ 410	Keith Atherton	.05	.02	.00
□ 411	Dusty Baker	.08	.03	.01
□ 412	Tim Birtsas	.15	.06	.01
□ 413	Bruce Bochte	.05	.02	.00
□ 414	Chris Codiroli	.05	.02	.00
□ 415	Dave Collins	.05	.02	.00
□ 416	Mike Davis	.05	.02	.00
□ 417	Alfredo Griffin	.08	.03	.01
□ 418	Mike Heath	.05	.02	.00
□ 419	Steve Henderson	.05	.02	.00
□ 420	Donnie Hill	.05	.02	.00
□ 421	Jay Howell	.08	.03	.01
□ 422	Tommy John	.12	.05	.01
□ 423	Dave Kingman	.12	.05	.01
□ 424	Bill Krueger	.05	.02	.00
□ 425	Rick Langford	.05	.02	.00
□ 426	Carney Lansford	.10	.04	.01
□ 427	Steve McCatty	.05	.02	.00
□ 428	Dwayne Murphy	.05	.02	.00
□ 429	Steve Ontiveros	.12	.05	.01
□ 430	Tony Phillips	.05	.02	.00
□ 431	Jose Rijo	.08	.03	.01
□ 432	Mickey Tettleton	.08	.03	.01
□ 433	Luis Aguayo	.05	.02	.00
□ 434	Larry Andersen	.05	.02	.00
□ 435	Steve Carlton	.25	.10	.02
□ 436	Don Carman	.25	.10	.02
□ 437	Tim Corcoran	.05	.02	.00
□ 438	Darren Daulton	.12	.05	.01
□ 439	John Denny	.08	.03	.01
□ 440	Tom Foley	.05	.02	.00
□ 441	Greg Gross	.05	.02	.00
□ 442	Kevin Gross	.05	.02	.00
□ 443	Von Hayes	.10	.04	.01
□ 444	Charles Hudson	.05	.02	.00
□ 445	Garry Maddox	.08	.03	.01
□ 446	Shane Rawley	.08	.03	.01
□ 447	Dave Rucker	.05	.02	.00
□ 448	John Russell	.05	.02	.00
□ 449	Juan Samuel	.12	.05	.01
□ 450	Mike Schmidt	.45	.18	.04
□ 451	Rick Schu	.05	.02	.00
□ 452	Dave Shipanoff	.10	.04	.01
□ 453	Dave Stewart	.12	.05	.01
□ 454	Jeff Stone	.05	.02	.00
□ 455	Kent Tekulve	.08	.03	.01
□ 456	Ozzie Virgil	.05	.02	.00
□ 457	Glenn Wilson	.08	.03	.01
□ 458	Jim Beattie	.05	.02	.00
□ 459	Karl Best	.08	.03	.01
□ 460	Barry Bonnell	.05	.02	.00
□ 461	Phil Bradley	.12	.05	.01
□ 462	Ivan Calderon	.65	.26	.06
□ 463	Al Cowens	.05	.02	.00

□ 464	Alvin Davis	.18	.08	.01
□ 465	Dave Henderson	.08	.03	.01
□ 466	Bob Kearney	.05	.02	.00
□ 467	Mark Langston	.18	.08	.01
□ 468	Bob Long	.05	.02	.00
□ 469	Mike Moore	.08	.03	.01
□ 470	Edwin Nunez	.05	.02	.00
□ 471	Spike Owen	.05	.02	.00
□ 472	Jack Perconte	.05	.02	.00
□ 473	Jim Presley	.15	.06	.01
□ 474	Donnie Scott	.05	.02	.00
□ 475	Bill Swift	.10	.04	.01
□ 476	Danny Tartabull	.75	.30	.07
□ 477	Gorman Thomas	.10	.04	.01
□ 478	Roy Thomas	.05	.02	.00
□ 479	Ed VandeBerg	.05	.02	.00
□ 480	Frank Wills	.08	.03	.01
□ 481	Matt Young	.05	.02	.00
□ 482	Ray Burris	.05	.02	.00
□ 483	Jaime Cocanower	.05	.02	.00
□ 484	Cecil Cooper	.10	.04	.01
□ 485	Danny Darwin	.05	.02	.00
□ 486	Rollie Fingers	.15	.06	.01
□ 487	Jim Gantner	.05	.02	.00
□ 488	Bob L. Gibson	.05	.02	.00
□ 489	Moose Haas	.05	.02	.00
□ 490	Teddy Higuera	1.25	.50	.12
□ 491	Paul Householder	.05	.02	.00
□ 492	Pete Ladd	.05	.02	.00
□ 493	Rick Manning	.05	.02	.00
□ 494	Bob McClure	.05	.02	.00
□ 495	Paul Molitor	.18	.08	.01
□ 496	Charlie Moore	.05	.02	.00
□ 497	Ben Oglivie	.08	.03	.01
□ 498	Randy Ready	.08	.03	.01
□ 499	Earnie Riles	.20	.08	.02
□ 500	Ed Romero	.05	.02	.00
□ 501	Bill Schroeder	.05	.02	.00
□ 502	Ray Searage	.05	.02	.00
□ 503	Ted Simmons	.10	.04	.01
□ 504	Pete Vuckovich	.08	.03	.01
□ 505	Rick Waits	.05	.02	.00
□ 506	Robin Yount	.30	.12	.03
□ 507	Len Barker	.05	.02	.00
□ 508	Steve Bedrosian	.12	.05	.01
□ 509	Bruce Benedict	.05	.02	.00
□ 510	Rick Camp	.05	.02	.00
□ 511	Rick Cerone	.05	.02	.00
□ 512	Chris Chambliss	.08	.03	.01
□ 513	Jeff Dedmon	.05	.02	.00
□ 514	Terry Forster	.08	.03	.01
□ 515	Gene Garber	.05	.02	.00
□ 516	Terry Harper	.05	.02	.00
□ 517	Bob Horner	.15	.06	.01
□ 518	Glenn Hubbard	.05	.02	.00
□ 519	Joe Johnson	.12	.05	.01
□ 520	Brad Komminsk	.05	.02	.00
□ 521	Rick Mahler	.05	.02	.00
□ 522	Dale Murphy	.50	.20	.05
□ 523	Ken Oberkfell	.05	.02	.00
□ 524	Pascual Perez	.08	.03	.01
□ 525	Gerald Perry	.12	.05	.01
□ 526	Rafael Ramirez	.05	.02	.00
□ 527	Steve Shields	.08	.03	.01
□ 528	Zane Smith	.10	.04	.01
□ 529	Bruce Sutter	.12	.05	.01
□ 530	Milt Thompson	.30	.12	.03
□ 531	Claudell Washington	.08	.03	.01
□ 532	Paul Zuvella	.05	.02	.00
□ 533	Vida Blue	.08	.03	.01
□ 534	Bob Brenly	.05	.02	.00
□ 535	Chris Brown	.40	.16	.04
□ 536	Chili Davis	.10	.04	.01
□ 537	Mark Davis	.08	.03	.01
□ 538	Rob Deer	.20	.08	.02
□ 539	Dan Driessen	.05	.02	.00
□ 540	Scott Garrelts	.08	.03	.01
□ 541	Dan Gladden	.08	.03	.01
□ 542	Jim Gott	.05	.02	.00
□ 543	David Green	.05	.02	.00
□ 544	Atlee Hammaker	.05	.02	.00
□ 545	Mike Jeffcoat	.05	.02	.00
□ 546	Mike Krukow	.05	.02	.00
□ 547	Dave LaPoint	.08	.03	.01
□ 548	Jeff Leonard	.08	.03	.01
□ 549	Greg Minton	.05	.02	.00
□ 550	Alex Trevino	.05	.02	.00
□ 551	Manny Trillo	.05	.02	.00
□ 552	Jose Uribe	.30	.12	.03
□ 553	Brad Wellman	.05	.02	.00
□ 554	Frank Williams	.05	.02	.00
□ 555	Joel Youngblood	.05	.02	.00
□ 556	Alan Bannister	.05	.02	.00
□ 557	Glenn Brummer	.05	.02	.00
□ 558	Steve Buechele	.25	.10	.02

□ 559	Jose Guzman	.25	.10	.0
□ 560	Toby Harrah	.08	.03	.0
□ 561	Greg Harris	.05	.02	.0
□ 562	Dwayne Henry	.08	.03	.0
□ 563	Burt Hooton	.05	.02	.0
□ 564	Charlie Hough	.08	.03	.0
□ 565	Mike Mason	.05	.02	.0
□ 566	Oddibe McDowell	.20	.08	.0
□ 567	Dickie Noles	.05	.02	.0
□ 568	Pete O'Brien	.10	.04	.0
□ 569	Larry Parrish	.08	.03	.0
□ 570	Dave Rozema	.05	.02	.0
□ 571	Dave Schmidt	.08	.03	.0
□ 572	Don Slaught	.05	.02	.0
□ 573	Wayne Tolleson	.05	.02	.0
□ 574	Duane Walker	.05	.02	.0
□ 575	Gary Ward	.08	.03	.0
□ 576	Chris Welsh	.05	.02	.0
□ 577	Curtis Wilkerson	.05	.02	.0
□ 578	George Wright	.05	.02	.0
□ 579	Chris Bando	.05	.02	.0
□ 580	Tony Bernazard	.05	.02	.0
□ 581	Brett Butler	.08	.03	.0
□ 582	Ernie Camacho	.05	.02	.0
□ 583	Joe Carter	.35	.14	.0
□ 584	Carmen Castillo	.05	.02	.0
□ 585	Jamie Easterly	.05	.02	.0
□ 586	Julio Franco	.10	.04	.0
□ 587	Mel Hall	.08	.03	.0
□ 588	Mike Hargrove	.05	.02	.0
□ 589	Neal Heaton	.05	.02	.0
□ 590	Brook Jacoby	.12	.05	.0
□ 591	Otis Nixon	.15	.06	.0
□ 592	Jerry Reed	.05	.02	.0
□ 593	Vern Ruhle	.05	.02	.0
□ 594	Pat Tabler	.08	.03	.0
□ 595	Rich Thompson	.05	.02	.0
□ 596	Andre Thornton	.08	.03	.0
□ 597	Dave Von Ohlen	.05	.02	.0
□ 598	George Vukovich	.05	.02	.0
□ 599	Tom Waddell	.05	.02	.0
□ 600	Curt Wardle	.05	.02	.0
□ 601	Jerry Willard	.05	.02	.0
□ 602	Bill Almon	.05	.02	.0
□ 603	Mike Bielecki	.05	.02	.0
□ 604	Sid Bream	.05	.02	.0
□ 605	Mike Brown OF	.05	.02	.0
□ 606	Pat Clements	.12	.05	.0
□ 607	Jose DeLeon	.05	.02	.0
□ 608	Denny Gonzalez	.05	.02	.0
□ 609	Cecilio Guante	.05	.02	.0
□ 610	Steve Kemp	.08	.03	.01
□ 611	Sam Khalifa	.08	.03	.01
□ 612	Lee Mazzilli	.05	.02	.0
□ 613	Larry McWilliams	.05	.02	.0
□ 614	Jim Morrison	.05	.02	.0
□ 615	Joe Orsulak	.12	.05	.01
□ 616	Tony Pena	.10	.04	.01
□ 617	Johnny Ray	.10	.04	.01
□ 618	Rick Reuschel	.08	.03	.01
□ 619	R.J. Reynolds	.05	.02	.0
□ 620	Rick Rhoden	.08	.03	.01
□ 621	Don Robinson	.05	.02	.0
□ 622	Jason Thompson	.05	.02	.0
□ 623	Lee Tunnell	.05	.02	.0
□ 624	Jim Winn	.05	.02	.0
□ 625	Marvell Wynne	.05	.02	.0
□ 626	Dwight Gooden IA	.40	.16	.04
□ 627	Don Mattingly IA	1.50	.60	.15
□ 628	4192 (Pete Rose)	.40	.16	.04
□ 629	3000 Career Hits Rod Carew	.20	.08	.02
□ 630	300 Career Wins Tom Seaver Phil Niekro	.15	.06	.01
□ 631	Ouch (Don Baylor)	.08	.03	.01
□ 632	Instant Offense Darryl Strawberry Tim Raines	.25	.10	.02
□ 633	Shortstops Supreme Cal Ripken Alan Trammell	.15	.06	.01
□ 634	Boggs and "Hero" Wade Boggs George Brett	.50	.20	.05
□ 635	Braves Dynamic Duo Bob Horner Dale Murphy	.20	.08	.02
□ 636	Cardinal Ignitors Willie McGee Vince Coleman	.20	.08	.02
□ 637	Terror on Basepaths Vince Coleman	.25	.10	.02
□ 638	Charlie Hustle / Dr.K Pete Rose	.75	.30	.07

		MINT	EXC	G-VG
639	Dwight Gooden 1984 and 1985 AL Batting Champs Wade Boggs Don Mattingly	1.75	.70	.17
640	NL West Sluggers Dale Murphy Steve Garvey Dave Parker	.20	.08	.02
641	Staff Aces Fernando Valenzuela Dwight Gooden	.30	.12	.03
642	Blue Jay Stoppers Jimmy Key Dave Stieb	.08	.03	.01
643	AL All-Star Backstops Carlton Fisk Rich Gedman	.08	.03	.01
644	Gene Walter and Benito Santiago	4.50	1.80	.45
645	Mike Woodard and Collin Ward	.12	.05	.01
646	Kal Daniels and Paul O'Neill	4.50	1.80	.45
647	Andres Galarraga and Fred Toliver	3.50	1.40	.35
648	Bob Kipper and Curt Ford	.12	.05	.01
649	Jose Canseco and Eric Plunk	35.00	14.00	3.50
650	Mark McLemore and Gus Polidor	.12	.05	.01
651	Rob Woodward and Mickey Brantley	.60	.24	.06
652	Billy Jo Robidoux and Mark Funderburk	.12	.05	.01
653	Cecil Fielder and Cory Snyder	2.50	1.00	.25
654	CL: Royals/Cardinals Blue Jays/Mets	.08	.01	.00
655	CL: Yankees/Dodgers Angels/Reds	.08	.01	.00
656	CL: White Sox/Tigers Expos/Orioles (279 Dennis, 280 Tippy)	.08	.01	.00
657	CL: Astros/Padres Red Sox/Cubs	.08	.01	.00
658	CL: Twins/A's Phillies/Mariners	.08	.01	.00
659	CL: Brewers/Braves Giants/Rangers	.08	.01	.00
660	CL: Indians/Pirates Special Cards	.08	.01	.00

1986 Fleer Wax Box Cards

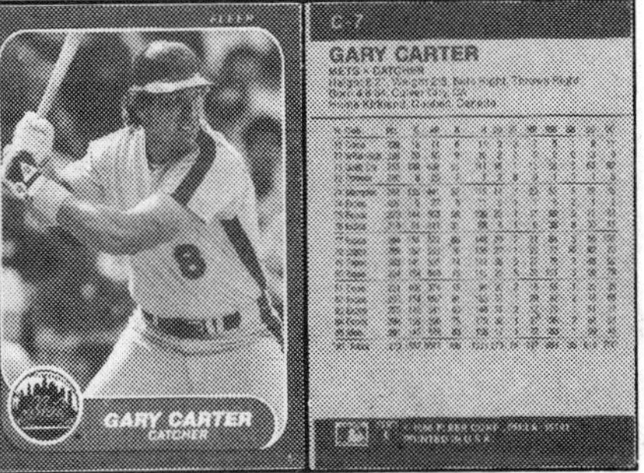

The cards in this 8-card set measure the standard 2 1/2" by 3 1/2" and were found on the bottom of the Fleer regular issue wax pack and cello pack boxes as four-card panel. Cards have essentially the same design as the 1986 Fleer regular issue set. These 8 cards (C1 to C8) are considered a separate set in their own right and are not typically included in a complete set of the regular issue 1986 Fleer cards. The value of the panel uncut is slightly greater, perhaps by 25% greater, than the value of the individual cards cut up carefully.

	MINT	EXC	G-VG
COMPLETE SET (8)	1.25	.50	.12
COMMON PLAYERS	.05	.02	.00
☐ C1 Royals Logo	.05	.02	.00
☐ C2 George Brett	.35	.14	.03
☐ C3 Ozzie Guillen	.15	.06	.01
☐ C4 Dale Murphy	.60	.24	.06
☐ C5 Cardinals Logo	.05	.02	.00
☐ C6 Tom Browning	.15	.06	.01
☐ C7 Gary Carter	.25	.10	.02
☐ C8 Carlton Fisk	.10	.04	.01

1986 Fleer All-Star Inserts

Fleer selected a 12-card (Major League) All-Star team to be included as inserts in their 39 cent wax packs and 59 cent cello packs. However they were randomly inserted in such a way that not all wax packs contain the insert. Cards measure 2 1/2" by 3 1/2" and feature attractive red backgrounds (American Leaguers) and blue backgrounds (National Leaguers). The 12 selections cover each position, left and right-handed starting pitchers, a reliever, and a designated hitter.

	MINT	EXC	G-VG
COMPLETE SET (12)	15.00	6.00	1.50
COMMON PLAYER (1-12)	.20	.08	.02
☐ 1 Don Mattingly First Base	7.50	3.00	.75
☐ 2 Tom Herr Second Base	.20	.08	.02
☐ 3 George Brett Third Base	1.00	.40	.10
☐ 4 Gary Carter Catcher	.75	.30	.07
☐ 5 Cal Ripken Shortstop	.75	.30	.07
☐ 6 Dave Parker Outfield	.30	.12	.03
☐ 7 Rickey Henderson Outfield	1.50	.60	.15
☐ 8 Pedro Guerrero Outfield	.30	.12	.03
☐ 9 Dan Quisenberry Relief Pitcher	.25	.10	.02
☐ 10 Dwight Gooden Right-Hand Pitcher	2.50	1.00	.25
☐ 11 Gorman Thomas Designated Hitter	.20	.08	.02
☐ 12 John Tudor Left-Hand Pitcher	.25	.10	.02

1986 Fleer Future HOF

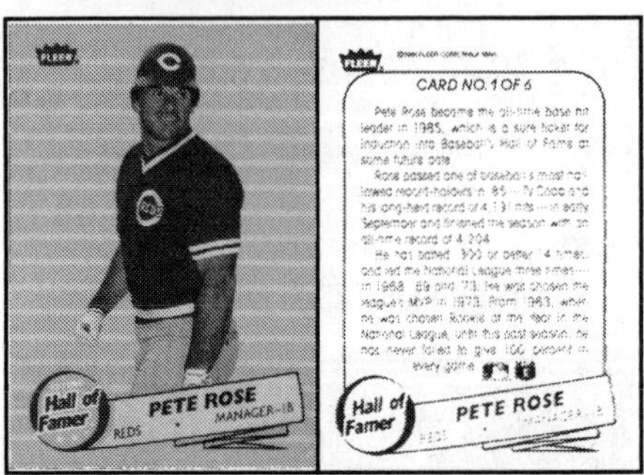

These attractive cards were issued as inserts with the Fleer three-packs. They are the same size as the regular issue (2 1/2" by 3 1/2") and feature players that Fleer predicts will be "Future Hall of Famers." The card backs describe career highlights, records, and honors won by the player. The cards are numbered on the back; Pete Rose is given the honor of being card #1.

	MINT	EXC	G-VG
COMPLETE SET (6)	6.00	2.40	.60
COMMON PLAYER (1-6)	1.00	.40	.10
□ 1 Pete Rose Cincinnati Reds	2.00	.80	.20
□ 2 Steve Carlton Philadelphia Phillies	1.00	.40	.10
□ 3 Tom Seaver Chicago White Sox	1.00	.40	.10
□ 4 Rod Carew California Angels	1.00	.40	.10
□ 5 Nolan Ryan Houston Astros	1.00	.40	.10
□ 6 Reggie Jackson California Angels	1.25	.50	.12

1986 Fleer League Leaders

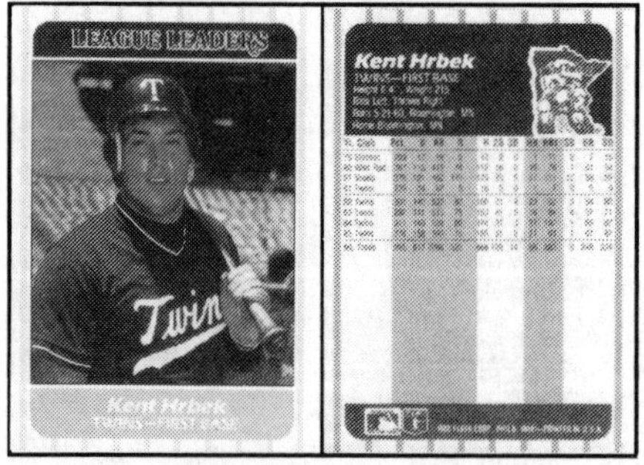

This 44-card set is also sometimes referred to as the Walgreen's set. Although the set was distributed through Walgreen's, there is no mention on the cards or box of that fact. The cards are easily recognizable by the fact that they contain the phrase "Fleer League Leaders" at the top of the obverse. Both sides of the cards are designed with a blue stripe on white pattern. The checklist for the set is given on the outside of the red, white, blue, and gold box in which the set was packaged. Cards are numbered on the back and measure the standard 2 1/2" by 3 1/2".

	MINT	EXC
COMPLETE SET (44)	5.00	2.00
COMMON PLAYER (1-44)	.10	.04
□ 1 Wade Boggs	.75	.30
□ 2 George Brett	.40	.16
□ 3 Jose Canseco	1.50	.60
□ 4 Rod Carew	.30	.12
□ 5 Gary Carter	.25	.10
□ 6 Jack Clark	.20	.08
□ 7 Vince Coleman	.35	.14
□ 8 Jose Cruz	.10	.04
□ 9 Alvin Davis	.15	.06
□ 10 Mariano Duncan	.10	.04
□ 11 Leon Durham	.10	.04
□ 12 Carlton Fisk	.15	.06
□ 13 Julio Franco	.10	.04
□ 14 Scott Garrelts	.10	.04
□ 15 Steve Garvey	.30	.12
□ 16 Dwight Gooden	.45	.18
□ 17 Ozzie Guillen	.20	.08
□ 18 Willie Hernandez	.10	.04
□ 19 Bob Horner	.15	.06
□ 20 Kent Hrbek	.20	.08
□ 21 Charlie Leibrandt	.10	.04
□ 22 Don Mattingly	1.00	.40
□ 23 Oddibe McDowell	.20	.08
□ 24 Willie McGee	.20	.08
□ 25 Keith Moreland	.10	.04
□ 26 Lloyd Moseby	.10	.04
□ 27 Dale Murphy	.45	.18
□ 28 Phil Niekro	.20	.08
□ 29 Joe Orsulak	.10	.04
□ 30 Dave Parker	.20	.08
□ 31 Lance Parrish	.20	.08
□ 32 Kirby Puckett	.40	.16
□ 33 Tim Raines	.30	.12
□ 34 Earnie Riles	.10	.04
□ 35 Cal Ripken	.30	.12
□ 36 Pete Rose	.60	.24
□ 37 Bret Saberhagen	.25	.10
□ 38 Juan Samuel	.15	.06
□ 39 Ryne Sandberg	.25	.10
□ 40 Tom Seaver	.30	.12
□ 41 Lee Smith	.10	.04
□ 42 Ozzie Smith	.20	.08
□ 43 Dave Stieb	.15	.06
□ 44 Robin Yount	.25	.10

1986 Fleer Limited Edition

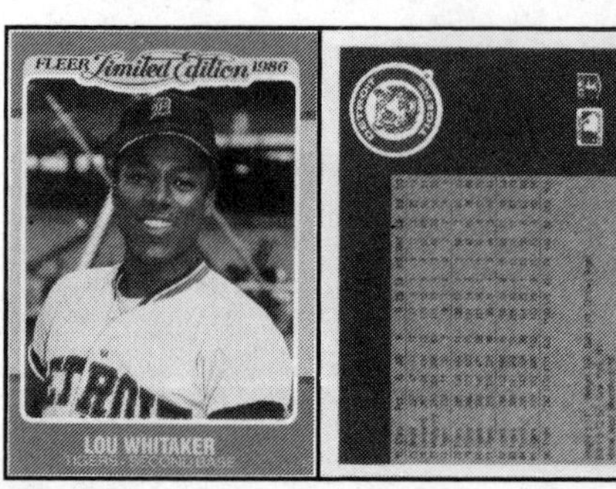

The 44-card boxed set was produced by Fleer for McCrory's. The cards are standard size 2 1/2" by 3 1/2" and have green and yellow borders. Card backs are printed in red and black on white card stock. Cards are numbered on the back; the back of the original box gives a complete checklist of the players in the set. The set box also contains six logo stickers.

	MINT	EXC
COMPLETE SET (44)	5.00	2.00
COMMON PLAYER (1-44)	.10	.04
□ 1 Doyle Alexander	.10	.04
□ 2 Joaquin Andujar	.10	.04
□ 3 Harold Baines	.15	.06

☐ 4	Wade Boggs	.75	.30	.07
☐ 5	Phil Bradley	.15	.06	.01
☐ 6	George Brett	.35	.14	.03
☐ 7	Hubie Brooks	.10	.04	.01
☐ 8	Chris Brown	.15	.06	.01
☐ 9	Tom Brunansky	.15	.06	.01
☐ 10	Gary Carter	.25	.10	.02
☐ 11	Vince Coleman	.30	.12	.03
☐ 12	Cecil Cooper	.15	.06	.01
☐ 13	Jose Cruz	.10	.04	.01
☐ 14	Mike Davis	.10	.04	.01
☐ 15	Carlton Fisk	.15	.06	.01
☐ 16	Julio Franco	.10	.04	.01
☐ 17	Damaso Garcia	.10	.04	.01
☐ 18	Rich Gedman	.10	.04	.01
☐ 19	Kirk Gibson	.35	.14	.03
☐ 20	Dwight Gooden	.50	.20	.05
☐ 21	Pedro Guerrero	.20	.08	.02
☐ 22	Tony Gwynn	.40	.16	.04
☐ 23	Rickey Henderson	.45	.18	.04
☐ 24	Orel Hershiser	.50	.20	.05
☐ 25	LaMarr Hoyt	.10	.04	.01
☐ 26	Reggie Jackson	.50	.20	.05
☐ 27	Don Mattingly	1.00	.40	.10
☐ 28	Oddibe McDowell	.15	.06	.01
☐ 29	Willie McGee	.20	.08	.02
☐ 30	Paul Molitor	.20	.08	.02
☐ 31	Dale Murphy	.45	.18	.04
☐ 32	Eddie Murray	.30	.12	.03
☐ 33	Dave Parker	.20	.08	.02
☐ 34	Tony Pena	.10	.04	.01
☐ 35	Jeff Reardon	.10	.04	.01
☐ 36	Cal Ripken	.30	.12	.03
☐ 37	Pete Rose	.60	.24	.06
☐ 38	Bret Saberhagen	.25	.10	.02
☐ 39	Juan Samuel	.15	.06	.01
☐ 40	Ryne Sandberg	.25	.10	.02
☐ 41	Mike Schmidt	.50	.20	.05
☐ 42	Lee Smith	.10	.04	.01
☐ 43	Don Sutton	.20	.08	.02
☐ 44	Lou Whitaker	.15	.06	.01

1986 Fleer Mini

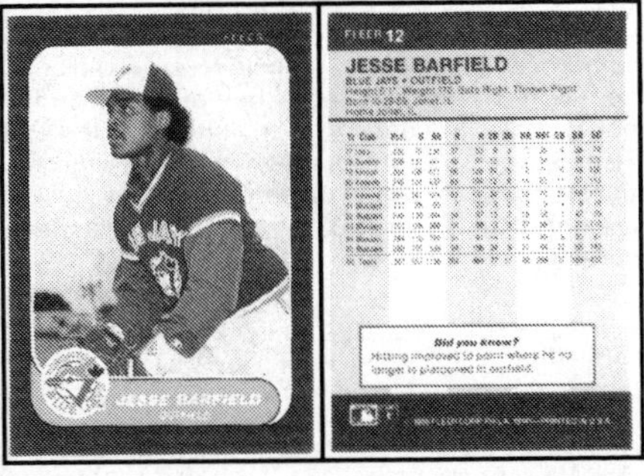

The Fleer "Classic Miniatures" set consists of 120 small cards with all new pictures of the players as compared to the 1986 Fleer regular issue. The cards are only 1 13/16" by 2 9/16", making them one of the smallest (in size) produced in recent memory. Card backs provide career year-by-year statistics. The complete set was distributed in a red, white, and silver box along with 18 logo stickers. The card numbering is done in team order as is the usual Fleer style.

	MINT	EXC	G-VG
COMPLETE SET (120)	10.00	4.00	1.00
COMMON PLAYER (1-120)	.05	.02	.00

☐ 1	George Brett	.30	.12	.03
☐ 2	Dan Quisenberry	.10	.04	.01
☐ 3	Bret Saberhagen	.20	.08	.02
☐ 4	Lonnie Smith	.05	.02	.00
☐ 5	Willie Wilson	.10	.04	.01
☐ 6	Jack Clark	.20	.08	.02
☐ 7	Vince Coleman	.30	.12	.03
☐ 8	Tom Herr	.05	.02	.00
☐ 9	Willie McGee	.15	.06	.01
☐ 10	Ozzie Smith	.20	.08	.02
☐ 11	John Tudor	.10	.04	.01
☐ 12	Jesse Barfield	.15	.06	.01
☐ 13	George Bell	.20	.08	.02
☐ 14	Tony Fernandez	.15	.06	.01
☐ 15	Damaso Garcia	.05	.02	.00
☐ 16	Dave Stieb	.10	.04	.01
☐ 17	Gary Carter	.25	.10	.02
☐ 18	Ron Darling	.15	.06	.01
☐ 19A	Dwight Gooden (R on Mets logo)	.90	.36	.09
☐ 19B	Dwight Gooden (no R on Mets logo)	1.00	.40	.10
☐ 20	Keith Hernandez	.20	.08	.02
☐ 21	Darryl Strawberry	.45	.18	.04
☐ 22	Ron Guidry	.15	.06	.01
☐ 23	Rickey Henderson	.35	.14	.03
☐ 24	Don Mattingly	1.50	.60	.15
☐ 25	Dave Righetti	.15	.06	.01
☐ 26	Dave Winfield	.20	.08	.02
☐ 27	Mariano Duncan	.05	.02	.00
☐ 28	Pedro Guerrero	.15	.06	.01
☐ 29	Bill Madlock	.05	.02	.00
☐ 30	Mike Marshall	.10	.04	.01
☐ 31	Fernando Valenzuela	.15	.06	.01
☐ 32	Reggie Jackson	.30	.12	.03
☐ 33	Gary Pettis	.05	.02	.00
☐ 34	Ron Romanick	.05	.02	.00
☐ 35	Don Sutton	.15	.06	.01
☐ 36	Mike Witt	.10	.04	.01
☐ 37	Buddy Bell	.10	.04	.01
☐ 38	Tom Browning	.10	.04	.01
☐ 39	Dave Parker	.15	.06	.01
☐ 40	Pete Rose	.65	.26	.06
☐ 41	Mario Soto	.05	.02	.00
☐ 42	Harold Baines	.10	.04	.01
☐ 43	Carlton Fisk	.10	.04	.01
☐ 44	Ozzie Guillen	.10	.04	.01
☐ 45	Ron Kittle	.10	.04	.01
☐ 46	Tom Seaver	.20	.08	.02
☐ 47	Kirk Gibson	.25	.10	.02
☐ 48	Jack Morris	.10	.04	.01
☐ 49	Lance Parrish	.10	.04	.01
☐ 50	Alan Trammell	.15	.06	.01
☐ 51	Lou Whitaker	.10	.04	.01
☐ 52	Hubie Brooks	.10	.04	.01
☐ 53	Andre Dawson	.25	.10	.02
☐ 54	Tim Raines	.20	.08	.02
☐ 55	Bryn Smith	.05	.02	.00
☐ 56	Tim Wallach	.10	.04	.01
☐ 57	Mike Boddicker	.10	.04	.01
☐ 58	Eddie Murray	.25	.10	.02
☐ 59	Cal Ripken	.25	.10	.02
☐ 60	John Shelby	.05	.02	.00
☐ 61	Mike Young	.05	.02	.00
☐ 62	Jose Cruz	.05	.02	.00
☐ 63	Glenn Davis	.15	.06	.01
☐ 64	Phil Garner	.05	.02	.00
☐ 65	Nolan Ryan	.25	.10	.02
☐ 66	Mike Scott	.15	.06	.01
☐ 67	Steve Garvey	.20	.08	.02
☐ 68	Goose Gossage	.10	.04	.01
☐ 69	Tony Gwynn	.30	.12	.03
☐ 70	Andy Hawkins	.05	.02	.00
☐ 71	Garry Templeton	.05	.02	.00
☐ 72	Wade Boggs	.90	.36	.09
☐ 73	Roger Clemens	.75	.30	.07
☐ 74	Dwight Evans	.15	.06	.01
☐ 75	Rich Gedman	.05	.02	.00
☐ 76	Jim Rice	.20	.08	.02
☐ 77	Shawon Dunston	.10	.04	.01
☐ 78	Leon Durham	.05	.02	.00
☐ 79	Keith Moreland	.05	.02	.00
☐ 80	Ryne Sandberg	.20	.08	.02
☐ 81	Rick Sutcliffe	.10	.04	.01
☐ 82	Bert Blyleven	.10	.04	.01
☐ 83	Tom Brunansky	.10	.04	.01
☐ 84	Kent Hrbek	.15	.06	.01
☐ 85	Kirby Puckett	.35	.14	.03
☐ 86	Bruce Bochte	.05	.02	.00
☐ 87	Jose Canseco	2.50	1.00	.25
☐ 88	Mike Davis	.05	.02	.00
☐ 89	Jay Howell	.05	.02	.00
☐ 90	Dwayne Murphy	.05	.02	.00
☐ 91	Steve Carlton	.20	.08	.02
☐ 92	Von Hayes	.10	.04	.01
☐ 93	Juan Samuel	.15	.06	.01
☐ 94	Mike Schmidt	.35	.14	.03
☐ 95	Glenn Wilson	.05	.02	.00
☐ 96	Phil Bradley	.10	.04	.01
☐ 97	Alvin Davis	.10	.04	.01
☐ 98	Jim Presley	.10	.04	.01
☐ 99	Danny Tartabull	.20	.08	.02
☐ 100	Cecil Cooper	.10	.04	.01
☐ 101	Paul Molitor	.15	.06	.01

□ 102 Ernie Riles	.05	.02	.00
□ 103 Robin Yount	.20	.08	.02
□ 104 Bob Horner	.10	.04	.01
□ 105 Dale Murphy	.35	.14	.03
□ 106 Bruce Sutter	.10	.04	.01
□ 107 Claudell Washington	.05	.02	.00
□ 108 Chris Brown	.10	.04	.01
□ 109 Chili Davis	.05	.02	.00
□ 110 Scott Garrelts	.05	.02	.00
□ 111 Oddibe McDowell	.10	.04	.01
□ 112 Pete O'Brien	.10	.04	.01
□ 113 Gary Ward	.05	.02	.00
□ 114 Brett Butler	.10	.04	.01
□ 115 Julio Franco	.10	.04	.01
□ 116 Brook Jacoby	.10	.04	.01
□ 117 Mike Brown OF	.05	.02	.00
□ 118 Joe Orsulak	.05	.02	.00
□ 119 Tony Pena	.05	.02	.00
□ 120 R.J. Reynolds	.05	.02	.00

1986 Fleer Sluggers/Pitchers

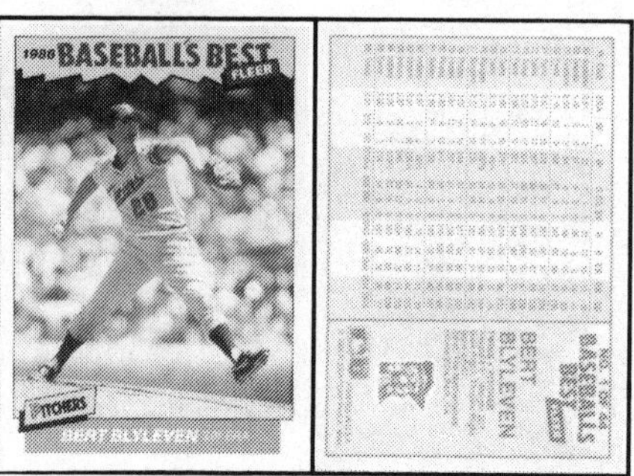

Fleer produced this 44-card boxed set although it was primarily distributed by Kress, McCrory, Newberry, T.G.Y., and other similar stores. The set features 22 sluggers and 22 pitchers and is subtitled "Baseball's Best". Cards are standard- size, 2 1/2" by 3 1/2", and were packaged in a red, white, blue, and yellow custom box along with six logo stickers. The set checklist is given on the back of the box.

	MINT	EXC	G-VG
COMPLETE SET (44)	5.00	2.00	.50
COMMON PLAYER (1-44)	.10	.04	.01
□ 1 Bert Blyleven	.15	.06	.01
□ 2 Wade Boggs	.75	.30	.07
□ 3 George Brett	.35	.14	.03
□ 4 Tom Browning	.10	.04	.01
□ 5 Jose Canseco	2.00	.80	.20
□ 6 Will Clark	.75	.30	.07
□ 7 Roger Clemens	.60	.24	.06
□ 8 Alvin Davis	.15	.06	.01
□ 9 Julio Franco	.15	.06	.01
□ 10 Kirk Gibson	.30	.12	.03
□ 11 Dwight Gooden	.50	.20	.05
□ 12 Goose Gossage	.15	.06	.01
□ 13 Pedro Guerrero	.20	.08	.02
□ 14 Ron Guidry	.15	.06	.01
□ 15 Tony Gwynn	.35	.14	.03
□ 16 Orel Hershiser	.50	.20	.05
□ 17 Kent Hrbek	.20	.08	.02
□ 18 Reggie Jackson	.40	.16	.04
□ 19 Wally Joyner	1.25	.50	.12
□ 20 Charlie Leibrandt	.10	.04	.01
□ 21 Don Mattingly	1.00	.40	.10
□ 22 Willie McGee	.20	.08	.02
□ 23 Jack Morris	.20	.08	.02
□ 24 Dale Murphy	.45	.18	.04
□ 25 Eddie Murray	.30	.12	.03
□ 26 Jeff Reardon	.10	.04	.01
□ 27 Rick Reuschel	.15	.06	.01
□ 28 Cal Ripken	.30	.12	.03
□ 29 Pete Rose	.60	.24	.06
□ 30 Nolan Ryan	.35	.14	.03
□ 31 Bret Saberhagen	.20	.08	.02
□ 32 Ryne Sandberg	.25	.10	.02
□ 33 Mike Schmidt	.50	.20	.05
□ 34 Tom Seaver	.30	.12	.0
□ 35 Bryn Smith	.10	.04	.0
□ 36 Mario Soto	.10	.04	.0
□ 37 Dave Stieb	.15	.06	.0
□ 38 Darryl Strawberry	.60	.24	.0
□ 39 Rick Sutcliffe	.15	.06	.0
□ 40 John Tudor	.15	.06	.0
□ 41 Fernando Valenzuela	.20	.08	.0
□ 42 Bobby Witt	.25	.10	.0
□ 43 Mike Witt	.15	.06	.0
□ 44 Robin Yount	.25	.10	.0

1986 Fleer Slug/Pitch Box Cards

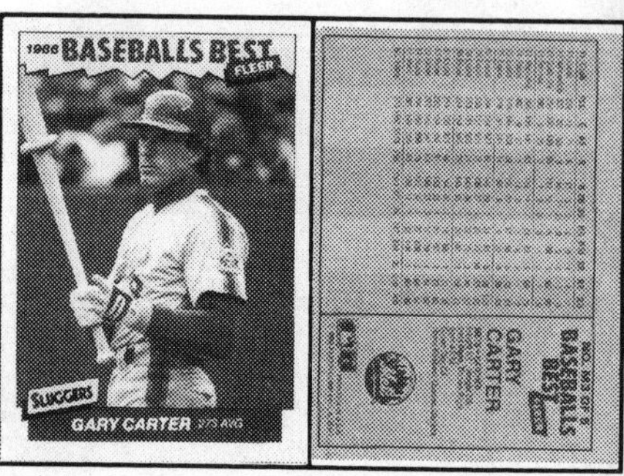

The cards in this 6-card set each measure the standard 2 1/2" by 3 1/2". Cards have essentially the same design as the 1986 Fleer Sluggers vs. Pitchers set of Baseball's Best. The cards were printed on the bottom of the counter display box which held 24 small boxed sets; hence theoretically these box cards are 1/24 as plentiful as the regular boxed set cards. These 6 cards, numbered M1 to M5 with one blank-back (unnumbered) card, are considered a separate set in their own right and are not typically included in a complete set of the 1986 Fleer Sluggers vs. Pitchers set of 44. The value of the panels uncut is slightly greater, perhaps by 25% greater, than the value of the individual cards cut up carefully.

	MINT	EXC	G-VG
COMPLETE SET	2.50	1.00	.25
COMMON PLAYERS	.10	.04	.01
□ M1 Harold Baines	.20	.08	.02
□ M2 Steve Carlton	.80	.32	.08
□ M3 Gary Carter	.60	.24	.06
□ M4 Vince Coleman	.80	.32	.08
□ M5 Kirby Puckett	1.00	.40	.10
□ xx Team Logo (unnumbered, blank back)	.10	.04	.01

1986 Fleer Sticker Cards

The stickers in this 132-sticker card set are standard card size, 2 1/2" by 3 1/2". The card photo on the front is surrounded by a yellow border and a cranberry frame. The backs are printed in blue and black on white card stock. The backs contain year by year statistical information. They are numbered on the back in the upper left hand corner.

	MINT	EXC	G-VG
COMPLETE SET (132)	24.00	10.00	2.40
COMMON PLAYER (1-132)	.05	.02	.00
□ 1 Harold Baines	.15	.06	.01
□ 2 Jesse Barfield	.20	.08	.02

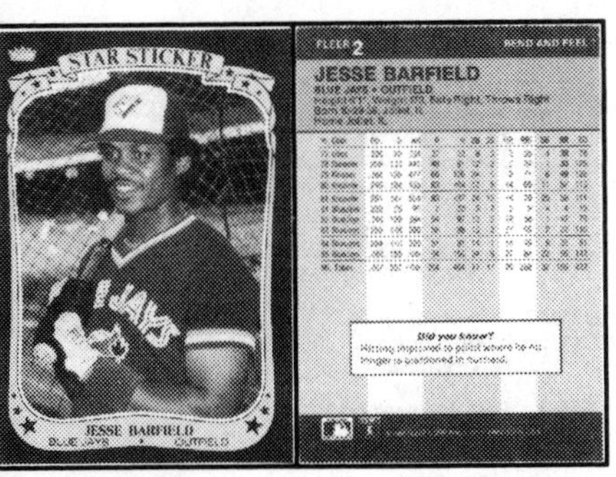

□ 3	Don Baylor	.10	.04	.01
□ 4	Juan Beniquez	.05	.02	.00
□ 5	Tim Birtsas	.05	.02	.00
□ 6	Bert Blyleven	.10	.04	.01
□ 7	Bruce Bochte	.05	.02	.00
□ 8	Wade Boggs	1.50	.60	.15
□ 9	Dennis Boyd	.10	.04	.01
□ 10	Phil Bradley	.10	.04	.01
□ 11	George Brett	.75	.30	.07
□ 12	Hubie Brooks	.10	.04	.01
□ 13	Chris Brown	.25	.10	.02
□ 14	Tom Browning	.15	.06	.01
□ 15	Tom Brunansky	.15	.06	.01
□ 16	Bill Buckner	.10	.04	.01
□ 17	Britt Burns	.05	.02	.00
□ 18	Brett Butler	.10	.04	.01
□ 19	Jose Canseco	4.00	1.60	.40
□ 20	Rod Carew	.40	.16	.04
□ 21	Steve Carlton	.40	.16	.04
□ 22	Don Carman	.15	.06	.01
□ 23	Gary Carter	.45	.18	.04
□ 24	Jack Clark	.30	.12	.03
□ 25	Vince Coleman	1.00	.40	.10
□ 26	Cecil Cooper	.10	.04	.01
□ 27	Jose Cruz	.05	.02	.00
□ 28	Ron Darling	.20	.08	.02
□ 29	Alvin Davis	.20	.08	.02
□ 30	Jody Davis	.10	.04	.01
□ 31	Mike Davis	.05	.02	.00
□ 32	Andre Dawson	.35	.14	.03
□ 33	Mariano Duncan	.15	.06	.01
□ 34	Shawon Dunston	.10	.04	.01
□ 35	Leon Durham	.05	.02	.00
□ 36	Darrell Evans	.10	.04	.01
□ 37	Tony Fernandez	.15	.06	.01
□ 38	Carlton Fisk	.20	.08	.02
□ 39	John Franco	.10	.04	.01
□ 40	Julio Franco	.10	.04	.01
□ 41	Damaso Garcia	.05	.02	.00
□ 42	Scott Garrelts	.05	.02	.00
□ 43	Steve Garvey	.50	.20	.05
□ 44	Rich Gedman	.10	.04	.01
□ 45	Kirk Gibson	.35	.14	.03
□ 46	Dwight Gooden	1.00	.40	.10
□ 47	Pedro Guerrero	.20	.08	.02
□ 48	Ron Guidry	.15	.06	.01
□ 49	Ozzie Guillen	.15	.06	.01
□ 50	Tony Gwynn	.45	.18	.04
□ 51	Andy Hawkins	.05	.02	.00
□ 52	Von Hayes	.10	.04	.01
□ 53	Rickey Henderson	.65	.26	.06
□ 54	Tom Henke	.10	.04	.01
□ 55	Keith Hernandez	.30	.12	.03
□ 56	Willie Hernandez	.10	.04	.01
□ 57	Tommy Herr	.05	.02	.00
□ 58	Orel Hershiser	.60	.24	.06
□ 59	Teddy Higuera	.60	.24	.06
□ 60	Bob Horner	.20	.08	.02
□ 61	Charlie Hough	.05	.02	.00
□ 62	Jay Howell	.05	.02	.00
□ 63	LaMarr Hoyt	.05	.02	.00
□ 64	Kent Hrbek	.20	.08	.02
□ 65	Reggie Jackson	.50	.20	.05
□ 66	Bob James	.05	.02	.00
□ 67	Dave Kingman	.10	.04	.01
□ 68	Ron Kittle	.10	.04	.01
□ 69	Charlie Leibrandt	.10	.04	.01
□ 70	Fred Lynn	.15	.06	.01
□ 71	Mike Marshall	.15	.06	.01
□ 72	Don Mattingly	2.50	1.00	.25
□ 73	Oddibe McDowell	.25	.10	.02
□ 74	Willie McGee	.20	.08	.02
□ 75	Scott McGregor	.10	.04	.01
□ 76	Paul Molitor	.25	.10	.02
□ 77	Charlie Moore	.05	.02	.00
□ 78	Keith Moreland	.10	.04	.01
□ 79	Jack Morris	.15	.06	.01
□ 80	Dale Murphy	.75	.30	.07
□ 81	Eddie Murray	.60	.24	.06
□ 82	Phil Niekro	.25	.10	.02
□ 83	Joe Orsulak	.10	.04	.01
□ 84	Dave Parker	.15	.06	.01
□ 85	Lance Parrish	.15	.06	.01
□ 86	Larry Parrish	.10	.04	.01
□ 87	Tony Pena	.10	.04	.01
□ 88	Gary Pettis	.10	.04	.01
□ 89	Jim Presley	.20	.08	.02
□ 90	Kirby Puckett	.90	.36	.09
□ 91	Dan Quisenberry	.15	.06	.01
□ 92	Tim Raines	.25	.10	.02
□ 93	Johnny Ray	.10	.04	.01
□ 94	Jeff Reardon	.15	.06	.01
□ 95	Rick Reuschel	.15	.06	.01
□ 96	Jim Rice	.25	.10	.02
□ 97	Dave Righetti	.15	.06	.01
□ 98	Earnie Riles	.10	.04	.01
□ 99	Cal Ripken	.45	.18	.04
□ 100	Ron Romanick	.05	.02	.00
□ 101	Pete Rose	1.00	.40	.10
□ 102	Nolan Ryan	.65	.26	.06
□ 103	Bret Saberhagen	.40	.16	.04
□ 104	Mark Salas	.10	.04	.01
□ 105	Juan Samuel	.20	.08	.02
□ 106	Ryne Sandberg	.40	.16	.04
□ 107	Mike Schmidt	.60	.24	.06
□ 108	Mike Scott	.20	.08	.02
□ 109	Tom Seaver	.35	.14	.03
□ 110	Bryn Smith	.05	.02	.00
□ 111	Dave Smith	.05	.02	.00
□ 112	Lonnie Smith	.05	.02	.00
□ 113	Ozzie Smith	.25	.10	.02
□ 114	Mario Soto	.05	.02	.00
□ 115	Dave Stieb	.10	.04	.01
□ 116	Darryl Strawberry	.75	.30	.07
□ 117	Bruce Sutter	.10	.04	.01
□ 118	Garry Templeton	.05	.02	.00
□ 119	Gorman Thomas	.10	.04	.01
□ 120	Andre Thornton	.05	.02	.00
□ 121	Alan Trammell	.25	.10	.02
□ 122	John Tudor	.15	.06	.01
□ 123	Fernando Valenzuela	.20	.08	.02
□ 124	Frank Viola	.20	.08	.02
□ 125	Gary Ward	.05	.02	.00
□ 126	Lou Whitaker	.15	.06	.01
□ 127	Frank White	.10	.04	.01
□ 128	Glenn Wilson	.05	.02	.00
□ 129	Willie Wilson	.15	.06	.01
□ 130	Dave Winfield	.35	.14	.03
□ 131	Robin Yount	.35	.14	.03
□ 132	Checklist Card Dwight Gooden Dale Murphy	1.50	.60	.15

1986 Fleer Sticker Wax Box

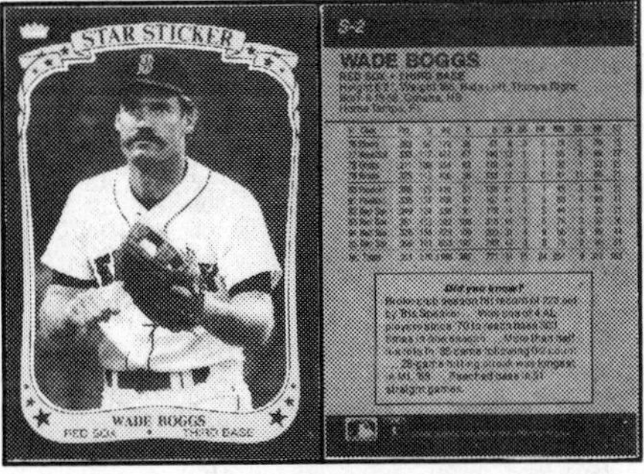

The bottoms of the Star Sticker wax boxes contained a set of four cards done in a similar format to the stickers; these cards (they are not stickers but truly cards) are numbered with the prefix S and are considered a separate set. Each individual card measures 2 1/2" by 3 1/2". The value of the panel uncut is slightly greater, perhaps by 25% greater, than the value of the individual cards cut up carefully.

	MINT	EXC	G-VG
COMPLETE SET (4)	1.50	.60	.15
COMMON PLAYER (S1-S4)	.10	.04	.01
□ S1 Team Logo (checklist back)	.10	.04	.01
□ S2 Wade Boggs	1.00	.40	.10
□ S3 Steve Garvey	.40	.16	.04
□ S4 Dave Winfield	.40	.16	.04

1986 Fleer Update

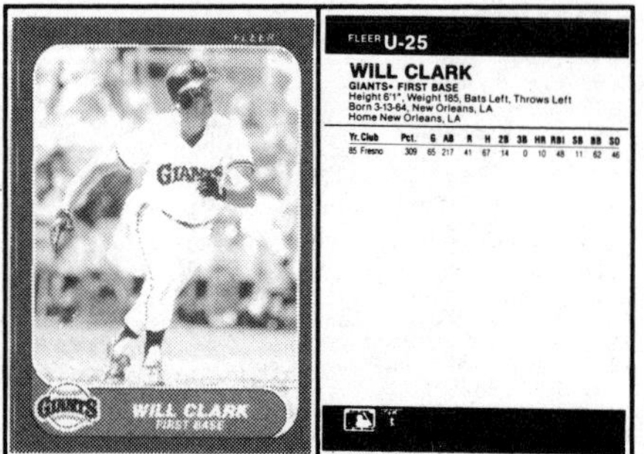

This 132-card set was distributed by Fleer to dealers as a complete set within a custom box. In addition to the complete set of 132 cards, the box also contains 25 Team Logo Stickers. The card fronts look very similar to the 1986 Fleer regular issue. The cards are numbered (with a U prefix) alphabetically according to player's last name. Cards measure the standard size, 2 1/2" by 3 1/2".

	MINT	EXC	G-VG
COMPLETE SET (132)	18.00	7.25	1.80
COMMON PLAYER (1-132)	.06	.02	.00
□ U1 Mike Aldrete	.30	.12	.03
□ U2 Andy Allanson	.15	.06	.01
□ U3 Neil Allen	.06	.02	.00
□ U4 Joaquin Andujar	.10	.04	.01
□ U5 Paul Assenmacher	.15	.06	.01
□ U6 Scott Bailes	.15	.06	.01
□ U7 Jay Baller	.06	.02	.00
□ U8 Scott Bankhead	.10	.04	.01
□ U9 Bill Bathe	.10	.04	.01
□ U10 Don Baylor	.10	.04	.01
□ U11 Billy Beane	.15	.06	.01
□ U12 Steve Bedrosian	.12	.05	.01
□ U13 Juan Beniquez	.06	.02	.00
□ U14 Barry Bonds	1.25	.50	.12
□ U15 Bobby Bonilla (wrong birthday)	1.25	.50	.12
□ U16 Rich Bordi	.06	.02	.00
□ U17 Bill Campbell	.06	.02	.00
□ U18 Tom Candiotti	.06	.02	.00
□ U19 John Cangelosi	.15	.06	.01
□ U20 Jose Canseco (headings on back for a pitcher)	7.50	3.00	.75
□ U21 Chuck Cary	.15	.06	.01
□ U22 Juan Castillo	.10	.04	.01
□ U23 Rick Cerone	.06	.02	.00
□ U24 John Cerutti	.20	.08	.02
□ U25 Will Clark	3.50	1.40	.35
□ U26 Mark Clear	.06	.02	.00
□ U27 Darnell Coles	.10	.04	.01
□ U28 Dave Collins	.06	.02	.00
□ U29 Tim Conroy	.06	.02	.00
□ U30 Ed Correa	.20	.08	.02
□ U31 Joe Cowley	.06	.02	.00
□ U32 Bill Dawley	.06	.02	.00
□ U33 Rob Deer	.20	.08	.02
□ U34 John Denny	.10	.04	.01
□ U35 Jim Deshaies	.30	.12	.03
□ U36 Doug Drabek	.30	.12	.03
□ U37 Mike Easler	.06	.02	.00
□ U38 Mark Eichhorn	.15	.06	.01
□ U39 Dave Engle	.06	.02	.0
□ U40 Mike Fischlin	.06	.02	.0
□ U41 Scott Fletcher	.15	.06	.0
□ U42 Terry Forster	.10	.04	.0
□ U43 Terry Francona	.06	.02	.0
□ U44 Andres Galarraga	.90	.36	.0
□ U45 Lee Guetterman	.20	.08	.0
□ U46 Bill Gullickson	.06	.02	.0
□ U47 Jackie Gutierrez	.06	.02	.0
□ U48 Moose Haas	.06	.02	.0
□ U49 Billy Hatcher	.20	.08	.0
□ U50 Mike Heath	.06	.02	.0
□ U51 Guy Hoffman	.06	.02	.0
□ U52 Tom Hume	.06	.02	.0
□ U53 Pete Incaviglia	.75	.30	.0
□ U54 Dane Iorg	.06	.02	.0
□ U55 Chris James	.75	.30	.0
□ U56 Stan Javier	.30	.12	.0
□ U57 Tommy John	.20	.08	.0
□ U58 Tracy Jones	.55	.22	.0
□ U59 Wally Joyner	2.50	1.00	.2
□ U60 Wayne Krenchicki	.06	.02	.0
□ U61 John Kruk	.45	.18	.0
□ U62 Mike LaCoss	.06	.02	.0
□ U63 Pete Ladd	.06	.02	.0
□ U64 Dave LaPoint	.10	.04	.0
□ U65 Mike LaValliere	.25	.10	.0
□ U66 Rudy Law	.06	.02	.0
□ U67 Dennis Leonard	.10	.04	.0
□ U68 Steve Lombardozzi	.10	.04	.0
□ U69 Aurelio Lopez	.06	.02	.0
□ U70 Mickey Mahler	.06	.02	.0
□ U71 Candy Maldonado	.10	.04	.0
□ U72 Roger Mason	.10	.04	.0
□ U73 Greg Mathews	.25	.10	.0
□ U74 Andy McGaffigan	.06	.02	.0
□ U75 Joel McKeon	.10	.04	.0
□ U76 Kevin Mitchell	.45	.18	.0
□ U77 Bill Mooneyham	.10	.04	.0
□ U78 Omar Moreno	.06	.02	.0
□ U79 Jerry Mumphrey	.06	.02	.0
□ U80 Al Newman	.10	.04	.0
□ U81 Phil Niekro	.30	.12	.0
□ U82 Randy Niemann	.06	.02	.0
□ U83 Juan Nieves	.20	.08	.0
□ U84 Bob Ojeda	.15	.06	.0
□ U85 Rick Ownbey	.06	.02	.0
□ U86 Tom Paciorek	.06	.02	.0
□ U87 David Palmer	.06	.02	.0
□ U88 Jeff Parrett	.30	.12	.03
□ U89 Pat Perry	.15	.06	.01
□ U90 Dan Plesac	.35	.14	.03
□ U91 Darrell Porter	.06	.02	.00
□ U92 Luis Quinones	.15	.06	.01
□ U93 Rey Quinones	.25	.10	.02
□ U94 Gary Redus	.06	.02	.00
□ U95 Jeff Reed	.10	.04	.01
□ U96 Bip Roberts	.10	.04	.01
□ U97 Billy Joe Robidoux	.10	.04	.01
□ U98 Gary Roenicke	.06	.02	.00
□ U99 Ron Roenicke	.06	.02	.00
□ U100 Angel Salazar	.06	.02	.00
□ U101 Joe Sambito	.06	.02	.00
□ U102 Billy Sample	.06	.02	.00
□ U103 Dave Schmidt	.10	.04	.01
□ U104 Ken Schrom	.06	.02	.00
□ U105 Ruben Sierra	1.75	.70	.17
□ U106 Ted Simmons	.20	.08	.02
□ U107 Sammy Stewart	.06	.02	.00
□ U108 Kurt Stillwell	.35	.14	.03
□ U109 Dale Sveum	.35	.14	.03
□ U110 Tim Teufel	.10	.04	.01
□ U111 Bob Tewksbury	.15	.06	.01
□ U112 Andres Thomas	.25	.10	.02
□ U113 Jason Thompson	.06	.02	.00
□ U114 Milt Thompson	.10	.04	.01
□ U115 Rob Thompson	.30	.12	.03
□ U116 Jay Tibbs	.06	.02	.00
□ U117 Fred Toliver	.10	.04	.01
□ U118 Wayne Tolleson	.06	.02	.00
□ U119 Alex Trevino	.06	.02	.00
□ U120 Manny Trillo	.06	.02	.00
□ U121 Ed VandeBerg	.06	.02	.00
□ U122 Ozzie Virgil	.06	.02	.00
□ U123 Tony Walker	.10	.04	.01
□ U124 Gene Walter	.10	.04	.01
□ U125 Duane Ward	.20	.08	.02
□ U126 Jerry Willard	.06	.02	.00
□ U127 Mitch Williams	.25	.10	.02
□ U128 Reggie Williams	.10	.04	.01
□ U129 Bobby Witt	.45	.18	.04
□ U130 Marvell Wynne	.06	.02	.00
□ U131 Steve Yeager	.06	.02	.00
□ U132 Checklist Card	.06	.01	.00

1987 Fleer

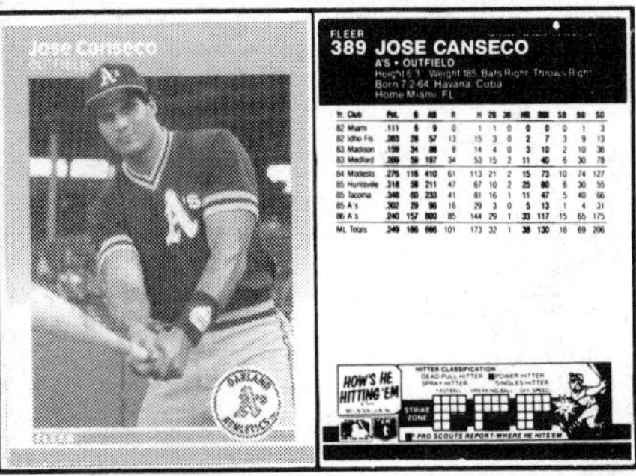

This 660-card set features a distinctive blue border which fades to white on the card fronts. The backs are printed in blue, red, and pink on white card stock. The bottom of the card back shows an innovative graph of the player's ability, e.g., "He's got the stuff" for pitchers and "How he's hitting 'em," for hitters. Cards are numbered on the back and are again the standard 2 1/2" by 3 1/2". Cards are again organized numerically by teams, i.e., World Champion Mets (1-25), Boston Red Sox (26-48), Houston Astros (49-72), California Angels (73- 95), New York Yankees (96-120), Texas Rangers (121-143), Detroit Tigers (144-168), Philadelphia Phillies (169-192), Cincinnati Reds (193-218), Toronto Blue Jays (219-240), Cleveland Indians (241-263), San Francisco Giants (264-288), St. Louis Cardinals (289-312), Montreal Expos (313-337), Milwaukee Brewers (338-361), Kansas City Royals (362-384), Oakland A's (385-410), San Diego Padres (411-435), Los Angeles Dodgers (436-460), Baltimore Orioles (461-483), Chicago White Sox (484-508), Atlanta Braves (509-532), Minnesota Twins (533-554), Chicago Cubs (555-578), Seattle Mariners (579-600), and Pittsburgh Pirates (601-624). The last 36 cards in the set consist of Specials (625-643), Rookie Pairs (644-653), and checklists (654-660).

	MINT	EXC	G-VG
COMPLETE SET (660)	45.00	18.00	4.50
COMMON PLAYER (1-660)	.04	.02	.00

	MINT	EXC	G-VG
□ 1 Rick Aguilera	.10	.03	.01
□ 2 Richard Anderson	.10	.04	.01
□ 3 Wally Backman	.07	.03	.01
□ 4 Gary Carter	.25	.10	.02
□ 5 Ron Darling	.18	.08	.01
□ 6 Len Dykstra	.12	.05	.01
□ 7 Kevin Elster	.65	.26	.06
□ 8 Sid Fernandez	.12	.05	.01
□ 9 Dwight Gooden	1.00	.40	.10
□ 10 Ed Hearn	.10	.04	.01
□ 11 Danny Heep	.04	.02	.00
□ 12 Keith Hernandez	.25	.10	.02
□ 13 Howard Johnson	.15	.06	.01
□ 14 Ray Knight	.07	.03	.01
□ 15 Lee Mazzilli	.04	.02	.00
□ 16 Roger McDowell	.07	.03	.01
□ 17 Kevin Mitchell	.30	.12	.03
□ 18 Randy Niemann	.04	.02	.00
□ 19 Bob Ojeda	.07	.03	.01
□ 20 Jesse Orosco	.04	.02	.00
□ 21 Rafael Santana	.04	.02	.00
□ 22 Doug Sisk	.04	.02	.00
□ 23 Darryl Strawberry	.80	.32	.08
□ 24 Tim Teufel	.04	.02	.00
□ 25 Mookie Wilson	.07	.03	.01
□ 26 Tony Armas	.07	.03	.01
□ 27 Marty Barrett	.10	.04	.01
□ 28 Don Baylor	.10	.04	.01
□ 29 Wade Boggs	1.50	.60	.15
□ 30 Oil Can Boyd	.07	.03	.01
□ 31 Bill Buckner	.07	.03	.01
□ 32 Roger Clemens	1.50	.60	.15
□ 33 Steve Crawford	.04	.02	.00
□ 34 Dwight Evans	.12	.05	.01
□ 35 Rich Gedman	.07	.03	.01
□ 36 Dave Henderson	.07	.03	.01
□ 37 Bruce Hurst	.12	.05	.01
□ 38 Tim Lollar	.04	.02	.00
□ 39 Al Nipper	.04	.02	.00
□ 40 Spike Owen	.04	.02	.00
□ 41 Jim Rice	.18	.08	.01
□ 42 Ed Romero	.04	.02	.00
□ 43 Joe Sambito	.04	.02	.00
□ 44 Calvin Schiraldi	.07	.03	.01
□ 45 Tom Seaver	.30	.12	.03
□ 46 Jeff Sellers	.15	.06	.01
□ 47 Bob Stanley	.04	.02	.00
□ 48 Sammy Stewart	.04	.02	.00
□ 49 Larry Andersen	.04	.02	.00
□ 50 Alan Ashby	.04	.02	.00
□ 51 Kevin Bass	.10	.04	.01
□ 52 Jeff Calhoun	.04	.02	.00
□ 53 Jose Cruz	.10	.04	.01
□ 54 Danny Darwin	.04	.02	.00
□ 55 Glenn Davis	.30	.12	.03
□ 56 Jim Deshaies	.25	.10	.02
□ 57 Bill Doran	.10	.04	.01
□ 58 Phil Garner	.04	.02	.00
□ 59 Billy Hatcher	.10	.04	.01
□ 60 Charlie Kerfeld	.04	.02	.00
□ 61 Bob Knepper	.07	.03	.01
□ 62 Dave Lopes	.07	.03	.01
□ 63 Aurelio Lopez	.04	.02	.00
□ 64 Jim Pankovits	.04	.02	.00
□ 65 Terry Puhl	.04	.02	.00
□ 66 Craig Reynolds	.04	.02	.00
□ 67 Nolan Ryan	.30	.12	.03
□ 68 Mike Scott	.25	.10	.02
□ 69 Dave Smith	.07	.03	.01
□ 70 Dickie Thon	.04	.02	.00
□ 71 Tony Walker	.10	.04	.01
□ 72 Denny Walling	.04	.02	.00
□ 73 Bob Boone	.10	.04	.01
□ 74 Rick Burleson	.07	.03	.01
□ 75 John Candelaria	.07	.03	.01
□ 76 Doug Corbett	.04	.02	.00
□ 77 Doug DeCinces	.07	.03	.01
□ 78 Brian Downing	.07	.03	.01
□ 79 Chuck Finley	.10	.04	.01
□ 80 Terry Forster	.07	.03	.01
□ 81 Bob Grich	.07	.03	.01
□ 82 George Hendrick	.07	.03	.01
□ 83 Jack Howell	.15	.06	.01
□ 84 Reggie Jackson	.35	.14	.03
□ 85 Ruppert Jones	.04	.02	.00
□ 86 Wally Joyner	1.75	.70	.17
□ 87 Gary Lucas	.04	.02	.00
□ 88 Kirk McCaskill	.04	.02	.00
□ 89 Donnie Moore	.04	.02	.00
□ 90 Gary Pettis	.04	.02	.00
□ 91 Vern Ruhle	.04	.02	.00
□ 92 Dick Schofield	.04	.02	.00
□ 93 Don Sutton	.12	.05	.01
□ 94 Rob Wilfong	.04	.02	.00
□ 95 Mike Witt	.10	.04	.01
□ 96 Doug Drabek	.25	.10	.02
□ 97 Mike Easler	.04	.02	.00
□ 98 Mike Fischlin	.04	.02	.00
□ 99 Brian Fisher	.04	.02	.00
□ 100 Ron Guidry	.12	.05	.01
□ 101 Rickey Henderson	.30	.12	.03
□ 102 Tommy John	.12	.05	.01
□ 103 Ron Kittle	.10	.04	.01
□ 104 Don Mattingly	2.50	1.00	.25
□ 105 Bobby Meacham	.04	.02	.00
□ 106 Joe Niekro	.10	.04	.01
□ 107 Mike Pagliarulo	.10	.04	.01
□ 108 Dan Pasqua	.10	.04	.01
□ 109 Willie Randolph	.07	.03	.01
□ 110 Dennis Rasmussen	.07	.03	.01
□ 111 Dave Righetti	.10	.04	.01
□ 112 Gary Roenicke	.04	.02	.00
□ 113 Rod Scurry	.04	.02	.00
□ 114 Bob Shirley	.04	.02	.00
□ 115 Joel Skinner	.04	.02	.00
□ 116 Tim Stoddard	.04	.02	.00
□ 117 Bob Tewksbury	.10	.04	.01
□ 118 Wayne Tolleson	.04	.02	.00
□ 119 Claudell Washington	.07	.03	.01
□ 120 Dave Winfield	.25	.10	.02
□ 121 Steve Buechele	.04	.02	.00
□ 122 Ed Correa	.20	.08	.02
□ 123 Scott Fletcher	.07	.03	.01
□ 124 Jose Guzman	.07	.03	.01
□ 125 Toby Harrah	.04	.02	.00
□ 126 Greg Harris	.04	.02	.00

□ 127	Charlie Hough	.07	.03	.01
□ 128	Pete Incaviglia	.75	.30	.07
□ 129	Mike Mason	.04	.02	.00
□ 130	Oddibe McDowell	.10	.04	.01
□ 131	Dave Mohorcic	.15	.06	.01
□ 132	Pete O'Brien	.10	.04	.01
□ 133	Tom Paciorek	.04	.02	.00
□ 134	Larry Parrish	.07	.03	.01
□ 135	Geno Petralli	.04	.02	.00
□ 136	Darrell Porter	.04	.02	.00
□ 137	Jeff Russell	.04	.02	.00
□ 138	Ruben Sierra	1.25	.50	.12
□ 139	Don Slaught	.04	.02	.00
□ 140	Gary Ward	.07	.03	.01
□ 141	Curtis Wilkerson	.04	.02	.00
□ 142	Mitch Williams	.20	.08	.02
□ 143	Bobby Witt	.35	.14	.03
□ 144	Dave Bergman	.04	.02	.00
□ 145	Tom Brookens	.04	.02	.00
□ 146	Bill Campbell	.04	.02	.00
□ 147	Chuck Cary	.15	.06	.01
□ 148	Darnell Coles	.07	.03	.01
□ 149	Dave Collins	.04	.02	.00
□ 150	Darrell Evans	.10	.04	.01
□ 151	Kirk Gibson	.25	.10	.02
□ 152	John Grubb	.04	.02	.00
□ 153	Willie Hernandez	.10	.04	.01
□ 154	Larry Herndon	.04	.02	.00
□ 155	Eric King	.15	.06	.01
□ 156	Chet Lemon	.04	.02	.00
□ 157	Dwight Lowry	.10	.04	.01
□ 158	Jack Morris	.12	.05	.01
□ 159	Randy O'Neal	.04	.02	.00
□ 160	Lance Parrish	.12	.05	.01
□ 161	Dan Petry	.07	.03	.01
□ 162	Pat Sheridan	.04	.02	.00
□ 163	Jim Slaton	.04	.02	.00
□ 164	Frank Tanana	.07	.03	.01
□ 165	Walt Terrell	.04	.02	.00
□ 166	Mark Thurmond	.04	.02	.00
□ 167	Alan Trammell	.18	.08	.01
□ 168	Lou Whitaker	.10	.04	.01
□ 169	Luis Aguayo	.04	.02	.00
□ 170	Steve Bedrosian	.10	.04	.01
□ 171	Don Carman	.04	.02	.00
□ 172	Darren Daulton	.04	.02	.00
□ 173	Greg Gross	.04	.02	.00
□ 174	Kevin Gross	.04	.02	.00
□ 175	Von Hayes	.10	.04	.01
□ 176	Charles Hudson	.04	.02	.00
□ 177	Tom Hume	.04	.02	.00
□ 178	Steve Jeltz	.04	.02	.00
□ 179	Mike Maddux	.15	.06	.01
□ 180	Shane Rawley	.07	.03	.01
□ 181	Gary Redus	.04	.02	.00
□ 182	Ron Roenicke	.04	.02	.00
□ 183	Bruce Ruffin	.20	.08	.02
□ 184	John Russell	.04	.02	.00
□ 185	Juan Samuel	.12	.05	.01
□ 186	Dan Schatzeder	.04	.02	.00
□ 187	Mike Schmidt	.35	.14	.03
□ 188	Rick Schu	.04	.02	.00
□ 189	Jeff Stone	.04	.02	.00
□ 190	Kent Tekulve	.04	.02	.00
□ 191	Milt Thompson	.07	.03	.01
□ 192	Glenn Wilson	.07	.03	.01
□ 193	Buddy Bell	.10	.04	.01
□ 194	Tom Browning	.12	.05	.01
□ 195	Sal Butera	.04	.02	.00
□ 196	Dave Concepcion	.10	.04	.01
□ 197	Kal Daniels	.90	.36	.09
□ 198	Eric Davis	1.50	.60	.15
□ 199	John Denny	.07	.03	.01
□ 200	Bo Diaz	.04	.02	.00
□ 201	Nick Esasky	.04	.02	.00
□ 202	John Franco	.10	.04	.01
□ 203	Bill Gullickson	.04	.02	.00
□ 204	Barry Larkin	1.25	.50	.12
□ 205	Eddie Milner	.04	.02	.00
□ 206	Rob Murphy	.25	.10	.02
□ 207	Ron Oester	.04	.02	.00
□ 208	Dave Parker	.12	.05	.01
□ 209	Tony Perez	.12	.05	.01
□ 210	Ted Power	.04	.02	.00
□ 211	Joe Price	.04	.02	.00
□ 212	Ron Robinson	.04	.02	.00
□ 213	Pete Rose	.60	.24	.06
□ 214	Mario Soto	.04	.02	.00
□ 215	Kurt Stillwell	.25	.10	.02
□ 216	Max Venable	.04	.02	.00
□ 217	Chris Welsh	.04	.02	.00
□ 218	Carl Willis	.07	.03	.01
□ 219	Jesse Barfield	.18	.08	.01
□ 220	George Bell	.25	.10	.02
□ 221	Bill Caudill	.04	.02	.00
□ 222	John Cerutti	.15	.06	.01
□ 223	Jim Clancy	.04	.02	.00
□ 224	Mark Eichhorn	.12	.05	.01
□ 225	Tony Fernandez	.12	.05	.01
□ 226	Damaso Garcia	.04	.02	.00
□ 227	Kelly Gruber ERR (wrong birth year)	.04	.02	.00
□ 228	Tom Henke	.07	.03	.01
□ 229	Garth Iorg	.04	.02	.00
□ 230	Joe Johnson	.04	.02	.00
□ 231	Cliff Johnson	.04	.02	.00
□ 232	Jimmy Key	.10	.04	.01
□ 233	Dennis Lamp	.04	.02	.00
□ 234	Rick Leach	.04	.02	.00
□ 235	Buck Martinez	.04	.02	.00
□ 236	Lloyd Moseby	.10	.04	.01
□ 237	Rance Mulliniks	.04	.02	.00
□ 238	Dave Stieb	.10	.04	.01
□ 239	Willie Upshaw	.04	.02	.00
□ 240	Ernie Whitt	.04	.02	.00
□ 241	Andy Allanson	.10	.04	.01
□ 242	Scott Bailes	.12	.05	.01
□ 243	Chris Bando	.04	.02	.00
□ 244	Tony Bernazard	.04	.02	.00
□ 245	John Butcher	.04	.02	.00
□ 246	Brett Butler	.07	.03	.01
□ 247	Ernie Camacho	.04	.02	.00
□ 248	Tom Candiotti	.04	.02	.00
□ 249	Joe Carter	.20	.08	.02
□ 250	Carmen Castillo	.04	.02	.00
□ 251	Julio Franco	.10	.04	.01
□ 252	Mel Hall	.07	.03	.01
□ 253	Brook Jacoby	.10	.04	.01
□ 254	Phil Niekro	.15	.06	.01
□ 255	Otis Nixon	.10	.04	.01
□ 256	Dickie Noles	.04	.02	.00
□ 257	Bryan Oelkers	.04	.02	.00
□ 258	Ken Schrom	.04	.02	.00
□ 259	Don Schulze	.04	.02	.00
□ 260	Cory Snyder	.80	.32	.08
□ 261	Pat Tabler	.10	.04	.01
□ 262	Andre Thornton	.07	.03	.01
□ 263	Rich Yett	.04	.02	.00
□ 264	Mike Aldrete	.25	.10	.02
□ 265	Juan Berenguer	.04	.02	.00
□ 266	Vida Blue	.07	.03	.01
□ 267	Bob Brenly	.04	.02	.00
□ 268	Chris Brown	.10	.04	.01
□ 269	Will Clark	2.50	1.00	.25
□ 270	Chili Davis	.10	.04	.01
□ 271	Mark Davis	.07	.03	.01
□ 272	Kelly Downs	.30	.12	.03
□ 273	Scott Garrelts	.04	.02	.00
□ 274	Dan Gladden	.07	.03	.01
□ 275	Mike Krukow	.04	.02	.00
□ 276	Randy Kutcher	.10	.04	.01
□ 277	Mike LaCoss	.04	.02	.00
□ 278	Jeff Leonard	.07	.03	.01
□ 279	Candy Maldonado	.07	.03	.01
□ 280	Roger Mason	.04	.02	.00
□ 281	Bob Melvin	.04	.02	.00
□ 282	Greg Minton	.04	.02	.00
□ 283	Jeff Robinson (Giants pitcher)	.07	.03	.01
□ 284	Harry Spilman	.04	.02	.00
□ 285	Robby Thompson	.25	.10	.02
□ 286	Jose Uribe	.04	.02	.00
□ 287	Frank Williams	.04	.02	.00
□ 288	Joel Youngblood	.04	.02	.00
□ 289	Jack Clark	.20	.08	.02
□ 290	Vince Coleman	.40	.16	.04
□ 291	Tim Conroy	.04	.02	.00
□ 292	Danny Cox	.07	.03	.01
□ 293	Ken Dayley	.04	.02	.00
□ 294	Curt Ford	.04	.02	.00
□ 295	Bob Forsch	.04	.02	.00
□ 296	Tom Herr	.07	.03	.01
□ 297	Ricky Horton	.04	.02	.00
□ 298	Clint Hurdle	.04	.02	.00
□ 299	Jeff Lahti	.04	.02	.00
□ 300	Steve Lake	.04	.02	.00
□ 301	Tito Landrum	.04	.02	.00
□ 302	Mike LaValliere	.20	.08	.02
□ 303	Greg Mathews	.20	.08	.02
□ 304	Willie McGee	.12	.05	.01
□ 305	Jose Oquendo	.04	.02	.00
□ 306	Terry Pendleton	.04	.02	.00
□ 307	Pat Perry	.04	.02	.00
□ 308	Ozzie Smith	.15	.06	.01
□ 309	Ray Soff	.07	.03	.01
□ 310	John Tudor	.10	.04	.01
□ 311	Andy Van Slyke ERR (Bats R, Throws L)	.20	.08	.02
□ 312	Todd Worrell	.20	.08	.02
□ 313	Dann Bilardello	.04	.02	.00

□ 314 Hubie Brooks .07 .03 .01
□ 315 Tim Burke .07 .03 .01
□ 316 Andre Dawson .30 .12 .03
□ 317 Mike Fitzgerald .04 .02 .00
□ 318 Tom Foley .04 .02 .00
□ 319 Andres Galarraga .35 .14 .03
□ 320 Joe Hesketh .04 .02 .00
□ 321 Wallace Johnson .04 .02 .00
□ 322 Wayne Krenchicki .04 .02 .00
□ 323 Vance Law .07 .03 .01
□ 324 Dennis Martinez .07 .03 .01
□ 325 Bob McClure .04 .02 .00
□ 326 Andy McGaffigan .04 .02 .00
□ 327 Al Newman .07 .03 .01
□ 328 Tim Raines .25 .10 .02
□ 329 Jeff Reardon .07 .03 .01
□ 330 Luis Rivera .07 .03 .01
□ 331 Bob Sebra .10 .04 .01
□ 332 Bryn Smith .04 .02 .00
□ 333 Jay Tibbs .04 .02 .00
□ 334 Tim Wallach .10 .04 .01
□ 335 Mitch Webster .04 .02 .00
□ 336 Jim Wohlford .04 .02 .00
□ 337 Floyd Youmans .07 .03 .01
□ 338 Chris Bosio .15 .06 .01
□ 339 Glenn Braggs .35 .14 .03
□ 340 Rick Cerone .04 .02 .00
□ 341 Mark Clear .04 .02 .00
□ 342 Bryan Clutterbuck .07 .03 .01
□ 343 Cecil Cooper .10 .04 .01
□ 344 Rob Deer .15 .06 .01
□ 345 Jim Gantner .04 .02 .00
□ 346 Ted Higuera .15 .06 .01
□ 347 John H. Johnson .04 .02 .00
□ 348 Tim Leary .30 .12 .03
□ 349 Rick Manning .04 .02 .00
□ 350 Paul Molitor .12 .05 .01
□ 351 Charlie Moore .04 .02 .00
□ 352 Juan Nieves .15 .06 .01
□ 353 Ben Oglivie .07 .03 .01
□ 354 Dan Plesac .30 .12 .03
□ 355 Ernest Riles .04 .02 .00
□ 356 Billy Jo Robidoux .04 .02 .00
□ 357 Bill Schroeder .04 .02 .00
□ 358 Dale Sveum .25 .10 .02
□ 359 Gorman Thomas .10 .04 .01
□ 360 Bill Wegman .07 .03 .01
□ 361 Robin Yount .25 .10 .02
□ 362 Steve Balboni .04 .02 .00
□ 363 Scott Bankhead .12 .05 .01
□ 364 Buddy Biancalana .04 .02 .00
□ 365 Bud Black .04 .02 .00
□ 366 George Brett .35 .14 .03
□ 367 Steve Farr .04 .02 .00
□ 368 Mark Gubicza .10 .04 .01
□ 369 Bo Jackson 1.25 .50 .12
□ 370 Danny Jackson .15 .06 .01
□ 371 Mike Kingery .12 .05 .01
□ 372 Rudy Law .04 .02 .00
□ 373 Charlie Leibrandt .04 .02 .00
□ 374 Dennis Leonard .04 .02 .00
□ 375 Hal McRae .07 .03 .01
□ 376 Jorge Orta .04 .02 .00
□ 377 Jamie Quirk .04 .02 .00
□ 378 Dan Quisenberry .10 .04 .01
□ 379 Bret Saberhagen .18 .08 .01
□ 380 Angel Salazar .04 .02 .00
□ 381 Lonnie Smith .04 .02 .00
□ 382 Jim Sundberg .04 .02 .00
□ 383 Frank White .07 .03 .01
□ 384 Willie Wilson .10 .04 .01
□ 385 Joaquin Andujar .07 .03 .01
□ 386 Doug Bair .04 .02 .00
□ 387 Dusty Baker .07 .03 .01
□ 388 Bruce Bochte .04 .02 .00
□ 389 Jose Canseco 6.00 2.40 .60
□ 390 Chris Codiroli .04 .02 .00
□ 391 Mike Davis .04 .02 .00
□ 392 Alfredo Griffin .07 .03 .01
□ 393 Moose Haas .04 .02 .00
□ 394 Donnie Hill .04 .02 .00
□ 395 Jay Howell .07 .03 .01
□ 396 Dave Kingman .10 .04 .01
□ 397 Carney Lansford .10 .04 .01
□ 398 Dave Leiper .07 .03 .01
□ 399 Bill Mooneyham .07 .03 .01
□ 400 Dwayne Murphy .04 .02 .00
□ 401 Steve Ontiveros .04 .02 .00
□ 402 Tony Phillips .04 .02 .00
□ 403 Eric Plunk .04 .02 .00
□ 404 Jose Rijo .07 .03 .01
□ 405 Terry Steinbach .45 .18 .04
□ 406 Dave Stewart .10 .04 .01
□ 407 Mickey Tettleton .04 .02 .00
□ 408 Dave Von Ohlen .04 .02 .00
□ 409 Jerry Willard .04 .02 .00
□ 410 Curt Young .04 .02 .00
□ 411 Bruce Bochy .04 .02 .00
□ 412 Dave Dravecky .04 .02 .00
□ 413 Tim Flannery .04 .02 .00
□ 414 Steve Garvey .30 .12 .03
□ 415 Goose Gossage .10 .04 .01
□ 416 Tony Gwynn .45 .18 .04
□ 417 Andy Hawkins .07 .03 .01
□ 418 LaMarr Hoyt .07 .03 .01
□ 419 Terry Kennedy .04 .02 .00
□ 420 John Kruk .35 .14 .03
□ 421 Dave LaPoint .07 .03 .01
□ 422 Craig Lefferts .04 .02 .00
□ 423 Carmelo Martinez .04 .02 .00
□ 424 Lance McCullers .07 .03 .01
□ 425 Kevin McReynolds .30 .12 .03
□ 426 Graig Nettles .10 .04 .01
□ 427 Bip Roberts .07 .03 .01
□ 428 Jerry Royster .04 .02 .00
□ 429 Benito Santiago .85 .34 .08
□ 430 Eric Show .07 .03 .01
□ 431 Bob Stoddard .04 .02 .00
□ 432 Garry Templeton .07 .03 .01
□ 433 Gene Walter .04 .02 .00
□ 434 Ed Whitson .04 .02 .00
□ 435 Marvell Wynne .04 .02 .00
□ 436 Dave Anderson .04 .02 .00
□ 437 Greg Brock .04 .02 .00
□ 438 Enos Cabell .04 .02 .00
□ 439 Mariano Duncan .04 .02 .00
□ 440 Pedro Guerrero .15 .06 .01
□ 441 Orel Hershiser .35 .14 .03
□ 442 Rick Honeycutt .04 .02 .00
□ 443 Ken Howell .04 .02 .00
□ 444 Ken Landreaux .04 .02 .00
□ 445 Bill Madlock .07 .03 .01
□ 446 Mike Marshall .10 .04 .01
□ 447 Len Matuszek .04 .02 .00
□ 448 Tom Niedenfuer .04 .02 .00
□ 449 Alejandro Pena .04 .02 .00
□ 450 Dennis Powell .04 .02 .00
□ 451 Jerry Reuss .04 .02 .00
□ 452 Bill Russell .04 .02 .00
□ 453 Steve Sax .15 .06 .01
□ 454 Mike Scioscia .04 .02 .00
□ 455 Franklin Stubbs .04 .02 .00
□ 456 Alex Trevino .04 .02 .00
□ 457 Fernando Valenzuela .18 .08 .01
□ 458 Ed VandeBerg .04 .02 .00
□ 459 Bob Welch .07 .03 .01
□ 460 Reggie Williams .07 .03 .01
□ 461 Don Aase .04 .02 .00
□ 462 Juan Beniquez .04 .02 .00
□ 463 Mike Boddicker .07 .03 .01
□ 464 Juan Bonilla .04 .02 .00
□ 465 Rich Bordi .04 .02 .00
□ 466 Storm Davis .07 .03 .01
□ 467 Rick Dempsey .04 .02 .00
□ 468 Ken Dixon .04 .02 .00
□ 469 Jim Dwyer .04 .02 .00
□ 470 Mike Flanagan .07 .03 .01
□ 471 Jackie Gutierrez .04 .02 .00
□ 472 Brad Havens .04 .02 .00
□ 473 Lee Lacy .04 .02 .00
□ 474 Fred Lynn .12 .05 .01
□ 475 Scott McGregor .07 .03 .01
□ 476 Eddie Murray .25 .10 .02
□ 477 Tom O'Malley .04 .02 .00
□ 478 Cal Ripken Jr. .25 .10 .02
□ 479 Larry Sheets .07 .03 .01
□ 480 John Shelby .04 .02 .00
□ 481 Nate Snell .04 .02 .00
□ 482 Jim Traber .07 .03 .01
□ 483 Mike Young .04 .02 .00
□ 484 Neil Allen .04 .02 .00
□ 485 Harold Baines .10 .04 .01
□ 486 Floyd Bannister .04 .02 .00
□ 487 Daryl Boston .04 .02 .00
□ 488 Ivan Calderon .12 .05 .01
□ 489 John Cangelosi .10 .04 .01
□ 490 Steve Carlton .20 .08 .02
□ 491 Joe Cowley .04 .02 .00
□ 492 Julio Cruz .04 .02 .00
□ 493 Bill Dawley .04 .02 .00
□ 494 Jose DeLeon .04 .02 .00
□ 495 Richard Dotson .07 .03 .01
□ 496 Carlton Fisk .12 .05 .01
□ 497 Ozzie Guillen .07 .03 .01
□ 498 Jerry Hairston .04 .02 .00
□ 499 Ron Hassey .04 .02 .00
□ 500 Tim Hulett .04 .02 .00
□ 501 Bob James .04 .02 .00
□ 502 Steve Lyons .04 .02 .00
□ 503 Joel McKeon .10 .04 .01

☐ 504 Gene Nelson .... .04 .02 .00
☐ 505 Dave Schmidt .... .04 .02 .00
☐ 506 Ray Searage .... .04 .02 .00
☐ 507 Bobby Thigpen .... .25 .10 .02
☐ 508 Greg Walker .... .07 .03 .01
☐ 509 Jim Acker .... .04 .02 .00
☐ 510 Doyle Alexander .... .07 .03 .01
☐ 511 Paul Assenmacher .... .07 .03 .01
☐ 512 Bruce Benedict .... .04 .02 .00
☐ 513 Chris Chambliss .... .07 .03 .01
☐ 514 Jeff Dedmon .... .04 .02 .00
☐ 515 Gene Garber .... .04 .02 .00
☐ 516 Ken Griffey .... .07 .03 .01
☐ 517 Terry Harper .... .04 .02 .00
☐ 518 Bob Horner .... .12 .05 .01
☐ 519 Glenn Hubbard .... .04 .02 .00
☐ 520 Rick Mahler .... .04 .02 .00
☐ 521 Omar Moreno .... .04 .02 .00
☐ 522 Dale Murphy .... .45 .18 .04
☐ 523 Ken Oberkfell .... .04 .02 .00
☐ 524 Ed Olwine .... .07 .03 .01
☐ 525 David Palmer .... .04 .02 .00
☐ 526 Rafael Ramirez .... .04 .02 .00
☐ 527 Billy Sample .... .04 .02 .00
☐ 528 Ted Simmons .... .10 .04 .01
☐ 529 Zane Smith .... .07 .03 .01
☐ 530 Bruce Sutter .... .10 .04 .01
☐ 531 Andres Thomas .... .20 .08 .02
☐ 532 Ozzie Virgil .... .04 .02 .00
☐ 533 Allan Anderson .... .35 .14 .03
☐ 534 Keith Atherton .... .04 .02 .00
☐ 535 Billy Beane .... .07 .03 .01
☐ 536 Bert Blyleven .... .10 .04 .01
☐ 537 Tom Brunansky .... .12 .05 .01
☐ 538 Randy Bush .... .07 .03 .01
☐ 539 George Frazier .... .04 .02 .00
☐ 540 Gary Gaetti .... .15 .06 .01
☐ 541 Greg Gagne .... .04 .02 .00
☐ 542 Mickey Hatcher .... .07 .03 .01
☐ 543 Neal Heaton .... .04 .02 .00
☐ 544 Kent Hrbek .... .15 .06 .01
☐ 545 Roy Lee Jackson .... .04 .02 .00
☐ 546 Tim Laudner .... .04 .02 .00
☐ 547 Steve Lombardozzi .... .04 .02 .00
☐ 548 Mark Portugal .... .07 .03 .01
☐ 549 Kirby Puckett .... .45 .18 .04
☐ 550 Jeff Reed .... .04 .02 .00
☐ 551 Mark Salas .... .04 .02 .00
☐ 552 Roy Smalley .... .04 .02 .00
☐ 553 Mike Smithson .... .04 .02 .00
☐ 554 Frank Viola .... .18 .08 .01
☐ 555 Thad Bosley .... .04 .02 .00
☐ 556 Ron Cey .... .07 .03 .01
☐ 557 Jody Davis .... .07 .03 .01
☐ 558 Ron Davis .... .04 .02 .00
☐ 559 Bob Dernier .... .04 .02 .00
☐ 560 Frank DiPino .... .04 .02 .00
☐ 561 Shawon Dunston UER .... .10 .04 .01
(wrong birth year
listed on card back)
☐ 562 Leon Durham .... .07 .03 .01
☐ 563 Dennis Eckersley .... .12 .05 .01
☐ 564 Terry Francona .... .04 .02 .00
☐ 565 Dave Gumpert .... .04 .02 .00
☐ 566 Guy Hoffman .... .04 .02 .00
☐ 567 Ed Lynch .... .04 .02 .00
☐ 568 Gary Matthews .... .07 .03 .01
☐ 569 Keith Moreland .... .04 .02 .00
☐ 570 Jamie Moyer .... .15 .06 .01
☐ 571 Jerry Mumphrey .... .04 .02 .00
☐ 572 Ryne Sandberg .... .20 .08 .02
☐ 573 Scott Sanderson .... .04 .02 .00
☐ 574 Lee Smith .... .07 .03 .01
☐ 575 Chris Speier .... .04 .02 .00
☐ 576 Rick Sutcliffe .... .10 .04 .01
☐ 577 Manny Trillo .... .04 .02 .00
☐ 578 Steve Trout .... .04 .02 .00
☐ 579 Karl Best .... .04 .02 .00
☐ 580 Scott Bradley .... .04 .02 .00
☐ 581 Phil Bradley .... .07 .03 .01
☐ 582 Mickey Brantley .... .07 .03 .01
☐ 583 Mike Brown .... .04 .02 .00
(Mariners pitcher)
☐ 584 Alvin Davis .... .10 .04 .01
☐ 585 Lee Guetterman .... .15 .06 .01
☐ 586 Mark Huismann .... .04 .02 .00
☐ 587 Bob Kearney .... .04 .02 .00
☐ 588 Pete Ladd .... .04 .02 .00
☐ 589 Mark Langston .... .10 .04 .01
☐ 590 Mike Moore .... .07 .03 .01
☐ 591 Mike Morgan .... .04 .02 .00
☐ 592 John Moses .... .04 .02 .00
☐ 593 Ken Phelps .... .10 .04 .01
☐ 594 Jim Presley .... .10 .04 .01
☐ 595 Rey Quinones ERR .... .20 .08 .02
(Quinonez on front)
☐ 596 Harold Reynolds .... .07 .03 .01
☐ 597 Billy Swift .... .04 .02 .00
☐ 598 Danny Tartabull .... .30 .12 .03
☐ 599 Steve Yeager .... .04 .02 .00
☐ 600 Matt Young .... .04 .02 .00
☐ 601 Bill Almon .... .04 .02 .00
☐ 602 Rafael Belliard .... .07 .03 .01
☐ 603 Mike Bielecki .... .04 .02 .00
☐ 604 Barry Bonds .... 1.00 .40 .10
☐ 605 Bobby Bonilla .... 1.00 .40 .10
☐ 606 Sid Bream .... .04 .02 .00
☐ 607 Mike Brown .... .04 .02 .00
(Pirates OF)
☐ 608 Pat Clements .... .04 .02 .00
☐ 609 Mike Diaz .... .10 .04 .01
☐ 610 Cecilio Guante .... .04 .02 .00
☐ 611 Barry Jones .... .12 .05 .01
☐ 612 Bob Kipper .... .04 .02 .00
☐ 613 Larry McWilliams .... .04 .02 .00
☐ 614 Jim Morrison .... .04 .02 .00
☐ 615 Joe Orsulak .... .04 .02 .00
☐ 616 Junior Ortiz .... .04 .02 .00
☐ 617 Tony Pena .... .07 .03 .01
☐ 618 Johnny Ray .... .07 .03 .01
☐ 619 Rick Reuschel .... .07 .03 .01
☐ 620 R.J. Reynolds .... .04 .02 .00
☐ 621 Rick Rhoden .... .07 .03 .01
☐ 622 Don Robinson .... .04 .02 .00
☐ 623 Bob Walk .... .07 .03 .01
☐ 624 Jim Winn .... .04 .02 .00
☐ 625 Youthful Power .... .60 .24 .06
Pete Incaviglia
Jose Canseco
☐ 626 300 Game Winners .... .10 .04 .01
Don Sutton
Phil Niekro
☐ 627 AL Firemen .... .07 .03 .01
Dave Righetti
Don Aase
☐ 628 Rookie All-Stars .... 1.25 .50 .12
Wally Joyner
Jose Canseco
☐ 629 Magic Mets .... .50 .20 .05
Gary Carter
Sid Fernandez
Dwight Gooden
Keith Hernandez
Darryl Strawberry
☐ 630 NL Best Righties .... .07 .03 .01
Mike Scott
Mike Krukow
☐ 631 Sensational Southpaws .. .10 .04 .01
Fernando Valenzuela
John Franco
☐ 632 Count'Em .... .10 .04 .01
Bob Horner
☐ 633 AL Pitcher's Nightmare .. .50 .20 .05
Jose Canseco
Jim Rice
Kirby Puckett
☐ 634 All-Star Battery .... .25 .10 .02
Gary Carter
Roger Clemens
☐ 635 4000 Strikeouts .... .15 .06 .01
Steve Carlton
☐ 636 Big Bats at First .... .15 .06 .01
Glenn Davis
Eddie Murray
☐ 637 On Base .... .35 .14 .03
Wade Boggs
Keith Hernandez
☐ 638 Sluggers Left Side .... 1.00 .40 .10
Don Mattingly
Darryl Strawberry
☐ 639 Former MVP's .... .12 .05 .01
Dave Parker
Ryne Sandberg
☐ 640 Dr. K , Super K .... .60 .24 .06
Dwight Gooden
Roger Clemens
☐ 641 AL West Stoppers .... .07 .03 .01
Mike Witt
Charlie Hough
☐ 642 Doubles and Triples .... .10 .04 .01
Juan Samuel
Tim Raines
☐ 643 Outfielders with Punch ... .10 .04 .01
Harold Baines
Jesse Barfield
☐ 644 Dave Clark and .... .90 .36 .09
Greg Swindell
☐ 645 Ron Karkovice and .... .12 .05 .01
Russ Morman
☐ 646 Devon White and .... .90 .36 .09
Willie Fraser

		MINT	EXC	G-VG
☐ 647	Mike Stanley and Jerry Browne	.12	.05	.01
☐ 648	Dave Magadan and Phil Lombardi	.45	.18	.04
☐ 649	Jose Gonzalez and Ralph Bryant	.25	.10	.02
☐ 650	Jimmy Jones and Randy Asadoor	.30	.12	.03
☐ 651	Tracy Jones and Marvin Freeman	.40	.16	.04
☐ 652	John Stefero and Kevin Seitzer	7.00	2.80	.70
☐ 653	Rob Nelson and Steve Fireovid	.15	.06	.01
☐ 654	CL: Mets/Red Sox Astros/Angels	.06	.01	.00
☐ 655	CL: Yankees/Rangers Tigers/Phillies	.06	.01	.00
☐ 656	CL: Reds/Blue Jays Indians/Giants ERR (230/231 wrong)	.06	.01	.00
☐ 657	CL: Cardinals/Expos Brewers/Royals	.06	.01	.00
☐ 658	CL: A's/Padres Dodgers/Orioles	.06	.01	.00
☐ 659	CL: White Sox/Braves Twins/Cubs	.06	.01	.00
☐ 660	CL: Mariners/Pirates Special Cards ERR (580/581 wrong)	.06	.01	.00

1987 Fleer Wax Box Cards

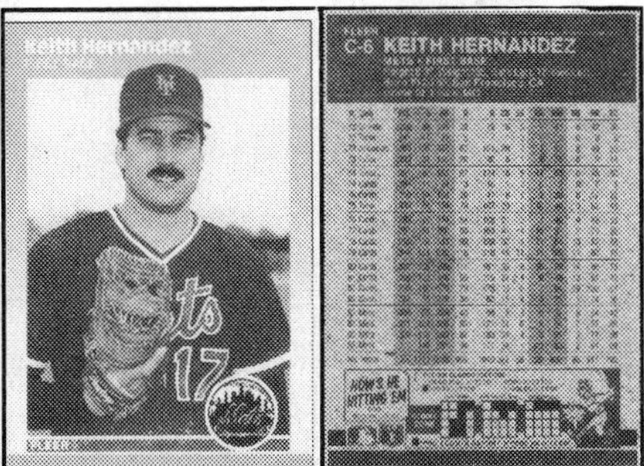

The cards in this 16-card set measure the standard 2 1/2" by 3 1/2". Cards have essentially the same design as the 1987 Fleer regular issue set. The cards were printed on the bottoms of the regular issue wax pack boxes. These 16 cards (C1 to C16) are considered a separate set in their own right and are not typically included in a complete set of the regular issue 1987 Fleer cards. The value of the panel uncut is slightly greater, perhaps by 25% greater, than the value of the individual cards cut up carefully.

	MINT	EXC	G-VG
COMPLETE SET (16)	4.00	1.60	.40
COMMON CARDS (C1-C16)	.05	.02	.00
☐ C1 Mets Logo	.05	.02	.00
☐ C2 Jesse Barfield	.15	.06	.01
☐ C3 George Brett	.35	.14	.03
☐ C4 Dwight Gooden	.60	.24	.06
☐ C5 Boston Logo	.05	.02	.00
☐ C6 Keith Hernandez	.20	.08	.02
☐ C7 Wally Joyner	.90	.36	.09
☐ C8 Dale Murphy	.45	.18	.04
☐ C9 Astros Logo	.05	.02	.00
☐ C10 Dave Parker	.15	.06	.01
☐ C11 Kirby Puckett	.50	.20	.05
☐ C12 Dave Righetti	.15	.06	.01
☐ C13 Angels Logo	.05	.02	.00
☐ C14 Ryne Sandberg	.25	.10	.02
☐ C15 Mike Schmidt	.45	.18	.04
☐ C16 Robin Yount	.25	.10	.02

1987 Fleer All-Star Inserts

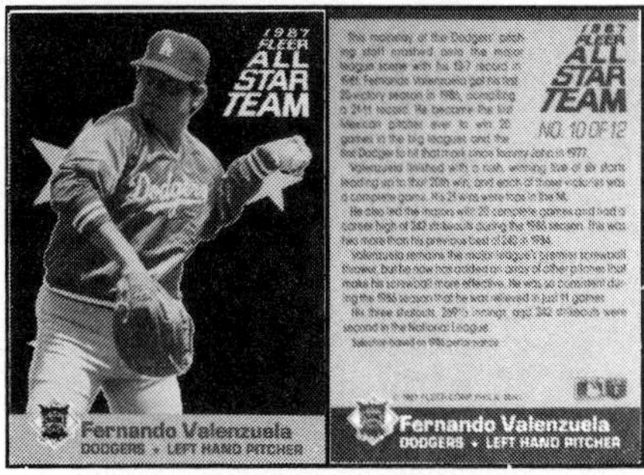

This 12-card set was distributed as an insert in packs of the Fleer regular issue. The cards are 2 1/2" by 3 1/2" and designed with a color player photo superimposed on a gray or black background with yellow stars. The player's name, team, and position are printed in orange on black or gray at the bottom of the obverse. The card backs are done predominantly in gray, red, and black. Cards are numbered on the back in the upper right hand corner.

	MINT	EXC	G-VG
COMPLETE SET (12)	12.50	5.00	1.25
COMMON PLAYER (1-12)	.20	.08	.02
☐ 1 Don Mattingly First Base	6.00	2.40	.60
☐ 2 Gary Carter Catcher	1.00	.40	.10
☐ 3 Tony Fernandez Shortstop	.40	.16	.04
☐ 4 Steve Sax Second Base	.40	.16	.04
☐ 5 Kirby Puckett Outfield	1.50	.60	.15
☐ 6 Mike Schmidt Third Base	1.50	.60	.15
☐ 7 Mike Easler Designated Hitter	.20	.08	.02
☐ 8 Todd Worrell Relief Pitcher	.40	.16	.04
☐ 9 George Bell Outfield	.50	.20	.05
☐ 10 Fernando Valenzuela Left Hand Starter	.50	.20	.05
☐ 11 Roger Clemens Right Hand Starter	2.00	.80	.20
☐ 12 Tim Raines Outfield	.75	.30	.07

1987 Fleer Headliners

This six-card set was distributed as a special insert in rack packs. The obverse features the player photo against a beige background with irregular red stripes. Cards are 2 1/2" by 3 1/2". The cards are numbered on the back.

	MINT	EXC	G-VG
COMPLETE SET (6)	6.00	2.40	.60
COMMON PLAYER (1-6)	.50	.20	.05

	MINT	EXC	G-VG
☐ 1 Wade Boggs Boston Red Sox	2.00	.80	.20
☐ 2 Jose Canseco Oakland Athletics	3.00	1.20	.30
☐ 3 Dwight Gooden New York Mets	1.00	.40	.10
☐ 4 Rickey Henderson New York Yankees	.75	.30	.07
☐ 5 Keith Hernandez New York Mets	.50	.20	.05
☐ 6 Jim Rice Boston Red Sox	.50	.20	.05

1987 Fleer Sticker Cards

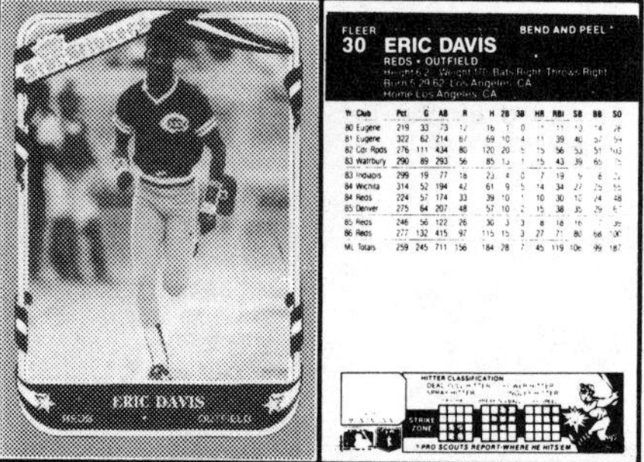

These Star Stickers were distributed as a separate issue by Fleer with five star stickers and a logo sticker in each wax pack. The 132-card (sticker) set features 2 1/2" by 3 1/2" full color fronts and even statistics on the sticker back, which is an indication that the Fleer Company understands that these stickers are rarely used as stickers but more like traditional cards. The card fronts are surrounded by a green border and the backs are printed in green and yellow on white card stock.

	MINT	EXC	G-VG
COMPLETE SET (132)	21.00	8.50	2.10
COMMON PLAYER (1-132)	.05	.02	.00

	MINT	EXC	G-VG
☐ 1 Don Aase	.05	.02	.00
☐ 2 Harold Baines	.10	.04	.01
☐ 3 Floyd Bannister	.05	.02	.00
☐ 4 Jesse Barfield	.15	.06	.01
☐ 5 Marty Barrett	.10	.04	.01
☐ 6 Kevin Bass	.05	.02	.00
☐ 7 Don Baylor	.10	.04	.01
☐ 8 Steve Bedrosian	.10	.04	.01
☐ 9 George Bell	.20	.08	.02
☐ 10 Bert Blyleven	.10	.04	.01
☐ 11 Mike Boddicker	.10	.04	.01
☐ 12 Wade Boggs	1.50	.60	.15
☐ 13 Phil Bradley	.10	.04	.01
☐ 14 Sid Bream	.05	.02	.00
☐ 15 George Brett	.45	.18	.04
☐ 16 Hubie Brooks	.05	.02	.00
☐ 17 Tom Brunansky	.10	.04	.01
☐ 18 Tom Candiotti	.05	.02	.00
☐ 19 Jose Canseco	2.50	1.00	.25
☐ 20 Gary Carter	.35	.14	.03
☐ 21 Joe Carter	.20	.08	.02
☐ 22 Will Clark	1.00	.40	.10
☐ 23 Mark Clear	.05	.02	.00
☐ 24 Roger Clemens	.75	.30	.07
☐ 25 Vince Coleman	.35	.14	.03
☐ 26 Jose Cruz	.05	.02	.00
☐ 27 Ron Darling	.15	.06	.0
☐ 28 Alvin Davis	.10	.04	.0
☐ 29 Chili Davis	.10	.04	.0
☐ 30 Eric Davis	1.00	.40	.1
☐ 31 Glenn Davis	.20	.08	.0
☐ 32 Mike Davis	.05	.02	.0
☐ 33 Andre Dawson	.35	.14	.0
☐ 34 Doug DeCinces	.05	.02	.0
☐ 35 Brian Downing	.05	.02	.0
☐ 36 Shawon Dunston	.10	.04	.0
☐ 37 Mark Eichhorn	.05	.02	.0
☐ 38 Dwight Evans	.20	.08	.0
☐ 39 Tony Fernandez	.15	.06	.0
☐ 40 Bob Forsch	.05	.02	.0
☐ 41 John Franco	.10	.04	.0
☐ 42 Julio Franco	.10	.04	.0
☐ 43 Gary Gaetti	.20	.08	.0
☐ 44 Gene Garber	.05	.02	.0
☐ 45 Scott Garrelts	.05	.02	.0
☐ 46 Steve Garvey	.45	.18	.0
☐ 47 Kirk Gibson	.35	.14	.0
☐ 48 Dwight Gooden	.75	.30	.0
☐ 49 Ken Griffey Sr.	.10	.04	.0
☐ 50 Ozzie Guillen	.10	.04	.0
☐ 51 Bill Gullickson	.05	.02	.0
☐ 52 Tony Gwynn	.45	.18	.0
☐ 53 Mel Hall	.05	.02	.0
☐ 54 Greg Harris	.05	.02	.0
☐ 55 Von Hayes	.10	.04	.0
☐ 56 Rickey Henderson	.50	.20	.0
☐ 57 Tom Henke	.10	.04	.0
☐ 58 Keith Hernandez	.25	.10	.0
☐ 59 Willie Hernandez	.10	.04	.0
☐ 60 Ted Higuera	.25	.10	.0
☐ 61 Bob Horner	.20	.08	.0
☐ 62 Charlie Hough	.05	.02	.0
☐ 63 Jay Howell	.05	.02	.0
☐ 64 Kent Hrbek	.20	.08	.0
☐ 65 Bruce Hurst	.20	.08	.0
☐ 66 Pete Incaviglia	.25	.10	.0
☐ 67 Bob James	.05	.02	.0
☐ 68 Wally Joyner	1.00	.40	.1
☐ 69 Mike Krukow	.05	.02	.0
☐ 70 Mark Langston	.10	.04	.0
☐ 71 Carney Lansford	.10	.04	.0
☐ 72 Fred Lynn	.15	.06	.0
☐ 73 Bill Madlock	.05	.02	.0
☐ 74 Don Mattingly	2.50	1.00	.25
☐ 75 Kirk McCaskill	.05	.02	.00
☐ 76 Lance McCullers	.05	.02	.00
☐ 77 Oddibe McDowell	.15	.06	.01
☐ 78 Paul Molitor	.20	.08	.02
☐ 79 Keith Moreland	.05	.02	.00
☐ 80 Jack Morris	.15	.06	.01
☐ 81 Jim Morrison	.05	.02	.00
☐ 82 Jerry Mumphrey	.05	.02	.00
☐ 83 Dale Murphy	.50	.20	.05
☐ 84 Eddie Murray	.40	.16	.04
☐ 85 Ben Oglivie	.05	.02	.00
☐ 86 Bob Ojeda	.10	.04	.01
☐ 87 Jesse Orosco	.05	.02	.00
☐ 88 Dave Parker	.15	.06	.01
☐ 89 Larry Parrish	.05	.02	.00
☐ 90 Tony Pena	.05	.02	.00
☐ 91 Jim Presley	.10	.04	.01
☐ 92 Kirby Puckett	.75	.30	.07
☐ 93 Dan Quisenberry	.10	.04	.01
☐ 94 Tim Raines	.30	.12	.03
☐ 95 Dennis Rasmussen	.10	.04	.01
☐ 96 Shane Rawley	.05	.02	.00
☐ 97 Johnny Ray	.10	.04	.01
☐ 98 Jeff Reardon	.10	.04	.01
☐ 99 Jim Rice	.25	.10	.02
☐ 100 Dave Righetti	.15	.06	.01
☐ 101 Cal Ripken Jr.	.40	.16	.04
☐ 102 Pete Rose	.75	.30	.07
☐ 103 Nolan Ryan	.50	.20	.05
☐ 104 Juan Samuel	.15	.06	.01
☐ 105 Ryne Sandberg	.25	.10	.02
☐ 106 Steve Sax	.15	.06	.01
☐ 107 Mike Schmidt	.60	.24	.06
☐ 108 Mike Scott	.20	.08	.02
☐ 109 Dave Smith	.05	.02	.00
☐ 110 Lee Smith	.10	.04	.01
☐ 111 Lonnie Smith	.05	.02	.00
☐ 112 Ozzie Smith	.20	.08	.02
☐ 113 Cory Snyder	.40	.16	.04
☐ 114 Darryl Strawberry	.60	.24	.06
☐ 115 Don Sutton	.20	.08	.02
☐ 116 Kent Tekulve	.05	.02	.00
☐ 117 Andres Thomas	.10	.04	.01
☐ 118 Alan Trammell	.25	.10	.02
☐ 119 John Tudor	.15	.06	.01
☐ 120 Fernando Valenzuela	.20	.08	.02
☐ 121 Bob Welch	.10	.04	.01

□ 122 Lou Whitaker	.15	.06	.01
□ 123 Frank White	.10	.04	.01
□ 124 Reggie Williams	.05	.02	.00
□ 125 Willie Wilson	.10	.04	.01
□ 126 Dave Winfield	.25	.10	.02
□ 127 Mike Witt	.10	.04	.01
□ 128 Todd Worrell	.20	.08	.02
□ 129 Curt Young	.05	.02	.00
□ 130 Robin Yount	.30	.12	.03
□ 131 Checklist Jose Canseco Don Mattingly	2.00	.80	.20
□ 132 Checklist Bo Jackson Eric Davis	1.00	.40	.10

1987 Fleer Sticker Wax Box

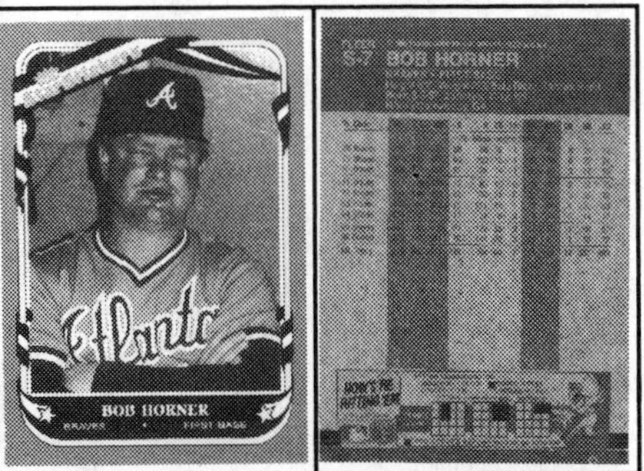

The bottoms of the Star Sticker wax boxes contained two different sets of four cards done in a similar format to the stickers; these cards (they are not stickers but truly cards) are numbered with the prefix S and are considered a separate set. The value of the panels uncut is slightly greater, perhaps by 25% greater, than the value of the individual cards cut up carefully.

	MINT	EXC	G-VG
COMPLETE SET (8)	2.50	1.00	.25
COMMON PLAYER (S1-S8)	.10	.04	.01
□ S1 Detroit Logo	.10	.04	.01
□ S2 Wade Boggs	.75	.30	.07
□ S3 Bert Blyleven	.15	.06	.01
□ S4 Jose Cruz	.15	.06	.01
□ S5 Glenn Davis	.20	.08	.02
□ S6 Phillies Logo	.10	.04	.01
□ S7 Bob Horner	.20	.08	.02
□ S8 Don Mattingly	1.50	.60	.15

1987 Fleer Award Winners

This small set of 44 cards was (mass)-produced for 7-Eleven stores by Fleer. The cards measure the standard 2 1/2" by 3 1/2" and feature full color fronts and yellow, white, and black backs. The card fronts are distinguished by their yellow frame around the player's full-color photo. The box for the cards describes the set as the "1987 Limited Edition Baseball's Award Winners." The checklist for the set is given on the back of the set box.

	MINT	EXC	G-VG
COMPLETE SET (44)	4.00	1.60	.40
COMMON PLAYER (1-44)	.10	.04	.01
□ 1 Marty Barrett	.10	.04	.01
□ 2 George Bell	.20	.08	.02
□ 3 Bert Blyleven	.15	.06	.01
□ 4 Bob Boone	.15	.06	.01

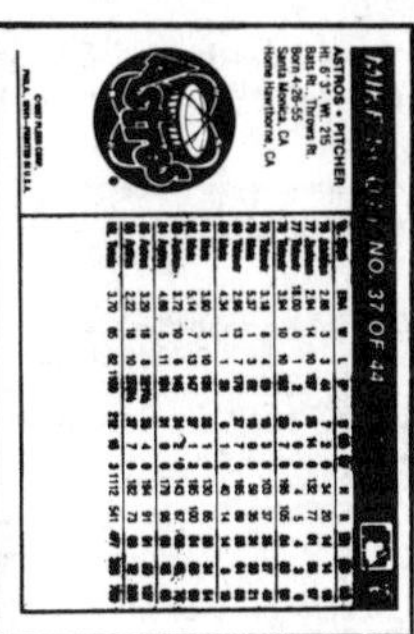

□ 5 John Candelaria	.10	.04	.01
□ 6 Jose Canseco	1.25	.50	.12
□ 7 Gary Carter	.25	.10	.02
□ 8 Joe Carter	.20	.08	.02
□ 9 Roger Clemens	.50	.20	.05
□ 10 Cecil Cooper	.10	.04	.01
□ 11 Eric Davis	.65	.26	.06
□ 12 Tony Fernandez	.15	.06	.01
□ 13 Scott Fletcher	.10	.04	.01
□ 14 Bob Forsch	.10	.04	.01
□ 15 Dwight Gooden	.45	.18	.04
□ 16 Ron Guidry	.15	.06	.01
□ 17 Ozzie Guillen	.15	.06	.01
□ 18 Bill Gullickson	.10	.04	.01
□ 19 Tony Gwynn	.40	.16	.04
□ 20 Bob Knepper	.10	.04	.01
□ 21 Ray Knight	.10	.04	.01
□ 22 Mark Langston	.15	.06	.01
□ 23 Candy Maldonado	.10	.04	.01
□ 24 Don Mattingly	1.00	.40	.10
□ 25 Roger McDowell	.15	.06	.01
□ 26 Dale Murphy	.45	.18	.04
□ 27 Dave Parker	.15	.06	.01
□ 28 Lance Parrish	.15	.06	.01
□ 29 Gary Pettis	.10	.04	.01
□ 30 Kirby Puckett	.50	.20	.05
□ 31 Johnny Ray	.15	.06	.01
□ 32 Dave Righetti	.15	.06	.01
□ 33 Cal Ripken	.35	.14	.03
□ 34 Bret Saberhagen	.20	.08	.02
□ 35 Ryne Sandberg	.30	.12	.03
□ 36 Mike Schmidt	.45	.18	.04
□ 37 Mike Scott	.20	.08	.02
□ 38 Ozzie Smith	.20	.08	.02
□ 39 Robbie Thompson	.15	.06	.01
□ 40 Fernando Valenzuela	.20	.08	.02
□ 41 Mitch Webster ER (Mike on front)	.20	.08	.02
□ 42 Frank White	.10	.04	.01
□ 43 Mike Witt	.15	.06	.01
□ 44 Todd Worrell	.20	.08	.02

1987 Fleer Exciting Stars

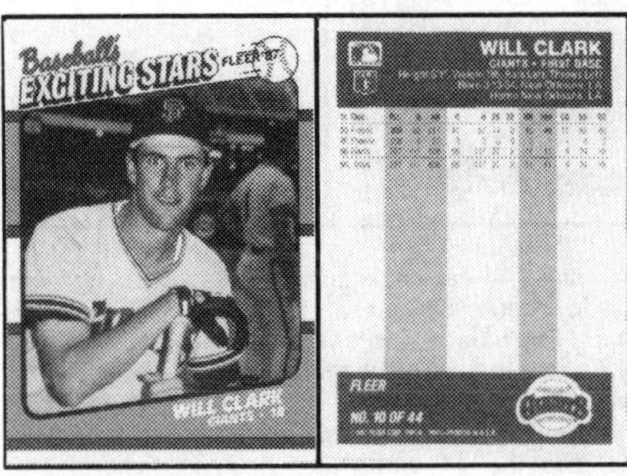

This small 44-card boxed set was produced by Fleer for distribution by the Cumberland Farm stores. The cards measure the standard 2 1/2" by 3 1/2" and feature full color fronts. The set is titled "Baseball's Exciting Stars." Each individual boxed set includes the 44 cards and 6 logo stickers. The checklist for the set is found on the back panel of the box.

	MINT	EXC	G-VG
COMPLETE SET (44)	5.00	2.00	.50
COMMON PLAYER (1-44)	.10	.04	.01

	MINT	EXC	G-VG
☐ 1 Don Aase	.10	.04	.01
☐ 2 Rick Aguilera	.15	.06	.01
☐ 3 Jesse Barfield	.20	.08	.02
☐ 4 Wade Boggs	.75	.30	.07
☐ 5 Dennis"Oil Can" Boyd	.15	.06	.01
☐ 6 Sid Bream	.10	.04	.01
☐ 7 Jose Canseco	1.25	.50	.12
☐ 8 Steve Carlton	.30	.12	.03
☐ 9 Gary Carter	.30	.12	.03
☐ 10 Will Clark	.65	.26	.06
☐ 11 Roger Clemens	.50	.20	.05
☐ 12 Danny Cox	.15	.06	.01
☐ 13 Alvin Davis	.15	.06	.01
☐ 14 Eric Davis	.65	.26	.06
☐ 15 Rob Deer	.15	.06	.01
☐ 16 Brian Downing	.10	.04	.01
☐ 17 Gene Garber	.10	.04	.01
☐ 18 Steve Garvey	.30	.12	.03
☐ 19 Dwight Gooden	.45	.18	.04
☐ 20 Mark Gubicza	.15	.06	.01
☐ 21 Mel Hall	.10	.04	.01
☐ 22 Terry Harper	.10	.04	.01
☐ 23 Von Hayes	.15	.06	.01
☐ 24 Rickey Henderson	.40	.16	.04
☐ 25 Tom Henke	.15	.06	.01
☐ 26 Willie Hernandez	.15	.06	.01
☐ 27 Ted Higuera	.25	.10	.02
☐ 28 Rick Honeycutt	.10	.04	.01
☐ 29 Kent Hrbek	.20	.08	.02
☐ 30 Wally Joyner	.60	.24	.06
☐ 31 Charlie Kerfeld	.10	.04	.01
☐ 32 Fred Lynn	.15	.06	.01
☐ 33 Don Mattingly	1.00	.40	.10
☐ 34 Tim Raines	.30	.12	.03
☐ 35 Dennis Rasmussen	.10	.04	.01
☐ 36 Johnny Ray	.15	.06	.01
☐ 37 Jim Rice	.20	.08	.02
☐ 38 Pete Rose	.65	.26	.06
☐ 39 Lee Smith	.10	.04	.01
☐ 40 Cory Snyder	.30	.12	.03
☐ 41 Darryl Strawberry	.60	.24	.06
☐ 42 Kent Tekulve	.10	.04	.01
☐ 43 Willie Wilson	.15	.06	.01
☐ 44 Bobby Witt	.15	.06	.01

1987 Fleer Game Winners

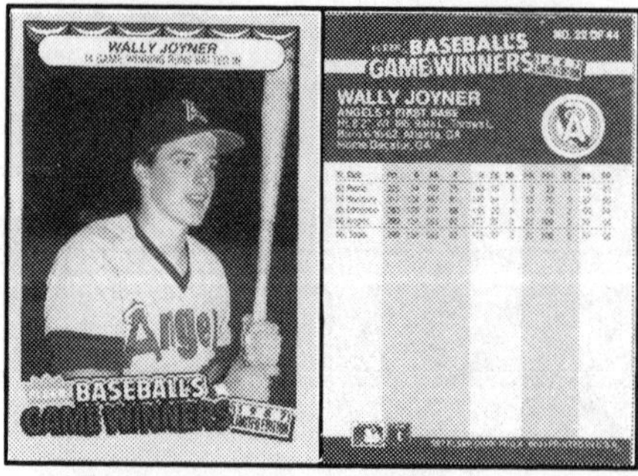

This small 44-card boxed set was produced by Fleer for distribution by several store chains, including Bi-Mart, Pay'n'Save, Mott's, M.E.Moses, and Winn's. The cards measure the standard 2 1/2" by 3 1/2" and feature full color fronts. The set is titled "Baseball's Game Winners. Each individual boxed set includes the 44 cards and 6 logo stickers. The checklist for the set is found on the back panel of the box.

	MINT	EXC	G-VG
COMPLETE SET (44)	4.00	1.60	.40
COMMON PLAYER (1-44)	.10	.04	.01

	MINT	EXC	G-VG
☐ 1 Harold Baines	.15	.06	.01
☐ 2 Don Baylor	.15	.06	.01
☐ 3 George Bell	.20	.08	.02
☐ 4 Tony Bernazard	.10	.04	.01
☐ 5 Wade Boggs	.75	.30	.07
☐ 6 George Brett	.40	.16	.04
☐ 7 Hubie Brooks	.10	.04	.01
☐ 8 Jose Canseco	1.25	.50	.12
☐ 9 Gary Carter	.30	.12	.03
☐ 10 Roger Clemens	.50	.20	.05
☐ 11 Eric Davis	.65	.26	.06
☐ 12 Glenn Davis	.20	.08	.02
☐ 13 Shawon Dunston	.15	.06	.01
☐ 14 Mark Eichhorn	.10	.04	.01
☐ 15 Gary Gaetti	.20	.08	.02
☐ 16 Steve Garvey	.30	.12	.03
☐ 17 Kirk Gibson	.30	.12	.03
☐ 18 Dwight Gooden	.45	.18	.04
☐ 19 Von Hayes	.15	.06	.01
☐ 20 Willie Hernandez	.15	.06	.01
☐ 21 Ted Higuera	.25	.10	.02
☐ 22 Wally Joyner	.50	.20	.05
☐ 23 Bob Knepper	.10	.04	.01
☐ 24 Mike Krukow	.10	.04	.01
☐ 25 Jeff Leonard	.10	.04	.01
☐ 26 Don Mattingly	1.00	.40	.10
☐ 27 Kirk McCaskill	.10	.04	.01
☐ 28 Kevin McReynolds	.25	.10	.02
☐ 29 Jim Morrison	.10	.04	.01
☐ 30 Dale Murphy	.45	.18	.04
☐ 31 Pete O'Brien	.15	.06	.01
☐ 32 Bob Ojeda	.15	.06	.01
☐ 33 Larry Parrish	.10	.04	.01
☐ 34 Ken Phelps	.10	.04	.01
☐ 35 Dennis Rasmussen	.10	.04	.01
☐ 36 Ernest Riles	.10	.04	.01
☐ 37 Cal Ripken	.35	.14	.03
☐ 38 Ron Robinson	.10	.04	.01
☐ 39 Steve Sax	.20	.08	.02
☐ 40 Mike Schmidt	.45	.18	.04
☐ 41 John Tudor	.15	.06	.01
☐ 42 Fernando Valenzuela	.20	.08	.02
☐ 43 Mike Witt	.15	.06	.01
☐ 44 Curt Young	.10	.04	.01

1987 Fleer Hottest Stars

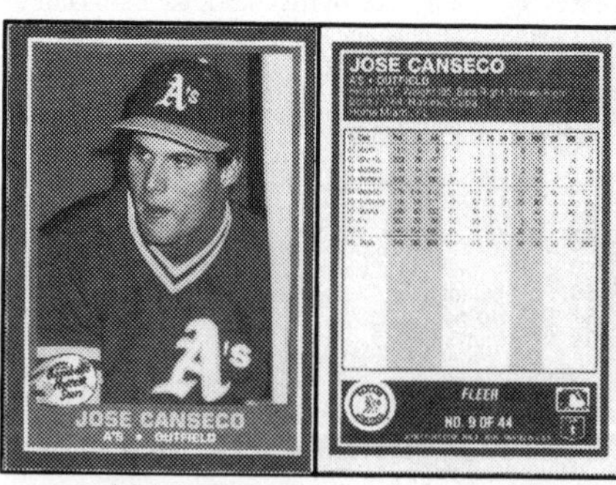

This 44-card boxed set was produced by Fleer for distribution by Revco stores all over the country. The cards measure the standard 2 1/2" by 3 1/2" and feature full color fronts and red, white, and black backs. The card fronts are easily distinguished by their solid red outside borders and and white and blue inner borders framing the player's picture. The box for the cards proclaims "1987 Limited Edition Baseball's Hottest Stars" and is styled in the same manner and color scheme as the cards themselves. The checklist for the set is given on the back of the set box.

	MINT	EXC	G-VG
COMPLETE SET (44)	5.00	2.00	.50
COMMON PLAYER (1-44)	.10	.04	.01

	MINT	EXC	G-VG
☐ 1 Joaquin Andujar	.10	.04	.01
☐ 2 Harold Baines	.15	.06	.01

☐ 3 Kevin Bass	.10	.04	.01
☐ 4 Don Baylor	.15	.06	.01
☐ 5 Barry Bonds	.25	.10	.02
☐ 6 George Brett	.45	.18	.04
☐ 7 Tom Brunansky	.15	.06	.01
☐ 8 Brett Butler	.15	.06	.01
☐ 9 Jose Canseco	1.25	.50	.12
☐ 10 Roger Clemens	.50	.20	.05
☐ 11 Ron Darling	.20	.08	.02
☐ 12 Eric Davis	.65	.26	.06
☐ 13 Andre Dawson	.25	.10	.02
☐ 14 Doug DeCinces	.10	.04	.01
☐ 15 Leon Durham	.10	.04	.01
☐ 16 Mark Eichhorn	.10	.04	.01
☐ 17 Scott Garrelts	.10	.04	.01
☐ 18 Dwight Gooden	.50	.20	.05
☐ 19 Dave Henderson	.10	.04	.01
☐ 20 Rickey Henderson	.40	.16	.04
☐ 21 Keith Hernandez	.25	.10	.02
☐ 22 Ted Higuera	.25	.10	.02
☐ 23 Bob Horner	.15	.06	.01
☐ 24 Pete Incaviglia	.25	.10	.02
☐ 25 Wally Joyner	.50	.20	.05
☐ 26 Mark Langston	.15	.06	.01
☐ 27 Don Mattingly ERR (Pirates logo on back)	1.25	.50	.12
☐ 28 Dale Murphy	.45	.18	.04
☐ 29 Kirk McCaskill	.10	.04	.01
☐ 30 Willie McGee	.20	.08	.02
☐ 31 Dave Righetti	.15	.06	.01
☐ 32 Pete Rose	.60	.24	.06
☐ 33 Bruce Ruffin	.10	.04	.01
☐ 34 Steve Sax	.20	.08	.02
☐ 35 Mike Schmidt	.45	.18	.04
☐ 36 Larry Sheets	.15	.06	.01
☐ 37 Eric Show	.10	.04	.01
☐ 38 Dave Smith	.10	.04	.01
☐ 39 Cory Snyder	.25	.10	.02
☐ 40 Frank Tanana	.15	.06	.01
☐ 41 Alan Trammell	.20	.08	.02
☐ 42 Reggie Williams	.10	.04	.01
☐ 43 Mookie Wilson	.10	.04	.01
☐ 44 Todd Worrell	.20	.08	.02

1987 Fleer League Leaders

This small set of 44 cards was produced for Walgreens by Fleer. The cards measure the standard 2 1/2" by 3 1/2" and feature full color fronts and red, white, and blue backs. The card fronts are easily distinguished by their light blue vertical stripes over a white background. The box for the cards proclaims a "Walgreens Exclusive" and is styled in the same manner and color scheme as the cards themselves. The checklist for the set is given on the back of the set box.

	MINT	EXC	G-VG
COMPLETE SET (44)	5.00	2.00	.50
COMMON PLAYER (1-44)	.10	.04	.01
☐ 1 Jesse Barfield	.20	.08	.02
☐ 2 Mike Boddicker	.15	.06	.01
☐ 3 Wade Boggs	.75	.30	.07
☐ 4 Phil Bradley	.15	.06	.01
☐ 5 George Brett	.45	.18	.04
☐ 6 Hubie Brooks	.10	.04	.01

☐ 7 Chris Brown	.10	.04	.01
☐ 8 Jose Canseco	1.25	.50	.12
☐ 9 Joe Carter	.20	.08	.02
☐ 10 Roger Clemens	.50	.20	.05
☐ 11 Vince Coleman	.35	.14	.03
☐ 12 Joe Cowley	.10	.04	.01
☐ 13 Kal Daniels	.30	.12	.03
☐ 14 Glenn Davis	.20	.08	.02
☐ 15 Jody Davis	.10	.04	.01
☐ 16 Darrell Evans	.15	.06	.01
☐ 17 Dwight Evans	.20	.08	.02
☐ 18 John Franco	.10	.04	.01
☐ 19 Julio Franco	.10	.04	.01
☐ 20 Dwight Gooden	.45	.18	.04
☐ 21 Goose Gossage	.15	.06	.01
☐ 22 Tom Herr	.10	.04	.01
☐ 23 Ted Higuera	.20	.08	.02
☐ 24 Bob Horner	.15	.06	.01
☐ 25 Pete Incaviglia	.20	.08	.02
☐ 26 Wally Joyner	.50	.20	.05
☐ 27 Dave Kingman	.15	.06	.01
☐ 28 Don Mattingly	1.00	.40	.10
☐ 29 Willie McGee	.20	.08	.02
☐ 30 Donnie Moore	.10	.04	.01
☐ 31 Keith Moreland	.10	.04	.01
☐ 32 Eddie Murray	.30	.12	.03
☐ 33 Mike Pagliarulo	.15	.06	.01
☐ 34 Larry Parrish	.10	.04	.01
☐ 35 Tony Pena	.10	.04	.01
☐ 36 Kirby Puckett	.50	.20	.05
☐ 37 Pete Rose	.60	.24	.06
☐ 38 Juan Samuel	.20	.08	.02
☐ 39 Ryne Sandberg	.25	.10	.02
☐ 40 Mike Schmidt	.45	.18	.04
☐ 41 Darryl Strawberry	.60	.24	.06
☐ 42 Greg Walker	.15	.06	.01
☐ 43 Bob Welch	.10	.04	.01
☐ 44 Todd Worrell	.20	.08	.02

1987 Fleer Baseball All-Stars

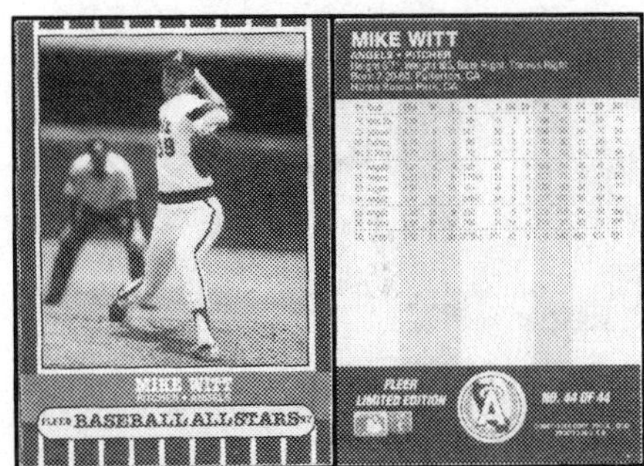

This small set of 44 cards was produced for Ben Franklin stores by Fleer. The cards measure the standard 2 1/2" by 3 1/2" and feature full color fronts and red, white, and blue backs. The card fronts are easily distinguished by their white vertical stripes over a bright red background. The box for the cards proclaims "Limited Edition Baseball All-Stars" and is styled in the same manner and color scheme as the cards themselves. The checklist for the set is given on the back of the set box.

	MINT	EXC	G-VG
COMPLETE SET (44)	5.00	2.00	.50
COMMON PLAYER (1-44)	.10	.04	.01
☐ 1 Harold Baines	.15	.06	.01
☐ 2 Jesse Barfield	.20	.08	.02
☐ 3 Wade Boggs	.75	.30	.07
☐ 4 Dennis "Oil Can" Boyd	.15	.06	.01
☐ 5 Scott Bradley	.10	.04	.01
☐ 6 Jose Canseco	1.25	.50	.12
☐ 7 Gary Carter	.30	.12	.03
☐ 8 Joe Carter	.20	.08	.02
☐ 9 Mark Clear	.10	.04	.01
☐ 10 Roger Clemens	.50	.20	.05
☐ 11 Jose Cruz	.10	.04	.01
☐ 12 Chili Davis	.10	.04	.01

No.	Player	MINT	EXC	G-VG
□ 13	Jody Davis	.10	.04	.01
□ 14	Rob Deer	.10	.04	.01
□ 15	Brian Downing	.10	.04	.01
□ 16	Sid Fernandez	.15	.06	.01
□ 17	John Franco	.10	.04	.01
□ 18	Andres Galarraga	.30	.12	.03
□ 19	Dwight Gooden	.45	.18	.04
□ 20	Tony Gwynn	.45	.18	.04
□ 21	Charlie Hough	.10	.04	.01
□ 22	Bruce Hurst	.20	.08	.02
□ 23	Wally Joyner	.50	.20	.05
□ 24	Carney Lansford	.15	.06	.01
□ 25	Fred Lynn	.15	.06	.01
□ 26	Don Mattingly	1.00	.40	.10
□ 27	Willie McGee	.20	.08	.02
□ 28	Jack Morris	.15	.06	.01
□ 29	Dale Murphy	.45	.18	.04
□ 30	Bob Ojeda	.10	.04	.01
□ 31	Tony Pena	.10	.04	.01
□ 32	Kirby Puckett	.50	.20	.05
□ 33	Dan Quisenberry	.15	.06	.01
□ 34	Tim Raines	.30	.12	.03
□ 35	Willie Randolph	.15	.06	.01
□ 36	Cal Ripken	.35	.14	.03
□ 37	Pete Rose	.50	.20	.05
□ 38	Nolan Ryan	.35	.14	.03
□ 39	Juan Samuel	.15	.06	.01
□ 40	Mike Schmidt	.45	.18	.04
□ 41	Ozzie Smith	.20	.08	.02
□ 42	Andres Thomas	.10	.04	.01
□ 43	Fernando Valenzuela	.20	.08	.02
□ 44	Mike Witt	.15	.06	.01

1987 Fleer Limited Edition

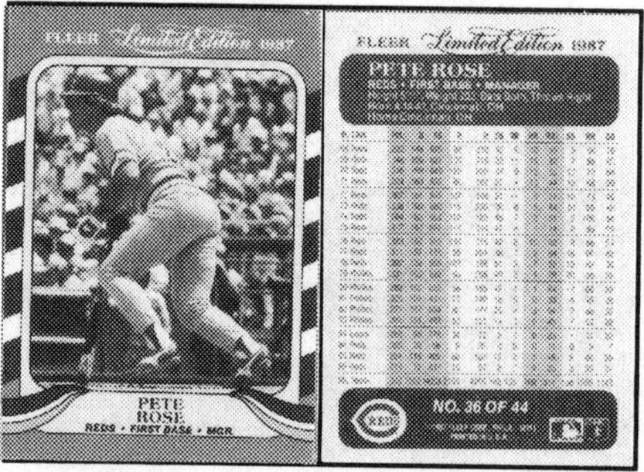

This 44-card boxed set was (mass) produced by Fleer for distribution by McCrory's and is sometimes referred to as the McCrory's set. The numerical checklist on the back of the box shows that the set is numbered alphabetically. The cards measure 2 1/2" by 3 1/2".

	MINT	EXC	G-VG
COMPLETE SET (44)	4.00	1.60	.40
COMMON PLAYER (1-44)	.05	.02	.00

No.	Player	MINT	EXC	G-VG
□ 1	Floyd Bannister	.05	.02	.00
□ 2	Marty Barrett	.10	.04	.01
□ 3	Steve Bedrosian	.10	.04	.01
□ 4	George Bell	.15	.06	.01
□ 5	George Brett	.30	.12	.03
□ 6	Jose Canseco	1.00	.40	.10
□ 7	Joe Carter	.15	.06	.01
□ 8	Will Clark	.40	.16	.04
□ 9	Roger Clemens	.60	.24	.06
□ 10	Vince Coleman	.25	.10	.02
□ 11	Glenn Davis	.15	.06	.01
□ 12	Mike Davis	.05	.02	.00
□ 13	Len Dykstra	.10	.04	.01
□ 14	John Franco	.05	.02	.00
□ 15	Julio Franco	.05	.02	.00
□ 16	Steve Garvey	.30	.12	.03
□ 17	Kirk Gibson	.30	.12	.03
□ 18	Dwight Gooden	.50	.20	.05
□ 19	Tony Gwynn	.40	.16	.04
□ 20	Keith Hernandez	.20	.08	.02
□ 21	Teddy Higuera	.15	.06	.01
□ 22	Kent Hrbek	.15	.06	.01
□ 23	Wally Joyner	.50	.20	.05
□ 24	Mike Krukow	.05	.02	.0
□ 25	Mike Marshall	.10	.04	.0
□ 26	Don Mattingly	1.00	.40	.1
□ 27	Oddibe McDowell	.10	.04	.0
□ 28	Jack Morris	.10	.04	.0
□ 29	Lloyd Moseby	.05	.02	.0
□ 30	Dale Murphy	.40	.16	.0
□ 31	Eddie Murray	.30	.12	.0
□ 32	Tony Pena	.05	.02	.0
□ 33	Jim Presley	.10	.04	.0
□ 34	Jeff Reardon	.05	.02	.0
□ 35	Jim Rice	.15	.06	.0
□ 36	Pete Rose	.50	.20	.0
□ 37	Mike Schmidt	.35	.14	.0
□ 38	Mike Scott	.15	.06	.0
□ 39	Lee Smith	.05	.02	.0
□ 40	Lonnie Smith	.05	.02	.0
□ 41	Gary Ward	.05	.02	.0
□ 42	Dave Winfield	.25	.10	.0
□ 43	Todd Worrell	.15	.06	.0
□ 44	Robin Yount	.25	.10	.0

1987 Fleer Limited Box Cards

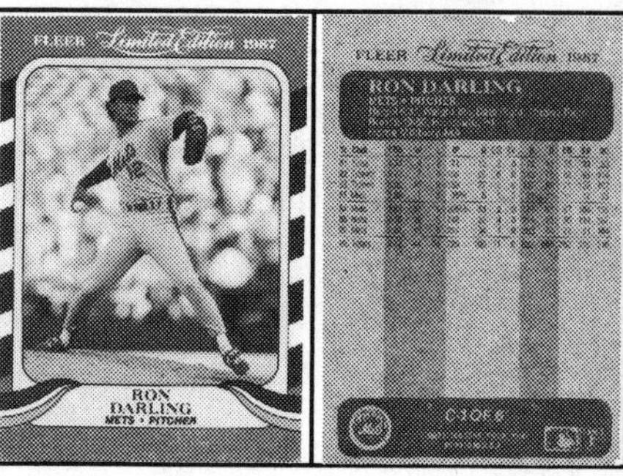

The cards in this 6-card set each measure the standard 2 1/2" by 3 1/2". Cards have essentially the same design as the 1987 Fleer Limited Edition cards which were distributed by McCrory's. The cards were printed on the bottom of the counter display box which held 24 small boxed sets; hence theoretically these box cards are 1/24 as plentiful as the regular boxed set cards. These 6 cards, numbered C1 to C6, are considered a separate set in their own right and are not typically included in a complete set of the 1987 Fleer Limited Edition set of 44. The value of the panels uncut is slightly greater, perhaps by 25% greater, than the value of the individual cards cut up carefully.

	MINT	EXC	G-VG
COMPLETE SET (6)	1.50	.60	.15
COMMON PLAYERS (C1-C6)	.10	.04	.01

No.	Player	MINT	EXC	G-VG
□ C1	Ron Darling (box bottom card)	.30	.12	.03
□ C2	Bill Buckner (box bottom card)	.20	.08	.02
□ C3	John Candelaria (box bottom card)	.20	.08	.02
□ C4	Jack Clark (box bottom card)	.50	.20	.05
□ C5	Bret Saberhagen (box bottom card)	.50	.20	.05
□ C6	Team Logo (box bottom card; checklist back)	.10	.04	.01

1987 Fleer Mini

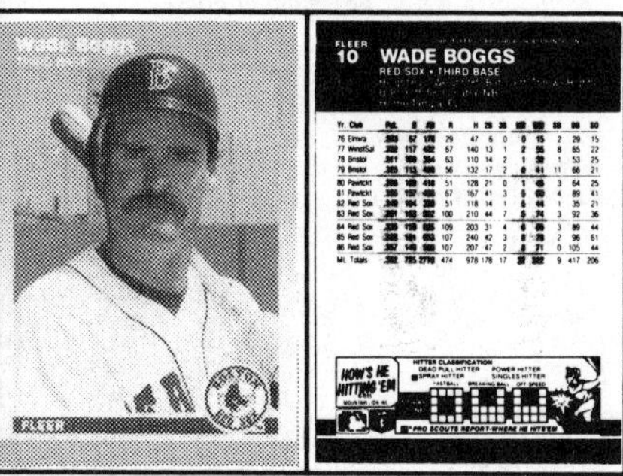

The 1987 Fleer "Classic Miniatures" set consists of 120 small cards with all new pictures of the players as compared to the 1987 Fleer regular issue. The cards are only 1 13/16" by 2 9/16", making them one of the smallest cards available. Card backs provide career year-by-year statistics. The complete set was distributed in a blue, red, white, and silver box along with 18 logo stickers. The card numbering is by alphabetical order.

	MINT	EXC	G-VG
COMPLETE SET (120)	9.00	3.75	.90
COMMON PLAYER (1-120)	.05	.02	.00
☐ 1 Don Aase	.05	.02	.00
☐ 2 Joaquin Andujar	.05	.02	.00
☐ 3 Harold Baines	.10	.04	.01
☐ 4 Jesse Barfield	.15	.06	.01
☐ 5 Kevin Bass	.05	.02	.00
☐ 6 Don Baylor	.10	.04	.01
☐ 7 George Bell	.20	.08	.02
☐ 8 Tony Bernazard	.05	.02	.00
☐ 9 Bert Blyleven	.10	.04	.01
☐ 10 Wade Boggs	.75	.30	.07
☐ 11 Phil Bradley	.10	.04	.01
☐ 12 Sid Bream	.05	.02	.00
☐ 13 George Brett	.35	.14	.03
☐ 14 Hubie Brooks	.05	.02	.00
☐ 15 Chris Brown	.10	.04	.01
☐ 16 Tom Candiotti	.05	.02	.00
☐ 17 Jose Canseco	1.25	.50	.12
☐ 18 Gary Carter	.25	.10	.02
☐ 19 Joe Carter	.15	.06	.01
☐ 20 Roger Clemens	.50	.20	.05
☐ 21 Vince Coleman	.20	.08	.02
☐ 22 Cecil Cooper	.10	.04	.01
☐ 23 Ron Darling	.15	.06	.01
☐ 24 Alvin Davis	.10	.04	.01
☐ 25 Chili Davis	.10	.04	.01
☐ 26 Eric Davis	.75	.30	.07
☐ 27 Glenn Davis	.15	.06	.01
☐ 28 Mike Davis	.05	.02	.00
☐ 29 Doug DeCinces	.05	.02	.00
☐ 30 Rob Deer	.10	.04	.01
☐ 31 Jim Deshaies	.05	.02	.00
☐ 32 Bo Diaz	.05	.02	.00
☐ 33 Richard Dotson	.05	.02	.00
☐ 34 Brian Downing	.05	.02	.00
☐ 35 Shawon Dunston	.10	.04	.01
☐ 36 Mark Eichhorn	.05	.02	.00
☐ 37 Dwight Evans	.10	.04	.01
☐ 38 Tony Fernandez	.10	.04	.01
☐ 39 Julio Franco	.10	.04	.01
☐ 40 Gary Gaetti	.15	.06	.01
☐ 41 Andres Galarraga	.25	.10	.02
☐ 42 Scott Garrelts	.05	.02	.00
☐ 43 Steve Garvey	.25	.10	.02
☐ 44 Kirk Gibson	.25	.10	.02
☐ 45 Dwight Gooden	.45	.18	.04
☐ 46 Ken Griffey Sr.	.05	.02	.00
☐ 47 Mark Gubicza	.10	.04	.01
☐ 48 Ozzie Guillen	.10	.04	.01
☐ 49 Bill Gullickson	.05	.02	.00
☐ 50 Tony Gwynn	.40	.16	.04
☐ 51 Von Hayes	.10	.04	.01
☐ 52 Rickey Henderson	.35	.14	.03
☐ 53 Keith Hernandez	.20	.08	.02
☐ 54 Willie Hernandez	.10	.04	.01
☐ 55 Ted Higuera	.15	.06	.01
☐ 56 Charlie Hough	.05	.02	.00
☐ 57 Kent Hrbek	.15	.06	.01
☐ 58 Pete Incaviglia	.20	.08	.02
☐ 59 Wally Joyner	.50	.20	.05
☐ 60 Bob Knepper	.05	.02	.00
☐ 61 Mike Krukow	.05	.02	.00
☐ 62 Mark Langston	.10	.04	.01
☐ 63 Carney Lansford	.10	.04	.01
☐ 64 Jim Lindeman	.05	.02	.00
☐ 65 Bill Madlock	.05	.02	.00
☐ 66 Don Mattingly	1.25	.50	.12
☐ 67 Kirk McCaskill	.05	.02	.00
☐ 68 Lance McCullers	.10	.04	.01
☐ 69 Keith Moreland	.05	.02	.00
☐ 70 Jack Morris	.15	.06	.01
☐ 71 Jim Morrison	.05	.02	.00
☐ 72 Lloyd Moseby	.10	.04	.01
☐ 73 Jerry Mumphrey	.05	.02	.00
☐ 74 Dale Murphy	.45	.18	.04
☐ 75 Eddie Murray	.35	.14	.03
☐ 76 Pete O'Brien	.10	.04	.01
☐ 77 Bob Ojeda	.10	.04	.01
☐ 78 Jesse Orosco	.05	.02	.00
☐ 79 Dan Pasqua	.10	.04	.01
☐ 80 Dave Parker	.15	.06	.01
☐ 81 Larry Parrish	.05	.02	.00
☐ 82 Jim Presley	.10	.04	.01
☐ 83 Kirby Puckett	.50	.20	.05
☐ 84 Dan Quisenberry	.10	.04	.01
☐ 85 Tim Raines	.30	.12	.03
☐ 86 Dennis Rasmussen	.10	.04	.01
☐ 87 Johnny Ray	.10	.04	.01
☐ 88 Jeff Reardon	.10	.04	.01
☐ 89 Jim Rice	.20	.08	.02
☐ 90 Dave Righetti	.10	.04	.01
☐ 91 Earnest Riles	.05	.02	.00
☐ 92 Cal Ripken	.30	.12	.03
☐ 93 Ron Robinson	.05	.02	.00
☐ 94 Juan Samuel	.10	.04	.01
☐ 95 Ryne Sandberg	.20	.08	.02
☐ 96 Steve Sax	.15	.06	.01
☐ 97 Mike Schmidt	.45	.18	.04
☐ 98 Ken Schrom	.05	.02	.00
☐ 99 Mike Scott	.20	.08	.02
☐ 100 Ruben Sierra	.40	.16	.04
☐ 101 Lee Smith	.10	.04	.01
☐ 102 Ozzie Smith	.15	.06	.01
☐ 103 Cory Snyder	.20	.08	.02
☐ 104 Kent Tekulve	.05	.02	.00
☐ 105 Andres Thomas	.05	.02	.00
☐ 106 Rob Thompson	.05	.02	.00
☐ 107 Alan Trammell	.20	.08	.02
☐ 108 John Tudor	.10	.04	.01
☐ 109 Fernando Valenzuela	.15	.06	.01
☐ 110 Greg Walker	.10	.04	.01
☐ 111 Mitch Webster	.05	.02	.00
☐ 112 Lou Whitaker	.10	.04	.01
☐ 113 Frank White	.05	.02	.00
☐ 114 Reggie Williams	.05	.02	.00
☐ 115 Glenn Wilson	.05	.02	.00
☐ 116 Willie Wilson	.10	.04	.01
☐ 117 Dave Winfield	.25	.10	.02
☐ 118 Mike Witt	.10	.04	.01
☐ 119 Todd Worrell	.15	.06	.01
☐ 120 Floyd Youmans	.05	.02	.00

1987 Fleer Record Setters

This 44-card boxed set was produced by Fleer for distribution by Eckerd's Drug Stores and is sometimes referred to as the Eckerd's set. Six team logo stickers are included in the box with the complete set. The numerical checklist on the back of the box shows that the set is numbered alphabetically. The cards measure 2 1/2" by 3 1/2".

	MINT	EXC	G-VG
COMPLETE SET (44)	5.00	2.00	.50
COMMON PLAYER (1-44)	.05	.02	.00
☐ 1 George Brett	.35	.14	.03
☐ 2 Chris Brown	.10	.04	.01
☐ 3 Jose Canseco UER (3 of 444 on back)	1.25	.50	.12
☐ 4 Roger Clemens	.60	.24	.06
☐ 5 Alvin Davis UER (5 of 441 on back, upside down one)	.10	.04	.01

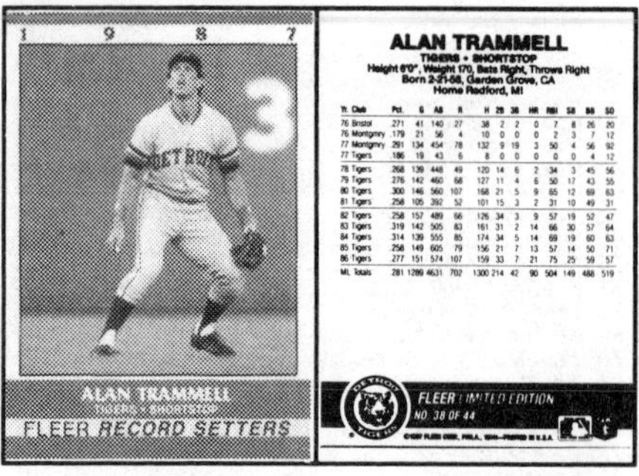

□ 6 Shawon Dunston	.10	.04	.01
□ 7 Tony Fernandez	.10	.04	.01
□ 8 Carlton Fisk UER (8 of 44' on back)	.10	.04	.01
□ 9 Gary Gaetti UER (9 of 444 on back)	.15	.06	.01
□ 10 Gene Garber	.05	.02	.00
□ 11 Rich Gedman	.05	.02	.00
□ 12 Dwight Gooden	.50	.20	.05
□ 13 Ozzie Guillen	.10	.04	.01
□ 14 Bill Gullickson	.05	.02	.00
□ 15 Billy Hatcher	.10	.04	.01
□ 16 Orel Hershiser	.45	.18	.04
□ 17 Wally Joyner	.50	.20	.05
□ 18 Ray Knight	.05	.02	.00
□ 19 Craig Lefferts	.05	.02	.00
□ 20 Don Mattingly	1.00	.40	.10
□ 21 Kevin Mitchell	.10	.04	.01
□ 22 Lloyd Moseby	.05	.02	.00
□ 23 Dale Murphy	.40	.16	.04
□ 24 Eddie Murray	.30	.12	.03
□ 25 Phil Niekro	.15	.06	.01
□ 26 Ben Oglivie	.05	.02	.00
□ 27 Jesse Orosco	.05	.02	.00
□ 28 Joe Orsulak	.05	.02	.00
□ 29 Larry Parrish	.05	.02	.00
□ 30 Tim Raines	.20	.08	.02
□ 31 Shane Rawley	.05	.02	.00
□ 32 Dave Righetti	.10	.04	.01
□ 33 Pete Rose	.60	.24	.06
□ 34 Steve Sax	.15	.06	.01
□ 35 Mike Schmidt	.35	.14	.03
□ 36 Mike Scott	.15	.06	.01
□ 37 Don Sutton	.15	.06	.01
□ 38 Alan Trammell	.20	.08	.02
□ 39 John Tudor	.10	.04	.01
□ 40 Gary Ward	.05	.02	.00
□ 41 Lou Whitaker	.10	.04	.01
□ 42 Willie Wilson	.10	.04	.01
□ 43 Todd Worrell	.15	.06	.01
□ 44 Floyd Youmans	.05	.02	.00

1987 Fleer Sluggers/Pitchers

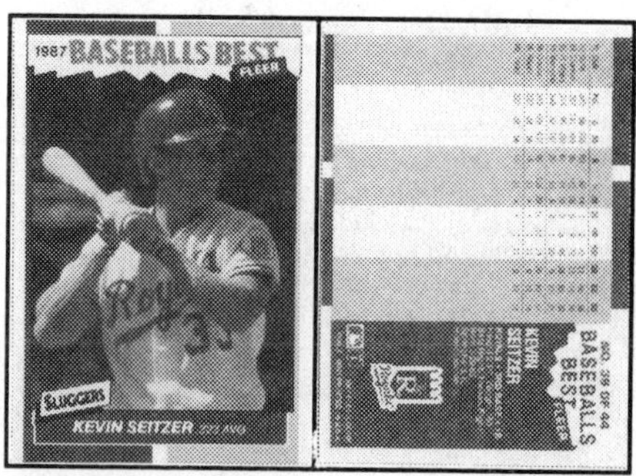

Fleer produced this 44-card boxed set although it was primarily distributed by McCrory, McLellan, Newberry, H.L.Green, T.G.Y., and other similar stores. The set features 28 sluggers and 16 pitchers and is subtitled "Baseball's Best". Cards are standard-size, 2 1/2" by 3 1/2", and were packaged in a red, white, blue, and yellow custom box along with six logo stickers. The set checklist is given on the back of the box. The checklist on the back of the set box misspells McGwire as McGuire.

	MINT	EXC	G-VG
COMPLETE SET (44)	5.00	2.00	.50
COMMON PLAYER (1-44)	.10	.04	.01
□ 1 Kevin Bass	.10	.04	.01
□ 2 Jesse Barfield	.15	.06	.01
□ 3 George Bell	.20	.08	.02
□ 4 Wade Boggs	.75	.30	.07
□ 5 Sid Bream	.10	.04	.01
□ 6 George Brett	.35	.14	.03
□ 7 Ivan Calderon	.15	.06	.01
□ 8 Jose Canseco	1.25	.50	.12
□ 9 Jack Clark	.20	.08	.02
□ 10 Roger Clemens	.50	.20	.05
□ 11 Eric Davis	.65	.26	.06
□ 12 Andre Dawson	.25	.10	.02
□ 13 Sid Fernandez	.15	.06	.01
□ 14 John Franco	.10	.04	.01
□ 15 Dwight Gooden	.40	.16	.04
□ 16 Pedro Guerrero	.20	.08	.02
□ 17 Tony Gwynn	.35	.14	.03
□ 18 Rickey Henderson	.40	.16	.04
□ 19 Tom Henke	.10	.04	.01
□ 20 Ted Higuera	.20	.08	.02
□ 21 Pete Incaviglia	.20	.08	.02
□ 22 Wally Joyner	.45	.18	.04
□ 23 Jeff Leonard	.10	.04	.01
□ 24 Joe Magrane	.15	.06	.01
□ 25 Don Mattingly	1.00	.40	.10
□ 26 Mark McGwire	1.00	.40	.10
□ 27 Jack Morris	.15	.06	.01
□ 28 Dale Murphy	.40	.16	.04
□ 29 Dave Parker	.15	.06	.01
□ 30 Ken Phelps	.10	.04	.01
□ 31 Kirby Puckett	.40	.16	.04
□ 32 Tim Raines	.25	.10	.02
□ 33 Jeff Reardon	.10	.04	.01
□ 34 Dave Righetti	.15	.06	.01
□ 35 Cal Ripken	.30	.12	.03
□ 36 Bret Saberhagen	.20	.08	.02
□ 37 Mike Schmidt	.40	.16	.04
□ 38 Mike Scott	.20	.08	.02
□ 39 Kevin Seitzer	.90	.36	.09
□ 40 Darryl Strawberry	.60	.24	.06
□ 41 Rick Sutcliffe	.15	.06	.01
□ 42 Pat Tabler	.15	.06	.01
□ 43 Fernando Valenzuela	.20	.08	.02
□ 44 Mike Witt	.15	.06	.01

1987 Fleer Slug/Pitch Box Cards

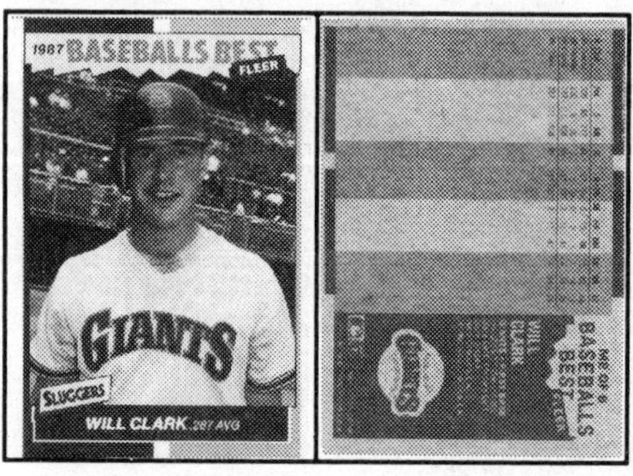

The cards in this 6-card set each measure the standard 2 1/2" by 3 1/2". Cards have essentially the same design as the 1987 Fleer Sluggers vs. Pitchers set of Baseball's Best. The cards were printed on the bottom of the counter display box which held 24 small boxed sets; hence theoretically these box cards are 1/24 as plentiful as the regular boxed set cards. These 6 cards, numbered M1 to M5 with one blank-back (unnumbered) card, are considered a separate set in their own right and are not typically included in a complete set of the 1987 Fleer Sluggers vs. Pitchers set of 44. The value of the panels uncut is slightly greater, perhaps by 25% greater, than the value of the individual cards cut up carefully.

	MINT	EXC	G-VG
COMPLETE SET (6)	2.00	.80	.20
COMMON PLAYERS (M1-M5)	.10	.04	.01
□ M1 Steve Bedrosian (box bottom card)	.20	.08	.02
□ M2 Will Clark (box bottom card)	1.00	.40	.10
□ M3 Vince Coleman (box bottom card)	.50	.20	.05
□ M4 Bo Jackson (box bottom card)	.60	.24	.06
□ M5 Cory Snyder (box bottom card)	.40	.16	.04
□ xx Team Logo (box bottom card, unnumbered, blank back)	.10	.04	.01

1987 Fleer Update

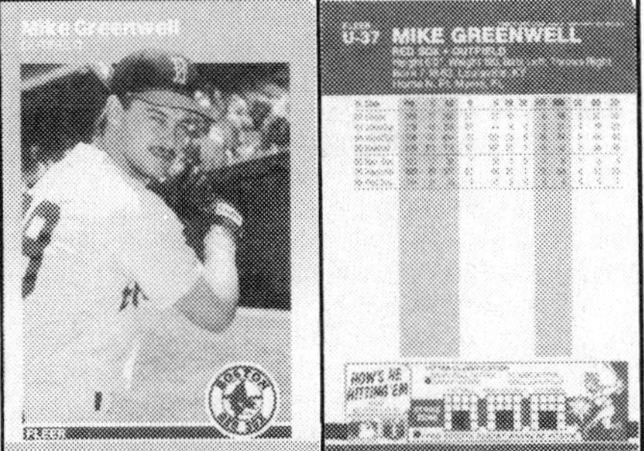

This 132-card set was distributed by Fleer to dealers as a complete set within a custom box. In addition to the complete set of 132 cards, the box also contains 25 Team Logo stickers.The card fronts look very similar to the 1987 Fleer regular issue. The cards are numbered (with a U prefix) alphabetically according to player's last name. Cards measure the standard size, 2 1/2" by 3 1/2". Fleer misalphabetized Jim Winn in their set numbering by putting him ahead of the next four players listed.

	MINT	EXC	G-VG
COMPLETE SET (132)	12.00	5.00	1.20
COMMON PLAYER (1-132)	.05	.02	.00
□ U1 Scott Bankhead	.10	.04	.01
□ U2 Eric Bell	.10	.04	.01
□ U3 Juan Beniquez	.05	.02	.00
□ U4 Juan Berenguer	.05	.02	.00
□ U5 Mike Birkbeck	.15	.06	.01
□ U6 Randy Bockus	.10	.04	.01
□ U7 Greg Booker	.05	.02	.00
□ U8 Thad Bosley	.05	.02	.00
□ U9 Greg Brock	.05	.02	.00
□ U10 Bob Brower	.15	.06	.01
□ U11 Chris Brown	.15	.06	.01
□ U12 Jerry Browne	.05	.02	.00
□ U13 Ralph Bryant	.10	.04	.01
□ U14 DeWayne Buice	.10	.04	.01
□ U15 Ellis Burks	1.75	.70	.17
□ U16 Casey Candaele	.10	.04	.01
□ U17 Steve Carlton	.30	.12	.03
□ U18 Juan Castillo	.05	.02	.00
□ U19 Chuck Crim	.10	.04	.01
□ U20 Mark Davidson	.15	.06	.01
□ U21 Mark Davis	.10	.04	.01
□ U22 Storm Davis	.10	.04	.01
□ U23 Bill Dawley	.05	.02	.00
□ U24 Andre Dawson	.35	.14	.03
□ U25 Brian Dayett	.05	.02	.00
□ U26 Rick Dempsey	.05	.02	.00
□ U27 Ken Dowell	.10	.04	.01
□ U28 Dave Dravecky	.05	.02	.00
□ U29 Mike Dunne	.30	.12	.03
□ U30 Dennis Eckersley	.30	.12	.03
□ U31 Cecil Fielder	.10	.04	.01
□ U32 Brian Fisher	.10	.04	.01
□ U33 Willie Fraser	.10	.04	.01
□ U34 Ken Gerhart	.15	.06	.01
□ U35 Jim Gott	.10	.04	.01
□ U36 Dan Gladden	.10	.04	.01
□ U37 Mike Greenwell	4.00	1.60	.40
□ U38 Cecelio Guante	.05	.02	.00
□ U39 Albert Hall	.05	.02	.00
□ U40 Atlee Hammaker	.05	.02	.00
□ U41 Mickey Hatcher	.10	.04	.01
□ U42 Mike Heath	.05	.02	.00
□ U43 Neal Heaton	.05	.02	.00
□ U44 Mike Henneman	.35	.14	.03
□ U45 Guy Hoffman	.10	.04	.01
□ U46 Charles Hudson	.05	.02	.00
□ U47 Chuck Jackson	.15	.06	.01
□ U48 Mike Jackson	.15	.06	.01
□ U49 Reggie Jackson	.40	.16	.04
□ U50 Chris James	.35	.14	.03
□ U51 Dion James	.10	.04	.01
□ U52 Stan Javier	.10	.04	.01
□ U53 Stan Jefferson	.25	.10	.02
□ U54 Jimmy Jones	.15	.06	.01
□ U55 Tracy Jones	.25	.10	.02
□ U56 Terry Kennedy	.10	.04	.01
□ U57 Mike Kingery	.10	.04	.01
□ U58 Ray Knight	.10	.04	.01
□ U59 Gene Larkin	.35	.14	.03
□ U60 Mike LaValliere	.10	.04	.01
□ U61 Jack Lazorko	.10	.04	.01
□ U62 Terry Leach	.15	.06	.01
□ U63 Rick Leach	.05	.02	.00
□ U64 Craig Lefferts	.05	.02	.00
□ U65 Jim Lindeman	.20	.08	.02
□ U66 Bill Long	.15	.06	.01
□ U67 Mike Loynd	.10	.04	.01
□ U68 Greg Maddux	.75	.30	.07
□ U69 Bill Madlock	.15	.06	.01
□ U70 Dave Magadan	.25	.10	.02
□ U71 Joe Magrane	.50	.20	.05
□ U72 Fred Manrique	.15	.06	.01
□ U73 Mike Mason	.05	.02	.00
□ U74 Lloyd McClendon	.10	.04	.01
□ U75 Fred McGriff	1.50	.60	.15
□ U76 Mark McGwire	2.50	1.00	.25
□ U77 Mark McLemore	.05	.02	.00
□ U78 Kevin McReynolds	.25	.10	.02
□ U79 Dave Meads	.10	.04	.01
□ U80 Greg Minton	.05	.02	.00
□ U81 John Mitchell	.15	.06	.01
□ U82 Kevin Mitchell	.15	.06	.01
□ U83 John Morris	.05	.02	.00
□ U84 Jeff Musselman	.15	.06	.01
□ U85 Randy Myers	.45	.18	.04
□ U86 Gene Nelson	.05	.02	.00
□ U87 Joe Niekro	.15	.06	.01
□ U88 Tom Nieto	.05	.02	.00
□ U89 Reid Nichols	.05	.02	.00
□ U90 Matt Nokes	.65	.26	.06
□ U91 Dickie Noles	.05	.02	.00
□ U92 Edwin Nunez	.05	.02	.00
□ U93 Jose Nunez	.15	.06	.01
□ U94 Paul O'Neill	.10	.04	.01
□ U95 Jim Paciorek	.10	.04	.01
□ U96 Lance Parrish	.15	.06	.01
□ U97 Bill Pecota	.15	.06	.01
□ U98 Tony Pena	.15	.06	.01
□ U99 Luis Polonia	.30	.12	.03
□ U100 Randy Ready	.10	.04	.01
□ U101 Jeff Reardon	.15	.06	.01
□ U102 Gary Redus	.05	.02	.00
□ U103 Rick Rhoden	.15	.06	.01
□ U104 Wally Ritchie	.10	.04	.01
□ U105 Jeff Robinson (wrong Jeff's stats on back)	.45	.18	.04
□ U106 Mark Salas	.05	.02	.00
□ U107 Dave Schmidt	.10	.04	.01
□ U108 Kevin Seitzer ERR (wrong birth year)	1.50	.60	.15
□ U109 John Shelby	.05	.02	.00
□ U110 John Smiley	.35	.14	.03
□ U111 Lary Sorensen	.05	.02	.00
□ U112 Chris Speier	.05	.02	.00
□ U113 Randy St.Claire	.05	.02	.00

		MINT	EXC	G-VG
☐ U114	Jim Sundberg	.05	.02	.00
☐ U115	B.J. Surhoff	.40	.16	.04
☐ U116	Greg Swindell	.40	.16	.04
☐ U117	Danny Tartabull	.40	.16	.04
☐ U118	Dorn Taylor	.10	.04	.01
☐ U119	Lee Tunnell	.05	.02	.00
☐ U120	Ed VandeBerg	.05	.02	.00
☐ U121	Andy Van Slyke	.20	.08	.02
☐ U122	Gary Ward	.10	.04	.01
☐ U123	Devon White	.35	.14	.03
☐ U124	Alan Wiggins	.05	.02	.00
☐ U125	Bill Wilkinson	.10	.04	.01
☐ U126	Jim Winn	.05	.02	.00
☐ U127	Frank Williams	.05	.02	.00
☐ U128	Kenny Williams	.20	.08	.02
☐ U129	Matt Williams	.45	.18	.04
☐ U130	Herm Willingham	.10	.04	.01
☐ U131	Matt Young	.05	.02	.00
☐ U132	Checklist	.05	.01	.00

1987 Fleer World Series

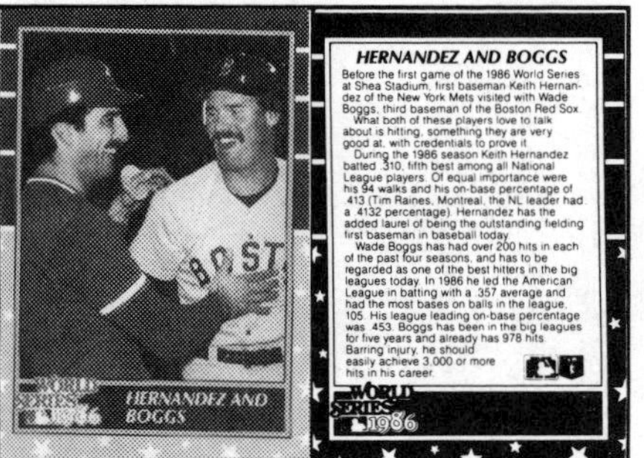

This 12-card set of 2 1/2" by 3 1/2" cards features highlights of the previous year's World Series between the Mets and the Red Sox. The sets were packaged as a complete set insert with the collated sets (of the 1987 Fleer regular issue) which were sold by Fleer directly to hobby card dealers; they were not available in the general retail candy store outlets.

	MINT	EXC	G-VG
COMPLETE SET (12)	4.00	1.60	.40
COMMON PLAYER (1-12)	.25	.10	.02
☐ 1 Bruce Hurst Left Hand Finesse Beats Mets	.35	.14	.03
☐ 2 Keith Hernandez and Wade Boggs	.60	.24	.06
☐ 3 Roger Clemens HOR	.75	.30	.07
☐ 4 Clutch Hitting (Gary Carter)	.45	.18	.04
☐ 5 Ron Darling Picks Up Slack	.35	.14	.03
☐ 6 Marty Barrett .433 Series BA	.35	.14	.03
☐ 7 Dwight Gooden	.60	.24	.06
☐ 8 Strategy at Work (Mets Conference)	.25	.10	.02
☐ 9 Dewey Evans (Congratulated by Rich Gedman)	.35	.14	.03
☐ 10 One Strike From Boston Victory (Dave Henderson)	.25	.10	.02
☐ 11 Series Home Run Duo (Ray Knight and Darryl Strawberry)	.35	.14	.03
☐ 12 Ray Knight (Series MVP)	.35	.14	.03

1988 Fleer

This 660-card set features a distinctive white background with red and blue diagonal stripes across the card. The backs are printed in gray and red on white card stock. The bottom of the card back shows an innovative breakdown of the player's demonstrated ability with respect to day, night, home, and road games. Cards are numbered on the back and are again the standard 2 1/2" by 3 1/2". Cards are again organized numerically by teams, i.e., World Champion Twins (1-25), St. Louis Cardinals (26-50), Detroit Tigers (51-75), San Francisco Giants (76-101), Toronto Blue Jays (102-126), New York Mets (127-154), Milwaukee Brewers (155-178), Montreal Expos (179-201), New York Yankees (202-226), Cincinnati Reds (227-250), Kansas City Royals (251- 274), Oakland A's (275-296), Philadelphia Phillies (297-320), Pittsburgh Pirates (321-342), Boston Red Sox (343-367), Seattle Mariners (368-390), Chicago White Sox (391-413), Chicago Cubs (414-436), Houston Astros (437-460), Texas Rangers (461-483), California Angels (484-507), Los Angeles Dodgers (508-530), Atlanta Braves (531-552), Baltimore Orioles (553-575), San Diego Padres (576-599), and Cleveland Indians (600-621). The last 39 cards in the set consist of Specials (622-640), Rookie Pairs (641-653), and checklists (654-660). Cards 90 and 91 are incorrectly numbered on the checklist card #654.

	MINT	EXC	G-VG
COMPLETE SET (660)	28.00	11.50	2.80
COMMON PLAYER (1-660)	.03	.01	.00
☐ 1 Keith Atherton	.03	.01	.00
☐ 2 Don Baylor	.08	.03	.01
☐ 3 Juan Berenguer	.03	.01	.00
☐ 4 Bert Blyleven	.08	.03	.01
☐ 5 Tom Brunansky	.10	.04	.01
☐ 6 Randy Bush	.03	.01	.00
☐ 7 Steve Carlton	.18	.08	.01
☐ 8 Mark Davidson	.12	.05	.01
☐ 9 George Frazier	.03	.01	.00
☐ 10 Gary Gaetti	.12	.05	.01
☐ 11 Greg Gagne	.03	.01	.00
☐ 12 Dan Gladden	.06	.02	.00
☐ 13 Kent Hrbek	.12	.05	.01
☐ 14 Gene Larkin	.25	.10	.02
☐ 15 Tim Laudner	.03	.01	.00
☐ 16 Steve Lombardozzi	.03	.01	.00
☐ 17 Al Newman	.03	.01	.00
☐ 18 Joe Niekro	.06	.02	.00
☐ 19 Kirby Puckett	.35	.14	.03
☐ 20 Jeff Reardon	.06	.02	.00
☐ 21A Dan Schatzeder ERR (misspelled Schatzader on card front)	.12	.05	.01
☐ 21B Dan Schatzeder COR	.06	.02	.00
☐ 22 Roy Smalley	.03	.01	.00
☐ 23 Mike Smithson	.03	.01	.00
☐ 24 Les Straker	.10	.04	.01
☐ 25 Frank Viola	.15	.06	.01

☐	26 Jack Clark	.15	.06	.01
☐	27 Vince Coleman	.20	.08	.02
☐	28 Danny Cox	.06	.02	.00
☐	29 Bill Dawley	.03	.01	.00
☐	30 Ken Dayley	.03	.01	.00
☐	31 Doug DeCinces	.06	.02	.00
☐	32 Curt Ford	.03	.01	.00
☐	33 Bob Forsch	.03	.01	.00
☐	34 David Green	.03	.01	.00
☐	35 Tom Herr	.06	.02	.00
☐	36 Ricky Horton	.03	.01	.00
☐	37 Lance Johnson	.20	.08	.02
☐	38 Steve Lake	.03	.01	.00
☐	39 Jim Lindeman	.08	.03	.01
☐	40 Joe Magrane	.30	.12	.03
☐	41 Greg Mathews	.03	.01	.00
☐	42 Willie McGee	.10	.04	.01
☐	43 John Morris	.03	.01	.00
☐	44 Jose Oquendo	.03	.01	.00
☐	45 Tony Pena	.06	.02	.00
☐	46 Terry Pendleton	.03	.01	.00
☐	47 Ozzie Smith	.12	.05	.01
☐	48 John Tudor	.08	.03	.01
☐	49 Lee Tunnell	.03	.01	.00
☐	50 Todd Worrell	.10	.04	.01
☐	51 Doyle Alexander	.03	.01	.00
☐	52 Dave Bergman	.03	.01	.00
☐	53 Tom Brookens	.03	.01	.00
☐	54 Darrell Evans	.08	.03	.01
☐	55 Kirk Gibson	.20	.08	.02
☐	56 Mike Heath	.03	.01	.00
☐	57 Mike Henneman	.20	.08	.02
☐	58 Willie Hernandez	.06	.02	.00
☐	59 Larry Herndon	.03	.01	.00
☐	60 Eric King	.03	.01	.00
☐	61 Chet Lemon	.03	.01	.00
☐	62 Scott Lusader	.15	.06	.01
☐	63 Bill Madlock	.06	.02	.00
☐	64 Jack Morris	.12	.05	.01
☐	65 Jim Morrison	.03	.01	.00
☐	66 Matt Nokes	.50	.20	.05
☐	67 Dan Petry	.03	.01	.00
☐	68A Jeff Robinson ERR Detroit Tigers (stats for other Jeff Robinson on card back)	.50	.20	.05
☐	68B Jeff Robinson COR Detroit Tigers	.40	.16	.04
☐	69 Pat Sheridan	.03	.01	.00
☐	70 Nate Snell	.03	.01	.00
☐	71 Frank Tanana	.06	.02	.00
☐	72 Walt Terrell	.03	.01	.00
☐	73 Mark Thurmond	.03	.01	.00
☐	74 Alan Trammell	.15	.06	.01
☐	75 Lou Whitaker	.10	.04	.01
☐	76 Mike Aldrete	.06	.02	.00
☐	77 Bob Brenly	.03	.01	.00
☐	78 Will Clark	.75	.30	.07
☐	79 Chili Davis	.06	.02	.00
☐	80 Kelly Downs	.03	.01	.00
☐	81 Dave Dravecky	.03	.01	.00
☐	82 Scott Garrelts	.03	.01	.00
☐	83 Atlee Hammaker	.03	.01	.00
☐	84 Dave Henderson	.03	.01	.00
☐	85 Mike Krukow	.03	.01	.00
☐	86 Mike LaCoss	.03	.01	.00
☐	87 Craig Lefferts	.03	.01	.00
☐	88 Jeff Leonard	.06	.02	.00
☐	89 Candy Maldonado	.06	.02	.00
☐	90 Ed Milner	.03	.01	.00
☐	91 Bob Melvin	.03	.01	.00
☐	92 Kevin Mitchell	.06	.02	.00
☐	93 Jon Perlman	.10	.04	.01
☐	94 Rick Reuschel	.06	.02	.00
☐	95 Don Robinson	.03	.01	.00
☐	96 Chris Speier	.03	.01	.00
☐	97 Harry Spilman	.03	.01	.00
☐	98 Robbie Thompson	.06	.02	.00
☐	99 Jose Uribe	.03	.01	.00
☐	100 Mark Wasinger	.15	.06	.01
☐	101 Matt Williams	.35	.14	.03
☐	102 Jesse Barfield	.15	.06	.01
☐	103 George Bell	.18	.08	.01
☐	104 Juan Beniquez	.03	.01	.00
☐	105 John Cerutti	.03	.01	.00
☐	106 Jim Clancy	.03	.01	.00
☐	107 Rob Ducey	.20	.08	.02
☐	108 Mark Eichhorn	.03	.01	.00
☐	109 Tony Fernandez	.10	.04	.01
☐	110 Cecil Fielder	.03	.01	.00
☐	111 Kelly Gruber	.03	.01	.00
☐	112 Tom Henke	.06	.02	.00
☐	113A Garth Iorg ERR (misspelled Iorq on card front)	.12	.05	.01
☐	113B Garth Iorg COR	.06	.02	.00
☐	114 Jimmy Key	.08	.03	.01
☐	115 Rick Leach	.03	.01	.00
☐	116 Manny Lee	.08	.03	.01
☐	117 Nelson Liriano	.15	.06	.01
☐	118 Fred McGriff	.70	.28	.07
☐	119 Lloyd Moseby	.08	.03	.01
☐	120 Rance Mulliniks	.03	.01	.00
☐	121 Jeff Musselman	.08	.03	.01
☐	122 Jose Nunez	.15	.06	.01
☐	123 Dave Stieb	.08	.03	.01
☐	124 Willie Upshaw	.03	.01	.00
☐	125 Duane Ward	.08	.03	.01
☐	126 Ernie Whitt	.03	.01	.00
☐	127 Rick Aguilera	.03	.01	.00
☐	128 Wally Backman	.03	.01	.00
☐	129 Mark Carreon	.12	.05	.01
☐	130 Gary Carter	.20	.08	.02
☐	131 David Cone	1.25	.50	.12
☐	132 Ron Darling	.12	.05	.01
☐	133 Len Dykstra	.08	.03	.01
☐	134 Sid Fernandez	.08	.03	.01
☐	135 Dwight Gooden	.60	.24	.06
☐	136 Keith Hernandez	.20	.08	.02
☐	137 Gregg Jefferies	7.50	3.00	.75
☐	138 Howard Johnson	.08	.03	.01
☐	139 Terry Leach	.06	.02	.00
☐	140 Barry Lyons	.10	.04	.01
☐	141 Dave Magadan	.08	.03	.01
☐	142 Roger McDowell	.06	.02	.00
☐	143 Kevin McReynolds	.15	.06	.01
☐	144 Keith Miller (New York Mets)	.20	.08	.02
☐	145 John Mitchell	.15	.06	.01
☐	146 Randy Myers	.25	.10	.02
☐	147 Bob Ojeda	.06	.02	.00
☐	148 Jesse Orosco	.03	.01	.00
☐	149 Rafael Santana	.03	.01	.00
☐	150 Doug Sisk	.03	.01	.00
☐	151 Darryl Strawberry	.45	.18	.04
☐	152 Tim Teufel	.03	.01	.00
☐	153 Gene Walter	.03	.01	.00
☐	154 Mookie Wilson	.03	.01	.00
☐	155 Jay Aldrich	.10	.04	.01
☐	156 Chris Bosio	.03	.01	.00
☐	157 Glenn Braggs	.08	.03	.01
☐	158 Greg Brock	.03	.01	.00
☐	159 Juan Castillo	.06	.02	.00
☐	160 Mark Clear	.03	.01	.00
☐	161 Cecil Cooper	.08	.03	.01
☐	162 Chuck Crim	.10	.04	.01
☐	163 Rob Deer	.08	.03	.01
☐	164 Mike Felder	.03	.01	.00
☐	165 Jim Gantner	.03	.01	.00
☐	166 Ted Higuera	.10	.04	.01
☐	167 Steve Kiefer	.06	.02	.00
☐	168 Rick Manning	.03	.01	.00
☐	169 Paul Molitor	.12	.05	.01
☐	170 Juan Nieves	.03	.01	.00
☐	171 Dan Plesac	.03	.01	.00
☐	172 Earnest Riles	.03	.01	.00
☐	173 Bill Schroeder	.03	.01	.00
☐	174 Steve Stanicek	.15	.06	.01
☐	175 B.J. Surhoff	.15	.06	.01
☐	176 Dale Sveum	.03	.01	.00
☐	177 Bill Wegman	.03	.01	.00
☐	178 Robin Yount	.25	.10	.02
☐	179 Hubie Brooks	.06	.02	.00
☐	180 Tim Burke	.03	.01	.00
☐	181 Casey Candaele	.03	.01	.00
☐	182 Mike Fitzgerald	.03	.01	.00
☐	183 Tom Foley	.03	.01	.00
☐	184 Andres Galarraga	.30	.12	.03
☐	185 Neal Heaton	.03	.01	.00
☐	186 Wallace Johnson	.03	.01	.00
☐	187 Vance Law	.06	.02	.00
☐	188 Dennis Martinez	.06	.02	.00
☐	189 Bob McClure	.03	.01	.00
☐	190 Andy McGaffigan	.03	.01	.00
☐	191 Reid Nichols	.03	.01	.00
☐	192 Pascual Perez	.06	.02	.00
☐	193 Tim Raines	.20	.08	.02
☐	194 Jeff Reed	.03	.01	.00
☐	195 Bob Sebra	.03	.01	.00
☐	196 Bryn Smith	.03	.01	.00
☐	197 Randy St.Claire	.03	.01	.00
☐	198 Tim Wallach	.08	.03	.01
☐	199 Mitch Webster	.03	.01	.00
☐	200 Herm Winningham	.03	.01	.00
☐	201 Floyd Youmans	.03	.01	.00
☐	202 Brad Arnsberg	.10	.04	.01
☐	203 Rick Cerone	.03	.01	.00
☐	204 Pat Clements	.03	.01	.00
☐	205 Henry Cotto	.03	.01	.00
☐	206 Mike Easler	.03	.01	.00

□ 207 Ron Guidry .08 .03 .01
□ 208 Bill Gullickson .03 .01 .00
□ 209 Rickey Henderson .25 .10 .02
□ 210 Charles Hudson .03 .01 .00
□ 211 Tommy John .10 .04 .01
□ 212 Roberto Kelly .35 .14 .03
□ 213 Ron Kittle .08 .03 .01
□ 214 Don Mattingly 1.50 .60 .15
□ 215 Bobby Meacham .03 .01 .00
□ 216 Mike Pagliarulo .08 .03 .01
□ 217 Dan Pasqua .06 .02 .00
□ 218 Willie Randolph .06 .02 .00
□ 219 Rick Rhoden .03 .01 .00
□ 220 Dave Righetti .08 .03 .01
□ 221 Jerry Royster .03 .01 .00
□ 222 Tim Stoddard .03 .01 .00
□ 223 Wayne Tolleson .03 .01 .00
□ 224 Gary Ward .03 .01 .00
□ 225 Claudell Washington .06 .02 .00
□ 226 Dave Winfield .25 .10 .02
□ 227 Buddy Bell .08 .03 .01
□ 228 Tom Browning .10 .04 .01
□ 229 Dave Concepcion .08 .03 .01
□ 230 Kal Daniels .18 .08 .01
□ 231 Eric Davis .80 .32 .08
□ 232 Bo Diaz .03 .01 .00
□ 233 Nick Esasky .03 .01 .00
□ 234 John Franco .06 .02 .00
□ 235 Guy Hoffman .03 .01 .00
□ 236 Tom Hume .03 .01 .00
□ 237 Tracy Jones .06 .02 .00
□ 238 Bill Landrum .10 .04 .01
□ 239 Barry Larkin .15 .06 .01
□ 240 Terry McGriff .10 .04 .01
□ 241 Rob Murphy .03 .01 .00
□ 242 Ron Oester .03 .01 .00
□ 243 Dave Parker .10 .04 .01
□ 244 Pat Perry .03 .01 .00
□ 245 Ted Power .03 .01 .00
□ 246 Dennis Rasmussen .06 .02 .00
□ 247 Ron Robinson .03 .01 .00
□ 248 Kurt Stillwell .06 .02 .00
□ 249 Jeff Treadway .30 .12 .03
□ 250 Frank Williams .03 .01 .00
□ 251 Steve Balboni .03 .01 .00
□ 252 Bud Black .03 .01 .00
□ 253 Thad Bosley .03 .01 .00
□ 254 George Brett .30 .12 .03
□ 255 John Davis .15 .06 .01
□ 256 Steve Farr .03 .01 .00
□ 257 Gene Garber .03 .01 .00
□ 258 Jerry Don Gleaton .03 .01 .00
□ 259 Mark Gubicza .08 .03 .01
□ 260 Bo Jackson .30 .12 .03
□ 261 Danny Jackson .15 .06 .01
□ 262 Ross Jones .10 .04 .01
□ 263 Charlie Leibrandt .03 .01 .00
□ 264 Bill Pecota .10 .04 .01
□ 265 Melido Perez .25 .10 .02
□ 266 Jamie Quirk .03 .01 .00
□ 267 Dan Quisenberry .08 .03 .01
□ 268 Bret Saberhagen .12 .05 .01
□ 269 Angel Salazar .03 .01 .00
□ 270 Kevin Seitzer UER .70 .28 .07
(wrong birth year)
□ 271 Danny Tartabull .20 .08 .02
□ 272 Gary Thurman .25 .10 .02
□ 273 Frank White .06 .02 .00
□ 274 Willie Wilson .06 .02 .00
□ 275 Tony Bernazard .03 .01 .00
□ 276 Jose Canseco 2.00 .80 .20
□ 277 Mike Davis .03 .01 .00
□ 278 Storm Davis .06 .02 .00
□ 279 Dennis Eckersley .12 .05 .01
□ 280 Alfredo Griffin .06 .02 .00
□ 281 Rick Honeycutt .03 .01 .00
□ 282 Jay Howell .03 .01 .00
□ 283 Reggie Jackson .30 .12 .03
□ 284 Dennis Lamp .03 .01 .00
□ 285 Carney Lansford .08 .03 .01
□ 286 Mark McGwire 1.25 .50 .12
□ 287 Dwayne Murphy .03 .01 .00
□ 288 Gene Nelson .03 .01 .00
□ 289 Steve Ontiveros .03 .01 .00
□ 290 Tony Phillips .03 .01 .00
□ 291 Eric Plunk .03 .01 .00
□ 292 Luis Polonia .25 .10 .02
□ 293 Rick Rodriguez .10 .04 .01
□ 294 Terry Steinbach .10 .04 .01
□ 295 Dave Stewart .08 .03 .01
□ 296 Curt Young .03 .01 .00
□ 297 Luis Aguayo .03 .01 .00
□ 298 Steve Bedrosian .08 .03 .01
□ 299 Jeff Calhoun .03 .01 .00
□ 300 Don Carman .03 .01 .00
□ 301 Todd Frohwirth .15 .06 .01
□ 302 Greg Gross .03 .01 .00
□ 303 Kevin Gross .03 .01 .00
□ 304 Von Hayes .08 .03 .01
□ 305 Keith Hughes .20 .08 .02
□ 306 Mike Jackson .15 .06 .01
□ 307 Chris James .15 .06 .01
□ 308 Steve Jeltz .03 .01 .00
□ 309 Mike Maddux .03 .01 .00
□ 310 Lance Parrish .10 .04 .01
□ 311 Shane Rawley .03 .01 .00
□ 312 Wally Ritchie .10 .04 .01
□ 313 Bruce Ruffin .03 .01 .00
□ 314 Juan Samuel .08 .03 .01
□ 315 Mike Schmidt .30 .12 .03
□ 316 Rick Schu .03 .01 .00
□ 317 Jeff Stone .03 .01 .00
□ 318 Kent Tekulve .03 .01 .00
□ 319 Milt Thompson .03 .01 .00
□ 320 Glenn Wilson .03 .01 .00
□ 321 Rafael Belliard .03 .01 .00
□ 322 Barry Bonds .20 .08 .02
□ 323 Bobby Bonilla UER .20 .08 .02
(wrong birth year)
□ 324 Sid Bream .03 .01 .00
□ 325 John Cangelosi .03 .01 .00
□ 326 Mike Diaz .03 .01 .00
□ 327 Doug Drabek .03 .01 .00
□ 328 Mike Dunne .20 .08 .02
□ 329 Brian Fisher .03 .01 .00
□ 330 Brett Gideon .12 .05 .01
□ 331 Terry Harper .03 .01 .00
□ 332 Bob Kipper .03 .01 .00
□ 333 Mike LaValliere .03 .01 .00
□ 334 Jose Lind .30 .12 .03
□ 335 Junior Ortiz .03 .01 .00
□ 336 Vincent Palacios .12 .05 .01
□ 337 Bob Patterson .10 .04 .01
□ 338 Al Pedrique .10 .04 .01
□ 339 R.J. Reynolds .03 .01 .00
□ 340 John Smiley .25 .10 .02
□ 341 Andy Van Slyke UER .15 .06 .01
(wrong batting and throwing listed)
□ 342 Bob Walk .06 .02 .00
□ 343 Marty Barrett .06 .02 .00
□ 344 Todd Benzinger .40 .16 .04
□ 345 Wade Boggs 1.00 .40 .10
□ 346 Tom Bolton .15 .06 .01
□ 347 Oil Can Boyd .06 .02 .00
□ 348 Ellis Burks 1.25 .50 .12
□ 349 Roger Clemens .75 .30 .07
□ 350 Steve Crawford .10 .04 .01
□ 351 Dwight Evans .10 .04 .01
□ 352 Wes Gardner .30 .12 .03
□ 353 Rich Gedman .06 .02 .00
□ 354 Mike Greenwell 2.00 .80 .20
□ 355 Sam Horn .35 .14 .03
□ 356 Bruce Hurst .10 .04 .01
□ 357 John Marzano .12 .05 .01
□ 358 Al Nipper .03 .01 .00
□ 359 Spike Owen .03 .01 .00
□ 360 Jody Reed .50 .20 .05
□ 361 Jim Rice .15 .06 .01
□ 362 Ed Romero .03 .01 .00
□ 363 Kevin Romine .12 .05 .01
□ 364 Joe Sambito .03 .01 .00
□ 365 Calvin Schiraldi .03 .01 .00
□ 366 Jeff Sellers .03 .01 .00
□ 367 Bob Stanley .03 .01 .00
□ 368 Scott Bankhead .03 .01 .00
□ 369 Phil Bradley .08 .03 .01
□ 370 Scott Bradley .03 .01 .00
□ 371 Mickey Brantley .06 .02 .00
□ 372 Mike Campbell .15 .06 .01
□ 373 Alvin Davis .08 .03 .01
□ 374 Lee Guetterman .03 .01 .00
□ 375 Dave Hengel .15 .06 .01
□ 376 Mike Kingery .03 .01 .00
□ 377 Mark Langston .08 .03 .01
□ 378 Edgar Martinez .25 .10 .02
□ 379 Mike Moore .06 .02 .00
□ 380 Mike Morgan .03 .01 .00
□ 381 John Moses .03 .01 .00
□ 382 Donnell Nixon .15 .06 .01
□ 383 Edwin Nunez .03 .01 .00
□ 384 Ken Phelps .06 .02 .00
□ 385 Jim Presley .08 .03 .01
□ 386 Rey Quinones .03 .01 .00
□ 387 Jerry Reed .03 .01 .00
□ 388 Harold Reynolds .03 .01 .00
□ 389 Dave Valle .06 .02 .00
□ 390 Bill Wilkinson .10 .04 .01
□ 391 Harold Baines .10 .04 .01
□ 392 Floyd Bannister .03 .01 .00

□ 393	Daryl Boston	.03	.01	.00
□ 394	Ivan Calderon	.08	.03	.01
□ 395	Jose DeLeon	.03	.01	.00
□ 396	Richard Dotson	.03	.01	.00
□ 397	Carlton Fisk	.10	.04	.01
□ 398	Ozzie Guillen	.06	.02	.00
□ 399	Ron Hassey	.03	.01	.00
□ 400	Donnie Hill	.03	.01	.00
□ 401	Bob James	.03	.01	.00
□ 402	Dave LaPoint	.06	.02	.00
□ 403	Bill Lindsey	.10	.04	.01
□ 404	Bill Long	.10	.04	.01
□ 405	Steve Lyons	.03	.01	.00
□ 406	Fred Manrique	.10	.04	.01
□ 407	Jack McDowell	.25	.10	.02
□ 408	Gary Redus	.03	.01	.00
□ 409	Ray Searage	.03	.01	.00
□ 410	Bobby Thigpen	.03	.01	.00
□ 411	Greg Walker	.06	.02	.00
□ 412	Kenny Williams	.20	.08	.02
□ 413	Jim Winn	.03	.01	.00
□ 414	Jody Davis	.06	.02	.00
□ 415	Andre Dawson	.25	.10	.02
□ 416	Brian Dayett	.03	.01	.00
□ 417	Bob Dernier	.03	.01	.00
□ 418	Frank DiPino	.03	.01	.00
□ 419	Shawon Dunston	.06	.02	.00
□ 420	Leon Durham	.06	.02	.00
□ 421	Les Lancaster	.10	.04	.01
□ 422	Ed Lynch	.03	.01	.00
□ 423	Greg Maddux	.45	.18	.04
□ 424	Dave Martinez	.10	.04	.01
□ 425A	Keith Moreland ERR (photo actually Jody Davis)	4.00	1.60	.40
□ 425B	Keith Moreland COR (bat on shoulder)	.15	.06	.01
□ 426	Jamie Moyer	.03	.01	.00
□ 427	Jerry Mumphrey	.03	.01	.00
□ 428	Paul Noce	.12	.05	.01
□ 429	Rafael Palmeiro	.70	.28	.07
□ 430	Wade Rowdon	.08	.03	.01
□ 431	Ryne Sandberg	.20	.08	.02
□ 432	Scott Sanderson	.03	.01	.00
□ 433	Lee Smith	.06	.02	.00
□ 434	Jim Sundberg	.03	.01	.00
□ 435	Rick Sutcliffe	.08	.03	.01
□ 436	Manny Trillo	.03	.01	.00
□ 437	Juan Agosto	.03	.01	.00
□ 438	Larry Andersen	.03	.01	.00
□ 439	Alan Ashby	.03	.01	.00
□ 440	Kevin Bass	.06	.02	.00
□ 441	Ken Caminiti	.20	.08	.02
□ 442	Rocky Childress	.10	.04	.01
□ 443	Jose Cruz	.06	.02	.00
□ 444	Danny Darwin	.03	.01	.00
□ 445	Glenn Davis	.15	.06	.01
□ 446	Jim Deshaies	.03	.01	.00
□ 447	Bill Doran	.06	.02	.00
□ 448	Ty Gainey	.06	.02	.00
□ 449	Billy Hatcher	.06	.02	.00
□ 450	Jeff Heathcock	.03	.01	.00
□ 451	Bob Knepper	.06	.02	.00
□ 452	Rob Mallicoat	.10	.04	.01
□ 453	Dave Meads	.08	.03	.01
□ 454	Craig Reynolds	.03	.01	.00
□ 455	Nolan Ryan	.30	.12	.03
□ 456	Mike Scott	.12	.05	.01
□ 457	Dave Smith	.03	.01	.00
□ 458	Denny Walling	.03	.01	.00
□ 459	Robbie Wine	.10	.04	.01
□ 460	Gerald Young	.30	.12	.03
□ 461	Bob Brower	.10	.04	.01
□ 462A	Jerry Browne ERR (photo actually Bob Brower, white player)	4.00	1.60	.40
□ 462B	Jerry Browne COR (black player)	.15	.06	.01
□ 463	Steve Buechele	.03	.01	.00
□ 464	Edwin Correa	.03	.01	.00
□ 465	Cecil Espy	.15	.06	.01
□ 466	Scott Fletcher	.03	.01	.00
□ 467	Jose Guzman	.03	.01	.00
□ 468	Greg Harris	.03	.01	.00
□ 469	Charlie Hough	.03	.01	.00
□ 470	Pete Incaviglia	.18	.08	.01
□ 471	Paul Kilgus	.15	.06	.01
□ 472	Mike Loynd	.03	.01	.00
□ 473	Oddibe McDowell	.08	.03	.01
□ 474	Dale Mohorcic	.03	.01	.00
□ 475	Pete O'Brien	.08	.03	.01
□ 476	Larry Parrish	.03	.01	.00
□ 477	Geno Petralli	.03	.01	.00
□ 478	Jeff Russell	.03	.01	.00
□ 479	Ruben Sierra	.20	.08	.02
□ 480	Mike Stanley	.03	.01	.00
□ 481	Curtis Wilkerson	.03	.01	.00
□ 482	Mitch Williams	.03	.01	.00
□ 483	Bobby Witt	.06	.02	.00
□ 484	Tony Armas	.06	.02	.00
□ 485	Bob Boone	.06	.02	.00
□ 486	Bill Buckner	.06	.02	.00
□ 487	DeWayne Buice	.12	.05	.01
□ 488	Brian Downing	.06	.02	.00
□ 489	Chuck Finley	.03	.01	.00
□ 490	Willie Fraser UER (wrong bio stats, for George Hendrick)	.03	.01	.00
□ 491	Jack Howell	.03	.01	.00
□ 492	Ruppert Jones	.03	.01	.00
□ 493	Wally Joyner	.45	.18	.04
□ 494	Jack Lazorko	.06	.02	.00
□ 495	Gary Lucas	.03	.01	.00
□ 496	Kirk McCaskill	.03	.01	.00
□ 497	Mark McLemore	.03	.01	.00
□ 498	Darrell Miller	.03	.01	.00
□ 499	Greg Minton	.03	.01	.00
□ 500	Donnie Moore	.03	.01	.00
□ 501	Gus Polidor	.03	.01	.00
□ 502	Johnny Ray	.06	.02	.00
□ 503	Mark Ryal	.06	.02	.00
□ 504	Dick Schofield	.03	.01	.00
□ 505	Don Sutton	.12	.05	.01
□ 506	Devon White	.15	.06	.01
□ 507	Mike Witt	.08	.03	.01
□ 508	Dave Anderson	.03	.01	.00
□ 509	Tim Belcher	.25	.10	.02
□ 510	Ralph Bryant	.03	.01	.00
□ 511	Tim Crews	.10	.04	.01
□ 512	Mike Devereaux	.30	.12	.03
□ 513	Mariano Duncan	.03	.01	.00
□ 514	Pedro Guerrero	.15	.06	.01
□ 515	Jeff Hamilton	.10	.04	.01
□ 516	Mickey Hatcher	.06	.02	.00
□ 517	Brad Havens	.03	.01	.00
□ 518	Orel Hershiser	.25	.10	.02
□ 519	Shawn Hillegas	.15	.06	.01
□ 520	Ken Howell	.03	.01	.00
□ 521	Tim Leary	.08	.03	.01
□ 522	Mike Marshall	.10	.04	.01
□ 523	Steve Sax	.15	.06	.01
□ 524	Mike Scioscia	.03	.01	.00
□ 525	Mike Sharperson	.06	.02	.00
□ 526	John Shelby	.03	.01	.00
□ 527	Franklin Stubbs	.03	.01	.00
□ 528	Fernando Valenzuela	.15	.06	.01
□ 529	Bob Welch	.06	.02	.00
□ 530	Matt Young	.03	.01	.00
□ 531	Jim Acker	.03	.01	.00
□ 532	Paul Assenmacher	.03	.01	.00
□ 533	Jeff Blauser	.20	.08	.02
□ 534	Joe Boever	.15	.06	.01
□ 535	Martin Clary	.06	.02	.00
□ 536	Kevin Coffman	.10	.04	.01
□ 537	Jeff Dedmon	.03	.01	.00
□ 538	Ronnie Gant	.70	.28	.07
□ 539	Tom Glavine	.20	.08	.02
□ 540	Ken Griffey	.06	.02	.00
□ 541	Albert Hall	.03	.01	.00
□ 542	Glenn Hubbard	.03	.01	.00
□ 543	Dion James	.03	.01	.00
□ 544	Dale Murphy	.30	.12	.03
□ 545	Ken Oberkfell	.03	.01	.00
□ 546	David Palmer	.03	.01	.00
□ 547	Gerald Perry	.08	.03	.01
□ 548	Charlie Puleo	.03	.01	.00
□ 549	Ted Simmons	.08	.03	.01
□ 550	Zane Smith	.06	.02	.00
□ 551	Andres Thomas	.03	.01	.00
□ 552	Ozzie Virgil	.03	.01	.00
□ 553	Don Aase	.03	.01	.00
□ 554	Jeff Ballard	.15	.06	.01
□ 555	Eric Bell	.06	.02	.00
□ 556	Mike Boddicker	.06	.02	.00
□ 557	Ken Dixon	.03	.01	.00
□ 558	Jim Dwyer	.03	.01	.00
□ 559	Ken Gerhart	.08	.03	.01
□ 560	Rene Gonzales	.12	.05	.01
□ 561	Mike Griffin	.03	.01	.00
□ 562	John Habyan UER (misspelled Hayban on both sides of card)	.08	.03	.01
□ 563	Terry Kennedy	.03	.01	.00
□ 564	Ray Knight	.06	.02	.00
□ 565	Lee Lacy	.03	.01	.00
□ 566	Fred Lynn	.12	.05	.01
□ 567	Eddie Murray	.20	.08	.02
□ 568	Tom Niedenfuer	.03	.01	.00
□ 569	Bill Ripken	.15	.06	.01

□ 570 Cal Ripken Jr.	.20	.08	.02
□ 571 Dave Schmidt	.03	.01	.00
□ 572 Larry Sheets	.08	.03	.01
□ 573 Pete Stanicek	.20	.08	.02
□ 574 Mark Williamson	.10	.04	.01
□ 575 Mike Young	.03	.01	.00
□ 576 Shawn Abner	.20	.08	.02
□ 577 Greg Booker	.03	.01	.00
□ 578 Chris Brown	.08	.03	.01
□ 579 Keith Comstock	.12	.05	.01
□ 580 Joey Cora	.12	.05	.01
□ 581 Mark Davis	.06	.02	.00
□ 582 Tim Flannery (with surfboard)	.03	.01	.00
□ 583 Goose Gossage	.08	.03	.01
□ 584 Mark Grant	.06	.02	.00
□ 585 Tony Gwynn	.35	.14	.03
□ 586 Andy Hawkins	.03	.01	.00
□ 587 Stan Jefferson	.25	.10	.02
□ 588 Jimmy Jones	.06	.02	.00
□ 589 John Kruk	.10	.04	.01
□ 590 Shane Mack	.18	.08	.01
□ 591 Carmelo Martinez	.03	.01	.00
□ 592 Lance McCullers	.06	.02	.00
□ 593 Eric Nolte	.15	.06	.01
□ 594 Randy Ready	.03	.01	.00
□ 595 Luis Salazar	.03	.01	.00
□ 596 Benito Santiago	.40	.16	.04
□ 597 Eric Show	.03	.01	.00
□ 598 Garry Templeton	.06	.02	.00
□ 599 Ed Whitson	.03	.01	.00
□ 600 Scott Bailes	.03	.01	.00
□ 601 Chris Bando	.03	.01	.00
□ 602 Jay Bell	.20	.08	.02
□ 603 Brett Butler	.06	.02	.00
□ 604 Tom Candiotti	.03	.01	.00
□ 605 Joe Carter	.12	.05	.01
□ 606 Carmen Castillo	.03	.01	.00
□ 607 Brian Dorsett	.12	.05	.01
□ 608 John Farrell	.25	.10	.02
□ 609 Julio Franco	.08	.03	.01
□ 610 Mel Hall	.06	.02	.00
□ 611 Tommy Hinzo	.10	.04	.01
□ 612 Brook Jacoby	.08	.03	.01
□ 613 Doug Jones	.35	.14	.03
□ 614 Ken Schrom	.03	.01	.00
□ 615 Cory Snyder	.20	.08	.02
□ 616 Sammy Stewart	.03	.01	.00
□ 617 Greg Swindell	.12	.05	.01
□ 618 Pat Tabler	.06	.02	.00
□ 619 Ed VandeBerg	.03	.01	.00
□ 620 Eddie Williams	.18	.08	.01
□ 621 Rich Yett	.03	.01	.00
□ 622 Slugging Sophomores Wally Joyner Cory Snyder	.12	.05	.01
□ 623 Dominican Dynamite George Bell Pedro Guerrero	.10	.04	.01
□ 624 Oakland's Power Team Mark McGwire Jose Canseco	.75	.30	.07
□ 625 Classic Relief Dave Righetti Dan Plesac	.10	.04	.01
□ 626 All Star Righties Bret Saberhagen Mike Witt Jack Morris	.10	.04	.01
□ 627 Game Closers John Franco Steve Bedrosian	.08	.03	.01
□ 628 Masters/Double Play Ozzie Smith Ryne Sandberg	.10	.04	.01
□ 629 Rookie Record Setter Mark McGwire	.40	.16	.04
□ 630 Changing the Guard Mike Greenwell Ellis Burks Todd Benzinger	.75	.30	.07
□ 631 NL Batting Champs Tony Gwynn Tim Raines	.18	.08	.01
□ 632 Pitching Magic Mike Scott Orel Hershiser	.15	.06	.01
□ 633 Big Bats at First Pat Tabler Mark McGwire	.30	.12	.03
□ 634 Hitting King/Thief Tony Gwynn Vince Coleman	.12	.05	.01
□ 635 Slugging Shortstops Tony Fernandez Cal Ripken Alan Trammell	.12	.05	.01
□ 636 Tried/True Sluggers Mike Schmidt Gary Carter	.12	.05	.01
□ 637 Crunch Time Darryl Strawberry Eric Davis	.35	.14	.03
□ 638 AL All-Stars Matt Nokes Kirby Puckett	.15	.06	.01
□ 639 NL All-Stars Keith Hernandez Dale Murphy	.12	.05	.01
□ 640 The O's Brothers Billy Ripken Cal Ripken	.08	.03	.01
□ 641 Mark Grace and Darrin Jackson	4.00	1.60	.40
□ 642 Damon Berryhill and Jeff Montgomery	.60	.24	.06
□ 643 Felix Fermin and Jesse Reid	.12	.05	.01
□ 644 Greg Myers and Greg Tabor	.20	.08	.02
□ 645 Joey Meyer and Jim Eppard	.35	.14	.03
□ 646 Adam Peterson and Randy Velarde	.20	.08	.02
□ 647 Peter Smith and Chris Gwynn	.40	.16	.04
□ 648 Tom Newell and Greg Jelks	.15	.06	.01
□ 649 Mario Diaz and Clay Parker	.20	.08	.02
□ 650 Jack Savage and Todd Simmons	.20	.08	.02
□ 651 John Burkett and Kirt Manwaring	.25	.10	.02
□ 652 Dave Otto and Walt Weiss	2.00	.80	.20
□ 653 Jeff King and Randell Byers	.25	.10	.02
□ 654 CL: Twins/Cards Tigers/Giants UER (90 Bob Melvin, 91 Eddie Milner)	.06	.01	.00
□ 655 CL: Blue Jays/Mets Brewers/Expos UER (Mets listed before Blue Jays on card)	.06	.01	.00
□ 656 CL: Yankees/Reds Royals/A's	.06	.01	.00
□ 657 CL: Phillies/Pirates Red Sox/Mariners	.06	.01	.00
□ 658 CL: White Sox/Cubs Astros/Rangers	.06	.01	.00
□ 659 CL: Angels/Dodgers Braves/Orioles	.06	.01	.00
□ 660 CL: Padres/Indians Rookies/Specials	.06	.01	.00

1988 Fleer Wax Box Cards

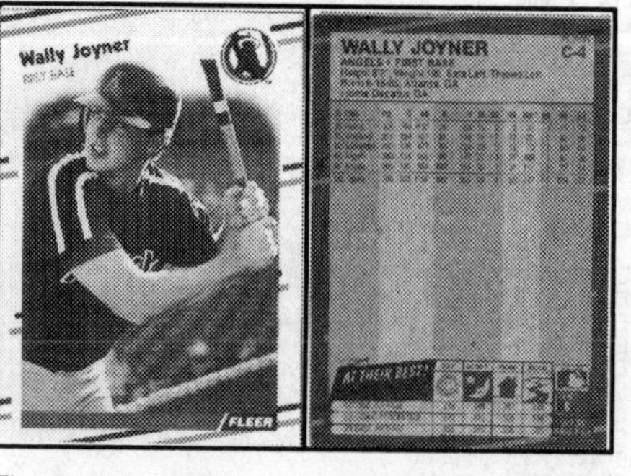

The cards in this 16-card set measure the standard 2 1/2" by 3 1/2". Cards have essentially the same design as the 1988 Fleer regular issue set. The cards were printed on the bottoms of the regular issue wax pack boxes. These 16 cards (C1 to C16) are considered a separate set in their own right and are not typically included in a complete set of the regular issue 1988 Fleer cards. The value of the panel uncut is slightly greater, perhaps by 25% greater, than the value of the individual cards cut up carefully.

	MINT	EXC	G-VG
COMPLETE SET (16)	3.00	1.20	.30
COMMON PLAYER (C1-C16)	.05	.02	.00
□ C1 Cardinals Logo	.05	.02	.00
□ C2 Dwight Evans	.10	.04	.01
□ C3 Andres Galarraga	.20	.08	.02
□ C4 Wally Joyner	.60	.24	.06
□ C5 Twins Logo	.05	.02	.00
□ C6 Dale Murphy	.35	.14	.03
□ C7 Kirby Puckett	.50	.20	.05
□ C8 Shane Rawley	.10	.04	.01
□ C9 Giants Logo	.05	.02	.00
□ C10 Ryne Sandberg	.25	.10	.02
□ C11 Mike Schmidt	.40	.16	.04
□ C12 Kevin Seitzer	.60	.24	.06
□ C13 Tigers Logo	.05	.02	.00
□ C14 Dave Stewart	.10	.04	.01
□ C15 Tim Wallach	.10	.04	.01
□ C16 Todd Worrell	.15	.06	.01

1988 Fleer All-Star Inserts

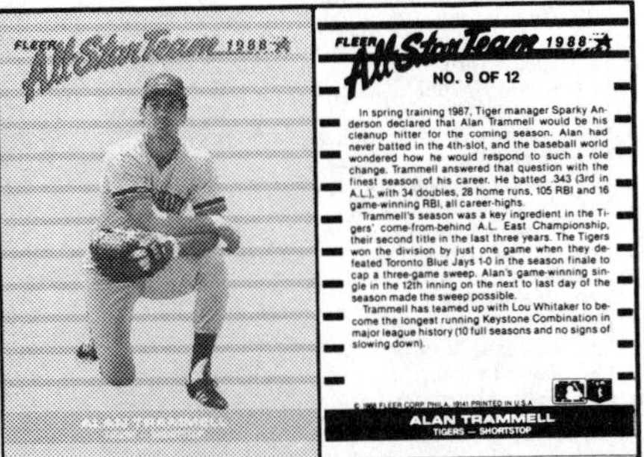

The cards in this 12-card set measure the standard 2 1/2" by 3 1/2". These cards were inserted (randomly) in wax and cello packs of the 1988 Fleer regular issue set. The cards show the player silhouetted against a light green background with dark green stripes. The player's name, team, and position are printed in yellow at the bottom of the obverse. The card backs are done predominantly in green, white, and black. Cards are numbered on the back. These 12 cards are considered a separate set in their own right and are not typically included in a complete set of the regular issue 1988 Fleer cards. The players are the "best" at each position, three pitchers, eight position players, and a designated hitter.

	MINT	EXC	G-VG
COMPLETE SET (12)	12.00	5.00	1.20
COMMON PLAYERS (1-12)	.25	.10	.02
□ 1 Matt Nokes Catcher	.60	.24	.06
□ 2 Tom Henke Relief Pitcher	.25	.10	.02
□ 3 Ted Higuera Left Hand Pitcher	.50	.20	.05
□ 4 Roger Clemens Right Hand Pitcher	2.00	.80	.20
□ 5 George Bell Outfielder	.60	.24	.06
□ 6 Andre Dawson Outfielder	.60	.24	.06
□ 7 Eric Davis Outfielder	2.00	.80	.20
□ 8 Wade Boggs Third Baseman	2.50	1.00	.25
□ 9 Alan Trammell Shortstop	.75	.30	.07
□ 10 Juan Samuel Second Baseman	.35	.14	.03
□ 11 Jack Clark First Baseman	.60	.24	.06
□ 12 Paul Molitor Designated Hitter	.50	.20	.05

1988 Fleer Headliners

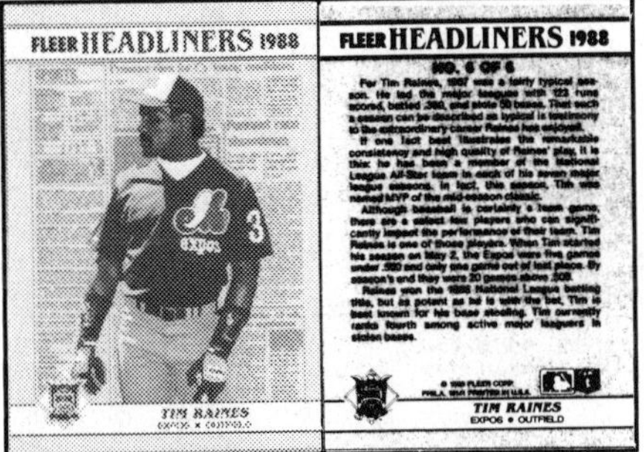

This six-card set was distributed as a special insert in rack packs. The obverse features the player photo superimposed on a gray newsprint background. Cards are 2 1/2" by 3 1/2". The cards are printed in red, black, and white on the back describing why that particular player made headlines the previous season. The cards are numbered on the back.

	MINT	EXC	G-VG
COMPLETE SET (6)	6.00	2.40	.60
COMMON PLAYER (1-6)	.50	.20	.05
□ 1 Don Mattingly New York Yankees	3.00	1.20	.30
□ 2 Mark McGwire Oakland Athletics	2.00	.80	.20
□ 3 Jack Morris Detroit Tigers	.50	.20	.05
□ 4 Darryl Strawberry New York Mets	1.00	.40	.10
□ 5 Dwight Gooden New York Mets	1.00	.40	.10
□ 6 Tim Raines Montreal Expos	.75	.30	.07

1988 Fleer Update

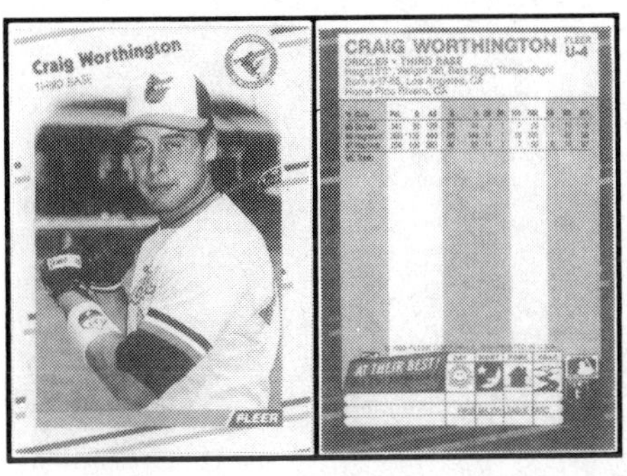

This 132-card set was distributed by Fleer to dealers as a complete set within a custom box. In addition to the complete set of 132 cards, the box also contains 25 Team Logo stickers.The card fronts look very similar to the 1987 Fleer regular issue. The cards are numbered (with a U prefix) alphabetically according to player's last name. Cards measure the standard size, 2 1/2" by 3 1/2". This was the first Fleer Update set to adopt the Fleer "alphabetical within team" numbering system.

	MINT	EXC	G-VG
COMPLETE SET (132)	12.00	5.00	1.20
COMMON PLAYER (1-132)	.05	.02	.00
☐ U1 Jose Bautista	.12	.05	.01
☐ U2 Joe Orsulak	.05	.02	.00
☐ U3 Doug Sisk	.05	.02	.00
☐ U4 Craig Worthington	.20	.08	.02
☐ U5 Mike Boddicker	.08	.03	.01
☐ U6 Rick Cerone	.05	.02	.00
☐ U7 Larry Parrish	.05	.02	.00
☐ U8 Lee Smith	.08	.03	.01
☐ U9 Mike Smithson	.05	.02	.00
☐ U10 John Trautwein	.12	.05	.01
☐ U11 Sherman Corbett	.15	.06	.01
☐ U12 Chili Davis	.08	.03	.01
☐ U13 Jim Eppard	.05	.02	.00
☐ U14 Bryan Harvey	.30	.12	.03
☐ U15 John Davis	.05	.02	.00
☐ U16 Dave Gallagher	.25	.10	.02
☐ U17 Ricky Horton	.05	.02	.00
☐ U18 Dan Pasqua	.08	.03	.01
☐ U19 Melido Perez	.20	.08	.02
☐ U20 Jose Segura	.12	.05	.01
☐ U21 Andy Allanson	.05	.02	.00
☐ U22 Jon Perlman	.05	.02	.00
☐ U23 Domingo Ramos	.08	.03	.01
☐ U24 Rick Rodriguez	.05	.02	.00
☐ U25 Willie Upshaw	.05	.02	.00
☐ U26 Paul Gibson	.15	.06	.01
☐ U27 Don Heinkel	.15	.06	.01
☐ U28 Ray Knight	.08	.03	.01
☐ U29 Gary Pettis	.08	.03	.01
☐ U30 Luis Salazar	.05	.02	.00
☐ U31 Mike MacFarlane	.20	.08	.02
☐ U32 Jeff Montgomery	.08	.03	.01
☐ U33 Ted Power	.05	.02	.00
☐ U34 Israel Sanchez	.12	.05	.01
☐ U35 Kurt Stillwell	.08	.03	.01
☐ U36 Pat Tabler	.08	.03	.01
☐ U37 Don August	.20	.08	.02
☐ U38 Darryl Hamilton	.25	.10	.02
☐ U39 Jeff Leonard	.08	.03	.01
☐ U40 Joey Meyer	.20	.08	.02
☐ U41 Allan Anderson	.10	.04	.01
☐ U42 Brian Harper	.05	.02	.00
☐ U43 Tom Herr	.08	.03	.01
☐ U44 Charlie Lea	.05	.02	.00
☐ U45 John Moses (listed as Hohn on checklist card)	.05	.02	.00
☐ U46 John Candelaria	.08	.03	.01
☐ U47 Jack Clark	.15	.06	.01
☐ U48 Richard Dotson	.08	.03	.01
☐ U49 Al Leiter	.45	.18	.04
☐ U50 Rafael Santana	.05	.02	.00
☐ U51 Don Slaught	.05	.02	.00
☐ U52 Todd Burns	.25	.10	.02
☐ U53 Dave Henderson	.08	.03	.01
☐ U54 Doug Jennings	.25	.10	.02
☐ U55 Dave Parker	.15	.06	.01
☐ U56 Walt Weiss	.75	.30	.07
☐ U57 Bob Welch	.08	.03	.01
☐ U58 Henry Cotto	.05	.02	.00
☐ U59 Mario Diaz UER (listed as Marion on card front)	.08	.03	.01
☐ U60 Mike Jackson	.08	.03	.01
☐ U61 Bill Swift	.08	.03	.01
☐ U62 Jose Cecena	.10	.04	.01
☐ U63 Ray Hayward	.10	.04	.01
☐ U64 Jim Steels UER (listed as Jim Steele on card back)	.10	.04	.01
☐ U65 Pat Borders	.20	.08	.02
☐ U66 Sil Campusano	.25	.10	.02
☐ U67 Mike Flanagan	.08	.03	.01
☐ U68 Todd Stottlemyre	.25	.10	.02
☐ U69 David Wells	.15	.06	.01
☐ U70 Jose Alvarez	.12	.05	.01
☐ U71 Paul Runge	.05	.02	.00
☐ U72 Cesar Jimenez (card was intended for German Jiminez, it's his photo)	.15	.06	.01
☐ U73 Pete Smith	.15	.06	.01
☐ U74 John Smoltz	.25	.10	.02
☐ U75 Damon Berryhill	.25	.10	.02
☐ U76 Goose Gossage	.10	.04	.01
☐ U77 Mark Grace	1.50	.60	.15
☐ U78 Darrin Jackson	.20	.08	.02
☐ U79 Vance Law	.08	.03	.01
☐ U80 Jeff Pico	.15	.06	.01
☐ U81 Gary Varsho	.25	.10	.02
☐ U82 Tim Birtsas	.05	.02	.00
☐ U83 Rob Dibble	.20	.08	.02
☐ U84 Danny Jackson	.20	.08	.02
☐ U85 Paul O'Neil	.08	.03	.01
☐ U86 Jose Rijo	.08	.03	.01
☐ U87 Chris Sabo	1.75	.70	.17
☐ U88 John Fishel	.20	.08	.02
☐ U89 Craig Biggio	.15	.06	.01
☐ U90 Terry Puhl	.05	.02	.00
☐ U91 Rafael Ramirez	.05	.02	.00
☐ U92 Louie Meadows	.12	.05	.01
☐ U93 Kirk Gibson	.25	.10	.02
☐ U94 Alfredo Griffin	.08	.03	.01
☐ U95 Jay Howell	.05	.02	.00
☐ U96 Jesse Orosco	.05	.02	.00
☐ U97 Alejandro Pena	.05	.02	.00
☐ U98 Tracy Woodson	.25	.10	.02
☐ U99 John Dopson	.20	.08	.02
☐ U100 Brian Holman	.20	.08	.02
☐ U101 Rex Hudler	.05	.02	.00
☐ U102 Jeff Parrett	.08	.03	.01
☐ U103 Nelson Santovenia	.15	.06	.01
☐ U104 Kevin Elster	.15	.06	.01
☐ U105 Jeff Innis	.20	.08	.02
☐ U106 Mackey Sasser	.25	.10	.02
☐ U107 Phil Bradley	.08	.03	.01
☐ U108 Danny Clay	.15	.06	.01
☐ U109 Greg Harris	.05	.02	.00
☐ U110 Ricky Jordan	2.25	.90	.22
☐ U111 David Palmer	.05	.02	.00
☐ U112 Jim Gott	.08	.03	.01
☐ U113 Tommy Gregg	.25	.10	.02
☐ U114 Barry Jones	.05	.02	.00
☐ U115 Randy Milligan	.25	.10	.02
☐ U116 Luis Alicea	.15	.06	.01
☐ U117 Tom Brunansky	.10	.04	.01
☐ U118 John Costello	.15	.06	.01
☐ U119 Jose DeLeon	.05	.02	.00
☐ U120 Bob Horner	.10	.04	.01
☐ U121 Scott Terry	.12	.05	.01
☐ U122 Roberto Alomar	.35	.14	.03
☐ U123 Dave Leiper	.05	.02	.00
☐ U124 Keith Moreland	.05	.02	.00
☐ U125 Mark Parent	.12	.05	.01
☐ U126 Dennis Rassmussen	.08	.03	.01
☐ U127 Randy Bockus	.05	.02	.00
☐ U128 Brett Butler	.08	.03	.01
☐ U129 Donell Nixon	.08	.03	.01
☐ U130 Earnest Riles	.05	.02	.00
☐ U131 Roger Samuels	.12	.05	.01
☐ U132 Checklist U1-U132	.05	.01	.00

1988 Fleer Award Winners

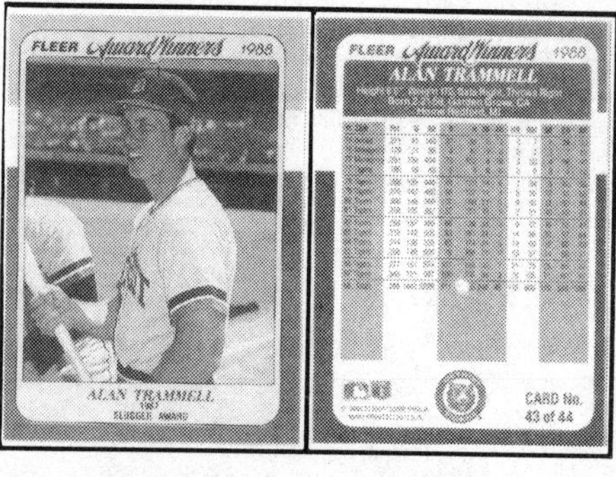

This small set of 44 cards was produced for 7- Eleven stores by Fleer. The cards measure the standard 2 1/2" by 3 1/2" and feature full color fronts and red, white, and blue backs. The card fronts are distinguished by the red, white, and blue frame around the player's full-color photo. The box for the cards describes the set as the "1988 Limited Edition

Baseball Award Winners." The checklist for the set is given on the back of the set box.

	MINT	EXC	G-VG
COMPLETE SET (44)	4.00	1.60	.40
COMMON PLAYER (1-44)	.05	.02	.00

	MINT	EXC	G-VG
☐ 1 Steve Bedrosian	.10	.04	.01
☐ 2 George Bell	.15	.06	.01
☐ 3 Wade Boggs	.65	.26	.06
☐ 4 Jose Canseco	1.00	.40	.10
☐ 5 Will Clark	.50	.20	.05
☐ 6 Roger Clemens	.50	.20	.05
☐ 7 Kal Daniels	.20	.08	.02
☐ 8 Eric Davis	.50	.20	.05
☐ 9 Andre Dawson	.20	.08	.02
☐ 10 Mike Dunne	.10	.04	.01
☐ 11 Dwight Evans	.10	.04	.01
☐ 12 Carlton Fisk	.10	.04	.01
☐ 13 Julio Franco	.05	.02	.00
☐ 14 Dwight Gooden	.35	.14	.03
☐ 15 Pedro Guerrero	.15	.06	.01
☐ 16 Tony Gwynn	.30	.12	.03
☐ 17 Orel Hershiser	.35	.14	.03
☐ 18 Tom Henke	.05	.02	.00
☐ 19 Ted Higuera	.10	.04	.01
☐ 20 Charlie Hough	.05	.02	.00
☐ 21 Wally Joyner	.35	.14	.03
☐ 22 Jimmy Key	.05	.02	.00
☐ 23 Don Mattingly	1.00	.40	.10
☐ 24 Mark McGwire	.65	.26	.06
☐ 25 Paul Molitor	.10	.04	.01
☐ 26 Jack Morris	.10	.04	.01
☐ 27 Dale Murphy	.35	.14	.03
☐ 28 Terry Pendleton	.05	.02	.00
☐ 29 Kirby Puckett	.35	.14	.03
☐ 30 Tim Raines	.20	.08	.02
☐ 31 Jeff Reardon	.05	.02	.00
☐ 32 Harold Reynolds	.05	.02	.00
☐ 33 Dave Righetti	.10	.04	.01
☐ 34 Benito Santiago	.25	.10	.02
☐ 35 Mike Schmidt	.35	.14	.03
☐ 36 Mike Scott	.15	.06	.01
☐ 37 Kevin Seitzer	.30	.12	.03
☐ 38 Larry Sheets	.10	.04	.01
☐ 39 Ozzie Smith	.15	.06	.01
☐ 40 Darryl Strawberry	.50	.20	.05
☐ 41 Rick Sutcliffe	.10	.04	.01
☐ 42 Danny Tartabull	.20	.08	.02
☐ 43 Alan Trammell	.15	.06	.01
☐ 44 Tim Wallach	.05	.02	.00

1988 Fleer Baseball All-Stars

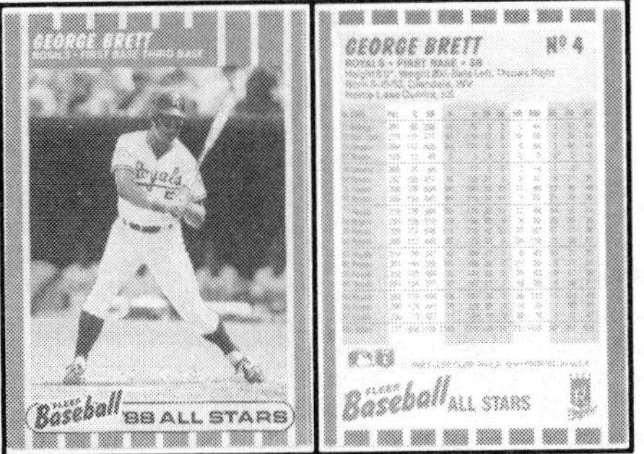

This small boxed set of 44 cards was produced exclusively for Ben Franklin Stores. The cards measure the standard 2 1/2" by 3 1/2" and feature full color fronts and white and blue backs. The card fronts are distinguished by the yellow and blue striped background behind the player's full-color photo. The box for the cards describes the set as the "1988 Fleer Baseball All-Stars." The checklist for the set is given on the back of the set box.

	MINT	EXC	G-VG
COMPLETE SET (44)	5.00	2.00	.50
COMMON PLAYER (1-44)	.10	.04	.01

	MINT	EXC	G-VG
☐ 1 George Bell	.20	.08	.02
☐ 2 Wade Boggs	.75	.30	.07
☐ 3 Bobby Bonilla	.20	.08	.02
☐ 4 George Brett	.40	.16	.04
☐ 5 Jose Canseco	1.25	.50	.12
☐ 6 Jack Clark	.20	.08	.02
☐ 7 Will Clark	.60	.24	.06
☐ 8 Roger Clemens	.60	.24	.06
☐ 9 Eric Davis	.60	.24	.06
☐ 10 Andre Dawson	.25	.10	.02
☐ 11 Julio Franco	.10	.04	.01
☐ 12 Dwight Gooden	.50	.20	.05
☐ 13 Tony Gwynn	.45	.18	.04
☐ 14 Orel Hershiser	.50	.20	.05
☐ 15 Teddy Higuera	.20	.08	.02
☐ 16 Charlie Hough	.10	.04	.01
☐ 17 Kent Hrbek	.20	.08	.02
☐ 18 Bruce Hurst	.20	.08	.02
☐ 19 Wally Joyner	.40	.16	.04
☐ 20 Mark Langston	.15	.06	.01
☐ 21 Dave LaPoint	.15	.06	.01
☐ 22 Candy Maldonado	.10	.04	.01
☐ 23 Don Mattingly	1.00	.40	.10
☐ 24 Roger McDowell	.15	.06	.01
☐ 25 Mark McGwire	.75	.30	.07
☐ 26 Jack Morris	.15	.06	.01
☐ 27 Dale Murphy	.40	.16	.04
☐ 28 Eddie Murray	.35	.14	.03
☐ 29 Matt Nokes	.25	.10	.02
☐ 30 Kirby Puckett	.40	.16	.04
☐ 31 Tim Raines	.25	.10	.02
☐ 32 Willie Randolph	.15	.06	.01
☐ 33 Jeff Reardon	.15	.06	.01
☐ 34 Nolan Ryan	.30	.12	.03
☐ 35 Juan Samuel	.15	.06	.01
☐ 36 Mike Schmidt	.40	.16	.04
☐ 37 Mike Scott	.15	.06	.01
☐ 38 Kevin Seitzer	.35	.14	.03
☐ 39 Ozzie Smith	.20	.08	.02
☐ 40 Darryl Strawberry	.60	.24	.06
☐ 41 Rick Sutcliffe	.15	.06	.01
☐ 42 Alan Trammell	.20	.08	.02
☐ 43 Tim Wallach	.10	.04	.01
☐ 44 Dave Winfield	.25	.10	.02

1988 Fleer Baseball MVP

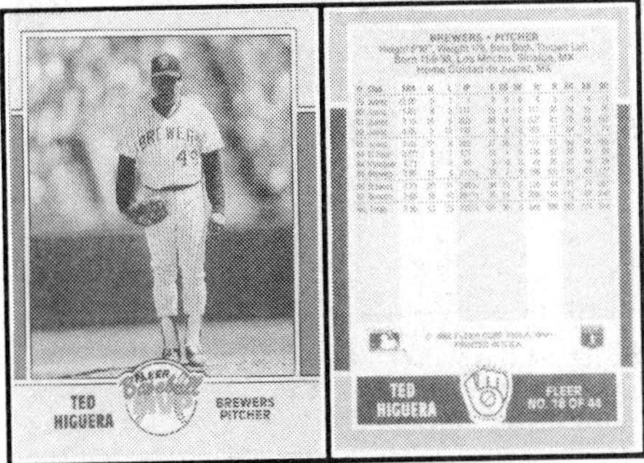

This small 44-card boxed set was produced by Fleer for distribution by the Toys'r'Us stores. The cards measure the standard 2 1/2" by 3 1/2" and feature full color fronts. The set is titled "Baseball MVP." Each individual boxed set includes the 44 cards and 6 logo stickers. The checklist for the set is found on the back panel of the box. The card fronts have a vanilla-yellow and blue border. The box refers to Toys'r'Us but there is no mention of Toys'r'Us anywhere on the cards themselves.

	MINT	EXC	G-VG
COMPLETE SET (44)	5.00	2.00	.50
COMMON PLAYER (1-44)	.10	.04	.01

	MINT	EXC	G-VG
☐ 1 George Bell	.20	.08	.02
☐ 2 Wade Boggs	.75	.30	.07
☐ 3 Jose Canseco	1.25	.50	.12
☐ 4 Ivan Calderon	.15	.06	.01
☐ 5 Will Clark	.60	.24	.06

☐ 6	Roger Clemens	.60	.24	.06
☐ 7	Vince Coleman	.25	.10	.02
☐ 8	Eric Davis	.60	.24	.06
☐ 9	Andre Dawson	.25	.10	.02
☐ 10	Dave Dravecky	.10	.04	.01
☐ 11	Mike Dunne	.15	.06	.01
☐ 12	Dwight Evans	.15	.06	.01
☐ 13	Sid Fernandez	.15	.06	.01
☐ 14	Tony Fernandez	.15	.06	.01
☐ 15	Julio Franco	.10	.04	.01
☐ 16	Dwight Gooden	.40	.16	.04
☐ 17	Tony Gwynn	.35	.14	.03
☐ 18	Ted Higuera	.20	.08	.02
☐ 19	Charlie Hough	.10	.04	.01
☐ 20	Wally Joyner	.40	.16	.04
☐ 21	Mark Langston	.15	.06	.01
☐ 22	Don Mattingly	1.00	.40	.10
☐ 23	Mark McGwire	.75	.30	.07
☐ 24	Jack Morris	.15	.06	.01
☐ 25	Dale Murphy	.40	.16	.04
☐ 26	Kirby Puckett	.40	.16	.04
☐ 27	Tim Raines	.25	.10	.02
☐ 28	Willie Randolph	.15	.06	.01
☐ 29	Ryne Sandberg	.25	.10	.02
☐ 30	Benito Santiago	.30	.12	.03
☐ 31	Mike Schmidt	.40	.16	.04
☐ 32	Mike Scott	.15	.06	.01
☐ 33	Kevin Seitzer	.35	.14	.03
☐ 34	Larry Sheets	.15	.06	.01
☐ 35	Ozzie Smith	.20	.08	.02
☐ 36	Dave Stewart	.15	.06	.01
☐ 37	Darryl Strawberry	.60	.24	.06
☐ 38	Rick Sutcliffe	.15	.06	.01
☐ 39	Alan Trammell	.20	.08	.02
☐ 40	Fernando Valenzuela	.20	.08	.02
☐ 41	Frank Viola	.20	.08	.02
☐ 42	Tim Wallach	.10	.04	.01
☐ 43	Dave Winfield	.25	.10	.02
☐ 44	Robin Yount	.25	.10	.02

1988 Fleer Exciting Stars

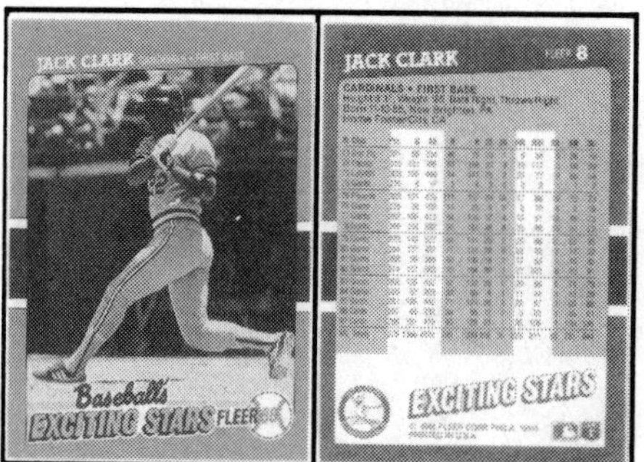

This small boxed set of 44 cards was produced exclusively for Cumberland Farm Stores. The cards measure the standard 2 1/2" by 3 1/2" and feature full color fronts and red, white, and blue backs. The card fronts are distinguished by the framing of the player's full-color photo with a blue border with a red and white bar stripe across the middle. The box for the cards describes the set as the "1988 Fleer Baseball's Exciting Stars." The checklist for the set is given on the back of the set box.

		MINT	EXC	G-VG
	COMPLETE SET (44)	5.00	2.00	.50
	COMMON PLAYER (1-44)	.10	.04	.01
☐ 1	Harold Baines	.15	.06	.01
☐ 2	Kevin Bass	.10	.04	.01
☐ 3	George Bell	.20	.08	.02
☐ 4	Wade Boggs	.75	.30	.07
☐ 5	Mickey Brantley	.15	.06	.01
☐ 6	Sid Bream	.10	.04	.01
☐ 7	Jose Canseco	1.25	.50	.12
☐ 8	Jack Clark	.20	.08	.02
☐ 9	Will Clark	.60	.24	.06
☐ 10	Roger Clemens	.60	.24	.06
☐ 11	Vince Coleman	.25	.10	.02
☐ 12	Eric Davis	.60	.24	.06
☐ 13	Andre Dawson	.25	.10	.02
☐ 14	Julio Franco	.15	.06	.01
☐ 15	Dwight Gooden	.50	.20	.05
☐ 16	Mike Greenwell	1.00	.40	.10
☐ 17	Tony Gwynn	.35	.14	.03
☐ 18	Von Hayes	.15	.06	.01
☐ 19	Tom Henke	.10	.04	.01
☐ 20	Orel Hershiser	.50	.20	.05
☐ 21	Teddy Higuera	.20	.08	.02
☐ 22	Brook Jacoby	.15	.06	.01
☐ 23	Wally Joyner	.40	.16	.04
☐ 24	Jimmy Key	.15	.06	.01
☐ 25	Don Mattingly	1.00	.40	.10
☐ 26	Mark McGwire	.75	.30	.07
☐ 27	Jack Morris	.15	.06	.01
☐ 28	Dale Murphy	.35	.14	.03
☐ 29	Matt Nokes	.30	.12	.03
☐ 30	Kirby Puckett	.40	.16	.04
☐ 31	Tim Raines	.25	.10	.02
☐ 32	Ryne Sandberg	.25	.10	.02
☐ 33	Benito Santiago	.30	.12	.03
☐ 34	Mike Schmidt	.40	.16	.04
☐ 35	Mike Scott	.15	.06	.01
☐ 36	Kevin Seitzer	.35	.14	.03
☐ 37	Larry Sheets	.15	.06	.01
☐ 38	Ruben Sierra	.20	.08	.02
☐ 39	Darryl Strawberry	.60	.24	.06
☐ 40	Rick Sutcliffe	.15	.06	.01
☐ 41	Danny Tartabull	.25	.10	.02
☐ 42	Alan Trammell	.20	.08	.02
☐ 43	Fernando Valenzuela	.15	.06	.01
☐ 44	Devon White	.20	.08	.02

1988 Fleer Hottest Stars

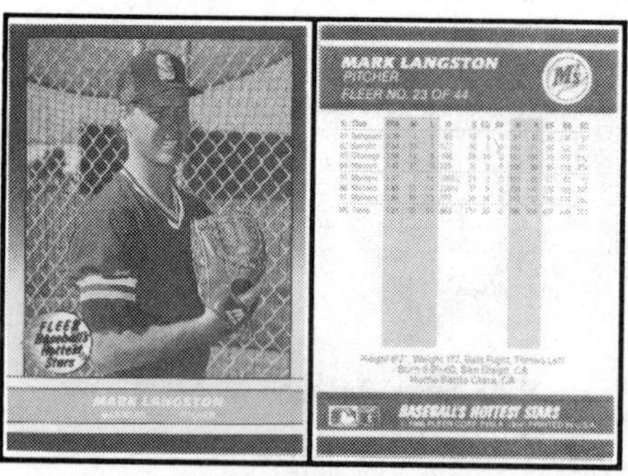

This 44-card boxed set was produced by Fleer for exclusive distribution by Revco Discount Drug stores all over the country. The cards measure the standard 2 1/2" by 3 1/2" and feature full color fronts and red, white, and blue backs. The card fronts are easily distinguished by the flaming baseball in the lower right corner which says "Fleer Baseball's Hottest Stars. The player's picture is framed in red fading from orange down to yellow. The box for the cards proclaims "1988 Limited Edition Baseball's Hottest Stars" and is styled in blue, red, and yellow. The checklist for the set is given on the back of the set box. The box refers to Revco but there is no mention of Revco anywhere on the cards themselves.

		MINT	EXC	G-VG
	COMPLETE SET (44)	5.00	2.00	.50
	COMMON PLAYER (1-44)	.10	.04	.01
☐ 1	George Bell	.20	.08	.02
☐ 2	Wade Boggs	.75	.30	.07
☐ 3	Bobby Bonilla	.20	.08	.02
☐ 4	George Brett	.35	.14	.03
☐ 5	Jose Canseco	1.25	.50	.12
☐ 6	Will Clark	.60	.24	.06
☐ 7	Roger Clemens	.60	.24	.06
☐ 8	Eric Davis	.60	.24	.06
☐ 9	Andre Dawson	.20	.08	.02
☐ 10	Tony Fernandez	.15	.06	.01
☐ 11	Julio Franco	.10	.04	.01

☐ 12 Gary Gaetti	.15	.06	.01
☐ 13 Dwight Gooden	.40	.16	.04
☐ 14 Mike Greenwell	1.00	.40	.10
☐ 15 Tony Gwynn	.35	.14	.03
☐ 16 Rickey Henderson	.35	.14	.03
☐ 17 Keith Hernandez	.20	.08	.02
☐ 18 Tom Herr	.10	.04	.01
☐ 19 Orel Hershiser	.50	.20	.05
☐ 20 Ted Higuera	.20	.08	.02
☐ 21 Wally Joyner	.40	.16	.04
☐ 22 Jimmy Key	.10	.04	.01
☐ 23 Mark Langston	.15	.06	.01
☐ 24 Don Mattingly	1.00	.40	.10
☐ 25 Jack McDowell	.20	.08	.02
☐ 26 Mark McGwire	.75	.30	.07
☐ 27 Kevin Mitchell	.10	.04	.01
☐ 28 Jack Morris	.15	.06	.01
☐ 29 Dale Murphy	.40	.16	.04
☐ 30 Kirby Puckett	.40	.16	.04
☐ 31 Tim Raines	.25	.10	.02
☐ 32 Shane Rawley	.10	.04	.01
☐ 33 Benito Santiago	.35	.14	.03
☐ 34 Mike Schmidt	.40	.16	.04
☐ 35 Mike Scott	.15	.06	.01
☐ 36 Kevin Seitzer	.35	.14	.03
☐ 37 Larry Sheets	.15	.06	.01
☐ 38 Ruben Sierra	.20	.08	.02
☐ 39 Dave Smith	.10	.04	.01
☐ 40 Ozzie Smith	.20	.08	.02
☐ 41 Darryl Strawberry	.60	.24	.06
☐ 42 Rick Sutcliffe	.15	.06	.01
☐ 43 Pat Tabler	.10	.04	.01
☐ 44 Alan Trammell	.20	.08	.02

1988 Fleer League Leaders

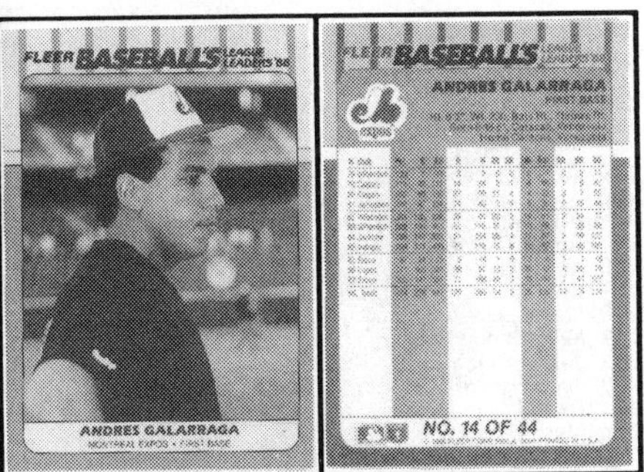

This small boxed set of 44 cards was produced exclusively for Walgreen Drug Stores. The cards measure the standard 2 1/2" by 3 1/2" and feature full color fronts and pink, white, and blue backs. The card fronts are distinguished by the blue solid and striped background behind the player's full-color photo. The box for the cards describes the set as the "1988 Fleer Baseball's League Leaders." The checklist for the set is given on the back of the set box.

	MINT	EXC	G-VG
COMPLETE SET (44)	5.00	2.00	.50
COMMON PLAYER (1-44)	.10	.04	.01
☐ 1 George Bell	.20	.08	.02
☐ 2 Wade Boggs	.75	.30	.07
☐ 3 Ivan Calderon	.15	.06	.01
☐ 4 Jose Canseco	1.25	.50	.12
☐ 5 Will Clark	.60	.24	.06
☐ 6 Roger Clemens	.60	.24	.06
☐ 7 Vince Coleman	.25	.10	.02
☐ 8 Eric Davis	.60	.24	.06
☐ 9 Andre Dawson	.25	.10	.02
☐ 10 Bill Doran	.15	.06	.01
☐ 11 Dwight Evans	.15	.06	.01
☐ 12 Julio Franco	.15	.06	.01
☐ 13 Gary Gaetti	.15	.06	.01
☐ 14 Andres Galarraga	.20	.08	.02
☐ 15 Dwight Gooden	.50	.20	.05
☐ 16 Tony Gwynn	.40	.16	.04
☐ 17 Tom Henke	.10	.04	.01
☐ 18 Keith Hernandez	.20	.08	.02
☐ 19 Orel Hershiser	.50	.20	.05
☐ 20 Ted Higuera	.20	.08	.02
☐ 21 Kent Hrbek	.20	.08	.02
☐ 22 Wally Joyner	.40	.16	.04
☐ 23 Jimmy Key	.10	.04	.01
☐ 24 Mark Langston	.15	.06	.01
☐ 25 Don Mattingly	1.00	.40	.10
☐ 26 Mark McGwire	.75	.30	.07
☐ 27 Paul Molitor	.20	.08	.02
☐ 28 Jack Morris	.15	.06	.01
☐ 29 Dale Murphy	.40	.16	.04
☐ 30 Kirby Puckett	.40	.16	.04
☐ 31 Tim Raines	.25	.10	.02
☐ 32 Rick Reuschel	.15	.06	.01
☐ 33 Bret Saberhagen	.20	.08	.02
☐ 34 Benito Santiago	.30	.12	.03
☐ 35 Mike Schmidt	.35	.14	.03
☐ 36 Mike Scott	.15	.06	.01
☐ 37 Kevin Seitzer	.35	.14	.03
☐ 38 Larry Sheets	.15	.06	.01
☐ 39 Ruben Sierra	.20	.08	.02
☐ 40 Darryl Strawberry	.60	.24	.06
☐ 41 Rick Sutcliffe	.15	.06	.01
☐ 42 Alan Trammell	.20	.08	.02
☐ 43 Andy Van Slyke	.20	.08	.02
☐ 44 Todd Worrell	.15	.06	.01

1988 Fleer Mini

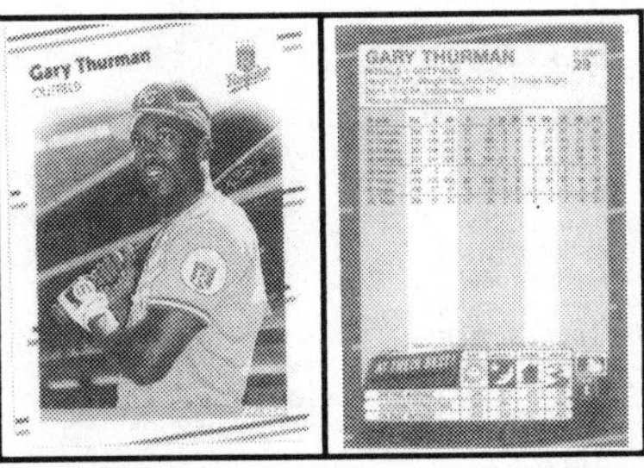

The 1988 Fleer "Classic Miniatures" set consists of 120 small cards with all new pictures of the players as compared to the 1988 Fleer regular issue. The cards are only 1 13/16" by 2 9/16", making them one of the smallest cards available. Card backs provide career year-by-year statistics. The complete set was distributed in a green, red, white, and silver box along with 18 logo stickers. The card numbering is by team order.

	MINT	EXC	G-VG
COMPLETE SET (120)	9.00	3.75	.90
COMMON PLAYER (1-120)	.05	.02	.00
☐ 1 Eddie Murray	.25	.10	.02
☐ 2 Dave Schmidt	.05	.02	.00
☐ 3 Larry Sheets	.10	.04	.01
☐ 4 Wade Boggs	.75	.30	.07
☐ 5 Roger Clemens	.50	.20	.05
☐ 6 Dwight Evans	.10	.04	.01
☐ 7 Mike Greenwell	.75	.30	.07
☐ 8 Sam Horn	.15	.06	.01
☐ 9 Lee Smith	.05	.02	.00
☐ 10 Brian Downing	.05	.02	.00
☐ 11 Wally Joyner	.45	.18	.04
☐ 12 Devon White	.20	.08	.02
☐ 13 Mike Witt	.10	.04	.01
☐ 14 Ivan Calderon	.10	.04	.01
☐ 15 Ozzie Guillen	.10	.04	.01
☐ 16 Jack McDowell	.10	.04	.01
☐ 17 Kenny Williams	.10	.04	.01
☐ 18 Joe Carter	.15	.06	.01
☐ 19 Julio Franco	.10	.04	.01
☐ 20 Pat Tabler	.05	.02	.00
☐ 21 Doyle Alexander	.05	.02	.00
☐ 22 Jack Morris	.15	.06	.01
☐ 23 Matt Nokes	.20	.08	.02
☐ 24 Walt Terrell	.05	.02	.00
☐ 25 Alan Trammell	.15	.06	.01
☐ 26 Bret Saberhagen	.20	.08	.02
☐ 27 Kevin Seitzer	.35	.14	.03

□ 28 Danny Tartabull	.25	.10	.02
□ 29 Gary Thurman	.15	.06	.01
□ 30 Ted Higuera	.10	.04	.01
□ 31 Paul Molitor	.15	.06	.01
□ 32 Dan Plesac	.05	.02	.00
□ 33 Robin Yount	.25	.10	.02
□ 34 Gary Gaetti	.15	.06	.01
□ 35 Kent Hrbek	.15	.06	.01
□ 36 Kirby Puckett	.40	.16	.04
□ 37 Jeff Reardon	.10	.04	.01
□ 38 Frank Viola	.15	.06	.01
□ 39 Jack Clark	.15	.06	.01
□ 40 Rickey Henderson	.35	.14	.03
□ 41 Don Mattingly	1.00	.40	.10
□ 42 Willie Randolph	.10	.04	.01
□ 43 Dave Righetti	.10	.04	.01
□ 44 Dave Winfield	.25	.10	.02
□ 45 Jose Canseco	1.25	.50	.12
□ 46 Mark McGwire	.75	.30	.07
□ 47 Dave Parker	.10	.04	.01
□ 48 Dave Stewart	.10	.04	.01
□ 49 Walt Weiss	.45	.18	.04
□ 50 Bob Welch	.05	.02	.00
□ 51 Mickey Brantley	.10	.04	.01
□ 52 Mark Langston	.10	.04	.01
□ 53 Harold Reynolds	.05	.02	.00
□ 54 Scott Fletcher	.05	.02	.00
□ 55 Charlie Hough	.05	.02	.00
□ 56 Pete Incaviglia	.20	.08	.02
□ 57 Larry Parrish	.05	.02	.00
□ 58 Ruben Sierra	.20	.08	.02
□ 59 George Bell	.20	.08	.02
□ 60 Mark Eichhorn	.05	.02	.00
□ 61 Tony Fernandez	.10	.04	.01
□ 62 Tom Henke	.05	.02	.00
□ 63 Jimmy Key	.10	.04	.01
□ 64 Dion James	.05	.02	.00
□ 65 Dale Murphy	.35	.14	.03
□ 66 Zane Smith	.05	.02	.00
□ 67 Andre Dawson	.20	.08	.02
□ 68 Mark Grace	1.25	.50	.12
□ 69 Jerry Mumphrey	.05	.02	.00
□ 70 Ryne Sandberg	.25	.10	.02
□ 71 Rick Sutcliffe	.10	.04	.01
□ 72 Kal Daniels	.20	.08	.02
□ 73 Eric Davis	.75	.30	.07
□ 74 John Franco	.05	.02	.00
□ 75 Ron Robinson	.05	.02	.00
□ 76 Jeff Treadway	.10	.04	.01
□ 77 Kevin Bass	.05	.02	.00
□ 78 Glenn Davis	.15	.06	.01
□ 79 Nolan Ryan	.25	.10	.02
□ 80 Mike Scott	.15	.06	.01
□ 81 Dave Smith	.05	.02	.00
□ 82 Kirk Gibson	.25	.10	.02
□ 83 Pedro Guerrero	.15	.06	.01
□ 84 Orel Hershiser	.50	.20	.05
□ 85 Steve Sax	.15	.06	.01
□ 86 Fernando Valenzuela	.15	.06	.01
□ 87 Tim Burke	.05	.02	.00
□ 88 Andres Galarraga	.25	.10	.02
□ 89 Neal Heaton	.05	.02	.00
□ 90 Tim Raines	.25	.10	.02
□ 91 Tim Wallach	.05	.02	.00
□ 92 Dwight Gooden	.45	.18	.04
□ 93 Keith Hernandez	.20	.08	.02
□ 94 Gregg Jefferies	2.50	1.00	.25
□ 95 Howard Johnson	.10	.04	.01
□ 96 Roger McDowell	.10	.04	.01
□ 97 Darryl Strawberry	.50	.20	.05
□ 98 Steve Bedrosian	.10	.04	.01
□ 99 Von Hayes	.10	.04	.01
□ 100 Shane Rawley	.05	.02	.00
□ 101 Juan Samuel	.10	.04	.01
□ 102 Mike Schmidt	.35	.14	.03
□ 103 Bobby Bonilla	.15	.06	.01
□ 104 Mike Dunne	.10	.04	.01
□ 105 Andy Van Slyke	.20	.08	.02
□ 106 Vince Coleman	.20	.08	.02
□ 107 Bob Horner	.15	.06	.01
□ 108 Willie McGee	.15	.06	.01
□ 109 Ozzie Smith	.15	.06	.01
□ 110 John Tudor	.10	.04	.01
□ 111 Todd Worrell	.15	.06	.01
□ 112 Tony Gwynn	.35	.14	.03
□ 113 John Kruk	.15	.06	.01
□ 114 Lance McCullers	.10	.04	.01
□ 115 Benito Santiago	.35	.14	.03
□ 116 Will Clark	.75	.30	.07
□ 117 Jeff Leonard	.05	.02	.00
□ 118 Candy Maldonado	.05	.02	.00
□ 119 Kirt Manwaring	.10	.04	.01
□ 120 Don Robinson	.05	.02	.00

1988 Fleer Record Setters

This small boxed set of 44 cards was produced exclusively for Eckerd's Drug Stores. The cards measure the standard 2 1/2" by 3 1/2" and feature full color fronts and red, white, and blue backs. The card fronts are distinguished by the red and blue frame around the player's full-color photo. The box for the cards describes the set as the "1988 Baseball Record Setters." The checklist for the set is given on the back of the set box.

	MINT	EXC	G-VG
COMPLETE SET (44)	5.00	2.00	.50
COMMON PLAYER (1-44)	.10	.04	.01
□ 1 Jesse Barfield	.20	.08	.02
□ 2 George Bell	.20	.08	.02
□ 3 Wade Boggs	.75	.30	.07
□ 4 Jose Canseco	1.25	.50	.12
□ 5 Jack Clark	.20	.08	.02
□ 6 Will Clark	.60	.24	.06
□ 7 Roger Clemens	.60	.24	.06
□ 8 Alvin Davis	.15	.06	.01
□ 9 Eric Davis	.60	.24	.06
□ 10 Andre Dawson	.25	.10	.02
□ 11 Mike Dunne	.15	.06	.01
□ 12 John Franco	.10	.04	.01
□ 13 Julio Franco	.10	.04	.01
□ 14 Dwight Gooden	.50	.20	.05
□ 15 Mark Gubicza (listed as Gubiczo on box checklist)	.15	.06	.01
□ 16 Ozzie Guillen	.15	.06	.01
□ 17 Tony Gwynn	.40	.16	.04
□ 18 Orel Hershiser	.50	.20	.05
□ 19 Teddy Higuera	.20	.08	.02
□ 20 Howard Johnson	.15	.06	.01
□ 21 Wally Joyner	.40	.16	.04
□ 22 Jimmy Key	.15	.06	.01
□ 23 Jeff Leonard	.10	.04	.01
□ 24 Don Mattingly	1.00	.40	.10
□ 25 Mark McGwire	.75	.30	.07
□ 26 Jack Morris	.15	.06	.01
□ 27 Dale Murphy	.40	.16	.04
□ 28 Larry Parrish	.10	.04	.01
□ 29 Kirby Puckett	.40	.16	.04
□ 30 Tim Raines	.25	.10	.02
□ 31 Harold Reynolds	.10	.04	.01
□ 32 Dave Righetti	.15	.06	.01
□ 33 Cal Ripken	.25	.10	.02
□ 34 Benito Santiago	.25	.10	.02
□ 35 Mike Schmidt	.35	.14	.03
□ 36 Mike Scott	.15	.06	.01
□ 37 Kevin Seitzer	.30	.12	.03
□ 38 Ozzie Smith	.20	.08	.02
□ 39 Darryl Strawberry	.60	.24	.06
□ 40 Rick Sutcliffe	.15	.06	.01
□ 41 Alan Trammell	.20	.08	.02
□ 42 Frank Viola	.20	.08	.02
□ 43 Mitch Williams	.10	.04	.01
□ 44 Todd Worrell	.15	.06	.01

1988 Fleer Sluggers/Pitchers

Fleer produced this 44-card boxed set although it was primarily distributed by McCrory, McLellan, J.J Newberry, H.L.Green, T.G.Y., and other similar stores. The set is subtitled "Baseball's Best". Cards are standard-size, 2 1/2" by 3 1/2", and were packaged in a green custom box along with six logo stickers. The set checklist is given on the back of the box. The bottoms of the boxes which held the individual set boxes also contained a panel of six cards; these box bottom cards were numbered C1 through C6.

	MINT	EXC	G-VG
COMPLETE SET (44)	5.00	2.00	.50
COMMON PLAYER (1-44)	.10	.04	.01
☐ 1 George Bell	.20	.08	.02
☐ 2 Wade Boggs	.75	.30	.07
☐ 3 Bobby Bonilla	.20	.08	.02
☐ 4 Tom Brunansky	.15	.06	.01
☐ 5 Ellis Burks	.60	.24	.06
☐ 6 Jose Canseco	1.25	.50	.12
☐ 7 Joe Carter	.20	.08	.02
☐ 8 Will Clark	.60	.24	.06
☐ 9 Roger Clemens	.60	.24	.06
☐ 10 Eric Davis	.60	.24	.06
☐ 11 Glenn Davis	.20	.08	.02
☐ 12 Andre Dawson	.25	.10	.02
☐ 13 Dennis Eckersley	.20	.08	.02
☐ 14 Andres Galarraga	.25	.10	.02
☐ 15 Dwight Gooden	.50	.20	.05
☐ 16 Pedro Guerrero	.20	.08	.02
☐ 17 Tony Gwynn	.35	.14	.03
☐ 18 Orel Hershiser	.50	.20	.05
☐ 19 Ted Higuera	.20	.08	.02
☐ 20 Pete Incaviglia	.20	.08	.02
☐ 21 Danny Jackson	.15	.06	.01
☐ 22 Doug Jennings	.15	.06	.01
☐ 23 Mark Langston	.15	.06	.01
☐ 24 Dave LaPoint	.10	.04	.01
☐ 25 Mike LaValliere	.10	.04	.01
☐ 26 Don Mattingly	1.00	.40	.10
☐ 27 Mark McGwire	.75	.30	.07
☐ 28 Dale Murphy	.40	.16	.04
☐ 29 Ken Phelps	.10	.04	.01
☐ 30 Kirby Puckett	.40	.16	.04
☐ 31 Johnny Ray	.15	.06	.01
☐ 32 Jeff Reardon	.15	.06	.01
☐ 33 Dave Righetti	.15	.06	.01
☐ 34 Cal Ripken	.30	.12	.03
☐ 35 Chris Sabo	.75	.30	.07
☐ 36 Mike Schmidt	.45	.18	.04
☐ 37 Mike Scott	.15	.06	.01
☐ 38 Kevin Seitzer	.35	.14	.03
☐ 39 Dave Stewart	.15	.06	.01
☐ 40 Darryl Strawberry	.60	.24	.06
☐ 41 Greg Swindell	.15	.06	.01
☐ 42 Frank Tanana	.10	.04	.01
☐ 43 Dave Winfield	.25	.10	.02
☐ 44 Todd Worrell	.15	.06	.01

1988 Fleer Slug/Pitch Box Cards

The cards in this 6-card set each measure the standard 2 1/2" by 3 1/2". Cards have essentially the same design as the 1988 Fleer Sluggers vs. Pitchers set of Baseball's Best. The cards were printed on the bottom of the counter display box which held 24 small boxed sets; hence theoretically these box cards are 1/24 as plentiful as the regular boxed set cards. These 6 cards, numbered C1 to C6 are considered a separate set in their own right and are not typically included in a complete set of the 1988 Fleer Sluggers vs. Pitchers set of 44. The value of the panels uncut is slightly greater, perhaps by 25% greater, than the value of the individual cards cut up carefully.

	MINT	EXC	G-VG
COMPLETE SET (6)	1.50	.60	.15
COMMON PLAYERS (C1-C6)	.10	.04	.01
☐ C1 Ron Darling (box bottom card)	.20	.08	.02
☐ C2 Rickey Henderson (box bottom card)	.65	.26	.06
☐ C3 Carney Lansford (box bottom card)	.15	.06	.01
☐ C4 Rafael Palmeiro (box bottom card)	.30	.12	.03
☐ C5 Frank Viola (box bottom card)	.30	.12	.03
☐ C6 Twins Logo (checklist back) (box bottom card)	.10	.04	.01

1988 Fleer Sticker Cards

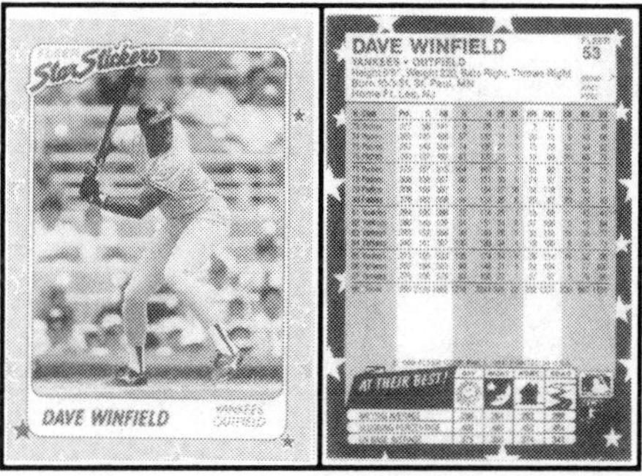

These Star Stickers were distributed as a separate issue by Fleer with five star stickers and a logo sticker in each wax pack. The 132-card (sticker) set features 2 1/2" by 3 1/2" full-color fronts and even statistics on the sticker back, which is an indication that the

Fleer Company understands that these stickers are rarely used as stickers but more like traditional cards. The card fronts are surrounded by a silver-gray border and the backs are printed in red and black on white card stock.

	MINT	EXC	G-VG
COMPLETE SET (132)	16.00	6.50	1.60
COMMON PLAYER (1-132)	.05	.02	.00

	MINT	EXC	G-VG
☐ 1 Mike Boddicker	.10	.04	.01
☐ 2 Eddie Murray	.25	.10	.02
☐ 3 Cal Ripken	.25	.10	.02
☐ 4 Larry Sheets	.10	.04	.01
☐ 5 Wade Boggs	1.50	.60	.15
☐ 6 Ellis Burks	1.00	.40	.10
☐ 7 Roger Clemens	1.00	.40	.10
☐ 8 Dwight Evans	.10	.04	.01
☐ 9 Mike Greenwell	1.00	.40	.10
☐ 10 Bruce Hurst	.15	.06	.01
☐ 11 Brian Downing	.05	.02	.00
☐ 12 Wally Joyner	.75	.30	.07
☐ 13 Mike Witt	.10	.04	.01
☐ 14 Ivan Calderon	.10	.04	.01
☐ 15 Jose DeLeon	.05	.02	.00
☐ 16 Ozzie Guillen	.10	.04	.01
☐ 17 Bobby Thigpen	.15	.06	.01
☐ 18 Joe Carter	.15	.06	.01
☐ 19 Julio Franco	.10	.04	.01
☐ 20 Brook Jacoby	.10	.04	.01
☐ 21 Cory Snyder	.25	.10	.02
☐ 22 Pat Tabler	.05	.02	.00
☐ 23 Doyle Alexander	.05	.02	.00
☐ 24 Kirk Gibson	.25	.10	.02
☐ 25 Mike Henneman	.15	.06	.01
☐ 26 Jack Morris	.15	.06	.01
☐ 27 Matt Nokes	.25	.10	.02
☐ 28 Walt Terrell	.05	.02	.00
☐ 29 Alan Trammell	.25	.10	.02
☐ 30 George Brett	.45	.18	.04
☐ 31 Charlie Leibrandt	.05	.02	.00
☐ 32 Bret Saberhagen	.25	.10	.02
☐ 33 Kevin Seitzer	.45	.18	.04
☐ 34 Danny Tartabull	.25	.10	.02
☐ 35 Frank White	.10	.04	.01
☐ 36 Rob Deer	.10	.04	.01
☐ 37 Ted Higuera	.15	.06	.01
☐ 38 Paul Molitor	.15	.06	.01
☐ 39 Dan Plesac	.10	.04	.01
☐ 40 Robin Yount	.25	.10	.02
☐ 41 Bert Blyleven	.10	.04	.01
☐ 42 Tom Brunansky	.15	.06	.01
☐ 43 Gary Gaetti	.15	.06	.01
☐ 44 Kent Hrbek	.20	.08	.02
☐ 45 Kirby Puckett	.60	.24	.06
☐ 46 Jeff Reardon	.10	.04	.01
☐ 47 Frank Viola	.15	.06	.01
☐ 48 Don Mattingly	2.00	.80	.20
☐ 49 Mike Pagliarulo	.10	.04	.01
☐ 50 Willie Randolph	.10	.04	.01
☐ 51 Rick Rhoden	.05	.02	.00
☐ 52 Dave Righetti	.15	.06	.01
☐ 53 Dave Winfield	.25	.10	.02
☐ 54 Jose Canseco	2.00	.80	.20
☐ 55 Carney Lansford	.10	.04	.01
☐ 56 Mark McGwire	1.00	.40	.10
☐ 57 Dave Stewart	.10	.04	.01
☐ 58 Curt Young	.05	.02	.00
☐ 59 Alvin Davis	.10	.04	.01
☐ 60 Mark Langston	.10	.04	.01
☐ 61 Ken Phelps	.10	.04	.01
☐ 62 Harold Reynolds	.05	.02	.00
☐ 63 Scott Fletcher	.05	.02	.00
☐ 64 Charlie Hough	.05	.02	.00
☐ 65 Pete Incaviglia	.20	.08	.02
☐ 66 Oddibe McDowell	.10	.04	.01
☐ 67 Pete O'Brien	.10	.04	.01
☐ 68 Larry Parrish	.05	.02	.00
☐ 69 Ruben Sierra	.20	.08	.02
☐ 70 Jesse Barfield	.15	.06	.01
☐ 71 George Bell	.20	.08	.02
☐ 72 Tony Fernandez	.15	.06	.01
☐ 73 Tom Henke	.05	.02	.00
☐ 74 Jimmy Key	.10	.04	.01
☐ 75 Lloyd Moseby	.10	.04	.01
☐ 76 Dion James	.05	.02	.00
☐ 77 Dale Murphy	.40	.16	.04
☐ 78 Zane Smith	.05	.02	.00
☐ 79 Andre Dawson	.25	.10	.02
☐ 80 Ryne Sandberg	.25	.10	.02
☐ 81 Rick Sutcliffe	.10	.04	.01
☐ 82 Kal Daniels	.20	.08	.02
☐ 83 Eric Davis	1.00	.40	.10
☐ 84 John Franco	.10	.04	.01
☐ 85 Kevin Bass	.05	.02	.00
☐ 86 Glenn Davis	.15	.06	.01
☐ 87 Bill Doran	.10	.04	.01
☐ 88 Nolan Ryan	.35	.14	.03
☐ 89 Mike Scott	.15	.06	.01
☐ 90 Dave Smith	.05	.02	.00
☐ 91 Pedro Guerrero	.20	.08	.02
☐ 92 Orel Hershiser	.50	.20	.05
☐ 93 Steve Sax	.15	.06	.01
☐ 94 Fernando Valenzuela	.15	.06	.01
☐ 95 Tim Burke	.05	.02	.00
☐ 96 Andres Galarraga	.25	.10	.02
☐ 97 Tim Raines	.25	.10	.02
☐ 98 Tim Wallach	.10	.04	.01
☐ 99 Mitch Webster	.05	.02	.00
☐ 100 Ron Darling	.15	.06	.01
☐ 101 Sid Fernandez	.10	.04	.01
☐ 102 Dwight Gooden	.50	.20	.05
☐ 103 Keith Hernandez	.25	.10	.02
☐ 104 Howard Johnson	.15	.06	.01
☐ 105 Roger McDowell	.10	.04	.01
☐ 106 Darryl Strawberry	.75	.30	.07
☐ 107 Steve Bedrosian	.10	.04	.01
☐ 108 Von Hayes	.10	.04	.01
☐ 109 Shane Rawley	.05	.02	.00
☐ 110 Juan Samuel	.15	.06	.01
☐ 111 Mike Schmidt	.50	.20	.05
☐ 112 Milt Thompson	.05	.02	.00
☐ 113 Sid Bream	.05	.02	.00
☐ 114 Bobby Bonilla	.15	.06	.01
☐ 115 Mike Dunne	.10	.04	.01
☐ 116 Any Van Slyke	.20	.08	.02
☐ 117 Vince Coleman	.20	.08	.02
☐ 118 Willie McGee	.15	.06	.01
☐ 119 Terry Pendleton	.05	.02	.00
☐ 120 Ozzie Smith	.15	.06	.01
☐ 121 John Tudor	.10	.04	.01
☐ 122 Todd Worrell	.15	.06	.01
☐ 123 Tony Gwynn	.45	.18	.04
☐ 124 John Kruk	.20	.08	.02
☐ 125 Benito Santiago	.50	.20	.05
☐ 126 Will Clark	.75	.30	.07
☐ 127 Dave Dravecky	.05	.02	.00
☐ 128 Jeff Leonard	.05	.02	.00
☐ 129 Candy Maldonado	.05	.02	.00
☐ 130 Rick Reuschel	.10	.04	.01
☐ 131 Don Robinson	.05	.02	.00
☐ 132 Checklist	.05	.02	.00

1988 Fleer Sticker Box Cards

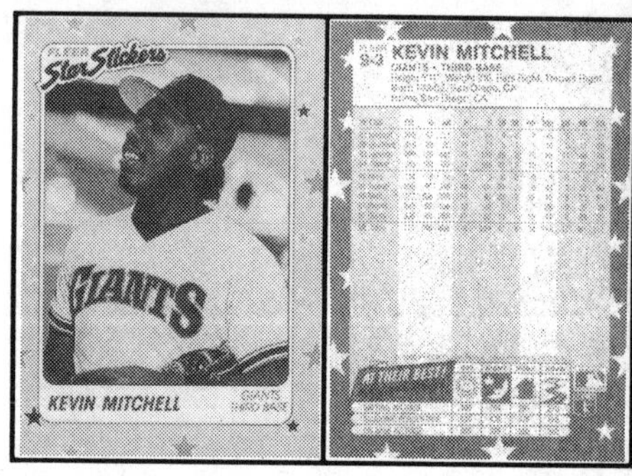

The bottoms of the Star Sticker wax boxes contained two different sets of four cards done in a similar format to the stickers; these cards (they are not stickers but truly cards) are numbered with the prefix S and are considered a separate set. The value of the panels uncut is slightly greater, perhaps by 25% greater, than the value of the individual cards cut up carefully.

	MINT	EXC	G-VG
COMPLETE SET (8)	2.00	.80	.20
COMMON PLAYER	.10	.04	.01
☐ S1 Don Baylor (wax box card)	.15	.06	.01
☐ S2 Gary Carter	.40	.16	.04

		MINT	EXC	G-VG
	(wax box card)			
☐ S3	Ron Guidry (wax box card)	.20	.08	.02
☐ S4	Rickey Henderson (wax box card)	.60	.24	.06
☐ S5	Kevin Mitchell (wax box card)	.20	.08	.02
☐ S6	Mark McGwire and Eric Davis (wax box card)	1.00	.40	.10
☐ S7	Giants Logo (wax box card)	.10	.04	.01
☐ S8	Detroit Logo (wax box card)	.10	.04	.01

1988 Fleer Superstars

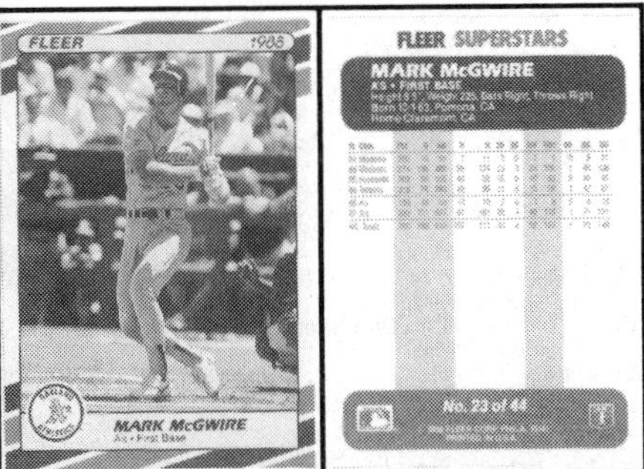

Fleer produced this 44-card boxed set although it was primarily distributed by McCrory, McLellan, J.J Newberry, H.L.Green, T.G.Y., and other similar stores. The set is subtitled "Fleer Superstars." Cards are standard-size, 2 1/2" by 3 1/2", and were packaged in a red, white, blue, and yellow custom box along with six logo stickers. The set checklist is given on the back of the box. The bottoms of the boxes which held the individual set boxes also contained a panel of six cards; these box bottom cards were numbered C1 through C6.

		MINT	EXC	G-VG
	COMPLETE SET (44)	4.00	1.60	.40
	COMMON PLAYER (1-44)	.05	.02	.00
☐ 1	Steve Bedrosian	.10	.04	.01
☐ 2	George Bell	.15	.06	.01
☐ 3	Wade Boggs	.60	.24	.06
☐ 4	Barry Bonds	.15	.06	.01
☐ 5	Jose Canseco	1.00	.40	.10
☐ 6	Joe Carter	.15	.06	.01
☐ 7	Jack Clark	.15	.06	.01
☐ 8	Will Clark	.50	.20	.05
☐ 9	Roger Clemens	.50	.20	.05
☐ 10	Alvin Davis	.10	.04	.01
☐ 11	Eric Davis	.50	.20	.05
☐ 12	Glenn Davis	.15	.06	.01
☐ 13	Andre Dawson	.20	.08	.02
☐ 14	Dwight Gooden	.40	.16	.04
☐ 15	Orel Hershiser	.40	.16	.04
☐ 16	Teddy Higuera	.15	.06	.01
☐ 17	Kent Hrbek	.15	.06	.01
☐ 18	Wally Joyner	.35	.14	.03
☐ 19	Jimmy Key	.10	.04	.01
☐ 20	John Kruk	.10	.04	.01
☐ 21	Jeff Leonard	.05	.02	.00
☐ 22	Don Mattingly	1.00	.40	.10
☐ 23	Mark McGwire	.65	.26	.06
☐ 24	Kevin McReynolds	.20	.08	.02
☐ 25	Dale Murphy	.35	.14	.03
☐ 26	Matt Nokes	.20	.08	.02
☐ 27	Terry Pendleton	.05	.02	.00
☐ 28	Kirby Puckett	.40	.16	.04
☐ 29	Tim Raines	.20	.08	.02
☐ 30	Rick Rhoden	.05	.02	.00
☐ 31	Cal Ripken Jr.	.25	.10	.02
☐ 32	Benito Santiago	.25	.10	.02
☐ 33	Mike Schmidt	.35	.14	.03
☐ 34	Mike Scott	.15	.06	.01
☐ 35	Kevin Seitzer	.35	.14	.03
☐ 36	Ruben Sierra	.20	.08	.02
☐ 37	Cory Snyder	.20	.08	.02
☐ 38	Darryl Strawberry	.50	.20	.05
☐ 39	Rick Sutcliffe	.10	.04	.01
☐ 40	Danny Tartabull	.20	.08	.02
☐ 41	Alan Trammell	.15	.06	.01
☐ 42	Kenny Williams	.10	.04	.01
☐ 43	Mike Witt	.10	.04	.01
☐ 44	Robin Yount	.20	.08	.02

1988 Fleer Superstars Box Cards

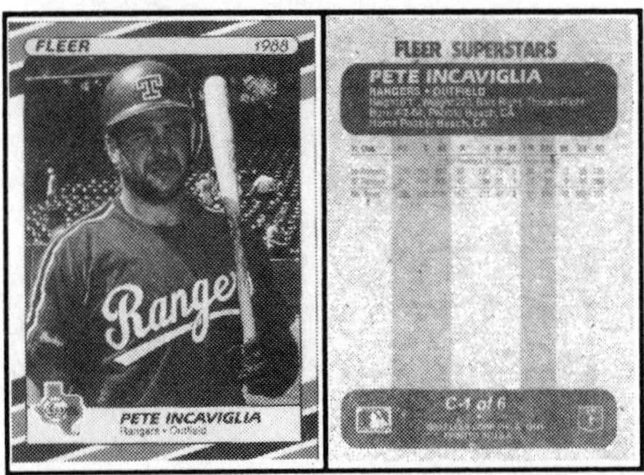

The cards in this 6-card set each measure the standard 2 1/2" by 3 1/2". Cards have essentially the same design as the 1988 Fleer Superstars set. The cards were printed on the bottom of the counter display box which held 24 small boxed sets; hence theoretically these box cards are 1/24 as plentiful as the regular boxed set cards. These 6 cards, numbered C1 to C6 are considered a separate set in their own right and are not typically included in a complete set of the 1988 Fleer Superstars set of 44. The value of the panels uncut is slightly greater, perhaps by 25% greater, than the value of the individual cards cut up carefully.

		MINT	EXC	G-VG
	COMPLETE SET (6)	1.50	.60	.15
	COMMON PLAYER (C1-C6)	.10	.04	.01
☐ C1	Pete Incaviglia (box bottom card)	.30	.12	.03
☐ C2	Rickey Henderson (box bottom card)	.75	.30	.07
☐ C3	Tony Fernandez (box bottom card)	.20	.08	.02
☐ C4	Shane Rawley (box bottom card)	.15	.06	.01
☐ C5	Ryne Sandberg (box bottom card)	.30	.12	.03
☐ C6	Cardinals Logo (checklist back) (box bottom card)	.10	.04	.01

1988 Fleer Team Leaders

This 44-card boxed set was produced by Fleer for exclusive distribution by Kay Bee Toys and is sometimes referred to as the Fleer Kay Bee set. Six team logo stickers are included in the box with the complete set. The numerical checklist on the back of the box shows that the set is numbered alphabetically. The cards measure 2 1/2" by 3 1/2" and have a distinctive red border on the fronts. The Kay Bee logo is printed in the lower right corner of the obverse of each card.

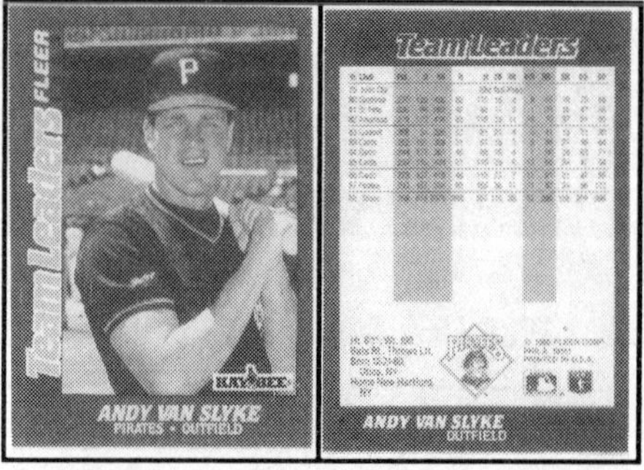

	MINT	EXC	G-VG
COMPLETE SET (44)	5.00	2.00	.50
COMMON PLAYER (1-44)	.10	.04	.01
□ 1 George Bell	.20	.08	.02
□ 2 Wade Boggs	.75	.30	.07
□ 3 Jose Canseco	1.25	.50	.12
□ 4 Will Clark	.60	.24	.06
□ 5 Roger Clemens	.60	.24	.06
□ 6 Eric Davis	.60	.24	.06
□ 7 Andre Dawson	.20	.08	.02
□ 8 Julio Franco	.10	.04	.01
□ 9 Andres Galarraga	.20	.08	.02
□ 10 Dwight Gooden	.50	.20	.05
□ 11 Tony Gwynn	.40	.16	.04
□ 12 Tom Henke	.10	.04	.01
□ 13 Orel Hershiser	.50	.20	.05
□ 14 Kent Hrbek	.20	.08	.02
□ 15 Ted Higuera	.15	.06	.01
□ 16 Wally Joyner	.40	.16	.04
□ 17 Jimmy Key	.10	.04	.01
□ 18 Mark Langston	.15	.06	.01
□ 19 Don Mattingly	1.00	.40	.10
□ 20 Willie McGee	.15	.06	.01
□ 21 Mark McGwire	.75	.30	.07
□ 22 Paul Molitor	.15	.06	.01
□ 23 Jack Morris	.15	.06	.01
□ 24 Dale Murphy	.35	.14	.03
□ 25 Larry Parrish	.10	.04	.01
□ 26 Kirby Puckett	.40	.16	.04
□ 27 Tim Raines	.25	.10	.02
□ 28 Jeff Reardon	.10	.04	.01
□ 29 Dave Righetti	.15	.06	.01
□ 30 Cal Ripken	.30	.12	.03
□ 31 Don Robinson	.10	.04	.01
□ 32 Bret Saberhagen	.20	.08	.02
□ 33 Juan Samuel	.15	.06	.01
□ 34 Mike Schmidt	.35	.14	.03
□ 35 Mike Scott	.15	.06	.01
□ 36 Kevin Seitzer	.35	.14	.03
□ 37 Dave Smith	.10	.04	.01
□ 38 Ozzie Smith	.20	.08	.02
□ 39 Zane Smith	.10	.04	.01
□ 40 Darryl Strawberry	.60	.24	.06
□ 41 Rick Sutcliffe	.15	.06	.01
□ 42 Bobby Thigpen	.15	.06	.01
□ 43 Alan Trammell	.20	.08	.02
□ 44 Andy Van Slyke	.20	.08	.02

1988 Fleer World Series

This 12-card set of 2 1/2" by 3 1/2" cards features highlights of the previous year's World Series between the Mets and the Red Sox. The sets were packaged as a complete set insert with the collated sets (of the 1988 Fleer regular issue) which were sold by Fleer directly to hobby card dealers; they were not available in the general retail candy store outlets.

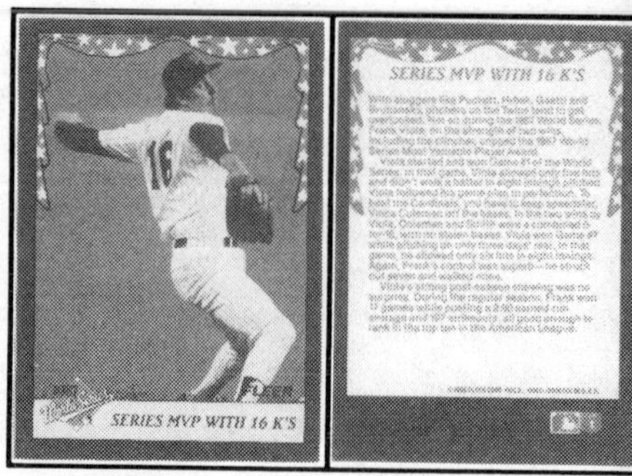

	MINT	EXC	G-VG
COMPLETE SET (12)	4.00	1.60	.40
COMMON PLAYER (1-12)	.25	.10	.02
□ 1 Dan Gladden Grand Hero Game 1	.25	.10	.02
□ 2 Randy Bush Cardinals "Bush" Wacked	.25	.10	.02
□ 3 John Tudor Masterful Performance in Game 3	.35	.14	.03
□ 4 Ozzie Smith The Wizard	.50	.20	.05
□ 5 Todd Worrell and Tony Pena Throw Smoke	.25	.10	.02
□ 6 Vince Coleman Cardinal Attack	.50	.20	.05
□ 7 Tom Herr/Dan Driessen Herr's Wallop	.25	.10	.02
□ 8 Kirby Puckett Kirby's Bat Comes Alive	.75	.30	.07
□ 9 Kent Hrbek Hrbek's Slam Forces Game 7	.35	.14	.03
□ 10 Tom Herr Out at First	.25	.10	.02
□ 11 Don Baylor Game 7's Play At The Plate	.25	.10	.02
□ 12 Frank Viola Series MVP, 16 K's	.60	.24	.06

1989 Fleer

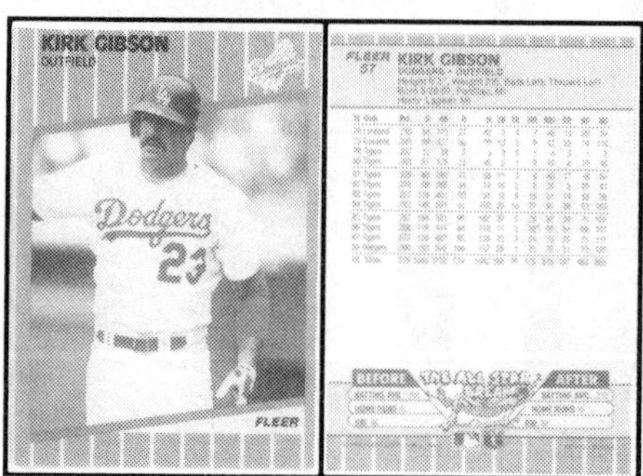

This 660-card set features a distinctive gray border background with white and yellow trim. The backs are printed in gray, black, and yellow on white card stock. The bottom of the card back shows an innovative breakdown of the player's demonstrated ability with respect to his performance before and after the All-Star break. Cards are numbered on the back and are again the standard 2 1/2" by 3 1/2". Cards are again organized numerically by teams. The last 33 cards in the set consist of Specials (628-639), Rookie Pairs (640-653), and checklists (654-660).

	MINT	EXC	G-VG
COMPLETE SET (660)	25.00	10.00	2.50
COMMON PLAYER (1-660)	.03	.01	.00

□ 1 Don Baylor .10 .03 .01
□ 2 Lance Blankenship .20 .08 .02
□ 3 Todd Burns .20 .08 .02
□ 4 Greg Cadaret .10 .04 .01
□ 5 Jose Canseco 1.00 .40 .10
□ 6 Storm Davis .06 .02 .00
□ 7 Dennis Eckersley .10 .04 .01
□ 8 Mike Gallego .03 .01 .00
□ 9 Ron Hassey .03 .01 .00
□ 10 Dave Henderson .06 .02 .00
□ 11 Rick Honeycutt .03 .01 .00
□ 12 Glenn Hubbard .03 .01 .00
□ 13 Stan Javier .03 .01 .00
□ 14 Doug Jennings .20 .08 .02
□ 15 Felix Jose .25 .10 .02
□ 16 Carney Lansford .06 .02 .00
□ 17 Mark McGwire .50 .20 .05
□ 18 Gene Nelson .03 .01 .00
□ 19 Dave Parker .08 .03 .01
□ 20 Eric Plunk .03 .01 .00
□ 21 Luis Polonia .03 .01 .00
□ 22 Terry Steinbach .08 .03 .01
□ 23 Dave Stewart .08 .03 .01
□ 24 Walt Weiss .35 .14 .03
□ 25 Bob Welch .06 .02 .00
□ 26 Curt Young .03 .01 .00
□ 27 Rick Aguilera .03 .01 .00
□ 28 Wally Backman .03 .01 .00
□ 29 Mark Carreon .03 .01 .00
□ 30 Gary Carter .15 .06 .01
□ 31 David Cone .30 .12 .03
□ 32 Ron Darling .08 .03 .01
□ 33 Len Dykstra .08 .03 .01
□ 34 Kevin Elster .06 .02 .00
□ 35 Sid Fernandez .08 .03 .01
□ 36 Dwight Gooden .30 .12 .03
□ 37 Keith Hernandez .12 .05 .01
□ 38 Gregg Jefferies 2.00 .80 .20
□ 39 Howard Johnson .08 .03 .01
□ 40 Terry Leach .06 .02 .00
□ 41 Dave Magadan .06 .02 .00
□ 42 Bob McClure .03 .01 .00
□ 43 Roger McDowell .06 .02 .00
□ 44 Kevin McReynolds .15 .06 .01
□ 45 Keith Miller .03 .01 .00
New York Mets
□ 46 Randy Myers .08 .03 .01
□ 47 Bob Ojeda .06 .02 .00
□ 48 Mackey Sasser .12 .05 .01
□ 49 Darryl Strawberry .35 .14 .03
□ 50 Tim Teufel .03 .01 .00
□ 51 Dave West .50 .20 .05
□ 52 Mookie Wilson .06 .02 .00
□ 53 Dave Anderson .03 .01 .00
□ 54 Tim Belcher .08 .03 .01
□ 55 Mike Davis .03 .01 .00
□ 56 Mike Devereaux .08 .03 .01
□ 57 Kirk Gibson .15 .06 .01
□ 58 Alfredo Griffin .06 .02 .00
□ 59 Chris Gwynn .08 .03 .01
□ 60 Jeff Hamilton .03 .01 .00
□ 61 Danny Heep .03 .01 .00
□ 62 Orel Hershiser .25 .10 .02
□ 63 Brian Holton .03 .01 .00
□ 64 Jay Howell .03 .01 .00
□ 65 Tim Leary .06 .02 .00
□ 66 Mike Marshall .08 .03 .01
□ 67 Ramon Martinez .35 .14 .03
□ 68 Jesse Orosco .03 .01 .00
□ 69 Alejandro Pena .03 .01 .00
□ 70 Steve Sax .10 .04 .01
□ 71 Mike Scioscia .03 .01 .00
□ 72 Mike Sharperson .03 .01 .00
□ 73 John Shelby .03 .01 .00
□ 74 Franklin Stubbs .03 .01 .00
□ 75 John Tudor .08 .03 .01
□ 76 Fernando Valenzuela .12 .05 .01
□ 77 Tracy Woodson .10 .04 .01
□ 78 Marty Barrett .06 .02 .00
□ 79 Todd Benzinger .06 .02 .00
□ 80 Mike Boddicker .06 .02 .00
□ 81 Wade Boggs .50 .20 .05
□ 82 "Oil Can" Boyd .06 .02 .00
□ 83 Ellis Burks .30 .12 .03
□ 84 Rick Cerone .03 .01 .00
□ 85 Roger Clemens .35 .14 .03
□ 86 Steve Curry .12 .05 .01
□ 87 Dwight Evans .08 .03 .01
□ 88 Wes Gardner .03 .01 .00
□ 89 Rich Gedman .06 .02 .00
□ 90 Mike Greenwell .75 .30 .07
□ 91 Bruce Hurst .10 .04 .01
□ 92 Dennis Lamp .03 .01 .00
□ 93 Spike Owen .03 .01 .00
□ 94 Larry Parrish .03 .01 .00
□ 95 Carlos Quintana .35 .14 .03
□ 96 Jody Reed .08 .03 .01
□ 97 Jim Rice .10 .04 .01
□ 98 Kevin Romine .03 .01 .00
□ 99 Lee Smith .06 .02 .00
□ 100 Mike Smithson .03 .01 .00
□ 101 Bob Stanley .03 .01 .00
□ 102 Allan Anderson .06 .02 .00
□ 103 Keith Atherton .03 .01 .00
□ 104 Juan Berenguer .03 .01 .00
□ 105 Bert Blyleven .08 .03 .01
□ 106 Eric Bullock .12 .05 .01
□ 107 Randy Bush .03 .01 .00
□ 108 John Christensen .03 .01 .00
□ 109 Mark Davidson .03 .01 .00
□ 110 Gary Gaetti .10 .04 .01
□ 111 Greg Gagne .03 .01 .00
□ 112 Dan Gladden .06 .02 .00
□ 113 German Gonzalez .10 .04 .01
□ 114 Brian Harper .03 .01 .00
□ 115 Tom Herr .06 .02 .00
□ 116 Kent Hrbek .10 .04 .01
□ 117 Gene Larkin .06 .02 .00
□ 118 Tim Laudner .03 .01 .00
□ 119 Charlie Lea .03 .01 .00
□ 120 Steve Lombardozzi .03 .01 .00
□ 121 John Moses .03 .01 .00
□ 122 Al Newman .03 .01 .00
□ 123 Mark Portugal .03 .01 .00
□ 124 Kirby Puckett .30 .12 .03
□ 125 Jeff Reardon .06 .02 .00
□ 126 Fred Toliver .03 .01 .00
□ 127 Frank Viola .15 .06 .01
□ 128 Doyle Alexander .06 .02 .00
□ 129 Dave Bergman .03 .01 .00
□ 130 Tom Brookens .03 .01 .00
□ 131 Paul Gibson .10 .04 .01
□ 132 Mike Heath .03 .01 .00
□ 133 Don Heinkel .10 .04 .01
□ 134 Mike Henneman .03 .01 .00
□ 135 Guillermo Hernandez .06 .02 .00
□ 136 Eric King .03 .01 .00
□ 137 Chet Lemon .06 .02 .00
□ 138 Fred Lynn .10 .04 .01
□ 139 Jack Morris .10 .04 .01
□ 140 Matt Nokes .10 .04 .01
□ 141 Gary Pettis .03 .01 .00
□ 142 Ted Power .03 .01 .00
□ 143 Jeff M. Robinson .08 .03 .01
Detroit Tigers
□ 144 Luis Salazar .03 .01 .00
□ 145 Steve Searcy .30 .12 .03
□ 146 Pat Sheridan .03 .01 .00
□ 147 Frank Tanana .06 .02 .00
□ 148 Alan Trammell .15 .06 .01
□ 149 Walt Terrell .03 .01 .00
□ 150 Jim Walewander .10 .04 .01
□ 151 Lou Whitaker .08 .03 .01
□ 152 Tim Birtsas .03 .01 .00
□ 153 Tom Browning .08 .03 .01
□ 154 Keith Brown .10 .04 .01
□ 155 Norm Charlton .10 .04 .01
□ 156 Dave Concepcion .08 .03 .01
□ 157 Kal Daniels .12 .05 .01
□ 158 Eric Davis .35 .14 .03
□ 159 Bo Diaz .03 .01 .00
□ 160 Rob Dibble .12 .05 .01
□ 161 Nick Esasky .03 .01 .00
□ 162 John Franco .08 .03 .01
□ 163 Danny Jackson .10 .04 .01
□ 164 Barry Larkin .10 .04 .01
□ 165 Rob Murphy .03 .01 .00
□ 166 Paul O'Neill .06 .02 .00
□ 167 Jeff Reed .03 .01 .00
□ 168 Jose Rijo .03 .01 .00
□ 169 Ron Robinson .03 .01 .00
□ 170 Chris Sabo 1.00 .40 .10
□ 171 Candy Sierra .10 .04 .01
□ 172 Van Snider .25 .10 .02
□ 173 Jeff Treadway .06 .02 .00
□ 174 Frank Williams .03 .01 .00
□ 175 Herm Winningham .03 .01 .00
□ 176 Jim Adduci .03 .01 .00
□ 177 Don August .06 .02 .00
□ 178 Mike Birkbeck .03 .01 .00
□ 179 Chris Bosio .03 .01 .00
□ 180 Glenn Braggs .03 .01 .00
□ 181 Greg Brock .03 .01 .00
□ 182 Mark Clear .03 .01 .00
□ 183 Chuck Crim .03 .01 .00
□ 184 Rob Deer .06 .02 .00
□ 185 Tom Filer .03 .01 .00
□ 186 Jim Gantner .03 .01 .00
□ 187 Darryl Hamilton .25 .10 .02
□ 188 Ted Higuera .08 .03 .01

☐ 189	Odell Jones	.03	.01	.00
☐ 190	Jeffrey Leonard	.06	.02	.00
☐ 191	Joey Meyer	.08	.03	.01
☐ 192	Paul Mirabella	.03	.01	.00
☐ 193	Paul Molitor	.10	.04	.01
☐ 194	Charlie O'Brien	.10	.04	.01
☐ 195	Dan Plesac	.06	.02	.00
☐ 196	Gary Sheffield	1.50	.60	.15
☐ 197	B.J. Surhoff	.08	.03	.01
☐ 198	Dale Sveum	.03	.01	.00
☐ 199	Bill Wegman	.03	.01	.00
☐ 200	Robin Yount	.15	.06	.01
☐ 201	Rafael Belliard	.03	.01	.00
☐ 202	Barry Bonds	.10	.04	.01
☐ 203	Bobby Bonilla	.10	.04	.01
☐ 204	Sid Bream	.03	.01	.00
☐ 205	Benny Distefano	.03	.01	.00
☐ 206	Doug Drabek	.03	.01	.00
☐ 207	Mike Dunne	.06	.02	.00
☐ 208	Felix Fermin	.03	.01	.00
☐ 209	Brian Fisher	.03	.01	.00
☐ 210	Jim Gott	.03	.01	.00
☐ 211	Bob Kipper	.03	.01	.00
☐ 212	Dave LaPoint	.03	.01	.00
☐ 213	Mike LaValliere	.03	.01	.00
☐ 214	Jose Lind	.03	.01	.00
☐ 215	Junior Ortiz	.03	.01	.00
☐ 216	Vicente Palacios	.03	.01	.00
☐ 217	Tom Prince	.08	.03	.01
☐ 218	Gary Redus	.03	.01	.00
☐ 219	R.J. Reynolds	.03	.01	.00
☐ 220	Jeff Robinson Pittsburgh Pirates	.03	.01	.00
☐ 221	John Smiley	.03	.01	.00
☐ 222	Andy Van Slyke	.12	.05	.01
☐ 223	Bob Walk	.06	.02	.00
☐ 224	Glenn Wilson	.03	.01	.00
☐ 225	Jesse Barfield	.10	.04	.01
☐ 226	George Bell	.12	.05	.01
☐ 227	Pat Borders	.12	.05	.01
☐ 228	John Cerutti	.03	.01	.00
☐ 229	Jim Clancy	.03	.01	.00
☐ 230	Mark Eichhorn	.03	.01	.00
☐ 231	Tony Fernandez	.08	.03	.01
☐ 232	Cecil Fielder	.03	.01	.00
☐ 233	Mike Flanagan	.03	.01	.00
☐ 234	Kelly Gruber	.03	.01	.00
☐ 235	Tom Henke	.06	.02	.00
☐ 236	Jimmy Key	.06	.02	.00
☐ 237	Rick Leach	.03	.01	.00
☐ 238	Manny Lee	.03	.01	.00
☐ 239	Nelson Liriano	.03	.01	.00
☐ 240	Fred McGriff	.15	.06	.01
☐ 241	Lloyd Moseby	.08	.03	.01
☐ 242	Rance Mulliniks	.03	.01	.00
☐ 243	Jeff Musselman	.03	.01	.00
☐ 244	Dave Stieb	.08	.03	.01
☐ 245	Todd Stottlemyre	.12	.05	.01
☐ 246	Duane Ward	.03	.01	.00
☐ 247	David Wells	.08	.03	.01
☐ 248	Ernie Whitt	.03	.01	.00
☐ 249	Luis Aguayo	.03	.01	.00
☐ 250	Neil Allen	.03	.01	.00
☐ 251	John Candelaria	.06	.02	.00
☐ 252	Jack Clark	.12	.05	.01
☐ 253	Richard Dotson	.06	.02	.00
☐ 254	Rickey Henderson	.20	.08	.02
☐ 255	Tommy John	.08	.03	.01
☐ 256	Roberto Kelly	.12	.05	.01
☐ 257	Al Leiter	.25	.10	.02
☐ 258	Don Mattingly	1.00	.40	.10
☐ 259	Dale Mohorcic	.03	.01	.00
☐ 260	Hal Morris	.15	.06	.01
☐ 261	Scott Nielsen	.03	.01	.00
☐ 262	Mike Pagliarulo	.06	.02	.00
☐ 263	Hipolito Pena	.12	.05	.01
☐ 264	Ken Phelps	.06	.02	.00
☐ 265	Willie Randolph	.06	.02	.00
☐ 266	Rick Rhoden	.06	.02	.00
☐ 267	Dave Righetti	.08	.03	.01
☐ 268	Rafael Santana	.03	.01	.00
☐ 269	Steve Shields	.03	.01	.00
☐ 270	Joel Skinner	.03	.01	.00
☐ 271	Don Slaught	.03	.01	.00
☐ 272	Claudell Washington	.06	.02	.00
☐ 273	Gary Ward	.03	.01	.00
☐ 274	Dave Winfield	.15	.06	.01
☐ 275	Luis Aquino	.03	.01	.00
☐ 276	Floyd Bannister	.03	.01	.00
☐ 277	George Brett	.20	.08	.02
☐ 278	Bill Buckner	.06	.02	.00
☐ 279	Nick Capra	.08	.03	.01
☐ 280	Jose DeJesus	.10	.04	.01
☐ 281	Steve Farr	.03	.01	.00
☐ 282	Jerry Don Gleaton	.03	.01	.00

☐ 283	Mark Gubicza	.08	.03
☐ 284	Tom Gordon	.25	.10
☐ 285	Bo Jackson	.20	.08
☐ 286	Charlie Leibrandt	.03	.01
☐ 287	Mike Macfarlane	.15	.06
☐ 288	Jeff Montgomery	.03	.01
☐ 289	Bill Pecota	.03	.01
☐ 290	Jamie Quirk	.03	.01
☐ 291	Bret Saberhagen	.10	.04
☐ 292	Kevin Seitzer	.18	.08
☐ 293	Kurt Stillwell	.03	.01
☐ 294	Pat Tabler	.06	.02
☐ 295	Danny Tartabull	.15	.06
☐ 296	Gary Thurman	.03	.01
☐ 297	Frank White	.06	.02
☐ 298	Willie Wilson	.08	.03
☐ 299	Roberto Alomar	.30	.12
☐ 300	Sandy Alomar Jr.	.90	.36
☐ 301	Chris Brown	.06	.02
☐ 302	Mike Brumley	.08	.03
☐ 303	Mark Davis	.06	.02
☐ 304	Mark Grant	.03	.01
☐ 305	Tony Gwynn	.20	.08
☐ 306	Greg W. Harris San Diego Padres	.20	.08
☐ 307	Andy Hawkins	.06	.02
☐ 308	Jimmy Jones	.06	.02
☐ 309	John Kruk	.06	.02
☐ 310	Dave Leiper	.03	.01
☐ 311	Carmelo Martinez	.03	.01
☐ 312	Lance McCullers	.06	.02
☐ 313	Keith Moreland	.03	.01
☐ 314	Dennis Rasmussen	.06	.02
☐ 315	Randy Ready	.03	.01
☐ 316	Benito Santiago	.18	.08
☐ 317	Eric Show	.06	.02
☐ 318	Todd Simmons	.06	.02
☐ 319	Garry Templeton	.06	.02
☐ 320	Dickie Thon	.03	.01
☐ 321	Ed Whitson	.03	.01
☐ 322	Marvell Wynne	.03	.01
☐ 323	Mike Aldrete	.03	.01
☐ 324	Brett Butler	.06	.02
☐ 325	Will Clark	.35	.14
☐ 326	Kelly Downs	.06	.02
☐ 327	Dave Dravecky	.03	.01
☐ 328	Scott Garrelts	.03	.01
☐ 329	Atlee Hammaker	.03	.01
☐ 330	Charlie Hayes	.12	.05
☐ 331	Mike Krukow	.03	.01
☐ 332	Craig Lefferts	.03	.01
☐ 333	Candy Maldonado	.06	.02
☐ 334	Kirt Manwaring	.03	.01
☐ 335	Bob Melvin	.03	.01
☐ 336	Kevin Mitchell	.06	.02
☐ 337	Donell Nixon	.03	.01
☐ 338	Tony Perezchica	.12	.05
☐ 339	Joe Price	.03	.01
☐ 340	Rick Reuschel	.06	.02
☐ 341	Earnest Riles	.03	.01
☐ 342	Don Robinson	.03	.01
☐ 343	Chris Speier	.03	.01
☐ 344	Robby Thompson	.03	.01
☐ 345	Jose Uribe	.03	.01
☐ 346	Matt Williams	.08	.03
☐ 347	Trevor Wilson	.15	.06
☐ 348	Juan Agosto	.03	.01
☐ 349	Larry Andersen	.03	.01
☐ 350	Alan Ashby	.03	.01
☐ 351	Kevin Bass	.06	.02
☐ 352	Buddy Bell	.08	.03
☐ 353	Craig Biggio	.15	.06
☐ 354	Danny Darwin	.03	.01
☐ 355	Glenn Davis	.10	.04
☐ 356	Jim Deshaies	.03	.01
☐ 357	Bill Doran	.06	.02
☐ 358	John Fishel	.15	.06
☐ 359	Billy Hatcher	.06	.02
☐ 360	Bob Knepper	.03	.01
☐ 361	Louie Meadows	.10	.04
☐ 362	Dave Meads	.03	.01
☐ 363	Jim Pankovits	.03	.01
☐ 364	Terry Puhl	.03	.01
☐ 365	Rafael Ramirez	.03	.01
☐ 366	Craig Reynolds	.03	.01
☐ 367	Mike Scott	.10	.04
☐ 368	Nolan Ryan	.20	.08
☐ 369	Dave Smith	.03	.01
☐ 370	Gerald Young	.06	.02
☐ 371	Hubie Brooks	.06	.02
☐ 372	Tim Burke	.03	.01
☐ 373	John Dopson	.15	.06
☐ 374	Mike Fitzgerald Montreal Expos	.03	.01
☐ 375	Tom Foley	.03	.01

376 Andres Galarraga	.12	.05	.01
377 Neal Heaton	.03	.01	.00
378 Joe Hesketh	.03	.01	.00
379 Brian Holman	.12	.05	.01
380 Rex Hudler	.03	.01	.00
381 Randy Johnson	.25	.10	.02
382 Wallace Johnson	.03	.01	.00
383 Tracy Jones	.06	.02	.00
384 Dave Martinez	.03	.01	.00
385 Dennis Martinez	.03	.01	.00
386 Andy McGaffigan	.03	.01	.00
387 Otis Nixon	.03	.01	.00
388 Johnny Paredes	.12	.05	.01
389 Jeff Parrett	.10	.04	.01
390 Pascual Perez	.06	.02	.00
391 Tim Raines	.15	.06	.01
392 Luis Rivera	.03	.01	.00
393 Nelson Santovenia	.12	.05	.01
394 Bryn Smith	.03	.01	.00
395 Tim Wallach	.08	.03	.01
396 Andy Allanson	.03	.01	.00
397 Rod Allen	.10	.04	.01
398 Scott Bailes	.03	.01	.00
399 Tom Candiotti	.03	.01	.00
400 Joe Carter	.10	.04	.01
401 Carmen Castillo	.03	.01	.00
402 Dave Clark	.06	.02	.00
403 John Farrell	.03	.01	.00
404 Julio Franco	.06	.02	.00
405 Don Gordon	.08	.03	.01
406 Mel Hall	.06	.02	.00
407 Brad Havens	.03	.01	.00
408 Brook Jacoby	.06	.02	.00
409 Doug Jones	.06	.02	.00
410 Jeff Kaiser	.10	.04	.01
411 Luis Medina	.45	.18	.04
412 Cory Snyder	.15	.06	.01
413 Greg Swindell	.10	.04	.01
414 Ron Tingley	.10	.04	.01
415 Willie Upshaw	.03	.01	.00
416 Ron Washington	.03	.01	.00
417 Rich Yett	.03	.01	.00
418 Damon Berryhill	.10	.04	.01
419 Mike Bielecki	.03	.01	.00
420 Doug Dascenzo	.15	.06	.01
421 Jody Davis	.06	.02	.00
422 Andre Dawson	.12	.05	.01
423 Frank DiPino	.03	.01	.00
424 Shawon Dunston	.06	.02	.00
425 "Goose" Gossage	.08	.03	.01
426 Mark Grace	.85	.34	.08
427 Mike Harkey	.50	.20	.05
428 Darrin Jackson	.08	.03	.01
429 Les Lancaster	.03	.01	.00
430 Vance Law	.03	.01	.00
431 Greg Maddux	.12	.05	.01
432 Jamie Moyer	.03	.01	.00
433 Al Nipper	.03	.01	.00
434 Rafael Palmeiro	.15	.06	.01
435 Pat Perry	.03	.01	.00
436 Jeff Pico	.10	.04	.01
437 Ryne Sandberg	.15	.06	.01
438 Calvin Schiraldi	.03	.01	.00
439 Rick Sutcliffe	.08	.03	.01
440 Manny Trillo	.03	.01	.00
441 Gary Varsho	.15	.06	.01
442 Mitch Webster	.03	.01	.00
443 Luis Alicea	.12	.05	.01
444 Tom Brunansky	.08	.03	.01
445 Vince Coleman	.15	.06	.01
446 John Costello	.12	.05	.01
447 Danny Cox	.06	.02	.00
448 Ken Dayley	.03	.01	.00
449 Jose DeLeon	.03	.01	.00
450 Curt Ford	.03	.01	.00
451 Pedro Guerrero	.10	.04	.01
452 Bob Horner	.08	.03	.01
453 Tim Jones	.15	.06	.01
454 Steve Lake	.03	.01	.00
455 Joe Magrane	.06	.02	.00
456 Greg Mathews	.03	.01	.00
457 Willie McGee	.08	.03	.01
458 Larry McWilliams	.03	.01	.00
459 Jose Oquendo	.03	.01	.00
460 Tony Pena	.06	.02	.00
461 Terry Pendleton	.03	.01	.00
462 Steve Peters	.15	.06	.01
463 Ozzie Smith	.12	.05	.01
464 Scott Terry	.03	.01	.00
465 Denny Walling	.03	.01	.00
466 Todd Worrell	.08	.03	.01
467 Tony Armas	.06	.02	.00
468 Dante Bichette	.20	.08	.02
469 Bob Boone	.06	.02	.00
470 Terry Clark	.15	.06	.01
471 Stew Cliburn	.03	.01	.00
472 Mike Cook	.12	.05	.01
473 Sherman Corbett	.12	.05	.01
474 Chili Davis	.06	.02	.00
475 Brian Downing	.06	.02	.00
476 Jim Eppard	.03	.01	.00
477 Chuck Finley	.03	.01	.00
478 Willie Fraser	.03	.01	.00
479 Bryan Harvey	.25	.10	.02
480 Jack Howell	.03	.01	.00
481 Wally Joyner	.20	.08	.02
482 Jack Lazorko	.03	.01	.00
483 Kirk McCaskill	.03	.01	.00
484 Mark McLemore	.03	.01	.00
485 Greg Minton	.03	.01	.00
486 Dan Petry	.03	.01	.00
487 Johnny Ray	.06	.02	.00
488 Dick Schofield	.03	.01	.00
489 Devon White	.08	.03	.01
490 Mike Witt	.08	.03	.01
491 Harold Baines	.08	.03	.01
492 Daryl Boston	.03	.01	.00
493 Ivan Calderon	.08	.03	.01
494 Mike Diaz	.03	.01	.00
495 Carlton Fisk	.08	.03	.01
496 Dave Gallagher	.15	.06	.01
497 Ozzie Guillen	.06	.02	.00
498 Shawn Hillegas	.03	.01	.00
499 Lance Johnson	.03	.01	.00
500 Barry Jones	.03	.01	.00
501 Bill Long	.03	.01	.00
502 Steve Lyons	.03	.01	.00
503 Fred Manrique	.03	.01	.00
504 Jack McDowell	.08	.03	.01
505 Donn Pall	.08	.03	.01
506 Kelly Paris	.03	.01	.00
507 Dan Pasqua	.06	.02	.00
508 Ken Patterson	.10	.04	.01
509 Melido Perez	.08	.03	.01
510 Jerry Reuss	.03	.01	.00
511 Mark Salas	.03	.01	.00
512 Bobby Thigpen	.06	.02	.00
513 Mike Woodard	.03	.01	.00
514 Bob Brower	.06	.02	.00
515 Steve Buechele	.03	.01	.00
516 Jose Cecena	.10	.04	.01
517 Cecil Espy	.08	.03	.01
518 Scott Fletcher	.03	.01	.00
519 Cecilio Guante	.03	.01	.00
520 Jose Guzman	.03	.01	.00
521 Ray Hayward	.08	.03	.01
522 Charlie Hough	.03	.01	.00
523 Pete Incaviglia	.10	.04	.01
524 Mike Jeffcoat	.03	.01	.00
525 Paul Kilgus	.03	.01	.00
526 Chad Kreuter	.20	.08	.02
527 Jeff Kunkel	.03	.01	.00
528 Oddibe McDowell	.06	.02	.00
529 Pete O'Brien	.06	.02	.00
530 Geno Petralli	.03	.01	.00
531 Jeff Russell	.03	.01	.00
532 Ruben Sierra	.12	.05	.01
533 Mike Stanley	.03	.01	.00
534 Ed VandeBerg	.03	.01	.00
535 Curtis Wilkerson	.03	.01	.00
536 Mitch Williams	.03	.01	.00
537 Bobby Witt	.06	.02	.00
538 Steve Balboni	.03	.01	.00
539 Scott Bankhead	.03	.01	.00
540 Scott Bradley	.03	.01	.00
541 Mickey Brantley	.06	.02	.00
542 Jay Buhner	.20	.08	.02
543 Mike Campbell	.03	.01	.00
544 Darnell Coles	.03	.01	.00
545 Henry Cotto	.03	.01	.00
546 Alvin Davis	.08	.03	.01
547 Mario Diaz	.03	.01	.00
548 Ken Griffey Jr.	1.25	.50	.12
549 Erik Hanson	.15	.06	.01
550 Mike Jackson	.03	.01	.00
551 Mark Langston	.08	.03	.01
552 Edgar Martinez	.10	.04	.01
553 Bill McGuire	.10	.04	.01
554 Mike Moore	.03	.01	.00
555 Jim Presley	.06	.02	.00
556 Rey Quinones	.03	.01	.00
557 Jerry Reed	.03	.01	.00
558 Harold Reynolds	.03	.01	.00
559 Mike Schooler	.12	.05	.01
560 Bill Swift	.03	.01	.00
561 Dave Valle	.03	.01	.00
562 Steve Bedrosian	.08	.03	.01
563 Phil Bradley	.06	.02	.00
564 Don Carman	.03	.01	.00
565 Bob Dernier	.03	.01	.00

☐ 566	Marvin Freeman	.03	.01	.00
☐ 567	Todd Frohwirth	.03	.01	.00
☐ 568	Greg Gross	.03	.01	.00
☐ 569	Kevin Gross	.03	.01	.00
☐ 570	Greg Harris	.03	.01	.00
	Philadelphia Phillies			
☐ 571	Von Hayes	.08	.03	.01
☐ 572	Chris James	.08	.03	.01
☐ 573	Steve Jeltz	.03	.01	.00
☐ 574	Ron Jones	.30	.12	.03
☐ 575	Ricky Jordan	1.25	.50	.12
☐ 576	Mike Maddux	.03	.01	.00
☐ 577	David Palmer	.03	.01	.00
☐ 578	Lance Parrish	.08	.03	.01
☐ 579	Shane Rawley	.03	.01	.00
☐ 580	Bruce Ruffin	.03	.01	.00
☐ 581	Juan Samuel	.08	.03	.01
☐ 582	Mike Schmidt	.20	.08	.02
☐ 583	Kent Tekulve	.03	.01	.00
☐ 584	Milt Thompson	.03	.01	.00
☐ 585	Jose Alvarez	.10	.04	.01
☐ 586	Paul Assenmacher	.03	.01	.00
☐ 587	Bruce Benedict	.03	.01	.00
☐ 588	Jeff Blauser	.03	.01	.00
☐ 589	Terry Blocker	.12	.05	.01
☐ 590	Ron Gant	.15	.06	.01
☐ 591	Tom Glavine	.03	.01	.00
☐ 592	Tommy Gregg	.10	.04	.01
☐ 593	Albert Hall	.03	.01	.00
☐ 594	Dion James	.03	.01	.00
☐ 595	Rick Mahler	.03	.01	.00
☐ 596	Dale Murphy	.25	.10	.02
☐ 597	Gerald Perry	.08	.03	.01
☐ 598	Charlie Puleo	.03	.01	.00
☐ 599	Ted Simmons	.08	.03	.01
☐ 600	Pete Smith	.03	.01	.00
☐ 601	Zane Smith	.03	.01	.00
☐ 602	John Smoltz	.25	.10	.02
☐ 603	Bruce Sutter	.08	.03	.01
☐ 604	Andres Thomas	.03	.01	.00
☐ 605	Ozzie Virgil	.03	.01	.00
☐ 606	Brady Anderson	.20	.08	.02
☐ 607	Jeff Ballard	.03	.01	.00
☐ 608	Jose Bautista	.10	.04	.01
☐ 609	Ken Gerhart	.03	.01	.00
☐ 610	Terry Kennedy	.03	.01	.00
☐ 611	Eddie Murray	.15	.06	.01
☐ 612	Carl Nichols	.08	.03	.01
☐ 613	Tom Niedenfuer	.03	.01	.00
☐ 614	Joe Orsulak	.03	.01	.00
☐ 615	Oswald Peraza	.10	.04	.01
☐ 616A	Bill Ripken ERR	20.00	8.00	1.00
	(Rick Face written			
	on knob of bat)			
☐ 616B	Bill Ripken COR	.15	.06	.01
☐ 617	Cal Ripken Jr.	.15	.06	.01
☐ 618	Dave Schmidt	.03	.01	.00
☐ 619	Rick Schu	.03	.01	.00
☐ 620	Larry Sheets	.06	.02	.00
☐ 621	Doug Sisk	.03	.01	.00
☐ 622	Pete Stanicek	.06	.02	.00
☐ 623	Mickey Tettleton	.03	.01	.00
☐ 624	Jay Tibbs	.03	.01	.00
☐ 625	Jim Traber	.06	.02	.00
☐ 626	Mark Williamson	.03	.01	.00
☐ 627	Craig Worthington	.30	.12	.03
☐ 628	Speed/Power	.35	.14	.03
	Jose Canseco			
☐ 629	Pitcher Perfect	.06	.02	.00
	Tom Browning			
☐ 630	Like Father/Like Sons	.20	.08	.02
	Roberto Alomar			
	Sandy Alomar Jr.			
☐ 631	NL All Stars	.12	.05	.01
	Will Clark			
	Rafael Palmeiro			
☐ 632	Homeruns - Coast to Coast	.20	.08	.02
	Darryl Strawberry			
	Will Clark			
☐ 633	Hot Corners - Hot Hitters	.20	.08	.02
	Wade Boggs			
	Carney Lansford			
☐ 634	Triple A's	.30	.12	.03
	Jose Canseco			
	Terry Steinbach			
	Mark McGwire			
☐ 635	Dual Heat	.15	.06	.01
	Mark Davis			
	Dwight Gooden			
☐ 636	NL Pitching Power	.12	.05	.01
	Danny Jackson			
	David Cone			
☐ 637	Cannon Arms	.15	.06	.01
	Chris Sabo			
	Bobby Bonilla			
☐ 638	Double Trouble	.08	.03	.0
	Andres Galarraga			
	Gerald Perry			
☐ 639	Power Center	.20	.08	.0
	Kirby Puckett			
	Eric Davis			
☐ 640	Steve Wilson and Cameron Drew	.25	.10	.0
☐ 641	Kevin Brown and Kevin Reimer	.20	.08	.0
☐ 642	Brad Pounders and Jerald Clark	.25	.10	.0
☐ 643	Mike Capel and Drew Hall	.20	.08	.0
☐ 644	Joe Girardi and Rolando Roomes	.20	.08	.0
☐ 645	Lenny Harris and Marty Brown	.20	.08	.0
☐ 646	Luis De Los Santos and Jim Campbell	.30	.12	.0
☐ 647	Randy Kramer and Miguel Garcia	.25	.10	.0
☐ 648	Torey Lovullo and Robert Palacios	.20	.08	.0
☐ 649	Jim Corsi and Bob Milacki	.25	.10	.0
☐ 650	Grady Hall and Mike Rochford	.20	.08	.0
☐ 651	Terry Taylor and Vance Lovelace	.25	.10	.0
☐ 652	Ken Hill and Dennis Cook	.20	.08	.0
☐ 653	Scott Service and Shane Turner	.20	.08	.0
☐ 654	CL: Oakland/Mets Dodgers/Red Sox	.06	.01	.0
☐ 655	CL: Twins/Tigers Reds/Brewers	.06	.01	.0
☐ 656	CL: Pirates/Blue Jays Yankees/Royals	.06	.01	.0
☐ 657	CL: Padres/Giants Astros/Expos	.06	.01	.0
☐ 658	CL: Indians/Cubs Cardinals/Angels	.06	.01	.0
☐ 659	CL: White Sox/Rangers Mariners/Phillies	.06	.01	.0
☐ 660	CL: Braves/Orioles Specials/Checklists	.06	.01	.0

1989 Fleer Wax Box Cards

The cards in this 28-card set measure the standard 2 1/2" by 3 1/2". Cards have essentially the same design as the 1989 Fleer regular issue set. The cards were printed on the bottoms of the regular issue wax pack boxes. These 28 cards (C1 to C28) are considered a separate set in their own right and are not typically included in a complete set of the regular issue 1989 Fleer cards. The value of the panel uncut is slightly greater, perhaps by 25% greater, than the value of the individual cards cut up carefully. The wax box cards are further distinguished by the gray card stock used.

	MINT	EXC	G-VG
COMPLETE SET (28)	5.00	2.00	.50
COMMON PLAYER (C1-C28)	.05	.02	.00

"Our dad makes us happy!"

And he makes his customers happy too! Send self-addressed stamped envelope for current price list to:

GARY WALTER BASEBALL CARDS
561 River Terrace
Toms River, NJ 08755
(201) 286-9007
Phone hours: Mon-Fri 8:00am-5:00pm

We specialize in mail order sales of current stars and rookies—one at a time or by the hundreds. Our staff of over 30 sorters, order-fillers, and shipping personnel is eager to help you build a collection or start an investment empire. We emphasize fast, friendly, and reliable service and make sure that every card that is sent out is packed with careful protection.

SEND FOR YOUR FREE PRICE LIST TODAY! HAPPY COLLECTING!

COMPLETE BASEBALL SETS

1989 Topps (792)	$22.00
1989 Fleer Factory (660)	25.00
1988 Topps (792)	25.00
1988 Score Factory (660)	20.00
1988 Fleer Factory (660)	30.00
1987 Topps Factory (792)	35.00
1987 Fleer Factory (660)	45.00
1987 Topps Traded Set (132)	10.00
1987 Fleer Traded Set (132)	10.00
1987 Donruss Opening Day Set	20.00
1987 Donruss Highlights	8.00
1987 or 1986 Topps Minis	6.00
1988, '87, '86, '85, '84, or '83 Donruss Action All Stars (60)	6.00
1987, '86, '85 Topps Glossy (22)	5.00
1987 Fleer Mini Set	7.50

COMPLETE BASEBALL SETS

1986 Fleer Mini Set (Canseco)	$12.00
1986 Topps Factory Set (660)	35.00
1986 Donruss Highlights	6.00
1985 Topps Pete Rose Set (120)	17.50
1984 Donruss Champions (60)	6.00
1985 Coca-Cola White Sox	8.00
1984 Drakes Big Hitters	6.00
1983 Topps Foldouts (85)	6.00
1982 Donruss Factory (660)	26.00
1982 Fleer (660)	25.00
1981 Donruss (605)	30.00
1981 Fleer (660)	27.50
1981 Topps (726)	75.00
1981 Topps Scratchoffs (108)	7.95
1981 Squirt Panel Set	15.00
1980 Topps Supers (60)	12.00

COMPLETE BASEBALL SETS

1980 Kelloggs 3D Set (60)	$16.00
1977 Rowe (64 Hall of Famers)	4.00
1974 Topps Traded Set (44)	10.00
1964 Topps Supers (60)	100.00
1948 Bowman Reprint Set	7.50
Twins Past Players (50)	10.50
1,000 Card Gards	10.00
100 9-pocket, top-load sheets	12.00
Deluxe Large Card Album	6.95
Rookie Card Checklist Book	4.00
32-page Price List (Free w/order)	.50

COMPLETE FOOTBALL SETS

1988 or 1987 Topps (396)	$14.00
1986 or 1985 Topps (396)	18.50
1982 or 1981 Topps (528)	22.00
1980 Topps Super (30)	8.00

COMPLETE BASKETBALL SETS

1981-82 Topps (198)	12.00
1979-80 Topps (132)	12.00
1978-79 Topps (132)	14.00
1977-78 Topps (132)	20.00
1976-77 Topps (144)	42.50

Add $1.50 shipping to all orders.
Wisconsin orders add sales tax.
Prices subject to change.
U.S. orders only.

SEND ALL MAIL ORDERS TO:
Tom Daniels/T&J Sports Cards
Box 191-A
Richland Center, WI 53581
Phone 608-647-6687

BASEBALL, FOOTBALL, HOCKEY
BASKETBALL AND NON-SPORT SETS AND SINGLES
ALSO UNOPENED BOXES - AUTOGRAPHS - SUPPLIES

15,000,000 Cards in stock

THE BASEBALL CARD SHOPPE

126 WESTGATE MALL
ODANA ROAD & WHITNEY WAY
MADISON, WI 53711

Hours: Monday - Friday 12-7
Saturday 10-5, Sunday 12-5

PHONE: 608-274-8498
BUY-SELL-TRADE

Tom & Anita Daniels, Owners — Erik Osterberg, Manager
Jeff Daniels — Ryan Erickson — Dave Deibert
Angie Keelan — Jenny Keelan

☐ C1 Mets Logo	.05	.02	.00
☐ C2 Wade Boggs	.50	.20	.05
☐ C3 George Brett	.30	.12	.03
☐ C4 Jose Canseco	1.00	.40	.10
☐ C5 A's Logo	.05	.02	.00
☐ C6 Will Clark	.50	.20	.05
☐ C7 David Cone	.25	.10	.02
☐ C8 Andres Galarraga	.20	.08	.02
☐ C9 Dodgers Logo	.05	.02	.00
☐ C10 Kirk Gibson	.25	.10	.02
☐ C11 Mike Greenwell	.65	.26	.06
☐ C12 Tony Gwynn	.30	.12	.03
☐ C13 Tigers Logo	.05	.02	.00
☐ C14 Orel Hershiser	.25	.10	.02
☐ C15 Danny Jackson	.10	.04	.01
☐ C16 Wally Joyner	.30	.12	.03
☐ C17 Red Sox Logo	.05	.02	.00
☐ C18 Yankees Logo	.05	.02	.00
☐ C19 Fred McGriff	.25	.10	.02
☐ C20 Kirby Puckett	.35	.14	.03
☐ C21 Chris Sabo	.50	.20	.05
☐ C22 Kevin Seitzer	.25	.10	.02
☐ C23 Pirates Logo	.05	.02	.00
☐ C24 Astros Logo	.05	.02	.00
☐ C25 Darryl Strawberry	.35	.14	.03
☐ C26 Alan Trammell	.20	.08	.02
☐ C27 Andy Van Slyke	.20	.08	.02
☐ C28 Frank Viola	.15	.06	.01

1989 Fleer All Star Inserts

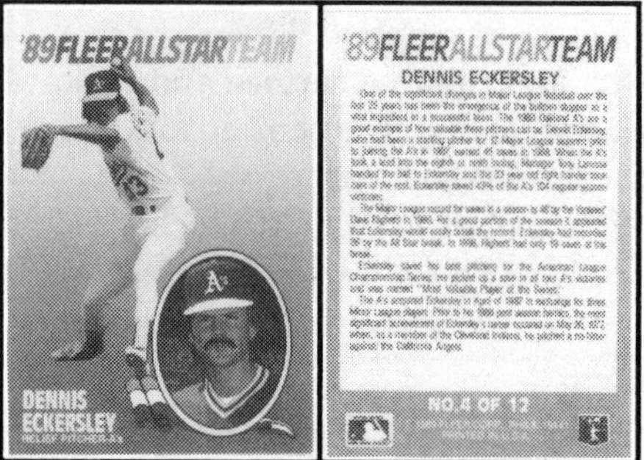

This twelve-card subset was randomly inserted in Fleer wax packs (15 regular cards) and Fleer value packs (36 regular cards). The players selected are the 1989 Fleer Major League All-Star team. One player has been selected for each position along with a DH and three pitchers. The cards are attractively designed and are standard size, 2 1/2" by 3 1/2". The cards are numbered on the backs and feature a distinctive green background on the card fronts.

	MINT	EXC	G-VG
COMPLETE SET (12)	12.00	5.00	1.20
COMMON PLAYER (1-12)	.30	.12	.03
☐ 1 Bobby Bonilla Third Baseman	.50	.20	.05
☐ 2 Jose Canseco Outfielder	3.50	1.40	.35
☐ 3 Will Clark First Baseman	1.25	.50	.12
☐ 4 Dennis Eckersley Relief Pitcher	.50	.20	.05
☐ 5 Julio Franco Second Baseman	.30	.12	.03
☐ 6 Mike Greenwell Outfielder	2.00	.80	.20
☐ 7 Orel Hershiser Righthand Pitcher	1.00	.40	.10
☐ 8 Paul Molitor Designated Hitter	.50	.20	.05
☐ 9 Mike Scioscia Catcher	.30	.12	.03
☐ 10 Darryl Strawberry Outfielder	1.25	.50	.12
☐ 11 Alan Trammell Shortstop	.50	.20	.05
☐ 12 Frank Viola Lefthand Pitcher	.50	.20	.05

1989 Fleer For The Record

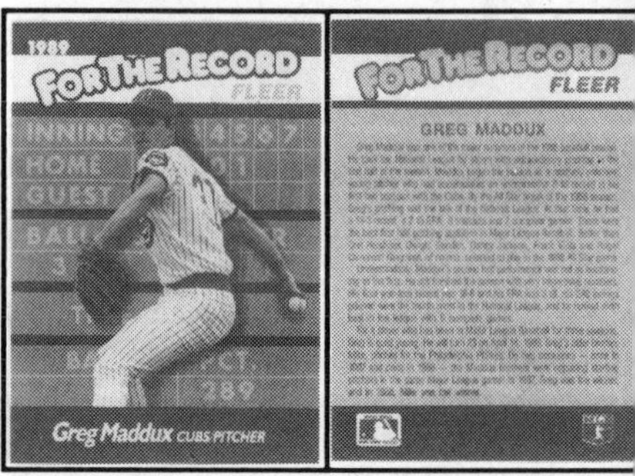

This six-card subset was distributed randomly (as ar insert) in Fleer rack packs. These cards are standarc size, 2 1/2" by 3 1/2" and are quite attractive. The set is subtitled "For The Record" anc commemorates record-breaking events for those players from the previous season. The cards are numbered on the backs. The card backs are printec in red, black, and gray on white card stock.

	MINT	EXC	G-V
COMPLETE SET (6)	5.50	2.20	.5
COMMON PLAYER (1-6)	.50	.20	.0
☐ 1 Wade Boggs Boston Red Sox	1.50	.60	.1
☐ 2 Roger Clemens Boston Red Sox	1.25	.50	.1
☐ 3 Andres Galarraga Montreal Expos	.50	.20	.0
☐ 4 Kirk Gibson Los Angeles Dodgers	1.00	.40	.1
☐ 5 Greg Maddux Chicago Cubs	.50	.20	.0
☐ 6 Don Mattingly New York Yankees	2.00	.80	.2

1989 Fleer World Series

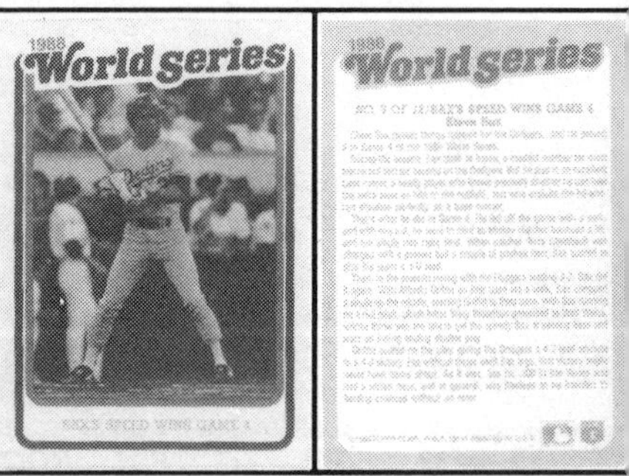

This 12-card set of 2 1/2" by 3 1/2" cards features highlights of the previous year's World Series between the Dodgers and the Athletics. The sets were packaged as a complete set insert with the collated sets (of the 1989 Fleer regular issue) which were sold by Fleer directly to hobby card dealers; they were not available in the general retail candy store outlets.

SURVEY CONTRIBUTORS: Prices typically increase over time, let us know of price changes you observe.

	MINT	EXC	G-VG
COMPLETE SET (12)	4.00	1.60	.40
COMMON PLAYER (1-12)	.25	.10	.02
□ 1 Mickey Hatcher Dodgers' Secret Weapon	.25	.10	.02
□ 2 Tim Belcher Rookie Starts Series	.25	.10	.02
□ 3 Jose Canseco Canseco Slams L.A.	.90	.35	.07
□ 4 Mike Scioscia Dramatic Comeback	.25	.10	.02
□ 5 Kirk Gibson Gibson Steals The Show	.50	.20	.04
□ 6 Orel Hershiser Bulldog	.50	.25	.05
□ 7 Mike Marshall One Swing, Three RBI's	.35	.15	.03
□ 8 Mark McGwire Game-Winning Home Run	.65	.30	.07
□ 9 Steve Sax Sax's Speed Wins Game 4	.35	.14	.03
□ 10 Walt Weiss Series Caps Award- Winning Year	.35	.15	.03
□ 11 Orel Hershiser Series MVP Uses Shutout Magic	.50	.25	.05
□ 12 Dodger Blue, World Champs	.25	.10	.02

1988 French Bray Orioles

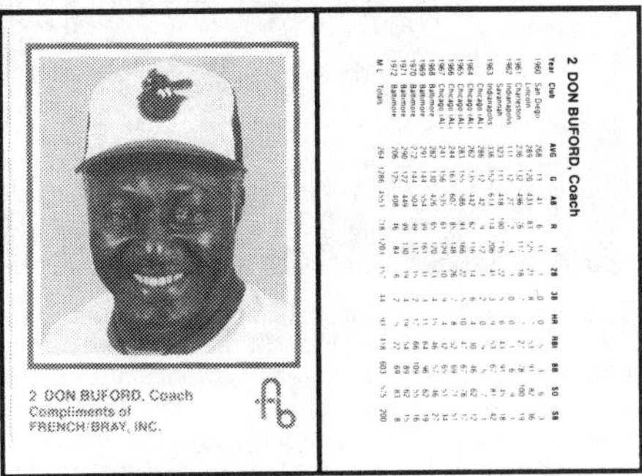

This set was distributed as a perforated set of 30 full-color cards attached to a large team photo on July 31, 1988, the Baltimore Orioles' Photo Card Day. The cards measure approximately 2 1/2" by 3 1/16". Card backs are simply done in black and white with statistics but no narrative or any personal information. Cards are unnumbered except for uniform number. Card front have a thin orange inner border and have the French Bray (Printing and Graphic Communication) logo in the lower right corner.

	MINT	EXC	G-VG
COMPLETE SET (30)	7.00	2.80	.70
COMMON PLAYER	.20	.08	.02
□ 2 Don Buford CO	.20	.08	.02
□ 6 Joe Orsulak	.20	.08	.02
□ 7 Bill Ripken	.40	.16	.04
□ 8 Cal Ripken	.75	.30	.07
□ 9 Jim Dwyer	.20	.08	.02
□ 10 Terry Crowley CO	.20	.08	.02
□ 12 Mike Morgan	.20	.08	.02
□ 14 Mickey Tettleton	.20	.08	.02
□ 15 Terry Kennedy	.30	.12	.03
□ 17 Pete Stanicek	.30	.12	.03
□ 18 Larry Sheets	.30	.12	.03
□ 19 Fred Lynn	.40	.16	.04
□ 20 Frank Robinson MG	.50	.20	.05
□ 23 Ozzie Peraza	.30	.12	.03
□ 24 Dave Schmidt	.30	.12	.03
□ 25 Rick Schu	.20	.08	.02
□ 28 Jim Traber	.30	.12	.03
□ 31 Herm Starrette CO	.20	.08	.02
□ 33 Eddie Murray	.75	.30	.07
□ 34 Jeff Ballard	.20	.08	.02
□ 38 Ken Gerhart	.30	.12	.03
□ 40 Minnie Mendoza CO	.20	.08	.02
□ 41 Don Aase	.20	.08	.02
□ 44 Elrod Hendricks CO	.20	.08	.02
□ 47 John Hart CO	.20	.08	.02
□ 48 Jose Bautista	.20	.08	.02
□ 49 Tom Niedenfuer	.20	.08	.02
□ 52 Mike Boddicker	.30	.12	.03
□ 53 Jay Tibbs	.20	.08	.02
□ 88 Rene Gonzales	.20	.08	.02

1928 Fro Joy

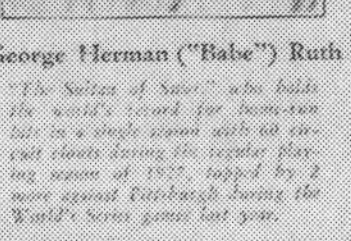

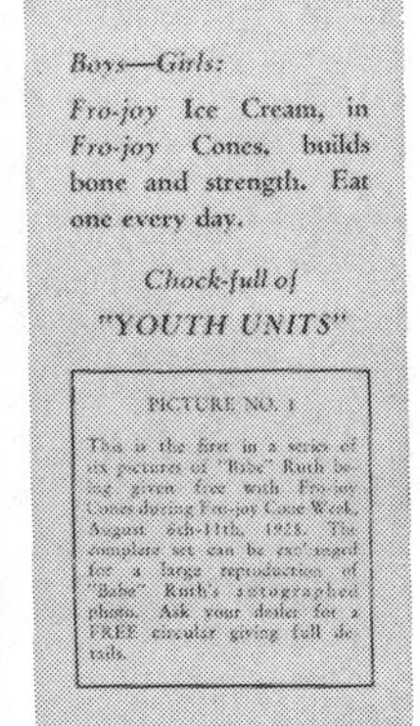

The cards in this 6-card set measure 2 1/16" by 4". The Fro Joy set of 1928 was designed to exploit the advertising potential of the mighty Babe Ruth. Six black and white cards explained specific baseball techniques while the reverse advertising extolled the virtues of Fro Joy ice cream and ice cream cones. Unfortunately this small set has been illegally reprinted and many of these virtually-worthless fakes have been introduced into the hobby. Be very careful before purchasing Fro- Joys; obtain a qualified opinion on authenticity from an experienced dealer (preferably one who is unrelated to the dealer trying to sell you his cards).

	NRMT	VG-E	GOOD
COMPLETE SET (6)	650.00	260.00	65.00
COMMON PLAYER (1-6)	100.00	40.00	10.00
□ 1 George Herman (Babe) Ruth	150.00	60.00	15.00
□ 2 Look Out, Mr. Pitcher	100.00	40.00	10.00
□ 3 Bang; The Babe Lines one out	100.00	40.00	10.00
□ 4 When the Babe Comes Out	100.00	40.00	10.00
□ 5 Babe Ruth's Grip	100.00	40.00	10.00
□ 6 Ruth is a Crack Fielder	100.00	40.00	10.00

1983 Gardner's Brewers

The cards in this 22-card set measure 2 1/2" by 3 1/2". The 1983 Gardner's Brewers set features Milwaukee Brewer players and manager Harvey Kuenn. Topps printed the set for the Madison (Wisconsin) bakery, hence, the backs are identical to

the 1983 Topps backs except for the card number. The fronts of the cards, however, feature all new photos and include the Gardner's logo and the Brewers' logo. Many of the cards are grease laden, as they were issued with packages of bread and hamburger and hot- dog buns.

	MINT	EXC	G-VG
COMPLETE SET (22)	24.00	10.00	2.40
COMMON PLAYER (1-22)	.40	.16	.04
□ 1 Harvey Kuenn MG	1.00	.40	.10
□ 2 Dwight Bernard	.50	.20	.05
□ 3 Mark Brouhard	.50	.20	.05
□ 4 Mike Caldwell	.75	.30	.07
□ 5 Cecil Cooper	1.50	.60	.15
□ 6 Marshall Edwards	.50	.20	.05
□ 7 Rollie Fingers	4.00	1.60	.40
□ 8 Jim Gantner	.75	.30	.07
□ 9 Moose Haas	.75	.30	.07
□ 10 Bob McClure	.50	.20	.05
□ 11 Paul Molitor	4.00	1.60	.40
□ 12 Don Money	.75	.30	.07
□ 13 Charlie Moore	.75	.30	.07
□ 14 Ben Oglivie	.75	.30	.07
□ 15 Ed Romero	.50	.20	.05
□ 16 Ted Simmons	1.50	.60	.15
□ 17 Jim Slaton	.75	.30	.07
□ 18 Don Sutton	3.00	1.20	.30
□ 19 Gorman Thomas	1.00	.40	.10
□ 20 Pete Vuckovich	.75	.30	.07
□ 21 Ned Yost	.50	.20	.05
□ 22 Robin Yount	7.50	3.00	.75

1984 Gardner's Brewers

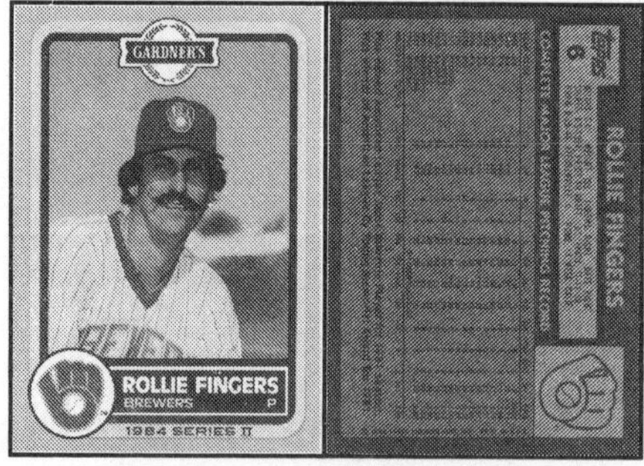

The cards in this 22-card set measure 2 1/2" by 3 1/2". For the second year in a row, the Gardner Bakery Company issued a set of cards available in packages of Gardner Bakery products. The set was manufactured by Topps, and the backs of the cards are identical to the Topps cards of this year except for the numbers. The Gardner logo appears on the fronts of the cards with the player's name, position abbreviation, the name Brewers, and the words 1984 Series II.

	MINT	EXC	G-VG
COMPLETE SET (22)	9.00	3.75	.90
COMMON PLAYER (1-22)	.30	.12	.03
□ 1 Rene Lachemann MG	.50	.20	.05
□ 2 Mark Brouhard	.30	.12	.03
□ 3 Mike Caldwell	.50	.20	.05
□ 4 Bobby Clark	.30	.12	.03
□ 5 Cecil Cooper	1.00	.40	.10
□ 6 Rollie Fingers	2.00	.80	.20
□ 7 Jim Gantner	.50	.20	.05
□ 8 Moose Haas	.40	.16	.04
□ 9 Roy Howell	.30	.12	.03
□ 10 Pete Ladd	.30	.12	.03
□ 11 Rick Manning	.30	.12	.03
□ 12 Bob McClure	.30	.12	.03
□ 13 Paul Molitor	2.00	.80	.20
□ 14 Charlie Moore	.40	.16	.04
□ 15 Ben Oglivie	.50	.20	.05
□ 16 Ed Romero	.30	.12	.03
□ 17 Ted Simmons	1.00	.40	.10
□ 18 Jim Sundberg	.40	.16	.04
□ 19 Don Sutton	1.75	.70	.17
□ 20 Tom Tellman	.30	.12	.03
□ 21 Pete Vuckovich	.50	.20	.05
□ 22 Robin Yount	3.50	1.40	.35

1985 Gardner's Brewers

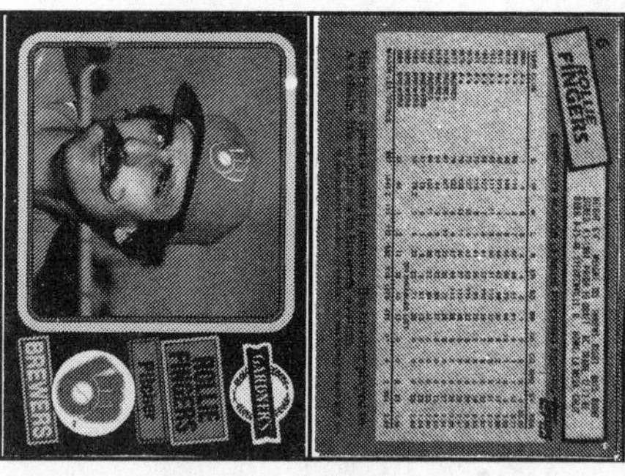

The cards in this 22-card set measure 2 1/2" by 3 1/2". For the third year in a row, the Gardner Bakery Company issued a set of cards available in packages of Gardner Bakery products. The set was manufactured by Topps, and the backs of the cards are identical to the Topps cards of this year except for the card numbers and copyright information. The Gardner logo appears on the fronts of the cards with the player's name, position abbreviation, and the name Brewers.

	MINT	EXC	G-VG
COMPLETE SET (22)	9.00	3.75	.90
COMMON PLAYER (1-22)	.30	.12	.03
□ 1 George Bamberger MG	.50	.20	.05
□ 2 Mark Brouhard	.30	.12	.03
□ 3 Bobby Clark	.30	.12	.03
□ 4 Jaime Cocanower	.30	.12	.03
□ 5 Cecil Cooper	1.00	.40	.10
□ 6 Rollie Fingers	2.00	.80	.20
□ 7 Jim Gantner	.50	.20	.05
□ 8 Moose Haas	.40	.16	.04
□ 9 Dion James	.40	.16	.04
□ 10 Pete Ladd	.30	.12	.03
□ 11 Rick Manning	.30	.12	.03
□ 12 Bob McClure	.30	.12	.03
□ 13 Paul Molitor	2.00	.80	.20
□ 14 Charlie Moore	.40	.16	.04
□ 15 Ben Oglivie	.40	.16	.04
□ 16 Chuck Porter	.30	.12	.03
□ 17 Ed Romero	.30	.12	.03
□ 18 Bill Schroeder	.40	.16	.04
□ 19 Ted Simmons	1.00	.40	.10
□ 20 Tom Tellman	.30	.12	.03
□ 21 Pete Vuckovich	.50	.20	.05
□ 22 Robin Yount	3.50	1.40	.35

1987 Gatorade Indians

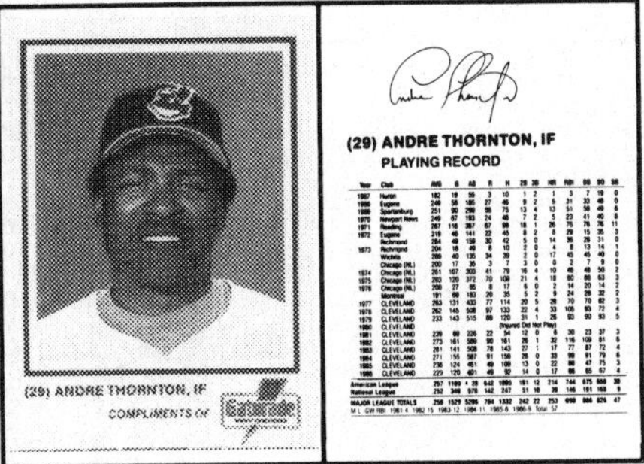

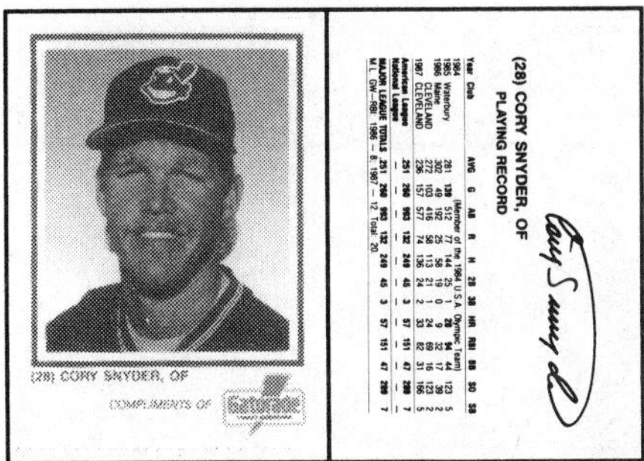

Gatorade sponsored this perforated set of 30 full-color cards of the Cleveland Indians. The cards measure 2 1/8" by 3" (or 3 1/8") and feature the Gatorade logo prominently on the fronts of the cards. The cards were distributed as a tri- folded sheet (each part approximately 9 5/8" by 11 3/16") on April 25th at the stadium during the game against the Yankees. The large team photo is approximately 11 3/16" by 9 5/8". Card backs for the individual players contain year-by-year stats for that player.

	MINT	EXC	G-VG
COMPLETE SET (30)	8.00	3.25	.80
COMMON PLAYER	.25	.10	.02
□ 2 Brett Butler	.50	.20	.05
□ 4 Tony Bernazard	.35	.14	.03
□ 6 Andy Allanson	.35	.14	.03
□ 7 Pat Corrales MG	.25	.10	.02
□ 8 Carmen Castillo	.25	.10	.02
□ 10 Pat Tabler	.35	.14	.03
□ 11 Jamie Easterly	.25	.10	.02
□ 12 Dave Clark	.35	.14	.03
□ 13 Ernie Camacho	.25	.10	.02
□ 14 Julio Franco	.50	.20	.05
□ 17 Junior Noboa	.25	.10	.02
□ 18 Ken Schrom	.25	.10	.02
□ 20 Otis Nixon	.25	.10	.02
□ 21 Greg Swindell	.50	.20	.05
□ 22 Frank Wills	.25	.10	.02
□ 23 Chris Bando	.25	.10	.02
□ 24 Rick Dempsey	.25	.10	.02
□ 26 Brook Jacoby	.50	.20	.05
□ 27 Mel Hall	.35	.14	.03
□ 28 Cory Snyder	.75	.30	.07
□ 29 Andre Thornton	.35	.14	.03
□ 30 Joe Carter	.75	.30	.07
□ 35 Phil Niekro	.75	.30	.07
□ 36 Ed VandeBerg	.25	.10	.02
□ 42 Rich Yett	.25	.10	.02
□ 43 Scott Bailes	.25	.10	.02
□ 46 Doug Jones	.50	.20	.05
□ 49 Tom Candiotti	.25	.10	.02
□ 54 Tom Waddell	.25	.10	.02
□ xx Indians MG/Coaches Bobby Bonds 25 Johnny Goryl 45 Pat Corrales MG 7 Doc Edwards 32 Jack Aker 1	.25	.10	.02
□ xx Team Photo (large size)	.75	.30	.07

1988 Gatorade Indians

This set was distributed as 30 perforated player cards attached to a large team photo of the Cleveland Indians. The cards measure approximately 2 1/4" by 3". Card backs are oriented either horizontally or vertically. Card backs are printed in red, blue, and black on white card stock. Card backs contain a facsimile autograph of the player. Cards are not arranged on the sheet in any order. The cards are unnumbered except for uniform number, which is given on the front and back of each card. The Gatorade logo is on the front of every card in the lower right corner.

	MINT	EXC	G-VG
COMPLETE SET (30)	6.00	2.40	.60
COMMON PLAYER	.20	.08	.02
□ 2 Tom Spencer CO	.20	.08	.02
□ 6 Andy Allanson	.20	.08	.02
□ 7 Luis Isaac CO	.20	.08	.02
□ 8 Carmen Castillo	.20	.08	.02
□ 9 Charlie Manuel CO	.20	.08	.02
□ 10 Pat Tabler	.30	.12	.03
□ 11 Doug Jones	.40	.16	.04
□ 14 Julio Franco	.40	.16	.04
□ 15 Ron Washington	.20	.08	.02
□ 16 Jay Bell	.30	.12	.03
□ 17 Bill Laskey	.20	.08	.02
□ 20 Willie Upshaw	.20	.08	.02
□ 21 Greg Swindell	.40	.16	.04
□ 23 Chris Bando	.20	.08	.02
□ 25 Dave Clark	.30	.12	.03
□ 26 Brook Jacoby	.30	.12	.03
□ 27 Mel Hall	.30	.12	.03
□ 28 Cory Snyder	.60	.24	.06
□ 30 Joe Carter	.60	.24	.06
□ 31 Dan Schatzeder	.20	.08	.02
□ 32 Doc Edwards MG	.20	.08	.02
□ 33 Ron Kittle	.30	.12	.03
□ 35 Mark Wiley CO	.20	.08	.02
□ 42 Rich Yett	.20	.08	.02
□ 43 Scott Bailes	.20	.08	.02
□ 45 John Goryl CO	.20	.08	.02
□ 47 Jeff Kaiser	.20	.08	.02
□ 49 Tom Candiotti	.20	.08	.02
□ 50 Jeff Dedmon	.20	.08	.02
□ 52 John Farrell	.30	.12	.03

1953 Glendale

The cards in this 28-card set measure 2 5/8" by 3 3/4". The 1953 Glendale Meats set of full-color, unnumbered cards features Detroit Tiger ballplayers exclusively and was distributed one per package of Glendale Meats in the Detroit area. The back contains the complete major and minor league record through the 1952 season. The scarcer cards of the set command higher prices, with the Houtteman card being the most difficult to find. There is an album associated with the set (which also is quite scarce now). The ACC designation for this scarce regional set is F151. Since the cards are unnumbered, they are ordered below alphabetically.

	NRMT	VG-E	GOOD
COMPLETE SET (28)	5000.00	2200.00	700.00
COMMON PLAYER (1-28)	125.00	50.00	12.50

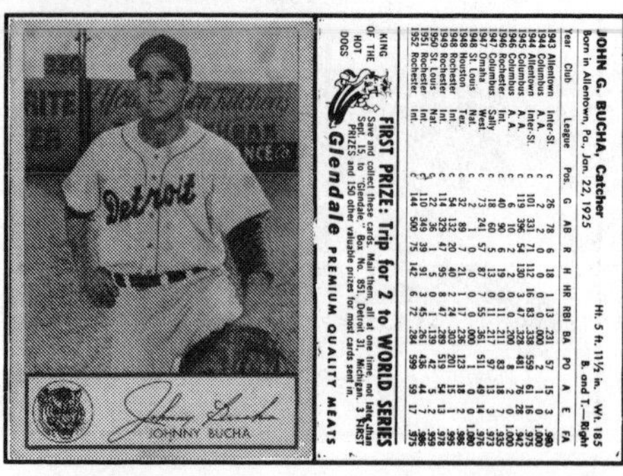

☐ 1	Matt Batts	125.00	50.00	12.50
☐ 2	Johnny Bucha	125.00	50.00	12.50
☐ 3	Frank Carswell	125.00	50.00	12.50
☐ 4	Jim Delsing	125.00	50.00	12.50
☐ 5	Walt Dropo	150.00	60.00	15.00
☐ 6	Hal Erickson	125.00	50.00	12.50
☐ 7	Paul Foytack	125.00	50.00	12.50
☐ 8	Owen Friend	125.00	50.00	12.50
☐ 9	Ned Garver	125.00	50.00	12.50
☐ 10	Joe Ginsberg	300.00	120.00	30.00
☐ 11	Ted Gray	125.00	50.00	12.50
☐ 12	Fred Hatfield	125.00	50.00	12.50
☐ 13	Ray Herbert	125.00	50.00	12.50
☐ 14	Bill Hitchcock	125.00	50.00	12.50
☐ 15	Bill Hoeft	200.00	80.00	20.00
☐ 16	Art Houtteman	2000.00	900.00	300.00
☐ 17	Milt Jordan	150.00	60.00	15.00
☐ 18	Harvey Kuenn	300.00	120.00	30.00
☐ 19	Don Lund	125.00	50.00	12.50
☐ 20	Dave Madison	125.00	50.00	12.50
☐ 21	Dick Marlowe	125.00	50.00	12.50
☐ 22	Pat Mullin	125.00	50.00	12.50
☐ 23	Bob Nieman	125.00	50.00	12.50
☐ 24	Johnny Pesky	125.00	50.00	12.50
☐ 25	Jerry Priddy	125.00	50.00	12.50
☐ 26	Steve Souchock	125.00	50.00	12.50
☐ 27	Russ Sullivan	125.00	50.00	12.50
☐ 28	Bill Wight	150.00	60.00	15.00

1961 Golden Press

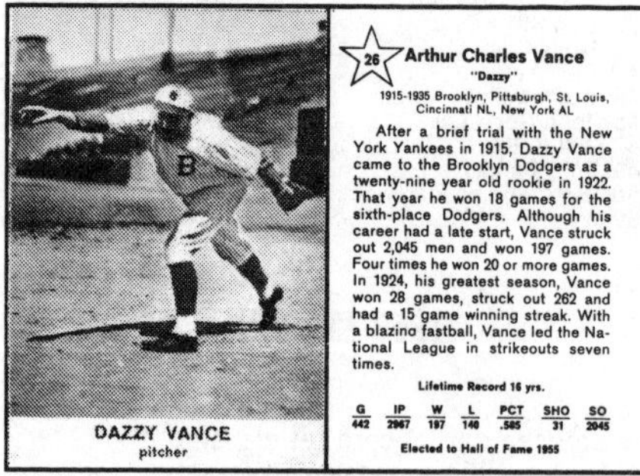

The cards in this 33-card set measure 2 1/2" by 3 1/2". The 1961 Golden Press set of full color cards features members of Baseball's Hall of Fame. The cards came in a booklet with perforations for punching the cards out of the book. The catalog designation is W524. The price for the full book intact is 25% higher than the complete set price listed.

	NRMT	VG-E	GOOD
COMPLETE SET (33)	45.00	18.00	4.50
COMMON PLAYER (1-33)	.50	.20	.05

☐ 1	Mel Ott	1.50	.60	.15
☐ 2	Grover C. Alexander	1.50	.60	.15
☐ 3	Babe Ruth	12.00	5.00	1.20
☐ 4	Hank Greenberg	.75	.30	.07
☐ 5	Bill Terry	.75	.30	.0
☐ 6	Carl Hubbell	.75	.30	.0
☐ 7	Rogers Hornsby	2.00	.80	.2
☐ 8	Dizzy Dean	3.50	1.40	.3
☐ 9	Joe DiMaggio	7.50	3.00	.7
☐ 10	Charlie Gehringer	.75	.30	.0
☐ 11	Gabby Hartnett	.50	.20	.0
☐ 12	Mickey Cochrane	.75	.30	.0
☐ 13	George Sisler	.65	.26	.0
☐ 14	Joe Cronin	.65	.26	.0
☐ 15	Pie Traynor	.65	.26	.0
☐ 16	Lou Gehrig	7.50	3.00	.7
☐ 17	Lefty Grove	1.25	.50	.1
☐ 18	Chief Bender	.50	.20	.05
☐ 19	Frankie Frisch	.65	.26	.06
☐ 20	Al Simmons	.50	.20	.05
☐ 21	Home Run Baker	.50	.20	.05
☐ 22	Jimmy Foxx	1.50	.60	.15
☐ 23	John McGraw	.75	.30	.07
☐ 24	Christy Mathewson	2.50	1.00	.25
☐ 25	Ty Cobb	7.50	3.00	.75
☐ 26	Dazzy Vance	.50	.20	.05
☐ 27	Bill Dickey	.75	.30	.07
☐ 28	Eddie Collins	.50	.20	.05
☐ 29	Walter Johnson	2.50	1.00	.25
☐ 30	Tris Speaker	1.25	.50	.12
☐ 31	Nap Lajoie	1.25	.50	.12
☐ 32	Honus Wagner	2.50	1.00	.25
☐ 33	Cy Young	1.50	.60	.15

1933 Goudey

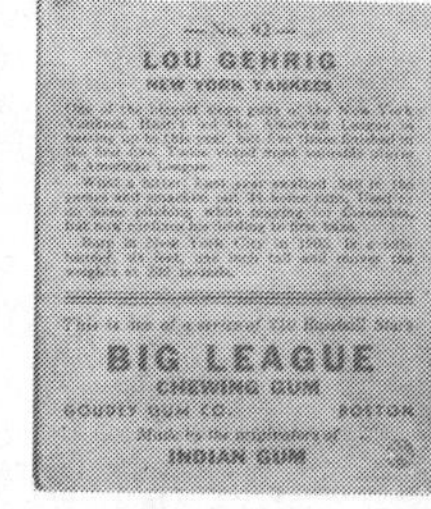

The cards in this 240-card set measure 2 3/8" by 2 7/8". The 1933 Goudey set, designated R319 by the ACC, was that company's first baseball issue. The four Babe Ruth and two Lou Gehrig cards in the set are extremely popular with collectors. Card number 106, Napoleon Lajoie, was not printed in 1933, and was circulated to a limited number of collectors in 1934 upon request (it was printed along with the 1934 Goudey cards). An album was offered to house the 1933 set. Several minor leaguers are depicted. Card number 1 (Bengough) is very rarely found in mint condition; in fact, as a general rule all the first series cards are more difficult to find in Mint condition. Players with more than one card are also sometimes differentiated below by their pose: BAT (Batting), FIELD (Fielding), PIT (Pitching), THROW (Throwing). One of the Babe Ruth cards was double printed (DP) apparently in place of the Lajoie and hence is easier to obtain than the others. Due to the scarcity of the Lajoie card, the set is considered complete at 239 cards and is priced as such below.

	NRMT	VG-E	GOOD
COMPLETE SET (239)	25000.00	9900.00	3300.00
COMMON PLAYER (1-40)	50.00	20.00	5.00
COMMON PLAYER (41-44)	40.00	16.00	4.00
COMMON PLAYER (45-52)	50.00	20.00	5.00
COMMON PLAYER (53-240)	40.00	16.00	4.00

☐ 1	Benny Bengough	1000.00	50.00	10.00
☐ 2	Dazzy Vance	100.00	40.00	10.00
☐ 3	Hugh Critz	50.00	20.00	5.00
☐ 4	Heine Schuble	50.00	20.00	5.00
☐ 5	Babe Herman	75.00	30.00	7.50
☐ 6	Jimmy Dykes	60.00	24.00	6.00

☐	7 Ted Lyons	100.00	40.00	10.00
☐	8 Roy Johnson	50.00	20.00	5.00
☐	9 Dave Harris	50.00	20.00	5.00
☐	10 Glenn Myatt	50.00	20.00	5.00
☐	11 Billy Rogell	50.00	20.00	5.00
☐	12 George Pipgras	50.00	20.00	5.00
☐	13 Lafayette Thompson	50.00	20.00	5.00
☐	14 Henry Johnson	50.00	20.00	5.00
☐	15 Victor Sorrell	50.00	20.00	5.00
☐	16 George Blaeholder	50.00	20.00	5.00
☐	17 Watson Clark	50.00	20.00	5.00
☐	18 Muddy Ruel	50.00	20.00	5.00
☐	19 Bill Dickey	200.00	80.00	20.00
☐	20 Bill Terry THROW	125.00	50.00	12.50
☐	21 Phil Collins	50.00	20.00	5.00
☐	22 Pie Traynor	125.00	50.00	12.50
☐	23 Kiki Cuyler	100.00	40.00	10.00
☐	24 Horace Ford	50.00	20.00	5.00
☐	25 Paul Waner	100.00	40.00	10.00
☐	26 Chalmer Cissell	50.00	20.00	5.00
☐	27 George Connally	50.00	20.00	5.00
☐	28 Dick Bartell	50.00	20.00	5.00
☐	29 Jimmy Foxx	200.00	80.00	20.00
☐	30 Frank Hogan	50.00	20.00	5.00
☐	31 Tony Lazzeri	75.00	30.00	7.50
☐	32 Bud Clancy	50.00	20.00	5.00
☐	33 Ralph Kress	50.00	20.00	5.00
☐	34 Bob O'Farrell	50.00	20.00	5.00
☐	35 Al Simmons	125.00	50.00	12.50
☐	36 Tommy Thevenow	50.00	20.00	5.00
☐	37 Jimmy Wilson	50.00	20.00	5.00
☐	38 Fred Bickell	50.00	20.00	5.00
☐	39 Mark Koenig	50.00	20.00	5.00
☐	40 Taylor Douthit	50.00	20.00	5.00
☐	41 Gus Mancuso	40.00	16.00	4.00
☐	42 Eddie Collins	80.00	32.00	8.00
☐	43 Lew Fonseca	40.00	16.00	4.00
☐	44 Jim Bottomley	80.00	32.00	8.00
☐	45 Larry Benton	50.00	20.00	5.00
☐	46 Ethan Allen	50.00	20.00	5.00
☐	47 Heine Manush BAT	100.00	40.00	10.00
☐	48 Marty McManus	50.00	20.00	5.00
☐	49 Frank Frisch	125.00	50.00	12.50
☐	50 Ed Brandt	50.00	20.00	5.00
☐	51 Charlie Grimm	60.00	24.00	6.00
☐	52 Andy Cohen	50.00	20.00	5.00
☐	53 Babe Ruth	3000.00	1200.00	300.00
☐	54 Ray Kremer	40.00	16.00	4.00
☐	55 Pat Malone	40.00	16.00	4.00
☐	56 Charlie Ruffing	90.00	36.00	9.00
☐	57 Earl Clark	40.00	16.00	4.00
☐	58 Lefty O'Doul	50.00	20.00	5.00
☐	59 Bing Miller	40.00	16.00	4.00
☐	60 Waite Hoyt	80.00	32.00	8.00
☐	61 Max Bishop	40.00	16.00	4.00
☐	62 Pepper Martin	50.00	20.00	5.00
☐	63 Joe Cronin BAT	90.00	36.00	9.00
☐	64 Burleigh Grimes	80.00	32.00	8.00
☐	65 Milt Gaston	40.00	16.00	4.00
☐	66 George Grantham	40.00	16.00	4.00
☐	67 Guy Bush	40.00	16.00	4.00
☐	68 Horace Lisenbee	40.00	16.00	4.00
☐	69 Randy Moore	40.00	16.00	4.00
☐	70 Floyd (Pete) Scott	40.00	16.00	4.00
☐	71 Robert J. Burke	40.00	16.00	4.00
☐	72 Owen Carroll	40.00	16.00	4.00
☐	73 Jess Haines	80.00	32.00	8.00
☐	74 Eppa Rixey	80.00	32.00	8.00
☐	75 Willie Kamm	40.00	16.00	4.00
☐	76 Mickey Cochrane	100.00	40.00	10.00
☐	77 Adam Comorosky	40.00	16.00	4.00
☐	78 Jack Quinn	40.00	16.00	4.00
☐	79 Red Faber	80.00	32.00	8.00
☐	80 Clyde Manion	40.00	16.00	4.00
☐	81 Sam Jones	40.00	16.00	4.00
☐	82 Dibrell Williams	40.00	16.00	4.00
☐	83 Pete Jablonowski	40.00	16.00	4.00
☐	84 Glenn Spencer	40.00	16.00	4.00
☐	85 Heine Sand	40.00	16.00	4.00
☐	86 Phil Todt	40.00	16.00	4.00
☐	87 Frank O'Rourke	40.00	16.00	4.00
☐	88 Russell Rollings	40.00	16.00	4.00
☐	89 Tris Speaker	200.00	80.00	20.00
☐	90 Jess Petty	40.00	16.00	4.00
☐	91 Tom Zachary	40.00	16.00	4.00
☐	92 Lou Gehrig	1250.00	500.00	150.00
☐	93 John Welch	40.00	16.00	4.00
☐	94 Bill Walker	40.00	16.00	4.00
☐	95 Alvin Crowder	40.00	16.00	4.00
☐	96 Willis Hudlin	40.00	16.00	4.00
☐	97 Joe Morrissey	40.00	16.00	4.00
☐	98 Walter Berger	40.00	16.00	4.00
☐	99 Tony Cuccinello	40.00	16.00	4.00
☐	100 George Uhle	40.00	16.00	4.00
☐	101 Richard Coffman	40.00	16.00	4.00
☐	102 Travis Jackson	80.00	32.00	8.00
☐	103 Earl Combs	80.00	32.00	8.00
☐	104 Fred Marberry	40.00	16.00	4.00
☐	105 Bernie Friberg	40.00	16.00	4.00
☐	106 Napoleon Lajoie (not issued until 1934)	10000.	4000.00	900.00
☐	107 Heine Manush	80.00	32.00	8.00
☐	108 Joe Kuhel	40.00	16.00	4.00
☐	109 Joe Cronin	90.00	36.00	9.00
☐	110 Goose Goslin	80.00	32.00	8.00
☐	111 Monte Weaver	40.00	16.00	4.00
☐	112 Fred Schulte	40.00	16.00	4.00
☐	113 Oswald Bluege	40.00	16.00	4.00
☐	114 Luke Sewell	40.00	16.00	4.00
☐	115 Cliff Heathcote	40.00	16.00	4.00
☐	116 Eddie Morgan	40.00	16.00	4.00
☐	117 Rabbit Maranville	80.00	32.00	8.00
☐	118 Val Picinich	40.00	16.00	4.00
☐	119 Rogers Hornsby FIELD	200.00	80.00	20.00
☐	120 Carl Reynolds	40.00	16.00	4.00
☐	121 Walter Stewart	40.00	16.00	4.00
☐	122 Alvin Crowder	40.00	16.00	4.00
☐	123 Jack Russell	40.00	16.00	4.00
☐	124 Earl Whitehill	40.00	16.00	4.00
☐	125 Bill Terry	125.00	50.00	12.50
☐	126 Joe Moore	40.00	16.00	4.00
☐	127 Mel Ott	150.00	60.00	15.00
☐	128 Chuck Klein	100.00	40.00	10.00
☐	129 Hal Schumacher PIT	40.00	16.00	4.00
☐	130 Fred Fitzsimmons	40.00	16.00	4.00
☐	131 Fred Frankhouse	40.00	16.00	4.00
☐	132 Jim Elliott	40.00	16.00	4.00
☐	133 Fred Lindstrom	80.00	32.00	8.00
☐	134 Sam Rice	80.00	32.00	8.00
☐	135 Woody English	40.00	16.00	4.00
☐	136 Flint Rhem	40.00	16.00	4.00
☐	137 Fred (Red) Lucas	40.00	16.00	4.00
☐	138 Herb Pennock	80.00	32.00	8.00
☐	139 Ben Cantwell	40.00	16.00	4.00
☐	140 Bump Hadley	40.00	16.00	4.00
☐	141 Ray Benge	40.00	16.00	4.00
☐	142 Paul Richards	50.00	20.00	5.00
☐	143 Glenn Wright	40.00	16.00	4.00
☐	144 Babe Ruth BAT DP	2400.00	900.00	250.00
☐	145 George Walberg	40.00	16.00	4.00
☐	146 Walter Stewart PIT	40.00	16.00	4.00
☐	147 Leo Durocher	80.00	32.00	8.00
☐	148 Eddie Farrell	40.00	16.00	4.00
☐	149 Babe Ruth	3000.00	1100.00	300.00
☐	150 Ray Kolp	40.00	16.00	4.00
☐	151 Jake Flowers	40.00	16.00	4.00
☐	152 Zack Taylor	40.00	16.00	4.00
☐	153 Buddy Myer	40.00	16.00	4.00
☐	154 Jimmy Foxx	200.00	80.00	20.00
☐	155 Joe Judge	40.00	16.00	4.00
☐	156 Danny MacFayden	40.00	16.00	4.00
☐	157 Sam Byrd	40.00	16.00	4.00
☐	158 Moe Berg	50.00	20.00	5.00
☐	159 Oswald Bluege	40.00	16.00	4.00
☐	160 Lou Gehrig	1250.00	500.00	150.00
☐	161 Al Spohrer	40.00	16.00	4.00
☐	162 Leo Mangum	40.00	16.00	4.00
☐	163 Luke Sewell	40.00	16.00	4.00
☐	164 Lloyd Waner	80.00	32.00	8.00
☐	165 Joe Sewell	80.00	32.00	8.00
☐	166 Sam West	40.00	16.00	4.00
☐	167 Jack Russell	40.00	16.00	4.00
☐	168 Goose Goslin	80.00	32.00	8.00
☐	169 Al Thomas	40.00	16.00	4.00
☐	170 Harry McCurdy	40.00	16.00	4.00
☐	171 Charlie Jamieson	40.00	16.00	4.00
☐	172 Billy Hargrave	40.00	16.00	4.00
☐	173 Roscoe Holm	40.00	16.00	4.00
☐	174 Warren(Curly) Ogden	40.00	16.00	4.00
☐	175 Dan Howley	40.00	16.00	4.00
☐	176 John Ogden	40.00	16.00	4.00
☐	177 Walter French	40.00	16.00	4.00
☐	178 Jackie Warner	40.00	16.00	4.00
☐	179 Fred Leach	40.00	16.00	4.00
☐	180 Eddie Moore	40.00	16.00	4.00
☐	181 Babe Ruth	3000.00	1100.00	300.00
☐	182 Andy High	40.00	16.00	4.00
☐	183 George Walberg	40.00	16.00	4.00
☐	184 Charley Berry	40.00	16.00	4.00
☐	185 Bob Smith	40.00	16.00	4.00
☐	186 John Schulte	40.00	16.00	4.00
☐	187 Heine Manush	80.00	32.00	8.00
☐	188 Rogers Hornsby	200.00	80.00	20.00
☐	189 Joe Cronin	90.00	36.00	9.00
☐	190 Fred Schulte	40.00	16.00	4.00
☐	191 Ben Chapman	50.00	20.00	5.00
☐	192 Walter Brown	40.00	16.00	4.00
☐	193 Lynford Lary	40.00	16.00	4.00
☐	194 Earl Averill	80.00	32.00	8.00

☐ 195	Evar Swanson	40.00	16.00	4.00
☐ 196	Leroy Mahaffey	40.00	16.00	4.00
☐ 197	Rick Ferrell	80.00	32.00	8.00
☐ 198	Jack Burns	40.00	16.00	4.00
☐ 199	Tom Bridges	40.00	16.00	4.00
☐ 200	Bill Hallahan	40.00	16.00	4.00
☐ 201	Ernie Orsatti	40.00	16.00	4.00
☐ 202	Gabby Hartnett	80.00	32.00	8.00
☐ 203	Lon Warneke	40.00	16.00	4.00
☐ 204	Riggs Stephenson	50.00	20.00	5.00
☐ 205	Heine Meine	40.00	16.00	4.00
☐ 206	Gus Suhr	40.00	16.00	4.00
☐ 207	Mel Ott BAT	150.00	60.00	15.00
☐ 208	Bernie James	40.00	16.00	4.00
☐ 209	Adolfo Luque	40.00	16.00	4.00
☐ 210	Virgil Davis	40.00	16.00	4.00
☐ 211	Hack Wilson	125.00	50.00	12.50
☐ 212	Billy Urbanski	40.00	16.00	4.00
☐ 213	Earl Adams	40.00	16.00	4.00
☐ 214	John Kerr	40.00	16.00	4.00
☐ 215	Russ Van Atta	40.00	16.00	4.00
☐ 216	Vernon Gomez	200.00	80.00	20.00
☐ 217	Frank Crosetti	80.00	32.00	8.00
☐ 218	Wes Ferrell	50.00	20.00	5.00
☐ 219	Mule Haas	40.00	16.00	4.00
☐ 220	Lefty Grove	250.00	100.00	25.00
☐ 221	Dale Alexander	40.00	16.00	4.00
☐ 222	Charley Gehringer	125.00	50.00	12.50
☐ 223	Dizzy Dean	450.00	180.00	45.00
☐ 224	Frank Demaree	40.00	16.00	4.00
☐ 225	Bill Jurges	40.00	16.00	4.00
☐ 226	Charley Root	40.00	16.00	4.00
☐ 227	Billy Herman	80.00	32.00	8.00
☐ 228	Tony Piet	40.00	16.00	4.00
☐ 229	Floyd(Arky) Vaughan	80.00	32.00	8.00
☐ 230	Carl Hubbell PIT	125.00	50.00	12.50
☐ 231	Joe Moore FIELD	40.00	16.00	4.00
☐ 232	Lefty O'Doul	50.00	20.00	5.00
☐ 233	Johnny Vergez	40.00	16.00	4.00
☐ 234	Carl Hubbell	125.00	50.00	12.50
☐ 235	Fred Fitzsimmons	50.00	20.00	5.00
☐ 236	George Davis	40.00	16.00	4.00
☐ 237	Gus Mancuso	40.00	16.00	4.00
☐ 238	Hugh Critz	40.00	16.00	4.00
☐ 239	Leroy Parmelee	40.00	16.00	4.00
☐ 240	Hal Schumacher	80.00	32.00	8.00

1934 Goudey

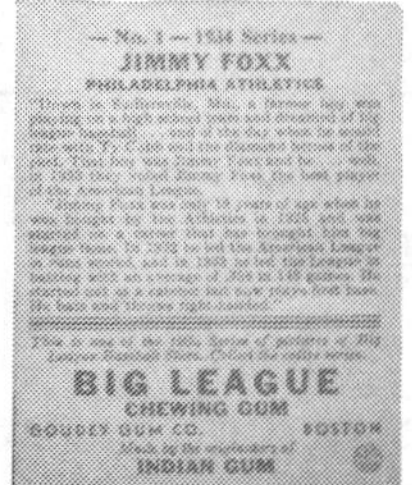

The cards in this 96-card set measure 2 3/8" by 2 7/8". The 1934 Goudey set of color cards carries the ACC catalog number R320. Cards 1-48 are considered to be the easiest to find (although card number 1, Foxx, is very scarce in mint condition) while 73-96 are much more difficult to find. Cards of this 1934 Goudey series are slightly less abundant than cards of the 1933 Goudey set. Of the 96 cards, 84 contain a "Lou Gehrig Says" line on the front in a blue design, while 12 of the high series contain a "Chuck Klein Says" line in a red design. These Chuck Klein cards are indicated in the checklist below by CK and are in fact the 12 National Leaguers in the high series.

	NRMT	VG-E	GOOD
COMPLETE SET (96)	11000.00	4750.00	1850.00
COMMON PLAYER (1-48)	40.00	16.00	4.00
COMMON PLAYER (49-72)	60.00	24.00	6.00
COMMON PLAYER (73-96)	150.00	60.00	15.00

☐ 1	Jimmy Foxx	500.00	125.00	25.00
☐ 2	Mickey Cochrane	100.00	40.00	10.00
☐ 3	Charlie Grimm	50.00	20.00	5.00
☐ 4	Woody English	40.00	16.00	4.00
☐ 5	Ed Brandt	40.00	16.00	4.00
☐ 6	Dizzy Dean	400.00	160.00	40.00
☐ 7	Leo Durocher	60.00	24.00	6.00
☐ 8	Tony Piet	40.00	16.00	4.00
☐ 9	Ben Chapman	50.00	20.00	5.00
☐ 10	Chuck Klein	80.00	32.00	8.00
☐ 11	Paul Waner	80.00	32.00	8.00
☐ 12	Carl Hubbell	100.00	40.00	10.00
☐ 13	Frank Frisch	100.00	40.00	10.00
☐ 14	Willie Kamm	40.00	16.00	4.00
☐ 15	Alvin Crowder	40.00	16.00	4.00
☐ 16	Joe Kuhel	40.00	16.00	4.00
☐ 17	Hugh Critz	40.00	16.00	4.00
☐ 18	Heinie Manush	80.00	32.00	8.00
☐ 19	Lefty Grove	150.00	60.00	15.00
☐ 20	Frank Hogan	40.00	16.00	4.00
☐ 21	Bill Terry	100.00	40.00	10.00
☐ 22	Arky Vaughan	80.00	32.00	8.00
☐ 23	Charlie Gehringer	100.00	40.00	10.00
☐ 24	Ray Benge	40.00	16.00	4.00
☐ 25	Roger Cramer	40.00	16.00	4.00
☐ 26	Gerald Walker	40.00	16.00	4.00
☐ 27	Luke Appling	80.00	32.00	8.00
☐ 28	Ed Coleman	40.00	16.00	4.00
☐ 29	Larry French	40.00	16.00	4.00
☐ 30	Julius Solters	40.00	16.00	4.00
☐ 31	Buck Jordan	40.00	16.00	4.00
☐ 32	Blondy Ryan	40.00	16.00	4.00
☐ 33	Frank Hurst	40.00	16.00	4.00
☐ 34	Chick Hafey	80.00	32.00	8.00
☐ 35	Ernie Lombardi	80.00	32.00	8.00
☐ 36	Walter Betts	40.00	16.00	4.00
☐ 37	Lou Gehrig	1750.00	750.00	200.00
☐ 38	Oral Hildebrand	40.00	16.00	4.00
☐ 39	Fred Walker	40.00	16.00	4.00
☐ 40	John Stone	40.00	16.00	4.00
☐ 41	George Earnshaw	40.00	16.00	4.00
☐ 42	John Allen	40.00	16.00	4.00
☐ 43	Dick Porter	40.00	16.00	4.00
☐ 44	Tom Bridges	40.00	16.00	4.00
☐ 45	Oscar Melillo	40.00	16.00	4.00
☐ 46	Joe Stripp	40.00	16.00	4.00
☐ 47	John Frederick	40.00	16.00	4.00
☐ 48	Tex Carleton	40.00	16.00	4.00
☐ 49	Sam Leslie	60.00	24.00	6.00
☐ 50	Walter Beck	60.00	24.00	6.00
☐ 51	Rip Collins	60.00	24.00	6.00
☐ 52	Herman Bell	60.00	24.00	6.00
☐ 53	George Watkins	60.00	24.00	6.00
☐ 54	Wesley Schulmerich	60.00	24.00	6.00
☐ 55	Ed Holley	60.00	24.00	6.00
☐ 56	Mark Koenig	60.00	24.00	6.00
☐ 57	Bill Swift	60.00	24.00	6.00
☐ 58	Earl Grace	60.00	24.00	6.00
☐ 59	Joe Mowry	60.00	24.00	6.00
☐ 60	Lynn Nelson	60.00	24.00	6.00
☐ 61	Lou Gehrig	2000.00	850.00	300.00
☐ 62	Hank Greenberg	150.00	60.00	15.00
☐ 63	Minter Hayes	60.00	24.00	6.00
☐ 64	Frank Grube	60.00	24.00	6.00
☐ 65	Cliff Bolton	60.00	24.00	6.00
☐ 66	Mel Harder	80.00	32.00	8.00
☐ 67	Bob Weiland	60.00	24.00	6.00
☐ 68	Bob Johnson	70.00	28.00	7.00
☐ 69	John Marcum	60.00	24.00	6.00
☐ 70	Pete Fox	60.00	24.00	6.00
☐ 71	Lyle Tinning	60.00	24.00	6.00
☐ 72	Arndt Jorgens	60.00	24.00	6.00
☐ 73	Ed Wells	150.00	60.00	15.00
☐ 74	Bob Boken	150.00	60.00	15.00
☐ 75	Bill Werber	150.00	60.00	15.00
☐ 76	Hal Trosky	150.00	60.00	15.00
☐ 77	Joe Vosmik	150.00	60.00	15.00
☐ 78	Pinky Higgins	175.00	70.00	18.00
☐ 79	Ed Durham	150.00	60.00	15.00
☐ 80	Marty McManus CK	150.00	60.00	15.00
☐ 81	Bob Brown CK	150.00	60.00	15.00
☐ 82	Bill Hallahan CK	150.00	60.00	15.00
☐ 83	Jim Mooney CK	150.00	60.00	15.00
☐ 84	Paul Derringer CK	175.00	70.00	18.00
☐ 85	Adam Comorosky CK	150.00	60.00	15.00
☐ 86	Lloyd Johnson CK	150.00	60.00	15.00
☐ 87	George Darrow CK	150.00	60.00	15.00
☐ 88	Homer Peel CK	150.00	60.00	15.00
☐ 89	Linus Frey CK	150.00	60.00	15.00
☐ 90	Ki-Ki Cuyler CK	300.00	120.00	30.00
☐ 91	Dolph Camilli CK	150.00	60.00	15.00
☐ 92	Steve Larkin	150.00	60.00	15.00
☐ 93	Fred Ostermueller	150.00	60.00	15.00
☐ 94	Red Rolfe	175.00	70.00	18.00
☐ 95	Myril Hoag	150.00	60.00	15.00
☐ 96	James DeShong	200.00	80.00	20.00

1935 Goudey

The cards in this 36-card set (the number of different front pictures) measure 2 3/8" by 2 7/8". The 1935 Goudey set is sometimes called the Goudey Puzzle Set, the Goudey 4-in-1's, or R321 (ACC). There are 36 different card fronts but 114 different front/back combinations. The card number in the checklist refers to the back puzzle number, as the backs can be arranged to form a puzzle picturing a player or team. To avoid the confusion caused by two different fronts having the same back number, the rarer cards have been arbitrarily given a "1" prefix. The scarcer puzzle cards are hence all listed at the numerical end of the list below, i.e. rare puzzle 1 is listed as number 11, rare puzzle 2 is listed as 12, etc. The BLUE in the checklist refers to a card with a blue border, as most cards have a red border. The set price below includes only the 36 different fronts, making no distinction as to which backs are present. The following is the list of the puzzle back pictures: 1) Detroit Tigers; 2) Chuck Klein; 3) Frankie Frisch; 4) Mickey Cochrane; 5) Joe Cronin; 6) Jimmy Foxx; 7) Al Simmons; 8) Cleveland Indians; and 9) Washington Senators.

	NRMT	VG-E	GOOD
COMPLETE SET (36)	3200.00	1400.00	375.00
COMMON CARDS (1-9)	30.00	12.00	3.00
COMMON CARDS (11-17)	45.00	18.00	4.50
□ 1A F.Frisch/Dizzy Dean Orsatti/Carleton	100.00	40.00	10.00
□ 1B Mahaffey/Jimmie Foxx Williams/Higgins	60.00	24.00	6.00
□ 1C Heine Manush/Lary Weaver/Hadley	35.00	14.00	3.50
□ 1D Cochrane/C.Gehringer Bridges/Rogell	60.00	24.00	6.00
□ 1E Paul Waner/Bush W.Hoyt/Lloyd Waner	60.00	24.00	6.00
□ 1F B.Grimes/Chuck Klein K.Cuyler/English	60.00	24.00	6.00
□ 1G Leslie/Frey Joe Stripp/Clark	30.00	12.00	3.00
□ 1H Piet/Comorosky Bottomley/Adams	35.00	14.00	3.50
□ 1I Earnshaw/Dykes Luke Sewell/Appling	35.00	14.00	3.50
□ 1J Babe Ruth/McManus Brandt/Maranville	600.00	240.00	60.00
□ 1K Bill Terry/Schumacher Mancuso/T.Jackson	60.00	24.00	6.00
□ 1L Kamm/Hildebrand Averill/Trosky	35.00	14.00	3.50
□ 2A F.Frisch/Dizzy Dean Orsatti/Carleton	100.00	40.00	10.00
□ 2B Mahaffey/Jimmie Foxx Williams/Higgins	60.00	24.00	6.00
□ 2C Heine Manush/Lary Weaver/Hadley	35.00	14.00	3.50
□ 2D Cochrane/C.Gehringer Bridges/Rogell	60.00	24.00	6.00
□ 2E Kamm/Hildebrand Earl Averill/Trosky	35.00	14.00	3.50
□ 2F Earnshaw/Dykes Luke Sewell/Appling	35.00	14.00	3.50
□ 3A Babe Ruth/McManus Brandt/Maranville	600.00	240.00	60.00
□ 3B Bill Terry/Schumacher Mancuso/T.Jackson	60.00	24.00	6.00
□ 3C Paul Waner/Bush W.Hoyt/Lloyd Waner	60.00	24.00	6.00
□ 3D B.Grimes/Chuck Klein K.Cuyler/English	60.00	24.00	6.00
□ 3E Leslie/Frey Joe Stripp/Clark	30.00	12.00	3.00
□ 3F Piet/Comorosky Jim Bottomley/Adams	35.00	14.00	3.50
□ 4A Critz/D.Bartell BLUE Mel Ott/Mancuso	60.00	24.00	6.00
□ 4B Pie Traynor/Lucas BLUE Tom Thevenow/Wright	35.00	14.00	3.50
□ 4C Berry/Burke BLUE Kress/Dazzy Vance	35.00	14.00	3.50
□ 4D R.Ruffing/Malone BLUE Lazzeri/Bill Dickey	100.00	40.00	10.00
□ 4E Moore/Hogan BLUE Frankhouse/Brandt	30.00	12.00	3.00
□ 4F Martin/O'Farrell BLUE Byrd/MacFayden	30.00	12.00	3.00
□ 5A Ruel/Al Simmons Kamm/M.Cochrane	60.00	24.00	6.00
□ 5B Willis Hudlin/Myatt Comorosky/Bottomley	35.00	14.00	3.50
□ 5C Paul Waner/Bush W.Hoyt/Lloyd Waner	60.00	24.00	6.00
□ 5D West/Oscar Melillo Blaeholder/Coffman	30.00	12.00	3.00
□ 5E Leslie/Frey Joe Stripp/Clark	30.00	12.00	3.00
□ 5F Schuble/Marberry Goose Goslin/Crowder	35.00	14.00	3.50
□ 6A Ruel/Al Simmons Kamm/M.Cochrane	60.00	24.00	6.00
□ 6B Willis Hudlin/Myatt Comorosky/Bottomley	35.00	14.00	3.50
□ 6C Wilson/Allen Jonnard/Brickell	30.00	12.00	3.00
□ 6D West/Oscar Melillo Blaeholder/Coffman	30.00	12.00	3.00
□ 6E Joe Cronin/Reynolds Bishop/Cissell	35.00	14.00	3.50
□ 6F Schuble/Marberry Goose Goslin/Crowder	35.00	14.00	3.50
□ 7A Critz/Bartell BLUE Mel Ott/Mancuso	60.00	24.00	6.00
□ 7B Pie Traynor/Lucas BLUE Tom Thevenow/Wright	35.00	14.00	3.50
□ 7C Berry/Burke BLUE Kress/Dazzy Vance	35.00	14.00	3.50
□ 7D R.Ruffing/Malone BLUE Lazzeri/Bill Dickey	100.00	40.00	10.00
□ 7E Moore/Hogan BLUE Frankhouse/Brandt	30.00	12.00	3.00
□ 7F Martin/O'Farrell BLUE Byrd/MacFayden	30.00	12.00	3.00
□ 8A M.Koenig/Fitzsimmons Benge/Zachary	30.00	12.00	3.00
□ 8B Hayes/Ted Lyons Haas/Zeke Bonura	35.00	14.00	3.50
□ 8C Burns/Rollie Hemsley Grube/Weiland	30.00	12.00	3.00
□ 8D Campbell/Meyers Goodman/Kampouris	30.00	12.00	3.00
□ 8E DeShong/Allen Red Rolfe/Walker	30.00	12.00	3.00
□ 8F P.Fox/Hank Greenberg Walker/Rowe	45.00	18.00	4.50
□ 8G Werber/Rick Ferrell W.Ferrell/Ostermueller	35.00	14.00	3.50
□ 8H Joe Kuhel/Whitehill Meyer/Stone	30.00	12.00	3.00
□ 8I J.Vosmik/Knickerbocker Mel Harder/Stewart	30.00	12.00	3.00
□ 8J Johnson/Coleman Marcum/Cramer	30.00	12.00	3.00
□ 8K Herman/Suhr Padden/Blanton	30.00	12.00	3.00
□ 8L Spohrer/Rhem Cantwell/Benton	30.00	12.00	3.00
□ 8M M.Koenig/Fitzsimmons Benge/Zachary	30.00	12.00	3.00
□ 9B Hayes/Ted Lyons Haas/Zeke Bonura	35.00	14.00	3.50
□ 9C Burns/Rollie Hemsley Grube/Weiland	30.00	12.00	3.00
□ 9D Campbell/Meyers Goodman/Kampouris	30.00	12.00	3.00
□ 9E DeShong/Allen Red Rolfe/Walker	30.00	12.00	3.00
□ 9F P.Fox/Hank Greenberg Walker/Rowe	45.00	18.00	4.50
□ 9G Werber/Rick Ferrell W.Ferrell/Ostermueller	35.00	14.00	3.50

□ 9H	Joe Kuhel/Whitehill Meyer/Stone	30.00	12.00	3.00
□ 9I	J.Vosmik/Knickerbocker Mel Harder/Stewart	30.00	12.00	3.00
□ 9J	Johnson/Coleman Marcum/Cramer	30.00	12.00	3.00
□ 9K	Herman/Suhr Padden/Blanton	30.00	12.00	3.00
□ 9L	Spohrer/Rhem Cantwell/Benton	30.00	12.00	3.00
□ 11E	Wilson/Allen Jonnard/Brickell	45.00	18.00	4.50
□ 11F	West/Melillo Blaeholder/Coffman	45.00	18.00	4.50
□ 11G	Joe Cronin/Reynolds Bishop/Cissel	50.00	20.00	5.00
□ 11H	Schuble/Marberry Goose Goslin/Crowder	50.00	20.00	5.00
□ 11J	Ruel/Al Simmons Kamm/M.Cochrane	75.00	30.00	7.50
□ 11K	Hudlin/Myatt Comorosky/Bottomley	50.00	20.00	5.00
□ 12A	Critz/Bartell BLUE Mel Ott/Mancuso	75.00	30.00	7.50
□ 12B	P.Traynor/Lucas BLUE Thevenow/Wright	50.00	20.00	5.00
□ 12C	Berry/Burke BLUE Kress/D.Vance	50.00	20.00	5.00
□ 12D	Ruffing/Malone BLUE Lazzeri/Bill Dickey	135.00	54.00	13.50
□ 12E	Moore/Hogan BLUE Frankhouse/Brandt	45.00	18.00	4.50
□ 12F	Martin/O'Farrell BLUE Byrd/MacFayden	45.00	18.00	4.50
□ 13A	Ruel/Al Simmons Kamm/M.Cochrane	75.00	30.00	7.50
□ 13B	Hudlin/Myatt Comorosky/Bottomley	50.00	20.00	5.00
□ 13C	Wilson/Allen Jonnard/Brickell	45.00	18.00	4.50
□ 13D	West/Oscar Melillo Blaeholder/Coffman	45.00	18.00	4.50
□ 13E	Joe Cronin/Reynolds Bishop/Cissell	50.00	20.00	5.00
□ 13F	Schuble/Marberry Goose Goslin/Crowder	50.00	20.00	5.00
□ 14A	Babe Ruth/McManus Brandt/Maranville	1000.00	400.00	125.00
□ 14B	Bill Terry/Schumacher Mancuso/T.Jackson	75.00	30.00	7.50
□ 14C	Paul Waner/Bush W.Hoyt/Lloyd Waner	75.00	30.00	7.50
□ 14D	B.Grimes/Chuck Klein K.Cuyler/English	75.00	30.00	7.50
□ 14E	Leslie/Frey Joe Stripp/Clark	45.00	18.00	4.50
□ 14F	Piet/Comorosky Jim Bottomley/Adams	50.00	20.00	5.00
□ 15A	Babe Ruth/McManus Brandt/Maranville	1000.00	400.00	125.00
□ 15B	Bill Terry/Schumacher Mancuso/T.Jackson	75.00	30.00	7.50
□ 15C	Wilson/Allen Jonnard/Brickell	45.00	18.00	4.50
□ 15D	B.Grimes/Chuck Klein K.Cuyler/English	75.00	30.00	7.50
□ 15E	Joe Cronin/Reynolds Bishop/Cissell	50.00	20.00	5.00
□ 15F	Piet/Comorosky Jim Bottomley/Adams	50.00	20.00	5.00
□ 16A	F.Frisch/Dizzy Dean E.Orsatti/Carleton	135.00	54.00	13.50
□ 16B	Mahaffey/Jimmie Foxx Williams/Higgins	75.00	30.00	7.50
□ 16C	Heine Manush/Lary Weaver/Hadley	50.00	20.00	5.00
□ 16D	Cochrane/C.Gehringer Tom Bridges/Rogell	75.00	30.00	7.50
□ 16E	Kamm/Hildebrand Earl Averill/Trosky	50.00	20.00	5.00
□ 16F	G.Earnshaw/Dykes Luke Sewell/Appling	50.00	20.00	5.00
□ 17A	F.Frisch/Dizzy Dean E.Orsatti/Carleton	135.00	54.00	13.50
□ 17B	Mahaffey/Jimmie Foxx Williams/Higgins	75.00	30.00	7.50
□ 17C	Heine Manush/Lary Weaver/Hadley	50.00	20.00	5.00
□ 17D	Cochrane/C.Gehringer Tom Bridges/Rogell	75.00	30.00	7.50
□ 17E	Kamm/Hildebrand Earl Averill/Trosky	50.00	20.00	5.00
□ 17F	G.Earnshaw/Dykes Luke Sewell/Appling	50.00	20.00	5.00

1936 Goudey

The cards in this 25-card black and white set measure 2 3/8" by 2 7/8". In contrast to the color artwork of its previous sets, the 1936 Goudey set contained a simple black and white player photograph. A facsimile autograph appeared within the picture area. Each card was issued with a number of different "game situation" backs, and there may be as many as 200 different front/back combinations. The ACC designation is R322.

	NRMT	VG-E	GOOD
COMPLETE SET (25)	1200.00	500.00	175.00
COMMON PLAYER (1-25)	30.00	12.00	3.00
□ 1 Wally Berger	35.00	14.00	3.50
□ 2 Zeke Bonura	30.00	12.00	3.00
□ 3 Stan Bordagaray	30.00	12.00	3.00
□ 4 Bill Brubaker	30.00	12.00	3.00
□ 5 Dolph Camilli	30.00	12.00	3.00
□ 6 Clyde Castleman	30.00	12.00	3.00
□ 7 Mickey Cochrane	125.00	50.00	12.50
□ 8 Joe Coscarart	30.00	12.00	3.00
□ 9 Frank Crosetti	45.00	18.00	4.50
□ 10 Kiki Cuyler	65.00	26.00	6.50
□ 11 Paul Derringer	35.00	14.00	3.50
□ 12 Jimmy Dykes	35.00	14.00	3.50
□ 13 Rick Ferrell	65.00	26.00	6.50
□ 14 Lefty Gomez	125.00	50.00	12.50
□ 15 Hank Greenberg	125.00	50.00	12.50
□ 16 Bucky Harris	55.00	22.00	5.50
□ 17 Rollie Hemsley	30.00	12.00	3.00
□ 18 Pinky Higgins	30.00	12.00	3.00
□ 19 Oral Hildebrand	30.00	12.00	3.00
□ 20 Chuck Klein	80.00	32.00	8.00
□ 21 Pepper Martin	35.00	14.00	3.50
□ 22 Bobo Newsom	35.00	14.00	3.50
□ 23 Joe Vosmik	30.00	12.00	3.00
□ 24 Paul Waner	70.00	28.00	7.00
□ 25 Bill Werber	30.00	12.00	3.00

1938 Goudey Heads Up

The cards in this 48-card set measure 2 3/8" by 2 7/8". The 1938 Goudey set is commonly referred to as the Heads-Up set, or R323 (ACC). These very popular but difficult to obtain cards came in two series of the same 24 players. The first series, numbers 241-264, is distinguished from the second series, numbers 265-288, in that the second contains etched cartoons and comments surrounding the player picture. Although the set starts with number 241, it is not a continuation of the 1933 Goudey set, but a separate set in its own right.

	NRMT	VG-E	GOOD
COMPLETE SET (48)	9500.00	4000.00	1250.00
COMMON PLAYER (241-264)	65.00	26.00	6.50
COMMON PLAYER (265-288)	75.00	30.00	7.50

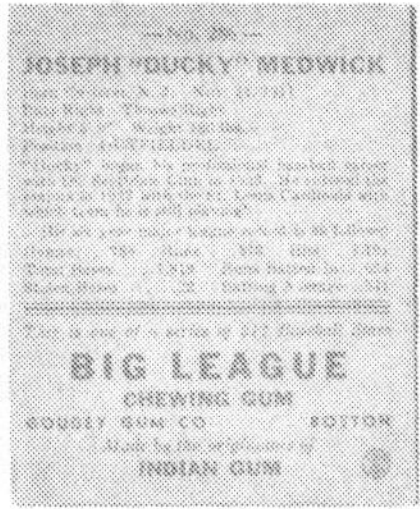

□ 241	Charlie Gehringer	250.00	100.00	25.00
□ 242	Pete Fox	65.00	26.00	6.50
□ 243	Joe Kuhel	65.00	26.00	6.50
□ 244	Frank Demaree	65.00	26.00	6.50
□ 245	Frank Pytlak	65.00	26.00	6.50
□ 246	Ernie Lombardi	125.00	50.00	12.50
□ 247	Joe Vosmik	65.00	26.00	6.50
□ 248	Dick Bartell	65.00	26.00	6.50
□ 249	Jimmie Foxx	300.00	120.00	30.00
□ 250	Joe DiMaggio	1800.00	800.00	200.00
□ 251	Bump Hadley	65.00	26.00	6.50
□ 252	Zeke Bonura	65.00	26.00	6.50
□ 253	Hank Greenberg	250.00	100.00	25.00
□ 254	Van Lingle Mungo	65.00	26.00	6.50
□ 255	Moose Solters	65.00	26.00	6.50
□ 256	Vernon Kennedy	65.00	26.00	6.50
□ 257	Al Lopez	125.00	50.00	12.50
□ 258	Bobby Doerr	200.00	80.00	20.00
□ 259	Billy Werber	65.00	26.00	6.50
□ 260	Rudy York	65.00	26.00	6.50
□ 261	Rip Radcliff	65.00	26.00	6.50
□ 262	Joe Medwick	175.00	70.00	18.00
□ 263	Marvin Owen	65.00	26.00	6.50
□ 264	Bob Feller	450.00	180.00	45.00
□ 265	Charlie Gehringer	300.00	120.00	30.00
□ 266	Pete Fox	75.00	30.00	7.50
□ 267	Joe Kuhel	75.00	30.00	7.50
□ 268	Frank Demaree	75.00	30.00	7.50
□ 269	Frank Pytlak	75.00	30.00	7.50
□ 270	Ernie Lombardi	150.00	60.00	15.00
□ 271	Joe Vosmik	75.00	30.00	7.50
□ 272	Dick Bartell	75.00	30.00	7.50
□ 273	Jimmie Foxx	350.00	140.00	35.00
□ 274	Joe DiMaggio	2100.00	900.00	250.00
□ 275	Bump Hadley	75.00	30.00	7.50
□ 276	Zeke Bonura	75.00	30.00	7.50
□ 277	Hank Greenberg	300.00	120.00	30.00
□ 278	Van Lingle Mungo	75.00	30.00	7.50
□ 279	Moose Solters	75.00	30.00	7.50
□ 280	Vernon Kennedy	75.00	30.00	7.50
□ 281	Al Lopez	150.00	60.00	15.00
□ 282	Bobby Doerr	225.00	90.00	22.00
□ 283	Billy Werber	75.00	30.00	7.50
□ 284	Rudy York	75.00	30.00	7.50
□ 285	Rip Radcliff	75.00	30.00	7.50
□ 286	Joe Medwick	200.00	80.00	20.00
□ 287	Marvin Owen	75.00	30.00	7.50
□ 288	Bob Feller	500.00	200.00	50.00

1981 Granny Goose

This set is the hardest to obtain of the three years Granny Goose issued cards of the Oakland A's. The Revering card was supposedly destroyed by the printer soon after he was traded away and hence is in shorter supply than the other 14 cards in the set. Wayne Gross is also supposedly available in lesser quantity compared to the other players. Cards are standard size (2 1/2" by 3 1/2") and were issued in bags of potato chips. Cards are numbered on the front and back by the player's uniform number.

	MINT	EXC	G-VG
COMPLETE SET (15)	70.00	28.00	7.00
COMMON PLAYER	1.00	.40	.10
□ 1 Billy Martin MG	5.00	2.00	.50
□ 2 Mike Heath	1.00	.40	.10

Rickey Henley Henderson
35 Outfield
Height: 5'10"
Weight: 198
Bats: Right
Throws: Left

In 1980 Rickey became the first American Leaguer and the 3rd in baseball history to steal 100 bases in a season. Rickey was 2nd in the league in walks with 117, and led the A's with 179 hits.

□ 5	Jeff Newman	1.00	.40	.10
□ 6	Mitchell Page	1.00	.40	.10
□ 8	Rob Picciolo	1.00	.40	.10
□ 10	Wayne Gross	6.00	2.40	.60
□ 13	Dave Revering SP	35.00	14.00	3.50
□ 17	Mike Norris	1.00	.40	.10
□ 20	Tony Armas	2.50	1.00	.25
□ 21	Dwayne Murphy	2.50	1.00	.25
□ 22	Rick Langford	1.50	.60	.15
□ 27	Matt Keough	1.00	.40	.10
□ 35	Rickey Henderson	20.00	8.00	2.00
□ 39	Dave McKay	1.00	.40	.10
□ 54	Steve McCatty	1.00	.40	.10

1982 Granny Goose

The cards in this 15-card set measure 2 1/2" by 3 1/2". Granny Goose Foods, Inc., a California based company, repeated its successful promotional idea of 1981 by issuing a new set of Oakland A's baseball cards for 1982. Each color player picture is surrounded by white borders and has trim and lettering done in Oakland's green and yellow colors. The cards are numbered according to the uniform number of the player, and the backs carry vital statistics done in black print on a white background. The cards were distributed in packages of potato chips and were also handed out on Fan Appreciation Day at the stadium. Although Picciolo was traded, his card was not withdrawn (as was Revering last year) and, therefore, its value is no greater than other cards in the set.

	MINT	EXC	G-VG
COMPLETE SET (15)	12.50	5.00	1.25
COMMON PLAYER (1-15)	.40	.16	.04
□ 1 Tony Armas	.75	.30	.07
□ 2 Wayne Gross	.40	.16	.04
□ 3 Mike Heath	.40	.16	.04
□ 4 Rickey Henderson	6.50	2.60	.65
□ 5 Cliff Johnson	.40	.16	.04
□ 6 Matt Keough	.40	.16	.04

☐ 7 Rick Langford	.40	.16	.04
☐ 8 Davey Lopes	.75	.30	.07
☐ 9 Billy Martin MG	1.50	.60	.15
☐ 10 Steve McCatty	.40	.16	.04
☐ 11 Dwayne Murphy	.75	.30	.07
☐ 12 Jeff Newman	.40	.16	.04
☐ 13 Mike Norris	.40	.16	.04
☐ 14 Rob Picciolo	.40	.16	.04
☐ 15 Fred Stanley	.40	.16	.04

1983 Granny Goose

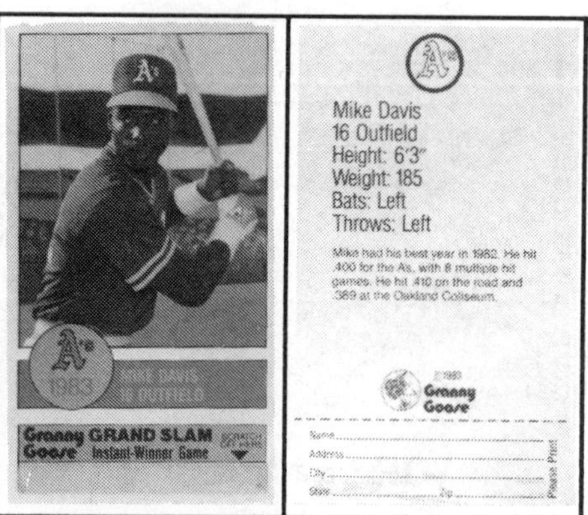

The cards in this 15-card set measure 2 1/2" by 4 1/4". The 1983 Granny Goose Potato Chips set again features Oakland A's players. The cards that were issued in bags of potato chips have a tear off coupon on the bottom with a scratch off section featuring prizes. In addition to their release in bags of potato chips, the Granny Goose cards were also given away to fans attending the Oakland game of July 3, 1983. These give away cards did not contain the coupon on the bottom. Prices listed below are for cards without the detachable tabs that came on the bottom of the cards; cards with tabs intact are valued 50% higher than the prices below.

	MINT	EXC	G-VG
COMPLETE SET (15)	9.00	3.75	.90
COMMON PLAYER	.40	.16	.04
☐ 2 Mike Heath	.40	.16	.04
☐ 4 Carney Lansford	1.00	.40	.10
☐ 10 Wayne Gross	.40	.16	.04
☐ 14 Steve Boros MG	.40	.16	.04
☐ 15 Davey Lopes	.75	.30	.07
☐ 16 Mike Davis	.75	.30	.07
☐ 17 Mike Norris	.40	.16	.04
☐ 21 Dwayne Murphy	.75	.30	.07
☐ 22 Rick Langford	.40	.16	.04
☐ 27 Matt Keough	.40	.16	.04
☐ 31 Tom Underwood	.40	.16	.04
☐ 33 Dave Beard	.40	.16	.04
☐ 35 Rickey Henderson	5.00	2.00	.50
☐ 39 Tom Burgmeier	.40	.16	.04
☐ 54 Steve McCatty	.40	.16	.04

1958 Hires

The cards in this 66-card set measure 2 5/16" by 3 1/2" or 2 5/16" by 7" with tabs. The 1958 Hires Root Beer set of numbered, colored cards was issued with detachable coupons as inserts with Hires Root Beer cartons. Cards with the coupon still intact are worth double the prices listed below. The card front picture is surrounded by a wood grain effect which makes it look like the player is seen through a knot hole. The numbering of this set is rather strange in that it begins with 10 and skips 69.

	NRMT	VG-E	GOOD
COMPLETE SET	875.00	360.00	90.00
COMMON PLAYER (10-76)	6.50	2.60	.65
☐ 10 Richie Ashburn	25.00	10.00	2.50
☐ 11 Chico Carrasquel	6.50	2.60	.65
☐ 12 Dave Philley	6.50	2.60	.65
☐ 13 Don Newcombe	11.00	4.50	1.10
☐ 14 Wally Post	6.50	2.60	.65
☐ 15 Rip Repulski	6.50	2.60	.65
☐ 16 Chico Fernandez	6.50	2.60	.65
☐ 17 Larry Doby	11.00	4.50	1.10
☐ 18 Hector Brown	6.50	2.60	.65
☐ 19 Danny O'Connell	6.50	2.60	.65
☐ 20 Granny Hamner	6.50	2.60	.65
☐ 21 Dick Groat	10.00	4.00	1.00
☐ 22 Ray Narleski	6.50	2.60	.65
☐ 23 Pee Wee Reese	40.00	16.00	4.00
☐ 24 Bob Friend	8.00	3.25	.80
☐ 25 Willie Mays	150.00	60.00	15.00
☐ 26 Bob Nieman	6.50	2.60	.65
☐ 27 Frank Thomas	8.00	3.25	.80
☐ 28 Curt Simmons	8.00	3.25	.80
☐ 29 Stan Lopata	6.50	2.60	.65
☐ 30 Bob Skinner	6.50	2.60	.65
☐ 31 Ron Kline	6.50	2.60	.65
☐ 32 Willie Miranda	6.50	2.60	.65
☐ 33 Bobby Avila	6.50	2.60	.65
☐ 34 Clem Labine	8.00	3.25	.80
☐ 35 Ray Jablonski	6.50	2.60	.65
☐ 36 Bill Mazeroski	12.00	5.00	1.20
☐ 37 Billy Gardner	6.50	2.60	.65
☐ 38 Pete Runnels	8.00	3.25	.80
☐ 39 Jack Sanford	6.50	2.60	.65
☐ 40 Dave Sisler	6.50	2.60	.65
☐ 41 Don Zimmer	10.00	4.00	1.00
☐ 42 Johnny Podres	10.00	4.00	1.00
☐ 43 Dick Farrell	6.50	2.60	.65
☐ 44 Hank Aaron	150.00	60.00	15.00
☐ 45 Bill Virdon	10.00	4.00	1.00
☐ 46 Bobby Thomson	10.00	4.00	1.00
☐ 47 Willard Nixon	6.50	2.60	.65
☐ 48 Billy Loes	6.50	2.60	.65
☐ 49 Hank Sauer	8.00	3.25	.80
☐ 50 Johnny Antonelli	8.00	3.25	.80
☐ 51 Daryl Spencer	6.50	2.60	.65
☐ 52 Ken Lehman	6.50	2.60	.65

☐ 53 Sammy White	6.50	2.60	.65
☐ 54 Charley Neal	8.00	3.25	.80
☐ 55 Don Drysdale	30.00	12.00	3.00
☐ 56 Jackie Jensen	11.00	4.50	1.10
☐ 57 Ray Katt	6.50	2.60	.65
☐ 58 Frank Sullivan	6.50	2.60	.65
☐ 59 Roy Face	8.00	3.25	.80
☐ 60 Willie Jones	6.50	2.60	.65
☐ 61 Duke Snider	75.00	30.00	7.50
☐ 62 Whitey Lockman	8.00	3.25	.80
☐ 63 Gino Cimoli	6.50	2.60	.65
☐ 64 Marv Grissom	6.50	2.60	.65
☐ 65 Gene Baker	6.50	2.60	.65
☐ 66 George Zuverink	6.50	2.60	.65
☐ 67 Ted Kluszewski	12.00	5.00	1.20
☐ 68 Jim Busby	6.50	2.60	.65
☐ 69 Not Issued	0.00	.00	.00
☐ 70 Curt Barclay	6.50	2.60	.65
☐ 71 Hank Foiles	6.50	2.60	.65
☐ 72 Gene Stephens	6.50	2.60	.65
☐ 73 Al Worthington	6.50	2.60	.65
☐ 74 Al Walker	6.50	2.60	.65
☐ 75 Bob Boyd	6.50	2.60	.65
☐ 76 Al Pilarcik	6.50	2.60	.65

1958 Hires Test

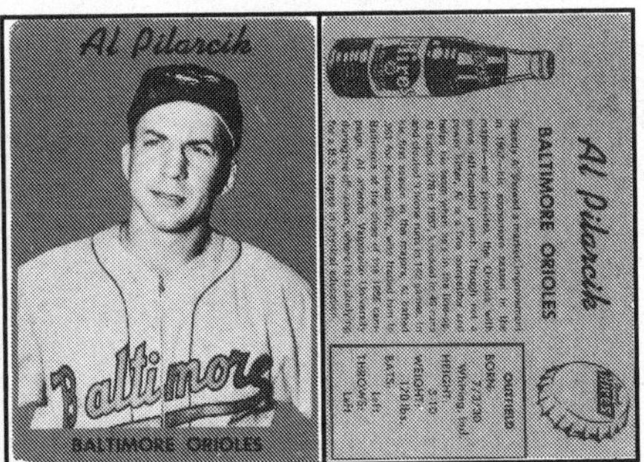

The cards in this 8-card test set measure 2 5/16" by 3 1/2" or 2 5/16" by 7" with tabs. The 1958 Hires Root Beer test set features unnumbered, color cards. The card front photos are shown on a yellow or orange back ground instead of the wood grain background used in the Hires regular set. The cards contain a detachable coupon just as the regular Hires issue does. Cards were test marketed on a very limited basis in a few cities. Cards with the coupon still intact are worth double the prices in the checklist below. The checklist below is ordered alphabetically.

	NRMT	VG-E	GOOD
COMPLETE SET (8)	800.00	300.00	100.00
COMMON PLAYER (1-8)	75.00	30.00	7.50
☐ 1 Johnny Antonelli	90.00	36.00	9.00
☐ 2 Jim Busby	75.00	30.00	7.50
☐ 3 Chico Fernandez	75.00	30.00	7.50
☐ 4 Bob Friend	90.00	36.00	9.00
☐ 5 Vern Law	90.00	36.00	9.00
☐ 6 Stan Lopata	75.00	30.00	7.50
☐ 7 Willie Mays	300.00	120.00	30.00
☐ 8 Al Pilarcik	75.00	30.00	7.50

1959 Home Run Derby

This 20-card set was produced in 1959 by American Motors to publicize a TV program. The cards are black and white and blank backed. The cards measure approximately 3 1/8" by 5 1/4". The cards are unnumbered and are ordered alphabetically below for convenience. During 1988, the 19 player cards in this set were publicly reprinted.

	NRMT	VG-E	GOOD
COMPLETE SET (20)	2400.00	1000.00	300.00
COMMON PLAYER (1-20)	40.00	16.00	4.00
☐ 1 Hank Aaron	275.00	110.00	27.00
☐ 2 Bob Allison	40.00	16.00	4.00
☐ 3 Ernie Banks	125.00	50.00	12.50
☐ 4 Ken Boyer	60.00	24.00	6.00
☐ 5 Bob Cerv	40.00	16.00	4.00
☐ 6 Rocky Colavito	60.00	24.00	6.00
☐ 7 Gil Hodges	90.00	36.00	9.00
☐ 8 Jackie Jensen	60.00	24.00	6.00
☐ 9 Al Kaline	150.00	60.00	15.00
☐ 10 Harmon Killebrew	125.00	50.00	12.50
☐ 11 Jim Lemon	40.00	16.00	4.00
☐ 12 Mickey Mantle	750.00	300.00	75.00
☐ 13 Ed Mathews	125.00	50.00	12.50
☐ 14 Willie Mays	275.00	110.00	27.00
☐ 15 Wally Post	40.00	16.00	4.00
☐ 16 Frank Robinson	125.00	50.00	12.50
☐ 17 Mark Scott (TV show host)	40.00	16.00	4.00
☐ 18 Duke Snider	200.00	80.00	20.00
☐ 19 Dick Stuart	40.00	16.00	4.00
☐ 20 Gus Triandos	40.00	16.00	4.00

1947 Homogenized Bond

The cards in this 48-card set measure 2 1/4" by 3 1/2". The 1947 W571/D305 Homogenized Bread are sets of unnumbered cards containing 44 baseball players and four boxers. The W571 set exists in two styles. Style one is identical to the D305 set except for the back printing while style two has perforated edges and movie stars depicted on the backs. The second style of W571 cards contains only 13 cards. The four boxers in the checklist below are indicated by BOX. The checklist below is ordered alphabetically. There are 24 cards in the set which were apparently produced in greater supply. These 24 (marked by DP below) are relatively more common than the other 24 cards in the set.

	NRMT	VG-E	GOOD
COMPLETE SET	450.00	180.00	55.00
COMMON PLAYER (1-48)	6.00	2.40	.60
COMMON BOXER	3.00	1.20	.30
COMMON DP BASEBALL	3.00	1.20	.30
COMMON DP BOXER	1.50	.60	.15
□ 1 Rex Barney	6.00	2.40	.60
□ 2 Larry Berra	30.00	12.00	3.00
□ 3 Ewell Blackwell DP	3.00	1.20	.30
□ 4 Lou Boudreau DP	7.50	3.00	.75
□ 5 Ralph Branca	7.50	3.00	.75
□ 6 Harry Brecheen DP	3.00	1.20	.30
□ 7 Primo Carnera BOX DP	1.50	.60	.15
□ 8 Marcel Cerdan BOX	3.00	1.20	.30
□ 9 Dom DiMaggio	9.00	3.75	.90
□ 10 Joe DiMaggio	75.00	30.00	7.50
□ 11 Bobby Doerr DP	7.50	3.00	.75
□ 12 Bruce Edwards	6.00	2.40	.60
□ 13 Bob Elliott DP	3.00	1.20	.30
□ 14 Del Ennis DP	3.00	1.20	.30
□ 15 Bob Feller DP	15.00	6.00	1.50
□ 16 Carl Furillo	9.00	3.75	.90
□ 17 Joe Gordon DP	3.00	1.20	.30
□ 18 Sid Gordon	6.00	2.40	.60
□ 19 Joe Hatten	6.00	2.40	.60
□ 20 Gil Hodges	20.00	8.00	2.00
□ 21 Tommy Holmes DP	3.00	1.20	.30
□ 22 Larry Jansen	6.00	2.40	.60
□ 23 Sheldon Jones	6.00	2.40	.60
□ 24 Edwin Joost	6.00	2.40	.60
□ 25 Charlie Keller	7.50	3.00	.75
□ 26 Ken Keltner DP	3.00	1.20	.30
□ 27 Buddy Kerr	6.00	2.40	.60
□ 28 Ralph Kiner DP	9.00	3.75	.90
□ 29 Jake LaMotta BOX	6.00	2.40	.60
□ 30 John Lindell	6.00	2.40	.60
□ 31 Whitey Lockman	6.00	2.40	.60
□ 32 Joe Louis BOX DP	7.50	3.00	.75
□ 33 Willard Marshall	6.00	2.40	.60
□ 34 Johnny Mize DP	9.00	3.75	.90
□ 35 Stan Musial DP	32.00	13.00	3.20
□ 36 Andy Pafko DP	3.00	1.20	.30
□ 37 Johnny Pesky DP	3.00	1.20	.30
□ 38 Pee Wee Reese	25.00	10.00	2.50
□ 39 Phil Rizzuto DP	12.00	5.00	1.20
□ 40 Aaron Robinson DP	3.00	1.20	.30
□ 41 Jackie Robinson DP	36.00	15.00	3.60
□ 42 John Sain DP	6.00	2.40	.60
□ 43 Enos Slaughter DP	9.00	3.75	.90
□ 44 Vern Stephens DP	3.00	1.20	.30
□ 45 George Tebbetts	6.00	2.40	.60
□ 46 Bobby Thomson	7.50	3.00	.75
□ 47 Johnny VanderMeer	7.50	3.00	.75
□ 48 Ted Williams DP	40.00	16.00	4.00

1975 Hostess

The cards in this 150-card set measure 2 1/4" by 3 1/4" individually or 3 1/4" by 7 1/4" as panels of three. The 1975 Hostess set was issued in panels of three cards each on the backs of family sized packages of Hostess cakes. Card number 125, Bill Madlock, was listed correctly as an infielder and incorrectly as a pitcher. Number 11, Burt Hooton, and number 89, Doug Rader, are spelled two different ways. Some panels are more scarce than others as they were issued only on the backs of less popular Hostess products. These scarcer panels are shown with asterisks in the checklist. Although complete panel prices are not explicitly listed, they would generally have a value 25% greater than the sum of the values of the individual players on that panel.

	NRMT	VG-E	GOOD
COMPLETE INDIV.SET	150.00	60.00	15.00
COMMON PLAYER (1-150)	.30	.12	.03
□ 1 Bob Tolan	.30	.12	.03
□ 2 Cookie Rojas	.40	.16	.04
□ 3 Darrell Evans	.60	.24	.06
□ 4 Sal Bando	.40	.16	.04
□ 5 Joe Morgan	2.00	.80	.20
□ 6 Mickey Lolich	.50	.20	.05
□ 7 Don Sutton	2.00	.80	.20
□ 8 Bill Melton	.30	.12	.03
□ 9 Tim Foli	.30	.12	.03
□ 10 Joe LaHoud	.30	.12	.03
□ 11A Bert Hooten (sic)	1.00	.40	.10
□ 11B Burt Hooton	1.00	.40	.10
□ 12 Paul Blair	.30	.12	.03
□ 13 Jim Barr	.30	.12	.03
□ 14 Toby Harrah	.40	.16	.04
□ 15 John Milner	.30	.12	.03
□ 16 Ken Holtzman	.40	.16	.04
□ 17 Cesar Cedeno	.40	.16	.04
□ 18 Dwight Evans	.75	.30	.07
□ 19 Willie McCovey	2.50	1.00	.25
□ 20 Tony Oliva	.60	.24	.06
□ 21 Manny Sanguillen	.40	.16	.04
□ 22 Mickey Rivers	.40	.16	.04
□ 23 Lou Brock	2.50	1.00	.25
□ 24 Graig Nettles (Craig on front)	1.50	.60	.15
□ 25 Jim Wynn	.40	.16	.04
□ 26 George Scott	.30	.12	.03
□ 27 Greg Luzinski	.50	.20	.05
□ 28 Bert Campaneris	.40	.16	.04
□ 29 Pete Rose	10.00	4.00	1.00
□ 30 Buddy Bell	.50	.20	.05
□ 31 Gary Matthews	.40	.16	.04
□ 32 Freddie Patek	.30	.12	.03
□ 33 Mike Lum	.30	.12	.03
□ 34 Ellie Rodriguez	.30	.12	.03
□ 35 Milt May (photo actually Lee May)	.50	.20	.05
□ 36 Willie Horton	.40	.16	.04
□ 37 Dave Winfield	3.50	1.40	.35
□ 38 Tom Grieve	.40	.16	.04
□ 39 Barry Foote	.30	.12	.03
□ 40 Joe Rudi	.40	.16	.04
□ 41 Bake McBride	.30	.12	.03
□ 42 Mike Cuellar	.40	.16	.04
□ 43 Garry Maddox	.40	.16	.04
□ 44 Carlos May	.30	.12	.03
□ 45 Bud Harrelson	.30	.12	.03
□ 46 Dave Chalk	.30	.12	.03
□ 47 Dave Concepcion	.50	.20	.05
□ 48 Carl Yastrzemski	7.00	2.80	.70
□ 49 Steve Garvey	4.00	1.60	.40
□ 50 Amos Otis	.40	.16	.04
□ 51 Rick Reuschel	.50	.20	.05
□ 52 Rollie Fingers	1.00	.40	.10
□ 53 Bob Watson	.40	.16	.04
□ 54 John Ellis	.30	.12	.03
□ 55 Bob Bailey	.30	.12	.03
□ 56 Rod Carew	4.00	1.60	.40
□ 57 Rich Hebner	.30	.12	.03
□ 58 Nolan Ryan	4.50	1.80	.45
□ 59 Reggie Smith	.50	.20	.05

☐ 60	Joe Coleman	.30	.12	.03
☐ 61	Ron Cey	.40	.16	.04
☐ 62	Darrell Porter	.40	.16	.04
☐ 63	Steve Carlton	4.00	1.60	.40
☐ 64	Gene Tenace	.30	.12	.03
☐ 65	Jose Cardenal	.30	.12	.03
☐ 66	Bill Lee	.40	.16	.04
☐ 67	Dave Lopes	.40	.16	.04
☐ 68	Wilbur Wood	.40	.16	.04
☐ 69	Steve Renko	.30	.12	.03
☐ 70	Joe Torre	.50	.20	.05
☐ 71	Ted Sizemore	.30	.12	.03
☐ 72	Bobby Grich	.40	.16	.04
☐ 73	Chris Speier	.30	.12	.03
☐ 74	Bert Blyleven	.60	.24	.06
☐ 75	Tom Seaver	4.00	1.60	.40
☐ 76	Nate Colbert	.30	.12	.03
☐ 77	Don Kessinger	.40	.16	.04
☐ 78	George Medich	.30	.12	.03
☐ 79	Andy Messersmith *	.50	.20	.05
☐ 80	Robin Yount *	8.00	3.25	.80
☐ 81	Al Oliver *	.90	.36	.09
☐ 82	Bill Singer *	.40	.16	.04
☐ 83	Johnny Bench *	5.50	2.20	.55
☐ 84	Gaylord Perry *	2.00	.80	.20
☐ 85	Dave Kingman *	.90	.36	.09
☐ 86	Ed Herrmann *	.40	.16	.04
☐ 87	Ralph Garr *	.40	.16	.04
☐ 88	Reggie Jackson *	6.00	2.40	.60
☐ 89A	Doug Radar ERR * (sic, Rader)	1.00	.40	.10
☐ 89B	Doug Rader COR *	2.00	.80	.20
☐ 90	Elliott Maddox *	.40	.16	.04
☐ 91	Bill Russell *	.50	.20	.05
☐ 92	John Mayberry *	.40	.16	.04
☐ 93	Dave Cash *	.40	.16	.04
☐ 94	Jeff Burroughs *	.40	.16	.04
☐ 95	Ted Simmons *	.80	.32	.08
☐ 96	Joe Decker *	.40	.16	.04
☐ 97	Bill Buckner *	.80	.32	.08
☐ 98	Bobby Darwin *	.40	.16	.04
☐ 99	Phil Niekro *	2.50	1.00	.25
☐ 100	Jim Sundberg	.40	.16	.04
☐ 101	Greg Gross	.30	.12	.03
☐ 102	Luis Tiant	.50	.20	.05
☐ 103	Glenn Beckert	.30	.12	.03
☐ 104	Hal McRae	.40	.16	.04
☐ 105	Mike Jorgensen	.30	.12	.03
☐ 106	Mike Hargrove	.40	.16	.04
☐ 107	Don Gullett	.40	.16	.04
☐ 108	Tito Fuentes	.30	.12	.03
☐ 109	John Grubb	.30	.12	.03
☐ 110	Jim Kaat	.75	.30	.07
☐ 111	Felix Millan	.30	.12	.03
☐ 112	Don Money	.30	.12	.03
☐ 113	Rick Monday	.40	.16	.04
☐ 114	Dick Bosman	.30	.12	.03
☐ 115	Roger Metzger	.30	.12	.03
☐ 116	Fergie Jenkins	.75	.30	.07
☐ 117	Dusty Baker	.50	.20	.05
☐ 118	Billy Champion *	.40	.16	.04
☐ 119	Bob Gibson *	3.00	1.20	.30
☐ 120	Bill Freehan *	.50	.20	.05
☐ 121	Cesar Geronimo	.30	.12	.03
☐ 122	Jorge Orta	.30	.12	.03
☐ 123	Cleon Jones	.30	.12	.03
☐ 124	Steve Busby	.40	.16	.04
☐ 125A	Bill Madlock ERR (pitcher)	1.50	.60	.15
☐ 125B	Bill Madlock COR (infielder)	1.50	.60	.15
☐ 126	Jim Palmer	2.50	1.00	.25
☐ 127	Tony Perez	.75	.30	.07
☐ 128	Larry Hisle	.40	.16	.04
☐ 129	Rusty Staub	.50	.20	.05
☐ 130	Hank Aaron *	7.00	2.80	.70
☐ 131	Rennie Stennett *	.40	.16	.04
☐ 132	Rico Petrocelli *	.50	.20	.05
☐ 133	Mike Schmidt	6.00	2.40	.60
☐ 134	Sparky Lyle	.50	.20	.05
☐ 135	Willie Stargell	2.50	1.00	.25
☐ 136	Ken Henderson	.30	.12	.03
☐ 137	Willie Montanez	.30	.12	.03
☐ 138	Thurman Munson	3.50	1.40	.35
☐ 139	Richie Zisk	.40	.16	.04
☐ 140	George Hendrick	.40	.16	.04
☐ 141	Bobby Murcer	.50	.20	.05
☐ 142	Lee May	.40	.16	.04
☐ 143	Carlton Fisk	.75	.30	.07
☐ 144	Brooks Robinson	3.00	1.20	.30
☐ 145	Bobby Bonds	.50	.20	.05
☐ 146	Gary Sutherland	.30	.12	.03
☐ 147	Oscar Gamble	.30	.12	.03
☐ 148	Jim Hunter	2.00	.80	.20
☐ 149	Tug McGraw	.50	.20	.05
☐ 150	Dave McNally	.40	.16	.04

1975 Hostess Twinkie

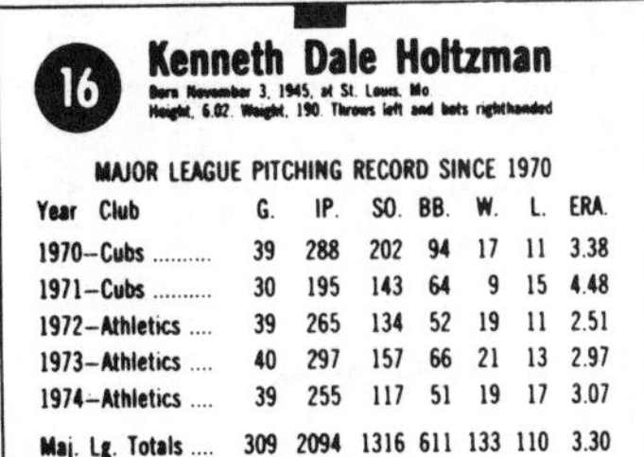
16 **Kenneth Dale Holtzman**

Born November 3, 1945, at St. Louis, Mo
Height, 6.02 Weight, 190 Throws left and bats righthanded

MAJOR LEAGUE PITCHING RECORD SINCE 1970

Year Club	G.	IP.	SO.	BB.	W.	L.	ERA.
1970–Cubs	39	288	202	94	17	11	3.38
1971–Cubs	30	195	143	64	9	15	4.48
1972–Athletics	39	265	134	52	19	11	2.51
1973–Athletics	40	297	157	66	21	13	2.97
1974–Athletics	39	255	117	51	19	17	3.07
Maj. Lg. Totals	309	2094	1316	611	133	110	3.30

The cards in this 60-card set measure 2 1/4" by 3 1/4". The 1975 Hostess Twinkie set was issued on a limited basis in the far western part of the country. The set contains the same numbers as the regular set to number 36; however, the set is skip numbered after number 36. The cards were issued as the backs for 25-cent Twinkies packs. The fronts are indistinguishable from the regular Hostess cards; however the card backs are different in that the Twinkie cards have a thick black bar in the middle of the reverse.

		NRMT	VG-E	GOOD
	COMPLETE SET (60)	75.00	30.00	7.50
	COMMON PLAYER	.60	.24	.06
☐ 1	Bob Tolan	.60	.24	.06
☐ 2	Cookie Rojas	.60	.24	.06
☐ 3	Darrell Evans	1.00	.40	.10
☐ 4	Sal Bando	.75	.30	.07
☐ 5	Joe Morgan	2.50	1.00	.25
☐ 6	Mickey Lolich	.90	.36	.09
☐ 7	Don Sutton	2.50	1.00	.25
☐ 8	Bill Melton	.60	.24	.06
☐ 9	Tim Foli	.60	.24	.06
☐ 10	Joe LaHoud	.60	.24	.06
☐ 11	Bert Hooten (sic)	1.00	.40	.10
☐ 12	Paul Blair	.60	.24	.06
☐ 13	Jim Barr	.60	.24	.06
☐ 14	Toby Harrah	.75	.30	.07
☐ 15	John Milner	.60	.24	.06
☐ 16	Ken Holtzman	.75	.30	.07
☐ 17	Cesar Cedeno	.75	.30	.07
☐ 18	Dwight Evans	1.25	.50	.12
☐ 19	Willie McCovey	3.00	1.20	.30
☐ 20	Tony Oliva	1.00	.40	.10
☐ 21	Manny Sanguillen	.75	.30	.07
☐ 22	Mickey Rivers	.75	.30	.07
☐ 23	Lou Brock	3.00	1.20	.30
☐ 24	Graig Nettles (Craig on front)	1.50	.60	.15
☐ 25	Jim Wynn	.75	.30	.07
☐ 26	George Scott	.60	.24	.06
☐ 27	Greg Luzinski	.90	.36	.09
☐ 28	Bert Campaneris	.75	.30	.07
☐ 29	Pete Rose	10.00	4.00	1.00
☐ 30	Buddy Bell	.90	.36	.09
☐ 31	Gary Matthews	.75	.30	.07
☐ 32	Freddie Patek	.60	.24	.06
☐ 33	Mike Lum	.60	.24	.06
☐ 34	Ellie Rodriguez	.60	.24	.06
☐ 35	Milt May (Lee May picture)	.90	.36	.09
☐ 36	Willie Horton	.75	.30	.07
☐ 40	Joe Rudi	.75	.30	.07
☐ 43	Garry Maddox	.75	.30	.07
☐ 46	Dave Chalk	.60	.24	.06
☐ 49	Steve Garvey	5.00	2.00	.50
☐ 52	Rollie Fingers	1.50	.60	.15
☐ 58	Nolan Ryan	5.00	2.00	.50
☐ 61	Ron Cey	.90	.36	.09
☐ 64	Gene Tenace	.60	.24	.06
☐ 65	Jose Cardenal	.60	.24	.06
☐ 67	Dave Lopes	.75	.30	.07
☐ 68	Wilbur Wood	.75	.30	.07
☐ 73	Chris Speier	.60	.24	.06
☐ 77	Don Kessinger	.75	.30	.07

□ 79 Andy Messersmith	.75	.30	.07
□ 80 Robin Yount	9.00	3.75	.90
□ 82 Bill Singer	.60	.24	.06
□ 103 Glenn Beckert	.60	.24	.06
□ 110 Jim Kaat	1.00	.40	.10
□ 112 Don Money	.60	.24	.06
□ 113 Rick Monday	.75	.30	.07
□ 122 Jorge Orta	.60	.24	.06
□ 125 Bill Madlock	1.00	.40	.10
□ 130 Hank Aaron	8.00	3.25	.80
□ 136 Ken Henderson	.60	.24	.06

1976 Hostess

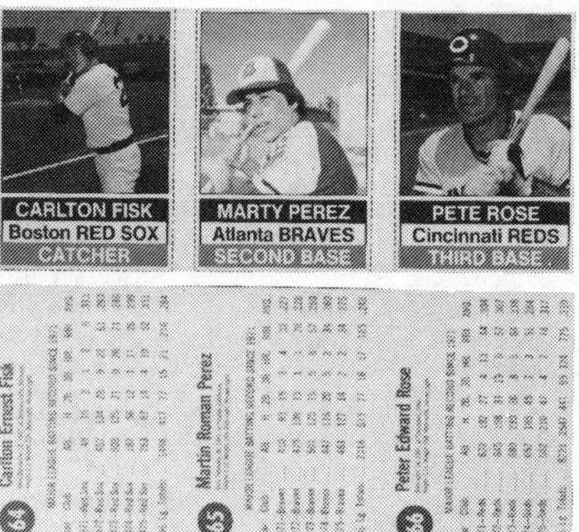

The cards in this 150-card set measure 2 1/4" by 3 1/4" individually or 3 1/4" by 7 1/4" as panels of three. The 1976 Hostess set contains color, numbered cards issued in panels of three cards each on family sized packages of Hostess cakes. Scarcer panels (those only found on less popular Hostess products) are listed in the checklist below with asterisks. Complete panels of three have a value 25% more than the sum of the individual cards on the panel. Nine additional numbers (151- 159) were apparently planned but never actually issued. These exist as proof cards and are quite scarce, e.g., 151 Ferguson Jenkins, 152 Mike Cuellar, 153 Tom Murphy, 154 Al Cowens, 155 Barry Foote, 156 Steve Carlton, 157 Richie Zisk, 158 Ken Holtzman, and 159 Cliff Johnson.

	NRMT	VG-E	GOOD
COMPLETE INDIV.SET(150)	150.00	60.00	15.00
COMMON PLAYER (1-150)	.30	.12	.03
□ 1 Fred Lynn	1.25	.50	.12
□ 2 Joe Morgan	2.00	.80	.20
□ 3 Phil Niekro	2.00	.80	.20
□ 4 Gaylord Perry	1.50	.60	.15
□ 5 Bob Watson	.40	.16	.04
□ 6 Bill Freehan	.50	.20	.05
□ 7 Lou Brock	2.50	1.00	.25
□ 8 Al Fitzmorris	.30	.12	.03
□ 9 Rennie Stennett	.30	.12	.03
□ 10 Tony Oliva	.60	.24	.06
□ 11 Robin Yount	3.50	1.40	.35
□ 12 Rick Manning	.30	.12	.03
□ 13 Bobby Grich	.40	.16	.04
□ 14 Terry Forster	.40	.16	.04
□ 15 Dave Kingman	.60	.24	.06
□ 16 Thurman Munson	3.50	1.40	.35
□ 17 Rick Reuschel	.50	.20	.05
□ 18 Bobby Bonds	.50	.20	.05
□ 19 Steve Garvey	4.00	1.60	.40
□ 20 Vida Blue	.40	.16	.04
□ 21 Dave Rader	.30	.12	.03
□ 22 Johnny Bench	4.00	1.60	.40
□ 23 Luis Tiant	.50	.20	.05
□ 24 Darrell Evans	.60	.24	.06
□ 25 Larry Dierker	.30	.12	.03
□ 26 Willie Horton	.40	.16	.04
□ 27 John Ellis	.30	.12	.03
□ 28 Al Cowens	.40	.16	.04
□ 29 Jerry Reuss	.40	.16	.04
□ 30 Reggie Smith	.50	.20	.05
□ 31 Bobby Darwin *	.40	.16	.04
□ 32 Fritz Peterson *	.40	.16	.04
□ 33 Rod Carew *	4.00	1.60	.40
□ 34 Carlos May *	.40	.16	.04
□ 35 Tom Seaver *	4.50	1.80	.45
□ 36 Brooks Robinson *	4.00	1.60	.40
□ 37 Jose Cardenal	.30	.12	.03
□ 38 Ron Blomberg	.30	.12	.03
□ 39 Leroy Stanton	.30	.12	.03
□ 40 Dave Cash	.30	.12	.03
□ 41 John Montefusco	.40	.16	.04
□ 42 Bob Tolan	.30	.12	.03
□ 43 Carl Morton	.30	.12	.03
□ 44 Rick Burleson	.40	.16	.04
□ 45 Don Gullett	.40	.16	.04
□ 46 Vern Ruhle	.30	.12	.03
□ 47 Cesar Cedeno	.40	.16	.04
□ 48 Toby Harrah	.40	.16	.04
□ 49 Willie Stargell	2.50	1.00	.25
□ 50 Al Hrabosky	.40	.16	.04
□ 51 Amos Otis	.40	.16	.04
□ 52 Bud Harrelson	.30	.12	.03
□ 53 Jim Hughes	.30	.12	.03
□ 54 George Scott	.30	.12	.03
□ 55 Mike Vail *	.40	.16	.04
□ 56 Jim Palmer *	3.00	1.20	.30
□ 57 Jorge Orta *	.40	.16	.04
□ 58 Chris Chambliss *	.50	.20	.05
□ 59 Dave Chalk *	.40	.16	.04
□ 60 Ray Burris *	.40	.16	.04
□ 61 Bert Campaneris *	.50	.20	.05
□ 62 Gary Carter *	6.00	2.40	.60
□ 63 Ron Cey *	.75	.30	.07
□ 64 Carlton Fisk *	1.00	.40	.10
□ 65 Marty Perez *	.40	.16	.04
□ 66 Pete Rose *	10.00	4.00	1.00
□ 67 Roger Metzger *	.40	.16	.04
□ 68 Jim Sundberg *	.40	.16	.04
□ 69 Ron LeFlore *	.40	.16	.04
□ 70 Ted Sizemore *	.40	.16	.04
□ 71 Steve Busby *	.50	.20	.05
□ 72 Manny Sanguillen *	.50	.20	.05
□ 73 Larry Hisle *	.40	.16	.04
□ 74 Pete Broberg *	.40	.16	.04
□ 75 Boog Powell *	.75	.30	.07
□ 76 Ken Singleton *	.60	.24	.06
□ 77 Rich Gossage *	1.25	.50	.12
□ 78 Jerry Grote *	.40	.16	.04
□ 79 Nolan Ryan *	5.00	2.00	.50
□ 80 Rick Monday *	.50	.20	.05
□ 81 Graig Nettles *	.75	.30	.07
□ 82 Chris Speier	.30	.12	.03
□ 83 Dave Winfield	3.00	1.20	.30
□ 84 Mike Schmidt	6.00	2.40	.60
□ 85 Buzz Capra	.30	.12	.03
□ 86 Tony Perez	.75	.30	.07
□ 87 Dwight Evans	.75	.30	.07
□ 88 Mike Hargrove	.30	.12	.03
□ 89 Joe Coleman	.30	.12	.03
□ 90 Greg Gross	.30	.12	.03
□ 91 John Mayberry	.40	.16	.04
□ 92 John Candelaria	.50	.20	.05
□ 93 Bake McBride	.30	.12	.03
□ 94 Hank Aaron	6.00	2.40	.60
□ 95 Buddy Bell	.50	.20	.05
□ 96 Steve Braun	.30	.12	.03
□ 97 Jon Matlack	.40	.16	.04
□ 98 Lee May	.40	.16	.04
□ 99 Wilbur Wood	.40	.16	.04
□ 100 Bill Madlock	.60	.24	.06
□ 101 Frank Tanana	.40	.16	.04
□ 102 Mickey Rivers	.40	.16	.04
□ 103 Mike Ivie	.30	.12	.03
□ 104 Rollie Fingers	1.00	.40	.10
□ 105 Dave Lopes	.40	.16	.04
□ 106 George Foster	.90	.36	.09
□ 107 Denny Doyle	.30	.12	.03
□ 108 Earl Williams	.30	.12	.03
□ 109 Tom Veryzer	.30	.12	.03
□ 110 J.R. Richard	.40	.16	.04
□ 111 Jeff Burroughs	.30	.12	.03
□ 112 Al Oliver	.75	.30	.07
□ 113 Ted Simmons	.75	.30	.07
□ 114 George Brett	7.00	2.80	.70
□ 115 Frank Duffy	.30	.12	.03
□ 116 Bert Blyleven	.50	.20	.05
□ 117 Darrell Porter	.30	.12	.03
□ 118 Don Baylor	.50	.20	.05
□ 119 Bucky Dent	.50	.20	.05
□ 120 Felix Millan	.30	.12	.03

□ 121	Mike Cuellar	.40	.16	.04
□ 122	Gene Tenace	.30	.12	.03
□ 123	Bobby Murcer	.50	.20	.05
□ 124	Willie McCovey	2.00	.80	.20
□ 125	Greg Luzinski	.50	.20	.05
□ 126	Larry Parrish	.60	.24	.06
□ 127	Jim Rice	4.00	1.60	.40
□ 128	Dave Concepcion	.50	.20	.05
□ 129	Jim Wynn	.40	.16	.04
□ 130	Tom Grieve	.40	.16	.04
□ 131	Mike Cosgrove	.30	.12	.03
□ 132	Dan Meyer	.30	.12	.03
□ 133	Dave Parker	2.00	.80	.20
□ 134	Don Kessinger	.40	.16	.04
□ 135	Hal McRae	.40	.16	.04
□ 136	Don Money	.30	.12	.03
□ 137	Dennis Eckersley	1.00	.40	.10
□ 138	Fergie Jenkins	.60	.24	.06
□ 139	Mike Torrez	.40	.16	.04
□ 140	Jerry Morales	.30	.12	.03
□ 141	Jim Hunter	2.00	.80	.20
□ 142	Gary Matthews	.40	.16	.04
□ 143	Randy Jones	.40	.16	.04
□ 144	Mike Jorgensen	.30	.12	.03
□ 145	Larry Bowa	.50	.20	.05
□ 146	Reggie Jackson	4.50	1.80	.45
□ 147	Steve Yeager	.30	.12	.03
□ 148	Dave May	.30	.12	.03
□ 149	Carl Yastrzemski	6.00	2.40	.60
□ 150	Cesar Geronimo	.30	.12	.03

1976 Hostess Twinkie

15 David Arthur Kingman

MAJOR LEAGUE BATTING RECORD SINCE 1971

Year Club	AB.	H.	2B.	3B.	HR.	RBI.	AVG.
1971–Giants	115	32	10	2	2	24	.278
1972–Giants	472	106	17	4	29	83	.225
1973–Giants	305	62	10	1	24	55	.203
1974–Giants	350	78	18	2	18	55	.223
1975–Mets	502	116	22	1	36	88	.231
Maj. Lg. Totals	1744	394	77	10	109	305	.226

The cards in this 60-card set measure 2 1/4" by 3 1/4". The 1976 Hostess Twinkies set contains the first 60 cards of the 1976 Hostess set. These cards were issued as backs on 25- cent Twinkie packages as in the 1975 Twinkies set. The fronts are indistinguishable from the regular Hostess cards; however the card backs are different in that the Twinkie cards have a thick black bar in the middle of the reverse.

		NRMT	VG-E	GOOD
	COMPLETE SET (60)	75.00	30.00	7.50
	COMMON PLAYER (1-60)	.60	.24	.06
□ 1	Fred Lynn	1.25	.50	.12
□ 2	Joe Morgan	2.50	1.00	.25
□ 3	Phil Niekro	2.00	.80	.20
□ 4	Gaylord Perry	1.50	.60	.15
□ 5	Bob Watson	.75	.30	.07
□ 6	Bill Freehan	.75	.30	.07
□ 7	Lou Brock	3.00	1.20	.30
□ 8	Al Fitzmorris	.60	.24	.06
□ 9	Rennie Stennett	.60	.24	.06
□ 10	Tony Oliva	1.00	.40	.10
□ 11	Robin Yount	3.50	1.40	.35
□ 12	Rick Manning	.60	.24	.06
□ 13	Bobby Grich	.75	.30	.07
□ 14	Terry Forster	.75	.30	.07
□ 15	Dave Kingman	.90	.36	.09
□ 16	Thurman Munson	3.50	1.40	.35
□ 17	Rick Reuschel	.90	.36	.09
□ 18	Bobby Bonds	.90	.36	.09
□ 19	Steve Garvey	4.50	1.80	.45
□ 20	Vida Blue	.75	.30	.07
□ 21	Dave Rader	.60	.24	.06
□ 22	Johnny Bench	4.50	1.80	.45
□ 23	Luis Tiant	.90	.36	.09
□ 24	Darrell Evans	1.00	.40	.10
□ 25	Larry Dierker	.60	.24	.06
□ 26	Willie Horton	.75	.30	.07
□ 27	John Ellis	.60	.24	.06
□ 28	Al Cowens	.75	.30	.07
□ 29	Jerry Reuss	.75	.30	.07
□ 30	Reggie Smith	.90	.36	.09
□ 31	Bobby Darwin	.60	.24	.06
□ 32	Fritz Peterson	.60	.24	.06
□ 33	Rod Carew	4.50	1.80	.45
□ 34	Carlos May	.60	.24	.06
□ 35	Tom Seaver	4.50	1.80	.45
□ 36	Brooks Robinson	4.00	1.60	.40
□ 37	Jose Cardenal	.60	.24	.06
□ 38	Ron Blomberg	.60	.24	.06
□ 39	Leroy Stanton	.60	.24	.06
□ 40	Dave Cash	.60	.24	.06
□ 41	John Montefusco	.75	.30	.07
□ 42	Bob Tolan	.60	.24	.06
□ 43	Carl Morton	.60	.24	.06
□ 44	Rick Burleson	.75	.30	.07
□ 45	Don Gullett	.75	.30	.07
□ 46	Vern Ruhle	.60	.24	.06
□ 47	Cesar Cedeno	.75	.30	.07
□ 48	Toby Harrah	.75	.30	.07
□ 49	Willie Stargell	2.50	1.00	.25
□ 50	Al Hrabosky	.75	.30	.07
□ 51	Amos Otis	.75	.30	.07
□ 52	Bud Harrelson	.60	.24	.06
□ 53	Jim Hughes	.60	.24	.06
□ 54	George Scott	.60	.24	.06
□ 55	Mike Vail	.60	.24	.06
□ 56	Jim Palmer	3.00	1.20	.30
□ 57	Jorge Orta	.60	.24	.06
□ 58	Chris Chambliss	.75	.30	.07
□ 59	Dave Chalk	.60	.24	.06
□ 60	Ray Burris	.60	.24	.06

1977 Hostess

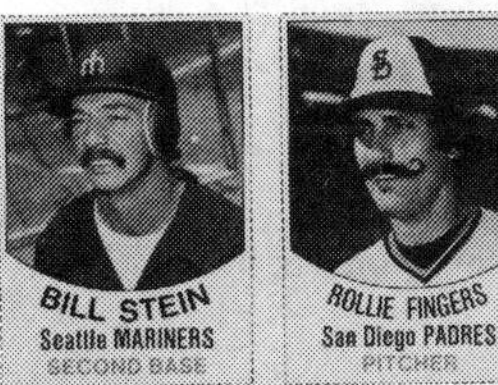

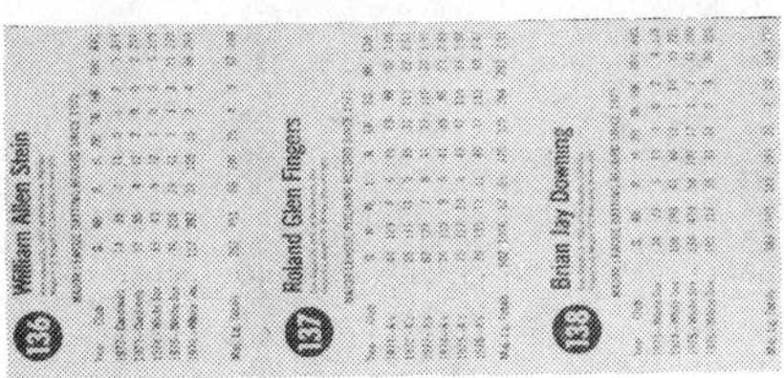

The cards in this 150-card set measure 2 1/4" by 3 1/4" individually or 3 1/4" by 7 1/4" as panels of three. The 1977 Hostess set contains color, numbered cards issued in panels of three cards each with Hostess family sized caked products. Scarcer panels are listed in the checklist below with asterisks. Although complete panel prices are not explicitly listed below, they would generally have a value 25% greater than the sum of the individual players on the panel. There were 10 additional cards proofed, but not produced or distributed; they are 151 Ed Kranepool, 152 Ross Grimsley, 153 Ken Brett, 154 Rowland Office, 155 Rick Wise, 156 Paul Splittorff, 157 Gerald Augustine, 158 Ken Forsch, 159 Jerry Reuss (Reuss is also #119), and 160 Nelson Briles. There is also a cmplete variation set that was available one card per Twinkie package. Common cards in this Twinkie set are worth double the prices listed below, although the stars are only worth about

20% more. The Twinkie cards are distinguished by the thick printing bar or band printed on the card backs just below the statistics.

	NRMT	VG-E	GOOD
COMPLETE INDIV. SET	150.00	60.00	15.00
COMMON PLAYER (1-150)	.30	.12	.03

	NRMT	VG-E	GOOD
□ 1 Jim Palmer	2.50	1.00	.25
□ 2 Joe Morgan	2.00	.80	.20
□ 3 Reggie Jackson	4.50	1.80	.45
□ 4 Carl Yastrzemski	6.00	2.40	.60
□ 5 Thurman Munson	3.50	1.40	.35
□ 6 Johnny Bench	4.00	1.60	.40
□ 7 Tom Seaver	3.50	1.40	.35
□ 8 Pete Rose	8.50	3.50	.85
□ 9 Rod Carew	3.50	1.40	.35
□ 10 Luis Tiant	.50	.20	.05
□ 11 Phil Garner	.30	.12	.03
□ 12 Sixto Lezcano	.30	.12	.03
□ 13 Mike Torrez	.30	.12	.03
□ 14 Dave Lopes	.40	.16	.04
□ 15 Doug DeCinces	.50	.20	.05
□ 16 Jim Spencer	.30	.12	.03
□ 17 Hal McRae	.40	.16	.04
□ 18 Mike Hargrove	.30	.12	.03
□ 19 Willie Montanez *	.40	.16	.04
□ 20 Roger Metzger *	.40	.16	.04
□ 21 Dwight Evans *	1.50	.60	.15
□ 22 Steve Rogers *	.75	.30	.07
□ 23 Jim Rice *	3.50	1.40	.35
□ 24 Pete Falcone *	.40	.16	.04
□ 25 Greg Luzinski *	.80	.32	.08
□ 26 Randy Jones *	.50	.20	.05
□ 27 Willie Stargell *	3.00	1.20	.30
□ 28 John Hiller *	.40	.16	.04
□ 29 Bobby Murcer *	.50	.20	.05
□ 30 Rick Monday *	.50	.20	.05
□ 31 John Montefusco *	.40	.16	.04
□ 32 Lou Brock *	3.00	1.20	.30
□ 33 Bill North *	.40	.16	.04
□ 34 Robin Yount *	3.00	1.20	.30
□ 35 Steve Garvey *	5.00	2.00	.50
□ 36 George Brett *	6.50	2.60	.65
□ 37 Toby Harrah *	.50	.20	.05
□ 38 Jerry Royster *	.40	.16	.04
□ 39 Bob Watson *	.40	.16	.04
□ 40 George Foster	.80	.32	.08
□ 41 Gary Carter	4.00	1.60	.40
□ 42 John Denny	.40	.16	.04
□ 43 Mike Schmidt	4.50	1.80	.45
□ 44 Dave Winfield	3.00	1.20	.30
□ 45 Al Oliver	.75	.30	.07
□ 46 Mark Fidrych	.50	.20	.05
□ 47 Larry Herndon	.30	.12	.03
□ 48 Dave Goltz	.30	.12	.03
□ 49 Jerry Morales	.30	.12	.03
□ 50 Ron LeFlore	.40	.16	.04
□ 51 Fred Lynn	1.00	.40	.10
□ 52 Vida Blue	.40	.16	.04
□ 53 Rick Manning	.30	.12	.03
□ 54 Bill Buckner	.50	.20	.05
□ 55 Lee May	.40	.16	.04
□ 56 John Mayberry	.40	.16	.04
□ 57 Darrell Chaney	.30	.12	.03
□ 58 Cesar Cedeno	.40	.16	.04
□ 59 Ken Griffey	.40	.16	.04
□ 60 Dave Kingman	.60	.24	.06
□ 61 Ted Simmons	.75	.30	.07
□ 62 Larry Bowa	.60	.24	.06
□ 63 Frank Tanana	.40	.16	.04
□ 64 Jason Thompson	.40	.16	.04
□ 65 Ken Brett	.30	.12	.03
□ 66 Roy Smalley	.40	.16	.04
□ 67 Ray Burris	.30	.12	.03
□ 68 Rick Burleson	.40	.16	.04
□ 69 Buddy Bell	.50	.20	.05
□ 70 Don Sutton	2.00	.80	.20
□ 71 Mark Belanger	.40	.16	.04
□ 72 Dennis Leonard	.40	.16	.04
□ 73 Gaylord Perry	1.50	.60	.15
□ 74 Dick Ruthven	.30	.12	.03
□ 75 Jose Cruz	.50	.20	.05
□ 76 Cesar Geronimo	.30	.12	.03
□ 77 Jerry Koosman	.50	.20	.05
□ 78 Garry Templeton	.80	.32	.08
□ 79 Jim Hunter	2.00	.80	.20
□ 80 John Candelaria	.50	.20	.05
□ 81 Nolan Ryan	4.00	1.60	.40
□ 82 Rusty Staub	.60	.24	.06
□ 83 Jim Barr	.30	.12	.03
□ 84 Butch Wynegar	.40	.16	.04
□ 85 Jose Cardenal	.30	.12	.03
□ 86 Claudell Washington	.50	.20	.05
□ 87 Bill Travers	.30	.12	.03
□ 88 Rick Waits	.30	.12	.03
□ 89 Ron Cey	.50	.20	.05
□ 90 Al Bumbry	.30	.12	.03
□ 91 Bucky Dent	.50	.20	.05
□ 92 Amos Otis	.40	.16	.04
□ 93 Tom Grieve	.40	.16	.04
□ 94 Enos Cabell	.30	.12	.03
□ 95 Dave Concepcion	.50	.20	.05
□ 96 Felix Millan	.30	.12	.03
□ 97 Bake McBride	.30	.12	.03
□ 98 Chris Chambliss	.40	.16	.04
□ 99 Butch Metzger	.30	.12	.03
□ 100 Rennie Stennett	.30	.12	.03
□ 101 Dave Roberts	.30	.12	.03
□ 102 Lyman Bostock	.40	.16	.04
□ 103 Rick Reuschel	.50	.20	.05
□ 104 Carlton Fisk	.80	.32	.08
□ 105 Jim Slaton	.30	.12	.03
□ 106 Dennis Eckersley	.75	.30	.07
□ 107 Ken Singleton	.50	.20	.05
□ 108 Ralph Garr	.30	.12	.03
□ 109 Freddie Patek *	.40	.16	.04
□ 110 Jim Sundberg *	.40	.16	.04
□ 111 Phil Niekro *	2.00	.80	.20
□ 112 J.R. Richard *	.50	.20	.05
□ 113 Gary Nolan *	.40	.16	.04
□ 114 Jon Matlack *	.50	.20	.05
□ 115 Keith Hernandez *	4.00	1.60	.40
□ 116 Graig Nettles *	1.00	.40	.10
□ 117 Steve Carlton *	3.50	1.40	.35
□ 118 Bill Madlock *	1.25	.50	.12
□ 119 Jerry Reuss *	.50	.20	.05
□ 120 Aurelio Rodriguez *	.40	.16	.04
□ 121 Dan Ford *	.40	.16	.04
□ 122 Ray Fosse *	.40	.16	.04
□ 123 George Hendrick *	.50	.20	.05
□ 124 Alan Ashby	.30	.12	.03
□ 125 Joe Lis	.30	.12	.03
□ 126 Sal Bando	.40	.16	.04
□ 127 Richie Zisk	.40	.16	.04
□ 128 Rich Gossage	.75	.30	.07
□ 129 Don Baylor	.50	.20	.05
□ 130 Dave McKay	.30	.12	.03
□ 131 Bob Grich	.40	.16	.04
□ 132 Dave Pagan	.30	.12	.03
□ 133 Dave Cash	.30	.12	.03
□ 134 Steve Braun	.30	.12	.03
□ 135 Dan Meyer	.30	.12	.03
□ 136 Bill Stein	.30	.12	.03
□ 137 Rollie Fingers	1.25	.50	.12
□ 138 Brian Downing	.50	.20	.05
□ 139 Bill Singer	.30	.12	.03
□ 140 Doyle Alexander	.50	.20	.05
□ 141 Gene Tenace	.30	.12	.03
□ 142 Gary Matthews	.40	.16	.04
□ 143 Don Gullett	.40	.16	.04
□ 144 Wayne Garland	.30	.12	.03
□ 145 Pete Broberg	.30	.12	.03
□ 146 Joe Rudi	.40	.16	.04
□ 147 Glenn Abbott	.30	.12	.03
□ 148 George Scott	.30	.12	.03
□ 149 Bert Campaneris	.40	.16	.04
□ 150 Andy Messersmith	.40	.16	.04

1978 Hostess

The cards in this 150-card set measure 2 1/4" by 3 1/4" individually or 3 1/4" by 7 1/4" as panels of three. The 1978 Hostess set contains full color, numbered cards issued in panels of three cards each on family packages of Hostess cake products. Scarcer panels are listed in the checklist with asterisks. The 1978 Hostess panels are considered by some collectors to be somewhat more difficult to obtain than Hostess panels of other years. Although complete panel prices are not explicitly listed below, they would generally have a value 25% greater than the sum of the individual players on the panel. There is additional interest in Eddie Murray #31 since this card corresponds to his "rookie' year in cards.

	NRMT	VG-E	GOOD
COMPLETE INDIV. SET	150.00	60.00	15.00
COMMON PLAYER (1-150)	.30	.12	.03

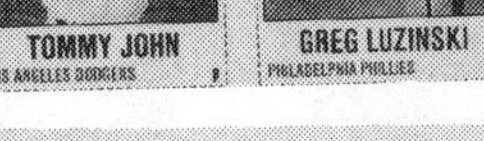

□	1	Butch Hobson	.30	.12	.03
□	2	George Foster	.80	.32	.08
□	3	Bob Forsch	.40	.16	.04
□	4	Tony Perez	.75	.30	.07
□	5	Bruce Sutter	.80	.32	.08
□	6	Hal McRae	.40	.16	.04
□	7	Tommy John	.90	.36	.09
□	8	Greg Luzinski	.50	.20	.05
□	9	Enos Cabell	.30	.12	.03
□	10	Doug DeCinces	.50	.20	.05
□	11	Willie Stargell	2.00	.80	.20
□	12	Ed Halicki	.30	.12	.03
□	13	Larry Hisle	.40	.16	.04
□	14	Jim Slaton	.30	.12	.03
□	15	Buddy Bell	.50	.20	.05
□	16	Earl Williams	.30	.12	.03
□	17	Glenn Abbott	.30	.12	.03
□	18	Dan Ford	.30	.12	.03
□	19	Gary Matthews	.40	.16	.04
□	20	Eric Soderholm	.30	.12	.03
□	21	Bump Wills	.30	.12	.03
□	22	Keith Hernandez	2.50	1.00	.25
□	23	Dave Cash	.30	.12	.03
□	24	George Scott	.30	.12	.03
□	25	Ron Guidry	1.50	.60	.15
□	26	Dave Kingman	.60	.24	.06
□	27	George Brett	5.00	2.00	.50
□	28	Bob Watson *	.40	.16	.04
□	29	Bob Boone *	.75	.30	.07
□	30	Reggie Smith *	.60	.24	.06
□	31	Eddie Murray *	11.00	4.50	1.10
□	32	Gary Lavelle *	.40	.16	.04
□	33	Rennie Stennett *	.40	.16	.04
□	34	Duane Kuiper *	.40	.16	.04
□	35	Sixto Lezcano *	.40	.16	.04
□	36	Dave Rozema *	.40	.16	.04
□	37	Butch Wynegar *	.50	.20	.05
□	38	Mitchell Page *	.40	.16	.04
□	39	Bill Stein *	.40	.16	.04
□	40	Elliott Maddox	.30	.12	.03
□	41	Mike Hargrove	.40	.16	.04
□	42	Bobby Bonds	.50	.20	.05
□	43	Garry Templeton	.50	.20	.05
□	44	Johnny Bench	4.00	1.60	.40
□	45	Jim Rice	3.00	1.20	.30
□	46	Bill Buckner	.50	.20	.05
□	47	Reggie Jackson	4.00	1.60	.40
□	48	Freddie Patek	.30	.12	.03
□	49	Steve Carlton	3.50	1.40	.35
□	50	Cesar Cedeno	.40	.16	.04
□	51	Steve Yeager	.30	.12	.03
□	52	Phil Garner	.30	.12	.03
□	53	Lee May	.40	.16	.04
□	54	Darrell Evans	.60	.24	.06
□	55	Steve Kemp	.40	.16	.04
□	56	Dusty Baker	.40	.16	.04
□	57	Ray Fosse	.30	.12	.03
□	58	Manny Sanguillen	.40	.16	.04
□	59	Tom Johnson	.30	.12	.03
□	60	Lee Stanton	.30	.12	.03
□	61	Jeff Burroughs	.40	.16	.04
□	62	Bobby Grich	.40	.16	.04
□	63	Dave Winfield	3.00	1.20	.30
□	64	Dan Driessen	.40	.16	.04
□	65	Ted Simmons	.75	.30	.07
□	66	Jerry Remy	.30	.12	.03
□	67	Al Cowens	.40	.16	.04
□	68	Sparky Lyle	.60	.24	.06
□	69	Manny Trillo	.40	.16	.04
□	70	Don Sutton	2.00	.80	.20
□	71	Larry Bowa	.60	.24	.06
□	72	Jose Cruz	.50	.20	.05
□	73	Willie McCovey	2.00	.80	.20
□	74	Bert Blyleven	.60	.24	.06
□	75	Ken Singleton	.50	.20	.05
□	76	Bill North	.30	.12	.03
□	77	Jason Thompson	.40	.16	.04
□	78	Dennis Eckersley	.60	.24	.06
□	79	Jim Sundberg	.40	.16	.04
□	80	Jerry Koosman	.50	.20	.05
□	81	Bruce Bochte	.30	.12	.03
□	82	George Hendrick	.40	.16	.04
□	83	Nolan Ryan	3.50	1.40	.35
□	84	Roy Howell	.30	.12	.03
□	85	Roger Metzger	.30	.12	.03
□	86	Doc Medich	.30	.12	.03
□	87	Joe Morgan	2.00	.80	.20
□	88	Dennis Leonard	.40	.16	.04
□	89	Willie Randolph	.75	.30	.07
□	90	Bobby Murcer	.50	.20	.05
□	91	Rick Manning	.30	.12	.03
□	92	J.R. Richard	.40	.16	.04
□	93	Ron Cey	.50	.20	.05
□	94	Sal Bando	.40	.16	.04
□	95	Ron LeFlore	.40	.16	.04
□	96	Dave Goltz	.30	.12	.03
□	97	Dan Meyer	.30	.12	.03
□	98	Chris Chambliss	.40	.16	.04
□	99	Biff Pocoroba	.30	.12	.03
□	100	Oscar Gamble	.40	.16	.04
□	101	Frank Tanana	.40	.16	.04
□	102	Len Randle	.30	.12	.03
□	103	Tommy Hutton	.30	.12	.03
□	104	John Candelaria	.50	.20	.05
□	105	George Orta	.30	.12	.03
□	106	Ken Reitz	.30	.12	.03
□	107	Bill Campbell	.30	.12	.03
□	108	Dave Concepcion	.50	.20	.05
□	109	Joe Ferguson	.30	.12	.03
□	110	Mickey Rivers	.40	.16	.04
□	111	Paul Splittorff	.40	.16	.04
□	112	Dave Lopes	.50	.20	.05
□	113	Mike Schmidt	5.00	2.00	.50
□	114	Joe Rudi	.40	.16	.04
□	115	Milt May	.30	.12	.03
□	116	Jim Palmer	2.00	.80	.20
□	117	Bill Madlock	.80	.32	.08
□	118	Roy Smalley	.40	.16	.04
□	119	Cecil Cooper	.90	.36	.09
□	120	Rick Langford	.30	.12	.03
□	121	Ruppert Jones	.40	.16	.04
□	122	Phil Niekro	1.50	.60	.15
□	123	Toby Harrah	.40	.16	.04
□	124	Chet Lemon	.40	.16	.04
□	125	Gene Tenace	.30	.12	.03
□	126	Steve Henderson	.30	.12	.03
□	127	Mike Torrez	.30	.12	.03
□	128	Pete Rose	8.50	3.50	.85
□	129	John Denny	.40	.16	.04
□	130	Darrell Porter	.40	.16	.04
□	131	Rick Reuschel	.50	.20	.05
□	132	Graig Nettles	.75	.30	.07
□	133	Garry Maddox	.40	.16	.04
□	134	Mike Flanagan	.40	.16	.04
□	135	Dave Parker	1.75	.70	.17
□	136	Terry Whitfield	.30	.12	.03
□	137	Wayne Garland	.30	.12	.03
□	138	Robin Yount	3.00	1.20	.30
□	139	Gaylord Perry	1.50	.60	.15
□	140	Rod Carew	3.50	1.40	.35
□	141	Greg Gross	.30	.12	.03
□	142	Barry Bonnell	.30	.12	.03
□	143	Willie Montanez	.30	.12	.03
□	144	Rollie Fingers	1.25	.50	.12
□	145	Lyman Bostock	.40	.16	.04
□	146	Gary Carter	3.50	1.40	.35
□	147	Ron Blomberg	.30	.12	.03
□	148	Bob Bailor	.30	.12	.03
□	149	Tom Seaver	3.50	1.40	.35
□	150	Thurman Munson	3.00	1.20	.30

1979 Hostess

The cards in this 150-card set measure 3 1/4" by 7 1/4" as panels of three. The 1979 Hostess set contains full color, numbered cards issued in panels of three cards each on the backs of family sized Hostess cake products. Scarcer panels are listed in

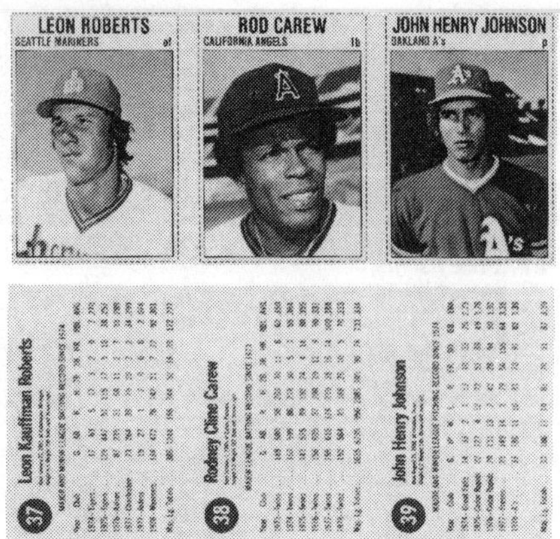

the checklist below with asterisks. Although complete panel prices are not explicitly listed below they would generally have a value 25% greater than the sum of the individual players on the panel. There is additional interest in Ozzie Smith #102 since this card corresponds to his "rookie' year in cards.

	NRMT	VG-E	GOOD
COMPLETE INDIV. SET	150.00	60.00	15.00
COMMON PLAYER (1-150)	.30	.12	.03
□ 1 John Denny	.40	.16	.04
□ 2 Jim Rice	3.00	1.20	.30
□ 3 Doug Bair	.30	.12	.03
□ 4 Darrell Porter	.40	.16	.04
□ 5 Ross Grimsley	.30	.12	.03
□ 6 Bobby Murcer	.50	.20	.05
□ 7 Lee Mazzilli	.30	.12	.03
□ 8 Steve Garvey	3.50	1.40	.35
□ 9 Mike Schmidt	4.50	1.80	.45
□ 10 Terry Whitfield	.30	.12	.03
□ 11 Jim Palmer	2.50	1.00	.25
□ 12 Omar Moreno	.30	.12	.03
□ 13 Duane Kuiper	.30	.12	.03
□ 14 Mike Caldwell	.40	.16	.04
□ 15 Steve Kemp	.40	.16	.04
□ 16 Dave Goltz	.30	.12	.03
□ 17 Mitchell Page	.30	.12	.03
□ 18 Bill Stein	.30	.12	.03
□ 19 Gene Tenace	.40	.16	.04
□ 20 Jeff Burroughs	.40	.16	.04
□ 21 Francisco Barrios	.30	.12	.03
□ 22 Mike Torrez	.30	.12	.03
□ 23 Ken Reitz	.30	.12	.03
□ 24 Gary Carter	3.50	1.40	.35
□ 25 Al Hrabosky	.40	.16	.04
□ 26 Thurman Munson	3.00	1.20	.30
□ 27 Bill Buckner	.50	.20	.05
□ 28 Ron Cey *	.60	.24	.06
□ 29 J.R. Richard *	.40	.16	.04
□ 30 Greg Luzinski *	.80	.32	.08
□ 31 Ed Ott *	.40	.16	.04
□ 32 Dennis Martinez *	.50	.20	.05
□ 33 Darrell Evans *	.60	.24	.06
□ 34 Ron LeFlore	.40	.16	.04
□ 35 Rick Waits	.30	.12	.03
□ 36 Cecil Cooper	.75	.30	.07
□ 37 Leon Roberts	.30	.12	.03
□ 38 Rod Carew	3.00	1.20	.30
□ 39 John Henry Johnson	.30	.12	.03
□ 40 Chet Lemon	.40	.16	.04
□ 41 Craig Swan	.30	.12	.03
□ 42 Gary Matthews	.40	.16	.04
□ 43 Lamar Johnson	.30	.12	.03
□ 44 Ted Simmons	.75	.30	.07
□ 45 Ken Griffey	.40	.16	.04
□ 46 Fred Patek	.30	.12	.03
□ 47 Frank Tanana	.40	.16	.04
□ 48 Goose Gossage	.80	.32	.08
□ 49 Burt Hooton	.30	.12	.03
□ 50 Ellis Valentine	.30	.12	.03
□ 51 Ken Forsch	.30	.12	.03
□ 52 Bob Knepper	.50	.20	.05
□ 53 Dave Parker	1.75	.70	.17
□ 54 Doug DeCinces	.50	.20	.05
□ 55 Robin Yount	3.00	1.20	.30
□ 56 Rusty Staub	.50	.20	.05
□ 57 Gary Alexander	.30	.12	.03
□ 58 Julio Cruz	.30	.12	.03
□ 59 Matt Keough	.30	.12	.03
□ 60 Roy Smalley	.30	.12	.03
□ 61 Joe Morgan	2.00	.80	.20
□ 62 Phil Niekro	2.00	.80	.20
□ 63 Don Baylor	.50	.20	.05
□ 64 Dwight Evans	.75	.30	.07
□ 65 Tom Seaver	3.00	1.20	.30
□ 66 George Hendrick	.40	.16	.04
□ 67 Rick Reuschel	.50	.20	.05
□ 68 George Brett	5.00	2.00	.50
□ 69 Lou Piniella	.50	.20	.05
□ 70 Enos Cabell	.30	.12	.03
□ 71 Steve Carlton	3.00	1.20	.30
□ 72 Reggie Smith	.50	.20	.05
□ 73 Rick Dempsey *	.50	.20	.05
□ 74 Vida Blue *	.50	.20	.05
□ 75 Phil Garner *	.40	.16	.04
□ 76 Rick Manning *	.40	.16	.04
□ 77 Mark Fidrych *	.50	.20	.05
□ 78 Mario Guerrero *	.40	.16	.04
□ 79 Bob Stinson *	.40	.16	.04
□ 80 Al Oliver *	.90	.36	.09
□ 81 Doug Flynn *	.40	.16	.04
□ 82 John Mayberry	.40	.16	.04
□ 83 Gaylord Perry	1.50	.60	.15
□ 84 Joe Rudi	.40	.16	.04
□ 85 Dave Concepcion	.50	.20	.05
□ 86 John Candelaria	.40	.16	.04
□ 87 Pete Vuckovich	.40	.16	.04
□ 88 Ivan DeJesus	.30	.12	.03
□ 89 Ron Guidry	1.50	.60	.15
□ 90 Hal McRae	.40	.16	.04
□ 91 Cesar Cedeno	.40	.16	.04
□ 92 Don Sutton	2.00	.80	.20
□ 93 Andre Thornton	.40	.16	.04
□ 94 Roger Erickson	.30	.12	.03
□ 95 Larry Hisle	.40	.16	.04
□ 96 Jason Thompson	.40	.16	.04
□ 97 Jim Sundberg	.40	.16	.04
□ 98 Bob Horner	2.00	.80	.20
□ 99 Ruppert Jones	.40	.16	.04
□ 100 Willie Montanez	.30	.12	.03
□ 101 Nolan Ryan	3.00	1.20	.30
□ 102 Ozzie Smith	6.50	2.60	.65
□ 103 Eric Soderholm	.30	.12	.03
□ 104 Willie Stargell	2.00	.80	.20
□ 105A Bob Bailor ERR (reverse negative)	.50	.20	.05
□ 105B Bob Bailor COR	.75	.30	.07
□ 106 Carlton Fisk	.90	.36	.09
□ 107 George Foster	.80	.32	.08
□ 108 Keith Hernandez	2.50	1.00	.25
□ 109 Dennis Leonard	.40	.16	.04
□ 110 Graig Nettles	.75	.30	.07
□ 111 Jose Cruz	.40	.16	.04
□ 112 Bobby Grich	.40	.16	.04
□ 113 Bob Boone	.60	.24	.06
□ 114 Dave Lopes	.40	.16	.04
□ 115 Eddie Murray	5.00	2.00	.50
□ 116 Jack Clark	2.50	1.00	.25
□ 117 Lou Whitaker	1.50	.60	.15
□ 118 Miguel Dilone	.30	.12	.03
□ 119 Sal Bando	.40	.16	.04
□ 120 Reggie Jackson	4.00	1.60	.40
□ 121 Dale Murphy	9.00	3.75	.90
□ 122 Jon Matlack	.40	.16	.04
□ 123 Bruce Bochte	.30	.12	.03
□ 124 John Stearns	.30	.12	.03
□ 125 Dave Winfield	3.00	1.20	.30
□ 126 Jorge Orta	.30	.12	.03
□ 127 Garry Templeton	.40	.16	.04
□ 128 Johnny Bench	3.50	1.40	.35
□ 129 Butch Hobson	.30	.12	.03
□ 130 Bruce Sutter	1.00	.40	.10
□ 131 Bucky Dent	.40	.16	.04
□ 132 Amos Otis	.40	.16	.04
□ 133 Bert Blyleven	.50	.20	.05
□ 134 Larry Bowa	.50	.20	.05
□ 135 Ken Singleton	.50	.20	.05
□ 136 Sixto Lezcano	.30	.12	.03
□ 137 Roy Howell	.30	.12	.03
□ 138 Bill Madlock	.80	.32	.08
□ 139 Dave Revering	.30	.12	.03
□ 140 Richie Zisk	.40	.16	.04
□ 141 Butch Wynegar	.40	.16	.04
□ 142 Alan Ashby	.30	.12	.03
□ 143 Sparky Lyle	.50	.20	.05
□ 144 Pete Rose	8.50	3.50	.85
□ 145 Dennis Eckersley	.60	.24	.06
□ 146 Dave Kingman	.60	.24	.06
□ 147 Buddy Bell	.50	.20	.05
□ 148 Mike Hargrove	.40	.16	.04
□ 149 Jerry Koosman	.50	.20	.05
□ 150 Toby Harrah	.40	.16	.04

1985 Hostess Braves

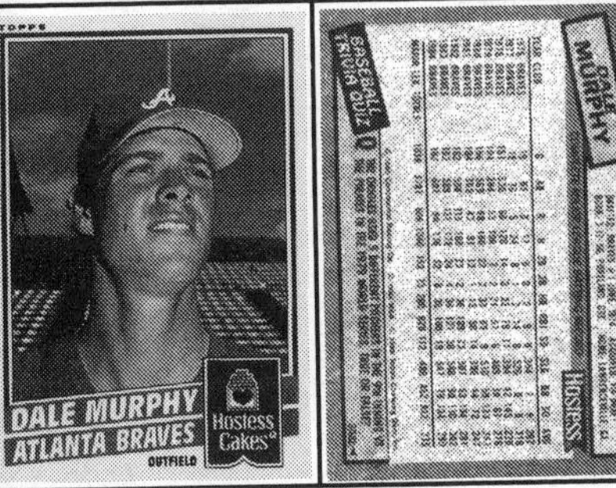

The cards in this 22-card set measure 2 1/2" by 3 1/2" and feature players of the Atlanta Braves. Cards were produced by Topps for Hostess (Continental Baking Co.) and are quite attractive. The card backs are similar in design to the 1985 Topps regular issue; however all photos are different from those that Topps used as these were apparently taken during Spring Training. Cards were available in boxes of Hostess products in packs of four (three players and a contest card).

	MINT	EXC	G-VG
COMPLETE SET (22)	8.00	3.25	.80
COMMON PLAYER (1-22)	.25	.10	.02
☐ 1 Eddie Haas MG	.25	.10	.02
☐ 2 Len Barker	.25	.10	.02
☐ 3 Steve Bedrosian	.60	.24	.06
☐ 4 Bruce Benedict	.25	.10	.02
☐ 5 Rick Camp	.25	.10	.02
☐ 6 Rick Cerone	.25	.10	.02
☐ 7 Chris Chambliss	.35	.14	.03
☐ 8 Terry Forster	.50	.20	.05
☐ 9 Gene Garber	.25	.10	.02
☐ 10 Albert Hall	.25	.10	.02
☐ 11 Bob Horner	.75	.30	.07
☐ 12 Glenn Hubbard	.35	.14	.03
☐ 13 Brad Komminsk	.25	.10	.02
☐ 14 Rick Mahler	.35	.14	.03
☐ 15 Craig McMurtry	.25	.10	.02
☐ 16 Dale Murphy	4.00	1.60	.40
☐ 17 Ken Oberkfell	.25	.10	.02
☐ 18 Pascual Perez	.35	.14	.03
☐ 19 Gerald Perry	.50	.20	.05
☐ 20 Rafael Ramirez	.25	.10	.02
☐ 21 Bruce Sutter	.60	.24	.06
☐ 22 Claudell Washington	.50	.20	.05

1953 Johnston Cookies

The cards in this 25-card set measure 2 9/16" by 3 5/8". The 1953 Johnston's Cookies set of numbered cards features Milwaukee Braves players only. This set is the most plentiful of the three Johnston's Cookies sets and no known scarcities exist. The ACC designation for this set is D356-1.

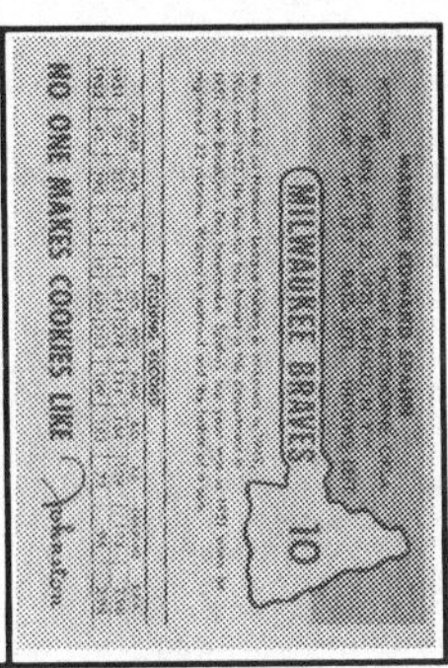

	NRMT	VG-E	GOOD
COMPLETE SET (25)	200.00	80.00	20.00
COMMON PLAYER (1-25)	6.00	2.40	.60
☐ 1 Charlie Grimm MG	7.00	2.80	.70
☐ 2 John Antonelli	7.00	2.80	.70
☐ 3 Vern Bickford	6.00	2.40	.60
☐ 4 Bob Buhl	6.00	2.40	.60
☐ 5 Lew Burdette	11.00	4.50	1.10
☐ 6 Dave Cole	6.00	2.40	.60
☐ 7 Ernie Johnson	6.00	2.40	.60
☐ 8 Dave Jolly	6.00	2.40	.60
☐ 9 Don Liddle	6.00	2.40	.60
☐ 10 Warren Spahn	32.00	13.00	3.20
☐ 11 Max Surkont	6.00	2.40	.60
☐ 12 Jim Wilson	6.00	2.40	.60
☐ 13 Sibbi Sisti	6.00	2.40	.60
☐ 14 Walker Cooper	6.00	2.40	.60
☐ 15 Del Crandall	7.00	2.80	.70
☐ 16 Ebba St.Claire	6.00	2.40	.60
☐ 17 Joe Adcock	8.00	3.25	.80
☐ 18 George Crowe	6.00	2.40	.60
☐ 19 Jack Dittmer	6.00	2.40	.60
☐ 20 Johnny Logan	7.00	2.80	.70
☐ 21 Ed Mathews	32.00	13.00	3.20
☐ 22 Bill Bruton	7.00	2.80	.70
☐ 23 Sid Gordon	6.00	2.40	.60
☐ 24 Andy Pafko	6.00	2.40	.60
☐ 25 Jim Pendleton	6.00	2.40	.60

1954 Johnston Cookies

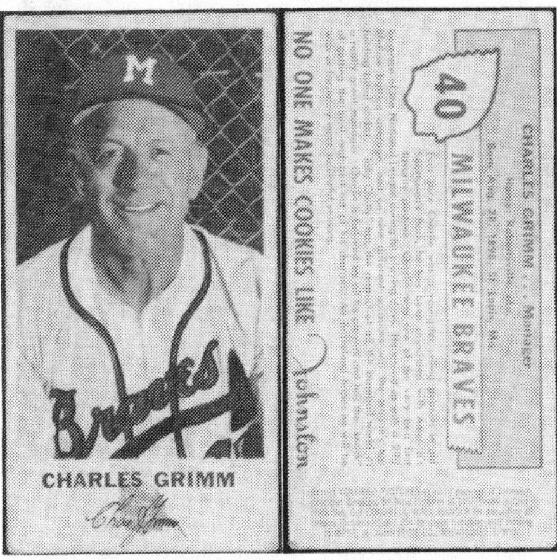

The cards in this 35-card set measure 2" by 3 7/8". The 1954 Johnston's Cookies set of color cards of Milwaukee Braves are numbered according to the player's uniform number, except for the non-players, Lacks and Taylor, who are found at the end of the set. The Bobby Thomson card was withdrawn early in the year after his injury and is scarce. The ACC catalog number for this set is D356-2.

	NRMT	VG-E	GOOD
COMPLETE SET (35)	700.00	320.00	90.00
COMMON PLAYER (1-50)	9.00	3.75	.90
☐ 1 Del Crandall	11.00	4.50	1.10
☐ 3 Jim Pendleton	9.00	3.75	.90
☐ 4 Danny O'Connell	9.00	3.75	.90
☐ 5 Hank Aaron	250.00	100.00	25.00

☐ 6 Jack Dittmer	9.00	3.75	.90
☐ 9 Joe Adcock	11.00	4.50	1.10
☐ 10 Bob Buhl	9.00	3.75	.90
☐ 11 Phil Paine	9.00	3.75	.90
☐ 12 Ben Johnson	9.00	3.75	.90
☐ 13 Sibbi Sisti	9.00	3.75	.90
☐ 15 Charles Gorin	9.00	3.75	.90
☐ 16 Chet Nichols	9.00	3.75	.90
☐ 17 Dave Jolly	9.00	3.75	.90
☐ 19 Jim Wilson	9.00	3.75	.90
☐ 20 Ray Crone	9.00	3.75	.90
☐ 21 Warren Spahn	40.00	16.00	4.00
☐ 22 Gene Conley	9.00	3.75	.90
☐ 23 Johnny Logan	11.00	4.50	1.10
☐ 24 Charlie White	9.00	3.75	.90
☐ 27 George Metkovich	9.00	3.75	.90
☐ 28 Johnny Cooney	9.00	3.75	.90
☐ 29 Paul Burris	9.00	3.75	.90
☐ 31 Bucky Walters	11.00	4.50	1.10
☐ 32 Ernie Johnson	9.00	3.75	.90
☐ 33 Lou Burdette	16.00	6.50	1.60
☐ 34 Bob Thomson	175.00	70.00	18.00
☐ 35 Bob Keely	9.00	3.75	.90
☐ 38 Bill Bruton	11.00	4.50	1.10
☐ 40 Charlie Grimm MG	11.00	4.50	1.10
☐ 41 Eddie Mathews	40.00	16.00	4.00
☐ 42 Sam Calderone	9.00	3.75	.90
☐ 47 Joey Jay	9.00	3.75	.90
☐ 48 Andy Pafko	9.00	3.75	.90
☐ 49 Dr. Charles Lacks (unnumbered)	9.00	3.75	.90
☐ 50 Joseph F. Taylor (unnumbered)	9.00	3.75	.90

1955 Johnston Cookies

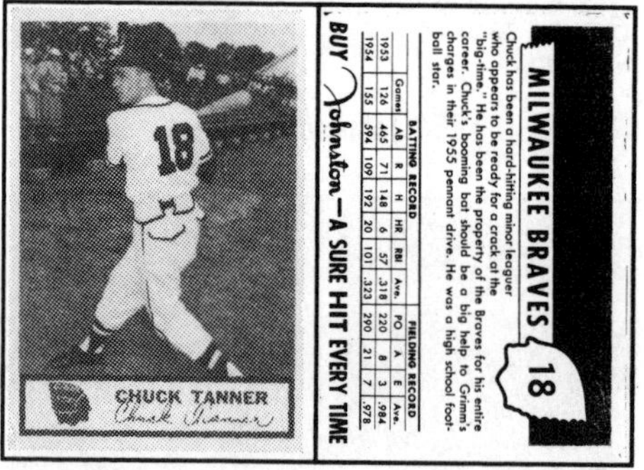

The cards in this 35-card set measure 2 3/4" by 4". This set of Milwaukee Braves issued in 1955 by Johnston Cookies are numbered by the uniform number of the player depicted, except for non-players Lacks, Lewis and Taylor. The cards were issued in strips of six which accounts for the rouletted edges found on single cards. They are larger in size than the two previous sets but are printed on thinner cardboard. Each player in the checklist has been marked to show on which panel or strip he appeared (Pafko appears twice). A complete panel of six cards is worth 25% more than the sum of the individual players. The ACC designation for this set is D356- 3.

	NRMT	VG-E	GOOD
COMPLETE SET (35)	750.00	300.00	75.00
COMMON PLAYER (1-51)	15.00	6.00	1.50
☐ 1 Del Crandall P1	18.00	7.25	1.80
☐ 3 Jim Pendleton P3	15.00	6.00	1.50
☐ 4 Danny O'Connell P1	15.00	6.00	1.50
☐ 6 Jack Dittmer P6	15.00	6.00	1.50
☐ 9 Joe Adcock P2	18.00	7.25	1.80
☐ 10 Bob Buhl P6	15.00	6.00	1.50
☐ 11 Phil Paine P5	15.00	6.00	1.50
☐ 12 Ray Crone P5	15.00	6.00	1.50
☐ 15 Charlie Gorin P1	15.00	6.00	1.50
☐ 16 Dave Jolly P4	15.00	6.00	1.50
☐ 17 Chet Nichols P2	15.00	6.00	1.50
☐ 18 Chuck Tanner P5	21.00	8.50	2.10
☐ 19 Jim Wilson P6	15.00	6.00	1.50
☐ 20 Dave Koslo P4	15.00	6.00	1.50
☐ 21 Warren Spahn P3	55.00	22.00	5.50
☐ 22 Gene Conley P3	15.00	6.00	1.50
☐ 23 Johnny Logan P4	18.00	7.25	1.80
☐ 24 Charlie White P2	15.00	6.00	1.50
☐ 28 Johnny Cooney P4	15.00	6.00	1.50
☐ 30 Roy Smalley P3	15.00	6.00	1.50
☐ 31 Bucky Walters P6	18.00	7.25	1.80
☐ 32 Ernie Johnson P5	15.00	6.00	1.50
☐ 33 Lew Burdette P1	27.00	11.00	2.70
☐ 34 Bobby Thomson P6	21.00	8.50	2.10
☐ 35 Bob Keely P1	15.00	6.00	1.50
☐ 38 Bill Bruton P4	18.00	7.25	1.80
☐ 39 George Crowe P3	15.00	6.00	1.50
☐ 40 Charlie Grimm MG P6	18.00	7.25	1.80
☐ 41 Eddie Mathews P5	55.00	22.00	5.50
☐ 44 Hank Aaron P1	225.00	90.00	22.00
☐ 47 Joey Jay P2	15.00	6.00	1.50
☐ 48 Andy Pafko P2 P4	15.00	6.00	1.50
☐ 49 Dr. Charles Leaks P2 (unnumbered)	15.00	6.00	1.50
☐ 50 Duffy Lewis P5 (unnumbered)	15.00	6.00	1.50
☐ 51 Joe Taylor P3 (unnumbered)	15.00	6.00	1.50

1955 Kahn's

The cards in this 6-card set measure 3 1/4" by 4". The 1955 Kahn's Wieners set received very limited distribution. The cards were supposedly given away at an amusement park. The set portrays the players in street clothes rather than in uniform and hence are sometimes referred to as "street clothes" Kahn's. All Kahn's sets from 1955 through 1963 are black and white and contain a 1/2" tab. Cards with the tab still intact are worth approximately 50% more than cards without the tab. Cards feature a facsimile autograph of the player on the front. Cards are blank-backed. Cincinnati Redlegs players only are featured.

	NRMT	VG-E	GOOD
COMPLETE SET (6)	2500.00	1100.00	300.00
COMMON PLAYER (1-6)	350.00	140.00	35.00
☐ 1 Gus Bell (street clothes)	600.00	240.00	60.00
☐ 2 Ted Kluszewski (street clothes)	500.00	200.00	50.00
☐ 3 Roy McMillan (street clothes)	350.00	140.00	35.00
☐ 4 Joe Nuxhall (street clothes)	350.00	140.00	35.00
☐ 5 Wally Post (street clothes)	350.00	140.00	35.00
☐ 6 Johnny Temple (street clothes)	350.00	140.00	35.00

1956 Kahn's

The cards in this 15-card set measure 3 1/4" by 4". The 1956 Kahn's set was the first set to be issued with Kahn's meat products. The cards are blank backed. The set is distinguished by the old style, short sleeve shirts on the players and the existence of backgounds (Kahn's cards of later years utilize a blank background). Cards which have the tab still intact are worth approximately 50% more than cards without the tab. Cincinnati Redlegs players only are featured.

	NRMT	VG-E	GOOD
COMPLETE SET (15)	1100.00	500.00	150.00
COMMON PLAYER (1-15)	60.00	24.00	6.00
□ 1 Ed Bailey	60.00	24.00	6.00
□ 2 Gus Bell	75.00	30.00	7.50
□ 3 Joe Black	75.00	30.00	7.50
□ 4 Smoky Burgess	75.00	30.00	7.50
□ 5 Art Fowler	60.00	24.00	6.00
□ 6 Hershel Freeman	60.00	24.00	6.00
□ 7 Ray Jablonski	60.00	24.00	6.00
□ 8 John Klippstein	60.00	24.00	6.00
□ 9 Ted Kluszewski	110.00	45.00	11.00
□ 10 Brooks Lawrence	60.00	24.00	6.00
□ 11 Roy McMillan	60.00	24.00	6.00
□ 12 Joe Nuxhall	75.00	30.00	7.50
□ 13 Wally Post	60.00	24.00	6.00
□ 14 Frank Robinson	225.00	90.00	22.00
□ 15 Johnny Temple	60.00	24.00	6.00

1957 Kahn's

The cards in this 29-card set measure 3 1/4" by 4". The 1957 Kahn's Wieners set contains black and white, blank backed, unnumbered cards. The set features the Cincinnati Redlegs and Pittsburgh Pirates only. The cards feature a light background. Each card features a facsimile autograph of the player on the front. The Groat card exists with a "Richard Groat" autograph and also exists with the printed name "Dick Groat" on the card. The ACC designation is D155-3.

	NRMT	VG-E	GOOD
COMPLETE SET (29)	2000.00	900.00	250.00
COMMON PLAYER (1-29)	50.00	20.00	5.00
□ 1 Tom Acker	50.00	20.00	5.00
□ 2 Ed Bailey	50.00	20.00	5.00
□ 3 Gus Bell	60.00	24.00	6.00
□ 4 Smoky Burgess	60.00	24.00	6.00
□ 5 Robert Clemente	400.00	160.00	40.00
□ 6 George Crowe	50.00	20.00	5.00
□ 7 Elroy Face	75.00	30.00	7.50
□ 8 Hershel Freeman	50.00	20.00	5.00
□ 9 Bob Friend	60.00	24.00	6.00
□ 10 Dick Groat	75.00	30.00	7.50
□ 11 Richard Groat	150.00	60.00	15.00
□ 12 Don Gross	50.00	20.00	5.00
□ 13 Warren Hacker	50.00	20.00	5.00
□ 14 Don Hoak	50.00	20.00	5.00
□ 15 Hal Jeffcoat	50.00	20.00	5.00
□ 16 Ron Kline	50.00	20.00	5.00
□ 17 John Klippstein	50.00	20.00	5.00
□ 18 Ted Kluszewski	100.00	40.00	10.00
□ 19 Brooks Lawrence	50.00	20.00	5.00
□ 20 Dale Long	60.00	24.00	6.00
□ 21 Bill Mazeroski	100.00	40.00	10.00
□ 22 Roy McMillan	50.00	20.00	5.00
□ 23 Joe Nuxhall	60.00	24.00	6.00
□ 24 Wally Post	50.00	20.00	5.00
□ 25 Frank Robinson	175.00	70.00	18.00
□ 26 John Temple	50.00	20.00	5.00
□ 27 Frank Thomas	60.00	24.00	6.00
□ 28 Bob Thurman	50.00	20.00	5.00
□ 29 Lee Walls	50.00	20.00	5.00

1958 Kahn's

IN BASEBALL
LEMENTE
in the majors,
So I arranged
from Puerto
ekend in New
ng to be there
irates playing
didn't get in
venth, when I
te, I could see
watching me
r the first time.
yer to help me
ed one pretty
were two runs
with two men
on base, tying the game up. I'll
always remember the expression of
happiness on my mother's face.
Compliments of Kahn's Wieners
"THE WIENER THE WORLD AWAITED"

The cards in this 29-card set measure 3 1/4" by 4". The 1958 Kahn's Wieners set of unnumbered, black and white cards features Cincinnati Redlegs,

Philadelphia Phillies, and Pittsburgh Pirates. The backs present a story for each player entitled "My Greatest Thrill in Baseball". A method of distinguishing 1958 Kahn's from 1959 Kahn's is that the word Wieners is found on the front of the 1958 but not on the front of the 1959 cards. Cards of Wally Post, Charlie Rabe, and Frank Thomas are somewhat more difficult to find and are marked with an asterisk in the checklist below.

	NRMT	VG-E	GOOD
COMPLETE SET (29)	2500.00	1000.00	300.00
COMMON PLAYER (1-29)	45.00	18.00	4.50
☐ 1 Ed Bailey	45.00	18.00	4.50
☐ 2 Gene Baker	45.00	18.00	4.50
☐ 3 Gus Bell	55.00	22.00	5.50
☐ 4 Smoky Burgess	55.00	22.00	5.50
☐ 5 Roberto Clemente	400.00	160.00	40.00
☐ 6 George Crowe	45.00	18.00	4.50
☐ 7 Elroy Face	70.00	28.00	7.00
☐ 8 Hank Foiles	45.00	18.00	4.50
☐ 9 Dee Fondy	45.00	18.00	4.50
☐ 10 Bob Friend	55.00	22.00	5.50
☐ 11 Dick Groat	70.00	28.00	7.00
☐ 12 Harvey Haddix	55.00	22.00	5.50
☐ 13 Don Hoak	45.00	18.00	4.50
☐ 14 Hal Jeffcoat	45.00	18.00	4.50
☐ 15 Ron Kline	45.00	18.00	4.50
☐ 16 Ted Kluszewski	90.00	36.00	9.00
☐ 17 Vernon Law	55.00	22.00	5.50
☐ 18 Brooks Lawrence	45.00	18.00	4.50
☐ 19 Bill Mazeroski	85.00	34.00	8.50
☐ 20 Roy McMillan	45.00	18.00	4.50
☐ 21 Joe Nuxhall	55.00	22.00	5.50
☐ 22 Wally Post *	250.00	100.00	25.00
☐ 23 John Powers	45.00	18.00	4.50
☐ 24 Bob Purkey	45.00	18.00	4.50
☐ 25 Charlie Rabe *	250.00	100.00	25.00
☐ 26 Frank Robinson	165.00	70.00	15.00
☐ 27 Bob Skinner	45.00	18.00	4.50
☐ 28 Johnny Temple	45.00	18.00	4.50
☐ 29 Frank Thomas *	250.00	100.00	25.00

1959 Kahn's

The cards in this 38-card set measure 3 1/4" by 4". The 1959 Kahn's set features Cincinnati, Cleveland, and Pittsburgh players. The backs feature stories entitled "The Toughest Play I have to Make," or "The Toughest Batter I Have To Face." The Brodowski card is very scarce while Haddix, Held and McLish are considered quite difficult to obtain; these scarcities are the asterisked cards in the checklist below.

	NRMT	VG-E	GOOD
COMPLETE SET (38)	3000.00	1200.00	350.00
COMMON PLAYER (1-38)	40.00	16.00	4.00
☐ 1 Ed Bailey	40.00	16.00	4.00
☐ 2 Gary Bell	40.00	16.00	4.00
☐ 3 Gus Bell	45.00	18.00	4.50
☐ 4 Dick Brodowski *	400.00	160.00	40.00
☐ 5 Smoky Burgess	45.00	18.00	4.50
☐ 6 Roberto Clemente	350.00	140.00	35.00
☐ 7 Rocky Colavito	75.00	30.00	7.50
☐ 8 Elroy Face	50.00	20.00	5.00
☐ 9 Bob Friend	45.00	18.00	4.50
☐ 10 Joe Gordon	45.00	18.00	4.50
☐ 11 Jim Grant	40.00	16.00	4.00
☐ 12 Dick Groat	60.00	24.00	6.00
☐ 13 Harvey Haddix * (blank back)	300.00	120.00	30.00
☐ 14 Woodie Held *	300.00	120.00	30.00
☐ 15 Don Hoak	40.00	16.00	4.00
☐ 16 Ron Kline	40.00	16.00	4.00
☐ 17 Ted Kluszewski	75.00	30.00	7.50
☐ 18 Vernon Law	45.00	18.00	4.50
☐ 19 Jerry Lynch	40.00	16.00	4.00
☐ 20 Billy Martin	90.00	36.00	9.00
☐ 21 Bill Mazeroski	75.00	30.00	7.50
☐ 22 Cal McLish *	300.00	120.00	30.00
☐ 23 Roy McMillan	40.00	16.00	4.00
☐ 24 Minnie Minoso	60.00	24.00	6.00
☐ 25 Russ Nixon	45.00	18.00	4.50
☐ 26 Joe Nuxhall	45.00	18.00	4.50
☐ 27 Jim Perry	45.00	18.00	4.50
☐ 28 Vada Pinson	60.00	24.00	6.00
☐ 29 Vic Power	40.00	16.00	4.00
☐ 30 Bob Purkey	40.00	16.00	4.00
☐ 31 Frank Robinson	150.00	60.00	15.00
☐ 32 Herb Score	60.00	24.00	6.00
☐ 33 Bob Skinner	40.00	16.00	4.00
☐ 34 George Strickland	40.00	16.00	4.00
☐ 35 Dick Stuart	45.00	18.00	4.50
☐ 36 Johnny Temple	40.00	16.00	4.00
☐ 37 Frank Thomas	45.00	18.00	4.50
☐ 38 George Witt	40.00	16.00	4.00

1960 Kahn's

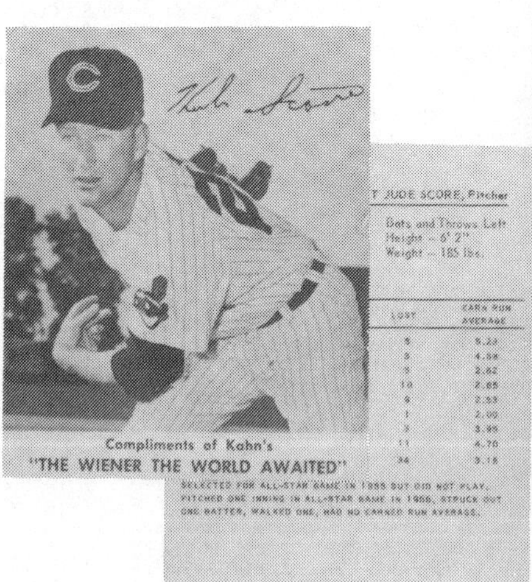

The cards in this 42-card set measure 3 1/4" by 4". The 1960 Kahn's set features players of the Chicago Cubs, Chicago White Sox, Cincinnati Redlegs, Cleveland Indians, Pittsburgh Pirates, and St. Louis Cardinals. The backs give vital player information and records through the 1959 season. Kline appears with either St. Louis or Pittsburgh. The Harvey Kuenn card (asterisked below) appears with a blank back, and is scarce.

	NRMT	VG-E	GOOD
COMPLETE SET (42)	1400.00	650.00	150.00
COMMON PLAYER (1-42)	20.00	8.00	2.00

□ 1 Ed Bailey	20.00	8.00	2.00
□ 2 Gary Bell	20.00	8.00	2.00
□ 3 Gus Bell	24.00	10.00	2.40
□ 4 Smoky Burgess	24.00	10.00	2.40
□ 5 Gino Cimoli	20.00	8.00	2.00
□ 6 Roberto Clemente	250.00	100.00	25.00
□ 7 Roy Face	28.00	11.50	2.80
□ 8 Tito Francona	24.00	10.00	2.40
□ 9 Bob Friend	24.00	10.00	2.40
□ 10 Jim Grant	20.00	8.00	2.00
□ 11 Dick Groat	28.00	11.50	2.80
□ 12 Harvey Haddix	24.00	10.00	2.40
□ 13 Woodie Held	20.00	8.00	2.00
□ 14 Bill Henry	20.00	8.00	2.00
□ 15 Don Hoak	20.00	8.00	2.00
□ 16 Jay Hook	20.00	8.00	2.00
□ 17 Eddie Kasko	20.00	8.00	2.00
□ 18A Ron Kline (Pittsburgh)	40.00	16.00	4.00
□ 18B Ron Kline (St. Louis)	40.00	16.00	4.00
□ 19 Ted Kluszewski	45.00	18.00	4.50
□ 20 Harvey Kuenn (blank back)	250.00	100.00	25.00
□ 21 Vernon Law	24.00	10.00	2.40
□ 22 Brooks Lawrence	20.00	8.00	2.00
□ 23 Jerry Lynch	20.00	8.00	2.00
□ 24 Billy Martin	45.00	18.00	4.50
□ 25 Bill Mazeroski	35.00	14.00	3.50
□ 26 Cal McLish	20.00	8.00	2.00
□ 27 Roy McMillan	20.00	8.00	2.00
□ 28 Don Newcombe	28.00	11.50	2.80
□ 29 Russ Nixon	24.00	10.00	2.40
□ 30 Joe Nuxhall	24.00	10.00	2.40
□ 31 Jim O'Toole	20.00	8.00	2.00
□ 32 Jim Perry	24.00	10.00	2.40
□ 33 Vada Pinson	28.00	11.50	2.80
□ 34 Vic Power	20.00	8.00	2.00
□ 35 Bob Purkey	20.00	8.00	2.00
□ 36 Frank Robinson	125.00	50.00	12.50
□ 37 Herb Score	28.00	11.50	2.80
□ 38 Bob Skinner	20.00	8.00	2.00
□ 39 Dick Stuart	24.00	10.00	2.40
□ 40 Johnny Temple	20.00	8.00	2.00
□ 41 Frank Thomas	24.00	10.00	2.40
□ 42 Lee Walls	20.00	8.00	2.00

1961 Kahn's

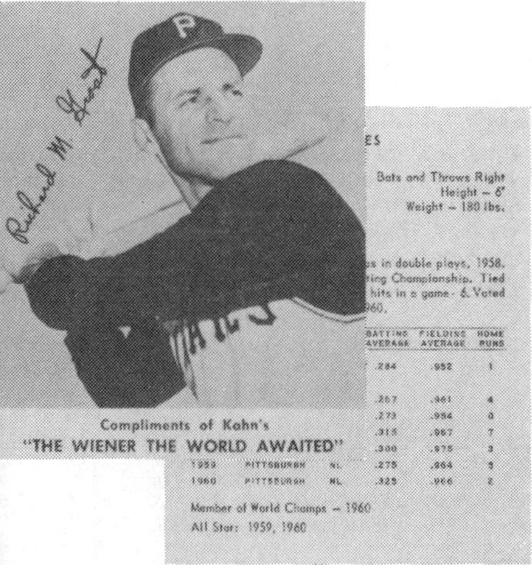

The cards in this 43-card set measure 3 1/4" by 4". The 1961 Kahn's Wieners set of black and white, unnumbered cards features players from Cincinnati, Cleveland, and Pittsburgh. This year was the first year Kahn's made complete sets available to the public; hence they are more available, especially in the better condition grades, than the Kahn's of the previous years. The backs give vital player information and year by year career statistics through 1960. The ACC designation is F155-7.

	NRMT	VG-E	GOOD
COMPLETE SET (43)	550.00	220.00	55.00
COMMON PLAYER (1-43)	10.00	4.00	1.00
□ 1 John Antonelli	11.00	4.50	1.10
□ 2 Ed Bailey	10.00	4.00	1.00
□ 3 Gary Bell	10.00	4.00	1.00
□ 4 Gus Bell	10.00	4.00	1.00
□ 5 Jim Brosnan	11.00	4.50	1.10
□ 6 Smoky Burgess	11.00	4.50	1.10
□ 7 Gino Cimoli	10.00	4.00	1.00
□ 8 Roberto Clemente	175.00	70.00	18.00
□ 9 Gordie Coleman	10.00	4.00	1.00
□ 10 Jimmy Dykes	11.00	4.50	1.10
□ 11 Roy Face	12.00	5.00	1.20
□ 12 Tito Francona	10.00	4.00	1.00
□ 13 Gene Freese	10.00	4.00	1.00
□ 14 Bob Friend	11.00	4.50	1.10
□ 15 Jim Grant	10.00	4.00	1.00
□ 16 Dick Groat	15.00	6.00	1.50
□ 17 Harvey Haddix	11.00	4.50	1.10
□ 18 Woodie Held	10.00	4.00	1.00
□ 19 Don Hoak	10.00	4.00	1.00
□ 20 Jay Hook	10.00	4.00	1.00
□ 21 Joey Jay	10.00	4.00	1.00
□ 22 Eddie Kasko	10.00	4.00	1.00
□ 23 Willie Kirkland	10.00	4.00	1.00
□ 24 Vernon Law	11.00	4.50	1.10
□ 25 Jerry Lynch	10.00	4.00	1.00
□ 26 Jim Maloney	12.00	5.00	1.20
□ 27 Bill Mazeroski	18.00	7.25	1.80
□ 28 Wilmer Mizell	10.00	4.00	1.00
□ 29 Rocky Nelson	10.00	4.00	1.00
□ 30 Jim O'Toole	10.00	4.00	1.00
□ 31 Jim Perry	11.00	4.50	1.10
□ 32 Bubba Phillips	10.00	4.00	1.00
□ 33 Vada Pinson	15.00	6.00	1.50
□ 34 Wally Post	10.00	4.00	1.00
□ 35 Vic Power	10.00	4.00	1.00
□ 36 Bob Purkey	10.00	4.00	1.00
□ 37 Frank Robinson	80.00	32.00	8.00
□ 38 John Romano	10.00	4.00	1.00
□ 39 Dick Schofield	10.00	4.00	1.00
□ 40 Bob Skinner	10.00	4.00	1.00
□ 41 Hal Smith	10.00	4.00	1.00
□ 42 Dick Stuart	11.00	4.50	1.10
□ 43 Johnny Temple	10.00	4.00	1.00

1962 Kahn's

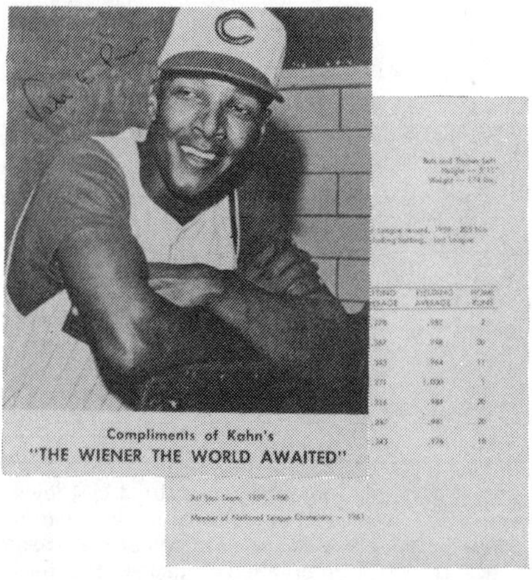

The cards in this 38-card set measure 3 1/4" by 4". The 1962 Kahn's Wieners set of black and white, unnumbered cards features Cincinnati, Cleveland, Minnesota, and Pittsburgh players. Card numbers 1 Bell, 33 Power, and 34 Purkey exist in two different forms; these variations are listed in the checklist below. The backs of the cards contain career information. The ACC designation is F155-8. The set price below includes the set with all variation cards.

	NRMT	VG-E	GOOD
COMPLETE SET (38)	900.00	400.00	100.00
COMMON PLAYER	9.00	3.75	.90
☐ 1A Gary Bell (with fat man)	90.00	36.00	9.00
☐ 1B Gary Bell (no fat man)	30.00	12.00	3.00
☐ 2 Jim Brosnan	10.00	4.00	1.00
☐ 3 Smoky Burgess	10.00	4.00	1.00
☐ 4 Chico Cardenas	9.00	3.75	.90
☐ 5 Roberto Clemente	135.00	54.00	13.50
☐ 6 Ty Cline	9.00	3.75	.90
☐ 7 Gordon Coleman	9.00	3.75	.90
☐ 8 Dick Donovan	10.00	4.00	1.00
☐ 9 John Edwards	9.00	3.75	.90
☐ 10 Tito Francona	9.00	3.75	.90
☐ 11 Gene Freese	9.00	3.75	.90
☐ 12 Bob Friend	10.00	4.00	1.00
☐ 13 Joe Gibbon	90.00	36.00	9.00
☐ 14 Jim Grant	9.00	3.75	.90
☐ 15 Dick Groat	12.00	5.00	1.20
☐ 16 Harvey Haddix	10.00	4.00	1.00
☐ 17 Woodie Held	9.00	3.75	.90
☐ 18 Bill Henry	9.00	3.75	.90
☐ 19 Don Hoak	9.00	3.75	.90
☐ 20 Ken Hunt	9.00	3.75	.90
☐ 21 Joey Jay	9.00	3.75	.90
☐ 22 Eddie Kasko	9.00	3.75	.90
☐ 23 Willie Kirkland	9.00	3.75	.90
☐ 24 Barry Latman	9.00	3.75	.90
☐ 25 Jerry Lynch	9.00	3.75	.90
☐ 26 Jim Maloney	10.00	4.00	1.00
☐ 27 Bill Mazeroski	15.00	6.00	1.50
☐ 28 Jim O'Toole	9.00	3.75	.90
☐ 29 Jim Perry	10.00	4.00	1.00
☐ 30 Bubba Phillips	9.00	3.75	.90
☐ 31 Vada Pinson	13.50	6.00	1.50
☐ 32 Wally Post	9.00	3.75	.90
☐ 33A Vic Power (Indians)	30.00	12.00	3.00
☐ 33B Vic Power (Twins)	90.00	36.00	9.00
☐ 34A Bob Purkey (with autograph)	30.00	12.00	3.00
☐ 34B Bob Purkey (no autograph)	90.00	36.00	9.00
☐ 35 Frank Robinson	65.00	26.00	6.50
☐ 36 John Romano	9.00	3.75	.90
☐ 37 Dick Stuart	10.00	4.00	1.00
☐ 38 Bill Virdon	13.50	6.00	1.50

1962 Kahn's Atlanta

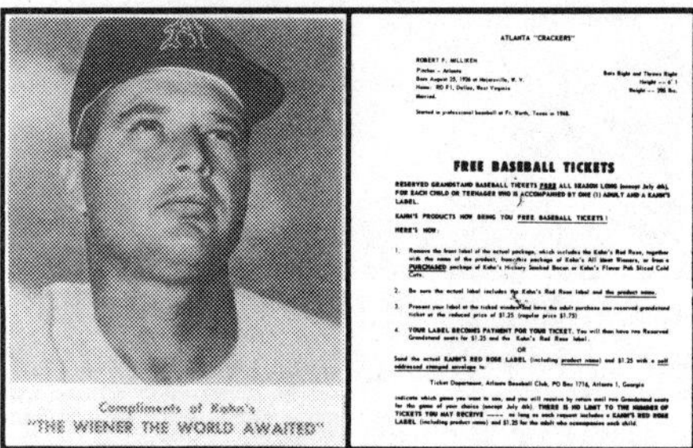

The cards in this 24-card set measure 3 1/4" by 4". The 1962 Kahn's Wieners Atlanta set features unnumbered, black and white cards of the Atlanta Crackers of the International League. The backs contain player statistical information as well as instructions on how to obtain free tickets. The ACC designation is F155-9.

	NRMT	VG-E	GOOD
COMPLETE SET (24)	300.00	120.00	30.00
COMMON PLAYER (1-24)	11.00	4.50	1.10
☐ 1 Jim Beauchamp	14.00	5.75	1.40
☐ 2 Gerry Buchek	11.00	4.50	1.10
☐ 3 Bob Burda	11.00	4.50	1.10
☐ 4 Dick Dietz	14.00	5.75	1.4
☐ 5 Bob Duliba	11.00	4.50	1.1
☐ 6 Harry Fanok	11.00	4.50	1.1
☐ 7 Phil Gagliano	14.00	5.75	1.4
☐ 8 John Glenn	11.00	4.50	1.1
☐ 9 Leroy Gregory	11.00	4.50	1.1
☐ 10 Dick Hughes	11.00	4.50	1.1
☐ 11 Johnny Kucks	14.00	5.75	1.4
☐ 12 Johnny Lewis	11.00	4.50	1.1
☐ 13 Tim McCarver	50.00	20.00	5.0
☐ 14 Bob Milliken	11.00	4.50	1.1
☐ 15 Joe Morgan	11.00	4.50	1.1
☐ 16 Ron Plaza	11.00	4.50	1.1
☐ 17 Bob Sadowski	11.00	4.50	1.1
☐ 18 Jim Saul	11.00	4.50	1.1
☐ 19 Willard Schmidt	11.00	4.50	1.1
☐ 20 Joe Schultz	11.00	4.50	1.1
☐ 21 Mike Shannon	21.00	8.50	2.1
☐ 22 Paul Toth	11.00	4.50	1.1
☐ 23 Lou Vickery	11.00	4.50	1.1
☐ 24 Fred Whitfield	14.00	5.75	1.4

1963 Kahn's

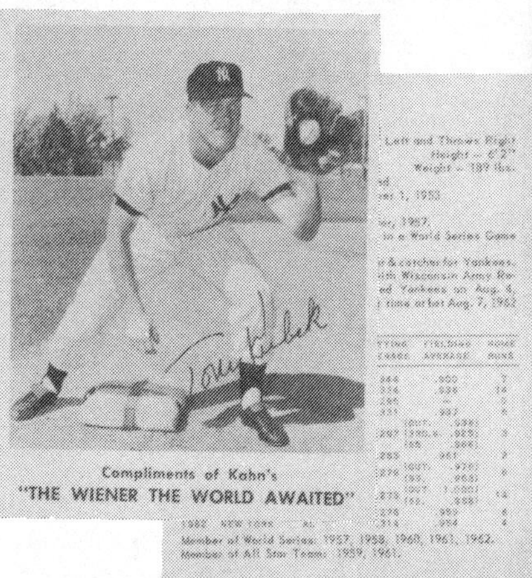

The cards in this 30-card set measure 3 1/4" by 4" The 1963 Kahn's Wieners set of black and white unnumbered cards features players from Cincinnati Cleveland, St. Louis, Pittsburgh and the New York Yankees. The cards feature a white border around the picture of the players. The backs contain career information. The ACC designation is F155-10.

	NRMT	VG-E	GOOD
COMPLETE SET (30)	450.00	180.00	45.0
COMMON PLAYER (1-30)	9.00	3.75	.9
☐ 1 Bob Bailey	9.00	3.75	.9
☐ 2 Don Blasingame	9.00	3.75	.9
☐ 3 Clete Boyer	12.00	5.00	1.2
☐ 4 Smoky Burgess	10.00	4.00	1.0
☐ 5 Chico Cardenas	9.00	3.75	.9
☐ 6 Roberto Clemente	135.00	54.00	13.5
☐ 7 Donn Clendenon	10.00	4.00	1.0
☐ 8 Gordon Coleman	9.00	3.75	.9
☐ 9 John Edwards	9.00	3.75	.9
☐ 10 Gene Freese	9.00	3.75	.9
☐ 11 Bob Friend	10.00	4.00	1.0
☐ 12 Joe Gibbon	9.00	3.75	.9
☐ 13 Dick Groat	13.50	6.00	1.5
☐ 14 Harvey Haddix	11.00	4.50	1.1
☐ 15 Elston Howard	16.00	6.50	1.6
☐ 16 Joey Jay	9.00	3.75	.9
☐ 17 Eddie Kasko	9.00	3.75	.9
☐ 18 Tony Kubek	20.00	8.00	2.0
☐ 19 Jerry Lynch	9.00	3.75	.9
☐ 20 Jim Maloney	10.00	4.00	1.0
☐ 21 Bill Mazeroski	16.00	6.50	1.6
☐ 22 Joe Nuxhall	10.00	4.00	1.0
☐ 23 Jim O'Toole	9.00	3.75	.9

□ 24 Vada Pinson	14.00	5.75	1.40
□ 25 Bob Purkey	9.00	3.75	.90
□ 26 Bobby Richardson	18.00	7.25	1.80
□ 27 Frank Robinson	65.00	26.00	6.50
□ 28 Bill Stafford	9.00	3.75	.90
□ 29 Ralph Terry	11.00	4.50	1.10
□ 30 Bill Virdon	12.00	5.00	1.20

1964 Kahn's

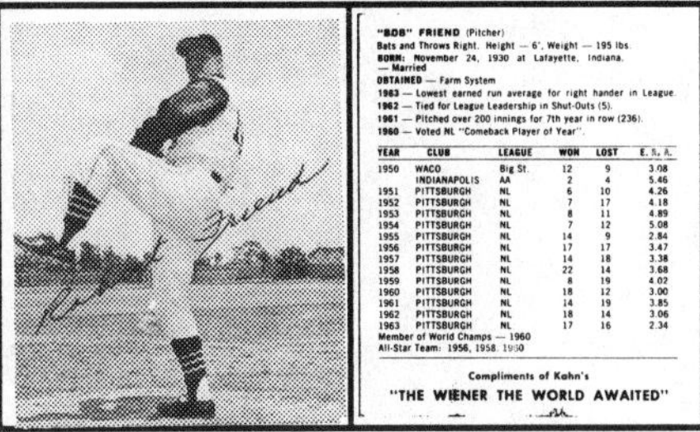

The cards in this 31-card set measure 3" by 3 1/2". The 1964 Kahn's set marks the beginning of the full color cards and the elimination of the tabs which existed on previous Kahn's cards. The set of unnumbered cards contains player information through the 1963 season on the backs. The set features Cincinnati, Cleveland and Pittsburgh players.

	NRMT	VG-E	GOOD
COMPLETE SET (31)	675.00	290.00	85.00
COMMON PLAYER (1-31)	9.00	3.75	.90
□ 1 Max Alvis	9.00	3.75	.90
□ 2 Bob Bailey	9.00	3.75	.90
□ 3 Chico Cardenas	9.00	3.75	.90
□ 4 Roberto Clemente	135.00	54.00	13.50
□ 5 Donn Clendenon	10.00	4.00	1.00
□ 6 Vic Davalillo	10.00	4.00	1.00
□ 7 Dick Donovan	9.00	3.75	.90
□ 8 John Edwards	9.00	3.75	.90
□ 9 Bob Friend	10.00	4.00	1.00
□ 10 Jim Grant	9.00	3.75	.90
□ 11 Tommy Harper	10.00	4.00	1.00
□ 12 Woodie Held	9.00	3.75	.90
□ 13 Joey Jay	9.00	3.75	.90
□ 14 Jack Kralick	9.00	3.75	.90
□ 15 Jerry Lynch	9.00	3.75	.90
□ 16 Jim Maloney	10.00	4.00	1.00
□ 17 Bill Mazeroski	16.00	6.50	1.60
□ 18 Alvin McBean	9.00	3.75	.90
□ 19 Joe Nuxhall	10.00	4.00	1.00
□ 20 Jim Pagliaroni	9.00	3.75	.90
□ 21 Vada Pinson	13.50	6.00	1.50
□ 22 Bob Purkey	9.00	3.75	.90
□ 23 Pedro Ramos	9.00	3.75	.90
□ 24 Frank Robinson	65.00	26.00	6.50
□ 25 John Romano	9.00	3.75	.90
□ 26 Pete Rose	350.00	140.00	35.00
□ 27 John Tsitouris	9.00	3.75	.90
□ 28 Bob Veale	10.00	4.00	1.00
□ 29 Bill Virdon	12.00	5.00	1.20
□ 30 Leon Wagner	9.00	3.75	.90
□ 31 Fred Whitfield	9.00	3.75	.90

1965 Kahn's

The cards in this 45-card set measure 3" by 3 1/2". The 1965 Kahn's set contains full color, unnumbered cards. The set features Cincinnati, Cleveland, Pittsburgh, and Milwaukee players. Backs contain statistical information through the 1964 season.

	NRMT	VG-E	GOOD
COMPLETE SET (45)	750.00	320.00	85.00
COMMON PLAYER (1-45)	9.00	3.75	.90
□ 1 Henry Aaron	125.00	50.00	12.50
□ 2 Max Alvis	9.00	3.75	.90
□ 3 Joe Azcue	9.00	3.75	.90
□ 4 Bob Bailey	9.00	3.75	.90
□ 5 Frank Bolling	9.00	3.75	.90
□ 6 Chico Cardenas	9.00	3.75	.90
□ 7 Rico Carty	12.50	5.00	1.25
□ 8 Donn Clendenon	10.00	4.00	1.00
□ 9 Tony Cloninger	9.00	3.75	.90
□ 10 Gordon Coleman	9.00	3.75	.90
□ 11 Vic Davalillo	9.00	3.75	.90
□ 12 John Edwards	9.00	3.75	.90
□ 13 Sammy Ellis	9.00	3.75	.90
□ 14 Bob Friend	10.00	4.00	1.00
□ 15 Tommy Harper	10.00	4.00	1.00
□ 16 Chuck Hinton	9.00	3.75	.90
□ 17 Dick Howser	15.00	6.00	1.50
□ 18 Joey Jay	9.00	3.75	.90
□ 19 Deron Johnson	10.00	4.00	1.00
□ 20 Jack Kralick	9.00	3.75	.90
□ 21 Denver LeMaster	9.00	3.75	.90
□ 22 Jerry Lynch	9.00	3.75	.90
□ 23 Jim Maloney	11.00	4.50	1.10
□ 24 Lee Maye	9.00	3.75	.90
□ 25 Bill Mazeroski	15.00	6.00	1.50
□ 26 Alvin McBean	9.00	3.75	.90
□ 27 Bill McCool	9.00	3.75	.90
□ 28 Sam McDowell	11.00	4.50	1.10
□ 29 Don McMahon	9.00	3.75	.90
□ 30 Denis Menke	9.00	3.75	.90
□ 31 Joe Nuxhall	10.00	4.00	1.00
□ 32 Gene Oliver	9.00	3.75	.90
□ 33 Jim O'Toole	9.00	3.75	.90
□ 34 Jim Pagliaroni	9.00	3.75	.90
□ 35 Vada Pinson	12.50	5.00	1.25
□ 36 Frank Robinson	65.00	26.00	6.50
□ 37 Pete Rose	225.00	90.00	22.00
□ 38 Willie Stargell	90.00	36.00	9.00
□ 39 Ralph Terry	12.00	5.00	1.20
□ 40 Luis Tiant	15.00	6.00	1.50
□ 41 Joe Torre	15.00	6.00	1.50
□ 42 John Tsitouris	9.00	3.75	.90
□ 43 Bob Veale	10.00	4.00	1.00
□ 44 Bill Virdon	12.00	5.00	1.20
□ 45 Leon Wagner	9.00	3.75	.90

1966 Kahn's

The cards in this 32-card set measure 2 13/16" by 4". 1966 Kahn's full color, unnumbered set features players from Atlanta, Cincinnati, Cleveland, and Pittsburgh. The set is identified by yellow and white vertical stripes and the name Kahn's written in red across a red rose at the top. The cards contain a 1 5/16" ad in the form of a tab. Cards with the ad (tab) are worth twice as much as cards without the ad, i.e., double the prices below.

	NRMT	VG-E	GOOD
COMPLETE SET (32)	375.00	160.00	45.00
COMMON PLAYER (1-32)	6.00	2.40	.60
□ 1 Henry Aaron (portrait, no wind-breaker under jersey	65.00	26.00	6.50
□ 2 Felipe Alou: Braves (full pose, batting screen in background)	7.50	3.00	.75

☐ 3 Max Alvis: Indians (kneeling, full pose, with bat, no patch on jersey)	6.00	2.40	.60
☐ 4 Bob Bailey	6.00	2.40	.60
☐ 5 Wade Blasingame	6.00	2.40	.60
☐ 6 Frank Bolling	6.00	2.40	.60
☐ 7 Chico Cardenas: Reds (fielding, feet at base)	6.00	2.40	.60
☐ 8 Roberto Clemente	60.00	24.00	6.00
☐ 9 Tony Cloninger: Braves (pitching, foulpole in background)	6.00	2.40	.60
☐ 10 Vic Davalillo	6.00	2.40	.60
☐ 11 John Edwards: Reds (catching)	6.00	2.40	.60
☐ 12 Sam Ellis: Reds (white hat)	6.00	2.40	.60
☐ 13 Pedro Gonzalez	6.00	2.40	.60
☐ 14 Tommy Harper: Reds (arm cocked)	6.00	2.40	.60
☐ 15 Deron Johnson: Reds (batting with batting cage in background)	6.00	2.40	.60
☐ 16 Mack Jones	6.00	2.40	.60
☐ 17 Denver Lemaster	6.00	2.40	.60
☐ 18 Jim Maloney: Reds (pitching, white hat)	7.50	3.00	.75
☐ 19 Bill Mazeroski: Pirates (throwing)	10.00	4.00	1.00
☐ 20 Bill McCool: Reds (white hat)	6.00	2.40	.60
☐ 21 Sam McDowell: Indians (kneeling)	7.50	3.00	.75
☐ 22 Denis Menke: Braves (white windbreaker under jersey)	6.00	2.40	.60
☐ 23 Joe Nuxhall	7.50	3.00	.75
☐ 24 Jim Pagliaroni: Pirates (catching)	6.00	2.40	.60
☐ 25 Milt Pappas	7.50	3.00	.75
☐ 26 Vada Pinson: Reds (fielding, ball on ground)	10.00	4.00	1.00
☐ 27 Pete Rose: Reds (with glove)	110.00	45.00	11.00
☐ 28 Sonny Siebert: Indians (pitching, signature at feet)	6.00	2.40	.60
☐ 29 Willie Stargell: Pirates (batting, clouds in sky)	40.00	16.00	4.00
☐ 30 Joe Torre: Braves (catching with hand on mask)	10.00	4.00	1.00
☐ 31 Bob Veale: Pirates (hands at knee with glasses)	7.50	3.00	.75
☐ 32 Fred Whitfield	6.00	2.40	.60

1967 Kahn's

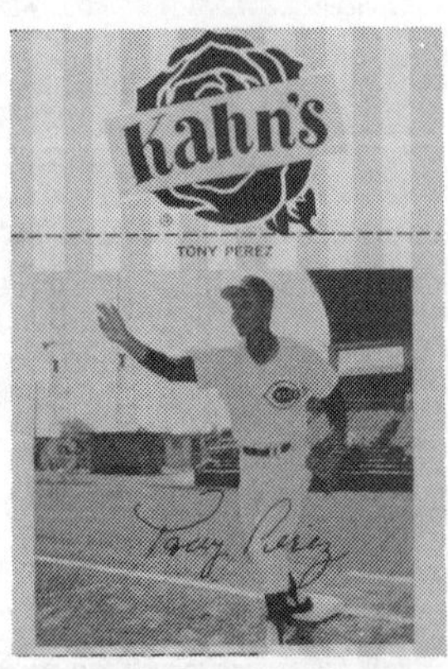

The cards in this 41-card set measure 2 13/16" b 4". The 1967 Kahn's set of full color, unnumbere cards is almost identical in style to the 1966 issue Different meat products had different backgroun colors (yellow and white stripes, red and whit stripes, etc.). The set features players from Atlant Cincinnati, Cleveland, New York Mets an Pittsburgh. Cards with the ads (see 1966 set) ar worth twice as much as cards without the ad, i.e double the prices below. The complete set pric below includes all variations.

	NRMT	VG-E	GOC
COMPLETE SET (51)	600.00	280.00	80.C
COMMON PLAYER (1-41)	6.00	2.40	.6
☐ 1A Henry Aaron: Braves (swinging pose, batting glove, ball, and hat on ground)	65.00	26.00	6.5
☐ 1B Henry Aaron: Braves (swinging pose, batting glove, ball, and hat on ground; Cut Along Dotted Lines printed on lower tab)	100.00	40.00	10.C
☐ 2 Gene Alley: Pirates (portrait)	6.00	2.40	.6
☐ 3 Felipe Alou: Braves (full pose, bat on shoulder)	7.50	3.00	.7
☐ 4A Matty Alou: Pirates (portrait with bat, "Matio Rojas Alou"; yellow stripes)	7.50	3.00	.7
☐ 4B Matty Alou: Pirates (portrait with bat, "Matio Rojas Alou"; red stripes)	10.00	4.00	1.0
☐ 5 Max Alvis: Indians (fielding, hands on knees)	6.00	2.40	.6
☐ 6A Ken Boyer (batting righthanded; autograph at waist)	10.00	4.00	1.0
☐ 6B Ken Boyer (batting righthanded; autograph at shoulders; Cut Along Dotted Lines printed on lower tab)	15.00	6.00	1.5
☐ 7 Chico Cardenas: Reds (fielding, hand on knee)	6.00	2.40	.6
☐ 8 Rico Carty	9.00	3.75	.9
☐ 9 Tony Cloninger: Braves (pitching, no foul-pole in background)	6.00	2.40	.6
☐ 10 Tommy Davis	9.00	3.75	.9
☐ 11 John Edwards: Reds (kneeling with bat)	6.00	2.40	.6
☐ 12A Sam Ellis: Reds (all red hat)	6.00	2.40	.6

□ 12B	Sam Ellis: Reds (all red hat) Cut Along Dotted Lines printed on lower tab)	9.00	3.75	.90
□ 13	Jack Fisher	6.00	2.40	.60
□ 14	Steve Hargan: Indians (pitching, no clouds, blue sky)	6.00	2.40	.60
□ 15	Tommy Harper: Reds (fielding, glove on ground)	6.00	2.40	.60
□ 16A	Tommy Helms (batting righthanded; top of bat visible)	6.00	2.40	.60
□ 16B	Tommy Helms (batting righthanded; bat chopped above hat; Cut Along Dotted Lines printed on lower tab)	9.00	3.75	.90
□ 17	Deron Johnson: Reds (batting, blue sky)	6.00	2.40	.60
□ 18	Ken Johnson	6.00	2.40	.60
□ 19	Cleon Jones	6.00	2.40	.60
□ 20A	Ed Kranepool (ready for throw; yellow stripes)	7.50	3.00	.75
□ 20B	Ed Kranepool (ready for throw; red stripes)	10.00	4.00	1.00
□ 21A	Jim Maloney: Reds (pitching, red hat, follow thru delivery; yellow stripes)	7.50	3.00	.75
□ 21B	Jim Maloney: Reds (pitching, red hat, follow thru delivery; red stripes)	10.00	4.00	1.00
□ 22	Lee May: Reds (hands on knee)	6.00	2.40	.60
□ 23A	Bill Mazeroski: Pirates (portrait; autograph below waist)	10.00	4.00	1.00
□ 23B	Bill Mazeroski: Pirates (portrait; autograph above waist; Cut Along Dotted Lines printed on lower tab)	15.00	6.00	1.50
□ 24	Bill McCool: Reds (red hat, left hand out)	6.00	2.40	.60
□ 25	Sam McDowell: Indians (pitching, left hand under glove)	7.50	3.00	.75
□ 26	Denis Menke: Braves (blue sleeves)	6.00	2.40	.60
□ 27	Jim Pagliaroni: Pirates (catching, no chest protector)	6.00	2.40	.60
□ 28	Don Pavletich	6.00	2.40	.60
□ 29	Tony Perez: Reds (throwing)	18.00	7.25	1.80
□ 30	Vada Pinson: Reds (ready to throw)	10.00	4.00	1.00
□ 31	Dennis Ribant	6.00	2.40	.60
□ 32	Pete Rose: Reds (batting)	100.00	40.00	10.00
□ 33	Art Shamsky: Reds	6.00	2.40	.60
□ 34	Bob Shaw	6.00	2.40	.60
□ 35	Sonny Siebert: Indians (pitching, signature at knees)	6.00	2.40	.60
□ 36	Willie Stargell: Pirates (batting, no clouds)	40.00	16.00	4.00
□ 37A	Joe Torre: Braves (catching, mask on ground)	10.00	4.00	1.00
□ 37B	Joe Torre: Braves (catching, mask on ground; Cut Along Dotted Lines printed on lower tab)	15.00	6.00	1.50
□ 38	Bob Veale: Pirates (portrait, hands not shown)	7.50	3.00	.75
□ 39	Leon Wagner: Indians (fielding)	6.00	2.40	.60
□ 40A	Fred Whitfield (batting lefthanded)	6.00	2.40	.60
□ 40B	Fred Whitfield (batting lefthanded; Cut Along Dotted Lines printed on lower tab)	9.00	3.75	.90
□ 41	Woody Woodward	7.50	3.00	.75

1968 Kahn's

The cards in this 50-card set contain two different sizes. The smaller of the two sizes, which contains 12 cards, is 2 13/16" by 3 1/4" with the ad tab and 2 13/16" by 1 7/8" without the ad tab. The larger size, which contains 38 cards, measures 2 13/16" by 3 7/8" with the ad tab and 2 13/16" by 2 11/16" without the ad tab. The 1968 Kahn's set of full color, blank backed, unnumbered cards features players from Atlanta, Chicago Cubs, Chicago White Sox, Cincinnati, Cleveland, Detroit, New York Mets, and Pittsburgh. In the set of 12, listed with the letter A in the checklist, Maloney exists with either yellow or yellow and green stripes at the top of the card. The large set of 38, listed with a letter B in the checklist, contains five cards which exist in two variations. The variations in this large set have either yellow or red stripes at the top of the cards, with Maloney being an exception. Maloney has either a yellow stripe or a Blue Mountain ad at the top. Cards with the ad tabs (see other Kahn's sets) are worth twice as much as cards without the ad, i.e., double the prices below.

		NRMT	VG-E	GOOD
COMPLETE SET (50)		550.00	230.00	70.00
COMMON PLAYER		6.00	2.40	.60
□ A1	Hank Aaron	65.00	26.00	6.50
□ A2	Gene Alley	6.00	2.40	.60
□ A3	Max Alvis	6.00	2.40	.60
□ A4	Clete Boyer	7.50	3.00	.75
□ A5	Chico Cardenas	6.00	2.40	.60
□ A6	Bill Freehan	9.00	3.75	.90
□ A7	Jim Maloney (2)	7.50	3.00	.75
□ A8	Lee May	6.00	2.40	.60
□ A9	Bill Mazeroski	10.00	4.00	1.00
□ A10	Vada Pinson	10.00	4.00	1.00
□ A11	Joe Torre	10.00	4.00	1.00
□ A12	Bob Veale	7.50	3.00	.75
□ B1	Hank Aaron: Braves (full pose, batting bat cocked)	65.00	26.00	6.50
□ B2	Tommy Agee	6.00	2.40	.60
□ B3	Gene Alley: Pirates (fielding, full pose)	6.00	2.40	.60
□ B4	Felipe Alou (full pose, batting, swinging, player in background)	7.50	3.00	.75
□ B5	Matty Alou: Pirates (portrait with bat, "Matio Alou" (2)	7.50	3.00	.75
□ B6	Max Alvis (fielding, glove on ground)	6.00	2.40	.60
□ B7	Gerry Arrigo: Reds (pitching, follow thru delivery)	6.00	2.40	.60
□ B8	John Bench	200.00	80.00	20.00
□ B9	Clete Boyer	7.50	3.00	.75
□ B10	Larry Brown	6.00	2.40	.60

☐ B11	Leo Cardenas: Reds (leaping in the air)	6.00	2.40	.60
☐ B12	Bill Freehan	7.50	3.00	.75
☐ B13	Steve Hargan: Indians (pitching, clouds in background)	6.00	2.40	.60
☐ B14	Joel Horlen: White Sox (portrait)	6.00	2.40	.60
☐ B15	Tony Horton: Indians (portrait, signed Anthony)	6.00	2.40	.60
☐ B16	Willie Horton	7.50	3.00	.75
☐ B17	Ferguson Jenkins	16.00	6.50	1.60
☐ B18	Deron Johnson: Braves	6.00	2.40	.60
☐ B19	Mack Jones: Reds	6.00	2.40	.60
☐ B20	Bob Lee	6.00	2.40	.60
☐ B21	Jim Maloney: Reds (red hat, pitching hands up) (2)	7.50	3.00	.75
☐ B22	Lee May: Reds (batting)	6.00	2.40	.60
☐ B23	Bill Mazeroski: Pirates (fielding, hands in front of body)	10.00	4.00	1.00
☐ B24	Dick McAuliffe	6.00	2.40	.60
☐ B25	Bill McCool (red hat, left hand down)	6.00	2.40	.60
☐ B26	Sam McDowell: Indians (pitching, left hand over glove (2)	7.50	3.00	.75
☐ B27	Tony Perez (fielding ball in glove (2)	18.00	7.25	1.80
☐ B28	Gary Peters: White Sox (portrait)	6.00	2.40	.60
☐ B29	Vada Pinson: Reds (batting)	10.00	4.00	1.00
☐ B30	Chico Ruiz	6.00	2.40	.60
☐ B31	Ron Santo: Cubs (batting, follow thru (2)	10.00	4.00	1.00
☐ B32	Art Shamsky: Mets	6.00	2.40	.60
☐ B33	Luis Tiant: Indians (hands over head)	9.00	3.75	.90
☐ B34	Joe Torre: Braves (batting)	10.00	4.00	1.00
☐ B35	Bob Veale: Pirates (hands chest high)	7.50	3.00	.75
☐ B36	Leon Wagner: Indians (batting)	6.00	2.40	.60
☐ B37	Billy Williams: Cubs (bat behind back)	30.00	12.00	3.00
☐ B38	Earl Wilson	6.00	2.40	.60

1969 Kahn's

The cards in this 25-card set contain two different sizes. The three small cards (see 1968 description) measure 2 13/16" by 3 1/4" and the 22 large cards (see 1968 description) measure 2 13/16" by 3 15/16". The 1969 Kahn's Wieners set of full color, unnumbered cards features players from Atlanta, Chicago Cubs, Chicago White Sox, Cincinnati, Cleveland, Pittsburgh, and St. Louis. The small cards have the letter A in the checklist while the large cards have the letter B in the checklist. Four of the larger cards exist in two variations (red or yellow color stripes at the top of the card). These variations are identified in the checklist below. Cards with the ad tabs (see other Kahn's sets) are worth twice as much as cards without the ad, i.e., double the prices below.

		NRMT	VG-E	GOOD
COMPLETE SET (25)		275.00	120.00	40.00
COMMON PLAYER		6.00	2.40	.60
☐ A1	Hank Aaron (portrait)	65.00	26.00	6.50
☐ A2	Jim Maloney (pitching, hands at side)	7.50	3.00	.75
☐ A3	Tony Perez (glove on)	15.00	6.00	1.50
☐ B1	Hank Aaron	65.00	26.00	6.50
☐ B2	Matty Alou (batting)	7.50	3.00	.75
☐ B3	Max Alvis ('69 patch)	6.00	2.40	.60
☐ B4	Gerry Arrigo (leg up)	6.00	2.40	.60
☐ B5	Steve Blass	7.50	3.00	.75
☐ B6	Clay Carroll	6.00	2.40	.60
☐ B7	Tony Cloninger: Reds	6.00	2.40	.60
☐ B8	George Culver	6.00	2.40	.60
☐ B9	Joel Horlen (pitching)	6.00	2.40	.60
☐ B10	Tony Horton (batting)	6.00	2.40	.60
☐ B11	Alex Johnson	6.00	2.40	.60
☐ B12	Jim Maloney	7.50	3.00	.75
☐ B13	Lee May (foot on bag) (2)	6.00	2.40	.60
☐ B14	Bill Mazeroski (hands on knees) (2)	10.00	4.00	1.00
☐ B15	Sam McDowell (leg up) (2)	7.50	3.00	.75
☐ B16	Tony Perez	15.00	6.00	1.50
☐ B17	Gary Peters (pitching)	6.00	2.40	.60
☐ B18	Ron Santo (emblem) (2)	10.00	4.00	1.00
☐ B19	Luis Tiant (glove at knee)	9.00	3.75	.90
☐ B20	Joe Torre: Cardinals	10.00	4.00	1.00
☐ B21	Bob Veale (hands at knees, no glasses)	7.50	3.00	.75
☐ B22	Billy Williams (bat behind head)	30.00	12.00	3.00

1987 Kahn's Weiners Reds

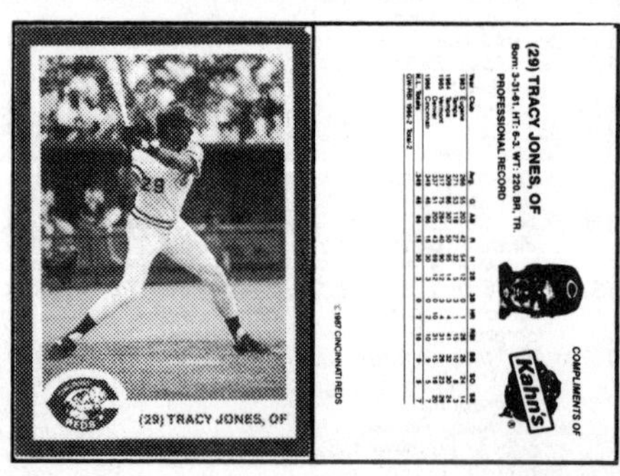

This 30-card set was issued to the first 20,000 fans at the August 2nd game between the Reds and the San Francisco Giants at Riverfront Stadium. Cards are standard size, 2 1/2" by 3 1/2". The cards are unnumbered except for uniform number and feature full-color photos bordered in red and white on the front. The Kahn's logo is printed in red in the corner of the reverse.

	MINT	EXC	G-VG
COMPLETE SET (30)	15.00	6.00	1.50
COMMON PLAYER	.40	.16	.04
☐ 6 Bo Diaz	.60	.24	.06
☐ 10 Terry Francona	.50	.20	.05
☐ 11 Kurt Stillwell	.60	.24	.06
☐ 12 Nick Esasky	.50	.20	.05
☐ 13 Dave Concepcion	.60	.24	.06
☐ 15 Barry Larkin	1.00	.40	.10
☐ 16 Ron Oester	.50	.20	.05
☐ 21 Paul O'Neill	.50	.20	.05
☐ 23 Lloyd McClendon	.40	.16	.04
☐ 25 Buddy Bell	.60	.24	.06
☐ 28 Kal Daniels	2.00	.80	.20
☐ 29 Tracy Jones	.75	.30	.07
☐ 30 Guy Hoffman	.40	.16	.04
☐ 31 John Franco	.75	.30	.07
☐ 32 Tom Browning	.60	.24	.06
☐ 33 Ron Robinson	.50	.20	.05
☐ 34 Bill Gullickson	.50	.20	.05
☐ 35 Pat Pacillo	.50	.20	.05
☐ 39 Dave Parker	.75	.30	.07
☐ 43 Bill Landrum	.40	.16	.04
☐ 44 Eric Davis	4.50	1.80	.45
☐ 46 Rob Murphy	.60	.24	.06
☐ 47 Frank Williams	.50	.20	.05
☐ 48 Ted Power	.40	.16	.04
☐ xx Pete Rose MG	1.50	.60	.15
☐ xx Coaches Card Scott Breeden Billy DeMars Tommy Helms Bruce Kimm Jim Lett Tony Perez	.50	.20	.05
☐ xx Ad Card Save 25 cents on Corn Dogs	.40	.16	.04
☐ xx Ad Card Save 30 cents on Smokeys	.40	.16	.04

1988 Kahn's Mets

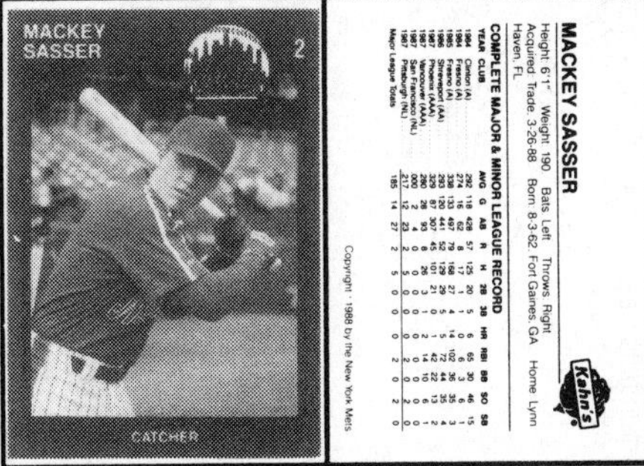

These 32-card sets were issued to the first 48,000 fans at the June 30th game between the Mets and the Houston Astros at Shea Stadium. The set includes 30 players, a team card, and a discount coupon card (to be redeemed at the grocery store). Cards are standard size, 2 1/2" by 3 1/2". The cards are unnumbered except for uniform number and feature full- color photos bordered in blue and orange on the front. The Kahn's logo is printed in red in the corner of the reverse.

	MINT	EXC	G-VG
COMPLETE SET (32)	12.50	5.00	1.25
COMMON PLAYER	.30	.12	.03
☐ 1 Mookie Wilson	.40	.16	.04
☐ 2 Mackey Sasser	.40	.16	.04
☐ 3 Bud Harrelson CO	.30	.12	.03
☐ 4 Lenny Dykstra	.40	.16	.04
☐ 5 Davey Johnson MG	.40	.16	.04
☐ 6 Wally Backman	.40	.16	.04
☐ 8 Gary Carter	.75	.30	.07
☐ 11 Tim Teufel	.30	.12	.03
☐ 12 Ron Darling	.60	.24	.06
☐ 13 Lee Mazzilli	.30	.12	.03
☐ 15 Rick Aguilera	.30	.12	.03
☐ 16 Dwight Gooden	1.00	.40	.10
☐ 17 Keith Hernandez	.75	.30	.07
☐ 18 Darryl Strawberry	1.25	.50	.12
☐ 19 Bob Ojeda	.40	.16	.04
☐ 20 Howard Johnson	.50	.20	.05
☐ 21 Kevin Elster	.40	.16	.04
☐ 22 Kevin McReynolds	1.00	.40	.10
☐ 26 Terry Leach	.30	.12	.03
☐ 28 Bill Robinson CO	.30	.12	.03
☐ 29 Dave Magadan	.40	.16	.04
☐ 30 Mel Stottlemyre CO	.30	.12	.03
☐ 31 Gene Walter	.30	.12	.03
☐ 33 Barry Lyons	.30	.12	.03
☐ 34 Sam Perlozzo CO	.30	.12	.03
☐ 42 Roger McDowell	.40	.16	.04
☐ 44 David Cone	1.00	.40	.10
☐ 48 Randy Myers	.50	.20	.05
☐ 50 Sid Fernandez	.50	.20	.05
☐ 52 Greg Pavlick	.30	.12	.03
☐ x Team Photo Card (unnumbered)	.30	.12	.03
☐ x Discount Coupon (unnumbered)	.30	.12	.03

1988 Kahn's Reds

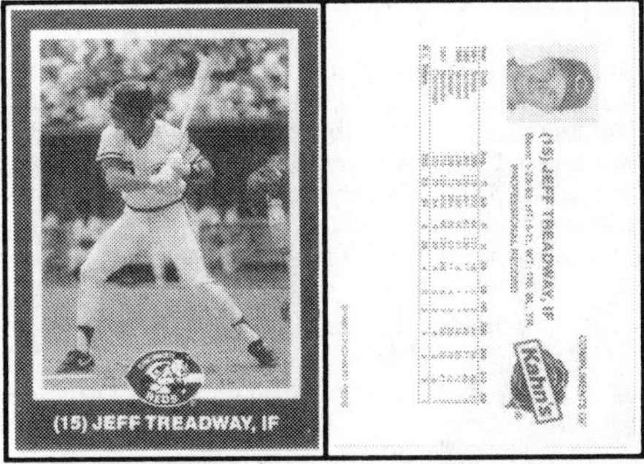

These 26-card sets were issued to fans at the August 14th game between the Reds and the Atlanta Braves at Riverfront Stadium. Cards are standard size, 2 1/2" by 3 1/2". The cards are unnumbered except for uniform number and feature full-color photos bordered in red and white on the front. The Kahn's logo is printed in red in the corner of the reverse. The cards are numbered below by uniform number which is listed parenthetically on the front of the cards.

	MINT	EXC	G-VG
COMPLETE SET (26)	15.00	6.00	1.50
COMMON PLAYER	.30	.12	.03
☐ 6 Bo Diaz	.30	.12	.03
☐ 8 Terry McGriff	.40	.16	.04
☐ 9 Eddie Milner	.30	.12	.03
☐ 10 Leon Durham	.40	.16	.04
☐ 11 Barry Larkin	.75	.30	.07
☐ 12 Nick Esasky	.40	.16	.04
☐ 13 Dave Concepcion	.40	.16	.04
☐ 14 Pete Rose MG	1.00	.40	.10
☐ 15 Jeff Treadway	.50	.20	.05
☐ 17 Chris Sabo	5.00	2.00	.50
☐ 20 Danny Jackson	.75	.30	.07
☐ 21 Paul O'Neill	.40	.16	.04
☐ 22 Dave Collins	.30	.12	.03
☐ 27 Jose Rijo	.30	.12	.03
☐ 28 Kal Daniels	.75	.30	.07
☐ 29 Tracy Jones	.40	.16	.04
☐ 30 Lloyd McClendon	.30	.12	.03
☐ 31 John Franco	.50	.20	.05
☐ 32 Tom Browning	.50	.20	.05
☐ 33 Ron Robinson	.30	.12	.03
☐ 40 Jack Armstrong	.40	.16	.04
☐ 44 Eric Davis	1.00	.40	.10

		MINT	EXC	G-VG
□ 46	Rob Murphy	.40	.16	.04
□ 47	Frank Williams	.30	.12	.03
□ 48	Tim Birtsas	.30	.12	.03
□ xx	Reds Coaches Lee May CO Tony Perez CO Bruce Kimm CO Tommy Helms CO Jim Lett CO Scott Breeden CO	.30	.12	.03

1986 Kay-Bee Young Stars

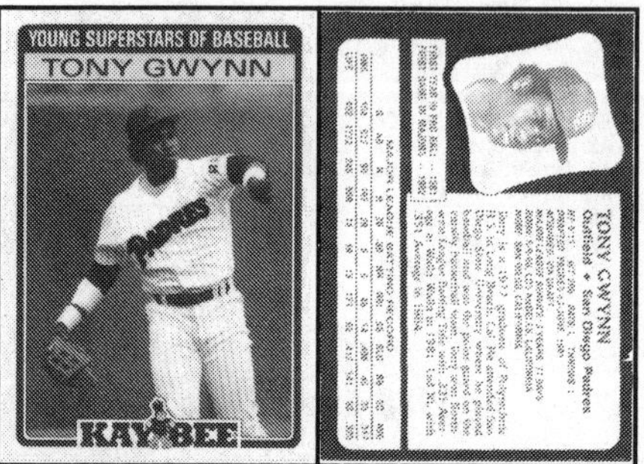

This 33-card, standard-sized (2 1/2" by 3 1/2") set was produced by Topps, although manufactured in Northern Ireland. This boxed set retailed in Kay-Bee stores for 1.99; the checklist was listed on the back of the box. The set is subtitled "Young Superstars of Baseball" and does indeed feature many young players. The cards are numbered on the back.

		MINT	EXC	G-VG
	COMPLETE SET (33)	4.50	1.80	.45
	COMMON PLAYER (1-33)	.10	.04	.01
□ 1	Rick Aguilera	.15	.06	.01
□ 2	Chris Brown	.15	.06	.01
□ 3	Tom Browning	.15	.06	.01
□ 4	Tom Brunansky	.15	.06	.01
□ 5	Vince Coleman	.25	.10	.02
□ 6	Ron Darling	.15	.06	.01
□ 7	Alvin Davis	.15	.06	.01
□ 8	Mariano Duncan	.10	.04	.01
□ 9	Shawon Dunston	.15	.06	.01
□ 10	Sid Fernandez	.15	.06	.01
□ 11	Tony Fernandez	.20	.08	.02
□ 12	Brian Fisher	.15	.06	.01
□ 13	John Franco	.15	.06	.01
□ 14	Julio Franco	.15	.06	.01
□ 16	Dwight Gooden	.75	.30	.07
□ 16	Ozzie Guillen	.15	.06	.01
□ 17	Tony Gwynn	.45	.18	.04
□ 18	Jimmy Key	.20	.08	.02
□ 19	Don Mattingly	1.00	.40	.10
□ 20	Oddibe McDowell	.15	.06	.01
□ 21	Roger McDowell	.15	.06	.01
□ 22	Dan Pasqua	.15	.06	.01
□ 23	Terry Pendleton	.10	.04	.01
□ 24	Jim Presley	.15	.06	.01
□ 25	Kirby Puckett	.50	.20	.05
□ 26	Earnie Riles	.10	.04	.01
□ 27	Bret Saberhagen	.20	.08	.02
□ 28	Mark Salas	.10	.04	.01
□ 29	Juan Samuel	.15	.06	.01
□ 30	Jeff Stone	.10	.04	.01
□ 31	Darryl Strawberry	.60	.24	.06
□ 32	Andy Van Slyke	.20	.08	.02
□ 33	Frank Viola	.20	.08	.02

FAMILY FUN: Attend a sports memorabilia show or convention in your area sometime this year. They are both interesting and enjoyable for all members of the family.

1987 Kay-Bee Superstars

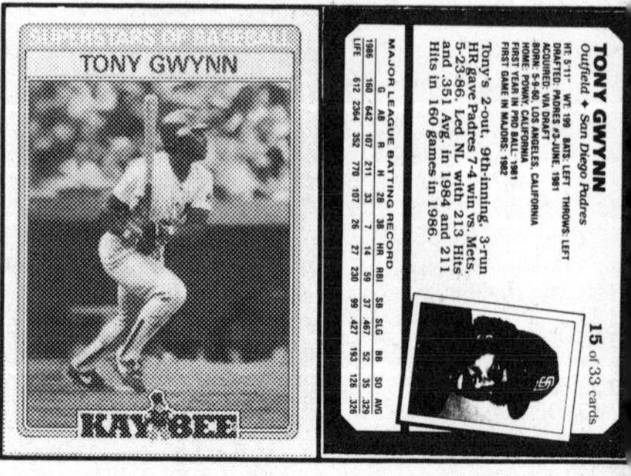

This small 33-card boxed set was produced by Topp for Kay-Bee Toy Stores. The set is subtitled "Supe Stars of Baseball" and measures the standard 2 1/2 by 3 1/2" with full-color fronts. The card backs ar printed in blue and black on white card stock. Th checklist for the set is printed on the back panel c the yellow box.

		MINT	EXC	G-V
	COMPLETE SET (33)	4.50	1.80	.4
	COMMON PLAYER (1-33)	.10	.04	.0
□ 1	Harold Baines	.10	.04	.0
□ 2	Jesse Barfield	.15	.06	.0
□ 3	Don Baylor	.10	.04	.0
□ 4	Wade Boggs	.60	.24	.0
□ 5	George Brett	.40	.16	.0
□ 6	Hubie Brooks	.10	.04	.0
□ 7	Jose Canseco	1.00	.40	.1
□ 8	Gary Carter	.20	.08	.0
□ 9	Joe Carter	.20	.08	.0
□ 10	Roger Clemens	.50	.20	.0
□ 11	Vince Coleman	.25	.10	.0
□ 12	Glenn Davis	.20	.08	.0
□ 13	Dwight Gooden	.40	.16	.0
□ 14	Pedro Guerrero	.20	.08	.0
□ 15	Tony Gwynn	.40	.16	.0
□ 16	Rickey Henderson	.35	.14	.0
□ 17	Keith Hernandez	.25	.10	.0
□ 18	Wally Joyner	.50	.20	.0
□ 19	Don Mattingly	.75	.30	.0
□ 20	Jack Morris	.20	.08	.0
□ 21	Dale Murphy	.40	.16	.0
□ 22	Eddie Murray	.30	.12	.0
□ 23	Dave Parker	.20	.08	.0
□ 24	Kirby Puckett	.40	.16	.0
□ 25	Tim Raines	.25	.10	.0
□ 26	Jim Rice	.20	.08	.0
□ 27	Dave Righetti	.15	.06	.0
□ 28	Ryne Sandberg	.25	.10	.0
□ 29	Mike Schmidt	.40	.16	.0
□ 30	Mike Scott	.20	.08	.0
□ 31	Darryl Strawberry	.40	.16	.0
□ 32	Fernando Valenzuela	.20	.08	.0
□ 33	Dave Winfield	.25	.10	.0

1988 Kay-Bee Superstars

This small 33-card boxed set was produced by Topps for Kay-Bee Toy Stores. The set is subtitlec "Superstars of Baseball" and measures the standarc 2 1/2" by 3 1/2" with full-color fronts. The carc backs are printed in blue and green on white carc stock. The checklist for the set is printed on the back panel of the box. These cards are numbered on the back.

	MINT	EXC	G-V(
COMPLETE SET (33)	4.00	1.60	.4(
COMMON PLAYER (1-33)	.10	.04	.0

☐ 1 George Bell	.20	.08	.02
☐ 2 Wade Boggs	.60	.24	.06
☐ 3 Jose Canseco	1.00	.40	.10
☐ 4 Joe Carter	.20	.08	.02
☐ 5 Jack Clark	.20	.08	.02
☐ 6 Alvin Davis	.15	.06	.01
☐ 7 Eric Davis	.60	.24	.06
☐ 8 Andre Dawson	.25	.10	.02
☐ 9 Darrell Evans	.10	.04	.01
☐ 10 Dwight Evans	.15	.06	.01
☐ 11 Gary Gaetti	.15	.06	.01
☐ 12 Pedro Guerrero	.20	.08	.02
☐ 13 Tony Gwynn	.35	.14	.03
☐ 14 Howard Johnson	.15	.06	.01
☐ 15 Wally Joyner	.40	.16	.04
☐ 16 Don Mattingly	1.00	.40	.10
☐ 17 Willie McGee	.20	.08	.02
☐ 18 Mark McGwire	.60	.24	.06
☐ 19 Paul Molitor	.20	.08	.02
☐ 20 Dale Murphy	.30	.12	.03
☐ 21 Dave Parker	.15	.06	.01
☐ 22 Lance Parrish	.15	.06	.01
☐ 23 Kirby Puckett	.40	.16	.04
☐ 24 Tim Raines	.30	.12	.03
☐ 25 Cal Ripken	.30	.12	.03
☐ 26 Juan Samuel	.15	.06	.01
☐ 27 Mike Schmidt	.40	.16	.04
☐ 28 Ruben Sierra	.20	.08	.02
☐ 29 Darryl Strawberry	.60	.24	.06
☐ 30 Danny Tartabull	.25	.10	.02
☐ 31 Alan Trammell	.20	.08	.02
☐ 32 Tim Wallach	.10	.04	.01
☐ 33 Dave Winfield	.25	.10	.02

1970 Kellogg's

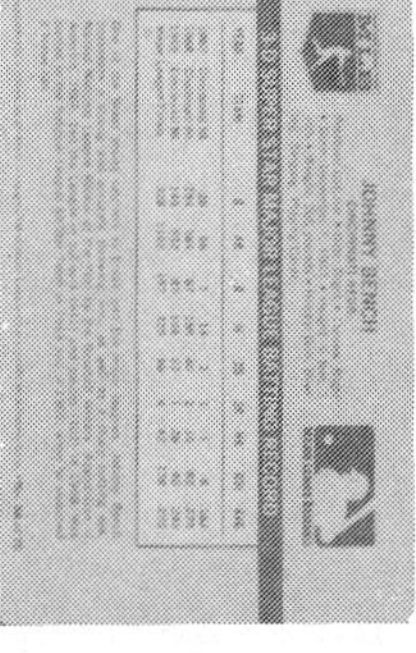

The cards in this 75-card set measure 2 1/4" by 3 1/2". The 1970 Kellogg's set was Kellogg's first venture into the baseball card producing field. The design incorporates a brilliant color photo of the player set against an indistinct background, which is then covered with a layer of plastic to simulate a 3-D look. Cards 16-30 seem to be in shorter supply than the other cards in the set.

	NRMT	VG-E	GOOD
COMPLETE SET (75)	90.00	32.00	8.00
COMMON PLAYER (1-75)	.75	.30	.07
☐ 1 Ed Kranepool	.75	.30	.07
☐ 2 Pete Rose	12.50	5.00	1.25
☐ 3 Cleon Jones	.75	.30	.07
☐ 4 Willie McCovey	3.00	1.20	.30
☐ 5 Mel Stottlemyre	1.00	.40	.10
☐ 6 Frank Howard	1.00	.40	.10
☐ 7 Tom Seaver	6.00	2.40	.60
☐ 8 Don Sutton	2.00	.80	.20
☐ 9 Jim Wynn	.75	.30	.07
☐ 10 Jim Maloney	1.00	.40	.10
☐ 11 Tommie Agee	.75	.30	.07
☐ 12 Willie Mays	9.00	3.75	.90
☐ 13 Juan Marichal	3.00	1.20	.30
☐ 14 Dave McNally	.75	.30	.07
☐ 15 Frank Robinson	3.50	1.40	.35
☐ 16 Carlos May	.75	.30	.07
☐ 17 Bill Singer	.75	.30	.07
☐ 18 Rick Reichardt	.75	.30	.07
☐ 19 Boog Powell	1.00	.40	.10
☐ 20 Gaylord Perry	3.00	1.20	.30
☐ 21 Brooks Robinson	5.00	2.00	.50
☐ 22 Luis Aparicio	3.50	1.40	.35
☐ 23 Joel Horlen	.75	.30	.07
☐ 24 Mike Epstein	.75	.30	.07
☐ 25 Tom Haller	.75	.30	.07
☐ 26 Willie Crawford	.75	.30	.07
☐ 27 Roberto Clemente	8.00	3.25	.80
☐ 28 Matty Alou	.75	.30	.07
☐ 29 Willie Stargell	4.00	1.60	.40
☐ 30 Tim Cullen	.75	.30	.07
☐ 31 Randy Hundley	.75	.30	.07
☐ 32 Reggie Jackson	7.00	2.80	.70
☐ 33 Rich Allen	1.00	.40	.10
☐ 34 Tim McCarver	1.25	.50	.12
☐ 35 Ray Culp	.75	.30	.07
☐ 36 Jim Fregosi	1.00	.40	.10
☐ 37 Billy Williams	3.00	1.20	.30
☐ 38 Johnny Odom	.75	.30	.07
☐ 39 Bert Campaneris	1.00	.40	.10
☐ 40 Ernie Banks	4.00	1.60	.40
☐ 41 Chris Short	.75	.30	.07
☐ 42 Ron Santo	1.00	.40	.10
☐ 43 Glenn Beckert	.75	.30	.07
☐ 44 Lou Brock	3.50	1.40	.35
☐ 45 Larry Hisle	.75	.30	.07
☐ 46 Reggie Smith	1.00	.40	.10
☐ 47 Rod Carew	4.00	1.60	.40
☐ 48 Curt Flood	1.00	.40	.10
☐ 49 Jim Lonborg	1.00	.40	.10
☐ 50 Sam McDowell	1.00	.40	.10
☐ 51 Sal Bando	1.00	.40	.10
☐ 52 Al Kaline	4.50	1.80	.45
☐ 53 Gary Nolan	.75	.30	.07
☐ 54 Rico Petrocelli	.75	.30	.07
☐ 55 Ollie Brown	.75	.30	.07
☐ 56 Luis Tiant	1.25	.50	.12
☐ 57 Bill Freehan	1.00	.40	.10
☐ 58 Johnny Bench	6.00	2.40	.60
☐ 59 Joe Pepitone	1.00	.40	.10
☐ 60 Bobby Murcer	1.25	.50	.12
☐ 61 Harmon Killebrew	3.00	1.20	.30
☐ 62 Don Wilson	.75	.30	.07
☐ 63 Tony Oliva	1.50	.60	.15
☐ 64 Jim Perry	1.00	.40	.10
☐ 65 Mickey Lolich	1.25	.50	.12
☐ 66 Jose Laboy	.75	.30	.07
☐ 67 Dean Chance	.75	.30	.07
☐ 68 Bud Harrelson	.75	.30	.07
☐ 69 Willie Horton	1.00	.40	.10
☐ 70 Wally Bunker	.75	.30	.07
☐ 71 Bob Gibson	3.50	1.40	.35
☐ 72 Joe Morgan	3.00	1.20	.30
☐ 73 Denny McLain	1.25	.50	.12
☐ 74 Tommy Harper	.75	.30	.07
☐ 75 Don Mincher	.75	.30	.07

1971 Kellogg's

The cards in this 75-card set measure 2 1/4" by 3 1/2". The 1971 set of 3-D cards marketed by the Kellogg Company is the scarcest of all that company's issues. It was distributed as single cards, one in each package of cereal, without the usual complete set mail-in offer. In addition, card dealers were unable to obtain this set in quantity, as they

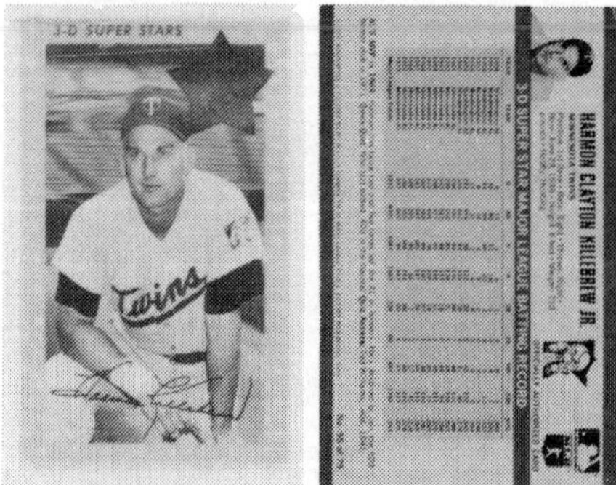

have in other years. All the cards are available with and without the copyright notice on the back; the version without carries a slight premium for most numbers. Prices listed below are for the more common variety with copyright.

	NRMT	VG-E	GOOD
COMPLETE SET (75)	650.00	260.00	65.00
COMMON PLAYER (1-75)	6.00	2.40	.60
□ 1 Wayne Simpson	6.00	2.40	.60
□ 2 Tom Seaver	25.00	10.00	2.50
□ 3 Jim Perry	7.00	2.80	.70
□ 4 Bob Robertson	6.00	2.40	.60
□ 5 Roberto Clemente	30.00	12.00	3.00
□ 6 Gaylord Perry	13.50	5.00	1.00
□ 7 Felipe Alou	7.00	2.80	.70
□ 8 Denis Menke	6.00	2.40	.60
□ 9 Don Kessinger	6.00	2.40	.60
□ 10 Willie Mays	32.00	13.00	3.20
□ 11 Jim Hickman	6.00	2.40	.60
□ 12 Tony Oliva	9.00	3.75	.90
□ 13 Manny Sanguillen	6.00	2.40	.60
□ 14 Frank Howard	7.00	2.80	.70
□ 15 Frank Robinson	16.00	6.50	1.60
□ 16 Willie Davis	7.00	2.80	.70
□ 17 Lou Brock	20.00	8.00	2.00
□ 18 Cesar Tovar	6.00	2.40	.60
□ 19 Luis Aparicio	13.50	5.00	1.00
□ 20 Boog Powell	9.00	3.75	.90
□ 21 Dick Selma	6.00	2.40	.60
□ 22 Danny Walton	6.00	2.40	.60
□ 23 Carl Morton	6.00	2.40	.60
□ 24 Sonny Siebert	6.00	2.40	.60
□ 25 Jim Merritt	6.00	2.40	.60
□ 26 Jose Cardenal	6.00	2.40	.60
□ 27 Don Mincher	6.00	2.40	.60
□ 28 Clyde Wright	6.00	2.40	.60
□ 29 Les Cain	6.00	2.40	.60
□ 30 Danny Cater	6.00	2.40	.60
□ 31 Don Sutton	13.50	5.00	1.00
□ 32 Chuck Dobson	6.00	2.40	.60
□ 33 Willie McCovey	16.00	6.50	1.60
□ 34 Mike Epstein	6.00	2.40	.60
□ 35 Paul Blair	6.00	2.40	.60
□ 36 Gary Nolan	6.00	2.40	.60
□ 37 Sam McDowell	7.00	2.80	.70
□ 38 Amos Otis	7.00	2.80	.70
□ 39 Ray Fosse	6.00	2.40	.60
□ 40 Mel Stottlemyre	7.00	2.80	.70
□ 41 Clarence Gaston	6.00	2.40	.60
□ 42 Dick Dietz	6.00	2.40	.60
□ 43 Roy White	7.00	2.80	.70
□ 44 Al Kaline	20.00	8.00	2.00
□ 45 Carlos May	6.00	2.40	.60
□ 46 Tommie Agee	6.00	2.40	.60
□ 47 Tommy Harper	6.00	2.40	.60
□ 48 Larry Dierker	6.00	2.40	.60
□ 49 Mike Cuellar	6.00	2.40	.60
□ 50 Ernie Banks	20.00	8.00	2.00
□ 51 Bob Gibson	16.00	6.50	1.60
□ 52 Reggie Smith	7.00	2.80	.70
□ 53 Matty Alou	7.00	2.80	.70
□ 54 Alex Johnson	6.00	2.40	.60
□ 55 Harmon Killebrew	16.00	6.50	1.60
□ 56 Bill Grabarkewitz	6.00	2.40	.60
□ 57 Richie Allen	9.00	3.75	.90
□ 58 Tony Perez	12.00	5.00	1.20
□ 59 Dave McNally	7.00	2.80	.70
□ 60 Jim Palmer	16.00	6.50	1.60
□ 61 Billy Williams	16.00	6.50	1.60
□ 62 Joe Torre	9.00	3.75	.9
□ 63 Jim Northrup	7.00	2.80	.7
□ 64 Jim Fregosi	7.00	2.80	.7
□ 65 Pete Rose	60.00	24.00	6.0
□ 66 Bud Harrelson	6.00	2.40	.6
□ 67 Tony Taylor	6.00	2.40	.6
□ 68 Willie Stargell	18.00	7.25	1.8
□ 69 Tony Horton	7.00	2.80	.7
□ 70 Claude Osteen	6.00	2.40	.6
□ 71 Glenn Beckert	6.00	2.40	.6
□ 72 Nate Colbert	6.00	2.40	.6
□ 73 Rick Monday	7.00	2.80	.7
□ 74 Tommy John	12.00	5.00	1.2
□ 75 Chris Short	6.00	2.40	.6

1972 Kellogg's

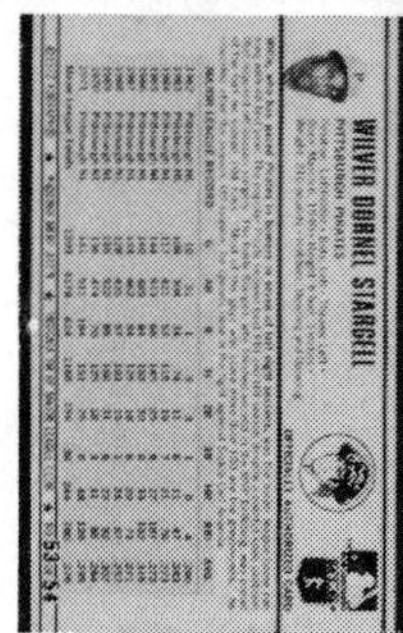

The cards in this 54-card set measure 2 1/8" by 3 1/4". The dimensions of the cards in the 1972 Kellogg's set were reduced in comparison to those of the 1971 series. In addition, the length of the set was set at 54 cards rather than the 75 of the previous year. The cards of this Kellogg's set are characterized by the diagonal bands found on the obverse.

	NRMT	VG-E	GOOD
COMPLETE SET (54)	50.00	20.00	5.00
COMMON PLAYER (1-54)	.50	.20	.05
□ 1 Tom Seaver	6.50	2.60	.65
□ 2 Amos Otis	.60	.24	.06
□ 3 Willie Davis	.60	.24	.06
□ 4 Wilbur Wood	.50	.20	.05
□ 5 Bill Parsons	.50	.20	.05
□ 6 Pete Rose	15.00	6.00	1.50
□ 7 Willie McCovey	3.00	1.20	.30
□ 8 Ferguson Jenkins	.80	.32	.08
□ 9 Vida Blue	.60	.24	.06
□ 10 Joe Torre	.80	.32	.08
□ 11 Merv Rettenmund	.50	.20	.05
□ 12 Bill Melton	.50	.20	.05
□ 13 Jim Palmer	3.00	1.20	.30
□ 14 Doug Rader	.60	.24	.06
□ 15 Dave Roberts	.50	.20	.05
□ 16 Bobby Murcer	.80	.32	.08
□ 17 Wes Parker	.60	.24	.06
□ 18 Joe Coleman	.50	.20	.05
□ 19 Manny Sanguillen	.50	.20	.05
□ 20 Reggie Jackson	6.50	2.60	.65
□ 21 Ralph Garr	.50	.20	.05
□ 22 Jim Hunter	2.50	1.00	.25
□ 23 Rick Wise	.50	.20	.05
□ 24 Glenn Beckert	.50	.20	.05
□ 25 Tony Oliva	1.00	.40	.10
□ 26 Bob Gibson	3.00	1.20	.30
□ 27 Mike Cuellar	.50	.20	.05
□ 28 Chris Speier	.50	.20	.05
□ 29 Dave McNally	.60	.24	.06
□ 30 Leo Cardenas	.50	.20	.05
□ 31 Bill Freehan	.60	.24	.06
□ 32 Bud Harrelson	.50	.20	.05
□ 33 Sam McDowell	.60	.24	.06
□ 34 Claude Osteen	.50	.20	.05
□ 35 Reggie Smith	.60	.24	.06
□ 36 Sonny Siebert	.50	.20	.05
□ 37 Lee May	.60	.24	.06
□ 38 Mickey Lolich	.80	.32	.08

☐ 39 Cookie Rojas	.60	.24	.06
☐ 40 Dick Drago	.50	.20	.05
☐ 41 Nate Colbert	.50	.20	.05
☐ 42 Andy Messersmith	.60	.24	.06
☐ 43 Dave Johnson	1.00	.40	.10
☐ 44 Steve Blass	.60	.24	.06
☐ 45 Bob Robertson	.50	.20	.05
☐ 46 Billy Williams	3.00	1.20	.30
☐ 47 Juan Marichal	3.00	1.20	.30
☐ 48 Lou Brock	3.50	1.40	.35
☐ 49 Roberto Clemente	7.00	2.80	.70
☐ 50 Mel Stottlemyre	.60	.24	.06
☐ 51 Don Wilson	.50	.20	.05
☐ 52 Sal Bando	.60	.24	.06
☐ 53 Willie Stargell	3.00	1.20	.30
☐ 54 Willie Mays	8.00	3.25	.80

1972 Kellogg's ATG

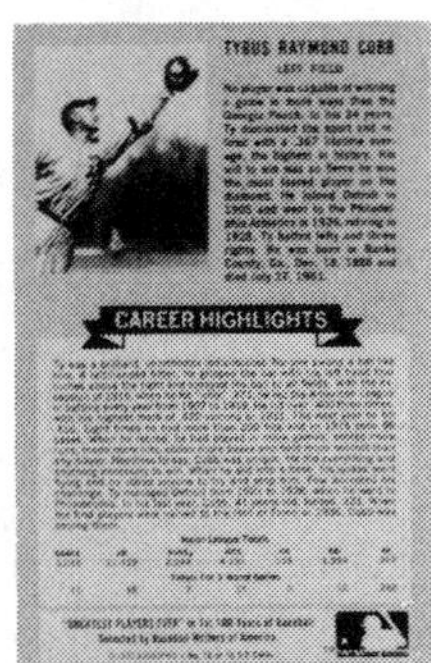

The cards in this 15-card set measure 2 1/4" by 3 1/2". The 1972 All-Time Greats 3-D set was issued with Kellogg's Danish Go Rounds. The set contains two different cards of Babe Ruth. The set is a reissue of a 1970 set issued by Rold Gold Pretzels to commemorate baseball's first 100 years. The Rold Gold cards are copyrighted 1970 on the reverse and are valued at approximately double the prices listed below.

	NRMT	VG-E	GOOD
COMPLETE SET (15)	12.50	5.00	1.25
COMMON PLAYER (1-15)	.40	.16	.04
☐ 1 Walter Johnson	1.00	.40	.10
☐ 2 Rogers Hornsby	.60	.24	.06
☐ 3 John McGraw	.40	.16	.04
☐ 4 Mickey Cochrane	.50	.20	.05
☐ 5 George Sisler	.50	.20	.05
☐ 6 Babe Ruth	3.00	1.20	.30
☐ 7 Lefty Grove	.60	.24	.06
☐ 8 Pie Traynor	.40	.16	.04
☐ 9 Honus Wagner	1.00	.40	.10
☐ 10 Eddie Collins	.40	.16	.04
☐ 11 Tris Speaker	.60	.24	.06
☐ 12 Cy Young	.60	.24	.06
☐ 13 Lou Gehrig	1.75	.70	.17
☐ 14 Babe Ruth	3.00	1.20	.30
☐ 15 Ty Cobb	1.75	.70	.17

1973 Kellogg's 2D

The cards in this 54-card set measure 2 1/4" by 3 1/2". The 1973 Kellogg's set is the only non 3-D set produced by the Kellogg Company. Apparently Kellogg's decided to have the cards produced through Visual Panographics rather than by Xograph as in the other years. The complete set could be

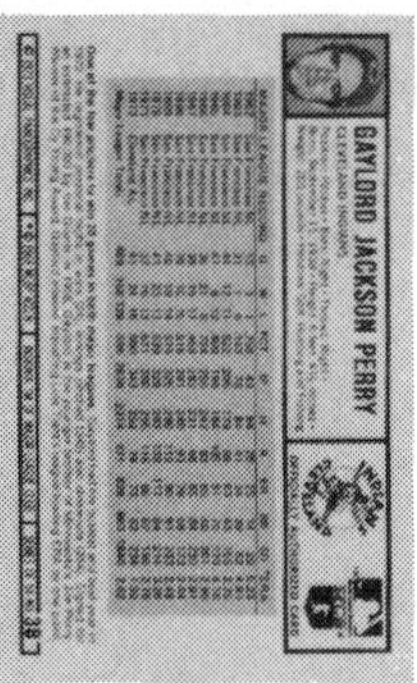

obtained from the company through a box-top redemption procedure. The card size is slightly larger than the previous year.

	NRMT	VG-E	GOOD
COMPLETE SET (54)	45.00	18.00	4.50
COMMON PLAYER (1-54)	.50	.20	.05
☐ 1 Amos Otis	.60	.24	.06
☐ 2 Ellie Rodriguez	.50	.20	.05
☐ 3 Mickey Lolich	.80	.32	.08
☐ 4 Tony Oliva	.80	.32	.08
☐ 5 Don Sutton	1.75	.70	.17
☐ 6 Pete Rose	12.00	5.00	1.20
☐ 7 Steve Carlton	4.00	1.60	.40
☐ 8 Bobby Bonds	.80	.32	.08
☐ 9 Wilbur Wood	.50	.20	.05
☐ 10 Billy Williams	2.50	1.00	.25
☐ 11 Steve Blass	.60	.24	.06
☐ 12 Jon Matlack	.50	.20	.05
☐ 13 Cesar Cedeno	.60	.24	.06
☐ 14 Bob Gibson	2.50	1.00	.25
☐ 15 Sparky Lyle	.80	.32	.08
☐ 16 Nolan Ryan	4.00	1.60	.40
☐ 17 Jim Palmer	2.50	1.00	.25
☐ 18 Ray Fosse	.50	.20	.05
☐ 19 Bobby Murcer	.60	.24	.06
☐ 20 Jim Hunter	2.00	.80	.20
☐ 21 Tom McCraw	.50	.20	.05
☐ 22 Reggie Jackson	5.00	2.00	.50
☐ 23 Bill Stoneman	.50	.20	.05
☐ 24 Lou Piniella	.60	.24	.06
☐ 25 Willie Stargell	3.50	1.40	.35
☐ 26 Dick Allen	.80	.32	.08
☐ 27 Carlton Fisk	1.25	.50	.12
☐ 28 Ferguson Jenkins	.80	.32	.08
☐ 29 Phil Niekro	2.00	.80	.20
☐ 30 Gary Nolan	.50	.20	.05
☐ 31 Joe Torre	.80	.32	.08
☐ 32 Bobby Tolan	.50	.20	.05
☐ 33 Nate Colbert	.50	.20	.05
☐ 34 Joe Morgan	2.50	1.00	.25
☐ 35 Bert Blyleven	.60	.24	.06
☐ 36 Joe Rudi	.60	.24	.06
☐ 37 Ralph Garr	.50	.20	.05
☐ 38 Gaylord Perry	1.75	.70	.17
☐ 39 Bobby Grich	.60	.24	.06
☐ 40 Lou Brock	2.50	1.00	.25
☐ 41 Pete Broberg	.50	.20	.05
☐ 42 Manny Sanguillen	.50	.20	.05
☐ 43 Willie Davis	.60	.24	.06
☐ 44 Dave Kingman	.80	.32	.08
☐ 45 Carlos May	.50	.20	.05
☐ 46 Tom Seaver	4.00	1.60	.40
☐ 47 Mike Cuellar	.50	.20	.05
☐ 48 Joe Coleman	.50	.20	.05
☐ 49 Claude Osteen	.50	.20	.05
☐ 50 Steve Kline	.50	.20	.05
☐ 51 Rod Carew	3.50	1.40	.35
☐ 52 Al Kaline	3.50	1.40	.35
☐ 53 Larry Dierker	.50	.20	.05
☐ 54 Ron Santo	.80	.32	.08

1974 Kellogg's

The cards in this 54-card set measure 2 1/8" by 3 1/4". In 1974 the Kellogg's set returned to its 3-D format; it also returned to the smaller-size card.

Complete sets could be obtained from the company through a box-top offer. The cards are numbered on the back.

	NRMT	VG-E	GOOD
COMPLETE SET (54)	40.00	16.00	4.00
COMMON PLAYER (1-54)	.35	.14	.03
☐ 1 Bob Gibson	2.50	1.00	.25
☐ 2 Rick Monday	.45	.18	.04
☐ 3 Joe Coleman	.35	.14	.03
☐ 4 Bert Campaneris	.45	.18	.04
☐ 5 Carlton Fisk	1.00	.40	.10
☐ 6 Jim Palmer	2.50	1.00	.25
☐ 7 Ron Santo	.60	.24	.06
☐ 8 Nolan Ryan	4.00	1.60	.40
☐ 9 Greg Luzinski	.60	.24	.06
☐ 10 Buddy Bell	.60	.24	.06
☐ 11 Bob Watson	.45	.18	.04
☐ 12 Bill Singer	.35	.14	.03
☐ 13 Dave May	.35	.14	.03
☐ 14 Jim Brewer	.35	.14	.03
☐ 15 Manny Sanguillen	.45	.18	.04
☐ 16 Jeff Burroughs	.45	.18	.04
☐ 17 Amos Otis	.45	.18	.04
☐ 18 Ed Goodson	.35	.14	.03
☐ 19 Nate Colbert	.35	.14	.03
☐ 20 Reggie Jackson	5.00	2.00	.50
☐ 21 Ted Simmons	.75	.30	.07
☐ 22 Bobby Murcer	.60	.24	.06
☐ 23 Willie Horton	.45	.18	.04
☐ 24 Orlando Cepeda	.75	.30	.07
☐ 25 Ron Hunt	.35	.14	.03
☐ 26 Wayne Twitchell	.35	.14	.03
☐ 27 Ron Fairly	.35	.14	.03
☐ 28 Johnny Bench	4.00	1.60	.40
☐ 29 John Mayberry	.35	.14	.03
☐ 30 Rod Carew	3.50	1.40	.35
☐ 31 Ken Holtzman	.45	.18	.04
☐ 32 Billy Williams	2.00	.80	.20
☐ 33 Dick Allen	.60	.24	.06
☐ 34 Wilbur Wood	.45	.18	.04
☐ 35 Danny Thompson	.35	.14	.03
☐ 36 Joe Morgan	2.00	.80	.20
☐ 37 Willie Stargell	2.50	1.00	.25
☐ 38 Pete Rose	11.00	4.50	1.10
☐ 39 Bobby Bonds	.60	.24	.06
☐ 40 Chris Speier	.35	.14	.03
☐ 41 Sparky Lyle	.60	.24	.06
☐ 42 Cookie Rojas	.45	.18	.04
☐ 43 Tommy Davis	.45	.18	.04
☐ 44 Jim Hunter	1.75	.70	.17
☐ 45 Willie Davis	.45	.18	.04
☐ 46 Bert Blyleven	.60	.24	.06
☐ 47 Pat Kelly	.35	.14	.03
☐ 48 Ken Singleton	.45	.18	.04
☐ 49 Manny Mota	.45	.18	.04
☐ 50 Dave Johnson	.75	.30	.07
☐ 51 Sal Bando	.45	.18	.04
☐ 52 Tom Seaver	4.00	1.60	.40
☐ 53 Felix Millan	.35	.14	.03
☐ 54 Ron Blomberg	.35	.14	.03

1975 Kellogg's

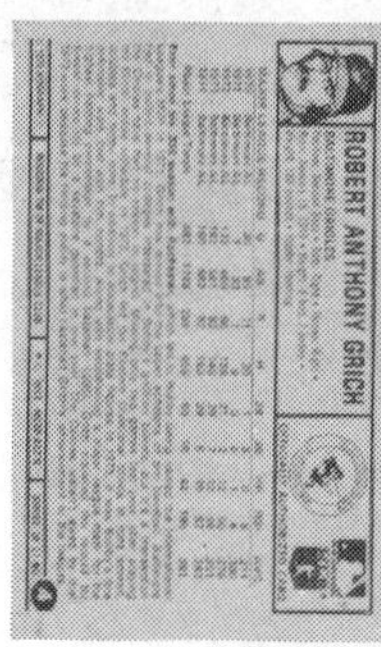

The cards in this 57-card set measure 2 1/8" by 3 1/4". The 1975 Kellogg's 3-D set could be obtained card by card in cereal boxes or as a set from a box-top offer from the company. Card number 44 Jim Hunter exists with the A's emblem or the Yankees emblem on the back of the card.

	NRMT	VG-E	GOOD
COMPLETE SET (57)	120.00	50.00	12.00
COMMON PLAYER (1-57)	.60	.24	.06
☐ 1 Roy White	.75	.30	.0
☐ 2 Ross Grimsley	.65	.26	.0
☐ 3 Reggie Smith	.75	.30	.0
☐ 4 Bob Grich	.75	.30	.07
☐ 5 Greg Gross	.65	.26	.06
☐ 6 Bob Watson	.75	.30	.07
☐ 7 Johnny Bench	7.50	3.00	.75
☐ 8 Jeff Burroughs	.75	.30	.07
☐ 9 Elliott Maddox	.65	.26	.06
☐ 10 Jon Matlack	.75	.30	.07
☐ 11 Pete Rose	18.00	7.25	1.80
☐ 12 Lee Stanton	.65	.26	.06
☐ 13 Bake McBride	.65	.26	.06
☐ 14 Jorge Orta	.65	.26	.06
☐ 15 Al Oliver	1.00	.40	.10
☐ 16 John Briggs	.65	.26	.06
☐ 17 Steve Garvey	6.50	2.60	.65
☐ 18 Brooks Robinson	5.00	2.00	.50
☐ 19 John Hiller	.75	.30	.07
☐ 20 Lynn McGlothen	.65	.26	.06
☐ 21 Cleon Jones	.65	.26	.06
☐ 22 Fergie Jenkins	1.25	.50	.12
☐ 23 Bill North	.65	.26	.06
☐ 24 Steve Busby	.75	.30	.07
☐ 25 Richie Zisk	.75	.30	.07
☐ 26 Nolan Ryan	7.50	3.00	.75
☐ 27 Joe Morgan	3.50	1.40	.35
☐ 28 Joe Rudi	.75	.30	.07
☐ 29 Jose Cardenal	.65	.26	.06
☐ 30 Andy Messersmith	.75	.30	.07
☐ 31 Willie Montanez	.65	.26	.06
☐ 32 Bill Buckner	1.00	.40	.10
☐ 33 Rod Carew	6.00	2.40	.60
☐ 34 Lou Piniella	.90	.36	.09
☐ 35 Ralph Garr	.75	.30	.07
☐ 36 Mike Marshall	.75	.30	.07
☐ 37 Garry Maddox	.75	.30	.07
☐ 38 Dwight Evans	1.50	.60	.15
☐ 39 Lou Brock	5.00	2.00	.50
☐ 40 Ken Singleton	.90	.36	.09
☐ 41 Steve Braun	.65	.26	.06
☐ 42 Rich Allen	1.00	.40	.10
☐ 43 John Grubb	.65	.26	.06
☐ 44 Jim Hunter (2)	4.00	1.60	.40
☐ 45 Gaylord Perry	2.50	1.00	.25
☐ 46 George Hendrick	.90	.36	.09
☐ 47 Sparky Lyle	.90	.36	.09
☐ 48 Dave Cash	.65	.26	.06
☐ 49 Luis Tiant	.90	.36	.09
☐ 50 Cesar Geronimo	.65	.26	.06
☐ 51 Carl Yastrzemski	15.00	6.00	1.50
☐ 52 Ken Brett	.65	.26	.06
☐ 53 Hal McRae	.75	.30	.07
☐ 54 Reggie Jackson	9.00	3.75	.90
☐ 55 Rollie Fingers	2.50	1.00	.25
☐ 56 Mike Schmidt	11.00	4.50	1.10
☐ 57 Richie Hebner	.65	.26	.06

1976 Kellogg's

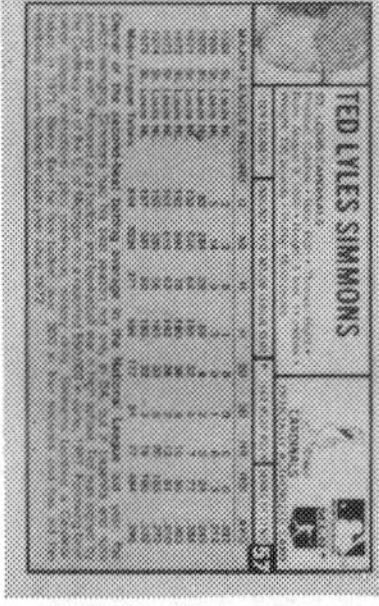

The cards in this 57-card set measure 2 1/8" by 3 1/4". The 1976 Kellogg's 3-D set could be obtained card by card in cereal boxes or as a set from the company for box-tops. Card number 6, that of Clay Carroll, exists with both a Reds or White Sox emblem on the back. Cards 1-3 (marked in the checklist below with SP) were apparently printed apart from the other 54 and are in shorter supply.

	NRMT	VG-E	GOOD
COMPLETE SET	60.00	24.00	6.00
COMMON PLAYER (1-3) SP	8.00	3.25	.80
COMMON PLAYER (4-57)	.40	.16	.04
□ 1 Steve Hargan SP	8.00	3.25	.80
□ 2 Claudell Washington SP	8.00	3.25	.80
□ 3 Don Gullett SP	8.00	3.25	.80
□ 4 Randy Jones	.50	.20	.05
□ 5 Jim Hunter	2.00	.80	.20
□ 6 Clay Carroll (2)	.60	.24	.06
□ 7 Joe Rudi	.50	.20	.05
□ 8 Reggie Jackson	5.00	2.00	.50
□ 9 Felix Millan	.40	.16	.04
□ 10 Jim Rice	3.00	1.20	.30
□ 11 Bert Blyleven	.60	.24	.06
□ 12 Ken Singleton	.50	.20	.05
□ 13 Don Sutton	1.50	.60	.15
□ 14 Joe Morgan	2.50	1.00	.25
□ 15 Dave Parker	1.50	.60	.15
□ 16 Dave Cash	.40	.16	.04
□ 17 Ron LeFlore	.40	.16	.04
□ 18 Greg Luzinski	.60	.24	.06
□ 19 Dennis Eckersley	1.25	.50	.12
□ 20 Bill Madlock	.80	.32	.08
□ 21 George Scott	.40	.16	.04
□ 22 Willie Stargell	2.50	1.00	.25
□ 23 Al Hrabosky	.50	.20	.05
□ 24 Carl Yastrzemski	6.00	2.40	.60
□ 25 Jim Kaat	.80	.32	.08
□ 26 Marty Perez	.40	.16	.04
□ 27 Bob Watson	.50	.20	.05
□ 28 Eric Soderholm	.40	.16	.04
□ 29 Bill Lee	.50	.20	.05
□ 30 Frank Tanana	.50	.20	.05
□ 31 Fred Lynn	1.50	.60	.15
□ 32 Tom Seaver	4.00	1.60	.40
□ 33 Steve Busby	.50	.20	.05
□ 34 Gary Carter	4.00	1.60	.40
□ 35 Rick Wise	.40	.16	.04
□ 36 Johnny Bench	4.00	1.60	.40
□ 37 Jim Palmer	2.00	.80	.20
□ 38 Bobby Murcer	.60	.24	.06
□ 39 Von Joshua	.40	.16	.04
□ 40 Lou Brock	2.50	1.00	.25
□ 41 Mickey Rivers (2)	.50	.20	.05
□ 42 Manny Sanguillen	.50	.20	.05
□ 43 Jerry Reuss	.40	.16	.04
□ 44 Ken Griffey	.50	.20	.05
□ 45 Jorge Orta	.40	.16	.04
□ 46 John Mayberry	.40	.16	.04
□ 47 Vida Blue (2)	.50	.20	.05
□ 48 Rod Carew	3.00	1.20	.30
□ 49 Jon Matlack	.50	.20	.05
□ 50 Boog Powell	.60	.24	.06
□ 51 Mike Hargrove	.50	.20	.05
□ 52 Paul Lindblad	.40	.16	.04
□ 53 Thurman Munson	3.50	1.40	.35
□ 54 Steve Garvey	3.50	1.40	.35
□ 55 Pete Rose	11.00	4.50	1.10
□ 56 Greg Gross	.40	.16	.04
□ 57 Ted Simmons	.80	.32	.08

1977 Kellogg's

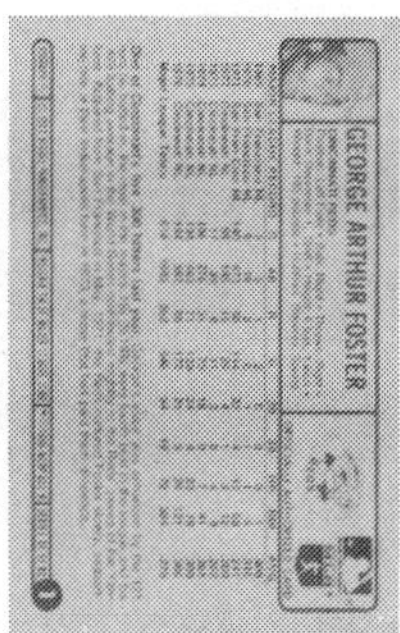

The cards in this 57-card set measure 2 1/8" by 3 1/4". The 1977 Kellogg's series of 3-D baseball player cards could be obtained card by card from cereal boxes or by sending in box-tops and money. Each player's picture appears in miniature form on the reverse, an idea begun in 1971 and replaced in subsequent years by the use of a picture of the Kellogg's mascot.

	NRMT	VG-E	GOOD
COMPLETE SET (57)	40.00	16.00	4.00
COMMON PLAYER (1-57)	.30	.12	.03
□ 1 George Foster	.80	.32	.08
□ 2 Bert Campaneris	.40	.16	.04
□ 3 Fergie Jenkins	.65	.26	.06
□ 4 Dock Ellis	.30	.12	.03
□ 5 John Montefusco	.30	.12	.03
□ 6 George Brett	6.00	2.40	.60
□ 7 John Candelaria	.40	.16	.04
□ 8 Fred Norman	.30	.12	.03
□ 9 Bill Travers	.30	.12	.03
□ 10 Hal McRae	.40	.16	.04
□ 11 Doug Rau	.30	.12	.03
□ 12 Greg Luzinski	.50	.20	.05
□ 13 Ralph Garr	.30	.12	.03
□ 14 Steve Garvey	3.50	1.40	.35
□ 15 Rick Manning	.30	.12	.03
□ 16 Lyman Bostock	.40	.16	.04
□ 17 Randy Jones	.30	.12	.03
□ 18 Ron Cey	.50	.20	.05
□ 19 Dave Parker	1.00	.40	.10
□ 20 Pete Rose	8.50	3.50	.85
□ 21 Wayne Garland	.30	.12	.03
□ 22 Bill North	.30	.12	.03
□ 23 Thurman Munson	2.50	1.00	.25
□ 24 Tom Poquette	.30	.12	.03
□ 25 Ron LeFlore	.40	.16	.04
□ 26 Mark Fidrych	.40	.16	.04
□ 27 Sixto Lezcano	.30	.12	.03
□ 28 Dave Winfield	2.50	1.00	.25
□ 29 Jerry Koosman	.40	.16	.04
□ 30 Mike Hargrove	.30	.12	.03
□ 31 Willie Montanez	.30	.12	.03
□ 32 Don Stanhouse	.30	.12	.03
□ 33 Jay Johnstone	.40	.16	.04
□ 34 Bake McBride	.30	.12	.03
□ 35 Dave Kingman	.60	.24	.06
□ 36 Fred Patek	.30	.12	.03
□ 37 Garry Maddox	.30	.12	.03
□ 38 Ken Reitz	.30	.12	.03
□ 39 Bobby Grich	.40	.16	.04
□ 40 Cesar Geronimo	.30	.12	.03
□ 41 Jim Lonborg	.40	.16	.04
□ 42 Ed Figueroa	.30	.12	.03
□ 43 Bill Madlock	.70	.28	.07
□ 44 Jerry Remy	.30	.12	.03
□ 45 Frank Tanana	.40	.16	.04
□ 46 Al Oliver	.70	.28	.07

☐ 47	Charlie Hough	.50	.20	.05
☐ 48	Lou Piniella	.50	.20	.05
☐ 49	Ken Griffey	.40	.16	.04
☐ 50	Jose Cruz	.50	.20	.05
☐ 51	Rollie Fingers	1.00	.40	.10
☐ 52	Chris Chambliss	.50	.20	.05
☐ 53	Rod Carew	3.00	1.20	.30
☐ 54	Andy Messersmith	.40	.16	.04
☐ 55	Mickey Rivers	.40	.16	.04
☐ 56	Butch Wynegar	.40	.16	.04
☐ 57	Steve Carlton	3.00	1.20	.30

1978 Kellogg's

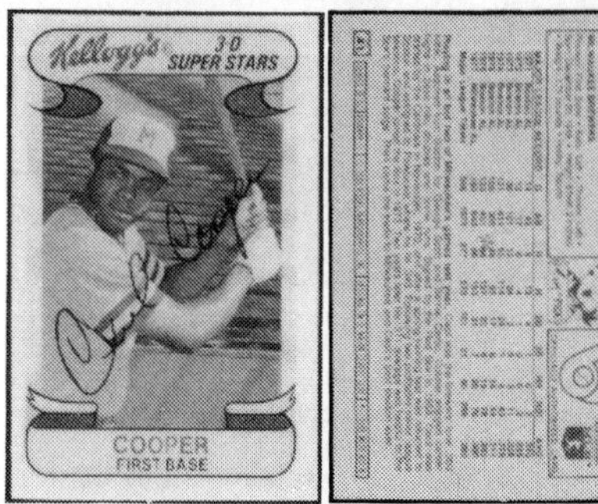

The cards in this 57-card set measure 2 1/8" by 3 1/4". This 1978 3-D Kellogg's series marks the first year in which Tony the Tiger appears on the reverse of each card next to the team and MLB logos. Once again the set could be obtained as individually wrapped cards in cereal boxes or as a set via a mail-in offer.

		NRMT	VG-E	GOOD
COMPLETE SET (57)		35.00	14.00	3.50
COMMON PLAYER (1-57)		.25	.10	.02
☐ 1	Steve Carlton	2.50	1.00	.25
☐ 2	Bucky Dent	.35	.14	.03
☐ 3	Mike Schmidt	4.00	1.60	.40
☐ 4	Ken Griffey	.35	.14	.03
☐ 5	Al Cowens	.25	.10	.02
☐ 6	George Brett	4.00	1.60	.40
☐ 7	Lou Brock	2.00	.80	.20
☐ 8	Rich Gossage	.70	.28	.07
☐ 9	Tom Johnson	.25	.10	.02
☐ 10	George Foster	.70	.28	.07
☐ 11	Dave Winfield	2.50	1.00	.25
☐ 12	Dan Meyer	.25	.10	.02
☐ 13	Chris Chambliss	.35	.14	.03
☐ 14	Paul Dade	.25	.10	.02
☐ 15	Jeff Burroughs	.25	.10	.02
☐ 16	Jose Cruz	.35	.14	.03
☐ 17	Mickey Rivers	.35	.14	.03
☐ 18	John Candelaria	.35	.14	.03
☐ 19	Ellis Valentine	.25	.10	.02
☐ 20	Hal McRae	.35	.14	.03
☐ 21	Dave Rozema	.25	.10	.02
☐ 22	Lenny Randle	.25	.10	.02
☐ 23	Willie McCovey	2.00	.80	.20
☐ 24	Ron Cey	.50	.20	.05
☐ 25	Eddie Murray	10.00	4.00	1.00
☐ 26	Larry Bowa	.40	.16	.04
☐ 27	Tom Seaver	3.50	1.40	.35
☐ 28	Garry Maddox	.35	.14	.03
☐ 29	Rod Carew	2.50	1.00	.25
☐ 30	Thurman Munson	3.00	1.20	.30
☐ 31	Gary Templeton	.50	.20	.05
☐ 32	Eric Soderholm	.25	.10	.02
☐ 33	Greg Luzinski	.50	.20	.05
☐ 34	Reggie Smith	.35	.14	.03
☐ 35	Dave Goltz	.25	.10	.02
☐ 36	Tommy John	.70	.28	.07
☐ 37	Ralph Garr	.25	.10	.02
☐ 38	Alan Bannister	.25	.10	.02
☐ 39	Bob Bailor	.25	.10	.02
☐ 40	Reggie Jackson	4.00	1.60	.40
☐ 41	Cecil Cooper	.50	.20	.05
☐ 42	Burt Hooton	.25	.10	.02
☐ 43	Sparky Lyle	.40	.16	.04
☐ 44	Steve Ontiveros	.25	.10	.02
☐ 45	Rick Reuschel	.50	.20	.05
☐ 46	Lyman Bostock	.35	.14	.03
☐ 47	Mitchell Page	.25	.10	.02
☐ 48	Bruce Sutter	.70	.28	.07
☐ 49	Jim Rice	2.00	.80	.20
☐ 50	Ken Forsch	.25	.10	.02
☐ 51	Nolan Ryan	3.00	1.20	.30
☐ 52	Dave Parker	1.25	.50	.12
☐ 53	Bert Blyleven	.50	.20	.05
☐ 54	Frank Tanana	.35	.14	.03
☐ 55	Ken Singleton	.35	.14	.03
☐ 56	Mike Hargrove	.35	.14	.03
☐ 57	Don Sutton	1.50	.60	.15

1979 Kellogg's

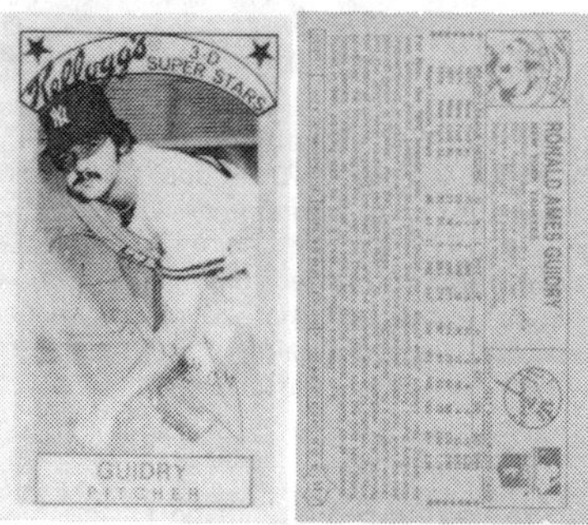

The cards in this 60-card set measure 1 15/16" by 3 1/4". The 1979 edition of Kellogg's 3-D baseball cards have a 3/16" reduced width from the previous year; a nicely designed curved panel above the picture gives this set a distinctive appearance. The set contains the largest number of cards issued in a Kellogg's set since the 1971 series.

		NRMT	VG-E	GOOD
COMPLETE SET (60)		25.00	10.00	2.50
COMMON PLAYER (1-60)		.20	.08	.02
☐ 1	Bruce Sutter	.50	.20	.05
☐ 2	Ted Simmons	.50	.20	.05
☐ 3	Ross Grimsley	.20	.08	.02
☐ 4	Wayne Nordhagen	.20	.08	.02
☐ 5	Jim Palmer	1.50	.60	.15
☐ 6	John Henry Johnson	.20	.08	.02
☐ 7	Jason Thompson	.20	.08	.02
☐ 8	Pat Zachry	.20	.08	.02
☐ 9	Dennis Eckersley	.75	.30	.07
☐ 10	Paul Splittorff	.20	.08	.02
☐ 11	Ron Guidry	1.25	.50	.12
☐ 12	Jeff Burroughs	.20	.08	.02
☐ 13	Rod Carew	2.50	1.00	.25
☐ 14	Buddy Bell	.30	.12	.03
☐ 15	Jim Rice	2.00	.80	.20
☐ 16	Garry Maddox	.20	.08	.02
☐ 17	Willie McCovey	1.50	.60	.15
☐ 18	Steve Carlton	2.50	1.00	.25
☐ 19	J.R. Richard	.30	.12	.03
☐ 20	Paul Molitor	1.25	.50	.12
☐ 21	Dave Parker	1.00	.40	.10
☐ 22	Pete Rose	6.50	2.60	.65
☐ 23	Vida Blue	.30	.12	.03
☐ 24	Richie Zisk	.20	.08	.02
☐ 25	Darrell Porter	.20	.08	.02
☐ 26	Dan Driessen	.20	.08	.02
☐ 27	Geoff Zahn	.20	.08	.02
☐ 28	Phil Niekro	1.25	.50	.12
☐ 29	Tom Seaver	3.00	1.20	.30
☐ 30	Fred Lynn	.70	.28	.07
☐ 31	Bill Bonham	.20	.08	.02
☐ 32	George Foster	.50	.20	.05
☐ 33	Terry Puhl	.20	.08	.02
☐ 34	John Candelaria	.30	.12	.03
☐ 35	Bob Knepper	.30	.12	.03
☐ 36	Fred Patek	.20	.08	.02
☐ 37	Chris Chambliss	.30	.12	.03
☐ 38	Bob Forsch	.20	.08	.02

		MINT	EXC	G-VG
□ 39	Ken Griffey	.30	.12	.03
□ 40	Jack Clark	1.50	.60	.15
□ 41	Dwight Evans	.80	.32	.08
□ 42	Lee Mazzilli	.20	.08	.02
□ 43	Mario Guerrero	.20	.08	.02
□ 44	Larry Bowa	.40	.16	.04
□ 45	Carl Yastrzemski	4.00	1.60	.40
□ 46	Reggie Jackson	3.50	1.40	.35
□ 47	Rick Reuschel	.40	.16	.04
□ 48	Mike Flanagan	.30	.12	.03
□ 49	Gaylord Perry	1.25	.50	.12
□ 50	George Brett	3.50	1.40	.35
□ 51	Craig Reynolds	.20	.08	.02
□ 52	Dave Lopes	.30	.12	.03
□ 53	Bill Almon	.20	.08	.02
□ 54	Roy Howell	.20	.08	.02
□ 55	Frank Tanana	.30	.12	.03
□ 56	Doug Rau	.20	.08	.02
□ 57	Rick Monday	.30	.12	.03
□ 58	Jon Matlack	.20	.08	.02
□ 59	Ron Jackson	.20	.08	.02
□ 60	Jim Sundberg	.20	.08	.02

1980 Kellogg's

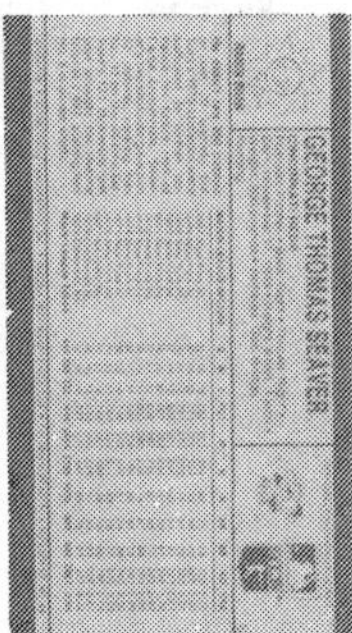

The cards in this 60-card set measure 1 7/8" by 3 1/4". The 1980 Kellogg's 3-D set is quite similar to, but smaller (narrower) than, the other recent Kellogg's issues. Sets could be obtained card by card from cereal boxes or as a set from a box- top offer from the company.

		MINT	EXC	G-VG
COMPLETE SET (60)		20.00	8.00	2.00
COMMON PLAYER (1-60)		.20	.08	.02
□ 1	Ross Grimsley	.20	.08	.02
□ 2	Mike Schmidt	3.50	1.40	.35
□ 3	Mike Flanagan	.30	.12	.03
□ 4	Ron Guidry	.70	.28	.07
□ 5	Bert Blyleven	.40	.16	.04
□ 6	Dave Kingman	.40	.16	.04
□ 7	Jeff Newman	.20	.08	.02
□ 8	Steve Rogers	.30	.12	.03
□ 9	George Brett	3.00	1.20	.30
□ 10	Bruce Sutter	.50	.20	.05
□ 11	Gorman Thomas	.30	.12	.03
□ 12	Darrell Porter	.20	.08	.02
□ 13	Roy Smalley	.20	.08	.02
□ 14	Steve Carlton	2.00	.80	.20
□ 15	Jim Palmer	1.50	.60	.15
□ 16	Bob Bailor	.20	.08	.02
□ 17	Jason Thompson	.20	.08	.02
□ 18	Graig Nettles	.40	.16	.04
□ 19	Ron Cey	.40	.16	.04
□ 20	Nolan Ryan	2.50	1.00	.25
□ 21	Ellis Valentine	.20	.08	.02
□ 22	Larry Hisle	.20	.08	.02
□ 23	Dave Parker	.70	.28	.07
□ 24	Eddie Murray	2.00	.80	.20
□ 25	Willie Stargell	1.50	.60	.15
□ 26	Reggie Jackson	2.50	1.00	.25
□ 27	Carl Yastrzemski	3.00	1.20	.30
□ 28	Andre Thornton	.20	.08	.02
□ 29	Dave Lopes	.30	.12	.03
□ 30	Ken Singleton	.30	.12	.03
□ 31	Steve Garvey	2.00	.80	.20
□ 32	Dave Winfield	2.00	.80	.20
□ 33	Steve Kemp	.30	.12	.03
□ 34	Claudell Washington	.30	.12	.03
□ 35	Pete Rose	5.00	2.00	.50
□ 36	Cesar Cedeno	.30	.12	.03
□ 37	John Stearns	.20	.08	.02
□ 38	Lee Mazzilli	.20	.08	.02
□ 39	Larry Bowa	.30	.12	.03
□ 40	Fred Lynn	.60	.24	.06
□ 41	Carlton Fisk	.60	.24	.06
□ 42	Vida Blue	.30	.12	.03
□ 43	Keith Hernandez	1.50	.60	.15
□ 44	Jim Rice	1.50	.60	.15
□ 45	Ted Simmons	.40	.16	.04
□ 46	Chet Lemon	.30	.12	.03
□ 47	Ferguson Jenkins	.50	.20	.05
□ 48	Gary Matthews	.30	.12	.03
□ 49	Tom Seaver	2.50	1.00	.25
□ 50	George Foster	.50	.20	.05
□ 51	Phil Niekro	1.00	.40	.10
□ 52	Johnny Bench	2.50	1.00	.25
□ 53	Buddy Bell	.40	.16	.04
□ 54	Lance Parrish	1.00	.40	.10
□ 55	Joaquin Andujar	.30	.12	.03
□ 56	Don Baylor	.30	.12	.03
□ 57	Jack Clark	1.00	.40	.10
□ 58	J.R. Richard	.30	.12	.03
□ 59	Bruce Bochte	.20	.08	.02
□ 60	Rod Carew	2.00	.80	.20

1981 Kellogg's

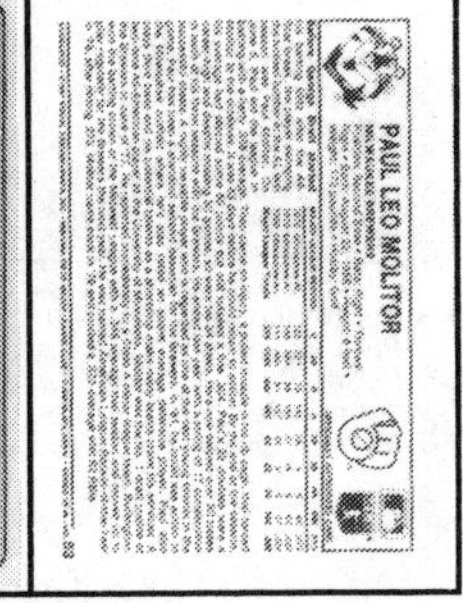

The cards in this 66-card set measure 2 1/2" by 3 1/2". The 1981 Kellogg's set witnessed an increase in both the size of the card and the size of the set. For the first time, cards were not packed in cereal sizes but available only by mail- in procedure. The offer for the card set was advertised on boxes of Kellogg's Corn Flakes. The cards were printed on a different stock than in previous years, presumably to prevent the cracking problem which has plagued all Kellogg's 3-D issues. At the end of the promotion, the remainder of the sets not distributed (to cereal-eaters), were ''sold" into the organized hobby, thus creating a situation where the set is relatively plentiful compared to other years of Kellogg's.

		MINT	EXC	G-VG
COMPLETE SET (66)		7.50	3.00	.75
COMMON PLAYER (1-66)		.07	.03	.01
□ 1	George Foster	.15	.06	.01
□ 2	Jim Palmer	.35	.14	.03
□ 3	Reggie Jackson	.80	.32	.08
□ 4	Al Oliver	.10	.04	.01
□ 5	Mike Schmidt	.90	.36	.09
□ 6	Nolan Ryan	.50	.20	.05
□ 7	Bucky Dent	.10	.04	.01
□ 8	George Brett	.90	.36	.09
□ 9	Jim Rice	.30	.12	.03
□ 10	Steve Garvey	.45	.18	.04
□ 11	Willie Stargell	.35	.14	.03
□ 12	Phil Niekro	.25	.10	.02
□ 13	Dave Parker	.20	.08	.02
□ 14	Cesar Cedeno	.10	.04	.01
□ 15	Don Baylor	.10	.04	.01
□ 16	J.R. Richard	.07	.03	.01

□ 17 Tony Perez	.10	.04	.01
□ 18 Eddie Murray	.60	.24	.06
□ 19 Chet Lemon	.07	.03	.01
□ 20 Ben Oglivie	.07	.03	.01
□ 21 Dave Winfield	.40	.16	.04
□ 22 Joe Morgan	.25	.10	.02
□ 23 Vida Blue	.10	.04	.01
□ 24 Willie Wilson	.10	.04	.01
□ 25 Steve Henderson	.07	.03	.01
□ 26 Rod Carew	.40	.16	.04
□ 27 Garry Templeton	.07	.03	.01
□ 28 Dave Concepcion	.10	.04	.01
□ 29 Dave Lopes	.07	.03	.01
□ 30 Ken Landreaux	.07	.03	.01
□ 31 Keith Hernandez	.35	.14	.03
□ 32 Cecil Cooper	.10	.04	.01
□ 33 Rickey Henderson	.60	.24	.06
□ 34 Frank White	.07	.03	.01
□ 35 George Hendrick	.07	.03	.01
□ 36 Reggie Smith	.10	.04	.01
□ 37 Tug McGraw	.10	.04	.01
□ 38 Tom Seaver	.50	.20	.05
□ 39 Ken Singleton	.10	.04	.01
□ 40 Fred Lynn	.15	.06	.01
□ 41 Rich Gossage	.10	.04	.01
□ 42 Terry Puhl	.07	.03	.01
□ 43 Larry Bowa	.15	.06	.01
□ 44 Phil Garner	.07	.03	.01
□ 45 Ron Guidry	.20	.08	.02
□ 46 Lee Mazzilli	.07	.03	.01
□ 47 Dave Kingman	.10	.04	.01
□ 48 Carl Yastrzemski	1.00	.40	.10
□ 49 Rick Burleson	.07	.03	.01
□ 50 Steve Carlton	.40	.16	.04
□ 51 Alan Trammell	.30	.12	.03
□ 52 Tommy John	.15	.06	.01
□ 53 Paul Molitor	.25	.10	.02
□ 54 Joe Charbonneau	.07	.03	.01
□ 55 Rick Langford	.07	.03	.01
□ 56 Bruce Sutter	.10	.04	.01
□ 57 Robin Yount	.25	.10	.02
□ 58 Steve Stone	.07	.03	.01
□ 59 Larry Gura	.07	.03	.01
□ 60 Mike Flanagan	.07	.03	.01
□ 61 Bob Horner	.20	.08	.02
□ 62 Bruce Bochte	.07	.03	.01
□ 63 Pete Rose	1.00	.40	.10
□ 64 Buddy Bell	.10	.04	.01
□ 65 Johnny Bench	.50	.20	.05
□ 66 Mike Hargrove	.07	.03	.01

1982 Kellogg's

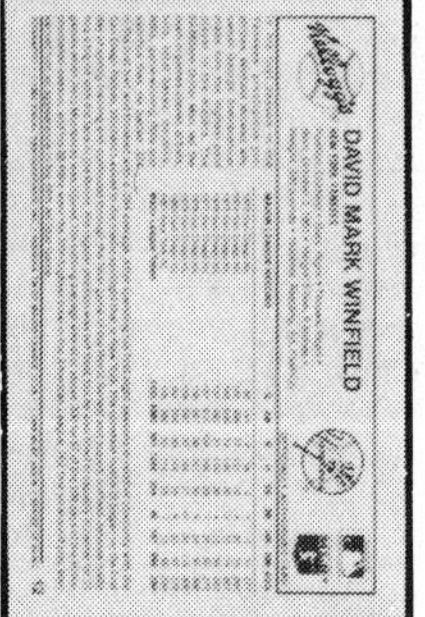

The cards in this 64-card set measure 2 1/8" by 3 1/4". The 1982 version of 3-D cards prepared for the Kellogg Company by Visual Panographics, Inc., is not only smaller in physical dimensions from the 1981 series (which was standard card size at 2 1/2" by 3 1/2") but is also two cards shorter in length (64 in '82 and 66 in '81). In addition, while retaining the policy of not inserting single cards into cereal packages and offering the sets through box-top mail-ins only, the Kellogg Company accepted box tops from four types of cereals, as opposed to only one type the previous year. Each card features a color 3- D ballplayer picture with a vertical line of white stars on each side set upon a blue background. The player's name and the word Kellogg's are printed in red on the obverse, and the card number is found on the bottom right of the reverse.

	MINT	EXC	G-VG
COMPLETE SET (64)	12.00	5.00	1.20
COMMON PLAYER (1-64)	.09	.04	.01
□ 1 Richie Zisk	.09	.04	.01
□ 2 Bill Buckner	.15	.06	.01
□ 3 George Brett	.90	.36	.09
□ 4 Rickey Henderson	.75	.30	.07
□ 5 Jack Morris	.15	.06	.01
□ 6 Ozzie Smith	.35	.14	.03
□ 7 Rollie Fingers	.15	.06	.01
□ 8 Tom Seaver	.60	.24	.06
□ 9 Fernando Valuenzuela	.40	.16	.04
□ 10 Hubie Brooks	.15	.06	.01
□ 11 Nolan Ryan	.65	.26	.06
□ 12 Dave Winfield	.35	.14	.03
□ 13 Bob Horner	.20	.08	.02
□ 14 Reggie Jackson	.75	.30	.07
□ 15 Burt Hooton	.09	.04	.01
□ 16 Mike Schmidt	.90	.36	.09
□ 17 Bruce Sutter	.15	.06	.01
□ 18 Pete Rose	1.00	.40	.10
□ 19 Dave Kingman	.15	.06	.01
□ 20 Neil Allen	.09	.04	.01
□ 21 Don Sutton	.30	.12	.03
□ 22 Dave Concepcion	.15	.06	.01
□ 23 Keith Hernandez	.30	.12	.03
□ 24 Gary Carter	.45	.18	.04
□ 25 Carlton Fisk	.20	.08	.02
□ 26 Ron Guidry	.20	.08	.02
□ 27 Steve Carlton	.35	.14	.03
□ 28 Robin Yount	.35	.14	.03
□ 29 John Castino	.09	.04	.01
□ 30 Johnny Bench	.50	.20	.05
□ 31 Bob Knepper	.15	.06	.01
□ 32 Rich Gossage	.15	.06	.01
□ 33 Buddy Bell	.15	.06	.01
□ 34 Art Howe	.15	.06	.01
□ 35 Tony Armas	.15	.06	.01
□ 36 Phil Niekro	.25	.10	.02
□ 37 Len Barker	.09	.04	.01
□ 38 Bob Grich	.15	.06	.01
□ 39 Steve Kemp	.09	.04	.01
□ 40 Kirk Gibson	.40	.16	.04
□ 41 Carney Lansford	.15	.06	.01
□ 42 Jim Palmer	.30	.12	.03
□ 43 Carl Yastrzemski	.85	.34	.08
□ 44 Rick Burleson	.09	.04	.01
□ 45 Dwight Evans	.20	.08	.02
□ 46 Ron Cey	.15	.06	.01
□ 47 Steve Garvey	.45	.18	.04
□ 48 Dave Parker	.20	.08	.02
□ 49 Mike Easler	.09	.04	.01
□ 50 Dusty Baker	.09	.04	.01
□ 51 Rod Carew	.40	.16	.04
□ 52 Chris Chambliss	.15	.06	.01
□ 53 Tim Raines	.45	.18	.04
□ 54 Chet Lemon	.09	.04	.01
□ 55 Bill Madlock	.15	.06	.01
□ 56 George Foster	.15	.06	.01
□ 57 Dwayne Murphy	.09	.04	.01
□ 58 Ken Singleton	.15	.06	.01
□ 59 Mike Norris	.09	.04	.01
□ 60 Cecil Cooper	.15	.06	.01
□ 61 Al Oliver	.15	.06	.01
□ 62 Willie Wilson	.15	.06	.01
□ 63 Vida Blue	.15	.06	.01
□ 64 Eddie Murray	.60	.24	.06

1983 Kellogg's

The cards in this 60-card set measure 1 7/8" by 3 1/4". For the 14th year in a row, the Kellogg Company issued a card set of Major League players. The set of 3-D cards contains the photo, player's autograph, Kellogg's logo, and name and position of the player on the front of the card. The backs feature the player's team logo, career statistics, player biography, and a narrative on the player's career.

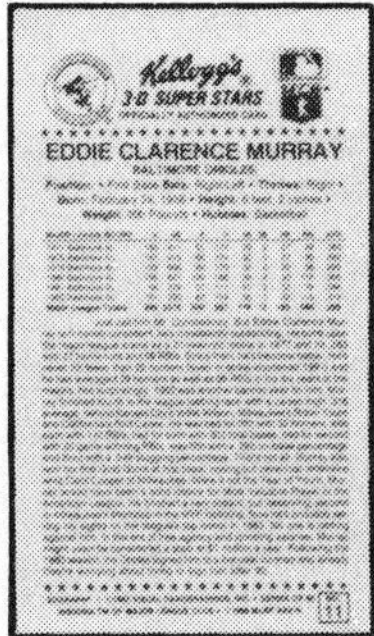

	MINT	EXC	G-VG
COMPLETE SET (60)	12.00	5.00	1.20
COMMON PLAYER (1-60)	.09	.04	.01
☐ 1 Rod Carew	.45	.18	.04
☐ 2 Rollie Fingers	.20	.08	.02
☐ 3 Reggie Jackson	.75	.30	.07
☐ 4 George Brett	.90	.36	.09
☐ 5 Hal McRae	.15	.06	.01
☐ 6 Pete Rose	1.00	.40	.10
☐ 7 Fernando Valenzuela	.35	.14	.03
☐ 8 Rickey Henderson	.75	.30	.07
☐ 9 Carl Yastrzemski	.75	.30	.07
☐ 10 Rich Gossage	.15	.06	.01
☐ 11 Eddie Murray	.50	.20	.05
☐ 12 Buddy Bell	.15	.06	.01
☐ 13 Jim Rice	.30	.12	.03
☐ 14 Robin Yount	.35	.14	.03
☐ 15 Dave Winfield	.35	.14	.03
☐ 16 Harold Baines	.20	.08	.02
☐ 17 Garry Templeton	.09	.04	.01
☐ 18 Bill Madlock	.15	.06	.01
☐ 19 Pete Vuckovich	.09	.04	.01
☐ 20 Pedro Guerrero	.25	.10	.02
☐ 21 Ozzie Smith	.30	.12	.03
☐ 22 George Foster	.15	.06	.01
☐ 23 Willie Wilson	.15	.06	.01
☐ 24 Johnny Ray	.15	.06	.01
☐ 25 George Hendrick	.09	.04	.01
☐ 26 Andre Thornton	.09	.04	.01
☐ 27 Leon Durham	.09	.04	.01
☐ 28 Cecil Cooper	.15	.06	.01
☐ 29 Don Baylor	.15	.06	.01
☐ 30 Lonnie Smith	.09	.04	.01
☐ 31 Nolan Ryan	.50	.20	.05
☐ 32 Dan Quisenberry	.15	.06	.01
☐ 33 Len Barker	.09	.04	.01
☐ 34 Neil Allen	.09	.04	.01
☐ 35 Jack Morris	.20	.08	.02
☐ 36 Dave Stieb	.15	.06	.01
☐ 37 Bruce Sutter	.15	.06	.01
☐ 38 Jim Sundberg	.09	.04	.01
☐ 39 Jim Palmer	.30	.12	.03
☐ 40 Lance Parrish	.20	.08	.02
☐ 41 Floyd Bannister	.09	.04	.01
☐ 42 Larry Gura	.09	.04	.01
☐ 43 Britt Burns	.09	.04	.01
☐ 44 Toby Harrah	.09	.04	.01
☐ 45 Steve Carlton	.35	.14	.03
☐ 46 Greg Minton	.09	.04	.01
☐ 47 Gorman Thomas	.15	.06	.01
☐ 48 Jack Clark	.25	.10	.02
☐ 49 Keith Hernandez	.30	.12	.03
☐ 50 Greg Luzinski	.15	.06	.01
☐ 51 Fred Lynn	.15	.06	.01
☐ 52 Dale Murphy	.75	.30	.07
☐ 53 Kent Hrbek	.30	.12	.03
☐ 54 Bob Horner	.20	.08	.02
☐ 55 Gary Carter	.45	.18	.04
☐ 56 Carlton Fisk	.15	.06	.01
☐ 57 Dave Concepcion	.15	.06	.01
☐ 58 Mike Schmidt	.85	.34	.08
☐ 59 Bill Buckner	.15	.06	.01
☐ 60 Bob Grich	.15	.06	.01

1982 K-Mart

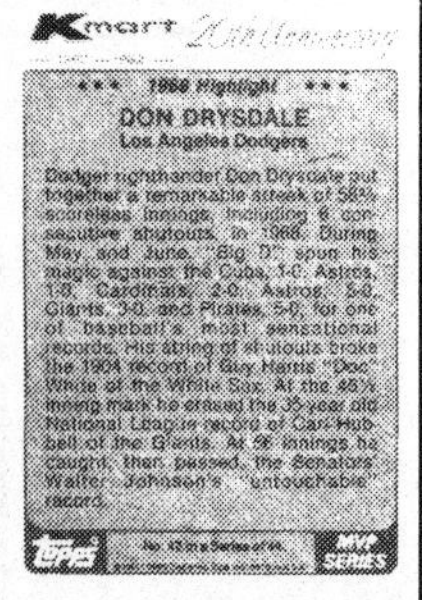

The cards in this 44-card set measure 2 1/2" by 3 1/2". This set was produced by Topps for K Mart's 20th Anniversary Celebration. The set features Topps cards of National and American League MVP's from 1962 through 1981. The backs highlight individual MVP winning performances. The dual National League MVP winners of 1979 and special cards commemorating the accomplishments of Drysdale (scoreless consecutive innings pitched streak), Aaron (home run record), and Rose (National League most hits lifetime record) round out the set. The 1975 Fred Lynn card is an original construction from the multi-player "Rookie Outfielders" card of Lynn of 1975. The Maury Wills card #2, similarly, was created after the fact as Maury was not originally included in the 1962 Topps set. The set was "Mass" produced for K-Mart distribution as a complete set in a box. Some collectors consider this to be one of the most plentiful sets ever produced.

	MINT	EXC	G-VG
COMPLETE SET (44)	1.00	.40	.10
COMMON PLAYER (1-44)	.01	.00	.00
☐ 1 Mickey Mantle: 62AL	.20	.08	.02
☐ 2 Maury Wills: 62NL	.02	.01	.00
☐ 3 Elston Howard: 63AL	.01	.00	.00
☐ 4 Sandy Koufax: 63NL	.05	.02	.00
☐ 5 Brooks Robinson: 64AL	.04	.02	.00
☐ 6 Ken Boyer: 64NL	.01	.00	.00
☐ 7 Zoilo Versalles: 65AL	.01	.00	.00
☐ 8 Willie Mays: 65NL	.07	.03	.01
☐ 9 Frank Robinson: 66AL	.03	.01	.00
☐ 10 Bob Clemente: 66NL	.05	.02	.00
☐ 11 Carl Yastrzemski: 67AL	.07	.03	.01
☐ 12 Orlando Cepeda: 67NL	.01	.00	.00
☐ 13 Denny McLain: 68AL	.01	.00	.00
☐ 14 Bob Gibson: 68NL	.03	.01	.00
☐ 15 Harmon Killebrew: 69AL	.02	.01	.00
☐ 16 Willie McCovey: 69NL	.03	.01	.00
☐ 17 Boog Powell: 70AL	.01	.00	.00
☐ 18 Johnny Bench: 70NL	.05	.02	.00
☐ 19 Vida Blue: 71AL	.01	.00	.00
☐ 20 Joe Torre: 71NL	.01	.00	.00
☐ 21 Rich Allen: 72AL	.01	.00	.00
☐ 22 Johnny Bench: 72NL	.05	.02	.00
☐ 23 Reggie Jackson: 73AL	.05	.02	.00
☐ 24 Pete Rose: 73NL	.10	.04	.01
☐ 25 Jeff Burroughs: 74AL	.01	.00	.00
☐ 26 Steve Garvey: 74NL	.04	.02	.00
☐ 27 Fred Lynn: 75AL	.02	.01	.00
☐ 28 Joe Morgan: 75NL	.02	.01	.00
☐ 29 Thurman Munson: 76AL	.04	.02	.00
☐ 30 Joe Morgan: 76NL	.02	.01	.00
☐ 31 Rod Carew: 77AL	.04	.02	.00
☐ 32 George Foster: 77NL	.01	.00	.00
☐ 33 Jim Rice: 78AL	.02	.01	.00
☐ 34 Dave Parker: 78NL	.01	.00	.00
☐ 35 Don Baylor: 79AL	.01	.00	.00
☐ 36 Keith Hernandez: 79NL	.02	.01	.00
☐ 37 Willie Stargell: 79NL	.03	.01	.00
☐ 38 George Brett: 80AL	.05	.02	.00
☐ 39 Mike Schmidt: 80NL	.06	.02	.00

□ 40 Rollie Fingers: 81AL	.02	.01	.00
□ 41 Mike Schmidt: 81NL	.06	.02	.00
□ 42 '68 HL: Don Drysdale (scoreless innings)	.02	.01	.00
□ 43 '74 HL: Hank Aaron (home run record)	.07	.03	.01
□ 44 '81 HL: Pete Rose (NL most hits)	.12	.05	.01

1987 K-Mart

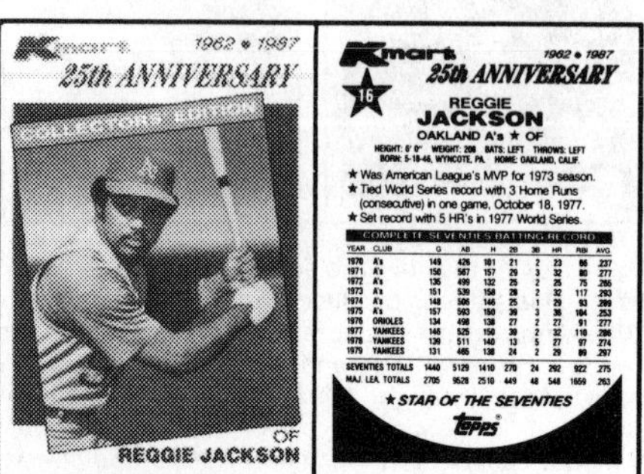

Topps produced this 33-card boxed set for K-Mart. The set celebrates K-Mart's 25th anniversary and is subtitled, "Stars of the Decades." Card fronts feature a color photo of the player oriented diagonally. Cards measure 2 1/2" by 3 1/2" and are numbered on the back. Card backs provide statistics for the player's best decade.

	MINT	EXC	G-VG
COMPLETE SET (33)	4.00	1.60	.40
COMMON PLAYER (1-33)	.10	.04	.01
□ 1 Hank Aaron	.30	.12	.03
□ 2 Roberto Clemente	.25	.10	.02
□ 3 Bob Gibson	.10	.04	.01
□ 4 Harmon Killebrew	.10	.04	.01
□ 5 Mickey Mantle	.75	.30	.07
□ 6 Juan Marichal	.10	.04	.01
□ 7 Roger Maris	.25	.10	.02
□ 8 Willie Mays	.30	.12	.03
□ 9 Brooks Robinson	.15	.06	.01
□ 10 Frank Robinson	.10	.04	.01
□ 11 Carl Yastrzemski	.30	.12	.03
□ 12 Johnny Bench	.20	.08	.02
□ 13 Lou Brock	.15	.06	.01
□ 14 Rod Carew	.15	.06	.01
□ 15 Steve Carlton	.15	.06	.01
□ 16 Reggie Jackson	.25	.10	.02
□ 17 Jim Palmer	.10	.04	.01
□ 18 Jim Rice	.10	.04	.01
□ 19 Pete Rose	.50	.20	.05
□ 20 Nolan Ryan	.25	.10	.02
□ 21 Tom Seaver	.25	.10	.02
□ 22 Willie Stargell	.15	.06	.01
□ 23 Wade Boggs	.60	.24	.06
□ 24 George Brett	.25	.10	.02
□ 25 Gary Carter	.15	.06	.01
□ 26 Dwight Gooden	.35	.14	.03
□ 27 Rickey Henderson	.30	.12	.03
□ 28 Don Mattingly	.75	.30	.07
□ 29 Dale Murphy	.25	.10	.02
□ 30 Eddie Murray	.20	.08	.02
□ 31 Mike Schmidt	.25	.10	.02
□ 32 Darryl Strawberry	.35	.14	.03
□ 33 Fernando Valenzuela	.15	.06	.01

1988 K-Mart Memorable Moments

Topps produced this 33-card boxed set exclusively for K-Mart. The set is subtitled, "Memorable Moments." Card fronts feature a color photo of the player with the K-Mart logo in lower right corner. Cards measure 2 1/2" by 3 1/2" and are numbered on the back. Card backs provide details for that player's "memorable moment." The set is packaged in a bright yellow and green box with a checklist on the back panel of the box.

	MINT	EXC	G-VG
COMPLETE SET (33)	4.00	1.60	.40
COMMON PLAYER (1-33)	.10	.04	.01
□ 1 George Bell	.15	.06	.01
□ 2 Wade Boggs	.50	.20	.05
□ 3 George Brett	.30	.12	.03
□ 4 Jose Canseco	.90	.36	.09
□ 5 Jack Clark	.15	.06	.01
□ 6 Will Clark	.40	.16	.04
□ 7 Roger Clemens	.40	.16	.04
□ 8 Vince Coleman	.20	.08	.02
□ 9 Andre Dawson	.20	.08	.02
□ 10 Dwight Gooden	.30	.12	.03
□ 11 Pedro Guerrero	.15	.06	.01
□ 12 Tony Gywnn	.30	.12	.03
□ 13 Rickey Henderson	.30	.12	.03
□ 14 Keith Hernandez	.20	.08	.02
□ 15 Don Mattingly	.60	.24	.06
□ 16 Mark McGwire	.50	.20	.05
□ 17 Paul Molitor	.15	.06	.01
□ 18 Dale Murphy	.30	.12	.03
□ 19 Tim Raines	.20	.08	.02
□ 20 Dave Righetti	.15	.06	.01
□ 21 Cal Ripken	.25	.10	.02
□ 22 Pete Rose	.60	.24	.06
□ 23 Nolan Ryan	.30	.12	.03
□ 24 Benny Santiago	.25	.10	.02
□ 25 Mike Schmidt	.30	.12	.03
□ 26 Mike Scott	.15	.06	.01
□ 27 Kevin Seitzer	.25	.10	.02
□ 28 Ozzie Smith	.20	.08	.02
□ 29 Darryl Strawberry	.35	.14	.03
□ 30 Rick Sutcliffe	.10	.04	.01
□ 31 Fernando Valenzuela	.15	.06	.01
□ 32 Todd Worrell	.10	.04	.01
□ 33 Robin Yount	.25	.10	.02

1960 Lake to Lake

The cards in this 28-card set measure 2 1/2" by 3 1/4". The 1960 Lake to Lake set of unnumbered, blue tinted cards features Milwaukee Braves players only. For some reason, this set of Braves does not include Eddie Mathews. The cards were issued on milk cartons by Lake to Lake Dairy. Most cards have staple holes in the upper right corner. The backs are in red and give details and prizes associated with the card promotion. Cards with staple holes can be considered very good to excellent at best. The ACC designation is F102-1. For some reason Eddie Mathews was not included in this set.

	NRMT	VG-E	GOOD
COMPLETE SET (28)	750.00	300.00	75.00
COMMON PLAYER (1-28)	10.00	4.00	1.00

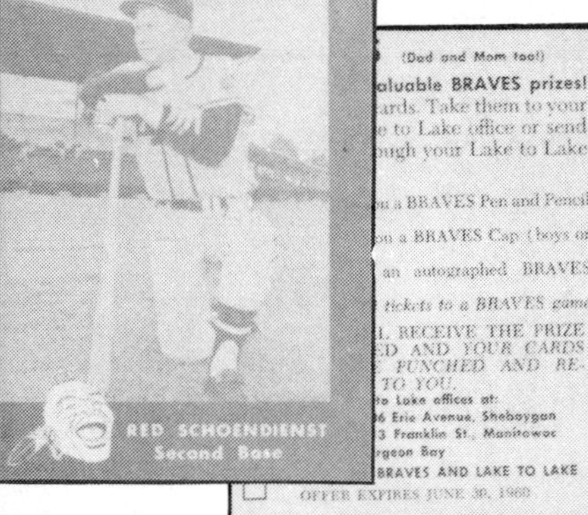

☐ 1 Hank Aaron	200.00	80.00	20.00
☐ 2 Joe Adcock	15.00	6.00	1.50
☐ 3 Ray Boone	100.00	40.00	10.00
☐ 4 Bill Bruton	200.00	80.00	20.00
☐ 5 Bob Buhl	10.00	4.00	1.00
☐ 6 Lew Burdette	15.00	6.00	1.50
☐ 7 Chuck Cottier	10.00	4.00	1.00
☐ 8 Wes Covington	10.00	4.00	1.00
☐ 9 Del Crandall	12.00	5.00	1.20
☐ 10 Chuck Dressen	10.00	4.00	1.00
☐ 11 Bob Giggie	10.00	4.00	1.00
☐ 12 Joey Jay	10.00	4.00	1.00
☐ 13 Johnny Logan	12.00	5.00	1.20
☐ 14 Felix Mantilla	10.00	4.00	1.00
☐ 15 Lee Maye	10.00	4.00	1.00
☐ 16 Don McMahon	10.00	4.00	1.00
☐ 17 George Myatt	10.00	4.00	1.00
☐ 18 Andy Pafko	10.00	4.00	1.00
☐ 19 Juan Pizarro	10.00	4.00	1.00
☐ 20 Mel Roach	10.00	4.00	1.00
☐ 21 Bob Rush	10.00	4.00	1.00
☐ 22 Bob Scheffing	10.00	4.00	1.00
☐ 23 Red Schoendienst	15.00	6.00	1.50
☐ 24 Warren Spahn	40.00	16.00	4.00
☐ 25 Al Spangler	10.00	4.00	1.00
☐ 26 Frank Torre	10.00	4.00	1.00
☐ 27 Carlton Willey	10.00	4.00	1.00
☐ 28 Whit Wyatt	10.00	4.00	1.00

1968 Laughlin World Series

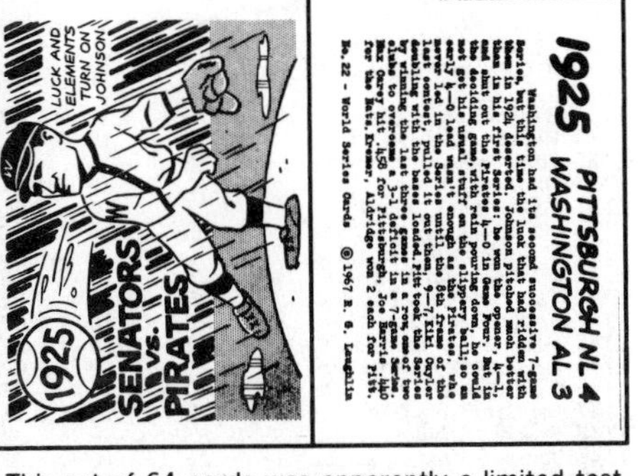

This set of 64 cards was apparently a limited test issue by sports artist R.G. Laughlin for the World Series set concept that was mass marketed by Fleer two and three years later. The cards are slightly oversized, 2 3/4" by 3 1/2" and are black and white on the front and red and white on the back. All the years are represented except for 1904 when no World Series was played. In the list below, the winning series team is listed first.

	NRMT	VG-E	GOOD
COMPLETE SET (64)	35.00	14.00	3.50
COMMON PLAYER (1-64)	.50	.20	.05
☐ 1 1903 Red Sox/Pirates	.50	.20	.05
☐ 2 1905 Giants/A's (Christy Mathewson)	.65	.26	.06
☐ 3 1906 White Sox/Cubs	.50	.20	.05
☐ 4 1907 Cubs/Tigers	.50	.20	.05
☐ 5 1908 Cubs/Tigers (Tinker/Evers/Chance)	.65	.26	.06
☐ 6 1909 Pirates/Tigers (Wagner/Cobb)	.85	.34	.08
☐ 7 1910 A's/Cubs	.50	.20	.05
☐ 8 1911 A's/Giants (John McGraw)	.65	.26	.06
☐ 9 1912 Red Sox/Giants	.50	.20	.05
☐ 10 1913 A's/Giants	.50	.20	.05
☐ 11 1914 Braves/A's	.50	.20	.05
☐ 12 1915 Red Sox/Phillies (Babe Ruth)	1.00	.40	.10
☐ 13 1916 Red Sox/Dodgers (Babe Ruth)	1.00	.40	.10
☐ 14 1917 White Sox/Giants	.50	.20	.05
☐ 15 1918 Red Sox/Cubs	.50	.20	.05
☐ 16 1919 Reds/White Sox	.50	.20	.05
☐ 17 1920 Indians/Dodgers	.50	.20	.05
☐ 18 1921 Giants/Yankees (Waite Hoyt)	.50	.20	.05
☐ 19 1922 Giants/Yankees (Frisch/Groh)	.50	.20	.05
☐ 20 1923 Yankees/Giants (Babe Ruth)	1.00	.40	.10
☐ 21 1924 Senators/Giants	.50	.20	.05
☐ 22 1925 Pirates/Senators (Walter Johnson)	.65	.26	.06
☐ 23 1926 Cardinals/Yankees (Alexander/Lazzeri)	.65	.26	.06
☐ 24 1927 Yankees/Pirates	.50	.20	.05
☐ 25 1928 Yankees/Cardinals (Ruth/Gehrig)	1.00	.40	.10
☐ 26 1929 A's/Cubs	.50	.20	.05
☐ 27 1930 A's/Cardinals	.50	.20	.05
☐ 28 1931 Cardinals/A's (Pepper Martin)	.50	.20	.05
☐ 29 1932 Yankees/Cubs (Babe Ruth)	1.00	.40	.10
☐ 30 1933 Giants/Senators (Mel Ott)	.65	.26	.06
☐ 31 1934 Cardinals/Tigers (Dizzy/Paul Dean)	.65	.26	.06
☐ 32 1935 Tigers/Cubs	.50	.20	.05
☐ 33 1936 Yankees/Giants	.50	.20	.05
☐ 34 1937 Yankees/Giants (Carl Hubbell)	.50	.20	.05
☐ 35 1938 Yankees/Cubs	.50	.20	.05
☐ 36 1939 Yankees/Reds (Joe DiMaggio)	.85	.34	.08
☐ 37 1940 Reds/Tigers	.50	.20	.05
☐ 38 1941 Yankees/Dodgers (Mickey Owen)	.50	.20	.05
☐ 39 1942 Cardinals/Yankees	.50	.20	.05
☐ 40 1943 Yankees/Cardinals (Joe McCarthy)	.50	.20	.05
☐ 41 1944 Cardinals/Browns	.50	.20	.05
☐ 42 1945 Tigers/Cubs (Hank Greenberg)	.50	.20	.05
☐ 43 1946 Cardinals/Red Sox (Enos Slaughter)	.50	.20	.05
☐ 44 1947 Yankees/Dodgers (Al Gionfriddo)	.50	.20	.05
☐ 45 1948 Indians/Braves (Bob Feller)	.65	.26	.06
☐ 46 1949 Yankees/Dodgers (Reynolds/Roe)	.50	.20	.05
☐ 47 1950 Yankees/Phillies	.50	.20	.05
☐ 48 1951 Yankees/Giants	.50	.20	.05
☐ 49 1952 Yankees/Dodgers (Mize/Snider)	.65	.26	.06
☐ 50 1953 Yankees/Dodgers (Casey Stengel)	.65	.26	.06
☐ 51 1954 Giants/Indians (Dusty Rhodes)	.50	.20	.05
☐ 52 1955 Dodgers/Yankees (Johnny Podres)	.50	.20	.05
☐ 53 1956 Yankees/Dodgers (Don Larsen)	.60	.24	.06
☐ 54 1957 Braves/Yankees (Lew Burdette)	.50	.20	.05
☐ 55 1958 Yankees/Braves (Hank Bauer)	.50	.20	.05
☐ 56 1959 Dodgers/Wh.Sox (Larry Sherry)	.50	.20	.05

□ 57 1960 Pirates/Yankees	.50	.20	.05
□ 58 1961 Yankees/Reds (Whitey Ford)	.50	.20	.05
□ 59 1962 Yankees/Giants	.50	.20	.05
□ 60 1963 Dodgers/Yankees (Sandy Koufax)	.65	.26	.06
□ 61 1964 Cardinals/Yankees (Mickey Mantle)	1.00	.40	.10
□ 62 1965 Dodgers/Twins	.50	.20	.05
□ 63 1966 Orioles/Dodgers	.50	.20	.05
□ 64 1967 Cardinals/Red Sox (Bob Gibson)	.65	.26	.06

1972 Laughlin Great Feats

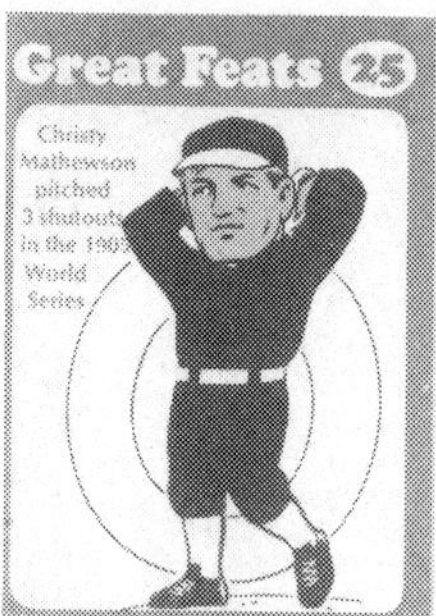

This set of 51 cards is printed on white card stock. Sports artist R.G. Laughlin 1972 is copyrighted only on the unnumbered title card but not on each card. The obverses are line drawings in black and white inside a red border. The cards measure approximately 2 9/16" by 3 9/16". The set features "Great Feats" from baseball's past. The cards are blank backed and hence are numbered and captioned on the front. There is a variation set with a blue border and colored in flesh tones in the players pictured; this variation is a little more attractive and hence is valued a little higher. The blue-bordered variation set has larger type in the captions; in fact, the type has been reset and there are some minor wording differences. The blue- bordered set is also 1/16" wider.

	NRMT	VG-E	GOOD
COMPLETE SET (51)	12.00	5.00	1.20
COMMON PLAYER (1-51)	.25	.10	.02
□ 1 Joe DiMaggio	.75	.30	.07
□ 2 Walter Johnson	.35	.14	.03
□ 3 Rudy York	.25	.10	.02
□ 4 Sandy Koufax	.35	.14	.03
□ 5 George Sisler	.25	.10	.02
□ 6 Iron Man McGinnity	.25	.10	.02
□ 7 Johnny VanderMeer	.25	.10	.02
□ 8 Lou Gehrig	.50	.20	.05
□ 9 Max Carey	.25	.10	.02
□ 10 Ed Delahanty	.25	.10	.02
□ 11 Pinky Higgins	.25	.10	.02
□ 12 Jack Chesbro	.25	.10	.02
□ 13 Jim Bottomley	.25	.10	.02
□ 14 Rube Marquard	.25	.10	.02
□ 15 Rogers Hornsby	.35	.14	.03
□ 16 Lefty Grove	.25	.10	.02
□ 17 Johnny Mize	.35	.14	.03
□ 18 Lefty Gomez	.25	.10	.02
□ 19 Jimmie Foxx	.35	.14	.03
□ 20 Casey Stengel	.35	.14	.03
□ 21 Dazzy Vance	.25	.10	.02
□ 22 Jerry Lynch	.25	.10	.02
□ 23 Hughie Jennings	.25	.10	.02
□ 24 Stan Musial	.35	.14	.03
□ 25 Christy Mathewson	.35	.14	.03
□ 26 Elroy Face	.25	.10	.02
□ 27 Hack Wilson	.25	.10	.02
□ 28 Smoky Burgess	.25	.10	.02
□ 29 Cy Young	.25	.10	.02
□ 30 Wilbert Robinson	.25	.10	.02
□ 31 Wee Willie Keeler	.25	.10	.02
□ 32 Babe Ruth	.75	.30	.07
□ 33 Mickey Mantle	.75	.30	.07
□ 34 Hub Leonard	.25	.10	.02
□ 35 Ty Cobb	.50	.20	.05
□ 36 Carl Hubbell	.25	.10	.02
□ 37 Joe Oeschger and Leon Cadore	.25	.10	.02
□ 38 Don Drysdale	.25	.10	.02
□ 39 Fred Toney and Hippo Vaughn	.25	.10	.02
□ 40 Joe Sewell	.25	.10	.02
□ 41 Grover C. Alexander	.25	.10	.02
□ 42 Joe Adcock	.25	.10	.02
□ 43 Eddie Collins	.25	.10	.02
□ 44 Bob Feller	.35	.14	.03
□ 45 Don Larsen	.25	.10	.02
□ 46 Dave Philley	.25	.10	.02
□ 47 Bill Fischer	.25	.10	.02
□ 48 Dale Long	.25	.10	.02
□ 49 Bill Wambsganss	.25	.10	.02
□ 50 Roger Maris	.35	.14	.03
□ x Title Card	.25	.10	.02

1974 Laughlin All-Star Games

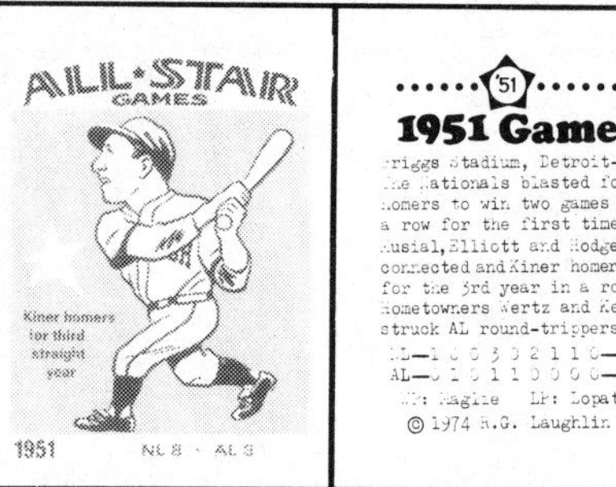

This set of 40 cards is printed on white card stock. Sports artist R.G. Laughlin 1974 is copyrighted at the bottom of the reverse of each card. The obverses are line drawings primarily in red, light blue, black, and white inside a white border. The cards measure approximately 2 11/16" by 3 3/8". The set features memorable moments from each year's All-Star Game(s). The cards are numbered on the back according to the last two digits of the year and captioned on the front. The backs are printed in blue on white stock.

	NRMT	VG-E	GOOD
COMPLETE SET (40)	10.00	4.00	1.00
COMMON PLAYER (33-73)	.25	.10	.02
□ 33 Babe's Homer	.75	.30	.07
□ 34 Hubbell Fans Five	.25	.10	.02
□ 35 Foxx Smashes Homer	.35	.14	.03
□ 36 Ol' Diz Fogs 'Em	.40	.16	.04
□ 37 Four Hits for Ducky	.25	.10	.02
□ 38 No-Hit Vandy	.25	.10	.02
□ 39 DiMaggio Homers	.50	.20	.05
□ 40 West's 3-Run Shot	.25	.10	.02
□ 41 Vaughan Busts Two	.25	.10	.02
□ 42 York's 2-Run Smash	.25	.10	.02
□ 43 Doerr 3-Run Blast	.25	.10	.02
□ 44 Cavarretta Reaches	.25	.10	.02
□ 46 Field Day for Ted	.40	.16	.04
□ 47 Big Cat Plants One	.25	.10	.02
□ 48 Raschi Pitches	.25	.10	.02
□ 49 Jackie Scores	.25	.10	.02
□ 50 Schoendienst Breaks	.25	.10	.02
□ 51 Kiner Homers	.25	.10	.02
□ 52 Sauer's Shot	.25	.10	.02
□ 53 Slaughter Hustles	.25	.10	.02
□ 54 Rosen Hits	.25	.10	.02
□ 55 Stan the Man's Homer	.35	.14	.03
□ 56 Ken Boyer Super	.25	.10	.02
□ 57 Kaline Hits	.35	.14	.03
□ 58 Only Nellie Gets Two	.25	.10	.02
□ 59 F.Robbie Perfect	.25	.10	.02
□ 60 Willie 3-for-4	.40	.16	.04
□ 61 Bunning Hitless	.25	.10	.02

☐ 62 Roberto Perfect	.35	.14	.03
☐ 63 Monster Strikeouts	.25	.10	.02
☐ 64 Callison's Homer	.25	.10	.02
☐ 65 Stargell Big Day	.25	.10	.02
☐ 66 Brooks Hits	.25	.10	.02
☐ 67 Fergie Fans Six	.25	.10	.02
☐ 68 Tom Terrific	.35	.14	.03
☐ 69 Stretch Belts Two	.25	.10	.02
☐ 70 Yaz Four Hits	.35	.14	.03
☐ 71 Reggie Unloads	.35	.14	.03
☐ 72 Henry Hammers	.35	.14	.03
☐ 73 Bonds Perfect	.25	.10	.02

1974 Laughlin Old Time Black Stars

26 RAYMOND (HOOKS) DANDRIDGE 3b

After a lifetime in Negro ball, Dandridge came close to major league stardom. Signed by Minne polis of the American Association in 1949, he hit .362 his first year in the AA and the next season was the league MVP. But he was already past 40; had he been younger he surely would have come to the majors. On the Millers Ray roomed with Willie Mays. Most of his career was spent as a top third baseman with the Newark Dodgers (later the Eagles). He also could handle shortstop and second.

This set of 36 cards is printed on flat (non- glossy) white card stock. Sports artist R.G. Laughlin's work is evident but there are no copyright notices or any mention of him anywhere on any of the cards in this set. The obverses are line drawings in tan and brown. The cards measure approximately 2 5/8" by 3 1/2". The set features outstanding black players form the past. The cards are numbered on the back. The backs are printed in brown on white stock.

	NRMT	VG-E	GOOD
COMPLETE SET (36)	12.00	5.00	1.20
COMMON PLAYER (1-36)	.35	.14	.03
☐ 1 Smokey Joe Williams	.50	.20	.05
☐ 2 Rap Dixon	.35	.14	.03
☐ 3 Oliver Marcelle	.35	.14	.03
☐ 4 Bingo DeMoss	.35	.14	.03
☐ 5 Willie Foster	.50	.20	.05
☐ 6 John Beckwith	.35	.14	.03
☐ 7 Floyd(Jelly) Gardner	.35	.14	.03
☐ 8 Josh Gibson	1.00	.40	.10
☐ 9 Jose Mendez	.35	.14	.03
☐ 10 Pete Hill	.35	.14	.03
☐ 11 Buck Leonard	.50	.20	.05
☐ 12 Jud Wilson	.35	.14	.03
☐ 13 Willie Wells	.50	.20	.05
☐ 14 Jimmie Lyons	.35	.14	.03
☐ 15 Satchel Paige	.75	.30	.07
☐ 16 Louis Santop	.35	.14	.03
☐ 17 Frank Grant	.35	.14	.03
☐ 18 Christobel Torrienti	.35	.14	.03
☐ 19 Bullet Rogon	.35	.14	.03
☐ 20 Dave Malarcher	.35	.14	.03
☐ 21 Spot Poles	.35	.14	.03
☐ 22 Home Run Johnson	.35	.14	.03
☐ 23 Charlie Grant	.35	.14	.03
☐ 24 Cool Papa Bell	.50	.20	.05
☐ 25 Cannonball Dick Redding	.35	.14	.03
☐ 26 Ray Dandridge	.50	.20	.05
☐ 27 Biz Mackey	.50	.20	.05
☐ 28 Fats Jenkins	.35	.14	.03
☐ 29 Martin Dihigo	.50	.20	.05
☐ 30 Mule Suttles	.35	.14	.03
☐ 31 Bill Monroe	.35	.14	.03
☐ 32 Dan McClellan	.35	.14	.03
☐ 33 John Henry Lloyd	.50	.20	.05
☐ 34 Oscar Charleston	.50	.20	.05
☐ 35 Andrew(Rube) Foster	.50	.20	.05
☐ 36 William(Judy) Johnson	.50	.20	.05

1974 Laughlin Sportslang

This set of 41 cards is printed on white card stock. Sports artist R.G. Laughlin 1974 is copyrighted at the bottom of every reverse. The obverses are drawings in red and blue on a white enamel card stock. The cards measure approximately 2 3/4" by 3 3/8". The set actually features the slang of several sports, not just baseball. The cards are numbered on the back and captioned on the front. The card back also provides an explanation of the slang term pictured on the card front.

	NRMT	VG-E	GOOD
COMPLETE SET (41)	7.50	3.00	.75
COMMON PLAYER (1-41)	.20	.08	.02
☐ 1 Bull Pen	.20	.08	.02
☐ 2 Charley Horse	.20	.08	.02
☐ 3 Derby	.20	.08	.02
☐ 4 Anchor Man	.20	.08	.02
☐ 5 Mascot	.20	.08	.02
☐ 6 Annie Oakley	.20	.08	.02
☐ 7 Taxi Squad	.20	.08	.02
☐ 8 Dukes	.20	.08	.02
☐ 9 Rookie	.20	.08	.02
☐ 10 Jinx	.20	.08	.02
☐ 11 Dark Horse	.20	.08	.02
☐ 12 Hat Trick	.20	.08	.02
☐ 13 Bell Wether	.20	.08	.02
☐ 14 Love	.20	.08	.02
☐ 15 Red Dog	.20	.08	.02
☐ 16 Barnstorm	.20	.08	.02
☐ 17 Bull's Eye	.20	.08	.02
☐ 18 Rabbit Punch	.20	.08	.02
☐ 19 The Upper Hand	.20	.08	.02
☐ 20 Handi Cap	.20	.08	.02
☐ 21 Marathon	.20	.08	.02
☐ 22 Southpaw	.20	.08	.02
☐ 23 Boner	.20	.08	.02
☐ 24 Gridiron	.20	.08	.02
☐ 25 Fan	.20	.08	.02
☐ 26 Moxie	.20	.08	.02
☐ 27 Birdie	.20	.08	.02
☐ 28 Sulky	.20	.08	.02
☐ 29 Dribble	.20	.08	.02
☐ 30 Donnybrook	.20	.08	.02
☐ 31 The Real McCoy	.20	.08	.02
☐ 32 Even Stephen	.20	.08	.02
☐ 33 Chinese Homer	.20	.08	.02
☐ 34 English	.20	.08	.02
☐ 35 Garrison Finish	.20	.08	.02
☐ 36 Foot in the Bucket	.20	.08	.02
☐ 37 Steeple Chase	.20	.08	.02
☐ 38 Long Shot	.20	.08	.02
☐ 39 Nip and Tuck	.20	.08	.02
☐ 40 Battery	.20	.08	.02
☐ xx Title Card (unnumbered)	.20	.08	.02

1975 Laughlin Batty Baseball

This set of 25 cards is printed on white card stock. Sports artist R.G. Laughlin 1975 is copyrighted on the title card. The obverses are line drawings primarily in orange, black, and white. The cards

measure approximately 2 9/16" by 3 7/16". The set features a card for each team with a depiction of a fractured nickname for the team. The cards are numbered on the front. The backs are blank, but on white stock.

	NRMT	VG-E	GOOD
COMPLETE SET (25)	4.50	1.80	.45
COMMON PLAYER	.20	.08	.02
☐ 1 Oakland Daze	.20	.08	.02
☐ 2 Boston Wet Sox	.20	.08	.02
☐ 3 Cincinnati Dreads	.20	.08	.02
☐ 4 Chicago Wide Sox	.20	.08	.02
☐ 5 Milwaukee Boozers	.20	.08	.02
☐ 6 Philadelphia Fillies	.20	.08	.02
☐ 7 Cleveland Engines	.20	.08	.02
☐ 8 New York Mitts	.20	.08	.02
☐ 9 Texas Ranchers	.20	.08	.02
☐ 10 San Francisco Gents	.20	.08	.02
☐ 11 Houston Disastros	.20	.08	.02
☐ 12 Chicago Clubs	.20	.08	.02
☐ 13 Minnesota Wins	.20	.08	.02
☐ 14 St. Louis Gardeners	.20	.08	.02
☐ 15 New York Yankers	.20	.08	.02
☐ 16 California Angles	.20	.08	.02
☐ 17 Pittsburgh Irates	.20	.08	.02
☐ 18 Los Angeles Smoggers	.20	.08	.02
☐ 19 Baltimore Oreos	.20	.08	.02
☐ 20 Montreal Expose	.20	.08	.02
☐ 21 San Diego Parties	.20	.08	.02
☐ 22 Detroit Taggers	.20	.08	.02
☐ 23 Kansas City Broils	.20	.08	.02
☐ 24 Atlanta Briefs	.20	.08	.02
☐ xx Title Card (unnumbered)	.20	.08	.02

1976 Laughlin Diamond Jubilee

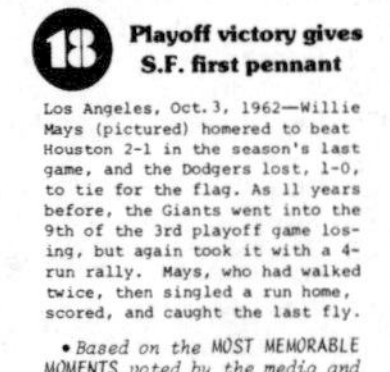

This set of 32 cards is printed on flat (non- glossy) white card stock. Sports artist R.Laughlin 1976 is copyrighted at the bottom of the reverse of each card. The obverses are line drawings primarily in red, blue, black, and white inside a red border. The cards measure approximately 2 13/16" by 3 15/16". The set features memorable moments voted by the media and fans in each major league city. The cards are numbered on the back and captioned on the front and the back. The backs are printed in dark blue on white stock.

	NRMT	VG-E	GOOD
COMPLETE SET (32)	10.00	4.00	1.00
COMMON PLAYER (1-32)	.30	.12	.03
☐ 1 Nolan Ryan	.60	.24	.06
☐ 2 Ernie Banks	.50	.20	.05
☐ 3 Mickey Lolich	.30	.12	.03
☐ 4 Sandy Koufax	.60	.24	.06
☐ 5 Frank Robinson	.40	.16	.04
☐ 6 Bill Mazeroski	.30	.12	.03
☐ 7 Jim Hunter	.40	.16	.04
☐ 8 Hank Aaron	.60	.24	.06
☐ 9 Carl Yastrzemski	.60	.24	.06
☐ 10 Jim Bunning	.30	.12	.03
☐ 11 Brooks Robinson	.40	.16	.04
☐ 12 John Vander Meer	.30	.12	.03
☐ 13 Harmon Killebrew	.40	.16	.04
☐ 14 Lou Brock	.30	.12	.03
☐ 15 Steve Busby	.30	.12	.03
☐ 16 Nate Colbert	.30	.12	.03
☐ 17 Don Larsen	.30	.12	.03
☐ 18 Willie Mays	.60	.24	.06
☐ 19 David Clyde	.30	.12	.03
☐ 20 Mack Jones	.30	.12	.03
☐ 21 Mike Hegan	.30	.12	.03
☐ 22 Jerry Koosman	.30	.12	.03
☐ 23 Early Wynn	.30	.12	.03
☐ 24 Nellie Fox	.30	.12	.03
☐ 25 Joe DiMaggio	.60	.24	.06
☐ 26 Jackie Robinson	.50	.20	.05
☐ 27 Ted Williams	.60	.24	.06
☐ 28 Lou Gehrig	.60	.24	.06
☐ 29 Bobby Thomson	.30	.12	.03
☐ 30 Roger Maris	.50	.20	.05
☐ 31 Harvey Haddix	.30	.12	.03
☐ 32 "Babe" Ruth	.75	.30	.07

1978 Laughlin Long Ago Black Stars

This set of 36 cards is printed on flat (non- glossy) white card stock. Sports artist R.G. Laughlin's work is evident and the reverse of each card indicates copyright by R.G. Laughlin 1978. The obverses are line drawings in light and dark green. The cards measure approximately 2 5/8" by 3 1/2". The set features outstanding black players form the past. The cards are numbered on the back. The backs are printed in black on white stock. This is not a reissue of the similar Laughlin set from 1974 Old Time Black Stars but is actually in effect a second series with all new players.

	NRMT	VG-E	GOOD
COMPLETE SET (36)	10.00	4.00	1.00
COMMON PLAYER (1-36)	.30	.12	.03
☐ 1 Ted Trent	.30	.12	.03
☐ 2 Larry Brown	.30	.12	.03
☐ 3 Newt Allen	.30	.12	.03
☐ 4 Norman Stearns	.30	.12	.03
☐ 5 Leon Day	.50	.20	.05
☐ 6 Dick Lundy	.30	.12	.03
☐ 7 Bruce Petway	.50	.20	.05
☐ 8 Bill Drake	.30	.12	.03
☐ 9 Chaney White	.30	.12	.03

□ 10 Webster McDonald	.30	.12	.03
□ 11 Tommy Butts	.30	.12	.03
□ 12 Ben Taylor	.30	.12	.03
□ 13 James (Joe) Greene	.30	.12	.03
□ 14 Dick Seay	.30	.12	.03
□ 15 Sammy Hughes	.30	.12	.03
□ 16 Ted Page	.50	.20	.05
□ 17 Willie Cornelius	.30	.12	.03
□ 18 Pat Patterson	.30	.12	.03
□ 19 Frank Wickware	.30	.12	.03
□ 20 Albert Haywood	.30	.12	.03
□ 21 Bill Holland	.30	.12	.03
□ 22 Sol White	.30	.12	.03
□ 23 Chet Brewer	.50	.20	.05
□ 24 Crush Holloway	.30	.12	.03
□ 25 George Johnson	.30	.12	.03
□ 26 George Scales	.30	.12	.03
□ 27 Dave Brown	.30	.12	.03
□ 28 John Donaldson	.30	.12	.03
□ 29 William Johnson	.30	.12	.03
□ 30 Bill Yancey	.30	.12	.03
□ 31 Sam Bankhead	.50	.20	.05
□ 32 Leroy Matlock	.30	.12	.03
□ 33 Quincy Troupe	.30	.12	.03
□ 34 Hilton Smith	.30	.12	.03
□ 35 Jim Crutchfield	.30	.12	.03
□ 36 Ted Radcliffe	.50	.20	.05

1980 Laughlin Famous Feats

This set of 40 cards is printed on white card stock. Sports artist R.G. Laughlin 1980 is copyrighted at the bottom ofevery obverse. The obverses are line drawings primarily in many colors. The cards measure approximately 2 1/2" by 3 1/2". The set is subtitled as the "Second Series" of Famous Feats. The cards are numbered on the front. The backs are blank, but on white stock.

	MINT	EXC	G-VG
COMPLETE SET (40)	6.00	2.40	.60
COMMON PLAYER (1-40)	.15	.06	.01
□ 1 Honus Wagner	.35	.14	.03
□ 2 Herb Pennock	.15	.06	.01
□ 3 Al Simmons	.15	.06	.01
□ 4 Hack Wilson	.15	.06	.01
□ 5 Dizzy Dean	.35	.14	.03
□ 6 Chuck Klein	.15	.06	.01
□ 7 Nellie Fox	.15	.06	.01
□ 8 Lefty Grove	.25	.10	.02
□ 9 George Sisler	.15	.06	.01
□ 10 Lou Gehrig	.35	.14	.03
□ 11 Rube Waddell	.15	.06	.01
□ 12 Max Carey	.15	.06	.01
□ 13 Thurman Munson	.25	.10	.02
□ 14 Mel Ott	.25	.10	.02
□ 15 Doc White	.15	.06	.01
□ 16 Babe Ruth	.50	.20	.05
□ 17 Schoolboy Rowe	.15	.06	.01
□ 18 Jackie Robinson	.35	.14	.03
□ 19 Joe Medwick	.15	.06	.01
□ 20 Casey Stengel	.25	.10	.02
□ 21 Roberto Clemente	.25	.10	.02
□ 22 Christy Mathewson	.25	.10	.02
□ 23 Jimmie Foxx	.25	.10	.02
□ 24 Joe Jackson	.35	.14	.03
□ 25 Walter Johnson	.25	.10	.02

□ 26 Tony Lazzeri	.15	.06	.01
□ 27 Hugh Casey	.15	.06	.01
□ 28 Ty Cobb	.35	.14	.03
□ 29 Stuffy McInnis	.15	.06	.01
□ 30 Cy Young	.25	.10	.02
□ 31 Lefty O'Doul	.15	.06	.01
□ 32 Eddie Collins	.15	.06	.01
□ 33 Joe McCarthy	.15	.06	.01
□ 34 Ed Walsh	.15	.06	.01
□ 35 George Burns	.15	.06	.01
□ 36 Walt Dropo	.15	.06	.01
□ 37 Connie Mack	.15	.06	.01
□ 38 Babe Adams	.15	.06	.01
□ 39 Roger Hornsby	.25	.10	.02
□ 40 Grover C. Alexander	.15	.06	.01

1980 Laughlin 300/400/500

This square (approximately 3 1/4" square) set of 30 players features members of the 300/400/500 club, namely, 300 pitching wins, batting .400 or better, or hitting 500 homers since 1900. Cards are blank backed but are numbered on the front. The cards feature the artwork of R.G. Laughlin for the player's body connected to an out of proportion head shot stock photo. This creates an effect faintly reminiscent of the Goudey Heads Up cards.

	NRMT	VG-E	GOOD
COMPLETE SET (30)	9.00	3.75	.90
COMMON PLAYER (1-30)	.30	.12	.03
□ 1 Title Card	.30	.12	.03
□ 2 Babe Ruth	.75	.30	.07
□ 3 Walter Johnson	.40	.16	.04
□ 4 Ty Cobb	.50	.20	.05
□ 5 Christy Mathewson	.40	.16	.04
□ 6 Ted Williams	.50	.20	.05
□ 7 Bill Terry	.30	.12	.03
□ 8 Grover C. Alexander	.30	.12	.03
□ 9 Napoleon Lajoie	.40	.16	.04
□ 10 Willie Mays	.50	.20	.05
□ 11 Cy Young	.40	.16	.04
□ 12 Mel Ott	.40	.16	.04
□ 13 Joe Jackson	.50	.20	.05
□ 14 Harmon Killebrew	.30	.12	.03
□ 15 Warren Spahn	.30	.12	.03
□ 16 Hank Aaron	.50	.20	.05
□ 17 Rogers Hornsby	.40	.16	.04
□ 18 Mickey Mantle	.75	.30	.07
□ 19 Lefty Grove	.40	.16	.04
□ 20 Ted Williams	.50	.20	.05
□ 21 Jimmie Foxx	.40	.16	.04
□ 22 Eddie Plank	.30	.12	.03
□ 23 Frank Robinson	.30	.12	.03
□ 24 George Sisler	.30	.12	.03
□ 25 Eddie Mathews	.30	.12	.03
□ 26 Early Wynn	.30	.12	.03
□ 27 Ernie Banks	.30	.12	.03
□ 28 Harry Heilmann	.30	.12	.03
□ 29 Lou Gehrig	.50	.20	.05
□ 30 Willie McCovey	.30	.12	.03

1948-49 Leaf

The cards in this 98-card set measure 2 3/8" by 2 7/8". The 1948-49 Leaf set was the first post-war baseball series issued in color. This effort was not entirely successful due to a lack of refinement which resulted in many color variations and cards out of register. In addition, the set was skip numbered from 1-168, with 49 of the 98 cards printed in limited quantities (marked with an asterisk in the checklist). Cards 102 and 136 have variations, and cards are sometimes found with overprinted or incorrect backs.

	NRMT	VG-E	GOOD
COMPLETE SET (98)	21500.	8000.	2500.
COMMON NUMBERS	16.50	7.00	1.50
COMMON * NUMBERS	325.00	130.00	32.00

		NRMT	VG-E	GOOD
□ 1	Joe DiMaggio	1000.00	300.00	60.00
□ 3	Babe Ruth	1200.00	500.00	150.00
□ 4	Stan Musial	250.00	100.00	25.00
□ 5	Virgil Trucks *	325.00	130.00	32.00
□ 8	Satchel Paige *	1650.00	700.00	200.00
□ 10	Dizzy Trout	16.50	7.00	1.50
□ 11	Phil Rizzuto	80.00	32.00	8.00
□ 13	Cass Michaels *	325.00	130.00	32.00
□ 14	Billy Johnson	16.50	7.00	1.50
□ 17	Frank Overmire	16.50	7.00	1.50
□ 19	Johnny Wyrostek *	325.00	130.00	32.00
□ 20	Hank Sauer *	350.00	140.00	35.00
□ 22	Al Evans	16.50	7.00	1.50
□ 26	Sam Chapman	16.50	7.00	1.50
□ 27	Mickey Harris	16.50	7.00	1.50
□ 28	Jim Hegan	16.50	7.00	1.50
□ 29	Elmer Valo	16.50	7.00	1.50
□ 30	Billy Goodman *	325.00	130.00	32.00
□ 31	Lou Brissie	16.50	7.00	1.50
□ 32	Warren Spahn	100.00	40.00	10.00
□ 33	Peanuts Lowrey *	325.00	130.00	32.00
□ 36	Al Zarilla *	325.00	130.00	32.00
□ 38	Ted Kluszewski	25.00	10.00	2.50
□ 39	Ewell Blackwell	20.00	8.00	2.00
□ 42	Kent Peterson	16.50	7.00	1.50
□ 43	Ed Stevens *	325.00	130.00	32.00
□ 45	Ken Keltner *	325.00	130.00	32.00
□ 46	Johnny Mize	65.00	26.00	6.50
□ 47	George Vico	16.50	7.00	1.50
□ 48	Johnny Schmitz *	325.00	130.00	32.00
□ 49	Del Ennis	16.50	7.00	1.50
□ 50	Dick Wakefield	16.50	7.00	1.50
□ 51	Al Dark *	375.00	150.00	37.00
□ 53	Johnny VanderMeer	25.00	10.00	2.50
□ 54	Bobby Adams *	325.00	130.00	32.00
□ 55	Tommy Henrich *	375.00	150.00	37.00
□ 56	Larry Jansen	16.50	7.00	1.50
□ 57	Bob McCall	16.50	7.00	1.50
□ 59	Luke Appling	40.00	16.00	4.00
□ 61	Jake Early	16.50	7.00	1.50
□ 62	Eddie Joost *	325.00	130.00	32.00
□ 63	Barney McCosky *	325.00	130.00	32.00
□ 65	Robert Elliott (misspelled Elliot on card front)	20.00	8.00	2.00
□ 66	Orval Grove *	325.00	130.00	32.00
□ 68	Eddie Miller *	325.00	130.00	32.00
□ 70	Honus Wagner	150.00	60.00	15.00
□ 72	Hank Edwards	16.50	7.00	1.50
□ 73	Pat Seerey	16.50	7.00	1.50
□ 75	Dom DiMaggio *	400.00	160.00	40.00
□ 76	Ted Williams	350.00	140.00	35.00
□ 77	Roy Smalley	16.50	7.00	1.50
□ 78	Hoot Evers *	325.00	130.00	32.00
□ 79	Jackie Robinson	250.00	100.00	25.00
□ 81	Whitey Kurowski *	325.00	130.00	32.00
□ 82	Johnny Lindell	16.50	7.00	1.50
□ 83	Bobby Doerr	65.00	26.00	6.50
□ 84	Sid Hudson	16.50	7.00	1.50
□ 85	Dave Philley *	325.00	130.00	32.00
□ 86	Ralph Weigel	16.50	7.00	1.50
□ 88	Frank Gustine *	325.00	130.00	32.00
□ 91	Ralph Kiner	65.00	26.00	6.50
□ 93	Bob Feller *	1000.00	400.00	125.00
□ 95	George Stirnweiss	16.50	7.00	1.50
□ 97	Marty Marion	20.00	8.00	2.00
□ 98	Hal Newhouser *	400.00	160.00	40.00
□ 102A	Gene Hermansk (sic)	150.00	60.00	15.00
□ 102B	Gene Hermanski	16.50	7.00	1.50
□ 104	Eddie Stewart *	175.00	70.00	18.00
□ 106	Lou Boudreau	65.00	26.00	6.50
□ 108	Matt Batts *	325.00	130.00	32.00
□ 111	Jerry Priddy	16.50	7.00	1.50
□ 113	Dutch Leonard *	325.00	130.00	32.00
□ 117	Joe Gordon	20.00	8.00	2.00
□ 120	George Kell *	550.00	220.00	55.00
□ 121	Johnny Pesky *	350.00	140.00	35.00
□ 123	Cliff Fannin *	325.00	130.00	32.00
□ 125	Andy Pafko	16.50	7.00	1.50
□ 127	Enos Slaughter *	550.00	220.00	55.00
□ 128	Buddy Rosar	16.50	7.00	1.50
□ 129	Kirby Higbe *	325.00	130.00	32.00
□ 131	Sid Gordon *	325.00	130.00	32.00
□ 133	Tommy Holmes *	350.00	140.00	35.00
□ 136A	Cliff Aberson (full sleeve)	16.50	7.00	1.50
□ 136B	Cliff Aberson (short sleeve)	65.00	26.00	6.50
□ 137	Harry Walker *	350.00	140.00	35.00
□ 138	Larry Doby *	400.00	160.00	40.00
□ 139	Johnny Hopp	16.50	7.00	1.50
□ 142	Danny Murtaugh *	350.00	140.00	35.00
□ 143	Dick Sisler *	325.00	130.00	32.00
□ 144	Bob Dillinger *	325.00	130.00	32.00
□ 146	Pete Reiser *	350.00	140.00	35.00
□ 149	Hank Majeski *	325.00	130.00	32.00
□ 153	Floyd Baker *	325.00	130.00	32.00
□ 158	Harry Brecheen *	325.00	130.00	32.00
□ 159	Mizell Platt	16.50	7.00	1.50
□ 160	Bob Scheffing *	325.00	130.00	32.00
□ 161	Vern Stephens *	350.00	140.00	35.00
□ 163	Fred Hutchinson *	375.00	150.00	37.00
□ 165	Dale Mitchell *	350.00	140.00	35.00
□ 168	Phil Cavarretta *	350.00	140.00	35.00

1960 Leaf

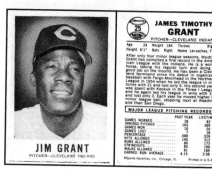

The cards in this 144-card set measure 2 1/2" by 3 1/2". The 1960 Leaf set was issued in a regular gum package style but with a marble instead of gum. The series was a joint production by Sports Novelties, Inc., and Leaf, two Chicago-based companies. Cards 73-144 are more difficult to find than the lower numbers. Photo variations exist (probably proof cards) for the seven cards listed with an asterisk and there is a well-known error card, number 25 showing Brooks Lawrence (in a Reds uniform) with Jim Grant's name on front, and Grant's biography and record on back. The corrected version with Grant's photo is the more difficult variety.

	NRMT	VG-E	GOOD
COMPLETE SET (144)	775.00	320.00	100.00
COMMON PLAYER (1-72)	1.00	.40	.10
COMMON PLAYER (73-144)	8.00	3.25	.80

	NRMT	VG-E	GOOD
□ 1 Luis Aparicio *	6.00	2.00	.40
□ 2 Woodson Held	1.00	.40	.10
□ 3 Frank Lary	1.00	.40	.10
□ 4 Camilo Pascual	1.00	.40	.10
□ 5 Juan Herrera	1.00	.40	.10
□ 6 Felipe Alou	1.25	.50	.12
□ 7 Benjamin Daniels	1.00	.40	.10
□ 8 Roger Craig	2.50	1.00	.25
□ 9 Edward Kasko	1.00	.40	.10
□ 10 Robert Anton Grim	1.25	.50	.12
□ 11 James Busby	1.00	.40	.10
□ 12 Kenton Boyer	2.50	1.00	.25
□ 13 Robert Boyd	1.00	.40	.10
□ 14 Samuel Jones	1.00	.40	.10
□ 15 Lawence Jackson	1.00	.40	.10
□ 16 Elroy Face	1.50	.60	.15
□ 17 Walter Moryn *	1.00	.40	.10
□ 18 James Gilliam	2.50	1.00	.25
□ 19 Donald Newcombe	1.50	.60	.15
□ 20 Glen Hobbie	1.00	.40	.10
□ 21 Pedro Ramos	1.00	.40	.10
□ 22 Rinold Duren	1.50	.60	.15
□ 23 Joseph Jay *	1.00	.40	.10
□ 24 Louis Berberet	1.00	.40	.10
□ 25A Jim Grant COR	15.00	6.00	1.50
□ 25B Jim Grant ERR (photo actually Brooks Lawrence)	10.00	4.00	1.00
□ 26 Thomas Borland	1.00	.40	.10
□ 27 Brooks Robinson	12.50	5.00	1.25
□ 28 Jerry Adair	1.00	.40	.10
□ 29 Ronald Jackson	1.00	.40	.10
□ 30 George Strickland	1.00	.40	.10
□ 31 Everett Rocky Bridges	1.00	.40	.10
□ 32 William Tuttle	1.00	.40	.10
□ 33 Kenneth Hunt	1.00	.40	.10
□ 34 Harold Griggs	1.00	.40	.10
□ 35 James Coates *	1.00	.40	.10
□ 36 Brooks Lawrence	1.00	.40	.10
□ 37 Edwin (Duke) Snider	16.00	6.50	1.60
□ 38 Albert Spangler	1.00	.40	.10
□ 39 James Owens	1.00	.40	.10
□ 40 William Virdon	1.50	.60	.15
□ 41 Ernest Broglio	1.00	.40	.10
□ 42 Andre Rodgers	1.00	.40	.10
□ 43 Julio Becquer	1.00	.40	.10
□ 44 Antonio(Tony) Taylor	1.00	.40	.10
□ 45 Gerald Lynch	1.00	.40	.10
□ 46 Cletis Boyer	1.50	.60	.15
□ 47 Jerry Lumpe	1.00	.40	.10
□ 48 Charles Maxwell	1.00	.40	.10
□ 49 James Perry	1.50	.60	.15
□ 50 Daniel McDevitt	1.00	.40	.10
□ 51 Juan Pizarro	1.00	.40	.10
□ 52 Dallas Green	3.00	1.20	.30
□ 53 Robert Friend	1.25	.50	.12
□ 54 Jack Sanford	1.00	.40	.10
□ 55 Manuel(Jim) Rivera	1.00	.40	.10
□ 56 Theodore Wills	1.00	.40	.10
□ 57 Milton Pappas	1.25	.50	.12
□ 58 Harold Smith *	1.25	.50	.12
□ 59 Roberto Avila	1.00	.40	.10
□ 60 Clement Labine	1.25	.50	.12
□ 61 Norman Rehm *	1.00	.40	.10
□ 62 John Gabler	1.00	.40	.10
□ 63 John Tsitouris	1.00	.40	.10
□ 64 David Sisler	1.00	.40	.10
□ 65 Victor Power	1.00	.40	.10
□ 66 Earl Battey	1.00	.40	.10
□ 67 Robert Purkey	1.00	.40	.10
□ 68 Myron(Moe) Drabowsky	1.00	.40	.10
□ 69 James(Hoyt) Wilhelm	6.00	2.40	.60
□ 70 Humberto Robinson	1.00	.40	.10
□ 71 Dorrel(Whitey) Herzog	2.50	1.00	.25
□ 72 Richard Donovan *	1.00	.40	.10
□ 73 Gordon Jones	8.00	3.25	.80
□ 74 Joe Hicks	8.00	3.25	.80
□ 75 Ray Culp	8.00	3.25	.80
□ 76 Dick Drott	8.00	3.25	.80
□ 77 Bob Duliba	8.00	3.25	.80
□ 78 Art Ditmar	8.00	3.25	.80
□ 79 Steve Korcheck	8.00	3.25	.80
□ 80 Henry Mason	8.00	3.25	.80
□ 81 Harry Simpson	8.00	3.25	.80
□ 82 Gene Green	8.00	3.25	.80
□ 83 Bob Shaw	8.00	3.25	.80
□ 84 Howard Reed	8.00	3.25	.80
□ 85 Dick Stigman	8.00	3.25	.80
□ 86 Rip Repulski	8.00	3.25	.80
□ 87 Seth Morehead	8.00	3.25	.80
□ 88 Camilo Carreon	8.00	3.25	.80
□ 89 John Blanchard	10.00	4.00	1.00
□ 90 Billy Hoeft	8.00	3.25	.80
□ 91 Fred Hopke	8.00	3.25	.80
□ 92 Joe Martin	8.00	3.25	.80
□ 93 Wally Shannon	8.00	3.25	.80
□ 94 Two Hal Smith's Hal R. Smith Hal W. Smith	15.00	6.00	1.50
□ 95 Al Schroll	8.00	3.25	.80
□ 96 John Kucks	10.00	4.00	1.00
□ 97 Tom Morgan	8.00	3.25	.80
□ 98 Willie Jones	8.00	3.25	.80
□ 99 Marshall Renfroe	8.00	3.25	.80
□ 100 Willie Tasby	8.00	3.25	.80
□ 101 Irv Noren	8.00	3.25	.80
□ 102 Russ Snyder	8.00	3.25	.80
□ 103 Bob Turley	12.00	5.00	1.20
□ 104 Jim Woods	8.00	3.25	.80
□ 105 Ronnie Kline	8.00	3.25	.80
□ 106 Steve Bilko	8.00	3.25	.80
□ 107 Elmer Valo	8.00	3.25	.80
□ 108 Tom McAvoy	8.00	3.25	.80
□ 109 Stan Williams	10.00	4.00	1.00
□ 110 Earl Averill Jr.	8.00	3.25	.80
□ 111 Lee Walls	8.00	3.25	.80
□ 112 Paul Richards MG	10.00	4.00	1.00
□ 113 Ed Sadowski	8.00	3.25	.80
□ 114 Stover McIlwain	8.00	3.25	.80
□ 115 Chuck Tanner (photo actually Ken Kuhn)	15.00	6.00	1.50
□ 116 Lou Klimchock	8.00	3.25	.80
□ 117 Neil Chrisley	8.00	3.25	.80
□ 118 John Callison	12.00	5.00	1.20
□ 119 Hal Smith	8.00	3.25	.80
□ 120 Carl Sawatski	8.00	3.25	.80
□ 121 Frank Leja	8.00	3.25	.80
□ 122 Earl Torgeson	8.00	3.25	.80
□ 123 Art Schult	8.00	3.25	.80
□ 124 Jim Brosnan	10.00	4.00	1.00
□ 125 George Anderson	20.00	8.00	2.00
□ 126 Joe Pignatano	8.00	3.25	.80
□ 127 Rocky Nelson	8.00	3.25	.80
□ 128 Orlando Cepeda	25.00	10.00	2.50
□ 129 Daryl Spencer	8.00	3.25	.80
□ 130 Ralph Lumenti	8.00	3.25	.80
□ 131 Sam Taylor	8.00	3.25	.80
□ 132 Harry Brecheen	8.00	3.25	.80
□ 133 Johnny Groth	8.00	3.25	.80
□ 134 Wayne Terwilliger	8.00	3.25	.80
□ 135 Kent Hadley	8.00	3.25	.80
□ 136 Faye Throneberry	8.00	3.25	.80
□ 137 Jack Meyer	8.00	3.25	.80
□ 138 Chuck Cottier	8.00	3.25	.80
□ 139 Joe DeMaestri	8.00	3.25	.80
□ 140 Gene Freese	8.00	3.25	.80
□ 141 Curt Flood	15.00	6.00	1.50
□ 142 Gino Cimoli	8.00	3.25	.80
□ 143 Clay Dalrymple	8.00	3.25	.80
□ 144 Jim Bunning	35.00	14.00	3.50

1960 MacGregor Staff

This 25-card set represents members of the MacGregor Sporting Goods Advisory Staff. Since the cards are unnumbered they ordered below in alphabetical order. The cards are blank backed and measure approximately 3 3/4" by 5". The photos are in black and white. The catalog designation for the set is H825-1. Cards have a facsimile autograph in white lettering on the front.

	NRMT	VG-E	GOOD
COMPLETE SET (25)	350.00	140.00	35.00
COMMON PLAYER (1-25)	6.00	2.40	.60
□ 1 Hank Aaron	80.00	32.00	8.00
□ 2 Richie Ashburn	12.50	5.00	1.25
□ 3 Gus Bell	6.00	2.40	.60
□ 4 Lou Berberet	6.00	2.40	.60
□ 5 Jerry Casale	6.00	2.40	.60
□ 6 Del Crandall	7.00	2.80	.70
□ 7 Art Ditmar	6.00	2.40	.60
□ 8 Gene Freese	6.00	2.40	.60
□ 9 James Gilliam	9.00	3.75	.90

☐ 10 Ted Kluszewski	11.00	4.50	1.10
☐ 11 Jim Landis	6.00	2.40	.60
☐ 12 Al Lopez	11.00	4.50	1.10
☐ 13 Willie Mays	80.00	32.00	8.00
☐ 14 Bill Mazeroski	9.00	3.75	.90
☐ 15 Mike McCormick	7.00	2.80	.70
☐ 16 Gil McDougald	10.00	4.00	1.00
☐ 17 Russ Nixon	7.00	2.80	.70
☐ 18 Bill Rigney	6.00	2.40	.60
☐ 19 Robin Roberts	20.00	8.00	2.00
☐ 20 Frank Robinson	35.00	14.00	3.50
☐ 21 John Roseboro	6.00	2.40	.60
☐ 22 Red Schoendienst	8.00	3.25	.80
☐ 23 Bill Skowron	12.00	5.00	1.20
☐ 24 Daryl Spencer	6.00	2.40	.60
☐ 25 Johnny Temple	6.00	2.40	.60

1965 MacGregor Staff

TONY OLIVA
MEMBER OF THE MacGregor/BRUNSWICK
ADVISORY STAFF

This 10-card set represents members of the MacGregor Sporting Goods Advisory Staff. Since the cards are unnumbered they ordered below in alphabetical order. The cards are blank backed and measure approximately 3 9/16" by 5 1/8". The photos are in black and white. The catalog designation for the set is H825-2.

	NRMT	VG-E	GOOD
COMPLETE SET (10)	150.00	60.00	15.00
COMMON PLAYER (1-10)	5.00	2.00	.50
☐ 1 Roberto Clemente	65.00	26.00	6.50
☐ 2 Al Downing	6.00	2.40	.60
☐ 3 Johnny Edwards	5.00	2.00	.50
☐ 4 Ron Hansen	5.00	2.00	.50
☐ 5 Deron Johnson	6.00	2.40	.60
☐ 6 Willie Mays	75.00	30.00	7.50
☐ 7 Tony Oliva	12.50	5.00	1.25
☐ 8 Claude Osteen	6.00	2.40	.60
☐ 9 Bobby Richardson	12.50	5.00	1.25
☐ 10 Zoilo Versalles	5.00	2.00	.50

1988 Mattingly Kit

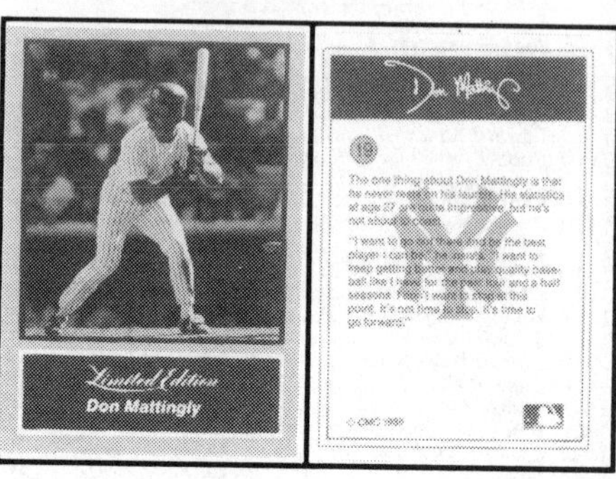

This 20-card set featuring Don Mattingly was distributed as part of a Collecting Kit produced by Collector's Marketing Corp. The cards themselves measure approximately 2 1/2" by 3 1/2" and have a light blue border. The card backs describe some aspect of Mattingly's career. Also in the kit were plastic sheets, a small album, a record, a booklet, and information on how to join Don's Fan Club. The set price below is for the whole kit as well as the cards.

	MINT	EXC	G-VG
COMPLETE SET (20)	10.00	4.00	1.00
COMMON PLAYER (1-20)	.60	.24	.06
☐ 1 Game Face	.60	.24	.06
☐ 2 Columbus Clippers	.60	.24	.06
☐ 3 1983 Spring Camp	.60	.24	.06
☐ 4 AL Batting Crown	.60	.24	.06
☐ 5 1981 All-Star Outfielder	.60	.24	.06
☐ 6 The Batting Tee	.60	.24	.06
☐ 7 AL MVP Honors	.60	.24	.06
☐ 8 Gold Glove Winner	.60	.24	.06
☐ 9 Batting Practice	.60	.24	.06
☐ 10 Yankee Records	.60	.24	.06
☐ 11 Baseball On His Mind	.60	.24	.06
☐ 12 Big Home Runs	.60	.24	.06
☐ 13 Hustle and Determination	.60	.24	.06
☐ 14 Delivering In The Clutch	.60	.24	.06
☐ 15 A Slick First Baseman	.60	.24	.06
☐ 16 Keep Playing Hard	.60	.24	.06
☐ 17 Mattingly's Eight-Game Streak	.60	.24	.06
☐ 18 The Textbook Swing	.60	.24	.06
☐ 19 It's Time To Go Forward	.60	.24	.06
☐ 20 Surehanded First Baseman	.60	.24	.06

1984 Mets Fan Club

The cards in this 8-player set measure 2 1/2" by 3 1/2". The sheets were produced by Topps for the New York Mets and feature only Mets. The full sheet measures 7 1/2" by 10 1/2". Cards are together on the sheet but are perforated for those collectors who want to separate the individual player cards. The middle (ninth) card is a Mets Fan club membership card which details various promotional days at Shea Stadium on the back. The cards are numbered on the back and printed in orange and blue.

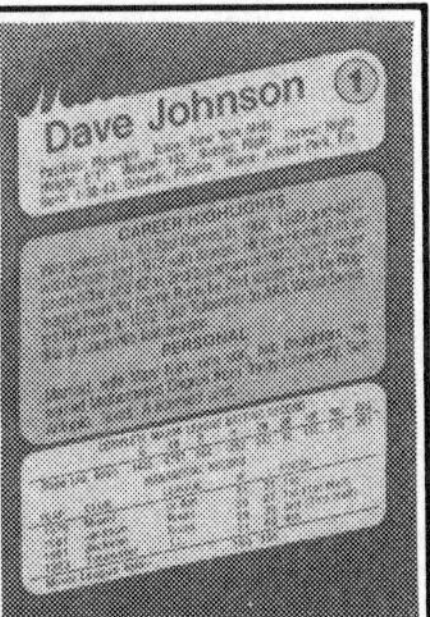

	MINT	EXC	G-VG
COMPLETE SET (8)	12.00	5.00	1.20
COMMON PLAYER	.50	.20	.05
□ 1 Dave Johnson MG	.65	.26	.06
□ 2 Ron Darling	1.50	.60	.15
□ 3 George Foster	1.00	.40	.10
□ 4 Keith Hernandez	2.50	1.00	.25
□ 5 Jesse Orosco	.50	.20	.05
□ 6 Rusty Staub	1.00	.40	.10
□ 7 Darryl Strawberry	8.00	3.25	.80
□ 8 Mookie Wilson	.65	.26	.06

1985 Mets Fan Club

The cards in this 8-player set measure 2 1/2" by 3 1/2". The sheets were produced by Topps for the New York Mets and feature only Mets. The full sheet measures 7 1/2" by 10 1/2". Cards are together on the sheet but are perforated for those collectors who want to separate the individual player cards. The middle (ninth) card is a Mets Fan club membership card. The set was available as a membership premium for joining the Junior Mets Fan Club for 4.00.

	MINT	EXC	G-VG
COMPLETE SET (8)	21.00	8.50	2.10
COMMON PLAYER	.50	.20	.05
□ 1 Wally Backman	.75	.30	.07
□ 2 Bruce Berenyi	.50	.20	.05
□ 3 Gary Carter	2.50	1.00	.25
□ 4 George Foster	1.25	.50	.12
□ 5 Dwight Gooden	11.00	4.50	1.10
□ 6 Keith Hernandez	2.50	1.00	.25
□ 7 Doug Sisk	.50	.20	.05
□ 8 Darryl Strawberry	6.00	2.40	.60

1986 Mets Fan Club

The cards in this 8-player set measure 2 1/2" by 3 1/2". The sheets were produced by Topps for the New York Mets and feature only Mets. The full sheet measures 7 1/2" by 10 1/2". Cards are together on the sheet but are perforated for those collectors who want to separate the individual player cards. The middle (ninth) card is a Mets Fan club membership card. The set was available as a membership premium for joining the Junior Mets Fan Club for 5.00.

	MINT	EXC	G-VG
COMPLETE SET (8)	15.00	6.00	1.50
COMMON PLAYER	.50	.20	.05
□ 1 Wally Backman	.75	.30	.07
□ 2 Gary Carter	2.50	1.00	.25

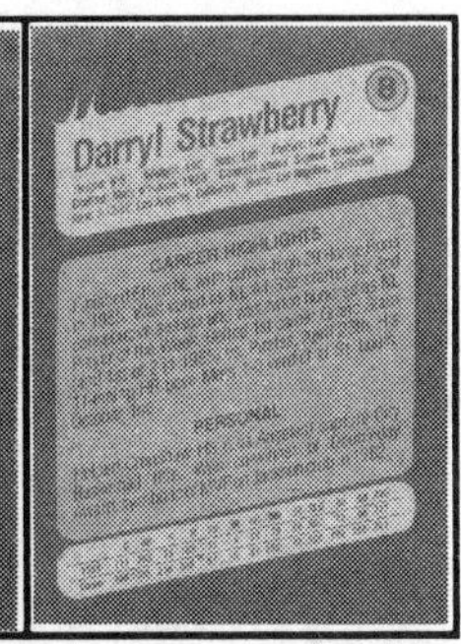

□ 3 Ron Darling	1.25	.50	.12
□ 4 Dwight Gooden	5.00	2.00	.50
□ 5 Keith Hernandez	2.50	1.00	.25
□ 6 Howard Johnson	1.25	.50	.12
□ 7 Roger McDowell	1.00	.40	.10
□ 8 Darryl Strawberry	5.00	2.00	.50

1987 Mets Fan Club

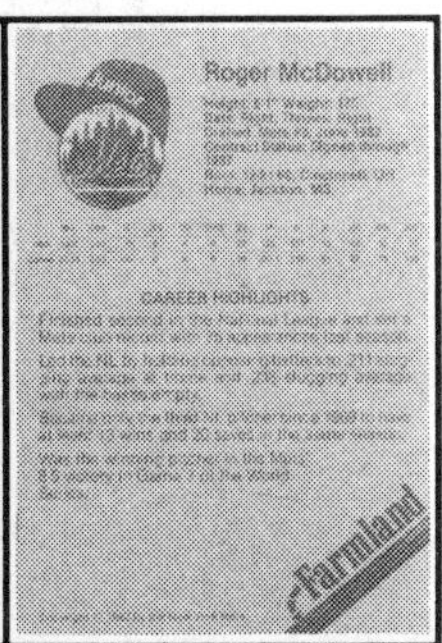

The cards in this 8-player set measure 2 1/2" by 3 1/2". The sheets were produced by Topps for the New York Mets and feature only Mets. The full sheet measures 7 1/2" by 10 1/2". Cards are together on the sheet but are perforated for those collectors who want to separate the individual player cards. The cards have an outer orange border. The set was available as a membership premium for joining the Junior Mets Fan Club for 6.00. The set and club were also sponsored by Farmland Dairies Milk. The cards are unnumbered on the back although they do contain the player's uniform number on the front.

	MINT	EXC	G-VG
COMPLETE SET (9)	10.00	4.00	1.00
COMMON PLAYER	.50	.20	.05
□ 1 Gary Carter 8	2.00	.80	.20
□ 2 Ron Darling 12	1.25	.50	.12
□ 3 Lenny Dykstra 4	.80	.32	.08
□ 4 Roger McDowell 42	.65	.26	.06
□ 5 Kevin McReynolds 22	2.50	1.00	.25
□ 6 Bob Ojeda 19	.65	.26	.06
□ 7 Darryl Strawberry 18	5.00	2.00	.50
□ 8 Mookie Wilson 1	.65	.26	.06
□ 9 Mets Team Card (1986 World Champs)	.50	.20	.05

FAMILY FUN: Have fun with all members of your family. Take them along to a sports collectibles convention in your area.

1988 Mets Fan Club

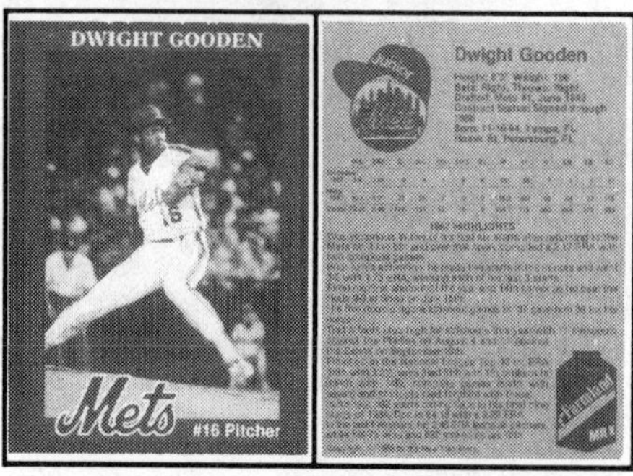

The cards in this 9-player set measure 2 1/2" by 3 1/2". The sheets were produced by Topps for the New York Mets and feature only Mets. The full sheet measures 7 1/2" by 10 1/2". Cards are together on the sheet but are perforated for those collectors who want to separate the individual player cards. The cards have an outer orange border and an inner dark blue border. The set was available as a membership premium for joining the Junior Mets Fan Club for 6.00. The set and club were also sponsored by Farmland Dairies Milk. The cards are unnumbered on the back although they do contain the player's uniform number on the front.

	MINT	EXC	G-VG
COMPLETE SET (9)	6.00	2.40	.60
COMMON PLAYER	.40	.16	.04
☐ 8 Gary Carter	.90	.36	.09
☐ 16 Dwight Gooden	.50	.20	.05
☐ 17 Keith Hernandez	.90	.36	.09
☐ 18 Darryl Strawberry	2.00	.80	.20
☐ 20 Howard Johnson	.60	.24	.06
☐ 21 Kevin Elster	.60	.24	.06
☐ 42 Roger McDowell	.40	.16	.04
☐ 48 Randy Myers	.50	.20	.05
☐ 50 Sid Fernandez	.60	.24	.06

1984 Milton Bradley

The cards in this 30-card set measure 2 1/2" by 3 1/2". This set of full color cards was produced by Topps for the Milton Bradley Co. The set was included in a board game entitled Championship Baseball. The fronts feature portraits of the players and the name, Championship Baseball, by Milton Bradley. The backs feature the Topps logo, statistics for the past year (pitchers' cards have career statistics), and dice rolls which are part of the board game. Pitcher cards have no dice roll charts. There are 15 players from each league. These unnumbered cards are listed below in alphabetical order. The cap logos and uniforms have been air-brushed to remove all team references.

	MINT	EXC	G-VG
COMPLETE SET (30)	9.00	3.75	.90
COMMON PLAYER (1-30)	.15	.06	.01
☐ 1 Wade Boggs	1.25	.50	.12
☐ 2 George Brett	.75	.30	.07
☐ 3 Rod Carew	.35	.14	.03
☐ 4 Steve Carlton	.35	.14	.03
☐ 5 Gary Carter	.35	.14	.03
☐ 6 Dave Concepcion	.15	.06	.01
☐ 7 Cecil Cooper	.15	.06	.01
☐ 8 Andre Dawson	.35	.14	.03
☐ 9 Carlton Fisk	.15	.06	.01
☐ 10 Steve Garvey	.45	.18	.04
☐ 11 Pedro Guerrero	.25	.10	.02
☐ 12 Ron Guidry	.25	.10	.02
☐ 13 Rickey Henderson	.75	.30	.07
☐ 14 Reggie Jackson	.75	.30	.07
☐ 15 Ron Kittle	.15	.06	.01
☐ 16 Bill Madlock	.15	.06	.01
☐ 17 Dale Murphy	.75	.30	.07
☐ 18 Al Oliver	.15	.06	.01
☐ 19 Darrell Porter	.15	.06	.01
☐ 20 Cal Ripken	.60	.24	.06
☐ 21 Pete Rose	1.00	.40	.10
☐ 22 Steve Sax	.35	.14	.03
☐ 23 Mike Schmidt	.75	.30	.07
☐ 24 Ted Simmons	.15	.06	.01
☐ 25 Ozzie Smith	.35	.14	.03
☐ 26 Dave Stieb	.15	.06	.01
☐ 27 Fernando Valenzuela	.25	.10	.02
☐ 28 Lou Whitaker	.25	.10	.02
☐ 29 Dave Winfield	.35	.14	.03
☐ 30 Robin Yount	.35	.14	.03

1987 MnM's Star Lineup

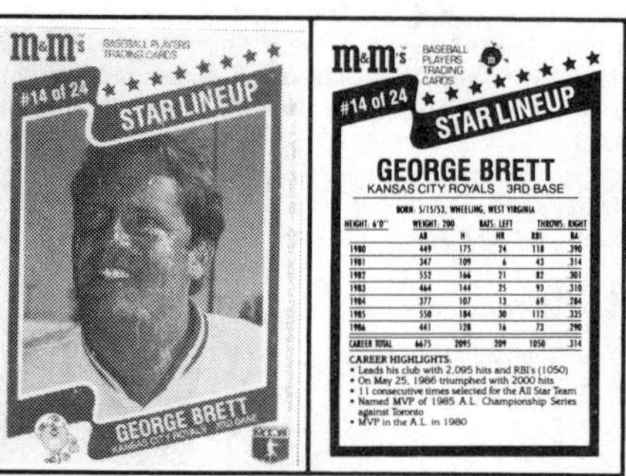

The Mars Candy Company is the sponsor of this 24-card set of cards. The cards were printed in perforated pairs. The pairs measure 5" by 3 1/2" whereas the individual cards measure the standard 2 1/2" by 3 1/2". The players are shown without team logos. The cards were designed and produced by MSA, Mike Schechter Associates. The cards are numbered on the front and back. The backs show statistics for every year since 1980 even if the player was not even playing during those earlier years. The values below are for individual players; panels intact would be valued at 25% more than the sum of the two individual players.

	MINT	EXC	G-VG
COMPLETE SET (24)	10.00	4.00	1.00
COMMON PLAYER (1-24)	.30	.12	.03
☐ 1 Wally Joyner	1.00	.40	.10
☐ 2 Tony Pena	.30	.12	.03
☐ 3 Mike Schmidt	.75	.30	.07
☐ 4 Ryne Sandberg	.75	.30	.07

□ 5 Wade Boggs	1.50	.60	.15
□ 6 Jack Morris	.50	.20	.05
□ 7 Roger Clemens	1.00	.40	.10
□ 8 Harold Baines	.40	.16	.04
□ 9 Dale Murphy	.75	.30	.07
□ 10 Jose Canseco	2.50	1.00	.25
□ 11 Don Mattingly	2.50	1.00	.25
□ 12 Gary Carter	.75	.30	.07
□ 13 Cal Ripken Jr.	.75	.30	.07
□ 14 George Brett	.75	.30	.07
□ 15 Kirby Puckett	1.00	.40	.10
□ 16 Joe Carter	.50	.20	.05
□ 17 Mike Witt	.30	.12	.03
□ 18 Mike Scott	.50	.20	.05
□ 19 Fernando Valenzuela	.50	.20	.05
□ 20 Steve Garvey	.75	.30	.07
□ 21 Steve Sax	.50	.20	.05
□ 22 Nolan Ryan	.75	.30	.07
□ 23 Tony Gwynn	.75	.30	.07
□ 24 Ozzie Smith	.50	.20	.05

1959 Morrell

The cards in this 12-card set measure 2 1/2" by 3 1/2". The 1959 Morrell Meats set of full color, unnumbered cards features Los Angeles Dodger players only. The photos used are the same as those selected for the Dodger team issue postcards in 1959. The Morrell Meats logo is on the backs of the cards. The Clem Labine card actually features a picture of Stan Williams and the Norm Larker card actually features a picture of Joe Pignatano. The ACC designation is F172-1.

	NRMT	VG-E	GOOD
COMPLETE SET (12)	800.00	320.00	80.00
COMMON PLAYER (1-12)	50.00	20.00	5.00
□ 1 Don Drysdale	100.00	40.00	10.00
□ 2 Carl Furillo	60.00	24.00	6.00
□ 3 Jim Gilliam	60.00	24.00	6.00
□ 4 Gil Hodges	100.00	40.00	10.00
□ 5 Sandy Koufax	150.00	60.00	15.00
□ 6 Clem Labine (photo actually Stan Williams)	50.00	20.00	5.00
□ 7 Norm Larker (photo actually Joe Pignatano)	50.00	20.00	5.00
□ 8 Charlie Neal	50.00	20.00	5.00
□ 9 Johnny Podres	60.00	24.00	6.00
□ 10 John Roseboro	50.00	20.00	5.00
□ 11 Duke Snider	150.00	60.00	15.00
□ 12 Don Zimmer	60.00	24.00	6.00

1960 Morrell

The cards in this 12-card set measure 2 1/2" by 3 1/2". The 1960 Morrell Meats set of full color, unnumbered cards is similar in format to the 1959 Morrell set but can be distinguished from the 1959 set by a red heart which appears in the Morrell logo on the back. The photos used are the same as those selected for the Dodger team issue postcards in 1960. The Furillo, Hodges, and Snider cards received limited distribution and are hence more scarce. The ACC designation is F172-2. The cards were printed in Japan.

	NRMT	VG-E	GOOD
COMPLETE SET (12)	575.00	250.00	75.00
COMMON PLAYER (1-12)	15.00	6.00	1.50
□ 1 Walt Alston MG	30.00	12.00	3.00
□ 2 Roger Craig	25.00	10.00	2.50
□ 3 Don Drysdale	45.00	18.00	4.50
□ 4 Carl Furillo SP	80.00	32.00	8.00
□ 5 Gil Hodges SP	135.00	54.00	13.50
□ 6 Sandy Koufax	80.00	32.00	8.00
□ 7 Wally Moon	15.00	6.00	1.50
□ 8 Charlie Neal	15.00	6.00	1.50
□ 9 Johnny Podres	20.00	8.00	2.00
□ 10 John Roseboro	15.00	6.00	1.50
□ 11 Larry Sherry	15.00	6.00	1.50
□ 12 Duke Snider SP	200.00	80.00	20.00

1961 Morrell

The cards in this 6-card set measure 2 1/2" by 3 1/2". The 1961 Morrell Meats set of full color, unnumbered cards features Los Angeles Dodger players only and contains statistical information on the backs of the cards in brown print. The ACC designation is F172-3.

	NRMT	VG-E	GOOD
COMPLETE SET (6)	175.00	70.00	25.00
COMMON PLAYER (1-6)	15.00	6.00	1.50
□ 1 Tommy Davis	20.00	8.00	2.00
□ 2 Don Drysdale	45.00	18.00	4.50
□ 3 Frank Howard	20.00	8.00	2.00
□ 4 Sandy Koufax	80.00	32.00	8.00
□ 5 Norm Larker	15.00	6.00	1.50
□ 6 Maury Wills	30.00	12.00	3.00

1983 Mother's Giants

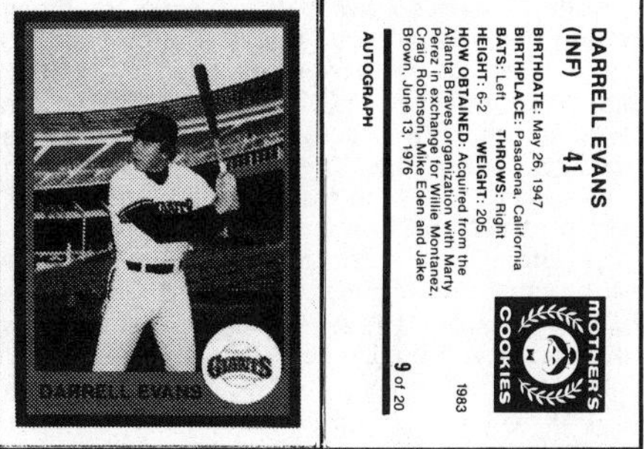

The cards in this 20-card set measure 2 1/2" by 3 1/2". For the first time in 30 years, Mother's Cookies issued a baseball card set. The full color set, produced by hobbyist Barry Colla, features San Francisco Giants players only. Fifteen cards were issued at the Astros vs. Giants game of August 7, 1983. Five of the cards were redeemable by sending in a coupon. The five additional cards received from redemption of the coupon were not guaranteed to be the five needed to complete the set. The fronts feature the player's photo, his name, and the Giants' logo, while the backs feature player biographies and the Mother's Cookies logo. The backs also contain a space in which to obtain the player's autograph.

	MINT	EXC	G-VG
COMPLETE SET (20)	15.00	6.00	1.50
COMMON PLAYER (1-20)	.50	.20	.05
□ 1 Frank Robinson MG	1.50	.60	.15
□ 2 Jack Clark	2.50	1.00	.25
□ 3 Chili Davis	1.50	.60	.15
□ 4 Johnnie LeMaster	.50	.20	.05
□ 5 Greg Minton	.60	.24	.06
□ 6 Bob Brenly	.75	.30	.07
□ 7 Fred Breining	.50	.20	.05
□ 8 Jeff Leonard	.90	.36	.09
□ 9 Darrell Evans	1.25	.50	.12
□ 10 Tom O'Malley	.50	.20	.05

□ 11 Duane Kuiper	.50	.20	.05
□ 12 Mike Krukow	.75	.30	.07
□ 13 Atlee Hammaker	.60	.24	.06
□ 14 Gary Lavelle	.60	.24	.06
□ 15 Bill Laskey	.50	.20	.05
□ 16 Max Venable	.50	.20	.05
□ 17 Joel Youngblood	.50	.20	.05
□ 18 Dave Bergman	.50	.20	.05
□ 19 Mike Vail	.50	.20	.05
□ 20 Andy McGaffigan	.50	.20	.05

1984 Mother's A's

The cards in this 28-card set measure 2 1/2" by 3 1/2". In 1984, the Los Angeles based Mother's Cookies Co. issued five sets of cards featuring players from major league teams. The Oakland A's set features current players depicted by photos. Similar to their 1952 and 1953 issues, the cards have rounded corners. The backs of the cards contain the Mother's Cookies logo. The cards were distributed in partial sets to fans at the respective stadiums of the teams involved. Whereas 20 cards were given to each patron, a redemption card, redeemable for eight more cards was included. Unfortunately, the eight cards received by redeeming the coupon were not necessarily the eight needed to complete a set. Hobbyist Barry Colla was involved in the production of these sets.

	MINT	EXC	G-VG
COMPLETE SET (28)	12.50	5.00	1.25
COMMON PLAYER (1-28)	.40	.16	.04
□ 1 Steve Boros MG	.40	.16	.04
□ 2 Rickey Henderson	3.50	1.40	.35
□ 3 Joe Morgan	1.50	.60	.15
□ 4 Dwayne Murphy	.60	.24	.06
□ 5 Mike Davis	.60	.24	.06
□ 6 Bruce Bochte	.40	.16	.04
□ 7 Carney Lansford	.80	.32	.08
□ 8 Steve McCatty	.40	.16	.04
□ 9 Mike Heath	.40	.16	.04
□ 10 Chris Codiroli	.40	.16	.04
□ 11 Bill Almon	.40	.16	.04
□ 12 Bill Caudill	.50	.20	.05
□ 13 Donnie Hill	.40	.16	.04
□ 14 Lary Sorensen	.40	.16	.04
□ 15 Dave Kingman	.80	.32	.08
□ 16 Garry Hancock	.40	.16	.04
□ 17 Jeff Burroughs	.50	.20	.05
□ 18 Tom Burgmeier	.40	.16	.04
□ 19 Jim Essian	.40	.16	.04
□ 20 Mike Warren	.40	.16	.04
□ 21 Davey Lopes	.50	.20	.05
□ 22 Ray Burris	.50	.20	.05
□ 23 Tony Phillips	.50	.20	.05
□ 24 Tim Conroy	.40	.16	.04
□ 25 Jeff Bettendorf	.40	.16	.04
□ 26 Keith Atherton	.40	.16	.04
□ 27 A's Coaches	.40	.16	.04
□ 28 A's Checklist	.40	.16	.04

1984 Mother's Astros

The cards in this 28-card set measure 2 1/2" by 3 1/2". In 1984, the Los Angeles based Mother's Cookies Co. issued five sets of cards featuring players from major league teams. The Houston Astros set features current players depicted by photos. Similar to their 1952 and 1953 issues, the cards have rounded corners. The backs of the cards contain the Mother's Cookies logo. The cards were distributed in partial sets to fans at the respective stadiums of the teams involved. Whereas 20 cards were given to each patron, a redemption card, redeemable for eight more cards was included. Unfortunately, the eight cards received by redeeming the coupon were not necessarily the eight needed to complete a set. Hobbyist Barry Colla was involved in the production of these sets.

	MINT	EXC	G-VG
COMPLETE SET (28)	11.00	4.50	1.10
COMMON PLAYER (1-28)	.30	.12	.03
□ 1 Nolan Ryan	3.50	1.40	.35
□ 2 Joe Niekro	.75	.30	.07
□ 3 Alan Ashby	.40	.16	.04
□ 4 Bill Doran	1.00	.40	.10
□ 5 Phil Garner	.40	.16	.04
□ 6 Ray Knight	.40	.16	.04
□ 7 Dickie Thon	.40	.16	.04
□ 8 Jose Cruz	.60	.24	.06
□ 9 Jerry Mumphrey	.30	.12	.03
□ 10 Terry Puhl	.40	.16	.04
□ 11 Enos Cabell	.30	.12	.03
□ 12 Harry Spilman	.30	.12	.03
□ 13 Dave Smith	.50	.20	.05
□ 14 Mike Scott	1.25	.50	.12
□ 15 Bob Lillis MG	.30	.12	.03
□ 16 Bob Knepper	.50	.20	.05
□ 17 Frank DiPino	.30	.12	.03
□ 18 Tom Wieghaus	.30	.12	.03
□ 19 Denny Walling	.30	.12	.03
□ 20 Tony Scott	.30	.12	.03
□ 21 Alan Bannister	.30	.12	.03
□ 22 Bill Dawley	.30	.12	.03
□ 23 Vern Ruhle	.30	.12	.03
□ 24 Mike LaCoss	.30	.12	.03
□ 25 Mike Madden	.30	.12	.03
□ 26 Craig Reynolds	.40	.16	.04
□ 27 Astros' Coaches	.30	.12	.03
□ 28 Astros' Checklist	.30	.12	.03

1984 Mother's Giants

The cards in this 28-card set measure 2 1/2" by 3 1/2". In 1984, the Los Angeles based Mother's Cookies Co. issued five sets of cards featuring players from major league teams. The San Francisco Giants set features previous Giant All-Star selections depicted by drawings. Similar to their 1952 and 1953

issues, the cards have rounded corners. The backs of the cards contain the Mother's Cookies logo. The cards were distributed in partial sets to fans at the respective stadiums of the teams involved. Whereas 20 cards were given to each patron, a redemption card, redeemable for eight more cards was included. Unfortunately, the eight cards received by redeeming the coupon were not necessarily the eight needed to complete a set. Hobbyist Barry Colla was involved in the production of these sets.

	MINT	EXC	G-VG
COMPLETE SET (28)	13.00	5.25	1.30
COMMON PLAYER (1-28)	.40	.16	.04
☐ 1 Willie Mays	3.00	1.20	.30
☐ 2 Willie McCovey	2.00	.80	.20
☐ 3 Juan Marichal	1.50	.60	.15
☐ 4 Gaylord Perry	1.25	.50	.12
☐ 5 Tom Haller	.40	.16	.04
☐ 6 Jim Davenport	.40	.16	.04
☐ 7 Jack Clark	1.25	.50	.12
☐ 8 Greg Minton	.40	.16	.04
☐ 9 Atlee Hammaker	.40	.16	.04
☐ 10 Gary Lavelle	.40	.16	.04
☐ 11 Orlando Cepeda	.90	.36	.09
☐ 12 Bobby Bonds	.60	.24	.06
☐ 13 John Antonelli	.40	.16	.04
☐ 14 Bob Schmidt (photo actually Wes Westrum)	.40	.16	.04
☐ 15 Sam Jones	.40	.16	.04
☐ 16 Mike McCormick	.40	.16	.04
☐ 17 Ed Bailey	.40	.16	.04
☐ 18 Stu Miller	.40	.16	.04
☐ 19 Felipe Alou	.50	.20	.05
☐ 20 Jim Ray Hart	.40	.16	.04
☐ 21 Dick Dietz	.40	.16	.04
☐ 22 Chris Speier	.40	.16	.04
☐ 23 Bobby Murcer	.60	.24	.06
☐ 24 John Montefusco	.40	.16	.04
☐ 25 Vida Blue	.50	.20	.05
☐ 26 Ed Whitson	.40	.16	.04
☐ 27 Darrell Evans	.75	.30	.07
☐ 28 Checklist	.40	.16	.04

1984 Mother's Mariners

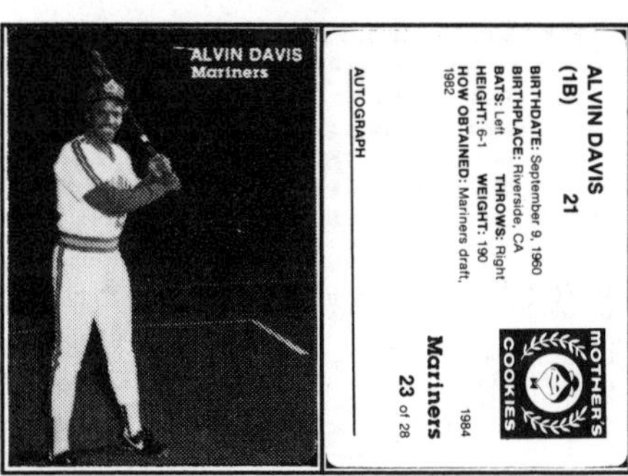

The cards in this 28-card set measure 2 1/2" by 3 1/2". In 1984, The Los Angeles-based Mother's Cookies Co. issued five sets of cards featuring players from major league teams. The Seattle Mariners set features current players depicted by photos. Similar to their 1952 and 1953 issues, the cards have rounded corners. The backs of the cards contain the Mother's Cookies logo. The cards were distributed in partial sets to fans at the respective stadiums of the teams involved. Whereas 20 cards were given to each patron, a redemption card, redeemable for eight more cards was included. Unfortunately, the eight cards received by redeeming the coupon were not necessarily the eight needed to complete a set. Hobbyist Barry Colla was involved in the production of these sets.

	MINT	EXC	G-VG
COMPLETE SET (28)	13.00	5.25	1.30
COMMON PLAYER (1-28)	.40	.16	.04
☐ 1 Del Crandall MG	.50	.20	.05
☐ 2 Barry Bonnell	.40	.16	.04
☐ 3 Dave Henderson	.75	.30	.07
☐ 4 Bob Kearney	.40	.16	.04
☐ 5 Mike Moore	.60	.24	.06
☐ 6 Spike Owen	.50	.20	.05
☐ 7 Gorman Thomas	.60	.24	.06
☐ 8 Ed VandeBerg	.40	.16	.04
☐ 9 Matt Young	.40	.16	.04
☐ 10 Larry Milbourne	.40	.16	.04
☐ 11 Dave Beard	.40	.16	.04
☐ 12 Jim Beattie	.40	.16	.04
☐ 13 Mark Langston	1.50	.60	.15
☐ 14 Orlando Mercado	.40	.16	.04
☐ 15 Jack Perconte	.40	.16	.04
☐ 16 Pat Putnam	.40	.16	.04
☐ 17 Paul Mirabella	.40	.16	.04
☐ 18 Domingo Ramos	.40	.16	.04
☐ 19 Al Cowens	.40	.16	.04
☐ 20 Mike Stanton	.40	.16	.04
☐ 21 Steve Henderson	.40	.16	.04
☐ 22 Bob Stoddard	.40	.16	.04
☐ 23 Alvin Davis	1.75	.70	.17
☐ 24 Phil Bradley	1.25	.50	.12
☐ 25 Roy Thomas	.40	.16	.04
☐ 26 Darnell Coles	.60	.24	.06
☐ 27 Mariners' Coaches	.40	.16	.04
☐ 28 Mariners' Checklist	.40	.16	.04

1984 Mother's Padres

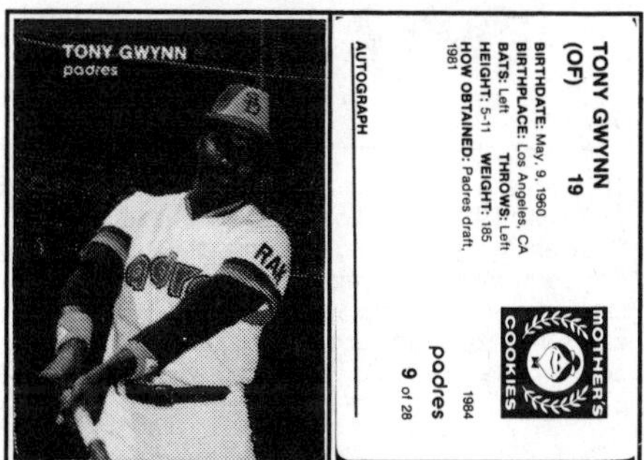

The cards in this 28-card set measure 2 1/2" by 3 1/2". In 1984, the Los Angeles based Mother's Cookies Co. issued five sets of cards featuring players from major league teams. The San Diego Padres set features current players depicted by photos. Similar to their 1952 and 1953 issues, the cards have rounded corners. The backs of the cards contain the Mother's Cookies logo. The cards were distributed in partial sets to fans at the respective stadiums of the teams involved. Whereas 20 cards were given to each patron, a redemption card, redeemable for eight more cards was included. Unfortunately, the eight cards received by redeeming the coupon were not necessarily the eight needed to complete a set. Hobbyist Barry Colla was involved in the production of these sets.

	MINT	EXC	G-VG
COMPLETE SET (28)	16.00	6.50	1.60
COMMON PLAYER (1-28)	.50	.20	.05
☐ 1 Dick Williams MG	.60	.24	.06
☐ 2 Rich Gossage	.90	.36	.09
☐ 3 Tim Lollar	.50	.20	.05
☐ 4 Eric Show	.75	.30	.07
☐ 5 Terry Kennedy	.60	.24	.06
☐ 6 Kurt Bevacqua	.50	.20	.05
☐ 7 Steve Garvey	2.00	.80	.20
☐ 8 Garry Templeton	.60	.24	.06
☐ 9 Tony Gwynn	3.50	1.40	.35
☐ 10 Alan Wiggins	.50	.20	.05
☐ 11 Dave Dravecky	.75	.30	.07
☐ 12 Tim Flannery	.50	.20	.05
☐ 13 Kevin McReynolds	2.50	1.00	.25
☐ 14 Bobby Brown	.50	.20	.05
☐ 15 Ed Whitson	.60	.24	.06
☐ 16 Doug Gwosdz	.50	.20	.05
☐ 17 Luis DeLeon	.50	.20	.05
☐ 18 Andy Hawkins	.60	.24	.06
☐ 19 Craig Lefferts	.50	.20	.05
☐ 20 Carmelo Martinez	.60	.24	.06
☐ 21 Sid Monge	.50	.20	.05
☐ 22 Graig Nettles	.75	.30	.07
☐ 23 Mario Ramirez	.50	.20	.05
☐ 24 Luis Salazar	.50	.20	.05
☐ 25 Champ Summers	.50	.20	.05
☐ 26 Mark Thurmond	.50	.20	.05
☐ 27 Padres' Coaches	.50	.20	.05
☐ 28 Padres' Checklist	.50	.20	.05

1985 Mother's A's

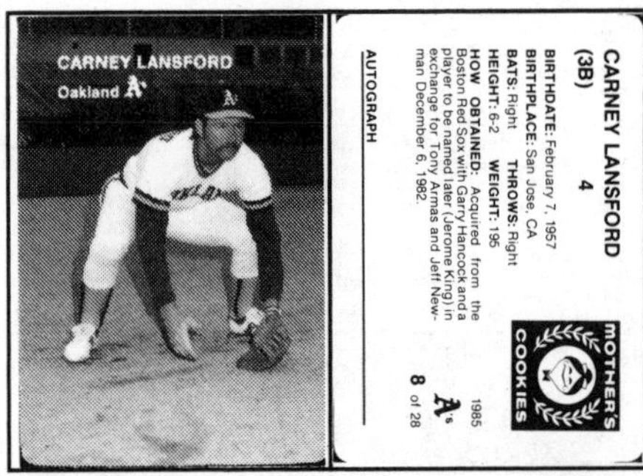

The cards in this 28-card set measure 2 1/2" by 3 1/2". In 1985, the Los Angeles based Mother's Cookies Co. again issued five sets of cards featuring players from major league teams. The Oakland A's set features current players depicted by photos on cards with rounded corners. The backs of the cards contain the Mother's Cookies logo. Cards were passed out at the stadium on July 6.

	MINT	EXC	G-VG
COMPLETE SET (28)	10.00	4.00	1.00
COMMON PLAYER (1-28)	.30	.12	.03
☐ 1 Jackie Moore MG	.30	.12	.03
☐ 2 Dave Kingman	.60	.24	.06
☐ 3 Don Sutton	1.25	.50	.12
☐ 4 Mike Heath	.30	.12	.03
☐ 5 Alfredo Griffin	.60	.24	.06
☐ 6 Dwayne Murphy	.40	.16	.04
☐ 7 Mike Davis	.50	.20	.05
☐ 8 Carney Lansford	.60	.24	.06
☐ 9 Chris Codiroli	.30	.12	.03
☐ 10 Bruce Bochte	.30	.12	.03
☐ 11 Mickey Tettleton	.30	.12	.0
☐ 12 Donnie Hill	.30	.12	.0
☐ 13 Rob Picciolo	.30	.12	.0
☐ 14 Dave Collins	.40	.16	.0
☐ 15 Dusty Baker	.40	.16	.0
☐ 16 Tim Conroy	.30	.12	.0
☐ 17 Keith Atherton	.30	.12	.0
☐ 18 Jay Howell	.50	.20	.0
☐ 19 Mike Warren	.30	.12	.0
☐ 20 Steve McCatty	.30	.12	.0
☐ 21 Bill Krueger	.30	.12	.0
☐ 22 Curt Young	.50	.20	.0
☐ 23 Dan Meyer	.30	.12	.0
☐ 24 Mike Gallego	.30	.12	.0
☐ 25 Jeff Kaiser	.30	.12	.0
☐ 26 Steve Henderson	.30	.12	.0
☐ 27 A's Coaches	.30	.12	.0
☐ 28 A's Checklist	.30	.12	.0

1985 Mother's Astros

The cards in this 28-card set measure 2 1/2" by 3 1/2". In 1985, the Los Angeles-based Mother's Cookies Co. again issued five sets of cards featuring players from major league teams. The Houston Astros set features current players depicted by photos on cards with rounded corners. The backs of the cards contain the Mother's Cookies logo. Cards were passed out at the stadium on July 13. The checklist card features the Astros logo on the obverse.

	MINT	EXC	G-VG
COMPLETE SET (28)	10.00	4.00	1.0
COMMON PLAYER (1-28)	.30	.12	.0
☐ 1 Bob Lillis MG	.30	.12	.0
☐ 2 Nolan Ryan	2.00	.80	.2
☐ 3 Phil Garner	.40	.16	.0
☐ 4 Jose Cruz	.60	.24	.0
☐ 5 Denny Walling	.30	.12	.0
☐ 6 Joe Niekro	.75	.30	.0
☐ 7 Terry Puhl	.40	.16	.0
☐ 8 Bill Doran	.75	.30	.0
☐ 9 Dickie Thon	.40	.16	.0
☐ 10 Enos Cabell	.30	.12	.03
☐ 11 Frank DiPino	.30	.12	.03
☐ 12 Julio Solano	.30	.12	.03
☐ 13 Alan Ashby	.40	.16	.0
☐ 14 Craig Reynolds	.30	.12	.0
☐ 15 Jerry Mumphrey	.30	.12	.0
☐ 16 Bill Dawley	.30	.12	.0
☐ 17 Mark Bailey	.30	.12	.0
☐ 18 Mike Scott	1.25	.50	.1
☐ 19 Harry Spilman	.30	.12	.0
☐ 20 Bob Knepper	.50	.20	.0
☐ 21 Dave Smith	.50	.20	.05
☐ 22 Kevin Bass	.60	.24	.06
☐ 23 Tim Tolman	.30	.12	.0
☐ 24 Jeff Calhoun	.30	.12	.03
☐ 25 Jim Pankovits	.30	.12	.03
☐ 26 Ron Mathis	.30	.12	.03
☐ 27 Astros' Coaches	.30	.12	.03
☐ 28 Astros' Checklist	.30	.12	.03

1985 Mother's Giants

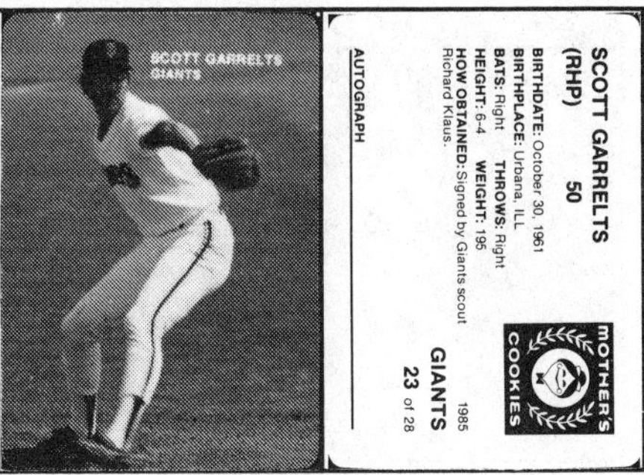

The cards in this 28-card set measure 2 1/2" by 3 1/2". In 1985, the Los Angeles based Mother's Cookies Co. again issued five sets of cards featuring players from major league teams. The San Francisco Giants set features current players depicted by photos on cards with rounded corners. The backs of the cards contain the Mother's Cookies logo. Cards were passed out at the stadium on June 30.

	MINT	EXC	G-VG
COMPLETE SET (28)	10.00	4.00	1.00
COMMON PLAYER (1-28)	.30	.12	.03
□ 1 Jim Davenport MG	.30	.12	.03
□ 2 Chili Davis	.75	.30	.07
□ 3 Dan Gladden	.60	.24	.06
□ 4 Jeff Leonard	.60	.24	.06
□ 5 Manny Trillo	.30	.12	.03
□ 6 Atlee Hammaker	.30	.12	.03
□ 7 Bob Brenly	.40	.16	.04
□ 8 Greg Minton	.40	.16	.04
□ 9 Bill Laskey	.30	.12	.03
□ 10 Vida Blue	.40	.16	.04
□ 11 Mike Krukow	.50	.20	.05
□ 12 Frank Williams	.30	.12	.03
□ 13 Jose Uribe	.50	.20	.05
□ 14 Johnnie LeMaster	.30	.12	.03
□ 15 Scot Thompson	.30	.12	.03
□ 16 Dave LaPoint	.40	.16	.04
□ 17 David Green	.30	.12	.03
□ 18 Chris Brown	.75	.30	.07
□ 19 Joel Youngblood	.30	.12	.03
□ 20 Mark Davis	.50	.20	.05
□ 21 Jim Gott	.40	.16	.04
□ 22 Doug Gwosdz	.30	.12	.03
□ 23 Scott Garrelts	.40	.16	.04
□ 24 Gary Rajsich	.30	.12	.03
□ 25 Rob Deer	.75	.30	.07
□ 26 Brad Wellman	.30	.12	.03
□ 27 Giants' Coaches	.30	.12	.03
□ 28 Giants' Checklist	.30	.12	.03

1985 Mother's Mariners

The cards in this 28-card set measure 2 1/2" by 3 1/2". In 1985, the Los Angeles based Mother's Cookies Co. again issued five sets of cards featuring players from major league teams. The Seattle Mariners set features current players depicted by photos on cards with rounded corners. The backs of the cards contain the Mother's Cookies logo. Cards were passed out at the stadium on August 10.

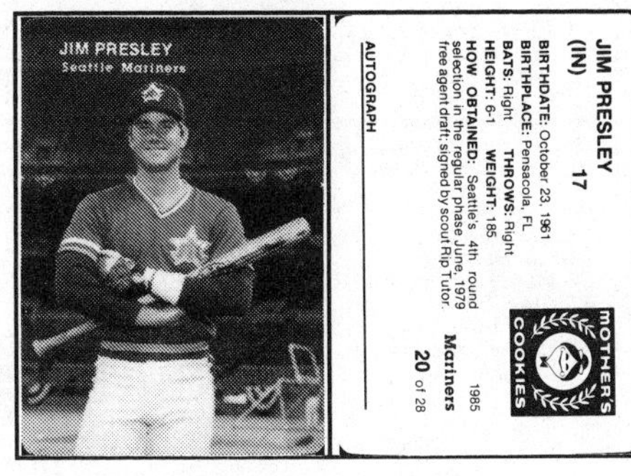

	MINT	EXC	G-VG
COMPLETE SET (28)	11.00	4.50	1.10
COMMON PLAYER (1-28)	.30	.12	.03
□ 1 Chuck Cottier MG	.30	.12	.03
□ 2 Alvin Davis	1.25	.50	.12
□ 3 Mark Langston	1.25	.50	.12
□ 4 Dave Henderson	.50	.20	.05
□ 5 Ed VandeBerg	.30	.12	.03
□ 6 Al Cowens	.30	.12	.03
□ 7 Spike Owen	.40	.16	.04
□ 8 Mike Moore	.50	.20	.05
□ 9 Gorman Thomas	.50	.20	.05
□ 10 Barry Bonnell	.30	.12	.03
□ 11 Jack Perconte	.30	.12	.03
□ 12 Domingo Ramos	.30	.12	.03
□ 13 Bob Kearney	.30	.12	.03
□ 14 Matt Young	.30	.12	.03
□ 15 Jim Beattie	.30	.12	.03
□ 16 Mike Stanton	.30	.12	.03
□ 17 David Valle	.30	.12	.03
□ 18 Ken Phelps	.60	.24	.06
□ 19 Salome Barojas	.30	.12	.03
□ 20 Jim Presley	1.25	.50	.12
□ 21 Phil Bradley	1.00	.40	.10
□ 22 Dave Geisel	.30	.12	.03
□ 23 Harold Reynolds	.75	.30	.07
□ 24 Ed Nunez	.40	.16	.04
□ 25 Mike Morgan	.30	.12	.03
□ 26 Ivan Calderon	.90	.36	.09
□ 27 Mariners Coaches	.30	.12	.03
□ 28 Checklist	.30	.12	.03

1985 Mother's Padres

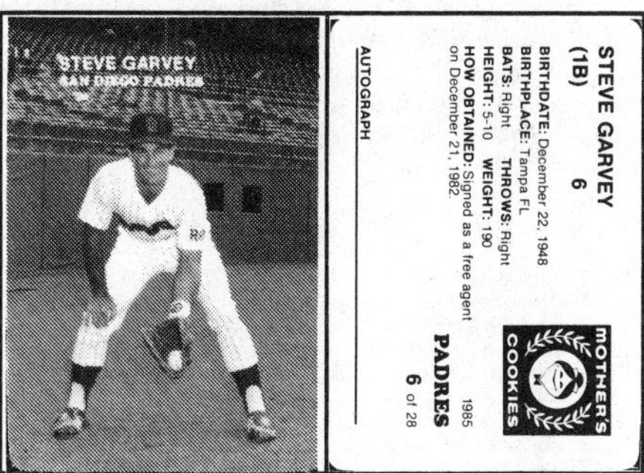

The cards in this 28-card set measure 2 1/2" by 3 1/2". In 1985, the Los Angeles based Mother's Cookies Co. again issued five sets of cards featuring players from major league teams. The San Diego Padres set features current players depicted by photos on cards with rounded corners. The backs of the cards contain the Mother's Cookies logo. Cards were passed out at the stadium on August 11.

	MINT	EXC	G-VG
COMPLETE SET (28)	11.00	4.50	1.10
COMMON PLAYER (1-28)	.30	.12	.03
□ 1 Dick Williams MG	.40	.16	.04
□ 2 Tony Gwynn	2.00	.80	.20
□ 3 Kevin McReynolds	1.50	.60	.15
□ 4 Graig Nettles	.75	.30	.07
□ 5 Rich Gossage	.75	.30	.07
□ 6 Steve Garvey	1.50	.60	.15
□ 7 Garry Templeton	.40	.16	.04
□ 8 Dave Dravecky	.50	.20	.05

		MINT	EXC	G-VG
☐ 9	Eric Show	.50	.20	.05
☐ 10	Terry Kennedy	.40	.16	.04
☐ 11	Luis DeLeon	.30	.12	.03
☐ 12	Bruce Bochy	.30	.12	.03
☐ 13	Andy Hawkins	.40	.16	.04
☐ 14	Kurt Bevacqua	.30	.12	.03
☐ 15	Craig Lefferts	.30	.12	.03
☐ 16	Mario Ramirez	.30	.12	.03
☐ 17	LaMarr Hoyt	.40	.16	.04
☐ 18	Jerry Royster	.30	.12	.03
☐ 19	Tim Stoddard	.30	.12	.03
☐ 20	Tim Flannery	.30	.12	.03
☐ 21	Mark Thurmond	.30	.12	.03
☐ 22	Greg Booker	.30	.12	.03
☐ 23	Bobby Brown	.30	.12	.03
☐ 24	Carmelo Martinez	.40	.16	.04
☐ 25	Al Bumbry	.30	.12	.03
☐ 26	Jerry Davis	.30	.12	.03
☐ 27	Padres' Coaches	.30	.12	.03
☐ 28	Padres' Checklist	.30	.12	.03

1986 Mother's A's

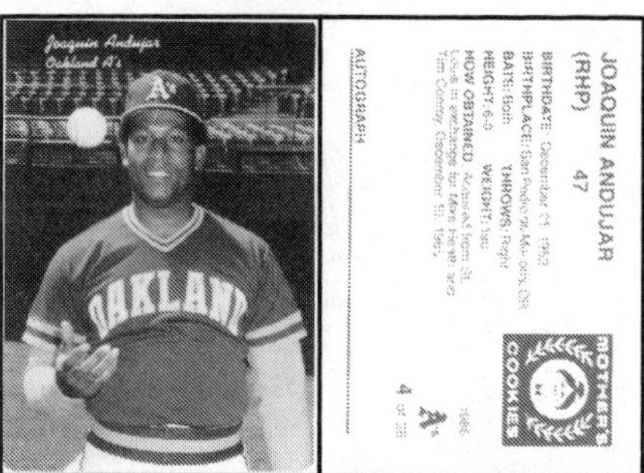

This set consists of 28 full-color, rounded- corner cards each measuring 2 1/2" by 3 1/2". Starter sets (only 20 cards but also including a certificate for eight more cards) were given out at the ballpark and collectors were encouraged to trade to fill in the rest of their set. The cards were originally given away on July 20th at Oakland Coliseum.

	MINT	EXC	G-VG
COMPLETE SET (28)	20.00	8.00	2.00
COMMON PLAYER (1-28)	.30	.12	.03

		MINT	EXC	G-VG
☐ 1	Jackie Moore MG	.30	.12	.03
☐ 2	Dave Kingman	.60	.24	.06
☐ 3	Dusty Baker	.40	.16	.04
☐ 4	Joaquin Andujar	.40	.16	.04
☐ 5	Alfredo Griffin	.50	.20	.05
☐ 6	Dwayne Murphy	.50	.20	.05
☐ 7	Mike Davis	.50	.20	.05
☐ 8	Carney Lansford	.50	.20	.05
☐ 9	Jose Canseco	12.50	5.00	1.25
☐ 10	Bruce Bochte	.30	.12	.03
☐ 11	Mickey Tettleton	.30	.12	.03
☐ 12	Donnie Hill	.30	.12	.03
☐ 13	Jose Rijo	.60	.24	.06
☐ 14	Rick Langford	.30	.12	.03
☐ 15	Chris Codiroli	.30	.12	.03
☐ 16	Moose Haas	.30	.12	.03
☐ 17	Keith Atherton	.30	.12	.03
☐ 18	Jay Howell	.40	.16	.04
☐ 19	Tony Phillips	.30	.12	.03
☐ 20	Steve Henderson	.30	.12	.03
☐ 21	Bill Krueger	.30	.12	.03
☐ 22	Steve Ontiveros	.30	.12	.03
☐ 23	Bill Bathe	.30	.12	.03
☐ 24	Ricky Peters	.30	.12	.03
☐ 25	Tim Birtsas	.30	.12	.03
☐ 26	A's Trainers and Equipment Mgrs	.30	.12	.03
☐ 27	A's Coaches	.30	.12	.03
☐ 28	Checklist card	.30	.12	.03

1986 Mother's Astros

This set consists of 28 full-color, rounded- corne cards each measuring 2 1/2" by 3 1/2". Starter set (only 20 cards but also including a certificate fo eight more cards) were given out at the ballpark an collectors were encouraged to trade to fill in the res of their set. Cards were originally given out at th Astrodome on July 10th. Since the 1986 All-Sta Game was held in Houston, the set features Astro All Stars since 1962 as painted by artist Richard Wallich

	MINT	EXC	G-V
COMPLETE SET (28)	9.00	3.75	.9
COMMON PLAYER (1-28)	.30	.12	.0

		MINT	EXC	G-V
☐ 1	Dick Farrell	.30	.12	.0
☐ 2	Hal Woodeshick	.30	.12	.0
☐ 3	Joe Morgan	1.00	.40	.1
☐ 4	Claude Raymond	.30	.12	.0
☐ 5	Mike Cuellar	.40	.16	.0
☐ 6	Rusty Staub	.60	.24	.0
☐ 7	Jimmy Wynn	.40	.16	.0
☐ 8	Larry Dierker	.40	.16	.0
☐ 9	Denis Menke	.30	.12	.0
☐ 10	Don Wilson	.30	.12	.0
☐ 11	Cesar Cedeno	.40	.16	.0
☐ 12	Lee May	.40	.16	.0
☐ 13	Bob Watson	.40	.16	.0
☐ 14	Ken Forsch	.30	.12	.0
☐ 15	Joaquin Andujar	.40	.16	.0
☐ 16	Terry Puhl	.40	.16	.0
☐ 17	Joe Niekro	.50	.20	.0
☐ 18	Craig Reynolds	.30	.12	.0
☐ 19	Joe Sambito	.30	.12	.0
☐ 20	Jose Cruz	.50	.20	.0
☐ 21	J.R. Richard	.40	.16	.0
☐ 22	Bob Knepper	.40	.16	.0
☐ 23	Nolan Ryan	1.50	.60	.1
☐ 24	Ray Knight	.40	.16	.0
☐ 25	Bill Dawley	.30	.12	.0
☐ 26	Dickie Thon	.30	.12	.0
☐ 27	Jerry Mumphrey	.30	.12	.0
☐ 28	Checklist card	.30	.12	.0

1986 Mother's Giants

This set consists of 28 full-color, rounded- corne cards each measuring 2 1/2" by 3 1/2". Starter set (only 20 cards but also including a certificate fo eight more cards) were given out at the ballpark an collectors were encouraged to trade to fill in the res of their set. Cards were originally given out a Candlestick Park on July 13th.

	MINT	EXC	G-V
COMPLETE SET (28)	11.00	4.50	1.1
COMMON PLAYER (1-28)	.30	.12	.0

		MINT	EXC	G-V
☐ 1	Roger Craig MG	.60	.24	.0
☐ 2	Chili Davis	.60	.24	.0
☐ 3	Dan Gladden	.50	.20	.0
☐ 4	Jeff Leonard	.50	.20	.0

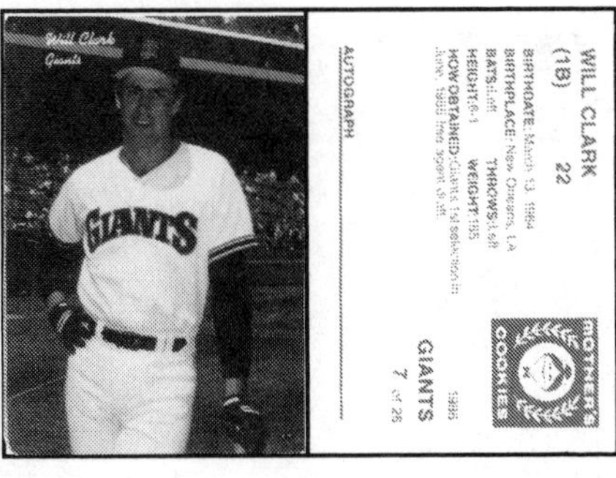

☐ 5 Bob Brenly	.40	.16	.04
☐ 6 Atlee Hammaker	.40	.16	.04
☐ 7 Will Clark	5.00	2.00	.50
☐ 8 Greg Minton	.40	.16	.04
☐ 9 Candy Maldonado	.60	.24	.06
☐ 10 Vida Blue	.40	.16	.04
☐ 11 Mike Krukow	.40	.16	.04
☐ 12 Bob Melvin	.30	.12	.03
☐ 13 Jose Uribe	.40	.16	.04
☐ 14 Dan Driessen	.30	.12	.03
☐ 15 Jeff Robinson	.50	.20	.05
☐ 16 Rob Thompson	.60	.24	.06
☐ 17 Mike LaCoss	.30	.12	.03
☐ 18 Chris Brown	.50	.20	.05
☐ 19 Scott Garrelts	.40	.16	.04
☐ 20 Mark Davis	.40	.16	.04
☐ 21 Jim Gott	.40	.16	.04
☐ 22 Brad Wellman	.30	.12	.03
☐ 23 Roger Mason	.30	.12	.03
☐ 24 Bill Laskey	.30	.12	.03
☐ 25 Brad Gulden	.30	.12	.03
☐ 26 Joel Youngblood	.30	.12	.03
☐ 27 Juan Berenguer	.30	.12	.03
☐ 28 Checklist card	.30	.12	.03

1986 Mother's Mariners

This set consists of 28 full-color, rounded- corner cards each measuring 2 1/2" by 3 1/2". Starter sets (only 20 cards but also including a certificate for eight more cards) were given out at the ballpark and collectors were encouraged to trade to fill in the rest of their set. Cards were originally given out on July 27th at the Seattle Kingdome.

	MINT	EXC	G-VG
COMPLETE SET (28)	9.00	3.75	.90
COMMON PLAYER (1-28)	.30	.12	.03
☐ 1 Dick Williams MG	.40	.16	.04
☐ 2 Alvin Davis	.75	.30	.07
☐ 3 Mark Langston	.75	.30	.07
☐ 4 Dave Henderson	.50	.20	.05
☐ 5 Steve Yeager	.30	.12	.03
☐ 6 Al Cowens	.30	.12	.03
☐ 7 Jim Presley	.65	.26	.06
☐ 8 Phil Bradley	.65	.26	.06
☐ 9 Gorman Thomas	.50	.20	.05
☐ 10 Barry Bonnell	.30	.12	.03
☐ 11 Milt Wilcox	.30	.12	.03
☐ 12 Domingo Ramos	.30	.12	.03
☐ 13 Pa[illegible] Mirabella	.30	.12	.03
☐ 14 Matt Young	.30	.12	.03
☐ 15 Ivan Calderon	.65	.26	.06
☐ 16 Bill Swift	.30	.12	.03
☐ 17 Pete Ladd	.30	.12	.03
☐ 18 Ken Phelps	.50	.20	.05
☐ 19 Karl Best	.30	.12	.03
☐ 20 Spike Owen	.40	.16	.04
☐ 21 Mike Moore	.50	.20	.05
☐ 22 Danny Tartabull	1.50	.60	.15
☐ 23 Bob Kearney	.30	.12	.03
☐ 24 Edwin Nunez	.30	.12	.03
☐ 25 Mike Morgan	.30	.12	.03
☐ 26 Roy Thomas	.30	.12	.03
☐ 27 Jim Beattie	.30	.12	.03
☐ 28 Checklist card	.30	.12	.03

1987 Mother's Cookies A's

This set consists of 28 full-color, rounded- corner cards each measuring 2 1/2" by 3 1/2". Starter sets (only 20 cards but also including a certificate for eight more cards) were given out at the ballpark and collectors were encouraged to trade to fill in the rest of their set. The cards were originally given away on July 5th at Oakland Coliseum during a game against the Boston Red Sox. This set is actually an All-Time All-Star set including every A's All-Star player since 1968 (when the franchise moved to Oakland). The vintage photos (each shot during the year of All-Star appearance) were taken from the collection of Doug McWilliams. The sets were supposedly given out free to the first 25,000 paid admissions at the game.

	MINT	EXC	G-VG
COMPLETE SET (28)	15.00	6.00	1.50
COMMON PLAYER (1-28)	.30	.12	.03
☐ 1 Bert Campaneris	.30	.12	.03
☐ 2 Rick Monday	.30	.12	.03
☐ 3 John Odom	.30	.12	.03
☐ 4 Sal Bando	.40	.16	.04
☐ 5 Reggie Jackson	1.50	.60	.15
☐ 6 Jim Hunter	1.00	.40	.10
☐ 7 Vida Blue	.40	.16	.04
☐ 8 Dave Duncan	.30	.12	.03
☐ 9 Joe Rudi	.40	.16	.04
☐ 10 Rollie Fingers	.80	.32	.08
☐ 11 Ken Holtzman	.30	.12	.03
☐ 12 Dick Williams	.40	.16	.04
☐ 13 Alvin Dark	.40	.16	.04
☐ 14 Gene Tenace	.30	.12	.03
☐ 15 Claudell Washington	.40	.16	.04
☐ 16 Phil Garner	.30	.12	.03
☐ 17 Wayne Gross	.30	.12	.03
☐ 18 Matt Keough	.30	.12	.03
☐ 19 Jeff Newman	.30	.12	.03
☐ 20 Rickey Henderson	1.50	.60	.15
☐ 21 Tony Armas	.40	.16	.04
☐ 22 Mike Norris	.30	.12	.03
☐ 23 Billy Martin	.50	.20	.05
☐ 24 Bill Caudill	.40	.16	.04
☐ 25 Jay Howell	.40	.16	.04

☐ 26 Jose Canseco	4.00	1.60	.40
☐ 27 Jose and Reggie	2.50	1.00	.25
☐ 28 Checklist Card	.30	.12	.03

1987 Mother's Cookies Astros

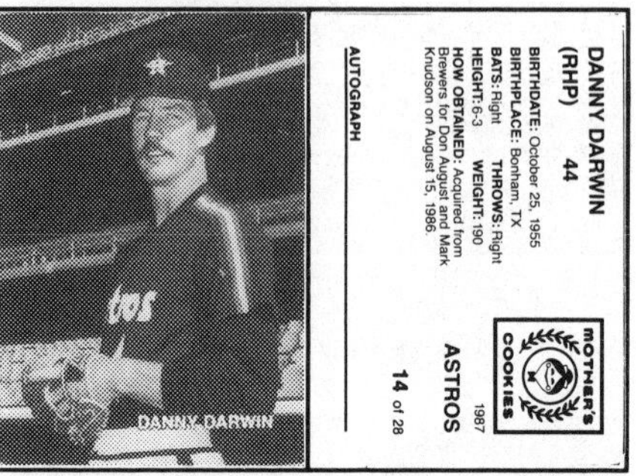

DANNY DARWIN
44
(RHP)
BIRTHDATE: October 25, 1955
BIRTHPLACE: Bonham, TX
BATS: Right THROWS: Right
HEIGHT: 6-3 WEIGHT: 190
HOW OBTAINED: Acquired from Brewers for Don August and Mark Knudson on August 15, 1986.
AUTOGRAPH
MOTHER'S COOKIES
1987
ASTROS
14 of 28

This set consists of 28 full-color, rounded- corner cards each measuring 2 1/2" by 3 1/2". Starter sets (only 20 cards but also including a certificate for eight more cards) were given out at the ballpark and collectors were encouraged to trade to fill in the rest of their set. Cards were originally given out at the Astrodome on July 17th during a game against the Phillies. Photos were taken by Barry Colla. The sets were supposedly given out free to the first 25,000 paid admissions at the game.

	MINT	EXC	G-VG
COMPLETE SET (28)	9.00	3.75	.90
COMMON PLAYER (1-28)	.30	.12	.03
☐ 1 Hal Lanier MG	.40	.16	.04
☐ 2 Mike Scott	1.00	.40	.10
☐ 3 Jose Cruz	.50	.20	.05
☐ 4 Bill Doran	.70	.28	.07
☐ 5 Bob Knepper	.40	.16	.04
☐ 6 Phil Garner	.40	.16	.04
☐ 7 Terry Puhl	.40	.16	.04
☐ 8 Nolan Ryan	2.00	.80	.20
☐ 9 Kevin Bass	.40	.16	.04
☐ 10 Glenn Davis	.90	.36	.09
☐ 11 Alan Ashby	.40	.16	.04
☐ 12 Charlie Kerfeld	.30	.12	.03
☐ 13 Denny Walling	.30	.12	.03
☐ 14 Danny Darwin	.30	.12	.03
☐ 15 Mark Bailey	.30	.12	.03
☐ 16 Davey Lopes	.40	.16	.04
☐ 17 Dave Meads	.30	.12	.03
☐ 18 Aurelio Lopez	.30	.12	.03
☐ 19 Craig Reynolds	.30	.12	.03
☐ 20 Dave Smith	.50	.20	.05
☐ 21 Larry Andersen	.30	.12	.03
☐ 22 Jim Pankovits	.30	.12	.03
☐ 23 Jim Deshaies	.40	.16	.04
☐ 24 Bert Pena	.30	.12	.03
☐ 25 Dickie Thon	.40	.16	.04
☐ 26 Billy Hatcher	.75	.30	.07
☐ 27 Astros' Coaches	.30	.12	.03
☐ 28 Checklist	.30	.12	.03

1987 Mother's Cookies Dodgers

This set consists of 28 full-color, rounded- corner cards each measuring 2 1/2" by 3 1/2". Starter sets (only 20 cards but also including a certificate for eight more cards) were given out at the ballpark and collectors were encouraged to trade to fill in the rest of their set. Cards were originally given out at Dodger Stadium on August 9th. Photos were taken by Barry Colla. The sets were supposedly given out free to all game attendees 14 years of age and under.

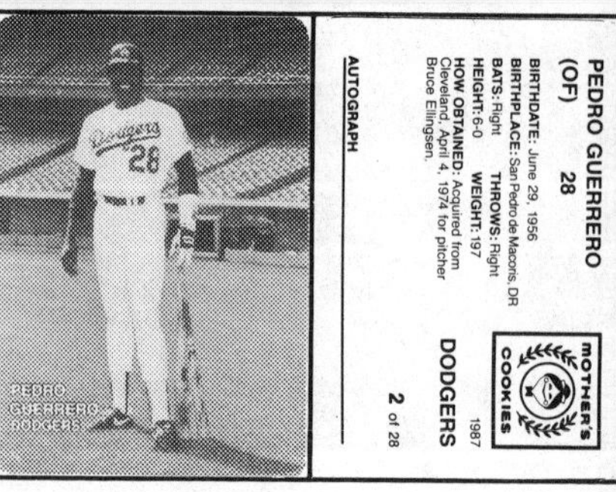

	MINT	EXC	G-VG
COMPLETE SET (28)	10.00	4.00	1.00
COMMON PLAYER (1-28)	.30	.12	.03
☐ 1 Tom Lasorda MG	.60	.24	.06
☐ 2 Pedro Guerrero	1.00	.40	.10
☐ 3 Steve Sax	.75	.30	.07
☐ 4 Fernando Valenzuela	1.00	.40	.10
☐ 5 Mike Marshall	.60	.24	.06
☐ 6 Orel Hershiser	1.50	.60	.15
☐ 7 Mariano Duncan	.40	.16	.04
☐ 8 Bill Madlock	.50	.20	.05
☐ 9 Bob Welch	.50	.20	.05
☐ 10 Mike Scioscia	.50	.20	.05
☐ 11 Mike Ramsey	.40	.16	.04
☐ 12 Matt Young	.30	.12	.03
☐ 13 Franklin Stubbs	.40	.16	.04
☐ 14 Tom Niedenfuer	.30	.12	.03
☐ 15 Reggie Williams	.30	.12	.03
☐ 16 Rick Honeycutt	.30	.12	.03
☐ 17 Dave Anderson	.30	.12	.03
☐ 18 Alejandro Pena	.40	.16	.04
☐ 19 Ken Howell	.30	.12	.03
☐ 20 Len Matuszek	.30	.12	.03
☐ 21 Tim Leary	.50	.20	.05
☐ 22 Tracy Woodson	.40	.16	.04
☐ 23 Alex Trevino	.30	.12	.03
☐ 24 Ken Landreaux	.30	.12	.03
☐ 25 Mickey Hatcher	.30	.12	.03
☐ 26 Brian Holton	.40	.16	.04
☐ 27 Dodgers' Coaches	.30	.12	.03
☐ 28 Checklist	.30	.12	.03

1987 Mother's Cookies Giants

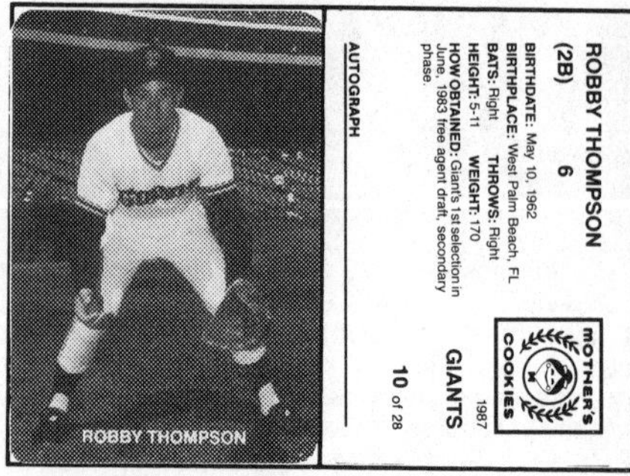

ROBBY THOMPSON
6
(2B)
BIRTHDATE: May 10, 1962
BIRTHPLACE: West Palm Beach, FL
BATS: Right THROWS: Right
HEIGHT: 5-11 WEIGHT: 170
HOW OBTAINED: Giant's 1st selection in June, 1983 free agent draft, secondary phase.
AUTOGRAPH
MOTHER'S COOKIES
1987
GIANTS
10 of 28
ROBBY THOMPSON

This set consists of 28 full-color, rounded- corner cards each measuring 2 1/2" by 3 1/2". Starter sets (only 20 cards but also including a certificate for eight more cards) were given out at the ballpark and collectors were encouraged to trade to fill in the rest of their set. Cards were originally given out at Candlestick Park on June 27th during a game against the Astros. Photos were taken by Dennis Desprois. The sets were supposedly given out free to the first 25,000 paid admissions at the game.

	MINT	EXC	G-VG
COMPLETE SET (28)	10.00	4.00	1.00
COMMON PLAYER (1-28)	.30	.12	.03
☐ 1 Roger Craig MG	.60	.24	.06
☐ 2 Will Clark	2.00	.80	.20
☐ 3 Chili Davis	.50	.20	.05
☐ 4 Bob Brenly	.40	.16	.04
☐ 5 Chris Brown	.50	.20	.05
☐ 6 Mike Krukow	.40	.16	.04
☐ 7 Candy Maldonado	.50	.20	.05
☐ 8 Jeffrey Leonard	.50	.20	.05
☐ 9 Greg Minton	.30	.12	.03
☐ 10 Robby Thompson	.50	.20	.05
☐ 11 Scott Garrelts	.40	.16	.04
☐ 12 Bob Melvin	.30	.12	.03
☐ 13 Jose Uribe	.40	.16	.04
☐ 14 Mark Davis	.40	.16	.04
☐ 15 Eddie Milner	.30	.12	.03
☐ 16 Harry Spilman	.30	.12	.03
☐ 17 Kelly Downs	.40	.16	.04
☐ 18 Chris Speier	.30	.12	.03
☐ 19 Jim Gott	.40	.16	.04
☐ 20 Joel Youngblood	.30	.12	.03
☐ 21 Mike LaCoss	.30	.12	.03
☐ 22 Matt Williams	.75	.30	.07
☐ 23 Roger Mason	.30	.12	.03
☐ 24 Mike Aldrete	.50	.20	.05
☐ 25 Jeff Robinson	.40	.16	.04
☐ 26 Mark Grant	.30	.12	.03
☐ 27 Giants' Coaches	.30	.12	.03
☐ 28 Checklist Card	.30	.12	.03

1987 Mother's Cookies Mariners

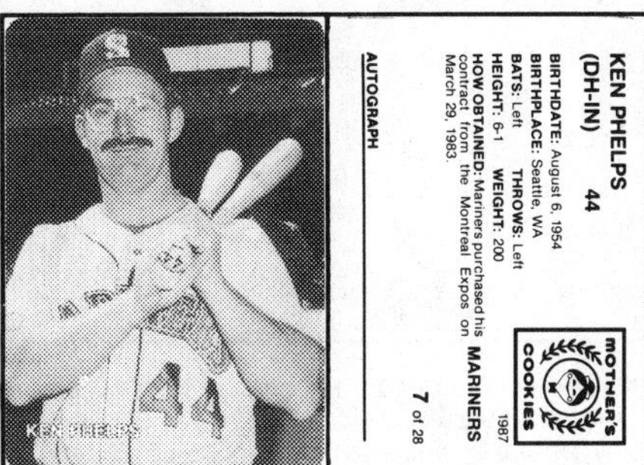

KEN PHELPS
KEN PHELPS
(DH-IN) 44
BIRTHDATE: August 6, 1954
BIRTHPLACE: Seattle, WA
BATS: Left THROWS: Left
HEIGHT: 6-1 WEIGHT: 200
HOW OBTAINED: Mariners purchased his contract from the Montreal Expos on March 29, 1983.
AUTOGRAPH
MOTHER'S COOKIES
1987 MARINERS
7 of 28

This set consists of 28 full-color, rounded- corner cards each measuring 2 1/2" by 3 1/2". Starter sets (only 20 cards but also including a certificate for eight more cards) were given out at the ballpark and collectors were encouraged to trade to fill in the rest of their set. Cards were originally given out on August 9th at the Seattle Kingdome. Photos were taken by Barry Colla. The sets were supposedly given out free to the first 20,000 paid admissions at the game.

	MINT	EXC	G-VG
COMPLETE SET (28)	9.00	3.75	.90
COMMON PLAYER (1-28)	.30	.12	.03
☐ 1 Dick Williams MG	.40	.16	.04
☐ 2 Alvin Davis	.60	.24	.06
☐ 3 Mike Moore	.40	.16	.04
☐ 4 Jim Presley	.60	.24	.06
☐ 5 Mark Langston	.75	.30	.07
☐ 6 Phil Bradley	.60	.24	.06
☐ 7 Ken Phelps	.50	.20	.05
☐ 8 Mike Morgan	.30	.12	.03
☐ 9 David Valle	.30	.12	.03
☐ 10 Harold Reynolds	.50	.20	.05
☐ 11 Edwin Nunez	.40	.16	.04
☐ 12 Bob Kearney	.30	.12	.03
☐ 13 Scott Bankhead	.40	.16	.04
☐ 14 Scott Bradley	.40	.16	.04
☐ 15 Mickey Brantley	.50	.20	.05
☐ 16 Mark Huismann	.30	.12	.03
☐ 17 Mike Kingery	.30	.12	.03
☐ 18 John Moses	.30	.12	.03
☐ 19 Donell Nixon	.30	.12	.03
☐ 20 Rey Quinones	.30	.12	.03
☐ 21 Domingo Ramos	.30	.12	.03
☐ 22 Jerry Reed	.30	.12	.03
☐ 23 Rich Renteria	.40	.16	.04
☐ 24 Rich Monteleone	.30	.12	.03
☐ 25 Mike Trujillo	.30	.12	.03
☐ 26 Bill Wilkinson	.30	.12	.03
☐ 27 John Christensen	.30	.12	.03
☐ 28 Checklist Card	.30	.12	.03

1987 Mother's Cookies McGwire

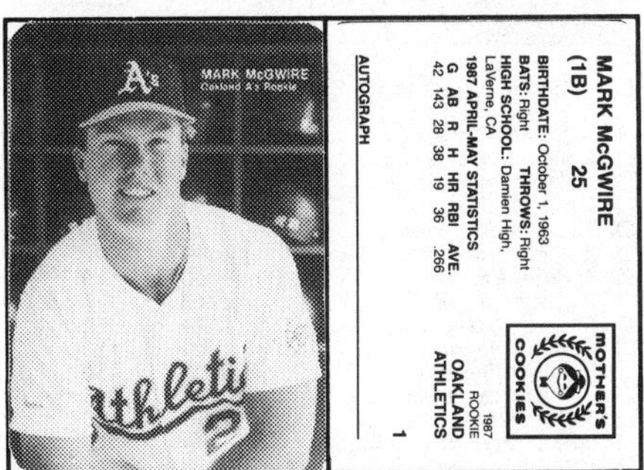

This set consists of 4 full-color, rounded-corner cards each measuring 2 1/2" by 3 1/2" and showing a different pose of A's slugging rookie Mark McGwire. Cards were originally given out at the national Card Collectors Convention in San Francisco. Later they were available through a mail-in offer involving collectors sending in two proofs-of-purchase from any Mother's Cookies products to get one free card. Photos were taken by Doug McWilliams. The cards are numbered on the back.

	MINT	EXC	G-VG
COMPLETE SET (4)	15.00	6.00	1.50
COMMON PLAYER (1-4)	4.00	1.60	.40
☐ 1 Mark McGwire close-up shot, head and shoulders	4.00	1.60	.40
☐ 2 Mark McGwire waist up, holding bat	4.50	1.80	.45
☐ 3 Mark McGwire batting stance, ready to swing	4.50	1.80	.45
☐ 4 Mark McGwire home run swing, follow through	5.00	2.00	.50

1987 Mother's Cookies Rangers

This set consists of 28 full-color, rounded- corner cards each measuring 2 1/2" by 3 1/2". Starter sets (only 20 cards but also including a certificate for eight more cards) were given out at the ballpark and collectors were encouraged to trade to fill in the rest of their set. Cards were originally given out on July 17th during the game against the Yankees. Photos were taken by Barry Colla. The sets were supposedly given out free to the first 25,000 paid admissions at the game.

	MINT	EXC	G-VG
COMPLETE SET (28)	9.00	3.75	.90
COMMON PLAYER (1-28)	.30	.12	.03

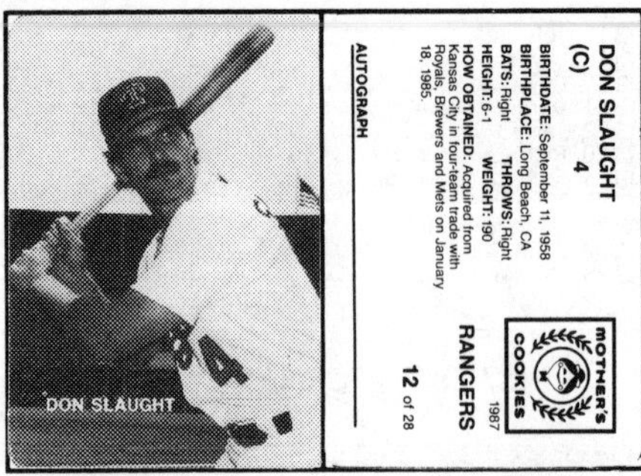

BIRTHDATE: September 11, 1958
BIRTHPLACE: Long Beach, CA

HOW OBTAINED: Acquired from Kansas City in four-team trade with Royals, Brewers and Mets on January 18, 1985.

☐ 1 Bobby Valentine MG	.50	.20	.05
☐ 2 Pete Incaviglia	.75	.30	.07
☐ 3 Charlie Hough	.50	.20	.05
☐ 4 Oddibe McDowell	.50	.20	.05
☐ 5 Larry Parrish	.40	.16	.04
☐ 6 Scott Fletcher	.50	.20	.05
☐ 7 Steve Buechele	.30	.12	.03
☐ 8 Tom Paciorek	.30	.12	.03
☐ 9 Pete O'Brien	.60	.24	.06
☐ 10 Darrell Porter	.40	.16	.04
☐ 11 Greg Harris	.30	.12	.03
☐ 12 Don Slaught	.40	.16	.04
☐ 13 Ruben Sierra	1.25	.50	.12
☐ 14 Curtis Wilkerson	.30	.12	.03
☐ 15 Dale Mohorcic	.50	.20	.05
☐ 16 Ron Meredith	.30	.12	.03
☐ 17 Mitch Williams	.40	.16	.04
☐ 18 Bob Brower	.40	.16	.04
☐ 19 Edwin Correa	.40	.16	.04
☐ 20 Geno Petralli	.30	.12	.03
☐ 21 Mike Loynd	.30	.12	.03
☐ 22 Jerry Browne	.30	.12	.03
☐ 23 Jose Guzman	.40	.16	.04
☐ 24 Jeff Kunkel	.30	.12	.03
☐ 25 Bobby Witt	.75	.30	.07
☐ 26 Jeff Russell	.40	.16	.04
☐ 27 Ranger's Trainers	.30	.12	.03
☐ 28 Checklist Card	.30	.12	.03

1988 Mother's Cookies A's

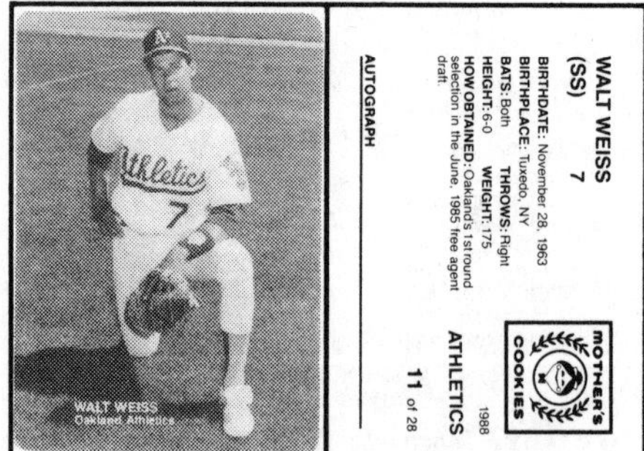

WALT WEISS
Oakland Athletics
WALT WEISS
(SS) 7
BIRTHDATE: November 28, 1963
BIRTHPLACE: Tuxedo, NY
BATS: Both THROWS: Right
HEIGHT: 6-0 WEIGHT: 175
HOW OBTAINED: Oakland's 1st round selection in the June, 1985 free agent draft.
AUTOGRAPH
MOTHER'S COOKIES
1988
ATHLETICS
11 of 28

This set consists of 28 full-color, rounded- corner cards each measuring 2 1/2" by 3 1/2". Starter sets (only 20 cards but also including a certificate for eight more cards) were given out at the ballpark and collectors were encouraged to trade to fill in the rest of their set. The cards were originally given away on July 23rd at Oakland Coliseum during a game. Short sets (20 cards plus certificate) were supposedly given out free to the first 35,000 paid admissions at the game.

	MINT	EXC	G-VG
COMPLETE SET (28)	12.50	5.00	1.25
COMMON PLAYER (1-28)	.30	.12	.03
☐ 1 Tony LaRussa MG	.50	.20	.05
☐ 2 Mark McGwire	2.00	.80	.20
☐ 3 Dave Stewart	.50	.20	.05
☐ 4 Terry Steinbach	.60	.24	.06
☐ 5 Dave Parker	.50	.20	.05
☐ 6 Carney Lansford	.50	.20	.05
☐ 7 Jose Canseco	3.00	1.20	.30
☐ 8 Don Baylor	.50	.20	.05
☐ 9 Bob Welch	.40	.16	.04
☐ 10 Dennis Eckersley	.75	.30	.07
☐ 11 Walt Weiss	1.00	.40	.10
☐ 12 Tony Phillips	.30	.12	.03
☐ 13 Steve Ontiveros	.30	.12	.03
☐ 14 Dave Henderson	.40	.16	.04
☐ 15 Stan Javier	.30	.12	.03
☐ 16 Ron Hassey	.30	.12	.03
☐ 17 Curt Young	.40	.16	.04
☐ 18 Glenn Hubbard	.30	.12	.03
☐ 19 Storm Davis	.50	.20	.05
☐ 20 Eric Plunk	.40	.16	.04
☐ 21 Matt Young	.30	.12	.03
☐ 22 Mike Gallego	.30	.12	.03
☐ 23 Rick Honeycutt	.30	.12	.03
☐ 24 Doug Jennings	.40	.16	.04
☐ 25 Gene Nelson	.40	.16	.04
☐ 26 Greg Cadaret	.30	.12	.03
☐ 27 Athletics Coaches	.30	.12	.03
☐ 28 Checklist Card	.30	.12	.03

1988 Mother's Cookies Astros

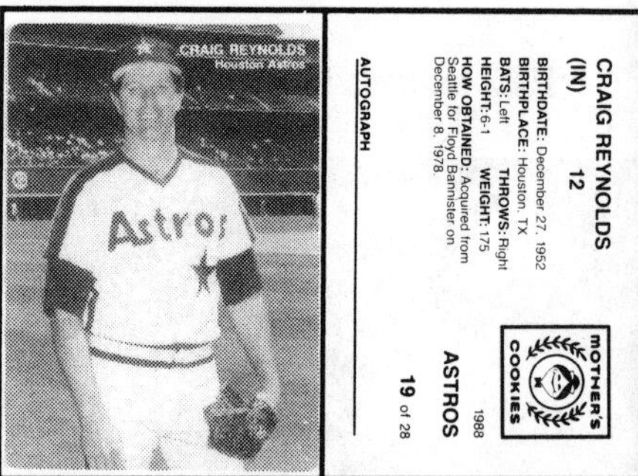

CRAIG REYNOLDS
Houston Astros
CRAIG REYNOLDS
(IN) 12
BIRTHDATE: December 27, 1952
BIRTHPLACE: Houston, TX
BATS: Left THROWS: Right
HEIGHT: 6-1 WEIGHT: 175
HOW OBTAINED: Acquired from Seattle for Floyd Bannister on December 8, 1978.
AUTOGRAPH
MOTHER'S COOKIES
1988
ASTROS
19 of 28

This set consists of 28 full-color, rounded- corner cards each measuring 2 1/2" by 3 1/2". Starter sets (only 20 cards but also including a certificate for eight more cards) were given out at the ballpark and collectors were encouraged to trade to fill in the rest of their set. Cards were originally given out at the Astrodome on August 26th during a game. The sets were supposedly given out free to the first 25,000 paid admissions at the game.

	MINT	EXC	G-VG
COMPLETE SET (28)	9.00	3.75	.90
COMMON PLAYER (1-28)	.30	.12	.03
☐ 1 Hal Lanier MG	.40	.16	.04
☐ 2 Mike Scott	1.00	.40	.10
☐ 3 Gerald Young	.50	.20	.05
☐ 4 Bill Doran	.60	.24	.06
☐ 5 Bob Knepper	.40	.16	.04
☐ 6 Billy Hatcher	.50	.20	.05
☐ 7 Terry Puhl	.40	.16	.04
☐ 8 Nolan Ryan	1.25	.50	.12
☐ 9 Kevin Bass	.50	.20	.05
☐ 10 Glenn Davis	.75	.30	.07
☐ 11 Alan Ashby	.40	.16	.04
☐ 12 Steve Henderson	.30	.12	.03
☐ 13 Denny Walling	.30	.12	.03
☐ 14 Danny Darwin	.30	.12	.03
☐ 15 Mark Bailey	.30	.12	.03
☐ 16 Ernie Camacho	.30	.12	.03
☐ 17 Rafael Ramirez	.40	.16	.04
☐ 18 Jeff Heathcock	.30	.12	.03
☐ 19 Craig Reynolds	.30	.12	.03
☐ 20 Dave Smith	.50	.20	.05
☐ 21 Larry Anderson	.30	.12	.03
☐ 22 Jim Pankovits	.30	.12	.03
☐ 23 Jim Deshaies	.40	.16	.04
☐ 24 Juan Agosto	.30	.12	.03

□ 25 Chuck Jackson	.40	.16	.04
□ 26 Joaquin Andujar	.40	.16	.04
□ 27 Astros' Coaches	.30	.12	.03
□ 28 Checklist	.30	.12	.03

1988 Mother's Cookies Will Clark

This regional set consists of 4 full-color, rounded-corner cards each measuring 2 1/2" by 3 1/2" and showing a different pose of Giants' slugging first baseman Will Clark. Cards were originally found in 18 oz. packages of "Big Bags" of Mother's Cookies at stores in the Northern California area in February and March of 1988. The cards are numbered on the back. Card backs are done in red and purple on white card stock.

	MINT	EXC	G-VG
COMPLETE SET (4)	10.00	4.00	1.00
COMMON PLAYER (1-4)	3.00	1.20	.30
□ 1 Will Clark Batting Pose, Waist Up	3.00	1.20	.30
□ 2 Will Clark Kneeling In On Deck Circle	3.00	1.20	.30
□ 3 Will Clark Follow Through Swing	3.00	1.20	.30
□ 4 Will Clark Starting Toward First Base	3.00	1.20	.30

1988 Mother's Cookies Dodgers

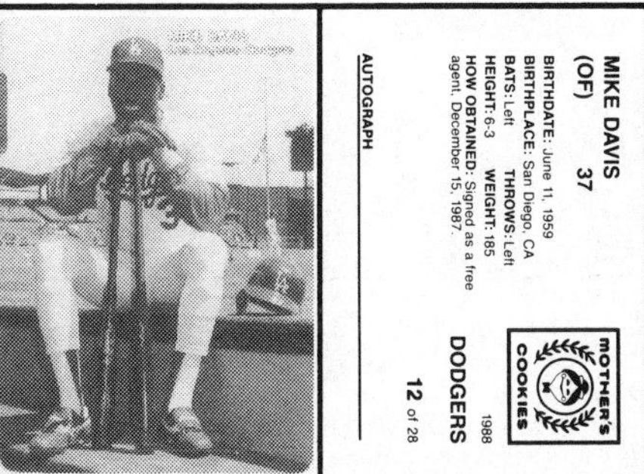

MIKE DAVIS
(OF) 37
BIRTHDATE: June 11, 1959
BIRTHPLACE: San Diego, CA
BATS: Left THROWS: Left
HEIGHT: 6-3 WEIGHT: 185
HOW OBTAINED: Signed as a free agent, December 15, 1987.
AUTOGRAPH
MOTHER'S COOKIES
1988
DODGERS
12 of 28

This set consists of 28 full-color, rounded- corner cards each measuring 2 1/2" by 3 1/2". Starter sets (only 20 cards but also including a certificate for eight more cards) were given out at the ballpark and collectors were encouraged to trade to fill in the rest of their set. Cards were originally given out at Dodger Stadium on July 31st. Photos were taken by Barry Colla. The sets were supposedly given out free to the first 25,000 game attendees 14 years of age and under.

	MINT	EXC	G-VG
COMPLETE SET (28)	12.00	5.00	1.20
COMMON PLAYER (1-28)	.30	.12	.03
□ 1 Tom Lasorda MG	.50	.20	.05
□ 2 Pedro Guerrero	.60	.24	.06
□ 3 Steve Sax	.60	.24	.06
□ 4 Fernando Valenzuela	.75	.30	.07
□ 5 Mike Marshall	.60	.24	.06
□ 6 Orel Hershiser	1.50	.60	.15
□ 7 Alfredo Griffin	.40	.16	.04
□ 8 Kirk Gibson	1.25	.50	.12
□ 9 Don Sutton	.60	.24	.06
□ 10 Mike Scioscia	.40	.16	.04
□ 11 Franklin Stubbs	.40	.16	.04
□ 12 Mike Davis	.40	.16	.04
□ 13 Jesse Orosco	.30	.12	.03
□ 14 John Shelby	.30	.12	.03
□ 15 Rick Dempsey	.30	.12	.03
□ 16 Jay Howell	.40	.16	.04
□ 17 Dave Anderson	.30	.12	.03
□ 18 Alejandro Pena	.40	.16	.04
□ 19 Jeff Hamilton	.40	.16	.04
□ 20 Danny Heep	.30	.12	.03
□ 21 Tim Leary	.50	.20	.05
□ 22 Brad Havens	.30	.12	.03
□ 23 Tim Belcher	.50	.20	.05
□ 24 Ken Howell	.30	.12	.03
□ 25 Mickey Hatcher	.30	.12	.03
□ 26 Brian Holton	.40	.16	.04
□ 27 Mike Devereaux	.50	.20	.05
□ 28 Checklist Card	.30	.12	.03

1988 Mother's Cookies Giants

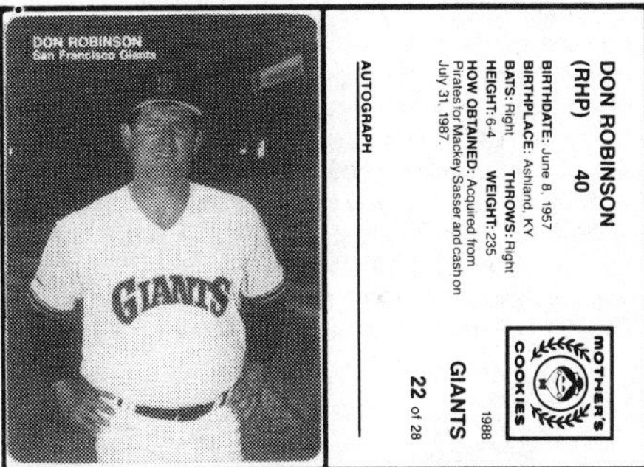

DON ROBINSON
San Francisco Giants
GIANTS
DON ROBINSON
(RHP) 40
BIRTHDATE: June 8, 1957
BIRTHPLACE: Ashland, KY
BATS: Right THROWS: Right
HEIGHT: 6-4 WEIGHT: 235
HOW OBTAINED: Acquired from Pirates for Mackey Sasser and cash on July 31, 1987.
AUTOGRAPH
MOTHER'S COOKIES
1988
GIANTS
22 of 28

This set consists of 28 full-color, rounded- corner cards each measuring 2 1/2" by 3 1/2". Starter sets (only 20 cards but also including a certificate for eight more cards) were given out at the ballpark and collectors were encouraged to trade to fill in the rest of their set. Cards were originally given out at Candlestick Park on July 30th during a game. Photos were taken by Dennis Desprois. The sets were supposedly given out free to the first 35,000 paid admissions at the game.

	MINT	EXC	G-VG
COMPLETE SET (28)	10.00	4.00	1.00
COMMON PLAYER (1-28)	.30	.12	.03
□ 1 Roger Craig MG	.50	.20	.05
□ 2 Will Clark	2.00	.80	.20
□ 3 Kevin Mitchell	.40	.16	.04
□ 4 Bob Brenly	.40	.16	.04
□ 5 Mike Aldrete	.40	.16	.04
□ 6 Mike Krukow	.40	.16	.04
□ 7 Candy Maldonado	.40	.16	.04
□ 8 Jeffrey Leonard	.40	.16	.04
□ 9 Dave Dravecky	.40	.16	.04
□ 10 Robby Thompson	.40	.16	.04
□ 11 Scott Garrelts	.40	.16	.04

		MINT	EXC	G-VG
□ 12	Bob Melvin	.30	.12	.03
□ 13	Jose Uribe	.40	.16	.04
□ 14	Brett Butler	.50	.20	.05
□ 15	Rick Reuschel	.50	.20	.05
□ 16	Harry Spilman	.30	.12	.03
□ 17	Kelly Downs	.40	.16	.04
□ 18	Chris Speier	.30	.12	.03
□ 19	Atlee Hammaker	.40	.16	.04
□ 20	Joel Youngblood	.30	.12	.03
□ 21	Mike LaCoss	.30	.12	.03
□ 22	Don Robinson	.40	.16	.04
□ 23	Mark Wasinger	.40	.16	.04
□ 24	Craig Lefferts	.30	.12	.03
□ 25	Phil Garner	.30	.12	.03
□ 26	Joe Price	.30	.12	.03
□ 27	Giants' Coaches	.30	.12	.03
□ 28	Checklist Card	.30	.12	.03

1988 Mother's Cookies Mariners

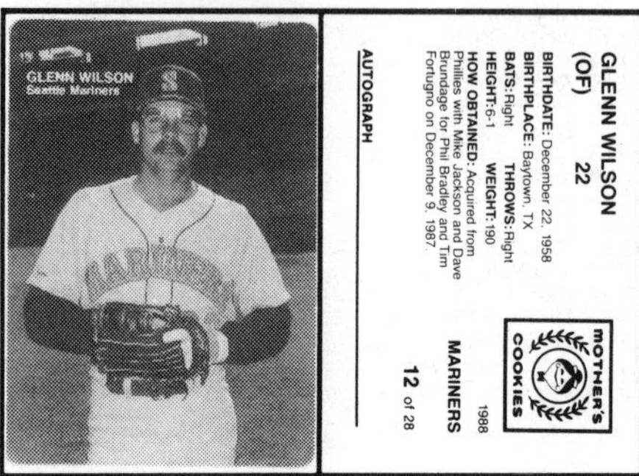

GLENN WILSON
Seattle Mariners
GLENN WILSON
(OF) 22
BIRTHDATE: December 22, 1958
BIRTHPLACE: Baytown, TX
BATS: Right THROWS: Right
HEIGHT: 6-1 WEIGHT: 190
HOW OBTAINED: Acquired from Phillies with Mike Jackson and Dave Brundage for Phil Bradley and Tim Fortugno on December 9, 1987.
AUTOGRAPH
MOTHER'S COOKIES
1988
MARINERS
12 of 28

This set consists of 28 full-color, rounded- corner cards each measuring 2 1/2" by 3 1/2". Starter sets (only 20 cards but also including a certificate for eight more cards) were given out at the ballpark and collectors were encouraged to trade to fill in the rest of their set. Cards were originally given out on August 14th at the Seattle Kingdome. Photos were taken by Barry Colla. The sets were supposedly given out free to the first 20,000 paid admissions at the game.

		MINT	EXC	G-VG
COMPLETE SET (28)		8.00	3.25	.80
COMMON PLAYER (1-28)		.30	.12	.03
□ 1	Dick Williams MG	.30	.12	.03
□ 2	Alvin Davis	.60	.24	.06
□ 3	Mike Moore	.50	.20	.05
□ 4	Jim Presley	.50	.20	.05
□ 5	Mark Langston	.60	.24	.06
□ 6	Henry Cotto	.30	.12	.03
□ 7	Ken Phelps	.50	.20	.05
□ 8	Steve Trout	.30	.12	.03
□ 9	David Valle	.30	.12	.03
□ 10	Harold Reynolds	.50	.20	.05
□ 11	Edwin Nunez	.30	.12	.03
□ 12	Glenn Wilson	.30	.12	.03
□ 13	Scott Bankhead	.40	.16	.04
□ 14	Scott Bradley	.40	.16	.04
□ 15	Mickey Brantley	.40	.16	.04
□ 16	Bruce Fields	.30	.12	.03
□ 17	Mike Kingery	.30	.12	.03
□ 18	Mike Campbell	.40	.16	.04
□ 19	Mike Jackson	.40	.16	.04
□ 20	Rey Quinones	.30	.12	.03
□ 21	Mario Diaz	.30	.12	.03
□ 22	Jerry Reed	.30	.12	.03
□ 23	Rich Renteria	.40	.16	.04
□ 24	Julio Solano	.30	.12	.03
□ 25	Bill Swift	.30	.12	.03
□ 26	Bill Wilkinson	.30	.12	.03
□ 27	Mariners Coaches	.30	.12	.03
□ 28	Checklist	.30	.12	.03

1988 Mother's Cookies McGwire

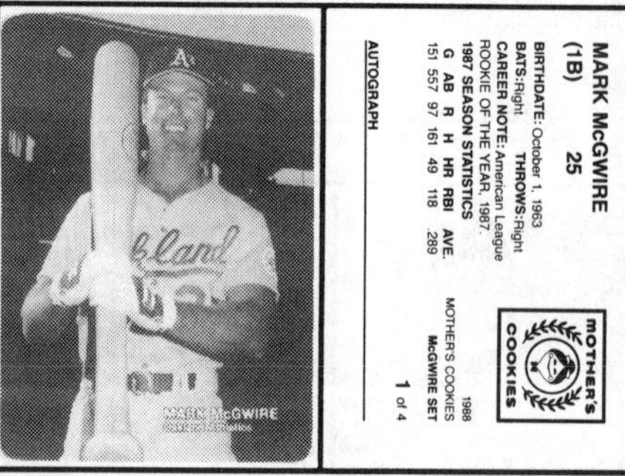

This regional set consists of 4 full-color, rounded-corner cards each measuring 2 1/2" by 3 1/2" and showing a different pose of Athletics' slugging first baseman Mark McGwire. Cards were originally found in 18 oz. packages of "Big Bags" of Mother's Cookies at stores in the Northern California area in February and March of 1988. The cards are numbered on the back. Card backs are done in red and purple on white card stock.

		MINT	EXC	G-VG
COMPLETE SET (4)		12.00	5.00	1.20
COMMON PLAYER (1-4)		4.00	1.60	.40
□ 1	Mark McGwire Holding Big Bat	4.00	1.60	.40
□ 2	Mark McGwire Fielding at First Base	4.00	1.60	.40
□ 3	Mark McGwire Kneeling In On Deck Circle	4.00	1.60	.40
□ 4	Mark McGwire Batting Pose, Waist Up	4.00	1.60	.40

1988 Mother's Cookies Rangers

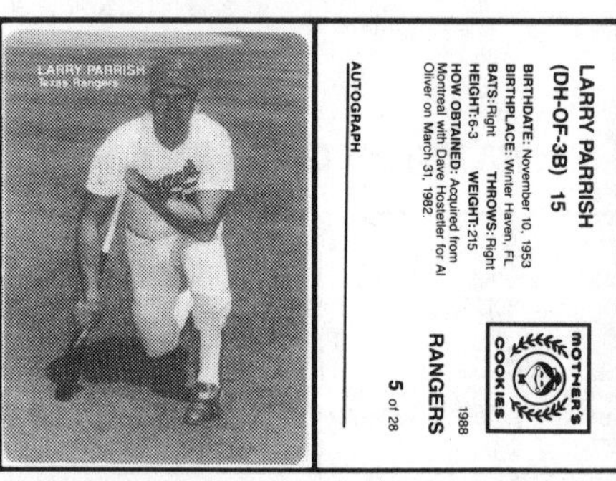

LARRY PARRISH
Texas Rangers
LARRY PARRISH
(DH-OF-3B) 15
BIRTHDATE: November 10, 1953
BIRTHPLACE: Winter Haven, FL
BATS: Right THROWS: Right
HEIGHT: 6-3 WEIGHT: 215
HOW OBTAINED: Acquired from Montreal with Dave Hostetler for Al Oliver on March 31, 1982.
AUTOGRAPH
MOTHER'S COOKIES
1988
RANGERS
5 of 28

This set consists of 28 full-color, rounded- corner cards each measuring 2 1/2" by 3 1/2". Starter sets (only 20 cards but also including a certificate for eight more cards) were given out at the ballpark and collectors were encouraged to trade to fill in the rest of their set. Cards were originally given out on August 7th. Photos were taken by Barry Colla. The sets were supposedly given out free to the first 25,000 paid admissions at the game.

	MINT	EXC	G-VG
COMPLETE SET (28)	8.00	3.25	.80
COMMON PLAYER (1-28)	.30	.12	.03

☐ 1 Bobby Valentine MG	.50	.20	.05
☐ 2 Pete Incaviglia	.60	.24	.06
☐ 3 Charlie Hough	.50	.20	.05
☐ 4 Oddibe McDowell	.50	.20	.05
☐ 5 Larry Parrish	.40	.16	.04
☐ 6 Scott Fletcher	.40	.16	.04
☐ 7 Steve Buechele	.30	.12	.03
☐ 8 Steve Kemp	.30	.12	.03
☐ 9 Pete O'Brien	.50	.20	.05
☐ 10 Ruben Sierra	.75	.30	.07
☐ 11 Mike Stanley	.40	.16	.04
☐ 12 Jose Cecena	.40	.16	.04
☐ 13 Cecil Espy	.40	.16	.04
☐ 14 Curtis Wilkerson	.30	.12	.03
☐ 15 Dale Mohorcic	.30	.12	.03
☐ 16 Ray Hayward	.30	.12	.03
☐ 17 Mitch Williams	.40	.16	.04
☐ 18 Bob Brower	.30	.12	.03
☐ 19 Paul Kilgus	.40	.16	.04
☐ 20 Geno Petralli	.30	.12	.03
☐ 21 James Steels	.30	.12	.03
☐ 22 Jerry Browne	.30	.12	.03
☐ 23 Jose Guzman	.40	.16	.04
☐ 24 DeWayne Vaughn	.30	.12	.03
☐ 25 Bobby Witt	.60	.24	.06
☐ 26 Jeff Russell	.40	.16	.04
☐ 27 Rangers Coaches	.30	.12	.03
☐ 28 Checklist Card	.30	.12	.03

1916 M101-4 Sporting News

J. CARLISLE SMITH
3rd B.—Boston Braves
163
THE SPORTING NEWS
"THE BASEBALL PAPER of the WORLD"
FIVE CENTS THE COPY
PUBLISHED WEEKLY the YEAR 'ROUND
SAMPLE COPY FREE ON REQUEST
C. C. SPINK & SON : ST. LOUIS, MO.

The cards in this 200-card set measure 1 5/8" by 3". Issued in 1916 as a premium offer, the M101-4 set features black and white photos of current ballplayers. Each card is numbered and the reverse carries Sporting News advertising. The fronts are the same as D329, H801-9 and the unclassified Famous and Barr set. Most of the players in this also appear in the M101-5 set. Those cards which are asterisked in the checklist below are those cards which do not appear in the companion M101-5 set issued the year before.

	NRMT	VG-E	GOOD
COMPLETE SET (200)	8000.00	3500.00	1000.00
COMMON PLAYER (1-200)	20.00	8.00	2.00
☐ 1 Babe Adams	20.00	8.00	2.00
☐ 2 Sam Agnew	20.00	8.00	2.00
☐ 3 Eddie Ainsmith	20.00	8.00	2.00
☐ 4 Grover Alexander	60.00	24.00	6.00
☐ 5 Leon Ames	20.00	8.00	2.00
☐ 6 Jimmy Archer	20.00	8.00	2.00
☐ 7 Jimmy Austin	20.00	8.00	2.00
☐ 8 H.D. Baird *	30.00	12.00	3.00
☐ 9 Frank Baker	40.00	16.00	4.00
☐ 10 Dave Bancroft	40.00	16.00	4.00
☐ 11 Jack Barry	20.00	8.00	2.00
☐ 12 Zinn Beck	20.00	8.00	2.00
☐ 13 Chief Bender *	50.00	20.00	5.00
☐ 14 Joe Benz	20.00	8.00	2.00
☐ 15 Bob Bescher	20.00	8.00	2.00
☐ 16 Al Betzel	20.00	8.00	2.00
☐ 17 Mordecai Brown	40.00	16.00	4.00
☐ 18 Eddie Burns	20.00	8.00	2.00
☐ 19 George Burns *	30.00	12.00	3.00
☐ 20 George J. Burns	20.00	8.00	2.00
☐ 21 Joe Bush	25.00	10.00	2.50
☐ 22 Donie Bush *	30.00	12.00	3.00
☐ 23 Art Butler	20.00	8.00	2.00
☐ 24 Bobbie Byrne	20.00	8.00	2.00
☐ 25 Forrest Cady *	30.00	12.00	3.00
☐ 26 Jim Callahan	20.00	8.00	2.00
☐ 27 Ray Caldwell	20.00	8.00	2.00
☐ 28 Max Carey	40.00	16.00	4.00
☐ 29 George Chalmers	20.00	8.00	2.00
☐ 30 Ray Chapman	25.00	10.00	2.50
☐ 31 Larry Cheney	20.00	8.00	2.00
☐ 32 Ed Cicotte	30.00	12.00	3.00
☐ 33 Tommy Clarke	20.00	8.00	2.00
☐ 34 Eddie Collins	50.00	20.00	5.00
☐ 35 Shano Collins	20.00	8.00	2.00
☐ 36 Charles Comiskey	40.00	16.00	4.00
☐ 37 Joe Connolly	20.00	8.00	2.00
☐ 38 Ty Cobb *	800.00	320.00	80.00
☐ 39 Harry Coveleskie	20.00	8.00	2.00
☐ 40 Gabby Cravath	25.00	10.00	2.50
☐ 41 Sam Crawford	40.00	16.00	4.00
☐ 42 Jean Dale	20.00	8.00	2.00
☐ 43 Jake Daubert	25.00	10.00	2.50
☐ 44 Charles Deal	20.00	8.00	2.00
☐ 45 Frank Demaree	20.00	8.00	2.00
☐ 46 Josh Devore *	30.00	12.00	3.00
☐ 47 William Doak	20.00	8.00	2.00
☐ 48 Bill Donovan	20.00	8.00	2.00
☐ 49 Red Dooin	20.00	8.00	2.00
☐ 50 Mike Doolan	20.00	8.00	2.00
☐ 51 Larry Doyle	20.00	8.00	2.00
☐ 52 Jean Dubuc	20.00	8.00	2.00
☐ 53 Oscar J. Dugey	20.00	8.00	2.00
☐ 54 John Evers	40.00	16.00	4.00
☐ 55 Red Faber	40.00	16.00	4.00
☐ 56 Happy Felsch	30.00	12.00	3.00
☐ 57 Bill Fischer	20.00	8.00	2.00
☐ 58 Ray Fisher	20.00	8.00	2.00
☐ 59 Max Flack	20.00	8.00	2.00
☐ 60 Art Fletcher	20.00	8.00	2.00
☐ 61 Eddie Foster	20.00	8.00	2.00
☐ 62 Jacques Fournier	20.00	8.00	2.00
☐ 63 Del Gainer	20.00	8.00	2.00
☐ 64 Chick Gandil *	40.00	16.00	4.00
☐ 65 Larry Gardner	20.00	8.00	2.00
☐ 66 Joe Gedeon	20.00	8.00	2.00
☐ 67 Gus Getz	20.00	8.00	2.00
☐ 68 George Gibson	20.00	8.00	2.00
☐ 69 Wilbur Good	20.00	8.00	2.00
☐ 70 Hank Gowdy	20.00	8.00	2.00
☐ 71 Jack Graney	20.00	8.00	2.00
☐ 72 Clark Griffith *	60.00	24.00	6.00
☐ 73 Tommy Griffith	20.00	8.00	2.00
☐ 74 Heine Groh	25.00	10.00	2.50
☐ 75 Earl Hamilton	20.00	8.00	2.00
☐ 76 Bob Harmon	20.00	8.00	2.00
☐ 77 Roy Hartzell	20.00	8.00	2.00
☐ 78 Claude Hendrix	20.00	8.00	2.00
☐ 79 Olaf Henriksen	20.00	8.00	2.00
☐ 80 John Henry	20.00	8.00	2.00
☐ 81 Buck Herzog	20.00	8.00	2.00
☐ 82 Hugh High	20.00	8.00	2.00
☐ 83 Dick Hoblitzell	20.00	8.00	2.00
☐ 84 Harry Hooper	40.00	16.00	4.00
☐ 85 Ivan Howard	20.00	8.00	2.00
☐ 86 Miller Huggins	40.00	16.00	4.00
☐ 87 Joe Jackson	750.00	300.00	75.00
☐ 88 William James	20.00	8.00	2.00
☐ 89 Harold Janvrin	20.00	8.00	2.00
☐ 90 Hughie Jennings	40.00	16.00	4.00
☐ 91 Walter Johnson	300.00	120.00	30.00
☐ 92 Fielder Jones	20.00	8.00	2.00
☐ 93 Joe Judge *	30.00	12.00	3.00
☐ 94 Benny Kauff	20.00	8.00	2.00
☐ 95 Bill Killifer	20.00	8.00	2.00
☐ 96 Ed Konetchy	20.00	8.00	2.00
☐ 97 Nap Lajoie	125.00	50.00	12.50
☐ 98 Jack Lapp	20.00	8.00	2.00
☐ 99 John Lavan	20.00	8.00	2.00
☐ 100 Jimmy Lavender	20.00	8.00	2.00
☐ 101 Nemo Leibold	20.00	8.00	2.00
☐ 102 Hub Leonard	20.00	8.00	2.00
☐ 103 Duffy Lewis	20.00	8.00	2.00
☐ 104 Hans Lobert	20.00	8.00	2.00
☐ 105 Tom Long	20.00	8.00	2.00
☐ 106 Fred Luderus	20.00	8.00	2.00
☐ 107 Connie Mack	75.00	30.00	7.50
☐ 108 Lee Magee	20.00	8.00	2.00
☐ 109 Sherry Magee *	30.00	12.00	3.00
☐ 110 Al Mamaux	20.00	8.00	2.00
☐ 111 Leslie Mann	20.00	8.00	2.00
☐ 112 Rabbit Maranville	40.00	16.00	4.00
☐ 113 Rube Marquard	40.00	16.00	4.00

□ 114	J.E. Mayer	20.00	8.00	2.00
□ 115	George McBride	20.00	8.00	2.00
□ 116	John McGraw	60.00	24.00	6.00
□ 117	Jack McInnis	25.00	10.00	2.50
□ 118	Fred Merkle	25.00	10.00	2.50
□ 119	Chief Meyers	20.00	8.00	2.00
□ 120	Clyde Milan	20.00	8.00	2.00
□ 121	John Miller *	30.00	12.00	3.00
□ 122	Otto Miller	20.00	8.00	2.00
□ 123	Willie Mitchell	20.00	8.00	2.00
□ 124	Fred Mollwitz	20.00	8.00	2.00
□ 125	Pat Moran	20.00	8.00	2.00
□ 126	Ray Morgan	20.00	8.00	2.00
□ 127	George Moriarty	20.00	8.00	2.00
□ 128	Guy Morton	20.00	8.00	2.00
□ 129	Mike Mowrey *	30.00	12.00	3.00
□ 130	Eddie Murphy	20.00	8.00	2.00
□ 131	Hy Myers	20.00	8.00	2.00
□ 132	Bert Niehoff	20.00	8.00	2.00
□ 133	Rube Oldring	20.00	8.00	2.00
□ 134	Oliver O'Mara	20.00	8.00	2.00
□ 135	Steve O'Neill	25.00	10.00	2.50
□ 136	Dode Paskert	20.00	8.00	2.00
□ 137	Roger Peckinpaugh	25.00	10.00	2.50
□ 138	Walter Pipp	30.00	12.00	3.00
□ 139	Del Pratt	20.00	8.00	2.00
□ 140	Pat Ragan *	30.00	12.00	3.00
□ 141	Bill Rariden	20.00	8.00	2.00
□ 142	Eppa Rixey	40.00	16.00	4.00
□ 143	Davey Robertson	20.00	8.00	2.00
□ 144	Wilbert Robinson	50.00	20.00	5.00
□ 145	Bob Roth	20.00	8.00	2.00
□ 146	Eddie Roush	40.00	16.00	4.00
□ 147	Clarence Rowland	20.00	8.00	2.00
□ 148	Nap Rucker	20.00	8.00	2.00
□ 149	Dick Rudolph	20.00	8.00	2.00
□ 150	Reb Russell	20.00	8.00	2.00
□ 151	Babe Ruth	1500.00	650.00	200.00
□ 152	Vic Saier	20.00	8.00	2.00
□ 153	Slim Sallee	20.00	8.00	2.00
□ 154	Ray Schalk	40.00	16.00	4.00
□ 155	Wally Schang	20.00	8.00	2.00
□ 156	Frank Schulte	20.00	8.00	2.00
□ 157	Everett Scott	25.00	10.00	2.50
□ 158	Jim Scott	20.00	8.00	2.00
□ 159	Tom Seaton	20.00	8.00	2.00
□ 160	Howard Shanks	20.00	8.00	2.00
□ 161	Bob Shawkey	25.00	10.00	2.50
□ 162	Ernie Shore	25.00	10.00	2.50
□ 163	Bert Shotton	20.00	8.00	2.00
□ 164	George Sisler	60.00	24.00	6.00
□ 165	J.C. Smith	20.00	8.00	2.00
□ 166	Fred Snodgrass	20.00	8.00	2.00
□ 167	George Stallings	20.00	8.00	2.00
□ 168	Oscar Stanage	20.00	8.00	2.00
□ 169	Charles Stengel	250.00	100.00	25.00
□ 170	Milton Stock	20.00	8.00	2.00
□ 171	Amos Strunk	20.00	8.00	2.00
□ 172	Billy Sullivan	25.00	10.00	2.50
□ 173	Jeff Tesreau	20.00	8.00	2.00
□ 174	Joe Tinker	40.00	16.00	4.00
□ 175	Fred Toney	20.00	8.00	2.00
□ 176	Terry Turner	20.00	8.00	2.00
□ 177	George Tyler *	30.00	12.00	3.00
□ 178	Jim Vaughn	20.00	8.00	2.00
□ 179	Bobby Veach	20.00	8.00	2.00
□ 180	James Viox	20.00	8.00	2.00
□ 181	Oscar Vitt	20.00	8.00	2.00
□ 182	Honus Wagner	300.00	120.00	30.00
□ 183	Clarence Walker	20.00	8.00	2.00
□ 184	Ed Walsh	40.00	16.00	4.00
□ 185	Bill Wambsganss *	30.00	12.00	3.00
□ 186	Buck Weaver	30.00	12.00	3.00
□ 187	Carl Weilman	20.00	8.00	2.00
□ 188	Zack Wheat	40.00	16.00	4.00
□ 189	George Whitted	20.00	8.00	2.00
□ 190	Fred Williams	20.00	8.00	2.00
□ 191	Arthur Wilson	20.00	8.00	2.00
□ 192	J.O. Wilson	20.00	8.00	2.00
□ 193	Ivy Wingo	20.00	8.00	2.00
□ 194	Meldon Wolfgang	20.00	8.00	2.00
□ 195	Joe Wood	30.00	12.00	3.00
□ 196	Steve Yerkes	20.00	8.00	2.00
□ 197	Pep Young * (Detroit Tigers)	30.00	12.00	3.00
□ 198	Rollie Zeider	20.00	8.00	2.00
□ 199	Heine Zimmerman	20.00	8.00	2.00
□ 200	Dutch Zwilling	20.00	8.00	2.00

1916 M101-5 Sporting News

The cards in this 200-card set measure 1 5/8 by 3". The 1916 M101-5 series of black and white, numbered baseball cards is essentially an updated version of M101-4. The set was offered as a marketing promotion by C.C. Spink and Son, publishers of The Sporting News ("The Baseball Paper of the World"). Most of the players in this also appear in the M101-4 set. Those cards which are asterisked in the checklist below are those cards which do not appear in the companion M101-4 set issued the year before.

		NRMT	VG-E	GOOD
COMPLETE SET (200)		8500.00	3700.00	1200.00
COMMON PLAYER (1-200)		20.00	8.00	2.00
□ 1	Babe Adams	20.00	8.00	2.00
□ 2	Sam Agnew	20.00	8.00	2.00
□ 3	Ed Ainsmith	20.00	8.00	2.00
□ 4	Grover Alexander	60.00	24.00	6.00
□ 5	Leon Ames	20.00	8.00	2.00
□ 6	Jimmy Archer	20.00	8.00	2.00
□ 7	Jimmy Austin	20.00	8.00	2.00
□ 8	Frank Baker	40.00	16.00	4.00
□ 9	Dave Bancroft	40.00	16.00	4.00
□ 10	Jack Barry	20.00	8.00	2.00
□ 11	Zinn Beck	20.00	8.00	2.00
□ 12	Luke Boone *	30.00	12.00	3.00
□ 13	Joe Benz	20.00	8.00	2.00
□ 14	Bob Bescher	20.00	8.00	2.00
□ 15	Al Betzel	20.00	8.00	2.00
□ 16	Roger Bresnahan *	50.00	20.00	5.00
□ 17	Eddie Burns	20.00	8.00	2.00
□ 18	G.J. Burns	20.00	8.00	2.00
□ 19	Joe Bush	25.00	10.00	2.50
□ 20	Owen Bush *	30.00	12.00	3.00
□ 21	Art Butler	20.00	8.00	2.00
□ 22	Bobby Byrne	20.00	8.00	2.00
□ 23	Mordecai Brown	40.00	16.00	4.00
□ 24	Jimmy Callahan	20.00	8.00	2.00
□ 25	Ray Caldwell	20.00	8.00	2.00
□ 26	Max Carey	40.00	16.00	4.00
□ 27	George Chalmers	20.00	8.00	2.00
□ 28	Frank Chance *	60.00	24.00	6.00
□ 29	Ray Chapman	25.00	10.00	2.50
□ 30	Larry Cheney	20.00	8.00	2.00
□ 31	Ed Cicotte	30.00	12.00	3.00
□ 32	Tommy Clarke	20.00	8.00	2.00
□ 33	Eddie Collins	50.00	20.00	5.00
□ 34	Shano Collins	20.00	8.00	2.00
□ 35	Charles Comiskey	40.00	16.00	4.00
□ 36	Joe Connolly	20.00	8.00	2.00
□ 37	L. Cook *	30.00	12.00	3.00
□ 38	Jack Coombs *	35.00	14.00	3.50
□ 39	Dan Costello *	30.00	12.00	3.00
□ 40	Harry Coveleskie	20.00	8.00	2.00
□ 41	Gavvy Cravath	25.00	10.00	2.50
□ 42	Sam Crawford	40.00	16.00	4.00
□ 43	Jean Dale	20.00	8.00	2.00
□ 44	Jake Daubert	25.00	10.00	2.50
□ 45	G.A. Davis Jr. *	30.00	12.00	3.00
□ 46	Charles Deal	20.00	8.00	2.00
□ 47	Frank Demaree	20.00	8.00	2.00
□ 48	Bill Doak	20.00	8.00	2.00
□ 49	Bill Donovan	20.00	8.00	2.00
□ 50	Red Dooin	20.00	8.00	2.00

□ 51 Mike Doolan 20.00 8.00 2.00
□ 52 Larry Doyle 20.00 8.00 2.00
□ 53 Jean Dubuc 20.00 8.00 2.00
□ 54 Oscar Dugey 20.00 8.00 2.00
□ 55 John Evers 40.00 16.00 4.00
□ 56 Red Faber 40.00 16.00 4.00
□ 57 Happy Felsch 30.00 12.00 3.00
□ 58 Bill Fischer 20.00 8.00 2.00
□ 59 Ray Fisher 20.00 8.00 2.00
□ 60 Max Flack 20.00 8.00 2.00
□ 61 Art Fletcher 20.00 8.00 2.00
□ 62 Eddie Foster 20.00 8.00 2.00
□ 63 Jacques Fournier 20.00 8.00 2.00
□ 64 Del Gainer 20.00 8.00 2.00
□ 65 Larry Gardner 20.00 8.00 2.00
□ 66 Joe Gedeon 20.00 8.00 2.00
□ 67 Gus Getz 20.00 8.00 2.00
□ 68 George Gibson 20.00 8.00 2.00
□ 69 Wilbur Good 20.00 8.00 2.00
□ 70 Hank Gowdy 20.00 8.00 2.00
□ 71 Jack Graney 20.00 8.00 2.00
□ 72 Tommy Griffith 20.00 8.00 2.00
□ 73 Heine Groh 25.00 10.00 2.50
□ 74 Earl Hamilton 20.00 8.00 2.00
□ 75 Bob Harmon 20.00 8.00 2.00
□ 76 Roy Hartzell 20.00 8.00 2.00
□ 77 Claude Hendrix 20.00 8.00 2.00
□ 78 Olaf Henriksen 20.00 8.00 2.00
□ 79 John Henry 20.00 8.00 2.00
□ 80 Buck Herzog 20.00 8.00 2.00
□ 81 Hugh High 20.00 8.00 2.00
□ 82 Dick Hoblitzell 20.00 8.00 2.00
□ 83 Harry Hooper 40.00 16.00 4.00
□ 84 Ivan Howard 20.00 8.00 2.00
□ 85 Miller Huggins 40.00 16.00 4.00
□ 86 Joe Jackson 750.00 300.00 75.00
□ 87 William James 20.00 8.00 2.00
□ 88 Harold Janvrin 20.00 8.00 2.00
□ 89 Hughie Jennings 40.00 16.00 4.00
□ 90 Walter Johnson 250.00 100.00 25.00
□ 91 Fielder Jones 20.00 8.00 2.00
□ 92 Benny Kauff 20.00 8.00 2.00
□ 93 Bill Killefer 20.00 8.00 2.00
□ 94 Ed Konetchy 20.00 8.00 2.00
□ 95 Napoleon Lajoie 125.00 50.00 12.50
□ 96 Jack Lapp 20.00 8.00 2.00
□ 97 John Lavan 20.00 8.00 2.00
□ 98 Jimmy Lavender 20.00 8.00 2.00
□ 99 Nemo Leibold 20.00 8.00 2.00
□ 100 Hub Leonard 20.00 8.00 2.00
□ 101 Duffy Lewis 20.00 8.00 2.00
□ 102 Hans Lobert 20.00 8.00 2.00
□ 103 Tom Long 20.00 8.00 2.00
□ 104 Fred Luderus 20.00 8.00 2.00
□ 105 Connie Mack 75.00 30.00 7.50
□ 106 Lee Magee 20.00 8.00 2.00
□ 107 Al Mamaux 20.00 8.00 2.00
□ 108 Leslie Mann 20.00 8.00 2.00
□ 109 Rabbit Maranville 40.00 16.00 4.00
□ 110 Rube Marquard 40.00 16.00 4.00
□ 111 Armando Marsans * 30.00 12.00 3.00
□ 112 J.E. Mayer 20.00 8.00 2.00
□ 113 George McBride 20.00 8.00 2.00
□ 114 John McGraw 60.00 24.00 6.00
□ 115 Jack McInnis 25.00 10.00 2.50
□ 116 Fred Merkle 25.00 10.00 2.50
□ 117 Chief Meyers 20.00 8.00 2.00
□ 118 Clyde Milan 20.00 8.00 2.00
□ 119 Otto Miller 20.00 8.00 2.00
□ 120 Willie Mitchell 20.00 8.00 2.00
□ 121 Fred Mollwitz 20.00 8.00 2.00
□ 122 J.H. Moran * 30.00 12.00 3.00
□ 123 Pat Moran 20.00 8.00 2.00
□ 124 Ray Morgan 20.00 8.00 2.00
□ 125 George Moriarty 20.00 8.00 2.00
□ 126 Guy Morton 20.00 8.00 2.00
□ 127 Eddie Murphy 20.00 8.00 2.00
□ 128 Jack Murray * 30.00 12.00 3.00
□ 129 Hy Myers 20.00 8.00 2.00
□ 130 Bert Niehoff 20.00 8.00 2.00
□ 131 Les Nunamaker * 30.00 12.00 3.00
□ 132 Rube Oldring 20.00 8.00 2.00
□ 133 Oliver O'Mara 20.00 8.00 2.00
□ 134 Steve O'Neill 25.00 10.00 2.50
□ 135 Dode Paskert 20.00 8.00 2.00
□ 136 Roger Peckinpaugh 25.00 10.00 2.50
□ 137 E.J. Pfeffer * 30.00 12.00 3.00
□ 138 George Pierce * 30.00 12.00 3.00
□ 139 Walter Pipp 30.00 12.00 3.00
□ 140 Del Pratt 20.00 8.00 2.00
□ 141 Bill Rariden 20.00 8.00 2.00
□ 142 Eppa Rixey 40.00 16.00 4.00
□ 143 Davey Robertson 20.00 8.00 2.00
□ 144 Wilbert Robinson 50.00 20.00 5.00
□ 145 Bob Roth 20.00 8.00 2.00
□ 146 Eddie Roush 40.00 16.00 4.00
□ 147 Clarence Rowland 20.00 8.00 2.00
□ 148 Nap Rucker 20.00 8.00 2.00
□ 149 Dick Rudolph 20.00 8.00 2.00
□ 150 Reb Russell 20.00 8.00 2.00
□ 151 Babe Ruth 2000.00 850.00 250.00
□ 152 Vic Saier 20.00 8.00 2.00
□ 153 Slim Sallee 20.00 8.00 2.00
□ 154 Germany Schaefer * 30.00 12.00 3.00
□ 155 Ray Schalk 40.00 16.00 4.00
□ 156 Wally Schang 20.00 8.00 2.00
□ 157 Chas. Schmidt * 30.00 12.00 3.00
□ 158 Frank Schulte 20.00 8.00 2.00
□ 159 Jim Scott 20.00 8.00 2.00
□ 160 Everett Scott 25.00 10.00 2.50
□ 161 Tom Seaton 20.00 8.00 2.00
□ 162 Howard Shanks 20.00 8.00 2.00
□ 163 Bob Shawkey 25.00 10.00 2.50
□ 164 Ernie Shore 25.00 10.00 2.50
□ 165 Bert Shotton 20.00 8.00 2.00
□ 166 George Sisler 60.00 24.00 6.00
□ 167 J.C. Smith 20.00 8.00 2.00
□ 168 Fred Snodgrass 20.00 8.00 2.00
□ 169 George Stallings 20.00 8.00 2.00
□ 170 Oscar Stanage 20.00 8.00 2.00
□ 171 Charles Stengel 250.00 100.00 25.00
□ 172 Milton Stock 20.00 8.00 2.00
□ 173 Amos Strunk 20.00 8.00 2.00
□ 174 Billy Sullivan 25.00 10.00 2.50
□ 175 Jeff Tesreau 20.00 8.00 2.00
□ 176 Jim Thorpe * 900.00 360.00 90.00
□ 177 Joe Tinker 40.00 16.00 4.00
□ 178 Fred Toney 20.00 8.00 2.00
□ 179 Terry Turner 20.00 8.00 2.00
□ 180 Jim Vaughn 20.00 8.00 2.00
□ 181 Bobby Veach 20.00 8.00 2.00
□ 182 James Viox 20.00 8.00 2.00
□ 183 Oscar Vitt 20.00 8.00 2.00
□ 184 Honus Wagner 300.00 120.00 30.00
□ 185 Clarence Walker 20.00 8.00 2.00
□ 186 Zack Wheat 40.00 16.00 4.00
□ 187 Ed Walsh 40.00 16.00 4.00
□ 188 Buck Weaver 30.00 12.00 3.00
□ 189 Carl Weilman 20.00 8.00 2.00
□ 190 George Whitted 20.00 8.00 2.00
□ 191 Fred Williams 20.00 8.00 2.00
□ 192 Arthur Wilson 20.00 8.00 2.00
□ 193 J.O. Wilson 20.00 8.00 2.00
□ 194 Ivy Wingo 20.00 8.00 2.00
□ 195 Meldon Wolfgang 20.00 8.00 2.00
□ 196 Joe Wood 30.00 12.00 3.00
□ 197 Steve Yerkes 20.00 8.00 2.00
□ 198 Rollie Zeider 20.00 8.00 2.00
□ 199 Heinie Zimmerman 20.00 8.00 2.00
□ 200 Dutch Zwilling 20.00 8.00 2.00

1911 M116 Sporting Life

The cards in this 288-card set measure 1 1/2" by 2 5/8". The Sporting Life set was offered as a premium to the publication's subscribers in 1911. Each of the 24 series of 12 cards came in an envelope printed with a list of the players within. Cards marked with an asterisk are also found with a special blue background and are worth double the listed price. McConnell appears with both Boston AL (common) and Chicago White Sox (scarce); McQuillan appears with Phillies (common) and Cincinnati (scarce).

Cards are numbered in the checklist below alphabetically within team. Teams are ordered alphabetically within league: Boston AL (1-19), Chicago AL (20-36), Cleveland (37-52), Detroit (53-73), New york AL (74-84), Philadelphia AL (85-105), St. Louis AL (106-120), Washington (121-134), Boston NL (135-147), Brooklyn (148-164), Chicago NL (165-185), Cincinnati (186-203), New york NL (204-223), Philadelphia NL (224-242), Pittsburgh (243-261), and St. Louis (262-279). Cards 280-288 feature minor leaguers and are somewhat more difficult to find since most are from the tougher higher series

	NRMT	VG-E	GOOD
COMPLETE SET	13000.00	5650.00	1800.00
COMMON MAJOR (1-279)	25.00	10.00	2.50
COMMON MINOR (280-288)	35.00	14.00	3.50

	No.	Player	NRMT	VG-E	GOOD
□	1	Frank Arellanes	25.00	10.00	2.50
□	2	Bill Carrigan	25.00	10.00	2.50
□	3	Ed Cicotte	35.00	14.00	3.50
□	4	Ray Collins S24	50.00	20.00	5.00
□	5	Pat Donahue	25.00	10.00	2.50
□	6	Donovan S21	50.00	20.00	5.00
□	7	Arthur Engle	25.00	10.00	2.50
□	8	Larry Gardner S24	50.00	20.00	5.00
□	9	Charles Hall	25.00	10.00	2.50
□	10	Harry Hooper S23	100.00	40.00	10.00
□	11	Edwin Karger	25.00	10.00	2.50
□	12	Harry Lord *	25.00	10.00	2.50
□	13	Thomas Madden S24	50.00	20.00	5.00
□	14A	Amby McConnell (Boston AL)	25.00	10.00	2.50
□	14B	Amby McConnell (Chicago AL)	750.00	300.00	75.00
□	15	Tris Speaker S23	250.00	100.00	25.00
□	16	Jake Stahl	35.00	14.00	3.50
□	17	John Thoney	25.00	10.00	2.50
□	18	Heine Wagner	25.00	10.00	2.50
□	19	Joe Wood S23	75.00	30.00	7.50
□	20	Blackburn	25.00	10.00	2.50
□	21	James J. Block S21	50.00	20.00	5.00
□	22	Dougherty	25.00	10.00	2.50
□	23	Hugh Duffy	75.00	30.00	7.50
□	24	Ed Hahn	25.00	10.00	2.50
□	25	Paul Meloan S24	50.00	20.00	5.00
□	26	Fred Parent	25.00	10.00	2.50
□	27	Frederick Payne S21	50.00	20.00	5.00
□	28	William Purtell	25.00	10.00	2.50
□	29	James Scott S23	50.00	20.00	5.00
□	30	F. Smith	25.00	10.00	2.50
□	31	Sullivan	25.00	10.00	2.50
□	32	Tannehill	25.00	10.00	2.50
□	33	Ed Walsh	50.00	20.00	5.00
□	34	Guy (Doc) White	25.00	10.00	2.50
□	35	I. Young	25.00	10.00	2.50
□	36	Dutch Zwilling S24	50.00	20.00	5.00
□	37	Harry Bemis	25.00	10.00	2.50
□	38	Charles Berger	25.00	10.00	2.50
□	39	Joseph Birmingham	25.00	10.00	2.50
□	40	Hugh Bradley	25.00	10.00	2.50
□	41	Clarke	25.00	10.00	2.50
□	42	Falkenberg	25.00	10.00	2.50
□	43	Elmer Flick	75.00	30.00	7.50
□	44	Addie Joss	75.00	30.00	7.50
□	45	Napoleon Lajoie *	125.00	50.00	12.50
□	46	Frederick Linke S20	50.00	20.00	5.00
□	47	B. Lord	25.00	10.00	2.50
□	48	McGuire	25.00	10.00	2.50
□	49	Niles	25.00	10.00	2.50
□	50	Stovall	25.00	10.00	2.50
□	51	Turner	25.00	10.00	2.50
□	52	Cy Young	125.00	50.00	12.50
□	53	Beckendorf	25.00	10.00	2.50
□	54	Bush	25.00	10.00	2.50
□	55	Ty Cobb *	900.00	360.00	90.00
□	56	Sam Crawford *	75.00	30.00	7.50
□	57	Jas. Delehanty	25.00	10.00	2.50
□	58	W. Donovan	25.00	10.00	2.50
□	59	Hugh Jennings *	60.00	24.00	6.00
□	60	D. Jones	25.00	10.00	2.50
□	61	T. Jones	25.00	10.00	2.50
□	62	Lathers S21	50.00	20.00	5.00
□	63	McIntyre	25.00	10.00	2.50
□	64	Moriarty	25.00	10.00	2.50
□	65	Mullin	25.00	10.00	2.50
□	66	O'Leary	25.00	10.00	2.50
□	67	Pernoll S23	50.00	20.00	5.00
□	68	Schmidt	25.00	10.00	2.50
□	69	Oscar Stanage	25.00	10.00	2.50
□	70	Stroud S21	50.00	20.00	5.00
□	71	Summers	25.00	10.00	2.50
□	72	Willett	25.00	10.00	2.50
□	73	Works	25.00	10.00	2.50
□	74	Austin S19	50.00	20.00	5.00
□	75	Hal Chase *	50.00	20.00	5.00
□	76	Cree	25.00	10.00	2.50
□	77	Criger	25.00	10.00	2.50
□	78	Ford S23	50.00	20.00	5.00
□	79	Gardner S23	50.00	20.00	5.00
□	80	Knight S19	50.00	20.00	5.00
□	81	LaPorte	25.00	10.00	2.50
□	82	Stallings	25.00	10.00	2.50
□	83	Sweeney S19	50.00	20.00	5.00
□	84	Wolter	25.00	10.00	2.50
□	85	Atkins S24	50.00	20.00	5.00
□	86	Frank Baker	75.00	30.00	7.50
□	87	Jack Barry	25.00	10.00	2.50
□	88	Chief Bender *	60.00	24.00	6.00
□	89	Eddie Collins *	75.00	30.00	7.50
□	90	Jack Coombs	35.00	14.00	3.50
□	91	H. Davis *	25.00	10.00	2.50
□	92	Dygert	25.00	10.00	2.50
□	93	Heitmuller	25.00	10.00	2.50
□	94	Hartsel	25.00	10.00	2.50
□	95	Krause	25.00	10.00	2.50
□	96	Lapp S24	50.00	20.00	5.00
□	97	Livingstone	25.00	10.00	2.50
□	98	Connie Mack	100.00	40.00	10.00
□	99	McInnes S24	50.00	20.00	5.00
□	100	Morgan	25.00	10.00	2.50
□	101	Murphy	25.00	10.00	2.50
□	102	Rube Oldring	25.00	10.00	2.50
□	103	Eddie Plank	100.00	40.00	10.00
□	104	Amos Strunk S24	50.00	20.00	5.00
□	105	Thomas *	25.00	10.00	2.50
□	106	Bailey	25.00	10.00	2.50
□	107	Criss S19	50.00	20.00	5.00
□	108	Graham	25.00	10.00	2.50
□	109	Hartzell	25.00	10.00	2.50
□	110	Hoffman	25.00	10.00	2.50
□	111	Howell	25.00	10.00	2.50
□	112	Lake S19	50.00	20.00	5.00
□	113	O'Conner	25.00	10.00	2.50
□	114	Pelty	25.00	10.00	2.50
□	115	Powell	25.00	10.00	2.50
□	116	Schweitzer	25.00	10.00	2.50
□	117	Stephens	25.00	10.00	2.50
□	118	Stone	25.00	10.00	2.50
□	119	Rube Waddell	75.00	30.00	7.50
□	120	Bobby Wallace	60.00	24.00	6.00
□	121	Conroy	25.00	10.00	2.50
□	122	Elberfeld	25.00	10.00	2.50
□	123	Foster	25.00	10.00	2.50
□	124	Gessler	25.00	10.00	2.50
□	125	Walter Johnson	300.00	120.00	30.00
□	126	Killifer S22	50.00	20.00	5.00
□	127	McAleer	25.00	10.00	2.50
□	128	McBride S21	50.00	20.00	5.00
□	129	Milan	25.00	10.00	2.50
□	130	Miller S23	50.00	20.00	5.00
□	131	Reisling	25.00	10.00	2.50
□	132	Schaefer	25.00	10.00	2.50
□	133	Street	25.00	10.00	2.50
□	134	Unglaub	25.00	10.00	2.50
□	135	Beck	25.00	10.00	2.50
□	136	Brown	25.00	10.00	2.50
□	137	Curtis S23	50.00	20.00	5.00
□	138	Ferguson	25.00	10.00	2.50
□	139	Samuel Frock S20	50.00	20.00	5.00
□	140	Graham	25.00	10.00	2.50
□	141	Buck Herzog	25.00	10.00	2.50
□	142	Lake	25.00	10.00	2.50
□	143	Bayard Sharpe S23	50.00	20.00	5.00
□	144	David Shean S20	50.00	20.00	5.00
□	145	C. Smith S22	50.00	20.00	5.00
□	146	H. Smith	25.00	10.00	2.50
□	147	Sweeney	25.00	10.00	2.50
□	148	Barger	25.00	10.00	2.50
□	149	Bell	25.00	10.00	2.50
□	150	Bergen	25.00	10.00	2.50
□	151	Burch	25.00	10.00	2.50
□	152	Dahlen	35.00	14.00	3.50
□	153	William Davidson S21	50.00	20.00	5.00
□	154	Frank Dessau S21	50.00	20.00	5.00
□	155	Erwin S20	50.00	20.00	5.00
□	156	Hummel	25.00	10.00	2.50
□	157	Hunter	25.00	10.00	2.50
□	158	Jordan *	25.00	10.00	2.50
□	159	Lennox	25.00	10.00	2.50
□	160	McElveen	25.00	10.00	2.50
□	161	McMillan	25.00	10.00	2.50
□	162	Nap Rucker	25.00	10.00	2.50
□	163	Scanlon	25.00	10.00	2.50
□	164	Wilhelm	25.00	10.00	2.50

□ 165	Archer S22	50.00	20.00	5.00
□ 166	Beaumont	25.00	10.00	2.50
□ 167	Mordecai Brown *	75.00	30.00	7.50
□ 168	Frank Chance *	100.00	40.00	10.00
□ 169	Johnny Evers	75.00	30.00	7.50
□ 170	Hofman	25.00	10.00	2.50
□ 171	Kane	25.00	10.00	2.50
□ 172	Kling	25.00	10.00	2.50
□ 173	Kroh	25.00	10.00	2.50
□ 174	McIntire	25.00	10.00	2.50
□ 175	Needham	25.00	10.00	2.50
□ 176	Overall	25.00	10.00	2.50
□ 177	Pfeffer S23	50.00	20.00	5.00
□ 178	Pfiester	25.00	10.00	2.50
□ 179	Ed Reulbach	25.00	10.00	2.50
□ 180	L. Richie	25.00	10.00	2.50
□ 181	Schulte	25.00	10.00	2.50
□ 182	Scheckard	25.00	10.00	2.50
□ 183	Harry Steinfeldt	25.00	10.00	2.50
□ 184	Joe Tinker	60.00	24.00	6.00
□ 185	Zimmerman S19	50.00	20.00	5.00
□ 186	Beebe	25.00	10.00	2.50
□ 187	Bescher	25.00	10.00	2.50
□ 188	Charles	25.00	10.00	2.50
□ 189	Tommy Clarke S20	50.00	20.00	5.00
□ 190	Downey	25.00	10.00	2.50
□ 191	Doyle	25.00	10.00	2.50
□ 192	Eagan	25.00	10.00	2.50
□ 193	Fromme	25.00	10.00	2.50
□ 194	Gaspar S19	50.00	20.00	5.00
□ 195	Clark Griffith	60.00	24.00	6.00
□ 196	Hoblitzel	25.00	10.00	2.50
□ 197	Hans Lobert	25.00	10.00	2.50
□ 198	McLean	25.00	10.00	2.50
□ 199	Mitchell	25.00	10.00	2.50
□ 200	Phelan S23	50.00	20.00	5.00
□ 201	Rowan	25.00	10.00	2.50
□ 202	Space	25.00	10.00	2.50
□ 203	Suggs	25.00	10.00	2.50
□ 204	Ames S22	50.00	20.00	5.00
□ 205	Bridwell	25.00	10.00	2.50
□ 206	Crandall	25.00	10.00	2.50
□ 207	Devlin	25.00	10.00	2.50
□ 208	Devore S19	50.00	20.00	5.00
□ 209	Doyle *	25.00	10.00	2.50
□ 210	Fletcher S22	50.00	20.00	5.00
□ 211	Christy Mathewson	300.00	120.00	30.00
□ 212	John McGraw	100.00	40.00	10.00
□ 213	Fred Merkle	35.00	14.00	3.50
□ 214	Murray	25.00	10.00	2.50
□ 215	Myers S23	50.00	20.00	5.00
□ 216	Raymond	25.00	10.00	2.50
□ 217	Schlei	25.00	10.00	2.50
□ 218	Seymour	25.00	10.00	2.50
□ 219	Shafer S19	50.00	20.00	5.00
□ 220	Fred Snodgrass	25.00	10.00	2.50
□ 221	Tenney *	25.00	10.00	2.50
□ 222	Wilson S23	50.00	20.00	5.00
□ 223	G. Wiltse	25.00	10.00	2.50
□ 224	Bates	25.00	10.00	2.50
□ 225	Bransfeld	25.00	10.00	2.50
□ 226	Dooin *	25.00	10.00	2.50
□ 227	Doolan	25.00	10.00	2.50
□ 228	Ewing	25.00	10.00	2.50
□ 229	Foxen	25.00	10.00	2.50
□ 230	Grant	25.00	10.00	2.50
□ 231	Jacklitsch	25.00	10.00	2.50
□ 232	Knabe	25.00	10.00	2.50
□ 233	Sherry Magee	25.00	10.00	2.50
□ 234A	McQuillan * (Philadelphia NL)	25.00	10.00	2.50
□ 234B	McQuillan (Cincinnati NL)	750.00	300.00	75.00
□ 235	Moore	25.00	10.00	2.50
□ 236	Moran	25.00	10.00	2.50
□ 237	Moren	25.00	10.00	2.50
□ 238	Dode Paskert S19	50.00	20.00	5.00
□ 239	Schettler S20	50.00	20.00	5.00
□ 240	Sparks	25.00	10.00	2.50
□ 241	Titus S23	50.00	20.00	5.00
□ 242A	Jimmy Walsh S20 dark background	75.00	30.00	7.50
□ 242B	Jimmy Walsh S22 white background	75.00	30.00	7.50
□ 243	Ed Abbaticchio	25.00	10.00	2.50
□ 244	Adams	25.00	10.00	2.50
□ 245	Byrne	25.00	10.00	2.50
□ 246	Camnitz	25.00	10.00	2.50
□ 247	Campbell S21	50.00	20.00	5.00
□ 248	Fred Clarke	75.00	30.00	7.50
□ 249	Flynn S20	50.00	20.00	5.00
□ 250	Gibson *	25.00	10.00	2.50
□ 251	Hyatt	25.00	10.00	2.50
□ 252	Leach *	25.00	10.00	2.50
□ 253	Leever	25.00	10.00	2.50
□ 254	Leifield	25.00	10.00	2.50
□ 255	Maddox	25.00	10.00	2.50
□ 256	Miller	25.00	10.00	2.50
□ 257	O'Conner	25.00	10.00	2.50
□ 258	Deacon Phillipe	35.00	14.00	3.50
□ 259	Simon S21	50.00	20.00	5.00
□ 260	Hans Wagner *	300.00	120.00	30.00
□ 261	Wilson	25.00	10.00	2.50
□ 262	Bliss S21	50.00	20.00	5.00
□ 263	Roger Bresnahan	50.00	20.00	5.00
□ 264	Bachman	25.00	10.00	2.50
□ 265	Corridon	25.00	10.00	2.50
□ 266	Demmitt S22	50.00	20.00	5.00
□ 267	Ellis	25.00	10.00	2.50
□ 268	Evans S23	50.00	20.00	5.00
□ 269	Harmon S20	50.00	20.00	5.00
□ 270	Miller Huggins	60.00	24.00	6.00
□ 271	Hulswitt	25.00	10.00	2.50
□ 272	Konetchy	25.00	10.00	2.50
□ 273	Lush	25.00	10.00	2.50
□ 274	Mattern	25.00	10.00	2.50
□ 275	Mowery S21	50.00	20.00	5.00
□ 276	Rebel Oakes S24	50.00	20.00	5.00
□ 277	Phelps	25.00	10.00	2.50
□ 278	Sallee	25.00	10.00	2.50
□ 279	Willis	35.00	14.00	3.50
□ 280	Coveleskie: Louisville S22	75.00	30.00	7.50
□ 281	Foster: Rochester S19	75.00	30.00	7.50
□ 282	Frill: Jersey City S20	75.00	30.00	7.50
□ 283	Hughes: Rochester S23	75.00	30.00	7.50
□ 284	Krueger: Sacramento S20	75.00	30.00	7.50
□ 285	Mitchell: Rochester S19	75.00	30.00	7.50
□ 286	O'Hara: Toronto	35.00	14.00	3.50
□ 287	Perring: Columbus S20	75.00	30.00	7.50
□ 288	Ray: Western League S24	75.00	30.00	7.50

N28 Allen and Ginter

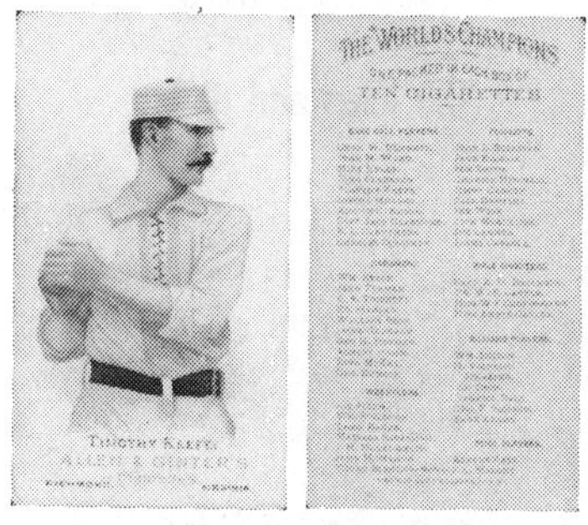

This 50-card set of The World's Champions was marketed by Allen and Ginter in 1887. The cards feature color lithographs of champion athletes from seven categories of sport, with baseball, rowing and boxing each having 10 individuals portrayed. Cards numbered 1 to 10 depict baseball players and cards numbered 11 to 20 depict popular boxers of the era. This set is called the first series although no such title appears on the cards. All 50 cards are checklisted on the reverse, and they are unnumbered. An album (ACC: A16) and an advertising banner (ACC: G20) were also issued in conjunction with this set.

	NRMT	VG-E	GOOD
COMPLETE SET (50)	5000.00	2200.00	600.00
COMMON BASEBALL (1-10)	175.00	70.00	18.00
COMMON BOXERS (11-20)	30.00	12.00	3.00
COMMON OTHERS (21-50)	12.00	5.00	1.20

□ 1	Adrian C. Anson	1000.00	400.00	125.00
□ 2	Chas. W. Bennett	175.00	70.00	18.00
□ 3	R.L. Caruthers	225.00	90.00	22.00

☐ 4 John Clarkson	400.00	160.00	40.00
☐ 5 Charles Comiskey	500.00	200.00	50.00
☐ 6 Capt. Jack Glasscock	225.00	90.00	22.00
☐ 7 Timothy Keefe	400.00	160.00	40.00
☐ 8 Mike Kelly	700.00	280.00	70.00
☐ 9 Joseph Mulvey	175.00	70.00	18.00
☐ 10 John M. Ward	500.00	200.00	50.00
☐ 11 Jimmy Carney	30.00	12.00	3.00
☐ 12 Jimmy Carroll	30.00	12.00	3.00
☐ 13 Jack Dempsey	60.00	24.00	6.00
☐ 14 Jake Kilrain	30.00	12.00	3.00
☐ 15 Joe Lannon	30.00	12.00	3.00
☐ 16 Jack McAuliffe	30.00	12.00	3.00
☐ 17 Charlie Mitchell	30.00	12.00	3.00
☐ 18 Jem Smith	30.00	12.00	3.00
☐ 19 John L. Sullivan	90.00	36.00	9.00
☐ 20 Ike Weir	30.00	12.00	3.00
☐ 21 Wm. Beach	12.00	5.00	1.20
☐ 22 Geo. Bubear	12.00	5.00	1.20
☐ 23 Jacob Gaudaur	12.00	5.00	1.20
☐ 24 Albert Hamm	12.00	5.00	1.20
☐ 25 Ed. Hanlan	12.00	5.00	1.20
☐ 26 Geo. H. Hosmer	12.00	5.00	1.20
☐ 27 John McKay	12.00	5.00	1.20
☐ 28 Wallace Ross	12.00	5.00	1.20
☐ 29 John Teemer	12.00	5.00	1.20
☐ 30 E.A. Trickett	12.00	5.00	1.20
☐ 31 Joe Acton	12.00	5.00	1.20
☐ 32 Theo. Bauer	12.00	5.00	1.20
☐ 33 Young Bibby (Geo. Mehling)	12.00	5.00	1.20
☐ 34 J.F. McLaughlin	12.00	5.00	1.20
☐ 35 John McMahon	12.00	5.00	1.20
☐ 36 Wm. Muldoon	12.00	5.00	1.20
☐ 37 Matsada Sorakichi	12.00	5.00	1.20
☐ 38 Capt. A.H. Bogardus	12.00	5.00	1.20
☐ 39 Dr. W.F. Carver	12.00	5.00	1.20
☐ 40 Hon. W.F. Cody (Buffalo Bill)	60.00	24.00	6.00
☐ 41 Miss Annie Oakley	40.00	16.00	4.00
☐ 42 Yank Adams	12.00	5.00	1.20
☐ 43 Maurice Daly	12.00	5.00	1.20
☐ 44 Jos. Dion	12.00	5.00	1.20
☐ 45 J. Schaefer	12.00	5.00	1.20
☐ 46 Wm. Sexton	12.00	5.00	1.20
☐ 47 Geo. F. Slosson	12.00	5.00	1.20
☐ 48 M. Vignaux	12.00	5.00	1.20
☐ 49 Albert Frey	12.00	5.00	1.20
☐ 50 J.L. Malone	12.00	5.00	1.20

N29 Allen and Ginter

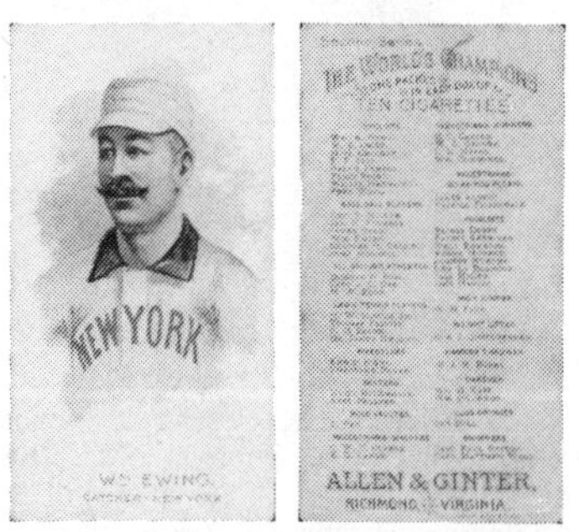

The second series of The World's Champions was probably issued in 1888. Like the first series, the cards are backlisted and unnumbered. However, there are 17 distinct categories of sports represented in this set, with only six baseball players portrayed (as opposed to 10 in the first series). Each card has a color lithograph of the individual set against a white background. An album (ACC: A17) and an advertising banner (ACC: G21) were issued in conjunction with the set. The numbering below is alphabetical within sport, e.g., baseball players (1-6), boxers (7-14), and other sports (15- 50).

	NRMT	VG-E	GOOD
COMPLETE SET (50)	4200.00	1800.00	500.00
COMMON BASEBALL (1-6)	500.00	200.00	50.00
COMMON BOXERS (7-14)	40.00	16.00	4.00
COMMON OTHERS (15-50)	20.00	8.00	2.00
☐ 1 Wm. Ewing	1000.00	400.00	100.00
☐ 2 Jas. H. Fogarty	500.00	200.00	50.00
☐ 3 Charles H. Getzin	500.00	200.00	50.00
☐ 4 Geo. F. Miller	500.00	200.00	50.00
☐ 5 John Morrell	500.00	200.00	50.00
☐ 6 James Ryan	500.00	200.00	50.00
☐ 7 Patsey Duffy	40.00	16.00	4.00
☐ 8 Billy Edwards	40.00	16.00	4.00
☐ 9 Jack Havlin	40.00	16.00	4.00
☐ 10 Patsey Kerrigan	40.00	16.00	4.00
☐ 11 Geo. La Blance	40.00	16.00	4.00
☐ 12 Jack McGee	40.00	16.00	4.00
☐ 13 Frank Murphy	40.00	16.00	4.00
☐ 14 Johnny Murphy	40.00	16.00	4.00
☐ 15 Capt. J.C. Daly	20.00	8.00	2.00
☐ 16 M.W. Ford	20.00	8.00	2.00
☐ 17 Duncan C. Ross	20.00	8.00	2.00
☐ 18 W.E. Crist	20.00	8.00	2.00
☐ 19 H.G. Crocken	20.00	8.00	2.00
☐ 20 Willie Harradon	20.00	8.00	2.00
☐ 21 F.F. Ives	20.00	8.00	2.00
☐ 22 Wm. A. Rowe	20.00	8.00	2.00
☐ 23 Percy Stone	20.00	8.00	2.00
☐ 24 Ralph Temple	20.00	8.00	2.00
☐ 25 Fred Wood	20.00	8.00	2.00
☐ 26 Dr. James Dwight	20.00	8.00	2.00
☐ 27 Thomas Pettit	20.00	8.00	2.00
☐ 28 R.D. Sears	20.00	8.00	2.00
☐ 29 H.W. Slocum Jr.	20.00	8.00	2.00
☐ 30 Theobaud Bauer	20.00	8.00	2.00
☐ 31 Edwin Bibby	20.00	8.00	2.00
☐ 32 Hugh McCormack	20.00	8.00	2.00
☐ 33 Axel Paulsen	20.00	8.00	2.00
☐ 34 T. Ray	20.00	8.00	2.00
☐ 35 C.W.V. Clarke	20.00	8.00	2.00
☐ 36 E.D. Lange	20.00	8.00	2.00
☐ 37 E.C. Carter	20.00	8.00	2.00
☐ 38 Wm. Cummings	20.00	8.00	2.00
☐ 39 W.G. George	20.00	8.00	2.00
☐ 40 L.E. Myers	20.00	8.00	2.00
☐ 41 James Albert	20.00	8.00	2.00
☐ 42 Patrick Fitzgerald	20.00	8.00	2.00
☐ 43 W.B. Page	20.00	8.00	2.00
☐ 44 C.A.J. Queckberner	20.00	8.00	2.00
☐ 45 W.J.M. Barry	20.00	8.00	2.00
☐ 46 Wm. G. East	20.00	8.00	2.00
☐ 47 Wm. O'Connor	20.00	8.00	2.00
☐ 48 Gus Hill	20.00	8.00	2.00
☐ 49 Capt. Paul Boyton	20.00	8.00	2.00
☐ 50 Capt. Matthew Webb	20.00	8.00	2.00

N43 Allen and Ginter

The primary designs of this 50-card set are identical to those of N29, but these are placed on a much larger card with extraneous background detail. The set was produced in 1888 by Allen and Ginter as inserts for a larger tobacco package than those in which sets N28 and N29 were marketed. Cards of this set, which is backlisted, are considered to be much scarcer than their counterparts in N29.

	NRMT	VG-E	GOOD
COMPLETE SET (50)	6000.00	2500.00	700.00
COMMON BASEBALL (1-6)	700.00	280.00	70.00
COMMON BOXERS (7-14)	60.00	24.00	6.00
COMMON OTHERS (15-50)	25.00	10.00	2.50
☐ 1 William Ewing	1250.00	500.00	150.00
☐ 2 Jas. J. Fogarty	700.00	280.00	70.00
☐ 3 Charles Getzein	700.00	280.00	70.00
☐ 4 Geo. F. Miller	700.00	280.00	70.00
☐ 5 John Morrell	700.00	280.00	70.00
☐ 6 James Ryan	700.00	280.00	70.00
☐ 7 Patsey Duffy	60.00	24.00	6.00
☐ 8 Billy Edwards	60.00	24.00	6.00
☐ 9 Jack Havlin	60.00	24.00	6.00
☐ 10 Patsey Kerrigan	60.00	24.00	6.00
☐ 11 George LaBlanche	60.00	24.00	6.00
☐ 12 Jack McGee	60.00	24.00	6.00
☐ 13 Frank Murphy	60.00	24.00	6.00
☐ 14 Johnny Murphy	60.00	24.00	6.00
☐ 15 James Albert	25.00	10.00	2.50
☐ 16 W.J.M. Barry	25.00	10.00	2.50
☐ 17 Theobaud Bauer	25.00	10.00	2.50

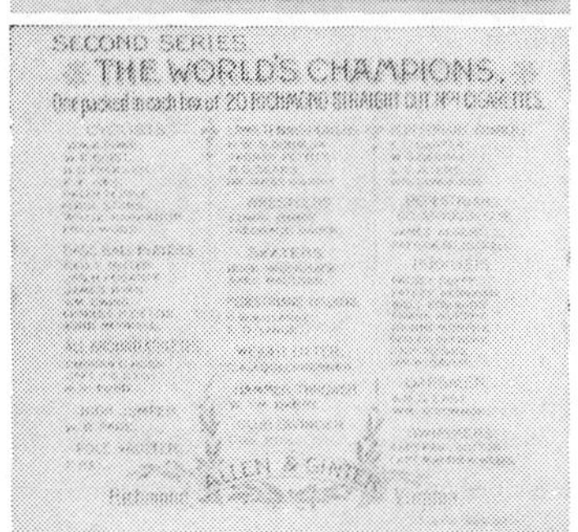

□ 18 Edwin Bibby	25.00	10.00	2.50
□ 19 Capt. Paul Boyton	25.00	10.00	2.50
□ 20 E.C. Carter	25.00	10.00	2.50
□ 21 C.W.V. Clarke	25.00	10.00	2.50
□ 22 W.E. Crist	25.00	10.00	2.50
□ 23 H.G. Crocker	25.00	10.00	2.50
□ 24 Wm. Cummings	25.00	10.00	2.50
□ 25 Capt. J.C. Daly	25.00	10.00	2.50
□ 26 Dr. James Dwight	25.00	10.00	2.50
□ 27 Wm. G. East	25.00	10.00	2.50
□ 28 Patrick Fitzgerald	25.00	10.00	2.50
□ 29 M.W. Ford	25.00	10.00	2.50
□ 30 W.G. George	25.00	10.00	2.50
□ 31 Willie Harradon	25.00	10.00	2.50
□ 32 Gus Hill	25.00	10.00	2.50
□ 33 F.F. Ives	25.00	10.00	2.50
□ 34 E.D. Lange	25.00	10.00	2.50
□ 35 Hugh McCormack	25.00	10.00	2.50
□ 36 L.E. Myers	25.00	10.00	2.50
□ 37 Wm. O'Connor	25.00	10.00	2.50
□ 38 W.B. Page	25.00	10.00	2.50
□ 39 Axel. Paulsen	25.00	10.00	2.50
□ 40 Thomas Pettitt	25.00	10.00	2.50
□ 41 C.A.J. Queckberner	25.00	10.00	2.50
□ 42 T. Ray	25.00	10.00	2.50
□ 43 Duncan C. Ross	25.00	10.00	2.50
□ 44 Wm. A. Rowe	25.00	10.00	2.50
□ 45 R.D. Sears	25.00	10.00	2.50
□ 46 H.W. Slocum Jr.	25.00	10.00	2.50
□ 47 Percy Stone	25.00	10.00	2.50
□ 48 Ralph Temple	25.00	10.00	2.50
□ 49 Capt. Matthew Webb	25.00	10.00	2.50
□ 50 Fred Wood	25.00	10.00	2.50

N162 Goodwin

This 50-card set issued by Goodwin was one of the major competitors to the N28 and N29 sets marketed by Allen and Ginter. It contains individuals representing 18 sports, with eight baseball players pictured. Each color card is backlisted and bears advertising for "Old Judge" and "Gypsy Queen" cigarettes on the front. The set was released to the public in 1888 and an album (ACC: A36) is associated with it as a premium issue.

	NRMT	VG-E	GOOD
COMPLETE SET (50)	6000.00	2500.00	700.00
COMMON BASEBALL (1-8)	300.00	120.00	30.00
COMMON BOXER	35.00	14.00	3.50
COMMON OTHERS	15.00	6.00	1.50
□ 1 Andrews: Phila.	300.00	120.00	30.00
□ 2 Anson: Chicago	1500.00	650.00	200.00
□ 3 Brouthers: Detroit	700.00	280.00	70.00
□ 4 Caruthers: Brooklyn	350.00	140.00	35.00
□ 5 Dunlap: Detroit	300.00	120.00	30.00
□ 6 Glasscock: Indianapolis	350.00	140.00	35.00
□ 7 Keefe: New York	700.00	280.00	70.00
□ 8 Kelly: Boston	1000.00	400.00	125.00
□ 9 Acton (Wrestler)	15.00	6.00	1.50
□ 10 Albert (Pedestrian)	15.00	6.00	1.50
□ 11 Beach (Oarsman)	15.00	6.00	1.50
□ 12 Beecher (Football)	100.00	40.00	10.00
□ 13 Beeckman (Lawn Tennis)	15.00	6.00	1.50
□ 14 Bogardus (Marksman)	15.00	6.00	1.50
□ 15 Buffalo Bill (Wild West Hunter)	60.00	24.00	6.00
□ 16 Daly (Billiards)	15.00	6.00	1.50
□ 17 Dempsey (Pugilist)	75.00	30.00	7.50
□ 18 D'oro (Pool)	15.00	6.00	1.50
□ 19 Dwight (Lawn Tennis)	15.00	6.00	1.50
□ 20 Fitzgerald (Pedestrian)	15.00	6.00	1.50
□ 21 Garrison (Jockey)	15.00	6.00	1.50
□ 22 Gaudaur (Oarsman)	15.00	6.00	1.50
□ 23 Hanlan (Oarsman)	15.00	6.00	1.50
□ 24 Kilrain (Pugilist)	35.00	14.00	3.50
□ 25 MacKenzie (Chess)	15.00	6.00	1.50
□ 26 McLaughlin (Jockey)	15.00	6.00	1.50
□ 27 Mitchell (Pugilist)	35.00	14.00	3.50
□ 28 Muldoon (Wrestler)	15.00	6.00	1.50
□ 29 Murphy (Jockey)	15.00	6.00	1.50
□ 30 Myers (Runner)	15.00	6.00	1.50
□ 31 Page (High Jumper)	15.00	6.00	1.50
□ 32 Prince (Bicyclist)	15.00	6.00	1.50
□ 33 Ross (Broadswordsman)	15.00	6.00	1.50
□ 34 Rowe (Bicyclist)	15.00	6.00	1.50
□ 35 Rowell (Pedestrian)	15.00	6.00	1.50
□ 36 Schaefer (Billiards)	15.00	6.00	1.50
□ 37 Sears (Lawn Tennis)	15.00	6.00	1.50
□ 38 Sexton (Billiards)	15.00	6.00	1.50
□ 39 Slosson (Billiards)	15.00	6.00	1.50
□ 40 Smith (Pugilist)	35.00	14.00	3.50
□ 41 Steinitz (Chess)	15.00	6.00	1.50
□ 42 Stevens (Bicyclist)	15.00	6.00	1.50
□ 43 Sullivan (Pugilist)	90.00	36.00	9.00
□ 44 Taylor (Lawn Tennis)	15.00	6.00	1.50
□ 45 Teemer (Oarsman)	15.00	6.00	1.50
□ 46 Vignaux (Billiards)	15.00	6.00	1.50
□ 47 Voss (Strongest Man in the World)	15.00	6.00	1.50
□ 48 Wood (Bicyclist)	15.00	6.00	1.50
□ 49 Wood (Jockey)	15.00	6.00	1.50
□ 50 Zukertort (Chess)	15.00	6.00	1.50

N172 Old Judge

The Goodwin Company's baseball series depicts hundreds of ballplayers from more than 40 major and minor league teams as well as boxers and wrestlers. The cards (approximately 1 1/2" by 2

1/2") are actually photographs from the Hall studio in New York which were pasted onto thick cardboard. The pictures are sepia in color with either a white or pink cast, and the cards are blank backed. They are found either numbered or unnumbered, with or without a copyright date, and with hand printed or machine printed names. All known cards have the name "Goodwin Co., New York" at the base. The cards were marketed during the period 1887-1890 in packs of "Old Judge" and "Gypsy Queen" cigarettes (cards marked with the latter brand are worth double the values listed below). They have been listed alphabetically and assigned numbers in the checklist below for simplicity's sake; the various poses known for some players also have not been listed for the same reason. Some of the players are pictured in horizontal (HOR) poses. In all, more than 2300 different Goodwin cards are known to collectors, with more being discovered every year. Cards from the "Spotted Tie" sub-series are denoted in the checklist below by SPOT.

	NRMT	VG-E	GOOD
COMPLETE SET	75000.	30000.	11000.
COMMON PLAYER	90.00	36.00	9.00
COMMON PLAYER (DOUBLE)	125.00	50.00	12.50
COMMON BROWNS CHAMP	150.00	60.00	15.00
COMMON PLAYER (PCL)	300.00	120.00	30.00
COMMON SPOTTED TIE	300.00	120.00	30.00

	No.	Player	NRMT	VG-E	GOOD
□	1	Gus Albert: Cleveland-Milwaukee	90.00	36.00	9.00
□	2	Charles Alcott: St. Louis Whites-Mansfield	90.00	36.00	9.00
□	3	Alexander: Des Moines	90.00	36.00	9.00
□	4	Myron Allen: K.C.	90.00	36.00	9.00
□	5	Bob Allen: Pitts.-Phila. N.L.	90.00	36.00	9.00
□	6	Uncle Bill Alvord: Toledo-Des Moines	90.00	36.00	9.00
□	7	Varney Anderson: St.Paul	90.00	36.00	9.00
□	8	Ed Andrews: Phila.	90.00	36.00	9.00
□	9	Andrews and Hoover: Philadelphia	125.00	50.00	12.50
□	10	Wally Andrews: Omaha	90.00	36.00	9.00
□	11	Bill Annis: Omaha-Worchester	90.00	36.00	9.00
□	12	Cap Anson: Chicago	900.00	400.00	100.00
□	13	Old Hoss Ardner: Kansas City-St. Joe	90.00	36.00	9.00
□	14	Tug Arundel: Indianapolis-Whites	90.00	36.00	9.00
□	15	Bakley: Jersey-Cleve.	90.00	36.00	9.00
□	16	Clarence Baldwin: Cincinnati	90.00	36.00	9.00
□	17	Mark (Fido) Baldwin: Chicago-Columbus	90.00	36.00	9.00
□	18	Lady Baldwin: Detroit	90.00	36.00	9.00
□	19	James Banning: Wash.	90.00	36.00	9.00
□	20	Samuel Barkley: Pittsburgh-K.C.	90.00	36.00	9.00
□	21	John Barnes: Mgr. St. Paul	90.00	36.00	9.00
□	22	Bald Billy Barnie: Mgr. Baltimore	125.00	50.00	12.50
□	23	Charles Bassett: Indianapolis-N.Y.	90.00	36.00	9.00
□	24	Charles Bastian: Phila.-Chicago	90.00	36.00	9.00
□	25	Bastian and Shriver: Philadelphia	125.00	50.00	12.50
□	26	Ollie Beard: Cinc.	90.00	36.00	9.00
□	27	Ebenezer Beatin: Cleve.	90.00	36.00	9.00
□	28	Jake Beckley: "Eagle Eye" Whites-Pittsburgh	350.00	140.00	35.00
□	29	Stephen Behel SPOT	300.00	120.00	30.00
□	30	Charles Bennett: Detroit-Boston	90.00	36.00	9.00
□	31	Louis Bierbauer: A's	90.00	36.00	9.00
□	32	Bierbauer and Gamble Athletics	125.00	50.00	12.50
□	33	Bill Bishop: Pittsburgh-Syracuse	90.00	36.00	9.00
□	34	William Blair: A's-Hamiltons	90.00	36.00	9.00
□	35	Ned Bligh: Columbus	90.00	36.00	9.00
□	36	Bogart: Indianapolis	90.00	36.00	9.00
□	37	Boyce: Washington	90.00	36.00	9.00
□	38	Jake Boyd: Maroons	90.00	36.00	9.00
□	39	Honest John Boyle: St. Louis-Chicago	90.00	36.00	9.00
□	40	Handsome Henry Boyle Indianapolis-N.Y.	90.00	36.00	9.00
□	41	Nick Bradley: K.C.- Worchester	90.00	36.00	9.00
□	42	George(Grin) Bradley Sioux City	90.00	36.00	9.00
□	43	Stephen Brady SPOT	300.00	120.00	30.00
□	44	Breckinridge: Sacramento PCL	300.00	120.00	30.00
□	45	Jim Brennan: Kansas City- A's	90.00	36.00	9.00
□	46	Timothy Brosnan: Minn.-Sioux City	90.00	36.00	9.00
□	47	Cal Broughton: Detroit-Boston	90.00	36.00	9.00
□	48	Big Dan Brouthers: Detroit-Boston	350.00	140.00	35.00
□	49	Thomas Brown: Pittsburgh-Boston	90.00	36.00	9.00
□	50	Brown: California-N.Y.	90.00	36.00	9.00
□	51	Pete Browning: "Gladiator" Louisville	150.00	60.00	15.00
□	52	Charles Brynan: Chicago-Des Moines	90.00	36.00	9.00
□	53	Al Buckenberger: Mgr. Columbus	90.00	36.00	9.00
□	54	Dick Buckley: Indianapolis-N.Y.	90.00	36.00	9.00
□	55	Charles Buffington: Philadelphia	90.00	36.00	9.00
□	56	Ernest Burch: Brooklyn-Whites	90.00	36.00	9.00
□	57	Bill Burdick: Omaha-Indianapolis	90.00	36.00	9.00
□	58	Black Jack Burdock: Boston-Brooklyn	90.00	36.00	9.00
□	59	Robert Burks: Sioux City	90.00	36.00	9.00
□	60	George(Watch) Burnham Mgr. Indianapolis	125.00	50.00	12.50
□	61	Burns: Omaha	90.00	36.00	9.00
□	62	Jimmy Burns: K.C.	90.00	36.00	9.00
□	63	Tommy (Oyster) Burns Baltimore-Brooklyn	90.00	36.00	9.00

□ 64	Thomas E. Burns: Chicago	90.00	36.00	9.00
□ 65A	Doc Bushong: Brook.	90.00	36.00	9.00
□ 65B	Doc Bushong: Browns Champ	150.00	60.00	15.00
□ 66	Patsy Cahill: Ind.	90.00	36.00	9.00
□ 67	Count Campau: Kansas City-Detroit	90.00	36.00	9.00
□ 68	Jimmy Canavan: Omaha	90.00	36.00	9.00
□ 69	Bart Cantz: Whites-Baltimore	90.00	36.00	9.00
□ 70	Handsome Jack Carney Washington	90.00	36.00	9.00
□ 71	Hick Carpenter Cincinnati	90.00	36.00	9.00
□ 72	Cliff Carroll: Wash.	90.00	36.00	9.00
□ 73	Scrappy Carroll: St.Paul-Chicago	90.00	36.00	9.00
□ 74	Frederick Carroll: Pitts.	90.00	36.00	9.00
□ 75	Jumbo Cartwright: Kansas City-St. Joe	90.00	36.00	9.00
□ 76A	Bob Caruthers: "Parisian" Brooklyn	80.00	32.00	8.00
□ 76B	Bob Caruthers: "Parisian" Browns Champs	200.00	80.00	20.00
□ 77	Daniel Casey: Phila.	90.00	36.00	9.00
□ 78	Icebox Chamberlain: St. Louis	90.00	36.00	9.00
□ 79	Cupid Childs: Phila.-Syracuse	90.00	36.00	9.00
□ 80	Bob Clark: Washington	90.00	36.00	9.00
□ 81	Owen Clark: Washington	90.00	36.00	9.00
□ 82	Clarke and Hughes: Brooklyn HOR	125.00	50.00	12.50
□ 83	William(Dad) Clarke: Chicago-Omaha	90.00	36.00	9.00
□ 84	John Clarkson: Chicago-Boston	350.00	140.00	35.00
□ 85	Jack Clements: Philadelphia	90.00	36.00	9.00
□ 86	Elmer Cleveland: Omaha-New York	90.00	36.00	9.00
□ 87	Monk Cline: K.C.-Sioux City	90.00	36.00	9.00
□ 88	Cody: Des Moines	90.00	36.00	9.00
□ 89	John Coleman: Pittsburgh - A's	90.00	36.00	9.00
□ 90	Bill Collins: New York-Newark	90.00	36.00	9.00
□ 91	Hub Collins: Louisville-Brooklyn	90.00	36.00	9.00
□ 92A	Charles Comiskey: Browns Champs	500.00	200.00	50.00
□ 92B	Commy Comiskey: St. Louis-Chicago	350.00	140.00	35.00
□ 93	Pete Connell: Des Moines	90.00	36.00	9.00
□ 94A	Roger Connor: All-Star	350.00	140.00	35.00
□ 94B	Roger Connor: New York	350.00	140.00	35.00
□ 95	Richard Conway: Boston-Worchester	90.00	36.00	9.00
□ 96	Peter Conway: Det.-Pitts.-Ind.	90.00	36.00	9.00
□ 97	James Conway: K.C.	90.00	36.00	9.00
□ 98	Paul Cook: Louisville	90.00	36.00	9.00
□ 99	Jimmy Cooney: Omaha-Chicago	90.00	36.00	9.00
□ 100	Larry Corcoran: Indianapolis-London	90.00	36.00	9.00
□ 101	Pop Corkhill: Cincinnnati-Brooklyn	90.00	36.00	9.00
□ 102	Roscoe Coughlin: Maroons-Chicago	90.00	36.00	9.00
□ 103	Cannon Ball Crane: New York	90.00	36.00	9.00
□ 104	Samuel Crane: Wash.	90.00	36.00	9.00
□ 105	Jack Crogan: Maroons	90.00	36.00	9.00
□ 106	John Crooks: Whites-Omaha	90.00	36.00	9.00
□ 107	Lave Cross: Louisville-A's-Phila.	90.00	36.00	9.00
□ 108	Bill Crossley: Milw.	90.00	36.00	9.00
□ 109A	Joe Crotty SPOT	300.00	120.00	30.00
□ 109B	Joe Crotty: Sioux City	90.00	36.00	9.00
□ 110	Billy Crowell: Cleveland-St. Joe	90.00	36.00	9.00
□ 111	Jim Cudworth: St. Louis-Worchester	90.00	36.00	9.00
□ 112	Bert Cunningham: Baltimore-Phila.	90.00	36.00	9.00
□ 113	Tacks Curtis: St. Joe	90.00	36.00	9.00
□ 114	Ed Cushman SPOT	300.00	120.00	30.00
□ 115	Tony Cusick: Mil.	90.00	36.00	9.00
□ 116	Dailey: Oakland PCL	300.00	120.00	30.00
□ 117	Edward Dailey: Phil.-Wash.-Columbus	90.00	36.00	9.00
□ 118	Bill Daley: Boston	90.00	36.00	9.00
□ 119	Con Daley: Boston-Indianapolis	90.00	36.00	9.00
□ 120	Abner Dalrymple: Pittsburgh-Denver	90.00	36.00	9.00
□ 121	Tom Daly: Chicago-Wash.-Cleve.	90.00	36.00	9.00
□ 122	James Daly: Minn.	90.00	36.00	9.00
□ 123	Law Daniels: K.C.	90.00	36.00	9.00
□ 124	Dell Darling: Chicago	90.00	36.00	9.00
□ 125	Wm. Darnbrough: Denver	90.00	36.00	9.00
□ 126	D. Davin: Milwaukee	90.00	36.00	9.00
□ 127	Jumbo Davis: K.C.	90.00	36.00	9.00
□ 128	Pat Dealey: Wash.	90.00	36.00	9.00
□ 129	Thomas Deasley: New York-Washington	90.00	36.00	9.00
□ 130	Edward Decker: Phil.	90.00	36.00	9.00
□ 131	Big Ed Delahanty: Philadelphia	450.00	180.00	45.00
□ 132	Jeremiah Denny: Indianapolis-New York	90.00	36.00	9.00
□ 133	James Devlin: St.L.	90.00	36.00	9.00
□ 134	Thomas Dolan: Whites-St. Louis-Denver	90.00	36.00	9.00
□ 135	Jack Donahue: San Francisco PCL	300.00	120.00	30.00
□ 136A	James Donahue SPOT	300.00	120.00	30.00
□ 136B	James Donahue: K.C.	90.00	36.00	9.00
□ 137	James Donnelly: Washington	90.00	36.00	9.00
□ 138	Dooley: Oakland PCL	300.00	120.00	30.00
□ 139	J. Doran: Omaha	90.00	36.00	9.00
□ 140	Michael Dorgan: N.Y.	90.00	36.00	9.00
□ 141	Doyle: San Fran. PCL	300.00	120.00	30.00
□ 142	Homerun Duffe: St.L.	90.00	36.00	9.00
□ 143	Hugh Duffy: Chicago	350.00	140.00	35.00
□ 144	Dan Dugdale: Maroons-Minneapolis	90.00	36.00	9.00
□ 145	Dugrahm: Maroons	90.00	36.00	9.00
□ 146	Duck Duke: Minn.	90.00	36.00	9.00
□ 147	Sure Shot Dunlap: Pittsburgh	90.00	36.00	9.00
□ 148	J. Dunn: Maroons	90.00	36.00	9.00
□ 149	Jesse(Cyclone)Duryea St. Paul-Cinc.	90.00	36.00	9.00
□ 150	John Dwyer: Chicago-Maroons	90.00	36.00	9.00
□ 151	Billy Earle: Cincinnati-St.Paul	90.00	36.00	9.00
□ 152	Buck Ebright: Wash.	90.00	36.00	9.00
□ 153	Red Ehret: Louisville	90.00	36.00	9.00
□ 154	R. Emmerke: Des Moines	90.00	36.00	9.00
□ 155	Dude Esterbrook: Louisville-Ind.-New York-All Star	90.00	36.00	9.00
□ 156	Henry Esterday: K.C.-Columbus	90.00	36.00	9.00
□ 157	Long John Ewing: Louisville-N.Y.	90.00	36.00	9.00
□ 158	Buck Ewing: New York	350.00	140.00	35.00
□ 159	Ewing and Mascot: New York	250.00	100.00	25.00
□ 160	Jay Faatz: Cleveland	90.00	36.00	9.00
□ 161	Clinkgers Fagan: Kansas City-Denver	90.00	36.00	9.00
□ 162	William Farmer: Pittsburgh-St. Paul	90.00	36.00	9.00
□ 163	Sidney Farrar: Philadelphia	90.00	36.00	9.00
□ 164	John(Moose) Farrell: Wash.-Baltimore	90.00	36.00	9.00
□ 165	Charles(Duke)Farrell Chicago	90.00	36.00	9.00
□ 166	Frank Fennelly: Cincinnati-A's	90.00	36.00	9.00

☐ 167	Chas. Ferguson: Phila.	90.00	36.00	9.00
☐ 168	Colonel Ferson: Washington	90.00	36.00	9.00
☐ 169	Wallace Fessenden: Umpire National	125.00	50.00	12.50
☐ 170	Jocko Fields: Pitts.	90.00	36.00	9.00
☐ 171	Fischer: Maroons	90.00	36.00	9.00
☐ 172	Thomas Flanigan: Cleve.-Sioux City	90.00	36.00	9.00
☐ 173	Silver Flint: Chicago	90.00	36.00	9.00
☐ 174	Thomas Flood: St. Joe	90.00	36.00	9.00
☐ 175	Flynn: Omaha	90.00	36.00	9.00
☐ 176	James Fogarty: Philadelphia	90.00	36.00	9.00
☐ 177	Frank(Monkey)Foreman Baltimore-Cinc.	90.00	36.00	9.00
☐ 178	Thomas Forster: Milwaukee-Hartford	90.00	36.00	9.00
☐ 179A	Elmer E. Foster SPOT	300.00	120.00	30.00
☐ 179B	Elmer Foster: New York-Chicago	90.00	36.00	9.00
☐ 180	F.W. Foster SPOT T.W. Forster (sic)	300.00	120.00	30.00
☐ 181A	Scissors Foutz: Browns Champ	150.00	60.00	15.00
☐ 181B	Scissors Foutz: Brooklyn	90.00	36.00	9.00
☐ 182	Julie Freeman: St.L.-Milwaukee	90.00	36.00	9.00
☐ 183	Will Fry: St. Joe	90.00	36.00	9.00
☐ 184	Fudger: Oakland PCL	300.00	120.00	30.00
☐ 185	William Fuller: Milwaukee	90.00	36.00	9.00
☐ 186	Shorty Fuller: St.Louis	90.00	36.00	9.00
☐ 187	Christopher Fullmer: Baltimore	90.00	36.00	9.00
☐ 188	Fullmer and Tucker: Baltimore HOR	125.00	50.00	12.50
☐ 189	Honest John Gaffney: Mgr. Washington	125.00	50.00	12.50
☐ 190	Pud Galvin: Pitts.	350.00	140.00	35.00
☐ 191	Robert Gamble: A's	90.00	36.00	9.00
☐ 192	Charles Ganzel: Detroit-Boston	90.00	36.00	9.00
☐ 193	Frank (Gid) Gardner: Phila.-Washington	90.00	36.00	9.00
☐ 194	Gardner and Murray: Washington HOR	125.00	50.00	12.50
☐ 195	Ed Gastfield: Omaha	90.00	36.00	9.00
☐ 196	Hank Gastreich: Columbus	90.00	36.00	9.00
☐ 197	Emil Geiss: Chicago	90.00	36.00	9.00
☐ 198	Frenchy Genins: Sioux City	90.00	36.00	9.00
☐ 199	William George: N.Y.	90.00	36.00	9.00
☐ 200	Move Up Joe Gerhardt All Star-Jersey City	90.00	36.00	9.00
☐ 201	Pretzels Getzein: Detroit-Ind.	90.00	36.00	9.00
☐ 202	Robert Gilks: Cleve.	90.00	36.00	9.00
☐ 203	Pete Gillespie: N.Y.	90.00	36.00	9.00
☐ 204	Barney Gilligan Washington-Detroit	90.00	36.00	9.00
☐ 205	Frank Gilmore: Wash.	90.00	36.00	9.00
☐ 206	Lee Gisbon: A's	90.00	36.00	9.00
☐ 207	Pebbly Jack Glasscock Indianapolis-N.Y.	125.00	50.00	12.50
☐ 208	Kid Gleason: Phila.	90.00	36.00	9.00
☐ 209A	Brother Bill Gleason A's-Louisville	90.00	36.00	9.00
☐ 209B	William Bill Gleason Browns Champs	150.00	60.00	15.00
☐ 210	Mouse Glenn: Sioux City	90.00	36.00	9.00
☐ 211	Walt Goldsby: Balt.	90.00	36.00	9.00
☐ 212	Michael Goodfellow: Cleveland-Detroit	90.00	36.00	9.00
☐ 213	George Pianolegs Gore New York	90.00	36.00	9.00
☐ 214	Frank Graves: Minn.	90.00	36.00	9.00
☐ 215	William Greenwood: Baltimore-Columbus	90.00	36.00	9.00
☐ 216	Michael Greer: Cleveland-Brooklyn	90.00	36.00	9.00
☐ 217	Mike Griffin: Baltimore-Phila NL	90.00	36.00	9.00
☐ 218	Clark Griffith: Milwaukee	350.00	140.00	35.00
☐ 219	Henry Gruber: Cleve.	90.00	36.00	9.00
☐ 220	Addison Gumbert: Chicago-Boston	90.00	36.00	9.00
☐ 221	Thomas Gunning: Philadelphia-A's	90.00	36.00	9.00
☐ 222	Joseph Gunson: K.C.	90.00	36.00	9.00
☐ 223	George Haddock: Washington	90.00	36.00	9.00
☐ 224	William Hafner: K.C.	90.00	36.00	9.00
☐ 225	Willie Hahm: Chicago Mascot	90.00	36.00	9.00
☐ 226	William Hallman: Philadelphia	90.00	36.00	9.00
☐ 227	Charlie Hallstrom: Minn.	90.00	36.00	9.00
☐ 228	Billy Hamilton: Kansas City-Phila.	400.00	160.00	40.00
☐ 229	Hamm and Williamson:	125.00	50.00	12.50
☐ 230A	Frank Hankinson: SPOT	300.00	120.00	30.00
☐ 230B	Frank Hankinson: Kansas City	90.00	36.00	9.00
☐ 231	Ned Hanlon: Det.-Boston-Pitts.	125.00	50.00	12.50
☐ 232	William Hanrahan: Maroons-Minn.	90.00	36.00	9.00
☐ 233	Hapeman: Sacramento PCL	300.00	120.00	30.00
☐ 234	Pa Harkins: Brooklyn-Baltimore	90.00	36.00	9.00
☐ 235	William Hart: Cinc.-Des Moines	90.00	36.00	9.00
☐ 236	Wm. Hasamdear: K.C.	90.00	36.00	9.00
☐ 237	Colonel Hatfield: New York	90.00	36.00	9.00
☐ 238	Egyptian Healey: Wash.-Indianapolis	90.00	36.00	9.00
☐ 239	J.C. Healy: Omaha-Denver	90.00	36.00	9.00
☐ 240	Guy Hecker: Louisville	90.00	36.00	9.00
☐ 241	Tony Hellman: Sioux City	90.00	36.00	9.00
☐ 242	Hardie Henderson: Brook.-Pitts.-Balt.	90.00	36.00	9.00
☐ 243	Henderson and Greer: Brooklyn	125.00	50.00	12.50
☐ 244	Moxie Hengle: Maroons-Minneapolis	90.00	36.00	9.00
☐ 245	John Henry: Phila.	90.00	36.00	9.00
☐ 246	Edward Herr: Whites-Milwaukee	90.00	36.00	9.00
☐ 247	Hunkey Hines: Whites	90.00	36.00	9.00
☐ 248	Paul Hines: Wash.-Indianapolis	90.00	36.00	9.00
☐ 249	Texas Wonder Hoffman: Denver	90.00	36.00	9.00
☐ 250	Eddie Hogan: Cleve.	90.00	36.00	9.00
☐ 251A	William Holbert SPOT	300.00	120.00	30.00
☐ 251B	William Holbert: Brooklyn-Mets-Jersey City	90.00	36.00	9.00
☐ 252	James(Bugs) Holliday: Des Moines-Cinc.	90.00	36.00	9.00
☐ 253	Charles Hoover: Maroons-Chi.-K.C.	90.00	36.00	9.00
☐ 254	Buster Hoover: Phila.-Toronto	90.00	36.00	9.00
☐ 255	Jack Horner: Milwaukee-New Haven	90.00	36.00	9.00
☐ 256	Horner and Warner: Milwaukee	125.00	50.00	12.50
☐ 257	Michael Horning: Boston-Balt.-N.Y.	90.00	36.00	9.00
☐ 258	Pete Hotaling: Cleveland	90.00	36.00	9.00
☐ 259	William Howes: Minn..-St. Paul	90.00	36.00	9.00
☐ 260	Dummy Hoy: Washington	200.00	80.00	20.00
☐ 261A	Nat Hudson: Browns Champ	150.00	60.00	15.00
☐ 261B	Nat Hudson: St. Louis	90.00	36.00	9.00
☐ 262	Mickey Hughes: Brk.	90.00	36.00	9.00
☐ 263	Hungler: Sioux City	90.00	36.00	9.00
☐ 264	Wild Bill Hutchinson: Chicago	90.00	36.00	9.00
☐ 265	John Irwin: Wash.-Wilkes Barre	90.00	36.00	9.00
☐ 266	Cutrate Irwin: Phila.-Boston-Wash.	90.00	36.00	9.00
☐ 267	A.C. Jantzen: Minn.	90.00	36.00	9.00
☐ 268	Frederick Jevne: Minn.-St. Paul	90.00	36.00	9.00
☐ 269	John Johnson:	90.00	36.00	9.00

	K.C.-Columbus			
□ 270	Richard Johnston: .... Boston	90.00	36.00	9.00
□ 271	Jordan: Minneapolis	90.00	36.00	9.00
□ 272	Heinie Kappell: .... Columbus-Cincinnati	90.00	36.00	9.00
□ 273	Keas: Milwaukee	90.00	36.00	9.00
□ 274	Sir Timothy Keefe: .... New York	350.00	140.00	35.00
□ 275	Keefe and Richardson .... Stealing 2nd Base New York HOR	250.00	100.00	25.00
□ 276	George Keefe: Wash.	90.00	36.00	9.00
□ 277	James Keenan: Cinc.	90.00	36.00	9.00
□ 278	Mike (King) Kelly .... "10,000" Chic-Boston	600.00	240.00	60.00
□ 279	Honest John Kelly: .... Mgr. Louisville	125.00	50.00	12.50
□ 280	Kelly: (Umpire) .... Western Association	125.00	50.00	12.50
□ 281	Charles Kelly: .... Philadelphia	90.00	36.00	9.00
□ 282	Kelly and Powell: .... Umpire and Manager Sioux City	125.00	50.00	12.50
□ 283A	Rudolph Kemmler: .... Browns Champ	150.00	60.00	15.00
□ 283B	Rudolph Kemmler: .... St. Paul	90.00	36.00	9.00
□ 284	Theodore Kennedy: .... Des Moines-Omaha	125.00	50.00	12.50
□ 285	J.J. Kenyon: .... Whites-Des Moines	90.00	36.00	9.00
□ 286	John Kerins: .... Louisville	90.00	36.00	9.00
□ 287	Matthew Kilroy: .... Baltimore-Boston	90.00	36.00	9.00
□ 288	Charles King: .... St.L.-Chi.	90.00	36.00	9.00
□ 289	Aug. Kloff: .... Minn.-St.Joe	90.00	36.00	9.00
□ 290	William Klusman: .... Milwaukee-Denver	90.00	36.00	9.00
□ 291	Phillip Knell: .... St. Joe-Phila.	90.00	36.00	9.00
□ 292	Fred Knouf: .... St. Louis	90.00	36.00	9.00
□ 293	Charles Kremmeyer: ...... Sacramento PCL	300.00	120.00	30.00
□ 294	William Krieg: .... Wash.-St. Joe-Minn.	90.00	36.00	9.00
□ 295	Krieg and Kloff: .... Minneapolis	125.00	50.00	12.50
□ 296	Gus Krock: Chicago	90.00	36.00	9.00
□ 297	Willie Kuehne: .... Pittsburgh	90.00	36.00	9.00
□ 298	Frederick Lange: .... Maroons	90.00	36.00	9.00
□ 299	Ted Larkin: A's	90.00	36.00	9.00
□ 300A	Arlie Latham: .... Browns Champ	175.00	70.00	18.00
□ 300B	Arlie Latham: .... St. Louis-Chicago	125.00	50.00	12.50
□ 301	John Lauer: .... Pittsburgh	90.00	36.00	9.00
□ 302	Lawless: Columbus	90.00	36.00	9.00
□ 303	John Leighton: Omaha ...	90.00	36.00	9.00
□ 304	Levy: San Fran. PCL	300.00	120.00	30.00
□ 305	Tom Loftus MG: .... Whites-Cleveland	90.00	36.00	9.00
□ 306	Lohbeck: Cleveland	90.00	36.00	9.00
□ 307	Herman(Germany)Long . Maroons-K.C.	90.00	36.00	9.00
□ 308	Danny Long: Oak. PCL ...	300.00	120.00	30.00
□ 309	Tom Lovett: .... Omaha-Brooklyn	90.00	36.00	9.00
□ 310	Bobby (Link) Lowe: .... Milwaukee	150.00	60.00	15.00
□ 311A	Jack Lynch SPOT	300.00	120.00	30.00
□ 311B	John Lynch: .... All Stars	90.00	36.00	9.00
□ 312	Dennis Lyons: A's	90.00	36.00	9.00
□ 313	Harry Lyons: St. L.	90.00	36.00	9.00
□ 314	Connie Mack: Wash.	750.00	300.00	75.00
□ 315	Joe (Reddie) Mack: .... Louisville	90.00	36.00	9.00
□ 316	James (Little Mack) .... Macullar: Des Moines-Milwaukee	90.00	36.00	9.00
□ 317	Kid Madden: Boston	90.00	36.00	9.00
□ 318	Daniel Mahoney: .... St. Joe	90.00	36.00	9.00
□ 319	Willard(Grasshopper) ...... Maines: St. Paul	90.00	36.00	9.00
□ 320	Fred Mann: .... St.Louis-Hartford	90.00	36.00	9.00
□ 321	Jimmy Manning: K.C.	90.00	36.00	9.00
□ 322	Charles(Lefty) Marr: .... Col.-Cinc.	90.00	36.00	9.00
□ 323	Mascot (Willie .... Breslin): New York	125.00	50.00	12.50
□ 324	Samuel Maskery: .... Milwaukee- Des Moines	90.00	36.00	9.00
□ 325	Bobby Mathews: A's	90.00	36.00	9.00
□ 326	Michael Mattimore: .... New York-A's	90.00	36.00	9.00
□ 327	Albert Maul: Pitts.	90.00	36.00	9.00
□ 328A	Albert Mays SPOT	300.00	120.00	30.00
□ 328B	Albert Mays: .... Columbus	90.00	36.00	9.00
□ 329	James McAleer: .... Cleveland	90.00	36.00	9.00
□ 330	Thomas McCarthy: .... Phila.-St. Louis	350.00	140.00	35.00
□ 331	John McCarthy: K.C.	90.00	36.00	9.00
□ 332	James McCauley: .... Maroons-Phila.	90.00	36.00	9.00
□ 333	William McClellan: .... Brooklyn-Denver	90.00	36.00	9.00
□ 334	John McCormack: .... Whites	90.00	36.00	9.00
□ 335	Big Jim McCormick: .... Chicago-Pittsburgh	90.00	36.00	9.00
□ 336	McCreachery: .... Mgr. Indianapolis	125.00	50.00	12.50
□ 337	Thomas McCullum: .... Minneapolis	90.00	36.00	9.00
□ 338	James(Chippy)McGarr: .. St. Louis-K.C.	90.00	36.00	9.00
□ 339	Jack McGeachy: Ind.	90.00	36.00	9.00
□ 340	John McGlone: .... Cleveland-Detroit	90.00	36.00	9.00
□ 341	James(Deacon)McGuire . Phila.-Toronto	90.00	36.00	9.00
□ 342	Bill (Gunner) .... McGunnigle: Mgr. Brooklyn	125.00	50.00	12.50
□ 343	Ed McKean: Cleveland ...	90.00	36.00	9.00
□ 344	Alex McKinnon: .... Pittsburgh	90.00	36.00	9.00
□ 345	Thomas McLaughlin .... SPOT	300.00	120.00	30.00
□ 346	John (Bid) McPhee: .... Cincinnati	90.00	36.00	9.00
□ 347	James McQuaid: .... Denver	90.00	36.00	9.00
□ 348	John McQuaid: .... Umpire Amer. Assoc.	125.00	50.00	12.50
□ 349	Jame McTamany: .... Brook.-Col.-K.C.	90.00	36.00	9.00
□ 350	George McVey: .... Mil.-Denver-St. Joe	90.00	36.00	9.00
□ 351	Meegan: San Fran. .... PCL	300.00	120.00	30.00
□ 352	John Messitt: Omaha	90.00	36.00	9.00
□ 353	George(Doggie)Miller ..... Pittsburgh	90.00	36.00	9.00
□ 354	Joseph Miller: .... Omaha-Minneapolis	90.00	36.00	9.00
□ 355	Jocko Milligan: .... St. Louis-Phila.	90.00	36.00	9.00
□ 356	E.L. Mills: .... Milwaukee	90.00	36.00	9.00
□ 357	Minnehan: .... Minneapolis	90.00	36.00	9.00
□ 358	Samuel Moffet: Ind.	90.00	36.00	9.00
□ 359	Honest Morrill: .... Boston-Washington	90.00	36.00	9.00
□ 360	Ed(Cannonball)Morris ..... Pittsburgh	90.00	36.00	9.00
□ 361	Morrisey: St. Paul	90.00	36.00	9.00
□ 362	Tony(Count) Mullane: ..... Cincinnati	125.00	50.00	12.50
□ 363	Joseph Mulvey: .... Philadelphia	90.00	36.00	9.00
□ 364	P.L. Murphy: .... St. Paul	90.00	36.00	9.00
□ 365	P.J. Murphy: .... New York	90.00	36.00	9.00
□ 366	Miah Murray: Wash.	90.00	36.00	9.00
□ 367	James (Truthful) .... Mutrie: Mgr. N.Y.	90.00	36.00	9.00
□ 368	George Myers: .... Indianapolis-Phila.	90.00	36.00	9.00
□ 369	Al (Cod) Myers: .... Washington	90.00	36.00	9.00
□ 370	Thomas Nagle: .... Omaha-Chi.	90.00	36.00	9.00

☐ 371	Billy Nash: Boston	90.00	36.00	9.00
☐ 372	Jack(Candy) Nelson: SPOT	300.00	120.00	30.00
☐ 373	Kid Nichols: Omaha	450.00	180.00	45.00
☐ 374	Samuel Nichols: Pittsburgh	90.00	36.00	9.00
☐ 375	J.W. Nicholson Maroons-Minn.	90.00	36.00	9.00
☐ 376	Tom(Parson)Nicholson Whites-Cleveland	90.00	36.00	9.00
☐ 377A	Nicholls Nicol Browns Champ	150.00	60.00	15.00
☐ 377B	Hugh Nicol: Cinc.	90.00	36.00	9.00
☐ 378	Nicol and Reilly Cincinnati	125.00	50.00	12.50
☐ 379	Frederick Nyce Whites-Burlington	90.00	36.00	9.00
☐ 380	Doc Oberlander Cleveland-Syracuse	90.00	36.00	9.00
☐ 381	Jack O'Brien Brooklyn-Baltimore	90.00	36.00	9.00
☐ 382	William O'Brien: Washington	90.00	36.00	9.00
☐ 383	O'Brien and Irwin:	125.00	50.00	12.50
☐ 384	Darby O'Brien: Brooklyn	90.00	36.00	9.00
☐ 385	John O'Brien: Cleve.	90.00	36.00	9.00
☐ 386	P.J. O'Connell: Omaha-Des Moines	90.00	36.00	9.00
☐ 387	John O'Connor: Cincinnati-Columbus	90.00	36.00	9.00
☐ 388	Hank O'Day: Washington-New York	90.00	36.00	9.00
☐ 389A	James O'Neil: St. Louis-Chicago	90.00	36.00	9.00
☐ 389B	James O'Neil: Browns Champs	150.00	60.00	15.00
☐ 390	O'Neill: Oakland PCL	300.00	120.00	30.00
☐ 391	Orator O'Rourke: New York	350.00	140.00	35.00
☐ 392	Thomas O'Rourke: Boston-Jersey City	90.00	36.00	9.00
☐ 393A	David Orr SPOT	300.00	120.00	30.00
☐ 393B	David Orr: All Star- Brooklyn-Columbus	90.00	36.00	9.00
☐ 394	Parsons: Minneapolis	90.00	36.00	9.00
☐ 395	Owen Patton: Minn.-Des Moines	90.00	36.00	9.00
☐ 396	James Peeples: Brooklyn-Columbus	90.00	36.00	9.00
☐ 397	Peeples and Henderson . Brooklyn	125.00	50.00	12.50
☐ 398	Hip Perrier: San Francisco PCL	300.00	120.00	30.00
☐ 399	Patrick Pettee: Milwaukee-London	90.00	36.00	9.00
☐ 400	Pettee and Lowe: Milwaukee	125.00	50.00	12.50
☐ 401	Bob Pettit: Chicago	90.00	36.00	9.00
☐ 402	Dandelion Pfeffer: Chi.	90.00	36.00	9.00
☐ 403	Dick Phelan: Des Moines	90.00	36.00	9.00
☐ 404	William Phillips: Brooklyn-Kansas City	90.00	36.00	9.00
☐ 405	Horace Phillips: Pittsburgh	90.00	36.00	9.00
☐ 406	John Pickett: St. Paul-K.C.-Phila.	90.00	36.00	9.00
☐ 407	George Pinkney: Brooklyn	90.00	36.00	9.00
☐ 408	Thomas Poorman: A's-Milwaukee	90.00	36.00	9.00
☐ 409	Henry Porter: Brooklyn-Kansas City	90.00	36.00	9.00
☐ 410	James Powell: Sioux City	90.00	36.00	9.00
☐ 411	Tom Powers: San Francisco PCL	300.00	120.00	30.00
☐ 412	Bill Blonie Purcell: Baltimore-A's	90.00	36.00	9.00
☐ 413	Thomas Quinn: Baltimore	90.00	36.00	9.00
☐ 414	Joseph Quinn: Des Moines-Boston	90.00	36.00	9.00
☐ 415	Old Hoss Radbourne: Boston	300.00	120.00	30.00
☐ 416	Shorty Radford: Brooklyn-Cleveland	90.00	36.00	9.00
☐ 417	Tom Ramsey: Louisville	90.00	36.00	9.00
☐ 418	Rehse: Minneapolis	90.00	36.00	9.00
☐ 419	Long John Reilly: Cincinnati	90.00	36.00	9.00
☐ 420	Charles Reilly: (Princeton) St.Paul	90.00	36.00	9.00
☐ 421	Charles Reynolds: Kansas City	90.00	36.00	9.00
☐ 422	Hardie Richardson Detroit-Boston	90.00	36.00	9.00
☐ 423	Danny Richardson: New York	90.00	36.00	9.00
☐ 424	Frank Ringo: St. Paul	90.00	36.00	9.00
☐ 425	Charles Ripslager SPOT	300.00	120.00	30.00
☐ 426	John Roach: New York	90.00	36.00	9.00
☐ 427	Wilbert Robinson (Uncle Robbie): A's	400.00	160.00	40.00
☐ 428	M.C. Robinson: Minn.	90.00	36.00	9.00
☐ 429A	Yank Robinson: St. Louis	90.00	36.00	9.00
☐ 429B	Wm.(Yank) Robinson: Browns Champs	150.00	60.00	15.00
☐ 430	George Rooks: Maroons-Detroit	90.00	36.00	9.00
☐ 431	James(Chief) Roseman SPOT	300.00	120.00	30.00
☐ 432	Davis Rowe: Mgr. K.C.-Denver	90.00	36.00	9.00
☐ 433	Jack Rowe: Detroit- Pittsburgh	90.00	36.00	9.00
☐ 434	Amos (Hoosier Thunderbolt) Rusie: Ind.-New York	500.00	200.00	50.00
☐ 435	James Ryan: Chicago	90.00	36.00	9.00
☐ 436	Henry Sage: Des Moines-Toledo	90.00	36.00	9.00
☐ 437	Sage and Van Dyke: Des Moines-Toledo	125.00	50.00	12.50
☐ 438	Frank Salee Omaha-Boston	90.00	36.00	9.00
☐ 439	Sanders: Omaha	90.00	36.00	9.00
☐ 440	Al (Ben) Sanders: Philadelphia	90.00	36.00	9.00
☐ 441	Frank Scheibeck: Detroit	90.00	36.00	9.00
☐ 442	Albert Schellhase: St. Joseph	90.00	36.00	9.00
☐ 443	William Schenkle: Milwaukee	90.00	36.00	9.00
☐ 444	Bill Schildknecht: Des Moines-Milwaukee	90.00	36.00	9.00
☐ 445	Gus "Pink Whiskers" Schmelz Mgr. Cincinnati	90.00	36.00	9.00
☐ 446	R. F. Schoch: Wash.	90.00	36.00	9.00
☐ 447	Lewis Schoeneck (Jumbo): Maroons-Indianapolis	90.00	36.00	9.00
☐ 448	Pop Schriver: Phila.	90.00	36.00	9.00
☐ 449	John Seery: Ind.	90.00	36.00	9.00
☐ 450	William Serad Cincinnati-Toronto	90.00	36.00	9.00
☐ 451	Edward Seward: A's	90.00	36.00	9.00
☐ 452	George(Orator)Shafer Des Moines	90.00	36.00	9.00
☐ 453	Frank Shafer: St. Paul	90.00	36.00	9.00
☐ 454	Daniel Shannon: Omaha-L'ville-Phila.	90.00	36.00	9.00
☐ 455	William Sharsig: Mgr. Athletics	125.00	50.00	12.50
☐ 456	Samuel Shaw: Baltimore-Newark	90.00	36.00	9.00
☐ 457	John Shaw: Minneapolis	90.00	36.00	9.00
☐ 458	William Shindle: Baltimore-Phila.	90.00	36.00	9.00
☐ 459	George Shock: Wash.	90.00	36.00	9.00
☐ 460	Otto Shomberg: Ind.	90.00	36.00	9.00
☐ 461	Lev Shreve: Ind.	90.00	36.00	9.00
☐ 462	Ed (Baldy) Silch: Brooklyn-Denver	90.00	36.00	9.00
☐ 463	Michael Slattery: New York	90.00	36.00	9.00
☐ 464	Sam(Skyrocket)Smith: Louisville	90.00	36.00	9.00
☐ 465	John "Phenomenal" Smith: Balt.-A's	200.00	80.00	20.00
☐ 466	Elmer Smith: Cincinnati	90.00	36.00	9.00
☐ 467	Fred (Sam) Smith: Des Moines	90.00	36.00	9.00
☐ 468	George(Germany)Smith . Brooklyn	90.00	36.00	9.00
☐ 469	Pop Smith: Pitt.-Bos.-Phila.	90.00	36.00	9.00

☐ 470	Nick Smith: St. Joe	90.00	36.00	9.00
☐ 471	Pop Snyder: Cleve.	90.00	36.00	9.00
☐ 472	P.T. Somers: St. Louis	90.00	36.00	9.00
☐ 473	Joe Sommer: Balt.	90.00	36.00	9.00
☐ 474	Pete Sommers: Chicago-New York	90.00	36.00	9.00
☐ 475	William Sowders: Boston-Pittsburgh	90.00	36.00	9.00
☐ 476	John Sowders: St. Paul-Kansas City	90.00	36.00	9.00
☐ 477	Charles Sprague: Maroons-Chi.-Cleve.	90.00	36.00	9.00
☐ 478	Edward Sproat: Whites	90.00	36.00	9.00
☐ 479	Harry Staley: Whites-Pittsburgh	90.00	36.00	9.00
☐ 480	Daniel Stearns: Des Moines-K.C.	90.00	36.00	9.00
☐ 481	Billy "Cannonball" Stemmyer: Boston-Cleveland	90.00	36.00	9.00
☐ 482	Stengel: Columbus	90.00	36.00	9.00
☐ 483	B.F. Stephens: Milw.	90.00	36.00	9.00
☐ 484	John C. Sterling: Minneapolis	90.00	36.00	9.00
☐ 485	Stockwell: S.F. PCL	300.00	120.00	30.00
☐ 486	Harry Stovey: A's-Boston	200.00	80.00	20.00
☐ 487	C. Scott Stratton: Louisville	90.00	36.00	9.00
☐ 488	Joseph Straus: Omaha-Milwaukee	90.00	36.00	9.00
☐ 489	John (Cub) Stricker: Cleveland	90.00	36.00	9.00
☐ 490	J.O. Struck: Milw.	90.00	36.00	9.00
☐ 491	Marty Sullivan: Chicago-Ind.	90.00	36.00	9.00
☐ 492	Michael Sullivan: A's	90.00	36.00	9.00
☐ 493	Billy Sunday: Chicago-Pittsburgh	250.00	100.00	25.00
☐ 494	Sy Sutcliffe: Cleve.	90.00	36.00	9.00
☐ 495	Ezra Sutton: Boston-Milwaukee	90.00	36.00	9.00
☐ 496	Ed Cyrus Swartwood: Brook.-D.Moines-Ham.	90.00	36.00	9.00
☐ 497	Parke Swartzel: K.C.	90.00	36.00	9.00
☐ 498	Peter Sweeney: Wash.	90.00	36.00	9.00
☐ 499	Sylvester: Sacra. PCL	300.00	120.00	30.00
☐ 500	Ed (Dimples) Tate: Boston-Baltimore	90.00	36.00	9.00
☐ 501	Patsy Tebeau: Chi.-Cleve.-Minn.	90.00	36.00	9.00
☐ 502	John Tener: Chicago	125.00	50.00	12.50
☐ 503	Bill (Adonis) Terry: Brooklyn	90.00	36.00	9.00
☐ 504	Big Sam Thompson: Detroit-Philadelphia	350.00	140.00	35.00
☐ 505	Silent Mike Tiernan: New York	90.00	36.00	9.00
☐ 506	Ledell Titcomb: N.Y.	90.00	36.00	9.00
☐ 507	Phillip Tomney: Louisville	90.00	36.00	9.00
☐ 508	Stephen Toole: Brooklyn-K.C.-Rochester	90.00	36.00	9.00
☐ 509	George Townsend: A's	90.00	36.00	9.00
☐ 510	William Traffley: Des Moines	90.00	36.00	9.00
☐ 511	George Treadway: St. Paul-Denver	90.00	36.00	9.00
☐ 512	Samuel Trott: Baltimore-Newark	90.00	36.00	9.00
☐ 513	Trott and Burns: Baltimore HOR	125.00	50.00	12.50
☐ 514	Tom(Foghorn) Tucker: Baltimore	90.00	36.00	9.00
☐ 515	William Tuckerman: St. Paul	90.00	36.00	9.00
☐ 516	Turner: Minneapolis	90.00	36.00	9.00
☐ 517	Lawrence Twitchell: Detroit-Cleveland	90.00	36.00	9.00
☐ 518	James Tyng: Phila.	90.00	36.00	9.00
☐ 519	William Van Dyke: Des Moines-Toledo	90.00	36.00	9.00
☐ 520	George Rip VanHaltren Chicago	90.00	36.00	9.00
☐ 521	Harry(Farmer)Vaughn: Louisville-New York	90.00	36.00	9.00
☐ 522	Peek-a-Boo Veach: St. Paul	90.00	36.00	9.00

☐ 523	Veach: Sacra. PCL	300.00	120.00	30.00
☐ 524	Leon Viau: Cincinnati	90.00	36.00	9.00
☐ 525	William Vinton: Minneapolis	90.00	36.00	9.00
☐ 526	Joseph Visner: Brooklyn	90.00	36.00	9.00
☐ 527	Christian VonDer Ahe Owner Browns Champs	225.00	90.00	22.00
☐ 528	Joseph Walsh: Omaha	90.00	36.00	9.00
☐ 529	John (Monte) Ward: New York	350.00	140.00	35.00
☐ 530	E.H. Warner: Milwaukee	90.00	36.00	9.00
☐ 531	William Watkins: Mgr. Detroit-Kansas City	125.00	50.00	12.50
☐ 532	Bill(Farmer) Weaver: Louisville	90.00	36.00	9.00
☐ 533	Charles Weber: Sioux City	90.00	36.00	9.00
☐ 534	George Weidman (Stump): Detroit-New York	90.00	36.00	9.00
☐ 535	William Weidner: Columbus	90.00	36.00	9.00
☐ 536A	Curtis Welch: Browns Champ	150.00	60.00	15.00
☐ 536B	Curtis Welch: A's	90.00	36.00	9.00
☐ 537	Welch and Gleason: Athletics	125.00	50.00	12.50
☐ 538	Smilin'Mickey Welch: All Star-New York	350.00	140.00	35.00
☐ 539	Jake Wells: K.C.	90.00	36.00	9.00
☐ 540	Frank Wells: Des Moines-Mil.	125.00	50.00	12.50
☐ 541	Joseph Werrick: Louisville-St. Paul	90.00	36.00	9.00
☐ 542	Milton(Buck) West: Minneapolis	90.00	36.00	9.00
☐ 543	Gus "Cannonball" Weyhing: A's	90.00	36.00	9.00
☐ 544	John Weyhing: Athletics-Columbus	90.00	36.00	9.00
☐ 545	Bobby Wheelock: Boston-Detroit	90.00	36.00	9.00
☐ 546	Whitacre: A's	90.00	36.00	9.00
☐ 547	Pat Whitaker: Balt.	90.00	36.00	9.00
☐ 548	Deacon White: Detroit-Pittsburgh	90.00	36.00	9.00
☐ 549	William White: Louisville	90.00	36.00	9.00
☐ 550	Jim "Grasshopper" Whitney: Wash.-Indianapolis	90.00	36.00	9.00
☐ 551	Arthur Whitney: Pittsburgh-New York	90.00	36.00	9.00
☐ 552	G.Whitney: St. Joseph	90.00	36.00	9.00
☐ 553	James Williams: Mgr. Cleveland	125.00	50.00	12.50
☐ 554	Ned Williamson: Chi.	125.00	50.00	12.50
☐ 555	Williamson and Mascot	125.00	50.00	12.50
☐ 556	C.H. Willis: Omaha	90.00	36.00	9.00
☐ 557	Walt Wilmot: Washington-Chicago	90.00	36.00	9.00
☐ 558	George Winkleman: Minneapolis-Hartford	90.00	36.00	9.00
☐ 559	Samuel Wise: Boston-Washington	90.00	36.00	9.00
☐ 560	William(Chicken)Wolf Louisville	90.00	36.00	9.00
☐ 561	George (Dandy) Wood: Philadelphia	90.00	36.00	9.00
☐ 562	Peter Wood: Phila.	90.00	36.00	9.00
☐ 563	Harry Wright: Mgr. Philadelphia	750.00	300.00	75.00
☐ 564	Charles(Chief)Zimmer Cleveland	90.00	36.00	9.00
☐ 565	Frank Zinn: Athletics	90.00	36.00	9.00

N184 Kimball's

This set of 50 color pictures of contemporary athletes was Kimball's answer to the sets produced by Allen , Ginter (N28 and N29) and Goodwin (N162).

Issued in 1888, the cards are backlisted but are not numbered. The cards are listed below in alphabetical order without regard to sport. There are four baseball players in the set. An album (ACC: A42) was offered as a premium in exchange for coupons found in the tobacco packages. The baseball players are noted in the checklist below by BB after their name.

	NRMT	VG-E	GOOD
COMPLETE SET (50)	2650.00	1000.00	325.00
COMMON BASEBALL	500.00	200.00	50.00
COMMON BOXER	40.00	16.00	4.00
COMMON OTHERS	20.00	8.00	2.00
□ 1 Wm. Beach	20.00	8.00	2.00
□ 2 Marve Beardsley	20.00	8.00	2.00
□ 3 Chas. P. Blatt	20.00	8.00	2.00
□ 4 Blondin	20.00	8.00	2.00
□ 5 Paul Boynton	20.00	8.00	2.00
□ 6 E.A.(Ernie) Burch BB	500.00	200.00	50.00
□ 7 Patsy Cardiff	20.00	8.00	2.00
□ 8 Phillip Casey	20.00	8.00	2.00
□ 9 J.C. Cockburn	20.00	8.00	2.00
□ 10 Dell Darling BB	500.00	200.00	50.00
□ 11 Jack Dempsey BOX	80.00	32.00	8.00
□ 12 Della Ferrell	20.00	8.00	2.00
□ 13 Clarence Freeman	20.00	8.00	2.00
□ 14 Louis George	20.00	8.00	2.00
□ 15 W.G. George	20.00	8.00	2.00
□ 16 George W. Hamilton	20.00	8.00	2.00
□ 17 Edward Hanlan	20.00	8.00	2.00
□ 18 C.H. Heins	20.00	8.00	2.00
□ 19 Hardie Henderson BB	500.00	200.00	50.00
□ 20 Thomas H. Hume	20.00	8.00	2.00
□ 21 J.H. Jordon	20.00	8.00	2.00
□ 22 Johnny Kane	20.00	8.00	2.00
□ 23 James McLaughlin	20.00	8.00	2.00
□ 24 John McPherson	20.00	8.00	2.00
□ 25 Joseph Morsler	20.00	8.00	2.00
□ 26 William Muldoon	20.00	8.00	2.00
□ 27 S. Muller	20.00	8.00	2.00
□ 28 Isaac Murphy	20.00	8.00	2.00
□ 29 John Murphy	20.00	8.00	2.00
□ 30 L.E. Myers	20.00	8.00	2.00
□ 31 Annie Oakley	40.00	16.00	4.00
□ 32 Daniel O'Leary	20.00	8.00	2.00
□ 33 James O'Neil BB	550.00	220.00	55.00
□ 34 Wm. Byrd Page	20.00	8.00	2.00
□ 35 Axel Paulsen	20.00	8.00	2.00
□ 36 Master Ray Perry	20.00	8.00	2.00
□ 37 Duncan C. Ross	20.00	8.00	2.00
□ 38 W.A. Rowe	20.00	8.00	2.00
□ 39 Jacob Schaefer	20.00	8.00	2.00
□ 40 M. Schloss	20.00	8.00	2.00
□ 41 Jem Smith	20.00	8.00	2.00
□ 42 Lillian Smith	20.00	8.00	2.00
□ 43 Hattie Stewart	20.00	8.00	2.00
□ 44 John L. Sullivan BOX	100.00	40.00	10.00
□ 45 Arthur Wallace	20.00	8.00	2.00
□ 46 Tommy Warren BOX	40.00	16.00	4.00
□ 47 Ada Webb	20.00	8.00	2.00
□ 48 John Wessels	20.00	8.00	2.00
□ 49 Clarence Whistler	20.00	8.00	2.00
□ 50 Charles Wood	20.00	8.00	2.00

N284 Buchner

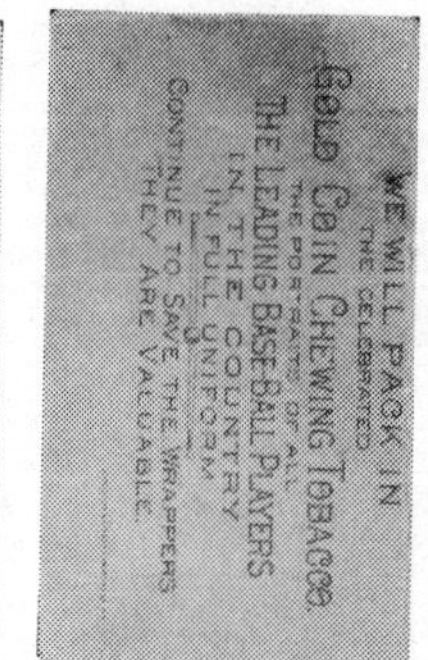

The baseball players found in this Buchner set are a part of a larger group of cards portraying policemen, jockeys and actors, all of which were issued with the tobacco brand "Gold Coin." Nine players from eight teams, plus four Brooklyn players, are all portrayed in identical poses according to position. St. Louis has 14 players depicted in poses which are not repeated. There are 53 additional cards which vary according to pose, team change, spelling, etc. In all, there are 118 individuals portrayed on 143 cards. The set was issued circa 1887. The cards are numbered below in alphabetical order within team with teams themselves listed in alphabetical order: Baltimore (1-4), Boston (5-13), Brooklyn (14-17), Chicago (18-26), Detroit (27-35), Indianapolis (36-47), LaCrosse (48-51), Milwaukee (52-55), New York Mets (56-63), New York (64-73), Philadelphia (74-83), Pittsburg (84-92), St. Louis (93-106), and Washington (107-117).

	NRMT	VG-E	GOOD
COMPLETE SET	11000.00	4750.00	1500.00
COMMON PLAYERS	70.00	28.00	7.00
COMMON ST. LOUIS	125.00	50.00	12.50
□ 1 Burns: Baltimore	70.00	28.00	7.00
□ 2 Fulmer: Baltimore	70.00	28.00	7.00
□ 3 Kilroy: Baltimore	70.00	28.00	7.00
□ 4 Purcell: Baltimore	70.00	28.00	7.00
□ 5 John Burdock: Boston	70.00	28.00	7.00
□ 6 Bill Daley: Boston	70.00	28.00	7.00
□ 7 Joe Hornung: Boston	70.00	28.00	7.00
□ 8 Johnston: Boston	70.00	28.00	7.00
□ 9A King Kelly: Boston (right field)	250.00	100.00	25.00
□ 9B King Kelly: Boston (catcher)	250.00	100.00	25.00
□ 10 Morrill (2): Boston	70.00	28.00	7.00
□ 11 Hoss Radbourn (2): Boston	175.00	70.00	18.00
□ 12 Sutton: Boston	70.00	28.00	7.00
□ 13 Wise: Boston	70.00	28.00	7.00
□ 14 McClellan: Brooklyn	70.00	28.00	7.00
□ 15 Peoples: Brooklyn	70.00	28.00	7.00
□ 16 Phillips: Brooklyn	70.00	28.00	7.00
□ 17 Porter: Brooklyn	70.00	28.00	7.00
□ 18 Adrian Anson (2): Chicago	350.00	140.00	35.00
□ 19 Burns: Chicago	70.00	28.00	7.00
□ 20 John Clarkson (2): Chicago	175.00	70.00	18.00
□ 21 Silver Flint: Chicago	70.00	28.00	7.00
□ 22 Pfeffer: Chicago	70.00	28.00	7.00
□ 23 Ryan: Chicago	70.00	28.00	7.00
□ 24 Billy Sullivan: Chicago	100.00	40.00	10.00
□ 25 Billy Sunday: Chicago	150.00	60.00	15.00
□ 26A Williamson: Chicago (shortstop)	70.00	28.00	7.00
□ 26B Williamson: Chicago (second base)	70.00	28.00	7.00

☐ 27	Bennett: Detroit	70.00	28.00	7.00
☐ 28A	Dan Brouthers: Detroit (fielding)	175.00	70.00	18.00
☐ 28B	Dan Brouthers: Detroit (batting)	175.00	70.00	18.00
☐ 29	Dunlap: Detroit	70.00	28.00	7.00
☐ 30	Getzein: Detroit	70.00	28.00	7.00
☐ 31	Hanlon: Detroit	70.00	28.00	7.00
☐ 32	Manning: Detoit	70.00	28.00	7.00
☐ 33	Richardson (2): Detroit	70.00	28.00	7.00
☐ 34	Sam Thompson (2): Detroit	175.00	70.00	18.00
☐ 35	White: Detroit	70.00	28.00	7.00
☐ 36	Arundel: Indianapolis	70.00	28.00	7.00
☐ 37	Bassett: Indianapolis	70.00	28.00	7.00
☐ 38	Boyle: Indianapolis	70.00	28.00	7.00
☐ 39	Cahill: Indianapolis	70.00	28.00	7.00
☐ 40	Denny (2): Indianapolis	70.00	28.00	7.00
☐ 41	Jack Glasscock (2): Indianapolis	80.00	32.00	8.00
☐ 42	Healy: Indianapolis	70.00	28.00	7.00
☐ 43	Meyers: Indianapolis	70.00	28.00	7.00
☐ 44	McGeachy: Indianapolis	70.00	28.00	7.00
☐ 45	Polhemus: Indianapolis	70.00	28.00	7.00
☐ 46	Seery (2): Indianapolis	70.00	28.00	7.00
☐ 47	Shomberg: Indianapolis	70.00	28.00	7.00
☐ 48	Corbett: Lacrosse	70.00	28.00	7.00
☐ 49	Crowley: Lacrosse	70.00	28.00	7.00
☐ 50	Kennedy: Lacrosse	70.00	28.00	7.00
☐ 51	Rooks: Lacrosse	70.00	28.00	7.00
☐ 52	Forster: Milwaukee	70.00	28.00	7.00
☐ 53	Hart: Milwaukee	70.00	28.00	7.00
☐ 54	Morrissy: Milwaukee	70.00	28.00	7.00
☐ 55	Strauss: Milwaukee	70.00	28.00	7.00
☐ 56	Cushmann: NY Mets	70.00	28.00	7.00
☐ 57	Jim Donahue: NY Mets	70.00	28.00	7.00
☐ 58	Esterbrooke (sic): NY Mets	70.00	28.00	7.00
☐ 59	Joe Gerhardt: NY Mets	70.00	28.00	7.00
☐ 60	Frank Hankinson: NY Mets	70.00	28.00	7.00
☐ 61	Jack Nelson: NY Mets	70.00	28.00	7.00
☐ 62	Dave Orr: NY Mets	70.00	28.00	7.00
☐ 63	James Rosemann: NY Mets	70.00	28.00	7.00
☐ 64	Roger Connor (2): New York	175.00	70.00	18.00
☐ 65	Deasley: New York	70.00	28.00	7.00
☐ 66A	Mike Dorgan: New York (fielding)	70.00	28.00	7.00
☐ 66B	Mike Dorgan: New York (batting)	70.00	28.00	7.00
☐ 67	Buck Ewing (2): New York	175.00	70.00	18.00
☐ 68A	Pete Gillespie: New York (fielding)	70.00	28.00	7.00
☐ 68B	Pete Gillespie: New York (batting)	70.00	28.00	7.00
☐ 69	George Gore: New York	70.00	28.00	7.00
☐ 70	Tim Keefe (2): New York	175.00	70.00	18.00
☐ 71	Jim O'Rourke: New York	175.00	70.00	18.00
☐ 72A	Danny Richardson: New York (third base)	70.00	28.00	7.00
☐ 72B	Danny Richardson: New York (second base)	70.00	28.00	7.00
☐ 73	John M. Ward (3): New York	175.00	70.00	18.00
☐ 74	Andrews (2): Philadelphia	70.00	28.00	7.00
☐ 75	Bastian: Philadelphia	70.00	28.00	7.00
☐ 76	Dan Casey: Philadelphia	70.00	28.00	7.00
☐ 77	Clements: Philadelphia	70.00	28.00	7.00
☐ 78	Sid Farrar: Philadelphia	70.00	28.00	7.00
☐ 79	Ferguson: Philadelphia	50.00	20.00	5.00
☐ 80	Fogerty: Philadelphia	70.00	28.00	7.00
☐ 81	Irwin: Philadelphia	70.00	28.00	7.00
☐ 82	Mulvey (2): Philadelphia	70.00	28.00	7.00
☐ 83A	Pete Wood: Philadelphia (fielding)	70.00	28.00	7.00
☐ 83B	Pete Wood: Philadelphia (stealing)	70.00	28.00	7.00
☐ 84	Barkley: Pittsburg	70.00	28.00	7.00
☐ 85	Beecher: Pittsburg	70.00	28.00	7.00
☐ 86	Brown: Pittsburg	70.00	28.00	7.00
☐ 87	Carroll: Pittsburg	70.00	28.00	7.00
☐ 88	Coleman: Pittsburg	70.00	28.00	7.00
☐ 89	McCormick: Pittsburg	70.00	28.00	7.00
☐ 90	Miller: Pittsburg	70.00	28.00	7.00
☐ 91	Smith: Pittsburg	70.00	28.00	7.00
☐ 92	Whitney: Pittsburg	70.00	28.00	7.00
☐ 93	Barkley: St. Louis	125.00	50.00	12.50
☐ 94	Bushong: St. Louis	125.00	50.00	12.50
☐ 95	Bob Carruthers (sic): St. Louis	150.00	60.00	15.00
☐ 96	Charles Comiskey: St. Louis	250.00	100.00	25.00
☐ 97	Dave Foutz: St. Louis	125.00	50.00	12.50
☐ 98	William Gleason: St. Louis	125.00	50.00	12.50
☐ 99	Arlie Latham: St. Louis	125.00	50.00	12.50
☐ 100	McGinnis: St. Louis	125.00	50.00	12.50
☐ 101	Hugh Nicol: St. Louis	125.00	50.00	12.50
☐ 102	James O'Neil: St. Louis	125.00	50.00	12.50
☐ 103	Robinson: St. Louis	125.00	50.00	12.50
☐ 104	Sullivan: St. Louis	125.00	50.00	12.50
☐ 105	Chris Von Der Ahe: St. Louis	175.00	70.00	18.00
☐ 106	Curt Welch: St. Louis	125.00	50.00	12.50
☐ 107	Carroll: Washington	70.00	28.00	7.00
☐ 108	Craig: Washington	70.00	28.00	7.00
☐ 109	Crane: Washington	70.00	28.00	7.00
☐ 110	Dailey: Washington	70.00	28.00	7.00
☐ 111	Donnelly: Washington	70.00	28.00	7.00
☐ 112	Farrell (2): Washington	70.00	28.00	7.00
☐ 113	Gilligan: Washington	70.00	28.00	7.00
☐ 114A	Hines: Washington (fielding)	70.00	28.00	7.00
☐ 114B	Hines: Washington (batting)	70.00	28.00	7.00
☐ 115	Myers: Washington	70.00	28.00	7.00
☐ 116	O'Brien: Washington	70.00	28.00	7.00
☐ 117	Whitney: Washington	70.00	28.00	7.00

N300 Mayo

The Mayo Tobacco Works of Richmond, Va., issued this set of 48 ballplayers about 1895. The cards contain sepia portraits although some pictures appear to be black and white. There are 40 different individuals known in the set; cards 1 to 28 appear in uniform, while the last twelve (29-40) appear in street clothes. Eight of the former also appear with variations in uniform. The player's name appears within the picture area and a "Mayo's Cut Plug" ad is printed in a panel at the base of the card.

	NRMT	VG-E	GOOD
COMPLETE SET (48)	12000.00	5400.00	1750.00
COMMON PLAYERS (1-28)	175.00	70.00	18.00
COMMON PLAYERS (29-40)	175.00	70.00	18.00
☐ 1 Cap Anson: Chicago	1000.00	400.00	125.00
☐ 2 Bannon RF: Boston	175.00	70.00	18.00
☐ 3A Dan Brouthers 1B: Baltimore	400.00	160.00	40.00
☐ 3B Dan Brouthers 1B: Louisville	450.00	180.00	45.00
☐ 4 John Clarkson P: St. Louis	400.00	160.00	40.00
☐ 5 T.W. Corcoran SS: Brooklyn	175.00	70.00	18.00
☐ 6 Cross 2B: Philadelphia	175.00	70.00	18.00
☐ 7 Hugh Duffy CF: Boston	400.00	160.00	40.00
☐ 8A Buck Ewing RF: Cincinnati	450.00	180.00	45.00
☐ 8B Buck Ewing RF: Cleveland	450.00	180.00	45.00
☐ 9 Dave Foutz 1B: Brooklyn	175.00	70.00	18.00
☐ 10 Ganzel C: Boston	175.00	70.00	18.00
☐ 11A Glasscock SS: Pittsburgh	200.00	80.00	20.00
☐ 11B Glasscock SS: Louisville	200.00	80.00	20.00
☐ 12 Griffin CF: Brooklyn	175.00	70.00	18.00
☐ 13A Haddock P: Philadelphia	175.00	70.00	18.00
☐ 13B Haddock P: no team	175.00	70.00	18.00
☐ 14 Joyce CF: Brooklyn	175.00	70.00	18.00
☐ 15 Wm. Kennedy P: Brooklyn	175.00	70.00	18.00
☐ 16A Tom F. Kinslow C: Pitts.	175.00	70.00	18.00
☐ 16B Tom F. Kinslow C: no team	175.00	70.00	18.00
☐ 17 Arlie Latham 3B: Cincinnati	175.00	70.00	18.00
☐ 18 Long SS: Boston	200.00	80.00	20.00
☐ 19 Lovett P: Boston	175.00	70.00	18.00
☐ 20 Lowe 2B: Boston	200.00	80.00	20.00
☐ 21 McCarthy LF: Boston	400.00	160.00	40.00
☐ 22 Murphy SS: New York	175.00	70.00	18.00
☐ 23 Billy Nash 3B: Boston	175.00	70.00	18.00
☐ 24 Nicols P: Boston	175.00	70.00	18.00
☐ 25A Pfeffer 2B: Louisville	175.00	70.00	18.00
☐ 25B Pfeffer (retired)	175.00	70.00	18.00
☐ 26A Amos Rusie P: New York	600.00	240.00	60.00
☐ 26B Amos Russie (sic) P: New York	500.00	200.00	50.00
☐ 27 Tucker 1B: Boston	175.00	70.00	18.00
☐ 28A John Ward 2B: New York	400.00	160.00	40.00
☐ 28B John Ward (retired)	450.00	180.00	45.00
☐ 29 Chas. S. Abbey CF: Washington	175.00	70.00	18.00
☐ 30 E.W. Cartwright FB: Washington	200.00	80.00	20.00
☐ 31 W. F. Dahlen SS: Chicago	200.00	80.00	20.00
☐ 32 T.P. Daly SB: Brooklyn	175.00	70.00	18.00
☐ 33 E.J. Delehanty LF: Phila.	500.00	200.00	50.00
☐ 34 W.W. Hallman SB: Phila.	175.00	70.00	18.00
☐ 35 W.R. Hamilton CF: Phila.	400.00	160.00	40.00
☐ 36 W. Robinson C: Baltimore	400.00	160.00	40.00
☐ 37 James Ryan RF: Chicago	175.00	70.00	18.00
☐ 38 Wm. Shindle TB: Brooklyn	175.00	70.00	18.00
☐ 39 Geo. J. Smith SS: Cinc.	175.00	70.00	18.00
☐ 40 Otis H. Stockdale P: Washington	175.00	70.00	18.00

1986 National Photo Royals

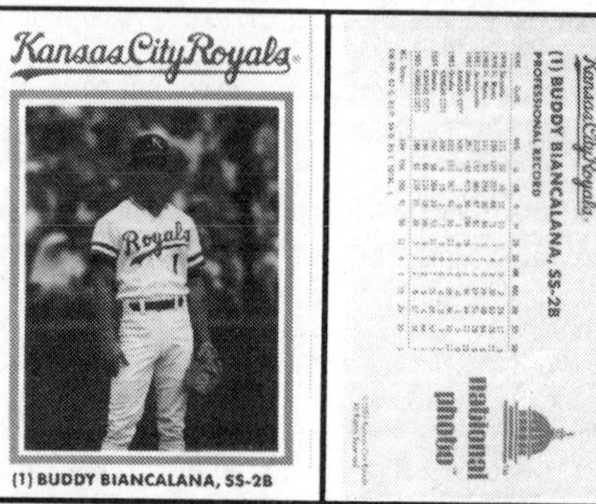

The set contains 24 cards which are numbered only by uniform number except for the checklist card and discount card, which entitles the bearer to a 40% discount at National Photo. Cards measure 2 7/8" by 4 1/4". Cards were distributed at the stadium on August 14th. The set was supposedly later available for 3.00 directly from the Royals.

	MINT	EXC	G-VG
COMPLETE SET (24)	10.00	4.00	1.00
COMMON PLAYER	.30	.12	.03
☐ 1 Buddy Biancalana	.30	.12	.03
☐ 3 Jorge Orta	.30	.12	.03
☐ 4 Greg Pryor	.30	.12	.03
☐ 5 George Brett	2.00	.80	.20
☐ 6 Willie Wilson	.60	.24	.06
☐ 8 Jim Sundberg	.30	.12	.03
☐ 10 Dick Howser MG	.60	.24	.06
☐ 11 Hal McRae	.40	.16	.04
☐ 20 Frank White	.60	.24	.06
☐ 21 Lonnie Smith	.40	.16	.04
☐ 22 Dennis Leonard	.50	.20	.05
☐ 23 Mark Gubicza	.60	.24	.06
☐ 24 Darryl Motley	.30	.12	.03
☐ 25 Danny Jackson	.75	.30	.07
☐ 26 Steve Farr	.30	.12	.03
☐ 29 Dan Quisenberry	.50	.20	.05
☐ 31 Bret Saberhagen	.75	.30	.07
☐ 35 Lynn Jones	.30	.12	.03
☐ 37 Charlie Leibrandt	.50	.20	.05
☐ 38 Mark Huismann	.30	.12	.03
☐ 40 Buddy Black	.40	.16	.04
☐ 45 Steve Balboni	.40	.16	.04
☐ xx Discount card (unnumbered)	.30	.12	.03
☐ xx Checklist card (unnumbered)	.30	.12	.03

1984 Nestle Dream Team

The cards in this 22-card set measure 2 1/2" by 3 1/2". In conjunction with Topps, the Nestle Company issued this set entitled the Dream Team. The fronts have the Nestle trademark in the upper frameline, and the backs are identical to the Topps cards of this year except for the number and the Nestle's logo. Cards 1-11 feature stars of the American League while cards 12-22 show National League stars. Each league's "Dream team" consists of eight position players and three pitchers. The cards were included with the Nestle chocolate bars as a pack of four (three player cards and a checklist header card. This set should not be confused with the Nestle 792 card (same player-number correspondence as 1984 Topps 792) set.

	MINT	EXC	G-VG
COMPLETE SET (22)	16.00	6.50	1.60
COMMON PLAYER (1-22)	.40	.16	.04
□ 1 Eddie Murray	1.50	.60	.15
□ 2 Lou Whitaker	.50	.20	.05
□ 3 George Brett	1.75	.70	.17
□ 4 Cal Ripken	1.50	.60	.15
□ 5 Jim Rice	.80	.32	.08
□ 6 Dave Winfield	1.00	.40	.10
□ 7 Lloyd Moseby	.40	.16	.04
□ 8 Lance Parrish	.60	.24	.06
□ 9 LaMarr Hoyt	.40	.16	.04
□ 10 Ron Guidry	.60	.24	.06
□ 11 Dan Quisenberry	.50	.20	.05
□ 12 Steve Garvey	1.25	.50	.12
□ 13 Johnny Ray	.40	.16	.04
□ 14 Mike Schmidt	1.75	.70	.17
□ 15 Ozzie Smith	.80	.32	.08
□ 16 Andre Dawson	.80	.32	.08
□ 17 Tim Raines	.80	.32	.08
□ 18 Dale Murphy	1.75	.70	.17
□ 19 Tony Pena	.40	.16	.04
□ 20 John Denny	.40	.16	.04
□ 21 Steve Carlton	.90	.36	.09
□ 22 Al Holland	.40	.16	.04
□ xx Checklist card (unnumbered)	.40	.16	.04

1984 Nestle 792

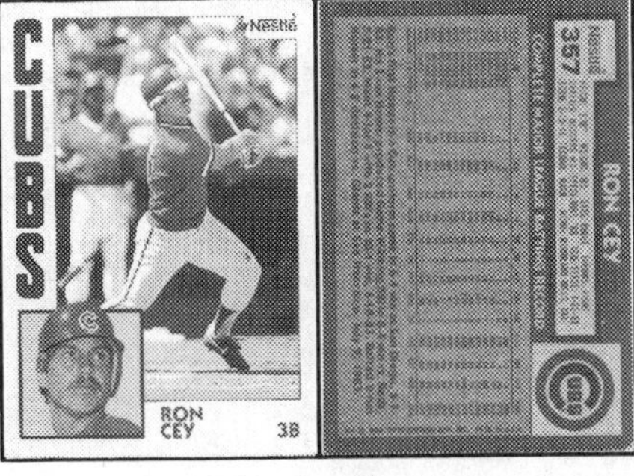

The cards in this 792-card set measure 2 1/2" by 3 1/2" and are extremely similar to the 1984 Topps regular issue (except for the Nestle logo instead of Topps logo on the front). In conjunction with Topps, the Nestle Company issued this set as six sheets available as a premium. The set was (as detailed on the back of the checklist card for the Nestle Dream Team cards) originally available from the Nestle Company in full sheets of 132 cards, 24" by 48", for 4.95 plus five Nestle candy wrappers per sheet. The backs are virtually identical to the Topps cards of this year, i.e., same player-number correspondence. These sheets have been cut up into individual cards and are available from a few dealers around the country. This is one of the few instances in this hobby where the complete uncut sheet is worth considerably less than the sum of the individual cards due to the expense required in having the sheet cut professionally (and precisely) into individual cards. Supposedly less than 5000 sets were printed. Since the checklist is exactly the same as that of the 1984 Topps, these Nestle cards are generally priced as a multiple of the corresponding Topps card. The list below shows only the major exceptions; cards (above common card price) not listed below are priced at five times the corresponding 1984 Topps price.

	MINT	EXC	G-VG
COMPLETE SET (792)	450.00	180.00	45.00
COMMON PLAYER (1-792)	.25	.10	.02
□ 8 Don Mattingly	150.00	60.00	15.00
□ 30 Wade Boggs	30.00	12.00	3.00
□ 100 Reggie Jackson	7.50	3.00	.75
□ 150 Dale Murphy	9.00	3.75	.90
□ 182 Darryl Strawberry	50.00	20.00	5.00
□ 230 Rickey Henderson	7.50	3.00	.75
□ 251 Tony Gwynn	10.00	4.00	1.00
□ 300 Pete Rose	15.00	6.00	1.50
□ 490 Cal Ripken	7.00	2.80	.70
□ 500 George Brett	7.00	2.80	.70
□ 596 Ryne Sandberg	9.00	3.75	.90
□ 700 Mike Schmidt	7.00	2.80	.70
□ 780 Steve Carlton	5.00	2.00	.50

1987 Nestle Dream Team

This 33-card set is, in a sense, three sets: Golden Era (1-11 gold), AL Modern Era (12-22 red), and NL Modern Era (23-33 blue). Cards are 2 1/2" by 3 1/2" and have color coded borders by era. The first 11 card photos are in black and white. The Nestle set was apparently not licensed by Major League Baseball and hence the team logos are not shown in the photos. Six-packs of certain Nestle candy bars contained three cards; cards were also available through a send-in offer.

	MINT	EXC	G-VG
COMPLETE SET (33)	7.00	2.80	.70
COMMON PLAYER (1-33)	.15	.06	.01
□ 1 Lou Gehrig	.50	.20	.05
□ 2 Rogers Hornsby	.25	.10	.02
□ 3 Pie Traynor	.15	.06	.01
□ 4 Honus Wagner	.25	.10	.02
□ 5 Babe Ruth	.80	.32	.08
□ 6 Tris Speaker	.25	.10	.02
□ 7 Ty Cobb	.50	.20	.05
□ 8 Mickey Cochrane	.25	.10	.02
□ 9 Walter Johnson	.35	.14	.03
□ 10 Carl Hubbell	.25	.10	.02
□ 11 Jimmy Foxx	.25	.10	.02
□ 12 Rod Carew	.25	.10	.02
□ 13 Nellie Fox	.15	.06	.01
□ 14 Brooks Robinson	.25	.10	.02
□ 15 Luis Aparicio	.15	.06	.01
□ 16 Frank Robinson	.25	.10	.02

□ 17 Mickey Mantle	1.00	.40	.10
□ 18 Ted Williams	.50	.20	.05
□ 19 Yogi Berra	.35	.14	.03
□ 20 Bob Feller	.35	.14	.03
□ 21 Whitey Ford	.35	.14	.03
□ 22 Harmon Killebrew	.25	.10	.02
□ 23 Stan Musial	.35	.14	.03
□ 24 Jackie Robinson	.45	.18	.04
□ 25 Eddie Mathews	.25	.10	.02
□ 26 Ernie Banks	.25	.10	.02
□ 27 Roberto Clemente	.35	.14	.03
□ 28 Willie Mays	.50	.20	.05
□ 29 Hank Aaron	.50	.20	.05
□ 30 Johnny Bench	.35	.14	.03
□ 31 Bob Gibson	.25	.10	.02
□ 32 Warren Spahn	.25	.10	.02
□ 33 Duke Snider	.35	.14	.03

1988 Nestle

This 44-card set was produced for Nestle by Mike Schechter Associates and was printed in Canada. Cards are 2 1/2" by 3 1/2" and have yellow borders. The Nestle set was apparently not licensed by Major League Baseball and hence the team logos are not shown in the photos. The cards are numbered on the back. The backs are printed in red and blue on white card stock.

	MINT	EXC	G-VG
COMPLETE SET (44)	16.50	7.00	1.00
COMMON PLAYER (1-44)	.25	.10	.02
□ 1 Roger Clemens	1.25	.50	.12
□ 2 Dale Murphy	.75	.30	.07
□ 3 Eric Davis	1.00	.40	.10
□ 4 Gary Gaetti	.35	.14	.03
□ 5 Ozzie Smith	.45	.18	.04
□ 6 Mike Schmidt	.75	.30	.07
□ 7 Ozzie Guillen	.25	.10	.02
□ 8 John Franco	.25	.10	.02
□ 9 Andre Dawson	.45	.18	.04
□ 10 Mark McGwire	1.25	.50	.12
□ 11 Bret Saberhagen	.35	.14	.03
□ 12 Benny Santiago	.45	.18	.04
□ 13 Jose Uribe	.25	.10	.02
□ 14 Will Clark	1.25	.50	.12
□ 15 Don Mattingly	1.75	.70	.17
□ 16 Juan Samuel	.25	.10	.02
□ 17 Jack Clark	.35	.14	.03
□ 18 Darryl Strawberry	1.25	.50	.12
□ 19 Bill Doran	.25	.10	.02
□ 20 Pete Incaviglia	.35	.14	.03
□ 21 Dwight Gooden	1.00	.40	.10
□ 22 Willie Randolph	.25	.10	.02
□ 23 Tim Wallach	.25	.10	.02
□ 24 Pedro Guerrero	.35	.14	.03
□ 25 Steve Bedrosian	.25	.10	.02
□ 26 Gary Carter	.45	.18	.04
□ 27 Jeff Reardon	.25	.10	.02
□ 28 Dave Righetti	.25	.10	.02
□ 29 Frank White	.25	.10	.02
□ 30 Buddy Bell	.25	.10	.02
□ 31 Tim Raines	.35	.14	.03
□ 32 Wade Boggs	1.50	.60	.15
□ 33 Dave Winfield	.60	.24	.06
□ 34 George Bell	.35	.14	.03
□ 35 Alan Trammell	.45	.18	.04
□ 36 Joe Carter	.35	.14	.03
□ 37 Jose Canseco	2.00	.80	.20
□ 38 Carlton Fisk	.35	.14	.03
□ 39 Kirby Puckett	1.00	.40	.10
□ 40 Tony Gwynn	.60	.24	.06
□ 41 Matt Nokes	.35	.14	.03
□ 42 Keith Hernandez	.35	.14	.03
□ 43 Nolan Ryan	.60	.24	.06
□ 44 Wally Joyner	.45	.18	.04

1954 N.Y. Journal American

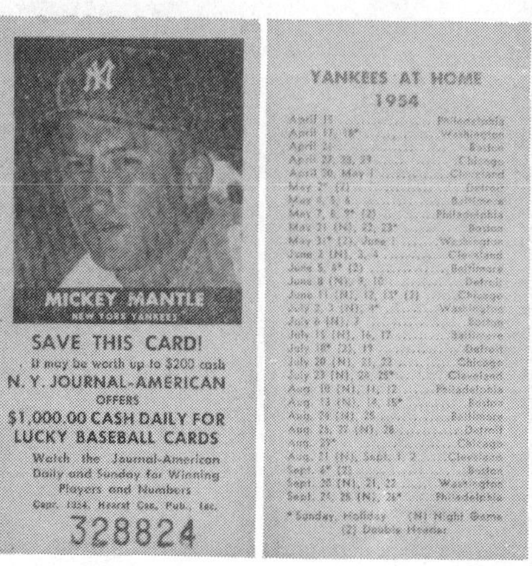

The cards in this 59-card set measure 2" by 4". The 1954 New York Journal American set contains black and white, unnumbered cards issued in conjunction with the newspaper. News stands were given boxes of cards to be distributed with purchases and each card had a serial number for redemption in the contest. The set spotlights New York teams only and carries game schedules on the reverse. The cards have been assigned numbers in the listing below alphabetically within team so that Brooklyn Dodgers are 1-19, New York Giants are 20-39, and New York Yankees are 40- 59. There is speculation that a 20th Dodger card may exist. The ACC designation for this set is M127.

	NRMT	VG-E	GOOD
COMPLETE SET (59)	1450.00	650.00	200.00
COMMON PLAYER (1-59)	8.00	3.25	.80
□ 1 Joe Black	10.00	4.00	1.00
□ 2 Roy Campanella	75.00	30.00	7.50
□ 3 Billy Cox	10.00	4.00	1.00
□ 4 Carl Erskine	12.00	5.00	1.20
□ 5 Carl Furillo	15.00	6.00	1.50
□ 6 Junior Gilliam	15.00	6.00	1.50
□ 7 Gil Hodges	30.00	12.00	3.00
□ 8 Jim Hughes	8.00	3.25	.80
□ 9 Clem Labine	10.00	4.00	1.00
□ 10 Billy Loes	8.00	3.25	.80
□ 11 Russ Meyer	8.00	3.25	.80
□ 12 Don Newcombe	15.00	6.00	1.50
□ 13 Ervin Palica	8.00	3.25	.80
□ 14 Pee Wee Reese	45.00	18.00	4.50
□ 15 Jackie Robinson	100.00	40.00	10.00
□ 16 Preacher Roe	15.00	6.00	1.50
□ 17 George Shuba	8.00	3.25	.80
□ 18 Duke Snider	75.00	30.00	7.50
□ 19 Dick Williams	10.00	4.00	1.00
□ 20 John Antonelli	10.00	4.00	1.00
□ 21 Alvin Dark	12.00	5.00	1.20
□ 22 Marv Grissom	8.00	3.25	.80
□ 23 Ruben Gomez	8.00	3.25	.80
□ 24 Jim Hearn	8.00	3.25	.80
□ 25 Bobby Hofman	8.00	3.25	.80
□ 26 Monte Irvin	25.00	10.00	2.50
□ 27 Larry Jansen	8.00	3.25	.80

□ 28 Ray Katt	8.00	3.25	.80
□ 29 Don Liddle	8.00	3.25	.80
□ 30 Whitey Lockman	10.00	4.00	1.00
□ 31 Sal Maglie	15.00	6.00	1.50
□ 32 Willie Mays	150.00	60.00	15.00
□ 33 Don Mueller	10.00	4.00	1.00
□ 34 Dusty Rhodes	10.00	4.00	1.00
□ 35 Hank Thompson	10.00	4.00	1.00
□ 36 Wes Westrum	8.00	3.25	.80
□ 37 Hoyt Wilhelm	30.00	12.00	3.00
□ 38 Davey Williams	10.00	4.00	1.00
□ 39 Al Worthington	8.00	3.25	.80
□ 40 Hank Bauer	15.00	6.00	1.50
□ 41 Yogi Berra	75.00	30.00	7.50
□ 42 Harry Byrd	8.00	3.25	.80
□ 43 Andy Carey	8.00	3.25	.80
□ 44 Jerry Coleman	10.00	4.00	1.00
□ 45 Joe Collins	10.00	4.00	1.00
□ 46 Whitey Ford	40.00	16.00	4.00
□ 47 Steve Kraly	8.00	3.25	.80
□ 48 Bob Kuzava	8.00	3.25	.80
□ 49 Frank Leja	8.00	3.25	.80
□ 50 Ed Lopat	15.00	6.00	1.50
□ 51 Mickey Mantle	350.00	140.00	35.00
□ 52 Gil McDougald	15.00	6.00	1.50
□ 53 Bill Miller	8.00	3.25	.80
□ 54 Tom Morgan	8.00	3.25	.80
□ 55 Irv Noren	8.00	3.25	.80
□ 56 Allie Reynolds	15.00	6.00	1.50
□ 57 Phil Rizzuto	30.00	12.00	3.00
□ 58 Eddie Robinson	8.00	3.25	.80
□ 59 Gene Woodling	10.00	4.00	1.00

1960 Nu-Card Hi-Lites

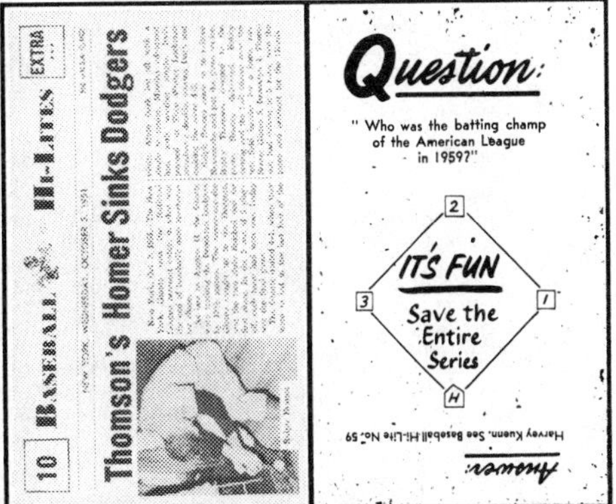

The cards in this 72-card set measure 3 1/4" by 5 3/8". In 1960, the Nu-Card Company introduced its Baseball Hi- Lites set of newspaper style cards. Each card singled out an individual baseball achievement with a picture and story. The reverses contain a baseball quiz. Cards 1-18 are more valuable if found printed totally in black on the front; these are copyrighted CVC as opposed to the NCI designation found on the red and black printed fronts.

	NRMT	VG-E	GOOD
COMPLETE SET (72)	160.00	65.00	20.00
COMMON PLAYER (1-72)	1.25	.50	.12
□ 1 Babe Hits 3 Homers In A Series Game	9.00	3.75	.90
□ 2 Podres Pitching Wins Series	1.25	.50	.12
□ 3 Bevans Pitches No Hitter, Almost	1.25	.50	.12
□ 4 Box Score Devised By Reporter	1.25	.50	.12
□ 5 VanderMeer Pitches Two No Hitters	1.25	.50	.12
□ 6 Indians Take Bums	1.25	.50	.12
□ 7 DiMag Comes Thru	7.50	3.00	.75
□ 8 Mathewson Pitches Three WS Shutouts	2.00	.80	.20
□ 9 Haddix Pitches 12 Perfect Innings	1.25	.50	.12
□ 10 Thomson's Homer Sinks Dodgers	2.00	.80	.20
□ 11 Hubbell Strikes Out Five A.L. Stars	1.25	.50	.12
□ 12 Pickoff Ends Series	1.25	.50	.12
□ 13 Cards Take Series From Yanks	1.25	.50	.12
□ 14 Dizzy And Daffy Dean Win Series	3.00	1.20	.30
□ 15 Owen Drops 3rd Strike	1.25	.50	.12
□ 16 Ruth Calls Shot	9.00	3.75	.90
□ 17 Merkle Pulls Boner	1.25	.50	.12
□ 18 Larsen Hurls Perfect World Series Game	2.00	.80	.20
□ 19 Bean Ball Ends Career of Mickey Cochrane	1.25	.50	.12
□ 20 Banks Belts 47 Homers Earns MVP	3.00	1.20	.30
□ 21 Stan Musial Hits Five Homers in One Day	4.00	1.60	.40
□ 22 Mickey Mantle Hits Longest Homer	10.00	4.00	1.00
□ 23 Sievers Captures Home Run Title	1.25	.50	.12
□ 24 Gehrig 2130 Consecutive Game Record Ends	5.00	2.00	.50
□ 25 Red Schoendienst Key Player Braves Pennant	1.25	.50	.12
□ 26 Midget Pinch-Hits For St. Louis	2.50	1.00	.25
□ 27 Willie Mays Makes Greatest Catch	5.00	2.00	.50
□ 28 Homer by Yogi Berra Puts Yanks In 1st	3.50	1.40	.35
□ 29 Campy NL MVP	4.00	1.60	.40
□ 30 Bob Turley Hurls Yankees To WS Champions	1.25	.50	.12
□ 31 Dodgers Take Series From Sox in Six	1.25	.50	.12
□ 32 Furillo Hero as Dodgers Beat Chicago in 3rd WS Game	1.25	.50	.12
□ 33 Adcock Gets 4 Homers And A Double	1.25	.50	.12
□ 34 Dickey Chosen All-Star Catcher	1.50	.60	.15
□ 35 Burdette Beats Yanks In Three WS Games	1.25	.50	.12
□ 36 Umpires Clear White Sox Bench	1.25	.50	.12
□ 37 Reese Honored As Greatest Dodger SS	3.00	1.20	.30
□ 38 Joe DiMaggio Hits In 56 Straight	7.50	3.00	.75
□ 39 Ted Williams Hits .406 For Season	5.00	2.00	.50
□ 40 Walter Johnson Pitches 56 Straight	2.50	1.00	.25
□ 41 Hodges Hits 4 Home Runs In Nite Game	1.50	.60	.15
□ 42 Greenberg Returns to Tigers From Army	1.50	.60	.15
□ 43 Ty Cobb Named Best Player Of All Time	7.50	3.00	.75
□ 44 Robin Roberts Wins 28 Games	2.00	.80	.20
□ 45 Rizzuto's Two Runs Save 1st Place	2.00	.80	.20
□ 46 Tigers Beat Out Senators For Pennant	1.25	.50	.12
□ 47 Babe Ruth Hits 60th Home Run	9.00	3.75	.90
□ 48 Cy Young Honored	2.00	.80	.20
□ 49 Killebrew Starts Spring Training	3.00	1.20	.30
□ 50 Mantle Hits Longest Homer at Stadium	10.00	4.00	1.00
□ 51 Braves Take Pennant	1.25	.50	.12
□ 52 Ted Williams Hero Of All-Star Game	5.00	2.00	.50
□ 53 Robinson Saves Dodgers For Play-off Series	4.00	1.60	.40
□ 54 Snodgrass Muffs Fly	1.25	.50	.12
□ 55 Snider Belts 2 Homers Ties Homer Record	3.50	1.40	.35
□ 56 Giants Win 26 Straight	1.25	.50	.12
□ 57 Ted Kluszewski Stars In 1st Series Win	1.50	.60	.15
□ 58 Ott Walks 5 Times In Single Game	1.50	.60	.15
□ 59 Harvey Kuenn Takes	1.25	.50	.12

A.L. Batting Title			
□ 60 Bob Feller Hurls 3rd No-Hitter of Career	3.50	1.40	.35
□ 61 Yanks Champs Again	1.25	.50	.12
□ 62 Aaron's Bat Beats Yankees In Series	5.00	2.00	.50
□ 63 Warren Spahn Beats Yanks in W.S.	2.50	1.00	.25
□ 64 Ump's Wrong Call Helps Dodgers Beat Yanks	1.25	.50	.12
□ 65 Kaline Hits 3 Homers Two In Same Inning	3.00	1.20	.30
□ 66 Bob Allison Named AL Rookie of the Year	1.25	.50	.12
□ 67 McCovey Blasts Way Into Giant Lineup	3.00	1.20	.30
□ 68 Colavito Hits Four Homers in One Game	1.50	.60	.15
□ 69 Erskine Sets Strike Out Record in World Series	1.25	.50	.12
□ 70 Sal Maglie Pitches No-Hit Game	1.25	.50	.12
□ 71 Early Wynn Victory Crushes Yanks	1.50	.60	.15
□ 72 Nellie Fox AL MVP	1.50	.60	.15

1961 Nu-Card Scoops

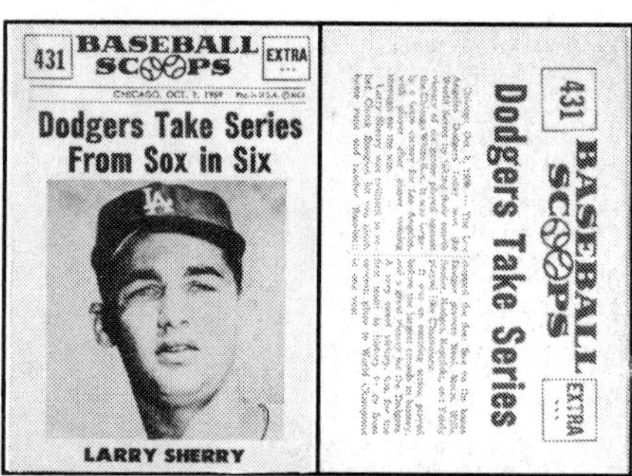

The cards in this 80-card set measure 2 1/2" by 3 1/2". This series depicts great moments in the history of individual ballplayers. Each card is designed as a miniature newspaper front-page, complete with data and picture. Both the number (401-480) and title are printed in red on the obverse, and the story is found on the back. An album was issued to hold the set. The set has been illegally reprinted, which has served to suppress the demand for the originals as well as the reprints.

	NRMT	VG-E	GOOD
COMPLETE SET (80)	80.00	30.00	10.00
COMMON PLAYER (401-480)	.40	.16	.04
□ 401 Jim Gentile	.40	.16	.04
□ 402 Warren Spahn (No-hitter)	1.50	.60	.15
□ 403 Bill Mazeroski	.75	.30	.07
□ 404 Willie Mays: (three triples)	4.00	1.60	.40
□ 405 Woodie Held	.40	.16	.04
□ 406 Vern Law	.40	.16	.04
□ 407 Pete Runnels	.40	.16	.04
□ 408 Lew Burdette (No-hitter)	.50	.20	.05
□ 409 Dick Stuart	.40	.16	.04
□ 410 Don Cardwell	.40	.16	.04
□ 411 Camilo Pascual	.40	.16	.04
□ 412 Ed Mathews	1.50	.60	.15
□ 413 Dick Groat	.60	.24	.06
□ 414 Gene Autry	1.50	.60	.15
□ 415 Bobby Richardson	.60	.24	.06
□ 416 Roger Maris	4.00	1.60	.40
□ 417 Fred Merkle	.40	.16	.04
□ 418 Don Larsen	.50	.20	.05
□ 419 Mickey Cochrane	.75	.30	.07
□ 420 Ernie Banks	2.00	.80	.20
□ 421 Stan Musial	3.50	1.40	.35
□ 422 Mickey Mantle (longest homer)	8.00	3.25	.80
□ 423 Roy Sievers	.40	.16	.04
□ 424 Lou Gehrig	4.00	1.60	.40
□ 425 Red Schoendienst	.50	.20	.05
□ 426 Eddie Gaedel	1.50	.60	.15
□ 427 Willie Mays (greatest catch)	4.00	1.60	.40
□ 428 Jackie Robinson	3.50	1.40	.35
□ 429 Roy Campanella	3.50	1.40	.35
□ 430 Bob Turley	.40	.16	.04
□ 431 Larry Sherry	.40	.16	.04
□ 432 Carl Furillo	.50	.20	.05
□ 433 Joe Adcock	.50	.20	.05
□ 434 Bill Dickey	.75	.30	.07
□ 435 Burdette 3 wins	.50	.20	.05
□ 436 Umpire Clears Bench	.40	.16	.04
□ 437 Pee Wee Reese	2.50	1.00	.25
□ 438 Joe DiMaggio (56 Game Hit Streak)	6.00	2.40	.60
□ 439 Ted Williams Hits .406	4.50	1.80	.45
□ 440 Walter Johnson	2.00	.80	.20
□ 441 Gil Hodges	1.50	.60	.15
□ 442 Hank Greenberg	1.00	.40	.10
□ 443 Ty Cobb	5.50	2.20	.55
□ 444 Robin Roberts	2.00	.80	.20
□ 445 Phil Rizzuto	1.50	.60	.15
□ 446 Hal Newhouser	.60	.24	.06
□ 447 Babe Ruth 60th Homer	7.50	3.00	.75
□ 448 Cy Young	1.50	.60	.15
□ 449 Harmon Killebrew	2.50	1.00	.25
□ 450 Mickey Mantle (longest homer)	8.00	3.25	.80
□ 451 Braves Take Pennant	.40	.16	.04
□ 452 Ted Williams (All-Star Hero)	4.50	1.80	.45
□ 453 Yogi Berra	3.50	1.40	.35
□ 454 Fred Snodgrass	.40	.16	.04
□ 455 Ruth 3 Homers	7.50	3.00	.75
□ 456 Giants 26 Game Streak	.40	.16	.04
□ 457 Ted Kluszewski	.75	.30	.07
□ 458 Mel Ott	1.00	.40	.10
□ 459 Harvey Kuenn	.60	.24	.06
□ 460 Bob Feller	2.50	1.00	.25
□ 461 Casey Stengel	1.50	.60	.15
□ 462 Hank Aaron	4.00	1.60	.40
□ 463 Spahn Beats Yanks	1.00	.40	.10
□ 464 Ump's Wrong Call	.40	.16	.04
□ 465 Al Kaline	2.50	1.00	.25
□ 466 Bob Allison	.40	.16	.04
□ 467 Joe DiMaggio (Four Homers)	6.00	2.40	.60
□ 468 Rocky Colavito	.60	.24	.06
□ 469 Carl Erskine	.50	.20	.05
□ 470 Sal Maglie	.50	.20	.05
□ 471 Early Wynn	1.25	.50	.12
□ 472 Nellie Fox	.75	.30	.07
□ 473 Marty Marion	.60	.24	.06
□ 474 Johnny Podres	.50	.20	.05
□ 475 Mickey Owen	.40	.16	.04
□ 476 Dean Brothers (Dizzy and Daffy)	2.00	.80	.20
□ 477 Christy Mathewson	2.00	.80	.20
□ 478 Harvey Haddix	.40	.16	.04
□ 479 Carl Hubbell	.60	.24	.06
□ 480 Bobby Thomson	.60	.24	.06

1952 Num Num

The cards in this 20-card set measure 3 1/2" by 4 1/2". The 1952 Num Num Potato Chips issue features black and white, numbered cards of the Cleveland Indians. Cards came with and without coupons (tabs). The cards were issued without coupons directly by the Cleveland baseball club. When the complete set was obtained the tabs were cut off and exchanged for an autographed baseball. Card Number 16, Kennedy, is rather scarce. Cards with the tabs still intact are worth approximately 25% more than the values listed below. The ACC designation for this set is F337-2.

	NRMT	VG-E	GOOD
COMPLETE SET (20)	700.00	300.00	90.00
COMMON PLAYER (1-20)	18.00	7.25	1.80

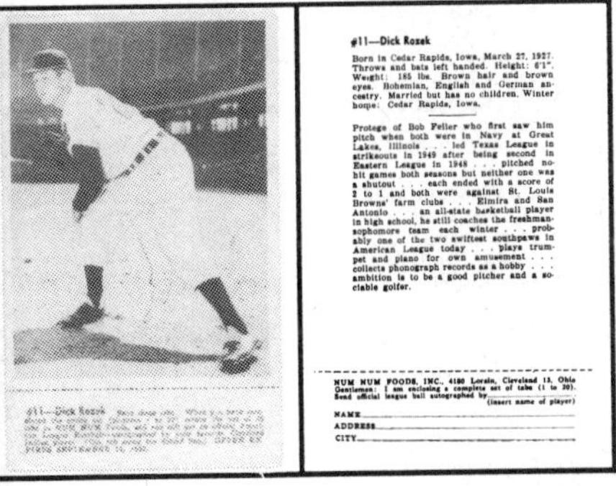

□ 1 Lou Brissie	18.00	7.25	1.80
□ 2 Jim Hegan	18.00	7.25	1.80
□ 3 Birdie Tebbetts	18.00	7.25	1.80
□ 4 Bob Lemon	45.00	18.00	4.50
□ 5 Bob Feller	75.00	30.00	7.50
□ 6 Early Wynn	45.00	18.00	4.50
□ 7 Mike Garcia	25.00	10.00	2.50
□ 8 Steve Gromek	18.00	7.25	1.80
□ 9 Bob Chakales	18.00	7.25	1.80
□ 10 Al Rosen	35.00	14.00	3.50
□ 11 Dick Rozek	18.00	7.25	1.80
□ 12 Luke Easter	18.00	7.25	1.80
□ 13 Ray Boone	18.00	7.25	1.80
□ 14 Bobby Avila	18.00	7.25	1.80
□ 15 Dale Mitchell	18.00	7.25	1.80
□ 16 Bob Kennedy	300.00	120.00	30.00
□ 17 Harry Simpson	18.00	7.25	1.80
□ 18 Larry Doby	35.00	14.00	3.50
□ 19 Sam Jones	18.00	7.25	1.80
□ 20 Al Lopez MG	45.00	18.00	4.50

1986 Oh Henry Indians

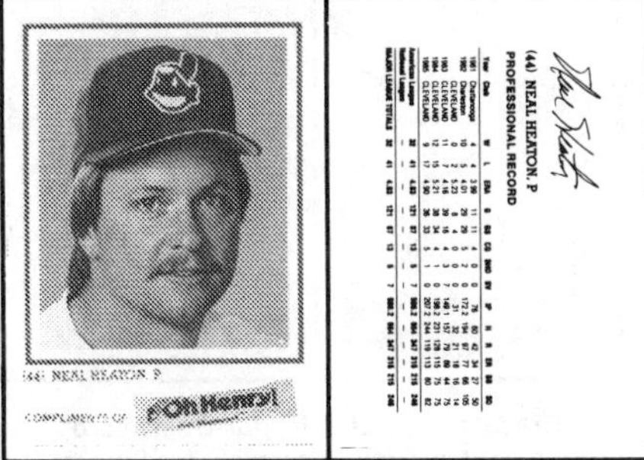

This 30-card set features Cleveland Indians and was distributed at the stadium to fans in attendance on Baseball Card Day. The cards were printed in one folded sheet which was perforated for easy separation into individual cards. The cards have white borders with a blue frame around each photo. The card backs include detailed career year-by-year statistics. The individual cards measure 2 1/4" by 3 1/8" and have full-color fronts.

	MINT	EXC	G-VG
COMPLETE SET (30)	10.00	4.00	1.00
COMMON PLAYER	.25	.10	.02
□ 2 Brett Butler	.50	.20	.05
□ 4 Tony Bernazard	.35	.14	.03
□ 6 Andy Allanson	.35	.14	.03
□ 7 Pat Corrales MG	.25	.10	.02
□ 8 Carmen Castillo	.25	.10	.02
□ 10 Pat Tabler	.50	.20	.05
□ 13 Ernie Camacho	.35	.14	.03
□ 14 Julio Franco	.75	.30	.07
□ 15 Dan Rohn	.25	.10	.02
□ 18 Ken Schrom	.25	.10	.02
□ 20 Otis Nixon	.25	.10	.02
□ 22 Fran Mullins	.25	.10	.02
□ 23 Chris Bando	.25	.10	.02
□ 24 Ed Williams	.35	.14	.03
□ 26 Brook Jacoby	.50	.20	.05
□ 27 Mel Hall	.35	.14	.03
□ 29 Andre Thornton	.50	.20	.05
□ 30 Joe Carter	1.00	.40	.10
□ 35 Phil Niekro	1.00	.40	.10
□ 36 Jamie Easterly	.25	.10	.02
□ 37 Don Schulze	.25	.10	.02
□ 42 Rick Yett	.25	.10	.02
□ 43 Scott Bailes	.25	.10	.02
□ 44 Neal Heaton	.25	.10	.02
□ 46 Jim Kern	.25	.10	.02
□ 48 Dickie Noles	.25	.10	.02
□ 49 Tom Candiotti	.25	.10	.02
□ 53 Reggie Ritter	.25	.10	.02
□ 54 Tom Waddell	.25	.10	.02
□ xx Coaching Staff Jack Aker Bobby Bonds Doc Edwards John Goryl	.25	.10	.02

1988 Pacific Eight Men Out

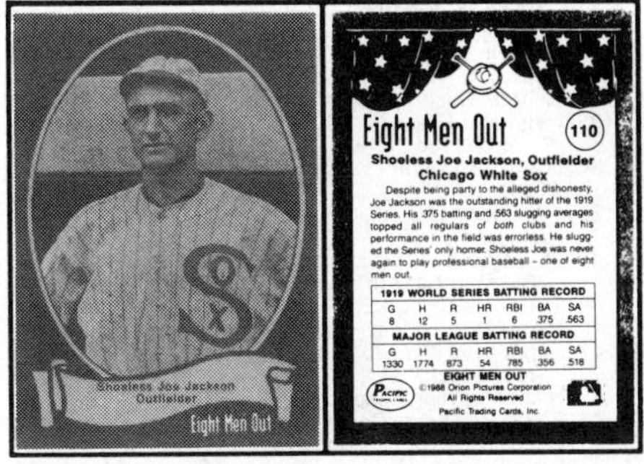

This set was produced by Mike Cramer's Pacific Trading Cards of Edmonds, Washington. The set was released in conjunction with the popular movie of the same name, which told the story of the "fix" of the 1919 World Series between the Cincinnati Reds and the Chicago "Black" Sox. The cards are standard size, 2 1/2" by 3 1/2" and have a raspberry-colored border on the card fronts as well as raspberry-colored print on the white card stock backs. The cards were available either as wax packs or as collated sets. Generally the cards relating to the movie (showing actors) are in full-color whereas the vintage photography showing the actual players involved is in a sepia tone.

	MINT	EXC	G-VG
COMPLETE SET (110)	10.00	4.00	1.00
COMMON PLAYER (1-110)	.10	.04	.01
□ 1 We're Going To See The Sox	.10	.04	.01
□ 2 White Sox Win The Pennant	.10	.04	.01
□ 3 The Series	.10	.04	.01
□ 4 1919 Chicago White Sox	.10	.04	.01
□ 5 The Black Sox Scandal	.10	.04	.01
□ 6 Eddie Cicotte 29-7 in 1919	.10	.04	.01
□ 7 "Buck's Their Favorite"	.10	.04	.01
□ 8 Eddie Collins	.20	.08	.02
□ 9 Michael Rooker as Chick Gandil	.10	.04	.01
□ 10 Charlie Sheen as Hap Felsch	.20	.08	.02
□ 11 James Read as	.10	.04	.01

Lefty Williams			
☐ 12 John Cusak as Buck Weaver	.10	.04	.01
☐ 13 D.B. Sweeney as Joe Jackson	.20	.08	.02
☐ 14 David Strathairn as Eddie Cicotte	.10	.04	.01
☐ 15 Perry Lang as Fred McMullin	.10	.04	.01
☐ 16 Don Harvey as Swede Risberg	.10	.04	.01
☐ 17 The Gambler Burns And Maharg	.10	.04	.01
☐ 18 "Sleepy"Bill Burns	.10	.04	.01
☐ 19 The Key is Cicotte	.10	.04	.01
☐ 20 C'moan Betsy	.10	.04	.01
☐ 21 The Fix	.10	.04	.01
☐ 22 Chick Approaches Cicotte	.10	.04	.01
☐ 23 Kid Gleason	.10	.04	.01
☐ 24 Charles Comiskey Owner	.10	.04	.01
☐ 25 Chick Gandil 1st Baseman	.10	.04	.01
☐ 26 Swede Risberg	.10	.04	.01
☐ 27 Sport Sullivan	.10	.04	.01
☐ 28 Abe Attell And Arnold Rothstein	.10	.04	.01
☐ 29 Hugh Fullerton Sportswriter	.10	.04	.01
☐ 30 Ring Lardner Sportswriter	.10	.04	.01
☐ 31 "Shoeless"Joe His Batting Eye	.20	.08	.02
☐ 32 "Shoeless Joe"	.30	.12	.03
☐ 33 Buck Can't Sleep	.10	.04	.01
☐ 34 George"Buck" Weaver	.10	.04	.01
☐ 35 Hugh and Ring Confront Kid	.10	.04	.01
☐ 36 Joe Doesn't Want To Play	.10	.04	.01
☐ 37 "Shoeless" Joe Jackson	.20	.08	.02
☐ 38 "Sore Arm, Cicotte," "Old Man Cicotte"	.10	.04	.01
☐ 39 The Fix Is On	.10	.04	.01
☐ 40 Buck Plays To Win	.10	.04	.01
☐ 41 Hap Makes A Great Catch	.10	.04	.01
☐ 42 Hugh and Ring Suspect	.10	.04	.01
☐ 43 Ray Gets Things Going	.10	.04	.01
☐ 44 Lefty Loses Game Two	.10	.04	.01
☐ 45 Lefty Crosses Up Catcher Ray Schalk	.10	.04	.01
☐ 46 Chick's RBI Wins Game Three	.10	.04	.01
☐ 47 Dickie Kerr Wins Game Three	.10	.04	.01
☐ 48 Chick Leaves Buck At Third	.10	.04	.01
☐ 49 Williams Loses Game Five	.10	.04	.01
☐ 50 Ray Schalk	.10	.04	.01
☐ 51 Schalk Blocks The Plate	.10	.04	.01
☐ 52 Schalk Is Thrown Out	.10	.04	.01
☐ 53 Chicago Stickball Game	.10	.04	.01
☐ 54 I'm Forever Blowing Ball Games	.10	.04	.01
☐ 55 Felsch Scores Jackson	.20	.08	.02
☐ 56 Kerr Wins Game Six	.10	.04	.01
☐ 57 Where The Money	.10	.04	.01
☐ 58 Cicotte Wins Game Seven	.10	.04	.01
☐ 59 Kid Watches Eddie	.10	.04	.01
☐ 60 Lefty Is Threatened	.10	.04	.01
☐ 61 James, Get Your Arm Ready, Fast	.10	.04	.01
☐ 62 Shoeless Joe's Home Run	.20	.08	.02
☐ 63 Buck Played His Best	.10	.04	.01
☐ 64 Hugh Exposes The Fix	.10	.04	.01
☐ 65 "Sign The Petition"	.10	.04	.01
☐ 66 Baseball Owners Hire A Commissioner	.10	.04	.01
☐ 67 Judge Kenesaw Mountain Landis	.10	.04	.01
☐ 68 Grand Jury Summoned	.10	.04	.01
☐ 69 "Say It Ain't So, Joe"	.10	.04	.01
☐ 70 The Swede's A Hard Guy	.10	.04	.01
☐ 71 Buck Loves The Game	.10	.04	.01
☐ 72 The Trial	.10	.04	.01
☐ 73 Kid Gleason Takes The Stand	.10	.04	.01
☐ 74 The Verdict	.10	.04	.01
☐ 75 Eight Men Out	.10	.04	.01
☐ 76 Oscar"Happy" Felsch	.20	.08	.02
☐ 77 Who's Joe Jackson	.20	.08	.02
☐ 78 Ban Johnson	.10	.04	.01
☐ 79 Judge Landis	.10	.04	.01
☐ 80 Charles Comiskey	.10	.04	.01
☐ 81 Heinie Groth	.10	.04	.01
☐ 82 Slim Sallee	.10	.04	.01
☐ 83 Dutch Ruether	.10	.04	.01
☐ 84 Edd Roush	.20	.08	.02
☐ 85 Morrie Rath	.10	.04	.01
☐ 86 Bill Rariden	.10	.04	.01
☐ 87 Jimmy Ring	.10	.04	.01
☐ 88 Greasy Neale	.10	.04	.01
☐ 89 Pat Moran	.10	.04	.01
☐ 90 Adolfo Luque	.10	.04	.01
☐ 91 Larry Kopf	.10	.04	.01
☐ 92 Ray Fisher	.10	.04	.01
☐ 93 Hod Eller	.10	.04	.01
☐ 94 Pat Duncan	.10	.04	.01
☐ 95 Jake Daubert	.10	.04	.01
☐ 96 Red Faber	.20	.08	.02
☐ 97 Dickie Kerr	.10	.04	.01
☐ 98 Shano Collins	.10	.04	.01
☐ 99 Eddie Collins	.20	.08	.02
☐ 100 Ray Schalk	.20	.08	.02
☐ 101 Nemo Leibold	.10	.04	.01
☐ 102 Kid Gleason	.10	.04	.01
☐ 103 Swede Risberg	.10	.04	.01
☐ 104 Eddie Cicotte	.10	.04	.01
☐ 105 Fred McMullin	.10	.04	.01
☐ 106 Chick Gandil	.10	.04	.01
☐ 107 Buck Weaver	.10	.04	.01
☐ 108 Lefty Williams	.10	.04	.01
☐ 109 Happy Felsch	.10	.04	.01
☐ 110 Joe Jackson	.30	.12	.03

1988 Pacific Legends

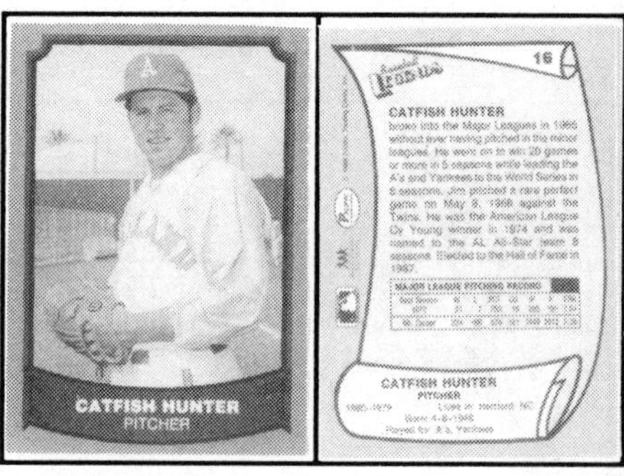

This attractive set of 110 full-color cards was produced by Mike Cramer's Pacific Trading Cards of Edmonds, Washington. The cards are silver bordered and are standard size, 2 1/2" by 3 1/2". Card backs are printed in yellow, black, and gray on white card stock. The cards were available either as wax packs or as collated sets. The players pictured in the set had retired many years before, but most are still well remembered. The statistics on the card backs give the player's career and "best season" statistics. The set was licensed by Major League Baseball Players Alumni.

	MINT	EXC	G-VG
COMPLETE SET (110)	10.00	4.00	1.00
COMMON PLAYER (1-110)	.05	.02	.00
☐ 1 Hank Aaron	.65	.26	.06
☐ 2 Red Schoendienst	.10	.04	.01
☐ 3 Brooks Robinson	.30	.12	.03
☐ 4 Luke Appling	.10	.04	.01
☐ 5 Gene Woodling	.05	.02	.00
☐ 6 Stan Musial	.50	.20	.05
☐ 7 Mickey Mantle	1.00	.40	.10
☐ 8 Richie Ashburn	.15	.06	.01

□ 9 Ralph Kiner .20 .08 .02
□ 10 Phil Rizzuto .15 .06 .01
□ 11 Harvey Haddix .05 .02 .00
□ 12 Ken Boyer .10 .04 .01
□ 13 Clete Boyer .05 .02 .00
□ 14 Ken Harrelson .10 .04 .01
□ 15 Robin Roberts .20 .08 .02
□ 16 Catfish Hunter .20 .08 .02
□ 17 Frank Howard .10 .04 .01
□ 18 Jim Perry .05 .02 .00
□ 19A Elston Howard ERR .10 .04 .01
(reversed negative)
□ 19B Elston Howard COR .10 .04 .01
□ 20 Jim Bouton .10 .04 .01
□ 21 Pee Wee Reese .20 .08 .02
□ 22A Mel Stottlemyre ERR .10 .04 .01
(spelled Stottlemyer on card front)
□ 22B Mel Stottlemyre COR .10 .04 .01
□ 23 Hank Sauer .05 .02 .00
□ 24 Willie Mays .65 .26 .06
□ 25 Tom Tresh .10 .04 .01
□ 26 Roy Sievers .05 .02 .00
□ 27 Leo Durocher .15 .06 .01
□ 28 Al Dark .05 .02 .00
□ 29 Tony Kubek .15 .06 .01
□ 30 Johnny VanderMeer .10 .04 .01
□ 31 Joe Adcock .05 .02 .00
□ 32 Bob Lemon .15 .06 .01
□ 33 Don Newcombe .10 .04 .01
□ 34 Thurman Munson .30 .12 .03
□ 35 Earl Battey .05 .02 .00
□ 36 Ernie Banks .30 .12 .03
□ 37 Matty Alou .05 .02 .00
□ 38 Dave McNally .05 .02 .00
□ 39 Mickey Lolich .10 .04 .01
□ 40 Jackie Robinson .30 .12 .03
□ 41 Allie Reynolds .10 .04 .01
□ 42A Don Larsen ERR .10 .04 .01
(misspelled Larson on card front)
□ 42B Don Larsen COR .10 .04 .01
□ 43 Fergie Jenkins .10 .04 .01
□ 44 Jim Gilliam .10 .04 .01
□ 45 Bobby Thomson .10 .04 .01
□ 46 Sparky Anderson .10 .04 .01
□ 47 Roy Campanella .30 .12 .03
□ 48 Marv Throneberry .10 .04 .01
□ 49 Bill Virdon .05 .02 .00
□ 50 Ted Williams .50 .20 .05
□ 51 Minnie Minoso .10 .04 .01
□ 52 Bob Turley .05 .02 .00
□ 53 Yogi Berra .30 .12 .03
□ 54 Juan Marichal .20 .08 .02
□ 55 Duke Snider .35 .14 .03
□ 56 Harvey Kuenn .10 .04 .01
□ 57 Nellie Fox .15 .06 .01
□ 58 Felipe Alou .05 .02 .00
□ 59 Tony Oliva .10 .04 .01
□ 60 Bill Mazeroski .10 .04 .01
□ 61 Bobby Shantz .05 .02 .00
□ 62 Mark Fidrych .05 .02 .00
□ 63 Johnny Mize .20 .08 .02
□ 64 Ralph Terry .10 .04 .01
□ 65 Gus Bell .05 .02 .00
□ 66 Jerry Koosman .10 .04 .01
□ 67 Mike McCormick .05 .02 .00
□ 68 Lou Burdette .10 .04 .01
□ 69 George Kell .20 .08 .02
□ 70 Vic Raschi .10 .04 .01
□ 71 Chuck Connors .20 .08 .02
□ 72 Ted Kluszewski .15 .06 .01
□ 73 Bobby Doerr .20 .08 .02
□ 74 Bobby Richardson .15 .06 .01
□ 75 Carl Erskine .10 .04 .01
□ 76 Hoyt Wilhelm .20 .08 .02
□ 77 Bob Purkey .05 .02 .00
□ 78 Bob Friend .05 .02 .00
□ 79 Monte Irvin .20 .08 .02
□ 80A Jim Lonborg ERR .10 .04 .01
(misspelled Longborg on card front)
□ 80B Jim Lonborg COR .10 .04 .01
□ 81 Wally Moon .05 .02 .00
□ 82 Moose Skowron .10 .04 .01
□ 83 Tommy Davis .10 .04 .01
□ 84 Enos Slaughter .20 .08 .02
□ 85 Sal Maglie .10 .04 .01
□ 86 Harmon Killebrew .20 .08 .02
□ 87 Gil Hodges .20 .08 .02
□ 88 Jim Kaat .10 .04 .01
□ 89 Roger Maris .40 .16 .04
□ 90 Billy Williams .20 .08 .02
□ 91 Luis Aparicio .20 .08 .02
□ 92 Jim Bunning .15 .06 .01
□ 93 Bill Freehan .10 .04 .01
□ 94 Orlando Cepeda .15 .06 .01
□ 95 Early Wynn .20 .08 .02
□ 96 Tug McGraw .10 .04 .01
□ 97 Ron Santo .10 .04 .01
□ 98 Del Crandall .05 .02 .00
□ 99 Sal Bando .05 .02 .00
□ 100 Joe DiMaggio .65 .26 .06
□ 101 Bob Feller .30 .12 .03
□ 102 Larry Doby .10 .04 .01
□ 103 Rollie Fingers .15 .06 .01
□ 104 Al Kaline .25 .10 .02
□ 105 Johnny Podres .10 .04 .01
□ 106 Lou Boudreau .20 .08 .02
□ 107 Zoilo Versalles .05 .02 .00
□ 108 Dick Groat .10 .04 .01
□ 109 Warren Spahn .25 .10 .02
□ 110 Johnny Bench .35 .14 .03

1988 Pepsi Tigers

This set of 25 cards features members of the Detroit Tigers and was sponsored by Pepsi Cola and Kroger. The cards are in full color on the fronts and measure approximately 2 7/8" by 4 1/4". The card backs contain complete Major and Minor League season-by-season statistics. The cards are unnumbered so they are listed below by uniform number, which is given on the card.

	MINT	EXC	G-VG
COMPLETE SET (25)	7.50	3.00	.75
COMMON PLAYER	.20	.08	.02

□ 1 Lou Whitaker .40 .16 .04
□ 2 Alan Trammell .75 .30 .07
□ 8 Mike Heath .20 .08 .02
□ 11 Sparky Anderson MG .30 .12 .03
□ 12 Luis Salazar .20 .08 .02
□ 14 Dave Bergman .20 .08 .02
□ 15 Pat Sheridan .20 .08 .02
□ 16 Tom Brookens .20 .08 .02
□ 19 Doyle Alexander .30 .12 .03
□ 21 Guillermo Hernandez .30 .12 .03
□ 22 Ray Knight .30 .12 .03
□ 24 Gary Pettis .30 .12 .03
□ 25 Eric King .20 .08 .02
□ 26 Frank Tanana .30 .12 .03
□ 31 Larry Herndon .20 .08 .02
□ 32 Jim Walewander .20 .08 .02
□ 33 Matt Nokes .40 .16 .04
□ 34 Chet Lemon .30 .12 .03
□ 35 Walt Terrell .30 .12 .03
□ 39 Mike Henneman .30 .12 .03
□ 41 Darrell Evans .40 .16 .04
□ 44 Jeff Robinson .40 .16 .04
□ 47 Jack Morris .50 .20 .05
□ 48 Paul Gibson .20 .08 .02
□ xx Tigers Coaches .20 .08 .02
Billy Consolo
Alex Grammas
Billy Muffett
Vada Pinson
Dick Tracewski

1939 Playball

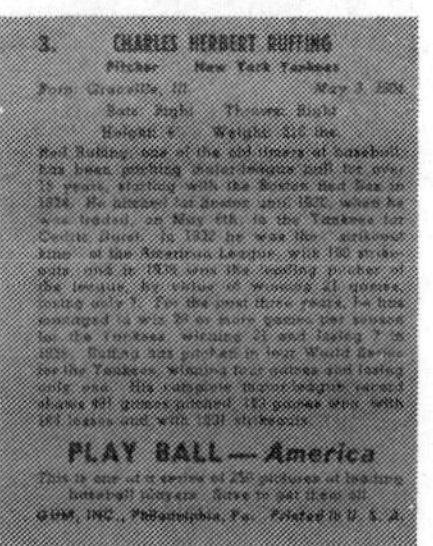

The cards in this 162-card set measure 2 1/2" by 3 1/8". Gum Incorporated introduced a brief (war-shortened) but innovative era of baseball card production with its set of 1939. The combination of actual player photos (black and white), large card size, and extensive biography proved extremely popular. Player names are found either entirely capitalized or with initial caps only, and a "sample card" overprint is not uncommon. Card number 126 was never issued, and cards 116-162 were produced in lesser quantities than 1-115. The ACC designation for this set is R334.

	NRMT	VG-E	GOOD
COMPLETE SET	6500.00	3000.00	900.00
COMMON PLAYER (1-115)	8.00	3.25	.80
COMMON PLAYER (116-162)	75.00	30.00	7.50

		NRMT	VG-E	GOOD
□ 1	Jake Powell	60.00	6.00	1.25
□ 2	Lee Grissom	8.00	3.25	.80
□ 3	Red Ruffing	50.00	20.00	5.00
□ 4	Eldon Auker	8.00	3.25	.80
□ 5	Luke Sewell	10.00	4.00	1.00
□ 6	Leo Durocher	40.00	16.00	4.00
□ 7	Bobby Doerr	45.00	18.00	4.50
□ 8	Henry Pippen	8.00	3.25	.80
□ 9	James Tobin	8.00	3.25	.80
□ 10	James DeShong	8.00	3.25	.80
□ 11	Johnny Rizzo	8.00	3.25	.80
□ 12	Hershel Martin	8.00	3.25	.80
□ 13	Luke Hamlin	8.00	3.25	.80
□ 14	Jim Tabor	8.00	3.25	.80
□ 15	Paul Derringer	12.00	5.00	1.20
□ 16	John Peacock	8.00	3.25	.80
□ 17	Emerson Dickman	8.00	3.25	.80
□ 18	Harry Danning	8.00	3.25	.80
□ 19	Paul Dean	15.00	6.00	1.50
□ 20	Joe Heving	8.00	3.25	.80
□ 21	Dutch Leonard	10.00	4.00	1.00
□ 22	Bucky Walters	10.00	4.00	1.00
□ 23	Burgess Whitehead	8.00	3.25	.80
□ 24	Richard Coffman	8.00	3.25	.80
□ 25	George Selkirk	15.00	6.00	1.50
□ 26	Joe DiMaggio	1000.00	450.00	125.00
□ 27	Fred Ostermueller	8.00	3.25	.80
□ 28	Sylvester Johnson	8.00	3.25	.80
□ 29	John (Jack) Wilson	8.00	3.25	.80
□ 30	Bill Dickey	100.00	40.00	10.00
□ 31	Sam West	8.00	3.25	.80
□ 32	Bob Seeds	8.00	3.25	.80
□ 33	Del Young	8.00	3.25	.80
□ 34	Frank Demaree	8.00	3.25	.80
□ 35	Bill Jurges	8.00	3.25	.80
□ 36	Frank McCormick	10.00	4.00	1.00
□ 37	Virgil Davis	8.00	3.25	.80
□ 38	Billy Myers	8.00	3.25	.80
□ 39	Rick Ferrell	45.00	18.00	4.50
□ 40	James Bagby Jr.	8.00	3.25	.80
□ 41	Lon Warneke	8.00	3.25	.80
□ 42	Arndt Jorgens	8.00	3.25	.80
□ 43	Melo Almada	8.00	3.25	.80
□ 44	Don Heffner	8.00	3.25	.80
□ 45	Merrill May	8.00	3.25	.80
□ 46	Morris Arnovich	8.00	3.25	.80
□ 47	Buddy Lewis	8.00	3.25	.80
□ 48	Lefty Gomez	80.00	32.00	8.00
□ 49	Eddie Miller	8.00	3.25	.80
□ 50	Charlie Gehringer	80.00	32.00	8.00
□ 51	Mel Ott	100.00	40.00	10.00
□ 52	Tommy Henrich	20.00	8.00	2.00
□ 53	Carl Hubbell	80.00	32.00	8.00
□ 54	Harry Gumpert	8.00	3.25	.80
□ 55	Arky Vaughan	45.00	18.00	4.50
□ 56	Hank Greenberg	100.00	40.00	10.00
□ 57	Buddy Hassett	8.00	3.25	.80
□ 58	Lou Chiozza	8.00	3.25	.80
□ 59	Ken Chase	8.00	3.25	.80
□ 60	Schoolboy Rowe	12.00	5.00	1.20
□ 61	Tony Cuccinello	8.00	3.25	.80
□ 62	Tom Carey	8.00	3.25	.80
□ 63	Emmett Mueller	8.00	3.25	.80
□ 64	Wally Moses	10.00	4.00	1.00
□ 65	Harry Craft	8.00	3.25	.80
□ 66	Jimmy Ripple	8.00	3.25	.80
□ 67	Ed Joost	8.00	3.25	.80
□ 68	Fred Sington	8.00	3.25	.80
□ 69	Elbie Fletcher	8.00	3.25	.80
□ 70	Fred Frankhouse	8.00	3.25	.80
□ 71	Monte Pearson	8.00	3.25	.80
□ 72	Debs Garms	8.00	3.25	.80
□ 73	Hal Schumacher	8.00	3.25	.80
□ 74	Cookie Lavagetto	10.00	4.00	1.00
□ 75	Stan Bordagaray	8.00	3.25	.80
□ 76	Goody Rosen	8.00	3.25	.80
□ 77	Lew Riggs	8.00	3.25	.80
□ 78	Julius Solters	8.00	3.25	.80
□ 79	Jo Jo Moore	8.00	3.25	.80
□ 80	Pete Fox	8.00	3.25	.80
□ 81	Babe Dahlgren	10.00	4.00	1.00
□ 82	Chuck Klein	65.00	26.00	6.50
□ 83	Gus Suhr	8.00	3.25	.80
□ 84	Skeeter Newsom	8.00	3.25	.80
□ 85	Johnny Cooney	8.00	3.25	.80
□ 86	Dolph Camilli	8.00	3.25	.80
□ 87	Milburn Schoffner	8.00	3.25	.80
□ 88	Charlie Keller	20.00	8.00	2.00
□ 89	Lloyd Waner	45.00	18.00	4.50
□ 90	Robert Klinger	8.00	3.25	.80
□ 91	John Knott	8.00	3.25	.80
□ 92	Ted Williams	1000.00	450.00	125.00
□ 93	Charles Gelbert	8.00	3.25	.80
□ 94	Heinie Manush	45.00	18.00	4.50
□ 95	Whit Wyatt	10.00	4.00	1.00
□ 96	Babe Phelps	8.00	3.25	.80
□ 97	Bob Johnson	10.00	4.00	1.00
□ 98	Pinky Whitney	8.00	3.25	.80
□ 99	Wally Berger	10.00	4.00	1.00
□ 100	Charles Myer	8.00	3.25	.80
□ 101	Roger Cramer	10.00	4.00	1.00
□ 102	Lem Young	8.00	3.25	.80
□ 103	Moe Berg	15.00	6.00	1.50
□ 104	Tom Bridges	10.00	4.00	1.00
□ 105	Rabbit McNair	8.00	3.25	.80
□ 106	Dolly Stark	10.00	4.00	1.00
□ 107	Joe Vosmik	8.00	3.25	.80
□ 108	Frank Hayes	8.00	3.25	.80
□ 109	Myril Hoag	8.00	3.25	.80
□ 110	Fred Fitzsimmons	8.00	3.25	.80
□ 111	Van Lingle Mungo	10.00	4.00	1.00
□ 112	Paul Waner	50.00	20.00	5.00
□ 113	Al Schacht	12.00	5.00	1.20
□ 114	Cecil Travis	8.00	3.25	.80
□ 115	Ralph Kress	8.00	3.25	.80
□ 116	Gene Desautels	75.00	30.00	7.50
□ 117	Wayne Ambler	75.00	30.00	7.50
□ 118	Lynn Nelson	75.00	30.00	7.50
□ 119	Will Hershberger	75.00	30.00	7.50
□ 120	Rabbit Warstler	75.00	30.00	7.50
□ 121	Bill Posedel	75.00	30.00	7.50
□ 122	George McQuinn	75.00	30.00	7.50
□ 123	Ray T. Davis	75.00	30.00	7.50
□ 124	Walter Brown	75.00	30.00	7.50
□ 125	Cliff Melton	75.00	30.00	7.50
□ 126	Not issued	0.00	.00	.00
□ 127	Gil Brack	75.00	30.00	7.50
□ 128	Joe Bowman	75.00	30.00	7.50
□ 129	Bill Swift	75.00	30.00	7.50
□ 130	Bill Brubaker	75.00	30.00	7.50
□ 131	Mort Cooper	90.00	36.00	9.00
□ 132	Jim Brown	75.00	30.00	7.50
□ 133	Lynn Myers	75.00	30.00	7.50
□ 134	Tot Presnell	75.00	30.00	7.50
□ 135	Mickey Owen	90.00	36.00	9.00
□ 136	Roy Bell	75.00	30.00	7.50
□ 137	Pete Appleton	75.00	30.00	7.50
□ 138	George Case	75.00	30.00	7.50
□ 139	Vito Tamulis	75.00	30.00	7.50
□ 140	Ray Hayworth	75.00	30.00	7.50
□ 141	Pete Coscarart	75.00	30.00	7.50
□ 142	Ira Hutchinson	75.00	30.00	7.50
□ 143	Earl Averill	200.00	80.00	20.00
□ 144	Zeke Bonura	75.00	30.00	7.50
□ 145	Hugh Mulcahy	75.00	30.00	7.50

	No.	Player	NRMT	VG-E	GOOD
□	146	Tom Sunkel	75.00	30.00	7.50
□	147	George Coffman	75.00	30.00	7.50
□	148	Bill Trotter	75.00	30.00	7.50
□	149	Max West	75.00	30.00	7.50
□	150	James Walkup	75.00	30.00	7.50
□	151	Hugh Casey	90.00	36.00	9.00
□	152	Roy Weatherly	75.00	30.00	7.50
□	153	Paul Trout	75.00	30.00	7.50
□	154	Johnny Hudson	75.00	30.00	7.50
□	155	Jimmy Outlaw	75.00	30.00	7.50
□	156	Ray Berres	75.00	30.00	7.50
□	157	Don Padgett	75.00	30.00	7.50
□	158	Bud Thomas	75.00	30.00	7.50
□	159	Red Evans	75.00	30.00	7.50
□	160	Gene Moore	75.00	30.00	7.50
□	161	Lonnie Frey	75.00	30.00	7.50
□	162	Whitey Moore	90.00	36.00	9.00

1940 Playball

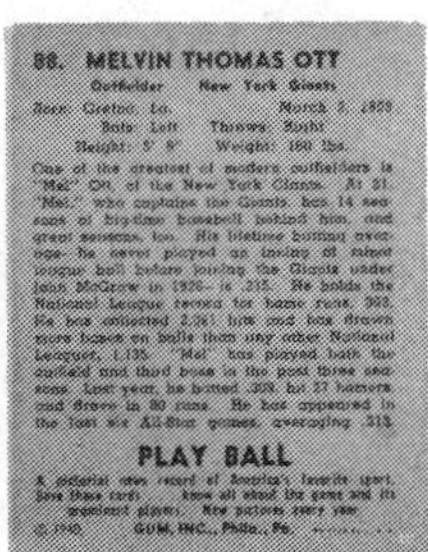
88. MELVIN THOMAS OTT

Outfielder New York Giants

PLAY BALL

GUM, INC., Phila., Pa.

The cards in this 240-card series measure 2 1/2" by 3 1/8". Gum Inc. improved upon its 1939 design by enclosing the 1940 black and white player photo with a frame line and printing the player's name in a panel below the picture (often using a nickname). The set included many Hall of Famers and Old Timers. Cards 181-240 are scarcer than cards 1-180. The backs contain an extensive biography and a dated copyright line. The ACC catalog number is R335.

	NRMT	VG-E	GOOD
COMPLETE SET (240)	9750.00	4500.00	1500.00
COMMON PLAYER (1-120)	10.00	4.00	1.00
COMMON PLAYER (121-180)	11.00	4.50	1.10
COMMON PLAYER (181-240)	40.00	16.00	4.00

	No.	Player	NRMT	VG-E	GOOD
□	1	Joe DiMaggio	1500.00	400.00	100.00
□	2	Art Jorgens	10.00	4.00	1.00
□	3	Babe Dahlgren	12.00	5.00	1.20
□	4	Tommy Henrich	20.00	8.00	2.00
□	5	Monte Pearson	12.00	5.00	1.20
□	6	Lefty Gomez	100.00	40.00	10.00
□	7	Bill Dickey	125.00	50.00	12.50
□	8	George Selkirk	15.00	6.00	1.50
□	9	Charlie Keller	20.00	8.00	2.00
□	10	Red Ruffing	60.00	24.00	6.00
□	11	Jake Powell	10.00	4.00	1.00
□	12	Johnny Schulte	10.00	4.00	1.00
□	13	Jack Knott	10.00	4.00	1.00
□	14	Rabbit McNair	10.00	4.00	1.00
□	15	George Case	10.00	4.00	1.00
□	16	Cecil Travis	10.00	4.00	1.00
□	17	Buddy Myer	10.00	4.00	1.00
□	18	Charlie Gelbert	10.00	4.00	1.00
□	19	Ken Chase	10.00	4.00	1.00
□	20	Buddy Lewis	10.00	4.00	1.00
□	21	Rick Ferrell	45.00	18.00	4.50
□	22	Sammy West	10.00	4.00	1.00
□	23	Dutch Leonard	12.00	5.00	1.20
□	24	Frank Hayes	10.00	4.00	1.00
□	25	Bob Johnson	12.00	5.00	1.20
□	26	Wally Moses	12.00	5.00	1.20
□	27	Ted Williams	700.00	280.00	70.00
□	28	Gene Desautels	10.00	4.00	1.00
□	29	Doc Cramer	12.00	5.00	1.20
□	30	Moe Berg	15.00	6.00	1.50
□	31	Jack Wilson	10.00	4.00	1.00
□	32	Jim Bagby	10.00	4.00	1.00
□	33	Fritz Ostermueller	10.00	4.00	1.00
□	34	John Peacock	10.00	4.00	1.00
□	35	Joe Heving	10.00	4.00	1.00
□	36	Jim Tabor	10.00	4.00	1.00
□	37	Emerson Dickman	10.00	4.00	1.00
□	38	Bobby Doerr	45.00	18.00	4.50
□	39	Tom Carey	10.00	4.00	1.00
□	40	Hank Greenberg	100.00	40.00	10.00
□	41	Charley Gehringer	90.00	36.00	9.00
□	42	Bud Thomas	10.00	4.00	1.00
□	43	Pete Fox	10.00	4.00	1.00
□	44	Dizzy Trout	12.00	5.00	1.20
□	45	Red Kress	10.00	4.00	1.00
□	46	Earl Averill	60.00	24.00	6.00
□	47	Ol' Os Vitt	10.00	4.00	1.00
□	48	Luke Sewell	12.00	5.00	1.20
□	49	Stormy Weatherly	10.00	4.00	1.00
□	50	Hal Trosky	12.00	5.00	1.20
□	51	Don Heffner	10.00	4.00	1.00
□	52	Myril Hoag	10.00	4.00	1.00
□	53	Mac McQuinn	10.00	4.00	1.00
□	54	Bill Trotter	10.00	4.00	1.00
□	55	Slick Coffman	10.00	4.00	1.00
□	56	Eddie Miller	10.00	4.00	1.00
□	57	Max West	10.00	4.00	1.00
□	58	Bill Posedel	10.00	4.00	1.00
□	59	Rabbit Warstler	10.00	4.00	1.00
□	60	John Cooney	10.00	4.00	1.00
□	61	Tony Cuccinello	10.00	4.00	1.00
□	62	Buddy Hassett	10.00	4.00	1.00
□	63	Pete Coscarart	10.00	4.00	1.00
□	64	Van Lingle Mungo	12.00	5.00	1.20
□	65	Fitz Fitzsimmons	10.00	4.00	1.00
□	66	Babe Phelps	10.00	4.00	1.00
□	67	Whit Wyatt	12.00	5.00	1.20
□	68	Dolph Camilli	10.00	4.00	1.00
□	69	Cookie Lavagetto	12.00	5.00	1.20
□	70	Hot Potato Hamlin	10.00	4.00	1.00
□	71	Mel Almada	10.00	4.00	1.00
□	72	Chuck Dressen	12.00	5.00	1.20
□	73	Bucky Walters	12.00	5.00	1.20
□	74	Duke Derringer	15.00	6.00	1.50
□	75	Buck McCormick	12.00	5.00	1.20
□	76	Lonny Frey	10.00	4.00	1.00
□	77	Bill Hershberger	10.00	4.00	1.00
□	78	Lew Riggs	10.00	4.00	1.00
□	79	Harry Wildfire Craft	10.00	4.00	1.00
□	80	Billy Myers	10.00	4.00	1.00
□	81	Wally Berger	12.00	5.00	1.20
□	82	Hank Gowdy	10.00	4.00	1.00
□	83	Cliff Melton	10.00	4.00	1.00
□	84	Jo Jo Moore	10.00	4.00	1.00
□	85	Hal Schumacher	12.00	5.00	1.20
□	86	Harry Gumbert	10.00	4.00	1.00
□	87	Carl Hubbell	90.00	36.00	9.00
□	88	Mel Ott	125.00	50.00	12.50
□	89	Bill Jurges	10.00	4.00	1.00
□	90	Frank Demaree	10.00	4.00	1.00
□	91	Suitcase Seeds	10.00	4.00	1.00
□	92	Whitey Whitehead	10.00	4.00	1.00
□	93	Harry Danning	10.00	4.00	1.00
□	94	Gus Suhr	10.00	4.00	1.00
□	95	Mul Mulcahy	10.00	4.00	1.00
□	96	Heinie Mueller	10.00	4.00	1.00
□	97	Morry Arnovich	10.00	4.00	1.00
□	98	Pinky May	10.00	4.00	1.00
□	99	Syl Johnson	10.00	4.00	1.00
□	100	Hersh Martin	10.00	4.00	1.00
□	101	Del Young	10.00	4.00	1.00
□	102	Chuck Klein	80.00	32.00	8.00
□	103	Elbie Fletcher	10.00	4.00	1.00
□	104	Big Poison Waner	60.00	24.00	6.00
□	105	Little Poison Waner	50.00	20.00	5.00
□	106	Pep Young	10.00	4.00	1.00
□	107	Arky Vaughan	45.00	18.00	4.50
□	108	Johnny Rizzo	10.00	4.00	1.00
□	109	Don Padgett	10.00	4.00	1.00
□	110	Tom Sunkel	10.00	4.00	1.00
□	111	Mickey Owen	12.00	5.00	1.20
□	112	Jimmy Brown	10.00	4.00	1.00
□	113	Mort Cooper	12.00	5.00	1.20
□	114	Lon Warneke	10.00	4.00	1.00
□	115	Mike Gonzales	10.00	4.00	1.00
□	116	Al Schacht	15.00	6.00	1.50
□	117	Dolly Stark	12.00	5.00	1.20
□	118	Schoolboy Hoyt	50.00	20.00	5.00
□	119	Ol Pete Alexander	80.00	32.00	8.00
□	120	Walter Johnson	150.00	60.00	15.00
□	121	Atley Donald	11.00	4.50	1.10
□	122	Sandy Sundra	11.00	4.50	1.10
□	123	Hildy Hildebrand	11.00	4.50	1.10
□	124	Colonel Earle Combs	75.00	30.00	7.50
□	125	Art Fletcher	11.00	4.50	1.10
□	126	Jake Solters	11.00	4.50	1.10
□	127	Muddy Ruel	11.00	4.50	1.10
□	128	Pete Appleton	11.00	4.50	1.10
□	129	Bucky Harris	45.00	18.00	4.50

□ 130 Deerfoot Milan	11.00	4.50	1.10
□ 131 Zeke Bonura	11.00	4.50	1.10
□ 132 Connie Mack	90.00	36.00	9.00
□ 133 Jimmie Foxx	150.00	60.00	15.00
□ 134 Joe Cronin	90.00	36.00	9.00
□ 135 Line Drive Nelson	11.00	4.50	1.10
□ 136 Cotton Pippen	11.00	4.50	1.10
□ 137 Bing Miller	11.00	4.50	1.10
□ 138 Beau Bell	11.00	4.50	1.10
□ 139 Elden Auker	11.00	4.50	1.10
□ 140 Dick Coffman	11.00	4.50	1.10
□ 141 Casey Stengel	125.00	50.00	12.50
□ 142 Highpockets Kelly	50.00	20.00	5.00
□ 143 Gene Moore	11.00	4.50	1.10
□ 144 Joe Vosmik	11.00	4.50	1.10
□ 145 Vito Tamulis	11.00	4.50	1.10
□ 146 Tot Pressnell	11.00	4.50	1.10
□ 147 Johnny Hudson	11.00	4.50	1.10
□ 148 Hugh Casey	11.00	4.50	1.10
□ 149 Pinky Shoffner	11.00	4.50	1.10
□ 150 Whitey Moore	11.00	4.50	1.10
□ 151 Edwin Joost	11.00	4.50	1.10
□ 152 Jimmy Wilson	11.00	4.50	1.10
□ 153 Bill McKechnie	45.00	18.00	4.50
□ 154 Jumbo Brown	11.00	4.50	1.10
□ 155 Ray Hayworth	11.00	4.50	1.10
□ 156 Daffy Dean	20.00	8.00	2.00
□ 157 Lou Chiozza	11.00	4.50	1.10
□ 158 Travis Jackson	50.00	20.00	5.00
□ 159 Pancho Snyder	11.00	4.50	1.10
□ 160 Hans Lobert	11.00	4.50	1.10
□ 161 Debs Garms	11.00	4.50	1.10
□ 162 Joe Bowman	11.00	4.50	1.10
□ 163 Spud Davis	11.00	4.50	1.10
□ 164 Ray Berres	11.00	4.50	1.10
□ 165 Bob Klinger	11.00	4.50	1.10
□ 166 Bill Brubaker	11.00	4.50	1.10
□ 167 Frankie Frisch	75.00	30.00	7.50
□ 168 Honus Wagner	150.00	60.00	15.00
□ 169 Gabby Street	10.00	4.00	1.00
□ 170 Tris Speaker	125.00	50.00	12.50
□ 171 Harry Heilmann	75.00	30.00	7.50
□ 172 Chief Bender	60.00	24.00	6.00
□ 173 Larry Lajoie	125.00	50.00	12.50
□ 174 Johnny Evers	60.00	24.00	6.00
□ 175 Christy Mathewson	150.00	60.00	15.00
□ 176 Heinie Manush	50.00	20.00	5.00
□ 177 Homerun Baker	60.00	24.00	6.00
□ 178 Max Carey	50.00	20.00	5.00
□ 179 George Sisler	75.00	30.00	7.50
□ 180 Mickey Cochrane	100.00	40.00	10.00
□ 181 Spud Chandler	50.00	20.00	5.00
□ 182 Knick Knickerbocker	40.00	16.00	4.00
□ 183 Marvin Breuer	40.00	16.00	4.00
□ 184 Mule Haas	40.00	16.00	4.00
□ 185 Joe Kuhel	40.00	16.00	4.00
□ 186 Taft Wright	40.00	16.00	4.00
□ 187 Jimmy Dykes	50.00	20.00	5.00
□ 188 Joe Krakauskas	40.00	16.00	4.00
□ 189 Jim Bloodworth	40.00	16.00	4.00
□ 190 Charley Berry	40.00	16.00	4.00
□ 191 John Babich	40.00	16.00	4.00
□ 192 Dick Siebert	40.00	16.00	4.00
□ 193 Chubby Dean	40.00	16.00	4.00
□ 194 Sam Chapman	40.00	16.00	4.00
□ 195 Dee Miles	40.00	16.00	4.00
□ 196 Nonny Nonnenkamp	40.00	16.00	4.00
□ 197 Lou Finney	40.00	16.00	4.00
□ 198 Denny Galehouse	40.00	16.00	4.00
□ 199 Pinky Higgins	40.00	16.00	4.00
□ 200 Soup Campbell	40.00	16.00	4.00
□ 201 Barney McCosky	40.00	16.00	4.00
□ 202 Al Milnar	40.00	16.00	4.00
□ 203 Bad News Hale	40.00	16.00	4.00
□ 204 Harry Eisenstat	40.00	16.00	4.00
□ 205 Rollie Hemsley	40.00	16.00	4.00
□ 206 Chet Laabs	40.00	16.00	4.00
□ 207 Gus Mancuso	40.00	16.00	4.00
□ 208 Lee Gamble	40.00	16.00	4.00
□ 209 Hy Vandenberg	40.00	16.00	4.00
□ 210 Bill Lohrman	40.00	16.00	4.00
□ 211 Pop Joiner	40.00	16.00	4.00
□ 212 Babe Young	40.00	16.00	4.00
□ 213 John Rucker	40.00	16.00	4.00
□ 214 Ken O'Dea	40.00	16.00	4.00
□ 215 Johnnie McCarthy	40.00	16.00	4.00
□ 216 Joe Marty	40.00	16.00	4.00
□ 217 Walter Beck	40.00	16.00	4.00
□ 218 Wally Millies	40.00	16.00	4.00
□ 219 Russ Bauers	40.00	16.00	4.00
□ 220 Mace Brown	40.00	16.00	4.00
□ 221 Lee Handley	40.00	16.00	4.00
□ 222 Max Butcher	40.00	16.00	4.00
□ 223 Hugh Jennings	80.00	32.00	8.00
□ 224 Pie Traynor	125.00	50.00	12.50
□ 225 Shoeless Joe Jackson	700.00	280.00	70.00
□ 226 Harry Hooper	80.00	32.00	8.00
□ 227 Pop Haines	80.00	32.00	8.00
□ 228 Charley Grimm	50.00	20.00	5.00
□ 229 Buck Herzog	40.00	16.00	4.00
□ 230 Red Faber	80.00	32.00	8.00
□ 231 Dolf Luque	40.00	16.00	4.00
□ 232 Goose Goslin	80.00	32.00	8.00
□ 233 Moose Earnshaw	40.00	16.00	4.00
□ 234 Frank(Husk) Chance	100.00	40.00	10.00
□ 235 John J. McGraw	125.00	50.00	12.50
□ 236 Jim Bottomley	80.00	32.00	8.00
□ 237 Wee Willie Keeler	100.00	40.00	10.00
□ 238 Tony Lazzeri	60.00	24.00	6.00
□ 239 George Uhle	40.00	16.00	4.00
□ 240 Bill Atwood	60.00	24.00	6.00

1941 Playball

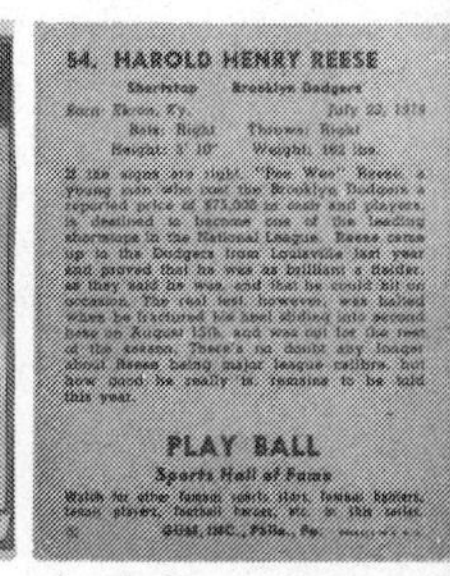

The cards in this 72-card set measure 2 1/2" by 3 1/8". Many of the cards in the 1941 Play Ball series are simply color versions of pictures appearing in the 1940 set. This was the only color baseball card set produced by Gum, Inc., and it carries the ACC designation R336. Card numbers 49-72 are slightly more difficult to obtain as they were not issued until 1942. In 1942, numbers 1-48 were also reissued but without the copyright date. The cards were also printed on paper without a cardboard backing; these are generally encountered in sheets or strips.

	NRMT	VG-E	GOOD
COMPLETE SET	6000.00	2700.00	900.00
COMMON PLAYER (1-48)	27.00	11.00	2.70
COMMON PLAYER (49-72)	35.00	14.00	3.50
□ 1 Eddie Miller	75.00	15.00	3.00
□ 2 Max West	27.00	11.00	2.70
□ 3 Bucky Walters	30.00	12.00	3.00
□ 4 Paul Derringer	35.00	14.00	3.50
□ 5 Buck McCormick	30.00	12.00	3.00
□ 6 Carl Hubbell	120.00	50.00	12.00
□ 7 Harry Danning	27.00	11.00	2.70
□ 8 Mel Ott	135.00	54.00	13.50
□ 9 Pinky May	27.00	11.00	2.70
□ 10 Arky Vaughan	60.00	24.00	6.00
□ 11 Debs Garms	27.00	11.00	2.70
□ 12 Jimmy Brown	27.00	11.00	2.70
□ 13 Jimmy Foxx	200.00	80.00	20.00
□ 14 Ted Williams	700.00	300.00	80.00
□ 15 Joe Cronin	75.00	30.00	7.50
□ 16 Hal Trosky	30.00	12.00	3.00
□ 17 Roy Weatherly	27.00	11.00	2.70
□ 18 Hank Greenberg	135.00	54.00	13.50
□ 19 Charlie Gehringer	120.00	50.00	12.00
□ 20 Red Ruffing	75.00	30.00	7.50
□ 21 Charlie Keller	40.00	16.00	4.00
□ 22 Indian Bob Johnson	35.00	14.00	3.50
□ 23 George McQuinn	27.00	11.00	2.70
□ 24 Dutch Leonard	30.00	12.00	3.00
□ 25 Gene Moore	27.00	11.00	2.70
□ 26 Harry Gumpert	27.00	11.00	2.70
□ 27 Babe Young	27.00	11.00	2.70
□ 28 Joe Marty	27.00	11.00	2.70
□ 29 Jack Wilson	27.00	11.00	2.70
□ 30 Lou Finney	27.00	11.00	2.70
□ 31 Joe Kuhel	27.00	11.00	2.70
□ 32 Taft Wright	27.00	11.00	2.70
□ 33 Al Milnar	27.00	11.00	2.70

☐ 34 Rollie Hemsley	27.00	11.00	2.70
☐ 35 Pinky Higgins	27.00	11.00	2.70
☐ 36 Barney McCosky	27.00	11.00	2.70
☐ 37 Bruce Campbell	27.00	11.00	2.70
☐ 38 Atley Donald	27.00	11.00	2.70
☐ 39 Tom Henrich	40.00	16.00	4.00
☐ 40 John Babich	27.00	11.00	2.70
☐ 41 Frank "Blimp" Hayes	27.00	11.00	2.70
☐ 42 Wally Moses	30.00	12.00	3.00
☐ 43 Al Brancato	27.00	11.00	2.70
☐ 44 Sam Chapman	27.00	11.00	2.70
☐ 45 Eldon Auker	27.00	11.00	2.70
☐ 46 Sid Hudson	27.00	11.00	2.70
☐ 47 Buddy Lewis	27.00	11.00	2.70
☐ 48 Cecil Travis	27.00	11.00	2.70
☐ 49 Babe Dahlgren	40.00	16.00	4.00
☐ 50 Johnny Cooney	35.00	14.00	3.50
☐ 51 Dolph Camilli	35.00	14.00	3.50
☐ 52 Kirby Higbe	35.00	14.00	3.50
☐ 53 Luke Hamlin	35.00	14.00	3.50
☐ 54 Pee Wee Reese	350.00	140.00	35.00
☐ 55 Whit Wyatt	40.00	16.00	4.00
☐ 56 Johnny VanderMeer	50.00	20.00	5.00
☐ 57 Moe Arnovich	35.00	14.00	3.50
☐ 58 Frank Demaree	35.00	14.00	3.50
☐ 59 Bill Jurges	35.00	14.00	3.50
☐ 60 Chuck Klein	100.00	40.00	10.00
☐ 61 Vince DiMaggio	125.00	50.00	12.50
☐ 62 Elbie Fletcher	35.00	14.00	3.50
☐ 63 Dom DiMaggio	125.00	50.00	12.50
☐ 64 Bobby Doerr	100.00	40.00	10.00
☐ 65 Tommy Bridges	40.00	16.00	4.00
☐ 66 Harland Clift	35.00	14.00	3.50
☐ 67 Walt Judnich	35.00	14.00	3.50
☐ 68 John Knott	35.00	14.00	3.50
☐ 69 George Case	35.00	14.00	3.50
☐ 70 Bill Dickey	250.00	100.00	25.00
☐ 71 Joe DiMaggio	1350.00	600.00	150.00
☐ 72 Lefty Gomez	250.00	75.00	15.00

1985 Polaroid Indians

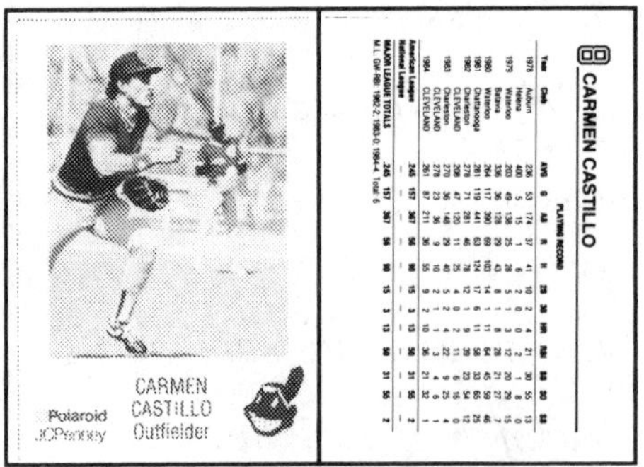
CARMEN CASTILLO
Polaroid
JCPenney
CARMEN
CASTILLO
Outfielder

This 32-card set features cards (each measuring 2 13/16" by 4 1/8") of the Cleveland Indians. The cards are unnumbered except for uniform number, as they are listed below. The set was also sponsored by J.C. Penney and was distributed at the stadium to fans in attendance on Baseball Card Day.

	MINT	EXC	G-VG
COMPLETE SET (32)	13.50	5.00	1.00
COMMON PLAYER	.35	.14	.03
☐ 2 Brett Butler	.75	.30	.07
☐ 4 Tony Bernazard	.45	.18	.04
☐ 8 Carmen Castillo	.35	.14	.03
☐ 10 Pat Tabler	.45	.18	.04
☐ 12 Benny Ayala	.35	.14	.03
☐ 13 Ernie Camacho	.35	.14	.03
☐ 14 Julio Franco	.75	.30	.07
☐ 16 Jerry Willard	.35	.14	.03
☐ 18 Pat Corrales MG	.35	.14	.03
☐ 20 Otis Nixon	.35	.14	.03
☐ 21 Mike Hargrove	.35	.14	.03
☐ 22 Mike Fischlin	.35	.14	.03
☐ 23 Chris Bando	.35	.14	.03
☐ 24 George Vukovich	.35	.14	.03
☐ 26 Brook Jacoby	.60	.24	.06
☐ 27 Mel Hall	.60	.24	.0
☐ 28 Bert Blyleven	.75	.30	.0
☐ 29 Andre Thornton	.60	.24	.0
☐ 30 Joe Carter	1.00	.40	.1
☐ 32 Rick Behenna	.35	.14	.0
☐ 33 Roy Smith	.35	.14	.0
☐ 35 Jerry Reed	.35	.14	.0
☐ 36 Jamie Easterly	.35	.14	.0
☐ 38 Dave Von Ohlen	.35	.14	.0
☐ 41 Rich Thompson	.35	.14	.0
☐ 43 Bryan Clark	.35	.14	.0
☐ 44 Neal Heaton	.45	.18	.0
☐ 48 Vern Ruhle	.35	.14	.0
☐ 49 Jeff Barkley	.35	.14	.0
☐ 50 Ramon Romero	.35	.14	.0
☐ 54 Tom Waddell	.35	.14	.0
☐ xx Coaching Staff	.35	.14	.0

Bobby Bonds
John Goryl
Don McMahon
Ed Napolean
Dennis Sommers

1979 Police Giants

#39 Bob Knepper
Pitcher
Giants

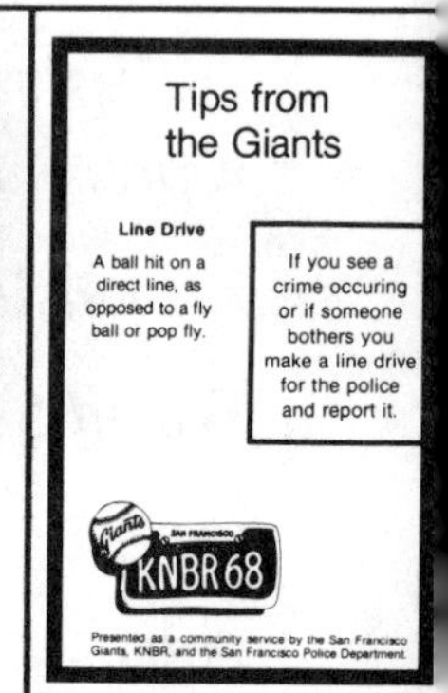
Tips from the Giants
Line Drive
A ball hit on a direct line, as opposed to a fly ball or pop fly.
If you see a crime occuring or if someone bothers you make a line drive for the police and report it.
KNBR 68
Presented as a community service by the San Francisco Giants, KNBR, and the San Francisco Police Department

The cards in this 30-card set measure 2 5/8" by 4 1/8". The 1979 Police Giants set features cards numbered by the player's uniform number. This full color set features the player's photo, the Giants' logo, and the player's name, number and position on the front of the cards. A facsimile autograph in an attractive blue ink is also contained on the front. The backs, printed in orange and black, feature Tips from the Giants, the Giants' and sponsoring radio station, KNBR, logos and a line listing the Giants, KNBR, and the San Francisco Police Department as sponsors of the set. The 15 cards which are shown with an asterisk below were available only from the Police. The other 15 cards were given away at the ballpark on June 17, 1979.

	NRMT	VG-E	GOOD
COMPLETE SET (30)	15.00	6.00	1.50
COMMON PLAYER	.35	.14	.03
☐ 1 Dave Bristol MG	.35	.14	.03
☐ 2 Marc Hill	.35	.14	.03
☐ 3 Mike Sadek *	.45	.18	.04
☐ 5 Tom Haller	.35	.14	.03
☐ 6 Joe Altobelli CO *	.45	.18	.04
☐ 8 Larry Shepard CO *	.45	.18	.04
☐ 9 Heity Cruz	.35	.14	.03
☐ 10 Johnnie LeMaster	.35	.14	.03
☐ 12 Jim Davenport	.45	.18	.04
☐ 14 Vida Blue	.45	.18	.04
☐ 15 Mike Ivie	.35	.14	.03
☐ 16 Roger Metzger	.35	.14	.03
☐ 17 Randy Moffitt	.35	.14	.03
☐ 18 Bill Madlock	.75	.30	.07
☐ 21 Rob Andrews *	.45	.18	.04
☐ 22 Jack Clark *	2.50	1.00	.25
☐ 25 Dave Roberts	.35	.14	.03
☐ 26 John Montefusco	.45	.18	.04

		MINT	EXC	G-VG
☐ 28	Ed Halicki *	.45	.18	.04
☐ 30	John Tamargo	.35	.14	.03
☐ 31	Larry Herndon	.45	.18	.04
☐ 36	Bill North *	.45	.18	.04
☐ 39	Bob Knepper *	.75	.30	.07
☐ 40	John Curtis *	.45	.18	.04
☐ 41	Darrell Evans *	1.25	.50	.12
☐ 43	Tom Griffin *	.45	.18	.04
☐ 44	Willie McCovey *	3.00	1.20	.30
☐ 45	Terry Whitfield *	.45	.18	.04
☐ 46	Gary Lavelle *	.45	.18	.04
☐ 49	Max Venable *	.45	.18	.04
☐ 41	Jerry Reuss	.35	.14	.03
☐ 43	Rick Sutcliffe	.65	.26	.06
☐ 44	Mickey Hatcher	.25	.10	.02
☐ 46	Burt Hooton	.25	.10	.02
☐ 49	Charlie Hough	.45	.18	.04
☐ xx	Team Card (unnumbered)	.25	.10	.02

1980 Police Dodgers

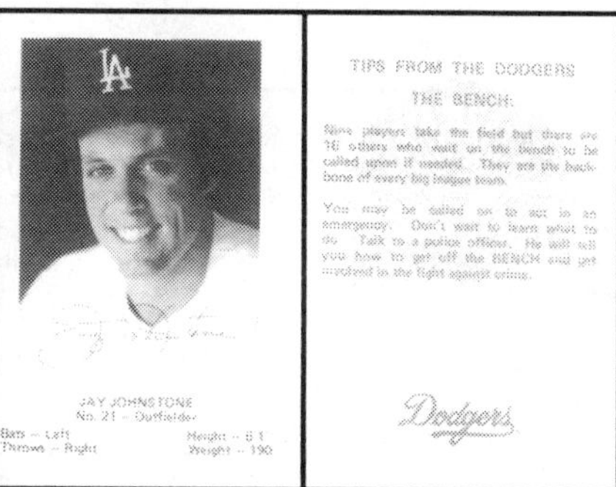

The cards in this 30-card set measure 2 13/16" by 4 1/8". The full color 1980 Police Los Angeles Dodgers set features the player's name, uniform number, position, and biographical data on the fronts in addition to the photo. The backs feature Tips from the Dodgers, the LAPD logo, and the Dodgers' logo. The cards are listed below according to uniform number.

		MINT	EXC	G-VG
	COMPLETE SET (30)	10.00	4.00	1.00
	COMMON PLAYER	.25	.10	.02
☐ 5	Johnny Oates	.25	.10	.02
☐ 6	Steve Garvey	1.25	.50	.12
☐ 7	Steve Yeager	.35	.14	.03
☐ 8	Reggie Smith	.35	.14	.03
☐ 9	Gary Thomasson	.25	.10	.02
☐ 10	Ron Cey	.45	.18	.04
☐ 12	Dusty Baker	.35	.14	.03
☐ 13	Joe Ferguson	.25	.10	.02
☐ 15	Davey Lopes	.35	.14	.03
☐ 16	Rick Monday	.35	.14	.03
☐ 18	Bill Russell	.35	.14	.03
☐ 20	Don Sutton	.85	.34	.08
☐ 21	Jay Johnstone	.35	.14	.03
☐ 23	Teddy Martinez	.25	.10	.02
☐ 27	Joe Beckwith	.25	.10	.02
☐ 28	Pedro Guerrero	1.00	.40	.10
☐ 29	Don Stanhouse	.25	.10	.02
☐ 30	Derrel Thomas	.25	.10	.02
☐ 31	Doug Rau	.25	.10	.02
☐ 34	Ken Brett	.25	.10	.02
☐ 35	Bob Welch	.45	.18	.04
☐ 37	Robert Castillo	.25	.10	.02
☐ 38	Dave Goltz	.25	.10	.02

1980 Police Giants

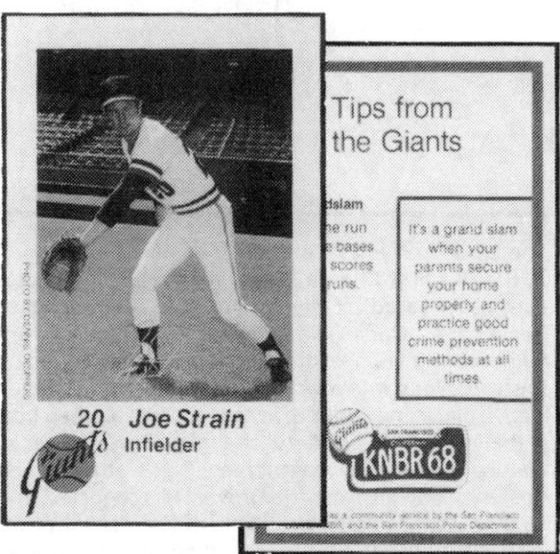

The cards in this 31-card set measure 2 5/8" by 4 1/8". The 1980 Police San Francisco Giants set features cards numbered by the player's uniform number. This full color set features the player's photo, the Giants' logo, and the player's name, number and position on the front of the cards. A facsimile autograph in an attractive blue ink is also contained on the front. The backs, printed in orange and black, feature Tips from the Giants, the Giants' and sponsoring radio station, KNBR, logos and a line listing the Giants, KNBR, and the San Francisco Police Department as sponsors of the set. The sets were given away at the ballpark on May 31, 1980.

		MINT	EXC	G-VG
	COMPLETE SET (31)	10.00	4.00	1.00
	COMMON PLAYER	.25	.10	.02
☐ 1	Dave Bristol MG	.25	.10	.02
☐ 2	Marc Hill	.25	.10	.02
☐ 3	Mike Sadek	.25	.10	.02
☐ 5	Jim Lefebvre	.45	.18	.04
☐ 6	Rennie Stennett	.25	.10	.02
☐ 7	Milt May	.25	.10	.02
☐ 8	Vern Benson CO	.25	.10	.02
☐ 9	Jim Wohlford	.25	.10	.02
☐ 10	Johnnie LeMaster	.25	.10	.02
☐ 12	Jim Davenport	.35	.14	.03
☐ 14	Vida Blue	.45	.18	.04
☐ 15	Mike Ivie	.25	.10	.02
☐ 16	Roger Metzger	.25	.10	.02
☐ 17	Randy Moffitt	.25	.10	.02
☐ 19	Al Holland	.25	.10	.02
☐ 20	Joe Strain	.25	.10	.02
☐ 22	Jack Clark	2.00	.80	.20
☐ 26	John Montefusco	.35	.14	.03
☐ 28	Ed Halicki	.25	.10	.02
☐ 31	Larry Herndon	.25	.10	.02
☐ 32	Ed Whitson	.35	.14	.03
☐ 36	Bill North	.25	.10	.02
☐ 38	Greg Minton	.35	.14	.03
☐ 39	Bob Knepper	.50	.20	.05
☐ 41	Darrell Evans	1.00	.40	.10
☐ 42	John Van Ornum	.25	.10	.02
☐ 43	Tom Griffin	.25	.10	.02
☐ 44	Willie McCovey	2.00	.80	.20
☐ 45	Terry Whitfield	.25	.10	.02
☐ 46	Gary Lavelle	.35	.14	.03
☐ 47	Don McMahon CO	.25	.10	.02

1981 Police Braves

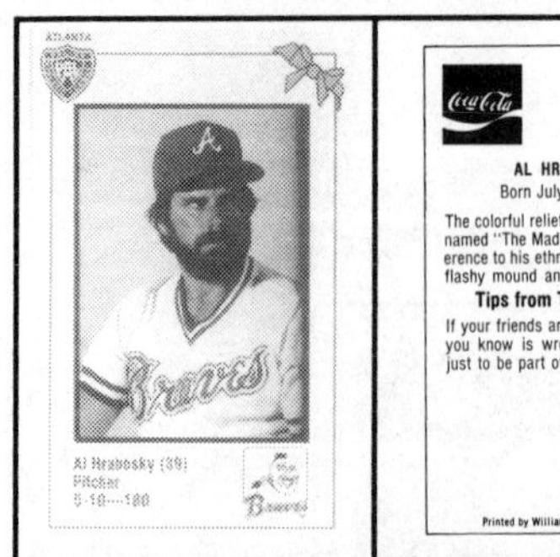

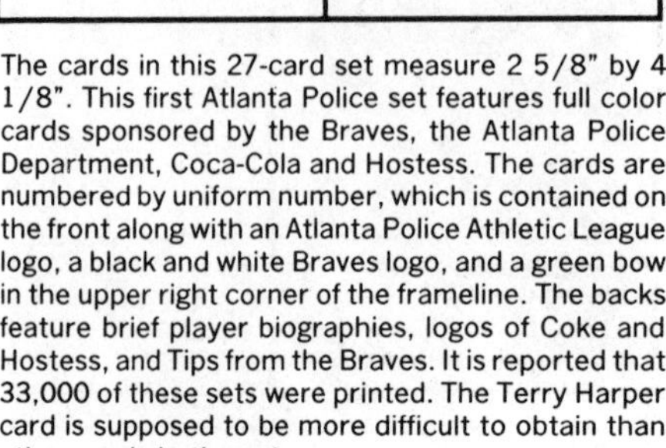

The cards in this 27-card set measure 2 5/8" by 4 1/8". This first Atlanta Police set features full color cards sponsored by the Braves, the Atlanta Police Department, Coca-Cola and Hostess. The cards are numbered by uniform number, which is contained on the front along with an Atlanta Police Athletic League logo, a black and white Braves logo, and a green bow in the upper right corner of the frameline. The backs feature brief player biographies, logos of Coke and Hostess, and Tips from the Braves. It is reported that 33,000 of these sets were printed. The Terry Harper card is supposed to be more difficult to obtain than other cards in the set.

	MINT	EXC	G-VG
COMPLETE SET (27)	11.00	4.50	1.10
COMMON PLAYER	.30	.12	.03
☐ 1 Jerry Royster	.30	.12	.03
☐ 3 Dale Murphy	3.50	1.40	.35
☐ 4 Biff Pocoroba	.30	.12	.03
☐ 5 Bob Horner	1.00	.40	.10
☐ 6 Bobby Cox MG	.30	.12	.03
☐ 9 Luis Gomez	.30	.12	.03
☐ 10 Chris Chambliss	.40	.16	.04
☐ 15 Bill Nahorodny	.30	.12	.03
☐ 16 Rafael Ramirez	.40	.16	.04
☐ 17 Glenn Hubbard	.30	.12	.03
☐ 18 Claudell Washington	.50	.20	.05
☐ 19 Terry Harper	.75	.30	.07
☐ 20 Bruce Benedict	.30	.12	.03
☐ 24 John Montefusco	.40	.16	.04
☐ 25 Rufino Linares	.30	.12	.03
☐ 26 Gene Garber	.40	.16	.04
☐ 30 Brian Asselstine	.30	.12	.03
☐ 34 Larry Bradford	.30	.12	.03
☐ 35 Phil Niekro	1.75	.70	.17
☐ 37 Rick Camp	.30	.12	.03
☐ 39 Al Hrabosky	.50	.20	.05
☐ 40 Tommy Boggs	.30	.12	.03
☐ 42 Rick Mahler	.40	.16	.04
☐ 44 Hank Aaron CO	2.50	1.00	.25
☐ 45 Ed Miller	.30	.12	.03
☐ 46 Gaylord Perry	1.50	.60	.15
☐ 49 Preston Hanna	.30	.12	.03

1981 Police Dodgers

The cards in this 32-card set measure 2 13/16" by 4 1/8". The full color set of 1981 Los Angeles Dodgers features the player's name, number, position and a line stating that the LAPD salutes the 1981 Dodgers, in addition to the player's photo. The backs feature the LAPD logo and short narratives, attributable to the player on the front of the card, revealing police associated tips. The cards of Ken Landreaux and Dave Stewart are reported to be

more difficult to obtain than other cards in this set due to the fact that they are replacements for Stanhouse (released 4/17/81) and Hatcher (traded for Landreaux 3/30/81). The complete set price below refers to all 32 cards, i.e., including the variations.

	MINT	EXC	G-VG
COMPLETE SET (32)	10.00	4.00	1.00
COMMON PLAYER	.25	.10	.02
☐ 2 Tom Lasorda MG	.50	.20	.05
☐ 3 Rudy Law	.25	.10	.02
☐ 6 Steve Garvey	1.25	.50	.12
☐ 7 Steve Yeager	.35	.14	.03
☐ 8 Reggie Smith	.35	.14	.03
☐ 10 Ron Cey	.45	.18	.04
☐ 12 Dusty Baker	.35	.14	.03
☐ 13 Joe Ferguson	.25	.10	.02
☐ 14 Mike Scioscia	.35	.14	.03
☐ 15 Davey Lopes	.35	.14	.03
☐ 16 Rick Monday	.35	.14	.03
☐ 18 Bill Russell	.35	.14	.03
☐ 21 Jay Johnstone	.35	.14	.03
☐ 26 Don Stanhouse	.50	.20	.05
☐ 27 Joe Beckwith	.25	.10	.02
☐ 28 Pedro Guerrero	.90	.36	.09
☐ 30 Derrel Thomas	.25	.10	.02
☐ 34 Fernando Valenzuela	2.00	.80	.20
☐ 35 Bob Welch	.35	.14	.03
☐ 36 Pepe Frias	.25	.10	.02
☐ 37 Robert Castillo	.25	.10	.02
☐ 38 Dave Goltz	.25	.10	.02
☐ 41 Jerry Reuss	.35	.14	.03
☐ 43 Rick Sutcliffe	.60	.24	.06
☐ 44A Mickey Hatcher	.50	.20	.05
☐ 44B Ken Landreaux	1.25	.50	.12
☐ 46 Burt Hooton	.25	.10	.02
☐ 48 Dave Stewart	1.50	.60	.15
☐ 51 Terry Forster	.35	.14	.03
☐ 57 Steve Howe	.25	.10	.02
☐ xx Team Photo (Checklist) (unnumbered)	.25	.10	.02
☐ xx Coaching Staff (unnumbered)	.25	.10	.02

1981 Police Mariners

The cards in this 16-card set measure 2 5/8" by 4 1/8". The full color Seattle Mariners Police set of this year was sponsored by the Washington State Crime Prevention Association, the Kiwanis Club, Coca-Cola and Ernst Home Centers. The fronts feature the player's name, his position, and the Seattle Mariners name in addition to the player's photo. The backs, in red and blue, feature Tips from the Mariners and the logos of the four sponsors of the set. The cards are numbered in the lower left corners of the backs.

	MINT	EXC	G-VG
COMPLETE SET (16)	5.00	2.00	.50
COMMON PLAYER (1-16)	.30	.12	.03

☐ 1 Jeff Burroughs	.40	.16	.04
☐ 2 Floyd Bannister	.50	.20	.05
☐ 3 Glenn Abbott	.30	.12	.03
☐ 4 Jim Anderson	.30	.12	.03
☐ 5 Danny Meyer	.30	.12	.03
☐ 6 Julio Cruz	.40	.16	.04
☐ 7 Dave Edler	.30	.12	.03
☐ 8 Kenny Clay	.30	.12	.03
☐ 9 Lenny Randle	.30	.12	.03
☐ 10 Mike Parrott	.30	.12	.03
☐ 11 Tom Paciorek	.40	.16	.04
☐ 12 Jerry Narron	.30	.12	.03
☐ 13 Richie Zisk	.40	.16	.04
☐ 14 Maury Wills MG	.75	.30	.07
☐ 15 Joe Simpson	.30	.12	.03
☐ 16 Shane Rawley	.50	.20	.05

1981 Police Royals

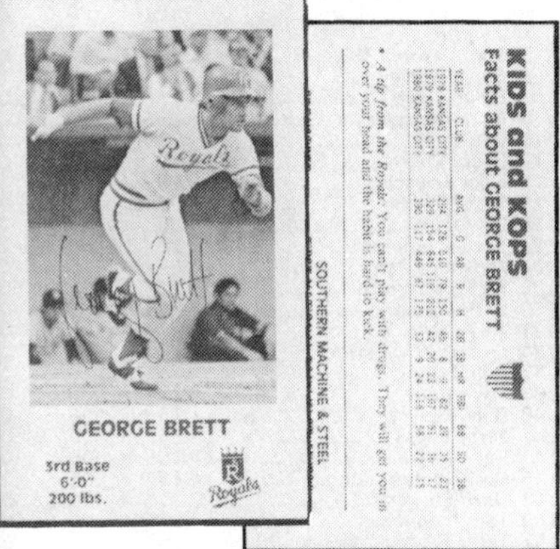

The cards in this 10-card set measure 2 1/2" by 4 1/8". The 1981 Police Kansas City Royals set features full color cards of Royals players. The fronts feature the player's name, position, height and weight, and the Royals' logo in addition to the photo and facsimile autograph of the player. The backs feature player statistics, Tips from the Royals, and identification of the sponsoring organizations.

	MINT	EXC	G-VG
COMPLETE SET (10)	35.00	14.00	3.50
COMMON PLAYER (1-10)	2.00	.80	.20
☐ 1 Willie Aikens	2.00	.80	.20
☐ 2 George Brett	15.00	6.00	1.50
☐ 3 Rich Gale	2.00	.80	.20
☐ 4 Clint Hurdle	2.00	.80	.20
☐ 5 Dennis Leonard	2.50	1.00	.25
☐ 6 Hal McRae	2.50	1.00	.25
☐ 7 Amos Otis	2.50	1.00	.25
☐ 8 U.L. Washington	2.00	.80	.20
☐ 9 Frank White	4.00	1.60	.40
☐ 10 Willie Wilson	5.00	2.00	.50

1982 Police Braves

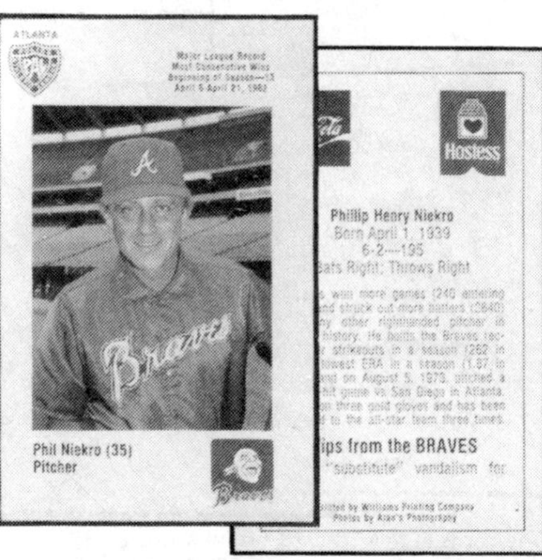

The cards in this 30-card set measure 2 5/8" by 4 1/8". The Atlanta Police Department followed up on their successful 1981 safety set by publishing a new Braves set for 1982. Featured in excellent color photos are manager Joe Torre, 24 players, and 5 coaches. The cards are numbered, by uniform number, on the front only, while the backs contain a short biography of the individual and a Tips from the Braves section. The logos for the Atlanta PAL and the Braves appear on the front; those of Coca-Cola and Hostess are found on the back. A line commemorating Atlanta's record-shattering, season-beginning win streak is located in the upper right corner on every card obverse. The player list on the reverse of the Torre card is a roster list and not a checklist for the set. There were 8,000 sets reportedly printed. The Bob Watson card is supposedly more difficult to obtain than others in this set.

	MINT	EXC	G-VG
COMPLETE SET (30)	18.00	7.25	1.80
COMMON PLAYER	.35	.14	.03
☐ 1 Jerry Royster	.35	.14	.03
☐ 3 Dale Murphy	6.00	2.40	.60
☐ 4 Biff Pocoroba	.35	.14	.03
☐ 5 Bob Horner	1.25	.50	.12
☐ 6 Randy Johnson	.35	.14	.03
☐ 8 Bob Watson	1.50	.60	.15
☐ 9 Joe Torre MG	.75	.30	.07
☐ 10 Chris Chambliss	.50	.20	.05
☐ 15 Claudell Washington	.50	.20	.05
☐ 16 Rafael Ramirez	.35	.14	.03
☐ 17 Glenn Hubbard	.35	.14	.03
☐ 20 Bruce Benedict	.35	.14	.03
☐ 22 Brett Butler	1.00	.40	.10
☐ 23 Tommy Aaron CO	.35	.14	.03
☐ 25 Rufino Linares	.35	.14	.03
☐ 26 Gene Garber	.50	.20	.05
☐ 27 Larry McWilliams	.35	.14	.03
☐ 28 Larry Whisenton	.35	.14	.03
☐ 32 Steve Bedrosian	1.00	.40	.10
☐ 35 Phil Niekro	2.50	1.00	.25
☐ 37 Rick Camp	.35	.14	.03
☐ 38 Joe Cowley	.35	.14	.03
☐ 39 Al Hrabosky	.50	.20	.05
☐ 42 Rick Mahler	.35	.14	.03
☐ 43 Bob Walk	.50	.20	.05
☐ 45 Bob Gibson CO	1.50	.60	.15
☐ 49 Preston Hanna	.35	.14	.03
☐ 52 Joe Pignatano CO	.35	.14	.03
☐ 53 Dal Maxvill CO	.35	.14	.03
☐ 54 Rube Walker CO	.35	.14	.03

1982 Police Brewers

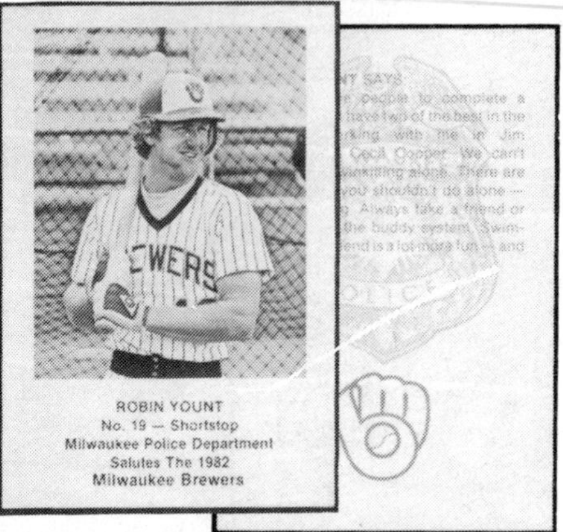

ROBIN YOUNT
No. 19 — Shortstop
Milwaukee Police Department
Salutes The 1982
Milwaukee Brewers

The cards in this 30-card set measure 2 13/16" by 4 1/8". The 1982 series of 30 Milwaukee Brewers baseball cards is noted for its excellent color photographs set upon a simple white background. The set was initially distributed at the stadium on May 5th, but was also handed out by several local police departments, and credit lines for the Wisconsin State Fair Park Police (no shield design on reverse), Milwaukee, Brookfield, and Wauwatosa PD's have already been found. The reverses feature advice concerning safety measures, social situations, and crime prevention (Romero card in both Spanish and English). The team card carries a checklist which lists the Brewer's coaches separately although they all appear on a single card; VP/GM Harry Dalton is not mentioned on this list but is included in the set.The prices below are for the basic set without regard to the Police Department listed on the backs. Cards from the more obscure corners and small towns of Wisconsin (where fewer cards were produced) will be valued higher.

	MINT	EXC	G-VG
COMPLETE SET (30)	10.00	4.00	1.00
COMMON PLAYER	.25	.10	.02
☐ 4 Paul Molitor	1.25	.50	.12
☐ 5 Ned Yost	.25	.10	.02
☐ 7 Don Money	.25	.10	.02
☐ 9 Larry Hisle	.25	.10	.02
☐ 10 Bob McClure	.25	.10	.02
☐ 11 Ed Romero	.25	.10	.02
☐ 13 Roy Howell	.25	.10	.02
☐ 15 Cecil Cooper	.50	.20	.05
☐ 17 Jim Gantner	.35	.14	.03
☐ 19 Robin Yount	1.75	.70	.17
☐ 20 Gorman Thomas	.50	.20	.05
☐ 22 Charlie Moore	.25	.10	.02
☐ 23 Ted Simmons	.50	.20	.05
☐ 24 Ben Oglivie	.35	.14	.03
☐ 26 Kevin Bass	.50	.20	.05
☐ 28 Jamie Easterly	.25	.10	.02
☐ 29 Mark Brouhard	.25	.10	.02
☐ 30 Moose Haas	.35	.14	.03
☐ 34 Rollie Fingers	.80	.32	.08
☐ 35 Randy Lerch	.25	.10	.02
☐ 41 Jim Slaton	.35	.14	.03
☐ 45 Doug Jones	.25	.10	.02
☐ 46 Jerry Augustine	.25	.10	.02
☐ 47 Dwight Bernard	.25	.10	.02
☐ 48 Mike Caldwell	.35	.14	.03
☐ 50 Pete Vuckovich	.35	.14	.03
☐ xx Team Card (unnumbered)	.25	.10	.02
☐ xx Harry Dalton GM (unnumbered)	.25	.10	.02
☐ xx Buck Rodgers MG (unnumbered)	.25	.10	.02
☐ xx Brewer Coaches (unnumbered)	.25	.10	.02

1982 Police Dodgers

FERNANDO VALENZUELA
No. 34 — PITCHER
The Los Angeles Police Department
presents the World Champion
Dodgers
FERNANDO VALENZUELA
Fernando Valenzuela, a 20 year old pitcher from the farm lands of Mexico, was pressed into action on Opening Day when the scheduled pitcher was forced out with an injury. Fernando calmly took over ignoring the pressure of the situation and displaying the skill, determination and confidence of a champion. He pitched a shutout and went on to win the Rookie of the Year and Cy Young Awards and helped lead the Dodgers to their World Championship.
When you face a tough situation remember Fernando Valenzuela and the team that wouldn't quit.
This is one of a series of 30 Dodger baseball cards that comes to you as a gift from your Los Angeles police officers.

The cards in this 30-card set measure 2 13/16" by 4 1/8". The 1982 Los Angeles Dodgers police set depicts the players and events of the 1981 season. There is a World Series trophy card, three cards commemorating the Division, League, and World Series wins, one manager card, and 25 player cards. The obverses have brilliant color photos set on white, and the player cards are numbered according to the uniform number of the individual. The reverses contain biographical material, information about stadium events, and a safety feature emphasizing "the team that wouldn't quit."

	MINT	EXC	G-VG
COMPLETE SET (30)	7.00	2.80	.70
COMMON PLAYER	.15	.06	.01
☐ 2 Tom Lasorda MG	.35	.14	.03
☐ 6 Steve Garvey	1.00	.40	.10
☐ 7 Steve Yeager	.25	.10	.02
☐ 8 Mark Belanger	.25	.10	.02
☐ 10 Ron Cey	.35	.14	.03
☐ 12 Dusty Baker	.25	.10	.02
☐ 14 Mike Scioscia	.25	.10	.02
☐ 16 Rick Monday	.25	.10	.02
☐ 18 Bill Russell	.25	.10	.02
☐ 21 Jay Johnstone	.25	.10	.02
☐ 26 Alejandro Pena	.35	.14	.03
☐ 28 Pedro Guerrero	.90	.36	.09
☐ 30 Derrel Thomas	.15	.06	.01
☐ 31 Jorge Orta	.15	.06	.01
☐ 34 Fernando Valenzuela	.90	.36	.09
☐ 35 Bob Welch	.25	.10	.02
☐ 38 Dave Goltz	.15	.06	.01
☐ 40 Ron Roenicke	.15	.06	.01
☐ 41 Jerry Reuss	.25	.10	.02
☐ 44 Ken Landreaux	.15	.06	.01
☐ 46 Burt Hooton	.15	.06	.01
☐ 48 Dave Stewart	.35	.14	.03
☐ 49 Tom Niedenfuer	.25	.10	.02
☐ 51 Terry Forster	.35	.14	.03
☐ 52 Steve Sax	.90	.36	.09
☐ 57 Steve Howe	.15	.06	.01
☐ xx World Series Trophy (checklist back) (unnumbered)	.15	.06	.01
☐ xx World Series Commemorative (unnumbered)	.15	.06	.01
☐ xx NL Champions (unnumbered)	.15	.06	.01
☐ xx Division Champs (unnumbered)	.15	.06	.01

1983 Police Braves

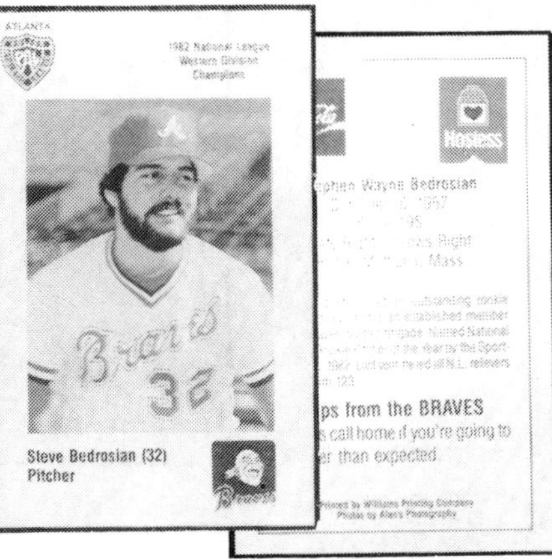

The cards in this 30-card set measure 2 5/8" by 4 1/8". For the third year in a row, the Atlanta Braves, in cooperation with the Atlanta Police Department, Coca-Cola, and Hostess, issued a full color safety set. The set features Joe Torre, five coaches, and 24 of the Atlanta Braves. Numbered only by uniform number, the statement that the Braves were the 1982 National League Western Division Champions is included on the fronts along with the Braves and Police Athletic biographies, a short narrative on the player, Tips from the Braves, and the Coke and Hostess logos.

	MINT	EXC	G-VG
COMPLETE SET (30)	12.00	5.00	1.20
COMMON PLAYER	.35	.14	.03
☐ 1 Jerry Royster	.35	.14	.03
☐ 3 Dale Murphy	4.00	1.60	.40
☐ 4 Biff Pocoroba	.35	.14	.03
☐ 5 Bob Horner	1.00	.40	.10
☐ 6 Randy Johnson	.35	.14	.03
☐ 8 Bob Watson	.50	.20	.05
☐ 9 Joe Torre MG	.60	.24	.06
☐ 10 Chris Chambliss	.50	.20	.05
☐ 11 Ken Smith	.35	.14	.03
☐ 15 Claudell Washington	.50	.20	.05
☐ 16 Rafael Ramirez	.35	.14	.03
☐ 17 Glenn Hubbard	.35	.14	.03
☐ 19 Terry Harper	.35	.14	.03
☐ 20 Bruce Benedict	.35	.14	.03
☐ 22 Brett Butler	.75	.30	.07
☐ 24 Larry Owen	.35	.14	.03
☐ 26 Gene Garber	.50	.20	.05
☐ 27 Pascual Perez	.75	.30	.07
☐ 29 Craig McMurtry	.35	.14	.03
☐ 32 Steve Bedrosian	.75	.30	.07
☐ 33 Pete Falcone	.35	.14	.03
☐ 35 Phil Niekro	1.50	.60	.15
☐ 36 Sonny Jackson CO	.35	.14	.03
☐ 37 Rick Camp	.35	.14	.03
☐ 45 Bob Gibson CO	1.50	.60	.15
☐ 49 Rick Behenna	.35	.14	.03
☐ 51 Terry Forster	.50	.20	.05
☐ 52 Joe Pignatano CO	.35	.14	.03
☐ 53 Dal Maxvill CO	.35	.14	.03
☐ 54 Rube Walker CO	.35	.14	.03

1983 Police Brewers

The cards in this 30-card set measure 2 13/16" by 4 1/8". The 1983 Police Milwaukee Brewers set contains full color cards issued by the Milwaukee Police Department in conjunction with the Brewers.

ROLLIE FINGERS SAYS:
My career total of saves was 301 at the beginning of the 1983 season. That's a Major League record that I'm proud of. To be #1 you have to put in a lot of hard work. Homework comes before playing with friends. Practice and exercise will help you more than laying around the house. Good habits add up to a healthy well rounded person who can be a winner at anything they pursue.

The cards are numbered on the fronts by the player uniform number and contain the line, "The Milwaukee Police Department Presents the 1983 Milwaukee Braves." The backs contain a brief narrative attributable to the player on the front, the Milwaukee Police logo, and a Milwaukee Brewers logo stating that they were the 1982 American League Champions. In all, 28 variations of these Police sets have been found to date. Prices below are for the basic set without regard to the Police Department listed on the backs of the cards; cards from the more obscure corners and small towns of Wisconsin (whose cards were produced in lesser quantities) will be valued higher.

	MINT	EXC	G-VG
COMPLETE SET (30)	7.00	2.80	.70
COMMON PLAYER	.20	.08	.02
☐ xx Dave Garcia CO	.20	.08	.02
☐ 4 Paul Molitor	.80	.32	.08
☐ 5 Ned Yost	.20	.08	.02
☐ 7 Don Money	.20	.08	.02
☐ 8 Rob Picciolo	.20	.08	.02
☐ 10 Bob McClure	.20	.08	.02
☐ 11 Ed Romero	.20	.08	.02
☐ 12 Larry Haney CO	.20	.08	.02
☐ 13 Roy Howell	.20	.08	.02
☐ 15 Cecil Cooper	.50	.20	.05
☐ 16 Marshall Edwards	.20	.08	.02
☐ 17 Jim Gantner	.30	.12	.03
☐ 18 Ron Hansen CO	.20	.08	.02
☐ 19 Robin Yount	1.00	.40	.10
☐ 20 Gorman Thomas	.40	.16	.04
☐ 21 Don Sutton	.80	.32	.08
☐ 22 Charlie Moore	.20	.08	.02
☐ 23 Ted Simmons	.50	.20	.05
☐ 24 Ben Oglivie	.30	.12	.03
☐ 26 Bob Skube	.20	.08	.02
☐ 27 Pete Ladd	.20	.08	.02
☐ 28 Jamie Easterly	.20	.08	.02
☐ 30 Moose Haas	.30	.12	.03
☐ 32 Harvey Kuenn MG	.40	.16	.04
☐ 34 Rollie Fingers	.80	.32	.08
☐ 40 Bob L. Gibson	.20	.08	.02
☐ 41 Jim Slaton	.20	.08	.02
☐ 42 Tom Tellmann	.20	.08	.02
☐ 45 Pat Dobson CO	.30	.12	.03
☐ 46 Jerry Augustine	.20	.08	.02
☐ 48 Mike Caldwell	.30	.12	.03
☐ 50 Pete Vuckovich	.30	.12	.03
☐ xx Team Photo (Checklist back) (unnumbered)	.20	.08	.02

1983 Police Dodgers

The cards in this 30-card set measure 2 13/16" by 4 1/8". The full color Police Los Angeles Dodgers set of 1983 features the player's name and uniform number on the front along with the Dodger's logo, the year, and the player's photo. The backs feature

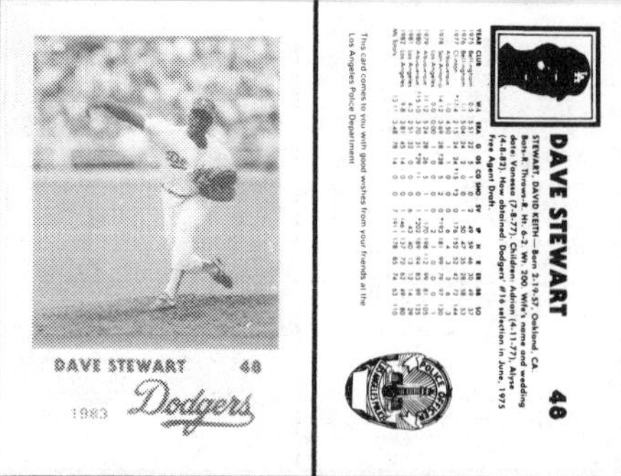

a small insert portrait picture of the player, player biographies, and career statistics. The logo of the Los Angeles Police Department, the sponsor of the set, is found on the backs of the cards.

	MINT	EXC	G-VG
COMPLETE SET (30)	6.00	2.40	.60
COMMON PLAYER	.15	.06	.01
□ 2 Tom Lasorda MG	.25	.10	.02
□ 3 Steve Sax	.60	.24	.06
□ 5 Mike Marshall	.60	.24	.06
□ 7 Steve Yeager	.25	.10	.02
□ 12 Dusty Baker	.25	.10	.02
□ 14 Mike Scioscia	.25	.10	.02
□ 16 Rick Monday	.25	.10	.02
□ 17 Greg Brock	.25	.10	.02
□ 18 Bill Russell	.25	.10	.02
□ 20 Candy Maldonado	.35	.14	.03
□ 21 Ricky Wright	.15	.06	.01
□ 22 Mark Bradley	.15	.06	.01
□ 23 Dave Sax	.15	.06	.01
□ 26 Alejandro Pena	.25	.10	.02
□ 27 Joe Beckwith	.15	.06	.01
□ 28 Pedro Guerrero	.75	.30	.07
□ 30 Derrel Thomas	.15	.06	.01
□ 34 Fernando Valenzuela	.75	.30	.07
□ 35 Bob Welch	.25	.10	.02
□ 38 Pat Zachry	.15	.06	.01
□ 40 Ron Roenicke	.15	.06	.01
□ 41 Jerry Reuss	.25	.10	.02
□ 43 Jose Morales	.15	.06	.01
□ 44 Ken Landreaux	.15	.06	.01
□ 46 Burt Hooton	.15	.06	.01
□ 47 Larry White	.15	.06	.01
□ 48 Dave Stewart	.25	.10	.02
□ 49 Tom Niedenfuer	.25	.10	.02
□ 57 Steve Howe	.15	.06	.01
□ xx Coaching Staff (unnumbered)	.15	.06	.01

1983 Police Royals

The cards in this 10-card set measure 2 1/2" by 4 1/8". The 1983 Police Kansas City Royals set features full color cards of Royals players. The fronts feature the player's name, height and weight, and the Royals' logo in addition to the player's photo and a facsimile autograph. The backs feature Kids and Cops Facts about the players, Tips from the Royals, and identification of the sponsors of the set. The cards are unnumbered.

	MINT	EXC	G-VG
COMPLETE SET (10)	30.00	12.00	3.00
COMMON PLAYER (1-10)	1.75	.70	.17
□ 1 Willie Aikens	1.75	.70	.17
□ 2 George Brett	12.00	5.00	1.20
□ 3 Dennis Leonard	2.50	1.00	.25
□ 4 Hal McRae	2.50	1.00	.25
□ 5 Amos Otis	2.50	1.00	.25
□ 6 Dan Quisenberry	3.00	1.20	.30
□ 7 U.L. Washington	1.75	.70	.17

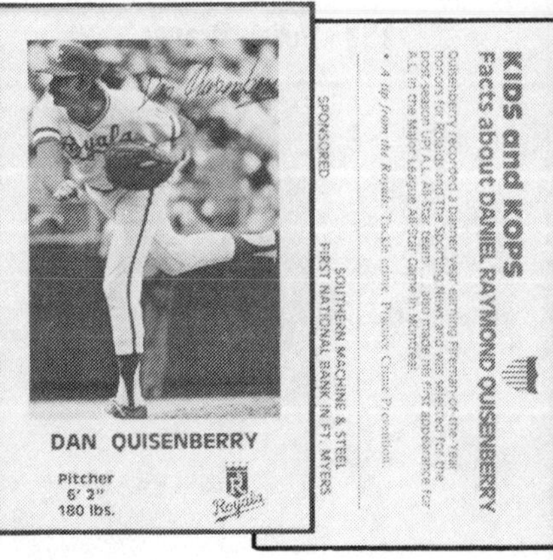

□ 8 John Wathan	2.50	1.00	.2
□ 9 Frank White	3.50	1.40	.3
□ 10 Willie Wilson	4.00	1.60	.4

1984 Police Braves

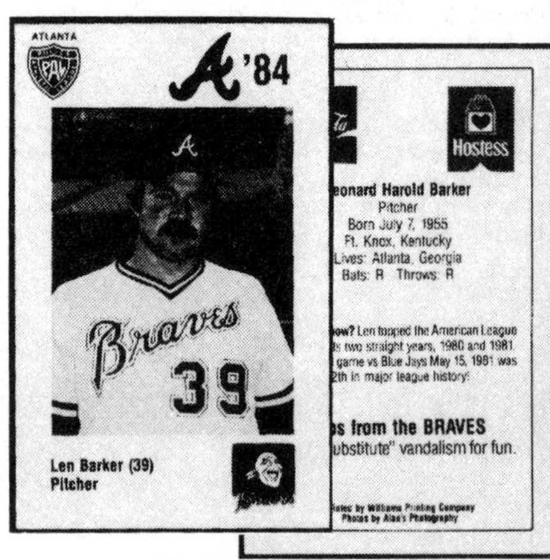

The cards in this 30-card set measure 2 5/8" by 4 1/8". For the fourth straight year, the Atlanta Police Department issued a full color set of Atlanta Braves. The cards were given out two per week by Atlanta police officers. In addition to the police department, the set was sponsored by Coke and Hostess. The backs of the cards of Perez and Ramirez are in Spanish. The Joe Torre card contains the checklist.

	MINT	EXC	G-VG
COMPLETE SET (30)	10.00	4.00	1.00
COMMON PLAYER	.30	.12	.03
□ 1 Jerry Royster	.30	.12	.03
□ 3 Dale Murphy	3.50	1.40	.35
□ 5 Bob Horner	.90	.36	.09
□ 6 Randy Johnson	.30	.12	.03
□ 8 Bob Watson	.40	.16	.04
□ 9 Joe Torre MG (checklist back)	.50	.20	.05
□ 10 Chris Chambliss	.40	.16	.04
□ 11 Mike Jorgensen	.30	.12	.03
□ 15 Claudell Washington	.50	.20	.05
□ 16 Rafael Ramirez	.30	.12	.03
□ 17 Glenn Hubbard	.30	.12	.03
□ 19 Terry Harper	.30	.12	.03
□ 20 Bruce Benedict	.30	.12	.03
□ 25 Alex Trevino	.30	.12	.03
□ 26 Gene Garber	.40	.16	.04
□ 27 Pascual Perez	.60	.24	.06

☐ 28 Gerald Perry	.75	.30	.07
☐ 29 Craig McMurtry	.30	.12	.03
☐ 31 Donnie Moore	.40	.16	.04
☐ 32 Steve Bedrosian	.75	.30	.07
☐ 33 Pete Falcone	.30	.12	.03
☐ 37 Rick Camp	.30	.12	.03
☐ 39 Len Barker	.30	.12	.03
☐ 42 Rick Mahler	.30	.12	.03
☐ 45 Bob Gibson CO	1.00	.40	.10
☐ 51 Terry Forster	.40	.16	.04
☐ 52 Joe Pignatano CO	.30	.12	.03
☐ 53 Dal Maxvill CO	.30	.12	.03
☐ 54 Rube Walker CO	.30	.12	.03
☐ 55 Luke Appling CO	.50	.20	.05

1984 Police Brewers

4 PAUL MOLITOR — IF
The Milwaukee Police Department
Presents The 1984
MILWAUKEE BREWERS

PAUL MOLITOR SAYS:
Stealing bases is part of the game of baseball. It helps win games, but no matter how good you are, you get caught sooner or later. Shoplifting is stealing and if you do it you will get caught. You'll embarass your family and friends and hurt your chances to be a winner in life. No one wants to be a loser. Don't take the chance.

The cards in this 30-card set measure 2 13/16" by 4 1/8". Again this year, the police departments in and around Milwaukee issued sets of the Milwaukee Brewers. Although each set contained the same players and numbers, the individual police departments placed their own name on the fronts of cards to show that they were the particular jurisdiction issuing the set. The backs contain the Brewers logo, a safety tip, and in some cases, a badge of the jurisdiction. To date, 59 variations of this set have been found. Prices below are for the basic set without regard to the Police Department issuing the cards; cards from the more obscure corners and small towns of Wisconsin will be valued higher. Cards are numbered by uniform number.

	MINT	EXC	G-VG
COMPLETE SET (30)	6.00	2.40	.60
COMMON PLAYER	.15	.06	.01
☐ 2 Randy Ready	.25	.10	.02
☐ 4 Paul Molitor	.75	.30	.07
☐ 8 Jim Sundberg	.25	.10	.02
☐ 9 Rene Lachemann MG	.15	.06	.01
☐ 10 Bob McClure	.15	.06	.01
☐ 11 Ed Romero	.15	.06	.01
☐ 13 Roy Howell	.15	.06	.01
☐ 14 Dion James	.25	.10	.02
☐ 15 Cecil Cooper	.45	.18	.04
☐ 17 Jim Gantner	.25	.10	.02
☐ 19 Robin Yount	.90	.36	.09
☐ 20 Don Sutton	.60	.24	.06
☐ 21 Bill Schroeder	.15	.06	.01
☐ 22 Charlie Moore	.15	.06	.01
☐ 23 Ted Simmons	.35	.14	.03
☐ 24 Ben Oglivie	.25	.10	.02
☐ 25 Bob Clark	.15	.06	.01
☐ 27 Pete Ladd	.15	.06	.01
☐ 28 Rick Manning	.15	.06	.01
☐ 29 Mark Brouhard	.15	.06	.01
☐ 30 Moose Haas	.15	.06	.01
☐ 34 Rollie Fingers	.60	.24	.06
☐ 42 Tom Tellmann	.15	.06	.01
☐ 43 Chuck Porter	.15	.06	.01
☐ 46 Jerry Augustine	.15	.06	.01
☐ 47 Jaime Cocanower	.15	.06	.01
☐ 48 Mike Caldwell	.25	.10	.02
☐ 50 Pete Vuckovich	.25	.10	.02

☐ xx Coaches Card (unnumbered)	.15	.06	.01
☐ xx Team Photo (Checklist back) (unnumbered)	.15	.06	.01

1984 Police Dodgers

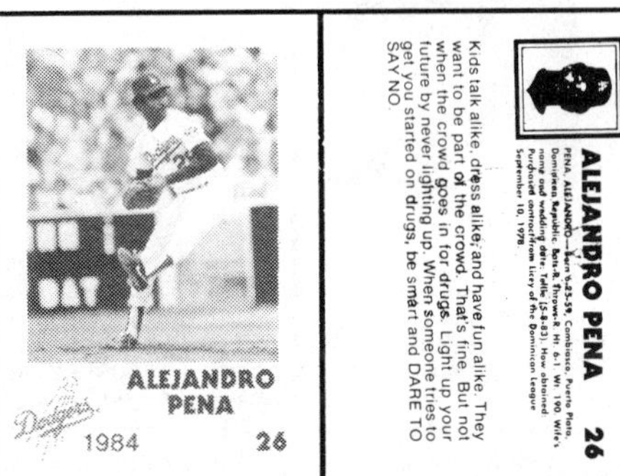

The cards in this 30-card set measure 2 13/16" by 4 1/8". For the fifth straight year, the Los Angeles Police Department sponsored a set of Dodger baseball cards. The set is numbered by player uniform number, which is featured on both the fronts and backs of the cards. The Dodgers' logo appears on the front, and the LAPD logo is superimposed on the backs of the cards. The backs are printed in Dodger blue ink and contain a small photo of the player on the front. Player biographical data and "Dare to Say No" antidrug information are featured on the back.

	MINT	EXC	G-VG
COMPLETE SET (30)	6.00	2.40	.60
COMMON PLAYER	.15	.06	.01
☐ 2 Tom Lasorda MG	.35	.14	.03
☐ 3 Steve Sax	.60	.24	.06
☐ 5 Mike Marshall	.60	.24	.06
☐ 7 Steve Yeager	.25	.10	.02
☐ 9 Greg Brock	.25	.10	.02
☐ 10 Dave Anderson	.15	.06	.01
☐ 14 Mike Scioscia	.25	.10	.02
☐ 16 Rick Monday	.25	.10	.02
☐ 17 Rafael Landestoy	.15	.06	.01
☐ 18 Bill Russell	.25	.10	.02
☐ 20 Candy Maldonado	.25	.10	.02
☐ 21 Bob Bailor	.15	.06	.01
☐ 25 German Rivera	.15	.06	.01
☐ 26 Alejandro Pena	.25	.10	.02
☐ 27 Carlos Diaz	.15	.06	.01
☐ 28 Pedro Guerrero	.75	.30	.07
☐ 31 Jack Fimple	.15	.06	.01
☐ 34 Fernando Valenzuela	.75	.30	.07
☐ 35 Bob Welch	.25	.10	.02
☐ 38 Pat Zachry	.15	.06	.01
☐ 40 Rick Honeycutt	.15	.06	.01
☐ 41 Jerry Reuss	.25	.10	.02
☐ 43 Jose Morales	.15	.06	.01
☐ 44 Ken Landreaux	.15	.06	.01
☐ 45 Terry Whitfield	.15	.06	.01
☐ 46 Burt Hooton	.15	.06	.01
☐ 49 Tom Niedenfuer	.25	.10	.02
☐ 55 Orel Hershiser	1.50	.60	.15
☐ 56 Richard Rodas	.15	.06	.01
☐ xx Coaching Staff (unnumbered)	.15	.06	.01

YOU CAN HELP: Your input is solicited for future editions of this guide. Write the author at 3410 MidCourt Suite 110, Carrollton, Texas 75006.

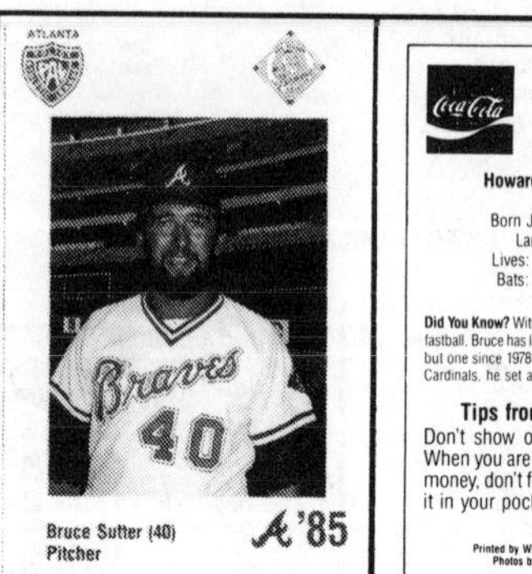

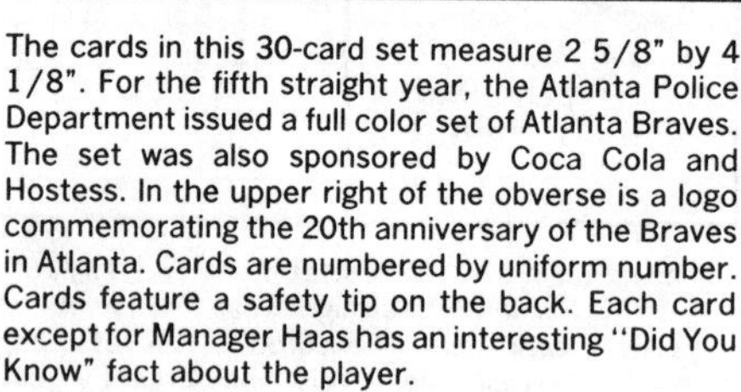

Coca-Cola
Hostess
Howard Bruce Sutter
Pitcher
Born January 8, 1953
Lancaster, Pa.
Lives: Kennesaw, Ga.
Bats: R Throws: R
Did You Know? With his devastating split-fingered fastball, Bruce has led the N.L. in saves every year but one since 1978! In fact, last season with the Cardinals, he set a new N.L. record with 45!
Tips from the BRAVES
Don't show off with your money. When you are going anywhere with money, don't flash your cash. Leave it in your pocket.
Printed by Williams Printing Company
Photos by Alan's Photography

The cards in this 30-card set measure 2 5/8" by 4 1/8". For the fifth straight year, the Atlanta Police Department issued a full color set of Atlanta Braves. The set was also sponsored by Coca Cola and Hostess. In the upper right of the obverse is a logo commemorating the 20th anniversary of the Braves in Atlanta. Cards are numbered by uniform number. Cards feature a safety tip on the back. Each card except for Manager Haas has an interesting "Did You Know" fact about the player.

	MINT	EXC	G-VG
COMPLETE SET (30)	10.00	4.00	1.00
COMMON PLAYER	.30	.12	.03
□ 2 Albert Hall	.40	.16	.04
□ 3 Dale Murphy	3.00	1.20	.30
□ 5 Rick Cerone	.30	.12	.03
□ 7 Bobby Wine CO	.30	.12	.03
□ 10 Chris Chambliss	.40	.16	.04
□ 11 Bob Horner	.90	.36	.09
□ 12 Paul Runge	.30	.12	.03
□ 15 Claudell Washington	.50	.20	.05
□ 16 Rafael Ramirez	.30	.12	.03
□ 17 Glenn Hubbard	.30	.12	.03
□ 18 Paul Zuvella	.30	.12	.03
□ 19 Terry Harper	.30	.12	.03
□ 20 Bruce Benedict	.30	.12	.03
□ 22 Eddie Haas MG	.30	.12	.03
□ 24 Ken Oberkfell	.30	.12	.03
□ 26 Gene Garber	.40	.16	.04
□ 27 Pascual Perez	.50	.20	.05
□ 28 Gerald Perry	.60	.24	.06
□ 29 Craig McMurtry	.30	.12	.03
□ 32 Steve Bedrosian	.60	.24	.06
□ 33 Johnny Sain CO	.50	.20	.05
□ 34 Zane Smith	.60	.24	.06
□ 36 Brad Komminsk	.30	.12	.03
□ 37 Rick Camp	.30	.12	.03
□ 39 Len Barker	.30	.12	.03
□ 40 Bruce Sutter	.50	.20	.05
□ 42 Rick Mahler	.30	.12	.03
□ 51 Terry Forster	.40	.16	.04
□ 52 Leo Mazzone CO	.30	.12	.03
□ 53 Bobby Dews CO	.30	.12	.03

1985 Police Brewers

48 Ray Burris P
The Chilton Police Department and
The Chilton Local Merchants, Service Clubs
and Financial Institutions
present the 1985
Milwaukee Brewers

Ray Burris says:
Our advance scouts are very importar to us. They check out opposing teams before we play them and give us tips on how to play individual ballplayers. They as our eyes and ears. You, too, can be a scout for the police in your neighborhoo You and your friends can prevent crime being the eyes and ears of your local police. Call them immediately to report anything unusual or suspicious that you see.

Watch the Friday Milwaukee Journal Sports Weekend Section for the 2 players featured on next week's baseball cards. You could win free tickets to a Brewer game!

The cards in this 30-card set measure 2 3/4" by 4 1/8". Again this year, the police departments in and around Milwaukee issued sets of the Milwaukee Brewers. The backs contain the Brewers logo, a safety tip, and in some cases, a badge of the jurisdiction. Prices below are for the basic set without regard to the Police Department issuing the cards; cards from the more obscure corners and small towns of Wisconsin (smaller production) will be valued higher. Cards are numbered by uniform number.

	MINT	EXC	G-V
COMPLETE SET (30)	6.00	2.40	.
COMMON PLAYER	.15	.06	.
□ 2 Randy Ready	.25	.10	.0
□ 4 Paul Molitor	.75	.30	.0
□ 5 Doug Loman	.25	.10	.0
□ 7 Paul Householder	.15	.06	.0
□ 10 Bob McClure	.15	.06	.0
□ 11 Ed Romero	.15	.06	.0
□ 14 Dion James	.25	.10	.0
□ 15 Cecil Cooper	.45	.18	.0
□ 17 Jim Gantner	.25	.10	.0
□ 18 Danny Darwin	.15	.06	.0
□ 19 Robin Yount	.90	.36	.0
□ 21 Bill Schroeder	.15	.06	.0
□ 22 Charlie Moore	.15	.06	.0
□ 23 Ted Simmons	.35	.14	.0
□ 24 Ben Oglivie	.25	.10	.0
□ 26 Brian Giles	.15	.06	.0
□ 27 Pete Ladd	.15	.06	.0
□ 28 Rick Manning	.15	.06	.0
□ 29 Mark Brouhard	.15	.06	.0
□ 30 Moose Haas	.15	.06	.0
□ 31 George Bamberger MG	.15	.06	.0
□ 34 Rollie Fingers	.60	.24	.0
□ 40 Bob L. Gibson	.15	.06	.0
□ 41 Ray Searage	.15	.06	.0
□ 47 Jaime Cocanower	.15	.06	.0
□ 48 Ray Burris	.15	.06	.0
□ 49 Ted Higuera	.90	.36	.0
□ 50 Pete Vuckovich	.25	.10	.0
□ xx Team Roster (unnumbered)	.15	.06	.0
□ xx Coaches (unnumbered)	.15	.06	.0
□ xx Newspaper Carrier (unnumbered)	.15	.06	.0

1986 Police Astros

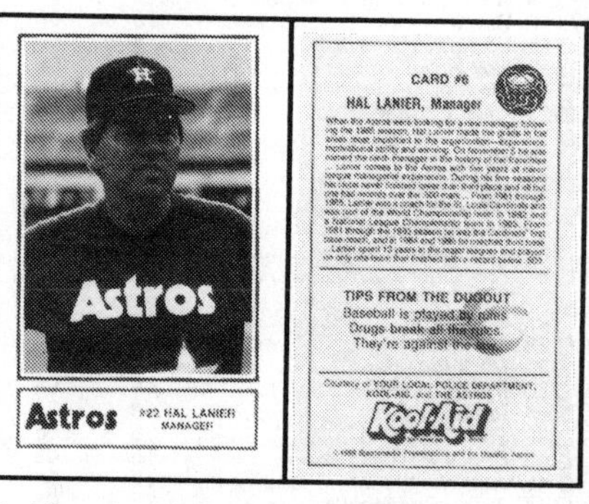

Astros
Astros
#22 HAL LANIER
MANAGER
CARD #6
HAL LANIER, Manager
TIPS FROM THE DUGOUT
Kool-Aid

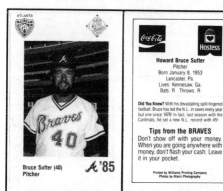

This 26-card safety set was also sponsored by Kool-Aid. The backs contain a biographical paragraph above a "Tip from the Dugout". The front features a full-color photo of the player, his name, and uniform number. The cards are numbered on the back and measure 2 5/8" by 4 1/8". The backs are printed in orange and blue on white card stock. Sets were distributed at the Astrodome on June 14th as well as given away throughout the summer by the Houston Police.

	MINT	EXC	G-VG
COMPLETE SET (26)	6.00	2.40	.60
COMMON PLAYER (1-26)	.15	.06	.01
□ 1 Jim Pankovits	.15	.06	.01
□ 2 Nolan Ryan	1.00	.40	.10
□ 3 Mike Scott	.65	.26	.06
□ 4 Kevin Bass	.40	.16	.04
□ 5 Bill Doran	.50	.20	.05
□ 6 Hal Lanier MG	.25	.10	.02
□ 7 Denny Walling	.15	.06	.01
□ 8 Alan Ashby	.25	.10	.02
□ 9 Phil Garner	.15	.06	.01
□ 10 Charlie Kerfeld	.15	.06	.01
□ 11 Dave Smith	.35	.14	.03
□ 12 Jose Cruz	.50	.20	.05
□ 13 Craig Reynolds	.15	.06	.01
□ 14 Mark Bailey	.15	.06	.01
□ 15 Bob Knepper	.35	.14	.03
□ 16 Julio Solano	.15	.06	.01
□ 17 Dickie Thon	.25	.10	.02
□ 18 Mike Madden	.15	.06	.01
□ 19 Jeff Calhoun	.15	.06	.01
□ 20 Tony Walker	.15	.06	.01
□ 21 Terry Puhl	.25	.10	.02
□ 22 Glenn Davis	.75	.30	.07
□ 23 Billy Hatcher	.35	.14	.03
□ 24 Jim Deshaies	.25	.10	.02
□ 25 Frank DiPino	.15	.06	.01
□ 26 Coaching Staff	.15	.06	.01

1986 Police Braves

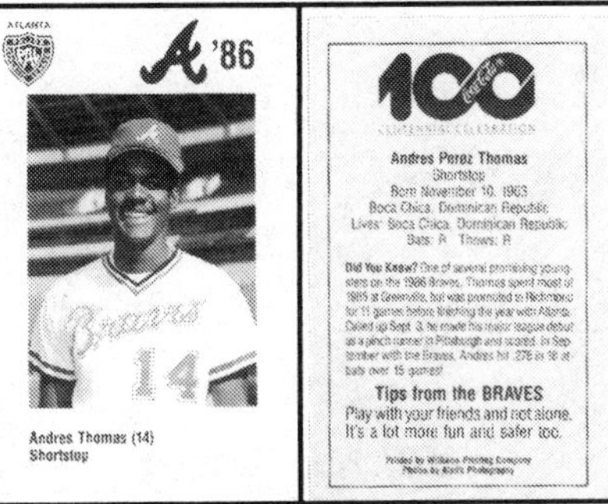

This 30-card safety set was also sponsored by Coca-Cola. The backs contain the usual biographical info and safety tip. The front features a full-color photo of the player, his name, and uniform number. The cards measure 2 5/8" by 4 1/8". Cards were freely distributed throughout the summer by the Police Departments in the Atlanta area. Cards are numbered below by uniform number.

	MINT	EXC	G-VG
COMPLETE SET (30)	10.00	4.00	1.00
COMMON PLAYER	.25	.10	.02
□ 2 Russ Nixon COA	.25	.10	.02
□ 3 Dale Murphy	2.50	1.00	.25
□ 4 Bob Skinner COA	.35	.14	.03
□ 5 Billy Sample	.25	.10	.02
□ 7 Chuck Tanner MG	.35	.14	.03
□ 8 Willie Stargell COA	1.00	.40	.10
□ 9 Ozzie Virgil	.35	.14	.03
□ 10 Chris Chambliss	.35	.14	.03
□ 11 Bob Horner	.70	.28	.07
□ 14 Andres Thomas	.50	.20	.05
□ 15 Claudell Washington	.35	.14	.03
□ 16 Rafael Ramirez	.25	.10	.02
□ 17 Glenn Hubbard	.25	.10	.02
□ 18 Omar Moreno	.25	.10	.02
□ 19 Terry Harper	.25	.10	.02
□ 20 Bruce Benedict	.25	.10	.02
□ 23 Ted Simmons	.45	.18	.04
□ 24 Ken Oberkfell	.25	.10	.02
□ 26 Gene Garber	.35	.14	.03
□ 29 Craig McMurtry	.25	.10	.02
□ 30 Paul Assenmacher	.25	.10	.02
□ 33 Johnny Sain COA	.45	.18	.04
□ 34 Zane Smith	.60	.24	.06
□ 38 Joe Johnson	.35	.14	.03
□ 40 Bruce Sutter	.45	.18	.04
□ 42 Rick Mahler	.45	.18	.04
□ 46 David Palmer	.35	.14	.03
□ 48 Duane Ward	.35	.14	.03
□ 49 Jeff Dedmon	.25	.10	.02
□ 52 Al Monchak COA	.25	.10	.02

1986 Police Brewers

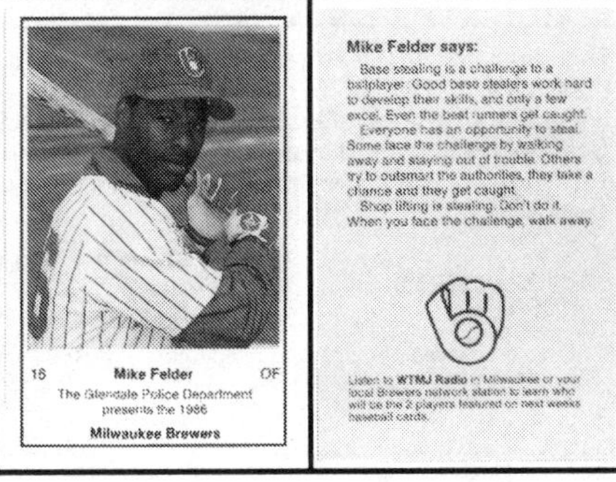

This 32-card safety set was also sponsored by WTMJ Radio and Kinney Shoes. The backs contain the usual biographical info and safety tip. The front features a full-color photo of the player, his name, position, and uniform number. The cards measure 2 5/8" by 4 1/8". Cards were freely distributed throughout the summer by the Police Departments in the Milwaukee area. Cards are numbered below by uniform number.

	MINT	EXC	G-VG
COMPLETE SET (32)	5.00	2.00	.50
COMMON PLAYER	.10	.04	.01
□ 1 Ernest Riles	.25	.10	.02
□ 2 Randy Ready	.15	.06	.01
□ 3 Juan Castillo	.15	.06	.01
□ 4 Paul Molitor	.60	.24	.06
□ 7 Paul Householder	.10	.04	.01
□ 8 Andy Etchebarren COA	.10	.04	.01
□ 10 Bob McClure	.15	.06	.01
□ 11 Rick Cerone	.10	.04	.01
□ 12 Larry Haney COA	.10	.04	.01
□ 13 Billy Jo Robidoux	.15	.06	.01
□ 15 Cecil Cooper	.35	.14	.03
□ 16 Mike Felder	.20	.08	.02
□ 17 Jim Gantner	.15	.06	.01
□ 18 Danny Darwin	.10	.04	.01
□ 19 Robin Yount	.75	.30	.07
□ 20 Juan Nieves	.20	.08	.02
□ 21 Bill Schroeder	.10	.04	.01
□ 22 Charlie Moore	.10	.04	.01
□ 24 Ben Oglivie	.20	.08	.02
□ 25 Mark Clear	.10	.04	.01
□ 28 Rick Manning	.10	.04	.01
□ 31 George Bamberger MG	.15	.06	.01
□ 33 Frank Howard COA	.15	.06	.01
□ 35 Tony Muser COA	.10	.04	.01
□ 37 Dan Plesac	.30	.12	.03
□ 38 Herm Starrette COA	.10	.04	.01
□ 39 Tim Leary	.10	.04	.01
□ 42 Tom Trebelhorn COA	.20	.08	.02
□ 45 Rob Deer	.40	.16	.04
□ 46 Bill Wegman	.15	.06	.01
□ 47 Jaime Cocanower	.10	.04	.01
□ 49 Teddy Higuera	.60	.24	.06

1986 Police Dodgers

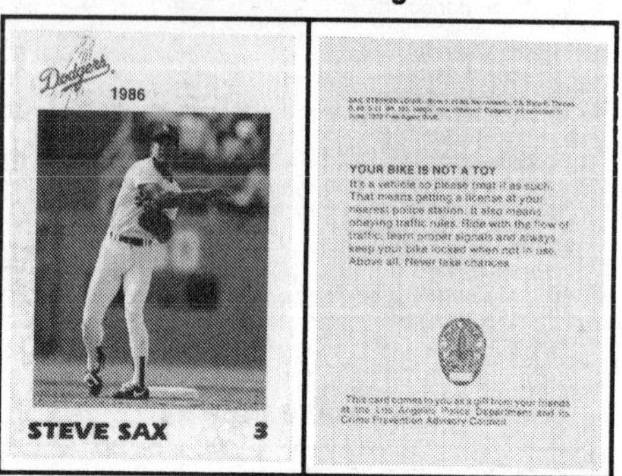

This 30-card set features full-color cards each measuring 2 13/16" by 4 1/8". The cards are unnumbered except for uniform numbers. The backs give a safety tip as well as a short capsule biography. The sets were given away at Dodger Stadium on May 18th.

	MINT	EXC	G-VG
COMPLETE SET (30)	5.00	2.00	.50
COMMON PLAYER	.10	.04	.01
☐ 2 Tom Lasorda MG	.25	.10	.02
☐ 3 Steve Sax	.50	.20	.05
☐ 5 Mike Marshall	.50	.20	.05
☐ 9 Greg Brock	.20	.08	.02
☐ 10 Dave Anderson	.10	.04	.01
☐ 12 Bill Madlock	.20	.08	.02
☐ 14 Mike Scioscia	.20	.08	.02
☐ 17 Len Matuszek	.10	.04	.01
☐ 18 Bill Russell	.20	.08	.02
☐ 22 Franklin Stubbs	.25	.10	.02
☐ 23 Enos Cabell	.10	.04	.01
☐ 25 Mariano Duncan	.15	.06	.01
☐ 26 Alejandro Pena	.20	.08	.02
☐ 27 Carlos Diaz	.10	.04	.01
☐ 28 Pedro Guerrero	.65	.26	.06
☐ 29 Alex Trevino	.10	.04	.01
☐ 31 Ed VandeBerg	.10	.04	.01
☐ 34 Fernando Valenzuela	.65	.26	.06
☐ 35 Bob Welch	.20	.08	.02
☐ 40 Rick Honeycutt	.10	.04	.01
☐ 41 Jerry Reuss	.15	.06	.01
☐ 43 Ken Howell	.10	.04	.01
☐ 44 Ken Landreaux	.10	.04	.01
☐ 45 Terry Whitfield	.10	.04	.01
☐ 48 Dennis Powell	.10	.04	.01
☐ 49 Tom Niedenfuer	.15	.06	.01
☐ 51 Reggie Williams	.10	.04	.01
☐ 55 Orel Hershiser	.90	.36	.09
☐ xx Coaching Staff (unnumbered) Don McMahon, Mark Cresse, Ben Hines, Ron Perranoski, Monty Basgall, Manny Mota, Joe Amalfitano	.10	.04	.01
☐ xx Team Photo (unnumbered) (checklist back)	.10	.04	.01

1987 Police Astros

This 26-card safety set was sponsored by the Astros, Deer Park Hospital, and Sportsmedia Presentations. The backs contain a biographical paragraph above a "Tip from the Dugout". The front features a full-color photo of the player, his name, position, and

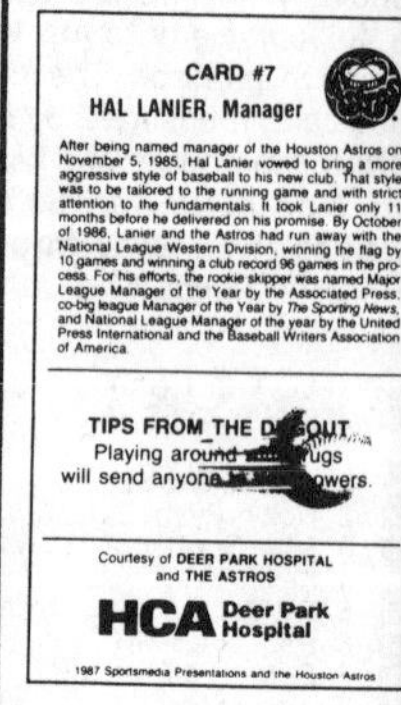

uniform number. The cards are numbered on the back and measure 2 5/8" by 4 1/8". The first twelve cards were distributed at the Astrodome on July 14th and the rest were given away later in the summer by the Deer Park Hospital.

	MINT	EXC	G-VG
COMPLETE SET (26)	5.00	2.00	.5
COMMON PLAYER (1-26)	.15	.06	.0
☐ 1 Larry Andersen	.15	.06	.0
☐ 2 Mark Bailey	.15	.06	.0
☐ 3 Jose Cruz	.35	.14	.0
☐ 4 Danny Darwin	.15	.06	.0
☐ 5 Bill Doran	.45	.18	.0
☐ 6 Billy Hatcher	.45	.18	.0
☐ 7 Hal Lanier MG	.25	.10	.0
☐ 8 Davey Lopes	.25	.10	.0
☐ 9 Dave Meads	.15	.06	.0
☐ 10 Craig Reynolds	.15	.06	.0
☐ 11 Mike Scott	.75	.30	.0
☐ 12 Denny Walling	.15	.06	.0
☐ 13 Aurelio Lopez	.15	.06	.01
☐ 14 Dickie Thon	.25	.10	.02
☐ 15 Terry Puhl	.25	.10	.02
☐ 16 Nolan Ryan	1.00	.40	.1
☐ 17 Dave Smith	.35	.14	.03
☐ 18 Julio Solano	.15	.06	.01
☐ 19 Jim Deshaies	.25	.10	.02
☐ 20 Bob Knepper	.25	.10	.02
☐ 21 Alan Ashby	.25	.10	.02
☐ 22 Kevin Bass	.35	.14	.03
☐ 23 Glenn Davis	.60	.24	.06
☐ 24 Phil Garner	.25	.10	.02
☐ 25 Jim Pankovits	.15	.06	.01
☐ 26 Coaching Staff	.15	.06	.01

1987 Police Brewers

20
Juan Nieves
P
The Milwaukee Police Department
Kinney Shoes and WTMJ Radio
present the 1987
Milwaukee Brewers

Juan Nieves says:

"Baseball players are constantly tempted by drug dealers. They love to hang around celebrities and try to get us to join them at parties. We learn to just to say no. We tell them to get lost or we'll call the police.

Call it what you want, pot, grass, speed, angel dust, or coke. It's dangerous stuff that can hurt you or even kill. If you're approached, just say no, and then call your local police or tell your parents."

Listen to WTMJ Radio in Milwaukee or your local Brewers network station to learn who will be the 2 players featured on next weeks baseball cards.

This 30-card safety set was also sponsored by WTMJ Radio and Kinney Shoes. The backs contain the usual biographical info and safety tip. The front features a full-color photo of the player, his name, position, and uniform number. The cards measure 2 5/8" by 4 1/8". Cards were freely distributed throughout the summer by the Police Departments in the Milwaukee area and throughout other parts of Wisconsin. Cards are numbered below by uniform number.

	MINT	EXC	G-VG
COMPLETE SET (30)	5.00	2.00	.50
COMMON PLAYER	.15	.06	.01
□ 1 Ernest Riles	.25	.10	.02
□ 2 Edgar Diaz	.25	.10	.02
□ 3 Juan Castillo	.15	.06	.01
□ 4 Paul Molitor	.75	.30	.07
□ 5 B.J. Surhoff	.60	.24	.06
□ 7 Dale Sveum	.35	.14	.03
□ 9 Greg Brock	.25	.10	.02
□ 13 Billy Jo Robidoux	.15	.06	.01
□ 14 Jim Paciorek	.15	.06	.01
□ 15 Cecil Cooper	.35	.14	.03
□ 16 Mike Felder	.15	.06	.01
□ 17 Jim Gantner	.25	.10	.02
□ 19 Robin Yount	.90	.36	.09
□ 20 Juan Nieves	.25	.10	.02
□ 21 Bill Schroeder	.15	.06	.01
□ 25 Mark Clear	.15	.06	.01
□ 26 Glenn Braggs	.35	.14	.03
□ 28 Rick Manning	.15	.06	.01
□ 29 Chris Bosio	.15	.06	.01
□ 32 Chuck Crim	.15	.06	.01
□ 34 Mark Ciardi	.15	.06	.01
□ 37 Dan Plesac	.35	.14	.03
□ 38 John Henry Johnson	.15	.06	.01
□ 40 Mike Birkbeck	.25	.10	.02
□ 42 Tom Trebelhorn MG	.25	.10	.02
□ 45 Rob Deer	.35	.14	.03
□ 46 Bill Wegman	.15	.06	.01
□ 49 Teddy Higuera	.45	.18	.04
□ xx Coaching Staff	.15	.06	.01
□ xx Brewers Team (Checklist on back)	.15	.06	.01

1987 Police Dodgers

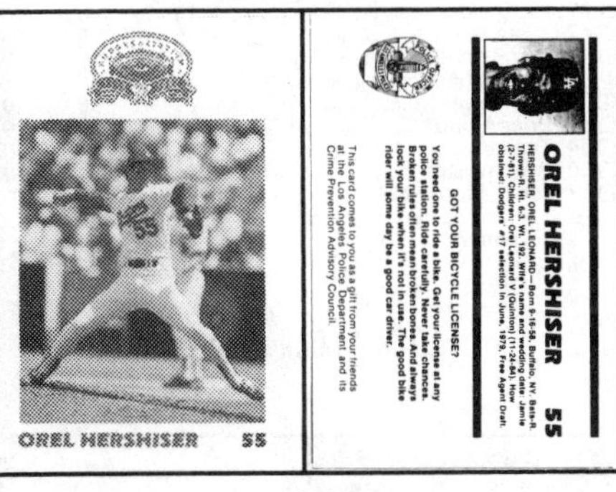

This 30-card set features full-color cards each measuring 2 13/16" by 4 1/8". The cards are unnumbered except for uniform numbers. The backs give a safety tip as well as a short capsule biography. Cards were given away at Dodger Stadium on April 24th and later during the summer by LAPD officers at a rate of two cards per week.

	MINT	EXC	G-VG
COMPLETE SET (30)	5.00	2.00	.50
COMMON PLAYER (1-30)	.15	.06	.01
□ 1 Tom Lasorda 2	.35	.14	.03
□ 2 Steve Sax 3	.50	.20	.05
□ 3 Mike Marshall 5	.50	.20	.05
□ 4 Dave Anderson 10	.15	.06	.01
□ 5 Bill Madlock 12	.25	.10	.02
□ 6 Mike Scioscia 14	.25	.10	.02
□ 7 Gilberto Reyes 15	.15	.06	.01
□ 8 Len Matuszek 17	.15	.06	.01
□ 9 Reggie Williams 21	.15	.06	.01
□ 10 Franklin Stubbs 22	.25	.10	.02
□ 11 Tim Leary 23	.35	.14	.03
□ 12 Mariano Duncan 25	.15	.06	.01
□ 13 Alejandro Pena 26	.25	.10	.02
□ 14 Pedro Guerrero 28	.65	.26	.06
□ 15 Alex Trevino 29	.15	.06	.01
□ 16 Jeff Hamilton 33	.25	.10	.02
□ 17 Fernando Valenzuela 34	.65	.26	.06
□ 18 Bob Welch 35	.25	.10	.02
□ 19 Matt Young 36	.15	.06	.01
□ 20 Rick Honeycutt 40	.15	.06	.01
□ 21 Jerry Reuss 41	.25	.10	.02
□ 22 Ken Howell 43	.15	.06	.01
□ 23 Ken Landreaux 44	.15	.06	.01
□ 24 Ralph Bryant 46	.15	.06	.01
□ 25 Jose Gonzalez 47	.25	.10	.02
□ 26 Tom Niedenfuer 49	.15	.06	.01
□ 27 Brian Holton 51	.15	.06	.01
□ 28 Orel Hershiser 55	.75	.30	.07
□ 29 Coaching Staff	.15	.06	.01
□ 30 Dodgers Stadium (25th Anniversary)	.15	.06	.01

1988 Police Astros

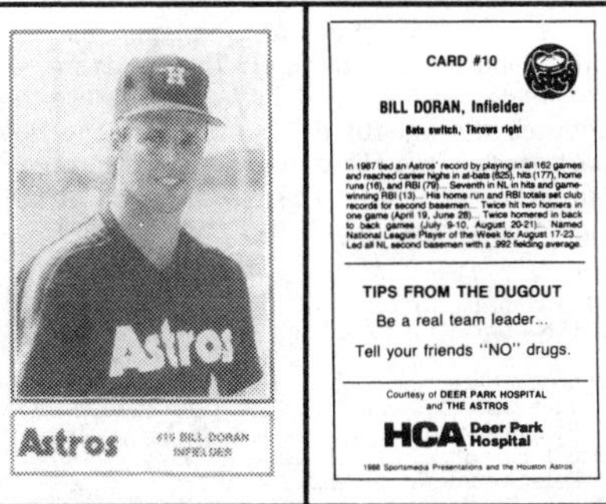

Astros
CARD #10
BILL DORAN, Infielder
Bats switch, Throws right
TIPS FROM THE DUGOUT
Be a real team leader...
Tell your friends "NO" drugs.
Courtesy of DEER PARK HOSPITAL and THE ASTROS
HCA Deer Park Hospital

This 26-card safety set was sponsored by the Astros, Deer Park Hospital, and Sportsmedia Presentations. The backs contain a biographical paragraph above "Tips from the Dugout". The front features a full-color photo of the player, his name, position, and uniform number. The cards are numbered on the back and measure 2 5/8" by 4 1/8". The sets were supposedly distributed to the first 15,000 youngsters attending the New York Mets game against the Astros at the Astrodome on July 9th.

	MINT	EXC	G-VG
COMPLETE SET (26)	7.50	3.00	.75
COMMON PLAYER (1-26)	.25	.10	.02
□ 1 Juan Agosto	.25	.10	.02
□ 2 Larry Andersen	.25	.10	.02
□ 3 Joaquin Andujar	.35	.14	.03
□ 4 Alan Ashby	.35	.14	.03
□ 5 Mark Bailey	.25	.10	.02
□ 6 Kevin Bass	.45	.18	.04
□ 7 Danny Darwin	.25	.10	.02
□ 8 Glenn Davis	.75	.30	.07
□ 9 Jim Deshaies	.35	.14	.03
□ 10 Bill Doran	.45	.18	.04
□ 11 Billy Hatcher	.45	.18	.04
□ 12 Jeff Heathcock	.25	.10	.02
□ 13 Steve Henderson	.25	.10	.02
□ 14 Chuck Jackson	.25	.10	.02
□ 15 Bob Knepper	.35	.14	.03
□ 16 Jim Pankovits	.25	.10	.02
□ 17 Terry Puhl	.35	.14	.03
□ 18 Rafael Ramirez	.25	.10	.02
□ 19 Craig Reynolds	.25	.10	.02
□ 20 Nolan Ryan	1.00	.40	.10
□ 21 Mike Scott	.75	.30	.07
□ 22 Dave Smith	.45	.18	.04
□ 23 Denny Walling	.25	.10	.02
□ 24 Gerald Young	.35	.14	.03
□ 25 Hal Lanier MG	.25	.10	.02
□ 26 Coaching Staff	.25	.10	.02

1988 Police Brewers

Greg Brock says:

"We all want to win. No one wants to be a loser. Winners are competitors because they give their best effort all the time. You can't ask for more.

If you give your best effort in school, study hard, and have good attendance, you'll be a winner too. You'll get your diploma and be ready to work in a respectable job."

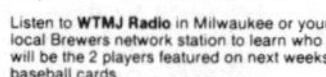

Listen to **WTMJ Radio** in Milwaukee or your local Brewers network station to learn who will be the 2 players featured on next weeks baseball cards.

This 30-card safety set was also sponsored by WTMJ Radio and Stadia Athletic Shoes. The backs contain the usual biographical info and safety tip. The front features a full-color photo of the player, his name, position, and uniform number. The cards measure approximately 2 7/8" by 4 1/8". Cards were freely distributed throughout the summer by the Police Departments in the Milwaukee area and throughout other parts of Wisconsin. Cards are numbered below by uniform number.

	MINT	EXC	G-VG
COMPLETE SET (30)	5.00	2.00	.50
COMMON PLAYER	.15	.06	.01
□ 1 Ernest Riles	.15	.06	.01
□ 3 Juan Castillo	.15	.06	.01
□ 4 Paul Molitor	.60	.24	.06
□ 5 B.J. Surhoff	.35	.14	.03
□ 7 Dale Sveum	.25	.10	.02
□ 9 Greg Brock	.25	.10	.02
□ 11 Charlie O'Brien	.15	.06	.01
□ 14 Jim Adduci	.25	.10	.02
□ 16 Mike Felder	.15	.06	.01
□ 17 Jim Gantner	.25	.10	.02
□ 19 Robin Yount	.75	.30	.07
□ 20 Juan Nieves	.25	.10	.02
□ 21 Bill Schroeder	.15	.06	.01
□ 23 Joey Meyer	.25	.10	.02
□ 25 Mark Clear	.15	.06	.01
□ 26 Glenn Braggs	.25	.10	.02
□ 28 Odell Jones	.15	.06	.01
□ 29 Chris Bosio	.15	.06	.01
□ 30 Steve Kiefer	.15	.06	.01
□ 32 Chuck Crim	.15	.06	.01
□ 33 Jay Aldrich	.15	.06	.01
□ 37 Dan Plesac	.35	.14	.03
□ 40 Mike Birkbeck	.25	.10	.02
□ 42 Tom Trebelhorn MG	.15	.06	.01
□ 43 Dave Stapleton	.15	.06	.01
□ 45 Rob Deer	.35	.14	.03
□ 46 Bill Wegman	.15	.06	.01
□ 49 Ted Higuera	.45	.18	.04
□ x Team Photo HOR (unnumbered)	.15	.06	.01
□ x Manager and Coaches HOR (unnumbered)	.15	.06	.01

1988 Police Dodgers

This 30-card set features full-color cards each measuring approximately 2 13/16" by 4 1/8". The cards are unnumbered except for uniform numbers. The backs give a safety tip as well as a short capsule biography. Cards were given during the summer by LAPD officers. The set is very similar to the 1987 set, the 1988 set is distinguished by the fact that it does not have the 25th anniversary (of Dodger Stadium) logo on the card front.

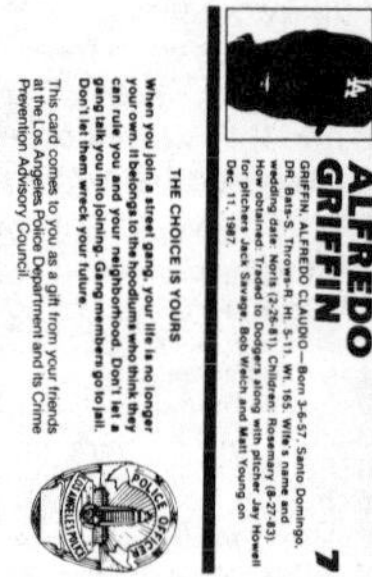

	MINT	EXC	G-VG
COMPLETE SET (30)	5.00	2.00	.50
COMMON PLAYER	.15	.06	.01
□ 2 Tom Lasorda MG	.35	.14	.03
□ 3 Steve Sax	.50	.20	.05
□ 5 Mike Marshall	.40	.16	.04
□ 7 Alfredo Griffin	.25	.10	.02
□ 9 Mickey Hatcher	.15	.06	.01
□ 10 Dave Anderson	.15	.06	.01
□ 12 Danny Heep	.15	.06	.01
□ 14 Mike Scioscia	.25	.10	.02
□ 20 Don Sutton	.50	.20	.05
□ 21 Tito Landrum and 17 Len Matuszak	.15	.06	.01
□ 22 Franklin Stubbs	.15	.06	.01
□ 23 Kirk Gibson	.75	.30	.07
□ 25 Marciano Duncan	.15	.06	.01
□ 26 Alejandro Pena	.25	.10	.02
□ 27 Mike Sharperson and 52 Tim Crews	.15	.06	.01
□ 28 Pedro Guerrero	.50	.20	.05
□ 29 Alex Trevino	.15	.06	.01
□ 31 John Shelby	.15	.06	.01
□ 33 Jeff Hamilton	.25	.10	.02
□ 34 Fernando Valenzuela	.50	.20	.05
□ 37 Mike Davis	.15	.06	.01
□ 41 Brad Havens	.15	.06	.01
□ 43 Ken Howell	.15	.06	.01
□ 47 Jesse Orosco	.15	.06	.01
□ 49 Tim Belcher and 57 Shawn Hillegas	.25	.10	.02
□ 50 Jay Howell	.15	.06	.01
□ 51 Brian Holton	.15	.06	.01
□ 54 Tim Leary	.25	.10	.02
□ 55 Orel Hershiser	.75	.30	.07
□ x Tom Lasorda MG and Coaches (unnumbered)	.35	.14	.03

1988 Police Tigers

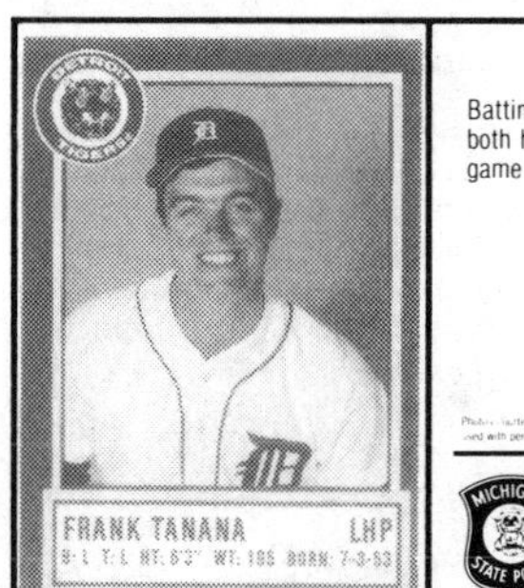

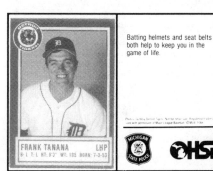

Batting helmets and seat belts both help to keep you in the game of life.

This set was sponsored by the Michigan State Police and the Detroit Tigers organization. There are 14 blue-bordered cards in the set; each card measures approximately 2 1/2" by 3 1/2". The cards are completely unnumbered as there is not even any reference to uniform numbers on the cards; the cards are listed below in alphabetical order.

	MINT	EXC	G-VG
COMPLETE SET (14)	20.00	8.00	2.00
COMMON PLAYER (1-14)	1.00	.40	.10
☐ 1 Doyle Alexander	1.25	.50	.12
☐ 2 Sparky Anderson MG	2.00	.80	.20
☐ 3 Dave Bergman	1.00	.40	.10
☐ 4 Tom Brookens	1.00	.40	.10
☐ 5 Darrell Evans	1.25	.50	.12
☐ 6 Larry Herndon	1.00	.40	.10
☐ 7 Chet Lemon	1.50	.60	.15
☐ 8 Jack Morris	2.50	1.00	.25
☐ 9 Matt Nokes	2.00	.80	.20
☐ 10 Jeff Robinson	2.00	.80	.20
☐ 11 Frank Tanana	1.25	.50	.12
☐ 12 Walt Terrell	1.00	.40	.10
☐ 13 Alan Trammell	3.50	1.40	.35
☐ 14 Lou Whitaker	2.00	.80	.20

1961 Post Cereal

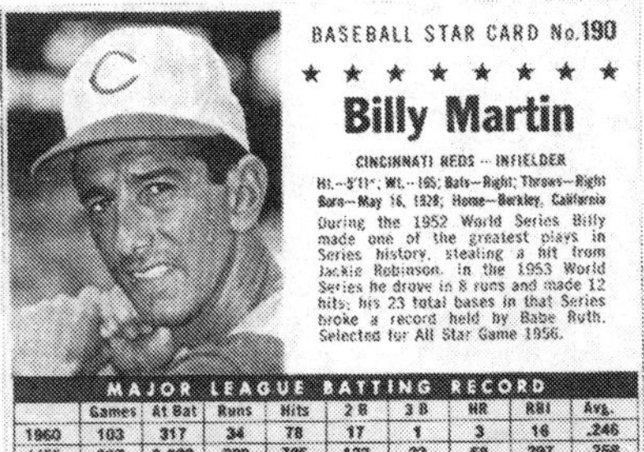

The cards in this 200-card set measure 2 1/2" by 3 1/2". The 1961 Post set was this company's first major set. The cards were available on thick cardbox stock, singly or in various panel sizes from cereal boxes (BOX), or in team sheets, printed on thinner cardboard stock, directly from the Post Cereal Company (COM). Many variations exist and are noted in the checklist below. There are many cards which were produced in lesser quantities; the prices below reflect the relative scarcity of the cards. Cards 10, 23, 70, 73, 94, 113, 135, 163, and 183 are examples of cards printed in limited quantities and hence commanding premium prices. The cards are numbered essentially in team groups, i.e., New York Yankees (1-18), Chicago White Sox (19-34), Detroit (35-46), Boston (47-56), Cleveland (57-67), Baltimore (68-80), Kansas City (81-90), Minnesota (91-100), Milwaukee (101-114), Philadelphia (115-124), Pittsburgh (125- 140), San Francisco (141-155), Los Angeles Dodgers (156-170), St. Louis (171-180), Cincinnati (181-190), and Chicago Cubs (191-200). The catalog number is F278-33. The complete set prices refer to both ways of collecting the set, all variations (357) or one of each player (200).

	NRMT	VG-E	GOOD
COMPLETE SET (357)	1650.00	700.00	200.00
COMPLETE SET (200)	1100.00	500.00	150.00
COMMON PLAYER (1-200)	1.25	.50	.12
☐ 1A Yogi Berra COM	15.00	6.00	1.50
☐ 1B Yogi Berra BOX	18.00	7.25	1.80
☐ 2A Elston Howard COM	2.00	.80	.20
☐ 2B Elston Howard BOX	3.00	1.20	.30
☐ 3A Bill Skowron COM	2.00	.80	.20
☐ 3B Bill Skowron BOX	1.50	.60	.15
☐ 4A Mickey Mantle COM	75.00	30.00	7.50
☐ 4B Mickey Mantle BOX	75.00	30.00	7.50
☐ 5 Bob Turley COM only	10.00	4.00	1.00
☐ 6A Whitey Ford COM	6.00	2.40	.60
☐ 6B Whitey Ford BOX	6.00	2.40	.60
☐ 7A Roger Maris COM	12.00	5.00	1.20
☐ 7B Roger Maris BOX	12.00	5.00	1.20
☐ 8A B.Richardson COM	2.00	.80	.20
☐ 8B B.Richardson BOX	1.50	.60	.15
☐ 9A Tony Kubek COM	2.00	.80	.20
☐ 9B Tony Kubek BOX	1.50	.60	.15
☐ 10 G.McDougald BOX only	25.00	10.00	2.50
☐ 11 Cletis Boyer BOX only	1.25	.50	.12
☐ 12A Hector Lopes COM	1.25	.50	.12
☐ 12B Hector Lopes BOX	1.25	.50	.12
☐ 13 Bob Cerv BOX only	1.25	.50	.12
☐ 14 Ryne Duren BOX only	1.25	.50	.12
☐ 15 Bobby Shantz BOX only	1.25	.50	.12
☐ 16 Art Ditmar BOX only	1.25	.50	.12
☐ 17 Jim Coates BOX only	1.25	.50	.12
☐ 18 J.Blanchard BOX only	1.25	.50	.12
☐ 19A Luis Aparicio COM	4.00	1.60	.40
☐ 19B Luis Aparicio BOX	3.50	1.40	.35
☐ 20A Nelson Fox COM	3.00	1.20	.30
☐ 20B Nelson Fox BOX	2.50	1.00	.25
☐ 21A Bill Pierce COM	3.00	1.20	.30
☐ 21B Bill Pierce BOX	5.00	2.00	.50
☐ 22A Early Wynn COM	6.00	2.40	.60
☐ 22B Early Wynn BOX	10.00	4.00	1.00
☐ 23 Bob Shaw BOX only	65.00	26.00	6.50
☐ 24A Al Smith COM	1.25	.50	.12
☐ 24B Al Smith BOX	2.50	1.00	.25
☐ 25A Minnie Minoso COM	2.00	.80	.20
☐ 25B Minnie Minoso BOX	2.00	.80	.20
☐ 26A Roy Sievers COM	1.25	.50	.12
☐ 26B Roy Sievers BOX	1.25	.50	.12
☐ 27A Jim Landis COM	2.00	.80	.20
☐ 27B Jim Landis BOX	2.00	.80	.20
☐ 28A Sherm Lollar COM	2.00	.80	.20
☐ 28B Sherm Lollar BOX	2.00	.80	.20
☐ 29 Gerry Staley BOX only	1.25	.50	.12
☐ 30A Gene Freese COM (Reds)	5.00	2.00	.50
☐ 30B Gene Freese BOX (White Sox)	1.25	.50	.12
☐ 31 Ted Kluszewski BOX only	1.25	.50	.12
☐ 32 Turk Lown BOX only	1.25	.50	.12
☐ 33A Jim Rivera COM	1.25	.50	.12
☐ 33B Jim Rivera BOX	1.25	.50	.12
☐ 34 F.Baumann BOX only	1.25	.50	.12
☐ 35A Al Kaline COM	10.00	4.00	1.00
☐ 35B Al Kaline BOX	12.50	5.00	1.25
☐ 36A Rocky Colavito COM	3.50	1.40	.35
☐ 36B Rocky Colavito BOX	4.00	1.60	.40
☐ 37A C.Maxwell COM	1.25	.50	.12
☐ 37B C.Maxwell BOX	2.50	1.00	.25
☐ 38A Frank Lary COM	1.25	.50	.12
☐ 38B Frank Lary BOX	1.25	.50	.12
☐ 39A Jim Bunning COM	2.50	1.00	.25
☐ 39B Jim Bunning BOX	2.50	1.00	.25
☐ 40A Norm Cash COM	1.25	.50	.12
☐ 40B Norm Cash BOX	1.25	.50	.12
☐ 41B Frank Bolling COM (Braves)	4.00	1.60	.40
☐ 41A Frank Bolling BOX (Tigers)	6.00	2.40	.60
☐ 42A Don Mossi COM	1.25	.50	.12
☐ 42B Don Mossi BOX	1.25	.50	.12
☐ 43A Lou Berberet COM	1.25	.50	.12
☐ 43B Lou Berberet BOX	1.25	.50	.12
☐ 44 Dave Sisler BOX only	1.25	.50	.12
☐ 45 Ed Yost BOX only	1.25	.50	.12
☐ 46 Pete Burnside BOX only	1.25	.50	.12
☐ 47A Pete Runnels COM	2.00	.80	.20
☐ 47B Pete Runnels BOX	3.00	1.20	.30
☐ 48A Frank Malzone COM	1.25	.50	.12
☐ 48B Frank Malzone BOX	1.25	.50	.12
☐ 49A Vic Wertz COM	3.50	1.40	.35
☐ 49B Vic Wertz BOX	4.00	1.60	.40
☐ 50A Tom Brewer COM	1.25	.50	.12
☐ 50B Tom Brewer BOX	2.00	.80	.20
☐ 51A Willie Tasby COM (Sold to Wash.)	5.00	2.00	.50
☐ 51B Willie Tasby BOX (no sale mention)	1.25	.50	.12
☐ 52A Russ Nixon COM	2.00	.80	.20
☐ 52B Russ Nixon BOX	2.00	.80	.20
☐ 53A Don Buddin COM	1.25	.50	.12
☐ 53B Don Buddin BOX	1.25	.50	.12
☐ 54A B.Monbouquette COM	1.25	.50	.12
☐ 54B B.Monbouquette BOX	1.25	.50	.12
☐ 55A Frank Sullivan COM (Phillies)	6.00	2.40	.60

☐ 55B Frank Sullivan BOX ...... 1.25 .50 .12
(Red Sox)
☐ 56A H.Sullivan COM .... 1.25 .50 .12
☐ 56B H.Sullivan BOX .... 1.25 .50 .12
☐ 57A Harvey Kuenn COM ..... 5.00 2.00 .50
(Giants)
☐ 57B Harvey Kuenn BOX ...... 3.00 1.20 .30
(Indians)
☐ 58A Gary Bell COM .... 2.50 1.00 .25
☐ 58B Gary Bell BOX .... 4.00 1.60 .40
☐ 59A Jim Perry COM .... 1.25 .50 .12
☐ 59B Jim Perry BOX .... 1.25 .50 .12
☐ 60A Jim Grant COM .... 2.00 .80 .20
☐ 60B Jim Grant BOX .... 3.00 1.20 .30
☐ 61A Johnny Temple COM ... 1.25 .50 .12
☐ 61B Johnny Temple BOX .... 1.25 .50 .12
☐ 62A Paul Foytack COM .... 1.25 .50 .12
☐ 62B Paul Foytack BOX .... 1.25 .50 .12
☐ 63A Vic Power COM .... 1.25 .50 .12
☐ 63B Vic Power BOX .... 1.25 .50 .12
☐ 64A Tito Francona COM ...... 1.25 .50 .12
☐ 64B Tito Francona BOX ...... 1.25 .50 .12
☐ 65A Ken Aspromonte COM . 6.00 2.40 .60
(Sold to L.A.)
☐ 65B Ken Aspromonte BOX .. 6.00 2.40 .60
(no sale mention)
☐ 66 Bob Wilson BOX only ...... 1.25 .50 .12
☐ 67A John Romano COM ...... 1.25 .50 .12
☐ 67B John Romano BOX ...... 1.25 .50 .12
☐ 68A Jim Gentile COM .... 2.00 .80 .20
☐ 68B Jim Gentile BOX .... 2.00 .80 .20
☐ 69A Gus Triandos COM .... 2.00 .80 .20
☐ 69B Gus Triandos BOX .... 3.00 1.20 .30
☐ 70 G.Woodling BOX only 25.00 10.00 2.50
☐ 71A Milt Pappas COM .... 2.00 .80 .20
☐ 71B Milt Pappas BOX .... 3.00 1.20 .30
☐ 72A Ron Hansen COM .... 2.00 .80 .20
☐ 72B Ron Hansen BOX .... 2.00 .80 .20
☐ 73 Chuck Estrada 65.00 26.00 6.50
COM only
☐ 74A Steve Barber COM .... 2.00 .80 .20
☐ 74B Steve Barber BOX .... 2.00 .80 .20
☐ 75A B.Robinson COM 10.00 4.00 1.00
☐ 75B B.Robinson BOX 12.50 5.00 1.25
☐ 76A Jackie Brandt COM ...... 1.25 .50 .12
☐ 76B Jackie Brandt BOX .... 1.25 .50 .12
☐ 77A Marv Breeding COM ..... 1.25 .50 .12
☐ 77B Marv Breeding BOX ..... 1.25 .50 .12
☐ 78 Hal Brown BOX only .... 1.25 .50 .12
☐ 79 Billy Klaus BOX only .... 1.25 .50 .12
☐ 80A Hoyt Wilhelm COM .... 6.00 2.40 .60
☐ 80B Hoyt Wilhelm BOX .... 4.00 1.60 .40
☐ 81A Jerry Lumpe COM .... 3.50 1.40 .35
☐ 81B Jerry Lumpe BOX .... 4.00 1.60 .40
☐ 82A Norm Siebern COM ...... 1.25 .50 .12
☐ 82B Norm Siebern BOX ...... 1.25 .50 .12
☐ 83A Bud Daley COM .... 3.00 1.20 .30
☐ 83B Bud Daley BOX .... 2.00 .80 .20
☐ 84A Bill Tuttle COM .... 1.25 .50 .12
☐ 84B Bill Tuttle BOX .... 2.00 .80 .20
☐ 85A M.Throneberry COM .... 2.00 .80 .20
☐ 85B M.Throneberry BOX ..... 2.00 .80 .20
☐ 86A Dick Williams COM .... 1.25 .50 .12
☐ 86B Dick Williams BOX .... 1.25 .50 .12
☐ 87A Ray Herbert COM .... 1.25 .50 .12
☐ 87B Ray Herbert BOX .... 1.25 .50 .12
☐ 88A Whitey Herzog COM ..... 1.25 .50 .12
☐ 88B Whitey Herzog BOX ..... 1.25 .50 .12
☐ 89A Ken Hamlin COM 10.00 4.00 1.00
(Sold to L.A.)
☐ 89B Ken Hamlin BOX .... 1.25 .50 .12
(no sale mention)
☐ 90A Hank Bauer COM .... 1.25 .50 .12
☐ 90B Hank Bauer BOX .... 1.25 .50 .12
☐ 91A Bob Allison COM .... 4.00 1.60 .40
(Minnesota)
☐ 91B Bob Allison BOX .... 4.00 1.60 .40
(Minneapolis)
☐ 92A Harmon Killebrew 12.00 5.00 1.20
(Minnesota) COM
☐ 92B Harmon Killebrew 15.00 6.00 1.50
(Minneapolis) BOX
☐ 93A Jim Lemon COM 15.00 6.00 1.50
(Minnesota)
☐ 93B Jim Lemon BOX 30.00 12.00 3.00
(Minneapolis)
☐ 94A Chuck Stobbs 100.00 40.00 10.00
(Minnesota)
COM only
☐ 95A Reno Bertoia COM .... 4.00 1.60 .40
(Minnesota)
☐ 95B Reno Bertoia BOX .... 1.25 .50 .12
(Minneapolis)
☐ 96A Billy Gardner COM .... 4.00 1.60 .40
(Minnesota)
☐ 96B Billy Gardner BOX .... 1.25 .50 .12
(Minneapolis)
☐ 97A Earl Battey COM .... 4.00 1.60 .40
(Minnesota)
☐ 97B Earl Battey BOX .... 1.25 .50 .12
(Minneapolis)
☐ 98A Pedro Ramos COM ...... 4.00 1.60 .40
(Minnesota)
☐ 98B Pedro Ramos BOX .... 1.25 .50 .12
(Minneapolis)
☐ 99A Camilo Pascual COM .... 4.00 1.60 .40
(Minnesota)
☐ 99B Camilo Pascual BOX .... 1.25 .50 .12
(Minneapolis)
☐ 100A Billy Consolo COM .... 4.00 1.60 .40
(Minnesota)
☐ 100B Billy Consolo BOX .... 1.25 .50 .12
(Minneapolis)
☐ 101A Warren Spahn COM 10.00 4.00 1.00
☐ 101B Warren Spahn BOX 12.50 5.00 1.25
☐ 102A Lew Burdette COM ...... 2.00 .80 .20
☐ 102B Lew Burdette BOX .... 2.00 .80 .20
☐ 103A Bob Buhl COM .... 1.25 .50 .12
☐ 103B Bob Buhl BOX .... 1.25 .50 .12
☐ 104A Joe Adcock COM .... 2.00 .80 .20
☐ 104B Joe Adcock BOX .... 3.00 1.20 .30
☐ 105A John Logan COM .... 2.00 .80 .20
☐ 105B John Logan BOX .... 3.00 1.20 .30
☐ 106 Ed Mathews COM only ... 21.00 8.50 2.10
☐ 107A Hank Aaron COM 18.00 7.25 1.80
☐ 107B Hank Aaron BOX 16.00 6.50 1.60
☐ 108A Wes Covington COM .... 1.25 .50 .12
☐ 108B Wes Covington BOX .... 1.25 .50 .12
☐ 109A Bill Bruton COM .... 4.00 1.60 .40
(Tigers)
☐ 109B Bill Bruton BOX .... 5.00 2.00 .50
(Braves)
☐ 110A Del Crandall COM .... 2.00 .80 .20
☐ 110B Del Crandall BOX .... 3.00 1.20 .30
☐ 111 Red Schoendienst .... 1.25 .50 .12
BOX only
☐ 112 Juan Pizarro .... 1.25 .50 .12
BOX only
☐ 113 Chuck Cottier .... 8.00 3.25 .80
BOX only
☐ 114 Al Spangler BOX only ..... 1.25 .50 .12
☐ 115A Dick Farrell COM .... 3.50 1.40 .35
☐ 115B Dick Farrell BOX .... 4.00 1.60 .40
☐ 116A Jim Owens COM .... 3.50 1.40 .35
☐ 116B Jim Owens BOX .... 4.00 1.60 .40
☐ 117A Robin Roberts COM ..... 6.00 2.40 .60
☐ 117B Robin Roberts BOX ...... 4.00 1.60 .40
☐ 118A Tony Taylor COM .... 1.25 .50 .12
☐ 118B Tony Taylor BOX .... 1.25 .50 .12
☐ 119A Lee Walls COM .... 1.25 .50 .12
☐ 119B Lee Walls BOX .... 1.25 .50 .12
☐ 120A Tony Curry COM .... 1.25 .50 .12
☐ 120B Tony Curry BOX .... 1.25 .50 .12
☐ 121A Pancho Herrera COM ... 1.25 .50 .12
☐ 121B Pancho Herrera BOX ... 1.25 .50 .12
☐ 122A Ken Walters COM .... 1.25 .50 .12
☐ 122B Ken Walters BOX .... 1.25 .50 .12
☐ 123A John Callison COM .... 1.25 .50 .12
☐ 123B John Callison BOX .... 1.25 .50 .12
☐ 124A Gene Conley COM .... 8.00 3.25 .80
(Red Sox)
☐ 124B Gene Conley BOX .... 1.25 .50 .12
(Phillies)
☐ 125A Bob Friend COM .... 2.00 .80 .20
☐ 125B Bob Friend BOX .... 3.00 1.20 .30
☐ 126A Vernon Law COM .... 2.00 .80 .20
☐ 126B Vernon Law BOX .... 3.00 1.20 .30
☐ 127A Dick Stuart COM .... 1.25 .50 .12
☐ 127B Dick Stuart BOX .... 1.25 .50 .12
☐ 128A Bill Mazeroski COM ...... 2.00 .80 .20
☐ 128B Bill Mazeroski BOX .... 1.25 .50 .12
☐ 129A Dick Groat COM .... 2.00 .80 .20
☐ 129B Dick Groat BOX .... 2.00 .80 .20
☐ 130A Don Hoak COM .... 1.25 .50 .12
☐ 130B Don Hoak BOX .... 1.25 .50 .12
☐ 131A Bob Skinner COM .... 1.25 .50 .12
☐ 131B Bob Skinner BOX .... 1.25 .50 .12
☐ 132A Bob Clemente COM 18.00 7.25 1.80
☐ 132B Bob Clemente BOX 21.00 8.50 2.10
☐ 133 Roy Face BOX only .... 2.50 1.00 .25
☐ 134 H.Haddix BOX only .... 1.25 .50 .12
☐ 135 Bill Virdon BOX only 25.00 10.00 2.50
☐ 136A Gino Cimoli COM .... 1.25 .50 .12
☐ 136B Gino Cimoli BOX .... 1.25 .50 .12
☐ 137 Rocky Nelson .... 1.25 .50 .12
BOX only
☐ 138A Smoky Burgess COM ... 1.25 .50 .12
☐ 138B Smoky Burgess BOX .... 1.25 .50 .12
☐ 139 Hal Smith BOX only .... 1.25 .50 .12
☐ 140 Wilmer Mizell .... 1.25 .50 .12

BOX only			
□ 141A M.McCormick COM	1.25	.50	.12
□ 141B M.McCormick BOX	1.25	.50	.12
□ 142A John Antonelli COM (Cleveland)	4.00	1.60	.40
□ 142B John Antonelli BOX (San Francisco)	3.00	1.20	.30
□ 143A Sam Jones COM	2.50	1.00	.25
□ 143B Sam Jones BOX	4.00	1.60	.40
□ 144A Orlando Cepeda COM	4.50	1.80	.45
□ 144B Orlando Cepeda BOX	5.00	2.00	.50
□ 145A Willie Mays COM	16.00	6.50	1.60
□ 145B Willie Mays BOX	16.00	6.50	1.60
□ 146A Willie Kirkland (Cleve.) COM	3.50	1.40	.35
□ 146B Willie Kirkland (San Fran.) BOX	3.00	1.20	.30
□ 147A Willie McCovey COM	7.00	2.80	.70
□ 147B Willie McCovey BOX	5.00	2.00	.50
□ 148A Don Blasingame COM	1.25	.50	.12
□ 148B Don Blasingame BOX	1.25	.50	.12
□ 149A Jim Davenport COM	1.25	.50	.12
□ 149B Jim Davenport BOX	1.25	.50	.12
□ 150A Hobie Landrith COM	1.25	.50	.12
□ 150B Hobie Landrith BOX	1.25	.50	.12
□ 151 Bob Schmidt BOX only	1.25	.50	.12
□ 152A Ed Bressoud COM	1.25	.50	.12
□ 152B Ed Bressoud BOX	1.25	.50	.12
□ 153A Andre Rodgers (no trade mention) BOX only	10.00	4.00	1.00
□ 153B Andre Rodgers (Traded to Milw.) BOX only	2.00	.80	.20
□ 154 Jack Sanford BOX only	1.25	.50	.12
□ 155 Billy O'Dell BOX only	1.25	.50	.12
□ 156A Norm Larker COM	2.00	.80	.20
□ 156B Norm Larker BOX	2.00	.80	.20
□ 157A Charlie Neal COM	1.25	.50	.12
□ 157B Charlie Neal BOX	1.25	.50	.12
□ 158A Jim Gilliam COM	2.00	.80	.20
□ 158B Jim Gilliam BOX	3.00	1.20	.30
□ 159A Wally Moon COM	1.25	.50	.12
□ 159B Wally Moon BOX	1.25	.50	.12
□ 160A Don Drysdale COM	6.00	2.40	.60
□ 160B Don Drysdale BOX	6.00	2.40	.60
□ 161A Larry Sherry COM	1.25	.50	.12
□ 161B Larry Sherry BOX	1.25	.50	.12
□ 162 Stan Williams BOX only	4.00	1.60	.40
□ 163 Mel Roach BOX only	45.00	18.00	4.50
□ 164A Maury Wills COM	3.50	1.40	.35
□ 164B Maury Wills BOX	3.00	1.20	.30
□ 165 Tommy Davis BOX only	1.25	.50	.12
□ 166A John Roseboro COM	1.25	.50	.12
□ 166B John Roseboro BOX	1.25	.50	.12
□ 167A Duke Snider COM	7.50	3.00	.75
□ 167B Duke Snider BOX	3.50	1.40	.35
□ 168A Gil Hodges COM	6.00	2.40	.60
□ 168B Gil Hodges BOX	3.50	1.40	.35
□ 169 John Podres BOX only	1.25	.50	.12
□ 170 Ed Roebuck BOX only	1.25	.50	.12
□ 171A Ken Boyer COM	5.00	2.00	.50
□ 171B Ken Boyer BOX	6.00	2.40	.60
□ 172A J.Cunningham COM	2.00	.80	.20
□ 172B J.Cunningham BOX	2.00	.80	.20
□ 173A Daryl Spencer COM	1.25	.50	.12
□ 173B Daryl Spencer BOX	1.25	.50	.12
□ 174A Larry Jackson COM	2.00	.80	.20
□ 174B Larry Jackson BOX	2.00	.80	.20
□ 175A Lindy McDaniel COM	1.25	.50	.12
□ 175B Lindy McDaniel BOX	1.25	.50	.12
□ 176A Bill White COM	2.00	.80	.20
□ 176B Bill White BOX	1.25	.50	.12
□ 177A Alex Grammas COM	1.25	.50	.12
□ 177B Alex Grammas BOX	1.25	.50	.12
□ 178A Curt Flood COM	2.00	.80	.20
□ 178B Curt Flood BOX	1.25	.50	.12
□ 179A Ernie Broglio COM	1.25	.50	.12
□ 179B Ernie Broglio BOX	1.25	.50	.12
□ 180A Hal Smith COM	1.25	.50	.12
□ 180B Hal Smith BOX	1.25	.50	.12
□ 181A Vada Pinson COM	2.00	.80	.20
□ 181B Vada Pinson BOX	1.25	.50	.12
□ 182A Frank Robinson COM	20.00	8.00	2.00
□ 182B Frank Robinson BOX	16.00	6.50	1.60
□ 183 Roy McMillan BOX only	45.00	18.00	4.50
□ 184A Bob Purkey COM	1.25	.50	.12
□ 184B Bob Purkey BOX	1.25	.50	.12
□ 185A Ed Kasko COM	1.25	.50	.12
□ 185B Ed Kasko BOX	1.25	.50	.12
□ 186A Gus Bell COM	2.00	.80	.20
□ 186B Gus Bell BOX	2.00	.80	.20
□ 187A Jerry Lynch COM	1.25	.50	.12
□ 187B Jerry Lynch BOX	1.25	.50	.12
□ 188A Ed Bailey COM	1.25	.50	.12
□ 188B Ed Bailey BOX	1.25	.50	.12
□ 189A Jim O'Toole COM	1.25	.50	.12
□ 189B Jim O'Toole BOX	1.25	.50	.12
□ 190A Billy Martin COM (Sold to Milw.)	5.00	2.00	.50
□ 190B Billy Martin BOX (no sale mention)	2.00	.80	.20
□ 191A Ernie Banks COM	9.00	3.75	.90
□ 191B Ernie Banks BOX	12.00	5.00	1.20
□ 192A Richie Ashburn COM	2.50	1.00	.25
□ 192B Richie Ashburn BOX	2.00	.80	.20
□ 193A Frank Thomas COM	8.00	3.25	.80
□ 193B Frank Thomas BOX	20.00	8.00	2.00
□ 194A Don Cardwell COM	2.00	.80	.20
□ 194B Don Cardwell BOX	2.00	.80	.20
□ 195A George Altman COM	1.25	.50	.12
□ 195B George Altman BOX	1.25	.50	.12
□ 196A Ron Santo COM	2.00	.80	.20
□ 196B Ron Santo BOX	1.25	.50	.12
□ 197A Glen Hobbie COM	1.25	.50	.12
□ 197B Glen Hobbie BOX	1.25	.50	.12
□ 198A Sam Taylor COM	1.25	.50	.12
□ 198B Sam Taylor BOX	1.25	.50	.12
□ 199A Jerry Kindall COM	1.25	.50	.12
□ 199B Jerry Kindall BOX	1.25	.50	.12
□ 200A Don Elston COM	1.25	.50	.12
□ 200B Don Elston BOX	1.25	.50	.12

1962 Post Cereal

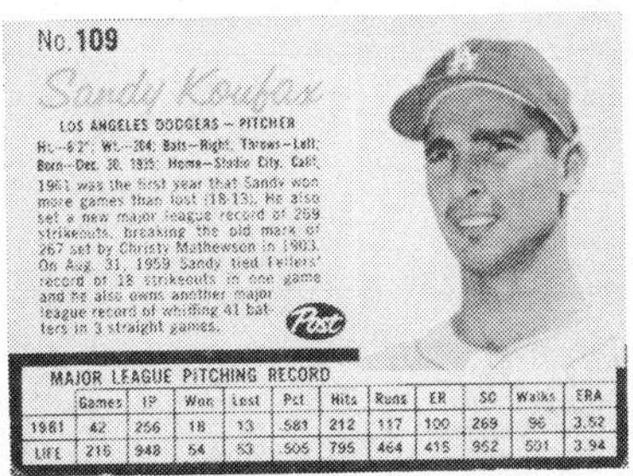

The cards in this 200-card series measure 2 1/2" by 3 1/2". The 1962 Post set is the easiest of the Post sets to complete. The cards are grouped numerically by team, for example, New York Yankees (1-13), Detroit (14-26), Baltimore (27-36), Cleveland (37-45), Chicago White Sox (46-55), Boston (56-64), Washington (65-73), Los Angeles Angels (74-82), Minnesota (83- 91), Kansas City (92-100), Los Angeles Dodgers (101-115), Cincinnati (116-130), San Francisco (131-144), Milwaukee (145- 157), St. Louis (158-168), Pittsburgh (169-181), Chicago Cubs (182-191), and Philadelphia (192-200). Cards 5B and 6B were printed on thin stock in a two card panel and distributed in a magazine promotion. The scarce cards are 55, 92, 101, 116, 121, and 140. The checklist for this set is the same as that of 1962 Jello and 1962 Post Canadian, but those sets are considered separate issues. The catalog number for this set is F278-37.

	NRMT	VG-E	GOOD
COMPLETE SET (200)	1000.00	400.00	150.00
COMMON PLAYER (1-200)	.90	.36	.09
□ 1 Bill Skowron	1.50	.60	.15
□ 2 Bobby Richardson	1.50	.60	.15
□ 3 Cletis Boyer	.90	.36	.09
□ 4 Tony Kubek	1.50	.60	.15
□ 5A Mickey Mantle	50.00	20.00	5.00
□ 5B Mickey Mantle AD	60.00	24.00	6.00
□ 6A Roger Maris	12.00	5.00	1.20
□ 6B Roger Maris AD	15.00	6.00	1.50
□ 7 Yogi Berra	10.00	4.00	1.00

☐ 8 Elston Howard .... 1.50 .60 .15
☐ 9 Whitey Ford .... 6.00 2.40 .60
☐ 10 Ralph Terry .... 1.50 .60 .15
☐ 11 John Blanchard .... .90 .36 .09
☐ 12 Luis Arroyo .... 1.50 .60 .15
☐ 13 Bill Stafford .... .90 .36 .09
☐ 14 Norm Cash .... 1.50 .60 .15
☐ 15 Jake Wood .... .90 .36 .09
☐ 16 Steve Boros .... .90 .36 .09
☐ 17 Chico Fernandez .... .90 .36 .09
☐ 18 Bill Bruton .... .90 .36 .09
☐ 19 Rocky Colavito .... 1.50 .60 .15
☐ 20 Al Kaline .... 7.00 2.80 .70
☐ 21 Dick Brown .... .90 .36 .09
☐ 22 Frank Lary .... .90 .36 .09
☐ 23 Don Mossi .... 1.50 .60 .15
☐ 24 Phil Regan .... .90 .36 .09
☐ 25 Charley Maxwell .... .90 .36 .09
☐ 26 Jim Bunning .... 3.00 1.20 .30
☐ 27A Jim Gentile .... 1.50 .60 .15
Home: Baltimore
☐ 27B Jim Gentile 9.00 3.75 .90
Home: San Lorenzo
☐ 28 Marv Breeding .... .90 .36 .09
☐ 29 Brooks Robinson .... 8.00 3.25 .80
☐ 30 Ron Hansen .... .90 .36 .09
☐ 31 Jackie Brandt .... .90 .36 .09
☐ 32 Dick Williams .... .90 .36 .09
☐ 33 Gus Triandos .... .90 .36 .09
☐ 34 Milt Pappas .... .90 .36 .09
☐ 35 Hoyt Wilhelm .... 5.00 2.00 .50
☐ 36 Chuck Estrada .... 4.00 1.60 .40
☐ 37 Vic Power .... .90 .36 .09
☐ 38 Johnny Temple .... .90 .36 .09
☐ 39 Bubba Phillips .... .90 .36 .09
☐ 40 Tito Francona .... .90 .36 .09
☐ 41 Willie Kirkland .... .90 .36 .09
☐ 42 John Romano .... .90 .36 .09
☐ 43 Jim Perry .... .90 .36 .09
☐ 44 Woodie Held .... .90 .36 .09
☐ 45 Chuck Essegian .... .90 .36 .09
☐ 46 Roy Sievers .... .90 .36 .09
☐ 47 Nellie Fox .... 2.00 .80 .20
☐ 48 Al Smith .... .90 .36 .09
☐ 49 Luis Aparicio .... 2.50 1.00 .25
☐ 50 Jim Landis .... .90 .36 .09
☐ 51 Minnie Minoso .... 1.50 .60 .15
☐ 52 Andy Carey .... .90 .36 .09
☐ 53 Sherman Lollar .... .90 .36 .09
☐ 54 Bill Pierce .... .90 .36 .09
☐ 55 Early Wynn 21.00 8.50 2.10
☐ 56 Chuck Schilling .... .90 .36 .09
☐ 57 Pete Runnels .... .90 .36 .09
☐ 58 Frank Malzone .... .90 .36 .09
☐ 59 Don Buddin .... .90 .36 .09
☐ 60 Gary Geiger .... .90 .36 .09
☐ 61 Carl Yastrzemski 27.00 11.00 2.70
☐ 62 Jackie Jensen .... .90 .36 .09
☐ 63 Jim Pagliaroni .... .90 .36 .09
☐ 64 Don Schwall .... .90 .36 .09
☐ 65 Dale Long .... .90 .36 .09
☐ 66 Chuck Cottier .... .90 .36 .09
☐ 67 Billy Klaus .... .90 .36 .09
☐ 68 Coot Veal .... .90 .36 .09
☐ 69 Marty Keough 25.00 10.00 2.50
☐ 70 Willie Tasby .... .90 .36 .09
☐ 71 Gene Woodling .... .90 .36 .09
☐ 72 Gene Green .... 1.50 .60 .15
☐ 73 Dick Donovan .... .90 .36 .09
☐ 74 Steve Bilko .... .90 .36 .09
☐ 75 Rocky Bridges .... .90 .36 .09
☐ 76 Eddie Yost .... .90 .36 .09
☐ 77 Leon Wagner .... .90 .36 .09
☐ 78 Albie Pearson .... .90 .36 .09
☐ 79 Ken Hunt .... .90 .36 .09
☐ 80 Earl Averill Jr. .... .90 .36 .09
☐ 81 Ryne Duren .... .90 .36 .09
☐ 82 Ted Kluszewski .... 2.00 .80 .20
☐ 83 Bob Allison 15.00 6.00 1.50
☐ 84 Billy Martin .... 2.00 .80 .20
☐ 85 Harmon Killebrew .... 5.00 2.00 .50
☐ 86 Zoilo Versalles .... .90 .36 .09
☐ 87 Lenny Green .... .90 .36 .09
☐ 88 Bill Tuttle .... .90 .36 .09
☐ 89 Jim Lemon .... .90 .36 .09
☐ 90 Earl Battey .... .90 .36 .09
☐ 91 Camilo Pascual .... .90 .36 .09
☐ 92 Norm Sieburn 40.00 16.00 4.00
☐ 93 Jerry Lumpe .... .90 .36 .09
☐ 94 Dick Howser .... 1.50 .60 .15
☐ 95A Gene Stephens .... 1.50 .60 .15
Born: Jan. 5
☐ 95B Gene Stephens .... 9.00 3.75 .90
Born: Jan. 20
☐ 96 Leo Posada .... .90 .36 .09
☐ 97 Joe Pignatano .... .90 .36 .09
☐ 98 Jim Archer .... .90 .36 .09
☐ 99 Haywood Sullivan .... .90 .36 .09
☐ 100 Art Ditmar .... .90 .36 .09
☐ 101 Gil Hodges 45.00 18.00 4.50
☐ 102 Charlie Neal .... .90 .36 .09
☐ 103 Daryl Spencer 15.00 6.00 1.50
☐ 104 Maury Wills .... 3.00 1.20 .30
☐ 105 Tommy Davis .... 1.50 .60 .15
☐ 106 Willie Davis .... .90 .36 .09
☐ 107 John Roseboro .... .90 .36 .09
☐ 108 John Podres .... 1.50 .60 .15
☐ 109A Sandy Koufax 15.00 6.00 1.50
☐ 109B Sandy Koufax 30.00 12.00 3.00
(with blue lines)
☐ 110 Don Drysdale .... 6.50 2.60 .65
☐ 111 Larry Sherry .... 2.50 1.00 .25
☐ 112 Jim Gilliam .... 1.50 .60 .15
☐ 113 Norm Larker 25.00 10.00 2.50
☐ 114 Duke Snider .... 5.00 2.00 .50
☐ 115 Stan Williams .... .90 .36 .09
☐ 116 Gordy Coleman 50.00 20.00 5.00
☐ 117 Don Blasingame .... .90 .36 .09
☐ 118 Gene Freese .... .90 .36 .09
☐ 119 Ed Kasko .... .90 .36 .09
☐ 120 Gus Bell .... .90 .36 .09
☐ 121 Vada Pinson .... 1.50 .60 .15
☐ 122 Frank Robinson 16.00 6.50 1.60
☐ 123 Bob Purkey .... .90 .36 .09
☐ 124A Joey Jay .... .90 .36 .09
☐ 124B Joey Jay 10.00 4.00 1.00
(with blue lines)
☐ 125 Jim Brosnan 20.00 8.00 2.00
☐ 126 Jim O'Toole .... .90 .36 .09
☐ 127 Jerry Lynch 40.00 16.00 4.00
☐ 128 Wally Post .... .90 .36 .09
☐ 129 Ken Hunt .... .90 .36 .09
☐ 130 Jerry Zimmerman .... .90 .36 .09
☐ 131 Willie McCovey 50.00 20.00 5.00
☐ 132 Jose Pagan .... .90 .36 .09
☐ 133 Felipe Alou .... .90 .36 .09
☐ 134 Jim Davenport .... .90 .36 .09
☐ 135 Harvey Kuenn .... 1.50 .60 .15
☐ 136 Orlando Cepeda .... 2.50 1.00 .25
☐ 137 Ed Bailey .... .90 .36 .09
☐ 138 Sam Jones .... .90 .36 .09
☐ 139 Mike McCormick .... .90 .36 .09
☐ 140 Juan Marichal 55.00 22.00 5.50
☐ 141 Jack Sanford .... .90 .36 .09
☐ 142 Willie Mays 21.00 8.50 2.10
☐ 143 Stu Miller .... 3.50 1.40 .35
☐ 144 Joe Amalfitano 10.00 4.00 1.00
☐ 145A Joe Adcock .... 1.50 .60 .15
☐ 145B Joe Adock (sic) ERR 30.00 12.00 3.00
☐ 146 Frank Bolling .... .90 .36 .09
☐ 147 Ed Mathews .... 5.00 2.00 .50
☐ 148 Roy McMillan .... .90 .36 .09
☐ 149 Hank Aaron 21.00 8.50 2.10
☐ 150 Gino Cimoli .... .90 .36 .09
☐ 151 Frank Thomas .... .90 .36 .09
☐ 152 Joe Torre .... 1.50 .60 .15
☐ 153 Lew Burdette .... 1.50 .60 .15
☐ 154 Bob Buhl .... .90 .36 .09
☐ 155 Carlton Willey .... .90 .36 .09
☐ 156 Lee Maye .... .90 .36 .09
☐ 157 Al Spangler .... .90 .36 .09
☐ 158 Bill White 25.00 10.00 2.50
☐ 159 Ken Boyer .... 2.00 .80 .20
☐ 160 Joe Cunningham .... .90 .36 .09
☐ 161 Carl Warwick .... .90 .36 .09
☐ 162 Carl Sawatski .... .90 .36 .09
☐ 163 Lindy McDaniel .... .90 .36 .09
☐ 164 Ernie Broglio .... .90 .36 .09
☐ 165 Larry Jackson .... .90 .36 .09
☐ 166 Curt Flood .... 1.50 .60 .15
☐ 167 Curt Simmons .... .90 .36 .09
☐ 168 Alex Grammas .... .90 .36 .09
☐ 169 Dick Stuart .... .90 .36 .09
☐ 170 Bill Mazeroski .... 1.50 .60 .15
☐ 171 Don Hoak .... .90 .36 .09
☐ 172 Dick Groat .... 1.50 .60 .15
☐ 173A Roberto Clemente 16.00 6.50 1.60
☐ 173B Roberto Clemente 40.00 16.00 4.00
(with blue lines)
☐ 174 Bob Skinner .... .90 .36 .09
☐ 175 Bill Virdon .... .90 .36 .09
☐ 176 Smoky Burgess .... .90 .36 .09
☐ 177 Elroy Face .... .90 .36 .09
☐ 178 Bob Friend .... .90 .36 .09
☐ 179 Vernon Law .... .90 .36 .09
☐ 180 Harvey Haddix .... .90 .36 .09
☐ 181 Hal Smith .... .90 .36 .09
☐ 182 Ed Bouchee .... .90 .36 .09
☐ 183 Don Zimmer .... .90 .36 .09
☐ 184 Ron Santo .... 1.50 .60 .15

185 Andre Rodgers	.90	.36	.09
186 Richie Ashburn	2.00	.80	.20
187 George Altman	1.50	.60	.15
188 Ernie Banks	6.50	2.60	.65
189 Sam Taylor	2.50	1.00	.25
190 Don Elston	.90	.36	.09
191 Jerry Kindall	.90	.36	.09
192 Pancho Herrera	.90	.36	.09
193 Tony Taylor	.90	.36	.09
194 Ruben Amaro	.90	.36	.09
195 Don Demeter	.90	.36	.09
196 Bobby Gene Smith	.90	.36	.09
197 Clay Dalrymple	.90	.36	.09
198 Robin Roberts	4.00	1.60	.40
199 Art Mahaffey	.90	.36	.09
200 John Buzhardt	.90	.36	.09

1963 Post Cereal

No. 134
Bob Purkey
CINCINNATI REDS — PITCHER
MAJOR LEAGUE PITCHING RECORD

The cards in this 200-card set measure 2 1/2" by 3 1/2". The players are grouped by team with American Leaguers comprising 1-100 and National Leaguers 101-200. The ordering of teams is as follows: Minnesota (1-11), New York Yankees, Los Angeles Angels (24-34), Chicago White Sox (35-45), Detroit (46- 56), Baltimore (57-66), Cleveland (67-76), Boston (77-84), Kansas City (85-92), Washington (93-100), San Francisco (101-112), Los Angeles Dodgers (113-124), Cincinnati (125-136), Pittsburgh (137- 147), Milwaukee (148-157), St. Louis (158-168), Chicago Cubs (169-176), Philadelphia (177-184), Houston (185-192), and New York Mets (193-200). In contrast to the 1962 issue, the 1963 Post baseball card series is very difficult to complete. There are many card scarcities reflected in the price list below. Cards of the Post set are easily confused with those of the 1963 Jello set, which are 1/4" narrower (a difference which is often eliminated by bad cutting). The catalog designation is F278- 38.

	NRMT	VG-E	GOOD
COMPLETE SET (200)	2700.00	1200.00	350.00
COMMON PLAYER (1-200)	1.50	.60	.15
1 Vic Power	2.00	.80	.20
2 Bernie Allen	1.50	.60	.15
3 Zoilo Versalles	2.50	1.00	.25
4 Rich Rollins	1.50	.60	.15
5 Harmon Killebrew	11.00	4.50	1.10
6 Lenny Green	30.00	12.00	3.00
7 Bob Allison	1.50	.60	.15
8 Earl Battey	2.50	1.00	.25
9 Camilo Pascual	1.50	.60	.15
10 Jim Kaat	2.50	1.00	.25
11 Jack Kralick	1.50	.60	.15
12 Bill Skowron	2.00	.80	.20
13 Bobby Richardson	2.50	1.00	.25
14 Cletis Boyer	2.00	.80	.20
15 Mickey Mantle	250.00	100.00	25.00
16 Roger Maris	125.00	50.00	12.50
17 Yogi Berra	11.00	4.50	1.10
18 Elston Howard	2.50	1.00	.25
19 Whitey Ford	7.00	2.80	.70
20 Ralph Terry	2.00	.80	.20
21 John Blanchard	1.50	.60	.15
22 Bill Stafford	1.50	.60	.15
23 Tom Tresh	2.00	.80	.20
24 Steve Bilko	2.50	1.00	.25
25 Bill Moran	1.50	.60	.15
26A Joe Koppe BA: .277	2.00	.80	.20
26B Joe Koppe BA: .227	8.00	3.25	.80
27 Felix Torres	1.50	.60	.15
28A Leon Wagner BA: .278	2.00	.80	.20
28B Leon Wagner BA: .272	8.00	3.25	.80
29 Albie Pearson	1.50	.60	.15
30 Lee Thomas (photo actually George Thomas)	60.00	24.00	6.00
31 Bob Rodgers	1.50	.60	.15
32 Dean Chance	1.50	.60	.15
33 Ken McBride	1.50	.60	.15
34 George Thomas (photo actually Lee Thomas)	1.50	.60	.15
35 Joe Cunningham	1.50	.60	.15
36 Nelson Fox	2.50	1.00	.25
37 Luis Aparicio	3.50	1.40	.35
38 Al Smith	25.00	10.00	2.50
39 Floyd Robinson	70.00	28.00	7.00
40 Jim Landis	1.50	.60	.15
41 Charlie Maxwell	1.50	.60	.15
42 Sherman Lollar	1.50	.60	.15
43 Early Wynn	4.00	1.60	.40
44 Juan Pizarro	1.50	.60	.15
45 Ray Herbert	1.50	.60	.15
46 Norm Cash	2.00	.80	.20
47 Steve Boros	1.50	.60	.15
48 Dick McAuliffe	16.00	6.50	1.60
49 Bill Bruton	2.50	1.00	.25
50 Rocky Colavito	2.50	1.00	.25
51 Al Kaline	10.00	4.00	1.00
52 Dick Brown	1.50	.60	.15
53 Jim Bunning	100.00	40.00	10.00
54 Hank Aguirre	1.50	.60	.15
55 Frank Lary	1.50	.60	.15
56 Don Mossi	1.50	.60	.15
57 Jim Gentile	1.50	.60	.15
58 Jackie Brandt	1.50	.60	.15
59 Brooks Robinson	9.00	3.75	.90
60 Ron Hansen	2.50	1.00	.25
61 Jerry Adair	125.00	50.00	12.50
62 John (Boog) Powell	2.50	1.00	.25
63 Russ Snyder	1.50	.60	.15
64 Steve Barber	1.50	.60	.15
65 Milt Pappas	1.50	.60	.15
66 Robin Roberts	4.00	1.60	.40
67 Tito Francona	1.50	.60	.15
68 Jerry Kindall	1.50	.60	.15
69 Woody Held	1.50	.60	.15
70 Bubba Phillips	10.00	4.00	1.00
71 Chuck Essegian	1.50	.60	.15
72 Willie Kirkland	1.50	.60	.15
73 Al Luplow	1.50	.60	.15
74 Ty Cline	1.50	.60	.15
75 Dick Donovan	1.50	.60	.15
76 John Romano	1.50	.60	.15
77 Pete Runnels	1.50	.60	.15
78 Ed Bressoud	1.50	.60	.15
79 Frank Malzone	1.50	.60	.15
80 Carl Yastrzemski	250.00	100.00	25.00
81 Gary Geiger	1.50	.60	.15
82 Lou Clinton	1.50	.60	.15
83 Earl Wilson	1.50	.60	.15
84 Bill Monbouquette	1.50	.60	.15
85 Norm Siebern	1.50	.60	.15
86 Jerry Lumpe	70.00	28.00	7.00
87 Manny Jimenez	70.00	28.00	7.00
88 Gino Cimoli	1.50	.60	.15
89 Ed Charles	1.50	.60	.15
90 Ed Rakow	1.50	.60	.15
91 Bob Del Greco	1.50	.60	.15
92 Haywood Sullivan	1.50	.60	.15
93 Chuck Hinton	1.50	.60	.15
94 Ken Retzer	1.50	.60	.15
95 Harry Bright	1.50	.60	.15
96 Bob Johnson	1.50	.60	.15
97 Dave Stenhouse	10.00	4.00	1.00
98 Chuck Cottier	16.00	6.50	1.60
99 Tom Cheney	1.50	.60	.15
100 Claude Osteen	10.00	4.00	1.00
101 Orlando Cepeda	2.50	1.00	.25
102 Charley Hiller	1.50	.60	.15
103 Jose Pagan	1.50	.60	.15
104 Jim Davenport	1.50	.60	.15
105 Harvey Kuenn	2.50	1.00	.25
106 Willie Mays	25.00	10.00	2.50

□ 107 Felipe Alou	1.50	.60	.15
□ 108 Tom Haller	70.00	28.00	7.00
□ 109 Juan Marichal	4.00	1.60	.40
□ 110 Jack Sanford	1.50	.60	.15
□ 111 Bill O'Dell	1.50	.60	.15
□ 112 Willie McCovey	4.50	1.80	.45
□ 113 Lee Walls	1.50	.60	.15
□ 114 Jim Gilliam	2.00	.80	.20
□ 115 Maury Wills	2.50	1.00	.25
□ 116 Ron Fairly	1.50	.60	.15
□ 117 Tommy Davis	2.00	.80	.20
□ 118 Duke Snider	6.00	2.40	.60
□ 119 Willie Davis	125.00	50.00	12.50
□ 120 John Roseboro	1.50	.60	.15
□ 121 Sandy Koufax	16.00	6.50	1.60
□ 122 Stan Williams	1.50	.60	.15
□ 123 Don Drysdale	4.50	1.80	.45
□ 124 Daryl Spencer	2.00	.80	.20
□ 125 Gordy Coleman	1.50	.60	.15
□ 126 Don Blasingame	1.50	.60	.15
□ 127 Leo Cardenas	1.50	.60	.15
□ 128 Eddie Kasko	125.00	50.00	12.50
□ 129 Jerry Lynch	10.00	4.00	1.00
□ 130 Vada Pinson	2.00	.80	.20
□ 131A Frank Robinson (no stripes)	8.00	3.25	.80
□ 131B Frank Robinson (stripes on hat)	12.00	5.00	1.20
□ 132 John Edwards	1.50	.60	.15
□ 133 Joey Jay	1.50	.60	.15
□ 134 Bob Purkey	1.50	.60	.15
□ 135 Marty Keough	15.00	6.00	1.50
□ 136 Jim O'Toole	1.50	.60	.15
□ 137 Dick Stuart	1.50	.60	.15
□ 138 Bill Mazeroski	2.00	.80	.20
□ 139 Dick Groat	2.00	.80	.20
□ 140 Don Hoak	21.00	8.50	2.10
□ 141 Bob Skinner	10.00	4.00	1.00
□ 142 Bill Virdon	2.00	.80	.20
□ 143 Roberto Clemente	16.00	6.50	1.60
□ 144 Smoky Burgess	2.00	.80	.20
□ 145 Bob Friend	1.50	.60	.15
□ 146 Al McBean	1.50	.60	.15
□ 147 Elroy Face	2.00	.80	.20
□ 148 Joe Adcock	2.00	.80	.20
□ 149 Frank Bolling	1.50	.60	.15
□ 150 Roy McMillan	1.50	.60	.15
□ 151 Eddie Mathews	8.00	3.25	.80
□ 152 Hank Aaron	75.00	30.00	7.50
□ 153 Del Crandall	25.00	10.00	2.50
□ 154A Bob Shaw COR	2.00	.80	.20
□ 154B Bob Shaw ERR (two "in 1959" in same sentence)	10.00	4.00	1.00
□ 155 Lew Burdette	2.00	.80	.20
□ 156 Joe Torre	2.00	.80	.20
□ 157 Tony Cloninger	1.50	.60	.15
□ 158 Bill White	2.00	.80	.20
□ 159 Julian Javier	1.50	.60	.15
□ 160 Ken Boyer	2.50	1.00	.25
□ 161 Julio Gotay	1.50	.60	.15
□ 162 Curt Flood	80.00	32.00	8.00
□ 163 Charlie James	2.50	1.00	.25
□ 164 Gene Oliver	1.50	.60	.15
□ 165 Ernie Broglio	1.50	.60	.15
□ 166 Bob Gibson	5.00	2.00	.50
□ 167A Lindy McDaniel (no asterisk)	5.00	2.00	.50
□ 167B Lindy McDaniel (asterisk traded line)	4.00	1.60	.40
□ 168 Ray Washburn	1.50	.60	.15
□ 169 Ernie Banks	6.00	2.40	.60
□ 170 Ron Santo	2.00	.80	.20
□ 171 George Altman	1.50	.60	.15
□ 172 Billy Williams	100.00	40.00	10.00
□ 173 Andre Rodgers	6.00	2.40	.60
□ 174 Ken Hubbs	16.00	6.50	1.60
□ 175 Don Landrum	1.50	.60	.15
□ 176 Dick Bertell	12.00	5.00	1.20
□ 177 Roy Sievers	1.50	.60	.15
□ 178 Tony Taylor	1.50	.60	.15
□ 179 John Callison	1.50	.60	.15
□ 180 Don Demeter	1.50	.60	.15
□ 181 Tony Gonzalez	8.00	3.25	.80
□ 182 Wes Covington	15.00	6.00	1.50
□ 183 Art Mahaffey	1.50	.60	.15
□ 184 Clay Dalrymple	1.50	.60	.15
□ 185 Al Spangler	2.50	1.00	.25
□ 186 Roman Mejias	1.50	.60	.15
□ 187 Bob Aspromonte	250.00	100.00	25.00
□ 188 Norm Larker	25.00	10.00	2.50
□ 189 Johnny Temple	1.50	.60	.15
□ 190 Carl Warwick	1.50	.60	.15
□ 191 Bob Lillis	1.50	.60	.15
□ 192 Dick Farrell	1.50	.60	.15
□ 193 Gil Hodges	4.50	1.80	.45
□ 194 Marv Throneberry	1.50	.60	.15
□ 195 Charlie Neal	6.00	2.40	.60
□ 196 Frank Thomas	125.00	50.00	12.50
□ 197 Richie Ashburn	16.00	6.50	1.60
□ 198 Felix Mantilla	1.50	.60	.15
□ 199 Rod Kanehl	12.00	5.00	1.20
□ 200 Roger Craig	2.00	.80	.20

1986 Quaker Granola

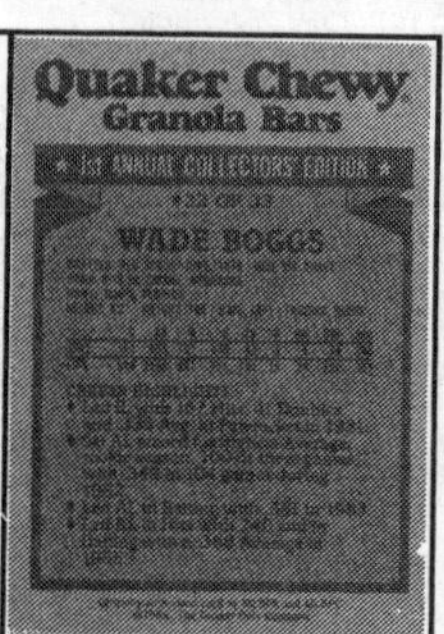

This set of 33 cards was available in packages of Quaker Oats Chewy Granola, three player cards plus a complete set offer card in each package. The set was also available through a mail-in offer where anyone sending in four UPC seals from Chewy Granola (before 12/31/86) would receive a complete set. The cards were produced by Topps for Quaker Oats and are 2 1/2" by 3 1/2". Card backs are printed in red and blue on gray card stock. The cards are numbered on the front and the back.

	MINT	EXC	G-VG
COMPLETE SET (33)	6.00	2.40	.60
COMMON PLAYER (1-33)	.10	.04	.01
□ 1 Willie McGee	.20	.08	.02
□ 2 Dwight Gooden	.50	.20	.05
□ 3 Vince Coleman	.30	.12	.03
□ 4 Gary Carter	.30	.12	.03
□ 5 Jack Clark	.20	.08	.02
□ 6 Steve Garvey	.30	.12	.03
□ 7 Tony Gwynn	.40	.16	.04
□ 8 Dale Murphy	.45	.18	.04
□ 9 Dave Parker	.15	.06	.01
□ 10 Tim Raines	.25	.10	.02
□ 11 Pete Rose	.60	.24	.06
□ 12 Nolan Ryan	.40	.16	.04
□ 13 Ryne Sandberg	.25	.10	.02
□ 14 Mike Schmidt	.45	.18	.04
□ 15 Ozzie Smith	.25	.10	.02
□ 16 Darryl Strawberry	.50	.20	.05
□ 17 Fernando Valenzuela	.25	.10	.02
□ 18 Don Mattingly	1.00	.40	.10
□ 19 Bret Saberhagen	.25	.10	.02
□ 20 Ozzie Guillen	.10	.04	.01
□ 21 Bert Blyleven	.10	.04	.01
□ 22 Wade Boggs	.75	.30	.07
□ 23 George Brett	.45	.18	.04
□ 24 Darrell Evans	.10	.04	.01
□ 25 Rickey Henderson	.50	.20	.05
□ 26 Reggie Jackson	.50	.20	.05
□ 27 Eddie Murray	.35	.14	.03
□ 28 Phil Niekro	.20	.08	.02
□ 29 Dan Quisenberry	.15	.06	.01
□ 30 Jim Rice	.25	.10	.02
□ 31 Cal Ripken	.30	.12	.03
□ 32 Tom Seaver	.30	.12	.03
□ 33 Dave Winfield	.30	.12	.03
□ 34 Offer Card for the complete set (unnumbered)	.03	.01	.00

SURVEY CONTRIBUTORS: Prices typically increase over time, let us know of price changes you observe.

1984 Ralston Purina

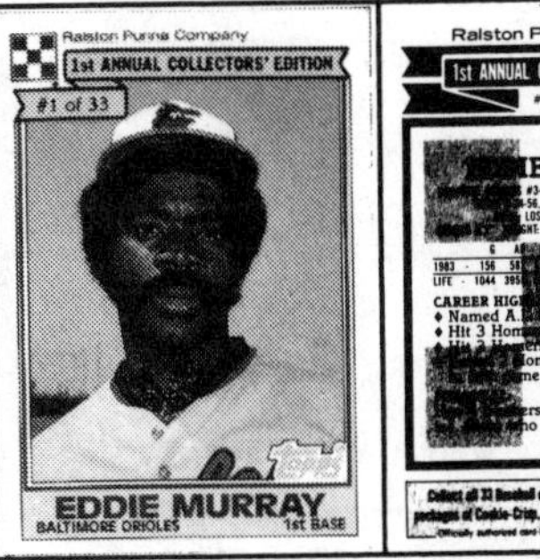
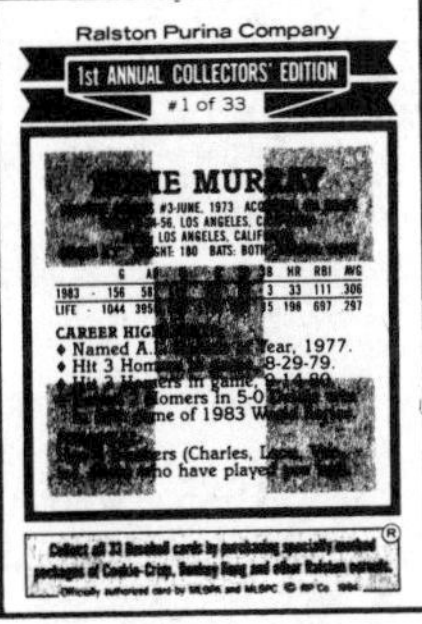

The cards in this 33-card set measure 2 1/2" by 3 1/2". In 1984 the Ralston Purina Company issued what it has entitled "The First Annual Collectors Edition of Baseball Cards." The cards feature portrait photos of the players rather than batting action shots. The Topps logo appears along with the Ralston logo on the front of the card. The backs are completely different from the Topps cards of this year; in fact, they contain neither a Topps logo nor a Topps copyright. Large quantities of these cards were obtained by card dealers for direct distribution into the organized hobby, hence the relatively low price of the set.

	MINT	EXC	G-VG
COMPLETE SET (33)	3.50	1.40	.35
COMMON PLAYER (1-33)	.05	.02	.00
☐ 1 Eddie Murray	.25	.10	.02
☐ 2 Ozzie Smith	.15	.06	.01
☐ 3 Ted Simmons	.05	.02	.00
☐ 4 Pete Rose	.50	.20	.05
☐ 5 Greg Luzinski	.05	.02	.00
☐ 6 Andre Dawson	.20	.08	.02
☐ 7 Dave Winfield	.20	.08	.02
☐ 8 Tom Seaver	.25	.10	.02
☐ 9 Jim Rice	.15	.06	.01
☐ 10 Fernando Valenzuela	.15	.06	.01
☐ 11 Wade Boggs	.50	.20	.05
☐ 12 Dale Murphy	.40	.16	.04
☐ 13 George Brett	.35	.14	.03
☐ 14 Nolan Ryan	.30	.12	.03
☐ 15 Rickey Henderson	.35	.14	.03
☐ 16 Steve Carlton	.20	.08	.02
☐ 17 Rod Carew	.25	.10	.02
☐ 18 Steve Garvey	.25	.10	.02
☐ 19 Reggie Jackson	.35	.14	.03
☐ 20 Dave Concepcion	.05	.02	.00
☐ 21 Robin Yount	.20	.08	.02
☐ 22 Mike Schmidt	.40	.16	.04
☐ 23 Jim Palmer	.20	.08	.02
☐ 24 Bruce Sutter	.10	.04	.01
☐ 25 Dan Quisenberry	.10	.04	.01
☐ 26 Bill Madlock	.05	.02	.00
☐ 27 Cecil Cooper	.05	.02	.00
☐ 28 Gary Carter	.25	.10	.02
☐ 29 Fred Lynn	.10	.04	.01
☐ 30 Pedro Guerrero	.15	.06	.01
☐ 31 Ron Guidry	.10	.04	.01
☐ 32 Keith Hernandez	.20	.08	.02
☐ 33 Carlton Fisk	.10	.04	.01

1987 Ralston Purina

The Ralston Purina Company issued a set of 15 cards picturing players without their respective team logos. The cards were distributed as inserts inside packages of certain flavors of Ralston Purina's breakfast cereals. The cards measure approximately 2 1/2" by 3 3/8" and are in full-color on the front.

The cards are numbered on the back in the lower right hand corner; the player's uniform number is prominently displayed on the front.

	MINT	EXC	G-VG
COMPLETE SET (15)	9.00	3.75	.90
COMMON PLAYER (1-15)	.35	.14	.03
☐ 1 Nolan Ryan	.75	.30	.07
☐ 2 Steve Garvey	.50	.20	.05
☐ 3 Wade Boggs	1.25	.50	.12
☐ 4 Dave Winfield	.50	.20	.05
☐ 5 Don Mattingly	2.00	.80	.20
☐ 6 Don Sutton	.35	.14	.03
☐ 7 Dave Parker	.35	.14	.03
☐ 8 Eddie Murray	.50	.20	.05
☐ 9 Gary Carter	.50	.20	.05
☐ 10 Roger Clemens	1.00	.40	.10
☐ 11 Fernando Valenzuela	.50	.20	.05
☐ 12 Cal Ripken	.50	.20	.05
☐ 13 Ozzie Smith	.50	.20	.05
☐ 14 Mike Schmidt	.65	.26	.06
☐ 15 Ryne Sandberg	.50	.20	.05

1983 Rangers Affiliated Food

The cards in this 28-card set measure 2 3/8" by 3 1/2". The Affiliated Food Stores chain of Arlington, Texas, produced this set of Texas Rangers late during the 1983 baseball season. Complete sets were given to children 13 and under at the September 3, 1983, Rangers game. The cards are numbered by uniform number and feature the player's name, card number, and the words "1983 Rangers" on the bottom front. The backs contain biographical data, career totals, a small black and white insert picture of the player, and the Affiliated Food Stores' logo. The coaches card is unnumbered.

	MINT	EXC	G-VG
COMPLETE SET (28)	5.50	2.20	.55
COMMON PLAYER	.15	.06	.01
☐ 1 Bill Stein	.15	.06	.01
☐ 2 Mike Richardt	.15	.06	.01

□ 3 Wayne Tolleson	.15	.06	.01
□ 5 Billy Sample	.15	.06	.01
□ 6 Bobby Jones	.15	.06	.01
□ 7 Bucky Dent	.35	.14	.03
□ 8 Bobby Johnson	.15	.06	.01
□ 9 Pete O'Brien	.75	.30	.07
□ 10 Jim Sundberg	.25	.10	.02
□ 11 Doug Rader MG	.25	.10	.02
□ 12 Dave Hostetler	.15	.06	.01
□ 14 Larry Biittner	.15	.06	.01
□ 15 Larry Parrish	.25	.10	.02
□ 17 Mickey Rivers	.25	.10	.02
□ 21 Odell Jones	.15	.06	.01
□ 24 Dave Schmidt	.25	.10	.02
□ 25 Buddy Bell	.50	.20	.05
□ 26 George Wright	.15	.06	.01
□ 28 Frank Tanana	.25	.10	.02
□ 29 John Butcher	.15	.06	.01
□ 32 John Matlack	.25	.10	.02
□ 40 Rick Honeycutt	.15	.06	.01
□ 41 Dave Tobik	.15	.06	.01
□ 44 Danny Darwin	.15	.06	.01
□ 46 Jim Anderson	.15	.06	.01
□ 48 Mike Smithson	.15	.06	.01
□ 49 Charlie Hough	.35	.14	.03
□ xx Rangers Coaches: (unnumbered) Wayne Terwilliger 42, Merv Rettenmund 22, Dick Such 52, Glenn Ezell 18, Rich Donnelly 37	.15	.06	.01

1984 Rangers Jarvis Press

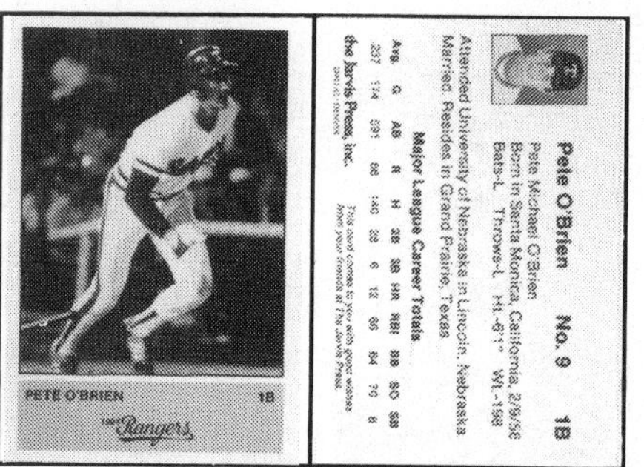

The cards in this 30-card set measure 2 1/2" by 3 1/2". The Jarvis Press of Dallas issued this full-color regional set of Texas Rangers. Cards are numbered on the front by the players uniform number. The cards were issued on an uncut sheet. Twenty-seven player cards, a manager card, a trainer card (unnumbered) and a coaches card (unnumbered) comprise this set. The backs are black and white and contain biographical information, statistics, and an additional photo of the player.

	MINT	EXC	G-VG
COMPLETE SET (30)	5.50	2.20	.55
COMMON PLAYER	.15	.06	.01
□ 1 Bill Stein	.15	.06	.01
□ 2 Alan Bannister	.15	.06	.01
□ 3 Wayne Tolleson	.15	.06	.01
□ 5 Billy Sample	.15	.06	.01
□ 6 Bobby Jones	.15	.06	.01
□ 7 Ned Yost	.15	.06	.01
□ 9 Pete O'Brien	.60	.24	.06
□ 11 Doug Rader MG	.25	.10	.02
□ 13 Tommy Dunbar	.15	.06	.01
□ 14 Jim Anderson	.15	.06	.01
□ 15 Larry Parrish	.25	.10	.02
□ 16 Mike Mason	.15	.06	.01
□ 17 Mickey Rivers	.25	.10	.02
□ 19 Curtis Wilkerson	.15	.06	.01
□ 20 Jeff Kunkel	.25	.10	.02
□ 21 Odell Jones	.15	.06	.01
□ 24 Dave Schmidt	.25	.10	.02
□ 25 Buddy Bell	.60	.24	.06
□ 26 George Wright	.15	.06	.01
□ 28 Frank Tanana	.25	.10	.02
□ 30 Marv Foley	.15	.06	.01
□ 31 Dave Stewart	.35	.14	.03
□ 32 Gary Ward	.15	.06	.01
□ 36 Dickie Noles	.15	.06	.01
□ 43 Donnie Scott	.15	.06	.01
□ 44 Danny Darwin	.15	.06	.01
□ 49 Charlie Hough	.35	.14	.03
□ 53 Joey McLaughlin	.15	.06	.01
□ xx Bill Ziegler (Trainer) (unnumbered)	.15	.06	.01
□ xx Rangers Coaches: (unnumbered) Merv Rettenmund 22, Rich Donnelly 37, Glenn Ezell 18, Dick Such 52, Wayne Terwilliger 42	.15	.06	.01

1985 Rangers Performance

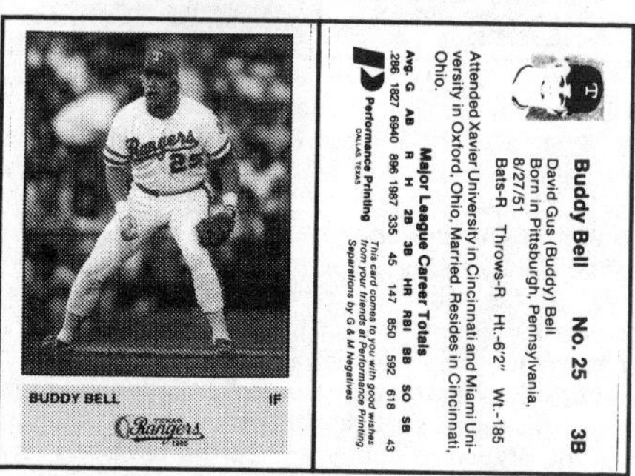

The cards in this 28-card set measure 2 3/8" by 3 1/2". Performance Printing sponsored this full-color regional set of Texas Rangers. Cards are numbered on the back by the players uniform number. The cards were also issued on an uncut sheet. Twenty-five player cards, a manager card, a trainer card (unnumbered) and a coaches card (unnumbered) comprise this set. The backs are black and white and contain biographical information, statistics, and an additional photo of the player.

	MINT	EXC	G-VG
COMPLETE SET (28)	5.50	2.20	.55
COMMON PLAYER	.15	.06	.01
□ 0 Oddibe McDowell	.60	.24	.06
□ 1 Bill Stein	.15	.06	.01
□ 2 Bobby Valentine MG	.35	.14	.03
□ 3 Wayne Tolleson	.15	.06	.01
□ 4 Don Slaught	.15	.06	.01
□ 5 Alan Bannister	.15	.06	.01
□ 6 Bobby Jones	.15	.06	.01
□ 7 Glenn Brummer	.15	.06	.01
□ 8 Luis Pujols	.15	.06	.01
□ 9 Pete O'Brien	.60	.24	.06
□ 11 Toby Harrah	.25	.10	.02
□ 13 Tommy Dunbar	.15	.06	.01
□ 15 Larry Parrish	.25	.10	.02
□ 16 Mike Mason	.15	.06	.01
□ 19 Curtis Wilkerson	.15	.06	.01
□ 24 Dave Schmidt	.25	.10	.02
□ 25 Buddy Bell	.50	.20	.05
□ 27 Greg Harris	.15	.06	.01
□ 30 Dave Rozema	.15	.06	.01
□ 32 Gary Ward	.15	.06	.01
□ 36 Dickie Noles	.15	.06	.01
□ 41 Chris Welsh	.15	.06	.01
□ 44 Cliff Johnson	.15	.06	.01
□ 46 Burt Hooton	.15	.06	.01
□ 48 Dave Stewart	.35	.14	.03
□ 49 Charlie Hough	.35	.14	.03
□ xx Trainers: Bill Ziegler, Danny Wheat (unnumbered)	.15	.06	.01
□ xx Rangers Coaches: (unnumbered) Art Howe 10, Rich Donnelly 37, Glenn Ezell 18, Tom House 35, Wayne Terwilliger 42	.15	.06	.01

1986 Rangers Performance

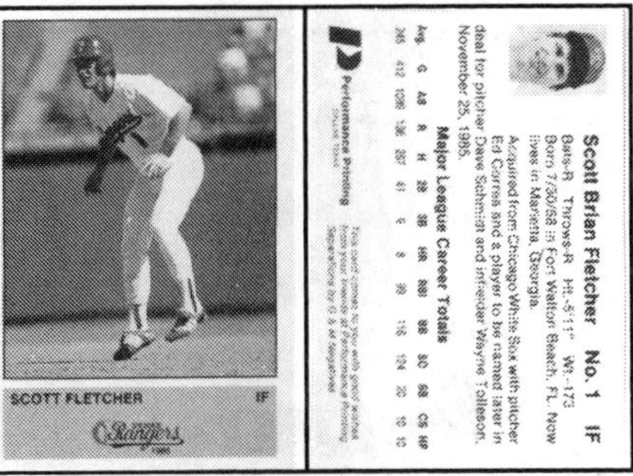

Performance Printing of Dallas produced a 28-card set of Texas Rangers which were given out at the stadium on August 23rd. Cards measure 2 3/8" by 3 1/2" and are in full color. The cards are unnumbered except for uniform number which is given on the card back. Card backs feature black printing on white card stock with a small picture of the player's head in the upper left corner. The set seems to be more desirable than the previous Ranger sets due to the Rangers' 1986 success which was directly related to their outstanding rookie crop.

	MINT	EXC	G-VG
COMPLETE SET (28)	7.50	3.00	.75
COMMON PLAYER	.10	.04	.01
□ 0 Oddibe McDowell	.40	.16	.04
□ 1 Scott Fletcher	.30	.12	.03
□ 2 Bobby Valentine MG	.25	.10	.02
□ 3 Ruben Sierra	1.25	.50	.12
□ 4 Don Slaught	.15	.06	.01
□ 9 Pete O'Brien	.50	.20	.05
□ 11 Toby Harrah	.20	.08	.02
□ 12 Geno Petralli	.10	.04	.01
□ 15 Larry Parrish	.20	.08	.02
□ 16 Mike Mason	.10	.04	.01
□ 17 Darrell Porter	.10	.04	.01
□ 18 Edwin Correa	.35	.14	.03
□ 19 Curtis Wilkerson	.10	.04	.01
□ 22 Steve Buechele	.20	.08	.02
□ 23 Jose Guzman	.35	.14	.03
□ 24 Ricky Wright	.10	.04	.01
□ 27 Greg Harris	.10	.04	.01
□ 28 Mitch Williams	.30	.12	.03
□ 29 Pete Incaviglia	1.00	.40	.10
□ 32 Gary Ward	.10	.04	.01
□ 34 Dale Mohorcic	.25	.10	.02
□ 40 Jeff Russell	.20	.08	.02
□ 44 Tom Paciorek	.10	.04	.01
□ 46 Mike Loynd	.20	.08	.02
□ 48 Bobby Witt	.60	.24	.06
□ 49 Charlie Hough	.30	.12	.03
□ xx Coaching Staff: (unnumbered) Art Howe 10, Joe Ferguson 13, Tim Foli 14, Tom Robson 31, Tom House 35	.10	.04	.01
□ xx Trainers: (unnumbered) Bill Zeigler, Danny Wheat	.10	.04	.01

1954 Red Heart

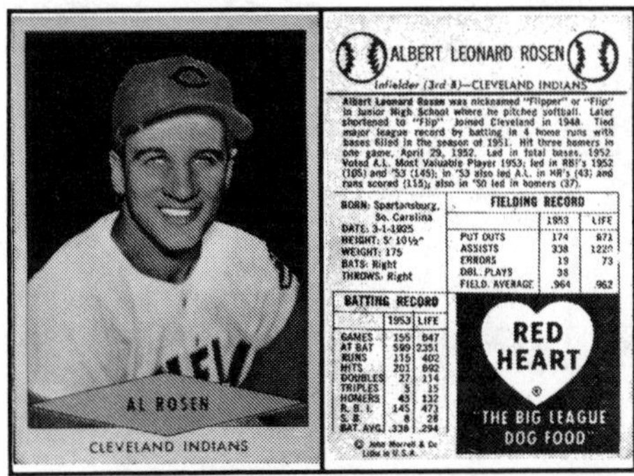

The cards in this 33-card set measure 2 5/8" by 3 3/4". The 1954 Red Heart baseball series was marketed by Red Heart dog food, which, incidentally, was a subsidiary of Morrell Meats. The set consists of three series of eleven unnumbered cards each of which could be ordered from the company via an offer (two can labels plus ten cents for each series) on the can label. Each series has a specific color background (red, green or blue) behind the color player photo. Cards with red backgrounds are considered scarcer and are marked with an asterisk in the checklist (which has been alphabetized and numbered for reference). The ACC designation is F156.

	NRMT	VG-E	GOOD
COMPLETE SET (33)	1400.00	600.00	175.00
COMMON PLAYER (1-33)	20.00	8.00	2.00
COMMON * (RED) PLAYER	30.00	12.00	3.00
□ 1 Richie Ashburn *	40.00	16.00	4.00
□ 2 Frank Baumholtz *	30.00	12.00	3.00
□ 3 Gus Bell	20.00	8.00	2.00
□ 4 Billy Cox	20.00	8.00	2.00
□ 5 Alvin Dark	25.00	10.00	2.50
□ 6 Carl Erskine *	35.00	14.00	3.50
□ 7 Ferris Fain	20.00	8.00	2.00
□ 8 Dee Fondy	20.00	8.00	2.00
□ 9 Nelson Fox	30.00	12.00	3.00
□ 10 Jim Gilliam	25.00	10.00	2.50
□ 11 Jim Hegan *	30.00	12.00	3.00
□ 12 George Kell	40.00	16.00	4.00
□ 13 Ralph Kiner *	50.00	20.00	5.00
□ 14 Ted Kluszewski *	40.00	16.00	4.00
□ 15 Harvey Kuenn	25.00	10.00	2.50
□ 16 Bob Lemon *	50.00	20.00	5.00
□ 17 Sherman Lollar	20.00	8.00	2.00
□ 18 Mickey Mantle	350.00	140.00	35.00
□ 19 Billy Martin	35.00	14.00	3.50
□ 20 Gil McDougald *	35.00	14.00	3.50
□ 21 Roy McMillan	20.00	8.00	2.00
□ 22 Minnie Minoso	25.00	10.00	2.50
□ 23 Stan Musial *	225.00	90.00	22.00
□ 24 Billy Pierce	25.00	10.00	2.50
□ 25 Al Rosen *	35.00	14.00	3.50
□ 26 Hank Sauer	20.00	8.00	2.00
□ 27 Red Schoendienst *	35.00	14.00	3.50
□ 28 Enos Slaughter	40.00	16.00	4.00
□ 29 Duke Snider	75.00	30.00	7.50
□ 30 Warren Spahn	40.00	16.00	4.00
□ 31 Sammy White	20.00	8.00	2.00
□ 32 Eddie Yost	20.00	8.00	2.00
□ 33 Gus Zernial	20.00	8.00	2.00

1952 Red Man

The cards in this 52-card set measure 3 1/2" by 4" (or 3 1/2" by 3 5/8" without the tab). This Red Man issue was the first nationally available tobacco issue

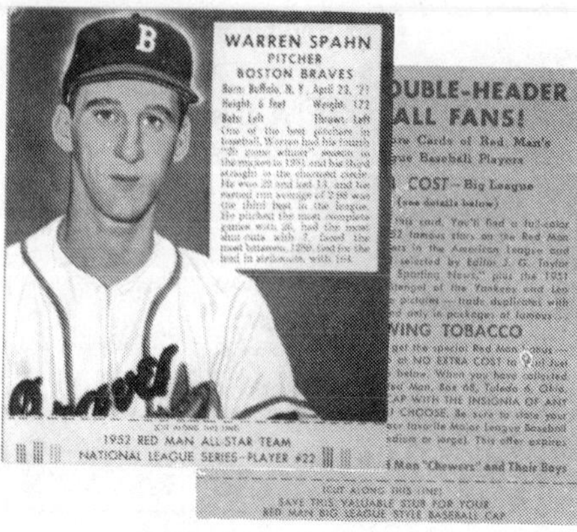

since the T cards of the teens early in this century. This 52 card set contains 26 top players from each league. Cards that have the tab (coupon) attached are generally worth triple the price of cards with the tab removed. Card numbers are located on the tabs. The prices listed below refer to cards without tabs.

	NRMT	VG-E	GOOD
COMPLETE SET (52)	450.00	180.00	45.00
COMMON PLAYER	4.00	1.60	.40
☐ AL1 Casey Stengel MG	15.00	6.00	1.50
☐ AL2 Roberto Avila	4.00	1.60	.40
☐ AL3 Yogi Berra	21.00	8.50	2.10
☐ AL4 Gil Coan	4.00	1.60	.40
☐ AL5 Dom DiMaggio	6.00	2.40	.60
☐ AL6 Larry Doby	5.00	2.00	.50
☐ AL7 Ferris Fain	4.00	1.60	.40
☐ AL8 Bob Feller	21.00	8.50	2.10
☐ AL9 Nelson Fox	7.50	3.00	.75
☐ AL10 Johnny Groth	4.00	1.60	.40
☐ AL11 Jim Hegan	4.00	1.60	.40
☐ AL12 Eddie Joost	4.00	1.60	.40
☐ AL13 George Kell	12.00	5.00	1.20
☐ AL14 Gil McDougald	6.00	2.40	.60
☐ AL15 Minnie Minoso	6.00	2.40	.60
☐ AL16 Billy Pierce	5.00	2.00	.50
☐ AL17 Bob Porterfield	4.00	1.60	.40
☐ AL18 Eddie Robinson	4.00	1.60	.40
☐ AL19 Saul Rogovin	4.00	1.60	.40
☐ AL20 Bobby Shantz	5.00	2.00	.50
☐ AL21 Vern Stephens	4.00	1.60	.40
☐ AL22 Vic Wertz	4.00	1.60	.40
☐ AL23 Ted Williams	60.00	24.00	6.00
☐ AL24 Early Wynn	12.00	5.00	1.20
☐ AL25 Eddie Yost	4.00	1.60	.40
☐ AL26 Gus Zernial	4.00	1.60	.40
☐ NL1 Leo Durocher MG	10.00	4.00	1.00
☐ NL2 Richie Ashburn	9.00	3.75	.90
☐ NL3 Ewell Blackwell	5.00	2.00	.50
☐ NL4 Cliff Chambers	4.00	1.60	.40
☐ NL5 Murray Dickson	4.00	1.60	.40
☐ NL6 Sid Gordon	4.00	1.60	.40
☐ NL7 Granny Hamner	4.00	1.60	.40
☐ NL8 Jim Hearn	4.00	1.60	.40
☐ NL9 Monte Irvin	11.00	4.50	1.10
☐ NL10 Larry Jansen	4.00	1.60	.40
☐ NL11 Willie Jones	4.00	1.60	.40
☐ NL12 Ralph Kiner	12.00	5.00	1.20
☐ NL13 Whitey Lockman	4.00	1.60	.40
☐ NL14 Sal Maglie	6.00	2.40	.60
☐ NL15 Willie Mays	45.00	18.00	4.50
☐ NL16 Stan Musial	40.00	16.00	4.00
☐ NL17 Pee Wee Reese	18.00	7.25	1.80
☐ NL18 Robin Roberts	12.00	5.00	1.20
☐ NL19 Al Schoendienst	6.00	2.40	.60
☐ NL20 Enos Slaughter	12.00	5.00	1.20
☐ NL21 Duke Snider	30.00	12.00	3.00
☐ NL22 Warren Spahn	12.00	5.00	1.20
☐ NL23 Ed Stanky	5.00	2.00	.50
☐ NL24 Bobby Thomson	6.00	2.40	.60
☐ NL25 Earl Torgeson	4.00	1.60	.40
☐ NL26 Wes Westrum	4.00	1.60	.40

1953 Red Man

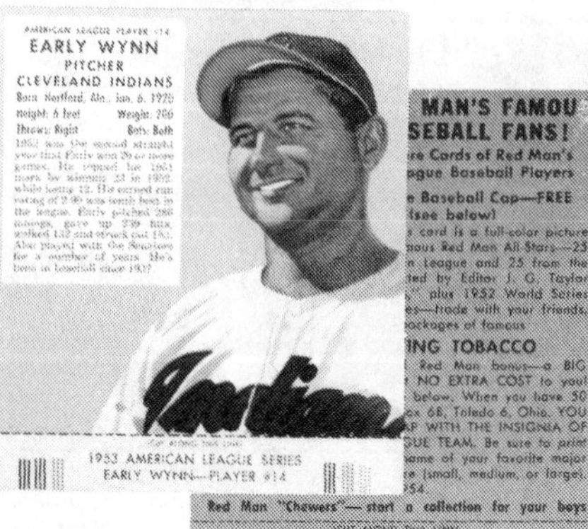

The cards in this 52-card set measure 3 1/2" by 4" (or 3 1/2" by 3 5/8" without the tab). The 1953 Red Man set contains 26 National League stars and 26 American League stars. Card numbers are located both on the write-up of the player and on the tab. Cards that have the tab (coupon) attached are generally worth triple the price of cards with the tab removed. The prices listed below refer to cards without tabs.

	NRMT	VG-E	GOOD
COMPLETE SET (52)	400.00	160.00	40.00
COMMON PLAYER	4.00	1.60	.40
☐ AL1 Casey Stengel MG	15.00	6.00	1.50
☐ AL2 Hank Bauer	6.00	2.40	.60
☐ AL3 Yogi Berra	21.00	8.50	2.10
☐ AL4 Walt Dropo	4.00	1.60	.40
☐ AL5 Nelson Fox	7.50	3.00	.75
☐ AL6 Jackie Jensen	6.00	2.40	.60
☐ AL7 Eddie Joost	4.00	1.60	.40
☐ AL8 George Kell	12.00	5.00	1.20
☐ AL9 Dale Mitchell	4.00	1.60	.40
☐ AL10 Phil Rizzuto	12.00	5.00	1.20
☐ AL11 Eddie Robinson	4.00	1.60	.40
☐ AL12 Gene Woodling	5.00	2.00	.50
☐ AL13 Gus Zernial	4.00	1.60	.40
☐ AL14 Early Wynn	12.00	5.00	1.20
☐ AL15 Joe Dobson	4.00	1.60	.40
☐ AL16 Billy Pierce	5.00	2.00	.50
☐ AL17 Bob Lemon	12.00	5.00	1.20
☐ AL18 Johnny Mize	12.00	5.00	1.20
☐ AL19 Bob Porterfield	4.00	1.60	.40
☐ AL20 Bobby Shantz	5.00	2.00	.50
☐ AL21 Mickey Vernon	5.00	2.00	.50
☐ AL22 Dom DiMaggio	6.00	2.40	.60
☐ AL23 Gil McDougald	6.00	2.40	.60
☐ AL24 Al Rosen	6.00	2.40	.60
☐ AL25 Mel Parnell	5.00	2.00	.50
☐ AL26 Bobby Avila	4.00	1.60	.40
☐ NL1 Charlie Dressen MG	5.00	2.00	.50
☐ NL2 Bobby Adams	4.00	1.60	.40
☐ NL3 Richie Ashburn	9.00	3.75	.90
☐ NL4 Joe Black	5.00	2.00	.50
☐ NL5 Roy Campanella	30.00	12.00	3.00
☐ NL6 Ted Kluszewski	6.00	2.40	.60
☐ NL7 Whitey Lockman	4.00	1.60	.40
☐ NL8 Sal Maglie	6.00	2.40	.60
☐ NL9 Andy Pafko	4.00	1.60	.40
☐ NL10 Pee Wee Reese	18.00	7.25	1.80
☐ NL11 Robin Roberts	12.00	5.00	1.20
☐ NL12 Al Schoendienst	6.00	2.40	.60
☐ NL13 Enos Slaughter	12.00	5.00	1.20
☐ NL14 Duke Snider	30.00	12.00	3.00
☐ NL15 Ralph Kiner	12.00	5.00	1.20
☐ NL16 Hank Sauer	4.00	1.60	.40
☐ NL17 Del Ennis	4.00	1.60	.40
☐ NL18 Granny Hamner	4.00	1.60	.40
☐ NL19 Warren Spahn	12.00	5.00	1.20
☐ NL20 Wes Westrum	4.00	1.60	.40
☐ NL21 Hoyt Wilhelm	12.00	5.00	1.20
☐ NL22 Murray Dickson	4.00	1.60	.40
☐ NL23 Warren Hacker	4.00	1.60	.40

☐ NL24 Gerry Staley	4.00	1.60	.40
☐ NL25 Bobby Thomson	6.00	2.40	.60
☐ NL26 Stan Musial	40.00	16.00	4.00

1954 Red Man

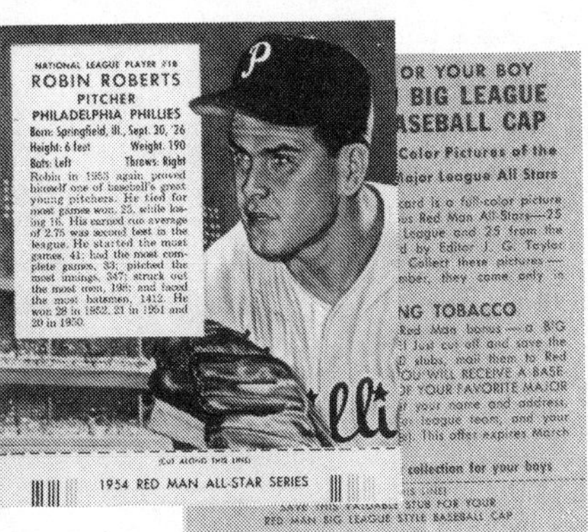

The cards in this 50-card set measure 3 1/2" by 4" (or 3 1/2" by 3 5/8" without the tab). The 1954 Red Man set witnessed a reduction to 25 players from each league. George Kell, Sam Mele, and Dave Philley are known to exist with two different teams. Card number 19 of the National League exists as Enos Slaughter and as Gus Bell. Card numbers are on the write-ups of the players. Cards that have the tab (coupon) attached are generally worth triple the price of cards with the tab removed. The prices listed below refer to cards without tabs. The complete set price below refers to all 54 cards including the four variations.

	NRMT	VG-E	GOOD
COMPLETE SET (54)	475.00	200.00	65.00
COMMON PLAYERS	4.00	1.60	.40
☐ AL1 Bobby Avila	4.00	1.60	.40
☐ AL2 Jim Busby	4.00	1.60	.40
☐ AL3 Nelson Fox	7.50	3.00	.75
☐ AL4A George Kell (Boston)	12.00	5.00	1.20
☐ AL4B George Kell (Chicago)	30.00	12.00	3.00
☐ AL5 Sherman Lollar	4.00	1.60	.40
☐ AL6A Sam Mele (Baltimore)	8.00	3.25	.80
☐ AL6B Sam Mele (Chicago)	20.00	8.00	2.00
☐ AL7 Minnie Minoso	6.00	2.40	.60
☐ AL8 Mel Parnell	5.00	2.00	.50
☐ AL9A Dave Philley (Cleveland)	8.00	3.25	.80
☐ AL9B Dave Philley (Philadelphia)	20.00	8.00	2.00
☐ AL10 Billy Pierce	5.00	2.00	.50
☐ AL11 Jim Piersall	6.00	2.40	.60
☐ AL12 Al Rosen	6.00	2.40	.60
☐ AL13 Mickey Vernon	5.00	2.00	.50
☐ AL14 Sammy White	4.00	1.60	.40
☐ AL15 Gene Woodling	5.00	2.00	.50
☐ AL16 Whitey Ford	16.00	6.50	1.60
☐ AL17 Phil Rizzuto	12.00	5.00	1.20
☐ AL18 Bob Porterfield	4.00	1.60	.40
☐ AL19 Chico Carrasquel	4.00	1.60	.40
☐ AL20 Yogi Berra	21.00	8.50	2.10
☐ AL21 Bob Lemon	12.00	5.00	1.20
☐ AL22 Ferris Fain	4.00	1.60	.40
☐ AL23 Hank Bauer	6.00	2.40	.60
☐ AL24 Jim Delsing	4.00	1.60	.40
☐ AL25 Gil McDougald	6.00	2.40	.60
☐ NL1 Richie Ashburn	9.00	3.75	.90
☐ NL2 Billy Cox	4.00	1.60	.40
☐ NL3 Del Crandall	4.00	1.60	.40
☐ NL4 Carl Erskine	5.00	2.00	.50
☐ NL5 Monte Irvin	11.00	4.50	1.10
☐ NL6 Ted Kluszewski	6.00	2.40	.60
☐ NL7 Don Mueller	4.00	1.60	.40
☐ NL8 Andy Pafko	4.00	1.60	.40
☐ NL9 Del Rice	4.00	1.60	.40
☐ NL10 Al Schoendienst	6.00	2.40	.60
☐ NL11 Warren Spahn	12.00	5.00	1.20
☐ NL12 Curt Simmons	5.00	2.00	.50
☐ NL13 Roy Campanella	30.00	12.00	3.00
☐ NL14 Jim Gilliam	6.00	2.40	.60
☐ NL15 Pee Wee Reese	18.00	7.25	1.80
☐ NL16 Duke Snider	30.00	12.00	3.00
☐ NL17 Rip Repulski	4.00	1.60	.40
☐ NL18 Robin Roberts	12.00	5.00	1.20
☐ NL19A Enos Slaughter	30.00	12.00	3.00
☐ NL19B Gus Bell	20.00	8.00	2.00
☐ NL20 Johnny Logan	4.00	1.60	.40
☐ NL21 John Antonelli	5.00	2.00	.50
☐ NL22 Gil Hodges	15.00	6.00	1.50
☐ NL23 Eddie Mathews	12.00	5.00	1.20
☐ NL24 Lew Burdette	5.00	2.00	.50
☐ NL25 Willie Mays	45.00	18.00	4.50

1955 Red Man

The cards in this 50-card set measure 3 1/2" by 4" (or 3 1/2" by 3 5/8" without the tab). The 1955 Red Man set contains 25 players from each league. Card numbers are on the write-ups of the players. Cards that have the tab (coupon) attached are generally worth triple the price of cards with the tab removed. The prices listed below refer to cards without tabs.

	NRMT	VG-E	GOOD
COMPLETE SET (50)	375.00	150.00	37.00
COMMON PLAYER	4.00	1.60	.40
☐ AL1 Ray Boone	4.00	1.60	.40
☐ AL2 Jim Busby	4.00	1.60	.40
☐ AL3 Whitey Ford	17.00	7.00	1.70
☐ AL4 Nelson Fox	7.50	3.00	.75
☐ AL5 Bob Grim	4.00	1.60	.40
☐ AL6 Jack Harshman	4.00	1.60	.40
☐ AL7 Jim Hegan	4.00	1.60	.40
☐ AL8 Bob Lemon	12.00	5.00	1.20
☐ AL9 Irv Noren	4.00	1.60	.40
☐ AL10 Bob Porterfield	4.00	1.60	.40
☐ AL11 Al Rosen	6.00	2.40	.60
☐ AL12 Mickey Vernon	5.00	2.00	.50
☐ AL13 Vic Wertz	4.00	1.60	.40
☐ AL14 Early Wynn	12.00	5.00	1.20
☐ AL15 Bobby Avila	4.00	1.60	.40
☐ AL16 Yogi Berra	21.00	8.50	2.10
☐ AL17 Joe Coleman	4.00	1.60	.40
☐ AL18 Larry Doby	5.00	2.00	.50
☐ AL19 Jackie Jensen	5.00	2.00	.50
☐ AL20 Pete Runnels	4.00	1.60	.40
☐ AL21 Jim Piersall	6.00	2.40	.60
☐ AL22 Hank Bauer	6.00	2.40	.60
☐ AL23 Chico Carrasquel	4.00	1.60	.40
☐ AL24 Minnie Minoso	6.00	2.40	.60
☐ AL25 Sandy Consuegra	4.00	1.60	.40
☐ NL1 Richie Ashburn	9.00	3.75	.90
☐ NL2 Del Crandall	4.00	1.60	.40

□NL3 Gil Hodges	15.00	6.00	1.50
□NL4 Brooks Lawrence	4.00	1.60	.40
□NL5 Johnny Logan	4.00	1.60	.40
□NL6 Sal Maglie	6.00	2.40	.60
□NL7 Willie Mays	45.00	18.00	4.50
□NL8 Don Mueller	4.00	1.60	.40
□NL9 Bill Sarni	4.00	1.60	.40
□NL10 Warren Spahn	12.00	5.00	1.20
□NL11 Hank Thompson	4.00	1.60	.40
□NL12 Hoyt Wilhelm	12.00	5.00	1.20
□NL13 John Antonelli	5.00	2.00	.50
□NL14 Carl Erskine	5.00	2.00	.50
□NL15 Granny Hamner	4.00	1.60	.40
□NL16 Ted Kluszewski	6.00	2.40	.60
□NL17 Pee Wee Reese	17.00	7.00	1.70
□NL18 Al Schoendienst	6.00	2.40	.60
□NL19 Duke Snider	30.00	12.00	3.00
□NL20 Frank Thomas	4.00	1.60	.40
□NL21 Ray Jablonski	4.00	1.60	.40
□NL22 Dusty Rhodes	4.00	1.60	.40
□NL23 Gus Bell	4.00	1.60	.40
□NL24 Curt Simmons	4.00	1.60	.40
□NL25 Marv Grissom	4.00	1.60	.40

1955 Rodeo Meats

The cards in this 47-card set measure 2 1/2" by 3 1/2". The 1955 Rodeo Meats set contains unnumbered, color cards of the first Kansas City A's team. There are many background color variations noted in the checklist, and the card reverses carry a scrapbook offer. The Grimes and Kryhoski cards listed in the scrapbook album were apparently never issued. The ACC catalog number is F152-1. The cards have been arranged in alphabetical order and assigned numbers for reference.

	NRMT	VG-E	GOOD
COMPLETE SET (47)	3500.00	1600.00	400.00
COMMON PLAYER (1-47)	60.00	24.00	6.00
□ 1 Joe Astroth	60.00	24.00	6.00
□ 2 Harold Bevan	90.00	36.00	9.00
□ 3 Charles Bishop	90.00	36.00	9.00
□ 4 Don Bollweg	90.00	36.00	9.00
□ 5 Lou Boudreau	175.00	70.00	18.00
□ 6 Cloyd Boyer (salmon)	60.00	24.00	6.00
□ 7 Cloyd Boyer (light blue)	90.00	36.00	9.00
□ 8 Ed Burtschy	125.00	50.00	12.50
□ 9 Art Ceccarelli	90.00	36.00	9.00
□10 Joe DeMaestri (yellow)	60.00	24.00	6.00
□11 Joe DeMaestri (green)	60.00	24.00	6.00
□12 Art Ditmar	60.00	24.00	6.00
□13 John Dixon	90.00	36.00	9.00
□14 Jim Finigan	60.00	24.00	6.00
□15 Marion Fricano	90.00	36.00	9.00
□16 Tom Gorman	60.00	24.00	6.00
□17 John Gray	90.00	36.00	9.00
□18 Ray Herbert	60.00	24.00	6.00
□19 Forest Jacobs	125.00	50.00	12.50
□20 Alex Kellner	60.00	24.00	6.00
□21 Harry Kraft	60.00	24.00	6.00
□22 Jack Littrell	60.00	24.00	6.00
□23 Hector Lopez	60.00	24.00	6.00
□24 Oscar Melillo	60.00	24.00	6.00
□25 Arnold Portocarrero (purple)	90.00	36.00	9.00
□26 Arnold Portocarrero (gray)	60.00	24.00	6.00
□27 Vic Power (yellow)	60.00	24.00	6.00
□28 Vic Power (pink)	90.00	36.00	9.00
□29 Vic Raschi	90.00	36.00	9.00
□30 Bill Renna (lavender)	60.00	24.00	6.00
□31 Bill Renna (dark pink)	90.00	36.00	9.00
□32 Al Robertson	90.00	36.00	9.00
□33 Johnny Sain	125.00	50.00	12.50
□35 Bobby Schantz ERR (misspelling)	150.00	60.00	15.00
□34 Bobby Shantz COR	125.00	50.00	12.50
□36 Wilmer Shantz (orange)	60.00	24.00	6.00
□37 Wilmer Shantz (lavender)	60.00	24.00	6.00
□38 Harry Simpson	60.00	24.00	6.00
□39 Enos Slaughter	200.00	80.00	20.00
□40 Lou Sleator	60.00	24.00	6.00
□41 George Susce	90.00	36.00	9.00
□42 Bob Trice	90.00	36.00	9.00
□43 Elmer Valo (yellow)	90.00	36.00	9.00
□44 Elmer Valo (green sky)	60.00	24.00	6.00
□45 Bill Wilson (yellow)	90.00	36.00	9.00
□46 Bill Wilson (lavender sky)	60.00	24.00	6.00
□47 Gus Zernial	60.00	24.00	6.00

1956 Rodeo Meats

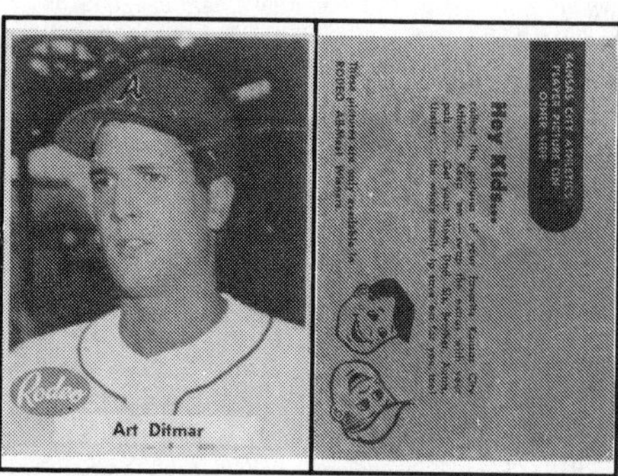

The cards in this 12-card set measure 2 1/2" by 3 1/2". The unnumbered, color cards of the 1956 Rodeo baseball series are easily distinguished from their 1955 counterparts by the absence of the scrapbook offer on the reverse. They were available only in packages of Rodeo All-Meat Wieners. The ACC designation is F152-2, and the cards have been assigned numbers in alphabetical order in the checklist below.

	NRMT	VG-E	GOOD
COMPLETE SET (12)	900.00	360.00	90.00
COMMON PLAYER (1-12)	60.00	24.00	6.00
□ 1 Joe Astroth	60.00	24.00	6.00
□ 2 Lou Boudreau	175.00	70.00	18.00
□ 3 Joe DeMaestri	60.00	24.00	6.00
□ 4 Art Ditmar	60.00	24.00	6.00
□ 5 Jim Finigan	60.00	24.00	6.00
□ 6 Hector Lopez	60.00	24.00	6.00
□ 7 Vic Power	60.00	24.00	6.00
□ 8 Bobby Shantz	100.00	40.00	10.00
□ 9 Harry Simpson	60.00	24.00	6.00
□10 Enos Slaughter	200.00	80.00	20.00
□11 Elmer Valo	60.00	24.00	6.00
□12 Gus Zernial	60.00	24.00	6.00

1958 S.F. Call-Bulletin

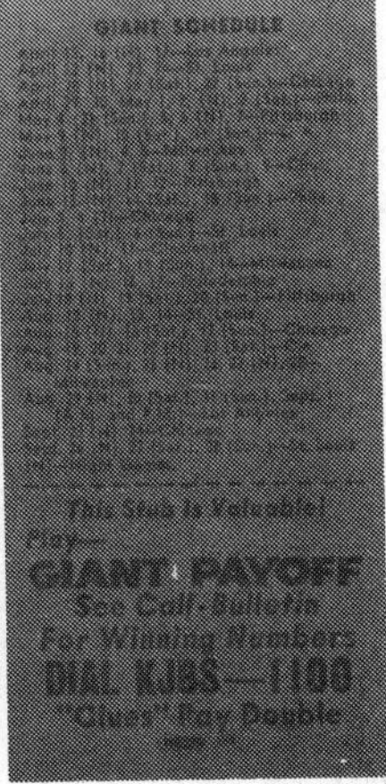

The cards in this 25-card set measure 2" by 4". The 1958 San Francisco Call-Bulletin set of unnumbered cards features black print on orange paper. These cards were given away as inserts in the San Francisco Call-Bulletin newspaper. The backs of the cards list the Giants home schedule and a radio station ad. The cards are entitled "Giant Payoff" and feature San Francisco Giant players only. The bottom part of the card (tab) could be detached as a ticket stub; hence, cards with the tab intact are worth approximately double the prices listed below. The ACC designation is M126. The Tom Bowers card was issued in very short supply; also Bressoud, Jablonski, and Kirkland are somewhat tougher to find than the others. All of these tougher cards are asterisked in the checklist below.

	NRMT	VG-E	GOOD
COMPLETE SET (25)	550.00	220.00	55.00
COMMON PLAYER (1-25)	6.00	2.40	.60
□ 1 John Antonelli	7.00	2.80	.70
□ 2 Curt Barclay	6.00	2.40	.60
□ 3 Tom Bowers *	200.00	80.00	20.00
□ 4 Ed Bressoud *	25.00	10.00	2.50
□ 5 Orlando Cepeda	35.00	14.00	3.50
□ 6 Ray Crone	6.00	2.40	.60
□ 7 Jim Davenport	7.00	2.80	.70
□ 8 Paul Giel	6.00	2.40	.60
□ 9 Ruben Gomez	6.00	2.40	.60
□ 10 Marv Grissom	6.00	2.40	.60
□ 11 Ray Jablonski *	12.00	5.00	1.20
□ 12 Willie Kirkland *	35.00	14.00	3.50
□ 13 Whitey Lockman	6.00	2.40	.60
□ 14 Willie Mays	150.00	60.00	15.00
□ 15 Mike McCormick	7.00	2.80	.70
□ 16 Stu Miller	7.00	2.80	.70
□ 17 Ray Monzant	6.00	2.40	.60
□ 18 Danny O'Connell	6.00	2.40	.60
□ 19 Bill Rigney	7.00	2.80	.70
□ 20 Hank Sauer	7.00	2.80	.70
□ 21 Bob Schmidt	6.00	2.40	.60
□ 22 Daryl Spencer	6.00	2.40	.60
□ 23 Valmy Thomas	6.00	2.40	.60
□ 24 Bobby Thomson	8.00	3.25	.80
□ 25 Al Worthington	6.00	2.40	.60

1988 Score

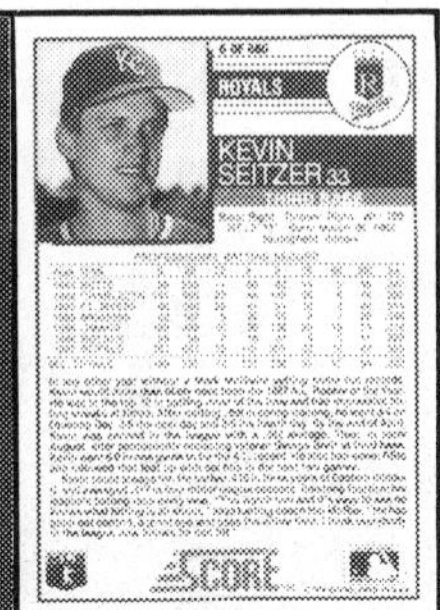

This 660-card set was distributed by Major League Marketing. Cards measure 2 1/2" by 3 1/2" and feature six distinctive border colors on the front. Highlights (652-660) and Rookie Prospects (623-647) are included in the set. Reggie Jackson's career is honored with a 5-card subset on cards 500- 504. The set is distinguished by the fact that each card back shows a full-color picture of the player.

	MINT	EXC	G-VG
COMPLETE SET (660)	24.00	10.00	2.40
COMMON PLAYER (1-660)	.03	.01	.00
□ 1 Don Mattingly	1.50	.35	.07
□ 2 Wade Boggs	.80	.32	.08
□ 3 Tim Raines	.20	.08	.02
□ 4 Andre Dawson	.20	.08	.02
□ 5 Mark McGwire	1.25	.50	.12
□ 6 Kevin Seitzer	1.00	.40	.10
□ 7 Wally Joyner	.40	.16	.04
□ 8 Jesse Barfield	.15	.06	.01
□ 9 Pedro Guerrero	.15	.06	.01
□ 10 Eric Davis	.65	.26	.06
□ 11 George Brett	.25	.10	.02
□ 12 Ozzie Smith	.12	.05	.01
□ 13 Rickey Henderson	.25	.10	.02
□ 14 Jim Rice	.15	.06	.01
□ 15 Matt Nokes	.45	.18	.04
□ 16 Mike Schmidt	.25	.10	.02
□ 17 Dave Parker	.10	.04	.01
□ 18 Eddie Murray	.20	.08	.02
□ 19 Andres Galarraga	.25	.10	.02
□ 20 Tony Fernandez	.10	.04	.01
□ 21 Kevin McReynolds	.15	.06	.01
□ 22 B.J. Surhoff	.10	.04	.01
□ 23 Pat Tabler	.06	.02	.00
□ 24 Kirby Puckett	.30	.12	.03
□ 25 Benny Santiago	.40	.16	.04
□ 26 Ryne Sandberg	.20	.08	.02
□ 27 Kelly Downs (Will Clark in background, out of focus)	.08	.03	.01
□ 28 Jose Cruz	.06	.02	.00
□ 29 Pete O'Brien	.08	.03	.01
□ 30 Mark Langston	.08	.03	.01
□ 31 Lee Smith	.06	.02	.00
□ 32 Juan Samuel	.10	.04	.01
□ 33 Kevin Bass	.06	.02	.00
□ 34 R.J. Reynolds	.03	.01	.00
□ 35 Steve Sax	.12	.05	.01
□ 36 John Kruk	.10	.04	.01
□ 37 Alan Trammell	.15	.06	.01
□ 38 Chris Bosio	.03	.01	.00
□ 39 Brook Jacoby	.08	.03	.01
□ 40 Willie McGee	.10	.04	.01
□ 41 Dave Magadan	.10	.04	.01
□ 42 Fred Lynn	.10	.04	.01
□ 43 Kent Hrbek	.12	.05	.01
□ 44 Brian Downing	.03	.01	.00
□ 45 Jose Canseco	1.50	.60	.15
□ 46 Jim Presley	.06	.02	.00
□ 47 Mike Stanley	.06	.02	.00
□ 48 Tony Pena	.06	.02	.00
□ 49 David Cone	.90	.36	.09
□ 50 Rick Sutcliffe	.08	.03	.01
□ 51 Doug Drabek	.03	.01	.00
□ 52 Bill Doran	.06	.02	.00
□ 53 Mike Scioscia	.03	.01	.00

☐ 54 Candy Maldonado .... .08 .03 .01
☐ 55 Dave Winfield .... .20 .08 .02
☐ 56 Lou Whitaker .... .10 .04 .01
☐ 57 Tom Henke .... .06 .02 .00
☐ 58 Ken Gerhart .... .06 .02 .00
☐ 59 Glenn Braggs .... .08 .03 .01
☐ 60 Julio Franco .... .08 .03 .01
☐ 61 Charlie Leibrandt .... .03 .01 .00
☐ 62 Gary Gaetti .... .12 .05 .01
☐ 63 Bob Boone .... .06 .02 .00
☐ 64 Luis Polonia .... .20 .08 .02
☐ 65 Dwight Evans .... .10 .04 .01
☐ 66 Phil Bradley .... .08 .03 .01
☐ 67 Mike Boddicker .... .06 .02 .00
☐ 68 Vince Coleman .... .20 .08 .02
☐ 69 Howard Johnson .... .08 .03 .01
☐ 70 Tim Wallach .... .08 .03 .01
☐ 71 Keith Moreland .... .03 .01 .00
☐ 72 Barry Larkin .... .12 .05 .01
☐ 73 Alan Ashby .... .03 .01 .00
☐ 74 Rick Rhoden .... .03 .01 .00
☐ 75 Darrell Evans .... .06 .02 .00
☐ 76 Dave Stieb .... .08 .03 .01
☐ 77 Dan Plesac .... .06 .02 .00
☐ 78 Will Clark .... .65 .26 .06
☐ 79 Frank White .... .06 .02 .00
☐ 80 Joe Carter .... .12 .05 .01
☐ 81 Mike Witt .... .08 .03 .01
☐ 82 Terry Steinbach .... .20 .08 .02
☐ 83 Alvin Davis .... .08 .03 .01
☐ 84 Tommy Herr .... .08 .03 .01
(Will Clark shown sliding into second)
☐ 85 Vance Law .... .03 .01 .00
☐ 86 Kal Daniels .... .20 .08 .02
☐ 87 Rick Honeycutt UER .... .03 .01 .00
(wrong years for stats on back)
☐ 88 Alfredo Griffin .... .06 .02 .00
☐ 89 Bret Saberhagen .... .12 .05 .01
☐ 90 Bert Blyleven .... .08 .03 .01
☐ 91 Jeff Reardon .... .06 .02 .00
☐ 92 Cory Snyder .... .20 .08 .02
☐ 93 Greg Walker .... .06 .02 .00
☐ 94 Joe Magrane .... .25 .10 .02
☐ 95 Rob Deer .... .08 .03 .01
☐ 96 Ray Knight .... .06 .02 .00
☐ 97 Casey Candaele .... .03 .01 .00
☐ 98 John Cerutti .... .03 .01 .00
☐ 99 Buddy Bell .... .08 .03 .01
☐ 100 Jack Clark .... .15 .06 .01
☐ 101 Eric Bell .... .03 .01 .00
☐ 102 Willie Wilson .... .08 .03 .01
☐ 103 Dave Schmidt .... .03 .01 .00
☐ 104 Dennis Eckersley .... .10 .04 .01
☐ 105 Don Sutton .... .12 .05 .01
☐ 106 Danny Tartabull .... .20 .08 .02
☐ 107 Fred McGriff .... .75 .30 .07
☐ 108 Les Straker .... .10 .04 .01
☐ 109 Lloyd Moseby .... .08 .03 .01
☐ 110 Roger Clemens .... .50 .20 .05
☐ 111 Glenn Hubbard .... .03 .01 .00
☐ 112 Ken Williams .... .20 .08 .02
☐ 113 Ruben Sierra .... .18 .08 .01
☐ 114 Stan Jefferson .... .18 .08 .01
☐ 115 Milt Thompson .... .03 .01 .00
☐ 116 Bobby Bonilla .... .18 .08 .01
☐ 117 Wayne Tolleson .... .03 .01 .00
☐ 118 Matt Williams .... .35 .14 .03
☐ 119 Chet Lemon .... .06 .02 .00
☐ 120 Dale Sveum .... .03 .01 .00
☐ 121 Dennis Boyd .... .06 .02 .00
☐ 122 Brett Butler .... .06 .02 .00
☐ 123 Terry Kennedy .... .03 .01 .00
☐ 124 Jack Howell .... .03 .01 .00
☐ 125 Curt Young .... .03 .01 .00
☐ 126A Dave Valle ERR .... .25 .10 .02
(misspelled Dale on card front)
☐ 126B Dave Valle COR .... .10 .04 .01
☐ 127 Curt Wilkerson .... .03 .01 .00
☐ 128 Tim Teufel .... .03 .01 .00
☐ 129 Ozzie Virgil .... .03 .01 .00
☐ 130 Brian Fisher .... .03 .01 .00
☐ 131 Lance Parrish .... .08 .03 .01
☐ 132 Tom Browning .... .08 .03 .01
☐ 133A Larry Andersen ERR .... .15 .06 .01
(misspelled Anderson on card front)
☐ 133B Larry Andersen COR .... .03 .01 .00
☐ 134A Bob Brenly ERR .... .15 .06 .01
(misspelled Brenley on card front)
☐ 134B Bob Brenly COR .... .08 .03 .01
☐ 135 Mike Marshall .... .08 .03 .01
☐ 136 Gerald Perry .... .08 .03 .01
☐ 137 Bobby Meacham .... .03 .01 .00
☐ 138 Larry Herndon .... .03 .01 .00
☐ 139 Fred Manrique .... .10 .04 .01
☐ 140 Charlie Hough .... .03 .01 .00
☐ 141 Ron Darling .... .10 .04 .01
☐ 142 Herm Winningham .... .03 .01 .00
☐ 143 Mike Diaz .... .03 .01 .00
☐ 144 Mike Jackson .... .12 .05 .01
☐ 145 Denny Walling .... .03 .01 .00
☐ 146 Rob Thompson .... .03 .01 .00
☐ 147 Franklin Stubbs .... .03 .01 .00
☐ 148 Albert Hall .... .03 .01 .00
☐ 149 Bobby Witt .... .06 .02 .00
☐ 150 Lance McCullers .... .06 .02 .00
☐ 151 Scott Bradley .... .03 .01 .00
☐ 152 Mark McLemore .... .03 .01 .00
☐ 153 Tim Laudner .... .03 .01 .00
☐ 154 Greg Swindell .... .10 .04 .01
☐ 155 Marty Barrett .... .06 .02 .00
☐ 156 Mike Heath .... .03 .01 .00
☐ 157 Gary Ward .... .03 .01 .00
☐ 158A Lee Mazzilli ERR .... .20 .08 .02
(misspelled Mazilli on card front)
☐ 158B Lee Mazzilli COR .... .08 .03 .01
☐ 159 Tom Foley .... .03 .01 .00
☐ 160 Robin Yount .... .20 .08 .02
☐ 161 Steve Bedrosian .... .08 .03 .01
☐ 162 Bob Walk .... .03 .01 .00
☐ 163 Nick Esasky .... .03 .01 .00
☐ 164 Ken Caminiti .... .20 .08 .02
☐ 165 Jose Uribe .... .03 .01 .00
☐ 166 Dave Anderson .... .03 .01 .00
☐ 167 Ed Whitson .... .03 .01 .00
☐ 168 Ernie Whitt .... .03 .01 .00
☐ 169 Cecil Cooper .... .08 .03 .01
☐ 170 Mike Pagliarulo .... .08 .03 .01
☐ 171 Pat Sheridan .... .03 .01 .00
☐ 172 Chris Bando .... .03 .01 .00
☐ 173 Lee Lacy .... .03 .01 .00
☐ 174 Steve Lombardozzi .... .03 .01 .00
☐ 175 Mike Greenwell .... 1.50 .60 .15
☐ 176 Greg Minton .... .03 .01 .00
☐ 177 Moose Haas .... .03 .01 .00
☐ 178 Mike Kingery .... .03 .01 .00
☐ 179 Greg Harris .... .03 .01 .00
☐ 180 Bo Jackson .... .35 .14 .03
☐ 181 Carmelo Martinez .... .03 .01 .00
☐ 182 Alex Trevino .... .03 .01 .00
☐ 183 Ron Oester .... .03 .01 .00
☐ 184 Danny Darwin .... .03 .01 .00
☐ 185 Mike Krukow .... .03 .01 .00
☐ 186 Rafael Palmeiro .... .50 .20 .05
☐ 187 Tim Burke .... .03 .01 .00
☐ 188 Roger McDowell .... .06 .02 .00
☐ 189 Garry Templeton .... .06 .02 .00
☐ 190 Terry Pendleton .... .03 .01 .00
☐ 191 Larry Parrish .... .03 .01 .00
☐ 192 Rey Quinones .... .03 .01 .00
☐ 193 Joaquin Andujar .... .06 .02 .00
☐ 194 Tom Brunansky .... .10 .04 .01
☐ 195 Donnie Moore .... .03 .01 .00
☐ 196 Dan Pasqua .... .06 .02 .00
☐ 197 Jim Gantner .... .03 .01 .00
☐ 198 Mark Eichhorn .... .03 .01 .00
☐ 199 John Grubb .... .03 .01 .00
☐ 200 Bill Ripken .... .15 .06 .01
☐ 201 Sam Horn .... .30 .12 .03
☐ 202 Todd Worrell .... .10 .04 .01
☐ 203 Terry Leach .... .08 .03 .01
☐ 204 Garth Iorg .... .03 .01 .00
☐ 205 Brian Dayett .... .03 .01 .00
☐ 206 Bo Diaz .... .03 .01 .00
☐ 207 Craig Reynolds .... .03 .01 .00
☐ 208 Brian Holton .... .08 .03 .01
☐ 209 Marvell Wynne UER .... .06 .02 .00
(misspelled Marvelle on card front)
☐ 210 Dave Concepcion .... .08 .03 .01
☐ 211 Mike Davis .... .03 .01 .00
☐ 212 Devon White .... .12 .05 .01
☐ 213 Mickey Brantley .... .08 .03 .01
☐ 214 Greg Gagne .... .03 .01 .00
☐ 215 Oddibe McDowell .... .08 .03 .01
☐ 216 Jimmy Key .... .08 .03 .01
☐ 217 Dave Bergman .... .03 .01 .00
☐ 218 Calvin Schiraldi .... .03 .01 .00
☐ 219 Larry Sheets .... .08 .03 .01
☐ 220 Mike Easler .... .03 .01 .00
☐ 221 Kurt Stillwell .... .03 .01 .00
☐ 222 Chuck Jackson .... .10 .04 .01
☐ 223 Dave Martinez .... .06 .02 .00
☐ 224 Tim Leary .... .08 .03 .01
☐ 225 Steve Garvey .... .25 .10 .02

□ 226	Greg Mathews	.03	.01	.00
□ 227	Doug Sisk	.03	.01	.00
□ 228	Dave Henderson	.06	.02	.00
□ 229	Jimmy Dwyer	.03	.01	.00
□ 230	Larry Owen	.03	.01	.00
□ 231	Andre Thornton	.03	.01	.00
□ 232	Mark Salas	.03	.01	.00
□ 233	Tom Brookens	.03	.01	.00
□ 234	Greg Brock	.03	.01	.00
□ 235	Rance Mulliniks	.03	.01	.00
□ 236	Bob Brower	.08	.03	.01
□ 237	Joe Niekro	.06	.02	.00
□ 238	Scott Bankhead	.03	.01	.00
□ 239	Doug DeCinces	.03	.01	.00
□ 240	Tommy John	.10	.04	.01
□ 241	Rich Gedman	.03	.01	.00
□ 242	Ted Power	.03	.01	.00
□ 243	Dave Meads	.10	.04	.01
□ 244	Jim Sundberg	.03	.01	.00
□ 245	Ken Oberkfell	.03	.01	.00
□ 246	Jimmy Jones	.10	.04	.01
□ 247	Ken Landreaux	.03	.01	.00
□ 248	Jose Oquendo	.03	.01	.00
□ 249	John Mitchell	.12	.05	.01
□ 250	Don Baylor	.08	.03	.01
□ 251	Scott Fletcher	.03	.01	.00
□ 252	Al Newman	.03	.01	.00
□ 253	Carney Lansford	.08	.03	.01
□ 254	Johnny Ray	.08	.03	.01
□ 255	Gary Pettis	.03	.01	.00
□ 256	Ken Phelps	.06	.02	.00
□ 257	Rick Leach	.03	.01	.00
□ 258	Tim Stoddard	.03	.01	.00
□ 259	Ed Romero	.03	.01	.00
□ 260	Sid Bream	.03	.01	.00
□ 261A	Tom Niedenfuer ERR (misspelled Neidenfuer on card front)	.15	.06	.01
□ 261B	Tom Niedenfuer COR	.06	.02	.00
□ 262	Rick Dempsey	.03	.01	.00
□ 263	Lonnie Smith	.03	.01	.00
□ 264	Bob Forsch	.03	.01	.00
□ 265	Barry Bonds	.18	.08	.01
□ 266	Willie Randolph	.08	.03	.01
□ 267	Mike Ramsey	.12	.05	.01
□ 268	Don Slaught	.03	.01	.00
□ 269	Mickey Tettleton	.03	.01	.00
□ 270	Jerry Reuss	.03	.01	.00
□ 271	Marc Sullivan	.03	.01	.00
□ 272	Jim Morrison	.03	.01	.00
□ 273	Steve Balboni	.03	.01	.00
□ 274	Dick Schofield	.03	.01	.00
□ 275	John Tudor	.08	.03	.01
□ 276	Gene Larkin	.20	.08	.02
□ 277	Harold Reynolds	.03	.01	.00
□ 278	Jerry Browne	.03	.01	.00
□ 279	Willie Upshaw	.03	.01	.00
□ 280	Ted Higuera	.10	.04	.01
□ 281	Terry McGriff	.08	.03	.01
□ 282	Terry Puhl	.03	.01	.00
□ 283	Mark Wasinger	.15	.06	.01
□ 284	Luis Salazar	.03	.01	.00
□ 285	Ted Simmons	.08	.03	.01
□ 286	John Shelby	.03	.01	.00
□ 287	John Smiley	.20	.08	.02
□ 288	Curt Ford	.03	.01	.00
□ 289	Steve Crawford	.03	.01	.00
□ 290	Dan Quisenberry	.08	.03	.01
□ 291	Alan Wiggins	.03	.01	.00
□ 292	Randy Bush	.03	.01	.00
□ 293	John Candelaria	.06	.02	.00
□ 294	Tony Phillips	.03	.01	.00
□ 295	Mike Morgan	.03	.01	.00
□ 296	Bill Wegman	.03	.01	.00
□ 297A	Terry Francona ERR (misspelled Franconia on card front)	.15	.06	.01
□ 297B	Terry Francona COR	.03	.01	.00
□ 298	Mickey Hatcher	.06	.02	.00
□ 299	Andres Thomas	.03	.01	.00
□ 300	Bob Stanley	.03	.01	.00
□ 301	Alfredo Pedrique	.10	.04	.01
□ 302	Jim Lindeman	.06	.02	.00
□ 303	Wally Backman	.06	.02	.00
□ 304	Paul O'Neill	.08	.03	.01
□ 305	Hubie Brooks	.06	.02	.00
□ 306	Steve Buechele	.03	.01	.00
□ 307	Bobby Thigpen	.06	.02	.00
□ 308	George Hendrick	.06	.02	.00
□ 309	John Moses	.03	.01	.00
□ 310	Ron Guidry	.08	.03	.01
□ 311	Bill Schroeder	.03	.01	.00
□ 312	Jose Nunez	.12	.05	.01
□ 313	Bud Black	.03	.01	.00
□ 314	Joe Sambito	.03	.01	.00
□ 315	Scott McGregor	.03	.01	.00
□ 316	Rafael Santana	.03	.01	.00
□ 317	Frank Williams	.03	.01	.00
□ 318	Mike Fitzgerald	.03	.01	.00
□ 319	Rick Mahler	.03	.01	.00
□ 320	Jim Gott	.03	.01	.00
□ 321	Mariano Duncan	.03	.01	.00
□ 322	Jose Guzman	.03	.01	.00
□ 323	Lee Guetterman	.03	.01	.00
□ 324	Dan Gladden	.06	.02	.00
□ 325	Gary Carter	.20	.08	.02
□ 326	Tracy Jones	.08	.03	.01
□ 327	Floyd Youmans	.03	.01	.00
□ 328	Bill Dawley	.03	.01	.00
□ 329	Paul Noce	.10	.04	.01
□ 330	Angel Salazar	.03	.01	.00
□ 331	Goose Gossage	.08	.03	.01
□ 332	George Frazier	.03	.01	.00
□ 333	Ruppert Jones	.03	.01	.00
□ 334	Billy Jo Robidoux	.03	.01	.00
□ 335	Mike Scott	.12	.05	.01
□ 336	Randy Myers	.15	.06	.01
□ 337	Bob Sebra	.03	.01	.00
□ 338	Eric Show	.03	.01	.00
□ 339	Mitch Williams	.03	.01	.00
□ 340	Paul Molitor	.10	.04	.01
□ 341	Gus Polidor	.03	.01	.00
□ 342	Steve Trout	.03	.01	.00
□ 343	Jerry Don Gleaton	.03	.01	.00
□ 344	Bob Knepper	.03	.01	.00
□ 345	Mitch Webster	.03	.01	.00
□ 346	John Morris	.03	.01	.00
□ 347	Andy Hawkins	.03	.01	.00
□ 348	Dave Leiper	.03	.01	.00
□ 349	Ernest Riles	.03	.01	.00
□ 350	Dwight Gooden	.40	.16	.04
□ 351	Dave Righetti	.08	.03	.01
□ 352	Pat Dodson	.08	.03	.01
□ 353	John Habyan	.08	.03	.01
□ 354	Jim Deshaies	.03	.01	.00
□ 355	Butch Wynegar	.03	.01	.00
□ 356	Bryn Smith	.03	.01	.00
□ 357	Matt Young	.03	.01	.00
□ 358	Tom Pagnozzi	.15	.06	.01
□ 359	Floyd Rayford	.03	.01	.00
□ 360	Darryl Strawberry	.35	.14	.03
□ 361	Sal Butera	.03	.01	.00
□ 362	Domingo Ramos	.03	.01	.00
□ 363	Chris Brown	.08	.03	.01
□ 364	Jose Gonzalez	.08	.03	.01
□ 365	Dave Smith	.03	.01	.00
□ 366	Andy McGaffigan	.03	.01	.00
□ 367	Stan Javier	.03	.01	.00
□ 368	Henry Cotto	.03	.01	.00
□ 369	Mike Birkbeck	.08	.03	.01
□ 370	Len Dykstra	.08	.03	.01
□ 371	Dave Collins	.03	.01	.00
□ 372	Spike Owen	.03	.01	.00
□ 373	Geno Petralli	.03	.01	.00
□ 374	Ron Karkovice	.03	.01	.00
□ 375	Shane Rawley	.03	.01	.00
□ 376	DeWayne Buice	.10	.04	.01
□ 377	Bill Pecota	.10	.04	.01
□ 378	Leon Durham	.06	.02	.00
□ 379	Ed Olwine	.03	.01	.00
□ 380	Bruce Hurst	.10	.04	.01
□ 381	Bob McClure	.03	.01	.00
□ 382	Mark Thurmond	.03	.01	.00
□ 383	Buddy Biancalana	.03	.01	.00
□ 384	Tim Conroy	.03	.01	.00
□ 385	Tony Gwynn	.30	.12	.03
□ 386	Greg Gross	.03	.01	.00
□ 387	Barry Lyons	.10	.04	.01
□ 388	Mike Felder	.03	.01	.00
□ 389	Pat Clements	.03	.01	.00
□ 390	Ken Griffey	.06	.02	.00
□ 391	Mark Davis	.06	.02	.00
□ 392	Jose Rijo	.06	.02	.00
□ 393	Mike Young	.03	.01	.00
□ 394	Willie Fraser	.03	.01	.00
□ 395	Dion James	.03	.01	.00
□ 396	Steve Shields	.03	.01	.00
□ 397	Randy St.Claire	.03	.01	.00
□ 398	Danny Jackson	.12	.05	.01
□ 399	Cecil Fielder	.03	.01	.00
□ 400	Keith Hernandez	.18	.08	.01
□ 401	Don Carman	.03	.01	.00
□ 402	Chuck Crim	.10	.04	.01
□ 403	Rob Woodward	.03	.01	.00
□ 404	Junior Ortiz	.03	.01	.00
□ 405	Glenn Wilson	.03	.01	.00
□ 406	Ken Howell	.03	.01	.00
□ 407	Jeff Kunkel	.03	.01	.00
□ 408	Jeff Reed	.03	.01	.00
□ 409	Chris James	.10	.04	.01

□ 410 Zane Smith .06 .02 .00
□ 411 Ken Dixon .03 .01 .00
□ 412 Ricky Horton .03 .01 .00
□ 413 Frank DiPino .03 .01 .00
□ 414 Shane Mack .12 .05 .01
□ 415 Danny Cox .06 .02 .00
□ 416 Andy Van Slyke .15 .06 .01
□ 417 Danny Heep .03 .01 .00
□ 418 John Cangelosi .03 .01 .00
□ 419A John Christensen ERR .15 .06 .01
(misspelled Christiansen on card front)
□ 419B John Christensen COR .03 .01 .00
□ 420 Joey Cora .12 .05 .01
□ 421 Mike LaValliere .03 .01 .00
□ 422 Kelly Gruber .03 .01 .00
□ 423 Bruce Benedict .03 .01 .00
□ 424 Len Matuszek .03 .01 .00
□ 425 Kent Tekulve .03 .01 .00
□ 426 Rafael Ramirez .03 .01 .00
□ 427 Mike Flanagan .03 .01 .00
□ 428 Mike Gallego .03 .01 .00
□ 429 Juan Castillo .06 .02 .00
□ 430 Neal Heaton .03 .01 .00
□ 431 Phil Garner .03 .01 .00
□ 432 Mike Dunne .15 .06 .01
□ 433 Wallace Johnson .03 .01 .00
□ 434 Jack O'Connor .03 .01 .00
□ 435 Steve Jeltz .03 .01 .00
□ 436 Donnell Nixon .12 .05 .01
□ 437 Jack Lazorko .03 .01 .00
□ 438 Keith Comstock .12 .05 .01
□ 439 Jeff Robinson .03 .01 .00
(Pirates pitcher)
□ 440 Graig Nettles .08 .03 .01
□ 441 Mel Hall .03 .01 .00
□ 442 Gerald Young .25 .10 .02
□ 443 Gary Redus .03 .01 .00
□ 444 Charlie Moore .03 .01 .00
□ 445 Bill Madlock .06 .02 .00
□ 446 Mark Clear .03 .01 .00
□ 447 Greg Booker .03 .01 .00
□ 448 Rick Schu .03 .01 .00
□ 449 Ron Kittle .08 .03 .01
□ 450 Dale Murphy .25 .10 .02
□ 451 Bob Dernier .03 .01 .00
□ 452 Dale Mohorcic .03 .01 .00
□ 453 Rafael Belliard .03 .01 .00
□ 454 Charlie Puleo .03 .01 .00
□ 455 Dwayne Murphy .03 .01 .00
□ 456 Jim Eisenreich .03 .01 .00
□ 457 David Palmer .03 .01 .00
□ 458 Dave Stewart .08 .03 .01
□ 459 Pasqual Perez .03 .01 .00
□ 460 Glenn Davis .12 .05 .01
□ 461 Dan Petry .03 .01 .00
□ 462 Jim Winn .03 .01 .00
□ 463 Darrell Miller .03 .01 .00
□ 464 Mike Moore .06 .02 .00
□ 465 Mike LaCoss .03 .01 .00
□ 466 Steve Farr .03 .01 .00
□ 467 Jerry Mumphrey .03 .01 .00
□ 468 Kevin Gross .03 .01 .00
□ 469 Bruce Bochy .03 .01 .00
□ 470 Orel Hershiser .20 .08 .02
□ 471 Eric King .03 .01 .00
□ 472 Ellis Burks 1.00 .40 .10
□ 473 Darren Daulton .03 .01 .00
□ 474 Mookie Wilson .06 .02 .00
□ 475 Frank Viola .15 .06 .01
□ 476 Ron Robinson .03 .01 .00
□ 477 Bob Melvin .03 .01 .00
□ 478 Jeff Musselman .08 .03 .01
□ 479 Charlie Kerfeld .03 .01 .00
□ 480 Richard Dotson .06 .02 .00
□ 481 Kevin Mitchell .06 .02 .00
□ 482 Gary Roenicke .03 .01 .00
□ 483 Tim Flannery .03 .01 .00
□ 484 Rich Yett .03 .01 .00
□ 485 Pete Incaviglia .15 .06 .01
□ 486 Rick Cerone .03 .01 .00
□ 487 Tony Armas .06 .02 .00
□ 488 Jerry Reed .03 .01 .00
□ 489 Davey Lopes .06 .02 .00
□ 490 Frank Tanana .06 .02 .00
□ 491 Mike Loynd .06 .02 .00
□ 492 Bruce Ruffin .03 .01 .00
□ 493 Chris Speier .03 .01 .00
□ 494 Tom Hume .03 .01 .00
□ 495 Jesse Orosco .03 .01 .00
□ 496 Robbie Wine UER .15 .06 .01
(misspelled Robby on card front)
□ 497 Jeff Montgomery .15 .06 .01
□ 498 Jeff Dedmon .03 .01 .00
□ 499 Luis Aguayo .03 .01 .00
□ 500 Reggie Jackson .25 .10 .02
(Oakland A's)
□ 501 Reggie Jackson .25 .10 .02
(Baltimore Orioles)
□ 502 Reggie Jackson .25 .10 .02
(New York Yankees)
□ 503 Reggie Jackson .20 .08 .02
(California Angels)
□ 504 Reggie Jackson .20 .08 .02
(Oakland A's)
□ 505 Billy Hatcher .06 .02 .00
□ 506 Ed Lynch .03 .01 .00
□ 507 Willie Hernandez .06 .02 .00
□ 508 Jose DeLeon .03 .01 .00
□ 509 Joel Youngblood .03 .01 .00
□ 510 Bob Welch .06 .02 .00
□ 511 Steve Ontiveros .03 .01 .00
□ 512 Randy Ready .03 .01 .00
□ 513 Juan Nieves .03 .01 .00
□ 514 Jeff Russell .03 .01 .00
□ 515 Von Hayes .08 .03 .01
□ 516 Mark Gubicza .08 .03 .01
□ 517 Ken Dayley .03 .01 .00
□ 518 Don Aase .03 .01 .00
□ 519 Rick Reuschel .06 .02 .00
□ 520 Mike Henneman .20 .08 .02
□ 521 Rick Aguilera .03 .01 .00
□ 522 Jay Howell .03 .01 .00
□ 523 Ed Correa .03 .01 .00
□ 524 Manny Trillo .03 .01 .00
□ 525 Kirk Gibson .20 .08 .02
□ 526 Wally Ritchie .10 .04 .01
□ 527 Al Nipper .03 .01 .00
□ 528 Atlee Hammaker .03 .01 .00
□ 529 Shawon Dunston .06 .02 .00
□ 530 Jim Clancy .03 .01 .00
□ 531 Tom Paciorek .03 .01 .00
□ 532 Joel Skinner .03 .01 .00
□ 533 Scott Garrelts .03 .01 .00
□ 534 Tom O'Malley .03 .01 .00
□ 535 John Franco .06 .02 .00
□ 536 Paul Kilgus .12 .05 .01
□ 537 Darrell Porter .03 .01 .00
□ 538 Walt Terrell .03 .01 .00
□ 539 Bill Long .10 .04 .01
□ 540 George Bell .18 .08 .01
□ 541 Jeff Sellers .03 .01 .00
□ 542 Joe Boever .10 .04 .01
□ 543 Steve Howe .03 .01 .00
□ 544 Scott Sanderson .03 .01 .00
□ 545 Jack Morris .10 .04 .01
□ 546 Todd Benzinger .30 .12 .03
□ 547 Steve Henderson .03 .01 .00
□ 548 Eddie Milner .03 .01 .00
□ 549 Jeff Robinson .35 .14 .03
(Tigers pitcher)
□ 550 Cal Ripken .20 .08 .02
□ 551 Jody Davis .06 .02 .00
□ 552 Kirk McCaskill .03 .01 .00
□ 553 Craig Lefferts .03 .01 .00
□ 554 Darnell Coles .03 .01 .00
□ 555 Phil Niekro .12 .05 .01
□ 556 Mike Aldrete .06 .02 .00
□ 557 Pat Perry .03 .01 .00
□ 558 Juan Agosto .03 .01 .00
□ 559 Rob Murphy .03 .01 .00
□ 560 Dennis Rasmussen .06 .02 .00
□ 561 Manny Lee .03 .01 .00
□ 562 Jeff Blauser .18 .08 .01
□ 563 Bob Ojeda .06 .02 .00
□ 564 Dave Dravecky .03 .01 .00
□ 565 Gene Garber .03 .01 .00
□ 566 Ron Roenicke .03 .01 .00
□ 567 Tommy Hinzo .10 .04 .01
□ 568 Eric Nolte .10 .04 .01
□ 569 Ed Hearn .03 .01 .00
□ 570 Mark Davidson .10 .04 .01
□ 571 Jim Walewander .15 .06 .01
□ 572 Donnie Hill .03 .01 .00
□ 573 Jamie Moyer .03 .01 .00
□ 574 Ken Schrom .03 .01 .00
□ 575 Nolan Ryan .25 .10 .02
□ 576 Jim Acker .03 .01 .00
□ 577 Jamie Quirk .03 .01 .00
□ 578 Jay Aldrich .10 .04 .01
□ 579 Claudell Washington .06 .02 .00
□ 580 Jeff Leonard .06 .02 .00
□ 581 Carmen Castillo .03 .01 .00
□ 582 Darryl Boston .03 .01 .00
□ 583 Jeff DeWillis .10 .04 .01
□ 584 John Marzano .08 .03 .01
□ 585 Bill Gullickson .03 .01 .00
□ 586 Andy Allanson .03 .01 .00
□ 587 Lee Tunnell .03 .01 .00

□ 588	Gene Nelson	.03	.01	.00
□ 589	Dave LaPoint	.03	.01	.00
□ 590	Harold Baines	.08	.03	.01
□ 591	Bill Buckner	.08	.03	.01
□ 592	Carlton Fisk	.10	.04	.01
□ 593	Rick Manning	.03	.01	.00
□ 594	Doug Jones	.25	.10	.02
□ 595	Tom Candiotti	.03	.01	.00
□ 596	Steve Lake	.03	.01	.00
□ 597	Jose Lind	.25	.10	.02
□ 598	Ross Jones	.10	.04	.01
□ 599	Gary Matthews	.03	.01	.00
□ 600	Fernando Valenzuela	.15	.06	.01
□ 601	Dennis Martinez	.06	.02	.00
□ 602	Les Lancaster	.10	.04	.01
□ 603	Ozzie Guillen	.06	.02	.00
□ 604	Tony Bernazard	.03	.01	.00
□ 605	Chili Davis	.06	.02	.00
□ 606	Roy Smalley	.03	.01	.00
□ 607	Ivan Calderon	.08	.03	.01
□ 608	Jay Tibbs	.03	.01	.00
□ 609	Guy Hoffman	.03	.01	.00
□ 610	Doyle Alexander	.06	.02	.00
□ 611	Mike Bielecki	.03	.01	.00
□ 612	Shawn Hillegas	.15	.06	.01
□ 613	Keith Atherton	.03	.01	.00
□ 614	Eric Plunk	.03	.01	.00
□ 615	Sid Fernandez	.08	.03	.01
□ 616	Dennis Lamp	.03	.01	.00
□ 617	Dave Engle	.03	.01	.00
□ 618	Harry Spilman	.03	.01	.00
□ 619	Don Robinson	.03	.01	.00
□ 620	John Farrell	.20	.08	.02
□ 621	Nelson Liriano	.12	.05	.01
□ 622	Floyd Bannister	.03	.01	.00
□ 623	Randy Milligan	.30	.12	.03
□ 624	Kevin Elster	.20	.08	.02
□ 625	Jody Reed	.35	.14	.03
□ 626	Shawn Abner	.20	.08	.02
□ 627	Kurt Manwaring	.20	.08	.02
□ 628	Pete Stanicek	.20	.08	.02
□ 629	Rob Ducey	.20	.08	.02
□ 630	Steve Kiefer	.06	.02	.00
□ 631	Gary Thurman	.20	.08	.02
□ 632	Darrel Akerfelds	.15	.06	.01
□ 633	Dave Clark	.12	.05	.01
□ 634	Roberto Kelly	.30	.12	.03
□ 635	Keith Hughes	.20	.08	.02
□ 636	John Davis	.15	.06	.01
□ 637	Mike Devereaux	.30	.12	.03
□ 638	Tom Glavine	.18	.08	.01
□ 639	Keith Miller (New York Mets)	.20	.08	.02
□ 640	Chris Gwynn UER (wrong batting and throwing on back)	.35	.14	.03
□ 641	Tim Crews	.12	.05	.01
□ 642	Mackey Sasser	.25	.10	.02
□ 643	Vincente Palacios	.12	.05	.01
□ 644	Kevin Romine	.08	.03	.01
□ 645	Gregg Jefferies	4.50	1.80	.45
□ 646	Jeff Treadway	.30	.12	.03
□ 647	Ronnie Gant	.45	.18	.04
□ 648	Mark McGwire and Matt Nokes (Rookie Sluggers)	.30	.12	.03
□ 649	Eric Davis and Tim Raines (Speed and Power)	.20	.08	.02
□ 650	Don Mattingly and Jack Clark	.40	.16	.04
□ 651	Tony Fernandez, Alan Trammell, and Cal Ripken	.10	.04	.01
□ 652	Vince Coleman HL 100 Stolen Bases	.12	.05	.01
□ 653	Kirby Puckett HL 10 Hits in a Row	.15	.06	.01
□ 654	Benito Santiago HL Hitting Streak	.12	.05	.01
□ 655	Juan Nieves HL No Hitter	.06	.02	.00
□ 656	Steve Bedrosian HL Saves Record	.06	.02	.00
□ 657	Mike Schmidt HL 500 Homers	.15	.06	.01
□ 658	Don Mattingly HL Home Run Streak	.40	.16	.04
□ 659	Mark McGwire HL Rookie HR Record	.35	.14	.03
□ 660	Paul Molitor HL Hitting Streak	.10	.04	.01

1988 Score Box Bottoms

There are six different wax box bottom panels each featuring three players and a trivia (related to a particular stadium for a given year) question. The players and trivia question cards are individually numbered. The trivia are numbered below with the prefix T in order to avoid confusion. The trivia cards are very unpopular with collectors since they do not picture any players. When panels of four are cut into individuals, the cards are standard size, 2/1/2" by 3 1/2". The card backs of the players feature the respective League logos most prominently.

		MINT	EXC	G-VG
COMPLETE SET (24)		2.00	.80	.20
COMMON PLAYER (1-18)		.06	.02	.00
COMMON TRIVIA (T1-T6)		.03	.01	.00
□ 1	Terry Kennedy	.06	.02	.00
□ 2	Don Mattingly	.50	.20	.05
□ 3	Willie Randolph	.10	.04	.01
□ 4	Wade Boggs	.35	.14	.03
□ 5	Cal Ripken	.20	.08	.02
□ 6	George Bell	.12	.05	.01
□ 7	Rickey Henderson	.20	.08	.02
□ 8	Dave Winfield	.20	.08	.02
□ 9	Bret Saberhagen	.12	.05	.01
□ 10	Gary Carter	.20	.08	.02
□ 11	Jack Clark	.12	.05	.01
□ 12	Ryne Sandberg	.12	.05	.01
□ 13	Mike Schmidt	.25	.10	.02
□ 14	Ozzie Smith	.12	.05	.01
□ 15	Eric Davis	.25	.10	.02
□ 16	Andre Dawson	.15	.06	.01
□ 17	Darryl Strawberry	.35	.14	.03
□ 18	Mike Scott	.10	.04	.01
□ T1	Fenway Park '60 Ted (Williams) Hits To The End	.06	.02	.00
□ T2	Comiskey Park '83 Grand Slam (Fred Lynn) Breaks Jinx	.03	.01	.00
□ T3	Anaheim Stadium '87 Old Rookie Record Falls (Mark McGwire)	.06	.02	.00
□ T4	Wrigley Field '38 Gabby (Hartnett) Gets Pennant Homer	.03	.01	.00
□ T5	Comiskey Park '50 Red (Schoendienst) Rips Winning HR	.03	.01	.00
□ T6	County Stadium '87 Rookie (John Farrell) Stops Hit Streak (Paul Molitor)	.03	.01	.00

1988 Score Young Superstars I

This attractive high-gloss 40-card set of "Young Superstars" was distributed in a small blue box which had the checklist of the set on a side panel of the box. The cards are in full color on the front and also have

a full-color small portrait on the card back. The cards are standard size, 2 1/2" by 3 1/2". The cards in this series are distinguishable from the cards in Series II by the fact that this series has a blue and green border on the card front instead of the (Series II) blue and pink border.

	MINT	EXC	G-VG
COMPLETE SET (40)	7.50	3.00	.75
COMMON PLAYER (1-40)	.10	.04	.01
□ 1 Mark McGwire	1.00	.40	.10
□ 2 Benito Santiago	.50	.20	.05
□ 3 Sam Horn	.30	.12	.03
□ 4 Chris Bosio	.10	.04	.01
□ 5 Matt Nokes	.30	.12	.03
□ 6 Ken Williams	.20	.08	.02
□ 7 Dion James	.10	.04	.01
□ 8 B.J. Surhoff	.20	.08	.02
□ 9 Joe Magrane	.20	.08	.02
□ 10 Kevin Seitzer	.50	.20	.05
□ 11 Stanley Jefferson	.15	.06	.01
□ 12 Devon White	.25	.10	.02
□ 13 Nelson Liriano	.10	.04	.01
□ 14 Chris James	.20	.08	.02
□ 15 Mike Henneman	.20	.08	.02
□ 16 Terry Steinbach	.25	.10	.02
□ 17 John Kruk	.25	.10	.02
□ 18 Matt Williams	.25	.10	.02
□ 19 Kelly Downs	.15	.06	.01
□ 20 Bill Ripken	.20	.08	.02
□ 21 Ozzie Guillen	.15	.06	.01
□ 22 Luis Polonia	.20	.08	.02
□ 23 Dave Magadan	.20	.08	.02
□ 24 Mike Greenwell	1.00	.40	.10
□ 25 Will Clark	.75	.30	.07
□ 26 Mike Dunn	.20	.08	.02
□ 27 Wally Joyner	.50	.20	.05
□ 28 Robby Thompson	.15	.06	.01
□ 29 Ken Caminiti	.20	.08	.02
□ 30 Jose Canseco	1.50	.60	.15
□ 31 Todd Benzinger	.25	.10	.02
□ 32 Pete Incaviglia	.30	.12	.03
□ 33 John Farrell	.15	.06	.01
□ 34 Casey Candaele	.10	.04	.01
□ 35 Mike Aldrete	.15	.06	.01
□ 36 Ruben Sierra	.30	.12	.03
□ 37 Ellis Burks	.50	.20	.05
□ 38 Tracy Jones	.20	.08	.02
□ 39 Kal Daniels	.35	.14	.03
□ 40 Cory Snyder	.30	.12	.03

1988 Score Young Superstars II

This attractive high-gloss 40-card set of "Young Superstars" was distributed in a small purple box which had the checklist of the set on a side panel of the box. The cards are in full color on the front and also have a full-color small portrait on the card back. The cards are standard size, 2 1/2" by 3 1/2". The cards in this series are distinguishable from the cards in Series I by the fact that this series has a blue and pink border on the card front instead of the (Series I) blue and green border.

	MINT	EXC	G-VG
COMPLETE SET (40)	6.00	2.40	.60
COMMON PLAYER (1-40)	.10	.04	.01
□ 1 Eric Davis	1.00	.40	.10
□ 2 Glenn Braggs	.20	.08	.02
□ 3 Dwight Gooden	.50	.20	.05
□ 4 Jose Lind	.20	.08	.02
□ 5 Danny Tartabull	.35	.14	.03
□ 6 Tony Fernandez	.30	.12	.03
□ 7 Julio Franco	.15	.06	.01
□ 8 Andres Galarraga	.35	.14	.03
□ 9 Bobby Bonilla	.25	.10	.02
□ 10 Rob Mallicoat	.10	.04	.01
□ 11 Gerald Young	.20	.08	.02
□ 12 Barry Bonds	.25	.10	.02
□ 13 Jerry Browne	.10	.04	.01
□ 14 Jeff Blauser	.20	.08	.02
□ 15 Mickey Brantley	.15	.06	.01
□ 16 Floyd Youmans	.10	.04	.01
□ 17 Bret Saberhagen	.20	.08	.02
□ 18 Shawon Dunston	.15	.06	.01
□ 19 Len Dykstra	.15	.06	.01
□ 20 Darryl Strawberry	.50	.20	.05
□ 21 Rick Aguilera	.15	.06	.01
□ 22 Ivan Calderon	.15	.06	.01
□ 23 Roger Clemens	.50	.20	.05
□ 24 Vince Coleman	.30	.12	.03
□ 25 Gary Thurman	.20	.08	.02
□ 26 Jeff Treadway	.25	.10	.02
□ 27 Oddibe McDowell	.15	.06	.01
□ 28 Fred McGriff	.50	.20	.05
□ 29 Mark McLemore	.10	.04	.01
□ 30 Jeff Musselman	.10	.04	.01
□ 31 Matt Williams	.25	.10	.02
□ 32 Dan Plesac	.15	.06	.01
□ 33 Juan Nieves	.15	.06	.01
□ 34 Barry Larkin	.25	.10	.02
□ 35 Greg Matthews	.20	.08	.02
□ 36 Shane Mack	.20	.08	.02
□ 37 Scott Bankhead	.15	.06	.01
□ 38 Eric Bell	.10	.04	.01
□ 39 Greg Swindell	.25	.10	.02
□ 40 Kevin Elster	.20	.08	.02

1988 Score Traded

This 110-card set featured traded players (1-65) and rookies (66-110) for the 1988 season. The cards are distinguishable from the regular Score set by the orange borders and by the fact that the numbering on the back has a T suffix. The cards are standard size, 2 1/2" by 3 1/2" and were distributed by Score as a collated set in a special collector box along with some trivia cards.

	MINT	EXC	G-VG
COMPLETE SET (110)	11.00	4.50	1.10
COMMON PLAYER (1-65)	.05	.02	.00
COMMON PLAYER (66-110)	.05	.02	.00
□ 1T Jack Clark	.15	.06	.01
□ 2T Danny Jackson	.15	.06	.01
□ 3T Brett Butler	.10	.04	.01
□ 4T Kurt Stillwell	.05	.02	.00

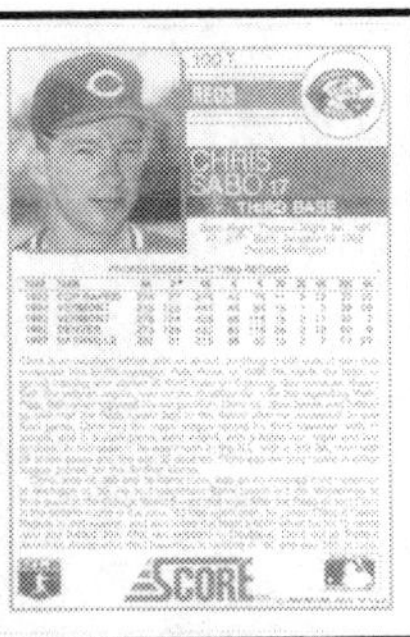

☐	5T Tom Brunansky	.10	.04	.01
☐	6T Dennis Lamp	.05	.02	.00
☐	7T Jose DeLeon	.05	.02	.00
☐	8T Tom Herr	.05	.02	.00
☐	9T Keith Moreland	.05	.02	.00
☐	10T Kirk Gibson	.20	.08	.02
☐	11T Bud Black	.05	.02	.00
☐	12T Rafael Ramirez	.05	.02	.00
☐	13T Luis Salazar	.05	.02	.00
☐	14T Goose Gossage	.10	.04	.01
☐	15T Bob Welch	.05	.02	.00
☐	16T Vance Law	.05	.02	.00
☐	17T Ray Knight	.05	.02	.00
☐	18T Dan Quisenberry	.10	.04	.01
☐	19T Don Slaught	.05	.02	.00
☐	20T Lee Smith	.10	.04	.01
☐	21T Rick Cerone	.05	.02	.00
☐	22T Pat Tabler	.05	.02	.00
☐	23T Larry McWilliams	.05	.02	.00
☐	24T Rick Horton	.05	.02	.00
☐	25T Craig Nettles	.10	.04	.01
☐	26T Dan Petry	.05	.02	.00
☐	27T Jose Rijo	.05	.02	.00
☐	28T Chili Davis	.10	.04	.01
☐	29T Dickie Thon	.05	.02	.00
☐	30T Mackey Sasser	.15	.06	.01
☐	31T Mickey Tettleton	.05	.02	.00
☐	32T Rick Dempsey	.05	.02	.00
☐	33T Ron Hassey	.05	.02	.00
☐	34T Phil Bradley	.10	.04	.01
☐	35T Jay Howell	.05	.02	.00
☐	36T Bill Buckner	.10	.04	.01
☐	37T Alfredo Griffin	.10	.04	.01
☐	38T Gary Pettis	.05	.02	.00
☐	39T Calvin Schiraldi	.05	.02	.00
☐	40T John Candelaria	.10	.04	.01
☐	41T Joe Orsulak	.05	.02	.00
☐	42T Willie Upshaw	.05	.02	.00
☐	43T Herm Winningham	.05	.02	.00
☐	44T Ron Kittle	.10	.04	.01
☐	45T Bob Dernier	.05	.02	.00
☐	46T Steve Balboni	.05	.02	.00
☐	47T Steve Shields	.05	.02	.00
☐	48T Henry Cotto	.05	.02	.00
☐	49T Dave Henderson	.10	.04	.01
☐	50T Dave Parker	.10	.04	.01
☐	51T Mike Young	.05	.02	.00
☐	52T Mark Salas	.05	.02	.00
☐	53T Mike Davis	.05	.02	.00
☐	54T Rafael Santana	.05	.02	.00
☐	55T Don Baylor	.10	.04	.01
☐	56T Dan Pasqua	.10	.04	.01
☐	57T Ernest Riles	.05	.02	.00
☐	58T Glenn Hubbard	.05	.02	.00
☐	59T Mike Smithson	.05	.02	.00
☐	60T Richard Dotson	.10	.04	.01
☐	61T Jerry Reuss	.05	.02	.00
☐	62T Mike Jackson	.10	.04	.01
☐	63T Floyd Bannister	.05	.02	.00
☐	64T Jesse Orosco	.05	.02	.00
☐	65T Larry Parrish	.05	.02	.00
☐	66T Jeff Bittiger	.15	.06	.01
☐	67T Ray Hayward	.12	.05	.01
☐	68T Ricky Jordan	2.00	.80	.20
☐	69T Tommy Gregg	.15	.06	.01
☐	70T Brady Anderson	.35	.14	.03
☐	71T Jeff Montgomery	.10	.04	.01
☐	72T Darryl Hamilton	.25	.10	.02
☐	73T Cecil Espy	.20	.08	.02
☐	74T Gregg Briley	.15	.06	.01
☐	75T Joey Meyer	.20	.08	.02
☐	76T Mike MacFarlane	.20	.08	.02
☐	77T Oswald Peraza	.15	.06	.01
☐	78T Jack Armstrong	.25	.10	.02
☐	79T Don Heinkel	.15	.06	.01
☐	80T Mark Grace	1.75	.70	.17
☐	81T Steve Curry	.15	.06	.01
☐	82T Damon Berryhill	.35	.14	.03
☐	83T Steve Ellsworth	.15	.06	.01
☐	84T Pete Smith	.15	.06	.01
☐	85T Jack McDowell	.25	.10	.02
☐	86T Rob Dibble	.15	.06	.01
☐	87T Brian Harvey	.30	.12	.03
☐	88T John Dopson	.20	.08	.02
☐	89T Dave Gallagher	.25	.10	.02
☐	90T Todd Stottlemyre	.25	.10	.02
☐	91T Mike Schooler	.15	.06	.01
☐	92T Don Gordon	.15	.06	.01
☐	93T Sil Campusano	.25	.10	.02
☐	94T Jeff Pico	.15	.06	.01
☐	95T Jay Buhner	.35	.14	.03
☐	96T Nelson Santovenia	.15	.06	.01
☐	97T Al Leiter	.40	.16	.04
☐	98T Luis Alicea	.15	.06	.01
☐	99T Pat Borders	.15	.06	.01
☐	100T Chris Sabo	2.00	.80	.20
☐	101T Tim Belcher	.25	.10	.02
☐	102T Walt Weiss	.75	.30	.07
☐	103T Craig Biggio	.15	.06	.01
☐	104T Don August	.15	.06	.01
☐	105T Roberto Alomar	.35	.14	.03
☐	106T Todd Burns	.25	.10	.02
☐	107T John Costello	.20	.08	.02
☐	108T Melido Perez	.25	.10	.02
☐	109T Darrin Jackson	.25	.10	.02
☐	110T Orestes Destrade	.25	.10	.02

1989 Score

This 660-card set was distributed by Major League Marketing. Cards measure 2 1/2" by 3 1/2" and feature six distinctive inner border (inside a white outer border) colors on the front. Highlights (652-660) and Rookie Prospects (621-651) are included in the set. The set is distinguished by the fact that each card back shows a full-color picture (portrait) of the player.

		MINT	EXC	G-VG
	COMPLETE SET (660)	23.00	9.50	2.30
	COMMON PLAYER (1-660)	.03	.01	.00
☐	1 Jose Canseco	1.00	.35	.07
☐	2 Andre Dawson	.12	.05	.01
☐	3 Mark McGwire	.40	.16	.04
☐	4 Benny Santiago	.12	.05	.01
☐	5 Rick Reuschel	.06	.02	.00
☐	6 Fred McGriff	.12	.05	.01
☐	7 Kal Daniels	.10	.04	.01
☐	8 Gary Gaetti	.10	.04	.01
☐	9 Ellis Burks	.20	.08	.02
☐	10 Darryl Strawberry	.30	.12	.03
☐	11 Julio Franco	.08	.03	.01
☐	12 Lloyd Moseby	.08	.03	.01
☐	13 Jeff Pico	.10	.04	.01
☐	14 Johnny Ray	.06	.02	.00
☐	15 Cal Ripken Jr.	.15	.06	.01
☐	16 Dick Schofield	.03	.01	.00
☐	17 Mel Hall	.03	.01	.00
☐	18 Bill Ripken	.03	.01	.00
☐	19 Brook Jacoby	.06	.02	.00
☐	20 Kirby Puckett	.20	.08	.02
☐	21 Bill Doran	.06	.02	.00

☐ 22	Pete O'Brien	.06	.02	.00
☐ 23	Matt Nokes	.10	.04	.01
☐ 24	Brian Fisher	.03	.01	.00
☐ 25	Jack Clark	.12	.05	.01
☐ 26	Gary Pettis	.03	.01	.00
☐ 27	Dave Valle	.03	.01	.00
☐ 28	Willie Wilson	.08	.03	.01
☐ 29	Curt Young	.03	.01	.00
☐ 30	Dale Murphy	.20	.08	.02
☐ 31	Barry Larkin	.10	.04	.01
☐ 32	Dave Stewart	.06	.02	.00
☐ 33	Mike LaValliere	.03	.01	.00
☐ 34	Glenn Hubbard	.03	.01	.00
☐ 35	Ryne Sandberg	.15	.06	.01
☐ 36	Tony Pena	.06	.02	.00
☐ 37	Greg Walker	.06	.02	.00
☐ 38	Von Hayes	.08	.03	.01
☐ 39	Kevin Mitchell	.06	.02	.00
☐ 40	Tim Raines	.12	.05	.01
☐ 41	Keith Hernandez	.12	.05	.01
☐ 42	Keith Moreland	.03	.01	.00
☐ 43	Ruben Sierra	.10	.04	.01
☐ 44	Chet Lemon	.06	.02	.00
☐ 45	Willie Randolph	.06	.02	.00
☐ 46	Andy Allanson	.03	.01	.00
☐ 47	Candy Maldonado	.06	.02	.00
☐ 48	Sid Bream	.03	.01	.00
☐ 49	Denny Walling	.03	.01	.00
☐ 50	Dave Winfield	.15	.06	.01
☐ 51	Alvin Davis	.08	.03	.01
☐ 52	Cory Snyder	.12	.05	.01
☐ 53	Hubie Brooks	.06	.02	.00
☐ 54	Chili Davis	.06	.02	.00
☐ 55	Kevin Seitzer	.15	.06	.01
☐ 56	Jose Uribe	.03	.01	.00
☐ 57	Tony Fernandez	.10	.04	.01
☐ 58	Tim Teufel	.03	.01	.00
☐ 59	Oddibe McDowell	.06	.02	.00
☐ 60	Les Lancaster	.03	.01	.00
☐ 61	Billy Hatcher	.06	.02	.00
☐ 62	Dan Gladden	.06	.02	.00
☐ 63	Marty Barrett	.03	.01	.00
☐ 64	Nick Esasky	.03	.01	.00
☐ 65	Wally Joyner	.15	.06	.01
☐ 66	Mike Greenwell	.50	.20	.05
☐ 67	Ken Williams	.03	.01	.00
☐ 68	Bob Horner	.08	.03	.01
☐ 69	Steve Sax	.10	.04	.01
☐ 70	Rickey Henderson	.20	.08	.02
☐ 71	Mitch Webster	.03	.01	.00
☐ 72	Rob Deer	.08	.03	.01
☐ 73	Jim Presley	.06	.02	.00
☐ 74	Albert Hall	.03	.01	.00
☐ 75	George Brett	.20	.08	.02
☐ 76	Brian Downing	.03	.01	.00
☐ 77	Dave Martinez	.03	.01	.00
☐ 78	Scott Fletcher	.03	.01	.00
☐ 79	Phil Bradley	.06	.02	.00
☐ 80	Ozzie Smith	.10	.04	.01
☐ 81	Larry Sheets	.06	.02	.00
☐ 82	Mike Aldrete	.03	.01	.00
☐ 83	Darnell Coles	.03	.01	.00
☐ 84	Len Dykstra	.06	.02	.00
☐ 85	Jim Rice	.10	.04	.01
☐ 86	Jeff Treadway	.06	.02	.00
☐ 87	Jose Lind	.03	.01	.00
☐ 88	Willie McGee	.08	.03	.01
☐ 89	Mickey Brantley	.06	.02	.00
☐ 90	Tony Gwynn	.15	.06	.01
☐ 91	R.J. Reynolds	.03	.01	.00
☐ 92	Milt Thompson	.03	.01	.00
☐ 93	Kevin McReynolds	.15	.06	.01
☐ 94	Eddie Murray	.15	.06	.01
☐ 95	Lance Parrish	.08	.03	.01
☐ 96	Ron Kittle	.06	.02	.00
☐ 97	Gerald Young	.06	.02	.00
☐ 98	Ernie Whitt	.03	.01	.00
☐ 99	Jeff Reed	.03	.01	.00
☐ 100	Don Mattingly	.75	.30	.07
☐ 101	Gerald Perry	.08	.03	.01
☐ 102	Vance Law	.03	.01	.00
☐ 103	John Shelby	.03	.01	.00
☐ 104	Chris Sabo	.75	.30	.07
☐ 105	Danny Tartabull	.12	.05	.01
☐ 106	Glenn Wilson	.03	.01	.00
☐ 107	Mark Davidson	.03	.01	.00
☐ 108	Dave Parker	.08	.03	.01
☐ 109	Eric Davis	.25	.10	.02
☐ 110	Alan Trammell	.12	.05	.01
☐ 111	Ozzie Virgil	.03	.01	.00
☐ 112	Frank Tanana	.03	.01	.00
☐ 113	Rafael Ramirez	.03	.01	.00
☐ 114	Dennis Martinez	.03	.01	.00
☐ 115	Jose DeLeon	.03	.01	.00
☐ 116	Bob Ojeda	.06	.02	.00

☐ 117	Doug Drabek	.03	.01
☐ 118	Andy Hawkins	.03	.01
☐ 119	Greg Maddux	.15	.06
☐ 120	Cecil Fielder	.03	.01
☐ 121	Mike Scioscia	.03	.01
☐ 122	Dan Petry	.03	.01
☐ 123	Terry Kennedy	.03	.01
☐ 124	Kelly Downs	.03	.01
☐ 125	Greg Gross	.03	.01
☐ 126	Fred Lynn	.08	.03
☐ 127	Barry Bonds	.10	.04
☐ 128	Harold Baines	.08	.03
☐ 129	Doyle Alexander	.03	.01
☐ 130	Kevin Elster	.06	.02
☐ 131	Mike Heath	.03	.01
☐ 132	Teddy Higuera	.08	.03
☐ 133	Charlie Leibrandt	.03	.01
☐ 134	Tim Laudner	.03	.01
☐ 135	Ray Knight	.06	.02
☐ 136	Howard Johnson	.08	.03
☐ 137	Terry Pendleton	.03	.01
☐ 138	Andy McGaffigan	.03	.01
☐ 139	Ken Oberkfell	.03	.01
☐ 140	Butch Wynegar	.03	.01
☐ 141	Rob Murphy	.03	.01
☐ 142	Rich Renteria	.10	.04
☐ 143	Jose Guzman	.03	.01
☐ 144	Andres Galarraga	.12	.05
☐ 145	Ricky Horton	.03	.01
☐ 146	Frank DiPino	.03	.01
☐ 147	Glenn Braggs	.06	.02
☐ 148	John Kruk	.06	.02
☐ 149	Mike Schmidt	.20	.08
☐ 150	Lee Smith	.06	.02
☐ 151	Robin Yount	.12	.05
☐ 152	Mark Eichhorn	.03	.01
☐ 153	DeWayne Buice	.03	.01
☐ 154	B.J. Surhoff	.06	.02
☐ 155	Vince Coleman	.12	.05
☐ 156	Tony Phillips	.03	.01
☐ 157	Willie Fraser	.03	.01
☐ 158	Lance McCullers	.06	.02
☐ 159	Greg Gagne	.03	.01
☐ 160	Jesse Barfield	.10	.04
☐ 161	Mark Langston	.08	.03
☐ 162	Kurt Stillwell	.03	.01
☐ 163	Dion James	.03	.01
☐ 164	Glenn Davis	.10	.04
☐ 165	Walt Weiss	.40	.16
☐ 166	Dave Concepcion	.08	.03
☐ 167	Alfredo Griffin	.06	.02
☐ 168	Don Heinkel	.10	.04
☐ 169	Luis Rivera	.03	.01
☐ 170	Shane Rawley	.03	.01
☐ 171	Darrell Evans	.06	.02
☐ 172	Robby Thompson	.03	.01
☐ 173	Jody Davis	.06	.02
☐ 174	Andy Van Slyke	.10	.04
☐ 175	Wade Boggs	.50	.20
☐ 176	Garry Templeton	.06	.02
☐ 177	Gary Redus	.03	.01
☐ 178	Craig Lefferts	.03	.01
☐ 179	Carney Lansford	.06	.02
☐ 180	Ron Darling	.08	.03
☐ 181	Kirk McCaskill	.03	.01
☐ 182	Tony Armas	.06	.02
☐ 183	Steve Farr	.03	.01
☐ 184	Tom Brunansky	.08	.03
☐ 185	Bryan Harvey	.25	.10
☐ 186	Mike Marshall	.08	.03
☐ 187	Bo Diaz	.03	.01
☐ 188	Willie Upshaw	.03	.01
☐ 189	Mike Pagliarulo	.06	.02
☐ 190	Mike Krukow	.03	.01
☐ 191	Tommy Herr	.06	.02
☐ 192	Jim Pankovits	.03	.01
☐ 193	Dwight Evans	.08	.03
☐ 194	Kelly Gruber	.03	.01
☐ 195	Bobby Bonilla	.10	.04
☐ 196	Wallace Johnson	.03	.01
☐ 197	Dave Stieb	.08	.03
☐ 198	Pat Borders	.12	.05
☐ 199	Rafael Palmeiro	.10	.04
☐ 200	Doc Gooden	.30	.12
☐ 201	Pete Incaviglia	.10	.04
☐ 202	Chris James	.08	.03
☐ 203	Marvell Wynne	.03	.01
☐ 204	Pat Sheridan	.03	.01
☐ 205	Don Baylor	.08	.03
☐ 206	Paul O'Neill	.06	.02
☐ 207	Pete Smith	.10	.04
☐ 208	Mark McLemore	.03	.01
☐ 209	Henry Cotto	.03	.01
☐ 210	Kirk Gibson	.15	.06
☐ 211	Claudell Washington	.06	.02

□ 212	Randy Bush	.03	.01	.00
□ 213	Joe Carter	.10	.04	.01
□ 214	Bill Buckner	.06	.02	.00
□ 215	Bert Blyleven	.06	.02	.00
□ 216	Brett Butler	.06	.02	.00
□ 217	Lee Mazzilli	.03	.01	.00
□ 218	Spike Owen	.03	.01	.00
□ 219	Bill Swift	.03	.01	.00
□ 220	Tim Wallach	.06	.02	.00
□ 221	David Cone	.20	.08	.02
□ 222	Don Carman	.03	.01	.00
□ 223	Rich Gossage	.08	.03	.01
□ 224	Bob Walk	.06	.02	.00
□ 225	Dave Righetti	.08	.03	.01
□ 226	Kevin Bass	.06	.02	.00
□ 227	Kevin Gross	.03	.01	.00
□ 228	Tim Burke	.03	.01	.00
□ 229	Rick Mahler	.03	.01	.00
□ 230	Lou Whitaker	.08	.03	.01
□ 231	Luis Alicea	.12	.05	.01
□ 232	Roberto Alomar	.20	.08	.02
□ 233	Bob Boone	.06	.02	.00
□ 234	Dickie Thon	.03	.01	.00
□ 235	Shawon Dunston	.06	.02	.00
□ 236	Pete Stanicek	.06	.02	.00
□ 237	Craig Biggio	.12	.05	.01
□ 238	Dennis Boyd	.06	.02	.00
□ 239	Tom Candiotti	.03	.01	.00
□ 240	Gary Carter	.15	.06	.01
□ 241	Mike Stanley	.03	.01	.00
□ 242	Ken Phelps	.06	.02	.00
□ 243	Chris Bosio	.03	.01	.00
□ 244	Les Straker	.03	.01	.00
□ 245	Dave Smith	.03	.01	.00
□ 246	John Candelaria	.06	.02	.00
□ 247	Joe Orsulak	.03	.01	.00
□ 248	Storm Davis	.06	.02	.00
□ 249	Floyd Bannister	.03	.01	.00
□ 250	Jack Morris	.10	.04	.01
□ 251	Bret Saberhagen	.10	.04	.01
□ 252	Tom Niedenfuer	.03	.01	.00
□ 253	Neal Heaton	.03	.01	.00
□ 254	Eric Show	.03	.01	.00
□ 255	Juan Samuel	.08	.03	.01
□ 256	Dale Sveum	.03	.01	.00
□ 257	Jim Gott	.03	.01	.00
□ 258	Scott Garrelts	.03	.01	.00
□ 259	Larry McWilliams	.03	.01	.00
□ 260	Steve Bedrosian	.08	.03	.01
□ 261	Jack Howell	.03	.01	.00
□ 262	Jay Tibbs	.03	.01	.00
□ 263	Jamie Moyer	.03	.01	.00
□ 264	Doug Sisk	.03	.01	.00
□ 265	Todd Worrell	.08	.03	.01
□ 266	John Farrell	.03	.01	.00
□ 267	Dave Collins	.03	.01	.00
□ 268	Sid Fernandez	.08	.03	.01
□ 269	Tom Brookens	.03	.01	.00
□ 270	Shane Mack	.06	.02	.00
□ 271	Paul Kilgus	.03	.01	.00
□ 272	Chuck Crim	.03	.01	.00
□ 273	Bob Knepper	.03	.01	.00
□ 274	Mike Moore	.03	.01	.00
□ 275	Guillermo Hernandez	.06	.02	.00
□ 276	Dennis Eckersley	.10	.04	.01
□ 277	Graig Nettles	.08	.03	.01
□ 278	Rich Dotson	.06	.02	.00
□ 279	Larry Herndon	.03	.01	.00
□ 280	Gene Larkin	.06	.02	.00
□ 281	Roger McDowell	.06	.02	.00
□ 282	Greg Swindell	.08	.03	.01
□ 283	Juan Agosto	.03	.01	.00
□ 284	Jeff Robinson Detroit Tigers	.08	.03	.01
□ 285	Mike Dunne	.08	.03	.01
□ 286	Greg Mathews	.03	.01	.00
□ 287	Kent Tekulve	.03	.01	.00
□ 288	Jerry Mumphrey	.03	.01	.00
□ 289	Jack McDowell	.12	.05	.01
□ 290	Frank Viola	.12	.05	.01
□ 291	Mark Gubicza	.08	.03	.01
□ 292	Dave Schmidt	.03	.01	.00
□ 293	Mike Henneman	.03	.01	.00
□ 294	Jimmy Jones	.06	.02	.00
□ 295	Charlie Hough	.03	.01	.00
□ 296	Rafael Santana	.03	.01	.00
□ 297	Chris Speier	.03	.01	.00
□ 298	Mike Witt	.06	.02	.00
□ 299	Pascual Perez	.06	.02	.00
□ 300	Nolan Ryan	.15	.06	.01
□ 301	Mitch Williams	.03	.01	.00
□ 302	Mookie Wilson	.03	.01	.00
□ 303	Mackey Sasser	.08	.03	.01
□ 304	John Cerutti	.03	.01	.00
□ 305	Jeff Reardon	.06	.02	.00
□ 306	Randy Myers	.06	.02	.00
□ 307	Greg Brock	.03	.01	.00
□ 308	Bob Welch	.06	.02	.00
□ 309	Jeff Robinson Pittsburgh Pirates	.03	.01	.00
□ 310	Harold Reynolds	.03	.01	.00
□ 311	Jim Walewander	.03	.01	.00
□ 312	Dave Magadan	.06	.02	.00
□ 313	Jim Gantner	.03	.01	.00
□ 314	Walt Terrell	.03	.01	.00
□ 315	Wally Backman	.03	.01	.00
□ 316	Luis Salazar	.03	.01	.00
□ 317	Rick Rhoden	.03	.01	.00
□ 318	Tom Henke	.03	.01	.00
□ 319	Mike Macfarlane	.12	.05	.01
□ 320	Dan Plesac	.06	.02	.00
□ 321	Calvin Schiraldi	.03	.01	.00
□ 322	Stan Javier	.03	.01	.00
□ 323	Devon White	.08	.03	.01
□ 324	Scott Bradley	.03	.01	.00
□ 325	Bruce Hurst	.08	.03	.01
□ 326	Manny Lee	.03	.01	.00
□ 327	Rick Aguilera	.03	.01	.00
□ 328	Bruce Ruffin	.03	.01	.00
□ 329	Ed Whitson	.03	.01	.00
□ 330	Bo Jackson	.20	.08	.02
□ 331	Ivan Calderon	.08	.03	.01
□ 332	Mickey Hatcher	.06	.02	.00
□ 333	Barry Jones	.03	.01	.00
□ 334	Ron Hassey	.03	.01	.00
□ 335	Bill Wegman	.03	.01	.00
□ 336	Damon Berryhill	.20	.08	.02
□ 337	Steve Ontiveros	.03	.01	.00
□ 338	Dan Pasqua	.06	.02	.00
□ 339	Bill Pecota	.03	.01	.00
□ 340	Greg Cadaret	.08	.03	.01
□ 341	Scott Bankhead	.03	.01	.00
□ 342	Ron Guidry	.08	.03	.01
□ 343	Danny Heep	.03	.01	.00
□ 344	Bob Brower	.06	.02	.00
□ 345	Rich Gedman	.06	.02	.00
□ 346	Nelson Santovenia	.10	.04	.01
□ 347	George Bell	.10	.04	.01
□ 348	Ted Power	.03	.01	.00
□ 349	Mark Grant	.03	.01	.00
□ 350	Roger Clemens	.25	.10	.02
□ 351	Bill Long	.03	.01	.00
□ 352	Jay Bell	.08	.03	.01
□ 353	Steve Balboni	.03	.01	.00
□ 354	Bob Kipper	.03	.01	.00
□ 355	Steve Jeltz	.03	.01	.00
□ 356	Jesse Orosco	.03	.01	.00
□ 357	Bob Dernier	.03	.01	.00
□ 358	Mickey Tettleton	.03	.01	.00
□ 359	Duane Ward	.03	.01	.00
□ 360	Darrin Jackson	.12	.05	.01
□ 361	Rey Quinones	.03	.01	.00
□ 362	Mark Grace	.75	.30	.07
□ 363	Steve Lake	.03	.01	.00
□ 364	Pat Perry	.03	.01	.00
□ 365	Terry Steinbach	.08	.03	.01
□ 366	Alan Ashby	.03	.01	.00
□ 367	Jeff Montgomery	.03	.01	.00
□ 368	Steve Buechele	.03	.01	.00
□ 369	Chris Brown	.06	.02	.00
□ 370	Orel Hershiser	.20	.08	.02
□ 371	Todd Benzinger	.06	.02	.00
□ 372	Ron Gant	.12	.05	.01
□ 373	Paul Assenmacher	.03	.01	.00
□ 374	Joey Meyer	.12	.05	.01
□ 375	Neil Allen	.03	.01	.00
□ 376	Mike Davis	.03	.01	.00
□ 377	Jeff Parrett	.08	.03	.01
□ 378	Jay Howell	.03	.01	.00
□ 379	Rafael Belliard	.03	.01	.00
□ 380	Luis Polonia	.03	.01	.00
□ 381	Keith Atherton	.03	.01	.00
□ 382	Kent Hrbek	.10	.04	.01
□ 383	Bob Stanley	.03	.01	.00
□ 384	Dave LaPoint	.03	.01	.00
□ 385	Rance Mulliniks	.03	.01	.00
□ 386	Melido Perez	.15	.06	.01
□ 387	Doug Jones	.06	.02	.00
□ 388	Steve Lyons	.03	.01	.00
□ 389	Alejandro Pena	.03	.01	.00
□ 390	Frank White	.06	.02	.00
□ 391	Pat Tabler	.06	.02	.00
□ 392	Eric Plunk	.03	.01	.00
□ 393	Mike Maddux	.03	.01	.00
□ 394	Allan Anderson	.06	.02	.00
□ 395	Bob Brenly	.03	.01	.00
□ 396	Rick Cerone	.03	.01	.00
□ 397	Scott Terry	.03	.01	.00
□ 398	Mike Jackson	.03	.01	.00
□ 399	Bobby Thigpen	.06	.02	.00

□ 400	Don Sutton	.10	.04	.01
□ 401	Cecil Espy	.10	.04	.01
□ 402	Junior Ortiz	.03	.01	.00
□ 403	Mike Smithson	.03	.01	.00
□ 404	Bud Black	.03	.01	.00
□ 405	Tom Foley	.03	.01	.00
□ 406	Andres Thomas	.03	.01	.00
□ 407	Rick Sutcliffe	.08	.03	.01
□ 408	Brian Harper	.03	.01	.00
□ 409	John Smiley	.03	.01	.00
□ 410	Juan Nieves	.03	.01	.00
□ 411	Shawn Abner	.06	.02	.00
□ 412	Wes Gardner	.08	.03	.01
□ 413	Darren Daulton	.03	.01	.00
□ 414	Juan Berenguer	.03	.01	.00
□ 415	Charles Hudson	.03	.01	.00
□ 416	Rick Honeycutt	.03	.01	.00
□ 417	Greg Booker	.03	.01	.00
□ 418	Tim Belcher	.08	.03	.01
□ 419	Don August	.06	.02	.00
□ 420	Dale Mohorcic	.03	.01	.00
□ 421	Steve Lombardozzi	.03	.01	.00
□ 422	Atlee Hammaker	.03	.01	.00
□ 423	Jerry Don Gleaton	.03	.01	.00
□ 424	Scott Bailes	.03	.01	.00
□ 425	Bruce Sutter	.08	.03	.01
□ 426	Randy Ready	.03	.01	.00
□ 427	Jerry Reed	.03	.01	.00
□ 428	Bryn Smith	.03	.01	.00
□ 429	Tim Leary	.06	.02	.00
□ 430	Mark Clear	.03	.01	.00
□ 431	Terry Leach	.06	.02	.00
□ 432	John Moses	.03	.01	.00
□ 433	Ozzie Guillen	.06	.02	.00
□ 434	Gene Nelson	.03	.01	.00
□ 435	Gary Ward	.03	.01	.00
□ 436	Luis Aguayo	.03	.01	.00
□ 437	Fernando Valenzuela	.10	.04	.01
□ 438	Jeff Russell	.03	.01	.00
□ 439	Cecilio Guante	.03	.01	.00
□ 440	Don Robinson	.03	.01	.00
□ 441	Rick Anderson	.03	.01	.00
□ 442	Tom Glavine	.03	.01	.00
□ 443	Daryl Boston	.03	.01	.00
□ 444	Joe Price	.03	.01	.00
□ 445	Stewart Cliburn	.03	.01	.00
□ 446	Manny Trillo	.03	.01	.00
□ 447	Joel Skinner	.03	.01	.00
□ 448	Charlie Puleo	.03	.01	.00
□ 449	Carlton Fisk	.08	.03	.01
□ 450	Will Clark	.25	.10	.02
□ 451	Otis Nixon	.03	.01	.00
□ 452	Rick Schu	.03	.01	.00
□ 453	Todd Stottlemyre	.12	.05	.01
□ 454	Tim Birtsas	.03	.01	.00
□ 455	Dave Gallagher	.15	.06	.01
□ 456	Barry Lyons	.03	.01	.00
□ 457	Fred Manrique	.03	.01	.00
□ 458	Ernest Riles	.03	.01	.00
□ 459	Doug Jennings	.20	.08	.02
□ 460	Joe Magrane	.06	.02	.00
□ 461	Jamie Quirk	.03	.01	.00
□ 462	Jack Armstrong	.20	.08	.02
□ 463	Bobby Witt	.06	.02	.00
□ 464	Keith Miller New York Mets	.03	.01	.00
□ 465	Todd Burns	.20	.08	.02
□ 466	John Dopson	.12	.05	.01
□ 467	Rich Yett	.03	.01	.00
□ 468	Craig Reynolds	.03	.01	.00
□ 469	Dave Bergman	.03	.01	.00
□ 470	Rex Hudler	.03	.01	.00
□ 471	Eric King	.03	.01	.00
□ 472	Joaquin Andujar	.06	.02	.00
□ 473	Sil Campusano	.25	.10	.02
□ 474	Terry Mulholland	.03	.01	.00
□ 475	Mike Flanagan	.06	.02	.00
□ 476	Greg Harris Philadelphia Phillies	.03	.01	.00
□ 477	Tommy John	.08	.03	.01
□ 478	Dave Anderson	.03	.01	.00
□ 479	Fred Toliver	.03	.01	.00
□ 480	Jimmy Key	.06	.02	.00
□ 481	Donell Nixon	.03	.01	.00
□ 482	Mark Portugal	.03	.01	.00
□ 483	Tom Pagnozzi	.03	.01	.00
□ 484	Jeff Kunkel	.03	.01	.00
□ 485	Frank Williams	.03	.01	.00
□ 486	Jody Reed	.08	.03	.01
□ 487	Roberto Kelly	.12	.05	.01
□ 488	Shawn Hillegas	.03	.01	.00
□ 489	Jerry Reuss	.03	.01	.00
□ 490	Mark Davis	.06	.02	.00
□ 491	Jeff Sellers	.03	.01	.00
□ 492	Zane Smith	.06	.02	.00
□ 493	Al Newman	.03	.01	.00
□ 494	Mike Young	.03	.01	.00
□ 495	Larry Parrish	.03	.01	.00
□ 496	Herm Winningham	.03	.01	.00
□ 497	Carmen Castillo	.03	.01	.00
□ 498	Joe Hesketh	.03	.01	.00
□ 499	Darrell Miller	.03	.01	.00
□ 500	Mike LaCoss	.03	.01	.00
□ 501	Charlie Lea	.03	.01	.00
□ 502	Bruce Benedict	.03	.01	.00
□ 503	Chuck Finley	.03	.01	.00
□ 504	Brad Wellman	.03	.01	.00
□ 505	Tim Crews	.03	.01	.00
□ 506	Ken Gerhart	.06	.02	.00
□ 507	Brian Holton	.03	.01	.00
□ 508	Dennis Lamp	.03	.01	.00
□ 509	Bobby Meacham	.03	.01	.00
□ 510	Tracy Jones	.06	.02	.00
□ 511	Mike Fitzgerald Montreal Expos	.03	.01	.00
□ 512	Jeff Bittiger	.12	.05	.01
□ 513	Tim Flannery	.03	.01	.00
□ 514	Ray Hayward	.08	.03	.01
□ 515	Dave Leiper	.03	.01	.00
□ 516	Rod Scurry	.03	.01	.00
□ 517	Carmelo Martinez	.03	.01	.00
□ 518	Curtis Wilkerson	.03	.01	.00
□ 519	Stan Jefferson	.08	.03	.01
□ 520	Dan Quisenberry	.08	.03	.01
□ 521	Lloyd McClendon	.08	.03	.01
□ 522	Steve Trout	.03	.01	.00
□ 523	Larry Andersen	.03	.01	.00
□ 524	Don Aase	.03	.01	.00
□ 525	Bob Forsch	.03	.01	.00
□ 526	Geno Petralli	.03	.01	.00
□ 527	Angel Salazar	.03	.01	.00
□ 528	Mike Schooler	.12	.05	.01
□ 529	Jose Oquendo	.03	.01	.00
□ 530	Jay Buhner	.15	.06	.01
□ 531	Tom Bolton	.10	.04	.01
□ 532	Al Nipper	.03	.01	.00
□ 533	Dave Henderson	.06	.02	.00
□ 534	John Costello	.12	.05	.01
□ 535	Donnie Moore	.03	.01	.00
□ 536	Mike Laga	.03	.01	.00
□ 537	Mike Gallego	.03	.01	.00
□ 538	Jim Clancy	.03	.01	.00
□ 539	Joel Youngblood	.03	.01	.00
□ 540	Rick Leach	.03	.01	.00
□ 541	Kevin Romine	.03	.01	.00
□ 542	Mark Salas	.03	.01	.00
□ 543	Greg Minton	.03	.01	.00
□ 544	Dave Palmer	.03	.01	.00
□ 545	Dwayne Murphy	.03	.01	.00
□ 546	Jim Deshaies	.03	.01	.00
□ 547	Don Gordon	.08	.03	.01
□ 548	Ricky Jordan	1.00	.40	.10
□ 549	Mike Boddicker	.06	.02	.00
□ 550	Mike Scott	.10	.04	.01
□ 551	Jeff Ballard	.08	.03	.01
□ 552	Jose Rijo	.03	.01	.00
□ 553	Danny Darwin	.03	.01	.00
□ 554	Tom Browning	.08	.03	.01
□ 555	Danny Jackson	.10	.04	.01
□ 556	Rick Dempsey	.03	.01	.00
□ 557	Jeffrey Leonard	.06	.02	.00
□ 558	Jeff Musselman	.03	.01	.00
□ 559	Ron Robinson	.03	.01	.00
□ 560	John Tudor	.08	.03	.01
□ 561	Don Slaught	.03	.01	.00
□ 562	Dennis Rasmussen	.06	.02	.00
□ 563	Brady Anderson	.20	.08	.02
□ 564	Pedro Guerrero	.10	.04	.01
□ 565	Paul Molitor	.10	.04	.01
□ 566	Terry Clark	.15	.06	.01
□ 567	Terry Puhl	.03	.01	.00
□ 568	Mike Campbell	.12	.05	.01
□ 569	Paul Mirabella	.03	.01	.00
□ 570	Jeff Hamilton	.03	.01	.00
□ 571	Oswald Peraza	.10	.04	.01
□ 572	Bob McClure	.03	.01	.00
□ 573	Jose Bautista	.10	.04	.01
□ 574	Alex Trevino	.03	.01	.00
□ 575	John Franco	.06	.02	.00
□ 576	Mark Parent	.10	.04	.01
□ 577	Nelson Liriano	.03	.01	.00
□ 578	Steve Shields	.03	.01	.00
□ 579	Odell Jones	.03	.01	.00
□ 580	Al Leiter	.20	.08	.02
□ 581	Dave Stapleton	.10	.04	.01
□ 582	World Series '88 Orel Hershiser Jose Canseco Kirk Gibson Dave Stewart	.15	.06	.01

No.	Player	MINT	EXC	G-VG
583	Donnie Hill	.03	.01	.00
584	Chuck Jackson	.03	.01	.00
585	Rene Gonzales	.10	.04	.01
586	Tracy Woodson	.08	.03	.01
587	Jim Adduci	.03	.01	.00
588	Mario Soto	.03	.01	.00
589	Jeff Blauser	.03	.01	.00
590	Jim Traber	.03	.01	.00
591	Jon Perlman	.08	.03	.01
592	Mark Williamson	.08	.03	.01
593	Dave Meads	.03	.01	.00
594	Jim Eisenreich	.03	.01	.00
595	Paul Gibson	.10	.04	.01
596	Mike Birkbeck	.03	.01	.00
597	Terry Francona	.03	.01	.00
598	Paul Zuvella	.03	.01	.00
599	Franklin Stubbs	.03	.01	.00
600	Gregg Jefferies	1.50	.60	.15
601	John Cangelosi	.03	.01	.00
602	Mike Sharperson	.03	.01	.00
603	Mike Diaz	.03	.01	.00
604	Gary Varsho	.15	.06	.01
605	Terry Blocker	.12	.05	.01
606	Charlie O'Brien	.10	.04	.01
607	Jim Eppard	.10	.04	.01
608	John Davis	.03	.01	.00
609	Ken Griffey Sr.	.06	.02	.00
610	Buddy Bell	.08	.03	.01
611	Ted Simmons	.08	.03	.01
612	Matt Williams	.08	.03	.01
613	Danny Cox	.06	.02	.00
614	Al Pedrique	.03	.01	.00
615	Ron Oester	.03	.01	.00
616	John Smoltz	.20	.08	.02
617	Bob Melvin	.03	.01	.00
618	Rob Dibble	.12	.05	.01
619	Kirt Manwaring	.03	.01	.00
620	Felix Fermin	.10	.04	.01
621	Doug Dascenzo	.15	.06	.01
622	Bill Brennan	.15	.06	.01
623	Carlos Quintana	.30	.12	.03
624	Mike Harkey	.50	.20	.05
625	Gary Sheffield	1.25	.50	.12
626	Tom Prince	.10	.04	.01
627	Steve Searcy	.25	.10	.02
628	Charlie Hayes	.15	.06	.01
629	Felix Jose	.25	.10	.02
630	Sandy Alomar	.90	.36	.09
631	Derek Lilliquist	.20	.08	.02
632	Geronimo Berroa	.20	.08	.02
633	Luis Medina	.40	.16	.04
634	Tom Gordon	.25	.10	.02
635	Ramon Martinez	.25	.10	.02
636	Craig Worthington	.25	.10	.02
637	Edgar Martinez	.12	.05	.01
638	Chad Kreuter	.20	.08	.02
639	Ron Jones	.30	.12	.03
640	Van Snider	.20	.08	.02
641	Lance Blankenship	.15	.06	.01
642	Dwight Smith	.20	.08	.02
643	Cameron Drew	.20	.08	.02
644	Jerald Clark	.20	.08	.02
645	Randy Johnson	.20	.08	.02
646	Norm Charlton	.12	.05	.01
647	Todd Frohwirth	.08	.03	.01
648	Luis De Los Santos	.25	.10	.02
649	Tim Jones	.15	.06	.01
650	Dave West	.40	.16	.04
651	Bob Milacki	.25	.10	.02
652	Wrigley Field HL (Let There Be Lights)	.06	.02	.00
653	Orel Hershiser HL (The Streak)	.15	.06	.01
654	Wade Boggs HL (Wade Whacks 'Em)	.20	.08	.02
655	Jose Canseco HL (One of a Kind)	.35	.14	.03
656	Doug Jones HL (Doug Sets Saves)	.06	.02	.00
657	Rickey Henderson HL (Rickey Rocks 'Em)	.12	.05	.01
658	Tom Browning HL (Tom Perfect Pitches)	.06	.02	.00
659	Mike Greenwell HL (Greenwell Gamers)	.25	.10	.02
660	Boston Red Sox HL (Joe Morgan MG, Sox Sock 'Em)	.06	.02	.00

1989 Score Hottest 100 Rookies

This set was distributed by Publications International in January 1989 through many retail stores and chains; the card set was packaged along with a colorful 48-page book for a suggested retail price of 12.95. The cards measure the standard 2 1/2" by 3 1/2" and show full color on both sides of the card. The cards were produced by Score as indicated on the card backs. The set is subtitled "Rising Star" on the reverse. The first six cards (#1-#6) of a 12-card set of Score's trivia cards, subtitled "Rookies to Remember" is included along with each set. The cards are numbered on the back. This set is distinguished by the sharp blue borders and the player's first initial inside a yellow triangle in the lower left corner of the obverse.

	MINT	EXC	G-VG
COMPLETE SET (100)	12.50	5.00	1.25
COMMON PLAYER (1-100)	.05	.02	.00

No.	Player	MINT	EXC	G-VG
1	Gregg Jefferies	1.50	.60	.15
2	Vicente Palacios	.05	.02	.00
3	Cameron Drew	.25	.10	.02
4	Doug Dascenzo	.15	.06	.01
5	Luis Medina	.35	.14	.03
6	Craig Worthington	.15	.06	.01
7	Rob Ducey	.10	.04	.01
8	Hal Morris	.15	.06	.01
9	Bill Brennan	.15	.06	.01
10	Gary Sheffield	1.00	.40	.10
11	Mike Devereaux	.15	.06	.01
12	Hensley Meulens	.75	.30	.07
13	Carlos Quintana	.25	.10	.02
14	Todd Frohwirth	.05	.02	.00
15	Scott Lusader	.05	.02	.00
16	Mark Carreon	.10	.04	.01
17	Torey Lovullo	.15	.06	.01
18	Randy Velarde	.05	.02	.00
19	Billy Bean	.05	.02	.00
20	Lance Blankenship	.15	.06	.01
21	Chris Gwynn	.15	.06	.01
22	Felix Jose	.25	.10	.02
23	Derek Lilliquist	.05	.02	.00
24	Gary Thurman	.10	.04	.01
25	Ron Jones	.15	.06	.01
26	Dave Justice	.10	.04	.01
27	Johnny Paredes	.05	.02	.00
28	Tim Jones	.10	.04	.01
29	Jose Gonzales	.10	.04	.01
30	Geronimo Berroa	.10	.04	.01
31	Trevor Wilson	.10	.04	.01
32	Morris Madden	.05	.02	.00
33	Lance Johnson	.10	.04	.01
34	Marvin Freeman	.05	.02	.00
35	Jose Cecena	.05	.02	.00
36	Jim Corsi	.10	.04	.01
37	Rolando Roomes	.15	.06	.01
38	Scott Medvin	.05	.02	.00
39	Charlie Hayes	.10	.04	.01
40	Edgar Martinez	.15	.06	.01
41	Van Snider	.15	.06	.01
42	John Fishel	.10	.04	.01
43	Bruce Fields	.05	.02	.00
44	Darryl Hamilton	.15	.06	.01
45	Tom Prince	.10	.04	.01
46	Kirt Manwaring	.15	.06	.01

☐	47 Steve Searcy	.25	.10	.02
☐	48 Mike Harkey	.50	.20	.05
☐	49 German Gonzalez	.05	.02	.00
☐	50 Tony Perezchica	.10	.04	.01
☐	51 Chad Krueter	.15	.06	.01
☐	52 Luis De los Santos	.25	.10	.02
☐	53 Steve Curry	.10	.04	.01
☐	54 Greg Briley	.05	.02	.00
☐	55 Ramon Martinez	.25	.10	.02
☐	56 Ron Tingley	.10	.04	.01
☐	57 Randy Kramer	.05	.02	.00
☐	58 Alex Madrid	.10	.04	.01
☐	59 Kevin Reimer	.05	.02	.00
☐	60 Dave Otto	.10	.04	.01
☐	61 Ken Patterson	.05	.02	.00
☐	62 Keith Miller	.10	.04	.01
☐	63 Randy Johnson	.20	.08	.02
☐	64 Dwight Smith	.05	.02	.00
☐	65 Eric Yelding	.10	.04	.01
☐	66 Bob Geren	.10	.04	.01
☐	67 Shane Turner	.15	.06	.01
☐	68 Tom Gordon	.25	.10	.02
☐	69 Jeff Huson	.10	.04	.01
☐	70 Marty Brown	.15	.06	.01
☐	71 Nelson Santovenia	.10	.04	.01
☐	72 Roberto Alomar	.20	.08	.02
☐	73 Mike Schooler	.15	.06	.01
☐	74 Pete Smith	.10	.04	.01
☐	75 John Costello	.15	.06	.01
☐	76 Chris Sabo	.50	.20	.05
☐	77 Damon Berryhill	.30	.12	.03
☐	78 Mark Grace	.75	.30	.07
☐	79 Melido Perez	.15	.06	.01
☐	80 Al Leiter	.25	.10	.02
☐	81 Todd Stottlemyre	.15	.06	.01
☐	82 Mackey Sasser	.15	.06	.01
☐	83 Don August	.15	.06	.01
☐	84 Jeff Treadway	.15	.06	.01
☐	85 Jody Reed	.15	.06	.01
☐	86 Mike Campbell	.10	.04	.01
☐	87 Ron Gant	.35	.14	.03
☐	88 Ricky Jordan	.75	.30	.07
☐	89 Terry Clark	.15	.06	.01
☐	90 Roberto Kelly	.15	.06	.01
☐	91 Pat Borders	.10	.04	.01
☐	92 Bryan Harvey	.15	.06	.01
☐	93 Joey Meyer	.15	.06	.01
☐	94 Tim Belcher	.15	.06	.01
☐	95 Walt Weiss	.45	.18	.04
☐	96 Dave Gallagher	.15	.06	.01
☐	97 Mike Macfarlane	.10	.04	.01
☐	98 Craig Biggio	.10	.04	.01
☐	99 Jack Armstrong	.15	.06	.01
☐	100 Todd Burns	.15	.06	.01

1989 Score Hottest 100 Stars

This set was distributed by Publications International in January 1989 through many retail stores and chains; the card set was packaged along with a colorful 48-page book for a suggested retail price of 12.95. The cards measure the standard 2 1/2" by 3 1/2" and show full color on both sides of the card. The cards were produced by Score as indicated on the card backs. The set is subtitled "Superstar" on the reverse. The last six cards (#7-#12) of a 12-card set of Score's trivia cards, subtitled "Rookies to Remember" is included along with each set. The cards are numbered on the back. This set is distinguished by the sharp red borders and the player's first initial inside a yellow triangle in the upper left corner of the obverse.

		MINT	EXC	G-V
	COMPLETE SET (100)	12.50	5.00	1.2
	COMMON PLAYER (1-100)	.05	.02	.0
☐	1 Jose Canseco	1.50	.60	.1
☐	2 David Cone	.35	.14	.0
☐	3 Dave Winfield	.35	.14	.0
☐	4 George Brett	.35	.14	.0
☐	5 Frank Viola	.25	.10	.0
☐	6 Cory Snyder	.25	.10	.0
☐	7 Alan Trammell	.25	.10	.0
☐	8 Dwight Evans	.15	.06	.0
☐	9 Tim Leary	.10	.04	.0
☐	10 Don Mattingly	1.00	.40	.1
☐	11 Kirby Puckett	.75	.30	.0
☐	12 Carney Lansford	.10	.04	.0
☐	13 Dennis Martinez	.05	.02	.0
☐	14 Kent Hrbek	.20	.08	.0
☐	15 Doc Gooden	.35	.14	.0
☐	16 Dennis Eckersley	.15	.06	.0
☐	17 Kevin Seitzer	.35	.14	.0
☐	18 Lee Smith	.05	.02	.0
☐	19 Danny Tartabull	.25	.10	.0
☐	20 Gerald Perry	.10	.04	.0
☐	21 Gary Gaetti	.15	.06	.0
☐	22 Rick Reuschel	.10	.04	.0
☐	23 Keith Hernandez	.20	.08	.0
☐	24 Jeff Reardon	.05	.02	.0
☐	25 Mark McGwire	.75	.30	.0
☐	26 Juan Samuel	.10	.04	.0
☐	27 Jack Clark	.15	.06	.0
☐	28 Robin Yount	.25	.10	.0
☐	29 Steve Bedrosian	.10	.04	.0
☐	30 Kirk Gibson	.30	.12	.0
☐	31 Barry Bonds	.25	.10	.02
☐	32 Dan Plesac	.10	.04	.01
☐	33 Steve Sax	.20	.08	.02
☐	34 Jeff Robinson	.10	.04	.01
☐	35 Orel Hershiser	.65	.26	.06
☐	36 Julio Franco	.10	.04	.01
☐	37 Dave Righetti	.10	.04	.01
☐	38 Bob Knepper	.05	.02	.00
☐	39 Carlton Fisk	.10	.04	.01
☐	40 Tony Gwynn	.30	.12	.03
☐	41 Doug Jones	.05	.02	.00
☐	42 Bobby Bonilla	.25	.10	.02
☐	43 Ellis Burks	.30	.12	.03
☐	44 Pedro Guerrero	.20	.08	.02
☐	45 Rickey Henderson	.25	.10	.02
☐	46 Glenn Davis	.20	.08	.02
☐	47 Benny Santiago	.25	.10	.02
☐	48 Greg Maddux	.15	.06	.01
☐	49 Teddy Higuera	.10	.04	.01
☐	50 Darryl Strawberry	.45	.18	.04
☐	51 Ozzie Guillen	.10	.04	.01
☐	52 Barry Larkin	.15	.06	.01
☐	53 Tony Fernandez	.15	.06	.01
☐	54 Ryne Sandberg	.20	.08	.02
☐	55 Joe Carter	.15	.06	.01
☐	56 Rafael Palmeiro	.15	.06	.01
☐	57 Paul Molitor	.15	.06	.01
☐	58 Eric Davis	.75	.30	.07
☐	59 Mike Henneman	.10	.04	.01
☐	60 Mike Scott	.15	.06	.01
☐	61 Tom Browning	.10	.04	.01
☐	62 Mark Davis	.05	.02	.00
☐	63 Tom Henke	.05	.02	.00
☐	64 Nolan Ryan	.35	.14	.03
☐	65 Fred McGriff	.50	.20	.05
☐	66 Dale Murphy	.40	.16	.04
☐	67 Mark Langston	.10	.04	.01
☐	68 Bobby Thigpen	.10	.04	.01
☐	69 Mark Gubicza	.10	.04	.01
☐	70 Mike Greenwell	1.00	.40	.10
☐	71 Ron Darling	.15	.06	.01
☐	72 Gerald Young	.10	.04	.01
☐	73 Wally Joyner	.35	.14	.03
☐	74 Andres Galarraga	.25	.10	.02
☐	75 Danny Jackson	.15	.06	.01
☐	76 Mike Schmidt	.40	.16	.04
☐	77 Cal Ripken Jr.	.25	.10	.02
☐	78 Alvin Davis	.10	.04	.01
☐	79 Bruce Hurst	.15	.06	.01
☐	80 Andre Dawson	.25	.10	.02
☐	81 Bob Boone	.10	.04	.01
☐	82 Harold Reynolds	.05	.02	.00
☐	83 Eddie Murray	.25	.10	.02

☐ 84 Robby Thompson	.10	.04	.01
☐ 85 Will Clark	.75	.30	.07
☐ 86 Vince Coleman	.20	.08	.02
☐ 87 Doug Drabek	.05	.02	.00
☐ 88 Ozzie Smith	.20	.08	.02
☐ 89 Bob Welch	.05	.02	.00
☐ 90 Roger Clemens	.60	.24	.06
☐ 91 George Bell	.20	.08	.02
☐ 92 Andy Van Slyke	.20	.08	.02
☐ 93 Willie McGee	.15	.06	.01
☐ 94 Todd Worrell	.15	.06	.01
☐ 95 Tim Raines	.25	.10	.02
☐ 96 Kevin McReynolds	.35	.14	.03
☐ 97 John Franco	.10	.04	.01
☐ 98 Jim Gott	.05	.02	.00
☐ 99 Johnny Ray	.05	.02	.00
☐ 100 Wade Boggs	1.00	.40	.10

1985 7-Eleven Twins

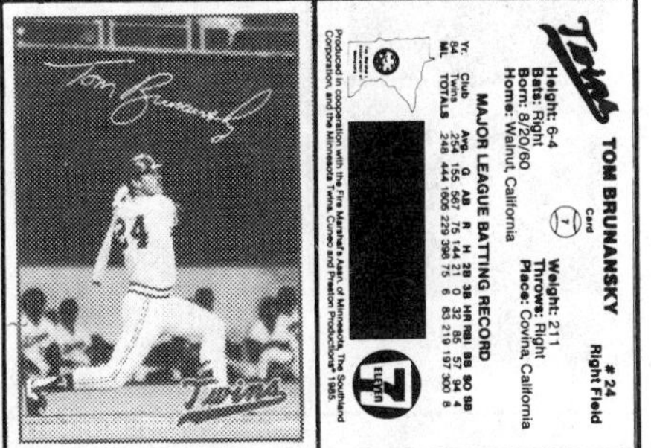

This 13-card set of Minnesota Twins was produced and distributed by the Twins in conjunction with the 7-Eleven stores and the Fire Marshall's Association. The cards measure approximately 2 1/2" by 3 1/2" and are in full color. Supposedly 20,000 sets of cards were distributed during the promotion which began on June 2nd and lasted throughout the month of July. The card backs have some statistics and a fire safety tip.

	MINT	EXC	G-VG
COMPLETE SET (13)	6.00	2.40	.60
COMMON PLAYER (1-13)	.25	.10	.02
☐ 1 Kirby Puckett	2.00	.80	.20
☐ 2 Frank Viola	1.00	.40	.10
☐ 3 Mickey Hatcher	.25	.10	.02
☐ 4 Kent Hrbek	1.00	.40	.10
☐ 5 John Butcher	.25	.10	.02
☐ 6 Roy Smalley	.25	.10	.02
☐ 7 Tom Brunansky	.50	.20	.05
☐ 8 Ron Davis	.25	.10	.02
☐ 9 Gary Gaetti	1.00	.40	.10
☐ 10 Tim Teufel	.25	.10	.02
☐ 11 Mike Smithson	.25	.10	.02
☐ 12 Tim Laudner	.35	.14	.03
☐ xx Checklist Card	.25	.10	.02

1984 Smokey Angels

The cards in this 32-card set measure 2 1/2" by 3 3/4" and feature the California Angels in full color. Sets were given out to persons 15 and under attending the June 16th game against the Indians. Unlike the Padres set of this year, Smokey the Bear is not featured on these cards. The player's photo, the Angels' logo, and the Smokey the Bear logo appear on the front, in addition to the California Department of Forestry and the U.S. Forest Service logos. The abbreviated backs contain short biographical data, career statistics, and an anti-wildfire hint from the player on the front. Since the cards are unnumbered, they are ordered and numbered below alphabetically by the player's name.

	MINT	EXC	G-VG
COMPLETE SET (32)	8.00	3.25	.80
COMMON PLAYER (1-32)	.20	.08	.02
☐ 1 Don Aase	.20	.08	.02
☐ 2 Juan Beniquez	.20	.08	.02
☐ 3 Bob Boone	.40	.16	.04
☐ 4 Rick Burleson	.30	.12	.03
☐ 5 Rod Carew	1.00	.40	.10
☐ 6 John Curtis	.20	.08	.02
☐ 7 Doug DeCinces	.30	.12	.03
☐ 8 Brian Downing	.40	.16	.04
☐ 9 Ken Forsch	.20	.08	.02
☐ 10 Bobby Grich	.30	.12	.03
☐ 11 Reggie Jackson	1.50	.60	.15
☐ 12 Ron Jackson	.20	.08	.02
☐ 13 Tommy John	.60	.24	.06
☐ 14 Curt Kaufman	.20	.08	.02
☐ 15 Bruce Kison	.20	.08	.02
☐ 16 Frank LaCorte	.20	.08	.02
☐ 17 Logo Card (Forestry Dept.)	.20	.08	.02
☐ 18 Fred Lynn	.50	.20	.05
☐ 19 John McNamara MG	.20	.08	.02
☐ 20 Jerry Narron	.20	.08	.02
☐ 21 Gary Pettis	.30	.12	.03
☐ 22 Rob Picciolo	.20	.08	.02
☐ 23 Ron Romanick	.20	.08	.02
☐ 24 Luis Sanchez	.20	.08	.02
☐ 25 Dick Schofield	.30	.12	.03
☐ 26 Daryl Sconiers	.20	.08	.02
☐ 27 Jim Slaton	.20	.08	.02
☐ 28 Smokey the Bear	.20	.08	.02
☐ 29 Ellis Valentine	.20	.08	.02
☐ 30 Rob Wilfong	.20	.08	.02
☐ 31 Mike Witt	.50	.20	.05
☐ 32 Geoff Zahn	.20	.08	.02

1984 Smokey Dodgers

This four-card set was not widely distributed and has not proven to be very popular with collectors. Cards were supposedly distributed by fire agencies in Southern California at fairs, mall displays, and special events. Cards are approximately 5" by 7" and feature a color picture of Smokey the Bear with a Dodger. The cards were printed on relatively thin card stock; printing on the back is black on white.

	MINT	EXC	G-VG
COMPLETE SET (4)	10.00	4.00	1.00
COMMON PLAYER (1-4)	1.00	.40	.10
☐ 1 Ken Landreaux with Smokey	2.00	.80	.20
☐ 2 Tom Niedenfuer with Smokey	2.00	.80	.20

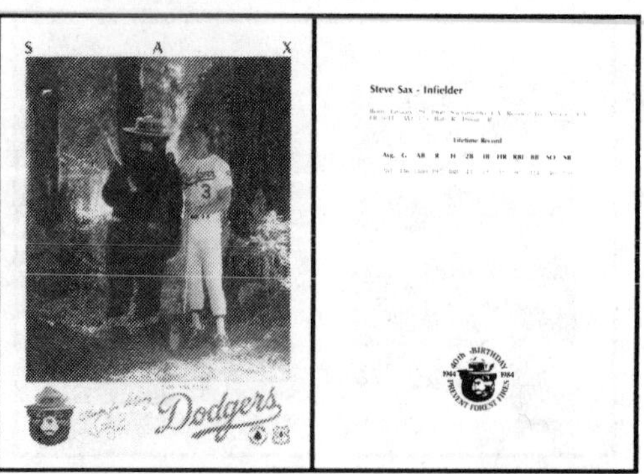

	MINT	EXC	G-VG
□ 3 Steve Sax with Smokey	6.00	2.40	.60
□ 4 Smokey the Bear (batting pose)	1.00	.40	.10

1984 Smokey Padres

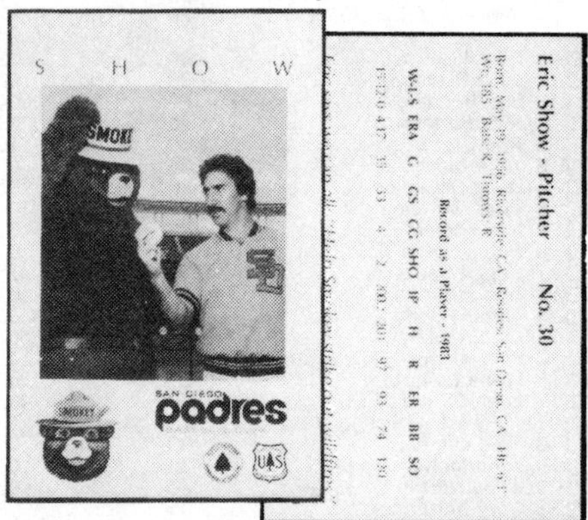

The cards in this 29-card set measure 2 1/2" by 3 3/4". This unnumbered, full color set features the Fire Prevention Bear and a Padres player, coach, manager, or associate on each card. The set was given out at the ballpark at the May 14th game against the Expos. Logos of the California Department of Forestry and the U.S. Forest Service appear in conjunction with a Smokey the Bear logo on the obverse. The set commemorates the 40th birthday of Smokey the Bear. The backs contain short biographical data, statistics and a fire prevention hint from the player pictured on the front.

	MINT	EXC	G-VG
COMPLETE SET (29)	9.00	3.75	.90
COMMON PLAYER (1-29)	.25	.10	.02
□ 1 Kurt Bevacqua	.25	.10	.02
□ 2 Bobby Brown	.25	.10	.02
□ 3 Dave Campbell (Broadcast Team)	.25	.10	.02
□ 4 The Chicken (Mascot)	.35	.14	.03
□ 5 Jerry Coleman (Broadcast Team)	.25	.10	.02
□ 6 Luis DeLeon	.25	.10	.02
□ 7 Dave Dravecky	.35	.14	.03
□ 8 Harry Dunlop CO	.25	.10	.02
□ 9 Tim Flannery	.25	.10	.02
□ 10 Steve Garvey	1.25	.50	.12
□ 11 Doug Gwosdz	.25	.10	.02
□ 12 Tony Gwynn	1.75	.70	.17
□ 13 Harold (Doug) Harvey (ex-UMP)	.25	.10	.02
□ 14 Terry Kennedy	.25	.10	.02
□ 15 Jack Krol COACH	.25	.10	.02
□ 16 Tim Lollar	.25	.10	.02
□ 17 Jack McKeon (VP for Baseball Operations)	.35	.14	.03
□ 18 Kevin McReynolds	1.25	.50	.12
□ 19 Sid Monge	.25	.10	.02
□ 20 Luis Salazar	.35	.14	.03
□ 21 Norm Sherry CO	.25	.10	.02
□ 22 Eric Show	.35	.14	.03
□ 23 Smokey the Bear	.25	.10	.02
□ 24 Garry Templeton	.35	.14	.03
□ 25 Mark Thurmond	.35	.14	.03
□ 26 Ozzie Virgil CO	.25	.10	.02
□ 27 Ed Whitson	.35	.14	.03
□ 28 Alan Wiggins	.25	.10	.02
□ 29 Dick Williams MG	.35	.14	.03

1985 Smokey Angels

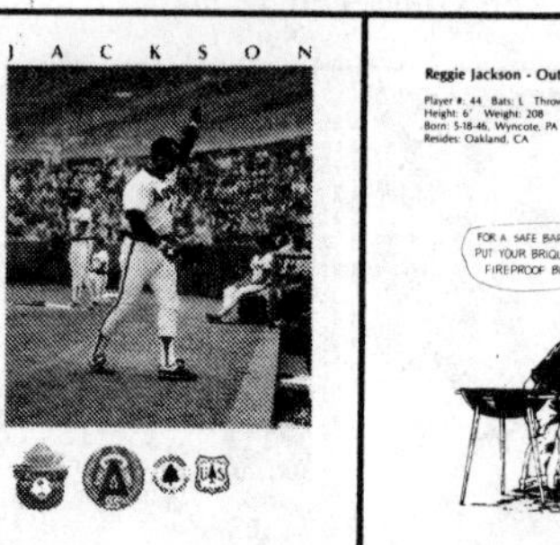

The cards in this 24-card set measure 4 1/4" by 6" and feature the California Angels in full color. The player's photo, the Angels' logo, and the Smokey the Bear logo appear on the front, in addition to the California Department of Forestry and the U.S. Forest Service logos. The abbreviated backs contain short biographical data and an anti-wildfire hint.

	MINT	EXC	G-VG
COMPLETE SET (24)	6.00	2.40	.60
COMMON PLAYER (1-24)	.20	.08	.02
□ 1 Mike Witt	.50	.20	.05
□ 2 Reggie Jackson	1.25	.50	.12
□ 3 Bob Boone	.40	.16	.04
□ 4 Mike Brown	.20	.08	.02
□ 5 Rod Carew	1.00	.40	.10
□ 6 Doug DeCinces	.30	.12	.03
□ 7 Brian Downing	.40	.16	.04
□ 8 Ken Forsch	.20	.08	.02
□ 9 Gary Pettis	.30	.12	.03
□ 10 Jerry Narron	.20	.08	.02
□ 11 Ron Romanick	.20	.08	.02
□ 12 Bobby Grich	.30	.12	.03
□ 13 Dick Schofield	.30	.12	.03
□ 14 Juan Beniquez	.20	.08	.02
□ 15 Geoff Zahn	.20	.08	.02
□ 16 Luis Sanchez	.20	.08	.02
□ 17 Jim Slaton	.20	.08	.02
□ 18 Doug Corbett	.20	.08	.02
□ 19 Ruppert Jones	.20	.08	.02
□ 20 Rob Wilfong	.20	.08	.02
□ 21 Donnie Moore	.20	.08	.02
□ 22 Pat Clements	.20	.08	.02
□ 23 Tommy John	.50	.20	.05
□ 24 Gene Mauch MG	.20	.08	.02

1986 Smokey Angels

The Forestry Service (in conjunction with the California Angels) produced this large, attractive 24-card set. The cards feature Smokey the Bear pictured in the upper right corner of the card. The card backs give a fire safety tip. The set was given

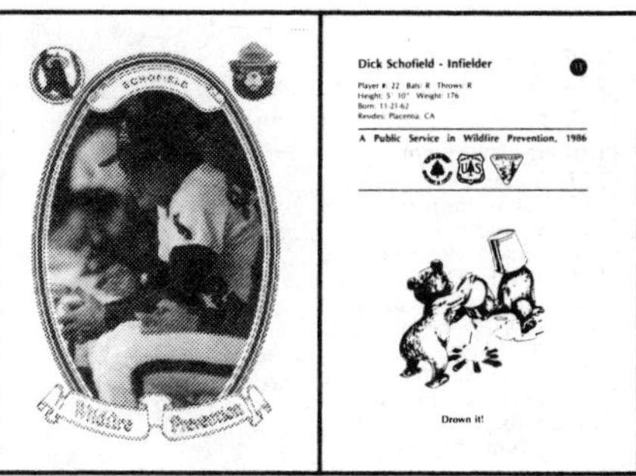

out free at Anaheim Stadium on August 9th. The cards measure 4 1/4" by 6" and are subtitled "Wildfire Prevention" on the front.

	MINT	EXC	G-VG
COMPLETE SET (24)	7.00	2.80	.70
COMMON PLAYER (1-24)	.20	.08	.02
□ 1 Mike Witt	.40	.16	.04
□ 2 Reggie Jackson	.90	.36	.09
□ 3 Bob Boone	.40	.16	.04
□ 4 Don Sutton	.60	.24	.06
□ 5 Kirk McCaskill	.30	.12	.03
□ 6 Doug DeCinces	.30	.12	.03
□ 7 Brian Downing	.30	.12	.03
□ 8 Doug Corbett	.20	.08	.02
□ 9 Gary Pettis	.30	.12	.03
□ 10 Jerry Narron	.20	.08	.02
□ 11 Ron Romanick	.20	.08	.02
□ 12 Bobby Grich	.30	.12	.03
□ 13 Dick Schofield	.30	.12	.03
□ 14 George Hendrick	.20	.08	.02
□ 15 Rick Burleson	.20	.08	.02
□ 16 John Candelaria	.30	.12	.03
□ 17 Jim Slaton	.20	.08	.02
□ 18 Darrell Miller	.20	.08	.02
□ 19 Ruppert Jones	.20	.08	.02
□ 20 Rob Wilfong	.20	.08	.02
□ 21 Donnie Moore	.20	.08	.02
□ 22 Wally Joyner	1.50	.60	.15
□ 23 Terry Forster	.20	.08	.02
□ 24 Gene Mauch MG	.20	.08	.02

1987 Smokey A's Colorgrams

These cards are actually pages of a booklet featuring members of the Oakland A's and Smokey's fire safety tips. The booklet has 12 pages each containing a black and white photo card (approximately 2 1/2" by 3 3/4") and a black and white player caricature (oversized head) postcard (approximately 3 3/4" by 5 5/8"). The cards are unnumbered but they have biographical information and a fire-prevention cartoon on the back of the card.

	MINT	EXC	G-VG
COMPLETE SET (12)	7.00	2.80	.70
COMMON PLAYER (1-12)	.50	.20	.05
□ 1 Joaquin Andujar	.50	.20	.05
□ 2 Jose Canseco	2.50	1.00	.25
□ 3 Mike Davis	.60	.24	.06
□ 4 Alfredo Griffin	.60	.24	.06
□ 5 Moose Haas	.50	.20	.05
□ 6 Jay Howell	.50	.20	.05
□ 7 Reggie Jackson	1.25	.50	.12
□ 8 Carney Lansford	.75	.30	.07
□ 9 Dwayne Murphy	.60	.24	.06
□ 10 Tony Phillips	.50	.20	.05
□ 11 Dave Stewart	.75	.30	.07
□ 12 Curt Young	.60	.24	.06

1987 Smokey AL

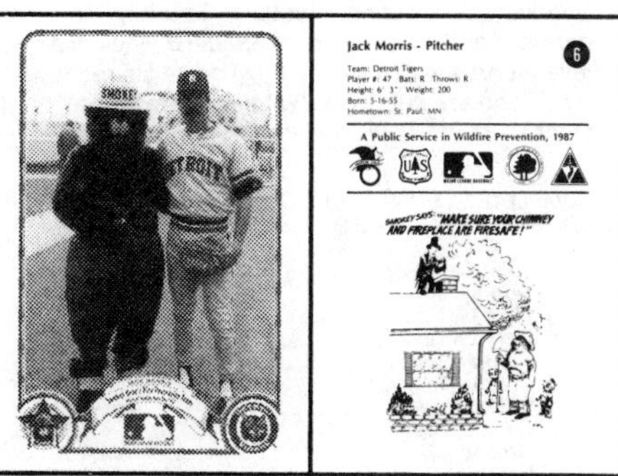

The U.S. Forestry Service (in conjunction with Major League Baseball) produced this large, attractive 14 player card set to commemorate the 43rd birthday of Smokey. The cards feature Smokey the Bear pictured on every card with the player. The card backs give a fire safety tip. The cards measure 4" by 6" and are subtitled "National Smokey Bear Day 1987" on the front. The cards were printed on an uncut (but perforated) sheet that measured 18" by 24".

	MINT	EXC	G-VG
COMPLETE SET (16)	5.00	2.00	.50
COMMON PLAYER (1-16)	.25	.10	.02
□ 1 Jose Canseco	2.00	.80	.20
□ 2 Dennis Oil Can Boyd	.25	.10	.02
□ 3 John Candelaria	.25	.10	.02
□ 4 Harold Baines	.35	.14	.03
□ 5 Joe Carter	.45	.18	.04
□ 6 Jack Morris	.45	.18	.04
□ 7 Buddy Biancalana	.25	.10	.02
□ 8 Kirby Puckett	1.00	.40	.10
□ 9 Mike Pagliarulo	.25	.10	.02
□ 10 Larry Sheets	.25	.10	.02
□ 11 Mike Moore	.25	.10	.02
□ 12 Charlie Hough	.25	.10	.02
□ 13 National Smokey Bear Day 1987	.25	.10	.02
□ 14 Tom Henke	.25	.10	.02
□ 15 Jim Gantner	.25	.10	.02
□ 16 American League Smokey Bear Day 1987	.25	.10	.02

1987 Smokey Angels

The U.S. Forestry Service (in conjunction with the California Angels) produced this large, attractive 24-card set to commemorate the 43rd birthday of

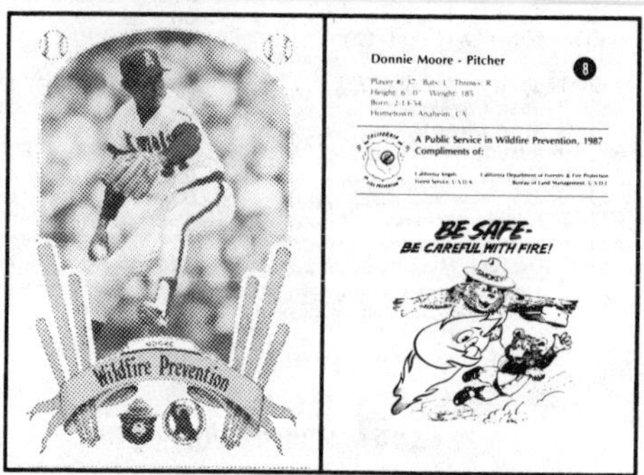

Smokey. The cards feature Smokey the Bear pictured at the bottom of every card. The card backs give a cartoon fire safety tip. The cards measure 4" by 6" and are subtitled "Wildfire Prevention" on the front.

	MINT	EXC	G-VG
COMPLETE SET (24)	7.00	2.80	.70
COMMON PLAYER (1-24)	.25	.10	.02
☐ 1 John Candelaria	.35	.14	.03
☐ 2 Don Sutton	.75	.30	.07
☐ 3 Mike Witt	.50	.20	.05
☐ 4 Gary Lucas	.25	.10	.02
☐ 5 Kirk McCaskill	.35	.14	.03
☐ 6 Chuck Finley	.25	.10	.02
☐ 7 Willie Fraser	.25	.10	.02
☐ 8 Donnie Moore	.25	.10	.02
☐ 9 Urbano Lugo	.25	.10	.02
☐ 10 Butch Wynegar	.25	.10	.02
☐ 11 Darrell Miller	.25	.10	.02
☐ 12 Wally Joyner	1.25	.50	.12
☐ 13 Mark McLemore	.25	.10	.02
☐ 14 Mark Ryal	.25	.10	.02
☐ 15 Dick Schofield	.35	.14	.03
☐ 16 Jack Howell	.35	.14	.03
☐ 17 Doug DeCinces	.35	.14	.03
☐ 18 Gus Polidor	.25	.10	.02
☐ 19 Brian Downing	.35	.14	.03
☐ 20 Gary Pettis	.35	.14	.03
☐ 21 Ruppert Jones	.25	.10	.02
☐ 22 George Hendrick	.25	.10	.02
☐ 23 Devon White	.90	.36	.09
☐ 24 Checklist Card	.25	.10	.02

1987 Smokey Braves

The U.S. Forestry Service (in conjunction with the Atlanta Braves) produced this large, attractive 27-card set to commemorate the 43rd birthday of Smokey. The cards feature Smokey the Bear pictured in the top right corner of every card. The card backs give a cartoon fire safety tip. The cards measure 4" by 6" and are subtitled "Wildfire Prevention" on the front. Distribution of the cards was gradual at the stadium throughout the summer. These large cards are numbered on the back.

	MINT	EXC	G-VG
COMPLETE SET (27)	12.00	5.00	1.20
COMMON PLAYER (1-26)	.35	.14	.03
☐ 1 Zane Smith	.60	.24	.06
☐ 2 Charlie Puleo	.35	.14	.03
☐ 3 Randy O'Neal	.35	.14	.03
☐ 4 David Palmer	.45	.18	.04
☐ 5 Rick Mahler	.45	.18	.04
☐ 6 Ed Olwine	.35	.14	.03
☐ 7 Jeff Dedmon	.35	.14	.03
☐ 8 Paul Assenmacher	.35	.14	.03
☐ 9 Gene Garber	.45	.18	.04
☐ 10 Jim Acker	.35	.14	.03
☐ 11 Bruce Benedict	.35	.14	.03
☐ 12 Ozzie Virgil	.45	.18	.0
☐ 13 Ted Simmons	.75	.30	.0
☐ 14 Dale Murphy	2.00	.80	.2
☐ 15 Graig Nettles	.60	.24	.0
☐ 16 Ken Oberkfell	.35	.14	.0
☐ 17 Gerald Perry	.75	.30	.0
☐ 18 Rafael Ramirez	.35	.14	.0
☐ 19 Ken Griffey	.45	.18	.0
☐ 20 Andres Thomas	.45	.18	.0
☐ 21 Glenn Hubbard	.35	.14	.0
☐ 22 Damaso Garcia	.35	.14	.0
☐ 23 Gary Roenicke	.35	.14	.0
☐ 24 Dion James	.35	.14	.0
☐ 25 Albert Hall	.35	.14	.0
☐ 26 Chuck Tanner MG	.35	.14	.0
☐ xx Smokey/Checklist (unnumbered)	.35	.14	.0

1987 Smokey Cardinals

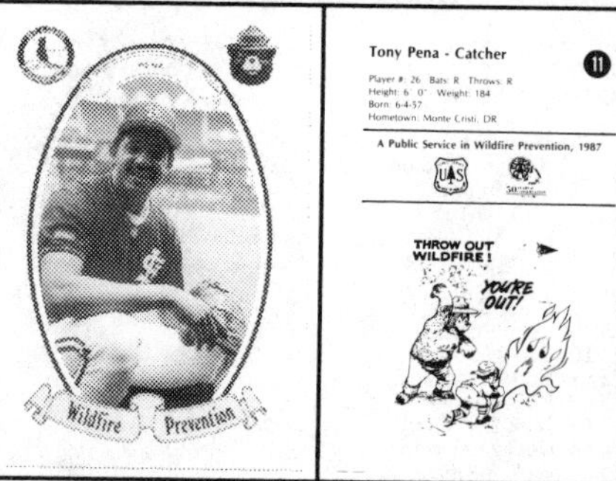

The U.S. Forestry Service (in conjunction with the St. Louis Cardinals) produced this large, attractive 25-card set to commemorate the 43rd birthday of Smokey. The cards feature Smokey the Bear pictured in the top right corner of every card. The card backs give a cartoon fire safety tip. The cards measure 4" by 6" and are subtitled "Wildfire Prevention" on the front. Sets were supposedly available from the Cardinals team for 3.50 postpaid. Also a limited number of 8 1/2" by 12" full-color team photos were available from the team to those who sent in a large SASE. The large team photo is not considered part of the complete set.

	MINT	EXC	G-VG
COMPLETE SET (25)	8.00	3.25	.80
COMMON PLAYER (1-25)	.25	.10	.02
☐ 1 Ray Soff	.25	.10	.02
☐ 2 Todd Worrell	.50	.20	.05
☐ 3 John Tudor	.50	.20	.05
☐ 4 Pat Perry	.25	.10	.02
☐ 5 Rick Horton	.25	.10	.02
☐ 6 Danny Cox	.35	.14	.03
☐ 7 Bob Forsch	.25	.10	.02
☐ 8 Greg Matthews	.35	.14	.03
☐ 9 Bill Dawley	.25	.10	.02
☐ 10 Steve Lake	.25	.10	.02
☐ 11 Tony Pena	.35	.14	.03
☐ 12 Tom Pagnozzi	.25	.10	.02
☐ 13 Jack Clark	.75	.30	.07
☐ 14 Jim Lindeman	.35	.14	.03
☐ 15 Mike Laga	.25	.10	.02
☐ 16 Terry Pendleton	.35	.14	.03
☐ 17 Ozzie Smith	1.00	.40	.10
☐ 18 Jose Oquendo	.35	.14	.03
☐ 19 Tom Lawless	.25	.10	.02
☐ 20 Tom Herr	.35	.14	.03
☐ 21 Curt Ford	.25	.10	.02
☐ 22 Willie McGee	.50	.20	.05
☐ 23 Tito Landrum	.25	.10	.02
☐ 24 Vince Coleman	.75	.30	.07
☐ 25 Whitey Herzog MG	.35	.14	.03
☐ xx Team Photo (large)	1.00	.40	.10

1987 Smokey Dodger All-Stars

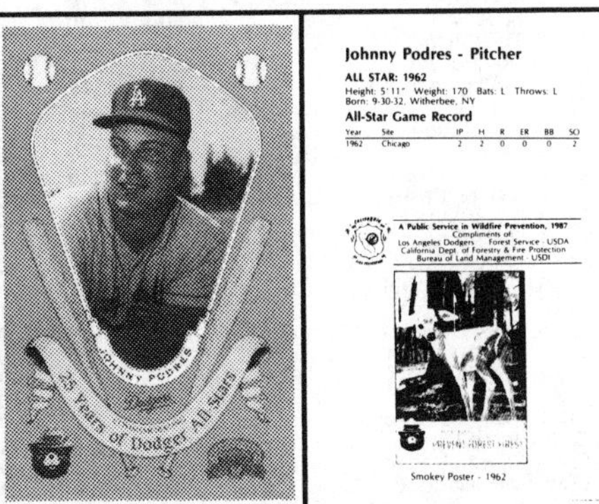

This 40-card set was issued by the U.S. Forestry Service to commemorate the Los Angeles Dodgers selected for the All-Star game over the past 25 years. The cards measure 2 1/2" by 3 3/4" and have full-color fronts. The card fronts are distinguished by their thick silver borders and the bats, balls, and stadium design layout. The 25th anniversary logo for Dodger Stadium is in the lower right corner of each card.

	MINT	EXC	G-VG
COMPLETE SET (40)	7.00	2.80	.70
COMMON PLAYER (1-40)	.15	.06	.01
☐ 1 Walt Alston	.35	.14	.03
☐ 2 Dusty Baker	.15	.06	.01
☐ 3 Jim Brewer	.15	.06	.01
☐ 4 Ron Cey	.25	.10	.02
☐ 5 Tommy Davis	.25	.10	.02
☐ 6 Willie Davis	.25	.10	.02
☐ 7 Don Drysdale	.75	.30	.07
☐ 8 Steve Garvey	.75	.30	.07
☐ 9 Bill Grabarkewitz	.15	.06	.01
☐ 10 Pedro Guerrero	.60	.24	.06
☐ 11 Tom Haller	.15	.06	.01
☐ 12 Orel Hershiser	1.00	.40	.10
☐ 13 Burt Hooton	.15	.06	.01
☐ 14 Steve Howe	.15	.06	.01
☐ 15 Tommy John	.25	.10	.02
☐ 16 Sandy Koufax	1.00	.40	.10
☐ 17 Tom Lasorda	.45	.18	.04
☐ 18 Jim Lefebvre	.15	.06	.01
☐ 19 Davey Lopes	.25	.10	.02
☐ 20 Mike Marshall (pitcher)	.25	.10	.02
☐ 21 Mike Marshall (outfielder)	.35	.14	.03
☐ 22 Andy Messersmith	.15	.06	.01
☐ 23 Rick Monday	.15	.06	.01
☐ 24 Manny Mota	.15	.06	.01
☐ 25 Claude Osteen	.15	.06	.01
☐ 26 Johnny Podres	.25	.10	.02
☐ 27 Phil Regan	.15	.06	.01
☐ 28 Jerry Reuss	.15	.06	.01
☐ 29 Rick Rhoden	.15	.06	.01
☐ 30 John Roseboro	.15	.06	.01
☐ 31 Bill Russell	.25	.10	.02
☐ 32 Steve Sax	.35	.14	.03
☐ 33 Bill Singer	.15	.06	.01
☐ 34 Reggie Smith	.25	.10	.02
☐ 35 Don Sutton	.50	.20	.05
☐ 36 Fernando Valenzuela	.50	.20	.05
☐ 37 Bob Welch	.25	.10	.02
☐ 38 Maury Wills	.35	.14	.03
☐ 39 Jim Wynn	.15	.06	.01
☐ 40 Checklist Card	.15	.06	.01

1987 Smokey National League

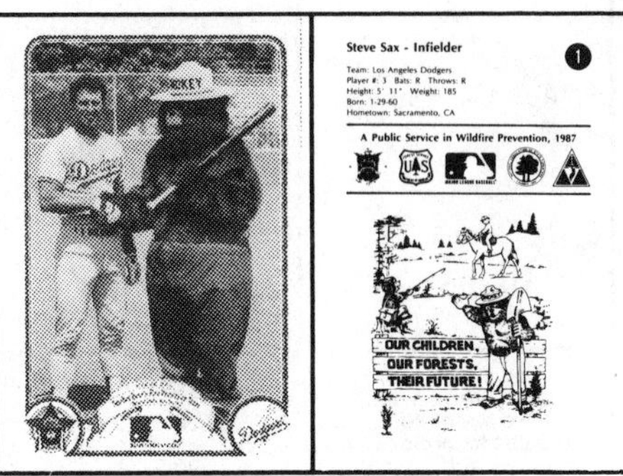

The U.S. Forestry Service (in conjunction with Major League Baseball) produced this large, attractive 14 player card set to commemorate the 43rd birthday of Smokey. The cards feature Smokey the Bear pictured on every card with the player. The card backs give a fire safety tip. The cards measure 4" by 6" and are subtitled "National Smokey Bear Day 1987" on the front. The set price below does not include the more difficult variation cards.

	MINT	EXC	G-VG
COMPLETE SET (15)	5.00	2.00	.50
COMMON PLAYER (1-15)	.25	.10	.02
☐ 1 Steve Sax	.50	.20	.05
☐ 2A Dale Murphy (holding bat)	1.50	.60	.15
☐ 2B Dale Murphy (no bat, arm around Smokey)	12.00	5.00	1.00
☐ 3A Jody Davis (kneeling with Smokey)	.35	.14	.03
☐ 3B Jody Davis (standing, shaking Smokey's hand)	8.00	3.60	.80
☐ 4 Bill Gullickson	.25	.10	.02
☐ 5 Mike Scott	.50	.20	.05
☐ 6 Roger McDowell	.35	.14	.03
☐ 7 Steve Bedrosian	.50	.20	.05
☐ 8 Johnny Ray	.35	.14	.03
☐ 9 Ozzie Smith	.75	.30	.07
☐ 10 Steve Garvey	.75	.30	.07
☐ 11 National Smokey Bear Day	.25	.10	.02
☐ 12 Mike Krukow	.25	.10	.02
☐ 13 Smokey the Bear	.25	.10	.02
☐ 14 Mike Fitzgerald	.25	.10	.02
☐ 15 National League Logo	.25	.10	.02

1987 Smokey Rangers

The U.S. Forestry Service (in conjunction with the Texas Rangers) produced this large, attractive 32-card set. The cards feature Smokey the Bear pictured in the upper-right corner of every player's card. The card backs give a cartoon fire safety tip. The cards measure approximately 4 1/4" by 6" and are subtitled "Wildfire Prevention" on the front. These large cards are numbered on the back. Cards 4 Mike Mason and 14 Tom Paciorek were withdrawn and were never formally released as part of the set and hence are quite scarce.

	MINT	EXC	G-VG
COMPLETE SET (32)	75.00	30.00	7.50
COMMON PLAYER (1-32)	.35	.14	.03
☐ 1 Charlie Hough	.65	.26	.06

	Player	MINT	EXC	G-VG
□ 2	Greg Harris	.35	.14	.03
□ 3	Jose Guzman	.50	.20	.05
□ 4	Mike Mason SP	30.00	12.00	3.00
□ 5	Dale Mohorcic	.50	.20	.05
□ 6	Bobby Witt	.90	.36	.09
□ 7	Mitch Williams	.50	.20	.05
□ 8	Geno Petralli	.35	.14	.03
□ 9	Don Slaught	.35	.14	.03
□ 10	Darrell Porter	.35	.14	.03
□ 11	Steve Buechele	.50	.20	.05
□ 12	Pete O'Brien	.65	.26	.06
□ 13	Scott Fletcher	.50	.20	.05
□ 14	Tom Paciorek	30.00	12.00	3.00
□ 15	Pete Incaviglia	.90	.36	.09
□ 16	Oddibe McDowell	.50	.20	.05
□ 17	Ruben Sierra	1.25	.50	.12
□ 18	Larry Parrish	.50	.20	.05
□ 19	Bobby Valentine MG	.65	.26	.06
□ 20	Tom House CO	.35	.14	.03
□ 21	Tom Robson CO	.35	.14	.03
□ 22	Edwin Correa	.50	.20	.05
□ 23	Mike Stanley	.50	.20	.05
□ 24	Joe Ferguson CO	.35	.14	.03
□ 25	Art Howe CO	.50	.20	.05
□ 26	Bob Brower	.50	.20	.05
□ 27	Mike Loynd	.35	.14	.03
□ 28	Curtis Wilkerson	.35	.14	.03
□ 29	Tim Foli CO	.35	.14	.03
□ 30	Dave Oliver	.35	.14	.03
□ 31	Jerry Browne	.35	.14	.03
□ 32	Jeff Russell	.50	.20	.05

1988 Smokey Angels

Dick Schofield - Infielder
16
Player #: 22 Bats: R Throws: R
Height: 5'10" Weight: 180
Born: 11-21-62, Springfield, IL
STRIKE OUT WILDFIRE!
A Public Service in Wildfire Prevention, 1988
Sale and/or Reproduction Prohibited. © 1988 MLB/USFS PL82-359

The U.S. Forestry Service (in conjunction with the California Angels) produced this attractive 25-card set. The cards feature Smokey the Bear pictured at the bottom of every card. The card backs give a cartoon fire safety tip. The cards measure approximately 2 1/2" by 3 1/2" and are in full color. The cards are numbered on the back. They were distributed during promotions on August 28, September 4, and September 18.

	MINT	EXC	G-VG
COMPLETE SET (25)	9.00	3.75	.90
COMMON PLAYER (1-24)	.30	.12	.03

	Player	MINT	EXC	G-VG
□ 1	Cookie Rojas MG	.30	.12	.03
□ 2	Johnny Ray	.50	.20	.05
□ 3	Jack Howell	.40	.16	.04
□ 4	Mike Witt	.50	.20	.05
□ 5	Tony Armas	.40	.16	.04
□ 6	Gus Polidor	.30	.12	.03
□ 7	DeWayne Buice	.40	.16	.04
□ 8	Dan Petry	.30	.12	.03
□ 9	Bob Boone	.50	.20	.05
□ 10	Chili Davis	.50	.20	.05
□ 11	Greg Minton	.40	.16	.04
□ 12	Kirk McCaskell	.40	.16	.04
□ 13	Devon White	.60	.24	.06
□ 14	Willie Fraser	.30	.12	.03
□ 15	Chuck Finley	.30	.12	.03
□ 16	Dick Schofield	.40	.16	.04
□ 17	Wally Joyner	1.00	.40	.10
□ 18	Brian Downing	.40	.16	.04
□ 19	Stewart Cliburn	.30	.12	.03
□ 20	Donnie Moore	.30	.12	.03
□ 21	Bryan Harvey	.50	.20	.05
□ 22	Mark McLemore	.30	.12	.03
□ 23	Butch Wynegar	.30	.12	.03
□ 24	George Hendrick	.30	.12	.03
□ xx	Checklist/Logo Card	.30	.12	.03

1988 Smokey Cardinals

Whitey Herzog - Manager
1
Player #:24
Height: 5'11" Weight: 195
Born: 11-9-31, New Athens, Il
Resides: Independence, MO
FIRE PREVENTION
A TEAM EFFORT
Whitey Herzog
Manager
A Public Service in Wildfire Prevention, 1988

The U.S. Forestry Service (in conjunction with the St. Louis Cardinals) produced this attractive 25-card set. The cards feature Smokey the Bear pictured in the lower right corner of every card. The card backs give a cartoon fire safety tip. The cards measure approximately 3" by 5" and are in full color. The cards are numbered on the backs. The sets were distributed on July 19th during the Cardinals' game against the Los Angeles Dodgers to fans 15 years of age and under.

	MINT	EXC	G-VG
COMPLETE SET (25)	9.00	3.75	.90
COMMON PLAYER (1-25)	.30	.12	.03

	Player	MINT	EXC	G-VG
□ 1	Whitey Herzog MG	.50	.20	.05
□ 2	Danny Cox	.40	.16	.04
□ 3	Ken Dayley	.30	.12	.03
□ 4	Jose DeLeon	.40	.16	.04
□ 5	Bob Forsch	.40	.16	.04
□ 6	Joe Magrane	.50	.20	.05
□ 7	Greg Mathews	.40	.16	.04
□ 8	Scott Terry	.40	.16	.04
□ 9	John Tudor	.50	.20	.05
□ 10	Todd Worrell	.50	.20	.05
□ 11	Steve Lake	.30	.12	.03
□ 12	Tom Pagnozzi	.30	.12	.03
□ 13	Tony Pena	.40	.16	.04
□ 14	Bob Horner	.50	.20	.05
□ 15	Tom Lawless	.30	.12	.03
□ 16	Jose Oquendo	.40	.16	.04
□ 17	Terry Pendleton	.40	.16	.04
□ 18	Ozzie Smith	.75	.30	.07
□ 19	Vince Coleman	.60	.24	.06
□ 20	Curt Ford	.30	.12	.03
□ 21	Willie McGee	.50	.20	.05
□ 22	Larry McWilliams	.30	.12	.03

☐ 23 Steve Peters	.40	.16	.04
☐ 24 Luis Alicea	.40	.16	.04
☐ 25 Tom Brunansky	.50	.20	.05

1988 Smokey Dodgers

This 32-card set was issued by the U.S. Forestry Service as a perforated sheet that could be separated into individual cards. The set commemorates Los Angeles Dodgers who hold various team and league records, i.e., "L.A. Dodgers Record-Breakers." The cards measure approximately 2 1/2" by 4" and have full-color fronts. The card fronts are distinguished by their thick light blue borders and the bats, balls, and stadium design layout. The sheets of cards were distributed at the Dodgers' Smokey Bear Day game on September 9th.

	MINT	EXC	G-VG
COMPLETE SET (32)	8.00	3.25	.80
COMMON PLAYER (1-32)	.20	.08	.02
☐ 1 Walter Alston	.50	.20	.05
☐ 2 John Roseboro	.20	.08	.02
☐ 3 Frank Howard	.30	.12	.03
☐ 4 Sandy Koufax	.75	.30	.07
☐ 5 Manny Mota	.30	.12	.03
☐ 6 Sandy Koufax, Jerry Reuss, and Bill Singer	.30	.12	.03
☐ 7 Maury Wills	.40	.16	.04
☐ 8 Tommy Davis	.30	.12	.03
☐ 9 Phil Regan	.20	.08	.02
☐ 10 Wes Parker	.20	.08	.02
☐ 11 Don Drysdale	.50	.20	.05
☐ 12 Willie Davis	.30	.12	.03
☐ 13 Bill Russell	.30	.12	.03
☐ 14 Jim Brewer	.20	.08	.02
☐ 15 Steve Garvey, Davey Lopes, Bill Russell, and Ron Cey	.30	.12	.03
☐ 16 Mike Marshall	.30	.12	.03
☐ 17 Steve Garvey	.50	.20	.05
☐ 18 Davey Lopes	.30	.12	.03
☐ 19 Burt Hooton	.20	.08	.02
☐ 20 Jim Wynn	.20	.08	.02
☐ 21 Dusty Baker, Ron Cey, Steve Garvey, and Reggie Smith	.30	.12	.03
☐ 22 Dusty Baker	.20	.08	.02
☐ 23 Tommy Lasorda	.50	.20	.05
☐ 24 Fernando Valenzuela	.50	.20	.05
☐ 25 Steve Sax	.40	.16	.04
☐ 26 Dodger Stadium	.20	.08	.02
☐ 27 Ron Cey	.30	.12	.03
☐ 28 Pedro Guerrero	.40	.16	.04
☐ 29 Mike Marshall	.30	.12	.03
☐ 30 Don Sutton	.40	.16	.04
☐ xx Checklist Card (unnumbered)	.20	.08	.02
☐ xx Smokey Bear (unnumbered)	.20	.08	.02

1988 Smokey Padres

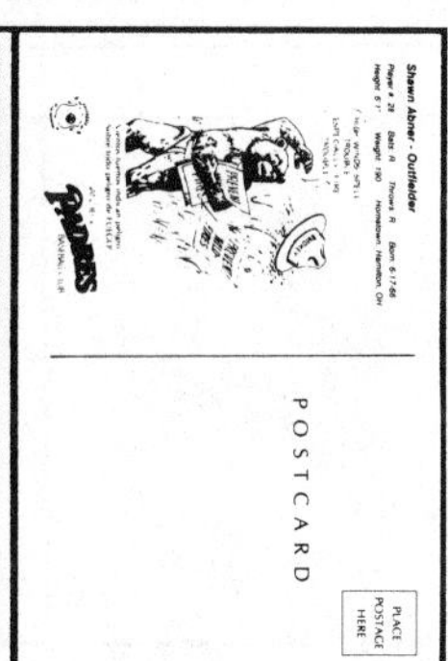

The cards in this 31-card set measure approximately 3 3/4" by 5 3/4". This unnumbered, full color set features the Fire Prevention Bear, Smokey, and a Padres player, coach, manager, or associate on each card. The set was given out at Jack Murphy Stadium to fans under the age of 14 during the Smokey Bear Day game promotion. The logo of the California Department of Forestry appears on the reverse in conjunction with a Smokey the Bear logo on the obverse. The backs contain short biographical data and a fire prevention hint from Smokey. The set is numbered below in alphabetical order. The card backs are actually postcards that can be addressed and mailed. Cards of Larry Bowa and Candy Sierra were printed but were not officially released since they were no longer members of the Padres by the time the cards were to be distributed.

	MINT	EXC	G-VG
COMPLETE SET (31)	12.50	5.00	1.25
COMMON PLAYER (1-31)	.35	.14	.03
☐ 1 Shawn Abner	.50	.20	.05
☐ 2 Roberto Alomar	.75	.30	.07
☐ 3 Sandy Alomar CO	.35	.14	.03
☐ 4 Greg Booker	.35	.14	.03
☐ 5 Chris Brown	.50	.20	.05
☐ 6 Mark Davis	.50	.20	.05
☐ 7 Pat Dobson CO	.35	.14	.03
☐ 8 Tim Flannery	.35	.14	.03
☐ 9 Mark Grant	.35	.14	.03
☐ 10 Tony Gwynn	1.25	.50	.12
☐ 11 Andy Hawkins	.50	.20	.05
☐ 12 Stan Jefferson	.50	.20	.05
☐ 13 Jimmy Jones	.50	.20	.05
☐ 14 John Kruk	.50	.20	.05
☐ 15 Dave Leiper	.35	.14	.03
☐ 16 Shane Mack	.50	.20	.05
☐ 17 Carmelo Martinez	.35	.14	.03
☐ 18 Lance McCullers	.50	.20	.05
☐ 19 Keith Moreland	.35	.14	.03
☐ 20 Eric Nolte	.35	.14	.03
☐ 21 Amos Otis CO	.35	.14	.03
☐ 22 Mark Parent	.35	.14	.03
☐ 23 Randy Ready	.35	.14	.03
☐ 24 Greg Riddoch	.35	.14	.03
☐ 25 Benito Santiago	1.00	.40	.10
☐ 26 Eric Show	.50	.20	.05
☐ 27 Denny Sommers CO	.35	.14	.03
☐ 28 Gary Templeton	.50	.20	.05
☐ 29 Dickie Thon	.50	.20	.05
☐ 30 Ed Whitson	.50	.20	.05
☐ 31 Marvell Wynne	.35	.14	.03

1988 Smokey Rangers

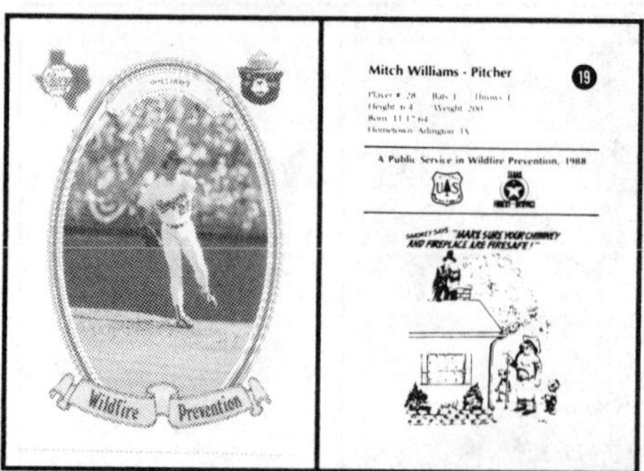

The cards in this 21-card set measure approximately 3 1/2" by 5". This numbered, full color set features the Fire Prevention Bear, Smokey, and a Rangers player (or manager) on each card. The set was given out at Arlington Stadium to fans during the Smokey Bear Day game promotion on August 7th. The logos of the Texas Forest Service and the U.S. Forestry Service appear on the reverse in conjunction with a Smokey the Bear logo on the obverse. The backs contain short biographical data and a fire prevention hint from Smokey.

	MINT	EXC	G-VG
COMPLETE SET (21)	8.00	3.25	.80
COMMON PLAYER (1-21)	.30	.12	.03
☐ 1 Tom O'Malley	.30	.12	.03
☐ 2 Pete O'Brien	.50	.20	.05
☐ 3 Geno Petralli	.30	.12	.03
☐ 4 Pete Incaviglia	.60	.24	.06
☐ 5 Oddibe McDowell	.50	.20	.05
☐ 6 Dal Mohorcic	.40	.16	.04
☐ 7 Bobby Witt	.60	.24	.06
☐ 8 Bobby Valentine MG	.50	.20	.05
☐ 9 Ruben Sierra	.60	.24	.06
☐ 10 Scott Fletcher	.40	.16	.04
☐ 11 Mike Stanley	.40	.16	.04
☐ 12 Steve Buechele	.30	.12	.03
☐ 13 Charlie Hough	.50	.20	.05
☐ 14 Larry Parrish	.40	.16	.04
☐ 15 Jerry Browne	.30	.12	.03
☐ 16 Bob Brower	.40	.16	.04
☐ 17 Jeff Russell	.40	.16	.04
☐ 18 Edwin Correa	.40	.16	.04
☐ 19 Mitch Williams	.40	.16	.04
☐ 20 Jose Guzman	.40	.16	.04
☐ 21 Curtis Wilkerson	.30	.12	.03

1988 Smokey Royals

This set of 28 cards features caricatures of the Kansas City Royals players. The cards are nunmbered on the back except for the unnumbered title/checklist card. The card set was distributed as a giveaway item at the stadium on August 14th to kids age 14 and under. The cards are approximately 3" by 5" and are in full color on the card fronts. The Smokey logo is in the upper right corner of every obverse.

	MINT	EXC	G-VG
COMPLETE SET (28)	9.00	3.75	.90
COMMON PLAYER (1-27)	.30	.12	.03
☐ 1 John Wathan MG	.30	.12	.03
☐ 2 Royals Coaches	.30	.12	.03
☐ 3 Willie Wilson	.50	.20	.05
☐ 4 Danny Tartabull	.75	.30	.07
☐ 5 Bo Jackson	.75	.30	.07
☐ 6 Gary Thurman	.40	.16	.04
☐ 7 Jerry Don Gleaton	.30	.12	.03
☐ 8 Floyd Bannister	.30	.12	.03
☐ 9 Buddy Black	.30	.12	.03
☐ 10 Steve Farr	.30	.12	.03
☐ 11 Gene Garber	.30	.12	.03
☐ 12 Mark Gubicza	.60	.24	.06
☐ 13 Charlie Liebrandt	.50	.20	.05
☐ 14 Ted Power	.30	.12	.03
☐ 15 Dan Quisenberry	.50	.20	.05
☐ 16 Bret Saberhagen	.75	.30	.07
☐ 17 Mike Macfarlane	.40	.16	.04
☐ 18 Scotti Madison	.30	.12	.03
☐ 19 Jamie Quirk	.30	.12	.03
☐ 20 George Brett	.90	.36	.09
☐ 21 Kevin Seitzer	.75	.30	.07
☐ 22 Bill Pecota	.30	.12	.03
☐ 23 Kurt Stillwell	.40	.16	.04
☐ 24 Brad Wellman	.30	.12	.03
☐ 25 Frank White	.50	.20	.05
☐ 26 Jim Eisenreich	.30	.12	.03
☐ 27 Smokey Bear	.30	.12	.03
☐ xx Checklist	.30	.12	.03

1988 Smokey Twins Colorgrams

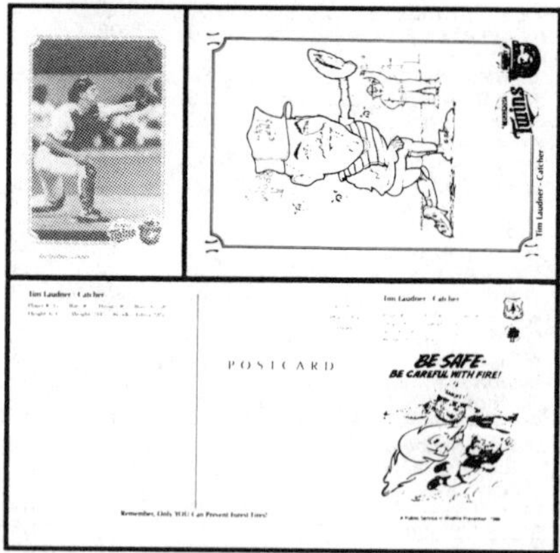

These cards are actually pages of a booklet featuring members of the Minnesota Twins and Smokey's fire safety tips. The booklet has 12 pages each containing a black and white photo card (approximately 2 1/2" by 3 3/4") and a black and white player caricature (oversized head) postcard (approximately 3 3/4" by 5 5/8"). The cards are unnumbered but they have biographical information and a fire-prevention cartoon on the back of the card.

	MINT	EXC	G-VG
COMPLETE SET (12)	9.00	3.75	.90
COMMON PLAYER (1-12)	.50	.20	.05
☐ 1 Frank Viola	1.00	.40	.10

□ 2 Gary Gaetti	1.00	.40	.10
□ 3 Kent Hrbek	1.00	.40	.10
□ 4 Jeff Reardon	.75	.30	.07
□ 5 Gene Larkin	.75	.30	.07
□ 6 Bert Blyleven	.75	.30	.07
□ 7 Tim Laudner	.60	.24	.06
□ 8 Greg Gagne	.50	.20	.05
□ 9 Randy Bush	.50	.20	.05
□ 10 Dan Gladden	.60	.24	.06
□ 11 Al Newman	.50	.20	.05
□ 12 Kirby Puckett	1.50	.60	.15

1986 Sportflics

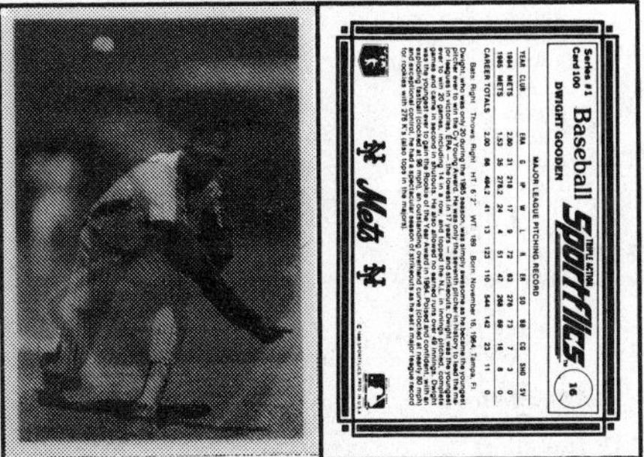

This 200-card set was marketed with 133 small trivia cards. This inaugural set for Sportflics was initially fairly well-received by the public. Sportflics was distributed by Major League Marketing; the company is also affiliated with Wrigley and Amurol. The set features 139 single player "magic motion" cards (which can be tilted to show three different pictures of the same player), 50 "Tri-Stars" (which show three different players), 10 "Big Six" cards (which show six players who share similar achievements), and one World Champs card featuring 12 members of the victorious Kansas City Royals. All cards measure 2 1/2" by 3 1/2".

	MINT	EXC	G-VG
COMPLETE SET (200)	36.00	15.00	3.60
COMMON PLAYER (1-200)	.12	.05	.01
□ 1 George Brett	1.25	.50	.12
□ 2 Don Mattingly	4.00	1.60	.40
□ 3 Wade Boggs	2.50	1.00	.25
□ 4 Eddie Murray	.80	.32	.08
□ 5 Dale Murphy	1.00	.40	.10
□ 6 Rickey Henderson	.90	.36	.09
□ 7 Harold Baines	.25	.10	.02
□ 8 Cal Ripken	.80	.32	.08
□ 9 Orel Hershiser	.80	.32	.08
□ 10 Bret Saberhagen	.40	.16	.04
□ 11 Tim Raines	.50	.20	.05
□ 12 Fernando Valenzuela	.40	.16	.04
□ 13 Tony Gwynn	.90	.36	.09
□ 14 Pedro Guerrero	.30	.12	.03
□ 15 Keith Hernandez	.40	.16	.04
□ 16 Ernie Riles	.25	.10	.02
□ 17 Jim Rice	.40	.16	.04
□ 18 Ron Guidry	.30	.12	.03
□ 19 Willie McGee	.40	.16	.04
□ 20 Ryne Sandberg	.75	.30	.07
□ 21 Kirk Gibson	.60	.24	.06
□ 22 Ozzie Guillen	.40	.16	.04
□ 23 Dave Parker	.30	.12	.03
□ 24 Vince Coleman	1.50	.60	.15
□ 25 Tom Seaver	.70	.28	.07
□ 26 Brett Butler	.20	.08	.02
□ 27 Steve Carlton	.50	.20	.05
□ 28 Gary Carter	.60	.24	.06
□ 29 Cecil Cooper	.20	.08	.02
□ 30 Jose Cruz	.15	.06	.01
□ 31 Alvin Davis	.20	.08	.02
□ 32 Dwight Evans	.25	.10	.02
□ 33 Julio Franco	.15	.06	.01
□ 34 Damaso Garcia	.12	.05	.01
□ 35 Steve Garvey	.75	.30	.07
□ 36 Kent Hrbek	.40	.16	.04
□ 37 Reggie Jackson	.90	.36	.09
□ 38 Fred Lynn	.30	.12	.03
□ 39 Paul Molitor	.40	.16	.04
□ 40 Jim Presley	.30	.12	.03
□ 41 Dave Righetti	.30	.12	.03
□ 42 Robin Yount	.45	.18	.04
□ 43 Nolan Ryan	.75	.30	.07
□ 44 Mike Schmidt	1.00	.40	.10
□ 45 Lee Smith	.15	.06	.01
□ 46 Rick Sutcliffe	.20	.08	.02
□ 47 Bruce Sutter	.25	.10	.02
□ 48 Lou Whitaker	.25	.10	.02
□ 49 Dave Winfield	.65	.26	.06
□ 50 Pete Rose	1.50	.60	.15
□ 51 NL MVPs	.80	.32	.08
Ryne Sandberg			
Steve Garvey			
Pete Rose			
□ 52 Slugging Stars	.40	.16	.04
George Brett			
Harold Baines			
Jim Rice			
□ 53 No-Hitters	.20	.08	.02
Phil Niekro			
Jerry Reuss			
Mike Witt			
□ 54 Big Hitters	.90	.36	.09
Don Mattingly			
Cal Ripken			
Robin Yount			
□ 55 Bullpen Aces	.20	.08	.02
Dan Quisenberry			
Goose Gossage			
Lee Smith			
□ 56 Rookies of The Year	.90	.36	.09
Darryl Strawberry			
Steve Sax			
Pete Rose			
□ 57 AL MVP's	.50	.20	.05
Cal Ripken			
Don Baylor			
Reggie Jackson			
□ 58 Repeat Batting Champs	.80	.32	.08
Dave Parker			
Bill Madlock			
Pete Rose			
□ 59 Cy Young Winners	.15	.06	.01
LaMarr Hoyt			
Mike Flanagan			
Ron Guidry			
□ 60 Double Award Winners	.30	.12	.03
Fernando Valenzuela			
Rick Sutcliffe			
Tom Seaver			
□ 61 Home Run Champs	.65	.26	.06
Reggie Jackson			
Jim Rice			
Tony Armas			
□ 62 NL MVP's	.85	.34	.08
Keith Hernandez			
Dale Murphy			
Mike Schmidt			
□ 63 AL MVP's	.50	.20	.05
Robin Yount			
George Brett			
Fred Lynn			
□ 64 Comeback Players	.15	.06	.01
Bert Blyleven			
Jerry Koosman			
John Denny			
□ 65 Cy Young Relievers	.20	.08	.02
Willie Hernandez			
Rollie Fingers			
Bruce Sutter			
□ 66 Rookies of The Year	.20	.08	.02
Bob Horner			
Andre Dawson			
Gary Matthews			
□ 67 Rookies of The Year	.30	.12	.03
Ron Kittle			
Carlton Fisk			
Tom Seaver			
□ 68 Home Run Champs	.30	.12	.03
Mike Schmidt			
George Foster			
Dave Kingman			
□ 69 Double Award Winners	.80	.32	.08
Cal Ripken			
Rod Carew			
Pete Rose			
□ 70 Cy Young Winners	.40	.16	.04
Rick Sutcliffe			
Steve Carlton			
Tom Seaver			

□ 71	Top Sluggers Reggie Jackson Fred Lynn Robin Yount	.40	.16	.04
□ 72	Rookies of The Year Dave Righetti Fernando Valenzuela Rick Sutcliffe	.25	.10	.02
□ 73	Rookies of The Year Fred Lynn Eddie Murray Cal Ripken	.60	.24	.06
□ 74	Rookies of The Year Alvin Davis Lou Whitaker Rod Carew	.25	.10	.02
□ 75	Batting Champs Don Mattingly Wade Boggs Carney Lansford	1.25	.50	.12
□ 76	Jesse Barfield	.40	.16	.04
□ 77	Phil Bradley	.30	.12	.03
□ 78	Chris Brown	.40	.16	.04
□ 79	Tom Browning	.30	.12	.03
□ 80	Tom Brunansky	.25	.10	.02
□ 81	Bill Buckner	.15	.06	.01
□ 82	Chili Davis	.20	.08	.02
□ 83	Mike Davis	.15	.06	.01
□ 84	Rich Gedman	.20	.08	.02
□ 85	Willie Hernandez	.15	.06	.01
□ 86	Ron Kittle	.20	.08	.02
□ 87	Lee Lacy	.12	.05	.01
□ 88	Bill Madlock	.15	.06	.01
□ 89	Mike Marshall	.20	.08	.02
□ 90	Keith Moreland	.12	.05	.01
□ 91	Graig Nettles	.20	.08	.02
□ 92	Lance Parrish	.30	.12	.03
□ 93	Kirby Puckett	1.00	.40	.10
□ 94	Juan Samuel	.30	.12	.03
□ 95	Steve Sax	.35	.14	.03
□ 96	Dave Stieb	.20	.08	.02
□ 97	Darryl Strawberry	1.25	.50	.12
□ 98	Willie Upshaw	.12	.05	.01
□ 99	Frank Viola	.35	.14	.03
□ 100	Dwight Gooden	1.25	.50	.12
□ 101	Joaquin Andujar	.15	.06	.01
□ 102	George Bell	.45	.18	.04
□ 103	Bert Blyleven	.20	.08	.02
□ 104	Mike Boddicker	.15	.06	.01
□ 105	Britt Burns	.12	.05	.01
□ 106	Rod Carew	.70	.28	.07
□ 107	Jack Clark	.35	.14	.03
□ 108	Danny Cox	.20	.08	.02
□ 109	Ron Darling	.40	.16	.04
□ 110	Andre Dawson	.50	.20	.05
□ 111	Leon Durham	.12	.05	.01
□ 112	Tony Fernandez	.30	.12	.03
□ 113	Tommy Herr	.12	.05	.01
□ 114	Teddy Higuera	.60	.24	.06
□ 115	Bob Horner	.25	.10	.02
□ 116	Dave Kingman	.20	.08	.02
□ 117	Jack Morris	.30	.12	.03
□ 118	Dan Quisenberry	.20	.08	.02
□ 119	Jeff Reardon	.20	.08	.02
□ 120	Bryn Smith	.12	.05	.01
□ 121	Ozzie Smith	.40	.16	.04
□ 122	John Tudor	.20	.08	.02
□ 123	Tim Wallach	.15	.06	.01
□ 124	Willie Wilson	.15	.06	.01
□ 125	Carlton Fisk	.25	.10	.02
□ 126	RBI Sluggers Gary Carter Al Oliver George Foster	.25	.10	.02
□ 127	Run Scorers Tim Raines Ryne Sandberg Keith Hernandez	.50	.20	.05
□ 128	Run Scorers Paul Molitor Cal Ripken Willie Wilson	.40	.16	.04
□ 129	No-Hitters John Candelaria Dennis Eckersley Bob Forsch	.15	.06	.01
□ 130	World Series MVP's Pete Rose Ron Cey Rollie Fingers	.60	.24	.06
□ 131	All-Star Game MVPs Dave Concepcion George Foster Bill Madlock	.15	.06	.01
□ 132	Cy Young Winners John Denny Fernando Valenzuela Vida Blue	.20	.08	.02
□ 133	Comeback Players Rich Dotson Joaquin Andujar Doyle Alexander	.15	.06	.01
□ 134	Big Winners Rick Sutcliffe Tom Seaver John Denny	.35	.14	.03
□ 135	Veteran Pitchers Tom Seaver Phil Niekro Don Sutton	.40	.16	.04
□ 136	Rookies of The Year Dwight Gooden Vince Coleman Alfredo Griffin	.90	.36	.09
□ 137	All-Star Game MVPs Gary Carter Fred Lynn Steve Garvey	.40	.16	.04
□ 138	Veteran Hitters Tony Perez Rusty Staub Pete Rose	.60	.24	.06
□ 139	Power Hitters Mike Schmidt Jim Rice George Foster	.50	.20	.05
□ 140	Batting Champs Tony Gwynn Al Oliver Bill Buckner	.25	.10	.02
□ 141	No-Hitters Nolan Ryan Jack Morris Dave Righetti	.35	.14	.03
□ 142	No-Hitters Tom Seaver Bert Blyleven Vida Blue	.30	.12	.03
□ 143	Strikeout Kings Nolan Ryan Fernando Valenzuela Dwight Gooden	.90	.36	.09
□ 144	Base Stealers Tim Raines Willie Wilson Davey Lopes	.30	.12	.03
□ 145	RBI Sluggers Tony Armas Cecil Cooper Eddie Murray	.35	.14	.03
□ 146	AL MVP's Rod Carew Jim Rice Rollie Fingers	.40	.16	.04
□ 147	World Series MVP's Alan Trammell Rick Dempsey Reggie Jackson	.35	.14	.03
□ 148	World Series MVP's Darrell Porter Pedro Guerrero Mike Schmidt	.40	.16	.04
□ 149	ERA Leaders Mike Boddicker Rick Sutcliffe Ron Guidry	.15	.06	.01
□ 150	Comeback Players Reggie Jackson Dave Kingman Fred Lynn	.35	.14	.03
□ 151	Buddy Bell	.15	.06	.01
□ 152	Dennis Boyd	.15	.06	.01
□ 153	Dave Concepcion	.15	.06	.01
□ 154	Brian Downing	.15	.06	.01
□ 155	Shawon Dunston	.25	.10	.02
□ 156	John Franco	.30	.12	.03
□ 157	Scott Garrelts	.15	.06	.01
□ 158	Bob James	.12	.05	.01
□ 159	Charlie Leibrandt	.15	.06	.01
□ 160	Oddibe McDowell	.40	.16	.04
□ 161	Roger McDowell	.40	.16	.04
□ 162	Mike Moore	.20	.08	.02
□ 163	Phil Niekro	.45	.18	.04
□ 164	Al Oliver	.15	.06	.01
□ 165	Tony Pena	.20	.08	.02
□ 166	Ted Power	.15	.06	.01
□ 167	Mike Scioscia	.15	.06	.01
□ 168	Mario Soto	.15	.06	.01
□ 169	Bob Stanley	.15	.06	.01
□ 170	Gary Templeton	.15	.06	.01

□ 171	Andre Thornton	.15	.06	.01
□ 172	Alan Trammell	.45	.18	.04
□ 173	Doug DeCinces	.20	.08	.02
□ 174	Greg Walker	.20	.08	.02
□ 175	Don Sutton	.40	.16	.04
□ 176	1985 Award Winners	1.00	.40	.10
	Ozzie Guillen			
	Bret Saberhagen			
	Don Mattingly			
	Vince Coleman			
	Dwight Gooden			
	Willie McGee			
□ 177	1985 Hot Rookies	.60	.24	.06
	Stew Cliburn			
	Brian Fisher			
	Joe Hesketh			
	Joe Orsulak			
	Mark Salas			
	Larry Sheets			
□ 178	1986 Rookies To Watch	12.50	5.00	1.25
	Jose Canseco			
	Mark Funderburk			
	Mike Greenwell			
	Steve Lombardozzi			
	Billy Joe Robidoux			
	Danny Tartabull			
□ 179	1985 Gold Glovers	.80	.32	.08
	George Brett			
	Ron Guidry			
	Keith Hernandez			
	Don Mattingly			
	Willie McGee			
	Dale Murphy			
□ 180	Active Lifetime .300	.80	.32	.08
	Wade Boggs			
	George Brett			
	Rod Carew			
	Cecil Cooper			
	Don Mattingly			
	Willie Wilson			
□ 181	Active Lifetime .300	.70	.28	.07
	Tony Gwynn			
	Bill Madlock			
	Pedro Guerrero			
	Dave Parker			
	Pete Rose			
	Keith Hernandez			
□ 182	1985 Milestones	.80	.32	.08
	Rod Carew			
	Phil Niekro			
	Pete Rose			
	Nolan Ryan			
	Tom Seaver			
	Matt Tallman (fan)			
□ 183	1985 Triple Crown	.80	.32	.08
	Wade Boggs			
	Darrell Evans			
	Don Mattingly			
	Willie McGee			
	Dale Murphy			
	Dave Parker			
□ 184	1985 Highlights	1.00	.40	.10
	Wade Boggs			
	Dwight Gooden			
	Rickey Henderson			
	Don Mattingly			
	Willie McGee			
	John Tudor			
□ 185	1985 20 Game Winners	.80	.32	.08
	Dwight Gooden			
	Ron Guidry			
	John Tudor			
	Joaquin Andujar			
	Bret Saberhagen			
	Tom Browning			
□ 186	World Series Champs	.40	.16	.04
	L. Smith, Dane Iorg			
	W. Wilson, Leibrandt			
	G. Brett, Saberhagen			
	Motley, Quisenberry			
	D. Jackson, Sundberg			
	S. Balboni, F. White			
□ 187	Hubie Brooks	.20	.08	.02
□ 188	Glenn Davis	.60	.24	.06
□ 189	Darrell Evans	.20	.08	.02
□ 190	Rich Gossage	.25	.10	.02
□ 191	Andy Hawkins	.15	.06	.01
□ 192	Jay Howell	.12	.05	.01
□ 193	LaMarr Hoyt	.15	.06	.01
□ 194	Davey Lopes	.12	.05	.01
□ 195	Mike Scott	.45	.18	.04
□ 196	Ted Simmons	.20	.08	.02
□ 197	Gary Ward	.12	.05	.01
□ 198	Bob Welch	.20	.08	.02
□ 199	Mike Young	.15	.06	.01
□ 200	Buddy Biancalana	.12	.05	.01

1986 Sportflics Decade Greats

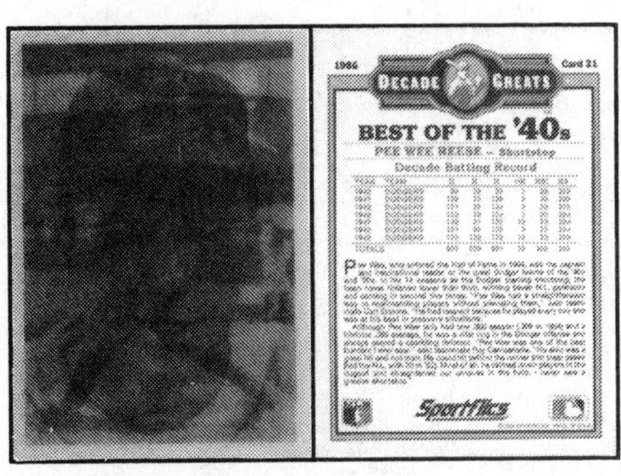

This set of 75 three-phase "animated" cards was produced by Sportflics and manufactured by Opti-Graphics of Arlington, Texas. Cards are standard size, 2 1/2" by 3 1/2", and feature both sepia (players of the '30s and '40s) and full color cards. The concept of the set was that the best players at each position for each decade (from the '30s to the '80s) were chosen. The bios were written by Les Woodcock. Also included with the set in the specially designed collector box are 51 trivia cards with historical questions about the six decades of All-Star games.

		MINT	EXC	G-VG
COMPLETE SET (75)		14.00	5.75	1.40
COMMON PLAYER (1-75)		.15	.06	.01
□ 1	Babe Ruth	3.00	1.20	.30
□ 2	Jimmie Foxx	.35	.14	.03
□ 3	Lefty Grove	.35	.14	.03
□ 4	Hank Greenberg	.35	.14	.03
□ 5	Al Simmons	.25	.10	.02
□ 6	Carl Hubbell	.25	.10	.02
□ 7	Joe Cronin	.25	.10	.02
□ 8	Mel Ott	.35	.14	.03
□ 9	Lefty Gomez	.25	.10	.02
□ 10	Lou Gehrig	1.00	.40	.10
	(Best '30s Player)			
□ 11	Pie Traynor	.25	.10	.02
□ 12	Charlie Gehringer	.25	.10	.02
□ 13	Best '30s Catchers	.25	.10	.02
	Bill Dickey			
	Mickey Cochrane			
	Gabby Hartnett			
□ 14	Best '30s Pitchers	.25	.10	.02
	Dizzy Dean			
	Red Ruffing			
	Paul Derringer			
□ 15	Best '30s Outfielders	.15	.06	.01
	Paul Waner			
	Joe Medwick			
	Earl Averill			
□ 16	Bob Feller	.75	.30	.07
□ 17	Lou Boudreau	.25	.10	.02
□ 18	Enos Slaughter	.25	.10	.02
□ 19	Hal Newhouser	.15	.06	.01
□ 20	Joe DiMaggio	1.50	.60	.15
□ 21	Pee Wee Reese	.45	.18	.04
□ 22	Phil Rizzuto	.35	.14	.03
□ 23	Ernie Lombardi	.15	.06	.01
□ 24	Best '40s Infielders	.25	.10	.02
	Johnny Mize			
	Joe Gordon			
	George Kell			
□ 25	Ted Williams	1.00	.40	.10
	(Best '40s Player)			
□ 26	Mickey Mantle	3.00	1.20	.30
□ 27	Warren Spahn	.35	.14	.03
□ 28	Jackie Robinson	.75	.30	.07
□ 29	Ernie Banks	.35	.14	.03
□ 30	Stan Musial	.75	.30	.07
	(Best '50s Player)			
□ 31	Yogi Berra	.75	.30	.07

□ 32 Duke Snider	.75	.30	.07
□ 33 Roy Campanella	.75	.30	.07
□ 34 Eddie Mathews	.35	.14	.03
□ 35 Ralph Kiner	.25	.10	.02
□ 36 Early Wynn	.25	.10	.02
□ 37 Double Play Duo	.25	.10	.02
Nellie Fox			
Luis Aparicio			
□ 38 Best '50s First Base	.15	.06	.01
Gil Hodges			
Ted Kluszewski			
Mickey Vernon			
□ 39 Best '50s Pitchers	.15	.06	.01
Bob Lemon			
Don Newcombe			
Robin Roberts			
□ 40 Henry Aaron	1.00	.40	.10
□ 41 Frank Robinson	.35	.14	.03
□ 42 Bob Gibson	.35	.14	.03
□ 43 Roberto Clemente	1.00	.40	.10
□ 44 Whitey Ford	.45	.18	.04
□ 45 Brooks Robinson	.50	.20	.05
□ 46 Juan Marichal	.25	.10	.02
□ 47 Carl Yastrzemski	1.00	.40	.10
□ 48 Best '60s First Base	.25	.10	.02
Willie McCovey			
Harmon Killebrew			
Orlando Cepeda			
□ 49 Best '60s Catchers	.15	.06	.01
Joe Torre			
Elston Howard			
Bill Freehan			
□ 50 Willie Mays	1.00	.40	.10
(Best '50s Player)			
□ 51 Best '60s Outfielders	.25	.10	.02
Al Kaline			
Tony Oliva			
Billy Williams			
□ 52 Tom Seaver	.75	.30	.07
□ 53 Reggie Jackson	1.00	.40	.10
□ 54 Steve Carlton	.75	.30	.07
□ 55 Mike Schmidt	1.00	.40	.10
□ 56 Joe Morgan	.35	.14	.03
□ 57 Jim Rice	.25	.10	.02
□ 58 Jim Palmer	.35	.14	.03
□ 59 Lou Brock	.35	.14	.03
□ 60 Pete Rose	1.25	.50	.12
(Best '70s Player)			
□ 61 Steve Garvey	.50	.20	.05
□ 62 Best '70s Catchers	.15	.06	.01
Thurman Munson			
Carlton Fisk			
Ted Simmons			
□ 63 Best '70s Pitchers	.25	.10	.02
Vida Blue			
Catfish Hunter			
Nolan Ryan			
□ 64 George Brett	1.00	.40	.10
□ 65 Don Mattingly	2.00	.80	.20
□ 66 Fernando Valenzuela	.25	.10	.02
□ 67 Dale Murphy	.75	.30	.07
□ 68 Wade Boggs	1.25	.50	.12
□ 69 Rickey Henderson	.90	.36	.09
□ 70 Eddie Murray	.60	.24	.06
(Best '80s Player)			
□ 71 Ron Guidry	.15	.06	.01
□ 72 Best '80s Catchers	.25	.10	.02
Gary Carter			
Lance Parrish			
Tony Pena			
□ 73 Best '80s Infielders	.25	.10	.02
Cal Ripken			
Lou Whitaker			
Robin Yount			
□ 74 Best '80s Outfielders	.25	.10	.02
Pedro Guerrero			
Tim Raines			
Dave Winfield			
□ 75 Dwight Gooden	.75	.30	.07

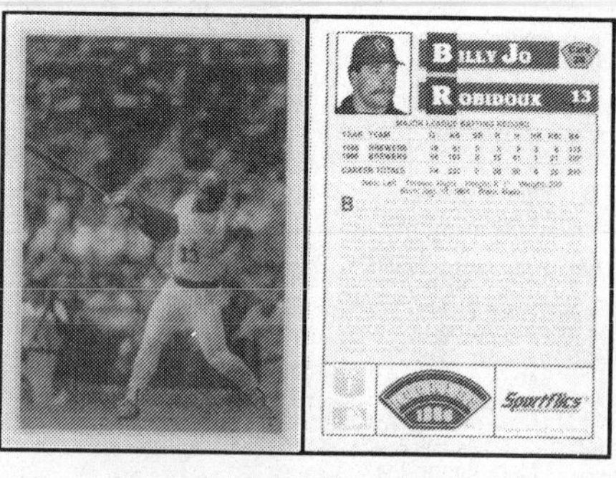

1986 Sportflics Rookies

This set of 50 three-phase "animated" cards features top rookies of 1986 as well as a few outstanding rookies from the past. These "Magic Motion" cards are standard size, 2 1/2" by 3 1/2", and feature a distinctive light blue border on the front of the card. Cards were distributed in a light blue box, which also contained 34 trivia cards, each measuring 1 3/4" by 2". There are 47 single player cards along with two Tri-Stars and one Big Six.

	MINT	EXC	G-VG
COMPLETE SET (50)	14.00	5.75	1.40
COMMON PLAYER (1-50)	.10	.04	.01
□ 1 John Kruk	.25	.10	.02
□ 2 Edwin Correa	.15	.06	.01
□ 3 Pete Incaviglia	.75	.30	.07
□ 4 Dale Sveum	.15	.06	.01
□ 5 Juan Nieves	.15	.06	.01
□ 6 Will Clark	2.50	1.00	.25
□ 7 Wally Joyner	2.00	.80	.20
□ 8 Lance McCullers	.15	.06	.01
□ 9 Scott Bailes	.15	.06	.01
□ 10 Dan Plesac	.20	.08	.02
□ 11 Jose Canseco	3.50	1.40	.35
□ 12 Bobby Witt	.25	.10	.02
□ 13 Barry Bonds	.75	.30	.07
□ 14 Andres Thomas	.20	.08	.02
□ 15 Jim Deshaies	.20	.08	.02
□ 16 Ruben Sierra	1.25	.50	.12
□ 17 Steve Lombardozzi	.10	.04	.01
□ 18 Cory Snyder	1.00	.40	.10
□ 19 Reggie Williams	.10	.04	.01
□ 20 Mitch Williams	.15	.06	.01
□ 21 Glenn Braggs	.25	.10	.02
□ 22 Danny Tartabull	.75	.30	.07
□ 23 Charlie Kerfeld	.15	.06	.01
□ 24 Paul Assenmacher	.15	.06	.01
□ 25 Robby Thompson	.25	.10	.02
□ 26 Bobby Bonilla	.75	.30	.07
□ 27 Andres Galarraga	.75	.30	.07
□ 28 Billy Jo Robidoux	.15	.06	.01
□ 29 Bruce Ruffin	.20	.08	.02
□ 30 Greg Swindell	.45	.18	.04
□ 31 John Cangelosi	.15	.06	.01
□ 32 Jim Traber	.10	.04	.01
□ 33 Russ Morman	.15	.06	.01
□ 34 Barry Larkin	.75	.30	.07
□ 35 Todd Worrell	.45	.18	.04
□ 36 John Cerutti	.15	.06	.01
□ 37 Mike Kingery	.10	.04	.01
□ 38 Mark Eichhorn	.20	.08	.02
□ 39 Scott Bankhead	.15	.06	.01
□ 40 Bo Jackson	1.00	.40	.10
□ 41 Greg Mathews	.25	.10	.02
□ 42 Eric King	.15	.06	.01
□ 43 Kal Daniels	1.00	.40	.10
□ 44 Calvin Schiraldi	.15	.06	.01
□ 45 Mickey Brantley	.20	.08	.02
□ 46 Tri-Stars	.50	.20	.05
Willie Mays			
Pete Rose			
Fred Lynn			
□ 47 Tri-Stars	.50	.20	.05
Tom Seaver			
Fern. Valenzuela			
Dwight Gooden			
□ 48 Big Six	.50	.20	.05
Eddie Murray			
Lou Whitaker			
Dave Righetti			
Steve Sax			
Cal Ripken Jr.			
Darryl Strawberry			
□ 49 Kevin Mitchell	.30	.12	.03
□ 50 Mike Diaz	.15	.06	.01

1987 Sportflics

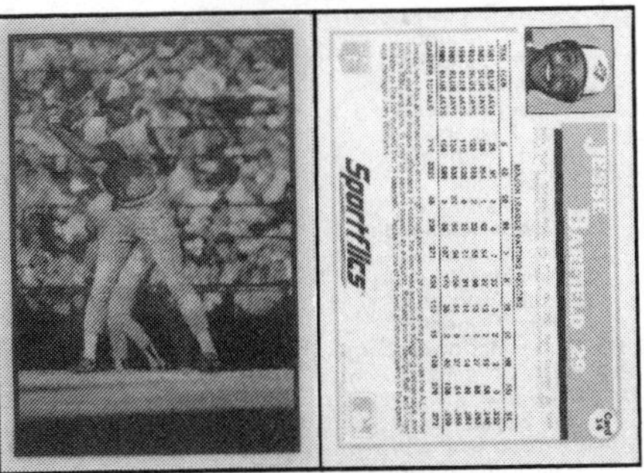

This 200-card set was produced by Sportflics and again features three sequence action pictures on each card. Cards measure 2 1/2" by 3 1/2" and are in full color. Also included with the cards were 136 small team logo and trivia cards. There are 165 individual players, 20 Tri-Stars (the top three players in each league at each position), and 15 other miscellaneous multi-player cards. The cards feature a red border on the front. A full-color face shot of the player is printed on the back of the card. Cards are numbered on the back in the upper right corner. The cards in the factory collated sets are copyrighted 1986, while the cards in the wax packs are copyrighted 1987 or show no copyright year on the back. Cards from wax packs with 1987 copyright are 1-35, 41-75, 81-115, 121-155, and 161-195; the rest of the numbers (when taken from wax packs) are found without a copyright year.

	MINT	EXC	G-VG
COMPLETE SET (200)	32.00	13.00	3.20
COMMON PLAYER (1-200)	.12	.05	.01
□ 1 Don Mattingly	3.00	1.20	.30
□ 2 Wade Boggs	2.00	.80	.20
□ 3 Dale Murphy	.90	.36	.09
□ 4 Rickey Henderson	.70	.28	.07
□ 5 George Brett	.70	.28	.07
□ 6 Eddie Murray	.60	.24	.06
□ 7 Kirby Puckett	.80	.32	.08
□ 8 Ryne Sandberg	.40	.16	.04
□ 9 Cal Ripken	.45	.18	.04
□ 10 Roger Clemens	1.25	.50	.12
□ 11 Ted Higuera	.30	.12	.03
□ 12 Steve Sax	.25	.10	.02
□ 13 Chris Brown	.15	.06	.01
□ 14 Jesse Barfield	.30	.12	.03
□ 15 Kent Hrbek	.30	.12	.03
□ 16 Robin Yount	.35	.14	.03
□ 17 Glenn Davis	.35	.14	.03
□ 18 Hubie Brooks	.15	.06	.01
□ 19 Mike Scott	.30	.12	.03
□ 20 Darryl Strawberry	.85	.34	.08
□ 21 Alvin Davis	.15	.06	.01
□ 22 Eric Davis	1.25	.50	.12
□ 23 Danny Tartabull	.45	.18	.04
□ 24A Cory Snyder ERR '86 ...	3.00	1.20	.30
(photo on front			
is Pat Tabler)			
□ 24B Cory Snyder ERR '87 ...	2.00	.80	.20
(photos on front and			
back are Pat Tabler)			
□ 24C Cory Snyder COR '86 ..	2.00	.80	.20
□ 25 Pete Rose	1.00	.40	.10
□ 26 Wally Joyner	1.25	.50	.12
□ 27 Pedro Guerrero	.25	.10	.02
□ 28 Tom Seaver	.60	.24	.06
□ 29 Bob Knepper	.15	.06	.01
□ 30 Mike Schmidt	.90	.36	.09
□ 31 Tony Gwynn	.75	.30	.07
□ 32 Don Slaught	.12	.05	.01
□ 33 Todd Worrell	.30	.12	.03
□ 34 Tim Raines	.35	.14	.03
□ 35 Dave Parker	.25	.10	.02
□ 36 Bob Ojeda	.15	.06	.01
□ 37 Pete Incaviglia	.60	.24	.06
□ 38 Bruce Hurst	.20	.08	.02
□ 39 Bobby Witt	.25	.10	.02
□ 40 Steve Garvey	.60	.24	.06
□ 41 Dave Winfield	.45	.18	.04
□ 42 Jose Cruz	.15	.06	.01
□ 43 Orel Hershiser	.65	.26	.06
□ 44 Reggie Jackson	.85	.34	.08
□ 45 Chili Davis	.15	.06	.01
□ 46 Robby Thompson	.20	.08	.02
□ 47 Dennis Boyd	.15	.06	.01
□ 48 Kirk Gibson	.45	.18	.04
□ 49 Fred Lynn	.20	.08	.02
□ 50 Gary Carter	.50	.20	.05
□ 51 George Bell	.35	.14	.03
□ 52 Pete O'Brien	.15	.06	.01
□ 53 Ron Darling	.25	.10	.02
□ 54 Paul Molitor	.30	.12	.03
□ 55 Mike Pagliarulo	.15	.06	.01
□ 56 Mike Boddicker	.15	.06	.01
□ 57 Dave Righetti	.20	.08	.02
□ 58 Len Dykstra	.20	.08	.02
□ 59 Mike Witt	.20	.08	.02
□ 60 Tony Bernazard	.12	.05	.01
□ 61 John Kruk	.25	.10	.02
□ 62 Mike Krukow	.15	.06	.01
□ 63 Sid Fernandez	.25	.10	.02
□ 64 Gary Gaetti	.30	.12	.03
□ 65 Vince Coleman	.50	.20	.05
□ 66 Pat Tabler	.15	.06	.01
□ 67 Mike Scioscia	.15	.06	.01
□ 68 Scott Garrelts	.12	.05	.01
□ 69 Brett Butler	.15	.06	.01
□ 70 Bill Buckner	.15	.06	.01
□ 71A Dennis Rasmussen	1.00	.40	.10
ERR '86 copyright			
(photo on back			
is John Montefusco)			
□ 71B Dennis Rasmussen	.50	.20	.05
COR '87 copyright			
(photo with mustache)			
□ 72 Tim Wallach	.15	.06	.01
□ 73 Bob Horner	.20	.08	.02
□ 74 Willie McGee	.25	.10	.02
□ 75 Tri-Stars	1.25	.50	.12
Don Mattingly			
Wally Joyner			
Eddie Murray			
□ 76 Jesse Orosco	.12	.05	.01
□ 77 Tri-Stars	.15	.06	.01
Todd Worrell			
Jeff Reardon			
Lee Smith			
□ 78 Candy Maldonado	.20	.08	.02
□ 79 Tri-Stars	.20	.08	.02
Ozzie Smith			
Hubie Brooks			
Shawon Dunston			
□ 80 Tri-Stars	1.00	.40	.10
George Bell			
Jose Canseco			
Jim Rice			
□ 81 Bert Blyleven	.20	.08	.02
□ 82 Mike Marshall	.20	.08	.02
□ 83 Ron Guidry	.20	.08	.02
□ 84 Julio Franco	.15	.06	.01
□ 85 Willie Wilson	.20	.08	.02
□ 86 Lee Lacy	.12	.05	.01
□ 87 Jack Morris	.30	.12	.03
□ 88 Ray Knight	.15	.06	.01
□ 89 Phil Bradley	.20	.08	.02
□ 90 Jose Canseco	3.00	1.20	.30
□ 91 Gary Ward	.12	.05	.01
□ 92 Mike Easler	.12	.05	.01
□ 93 Tony Pena	.15	.06	.01
□ 94 Dave Smith	.15	.06	.01
□ 95 Will Clark	1.50	.60	.15
□ 96 Lloyd Moseby	.15	.06	.01
□ 97 Jim Rice	.35	.14	.03
□ 98 Shawon Dunston	.20	.08	.02
□ 99 Don Sutton	.35	.14	.03
□ 100 Dwight Gooden	.85	.34	.08
□ 101 Lance Parrish	.25	.10	.02
□ 102 Mark Langston	.25	.10	.02
□ 103 Floyd Youmans	.20	.08	.02
□ 104 Lee Smith	.15	.06	.01
□ 105 Willie Hernandez	.20	.08	.02
□ 106 Doug DeCinces	.15	.06	.01
□ 107 Ken Schrom	.12	.05	.01
□ 108 Don Carman	.12	.05	.01
□ 109 Brook Jacoby	.20	.08	.02
□ 110 Steve Bedrosian	.25	.10	.02
□ 111 Tri-Stars	.60	.24	.06
Roger Clemens			
Jack Morris			

Ted Higuera
□ 112 Tri-Stars .... .15 .06 .01
Marty Barrett
Tony Bernazard
Lou Whitaker
□ 113 Tri-Stars .... .30 .12 .03
Cal Ripken
Scott Fletcher
Tony Fernandez
□ 114 Tri-Stars .... .90 .36 .09
Wade Boggs
George Brett
Gary Gaetti
□ 115 Tri-Stars .... .45 .18 .04
Mike Schmidt
Chris Brown
Tim Wallach
□ 116 Tri-Stars .... .25 .10 .02
Ryne Sandberg
Johnny Ray
Bill Doran
□ 117 Tri-Stars .... .30 .12 .03
Dave Parker
Tony Gwynn
Kevin Bass
□ 118 Big Six Rookies .... 2.50 1.00 .25
Ty Gainey
Terry Steinbach
David Clark
Pat Dodson
Phil Lombardi
Benito Santiago
□ 119 Hi-Lite Tri-Stars .... .30 .12 .03
Dave Righetti
Fernando Valenzuela
Mike Scott
□ 120 Tri-Stars .... .60 .24 .06
Fernando Valenzuela
Mike Scott
Dwight Gooden
□ 121 Johnny Ray .... .15 .06 .01
□ 122 Keith Moreland .... .12 .05 .01
□ 123 Juan Samuel .... .20 .08 .02
□ 124 Wally Backman .... .12 .05 .01
□ 125 Nolan Ryan .... .75 .30 .07
□ 126 Greg Harris .... .12 .05 .01
□ 127 Kirk McCaskill .... .15 .06 .01
□ 128 Dwight Evans .... .25 .10 .02
□ 129 Rick Rhoden .... .15 .06 .01
□ 130 Bill Madlock .... .15 .06 .01
□ 131 Oddibe McDowell .... .20 .08 .02
□ 132 Darrell Evans .... .20 .08 .02
□ 133 Keith Hernandez .... .30 .12 .03
□ 134 Tom Brunansky .... .20 .08 .02
□ 135 Kevin McReynolds .... .60 .24 .06
□ 136 Scott Fletcher .... .15 .06 .01
□ 137 Lou Whitaker .... .20 .08 .02
□ 138 Carney Lansford .... .20 .08 .02
□ 139 Andre Dawson .... .35 .14 .03
□ 140 Carlton Fisk .... .25 .10 .02
□ 141 Buddy Bell .... .15 .06 .01
□ 142 Ozzie Smith .... .40 .16 .04
□ 143 Dan Pasqua .... .20 .08 .02
□ 144 Kevin Mitchell .... .25 .10 .02
□ 145 Bret Saberhagen .... .30 .12 .03
□ 146 Charlie Kerfeld .... .15 .06 .01
□ 147 Phil Niekro .... .35 .14 .03
□ 148 John Candelaria .... .15 .06 .01
□ 149 Rich Gedman .... .15 .06 .01
□ 150 Fernando Valenzuela ...... .35 .14 .03
□ 151 Tri-Stars .... .25 .10 .02
Gary Carter
Mike Scioscia
Tony Pena
□ 152 Tri-Stars .... .45 .18 .04
Tim Raines
Jose Cruz
Vince Coleman
□ 153 Tri-Stars .... .35 .14 .03
Jesse Barfield
Harold Baines
Dave Winfield
□ 154 Tri-Stars .... .20 .08 .02
Lance Parrish
Don Slaught
Rich Gedman
□ 155 Tri-Stars .... .80 .32 .08
Dale Murphy
Kevin McReynolds
Eric Davis
□ 156 Hi-Lite Tri-Stars .... .45 .18 .04
Don Sutton
Mike Schmidt
Jim Deshaies
□ 157 Speedburners .... .35 .14 .03
Rickey Henderson
John Cangelosi
Gary Pettis
□ 158 Big Six Rookies .... 3.00 1.20 .30
Randy Asadoor
Casey Candaele
Kevin Seitzer
Rafael Palmeiro
Tim Pyznarski
Dave Cochrane
□ 159 Big Six .... 2.00 .80 .20
Don Mattingly
Rickey Henderson
Roger Clemens
Dale Murphy
Eddie Murray
Dwight Gooden
□ 160 Roger McDowell .... .20 .08 .02
□ 161 Brian Downing .... .15 .06 .01
□ 162 Bill Doran .... .20 .08 .02
□ 163 Don Baylor .... .20 .08 .02
□ 164A Alfredo Griffin ERR .... .25 .10 .02
(no uniform number
on card back) '87
□ 164A Alfredo Griffin .... .25 .10 .02
COR '86
□ 165 Don Aase .... .12 .05 .01
□ 166 Glenn Wilson .... .15 .06 .01
□ 167 Dan Quisenberry .... .20 .08 .02
□ 168 Frank White .... .15 .06 .01
□ 169 Cecil Cooper .... .15 .06 .01
□ 170 Jody Davis .... .20 .08 .02
□ 171 Harold Baines .... .25 .10 .02
□ 172 Rob Deer .... .25 .10 .02
□ 173 John Tudor .... .25 .10 .02
□ 174 Larry Parrish .... .12 .05 .01
□ 175 Kevin Bass .... .20 .08 .02
□ 176 Joe Carter .... .40 .16 .04
□ 177 Mitch Webster .... .15 .06 .01
□ 178 Dave Kingman .... .20 .08 .02
□ 179 Jim Presley .... .25 .10 .02
□ 180 Mel Hall .... .20 .08 .02
□ 181 Shane Rawley .... .15 .06 .01
□ 182 Marty Barrett .... .25 .10 .02
□ 183 Damaso Garcia .... .12 .05 .01
□ 184 Bobby Grich .... .20 .08 .02
□ 185 Leon Durham .... .12 .05 .01
□ 186 Ozzie Guillen .... .20 .08 .02
□ 187 Tony Fernandez .... .30 .12 .03
□ 188 Alan Trammell .... .35 .14 .03
□ 189 Jim Clancy .... .12 .05 .01
□ 190 Bo Jackson .... 1.25 .50 .12
□ 191 Bob Forsch .... .12 .05 .01
□ 192 John Franco .... .20 .08 .02
□ 193 Von Hayes .... .20 .08 .02
□ 194 Tri-Stars .... .15 .06 .01
Don Aase
Dave Righetti
Mark Eichhorn
□ 195 Tri-Stars .... .60 .24 .06
Keith Hernandez
Will Clark
Glenn Davis
□ 196 Hi-Lite Tri-Stars .... .50 .20 .05
Roger Clemens
Joe Cowley
Bob Horner
□ 197 Big Six .... .90 .36 .09
George Brett
Hubie Brooks
Tony Gwynn
Ryne Sandberg
Tim Raines
Wade Boggs
□ 198 Tri-Stars .... .50 .20 .05
Kirby Puckett
Rickey Henderson
Fred Lynn
□ 199 Speedburners .... .90 .36 .09
Tim Raines
Vince Coleman
Eric Davis
□ 200 Steve Carlton .... .40 .16 .04

1987 Sportflics Dealer Panels

These "Magic Motion" card panels of four were issued only to dealers who were ordering other Sportflics product in quantity. If cut into individual

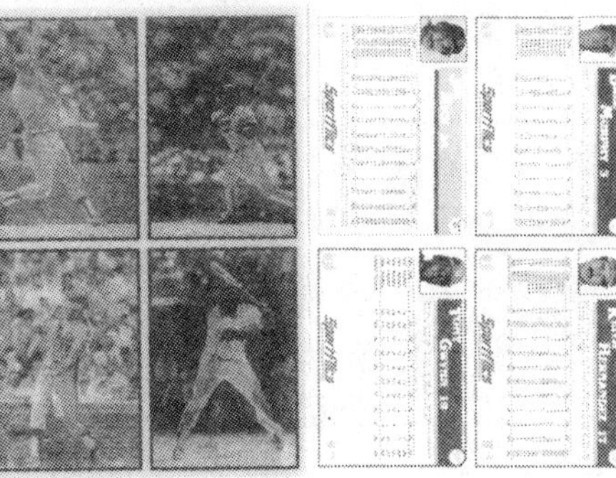

cards, the interior white borders will be slightly narrower than the regular issue Sportflics since the panels of four measure a shade under 4 7/8" by 6 7/8". The cards have a 1986 copyright on the back same as the factory collated sets. Other than the slight difference in size, these cards are essentially styled the same as the regular issue of 1987 Sportflics. This set of sixteen top players was accompanied by the inclusion of four smaller panels of four team logo/team fact cards. The 16 small team cards correspond directly to the 16 players in the sets. The checklist below prices the panels and gives the card number for each player, which is the same as the player's card number in the Sportflics regular set.

	MINT	EXC	G-VG
COMPLETE SET (4)	12.00	5.00	1.20
COMMON PANEL (1-4)	3.00	1.20	.30
□ 1 Don Mattingly 1 Roger Clemens 10 Mike Schmidt 30 Tim Raines 34	5.00	2.00	.50
□ 2 Wade Boggs 2 Eddie Murray 6 Wally Joyner 26 Fern.Valenzuela 150	4.00	1.60	.40
□ 3 Dale Murphy 3 Tony Gwynn 31 Jim Rice 97 Keith Hernandez 133	3.00	1.20	.30
□ 4 Rickey Henderson 4 George Brett 5 Cal Ripken 9 Dwight Gooden 100	3.00	1.20	.30

1987 Sportflics Team Preview

This 26-card set features a card for each Major League team. Each card shows 12 different players on that team via four "Magic Motion" trios. The cards are numbered on the backs. The narrative on the back gives Outlook, Newcomers to Watch, and Summary for each team. The list of players appearing on the front is given at the bottom of the reverse of each card. Cards are standard size, 2 1/2" by 3 1/2". The was distributed as a complete set in its own box along with 26 team logo trivia cards measuring 1 3/4" by 2".

	MINT	EXC	G-VG
COMPLETE SET (26)	7.00	2.80	.70
COMMON PLAYER (1-26)	.50	.20	.05
□ 1 Texas Rangers	.50	.20	.05
□ 2 New York Mets	.60	.24	.06
□ 3 Cleveland Indians	.50	.20	.05
□ 4 Cincinnati Reds	.60	.24	.06
□ 5 Toronto Blue Jays	.50	.20	.05
□ 6 Philadelphia Phillies	.50	.20	.05
□ 7 New York Yankees	.60	.24	.06
□ 8 Houston Astros	.50	.20	.05
□ 9 Boston Red Sox	.60	.24	.06
□ 10 San Francisco Giants	.50	.20	.05
□ 11 California Angels	.50	.20	.05
□ 12 St. Louis Cardinals	.60	.24	.06
□ 13 Kansas City Royals	.60	.24	.06
□ 14 Los Angeles Dodgers	.60	.24	.06
□ 15 Detroit Tigers	.60	.24	.06
□ 16 San Diego Padres	.50	.20	.05
□ 17 Minnesota Twins	.60	.24	.06
□ 18 Pittsburgh Pirates	.50	.20	.05
□ 19 Milwaukee Brewers	.50	.20	.05
□ 20 Montreal Expos	.50	.20	.05
□ 21 Baltimore Orioles	.60	.24	.06
□ 22 Chicago Cubs	.50	.20	.05
□ 23 Oakland Athletics	.60	.24	.06
□ 24 Atlanta Braves	.50	.20	.05
□ 25 Seattle Mariners	.50	.20	.05
□ 26 Chicago White Sox	.50	.20	.05

1987 Sportflics Rookie Packs

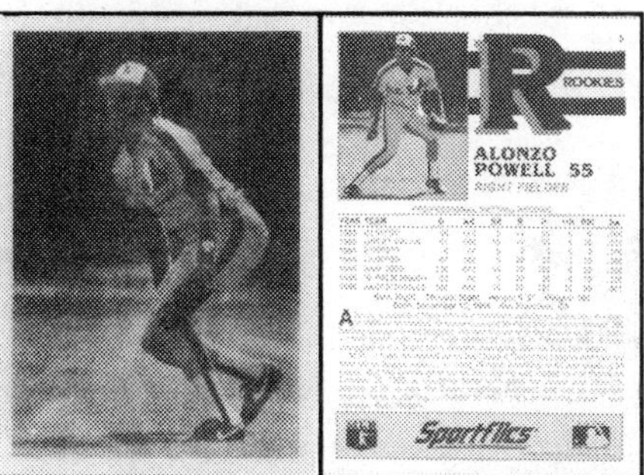

This two pack set consists of 10 "rookie" players and 2 trivia cards. Each of the two different packs had half the set and the outside of the wrapper told which cards were inside. The cards are all 2 1/2" by 3 1/2". The set includes the first major league baseball cards ever of Alonzo Powell, John Smiley, and Brick Smith. Dealers received one rookie pack with every Team Preview set they ordered. The card backs also feature a full-color small photo of the player.

	MINT	EXC	G-VG
COMPLETE SET (10)	7.00	2.80	.70
COMMON PLAYER (1-10)	.40	.16	.04
□ 1 Terry Steinbach (pack two)	1.00	.40	.10
□ 2 Rafael Palmeiro (pack one)	1.25	.50	.12
□ 3 Dave Magadan (pack two)	.75	.30	.07
□ 4 Marvin Freeman (pack two)	.40	.16	.04
□ 5 Brick Smith	.40	.16	.04

		MINT	EXC	G-VG
	(pack two)			
□ 6	B.J. Surhoff	.75	.30	.07
	(pack one)			
□ 7	John Smiley	.75	.30	.07
	(pack one)			
□ 8	Alonzo Powell	.40	.16	.04
	(pack two)			
□ 9	Benny Santiago	2.50	1.00	.25
	(pack one)			
□ 10	Devon White	1.25	.50	.12
	(pack one)			

1987 Sportflics Rookies I

These "Magic Motion" cards were issued as a series of 25 cards packaged in its own complete set box, along with 17 trivia cards. Cards are 2 1/2" by 3 1/2." The three front photos show the player in two action poses and one portrait pose. The card backs also provide a full-color photo (1 3/8" by 2 1/4") of the player as well as the usual statistics and biographical notes. The front photos are framed by a wide, round-cornered, red border and have the player's name and uniform number at the bottom.

		MINT	EXC	G-VG
	COMPLETE SET (25)	7.50	3.00	.75
	COMMON PLAYER (1-25)	.12	.05	.01
□ 1	Eric Bell	.12	.05	.01
□ 2	Chris Bosio	.12	.05	.01
□ 3	Bob Brower	.12	.05	.01
□ 4	Jerry Browne	.12	.05	.01
□ 5	Ellis Burks	1.00	.40	.10
□ 6	Casey Candaele	.12	.05	.01
□ 7	Ken Gerhart	.12	.05	.01
□ 8	Mike Greenwell	2.00	.80	.20
□ 9	Stan Jefferson	.25	.10	.02
□ 10	Dave Magadan	.35	.14	.03
□ 11	Joe Magrane	.35	.14	.03
□ 12	Fred McGriff	1.00	.40	.10
□ 13	Mark McGwire	1.75	.70	.17
□ 14	Mark McLemore	.12	.05	.01
□ 15	Jeff Musselman	.12	.05	.01
□ 16	Matt Nokes	.50	.20	.05
□ 17	Paul O'Neill	.25	.10	.02
□ 18	Luis Polonia	.25	.10	.02
□ 19	Benny Santiago	1.00	.40	.10
□ 20	Kevin Seitzer	1.50	.60	.15
□ 21	John Smiley	.30	.12	.03
□ 22	Terry Steinbach	.50	.20	.05
□ 23	B.J. Surhoff	.35	.14	.03
□ 24	Devon White	.50	.20	.05
□ 25	Matt Williams	.35	.14	.03

1987 Sportflics Rookies II

These "Magic Motion" cards were issued as a series of 25 cards packaged in its own complete set box along with 17 trivia cards. Cards are 2 1/2" by 3 1/2." In this second set the card numbering begins

with number 26. The three front photos show the player in two action poses and one portrait pose. The card backs also provide a full-color photo (1 3/8" by 2 1/4") of the player as well as the usual statistics and biographical notes. The front photos are framed by a wide, round-cornered, red border and have the player's name and uniform number at the bottom.

		MINT	EXC	G-VG
	COMPLETE SET (25)	5.00	2.00	.50
	COMMON PLAYER (26-50)	.12	.05	.01
□ 26	DeWayne Buice	.15	.06	.01
□ 27	Willie Fraser	.12	.05	.01
□ 28	Billy Ripken	.25	.10	.02
□ 29	Mike Henneman	.25	.10	.02
□ 30	Shawn Hillegas	.12	.05	.01
□ 31	Shane Mack	.20	.08	.02
□ 32	Rafael Palmeiro	.60	.24	.06
□ 33	Mike Jackson	.12	.05	.01
□ 34	Gene Larkin	.30	.12	.03
□ 35	Jimmy Jones	.12	.05	.01
□ 36	Gerald Young	.35	.14	.03
□ 37	Ken Caminiti	.25	.10	.02
□ 38	Sam Horn	.50	.20	.05
□ 39	David Cone	1.00	.40	.10
□ 40	Mike Dunne	.30	.12	.03
□ 41	Ken Williams	.25	.10	.02
□ 42	John Morris	.12	.05	.01
□ 43	Jim Lindeman	.20	.08	.02
□ 44	Todd Benzinger	.35	.14	.03
□ 45	Mike Stanley	.20	.08	.02
□ 46	Les Straker	.20	.08	.02
□ 47	Jeff Robinson	.35	.14	.03
□ 48	Jeff Blauser	.25	.10	.02
□ 49	John Marzano	.25	.10	.02
□ 50	Keith Miller	.25	.10	.02

1988 Sportflics

This 225-card set was produced by Sportflics and again features three sequence action pictures on each card. Cards measure 2 1/2" by 3 1/2" and are in full color. There are 219 individual players, 3 Highlights trios, and 3 Rookie Prospect trio cards. The cards feature a red border on the front. A fullolor action picture of the player is printed on the ack of the card. Cards are numbered on the back 1 the lower right corner.

	MINT	EXC	G-VG
OMPLETE SET (225)	33.00	12.00	3.00
OMMON PLAYER (1-225)	.12	.05	.01
1 Don Mattingly	2.50	1.00	.25
2 Tim Raines	.40	.16	.04
3 Andre Dawson	.40	.16	.04
4 George Bell	.35	.14	.03
5 Joe Carter	.30	.12	.03
6 Matt Nokes	.50	.20	.05
7 Dave Winfield	.40	.16	.04
8 Kirby Puckett	.70	.28	.07
9 Will Clark	.90	.36	.09
10 Eric Davis	.90	.36	.09
11 Rickey Henderson	.65	.26	.06
12 Ryne Sandberg	.40	.16	.04
13 Jesse Barfield UER (misspelled Jessie on card back)	.30	.12	.03
14 Ozzie Guillen	.20	.08	.02
15 Bret Saberhagen	.25	.10	.02
16 Tony Gwynn	.50	.20	.05
17 Kevin Seitzer	.90	.36	.09
18 Jack Clark	.30	.12	.03
19 Danny Tartabull	.40	.16	.04
20 Ted Higuera	.25	.10	.02
21 Charlie Leibrandt UER (misspelled Liebrandt on card front)	.15	.06	.01
22 Benny Santiago	.75	.30	.07
23 Fred Lynn	.25	.10	.02
24 Rob Thompson	.15	.06	.01
25 Alan Trammell	.35	.14	.03
26 Tony Fernandez	.25	.10	.02
27 Rick Sutcliffe	.20	.08	.02
28 Gary Carter	.35	.14	.03
29 Cory Snyder	.40	.16	.04
30 Lou Whitaker	.20	.08	.02
31 Keith Hernandez	.30	.12	.03
32 Mike Witt	.20	.08	.02
33 Harold Baines	.20	.08	.02
34 Robin Yount	.40	.16	.04
35 Mike Schmidt	.65	.26	.06
36 Dion James	.12	.05	.01
37 Tom Candiotti	.12	.05	.01
38 Tracy Jones	.20	.08	.02
39 Nolan Ryan	.60	.24	.06
40 Fernando Valenzuela	.35	.14	.03
41 Vance Law	.12	.05	.01
42 Roger McDowell	.20	.08	.02
43 Carlton Fisk	.25	.10	.02
44 Scott Garrelts	.12	.05	.01
45 Lee Guetterman	.12	.05	.01
46 Mark Langston	.25	.10	.02
47 Willie Randolph	.20	.08	.02
48 Bill Doran	.20	.08	.02
49 Larry Parrish	.12	.05	.01
50 Wade Boggs	1.25	.50	.12
51 Shane Rawley	.12	.05	.01
52 Alvin Davis	.15	.06	.01
53 Jeff Reardon	.15	.06	.01
54 Jim Presley	.15	.06	.01
55 Kevin Bass	.15	.06	.01
56 Kevin McReynolds	.45	.18	.04
57 B.J. Surhoff	.20	.08	.02
58 Julio Franco	.15	.06	.01
59 Eddie Murray	.50	.20	.05
60 Jody Davis	.15	.06	.01
61 Todd Worrell	.20	.08	.02
62 Von Hayes	.20	.08	.02
63 Billy Hatcher	.20	.08	.02
64 John Kruk	.25	.10	.02
65 Tom Henke	.15	.06	.01
66 Mike Scott	.30	.12	.03
67 Vince Coleman	.40	.16	.04
68 Ozzie Smith	.35	.14	.03
69 Ken Williams	.25	.10	.02
70 Steve Bedrosian	.20	.08	.02
71 Luis Polonia	.25	.10	.02
72 Brook Jacoby	.15	.06	.01
73 Ron Darling	.25	.10	.02
74 Lloyd Moseby	.15	.06	.01
75 Wally Joyner	.60	.24	.06
76 Dan Quisenberry	.20	.08	.02
77 Scott Fletcher	.15	.06	.01
78 Kirk McCaskill	.12	.05	.01
79 Paul Molitor	.30	.12	.03
80 Mike Aldrete	.20	.08	.02
81 Neal Heaton	.12	.05	.01
82 Jeffrey Leonard	.15	.06	.01
83 Dave Magadan	.20	.08	.02
84 Danny Cox	.20	.08	.02
85 Lance McCullers	.15	.06	.01
86 Jay Howell	.12	.05	.01
87 Charlie Hough	.12	.05	.01
88 Gene Garber	.12	.05	.01
89 Jesse Orosco	.12	.05	.01
90 Don Robinson	.12	.05	.01
91 Willie McGee	.25	.10	.02
92 Bert Blyleven	.20	.08	.02
93 Phil Bradley	.20	.08	.02
94 Terry Kennedy	.12	.05	.01
95 Kent Hrbek	.30	.12	.03
96 Juan Samuel	.25	.10	.02
97 Pedro Guerrero	.30	.12	.03
98 Sid Bream	.12	.05	.01
99 Devon White	.30	.12	.03
100 Mark McGwire	1.00	.40	.10
101 Dave Parker	.25	.10	.02
102 Glenn Davis	.30	.12	.03
103 Greg Walker	.20	.08	.02
104 Rick Rhoden	.15	.06	.01
105 Mitch Webster	.12	.05	.01
106 Lenny Dykstra	.20	.08	.02
107 Gene Larkin	.20	.08	.02
108 Floyd Youmans	.12	.05	.01
109 Andy Van Slyke	.35	.14	.03
110 Mike Scioscia	.15	.06	.01
111 Kirk Gibson	.40	.16	.04
112 Kal Daniels	.40	.16	.04
113 Ruben Sierra	.45	.18	.04
114 Sam Horn	.40	.16	.04
115 Ray Knight	.15	.06	.01
116 Jimmy Key	.15	.06	.01
117 Bo Diaz	.12	.05	.01
118 Mike Greenwell	1.25	.50	.12
119 Barry Bonds	.35	.14	.03
120 Reggie Jackson UER (463 lifetime homers)	.50	.20	.05
121 Mike Pagliarulo	.20	.08	.02
122 Tommy John	.20	.08	.02
123 Bill Madlock	.15	.06	.01
124 Ken Caminiti	.25	.10	.02
125 Gary Ward	.12	.05	.01
126 Candy Maldonado	.15	.06	.01
127 Harold Reynolds	.15	.06	.01
128 Joe Magrane	.35	.14	.03
129 Mike Henneman	.25	.10	.02
130 Jim Gantner	.12	.05	.01
131 Bobby Bonilla	.35	.14	.03
132 John Farrell	.35	.14	.03
133 Frank Tanana	.12	.05	.01
134 Zane Smith	.20	.08	.02
135 Dave Righetti	.20	.08	.02
136 Rick Reuschel	.20	.08	.02
137 Dwight Evans	.25	.10	.02
138 Howard Johnson	.25	.10	.02
139 Terry Leach	.20	.08	.02
140 Casey Candaele	.15	.06	.01
141 Tom Herr	.15	.06	.01
142 Tony Pena	.15	.06	.01
143 Lance Parrish	.25	.10	.02
144 Ellis Burks	1.00	.40	.10
145 Pete O'Brien	.20	.08	.02
146 Mike Boddicker	.15	.06	.01
147 Buddy Bell	.15	.06	.01
148 Bo Jackson	.50	.20	.05
149 Frank White	.15	.06	.01
150 George Brett	.50	.20	.05
151 Tim Wallach	.15	.06	.01
152 Cal Ripken Jr.	.40	.16	.04
153 Brett Butler	.15	.06	.01
154 Gary Gaetti	.30	.12	.03
155 Darryl Strawberry	.70	.28	.07
156 Alredo Griffin	.15	.06	.01
157 Marty Barrett	.20	.08	.02
158 Jim Rice	.30	.12	.03
159 Terry Pendleton	.15	.06	.01
160 Orel Hershiser	.65	.26	.06
161 Larry Sheets	.20	.08	.02
162 Dave Stewart UER (Braves logo)	.25	.10	.02
163 Shawon Dunston	.20	.08	.02
164 Keith Moreland	.12	.05	.01
165 Ken Oberkfell	.12	.05	.01
166 Ivan Calderon	.20	.08	.02
167 Bob Welch	.20	.08	.02
168 Fred McGriff	.50	.20	.05
169 Pete Incaviglia	.35	.14	.03
170 Dale Murphy	.60	.24	.06
171 Mike Dunne	.25	.10	.02
172 Chili Davis	.20	.08	.02
173 Milt Thompson	.15	.06	.01
174 Terry Steinbach	.25	.10	.02
175 Oddibe McDowell	.20	.08	.02

□ 176 Jack Morris	.25	.10	.02
□ 177 Sid Fernandez	.20	.08	.02
□ 178 Ken Griffey	.15	.06	.01
□ 179 Lee Smith	.15	.06	.01
□ 180 Highlights 1987 Kirby Puckett Juan Nieves Mike Schmidt	.35	.14	.03
□ 181 Brian Downing	.15	.06	.01
□ 182 Andres Galarraga	.45	.18	.04
□ 183 Rob Deer	.20	.08	.02
□ 184 Greg Brock	.12	.05	.01
□ 185 Doug DeCinces	.12	.05	.01
□ 186 Johnny Ray	.12	.05	.01
□ 187 Hubie Brooks	.15	.06	.01
□ 188 Darrell Evans	.15	.06	.01
□ 189 Mel Hall	.15	.06	.01
□ 190 Jim Deshaies	.12	.05	.01
□ 191 Dan Plesac	.20	.08	.02
□ 192 Willie Wilson	.20	.08	.02
□ 193 Mike LaValliere	.12	.05	.01
□ 194 Tom Brunansky	.25	.10	.02
□ 195 John Franco	.20	.08	.02
□ 196 Frank Viola	.35	.14	.03
□ 197 Bruce Hurst	.25	.10	.02
□ 198 John Tudor	.20	.08	.02
□ 199 Bob Forsch	.12	.05	.01
□ 200 Dwight Gooden	.70	.28	.07
□ 201 Jose Canseco	1.75	.70	.17
□ 202 Carney Lansford	.20	.08	.02
□ 203 Kelly Downs	.15	.06	.01
□ 204 Glenn Wilson	.15	.06	.01
□ 205 Pat Tabler	.15	.06	.01
□ 206 Mike Davis	.15	.06	.01
□ 207 Roger Clemens	.90	.36	.09
□ 208 Dave Smith	.15	.06	.01
□ 209 Curt Young	.15	.06	.01
□ 210 Mark Eichhorn	.15	.06	.01
□ 211 Juan Nieves	.15	.06	.01
□ 212 Bob Boone	.15	.06	.01
□ 213 Don Sutton	.30	.12	.03
□ 214 Willie Upshaw	.12	.05	.01
□ 215 Jim Clancy	.12	.05	.01
□ 216 Bill Ripken	.25	.10	.02
□ 217 Ozzie Virgil	.12	.05	.01
□ 218 Dave Concepcion	.15	.06	.01
□ 219 Alan Ashby	.12	.05	.01
□ 220 Mike Marshall	.20	.08	.02
□ 221 Highlights 1987 Mark McGwire Paul Molitor Vince Coleman	.60	.24	.06
□ 222 Highlights 1987 Benito Santiago Steve Bedrosian Don Mattingly	.75	.30	.07
□ 223 Rookie Prospects Shawn Abner Jay Buhner Gary Thurman	1.00	.40	.10
□ 224 Rookie Prospects Tim Crews Vincente Palacios John Davis	.40	.16	.04
□ 225 Rookie Prospects Jody Reed Jeff Treadway Keith Miller	.75	.30	.07

1988 Sportflics Gamewinners

This 25-card set of "Gamewinners" was distributed in a green and yellow box along with 17 trivia cards by Weiser Card Company of New Jersey. The 25 players selected for the set show a strong New York preference. The set was ostensibly produced for use as a youth organizational fund raiser. The cards are the standard size, 2 1/2" by 3 1/2" and are done in the typical Sportflics' Magic Motion (three picture) style. The cards are numbered on the back.

	MINT	EXC	G-VG
COMPLETE SET (25)	10.00	4.00	1.00
COMMON PLAYER (1-25)	.20	.08	.02
□ 1 Don Mattingly	1.25	.50	.12
□ 2 Mark McGwire	.80	.32	.08

□ 3 Wade Boggs	1.00	.40	.10
□ 4 Will Clark	.80	.32	.08
□ 5 Eric Davis	.80	.32	.08
□ 6 Willie Randolph	.20	.08	.02
□ 7 Dave Winfield	.40	.16	.04
□ 8 Rickey Henderson	.50	.20	.05
□ 9 Dwight Gooden	.50	.20	.05
□ 10 Benny Santiago	.50	.20	.05
□ 11 Keith Hernandez	.40	.16	.04
□ 12 Juan Samuel	.30	.12	.03
□ 13 Kevin Seitzer	.50	.20	.05
□ 14 Gary Carter	.40	.16	.04
□ 15 Darryl Strawberry	.80	.32	.08
□ 16 Rick Rhoden	.20	.08	.02
□ 17 Howard Johnson	.30	.12	.03
□ 18 Matt Nokes	.40	.16	.04
□ 19 Dave Righetti	.30	.12	.03
□ 20 Roger Clemens	.80	.32	.08
□ 21 Mike Schmidt	.60	.24	.06
□ 22 Kevin McReynolds	.50	.20	.05
□ 23 Mike Pagliarulo	.30	.12	.03
□ 24 Kevin Elster	.30	.12	.03
□ 25 Jack Clark	.40	.16	.04

1989 Sportflics

This 225-card set was produced by Sportflics (distributed by Major League Marketing) and again features three sequence action pictures on each card. Cards measure 2 1/2" by 3 1/2" and are in full color. There are 219 individual players, 2 Highlights trios, and 3 Rookie Prospect trio cards. The cards feature a white border on the front with red and blue inner trim colors. A full-color action picture of the player is printed on the back of the card. Cards are numbered on the back in the lower right corner.

	MINT	EXC	G-VG
COMPLETE SET (225)	33.00	11.00	3.00
COMMON PLAYER (1-225)	.10	.04	.01
□ 1 Jose Canseco	1.50	.60	.15
□ 2 Wally Joyner	.50	.20	.05
□ 3 Roger Clemens	.75	.30	.07
□ 4 Greg Swindell	.25	.10	.02
□ 5 Jack Morris	.20	.08	.02
□ 6 Mickey Brantley	.15	.06	.01

□ 7 Jim Presley .15 .06 .01
□ 8 Pete O'Brien .15 .06 .01
□ 9 Jesse Barfield .25 .10 .02
□ 10 Frank Viola .20 .08 .02
□ 11 Kevin Bass .10 .04 .01
□ 12 Glenn Wilson .10 .04 .01
□ 13 Chris Sabo .60 .24 .06
□ 14 Fred McGriff .50 .20 .05
□ 15 Mark Grace .75 .30 .07
□ 16 Devon White .20 .08 .02
□ 17 Juan Samuel .15 .06 .01
□ 18 Lou Whitaker .15 .06 .01
□ 19 Greg Walker .15 .06 .01
□ 20 Roberto Alomar .25 .10 .02
□ 21 Mike Schmidt .60 .24 .06
□ 22 Benny Santiago .50 .20 .05
□ 23 Dave Stewart .15 .06 .01
□ 24 Dave Winfield .40 .16 .04
□ 25 George Bell .20 .08 .02
□ 26 Jack Clark .20 .08 .02
□ 27 Doug Drabek .10 .04 .01
□ 28 Ron Gant .30 .12 .03
□ 29 Glenn Braggs .15 .06 .01
□ 30 Rafael Palmeiro .30 .12 .03
□ 31 Brett Butler .15 .06 .01
□ 32 Ron Darling .20 .08 .02
□ 33 Alvin Davis .15 .06 .01
□ 34 Bob Walk .10 .04 .01
□ 35 Dave Stieb .15 .06 .01
□ 36 Orel Hershiser .75 .30 .07
□ 37 John Farrell .15 .06 .01
□ 38 Doug Jones .15 .06 .01
□ 39 Kelly Downs .15 .06 .01
□ 40 Bob Boone .15 .06 .01
□ 41 Gary Sheffield 1.25 .50 .12
□ 42 Doug Dascenzo .20 .08 .02
□ 43 Chad Kreuter .20 .08 .02
□ 44 Ricky Jordan 1.00 .40 .10
□ 45 Dave West .50 .20 .05
□ 46 Danny Tartabull .30 .12 .03
□ 47 Teddy Higuera .20 .08 .02
□ 48 Gary Gaetti .20 .08 .02
□ 49 Dave Parker .20 .08 .02
□ 50 Don Mattingly 1.25 .50 .12
□ 51 David Cone .50 .20 .05
□ 52 Kal Daniels .30 .12 .03
□ 53 Carney Lansford .15 .06 .01
□ 54 Mike Marshall .20 .08 .02
□ 55 Kevin Seitzer .35 .14 .03
□ 56 Mike Henneman .15 .06 .01
□ 57 Bill Doran .15 .06 .01
□ 58 Steve Sax .20 .08 .02
□ 59 Lance Parrish .15 .06 .01
□ 60 Keith Hernandez .25 .10 .02
□ 61 Jose Uribe .10 .04 .01
□ 62 Jose Lind .15 .06 .01
□ 63 Steve Bedrosian .15 .06 .01
□ 64 George Brett .30 .12 .03
□ 65 Kirk Gibson .30 .12 .03
□ 66 Cal Ripken Jr. .25 .10 .02
□ 67 Mitch Webster .10 .04 .01
□ 68 Fred Lynn .20 .08 .02
□ 69 Eric Davis .75 .30 .07
□ 70 Bo Jackson .60 .24 .06
□ 71 Kevin Elster .20 .08 .02
□ 72 Rick Reuschel .15 .06 .01
□ 73 Tim Burke .10 .04 .01
□ 74 Mark Davis .15 .06 .01
□ 75 Claudell Washington .15 .06 .01
□ 76 Lance McCullers .15 .06 .01
□ 77 Mike Moore .15 .06 .01
□ 78 Robby Thompson .15 .06 .01
□ 79 Roger McDowell .15 .06 .01
□ 80 Danny Jackson .20 .08 .02
□ 81 Tim Leary .15 .06 .01
□ 82 Bobby Witt .20 .08 .02
□ 83 Jim Gott .10 .04 .01
□ 84 Andy Hawkins .15 .06 .01
□ 85 Ozzie Guillen .15 .06 .01
□ 86 John Tudor .15 .06 .01
□ 87 Todd Burns .20 .08 .02
□ 88 Dave Gallagher .15 .06 .01
□ 89 Jay Buhner .20 .08 .02
□ 90 Gregg Jefferies 1.50 .60 .15
□ 91 Bob Welch .10 .04 .01
□ 92 Charlie Hough .10 .04 .01
□ 93 Tony Fernandez .20 .08 .02
□ 94 Ozzie Virgil .10 .04 .01
□ 95 Andre Dawson .25 .10 .02
□ 96 Hubie Brooks .15 .06 .01
□ 97 Kevin McReynolds .35 .14 .03
□ 98 Mike LaValliere .10 .04 .01
□ 99 Terry Pendleton .15 .06 .01
□ 100 Wade Boggs 1.00 .40 .10
□ 101 Dennis Eckersley .20 .08 .02
□ 102 Mark Gubicza .15 .06 .01
□ 103 Frank Tanana .15 .06 .01
□ 104 Joe Carter .25 .10 .02
□ 105 Ozzie Smith .25 .10 .02
□ 106 Dennis Martinez .10 .04 .01
□ 107 Jeff Treadway .15 .06 .01
□ 108 Greg Maddux .20 .08 .02
□ 109 Bret Saberhagen .25 .10 .02
□ 110 Dale Murphy .35 .14 .03
□ 111 Rob Deer .15 .06 .01
□ 112 Pete Incaviglia .30 .12 .03
□ 113 Vince Coleman .25 .10 .02
□ 114 Tim Wallach .15 .06 .01
□ 115 Nolan Ryan .35 .14 .03
□ 116 Walt Weiss .45 .18 .04
□ 117 Brian Downing .15 .06 .01
□ 118 Melido Perez .20 .08 .02
□ 119 Terry Steinbach .20 .08 .02
□ 120 Mike Scott .20 .08 .02
□ 121 Tim Belcher .20 .08 .02
□ 122 Mike Boddicker .15 .06 .01
□ 123 Len Dykstra .20 .08 .02
□ 124 Fernando Valenzuela .25 .10 .02
□ 125 Gerald Young .20 .08 .02
□ 126 Tom Henke .15 .06 .01
□ 127 Dave Henderson .15 .06 .01
□ 128 Dan Plesac .15 .06 .01
□ 129 Chili Davis .15 .06 .01
□ 130 Bryan Harvey .20 .08 .02
□ 131 Don August .15 .06 .01
□ 132 Mike Harkey .50 .20 .05
□ 133 Luis Polonia .15 .06 .01
□ 134 Craig Worthington .20 .08 .02
□ 135 Joey Meyer .15 .06 .01
□ 136 Barry Larkin .20 .08 .02
□ 137 Glenn Davis .20 .08 .02
□ 138 Mike Scioscia .10 .04 .01
□ 139 Andres Galarraga .25 .10 .02
□ 140 Doc Gooden .50 .20 .05
□ 141 Keith Moreland .10 .04 .01
□ 142 Kevin Mitchell .15 .06 .01
□ 143 Mike Greenwell 1.00 .40 .10
□ 144 Mel Hall .15 .06 .01
□ 145 Rickey Henderson .50 .20 .05
□ 146 Barry Bonds .25 .10 .02
□ 147 Eddie Murray .45 .18 .04
□ 148 Lee Smith .15 .06 .01
□ 149 Julio Franco .15 .06 .01
□ 150 Tim Raines .25 .10 .02
□ 151 Mitch Williams .15 .06 .01
□ 152 Tim Laudner .10 .04 .01
□ 153 Mike Pagliarulo .15 .06 .01
□ 154 Floyd Bannister .10 .04 .01
□ 155 Gary Carter .30 .12 .03
□ 156 Kirby Puckett .65 .26 .06
□ 157 Harold Baines .15 .06 .01
□ 158 Dave Righetti .15 .06 .01
□ 159 Mark Langston .15 .06 .01
□ 160 Tony Gwynn .35 .14 .03
□ 161 Tom Brunansky .15 .06 .01
□ 162 Vance Law .10 .04 .01
□ 163 Kelly Gruber .10 .04 .01
□ 164 Gerald Perry .20 .08 .02
□ 165 Harold Reynolds .15 .06 .01
□ 166 Andy Van Slyke .25 .10 .02
□ 167 Jimmy Key .15 .06 .01
□ 168 Jeff Reardon .15 .06 .01
□ 169 Milt Thompson .10 .04 .01
□ 170 Will Clark .75 .30 .07
□ 171 Chet Lemon .10 .04 .01
□ 172 Pat Tabler .10 .04 .01
□ 173 Jim Rice .20 .08 .02
□ 174 Billy Hatcher .15 .06 .01
□ 175 Bruce Hurst .20 .08 .02
□ 176 John Franco .15 .06 .01
□ 177 Van Snider .20 .08 .02
□ 178 Ron Jones .20 .08 .02
□ 179 Jerald Clark .20 .08 .02
□ 180 Tom Browning .20 .08 .02
□ 181 Von Hayes .15 .06 .01
□ 182 Bobby Bonilla .25 .10 .02
□ 183 Todd Worrell .15 .06 .01
□ 184 John Kruk .15 .06 .01
□ 185 Scott Fletcher .15 .06 .01
□ 186 Willie Wilson .15 .06 .01
□ 187 Jody Davis .15 .06 .01
□ 188 Kent Hrbek .20 .08 .02
□ 189 Ruben Sierra .20 .08 .02
□ 190 Shawon Dunston .15 .06 .01
□ 191 Ellis Burks .25 .10 .02
□ 192 Brook Jacoby .15 .06 .01
□ 193 Jeff Robinson .15 .06 .01
Detroit Tigers
□ 194 Rich Dotson .15 .06 .01
□ 195 Johnny Ray .10 .04 .01

□ 196	Cory Snyder	.25	.10	.02
□ 197	Mike Witt	.15	.06	.01
□ 198	Marty Barrett	.15	.06	.01
□ 199	Robin Yount	.30	.12	.03
□ 200	Mark McGwire	.75	.30	.07
□ 201	Ryne Sandberg	.25	.10	.02
□ 202	John Candelaria	.15	.06	.01
□ 203	Matt Nokes	.20	.08	.02
□ 204	Dwight Evans	.20	.08	.02
□ 205	Darryl Strawberry	.75	.30	.07
□ 206	Willie McGee	.20	.08	.02
□ 207	Bobby Thigpen	.15	.06	.01
□ 208	B.J. Surhoff	.15	.06	.01
□ 209	Paul Molitor	.20	.08	.02
□ 210	Jody Reed	.20	.08	.02
□ 211	Doyle Alexander	.15	.06	.01
□ 212	Dennis Rasmussen	.15	.06	.01
□ 213	Kevin Gross	.15	.06	.01
□ 214	Kirk McCaskill	.15	.06	.01
□ 215	Alan Trammell	.25	.10	.02
□ 216	Damon Berryhill	.20	.08	.02
□ 217	Rick Sutcliffe	.15	.06	.01
□ 218	Don Slaught	.10	.04	.01
□ 219	Carlton Fisk	.20	.08	.02
□ 220	Allan Anderson	.20	.08	.02
□ 221	Jose Canseco Wade Boggs Mike Greenwell	1.50	.60	.15
□ 222	Orel Hershiser Dennis Eckersley Tom Browning	.50	.20	.05
□ 223	Gary Sheffield Gregg Jefferies Sandy Alomar	2.50	1.00	.25
□ 224	Bob Milacki Randy Johnson Ramon Martinez	.50	.20	.05
□ 225	Cameron Drew Geronimo Berroa Ron Jones	.50	.20	.05

1981 Squirt

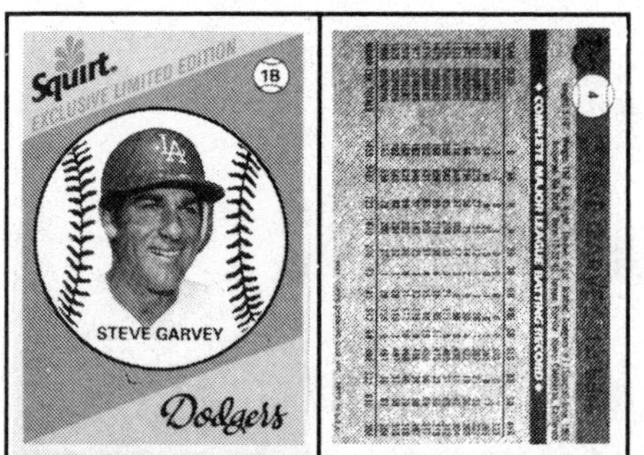

The cards in this 22-panel set consist of 33 different individual cards, each measuring 2 1/2" by 3 1/2" while the panels measure 2 1/2" by 10 1/2"as the 1981 Squirt cards were issued individually as well as in two card panels. Cards numbered 1-11 appear twice, whereas cards 12-33 appear only once in the 22-panel set. The pattern for pairings was 1/12 and 1/23, 2/13 and 2/24, 3/14 and 3/25, and so forth on up to 11/22 and 11/33. Two card panels have a value equal to the sum of the individual cards on the panel. Supposedly panels 4/15, 4/26, 5/27, and 6/28 are more difficult to find than the other panels and are marked as SP in the checklist below.

	MINT	EXC	G-VG
COMPLETE PANEL SET	18.00	7.25	1.80
COMPLETE IND. SET	10.00	4.00	1.00
COMMON PANEL	.40	.16	.04
COMMON PLAYER (1-11) DP	.20	.08	.02
COMMON PLAYER (12-33)	.20	.08	.02

□ 1	George Brett DP	.50	.20	.05
□ 2	George Foster DP	.20	.08	.02
□ 3	Ben Oglivie DP	.20	.08	.02
□ 4	Steve Garvey DP	.75	.30	.07
□ 5	Reggie Jackson DP	.75	.30	.07
□ 6	Bill Buckner DP	.20	.08	.02
□ 7	Jim Rice DP	.25	.10	.02
□ 8	Mike Schmidt DP	.60	.24	.06
□ 9	Rod Carew DP	.45	.18	.04
□ 10	Dave Parker DP	.20	.08	.02
□ 11	Pete Rose DP	.90	.36	.09
□ 12	Garry Templeton	.20	.08	.02
□ 13	Rick Burleson	.20	.08	.02
□ 14	Dave Kingman	.20	.08	.02
□ 15	Eddie Murray SP	3.50	1.40	.35
□ 16	Don Sutton	.60	.24	.06
□ 17	Dusty Baker	.20	.08	.02
□ 18	Jack Clark	.50	.20	.05
□ 19	Dave Winfield	1.00	.40	.10
□ 20	Johnny Bench	1.00	.40	.10
□ 21	Lee Mazzilli	.20	.08	.02
□ 22	Al Oliver	.20	.08	.02
□ 23	Jerry Mumphrey	.20	.08	.02
□ 24	Tony Armas	.20	.08	.02
□ 25	Fred Lynn	.30	.12	.03
□ 26	Ron LeFlore SP	1.00	.40	.10
□ 27	Steve Kemp SP	1.00	.40	.10
□ 28	Rickey Henderson SP	3.50	1.40	.35
□ 29	John Castino	.20	.08	.02
□ 30	Cecil Cooper	.20	.08	.02
□ 31	Bruce Bochte	.20	.08	.02
□ 32	Joe Charboneau	.20	.08	.02
□ 33	Chet Lemon	.20	.08	.02

1982 Squirt

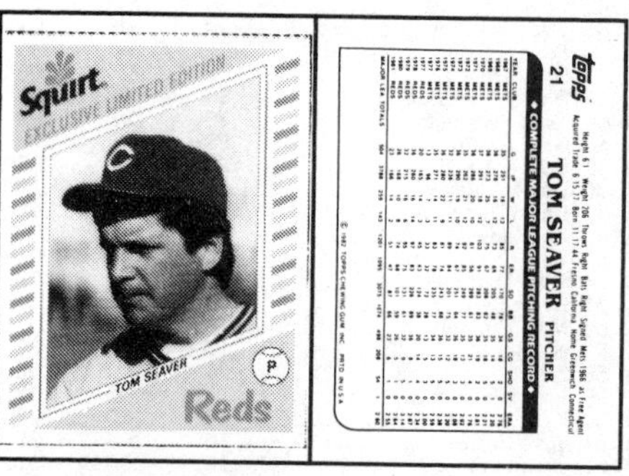

The cards in this 22-card set measure 2 1/2" by 3 1/2". Although the 1982 "Exclusive Limited Edition" was prepared for Squirt by Topps, the format and pictures are completely different from the regular Topps cards of this year. Each color picture is obliquely cut and the word Squirt is printed in red in the top left corner. The cards are numbered 1 through 22 and the reverses are yellow and black on white. The cards were issued on four types of panels: (1) yellow attachment card at top with picture card in center and scratch-off game at bottom; (2) yellow attachment card at top with scratch-off game in center and picture card at bottom; (3) white attachment card at top with "Collect all 22" panel in center and picture card at bottom; (4) two card panel with attachment card at top. The two card panels have parallel cards; that is, numbers 1 and 12 together, numbers 2 and 13 together, etc. Two card panels have a value equal to the sum of the individual cards on the panel. The two types (1 and 2) with the scratch-off games are more slightly difficult to obtain than the other two types and hence command prices double those below.

	MINT	EXC	G-VG
COMPLETE SET (22)	5.00	2.00	.50
COMMON PLAYER (1-22)	.15	.06	.01

□ 1	Cecil Cooper	.20	.08	.02
□ 2	Jerry Remy	.15	.06	.01

No.	Player	NRMT	VG-E	GOOD
☐ 3	George Brett	.75	.30	.07
☐ 4	Alan Trammell	.35	.14	.03
☐ 5	Reggie Jackson	.75	.30	.07
☐ 6	Kirk Gibson	.45	.18	.04
☐ 7	Dave Winfield	.45	.18	.04
☐ 8	Carlton Fisk	.25	.10	.02
☐ 9	Ron Guidry	.20	.08	.02
☐ 10	Dennis Leonard	.15	.06	.01
☐ 11	Rollie Fingers	.25	.10	.02
☐ 12	Pete Rose	1.00	.40	.10
☐ 13	Phil Garner	.15	.06	.01
☐ 14	Mike Schmidt	.75	.30	.07
☐ 15	Dave Concepcion	.15	.06	.01
☐ 16	George Hendrick	.15	.06	.01
☐ 17	Andre Dawson	.35	.14	.03
☐ 18	George Foster	.20	.08	.02
☐ 19	Gary Carter	.45	.18	.04
☐ 20	Fernando Valenzuela	.30	.12	.03
☐ 21	Tom Seaver	.55	.22	.05
☐ 22	Bruce Sutter	.20	.08	.02

1976 SSPC

CINCINNATI 10 REDS

Manager
5'9", 170 lbs.
Bn. 2/22/34
BR-TR

GEORGE LEE (SPARKY) ANDERSON

Prior to '75, Sparky had all kinds of success as Red's skipper - 3 divisional titles and 2 N.L. Championships in 5 seasons, but he'd never reached his goal of a World's Championship. Finally, last year, he guided Cincinnati to 108 wins, a sweep in the playoffs, and a 7-game Series victory over Boston. A second baseman in his playing days, he started in the Dodgers' chain in '53, and spent '59 as the Phillies' regular second sacker, finishing with a .218 average in his only big league season. Returned to the minors and became a skipper in '64, and won 4 titles before joining the Padres as a coach in '69. Joined Reds in '70.

CARD # 22 SSPC 1975

The cards in this 630-card set measure 2 1/2" by 3 1/2". The 1976 "Pure Card" set issued by TCMA derives its name from the lack of borders, logos, signatures, etc., which often clutter up the picture areas of some baseball sets. It differs from other sets produced by this company in that it cannot be reissued due to an agreement entered into by the manufacturer. Thus, while not technically a legitimate issue, it is significant because it cannot be reprinted, unlike other collector issues. There are no scarcities known. The cards are numbered in team groups, i.e., Atlanta (1-21), Cincinnati (22-46), Houston (47- 65), Los Angeles (66-91), San Francisco (92-113), San Diego (114- 133), Chicago White Sox (134-158), Kansas City (159-195), California (186-204), Minnesota (205-225), Milwaukee (226-251), Texas (252-273), St. Louis (274-300), Chicago Cubs (301-321), Montreal (322-351), Detroit (352-373), Baltimore (374-401), Boston (402-424), New York Yankees (425-455), Philadelphia (456- 477), Oakland (478-503), Cleveland (504-532), New York Mets (533- 560), and Pittsburgh (561-586). The rest of the numbers are filled in with checklists (589-595), miscellaneous players, and a heavy dose of coaches.

No.	Player	NRMT	VG-E	GOOD
	COMPLETE SET (630)	60.00	24.00	6.00
	COMMON PLAYER (1-630)	.10	.04	.01
☐ 1	Buzz Capra	.10	.04	.01
☐ 2	Tom House	.15	.06	.01
☐ 3	Max Leon	.10	.04	.01
☐ 4	Carl Morton	.10	.04	.01
☐ 5	Phil Niekro	2.00	.80	.20
☐ 6	Mike Thompson	.10	.04	.01
☐ 7	Elias Sosa	.10	.04	.01
☐ 8	Larvell Blanks	.10	.04	.01
☐ 9	Darrell Evans	.35	.14	.03
☐ 10	Rod Gilbreath	.10	.04	.01
☐ 11	Mike Lum	.10	.04	.01
☐ 12	Craig Robinson	.10	.04	.01
☐ 13	Earl Williams	.10	.04	.01
☐ 14	Vic Correll	.10	.04	.01
☐ 15	Biff Pocoroba	.10	.04	.01
☐ 16	Dusty Baker	.20	.08	.02
☐ 17	Ralph Garr	.15	.06	.01
☐ 18	Cito Gaston	.10	.04	.01
☐ 19	Dave May	.10	.04	.01
☐ 20	Rowland Office	.10	.04	.01
☐ 21	Bob Beall	.10	.04	.01
☐ 22	Sparky Anderson MG	.30	.12	.03
☐ 23	Jack Billingham	.10	.04	.01
☐ 24	Pedro Borbon	.10	.04	.01
☐ 25	Clay Carroll	.10	.04	.01
☐ 26	Pat Darcy	.10	.04	.01
☐ 27	Don Gullett	.15	.06	.01
☐ 28	Clay Kirby	.10	.04	.01
☐ 29	Gary Nolan	.10	.04	.01
☐ 30	Fred Norman	.10	.04	.01
☐ 31	Johnny Bench	5.00	2.00	.50
☐ 32	Bill Plummer	.10	.04	.01
☐ 33	Darrel Chaney	.10	.04	.01
☐ 34	Dave Concepcion	.25	.10	.02
☐ 35	Terry Crowley	.10	.04	.01
☐ 36	Dan Driessen	.15	.06	.01
☐ 37	Doug Flynn	.10	.04	.01
☐ 38	Joe Morgan	2.00	.80	.20
☐ 39	Tony Perez	.75	.30	.07
☐ 40	Ken Griffey	.25	.10	.02
☐ 41	Pete Rose	10.00	4.00	1.00
☐ 42	Ed Armbrister	.10	.04	.01
☐ 43	John Vukovich	.10	.04	.01
☐ 44	George Foster	.85	.34	.08
☐ 45	Cesar Geronimo	.10	.04	.01
☐ 46	Merv Rettenmund	.10	.04	.01
☐ 47	Jim Crawford	.10	.04	.01
☐ 48	Ken Forsch	.10	.04	.01
☐ 49	Doug Konieczny	.10	.04	.01
☐ 50	Joe Niekro	.30	.12	.03
☐ 51	Cliff Johnson	.10	.04	.01
☐ 52	Skip Jutze	.10	.04	.01
☐ 53	Milt May	.10	.04	.01
☐ 54	Rob Andrews	.10	.04	.01
☐ 55	Ken Boswell	.10	.04	.01
☐ 56	Tommy Helms	.10	.04	.01
☐ 57	Roger Metzger	.10	.04	.01
☐ 58	Larry Milbourne	.10	.04	.01
☐ 59	Doug Rader	.20	.08	.02
☐ 60	Bob Watson	.15	.06	.01
☐ 61	Enos Cabell	.10	.04	.01
☐ 62	Jose Cruz	.35	.14	.03
☐ 63	Cesar Cedeno	.20	.08	.02
☐ 64	Greg Gross	.10	.04	.01
☐ 65	Wilbur Howard	.10	.04	.01
☐ 66	Al Downing	.10	.04	.01
☐ 67	Burt Hooton	.10	.04	.01
☐ 68	Charlie Hough	.20	.08	.02
☐ 69	Tommy John	.70	.28	.07
☐ 70	Andy Messersmith	.15	.06	.01
☐ 71	Doug Rau	.10	.04	.01
☐ 72	Rick Rhoden	.25	.10	.02
☐ 73	Don Sutton	1.25	.50	.12
☐ 74	Rick Auerbach	.10	.04	.01
☐ 75	Ron Cey	.45	.18	.04
☐ 76	Ivan DeJesus	.10	.04	.01
☐ 77	Steve Garvey	4.00	1.60	.40
☐ 78	Lee Lacy	.10	.04	.01
☐ 79	Dave Lopes	.20	.08	.02
☐ 80	Ken McMullen	.10	.04	.01
☐ 81	Joe Ferguson	.10	.04	.01
☐ 82	Paul Powell	.10	.04	.01
☐ 83	Steve Yeager	.10	.04	.01
☐ 84	Willie Crawford	.10	.04	.01
☐ 85	Henry Cruz	.10	.04	.01
☐ 86	Charlie Manuel	.10	.04	.01
☐ 87	Manny Mota	.15	.06	.01
☐ 88	Tom Paciorek	.10	.04	.01
☐ 89	Jim Wynn	.15	.06	.01
☐ 90	Walt Alston MG	.60	.24	.06
☐ 91	Bill Buckner	.40	.16	.04
☐ 92	Jim Barr	.10	.04	.01
☐ 93	Mike Caldwell	.10	.04	.01
☐ 94	John D'Acquisto	.10	.04	.01
☐ 95	Dave Heaverlo	.10	.04	.01
☐ 96	Gary Lavelle	.10	.04	.01
☐ 97	John Montefusco	.15	.06	.01
☐ 98	Charlie Williams	.10	.04	.01
☐ 99	Chris Arnold	.10	.04	.01
☐ 100	Marc Hill	.10	.04	.01
☐ 101	Dave Rader	.10	.04	.01
☐ 102	Bruce Miller	.10	.04	.01
☐ 103	Willie Montanez	.10	.04	.01
☐ 104	Steve Ontiveros	.10	.04	.01
☐ 105	Chris Speier	.10	.04	.01

□ 106 Derrel Thomas	.10	.04	.01
□ 107 Gary Thomasson	.10	.04	.01
□ 108 Glenn Adams	.10	.04	.01
□ 109 Von Joshua	.10	.04	.01
□ 110 Gary Matthews	.20	.08	.02
□ 111 Bobby Murcer	.40	.16	.04
□ 112 Horace Speed	.10	.04	.01
□ 113 Wes Westrum MG	.10	.04	.01
□ 114 Rich Folkers	.10	.04	.01
□ 115 Alan Foster	.10	.04	.01
□ 116 Dave Freisleben	.10	.04	.01
□ 117 Dan Frisella	.10	.04	.01
□ 118 Randy Jones	.15	.06	.01
□ 119 Dan Spillner	.10	.04	.01
□ 120 Larry Hardy	.10	.04	.01
□ 121 Randy Hundley	.10	.04	.01
□ 122 Fred Kendall	.10	.04	.01
□ 123 John McNamara MG	.15	.06	.01
□ 124 Tito Fuentes	.10	.04	.01
□ 125 Enzo Hernandez	.10	.04	.01
□ 126 Steve Huntz	.10	.04	.01
□ 127 Mike Ivie	.10	.04	.01
□ 128 Hector Torres	.10	.04	.01
□ 129 Ted Kubiak	.10	.04	.01
□ 130 John Grubb	.10	.04	.01
□ 131 John Scott	.10	.04	.01
□ 132 Bob Tolan	.10	.04	.01
□ 133 Dave Winfield	3.50	1.40	.35
□ 134 Bill Gogolewski	.10	.04	.01
□ 135 Dan Osborn	.10	.04	.01
□ 136 Jim Kaat	.60	.24	.06
□ 137 Claude Osteen	.15	.06	.01
□ 138 Cecil Upshaw	.10	.04	.01
□ 139 Wilbur Wood	.15	.06	.01
□ 140 Lloyd Allen	.10	.04	.01
□ 141 Brian Downing	.25	.10	.02
□ 142 Jim Essian	.10	.04	.01
□ 143 Bucky Dent	.25	.10	.02
□ 144 Jorge Orta	.10	.04	.01
□ 145 Lee Richard	.10	.04	.01
□ 146 Bill Stein	.10	.04	.01
□ 147 Ken Henderson	.10	.04	.01
□ 148 Carlos May	.10	.04	.01
□ 149 Nyls Nyman	.10	.04	.01
□ 150 Bob Coluccio	.10	.04	.01
□ 151 Chuck Tanner MG	.15	.06	.01
□ 152 Pat Kelly	.10	.04	.01
□ 153 Jerry Hairston	.10	.04	.01
□ 154 Pete Varney	.10	.04	.01
□ 155 Bill Melton	.10	.04	.01
□ 156 Rich Gossage	.85	.34	.08
□ 157 Terry Forster	.20	.08	.02
□ 158 Rich Hinton	.10	.04	.01
□ 159 Nelson Briles	.15	.06	.01
□ 160 Al Fitzmorris	.10	.04	.01
□ 161 Steve Mingori	.10	.04	.01
□ 162 Marty Pattin	.10	.04	.01
□ 163 Paul Splittorff	.15	.06	.01
□ 164 Dennis Leonard	.20	.08	.02
□ 165 Buck Martinez	.10	.04	.01
□ 166 Bob Stinson	.10	.04	.01
□ 167 George Brett	7.00	2.80	.70
□ 168 Harmon Killebrew	2.50	1.00	.25
□ 169 John Mayberry	.15	.06	.01
□ 170 Fred Patek	.15	.06	.01
□ 171 Cookie Rojas	.15	.06	.01
□ 172 Rodney Scott	.10	.04	.01
□ 173 Tony Solaita	.10	.04	.01
□ 174 Frank White	.30	.12	.03
□ 175 Al Cowens	.15	.06	.01
□ 176 Hal McRae	.20	.08	.02
□ 177 Amos Otis	.25	.10	.02
□ 178 Vada Pinson	.35	.14	.03
□ 179 Jim Wohlford	.10	.04	.01
□ 180 Doug Bird	.10	.04	.01
□ 181 Mark Littell	.10	.04	.01
□ 182 Bob McClure	.10	.04	.01
□ 183 Steve Busby	.15	.06	.01
□ 184 Fran Healy	.10	.04	.01
□ 185 Whitey Herzog MG	.25	.10	.02
□ 186 Andy Hassler	.10	.04	.01
□ 187 Nolan Ryan	4.50	1.80	.45
□ 188 Bill Singer	.10	.04	.01
□ 189 Frank Tanana	.15	.06	.01
□ 190 Ed Figueroa	.10	.04	.01
□ 191 Dave Collins	.15	.06	.01
□ 192 Dick Williams	.15	.06	.01
□ 193 Ellie Rodriguez	.10	.04	.01
□ 194 Dave Chalk	.10	.04	.01
□ 195 Winston Llenas	.10	.04	.01
□ 196 Rudy Meoli	.10	.04	.01
□ 197 Orlando Ramirez	.10	.04	.01
□ 198 Jerry Remy	.10	.04	.01
□ 199 Billy Smith	.10	.04	.01
□ 200 Bruce Bochte	.10	.04	.01
□ 201 Joe Lahoud	.10	.04	.01
□ 202 Morris Nettles	.10	.04	.01
□ 203 Mickey Rivers	.25	.10	.02
□ 204 Leroy Stanton	.10	.04	.01
□ 205 Vic Albury	.10	.04	.01
□ 206 Tom Burgmeier	.10	.04	.01
□ 207 Bill Butler	.10	.04	.01
□ 208 Bill Campbell	.10	.04	.01
□ 209 Ray Corbin	.10	.04	.01
□ 210 Joe Decker	.10	.04	.01
□ 211 Jim Hughes	.10	.04	.01
□ 212 Ed Bane (photo actually Mike Pazik)	.10	.04	.01
□ 213 Glenn Borgman	.10	.04	.01
□ 214 Rod Carew	4.00	1.60	.40
□ 215 Steve Brye	.10	.04	.01
□ 216 Dan Ford	.10	.04	.01
□ 217 Tony Oliva	.75	.30	.07
□ 218 Dave Goltz	.10	.04	.01
□ 219 Bert Blyleven	.45	.18	.04
□ 220 Larry Hisle	.15	.06	.01
□ 221 Steve Braun	.10	.04	.01
□ 222 Jerry Terrell	.10	.04	.01
□ 223 Eric Soderholm	.10	.04	.01
□ 224 Phil Roof	.10	.04	.01
□ 225 Danny Thompson	.10	.04	.01
□ 226 Jim Colborn	.10	.04	.01
□ 227 Tom Murphy	.10	.04	.01
□ 228 Ed Rodriquez	.10	.04	.01
□ 229 Jim Slaton	.10	.04	.01
□ 230 Ed Spraque	.10	.04	.01
□ 231 Charlie Moore	.10	.04	.01
□ 232 Darrell Porter	.15	.06	.01
□ 233 Kurt Bevacqua	.10	.04	.01
□ 234 Pedro Garcia	.10	.04	.01
□ 235 Mike Hegan	.10	.04	.01
□ 236 Don Money	.15	.06	.01
□ 237 George Scott	.15	.06	.01
□ 238 Robin Yount	3.50	1.40	.35
□ 239 Hank Aaron	7.00	2.80	.70
□ 240 Rob Ellis	.10	.04	.01
□ 241 Sixto Lezcano	.10	.04	.01
□ 242 Bob Mitchell	.10	.04	.01
□ 243 Gorman Thomas	.35	.14	.03
□ 244 Bill Travers	.10	.04	.01
□ 245 Pete Broberg	.10	.04	.01
□ 246 Bill Sharp	.10	.04	.01
□ 247 Bobby Darwin	.10	.04	.01
□ 248 Rick Austin (photo actually Larry Anderson)	.10	.04	.01
□ 249 Larry Anderson (photo actually Rick Austin)	.10	.04	.01
□ 250 Tom Bianco	.10	.04	.01
□ 251 L. Currence	.10	.04	.01
□ 252 Steve Foucault	.10	.04	.01
□ 253 Bill Hands	.10	.04	.01
□ 254 Steve Hargan	.10	.04	.01
□ 255 Fergie Jenkins	.60	.24	.06
□ 256 Bob Sheldon	.10	.04	.01
□ 257 Jim Umbarger	.10	.04	.01
□ 258 Clyde Wright	.10	.04	.01
□ 259 Bill Fahey	.10	.04	.01
□ 260 Jim Sundberg	.15	.06	.01
□ 261 Leo Cardenas	.10	.04	.01
□ 262 Jim Fregosi	.20	.08	.02
□ 263 Mike Hargrove	.15	.06	.01
□ 264 Toby Harrah	.20	.08	.02
□ 265 Roy Howell	.10	.04	.01
□ 266 Lenny Randle	.10	.04	.01
□ 267 Roy Smalley	.20	.08	.02
□ 268 Jim Spencer	.10	.04	.01
□ 269 Jeff Burroughs	.15	.06	.01
□ 270 Tom Grieve	.20	.08	.02
□ 271 Joe Lovitto	.10	.04	.01
□ 272 Frank Lucchesi MG	.10	.04	.01
□ 273 Dave Nelson	.10	.04	.01
□ 274 Ted Simmons	.50	.20	.05
□ 275 Lou Brock	3.00	1.20	.30
□ 276 Ron Fairly	.15	.06	.01
□ 277 Bake McBride	.15	.06	.01
□ 278 Reggie Smith	.25	.10	.02
□ 279 Willie Davis	.15	.06	.01
□ 280 Ken Reitz	.10	.04	.01
□ 281 Buddy Bradford	.10	.04	.01
□ 282 Luis Melendez	.10	.04	.01
□ 283 Mike Tyson	.10	.04	.01
□ 284 Ted Sizemore	.10	.04	.01
□ 285 Mario Guerrero	.10	.04	.01
□ 286 Larry Lintz	.10	.04	.01
□ 287 Ken Rudolph	.10	.04	.01
□ 288 Dick Billings	.10	.04	.01
□ 289 Jerry Mumphrey	.10	.04	.01

☐ 290	Mike Wallace	.10	.04	.01
☐ 291	Al Hrabosky	.15	.06	.01
☐ 292	Ken Reynolds	.10	.04	.01
☐ 293	Mike Garman	.10	.04	.01
☐ 294	Bob Forsch	.15	.06	.01
☐ 295	John Denny	.20	.08	.02
☐ 296	Harry Rasmussen	.10	.04	.01
☐ 297	Lynn McGlothen	.10	.04	.01
☐ 298	Mike Barlow	.10	.04	.01
☐ 299	Greg Terlecky	.10	.04	.01
☐ 300	Red Schoendienst MG	.20	.08	.02
☐ 301	Rick Reuschel	.30	.12	.03
☐ 302	Steve Stone	.20	.08	.02
☐ 303	Bill Bonham	.10	.04	.01
☐ 304	Oscar Zamora	.10	.04	.01
☐ 305	Ken Frailing	.10	.04	.01
☐ 306	Milt Wilcox	.10	.04	.01
☐ 307	Darold Knowles	.10	.04	.01
☐ 308	Jim Marshall	.10	.04	.01
☐ 309	Bill Madlock	.75	.30	.07
☐ 310	Jose Cardenal	.10	.04	.01
☐ 311	Rick Monday	.15	.06	.01
☐ 312	Jerry Morales	.10	.04	.01
☐ 313	Tim Hosley	.10	.04	.01
☐ 314	Gene Hiser	.10	.04	.01
☐ 315	Don Kessinger	.20	.08	.02
☐ 316	Manny Trillo	.15	.06	.01
☐ 317	Pete LaCock	.10	.04	.01
☐ 318	George Mitterwald	.10	.04	.01
☐ 319	Steve Swisher	.10	.04	.01
☐ 320	Rob Sperring	.10	.04	.01
☐ 321	Vic Harris	.10	.04	.01
☐ 322	Ron Dunn	.10	.04	.01
☐ 323	Jose Morales	.10	.04	.01
☐ 324	Pete Mackanin	.10	.04	.01
☐ 325	Jim Cox	.10	.04	.01
☐ 326	Larry Parrish	.40	.16	.04
☐ 327	Mike Jorgensen	.10	.04	.01
☐ 328	Tim Foli	.10	.04	.01
☐ 329	Hal Breeden	.10	.04	.01
☐ 330	Nate Colbert	.10	.04	.01
☐ 331	Pepe Frias	.10	.04	.01
☐ 332	Pat Scanlon	.10	.04	.01
☐ 333	Bob Bailey	.10	.04	.01
☐ 334	Gary Carter	4.50	1.80	.45
☐ 335	Pepe Mangual	.10	.04	.01
☐ 336	Larry Biittner	.10	.04	.01
☐ 337	Jim Lyttle	.10	.04	.01
☐ 338	Gary Roenicke	.10	.04	.01
☐ 339	Tony Scott	.10	.04	.01
☐ 340	Jerry White	.10	.04	.01
☐ 341	Jim Dwyer	.10	.04	.01
☐ 342	Ellis Valentine	.10	.04	.01
☐ 343	Fred Scherman	.10	.04	.01
☐ 344	Dennis Blair	.10	.04	.01
☐ 345	Woodie Fryman	.10	.04	.01
☐ 346	Chuck Taylor	.10	.04	.01
☐ 347	Dan Warthen	.10	.04	.01
☐ 348	Dan Carrithers	.10	.04	.01
☐ 349	Steve Rogers	.15	.06	.01
☐ 350	Dale Murray	.10	.04	.01
☐ 351	Duke Snider	2.00	.80	.20
☐ 352	Ralph Houk MG	.20	.08	.02
☐ 353	John Hiller	.15	.06	.01
☐ 354	Mickey Lolich	.30	.12	.03
☐ 355	Dave Lemancyzk	.10	.04	.01
☐ 356	Lerrin LaGrow	.10	.04	.01
☐ 357	Fred Arroyo	.10	.04	.01
☐ 358	Joe Coleman	.10	.04	.01
☐ 359	Ben Oglivie	.20	.08	.02
☐ 360	Willie Horton	.15	.06	.01
☐ 361	John Knox	.10	.04	.01
☐ 362	Leon Roberts	.10	.04	.01
☐ 363	Ron LeFlore	.15	.06	.01
☐ 364	G. Sutherland	.10	.04	.01
☐ 365	Dan Meyer	.10	.04	.01
☐ 366	Aurelio Rodriguez	.10	.04	.01
☐ 367	Tom Veryzer	.10	.04	.01
☐ 368	Jack Pierce	.10	.04	.01
☐ 369	Gene Michael	.15	.06	.01
☐ 370	Billy Baldwin	.10	.04	.01
☐ 371	Gates Brown	.15	.06	.01
☐ 372	Mickey Stanley	.15	.06	.01
☐ 373	Terry Humphrey	.10	.04	.01
☐ 374	Doyle Alexander	.25	.10	.02
☐ 375	Mike Cuellar	.15	.06	.01
☐ 376	Wayne Garland	.10	.04	.01
☐ 377	Ross Grimsley	.10	.04	.01
☐ 378	Grant Jackson	.10	.04	.01
☐ 379	Dyar Miller	.10	.04	.01
☐ 380	Jim Palmer	3.00	1.20	.30
☐ 381	Mike Torrez	.15	.06	.01
☐ 382	Mike Willis	.10	.04	.01
☐ 383	Dave Duncan	.10	.04	.01
☐ 384	Ellie Hendricks	.10	.04	.01
☐ 385	Jim Hutto	.10	.04	.01
☐ 386	Bob Bailor	.10	.04	.01
☐ 387	Doug DeCinces	.35	.14	.03
☐ 388	Bob Grich	.30	.12	.03
☐ 389	Lee May	.20	.08	.02
☐ 390	Tony Muser	.10	.04	.01
☐ 391	Tim Nordbrook	.10	.04	.01
☐ 392	Brooks Robinson	3.50	1.40	.35
☐ 393	Royle Stillman	.10	.04	.01
☐ 394	Don Baylor	.35	.14	.03
☐ 395	Paul Blair	.15	.06	.01
☐ 396	Al Bumbry	.10	.04	.01
☐ 397	Larry Harlow	.10	.04	.01
☐ 398	Tommy Davis	.20	.08	.02
☐ 399	Jim Northrup	.15	.06	.01
☐ 400	Ken Singleton	.30	.12	.03
☐ 401	Tom Shopay	.10	.04	.01
☐ 402	Fred Lynn	1.00	.40	.10
☐ 403	Carlton Fisk	1.00	.40	.10
☐ 404	Cecil Cooper	.50	.20	.05
☐ 405	Jim Rice	3.00	1.20	.30
☐ 406	Juan Beniquez	.15	.06	.01
☐ 407	Denny Doyle	.10	.04	.01
☐ 408	Dwight Evans	.90	.36	.09
☐ 409	Carl Yastrzemski	8.00	3.25	.80
☐ 410	Rick Burleson	.15	.06	.01
☐ 411	Bernie Carbo	.10	.04	.01
☐ 412	Doug Griffin	.10	.04	.01
☐ 413	Rico Petrocelli	.15	.06	.01
☐ 414	Bob Montgomery	.10	.04	.01
☐ 415	Tim Blackwell	.10	.04	.01
☐ 416	Rick Miller	.10	.04	.01
☐ 417	Darrell Johnson	.10	.04	.01
☐ 418	Jim Burton	.10	.04	.01
☐ 419	Jim Willoughby	.10	.04	.01
☐ 420	Rogelio Moret	.10	.04	.01
☐ 421	Bill Lee	.15	.06	.01
☐ 422	Dick Drago	.10	.04	.01
☐ 423	Diego Segui	.10	.04	.01
☐ 424	Luis Tiant	.30	.12	.03
☐ 425	Jim Hunter	2.00	.80	.20
☐ 426	Rick Sawyer	.10	.04	.01
☐ 427	Rudy May	.10	.04	.01
☐ 428	Dick Tidrow	.10	.04	.01
☐ 429	Sparky Lyle	.35	.14	.03
☐ 430	Doc Medich	.10	.04	.01
☐ 431	Pat Dobson	.15	.06	.01
☐ 432	Dave Pagan	.10	.04	.01
☐ 433	Thurman Munson	3.00	1.20	.30
☐ 434	Chris Chambliss	.20	.08	.02
☐ 435	Roy White	.15	.06	.01
☐ 436	Walt Williams	.10	.04	.01
☐ 437	Graig Nettles	.75	.30	.07
☐ 438	Rick Dempsey	.15	.06	.01
☐ 439	Bobby Bonds	.35	.14	.03
☐ 440	Ed Herrmann	.10	.04	.01
☐ 441	Sandy Alomar	.15	.06	.01
☐ 442	Fred Stanley	.10	.04	.01
☐ 443	Terry Whitfield	.10	.04	.01
☐ 444	Rich Bladt	.10	.04	.01
☐ 445	Lou Piniella	.30	.12	.03
☐ 446	Rich Coggins	.10	.04	.01
☐ 447	Ed Brinkman	.10	.04	.01
☐ 448	Jim Mason	.10	.04	.01
☐ 449	Larry Murray	.10	.04	.01
☐ 450	Ron Blomberg	.10	.04	.01
☐ 451	Elliott Maddox	.10	.04	.01
☐ 452	Kerry Dineen	.10	.04	.01
☐ 453	Billy Martin MG	.60	.24	.06
☐ 454	Dave Bergman	.10	.04	.01
☐ 455	Otto Velez	.10	.04	.01
☐ 456	Joe Hoerner	.10	.04	.01
☐ 457	Tug McGraw	.35	.14	.03
☐ 458	Gene Garber	.15	.06	.01
☐ 459	Steve Carlton	3.00	1.20	.30
☐ 460	Larry Christenson	.10	.04	.01
☐ 461	Tom Underwood	.10	.04	.01
☐ 462	Jim Lonborg	.15	.06	.01
☐ 463	Jay Johnstone	.20	.08	.02
☐ 464	Larry Bowa	.35	.14	.03
☐ 465	Dave Cash	.10	.04	.01
☐ 466	Ollie Brown	.10	.04	.01
☐ 467	Greg Luzinski	.30	.12	.03
☐ 468	Johnny Oates	.10	.04	.01
☐ 469	Mike Anderson	.10	.04	.01
☐ 470	Mike Schmidt	7.00	2.80	.70
☐ 471	Bob Boone	.25	.10	.02
☐ 472	Tom Hutton	.10	.04	.01
☐ 473	Rich Allen	.40	.16	.04
☐ 474	Tony Taylor	.10	.04	.01
☐ 475	Jerry Martin	.10	.04	.01
☐ 476	Danny Ozark MG	.10	.04	.01
☐ 477	Dick Ruthven	.10	.04	.01
☐ 478	Jim Todd	.10	.04	.01
☐ 479	Paul Lindblad	.10	.04	.01

☐ 480	Rollie Fingers	1.25	.50	.12
☐ 481	Vida Blue	.25	.10	.02
☐ 482	Ken Holtzman	.15	.06	.01
☐ 483	Dick Bosman	.10	.04	.01
☐ 484	Sonny Siebert	.10	.04	.01
☐ 485	Glenn Abbott	.10	.04	.01
☐ 486	Stan Bahnsen	.10	.04	.01
☐ 487	Mike Norris	.15	.06	.01
☐ 488	Alvin Dark MG	.15	.06	.01
☐ 489	Claudell Washington	.25	.10	.02
☐ 490	Joe Rudi	.15	.06	.01
☐ 491	Bill North	.10	.04	.01
☐ 492	Bert Campaneris	.20	.08	.02
☐ 493	Gene Tenace	.15	.06	.01
☐ 494	Reggie Jackson	6.00	2.40	.60
☐ 495	Phil Garner	.15	.06	.01
☐ 496	Billy Williams	2.00	.80	.20
☐ 497	Sal Bando	.20	.08	.02
☐ 498	Jim Holt	.10	.04	.01
☐ 499	Ted Martinez	.10	.04	.01
☐ 500	Ray Fosse	.10	.04	.01
☐ 501	Matt Alexander	.10	.04	.01
☐ 502	Larry Haney	.10	.04	.01
☐ 503	Angel Mangual	.10	.04	.01
☐ 504	Fred Beene	.10	.04	.01
☐ 505	Tom Buskey	.10	.04	.01
☐ 506	Dennis Eckersley	1.00	.40	.10
☐ 507	Roric Harrison	.10	.04	.01
☐ 508	Don Hood	.10	.04	.01
☐ 509	Jim Kern	.10	.04	.01
☐ 510	Dave LaRoche	.10	.04	.01
☐ 511	Fritz Peterson	.10	.04	.01
☐ 512	Jim Strickland	.10	.04	.01
☐ 513	Rick Waits	.10	.04	.01
☐ 514	Alan Ashby	.10	.04	.01
☐ 515	John Ellis	.10	.04	.01
☐ 516	Rick Cerone	.10	.04	.01
☐ 517	Buddy Bell	.40	.16	.04
☐ 518	Jack Brohamer	.10	.04	.01
☐ 519	Rico Carty	.15	.06	.01
☐ 520	Ed Crosby	.10	.04	.01
☐ 521	Frank Duffy	.10	.04	.01
☐ 522	Duane Kuiper	.10	.04	.01
	(photo actually			
	Rick Manning)			
☐ 523	Joe Lis	.10	.04	.01
☐ 524	Boog Powell	.60	.24	.06
☐ 525	Frank Robinson	2.00	.80	.20
☐ 526	Oscar Gamble	.15	.06	.01
☐ 527	George Hendrick	.15	.06	.01
☐ 528	John Lowenstein	.10	.04	.01
☐ 529	Rick Manning	.10	.04	.01
	(photo actually			
	Duane Kuiper)			
☐ 530	Tommy Smith	.10	.04	.01
☐ 531	Charlie Spikes	.10	.04	.01
☐ 532	Steve Kline	.10	.04	.01
☐ 533	Ed Kranepool	.15	.06	.01
☐ 534	Mike Vail	.10	.04	.01
☐ 535	Del Unser	.10	.04	.01
☐ 536	Felix Millan	.10	.04	.01
☐ 537	Rusty Staub	.35	.14	.03
☐ 538	Jesus Alou	.10	.04	.01
☐ 539	Wayne Garrett	.10	.04	.01
☐ 540	Mike Phillips	.10	.04	.01
☐ 541	Joe Torre	.40	.16	.04
☐ 542	Dave Kingman	.70	.28	.07
☐ 543	Gene Clines	.10	.04	.01
☐ 544	Jack Heidemann	.10	.04	.01
☐ 545	Bud Harrelson	.15	.06	.01
☐ 546	John Stearns	.15	.06	.01
☐ 547	John Milner	.10	.04	.01
☐ 548	Bob Apodaca	.10	.04	.01
☐ 549	Skip Lockwood	.10	.04	.01
☐ 550	Ken Sanders	.10	.04	.01
☐ 551	Tom Seaver	4.00	1.60	.40
☐ 552	Rick Baldwin	.10	.04	.01
☐ 553	Hank Webb	.10	.04	.01
☐ 554	Jon Matlack	.15	.06	.01
☐ 555	Randy Tate	.10	.04	.01
☐ 556	Tom Hall	.10	.04	.01
☐ 557	George Stone	.10	.04	.01
☐ 558	Craig Swan	.15	.06	.01
☐ 559	Jerry Cram	.10	.04	.01
☐ 560	Roy Staiger	.10	.04	.01
☐ 561	Kent Tekulve	.20	.08	.02
☐ 562	Jerry Reuss	.15	.06	.01
☐ 563	John Candelaria	.25	.10	.02
☐ 564	Larry Demery	.10	.04	.01
☐ 565	Dave Giusti	.15	.06	.01
☐ 566	Jim Rooker	.10	.04	.01
☐ 567	Ramon Hernandez	.10	.04	.01
☐ 568	Bruce Kison	.10	.04	.01
☐ 569	Ken Brett	.10	.04	.01
☐ 570	Bob Moose	.15	.06	.01
☐ 571	Manny Sanguillen	.20	.08	.0
☐ 572	Dave Parker	1.50	.60	.1
☐ 573	Willie Stargell	2.50	1.00	.2
☐ 574	Richie Zisk	.15	.06	.0
☐ 575	Rennie Stennett	.10	.04	.0
☐ 576	Al Oliver	.70	.28	.0
☐ 577	Bill Robinson	.20	.08	.0
☐ 578	Bob Robertson	.10	.04	.0
☐ 579	Rich Hebner	.10	.04	.0
☐ 580	Ed Kirkpatrick	.10	.04	.0
☐ 581	Duffy Dyer	.10	.04	.0
☐ 582	Craig Reynolds	.10	.04	.0
☐ 583	Frank Taveras	.10	.04	.0
☐ 584	Willie Randolph	1.00	.40	.1
☐ 585	Art Howe	.20	.08	.0
☐ 586	Danny Murtaugh MG	.10	.04	.0
☐ 587	Rick McKinney	.10	.04	.0
☐ 588	Ed Goodson	.10	.04	.0
☐ 589	Checklist 1	1.00	.25	.0
	George Brett			
	Al Cowens			
☐ 590	Checklist 2	1.00	.25	.0
	Keith Hernandez			
	Lou Brock			
☐ 591	Checklist 3	.50	.10	.0
	Jerry Koosman			
	Duke Snider			
☐ 592	Checklist 4	.25	.05	.0
	Maury Wills			
	John Knox			
☐ 593	Checklist 5	1.25	.30	.0
	Jim Hunter			
	Nolan Ryan			
☐ 594	Checklist 6	.30	.06	.0
	Ralph Branca			
	Carl Erskine			
	Pee Wee Reese			
☐ 595	Checklist 7	.75	.15	.0
	Willie Mays			
	Herb Score			
☐ 596	Larry Cox	.10	.04	.0
☐ 597	Gene Mauch MG	.15	.06	.0
☐ 598	Whitey Wietelmann	.10	.04	.0
☐ 599	Wayne Simpson	.10	.04	.0
☐ 600	Mel Thomason	.10	.04	.0
☐ 601	Ike Hampton	.10	.04	.0
☐ 602	Ken Crosby	.10	.04	.0
☐ 603	Ralph Rowe	.10	.04	.0
☐ 604	Jim Tyrone	.10	.04	.0
☐ 605	Mick Kelleher	.10	.04	.0
☐ 606	Mario Mendoza	.10	.04	.0
☐ 607	Mike Rogodzinski	.10	.04	.0
☐ 608	Bob Gallagher	.10	.04	.0
☐ 609	Jerry Koosman	.20	.08	.0
☐ 610	Joe Frazier	.10	.04	.0
☐ 611	Karl Kuehl	.10	.04	.0
☐ 612	Frank LaCorte	.10	.04	.0
☐ 613	Ray Bare	.10	.04	.0
☐ 614	Billy Muffett	.10	.04	.0
☐ 615	Bill Laxton	.10	.04	.0
☐ 616	Willie Mays	5.00	2.00	.5
☐ 617	Phil Cavarretta CO	.15	.06	.0
☐ 618	Ted Kluszewski CO	.30	.12	.0
☐ 619	Elston Howard CO	.35	.14	.0
☐ 620	Alex Grammas CO	.10	.04	.0
☐ 621	Mickey Vernon CO	.15	.06	.0
☐ 622	Dick Sisler CO	.10	.04	.0
☐ 623	Harvey Haddix CO	.15	.06	.0
☐ 624	Bobby Winkles CO	.10	.04	.0
☐ 625	John Pesky CO	.10	.04	.0
☐ 626	Jim Davenport CO	.15	.06	.0
☐ 627	Dave Tomlin	.10	.04	.0
☐ 628	Roger Craig CO	.35	.14	.0
☐ 629	Joe Amalfitano CO	.10	.04	.0
☐ 630	Jim Reese CO	.15	.06	.0

1953 Stahl Meyer

The cards in this 9-card set measure 3 1/4" by 4 1/2". The 1953 Stahl Meyer set of full color, unnumbered cards includes three players from each of the three New York teams. The cards have white borders. The Lockman card is the most plentiful of any card in the set. Some batting and fielding statistics and short biography are included on the back. The cards are ordered in the checklist below by alphabetical order without regard to team affiliation.

	NRMT	VG-E	GOOD
COMPLETE SET	3000.00	1200.00	400.00
COMMON PLAYER (1-9)	100.00	40.00	10.00
□ 1 Hank Bauer	125.00	50.00	12.50
□ 2 Roy Campanella	450.00	180.00	45.00
□ 3 Gil Hodges	250.00	100.00	25.00
□ 4 Monte Irvin	175.00	70.00	18.00
□ 5 Whitey Lockman	100.00	40.00	10.00
□ 6 Mickey Mantle	1650.00	700.00	200.00
□ 7 Phil Rizzuto	250.00	100.00	25.00
□ 8 Duke Snider	450.00	180.00	45.00
□ 9 Bobby Thomson	125.00	50.00	12.50

1954 Stahl Meyer

The cards in this 12-card set measure 3 1/4" by 4 1/2". The 1954 Stahl Meyer set of full color, unnumbered cards includes four players from each of the three New York teams. The cards have yellow borders and the backs, oriented horizontally, include an ad for a baseball kit and the player's statistics. No player biography is included on the back. The cards are ordered in the checklist below by alphabetical order without regard to team affiliation.

	NRMT	VG-E	GOOD
COMPLETE SET	4500.00	2000.00	600.00
COMMON PLAYER (1-12)	125.00	50.00	12.50
□ 1 Hank Bauer	150.00	60.00	15.00
□ 2 Carl Erskine	150.00	60.00	15.00
□ 3 Gil Hodges	250.00	100.00	25.00
□ 4 Monte Irvin	200.00	80.00	20.00
□ 5 Whitey Lockman	125.00	50.00	12.50
□ 6 Mickey Mantle	2000.00	800.00	250.00
□ 7 Willie Mays	1000.00	400.00	125.00
□ 8 Gil McDougald	150.00	60.00	15.00
□ 9 Don Mueller	125.00	50.00	12.50
□ 10 Don Newcombe	150.00	60.00	15.00
□ 11 Phil Rizzuto	250.00	100.00	25.00
□ 12 Duke Snider	450.00	180.00	45.00

1955 Stahl Meyer

The cards in this 12 card set measure 3 1/4" by 4 1/2". The 1955 Stahl Meyer set of full color, unnumbered cards contains four players each from the three New York teams. As in the 1954 set, the cards have yellow borders; however, the back of the cards contain a sketch of Mickey Mantle with an ad for a baseball cap or a pennant. The cards are ordered in the checklist below by alphabetical order without regard to team affiliation.

	NRMT	VG-E	GOOD
COMPLETE SET	3500.00	1500.00	450.00
COMMON PLAYER (1-12)	125.00	50.00	12.50
□ 1 Hank Bauer	150.00	60.00	15.00
□ 2 Carl Erskine	150.00	60.00	15.00
□ 3 Gil Hodges	250.00	100.00	25.00
□ 4 Monte Irvin	200.00	80.00	20.00
□ 5 Whitey Lockman	125.00	50.00	12.50
□ 6 Mickey Mantle	2000.00	800.00	250.00
□ 7 Gil McDougald	150.00	60.00	15.00
□ 8 Don Mueller	125.00	50.00	12.50
□ 9 Don Newcombe	150.00	60.00	15.00
□ 10 Dusty Rhodes	125.00	50.00	12.50
□ 11 Phil Rizzuto	250.00	100.00	25.00
□ 12 Duke Snider	450.00	180.00	45.00

1962 Sugardale

The cards in this 22-card set measure 3 3/4" by 5 1/8". The 1962 Sugardale Meats set of black and white, numbered and lettered cards features the Cleveland Indians and the Pittsburgh Pirates. The Indians are numbered while the Pirates are lettered. The backs, in red print, give player tips. The Bob Nieman card was just recently discovered and is quite scarce. The catalog designation is F174-1.

	NRMT	VG-E	GOOD
COMPLETE SET (22)	1400.00	500.00	175.00
COMMON PLAYER (1-19)	40.00	16.00	4.00
COMMON PLAYER (A-D)	60.00	24.00	6.00
□ 1 Barry Latman	40.00	16.00	4.00
□ 2 Gary Bell	40.00	16.00	4.00
□ 3 Dick Donovan	40.00	16.00	4.00
□ 4 Frank Funk	40.00	16.00	4.00
□ 5 Jim Perry	60.00	24.00	6.00
□ 6 not issued	0.00	.00	.00
□ 7 John Romano	40.00	16.00	4.00
□ 8 Ty Cline	40.00	16.00	4.00
□ 9 Tito Francona	40.00	16.00	4.00
□ 10 Bob Nieman	200.00	80.00	20.00
□ 11 Willie Kirkland	40.00	16.00	4.00
□ 12 Woody Held	40.00	16.00	4.00
□ 13 Jerry Kindall	40.00	16.00	4.00
□ 14 Bubba Phillips	40.00	16.00	4.00
□ 15 Mel Harder	40.00	16.00	4.00
□ 16 Salty Parker	40.00	16.00	4.00
□ 17 Ray Katt	40.00	16.00	4.00
□ 18 Mel McGaha	40.00	16.00	4.00
□ 19 Pedro Ramos	40.00	16.00	4.00
□ A Dick Groat	80.00	32.00	8.00
□ B Robert Clemente	500.00	200.00	50.00
□ C Don Hoak	60.00	24.00	6.00
□ D Dick Stuart	70.00	28.00	7.00

1963 Sugardale

The cards in this 31-card set measure 3 3/4" by 5 1/8". The 1963 Sugardale Meats set of 31 black and white, numbered cards features the Cleveland Indians and Pittsburgh Pirates. The backs are printed in red and give player tips. The 1963 Sugardale set can be distinguished from the 1962 Sugardale set by examining the biographies on the card for mention of the 1962 season. The Perry and Skinner cards were withdrawn after June trades and are difficult to obtain.

	NRMT	VG-E	GOOD
COMPLETE SET (31)	1400.00	500.00	175.00
COMMON PLAYER (1-33)	40.00	16.00	4.00
COMMON PLAYER (34-38)	60.00	24.00	6.00
□ 1 Barry Latman	40.00	16.00	4.00
□ 2 Gary Bell	40.00	16.00	4.00
□ 3 Dick Donovan	40.00	16.00	4.00
□ 4 Joe Adcock	60.00	24.00	6.00
□ 5 Jim Perry	150.00	60.00	15.00
□ 6 Not issued	0.00	.00	.00
□ 7 John Romano	40.00	16.00	4.00
□ 8 Mike de la Hoz	40.00	16.00	4.00
□ 9 Tito Francona	40.00	16.00	4.00
□ 10 Gene Green	40.00	16.00	4.00
□ 11 Willie Kirkland	40.00	16.00	4.00
□ 12 Woody Held	40.00	16.00	4.00
□ 13 Jerry Kindall	40.00	16.00	4.00
□ 14 Max Alvis	40.00	16.00	4.00
□ 15 Mel Harder	40.00	16.00	4.00
□ 16 George Strickland	40.00	16.00	4.00
□ 17 Elmer Valo	40.00	16.00	4.00
□ 18 Birdie Tebbetts	40.00	16.00	4.00
□ 19 Pedro Ramos	40.00	16.00	4.00
□ 20 Al Luplow	40.00	16.00	4.00
□ 21 Not issued	0.00	.00	.00
□ 22 Not issued	0.00	.00	.00
□ 23 Jim Grant	40.00	16.00	4.00

□ 24 Victor Davalillo	40.00	16.00	4.00
□ 25 Jerry Walker	40.00	16.00	4.00
□ 26 Sam McDowell	60.00	24.00	6.00
□ 27 Fred Whitfield	40.00	16.00	4.00
□ 28 Jack Kralick	40.00	16.00	4.00
□ 29 Not issued	0.00	.00	.00
□ 30 Not issued	0.00	.00	.00
□ 31 Not issued	0.00	.00	.00
□ 32 Not issued	0.00	.00	.00
□ 33 Bob Allen	40.00	16.00	4.00
□ 34 Don Cardwell	60.00	24.00	6.00
□ 35 Bob Skinner	200.00	80.00	20.00
□ 36 Don Schwall	60.00	24.00	6.00
□ 37 Jim Pagliaroni	60.00	24.00	6.00
□ 38 Dick Schofield	60.00	24.00	6.00

1948 Swell Sport Thrills

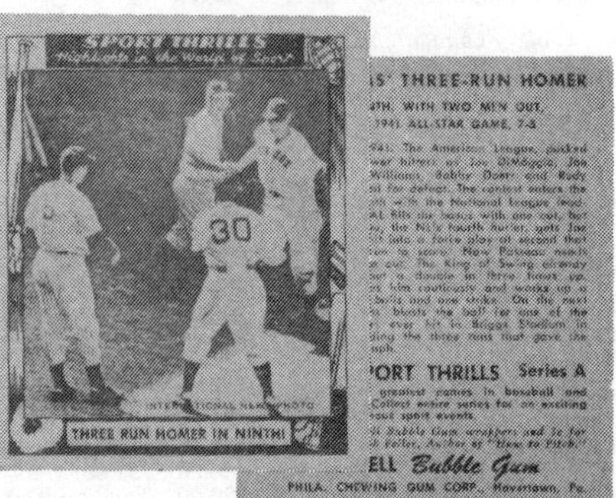

The cards in this 20-card set measure 2 1/2" by 3". The 1948 Swell Gum Sports Thrills set of black and white, numbered cards highlights events from baseball history. The cards have picture framed borders with the title "Sports Thrills Highlights in the World of Sport" on the front. The backs of the cards give the story of the event pictured on the front. Cards numbered 9, 11, 16, and 20 are more difficult to obtain than the other cards in this set. The ACC designation is R448.

	NRMT	VG-E	GOOD
COMPLETE SET (20)	650.00	280.00	80.00
COMMON PLAYER (1-20)	13.50	6.00	1.20
□ 1 Greatest Single Inning Athletics' 10 Run Rally	13.50	6.00	1.20
□ 2 Amazing Record: Reiser's Debut With Dodgers	13.50	6.00	1.20
□ 3 Dramatic Debut: Jackie Robinson ROY	100.00	40.00	10.00
□ 4 Greatest Pitcher of Them All: W.Johnson	40.00	16.00	4.00
□ 5 Three Strikes Not Out: Lost Third Strike Changes Tide of 1941 World Series	13.50	6.00	1.20
□ 6 Home Run Wins Series: Bill Dickey's Last Home Run	20.00	8.00	2.00
□ 7 Never Say Die Pitcher: Schumacher Pitching	13.50	6.00	1.20
□ 8 Five Strikeouts: Nationals Lose All Star Game (Hubbell)	20.00	8.00	2.00
□ 9 Greatest Catch: Al Gionfriddo's Catch	25.00	10.00	2.50
□ 10 No Hits No Runs: VanderMeer Comes Back	20.00	8.00	2.00
□ 11 Bases Loaded: Alexander The Great	30.00	12.00	3.00
□ 12 Most Dramatic Homer: Babe Ruth Points	125.00	50.00	12.50
□ 13 Winning Run: Bridges' Pitching and Goslin's Single Wins 1935 World Series	13.50	6.00	1.20
□ 14 Great Slugging: Lou Gehrig's Four Homers	90.00	36.00	9.00
□ 15 Four Men To Stop Him: DiMaggio's Bat Streak	30.00	12.00	3.00
□ 16 Three Run Homer in Ninth: Williams' Homer	100.00	40.00	10.00
□ 17 Football Block: Lindell's Football Block Paves Way For Yank's Series Victory	13.50	6.00	1.20
□ 18 Home Run To Fame: Reese's Grand Slam	35.00	14.00	3.50
□ 19 Strikeout Record: Feller Whiffs Five	35.00	14.00	3.50
□ 20 Rifle Arm: Furillo	35.00	14.00	3.50

1957 Swifts Franks

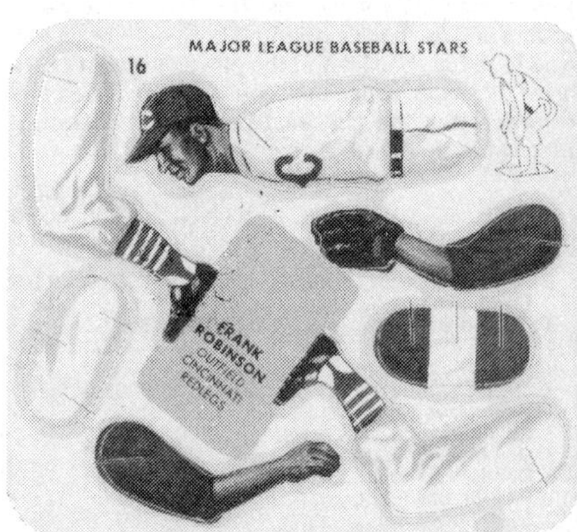

The cards in this 18-card set measure 3 1/2" by 4". These full color, numbered cards issued in 1957 by the Swift Company are die-cut. Each card consists of several pieces which can be punched out and assembled to form a stand-up model of the player. The cards and a game board were available directly from the company. The ACC designation is F162.

	NRMT	VG-E	GOOD
COMPLETE SET (18)	1350.00	600.00	150.00
COMMON PLAYER (1-18)	40.00	16.00	4.00
□ 1 John Podres	50.00	20.00	5.00
□ 2 Gus Triandos	40.00	16.00	4.00
□ 3 Dale Long	40.00	16.00	4.00
□ 4 Billy Pierce	50.00	20.00	5.00
□ 5 Ed Bailey	40.00	16.00	4.00
□ 6 Vic Wertz	40.00	16.00	4.00
□ 7 Nelson Fox	80.00	32.00	8.00
□ 8 Ken Boyer	80.00	32.00	8.00
□ 9 Gil McDougald	60.00	24.00	6.00
□ 10 Junior Gilliam	60.00	24.00	6.00
□ 11 Eddie Yost	40.00	16.00	4.00
□ 12 Johnny Logan	40.00	16.00	4.00
□ 13 Hank Aaron	400.00	160.00	40.00
□ 14 Bill Tuttle	40.00	16.00	4.00
□ 15 Jackie Jensen	60.00	24.00	6.00
□ 16 Frank Robinson	135.00	54.00	13.50
□ 17 Richie Ashburn	100.00	40.00	10.00
□ 18 Rocky Colavito	80.00	32.00	8.00

ADVERTISER INDEX: Found at the end of the Table of Contents. Be sure to let our advertisers know that you saw their ad in this publication.

1986 Texas Gold Reds

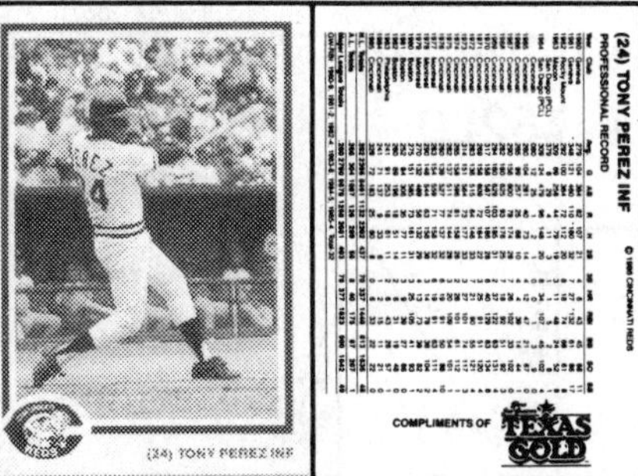

Texas Gold Ice Cream is the sponsor of this 28- card set of Cincinnati Reds. The cards are 2 1/2" by 3 1/2" and feature player photos in full color with a red and white border on the front of the card. The set was distributed to fans attending the Reds game at Riverfront Stadium on September 19th. The card backs contain the player's career statistics, uniform number, name, position, and the Texas Gold logo.

		MINT	EXC	G-VG
	COMPLETE SET (28)	21.00	8.50	2.10
	COMMON PLAYER	.30	.12	.03
☐ 6	Bo Diaz	.30	.12	.03
☐ 9	Max Venable	.30	.12	.03
☐ 11	Kurt Stillwell	.40	.16	.04
☐ 12	Nick Esasky	.30	.12	.03
☐ 13	Dave Concepcion	.50	.20	.05
☐ 14A	Pete Rose INF	2.00	.80	.20
☐ 14B	Pete Rose MG	2.00	.80	.20
☐ 14C	Pete Rose (commemorative)	2.00	.80	.20
☐ 16	Ron Oester	.30	.12	.03
☐ 20	Eddie Milner	.30	.12	.03
☐ 22	Sal Butera	.30	.12	.03
☐ 24	Tony Perez	.75	.30	.07
☐ 25	Buddy Bell	.50	.20	.05
☐ 28	Kal Daniels	2.50	1.00	.25
☐ 29	Tracy Jones	.75	.30	.07
☐ 31	John Franco	.75	.30	.07
☐ 32	Tom Browning	.60	.24	.06
☐ 33	Ron Robinson	.40	.16	.04
☐ 34	Bill Gullickson	.40	.16	.04
☐ 36	Mario Soto	.40	.16	.04
☐ 39	Dave Parker	.75	.30	.07
☐ 40	John Denny	.40	.16	.04
☐ 44	Eric Davis	5.00	2.00	.50
☐ 45	Chris Welsh	.30	.12	.03
☐ 48	Ted Power	.30	.12	.03
☐ 49	Joe Price	.30	.12	.03
☐ xx	Reds Coaches George Scherger Bruce Kimm Billy DeMars Tommy Helms Scott Breeden Jim Lett	.30	.12	.03
☐ xx	Preferred Customer Card (Discount Coupon)	.30	.12	.03

1947 Tip Top

The cards in this 163-card set measure 2 1/4" by 3". The 1947 Tip Top Bread issue contains unnumbered cards with black and white player photos. The set is of interest to baseball historians in that it contains cards of many players not appearing in any other card sets. The cards were issued locally for the eleven following teams: Red Sox (1-15), White Sox (16- 30), Tigers (31-45), Yankees (46-60), Browns

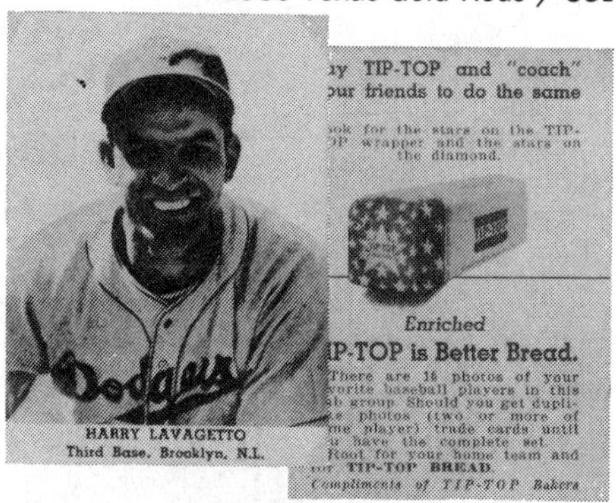

(61-75), Braves (76- 90), Dodgers (91-104), Cubs (105-119), Giants (120-135), Pirates (136-149), and Cardinals (150-164). Players of the Red Sox, Tigers, White Sox, Braves, and the Cubs are scarcer than those of the other teams; players from these tougher teams are marked by SP below to indicate their scarcity. The ACC designation is D323.

		NRMT	VG-E	GOOD
	COMPLETE SET (163)	8000.00	3600.00	1150.00
	COMMON PLAYER (1-164)	22.00	8.50	2.10
☐ 1	Leon Culberson SP	60.00	24.00	6.00
☐ 2	Dom DiMaggio SP	100.00	40.00	10.00
☐ 3	Joe Dobson SP	60.00	24.00	6.00
☐ 4	Bob Doerr SP	150.00	60.00	15.00
☐ 5	Dave(Boo) Ferris SP	60.00	24.00	6.00
☐ 6	Mickey Harris SP	60.00	24.00	6.00
☐ 7	Frank Hayes SP	60.00	24.00	6.00
☐ 8	Cecil Hughson SP	60.00	24.00	6.00
☐ 9	Earl Johnson SP	60.00	24.00	6.00
☐ 10	Roy Partee SP	60.00	24.00	6.00
☐ 11	Johnny Pesky SP	75.00	30.00	7.50
☐ 12	Rip Russell SP	60.00	24.00	6.00
☐ 13	Hal Wagner SP	60.00	24.00	6.00
☐ 14	Rudy York SP	75.00	30.00	7.50
☐ 15	Bill Zuber SP	60.00	24.00	6.00
☐ 16	Floyd Baker SP	60.00	24.00	6.00
☐ 17	Earl Caldwell SP	60.00	24.00	6.00
☐ 18	Lloyd Christopher SP	60.00	24.00	6.00
☐ 19	George Dickey SP	60.00	24.00	6.00
☐ 20	Ralph Hodgin SP	60.00	24.00	6.00
☐ 21	Bob Kennedy SP	60.00	24.00	6.00
☐ 22	Joe Kuhel SP	60.00	24.00	6.00
☐ 23	Thornton Lee SP	60.00	24.00	6.00
☐ 24	Ed Lopat SP	100.00	40.00	10.00
☐ 25	Cass Michaels SP	60.00	24.00	6.00
☐ 26	John Rigney SP	60.00	24.00	6.00
☐ 27	Mike Tresh SP	60.00	24.00	6.00
☐ 28	Thurman Tucker SP	60.00	24.00	6.00
☐ 29	Jack Wallasca SP	60.00	24.00	6.00
☐ 30	Taft Wright SP	60.00	24.00	6.00
☐ 31	Walter(Hoot)Evers SP	60.00	24.00	6.00
☐ 32	John Gorsica SP	60.00	24.00	6.00
☐ 33	Fred Hutchinson SP	75.00	30.00	7.50
☐ 34	George Kell SP	250.00	100.00	25.00
☐ 35	Eddie Lake SP	60.00	24.00	6.00
☐ 36	Ed Mayo SP	60.00	24.00	6.00
☐ 37	Arthur Mills SP	60.00	24.00	6.00
☐ 38	Pat Mullin SP	60.00	24.00	6.00
☐ 39	James Outlaw SP	60.00	24.00	6.00
☐ 40	Frank(Stub) Overmire	60.00	24.00	6.00
☐ 41	Bob Swift SP	60.00	24.00	6.00
☐ 42	Birdie Tebbetts SP	60.00	24.00	6.00
☐ 43	Paul(Diz) Trout SP	75.00	30.00	7.50
☐ 44	Virgil Trucks SP	75.00	30.00	7.50
☐ 45	Dick Wakefield SP	60.00	24.00	6.00
☐ 46	Larry Berra	150.00	60.00	15.00
☐ 47	Floyd(Bill) Bevans	22.00	8.50	2.10
☐ 48	Bobby Brown	40.00	16.00	4.00
☐ 49	Thomas Byrne	22.00	8.50	2.10
☐ 50	Frank Crosetti	40.00	16.00	4.00
☐ 51	Tom Henrich	40.00	16.00	4.00
☐ 52	Charlie Keller	30.00	12.00	3.00
☐ 53	Johnny Lindell	22.00	8.50	2.10
☐ 54	Joe Page	22.00	8.50	2.10
☐ 55	Mel Queen	22.00	8.50	2.10
☐ 56	Allie Reynolds	40.00	16.00	4.00
☐ 57	Phil Rizzuto	100.00	40.00	10.00
☐ 58	Aaron Robinson	22.00	8.50	2.10
☐ 59	George Stirnweiss	22.00	8.50	2.10

Store #1
Webb Chapel Village
Shopping Center #231
1-214-243-5271
11-7 Mon-Sat
Closed Sun.

FIRST BASE

231 Webb Chapel Village
Dallas, Texas 75229

Store #2
Audelia Plaza #102
1-214-341-9919
11-6 Mon-Sat
Closed Sun.

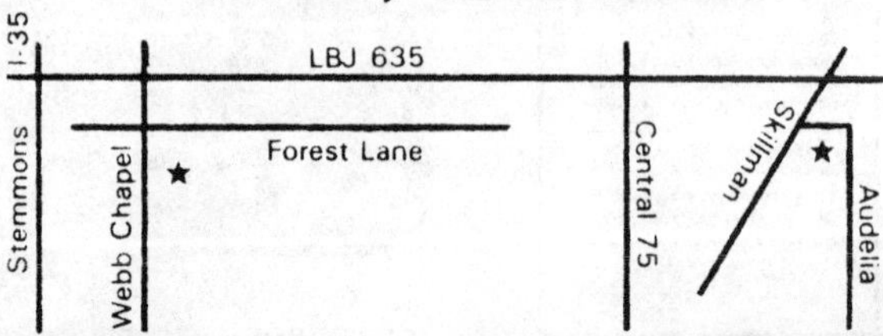

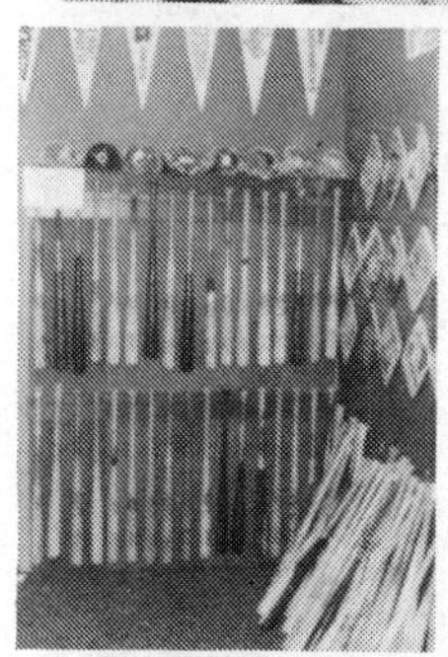

We are located on the southeast corner of Webb Chapel and Forest just 15 minutes from the airport. Our large (1,650-square foot showroom) store is convenient to all parts of Dallas, being only one block south of the LBJ (I-635) Freeway at the Webb Chapel exit. Many collectors and dealers have told us that our store is the most complete they've ever seen. Just look on the opposite page for a few of our offers. We want you for a customer -- please stop in and see for yourself. Also visit our new convenient location in the Audelia Plaza Shopping Center.

FIRST BASE

Sincerely,

Wayne Grove
Gervise Ford

P.S. We are always interested in buying your cards — let us know what you have.

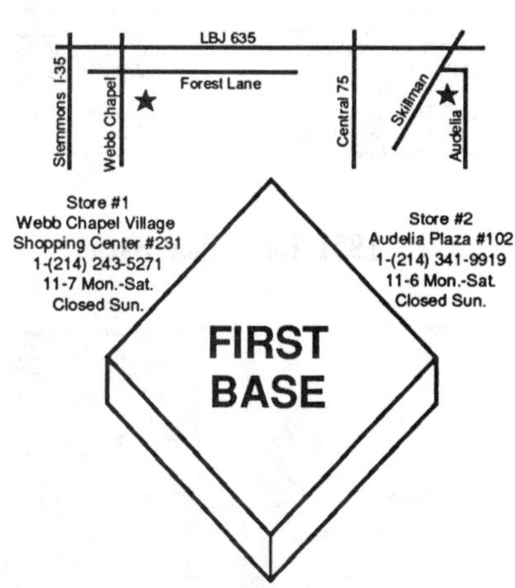

BASEBALL CARD LOTS

1959 Topps 25 diff (f-vg) $15.95
1960 Topps 25 diff (f-vg) 10.95
1961 Topps 25 diff (f-vg) 8.95
1962 Topps 25 diff (f-vg) 8.95
1963 Topps 25 diff (f-vg) 8.95
1964 Topps 25 diff (f-vg) 6.95
1965 Topps 25 diff (f-vg) 6.95
1966 Topps 25 diff (f-vg) 4.95
1967 Topps 25 diff (f-vg) 4.95
1968 Topps 25 diff (f-vg) 4.95
1969 Topps 25 diff (f-vg) 4.95
1970 Topps 25 diff (f-vg) 2.95
1971 Topps 25 diff (f-vg) 2.95
1972 Topps 25 diff (f-vg) 2.95
1973 Topps 25 diff (f-vg) 2.95
1974 Topps 25 diff (f-vg) 2.95
1975 Topps 50 diff (f-vg) 5.95
1976 Topps 50 diff (f-vg) 3.95
1977 Topps 50 diff (f-vg) 3.95
1978 Topps 50 diff (f-vg) 2.95
1979 Topps 50 diff (f-vg) 2.95
1980 Topps 50 diff (f-vg) 2.95
1981 Donruss 50 diff (ex-m) 2.50
1981 Fleer 50 diff (ex-m) 2.50
1982 Fleer 50 diff (ex-m) 2.50

FOOTBALL CARD LOTS

1969 Topps 25 diff (f-vg) $4.95
1970 Topps 25 diff (f-vg) 3.95
1971 Topps 25 diff (f-vg) 2.95
1972 Topps 25 diff (f-vg) 2.95
1973 Topps 25 diff (f-vg) 2.35
1974 Topps 25 diff (f-vg) 2.35
1975 Topps 25 diff (f-vg) 2.00
1976 Topps 25 diff (f-vg) 2.00
1977 Topps 25 diff (f-vg) 2.00
1978 Topps 50 diff (f-vg) 3.00
1979 Topps 50 diff (f-vg) 3.00
1980 Topps 50 diff (f-vg) 2.50

ORDERING INSTRUCTIONS

Offers expire March 1990 while supply lasts. Please include $2.00 per order for postage and handling.

Send orders to:

FIRST BASE
231 Webb Chapel Village
Dallas, Texas 75229
(214) 243-5271

Our current price lists sent free with orders. To receive price lists without ordering send $1.00 or a **large** self addressed stamped (65¢ in stamps) envelope to the above address.

SPECIAL OFFERS

#1: Type Set: One card from each year of Topps baseball 1952 through 1988, our choice of cards, Good to EX, 37 cards for $24.95.
#2: Baseball cigarette card from 1910, our choice (Good to VG) — $5.95.
#3: Robert Redford Poster as "The Natural" - $6.95.
#4: 25 Diff. 1964 Topps Giant Baseball Cards ex-mint — $6.00.
#5: 1982 Topps Baseball Stickers (48 Diff.) — $2.50.
#6: 1989 Score "A Year to Remember" Trivia Cards. Complete Set of 56 — $3.95.
#7: 1985 Circle K All-Time Home Run Kings. Complete Set of 33 — $5.95.
#8: 1982 K-Mart Baseball Set of 33 — $2.50.
#9: 66 Diff. 1981-82 Topps Basketball cards in excellent to mint condition including Stars — $5.95.
#10: Super Bowl XX Game Program — $6.00.
#11: 1986 McDonalds Dallas Cowboys Football Card Set of 25 with Herschel Walker — $9.95.
#12: 1986 McDonalds NFL All-Stars Football Card Set of 24 — $3.95.
#13: Dallas Cowboys Police/Safety Sets: 1979 (15) — $14.95, 1980 (14) — $9.95, 1981 (14) — $9.95, 1983 (28) — $9.95.
#14: Dallas Cowboys Media Guides (not issued to the public) 1988 edition $5.00, 1987 edition $5.00, 1986 edition $5.00, 1985 edition $5.00.

□ 60 Charles Wensloff	22.00	8.50	2.10
□ 61 John Berardino	22.00	8.50	2.10
□ 62 Clifford Fannin	22.00	8.50	2.10
□ 63 Dennis Galehouse	22.00	8.50	2.10
□ 64 Jeff Heath	22.00	8.50	2.10
□ 65 Walter Judnich	22.00	8.50	2.10
□ 66 Jack Kramer	22.00	8.50	2.10
□ 67 Paul Lehner	22.00	8.50	2.10
□ 68 Lester Moss	22.00	8.50	2.10
□ 69 Bob Muncrief	22.00	8.50	2.10
□ 70 Nelson Potter	22.00	8.50	2.10
□ 71 Fred Sanford	22.00	8.50	2.10
□ 72 Joe Schultz	22.00	8.50	2.10
□ 73 Vern Stephens	30.00	12.00	3.00
□ 74 Jerry Witte	22.00	8.50	2.10
□ 75 Al Zarilla	22.00	8.50	2.10
□ 76 Charles Barrett SP	60.00	24.00	6.00
□ 77 Hank Camelli SP	60.00	24.00	6.00
□ 78 Dick Culler SP	60.00	24.00	6.00
□ 79 Nanny Fernandez SP	75.00	30.00	7.50
□ 80 Si Johnson SP	60.00	24.00	6.00
□ 81 Danny Litwhiler SP	60.00	24.00	6.00
□ 82 Phil Masi SP	60.00	24.00	6.00
□ 83 Carvel Rowell SP	60.00	24.00	6.00
□ 84 Connie Ryan SP	60.00	24.00	6.00
□ 85 John Sain SP	100.00	40.00	10.00
□ 86 Ray Sanders SP	60.00	24.00	6.00
□ 87 Sibby Sisti SP	60.00	24.00	6.00
□ 88 Billy Southworth SP	60.00	24.00	6.00
□ 89 Warren Spahn SP	300.00	120.00	30.00
□ 90 Ed Wright SP	60.00	24.00	6.00
□ 91 Bob Bragan	22.00	8.50	2.10
□ 92 Ralph Branca	30.00	12.00	3.00
□ 93 Hugh Casey	22.00	8.50	2.10
□ 94 Bruce Edwards	22.00	8.50	2.10
□ 95 Hal Gregg	22.00	8.50	2.10
□ 96 Joe Hatten	22.00	8.50	2.10
□ 97 Gene Hermanski	22.00	8.50	2.10
□ 98 John Jorgensen	22.00	8.50	2.10
□ 99 Harry Lavagetto	22.00	8.50	2.10
□ 100 Vic Lombardi	22.00	8.50	2.10
□ 101 Frank Melton	22.00	8.50	2.10
□ 102 Ed Miksis	22.00	8.50	2.10
□ 103 Marv Rackley	22.00	8.50	2.10
□ 104 Ed Stevens	22.00	8.50	2.10
□ 105 Phil Cavarretta SP	100.00	40.00	10.00
□ 106 Bob Chipman SP	60.00	24.00	6.00
□ 107 Stanley Hack SP	60.00	24.00	6.00
□ 108 Don Johnson SP	60.00	24.00	6.00
□ 109 Emil Kush SP	60.00	24.00	6.00
□ 110 Bill Lee SP	60.00	24.00	6.00
□ 111 Mickey Livingston SP	60.00	24.00	6.00
□ 112 Harry Lowrey SP	60.00	24.00	6.00
□ 113 Clyde McCullough SP	60.00	24.00	6.00
□ 114 Andy Pafko SP	60.00	24.00	6.00
□ 115 Marv Rickert SP	60.00	24.00	6.00
□ 116 John Schmitz SP	60.00	24.00	6.00
□ 117 Bobby Sturgeon SP	60.00	24.00	6.00
□ 118 Ed Waitkus SP	60.00	24.00	6.00
□ 119 Henry Wyse SP	60.00	24.00	6.00
□ 120 Bill Ayers	22.00	8.50	2.10
□ 121 Robert Blattner	22.00	8.50	2.10
□ 122 Mike Budnick	22.00	8.50	2.10
□ 123 Sid Gordon	22.00	8.50	2.10
□ 124 Clinton Hartung	22.00	8.50	2.10
□ 125 Monte Kennedy	22.00	8.50	2.10
□ 126 Dave Koslo	22.00	8.50	2.10
□ 127 Carroll Lockman	25.00	10.00	2.50
□ 128 Jack Lohrke	22.00	8.50	2.10
□ 129 Ernie Lombardi	50.00	20.00	5.00
□ 130 Willard Marshall	22.00	8.50	2.10
□ 131 John Mize	75.00	30.00	7.50
□ 132 Eugene Thompson (does not exist)	0.00	.00	.00
□ 133 Ken Trinkle	22.00	8.50	2.10
□ 134 Bill Voiselle	22.00	8.50	2.10
□ 135 Mickey Witek	22.00	8.50	2.10
□ 136 Eddie Basinski	22.00	8.50	2.10
□ 137 Ernie Bonham	22.00	8.50	2.10
□ 138 Billy Cox	25.00	10.00	2.50
□ 139 Elbie Fletcher	22.00	8.50	2.10
□ 140 Frank Gustine	22.00	8.50	2.10
□ 141 Kirby Higbe	22.00	8.50	2.10
□ 142 Leroy Jarvis	22.00	8.50	2.10
□ 143 Ralph Kiner	75.00	30.00	7.50
□ 144 Fred Ostermueller	22.00	8.50	2.10
□ 145 Preacher Roe	40.00	16.00	4.00
□ 146 Jim Russell	22.00	8.50	2.10
□ 147 Rip Sewell	25.00	10.00	2.50
□ 148 Nick Strincevich	22.00	8.50	2.10
□ 149 Honus Wagner	100.00	40.00	10.00
□ 150 Alpha Brazle	22.00	8.50	2.10
□ 151 Ken Burkhart	22.00	8.50	2.10
□ 152 Bernard Creger	22.00	8.50	2.10
□ 153 Joffre Cross	22.00	8.50	2.10
□ 154 Charles E. Diering	22.00	8.50	2.10
□ 155 Ervin Dusak	22.00	8.50	2.10
□ 156 Joe Garagiola	75.00	30.00	7.50
□ 157 Tony Kaufmann	22.00	8.50	2.10
□ 158 George Kurowski	22.00	8.50	2.10
□ 159 Marty Marion	40.00	16.00	4.00
□ 160 George Munger	22.00	8.50	2.10
□ 161 Del Rice	22.00	8.50	2.10
□ 162 Dick Sisler	22.00	8.50	2.10
□ 163 Enos Slaughter	75.00	30.00	7.50
□ 164 Ted Wilks	22.00	8.50	2.10

1951 Topps Blue Backs

The cards in this 52-card set measure 2" by 2 5/8". The 1951 Topps series of blue backed baseball cards could be used to play a baseball game by shuffling the cards and drawing them from a pile. These cards were marketed with a piece of caramel candy, which often melted or was squashed in such a way as to damage the card and wrapper (despite the fact that a paper shield was inserted between candy and card). Blue Backs are more difficult to obtain than the similarly styled Red Backs. The set is denoted on the cards as "Set B" and the Red Back set is correspondingly Set A. Appropriately leading off the set is Eddie Yost.

	NRMT	VG-E	GOOD
COMPLETE SET (52)	1250.00	500.00	150.00
COMMON PLAYER (1-52)	20.00	8.00	2.00
□ 1 Eddie Yost	22.50	9.00	2.00
□ 2 Hank Majeski	20.00	8.00	2.00
□ 3 Richie Ashburn	45.00	18.00	4.50
□ 4 Del Ennis	22.50	9.00	2.00
□ 5 Johnny Pesky	22.50	9.00	2.00
□ 6 Al Schoendienst	30.00	12.00	3.00
□ 7 Gerry Staley	20.00	8.00	2.00
□ 8 Dick Sisler	20.00	8.00	2.00
□ 9 Johnny Sain	30.00	12.00	3.00
□ 10 Joe Page	22.50	9.00	2.00
□ 11 Johnny Groth	20.00	8.00	2.00
□ 12 Sam Jethroe	20.00	8.00	2.00
□ 13 Mickey Vernon	22.50	9.00	2.00
□ 14 Red Munger	20.00	8.00	2.00
□ 15 Eddie Joost	20.00	8.00	2.00
□ 16 Murry Dickson	20.00	8.00	2.00
□ 17 Roy Smalley	20.00	8.00	2.00
□ 18 Ned Garver	20.00	8.00	2.00
□ 19 Phil Masi	20.00	8.00	2.00
□ 20 Ralph Branca	27.00	11.00	2.70
□ 21 Billy Johnson	20.00	8.00	2.00
□ 22 Bob Kuzava	20.00	8.00	2.00
□ 23 Dizzy Trout	20.00	8.00	2.00
□ 24 Sherman Lollar	22.50	9.00	2.00
□ 25 Sam Mele	20.00	8.00	2.00
□ 26 Chico Carrasquel	20.00	8.00	2.00
□ 27 Andy Pafko	20.00	8.00	2.00
□ 28 Harry Brecheen	20.00	8.00	2.00
□ 29 Granville Hamner	20.00	8.00	2.00
□ 30 Enos Slaughter	55.00	22.00	5.50
□ 31 Lou Brissie	20.00	8.00	2.00
□ 32 Bob Elliott	22.50	9.00	2.00
□ 33 Don Lenhardt	20.00	8.00	2.00
□ 34 Earl Torgeson	20.00	8.00	2.00
□ 35 Tommy Byrne	22.50	9.00	2.00
□ 36 Cliff Fannin	20.00	8.00	2.00
□ 37 Bobby Doerr	50.00	20.00	5.00
□ 38 Irv Noren	20.00	8.00	2.00

□ 39 Ed Lopat	30.00	12.00	3.00
□ 40 Vic Wertz	22.50	9.00	2.00
□ 41 Johnny Schmitz	20.00	8.00	2.00
□ 42 Bruce Edwards	20.00	8.00	2.00
□ 43 Willie Jones	20.00	8.00	2.00
□ 44 Johnny Wyrostek	20.00	8.00	2.00
□ 45 Billy Pierce	27.00	11.00	2.70
□ 46 Gerry Priddy	20.00	8.00	2.00
□ 47 Herman Wehmeier	20.00	8.00	2.00
□ 48 Billy Cox	22.50	9.00	2.00
□ 49 Henry Sauer	22.50	9.00	2.00
□ 50 Johnny Mize	60.00	24.00	6.00
□ 51 Eddie Waitkus	20.00	8.00	2.00
□ 52 Sam Chapman	20.00	8.00	2.00

1951 Topps Red Backs

The cards in this 52-card set measure 2" by 2 5/8". The 1951 Topps Red Back set is identical in style to the Blue Back set of the same year. The cards have rounded corners and were designed to be used as a baseball game. Zernial, number 36, is listed with either the White Sox or Athletics, and Holmes, number 52, with either the Braves or Hartford. The set is denoted on the cards as "Set A" and the Blue Back set is correspondingly Set B.

	NRMT	VG-E	GOOD
COMPLETE SET (52)	350.00	140.00	35.00
COMMON PLAYER (1-52)	3.50	1.40	.35
□ 1 Yogi Berra	45.00	15.00	3.00
□ 2 Sid Gordon	3.50	1.40	.35
□ 3 Ferris Fain	3.50	1.40	.35
□ 4 Vern Stephens	3.50	1.40	.35
□ 5 Phil Rizzuto	15.00	6.00	1.50
□ 6 Allie Reynolds	6.50	2.60	.65
□ 7 Howie Pollet	3.50	1.40	.35
□ 8 Early Wynn	10.00	4.00	1.00
□ 9 Roy Sievers	3.50	1.40	.35
□ 10 Mel Parnell	3.50	1.40	.35
□ 11 Gene Hermanski	3.50	1.40	.35
□ 12 Jim Hegan	3.50	1.40	.35
□ 13 Dale Mitchell	3.50	1.40	.35
□ 14 Wayne Terwilliger	3.50	1.40	.35
□ 15 Ralph Kiner	12.00	5.00	1.20
□ 16 Preacher Roe	6.00	2.40	.60
□ 17 Dave (Gus) Bell	5.00	2.00	.50
□ 18 Gerry Coleman	3.50	1.40	.35
□ 19 Dick Kokos	3.50	1.40	.35
□ 20 Dom DiMaggio	6.00	2.40	.60
□ 21 Larry Jansen	3.50	1.40	.35
□ 22 Bob Feller	20.00	8.00	2.00
□ 23 Ray Boone	5.00	2.00	.50
□ 24 Hank Bauer	6.50	2.60	.65
□ 25 Cliff Chambers	3.50	1.40	.35
□ 26 Luke Easter	3.50	1.40	.35
□ 27 Wally Westlake	3.50	1.40	.35
□ 28 Elmer Valo	3.50	1.40	.35
□ 29 Bob Kennedy	3.50	1.40	.35
□ 30 Warren Spahn	18.00	7.25	1.80
□ 31 Gil Hodges	15.00	6.00	1.50
□ 32 Henry Thompson	3.50	1.40	.35
□ 33 William Werle	3.50	1.40	.35
□ 34 Grady Hatton	3.50	1.40	.35
□ 35 Al Rosen	6.50	2.60	.65
□ 36A Gus Zernial (Chicago)	13.50	6.00	1.00
□ 36B Gus Zernial (Philadelphia)	10.00	4.00	1.00
□ 37 Wes Westrum	3.00	1.20	.30
□ 38 Duke Snider	30.00	12.00	3.00
□ 39 Ted Kluszewski	6.50	2.60	.65
□ 40 Mike Garcia	3.50	1.40	.35
□ 41 Whitey Lockman	3.50	1.40	.35
□ 42 Ray Scarborough	3.50	1.40	.35
□ 43 Maurice McDermott	3.50	1.40	.35
□ 44 Sid Hudson	3.50	1.40	.35
□ 45 Andy Seminick	3.50	1.40	.35
□ 46 Billy Goodman	3.50	1.40	.35
□ 47 Tommy Glaviano	3.50	1.40	.35
□ 48 Eddie Stanky	3.50	1.40	.35
□ 49 Al Zarilla	3.50	1.40	.35
□ 50 Monte Irvin	18.00	7.25	1.80
□ 51 Eddie Robinson	3.50	1.40	.35
□ 52A Tommy Holmes (Boston)	15.00	6.00	1.50
□ 52B Tommy Holmes (Hartford)	10.00	4.00	1.00

1951 Topps Teams

The cards in this 9-card set measure 2 1/16" by 5 1/4". These unnumbered team cards issued by Topps in 1951 carry black and white photographs framed by a yellow border. They are found with or without "1950" printed in the name panel before the team name (no difference in value for either variety). These cards were issued in the same 5 cent wrapper as the Connie Mack and Current All Stars. They have been assigned reference numbers in the checklist alphabetically by team city and name.

	NRMT	VG-E	GOOD
COMPLETE SET (9)	1250.00	500.00	150.00
COMMON TEAM (1-9)	100.00	40.00	10.00
□ 1 Boston Red Sox	200.00	80.00	20.00
□ 2 Brooklyn Dodgers	150.00	60.00	15.00
□ 3 Chicago White Sox	150.00	60.00	15.00
□ 4 Cincinnati Reds	120.00	50.00	12.00
□ 5 New York Giants	150.00	60.00	15.00
□ 6 Philadelphia Athletics	100.00	40.00	10.00
□ 7 Philadelphia Phillies	120.00	50.00	12.00
□ 8 St. Louis Cardinals	200.00	80.00	20.00
□ 9 Washington Senators	100.00	40.00	10.00

1951 Topps Connie Mack

The cards in this 11-card set measure 2 1/16" by 5 1/4". The series of die-cut cards which comprise the set entitled Connie Mack All-Stars was one of Topps' most distinctive and fragile card designs. Printed on thin cardboard, these elegant cards were protected in the wrapper by panels of accompanying Red Backs, but once removed were easily damaged (after all, they were intended to be folded and used as toy figures). Cards without tops have a value less than one-half of that listed below. The cards are unnumbered and are listed below in alphabetical order.

	NRMT	VG-E	GOOD
COMPLETE SET (11)	3500.00	1500.00	350.00
COMMON PLAYER (1-11)	100.00	40.00	10.00
□ 1 Grover C. Alexander	300.00	120.00	30.00
□ 2 Mickey Cochrane	200.00	80.00	20.00
□ 3 Ed Collins	125.00	50.00	12.50
□ 4 Jimmy Collins	100.00	40.00	10.00
□ 5 Lou Gehrig	800.00	320.00	80.00
□ 6 Walter Johnson	400.00	160.00	40.00
□ 7 Connie Mack	200.00	80.00	20.00
□ 8 Christy Mathewson	200.00	80.00	20.00
□ 9 Babe Ruth	1000.00	400.00	100.00
□ 10 Tris Speaker	125.00	50.00	12.50
□ 11 Honus Wagner	200.00	80.00	20.00

1951 Topps Current AS

The cards in this 11-card set measure 2 1/16" by 5 1/4". The 1951 Topps Current All-Star series is probably the rarest of all legitimate, nationally issued, post war baseball issues. The set price listed below does not include the prices for the cards of Konstanty, Roberts and Stanky, which likely never were released to the public in gum packs. These three cards (SP in the checklist below) were probably obtained directly from the company and exist in extremely limited numbers. As with the Connie Mack set, cards without the die-cut background are worth half of the value listed below. The cards are unnumbered and are listed below in alphabetical order.

	NRMT	VG-E	GOOD
COMPLETE SET (8)	3000.00	1200.00	300.00
COMMON PLAYER (1-11)	150.00	60.00	15.00
□ 1 Yogi Berra	750.00	300.00	75.00
□ 2 Larry Doby	200.00	80.00	20.00
□ 3 Walt Dropo	250.00	100.00	25.00
□ 4 Hoot Evers	150.00	60.00	15.00
□ 5 George Kell	400.00	160.00	40.00
□ 6 Ralph Kiner	450.00	180.00	45.00
□ 7 Jim Konstanty SP	8000.00	4000.00	900.00
□ 8 Bob Lemon	400.00	160.00	40.00
□ 9 Phil Rizzuto	400.00	160.00	40.00
□ 10 Robin Roberts SP	9000.00	4000.00	900.00
□ 11 Eddie Stanky SP	8000.00	4000.00	900.00

1952 Topps

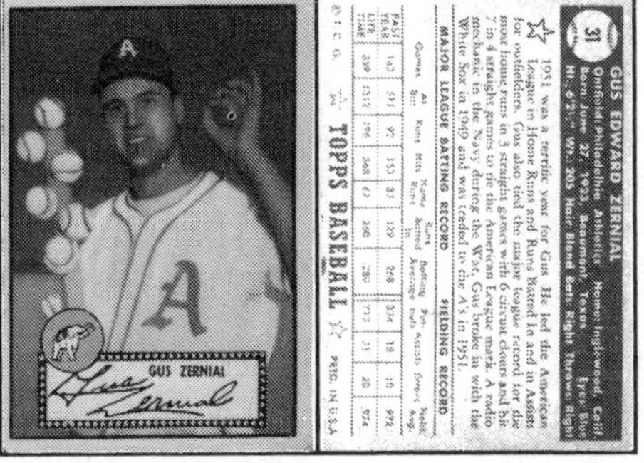

The cards in this 407-card set measure 2 5/8" by 3 3/4". The 1952 Topps set is Topps' first truly major set. Card numbers 1 to 80 were issued with red or black backs, both of which are less plentiful than card numbers 81 to 250. In fact the first series is considered the most difficult with respect to finding Mint condition cards. Card number 48 (Joe Page) and number 49 (Johnny Sain) can be found with each other's write-up on their back. Card numbers 251 to 310 are somewhat scarce and numbers 311 to 407 are quite scarce. Cards 281-300 were single printed compared to the other cards in the next to last series. Cards 311-313 were double printed on the last high number printing sheet. The key card in the set is obviously Mickey Mantle #311, Mickey's first of many Topps cards.

	NRMT	VG-E	GOOD
COMPLETE SET (407)	37500.	14000.	5000.
COMMON PLAYER (1-80)	50.00	20.00	5.00
COMMON PLAYER (81-250)	20.00	8.00	2.00
COMMON PLAYER (251-280)	40.00	16.00	4.00
COMMON PLAYER (281-300)	50.00	20.00	5.00
COMMON PLAYER (301-310)	40.00	16.00	4.00
COMMON PLAYER (311-407)	150.00	60.00	15.00
□ 1 Andy Pafko	900.00	40.00	8.00
□ 2 James Pete Runnels	55.00	22.00	5.50
□ 3 Henry Thompson	55.00	22.00	5.50
□ 4 Don Lenhardt	50.00	20.00	5.00
□ 5 Larry Jansen	50.00	20.00	5.00
□ 6 Grady Hatton	50.00	20.00	5.00
□ 7 Wayne Terwilliger	50.00	20.00	5.00
□ 8 Fred Marsh	50.00	20.00	5.00
□ 9 Robert Hogue	50.00	20.00	5.00
□ 10 Al Rosen	70.00	28.00	7.00
□ 11 Phil Rizzuto	135.00	54.00	13.50
□ 12 Romanus Basgall	50.00	20.00	5.00
□ 13 Johnny Wyrostek	50.00	20.00	5.00
□ 14 Bob Elliott	55.00	22.00	5.50
□ 15 Johnny Pesky	55.00	22.00	5.50
□ 16 Gene Hermanski	50.00	20.00	5.00
□ 17 Jim Hegan	55.00	22.00	5.50
□ 18 Merrill Combs	50.00	20.00	5.00
□ 19 Johnny Bucha	50.00	20.00	5.00
□ 20 Billy Loes	80.00	32.00	8.00
□ 21 Ferris Fain	55.00	22.00	5.50
□ 22 Dom DiMaggio	75.00	30.00	7.50
□ 23 Billy Goodman	55.00	22.00	5.50
□ 24 Luke Easter	55.00	22.00	5.50
□ 25 John Groth	50.00	20.00	5.00
□ 26 Monte Irvin	90.00	36.00	9.00
□ 27 Sam Jethroe	50.00	20.00	5.00
□ 28 Jerry Priddy	50.00	20.00	5.00
□ 29 Ted Kluszewski	70.00	28.00	7.00
□ 30 Mel Parnell	55.00	22.00	5.50
□ 31 Gus Zernial	60.00	24.00	6.00
□ 32 Eddie Robinson	50.00	20.00	5.00
□ 33 Warren Spahn	150.00	60.00	15.00
□ 34 Elmer Valo	50.00	20.00	5.00
□ 35 Hank Sauer	60.00	24.00	6.00
□ 36 Gil Hodges	125.00	50.00	11.00
□ 37 Duke Snider	250.00	100.00	22.00
□ 38 Wally Westlake	50.00	20.00	5.00
□ 39 Dizzy Trout	55.00	22.00	5.50
□ 40 Irv Noren	50.00	20.00	5.00
□ 41 Bob Wellman	50.00	20.00	5.00
□ 42 Lou Kretlow	50.00	20.00	5.00
□ 43 Ray Scarborough	50.00	20.00	5.00
□ 44 Con Dempsey	50.00	20.00	5.00
□ 45 Eddie Joost	50.00	20.00	5.00
□ 46 Gordon Goldsberry	50.00	20.00	5.00
□ 47 Willie Jones	50.00	20.00	5.00
□ 48A Joe Page COR	65.00	26.00	6.50
□ 48B Joe Page ERR (bio for Sain)	275.00	110.00	27.00
□ 49A Johnny Sain COR	80.00	32.00	8.00
□ 49B Johnny Sain ERR (bio for Page)	275.00	110.00	27.00
□ 50 Marv Rickert	50.00	20.00	5.00
□ 51 Jim Russell	50.00	20.00	5.00
□ 52 Don Mueller	60.00	24.00	6.00
□ 53 Chris Van Cuyk	50.00	20.00	5.00
□ 54 Leo Kiely	50.00	20.00	5.00
□ 55 Ray Boone	55.00	22.00	5.50
□ 56 Thomas Glaviano	50.00	20.00	5.00
□ 57 Ed Lopat	85.00	34.00	8.50
□ 58 Bob Mahoney	50.00	20.00	5.00
□ 59 Robin Roberts	110.00	45.00	11.00
□ 60 Sid Hudson	50.00	20.00	5.00
□ 61 Tookie Gilbert	50.00	20.00	5.00
□ 62 Chuck Stobbs	50.00	20.00	5.00
□ 63 Howie Pollet	50.00	20.00	5.00
□ 64 Roy Sievers	55.00	22.00	5.50
□ 65 Enos Slaughter	110.00	45.00	11.00
□ 66 Preacher Roe	85.00	34.00	8.50
□ 67 Allie Reynolds	90.00	36.00	9.00
□ 68 Cliff Chambers	50.00	20.00	5.00
□ 69 Virgil Stallcup	50.00	20.00	5.00
□ 70 Al Zarilla	50.00	20.00	5.00
□ 71 Tom Upton	50.00	20.00	5.00
□ 72 Karl Olson	50.00	20.00	5.00
□ 73 William Werle	50.00	20.00	5.00
□ 74 Andy Hansen	50.00	20.00	5.00
□ 75 Wes Westrum	50.00	20.00	5.00
□ 76 Eddie Stanky	55.00	22.00	5.50
□ 77 Bob Kennedy	50.00	20.00	5.00
□ 78 Ellis Kinder	50.00	20.00	5.00
□ 79 Gerald Staley	50.00	20.00	5.00
□ 80 Herman Wehmeier	50.00	20.00	5.00
□ 81 Vernon Law	27.00	11.00	2.70
□ 82 Duane Pillette	20.00	8.00	2.00
□ 83 Billy Johnson	20.00	8.00	2.00
□ 84 Vern Stephens	22.00	9.00	2.20
□ 85 Bob Kuzava	20.00	8.00	2.00
□ 86 Ted Gray	20.00	8.00	2.00

□ 87	Dale Coogan	20.00	8.00	2.00
□ 88	Bob Feller	110.00	45.00	11.00
□ 89	Johnny Lipon	20.00	8.00	2.00
□ 90	Mickey Grasso	20.00	8.00	2.00
□ 91	Red Schoendienst	32.00	13.00	3.20
□ 92	Dale Mitchell	28.00	11.50	2.80
□ 93	Al Sima	20.00	8.00	2.00
□ 94	Sam Mele	20.00	8.00	2.00
□ 95	Ken Holcombe	20.00	8.00	2.00
□ 96	Willard Marshall	20.00	8.00	2.00
□ 97	Earl Torgeson	20.00	8.00	2.00
□ 98	Billy Pierce	25.00	10.00	2.50
□ 99	Gene Woodling	45.00	18.00	4.50
□ 100	Del Rice	20.00	8.00	2.00
□ 101	Max Lanier	20.00	8.00	2.00
□ 102	Bill Kennedy	20.00	8.00	2.00
□ 103	Cliff Mapes	20.00	8.00	2.00
□ 104	Don Kolloway	20.00	8.00	2.00
□ 105	John Pramesa	20.00	8.00	2.00
□ 106	Mickey Vernon	22.00	9.00	2.20
□ 107	Connie Ryan	20.00	8.00	2.00
□ 108	Jim Konstanty	24.00	10.00	2.40
□ 109	Ted Wilks	20.00	8.00	2.00
□ 110	Dutch Leonard	20.00	8.00	2.00
□ 111	Peanuts Lowrey	20.00	8.00	2.00
□ 112	Henry Majeski	20.00	8.00	2.00
□ 113	Dick Sisler	20.00	8.00	2.00
□ 114	Willard Ramsdell	20.00	8.00	2.00
□ 115	Red Munger	20.00	8.00	2.00
□ 116	Carl Scheib	20.00	8.00	2.00
□ 117	Sherman Lollar	22.00	9.00	2.20
□ 118	Ken Raffensberger	20.00	8.00	2.00
□ 119	Mickey McDermott	20.00	8.00	2.00
□ 120	Bob Chakales	20.00	8.00	2.00
□ 121	Gus Niarhos	20.00	8.00	2.00
□ 122	Jackie Jensen	60.00	24.00	6.00
□ 123	Eddie Yost	20.00	8.00	2.00
□ 124	Monte Kennedy	20.00	8.00	2.00
□ 125	Bill Rigney	20.00	8.00	2.00
□ 126	Fred Hutchinson	25.00	10.00	2.50
□ 127	Paul Minner	20.00	8.00	2.00
□ 128	Don Bollweg	20.00	8.00	2.00
□ 129	Johnny Mize	70.00	28.00	7.00
□ 130	Sheldon Jones	20.00	8.00	2.00
□ 131	Morris Martin	20.00	8.00	2.00
□ 132	Clyde Klutz	20.00	8.00	2.00
□ 133	Al Widmar	20.00	8.00	2.00
□ 134	Joe Tipton	20.00	8.00	2.00
□ 135	Dixie Howell	20.00	8.00	2.00
□ 136	Johnny Schmitz	20.00	8.00	2.00
□ 137	Roy McMillan	20.00	8.00	2.00
□ 138	Bill MacDonald	20.00	8.00	2.00
□ 139	Ken Wood	20.00	8.00	2.00
□ 140	Johnny Antonelli	22.00	9.00	2.20
□ 141	Clint Hartung	20.00	8.00	2.00
□ 142	Harry Perkowski	20.00	8.00	2.00
□ 143	Les Moss	20.00	8.00	2.00
□ 144	Ed Blake	20.00	8.00	2.00
□ 145	Joe Haynes	20.00	8.00	2.00
□ 146	Frank House	20.00	8.00	2.00
□ 147	Bob Young	20.00	8.00	2.00
□ 148	Johnny Klippstein	20.00	8.00	2.00
□ 149	Dick Kryhoski	20.00	8.00	2.00
□ 150	Ted Beard	20.00	8.00	2.00
□ 151	Wally Post	22.00	9.00	2.20
□ 152	Al Evans	20.00	8.00	2.00
□ 153	Bob Rush	20.00	8.00	2.00
□ 154	Joe Muir	20.00	8.00	2.00
□ 155	Frank Overmire	20.00	8.00	2.00
□ 156	Frank Hiller	20.00	8.00	2.00
□ 157	Bob Usher	20.00	8.00	2.00
□ 158	Eddie Waitkus	20.00	8.00	2.00
□ 159	Saul Rogovin	20.00	8.00	2.00
□ 160	Owen Friend	20.00	8.00	2.00
□ 161	Bud Byerly	20.00	8.00	2.00
□ 162	Del Crandall	22.00	9.00	2.20
□ 163	Stan Rojek	20.00	8.00	2.00
□ 164	Walt Dubiel	20.00	8.00	2.00
□ 165	Eddie Kazak	20.00	8.00	2.00
□ 166	Paul LaPalme	20.00	8.00	2.00
□ 167	Bill Howerton	20.00	8.00	2.00
□ 168	Charlie Silvera	22.00	9.00	2.20
□ 169	Howie Judson	20.00	8.00	2.00
□ 170	Gus Bell	22.00	9.00	2.20
□ 171	Ed Erautt	20.00	8.00	2.00
□ 172	Eddie Miksis	20.00	8.00	2.00
□ 173	Roy Smalley	20.00	8.00	2.00
□ 174	Clarence Marshall	20.00	8.00	2.00
□ 175	Billy Martin	200.00	80.00	20.00
□ 176	Hank Edwards	20.00	8.00	2.00
□ 177	Bill Wight	20.00	8.00	2.00
□ 178	Cass Michaels	20.00	8.00	2.00
□ 179	Frank Smith	20.00	8.00	2.00
□ 180	Charley Maxwell	20.00	8.00	2.00
□ 181	Bob Swift	20.00	8.00	2.00
□ 182	Billy Hitchcock	20.00	8.00	2.00
□ 183	Erv Dusak	20.00	8.00	2.00
□ 184	Bob Ramazotti	20.00	8.00	2.00
□ 185	Bill Nicholson	20.00	8.00	2.00
□ 186	Walt Masterson	20.00	8.00	2.00
□ 187	Bob Miller	20.00	8.00	2.00
□ 188	Clarence Podbielan	20.00	8.00	2.00
□ 189	Pete Reiser	25.00	10.00	2.50
□ 190	Don Johnson	20.00	8.00	2.00
□ **191**	**Yogi Berra**	**250.00**	**100.00**	**22.00**
□ 192	Myron Ginsberg	20.00	8.00	2.00
□ 193	Harry Simpson	20.00	8.00	2.00
□ 194	Joe Hatton	20.00	8.00	2.00
□ 195	Minnie Minoso	50.00	20.00	5.00
□ 196	Solly Hemus	20.00	8.00	2.00
□ 197	George Strickland	20.00	8.00	2.00
□ 198	Phil Haugstad	20.00	8.00	2.00
□ 199	George Zuverink	20.00	8.00	2.00
□ 200	Ralph Houk	60.00	24.00	6.00
□ 201	Alex Kellner	20.00	8.00	2.00
□ 202	Joe Collins	25.00	10.00	2.50
□ 203	Curt Simmons	25.00	10.00	2.50
□ 204	Ron Northey	20.00	8.00	2.00
□ 205	Clyde King	22.00	9.00	2.20
□ 206	Joe Ostrowski	20.00	8.00	2.00
□ 207	Mickey Harris	20.00	8.00	2.00
□ 208	Marlin Stuart	20.00	8.00	2.00
□ 209	Howie Fox	20.00	8.00	2.00
□ 210	Dick Fowler	20.00	8.00	2.00
□ 211	Ray Coleman	20.00	8.00	2.00
□ 212	Ned Garver	20.00	8.00	2.00
□ 213	Nippy Jones	20.00	8.00	2.00
□ 214	Johnny Hopp	22.00	9.00	2.20
□ 215	Hank Bauer	40.00	16.00	4.00
□ 216	Richie Ashburn	45.00	18.00	4.50
□ 217	Snuffy Stirnweiss	22.00	9.00	2.20
□ 218	Clyde McCullough	20.00	8.00	2.00
□ 219	Bobby Shantz	27.00	11.00	2.70
□ 220	Joe Presko	20.00	8.00	2.00
□ 221	Granny Hamner	20.00	8.00	2.00
□ 222	Hoot Evers	20.00	8.00	2.00
□ 223	Del Ennis	22.00	9.00	2.20
□ 224	Bruce Edwards	20.00	8.00	2.00
□ 225	Frank Baumholtz	20.00	8.00	2.00
□ 226	Dave Philley	20.00	8.00	2.00
□ 227	Joe Garagiola	60.00	24.00	6.00
□ 228	Al Brazle	20.00	8.00	2.00
□ 229	Gene Bearden	20.00	8.00	2.00
□ 230	Matt Batts	20.00	8.00	2.00
□ 231	Sam Zoldak	20.00	8.00	2.00
□ 232	Billy Cox	24.00	10.00	2.40
□ 233	Bob Friend	25.00	10.00	2.50
□ 234	Steve Souchock	20.00	8.00	2.00
□ 235	Walt Dropo	22.00	9.00	2.20
□ 236	Ed Fitzgerald	20.00	8.00	2.00
□ 237	Jerry Coleman	25.00	10.00	2.50
□ 238	Art Houtteman	20.00	8.00	2.00
□ 239	Rocky Bridges	20.00	8.00	2.00
□ 240	Jack Phillips	20.00	8.00	2.00
□ 241	Tommy Byrne	22.00	9.00	2.20
□ 242	Tom Poholsky	20.00	8.00	2.00
□ 243	Larry Doby	30.00	12.00	3.00
□ 244	Vic Wertz	22.00	9.00	2.20
□ 245	Sherry Robertson	20.00	8.00	2.00
□ 246	George Kell	60.00	24.00	6.00
□ 247	Randy Gumpert	20.00	8.00	2.00
□ 248	Frank Shea	20.00	8.00	2.00
□ 249	Bobby Adams	20.00	8.00	2.00
□ 250	Carl Erskine	50.00	20.00	5.00
□ 251	Chico Carrasquel	40.00	16.00	4.00
□ 252	Vern Bickford	40.00	16.00	4.00
□ 253	Johnny Berardino	50.00	20.00	5.00
□ 254	Joe Dobson	40.00	16.00	4.00
□ 255	Clyde Vollmer	40.00	16.00	4.00
□ 256	Pete Suder	40.00	16.00	4.00
□ 257	Bobby Avila	45.00	18.00	4.50
□ 258	Steve Gromek	40.00	16.00	4.00
□ 259	Bob Addis	40.00	16.00	4.00
□ 260	Pete Castiglione	40.00	16.00	4.00
□ 261	Willie Mays	1000.00	400.00	100.00
□ 262	Virgil Trucks	45.00	18.00	4.50
□ 263	Harry Brecheen	40.00	16.00	4.00
□ 264	Roy Hartsfield	40.00	16.00	4.00
□ 265	Chuck Diering	40.00	16.00	4.00
□ 266	Murry Dickson	40.00	16.00	4.00
□ 267	Sid Gordon	40.00	16.00	4.00
□ 268	Bob Lemon	150.00	60.00	15.00
□ 269	Willard Nixon	40.00	16.00	4.00
□ 270	Lou Brissie	40.00	16.00	4.00
□ 271	Jim Delsing	40.00	16.00	4.00
□ 272	Mike Garcia	50.00	20.00	5.00
□ 273	Erv Palica	40.00	16.00	4.00
□ 274	Ralph Branca	75.00	30.00	7.50
□ 275	Pat Mullin	40.00	16.00	4.00
□ 276	Jim Wilson	40.00	16.00	4.00

□ 277 Early Wynn 150.00 60.00 15.00
□ 278 Al Clark 40.00 16.00 4.00
□ 279 Ed Stewart 40.00 16.00 4.00
□ 280 Cloyd Boyer 45.00 18.00 4.50
□ 281 Tommy Brown SP 50.00 20.00 5.00
□ 282 Birdie Tebbetts SP 55.00 22.00 5.50
□ 283 Philip Masi SP 50.00 20.00 5.00
□ 284 Hank Arft SP 50.00 20.00 5.00
□ 285 Cliff Fannin SP 50.00 20.00 5.00
□ 286 Joe DeMaestri SP 50.00 20.00 5.00
□ 287 Steve Bilko SP 50.00 20.00 5.00
□ 288 Chet Nichols SP 50.00 20.00 5.00
□ 289 Tommy Holmes SP 55.00 22.00 5.50
□ 290 Joe Astroth SP 50.00 20.00 5.00
□ 291 Gil Coan SP 50.00 20.00 5.00
□ 292 Floyd Baker SP 50.00 20.00 5.00
□ 293 Sibby Sisti SP 50.00 20.00 5.00
□ 294 Walker Cooper SP 50.00 20.00 5.00
□ 295 Phil Cavarretta SP 60.00 24.00 6.00
□ 296 Red Rolfe SP 60.00 24.00 6.00
□ 297 Andy Seminick SP 50.00 20.00 5.00
□ 298 Bob Ross SP 50.00 20.00 5.00
□ 299 Ray Murray SP 50.00 20.00 5.00
□ 300 Barney McCosky SP 50.00 20.00 5.00
□ 301 Bob Porterfield 40.00 16.00 4.00
□ 302 Max Surkont 40.00 16.00 4.00
□ 303 Harry Dorish 40.00 16.00 4.00
□ 304 Sam Dente 40.00 16.00 4.00
□ 305 Paul Richards 50.00 20.00 5.00
□ 306 Lou Sleater 40.00 16.00 4.00
□ 307 Frank Campos 40.00 16.00 4.00
□ 308 Luis Aloma 40.00 16.00 4.00
□ 309 Jim Busby 40.00 16.00 4.00
□ 310 George Metkovich 60.00 24.00 6.00
□ 311 Mickey Mantle DP 6500.00 2000.00 500.00
□ 312 Jackie Robinson DP 800.00 320.00 80.00
□ 313 Bobby Thomson DP 175.00 70.00 18.00
□ 314 Roy Campanella 1250.00 500.00 100.00
□ 315 Leo Durocher 250.00 100.00 25.00
□ 316 Dave Williams 175.00 70.00 18.00
□ 317 Conrado Marrerro 150.00 60.00 15.00
□ 318 Harold Gregg 150.00 60.00 15.00
□ 319 Al Walker 150.00 60.00 15.00
□ 320 John Rutherford 150.00 60.00 15.00
□ 321 Joe Black 200.00 80.00 20.00
□ 322 Randy Jackson 150.00 60.00 15.00
□ 323 Bubba Church 150.00 60.00 15.00
□ 324 Warren Hacker 150.00 60.00 15.00
□ 325 Bill Serena 150.00 60.00 15.00
□ 326 George Shuba 175.00 70.00 18.00
□ 327 Al Wilson 150.00 60.00 15.00
□ 328 Bob Borkowski 150.00 60.00 15.00
□ 329 Ike Delock 150.00 60.00 15.00
□ 330 Turk Lown 150.00 60.00 15.00
□ 331 Tom Morgan 150.00 60.00 15.00
□ 332 Anthony Bartirome 150.00 60.00 15.00
□ 333 Pee Wee Reese 600.00 240.00 60.00
□ 334 Wilmer Mizell 150.00 60.00 15.00
□ 335 Ted Lepcio 150.00 60.00 15.00
□ 336 Dave Koslo 150.00 60.00 15.00
□ 337 Jim Hearn 150.00 60.00 15.00
□ 338 Sal Yvars 150.00 60.00 15.00
□ 339 Russ Meyer 150.00 60.00 15.00
□ 340 Bob Hooper 150.00 60.00 15.00
□ 341 Hal Jeffcoat 150.00 60.00 15.00
□ 342 Clem Labine 175.00 70.00 18.00
□ 343 Dick Gernert 150.00 60.00 15.00
□ 344 Ewell Blackwell 175.00 70.00 18.00
□ 345 Sammy White 150.00 60.00 15.00
□ 346 George Spencer 150.00 60.00 15.00
□ 347 Joe Adcock 200.00 80.00 20.00
□ 348 Robert Kelly 150.00 60.00 15.00
□ 349 Bob Cain 150.00 60.00 15.00
□ 350 Cal Abrams 150.00 60.00 15.00
□ 351 Alvin Dark 200.00 80.00 20.00
□ 352 Karl Drews 150.00 60.00 15.00
□ 353 Bobby Del Greco 150.00 60.00 15.00
□ 354 Fred Hatfield 150.00 60.00 15.00
□ 355 Bobby Morgan 150.00 60.00 15.00
□ 356 Toby Atwell 150.00 60.00 15.00
□ 357 Smoky Burgess 175.00 70.00 18.00
□ 358 John Kucab 150.00 60.00 15.00
□ 359 Dee Fondy 150.00 60.00 15.00
□ 360 George Crowe 150.00 60.00 15.00
□ 361 William Posedel 150.00 60.00 15.00
□ 362 Ken Heintzelman 150.00 60.00 15.00
□ 363 Dick Rozek 150.00 60.00 15.00
□ 364 Clyde Sukeforth 150.00 60.00 15.00
□ 365 Cookie Lavagetto 150.00 60.00 15.00
□ 366 Dave Madison 150.00 60.00 15.00
□ 367 Ben Thorpe 150.00 60.00 15.00
□ 368 Ed Wright 150.00 60.00 15.00
□ 369 Dick Groat 250.00 100.00 25.00
□ 370 Billy Hoeft 150.00 60.00 15.00
□ 371 Bobby Hofman 150.00 60.00 15.00
□ 372 Gil McDougald 275.00 110.00 27.00
□ 373 Jim Turner COA 175.00 70.00 18.00
□ 374 John Benton 150.00 60.00 15.00
□ 375 John Merson 150.00 60.00 15.00
□ 376 Faye Throneberry 150.00 60.00 15.00
□ 377 Chuck Dressen MG 175.00 70.00 18.00
□ 378 Leroy Fusselman 150.00 60.00 15.00
□ 379 Joseph Rossi 150.00 60.00 15.00
□ 380 Clem Koshorek 150.00 60.00 15.00
□ 381 Milton Stock 150.00 60.00 15.00
□ 382 Sam Jones 175.00 70.00 18.00
□ 383 Del Wilber 150.00 60.00 15.00
□ 384 Frank Crosetti COA 250.00 100.00 25.00
□ 385 Herman Franks 175.00 70.00 18.00
□ 386 John Yuhas 150.00 60.00 15.00
□ 387 William Meyer 150.00 60.00 15.00
□ 388 Bob Chipman 150.00 60.00 15.00
□ 389 Ben Wade 150.00 60.00 15.00
□ 390 Glenn Nelson 150.00 60.00 15.00
□ 391 Ben Chapman 150.00 60.00 15.00
(photo actually
Sam Chapman)
□ 392 Hoyt Wilhelm 425.00 170.00 42.00
□ 393 Ebba St.Claire 150.00 60.00 15.00
□ 394 Billy Herman COA 225.00 90.00 22.00
□ 395 Jake Pitler COA 150.00 60.00 15.00
□ 396 Dick Williams 200.00 80.00 20.00
□ 397 Forrest Main 150.00 60.00 15.00
□ 398 Hal Rice 150.00 60.00 15.00
□ 399 Jim Fridley 150.00 60.00 15.00
□ 400 Bill Dickey COA 500.00 200.00 50.00
□ 401 Bob Schultz 150.00 60.00 15.00
□ 402 Earl Harrist 150.00 60.00 15.00
□ 403 Bill Miller 150.00 60.00 15.00
□ 404 Dick Brodowski 150.00 60.00 15.00
□ 405 Ed Pellagrini 150.00 60.00 15.00
□ 406 Joe Nuxhall 200.00 80.00 20.00
□ 407 Eddie Mathews 1500.00 400.00 80.00

1953 Topps

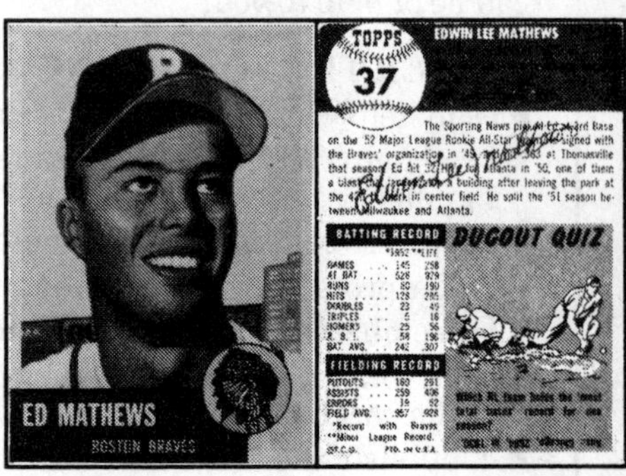

The cards in this 274-card set measure 2 5/8" by 3/3/4". Although the last card is numbered 280, there are only 274 cards in the set since numbers 253, 261, 267, 268, 271, and 275 were never issued. The 1953 Topps series contains line drawings of players in full color. The name and team panel at the card base is easily damaged, making it very difficult to complete a mint set. The high number series, 221 to 280, was produced in shorter supply late in the year and hence is more difficult to complete than the lower numbers. The key cards in the set are Mickey Mantle #82 and Willie Mays #244. There are a number of double-printed cards (actually not double but 50% more of each of these numbers were printed compared to the other cards in the series) indicated by DP in the checklist below. In addition there are five numbers which were printed in with the more plentiful series 166-220; these cards (94, 107, 131, 145, and 156) are also indicated by DP in the checklist below. There were some three-card advertising panels produced by Topps; the players include Johnny Mize, Clem Koshorek, and Toby Atwell and Mickey Mantle, Johnny Wyrostek, and Sal

Yvars. When cut apart, these advertising cards are distinguished by the non-standard card back, i.e., part of an advertisement for the 1953 Topps set instead of the typical statistics and biographical information about the player pictured.

	NRMT	VG-E	GOOD
COMPLETE SET (274)	10500.00	4500.00	1500.00
COMMON PLAYER (1-165)	20.00	8.00	2.00
COMMON DP (1-165)	12.00	5.00	1.20
COMMON PLAYER (166-220)	12.00	5.00	1.20
COMMON PLAYER (221-280)	60.00	24.00	6.00
COMMON DP (221-280)	30.00	12.00	3.00

	NRMT	VG-E	GOOD
□ 1 Jackie Robinson DP	400.00	100.00	20.00
□ 2 Luke Easter DP	12.00	5.00	1.20
□ 3 George Crowe DP	12.00	5.00	1.20
□ 4 Ben Wade	20.00	8.00	2.00
□ 5 Joe Dobson	20.00	8.00	2.00
□ 6 Sam Jones	20.00	8.00	2.00
□ 7 Bob Borkowski DP	12.00	5.00	1.20
□ 8 Clem Koshorek DP	12.00	5.00	1.20
□ 9 Joe Collins	27.00	11.00	2.70
□ 10 Smoky Burgess	22.00	9.00	2.20
□ 11 Sal Yvars	20.00	8.00	2.00
□ 12 Howie Judson DP	12.00	5.00	1.20
□ 13 Conrado Marrero DP	12.00	5.00	1.20
□ 14 Clem Labine	27.00	11.00	2.70
□ 15 Bobo Newsom	22.00	9.00	2.20
□ 16 Peanuts Lowrey	20.00	8.00	2.00
□ 17 Billy Hitchcock	20.00	8.00	2.00
□ 18 Ted Lepcio DP	12.00	5.00	1.20
□ 19 Mel Parnell DP	14.00	5.75	1.40
□ 20 Hank Thompson	22.00	9.00	2.20
□ 21 Billy Johnson	20.00	8.00	2.00
□ 22 Howie Fox	20.00	8.00	2.00
□ 23 Toby Atwell DP	12.00	5.00	1.20
□ 24 Ferris Fain	22.00	9.00	2.20
□ 25 Ray Boone	22.00	9.00	2.20
□ 26 Dale Mitchell DP	14.00	5.75	1.40
□ 27 Roy Campanella DP	135.00	54.00	13.50
□ 28 Eddie Pellagrini	20.00	8.00	2.00
□ 29 Hal Jeffcoat	20.00	8.00	2.00
□ 30 Willard Nixon	20.00	8.00	2.00
□ 31 Ewell Blackwell	27.00	11.00	2.70
□ 32 Clyde Vollmer	20.00	8.00	2.00
□ 33 Bob Kennedy DP	12.00	5.00	1.20
□ 34 George Shuba	22.00	9.00	2.20
□ 35 Irv Noren DP	12.00	5.00	1.20
□ 36 Johnny Groth DP	12.00	5.00	1.20
□ 37 Eddie Mathews DP	70.00	28.00	7.00
□ 38 Jim Hearn DP	12.00	5.00	1.20
□ 39 Eddie Miksis	20.00	8.00	2.00
□ 40 John Lipon	20.00	8.00	2.00
□ 41 Enos Slaughter	55.00	22.00	5.50
□ 42 Gus Zernial DP	10.00	4.00	1.00
□ 43 Gil McDougald	30.00	12.00	3.00
□ 44 Ellis Kinder	20.00	8.00	2.00
□ 45 Grady Hatton DP	12.00	5.00	1.20
□ 46 Johnny Klippstein DP	12.00	5.00	1.20
□ 47 Bubba Church DP	12.00	5.00	1.20
□ 48 Bob Del Greco DP	12.00	5.00	1.20
□ 49 Faye Throneberry DP	12.00	5.00	1.20
□ 50 Chuck Dressen MG DP	14.00	5.75	1.40
□ 51 Frank Campos DP	12.00	5.00	1.20
□ 52 Ted Gray DP	12.00	5.00	1.20
□ 53 Sherm Lollar DP	14.00	5.75	1.40
□ 54 Bob Feller	80.00	32.00	8.00
□ 55 Maurice McDermott DP	12.00	5.00	1.20
□ 56 Jerry Staley DP	12.00	5.00	1.20
□ 57 Carl Scheib DP	12.00	5.00	1.20
□ 58 George Metkovich	20.00	8.00	2.00
□ 59 Karl Drews DP	12.00	5.00	1.20
□ 60 Cloyd Boyer DP	12.00	5.00	1.20
□ 61 Early Wynn	55.00	22.00	5.50
□ 62 Monte Irvin DP	27.00	11.00	2.70
□ 63 Gus Niarhos DP	12.00	5.00	1.20
□ 64 Dave Philley	20.00	8.00	2.00
□ 65 Earl Harrist	20.00	8.00	2.00
□ 66 Minnie Minoso	27.00	11.00	2.70
□ 67 Roy Sievers DP	14.00	5.75	1.40
□ 68 Del Rice	20.00	8.00	2.00
□ 69 Dick Brodowski DP	12.00	5.00	1.20
□ 70 Ed Yuhas	20.00	8.00	2.00
□ 71 Tony Bartirome	20.00	8.00	2.00
□ 72 Fred Hutchinson	22.00	9.00	2.20
□ 73 Eddie Robinson	20.00	8.00	2.00
□ 74 Joe Rossi	20.00	8.00	2.00
□ 75 Mike Garcia	22.00	9.00	2.20
□ 76 Pee Wee Reese	90.00	36.00	9.00
□ 77 Johnny Mize DP	45.00	18.00	4.50
□ 78 Al(Red) Schoendienst	30.00	12.00	3.00
□ 79 Johnny Wyrostek DP	12.00	5.00	1.20
□ 80 Jim Hegan	22.00	9.00	2.20
□ 81 Joe Black	30.00	12.00	3.00
□ 82 Mickey Mantle	1750.00	650.00	150.00
□ 83 Howie Pollet	20.00	8.00	2.00
□ 84 Bob Hooper DP	12.00	5.00	1.20
□ 85 Bobby Morgan DP	12.00	5.00	1.20
□ 86 Billy Martin	65.00	26.00	6.50
□ 87 Ed Lopat	32.00	13.00	3.20
□ 88 Willie Jones DP	12.00	5.00	1.20
□ 89 Chuck Stobbs DP	12.00	5.00	1.20
□ 90 Hank Edwards DP	12.00	5.00	1.20
□ 91 Ebba St.Claire DP	12.00	5.00	1.20
□ 92 Paul Minner DP	12.00	5.00	1.20
□ 93 Hal Rice DP	12.00	5.00	1.20
□ 94 Bill Kennedy DP	12.00	5.00	1.20
□ 95 Willard Marshall DP	12.00	5.00	1.20
□ 96 Virgil Trucks	22.00	9.00	2.20
□ 97 Don Kolloway DP	12.00	5.00	1.20
□ 98 Cal Abrams DP	12.00	5.00	1.20
□ 99 Dave Madison	20.00	8.00	2.00
□ 100 Bill Miller	20.00	8.00	2.00
□ 101 Ted Wilks	20.00	8.00	2.00
□ 102 Connie Ryan DP	12.00	5.00	1.20
□ 103 Joe Astroth DP	12.00	5.00	1.20
□ 104 Yogi Berra	135.00	54.00	13.50
□ 105 Joe Nuxhall DP	14.00	5.75	1.40
□ 106 Johnny Antonelli	22.00	9.00	2.20
□ 107 Danny O'Connell DP	12.00	5.00	1.20
□ 108 Bob Porterfield DP	12.00	5.00	1.20
□ 109 Alvin Dark	25.00	10.00	2.50
□ 110 Herman Wehmeier DP	12.00	5.00	1.20
□ 111 Hank Sauer DP	14.00	5.75	1.40
□ 112 Ned Garver DP	12.00	5.00	1.20
□ 113 Jerry Priddy	20.00	8.00	2.00
□ 114 Phil Rizzuto	65.00	26.00	6.50
□ 115 George Spencer	20.00	8.00	2.00
□ 116 Frank Smith DP	12.00	5.00	1.20
□ 117 Sid Gordon DP	12.00	5.00	1.20
□ 118 Gus Bell DP	14.00	5.75	1.40
□ 119 Johnny Sain	32.00	13.00	3.20
□ 120 Davey Williams	25.00	10.00	2.50
□ 121 Walt Dropo	22.00	9.00	2.20
□ 122 Elmer Valo	20.00	8.00	2.00
□ 123 Tommy Byrne DP	14.00	5.75	1.40
□ 124 Sibby Sisti DP	12.00	5.00	1.20
□ 125 Dick Williams DP	15.00	6.00	1.50
□ 126 Bill Connelly DP	12.00	5.00	1.20
□ 127 Clint Courtney DP	12.00	5.00	1.20
□ 128 Wilmer Mizell DP	12.00	5.00	1.20
□ 129 Keith Thomas	20.00	8.00	2.00
□ 130 Turk Lown DP	12.00	5.00	1.20
□ 131 Harry Byrd DP	12.00	5.00	1.20
□ 132 Tom Morgan	20.00	8.00	2.00
□ 133 Gil Coan	20.00	8.00	2.00
□ 134 Rube Walker	22.00	9.00	2.20
□ 135 Al Rosen DP	25.00	10.00	2.50
□ 136 Ken Heintzelman DP	12.00	5.00	1.20
□ 137 John Rutherford DP	12.00	5.00	1.20
□ 138 George Kell	45.00	18.00	4.50
□ 139 Sammy White	20.00	8.00	2.00
□ 140 Tommy Glaviano	20.00	8.00	2.00
□ 141 Allie Reynolds DP	25.00	10.00	2.50
□ 142 Vic Wertz	22.00	9.00	2.20
□ 143 Billy Pierce	27.00	11.00	2.70
□ 144 Bob Schultz DP	12.00	5.00	1.20
□ 145 Harry Dorish DP	12.00	5.00	1.20
□ 146 Granny Hamner	20.00	8.00	2.00
□ 147 Warren Spahn	80.00	32.00	8.00
□ 148 Mickey Grasso	20.00	8.00	2.00
□ 149 Dom DiMaggio DP	25.00	10.00	2.50
□ 150 Harry Simpson DP	12.00	5.00	1.20
□ 151 Hoyt Wilhelm	50.00	20.00	5.00
□ 152 Bob Adams DP	12.00	5.00	1.20
□ 153 Andy Seminick DP	12.00	5.00	1.20
□ 154 Dick Groat	27.00	11.00	2.70
□ 155 Dutch Leonard	20.00	8.00	2.00
□ 156 Jim Rivera DP	12.00	5.00	1.20
□ 157 Bob Addis DP	12.00	5.00	1.20
□ 158 Johnny Logan	22.00	9.00	2.20
□ 159 Wayne Terwilliger DP	12.00	5.00	1.20
□ 160 Bob Young	20.00	8.00	2.00
□ 161 Vern Bickford DP	12.00	5.00	1.20
□ 162 Ted Kluszewski	32.00	13.00	3.20
□ 163 Fred Hatfield DP	12.00	5.00	1.20
□ 164 Frank Shea DP	12.00	5.00	1.20
□ 165 Billy Hoeft	20.00	8.00	2.00
□ 166 Billy Hunter	12.00	5.00	1.20
□ 167 Art Schult	12.00	5.00	1.20
□ 168 Willard Schmidt	12.00	5.00	1.20
□ 169 Dizzy Trout	12.00	5.00	1.20
□ 170 Bill Werle	12.00	5.00	1.20
□ 171 Bill Glynn	12.00	5.00	1.20
□ 172 Rip Repulski	12.00	5.00	1.20
□ 173 Preston Ward	12.00	5.00	1.20
□ 174 Billy Loes	14.00	5.75	1.40

□ 175 Ron Kline	12.00	5.00	1.20
□ 176 Don Hoak	14.00	5.75	1.40
□ 177 Jim Dyck	12.00	5.00	1.20
□ 178 Jim Waugh	12.00	5.00	1.20
□ 179 Gene Hermanski	12.00	5.00	1.20
□ 180 Virgil Stallcup	12.00	5.00	1.20
□ 181 Al Zarilla	12.00	5.00	1.20
□ 182 Bobby Hofman	12.00	5.00	1.20
□ 183 Stu Miller	12.00	5.00	1.20
□ 184 Hal Brown	12.00	5.00	1.20
□ 185 Jim Pendleton	12.00	5.00	1.20
□ 186 Charlie Bishop	12.00	5.00	1.20
□ 187 Jim Fridley	12.00	5.00	1.20
□ 188 Andy Carey	14.00	5.75	1.40
□ 189 Ray Jablonski	12.00	5.00	1.20
□ 190 Dixie Walker	12.00	5.00	1.20
□ 191 Ralph Kiner	40.00	16.00	4.00
□ 192 Wally Westlake	12.00	5.00	1.20
□ 193 Mike Clark	12.00	5.00	1.20
□ 194 Eddie Kazak	12.00	5.00	1.20
□ 195 Ed McGhee	12.00	5.00	1.20
□ 196 Bob Keegan	12.00	5.00	1.20
□ 197 Del Crandall	14.00	5.75	1.40
□ 198 Forrest Main	12.00	5.00	1.20
□ 199 Marion Fricano	12.00	5.00	1.20
□ 200 Gordon Goldsberry	12.00	5.00	1.20
□ 201 Paul LaPalme	12.00	5.00	1.20
□ 202 Carl Sawatski	12.00	5.00	1.20
□ 203 Cliff Fannin	12.00	5.00	1.20
□ 204 Dick Bokelman	12.00	5.00	1.20
□ 205 Vern Benson	12.00	5.00	1.20
□ 206 Ed Bailey	14.00	5.75	1.40
□ 207 Whitey Ford	70.00	28.00	7.00
□ 208 Jim Wilson	12.00	5.00	1.20
□ 209 Jim Greengrass	12.00	5.00	1.20
□ 210 Bob Cerv	14.00	5.75	1.40
□ 211 J.W. Porter	12.00	5.00	1.20
□ 212 Jack Dittmer	12.00	5.00	1.20
□ 213 Ray Scarborough	12.00	5.00	1.20
□ 214 Bill Bruton	14.00	5.75	1.40
□ 215 Gene Conley	14.00	5.75	1.40
□ 216 Jim Hughes	12.00	5.00	1.20
□ 217 Murray Wall	12.00	5.00	1.20
□ 218 Les Fusselman	12.00	5.00	1.20
□ 219 Pete Runnels (photo actually Don Johnson)	12.00	5.00	1.20
□ 220 Satchel Paige UER (misspelled Satchell on card front)	275.00	110.00	27.00
□ 221 Bob Milliken	60.00	24.00	6.00
□ 222 Vic Janowicz DP	30.00	12.00	3.00
□ 223 Johnny O'Brien DP	30.00	12.00	3.00
□ 224 Lou Sleater DP	30.00	12.00	3.00
□ 225 Bobby Shantz	75.00	30.00	7.50
□ 226 Ed Erautt	60.00	24.00	6.00
□ 227 Morris Martin	60.00	24.00	6.00
□ 228 Hal Newhouser	90.00	36.00	9.00
□ 229 Rockey Krsnich	60.00	24.00	6.00
□ 230 Johnny Lindell DP	30.00	12.00	3.00
□ 231 Solly Hemus DP	30.00	12.00	3.00
□ 232 Dick Kokos	60.00	24.00	6.00
□ 233 Al Aber	60.00	24.00	6.00
□ 234 Ray Murray DP	30.00	12.00	3.00
□ 235 John Hetki DP	30.00	12.00	3.00
□ 236 Harry Perkowski DP	30.00	12.00	3.00
□ 237 Bud Podbielan DP	30.00	12.00	3.00
□ 238 Cal Hogue DP	30.00	12.00	3.00
□ 239 Jim Delsing	60.00	24.00	6.00
□ 240 Freddie Marsh	60.00	24.00	6.00
□ 241 Al Sima DP	30.00	12.00	3.00
□ 242 Charlie Silvera	60.00	24.00	6.00
□ 243 Carlos Bernier DP	30.00	12.00	3.00
□ 244 Willie Mays	1400.00	500.00	125.00
□ 245 Bill Norman	60.00	24.00	6.00
□ 246 Roy Face DP	60.00	24.00	6.00
□ 247 Mike Sandlock DP	30.00	12.00	3.00
□ 248 Gene Stephens DP	30.00	12.00	3.00
□ 249 Eddie O'Brien	60.00	24.00	6.00
□ 250 Bob Wilson	60.00	24.00	6.00
□ 251 Sid Hudson	60.00	24.00	6.00
□ 252 Henry Foiles	60.00	24.00	6.00
□ 253 Does not exist	0.00	.00	.00
□ 254 Preacher Roe DP	60.00	24.00	6.00
□ 255 Dixie Howell	60.00	24.00	6.00
□ 256 Les Peden	60.00	24.00	6.00
□ 257 Bob Boyd	60.00	24.00	6.00
□ 258 Jim Gilliam	275.00	110.00	27.00
□ 259 Roy McMillan DP	30.00	12.00	3.00
□ 260 Sam Calderone	75.00	30.00	7.50
□ 261 Does not exist	0.00	.00	.00
□ 262 Bob Oldis	60.00	24.00	6.00
□ 263 Johnny Podres	250.00	100.00	25.00
□ 264 Gene Woodling DP	60.00	24.00	6.00
□ 265 Jackie Jensen	100.00	40.00	10.00
□ 266 Bob Cain	60.00	24.00	6.00
□ 267 Does not exist	0.00	.00	.00
□ 268 Does not exist	0.00	.00	.00
□ 269 Duane Pillette	60.00	24.00	6.00
□ 270 Vern Stephens	75.00	30.00	7.50
□ 271 Does not exist	0.00	.00	.00
□ 272 Bill Antonello	60.00	24.00	6.00
□ 273 Harvey Haddix	90.00	36.00	9.00
□ 274 John Riddle	60.00	24.00	6.00
□ 275 Does not exist	0.00	.00	.00
□ 276 Ken Raffensberger	60.00	24.00	6.00
□ 277 Don Lund	60.00	24.00	6.00
□ 278 Willie Miranda	75.00	30.00	7.50
□ 279 Joe Coleman DP	30.00	12.00	3.00
□ 280 Milt Bolling	225.00	35.00	7.00

1954 Topps

The cards in this 250-card set measure 2 5/8" by 3 3/4". Each of the cards in the 1954 Topps set contains a large "head" shot of the player in color plus a smaller full-length photo in black and white set against a color background. This series contains the rookie cards of Hank Aaron, Ernie Banks, and Al Kaline and two separate cards of Ted Williams (number 1 and number 250). Conspicuous by his absence is Mickey Mantle who apparently was the exclusive property of Bowman during 1954 (and 1955).

	NRMT	VG-E	GOOD
COMPLETE SET (250)	6000.00	2500.00	900.00
COMMON PLAYER (1-50)	7.00	2.80	.70
COMMON PLAYER (51-75)	18.00	7.25	1.80
COMMON PLAYER (76-125)	8.00	3.25	.80
COMMON PLAYER (126-250)	10.00	4.00	1.00
□ 1 Ted Williams	500.00	125.00	25.00
□ 2 Gus Zernial	8.00	3.25	.80
□ 3 Monte Irvin	21.00	8.50	2.10
□ 4 Hank Sauer	8.00	3.25	.80
□ 5 Ed Lopat	14.00	5.75	1.40
□ 6 Pete Runnels	8.00	3.25	.80
□ 7 Ted Kluszewski	13.00	5.25	1.30
□ 8 Bob Young	7.00	2.80	.70
□ 9 Harvey Haddix	8.00	3.25	.80
□ 10 Jackie Robinson	175.00	70.00	18.00
□ 11 Paul Leslie Smith	7.00	2.80	.70
□ 12 Del Crandall	8.00	3.25	.80
□ 13 Billy Martin	45.00	18.00	4.50
□ 14 Preacher Roe	13.00	5.25	1.30
□ 15 Al Rosen	12.00	5.00	1.20
□ 16 Vic Janowicz	8.00	3.25	.80
□ 17 Phil Rizzuto	45.00	18.00	4.50
□ 18 Walt Dropo	7.00	2.80	.70
□ 19 Johnny Lipon	7.00	2.80	.70
□ 20 Warren Spahn	55.00	22.00	5.50
□ 21 Bobby Shantz	9.00	3.75	.90
□ 22 Jim Greengrass	7.00	2.80	.70
□ 23 Luke Easter	8.00	3.25	.80
□ 24 Granny Hamner	7.00	2.80	.70
□ 25 Harvey Kuenn	20.00	8.00	2.00
□ 26 Ray Jablonski	7.00	2.80	.70
□ 27 Ferris Fain	8.00	3.25	.80
□ 28 Paul Minner	7.00	2.80	.70
□ 29 Jim Hegan	8.00	3.25	.80
□ 30 Eddie Mathews	45.00	18.00	4.50
□ 31 Johnny Klippstein	7.00	2.80	.70

□ 32	Duke Snider	100.00	40.00	10.00
□ 33	Johnny Schmitz	7.00	2.80	.70
□ 34	Jim Rivera	7.00	2.80	.70
□ 35	Jim Gilliam	13.00	5.25	1.30
□ 36	Hoyt Wilhelm	24.00	10.00	2.40
□ 37	Whitey Ford	55.00	22.00	5.50
□ 38	Eddie Stanky	8.00	3.25	.80
□ 39	Sherm Lollar	8.00	3.25	.80
□ 40	Mel Parnell	8.00	3.25	.80
□ 41	Willie Jones	7.00	2.80	.70
□ 42	Don Mueller	8.00	3.25	.80
□ 43	Dick Groat	9.00	3.75	.90
□ 44	Ned Garver	7.00	2.80	.70
□ 45	Richie Ashburn	16.00	6.50	1.60
□ 46	Ken Raffensberger	7.00	2.80	.70
□ 47	Ellis Kinder	7.00	2.80	.70
□ 48	Billy Hunter	7.00	2.80	.70
□ 49	Ray Murray	7.00	2.80	.70
□ 50	Yogi Berra	150.00	60.00	15.00
□ 51	Johnny Lindell	18.00	7.25	1.80
□ 52	Vic Power	20.00	8.00	2.00
□ 53	Jack Dittmer	18.00	7.25	1.80
□ 54	Vern Stephens	22.00	9.00	2.20
□ 55	Phil Cavarretta	22.00	9.00	2.20
□ 56	Willie Miranda	18.00	7.25	1.80
□ 57	Luis Aloma	18.00	7.25	1.80
□ 58	Bob Wilson	18.00	7.25	1.80
□ 59	Gene Conley	20.00	8.00	2.00
□ 60	Frank Baumholtz	18.00	7.25	1.80
□ 61	Bob Cain	18.00	7.25	1.80
□ 62	Eddie Robinson	20.00	8.00	2.00
□ 63	Johnny Pesky	20.00	8.00	2.00
□ 64	Hank Thompson	22.00	9.00	2.20
□ 65	Bob Swift	18.00	7.25	1.80
□ 66	Ted Lepcio	18.00	7.25	1.80
□ 67	Jim Willis	18.00	7.25	1.80
□ 68	Sam Calderone	18.00	7.25	1.80
□ 69	Bud Podbielan	18.00	7.25	1.80
□ 70	Larry Doby	30.00	12.00	3.00
□ 71	Frank Smith	18.00	7.25	1.80
□ 72	Preston Ward	18.00	7.25	1.80
□ 73	Wayne Terwilliger	18.00	7.25	1.80
□ 74	Bill Taylor	18.00	7.25	1.80
□ 75	Fred Haney	18.00	7.25	1.80
□ 76	Bob Scheffing	8.00	3.25	.80
□ 77	Ray Boone	9.00	3.75	.90
□ 78	Ted Kazanski	8.00	3.25	.80
□ 79	Andy Pafko	9.00	3.75	.90
□ 80	Jackie Jensen	12.00	5.00	1.20
□ 81	Dave Hoskins	8.00	3.25	.80
□ 82	Milt Bolling	8.00	3.25	.80
□ 83	Joe Collins	10.00	4.00	1.00
□ 84	Dick Cole	8.00	3.25	.80
□ 85	Bob Turley	15.00	6.00	1.50
□ 86	Billy Herman	15.00	6.00	1.50
□ 87	Roy Face	12.00	5.00	1.20
□ 88	Matt Batts	8.00	3.25	.80
□ 89	Howie Pollet	8.00	3.25	.80
□ 90	Willie Mays	250.00	100.00	25.00
□ 91	Bob Oldis	8.00	3.25	.80
□ 92	Wally Westlake	8.00	3.25	.80
□ 93	Sid Hudson	8.00	3.25	.80
□ 94	Ernie Banks	500.00	200.00	50.00
□ 95	Hal Rice	8.00	3.25	.80
□ 96	Charlie Silvera	8.00	3.25	.80
□ 97	Jerald Hal Lane	8.00	3.25	.80
□ 98	Joe Black	11.00	4.50	1.10
□ 99	Bobby Hofman	8.00	3.25	.80
□ 100	Bob Keegan	8.00	3.25	.80
□ 101	Gene Woodling	11.00	4.50	1.10
□ 102	Gil Hodges	45.00	18.00	4.50
□ 103	Jim Lemon	9.00	3.75	.90
□ 104	Mike Sandlock	8.00	3.25	.80
□ 105	Andy Carey	10.00	4.00	1.00
□ 106	Dick Kokos	8.00	3.25	.80
□ 107	Duane Pillette	8.00	3.25	.80
□ 108	Thornton Kipper	8.00	3.25	.80
□ 109	Bill Bruton	9.00	3.75	.90
□ 110	Harry Dorish	8.00	3.25	.80
□ 111	Jim Delsing	8.00	3.25	.80
□ 112	Bill Renna	8.00	3.25	.80
□ 113	Bob Boyd	8.00	3.25	.80
□ 114	Dean Stone	8.00	3.25	.80
□ 115	Rip Repulski	8.00	3.25	.80
□ 116	Steve Bilko	8.00	3.25	.80
□ 117	Solly Hemus	8.00	3.25	.80
□ 118	Carl Scheib	8.00	3.25	.80
□ 119	Johnny Antonelli	10.00	4.00	1.00
□ 120	Roy McMillan	8.00	3.25	.80
□ 121	Clem Labine	10.00	4.00	1.00
□ 122	Johnny Logan	9.00	3.75	.90
□ 123	Bobby Adams	8.00	3.25	.80
□ 124	Marion Fricano	8.00	3.25	.80
□ 125	Harry Perkowski	8.00	3.25	.80
□ 126	Ben Wade	10.00	4.00	1.00
□ 127	Steve O'Neill	10.00	4.00	1.00
□ 128	Hank Aaron	800.00	320.00	80.00
□ 129	Forrest Jacobs	10.00	4.00	1.00
□ 130	Hank Bauer	16.50	7.00	1.50
□ 131	Reno Bertoia	10.00	4.00	1.00
□ 132	Tom Lasorda	125.00	50.00	12.50
□ 133	Dave Baker	10.00	4.00	1.00
□ 134	Cal Hogue	10.00	4.00	1.00
□ 135	Joe Presko	10.00	4.00	1.00
□ 136	Connie Ryan	10.00	4.00	1.00
□ 137	Wally Moon	15.00	6.00	1.50
□ 138	Bob Borkowski	10.00	4.00	1.00
□ 139	The O'Briens Johnny O'Brien Eddie O'Brien	15.00	6.00	1.50
□ 140	Tom Wright	10.00	4.00	1.00
□ 141	Joey Jay	11.00	4.50	1.10
□ 142	Tom Poholsky	10.00	4.00	1.00
□ 143	Ralston Hemsley	10.00	4.00	1.00
□ 144	Bill Werle	10.00	4.00	1.00
□ 145	Elmer Valo	10.00	4.00	1.00
□ 146	Don Johnson	10.00	4.00	1.00
□ 147	Johnny Riddle	10.00	4.00	1.00
□ 148	Bob Trice	10.00	4.00	1.00
□ 149	Al Robertson	10.00	4.00	1.00
□ 150	Dick Kryhoski	10.00	4.00	1.00
□ 151	Alex Grammas	10.00	4.00	1.00
□ 152	Michael Blyzka	10.00	4.00	1.00
□ 153	Al Walker	11.00	4.50	1.10
□ 154	Mike Fornieles	10.00	4.00	1.00
□ 155	Bob Kennedy	10.00	4.00	1.00
□ 156	Joe Coleman	10.00	4.00	1.00
□ 157	Don Lenhardt	10.00	4.00	1.00
□ 158	Peanuts Lowrey	10.00	4.00	1.00
□ 159	Dave Philley	10.00	4.00	1.00
□ 160	Ralph Kress	10.00	4.00	1.00
□ 161	John Hetki	10.00	4.00	1.00
□ 162	Herman Wehmeier	10.00	4.00	1.00
□ 163	Frank House	10.00	4.00	1.00
□ 164	Stu Miller	10.00	4.00	1.00
□ 165	Jim Pendleton	10.00	4.00	1.00
□ 166	Johnny Podres	20.00	8.00	2.00
□ 167	Don Lund	10.00	4.00	1.00
□ 168	Morrie Martin	10.00	4.00	1.00
□ 169	Jim Hughes	10.00	4.00	1.00
□ 170	James(Dusty) Rhodes	12.00	5.00	1.20
□ 171	Leo Kiely	10.00	4.00	1.00
□ 172	Harold Brown	10.00	4.00	1.00
□ 173	Jack Harshman	10.00	4.00	1.00
□ 174	Tom Qualters	10.00	4.00	1.00
□ 175	Frank Leja	11.00	4.50	1.10
□ 176	Robert Keeley	10.00	4.00	1.00
□ 177	Bob Milliken	10.00	4.00	1.00
□ 178	Bill Glynn	10.00	4.00	1.00
□ 179	Gair Allie	10.00	4.00	1.00
□ 180	Wes Westrum	11.00	4.50	1.10
□ 181	Mel Roach	10.00	4.00	1.00
□ 182	Chuck Harmon	10.00	4.00	1.00
□ 183	Earle Combs	15.00	6.00	1.50
□ 184	Ed Bailey	10.00	4.00	1.00
□ 185	Chuck Stobbs	10.00	4.00	1.00
□ 186	Karl Olson	10.00	4.00	1.00
□ 187	Henry Manush	15.00	6.00	1.50
□ 188	Dave Jolly	10.00	4.00	1.00
□ 189	Floyd Ross	10.00	4.00	1.00
□ 190	Ray Herbert	10.00	4.00	1.00
□ 191	John(Dick) Schofield	11.00	4.50	1.10
□ 192	Ellis Deal	10.00	4.00	1.00
□ 193	Johnny Hopp	12.00	5.00	1.20
□ 194	Bill Sarni	10.00	4.00	1.00
□ 195	Billy Consolo	10.00	4.00	1.00
□ 196	Stan Jok	10.00	4.00	1.00
□ 197	Lynwood Rowe	12.00	5.00	1.20
□ 198	Carl Sawatski	10.00	4.00	1.00
□ 199	Glenn(Rocky) Nelson	10.00	4.00	1.00
□ 200	Larry Jansen	11.00	4.50	1.10
□ 201	Al Kaline	500.00	200.00	50.00
□ 202	Bob Purkey	10.00	4.00	1.00
□ 203	Harry Brecheen	11.00	4.50	1.10
□ 204	Angel Scull	10.00	4.00	1.00
□ 205	Johnny Sain	20.00	8.00	2.00
□ 206	Ray Crone	10.00	4.00	1.00
□ 207	Tom Oliver	10.00	4.00	1.00
□ 208	Grady Hatton	10.00	4.00	1.00
□ 209	Chuck Thompson	10.00	4.00	1.00
□ 210	Bob Buhl	12.00	5.00	1.20
□ 211	Don Hoak	11.00	4.50	1.10
□ 212	Bob Micelotta	10.00	4.00	1.00
□ 213	Johnny Fitzpatrick	10.00	4.00	1.00
□ 214	Arnie Portocarrero	10.00	4.00	1.00
□ 215	Warren McGhee	10.00	4.00	1.00
□ 216	Al Sima	10.00	4.00	1.00
□ 217	Paul Schreiber	10.00	4.00	1.00
□ 218	Fred Marsh	10.00	4.00	1.00
□ 219	Chuck Kress	10.00	4.00	1.00

□ 220 Ruben Gomez	10.00	4.00	1.00
□ 221 Dick Brodowski	10.00	4.00	1.00
□ 222 Bill Wilson	10.00	4.00	1.00
□ 223 Joe Haynes	10.00	4.00	1.00
□ 224 Dick Weik	10.00	4.00	1.00
□ 225 Don Liddle	10.00	4.00	1.00
□ 226 Jehosie Heard	10.00	4.00	1.00
□ 227 Colonel Mills	10.00	4.00	1.00
□ 228 Gene Hermanski	10.00	4.00	1.00
□ 229 Bob Talbot	10.00	4.00	1.00
□ 230 Bob Kuzava	12.00	5.00	1.20
□ 231 Roy Smalley	11.00	4.50	1.10
□ 232 Lou Limmer	10.00	4.00	1.00
□ 233 Augie Galan	10.00	4.00	1.00
□ 234 Jerry Lynch	12.00	5.00	1.20
□ 235 Vernon Law	14.00	5.75	1.40
□ 236 Paul Penson	10.00	4.00	1.00
□ 237 Dominic Ryba	10.00	4.00	1.00
□ 238 Al Aber	10.00	4.00	1.00
□ 239 Bill Skowron	40.00	16.00	4.00
□ 240 Sam Mele	10.00	4.00	1.00
□ 241 Robert Miller	10.00	4.00	1.00
□ 242 Curt Roberts	10.00	4.00	1.00
□ 243 Ray Blades	10.00	4.00	1.00
□ 244 Leroy Wheat	10.00	4.00	1.00
□ 245 Roy Sievers	12.00	5.00	1.20
□ 246 Howie Fox	10.00	4.00	1.00
□ 247 Ed Mayo	10.00	4.00	1.00
□ 248 Al Smith	12.00	5.00	1.20
□ 249 Wilmer Mizell	12.00	5.00	1.20
□ 250 Ted Williams	500.00	150.00	30.00

1955 Topps

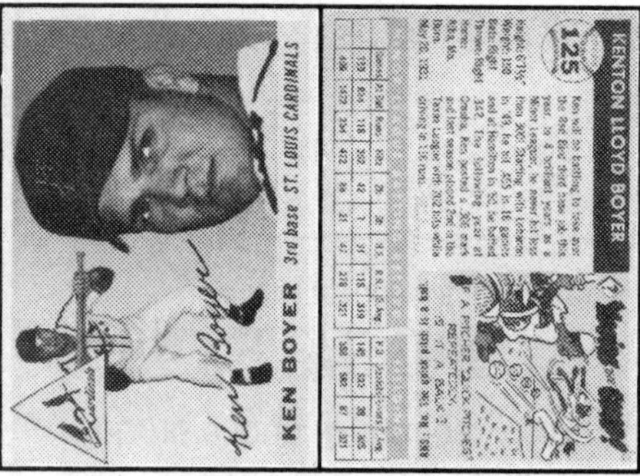

The cards in this 206-card set measure 2 5/8" by 3 3/4". Both the large "head" shot and the smaller full-length photos used on each card of the 1955 Topps set are in color. The card fronts were designed horizontally for the first time in Topps' history. The first card features Dusty Rhodes, hitting star for the Giants' 1954 World Series sweep over the Indians. A "high" series, 161 to 210, is more difficult to find than cards 1 to 160. Numbers 175, 186, 203, and 209 were never issued. To fill in for the four cards not issued in the high number series, Topps double printed four players, those appearing on cards 170, 172, 184, and 188.

	NRMT	VG-E	GOOD
COMPLETE SET (206)	4250.00	1900.00	650.00
COMMON PLAYER (1-150)	5.00	2.00	.50
COMMON PLAYER (151-160)	10.00	4.00	1.00
COMMON PLAYER (161-210)	12.50	5.00	1.25
□ 1 Dusty Rhodes	25.00	5.00	1.00
□ 2 Ted Williams	200.00	80.00	20.00
□ 3 Art Fowler	5.00	2.00	.50
□ 4 Al Kaline	80.00	32.00	8.00
□ 5 Jim Gilliam	9.00	3.75	.90
□ 6 Stan Hack	5.50	2.20	.55
□ 7 Jim Hegan	5.50	2.20	.55
□ 8 Harold Smith	5.00	2.00	.50
□ 9 Robert Miller	5.00	2.00	.50
□ 10 Bob Keegan	5.00	2.00	.50
□ 11 Ferris Fain	5.50	2.20	.55
□ 12 Vernon Thies	5.00	2.00	.50
□ 13 Fred Marsh	5.00	2.00	.50
□ 14 Jim Finigan	5.00	2.00	.50
□ 15 Jim Pendleton	5.00	2.00	.50
□ 16 Roy Sievers	5.50	2.20	.55
□ 17 Bobby Hofman	5.00	2.00	.50
□ 18 Russ Kemmerer	5.00	2.00	.50
□ 19 Billy Herman	9.00	3.75	.90
□ 20 Andy Carey	7.00	2.80	.70
□ 21 Alex Grammas	5.00	2.00	.50
□ 22 Bill Skowron	10.00	4.00	1.00
□ 23 Jack Parks	5.00	2.00	.50
□ 24 Hal Newhouser	8.00	3.25	.80
□ 25 John Podres	10.00	4.00	1.00
□ 26 Dick Groat	7.50	3.00	.75
□ 27 Bill Gardner	5.50	2.20	.55
□ 28 Ernie Banks	65.00	26.00	6.50
□ 29 Herman Wehmeier	5.00	2.00	.50
□ 30 Vic Power	5.50	2.20	.55
□ 31 Warren Spahn	36.00	15.00	3.60
□ 32 Warren McGhee	5.00	2.00	.50
□ 33 Tom Qualters	5.00	2.00	.50
□ 34 Wayne Terwilliger	5.00	2.00	.50
□ 35 Dave Jolly	5.00	2.00	.50
□ 36 Leo Kiely	5.00	2.00	.50
□ 37 Joe Cunningham	5.50	2.20	.55
□ 38 Bob Turley	9.00	3.75	.90
□ 39 Bill Glynn	5.00	2.00	.50
□ 40 Don Hoak	5.50	2.20	.55
□ 41 Chuck Stobbs	5.00	2.00	.50
□ 42 John(Windy) McCall	5.00	2.00	.50
□ 43 Harvey Haddix	5.50	2.20	.55
□ 44 Harold Valentine	5.00	2.00	.50
□ 45 Hank Sauer	5.50	2.20	.55
□ 46 Ted Kazanski	5.00	2.00	.50
□ 47 Hank Aaron	200.00	80.00	20.00
□ 48 Bob Kennedy	5.00	2.00	.50
□ 49 J.W. Porter	5.00	2.00	.50
□ 50 Jackie Robinson	135.00	54.00	13.50
□ 51 Jim Hughes	5.00	2.00	.50
□ 52 Bill Tremel	5.00	2.00	.50
□ 53 Bill Taylor	5.00	2.00	.50
□ 54 Lou Limmer	5.00	2.00	.50
□ 55 Rip Repulski	5.00	2.00	.50
□ 56 Ray Jablonski	5.00	2.00	.50
□ 57 Billy O'Dell	5.00	2.00	.50
□ 58 Jim Rivera	5.00	2.00	.50
□ 59 Gair Allie	5.00	2.00	.50
□ 60 Dean Stone	5.00	2.00	.50
□ 61 Forrest Jacobs	5.00	2.00	.50
□ 62 Thornton Kipper	5.00	2.00	.50
□ 63 Joe Collins	6.00	2.40	.60
□ 64 Gus Triandos	6.00	2.40	.60
□ 65 Ray Boone	5.50	2.20	.55
□ 66 Ron Jackson	5.00	2.00	.50
□ 67 Wally Moon	6.00	2.40	.60
□ 68 Jim Davis	5.00	2.00	.50
□ 69 Ed Bailey	5.50	2.20	.55
□ 70 Al Rosen	8.00	3.25	.80
□ 71 Ruben Gomez	5.00	2.00	.50
□ 72 Karl Olson	5.00	2.00	.50
□ 73 Jack Shepard	5.00	2.00	.50
□ 74 Robert Borkowski	5.00	2.00	.50
□ 75 Sandy Amoros	8.00	3.25	.80
□ 76 Howie Pollet	5.00	2.00	.50
□ 77 Arnold Portocarrero	5.00	2.00	.50
□ 78 Gordon Jones	5.00	2.00	.50
□ 79 Clyde Schell	5.00	2.00	.50
□ 80 Bob Grim	8.00	3.25	.80
□ 81 Gene Conley	5.50	2.20	.55
□ 82 Chuck Harmon	5.00	2.00	.50
□ 83 Tom Brewer	5.00	2.00	.50
□ 84 Camilo Pascual	7.00	2.80	.70
□ 85 Don Mossi	7.00	2.80	.70
□ 86 Bill Wilson	5.00	2.00	.50
□ 87 Frank House	5.00	2.00	.50
□ 88 Bob Skinner	6.00	2.40	.60
□ 89 Joe Frazier	5.00	2.00	.50
□ 90 Karl Spooner	5.00	2.00	.50
□ 91 Milt Bolling	5.00	2.00	.50
□ 92 Don Zimmer	11.00	4.50	1.10
□ 93 Steve Bilko	5.00	2.00	.50
□ 94 Reno Bertoia	5.00	2.00	.50
□ 95 Preston Ward	5.00	2.00	.50
□ 96 Chuck Bishop	5.00	2.00	.50
□ 97 Carlos Paula	5.00	2.00	.50
□ 98 John Riddle	5.00	2.00	.50
□ 99 Frank Leja	5.00	2.00	.50
□ 100 Monte Irvin	17.00	7.00	1.70
□ 101 Johnny Gray	5.00	2.00	.50
□ 102 Wally Westlake	5.00	2.00	.50
□ 103 Chuck White	5.00	2.00	.50
□ 104 Jack Harshman	5.00	2.00	.50
□ 105 Chuck Diering	5.00	2.00	.50
□ 106 Frank Sullivan	5.00	2.00	.50

BASEBALL CARD LOTS

VG Condition or Better	100 Diff.	200 Diff.	My Choice of #'s	100 Diff.	200 Diff.
1955B	300.00		1965	36.00	70.00
1956	300.00		1966	36.00	70.00
1957	210.00		1967	36.00	70.00
1958	120.00		1968	30.00	55.00
1959	120.00	230.00	1969	30.00	55.00
1960	75.00	145.00	1970	22.00	40.00
1961	60.00	115.00	1971	22.00	40.00
1962	60.00	115.00	1972	22.00	40.00
1963	36.00		1973-76	18.00	35.00
1964	36.00	70.00	1976-80	10.00	18.00

Bowman	25 Diff.	50 Diff.	Topps	25 Diff.	50 Diff.
1950	180.00	360.00	1952	390.00	750.00
1951	180.00	360.00	1953	230.00	450.00
1952	180.00	360.00	1954	125.00	240.00
1953	380.00	750.00	1955	95.00	180.00
1954	90.00	180.00	1956	80.00	155.00
1955	80.00	155.00	1957	60.00	110.00

SPECIALS - POSTPAID

250 Assorted 1958-62 VG	215.00	500	420.00
250 Assorted 1960-69 VG	110.00	500	200.00
250 Assorted 1970-79 VG	35.00	500	65.00
250 Assorted 1980-84 VG	15.00	500	28.00

Also send for Free Retail Price List on Stars and Commons.

Postage & Handling: 1.75 first 100 cards
.50 each add. 100 cards

Hi Numbers VG Condition
My Choice of #'s

	10		20	40
1957	70.00	1965	34.00	
1959	45.00	1968	9.00	16.00
1960	40.00	1970	24.00	46.00
1962	40.00	1971	24.00	46.00
1963	40.00	1972	24.00	46.00
		1973	18.00	34.00

BILL HENDERSON'S CARDS
2320 Ruger Ave., BLK-3
Janesville, WI 53545
1-608-755-0922

BASEBALL CARDS ON APPROVAL

I fill wantlists of baseball and football cards and will send you your order on approval (excluding complete sets). If the cards are satisfactory, then send payment. If they are unsatisfactory just return them, securely packaged with my original invoice. Send your wantlists in *numerical order* by year. Orders **over $25** will be discounted at least 10 percent and will be sent U.P.S. postpaid. Orders **under $25** will have mailing costs added. Minimum order is **$5** and no "mint only" orders please. Same-day service and satisfaction are always my guarantee. Your *first* order with me *must* include your street address for U.P.S shipping, your phone number, an SASE and a price limit for how much you want to spend. A deposit may be required on certain orders.

I also sell complete sets, 1981 to present, and bricks (lots) in most years. Send SASE for my pricelist. I also have a huge inventory of lesser condition (F-VG) cards that are reasonably priced.

Yes! We buy collections!

Baseball Cards-Plus
Dave Shore
5589 Clairemont Mesa Blvd
Suite A, Dept. PG11
San Diego, CA 92117
(619)565-CARD

We need small or large amounts of:

- Unopened Material
- Star & Rookie Cards
- Sets, Collections
- Commons from 1969 & Earlier

Send cards insured with price and phone number for immediate payment or send descriptive list and phone number for offer. You'll get prompt, fair service.

Dave Woodruff
Mt. Shasta Mall
900 Dana Drive, B-2
Redding, CA 96003
916-222-2343

□ 107 Curt Roberts	5.00	2.00	.50
□ 108 Al Walker	5.00	2.00	.50
□ 109 Ed Lopat	11.00	4.50	1.10
□ 110 Gus Zernial	5.50	2.20	.55
□ 111 Bob Milliken	5.00	2.00	.50
□ 112 Nelson King	5.00	2.00	.50
□ 113 Harry Brecheen	5.00	2.00	.50
□ 114 Louis Ortiz	5.00	2.00	.50
□ 115 Ellis Kinder	5.00	2.00	.50
□ 116 Tom Hurd	5.00	2.00	.50
□ 117 Mel Roach	5.00	2.00	.50
□ 118 Bob Purkey	5.00	2.00	.50
□ 119 Bob Lennon	5.00	2.00	.50
□ 120 Ted Kluszewski	10.00	4.00	1.00
□ 121 Bill Renna	5.00	2.00	.50
□ 122 Carl Sawatski	5.00	2.00	.50
□ 123 Sandy Koufax	450.00	180.00	45.00
□ 124 Harmon Killebrew	225.00	90.00	22.00
□ 125 Ken Boyer	30.00	12.00	3.00
□ 126 Dick Hall	5.00	2.00	.50
□ 127 Dale Long	5.50	2.20	.55
□ 128 Ted Lepcio	5.00	2.00	.50
□ 129 Elvin Tappe	5.00	2.00	.50
□ 130 Mayo Smith MG	5.00	2.00	.50
□ 131 Grady Hatton	5.00	2.00	.50
□ 132 Bob Trice	5.00	2.00	.50
□ 133 Dave Hoskins	5.00	2.00	.50
□ 134 Joe Jay	5.00	2.00	.50
□ 135 Johnny O'Brien	5.00	2.00	.50
□ 136 Vernon Stewart	5.00	2.00	.50
□ 137 Harry Elliott	5.00	2.00	.50
□ 138 Ray Herbert	5.00	2.00	.50
□ 139 Steve Kraly	5.00	2.00	.50
□ 140 Mel Parnell	5.50	2.20	.55
□ 141 Tom Wright	5.00	2.00	.50
□ 142 Gerry Lynch	5.50	2.20	.55
□ 143 John(Dick) Schofield	5.50	2.20	.55
□ 144 John(Joe) Amalfitano	5.00	2.00	.50
□ 145 Elmer Valo	5.00	2.00	.50
□ 146 Dick Donovan	5.00	2.00	.50
□ 147 Hugh Pepper	5.00	2.00	.50
□ 148 Hector Brown	5.00	2.00	.50
□ 149 Ray Crone	5.00	2.00	.50
□ 150 Michael Higgins	5.00	2.00	.50
□ 151 Ralph Kress	10.00	4.00	1.00
□ 152 Harry Agganis	50.00	20.00	5.00
□ 153 Bud Podbielan	10.00	4.00	1.00
□ 154 Willie Miranda	10.00	4.00	1.00
□ 155 Eddie Mathews	70.00	28.00	7.00
□ 156 Joe Black	15.00	6.00	1.50
□ 157 Robert Miller	10.00	4.00	1.00
□ 158 Tommy Carroll	12.00	5.00	1.20
□ 159 Johnny Schmitz	10.00	4.00	1.00
□ 160 Ray Narleski	12.00	5.00	1.20
□ 161 Chuck Tanner	16.00	6.50	1.60
□ 162 Joe Coleman	12.50	5.00	1.25
□ 163 Faye Throneberry	12.50	5.00	1.25
□ 164 Roberto Clemente	750.00	300.00	75.00
□ 165 Don Johnson	12.50	5.00	1.25
□ 166 Hank Bauer	21.00	8.50	2.10
□ 167 Thomas Casagrande	12.50	5.00	1.25
□ 168 Duane Pillette	12.50	5.00	1.25
□ 169 Bob Oldis	12.50	5.00	1.25
□ 170 Jim Pearce DP	7.50	3.00	.75
□ 171 Dick Brodowski	12.50	5.00	1.25
□ 172 Frank Baumholtz DP	7.50	3.00	.75
□ 173 Johnny Kline	12.50	5.00	1.25
□ 174 Rudy Minarcin	12.50	5.00	1.25
□ 175 Does not exist	0.00	.00	.00
□ 176 Norm Zauchin	12.50	5.00	1.25
□ 177 Al Robertson	12.50	5.00	1.25
□ 178 Bobby Adams	12.50	5.00	1.25
□ 179 Jim Bolger	12.50	5.00	1.25
□ 180 Clem Labine	16.00	6.50	1.60
□ 181 Roy McMillan	12.50	5.00	1.25
□ 182 Humberto Robinson	12.50	5.00	1.25
□ 183 Anthony Jacobs	12.50	5.00	1.25
□ 184 Harry Perkowski DP	7.50	3.00	.75
□ 185 Don Ferrarese	12.50	5.00	1.25
□ 186 Does not exist	0.00	.00	.00
□ 187 Gil Hodges	100.00	40.00	10.00
□ 188 Charlie Silvera DP	7.50	3.00	.75
□ 189 Phil Rizzuto	100.00	40.00	10.00
□ 190 Gene Woodling	16.00	6.50	1.60
□ 191 Eddie Stanky	16.00	6.50	1.60
□ 192 Jim Delsing	12.50	5.00	1.25
□ 193 Johnny Sain	21.00	8.50	2.10
□ 194 Willie Mays	350.00	140.00	35.00
□ 195 Ed Roebuck	16.00	6.50	1.60
□ 196 Gale Wade	12.50	5.00	1.25
□ 197 Al Smith	14.00	5.75	1.40
□ 198 Yogi Berra	160.00	65.00	16.00
□ 199 Odbert Hamric	12.50	5.00	1.25
□ 200 Jackie Jensen	30.00	12.00	3.00
□ 201 Sherman Lollar	14.00	5.75	1.40
□ 202 Jim Owens	12.50	5.00	1.25
□ 203 Does not exist	0.00	.00	.00
□ 204 Frank Smith	12.50	5.00	1.25
□ 205 Gene Freese	12.50	5.00	1.25
□ 206 Pete Daley	12.50	5.00	1.25
□ 207 Bill Consolo	12.50	5.00	1.25
□ 208 Ray Moore	12.50	5.00	1.25
□ 209 Does not exist	0.00	.00	.00
□ 210 Duke Snider	375.00	100.00	20.00

1955 Topps Double Header

The cards in ths 66-card set measure 2 1/16" by 4 7/8". Borrowing a design from the T201 Mecca series, Topps issued a 132-player "Double Header" set in a separate wrapper in 1955. Each player is numbered in the biographical section on the reverse. When open, with perforated flap up, one player is revealed; when the flap is lowered, or closed, the player design on top incorporates a portion of the inside player artwork. When the cards are placed side by side, a continuous ballpark background is formed. Some cards have been found without perforations, and all players pictured appear in the low series of the 1955 regular issue.

	NRMT	VG-E	GOOD
COMPLETE SET (66)	2000.00	850.00	250.00
COMMON PAIR (1-132)	20.00	8.00	2.00
□ 1 Al Rosen and 2 Chuck Diering	22.00	9.00	2.20
□ 3 Monte Irvin and 4 Russ Kemmerer	27.00	11.00	2.70
□ 5 Ted Kazanski and 6 Gordon Jones	20.00	8.00	2.00
□ 7 Bill Taylor and 8 Billy O'Dell	20.00	8.00	2.00
□ 9 J.W. Porter and 10 Thornton Kipper	20.00	8.00	2.00
□ 11 Curt Roberts and 12 Arnie Portocarrero	20.00	8.00	2.00
□ 13 Wally Westlake and 14 Frank House	20.00	8.00	2.00
□ 15 Rube Walker and 16 Lou Limmer	20.00	8.00	2.00
□ 17 Dean Stone and 18 Charlie White	20.00	8.00	2.00
□ 19 Karl Spooner and 20 Jim Hughes	20.00	8.00	2.00
□ 21 Bill Skowron and 22 Frank Sullivan	22.00	9.00	2.20
□ 23 Jack Shepard and 24 Stan Hack	20.00	8.00	2.00
□ 25 Jackie Robinson and 26 Don Hoak	110.00	45.00	11.00

		NRMT	VG-E	GOOD
□	27 Dusty Rhodes and	20.00	8.00	2.00
	28 Jim Davis			
□	29 Vic Power and	20.00	8.00	2.00
	30 Ed Bailey			
□	31 Howie Pollet and	90.00	36.00	9.00
	32 Ernie Banks			
□	33 Jim Pendleton and	20.00	8.00	2.00
	34 Gene Conley			
□	35 Karl Olson and	20.00	8.00	2.00
	36 Andy Carey			
□	37 Wally Moon and	20.00	8.00	2.00
	38 Joe Cunningham			
□	39 Freddie Marsh and	20.00	8.00	2.00
	40 Vernon Thies			
□	41 Eddie Lopat and	22.00	9.00	2.20
	42 Harvey Haddix			
□	43 Leo Kiely and	20.00	8.00	2.00
	44 Chuck Stobbs			
□	45 Al Kaline and	100.00	40.00	10.00
	46 Harold Valentine			
□	47 Forrest Jacobs and	20.00	8.00	2.00
	48 Johnny Gray			
□	49 Ron Jackson and	20.00	8.00	2.00
	50 Jim Finigan			
□	51 Ray Jablonski and	20.00	8.00	2.00
	52 Bob Keegan			
□	53 Billy Herman and	27.00	11.00	2.70
	54 Sandy Amoros			
□	55 Chuck Harmon and	20.00	8.00	2.00
	56 Bob Skinner			
□	57 Dick Hall and	20.00	8.00	2.00
	58 Bob Grim			
□	59 Billy Glynn and	20.00	8.00	2.00
	60 Bob Miller			
□	61 Billy Gardner and	20.00	8.00	2.00
	62 John Hetki			
□	63 Bob Borkowski and	22.00	9.00	2.20
	64 Bob Turley			
□	65 Joe Collins and	20.00	8.00	2.00
	66 Jack Harshman			
□	67 Jim Hegan and	20.00	8.00	2.00
	68 Jack Parks			
□	69 Ted Williams and	175.00	70.00	18.00
	70 Mayo Smith			
□	71 Gair Allie and	20.00	8.00	2.00
	72 Grady Hatton			
□	73 Jerry Lynch and	20.00	8.00	2.00
	74 Harry Brecheen			
□	75 Tom Wright and	20.00	8.00	2.00
	76 Vernon Stewart			
□	77 Dave Hoskins and	20.00	8.00	2.00
	78 Warren McGhee			
□	79 Roy Sievers and	20.00	8.00	2.00
	80 Art Fowler			
□	81 Danny Schell and	20.00	8.00	2.00
	82 Gus Triandos			
□	83 Joe Frazier and	20.00	8.00	2.00
	84 Don Mossi			
□	85 Elmer Valo and	20.00	8.00	2.00
	86 Hector Brown			
□	87 Bob Kennedy and	20.00	8.00	2.00
	88 Windy McCall			
□	89 Ruben Gomez and	20.00	8.00	2.00
	90 Jim Rivera			
□	91 Louis Ortiz and	20.00	8.00	2.00
	92 Milt Bolling			
□	93 Carl Sawatski and	20.00	8.00	2.00
	94 El Tappe			
□	95 Dave Jolly and	20.00	8.00	2.00
	96 Bobby Hofman			
□	97 Preston Ward and	20.00	8.00	2.00
	98 Don Zimmer			
□	99 Bill Renna and	22.00	9.00	2.20
	100 Dick Groat			
□	101 Bill Wilson and	20.00	8.00	2.00
	102 Bill Tremel			
□	103 Hank Sauer and	22.00	9.00	2.20
	104 Camilo Pascual			
□	105 Hank Aaron and	200.00	80.00	20.00
	106 Ray Herbert			
□	107 Alex Grammas and	20.00	8.00	2.00
	108 Tom Qualters			
□	109 Hal Newhouser and	22.00	9.00	2.20
	110 Chuck Bishop			
□	111 Harmon Killebrew	90.00	36.00	9.00
	112 John Podres			
□	113 Ray Boone and	20.00	8.00	2.00
	114 Bob Purkey			
□	115 Dale Long and	20.00	8.00	2.00
	116 Ferris Fain			
□	117 Steve Bilko and	20.00	8.00	2.00
	118 Bob Milliken			
□	119 Mel Parnell and	20.00	8.00	2.00
	120 Tom Hurd			
□	121 Ted Kluszewski and	22.00	9.00	2.20
	122 Jim Owens			
□	123 Gus Zernial and	20.00	8.00	2.00
	124 Bob Trice			
□	125 Rip Repulski and	20.00	8.00	2.00
	126 Ted Lepcio			
□	127 Warren Spahn and	80.00	32.00	8.00
	128 Tom Brewer			
□	129 Jim Gilliam and	22.00	9.00	2.20
	130 Ellis Kinder			
□	131 Herm Wehmeier and	20.00	8.00	2.00
	132 Wayne Terwilliger			

1956 Topps

The cards in this 340-card set measure 2 5/8" by 3 3/4". Following up with another horizontally oriented card in 1956, Topps improved the format by layering the color "head" shot onto an actual action sequence involving the player. Cards 1 to 180 come with either white or gray backs: in the 1 to 100 sequence, gray backs are less common (worth about 10% more) and in the 101 to 180 sequence, white backs are less common (worth 30% more). The team cards used for the first time in a regular set by Topps, are found dated 1955, or undated, with the team name appearing on either side. The two unnumbered checklist cards are highly prized (must be unmarked to qualify as excellent or mint). The complete set price below does not include the unnumbered checklist cards or any of the variations.

	NRMT	VG-E	GOOD
COMPLETE SET (340)	4250.00	1900.00	650.00
COMMON PLAYER (1-100)	4.00	1.60	.40
COMMON PLAYER (101-180)	5.00	2.00	.50
COMMON PLAYER (181-260)	9.00	3.75	.90
COMMON PLAYER (261-340)	6.00	2.40	.60

		NRMT	VG-E	GOOD
□	1 William Harridge	75.00	7.50	1.50
	(AL President)			
□	2 Warren Giles DP	10.00	4.00	1.00
	(NL President)			
□	3 Elmer Valo	4.00	1.60	.40
□	4 Carlos Paula	4.00	1.60	.40
□	5 Ted Williams	175.00	70.00	18.00
□	6 Ray Boone	4.00	1.60	.40
□	7 Ron Negray	4.00	1.60	.40
□	8 Walter Alston MG	18.00	7.25	1.80
□	9 Ruben Gomez	4.00	1.60	.40
□	10 Warren Spahn DP	27.00	11.00	2.70
□	11A Chicago Cubs	8.00	3.25	.80
	(centered)			
□	11B Cubs Team	30.00	12.00	3.00
	(dated 1955)			
□	11C Cubs Team	10.00	4.00	1.00
	(name at far left)			
□	12 Andy Carey	5.00	2.00	.50
□	13 Roy Face	6.00	2.40	.60
□	14 Ken Boyer	9.00	3.75	.90
□	15 Ernie Banks DP	40.00	16.00	4.00
□	16 Hector Lopez	4.00	1.60	.40
□	17 Gene Conley	4.00	1.60	.40
□	18 Dick Donovan	4.00	1.60	.40
□	19 Chuck Diering	4.00	1.60	.40

□ 20 Al Kaline 50.00 20.00 5.00
□ 21 Joe Collins .... 5.00 2.00 .50
□ 22 Jim Finigan .... 4.00 1.60 .40
□ 23 Fred Marsh .... 4.00 1.60 .40
□ 24 Dick Groat .... 6.00 2.40 .60
□ 25 Ted Kluszewski .... 9.00 3.75 .90
□ 26 Grady Hatton .... 4.00 1.60 .40
□ 27 Nelson Burbrink .... 4.00 1.60 .40
□ 28 Bobby Hofman .... 4.00 1.60 .40
□ 29 Jack Harshman .... 4.00 1.60 .40
□ 30 Jackie Robinson DP 100.00 40.00 10.00
□ 31 Hank Aaron DP 135.00 54.00 13.50
(small photo
actually W.Mays)
□ 32 Frank House .... 4.00 1.60 .40
□ 33 Roberto Clemente 175.00 70.00 18.00
□ 34 Tom Brewer .... 4.00 1.60 .40
□ 35 Al Rosen DP .... 7.00 2.80 .70
□ 36 Rudy Minarcin .... 4.00 1.60 .40
□ 37 Alex Grammas .... 4.00 1.60 .40
□ 38 Bob Kennedy .... 4.00 1.60 .40
□ 39 Don Mossi .... 5.00 2.00 .50
□ 40 Bob Turley .... 7.00 2.80 .70
□ 41 Hank Sauer .... 5.00 2.00 .50
□ 42 Sandy Amoros .... 5.00 2.00 .50
□ 43 Ray Moore .... 4.00 1.60 .40
□ 44 Windy McCall .... 4.00 1.60 .40
□ 45 Gus Zernial .... 4.00 1.60 .40
□ 46 Gene Freese .... 4.00 1.60 .40
□ 47 Art Fowler .... 4.00 1.60 .40
□ 48 Jim Hegan .... 4.00 1.60 .40
□ 49 Pedro Ramos .... 4.00 1.60 .40
□ 50 Dusty Rhodes .... 5.00 2.00 .50
□ 51 Ernie Oravetz .... 4.00 1.60 .40
□ 52 Bob Grim .... 5.00 2.00 .50
□ 53 Arnie Portocarrero .... 4.00 1.60 .40
□ 54 Bob Keegan .... 4.00 1.60 .40
□ 55 Wally Moon .... 6.00 2.40 .60
□ 56 Dale Long .... 5.00 2.00 .50
□ 57 Duke Maas .... 4.00 1.60 .40
□ 58 Ed Roebuck .... 5.00 2.00 .50
□ 59 Jose Santiago .... 4.00 1.60 .40
□ 60 Mayo Smith MG .... 4.00 1.60 .40
□ 61 Bill Skowron .... 8.00 3.25 .80
□ 62 Hal Smith .... 4.00 1.60 .40
□ 63 Roger Craig 12.00 5.00 1.20
□ 64 Luis Arroyo .... 5.00 2.00 .50
□ 65 Johnny O'Brien .... 4.00 1.60 .40
□ 66 Bob Speake .... 4.00 1.60 .40
□ 67 Vic Power .... 4.00 1.60 .40
□ 68 Chuck Stobbs .... 4.00 1.60 .40
□ 69 Chuck Tanner .... 6.00 2.40 .60
□ 70 Jim Rivera .... 4.00 1.60 .40
□ 71 Frank Sullivan .... 4.00 1.60 .40
□ 72A Phillies Team DP .... 6.00 2.40 .60
(centered)
□ 72B Phillies Team 30.00 12.00 3.00
(dated 1955)
□ 72C Phillies Team 10.00 4.00 1.00
(name at far left)
□ 73 Wayne Terwilliger .... 4.00 1.60 .40
□ 74 Jim King .... 4.00 1.60 .40
□ 75 Roy Sievers .... 5.00 2.00 .50
□ 76 Ray Crone .... 4.00 1.60 .40
□ 77 Harvey Haddix .... 5.00 2.00 .50
□ 78 Herman Wehmeier .... 4.00 1.60 .40
□ 79 Sandy Koufax 175.00 70.00 18.00
□ 80 Gus Triandos .... 5.00 2.00 .50
□ 81 Wally Westlake .... 4.00 1.60 .40
□ 82 Bill Renna .... 4.00 1.60 .40
□ 83 Karl Spooner .... 5.00 2.00 .50
□ 84 Babe Birrer .... 4.00 1.60 .40
□ 85A Cleveland Indians .... 8.00 3.25 .80
(centered)
□ 85B Indians Team 30.00 12.00 3.00
(dated 1955)
□ 85C Indians Team 10.00 4.00 1.00
(name at far left)
□ 86 Ray Jablonski .... 4.00 1.60 .40
□ 87 Dean Stone .... 4.00 1.60 .40
□ 88 Johnny Kucks .... 5.00 2.00 .50
□ 89 Norm Zauchin .... 4.00 1.60 .40
□ 90A Cincinnati Redlegs .... 8.00 3.25 .80
Team (centered)
□ 90B Reds Team 30.00 12.00 3.00
(dated 1955)
□ 90C Reds Team 10.00 4.00 1.00
(name at far left)
□ 91 Gail Harris .... 4.00 1.60 .40
□ 92 Bob(Red) Wilson .... 4.00 1.60 .40
□ 93 George Susce .... 4.00 1.60 .40
□ 94 Ron Kline .... 4.00 1.60 .40
□ 95A Milwaukee Braves .... 8.00 3.25 .80
Team (centered)
□ 95B Braves Team 30.00 12.00 3.00
(dated 1955)
□ 95C Braves Team 10.00 4.00 1.00
(name at far left)
□ 96 Bill Tremel .... 4.00 1.60 .40
□ 97 Jerry Lynch .... 4.00 1.60 .40
□ 98 Camilo Pascual .... 5.00 2.00 .50
□ 99 Don Zimmer .... 7.00 2.80 .70
□ 100A Baltimore Orioles .... 8.00 3.25 .80
Team (centered)
□ 100B Orioles Team 30.00 12.00 3.00
(dated 1955)
□ 100C Orioles Team 10.00 4.00 1.00
(name at far left)
□ 101 Roy Campanella 90.00 36.00 9.00
□ 102 Jim Davis .... 5.00 2.00 .50
□ 103 Willie Miranda .... 5.00 2.00 .50
□ 104 Bob Lennon .... 5.00 2.00 .50
□ 105 Al Smith .... 5.00 2.00 .50
□ 106 Joe Astroth .... 5.00 2.00 .50
□ 107 Eddie Mathews 32.00 13.00 3.20
□ 108 Laurin Pepper .... 5.00 2.00 .50
□ 109 Enos Slaughter 21.00 8.50 2.10
□ 110 Yogi Berra 90.00 36.00 9.00
□ 111 Boston Red Sox 12.50 5.00 1.25
Team Card
□ 112 Dee Fondy .... 5.00 2.00 .50
□ 113 Phil Rizzuto 30.00 12.00 3.00
□ 114 Jim Owens .... 5.00 2.00 .50
□ 115 Jackie Jensen .... 9.00 3.75 .90
□ 116 Eddie O'Brien .... 5.00 2.00 .50
□ 117 Virgil Trucks .... 6.00 2.40 .60
□ 118 Nellie Fox 12.00 5.00 1.20
□ 119 Larry Jackson .... 5.00 2.00 .50
□ 120 Richie Ashburn 13.00 5.25 1.30
□ 121 Pittsburgh Pirates 10.00 4.00 1.00
Team Card
□ 122 Willard Nixon .... 5.00 2.00 .50
□ 123 Roy McMillan .... 5.00 2.00 .50
□ 124 Don Kaiser .... 5.00 2.00 .50
□ 125 Minnie Minoso .... 9.00 3.75 .90
□ 126 Jim Brady .... 5.00 2.00 .50
□ 127 Willie Jones .... 5.00 2.00 .50
□ 128 Eddie Yost .... 5.00 2.00 .50
□ 129 Jake Martin .... 5.00 2.00 .50
□ 130 Willie Mays 200.00 80.00 20.00
□ 131 Bob Roselli .... 5.00 2.00 .50
□ 132 Bobby Avila .... 6.00 2.40 .60
□ 133 Ray Narleski .... 5.00 2.00 .50
□ 134 St. Louis Cardinals 10.00 4.00 1.00
Team Card
□ 135 Mickey Mantle 700.00 280.00 70.00
□ 136 Johnny Logan .... 6.00 2.40 .60
□ 137 Al Silvera .... 5.00 2.00 .50
□ 138 Johnny Antonelli .... 7.00 2.80 .70
□ 139 Tommy Carroll .... 6.00 2.40 .60
□ 140 Herb Score 11.00 4.50 1.10
□ 141 Joe Frazier .... 5.00 2.00 .50
□ 142 Gene Baker .... 5.00 2.00 .50
□ 143 Jim Piersall .... 8.00 3.25 .80
□ 144 Leroy Powell .... 5.00 2.00 .50
□ 145 Gil Hodges 28.00 11.50 2.80
□ 146 Washington Nationals .... 9.00 3.75 .90
Team Card
□ 147 Earl Torgeson .... 5.00 2.00 .50
□ 148 Alvin Dark .... 8.00 3.25 .80
□ 149 Dixie Howell .... 5.00 2.00 .50
□ 150 Duke Snider 80.00 32.00 8.00
□ 151 Spook Jacobs .... 5.00 2.00 .50
□ 152 Billy Hoeft .... 5.00 2.00 .50
□ 153 Frank Thomas .... 6.00 2.40 .60
□ 154 Dave Pope .... 5.00 2.00 .50
□ 155 Harvey Kuenn .... 8.00 3.25 .80
□ 156 Wes Westrum .... 6.00 2.40 .60
□ 157 Dick Brodowski .... 5.00 2.00 .50
□ 158 Wally Post .... 6.00 2.40 .60
□ 159 Clint Courtney .... 5.00 2.00 .50
□ 160 Billy Pierce .... 7.00 2.80 .70
□ 161 Joe DeMaestri .... 5.00 2.00 .50
□ 162 Dave(Gus) Bell .... 6.00 2.40 .60
□ 163 Gene Woodling .... 7.00 2.80 .70
□ 164 Harmon Killebrew 50.00 20.00 5.00
□ 165 Red Schoendienst .... 9.00 3.75 .90
□ 166 Brooklyn Dodgers 110.00 45.00 11.00
Team Card
□ 167 Harry Dorish .... 5.00 2.00 .50
□ 168 Sammy White .... 5.00 2.00 .50
□ 169 Bob Nelson .... 5.00 2.00 .50
□ 170 Bill Virdon .... 8.00 3.25 .80
□ 171 Jim Wilson .... 5.00 2.00 .50
□ 172 Frank Torre .... 5.00 2.00 .50
□ 173 Johnny Podres 11.00 4.50 1.10
□ 174 Glen Gorbous .... 5.00 2.00 .50
□ 175 Del Crandall .... 6.00 2.40 .60
□ 176 Alex Kellner .... 5.00 2.00 .50
□ 177 Hank Bauer 10.00 4.00 1.00

□ 178 Joe Black 7.00 2.80 .70
□ 179 Harry Chiti 5.00 2.00 .50
□ 180 Robin Roberts 21.00 8.50 2.10
□ 181 Billy Martin 45.00 18.00 4.50
□ 182 Paul Minner 9.00 3.75 .90
□ 183 Stan Lopata 9.00 3.75 .90
□ 184 Don Bessent 9.00 3.75 .90
□ 185 Bill Bruton 9.00 3.75 .90
□ 186 Ron Jackson 9.00 3.75 .90
□ 187 Early Wynn 25.00 10.00 2.50
□ 188 Chicago White Sox 18.00 7.25 1.80
Team Card
□ 189 Ned Garver 9.00 3.75 .90
□ 190 Carl Furillo 18.00 7.25 1.80
□ 191 Frank Lary 12.00 5.00 1.20
□ 192 Smoky Burgess 12.00 5.00 1.20
□ 193 Wilmer Mizell 9.00 3.75 .90
□ 194 Monte Irvin 22.00 9.00 2.20
□ 195 George Kell 25.00 10.00 2.50
□ 196 Tom Poholsky 9.00 3.75 .90
□ 197 Granny Hamner 9.00 3.75 .90
□ 198 Ed Fitzgerald 9.00 3.75 .90
□ 199 Hank Thompson 11.00 4.50 1.10
□ 200 Bob Feller 75.00 30.00 7.50
□ 201 Rip Repulski 9.00 3.75 .90
□ 202 Jim Hearn 9.00 3.75 .90
□ 203 Bill Tuttle 9.00 3.75 .90
□ 204 Art Swanson 9.00 3.75 .90
□ 205 Whitey Lockman 10.00 4.00 1.00
□ 206 Erv Palica 9.00 3.75 .90
□ 207 Jim Small 9.00 3.75 .90
□ 208 Elston Howard 25.00 10.00 2.50
□ 209 Max Surkont 9.00 3.75 .90
□ 210 Mike Garcia 11.00 4.50 1.10
□ 211 Murry Dickson 9.00 3.75 .90
□ 212 Johnny Temple 11.00 4.50 1.10
□ 213 Detroit Tigers 25.00 10.00 2.50
Team Card
□ 214 Bob Rush 9.00 3.75 .90
□ 215 Tommy Byrne 11.00 4.50 1.10
□ 216 Jerry Schoonmaker 9.00 3.75 .90
□ 217 Billy Klaus 9.00 3.75 .90
□ 218 Joe Nuxall 11.00 4.50 1.10
(sic, Nuxhall)
□ 219 Lew Burdette 15.00 6.00 1.50
□ 220 Del Ennis 11.00 4.50 1.10
□ 221 Bob Friend 11.00 4.50 1.10
□ 222 Dave Philley 9.00 3.75 .90
□ 223 Randy Jackson 9.00 3.75 .90
□ 224 Bud Podbielan 9.00 3.75 .90
□ 225 Gil McDougald 18.00 7.25 1.80
□ 226 New York Giants 40.00 16.00 4.00
Team Card
□ 227 Russ Meyer 9.00 3.75 .90
□ 228 Mickey Vernon 12.00 5.00 1.20
□ 229 Harry Brecheen 10.00 4.00 1.00
□ 230 Chico Carrasquel 9.00 3.75 .90
□ 231 Bob Hale 9.00 3.75 .90
□ 232 Toby Atwell 9.00 3.75 .90
□ 233 Carl Erskine 16.00 6.50 1.60
□ 234 Pete Runnels 11.00 4.50 1.10
□ 235 Don Newcombe 25.00 10.00 2.50
□ 236 Kansas City Athletics 15.00 6.00 1.50
Team Card
□ 237 Jose Valdivielso 9.00 3.75 .90
□ 238 Walt Dropo 11.00 4.50 1.10
□ 239 Harry Simpson 9.00 3.75 .90
□ 240 Whitey Ford 75.00 30.00 7.50
□ 241 Don Mueller 11.00 4.50 1.10
□ 242 Hershell Freeman 9.00 3.75 .90
□ 243 Sherm Lollar 11.00 4.50 1.10
□ 244 Bob Buhl 9.00 3.75 .90
□ 245 Billy Goodman 11.00 4.50 1.10
□ 246 Tom Gorman 9.00 3.75 .90
□ 247 Bill Sarni 9.00 3.75 .90
□ 248 Bob Porterfield 9.00 3.75 .90
□ 249 Johnny Klippstein 9.00 3.75 .90
□ 250 Larry Doby 15.00 6.00 1.50
□ 251 New York Yankees 120.00 50.00 12.00
Team Card
□ 252 Vern Law 11.00 4.50 1.10
□ 253 Irv Noren 11.00 4.50 1.10
□ 254 George Crowe 9.00 3.75 .90
□ 255 Bob Lemon 25.00 10.00 2.50
□ 256 Tom Hurd 9.00 3.75 .90
□ 257 Bobby Thomson 14.00 5.75 1.40
□ 258 Art Ditmar 11.00 4.50 1.10
□ 259 Sam Jones 11.00 4.50 1.10
□ 260 Pee Wee Reese 85.00 34.00 8.50
□ 261 Bobby Shantz 10.00 4.00 1.00
□ 262 Howie Pollet 6.00 2.40 .60
□ 263 Bob Miller 6.00 2.40 .60
□ 264 Ray Monzant 6.00 2.40 .60
□ 265 Sandy Consuegra 6.00 2.40 .60
□ 266 Don Ferrarese 6.00 2.40 .60
□ 267 Bob Nieman 6.00 2.40 .60
□ 268 Dale Mitchell 7.00 2.80 .70
□ 269 Jack Meyer 6.00 2.40 .60
□ 270 Billy Loes 7.00 2.80 .70
□ 271 Foster Castleman 6.00 2.40 .60
□ 272 Danny O'Connell 6.00 2.40 .60
□ 273 Walker Cooper 6.00 2.40 .60
□ 274 Frank Baumholtz 6.00 2.40 .60
□ 275 Jim Greengrass 6.00 2.40 .60
□ 276 George Zuverink 6.00 2.40 .60
□ 277 Daryl Spencer 6.00 2.40 .60
□ 278 Chet Nichols 6.00 2.40 .60
□ 279 Johnny Groth 6.00 2.40 .60
□ 280 Jim Gilliam 10.00 4.00 1.00
□ 281 Art Houtteman 6.00 2.40 .60
□ 282 Warren Hacker 6.00 2.40 .60
□ 283 Hal Smith 6.00 2.40 .60
□ 284 Ike Delock 6.00 2.40 .60
□ 285 Eddie Miksis 6.00 2.40 .60
□ 286 Bill Wight 6.00 2.40 .60
□ 287 Bobby Adams 6.00 2.40 .60
□ 288 Bob Cerv 9.00 3.75 .90
□ 289 Hal Jeffcoat 6.00 2.40 .60
□ 290 Curt Simmons 8.00 3.25 .80
□ 291 Frank Kellert 6.00 2.40 .60
□ 292 Luis Aparicio 80.00 32.00 8.00
□ 293 Stu Miller 6.00 2.40 .60
□ 294 Ernie Johnson 6.00 2.40 .60
□ 295 Clem Labine 8.00 3.25 .80
□ 296 Andy Seminick 6.00 2.40 .60
□ 297 Bob Skinner 7.00 2.80 .70
□ 298 Johnny Schmitz 6.00 2.40 .60
□ 299 Charlie Neal 12.00 5.00 1.20
□ 300 Vic Wertz 7.00 2.80 .70
□ 301 Marv Grissom 6.00 2.40 .60
□ 302 Eddie Robinson 6.00 2.40 .60
□ 303 Jim Dyck 6.00 2.40 .60
□ 304 Frank Malzone 12.00 5.00 1.20
□ 305 Brooks Lawrence 6.00 2.40 .60
□ 306 Curt Roberts 6.00 2.40 .60
□ 307 Hoyt Wilhelm 25.00 10.00 2.50
□ 308 Chuck Harmon 6.00 2.40 .60
□ 309 Don Blasingame 6.00 2.40 .60
□ 310 Steve Gromek 6.00 2.40 .60
□ 311 Hal Naragon 6.00 2.40 .60
□ 312 Andy Pafko 7.00 2.80 .70
□ 313 Gene Stephens 6.00 2.40 .60
□ 314 Hobie Landrith 6.00 2.40 .60
□ 315 Milt Bolling 6.00 2.40 .60
□ 316 Jerry Coleman 8.00 3.25 .80
□ 317 Al Aber 6.00 2.40 .60
□ 318 Fred Hatfield 6.00 2.40 .60
□ 319 Jack Crimian 6.00 2.40 .60
□ 320 Joe Adcock 8.00 3.25 .80
□ 321 Jim Konstanty 7.00 2.80 .70
□ 322 Karl Olson 6.00 2.40 .60
□ 323 Willard Schmidt 6.00 2.40 .60
□ 324 Rocky Bridges 6.00 2.40 .60
□ 325 Don Liddle 6.00 2.40 .60
□ 326 Connie Johnson 6.00 2.40 .60
□ 327 Bob Wiesler 6.00 2.40 .60
□ 328 Preston Ward 6.00 2.40 .60
□ 329 Lou Berberet 6.00 2.40 .60
□ 330 Jim Busby 6.00 2.40 .60
□ 331 Dick Hall 6.00 2.40 .60
□ 332 Don Larsen 15.00 6.00 1.50
□ 333 Rube Walker 7.00 2.80 .70
□ 334 Bob Miller 6.00 2.40 .60
□ 335 Don Hoak 7.00 2.80 .70
□ 336 Ellis Kinder 6.00 2.40 .60
□ 337 Bobby Morgan 6.00 2.40 .60
□ 338 Jim Delsing 6.00 2.40 .60
□ 339 Rance Pless 6.00 2.40 .60
□ 340 Mickey McDermott 15.00 4.00 .80
□ 341 Checklist 1/3 175.00 35.00 5.00
(unnumbered)
□ 342 Checklist 2/4 175.00 35.00 5.00
(unnumbered)

1957 Topps

The cards in this 407-card set measure 2 1/2" by 3 1/2". In 1957, Topps returned to the vertical obverse, adopted what we now call the standard card size, and used a large, uncluttered color photo for the first time since 1952. Cards in the series 265 to 352 and the unnumbered checklist cards are scarcer than other cards in the set. The first star

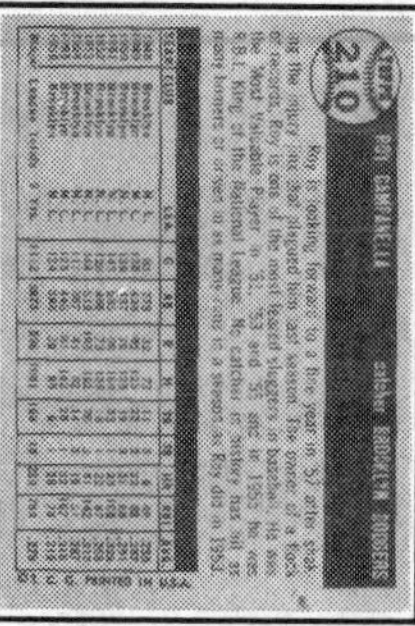

combination cards, #400 and #407, are quite popular with collectors. They feature the big stars of the previous season's World Series teams, the Dodgers (Furillo, Hodges, Campanella, and Snider) and Yankees (Berra and Mantle). The complete set price below does not include the unnumbered checklist cards.

	NRMT	VG-E	GOOD
COMPLETE SET (407)	5250.00	2400.00	800.00
COMMON PLAYER (1-88)	4.00	1.60	.40
COMMON PLAYER (89-264)	3.00	1.20	.30
COMMON PLAYER (265-352)	12.50	5.00	1.25
COMMON PLAYER (353-407)	3.50	1.40	.35

	#	Player	NRMT	VG-E	GOOD
□	1	Ted Williams	350.00	80.00	20.00
□	2	Yogi Berra	80.00	32.00	8.00
□	3	Dale Long	5.00	2.00	.50
□	4	Johnny Logan	5.00	2.00	.50
□	5	Sal Maglie	6.00	2.40	.60
□	6	Hector Lopez	4.00	1.60	.40
□	7	Luis Aparicio	20.00	8.00	2.00
□	8	Don Mossi	5.00	2.00	.50
□	9	Johnny Temple	5.00	2.00	.50
□	10	Willie Mays	150.00	60.00	15.00
□	11	George Zuverink	4.00	1.60	.40
□	12	Dick Groat	6.00	2.40	.60
□	13	Wally Burnette	4.00	1.60	.40
□	14	Bob Nieman	4.00	1.60	.40
□	15	Robin Roberts	16.00	6.50	1.60
□	16	Walt Moryn	4.00	1.60	.40
□	17	Billy Gardner	5.00	2.00	.50
□	18	Don Drysdale	125.00	50.00	12.50
□	19	Bob Wilson	4.00	1.60	.40
□	20	Hank Aaron (reverse negative photo on front)	175.00	70.00	18.00
□	21	Frank Sullivan	4.00	1.60	.40
□	22	Jerry Snyder (photo actually Ed Fitzgerald)	4.00	1.60	.40
□	23	Sherm Lollar	5.00	2.00	.50
□	24	Bill Mazeroski	21.00	8.50	2.10
□	25	Whitey Ford	36.00	15.00	3.60
□	26	Bob Boyd	4.00	1.60	.40
□	27	Ted Kazanski	4.00	1.60	.40
□	28	Gene Conley	4.00	1.60	.40
□	29	Whitey Herzog	16.00	6.50	1.60
□	30	Pee Wee Reese	36.00	15.00	3.60
□	31	Ron Northey	4.00	1.60	.40
□	32	Hershell Freeman	4.00	1.60	.40
□	33	Jim Small	4.00	1.60	.40
□	34	Tom Sturdivant	4.00	1.60	.40
□	35	Frank Robinson	135.00	54.00	13.50
□	36	Bob Grim	5.00	2.00	.50
□	37	Frank Torre	4.00	1.60	.40
□	38	Nellie Fox	10.00	4.00	1.00
□	39	Al Worthington	4.00	1.60	.40
□	40	Early Wynn	14.00	5.75	1.40
□	41	Hal W. Smith	4.00	1.60	.40
□	42	Dee Fondy	4.00	1.60	.40
□	43	Connie Johnson	4.00	1.60	.40
□	44	Joe DeMaestri	4.00	1.60	.40
□	45	Carl Furillo	9.00	3.75	.90
□	46	Robert J. Miller	4.00	1.60	.40
□	47	Don Blasingame	4.00	1.60	.40
□	48	Bill Bruton	5.00	2.00	.50
□	49	Daryl Spencer	4.00	1.60	.40
□	50	Herb Score	6.00	2.40	.60
□	51	Clint Courtney	4.00	1.60	.40
□	52	Lee Walls	4.00	1.60	.40
□	53	Clem Labine	5.00	2.00	.50
□	54	Elmer Valo	4.00	1.60	.40
□	55	Ernie Banks	40.00	16.00	4.00
□	56	Dave Sisler	4.00	1.60	.40
□	57	Jim Lemon	4.00	1.60	.40
□	58	Ruben Gomez	4.00	1.60	.40
□	59	Dick Williams	5.00	2.00	.50
□	60	Billy Hoeft	4.00	1.60	.40
□	61	James "Dusty" Rhodes	5.00	2.00	.50
□	62	Billy Martin	28.00	11.50	2.80
□	63	Ike Delock	4.00	1.60	.40
□	64	Pete Runnels	5.00	2.00	.50
□	65	Wally Moon	5.00	2.00	.50
□	66	Brooks Lawrence	4.00	1.60	.40
□	67	Chico Carrasquel	4.00	1.60	.40
□	68	Ray Crone	4.00	1.60	.40
□	69	Roy McMillan	4.00	1.60	.40
□	70	Richie Ashburn	10.00	4.00	1.00
□	71	Murry Dickson	4.00	1.60	.40
□	72	Bill Tuttle	4.00	1.60	.40
□	73	George Crowe	4.00	1.60	.40
□	74	Vito Valentinetti	4.00	1.60	.40
□	75	Jim Piersall	6.00	2.40	.60
□	76	Roberto Clemente	100.00	40.00	10.00
□	77	Paul Foytack	4.00	1.60	.40
□	78	Vic Wertz	5.00	2.00	.50
□	79	Lindy McDaniel	5.00	2.00	.50
□	80	Gil Hodges	25.00	10.00	2.50
□	81	Herman Wehmeier	4.00	1.60	.40
□	82	Elston Howard	9.00	3.75	.90
□	83	Lou Skizas	4.00	1.60	.40
□	84	Moe Drabowsky	4.00	1.60	.40
□	85	Larry Doby	6.00	2.40	.60
□	86	Bill Sarni	4.00	1.60	.40
□	87	Tom Gorman	4.00	1.60	.40
□	88	Harvey Kuenn	7.00	2.80	.70
□	89	Roy Sievers	4.00	1.60	.40
□	90	Warren Spahn	35.00	14.00	3.50
□	91	Mack Burk	3.00	1.20	.30
□	92	Mickey Vernon	4.00	1.60	.40
□	93	Hal Jeffcoat	3.00	1.20	.30
□	94	Bobby Del Greco	3.00	1.20	.30
□	95	Mickey Mantle	700.00	280.00	70.00
□	96	Hank Aguirre	3.00	1.20	.30
□	97	New York Yankees Team Card	25.00	10.00	2.50
□	98	Alvin Dark	5.00	2.00	.50
□	99	Bob Keegan	3.00	1.20	.30
□	100	Giles and Harridge League Presidents	5.00	2.00	.50
□	101	Chuck Stobbs	3.00	1.20	.30
□	102	Ray Boone	4.00	1.60	.40
□	103	Joe Nuxhall	4.00	1.60	.40
□	104	Hank Foiles	3.00	1.20	.30
□	105	Johnny Antonelli	4.00	1.60	.40
□	106	Ray Moore	3.00	1.20	.30
□	107	Jim Rivera	3.00	1.20	.30
□	108	Tommy Byrne	4.00	1.60	.40
□	109	Hank Thompson	4.00	1.60	.40
□	110	Bill Virdon	5.00	2.00	.50
□	111	Hal R. Smith	3.00	1.20	.30
□	112	Tom Brewer	3.00	1.20	.30
□	113	Wilmer Mizell	3.00	1.20	.30
□	114	Milwaukee Braves Team Card	7.00	2.80	.70
□	115	Jim Gilliam	7.50	3.00	.75
□	116	Mike Fornieles	3.00	1.20	.30
□	117	Joe Adcock	4.00	1.60	.40
□	118	Bob Porterfield	3.00	1.20	.30
□	119	Stan Lopata	3.00	1.20	.30
□	120	Bob Lemon	14.00	5.75	1.40
□	121	Cletis Boyer	8.00	3.25	.80
□	122	Ken Boyer	6.50	2.60	.65
□	123	Steve Ridzik	3.00	1.20	.30
□	124	Dave Philley	3.00	1.20	.30
□	125	Al Kaline	40.00	16.00	4.00
□	126	Bob Wiesler	3.00	1.20	.30
□	127	Bob Buhl	3.00	1.20	.30
□	128	Ed Bailey	3.00	1.20	.30
□	129	Saul Rogovin	3.00	1.20	.30
□	130	Don Newcombe	7.00	2.80	.70
□	131	Milt Bolling	3.00	1.20	.30
□	132	Art Ditmar	3.00	1.20	.30
□	133	Del Crandall	4.00	1.60	.40
□	134	Don Kaiser	3.00	1.20	.30
□	135	Bill Skowron	9.00	3.75	.90
□	136	Jim Hegan	4.00	1.60	.40
□	137	Bob Rush	3.00	1.20	.30
□	138	Minnie Minoso	6.50	2.60	.65
□	139	Lou Kretlow	3.00	1.20	.30
□	140	Frank Thomas	4.00	1.60	.40
□	141	Al Aber	3.00	1.20	.30
□	142	Charley Thompson	3.00	1.20	.30
□	143	Andy Pafko	3.00	1.20	.30
□	144	Ray Narleski	3.00	1.20	.30
□	145	Al Smith	3.00	1.20	.30

□ 146 Don Ferrarese	3.00	1.20	.30
□ 147 Al Walker	3.00	1.20	.30
□ 148 Don Mueller	4.00	1.60	.40
□ 149 Bob Kennedy	3.00	1.20	.30
□ 150 Bob Friend	4.00	1.60	.40
□ 151 Willie Miranda	3.00	1.20	.30
□ 152 Jack Harshman	3.00	1.20	.30
□ 153 Karl Olson	3.00	1.20	.30
□ 154 Red Schoendienst	6.50	2.60	.65
□ 155 Jim Brosnan	4.00	1.60	.40
□ 156 Gus Triandos	4.00	1.60	.40
□ 157 Wally Post	4.00	1.60	.40
□ 158 Curt Simmons	4.00	1.60	.40
□ 159 Solly Drake	3.00	1.20	.30
□ 160 Billy Pierce	4.00	1.60	.40
□ 161 Pittsburgh Pirates Team Card	5.00	2.00	.50
□ 162 Jack Meyer	3.00	1.20	.30
□ 163 Sammy White	3.00	1.20	.30
□ 164 Tommy Carroll	3.00	1.20	.30
□ 165 Ted Kluszewski	9.00	3.75	.90
□ 166 Elroy Face	5.00	2.00	.50
□ 167 Vic Power	4.00	1.60	.40
□ 168 Frank Lary	4.00	1.60	.40
□ 169 Herb Plews	3.00	1.20	.30
□ 170 Duke Snider	70.00	28.00	7.00
□ 171 Boston Red Sox Team Card	6.50	2.60	.65
□ 172 Gene Woodling	5.00	2.00	.50
□ 173 Roger Craig	7.50	3.00	.75
□ 174 Willie Jones	3.00	1.20	.30
□ 175 Don Larsen	7.00	2.80	.70
□ 176 Gene Baker	3.00	1.20	.30
□ 177 Eddie Yost	3.00	1.20	.30
□ 178 Don Bessent	3.00	1.20	.30
□ 179 Ernie Oravetz	3.00	1.20	.30
□ 180 Dave (Gus) Bell	4.00	1.60	.40
□ 181 Dick Donovan	3.00	1.20	.30
□ 182 Hobie Landrith	3.00	1.20	.30
□ 183 Chicago Cubs Team Card	6.00	2.40	.60
□ 184 Tito Francona	4.00	1.60	.40
□ 185 Johnny Kucks	4.00	1.60	.40
□ 186 Jim King	3.00	1.20	.30
□ 187 Virgil Trucks	4.00	1.60	.40
□ 188 Felix Mantilla	3.00	1.20	.30
□ 189 Willard Nixon	3.00	1.20	.30
□ 190 Randy Jackson	3.00	1.20	.30
□ 191 Joe Margoneri	3.00	1.20	.30
□ 192 Gerry Coleman	4.00	1.60	.40
□ 193 Del Rice	3.00	1.20	.30
□ 194 Hal Brown	3.00	1.20	.30
□ 195 Bobby Avila	3.00	1.20	.30
□ 196 Larry Jackson	3.00	1.20	.30
□ 197 Hank Sauer	4.00	1.60	.40
□ 198 Detroit Tigers Team Card	7.50	3.00	.75
□ 199 Vern Law	4.00	1.60	.40
□ 200 Gil McDougald	7.50	3.00	.75
□ 201 Sandy Amoros	4.00	1.60	.40
□ 202 Dick Gernert	3.00	1.20	.30
□ 203 Hoyt Wilhelm	13.00	5.25	1.30
□ 204 Kansas City Athletics Team Card	5.00	2.00	.50
□ 205 Charlie Maxwell	3.00	1.20	.30
□ 206 Willard Schmidt	3.00	1.20	.30
□ 207 Gordon(Billy) Hunter	3.00	1.20	.30
□ 208 Lou Burdette	5.00	2.00	.50
□ 209 Bob Skinner	4.00	1.60	.40
□ 210 Roy Campanella	65.00	26.00	6.50
□ 211 Camilo Pascual	4.00	1.60	.40
□ 212 Rocco Colavito	30.00	12.00	3.00
□ 213 Les Moss	3.00	1.20	.30
□ 214 Philadelphia Phillies Team Card	5.00	2.00	.50
□ 215 Enos Slaughter	14.00	5.75	1.40
□ 216 Marv Grissom	3.00	1.20	.30
□ 217 Gene Stephens	3.00	1.20	.30
□ 218 Ray Jablonski	3.00	1.20	.30
□ 219 Tom Acker	3.00	1.20	.30
□ 220 Jackie Jensen	5.50	2.20	.55
□ 221 Dixie Howell	3.00	1.20	.30
□ 222 Alex Grammas	3.00	1.20	.30
□ 223 Frank House	3.00	1.20	.30
□ 224 Marv Blaylock	3.00	1.20	.30
□ 225 Harry Simpson	3.00	1.20	.30
□ 226 Preston Ward	3.00	1.20	.30
□ 227 Gerry Staley	3.00	1.20	.30
□ 228 Smoky Burgess	4.00	1.60	.40
□ 229 George Susce	3.00	1.20	.30
□ 230 George Kell	13.00	5.25	1.30
□ 231 Solly Hemus	3.00	1.20	.30
□ 232 Whitey Lockman	4.00	1.60	.40
□ 233 Art Fowler	3.00	1.20	.30
□ 234 Dick Cole	3.00	1.20	.30
□ 235 Tom Poholsky	3.00	1.20	.30
□ 236 Joe Ginsberg	3.00	1.20	.30
□ 237 Foster Castleman	3.00	1.20	.30
□ 238 Eddie Robinson	3.00	1.20	.30
□ 239 Tom Morgan	3.00	1.20	.30
□ 240 Hank Bauer	7.50	3.00	.75
□ 241 Joe Lonnett	3.00	1.20	.30
□ 242 Charlie Neal	4.00	1.60	.40
□ 243 St. Louis Cardinals Team Card	7.00	2.80	.70
□ 244 Billy Loes	4.00	1.60	.40
□ 245 Rip Repulski	3.00	1.20	.30
□ 246 Jose Valdivielso	3.00	1.20	.30
□ 247 Turk Lown	3.00	1.20	.30
□ 248 Jim Finigan	3.00	1.20	.30
□ 249 Dave Pope	3.00	1.20	.30
□ 250 Ed Mathews	21.00	8.50	2.10
□ 251 Baltimore Orioles Team Card	6.00	2.40	.60
□ 252 Carl Erskine	6.50	2.60	.65
□ 253 Gus Zernial	4.00	1.60	.40
□ 254 Ron Negray	3.00	1.20	.30
□ 255 Charlie Silvera	3.00	1.20	.30
□ 256 Ron Kline	3.00	1.20	.30
□ 257 Walt Dropo	3.00	1.20	.30
□ 258 Steve Gromek	3.00	1.20	.30
□ 259 Eddie O'Brien	3.00	1.20	.30
□ 260 Del Ennis	4.00	1.60	.40
□ 261 Bob Chakales	3.00	1.20	.30
□ 262 Bobby Thomson	5.00	2.00	.50
□ 263 George Strickland	3.00	1.20	.30
□ 264 Bob Turley	6.50	2.60	.65
□ 265 Harvey Haddix	16.00	6.50	1.60
□ 266 Ken Kuhn	12.50	5.00	1.25
□ 267 Danny Kravitz	12.50	5.00	1.25
□ 268 Joe Collum	12.50	5.00	1.25
□ 269 Bob Cerv	14.00	5.75	1.40
□ 270 Washington Senators Team Card	20.00	8.00	2.00
□ 271 Danny O'Connell	12.50	5.00	1.25
□ 272 Bobby Shantz	20.00	8.00	2.00
□ 273 Jim Davis	12.50	5.00	1.25
□ 274 Don Hoak	14.00	5.75	1.40
□ 275 Cleveland Indians Team Card	20.00	8.00	2.00
□ 276 Jim Pyburn	12.50	5.00	1.25
□ 277 Johnny Podres	50.00	20.00	5.00
□ 278 Fred Hatfield	12.50	5.00	1.25
□ 279 Bob Thurman	12.50	5.00	1.25
□ 280 Alex Kellner	12.50	5.00	1.25
□ 281 Gail Harris	12.50	5.00	1.25
□ 282 Jack Dittmer	12.50	5.00	1.25
□ 283 Wes Covington	14.00	5.75	1.40
□ 284 Don Zimmer	16.00	6.50	1.60
□ 285 Ned Garver	12.50	5.00	1.25
□ 286 Bobby Richardson	80.00	32.00	8.00
□ 287 Sam Jones	14.00	5.75	1.40
□ 288 Ted Lepcio	12.50	5.00	1.25
□ 289 Jim Bolger	12.50	5.00	1.25
□ 290 Andy Carey	14.00	5.75	1.40
□ 291 Windy McCall	12.50	5.00	1.25
□ 292 Billy Klaus	12.50	5.00	1.25
□ 293 Ted Abernathy	12.50	5.00	1.25
□ 294 Rocky Bridges	12.50	5.00	1.25
□ 295 Joe Collins	14.00	5.75	1.40
□ 296 Johnny Klippstein	12.50	5.00	1.25
□ 297 Jack Crimian	12.50	5.00	1.25
□ 298 Irv Noren	12.50	5.00	1.25
□ 299 Chuck Harmon	12.50	5.00	1.25
□ 300 Mike Garcia	14.00	5.75	1.40
□ 301 Sammy Esposito	12.50	5.00	1.25
□ 302 Sandy Koufax	300.00	120.00	30.00
□ 303 Billy Goodman	14.00	5.75	1.40
□ 304 Joe Cunningham	14.00	5.75	1.40
□ 305 Chico Fernandez	12.50	5.00	1.25
□ 306 Darrell Johnson	14.00	5.75	1.40
□ 307 Jack D. Phillips	12.50	5.00	1.25
□ 308 Richard Hall	12.50	5.00	1.25
□ 309 Jim Busby	12.50	5.00	1.25
□ 310 Max Surkont	12.50	5.00	1.25
□ 311 Al Pilarcik	12.50	5.00	1.25
□ 312 Tony Kubek	90.00	36.00	9.00
□ 313 Mel Parnell	14.00	5.75	1.40
□ 314 Ed Bouchee	12.50	5.00	1.25
□ 315 Lou Berberet	12.50	5.00	1.25
□ 316 Billy O'Dell	12.50	5.00	1.25
□ 317 New York Giants Team Card	40.00	16.00	4.00
□ 318 Mickey McDermott	12.50	5.00	1.25
□ 319 Gino Cimoli	14.00	5.75	1.40
□ 320 Neil Chrisley	12.50	5.00	1.25
□ 321 John (Red) Murff	12.50	5.00	1.25
□ 322 Cincinnati Reds Team Card	40.00	16.00	4.00
□ 323 Wes Westrum	14.00	5.75	1.40

□ 324 Brooklyn Dodgers	80.00	32.00	8.00
Team Card			
□ 325 Frank Bolling	12.50	5.00	1.25
□ 326 Pedro Ramos	12.50	5.00	1.25
□ 327 Jim Pendleton	12.50	5.00	1.25
□ 328 Brooks Robinson	300.00	120.00	30.00
□ 329 Chicago White Sox	20.00	8.00	2.00
Team Card			
□ 330 Jim Wilson	12.50	5.00	1.25
□ 331 Ray Katt	12.50	5.00	1.25
□ 332 Bob Bowman	12.50	5.00	1.25
□ 333 Ernie Johnson	12.50	5.00	1.25
□ 334 Jerry Schoonmaker	12.50	5.00	1.25
□ 335 Granny Hamner	12.50	5.00	1.25
□ 336 Haywood Sullivan	14.00	5.75	1.40
□ 337 Rene Valdes	12.50	5.00	1.25
□ 338 Jim Bunning	100.00	40.00	10.00
□ 339 Bob Speake	12.50	5.00	1.25
□ 340 Bill Wight	12.50	5.00	1.25
□ 341 Don Gross	12.50	5.00	1.25
□ 342 Gene Mauch	16.00	6.50	1.60
□ 343 Taylor Phillips	12.50	5.00	1.25
□ 344 Paul LaPalme	12.50	5.00	1.25
□ 345 Paul Smith	12.50	5.00	1.25
□ 346 Dick Littlefield	12.50	5.00	1.25
□ 347 Hal Naragon	12.50	5.00	1.25
□ 348 Jim Hearn	12.50	5.00	1.25
□ 349 Nellie King	12.50	5.00	1.25
□ 350 Eddie Miksis	12.50	5.00	1.25
□ 351 Dave Hillman	12.50	5.00	1.25
□ 352 Ellis Kinder	12.50	5.00	1.25
□ 353 Cal Neeman	3.50	1.40	.35
□ 354 W. (Rip) Coleman	3.50	1.40	.35
□ 355 Frank Malzone	4.50	1.80	.45
□ 356 Faye Throneberry	3.50	1.40	.35
□ 357 Earl Torgeson	3.50	1.40	.35
□ 358 Gerry Lynch	4.50	1.80	.45
□ 359 Tom Cheney	3.50	1.40	.35
□ 360 Johnny Groth	3.50	1.40	.35
□ 361 Curt Barclay	3.50	1.40	.35
□ 362 Roman Mejias	3.50	1.40	.35
□ 363 Eddie Kasko	3.50	1.40	.35
□ 364 Cal McLish	3.50	1.40	.35
□ 365 Ozzie Virgil	3.50	1.40	.35
□ 366 Ken Lehman	3.50	1.40	.35
□ 367 Ed Fitzgerald	3.50	1.40	.35
□ 368 Bob Purkey	3.50	1.40	.35
□ 369 Milt Graff	3.50	1.40	.35
□ 370 Warren Hacker	3.50	1.40	.35
□ 371 Bob Lennon	3.50	1.40	.35
□ 372 Norm Zauchin	3.50	1.40	.35
□ 373 Pete Whisenant	3.50	1.40	.35
□ 374 Don Cardwell	3.50	1.40	.35
□ 375 Jim Landis	3.50	1.40	.35
□ 376 Don Elston	3.50	1.40	.35
□ 377 Andre Rodgers	3.50	1.40	.35
□ 378 Elmer Singleton	3.50	1.40	.35
□ 379 Don Lee	3.50	1.40	.35
□ 380 Walker Cooper	3.50	1.40	.35
□ 381 Dean Stone	3.50	1.40	.35
□ 382 Jim Brideweser	3.50	1.40	.35
□ 383 Juan Pizarro	3.50	1.40	.35
□ 384 Bobby G. Smith	3.50	1.40	.35
□ 385 Art Houtteman	3.50	1.40	.35
□ 386 Lyle Luttrell	3.50	1.40	.35
□ 387 Jack Sanford	6.00	2.40	.60
□ 388 Pete Daley	3.50	1.40	.35
□ 389 Dave Jolly	3.50	1.40	.35
□ 390 Reno Bertoia	3.50	1.40	.35
□ 391 Ralph Terry	8.00	3.25	.80
□ 392 Chuck Tanner	5.00	2.00	.50
□ 393 Raul Sanchez	3.50	1.40	.35
□ 394 Luis Arroyo	4.50	1.80	.45
□ 395 J.M.(Bubba) Phillips	3.50	1.40	.35
□ 396 K. (Casey) Wise	3.50	1.40	.35
□ 397 Roy Smalley	3.50	1.40	.35
□ 398 Al Cicotte	4.50	1.80	.45
□ 399 Bill Consolo	3.50	1.40	.35
□ 400 Dodgers' Sluggers	150.00	60.00	15.00
Carl Furillo			
Gil Hodges			
Roy Campanella			
Duke Snider			
□ 401 Earl Battey	4.50	1.80	.45
□ 402 Jim Pisani	3.50	1.40	.35
□ 403 Richard Hyde	3.50	1.40	.35
□ 404 Harry Anderson	3.50	1.40	.35
□ 405 Duke Maas	3.50	1.40	.35
□ 406 Bob Hale	3.50	1.40	.35
□ 407 Yankee Power Hitters	250.00	100.00	25.00
Mickey Mantle			
Yogi Berra			
□ 408 Checklist 1/2	80.00	10.00	2.00
(unnumbered)			
□ 409 Checklist 2/3	125.00	15.00	3.00
(unnumbered)			
□ 410 Checklist 3/4	250.00	35.00	5.00
(unnumbered)			
□ 411 Checklist 4/5	400.00	50.00	8.00
(unnumbered)			

1958 Topps

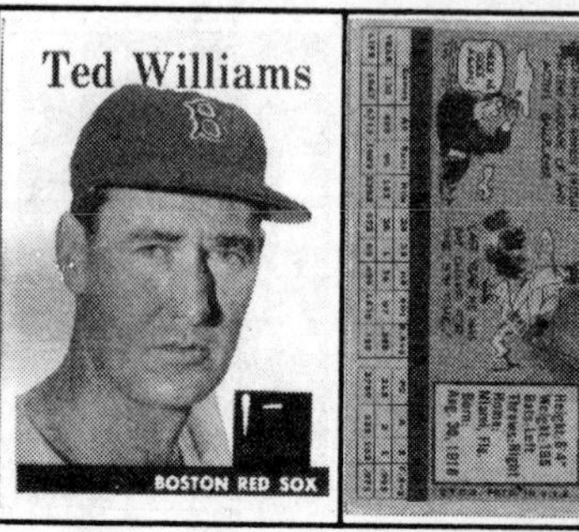

The cards in this 494-card set measure 2 1/2" by 3 1/2". Although the last card is numbered 495, number 145 was not issued, bringing the set total to 494 cards. The 1958 Topps set contains the first Sport Magazine All-Star Selection series (475-495) and expanded use of combination cards. The team cards carried series checklists on back (Milwaukee, Detroit, Baltimore, and Cincinnati are also found with players listed alphabetically). Cards with the scarce yellow name (YL) or team (YT) lettering as opposed to the common white lettering are noted in the checklist. In the last series cards of Stan Musial and Mickey Mantle were triple printed; the cards they replaced (443, 446, 450, and 462) on the printing sheet were hence printed in shorter supply than other cards in the last series and are marked with an SP in the list below.

	NRMT	VG-E	GOOD
COMPLETE SET (494)	3250.00	1400.00	500.00
COMMON PLAYER (1-110)	3.00	1.20	.30
COMMON PLAYER (111-198)	2.25	.90	.22
COMMON PLAYER (199-352)	2.00	.80	.20
COMMON PLAYER (353-440)	2.00	.80	.20
COMMON PLAYER (441-474)	1.75	.70	.17
COMMON PLAYER (475-495)	2.00	.80	.20
□ 1 Ted Williams	300.00	75.00	15.00
□ 2A Bob Lemon	13.00	5.25	1.30
□ 2B Bob Lemon YT	30.00	12.00	3.00
□ 3 Alex Kellner	3.00	1.20	.30
□ 4 Hank Foiles	3.00	1.20	.30
□ 5 Willie Mays	125.00	50.00	12.50
□ 6 George Zuverink	3.00	1.20	.30
□ 7 Dale Long	4.00	1.60	.40
□ 8A Eddie Kasko	3.00	1.20	.30
□ 8B Eddie Kasko YL	20.00	8.00	2.00
□ 9 Hank Bauer	6.00	2.40	.60
□ 10 Lou Burdette	5.00	2.00	.50
□ 11A Jim Rivera	3.00	1.20	.30
□ 11B Jim Rivera YT	15.00	6.00	1.50
□ 12 George Crowe	3.00	1.20	.30
□ 13A Billy Hoeft	3.00	1.20	.30
□ 13B Billy Hoeft YL	20.00	8.00	2.00
□ 14 Rip Repulski	3.00	1.20	.30
□ 15 Jim Lemon	4.00	1.60	.40
□ 16 Charley Neal	4.00	1.60	.40
□ 17 Felix Mantilla	3.00	1.20	.30
□ 18 Frank Sullivan	3.00	1.20	.30
□ 19 New York Giants	12.00	3.00	.60
Team Card			
(checklist on back)			
□ 20A Gil McDougald	7.00	2.80	.70
□ 20B Gil McDougald YL	25.00	10.00	2.50
□ 21 Curt Barclay	3.00	1.20	.30
□ 22 Hal Naragon	3.00	1.20	.30
□ 23A Bill Tuttle	3.00	1.20	.30

☐	23B	Bill Tuttle YL	20.00	8.00	2.00
☐	24A	Hobie Landrith	3.00	1.20	.30
☐	24B	Hobie Landrith YL	20.00	8.00	2.00
☐	25	Don Drysdale	25.00	10.00	2.50
☐	26	Ron Jackson	3.00	1.20	.30
☐	27	Bud Freeman	3.00	1.20	.30
☐	28	Jim Busby	3.00	1.20	.30
☐	29	Ted Lepcio	3.00	1.20	.30
☐	30A	Hank Aaron	125.00	50.00	12.50
☐	30B	Hank Aaron YL	200.00	80.00	20.00
☐	31	Tex Clevenger	3.00	1.20	.30
☐	32A	J.W. Porter	3.00	1.20	.30
☐	32B	J.W. Porter YL	20.00	8.00	2.00
☐	33A	Cal Neeman	3.00	1.20	.30
☐	33B	Cal Neeman YT	15.00	6.00	1.50
☐	34	Bob Thurman	3.00	1.20	.30
☐	35A	Don Mossi	4.00	1.60	.40
☐	35B	Don Mossi YT	15.00	6.00	1.50
☐	36	Ted Kazanski	3.00	1.20	.30
☐	37	Mike McCormick (photo actually Ray Monzant)	4.00	1.60	.40
☐	38	Dick Gernert	3.00	1.20	.30
☐	39	Bob Martyn	3.00	1.20	.30
☐	40	George Kell	12.00	5.00	1.20
☐	41	Dave Hillman	3.00	1.20	.30
☐	42	John Roseboro	5.00	2.00	.50
☐	43	Sal Maglie	5.00	2.00	.50
☐	44	Washington Senators Team Card (checklist on back)	5.00	1.50	.30
☐	45	Dick Groat	5.00	2.00	.50
☐	46A	Lou Sleater	3.00	1.20	.30
☐	46B	Lou Sleater YL	20.00	8.00	2.00
☐	47	Roger Maris	300.00	120.00	30.00
☐	48	Chuck Harmon	3.00	1.20	.30
☐	49	Smoky Burgess	4.00	1.60	.40
☐	50A	Billy Pierce	5.00	2.00	.50
☐	50B	Billy Pierce YT	20.00	8.00	2.00
☐	51	Del Rice	3.00	1.20	.30
☐	52A	Bob Clemente	65.00	26.00	6.50
☐	52B	Bob Clemente YT	125.00	50.00	12.50
☐	53A	Morrie Martin	3.00	1.20	.30
☐	53B	Morrie Martin YL	20.00	8.00	2.00
☐	54	Norm Siebern	3.00	1.20	.30
☐	55	Chico Carrasquel	3.00	1.20	.30
☐	56	Bill Fischer	3.00	1.20	.30
☐	57A	Tim Thompson	3.00	1.20	.30
☐	57B	Tim Thompson YL	20.00	8.00	2.00
☐	58A	Art Schult	3.00	1.20	.30
☐	58B	Art Schult YT	15.00	6.00	1.50
☐	59	Dave Sisler	3.00	1.20	.30
☐	60A	Del Ennis	4.00	1.60	.40
☐	60B	Del Ennis YL	20.00	8.00	2.00
☐	61A	Darrell Johnson	4.00	1.60	.40
☐	61B	Darrell Johnson YL	20.00	8.00	2.00
☐	62	Joe DeMaestri	3.00	1.20	.30
☐	63	Joe Nuxhall	4.00	1.60	.40
☐	64	Joe Lonnett	3.00	1.20	.30
☐	65A	Von McDaniel	3.00	1.20	.30
☐	65B	Von McDaniel YL	20.00	8.00	2.00
☐	66	Lee Walls	3.00	1.20	.30
☐	67	Joe Ginsberg	3.00	1.20	.30
☐	68	Daryl Spencer	3.00	1.20	.30
☐	69	Wally Burnette	3.00	1.20	.30
☐	70A	Al Kaline	35.00	14.00	3.50
☐	70B	Al Kaline YL	70.00	28.00	7.00
☐	71	Dodgers Team (checklist on back)	15.00	3.50	.75
☐	72	Bud Byerly	3.00	1.20	.30
☐	73	Pete Daley	3.00	1.20	.30
☐	74	Roy Face	5.00	2.00	.50
☐	75	Gus Bell	4.00	1.60	.40
☐	76A	Dick Farrell	4.00	1.60	.40
☐	76B	Dick Farrell YT	20.00	8.00	2.00
☐	77A	Don Zimmer	5.00	2.00	.50
☐	77B	Don Zimmer YT	20.00	8.00	2.00
☐	78A	Ernie Johnson	3.00	1.20	.30
☐	78B	Ernie Johnson YL	20.00	8.00	2.00
☐	79A	Dick Williams	4.00	1.60	.40
☐	79B	Dick Williams YT	20.00	8.00	2.00
☐	80	Dick Drott	3.00	1.20	.30
☐	81A	Steve Boros	4.00	1.60	.40
☐	81B	Steve Boros YT	20.00	8.00	2.00
☐	82	Ronnie Kline	3.00	1.20	.30
☐	83	Bob Hazle	4.00	1.60	.40
☐	84	Billy O'Dell	3.00	1.20	.30
☐	85A	Luis Aparicio	14.00	5.75	1.40
☐	85B	Luis Aparicio YT	30.00	12.00	3.00
☐	86	Valmy Thomas	3.00	1.20	.30
☐	87	Johnny Kucks	3.00	1.20	.30
☐	88	Duke Snider	45.00	18.00	4.00
☐	89	Billy Klaus	3.00	1.20	.30
☐	90	Robin Roberts	12.00	5.00	1.20
☐	91	Chuck Tanner	4.00	1.60	.40
☐	92A	Clint Courtney	3.00	1.20	.30
☐	92B	Clint Courtney YL	20.00	8.00	2.00
☐	93	Sandy Amoros	4.00	1.60	.40
☐	94	Bob Skinner	3.00	1.20	.30
☐	95	Frank Bolling	3.00	1.20	.30
☐	96	Joe Durham	3.00	1.20	.30
☐	97A	Larry Jackson	3.00	1.20	.30
☐	97B	Larry Jackson YL	20.00	8.00	2.00
☐	98A	Billy Hunter	3.00	1.20	.30
☐	98B	Billy Hunter YL	20.00	8.00	2.00
☐	99	Bobby Adams	3.00	1.20	.30
☐	100A	Early Wynn	12.00	5.00	1.20
☐	100B	Early Wynn YT	30.00	12.00	3.00
☐	101A	Bobby Richardson	10.00	4.00	1.00
☐	101B	Bobby Richardson YL	30.00	12.00	3.00
☐	102	George Strickland	3.00	1.20	.30
☐	103	Jerry Lynch	3.00	1.20	.30
☐	104	Jim Pendleton	3.00	1.20	.30
☐	105	Billy Gardner	4.00	1.60	.40
☐	106	Dick Schofield	3.00	1.20	.30
☐	107	Ossie Virgil	3.00	1.20	.30
☐	108A	Jim Landis	3.00	1.20	.30
☐	108B	Jim Landis YT	15.00	6.00	1.50
☐	109	Herb Plews	3.00	1.20	.30
☐	110	Johnny Logan	4.00	1.60	.40
☐	111	Stu Miller	2.25	.90	.22
☐	112	Gus Zernial	3.00	1.20	.30
☐	113	Jerry Walker	2.25	.90	.22
☐	114	Irv Noren	2.25	.90	.22
☐	115	Jim Bunning	10.00	4.00	1.00
☐	116	Dave Philley	2.25	.90	.22
☐	117	Frank Torre	2.25	.90	.22
☐	118	Harvey Haddix	3.50	1.40	.35
☐	119	Harry Chiti	2.25	.90	.22
☐	120	Johnny Podres	6.00	2.40	.60
☐	121	Eddie Miksis	2.25	.90	.22
☐	122	Walt Moryn	2.25	.90	.22
☐	123	Dick Tomanek	2.25	.90	.22
☐	124	Bobby Usher	2.25	.90	.22
☐	125	Al Dark	3.50	1.40	.35
☐	126	Stan Palys	2.25	.90	.22
☐	127	Tom Sturdivant	3.00	1.20	.30
☐	128	Willie Kirkland	3.00	1.20	.30
☐	129	Jim Derrington	2.25	.90	.22
☐	130	Jackie Jensen	6.00	2.40	.60
☐	131	Bob Henrich	2.25	.90	.22
☐	132	Vernon Law	3.00	1.20	.30
☐	133	Russ Nixon	4.00	1.60	.40
☐	134	Philadelphia Phillies Team Card (checklist on back)	5.00	1.50	.30
☐	135	Mike(Moe) Drabowsky	3.00	1.20	.30
☐	136	Jim Finigan	2.25	.90	.22
☐	137	Russ Kemmerer	2.25	.90	.22
☐	138	Earl Torgeson	2.25	.90	.22
☐	139	George Brunet	2.25	.90	.22
☐	140	Wes Covington	3.00	1.20	.30
☐	141	Ken Lehman	2.25	.90	.22
☐	142	Enos Slaughter	13.00	5.25	1.30
☐	143	Billy Muffett	2.25	.90	.22
☐	144	Bobby Morgan	2.25	.90	.22
☐	145	Never issued	0.00	.00	.00
☐	146	Dick Gray	2.25	.90	.22
☐	147	Don McMahon	3.00	1.20	.30
☐	148	Billy Consolo	2.25	.90	.22
☐	149	Tom Acker	2.25	.90	.22
☐	150	Mickey Mantle	450.00	180.00	45.00
☐	151	Buddy Pritchard	2.25	.90	.22
☐	152	Johnny Antonelli	3.00	1.20	.30
☐	153	Les Moss	2.25	.90	.22
☐	154	Harry Byrd	2.25	.90	.22
☐	155	Hector Lopez	2.25	.90	.22
☐	156	Dick Hyde	2.25	.90	.22
☐	157	Dee Fondy	2.25	.90	.22
☐	158	Cleveland Indians Team Card (checklist on back)	5.00	1.50	.30
☐	159	Taylor Phillips	2.25	.90	.22
☐	160	Don Hoak	3.00	1.20	.30
☐	161	Don Larsen	5.00	2.00	.50
☐	162	Gil Hodges	16.00	6.50	1.60
☐	163	Jim Wilson	2.25	.90	.22
☐	164	Bob Taylor	2.25	.90	.22
☐	165	Bob Nieman	2.25	.90	.22
☐	166	Danny O'Connell	2.25	.90	.22
☐	167	Frank Baumann	2.25	.90	.22
☐	168	Joe Cunningham	3.00	1.20	.30
☐	169	Ralph Terry	4.00	1.60	.40
☐	170	Vic Wertz	3.00	1.20	.30
☐	171	Harry Anderson	2.25	.90	.22
☐	172	Don Gross	2.25	.90	.22
☐	173	Eddie Yost	2.25	.90	.22
☐	174	Athletics Team (checklist on back)	5.00	1.50	.30
☐	175	Marv Throneberry	6.00	2.40	.60

☐ 176	Bob Buhl	2.25	.90	.22
☐ 177	Al Smith	2.25	.90	.22
☐ 178	Ted Kluszewski	6.50	2.60	.65
☐ 179	Willie Miranda	2.25	.90	.22
☐ 180	Lindy McDaniel	3.00	1.20	.30
☐ 181	Willie Jones	2.25	.90	.22
☐ 182	Joe Caffie	2.25	.90	.22
☐ 183	Dave Jolly	2.25	.90	.22
☐ 184	Elvin Tappe	2.25	.90	.22
☐ 185	Ray Boone	3.00	1.20	.30
☐ 186	Jack Meyer	2.25	.90	.22
☐ 187	Sandy Koufax	75.00	30.00	7.50
☐ 188	Milt Bolling (photo actually Lou Berberet)	2.25	.90	.22
☐ 189	George Susce	2.25	.90	.22
☐ 190	Red Schoendienst	4.50	1.80	.45
☐ 191	Art Ceccarelli	2.25	.90	.22
☐ 192	Milt Graff	2.25	.90	.22
☐ 193	Jerry Lumpe	2.25	.90	.22
☐ 194	Roger Craig	5.50	2.20	.55
☐ 195	Whitey Lockman	3.00	1.20	.30
☐ 196	Mike Garcia	3.00	1.20	.30
☐ 197	Haywood Sullivan	3.00	1.20	.30
☐ 198	Bill Virdon	3.50	1.40	.35
☐ 199	Don Blasingame	2.00	.80	.20
☐ 200	Bob Keegan	2.00	.80	.20
☐ 201	Jim Bolger	2.00	.80	.20
☐ 202	Woody Held	2.00	.80	.20
☐ 203	Al Walker	2.00	.80	.20
☐ 204	Leo Kiely	2.00	.80	.20
☐ 205	Johnny Temple	2.50	1.00	.25
☐ 206	Bob Shaw	2.00	.80	.20
☐ 207	Solly Hemus	2.00	.80	.20
☐ 208	Cal McLish	2.00	.80	.20
☐ 209	Bob Anderson	2.00	.80	.20
☐ 210	Wally Moon	3.00	1.20	.30
☐ 211	Pete Burnside	2.00	.80	.20
☐ 212	Bubba Phillips	2.00	.80	.20
☐ 213	Red Wilson	2.00	.80	.20
☐ 214	Willard Schmidt	2.00	.80	.20
☐ 215	Jim Gilliam	6.00	2.40	.60
☐ 216	St. Louis Cardinals Team Card (checklist on back)	5.00	1.50	.30
☐ 217	Jack Harshman	2.00	.80	.20
☐ 218	Dick Rand	2.00	.80	.20
☐ 219	Camilo Pascual	2.50	1.00	.25
☐ 220	Tom Brewer	2.00	.80	.20
☐ 221	Jerry Kindall	2.50	1.00	.25
☐ 222	Bud Daley	2.00	.80	.20
☐ 223	Andy Pafko	2.50	1.00	.25
☐ 224	Bob Grim	2.50	1.00	.25
☐ 225	Billy Goodman	2.50	1.00	.25
☐ 226	Bob Smith	2.00	.80	.20
☐ 227	Gene Stephens	2.00	.80	.20
☐ 228	Duke Maas	2.00	.80	.20
☐ 229	Frank Zupo	2.00	.80	.20
☐ 230	Richie Ashburn	8.00	3.25	.80
☐ 231	Lloyd Merritt	2.00	.80	.20
☐ 232	Reno Bertoia	2.00	.80	.20
☐ 233	Mickey Vernon	2.50	1.00	.25
☐ 234	Carl Sawatski	2.00	.80	.20
☐ 235	Tom Gorman	2.00	.80	.20
☐ 236	Ed Fitzgerald	2.00	.80	.20
☐ 237	Bill Wight	2.00	.80	.20
☐ 238	Bill Mazeroski	7.00	2.80	.70
☐ 239	Chuck Stobbs	2.00	.80	.20
☐ 240	Moose Skowron	7.50	3.00	.75
☐ 241	Dick Littlefield	2.00	.80	.20
☐ 242	Johnny Klippstein	2.00	.80	.20
☐ 243	Larry Raines	2.00	.80	.20
☐ 244	Don Demeter	2.00	.80	.20
☐ 245	Frank Lary	2.50	1.00	.25
☐ 246	New York Yankees Team Card (checklist on back)	25.00	6.00	1.00
☐ 247	Casey Wise	2.00	.80	.20
☐ 248	Herm Wehmeier	2.00	.80	.20
☐ 249	Ray Moore	2.00	.80	.20
☐ 250	Roy Sievers	2.50	1.00	.25
☐ 251	Warren Hacker	2.00	.80	.20
☐ 252	Bob Trowbridge	2.00	.80	.20
☐ 253	Don Mueller	2.50	1.00	.25
☐ 254	Alex Grammas	2.00	.80	.20
☐ 255	Bob Turley	6.00	2.40	.60
☐ 256	Chicago White Sox Team Card (checklist on back)	5.00	1.50	.30
☐ 257	Hal Smith	2.00	.80	.20
☐ 258	Carl Erskine	5.00	2.00	.50
☐ 259	Al Pilarcik	2.00	.80	.20
☐ 260	Frank Malzone	3.00	1.20	.30
☐ 261	Turk Lown	2.00	.80	.20
☐ 262	Johnny Groth	2.00	.80	.20
☐ 263	Eddie Bressoud	2.00	.80	.20
☐ 264	Jack Sanford	2.50	1.00	.25
☐ 265	Pete Runnels	2.50	1.00	.25
☐ 266	Connie Johnson	2.00	.80	.20
☐ 267	Sherm Lollar	2.50	1.00	.25
☐ 268	Granny Hamner	2.00	.80	.20
☐ 269	Paul Smith	2.00	.80	.20
☐ 270	Warren Spahn	22.00	9.00	2.20
☐ 271	Billy Martin	7.00	2.80	.70
☐ 272	Ray Crone	2.00	.80	.20
☐ 273	Hal Smith	2.00	.80	.20
☐ 274	Rocky Bridges	2.00	.80	.20
☐ 275	Elston Howard	6.50	2.60	.65
☐ 276	Bobby Avila	2.50	1.00	.25
☐ 277	Virgil Trucks	2.50	1.00	.25
☐ 278	Mack Burk	2.00	.80	.20
☐ 279	Bob Boyd	2.00	.80	.20
☐ 280	Jim Piersall	4.50	1.80	.45
☐ 281	Sam Taylor	2.00	.80	.20
☐ 282	Paul Foytack	2.00	.80	.20
☐ 283	Ray Shearer	2.00	.80	.20
☐ 284	Ray Katt	2.00	.80	.20
☐ 285	Frank Robinson	40.00	16.00	4.00
☐ 286	Gino Cimoli	2.50	1.00	.25
☐ 287	Sam Jones	2.50	1.00	.25
☐ 288	Harmon Killebrew	25.00	10.00	2.50
☐ 289	Series Hurling Rivals Lou Burdette Bobby Shantz	3.50	1.40	.35
☐ 290	Dick Donovan	2.00	.80	.20
☐ 291	Don Landrum	2.00	.80	.20
☐ 292	Ned Garver	2.00	.80	.20
☐ 293	Gene Freese	2.00	.80	.20
☐ 294	Hal Jeffcoat	2.00	.80	.20
☐ 295	Minnie Minoso	4.50	1.80	.45
☐ 296	Ryne Duren	6.50	2.60	.65
☐ 297	Don Buddin	2.00	.80	.20
☐ 298	Jim Hearn	2.00	.80	.20
☐ 299	Harry Simpson	2.00	.80	.20
☐ 300	Harridge and Giles League Presidents	4.00	1.60	.40
☐ 301	Randy Jackson	2.00	.80	.20
☐ 302	Mike Baxes	2.00	.80	.20
☐ 303	Neil Chrisley	2.00	.80	.20
☐ 304	Tigers' Big Bats Harvey Kuenn Al Kaline	6.50	2.60	.65
☐ 305	Clem Labine	3.00	1.20	.30
☐ 306	Whammy Douglas	2.00	.80	.20
☐ 307	Brooks Robinson	45.00	18.00	4.50
☐ 308	Paul Giel	2.00	.80	.20
☐ 309	Gail Harris	2.00	.80	.20
☐ 310	Ernie Banks	35.00	14.00	3.50
☐ 311	Bob Purkey	2.00	.80	.20
☐ 312	Boston Red Sox Team Card (checklist on back)	7.00	2.00	.40
☐ 313	Bob Rush	2.00	.80	.20
☐ 314	Dodgers' Boss and Power: Duke Snider Walt Alston	12.50	5.00	1.25
☐ 315	Bob Friend	3.00	1.20	.30
☐ 316	Tito Francona	2.00	.80	.20
☐ 317	Albie Pearson	3.00	1.20	.30
☐ 318	Frank House	2.00	.80	.20
☐ 319	Lou Skizas	2.00	.80	.20
☐ 320	Whitey Ford	27.00	11.00	2.70
☐ 321	Sluggers Supreme Ted Kluszewski Ted Williams	18.00	7.25	1.80
☐ 322	Harding Peterson	2.00	.80	.20
☐ 323	Elmer Valo	2.00	.80	.20
☐ 324	Hoyt Wilhelm	12.00	5.00	1.20
☐ 325	Joe Adcock	3.00	1.20	.30
☐ 326	Bob Miller	2.00	.80	.20
☐ 327	Chicago Cubs Team Card (checklist on back)	5.00	1.50	.30
☐ 328	Ike Delock	2.00	.80	.20
☐ 329	Bob Cerv	2.50	1.00	.25
☐ 330	Ed Bailey	2.50	1.00	.25
☐ 331	Pedro Ramos	2.00	.80	.20
☐ 332	Jim King	2.00	.80	.20
☐ 333	Andy Carey	3.00	1.20	.30
☐ 334	Mound Aces Bob Friend Billy Pierce	3.00	1.20	.30
☐ 335	Ruben Gomez	2.00	.80	.20
☐ 336	Bert Hamric	2.00	.80	.20
☐ 337	Hank Aguirre	2.00	.80	.20
☐ 338	Walt Dropo	2.00	.80	.20
☐ 339	Fred Hatfield	2.00	.80	.20
☐ 340	Don Newcombe	5.00	2.00	.50
☐ 341	Pittsburgh Pirates Team Card	5.00	1.50	.30

	(checklist on back)			
□ 342	Jim Brosnan	2.50	1.00	.25
□ 343	Orlando Cepeda	30.00	12.00	3.00
□ 344	Bob Porterfield	2.00	.80	.20
□ 345	Jim Hegan	2.50	1.00	.25
□ 346	Steve Bilko	2.00	.80	.20
□ 347	Don Rudolph	2.00	.80	.20
□ 348	Chico Fernandez	2.00	.80	.20
□ 349	Murry Dickson	2.00	.80	.20
□ 350	Ken Boyer	4.50	1.80	.45
□ 351	Braves Fence Busters	16.00	6.50	1.60
	Del Crandall			
	Eddie Mathews			
	Hank Aaron			
	Joe Adcock			
□ 352	Herb Score	3.50	1.40	.35
□ 353	Stan Lopata	2.00	.80	.20
□ 354	Art Ditmar	2.50	1.00	.25
□ 355	Bill Bruton	2.50	1.00	.25
□ 356	Bob Malkmus	2.00	.80	.20
□ 357	Danny McDevitt	2.00	.80	.20
□ 358	Gene Baker	2.00	.80	.20
□ 359	Billy Loes	2.00	.80	.20
□ 360	Roy McMillan	2.00	.80	.20
□ 361	Mike Fornieles	2.00	.80	.20
□ 362	Ray Jablonski	2.00	.80	.20
□ 363	Don Elston	2.00	.80	.20
□ 364	Earl Battey	2.50	1.00	.25
□ 365	Tom Morgan	2.00	.80	.20
□ 366	Gene Green	2.00	.80	.20
□ 367	Jack Urban	2.00	.80	.20
□ 368	Rocky Colavito	7.50	3.00	.75
□ 369	Ralph Lumenti	2.00	.80	.20
□ 370	Yogi Berra	50.00	20.00	5.00
□ 371	Marty Keough	2.00	.80	.20
□ 372	Don Cardwell	2.00	.80	.20
□ 373	Joe Pignatano	2.00	.80	.20
□ 374	Brooks Lawrence	2.00	.80	.20
□ 375	Pee Wee Reese	28.00	11.50	2.80
□ 376	Charley Rabe	2.00	.80	.20
□ 377A	Milwaukee Braves	6.00	2.40	.60
	Team Card			
	(alphabetical)			
□ 377B	Milwaukee Team	45.00	5.00	1.00
	numerical checklist			
□ 378	Hank Sauer	2.50	1.00	.25
□ 379	Ray Herbert	2.00	.80	.20
□ 380	Charley Maxwell	2.00	.80	.20
□ 381	Hal Brown	2.00	.80	.20
□ 382	Al Cicotte	2.50	1.00	.25
□ 383	Lou Berberet	2.00	.80	.20
□ 384	John Goryl	2.00	.80	.20
□ 385	Wilmer Mizell	2.00	.80	.20
□ 386	Birdie's Sluggers	6.00	2.40	.60
	Ed Bailey			
	Birdie Tebbetts			
	Frank Robinson			
□ 387	Wally Post	2.50	1.00	.25
□ 388	Billy Moran	2.00	.80	.20
□ 389	Bill Taylor	2.00	.80	.20
□ 390	Del Crandall	2.50	1.00	.25
□ 391	Dave Melton	2.00	.80	.20
□ 392	Bennie Daniels	2.00	.80	.20
□ 393	Tony Kubek	11.00	4.50	1.10
□ 394	Jim Grant	2.50	1.00	.25
□ 395	Willard Nixon	2.00	.80	.20
□ 396	Dutch Dotterer	2.00	.80	.20
□ 397A	Detroit Tigers	6.00	2.40	.60
	Team Card			
	(alphabetical)			
□ 397B	Detroit Team	45.00	5.00	1.00
	numerical checklist			
□ 398	Gene Woodling	3.00	1.20	.30
□ 399	Marv Grissom	2.00	.80	.20
□ 400	Nellie Fox	7.50	3.00	.75
□ 401	Don Bessent	2.50	1.00	.25
□ 402	Bobby Gene Smith	2.00	.80	.20
□ 403	Steve Korcheck	2.00	.80	.20
□ 404	Curt Simmons	2.50	1.00	.25
□ 405	Ken Aspromonte	2.00	.80	.20
□ 406	Vic Power	2.50	1.00	.25
□ 407	Carlton Willey	2.00	.80	.20
□ 408A	Baltimore Orioles	6.00	2.40	.60
	Team Card			
	(alphabetical)			
□ 408B	Baltimore Team	45.00	5.00	1.00
	numerical checklist			
□ 409	Frank Thomas	2.50	1.00	.25
□ 410	Murray Wall	2.00	.80	.20
□ 411	Tony Taylor	2.00	.80	.20
□ 412	Jerry Staley	2.00	.80	.20
□ 413	Jim Davenport	2.50	1.00	.25
□ 414	Sammy White	2.00	.80	.20
□ 415	Bob Bowman	2.00	.80	.20
□ 416	Foster Castleman	2.00	.80	.20
□ 417	Carl Furillo	6.00	2.40	.60
□ 418	World Series Batting	100.00	40.00	10.00
	Foes: Mickey Mantle			
	Hank Aaron			
□ 419	Bobby Shantz	4.00	1.60	.40
□ 420	Vada Pinson	12.00	5.00	1.20
□ 421	Dixie Howell	2.00	.80	.20
□ 422	Norm Zauchin	2.00	.80	.20
□ 423	Phil Clark	2.00	.80	.20
□ 424	Larry Doby	4.00	1.60	.40
□ 425	Sammy Esposito	2.00	.80	.20
□ 426	Johnny O'Brien	2.00	.80	.20
□ 427	Al Worthington	2.00	.80	.20
□ 428A	Cincinnati Reds	6.00	2.40	.60
	Team Card			
	(alphabetical)			
□ 428B	Cincinnati Team	45.00	5.00	1.00
	numerical checklist			
□ 429	Gus Triandos	2.50	1.00	.25
□ 430	Bobby Thomson	3.50	1.40	.35
□ 431	Gene Conley	2.00	.80	.20
□ 432	John Powers	2.00	.80	.20
□ 433A	Pancho Herrer ERR	400.00	160.00	40.00
□ 433B	Pancho Herrera COR	2.50	1.00	.25
□ 434	Harvey Kuenn	4.50	1.80	.45
□ 435	Ed Roebuck	2.50	1.00	.25
□ 436	Rival Fence Busters	40.00	16.00	4.00
	Willie Mays			
	Duke Snider			
□ 437	Bob Speake	2.00	.80	.20
□ 438	Whitey Herzog	4.00	1.60	.40
□ 439	Ray Narleski	2.00	.80	.20
□ 440	Eddie Mathews	20.00	8.00	2.00
□ 441	Jim Marshall	1.75	.70	.17
□ 442	Phil Paine	1.75	.70	.17
□ 443	Billy Harrell SP	7.50	3.00	.75
□ 444	Danny Kravitz	1.75	.70	.17
□ 445	Bob Smith	1.75	.70	.17
□ 446	Carroll Hardy SP	7.50	3.00	.75
□ 447	Ray Monzant	1.75	.70	.17
□ 448	Charlie Lau	4.00	1.60	.40
□ 449	Gene Fodge	1.75	.70	.17
□ 450	Preston Ward SP	7.50	3.00	.75
□ 451	Joe Taylor	1.75	.70	.17
□ 452	Roman Mejias	1.75	.70	.17
□ 453	Tom Qualters	1.75	.70	.17
□ 454	Harry Hanebrink	1.75	.70	.17
□ 455	Hal Griggs	1.75	.70	.17
□ 456	Dick Brown	1.75	.70	.17
□ 457	Milt Pappas	3.50	1.40	.35
□ 458	Julio Becquer	1.75	.70	.17
□ 459	Ron Blackburn	1.75	.70	.17
□ 460	Chuck Essegian	1.75	.70	.17
□ 461	Ed Mayer	1.75	.70	.17
□ 462	Gary Geiger SP	7.50	3.00	.75
□ 463	Vito Valentinetti	1.75	.70	.17
□ 464	Curt Flood	10.00	4.00	1.00
□ 465	Arnie Portocarrero	1.75	.70	.17
□ 466	Pete Whisenant	1.75	.70	.17
□ 467	Glen Hobbie	1.75	.70	.17
□ 468	Bob Schmidt	1.75	.70	.17
□ 469	Don Ferrarese	1.75	.70	.17
□ 470	R.C. Stevens	1.75	.70	.17
□ 471	Lenny Green	1.75	.70	.17
□ 472	Joey Jay	2.50	1.00	.25
□ 473	Bill Renna	1.75	.70	.17
□ 474	Roman Semproch	1.75	.70	.17
□ 475	Haney/Stengel AS	12.50	4.00	.80
	(checklist back)			
□ 476	Stan Musial AS TP	21.00	8.50	2.10
□ 477	Bill Skowron AS	3.50	1.40	.35
□ 478	Johnny Temple AS	2.00	.80	.20
□ 479	Nellie Fox AS	4.50	1.80	.45
□ 480	Eddie Mathews AS	9.00	3.75	.90
□ 481	Frank Malzone AS	2.00	.80	.20
□ 482	Ernie Banks AS	11.00	4.50	1.10
□ 483	Luis Aparicio AS	7.00	2.80	.70
□ 484	Frank Robinson AS	10.00	4.00	1.00
□ 485	Ted Williams AS	40.00	16.00	4.00
□ 486	Willie Mays AS	25.00	10.00	2.50
□ 487	Mickey Mantle AS TP	50.00	20.00	5.00
□ 488	Hank Aaron AS	25.00	10.00	2.50
□ 489	Jackie Jensen AS	3.00	1.20	.30
□ 490	Ed Bailey AS	2.00	.80	.20
□ 491	Sherm Lollar AS	2.00	.80	.20
□ 492	Bob Friend AS	2.00	.80	.20
□ 493	Bob Turley AS	2.50	1.00	.25
□ 494	Warren Spahn AS	10.00	4.00	1.00
□ 495	Herb Score AS	4.00	1.60	.40

FAMILY FUN: Take along a family member with you to a sports show.

1959 Topps

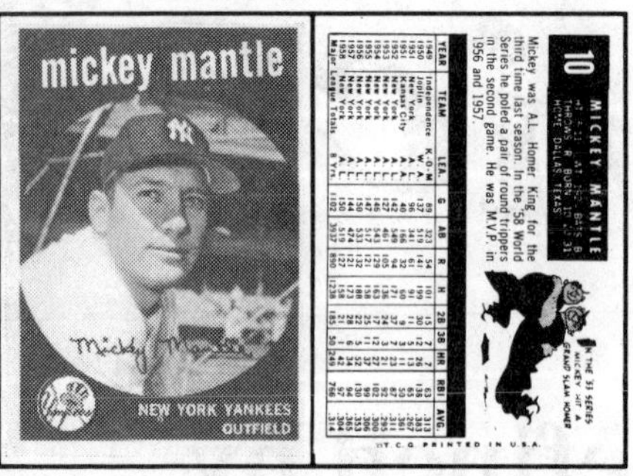

The cards in this 572-card set measure 2 1/2" by 3 1/2". The 1959 Topps set contains bust pictures of the players in a colored circle. Card numbers 551 to 572 are Sporting News All-Star Selections. High numbers 507 to 572 have the card number in a black background on the reverse rather than a green background as in the lower numbers. The high numbers are more difficult to obtain. Several cards in the 300's exist with or without an extra traded or option line on the back of the card. Cards 199 to 286 exist with either white or gray backs. Cards 461 to 470 contain "Highlights" while cards 116 to 146 give an alphabetically ordered listing of "Rookie Prospects." These Rookie Prospects (RP) were Topps' first organized inclusion of untested "Rookie" cards. Card 440 features Lew Burdette erroneously posing as a left handed pitcher. There were some three-card advertising panels produced by Topps; the players included are from the first series; one panel shows Don McMahon, Red Wilson, and Bob Boyd on the front with Ted Kluszewski's reverse on one of the backs. When cut apart, these advertising cards are distinguished by the non-standard card back, i.e., part of an advertisement for the 1959 Topps set instead of the typical statistics and biographical information about the player pictured.

	NRMT	VG-E	GOOD
COMPLETE SET (572)	3250.00	1400.00	500.00
COMMON PLAYER (1-110)	2.25	.90	.22
COMMON PLAYER (111-506)	1.75	.70	.17
COMMON PLAYER (507-550)	7.50	3.00	.75
COMMON PLAYER (551-572)	9.00	3.75	.90

		NRMT	VG-E	GOOD
☐ 1	Ford Frick	35.00	3.50	.70
☐ 2	Eddie Yost	2.25	.90	.22
☐ 3	Don McMahon	2.25	.90	.22
☐ 4	Albie Pearson	2.25	.90	.22
☐ 5	Dick Donovan	2.25	.90	.22
☐ 6	Alex Grammas	2.25	.90	.22
☐ 7	Al Pilarcik	2.25	.90	.22
☐ 8	Phillies Team (checklist on back)	6.50	1.50	.25
☐ 9	Paul Giel	2.25	.90	.22
☐ 10	Mickey Mantle	300.00	120.00	30.00
☐ 11	Billy Hunter	2.25	.90	.22
☐ 12	Vern Law	3.00	1.20	.30
☐ 13	Dick Gernert	2.25	.90	.22
☐ 14	Pete Whisenant	2.25	.90	.22
☐ 15	Dick Drott	2.25	.90	.22
☐ 16	Joe Pignatano	2.25	.90	.22
☐ 17	Danny's Stars Frank Thomas Danny Murtaugh Ted Kluszewski	3.50	1.40	.35
☐ 18	Jack Urban	2.25	.90	.22
☐ 19	Eddie Bressoud	2.25	.90	.22
☐ 20	Duke Snider	40.00	16.00	4.00
☐ 21	Connie Johnson	2.25	.90	.22
☐ 22	Al Smith	2.25	.90	.22
☐ 23	Murry Dickson	2.25	.90	.22
☐ 24	Red Wilson	2.25	.90	.22
☐ 25	Don Hoak	3.00	1.20	.30
☐ 26	Chuck Stobbs	2.25	.90	.22
☐ 27	Andy Pafko	3.00	1.20	.30
☐ 28	Al Worthington	2.25	.90	.22
☐ 29	Jim Bolger	2.25	.90	.22
☐ 30	Nellie Fox	7.00	2.80	.70
☐ 31	Ken Lehman	2.25	.90	.22
☐ 32	Don Buddin	2.25	.90	.22
☐ 33	Ed Fitzgerald	2.25	.90	.22
☐ 34	Pitchers Beware Al Kaline Charley Maxwell	6.00	2.40	.60
☐ 35	Ted Kluszewski	5.00	2.00	.50
☐ 36	Hank Aguirre	2.25	.90	.22
☐ 37	Gene Green	2.25	.90	.22
☐ 38	Morrie Martin	2.25	.90	.22
☐ 39	Ed Bouchee	2.25	.90	.22
☐ 40	Warren Spahn	25.00	10.00	2.50
☐ 41	Bob Martyn	2.25	.90	.22
☐ 42	Murray Wall	2.25	.90	.22
☐ 43	Steve Bilko	2.25	.90	.22
☐ 44	Vito Valentinetti	2.25	.90	.22
☐ 45	Andy Carey	3.50	1.40	.35
☐ 46	Bill R. Henry	2.25	.90	.22
☐ 47	Jim Finigan	2.25	.90	.22
☐ 48	Orioles Team (checklist on back)	6.50	1.50	.25
☐ 49	Bill Hall	2.25	.90	.22
☐ 50	Willie Mays	90.00	36.00	9.00
☐ 51	Rip Coleman	2.25	.90	.22
☐ 52	Coot Veal	2.25	.90	.22
☐ 53	Stan Williams	2.25	.90	.22
☐ 54	Mel Roach	2.25	.90	.22
☐ 55	Tom Brewer	2.25	.90	.22
☐ 56	Carl Sawatski	2.25	.90	.22
☐ 57	Al Cicotte	2.25	.90	.22
☐ 58	Eddie Miksis	2.25	.90	.22
☐ 59	Irv Noren	2.25	.90	.22
☐ 60	Bob Turley	4.50	1.80	.45
☐ 61	Dick Brown	2.25	.90	.22
☐ 62	Tony Taylor	2.25	.90	.22
☐ 63	Jim Hearn	2.25	.90	.22
☐ 64	Joe DeMaestri	2.25	.90	.22
☐ 65	Frank Torre	2.25	.90	.22
☐ 66	Joe Ginsberg	2.25	.90	.22
☐ 67	Brooks Lawrence	2.25	.90	.22
☐ 68	Dick Schofield	2.25	.90	.22
☐ 69	Giants Team (checklist on back)	6.50	1.50	.25
☐ 70	Harvey Kuenn	4.00	1.60	.40
☐ 71	Don Bessent	2.25	.90	.22
☐ 72	Bill Renna	2.25	.90	.22
☐ 73	Ron Jackson	2.25	.90	.22
☐ 74	Directing Power Jim Lemon Cookie Lavagetto Roy Sievers	3.00	1.20	.30
☐ 75	Sam Jones	3.00	1.20	.30
☐ 76	Bobby Richardson	7.00	2.80	.70
☐ 77	John Goryl	2.25	.90	.22
☐ 78	Pedro Ramos	2.25	.90	.22
☐ 79	Harry Chiti	2.25	.90	.22
☐ 80	Minnie Minoso	4.50	1.80	.45
☐ 81	Hal Jeffcoat	2.25	.90	.22
☐ 82	Bob Boyd	2.25	.90	.22
☐ 83	Bob Smith	2.25	.90	.22
☐ 84	Reno Bertoia	2.25	.90	.22
☐ 85	Harry Anderson	2.25	.90	.22
☐ 86	Bob Keegan	2.25	.90	.22
☐ 87	Danny O'Connell	2.25	.90	.22
☐ 88	Herb Score	3.50	1.40	.35
☐ 89	Billy Gardner	3.00	1.20	.30
☐ 90	Bill Skowron	7.00	2.80	.70
☐ 91	Herb Moford	2.25	.90	.22
☐ 92	Dave Philley	2.25	.90	.22
☐ 93	Julio Becquer	2.25	.90	.22
☐ 94	White Sox Team (checklist on back)	6.50	1.50	.25
☐ 95	Carl Willey	2.25	.90	.22
☐ 96	Lou Berberet	2.25	.90	.22
☐ 97	Jerry Lynch	2.25	.90	.22
☐ 98	Arnie Portocarrero	2.25	.90	.22
☐ 99	Ted Kazanski	2.25	.90	.22
☐ 100	Bob Cerv	3.00	1.20	.30
☐ 101	Alex Kellner	2.25	.90	.22
☐ 102	Felipe Alou	6.00	2.40	.60
☐ 103	Billy Goodman	3.00	1.20	.30
☐ 104	Del Rice	2.25	.90	.22
☐ 105	Lee Walls	2.25	.90	.22
☐ 106	Hal Woodeshick	2.25	.90	.22
☐ 107	Norm Larker	3.00	1.20	.30
☐ 108	Zack Monroe	2.25	.90	.22
☐ 109	Bob Schmidt	2.25	.90	.22
☐ 110	George Witt	2.25	.90	.22
☐ 111	Redlegs Team (checklist on back)	6.00	1.50	.25

□ 112 Billy Consolo	1.75	.70	.17
□ 113 Taylor Phillips	1.75	.70	.17
□ 114 Earl Battey	1.75	.70	.17
□ 115 Mickey Vernon	2.50	1.00	.25
□ 116 Bob Allison RP	4.50	1.80	.45
□ 117 John Blanchard RP	2.50	1.00	.25
□ 118 John Buzhardt RP	1.75	.70	.17
□ 119 John Callison RP	3.50	1.40	.35
□ 120 Chuck Coles RP	1.75	.70	.17
□ 121 Bob Conley RP	1.75	.70	.17
□ 122 Bennie Daniels RP	1.75	.70	.17
□ 123 Don Dillard RP	1.75	.70	.17
□ 124 Dan Dobbek RP	1.75	.70	.17
□ 125 Ron Fairly RP	3.50	1.40	.35
□ 126 Ed Haas RP	2.50	1.00	.25
□ 127 Kent Hadley RP	1.75	.70	.17
□ 128 Bob Hartman RP	1.75	.70	.17
□ 129 Frank Herrera RP	1.75	.70	.17
□ 130 Lou Jackson RP	1.75	.70	.17
□ 131 Deron Johnson RP	2.50	1.00	.25
□ 132 Don Lee RP	1.75	.70	.17
□ 133 Bob Lillis RP	2.50	1.00	.25
□ 134 Jim McDaniel RP	1.75	.70	.17
□ 135 Gene Oliver RP	1.75	.70	.17
□ 136 Jim O'Toole RP	2.50	1.00	.25
□ 137 Dick Ricketts RP	1.75	.70	.17
□ 138 John Romano RP	2.50	1.00	.25
□ 139 Ed Sadowski RP	1.75	.70	.17
□ 140 Charlie Secrest RP	1.75	.70	.17
□ 141 Joe Shipley RP	1.75	.70	.17
□ 142 Dick Stigman RP	1.75	.70	.17
□ 143 Willie Tasby RP	1.75	.70	.17
□ 144 Jerry Walker RP	1.75	.70	.17
□ 145 Dom Zanni RP	1.75	.70	.17
□ 146 Jerry Zimmerman RP	1.75	.70	.17
□ 147 Cubs Clubbers Dale Long Ernie Banks Walt Moryn	6.50	2.60	.65
□ 148 Mike McCormick	2.50	1.00	.25
□ 149 Jim Bunning	8.00	3.25	.80
□ 150 Stan Musial	85.00	34.00	8.50
□ 151 Bob Malkmus	1.75	.70	.17
□ 152 Johnny Klippstein	1.75	.70	.17
□ 153 Jim Marshall	1.75	.70	.17
□ 154 Ray Herbert	1.75	.70	.17
□ 155 Enos Slaughter	12.00	5.00	1.20
□ 156 Ace Hurlers Billy Pierce Robin Roberts	3.50	1.40	.35
□ 157 Felix Mantilla	1.75	.70	.17
□ 158 Walt Dropo	1.75	.70	.17
□ 159 Bob Shaw	1.75	.70	.17
□ 160 Dick Groat	3.50	1.40	.35
□ 161 Frank Baumann	1.75	.70	.17
□ 162 Bobby G. Smith	1.75	.70	.17
□ 163 Sandy Koufax	70.00	28.00	7.00
□ 164 Johnny Groth	1.75	.70	.17
□ 165 Bill Bruton	1.75	.70	.17
□ 166 Destruction Crew Minnie Minoso Rocky Colavito (misspelled Colovito on card back) Larry Doby	3.00	1.20	.30
□ 167 Duke Maas	1.75	.70	.17
□ 168 Carroll Hardy	1.75	.70	.17
□ 169 Ted Abernathy	1.75	.70	.17
□ 170 Gene Woodling	2.50	1.00	.25
□ 171 Willard Schmidt	1.75	.70	.17
□ 172 Athletics Team (checklist on back)	6.00	1.50	.25
□ 173 Bill Monbouquette	1.75	.70	.17
□ 174 Jim Pendleton	1.75	.70	.17
□ 175 Dick Farrell	1.75	.70	.17
□ 176 Preston Ward	1.75	.70	.17
□ 177 John Briggs	1.75	.70	.17
□ 178 Ruben Amaro	1.75	.70	.17
□ 179 Don Rudolph	1.75	.70	.17
□ 180 Yogi Berra	40.00	16.00	4.00
□ 181 Bob Porterfield	1.75	.70	.17
□ 182 Milt Graff	1.75	.70	.17
□ 183 Stu Miller	1.75	.70	.17
□ 184 Harvey Haddix	2.50	1.00	.25
□ 185 Jim Busby	1.75	.70	.17
□ 186 Mudcat Grant	1.75	.70	.17
□ 187 Bubba Phillips	1.75	.70	.17
□ 188 Juan Pizarro	1.75	.70	.17
□ 189 Neil Chrisley	1.75	.70	.17
□ 190 Bill Virdon	3.00	1.20	.30
□ 191 Russ Kemmerer	1.75	.70	.17
□ 192 Charlie Beamon	1.75	.70	.17
□ 193 Sammy Taylor	1.75	.70	.17
□ 194 Jim Brosnan	1.75	.70	.17
□ 195 Rip Repulski	1.75	.70	.17
□ 196 Billy Moran	1.75	.70	.17
□ 197 Ray Semproch	1.75	.70	.17
□ 198 Jim Davenport	2.50	1.00	.25
□ 199 Leo Kiely	1.75	.70	.17
□ 200 Warren Giles (NL President)	4.00	1.60	.40
□ 201 Tom Acker	1.75	.70	.17
□ 202 Roger Maris	85.00	34.00	8.50
□ 203 Ossie Virgil	1.75	.70	.17
□ 204 Casey Wise	1.75	.70	.17
□ 205 Don Larsen	4.00	1.60	.40
□ 206 Carl Furillo	4.50	1.80	.45
□ 207 George Strickland	1.75	.70	.17
□ 208 Willie Jones	1.75	.70	.17
□ 209 Lenny Green	1.75	.70	.17
□ 210 Ed Bailey	1.75	.70	.17
□ 211 Bob Blaylock	1.75	.70	.17
□ 212 Fence Busters Hank Aaron Eddie Mathews	16.00	6.50	1.60
□ 213 Jim Rivera	1.75	.70	.17
□ 214 Marcelino Solis	1.75	.70	.17
□ 215 Jim Lemon	1.75	.70	.17
□ 216 Andre Rodgers	1.75	.70	.17
□ 217 Carl Erskine	3.50	1.40	.35
□ 218 Roman Mejias	1.75	.70	.17
□ 219 George Zuverink	1.75	.70	.17
□ 220 Frank Malzone	2.50	1.00	.25
□ 221 Bob Bowman	1.75	.70	.17
□ 222 Bobby Shantz	3.00	1.20	.30
□ 223 Cardinals Team (checklist on back)	6.00	1.50	.25
□ 224 Claude Osteen	3.00	1.20	.30
□ 225 Johnny Logan	2.50	1.00	.25
□ 226 Art Ceccarelli	1.75	.70	.17
□ 227 Hal W. Smith	1.75	.70	.17
□ 228 Don Gross	1.75	.70	.17
□ 229 Vic Power	1.75	.70	.17
□ 230 Bill Fischer	1.75	.70	.17
□ 231 Ellis Burton	1.75	.70	.17
□ 232 Eddie Kasko	1.75	.70	.17
□ 233 Paul Foytack	1.75	.70	.17
□ 234 Chuck Tanner	2.50	1.00	.25
□ 235 Valmy Thomas	1.75	.70	.17
□ 236 Ted Bowsfield	1.75	.70	.17
□ 237 Run Preventers Gil McDougald Bob Turley Bobby Richardson	4.50	1.80	.45
□ 238 Gene Baker	1.75	.70	.17
□ 239 Bob Trowbridge	1.75	.70	.17
□ 240 Hank Bauer	4.50	1.80	.45
□ 241 Billy Muffett	1.75	.70	.17
□ 242 Ron Samford	1.75	.70	.17
□ 243 Marv Grissom	1.75	.70	.17
□ 244 Ted Gray	1.75	.70	.17
□ 245 Ned Garver	1.75	.70	.17
□ 246 J.W. Porter	1.75	.70	.17
□ 247 Don Ferrarese	1.75	.70	.17
□ 248 Red Sox Team (checklist on back)	6.50	1.50	.25
□ 249 Bobby Adams	1.75	.70	.17
□ 250 Billy O'Dell	1.75	.70	.17
□ 251 Clete Boyer	3.50	1.40	.35
□ 252 Ray Boone	2.50	1.00	.25
□ 253 Seth Morehead	1.75	.70	.17
□ 254 Zeke Bella	1.75	.70	.17
□ 255 Del Ennis	2.50	1.00	.25
□ 256 Jerry Davie	1.75	.70	.17
□ 257 Leon Wagner	1.75	.70	.17
□ 258 Fred Kipp	1.75	.70	.17
□ 259 Jim Pisoni	1.75	.70	.17
□ 260 Early Wynn	12.00	5.00	1.20
□ 261 Gene Stephens	1.75	.70	.17
□ 262 Hitters' Foes Johnny Podres Clem Labine Don Drysdale	4.50	1.80	.45
□ 263 Bud Daley	1.75	.70	.17
□ 264 Chico Carrasquel	1.75	.70	.17
□ 265 Ron Kline	1.75	.70	.17
□ 266 Woody Held	1.75	.70	.17
□ 267 John Romonosky	1.75	.70	.17
□ 268 Tito Francona	2.50	1.00	.25
□ 269 Jack Meyer	1.75	.70	.17
□ 270 Gil Hodges	12.50	5.00	1.25
□ 271 Orlando Pena	1.75	.70	.17
□ 272 Jerry Lumpe	1.75	.70	.17
□ 273 Joey Jay	1.75	.70	.17
□ 274 Jerry Kindall	2.50	1.00	.25
□ 275 Jack Sanford	2.50	1.00	.25
□ 276 Pete Daley	1.75	.70	.17
□ 277 Turk Lown	1.75	.70	.17
□ 278 Chuck Essegian	2.50	1.00	.25
□ 279 Ernie Johnson	1.75	.70	.17

□ 280	Frank Bolling	1.75	.70	.17
□ 281	Walt Craddock	1.75	.70	.17
□ 282	R.C. Stevens	1.75	.70	.17
□ 283	Russ Heman	1.75	.70	.17
□ 284	Steve Korcheck	1.75	.70	.17
□ 285	Joe Cunningham	2.50	1.00	.25
□ 286	Dean Stone	1.75	.70	.17
□ 287	Don Zimmer	3.50	1.40	.35
□ 288	Dutch Dotterer	1.75	.70	.17
□ 289	Johnny Kucks	2.50	1.00	.25
□ 290	Wes Covington	2.50	1.00	.25
□ 291	Pitching Partners Pedro Ramos Camilo Pascual	2.50	1.00	.25
□ 292	Dick Williams	2.50	1.00	.25
□ 293	Ray Moore	1.75	.70	.17
□ 294	Hank Foiles	1.75	.70	.17
□ 295	Billy Martin	6.50	2.60	.65
□ 296	Ernie Broglio	2.50	1.00	.25
□ 297	Jackie Brandt	1.75	.70	.17
□ 298	Tex Clevenger	1.75	.70	.17
□ 299	Billy Klaus	1.75	.70	.17
□ 300	Richie Ashburn	7.00	2.80	.70
□ 301	Earl Averill	1.75	.70	.17
□ 302	Don Mossi	2.50	1.00	.25
□ 303	Marty Keough	1.75	.70	.17
□ 304	Cubs Team (checklist on back)	6.00	1.50	.25
□ 305	Curt Raydon	1.75	.70	.17
□ 306	Jim Gilliam	4.50	1.80	.45
□ 307	Curt Barclay	1.75	.70	.17
□ 308	Norm Siebern	1.75	.70	.17
□ 309	Sal Maglie	3.50	1.40	.35
□ 310	Luis Aparicio	11.00	4.50	1.10
□ 311	Norm Zauchin	1.75	.70	.17
□ 312	Don Newcombe	3.00	1.20	.30
□ 313	Frank House	1.75	.70	.17
□ 314	Don Cardwell	1.75	.70	.17
□ 315	Joe Adcock	3.00	1.20	.30
□ 316A	Ralph Lumenti (option) (photo actually Camilo Pascual)	1.75	.70	.17
□ 316B	Ralph Lumenti (no option) (photo actually Camilo Pascual)	75.00	30.00	7.50
□ 317	Hitting Kings Willie Mays Richie Ashburn	12.50	5.00	1.25
□ 318	Rocky Bridges	1.75	.70	.17
□ 319	Dave Hillman	1.75	.70	.17
□ 320	Bob Skinner	2.50	1.00	.25
□ 321A	Bob Giallombardo (option)	1.75	.70	.17
□ 321B	Bob Giallombardo (no option)	75.00	30.00	7.50
□ 322A	Harry Hanebrink (traded)	1.75	.70	.17
□ 322B	Harry Hanebrink (no trade)	75.00	30.00	7.50
□ 323	Frank Sullivan	1.75	.70	.17
□ 324	Don Demeter	1.75	.70	.17
□ 325	Ken Boyer	4.00	1.60	.40
□ 326	Marv Throneberry	3.00	1.20	.30
□ 327	Gary Bell	1.75	.70	.17
□ 328	Lou Skizas	1.75	.70	.17
□ 329	Tigers Team (checklist on back)	6.50	1.50	.25
□ 330	Gus Triandos	2.50	1.00	.25
□ 331	Steve Boros	2.50	1.00	.25
□ 332	Ray Monzant	1.75	.70	.17
□ 333	Harry Simpson	1.75	.70	.17
□ 334	Glen Hobbie	1.75	.70	.17
□ 335	Johnny Temple	2.50	1.00	.25
□ 336A	Billy Loes (with traded line)	1.75	.70	.17
□ 336B	Billy Loes (no trade)	75.00	30.00	7.50
□ 337	George Crowe	1.75	.70	.17
□ 338	Sparky Anderson	11.00	4.50	1.10
□ 339	Roy Face	3.50	1.40	.35
□ 340	Roy Sievers	2.50	1.00	.25
□ 341	Tom Qualters	1.75	.70	.17
□ 342	Ray Jablonski	1.75	.70	.17
□ 343	Billy Hoeft	1.75	.70	.17
□ 344	Russ Nixon	2.50	1.00	.25
□ 345	Gil McDougald	4.50	1.80	.45
□ 346	Batter Bafflers Dave Sisler Tom Brewer	2.50	1.00	.25
□ 347	Bob Buhl	1.75	.70	.17
□ 348	Ted Lepcio	1.75	.70	.17
□ 349	Hoyt Wilhelm	11.00	4.50	1.10
□ 350	Ernie Banks	30.00	12.00	3.00
□ 351	Earl Torgeson	1.75	.70	.17
□ 352	Robin Roberts	12.00	5.00	1.20
□ 353	Curt Flood	3.50	1.40	.35
□ 354	Pete Burnside	1.75	.70	.17
□ 355	Jim Piersall	3.00	1.20	.30
□ 356	Bob Mabe	1.75	.70	.17
□ 357	Dick Stuart	2.50	1.00	.25
□ 358	Ralph Terry	2.50	1.00	.25
□ 359	Bill White	6.00	2.40	.60
□ 360	Al Kaline	30.00	12.00	3.00
□ 361	Willard Nixon	1.75	.70	.17
□ 362A	Dolan Nichols (with option line)	1.75	.70	.17
□ 362B	Dolan Nichols (no option)	75.00	30.00	7.50
□ 363	Bobby Avila	1.75	.70	.17
□ 364	Danny McDevitt	1.75	.70	.17
□ 365	Gus Bell	2.50	1.00	.25
□ 366	Humberto Robinson	1.75	.70	.17
□ 367	Cal Neeman	1.75	.70	.17
□ 368	Don Mueller	2.50	1.00	.25
□ 369	Dick Tomanek	1.75	.70	.17
□ 370	Pete Runnels	2.50	1.00	.25
□ 371	Dick Brodowski	1.75	.70	.17
□ 372	Jim Hegan	2.50	1.00	.25
□ 373	Herb Plews	1.75	.70	.17
□ 374	Art Ditmar	1.75	.70	.17
□ 375	Bob Nieman	1.75	.70	.17
□ 376	Hal Naragon	1.75	.70	.17
□ 377	John Antonelli	2.50	1.00	.25
□ 378	Gail Harris	1.75	.70	.17
□ 379	Bob Miller	1.75	.70	.17
□ 380	Hank Aaron	70.00	28.00	7.00
□ 381	Mike Baxes	1.75	.70	.17
□ 382	Curt Simmons	2.50	1.00	.25
□ 383	Words of Wisdom Don Larsen Casey Stengel	6.00	2.40	.60
□ 384	Dave Sisler	1.75	.70	.17
□ 385	Sherm Lollar	2.50	1.00	.25
□ 386	Jim Delsing	1.75	.70	.17
□ 387	Don Drysdale	16.00	6.50	1.60
□ 388	Bob Will	1.75	.70	.17
□ 389	Joe Nuxhall	2.50	1.00	.25
□ 390	Orlando Cepeda	7.00	2.80	.70
□ 391	Milt Pappas	2.50	1.00	.25
□ 392	Whitey Herzog	3.50	1.40	.35
□ 393	Frank Lary	2.50	1.00	.25
□ 394	Randy Jackson	1.75	.70	.17
□ 395	Elston Howard	4.50	1.80	.45
□ 396	Bob Rush	1.75	.70	.17
□ 397	Senators Team (checklist on back)	6.00	1.50	.25
□ 398	Wally Post	2.50	1.00	.25
□ 399	Larry Jackson	1.75	.70	.17
□ 400	Jackie Jensen	3.50	1.40	.35
□ 401	Ron Blackburn	1.75	.70	.17
□ 402	Hector Lopez	1.75	.70	.17
□ 403	Clem Labine	2.50	1.00	.25
□ 404	Hank Sauer	2.50	1.00	.25
□ 405	Roy McMillan	1.75	.70	.17
□ 406	Solly Drake	1.75	.70	.17
□ 407	Moe Drabowsky	1.75	.70	.17
□ 408	Keystone Combo Nellie Fox Luis Aparicio	5.50	2.20	.55
□ 409	Gus Zernial	2.50	1.00	.25
□ 410	Billy Pierce	3.00	1.20	.30
□ 411	Whitey Lockman	2.50	1.00	.25
□ 412	Stan Lopata	1.75	.70	.17
□ 413	Camilo Pascual (listed as Camillo on front)	2.50	1.00	.25
□ 414	Dale Long	2.50	1.00	.25
□ 415	Bill Mazeroski	4.50	1.80	.45
□ 416	Haywood Sullivan	2.50	1.00	.25
□ 417	Virgil Trucks	2.50	1.00	.25
□ 418	Gino Cimoli	1.75	.70	.17
□ 419	Braves Team (checklist on back)	6.50	1.50	.25
□ 420	Rocky Colavito	4.50	1.80	.45
□ 421	Herman Wehmeier	1.75	.70	.17
□ 422	Hobie Landrith	1.75	.70	.17
□ 423	Bob Grim	2.50	1.00	.25
□ 424	Ken Aspromonte	1.75	.70	.17
□ 425	Del Crandall	2.50	1.00	.25
□ 426	Jerry Staley	1.75	.70	.17
□ 427	Charlie Neal	2.50	1.00	.25
□ 428	Buc Hill Aces Ron Kline Bob Friend Vernon Law Roy Face	3.00	1.20	.30
□ 429	Bobby Thomson	3.00	1.20	.30
□ 430	Whitey Ford	24.00	10.00	2.40

□ 431	Whammy Douglas	1.75	.70	.17
□ 432	Smoky Burgess	2.50	1.00	.25
□ 433	Billy Harrell	1.75	.70	.17
□ 434	Hal Griggs	1.75	.70	.17
□ 435	Frank Robinson	25.00	10.00	2.50
□ 436	Granny Hamner	1.75	.70	.17
□ 437	Ike Delock	1.75	.70	.17
□ 438	Sammy Esposito	1.75	.70	.17
□ 439	Brooks Robinson	30.00	12.00	3.00
□ 440	Lou Burdette	4.50	1.80	.45
	(posing as if lefthanded)			
□ 441	John Roseboro	2.50	1.00	.25
□ 442	Ray Narleski	1.75	.70	.17
□ 443	Daryl Spencer	1.75	.70	.17
□ 444	Ron Hansen	2.50	1.00	.25
□ 445	Cal McLish	1.75	.70	.17
□ 446	Rocky Nelson	1.75	.70	.17
□ 447	Bob Anderson	1.75	.70	.17
□ 448	Vada Pinson	3.50	1.40	.35
□ 449	Tom Gorman	1.75	.70	.17
□ 450	Eddie Mathews	18.00	7.25	1.80
□ 451	Jimmy Constable	1.75	.70	.17
□ 452	Chico Fernandez	1.75	.70	.17
□ 453	Les Moss	1.75	.70	.17
□ 454	Phil Clark	1.75	.70	.17
□ 455	Larry Doby	3.00	1.20	.30
□ 456	Jerry Casale	1.75	.70	.17
□ 457	Dodgers Team	12.00	3.00	.50
	(checklist on back)			
□ 458	Gordon Jones	1.75	.70	.17
□ 459	Bill Tuttle	1.75	.70	.17
□ 460	Bob Friend	2.50	1.00	.25
□ 461	Mantle Hits Homer	25.00	10.00	2.50
□ 462	Colavito's Catch	3.00	1.20	.30
□ 463	Kaline Batting Champ	6.50	2.60	.65
□ 464	Mays' Series Catch	14.00	5.75	1.40
□ 465	Sievers Sets Mark	2.50	1.00	.25
□ 466	Pierce All-Star	2.50	1.00	.25
□ 467	Aaron Clubs Homer	14.00	5.75	1.40
□ 468	Snider's Play	8.00	3.25	.80
□ 469	Hustler Banks	7.00	2.80	.70
□ 470	Musial's 3000 Hit	10.00	4.00	1.00
□ 471	Tom Sturdivant	1.75	.70	.17
□ 472	Gene Freese	1.75	.70	.17
□ 473	Mike Fornieles	1.75	.70	.17
□ 474	Moe Thacker	1.75	.70	.17
□ 475	Jack Harshman	1.75	.70	.17
□ 476	Indians Team	6.00	1.50	.25
	(checklist on back)			
□ 477	Barry Latman	1.75	.70	.17
□ 478	Bob Clemente	50.00	20.00	5.00
□ 479	Lindy McDaniel	2.50	1.00	.25
□ 480	Red Schoendienst	3.50	1.40	.35
□ 481	Charlie Maxwell	1.75	.70	.17
□ 482	Russ Meyer	1.75	.70	.17
□ 483	Clint Courtney	1.75	.70	.17
□ 484	Willie Kirkland	1.75	.70	.17
□ 485	Ryne Duren	3.00	1.20	.30
□ 486	Sammy White	1.75	.70	.17
□ 487	Hal Brown	1.75	.70	.17
□ 488	Walt Moryn	1.75	.70	.17
□ 489	John Powers	1.75	.70	.17
□ 490	Frank Thomas	2.50	1.00	.25
□ 491	Don Blasingame	1.75	.70	.17
□ 492	Gene Conley	1.75	.70	.17
□ 493	Jim Landis	1.75	.70	.17
□ 494	Don Pavletich	1.75	.70	.17
□ 495	Johnny Podres	3.50	1.40	.35
□ 496	Wayne Terwilliger	1.75	.70	.17
□ 497	Hal R. Smith	1.75	.70	.17
□ 498	Dick Hyde	1.75	.70	.17
□ 499	Johnny O'Brien	1.75	.70	.17
□ 500	Vic Wertz	2.50	1.00	.25
□ 501	Bob Tiefenauer	1.75	.70	.17
□ 502	Alvin Dark	3.00	1.20	.30
□ 503	Jim Owens	1.75	.70	.17
□ 504	Ossie Alvarez	1.75	.70	.17
□ 505	Tony Kubek	7.50	3.00	.75
□ 506	Bob Purkey	1.75	.70	.17
□ 507	Bob Hale	7.50	3.00	.75
□ 508	Art Fowler	7.50	3.00	.75
□ 509	Norm Cash	20.00	8.00	2.00
□ 510	Yankees Team	36.00	6.50	1.25
	(checklist on back)			
□ 511	George Susce	7.50	3.00	.75
□ 512	George Altman	7.50	3.00	.75
□ 513	Tommy Carroll	7.50	3.00	.75
□ 514	Bob Gibson	225.00	90.00	22.00
□ 515	Harmon Killebrew	50.00	20.00	5.00
□ 516	Mike Garcia	9.00	3.75	.90
□ 517	Joe Koppe	7.50	3.00	.75
□ 518	Mike Cueller	12.00	5.00	1.20
	(sic, Cuellar)			
□ 519	Infield Power	10.00	4.00	1.00
	Pete Runnels			
	Dick Gernert			
	Frank Malzone			
□ 520	Don Elston	7.50	3.00	.75
□ 521	Gary Geiger	7.50	3.00	.75
□ 522	Gene Snyder	7.50	3.00	.75
□ 523	Harry Bright	7.50	3.00	.75
□ 524	Larry Osborne	7.50	3.00	.75
□ 525	Jim Coates	7.50	3.00	.75
□ 526	Bob Speake	7.50	3.00	.75
□ 527	Solly Hemus	7.50	3.00	.75
□ 528	Pirates Team	21.00	2.50	.50
	(checklist on back)			
□ 529	George Bamberger	12.00	5.00	1.20
□ 530	Wally Moon	10.00	4.00	1.00
□ 531	Ray Webster	7.50	3.00	.75
□ 532	Mark Freeman	7.50	3.00	.75
□ 533	Darrell Johnson	9.00	3.75	.90
□ 534	Faye Throneberry	7.50	3.00	.75
□ 535	Ruben Gomez	7.50	3.00	.75
□ 536	Danny Kravitz	7.50	3.00	.75
□ 537	Rudolph Arias	7.50	3.00	.75
□ 538	Chick King	7.50	3.00	.75
□ 539	Gary Blaylock	7.50	3.00	.75
□ 540	Willie Miranda	7.50	3.00	.75
□ 541	Bob Thurman	7.50	3.00	.75
□ 542	Jim Perry	12.00	5.00	1.20
□ 543	Corsair Trio	30.00	12.00	3.00
	Bob Skinner			
	Bill Virdon			
	Roberto Clemente			
□ 544	Lee Tate	7.50	3.00	.75
□ 545	Tom Morgan	7.50	3.00	.75
□ 546	Al Schroll	7.50	3.00	.75
□ 547	Jim Baxes	7.50	3.00	.75
□ 548	Elmer Singleton	7.50	3.00	.75
□ 549	Howie Nunn	7.50	3.00	.75
□ 550	Roy Campanella	80.00	32.00	8.00
	(Symbol of Courage)			
□ 551	Fred Haney MG AS	9.00	3.75	.90
□ 552	Casey Stengel MG AS	18.00	7.25	1.80
□ 553	Orlando Cepeda AS	12.00	5.00	1.20
□ 554	Bill Skowron AS	10.00	4.00	1.00
□ 555	Bill Mazeroski AS	10.00	4.00	1.00
□ 556	Nellie Fox AS	12.00	5.00	1.20
□ 557	Ken Boyer AS	10.00	4.00	1.00
□ 558	Frank Malzone AS	9.00	3.75	.90
□ 559	Ernie Banks AS	25.00	10.00	2.50
□ 560	Luis Aparicio AS	15.00	6.00	1.50
□ 561	Hank Aaron AS	60.00	24.00	6.00
□ 562	Al Kaline AS	28.00	11.50	2.80
□ 563	Willie Mays AS	60.00	24.00	6.00
□ 564	Mickey Mantle AS	150.00	60.00	15.00
□ 565	Wes Covington AS	9.00	3.75	.90
□ 566	Roy Sievers AS	9.00	3.75	.90
□ 567	Del Crandall AS	9.00	3.75	.90
□ 568	Gus Triandos AS	9.00	3.75	.90
□ 569	Bob Friend AS	9.00	3.75	.90
□ 570	Bob Turley AS	10.00	4.00	1.00
□ 571	Warren Spahn AS	25.00	10.00	2.50
□ 572	Billy Pierce AS	10.00	4.00	1.00

1960 Topps

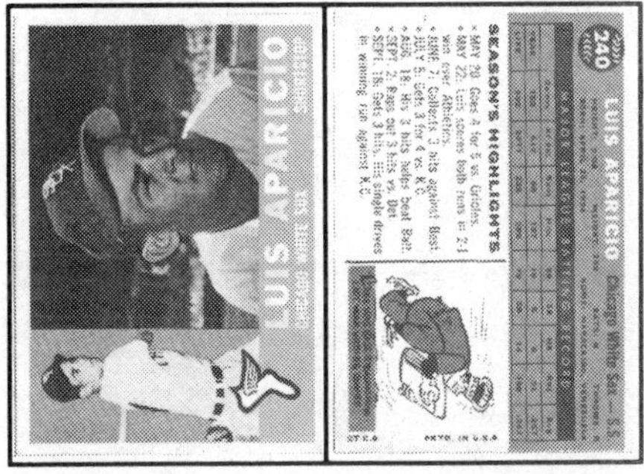

The cards in this 572-card set measure 2 1/2" by 3 1/2". The 1960 Topps set is the only Topps standard size issue to use a horizontally oriented front. World Series cards appeared for the first time (385 to 391), and there is a Rookie Prospect (RP) series (117-

148), the most famous of which is Carl Yastrzemski, and a Sport Magazine All-Star Selection (AS) series (553-572). There are 16 manager cards listed alphabetically from 212 through 227. The coaching staff of each team was also afforded their own card in a 16-card subset (455-470). Cards 375 to 440 come with either gray or white backs, and the high series (507-572) were printed on a more limited basis than the rest of the set. The team cards have series checklists on the reverse.

	NRMT	VG-E	GOOD
COMPLETE SET (572)	3000.00	1350.00	450.00
COMMON PLAYER (1-286)	1.25	.50	.12
COMMON PLAYER (287-440)	1.50	.60	.15
COMMON PLAYER (441-506)	2.50	1.00	.25
COMMON PLAYER (507-552)	7.00	2.80	.70
COMMON PLAYER (553-572)	8.00	3.25	.80

		NRMT	VG-E	GOOD
□ 1	Early Wynn	25.00	5.00	1.00
□ 2	Roman Mejias	1.25	.50	.12
□ 3	Joe Adcock	1.75	.70	.17
□ 4	Bob Purkey	1.25	.50	.12
□ 5	Wally Moon	1.75	.70	.17
□ 6	Lou Berberet	1.25	.50	.12
□ 7	Master and Mentor Willie Mays Bill Rigney	8.00	3.25	.80
□ 8	Bud Daley	1.25	.50	.12
□ 9	Faye Throneberry	1.25	.50	.12
□ 10	Ernie Banks	21.00	8.50	2.10
□ 11	Norm Siebern	1.25	.50	.12
□ 12	Milt Pappas	1.75	.70	.17
□ 13	Wally Post	1.25	.50	.12
□ 14	Jim Grant	1.25	.50	.12
□ 15	Pete Runnels	1.75	.70	.17
□ 16	Ernie Broglio	1.75	.70	.17
□ 17	Johnny Callison	1.75	.70	.17
□ 18	Dodgers Team (checklist on back)	9.00	2.50	.50
□ 19	Felix Mantilla	1.25	.50	.12
□ 20	Roy Face	2.50	1.00	.25
□ 21	Dutch Dotterer	1.25	.50	.12
□ 22	Rocky Bridges	1.25	.50	.12
□ 23	Eddie Fisher	1.25	.50	.12
□ 24	Dick Gray	1.25	.50	.12
□ 25	Roy Sievers	1.75	.70	.17
□ 26	Wayne Terwilliger	1.25	.50	.12
□ 27	Dick Drott	1.25	.50	.12
□ 28	Brooks Robinson	24.00	10.00	2.40
□ 29	Clem Labine	1.75	.70	.17
□ 30	Tito Francona	1.75	.70	.17
□ 31	Sammy Esposito	1.25	.50	.12
□ 32	Sophomore Stalwarts Jim O'Toole Vada Pinson	1.75	.70	.17
□ 33	Tom Morgan	1.25	.50	.12
□ 34	George Anderson	3.50	1.40	.35
□ 35	Whitey Ford	21.00	8.50	2.10
□ 36	Russ Nixon	1.75	.70	.17
□ 37	Bill Bruton	1.25	.50	.12
□ 38	Jerry Casale	1.25	.50	.12
□ 39	Earl Averill	1.25	.50	.12
□ 40	Joe Cunningham	1.75	.70	.17
□ 41	Barry Latman	1.25	.50	.12
□ 42	Hobie Landrith	1.25	.50	.12
□ 43	Senators Team (checklist on back)	4.00	1.00	.20
□ 44	Bobby Locke	1.25	.50	.12
□ 45	Roy McMillan	1.25	.50	.12
□ 46	Jerry Fisher	1.25	.50	.12
□ 47	Don Zimmer	2.50	1.00	.25
□ 48	Hal W. Smith	1.25	.50	.12
□ 49	Curt Raydon	1.25	.50	.12
□ 50	Al Kaline	21.00	8.50	2.10
□ 51	Jim Coates	1.25	.50	.12
□ 52	Dave Philley	1.25	.50	.12
□ 53	Jackie Brandt	1.25	.50	.12
□ 54	Mike Fornieles	1.25	.50	.12
□ 55	Bill Mazeroski	3.00	1.20	.30
□ 56	Steve Korcheck	1.25	.50	.12
□ 57	Win Savers Turk Lown Jerry Staley	1.75	.70	.17
□ 58	Gino Cimoli	1.25	.50	.12
□ 59	Juan Pizarro	1.25	.50	.12
□ 60	Gus Triandos	1.75	.70	.17
□ 61	Eddie Kasko	1.25	.50	.12
□ 62	Roger Craig	3.50	1.40	.35
□ 63	George Strickland	1.25	.50	.12
□ 64	Jack Meyer	1.25	.50	.12
□ 65	Elston Howard	4.00	1.60	.40
□ 66	Bob Trowbridge	1.25	.50	.12
□ 67	Jose Pagan	1.25	.50	.12
□ 68	Dave Hillman	1.25	.50	.12
□ 69	Billy Goodman	1.75	.70	.17
□ 70	Lew Burdette	2.50	1.00	.25
□ 71	Marty Keough	1.25	.50	.12
□ 72	Tigers Team (checklist on back)	6.50	1.50	.25
□ 73	Bob Gibson	25.00	10.00	2.50
□ 74	Walt Moryn	1.25	.50	.12
□ 75	Vic Power	1.25	.50	.12
□ 76	Bill Fischer	1.25	.50	.12
□ 77	Hank Foiles	1.25	.50	.12
□ 78	Bob Grim	1.25	.50	.12
□ 79	Walt Dropo	1.25	.50	.12
□ 80	Johnny Antonelli	1.75	.70	.17
□ 81	Russ Snyder	1.25	.50	.12
□ 82	Ruben Gomez	1.25	.50	.12
□ 83	Tony Kubek	4.00	1.60	.40
□ 84	Hal R. Smith	1.25	.50	.12
□ 85	Frank Lary	1.75	.70	.17
□ 86	Dick Gernert	1.25	.50	.12
□ 87	John Romonosky	1.25	.50	.12
□ 88	John Roseboro	1.75	.70	.17
□ 89	Hal Brown	1.25	.50	.12
□ 90	Bobby Avila	1.25	.50	.12
□ 91	Bennie Daniels	1.25	.50	.12
□ 92	Whitey Herzog	3.50	1.40	.35
□ 93	Art Schult	1.25	.50	.12
□ 94	Leo Kiely	1.25	.50	.12
□ 95	Frank Thomas	1.75	.70	.17
□ 96	Ralph Terry	2.50	1.00	.25
□ 97	Ted Lepcio	1.25	.50	.12
□ 91	Gordon Jones	1.25	.50	.12
□ 99	Lenny Green	1.25	.50	.12
□ 100	Nellie Fox	4.50	1.80	.45
□ 101	Bob Miller	1.25	.50	.12
□ 102	Kent Hadley	1.25	.50	.12
□ 103	Dick Farrell	1.25	.50	.12
□ 104	Dick Schofield	1.25	.50	.12
□ 105	Larry Sherry	2.50	1.00	.25
□ 106	Billy Gardner	1.25	.50	.12
□ 107	Carlton Willey	1.25	.50	.12
□ 108	Pete Daley	1.25	.50	.12
□ 109	Clete Boyer	2.50	1.00	.25
□ 110	Cal McLish	1.25	.50	.12
□ 111	Vic Wertz	1.75	.70	.17
□ 112	Jack Harshman	1.25	.50	.12
□ 113	Bob Skinner	1.75	.70	.17
□ 114	Ken Aspromonte	1.25	.50	.12
□ 115	Fork and Knuckler Roy Face Hoyt Wilhelm	3.50	1.40	.35
□ 116	Jim Rivera	1.25	.50	.12
□ 117	Tom Borland RP	1.25	.50	.12
□ 118	Bob Bruce RP	1.25	.50	.12
□ 119	Chico Cardenas RP	1.75	.70	.17
□ 120	Duke Carmel RP	1.25	.50	.12
□ 121	Camilo Carreon RP	1.75	.70	.17
□ 122	Don Dillard RP	1.25	.50	.12
□ 123	Dan Dobbek RP	1.25	.50	.12
□ 124	Jim Donohue RP	1.25	.50	.12
□ 125	Dick Ellsworth RP	1.75	.70	.17
□ 126	Chuck Estrada RP	1.75	.70	.17
□ 127	Ron Hansen RP	1.75	.70	.17
□ 128	Bill Harris RP	1.25	.50	.12
□ 129	Bob Hartman RP	1.25	.50	.12
□ 130	Frank Herrera RP	1.25	.50	.12
□ 131	Ed Hobaugh RP	1.25	.50	.12
□ 132	Frank Howard RP	8.00	3.25	.80
□ 133	Manuel Javier RP (sic, Julian)	1.75	.70	.17
□ 134	Deron Johnson RP	1.75	.70	.17
□ 135	Ken Johnson RP	1.25	.50	.12
□ 136	Jim Kaat RP	20.00	8.00	2.00
□ 137	Lou Klimchock RP	1.25	.50	.12
□ 138	Art Mahaffey RP	1.75	.70	.17
□ 139	Carl Mathias RP	1.25	.50	.12
□ 140	Julio Navarro RP	1.75	.70	.17
□ 141	Jim Proctor RP	1.25	.50	.12
□ 142	Bill Short RP	1.75	.70	.17
□ 143	Al Spangler RP	1.25	.50	.12
□ 144	Al Stieglitz RP	1.25	.50	.12
□ 145	Jim Umbricht RP	1.25	.50	.12
□ 146	Ted Wieand RP	1.25	.50	.12
□ 147	Bob Will RP	1.25	.50	.12
□ 148	Carl Yastrzemski RP	250.00	100.00	25.00
□ 149	Bob Nieman	1.25	.50	.12
□ 150	Billy Pierce	2.50	1.00	.25
□ 151	Giants Team (checklist on back)	5.00	1.00	.20
□ 152	Gail Harris	1.25	.50	.12
□ 153	Bobby Thomson	2.50	1.00	.25
□ 154	Jim Davenport	1.75	.70	.17
□ 155	Charlie Neal	1.75	.70	.17

□ 156 Art Ceccarelli .... 1.25 .50 .12
□ 157 Rocky Nelson .... 1.25 .50 .12
□ 158 Wes Covington .... 1.75 .70 .17
□ 159 Jim Piersall .... 2.50 1.00 .25
□ 160 Rival All-Stars 25.00 10.00 2.50
Mickey Mantle
Ken Boyer
□ 161 Ray Narleski .... 1.25 .50 .12
□ 162 Sammy Taylor .... 1.25 .50 .12
□ 163 Hector Lopez .... 1.25 .50 .12
□ 164 Reds Team .... 5.00 1.00 .20
(checklist on back)
□ 165 Jack Sanford .... 1.75 .70 .17
□ 166 Chuck Essegian .... 1.25 .50 .12
□ 167 Valmy Thomas .... 1.25 .50 .12
□ 168 Alex Grammas .... 1.25 .50 .12
□ 169 Jake Striker .... 1.25 .50 .12
□ 170 Del Crandall .... 1.75 .70 .17
□ 171 Johnny Groth .... 1.25 .50 .12
□ 172 Willie Kirkland .... 1.25 .50 .12
□ 173 Billy Martin .... 5.50 2.20 .55
□ 174 Indians Team .... 4.00 1.00 .20
(checklist on back)
□ 175 Pedro Ramos .... 1.25 .50 .12
□ 176 Vada Pinson .... 3.00 1.20 .30
□ 177 Johnny Kucks .... 1.25 .50 .12
□ 178 Woody Held .... 1.25 .50 .12
□ 179 Rip Coleman .... 1.25 .50 .12
□ 180 Harry Simpson .... 1.25 .50 .12
□ 181 Billy Loes .... 1.25 .50 .12
□ 182 Glen Hobbie .... 1.25 .50 .12
□ 183 Eli Grba .... 1.25 .50 .12
□ 184 Gary Geiger .... 1.25 .50 .12
□ 185 Jim Owens .... 1.25 .50 .12
□ 186 Dave Sisler .... 1.25 .50 .12
□ 187 Jay Hook .... 1.25 .50 .12
□ 188 Dick Williams .... 1.75 .70 .17
□ 189 Don McMahon .... 1.25 .50 .12
□ 190 Gene Woodling .... 1.75 .70 .17
□ 191 Johnny Klippstein .... 1.25 .50 .12
□ 192 Danny O'Connell .... 1.25 .50 .12
□ 193 Dick Hyde .... 1.25 .50 .12
□ 194 Bobby Gene Smith .... 1.25 .50 .12
□ 195 Lindy McDaniel .... 1.75 .70 .17
□ 196 Andy Carey .... 1.75 .70 .17
□ 197 Ron Kline .... 1.25 .50 .12
□ 198 Jerry Lynch .... 1.25 .50 .12
□ 199 Dick Donovan .... 1.25 .50 .12
□ 200 Willie Mays 70.00 28.00 7.00
□ 201 Larry Osborne .... 1.25 .50 .12
□ 202 Fred Kipp .... 1.25 .50 .12
□ 203 Sammy White .... 1.25 .50 .12
□ 204 Ryne Duren .... 2.50 1.00 .25
□ 205 Johnny Logan .... 1.75 .70 .17
□ 206 Claude Osteen .... 1.75 .70 .17
□ 207 Bob Boyd .... 1.25 .50 .12
□ 208 White Sox Team .... 4.00 1.00 .20
(checklist on back)
□ 209 Ron Blackburn .... 1.25 .50 .12
□ 210 Harmon Killebrew 16.00 6.50 1.60
□ 211 Taylor Phillips .... 1.25 .50 .12
□ 212 Walt Alston MG .... 6.00 2.40 .60
□ 213 Chuck Dressen MG .... 1.75 .70 .17
□ 214 Jimmy Dykes MG .... 1.75 .70 .17
□ 215 Bob Elliott MG .... 1.25 .50 .12
□ 216 Joe Gordon MG .... 1.75 .70 .17
□ 217 Charlie Grimm MG .... 1.75 .70 .17
□ 218 Solly Hemus MG .... 1.25 .50 .12
□ 219 Fred Hutchinson MG .... 1.75 .70 .17
□ 220 Billy Jurges MG .... 1.25 .50 .12
□ 221 Cookie Lavagetto MG .... 1.25 .50 .12
□ 222 Al Lopez MG .... 5.00 2.00 .50
□ 223 Danny Murtaugh MG .... 1.75 .70 .17
□ 224 Paul Richards MG .... 1.75 .70 .17
□ 225 Bill Rigney MG .... 1.75 .70 .17
□ 226 Eddie Sawyer MG .... 1.75 .70 .17
□ 227 Casey Stengel MG 12.00 5.00 1.20
□ 228 Ernie Johnson .... 1.25 .50 .12
□ 229 Joe M. Morgan .... 4.50 1.80 .45
□ 230 Mound Magicians .... 5.00 2.00 .50
Lou Burdette
Warren Spahn
Bob Buhl
□ 231 Hal Naragon .... 1.25 .50 .12
□ 232 Jim Busby .... 1.25 .50 .12
□ 233 Don Elston .... 1.25 .50 .12
□ 234 Don Demeter .... 1.25 .50 .12
□ 235 Gus Bell .... 1.75 .70 .17
□ 236 Dick Ricketts .... 1.25 .50 .12
□ 237 Elmer Valo .... 1.25 .50 .12
□ 238 Danny Kravitz .... 1.25 .50 .12
□ 239 Joe Shipley .... 1.25 .50 .12
□ 240 Luis Aparicio 10.00 4.00 1.00
□ 241 Albie Pearson .... 1.25 .50 .12
□ 242 Cardinals Team .... 4.50 1.00 .20
(checklist on back)
□ 243 Bubba Phillips .... 1.25 .50 .12
□ 244 Hal Griggs .... 1.25 .50 .12
□ 245 Eddie Yost .... 1.25 .50 .12
□ 246 Lee Maye .... 1.25 .50 .12
□ 247 Gil McDougald .... 3.50 1.40 .35
□ 248 Del Rice .... 1.25 .50 .12
□ 249 Earl Wilson .... 1.75 .70 .17
□ 250 Stan Musial 65.00 26.00 6.50
□ 251 Bob Malkmus .... 1.25 .50 .12
□ 252 Ray Herbert .... 1.25 .50 .12
□ 253 Eddie Bressoud .... 1.25 .50 .12
□ 254 Arnie Portocarrero .... 1.25 .50 .12
□ 255 Jim Gilliam .... 3.50 1.40 .35
□ 256 Dick Brown .... 1.25 .50 .12
□ 257 Gordy Coleman .... 1.75 .70 .17
□ 258 Dick Groat .... 3.00 1.20 .30
□ 259 George Altman .... 1.25 .50 .12
□ 260 Power Plus .... 1.75 .70 .17
Rocky Colavito
Tito Francona
□ 261 Pete Burnside .... 1.25 .50 .12
□ 262 Hank Bauer .... 2.50 1.00 .25
□ 263 Darrell Johnson .... 1.75 .70 .17
□ 264 Robin Roberts 11.00 4.50 1.10
□ 265 Rip Repulski .... 1.25 .50 .12
□ 266 Joey Jay .... 1.25 .50 .12
□ 267 Jim Marshall .... 1.25 .50 .12
□ 268 Al Worthington .... 1.25 .50 .12
□ 269 Gene Green .... 1.25 .50 .12
□ 270 Bob Turley .... 2.50 1.00 .25
□ 271 Julio Becquer .... 1.25 .50 .12
□ 272 Fred Green .... 1.25 .50 .12
□ 273 Neil Chrisley .... 1.25 .50 .12
□ 274 Tom Acker .... 1.25 .50 .12
□ 275 Curt Flood .... 2.50 1.00 .25
□ 276 Ken McBride .... 1.25 .50 .12
□ 277 Harry Bright .... 1.25 .50 .12
□ 278 Stan Williams .... 1.25 .50 .12
□ 279 Chuck Tanner .... 1.75 .70 .17
□ 280 Frank Sullivan .... 1.25 .50 .12
□ 281 Ray Boone .... 1.75 .70 .17
□ 282 Joe Nuxhall .... 1.75 .70 .17
□ 283 John Blanchard .... 1.75 .70 .17
□ 284 Don Gross .... 1.25 .50 .12
□ 285 Harry Anderson .... 1.25 .50 .12
□ 286 Ray Semproch .... 1.25 .50 .12
□ 287 Felipe Alou .... 2.50 1.00 .25
□ 288 Bob Mabe .... 1.50 .60 .15
□ 289 Willie Jones .... 1.50 .60 .15
□ 290 Jerry Lumpe .... 1.50 .60 .15
□ 291 Bob Keegan .... 1.50 .60 .15
□ 292 Dodger Backstops .... 2.00 .80 .20
Joe Pignatano
John Roseboro
□ 293 Gene Conley .... 1.50 .60 .15
□ 294 Tony Taylor .... 1.50 .60 .15
□ 295 Gil Hodges 11.00 4.50 1.10
□ 296 Nelson Chittum .... 1.50 .60 .15
□ 297 Reno Bertoia .... 1.50 .60 .15
□ 298 George Witt .... 1.50 .60 .15
□ 299 Earl Torgeson .... 1.50 .60 .15
□ 300 Hank Aaron 75.00 30.00 7.50
□ 301 Jerry Davie .... 1.50 .60 .15
□ 302 Phillies Team .... 4.50 1.25 .20
(checklist on back)
□ 303 Billy O'Dell .... 1.50 .60 .15
□ 304 Joe Ginsberg .... 1.50 .60 .15
□ 305 Richie Ashburn .... 5.50 2.20 .55
□ 306 Frank Baumann .... 1.50 .60 .15
□ 307 Gene Oliver .... 1.50 .60 .15
□ 308 Dick Hall .... 1.50 .60 .15
□ 309 Bob Hale .... 1.50 .60 .15
□ 310 Frank Malzone .... 2.00 .80 .20
□ 311 Raul Sanchez .... 1.50 .60 .15
□ 312 Charley Lau .... 2.00 .80 .20
□ 313 Turk Lown .... 1.50 .60 .15
□ 314 Chico Fernandez .... 1.50 .60 .15
□ 315 Bobby Shantz .... 2.50 1.00 .25
□ 316 Willie McCovey 90.00 36.00 9.00
□ 317 Pumpsie Green .... 1.50 .60 .15
□ 318 Jim Baxes .... 1.50 .60 .15
□ 319 Joe Koppe .... 1.50 .60 .15
□ 320 Bob Allison .... 2.00 .80 .20
□ 321 Ron Fairly .... 2.00 .80 .20
□ 322 Willie Tasby .... 1.50 .60 .15
□ 323 John Romano .... 1.50 .60 .15
□ 324 Jim Perry .... 2.50 1.00 .25
□ 325 Jim O'Toole .... 2.00 .80 .20
□ 326 Bob Clemente 60.00 24.00 6.00
□ 327 Ray Sadecki .... 1.50 .60 .15
□ 328 Earl Battey .... 1.50 .60 .15
□ 329 Zack Monroe .... 1.50 .60 .15
□ 330 Harvey Kuenn .... 2.50 1.00 .25
□ 331 Henry Mason .... 1.50 .60 .15

☐ 332	Yankees Team (checklist on back)	16.00	4.00	1.00
☐ 333	Danny McDevitt	1.50	.60	.15
☐ 334	Ted Abernathy	1.50	.60	.15
☐ 335	Red Schoendienst	3.00	1.20	.30
☐ 336	Ike Delock	1.50	.60	.15
☐ 337	Cal Neeman	1.50	.60	.15
☐ 338	Ray Monzant	1.50	.60	.15
☐ 339	Harry Chiti	1.50	.60	.15
☐ 340	Harvey Haddix	2.00	.80	.20
☐ 341	Carroll Hardy	1.50	.60	.15
☐ 342	Casey Wise	1.50	.60	.15
☐ 343	Sandy Koufax	60.00	24.00	6.00
☐ 344	Clint Courtney	1.50	.60	.15
☐ 345	Don Newcombe	2.50	1.00	.25
☐ 346	J.C. Martin (face actually Gary Peters)	1.50	.60	.15
☐ 347	Ed Bouchee	1.50	.60	.15
☐ 348	Barry Shetrone	1.50	.60	.15
☐ 349	Moe Drabowsky	1.50	.60	.15
☐ 350	Mickey Mantle	300.00	120.00	30.00
☐ 351	Don Nottebart	1.50	.60	.15
☐ 352	Cincy Clouters Gus Bell Frank Robinson Jerry Lynch	3.50	1.40	.35
☐ 353	Don Larsen	2.50	1.00	.25
☐ 354	Bob Lillis	2.00	.80	.20
☐ 355	Bill White	2.50	1.00	.25
☐ 356	Joe Amalfitano	1.50	.60	.15
☐ 357	Al Schroll	1.50	.60	.15
☐ 358	Joe DeMaestri	1.50	.60	.15
☐ 359	Buddy Gilbert	1.50	.60	.15
☐ 360	Herb Score	2.00	.80	.20
☐ 361	Bob Oldis	1.50	.60	.15
☐ 362	Russ Kemmerer	1.50	.60	.15
☐ 363	Gene Stephens	1.50	.60	.15
☐ 364	Paul Foytack	1.50	.60	.15
☐ 365	Minnie Minoso	3.50	1.40	.35
☐ 366	Dallas Green	6.50	2.60	.65
☐ 367	Bill Tuttle	1.50	.60	.15
☐ 368	Daryl Spencer	1.50	.60	.15
☐ 369	Billy Hoeft	1.50	.60	.15
☐ 370	Bill Skowron	4.50	1.80	.45
☐ 371	Bud Byerly	1.50	.60	.15
☐ 372	Frank House	1.50	.60	.15
☐ 373	Don Hoak	1.50	.60	.15
☐ 374	Bob Buhl	1.50	.60	.15
☐ 375	Dale Long	2.00	.80	.20
☐ 376	John Briggs	1.50	.60	.15
☐ 377	Roger Maris	75.00	30.00	7.50
☐ 378	Stu Miller	1.50	.60	.15
☐ 379	Red Wilson	1.50	.60	.15
☐ 380	Bob Shaw	1.50	.60	.15
☐ 381	Braves Team (checklist on back)	4.50	1.25	.20
☐ 382	Ted Bowsfield	1.50	.60	.15
☐ 383	Leon Wagner	1.50	.60	.15
☐ 384	Don Cardwell	1.50	.60	.15
☐ 385	World Series Game 1 Neal Steals Second	2.50	1.00	.25
☐ 386	World Series Game 2 Neal Belts 2nd Homer	2.50	1.00	.25
☐ 387	World Series Game 3 Furillo Breaks Game	3.00	1.20	.30
☐ 388	World Series Game 4 Hodges' Homer	4.00	1.60	.40
☐ 389	World Series Game 5 Luis Swipes Base	4.00	1.60	.40
☐ 390	World Series Game 6 Scrambling After Ball	2.50	1.00	.25
☐ 391	World Series Summary The Champs Celebrate	2.50	1.00	.25
☐ 392	Tex Clevenger	1.50	.60	.15
☐ 393	Smoky Burgess	2.00	.80	.20
☐ 394	Norm Larker	1.50	.60	.15
☐ 395	Hoyt Wilhelm	11.00	4.50	1.10
☐ 396	Steve Bilko	1.50	.60	.15
☐ 397	Don Blasingame	1.50	.60	.15
☐ 398	Mike Cuellar	2.00	.80	.20
☐ 399	Young Hill Stars Milt Pappas Jack Fisher Jerry Walker	2.00	.80	.20
☐ 400	Rocky Colavito	3.50	1.40	.35
☐ 401	Bob Duliba	1.50	.60	.15
☐ 402	Dick Stuart	2.00	.80	.20
☐ 403	Ed Sadowski	1.50	.60	.15
☐ 404	Bob Rush	1.50	.60	.15
☐ 405	Bobby Richardson	4.50	1.80	.45
☐ 406	Billy Klaus	1.50	.60	.15
☐ 407	Gary Peters (face actually J.C. Martin)	2.00	.80	.20

☐ 408	Carl Furillo	3.50	1.40	.35
☐ 409	Ron Samford	1.50	.60	.15
☐ 410	Sam Jones	2.00	.80	.20
☐ 411	Ed Bailey	1.50	.60	.15
☐ 412	Bob Anderson	1.50	.60	.15
☐ 413	Athletics Team (checklist on back)	4.00	1.00	.20
☐ 414	Don Williams	1.50	.60	.15
☐ 415	Bob Cerv	2.00	.80	.20
☐ 416	Humberto Robinson	1.50	.60	.15
☐ 417	Chuck Cottier	2.00	.80	.20
☐ 418	Don Mossi	2.00	.80	.20
☐ 419	George Crowe	1.50	.60	.15
☐ 420	Eddie Mathews	18.00	7.25	1.80
☐ 421	Duke Maas	1.50	.60	.15
☐ 422	John Powers	1.50	.60	.15
☐ 423	Ed Fitzgerald	1.50	.60	.15
☐ 424	Pete Whisenant	1.50	.60	.15
☐ 425	Johnny Podres	3.00	1.20	.30
☐ 426	Ron Jackson	1.50	.60	.15
☐ 427	Al Grunwald	1.50	.60	.15
☐ 428	Al Smith	1.50	.60	.15
☐ 429	AL Kings Nellie Fox Harvey Kuenn	3.00	1.20	.30
☐ 430	Art Ditmar	1.50	.60	.15
☐ 431	Andre Rodgers	1.50	.60	.15
☐ 432	Chuck Stobbs	1.50	.60	.15
☐ 433	Irv Noren	1.50	.60	.15
☐ 434	Brooks Lawrence	1.50	.60	.15
☐ 435	Gene Freese	1.50	.60	.15
☐ 436	Marv Throneberry	2.50	1.00	.25
☐ 437	Bob Friend	2.00	.80	.20
☐ 438	Jim Coker	1.50	.60	.15
☐ 439	Tom Brewer	1.50	.60	.15
☐ 440	Jim Lemon	1.50	.60	.15
☐ 441	Gary Bell	2.50	1.00	.25
☐ 442	Joe Pignatano	2.50	1.00	.25
☐ 443	Charley Maxwell	2.50	1.00	.25
☐ 444	Jerry Kindall	2.50	1.00	.25
☐ 445	Warren Spahn	21.00	8.50	2.10
☐ 446	Ellis Burton	2.50	1.00	.25
☐ 447	Ray Moore	2.50	1.00	.25
☐ 448	Jim Gentile	3.50	1.40	.35
☐ 449	Jim Brosnan	2.50	1.00	.25
☐ 450	Orlando Cepeda	6.50	2.60	.65
☐ 451	Curt Simmons	3.00	1.20	.30
☐ 452	Ray Webster	2.50	1.00	.25
☐ 453	Vern Law	3.50	1.40	.35
☐ 454	Hal Woodeshick	2.50	1.00	.25
☐ 455	Baltimore Coaches Eddie Robinson Harry Brecheen Luman Harris	3.50	1.40	.35
☐ 456	Red Sox Coaches Rudy York Billy Herman Sal Maglie Del Baker	4.00	1.60	.40
☐ 457	Cubs Coaches Charlie Root Lou Klein Elvin Tappe	3.50	1.40	.35
☐ 458	White Sox Coaches Johnny Cooney Don Gutteridge Tony Cuccinello Ray Berres	3.50	1.40	.35
☐ 459	Reds Coaches Reggie Otero Cot Deal Wally Moses	3.50	1.40	.35
☐ 460	Indians Coaches Mel Harder Jo-Jo White Bob Lemon Ralph(Red) Kress	4.00	1.60	.40
☐ 461	Tigers Coaches Tom Ferrick Luke Appling Billy Hitchcock	4.00	1.60	.40
☐ 462	Athletics Coaches Fred Fitzsimmons Don Heffner Walker Cooper	3.50	1.40	.35
☐ 463	Dodgers Coaches Bobby Bragan Pete Reiser Joe Becker Greg Mulleavy	4.00	1.60	.40
☐ 464	Braves Coaches Bob Scheffing Whitlow Wyatt Andy Pafko George Myatt	3.50	1.40	.35

□ 465	Yankees Coaches	7.00	2.80	.70
	Bill Dickey			
	Ralph Houk			
	Frank Crosetti			
	Ed Lopat			
□ 466	Phillies Coaches	3.50	1.40	.35
	Ken Silvestri			
	Dick Carter			
	Andy Cohen			
□ 467	Pirates Coaches	3.50	1.40	.35
	Mickey Vernon			
	Frank Oceak			
	Sam Narron			
	Bill Burwell			
□ 468	Cardinals Coaches	3.50	1.40	.35
	Johnny Keane			
	Howie Pollet			
	Ray Katt			
	Harry Walker			
□ 469	Giants Coaches	3.50	1.40	.35
	Wes Westrum			
	Salty Parker			
	Bill Posedel			
□ 470	Senators Coaches	3.50	1.40	.35
	Bob Swift			
	Ellis Clary			
	Sam Mele			
□ 471	Ned Garver	2.50	1.00	.25
□ 472	Alvin Dark	3.50	1.40	.35
□ 473	Al Cicotte	2.50	1.00	.25
□ 474	Haywood Sullivan	3.00	1.20	.30
□ 475	Don Drysdale	18.00	7.25	1.80
□ 476	Lou Johnson	2.50	1.00	.25
□ 477	Don Ferrarese	2.50	1.00	.25
□ 478	Frank Torre	2.50	1.00	.25
□ 479	Georges Maranda	2.50	1.00	.25
□ 480	Yogi Berra	40.00	16.00	4.00
□ 481	Wes Stock	2.50	1.00	.25
□ 482	Frank Bolling	2.50	1.00	.25
□ 483	Camilo Pascual	3.00	1.20	.30
□ 484	Pirates Team	12.50	4.00	1.00
	(checklist on back)			
□ 485	Ken Boyer	5.00	2.00	.50
□ 486	Bobby Del Greco	2.50	1.00	.25
□ 487	Tom Sturdivant	2.50	1.00	.25
□ 488	Norm Cash	4.00	1.60	.40
□ 489	Steve Ridzik	2.50	1.00	.25
□ 490	Frank Robinson	25.00	10.00	2.50
□ 491	Mel Roach	2.50	1.00	.25
□ 492	Larry Jackson	2.50	1.00	.25
□ 493	Duke Snider	33.00	13.00	3.00
□ 494	Orioles Team	7.50	2.00	.40
	(checklist on back)			
□ 495	Sherm Lollar	3.00	1.20	.30
□ 496	Bill Virdon	3.50	1.40	.35
□ 497	John Tsitouris	2.50	1.00	.25
□ 498	Al Pilarcik	2.50	1.00	.25
□ 499	Johnny James	2.50	1.00	.25
□ 500	Johnny Temple	3.00	1.20	.30
□ 501	Bob Schmidt	2.50	1.00	.25
□ 502	Jim Bunning	7.50	3.00	.75
□ 503	Don Lee	2.50	1.00	.25
□ 504	Seth Morehead	2.50	1.00	.25
□ 505	Ted Kluszewski	4.50	1.80	.45
□ 506	Lee Walls	2.50	1.00	.25
□ 507	Dick Stigman	7.00	2.80	.70
□ 508	Billy Consolo	7.00	2.80	.70
□ 509	Tommy Davis	12.00	5.00	1.20
□ 510	Jerry Staley	7.00	2.80	.70
□ 511	Ken Walters	7.00	2.80	.70
□ 512	Joe Gibbon	7.00	2.80	.70
□ 513	Chicago Cubs	17.00	5.00	1.00
	Team Card			
	(checklist on back)			
□ 514	Steve Barber	7.00	2.80	.70
□ 515	Stan Lopata	7.00	2.80	.70
□ 516	Marty Kutyna	7.00	2.80	.70
□ 517	Charlie James	7.00	2.80	.70
□ 518	Tony Gonzalez	7.00	2.80	.70
□ 519	Ed Roebuck	7.00	2.80	.70
□ 520	Don Buddin	7.00	2.80	.70
□ 521	Mike Lee	7.00	2.80	.70
□ 522	Ken Hunt	7.00	2.80	.70
□ 523	Clay Dalrymple	7.00	2.80	.70
□ 524	Bill Henry	7.00	2.80	.70
□ 525	Marv Breeding	7.00	2.80	.70
□ 526	Paul Giel	7.00	2.80	.70
□ 527	Jose Valdivielso	7.00	2.80	.70
□ 528	Ben Johnson	7.00	2.80	.70
□ 529	Norm Sherry	8.00	3.25	.80
□ 530	Mike McCormick	8.00	3.25	.80
□ 531	Sandy Amoros	8.00	3.25	.80
□ 532	Mike Garcia	10.00	4.00	1.00
□ 533	Lu Clinton	7.00	2.80	.70
□ 534	Ken MacKenzie	7.00	2.80	.70
□ 535	Whitey Lockman	8.00	3.25	.80
□ 536	Wynn Hawkins	7.00	2.80	.70
□ 537	Boston Red Sox	17.00	5.00	1.00
	Team Card			
	(checklist on back)			
□ 538	Frank Barnes	7.00	2.80	.70
□ 539	Gene Baker	7.00	2.80	.70
□ 540	Jerry Walker	7.00	2.80	.70
□ 541	Tony Curry	7.00	2.80	.70
□ 542	Ken Hamlin	7.00	2.80	.70
□ 543	Elio Chacon	7.00	2.80	.70
□ 544	Bill Monbouquette	8.00	3.25	.80
□ 545	Carl Sawatski	7.00	2.80	.70
□ 546	Hank Aguirre	7.00	2.80	.70
□ 547	Bob Aspromonte	7.00	2.80	.70
□ 548	Don Mincher	8.00	3.25	.80
□ 549	John Buzhardt	7.00	2.80	.70
□ 550	Jim Landis	7.00	2.80	.70
□ 551	Ed Rakow	7.00	2.80	.70
□ 552	Walt Bond	7.00	2.80	.70
□ 553	Bill Skowron AS	9.00	3.75	.90
□ 554	Willie McCovey AS	32.00	13.00	3.20
□ 555	Nellie Fox AS	12.00	5.00	1.20
□ 556	Charlie Neal AS	8.00	3.25	.80
□ 557	Frank Malzone AS	8.00	3.25	.80
□ 558	Eddie Mathews AS	21.00	8.50	2.10
□ 559	Luis Aparicio AS	16.00	6.50	1.60
□ 560	Ernie Banks AS	28.00	11.50	2.80
□ 561	Al Kaline AS	28.00	11.50	2.80
□ 562	Joe Cunningham AS	8.00	3.25	.80
□ 563	Mickey Mantle AS	150.00	60.00	15.00
□ 564	Willie Mays AS	65.00	26.00	6.50
□ 565	Roger Maris AS	55.00	22.00	5.50
□ 566	Hank Aaron AS	65.00	26.00	6.50
□ 567	Sherm Lollar AS	8.00	3.25	.80
□ 568	Del Crandall AS	8.00	3.25	.80
□ 569	Camilo Pascual AS	8.00	3.25	.80
□ 570	Don Drysdale AS	20.00	8.00	2.00
□ 571	Billy Pierce AS	8.00	3.25	.80
□ 572	Johnny Antonelli AS	10.00	4.00	1.00

1961 Topps

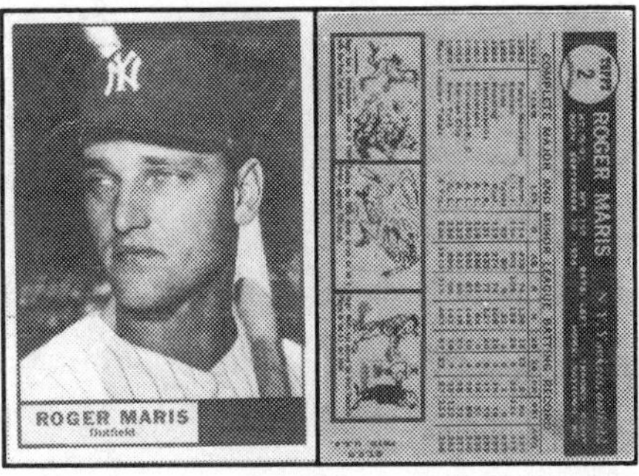

The cards in this 587-card set measure 2 1/2" by 3 1/2". In 1961, Topps returned to the vertical obverse format. Introduced for the first time were "League Leaders" (41 to 50) and separate, numbered checklist cards. Two number 463's exist: the Braves team card carrying that number was meant to be number 426. There are three versions of the second series checklist card #98; the variations are distinguished by the color of the "CHECKLIST" headline on the front of the card, the color of the printing of the card number on the bottom of the reverse, and the presence of the copyright notice running vertically on the card back. There are two groups of managers (131-139 and 219-226) as well as separate series of World Series cards (306-313), Baseball Thrills (401 to 410), previous MVP's (AL 471-478 and NL 479-486) and Sporting News All-Stars (566 to 589). The usual last series scarcity (523 to 589) exists. The set actually totals 587 cards since numbers 587 and 588 were never issued.

	NRMT	VG-E	GOOD
COMPLETE SET (587)	4000.00	1800.00	800.00
COMMON PLAYER (1-110)	.85	.34	.08
COMMON PLAYER (111-370)	1.00	.40	.10
COMMON PLAYER (371-446)	1.25	.50	.12
COMMON PLAYER (447-522)	1.75	.70	.17
COMMON PLAYER (523-565)	16.00	6.50	1.60
COMMON PLAYER (566-589)	18.00	7.25	1.80

	NRMT	VG-E	GOOD
☐ 1 Dick Groat	10.00	1.00	.20
☐ 2 Roger Maris	75.00	30.00	7.00
☐ 3 John Buzhardt	.85	.34	.08
☐ 4 Lenny Green	.85	.34	.08
☐ 5 John Romano	.85	.34	.08
☐ 6 Ed Roebuck	.85	.34	.08
☐ 7 White Sox Team	2.00	.80	.20
☐ 8 Dick Williams	1.50	.60	.15
☐ 9 Bob Purkey	.85	.34	.08
☐ 10 Brooks Robinson	20.00	8.00	2.00
☐ 11 Curt Simmons	1.25	.50	.12
☐ 12 Moe Thacker	.85	.34	.08
☐ 13 Chuck Cottier	.85	.34	.08
☐ 14 Don Mossi	1.25	.50	.12
☐ 15 Willie Kirkland	.85	.34	.08
☐ 16 Billy Muffett	.85	.34	.08
☐ 17 Checklist 1	4.50	.50	.10
☐ 18 Jim Grant	.85	.34	.08
☐ 19 Cletis Boyer	1.50	.60	.15
☐ 20 Robin Roberts	10.00	4.00	1.00
☐ 21 Zorro Versalles	1.25	.50	.12
☐ 22 Clem Labine	1.50	.60	.15
☐ 23 Don Demeter	.85	.34	.08
☐ 24 Ken Johnson	.85	.34	.08
☐ 25 Reds' Heavy Artillery	3.50	1.40	.35
Vada Pinson			
Gus Bell			
Frank Robinson			
☐ 26 Wes Stock	1.25	.50	.12
☐ 27 Jerry Kindall	.85	.34	.08
☐ 28 Hector Lopez	.85	.34	.08
☐ 29 Don Nottebart	.85	.34	.08
☐ 30 Nellie Fox	4.00	1.60	.40
☐ 31 Bob Schmidt	.85	.34	.08
☐ 32 Ray Sadecki	.85	.34	.08
☐ 33 Gary Geiger	.85	.34	.08
☐ 34 Wynn Hawkins	.85	.34	.08
☐ 35 Ron Santo	8.00	3.25	.80
☐ 36 Jack Kralick	.85	.34	.08
☐ 37 Charley Maxwell	.85	.34	.08
☐ 38 Bob Lillis	1.25	.50	.12
☐ 39 Leo Posada	.85	.34	.08
☐ 40 Bob Turley	2.00	.80	.20
☐ 41 NL Batting Leaders	2.50	1.00	.25
Dick Groat			
Norm Larker			
Willie Mays			
Roberto Clemente			
☐ 42 AL Batting Leaders	1.50	.60	.15
Pete Runnels			
Al Smith			
Minnie Minoso			
Bill Skowron			
☐ 43 NL Home Run Leaders	5.00	2.00	.50
Ernie Banks			
Hank Aaron			
Ed Mathews			
Ken Boyer			
☐ 44 AL Home Run Leaders	12.00	5.00	1.20
Mickey Mantle			
Roger Maris			
Jim Lemon			
Rocky Colavito			
☐ 45 NL ERA Leaders	1.50	.60	.15
Mike McCormick			
Ernie Broglio			
Don Drysdale			
Bob Friend			
Stan Williams			
☐ 46 AL ERA Leaders	1.50	.60	.15
Frank Baumann			
Jim Bunning			
Art Ditmar			
H. Brown			
☐ 47 NL Pitching Leaders	1.50	.60	.15
Ernie Broglio			
Warren Spahn			
Vern Law			
Lou Burdette			
☐ 48 AL Pitching Leaders	1.50	.60	.15
Chuck Estrada			
Jim Perry			
Bud Daley			
Art Ditmar			
Frank Lary			
Milt Pappas			
☐ 49 NL Strikeout Leaders	2.50	1.00	.2
Don Drysdale			
Sandy Koufax			
Sam Jones			
Ernie Broglio			
☐ 50 AL Strikeout Leaders	1.50	.60	.1
Jim Bunning			
Pedro Ramos			
Early Wynn			
Frank Lary			
☐ 51 Detroit Tigers Team Card	2.00	.80	.2
☐ 52 George Crowe	.85	.34	.0
☐ 53 Russ Nixon	1.25	.50	.1
☐ 54 Earl Francis	.85	.34	.0
☐ 55 Jim Davenport	1.25	.50	.1
☐ 56 Russ Kemmerer	.85	.34	.0
☐ 57 Marv Throneberry	1.50	.60	.1
☐ 58 Joe Schaffernoth	.85	.34	.0
☐ 59 Jim Woods	.85	.34	.08
☐ 60 Woodie Held	.85	.34	.08
☐ 61 Ron Piche	.85	.34	.08
☐ 62 Al Pilarcik	.85	.34	.08
☐ 63 Jim Kaat	6.00	2.40	.6
☐ 64 Alex Grammas	.85	.34	.0
☐ 65 Ted Kluszewski	3.50	1.40	.3
☐ 66 Billy Henry	.85	.34	.0
☐ 67 Ossie Virgil	.85	.34	.0
☐ 68 Deron Johnson	1.25	.50	.1
☐ 69 Earl Wilson	.85	.34	.0
☐ 70 Bill Virdon	1.50	.60	.1
☐ 71 Jerry Adair	.85	.34	.08
☐ 72 Stu Miller	.85	.34	.08
☐ 73 Al Spangler	.85	.34	.08
☐ 74 Joe Pignatano	.85	.34	.08
☐ 75 Lindy Shows Larry	1.25	.50	.1
Lindy McDaniel			
Larry Jackson			
☐ 76 Harry Anderson	.85	.34	.08
☐ 77 Dick Stigman	.85	.34	.08
☐ 78 Lee Walls	.85	.34	.08
☐ 79 Joe Ginsberg	.85	.34	.08
☐ 80 Harmon Killebrew	14.00	5.75	1.40
☐ 81 Tracy Stallard	.85	.34	.08
☐ 82 Joe Christopher	.85	.34	.08
☐ 83 Bob Bruce	.85	.34	.08
☐ 84 Lee Maye	.85	.34	.08
☐ 85 Jerry Walker	.85	.34	.08
☐ 86 Los Angeles Dodgers Team Card	3.00	1.20	.30
☐ 87 Joe Amalfitano	.85	.34	.08
☐ 88 Richie Ashburn	4.00	1.60	.40
☐ 89 Billy Martin	4.50	1.80	.45
☐ 90 Jerry Staley	.85	.34	.08
☐ 91 Walt Moryn	.85	.34	.08
☐ 92 Hal Naragon	.85	.34	.08
☐ 93 Tony Gonzalez	.85	.34	.08
☐ 94 John Kucks	.85	.34	.08
☐ 95 Norm Cash	2.50	1.00	.25
☐ 96 Bill O'Dell	.85	.34	.08
☐ 97 Jerry Lynch	.85	.34	.08
☐ 98A Checklist 2 (red "Checklist", 98 black on white)	4.50	.50	.10
☐ 98B Checklist 2 (yellow "Checklist", 98 black on white)	4.50	.50	.10
☐ 98C Checklist 2 (yellow "Checklist", 98 white on black, no copyright)	4.50	.50	.10
☐ 99 Don Buddin	.85	.34	.08
☐ 100 Harvey Haddix	1.50	.60	.15
☐ 101 Bubba Phillips	.85	.34	.08
☐ 102 Gene Stephens	.85	.34	.08
☐ 103 Ruben Amaro	.85	.34	.08
☐ 104 John Blanchard	1.25	.50	.12
☐ 105 Carl Willey	.85	.34	.08
☐ 106 Whitey Herzog	2.50	1.00	.25
☐ 107 Seth Morehead	.85	.34	.08
☐ 108 Dan Dobbek	.85	.34	.08
☐ 109 John Podres	2.50	1.00	.25
☐ 110 Vada Pinson	2.50	1.00	.25
☐ 111 Jack Meyer	1.00	.40	.10
☐ 112 Chico Fernandez	1.00	.40	.10
☐ 113 Mike Fornieles	1.00	.40	.10
☐ 114 Hobie Landrith	1.00	.40	.10
☐ 115 Johnny Antonelli	1.50	.60	.15
☐ 116 Joe DeMaestri	1.00	.40	.10
☐ 117 Dale Long	1.25	.50	.12
☐ 118 Chris Cannizzaro	1.00	.40	.10
☐ 119 A's Big Armor	1.25	.50	.12
Norm Siebern			

Hank Bauer			
Jerry Lumpe			
□ 120 Eddie Mathews	14.00	5.75	1.40
□ 121 Eli Grba	1.00	.40	.10
□ 122 Chicago Cubs Team Card	2.25	.90	.22
□ 123 Billy Gardner	1.25	.50	.12
□ 124 J.C. Martin	1.00	.40	.10
□ 125 Steve Barber	1.00	.40	.10
□ 126 Dick Stuart	1.50	.60	.15
□ 127 Ron Kline	1.00	.40	.10
□ 128 Rip Repulski	1.00	.40	.10
□ 129 Ed Hobaugh	1.00	.40	.10
□ 130 Norm Larker	1.25	.50	.12
□ 131 Paul Richards MG	1.25	.50	.12
□ 132 Al Lopez MG	3.50	1.40	.35
□ 133 Ralph Houk MG	2.50	1.00	.25
□ 134 Mickey Vernon MG	1.25	.50	.12
□ 135 Fred Hutchinson MG	1.25	.50	.12
□ 136 Walt Alston MG	4.00	1.60	.40
□ 137 Chuck Dressen MG	1.25	.50	.12
□ 138 Danny Murtaugh MG	1.25	.50	.12
□ 139 Solly Hemus MG	1.25	.50	.12
□ 140 Gus Triandos	1.25	.50	.12
□ 141 Billy Williams	50.00	20.00	5.00
□ 142 Luis Arroyo	1.25	.50	.12
□ 143 Russ Snyder	1.00	.40	.10
□ 144 Jim Coker	1.00	.40	.10
□ 145 Bob Buhl	1.00	.40	.10
□ 146 Marty Keough	1.00	.40	.10
□ 147 Ed Rakow	1.00	.40	.10
□ 148 Julian Javier	1.25	.50	.12
□ 149 Bob Oldis	1.00	.40	.10
□ 150 Willie Mays	70.00	28.00	7.00
□ 151 Jim Donohue	1.00	.40	.10
□ 152 Earl Torgeson	1.00	.40	.10
□ 153 Don Lee	1.00	.40	.10
□ 154 Bobby Del Greco	1.00	.40	.10
□ 155 Johnny Temple	1.25	.50	.12
□ 156 Ken Hunt	1.00	.40	.10
□ 157 Cal McLish	1.00	.40	.10
□ 158 Pete Daley	1.00	.40	.10
□ 159 Orioles Team	2.25	.90	.22
□ 160 Whitey Ford	21.00	8.50	2.10
□ 161 Sherman Jones (photo actually Eddie Fisher)	1.00	.40	.10
□ 162 Jay Hook	1.00	.40	.10
□ 163 Ed Sadowski	1.00	.40	.10
□ 164 Felix Mantilla	1.00	.40	.10
□ 165 Gino Cimoli	1.00	.40	.10
□ 166 Danny Kravitz	1.00	.40	.10
□ 167 San Francisco Giants Team Card	2.25	.90	.22
□ 168 Tommy Davis	2.50	1.00	.25
□ 169 Don Elston	1.00	.40	.10
□ 170 Al Smith	1.00	.40	.10
□ 171 Paul Foytack	1.00	.40	.10
□ 172 Don Dillard	1.00	.40	.10
□ 173 Beantown Bombers	1.50	.60	.15
Frank Malzone			
Vic Wertz			
Jackie Jensen			
□ 174 Ray Semproch	1.00	.40	.10
□ 175 Gene Freese	1.00	.40	.10
□ 176 Ken Aspromonte	1.00	.40	.10
□ 177 Don Larsen	1.75	.70	.17
□ 178 Bob Nieman	1.00	.40	.10
□ 179 Joe Koppe	1.00	.40	.10
□ 180 Bobby Richardson	4.00	1.60	.40
□ 181 Fred Green	1.00	.40	.10
□ 182 Dave Nicholson	1.00	.40	.10
□ 183 Andre Rodgers	1.00	.40	.10
□ 184 Steve Bilko	1.00	.40	.10
□ 185 Herb Score	1.75	.70	.17
□ 186 Elmer Valo	1.00	.40	.10
□ 187 Billy Klaus	1.00	.40	.10
□ 188 Jim Marshall	1.00	.40	.10
□ 189 Checklist 3	5.00	.50	.10
□ 190 Stan Williams	1.00	.40	.10
□ 191 Mike De La Hoz	1.00	.40	.10
□ 192 Dick Brown	1.00	.40	.10
□ 193 Gene Conley	1.00	.40	.10
□ 194 Gordy Coleman	1.25	.50	.12
□ 195 Jerry Casale	1.00	.40	.10
□ 196 Ed Bouchee	1.00	.40	.10
□ 197 Dick Hall	1.00	.40	.10
□ 198 Carl Sawatski	1.00	.40	.10
□ 199 Bob Boyd	1.00	.40	.10
□ 200 Warren Spahn	15.00	6.00	1.50
□ 201 Pete Whisenant	1.00	.40	.10
□ 202 Al Neiger	1.00	.40	.10
□ 203 Eddie Bressoud	1.00	.40	.10
□ 204 Bob Skinner	1.25	.50	.12
□ 205 Billy Pierce	1.50	.60	.15
□ 206 Gene Green	1.00	.40	.10
□ 207 Dodger Southpaws	9.00	3.75	.90
Sandy Koufax			
Johnny Podres			
□ 208 Larry Osborne	1.00	.40	.10
□ 209 Ken McBride	1.00	.40	.10
□ 210 Pete Runnels	1.25	.50	.12
□ 211 Bob Gibson	16.00	6.50	1.60
□ 212 Haywood Sullivan	1.25	.50	.12
□ 213 Bill Stafford	1.25	.50	.12
□ 214 Danny Murphy	1.00	.40	.10
□ 215 Gus Bell	1.25	.50	.12
□ 216 Ted Bowsfield	1.00	.40	.10
□ 217 Mel Roach	1.00	.40	.10
□ 218 Hal Brown	1.00	.40	.10
□ 219 Gene Mauch MG	1.50	.60	.15
□ 220 Alvin Dark MG	1.50	.60	.15
□ 221 Mike Higgins MG	1.25	.50	.12
□ 222 Jimmy Dykes MG	1.25	.50	.12
□ 223 Bob Scheffing MG	1.00	.40	.10
□ 224 Joe Gordon MG	1.25	.50	.12
□ 225 Bill Rigney MG	1.00	.40	.10
□ 226 Harry Lavagetto MG	1.25	.50	.12
□ 227 Juan Pizarro	1.00	.40	.10
□ 228 New York Yankees Team Card	12.00	5.00	1.20
□ 229 Rudy Hernandez	1.00	.40	.10
□ 230 Don Hoak	1.25	.50	.12
□ 231 Dick Drott	1.00	.40	.10
□ 232 Bill White	1.50	.60	.15
□ 233 Joey Jay	1.00	.40	.10
□ 234 Ted Lepcio	1.00	.40	.10
□ 235 Camilo Pascual	1.25	.50	.12
□ 236 Don Gile	1.00	.40	.10
□ 237 Billy Loes	1.00	.40	.10
□ 238 Jim Gilliam	2.50	1.00	.25
□ 239 Dave Sisler	1.00	.40	.10
□ 240 Ron Hansen	1.00	.40	.10
□ 241 Al Cicotte	1.00	.40	.10
□ 242 Hal Smith	1.00	.40	.10
□ 243 Frank Lary	1.25	.50	.12
□ 244 Chico Cardenas	1.00	.40	.10
□ 245 Joe Adcock	1.50	.60	.15
□ 246 Bob Davis	1.00	.40	.10
□ 247 Billy Goodman	1.25	.50	.12
□ 248 Ed Keegan	1.00	.40	.10
□ 249 Cincinnati Reds Team Card	2.75	1.10	.27
□ 250 Buc Hill Aces	1.50	.60	.15
Vern Law			
Roy Face			
□ 251 Bill Bruton	1.25	.50	.12
□ 252 Bill Short	1.00	.40	.10
□ 253 Sammy Taylor	1.00	.40	.10
□ 254 Ted Sadowski	1.00	.40	.10
□ 255 Vic Power	1.00	.40	.10
□ 256 Billy Hoeft	1.00	.40	.10
□ 257 Carroll Hardy	1.00	.40	.10
□ 258 Jack Sanford	1.50	.60	.15
□ 259 John Schaive	1.00	.40	.10
□ 260 Don Drysdale	13.00	5.25	1.30
□ 261 Charlie Lau	1.50	.60	.15
□ 262 Tony Curry	1.00	.40	.10
□ 263 Ken Hamlin	1.00	.40	.10
□ 264 Glen Hobbie	1.00	.40	.10
□ 265 Tony Kubek	4.50	1.80	.45
□ 266 Lindy McDaniel	1.25	.50	.12
□ 267 Norm Siebern	1.00	.40	.10
□ 268 Ike Delock	1.00	.40	.10
□ 269 Harry Chiti	1.00	.40	.10
□ 270 Bob Friend	1.25	.50	.12
□ 271 Jim Landis	1.00	.40	.10
□ 272 Tom Morgan	1.00	.40	.10
□ 273 Checklist 4	5.00	.50	.10
□ 274 Gary Bell	1.00	.40	.10
□ 275 Gene Woodling	1.50	.60	.15
□ 276 Ray Rippelmeyer	1.00	.40	.10
□ 277 Hank Foiles	1.00	.40	.10
□ 278 Don McMahon	1.25	.50	.12
□ 279 Jose Pagan	1.00	.40	.10
□ 280 Frank Howard	2.50	1.00	.25
□ 281 Frank Sullivan	1.00	.40	.10
□ 282 Faye Throneberry	1.00	.40	.10
□ 283 Bob Anderson	1.00	.40	.10
□ 284 Dick Gernert	1.00	.40	.10
□ 285 Sherm Lollar	1.25	.50	.12
□ 286 George Witt	1.00	.40	.10
□ 287 Carl Yastrzemski	125.00	50.00	12.50
□ 288 Albie Pearson	1.00	.40	.10
□ 289 Ray Moore	1.00	.40	.10
□ 290 Stan Musial	60.00	24.00	6.00
□ 291 Tex Clevenger	1.00	.40	.10
□ 292 Jim Baumer	1.00	.40	.10
□ 293 Tom Sturdivant	1.00	.40	.10
□ 294 Don Blasingame	1.00	.40	.10

□ 295 Milt Pappas	1.25	.50	.12
□ 296 Wes Covington	1.25	.50	.12
□ 297 Athletics Team	2.00	.80	.20
□ 298 Jim Golden	1.00	.40	.10
□ 299 Clay Dalrymple	1.00	.40	.10
□ 300 Mickey Mantle	300.00	120.00	30.00
□ 301 Chet Nichols	1.00	.40	.10
□ 302 Al Heist	1.00	.40	.10
□ 303 Gary Peters	1.25	.50	.12
□ 304 Rocky Nelson	1.00	.40	.10
□ 305 Mike McCormick	1.25	.50	.12
□ 306 World Series Game 1	2.50	1.00	.25
Virdon Saves Game			
□ 307 World Series Game 2	20.00	8.00	2.00
Mantle 2 Homers			
□ 308 World Series Game 3	3.50	1.40	.35
Richardson is Hero			
□ 309 World Series Game 4	2.50	1.00	.25
Cimoli Safe			
□ 310 World Series Game 5	3.00	1.20	.30
Face Saves the Day			
□ 311 World Series Game 6	5.00	2.00	.50
Ford Second Shutout			
□ 312 World Series Game 7	4.00	1.60	.40
Mazeroski's Homer			
□ 313 World Series Summary	2.50	1.00	.25
Pirates Celebrate			
□ 314 Bob Miller	1.00	.40	.10
□ 315 Earl Battey	1.00	.40	.10
□ 316 Bobby Gene Smith	1.00	.40	.10
□ 317 Jim Brewer	1.00	.40	.10
□ 318 Danny O'Connell	1.00	.40	.10
□ 319 Valmy Thomas	1.00	.40	.10
□ 320 Lou Burdette	2.00	.80	.20
□ 321 Marv Breeding	1.00	.40	.10
□ 322 Bill Kunkel	1.50	.60	.15
□ 323 Sammy Esposito	1.00	.40	.10
□ 324 Hank Aguirre	1.00	.40	.10
□ 325 Wally Moon	1.50	.60	.15
□ 326 Dave Hillman	1.00	.40	.10
□ 327 Matty Alou	2.50	1.00	.25
□ 328 Jim O'Toole	1.25	.50	.12
□ 329 Julio Becquer	1.00	.40	.10
□ 330 Rocky Colavito	3.00	1.20	.30
□ 331 Ned Garver	1.00	.40	.10
□ 332 Dutch Dotterer	1.25	.50	.12
(photo actually			
Tommy Dotterer,			
Dutch's brother)			
□ 333 Fritz Brickell	1.00	.40	.10
□ 334 Walt Bond	1.00	.40	.10
□ 335 Frank Bolling	1.00	.40	.10
□ 336 Don Mincher	1.25	.50	.12
□ 337 Al's Aces	3.50	1.40	.35
Early Wynn			
Al Lopez			
Herb Score			
□ 338 Don Landrum	1.00	.40	.10
□ 339 Gene Baker	1.00	.40	.10
□ 340 Vic Wertz	1.25	.50	.12
□ 341 Jim Owens	1.00	.40	.10
□ 342 Clint Courtney	1.00	.40	.10
□ 343 Earl Robinson	1.00	.40	.10
□ 344 Sandy Koufax	55.00	22.00	5.50
□ 345 Jim Piersall	2.00	.80	.20
□ 346 Howie Nunn	1.00	.40	.10
□ 347 St. Louis Cardinals	2.25	.90	.22
Team Card			
□ 348 Steve Boros	1.25	.50	.12
□ 349 Danny McDevitt	1.00	.40	.10
□ 350 Ernie Banks	18.00	7.25	1.80
□ 351 Jim King	1.00	.40	.10
□ 352 Bob Shaw	1.00	.40	.10
□ 353 Howie Bedell	1.00	.40	.10
□ 354 Billy Harrell	1.00	.40	.10
□ 355 Bob Allison	1.25	.50	.12
□ 356 Ryne Duren	1.50	.60	.15
□ 357 Daryl Spencer	1.00	.40	.10
□ 358 Earl Averill	1.00	.40	.10
□ 359 Dallas Green	3.00	1.20	.30
□ 360 Frank Robinson	20.00	8.00	2.00
□ 361A Checklist 5	5.00	1.00	.20
(no ad on back)			
□ 361B Checklist 5	10.00	2.00	.40
(Special Feature			
ad on back)			
□ 362 Frank Funk	1.00	.40	.10
□ 363 John Roseboro	1.25	.50	.12
□ 364 Moe Drabowsky	1.00	.40	.10
□ 365 Jerry Lumpe	1.00	.40	.10
□ 366 Eddie Fisher	1.00	.40	.10
□ 367 Jim Rivera	1.00	.40	.10
□ 368 Bennie Daniels	1.00	.40	.10
□ 369 Dave Philley	1.00	.40	.10
□ 370 Roy Face	2.25	.90	.22

□ 371 Bill Skowron SP	6.50	2.60	.65
□ 372 Bob Hendley	1.25	.50	.12
□ 373 Boston Red Sox	2.50	1.00	.25
Team Card			
□ 374 Paul Giel	1.25	.50	.12
□ 375 Ken Boyer	4.00	1.60	.40
□ 376 Mike Roarke	1.25	.50	.12
□ 377 Ruben Gomez	1.25	.50	.12
□ 378 Wally Post	1.25	.50	.12
□ 379 Bobby Shantz	2.50	1.00	.25
□ 380 Minnie Minoso	3.00	1.20	.30
□ 381 Dave Wickersham	1.25	.50	.12
□ 382 Frank Thomas	1.75	.70	.17
□ 383 Frisco First Liners	1.75	.70	.17
Mike McCormick			
Jack Sanford			
Billy O'Dell			
□ 384 Chuck Essegian	1.75	.70	.17
□ 385 Jim Perry	2.00	.80	.20
□ 386 Joe Hicks	1.25	.50	.12
□ 387 Duke Maas	1.25	.50	.12
□ 388 Bob Clemente	50.00	20.00	5.00
□ 389 Ralph Terry	2.00	.80	.20
□ 390 Del Crandall	1.75	.70	.17
□ 391 Winston Brown	1.25	.50	.12
□ 392 Reno Bertoia	1.25	.50	.12
□ 393 Batter Bafflers	1.75	.70	.17
Don Cardwell			
Glen Hobbie			
□ 394 Ken Walters	1.25	.50	.12
□ 395 Chuck Estrada	1.75	.70	.17
□ 396 Bob Aspromonte	1.25	.50	.12
□ 397 Hal Woodeshick	1.25	.50	.12
□ 398 Hank Bauer	2.00	.80	.20
□ 399 Cliff Cook	1.25	.50	.12
□ 400 Vern Law	2.00	.80	.20
□ 401 Ruth 60th Homer	12.00	5.00	1.20
□ 402 Perfect Game	5.00	2.00	.50
(Don Larsen)			
□ 403 26 Inning Tie	2.00	.80	.20
□ 404 Hornsby .424 Average	3.00	1.20	.30
□ 405 Gehrig's Streak	7.00	2.80	.70
□ 406 Mantle 565 Ft. Homer	21.00	8.50	2.10
□ 407 Chesbro Wins 41	2.00	.80	.20
□ 408 Mathewson Fans 267	3.00	1.20	.30
□ 409 Johnson Shutouts	3.00	1.20	.30
□ 410 Haddix 12 Perfect	2.00	.80	.20
Innings			
□ 411 Tony Taylor	1.25	.50	.12
□ 412 Larry Sherry	1.75	.70	.17
□ 413 Eddie Yost	1.25	.50	.12
□ 414 Dick Donovan	1.25	.50	.12
□ 415 Hank Aaron	75.00	30.00	7.50
□ 416 Dick Howser	7.00	2.80	.70
□ 417 Juan Marichal	75.00	30.00	7.50
□ 418 Ed Bailey	1.25	.50	.12
□ 419 Tom Borland	1.25	.50	.12
□ 420 Ernie Broglio	1.75	.70	.17
□ 421 Ty Cline	1.25	.50	.12
□ 422 Bud Daley	1.25	.50	.12
□ 423 Charlie Neal SP	3.50	1.40	.35
□ 424 Turk Lown	1.25	.50	.12
□ 425 Yogi Berra	40.00	16.00	4.00
□ 426 Milwaukee Braves	6.00	2.40	.60
Team Card			
(back numbered 463)			
□ 427 Dick Ellsworth	2.00	.80	.20
□ 428 Ray Barker SP	3.00	1.20	.30
□ 429 Al Kaline	25.00	10.00	2.50
□ 430 Bill Mazeroski SP	6.50	2.60	.65
□ 431 Chuck Stobbs	1.25	.50	.12
□ 432 Coot Veal	1.25	.50	.12
□ 433 Art Mahaffey	1.25	.50	.12
□ 434 Tom Brewer	1.25	.50	.12
□ 435 Orlando Cepeda	4.50	1.80	.45
□ 436 Jim Maloney	4.50	1.80	.45
□ 437A Checklist 6	6.00	.60	.10
440 Louis Aparicio			
□ 437B Checklist 6	6.00	.60	.10
440 Luis Aparicio			
□ 438 Curt Flood	2.50	1.00	.25
□ 439 Phil Regan	1.75	.70	.17
□ 440 Luis Aparicio	10.00	4.00	1.00
□ 441 Dick Bertell	1.25	.50	.12
□ 442 Gordon Jones	1.25	.50	.12
□ 443 Duke Snider	25.00	10.00	2.50
□ 444 Joe Nuxhall	1.75	.70	.17
□ 445 Frank Malzone	2.00	.80	.20
□ 446 Bob Taylor	1.25	.50	.12
□ 447 Harry Bright	1.75	.70	.17
□ 448 Del Rice	1.75	.70	.17
□ 449 Bob Bolin	1.75	.70	.17
□ 450 Jim Lemon	2.50	1.00	.25
□ 451 Power for Ernie	2.50	1.00	.25
Daryl Spencer			

	Bill White Ernie Broglio			
□ 452	Bob Allen	1.75	.70	.17
□ 453	Dick Schofield	1.75	.70	.17
□ 454	Pumpsie Green	1.75	.70	.17
□ 455	Early Wynn	10.00	4.00	1.00
□ 456	Hal Bevan	1.75	.70	.17
□ 457	John James	1.75	.70	.17
□ 458	Willie Tasby	1.75	.70	.17
□ 459	Terry Fox	1.75	.70	.17
□ 460	Gil Hodges	10.00	4.00	1.00
□ 461	Smoky Burgess	2.50	1.00	.25
□ 462	Lou Klimchock	1.75	.70	.17
□ 463	Jack Fisher (See also 426)	2.50	1.00	.25
□ 464	Leroy Thomas	3.00	1.20	.30
□ 465	Roy McMillan	1.75	.70	.17
□ 466	Ron Moeller	1.75	.70	.17
□ 467	Cleveland Indians Team Card	3.50	1.40	.35
□ 468	John Callison	2.50	1.00	.25
□ 469	Ralph Lumenti	1.75	.70	.17
□ 470	Roy Sievers	2.50	1.00	.25
□ 471	Phil Rizzuto MVP	10.00	4.00	.90
□ 472	Yogi Berra MVP	27.00	11.00	2.50
□ 473	Bob Shantz MVP	2.50	1.00	.25
□ 474	Al Rosen MVP	3.00	1.20	.25
□ 475	Mickey Mantle MVP	75.00	30.00	7.50
□ 476	Jackie Jensen MVP	3.00	1.20	.25
□ 477	Nellie Fox MVP	3.50	1.50	.30
□ 478	Roger Maris MVP	27.00	11.00	2.50
□ 479	Jim Konstanty MVP	2.50	1.00	.25
□ 480	Roy Campanella MVP	21.00	8.00	2.00
□ 481	Hank Sauer MVP	2.50	1.00	.25
□ 482	Willie Mays MVP	30.00	12.00	2.70
□ 483	Don Newcombe MVP	3.00	1.20	.25
□ 484	Hank Aaron MVP	30.00	12.00	2.70
□ 485	Ernie Banks MVP	11.00	4.50	1.00
□ 486	Dick Groat MVP	2.50	1.00	.25
□ 487	Gene Oliver	1.75	.70	.17
□ 488	Joe McClain	1.75	.70	.17
□ 489	Walt Dropo	1.75	.70	.17
□ 490	Jim Bunning	7.00	2.80	.70
□ 491	Philadelphia Phillies Team Card	3.50	1.40	.35
□ 492	Ron Fairly	2.50	1.00	.25
□ 493	Don Zimmer	3.00	1.20	.30
□ 494	Tom Cheney	1.75	.70	.17
□ 495	Elston Howard	4.00	1.60	.40
□ 496	Ken Mackenzie	1.75	.70	.17
□ 497	Willie Jones	1.75	.70	.17
□ 498	Ray Herbert	1.75	.70	.17
□ 499	Chuck Schilling	1.75	.70	.17
□ 500	Harvey Kuenn	3.00	1.20	.30
□ 501	John DeMerit	1.75	.70	.17
□ 502	Clarence Coleman	1.75	.70	.17
□ 503	Tito Francona	2.50	1.00	.25
□ 504	Billy Consolo	1.75	.70	.17
□ 505	Red Schoendienst	3.00	1.20	.30
□ 506	Willie Davis	5.00	2.00	.50
□ 507	Pete Burnside	1.75	.70	.17
□ 508	Rocky Bridges	1.75	.70	.17
□ 509	Camilo Carreon	1.75	.70	.17
□ 510	Art Ditmar	1.75	.70	.17
□ 511	Joe M. Morgan	3.50	1.40	.35
□ 512	Bob Will	1.75	.70	.17
□ 513	Jim Brosnan	2.50	1.00	.25
□ 514	Jake Wood	1.75	.70	.17
□ 515	Jackie Brandt	1.75	.70	.17
□ 516	Checklist 7	7.00	.75	.15
□ 517	Willie McCovey	35.00	14.00	3.50
□ 518	Andy Carey	2.50	1.00	.25
□ 519	Jim Pagliaroni	1.75	.70	.17
□ 520	Joe Cunningham	2.50	1.00	.25
□ 521	Brother Battery Norm Sherry Larry Sherry	2.50	1.00	.25
□ 522	Dick Farrell	2.50	1.00	.25
□ 523	Joe Gibbon	16.00	6.50	1.60
□ 524	John Logan	18.00	7.25	1.80
□ 525	Ron Perranoski	18.00	7.25	1.80
□ 526	R.C. Stevens	16.00	6.50	1.60
□ 527	Gene Leek	16.00	6.50	1.60
□ 528	Pedro Ramos	16.00	6.50	1.60
□ 529	Bob Roselli	16.00	6.50	1.60
□ 530	Bob Malkmus	16.00	6.50	1.60
□ 531	Jim Coates	16.00	6.50	1.60
□ 532	Bob Hale	16.00	6.50	1.60
□ 533	Jack Curtis	16.00	6.50	1.60
□ 534	Eddie Kasko	16.00	6.50	1.60
□ 535	Larry Jackson	16.00	6.50	1.60
□ 536	Bill Tuttle	16.00	6.50	1.60
□ 537	Bobby Locke	16.00	6.50	1.60
□ 538	Chuck Hiller	16.00	6.50	1.60
□ 539	John Klippstein	16.00	6.50	1.60
□ 540	Jackie Jensen	24.00	10.00	2.4
□ 541	Roland Sheldon	16.00	6.50	1.6
□ 542	Minnesota Twins Team Card	35.00	14.00	3.5
□ 543	Roger Craig	24.00	10.00	2.4
□ 544	George Thomas	16.00	6.50	1.6
□ 545	Hoyt Wilhelm	50.00	20.00	5.0
□ 546	Marty Kutyna	16.00	6.50	1.6
□ 547	Leon Wagner	16.00	6.50	1.6
□ 548	Ted Wills	16.00	6.50	1.6
□ 549	Hal R. Smith	16.00	6.50	1.6
□ 550	Frank Baumann	16.00	6.50	1.6
□ 551	George Altman	16.00	6.50	1.6
□ 552	Jim Archer	16.00	6.50	1.6
□ 553	Bill Fischer	16.00	6.50	1.6
□ 554	Pittsburgh Pirates Team Card	30.00	12.00	3.0
□ 555	Sam Jones	18.00	7.25	1.8
□ 556	Ken R. Hunt	16.00	6.50	1.6
□ 557	Jose Valdivielso	16.00	6.50	1.6
□ 558	Don Ferrarese	16.00	6.50	1.6
□ 559	Jim Gentile	18.00	7.25	1.8
□ 560	Barry Latman	16.00	6.50	1.6
□ 561	Charley James	16.00	6.50	1.6
□ 562	Bill Monbouquette	16.00	6.50	1.6
□ 563	Bob Cerv	18.00	7.25	1.8
□ 564	Don Cardwell	16.00	6.50	1.6
□ 565	Felipe Alou	18.00	7.25	1.8
□ 566	Paul Richards MG AS	18.00	7.25	1.80
□ 567	Danny Murtaugh MG AS	18.00	7.25	1.8
□ 568	Bill Skowron AS	20.00	8.00	2.0
□ 569	Frank Herrera AS	18.00	7.25	1.8
□ 570	Nellie Fox AS	25.00	10.00	2.5
□ 571	Bill Mazeroski AS	20.00	8.00	2.0
□ 572	Brooks Robinson AS	60.00	24.00	6.0
□ 573	Ken Boyer AS	20.00	8.00	2.0
□ 574	Luis Aparicio AS	35.00	14.00	3.5
□ 575	Ernie Banks AS	60.00	24.00	6.0
□ 576	Roger Maris AS	70.00	28.00	7.0
□ 577	Hank Aaron AS	125.00	50.00	12.5
□ 578	Mickey Mantle AS	300.00	120.00	30.0
□ 579	Willie Mays AS	125.00	50.00	12.50
□ 580	Al Kaline AS	65.00	26.00	6.50
□ 581	Frank Robinson AS	60.00	24.00	6.00
□ 582	Earl Battey AS	18.00	7.25	1.80
□ 583	Del Crandall AS	18.00	7.25	1.80
□ 584	Jim Perry AS	18.00	7.25	1.80
□ 585	Bob Friend AS	18.00	7.25	1.80
□ 586	Whitey Ford AS	60.00	24.00	6.00
□ 587	Does not exist	0.00	.00	.00
□ 588	Does not exist	0.00	.00	.00
□ 589	Warren Spahn AS	100.00	30.00	6.00

1962 Topps

The cards in this 598-card set measure 2 1/2" by 3 1/2". The 1962 Topps set contains a mini-series spotlighting Babe Ruth (135 to 144). Other subsets in the set include League Leaders (51-60), World Series cards (232-237), In Action cards (311-319), NL All Stars (390-399), AL All Stars (466-475), and Rookie Prospects (591-598). The second series had two distinct printings which are distinguishable by numerous color and pose variations. Card number 139 exists as A: Babe Ruth Special card, B: Hal Reniff with arms over head, or C: Hal Reniff in the same pose as card number 159. In addition, two poses exist for players depicted on card numbers 129, 132, 134, 147, 174, 176, and 190. The high number series, 523 to 598, is somewhat more difficult to obtain than other cards in the set. The set price listed does not include the pose variations (see checklist below for individual values).

	NRMT	VG-E	GOOD
COMPLETE SET	3600.00	1600.00	575.00
COMMON PLAYER (1-109)	.85	.34	.08
COMMON PLAYER (110-196)	.85	.34	.08
COMMON PLAYER (197-283)	1.00	.40	.10
COMMON PLAYER (284-370)	1.25	.50	.12
COMMON PLAYER (371-446)	1.75	.70	.17
COMMON PLAYER (447-522)	2.25	.90	.22
COMMON PLAYER (523-590)	8.00	3.25	.80
COMMON PLAYER (591-598)	12.00	5.00	1.20

	NRMT	VG-E	GOOD
☐ 1 Roger Maris	150.00	30.00	6.00
☐ 2 Jim Brosnan	1.00	.40	.10
☐ 3 Pete Runnels	1.00	.40	.10
☐ 4 John DeMerit	.85	.34	.08
☐ 5 Sandy Koufax	50.00	20.00	5.00
☐ 6 Marv Breeding	.85	.34	.08
☐ 7 Frank Thomas	1.00	.40	.10
☐ 8 Ray Herbert	.85	.34	.08
☐ 9 Jim Davenport	1.00	.40	.10
☐ 10 Bob Clemente	50.00	20.00	5.00
☐ 11 Tom Morgan	.85	.34	.08
☐ 12 Harry Craft MG	.85	.34	.08
☐ 13 Dick Howser	2.00	.80	.20
☐ 14 Bill White	1.50	.60	.15
☐ 15 Dick Donovan	.85	.34	.08
☐ 16 Darrell Johnson	1.00	.40	.10
☐ 17 John Callison	1.00	.40	.10
☐ 18 Managers' Dream Mickey Mantle Willie Mays	80.00	32.00	8.00
☐ 19 Ray Washburn	.85	.34	.08
☐ 20 Rocky Colavito	2.50	1.00	.25
☐ 21 Jim Kaat	3.50	1.40	.35
☐ 22A Checklist 1 COR	4.00	.40	.08
☐ 22B Checklist 1 ERR (121-176 on back)	5.00	.50	.10
☐ 23 Norm Larker	1.00	.40	.10
☐ 24 Tigers Team	2.00	.80	.20
☐ 25 Ernie Banks	14.00	5.75	1.40
☐ 26 Chris Cannizzaro	.85	.34	.08
☐ 27 Chuck Cottier	1.00	.40	.10
☐ 28 Minnie Minoso	2.00	.80	.20
☐ 29 Casey Stengel MG	12.00	5.00	1.20
☐ 30 Ed Mathews	12.00	5.00	1.20
☐ 31 Tom Tresh	6.00	2.40	.60
☐ 32 John Roseboro	1.00	.40	.10
☐ 33 Don Larsen	1.50	.60	.15
☐ 34 Johnny Temple	1.00	.40	.10
☐ 35 Don Schwall	1.00	.40	.10
☐ 36 Don Leppert	.85	.34	.08
☐ 37 Tribe Hill Trio Barry Latman Dick Stigman Jim Perry	1.00	.40	.10
☐ 38 Gene Stephens	.85	.34	.08
☐ 39 Joe Koppe	.85	.34	.08
☐ 40 Orlando Cepeda	4.00	1.60	.40
☐ 41 Cliff Cook	.85	.34	.08
☐ 42 Jim King	.85	.34	.08
☐ 43 Los Angeles Dodgers Team Card	3.00	1.20	.30
☐ 44 Don Taussig	.85	.34	.08
☐ 45 Brooks Robinson	14.00	5.75	1.40
☐ 46 Jack Baldschun	.85	.34	.08
☐ 47 Bob Will	.85	.34	.08
☐ 48 Ralph Terry	1.50	.60	.15
☐ 49 Hal Jones	.85	.34	.08
☐ 50 Stan Musial	45.00	18.00	4.50
☐ 51 AL Batting Leaders Norm Cash Jim Piersall Al Kaline Elston Howard	1.50	.60	.15
☐ 52 NL Batting Leaders Bob Clemente Vada Pinson Ken Boyer Wally Moon	2.00	.80	.20
☐ 53 AL Home Run Leaders Roger Maris Mickey Mantle Jim Gentile Harmon Killebrew	12.00	5.00	1.20
☐ 54 NL Home Run Leaders Orlando Cepeda Willie Mays Frank Robinson	3.00	1.20	.30
☐ 55 AL ERA Leaders Dick Donovan Bill Stafford Don Mossi Milt Pappas	1.50	.60	.15
☐ 56 NL ERA Leaders Warren Spahn Jim O'Toole Curt Simmons Mike McCormick	1.50	.60	.15
☐ 57 AL Wins Leaders Whitey Ford Frank Lary Steve Barber Jim Bunning	1.50	.60	.15
☐ 58 NL Wins Leaders Warren Spahn Joe Jay Jim O'Toole	1.50	.60	.15
☐ 59 AL Strikeout Leaders Camilo Pascual Whitey Ford Jim Bunning Juan Pizzaro	1.50	.60	.15
☐ 60 NL Strikeout Leaders Sandy Koufax Stan Williams Don Drysdale Jim O'Toole	2.50	1.00	.25
☐ 61 Cardinals Team	2.00	.80	.20
☐ 62 Steve Boros	1.00	.40	.10
☐ 63 Tony Cloninger	.85	.34	.08
☐ 64 Russ Snyder	.85	.34	.08
☐ 65 Bobby Richardson	3.50	1.40	.35
☐ 66 Cuno Barragon	.85	.34	.08
☐ 67 Harvey Haddix	1.50	.60	.15
☐ 68 Ken Hunt	.85	.34	.08
☐ 69 Phil Ortega	.85	.34	.08
☐ 70 Harmon Killebrew	12.00	5.00	1.20
☐ 71 Dick LeMay	.85	.34	.08
☐ 72 Bob's Pupils Steve Boros Bob Scheffing Jake Wood	1.00	.40	.10
☐ 73 Nellie Fox	3.50	1.40	.35
☐ 74 Bob Lillis	1.00	.40	.10
☐ 75 Milt Pappas	1.00	.40	.10
☐ 76 Howie Bedell	.85	.34	.08
☐ 77 Tony Taylor	.85	.34	.08
☐ 78 Gene Green	.85	.34	.08
☐ 79 Ed Hobaugh	.85	.34	.08
☐ 80 Vada Pinson	2.00	.80	.20
☐ 81 Jim Pagliaroni	.85	.34	.08
☐ 82 Deron Johnson	1.00	.40	.10
☐ 83 Larry Jackson	.85	.34	.08
☐ 84 Lenny Green	.85	.34	.08
☐ 85 Gil Hodges	9.00	3.75	.90
☐ 86 Donn Clendenon	1.50	.60	.15
☐ 87 Mike Roarke	1.00	.40	.10
☐ 88 Ralph Houk MG	1.50	.60	.15
☐ 89 Barney Schultz	.85	.34	.08
☐ 90 Jim Piersall	1.50	.60	.15
☐ 91 J.C. Martin	.85	.34	.08
☐ 92 Sam Jones	1.00	.40	.10
☐ 93 John Blanchard	1.50	.60	.15
☐ 94 Jay Hook	.85	.34	.08
☐ 95 Don Hoak	1.00	.40	.10
☐ 96 Eli Grba	.85	.34	.08
☐ 97 Tito Francona	1.00	.40	.10
☐ 98 Checklist 2	4.00	.40	.08
☐ 99 John (Boog) Powell	9.00	3.75	.90
☐ 100 Warren Spahn	12.00	5.00	1.20
☐ 101 Carroll Hardy	.85	.34	.08
☐ 102 Al Schroll	.85	.34	.08
☐ 103 Don Blasingame	.85	.34	.08
☐ 104 Ted Savage	.85	.34	.08
☐ 105 Don Mossi	1.00	.40	.10
☐ 106 Carl Sawatski	.85	.34	.08
☐ 107 Mike McCormick	1.00	.40	.10
☐ 108 Willie Davis	1.50	.60	.15
☐ 109 Bob Shaw	.85	.34	.08
☐ 110 Bill Skowron	3.50	1.40	.35
☐ 111 Dallas Green	2.00	.80	.20
☐ 112 Hank Foiles	.85	.34	.08
☐ 113 Chicago White Sox Team Card	2.00	.80	.20
☐ 114 Howie Koplitz	.85	.34	.08
☐ 115 Bob Skinner	1.00	.40	.10
☐ 116 Herb Score	1.50	.60	.15
☐ 117 Gary Geiger	.85	.34	.08
☐ 118 Julian Javier	1.00	.40	.10
☐ 119 Danny Murphy	.85	.34	.08
☐ 120 Bob Purkey	.85	.34	.08

□ 121 Billy Hitchcock MG	.85	.34	.08
□ 122 Norm Bass	.85	.34	.08
□ 123 Mike De La Hoz	.85	.34	.08
□ 124 Bill Pleis	.85	.34	.08
□ 125 Gene Woodling	1.25	.50	.12
□ 126 Al Cicotte	.85	.34	.08
□ 127 Pride of A's	1.25	.50	.12
Norm Siebern			
Hank Bauer			
Jerry Lumpe			
□ 128 Art Fowler	.85	.34	.08
□ 129A Lee Walls	.85	.34	.08
(facing right)			
□ 129B Lee Walls	10.00	4.00	1.00
(face left)			
□ 130 Frank Bolling	.85	.34	.08
□ 131 Pete Richert	.85	.34	.08
□ 132A Angels Team	2.00	.80	.20
(without photo)			
□ 132B Angels Team	10.00	4.00	1.00
(with photo)			
□ 133 Felipe Alou	1.50	.60	.15
□ 134A Billy Hoeft	.85	.34	.08
(facing right)			
□ 134B Billy Hoeft	10.00	4.00	1.00
(facing straight)			
□ 135 Babe Ruth Special 1	6.00	2.40	.60
Babe as a Boy			
□ 136 Babe Ruth Special 2	6.00	2.40	.60
Babe Joins Yanks			
□ 137 Babe Ruth Special 3	6.00	2.40	.60
Babe with Huggins			
□ 138 Babe Ruth Special 4	6.00	2.40	.60
Famous Slugger			
□ 139A Babe Ruth Special 5	9.00	3.75	.90
□ 139B Hal Reniff PORT	10.00	4.00	1.00
□ 139C Hal Reniff	40.00	16.00	4.00
(pitching)			
□ 140 Babe Ruth Special 6	8.00	3.25	.80
Gehrig and Ruth			
□ 141 Babe Ruth Special 7	6.00	2.40	.60
Twilight Years			
□ 142 Babe Ruth Special 8	6.00	2.40	.60
Coaching Dodgers			
□ 143 Babe Ruth Special 9	6.00	2.40	.60
Greatest Sports Hero			
□ 144 Babe Ruth Special 10	6.00	2.40	.60
Farewell Speech			
□ 145 Barry Latman	.85	.34	.08
□ 146 Don Demeter	.85	.34	.08
□ 147A Bill Kunkel PORT	.85	.34	.08
□ 147B Bill Kunkel	10.00	4.00	1.00
(pitching pose)			
□ 148 Wally Post	1.00	.40	.10
□ 149 Bob Duliba	.85	.34	.08
□ 150 Al Kaline	15.00	6.00	1.50
□ 151 Johnny Klippstein	.85	.34	.08
□ 152 Mickey Vernon	1.25	.50	.12
□ 153 Pumpsie Green	.85	.34	.08
□ 154 Lee Thomas	1.50	.60	.15
□ 155 Stu Miller	.85	.34	.08
□ 156 Merritt Ranew	.85	.34	.08
□ 157 Wes Covington	1.00	.40	.10
□ 158 Braves Team	2.00	.80	.20
□ 159 Hal Reniff	1.50	.60	.15
□ 160 Dick Stuart	1.25	.50	.12
□ 161 Frank Baumann	.85	.34	.08
□ 162 Sammy Drake	.85	.34	.08
□ 163 Hot Corner Guard	1.25	.50	.12
Billy Gardner			
Cletis Boyer			
□ 164 Hal Naragon	.85	.34	.08
□ 165 Jackie Brandt	.85	.34	.08
□ 166 Don Lee	.85	.34	.08
□ 167 Tim McCarver	12.00	5.00	1.20
□ 168 Leo Posada	.85	.34	.08
□ 169 Bob Cerv	1.00	.40	.10
□ 170 Ron Santo	2.50	1.00	.25
□ 171 Dave Sisler	.85	.34	.08
□ 172 Fred Hutchinson MG	1.25	.50	.12
□ 173 Chico Fernandez	.85	.34	.08
□ 174A Carl Willey	.85	.34	.08
(capless)			
□ 174B Carl Willey	10.00	4.00	1.00
(with cap)			
□ 175 Frank Howard	2.00	.80	.20
□ 176A Eddie Yost PORT	.85	.34	.08
□ 176B Eddie Yost BATTING	10.00	4.00	1.00
□ 177 Bobby Shantz	1.50	.60	.15
□ 178 Camilo Carreon	.85	.34	.08
□ 179 Tom Sturdivant	.85	.34	.08
□ 180 Bob Allison	1.25	.50	.12
□ 181 Paul Brown	.85	.34	.08
□ 182 Bob Nieman	.85	.34	.08
□ 183 Roger Craig	2.00	.80	.20
□ 184 Haywood Sullivan	1.00	.40	.10
□ 185 Roland Sheldon	.85	.34	.08
□ 186 Mack Jones	.85	.34	.08
□ 187 Gene Conley	.85	.34	.08
□ 188 Chuck Hiller	.85	.34	.08
□ 189 Dick Hall	.85	.34	.08
□ 190A Wally Moon PORT	1.00	.40	.10
□ 190B Wally Moon BATTING	10.00	4.00	1.00
□ 191 Jim Brewer	.85	.34	.08
□ 192A Checklist 3	4.00	.40	.08
(without comma)			
□ 192B Checklist 3	6.00	.60	.12
(comma after Checklist)			
□ 193 Eddie Kasko	.85	.34	.08
□ 194 Dean Chance	1.50	.60	.15
□ 195 Joe Cunningham	1.00	.40	.10
□ 196 Terry Fox	.85	.34	.08
□ 197 Daryl Spencer	1.00	.40	.10
□ 198 Johnny Keane MG	1.50	.60	.15
□ 199 Gaylord Perry	75.00	30.00	7.50
□ 200 Mickey Mantle	350.00	140.00	35.00
□ 201 Ike Delock	1.00	.40	.10
□ 202 Carl Warwick	1.00	.40	.10
□ 203 Jack Fisher	1.00	.40	.10
□ 204 Johnny Weekly	1.00	.40	.10
□ 205 Gene Freese	1.00	.40	.10
□ 206 Senators Team	2.00	.80	.20
□ 207 Pete Burnside	1.00	.40	.10
□ 208 Billy Martin	5.00	2.00	.50
□ 209 Jim Fregosi	5.00	2.00	.50
□ 210 Roy Face	2.00	.80	.20
□ 211 Midway Masters	1.25	.50	.12
Frank Bolling			
Roy McMillan			
□ 212 Jim Owens	1.00	.40	.10
□ 213 Richie Ashburn	4.00	1.60	.40
□ 214 Dom Zanni	1.00	.40	.10
□ 215 Woody Held	1.00	.40	.10
□ 216 Ron Kline	1.00	.40	.10
□ 217 Walt Alston MG	4.00	1.60	.40
□ 218 Joe Torre	10.00	4.00	1.00
□ 219 Al Downing	3.00	1.20	.30
□ 220 Roy Sievers	1.25	.50	.12
□ 221 Bill Short	1.00	.40	.10
□ 222 Jerry Zimmerman	1.00	.40	.10
□ 223 Alex Grammas	1.00	.40	.10
□ 224 Don Rudolph	1.00	.40	.10
□ 225 Frank Malzone	1.25	.50	.12
□ 226 San Francisco Giants	2.00	.80	.20
Team Card			
□ 227 Bob Tiefenauer	1.00	.40	.10
□ 228 Dale Long	1.25	.50	.12
□ 229 Jesus McFarlane	1.00	.40	.10
□ 230 Camilo Pascual	1.25	.50	.12
□ 231 Ernie Bowman	1.00	.40	.10
□ 232 World Series Game 1	2.25	.90	.22
Yanks win opener			
□ 233 World Series Game 2	2.25	.90	.22
Jay ties it up			
□ 234 World Series Game 3	7.50	3.00	.75
Maris wins in 9th			
□ 235 World Series Game 4	5.00	2.00	.50
Ford sets new mark			
□ 236 World Series Game 5	2.25	.90	.22
Yanks crush Reds			
□ 237 World Series Summary	2.25	.90	.22
Yanks celebrate			
□ 238 Norm Sherry	1.25	.50	.12
□ 239 Cecil Butler	1.00	.40	.10
□ 240 George Altman	1.00	.40	.10
□ 241 Johnny Kucks	1.00	.40	.10
□ 242 Mel McGaha	1.00	.40	.10
□ 243 Robin Roberts	10.00	4.00	1.00
□ 244 Don Gile	1.00	.40	.10
□ 245 Ron Hansen	1.00	.40	.10
□ 246 Art Ditmar	1.00	.40	.10
□ 247 Joe Pignatano	1.00	.40	.10
□ 248 Bob Aspromonte	1.00	.40	.10
□ 249 Ed Keegan	1.00	.40	.10
□ 250 Norm Cash	2.50	1.00	.25
□ 251 New York Yankees	10.00	4.00	1.00
Team Card			
□ 252 Earl Francis	1.00	.40	.10
□ 253 Harry Chiti	1.00	.40	.10
□ 254 Gordon Windhorn	1.00	.40	.10
□ 255 Juan Pizarro	1.00	.40	.10
□ 256 Elio Chacon	1.00	.40	.10
□ 257 Jack Spring	1.00	.40	.10
□ 258 Marty Keough	1.00	.40	.10
□ 259 Lou Klimchock	1.00	.40	.10
□ 260 Billy Pierce	1.50	.60	.15
□ 261 George Alusik	1.00	.40	.10
□ 262 Bob Schmidt	1.00	.40	.10
□ 263 The Right Pitch	1.25	.50	.12

Bob Purkey
Jim Turner
Joe Jay
□ 264 Dick Ellsworth .... 1.25 .50 .12
□ 265 Joe Adcock .... 1.50 .60 .15
□ 266 John Anderson .... 1.00 .40 .10
□ 267 Dan Dobbek .... 1.00 .40 .10
□ 268 Ken McBride .... 1.00 .40 .10
□ 269 Bob Oldis .... 1.00 .40 .10
□ 270 Dick Groat .... 2.00 .80 .20
□ 271 Ray Rippelmeyer .... 1.00 .40 .10
□ 272 Earl Robinson .... 1.00 .40 .10
□ 273 Gary Bell .... 1.00 .40 .10
□ 274 Sammy Taylor .... 1.00 .40 .10
□ 275 Norm Siebern .... 1.00 .40 .10
□ 276 Hal Kolstad .... 1.00 .40 .10
□ 277 Checklist 4 .... 4.50 .50 .10
□ 278 Ken Johnson .... 1.00 .40 .10
□ 279 Hobie Landrith .... 1.00 .40 .10
□ 280 Johnny Podres .... 2.50 1.00 .25
□ 281 Jake Gibbs .... 1.25 .50 .12
□ 282 Dave Hillman .... 1.00 .40 .10
□ 283 Charlie Smith .... 1.00 .40 .10
□ 284 Ruben Amaro .... 1.25 .50 .12
□ 285 Curt Simmons .... 1.75 .70 .17
□ 286 Al Lopez MG .... 3.00 1.20 .30
□ 287 George Witt .... 1.25 .50 .12
□ 288 Billy Williams 16.00 6.50 1.60
□ 289 Mike Krsnich .... 1.25 .50 .12
□ 290 Jim Gentile .... 1.75 .70 .17
□ 291 Hal Stowe .... 1.25 .50 .12
□ 292 Jerry Kindall .... 1.25 .50 .12
□ 293 Bob Miller .... 1.25 .50 .12
□ 294 Phillies Team .... 2.50 1.00 .25
□ 295 Vern Law .... 1.75 .70 .17
□ 296 Ken Hamlin .... 1.25 .50 .12
□ 297 Ron Perranoski .... 1.75 .70 .17
□ 298 Bill Tuttle .... 1.25 .50 .12
□ 299 Don Wert .... 1.25 .50 .12
□ 300 Willie Mays 80.00 32.00 8.00
□ 301 Galen Cisco .... 1.25 .50 .12
□ 302 Johnny Edwards .... 1.25 .50 .12
□ 303 Frank Torre .... 1.25 .50 .12
□ 304 Dick Farrell .... 1.25 .50 .12
□ 305 Jerry Lumpe .... 1.25 .50 .12
□ 306 Redbird Rippers .... 1.75 .70 .17
Lindy McDaniel
Larry Jackson
□ 307 Jim Grant .... 1.25 .50 .12
□ 308 Neil Chrisley .... 1.25 .50 .12
□ 309 Moe Morhardt .... 1.25 .50 .12
□ 310 Whitey Ford 20.00 8.00 2.00
□ 311 Tony Kubek IA .... 2.50 1.00 .25
□ 312 Warren Spahn IA .... 6.00 2.40 .60
□ 313 Roger Maris IA 12.50 5.00 1.25
□ 314 Rocky Colavito IA .... 2.50 1.00 .25
□ 315 Whitey Ford IA .... 6.00 2.40 .60
□ 316 Harmon Killebrew IA .... 5.00 2.00 .50
□ 317 Stan Musial IA 10.00 4.00 1.00
□ 318 Mickey Mantle IA 35.00 14.00 3.50
□ 319 Mike McCormick IA .... 1.75 .70 .17
□ 320 Hank Aaron 80.00 32.00 8.00
□ 321 Lee Stange .... 1.25 .50 .12
□ 322 Alvin Dark .... 1.75 .70 .17
□ 323 Don Landrum .... 1.25 .50 .12
□ 324 Joe McClain .... 1.25 .50 .12
□ 325 Luis Aparicio 10.00 4.00 1.00
□ 326 Tom Parsons .... 1.25 .50 .12
□ 327 Ozzie Virgil .... 1.25 .50 .12
□ 328 Ken Walters .... 1.25 .50 .12
□ 329 Bob Bolin .... 1.25 .50 .12
□ 330 John Romano .... 1.25 .50 .12
□ 331 Moe Drabowsky .... 1.25 .50 .12
□ 332 Don Buddin .... 1.25 .50 .12
□ 333 Frank Cipriani .... 1.25 .50 .12
□ 334 Boston Red Sox .... 2.50 1.00 .25
Team Card
□ 335 Bill Bruton .... 1.75 .70 .17
□ 336 Billy Muffett .... 1.25 .50 .12
□ 337 Jim Marshall .... 1.25 .50 .12
□ 338 Billy Gardner .... 1.75 .70 .17
□ 339 Jose Valdivielso .... 1.25 .50 .12
□ 340 Don Drysdale 18.00 7.25 1.80
□ 341 Mike Hershberger .... 1.25 .50 .12
□ 342 Ed Rakow .... 1.25 .50 .12
□ 343 Albie Pearson .... 1.25 .50 .12
□ 344 Ed Bauta .... 1.25 .50 .12
□ 345 Chuck Schilling .... 1.25 .50 .12
□ 346 Jack Kralick .... 1.25 .50 .12
□ 347 Chuck Hinton .... 1.25 .50 .12
□ 348 Larry Burright .... 1.25 .50 .12
□ 349 Paul Foytack .... 1.25 .50 .12
□ 350 Frank Robinson 18.00 7.25 1.80
□ 351 Braves' Backstops .... 1.75 .70 .17
Joe Torre
Del Crandall
□ 352 Frank Sullivan .... 1.25 .50 .12
□ 353 Bill Mazeroski .... 3.00 1.20 .30
□ 354 Roman Mejias .... 1.25 .50 .12
□ 355 Steve Barber .... 1.25 .50 .12
□ 356 Tom Haller .... 1.75 .70 .17
□ 357 Jerry Walker .... 1.25 .50 .12
□ 358 Tommy Davis .... 2.50 1.00 .25
□ 359 Bobby Locke .... 1.25 .50 .12
□ 360 Yogi Berra 40.00 16.00 4.00
□ 361 Bob Hendley .... 1.25 .50 .12
□ 362 Ty Cline .... 1.25 .50 .12
□ 363 Bob Roselli .... 1.25 .50 .12
□ 364 Ken Hunt .... 1.25 .50 .12
□ 365 Charlie Neal .... 1.75 .70 .17
□ 366 Phil Regan .... 1.75 .70 .17
□ 367 Checklist 5 .... 4.50 .50 .10
□ 368 Bob Tillman .... 1.25 .50 .12
□ 369 Ted Bowsfield .... 1.25 .50 .12
□ 370 Ken Boyer .... 3.50 1.40 .35
□ 371 Earl Battey .... 1.75 .70 .17
□ 372 Jack Curtis .... 1.75 .70 .17
□ 373 Al Heist .... 1.75 .70 .17
□ 374 Gene Mauch .... 2.50 1.00 .25
□ 375 Ron Fairly .... 1.75 .70 .17
□ 376 Bud Daley .... 1.75 .70 .17
□ 377 John Orsino .... 1.75 .70 .17
□ 378 Bennie Daniels .... 1.75 .70 .17
□ 379 Chuck Essegian .... 1.75 .70 .17
□ 380 Lou Burdette .... 3.00 1.20 .30
□ 381 Chico Cardenas .... 1.75 .70 .17
□ 382 Dick Williams .... 2.50 1.00 .25
□ 383 Ray Sadecki .... 1.75 .70 .17
□ 384 K.C. Athletics .... 3.50 1.40 .35
Team Card
□ 385 Early Wynn 10.00 4.00 1.00
□ 386 Don Mincher .... 2.50 1.00 .25
□ 387 Lou Brock 80.00 32.00 8.00
□ 388 Ryne Duren .... 2.50 1.00 .25
□ 389 Smoky Burgess .... 2.50 1.00 .25
□ 390 Orlando Cepeda AS .... 3.50 1.40 .35
□ 391 Bill Mazeroski AS .... 3.00 1.20 .30
□ 392 Ken Boyer AS .... 3.00 1.20 .30
□ 393 Roy McMillan AS .... 2.50 1.00 .25
□ 394 Hank Aaron AS 22.00 9.00 2.20
□ 395 Willie Mays AS 22.00 9.00 2.20
□ 396 Frank Robinson AS .... 8.50 3.50 .85
□ 397 John Roseboro AS .... 2.50 1.00 .25
□ 398 Don Drysdale AS .... 7.00 2.80 .70
□ 399 Warren Spahn AS .... 8.00 3.25 .80
□ 400 Elston Howard .... 5.00 2.00 .50
□ 401 AL/NL Homer Kings 18.00 7.25 1.80
Roger Maris
Orlando Cepeda
□ 402 Gino Cimoli .... 1.75 .70 .17
□ 403 Chet Nichols .... 1.75 .70 .17
□ 404 Tim Harkness .... 1.75 .70 .17
□ 405 Jim Perry .... 2.50 1.00 .25
□ 406 Bob Taylor .... 1.75 .70 .17
□ 407 Hank Aguirre .... 1.75 .70 .17
□ 408 Gus Bell .... 1.75 .70 .17
□ 409 Pittsburgh Pirates .... 3.50 1.40 .35
Team Card
□ 410 Al Smith .... 1.75 .70 .17
□ 411 Danny O'Connell .... 1.75 .70 .17
□ 412 Charlie James .... 1.75 .70 .17
□ 413 Matty Alou .... 2.50 1.00 .25
□ 414 Joe Gaines .... 1.75 .70 .17
□ 415 Bill Virdon .... 3.00 1.20 .30
□ 416 Bob Scheffing MG .... 1.75 .70 .17
□ 417 Joe Azcue .... 1.75 .70 .17
□ 418 Andy Carey .... 1.75 .70 .17
□ 419 Bob Bruce .... 1.75 .70 .17
□ 420 Gus Triandos .... 2.50 1.00 .25
□ 421 Ken MacKenzie .... 1.75 .70 .17
□ 422 Steve Bilko .... 1.75 .70 .17
□ 423 Rival League .... 4.00 1.60 .40
Relief Aces:
Roy Face
Hoyt Wilhelm
□ 424 Al McBean .... 1.75 .70 .17
□ 425 Carl Yastrzemski 135.00 54.00 13.50
□ 426 Bob Farley .... 1.75 .70 .17
□ 427 Jake Wood .... 1.75 .70 .17
□ 428 Joe Hicks .... 1.75 .70 .17
□ 429 Billy O'Dell .... 1.75 .70 .17
□ 430 Tony Kubek .... 7.00 2.80 .70
□ 431 Bob Rodgers .... 3.50 1.40 .35
□ 432 Jim Pendleton .... 1.75 .70 .17
□ 433 Jim Archer .... 1.75 .70 .17
□ 434 Clay Dalrymple .... 1.75 .70 .17
□ 435 Larry Sherry .... 2.50 1.00 .25
□ 436 Felix Mantilla .... 1.75 .70 .17
□ 437 Ray Moore .... 1.75 .70 .17
□ 438 Dick Brown .... 1.75 .70 .17

□ 439 Jerry Buchek 1.75 .70 .17
□ 440 Joey Jay 1.75 .70 .17
□ 441 Checklist 6 5.00 .50 .10
□ 442 Wes Stock 2.50 1.00 .25
□ 443 Del Crandall 2.50 1.00 .25
□ 444 Ted Wills 1.75 .70 .17
□ 445 Vic Power 1.75 .70 .17
□ 446 Don Elston 1.75 .70 .17
□ 447 Willie Kirkland 2.25 .90 .22
□ 448 Joe Gibbon 2.25 .90 .22
□ 449 Jerry Adair 2.25 .90 .22
□ 450 Jim O'Toole 3.00 1.20 .30
□ 451 Jose Tartabull 2.25 .90 .22
□ 452 Earl Averill 2.25 .90 .22
□ 453 Cal McLish 2.25 .90 .22
□ 454 Floyd Robinson 2.25 .90 .22
□ 455 Luis Arroyo 3.00 1.20 .30
□ 456 Joe Amalfitano 2.25 .90 .22
□ 457 Lou Clinton 2.25 .90 .22
□ 458A Bob Buhl 2.25 .90 .22
(Braves cap emblem)
□ 458B Bob Buhl 35.00 14.00 3.50
(no emblem on cap)
□ 459 Ed Bailey 2.25 .90 .22
□ 460 Jim Bunning 7.00 2.80 .70
□ 461 Ken Hubbs 6.50 2.60 .65
□ 462A Willie Tasby 2.25 .90 .22
(Senators cap emblem)
□ 462B Willie Tasby 35.00 14.00 3.50
(no emblem on cap)
□ 463 Hank Bauer 3.00 1.20 .30
□ 464 Al Jackson 2.25 .90 .22
□ 465 Reds Team 4.50 1.80 .45
□ 466 Norm Cash AS 3.50 1.40 .35
□ 467 Chuck Schilling AS 3.00 1.20 .30
□ 468 Brooks Robinson AS 10.00 4.00 1.00
□ 469 Luis Aparicio AS 6.00 2.40 .60
□ 470 Al Kaline AS 10.00 4.00 1.00
□ 471 Mickey Mantle AS 75.00 30.00 7.50
□ 472 Rocky Colavito AS 3.50 1.40 .35
□ 473 Elston Howard AS 3.50 1.40 .35
□ 474 Frank Lary AS 3.00 1.20 .30
□ 475 Whitey Ford AS 9.00 3.75 .90
□ 476 Orioles Team 4.50 1.80 .45
□ 477 Andre Rodgers 2.25 .90 .22
□ 478 Don Zimmer 4.00 1.60 .40
□ 479 Joel Horlen 3.00 1.20 .30
□ 480 Harvey Kuenn 3.50 1.40 .35
□ 481 Vic Wertz 3.00 1.20 .30
□ 482 Sam Mele MG 2.25 .90 .22
□ 483 Don McMahon 2.25 .90 .22
□ 484 Dick Schofield 2.25 .90 .22
□ 485 Pedro Ramos 2.25 .90 .22
□ 486 Jim Gilliam 5.00 2.00 .50
□ 487 Jerry Lynch 2.25 .90 .22
□ 488 Hal Brown 2.25 .90 .22
□ 489 Julio Gotay 2.25 .90 .22
□ 490 Clete Boyer 3.50 1.40 .35
□ 491 Leon Wagner 2.25 .90 .22
□ 492 Hal W. Smith 2.25 .90 .22
□ 493 Danny McDevitt 2.25 .90 .22
□ 494 Sammy White 2.25 .90 .22
□ 495 Don Cardwell 2.25 .90 .22
□ 496 Wayne Causey 2.25 .90 .22
□ 497 Ed Bouchee 2.25 .90 .22
□ 498 Jim Donohue 2.25 .90 .22
□ 499 Zoilo Versalles 2.25 .90 .22
□ 500 Duke Snider 30.00 12.00 3.00
□ 501 Claude Osteen 3.00 1.20 .30
□ 502 Hector Lopez 2.25 .90 .22
□ 503 Danny Murtaugh MG 2.25 .90 .22
□ 504 Eddie Bressoud 2.25 .90 .22
□ 505 Juan Marichal 21.00 8.50 2.10
□ 506 Charlie Maxwell 2.25 .90 .22
□ 507 Ernie Broglio 2.25 .90 .22
□ 508 Gordy Coleman 3.00 1.20 .30
□ 509 Dave Giusti 3.00 1.20 .30
□ 510 Jim Lemon 3.00 1.20 .30
□ 511 Bubba Phillips 2.25 .90 .22
□ 512 Mike Fornieles 2.25 .90 .22
□ 513 Whitey Herzog 4.00 1.60 .40
□ 514 Sherm Lollar 3.00 1.20 .30
□ 515 Stan Williams 2.25 .90 .22
□ 516 Checklist 7 8.00 .80 .10
□ 517 Dave Wickersham 2.25 .90 .22
□ 518 Lee Maye 2.25 .90 .22
□ 519 Bob Johnson 2.25 .90 .22
□ 520 Bob Friend 3.00 1.20 .30
□ 521 Jacke Davis 2.25 .90 .22
□ 522 Lindy McDaniel 3.00 1.20 .30
□ 523 Russ Nixon 10.00 4.00 1.00
□ 524 Howie Nunn 8.00 3.25 .80
□ 525 George Thomas 8.00 3.25 .80
□ 526 Hal Woodeshick 8.00 3.25 .80
□ 527 Dick McAuliffe 10.00 4.00 1.00
□ 528 Turk Lown 8.00 3.25 .80
□ 529 John Schaive 8.00 3.25 .80
□ 530 Bob Gibson 85.00 34.00 8.50
□ 531 Bobby G. Smith 8.00 3.25 .80
□ 532 Dick Stigman 8.00 3.25 .80
□ 533 Charley Lau 10.00 4.00 1.00
□ 534 Tony Gonzalez 8.00 3.25 .80
□ 535 Ed Roebuck 8.00 3.25 .80
□ 536 Dick Gernert 8.00 3.25 .80
□ 537 Cleveland Indians 15.00 6.00 1.50
Team Card
□ 538 Jack Sanford 10.00 4.00 1.00
□ 539 Billy Moran 8.00 3.25 .80
□ 540 Jim Landis 8.00 3.25 .80
□ 541 Don Nottebart 8.00 3.25 .80
□ 542 Dave Philley 8.00 3.25 .80
□ 543 Bob Allen 8.00 3.25 .80
□ 544 Willie McCovey 85.00 34.00 8.50
□ 545 Hoyt Wilhelm 40.00 16.00 4.00
□ 546 Moe Thacker 8.00 3.25 .80
□ 547 Don Ferrarese 8.00 3.25 .80
□ 548 Bobby Del Greco 8.00 3.25 .80
□ 549 Bill Rigney MG 8.00 3.25 .80
□ 550 Art Mahaffey 8.00 3.25 .80
□ 551 Harry Bright 8.00 3.25 .80
□ 552 Chicago Cubs 15.00 6.00 1.50
Team Card
□ 553 Jim Coates 8.00 3.25 .80
□ 554 Bubba Morton 8.00 3.25 .80
□ 555 John Buzhardt 8.00 3.25 .80
□ 556 Al Spangler 8.00 3.25 .80
□ 557 Bob Anderson 8.00 3.25 .80
□ 558 John Goryl 8.00 3.25 .80
□ 559 Mike Higgins MG 8.00 3.25 .80
□ 560 Chuck Estrada 10.00 4.00 1.00
□ 561 Gene Oliver 8.00 3.25 .80
□ 562 Bill Henry 8.00 3.25 .80
□ 563 Ken Aspromonte 8.00 3.25 .80
□ 564 Bob Grim 8.00 3.25 .80
□ 565 Jose Pagan 8.00 3.25 .80
□ 566 Marty Kutyna 8.00 3.25 .80
□ 567 Tracy Stallard 8.00 3.25 .80
□ 568 Jim Golden 8.00 3.25 .80
□ 569 Ed Sadowski 8.00 3.25 .80
□ 570 Bill Stafford 8.00 3.25 .80
□ 571 Billy Klaus 8.00 3.25 .80
□ 572 Bob G. Miller 8.00 3.25 .80
□ 573 Johnny Logan 10.00 4.00 1.00
□ 574 Dean Stone 8.00 3.25 .80
□ 575 Red Schoendienst 12.00 5.00 1.20
□ 576 Russ Kemmerer 8.00 3.25 .80
□ 577 Dave Nicholson 8.00 3.25 .80
□ 578 Jim Duffalo 8.00 3.25 .80
□ 579 Jim Schaffer 8.00 3.25 .80
□ 580 Bill Monbouquette 8.00 3.25 .80
□ 581 Mel Roach 8.00 3.25 .80
□ 582 Ron Piche 8.00 3.25 .80
□ 583 Larry Osborne 8.00 3.25 .80
□ 584 Minnesota Twins 15.00 6.00 1.50
Team Card
□ 585 Glen Hobbie 8.00 3.25 .80
□ 586 Sam Esposito 8.00 3.25 .80
□ 587 Frank Funk 8.00 3.25 .80
□ 588 Birdie Tebbetts MG 8.00 3.25 .80
□ 589 Bob Turley 12.00 5.00 1.20
□ 590 Curt Flood 12.00 5.00 1.20
□ 591 Rookie Pitchers 25.00 10.00 2.50
Sam McDowell
Ron Taylor
Ron Nischwitz
Art Quirk
Dick Radatz
□ 592 Rookie Pitchers 40.00 16.00 4.00
Dan Pfister
Bo Belinsky
Dave Stenhouse
Jim Bouton
Joe Bonikowski
□ 593 Rookie Pitchers 20.00 8.00 2.00
Jack Lamabe
Craig Anderson
Jack Hamilton
Bob Moorhead
Bob Veale
□ 594 Rookie Catchers 110.00 45.00 11.00
Doc Edwards
Ken Retzer
Bob Uecker
Doug Camilli
Don Pavletich
□ 595 Rookie Infielders 12.00 5.00 1.20
Bob Sadowski
Felix Torres
Marlan Coughtry
Ed Charles

☐ 596	Rookie Infielders	25.00	10.00	2.50
	Bernie Allen			
	Joe Pepitone			
	Phil Linz			
	Rich Rollins			
☐ 597	Rookie Infielders	12.00	5.00	1.20
	Jim McKnight			
	Rod Kanehl			
	Amado Samuel			
	Denis Menke			
☐ 598	Rookie Outfielders	20.00	6.00	1.25
	Al Luplow			
	Manny Jimenez			
	Howie Goss			
	Jim Hickman			
	Ed Olivares			

1963 Topps

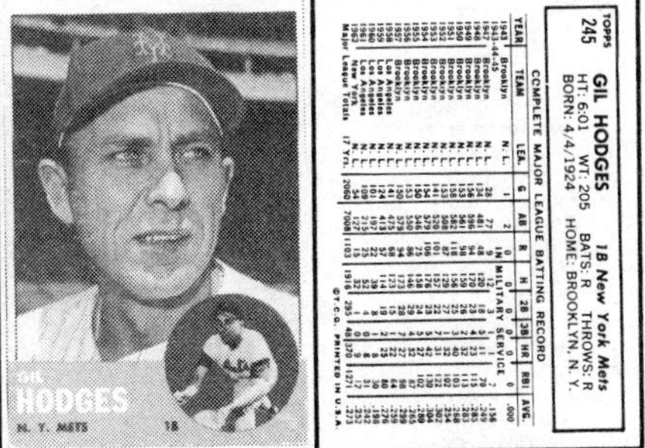

The cards in this 576-card set measure 2 1/2" by 3 1/2". The sharp color photographs of the 1963 set are a vivid contrast to the drab pictures of 1962. In addition to the "League Leaders" series (1-10) and World Series cards (142-148), the seventh and last series of cards (507-576) contains seven rookie cards (each depicting four players). This set has gained special prominence in recent years since it contains the rookie card of Pete Rose, #537.

	NRMT	VG-E	GOOD
COMPLETE SET (576)	3400.00	1500.00	500.00
COMMON PLAYER (1-109)	.50	.20	.05
COMMON PLAYER (110-196)	.60	.24	.06
COMMON PLAYER (197-283)	.75	.30	.07
COMMON PLAYER (284-446)	1.00	.40	.10
COMMON PLAYER (447-506)	6.00	2.40	.60
COMMON PLAYER (507-576)	4.00	1.60	.40

☐ 1	NL Batting Leaders	16.00	2.50	.50
	Tommy Davis			
	Frank Robinson			
	Stan Musial			
	Hank Aaron			
	Bill White			
☐ 2	AL Batting Leaders	7.50	3.00	.60
	Pete Runnels			
	Mickey Mantle			
	Floyd Robinson			
	Norm Siebern			
	Chuck Hinton			
☐ 3	NL Home Run Leaders	7.50	3.00	.60
	Willie Mays			
	Hank Aaron			
	Frank Robinson			
	Orlando Cepeda			
	Ernie Banks			
☐ 4	AL Home Run Leaders	2.50	1.00	.20
	Harmon Killebrew			
	Norm Cash			
	Rocky Colavito			
	Roger Maris			
	Jim Gentile			
	Leon Wagner			
☐ 5	NL ERA Leaders	2.50	1.00	.20
	Sandy Koufax			
	Bob Shaw			
	Bob Purkey			
	Bob Gibson			
	Don Drysdale			
☐ 6	AL ERA Leaders	2.00	.90	.15
	Hank Aguirre			
	Robin Roberts			
	Whitey Ford			
	Eddie Fisher			
	Dean Chance			
☐ 7	AL Pitching Leaders	1.50	.60	.15
	Don Drysdale			
	Jack Sanford			
	Bob Purkey			
	Billy O'Dell			
	Art Mahaffey			
	Joe Jay			
☐ 8	AL Pitching Leaders	1.50	.60	.15
	Ralph Terry			
	Dick Donovan			
	Ray Herbert			
	Jim Bunning			
	Camilo Pascual			
☐ 9	NL Strikeout Leaders	3.00	1.20	.30
	Don Drysdale			
	Sandy Koufax			
	Bob Gibson			
	Billy O'Dell			
	Dick Farrell			
☐ 10	AL Strikeout Leaders	1.50	.60	.15
	Camilo Pascual			
	Jim Bunning			
	Ralph Terry			
	Juan Pizarro			
	Jim Kaat			
☐ 11	Lee Walls	.50	.20	.05
☐ 12	Steve Barber	.50	.20	.05
☐ 13	Philadelphia Phillies Team Card	1.00	.40	.10
☐ 14	Pedro Ramos	.50	.20	.05
☐ 15	Ken Hubbs	1.50	.60	.15
☐ 16	Al Smith	.50	.20	.05
☐ 17	Ryne Duren	1.00	.40	.10
☐ 18	Buc Blasters	6.50	2.60	.65
	Smoky Burgess			
	Dick Stuart			
	Bob Clemente			
	Bob Skinner			
☐ 19	Pete Burnside	.50	.20	.05
☐ 20	Tony Kubek	3.00	1.20	.30
☐ 21	Marty Keough	.50	.20	.05
☐ 22	Curt Simmons	.75	.30	.07
☐ 23	Ed Lopat MG	1.00	.40	.10
☐ 24	Bob Bruce	.50	.20	.05
☐ 25	Al Kaline	14.00	5.75	1.40
☐ 26	Ray Moore	.50	.20	.05
☐ 27	Choo Choo Coleman	.50	.20	.05
☐ 28	Mike Fornieles	.50	.20	.05
☐ 29A	1963 Rookie Stars	1.25	.50	.12
	Sammy Ellis			
	Ray Culp			
	John Boozer			
	Jesse Gonder			
☐ 29B	1962 Rookie Stars	4.00	1.60	.40
	Sammy Ellis			
	Ray Culp			
	John Boozer			
	Jesse Gonder			
☐ 30	Harvey Kuenn	1.00	.40	.10
☐ 31	Cal Koonce	.50	.20	.05
☐ 32	Tony Gonzalez	.50	.20	.05
☐ 33	Bo Belinsky	.75	.30	.07
☐ 34	Dick Schofield	.50	.20	.05
☐ 35	John Buzhardt	.50	.20	.05
☐ 36	Jerry Kindall	.50	.20	.05
☐ 37	Jerry Lynch	.50	.20	.05
☐ 38	Bud Daley	.50	.20	.05
☐ 39	Angels Team	1.00	.40	.10
☐ 40	Vic Power	.50	.20	.05
☐ 41	Charley Lau	1.00	.40	.10
☐ 42	Stan Williams	.50	.20	.05
☐ 43	Veteran Masters	3.00	1.20	.30
	Casey Stengel			
	Gene Woodling			
☐ 44	Terry Fox	.50	.20	.05
☐ 45	Bob Aspromonte	.50	.20	.05
☐ 46	Tommy Aaron	.75	.30	.07
☐ 47	Don Lock	.50	.20	.05
☐ 48	Birdie Tebbetts MG	.50	.20	.05
☐ 49	Dal Maxvill	.75	.30	.07
☐ 50	Billy Pierce	1.00	.40	.10
☐ 51	George Alusik	.50	.20	.05
☐ 52	Chuck Schilling	.50	.20	.05
☐ 53	Joe Moeller	.50	.20	.05
☐ 54A	1963 Rookie Stars	3.50	1.40	.35
	Nelson Mathews			
	Harry Fanok			
	Jack Cullen			

Dave DeBusschere
□ 54B 1962 Rookie Stars .... 7.00 2.80 .70
Nelson Mathews
Harry Fanok
Jack Cullen
Dave DeBusschere
□ 55 Bill Virdon .... 1.00 .40 .10
□ 56 Dennis Bennett .... .50 .20 .05
□ 57 Billy Moran .... .50 .20 .05
□ 58 Bob Will .... .50 .20 .05
□ 59 Craig Anderson .... .50 .20 .05
□ 60 Elston Howard .... 3.50 1.40 .35
□ 61 Ernie Bowman .... .50 .20 .05
□ 62 Bob Hendley .... .50 .20 .05
□ 63 Reds Team .... 1.00 .40 .10
□ 64 Dick McAuliffe .... .75 .30 .07
□ 65 Jackie Brandt .... .50 .20 .05
□ 66 Mike Joyce .... .50 .20 .05
□ 67 Ed Charles .... .50 .20 .05
□ 68 Friendly Foes .... 6.50 2.60 .65
Duke Snider
Gil Hodges
□ 69 Bud Zipfel .... .50 .20 .05
□ 70 Jim O'Toole .... .75 .30 .07
□ 71 Bobby Wine .... .75 .30 .07
□ 72 Johnny Romano .... .50 .20 .05
□ 73 Bobby Bragan MG .... .50 .20 .05
□ 74 Denny Lemaster .... .50 .20 .05
□ 75 Bob Allison .... .75 .30 .07
□ 76 Earl Wilson .... .50 .20 .05
□ 77 Al Spangler .... .50 .20 .05
□ 78 Marv Throneberry .... 1.00 .40 .10
□ 79 Checklist 1 .... 3.50 .35 .07
□ 80 Jim Gilliam .... 2.00 .80 .20
□ 81 Jim Schaffer .... .50 .20 .05
□ 82 Ed Rakow .... .50 .20 .05
□ 83 Charley James .... .50 .20 .05
□ 84 Ron Kline .... .50 .20 .05
□ 85 Tom Haller .... .75 .30 .07
□ 86 Charley Maxwell .... .50 .20 .05
□ 87 Bob Veale .... .75 .30 .07
□ 88 Ron Hansen .... .50 .20 .05
□ 89 Dick Stigman .... .50 .20 .05
□ 90 Gordy Coleman .... .75 .30 .07
□ 91 Dallas Green .... 1.50 .60 .15
□ 92 Hector Lopez .... .50 .20 .05
□ 93 Galen Cisco .... .50 .20 .05
□ 94 Bob Schmidt .... .50 .20 .05
□ 95 Larry Jackson .... .50 .20 .05
□ 96 Lou Clinton .... .50 .20 .05
□ 97 Bob Duliba .... .50 .20 .05
□ 98 George Thomas .... .50 .20 .05
□ 99 Jim Umbricht .... .50 .20 .05
□ 100 Joe Cunningham .... .75 .30 .07
□ 101 Joe Gibbon .... .50 .20 .05
□ 102A Checklist 2 .... 4.00 .40 .08
(red on yellow)
□ 102B Checklist 2 .... 6.00 .60 .10
(white on red)
□ 103 Chuck Essegian .... .50 .20 .05
□ 104 Lew Krausse .... .50 .20 .05
□ 105 Ron Fairly .... .75 .30 .07
□ 106 Bobby Bolin .... .50 .20 .05
□ 107 Jim Hickman .... .50 .20 .05
□ 108 Hoyt Wilhelm .... 7.00 2.80 .70
□ 109 Lee Maye .... .50 .20 .05
□ 110 Rich Rollins .... .60 .24 .06
□ 111 Al Jackson .... .60 .24 .06
□ 112 Dick Brown .... .60 .24 .06
□ 113 Don Landrum .... 1.00 .40 .10
(photo actually
Ron Santo)
□ 114 Dan Osinski .... .60 .24 .06
□ 115 Carl Yastrzemski 60.00 24.00 6.00
□ 116 Jim Brosnan .... .75 .30 .07
□ 117 Jacke Davis .... .60 .24 .06
□ 118 Sherm Lollar .... .75 .30 .07
□ 119 Bob Lillis .... .75 .30 .07
□ 120 Roger Maris 35.00 14.00 3.50
□ 121 Jim Hannan .... .60 .24 .06
□ 122 Julio Gotay .... .60 .24 .06
□ 123 Frank Howard .... 1.75 .70 .17
□ 124 Dick Howser .... 1.25 .50 .12
□ 125 Robin Roberts .... 8.00 3.25 .80
□ 126 Bob Uecker 25.00 10.00 2.50
□ 127 Bill Tuttle .... .60 .24 .06
□ 128 Matty Alou .... .75 .30 .07
□ 129 Gary Bell .... .60 .24 .06
□ 130 Dick Groat .... 1.00 .40 .10
□ 131 Washington Senators .... 1.25 .50 .12
Team Card
□ 132 Jack Hamilton .... .60 .24 .06
□ 133 Gene Freese .... .60 .24 .06
□ 134 Bob Scheffing MG .... .60 .24 .06
□ 135 Richie Ashburn .... 3.50 1.40 .35
□ 136 Ike Delock .... .60 .24 .06
□ 137 Mack Jones .... .60 .24 .06
□ 138 Pride of NL 20.00 8.00 2.00
Willie Mays
Stan Musial
□ 139 Earl Averill .... .60 .24 .06
□ 140 Frank Lary .... .75 .30 .07
□ 141 Manny Mota .... 3.50 1.40 .35
□ 142 World Series Game 1 .... 3.50 1.40 .35
Ford wins
series opener
□ 143 World Series Game 2 .... 2.00 .80 .20
Sanford flashes
shutout magic
□ 144 World Series Game 3 .... 6.00 2.40 .60
Maris sparks
Yankee rally
□ 145 World Series Game 4 .... 2.00 .80 .20
Hiller blasts
grand slammer
□ 146 World Series Game 5 .... 2.00 .80 .20
Tresh's homer
defeats Giants
□ 147 World Series Game 6 .... 2.00 .80 .20
Pierce stars in
3 hit victory
□ 148 World Series Game 7 .... 2.00 .80 .20
Yanks celebrate
as Terry wins
□ 149 Marv Breeding .... .60 .24 .06
□ 150 Johnny Podres .... 1.75 .70 .17
□ 151 Pirates Team .... 1.25 .50 .12
□ 152 Ron Nischwitz .... .60 .24 .06
□ 153 Hal Smith .... .60 .24 .06
□ 154 Walt Alston MG .... 3.00 1.20 .30
□ 155 Bill Stafford .... .60 .24 .06
□ 156 Roy McMillan .... .60 .24 .06
□ 157 Diego Segui .... .60 .24 .06
□ 158 Rookie Stars .... 1.00 .40 .10
Rogelio Alvares
Dave Roberts
Tommy Harper
Bob Saverine
□ 159 Jim Pagliaroni .... .60 .24 .06
□ 160 Juan Pizarro .... .60 .24 .06
□ 161 Frank Torre .... .60 .24 .06
□ 162 Twins Team .... 1.25 .50 .12
□ 163 Don Larsen .... 1.25 .50 .12
□ 164 Bubba Morton .... .60 .24 .06
□ 165 Jim Kaat .... 3.00 1.20 .30
□ 166 Johnny Keane MG .... 1.00 .40 .10
□ 167 Jim Fregosi .... 1.50 .60 .15
□ 168 Russ Nixon .... 1.00 .40 .10
□ 169 Rookie Stars 16.00 6.50 1.60
Dick Egan
Julio Navarro
Tommie Sisk
Gaylord Perry
□ 170 Joe Adcock .... .75 .30 .07
□ 171 Steve Hamilton .... .60 .24 .06
□ 172 Gene Oliver .... .60 .24 .06
□ 173 Bombers' Best 30.00 12.00 3.00
Tom Tresh
Mickey Mantle
Bobby Richardson
□ 174 Larry Burright .... .60 .24 .06
□ 175 Bob Buhl .... .60 .24 .06
□ 176 Jim King .... .60 .24 .06
□ 177 Bubba Phillips .... .60 .24 .06
□ 178 Johnny Edwards .... .60 .24 .06
□ 179 Ron Piche .... .60 .24 .06
□ 180 Bill Skowron .... 1.50 .60 .15
□ 181 Sammy Esposito .... .60 .24 .06
□ 182 Albie Pearson .... .60 .24 .06
□ 183 Joe Pepitone .... 2.50 1.00 .25
□ 184 Vern Law .... .75 .30 .07
□ 185 Chuck Hiller .... .60 .24 .06
□ 186 Jerry Zimmerman .... .60 .24 .06
□ 187 Willie Kirkland .... .60 .24 .06
□ 188 Eddie Bressoud .... .60 .24 .06
□ 189 Dave Giusti .... .75 .30 .07
□ 190 Minnie Minoso .... 1.75 .70 .17
□ 191 Checklist 3 .... 4.00 .40 .08
□ 192 Clay Dalrymple .... .60 .24 .06
□ 193 Andre Rodgers .... .60 .24 .06
□ 194 Joe Nuxhall .... .75 .30 .07
□ 195 Manny Jimenez .... .60 .24 .06
□ 196 Doug Camilli .... .60 .24 .06
□ 197 Roger Craig .... 1.75 .70 .17
□ 198 Lenny Green .... .75 .30 .07
□ 199 Joe Amalfitano .... .75 .30 .07
□ 200 Mickey Mantle 300.00 120.00 30.00
□ 201 Cecil Butler .... .75 .30 .07
□ 202 Boston Red Sox .... 1.75 .70 .17
Team Card

□ 203 Chico Cardenas	.75	.30	.07
□ 204 Don Nottebart	.75	.30	.07
□ 205 Luis Aparicio	8.00	3.25	.80
□ 206 Ray Washburn	.75	.30	.07
□ 207 Ken Hunt	.75	.30	.07
□ 208 Rookie Stars	.75	.30	.07
Ron Herbel			
John Miller			
Wally Wolf			
Ron Taylor			
□ 209 Hobie Landrith	.75	.30	.07
□ 210 Sandy Koufax	70.00	28.00	7.00
□ 211 Fred Whitfield	.75	.30	.07
□ 212 Glen Hobbie	.75	.30	.07
□ 213 Billy Hitchcock MG	.75	.30	.07
□ 214 Orlando Pena	.75	.30	.07
□ 215 Bob Skinner	.75	.30	.07
□ 216 Gene Conley	.75	.30	.07
□ 217 Joe Christopher	.75	.30	.07
□ 218 Tiger Twirlers	1.50	.60	.15
Frank Lary			
Don Mossi			
Jim Bunning			
□ 219 Chuck Cottier	.75	.30	.07
□ 220 Camilo Pascual	1.00	.40	.10
□ 221 Cookie Rojas	2.00	.80	.20
□ 222 Cubs Team	1.75	.70	.17
□ 223 Eddie Fisher	.75	.30	.07
□ 224 Mike Roarke	.75	.30	.07
□ 225 Joey Jay	.75	.30	.07
□ 226 Julian Javier	1.00	.40	.10
□ 227 Jim Grant	.75	.30	.07
□ 228 Rookie Stars	21.00	8.50	2.10
Max Alvis			
Bob Bailey			
Pedro Oliva			
Ed Kranepool			
□ 229 Willie Davis	1.50	.60	.15
□ 230 Pete Runnels	1.00	.40	.10
□ 231 Eli Grba	1.00	.40	.10
(large photo is			
Ryne Duren)			
□ 232 Frank Malzone	1.00	.40	.10
□ 233 Casey Stengel MG	10.00	4.00	1.00
□ 234 Dave Nicholson	.75	.30	.07
□ 235 Billy O'Dell	.75	.30	.07
□ 236 Bill Bryan	.75	.30	.07
□ 237 Jim Coates	.75	.30	.07
□ 238 Lou Johnson	.75	.30	.07
□ 239 Harvey Haddix	1.25	.50	.12
□ 240 Rocky Colavito	2.50	1.00	.25
□ 241 Bob Smith	.75	.30	.07
□ 242 Power Plus	11.00	4.50	1.10
Ernie Banks			
Hank Aaron			
□ 243 Don Leppert	.75	.30	.07
□ 244 John Tsitouris	.75	.30	.07
□ 245 Gil Hodges	8.00	3.25	.80
□ 246 Lee Stange	.75	.30	.07
□ 247 Yankees Team	8.00	3.25	.80
□ 248 Tito Francona	1.00	.40	.10
□ 249 Leo Burke	.75	.30	.07
□ 250 Stan Musial	60.00	24.00	6.00
□ 251 Jack Lamabe	.75	.30	.07
□ 252 Ron Santo	2.00	.80	.20
□ 253 Rookie Stars	.75	.30	.07
Len Gabrielson			
Pete Jernigan			
John Wojcik			
Deacon Jones			
□ 254 Mike Hershberger	.75	.30	.07
□ 255 Bob Shaw	.75	.30	.07
□ 256 Jerry Lumpe	.75	.30	.07
□ 257 Hank Aguirre	.75	.30	.07
□ 258 Al Dark MG	1.25	.50	.12
□ 259 John Logan	1.00	.50	.10
□ 260 Jim Gentile	1.25	.50	.12
□ 261 Bob Miller	.75	.30	.07
□ 262 Ellis Burton	.75	.30	.07
□ 263 Dave Stenhouse	.75	.30	.07
□ 264 Phil Linz	1.25	.50	.12
□ 265 Vada Pinson	2.00	.80	.20
□ 266 Bob Allen	.75	.30	.07
□ 267 Carl Sawatski	.75	.30	.07
□ 268 Don Demeter	.75	.30	.07
□ 269 Don Mincher	1.00	.40	.10
□ 270 Felipe Alou	1.50	.60	.15
□ 271 Dean Stone	.75	.30	.07
□ 272 Danny Murphy	.75	.30	.07
□ 273 Sammy Taylor	.75	.30	.07
□ 274 Checklist 4	4.00	.40	.08
□ 275 Eddie Mathews	11.00	4.50	1.10
□ 276 Barry Shetrone	.75	.30	.07
□ 277 Dick Farrell	.75	.30	.07
□ 278 Chico Fernandez	.75	.30	.07
□ 279 Wally Moon	1.00	.40	.10
□ 280 Bob Rodgers	1.75	.70	.17
□ 281 Tom Sturdivant	.75	.30	.07
□ 282 Bobby Del Greco	.75	.30	.07
□ 283 Roy Sievers	1.50	.60	.15
□ 284 Dave Sisler	1.00	.40	.10
□ 285 Dick Stuart	1.50	.60	.15
□ 286 Stu Miller	1.00	.40	.10
□ 287 Dick Bertell	1.00	.40	.10
□ 288 Chicago White Sox	2.00	.80	.20
Team Card			
□ 289 Hal Brown	1.00	.40	.10
□ 290 Bill White	2.00	.80	.20
□ 291 Don Rudolph	1.00	.40	.10
□ 292 Pumpsie Green	1.00	.40	.10
□ 293 Bill Pleis	1.00	.40	.10
□ 294 Bill Rigney MG	1.00	.40	.10
□ 295 Ed Roebuck	1.00	.40	.10
□ 296 Doc Edwards	1.00	.40	.10
□ 297 Jim Golden	1.00	.40	.10
□ 298 Don Dillard	1.00	.40	.10
□ 299 Rookie Stars	1.00	.40	.10
Dave Morehead			
Bob Dustal			
Tom Butters			
Dan Schneider			
□ 300 Willie Mays	80.00	32.00	8.00
□ 301 Bill Fischer	1.00	.40	.10
□ 302 Whitey Herzog	2.50	1.00	.25
□ 303 Earl Francis	1.00	.40	.10
□ 304 Harry Bright	1.00	.40	.10
□ 305 Don Hoak	1.50	.60	.15
□ 306 Star Receivers	2.00	.80	.20
Earl Battey			
Elston Howard			
□ 307 Chet Nichols	1.00	.40	.10
□ 308 Camilo Carreon	1.00	.40	.10
□ 309 Jim Brewer	1.00	.40	.10
□ 310 Tommy Davis	2.00	.80	.20
□ 311 Joe McClain	1.00	.40	.10
□ 312 Houston Colts	6.00	2.40	.60
Team Card			
□ 313 Ernie Broglio	1.00	.40	.10
□ 314 John Goryl	1.00	.40	.10
□ 315 Ralph Terry	1.50	.60	.15
□ 316 Norm Sherry	1.00	.40	.10
□ 317 Sam McDowell	2.00	.80	.20
□ 318 Gene Mauch MG	1.50	.60	.15
□ 319 Joe Gaines	1.00	.40	.10
□ 320 Warren Spahn	15.00	6.00	1.50
□ 321 Gino Cimoli	1.00	.40	.10
□ 322 Bob Turley	2.00	.80	.20
□ 323 Bill Mazeroski	2.50	1.00	.25
□ 324 Rookie Stars	2.00	.80	.20
George Williams			
Pete Ward			
Phil Ward			
Vic Davalillo			
□ 325 Jack Sanford	1.50	.60	.15
□ 326 Hank Foiles	1.00	.40	.10
□ 327 Paul Foytack	1.00	.40	.10
□ 328 Dick Williams	1.50	.60	.15
□ 329 Lindy McDaniel	1.50	.60	.15
□ 330 Chuck Hinton	1.00	.40	.10
□ 331 Series Foes	1.50	.60	.15
Bill Stafford			
Bill Pierce			
□ 332 Joel Horlen	1.00	.40	.10
□ 333 Carl Warwick	1.00	.40	.10
□ 334 Wynn Hawkins	1.00	.40	.10
□ 335 Leon Wagner	1.00	.40	.10
□ 336 Ed Bauta	1.00	.40	.10
□ 337 Dodgers Team	6.00	2.40	.60
□ 338 Russ Kemmerer	1.00	.40	.10
□ 339 Ted Bowsfield	1.00	.40	.10
□ 340 Yogi Berra	35.00	14.00	3.50
□ 341 Jack Baldschun	1.00	.40	.10
□ 342 Gene Woodling	1.50	.60	.15
□ 343 Johnny Pesky MG	1.50	.60	.15
□ 344 Don Schwall	1.50	.60	.15
□ 345 Brooks Robinson	27.00	11.00	2.70
□ 346 Billy Hoeft	1.00	.40	.10
□ 347 Joe Torre	3.50	1.40	.35
□ 348 Vic Wertz	1.50	.60	.15
□ 349 Zoilo Versailles	1.00	.40	.10
□ 350 Bob Purkey	1.00	.40	.10
□ 351 Al Luplow	1.00	.40	.10
□ 352 Ken Johnson	1.00	.40	.10
□ 353 Billy Williams	11.00	4.50	1.10
□ 354 Dom Zanni	1.00	.40	.10
□ 355 Dean Chance	1.50	.60	.15
□ 356 John Schaive	1.00	.40	.10
□ 357 George Altman	1.00	.40	.10
□ 358 Milt Pappas	1.50	.60	.15
□ 359 Haywood Sullivan	1.50	.60	.15

□ 360	Don Drysdale	12.00	5.00	1.20
□ 361	Cletis Boyer	2.00	.80	.20
□ 362	Checklist 5	4.00	.40	.08
□ 363	Dick Radatz	2.00	.80	.20
□ 364	Howie Goss	1.00	.40	.10
□ 365	Jim Bunning	5.00	2.00	.50
□ 366	Tony Taylor	1.00	.40	.10
□ 367	Tony Cloninger	1.00	.40	.10
□ 368	Ed Bailey	1.00	.40	.10
□ 369	Jim Lemon MG	1.50	.60	.15
□ 370	Dick Donovan	1.00	.40	.10
□ 371	Rod Kanehl	1.00	.40	.10
□ 372	Don Lee	1.00	.40	.10
□ 373	Jim Campbell	1.00	.40	.10
□ 374	Claude Osteen	1.50	.60	.15
□ 375	Ken Boyer	2.50	1.00	.25
□ 376	John Wyatt	1.00	.40	.10
□ 377	Baltimore Orioles Team Card	2.00	.80	.20
□ 378	Bill Henry	1.00	.40	.10
□ 379	Bob Anderson	1.00	.40	.10
□ 380	Ernie Banks	25.00	10.00	2.50
□ 381	Frank Baumann	1.00	.40	.10
□ 382	Ralph Houk MG	1.50	.60	.15
□ 383	Pete Richert	1.00	.40	.10
□ 384	Bob Tillman	1.00	.40	.10
□ 385	Art Mahaffey	1.00	.40	.10
□ 386	Rookie Stars Ed Kirkpatrick John Bateman Larry Bearnarth Garry Roggenburk	1.50	.60	.15
□ 387	Al McBean	1.00	.40	.10
□ 388	Jim Davenport	1.50	.60	.15
□ 389	Frank Sullivan	1.00	.40	.10
□ 390	Hank Aaron	80.00	32.00	8.00
□ 391	B. Dailey	1.00	.40	.10
□ 392	Tribe Thumpers Johnny Romano Tito Francona	1.50	.60	.15
□ 393	Ken MacKenzie	1.00	.40	.10
□ 394	Tim McCarver	4.00	1.60	.40
□ 395	Don McMahon	1.50	.60	.15
□ 396	Joe Koppe	1.00	.40	.10
□ 397	Kansas City Athletics Team Card	2.00	.80	.20
□ 398	Boog Powell	4.00	1.60	.40
□ 399	Dick Ellsworth	1.50	.60	.15
□ 400	Frank Robinson	25.00	10.00	2.50
□ 401	Jim Bouton	3.50	1.40	.35
□ 402	Mickey Vernon	1.50	.60	.15
□ 403	Ron Perranoski	1.50	.60	.15
□ 404	Bob Oldis	1.00	.40	.10
□ 405	Floyd Robinson	1.00	.40	.10
□ 406	Howie Koplitz	1.00	.40	.10
□ 407	Rookie Stars Frank Kostro Chico Ruiz Larry Elliot Dick Simpson	1.00	.40	.10
□ 408	Billy Gardner	1.00	.40	.10
□ 409	Roy Face	2.00	.80	.20
□ 410	Earl Battey	1.50	.60	.15
□ 411	Jim Constable	1.00	.40	.10
□ 412	Dodger Big Three Johnny Podres Don Drysdale Sandy Koufax	20.00	8.00	2.00
□ 413	Jerry Walker	1.00	.40	.10
□ 414	Ty Cline	1.00	.40	.10
□ 415	Bob Gibson	20.00	8.00	2.00
□ 416	Alex Grammas	1.00	.40	.10
□ 417	Giants Team	2.00	.80	.20
□ 418	John Orsino	1.00	.40	.10
□ 419	Tracy Stallard	1.00	.40	.10
□ 420	Bobby Richardson	4.00	1.60	.40
□ 421	Tom Morgan	1.00	.40	.10
□ 422	Fred Hutchinson MG	1.50	.60	.15
□ 423	Ed Hobaugh	1.00	.40	.10
□ 424	Charley Smith	1.00	.40	.10
□ 425	Smoky Burgess	1.50	.60	.15
□ 426	Barry Latman	1.00	.40	.10
□ 427	Bernie Allen	1.00	.40	.10
□ 428	Carl Boles	1.00	.40	.10
□ 429	Lou Burdette	2.00	.80	.20
□ 430	Norm Siebern	1.00	.40	.10
□ 431A	Checklist 6 (white on red)	4.00	.40	.08
□ 431B	Checklist 6 (black on orange)	8.00	.80	.15
□ 432	Roman Mejias	1.00	.40	.10
□ 433	Denis Menke	1.00	.40	.10
□ 434	John Callison	1.50	.60	.15
□ 435	Woody Held	1.00	.40	.10
□ 436	Tim Harkness	1.00	.40	.10
□ 437	Bill Bruton	1.00	.40	.10
□ 438	Wes Stock	1.00	.40	.10
□ 439	Don Zimmer	2.00	.80	.20
□ 440	Juan Marichal	16.00	6.50	1.60
□ 441	Lee Thomas	2.00	.80	.20
□ 442	J.C. Hartman	1.00	.40	.10
□ 443	Jim Piersall	2.00	.80	.20
□ 444	Jim Maloney	2.00	.80	.20
□ 445	Norm Cash	2.50	1.00	.25
□ 446	Whitey Ford	25.00	10.00	2.50
□ 447	Felix Mantilla	6.00	2.40	.60
□ 448	Jack Kralick	6.00	2.40	.60
□ 449	Jose Tartabull	6.00	2.40	.60
□ 450	Bob Friend	7.00	2.80	.70
□ 451	Indians Team	11.00	4.50	1.10
□ 452	Buddy Schultz	6.00	2.40	.60
□ 453	Jake Wood	6.00	2.40	.60
□ 454A	Art Fowler (card number on white background)	6.00	2.40	.60
□ 454B	Art Fowler (card number on orange background)	10.00	4.00	1.00
□ 455	Ruben Amaro	6.00	2.40	.60
□ 456	Jim Coker	6.00	2.40	.60
□ 457	Tex Clevenger	6.00	2.40	.60
□ 458	Al Lopez MG	11.00	4.50	1.10
□ 459	Dick LeMay	6.00	2.40	.60
□ 460	Del Crandall	7.00	2.80	.70
□ 461	Norm Bass	6.00	2.40	.60
□ 462	Wally Post	6.00	2.40	.60
□ 463	Joe Schaffernoth	6.00	2.40	.60
□ 464	Ken Aspromonte	6.00	2.40	.60
□ 465	Chuck Estrada	7.00	2.80	.70
□ 466	Rookie Stars SP Nate Oliver Tony Martinez Bill Freehan Jerry Robinson	20.00	8.00	2.00
□ 467	Phil Ortega	6.00	2.40	.60
□ 468	Carroll Hardy	6.00	2.40	.60
□ 469	Jay Hook	6.00	2.40	.60
□ 470	Tom Tresh SP	20.00	8.00	2.00
□ 471	Ken Retzer	6.00	2.40	.60
□ 472	Lou Brock	75.00	30.00	7.50
□ 473	New York Mets Team Card	20.00	8.00	2.00
□ 474	Jack Fisher	6.00	2.40	.60
□ 475	Gus Triandos	7.00	2.80	.70
□ 476	Frank Funk	6.00	2.40	.60
□ 477	Donn Clendenon	7.00	2.80	.70
□ 478	Paul Brown	6.00	2.40	.60
□ 479	Ed Brinkman	6.00	2.40	.60
□ 480	Bill Monbouquette	6.00	2.40	.60
□ 481	Bill Taylor	6.00	2.40	.60
□ 482	Felix Torres	6.00	2.40	.60
□ 483	Jim Owens	6.00	2.40	.60
□ 484	Dale Long	7.00	2.80	.70
□ 485	Jim Landis	6.00	2.40	.60
□ 486	Ray Sadecki	6.00	2.40	.60
□ 487	John Roseboro	7.00	2.80	.70
□ 488	Jerry Adair	6.00	2.40	.60
□ 489	Paul Toth	6.00	2.40	.60
□ 490	Willie McCovey	60.00	24.00	6.00
□ 491	Harry Craft MG	6.00	2.40	.60
□ 492	Dave Wickersham	6.00	2.40	.60
□ 493	Walt Bond	6.00	2.40	.60
□ 494	Phil Regan	7.00	2.80	.70
□ 495	Frank Thomas	7.00	2.80	.70
□ 496	Rookie Stars Steve Dalkowski Fred Newman Jack Smith Carl Bouldin	7.00	2.80	.70
□ 497	Bennie Daniels	6.00	2.40	.60
□ 498	Ed Kasko	6.00	2.40	.60
□ 499	J.C. Martin	6.00	2.40	.60
□ 500	Harmon Killebrew	40.00	16.00	4.00
□ 501	Joe Azcue	6.00	2.40	.60
□ 502	Daryl Spencer	6.00	2.40	.60
□ 503	Braves Team	11.00	4.50	1.10
□ 504	Bob Johnson	6.00	2.40	.60
□ 505	Curt Flood	11.00	4.50	1.10
□ 506	Gene Green	6.00	2.40	.60
□ 507	Rollie Sheldon	4.00	1.60	.40
□ 508	Ted Savage	4.00	1.60	.40
□ 509A	Checklist 7 (copyright centered)	12.00	1.50	.15
□ 509B	Checklist 7 (copyright to right)	12.00	1.50	.15
□ 510	Ken McBride	4.00	1.60	.40
□ 511	Charlie Neal	5.00	2.00	.50
□ 512	Cal McLish	4.00	1.60	.40
□ 513	Gary Geiger	4.00	1.60	.40
□ 514	Larry Osborne	4.00	1.60	.40

□ 515	Don Elston	4.00	1.60	.40
□ 516	Purnell Goldy	4.00	1.60	.40
□ 517	Hal Woodeshick	4.00	1.60	.40
□ 518	Don Blasingame	4.00	1.60	.40
□ 519	Claude Raymond	4.00	1.60	.40
□ 520	Orlando Cepeda	11.00	4.50	1.10
□ 521	Dan Pfister	4.00	1.60	.40
□ 522	Rookie Stars	6.00	2.40	.60
	Mel Nelson			
	Gary Peters			
	Jim Roland			
	Art Quirk			
□ 523	Bill Kunkel	5.00	2.00	.50
□ 524	Cardinals Team	9.00	3.75	.90
□ 525	Nellie Fox	8.50	3.50	.85
□ 526	Dick Hall	4.00	1.60	.40
□ 527	Ed Sadowski	4.00	1.60	.40
□ 528	Carl Willey	4.00	1.60	.40
□ 529	Wes Covington	5.00	2.00	.50
□ 530	Don Mossi	5.00	2.00	.50
□ 531	Sam Mele MG	4.00	1.60	.40
□ 532	Steve Boros	5.00	2.00	.50
□ 533	Bobby Shantz	6.00	2.40	.60
□ 534	Ken Walters	4.00	1.60	.40
□ 535	Jim Perry	6.00	2.40	.60
□ 536	Norm Larker	5.00	2.00	.50
□ 537	Rookie Stars	600.00	240.00	60.00
	Pedro Gonzales			
	Ken McMullen			
	Al Weis			
	Pete Rose			
□ 538	George Brunet	4.00	1.60	.40
□ 539	Wayne Causey	4.00	1.60	.40
□ 540	Bob Clemente	110.00	45.00	11.00
□ 541	Ron Moeller	4.00	1.60	.40
□ 542	Lou Klimchock	4.00	1.60	.40
□ 543	Russ Snyder	4.00	1.60	.40
□ 544	Rookie Stars	25.00	10.00	2.50
	Duke Carmel			
	Bill Haas			
	Rusty Staub			
	Dick Phillips			
□ 545	Jose Pagan	4.00	1.60	.40
□ 546	Hal Reniff	4.00	1.60	.40
□ 547	Gus Bell	5.00	2.00	.50
□ 548	Tom Satriano	4.00	1.60	.40
□ 549	Rookie Stars	4.00	1.60	.40
	Marcelino Lopez			
	Pete Lovrich			
	Paul Ratliff			
	Elmo Plaskett			
□ 550	Duke Snider	50.00	20.00	5.00
□ 551	Billy Klaus	4.00	1.60	.40
□ 552	Detroit Tigers	16.00	6.50	1.60
	Team Card			
□ 553	Rookie Stars	150.00	60.00	15.00
	Brock Davis			
	Jim Gosger			
	Willie Stargell			
	John Herrnstein			
□ 554	Hank Fischer	4.00	1.60	.40
□ 555	John Blanchard	5.00	2.00	.50
□ 556	Al Worthington	4.00	1.60	.40
□ 557	Cuno Barragan	4.00	1.60	.40
□ 558	Rookie Stars	4.00	1.60	.40
	Bill Faul			
	Ron Hunt			
	Al Moran			
	Bob Lipski			
□ 559	Danny Murtaugh MG	4.00	1.60	.40
□ 560	Ray Herbert	4.00	1.60	.40
□ 561	Mike De La Hoz	4.00	1.60	.40
□ 562	Rookie Stars	8.00	3.25	.80
	Randy Cardinal			
	Dave McNally			
	Ken Rowe			
	Don Rowe			
□ 563	Mike McCormick	5.00	2.00	.50
□ 564	George Banks	4.00	1.60	.40
□ 565	Larry Sherry	5.00	2.00	.50
□ 566	Cliff Cook	4.00	1.60	.40
□ 567	Jim Duffalo	4.00	1.60	.40
□ 568	Bob Sadowski	4.00	1.60	.40
□ 569	Luis Arroyo	5.00	2.00	.50
□ 570	Frank Bolling	4.00	1.60	.40
□ 571	John Klippstein	4.00	1.60	.40
□ 572	Jack Spring	4.00	1.60	.40
□ 573	Coot Veal	4.00	1.60	.40
□ 574	Hal Kolstad	4.00	1.60	.40
□ 575	Don Cardwell	4.00	1.60	.40
□ 576	Johnny Temple	6.50	2.00	.40

1964 Topps

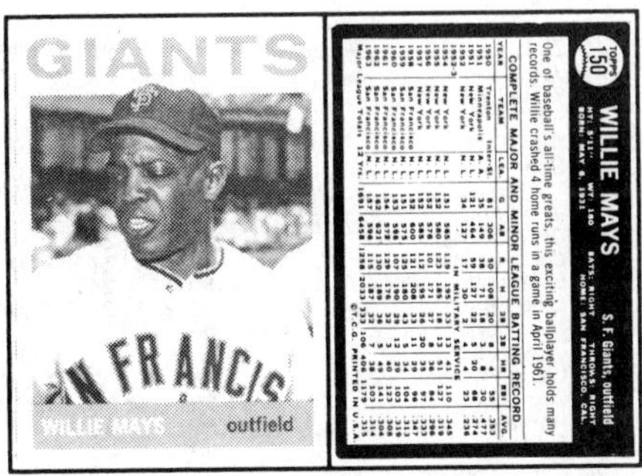

The cards in this 587-card set measure 2 1/2" by 3 1/2". Players in the 1964 Topps baseball series were easy to sort by team due to the giant block lettering found at the top of each card. The name and position of the player are found underneath the picture and the card is numbered in a ball design on the orange-colored back. The usual last series scarcity holds for this set (523 to 587). Subsets within this set include League Leaders (1-12) and World Series cards (136-140).

		NRMT	VG-E	GOOD
	COMPLETE SET (587)	2000.00	900.00	300.00
	COMMON PLAYER (1-370)	.60	.24	.06
	COMMON PLAYER (371-522)	1.00	.40	.10
	COMMON PLAYER (523-587)	3.50	1.40	.35
□ 1	NL ERA Leaders	9.00	1.50	.30
	Sandy Koufax			
	Dick Ellsworth			
	Bob Friend			
□ 2	AL ERA Leaders	1.50	.60	.15
	Gary Peters			
	Juan Pizarro			
	Camilo Pascual			
□ 3	NL Pitching Leaders	5.00	2.00	.40
	Sandy Koufax			
	Juan Marichal			
	Warren Spahn			
	Jim Maloney			
□ 4	AL Pitching Leaders	1.50	.60	.15
	Whitey Ford			
	Camilo Pascual			
	Jim Bouton			
□ 5	NL Strikeout Leaders	4.00	1.60	.35
	Sandy Koufax			
	Jim Maloney			
	Don Drysdale			
□ 6	AL Strikeout Leaders	1.50	.60	.15
	Camilo Pascual			
	Jim Bunning			
	Dick Stigman			
□ 7	NL Batting Leaders	3.00	1.20	.25
	Tommy Davis			
	Bob Clemente			
	Dick Groat			
	Hank Aaron			
□ 8	AL Batting Leaders	4.00	1.60	.35
	Carl Yastrzemski			
	Al Kaline			
	Rich Rollins			
□ 9	NL Home Run Leaders	7.50	3.00	.60
	Hank Aaron			
	Willie McCovey			
	Willie Mays			
	Orlando Cepeda			
□ 10	AL Home Run Leaders	1.50	.60	.15
	Harmon Killebrew			
	Dick Stuart			
	Bob Allison			
□ 11	NL RBI Leaders	2.50	1.00	.20
	Hank Aaron			
	Ken Boyer			
	Bill White			
□ 12	AL RBI Leaders	2.00	.80	.20
	Dick Stuart			
	Al Kaline			

Harmon Killebrew			
□ 13 Hoyt Wilhelm	6.50	2.60	.65
□ 14 Dodgers Rookies	.60	.24	.06
Dick Nen			
Nick Willhite			
□ 15 Zoilo Versalles	.60	.24	.06
□ 16 John Boozer	.60	.24	.06
□ 17 Willie Kirkland	.60	.24	.06
□ 18 Billy O'Dell	.60	.24	.06
□ 19 Don Wert	.60	.24	.06
□ 20 Bob Friend	.75	.30	.07
□ 21 Yogi Berra	25.00	10.00	2.50
□ 22 Jerry Adair	.60	.24	.06
□ 23 Chris Zachary	.60	.24	.06
□ 24 Carl Sawatski	.60	.24	.06
□ 25 Bill Monbouquette	.60	.24	.06
□ 26 Gino Cimoli	.60	.24	.06
□ 27 New York Mets	2.00	.80	.20
Team Card			
□ 28 Claude Osteen	.75	.30	.07
□ 29 Lou Brock	21.00	8.50	2.10
□ 30 Ron Perranoski	.75	.30	.07
□ 31 Dave Nicholson	.60	.24	.06
□ 32 Dean Chance	1.00	.40	.10
□ 33 Reds Rookies	.75	.30	.07
Sammy Ellis			
Mel Queen			
□ 34 Jim Perry	1.00	.40	.10
□ 35 Eddie Mathews	9.00	3.75	.90
□ 36 Hal Reniff	.60	.24	.06
□ 37 Smoky Burgess	.75	.30	.07
□ 38 Jim Wynn	1.50	.60	.15
□ 39 Hank Aguirre	.60	.24	.06
□ 40 Dick Groat	1.00	.40	.10
□ 41 Friendly Foes	3.00	1.20	.30
Willie McCovey			
Leon Wagner			
□ 42 Moe Drabowsky	.60	.24	.06
□ 43 Roy Sievers	.75	.30	.07
□ 44 Duke Carmel	.60	.24	.06
□ 45 Milt Pappas	.75	.30	.07
□ 46 Ed Brinkman	.60	.24	.06
□ 47 Giants Rookies	1.00	.40	.10
Jesus Alou			
Ron Herbel			
□ 48 Bob Perry	.60	.24	.06
□ 49 Bill Henry	.60	.24	.06
□ 50 Mickey Mantle	200.00	80.00	20.00
□ 51 Pete Richert	.60	.24	.06
□ 52 Chuck Hinton	.60	.24	.06
□ 53 Denis Menke	.60	.24	.06
□ 54 Sam Mele MG	.60	.24	.06
□ 55 Ernie Banks	12.00	5.00	1.20
□ 56 Hal Brown	.60	.24	.06
□ 57 Tim Harkness	.60	.24	.06
□ 58 Don Demeter	.60	.24	.06
□ 59 Ernie Broglio	.60	.24	.06
□ 60 Frank Malzone	.75	.30	.07
□ 61 Angel Backstops	1.00	.40	.10
Bob Rodgers			
Ed Sadowski			
□ 62 Ted Savage	.60	.24	.06
□ 63 John Orsino	.60	.24	.06
□ 64 Ted Abernathy	.60	.24	.06
□ 65 Felipe Alou	1.00	.40	.10
□ 66 Eddie Fisher	.60	.24	.06
□ 67 Tigers Team	1.50	.60	.15
□ 68 Willie Davis	1.00	.40	.10
□ 69 Clete Boyer	1.00	.40	.10
□ 70 Joe Torre	1.75	.70	.17
□ 71 Jack Spring	.60	.24	.06
□ 72 Chico Cardenas	.60	.24	.06
□ 73 Jimmie Hall	1.00	.40	.10
□ 74 Pirates Rookies	.60	.24	.06
Bob Priddy			
Tom Butters			
□ 75 Wayne Causey	.60	.24	.06
□ 76 Checklist 1	3.00	.30	.06
□ 77 Jerry Walker	.60	.24	.06
□ 78 Merritt Ranew	.60	.24	.06
□ 79 Bob Heffner	.60	.24	.06
□ 80 Vada Pinson	1.50	.60	.15
□ 81 All-Star Vets	4.00	1.60	.40
Nellie Fox			
Harmon Killebrew			
□ 82 Jim Davenport	.75	.30	.07
□ 83 Gus Triandos	.75	.30	.07
□ 84 Carl Willey	.60	.24	.06
□ 85 Pete Ward	.60	.24	.06
□ 86 Al Downing	.75	.30	.07
□ 87 St. Louis Cardinals	1.50	.60	.15
Team Card			
□ 88 John Roseboro	.75	.30	.07
□ 89 Boog Powell	2.00	.80	.20
□ 90 Earl Battey	.75	.30	.07
□ 91 Bob Bailey	.60	.24	.06
□ 92 Steve Ridzik	.60	.24	.06
□ 93 Gary Geiger	.60	.24	.06
□ 94 Braves Rookies	.60	.24	.06
Jim Britton			
Larry Maxie			
□ 95 George Altman	.60	.24	.06
□ 96 Bob Buhl	.60	.24	.06
□ 97 Jim Fregosi	1.00	.40	.10
□ 98 Bill Bruton	.60	.24	.06
□ 99 Al Stanek	.60	.24	.06
□ 100 Elston Howard	2.50	1.00	.25
□ 101 Walt Alston MG	2.50	1.00	.25
□ 102 Checklist 2	3.00	.30	.06
□ 103 Curt Flood	1.50	.60	.15
□ 104 Art Mahaffey	.60	.24	.06
□ 105 Woody Held	.60	.24	.06
□ 106 Joe Nuxhall	.75	.30	.07
□ 107 White Sox Rookies	.60	.24	.06
Bruce Howard			
Frank Kreutzer			
□ 108 John Wyatt	.60	.24	.06
□ 109 Rusty Staub	4.50	1.80	.45
□ 110 Albie Pearson	.60	.24	.06
□ 111 Don Elston	.60	.24	.06
□ 112 Bob Tillman	.60	.24	.06
□ 113 Grover Powell	.60	.24	.06
□ 114 Don Lock	.60	.24	.06
□ 115 Frank Bolling	.60	.24	.06
□ 116 Twins Rookies	7.00	2.80	.70
Jay Ward			
Tony Oliva			
□ 117 Earl Francis	.60	.24	.06
□ 118 John Blanchard	.75	.30	.07
□ 119 Gary Kolb	.60	.24	.06
□ 120 Don Drysdale	8.50	3.50	.85
□ 121 Pete Runnels	.75	.30	.07
□ 122 Don McMahon	.75	.30	.07
□ 123 Jose Pagan	.60	.24	.06
□ 124 Orlando Pena	.60	.24	.06
□ 125 Pete Rose	165.00	65.00	15.00
□ 126 Russ Snyder	.60	.24	.06
□ 127 Angels Rookies	.60	.24	.06
Aubrey Gatewood			
Dick Simpson			
□ 128 Mickey Lolich	7.50	3.00	.75
□ 129 Amado Samuel	.60	.24	.06
□ 130 Gary Peters	.75	.30	.07
□ 131 Steve Boros	.75	.30	.07
□ 132 Braves Team	1.50	.60	.15
□ 133 Jim Grant	.60	.24	.06
□ 134 Don Zimmer	1.00	.40	.10
□ 135 Johnny Callison	.75	.30	.07
□ 136 World Series Game 1	6.50	2.60	.65
Koufax strikes out 15			
□ 137 World Series Game 2	2.00	.80	.20
Davis sparks rally			
□ 138 World Series Game 3	2.00	.80	.20
LA 3 straight			
□ 139 World Series Game 4	2.00	.80	.20
Sealing Yanks doom			
□ 140 World Series Summary	2.00	.80	.20
Dodgers celebrate			
□ 141 Danny Murtaugh MG	.60	.24	.06
□ 142 John Bateman	.60	.24	.06
□ 143 Bubba Phillips	.60	.24	.06
□ 144 Al Worthington	.60	.24	.06
□ 145 Norm Siebern	.60	.24	.06
□ 146 Indians Rookies	30.00	12.00	3.00
Tommy John			
Bob Chance			
□ 147 Ray Sadecki	.60	.24	.06
□ 148 J.C. Martin	.60	.24	.06
□ 149 Paul Foytack	.60	.24	.06
□ 150 Willie Mays	50.00	20.00	5.00
□ 151 Athletics Team	1.25	.50	.12
□ 152 Denny Lemaster	.60	.24	.06
□ 153 Dick Williams	.75	.30	.07
□ 154 Dick Tracewski	.60	.24	.06
□ 155 Duke Snider	16.00	6.50	1.60
□ 156 Bill Dailey	.60	.24	.06
□ 157 Gene Mauch MG	.75	.30	.07
□ 158 Ken Johnson	.60	.24	.06
□ 159 Charlie Dees	.60	.24	.06
□ 160 Ken Boyer	3.50	1.40	.35
□ 161 Dave McNally	1.50	.60	.15
□ 162 Hitting Area	1.00	.40	.10
Dick Sisler			
Vada Pinson			
□ 163 Donn Clendenon	.75	.30	.07
□ 164 Bud Daley	.60	.24	.06
□ 165 Jerry Lumpe	.60	.24	.06
□ 166 Marty Keough	.60	.24	.06
□ 167 Senators Rookies	18.00	7.25	1.80
Mike Brumley			

	Lou Piniella			
☐ 168	Al Weis	.60	.24	.06
☐ 169	Del Crandall	.75	.30	.07
☐ 170	Dick Radatz	1.00	.40	.10
☐ 171	Ty Cline	.60	.24	.06
☐ 172	Indians Team	1.25	.50	.12
☐ 173	Ryne Duren	1.00	.40	.10
☐ 174	Doc Edwards	1.50	.60	.15
☐ 175	Billy Williams	9.00	3.75	.90
☐ 176	Tracy Stallard	.60	.24	.06
☐ 177	Harmon Killebrew	9.00	3.75	.90
☐ 178	Hank Bauer MG	1.00	.40	.10
☐ 179	Carl Warwick	.60	.24	.06
☐ 180	Tommy Davis	1.00	.40	.10
☐ 181	Dave Wickersham	.60	.24	.06
☐ 182	Sox Sockers	7.50	3.00	.75
	Carl Yastrzemski			
	Chuck Schilling			
☐ 183	Ron Taylor	.60	.24	.06
☐ 184	Al Luplow	.60	.24	.06
☐ 185	Jim O'Toole	.75	.30	.07
☐ 186	Roman Mejias	.60	.24	.06
☐ 187	Ed Roebuck	.60	.24	.06
☐ 188	Checklist 3	3.00	.30	.06
☐ 189	Bob Hendley	.60	.24	.06
☐ 190	Bobby Richardson	3.50	1.40	.35
☐ 191	Clay Dalrymple	.60	.24	.06
☐ 192	Cubs Rookies	.60	.24	.06
	John Boccabella			
	Billy Cowan			
☐ 193	Jerry Lynch	.60	.24	.06
☐ 194	John Goryl	.60	.24	.06
☐ 195	Floyd Robinson	.60	.24	.06
☐ 196	Jim Gentile	.75	.30	.07
☐ 197	Frank Lary	.75	.30	.07
☐ 198	Len Gabrielson	.60	.24	.06
☐ 199	Joe Azcue	.60	.24	.06
☐ 200	Sandy Koufax	50.00	20.00	5.00
☐ 201	Orioles Rookies	.75	.30	.07
	Sam Bowens			
	Wally Bunker			
☐ 202	Galen Cisco	.60	.24	.06
☐ 203	John Kennedy	.60	.24	.06
☐ 204	Matty Alou	.75	.30	.07
☐ 205	Nellie Fox	3.00	1.20	.30
☐ 206	Steve Hamilton	.60	.24	.06
☐ 207	Fred Hutchinson MG	.75	.30	.07
☐ 208	Wes Covington	.75	.30	.07
☐ 209	Bob Allen	.60	.24	.06
☐ 210	Carl Yastrzemski	60.00	24.00	6.00
☐ 211	Jim Coker	.60	.24	.06
☐ 212	Pete Lovrich	.60	.24	.06
☐ 213	Angels Team	1.25	.50	.12
☐ 214	Ken McMullen	.75	.30	.07
☐ 215	Ray Herbert	.60	.24	.06
☐ 216	Mike De La Hoz	.60	.24	.06
☐ 217	Jim King	.60	.24	.06
☐ 218	Hank Fischer	.60	.24	.06
☐ 219	Young Aces	1.50	.60	.15
	Al Downing			
	Jim Bouton			
☐ 220	Dick Ellsworth	.75	.30	.07
☐ 221	Bob Saverine	.60	.24	.06
☐ 222	Billy Pierce	1.00	.40	.10
☐ 223	George Banks	.60	.24	.06
☐ 224	Tommie Sisk	.60	.24	.06
☐ 225	Roger Maris	35.00	14.00	3.50
☐ 226	Colts Rookies	.75	.30	.07
	Gerald Grote			
	Larry Yellen			
☐ 227	Barry Latman	.60	.24	.06
☐ 228	Felix Mantilla	.60	.24	.06
☐ 229	Charley Lau	1.00	.40	.10
☐ 230	Brooks Robinson	20.00	8.00	2.00
☐ 231	Dick Calmus	.60	.24	.06
☐ 232	Al Lopez MG	2.00	.80	.20
☐ 233	Hal Smith	.60	.24	.06
☐ 234	Gary Bell	.60	.24	.06
☐ 235	Ron Hunt	.60	.24	.06
☐ 236	Bill Faul	.60	.24	.06
☐ 237	Cubs Team	1.25	.50	.12
☐ 238	Roy McMillan	.60	.24	.06
☐ 239	Herm Starrette	.60	.24	.06
☐ 240	Bill White	1.00	.40	.10
☐ 241	Jim Owens	.60	.24	.06
☐ 242	Harvey Kuenn	1.25	.50	.12
☐ 243	Phillies Rookies	10.00	4.00	1.00
	Richie Allen			
	John Herrnstein			
☐ 244	Tony LaRussa	6.00	2.40	.60
☐ 245	Dick Stigman	.60	.24	.06
☐ 246	Manny Mota	1.00	.40	.10
☐ 247	Dave DeBusschere	2.50	1.00	.25
☐ 248	Johnny Pesky MG	.75	.30	.07
☐ 249	Doug Camilli	.60	.24	.06
☐ 250	Al Kaline	14.00	5.75	1.40
☐ 251	Choo Choo Coleman	.60	.24	.06
☐ 252	Ken Aspromonte	.60	.24	.06
☐ 253	Wally Post	.60	.24	.06
☐ 254	Don Hoak	.60	.24	.06
☐ 255	Lee Thomas	1.00	.40	.10
☐ 256	Johnny Weekly	.60	.24	.06
☐ 257	San Francisco Giants	1.50	.60	.15
	Team Card			
☐ 258	Garry Roggenburk	.60	.24	.06
☐ 259	Harry Bright	.60	.24	.06
☐ 260	Frank Robinson	12.00	5.00	1.20
☐ 261	Jim Hannan	.60	.24	.06
☐ 262	Cards Rookies	2.50	1.00	.25
	Mike Shannon			
	Harry Fanok			
☐ 263	Chuck Estrada	.75	.30	.07
☐ 264	Jim Landis	.60	.24	.06
☐ 265	Jim Bunning	3.50	1.40	.35
☐ 266	Gene Freese	.60	.24	.06
☐ 267	Wilbur Wood	1.25	.50	.12
☐ 268	Bill's Got It	.75	.30	.07
	Danny Murtaugh			
	Bill Virdon			
☐ 269	Ellis Burton	.60	.24	.06
☐ 270	Rich Rollins	.75	.30	.07
☐ 271	Bob Sadowski	.60	.24	.06
☐ 272	Jake Wood	.60	.24	.06
☐ 273	Mel Nelson	.60	.24	.06
☐ 274	Checklist 4	3.00	.30	.06
☐ 275	John Tsitouris	.60	.24	.06
☐ 276	Jose Tartabull	.60	.24	.06
☐ 277	Ken Retzer	.60	.24	.06
☐ 278	Bobby Shantz	1.00	.40	.10
☐ 279	Joe Koppe (glove	.75	.30	.07
	on wrong hand)			
☐ 280	Juan Marichal	8.00	3.25	.80
☐ 281	Yankees Rookies	.75	.30	.07
	Jake Gibbs			
	Tom Metcalf			
☐ 282	Bob Bruce	.60	.24	.06
☐ 283	Tom McCraw	.75	.30	.07
☐ 284	Dick Schofield	.60	.24	.06
☐ 285	Robin Roberts	7.50	3.00	.75
☐ 286	Don Landrum	.60	.24	.06
☐ 287	Red Sox Rookies	7.50	3.00	.75
	Tony Conigliaro			
	Bill Spanswick			
☐ 288	Al Moran	.60	.24	.06
☐ 289	Frank Funk	.60	.24	.06
☐ 290	Bob Allison	.75	.30	.07
☐ 291	Phil Ortega	.60	.24	.06
☐ 292	Mike Roarke	.60	.24	.06
☐ 293	Phillies Team	1.25	.50	.12
☐ 294	Ken L. Hunt	.60	.24	.06
☐ 295	Roger Craig	1.50	.60	.15
☐ 296	Ed Kirkpatrick	.60	.24	.06
☐ 297	Ken MacKenzie	.60	.24	.06
☐ 298	Harry Craft MG	.60	.24	.06
☐ 299	Bill Stafford	.60	.24	.06
☐ 300	Hank Aaron	50.00	20.00	5.00
☐ 301	Larry Brown	.60	.24	.06
☐ 302	Dan Pfister	.60	.24	.06
☐ 303	Jim Campbell	.60	.24	.06
☐ 304	Bob Johnson	.60	.24	.06
☐ 305	Jack Lamabe	.60	.24	.06
☐ 306	Giant Gunners	11.00	4.50	1.10
	Willie Mays			
	Orlando Cepeda			
☐ 307	Joe Gibbon	.60	.24	.06
☐ 308	Gene Stephens	.60	.24	.06
☐ 309	Paul Toth	.60	.24	.06
☐ 310	Jim Gilliam	2.00	.80	.20
☐ 311	Tom Brown	.60	.24	.06
☐ 312	Tigers Rookies	.60	.24	.06
	Fritz Fisher			
	Fred Gladding			
☐ 313	Chuck Hiller	.60	.24	.06
☐ 314	Jerry Buchek	.60	.24	.06
☐ 315	Bo Belinsky	.75	.30	.07
☐ 316	Gene Oliver	.60	.24	.06
☐ 317	Al Smith	.60	.24	.06
☐ 318	Minnesota Twins	1.25	.50	.12
	Team Card			
☐ 319	Paul Brown	.60	.24	.06
☐ 320	Rocky Colavito	2.00	.80	.20
☐ 321	Bob Lillis	.75	.30	.07
☐ 322	George Brunet	.60	.24	.06
☐ 323	John Buzhardt	.60	.24	.06
☐ 324	Casey Stengel MG	9.00	3.75	.90
☐ 325	Hector Lopez	.60	.24	.06
☐ 326	Ron Brand	.60	.24	.06
☐ 327	Don Blasingame	.60	.24	.06
☐ 328	Bob Shaw	.60	.24	.06
☐ 329	Russ Nixon	1.00	.40	.10

□ 330 Tommy Harper	.75	.30	.07
□ 331 AL Bombers	50.00	20.00	5.00
Roger Maris			
Norm Cash			
Mickey Mantle			
Al Kaline			
□ 332 Ray Washburn	.60	.24	.06
□ 333 Billy Moran	.60	.24	.06
□ 334 Lew Krausse	.60	.24	.06
□ 335 Don Mossi	.75	.30	.07
□ 336 Andre Rodgers	.60	.24	.06
□ 337 Dodgers Rookies	2.00	.80	.20
Al Ferrara			
Jeff Torborg			
□ 338 Jack Kralick	.60	.24	.06
□ 339 Walt Bond	.60	.24	.06
□ 340 Joe Cunningham	.75	.30	.07
□ 341 Jim Roland	.60	.24	.06
□ 342 Willie Stargell	30.00	12.00	3.00
□ 343 Senators Team	1.25	.50	.12
□ 344 Phil Linz	.75	.30	.07
□ 345 Frank Thomas	.75	.30	.07
□ 346 Joey Jay	.60	.24	.06
□ 347 Bobby Wine	.60	.24	.06
□ 348 Ed Lopat MG	1.00	.40	.10
□ 349 Art Fowler	.60	.24	.06
□ 350 Willie McCovey	12.50	5.00	1.25
□ 351 Dan Schneider	.60	.24	.06
□ 352 Eddie Bressoud	.60	.24	.06
□ 353 Wally Moon	1.00	.40	.10
□ 354 Dave Giusti	.75	.30	.07
□ 355 Vic Power	.60	.24	.06
□ 356 Reds Rookies	.75	.30	.07
Bill McCool			
Chico Ruiz			
□ 357 Charley James	.60	.24	.06
□ 358 Ron Kline	.60	.24	.06
□ 359 Jim Schaffer	.60	.24	.06
□ 360 Joe Pepitone	1.50	.60	.15
□ 361 Jay Hook	.60	.24	.06
□ 362 Checklist 5	3.00	.30	.06
□ 363 Dick McAuliffe	.75	.30	.07
□ 364 Joe Gaines	.60	.24	.06
□ 365 Cal McLish	.60	.24	.06
□ 366 Nelson Mathews	.60	.24	.06
□ 367 Fred Whitfield	.60	.24	.06
□ 368 White Sox Rookies	1.00	.40	.10
Fritz Ackley			
Don Buford			
□ 369 Jerry Zimmerman	.60	.24	.06
□ 370 Hal Woodeshick	.60	.24	.06
□ 371 Frank Howard	2.00	.80	.20
□ 372 Howie Koplitz	1.00	.40	.10
□ 373 Pirates Team	2.00	.80	.20
□ 374 Bobby Bolin	1.00	.40	.10
□ 375 Ron Santo	2.00	.80	.20
□ 376 Dave Morehead	1.00	.40	.10
□ 377 Bob Skinner	1.00	.40	.10
□ 378 Braves Rookies	2.00	.80	.20
Woody Woodward			
Jack Smith			
□ 379 Tony Gonzalez	1.00	.40	.10
□ 380 Whitey Ford	14.00	5.75	1.40
□ 381 Bob Taylor	1.00	.40	.10
□ 382 Wes Stock	1.00	.40	.10
□ 383 Bill Rigney MG	1.00	.40	.10
□ 384 Ron Hansen	1.00	.40	.10
□ 385 Curt Simmons	1.50	.60	.15
□ 386 Lenny Green	1.00	.40	.10
□ 387 Terry Fox	1.00	.40	.10
□ 388 A's Rookies	1.00	.40	.10
John O'Donoghue			
George Williams			
□ 389 Jim Umbricht	1.00	.40	.10
□ 390 Orlando Cepeda	4.50	1.80	.45
□ 391 Sam McDowell	2.00	.80	.20
□ 392 Jim Pagliaroni	1.00	.40	.10
□ 393 Casey Teaches	3.50	1.40	.35
Casey Stengel			
Ed Kranepool			
□ 394 Bob Miller	1.00	.40	.10
□ 395 Tom Tresh	2.00	.80	.20
□ 396 Dennis Bennett	1.00	.40	.10
□ 397 Chuck Cottier	1.00	.40	.10
□ 398 Mets Rookies	1.00	.40	.10
Bill Haas			
Dick Smith			
□ 399 Jackie Brandt	1.00	.40	.10
□ 400 Warren Spahn	13.00	5.25	1.30
□ 401 Charlie Maxwell	1.00	.40	.10
□ 402 Tom Sturdivant	1.00	.40	.10
□ 403 Reds Team	2.00	.80	.20
□ 404 Tony Martinez	1.00	.40	.10
□ 405 Ken McBride	1.00	.40	.10
□ 406 Al Spangler	1.00	.40	.10

□ 407 Bill Freehan	3.00	1.20	.30
□ 408 Cubs Rookies	1.00	.40	.10
Jim Stewart			
Fred Burdette			
□ 409 Bill Fischer	1.00	.40	.10
□ 410 Dick Stuart	1.50	.60	.15
□ 411 Lee Walls	1.00	.40	.10
□ 412 Ray Culp	1.00	.40	.10
□ 413 Johnny Keane MG	1.50	.60	.15
□ 414 Jack Sanford	1.50	.60	.15
□ 415 Tony Kubek	5.00	2.00	.50
□ 416 Lee Maye	1.00	.40	.10
□ 417 Don Cardwell	1.00	.40	.10
□ 418 Orioles Rookies	1.50	.60	.15
Darold Knowles			
Les Narum			
□ 419 Ken Harrelson	4.50	1.80	.45
□ 420 Jim Maloney	2.00	.80	.20
□ 421 Camilo Carreon	1.00	.40	.10
□ 422 Jack Fisher	1.00	.40	.10
□ 423 Tops in NL	36.00	15.00	3.60
Hank Aaron			
Willie Mays			
□ 424 Dick Bertell	1.00	.40	.10
□ 425 Norm Cash	2.00	.80	.20
□ 426 Bob Rodgers	2.00	.80	.20
□ 427 Don Rudolph	1.00	.40	.10
□ 428 Red Sox Rookies	1.00	.40	.10
Archie Skeen			
Pete Smith			
□ 429 Tim McCarver	3.50	1.40	.35
□ 430 Juan Pizarro	1.00	.40	.10
□ 431 George Alusik	1.00	.40	.10
□ 432 Ruben Amaro	1.00	.40	.10
□ 433 Yankees Team	8.00	3.25	.80
□ 434 Don Nottebart	1.00	.40	.10
□ 435 Vic Davalillo	1.50	.60	.15
□ 436 Charlie Neal	1.50	.60	.15
□ 437 Ed Bailey	1.00	.40	.10
□ 438 Checklist 6	4.00	.40	.08
□ 439 Harvey Haddix	1.50	.60	.15
□ 440 Bob Clemente	45.00	18.00	4.50
□ 441 Bob Duliba	1.00	.40	.10
□ 442 Pumpsie Green	1.00	.40	.10
□ 443 Chuck Dressen MG	1.00	.40	.10
□ 444 Larry Jackson	1.00	.40	.10
□ 445 Bill Skowron	2.00	.80	.20
□ 446 Julian Javier	1.50	.60	.15
□ 447 Ted Bowsfield	1.00	.40	.10
□ 448 Cookie Rojas	1.50	.60	.15
□ 449 Deron Johnson	1.00	.40	.10
□ 450 Steve Barber	1.00	.40	.10
□ 451 Joe Amalfitano	1.00	.40	.10
□ 452 Giants Rookies	2.00	.80	.20
Gil Garrido			
Jim Ray Hart			
□ 453 Frank Baumann	1.00	.40	.10
□ 454 Tommie Aaron	1.50	.60	.15
□ 455 Bernie Allen	1.00	.40	.10
□ 456 Dodgers Rookies	2.50	1.00	.25
Wes Parker			
John Werhas			
□ 457 Jesse Gonder	1.00	.40	.10
□ 458 Ralph Terry	1.50	.60	.15
□ 459 Red Sox Rookies	1.00	.40	.10
Pete Charton			
Dalton Jones			
□ 460 Bob Gibson	17.00	7.00	1.70
□ 461 George Thomas	1.00	.40	.10
□ 462 Birdie Tebbetts MG	1.00	.40	.10
□ 463 Don Leppert	1.00	.40	.10
□ 464 Dallas Green	2.50	1.00	.25
□ 465 Mike Hershberger	1.00	.40	.10
□ 466 A's Rookies	1.50	.60	.15
Dick Green			
Aurelio Monteagudo			
□ 467 Bob Aspromonte	1.00	.40	.10
□ 468 Gaylord Perry	17.00	7.00	1.70
□ 469 Cubs Rookies	1.50	.60	.15
Fred Norman			
Sterling Slaughter			
□ 470 Jim Bouton	3.00	1.20	.30
□ 471 Gates Brown	2.00	.80	.20
□ 472 Vern Law	1.50	.60	.15
□ 473 Baltimore Orioles	2.00	.80	.20
Team Card			
□ 474 Larry Sherry	1.50	.60	.15
□ 475 Ed Charles	1.00	.40	.10
□ 476 Braves Rookies	5.00	2.00	.50
Rico Carty			
Dick Kelley			
□ 477 Mike Joyce	1.00	.40	.10
□ 478 Dick Howser	2.00	.80	.20
□ 479 Cardinals Rookies	1.00	.40	.10
Dave Bakenhaster			

Johnny Lewis			
□ 480 Bob Purkey	1.00	.40	.10
□ 481 Chuck Schilling	1.00	.40	.10
□ 482 Phillies Rookies	2.00	.80	.20
John Briggs			
Danny Cater			
□ 483 Fred Valentine	1.00	.40	.10
□ 484 Bill Pleis	1.00	.40	.10
□ 485 Tom Haller	1.50	.60	.15
□ 486 Bob Kennedy MG	1.00	.40	.10
□ 487 Mike McCormick	1.50	.60	.15
□ 488 Yankees Rookies	1.00	.40	.10
Pete Mikkelsen			
Bob Meyer			
□ 489 Julio Navarro	1.00	.40	.10
□ 490 Ron Fairly	1.50	.60	.15
□ 491 Ed Rakow	1.00	.40	.10
□ 492 Colts Rookies	1.00	.40	.10
Jim Beauchamp			
Mike White			
□ 493 Don Lee	1.00	.40	.10
□ 494 Al Jackson	1.00	.40	.10
□ 495 Bill Virdon	2.00	.80	.20
□ 496 White Sox Team	2.00	.80	.20
□ 497 Jeoff Long	1.00	.40	.10
□ 498 Dave Stenhouse	1.00	.40	.10
□ 499 Indians Rookies	1.00	.40	.10
Chico Salmon			
Gordon Seyfried			
□ 500 Camilo Pascual	1.50	.60	.15
□ 501 Bob Veale	1.50	.60	.15
□ 502 Angels Rookies	1.50	.60	.15
Bobby Knoop			
Bob Lee			
□ 503 Earl Wilson	1.00	.40	.10
□ 504 Claude Raymond	1.00	.40	.10
□ 505 Stan Williams	1.00	.40	.10
□ 506 Bobby Bragan MG	1.00	.40	.10
□ 507 John Edwards	1.00	.40	.10
□ 508 Diego Segui	1.00	.40	.10
□ 509 Pirates Rookies	2.00	.80	.20
Gene Alley			
Orlando McFarlane			
□ 510 Lindy McDaniel	1.50	.60	.15
□ 511 Lou Jackson	1.00	.40	.10
□ 512 Tigers Rookies	5.00	2.00	.50
Willie Horton			
Joe Sparma			
□ 513 Don Larsen	2.00	.80	.20
□ 514 Jim Hickman	1.00	.40	.10
□ 515 Johnny Romano	1.00	.40	.10
□ 516 Twins Rookies	1.00	.40	.10
Jerry Arrigo			
Dwight Siebler			
□ 517A Checklist 7 COR	5.00	.50	.10
(correct numbering on back)			
□ 517B Checklist 7 ERR	8.00	.80	.20
(incorrect numbering sequence on back)			
□ 518 Carl Bouldin	1.00	.40	.10
□ 519 Charlie Smith	1.00	.40	.10
□ 520 Jack Baldschun	1.00	.40	.10
□ 521 Tom Satriano	1.00	.40	.10
□ 522 Bob Tiefenauer	1.00	.40	.10
□ 523 Lou Burdette	6.00	2.40	.60
(pitching lefty)			
□ 524 Reds Rookies	3.50	1.40	.35
Jim Dickson			
Bobby Klaus			
□ 525 Al McBean	3.50	1.40	.35
□ 526 Lou Clinton	3.50	1.40	.35
□ 527 Larry Bearnarth	3.50	1.40	.35
□ 528 A's Rookies	4.50	1.80	.45
Dave Duncan			
Tommie Reynolds			
□ 529 Alvin Dark MG	4.50	1.80	.45
□ 530 Leon Wagner	3.50	1.40	.35
□ 531 Los Angeles Dodgers Team Card	8.00	3.25	.80
□ 532 Twins Rookies	3.50	1.40	.35
Bud Bloomfield			
(Bloomfield photo actually Jay Ward)			
Joe Nossek			
□ 533 Johnny Klippstein	3.50	1.40	.35
□ 534 Gus Bell	4.50	1.80	.45
□ 535 Phil Regan	4.50	1.80	.45
□ 536 Mets Rookies	3.50	1.40	.35
Larry Elliot			
John Stephenson			
□ 537 Dan Osinski	3.50	1.40	.35
□ 538 Minnie Minoso	6.00	2.40	.60
□ 539 Roy Face	4.50	1.80	.45
□ 540 Luis Aparicio	12.50	5.00	1.25
□ 541 Braves Rookies	80.00	32.00	8.00
Phil Roof			
Phil Niekro			
□ 542 Don Mincher	4.50	1.80	.45
□ 543 Bob Uecker	45.00	18.00	4.50
□ 544 Colts Rookies	4.50	1.80	.45
Steve Hertz			
Joe Hoerner			
□ 545 Max Alvis	3.50	1.40	.35
□ 546 Joe Christopher	3.50	1.40	.35
□ 547 Gil Hodges	9.00	3.75	.90
□ 548 NL Rookies	3.50	1.40	.35
Wayne Schurr			
Paul Speckenbach			
□ 549 Joe Moeller	3.50	1.40	.35
□ 550 Ken Hubbs	8.00	3.25	.80
(in memoriam)			
□ 551 Billy Hoeft	3.50	1.40	.35
□ 552 Indians Rookies	4.50	1.80	.45
Tom Kelley			
Sonny Siebert			
□ 553 Jim Brewer	3.50	1.40	.35
□ 554 Hank Foiles	3.50	1.40	.35
□ 555 Lee Stange	3.50	1.40	.35
□ 556 Mets Rookies	3.50	1.40	.35
Steve Dillon			
Ron Locke			
□ 557 Leo Burke	3.50	1.40	.35
□ 558 Don Schwall	3.50	1.40	.35
□ 559 Dick Phillips	3.50	1.40	.35
□ 560 Dick Farrell	3.50	1.40	.35
□ 561 Phillies Rookies	4.50	1.80	.45
Dave Bennett			
(19 ... is 18)			
Rick Wise			
□ 562 Pedro Ramos	3.50	1.40	.35
□ 563 Dal Maxvill	3.50	1.40	.35
□ 564 AL Rookies	3.50	1.40	.35
Joe McCabe			
Jerry McNertney			
□ 565 Stu Miller	3.50	1.40	.35
□ 566 Ed Kranepool	4.50	1.80	.45
□ 567 Jim Kaat	8.00	3.25	.80
□ 568 NL Rookies	3.50	1.40	.35
Phil Gagliano			
Cap Peterson			
□ 569 Fred Newman	3.50	1.40	.35
□ 570 Bill Mazeroski	6.00	2.40	.60
□ 571 Gene Conley	3.50	1.40	.35
□ 572 AL Rookies	3.50	1.40	.35
Dave Gray			
Dick Egan			
□ 573 Jim Duffalo	3.50	1.40	.35
□ 574 Manny Jimenez	3.50	1.40	.35
□ 575 Tony Cloninger	3.50	1.40	.35
□ 576 Mets Rookies	3.50	1.40	.35
Jerry Hinsley			
Bill Wakefield			
□ 577 Gordy Coleman	3.50	1.40	.35
□ 578 Glen Hobbie	3.50	1.40	.35
□ 579 Red Sox Team	8.00	3.25	.80
□ 580 Johnny Podres	5.50	2.20	.55
□ 581 Yankees Rookies	3.50	1.40	.35
Pedro Gonzalez			
Archie Moore			
□ 582 Rod Kanehl	3.50	1.40	.35
□ 583 Tito Francona	4.50	1.80	.45
□ 584 Joel Horlen	4.50	1.80	.45
□ 585 Tony Taylor	3.50	1.40	.35
□ 586 Jim Piersall	5.50	2.20	.55
□ 587 Bennie Daniels	4.50	1.80	.45

1964 Topps Giants

The cards in this 60-card set measure 3 1/8" by 5 1/4". The 1964 Topps Giants are postcard size cards containing color player photographs. They are numbered on the backs, which also contain biographical information presented in a newspaper format. These "giant size" cards were distributed in both cellophane and waxed gum packs apart from the Topps regular issue of 1964. Cards 3, 28, 42, 45, 47, 51 and 60 slightly more difficult to find and are indicated by SP in the checklist below.

	NRMT	VG-E	GOOD
COMPLETE SET (60)	65.00	26.00	6.50
COMMON PLAYER (1-60)	.10	.04	.01

☐ 1 Gary Peters	.10	.04	.01
☐ 2 Ken Johnson	.10	.04	.01
☐ 3 Sandy Koufax SP	12.50	5.00	1.25
☐ 4 Bob Bailey	.10	.04	.01
☐ 5 Milt Pappas	.10	.04	.01
☐ 6 Ron Hunt	.10	.04	.01
☐ 7 Whitey Ford	1.50	.60	.15
☐ 8 Roy McMillan	.10	.04	.01
☐ 9 Rocky Colavito	.30	.12	.03
☐ 10 Jim Bunning	.50	.20	.05
☐ 11 Bob Clemente	3.50	1.40	.35
☐ 12 Al Kaline	2.00	.80	.20
☐ 13 Nellie Fox	.30	.12	.03
☐ 14 Tony Gonzalez	.10	.04	.01
☐ 15 Jim Gentile	.10	.04	.01
☐ 16 Dean Chance	.10	.04	.01
☐ 17 Dick Ellsworth	.10	.04	.01
☐ 18 Jim Fregosi	.15	.06	.01
☐ 19 Dick Groat	.15	.06	.01
☐ 20 Chuck Hinton	.10	.04	.01
☐ 21 Elston Howard	.30	.12	.03
☐ 22 Dick Farrell	.10	.04	.01
☐ 23 Albie Pearson	.10	.04	.01
☐ 24 Frank Howard	.20	.08	.02
☐ 25 Mickey Mantle	8.00	3.25	.80
☐ 26 Joe Torre	.25	.10	.02
☐ 27 Eddie Brinkman	.10	.04	.01
☐ 28 Bob Friend SP	4.00	1.60	.40
☐ 29 Frank Robinson	1.50	.60	.15
☐ 30 Bill Freehan	.15	.06	.01
☐ 31 Warren Spahn	1.50	.60	.15
☐ 32 Camilo Pascual	.10	.04	.01
☐ 33 Pete Ward	.10	.04	.01
☐ 34 Jim Maloney	.10	.04	.01
☐ 35 Dave Wickersham	.10	.04	.01
☐ 36 Johnny Callison	.10	.04	.01
☐ 37 Juan Marichal	1.25	.50	.12
☐ 38 Harmon Killebrew	1.50	.60	.15
☐ 39 Luis Aparicio	1.25	.50	.12
☐ 40 Dick Radatz	.10	.04	.01
☐ 41 Bob Gibson	1.50	.60	.15
☐ 42 Dick Stuart SP	4.00	1.60	.40
☐ 43 Tommy Davis	.15	.06	.01
☐ 44 Tony Oliva	.30	.12	.03
☐ 45 Wayne Causey SP	4.00	1.60	.40
☐ 46 Max Alvis	.10	.04	.01
☐ 47 Galen Cisco SP	4.00	1.60	.40
☐ 48 Carl Yastrzemski	3.50	1.40	.35
☐ 49 Hank Aaron	3.50	1.40	.35
☐ 50 Brooks Robinson	2.50	1.00	.25
☐ 51 Willie Mays SP	12.50	5.00	1.25
☐ 52 Billy Williams	1.25	.50	.12
☐ 53 Juan Pizarro	.10	.04	.01
☐ 54 Leon Wagner	.10	.04	.01
☐ 55 Orlando Cepeda	.35	.14	.03
☐ 56 Vada Pinson	.20	.08	.02
☐ 57 Ken Boyer	.20	.08	.02
☐ 58 Ron Santo	.20	.08	.02
☐ 59 John Romano	.10	.04	.01
☐ 60 Bill Skowron SP	4.00	1.60	.40

1964 Topps Stand Ups

In 1964 Topps produced a die-cut "Stand-Up" card design for the first time since their Connie Mack and Current All Stars of 1951. The cards have full-length, color player photos set against a green and yellow background. Of the 77 cards in the set, 22 were single printed and these are marked in the checklist below with an SP. These unnumbered cards are standard-size (2 1/2" by 3 1/2"), blank backed, and have been numbered here for reference in alphabetical order of players.

	NRMT	VG-E	GOOD
COMPLETE SET (77)	1500.00	650.00	175.00
COMMON PLAYER (1-77)	3.00	1.20	.30
COMMON PLAYER SP	16.00	6.50	1.60
☐ 1 Hank Aaron	75.00	30.00	7.50
☐ 2 Hank Aguirre	3.00	1.20	.30
☐ 3 George Altman	3.00	1.20	.30
☐ 4 Max Alvis	3.00	1.20	.30
☐ 5 Bob Aspromonte	3.00	1.20	.30
☐ 6 Jack Baldschun SP	16.00	6.50	1.60
☐ 7 Ernie Banks	30.00	12.00	3.00
☐ 8 Steve Barber	3.00	1.20	.30
☐ 9 Earl Battey	3.00	1.20	.30
☐ 10 Ken Boyer	4.00	1.60	.40
☐ 11 Ernie Broglio	3.00	1.20	.30
☐ 12 John Callison	3.00	1.20	.30
☐ 13 Norm Cash SP	20.00	8.00	2.00
☐ 14 Wayne Causey	3.00	1.20	.30
☐ 15 Orlando Cepeda	5.00	2.00	.50
☐ 16 Ed Charles	3.00	1.20	.30
☐ 17 Bob Clemente	55.00	22.00	5.50
☐ 18 Donn Clendenon SP	16.00	6.50	1.60
☐ 19 Rocky Colavito	4.00	1.60	.40
☐ 20 Ray Culp SP	16.00	6.50	1.60
☐ 21 Tommy Davis	4.00	1.60	.40
☐ 22 Don Drysdale SP	65.00	26.00	6.50
☐ 23 Dick Ellsworth	3.00	1.20	.30
☐ 24 Dick Farrell	3.00	1.20	.30
☐ 25 Jim Fregosi	4.00	1.60	.40
☐ 26 Bob Friend	3.00	1.20	.30
☐ 27 Jim Gentile	3.00	1.20	.30
☐ 28 Jesse Gonder SP	16.00	6.50	1.60
☐ 29 Tony Gonzalez SP	16.00	6.50	1.60
☐ 30 Dick Groat	3.00	1.20	.30
☐ 31 Woody Held	3.00	1.20	.30
☐ 32 Chuck Hinton	3.00	1.20	.30
☐ 33 Elston Howard	4.00	1.60	.40
☐ 34 Frank Howard SP	20.00	8.00	2.00
☐ 35 Ron Hunt	3.00	1.20	.30
☐ 36 Al Jackson	3.00	1.20	.30
☐ 37 Ken Johnson	3.00	1.20	.30
☐ 38 Al Kaline	35.00	14.00	3.50
☐ 39 Harmon Killebrew	25.00	10.00	2.50
☐ 40 Sandy Koufax	50.00	20.00	5.00
☐ 41 Don Lock SP	16.00	6.50	1.60
☐ 42 Jerry Lumpe SP	16.00	6.50	1.60
☐ 43 Jim Maloney	3.00	1.20	.30
☐ 44 Frank Malzone	3.00	1.20	.30
☐ 45 Mickey Mantle	300.00	120.00	30.00
☐ 46 Juan Marichal SP	65.00	26.00	6.50
☐ 47 Eddie Mathews SP	75.00	30.00	7.50
☐ 48 Willie Mays	75.00	30.00	7.50
☐ 49 Bill Mazeroski	3.50	1.40	.35

□ 50 Ken McBride	3.00	1.20	.30
□ 51 Willie McCovey SP	75.00	30.00	7.50
□ 52 Claude Osteen	3.00	1.20	.30
□ 53 Jim O'Toole	3.00	1.20	.30
□ 54 Camilo Pascual	3.00	1.20	.30
□ 55 Albie Pearson SP	16.00	6.50	1.60
□ 56 Gary Peters	3.00	1.20	.30
□ 57 Vada Pinson	4.00	1.60	.40
□ 58 Juan Pizarro	3.00	1.20	.30
□ 59 Boog Powell	4.00	1.60	.40
□ 60 Bobby Richardson	5.00	2.00	.50
□ 61 Brooks Robinson	35.00	14.00	3.50
□ 62 Floyd Robinson	3.00	1.20	.30
□ 63 Frank Robinson	25.00	10.00	2.50
□ 64 Ed Roebuck SP	16.00	6.50	1.60
□ 65 Rich Rollins	3.00	1.20	.30
□ 66 John Romano	3.00	1.20	.30
□ 67 Ron Santo SP	20.00	8.00	2.00
□ 68 Norm Siebern	3.00	1.20	.30
□ 69 Warren Spahn SP	75.00	30.00	7.50
□ 70 Dick Stuart SP	16.00	6.50	1.60
□ 71 Lee Thomas	3.00	1.20	.30
□ 72 Joe Torre	5.00	2.00	.50
□ 73 Pete Ward	3.00	1.20	.30
□ 74 Bill White SP	20.00	8.00	2.00
□ 75 Billy Williams SP	65.00	26.00	6.50
□ 76 Hal Woodeshick SP	16.00	6.50	1.60
□ 77 Carl Yastrzemski SP	300.00	120.00	30.00

1965 Topps

The cards in this 598-card set measure 2 1/2" by 3 1/2". The cards comprising the 1965 Topps set have team names located within a distinctive pennant design below the picture. The cards have blue borders on the reverse and were issued by series. Cards 523 to 598 are more difficult to obtain than all other series. In addition, the sixth series (447-522) is more difficult to obtain than series one through five. Featured subsets within this set include League Leaders (1-12) and World Series cards (132-139). Key cards in this set include Steve Carlton's rookie and Pete Rose.

	NRMT	VG-E	GOOD
COMPLETE SET (598)	2200.00	950.00	325.00
COMMON PLAYER (1-196)	.45	.18	.04
COMMON PLAYER (197-283)	.75	.30	.07
COMMON PLAYER (284-370)	.75	.30	.07
COMMON PLAYER (371-446)	.85	.34	.08
COMMON PLAYER (447-522)	1.50	.60	.15
COMMON PLAYER (523-598)	3.00	1.20	.30

□ 1 AL Batting Leaders	7.50	1.00	.20
Tony Oliva			
Elston Howard			
Brooks Robinson			
□ 2 NL Batting Leaders	4.50	1.80	.45
Bob Clemente			
Hank Aaron			
Rico Carty			
□ 3 AL Home Run Leaders	7.50	3.00	.75
Harmon Killebrew			
Mickey Mantle			
Boog Powell			
□ 4 NL Home Run Leaders	4.00	1.60	.40
Willie Mays			
Billy Williams			
Jim Ray Hart			
Orlando Cepeda			
Johnny Callison			
□ 5 AL RBI Leaders	7.50	3.00	.75
Brooks Robinson			
Harmon Killebrew			
Mickey Mantle			
Dick Stuart			
□ 6 NL RBI Leaders	2.00	.80	.20
Ken Boyer			
Willie Mays			
Ron Santo			
□ 7 AL ERA Leaders	1.25	.50	.12
Dean Chance			
Joel Horlen			
□ 8 NL ERA Leaders	5.00	2.00	.50
Sandy Koufax			
Don Drysdale			
□ 9 AL Pitching Leaders	1.25	.50	.12
Dean Chance			
Gary Peters			
Dave Wickersham			
Juan Pizarro			
Wally Bunker			
□ 10 NL Pitching Leaders	1.25	.50	.12
Larry Jackson			
Ray Sadecki			
Juan Marichal			
□ 11 AL Strikeout Leaders	1.25	.50	.12
Al Downing			
Dean Chance			
Camilo Pascual			
□ 12 NL Strikeout Leaders	2.00	.80	.20
Bob Veale			
Don Drysdale			
Bob Gibson			
□ 13 Pedro Ramos	.45	.18	.04
□ 14 Len Gabrielson	.45	.18	.04
□ 15 Robin Roberts	6.50	2.60	.65
□ 16 Houston Rookies	40.00	16.00	4.00
Joe Morgan			
Sonny Jackson			
□ 17 John Romano	.45	.18	.04
□ 18 Bill McCool	.45	.18	.04
□ 19 Gates Brown	.75	.30	.07
□ 20 Jim Bunning	3.50	1.40	.35
□ 21 Don Blasingame	.45	.18	.04
□ 22 Charlie Smith	.45	.18	.04
□ 23 Bob Tiefenauer	.45	.18	.04
□ 24 Minnesota Twins Team Card	2.00	.80	.20
□ 25 Al McBean	.45	.18	.04
□ 26 Bob Knoop	.45	.18	.04
□ 27 Dick Bertell	.45	.18	.04
□ 28 Barney Schultz	.45	.18	.04
□ 29 Felix Mantilla	.45	.18	.04
□ 30 Jim Bouton	1.50	.60	.15
□ 31 Mike White	.45	.18	.04
□ 32 Herman Franks MG	.45	.18	.04
□ 33 Jackie Brandt	.45	.18	.04
□ 34 Cal Koonce	.45	.18	.04
□ 35 Ed Charles	.45	.18	.04
□ 36 Bobby Wine	.45	.18	.04
□ 37 Fred Gladding	.45	.18	.04
□ 38 Jim King	.45	.18	.04
□ 39 Gerry Arrigo	.45	.18	.04
□ 40 Frank Howard	1.25	.50	.12
□ 41 White Sox Rookies	.45	.18	.04
Bruce Howard			
Marv Staehle			
□ 42 Earl Wilson	.45	.18	.04
□ 43 Mike Shannon	1.00	.40	.10
□ 44 Wade Blasingame	.45	.18	.04
□ 45 Roy McMillan	.45	.18	.04
□ 46 Bob Lee	.45	.18	.04
□ 47 Tommy Harper	.75	.30	.07
□ 48 Claude Raymond	.45	.18	.04
□ 49 Orioles Rookies	1.00	.40	.10
Curt Blefary			
John Miller			
□ 50 Juan Marichal	7.50	3.00	.75
□ 51 Bill Bryan	.45	.18	.04
□ 52 Ed Roebuck	.45	.18	.04
□ 53 Dick McAuliffe	.75	.30	.07
□ 54 Joe Gibbon	.45	.18	.04
□ 55 Tony Conigliaro	3.00	1.20	.30
□ 56 Ron Kline	.45	.18	.04
□ 57 Cardinals Team	1.25	.50	.12
□ 58 Fred Talbot	.45	.18	.04
□ 59 Nate Oliver	.45	.18	.04
□ 60 Jim O'Toole	.45	.18	.04
□ 61 Chris Cannizzaro	.45	.18	.04
□ 62 Jim Katt (sic, Kaat)	4.00	1.60	.40
□ 63 Ty Cline	.45	.18	.04

□ 64 Lou Burdette	1.00	.40	.10
□ 65 Tony Kubek	3.00	1.20	.30
□ 66 Bill Rigney MG	.45	.18	.04
□ 67 Harvey Haddix	.75	.30	.07
□ 68 Del Crandall	.75	.30	.07
□ 69 Bill Virdon	1.00	.40	.10
□ 70 Bill Skowron	1.25	.50	.12
□ 71 John O'Donoghue	.45	.18	.04
□ 72 Tony Gonzalez	.45	.18	.04
□ 73 Dennis Ribant	.45	.18	.04
□ 74 Red Sox Rookies Rico Petrocelli Jerry Stephenson	3.00	1.20	.30
□ 75 Deron Johnson	.75	.30	.07
□ 76 Sam McDowell	.75	.30	.07
□ 77 Doug Camilli	.45	.18	.04
□ 78 Dal Maxvill	.75	.30	.07
□ 79 Checklist 1	3.00	.30	.06
□ 80 Turk Farrell	.45	.18	.04
□ 81 Don Buford	.75	.30	.07
□ 82 Braves Rookies Santos Alomar John Braun	1.00	.40	.10
□ 83 George Thomas	.45	.18	.04
□ 84 Ron Herbel	.45	.18	.04
□ 85 Willie Smith	.45	.18	.04
□ 86 Les Narum	.45	.18	.04
□ 87 Nelson Mathews	.45	.18	.04
□ 88 Jack Lamabe	.45	.18	.04
□ 89 Mike Hershberger	.45	.18	.04
□ 90 Rich Rollins	.75	.30	.07
□ 91 Cubs Team	1.25	.50	.12
□ 92 Dick Howser	1.25	.50	.12
□ 93 Jack Fisher	.45	.18	.04
□ 94 Charlie Lau	.75	.30	.07
□ 95 Bill Mazeroski	1.50	.60	.15
□ 96 Sonny Siebert	.75	.30	.07
□ 97 Pedro Gonzalez	.45	.18	.04
□ 98 Bob Miller	.45	.18	.04
□ 99 Gil Hodges MG	5.00	2.00	.50
□ 100 Ken Boyer	2.00	.80	.20
□ 101 Fred Newman	.45	.18	.04
□ 102 Steve Boros	.75	.30	.07
□ 103 Harvey Kuenn	1.00	.40	.10
□ 104 Checklist 2	3.00	.30	.06
□ 105 Chico Salmon	.45	.18	.04
□ 106 Gene Oliver	.45	.18	.04
□ 107 Phillies Rookies Pat Corrales Costen Shockley	1.75	.70	.17
□ 108 Don Mincher	.75	.30	.07
□ 109 Walt Bond	.45	.18	.04
□ 110 Ron Santo	1.25	.50	.12
□ 111 Lee Thomas	1.00	.40	.10
□ 112 Derrell Griffith	.45	.18	.04
□ 113 Steve Barber	.45	.18	.04
□ 114 Jim Hickman	.45	.18	.04
□ 115 Bobby Richardson	2.50	1.00	.25
□ 116 Cardinals Rookies Dave Dowling Bob Tolan	1.00	.40	.10
□ 117 Wes Stock	.45	.18	.04
□ 118 Hal Lanier	1.50	.60	.15
□ 119 John Kennedy	.45	.18	.04
□ 120 Frank Robinson	10.00	4.00	1.00
□ 121 Gene Alley	.75	.30	.07
□ 122 Bill Pleis	.45	.18	.04
□ 123 Frank Thomas	.75	.30	.07
□ 124 Tom Satriano	.45	.18	.04
□ 125 Juan Pizarro	.45	.18	.04
□ 126 Dodgers Team	3.50	1.40	.35
□ 127 Frank Lary	.75	.30	.07
□ 128 Vic Davalillo	.75	.30	.07
□ 129 Bennie Daniels	.45	.18	.04
□ 130 Al Kaline	13.00	5.25	1.30
□ 131 Johnny Keane MG	.75	.30	.07
□ 132 World Series Game 1 Cards take opener	1.75	.70	.17
□ 133 World Series Game 2 Stottlemyre wins	1.75	.70	.17
□ 134 World Series Game 3 Mantle's homer	20.00	8.00	2.00
□ 135 World Series Game 4 Boyer's grand-slam	2.50	1.00	.25
□ 136 World Series Game 5 10th inning triumph	1.75	.70	.17
□ 137 World Series Game 6 Bouton wins again	2.50	1.00	.25
□ 138 World Series Game 7 Gibson wins finale	3.50	1.40	.35
□ 139 World Series Summary Cards celebrate	1.75	.70	.17
□ 140 Dean Chance	.75	.30	.07
□ 141 Charlie James	.45	.18	.04
□ 142 Bill Monbouquette	.45	.18	.04
□ 143 Pirates Rookies John Gelnar Jerry May	.45	.18	.04
□ 144 Ed Kranepool	1.00	.40	.10
□ 145 Luis Tiant	7.50	3.00	.75
□ 146 Ron Hansen	.45	.18	.04
□ 147 Dennis Bennett	.45	.18	.04
□ 148 Willie Kirkland	.45	.18	.04
□ 149 Wayne Schurr	.45	.18	.04
□ 150 Brooks Robinson	14.00	5.75	1.40
□ 151 Athletics Team	1.00	.40	.10
□ 152 Phil Ortega	.45	.18	.04
□ 153 Norm Cash	1.50	.60	.15
□ 154 Bob Humphreys	.45	.18	.04
□ 155 Roger Maris	32.00	13.00	3.20
□ 156 Bob Sadowski	.45	.18	.04
□ 157 Zoilo Versalles	.75	.30	.07
□ 158 Dick Sisler	.45	.18	.04
□ 159 Jim Duffalo	.45	.18	.04
□ 160 Bob Clemente	30.00	12.00	3.00
□ 161 Frank Baumann	.45	.18	.04
□ 162 Russ Nixon	1.00	.40	.10
□ 163 John Briggs	.45	.18	.04
□ 164 Al Spangler	.45	.18	.04
□ 165 Dick Ellsworth	.75	.30	.07
□ 166 Indians Rookies George Culver Tommie Agee	1.00	.40	.10
□ 167 Bill Wakefield	.45	.18	.04
□ 168 Dick Green	.45	.18	.04
□ 169 Dave Vineyard	.45	.18	.04
□ 170 Hank Aaron	42.00	18.00	4.00
□ 171 Jim Roland	.45	.18	.04
□ 172 Jim Piersall	1.00	.40	.10
□ 173 Detroit Tigers Team Card	1.50	.60	.15
□ 174 Joey Jay	.45	.18	.04
□ 175 Bob Aspromonte	.45	.18	.04
□ 176 Willie McCovey	9.00	3.75	.90
□ 177 Pete Mikkelsen	.45	.18	.04
□ 178 Dalton Jones	.45	.18	.04
□ 179 Hal Woodeshick	.45	.18	.04
□ 180 Bob Allison	.75	.30	.07
□ 181 Senators Rookies Don Loun Joe McCabe	.45	.18	.04
□ 182 Mike De La Hoz	.45	.18	.04
□ 183 Dave Nicholson	.45	.18	.04
□ 184 John Boozer	.45	.18	.04
□ 185 Max Alvis	.45	.18	.04
□ 186 Bill Cowan	.45	.18	.04
□ 187 Casey Stengel MG	8.00	3.25	.80
□ 188 Sam Bowens	.45	.18	.04
□ 189 Checklist 3	3.00	.30	.06
□ 190 Bill White	1.00	.40	.10
□ 191 Phil Regan	.75	.30	.07
□ 192 Jim Coker	.45	.18	.04
□ 193 Gaylord Perry	8.00	3.25	.80
□ 194 Rookie Stars Bill Kelso Rick Reichardt	.75	.30	.07
□ 195 Bob Veale	.75	.30	.07
□ 196 Ron Fairly	.75	.30	.07
□ 197 Diego Segui	.75	.30	.07
□ 198 Smoky Burgess	1.00	.40	.10
□ 199 Bob Heffner	.75	.30	.07
□ 200 Joe Torre	1.75	.70	.17
□ 201 Twins Rookies Sandy Valdespino Cesar Tovar	1.00	.40	.10
□ 202 Leo Burke	.75	.30	.07
□ 203 Dallas Green	2.00	.80	.20
□ 204 Russ Snyder	.75	.30	.07
□ 205 Warren Spahn	10.00	4.00	1.00
□ 206 Willie Horton	1.50	.60	.15
□ 207 Pete Rose	150.00	60.00	15.00
□ 208 Tommy John	7.50	3.00	.75
□ 209 Pirates Team	1.50	.60	.15
□ 210 Jim Fregosi	1.50	.60	.15
□ 211 Steve Ridzik	.75	.30	.07
□ 212 Ron Brand	.75	.30	.07
□ 213 Jim Davenport	1.00	.40	.10
□ 214 Bob Purkey	.75	.30	.07
□ 215 Pete Ward	.75	.30	.07
□ 216 Al Worthington	.75	.30	.07
□ 217 Walt Alston MG	2.50	1.00	.25
□ 218 Dick Schofield	.75	.30	.07
□ 219 Bob Meyer	.75	.30	.07
□ 220 Billy Williams	7.50	3.00	.75
□ 221 John Tsitouris	.75	.30	.07
□ 222 Bob Tillman	.75	.30	.07
□ 223 Dan Osinski	.75	.30	.07
□ 224 Bob Chance	.75	.30	.07
□ 225 Bo Belinsky	1.00	.40	.10
□ 226 Yankees Rookies	1.00	.40	.10

	Elvio Jimenez			
	Jake Gibbs			
□ 227	Bobby Klaus	.75	.30	.07
□ 228	Jack Sanford	1.00	.40	.10
□ 229	Lou Clinton	.75	.30	.07
□ 230	Ray Sadecki	.75	.30	.07
□ 231	Jerry Adair	.75	.30	.07
□ 232	Steve Blass	1.50	.60	.15
□ 233	Don Zimmer	1.50	.60	.15
□ 234	White Sox Team	1.50	.60	.15
□ 235	Chuck Hinton	.75	.30	.07
□ 236	Denny McLain	9.00	3.75	.90
□ 237	Bernie Allen	.75	.30	.07
□ 238	Joe Moeller	.75	.30	.07
□ 239	Doc Edwards	1.50	.60	.15
□ 240	Bob Bruce	.75	.30	.07
□ 241	Mack Jones	.75	.30	.07
□ 242	George Brunet	.75	.30	.07
□ 243	Reds Rookies	1.50	.60	.15
	Ted Davidson			
	Tommy Helms			
□ 244	Lindy McDaniel	1.00	.40	.10
□ 245	Joe Pepitone	1.50	.60	.15
□ 246	Tom Butters	.75	.30	.07
□ 247	Wally Moon	1.00	.40	.10
□ 248	Gus Triandos	1.00	.40	.10
□ 249	Dave McNally	1.50	.60	.15
□ 250	Willie Mays	60.00	24.00	6.00
□ 251	Billy Herman MG	2.00	.80	.20
□ 252	Pete Richert	.75	.30	.07
□ 253	Danny Cater	1.00	.40	.10
□ 254	Roland Sheldon	.75	.30	.07
□ 255	Camilo Pascual	1.00	.40	.10
□ 256	Tito Francona	1.00	.40	.10
□ 257	Jim Wynn	1.50	.60	.15
□ 258	Larry Bearnarth	.75	.30	.07
□ 259	Tigers Rookies	1.50	.60	.15
	Jim Northrup			
	Ray Oyler			
□ 260	Don Drysdale	8.50	3.50	.85
□ 261	Duke Carmel	.75	.30	.07
□ 262	Bud Daley	.75	.30	.07
□ 263	Marty Keough	.75	.30	.07
□ 264	Bob Buhl	.75	.30	.07
□ 265	Jim Pagliaroni	.75	.30	.07
□ 266	Bert Campaneris	3.00	1.20	.30
□ 267	Senators Team	1.50	.60	.15
□ 268	Ken McBride	.75	.30	.07
□ 269	Frank Bolling	.75	.30	.07
□ 270	Milt Pappas	1.00	.40	.10
□ 271	Don Wert	.75	.30	.07
□ 272	Chuck Schilling	.75	.30	.07
□ 273	Checklist 4	3.00	.30	.06
□ 274	Lum Harris MG	.75	.30	.07
□ 275	Dick Groat	1.50	.60	.15
□ 276	Hoyt Wilhelm	6.50	2.60	.65
□ 277	Johnny Lewis	.75	.30	.07
□ 278	Ken Retzer	.75	.30	.07
□ 279	Dick Tracewski	.75	.30	.07
□ 280	Dick Stuart	1.00	.40	.10
□ 281	Bill Stafford	.75	.30	.07
□ 282	Giants Rookies	1.00	.40	.10
	Dick Estelle			
	Masanori Murakami			
□ 283	Fred Whitfield	.75	.30	.07
□ 284	Nick Willhite	.75	.30	.07
□ 285	Ron Hunt	.75	.30	.07
□ 286	Athletics Rookies	.75	.30	.07
	Jim Dickson			
	Aurelio Monteagudo			
□ 287	Gary Kolb	.75	.30	.07
□ 288	Jack Hamilton	.75	.30	.07
□ 289	Gordy Coleman	1.00	.40	.10
□ 290	Wally Bunker	1.00	.40	.10
□ 291	Jerry Lynch	.75	.30	.07
□ 292	Larry Yellen	.75	.30	.07
□ 293	Angels Team	1.50	.60	.15
□ 294	Tim McCarver	2.50	1.00	.25
□ 295	Dick Radatz	1.00	.40	.10
□ 296	Tony Taylor	.75	.30	.07
□ 297	Dave Debusschere	2.50	1.00	.25
□ 298	Jim Stewart	.75	.30	.07
□ 299	Jerry Zimmerman	.75	.30	.07
□ 300	Sandy Koufax	50.00	20.00	5.00
□ 301	Birdie Tebbetts MG	.75	.30	.07
□ 302	Al Stanek	.75	.30	.07
□ 303	John Orsino	.75	.30	.07
□ 304	Dave Stenhouse	.75	.30	.07
□ 305	Rico Carty	1.25	.50	.12
□ 306	Bubba Phillips	.75	.30	.07
□ 307	Barry Latman	.75	.30	.07
□ 308	Mets Rookies	1.00	.40	.10
	Cleon Jones			
	Tom Parsons			
□ 309	Steve Hamilton	.75	.30	.07
□ 310	Johnny Callison	1.00	.40	.10
□ 311	Orlando Pena	.75	.30	.07
□ 312	Joe Nuxhall	1.00	.40	.10
□ 313	Jim Schaffer	.75	.30	.07
□ 314	Sterling Slaughter	.75	.30	.07
□ 315	Frank Malzone	1.00	.40	.10
□ 316	Reds Team	1.50	.60	.15
□ 317	Don McMahon	.75	.30	.07
□ 318	Matty Alou	1.25	.50	.12
□ 319	Ken McMullen	.75	.30	.07
□ 320	Bob Gibson	12.00	5.00	1.20
□ 321	Rusty Staub	3.00	1.20	.30
□ 322	Rick Wise	1.00	.40	.10
□ 323	Hank Bauer MG	1.00	.40	.10
□ 324	Bobby Locke	.75	.30	.07
□ 325	Donn Clendenon	1.00	.40	.10
□ 326	Dwight Siebler	.75	.30	.07
□ 327	Denis Menke	.75	.30	.07
□ 328	Eddie Fisher	.75	.30	.07
□ 329	Hawk Taylor	.75	.30	.07
□ 330	Whitey Ford	12.00	5.00	1.20
□ 331	Dodgers Rookies	1.00	.40	.10
	Al Ferrara			
	John Purdin			
□ 332	Ted Abernathy	.75	.30	.07
□ 333	Tom Reynolds	.75	.30	.07
□ 334	Vic Roznovsky	.75	.30	.07
□ 335	Mickey Lolich	2.50	1.00	.25
□ 336	Woody Held	.75	.30	.07
□ 337	Mike Cuellar	1.50	.60	.15
□ 338	Philadelphia Phillies	1.50	.60	.15
	Team Card			
□ 339	Ryne Duren	1.00	.40	.10
□ 340	Tony Oliva	4.00	1.60	.40
□ 341	Bob Bolin	.75	.30	.07
□ 342	Bob Rodgers	1.50	.60	.15
□ 343	Mike McCormick	1.00	.40	.10
□ 344	Wes Parker	1.25	.50	.12
□ 345	Floyd Robinson	.75	.30	.07
□ 346	Bobby Bragan MG	.75	.30	.07
□ 347	Roy Face	1.50	.60	.15
□ 348	George Banks	.75	.30	.07
□ 349	Larry Miller	.75	.30	.07
□ 350	Mickey Mantle	375.00	150.00	37.00
□ 351	Jim Perry	1.00	.40	.10
□ 352	Alex Johnson	1.00	.40	.10
□ 353	Jerry Lumpe	.75	.30	.07
□ 354	Cubs Rookies	.75	.30	.07
	Billy Ott			
	Jack Warner			
□ 355	Vada Pinson	1.50	.60	.15
□ 356	Bill Spanswick	.75	.30	.07
□ 357	Carl Warwick	.75	.30	.07
□ 358	Albie Pearson	.75	.30	.07
□ 359	Ken Johnson	.75	.30	.07
□ 360	Orlando Cepeda	4.00	1.60	.40
□ 361	Checklist 5	3.00	.30	.06
□ 362	Don Schwall	.75	.30	.07
□ 363	Bob Johnson	.75	.30	.07
□ 364	Galen Cisco	.75	.30	.07
□ 365	Jim Gentile	1.00	.40	.10
□ 366	Dan Schneider	.75	.30	.07
□ 367	Leon Wagner	.75	.30	.07
□ 368	White Sox Rookies	1.00	.40	.10
	Ken Berry			
	Joel Gibson			
□ 369	Phil Linz	1.00	.40	.10
□ 370	Tommy Davis	1.50	.60	.15
□ 371	Frank Kreutzer	.85	.34	.08
□ 372	Clay Dalrymple	.85	.34	.08
□ 373	Curt Simmons	1.00	.40	.10
□ 374	Angels Rookies	1.00	.40	.10
	Jose Cardenal			
	Dick Simpson			
□ 375	Dave Wickersham	.85	.34	.08
□ 376	Jim Landis	.85	.34	.08
□ 377	Willie Stargell	20.00	8.00	2.00
□ 378	Chuck Estrada	1.00	.40	.10
□ 379	Giants Team	1.75	.70	.17
□ 380	Rocky Colavito	2.00	.80	.20
□ 381	Al Jackson	.85	.34	.08
□ 382	J.C. Martin	.85	.34	.08
□ 383	Felipe Alou	1.00	.40	.10
□ 384	John Klippstein	.85	.34	.08
□ 385	Carl Yastrzemski	55.00	22.00	5.50
□ 386	Cubs Rookies	1.00	.40	.10
	Paul Jaeckel			
	Fred Norman			
□ 387	John Podres	1.50	.60	.15
□ 388	John Blanchard	1.00	.40	.10
□ 389	Don Larsen	1.50	.60	.15
□ 390	Bill Freehan	2.25	.90	.22
□ 391	Mel McGaha MG	.85	.34	.08
□ 392	Bob Friend	1.00	.40	.10
□ 393	Ed Kirkpatrick	.85	.34	.08

☐ 394	Jim Hannan	.85	.34	.08
☐ 395	Jim Ray Hart	1.00	.40	.10
☐ 396	Frank Bertaina	.85	.34	.08
☐ 397	Jerry Buchek	.85	.34	.08
☐ 398	Reds Rookies	1.00	.40	.10
	Dan Neville			
	Art Shamsky			
☐ 399	Ray Herbert	.85	.34	.08
☐ 400	Harmon Killebrew	10.00	4.00	1.00
☐ 401	Carl Willey	.85	.34	.08
☐ 402	Joe Amalfitano	.85	.34	.08
☐ 403	Boston Red Sox	1.75	.70	.17
	Team Card			
☐ 404	Stan Williams	1.00	.40	.10
☐ 405	John Roseboro	1.00	.40	.10
☐ 406	Ralph Terry	1.25	.50	.12
☐ 407	Lee Maye	.85	.34	.08
☐ 408	Larry Sherry	1.00	.40	.10
☐ 409	Astros Rookies	1.25	.50	.12
	Jim Beauchamp			
	Larry Dierker			
☐ 410	Luis Aparicio	7.00	2.80	.70
☐ 411	Roger Craig	2.00	.80	.20
☐ 412	Bob Bailey	.85	.34	.08
☐ 413	Hal Reniff	.85	.34	.08
☐ 414	Al Lopez MG	2.50	1.00	.25
☐ 415	Curt Flood	1.75	.70	.17
☐ 416	Jim Brewer	.85	.34	.08
☐ 417	Ed Brinkman	.85	.34	.08
☐ 418	John Edwards	.85	.34	.08
☐ 419	Ruben Amaro	.85	.34	.08
☐ 420	Larry Jackson	.85	.34	.08
☐ 421	Twins Rookies	.85	.34	.08
	Gary Dotter			
	Jay Ward			
☐ 422	Aubrey Gatewood	.85	.34	.08
☐ 423	Jesse Gonder	.85	.34	.08
☐ 424	Gary Bell	.85	.34	.08
☐ 425	Wayne Causey	.85	.34	.08
☐ 426	Braves Team	1.75	.70	.17
☐ 427	Bob Saverine	.85	.34	.08
☐ 428	Bob Shaw	.85	.34	.08
☐ 429	Don Demeter	.85	.34	.08
☐ 430	Gary Peters	1.00	.40	.10
☐ 431	Cards Rookies	1.50	.60	.15
	Nelson Briles			
	Wayne Spiezio			
☐ 432	Jim Grant	.85	.34	.08
☐ 433	John Bateman	.85	.34	.08
☐ 434	Dave Morehead	.85	.34	.08
☐ 435	Willie Davis	1.25	.50	.12
☐ 436	Don Elston	.85	.34	.08
☐ 437	Chico Cardenas	.85	.34	.08
☐ 438	Harry Walker MG	1.00	.40	.10
☐ 439	Moe Drabowsky	.85	.34	.08
☐ 440	Tom Tresh	1.50	.60	.15
☐ 441	Denny Lemaster	.85	.34	.08
☐ 442	Vic Power	.85	.34	.08
☐ 443	Checklist 6	3.50	.40	.07
☐ 444	Bob Hendley	.85	.34	.08
☐ 445	Don Lock	.85	.34	.08
☐ 446	Art Mahaffey	.85	.34	.08
☐ 447	Julian Javier	2.00	.80	.20
☐ 448	Lee Stange	1.50	.60	.15
☐ 449	Mets Rookies	1.50	.60	.15
	Jerry Hinsley			
	Gary Kroll			
☐ 450	Elston Howard	3.50	1.40	.35
☐ 451	Jim Owens	1.50	.60	.15
☐ 452	Gary Geiger	1.50	.60	.15
☐ 453	Dodgers Rookies	2.00	.80	.20
	Willie Crawford			
	John Werhas			
☐ 454	Ed Rakow	1.50	.60	.15
☐ 455	Norm Siebern	1.50	.60	.15
☐ 456	Bill Henry	1.50	.60	.15
☐ 457	Bob Kennedy MG	1.50	.60	.15
☐ 458	John Buzhardt	1.50	.60	.15
☐ 459	Frank Kostro	1.50	.60	.15
☐ 460	Richie Allen	4.00	1.60	.40
☐ 461	Braves Rookies	25.00	10.00	2.50
	Clay Carroll			
	Phil Niekro			
☐ 462	Lew Krausse	1.50	.60	.15
	(photo actually			
	Pete Lovrich)			
☐ 463	Manny Mota	2.00	.80	.20
☐ 464	Ron Piche	1.50	.60	.15
☐ 465	Tom Haller	2.00	.80	.20
☐ 466	Senators Rookies	1.50	.60	.15
	Pete Craig			
	Dick Nen			
☐ 467	Ray Washburn	1.50	.60	.15
☐ 468	Larry Brown	1.50	.60	.15
☐ 469	Don Nottebart	1.50	.60	.15
☐ 470	Yogi Berra MG	30.00	12.00	3.00
☐ 471	Bill Hoeft	1.50	.60	.15
☐ 472	Don Pavletich	1.50	.60	.15
☐ 473	Orioles Rookies	8.00	3.25	.80
	Paul Blair			
	Dave Johnson			
☐ 474	Cookie Rojas	2.00	.80	.20
☐ 475	Clete Boyer	2.50	1.00	.25
☐ 476	Billy O'Dell	1.50	.60	.15
☐ 477	Cards Rookies	150.00	60.00	15.00
	Fritz Ackley			
	Steve Carlton			
☐ 478	Wilbur Wood	2.00	.80	.20
☐ 479	Ken Harrelson	3.00	1.20	.30
☐ 480	Joel Horlen	1.50	.60	.15
☐ 481	Cleveland Indians	3.00	1.20	.30
	Team Card			
☐ 482	Bob Priddy	1.50	.60	.15
☐ 483	George Smith	1.50	.60	.15
☐ 484	Ron Perranoski	2.00	.80	.20
☐ 485	Nellie Fox	4.00	1.60	.40
☐ 486	Angels Rookies	1.50	.60	.15
	Tom Egan			
	Pat Rogan			
☐ 487	Woody Woodward	2.00	.80	.20
☐ 488	Ted Wills	1.50	.60	.15
☐ 489	Gene Mauch MG	2.00	.80	.20
☐ 490	Earl Battey	1.50	.60	.15
☐ 491	Tracy Stallard	1.50	.60	.15
☐ 492	Gene Freese	1.50	.60	.15
☐ 493	Tigers Rookies	1.50	.60	.15
	Bill Roman			
	Bruce Brubaker			
☐ 494	Jay Ritchie	1.50	.60	.15
☐ 495	Joe Christopher	1.50	.60	.15
☐ 496	Joe Cunningham	2.00	.80	.20
☐ 497	Giants Rookies	2.00	.80	.20
	Ken Henderson			
	Jack Hiatt			
☐ 498	Gene Stephens	1.50	.60	.15
☐ 499	Stu Miller	1.50	.60	.15
☐ 500	Ed Mathews	16.00	6.50	1.60
☐ 501	Indians Rookies	1.50	.60	.15
	Ralph Gagliano			
	Jim Rittwage			
☐ 502	Don Cardwell	1.50	.60	.15
☐ 503	Phil Gagliano	1.50	.60	.15
☐ 504	Jerry Grote	1.50	.60	.15
☐ 505	Ray Culp	1.50	.60	.15
☐ 506	Sam Mele MG	1.50	.60	.15
☐ 507	Sam Ellis	1.50	.60	.15
☐ 508	Checklist 7	5.00	.50	.10
☐ 509	Red Sox Rookies	1.50	.60	.15
	Bob Guindon			
	Gerry Vezendy			
☐ 510	Ernie Banks	27.00	11.00	2.70
☐ 511	Ron Locke	1.50	.60	.15
☐ 512	Cap Peterson	1.50	.60	.15
☐ 513	New York Yankees	7.50	3.00	.75
	Team Card			
☐ 514	Joe Azcue	1.50	.60	.15
☐ 515	Vern Law	2.00	.80	.20
☐ 516	Al Weis	1.50	.60	.15
☐ 517	Angels Rookies	1.50	.60	.15
	Paul Schaal			
	Jack Warner			
☐ 518	Ken Rowe	1.50	.60	.15
☐ 519	Bob Uecker	40.00	16.00	4.00
☐ 520	Tony Cloninger	1.50	.60	.15
☐ 521	Phillies Rookies	1.50	.60	.15
	Dave Bennett			
	Morrie Stevens			
☐ 522	Hank Aguirre	1.50	.60	.15
☐ 523	Mike Brumley	3.00	1.20	.30
☐ 524	Dave Giusti	3.00	1.20	.30
☐ 525	Ed Bressoud	3.00	1.20	.30
☐ 526	Athletics Rookies	60.00	24.00	6.00
	Rene Lachemann			
	Johnny Odom			
	Jim Hunter ERR			
	("Tim" on back)			
	Skip Lockwood			
☐ 527	Jeff Torborg	4.00	1.60	.40
☐ 528	George Altman	3.00	1.20	.30
☐ 529	Jerry Fosnow	3.00	1.20	.30
☐ 530	Jim Maloney	4.00	1.60	.40
☐ 531	Chuck Hiller	3.00	1.20	.30
☐ 532	Hector Lopez	3.00	1.20	.30
☐ 533	Mets Rookies	13.50		
	Dan Napoleon			
	Ron Swoboda			
	Tug McGraw			
	Jim Bethke			
☐ 534	John Herrnstein	3.00	1.20	.30
☐ 535	Jack Kralick	3.00	1.20	.30

□ 536	Andre Rodgers	3.00	1.20	.30
□ 537	Angels Rookies	4.00	1.60	.40
	Marcelino Lopes			
	Phil Roof			
	Rudy May			
□ 538	Chuck Dressen MG	3.00	1.20	.30
□ 539	Herm Starrette	3.00	1.20	.30
□ 540	Lou Brock	30.00	12.00	3.00
□ 541	White Sox Rookies	3.00	1.20	.30
	Greg Bollo			
	Bob Locker			
□ 542	Lou Klimchock	3.00	1.20	.30
□ 543	Ed Connolly	3.00	1.20	.30
□ 544	Howie Reed	3.00	1.20	.30
□ 545	Jesus Alou	3.00	1.20	.30
□ 546	Indians Rookies	3.00	1.20	.30
	Bill Davis			
	Mike Hedlund			
	Ray Barker			
	Floyd Weaver			
□ 547	Jake Wood	3.00	1.20	.30
□ 548	Dick Stigman	3.00	1.20	.30
□ 549	Cubs Rookies	5.00	2.00	.50
	Roberto Pena			
	Glenn Beckert			
□ 550	Mel Stottlemyre	12.00	5.00	1.20
□ 551	New York Mets	8.00	3.25	.80
	Team Card			
□ 552	Julio Gotay	3.00	1.20	.30
□ 553	Astros Rookies	3.00	1.20	.30
	Dan Coombs			
	Gene Ratliff			
	Jack McClure			
□ 554	Chico Ruiz	3.00	1.20	.30
□ 555	Jack Baldschun	3.00	1.20	.30
□ 556	Red Schoendienst MG	5.00	2.00	.50
□ 557	Jose Santiago	3.00	1.20	.30
□ 558	Tom Sisk	3.00	1.20	.30
□ 559	Ed Bailey	3.00	1.20	.30
□ 560	Boog Powell	5.00	2.00	.50
□ 561	Dodgers Rookies	6.50	2.60	.65
	Dennis Daboll			
	Mike Kekich			
	Hector Valle			
	Jim Lefebvre			
□ 562	Bill Moran	3.00	1.20	.30
□ 563	Julio Navarro	3.00	1.20	.30
□ 564	Mel Nelson	3.00	1.20	.30
□ 565	Ernie Broglio	3.00	1.20	.30
□ 566	Yankees Rookies	3.00	1.20	.30
	Gil Blanco			
	Ross Moschitto			
	Art Lopez			
□ 567	Tommie Aaron	4.00	1.60	.40
□ 568	Ron Taylor	3.00	1.20	.30
□ 569	Gino Cimoli	3.00	1.20	.30
□ 570	Claude Osteen	4.00	1.60	.40
□ 571	Ossie Virgil	3.00	1.20	.30
□ 572	Baltimore Orioles	6.00	2.40	.60
	Team Card			
□ 573	Red Sox Rookies	6.00	2.40	.60
	Jim Lonborg			
	Gerry Moses			
	Bill Schlesinger			
	Mike Ryan			
□ 574	Roy Sievers	4.00	1.60	.40
□ 575	Jose Pagan	3.00	1.20	.30
□ 576	Terry Fox	3.00	1.20	.30
□ 577	AL Rookie Stars	3.00	1.20	.30
	Darold Knowles			
	Don Buschhorn			
	Richie Scheinblum			
□ 578	Camilo Carreon	3.00	1.20	.30
□ 579	Dick Smith	3.00	1.20	.30
□ 580	Jimmie Hall	4.00	1.60	.40
□ 581	NL Rookie Stars	45.00	18.00	4.50
	Tony Perez			
	Dave Ricketts			
	Kevin Collins			
□ 582	Bob Schmidt	3.00	1.20	.30
□ 583	Wes Covington	3.00	1.20	.30
□ 584	Harry Bright	3.00	1.20	.30
□ 585	Hank Fischer	3.00	1.20	.30
□ 586	Tom McCraw	3.00	1.20	.30
□ 587	Joe Sparma	3.00	1.20	.30
□ 588	Len Green	3.00	1.20	.30
□ 589	Giants Rookies	3.00	1.20	.30
	Frank Linzy			
	Bob Schroder			
□ 590	John Wyatt	3.00	1.20	.30
□ 591	Bob Skinner	3.00	1.20	.30
□ 592	Frank Bork	3.00	1.20	.30
□ 593	Tigers Rookies	3.00	1.20	.30
	Jackie Moore			
	John Sullivan			
□ 594	Joe Gaines	3.00	1.20	.3
□ 595	Don Lee	3.00	1.20	.3
□ 596	Don Landrum	3.00	1.20	.3
□ 597	Twins Rookies	3.00	1.20	.3
	Joe Nossek			
	John Sevcik			
	Dick Reese			
□ 598	Al Downing	4.50	1.50	.3

1966 Topps

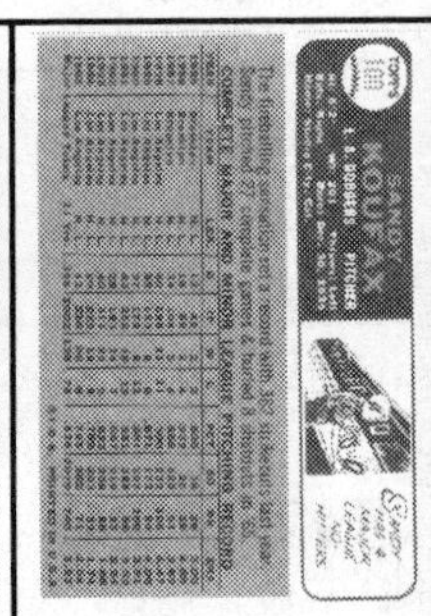

The cards in this 598-card set measure 2 1/2" by 3 1/2". There are the same number of cards as in the 1965 set. Once again, the seventh series cards (523 to 598) are considered more difficult to obtain than any other series' cards in the set. The only featured subset within this set is League Leaders (215- 226). Noteworthy rookie cards in the set include Jim Palmer (126) and Don Sutton (288). Palmer is described in the bio (on his card back) as a lefthander.

		NRMT	VG-E	GOO
COMPLETE SET (598)		2900.00	1250.00	400.0
COMMON PLAYER (1-110)		.40	.16	.0
COMMON PLAYER (111-370)		.60	.24	.0
COMMON PLAYER (371-446)		.85	.34	.0
COMMON PLAYER (447-522)		2.50	1.00	.2
COMMON PLAYER (523-598)		12.00	5.00	1.2
□ 1	Willie Mays	100.00	25.00	5.0
□ 2	Ted Abernathy	.40	.16	.0
□ 3	Sam Mele MG	.40	.16	.0
□ 4	Ray Culp	.40	.16	.0
□ 5	Jim Fregosi	1.00	.40	.1
□ 6	Chuck Schilling	.40	.16	.0
□ 7	Tracy Stallard	.40	.16	.0
□ 8	Floyd Robinson	.40	.16	.0
□ 9	Clete Boyer	.75	.30	.0
□ 10	Tony Cloninger	.40	.16	.0
□ 11	Senators Rookies	.40	.16	.0
	Brant Alyea			
	Pete Craig			
□ 12	John Tsitouris	.40	.16	.0
□ 13	Lou Johnson	.40	.16	.0
□ 14	Norm Siebern	.40	.16	.0
□ 15	Vern Law	.75	.30	.0
□ 16	Larry Brown	.40	.16	.0
□ 17	John Stephenson	.40	.16	.0
□ 18	Roland Sheldon	.40	.16	.0
□ 19	San Francisco Giants	1.00	.40	.1
	Team Card			
□ 20	Willie Horton	1.00	.40	.1
□ 21	Don Nottebart	.40	.16	.0
□ 22	Joe Nossek	.40	.16	.0
□ 23	Jack Sanford	.40	.16	.0
□ 24	Don Kessinger	1.25	.50	.1
□ 25	Pete Ward	.40	.16	.0
□ 26	Ray Sadecki	.40	.16	.0
□ 27	Orioles Rookies	.75	.30	.0
	Darold Knowles			
	Andy Etchebarren			
□ 28	Phil Niekro	12.00	5.00	1.2
□ 29	Mike Brumley	.40	.16	.0
□ 30	Pete Rose	60.00	24.00	6.0
□ 31	Jack Cullen	.40	.16	.0
□ 32	Adolfo Phillips	.40	.16	.0
□ 33	Jim Pagliaroni	.40	.16	.0

□ 34	Checklist 1	3.00	.30	.06
□ 35	Ron Swoboda	.75	.30	.07
□ 36	Jim Hunter	14.00	5.75	1.40
□ 37	Billy Herman MG	1.25	.50	.12
□ 38	Ron Nischwitz	.40	.16	.04
□ 39	Ken Henderson	.40	.16	.04
□ 40	Jim Grant	.40	.16	.04
□ 41	Don LeJohn	.40	.16	.04
□ 42	Aubrey Gatewood	.40	.16	.04
□ 43	Don Landrum	.40	.16	.04
□ 44	Indians Rookies Bill Davis Tom Kelley	.40	.16	.04
□ 45	Jim Gentile	.75	.30	.07
□ 46	Howie Koplitz	.40	.16	.04
□ 47	J.C. Martin	.40	.16	.04
□ 48	Paul Blair	.75	.30	.07
□ 49	Woody Woodward	.40	.16	.04
□ 50	Mickey Mantle	175.00	70.00	18.00
□ 51	Gordon Richardson	.40	.16	.04
□ 52	Power Plus Wes Covington Johnny Callison	.75	.30	.07
□ 53	Bob Duliba	.40	.16	.04
□ 54	Jose Pagan	.40	.16	.04
□ 55	Ken Harrelson	1.00	.40	.10
□ 56	Sandy Valdespino	.40	.16	.04
□ 57	Jim Lefebvre	1.00	.40	.10
□ 58	Dave Wickersham	.40	.16	.04
□ 59	Reds Team	1.00	.40	.10
□ 60	Curt Flood	1.00	.40	.10
□ 61	Bob Bolin	.40	.16	.04
□ 62A	Merritt Ranew (with sold line)	.40	.16	.04
□ 62B	Merritt Ranew (without sold line)	25.00	10.00	2.50
□ 63	Jim Stewart	.40	.16	.04
□ 64	Bob Bruce	.40	.16	.04
□ 65	Leon Wagner	.40	.16	.04
□ 66	Al Weis	.40	.16	.04
□ 67	Mets Rookies Cleon Jones Dick Selma	.75	.30	.07
□ 68	Hal Reniff	.40	.16	.04
□ 69	Ken Hamlin	.40	.16	.04
□ 70	Carl Yastrzemski	45.00	18.00	4.50
□ 71	Frank Carpin	.40	.16	.04
□ 72	Tony Perez	8.00	3.25	.80
□ 73	Jerry Zimmerman	.40	.16	.04
□ 74	Don Mossi	.75	.30	.07
□ 75	Tommy Davis	1.00	.40	.10
□ 76	Red Schoendienst MG	1.00	.40	.10
□ 77	Johnny Orsino	.40	.16	.04
□ 78	Frank Linzy	.40	.16	.04
□ 79	Joe Pepitone	1.00	.40	.10
□ 80	Richie Allen	1.50	.60	.15
□ 81	Ray Oyler	.40	.16	.04
□ 82	Bob Hendley	.40	.16	.04
□ 83	Albie Pearson	.40	.16	.04
□ 84	Braves Rookies Jim Beauchamp Dick Kelley	.40	.16	.04
□ 85	Eddie Fisher	.40	.16	.04
□ 86	John Bateman	.40	.16	.04
□ 87	Dan Napoleon	.40	.16	.04
□ 88	Fred Whitfield	.40	.16	.04
□ 89	Ted Davidson	.40	.16	.04
□ 90	Luis Aparicio	6.50	2.60	.65
□ 91A	Bob Uecker (with traded line)	12.50	5.00	1.25
□ 91B	Bob Uecker (no traded line)	60.00	24.00	6.00
□ 92	Yankees Team	3.00	1.20	.30
□ 93	Jim Lonborg	.75	.30	.07
□ 94	Matty Alou	.75	.30	.07
□ 95	Pete Richert	.40	.16	.04
□ 96	Felipe Alou	.75	.30	.07
□ 97	Jim Merritt	.40	.16	.04
□ 98	Don Demeter	.40	.16	.04
□ 99	Buc Belters Willie Stargell Donn Clendenon	3.00	1.20	.30
□ 100	Sandy Koufax	40.00	16.00	4.00
□ 101A	Checklist 2 (115 Bill Henry)	4.00	.40	.08
□ 101B	Checklist 2 (115 W. Spahn)	8.00	.80	.15
□ 102	Ed Kirkpatrick	.40	.16	.04
□ 103A	Dick Groat (with traded line)	1.00	.40	.10
□ 103B	Dick Groat (no traded line)	25.00	10.00	2.50
□ 104A	Alex Johnson (with traded line)	.75	.30	.07
□ 104B	Alex Johnson (no traded line)	25.00	10.00	2.50
□ 105	Milt Pappas	.75	.30	.07
□ 106	Rusty Staub	1.50	.60	.15
□ 107	A's Rookies Larry Stahl Ron Tompkins	.40	.16	.04
□ 108	Bobby Klaus	.40	.16	.04
□ 109	Ralph Terry	.75	.30	.07
□ 110	Ernie Banks	11.00	4.50	1.10
□ 111	Gary Peters	.75	.30	.07
□ 112	Manny Mota	.75	.30	.07
□ 113	Hank Aguirre	.60	.24	.06
□ 114	Jim Gosger	.60	.24	.06
□ 115	Bill Henry	.60	.24	.06
□ 116	Walt Alston MG	2.50	1.00	.25
□ 117	Jake Gibbs	.75	.30	.07
□ 118	Mike McCormick	.75	.30	.07
□ 119	Art Shamsky	.60	.24	.06
□ 120	Harmon Killebrew	10.00	4.00	1.00
□ 121	Ray Herbert	.60	.24	.06
□ 122	Joe Gaines	.60	.24	.06
□ 123	Pirates Rookies Frank Bork Jerry May	.60	.24	.06
□ 124	Tug McGraw	2.50	1.00	.25
□ 125	Lou Brock	11.00	4.50	1.10
□ 126	Jim Palmer	75.00	30.00	7.50
□ 127	Ken Berry	.60	.24	.06
□ 128	Jim Landis	.60	.24	.06
□ 129	Jack Kralick	.60	.24	.06
□ 130	Joe Torre	1.25	.50	.12
□ 131	Angels Team	1.25	.50	.12
□ 132	Orlando Cepeda	3.00	1.20	.30
□ 133	Don McMahon	.60	.24	.06
□ 134	Wes Parker	.75	.30	.07
□ 135	Dave Morehead	.60	.24	.06
□ 136	Woody Held	.60	.24	.06
□ 137	Pat Corrales	.75	.30	.07
□ 138	Roger Repoz	.60	.24	.06
□ 139	Cubs Rookies Byron Browne Don Young	.60	.24	.06
□ 140	Jim Maloney	1.00	.40	.10
□ 141	Tom McCraw	.60	.24	.06
□ 142	Don Dennis	.60	.24	.06
□ 143	Jose Tartabull	.60	.24	.06
□ 144	Don Schwall	.60	.24	.06
□ 145	Bill Freehan	1.25	.50	.12
□ 146	George Altman	.60	.24	.06
□ 147	Lum Harris MG	.60	.24	.06
□ 148	Bob Johnson	.60	.24	.06
□ 149	Dick Nen	.60	.24	.06
□ 150	Rocky Colavito	1.50	.60	.15
□ 151	Gary Wagner	.60	.24	.06
□ 152	Frank Malzone	.75	.30	.07
□ 153	Rico Carty	1.00	.40	.10
□ 154	Chuck Hiller	.60	.24	.06
□ 155	Marcelino Lopez	.60	.24	.06
□ 156	Double Play Combo Dick Schofield Hal Lanier	.75	.30	.07
□ 157	Rene Lachemann	1.00	.40	.10
□ 158	Jim Brewer	.60	.24	.06
□ 159	Chico Ruiz	.60	.24	.06
□ 160	Whitey Ford	11.00	4.50	1.10
□ 161	Jerry Lumpe	.60	.24	.06
□ 162	Lee Maye	.60	.24	.06
□ 163	Tito Francona	.75	.30	.07
□ 164	White Sox Rookies Tommie Agee Marv Staehle	.75	.30	.07
□ 165	Don Lock	.60	.24	.06
□ 166	Chris Krug	.60	.24	.06
□ 167	Boog Powell	1.75	.70	.17
□ 168	Dan Osinski	.60	.24	.06
□ 169	Duke Sims	.60	.24	.06
□ 170	Cookie Rojas	.75	.30	.07
□ 171	Nick Willhite	.60	.24	.06
□ 172	Mets Team	1.50	.60	.15
□ 173	Al Spangler	.60	.24	.06
□ 174	Ron Taylor	.60	.24	.06
□ 175	Bert Campaneris	.75	.30	.07
□ 176	Jim Davenport	.75	.30	.07
□ 177	Hector Lopez	.60	.24	.06
□ 178	Bob Tillman	.60	.24	.06
□ 179	Cards Rookies Dennis Aust Bob Tolan	.75	.30	.07
□ 180	Vada Pinson	1.25	.50	.12
□ 181	Al Worthington	.60	.24	.06
□ 182	Jerry Lynch	.60	.24	.06
□ 183	Checklist 3	3.00	.30	.06
□ 184	Denis Menke	.60	.24	.06
□ 185	Bob Buhl	.60	.24	.06
□ 186	Ruben Amaro	.60	.24	.06

□ 187 Chuck Dressen MG	.75	.30	.07
□ 188 Al Luplow	.60	.24	.06
□ 189 John Roseboro	.75	.30	.07
□ 190 Jimmie Hall	.75	.30	.07
□ 191 Darrell Sutherland	.60	.24	.06
□ 192 Vic Power	.60	.24	.06
□ 193 Dave McNally	1.00	.40	.10
□ 194 Senators Team	1.25	.50	.12
□ 195 Joe Morgan	12.50	5.00	1.25
□ 196 Don Pavletich	.60	.24	.06
□ 197 Sonny Siebert	.75	.30	.07
□ 198 Mickey Stanley	1.00	.40	.10
□ 199 Chisox Clubbers	.75	.30	.07
Bill Skowron			
Johnny Romano			
Floyd Robinson			
□ 200 Eddie Mathews	9.00	3.75	.90
□ 201 Jim Dickson	.60	.24	.06
□ 202 Clay Dalrymple	.60	.24	.06
□ 203 Jose Santiago	.60	.24	.06
□ 204 Cubs Team	1.25	.50	.12
□ 205 Tom Tresh	1.25	.50	.12
□ 206 Al Jackson	.60	.24	.06
□ 207 Frank Quilici	.60	.24	.06
□ 208 Bob Miller	.60	.24	.06
□ 209 Tigers Rookies	1.25	.50	.12
Fritz Fisher			
John Hiller			
□ 210 Bill Mazeroski	1.50	.60	.15
□ 211 Frank Kreutzer	.60	.24	.06
□ 212 Ed Kranepool	.75	.30	.07
□ 213 Fred Newman	.60	.24	.06
□ 214 Tommy Harper	.75	.30	.07
□ 215 NL Batting Leaders	10.00	4.00	1.00
Bob Clemente			
Hank Aaron			
Willie Mays			
□ 216 AL Batting Leaders	2.50	1.00	.25
Tony Oliva			
Carl Yastrzemski			
Vic Davalillo			
□ 217 NL Home Run Leaders	7.50	3.00	.75
Willie Mays			
Willie McCovey			
Billy Williams			
□ 218 AL Home Run Leaders	1.50	.60	.15
Tony Conigliaro			
Norm Cash			
Willie Horton			
□ 219 NL RBI Leaders	2.50	1.00	.25
Deron Johnson			
Frank Robinson			
Willie Mays			
□ 220 AL RBI Leaders	1.50	.60	.15
Rocky Colavito			
Willie Horton			
Tony Oliva			
□ 221 NL ERA Leaders	2.50	1.00	.25
Sandy Koufax			
Juan Marichal			
Vern Law			
□ 222 AL ERA Leaders	1.50	.60	.15
Sam McDowell			
Eddie Fisher			
Sonny Siebert			
□ 223 NL Pitching Leaders	2.50	1.00	.25
Sandy Koufax			
Tony Cloninger			
Don Drysdale			
□ 224 AL Pitching Leaders	1.50	.60	.15
Jim Grant			
Mel Stottlemyre			
Jim Kaat			
□ 225 NL Strikeout Leaders	3.00	1.20	.30
Sandy Koufax			
Bob Veale			
Bob Gibson			
□ 226 AL Strikeout Leaders	1.50	.60	.15
Sam McDowell			
Mickey Lolich			
Dennis McLain			
Sonny Siebert			
□ 227 Russ Nixon	1.00	.40	.10
□ 228 Larry Dierker	.75	.30	.07
□ 229 Hank Bauer MG	1.00	.40	.10
□ 230 Johnny Callison	.75	.30	.07
□ 231 Floyd Weaver	.60	.24	.06
□ 232 Glenn Beckert	.75	.30	.07
□ 233 Dom Zanni	.60	.24	.06
□ 234 Yankees Rookies	3.50	1.40	.35
Rich Beck			
Roy White			
□ 235 Don Cardwell	.60	.24	.06
□ 236 Mike Hershberger	.60	.24	.06
□ 237 Billy O'Dell	.60	.24	.06

□ 238 Dodgers Team	2.00	.80	.2
□ 239 Orlando Pena	.60	.24	.0
□ 240 Earl Battey	.75	.30	.0
□ 241 Dennis Ribant	.60	.24	.0
□ 242 Jesus Alou	.60	.24	.0
□ 243 Nelson Briles	.75	.30	.0
□ 244 Astros Rookies	.60	.24	.0
Chuck Harrison			
Sonny Jackson			
□ 245 John Buzhardt	.60	.24	.0
□ 246 Ed Bailey	.60	.24	.0
□ 247 Carl Warwick	.60	.24	.0
□ 248 Pete Mikkelsen	.60	.24	.0
□ 249 Bill Rigney MG	.60	.24	.0
□ 250 Sammy Ellis	.60	.24	.0
□ 251 Ed Brinkman	.60	.24	.0
□ 252 Denny Lemaster	.60	.24	.0
□ 253 Don Wert	.60	.24	.0
□ 254 Phillies Rookies	20.00	8.00	2.0
Ferguson Jenkins			
Bill Sorrell			
□ 255 Willie Stargell	12.50	5.00	1.2
□ 256 Lew Krausse	.60	.24	.0
□ 257 Jeff Torborg	1.25	.50	.1
□ 258 Dave Giusti	.75	.30	.0
□ 259 Boston Red Sox	1.25	.50	.1
Team Card			
□ 260 Bob Shaw	.60	.24	.0
□ 261 Ron Hansen	.60	.24	.0
□ 262 Jack Hamilton	.60	.24	.0
□ 263 Tom Egan	.60	.24	.0
□ 264 Twins Rookies	.60	.24	.0
Andy Kosco			
Ted Uhlaender			
□ 265 Stu Miller	.60	.24	.0
□ 266 Pedro Gonzalez	.60	.24	.0
(misspelled Gonzales			
on card back)			
□ 267 Joe Sparma	.60	.24	.0
□ 268 John Blanchard	.75	.30	.0
□ 269 Don Heffner MG	.60	.24	.0
□ 270 Claude Osteen	.75	.30	.0
□ 271 Hal Lanier	.75	.30	.0
□ 272 Jack Baldschun	.60	.24	.0
□ 273 Astro Aces	1.00	.40	.1
Bob Aspromonte			
Rusty Staub			
□ 274 Buster Narum	.60	.24	.0
□ 275 Tim McCarver	1.75	.70	.1
□ 276 Jim Bouton	1.50	.60	.1
□ 277 George Thomas	.60	.24	.0
□ 278 Cal Koonce	.60	.24	.0
□ 279 Checklist 4	3.00	.30	.0
□ 280 Bobby Knoop	.60	.24	.0
□ 281 Bruce Howard	.60	.24	.0
□ 282 Johnny Lewis	.60	.24	.0
□ 283 Jim Perry	.75	.30	.0
□ 284 Bobby Wine	.60	.24	.0
□ 285 Luis Tiant	1.75	.70	.1
□ 286 Gary Geiger	.60	.24	.0
□ 287 Jack Aker	.60	.24	.0
□ 288 Dodgers Rookies	60.00	24.00	6.0
Bill Singer			
Don Sutton			
□ 289 Larry Sherry	.75	.30	.0
□ 290 Ron Santo	1.25	.50	.1
□ 291 Moe Drabowsky	.60	.24	.0
□ 292 Jim Coker	.60	.24	.0
□ 293 Mike Shannon	1.00	.40	.1
□ 294 Steve Ridzik	.60	.24	.0
□ 295 Jim Ray Hart	.75	.30	.0
□ 296 Johnny Keane MG	.75	.30	.0
□ 297 Jim Owens	.60	.24	.0
□ 298 Rico Petrocelli	1.00	.40	.1
□ 299 Lou Burdette	1.25	.50	.1
□ 300 Bob Clemente	50.00	20.00	5.0
□ 301 Greg Bollo	.60	.24	.0
□ 302 Ernie Bowman	.60	.24	.0
□ 303 Cleveland Indians	1.25	.50	.1
Team Card			
□ 304 John Herrnstein	.60	.24	.0
□ 305 Camilo Pascual	.75	.30	.0
□ 306 Ty Cline	.60	.24	.0
□ 307 Clay Carroll	.60	.24	.0
□ 308 Tom Haller	.75	.30	.0
□ 309 Diego Segui	.60	.24	.0
□ 310 Frank Robinson	18.00	7.25	1.8
□ 311 Reds Rookies	.75	.30	.0
Tommy Helms			
Dick Simpson			
□ 312 Bob Saverine	.60	.24	.0
□ 313 Chris Zachary	.60	.24	.0
□ 314 Hector Valle	.60	.24	.0
□ 315 Norm Cash	1.50	.60	.1
□ 316 Jack Fisher	.60	.24	.0

☐ 317	Dalton Jones	.60	.24	.06
☐ 318	Harry Walker MG	.60	.24	.06
☐ 319	Gene Freese	.60	.24	.06
☐ 320	Bob Gibson	12.00	5.00	1.20
☐ 321	Rick Reichardt	.60	.24	.06
☐ 322	Bill Faul	.60	.24	.06
☐ 323	Ray Barker	.60	.24	.06
☐ 324	John Boozer	.60	.24	.06
☐ 325	Vic Davalillo	.75	.30	.07
☐ 326	Braves Team	1.25	.50	.12
☐ 327	Bernie Allen	.60	.24	.06
☐ 328	Jerry Grote	.60	.24	.06
☐ 329	Pete Charton	.60	.24	.06
☐ 330	Ron Fairly	.75	.30	.07
☐ 331	Ron Herbel	.60	.24	.06
☐ 332	Bill Bryan	.60	.24	.06
☐ 333	Senators Rookies	.60	.24	.06
	Joe Coleman			
	Jim French			
☐ 334	Marty Keough	.60	.24	.06
☐ 335	Juan Pizarro	.60	.24	.06
☐ 336	Gene Alley	.75	.30	.07
☐ 337	Fred Gladding	.60	.24	.06
☐ 338	Dal Maxvill	.60	.24	.06
☐ 339	Del Crandall	.75	.30	.07
☐ 340	Dean Chance	.75	.30	.07
☐ 341	Wes Westrum MG	.60	.24	.06
☐ 342	Bob Humphreys	.60	.24	.06
☐ 343	Joe Christopher	.60	.24	.06
☐ 344	Steve Blass	.75	.30	.07
☐ 345	Bob Allison	.75	.30	.07
☐ 346	Mike De La Hoz	.60	.24	.06
☐ 347	Phil Regan	.75	.30	.07
☐ 348	Orioles Team	1.25	.50	.12
☐ 349	Cap Peterson	.60	.24	.06
☐ 350	Mel Stottlemyre	2.50	1.00	.25
☐ 351	Fred Valentine	.60	.24	.06
☐ 352	Bob Aspromonte	.60	.24	.06
☐ 353	Al McBean	.60	.24	.06
☐ 354	Smoky Burgess	.75	.30	.07
☐ 355	Wade Blasingame	.60	.24	.06
☐ 356	Red Sox Rookies	.60	.24	.06
	Owen Johnson			
	Ken Sanders			
☐ 357	Gerry Arrigo	.60	.24	.06
☐ 358	Charlie Smith	.60	.24	.06
☐ 359	Johnny Briggs	.60	.24	.06
☐ 360	Ron Hunt	.60	.24	.06
☐ 361	Tom Satriano	.60	.24	.06
☐ 362	Gates Brown	.75	.30	.07
☐ 363	Checklist 5	3.00	.30	.06
☐ 364	Nate Oliver	.60	.24	.06
☐ 365	Roger Maris	35.00	14.00	3.50
☐ 366	Wayne Causey	.60	.24	.06
☐ 367	Mel Nelson	.60	.24	.06
☐ 368	Charlie Lau	.75	.30	.07
☐ 369	Jim King	.60	.24	.06
☐ 370	Chico Cardenas	.60	.24	.06
☐ 371	Lee Stange	.85	.34	.08
☐ 372	Harvey Kuenn	1.50	.60	.15
☐ 373	Giants Rookies	.85	.34	.08
	Jack Hiatt			
	Dick Estelle			
☐ 374	Bob Locker	.85	.34	.08
☐ 375	Donn Clendenon	1.00	.40	.10
☐ 376	Paul Schaal	.85	.34	.08
☐ 377	Turk Farrell	1.00	.40	.10
☐ 378	Dick Tracewski	.85	.34	.08
☐ 379	Cardinal Team	1.75	.70	.17
☐ 380	Tony Conigliaro	3.50	1.40	.35
☐ 381	Hank Fischer	.85	.34	.08
☐ 382	Phil Roof	.85	.34	.08
☐ 383	Jack Brandt	.85	.34	.08
☐ 384	Al Downing	1.00	.40	.10
☐ 385	Ken Boyer	2.00	.80	.20
☐ 386	Gil Hodges MG	4.50	1.80	.45
☐ 387	Howie Reed	.85	.34	.08
☐ 388	Don Mincher	1.00	.40	.10
☐ 389	Jim O'Toole	.85	.34	.08
☐ 390	Brooks Robinson	12.00	5.00	1.20
☐ 391	Chuck Hinton	.85	.34	.08
☐ 392	Cubs Rookies	1.25	.50	.12
	Bill Hands			
	Randy Hundley			
☐ 393	George Brunet	.85	.34	.08
☐ 394	Ron Brand	.85	.34	.08
☐ 395	Len Gabrielson	.85	.34	.08
☐ 396	Jerry Stephenson	.85	.34	.08
☐ 397	Bill White	1.25	.50	.12
☐ 398	Danny Cater	1.00	.40	.10
☐ 399	Ray Washburn	.85	.34	.08
☐ 400	Zoilo Versalles	.85	.34	.08
☐ 401	Ken McMullen	.85	.34	.08
☐ 402	Jim Hickman	.85	.34	.08
☐ 403	Fred Talbot	.85	.34	.08
☐ 404	Pittsburgh Pirates	1.75	.70	.17
	Team Card			
☐ 405	Elston Howard	2.50	1.00	.25
☐ 406	Joey Jay	.85	.34	.08
☐ 407	John Kennedy	.85	.34	.08
☐ 408	Lee Thomas	1.25	.50	.12
☐ 409	Billy Hoeft	.85	.34	.08
☐ 410	Al Kaline	13.00	5.25	1.30
☐ 411	Gene Mauch MG	1.00	.40	.10
☐ 412	Sam Bowens	.85	.34	.08
☐ 413	John Romano	.85	.34	.08
☐ 414	Dan Coombs	.85	.34	.08
☐ 415	Max Alvis	.85	.34	.08
☐ 416	Phil Ortega	.85	.34	.08
☐ 417	Angels Rookies	.85	.34	.08
	Jim McGlothlin			
	Ed Sukla			
☐ 418	Phil Gagliano	.85	.34	.08
☐ 419	Mike Ryan	.85	.34	.08
☐ 420	Juan Marichal	7.50	3.00	.75
☐ 421	Roy McMillan	.85	.34	.08
☐ 422	Ed Charles	.85	.34	.08
☐ 423	Ernie Broglio	.85	.34	.08
☐ 424	Reds Rookies	2.00	.80	.20
	Lee May			
	Darrell Osteen			
☐ 425	Bob Veale	1.00	.40	.10
☐ 426	White Sox Team	1.75	.70	.17
☐ 427	John Miller	.85	.34	.08
☐ 428	Sandy Alomar	1.00	.40	.10
☐ 429	Bill Monbouquette	.85	.34	.08
☐ 430	Don Drysdale	8.00	3.25	.80
☐ 431	Walt Bond	.85	.34	.08
☐ 432	Bob Heffner	.85	.34	.08
☐ 433	Alvin Dark MG	1.25	.50	.12
☐ 434	Willie Kirkland	.85	.34	.08
☐ 435	Jim Bunning	4.50	1.80	.45
☐ 436	Julian Javier	1.00	.40	.10
☐ 437	Al Stanek	.85	.34	.08
☐ 438	Willie Smith	.85	.34	.08
☐ 439	Pedro Ramos	.85	.34	.08
☐ 440	Deron Johnson	1.00	.40	.10
☐ 441	Tommie Sisk	.85	.34	.08
☐ 442	Orioles Rookies	.85	.34	.08
	Ed Barnowski			
	Eddie Watt			
☐ 443	Bill Wakefield	.85	.34	.08
☐ 444	Checklist 6	4.00	.40	.08
☐ 445	Jim Kaat	4.00	1.60	.40
☐ 446	Mack Jones	.85	.34	.08
☐ 447	Dick Ellsworth	3.50	1.40	.35
	(photo actually			
	Ken Hubbs)			
☐ 448	Eddie Stanky MG	3.50	1.40	.35
☐ 449	Joe Moeller	2.50	1.00	.25
☐ 450	Tony Oliva	5.00	2.00	.50
☐ 451	Barry Latman	2.50	1.00	.25
☐ 452	Joe Azcue	2.50	1.00	.25
☐ 453	Ron Kline	2.50	1.00	.25
☐ 454	Jerry Buchek	2.50	1.00	.25
☐ 455	Mickey Lolich	4.00	1.60	.40
☐ 456	Red Sox Rookies	2.50	1.00	.25
	Darrell Brandon			
	Joe Foy			
☐ 457	Joe Gibbon	2.50	1.00	.25
☐ 458	Manny Jiminez	2.50	1.00	.25
☐ 459	Bill McCool	2.50	1.00	.25
☐ 460	Curt Blefary	2.50	1.00	.25
☐ 461	Roy Face	3.50	1.40	.35
☐ 462	Bob Rodgers	3.50	1.40	.35
☐ 463	Philadelphia Phillies	5.00	2.00	.50
	Team Card			
☐ 464	Larry Bearnarth	2.50	1.00	.25
☐ 465	Don Buford	2.50	1.00	.25
☐ 466	Ken Johnson	2.50	1.00	.25
☐ 467	Vic Roznovsky	2.50	1.00	.25
☐ 468	Johnny Podres	4.00	1.60	.40
☐ 469	Yankees Rookies	9.00	3.75	.90
	Bobby Murcer			
	Dooley Womack			
☐ 470	Sam McDowell	3.50	1.40	.35
☐ 471	Bob Skinner	2.50	1.00	.25
☐ 472	Terry Fox	2.50	1.00	.25
☐ 473	Rich Rollins	2.50	1.00	.25
☐ 474	Dick Schofield	2.50	1.00	.25
☐ 475	Dick Radatz	2.50	1.00	.25
☐ 476	Bobby Bragan MG	2.50	1.00	.25
☐ 477	Steve Barber	2.50	1.00	.25
☐ 478	Tony Gonzalez	2.50	1.00	.25
☐ 479	Jim Hannan	2.50	1.00	.25
☐ 480	Dick Stuart	2.50	1.00	.25
☐ 481	Bob Lee	2.50	1.00	.25
☐ 482	Cubs Rookies	2.50	1.00	.25
	John Boccabella			
	Dave Dowling			

□ 483	Joe Nuxhall	3.50	1.40	.35
□ 484	Wes Covington	2.50	1.00	.25
□ 485	Bob Bailey	2.50	1.00	.25
□ 486	Tommy John	7.50	3.00	.75
□ 487	Al Ferrara	2.50	1.00	.25
□ 488	George Banks	2.50	1.00	.25
□ 489	Curt Simmons	3.50	1.40	.35
□ 490	Bobby Richardson	7.50	3.00	.75
□ 491	Dennis Bennett	2.50	1.00	.25
□ 492	Athletics Team	5.00	2.00	.50
□ 493	Johnny Klippstein	2.50	1.00	.25
□ 494	Gordy Coleman	2.50	1.00	.25
□ 495	Dick McAuliffe	3.50	1.40	.35
□ 496	Lindy McDaniel	3.50	1.40	.35
□ 497	Chris Cannizzaro	2.50	1.00	.25
□ 498	Pirates Rookies	3.50	1.40	.35
	Luke Walker			
	Woody Fryman			
□ 499	Wally Bunker	2.50	1.00	.25
□ 500	Hank Aaron	65.00	26.00	6.50
□ 501	John O'Donoghue	2.50	1.00	.25
□ 502	Lenny Green	2.50	1.00	.25
□ 503	Steve Hamilton	2.50	1.00	.25
□ 504	Grady Hatton MG	2.50	1.00	.25
□ 505	Jose Cardenal	2.50	1.00	.25
□ 506	Bo Belinsky	3.50	1.40	.35
□ 507	Johnny Edwards	2.50	1.00	.25
□ 508	Steve Hargan	2.50	1.00	.25
□ 509	Jake Wood	2.50	1.00	.25
□ 510	Hoyt Wilhelm	11.00	4.50	1.10
□ 511	Giants Rookies	2.50	1.00	.25
	Bob Barton			
	Tito Fuentes			
□ 512	Dick Stigman	2.50	1.00	.25
□ 513	Camilo Carreon	2.50	1.00	.25
□ 514	Hal Woodeshick	2.50	1.00	.25
□ 515	Frank Howard	3.50	1.40	.35
□ 516	Eddie Bressoud	2.50	1.00	.25
□ 517A	Checklist 7	8.00	.75	.15
	529 White Sox Rookies			
	544 Cardinals Rookies			
□ 517B	Checklist 7	8.00	.75	.15
	529 W. Sox Rookies			
	544 Cards Rookies			
□ 518	Braves Rookies	2.50	1.00	.25
	Herb Hippauf			
	Arnie Umbach			
□ 519	Bob Friend	3.50	1.40	.35
□ 520	Jim Wynn	3.50	1.40	.35
□ 521	John Wyatt	2.50	1.00	.25
□ 522	Phil Linz	3.50	1.40	.35
□ 523	Bob Sadowski	12.00	5.00	1.20
□ 524	Giants Rookies SP	20.00	8.00	2.00
	Ollie Brown			
	Don Mason			
□ 525	Gary Bell SP	20.00	8.00	2.00
□ 526	Twins Team SP	40.00	16.00	4.00
□ 527	Julio Navarro	12.00	5.00	1.20
□ 528	Jesse Gonder SP	20.00	8.00	2.00
□ 529	White Sox Rookies	15.00	6.00	1.50
	Lee Elia			
	Dennis Higgins			
	Bill Voss			
□ 530	Robin Roberts	35.00	14.00	3.50
□ 531	Joe Cunningham SP	20.00	8.00	2.00
□ 532	Aurelio Monteagudo SP	20.00	8.00	2.00
□ 533	Jerry Adair SP	20.00	8.00	2.00
□ 534	Mets Rookies	12.00	5.00	1.20
	Dave Eilers			
	Rob Gardner			
□ 535	Willie Davis	18.00	7.25	1.80
□ 536	Dick Egan	12.00	5.00	1.20
□ 537	Herman Franks MG	12.00	5.00	1.20
□ 538	Bob Allen	12.00	5.00	1.20
□ 539	Astros Rookies	12.00	5.00	1.20
	Bill Heath			
	Carroll Sembera			
□ 540	Denny McLain SP	40.00	16.00	4.00
□ 541	Gene Oliver	12.00	5.00	1.20
□ 542	George Smith	12.00	5.00	1.20
□ 543	Roger Craig SP	25.00	10.00	2.50
□ 544	Cardinals Rookies SP	20.00	8.00	2.00
	Joe Hoerner			
	George Kernek			
	Jimmy Williams			
□ 545	Dick Green SP	20.00	8.00	2.00
□ 546	Dwight Siebler	12.00	5.00	1.20
□ 547	Horace Clarke SP	30.00	12.00	3.00
□ 548	Gary Kroll SP	20.00	8.00	2.00
□ 549	Senators Rookies	12.00	5.00	1.20
	Al Closter			
	Casey Cox			
□ 550	Willie McCovey	90.00	36.00	9.00
□ 551	Bob Purkey SP	20.00	8.00	2.00
□ 552	Birdie Tebbetts MG	12.00	5.00	1.20

□ 553	Rookie Stars	12.00	5.00	1.20
	Pat Garrett			
	Jackie Warner			
□ 554	Jim Northrup	14.00	5.75	1.40
□ 555	Ron Perranoski SP	20.00	8.00	2.00
□ 556	Mel Queen SP	20.00	8.00	2.00
□ 557	Felix Mantilla	12.00	5.00	1.20
□ 558	Red Sox Rookies	16.00	6.50	1.60
	Guido Grilli			
	Pete Magrini			
	George Scott			
□ 559	Roberto Pena	12.00	5.00	1.20
□ 560	Joel Horlen	12.00	5.00	1.20
□			12.00	3.00
□ 562	Russ Snyder	12.00	5.00	1.20
□ 563	Twins Rookies	12.00	5.00	1.20
	Pete Cimino			
	Cesar Tovar			
□ 564	Bob Chance SP	20.00	8.00	2.00
□ 565	Jimmy Piersall SP	25.00	10.00	2.50
□ 566	Mike Cuellar SP	25.00	10.00	2.50
□ 567	Dick Howser SP	25.00	10.00	2.50
□ 568	Athletics Rookies	12.00	5.00	1.20
	Paul Lindblad			
	Rod Stone			
□ 569	Orlando McFarlane SP	20.00	8.00	2.00
□ 570	Art Mahaffey SP	20.00	8.00	2.00
□ 571	Dave Roberts SP	20.00	8.00	2.00
□ 572	Bob Priddy	12.00	5.00	1.20
□ 573	Derrell Griffith	12.00	5.00	1.20
□ 574	Mets Rookies	12.00	5.00	1.20
	Bill Hepler			
	Bill Murphy			
□ 575	Earl Wilson	12.00	5.00	1.20
□ 576	Dave Nicholson	12.00	5.00	1.20
□ 577	Jack Lamabe SP	20.00	8.00	2.00
□ 578	Chi Chi Olivo SP	20.00	8.00	2.00
□ 579	Orioles Rookies	16.00	6.50	1.60
	Frank Bertaina			
	Gene Brabender			
	Dave Johnson			
□ 580	Billy Williams	50.00	20.00	5.00
□ 581	Tony Martinez	12.00	5.00	1.20
□ 582	Garry Roggenburk	12.00	5.00	1.20
□ 583	Tigers Team SP	75.00	30.00	7.50
□ 584	Yankees Rookies	12.00	5.00	1.20
	Frank Fernandez			
	Fritz Peterson			
□ 585	Tony Taylor	12.00	5.00	1.20
□ 586	Claude Raymond	12.00	5.00	1.20
□ 587	Dick Bertell	12.00	5.00	1.20
□ 588	Athletics Rookies	12.00	5.00	1.20
	Chuck Dobson			
	Ken Suarez			
□ 589	Lou Klimchock	12.00	5.00	1.20
□ 590	Bill Skowron SP	35.00	14.00	3.50
□ 591	NL Rookies SP	20.00	8.00	2.00
	Bart Shirley			
	Grant Jackson			
□ 592	Andre Rodgers	12.00	5.00	1.20
□ 593	Doug Camilli SP	20.00	8.00	2.00
□ 594	Chico Salmon	12.00	5.00	1.20
□ 595	Larry Jackson	12.00	5.00	1.20
□ 596	Astros Rookies SP	20.00	8.00	2.00
	Nate Colbert			
	Greg Sims			
□ 597	John Sullivan	12.00	5.00	1.20
□ 598	Gaylord Perry SP	200.00	50.00	10.00

1967 Topps

The cards in this 609-card set measure 2 1/2" by 3 1/2". The 1967 Topps series is considered by some collectors to be one of the company's finest accomplishments in baseball card production. Excellent color photographs are combined with easy- to-read backs. Cards 458 to 533 are slightly harder to find than numbers 1 to 457, and the inevitable (difficult to find) high series (534 to 609) exists. Each checklist card features a small circular picture of a popular player included in that series. Printing discrepancies resulted in some high series cards being in short supply. Featured subsets within this set include World Series cards (151-155) and League Leaders (233-244). Although there are

several relatively expensive cards in this popular set, the key cards in the set are undoubtedly the Tom Seaver rookie card (581) and the Rod Carew rookie card (569).

	NRMT	VG-E	GOOD
COMPLETE SET	2800.00	1250.00	400.00
COMMON PLAYER (1-110)	.45	.18	.04
COMMON PLAYER (111-370)	.60	.24	.06
COMMON PLAYER (371-457)	.85	.34	.08
COMMON PLAYER (458-533)	2.50	1.00	.25
COMMON PLAYER (534-609)	6.00	2.40	.60

	No.	Player	NRMT	VG-E	GOOD
□	1	The Champs	8.00	2.00	.40
		Frank Robinson			
		Hank Bauer			
		Brooks Robinson			
□	2	Jack Hamilton	.45	.18	.04
□	3	Duke Sims	.45	.18	.04
□	4	Hal Lanier	.75	.30	.07
□	5	Whitey Ford UER	10.00	4.00	1.00
		(1953 listed as			
		1933 in stats on back)			
□	6	Dick Simpson	.45	.18	.04
□	7	Don McMahon	.45	.18	.04
□	8	Chuck Harrison	.45	.18	.04
□	9	Ron Hansen	.45	.18	.04
□	10	Matty Alou	.75	.30	.07
□	11	Barry Moore	.45	.18	.04
□	12	Dodgers Rookies	.75	.30	.07
		Jim Campanis			
		Bill Singer			
□	13	Joe Sparma	.45	.18	.04
□	14	Phil Linz	.75	.30	.07
□	15	Earl Battey	.45	.18	.04
□	16	Bill Hands	.45	.18	.04
□	17	Jim Gosger	.45	.18	.04
□	18	Gene Oliver	.45	.18	.04
□	19	Jim McGlothlin	.45	.18	.04
□	20	Orlando Cepeda	4.00	1.60	.40
□	21	Dave Bristol MG	.45	.18	.04
□	22	Gene Brabender	.45	.18	.04
□	23	Larry Elliot	.45	.18	.04
□	24	Bob Allen	.45	.18	.04
□	25	Elston Howard	2.00	.80	.20
□	26A	Bob Priddy	.45	.18	.04
		(with traded line)			
□	26B	Bob Priddy	25.00	10.00	2.50
		(no traded line)			
□	27	Bob Saverine	.45	.18	.04
□	28	Barry Latman	.45	.18	.04
□	29	Tommy McCraw	.45	.18	.04
□	30	Al Kaline	10.00	4.00	1.00
□	31	Jim Brewer	.45	.18	.04
□	32	Bob Bailey	.45	.18	.04
□	33	Athletic Rookies	1.50	.60	.15
		Sal Bando			
		Randy Schwartz			
□	34	Pete Cimino	.45	.18	.04
□	35	Rico Carty	.75	.30	.07
□	36	Bob Tillman	.45	.18	.04
□	37	Rick Wise	.75	.30	.07
□	38	Bob Johnson	.45	.18	.04
□	39	Curt Simmons	.75	.30	.07
□	40	Rick Reichardt	.45	.18	.04
□	41	Joe Hoerner	.45	.18	.04
□	42	Mets Team	1.50	.60	.15
□	43	Chico Salmon	.45	.18	.04
□	44	Joe Nuxhall	.75	.30	.07
□	45	Roger Maris	22.00	9.00	2.20
□	46	Lindy McDaniel	.75	.30	.07
□	47	Ken McMullen	.45	.18	.04
□	48	Bill Freehan	1.00	.40	.10
□	49	Roy Face	.75	.30	.07
□	50	Tony Oliva	2.50	1.00	.25
□	51	Astros Rookies	.45	.18	.04
		Dave Adlesh			
		Wes Bales			
□	52	Dennis Higgins	.45	.18	.04
□	53	Clay Dalrymple	.45	.18	.04
□	54	Dick Green	.45	.18	.04
□	55	Don Drysdale	7.50	3.00	.75
□	56	Jose Tartabull	.45	.18	.04
□	57	Pat Jarvis	.45	.18	.04
□	58	Paul Schaal	.45	.18	.04
□	59	Ralph Terry	.75	.30	.07
□	60	Luis Aparicio	5.50	2.20	.55
□	61	Gordy Coleman	.45	.18	.04
□	62	Checklist 1	2.50	.25	.05
		Frank Robinson			
□	63	Cards' Clubbers	4.50	1.80	.45
		Lou Brock			
		Curt Flood			
□	64	Fred Valentine	.45	.18	.04
□	65	Tom Haller	.75	.30	.07
□	66	Manny Mota	.75	.30	.07
□	67	Ken Berry	.45	.18	.04
□	68	Bob Buhl	.45	.18	.04
□	69	Vic Davalillo	.45	.18	.04
□	70	Ron Santo	1.00	.40	.10
□	71	Camilo Pascual	.75	.30	.07
□	72	Tigers Rookies	.75	.30	.07
		George Korince			
		(Photo actually			
		James Murray Brown)			
		John (Tom) Matchick			
□	73	Rusty Staub	1.50	.60	.15
□	74	Wes Stock	.45	.18	.04
□	75	George Scott	.75	.30	.07
□	76	Jim Barbieri	.45	.18	.04
□	77	Dooley Womack	.45	.18	.04
□	78	Pat Corrales	.75	.30	.07
□	79	Bubba Morton	.45	.18	.04
□	80	Jim Maloney	.75	.30	.07
□	81	Eddie Stanky MG	.75	.30	.07
□	82	Steve Barber	.45	.18	.04
□	83	Ollie Brown	.45	.18	.04
□	84	Tommie Sisk	.45	.18	.04
□	85	Johnny Callison	.75	.30	.07
□	86A	Mike McCormick	.75	.30	.07
		(with traded line)			
□	86B	Mike McCormick	25.00	10.00	2.50
		(no traded line)			
□	87	George Altman	.45	.18	.04
□	88	Mickey Lolich	1.50	.60	.15
□	89	Felix Millan	.45	.18	.04
□	90	Jim Nash	.45	.18	.04
□	91	Johnny Lewis	.45	.18	.04
□	92	Ray Washburn	.45	.18	.04
□	93	Yankees Rookies	2.50	1.00	.25
		Stan Bahnsen			
		Bobby Murcer			
□	94	Ron Fairly	.75	.30	.07
□	95	Sonny Siebert	.75	.30	.07
□	96	Art Shamsky	.45	.18	.04
□	97	Mike Cuellar	.75	.30	.07
□	98	Rich Rollins	.75	.30	.07
□	99	Lee Stange	.45	.18	.04
□	100	Frank Robinson	9.00	3.75	.90
□	101	Ken Johnson	.45	.18	.04
□	102	Philadelphia Phillies	1.00	.40	.10
		Team Card			
□	103	Checklist 2	5.00	1.00	.20
		Mickey Mantle			
□	104	Minnie Rojas	.45	.18	.04
□	105	Ken Boyer	1.50	.60	.15
□	106	Randy Hundley	.45	.18	.04
□	107	Joel Horlen	.45	.18	.04
□	108	Alex Johnson	.75	.30	.07
□	109	Tribe Thumpers	1.00	.40	.10
		Rocky Colavito			
		Leon Wagner			
□	110	Jack Aker	.45	.18	.04
□	111	John Kennedy	.60	.24	.06
□	112	Dave Wickersham	.60	.24	.06
□	113	Dave Nicholson	.60	.24	.06
□	114	Jack Baldschun	.60	.24	.06
□	115	Paul Casanova	.60	.24	.06
□	116	Herman Franks MG	.60	.24	.06
□	117	Darrell Brandon	.60	.24	.06
□	118	Bernie Allen	.60	.24	.06
□	119	Wade Blasingame	.60	.24	.06
□	120	Floyd Robinson	.60	.24	.06
□	121	Eddie Bressoud	.60	.24	.06
□	122	George Brunet	.60	.24	.06
□	123	Pirates Rookies	.75	.30	.07
		Jim Price			
		Luke Walker			

Card	Player			
□ 124	Jim Stewart	.60	.24	.06
□ 125	Moe Drabowsky	.60	.24	.06
□ 126	Tony Taylor	.60	.24	.06
□ 127	John O'Donoghue	.60	.24	.06
□ 128	Ed Spiezio	.60	.24	.06
□ 129	Phil Roof	.60	.24	.06
□ 130	Phil Regan	.75	.30	.07
□ 131	Yankees Team	3.00	1.20	.30
□ 132	Ozzie Virgil	.60	.24	.06
□ 133	Ron Kline	.60	.24	.06
□ 134	Gates Brown	.75	.30	.07
□ 135	Deron Johnson	.75	.30	.07
□ 136	Carroll Sembera	.60	.24	.06
□ 137	Twins Rookies	.60	.24	.06
	Ron Clark			
	Jim Ollum			
□ 138	Dick Kelley	.60	.24	.06
□ 139	Dalton Jones	.60	.24	.06
□ 140	Willie Stargell	11.00	4.50	1.10
□ 141	John Miller	.60	.24	.06
□ 142	Jackie Brandt	.60	.24	.06
□ 143	Sox Sockers	.75	.30	.07
	Pete Ward			
	Don Buford			
□ 144	Bill Hepler	.60	.24	.06
□ 145	Larry Brown	.60	.24	.06
□ 146	Steve Carlton	50.00	20.00	5.00
□ 147	Tom Egan	.60	.24	.06
□ 148	Adolfo Phillips	.60	.24	.06
□ 149	Joe Moeller	.60	.24	.06
□ 150	Mickey Mantle	200.00	80.00	20.00
□ 151	World Series Game 1	1.75	.70	.17
	Moe mows down 11			
□ 152	World Series Game 2	3.50	1.40	.35
	Palmer blanks Dodgers			
□ 153	World Series Game 3	1.75	.70	.17
	Blair's homer			
	defeats L.A.			
□ 154	World Series Game 4	1.75	.70	.17
	Orioles 4 straight			
□ 155	World Series Summary	1.75	.70	.17
	Winners celebrate			
□ 156	Ron Herbel	.60	.24	.06
□ 157	Danny Cater	.60	.24	.06
□ 158	Jimmie Coker	.60	.24	.06
□ 159	Bruce Howard	.60	.24	.06
□ 160	Willie Davis	1.00	.40	.10
□ 161	Dick Williams MG	.75	.30	.07
□ 162	Billy O'Dell	.60	.24	.06
□ 163	Vic Roznovsky	.60	.24	.06
□ 164	Dwight Siebler	.60	.24	.06
□ 165	Cleon Jones	.60	.24	.06
□ 166	Eddie Mathews	8.00	3.25	.80
□ 167	Senators Rookies	.60	.24	.06
	Joe Coleman			
	Tim Cullen			
□ 168	Ray Culp	.60	.24	.06
□ 169	Horace Clarke	.75	.30	.07
□ 170	Dick McAuliffe	.75	.30	.07
□ 171	Cal Koonce	.60	.24	.06
□ 172	Bill Heath	.60	.24	.06
□ 173	St. Louis Cardinals	1.25	.50	.12
	Team Card			
□ 174	Dick Radatz	.75	.30	.07
□ 175	Bobby Knoop	.60	.24	.06
□ 176	Sammy Ellis	.60	.24	.06
□ 177	Tito Fuentes	.60	.24	.06
□ 178	John Buzhardt	.60	.24	.06
□ 179	Braves Rookies	.60	.24	.06
	Charles Vaughan			
	Cecil Upshaw			
□ 180	Curt Blefary	.75	.30	.07
□ 181	Terry Fox	.60	.24	.06
□ 182	Ed Charles	.60	.24	.06
□ 183	Jim Pagliaroni	.60	.24	.06
□ 184	George Thomas	.60	.24	.06
□ 185	Ken Holtzman	1.50	.60	.15
□ 186	Mets Maulers	1.00	.40	.10
	Ed Kranepool			
	Ron Swoboda			
□ 187	Pedro Ramos	.60	.24	.06
□ 188	Ken Harrelson	1.25	.50	.12
□ 189	Chuck Hinton	.60	.24	.06
□ 190	Turk Farrell	.60	.24	.06
□ 191A	Checklist 3	3.00	.30	.06
	(214 Tom Kelley)			
	(Willie Mays)			
□ 191B	Checklist 3	6.00	.60	.12
	(214 Dick Kelley)			
	(Willie Mays)			
□ 192	Fred Gladding	.60	.24	.06
□ 193	Jose Cardenal	.60	.24	.06
□ 194	Bob Allison	.75	.30	.07
□ 195	Al Jackson	.60	.24	.06
□ 196	Johnny Romano	.60	.24	.06

□ 197	Ron Perranoski	.75	.30	.07
□ 198	Chuck Hiller	.60	.24	.06
□ 199	Billy Hitchcock MG	.60	.24	.06
□ 200	Willie Mays	45.00	18.00	4.50
□ 201	Hal Reniff	.60	.24	.06
□ 202	Johnny Edwards	.60	.24	.06
□ 203	Al McBean	.60	.24	.06
□ 204	Orioles Rookies	.75	.30	.07
	Mike Epstein			
	Tom Phoebus			
□ 205	Dick Groat	1.00	.40	.10
□ 206	Dennis Bennett	.60	.24	.06
□ 207	John Orsino	.60	.24	.06
□ 208	Jack Lamabe	.60	.24	.06
□ 209	Joe Nossek	.60	.24	.06
□ 210	Bob Gibson	9.00	3.75	.90
□ 211	Twins Team	1.25	.50	.12
□ 212	Chris Zachary	.60	.24	.06
□ 213	Jay Johnstone	1.00	.40	.10
□ 214	Dick Kelley	.60	.24	.06
□ 215	Ernie Banks	9.00	3.75	.90
□ 216	Bengal Belters	3.50	1.40	.35
	Norm Cash			
	Al Kaline			
□ 217	Rob Gardner	.60	.24	.06
□ 218	Wes Parker	.75	.30	.07
□ 219	Clay Carroll	.60	.24	.06
□ 220	Jim Ray Hart	.75	.30	.07
□ 221	Woodie Fryman	.75	.30	.07
□ 222	Reds Rookies	1.00	.40	.10
	Darrell Osteen			
	Lee May			
□ 223	Mike Ryan	.60	.24	.06
□ 224	Walt Bond	.60	.24	.06
□ 225	Mel Stottlemyre	1.50	.60	.15
□ 226	Julian Javier	.75	.30	.07
□ 227	Paul Lindblad	.60	.24	.06
□ 228	Gil Hodges MG	4.00	1.60	.40
□ 229	Larry Jackson	.60	.24	.06
□ 230	Boog Powell	1.75	.70	.17
□ 231	John Bateman	.60	.24	.06
□ 232	Don Buford	.75	.30	.07
□ 233	AL ERA Leaders	1.50	.60	.15
	Gary Peters			
	Joel Horlen			
	Steve Hargan			
□ 234	NL ERA Leaders	4.00	1.60	.40
	Sandy Koufax			
	Mike Cuellar			
	Juan Marichal			
□ 235	AL Pitching Leaders	1.50	.60	.15
	Jim Kaat			
	Denny McLain			
	Earl Wilson			
□ 236	NL Pitching Leaders	8.00	3.25	.80
	Sandy Koufax			
	Juan Marichal			
	Bob Gibson			
	Gaylord Perry			
□ 237	AL Strikeout Leaders	1.50	.60	.15
	Sam McDowell			
	Jim Kaat			
	Earl Wilson			
□ 238	NL Strikeout Leaders	2.50	1.00	.25
	Sandy Koufax			
	Jim Bunning			
	Bob Veale			
□ 239	AL Batting Leaders	3.50	1.40	.35
	Frank Robinson			
	Tony Oliva			
	Al Kaline			
□ 240	NL Batting Leaders	1.50	.60	.15
	Matty Alou			
	Felipe Alou			
	Rico Carty			
□ 241	AL RBI Leaders	2.50	1.00	.25
	Frank Robinson			
	Harmon Killebrew			
	Boog Powell			
□ 242	NL RBI Leaders	4.00	1.60	.40
	Hank Aaron			
	Bob Clemente			
	Richie Allen			
□ 243	AL Home Run Leaders	2.50	1.00	.25
	Frank Robinson			
	Harmon Killebrew			
	Boog Powell			
□ 244	NL Home Run Leaders	4.00	1.60	.40
	Hank Aaron			
	Richie Allen			
	Willie Mays			
□ 245	Curt Flood	1.25	.50	.12
□ 246	Jim Perry	.75	.30	.07
□ 247	Jerry Lumpe	.60	.24	.06
□ 248	Gene Mauch MG	.75	.30	.07

□ 249 Nick Willhite	.60	.24	.06
□ 250 Hank Aaron	45.00	18.00	4.50
□ 251 Woody Held	.60	.24	.06
□ 252 Bob Bolin	.60	.24	.06
□ 253 Indians Rookies	.60	.24	.06
Bill Davis			
Gus Gil			
□ 254 Milt Pappas	.75	.30	.07
□ 255 Frank Howard	1.25	.50	.12
□ 256 Bob Hendley	.60	.24	.06
□ 257 Charlie Smith	.60	.24	.06
□ 258 Lee Maye	.60	.24	.06
□ 259 Don Dennis	.60	.24	.06
□ 260 Jim Lefebvre	1.00	.40	.10
□ 261 John Wyatt	.60	.24	.06
□ 262 Athletics Team	1.25	.50	.12
□ 263 Hank Aguirre	.60	.24	.06
□ 264 Ron Swoboda	.75	.30	.07
□ 265 Lou Burdette	1.25	.50	.12
□ 266 Pitt Power	3.50	1.40	.35
Willie Stargell			
Donn Clendenon			
□ 267 Don Schwall	.60	.24	.06
□ 268 Johnny Briggs	.60	.24	.06
□ 269 Don Nottebart	.60	.24	.06
□ 270 Zoilo Versalles	.60	.24	.06
□ 271 Eddie Watt	.60	.24	.06
□ 272 Cubs Rookies	.60	.24	.06
Bill Connors			
Dave Dowling			
□ 273 Dick Lines	.60	.24	.06
□ 274 Bob Aspromonte	.60	.24	.06
□ 275 Fred Whitfield	.60	.24	.06
□ 276 Bruce Brubaker	.60	.24	.06
□ 277 Steve Whitaker	.60	.24	.06
□ 278 Checklist 4	2.50	.25	.05
Jim Kaat			
□ 279 Frank Linzy	.60	.24	.06
□ 280 Tony Conigliaro	2.50	1.00	.25
□ 281 Bob Rodgers	1.00	.40	.10
□ 282 John Odom	.60	.24	.06
□ 283 Gene Alley	.75	.30	.07
□ 284 Johnny Podres	1.25	.50	.12
□ 285 Lou Brock	11.00	4.50	1.10
□ 286 Wayne Causey	.60	.24	.06
□ 287 Mets Rookies	.60	.24	.06
Greg Goossen			
Bart Shirley			
□ 288 Denny Lemaster	.60	.24	.06
□ 289 Tom Tresh	1.25	.50	.12
□ 290 Bill White	1.00	.40	.10
□ 291 Jim Hannan	.60	.24	.06
□ 292 Don Pavletich	.60	.24	.06
□ 293 Ed Kirkpatrick	.60	.24	.06
□ 294 Walt Alston MG	2.50	1.00	.25
□ 295 Sam McDowell	1.00	.40	.10
□ 296 Glenn Beckert	.75	.30	.07
□ 297 Dave Morehead	.60	.24	.06
□ 298 Ron Davis	.60	.24	.06
□ 299 Norm Siebern	.60	.24	.06
□ 300 Jim Kaat	3.00	1.20	.30
□ 301 Jesse Gonder	.60	.24	.06
□ 302 Orioles Team	1.25	.50	.12
□ 303 Gil Blanco	.60	.24	.06
□ 304 Phil Gagliano	.60	.24	.06
□ 305 Earl Wilson	.60	.24	.06
□ 306 Bud Harrelson	.75	.30	.07
□ 307 Jim Beauchamp	.60	.24	.06
□ 308 Al Downing	.75	.30	.07
□ 309 Hurlers Beware	1.00	.40	.10
Johnny Callison			
Richie Allen			
□ 310 Gary Peters	.75	.30	.07
□ 311 Ed Brinkman	.60	.24	.06
□ 312 Don Mincher	.75	.30	.07
□ 313 Bob Lee	.60	.24	.06
□ 314 Red Sox Rookies	3.00	1.20	.30
Mike Andrews			
Reggie Smith			
□ 315 Billy Williams	6.00	2.40	.60
□ 316 Jack Kralick	.60	.24	.06
□ 317 Cesar Tovar	.60	.24	.06
□ 318 Dave Giusti	.60	.24	.06
□ 319 Paul Blair	.75	.30	.07
□ 320 Gaylord Perry	6.00	2.40	.60
□ 321 Mayo Smith MG	.60	.24	.06
□ 322 Jose Pagan	.60	.24	.06
□ 323 Mike Hershberger	.60	.24	.06
□ 324 Hal Woodeshick	.60	.24	.06
□ 325 Chico Cardenas	.60	.24	.06
□ 326 Bob Uecker	15.00	6.00	1.50
□ 327 California Angels	1.25	.50	.12
Team Card			
□ 328 Clete Boyer	1.00	.40	.10
□ 329 Charlie Lau	.75	.30	.07
□ 330 Claude Osteen	.75	.30	.07
□ 331 Joe Foy	.60	.24	.06
□ 332 Jesus Alou	.60	.24	.06
□ 333 Fergie Jenkins	5.00	2.00	.50
□ 334 Twin Terrors	3.00	1.20	.30
Bob Allison			
Harmon Killebrew			
□ 335 Bob Veale	.75	.30	.07
□ 336 Joe Azcue	.60	.24	.06
□ 337 Joe Morgan	6.50	2.60	.65
□ 338 Bob Locker	.60	.24	.06
□ 339 Chico Ruiz	.60	.24	.06
□ 340 Joe Pepitone	1.25	.50	.12
□ 341 Giants Rookies	.60	.24	.06
Dick Dietz			
Bill Sorrell			
□ 342 Hank Fischer	.60	.24	.06
□ 343 Tom Satriano	.60	.24	.06
□ 344 Ossie Chavarria	.60	.24	.06
□ 345 Stu Miller	.60	.24	.06
□ 346 Jim Hickman	.60	.24	.06
□ 347 Grady Hatton MG	.60	.24	.06
□ 348 Tug McGraw	1.25	.50	.12
□ 349 Bob Chance	.60	.24	.06
□ 350 Joe Torre	1.50	.60	.15
□ 351 Vern Law	.75	.30	.07
□ 352 Ray Oyler	.60	.24	.06
□ 353 Bill McCool	.60	.24	.06
□ 354 Cubs Team	1.25	.50	.12
□ 355 Carl Yastrzemski	80.00	32.00	8.00
□ 356 Larry Jaster	.60	.24	.06
□ 357 Bill Skowron	1.00	.40	.10
□ 358 Ruben Amaro	.60	.24	.06
□ 359 Dick Ellsworth	.75	.30	.07
□ 360 Leon Wagner	.60	.24	.06
□ 361 Checklist 5	3.00	.30	.06
Roberto Clemente			
□ 362 Darold Knowles	.60	.24	.06
□ 363 Dave Johnson	1.75	.70	.17
□ 364 Claude Raymond	.60	.24	.06
□ 365 John Roseboro	.75	.30	.07
□ 366 Andy Kosco	.60	.24	.06
□ 367 Angels Rookies	.60	.24	.06
Bill Kelso			
Don Wallace			
□ 368 Jack Hiatt	.60	.24	.06
□ 369 Jim Hunter	8.00	3.25	.80
□ 370 Tommy Davis	1.00	.40	.10
□ 371 Jim Lonborg	1.75	.70	.17
□ 372 Mike De La Hoz	.85	.34	.08
□ 373 White Sox Rookies	.85	.34	.08
Duane Josephson			
Fred Klages			
□ 374 Mel Queen	.85	.34	.08
□ 375 Jake Gibbs	1.00	.40	.10
□ 376 Don Lock	.85	.34	.08
□ 377 Luis Tiant	2.00	.80	.20
□ 378 Detroit Tigers	1.75	.70	.17
Team Card			
□ 379 Jerry May	.85	.34	.08
□ 380 Dean Chance	1.00	.40	.10
□ 381 Dick Schofield	.85	.34	.08
□ 382 Dave McNally	1.25	.50	.12
□ 383 Ken Henderson	.85	.34	.08
□ 384 Cardinals Rookies	.85	.34	.08
Jim Cosman			
Dick Hughes			
□ 385 Jim Fregosi	1.50	.60	.15
(batting wrong)			
□ 386 Dick Selma	.85	.34	.08
□ 387 Cap Peterson	.85	.34	.08
□ 388 Arnold Earley	.85	.34	.08
□ 389 Al Dark MG	1.25	.50	.12
□ 390 Jim Wynn	1.25	.50	.12
□ 391 Wilbur Wood	1.00	.40	.10
□ 392 Tommy Harper	1.00	.40	.10
□ 393 Jim Bouton	1.75	.70	.17
□ 394 Jake Wood	.85	.34	.08
□ 395 Chris Short	.85	.34	.08
□ 396 Atlanta Aces	1.00	.40	.10
Denis Menke			
Tony Cloninger			
□ 397 Willie Smith	.85	.34	.08
□ 398 Jeff Torborg	1.25	.50	.12
□ 399 Al Worthington	.85	.34	.08
□ 400 Bob Clemente	35.00	14.00	3.50
□ 401 Jim Coates	.85	.34	.08
□ 402 Phillies Rookies	1.00	.40	.10
Grant Jackson			
Billy Wilson			
□ 403 Dick Nen	.85	.34	.08
□ 404 Nelson Briles	1.00	.40	.10
□ 405 Russ Snyder	.85	.34	.08
□ 406 Lee Elia	1.50	.60	.15
□ 407 Reds Team	1.75	.70	.17

□ 408	Jim Northrup	1.00	.40	.10
□ 409	Ray Sadecki	.85	.34	.08
□ 410	Lou Johnson	.85	.34	.08
□ 411	Dick Howser	1.50	.60	.15
□ 412	Astros Rookies	1.75	.70	.17
	Norm Miller			
	Doug Rader			
□ 413	Jerry Grote	.85	.34	.08
□ 414	Casey Cox	.85	.34	.08
□ 415	Sonny Jackson	.85	.34	.08
□ 416	Roger Repoz	.85	.34	.08
□ 417	Bob Bruce	.85	.34	.08
□ 418	Sam Mele MG	.85	.34	.08
□ 419	Don Kessinger	1.25	.50	.12
□ 420	Denny McLain	2.50	1.00	.25
□ 421	Dal Maxvill	1.00	.40	.10
□ 422	Hoyt Wilhelm	6.50	2.60	.65
□ 423	Fence Busters	10.00	4.00	1.00
	Willie Mays			
	Willie McCovey			
□ 424	Pedro Gonzales	.85	.34	.08
□ 425	Pete Mikkelsen	.85	.34	.08
□ 426	Lou Clinton	.85	.34	.08
□ 427	Ruben Gomez	.85	.34	.08
□ 428	Dodgers Rookies	1.25	.50	.12
	Tom Hutton			
	Gene Michael			
□ 429	Garry Roggenburk	.85	.34	.08
□ 430	Pete Rose	75.00	30.00	7.50
□ 431	Ted Uhlaender	.85	.34	.08
□ 432	Jimmie Hall	1.00	.40	.10
□ 433	Al Luplow	.85	.34	.08
□ 434	Eddie Fisher	.85	.34	.08
□ 435	Mack Jones	.85	.34	.08
□ 436	Pete Ward	.85	.34	.08
□ 437	Senators Team	1.75	.70	.17
□ 438	Chuck Dobson	.85	.34	.08
□ 439	Byron Browne	.85	.34	.08
□ 440	Steve Hargan	.85	.34	.08
□ 441	Jim Davenport	1.00	.40	.10
□ 442	Yankees Rookies	1.50	.60	.15
	Bill Robinson			
	Joe Verbanic			
□ 443	Tito Francona	1.00	.40	.10
□ 444	George Smith	.85	.34	.08
□ 445	Don Sutton	15.00	6.00	1.50
□ 446	Russ Nixon	1.25	.50	.12
□ 447	Bo Belinsky	1.25	.50	.12
□ 448	Harry Walker MG	.85	.34	.08
□ 449	Orlando Pena	.85	.34	.08
□ 450	Richie Allen	2.50	1.00	.25
□ 451	Fred Newman	.85	.34	.08
□ 452	Ed Kranepool	1.25	.50	.12
□ 453	Aurelio Monteagudo	.85	.34	.08
□ 454A	Checklist 6	3.50	.40	.10
	Juan Marichal			
	(missing left ear)			
□ 454B	Checklist 6	6.00	.60	.15
	Juan Marichal			
	(left ear showing)			
□ 455	Tommy Agee	1.00	.40	.10
□ 456	Phil Niekro	7.50	3.00	.75
□ 457	Andy Etchebarren	.85	.34	.08
□ 458	Lee Thomas	3.50	1.40	.35
□ 459	Senators Rookies	2.50	1.00	.25
	Dick Bosman			
	Pete Craig			
□ 460	Harmon Killebrew	20.00	8.00	2.00
□ 461	Bob Miller	2.50	1.00	.25
□ 462	Bob Barton	2.50	1.00	.25
□ 463	Hill Aces	3.50	1.40	.35
	Sam McDowell			
	Sonny Siebert			
□ 464	Dan Coombs	2.50	1.00	.25
□ 465	Willie Horton	3.50	1.40	.35
□ 466	Bobby Wine	2.50	1.00	.25
□ 467	Jim O'Toole	2.50	1.00	.25
□ 468	Ralph Houk MG	3.50	1.40	.35
□ 469	Len Gabrielson	2.50	1.00	.25
□ 470	Bob Shaw	2.50	1.00	.25
□ 471	Rene Lachemann	3.50	1.40	.35
□ 472	Rookies Pirates	2.50	1.00	.25
	John Gelnar			
	George Spriggs			
□ 473	Jose Santiago	2.50	1.00	.25
□ 474	Bob Tolan	2.50	1.00	.25
□ 475	Jim Palmer	35.00	14.00	3.50
□ 476	Tony Perez SP	35.00	14.00	3.50
□ 477	Braves Team	5.00	2.00	.50
□ 478	Bob Humphreys	2.50	1.00	.25
□ 479	Gary Bell	2.50	1.00	.25
□ 480	Willie McCovey	20.00	8.00	2.00
□ 481	Leo Durocher MG	5.00	2.00	.50
□ 482	Bill Monbouquette	2.50	1.00	.25
□ 483	Jim Landis	2.50	1.00	.25
□ 484	Jerry Adair	2.50	1.00	.25
□ 485	Tim McCarver	6.50	2.60	.65
□ 486	Twins Rookies	3.50	1.40	.35
	Rich Reese			
	Bill Whitby			
□ 487	Tommie Reynolds	2.50	1.00	.25
□ 488	Gerry Arrigo	2.50	1.00	.25
□ 489	Doug Clemens	2.50	1.00	.25
□ 490	Tony Cloninger	2.50	1.00	.25
□ 491	Sam Bowens	2.50	1.00	.25
□ 492	Pittsburgh Pirates	5.00	2.00	.50
	Team Card			
□ 493	Phil Ortega	2.50	1.00	.25
□ 494	Bill Rigney MG	2.50	1.00	.25
□ 495	Fritz Peterson	2.50	1.00	.25
□ 496	Orlando McFarlane	2.50	1.00	.25
□ 497	Ron Campbell	2.50	1.00	.25
□ 498	Larry Dierker	2.50	1.00	.25
□ 499	Indians Rookies	2.50	1.00	.25
	George Culver			
	Jose Vidal			
□ 500	Juan Marichal	12.50	5.00	1.25
□ 501	Jerry Zimmerman	2.50	1.00	.25
□ 502	Derrell Griffith	2.50	1.00	.25
□ 503	Los Angeles Dodgers	7.50	3.00	.75
	Team Card			
□ 504	Orlando Martinez	2.50	1.00	.25
□ 505	Tommy Helms	3.50	1.40	.35
□ 506	Smoky Burgess	3.50	1.40	.35
□ 507	Orioles Rookies	2.50	1.00	.25
	Ed Barnowski			
	Larry Haney			
□ 508	Dick Hall	2.50	1.00	.25
□ 509	Jim King	2.50	1.00	.25
□ 510	Bill Mazeroski	5.00	2.00	.50
□ 511	Don Wert	2.50	1.00	.25
□ 512	Red Schoendienst MG	5.00	2.00	.50
□ 513	Marcelino Lopez	2.50	1.00	.25
□ 514	John Werhas	2.50	1.00	.25
□ 515	Bert Campaneris	3.50	1.40	.35
□ 516	Giants Team	5.00	2.00	.50
□ 517	Fred Talbot	2.50	1.00	.25
□ 518	Denis Menke	2.50	1.00	.25
□ 519	Ted Davidson	2.50	1.00	.25
□ 520	Max Alvis	2.50	1.00	.25
□ 521	Bird Bombers	3.50	1.40	.35
	Boog Powell			
	Curt Blefary			
□ 522	John Stephenson	2.50	1.00	.25
□ 523	Jim Merritt	2.50	1.00	.25
□ 524	Felix Mantilla	2.50	1.00	.25
□ 525	Ron Hunt	2.50	1.00	.25
□ 526	Tigers Rookies	3.50	1.40	.35
	Pat Dobson			
	George Korince			
	(See 67T-72)			
□ 527	Dennis Ribant	2.50	1.00	.25
□ 528	Rico Petrocelli	3.50	1.40	.35
□ 529	Gary Wagner	2.50	1.00	.25
□ 530	Felipe Alou	3.50	1.40	.35
□ 531	Checklist 7	6.00	.60	.10
	Brooks Robinson			
□ 532	Jim Hicks	2.50	1.00	.25
□ 533	Jack Fisher	2.50	1.00	.25
□ 534	Hank Bauer MG	10.00	4.00	1.00
□ 535	Donn Clendenon SP	15.00	6.00	1.50
□ 536	Cubs Rookies	18.00	7.25	1.80
	Joe Niekro			
	Paul Popovich			
□ 537	Chuck Estrada	6.00	2.40	.60
□ 538	J.C. Martin	6.00	2.40	.60
□ 539	Dick Egan	6.00	2.40	.60
□ 540	Norm Cash SP	20.00	8.00	2.00
□ 541	Joe Gibbon	6.00	2.40	.60
□ 542	Athletics Rookies	10.00	4.00	1.00
	Rick Monday			
	Tony Pierce			
□ 543	Dan Schneider	6.00	2.40	.60
□ 544	Cleveland Indians	15.00	6.00	1.50
	Team Card			
□ 545	Jim Grant	6.00	2.40	.60
□ 546	Woody Woodward	6.00	2.40	.60
□ 547	Red Sox Rookies	6.00	2.40	.60
	Russ Gibson			
	Bill Rohr			
□ 548	Tony Gonzalez	6.00	2.40	.60
□ 549	Jack Sanford	6.00	2.40	.60
□ 550	Vada Pinson	10.00	4.00	1.00
□ 551	Doug Camilli	6.00	2.40	.60
□ 552	Ted Savage	6.00	2.40	.60
□ 553	Yankees Rookies SP	15.00	6.00	1.50
	Mike Hegan			
	Thad Tillotson			
□ 554	Andre Rodgers	6.00	2.40	.60
□ 555	Don Cardwell	6.00	2.40	.60

□ 556	Al Weis	6.00	2.40	.60
□ 557	Al Ferrara SP	15.00	6.00	1.50
□ 558	Orioles Rookies SP	20.00	8.00	2.00
	Mark Belanger			
	Bill Dillman			
□ 559	Dick Tracewski	6.00	2.40	.60
□ 560	Jim Bunning SP	35.00	14.00	3.50
□ 561	Sandy Alomar SP	15.00	6.00	1.50
□ 562	Steve Blass	6.00	2.40	.60
□ 563	Joe Adcock SP	15.00	6.00	1.50
□ 564	Astros Rookies	6.00	2.40	.60
	Alonzo Harris			
	Aaron Pointer			
□ 565	Lew Krausse	6.00	2.40	.60
□ 566	Gary Geiger	6.00	2.40	.60
□ 567	Steve Hamilton SP	15.00	6.00	1.50
□ 568	John Sullivan	6.00	2.40	.60
□ 569	AL Rookies	175.00	70.00	18.00
	Rod Carew			
	Hank Allen			
□ 570	Maury Wills SP	75.00	30.00	7.50
□ 571	Larry Sherry	6.00	2.40	.60
□ 572	Don Demeter SP	15.00	6.00	1.50
□ 573	Chicago White Sox	15.00	6.00	1.50
	Team Card			
□ 574	Jerry Buchek SP	15.00	6.00	1.50
□ 575	Dave Boswell	6.00	2.40	.60
□ 576	NL Rookies SP	15.00	6.00	1.50
	Ramon Hernandez			
	Norm Gigon			
□ 577	Bill Short	6.00	2.40	.60
□ 578	John Boccabella	6.00	2.40	.60
□ 579	Bill Henry	6.00	2.40	.60
□ 580	Rocky Colavito SP	25.00	10.00	2.50
□ 581	Mets Rookies SP	550.00	220.00	55.00
	Bill Denehy			
	Tom Seaver			
□ 582	Jim Owens	6.00	2.40	.60
□ 583	Ray Barker SP	15.00	6.00	1.50
□ 584	Jim Piersall SP	20.00	8.00	2.00
□ 585	Wally Bunker	6.00	2.40	.60
□ 586	Manny Jimenez SP	15.00	6.00	1.50
□ 587	NL Rookies SP	20.00	8.00	2.00
	Don Shaw			
	Gary Sutherland			
□ 588	Johnny Klippstein	6.00	2.40	.60
□ 589	Dave Ricketts	6.00	2.40	.60
□ 590	Pete Richert	6.00	2.40	.60
□ 591	Ty Cline	6.00	2.40	.60
□ 592	NL Rookies SP	15.00	6.00	1.50
	Jim Shellenback			
	Ron Willis			
□ 593	Wes Westrum MG	6.00	2.40	.60
□ 594	Dan Osinski	6.00	2.40	.60
□ 595	Cookie Rojas SP	15.00	6.00	1.50
□ 596	Galen Cisco	6.00	2.40	.60
□ 597	Ted Abernathy	6.00	2.40	.60
□ 598	White Sox Rookies SP	15.00	6.00	1.50
	Walt Williams			
	Ed Stroud			
□ 599	Bob Duliba	6.00	2.40	.60
□ 600	Brooks Robinson SP	180.00	75.00	18.00
□ 601	Bill Bryan	6.00	2.40	.60
□ 602	Juan Pizarro	6.00	2.40	.60
□ 603	Athletics Rookies	6.00	2.40	.60
	Tim Talton			
	Ramon Webster			
□ 604	Red Sox Team SP	50.00	20.00	5.00
□ 605	Mike Shannon SP	20.00	8.00	2.00
□ 606	Ron Taylor	6.00	2.40	.60
□ 607	Mickey Stanley SP	20.00	8.00	2.00
□ 608	Cubs Rookies	6.00	2.40	.60
	Rich Nye			
	John Upham			
□ 609	Tommy John SP	80.00	32.00	8.00

1968 Topps

The cards in this 598-card set measure 2 1/2" by 3 1/2". The 1968 Topps set includes Sporting News All-Star Selections as card numbers 361 to 380. Other subsets in the set include League Leaders (1-12) and World Series cards (151-158). The front of each checklist card features a picture of a popular player inside a circle. High numbers 534 to 598 are slightly more difficult to obtain. The first series looks different from the other series as it has a lighter, wider mesh background on the card front. The later series all had a much darker, finer mesh pattern. Key cards in the set are the rookie cards of Johnny Bench (247) and Nolan Ryan (177).

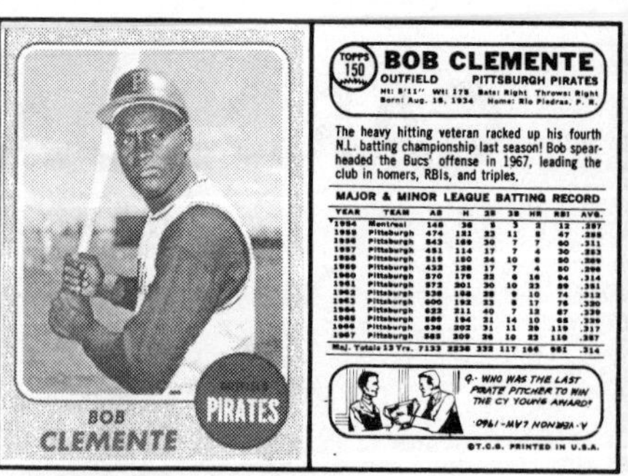

	NRMT	VG-E	GOOD
COMPLETE SET (598)	1350.00	550.00	175.00
COMMON PLAYER (1-110)	.50	.20	.05
COMMON PLAYER (111-457)	.40	.16	.04
COMMON PLAYER (458-533)	.65	.26	.06
COMMON PLAYER (534-598)	.70	.28	.07

□ 1	NL Batting Leaders	6.00	1.00	.20
	Bob Clemente			
	Tony Gonzales			
	Matty Alou			
□ 2	AL Batting Leaders	5.00	2.00	.45
	Carl Yastrzemski			
	Frank Robinson			
	Al Kaline			
□ 3	NL RBI Leaders	3.50	1.50	.30
	Orlando Cepeda			
	Bob Clemente			
	Hank Aaron			
□ 4	AL RBI Leaders	5.00	2.00	.45
	Carl Yastrzemski			
	Harmon Killebrew			
	Frank Robinson			
□ 5	NL Home Run Leaders	2.50	1.00	.25
	Hank Aaron			
	Jim Wynn			
	Ron Santo			
	Willie McCovey			
□ 6	NL Home Run Leaders	3.50	1.40	.35
	Carl Yastrzemski			
	Harmon Killebrew			
	Frank Howard			
□ 7	NL ERA Leaders	1.25	.50	.12
	Phil Niekro			
	Jim Bunning			
	Chris Short			
□ 8	AL ERA Leaders	1.00	.40	.10
	Joel Horlen			
	Gary Peters			
	Sonny Siebert			
□ 9	NL Pitching Leaders	1.25	.50	.12
	Mike McCormick			
	Ferguson Jenkins			
	Jim Bunning			
	Claude Osteen			
□ 10	AL Pitching Leaders	1.00	.40	.10
	Jim Lonborg			
	Earl Wilson			
	Dean Chance			
□ 11	NL Strikeout Leaders	1.50	.60	.15
	Jim Bunning			
	Ferguson Jenkins			
	Gaylord Perry			
□ 12	AL Strikeout Leaders	1.00	.40	.10
	Jim Lonborg			
	Sam McDowell			
	Dean Chance			
□ 13	Chuck Hartenstein	.50	.20	.05
□ 14	Jerry McNertney	.50	.20	.05
□ 15	Ron Hunt	.50	.20	.05
□ 16	Indians Rookies	2.00	.80	.20
	Lou Piniella			
	Richie Scheinblum			
□ 17	Dick Hall	.50	.20	.05
□ 18	Mike Hershberger	.50	.20	.05
□ 19	Juan Pizarro	.50	.20	.05
□ 20	Brooks Robinson	9.00	3.75	.90
□ 21	Ron Davis	.50	.20	.05

☐ 22	Pat Dobson	.60	.24	.06
☐ 23	Chico Cardenas	.50	.20	.05
☐ 24	Bobby Locke	.50	.20	.05
☐ 25	Julian Javier	.60	.24	.06
☐ 26	Darrell Brandon	.50	.20	.05
☐ 27	Gil Hodges MG	3.50	1.40	.35
☐ 28	Ted Uhlaender	.50	.20	.05
☐ 29	Joe Verbanic	.50	.20	.05
☐ 30	Joe Torre	1.00	.40	.10
☐ 31	Ed Stroud	.50	.20	.05
☐ 32	Joe Gibbon	.50	.20	.05
☐ 33	Pete Ward	.50	.20	.05
☐ 34	Al Ferrara	.50	.20	.05
☐ 35	Steve Hargan	.50	.20	.05
☐ 36	Pirates Rookies Bob Moose Bob Robertson	.75	.30	.07
☐ 37	Billy Williams	5.50	2.20	.55
☐ 38	Tony Pierce	.50	.20	.05
☐ 39	Cookie Rojas	.60	.24	.06
☐ 40	Denny McLain	3.00	1.20	.30
☐ 41	Julio Gotay	.50	.20	.05
☐ 42	Larry Haney	.50	.20	.05
☐ 43	Gary Bell	.50	.20	.05
☐ 44	Frank Kostro	.50	.20	.05
☐ 45	Tom Seaver	75.00	30.00	7.50
☐ 46	Dave Ricketts	.50	.20	.05
☐ 47	Ralph Houk MG	.75	.30	.07
☐ 48	Ted Davidson	.50	.20	.05
☐ 49A	Eddie Brinkman (white team name)	.50	.20	.05
☐ 49B	Eddie Brinkman (yellow team name)	40.00	16.00	4.00
☐ 50	Willie Mays	36.00	15.00	3.60
☐ 51	Bob Locker	.50	.20	.05
☐ 52	Hawk Taylor	.50	.20	.05
☐ 53	Gene Alley	.60	.24	.06
☐ 54	Stan Williams	.50	.20	.05
☐ 55	Felipe Alou	.60	.24	.06
☐ 56	Orioles Rookies Dave Leonhard Dave May	.60	.24	.06
☐ 57	Dan Schneider	.50	.20	.05
☐ 58	Eddie Mathews	7.00	2.80	.70
☐ 59	Don Lock	.50	.20	.05
☐ 60	Ken Holtzman	.75	.30	.07
☐ 61	Reggie Smith	1.00	.40	.10
☐ 62	Chuck Dobson	.50	.20	.05
☐ 63	Dick Kenworthy	.50	.20	.05
☐ 64	Jim Merritt	.50	.20	.05
☐ 65	John Roseboro	.60	.24	.06
☐ 66A	Casey Cox (white team name)	.50	.20	.05
☐ 66B	Casey Cox (yellow team name)	40.00	16.00	4.00
☐ 67	Checklist 1 Jim Kaat5	2.50	.25	.05
☐ 68	Ron Willis	.50	.20	.05
☐ 69	Tom Tresh	.75	.30	.07
☐ 70	Bob Veale	.60	.24	.06
☐ 71	Vern Fuller	.50	.20	.05
☐ 72	Tommy John	3.50	1.40	.35
☐ 73	Jim Ray Hart	.60	.24	.06
☐ 74	Milt Pappas	.60	.24	.06
☐ 75	Don Mincher	.60	.24	.06
☐ 76	Braves Rookies Jim Britton Ron Reed	.60	.24	.06
☐ 77	Don Wilson	.50	.20	.05
☐ 78	Jim Northrup	.75	.30	.07
☐ 79	Ted Kubiak	.50	.20	.05
☐ 80	Rod Carew	40.00	16.00	4.00
☐ 81	Larry Jackson	.50	.20	.05
☐ 82	Sam Bowens	.50	.20	.05
☐ 83	John Stephenson	.50	.20	.05
☐ 84	Bob Tolan	.60	.24	.06
☐ 85	Gaylord Perry	5.00	2.00	.50
☐ 86	Willie Stargell	8.00	3.25	.80
☐ 87	Dick Williams MG	.60	.24	.06
☐ 88	Phil Regan	.60	.24	.06
☐ 89	Jake Gibbs	.50	.20	.05
☐ 90	Vada Pinson	1.00	.40	.10
☐ 91	Jim Ollom	.50	.20	.05
☐ 92	Ed Kranepool	.60	.24	.06
☐ 93	Tony Cloninger	.50	.20	.05
☐ 94	Lee Maye	.50	.20	.05
☐ 95	Bob Aspromonte	.50	.20	.05
☐ 96	Senator Rookies Frank Coggins Dick Nold	.50	.20	.05
☐ 97	Tom Phoebus	.50	.20	.05
☐ 98	Gary Sutherland	.50	.20	.05
☐ 99	Rocky Colavito	1.25	.50	.12
☐ 100	Bob Gibson	10.00	4.00	1.00
☐ 101	Glenn Beckert	.60	.24	.06

☐ 102	Jose Cardenal	.50	.20	.05
☐ 103	Don Sutton	5.00	2.00	.50
☐ 104	Dick Dietz	.50	.20	.05
☐ 105	Al Downing	.60	.24	.06
☐ 106	Dalton Jones	.50	.20	.05
☐ 107A	Checklist 2 Juan Marichal (tan wide mesh)	2.50	.25	.05
☐ 107B	Checklist 2 Juan Marichal (brown fine mesh)	2.50	.25	.05
☐ 108	Don Pavletich	.50	.20	.05
☐ 109	Bert Campaneris	.75	.30	.07
☐ 110	Hank Aaron	36.00	15.00	3.60
☐ 111	Rich Reese	.60	.24	.06
☐ 112	Woody Fryman	.40	.16	.04
☐ 113	Tigers Rookies Tom Matchick Daryl Patterson	.40	.16	.04
☐ 114	Ron Swoboda	.60	.24	.06
☐ 115	Sam McDowell	.75	.30	.07
☐ 116	Ken McMullen	.40	.16	.04
☐ 117	Larry Jaster	.40	.16	.04
☐ 118	Mark Belanger	1.00	.40	.10
☐ 119	Ted Savage	.40	.16	.04
☐ 120	Mel Stottlemyre	1.00	.40	.10
☐ 121	Jimmie Hall	.60	.24	.06
☐ 122	Gene Mauch MG	.60	.24	.06
☐ 123	Jose Santiago	.40	.16	.04
☐ 124	Nate Oliver	.40	.16	.04
☐ 125	Joe Horlen	.40	.16	.04
☐ 126	Bob Etheridge	.40	.16	.04
☐ 127	Paul Lindblad	.40	.16	.04
☐ 128	Astros Rookies Tom Dukes Alonzo Harris	.40	.16	.04
☐ 129	Mickey Stanley	.60	.24	.06
☐ 130	Tony Perez	4.00	1.60	.40
☐ 131	Frank Bertaina	.40	.16	.04
☐ 132	Bud Harrelson	.60	.24	.06
☐ 133	Fred Whitfield	.40	.16	.04
☐ 134	Pat Jarvis	.40	.16	.04
☐ 135	Paul Blair	.60	.24	.06
☐ 136	Randy Hundley	.60	.24	.06
☐ 137	Twins Team	1.00	.40	.10
☐ 138	Ruben Amaro	.40	.16	.04
☐ 139	Chris Short	.40	.16	.04
☐ 140	Tony Conigliaro	1.50	.60	.15
☐ 141	Dal Maxvill	.60	.24	.06
☐ 142	White Sox Rookies Buddy Bradford Bill Voss	.40	.16	.04
☐ 143	Pete Cimino	.40	.16	.04
☐ 144	Joe Morgan	4.50	1.80	.45
☐ 145	Don Drysdale	6.50	2.60	.65
☐ 146	Sal Bando	.75	.30	.07
☐ 147	Frank Linzy	.40	.16	.04
☐ 148	Dave Bristol MG	.40	.16	.04
☐ 149	Bob Saverine	.40	.16	.04
☐ 150	Bob Clemente	24.00	10.00	2.40
☐ 151	World Series Game 1 Brock socks 4 hits in opener	3.00	1.20	.30
☐ 152	World Series Game 2 Yaz smashes 2 homers	5.00	2.00	.50
☐ 153	World Series Game 3 Briles cools Boston	1.75	.70	.17
☐ 154	World Series Game 4 Gibson hurls shutout	3.00	1.20	.30
☐ 155	World Series Game 5 Lonborg wins again	1.75	.70	.17
☐ 156	World Series Game 6 Petrocelli 2 homers	1.75	.70	.17
☐ 157	World Series Game 7 St. Louis wins it	1.75	.70	.17
☐ 158	World Series Summary Cardinals celebrate	1.75	.70	.17
☐ 159	Don Kessinger	.60	.24	.06
☐ 160	Earl Wilson	.40	.16	.04
☐ 161	Norm Miller	.40	.16	.04
☐ 162	Cards Rookies Hal Gilson Mike Torrez	.75	.30	.07
☐ 163	Gene Brabender	.40	.16	.04
☐ 164	Ramon Webster	.40	.16	.04
☐ 165	Tony Oliva	2.25	.90	.22
☐ 166	Claude Raymond	.40	.16	.04
☐ 167	Elston Howard	2.25	.90	.22
☐ 168	Dodgers Team	1.50	.60	.15
☐ 169	Bob Bolin	.40	.16	.04
☐ 170	Jim Fregosi	.75	.30	.07
☐ 171	Don Nottebart	.40	.16	.04
☐ 172	Walt Williams	.40	.16	.04
☐ 173	John Boozer	.40	.16	.04
☐ 174	Bob Tillman	.40	.16	.04

☐ 175	Maury Wills	3.50	1.40	.35
☐ 176	Bob Allen	.40	.16	.04
☐ 177	Mets Rookies Jerry Koosman Nolan Ryan	200.00	80.00	20.00
☐ 178	Don Wert	.40	.16	.04
☐ 179	Bill Stoneman	.40	.16	.04
☐ 180	Curt Flood	1.00	.40	.10
☐ 181	Jerry Zimmerman	.40	.16	.04
☐ 182	Dave Giusti	.60	.24	.06
☐ 183	Bob Kennedy MG	.40	.16	.04
☐ 184	Lou Johnson	.40	.16	.04
☐ 185	Tom Haller	.60	.24	.06
☐ 186	Eddie Watt	.40	.16	.04
☐ 187	Sonny Jackson	.40	.16	.04
☐ 188	Cap Peterson	.40	.16	.04
☐ 189	Bill Landis	.40	.16	.04
☐ 190	Bill White	.75	.30	.07
☐ 191	Dan Frisella	.40	.16	.04
☐ 192	Checklist 3 Carl Yastrzemski	3.00	.50	.10
☐ 193	Jack Hamilton	.40	.16	.04
☐ 194	Don Buford	.60	.24	.06
☐ 195	Joe Pepitone	1.00	.40	.10
☐ 196	Gary Nolan	.40	.16	.04
☐ 197	Larry Brown	.40	.16	.04
☐ 198	Roy Face	.75	.30	.07
☐ 199	A's Rookies Roberto Rodriquez Darrell Osteen	.40	.16	.04
☐ 200	Orlando Cepeda	3.00	1.20	.30
☐ 201	Mike Marshall	1.25	.50	.12
☐ 202	Adolfo Phillips	.40	.16	.04
☐ 203	Dick Kelley	.40	.16	.04
☐ 204	Andy Etchebarren	.40	.16	.04
☐ 205	Juan Marichal	5.00	2.00	.50
☐ 206	Cal Ermer MG	.40	.16	.04
☐ 207	Carroll Sembera	.40	.16	.04
☐ 208	Willie Davis	.75	.30	.07
☐ 209	Tim Cullen	.40	.16	.04
☐ 210	Gary Peters	.60	.24	.06
☐ 211	J.C. Martin	.40	.16	.04
☐ 212	Dave Morehead	.40	.16	.04
☐ 213	Chico Ruiz	.40	.16	.04
☐ 214	Yankees Rookies Stan Bahnsen Frank Fernandez	.75	.30	.07
☐ 215	Jim Bunning	3.00	1.20	.30
☐ 216	Bubba Morton	.40	.16	.04
☐ 217	Turk Farrell	.40	.16	.04
☐ 218	Ken Suarez	.40	.16	.04
☐ 219	Rob Gardner	.40	.16	.04
☐ 220	Harmon Killebrew	7.50	3.00	.75
☐ 221	Braves Team	1.00	.40	.10
☐ 222	Jim Hardin	.40	.16	.04
☐ 223	Ollie Brown	.40	.16	.04
☐ 224	Jack Aker	.40	.16	.04
☐ 225	Richie Allen	1.50	.60	.15
☐ 226	Jimmie Price	.40	.16	.04
☐ 227	Joe Hoerner	.40	.16	.04
☐ 228	Dodgers Rookies Jack Billingham Jim Fairey	.60	.24	.06
☐ 229	Fred Klages	.40	.16	.04
☐ 230	Pete Rose	45.00	18.00	4.50
☐ 231	Dave Baldwin	.40	.16	.04
☐ 232	Denis Menke	.40	.16	.04
☐ 233	George Scott	.60	.24	.06
☐ 234	Bill Monbouquette	.40	.16	.04
☐ 235	Ron Santo	1.00	.40	.10
☐ 236	Tug McGraw	1.00	.40	.10
☐ 237	Alvin Dark MG	.60	.24	.06
☐ 238	Tom Satriano	.40	.16	.04
☐ 239	Bill Henry	.40	.16	.04
☐ 240	Al Kaline	10.00	4.00	1.00
☐ 241	Felix Millan	.40	.16	.04
☐ 242	Moe Drabowsky	.40	.16	.04
☐ 243	Rich Rollins	.60	.24	.06
☐ 244	John Donaldson	.40	.16	.04
☐ 245	Tony Gonzalez	.40	.16	.04
☐ 246	Fritz Peterson	.40	.16	.04
☐ 247	Reds Rookies Johnny Bench Ron Tompkins	200.00	80.00	20.00
☐ 248	Fred Valentine	.40	.16	.04
☐ 249	Bill Singer	.40	.16	.04
☐ 250	Carl Yastrzemski	30.00	12.00	3.00
☐ 251	Manny Sanguillen	2.00	.80	.20
☐ 252	Angels Team	1.00	.40	.10
☐ 253	Dick Hughes	.40	.16	.04
☐ 254	Cleon Jones	.40	.16	.04
☐ 255	Dean Chance	.75	.30	.07
☐ 256	Norm Cash	1.50	.60	.15
☐ 257	Phil Niekro	4.50	1.80	.45
☐ 258	Cubs Rookies Jose Arcia Bill Schlesinger	.40	.16	.04
☐ 259	Ken Boyer	1.25	.50	.12
☐ 260	Jim Wynn	.75	.30	.07
☐ 261	Dave Duncan	.40	.16	.04
☐ 262	Rick Wise	.60	.24	.06
☐ 263	Horace Clarke	.60	.24	.06
☐ 264	Ted Abernathy	.40	.16	.04
☐ 265	Tommy Davis	.75	.30	.07
☐ 266	Paul Popovich	.40	.16	.04
☐ 267	Herman Franks MG	.40	.16	.04
☐ 268	Bob Humphreys	.40	.16	.04
☐ 269	Bob Tiefenauer	.40	.16	.04
☐ 270	Matty Alou	.60	.24	.06
☐ 271	Bobby Knoop	.40	.16	.04
☐ 272	Ray Culp	.40	.16	.04
☐ 273	Dave Johnson	1.00	.40	.10
☐ 274	Mike Cuellar	.75	.30	.07
☐ 275	Tim McCarver	1.50	.60	.15
☐ 276	Jim Roland	.40	.16	.04
☐ 277	Jerry Buchek	.40	.16	.04
☐ 278	Checklist 4 Orlando Cepeda	2.50	.50	.10
☐ 279	Bill Hands	.40	.16	.04
☐ 280	Mickey Mantle	175.00	70.00	18.00
☐ 281	Jim Campanis	.40	.16	.04
☐ 282	Rick Monday	.75	.30	.07
☐ 283	Mel Queen	.40	.16	.04
☐ 284	John Briggs	.40	.16	.04
☐ 285	Dick McAuliffe	.60	.24	.06
☐ 286	Cecil Upshaw	.40	.16	.04
☐ 287	White Sox Rookies Mickey Abarbanel Cisco Carlos	.40	.16	.04
☐ 288	Dave Wickersham	.40	.16	.04
☐ 289	Woody Held	.40	.16	.04
☐ 290	Willie McCovey	7.00	2.80	.70
☐ 291	Dick Lines	.40	.16	.04
☐ 292	Art Shamsky	.40	.16	.04
☐ 293	Bruce Howard	.40	.16	.04
☐ 294	Red Schoendienst MG	1.00	.40	.10
☐ 295	Sonny Siebert	.60	.24	.06
☐ 296	Byron Browne	.40	.16	.04
☐ 297	Russ Gibson	.40	.16	.04
☐ 298	Jim Brewer	.40	.16	.04
☐ 299	Gene Michael	.60	.24	.06
☐ 300	Rusty Staub	1.25	.50	.12
☐ 301	Twins Rookies George Mitterwald Rick Renick	.40	.16	.04
☐ 302	Gerry Arrigo	.40	.16	.04
☐ 303	Dick Green	.40	.16	.04
☐ 304	Sandy Valdespino	.40	.16	.04
☐ 305	Minnie Rojas	.40	.16	.04
☐ 306	Mike Ryan	.40	.16	.04
☐ 307	John Hiller	.75	.30	.07
☐ 308	Pirates Team	1.00	.40	.10
☐ 309	Ken Henderson	.40	.16	.04
☐ 310	Luis Aparicio	5.00	2.00	.50
☐ 311	Jack Lamabe	.40	.16	.04
☐ 312	Curt Blefary	.40	.16	.04
☐ 313	Al Weis	.40	.16	.04
☐ 314	Red Sox Rookies Bill Rohr George Spriggs	.40	.16	.04
☐ 315	Zoilo Versalles	.40	.16	.04
☐ 316	Steve Barber	.40	.16	.04
☐ 317	Ron Brand	.40	.16	.04
☐ 318	Chico Salmon	.40	.16	.04
☐ 319	George Culver	.40	.16	.04
☐ 320	Frank Howard	1.00	.40	.10
☐ 321	Leo Durocher MG	1.50	.60	.15
☐ 322	Dave Boswell	.40	.16	.04
☐ 323	Deron Johnson	.60	.24	.06
☐ 324	Jim Nash	.40	.16	.04
☐ 325	Manny Mota	.60	.24	.06
☐ 326	Denny Ribant	.40	.16	.04
☐ 327	Tony Taylor	.40	.16	.04
☐ 328	Angels Rookies Chuck Vinson Jim Weaver	.40	.16	.04
☐ 329	Duane Josephson	.40	.16	.04
☐ 330	Roger Maris	18.00	7.25	1.80
☐ 331	Dan Osinski	.40	.16	.04
☐ 332	Doug Rader	.75	.30	.07
☐ 333	Ron Herbel	.40	.16	.04
☐ 334	Orioles Team	1.00	.40	.10
☐ 335	Bob Allison	.75	.30	.07
☐ 336	John Purdin	.40	.16	.04
☐ 337	Bill Robinson	.75	.30	.07
☐ 338	Bob Johnson	.40	.16	.04
☐ 339	Rich Nye	.40	.16	.04
☐ 340	Max Alvis	.40	.16	.04
☐ 341	Jim Lemon MG	.60	.24	.06
☐ 342	Ken Johnson	.40	.16	.04

□ 343 Jim Gosger	.40	.16	.04
□ 344 Donn Clendenon	.60	.24	.06
□ 345 Bob Hendley	.40	.16	.04
□ 346 Jerry Adair	.40	.16	.04
□ 347 George Brunet	.40	.16	.04
□ 348 Phillies Rookies Larry Colton Dick Thoenen	.40	.16	.04
□ 349 Ed Spiezio	.40	.16	.04
□ 350 Hoyt Wilhelm	5.00	2.00	.50
□ 351 Bob Barton	.40	.16	.04
□ 352 Jackie Hernandez	.40	.16	.04
□ 353 Mack Jones	.40	.16	.04
□ 354 Pete Richert	.40	.16	.04
□ 355 Ernie Banks	8.00	3.25	.80
□ 356A Checklist 5 Ken Holtzman (head centered within circle)	2.50	.50	.10
□ 356B Checklist 5 Ken Holtzman (head shifted right within circle)	2.50	.50	.10
□ 357 Len Gabrielson	.40	.16	.04
□ 358 Mike Epstein	.40	.16	.04
□ 359 Joe Moeller	.40	.16	.04
□ 360 Willie Horton	.75	.30	.07
□ 361 Harmon Killebrew AS	4.00	1.60	.40
□ 362 Orlando Cepeda AS	1.25	.50	.12
□ 363 Rod Carew AS	7.00	2.80	.70
□ 364 Joe Morgan AS	2.50	1.00	.25
□ 365 Brooks Robinson AS	4.50	1.80	.45
□ 366 Ron Santo AS	.75	.30	.07
□ 367 Jim Fregosi AS	.60	.24	.06
□ 368 Gene Alley AS	.60	.24	.06
□ 369 Carl Yastrzemski AS	8.50	3.50	.85
□ 370 Hank Aaron AS	8.50	3.50	.85
□ 371 Tony Oliva AS	1.00	.40	.10
□ 372 Lou Brock AS	4.00	1.60	.40
□ 373 Frank Robinson AS	4.00	1.60	.40
□ 374 Bob Clemente AS	7.50	3.00	.75
□ 375 Bill Freehan AS	.75	.30	.07
□ 376 Tim McCarver AS	1.00	.40	.10
□ 377 Joe Horlen AS	.60	.24	.06
□ 378 Bob Gibson AS	4.00	1.60	.40
□ 379 Gary Peters AS	.60	.24	.06
□ 380 Ken Holtzman AS	.60	.24	.06
□ 381 Boog Powell	1.50	.60	.15
□ 382 Ramon Hernandez	.40	.16	.04
□ 383 Steve Whitaker	.40	.16	.04
□ 384 Reds Rookies Bill Henry Hal McRae	3.50	1.40	.35
□ 385 Jim Hunter	6.00	2.40	.60
□ 386 Greg Goossen	.40	.16	.04
□ 387 Joe Foy	.40	.16	.04
□ 388 Ray Washburn	.40	.16	.04
□ 389 Jay Johnstone	.75	.30	.07
□ 390 Bill Mazeroski	1.00	.40	.10
□ 391 Bob Priddy	.40	.16	.04
□ 392 Grady Hatton MG	.40	.16	.04
□ 393 Jim Perry	.75	.30	.07
□ 394 Tommie Aaron	.60	.24	.06
□ 395 Camilo Pascual	.60	.24	.06
□ 396 Bobby Wine	.40	.16	.04
□ 397 Vic Davalillo	.60	.24	.06
□ 398 Jim Grant	.40	.16	.04
□ 399 Ray Oyler	.40	.16	.04
□ 400A Mike McCormick (yellow letters)	.60	.24	.06
□ 400B Mike McCormick (team name in white letters)	20.00	8.00	2.00
□ 401 Mets Team	1.25	.50	.12
□ 402 Mike Hegan	.40	.16	.04
□ 403 John Buzhardt	.40	.16	.04
□ 404 Floyd Robinson	.40	.16	.04
□ 405 Tommy Helms	.60	.24	.06
□ 406 Dick Ellsworth	.60	.24	.06
□ 407 Gary Kolb	.40	.16	.04
□ 408 Steve Carlton	30.00	12.00	3.00
□ 409 Orioles Rookies Frank Peters Don Stone	.40	.16	.04
□ 410 Ferguson Jenkins	3.00	1.20	.30
□ 411 Ron Hansen	.40	.16	.04
□ 412 Clay Carroll	.40	.16	.04
□ 413 Tommy McCraw	.40	.16	.04
□ 414 Mickey Lolich	1.75	.70	.17
□ 415 Johnny Callison	.60	.24	.06
□ 416 Bill Rigney MG	.40	.16	.04
□ 417 Willie Crawford	.40	.16	.04
□ 418 Eddie Fisher	.40	.16	.04
□ 419 Jack Hiatt	.40	.16	.04
□ 420 Cesar Tovar	.40	.16	.04
□ 421 Ron Taylor	.40	.16	.04
□ 422 Rene Lachemann	.75	.30	.07
□ 423 Fred Gladding	.40	.16	.04
□ 424 Chicago White Sox Team Card	1.00	.40	.10
□ 425 Jim Maloney	.60	.24	.06
□ 426 Hank Allen	.40	.16	.04
□ 427 Dick Calmus	.40	.16	.04
□ 428 Vic Roznovsky	.40	.16	.04
□ 429 Tommie Sisk	.40	.16	.04
□ 430 Rico Petrocelli	.60	.24	.06
□ 431 Dooley Womack	.40	.16	.04
□ 432 Indians Rookies Bill Davis Jose Vidal	.40	.16	.04
□ 433 Bob Rodgers	.75	.30	.07
□ 434 Ricardo Joseph	.40	.16	.04
□ 435 Ron Perranoski	.60	.24	.06
□ 436 Hal Lanier	.60	.24	.06
□ 437 Don Cardwell	.40	.16	.04
□ 438 Lee Thomas	.75	.30	.07
□ 439 Luman Harris MG	.40	.16	.04
□ 440 Claude Osteen	.60	.24	.06
□ 441 Alex Johnson	.60	.24	.06
□ 442 Dick Bosman	.40	.16	.04
□ 443 Joe Azcue	.40	.16	.04
□ 444 Jack Fisher	.40	.16	.04
□ 445 Mike Shannon	.75	.30	.07
□ 446 Ron Kline	.40	.16	.04
□ 447 Tigers Rookies George Korince Fred Lasher	.40	.16	.04
□ 448 Gary Wagner	.40	.16	.04
□ 449 Gene Oliver	.40	.16	.04
□ 450 Jim Kaat	3.00	1.20	.30
□ 451 Al Spangler	.40	.16	.04
□ 452 Jesus Alou	.40	.16	.04
□ 453 Sammy Ellis	.40	.16	.04
□ 454A Checklist 6 Frank Robinson (cap complete within circle)	2.50	.50	.10
□ 454B Checklist 6 Frank Robinson (cap partially within circle)	2.50	.50	.10
□ 455 Rico Carty	.75	.30	.07
□ 456 John O'Donoghue	.40	.16	.04
□ 457 Jim Lefebvre	.75	.30	.07
□ 458 Lew Krausse	.65	.26	.06
□ 459 Dick Simpson	.65	.26	.06
□ 460 Jim Lonborg	1.00	.40	.10
□ 461 Chuck Hiller	.65	.26	.06
□ 462 Barry Moore	.65	.26	.06
□ 463 Jim Schaffer	.65	.26	.06
□ 464 Don McMahon	.65	.26	.06
□ 465 Tommie Agee	.65	.26	.06
□ 466 Bill Dillman	.65	.26	.06
□ 467 Dick Howser	1.00	.40	.10
□ 468 Larry Sherry	.65	.26	.06
□ 469 Ty Cline	.65	.26	.06
□ 470 Bill Freehan	1.50	.60	.15
□ 471 Orlando Pena	.65	.26	.06
□ 472 Walt Alston MG	2.00	.80	.20
□ 473 Al Worthington	.65	.26	.06
□ 474 Paul Schaal	.65	.26	.06
□ 475 Joe Niekro	1.50	.60	.15
□ 476 Woody Woodward	.65	.26	.06
□ 477 Philadelphia Phillies Team Card	1.50	.60	.15
□ 478 Dave McNally	1.00	.40	.10
□ 479 Phil Gagliano	.65	.26	.06
□ 480 Manager's Dream Tony Oliva Chico Cardenas Bob Clemente	8.00	3.25	.80
□ 481 John Wyatt	.65	.26	.06
□ 482 Jose Pagan	.65	.26	.06
□ 483 Darold Knowles	.65	.26	.06
□ 484 Phil Roof	.65	.26	.06
□ 485 Ken Berry	.65	.26	.06
□ 486 Cal Koonce	.65	.26	.06
□ 487 Lee May	1.00	.40	.10
□ 488 Dick Tracewski	.65	.26	.06
□ 489 Wally Bunker	.65	.26	.06
□ 490 Super Stars Harmon Killebrew Willie Mays Mickey Mantle	35.00	14.00	3.50
□ 491 Denny Lemaster	.65	.26	.06
□ 492 Jeff Torborg	1.00	.40	.10
□ 493 Jim McGlothlin	.65	.26	.06
□ 494 Ray Sadecki	.65	.26	.06
□ 495 Leon Wagner	.65	.26	.06
□ 496 Steve Hamilton	.65	.26	.06

□ 497	Cards Team	1.50	.60	.15
□ 498	Bill Bryan	.65	.26	.06
□ 499	Steve Blass	1.00	.40	.10
□ 500	Frank Robinson	10.00	4.00	1.00
□ 501	John Odom	.65	.26	.06
□ 502	Mike Andrews	.65	.26	.06
□ 503	Al Jackson	.65	.26	.06
□ 504	Russ Snyder	.65	.26	.06
□ 505	Joe Sparma	.65	.26	.06
□ 506	Clarence Jones	.65	.26	.06
□ 507	Wade Blasingame	.65	.26	.06
□ 508	Duke Sims	.65	.26	.06
□ 509	Dennis Higgins	.65	.26	.06
□ 510	Ron Fairly	1.00	.40	.10
□ 511	Bill Kelso	.65	.26	.06
□ 512	Grant Jackson	.65	.26	.06
□ 513	Hank Bauer MG	1.00	.40	.10
□ 514	Al McBean	.65	.26	.06
□ 515	Russ Nixon	1.00	.40	.10
□ 516	Pete Mikkelsen	.65	.26	.06
□ 517	Diego Segui	.65	.26	.06
□ 518A	Checklist 7	3.00	.50	.10
	(539 ML Rookies)			
	(Clete Boyer)			
□ 518B	Checklist 7	6.00	1.00	.20
	(539 AL Rookies)			
	(Clete Boyer)			
□ 519	Jerry Stephenson	.65	.26	.06
□ 520	Lou Brock	10.00	4.00	1.00
□ 521	Don Shaw	.65	.26	.06
□ 522	Wayne Causey	.65	.26	.06
□ 523	John Tsitouris	.65	.26	.06
□ 524	Andy Kosco	.65	.26	.06
□ 525	Jim Davenport	1.00	.40	.10
□ 526	Bill Denehy	.65	.26	.06
□ 527	Tito Francona	1.00	.40	.10
□ 528	Tigers Team	7.00	2.80	.70
□ 529	Bruce Von Hoff	.65	.26	.06
□ 530	Bird Belters	5.00	2.00	.50
	Brooks Robinson			
	Frank Robinson			
□ 531	Chuck Hinton	.65	.26	.06
□ 532	Luis Tiant	1.50	.60	.15
□ 533	Wes Parker	1.00	.40	.10
□ 534	Bob Miller	.70	.28	.07
□ 535	Danny Cater	.70	.28	.07
□ 536	Bill Short	.70	.28	.07
□ 537	Norm Siebern	.70	.28	.07
□ 538	Manny Jimenez	.70	.28	.07
□ 539	Major League Rookies	1.00	.40	.10
	Jim Ray			
	Mike Ferraro			
□ 540	Nelson Briles	1.00	.40	.10
□ 541	Sandy Alomar	.70	.28	.07
□ 542	John Boccabella	.70	.28	.07
□ 543	Bob Lee	.70	.28	.07
□ 544	Mayo Smith MG	.70	.28	.07
□ 545	Lindy McDaniel	1.00	.40	.10
□ 546	Roy White	1.25	.50	.12
□ 547	Dan Coombs	.70	.28	.07
□ 548	Bernie Allen	.70	.28	.07
□ 549	Orioles Rookies	.70	.28	.07
	Curt Motton			
	Roger Nelson			
□ 550	Clete Boyer	1.25	.50	.12
□ 551	Darrell Sutherland	.70	.28	.07
□ 552	Ed Kirkpatrick	.70	.28	.07
□ 553	Hank Aguirre	.70	.28	.07
□ 554	A's Team	1.50	.60	.15
□ 555	Jose Tartabull	.70	.28	.07
□ 556	Dick Selma	.70	.28	.07
□ 557	Frank Quilici	.70	.28	.07
□ 558	John Edwards	.70	.28	.07
□ 559	Pirates Rookies	1.00	.40	.10
	Carl Taylor			
	Luke Walker			
□ 560	Paul Casanova	.70	.28	.07
□ 561	Lee Elia	1.00	.40	.10
□ 562	Jim Bouton	1.50	.60	.15
□ 563	Ed Charles	.70	.28	.07
□ 564	Ed Stanky MG	1.00	.40	.10
□ 565	Larry Dierker	1.00	.40	.10
□ 566	Ken Harrelson	1.50	.60	.15
□ 567	Clay Dalrymple	.70	.28	.07
□ 568	Willie Smith	.70	.28	.07
□ 569	NL Rookies	.70	.28	.07
	Ivan Murrell			
	Les Rohr			
□ 570	Rick Reichardt	.70	.28	.07
□ 571	Tony LaRussa	1.50	.60	.15
□ 572	Don Bosch	.70	.28	.07
□ 573	Joe Coleman	.70	.28	.07
□ 574	Cincinnati Reds	1.50	.60	.15
	Team Card			
□ 575	Jim Palmer	15.00	6.00	1.50
□ 576	Dave Adlesh	.70	.28	.07
□ 577	Fred Talbot	.70	.28	.07
□ 578	Orlando Martinez	.70	.28	.07
□ 579	NL Rookies	1.00	.40	.10
	Larry Hisle			
	Mike Lum			
□ 580	Bob Bailey	.70	.28	.07
□ 581	Garry Roggenburk	.70	.28	.07
□ 582	Jerry Grote	.70	.28	.07
□ 583	Gates Brown	1.00	.40	.10
□ 584	Larry Shepard MG	.70	.28	.07
□ 585	Wilbur Wood	1.00	.40	.10
□ 586	Jim Pagliaroni	.70	.28	.07
□ 587	Roger Repoz	.70	.28	.07
□ 588	Dick Schofield	.70	.28	.07
□ 589	Twins Rookies	.70	.28	.07
	Ron Clark			
	Moe Ogier			
□ 590	Tommy Harper	1.00	.40	.10
□ 591	Dick Nen	.70	.28	.07
□ 592	John Bateman	.70	.28	.07
□ 593	Lee Stange	.70	.28	.07
□ 594	Phil Linz	1.00	.40	.10
□ 595	Phil Ortega	.70	.28	.07
□ 596	Charlie Smith	.70	.28	.07
□ 597	Bill McCool	.70	.28	.07
□ 598	Jerry May	1.50	.40	.08

1968 Topps Game

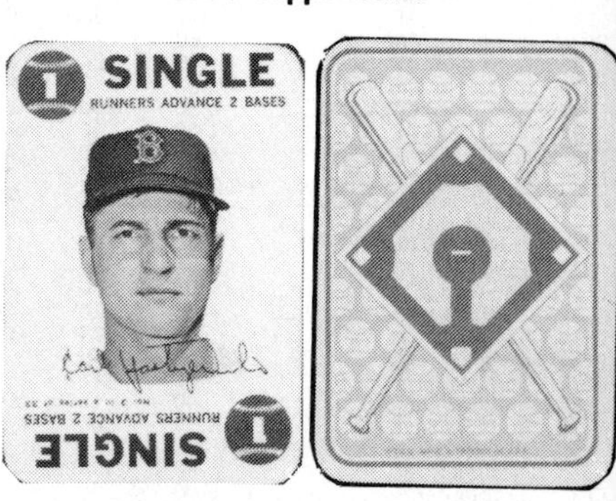

The cards in this 33-card set measure 2 1/4" by 3 1/4". This "Game" card set of players, issued as inserts with the regular 1968 Topps baseball series, was patterned directly after the Red Back and Blue Back sets of 1951. Each card has a color player photo set upon a pure white background, with a facsimile autograph underneath the picture. The cards have blue backs, and were also sold in boxed sets on a limited basis.

		NRMT	VG-E	GOOD
COMPLETE SET (33)		50.00	20.00	5.00
COMMON PLAYER (1-33)		.30	.12	.03
□ 1	Matty Alou	.30	.12	.03
□ 2	Mickey Mantle	12.00	5.00	1.20
□ 3	Carl Yastrzemski	7.50	3.00	.75
□ 4	Hank Aaron	5.00	2.00	.50
□ 5	Harmon Killebrew	2.00	.80	.20
□ 6	Roberto Clemente	4.50	1.80	.45
□ 7	Frank Robinson	2.50	1.00	.25
□ 8	Willie Mays	5.00	2.00	.50
□ 9	Brooks Robinson	3.00	1.20	.30
□ 10	Tommy Davis	.30	.12	.03
□ 11	Bill Freehan	.40	.16	.04
□ 12	Claude Osteen	.30	.12	.03
□ 13	Gary Peters	.30	.12	.03
□ 14	Jim Lonborg	.30	.12	.03
□ 15	Steve Hargan	.30	.12	.03
□ 16	Dean Chance	.30	.12	.03
□ 17	Mike McCormick	.30	.12	.03
□ 18	Tim McCarver	.50	.20	.05
□ 19	Ron Santo	.40	.16	.04
□ 20	Tony Gonzalez	.30	.12	.03
□ 21	Frank Howard	.40	.16	.04
□ 22	George Scott	.30	.12	.03
□ 23	Rich Allen	.40	.16	.04

□ 24 Jim Wynn	.30	.12	.03
□ 25 Gene Alley	.30	.12	.03
□ 26 Rick Monday	.30	.12	.03
□ 27 Al Kaline	3.00	1.20	.30
□ 28 Rusty Staub	.50	.20	.05
□ 29 Rod Carew	3.50	1.40	.35
□ 30 Pete Rose	9.00	3.75	.90
□ 31 Joe Torre	.50	.20	.05
□ 32 Orlando Cepeda	.50	.20	.05
□ 33 Jim Fregosi	.40	.16	.04

1969 Topps

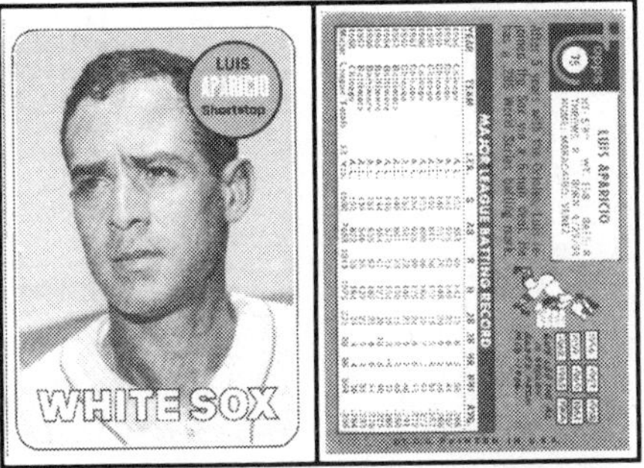

The cards in this 664-card set measure 2 1/2" by 3 1/2". The 1969 Topps set includes Sporting News All-Star Selections as card numbers 416 to 435. Other popular subsets within this set include League Leaders (1-12) and World Series cards (162-169). The fifth series contains several variations; the more difficult variety consists of cards with the player's first name, last name, and/or position in white letters instead of lettering in some other color. These are designated in the checklist below by WL (white letters). Each checklist card features a different popular player's picture inside a circle on the front of the checklist card. Two different poses of Clay Dalrymple and Donn Clendenon exist as indicated in the checklist.

	NRMT	VG-E	GOOD
COMPLETE SET (664)	1300.00	600.00	175.00
COMMON PLAYER (1-218)	.40	.16	.04
COMMON PLAYER (219-327)	.75	.30	.07
COMMON PLAYER (328-512)	.40	.16	.04
COMMON PLAYER (513-588)	.50	.20	.05
COMMON PLAYER (589-664)	.65	.26	.06
□ 1 AL Batting Leaders	5.00	1.00	.20
Carl Yastrzemski			
Danny Cater			
Tony Oliva			
□ 2 NL Batting Leaders	3.00	1.20	.30
Pete Rose			
Matty Alou			
Felipe Alou			
□ 3 AL RBI Leaders	1.25	.50	.12
Ken Harrelson			
Frank Howard			
Jim Northrup			
□ 4 NL RBI Leaders	2.00	.80	.20
Willie McCovey			
Ron Santo			
Billy Williams			
□ 5 AL Home Run Leaders	1.25	.50	.12
Frank Howard			
Willie Horton			
Ken Harrelson			
□ 6 NL Home Run Leaders	2.00	.80	.20
Willie McCovey			
Richie Allen			
Ernie Banks			
□ 7 AL ERA Leaders	1.25	.50	.12
Luis Tiant			
Sam McDowell			
Dave McNally			
□ 8 NL ERA Leaders	1.25	.50	.12
Bob Gibson			
Bobby Bolin			
Bob Veale			
□ 9 AL Pitching Leaders	1.25	.50	.12
Denny McLain			
Dave McNally			
Luis Tiant			
Mel Stottlemyre			
□ 10 NL Pitching Leaders	2.00	.80	.20
Juan Marichal			
Bob Gibson			
Fergie Jenkins			
□ 11 AL Strikeout Leaders	1.25	.50	.12
Sam McDowell			
Denny McLain			
Luis Tiant			
□ 12 NL Strikeout Leaders	1.25	.50	.12
Bob Gibson			
Fergie Jenkins			
Bill Singer			
□ 13 Mickey Stanley	.60	.24	.06
□ 14 Al McBean	.40	.16	.04
□ 15 Boog Powell	1.50	.60	.15
□ 16 Giants Rookies	.40	.16	.04
Cesar Gutierrez			
Rich Robertson			
□ 17 Mike Marshall	.75	.30	.07
□ 18 Dick Schofield	.40	.16	.04
□ 19 Ken Suarez	.40	.16	.04
□ 20 Ernie Banks	7.50	3.00	.75
□ 21 Jose Santiago	.40	.16	.04
□ 22 Jesus Alou	.40	.16	.04
□ 23 Lew Krausse	.40	.16	.04
□ 24 Walt Alston MG	1.50	.60	.15
□ 25 Roy White	.75	.30	.07
□ 26 Clay Carroll	.40	.16	.04
□ 27 Bernie Allen	.40	.16	.04
□ 28 Mike Ryan	.40	.16	.04
□ 29 Dave Morehead	.40	.16	.04
□ 30 Bob Allison	.60	.24	.06
□ 31 Mets Rookies	1.25	.50	.12
Gary Gentry			
Amos Otis			
□ 32 Sammy Ellis	.40	.16	.04
□ 33 Wayne Causey	.40	.16	.04
□ 34 Gary Peters	.60	.24	.06
□ 35 Joe Morgan	4.50	1.80	.45
□ 36 Luke Walker	.40	.16	.04
□ 37 Curt Motton	.40	.16	.04
□ 38 Zoilo Versalles	.40	.16	.04
□ 39 Dick Hughes	.40	.16	.04
□ 40 Mayo Smith MG	.40	.16	.04
□ 41 Bob Barton	.40	.16	.04
□ 42 Tommy Harper	.60	.24	.06
□ 43 Joe Niekro	1.00	.40	.10
□ 44 Danny Cater	.40	.16	.04
□ 45 Maury Wills	2.00	.80	.20
□ 46 Fritz Peterson	.40	.16	.04
□ 47A Paul Popovich	.40	.16	.04
(no helmet emblem)			
□ 47B Paul Popovich	12.00	5.00	1.20
(C emblem on helmet)			
□ 48 Brant Alyea	.40	.16	.04
□ 49A Royals Rookies	.40	.16	.04
Steve Jones			
E. Rodriguez "g"			
□ 49B Royals Rookies	12.00	5.00	1.20
Steve Jones			
E. Rodriquez "q"			
□ 50 Bob Clemente	22.00	9.00	2.20
□ 51 Woody Fryman	.40	.16	.04
□ 52 Mike Andrews	.40	.16	.04
□ 53 Sonny Jackson	.40	.16	.04
□ 54 Cisco Carlos	.40	.16	.04
□ 55 Jerry Grote	.40	.16	.04
□ 56 Rich Reese	.40	.16	.04
□ 57 Checklist 1	2.00	.30	.06
Denny McLain			
□ 58 Fred Gladding	.40	.16	.04
□ 59 Jay Johnstone	.75	.30	.07
□ 60 Nelson Briles	.60	.24	.06
□ 61 Jimmie Hall	.60	.24	.06
□ 62 Chico Salmon	.40	.16	.04
□ 63 Jim Hickman	.40	.16	.04
□ 64 Bill Monbouquette	.40	.16	.04
□ 65 Willie Davis	.75	.30	.07
□ 66 Orioles Rookies	.60	.24	.06
Mike Adamson			
Merv Rettenmund			
□ 67 Bill Stoneman	.40	.16	.04
□ 68 Dave Duncan	.40	.16	.04
□ 69 Steve Hamilton	.40	.16	.04
□ 70 Tommy Helms	.60	.24	.06
□ 71 Steve Whitaker	.40	.16	.04
□ 72 Ron Taylor	.40	.16	.04

□ 73 Johnny Briggs	.40	.16	.04
□ 74 Preston Gomez MG	.40	.16	.04
□ 75 Luis Aparicio	5.00	2.00	.50
□ 76 Norm Miller	.40	.16	.04
□ 77A Ron Perranoski (no emblem on cap)	.60	.24	.06
□ 77B Ron Perranoski (LA on cap)	12.00	5.00	1.20
□ 78 Tom Satriano	.40	.16	.04
□ 79 Milt Pappas	.60	.24	.06
□ 80 Norm Cash	1.00	.40	.10
□ 81 Mel Queen	.40	.16	.04
□ 82 Pirates Rookies Rich Hebner Al Oliver	8.00	3.25	.80
□ 83 Mike Ferraro	.60	.24	.06
□ 84 Bob Humphreys	.40	.16	.04
□ 85 Lou Brock	7.50	3.00	.75
□ 86 Pete Richert	.40	.16	.04
□ 87 Horace Clarke	.40	.16	.04
□ 88 Rich Nye	.40	.16	.04
□ 89 Russ Gibson	.40	.16	.04
□ 90 Jerry Koosman	1.50	.60	.15
□ 91 Al Dark MG	.60	.24	.06
□ 92 Jack Billingham	.40	.16	.04
□ 93 Joe Foy	.40	.16	.04
□ 94 Hank Aguirre	.40	.16	.04
□ 95 Johnny Bench	70.00	28.00	7.00
□ 96 Denver Lemaster	.40	.16	.04
□ 97 Buddy Bradford	.40	.16	.04
□ 98 Dave Giusti	.60	.24	.06
□ 99A Twins Rookies Danny Morris Graig Nettles (no loop)	15.00	6.00	1.50
□ 99B Twins Rookies (errant loop in upper left corner of obverse)	30.00	12.00	3.00
□ 100 Hank Aaron	30.00	12.00	3.00
□ 101 Daryl Patterson	.40	.16	.04
□ 102 Jim Davenport	.60	.24	.06
□ 103 Roger Repoz	.40	.16	.04
□ 104 Steve Blass	.60	.24	.06
□ 105 Rick Monday	.60	.24	.06
□ 106 Jim Hannan	.40	.16	.04
□ 107A Checklist 2 (161 Jim Purdin) (Bob Gibson)	2.00	.25	.05
□ 107B Checklist 2 (161 John Purdin) (Bob Gibson)	5.00	.50	.10
□ 108 Tony Taylor	.40	.16	.04
□ 109 Jim Lonborg	.75	.30	.07
□ 110 Mike Shannon	.75	.30	.07
□ 111 Johnny Morris	.40	.16	.04
□ 112 J.C. Martin	.40	.16	.04
□ 113 Dave May	.40	.16	.04
□ 114 Yankees Rookies Alan Closter John Cumberland	.40	.16	.04
□ 115 Bill Hands	.40	.16	.04
□ 116 Chuck Harrison	.40	.16	.04
□ 117 Jim Fairey	.40	.16	.04
□ 118 Stan Williams	.40	.16	.04
□ 119 Doug Rader	.60	.24	.06
□ 120 Pete Rose	30.00	12.00	3.00
□ 121 Joe Grzenda	.40	.16	.04
□ 122 Ron Fairly	.60	.24	.06
□ 123 Wilbur Wood	.60	.24	.06
□ 124 Hank Bauer MG	.60	.24	.06
□ 125 Ray Sadecki	.40	.16	.04
□ 126 Dick Tracewski	.40	.16	.04
□ 127 Kevin Collins	.40	.16	.04
□ 128 Tommie Aaron	.60	.24	.06
□ 129 Bill McCool	.40	.16	.04
□ 130 Carl Yastrzemski	25.00	10.00	2.50
□ 131 Chris Cannizzaro	.40	.16	.04
□ 132 Dave Baldwin	.40	.16	.04
□ 133 Johnny Callison	.60	.24	.06
□ 134 Jim Weaver	.40	.16	.04
□ 135 Tommy Davis	.75	.30	.07
□ 136 Cards Rookies Steve Huntz Mike Torrez	.60	.24	.06
□ 137 Wally Bunker	.40	.16	.04
□ 138 John Bateman	.40	.16	.04
□ 139 Andy Kosco	.40	.16	.04
□ 140 Jim Lefebvre	.75	.30	.07
□ 141 Bill Dillman	.40	.16	.04
□ 142 Woody Woodward	.60	.24	.06
□ 143 Joe Nossek	.40	.16	.04
□ 144 Bob Hendley	.40	.16	.04
□ 145 Max Alvis	.40	.16	.04
□ 146 Jim Perry	.75	.30	.07
□ 147 Leo Durocher MG	1.25	.50	.12
□ 148 Lee Stange	.40	.16	.04
□ 149 Ollie Brown	.40	.16	.04
□ 150 Denny McLain	2.00	.80	.20
□ 151A Clay Dalrymple (Portrait, Orioles)	.40	.16	.04
□ 151B Clay Dalrymple (Catching, Phillies)	12.00	5.00	1.20
□ 152 Tommie Sisk	.40	.16	.04
□ 153 Ed Brinkman	.40	.16	.04
□ 154 Jim Britton	.40	.16	.04
□ 155 Pete Ward	.40	.16	.04
□ 156 Houston Rookies Hal Gilson Leon McFadden	.40	.16	.04
□ 157 Bob Rodgers	.75	.30	.07
□ 158 Joe Gibbon	.40	.16	.04
□ 159 Jerry Adair	.40	.16	.04
□ 160 Vada Pinson	1.00	.40	.10
□ 161 John Purdin	.40	.16	.04
□ 162 World Series Game 1 Gibson fans 17	3.00	1.20	.30
□ 163 World Series Game 2 Tiger homers deck the Cards	1.75	.70	.17
□ 164 World Series Game 3 McCarver's homer	2.00	.80	.20
□ 165 World Series Game 4 Brock lead-off homer	3.00	1.20	.30
□ 166 World Series Game 5 Kaline's key hit	4.00	1.60	.40
□ 167 World Series Game 6 Northrup grandslam	1.75	.70	.17
□ 168 World Series Game 7 Lolich outduels Bob Gibson	3.00	1.20	.30
□ 169 World Series Summary Tigers celebrate	1.75	.70	.17
□ 170 Frank Howard	1.00	.40	.10
□ 171 Glenn Beckert	.60	.24	.06
□ 172 Jerry Stephenson	.40	.16	.04
□ 173 White Sox Rookies Bob Christian Gerry Nyman	.40	.16	.04
□ 174 Grant Jackson	.40	.16	.04
□ 175 Jim Bunning	2.50	1.00	.25
□ 176 Joe Azcue	.40	.16	.04
□ 177 Ron Reed	.40	.16	.04
□ 178 Ray Oyler	.40	.16	.04
□ 179 Don Pavletich	.40	.16	.04
□ 180 Willie Horton	.60	.24	.06
□ 181 Mel Nelson	.40	.16	.04
□ 182 Bill Rigney MG	.40	.16	.04
□ 183 Don Shaw	.40	.16	.04
□ 184 Roberto Pena	.40	.16	.04
□ 185 Tom Phoebus	.40	.16	.04
□ 186 John Edwards	.40	.16	.04
□ 187 Leon Wagner	.40	.16	.04
□ 188 Rick Wise	.60	.24	.06
□ 189 Red Sox Rookies Joe Lahoud John Thibodeau	.40	.16	.04
□ 190 Willie Mays	30.00	12.00	3.00
□ 191 Lindy McDaniel	.60	.24	.06
□ 192 Jose Pagan	.40	.16	.04
□ 193 Don Cardwell	.40	.16	.04
□ 194 Ted Uhlaender	.40	.16	.04
□ 195 John Odom	.40	.16	.04
□ 196 Lum Harris MG	.40	.16	.04
□ 197 Dick Selma	.40	.16	.04
□ 198 Willie Smith	.40	.16	.04
□ 199 Jim French	.40	.16	.04
□ 200 Bob Gibson	7.00	2.80	.70
□ 201 Russ Snyder	.40	.16	.04
□ 202 Don Wilson	.40	.16	.04
□ 203 Dave Johnson	1.00	.40	.10
□ 204 Jack Hiatt	.40	.16	.04
□ 205 Rick Reichardt	.40	.16	.04
□ 206 Phillies Rookies Larry Hisle Barry Lersch	.60	.24	.06
□ 207 Roy Face	.75	.30	.07
□ 208A Donn Clendenon (Houston)	.60	.24	.06
□ 208B Donn Clendenon (Expos)	12.00	5.00	1.20
□ 209 Larry Haney (reverse negative)	.40	.16	.04
□ 210 Felix Millan	.40	.16	.04
□ 211 Galen Cisco	.40	.16	.04
□ 212 Tom Tresh	.60	.24	.06
□ 213 Gerry Arrigo	.40	.16	.04
□ 214 Checklist 3 With 69T deckle CL on back (no player)	2.00	.25	.05

□ 215	Rico Petrocelli	.60	.24	.06
□ 216	Don Sutton	4.00	1.60	.40
□ 217	John Donaldson	.40	.16	.04
□ 218	John Roseboro	.60	.24	.06
□ 219	Freddie Patek	1.00	.40	.10
□ 220	Sam McDowell	1.25	.50	.12
□ 221	Art Shamsky	.75	.30	.07
□ 222	Duane Josephson	.75	.30	.07
□ 223	Tom Dukes	.75	.30	.07
□ 224	Angels Rookies	.75	.30	.07
	Bill Harrelson			
	Steve Kealey			
□ 225	Don Kessinger	1.00	.40	.10
□ 226	Bruce Howard	.75	.30	.07
□ 227	Frank Johnson	.75	.30	.07
□ 228	Dave Leonhard	.75	.30	.07
□ 229	Don Lock	.75	.30	.07
□ 230	Rusty Staub	1.50	.60	.15
□ 231	Pat Dobson	1.00	.40	.10
□ 232	Dave Ricketts	.75	.30	.07
□ 233	Steve Barber	.75	.30	.07
□ 234	Dave Bristol MG	.75	.30	.07
□ 235	Jim Hunter	7.50	3.00	.75
□ 236	Manny Mota	1.00	.40	.10
□ 237	Bobby Cox	1.00	.40	.10
□ 238	Ken Johnson	.75	.30	.07
□ 239	Bob Taylor	.75	.30	.07
□ 240	Ken Harrelson	1.25	.50	.12
□ 241	Jim Brewer	.75	.30	.07
□ 242	Frank Kostro	.75	.30	.07
□ 243	Ron Kline	.75	.30	.07
□ 244	Indians Rookies	1.00	.40	.10
	Ray Fosse			
	George Woodson			
□ 245	Ed Charles	.75	.30	.07
□ 246	Joe Coleman	.75	.30	.07
□ 247	Gene Oliver	.75	.30	.07
□ 248	Bob Priddy	.75	.30	.07
□ 249	Ed Spiezio	.75	.30	.07
□ 250	Frank Robinson	11.00	4.50	1.10
□ 251	Ron Herbel	.75	.30	.07
□ 252	Chuck Cottier	.75	.30	.07
□ 253	Jerry Johnson	.75	.30	.07
□ 254	Joe Schultz	.75	.30	.07
□ 255	Steve Carlton	25.00	10.00	2.50
□ 256	Gates Brown	1.00	.40	.10
□ 257	Jim Ray	.75	.30	.07
□ 258	Jackie Hernandez	.75	.30	.07
□ 259	Bill Short	.75	.30	.07
□ 260	Reggie Jackson	250.00	100.00	25.00
□ 261	Bob Johnson	.75	.30	.07
□ 262	Mike Kekich	.75	.30	.07
□ 263	Jerry May	.75	.30	.07
□ 264	Bill Landis	.75	.30	.07
□ 265	Chico Cardenas	.75	.30	.07
□ 266	Dodger Rookies	.75	.30	.07
	Tom Hutton			
	Alan Foster			
□ 267	Vicente Romo	.75	.30	.07
□ 268	Al Spangler	.75	.30	.07
□ 269	Al Weis	.75	.30	.07
□ 270	Mickey Lolich	1.75	.70	.17
□ 271	Larry Stahl	.75	.30	.07
□ 272	Ed Stroud	.75	.30	.07
□ 273	Ron Willis	.75	.30	.07
□ 274	Clyde King MG	.75	.30	.07
□ 275	Vic Davalillo	1.00	.40	.10
□ 276	Gary Wagner	.75	.30	.07
□ 277	Elrod Hendricks	.75	.30	.07
□ 278	Gary Geiger	1.00	.40	.10
	(Batting wrong)			
□ 279	Roger Nelson	.75	.30	.07
□ 280	Alex Johnson	1.00	.40	.10
□ 281	Ted Kubiak	.75	.30	.07
□ 282	Pat Jarvis	.75	.30	.07
□ 283	Sandy Alomar	.75	.30	.07
□ 284	Expos Rookies	.75	.30	.07
	Jerry Robertson			
	Mike Wegener			
□ 285	Don Mincher	1.00	.40	.10
□ 286	Dock Ellis	1.00	.40	.10
□ 287	Jose Tartabull	.75	.30	.07
□ 288	Ken Holtzman	1.00	.40	.10
□ 289	Bart Shirley	.75	.30	.07
□ 290	Jim Kaat	3.50	1.40	.35
□ 291	Vern Fuller	.75	.30	.07
□ 292	Al Downing	1.00	.40	.10
□ 293	Dick Dietz	.75	.30	.07
□ 294	Jim Lemon MG	.75	.30	.07
□ 295	Tony Perez	4.00	1.60	.40
□ 296	Andy Messersmith	1.50	.60	.15
□ 297	Deron Johnson	1.00	.40	.10
□ 298	Dave Nicholson	.75	.30	.07
□ 299	Mark Belanger	1.00	.40	.10
□ 300	Felipe Alou	1.00	.40	.10
□ 301	Darrell Brandon	.75	.30	.07
□ 302	Jim Pagliaroni	.75	.30	.07
□ 303	Cal Koonce	.75	.30	.07
□ 304	Padres Rookies	1.00	.40	.10
	Bill Davis			
	Clarence Gaston			
□ 305	Dick McAuliffe	1.00	.40	.10
□ 306	Jim Grant	.75	.30	.07
□ 307	Gary Kolb	.75	.30	.07
□ 308	Wade Blasingame	.75	.30	.07
□ 309	Walt Williams	.75	.30	.07
□ 310	Tom Haller	1.00	.40	.10
□ 311	Sparky Lyle	3.50	1.40	.35
□ 312	Lee Elia	1.00	.40	.10
□ 313	Bill Robinson	1.00	.40	.10
□ 314	Checklist 4	2.50	.25	.05
	Don Drysdale			
□ 315	Eddie Fisher	.75	.30	.07
□ 316	Hal Lanier	1.00	.40	.10
□ 317	Bruce Look	.75	.30	.07
□ 318	Jack Fisher	.75	.30	.07
□ 319	Ken McMullen	.75	.30	.07
□ 320	Dal Maxvill	.75	.30	.07
□ 321	Jim McAndrew	.75	.30	.07
□ 322	Jose Vidal	.75	.30	.07
□ 323	Larry Miller	.75	.30	.07
□ 324	Tiger Rookies	.75	.30	.07
	Les Cain			
	Dave Campbell			
□ 325	Jose Cardenal	.75	.30	.07
□ 326	Gary Sutherland	.75	.30	.07
□ 327	Willie Crawford	.75	.30	.07
□ 328	Joe Horlen	.40	.16	.04
□ 329	Rick Joseph	.40	.16	.04
□ 330	Tony Conigliaro	1.25	.50	.12
□ 331	Braves Rookies	.60	.24	.06
	Gil Garrido			
	Tom House			
□ 332	Fred Talbot	.40	.16	.04
□ 333	Ivan Murrell	.40	.16	.04
□ 334	Phil Roof	.40	.16	.04
□ 335	Bill Mazeroski	1.00	.40	.10
□ 336	Jim Roland	.40	.16	.04
□ 337	Marty Martinez	.40	.16	.04
□ 338	Del Unser	.40	.16	.04
□ 339	Reds Rookies	.40	.16	.04
	Steve Mingori			
	Jose Pena			
□ 340	Dave McNally	.75	.30	.07
□ 341	Dave Adlesh	.40	.16	.04
□ 342	Bubba Morton	.40	.16	.04
□ 343	Dan Frisella	.40	.16	.04
□ 344	Tom Matchick	.40	.16	.04
□ 345	Frank Linzy	.40	.16	.04
□ 346	Wayne Comer	.40	.16	.04
□ 347	Randy Hundley	.60	.24	.06
□ 348	Steve Hargan	.40	.16	.04
□ 349	Dick Williams MG	.60	.24	.06
□ 350	Richie Allen	1.00	.40	.10
□ 351	Carroll Sembera	.40	.16	.04
□ 352	Paul Schaal	.40	.16	.04
□ 353	Jeff Torborg	.60	.24	.06
□ 354	Nate Oliver	.40	.16	.04
□ 355	Phil Niekro	4.00	1.60	.40
□ 356	Frank Quilici MG	.40	.16	.04
□ 357	Carl Taylor	.40	.16	.04
□ 358	Athletics Rookies	.40	.16	.04
	George Lauzerique			
	Roberto Rodriquez			
□ 359	Dick Kelley	.40	.16	.04
□ 360	Jim Wynn	.60	.24	.06
□ 361	Gary Holman	.40	.16	.04
□ 362	Jim Maloney	.60	.24	.06
□ 363	Russ Nixon	.60	.24	.06
□ 364	Tommie Agee	.60	.24	.06
□ 365	Jim Fregosi	.75	.30	.07
□ 366	Bo Belinsky	.60	.24	.06
□ 367	Lou Johnson	.40	.16	.04
□ 368	Vic Roznovsky	.40	.16	.04
□ 369	Bob Skinner	.40	.16	.04
□ 370	Juan Marichal	4.50	1.80	.45
□ 371	Sal Bando	.75	.30	.07
□ 372	Adolfo Phillips	.40	.16	.04
□ 373	Fred Lasher	.40	.16	.04
□ 374	Bob Tillman	.40	.16	.04
□ 375	Harmon Killebrew	10.00	4.00	1.00
□ 376	Royals Rookies	.40	.16	.04
	Mike Fiore			
	Jim Rooker			
□ 377	Gary Bell	.40	.16	.04
□ 378	Jose Herrera	.40	.16	.04
□ 379	Ken Boyer	1.00	.40	.10
□ 380	Stan Bahnsen	.40	.16	.04
□ 381	Ed Kranepool	.60	.24	.06
□ 382	Pat Corrales	.60	.24	.06

☐ 383 Casey Cox	.40	.16	.04
☐ 384 Larry Shepard MG	.40	.16	.04
☐ 385 Orlando Cepeda	2.50	1.00	.25
☐ 386 Jim McGlothlin	.40	.16	.04
☐ 387 Bobby Klaus	.40	.16	.04
☐ 388 Tom McCraw	.40	.16	.04
☐ 389 Dan Coombs	.40	.16	.04
☐ 390 Bill Freehan	1.00	.40	.10
☐ 391 Ray Culp	.40	.16	.04
☐ 392 Bob Burda	.40	.16	.04
☐ 393 Gene Brabender	.40	.16	.04
☐ 394 Pilots Rookies Lou Piniella Marv Staehle	2.25	.90	.22
☐ 395 Chris Short	.40	.16	.04
☐ 396 Jim Campanis	.40	.16	.04
☐ 397 Chuck Dobson	.40	.16	.04
☐ 398 Tito Francona	.60	.24	.06
☐ 399 Bob Bailey	.40	.16	.04
☐ 400 Don Drysdale	6.50	2.60	.65
☐ 401 Jake Gibbs	.40	.16	.04
☐ 402 Ken Boswell	.40	.16	.04
☐ 403 Bob Miller	.40	.16	.04
☐ 404 Cubs Rookies Vic LaRose Gary Ross	.40	.16	.04
☐ 405 Lee May	.60	.24	.06
☐ 406 Phil Ortega	.40	.16	.04
☐ 407 Tom Egan	.40	.16	.04
☐ 408 Nate Colbert	.40	.16	.04
☐ 409 Bob Moose	.40	.16	.04
☐ 410 Al Kaline	8.00	3.25	.80
☐ 411 Larry Dierker	.60	.24	.06
☐ 412 Checklist 5 Mickey Mantle	5.00	1.00	.20
☐ 413 Roland Sheldon	.40	.16	.04
☐ 414 Duke Sims	.40	.16	.04
☐ 415 Ray Washburn	.40	.16	.04
☐ 416 Willie McCovey AS	4.00	1.60	.40
☐ 417 Ken Harrelson AS	.60	.24	.06
☐ 418 Tommy Helms AS	.60	.24	.06
☐ 419 Rod Carew AS	5.00	2.00	.50
☐ 420 Ron Santo AS	.75	.30	.07
☐ 421 Brooks Robinson AS	4.00	1.60	.40
☐ 422 Don Kessinger AS	.60	.24	.06
☐ 423 Bert Campaneris AS	.60	.24	.06
☐ 424 Pete Rose AS	10.00	4.00	1.00
☐ 425 Carl Yastrzemski AS	8.00	3.25	.80
☐ 426 Curt Flood AS	.75	.30	.07
☐ 427 Tony Oliva AS	1.00	.40	.10
☐ 428 Lou Brock AS	4.00	1.60	.40
☐ 429 Willie Horton AS	.60	.24	.06
☐ 430 Johnny Bench AS	10.00	4.00	1.00
☐ 431 Bill Freehan AS	.75	.30	.07
☐ 432 Bob Gibson AS	3.50	1.40	.35
☐ 433 Denny McLain AS	.75	.30	.07
☐ 434 Jerry Koosman AS	.60	.24	.06
☐ 435 Sam McDowell AS	.60	.24	.06
☐ 436 Gene Alley	.60	.24	.06
☐ 437 Luis Alcaraz	.40	.16	.04
☐ 438 Gary Waslewski	.40	.16	.04
☐ 439 White Sox Rookies Ed Herrmann Dan Lazar	.40	.16	.04
☐ 440A Willie McCovey	11.00	4.50	1.10
☐ 440B Willie McCovey WL (McCovey white)	75.00	30.00	7.50
☐ 441A Dennis Higgins	.40	.16	.04
☐ 441B Dennis Higgins WL (Higgins white)	12.00	5.00	1.20
☐ 442 Ty Cline	.40	.16	.04
☐ 443 Don Wert	.40	.16	.04
☐ 444A Joe Moeller	.40	.16	.04
☐ 444B Joe Moeller WL (Moeller white)	12.00	5.00	1.20
☐ 445 Bobby Knoop	.40	.16	.04
☐ 446 Claude Raymond	.40	.16	.04
☐ 447A Ralph Houk MG	.75	.30	.07
☐ 447B Ralph Houk WL MG (Houk white)	12.00	5.00	1.20
☐ 448 Bob Tolan	.60	.24	.06
☐ 449 Paul Lindblad	.40	.16	.04
☐ 450 Billy Williams	4.50	1.80	.45
☐ 451A Rich Rollins	.60	.24	.06
☐ 451B Rich Rollins WL (Rich and 3B white)	12.00	5.00	1.20
☐ 452A Al Ferrara	.40	.16	.04
☐ 452B Al Ferrara WL (Al and OF white)	12.00	5.00	1.20
☐ 453 Mike Cuellar	1.00	.40	.10
☐ 454A Phillies Rookies Larry Colton Don Money	.60	.24	.06
☐ 454B Phillies Rookies WL Larry Colton Don Money (names in white)	12.00	5.00	1.20
☐ 455 Sonny Siebert	.60	.24	.06
☐ 456 Bud Harrelson	.60	.24	.06
☐ 457 Dalton Jones	.40	.16	.04
☐ 458 Curt Blefary	.40	.16	.04
☐ 459 Dave Boswell	.40	.16	.04
☐ 460 Joe Torre	1.00	.40	.10
☐ 461A Mike Epstein	.40	.16	.04
☐ 461B Mike Epstein WL (Epstein white)	12.00	5.00	1.20
☐ 462 Red Schoendienst MG	1.00	.40	.10
☐ 463 Dennis Ribant	.40	.16	.04
☐ 464A Dave Marshall	.40	.16	.04
☐ 464B Dave Marshall WL (Marshall white)	12.00	5.00	1.20
☐ 465 Tommy John	3.50	1.40	.35
☐ 466 John Boccabella	.40	.16	.04
☐ 467 Tom Reynolds	.40	.16	.04
☐ 468A Pirates Rookies Bruce Dal Canton Bob Robertson	.40	.16	.04
☐ 468B Pirates Rookies WL Bruce Dal Canton Bob Robertson (names in white)	12.00	5.00	1.20
☐ 469 Chico Ruiz	.40	.16	.04
☐ 470A Mel Stottlemyre	1.00	.40	.10
☐ 470B Mel Stottlemyre WL (Stottlemyre white)	15.00	6.00	1.50
☐ 471A Ted Savage	.40	.16	.04
☐ 471B Ted Savage WL (Savage white)	12.00	5.00	1.20
☐ 472 Jim Price	.40	.16	.04
☐ 473A Jose Arcia	.40	.16	.04
☐ 473B Jose Arcia WL (Jose and 2B white)	12.00	5.00	1.20
☐ 474 Tom Murphy	.40	.16	.04
☐ 475 Tim McCarver	1.25	.50	.12
☐ 476A Boston Rookies Ken Brett Gerry Moses	.60	.24	.06
☐ 476B Boston Rookies WL Ken Brett Gerry Moses (names in white)	12.00	5.00	1.20
☐ 477 Jeff James	.40	.16	.04
☐ 478 Don Buford	.60	.24	.06
☐ 479 Richie Scheinblum	.40	.16	.04
☐ 480 Tom Seaver	50.00	20.00	5.00
☐ 481 Bill Melton	.40	.16	.04
☐ 482A Jim Gosger	.40	.16	.04
☐ 482B Jim Gosger WL (Jim and OF white)	12.00	5.00	1.20
☐ 483 Ted Abernathy	.40	.16	.04
☐ 484 Joe Gordon MG	.60	.24	.06
☐ 485A Gaylord Perry	5.50	2.20	.55
☐ 485B Gaylord Perry WL (Perry white)	45.00	18.00	4.50
☐ 486A Paul Casanova	.40	.16	.04
☐ 486B Paul Casanova WL (Casanova white)	12.00	5.00	1.20
☐ 487 Denis Menke	.40	.16	.04
☐ 488 Joe Sparma	.40	.16	.04
☐ 489 Clete Boyer	.60	.24	.06
☐ 490 Matty Alou	.60	.24	.06
☐ 491A Twins Rookies Jerry Crider George Mitterwald	.40	.16	.04
☐ 491B Twins Rookies WL Jerry Crider George Mitterwald (names in white)	12.00	5.00	1.20
☐ 492 Tony Cloninger	.40	.16	.04
☐ 493A Wes Parker	.60	.24	.06
☐ 493B Wes Parker WL (Parker white)	12.00	5.00	1.20
☐ 494 Ken Berry	.40	.16	.04
☐ 495 Bert Campaneris	.75	.30	.07
☐ 496 Larry Jaster	.40	.16	.04
☐ 497 Julian Javier	.60	.24	.06
☐ 498 Juan Pizarro	.40	.16	.04
☐ 499 Astro Rookies Don Bryant Steve Shea	.40	.16	.04
☐ 500A Mickey Mantle	150.00	60.00	15.00
☐ 500B Mickey Mantle WL (Mantle white)	500.00	200.00	50.00
☐ 501A Tony Gonzalez	.40	.16	.04
☐ 501B Tony Gonzalez WL (Tony and OF white)	12.00	5.00	1.20
☐ 502 Minnie Rojas	.40	.16	.04
☐ 503 Larry Brown	.40	.16	.04
☐ 504 Checklist 6 Brooks Robinson	2.50	.30	.05

☐ 505A	Bobby Bolin	.40	.16	.04
☐ 505B	Bobby Bolin WL	12.00	5.00	1.20
	(Bolin white)			
☐ 506	Paul Blair	.60	.24	.06
☐ 507	Cookie Rojas	.60	.24	.06
☐ 508	Moe Drabowsky	.40	.16	.04
☐ 509	Manny Sanguillen	.75	.30	.07
☐ 510	Rod Carew	25.00	10.00	2.50
☐ 511A	Diego Segui	.40	.16	.04
☐ 511B	Diego Segui WL	12.00	5.00	1.20
	(Diego and P white)			
☐ 512	Cleon Jones	.40	.16	.04
☐ 513	Camilo Pascual	.75	.30	.07
☐ 514	Mike Lum	.50	.20	.05
☐ 515	Dick Green	.50	.20	.05
☐ 516	Earl Weaver MG	4.00	1.60	.40
☐ 517	Mike McCormick	.75	.30	.07
☐ 518	Fred Whitfield	.50	.20	.05
☐ 519	Yankees Rookies	.50	.20	.05
	Gerry Kenney			
	Len Boehmer			
☐ 520	Bob Veale	.75	.30	.07
☐ 521	George Thomas	.50	.20	.05
☐ 522	Joe Hoerner	.50	.20	.05
☐ 523	Bob Chance	.50	.20	.05
☐ 524	Expos Rookies	.50	.20	.05
	Jose Laboy			
	Floyd Wicker			
☐ 525	Earl Wilson	.50	.20	.05
☐ 526	Hector Torres	.50	.20	.05
☐ 527	Al Lopez MG	2.00	.80	.20
☐ 528	Claude Osteen	.75	.30	.07
☐ 529	Ed Kirkpatrick	.50	.20	.05
☐ 530	Cesar Tovar	.50	.20	.05
☐ 531	Dick Farrell	.50	.20	.05
☐ 532	Bird Hill Aces	.75	.30	.07
	Tom Phoebus			
	Jim Hardin			
	Dave McNally			
	Mike Cuellar			
☐ 533	Nolan Ryan	70.00	28.00	7.00
☐ 534	Jerry McNertney	.50	.20	.05
☐ 535	Phil Regan	.75	.30	.07
☐ 536	Padres Rookies	.50	.20	.05
	Danny Breeden			
	Dave Roberts			
☐ 537	Mike Paul	.50	.20	.05
☐ 538	Charlie Smith	.50	.20	.05
☐ 539	Ted Shows How	3.50	1.40	.35
	Mike Epstein			
	Ted Williams			
☐ 540	Curt Flood	1.00	.40	.10
☐ 541	Joe Verbanic	.50	.20	.05
☐ 542	Bob Aspromonte	.50	.20	.05
☐ 543	Fred Newman	.50	.20	.05
☐ 544	Tigers Rookies	.50	.20	.05
	Mike Kilkenny			
	Ron Woods			
☐ 545	Willie Stargell	10.00	4.00	1.00
☐ 546	Jim Nash	.50	.20	.05
☐ 547	Billy Martin MG	2.50	1.00	.25
☐ 548	Bob Locker	.50	.20	.05
☐ 549	Ron Brand	.50	.20	.05
☐ 550	Brooks Robinson	10.00	4.00	1.00
☐ 551	Wayne Granger	.50	.20	.05
☐ 552	Dodgers Rookies	.75	.30	.07
	Ted Sizemore			
	Bill Sudakis			
☐ 553	Ron Davis	.50	.20	.05
☐ 554	Frank Bertaina	.50	.20	.05
☐ 555	Jim Ray Hart	.75	.30	.07
☐ 556	A's Stars	.75	.30	.07
	Sal Bando			
	Bert Campaneris			
	Danny Cater			
☐ 557	Frank Fernandez	.50	.20	.05
☐ 558	Tom Burgmeier	.75	.30	.07
☐ 559	Cardinals Rookies	.50	.20	.05
	Joe Hague			
	Jim Hicks			
☐ 560	Luis Tiant	1.25	.50	.12
☐ 561	Ron Clark	.50	.20	.05
☐ 562	Bob Watson	2.50	1.00	.25
☐ 563	Martin Pattin	.50	.20	.05
☐ 564	Gil Hodges MG	6.00	2.40	.60
☐ 565	Hoyt Wilhelm	5.50	2.20	.55
☐ 566	Ron Hansen	.50	.20	.05
☐ 567	Pirates Rookies	.50	.20	.05
	Elvio Jimenez			
	Jim Shellenback			
☐ 568	Cecil Upshaw	.50	.20	.05
☐ 569	Billy Harris	.50	.20	.05
☐ 570	Ron Santo	1.00	.40	.10
☐ 571	Cap Peterson	.50	.20	.05
☐ 572	Giants Heroes	6.50	2.60	.65
	Willie McCovey			
	Juan Marichal			
☐ 573	Jim Palmer	12.00	5.00	1.20
☐ 574	George Scott	.75	.30	.07
☐ 575	Bill Singer	.75	.30	.07
☐ 576	Phillies Rookies	.50	.20	.05
	Ron Stone			
	Bill Wilson			
☐ 577	Mike Hegan	.50	.20	.05
☐ 578	Don Bosch	.50	.20	.05
☐ 579	Dave Nelson	.50	.20	.05
☐ 580	Jim Northrup	.75	.30	.07
☐ 581	Gary Nolan	.50	.20	.05
☐ 582A	Checklist 7	2.50	.30	.05
	(white circle on back)			
	(Tony Oliva)			
☐ 582B	Checklist 7	4.00	.40	.07
	(red circle on back)			
	(Tony Oliva)			
☐ 583	Clyde Wright	.50	.20	.05
☐ 584	Don Mason	.50	.20	.05
☐ 585	Ron Swoboda	.75	.30	.07
☐ 586	Tim Cullen	.50	.20	.05
☐ 587	Joe Rudi	1.50	.60	.15
☐ 588	Bill White	1.00	.40	.10
☐ 589	Joe Pepitone	1.00	.40	.10
☐ 590	Rico Carty	1.00	.40	.10
☐ 591	Mike Hedlund	.65	.26	.06
☐ 592	Padres Rookies	.65	.26	.06
	Rafael Robles			
	Al Santorini			
☐ 593	Don Nottebart	.65	.26	.06
☐ 594	Dooley Womack	.65	.26	.06
☐ 595	Lee Maye	.65	.26	.06
☐ 596	Chuck Hartenstein	.65	.26	.06
☐ 597	A.L. Rookies	20.00	8.00	2.00
	Bob Floyd			
	Larry Burchart			
	Rollie Fingers			
☐ 598	Ruben Amaro	.65	.26	.06
☐ 599	John Boozer	.65	.26	.06
☐ 600	Tony Oliva	2.25	.90	.22
☐ 601	Tug McGraw	1.50	.60	.15
☐ 602	Cubs Rookies	.65	.26	.06
	Alec Distaso			
	Don Young			
	Jim Qualls			
☐ 603	Joe Keough	.65	.26	.06
☐ 604	Bobby Etheridge	.65	.26	.06
☐ 605	Dick Ellsworth	.65	.26	.06
☐ 606	Gene Mauch MG	1.00	.40	.10
☐ 607	Dick Bosman	.65	.26	.06
☐ 608	Dick Simpson	.65	.26	.06
☐ 609	Phil Gagliano	.65	.26	.06
☐ 610	Jim Hardin	.65	.26	.06
☐ 611	Braves Rookies	1.00	.40	.10
	Bob Didier			
	Walt Hriniak			
	Gary Neibauer			
☐ 612	Jack Aker	.65	.26	.06
☐ 613	Jim Beauchamp	.65	.26	.06
☐ 614	Houston Rookies	.65	.26	.06
	Tom Griffin			
	Skip Guinn			
☐ 615	Len Gabrielson	.65	.26	.06
☐ 616	Don McMahon	.65	.26	.06
☐ 617	Jesse Gonder	.65	.26	.06
☐ 618	Ramon Webster	.65	.26	.06
☐ 619	Royals Rookies	1.00	.40	.10
	Bill Butler			
	Pat Kelly			
	Juan Rios			
☐ 620	Dean Chance	1.00	.40	.10
☐ 621	Bill Voss	.65	.26	.06
☐ 622	Dan Osinski	.65	.26	.06
☐ 623	Hank Allen	.65	.26	.06
☐ 624	NL Rookies	.65	.26	.06
	Darrel Chaney			
	Duffy Dyer			
	Terry Harmon			
☐ 625	Mack Jones	.65	.26	.06
	(Batting wrong)			
☐ 626	Gene Michael	1.00	.40	.10
☐ 627	George Stone	.65	.26	.06
☐ 628	Red Sox Rookies	1.00	.40	.10
	Bill Conigliaro			
	Syd O'Brien			
	Fred Wenz			
☐ 629	Jack Hamilton	.65	.26	.06
☐ 630	Bobby Bonds	8.00	3.25	.80
☐ 631	John Kennedy	.65	.26	.06
☐ 632	Jon Warden	.65	.26	.06
☐ 633	Harry Walker MG	.65	.26	.06
☐ 634	Andy Etchebarren	.65	.26	.06
☐ 635	George Culver	.65	.26	.06

☐ 636	Woodie Held	.65	.26	.06
☐ 637	Padres Rookies	.65	.26	.06
	Jerry DaVanon			
	Frank Reberger			
	Clay Kirby			
☐ 638	Ed Sprague	.65	.26	.06
☐ 639	Barry Moore	.65	.26	.06
☐ 640	Fergie Jenkins	3.00	1.20	.30
☐ 641	NL Rookies	.65	.26	.06
	Bobby Darwin			
	John Miller			
	Tommy Dean			
☐ 642	John Hiller	1.00	.40	.10
☐ 643	Billy Cowan	.65	.26	.06
☐ 644	Chuck Hinton	.65	.26	.06
☐ 645	George Brunet	.65	.26	.06
☐ 646	Expos Rookies	.65	.26	.06
	Dan McGinn			
	Carl Morton			
☐ 647	Dave Wickersham	.65	.26	.06
☐ 648	Bobby Wine	.65	.26	.06
☐ 649	Al Jackson	.65	.26	.06
☐ 650	Ted Williams MG	6.00	2.40	.60
☐ 651	Gus Gil	.65	.26	.06
☐ 652	Eddie Watt	.65	.26	.06
☐ 653	Aurelio Rodriguez	1.50	.60	.15
	(photo actually			
	Angels' batboy)			
☐ 654	White Sox Rookies	1.00	.40	.10
	Carlos May			
	Don Secrist			
	Rich Morales			
☐ 655	Mike Hershberger	.65	.26	.06
☐ 656	Dan Schneider	.65	.26	.06
☐ 657	Bobby Murcer	1.25	.50	.12
☐ 658	AL Rookies	.65	.26	.06
	Tom Hall			
	Bill Burbach			
	Jim Miles			
☐ 659	Johnny Podres	1.25	.50	.12
☐ 660	Reggie Smith	1.50	.60	.15
☐ 661	Jim Merritt	.65	.26	.06
☐ 662	Royals Rookies	1.00	.40	.10
	Dick Drago			
	George Spriggs			
	Bob Oliver			
☐ 663	Dick Radatz	1.00	.40	.10
☐ 664	Ron Hunt	1.00	.40	.10

1969 Topps Deckle

The cards in this 33-card set measure 2 1/4" by 3 1/4". This unusual black and white insert set derives its name from the serrated border, or edge, of the cards. The cards were included as inserts in the regularly issued Topps baseball series of 1969. Card number 11 is found with either Hoyt Wilhelm or Jim Wynn, and number 22 with either Rusty Staub or Joe Foy. The set price below does include all variations.

		NRMT	VG-E	GOOD
COMPLETE SET (35)		50.00	20.00	5.00
COMMON PLAYER (1-33)		.30	.12	.03
☐ 1	Brooks Robinson	2.50	1.00	.25
☐ 2	Boog Powell	.50	.20	.05
☐ 3	Ken Harrelson	.40	.16	.04
☐ 4	Carl Yastrzemski	4.50	1.80	.45
☐ 5	Jim Fregosi	.40	.16	.04
☐ 6	Luis Aparicio	1.00	.40	.10
☐ 7	Luis Tiant	.40	.16	.04
☐ 8	Denny McLain	.40	.16	.04
☐ 9	Willie Horton	.30	.12	.03
☐ 10	Bill Freehan	.30	.12	.03
☐ 11A	Hoyt Wilhelm	5.00	2.00	.50
☐ 11B	Jim Wynn	6.00	2.40	.60
☐ 12	Rod Carew	3.50	1.40	.35
☐ 13	Mel Stottlemyre	.30	.12	.03
☐ 14	Rick Monday	.30	.12	.03
☐ 15	Tommy Davis	.30	.12	.03
☐ 16	Frank Howard	.40	.16	.04
☐ 17	Felipe Alou	.30	.12	.03
☐ 18	Don Kessinger	.30	.12	.03
☐ 19	Ron Santo	.40	.16	.04
☐ 20	Tommy Helms	.30	.12	.03
☐ 21	Pete Rose	8.00	3.25	.80
☐ 22A	Rusty Staub	2.50	1.00	.25
☐ 22B	Joe Foy	6.00	2.40	.60
☐ 23	Tom Haller	.30	.12	.03
☐ 24	Maury Wills	.60	.24	.06
☐ 25	Jerry Koosman	.40	.16	.04
☐ 26	Richie Allen	.40	.16	.04
☐ 27	Bob Clemente	3.50	1.40	.35
☐ 28	Curt Flood	.40	.16	.04
☐ 29	Bob Gibson	1.75	.70	.17
☐ 30	Al Ferrara	.30	.12	.03
☐ 31	Willie McCovey	2.00	.80	.20
☐ 32	Juan Marichal	1.75	.70	.17
☐ 33	Willie Mays	4.00	1.60	.40

1969 Topps Super

The cards in this 66-card set measure 2 1/4" by 3 1/4". This beautiful Topps set was released independently of the regular baseball series of 1969. It is referred to as "Super Baseball" on the back of the card, a title which was also used for the postcard-size cards issued in 1970 and 1971. Complete sheets, and cards with square corners cut from these sheets, are sometimes encountered.

		NRMT	VG-E	GOOD
COMPLETE SET (66)		3300.00	1500.00	375.00
COMMON PLAYER (1-66)		8.00	3.25	.80
☐ 1	Dave McNally	10.00	4.00	1.00
☐ 2	Frank Robinson	125.00	50.00	12.50
☐ 3	Brooks Robinson	175.00	70.00	18.00
☐ 4	Ken Harrelson	10.00	4.00	1.00
☐ 5	Carl Yastrzemski	350.00	140.00	35.00
☐ 6	Ray Culp	8.00	3.25	.80
☐ 7	Jim Fregosi	10.00	4.00	1.00
☐ 8	Rick Reichardt	8.00	3.25	.80
☐ 9	Vic Davalillo	8.00	3.25	.80
☐ 10	Luis Aparicio	50.00	20.00	5.00
☐ 11	Pete Ward	8.00	3.25	.80
☐ 12	Joe Horlen	8.00	3.25	.80
☐ 13	Luis Tiant	12.00	5.00	1.20
☐ 14	Sam McDowell	10.00	4.00	1.00
☐ 15	Jose Cardenal	8.00	3.25	.80
☐ 16	Willie Horton	10.00	4.00	1.00
☐ 17	Denny McLain	12.00	5.00	1.20
☐ 18	Bill Freehan	10.00	4.00	1.00
☐ 19	Harmon Killebrew	75.00	30.00	7.50

☐ 20	Tony Oliva	15.00	6.00	1.50
☐ 21	Dean Chance	8.00	3.25	.80
☐ 22	Joe Foy	8.00	3.25	.80
☐ 23	Roger Nelson	8.00	3.25	.80
☐ 24	Mickey Mantle	650.00	260.00	65.00
☐ 25	Mel Stottlemyre	10.00	4.00	1.00
☐ 26	Roy White	10.00	4.00	1.00
☐ 27	Rick Monday	10.00	4.00	1.00
☐ 28	Reggie Jackson	350.00	140.00	35.00
☐ 29	Bert Campaneris	8.00	3.25	.80
☐ 30	Frank Howard	10.00	4.00	1.00
☐ 31	Camilo Pascual	8.00	3.25	.80
☐ 32	Tommy Davis	10.00	4.00	1.00
☐ 33	Don Mincher	8.00	3.25	.80
☐ 34	Hank Aaron	300.00	120.00	30.00
☐ 35	Felipe Alou	8.00	3.25	.80
☐ 36	Joe Torre	12.00	5.00	1.20
☐ 37	Fergie Jenkins	15.00	6.00	1.50
☐ 38	Ron Santo	10.00	4.00	1.00
☐ 39	Billy Williams	50.00	20.00	5.00
☐ 40	Tommy Helms	8.00	3.25	.80
☐ 41	Pete Rose	500.00	200.00	50.00
☐ 42	Joe Morgan	50.00	20.00	5.00
☐ 43	Jim Wynn	8.00	3.25	.80
☐ 44	Curt Blefary	8.00	3.25	.80
☐ 45	Willie Davis	10.00	4.00	1.00
☐ 46	Don Drysdale	50.00	20.00	5.00
☐ 47	Tom Haller	8.00	3.25	.80
☐ 48	Rusty Staub	12.00	5.00	1.20
☐ 49	Maury Wills	15.00	6.00	1.50
☐ 50	Cleon Jones	8.00	3.25	.80
☐ 51	Jerry Koosman	10.00	4.00	1.00
☐ 52	Tom Seaver	175.00	70.00	18.00
☐ 53	Richie Allen	12.00	5.00	1.20
☐ 54	Chris Short	8.00	3.25	.80
☐ 55	Cookie Rojas	8.00	3.25	.80
☐ 56	Matty Alou	8.00	3.25	.80
☐ 57	Steve Blass	8.00	3.25	.80
☐ 58	Bob Clemente	200.00	80.00	20.00
☐ 59	Curt Flood	15.00	6.00	1.50
☐ 60	Bob Gibson	75.00	30.00	7.50
☐ 61	Tim McCarver	15.00	6.00	1.50
☐ 62	Dick Selma	8.00	3.25	.80
☐ 63	Ollie Brown	8.00	3.25	.80
☐ 64	Juan Marichal	75.00	30.00	7.50
☐ 65	Willie Mays	300.00	120.00	30.00
☐ 66	Willie McCovey	100.00	40.00	10.00

1970 Topps

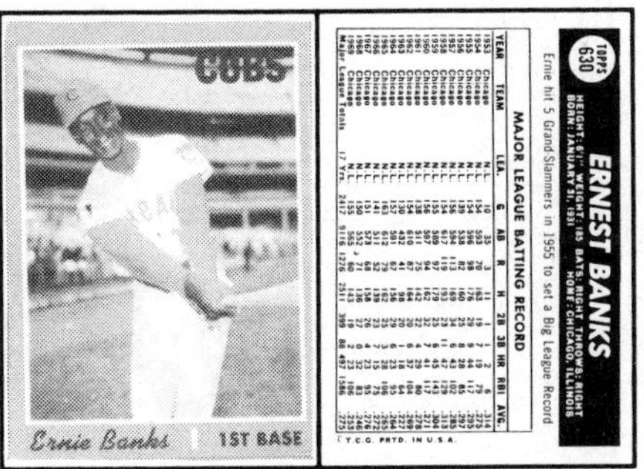

The cards in this 720-card set measure 2 1/2" by 3 1/2". The Topps set for 1970 has color photos surrounded by white frame lines and gray borders. The backs have a blue biographical section and a yellow record section. All-Star selections are featured on cards 450 to 469. Other topical subsets within this set include League Leaders (61-72), Playoffs cards (195-202), and World Series cards (305-310). There are graduations of scarcity, terminating in the high series (634- 720), which are outlined in the value summary.

	NRMT	VG-E	GOOD
COMPLETE SET (720)	1250.00	500.00	175.00
COMMON PLAYER (1-132)	.25	.10	.02
COMMON PLAYER (133-263)	.30	.12	.03
COMMON PLAYER (264-459)	.35	.14	.03
COMMON PLAYER (460-546)	.50	.20	.05
COMMON PLAYER (547-633)	.85	.34	.08
COMMON PLAYER (634-720)	2.00	.80	.20

☐ 1	New York Mets Team Card	6.00	1.00	.20
☐ 2	Diego Segui	.25	.10	.02
☐ 3	Darrel Chaney	.25	.10	.02
☐ 4	Tom Egan	.25	.10	.02
☐ 5	Wes Parker	.40	.16	.04
☐ 6	Grant Jackson	.25	.10	.02
☐ 7	Indians Rookies	.25	.10	.02
	Gary Boyd			
	Russ Nagelson			
☐ 8	Jose Martinez	.25	.10	.02
☐ 9	Checklist 1	1.50	.20	.04
☐ 10	Carl Yastrzemski	24.00	10.00	2.40
☐ 11	Nate Colbert	.25	.10	.02
☐ 12	John Hiller	.40	.16	.04
☐ 13	Jack Hiatt	.25	.10	.02
☐ 14	Hank Allen	.25	.10	.02
☐ 15	Larry Dierker	.40	.16	.04
☐ 16	Charlie Metro MG	.25	.10	.02
☐ 17	Hoyt Wilhelm	3.50	1.40	.35
☐ 18	Carlos May	.25	.10	.02
☐ 19	John Boccabella	.25	.10	.02
☐ 20	Dave McNally	.40	.16	.04
☐ 21	A's Rookies	2.00	.80	.20
	Vida Blue			
	Gene Tenace			
☐ 22	Ray Washburn	.25	.10	.02
☐ 23	Bill Robinson	.40	.16	.04
☐ 24	Dick Selma	.25	.10	.02
☐ 25	Cesar Tovar	.25	.10	.02
☐ 26	Tug McGraw	.75	.30	.07
☐ 27	Chuck Hinton	.25	.10	.02
☐ 28	Billy Wilson	.25	.10	.02
☐ 29	Sandy Alomar	.25	.10	.02
☐ 30	Matty Alou	.40	.16	.04
☐ 31	Marty Pattin	.25	.10	.02
☐ 32	Harry Walker MG	.25	.10	.02
☐ 33	Don Wert	.25	.10	.02
☐ 34	Willie Crawford	.25	.10	.02
☐ 35	Joe Horlen	.25	.10	.02
☐ 36	Red Rookies	.40	.16	.04
	Danny Breeden			
	Bernie Carbo			
☐ 37	Dick Drago	.25	.10	.02
☐ 38	Mack Jones	.25	.10	.02
☐ 39	Mike Nagy	.25	.10	.02
☐ 40	Rich Allen	.75	.30	.07
☐ 41	George Lauzerique	.25	.10	.02
☐ 42	Tito Fuentes	.25	.10	.02
☐ 43	Jack Aker	.25	.10	.02
☐ 44	Roberto Pena	.25	.10	.02
☐ 45	Dave Johnson	.60	.24	.06
☐ 46	Ken Rudolph	.25	.10	.02
☐ 47	Bob Miller	.25	.10	.02
☐ 48	Gil Garrido	.25	.10	.02
☐ 49	Tim Cullen	.25	.10	.02
☐ 50	Tommie Agee	.25	.10	.02
☐ 51	Bob Christian	.25	.10	.02
☐ 52	Bruce Dal Canton	.25	.10	.02
☐ 53	John Kennedy	.25	.10	.02
☐ 54	Jeff Torborg	.40	.16	.04
☐ 55	John Odom	.25	.10	.02
☐ 56	Phillies Rookies	.25	.10	.02
	Joe Lis			
	Scott Reid			
☐ 57	Pat Kelly	.25	.10	.02
☐ 58	Dave Marshall	.25	.10	.02
☐ 59	Dick Ellsworth	.40	.16	.04
☐ 60	Jim Wynn	.40	.16	.04
☐ 61	NL Batting Leaders	3.00	1.20	.30
	Pete Rose			
	Bob Clemente			
	Cleon Jones			
☐ 62	AL Batting Leaders	1.25	.50	.12
	Rod Carew			
	Reggie Smith			
	Tony Oliva			
☐ 63	NL RBI Leaders	1.25	.50	.12
	Willie McCovey			
	Ron Santo			
	Tony Perez			
☐ 64	AL RBI Leaders	1.75	.70	.17
	Harmon Killebrew			
	Boog Powell			
	Reggie Jackson			
☐ 65	NL Home Run Leaders	2.00	.80	.20
	Willie McCovey			
	Hank Aaron			
	Lee May			
☐ 66	AL Home Run Leaders	2.00	.80	.20
	Harmon Killebrew			

Frank Howard			
Reggie Jackson			
☐ 67 NL ERA Leaders	3.50	1.40	.35
Juan Marichal			
Steve Carlton			
Bob Gibson			
☐ 68 AL ERA Leaders	1.25	.50	.12
Dick Bosman			
Jim Palmer			
Mike Cuellar			
☐ 69 NL Pitching Leaders	2.50	1.00	.25
Tom Seaver			
Phil Niekro			
Fergie Jenkins			
Juan Marichal			
☐ 70 AL Pitching Leaders	1.25	.50	.12
Dennis McLain			
Mike Cuellar			
Dave Boswell			
Dave McNally			
Jim Perry			
Mel Stottlemyre			
☐ 71 NL Strikeout Leaders	1.25	.50	.12
Fergie Jenkins			
Bob Gibson			
Bill Singer			
☐ 72 AL Strikeout Leaders	1.25	.50	.12
Sam McDowell			
Mickey Lolich			
Andy Messersmith			
☐ 73 Wayne Granger	.25	.10	.02
☐ 74 Angels Rookies	.25	.10	.02
Greg Washburn			
Wally Wolf			
☐ 75 Jim Kaat	2.00	.80	.20
☐ 76 Carl Taylor	.25	.10	.02
☐ 77 Frank Linzy	.25	.10	.02
☐ 78 Joe Lahoud	.25	.10	.02
☐ 79 Clay Kirby	.25	.10	.02
☐ 80 Don Kessinger	.40	.16	.04
☐ 81 Dave May	.25	.10	.02
☐ 82 Frank Fernandez	.25	.10	.02
☐ 83 Don Cardwell	.25	.10	.02
☐ 84 Paul Casanova	.25	.10	.02
☐ 85 Max Alvis	.25	.10	.02
☐ 86 Lum Harris MG	.25	.10	.02
☐ 87 Steve Renko	.25	.10	.02
☐ 88 Pilots Rookies	.25	.10	.02
Miguel Fuentes			
Dick Baney			
☐ 89 Juan Rios	.25	.10	.02
☐ 90 Tim McCarver	.75	.30	.07
☐ 91 Rich Morales	.25	.10	.02
☐ 92 George Culver	.25	.10	.02
☐ 93 Rick Renick	.25	.10	.02
☐ 94 Fred Patek	.40	.16	.04
☐ 95 Earl Wilson	.25	.10	.02
☐ 96 Cardinals Rookies	2.25	.90	.22
Leron Lee			
Jerry Reuss			
☐ 97 Joe Moeller	.25	.10	.02
☐ 98 Gates Brown	.40	.16	.04
☐ 99 Bobby Pfeil	.25	.10	.02
☐ 100 Mel Stottlemyre	.60	.24	.06
☐ 101 Bobby Floyd	.25	.10	.02
☐ 102 Joe Rudi	.40	.16	.04
☐ 103 Frank Reberger	.25	.10	.02
☐ 104 Gerry Moses	.25	.10	.02
☐ 105 Tony Gonzalez	.25	.10	.02
☐ 106 Darold Knowles	.25	.10	.02
☐ 107 Bobby Etheridge	.25	.10	.02
☐ 108 Tom Burgmeier	.25	.10	.02
☐ 109 Expos Rookies	.40	.16	.04
Garry Jestadt			
Carl Morton			
☐ 110 Bob Moose	.25	.10	.02
☐ 111 Mike Hegan	.25	.10	.02
☐ 112 Dave Nelson	.25	.10	.02
☐ 113 Jim Ray	.25	.10	.02
☐ 114 Gene Michael	.40	.16	.04
☐ 115 Alex Johnson	.40	.16	.04
☐ 116 Sparky Lyle	.75	.30	.07
☐ 117 Don Young	.25	.10	.02
☐ 118 George Mitterwald	.25	.10	.02
☐ 119 Chuck Taylor	.25	.10	.02
☐ 120 Sal Bando	.60	.24	.06
☐ 121 Orioles Rookies	.40	.16	.04
Fred Beene			
Terry Crowley			
☐ 122 George Stone	.25	.10	.02
☐ 123 Don Gutteridge	.25	.10	.02
☐ 124 Larry Jaster	.25	.10	.02
☐ 125 Deron Johnson	.25	.10	.02
☐ 126 Marty Martinez	.25	.10	.02
☐ 127 Joe Coleman	.25	.10	.02
☐ 128 Checklist 2	1.50	.20	.04
☐ 129 Jimmie Price	.25	.10	.02
☐ 130 Ollie Brown	.25	.10	.02
☐ 131 Dodgers Rookies	.25	.10	.02
Ray Lamb			
Bob Stinson			
☐ 132 Jim McGlothlin	.25	.10	.02
☐ 133 Clay Carroll	.30	.12	.03
☐ 134 Danny Walton	.30	.12	.03
☐ 135 Dick Dietz	.30	.12	.03
☐ 136 Steve Hargan	.30	.12	.03
☐ 137 Art Shamsky	.30	.12	.03
☐ 138 Joe Foy	.30	.12	.03
☐ 139 Rich Nye	.30	.12	.03
☐ 140 Reggie Jackson	50.00	20.00	5.00
☐ 141 Pirates Rookies	.50	.20	.05
Dave Cash			
Johnny Jeter			
☐ 142 Fritz Peterson	.30	.12	.03
☐ 143 Phil Gagliano	.30	.12	.03
☐ 144 Ray Culp	.30	.12	.03
☐ 145 Rico Carty	.50	.20	.05
☐ 146 Danny Murphy	.30	.12	.03
☐ 147 Angel Hermoso	.30	.12	.03
☐ 148 Earl Weaver MG	1.00	.40	.10
☐ 149 Billy Champion	.30	.12	.03
☐ 150 Harmon Killebrew	5.00	2.00	.50
☐ 151 Dave Roberts	.30	.12	.03
☐ 152 Ike Brown	.30	.12	.03
☐ 153 Gary Gentry	.30	.12	.03
☐ 154 Senators Rookies	.30	.12	.03
Jim Miles			
Jan Dukes			
☐ 155 Denis Menke	.30	.12	.03
☐ 156 Eddie Fisher	.30	.12	.03
☐ 157 Manny Mota	.50	.20	.05
☐ 158 Jerry McNertney	.30	.12	.03
☐ 159 Tommy Helms	.50	.20	.05
☐ 160 Phil Niekro	3.50	1.40	.35
☐ 161 Richie Scheinblum	.30	.12	.03
☐ 162 Jerry Johnson	.30	.12	.03
☐ 163 Syd O'Brien	.30	.12	.03
☐ 164 Ty Cline	.30	.12	.03
☐ 165 Ed Kirkpatrick	.30	.12	.03
☐ 166 Al Oliver	2.00	.80	.20
☐ 167 Bill Burbach	.30	.12	.03
☐ 168 Dave Watkins	.30	.12	.03
☐ 169 Tom Hall	.30	.12	.03
☐ 170 Billy Williams	4.00	1.60	.40
☐ 171 Jim Nash	.30	.12	.03
☐ 172 Braves Rookies	1.00	.40	.10
Garry Hill			
Ralph Garr			
☐ 173 Jim Hicks	.30	.12	.03
☐ 174 Ted Sizemore	.50	.20	.05
☐ 175 Dick Bosman	.30	.12	.03
☐ 176 Jim Ray Hart	.50	.20	.05
☐ 177 Jim Northrup	.50	.20	.05
☐ 178 Denny Lemaster	.30	.12	.03
☐ 179 Ivan Murrell	.30	.12	.03
☐ 180 Tommy John	2.25	.90	.22
☐ 181 Sparky Anderson MG	1.00	.40	.10
☐ 182 Dick Hall	.30	.12	.03
☐ 183 Jerry Grote	.30	.12	.03
☐ 184 Ray Fosse	.30	.12	.03
☐ 185 Don Mincher	.50	.20	.05
☐ 186 Rick Joseph	.30	.12	.03
☐ 187 Mike Hedlund	.30	.12	.03
☐ 188 Manny Sanguillen	.50	.20	.05
☐ 189 Yankees Rookies	35.00	14.00	3.50
Thurman Munson			
Dave McDonald			
☐ 190 Joe Torre	1.00	.40	.10
☐ 191 Vicente Romo	.30	.12	.03
☐ 192 Jim Qualls	.30	.12	.03
☐ 193 Mike Wegener	.30	.12	.03
☐ 194 Chuck Manuel	.30	.12	.03
☐ 195 NL Playoff Game 1	3.00	1.20	.30
Seaver wins opener			
☐ 196 NL Playoff Game 2	1.25	.50	.12
Mets show muscle			
☐ 197 NL Playoff Game 3	3.00	1.20	.30
Ryan saves the day			
☐ 198 NL Playoff Summary	1.25	.50	.12
Mets celebrate			
☐ 199 AL Playoff Game 1	1.25	.50	.12
Orioles win squeaker (Cuellar)			
☐ 200 AL Playoff Game 2	1.25	.50	.12
Powell scores winning run			
☐ 201 AL Playoff Game 3	1.25	.50	.12
Birds wrap it up			
☐ 202 AL Playoff Summary	1.25	.50	.12
Orioles celebrate			

□ 203	Rudy May	.30	.12	.03
□ 204	Len Gabrielson	.30	.12	.03
□ 205	Bert Campaneris	.50	.20	.05
□ 206	Clete Boyer	.50	.20	.05
□ 207	Tigers Rookies	.30	.12	.03
	Norman McRae			
	Bob Reed			
□ 208	Fred Gladding	.30	.12	.03
□ 209	Ken Suarez	.30	.12	.03
□ 210	Juan Marichal	4.00	1.60	.40
□ 211	Ted Williams MG	5.00	2.00	.50
□ 212	Al Santorini	.30	.12	.03
□ 213	Andy Etchebarren	.30	.12	.03
□ 214	Ken Boswell	.30	.12	.03
□ 215	Reggie Smith	.75	.30	.07
□ 216	Chuck Hartenstein	.30	.12	.03
□ 217	Ron Hansen	.30	.12	.03
□ 218	Ron Stone	.30	.12	.03
□ 219	Jerry Kenney	.30	.12	.03
□ 220	Steve Carlton	12.00	5.00	1.20
□ 221	Ron Brand	.30	.12	.03
□ 222	Jim Rooker	.30	.12	.03
□ 223	Nate Oliver	.30	.12	.03
□ 224	Steve Barber	.30	.12	.03
□ 225	Lee May	.50	.20	.05
□ 226	Ron Perranoski	.50	.20	.05
□ 227	Astros Rookies	1.00	.40	.10
	John Mayberry			
	Bob Watkins			
□ 228	Aurelio Rodriguez	.30	.12	.03
□ 229	Rich Robertson	.30	.12	.03
□ 230	Brooks Robinson	7.00	2.80	.70
□ 231	Luis Tiant	1.00	.40	.10
□ 232	Bob Didier	.30	.12	.03
□ 233	Lew Krausse	.30	.12	.03
□ 234	Tommy Dean	.30	.12	.03
□ 235	Mike Epstein	.30	.12	.03
□ 236	Bob Veale	.50	.20	.05
□ 237	Russ Gibson	.30	.12	.03
□ 238	Jose Laboy	.30	.12	.03
□ 239	Ken Berry	.30	.12	.03
□ 240	Fergie Jenkins	2.25	.90	.22
□ 241	Royals Rookies	.30	.12	.03
	Al Fitzmorris			
	Scott Northey			
□ 242	Walter Alston MG	1.50	.60	.15
□ 243	Joe Sparma	.30	.12	.03
□ 244A	Checklist 3	2.00	.30	.05
	(red bat on front)			
□ 244B	Checklist 3	2.50	.30	.05
	(brown bat on front)			
□ 245	Leo Cardenas	.30	.12	.03
□ 246	Jim McAndrew	.30	.12	.03
□ 247	Lou Klimchock	.30	.12	.03
□ 248	Jesus Alou	.30	.12	.03
□ 249	Bob Locker	.30	.12	.03
□ 250	Willie McCovey	6.00	2.40	.60
□ 251	Dick Schofield	.30	.12	.03
□ 252	Lowell Palmer	.30	.12	.03
□ 253	Ron Woods	.30	.12	.03
□ 254	Camilo Pascual	.50	.20	.05
□ 255	Jim Spencer	.30	.12	.03
□ 256	Vic Davalillo	.30	.12	.03
□ 257	Dennis Higgins	.30	.12	.03
□ 258	Paul Popovich	.30	.12	.03
□ 259	Tommie Reynolds	.30	.12	.03
□ 260	Claude Osteen	.50	.20	.05
□ 261	Curt Motton	.30	.12	.03
□ 262	Padres Rookies	.50	.20	.05
	Jerry Morales			
	Jim Williams			
□ 263	Duane Josephson	.30	.12	.03
□ 264	Rich Hebner	.75	.30	.07
□ 265	Randy Hundley	.50	.20	.05
□ 266	Wally Bunker	.35	.14	.03
□ 267	Twins Rookies	.35	.14	.03
	Herman Hill			
	Paul Ratliff			
□ 268	Claude Raymond	.35	.14	.03
□ 269	Cesar Gutierrez	.35	.14	.03
□ 270	Chris Short	.35	.14	.03
□ 271	Greg Goossen	.35	.14	.03
□ 272	Hector Torres	.35	.14	.03
□ 273	Ralph Houk MG	.50	.20	.05
□ 274	Gerry Arrigo	.35	.14	.03
□ 275	Duke Sims	.35	.14	.03
□ 276	Ron Hunt	.35	.14	.03
□ 277	Paul Doyle	.35	.14	.03
□ 278	Tommie Aaron	.50	.20	.05
□ 279	Bill Lee	.75	.30	.07
□ 280	Donn Clendenon	.50	.20	.05
□ 281	Casey Cox	.35	.14	.03
□ 282	Steve Huntz	.35	.14	.03
□ 283	Angel Bravo	.35	.14	.03
□ 284	Jack Baldschun	.35	.14	.03
□ 285	Paul Blair	.50	.20	.05
□ 286	Dodgers Rookies	5.00	2.00	.50
	Jack Jenkins			
	Bill Buckner			
□ 287	Fred Talbot	.35	.14	.03
□ 288	Larry Hisle	.50	.20	.05
□ 289	Gene Brabender	.35	.14	.03
□ 290	Rod Carew	14.00	5.75	1.40
□ 291	Leo Durocher MG	1.25	.50	.12
□ 292	Eddie Leon	.35	.14	.03
□ 293	Bob Bailey	.35	.14	.03
□ 294	Jose Azcue	.35	.14	.03
□ 295	Cecil Upshaw	.35	.14	.03
□ 296	Woody Woodward	.50	.20	.05
□ 297	Curt Blefary	.35	.14	.03
□ 298	Ken Henderson	.35	.14	.03
□ 299	Buddy Bradford	.35	.14	.03
□ 300	Tom Seaver	30.00	12.00	3.00
□ 301	Chico Salmon	.35	.14	.03
□ 302	Jeff James	.35	.14	.03
□ 303	Brant Alyea	.35	.14	.03
□ 304	Bill Russell	1.50	.60	.15
□ 305	World Series Game 1	1.25	.50	.12
	Buford leadoff homer			
□ 306	World Series Game 2	1.25	.50	.12
	Clendenon's homer			
	breaks ice			
□ 307	World Series Game 3	1.25	.50	.12
	Agee's catch			
	saves the day			
□ 308	World Series Game 4	1.25	.50	.12
	Martin's bunt			
	ends deadlock			
□ 309	World Series Game 5	1.25	.50	.12
	Koosman shuts door			
□ 310	World Series Summary	1.25	.50	.12
	Mets whoop it up			
□ 311	Dick Green	.35	.14	.03
□ 312	Mike Torrez	.50	.20	.05
□ 313	Mayo Smith MG	.35	.14	.03
□ 314	Bill McCool	.35	.14	.03
□ 315	Luis Aparicio	3.50	1.40	.35
□ 316	Skip Guinn	.35	.14	.03
□ 317	Red Sox Rookies	.50	.20	.05
	Billy Conigliaro			
	Luis Alvarado			
□ 318	Willie Smith	.35	.14	.03
□ 319	Clay Dalrymple	.35	.14	.03
□ 320	Jim Maloney	.50	.20	.05
□ 321	Lou Piniella	1.00	.40	.10
□ 322	Luke Walker	.35	.14	.03
□ 323	Wayne Comer	.35	.14	.03
□ 324	Tony Taylor	.35	.14	.03
□ 325	Dave Boswell	.35	.14	.03
□ 326	Bill Voss	.35	.14	.03
□ 327	Hal King	.35	.14	.03
□ 328	George Brunet	.35	.14	.03
□ 329	Chris Cannizzaro	.35	.14	.03
□ 330	Lou Brock	5.00	2.00	.50
□ 331	Chuck Dobson	.35	.14	.03
□ 332	Bobby Wine	.35	.14	.03
□ 333	Bobby Murcer	1.00	.40	.10
□ 334	Phil Regan	.50	.20	.05
□ 335	Bill Freehan	.75	.30	.07
□ 336	Del Unser	.35	.14	.03
□ 337	Mike McCormick	.50	.20	.05
□ 338	Paul Schaal	.35	.14	.03
□ 339	Johnny Edwards	.35	.14	.03
□ 340	Tony Conigliaro	1.00	.40	.10
□ 341	Bill Sudakis	.35	.14	.03
□ 342	Wilbur Wood	.50	.20	.05
□ 343A	Checklist 4	2.00	.30	.05
	(red bat on front)			
□ 343B	Checklist 4	2.50	.30	.05
	(brown bat on front)			
□ 344	Marcelino Lopez	.35	.14	.03
□ 345	Al Ferrara	.35	.14	.03
□ 346	Red Schoendienst MG	.75	.30	.07
□ 347	Russ Snyder	.35	.14	.03
□ 348	Mets Rookies	.35	.14	.03
	Mike Jorgensen			
	Jesse Hudson			
□ 349	Steve Hamilton	.35	.14	.03
□ 350	Roberto Clemente	22.00	9.00	2.20
□ 351	Tom Murphy	.35	.14	.03
□ 352	Bob Barton	.35	.14	.03
□ 353	Stan Williams	.35	.14	.03
□ 354	Amos Otis	.75	.30	.07
□ 355	Doug Rader	.50	.20	.05
□ 356	Fred Lasher	.35	.14	.03
□ 357	Bob Burda	.35	.14	.03
□ 358	Pedro Borbon	.35	.14	.03
□ 359	Phil Roof	.35	.14	.03
□ 360	Curt Flood	.75	.30	.07
□ 361	Ray Jarvis	.35	.14	.03

☐ 362 Joe Hague .35 .14 .03
☐ 363 Tom Shopay .35 .14 .03
☐ 364 Dan McGinn .35 .14 .03
☐ 365 Zoilo Versalles .35 .14 .03
☐ 366 Barry Moore .35 .14 .03
☐ 367 Mike Lum .35 .14 .03
☐ 368 Ed Herrmann .35 .14 .03
☐ 369 Alan Foster .35 .14 .03
☐ 370 Tommy Harper .50 .20 .05
☐ 371 Rod Gaspar .35 .14 .03
☐ 372 Dave Giusti .50 .20 .05
☐ 373 Roy White .50 .20 .05
☐ 374 Tommie Sisk .35 .14 .03
☐ 375 Johnny Callison .50 .20 .05
☐ 376 Lefty Phillips MG .35 .14 .03
☐ 377 Bill Butler .35 .14 .03
☐ 378 Jim Davenport .50 .20 .05
☐ 379 Tom Tischinski .35 .14 .03
☐ 380 Tony Perez 3.00 1.20 .30
☐ 381 Athletics Rookies .35 .14 .03
Bobby Brooks
Mike Olivo
☐ 382 Jack DiLauro .35 .14 .03
☐ 383 Mickey Stanley .50 .20 .05
☐ 384 Gary Neibauer .35 .14 .03
☐ 385 George Scott .50 .20 .05
☐ 386 Bill Dillman .35 .14 .03
☐ 387 Baltimore Orioles 1.00 .40 .10
Team Card
☐ 388 Byron Browne .35 .14 .03
☐ 389 Jim Shellenback .35 .14 .03
☐ 390 Willie Davis .75 .30 .07
☐ 391 Larry Brown .35 .14 .03
☐ 392 Walt Hriniak .50 .20 .05
☐ 393 John Gelnar .35 .14 .03
☐ 394 Gil Hodges MG 3.50 1.40 .35
☐ 395 Walt Williams .35 .14 .03
☐ 396 Steve Blass .50 .20 .05
☐ 397 Roger Repoz .35 .14 .03
☐ 398 Bill Stoneman .35 .14 .03
☐ 399 New York Yankees 1.50 .60 .15
Team Card
☐ 400 Denny McLain 1.00 .40 .10
☐ 401 Giants Rookies .35 .14 .03
John Harrell
Bernie Williams
☐ 402 Ellie Rodriguez .35 .14 .03
☐ 403 Jim Bunning 2.50 1.00 .25
☐ 404 Rich Reese .35 .14 .03
☐ 405 Bill Hands .35 .14 .03
☐ 406 Mike Andrews .35 .14 .03
☐ 407 Bob Watson .75 .30 .07
☐ 408 Paul Lindblad .35 .14 .03
☐ 409 Bob Tolan .50 .20 .05
☐ 410 Boog Powell 2.00 .80 .20
☐ 411 Los Angeles Dodgers 1.25 .50 .12
Team Card
☐ 412 Larry Burchart .35 .14 .03
☐ 413 Sonny Jackson .35 .14 .03
☐ 414 Paul Edmondson .35 .14 .03
☐ 415 Julian Javier .50 .20 .05
☐ 416 Joe Verbanic .35 .14 .03
☐ 417 John Bateman .35 .14 .03
☐ 418 John Donaldson .35 .14 .03
☐ 419 Ron Taylor .35 .14 .03
☐ 420 Ken McMullen .35 .14 .03
☐ 421 Pat Dobson .50 .20 .05
☐ 422 Royals Team 1.00 .40 .10
☐ 423 Jerry May .35 .14 .03
☐ 424 Mike Kilkenny .35 .14 .03
(inconsistent design,
card # in white circle)
☐ 425 Bobby Bonds 2.00 .80 .20
☐ 426 Bill Rigney MG .35 .14 .03
☐ 427 Fred Norman .35 .14 .03
☐ 428 Don Buford .50 .20 .05
☐ 429 Cubs Rookies .35 .14 .03
Randy Bobb
Jim Cosman
☐ 430 Andy Messersmith .50 .20 .05
☐ 431 Ron Swoboda .50 .20 .05
☐ 432A Checklist 5 2.00 .30 .05
("Baseball" in
yellow letters)
☐ 432B Checklist 5 2.50 .30 .05
("Baseball" in
white letters)
☐ 433 Ron Bryant .35 .14 .03
☐ 434 Felipe Alou .50 .20 .05
☐ 435 Nelson Briles .50 .20 .05
☐ 436 Philadelphia Phillies 1.00 .40 .10
Team Card
☐ 437 Danny Cater .35 .14 .03
☐ 438 Pat Jarvis .35 .14 .03
☐ 439 Lee Maye .35 .14 .03
☐ 440 Bill Mazeroski 1.00 .40 .10
☐ 441 John O'Donoghue .35 .14 .03
☐ 442 Gene Mauch MG .50 .20 .05
☐ 443 Al Jackson .35 .14 .03
☐ 444 White Sox Rookies .35 .14 .03
Billy Farmer
John Matias
☐ 445 Vada Pinson 1.00 .40 .10
☐ 446 Billy Grabarkewitz .35 .14 .03
☐ 447 Lee Stange .35 .14 .03
☐ 448 Houston Astros 1.00 .40 .10
Team Card
☐ 449 Jim Palmer 8.00 3.25 .80
☐ 450 Willie McCovey AS 3.50 1.40 .35
☐ 451 Boog Powell AS .75 .30 .07
☐ 452 Felix Millan AS .50 .20 .05
☐ 453 Rod Carew AS 4.50 1.80 .45
☐ 454 Ron Santo AS .50 .20 .05
☐ 455 Brooks Robinson AS 3.50 1.40 .35
☐ 456 Don Kessinger AS .50 .20 .05
☐ 457 Rico Petrocelli AS .50 .20 .05
☐ 458 Pete Rose AS 9.00 3.75 .90
☐ 459 Reggie Jackson AS 8.00 3.25 .80
☐ 460 Matty Alou AS .75 .30 .07
☐ 461 Carl Yastrzemski AS 6.00 2.40 .60
☐ 462 Hank Aaron AS 6.00 2.40 .60
☐ 463 Frank Robinson AS 3.50 1.40 .35
☐ 464 Johnny Bench AS 6.00 2.40 .60
☐ 465 Bill Freehan AS .75 .30 .07
☐ 466 Juan Marichal AS 3.00 1.20 .30
☐ 467 Denny McLain AS .75 .30 .07
☐ 468 Jerry Koosman AS .75 .30 .07
☐ 469 Sam McDowell AS .75 .30 .07
☐ 470 Willie Stargell 6.00 2.40 .60
☐ 471 Chris Zachary .50 .20 .05
☐ 472 Braves Team 1.00 .40 .10
☐ 473 Don Bryant .50 .20 .05
☐ 474 Dick Kelley .50 .20 .05
☐ 475 Dick McAuliffe .75 .30 .07
☐ 476 Don Shaw .50 .20 .05
☐ 477 Orioles Rookies .50 .20 .05
Al Severinsen
Roger Freed
☐ 478 Bob Heise .50 .20 .05
☐ 479 Dick Woodson .50 .20 .05
☐ 480 Glen Beckert .75 .30 .07
☐ 481 Jose Tartabull .50 .20 .05
☐ 482 Tom Hilgendorf .50 .20 .05
☐ 483 Gail Hopkins .50 .20 .05
☐ 484 Gary Nolan .50 .20 .05
☐ 485 Jay Johnstone .75 .30 .07
☐ 486 Terry Harmon .50 .20 .05
☐ 487 Cisco Carlos .50 .20 .05
☐ 488 J.C. Martin .50 .20 .05
☐ 489 Eddie Kasko MG .50 .20 .05
☐ 490 Bill Singer .50 .20 .05
☐ 491 Graig Nettles 4.00 1.60 .40
☐ 492 Astros Rookies .50 .20 .05
Keith Lampard
Scipio Spinks
☐ 493 Lindy McDaniel .75 .30 .07
☐ 494 Larry Stahl .50 .20 .05
☐ 495 Dave Morehead .50 .20 .05
☐ 496 Steve Whitaker .50 .20 .05
☐ 497 Eddie Watt .50 .20 .05
☐ 498 Al Weis .50 .20 .05
☐ 499 Skip Lockwood .50 .20 .05
☐ 500 Hank Aaron 25.00 10.00 2.50
☐ 501 Chicago White Sox 1.00 .40 .10
Team Card
☐ 502 Rollie Fingers 4.50 1.80 .45
☐ 503 Dal Maxvill .75 .30 .07
☐ 504 Don Pavletich .50 .20 .05
☐ 505 Ken Holtzman .75 .30 .07
☐ 506 Ed Stroud .50 .20 .05
☐ 507 Pat Corrales .75 .30 .07
☐ 508 Joe Niekro 1.00 .40 .10
☐ 509 Montreal Expos 1.00 .40 .10
Team Card
☐ 510 Tony Oliva 1.50 .60 .15
☐ 511 Joe Hoerner .50 .20 .05
☐ 512 Billy Harris .50 .20 .05
☐ 513 Preston Gomez MG .50 .20 .05
☐ 514 Steve Hovley .50 .20 .05
☐ 515 Don Wilson .50 .20 .05
☐ 516 Yankees Rookies .50 .20 .05
John Ellis
Jim Lyttle
☐ 517 Joe Gibbon .50 .20 .05
☐ 518 Bill Melton .50 .20 .05
☐ 519 Don McMahon .50 .20 .05
☐ 520 Willie Horton .75 .30 .07
☐ 521 Cal Koonce .50 .20 .05
☐ 522 Angels Team 1.00 .40 .10

□ 523 Jose Pena	.50	.20	.05
□ 524 Alvin Dark MG	.75	.30	.07
□ 525 Jerry Adair	.50	.20	.05
□ 526 Ron Herbel	.50	.20	.05
□ 527 Don Bosch	.50	.20	.05
□ 528 Elrod Hendricks	.50	.20	.05
□ 529 Bob Aspromonte	.50	.20	.05
□ 530 Bob Gibson	7.00	2.80	.70
□ 531 Ron Clark	.50	.20	.05
□ 532 Danny Murtaugh MG	.50	.20	.05
□ 533 Buzz Stephen	.50	.20	.05
□ 534 Twins Team	1.00	.40	.10
□ 535 Andy Kosco	.50	.20	.05
□ 536 Mike Kekich	.50	.20	.05
□ 537 Joe Morgan	3.50	1.40	.35
□ 538 Bob Humphreys	.50	.20	.05
□ 539 Phillies Rookies Dennis Doyle Larry Bowa	4.00	1.60	.40
□ 540 Gary Peters	.50	.20	.05
□ 541 Bill Heath	.50	.20	.05
□ 542 Checklist 6	2.50	.30	.06
□ 543 Clyde Wright	.50	.20	.05
□ 544 Cincinnati Reds Team Card	1.25	.50	.12
□ 545 Ken Harrelson	1.00	.40	.10
□ 546 Ron Reed	.50	.20	.05
□ 547 Rick Monday	1.00	.40	.10
□ 548 Howie Reed	.85	.34	.08
□ 549 Cardinals Team	1.50	.60	.15
□ 550 Frank Howard	1.50	.60	.15
□ 551 Dock Ellis	.85	.34	.08
□ 552 Royals Rookies Don O'Riley Dennis Paepke Fred Rico	.85	.34	.08
□ 553 Jim Lefebvre	1.25	.50	.12
□ 554 Tom Timmermann	.85	.34	.08
□ 555 Orlando Cepeda	3.00	1.20	.30
□ 556 Dave Bristol MG	.85	.34	.08
□ 557 Ed Kranepool	1.25	.50	.12
□ 558 Vern Fuller	.85	.34	.08
□ 559 Tommy Davis	1.25	.50	.12
□ 560 Gaylord Perry	5.00	2.00	.50
□ 561 Tom McCraw	.85	.34	.08
□ 562 Ted Abernathy	.85	.34	.08
□ 563 Boston Red Sox Team Card	1.50	.60	.15
□ 564 Johnny Briggs	.85	.34	.08
□ 565 Jim Hunter	6.00	2.40	.60
□ 566 Gene Alley	1.25	.50	.12
□ 567 Bob Oliver	.85	.34	.08
□ 568 Stan Bahnsen	.85	.34	.08
□ 569 Cookie Rojas	1.25	.50	.12
□ 570 Jim Fregosi	1.25	.50	.12
□ 571 Jim Brewer	.85	.34	.08
□ 572 Frank Quilici MG	.85	.34	.08
□ 573 Padres Rookies Mike Corkins Rafael Robles Ron Slocum	.85	.34	.08
□ 574 Bobby Bolin	.85	.34	.08
□ 575 Cleon Jones	.85	.34	.08
□ 576 Milt Pappas	1.25	.50	.12
□ 577 Bernie Allen	.85	.34	.08
□ 578 Tom Griffin	.85	.34	.08
□ 579 Detroit Tigers Team Card	2.00	.80	.17
□ 580 Pete Rose	75.00	30.00	7.50
□ 581 Tom Satriano	.85	.34	.08
□ 582 Mike Paul	.85	.34	.08
□ 583 Hal Lanier	1.25	.50	.12
□ 584 Al Downing	1.25	.50	.12
□ 585 Rusty Staub	1.75	.70	.17
□ 586 Rickey Clark	.85	.34	.08
□ 587 Jose Arcia	.85	.34	.08
□ 588A Checklist 7 (666 Adolpho)	3.00	.40	.07
□ 588B Checklist 7 (666 Adolfo)	6.00	.60	.10
□ 589 Joe Keough	.85	.34	.08
□ 590 Mike Cuellar	1.25	.50	.12
□ 591 Mike Ryan	.85	.34	.08
□ 592 Daryl Patterson	.85	.34	.08
□ 593 Chicago Cubs Team Card	1.50	.60	.15
□ 594 Jake Gibbs	.85	.34	.08
□ 595 Maury Wills	2.25	.90	.22
□ 596 Mike Hershberger	.85	.34	.08
□ 597 Sonny Siebert	1.25	.50	.12
□ 598 Joe Pepitone	1.25	.50	.12
□ 599 Senators Rookies Dick Stelmaszek Gene Martin Dick Such	.85	.34	.08

□ 600 Willie Mays	32.00	13.00	3.20
□ 601 Pete Richert	.85	.34	.08
□ 602 Ted Savage	.85	.34	.08
□ 603 Ray Oyler	.85	.34	.08
□ 604 Clarence Gaston	.85	.34	.08
□ 605 Rick Wise	1.25	.50	.12
□ 606 Chico Ruiz	.85	.34	.08
□ 607 Gary Waslewski	.85	.34	.08
□ 608 Pittsburgh Pirates Team Card	1.75	.70	.15
□ 609 Buck Martinez	.85	.34	.08
□ 610 Jerry Koosman	1.50	.60	.15
□ 611 Norm Cash	1.50	.60	.15
□ 612 Jim Hickman	.85	.34	.08
□ 613 Dave Baldwin	.85	.34	.08
□ 614 Mike Shannon	1.25	.50	.12
□ 615 Mark Belanger	1.25	.50	.12
□ 616 Jim Merritt	.85	.34	.08
□ 617 Jim French	.85	.34	.08
□ 618 Billy Wynne	.85	.34	.08
□ 619 Norm Miller	.85	.34	.08
□ 620 Jim Perry	1.50	.60	.15
□ 621 Braves Rookies Mike McQueen Darrell Evans Rick Kester	10.00	4.00	1.00
□ 622 Don Sutton	5.50	2.20	.55
□ 623 Horace Clarke	.85	.34	.08
□ 624 Clyde King MG	.85	.34	.08
□ 625 Dean Chance	1.25	.50	.12
□ 626 Dave Ricketts	.85	.34	.08
□ 627 Gary Wagner	.85	.34	.08
□ 628 Wayne Garrett	.85	.34	.08
□ 629 Merv Rettenmund	.85	.34	.08
□ 630 Ernie Banks	12.00	5.00	1.20
□ 631 Oakland Athletics Team Card	1.50	.60	.15
□ 632 Gary Sutherland	.85	.34	.08
□ 633 Roger Nelson	.85	.34	.08
□ 634 Bud Harrelson	2.50	1.00	.25
□ 635 Bob Allison	2.50	1.00	.25
□ 636 Jim Stewart	2.00	.80	.20
□ 637 Cleveland Indians Team Card	4.00	1.60	.40
□ 638 Frank Bertaina	2.00	.80	.20
□ 639 Dave Campbell	2.00	.80	.20
□ 640 Al Kaline	25.00	10.00	2.50
□ 641 Al McBean	2.00	.80	.20
□ 642 Angels Rookies Greg Garrett Gordon Lund Jarvis Tatum	2.00	.80	.20
□ 643 Jose Pagan	2.00	.80	.20
□ 644 Gerry Nyman	2.00	.80	.20
□ 645 Don Money	2.50	1.00	.25
□ 646 Jim Britton	2.00	.80	.20
□ 647 Tom Matchick	2.00	.80	.20
□ 648 Larry Haney	2.00	.80	.20
□ 649 Jimmie Hall	2.50	1.00	.25
□ 650 Sam McDowell	3.00	1.20	.30
□ 651 Jim Gosger	2.00	.80	.20
□ 652 Rich Rollins	2.50	1.00	.25
□ 653 Moe Drabowsky	2.00	.80	.20
□ 654 NL Rookies Oscar Gamble Boots Day Angel Mangual	3.50	1.40	.35
□ 655 John Roseboro	2.50	1.00	.25
□ 656 Jim Hardin	2.00	.80	.20
□ 657 San Diego Padres Team Card	4.50	1.80	.45
□ 658 Ken Tatum	2.00	.80	.20
□ 659 Pete Ward	2.00	.80	.20
□ 660 Johnny Bench	90.00	36.00	9.00
□ 661 Jerry Robertson	2.00	.80	.20
□ 662 Frank Lucchesi MG	2.00	.80	.20
□ 663 Tito Francona	2.50	1.00	.25
□ 664 Bob Robertson	2.50	1.00	.25
□ 665 Jim Lonborg	2.50	1.00	.25
□ 666 Adolpho Phillips	2.00	.80	.20
□ 667 Bob Meyer	2.00	.80	.20
□ 668 Bob Tillman	2.00	.80	.20
□ 669 White Sox Rookies Bart Johnson Dan Lazar Mickey Scott	2.00	.80	.20
□ 670 Ron Santo	4.00	1.60	.40
□ 671 Jim Campanis	2.00	.80	.20
□ 672 Leon McFadden	2.00	.80	.20
□ 673 Ted Uhlaender	2.00	.80	.20
□ 674 Dave Leonhard	2.00	.80	.20
□ 675 Jose Cardenal	2.00	.80	.20
□ 676 Senators Team	4.00	1.60	.40
□ 677 Woodie Fryman	2.00	.80	.20
□ 678 Dave Duncan	2.00	.80	.20

□ 679	Ray Sadecki	2.00	.80	.20
□ 680	Rico Petrocelli	2.50	1.00	.25
□ 681	Bob Garibaldi	2.00	.80	.20
□ 682	Dalton Jones	2.00	.80	.20
□ 683	Reds Rookies	4.00	1.60	.40
	Vern Geishert			
	Hal McRae			
	Wayne Simpson			
□ 684	Jack Fisher	2.00	.80	.20
□ 685	Tom Haller	2.50	1.00	.25
□ 686	Jackie Hernandez	2.00	.80	.20
□ 687	Bob Priddy	2.00	.80	.20
□ 688	Ted Kubiak	2.00	.80	.20
□ 689	Frank Tepedino	2.00	.80	.20
□ 690	Ron Fairly	2.50	1.00	.25
□ 691	Joe Grzenda	2.00	.80	.20
□ 692	Duffy Dyer	2.00	.80	.20
□ 693	Bob Johnson	2.00	.80	.20
□ 694	Gary Ross	2.00	.80	.20
□ 695	Bobby Knoop	2.00	.80	.20
□ 696	San Francisco Giants	4.00	1.60	.40
	Team Card			
□ 697	Jim Hannan	2.00	.80	.20
□ 698	Tom Tresh	4.00	1.60	.40
□ 699	Hank Aguirre	2.00	.80	.20
□ 700	Frank Robinson	25.00	10.00	2.50
□ 701	Jack Billingham	2.00	.80	.20
□ 702	AL Rookies	2.00	.80	.20
	Bob Johnson			
	Ron Klimkowski			
	Bill Zepp			
□ 703	Lou Marone	2.00	.80	.20
□ 704	Frank Baker	2.00	.80	.20
□ 705	Tony Cloninger	2.00	.80	.20
□ 706	John McNamara MG	4.00	1.60	.40
□ 707	Kevin Collins	2.00	.80	.20
□ 708	Jose Santiago	2.00	.80	.20
□ 709	Mike Fiore	2.00	.80	.20
□ 710	Felix Millan	2.00	.80	.20
□ 711	Ed Brinkman	2.00	.80	.20
□ 712	Nolan Ryan	65.00	26.00	6.50
□ 713	Pilots Team	9.00	3.75	.90
□ 714	Al Spangler	2.00	.80	.20
□ 715	Mickey Lolich	4.50	1.80	.45
□ 716	Cardinals Rookies	2.50	1.00	.25
	Sal Campisi			
	Reggie Cleveland			
	Santiago Guzman			
□ 717	Tom Phoebus	2.00	.80	.20
□ 718	Ed Spiezio	2.00	.80	.20
□ 719	Jim Roland	2.00	.80	.20
□ 720	Rick Reichardt	3.00	1.00	.20

1971 Topps

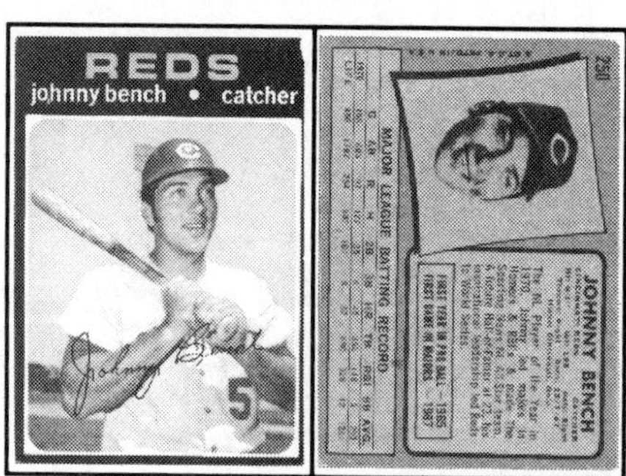

The cards in this 752-card set measure 2 1/2" by 3 1/2". The 1971 Topps set is a challenge to complete in strict mint condition because the black obverse border is easily scratched and damaged. An unusual feature of this set is that the player is also pictured in black and white on the back of the card. Featured subsets within this set include League Leaders (61-72), Playoffs cards (195-202), and World Series cards (327- 332). Cards 524-643 and the last series (644-752) are somewhat scarce.

	NRMT	VG-E	GOOD
COMPLETE SET (752)	1200.00	500.00	175.00
COMMON PLAYER (1-263)	.30	.12	.03
COMMON PLAYER (264-393)	.35	.14	.03
COMMON PLAYER (394-523)	.45	.18	.04
COMMON PLAYER (524-643)	.85	.34	.08
COMMON PLAYER (644-752)	2.00	.80	.20

□ 1	Baltimore Orioles	5.00	1.00	.20
	Team Card			
□ 2	Dock Ellis	.30	.12	.03
□ 3	Dick McAuliffe	.30	.12	.03
□ 4	Vic Davalillo	.30	.12	.03
□ 5	Thurman Munson	16.00	6.50	1.60
□ 6	Ed Spiezio	.30	.12	.03
□ 7	Jim Holt	.30	.12	.03
□ 8	Mike McQueen	.30	.12	.03
□ 9	George Scott	.50	.20	.05
□ 10	Claude Osteen	.50	.20	.05
□ 11	Elliott Maddox	.30	.12	.03
□ 12	Johnny Callison	.50	.20	.05
□ 13	White Sox Rookies	.30	.12	.03
	Charlie Brinkman			
	Dick Moloney			
□ 14	Dave Concepcion	5.00	2.00	.50
□ 15	Andy Messersmith	.50	.20	.05
□ 16	Ken Singleton	1.50	.60	.15
□ 17	Billy Sorrell	.30	.12	.03
□ 18	Norm Miller	.30	.12	.03
□ 19	Skip Pitlock	.30	.12	.03
□ 20	Reggie Jackson	27.00	11.00	2.70
□ 21	Dan McGinn	.30	.12	.03
□ 22	Phil Roof	.30	.12	.03
□ 23	Oscar Gamble	.50	.20	.05
□ 24	Rich Hand	.30	.12	.03
□ 25	Clarence Gaston	.50	.20	.05
□ 26	Bert Blyleven	10.00	4.00	1.00
□ 27	Pirates Rookies	.30	.12	.03
	Fred Cambria			
	Gene Clines			
□ 28	Ron Klimkowski	.30	.12	.03
□ 29	Don Buford	.50	.20	.05
□ 30	Phil Niekro	3.50	1.40	.35
□ 31	Eddie Kasko MG	.30	.12	.03
□ 32	Jerry DaVanon	.30	.12	.03
□ 33	Del Unser	.30	.12	.03
□ 34	Sandy Vance	.30	.12	.03
□ 35	Lou Piniella	.75	.30	.07
□ 36	Dean Chance	.50	.20	.05
□ 37	Rich McKinney	.30	.12	.03
□ 38	Jim Colborn	.30	.12	.03
□ 39	Tiger Rookies	.30	.12	.03
	Lerrin LaGrow			
	Gene Lamont			
□ 40	Lee May	.50	.20	.05
□ 41	Rick Austin	.30	.12	.03
□ 42	Boots Day	.30	.12	.03
□ 43	Steve Kealey	.30	.12	.03
□ 44	Johnny Edwards	.30	.12	.03
□ 45	Jim Hunter	4.00	1.60	.40
□ 46	Dave Campbell	.30	.12	.03
□ 47	Johnny Jeter	.30	.12	.03
□ 48	Dave Baldwin	.30	.12	.03
□ 49	Don Money	.50	.20	.05
□ 50	Willie McCovey	5.00	2.00	.50
□ 51	Steve Kline	.30	.12	.03
□ 52	Braves Rookies	.50	.20	.05
	Oscar Brown			
	Earl Williams			
□ 53	Paul Blair	.50	.20	.05
□ 54	Checklist 1	1.50	.20	.04
□ 55	Steve Carlton	12.00	5.00	1.20
□ 56	Duane Josephson	.30	.12	.03
□ 57	Von Joshua	.30	.12	.03
□ 58	Bill Lee	.50	.20	.05
□ 59	Gene Mauch MG	.50	.20	.05
□ 60	Dick Bosman	.30	.12	.03
□ 61	AL Batting Leaders	1.50	.60	.15
	Alex Johnson			
	Carl Yastrzemski			
	Tony Oliva			
□ 62	NL Batting Leaders	1.00	.40	.10
	Rico Carty			
	Joe Torre			
	Manny Sanguillen			
□ 63	AL RBI Leaders	1.00	.40	.10
	Frank Howard			
	Tony Conigliaro			
	Boog Powell			
□ 64	NL RBI Leaders	1.75	.70	.17
	Johnny Bench			
	Tony Perez			
	Billy Williams			
□ 65	AL HR Leaders	1.50	.60	.15
	Frank Howard			
	Harmon Killebrew			
	Carl Yastrzemski			

San Diego Sports Collectibles

THE WEST COAST'S LARGEST BASEBALL CARD STORE

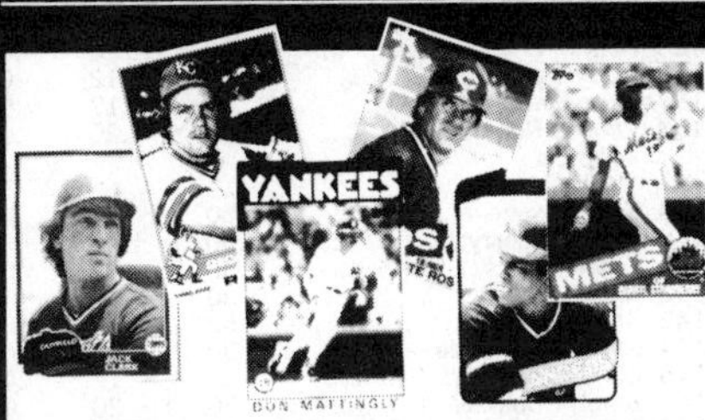

500 ORIGINAL OLD BASEBALL CARDS!

SPECIAL ½ PRICE INTRODUCTORY OFFER FOR TOPPS, FLEER & DONRUSS CARDS 1970s-1980s

GREAT STARTER LOT! Each lot includes 25 of the game's greatest superstars such as Bench, Brett, Boggs, Carew, Carlton, Carter, Clark, Clemens, Coleman, Davis, Dawson, Evans, Fisk, Garvey, Gibson, Gooden, Guerrero, Guidry, Gwynn, Henderson, Hernandez, Hershiser, Hrbek, Hunter, Jackson, Lynn, Madlock, Mattingly, McGee, Molitor, Morgan Murphy, Murray, Nettles, Niekro, Palmer, Parker, Perez, Puckett, Raines, Rice, Ripken, Rose, Ryan, Schmidt, Seaver, Smith, Stargell, Strawberry, Sutton, Trammell, Valenzuela, Yaz, Winfield, Yount and many more. Limit: 3 lots per customer. **Excellent to mint condition.**

ONLY $28.95 POSTPAID

PLUS...Our 56 page illustrated catalogue

FAST, FRIENDLY RELIABLE SERVICE • MILLIONS OF CARDS IN STOCK

BASEBALL SETS

	1981	1982	1983	1984	1985	1986	1987	1988	1989
TOPPS	85.00	85.00	105.00	105.00	105.00	34.50	29.95	24.95	22.95
DONRUSS	29.95	29.50	55.00	245.00	175.00	150.00	44.50	34.50	29.95
FLEER	29.95	29.50	55.00	95.00	115.00	105.00	44.50	39.50	29.95
TRADED TOPPS	39.50	39.50	79.50	89.00	19.95	19.50	13.95	18.95	—

SATISFACTION GUARANTEED OR YOUR MONEY BACK

PRICES SUBJECT TO CHANGE WITHOUT NOTICE

SCORE 1989 .... $19.95
SCORE 1988 .... 21.95
SPORTFLIC 1988 .... 39.95
SPORTFLIC 1987 .... 39.95
SPORTFLIC 1986 .... 59.95
TOPPS 1980 .... 185.00

TOPPS 1979 .... $175.00
TOPPS 1978 .... 245.00
TOPPS 1977 .... 325.00
TOPPS 1976 .... 325.00
TOPPS 1975 .... 650.00
FLEER 1988 (Traded) 11.95

FLEER 1987 (Traded) $13.95
FLEER 1986 (Traded) 19.95
FLEER 1985 (Traded) 19.95
FLEER 1984 (Traded) 329.00
DONRUSS 1988 Rookies 8.95
DONRUSS 1987 Rookies 15.95

DONRUSS 1986 Rookies $27.50
DONRUSS 1987 Hi-Lights 8.95
DONRUSS 1986 Hi-Lights 11.95
DONRUSS 1985 Hi-Lights 34.50
TOPPS 1988 Rookies 5.95
TOPPS 1987 Rookies 5.95

TOPPS 1988 Hi-Lights $5.95
TOPPS 1987 Hi-Lights 5.95
TOPPS 1988 Superstars 5.95
TOPPS 1987 Superstars 5.95
TOPPS 1988 Big Cards 45.00
FLEER 1988 World Series 7.75

☎ ORDER TOLL FREE 1-800-227-0483 ☎

UNOPENED FACTORY SEALED BOXES FROM TOPPS

1989 1000 Unsearched Cards .. $23.95 1988 1000 Unsearched Cards .. $24.95 1987 1000 Unsearched Cards .. $32.95 1986 1000 Unsearched Cards .. $36.95

BASEBALL CARD COLLECTORS KIT ONLY $19.95

- 3" Supreme Double Foam-Padded Album easily holds complete sets of Topps, Donruss or Fleer.
- 7 Double Polished Clear Pages, protect your valuable cards with these 9 pockets per page.
- 105 authentic, guaranteed unsearched Baseball Cards. 7 Topps or Donruss Wax Packs (unopened).
- 15 Donruss All Star Cards.
- 15 Donruss All Star Pop Up Cards.
- 15 Super Clear Individual Card Holders.
- Sports Collectors Digest Baseball Card Price Guide.
- BIG STARS CAN BE FOUND: Don Mattingly, Ozzie Smith, Mike Schmidt, Roger Clemens, Mark McGwire and more!
- **OVER 160 PIECES INCLUDED!** Please add $3.95 Ship. & Hand.

ALL TIME TEAMS

12 cards of each team featuring that club's best players at each position.

American League
Yankees $1.95
Red Sox 1.75
Indians 1.75
Blue Jays 1.75
Tigers $1.95
Orioles 1.75
Brewers 1.75
Royals 1.75
Rangers 1.75
Angels $1.75
Athletics 1.75
White Sox 1.75
Twins 1.75
Mariners 1.75

National League:
Mets $1.95
Cubs 1.95
Pirates 1.75
Cardinals 1.75
Phillies $1.75
Expos 1.75
Astros 1.75
Dodgers 1.95
Padres 1.75
Braves $1.75
Giants 1.95
Reds 1.75

Order All 26 Teams For Only $39.95

CLASSIC REPRINT SETS:

1888 Allen & Ginter .... $ 6.95
19th Century Tobacco 5.00
1910 T-206 (523 Cards) 49.95
1911 Mecca T-201 .... 14.95
1919 Black Sox Set 3.95
1933 Sport King 6.95

1934 Goudey Gum $10.95
1935 Goudey Gum 5.00
1936 Diamond Stars 10.00
1937 Diamond Stars 3.00
1938 Goudey Gum 7.00
1940 Playball Gum 27.50

1941 Playball Gum .... $ 9.95
1948 Bowman 7.95
1949 Bowman 29.95
1949 Bowman (P.C.L.) 5.95
1951 Bowman 39.95
1954 Red Heart Dog Food .. 9.95

1933 SPORT KING

1934 GOUDEY

1951 BOWMAN

N.F.L. SETS

TOPPS 1981 NFL $16.95
TOPPS 1982 NFL 19.95
TOPPS 1983 NFL 18.95
TOPPS 1984 NFL $17.95
TOPPS 1985 NFL $13.95
TOPPS 1986 NFL 13.95
TOPPS 1987 NFL 13.95
TOPPS 1988 NFL 13.95

BASEBALL CARD PRICE GUIDE

Contains over 175,000 prices for virtually all baseball cards in existence $12.95

MAIL ORDER INSTRUCTIONS

CREDIT CARD HOLDERS CALL FREE FOR INSTANT SERVICE
8:30 AM - 5 PM WEST COAST TIME MON-SUN Call Toll Free
☎ 1-800-227-0483 orders only ☎
All other inquiries call (619) 236-0600

SAN DIEGO SPORTS COLLECTIBLES
1845 Fifth Avenue, Dept. B-11
San Diego, California 92101

Shipping and Insurance
Baseball Cards

1-25 cards	$1.95
26-100	$2.50
101-800	$4.95
801 or more	$9.95
Complete Sets	$2.95

California residents please add 6½% sales tax.

SEND FOR HOBBY'S FINEST & MOST COMPLETE 56 PG. ILLUSTRATED CATALOGUE

Lists over 15,000 Old Baseball Cards & Sets. To receive next 3 issues send $1.00 or 5 stamps.

☐ 66 NL HR Leaders .... 1.75 .70 .17
Johnny Bench
Billy Williams
Tony Perez
☐ 67 AL ERA Leaders .... 1.00 .40 .10
Diego Segui
Jim Palmer
Clyde Wright
☐ 68 NL ERA Leaders .... 1.00 .40 .10
Tom Seaver
Wayne Simpson
Luke Walker
☐ 69 AL Pitching Leaders .... 1.00 .40 .10
Mike Cuellar
Dave McNally
Jim Perry
☐ 70 NL Pitching Leaders .... 1.50 .60 .15
Bob Gibson
Gaylord Perry
Fergie Jenkins
☐ 71 AL Strikeout Leaders ..... 1.00 .40 .10
Sam McDowell
Mickey Lolich
Bob Johnson
☐ 72 NL Strikeout Leaders ..... 1.50 .60 .15
Tom Seaver
Bob Gibson
Fergie Jenkins
☐ 73 George Brunet .... .30 .12 .03
☐ 74 Twins Rookies .... .30 .12 .03
Pete Hamm
Jim Nettles
☐ 75 Gary Nolan .... .30 .12 .03
☐ 76 Ted Savage .... .30 .12 .03
☐ 77 Mike Compton .... .30 .12 .03
☐ 78 Jim Spencer .... .30 .12 .03
☐ 79 Wade Blasingame .... .30 .12 .03
☐ 80 Bill Melton .... .30 .12 .03
☐ 81 Felix Millan .... .30 .12 .03
☐ 82 Casey Cox .... .30 .12 .03
☐ 83 Met Rookies .... .50 .20 .05
Tim Foli
Randy Bobb
☐ 84 Marcel Lachemann .... .50 .20 .05
☐ 85 Bill Grabarkewitz .... .30 .12 .03
☐ 86 Mike Kilkenny .... .30 .12 .03
☐ 87 Jack Heidemann .... .30 .12 .03
☐ 88 Hal King .... .30 .12 .03
☐ 89 Ken Brett .... .50 .20 .05
☐ 90 Joe Pepitone .... .75 .30 .07
☐ 91 Bob Lemon MG .... 1.25 .50 .12
☐ 92 Fred Wenz .... .30 .12 .03
☐ 93 Senators Rookies .... .30 .12 .03
Norm McRae
Denny Riddleberger
☐ 94 Don Hahn .... .30 .12 .03
☐ 95 Luis Tiant .... .75 .30 .07
☐ 96 Joe Hague .... .30 .12 .03
☐ 97 Floyd Wicker .... .30 .12 .03
☐ 98 Joe Decker .... .30 .12 .03
☐ 99 Mark Belanger .... .50 .20 .05
☐ 100 Pete Rose 45.00 18.00 4.50
☐ 101 Les Cain .... .30 .12 .03
☐ 102 Astros Rookies .... 1.00 .40 .10
Ken Forsch
Larry Howard
☐ 103 Rich Severson .... .30 .12 .03
☐ 104 Dan Frisella .... .30 .12 .03
☐ 105 Tony Conigliaro .... 1.00 .40 .10
☐ 106 Tom Dukes .... .30 .12 .03
☐ 107 Roy Foster .... .30 .12 .03
☐ 108 John Cumberland .... .30 .12 .03
☐ 109 Steve Hovley .... .30 .12 .03
☐ 110 Bill Mazeroski .... .75 .30 .07
☐ 111 Yankee Rookies .... .30 .12 .03
Loyd Colson
Bobby Mitchell
☐ 112 Manny Mota .... .50 .20 .05
☐ 113 Jerry Crider .... .30 .12 .03
☐ 114 Billy Conigliaro .... .50 .20 .05
☐ 115 Donn Clendenon .... .50 .20 .05
☐ 116 Ken Sanders .... .30 .12 .03
☐ 117 Ted Simmons .... 7.00 2.80 .70
☐ 118 Cookie Rojas .... .50 .20 .05
☐ 119 Frank Lucchesi MG .... .30 .12 .03
☐ 120 Willie Horton .... .50 .20 .05
☐ 121 Cubs Rookies .... .30 .12 .03
Jim Dunegan
Roe Skidmore
☐ 122 Eddie Watt .... .30 .12 .03
☐ 123A Checklist 2 .... 2.00 .30 .04
(card number
at bottom right)
☐ 123B Checklist 2 .... 2.50 .30 .05
(card number
centered)
☐ 124 Don Gullett .... .50 .20 .05
☐ 125 Ray Fosse .... .30 .12 .03
☐ 126 Danny Coombs .... .30 .12 .03
☐ 127 Danny Thompson .... .30 .12 .03
☐ 128 Frank Johnson .... .30 .12 .03
☐ 129 Aurelio Monteagudo .... .30 .12 .03
☐ 130 Denis Menke .... .30 .12 .03
☐ 131 Curt Blefary .... .30 .12 .03
☐ 132 Jose Laboy .... .30 .12 .03
☐ 133 Mickey Lolich .... 1.00 .40 .10
☐ 134 Jose Arcia .... .30 .12 .03
☐ 135 Rick Monday .... .50 .20 .05
☐ 136 Duffy Dyer .... .30 .12 .03
☐ 137 Marcelino Lopez .... .30 .12 .03
☐ 138 Phillies Rookies .... .50 .20 .05
Joe Lis
Willie Montanez
☐ 139 Paul Casanova .... .30 .12 .03
☐ 140 Gaylord Perry .... 3.50 1.40 .35
☐ 141 Frank Quilici .... .30 .12 .03
☐ 142 Mack Jones .... .30 .12 .03
☐ 143 Steve Blass .... .50 .20 .05
☐ 144 Jackie Hernandez .... .30 .12 .03
☐ 145 Bill Singer .... .30 .12 .03
☐ 146 Ralph Houk MG .... .50 .20 .05
☐ 147 Bob Priddy .... .30 .12 .03
☐ 148 John Mayberry .... .50 .20 .05
☐ 149 Mike Hershberger .... .30 .12 .03
☐ 150 Sam McDowell .... .50 .20 .05
☐ 151 Tommy Davis .... .50 .20 .05
☐ 152 Angels Rookies .... .30 .12 .03
Lloyd Allen
Winston Llenas
☐ 153 Gary Ross .... .30 .12 .03
☐ 154 Cesar Gutierrez .... .30 .12 .03
☐ 155 Ken Henderson .... .30 .12 .03
☐ 156 Bart Johnson .... .30 .12 .03
☐ 157 Bob Bailey .... .30 .12 .03
☐ 158 Jerry Reuss .... .75 .30 .07
☐ 159 Jarvis Tatum .... .30 .12 .03
☐ 160 Tom Seaver 21.00 8.50 2.10
☐ 161 Coin Checklist .... 1.50 .20 .04
☐ 162 Jack Billingham .... .30 .12 .03
☐ 163 Buck Martinez .... .30 .12 .03
☐ 164 Reds Rookies .... .50 .20 .05
Frank Duffy
Milt Wilcox
☐ 165 Cesar Tovar .... .30 .12 .03
☐ 166 Joe Hoerner .... .30 .12 .03
☐ 167 Tom Grieve .... .75 .30 .07
☐ 168 Bruce Dal Canton .... .30 .12 .03
☐ 169 Ed Herrmann .... .30 .12 .03
☐ 170 Mike Cuellar .... .50 .20 .05
☐ 171 Bobby Wine .... .30 .12 .03
☐ 172 Duke Sims .... .30 .12 .03
☐ 173 Gil Garrido .... .30 .12 .03
☐ 174 Dave LaRoche .... .30 .12 .03
☐ 175 Jim Hickman .... .30 .12 .03
☐ 176 Red Sox Rookies .... .30 .12 .03
Bob Montgomery
Doug Griffin
☐ 177 Hal McRae .... .75 .30 .07
☐ 178 Dave Duncan .... .30 .12 .03
☐ 179 Mike Corkins .... .30 .12 .03
☐ 180 Al Kaline .... 6.50 2.60 .65
☐ 181 Hal Lanier .... .50 .20 .05
☐ 182 Al Downing .... .50 .20 .05
☐ 183 Gil Hodges MG .... 3.00 1.20 .30
☐ 184 Stan Bahnsen .... .30 .12 .03
☐ 185 Julian Javier .... .50 .20 .05
☐ 186 Bob Spence .... .30 .12 .03
☐ 187 Ted Abernathy .... .30 .12 .03
☐ 188 Dodgers Rookies .... 2.00 .80 .20
Bob Valentine
Mike Strahler
☐ 189 George Mitterwald .... .30 .12 .03
☐ 190 Bob Tolan .... .50 .20 .05
☐ 191 Mike Andrews .... .30 .12 .03
☐ 192 Billy Wilson .... .30 .12 .03
☐ 193 Bob Grich .... 1.75 .70 .17
☐ 194 Mike Lum .... .30 .12 .03
☐ 195 AL Playoff Game 1 .... 1.25 .50 .12
Powell muscles Twins
☐ 196 AL Playoff Game 2 .... 1.25 .50 .12
McNally makes it
two straight
☐ 197 AL Playoff Game 3 .... 2.00 .80 .20
Palmer mows'em down
☐ 198 AL Playoff Summary ...... 1.25 .50 .12
Orioles celebrate
☐ 199 NL Playoff Game 1 .... 1.25 .50 .12
Cline pinch-triple
decides it
☐ 200 NL Playoff Game 2 .... 1.25 .50 .12

	Tolan scores for third time			
□ 201	NL Playoff Game 3	1.25	.50	.12
	Cline scores winning run			
□ 202	NL Playoff Summary	1.25	.50	.12
	Reds celebrate			
□ 203	Larry Gura	.75	.30	.07
□ 204	Brewers Rookies	.30	.12	.03
	Bernie Smith			
	George Kopacz			
□ 205	Gerry Moses	.30	.12	.03
□ 206	Checklist 3	1.50	.20	.04
□ 207	Alan Foster	.30	.12	.03
□ 208	Billy Martin MG	2.00	.80	.20
□ 209	Steve Renko	.30	.12	.03
□ 210	Rod Carew	15.00	6.00	1.50
□ 211	Phil Hennigan	.30	.12	.03
□ 212	Rich Hebner	.50	.20	.05
□ 213	Frank Baker	.30	.12	.03
□ 214	Al Ferrara	.30	.12	.03
□ 215	Diego Segui	.30	.12	.03
□ 216	Cards Rookies	.30	.12	.03
	Reggie Cleveland			
	Luis Melendez			
□ 217	Ed Stroud	.30	.12	.03
□ 218	Tony Cloninger	.30	.12	.03
□ 219	Elrod Hendricks	.30	.12	.03
□ 220	Ron Santo	.75	.30	.07
□ 221	Dave Morehead	.30	.12	.03
□ 222	Bob Watson	.50	.20	.05
□ 223	Cecil Upshaw	.30	.12	.03
□ 224	Alan Gallagher	.30	.12	.03
□ 225	Gary Peters	.35	.14	.03
□ 226	Bill Russell	.75	.30	.07
□ 227	Floyd Weaver	.30	.12	.03
□ 228	Wayne Garrett	.30	.12	.03
□ 229	Jim Hannan	.30	.12	.03
□ 230	Willie Stargell	6.00	2.40	.60
□ 231	Indians Rookies	.50	.20	.05
	Vince Colbert			
	John Lowenstein			
□ 232	John Strohmayer	.30	.12	.03
□ 233	Larry Bowa	1.75	.70	.17
□ 234	Jim Lyttle	.30	.12	.03
□ 235	Nate Colbert	.30	.12	.03
□ 236	Bob Humphreys	.30	.12	.03
□ 237	Cesar Cedeno	1.25	.50	.12
□ 238	Chuck Dobson	.30	.12	.03
□ 239	Red Schoendienst MG	.75	.30	.07
□ 240	Clyde Wright	.30	.12	.03
□ 241	Dave Nelson	.30	.12	.03
□ 242	Jim Ray	.30	.12	.03
□ 243	Carlos May	.30	.12	.03
□ 244	Bob Tillman	.30	.12	.03
□ 245	Jim Kaat	1.75	.70	.17
□ 246	Tony Taylor	.30	.12	.03
□ 247	Royals Rookies	.75	.30	.07
	Jerry Cram			
	Paul Splittorff			
□ 248	Hoyt Wilhelm	3.50	1.40	.35
□ 249	Chico Salmon	.30	.12	.03
□ 250	Johnny Bench	27.00	11.00	2.70
□ 251	Frank Reberger	.30	.12	.03
□ 252	Eddie Leon	.30	.12	.03
□ 253	Bill Sudakis	.30	.12	.03
□ 254	Cal Koonce	.30	.12	.03
□ 255	Bob Robertson	.30	.12	.03
□ 256	Tony Gonzalez	.30	.12	.03
□ 257	Nelson Briles	.50	.20	.05
□ 258	Dick Green	.30	.12	.03
□ 259	Dave Marshall	.30	.12	.03
□ 260	Tommy Harper	.50	.20	.05
□ 261	Darold Knowles	.30	.12	.03
□ 262	Padres Rookies	.30	.12	.03
	Jim Williams			
	Dave Robinson			
□ 263	John Ellis	.30	.12	.03
□ 264	Joe Morgan	3.50	1.40	.35
□ 265	Jim Northrup	.50	.20	.05
□ 266	Bill Stoneman	.35	.14	.03
□ 267	Rich Morales	.35	.14	.03
□ 268	Phillies Team	1.00	.40	.10
□ 269	Gail Hopkins	.35	.14	.03
□ 270	Rico Carty	.75	.30	.07
□ 271	Bill Zepp	.35	.14	.03
□ 272	Tommy Helms	.50	.20	.05
□ 273	Pete Richert	.35	.14	.03
□ 274	Ron Slocum	.35	.14	.03
□ 275	Vada Pinson	1.00	.40	.10
□ 276	Giants Rookies	4.50	1.80	.45
	Mike Davison			
	George Foster			
□ 277	Gary Waslewski	.35	.14	.03
□ 278	Jerry Grote	.35	.14	.03

□ 279	Lefty Phillips MG	.35	.14	.03
□ 280	Fergie Jenkins	2.50	1.00	.25
□ 281	Danny Walton	.35	.14	.03
□ 282	Jose Pagan	.35	.14	.03
□ 283	Dick Such	.35	.14	.03
□ 284	Jim Gosger	.35	.14	.03
□ 285	Sal Bando	.50	.20	.05
□ 286	Jerry McNertney	.35	.14	.03
□ 287	Mike Fiore	.35	.14	.03
□ 288	Joe Moeller	.35	.14	.03
□ 289	White Sox Team	1.00	.40	.10
□ 290	Tony Oliva	1.75	.70	.17
□ 291	George Culver	.35	.14	.03
□ 292	Jay Johnstone	.75	.30	.07
□ 293	Pat Corrales	.50	.20	.05
□ 294	Steve Dunning	.35	.14	.03
□ 295	Bobby Bonds	1.50	.60	.15
□ 296	Tom Timmermann	.35	.14	.03
□ 297	Johnny Briggs	.35	.14	.03
□ 298	Jim Nelson	.35	.14	.03
□ 299	Ed Kirkpatrick	.35	.14	.03
□ 300	Brooks Robinson	7.00	2.80	.70
□ 301	Earl Wilson	.35	.14	.03
□ 302	Phil Gagliano	.35	.14	.03
□ 303	Lindy McDaniel	.50	.20	.05
□ 304	Ron Brand	.35	.14	.03
□ 305	Reggie Smith	.75	.30	.07
□ 306	Jim Nash	.35	.14	.03
□ 307	Don Wert	.35	.14	.03
□ 308	St. Louis Cardinals	1.00	.40	.10
	Team Card			
□ 309	Dick Ellsworth	.50	.20	.05
□ 310	Tommie Agee	.50	.20	.05
□ 311	Lee Stange	.35	.14	.03
□ 312	Harry Walker MG	.35	.14	.03
□ 313	Tom Hall	.35	.14	.03
□ 314	Jeff Torborg	.50	.20	.05
□ 315	Ron Fairly	.50	.20	.05
□ 316	Fred Scherman	.35	.14	.03
□ 317	Athletic Rookies	.35	.14	.03
	Jim Driscoll			
	Angel Mangual			
□ 318	Rudy May	.35	.14	.03
□ 319	Ty Cline	.35	.14	.03
□ 320	Dave McNally	.50	.20	.05
□ 321	Tom Matchick	.35	.14	.03
□ 322	Jim Beauchamp	.35	.14	.03
□ 323	Billy Champion	.35	.14	.03
□ 324	Graig Nettles	2.25	.90	.22
□ 325	Juan Marichal	4.00	1.60	.40
□ 326	Richie Scheinblum	.35	.14	.03
□ 327	World Series Game 1	1.25	.50	.12
	Powell homers to opposite field			
□ 328	World Series Game 2	1.25	.50	.12
	Don Buford			
□ 329	World Series Game 3	2.00	.80	.20
	Frank Robinson shows muscle			
□ 330	World Series Game 4	1.25	.50	.12
	Reds stay alive			
□ 331	World Series Game 5	2.00	.80	.20
	Brooks Robinson commits robbery			
□ 332	World Series Summary	1.25	.50	.12
	Orioles celebrate			
□ 333	Clay Kirby	.35	.14	.03
□ 334	Roberto Pena	.35	.14	.03
□ 335	Jerry Koosman	.75	.30	.07
□ 336	Detroit Tigers	1.00	.40	.10
	Team Card			
□ 337	Jesus Alou	.35	.14	.03
□ 338	Gene Tenace	.50	.20	.05
□ 339	Wayne Simpson	.35	.14	.03
□ 340	Rico Petrocelli	.50	.20	.05
□ 341	Steve Garvey	75.00	30.00	7.50
□ 342	Frank Tepedino	.35	.14	.03
□ 343	Pirates Rookies	.35	.14	.03
	Ed Acosta			
	Milt May			
□ 344	Ellie Rodriguez	.35	.14	.03
□ 345	Joe Horlen	.35	.14	.03
□ 346	Lum Harris MG	.35	.14	.03
□ 347	Ted Uhlaender	.35	.14	.03
□ 348	Fred Norman	.35	.14	.03
□ 349	Rich Reese	.35	.14	.03
□ 350	Billy Williams	4.00	1.60	.40
□ 351	Jim Shellenback	.35	.14	.03
□ 352	Denny Doyle	.35	.14	.03
□ 353	Carl Taylor	.35	.14	.03
□ 354	Don McMahon	.35	.14	.03
□ 355	Bud Harrelson	.50	.20	.05
□ 356	Bob Locker	.35	.14	.03
□ 357	Reds Team	1.00	.40	.10
□ 358	Danny Cater	.35	.14	.03

□ 359 Ron Reed	.35	.14	.03
□ 360 Jim Fregosi	.75	.30	.07
□ 361 Don Sutton	3.50	1.40	.35
□ 362 Orioles Rookies	.35	.14	.03
Mike Adamson			
Roger Freed			
□ 363 Mike Nagy	.35	.14	.03
□ 364 Tommy Dean	.35	.14	.03
□ 365 Bob Johnson	.35	.14	.03
□ 366 Ron Stone	.35	.14	.03
□ 367 Dalton Jones	.35	.14	.03
□ 368 Bob Veale	.50	.20	.05
□ 369 Checklist 4	1.50	.20	.04
□ 370 Joe Torre	2.00	.80	.20
□ 371 Jack Hiatt	.35	.14	.03
□ 372 Lew Krausse	.35	.14	.03
□ 373 Tom McCraw	.35	.14	.03
□ 374 Clete Boyer	.50	.20	.05
□ 375 Steve Hargan	.35	.14	.03
□ 376 Expos Rookies	.35	.14	.03
Clyde Mashore			
Ernie McAnally			
□ 377 Greg Garrett	.35	.14	.03
□ 378 Tito Fuentes	.35	.14	.03
□ 379 Wayne Granger	.35	.14	.03
□ 380 Ted Williams MG	5.00	2.00	.50
□ 381 Fred Gladding	.35	.14	.03
□ 382 Jake Gibbs	.35	.14	.03
□ 383 Rod Gaspar	.35	.14	.03
□ 384 Rollie Fingers	3.00	1.20	.30
□ 385 Maury Wills	1.50	.60	.15
□ 386 Red Sox Team	1.00	.40	.10
□ 387 Ron Herbel	.35	.14	.03
□ 388 Al Oliver	1.75	.70	.17
□ 389 Ed Brinkman	.35	.14	.03
□ 390 Glenn Beckert	.50	.20	.05
□ 391 Twins Rookies	.50	.20	.05
Steve Brye			
Cotton Nash			
□ 392 Grant Jackson	.35	.14	.03
□ 393 Merv Rettenmund	.35	.14	.03
□ 394 Clay Carroll	.45	.18	.04
□ 395 Roy White	.60	.24	.06
□ 396 Dick Schofield	.45	.18	.04
□ 397 Alvin Dark MG	.60	.24	.06
□ 398 Howie Reed	.45	.18	.04
□ 399 Jim French	.45	.18	.04
□ 400 Hank Aaron	21.00	8.50	2.10
□ 401 Tom Murphy	.45	.18	.04
□ 402 Dodgers Team	1.00	.40	.10
□ 403 Joe Coleman	.45	.18	.04
□ 404 Astros Rookies	.45	.18	.04
Buddy Harris			
Roger Metzger			
□ 405 Leo Cardenas	.45	.18	.04
□ 406 Ray Sadecki	.45	.18	.04
□ 407 Joe Rudi	.60	.24	.06
□ 408 Rafael Robles	.45	.18	.04
□ 409 Don Pavletich	.45	.18	.04
□ 410 Ken Holtzman	.60	.24	.06
□ 411 George Spriggs	.45	.18	.04
□ 412 Jerry Johnson	.45	.18	.04
□ 413 Pat Kelly	.45	.18	.04
□ 414 Woodie Fryman	.45	.18	.04
□ 415 Mike Hegan	.45	.18	.04
□ 416 Gene Alley	.60	.24	.06
□ 417 Dick Hall	.45	.18	.04
□ 418 Adolfo Phillips	.45	.18	.04
□ 419 Ron Hansen	.45	.18	.04
□ 420 Jim Merritt	.45	.18	.04
□ 421 John Stephenson	.45	.18	.04
□ 422 Frank Bertaina	.45	.18	.04
□ 423 Tigers Rookies	.45	.18	.04
Dennis Saunders			
Tim Marting			
□ 424 R. Rodriquez	.45	.18	.04
□ 425 Doug Rader	.60	.24	.06
□ 426 Chris Cannizzaro	.45	.18	.04
□ 427 Bernie Allen	.45	.18	.04
□ 428 Jim McAndrew	.45	.18	.04
□ 429 Chuck Hinton	.45	.18	.04
□ 430 Wes Parker	.60	.24	.06
□ 431 Tom Burgmeier	.45	.18	.04
□ 432 Bob Didier	.45	.18	.04
□ 433 Skip Lockwood	.45	.18	.04
□ 434 Gary Sutherland	.45	.18	.04
□ 435 Jose Cardenal	.45	.18	.04
□ 436 Wilbur Wood	.60	.24	.06
□ 437 Danny Murtaugh MG	.45	.18	.04
□ 438 Mike McCormick	.60	.24	.06
□ 439 Phillies Rookies	2.25	.90	.22
Greg Luzinski			
Scott Reid			
□ 440 Bert Campaneris	.60	.24	.06
□ 441 Milt Pappas	.60	.24	.06
□ 442 California Angels	1.00	.40	.10
Team Card			
□ 443 Rich Robertson	.45	.18	.04
□ 444 Jimmie Price	.45	.18	.04
□ 445 Art Shamsky	.45	.18	.04
□ 446 Bobby Bolin	.45	.18	.04
□ 447 Cesar Geronimo	.45	.18	.04
□ 448 Dave Roberts	.45	.18	.04
□ 449 Brant Alyea	.45	.18	.04
□ 450 Bob Gibson	6.50	2.60	.65
□ 451 Joe Keough	.45	.18	.04
□ 452 John Boccabella	.45	.18	.04
□ 453 Terry Crowley	.45	.18	.04
□ 454 Mike Paul	.45	.18	.04
□ 455 Don Kessinger	.60	.24	.06
□ 456 Bob Meyer	.45	.18	.04
□ 457 Willie Smith	.45	.18	.04
□ 458 White Sox Rookies	.45	.18	.04
Ron Lolich			
Dave Lemonds			
□ 459 Jim Lefebvre	.75	.30	.07
□ 460 Fritz Peterson	.45	.18	.04
□ 461 Jim Ray Hart	.60	.24	.06
□ 462 Senators Team	1.00	.40	.10
□ 463 Tom Kelley	.45	.18	.04
□ 464 Aurelio Rodriguez	.45	.18	.04
□ 465 Tim McCarver	1.00	.40	.10
□ 466 Ken Berry	.45	.18	.04
□ 467 Al Santorini	.45	.18	.04
□ 468 Frank Fernandez	.45	.18	.04
□ 469 Bob Aspromonte	.45	.18	.04
□ 470 Bob Oliver	.45	.18	.04
□ 471 Tom Griffin	.45	.18	.04
□ 472 Ken Rudolph	.45	.18	.04
□ 473 Gary Wagner	.45	.18	.04
□ 474 Jim Fairey	.45	.18	.04
□ 475 Ron Perranoski	.60	.24	.06
□ 476 Dal Maxvill	.60	.24	.06
□ 477 Earl Weaver MG	1.00	.40	.10
□ 478 Bernie Carbo	.45	.18	.04
□ 479 Dennis Higgins	.45	.18	.04
□ 480 Manny Sanguillen	.60	.24	.06
□ 481 Daryl Patterson	.45	.18	.04
□ 482 Padres Team	1.00	.40	.10
□ 483 Gene Michael	.60	.24	.06
□ 484 Don Wilson	.45	.18	.04
□ 485 Ken McMullen	.45	.18	.04
□ 486 Steve Huntz	.45	.18	.04
□ 487 Paul Schaal	.45	.18	.04
□ 488 Jerry Stephenson	.45	.18	.04
□ 489 Luis Alvarado	.45	.18	.04
□ 490 Deron Johnson	.45	.18	.04
□ 491 Jim Hardin	.45	.18	.04
□ 492 Ken Boswell	.45	.18	.04
□ 493 Dave May	.45	.18	.04
□ 494 Braves Rookies	.60	.24	.06
Ralph Garr			
Rick Kester			
□ 495 Felipe Alou	.60	.24	.06
□ 496 Woody Woodward	.60	.24	.06
□ 497 Horacio Pina	.45	.18	.04
□ 498 John Kennedy	.45	.18	.04
□ 499 Checklist 5	1.50	.20	.04
□ 500 Jim Perry	.75	.30	.07
□ 501 Andy Etchebarren	.45	.18	.04
□ 502 Cubs Team	1.00	.40	.10
□ 503 Gates Brown	.60	.24	.06
□ 504 Ken Wright	.45	.18	.04
□ 505 Ollie Brown	.45	.18	.04
□ 506 Bobby Knoop	.45	.18	.04
□ 507 George Stone	.45	.18	.04
□ 508 Roger Repoz	.45	.18	.04
□ 509 Jim Grant	.45	.18	.04
□ 510 Ken Harrelson	1.00	.40	.10
□ 511 Chris Short	.45	.18	.04
□ 512 Red Sox Rookies	.45	.18	.04
Dick Mills			
Mike Garman			
□ 513 Nolan Ryan	27.00	11.00	2.70
□ 514 Ron Woods	.45	.18	.04
□ 515 Carl Morton	.45	.18	.04
□ 516 Ted Kubiak	.45	.18	.04
□ 517 Charlie Fox MG	.45	.18	.04
□ 518 Joe Grzenda	.45	.18	.04
□ 519 Willie Crawford	.45	.18	.04
□ 520 Tommy John	2.50	1.00	.25
□ 521 Leron Lee	.45	.18	.04
□ 522 Twins Team	1.00	.40	.10
□ 523 John Odom	.45	.18	.04
□ 524 Mickey Stanley	1.00	.40	.10
□ 525 Ernie Banks	11.00	4.50	1.10
□ 526 Ray Jarvis	.85	.34	.08
□ 527 Cleon Jones	.85	.34	.08
□ 528 Wally Bunker	.85	.34	.08
□ 529 NL Rookie Infielders	3.50	1.40	.35

	Enzo Hernandez			
	Bill Buckner			
	Marty Perez			
□ 530	Carl Yastrzemski	32.00	13.00	3.20
□ 531	Mike Torrez	1.00	.40	.10
□ 532	Bill Rigney MG	.85	.34	.08
□ 533	Mike Ryan	.85	.34	.08
□ 534	Luke Walker	.85	.34	.08
□ 535	Curt Flood	1.25	.50	.12
□ 536	Claude Raymond	.85	.34	.08
□ 537	Tom Egan	.85	.34	.08
□ 538	Angel Bravo	.85	.34	.08
□ 539	Larry Brown	.85	.34	.08
□ 540	Larry Dierker	1.00	.40	.10
□ 541	Bob Burda	.85	.34	.08
□ 542	Bob Miller	.85	.34	.08
□ 543	New York Yankees Team Card	2.50	1.00	.25
□ 544	Vida Blue	3.00	1.20	.30
□ 545	Dick Dietz	.85	.34	.08
□ 546	John Matias	.85	.34	.08
□ 547	Pat Dobson	1.00	.40	.10
□ 548	Don Mason	.85	.34	.08
□ 549	Jim Brewer	.85	.34	.08
□ 550	Harmon Killebrew	10.00	4.00	1.00
□ 551	Frank Linzy	.85	.34	.08
□ 552	Buddy Bradford	.85	.34	.08
□ 553	Kevin Collins	.85	.34	.08
□ 554	Lowell Palmer	.85	.34	.08
□ 555	Walt Williams	.85	.34	.08
□ 556	Jim McGlothlin	.85	.34	.08
□ 557	Tom Satriano	.85	.34	.08
□ 558	Hector Torres	.85	.34	.08
□ 559	AL Rookie Pitchers	.85	.34	.08
	Terry Cox			
	Bill Gogolewski			
	Gary Jones			
□ 560	Rusty Staub	2.00	.80	.20
□ 561	Syd O'Brien	.85	.34	.08
□ 562	Dave Giusti	1.00	.40	.10
□ 563	Giants Team	1.75	.70	.17
□ 564	Al Fitzmorris	.85	.34	.08
□ 565	Jim Wynn	1.25	.50	.12
□ 566	Tim Cullen	.85	.34	.08
□ 567	Walt Alston MG	2.50	1.00	.25
□ 568	Sal Campisi	.85	.34	.08
□ 569	Ivan Murrell	.85	.34	.08
□ 570	Jim Palmer	9.00	3.75	.90
□ 571	Ted Sizemore	1.00	.40	.10
□ 572	Jerry Kenney	.85	.34	.08
□ 573	Ed Kranepool	1.00	.40	.10
□ 574	Jim Bunning	2.50	1.00	.25
□ 575	Bill Freehan	1.50	.60	.15
□ 576	Cubs Rookies	.85	.34	.08
	Adrian Garrett			
	Brock Davis			
	Garry Jestadt			
□ 577	Jim Lonborg	1.25	.50	.12
□ 578	Ron Hunt	.85	.34	.08
□ 579	Marty Pattin	.85	.34	.08
□ 580	Tony Perez	3.00	1.20	.30
□ 581	Roger Nelson	.85	.34	.08
□ 582	Dave Cash	1.00	.40	.10
□ 583	Ron Cook	.85	.34	.08
□ 584	Indians Team	1.75	.70	.17
□ 585	Willie Davis	1.25	.50	.12
□ 586	Dick Woodson	.85	.34	.08
□ 587	Sonny Jackson	.85	.34	.08
□ 588	Tom Bradley	.85	.34	.08
□ 589	Bob Barton	.85	.34	.08
□ 590	Alex Johnson	1.00	.40	.10
□ 591	Jackie Brown	.85	.34	.08
□ 592	Randy Hundley	1.00	.40	.10
□ 593	Jack Aker	.85	.34	.08
□ 594	Cards Rookies	1.50	.60	.15
	Bob Chlupsa			
	Bob Stinson			
	Al Hrabosky			
□ 595	Dave Johnson	2.00	.80	.20
□ 596	Mike Jorgensen	.85	.34	.08
□ 597	Ken Suarez	.85	.34	.08
□ 598	Rick Wise	1.00	.40	.10
□ 599	Norm Cash	1.50	.60	.15
□ 600	Willie Mays	32.00	13.00	3.20
□ 601	Ken Tatum	.85	.34	.08
□ 602	Marty Martinez	.85	.34	.08
□ 603	Pirates Team	1.75	.70	.17
□ 604	John Gelnar	.85	.34	.08
□ 605	Orlando Cepeda	3.00	1.20	.30
□ 606	Chuck Taylor	.85	.34	.08
□ 607	Paul Ratliff	.85	.34	.08
□ 608	Mike Wegener	.85	.34	.08
□ 609	Leo Durocher MG	1.75	.70	.17
□ 610	Amos Otis	1.25	.50	.12
□ 611	Tom Phoebus	.85	.34	.08
□ 612	Indians Rookies	.85	.34	.08
	Lou Camilli			
	Ted Ford			
	Steve Mingori			
□ 613	Pedro Borbon	.85	.34	.08
□ 614	Billy Cowan	.85	.34	.08
□ 615	Mel Stottlemyre	1.50	.60	.15
□ 616	Larry Hisle	1.00	.40	.10
□ 617	Clay Dalrymple	.85	.34	.08
□ 618	Tug McGraw	1.50	.60	.15
□ 619A	Checklist 6 (copyright on back)	2.50	.30	.06
□ 619B	Checklist 6 (no copyright)	3.50	.40	.08
□ 620	Frank Howard	1.50	.60	.15
□ 621	Ron Bryant	.85	.34	.08
□ 622	Joe Lahoud	.85	.34	.08
□ 623	Pat Jarvis	.85	.34	.08
□ 624	Athletics Team	1.75	.70	.17
□ 625	Lou Brock	10.00	4.00	1.00
□ 626	Freddie Patek	1.00	.40	.10
□ 627	Steve Hamilton	.85	.34	.08
□ 628	John Bateman	.85	.34	.08
□ 629	John Hiller	1.00	.40	.10
□ 630	Roberto Clemente	22.00	9.00	2.20
□ 631	Eddie Fisher	.85	.34	.08
□ 632	Darrel Chaney	.85	.34	.08
□ 633	AL Rookie Outfielders	.85	.34	.08
	Bobby Brooks			
	Pete Koegel			
	Scott Northey			
□ 634	Phil Regan	1.00	.40	.10
□ 635	Bobby Murcer	1.75	.70	.17
□ 636	Denny Lemaster	.85	.34	.08
□ 637	Dave Bristol MG	.85	.34	.08
□ 638	Stan Williams	.85	.34	.08
□ 639	Tom Haller	1.00	.40	.10
□ 640	Frank Robinson	12.00	5.00	1.20
□ 641	New York Mets Team Card	3.00	1.20	.30
□ 642	Jim Roland	.85	.34	.08
□ 643	Rick Reichardt	.85	.34	.08
□ 644	Jim Stewart	2.00	.80	.20
□ 645	Jim Maloney	2.50	1.00	.25
□ 646	Bobby Floyd	2.00	.80	.20
□ 647	Juan Pizarro	2.00	.80	.20
□ 648	Mets Rookies	4.00	1.60	.40
	Rich Folkers			
	Ted Martinez			
	John Matlack			
□ 649	Sparky Lyle	3.50	1.40	.35
□ 650	Rich Allen	7.00	2.80	.70
□ 651	Jerry Robertson	2.00	.80	.20
□ 652	Braves Team	4.00	1.60	.40
□ 653	Russ Snyder	2.00	.80	.20
□ 654	Don Shaw	2.00	.80	.20
□ 655	Mike Epstein	2.00	.80	.20
□ 656	Gerry Nyman	2.00	.80	.20
□ 657	Jose Azcue	2.00	.80	.20
□ 658	Paul Lindblad	2.00	.80	.20
□ 659	Byron Browne	2.00	.80	.20
□ 660	Ray Culp	2.00	.80	.20
□ 661	Chuck Tanner MG	3.00	1.20	.30
□ 662	Mike Hedlund	2.00	.80	.20
□ 663	Marv Staehle	2.00	.80	.20
□ 664	Rookie Pitchers	2.50	1.00	.25
	Archie Reynolds			
	Bob Reynolds			
	Ken Reynolds			
□ 665	Ron Swoboda	2.50	1.00	.25
□ 666	Gene Brabender	2.00	.80	.20
□ 667	Pete Ward	2.00	.80	.20
□ 668	Gary Neibauer	2.00	.80	.20
□ 669	Ike Brown	2.00	.80	.20
□ 670	Bill Hands	2.00	.80	.20
□ 671	Bill Voss	2.00	.80	.20
□ 672	Ed Crosby	2.00	.80	.20
□ 673	Gerry Janeski	2.00	.80	.20
□ 674	Montreal Expos Team Card	4.50	1.80	.45
□ 675	Dave Boswell	2.00	.80	.20
□ 676	Tommie Reynolds	2.00	.80	.20
□ 677	Jack DiLauro	2.00	.80	.20
□ 678	George Thomas	2.00	.80	.20
□ 679	Don O'Riley	2.00	.80	.20
□ 680	Don Mincher	2.50	1.00	.25
□ 681	Bill Butler	2.00	.80	.20
□ 682	Terry Harmon	2.00	.80	.20
□ 683	Bill Burbach	2.00	.80	.20
□ 684	Curt Motton	2.00	.80	.20
□ 685	Moe Drabowsky	2.00	.80	.20
□ 686	Chico Ruiz	2.00	.80	.20
□ 687	Ron Taylor	2.00	.80	.20
□ 688	Sparky Anderson MG	4.50	1.80	.45
□ 689	Frank Baker	2.00	.80	.20

□690	Bob Moose	2.00	.80	.20
□691	Bob Heise	2.00	.80	.20
□692	AL Rookie Pitchers Hal Haydel Rogelio Moret Wayne Twitchell	2.00	.80	.20
□693	Jose Pena	2.00	.80	.20
□694	Rick Renick	2.00	.80	.20
□695	Joe Niekro	4.00	1.60	.40
□696	Jerry Morales	2.50	1.00	.25
□697	Rickey Clark	2.00	.80	.20
□698	Milwaukee Brewers Team Card	4.50	1.80	.45
□699	Jim Britton	2.00	.80	.20
□700	Boog Powell	5.00	2.00	.50
□701	Bob Garibaldi	2.00	.80	.20
□702	Milt Ramirez	2.00	.80	.20
□703	Mike Kekich	2.00	.80	.20
□704	J.C. Martin	2.00	.80	.20
□705	Dick Selma	2.00	.80	.20
□706	Joe Foy	2.00	.80	.20
□707	Fred Lasher	2.00	.80	.20
□708	Russ Nagelson	2.00	.80	.20
□709	Rookie Outfielders Dusty Baker Don Baylor Tom Paciorek	18.00	7.25	1.80
□710	Sonny Siebert	2.50	1.00	.25
□711	Larry Stahl	2.00	.80	.20
□712	Jose Martinez	2.00	.80	.20
□713	Mike Marshall	2.50	1.00	.25
□714	Dick Williams MG	2.50	1.00	.25
□715	Horace Clarke	2.00	.80	.20
□716	Dave Leonhard	2.00	.80	.20
□717	Tommie Aaron	2.50	1.00	.25
□718	Billy Wynne	2.00	.80	.20
□719	Jerry May	2.00	.80	.20
□720	Matty Alou	2.50	1.00	.25
□721	John Morris	2.00	.80	.20
□722	Houston Astros Team Card	4.00	1.60	.40
□723	Vicente Romo	2.00	.80	.20
□724	Tom Tischinski	2.00	.80	.20
□725	Gary Gentry	2.00	.80	.20
□726	Paul Popovich	2.00	.80	.20
□727	Ray Lamb	2.00	.80	.20
□728	NL Rookie Outfielders Wayne Redmond Keith Lampard Bernie Williams	2.00	.80	.20
□729	Dick Billings	2.00	.80	.20
□730	Jim Rooker	2.00	.80	.20
□731	Jim Qualls	2.00	.80	.20
□732	Bob Reed	2.00	.80	.20
□733	Lee Maye	2.00	.80	.20
□734	Rob Gardner	2.00	.80	.20
□735	Mike Shannon	3.50	1.40	.35
□736	Mel Queen	2.00	.80	.20
□737	Preston Gomez MG	2.00	.80	.20
□738	Russ Gibson	2.00	.80	.20
□739	Barry Lersch	2.00	.80	.20
□740	Luis Aparicio	10.00	4.00	1.00
□741	Skip Guinn	2.00	.80	.20
□742	Kansas City Royals Team Card	4.00	1.60	.40
□743	John O'Donoghue	2.00	.80	.20
□744	Chuck Manuel	2.00	.80	.20
□745	Sandy Alomar	2.00	.80	.20
□746	Andy Kosco	2.00	.80	.20
□747	NL Rookie Pitchers Al Severinsen Scipio Spinks Balor Moore	2.00	.80	.20
□748	John Purdin	2.00	.80	.20
□749	Ken Szotkiewicz	2.00	.80	.20
□750	Denny McLain	5.00	2.00	.50
□751	Al Weis	2.00	.80	.20
□752	Dick Drago	3.00	1.00	.20

1972 Topps

The cards in this 787-card set measure 2 1/2" by 3 1/2". The 1972 Topps set contained the most cards ever for a Topps set to that point in time. Features appearing for the first time were "Boyhood Photos" (KP: 341-348 and 491-498), Awards and Trophy cards (621-626), "In Action" (distributed throughout the set) and "Traded Cards" (TR: 751-757). Other

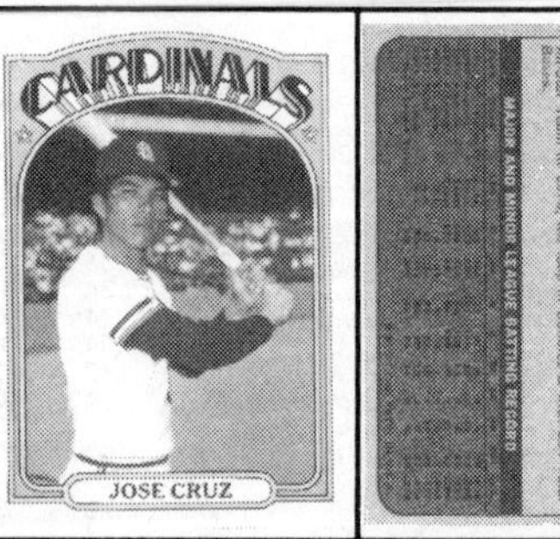

subsets included League Leaders (85-96), Playoffs cards (221-222), and World Series cards (223-230). The curved lines of the color picture are a departure from the rectangular designs of other years. There is a series of intermediate scarcity (526-656) and the usual high numbers (657-787).

		NRMT	VG-E	GOOD
	COMPLETE SET (787)	1300.00	500.00	175.00
	COMMON PLAYER (1-132)	.25	.10	.02
	COMMON PLAYER (133-263)	.30	.12	.03
	COMMON PLAYER (264-394)	.35	.14	.03
	COMMON PLAYER (395-525)	.40	.16	.04
	COMMON PLAYER (526-656)	.85	.34	.08
	COMMON PLAYER (657-787)	2.00	.80	.20
□ 1	Pittsburgh Pirates Team Card	4.00	.60	.12
□ 2	Ray Culp	.25	.10	.02
□ 3	Bob Tolan	.40	.16	.04
□ 4	Checklist 1	1.25	.15	.03
□ 5	John Bateman	.25	.10	.02
□ 6	Fred Scherman	.25	.10	.02
□ 7	Enzo Hernandez	.25	.10	.02
□ 8	Ron Swoboda	.40	.16	.04
□ 9	Stan Williams	.25	.10	.02
□ 10	Amos Otis	.40	.16	.04
□ 11	Bobby Valentine	.75	.30	.07
□ 12	Jose Cardenal	.25	.10	.02
□ 13	Joe Grzenda	.25	.10	.02
□ 14	Phillies Rookies Pete Koegel Mike Anderson Wayne Twitchell	.25	.10	.02
□ 15	Walt Williams	.25	.10	.02
□ 16	Mike Jorgensen	.25	.10	.02
□ 17	Dave Duncan	.25	.10	.02
□ 18A	Juan Pizarro (yellow underline C and S of Cubs)	.25	.10	.02
□ 18B	Juan Pizarro (green underline C and S of Cubs)	5.00	2.00	.50
□ 19	Billy Cowan	.25	.10	.02
□ 20	Don Wilson	.25	.10	.02
□ 21	Braves Team	.60	.24	.06
□ 22	Rob Gardner	.25	.10	.02
□ 23	Ted Kubiak	.25	.10	.02
□ 24	Ted Ford	.25	.10	.02
□ 25	Bill Singer	.40	.16	.04
□ 26	Andy Etchebarren	.25	.10	.02
□ 27	Bob Johnson	.25	.10	.02
□ 28	Twins Rookies Bob Gebhard Steve Brye Hal Haydel	.25	.10	.02
□ 29A	Bill Bonham (yellow underline C and S of Cubs)	.25	.10	.02
□ 29B	Bill Bonham (green underline C and S of Cubs)	5.00	2.00	.50
□ 30	Rico Petrocelli	.40	.16	.04
□ 31	Cleon Jones	.25	.10	.02
□ 32	Jones In Action	.25	.10	.02
□ 33	Billy Martin MG	1.50	.60	.15
□ 34	Martin In Action	.60	.24	.06
□ 35	Jerry Johnson	.25	.10	.02
□ 36	Johnson In Action	.25	.10	.02
□ 37	Carl Yastrzemski	15.00	6.00	1.50
□ 38	Yastrzemski In Action	6.00	2.40	.60
□ 39	Bob Barton	.25	.10	.02

☐ 40 Barton In Action .25 .10 .02
☐ 41 Tommy Davis .40 .16 .04
☐ 42 Davis In Action .25 .10 .02
☐ 43 Rick Wise .25 .10 .02
☐ 44 Wise In Action .25 .10 .02
☐ 45A Glenn Beckert .40 .16 .04
(yellow underline
C and S of Cubs)
☐ 45B Glenn Beckert 5.00 2.00 .50
(green underline
C and S of Cubs)
☐ 46 Beckert In Action .25 .10 .02
☐ 47 John Ellis .25 .10 .02
☐ 48 Ellis In Action .25 .10 .02
☐ 49 Willie Mays 15.00 6.00 1.50
☐ 50 Mays In Action 6.00 2.40 .60
☐ 51 Harmon Killebrew 4.00 1.60 .40
☐ 52 Killebrew In Action 1.50 .60 .15
☐ 53 Bud Harrelson .40 .16 .04
☐ 54 Harrelson In Action .25 .10 .02
☐ 55 Clyde Wright .25 .10 .02
☐ 56 Rich Chiles .25 .10 .02
☐ 57 Bob Oliver .25 .10 .02
☐ 58 Ernie McAnally .25 .10 .02
☐ 59 Fred Stanley .25 .10 .02
☐ 60 Manny Sanguillen .40 .16 .04
☐ 61 Cubs Rookies .60 .24 .06
Burt Hooton
Gene Hiser
Earl Stephenson
☐ 62 Angel Mangual .25 .10 .02
☐ 63 Duke Sims .25 .10 .02
☐ 64 Pete Broberg .25 .10 .02
☐ 65 Cesar Cedeno .60 .24 .06
☐ 66 Ray Corbin .25 .10 .02
☐ 67 Red Schoendienst MG .60 .24 .06
☐ 68 Jim York .25 .10 .02
☐ 69 Roger Freed .25 .10 .02
☐ 70 Mike Cuellar .40 .16 .04
☐ 71 Angels Team .60 .24 .06
☐ 72 Bruce Kison .60 .24 .06
☐ 73 Steve Huntz .25 .10 .02
☐ 74 Cecil Upshaw .25 .10 .02
☐ 75 Bert Campaneris .40 .16 .04
☐ 76 Don Carrithers .25 .10 .02
☐ 77 Ron Theobald .25 .10 .02
☐ 78 Steve Arlin .25 .10 .02
☐ 79 Red Sox Rookies 20.00 8.00 2.00
Mike Garman
Cecil Cooper
Carlton Fisk
☐ 80 Tony Perez 2.00 .80 .20
☐ 81 Mike Hedlund .25 .10 .02
☐ 82 Ron Woods .25 .10 .02
☐ 83 Dalton Jones .25 .10 .02
☐ 84 Vince Colbert .25 .10 .02
☐ 85 NL Batting Leaders .75 .30 .07
Joe Torre
Ralph Garr
Glenn Beckert
☐ 86 AL Batting Leaders .75 .30 .07
Tony Oliva
Bobby Murcer
Merv Rettenmund
☐ 87 NL RBI Leaders 1.50 .60 .15
Joe Torre
Willie Stargell
Hank Aaron
☐ 88 AL RBI Leaders 1.25 .50 .12
Harmon Killebrew
Frank Robinson
Reggie Smith
☐ 89 NL Home Run Leaders 1.50 .60 .15
Willie Stargell
Hank Aaron
Lee May
☐ 90 AL Home Run Leaders 1.00 .40 .10
Bill Melton
Norm Cash
Reggie Jackson
☐ 91 NL ERA Leaders 1.00 .40 .10
Tom Seaver
Dave Roberts
(photo actually
Danny Coombs)
Don Wilson
☐ 92 AL ERA Leaders .75 .30 .07
Vida Blue
Wilbur Wood
Jim Palmer
☐ 93 NL Pitching Leaders 1.50 .60 .15
Fergie Jenkins
Steve Carlton
Al Downing
Tom Seaver

☐ 94 AL Pitching Leaders .75 .30 .07
Mickey Lolich
Vida Blue
Wilbur Wood NL
Strikeout Leaders 1.00 .40 .10
Tom Seaver
Fergie Jenkins
Bill Stoneman
☐ 96 AL Strikeout Leaders .75 .30 .07
Mickey Lolich
Vida Blue
Joe Coleman
☐ 97 Tom Kelley .25 .10 .02
☐ 98 Chuck Tanner MG .40 .16 .04
☐ 99 Ross Grimsley .25 .10 .02
☐ 100 Frank Robinson 4.00 1.60 .40
☐ 101 Astros Rookies 1.50 .60 .15
Bill Greif
J.R. Richard
Ray Busse
☐ 102 Lloyd Allen .25 .10 .02
☐ 103 Checklist 2 1.25 .20 .03
☐ 104 Toby Harrah 1.25 .50 .12
☐ 105 Gary Gentry .25 .10 .02
☐ 106 Brewers Team .60 .24 .06
☐ 107 Jose Cruz 1.50 .60 .15
☐ 108 Gary Waslewski .25 .10 .02
☐ 109 Jerry May .25 .10 .02
☐ 110 Ron Hunt .25 .10 .02
☐ 111 Jim Grant .25 .10 .02
☐ 112 Greg Luzinski 1.00 .40 .10
☐ 113 Rogelio Moret .25 .10 .02
☐ 114 Bill Buckner 1.50 .60 .15
☐ 115 Jim Fregosi .40 .16 .04
☐ 116 Ed Farmer .25 .10 .02
☐ 117A Cleo James .25 .10 .02
(yellow underline
C and S of Cubs)
☐ 117B Cleo James 5.00 2.00 .50
(green underline
C and S of Cubs)
☐ 118 Skip Lockwood .25 .10 .02
☐ 119 Marty Perez .25 .10 .02
☐ 120 Bill Freehan .60 .24 .06
☐ 121 Ed Sprague .25 .10 .02
☐ 122 Larry Biittner .25 .10 .02
☐ 123 Ed Acosta .25 .10 .02
☐ 124 Yankees Rookies .25 .10 .02
Alan Closter
Rusty Torres
Roger Hambright
☐ 125 Dave Cash .40 .16 .04
☐ 126 Bart Johnson .25 .10 .02
☐ 127 Duffy Dyer .25 .10 .02
☐ 128 Eddie Watt .25 .10 .02
☐ 129 Charlie Fox MG .25 .10 .02
☐ 130 Bob Gibson 4.00 1.60 .40
☐ 131 Jim Nettles .25 .10 .02
☐ 132 Joe Morgan 2.50 1.00 .25
☐ 133 Joe Keough .30 .12 .03
☐ 134 Carl Morton .30 .12 .03
☐ 135 Vada Pinson .75 .30 .07
☐ 136 Darrell Chaney .30 .12 .03
☐ 137 Dick Williams MG .50 .20 .05
☐ 138 Mike Kekich .30 .12 .03
☐ 139 Tim McCarver .75 .30 .07
☐ 140 Pat Dobson .50 .20 .05
☐ 141 Mets Rookies .50 .20 .05
Buzz Capra
Leroy Stanton
Jon Matlack
☐ 142 Chris Chambliss 1.50 .60 .15
☐ 143 Garry Jestadt .30 .12 .03
☐ 144 Marty Pattin .30 .12 .03
☐ 145 Don Kessinger .50 .20 .05
☐ 146 Steve Kealey .30 .12 .03
☐ 147 Dave Kingman 4.50 1.80 .45
☐ 148 Dick Billings .30 .12 .03
☐ 149 Gary Neibauer .30 .12 .03
☐ 150 Norm Cash 1.00 .40 .10
☐ 151 Jim Brewer .30 .12 .03
☐ 152 Gene Clines .30 .12 .03
☐ 153 Rick Auerbach .30 .12 .03
☐ 154 Ted Simmons 1.50 .60 .15
☐ 155 Larry Dierker .50 .20 .05
☐ 156 Minnesota Twins .75 .30 .07
Team Card
☐ 157 Don Gullett .50 .20 .05
☐ 158 Jerry Kenney .30 .12 .03
☐ 159 John Boccabella .30 .12 .03
☐ 160 Andy Messersmith .50 .20 .05
☐ 161 Brock Davis .30 .12 .03
☐ 162 Brewers Rookies 1.00 .40 .10
Jerry Bell

Darrell Porter
Bob Reynolds
(Porter and Bell
photos switched)
☐ 163 Tug McGraw .75 .30 .07
☐ 164 McGraw In Action .50 .20 .05
☐ 165 Chris Speier .60 .24 .06
☐ 166 Speier In Action .30 .12 .03
☐ 167 Deron Johnson .30 .12 .03
☐ 168 Johnson In Action .30 .12 .03
☐ 169 Vida Blue .75 .30 .07
☐ 170 Blue In Action .50 .20 .05
☐ 171 Darrell Evans 1.50 .60 .15
☐ 172 Evans In Action .50 .20 .05
☐ 173 Clay Kirby .30 .12 .03
☐ 174 Kirby In Action .30 .12 .03
☐ 175 Tom Haller .30 .12 .03
☐ 176 Haller In Action .30 .12 .03
☐ 177 Paul Schaal .30 .12 .03
☐ 178 Schaal In Action .30 .12 .03
☐ 179 Dock Ellis .30 .12 .03
☐ 180 Ellis In Action .30 .12 .03
☐ 181 Ed Kranepool .50 .20 .05
☐ 182 Kranepool In Action .30 .12 .03
☐ 183 Bill Melton .30 .12 .03
☐ 184 Melton In Action .30 .12 .03
☐ 185 Ron Bryant .30 .12 .03
☐ 186 Bryant In Action .30 .12 .03
☐ 187 Gates Brown .50 .20 .05
☐ 188 Frank Lucchesi MG .30 .12 .03
☐ 189 Gene Tenace .50 .20 .05
☐ 190 Dave Giusti .50 .20 .05
☐ 191 Jeff Burroughs .75 .30 .07
☐ 192 Cubs Team .75 .30 .07
☐ 193 Kurt Bevacqua .30 .12 .03
☐ 194 Fred Norman .30 .12 .03
☐ 195 Orlando Cepeda 1.75 .70 .17
☐ 196 Mel Queen .30 .12 .03
☐ 197 Johnny Briggs .30 .12 .03
☐ 198 Dodgers Rookies 1.50 .60 .15
Charlie Hough
Bob O'Brien
Mike Strahler
☐ 199 Mike Fiore .30 .12 .03
☐ 200 Lou Brock 4.00 1.60 .40
☐ 201 Phil Roof .30 .12 .03
☐ 202 Scipio Spinks .30 .12 .03
☐ 203 Ron Blomberg .30 .12 .03
☐ 204 Tommy Helms .50 .20 .05
☐ 205 Dick Drago .30 .12 .03
☐ 206 Dal Maxvill .50 .20 .05
☐ 207 Tom Egan .30 .12 .03
☐ 208 Milt Pappas .50 .20 .05
☐ 209 Joe Rudi .50 .20 .05
☐ 210 Denny McLain 1.00 .40 .10
☐ 211 Gary Sutherland .30 .12 .03
☐ 212 Grant Jackson .30 .12 .03
☐ 213 Angels Rookies .30 .12 .03
Billy Parker
Art Kusnyer
Tom Silverio
☐ 214 Mike McQueen .30 .12 .03
☐ 215 Alex Johnson .50 .20 .05
☐ 216 Joe Niekro .75 .30 .07
☐ 217 Roger Metzger .30 .12 .03
☐ 218 Eddie Kasko MG .30 .12 .03
☐ 219 Rennie Stennett .50 .20 .05
☐ 220 Jim Perry .75 .30 .07
☐ 221 NL Playoffs .75 .30 .07
Bucs champs
☐ 222 AL Playoffs 1.50 .60 .15
Orioles champs
(Brooks Robinson)
☐ 223 World Series Game 1 .75 .30 .07
(McNally pitching)
☐ 224 World Series Game 2 .75 .30 .07
(Dave Johnson and
Mark Belanger)
☐ 225 World Series Game 3 .75 .30 .07
(Sanguillen scoring)
☐ 226 World Series Game 4 2.25 .90 .22
(Clemente on 2nd)
☐ 227 World Series Game 5 .75 .30 .07
(Briles pitching)
☐ 228 World Series Game 6 1.00 .40 .10
(Frank Robinson and
Manny Sanguillen)
☐ 229 World Series Game 7 .75 .30 .07
(Blass pitching)
☐ 230 World Series Summary .75 .30 .07
Pirates celebrate
☐ 231 Casey Cox .30 .12 .03
☐ 232 Giants Rookies .30 .12 .03
Chris Arnold
Jim Barr
Dave Rader
☐ 233 Jay Johnstone .50 .20 .05
☐ 234 Ron Taylor .30 .12 .03
☐ 235 Merv Rettenmund .30 .12 .03
☐ 236 Jim McGlothlin .30 .12 .03
☐ 237 Yankees Team 1.00 .40 .10
☐ 238 Leron Lee .30 .12 .03
☐ 239 Tom Timmermann .30 .12 .03
☐ 240 Rich Allen 1.50 .60 .15
☐ 241 Rollie Fingers 2.50 1.00 .25
☐ 242 Don Mincher .30 .12 .03
☐ 243 Frank Linzy .30 .12 .03
☐ 244 Steve Braun .30 .12 .03
☐ 245 Tommie Agee .30 .12 .03
☐ 246 Tom Burgmeier .30 .12 .03
☐ 247 Milt May .30 .12 .03
☐ 248 Tom Bradley .30 .12 .03
☐ 249 Harry Walker MG .30 .12 .03
☐ 250 Boog Powell 1.00 .40 .10
☐ 251 Checklist 3 1.25 .15 .03
☐ 252 Ken Reynolds .30 .12 .03
☐ 253 Sandy Alomar .30 .12 .03
☐ 254 Boots Day .30 .12 .03
☐ 255 Jim Lonborg .50 .20 .05
☐ 256 George Foster 1.50 .60 .15
☐ 257 Tigers Rookies .30 .12 .03
Jim Foor
Tim Hosley
Paul Jata
☐ 258 Randy Hundley .30 .12 .03
☐ 259 Sparky Lyle .75 .30 .07
☐ 260 Ralph Garr .50 .20 .05
☐ 261 Steve Mingori .30 .12 .03
☐ 262 San Diego Padres .75 .30 .07
Team Card
☐ 263 Felipe Alou .50 .20 .05
☐ 264 Tommy John 2.00 .80 .20
☐ 265 Wes Parker .50 .20 .05
☐ 266 Bobby Bolin .35 .14 .03
☐ 267 Dave Concepcion 1.50 .60 .15
☐ 268 A's Rookies .35 .14 .03
Dwain Anderson
Chris Floethe
☐ 269 Don Hahn .35 .14 .03
☐ 270 Jim Palmer 4.00 1.60 .40
☐ 271 Ken Rudolph .35 .14 .03
☐ 272 Mickey Rivers 1.00 .40 .10
☐ 273 Bobby Floyd .35 .14 .03
☐ 274 Al Severinsen .35 .14 .03
☐ 275 Cesar Tovar .35 .14 .03
☐ 276 Gene Mauch MG .50 .20 .05
☐ 277 Elliot Maddox .35 .14 .03
☐ 278 Dennis Higgins .35 .14 .03
☐ 279 Larry Brown .35 .14 .03
☐ 280 Willie McCovey 4.00 1.60 .40
☐ 281 Bill Parsons .35 .14 .03
☐ 282 Astros Team .75 .30 .07
☐ 283 Darrell Brandon .35 .14 .03
☐ 284 Ike Brown .35 .14 .03
☐ 285 Gaylord Perry 4.00 1.60 .40
☐ 286 Gene Alley .50 .20 .05
☐ 287 Jim Hardin .35 .14 .03
☐ 288 Johnny Jeter .35 .14 .03
☐ 289 Syd O'Brien .35 .14 .03
☐ 290 Sonny Siebert .50 .20 .05
☐ 291 Hal McRae .75 .30 .07
☐ 292 McRae In Action .50 .20 .05
☐ 293 Danny Frisella .35 .14 .03
☐ 294 Frisella In Action .35 .14 .03
☐ 295 Dick Dietz .35 .14 .03
☐ 296 Dietz In Action .35 .14 .03
☐ 297 Claude Osteen .50 .20 .05
☐ 298 Osteen In Action .35 .14 .03
☐ 299 Hank Aaron 15.00 6.00 1.50
☐ 300 Aaron in Action 6.00 2.40 .60
☐ 301 George Mitterwald .35 .14 .03
☐ 302 Mitterwald In Action .35 .14 .03
☐ 303 Joe Pepitone .50 .20 .05
☐ 304 Pepitone In Action .35 .14 .03
☐ 305 Ken Boswell .35 .14 .03
☐ 306 Boswell In Action .35 .14 .03
☐ 307 Steve Renko .35 .14 .03
☐ 308 Renko In Action .35 .14 .03
☐ 309 Roberto Clemente 13.00 5.25 1.30
☐ 310 Clemente In Action 5.00 2.00 .50
☐ 311 Clay Carroll .35 .14 .03
☐ 312 Carroll In Action .35 .14 .03
☐ 313 Luis Aparicio 3.00 1.20 .30
☐ 314 Aparicio In Action 1.25 .50 .12
☐ 315 Paul Splittorff .50 .20 .05
☐ 316 Cardinals Rookies .50 .20 .05
Jim Bibby
Jorge Roque
Santiago Guzman
☐ 317 Rich Hand .35 .14 .03

□ 318	Sonny Jackson	.35	.14	.03
□ 319	Aurelio Rodriguez	.35	.14	.03
□ 320	Steve Blass	.50	.20	.05
□ 321	Joe Lahoud	.35	.14	.03
□ 322	Jose Pena	.35	.14	.03
□ 323	Earl Weaver MG	.75	.30	.07
□ 324	Mike Ryan	.35	.14	.03
□ 325	Mel Stottlemyre	.75	.30	.07
□ 326	Pat Kelly	.35	.14	.03
□ 327	Steve Stone	.75	.30	.07
□ 328	Red Sox Team	.75	.30	.07
□ 329	Roy Foster	.35	.14	.03
□ 330	Jim Hunter	3.00	1.20	.30
□ 331	Stan Swanson	.35	.14	.03
□ 332	Buck Martinez	.35	.14	.03
□ 333	Steve Barber	.35	.14	.03
□ 334	Rangers Rookies	.35	.14	.03
	Bill Fahey			
	Jim Mason			
	Tom Ragland			
□ 335	Bill Hands	.35	.14	.03
□ 336	Marty Martinez	.35	.14	.03
□ 337	Mike Kilkenny	.35	.14	.03
□ 338	Bob Grich	.75	.30	.07
□ 339	Ron Cook	.35	.14	.03
□ 340	Roy White	.50	.20	.05
□ 341	KP: Joe Torre	.50	.20	.05
□ 342	KP: Wilbur Wood	.35	.14	.03
□ 343	KP: Willie Stargell	1.00	.40	.10
□ 344	KP: Dave McNally	.35	.14	.03
□ 345	KP: Rick Wise	.35	.14	.03
□ 346	KP: Jim Fregosi	.50	.20	.05
□ 347	KP: Tom Seaver	1.50	.60	.15
□ 348	KP: Sal Bando	.35	.14	.03
□ 349	Al Fitzmorris	.35	.14	.03
□ 350	Frank Howard	.75	.30	.07
□ 351	Braves Rookies	.50	.20	.05
	Tom House			
	Rick Kester			
	Jimmy Britton			
□ 352	Dave LaRoche	.35	.14	.03
□ 353	Art Shamsky	.35	.14	.03
□ 354	Tom Murphy	.35	.14	.03
□ 355	Bob Watson	.50	.20	.05
□ 356	Gerry Moses	.35	.14	.03
□ 357	Woodie Fryman	.35	.14	.03
□ 358	Sparky Anderson MG	1.00	.40	.10
□ 359	Don Pavletich	.35	.14	.03
□ 360	Dave Roberts	.35	.14	.03
□ 361	Mike Andrews	.35	.14	.03
□ 362	New York Mets	1.00	.40	.10
	Team Card			
□ 363	Ron Klimkowski	.35	.14	.03
□ 364	Johnny Callison	.50	.20	.05
□ 365	Dick Bosman	.35	.14	.03
□ 366	Jimmy Rosario	.35	.14	.03
□ 367	Ron Perranoski	.50	.20	.05
□ 368	Danny Thompson	.35	.14	.03
□ 369	Jim Lefebvre	.75	.30	.07
□ 370	Don Buford	.50	.20	.05
□ 371	Denny Lemaster	.35	.14	.03
□ 372	Royals Rookies	.35	.14	.03
	Lance Clemons			
	Monty Montgomery			
□ 373	John Mayberry	.50	.20	.05
□ 374	Jack Heidemann	.35	.14	.03
□ 375	Reggie Cleveland	.35	.14	.03
□ 376	Andy Kosco	.35	.14	.03
□ 377	Terry Harmon	.35	.14	.03
□ 378	Checklist 4	1.25	.15	.03
□ 379	Ken Berry	.35	.14	.03
□ 380	Earl Williams	.35	.14	.03
□ 381	Chicago White Sox	.75	.30	.07
	Team Card			
□ 382	Joe Gibbon	.35	.14	.03
□ 383	Brant Alyea	.35	.14	.03
□ 384	Dave Campbell	.35	.14	.03
□ 385	Mickey Stanley	.50	.20	.05
□ 386	Jim Colborn	.35	.14	.03
□ 387	Horace Clarke	.35	.14	.03
□ 388	Charlie Williams	.35	.14	.03
□ 389	Bill Rigney MG	.35	.14	.03
□ 390	Willie Davis	.50	.20	.05
□ 391	Ken Sanders	.35	.14	.03
□ 392	Pirates Rookies	.75	.30	.07
	Fred Cambria			
	Richie Zisk			
□ 393	Curt Motton	.35	.14	.03
□ 394	Ken Forsch	.50	.20	.05
□ 395	Matty Alou	.60	.24	.06
□ 396	Paul Lindblad	.45	.18	.04
□ 397	Philadelphia Phillies	.90	.36	.09
	Team Card			
□ 398	Larry Hisle	.60	.24	.06
□ 399	Milt Wilcox	.60	.24	.06
□ 400	Tony Oliva	1.50	.60	.15
□ 401	Jim Nash	.45	.18	.04
□ 402	Bobby Heise	.45	.18	.04
□ 403	John Cumberland	.45	.18	.04
□ 404	Jeff Torborg	.60	.24	.06
□ 405	Ron Fairly	.60	.24	.06
□ 406	George Hendrick	1.00	.40	.10
□ 407	Chuck Taylor	.45	.18	.04
□ 408	Jim Northrup	.60	.24	.06
□ 409	Frank Baker	.45	.18	.04
□ 410	Fergie Jenkins	1.75	.70	.17
□ 411	Bob Montgomery	.45	.18	.04
□ 412	Dick Kelley	.45	.18	.04
□ 413	White Sox Rookies	.45	.18	.04
	Don Eddy			
	Dave Lemonds			
□ 414	Bob Miller	.45	.18	.04
□ 415	Cookie Rojas	.60	.24	.06
□ 416	Johnny Edwards	.45	.18	.04
□ 417	Tom Hall	.45	.18	.04
□ 418	Tom Shopay	.45	.18	.04
□ 419	Jim Spencer	.45	.18	.04
□ 420	Steve Carlton	13.00	5.25	1.30
□ 421	Ellie Rodriguez	.45	.18	.04
□ 422	Ray Lamb	.45	.18	.04
□ 423	Oscar Gamble	.60	.24	.06
□ 424	Bill Gogolewski	.45	.18	.04
□ 425	Ken Singleton	.90	.36	.09
□ 426	Singleton In Action	.60	.24	.06
□ 427	Tito Fuentes	.45	.18	.04
□ 428	Fuentes In Action	.45	.18	.04
□ 429	Bob Robertson	.45	.18	.04
□ 430	Robertson In Action	.45	.18	.04
□ 431	Clarence Gaston	.45	.18	.04
□ 432	Gaston In Action	.45	.18	.04
□ 433	Johnny Bench	20.00	8.00	2.00
□ 434	Bench In Action	8.00	3.25	.80
□ 435	Reggie Jackson	18.00	7.25	1.80
□ 436	Jackson In Action	7.00	2.80	.70
□ 437	Maury Wills	1.25	.50	.12
□ 438	Wills In Action	.60	.24	.06
□ 439	Billy Williams	3.00	1.20	.30
□ 440	Williams In Action	1.25	.50	.12
□ 441	Thurman Munson	10.00	4.00	1.00
□ 442	Munson In Action	4.00	1.60	.40
□ 443	Ken Henderson	.45	.18	.04
□ 444	Henderson In Action	.45	.18	.04
□ 445	Tom Seaver	13.00	5.25	1.30
□ 446	Seaver In Action	5.00	2.00	.50
□ 447	Willie Stargell	4.50	1.80	.45
□ 448	Stargell In Action	1.75	.70	.17
□ 449	Bob Lemon MG	1.00	.40	.10
□ 450	Mickey Lolich	1.00	.40	.10
□ 451	Tony LaRussa	.75	.30	.07
□ 452	Ed Herrmann	.45	.18	.04
□ 453	Barry Lersch	.45	.18	.04
□ 454	Oakland A's	1.00	.40	.10
	Team Card			
□ 455	Tommy Harper	.60	.24	.06
□ 456	Mark Belanger	.60	.24	.06
□ 457	Padres Rookies	.60	.24	.06
	Darcy Fast			
	Derrel Thomas			
	Mike Ivie			
□ 458	Aurelio Monteagudo	.45	.18	.04
□ 459	Rick Renick	.45	.18	.04
□ 460	Al Downing	.60	.24	.06
□ 461	Tim Cullen	.45	.18	.04
□ 462	Rickey Clark	.45	.18	.04
□ 463	Bernie Carbo	.45	.18	.04
□ 464	Jim Roland	.45	.18	.04
□ 465	Gil Hodges MG	2.50	1.00	.25
□ 466	Norm Miller	.45	.18	.04
□ 467	Steve Kline	.45	.18	.04
□ 468	Richie Scheinblum	.45	.18	.04
□ 469	Ron Herbel	.45	.18	.04
□ 470	Ray Fosse	.45	.18	.04
□ 471	Luke Walker	.45	.18	.04
□ 472	Phil Gagliano	.45	.18	.04
□ 473	Dan McGinn	.45	.18	.04
□ 474	Orioles Rookies	2.00	.80	.20
	Don Baylor			
	Roric Harrison			
	Johnny Oates			
□ 475	Gary Nolan	.45	.18	.04
□ 476	Lee Richard	.45	.18	.04
□ 477	Tom Phoebus	.45	.18	.04
□ 478	Checklist 5	1.25	.15	.03
□ 479	Don Shaw	.45	.18	.04
□ 480	Lee May	.60	.24	.06
□ 481	Billy Conigliaro	.60	.24	.06
□ 482	Joe Hoerner	.45	.18	.04
□ 483	Ken Suarez	.45	.18	.04
□ 484	Lum Harris MG	.45	.18	.04
□ 485	Phil Regan	.60	.24	.06

□ 486 John Lowenstein	.45	.18	.04
□ 487 Tigers Team	1.00	.40	.10
□ 488 Mike Nagy	.45	.18	.04
□ 489 Expos Rookies	.45	.18	.04
Terry Humphrey			
Keith Lampard			
□ 490 Dave McNally	.60	.24	.06
□ 491 KP: Lou Piniella	.60	.24	.06
□ 492 KP: Mel Stottlemyre	.45	.18	.04
□ 493 KP: Bob Bailey	.45	.18	.04
□ 494 KP: Willie Horton	.45	.18	.04
□ 495 KP: Bill Melton	.45	.18	.04
□ 496 KP: Bud Harrelson	.45	.18	.04
□ 497 KP: Jim Perry	.45	.18	.04
□ 498 KP: Brooks Robinson	1.50	.60	.15
□ 499 Vicente Romo	.45	.18	.04
□ 500 Joe Torre	1.00	.40	.10
□ 501 Pete Hamm	.45	.18	.04
□ 502 Jackie Hernandez	.45	.18	.04
□ 503 Gary Peters	.60	.24	.06
□ 504 Ed Spiezio	.45	.18	.04
□ 505 Mike Marshall	.60	.24	.06
□ 506 Indians Rookies	.60	.24	.06
Terry Ley			
Jim Moyer			
Dick Tidrow			
□ 507 Fred Gladding	.45	.18	.04
□ 508 Ellie Hendricks	.45	.18	.04
□ 509 Don McMahon	.45	.18	.04
□ 510 Ted Williams MG	5.00	2.00	.50
□ 511 Tony Taylor	.45	.18	.04
□ 512 Paul Popovich	.45	.18	.04
□ 513 Lindy McDaniel	.60	.24	.06
□ 514 Ted Sizemore	.45	.18	.04
□ 515 Bert Blyleven	3.50	1.40	.35
□ 516 Oscar Brown	.45	.18	.04
□ 517 Ken Brett	.60	.24	.06
□ 518 Wayne Garrett	.45	.18	.04
□ 519 Ted Abernathy	.45	.18	.04
□ 520 Larry Bowa	1.50	.60	.15
□ 521 Alan Foster	.45	.18	.04
□ 522 Dodgers Team	1.25	.50	.12
□ 523 Chuck Dobson	.45	.18	.04
□ 524 Reds Rookies	.45	.18	.04
Ed Armbrister			
Mel Behney			
□ 525 Carlos May	.45	.18	.04
□ 526 Bob Bailey	.85	.34	.08
□ 527 Dave Leonhard	.85	.34	.08
□ 528 Ron Stone	.85	.34	.08
□ 529 Dave Nelson	.85	.34	.08
□ 530 Don Sutton	3.50	1.40	.35
□ 531 Freddie Patek	1.00	.40	.10
□ 532 Fred Kendall	.85	.34	.08
□ 533 Ralph Houk MG	1.00	.40	.10
□ 534 Jim Hickman	.85	.34	.08
□ 535 Ed Brinkman	.85	.34	.08
□ 536 Doug Rader	1.00	.40	.10
□ 537 Bob Locker	.85	.34	.08
□ 538 Charlie Sands	.85	.34	.08
□ 539 Terry Forster	1.50	.60	.15
□ 540 Felix Millan	.85	.34	.08
□ 541 Roger Repoz	.85	.34	.08
□ 542 Jack Billingham	.85	.34	.08
□ 543 Duane Josephson	.85	.34	.08
□ 544 Ted Martinez	.85	.34	.08
□ 545 Wayne Granger	.85	.34	.08
□ 546 Joe Hague	.85	.34	.08
□ 547 Indians Team	1.75	.70	.17
□ 548 Frank Reberger	.85	.34	.08
□ 549 Dave May	.85	.34	.08
□ 550 Brooks Robinson	10.00	4.00	1.00
□ 551 Ollie Brown	.85	.34	.08
□ 552 Brown In Action	.85	.34	.08
□ 553 Wilbur Wood	1.00	.40	.10
□ 554 Wood In Action	.85	.34	.08
□ 555 Ron Santo	1.50	.60	.15
□ 556 Santo In Action	1.00	.40	.10
□ 557 John Odom	.85	.34	.08
□ 558 Odom In Action	.85	.34	.08
□ 559 Pete Rose	60.00	24.00	6.00
□ 560 Rose In Action	20.00	8.00	2.00
□ 561 Leo Cardenas	.85	.34	.08
□ 562 Cardenas In Action	.85	.34	.08
□ 563 Ray Sadecki	.85	.34	.08
□ 564 Sadecki In Action	.85	.34	.08
□ 565 Reggie Smith	1.25	.50	.12
□ 566 Smith In Action	.85	.34	.08
□ 567 Juan Marichal	4.50	1.80	.45
□ 568 Marichal In Action	1.75	.70	.17
□ 569 Ed Kirkpatrick	.85	.34	.08
□ 570 Kirkpatrick In Action	.85	.34	.08
□ 571 Nate Colbert	.85	.34	.08
□ 572 Colbert In Action	.85	.34	.08
□ 573 Fritz Peterson	.85	.34	.08
□ 574 Peterson In Action	.85	.34	.08
□ 575 Al Oliver	1.75	.70	.17
□ 576 Leo Durocher MG	1.50	.60	.15
□ 577 Mike Paul	.85	.34	.08
□ 578 Billy Grabarkewitz	.85	.34	.08
□ 579 Doyle Alexander	3.00	1.20	.30
□ 580 Lou Piniella	2.00	.80	.20
□ 581 Wade Blasingame	.85	.34	.08
□ 582 Montreal Expos	1.75	.70	.17
Team Card			
□ 583 Darold Knowles	.85	.34	.08
□ 584 Jerry McNertney	.85	.34	.08
□ 585 George Scott	1.00	.40	.10
□ 586 Denis Menke	.85	.34	.08
□ 587 Billy Wilson	.85	.34	.08
□ 588 Jim Holt	.85	.34	.08
□ 589 Hal Lanier	1.00	.40	.10
□ 590 Graig Nettles	2.50	1.00	.25
□ 591 Paul Casanova	.85	.34	.08
□ 592 Lew Krausse	.85	.34	.08
□ 593 Rich Morales	.85	.34	.08
□ 594 Jim Beauchamp	.85	.34	.08
□ 595 Nolan Ryan	21.00	8.50	2.10
□ 596 Manny Mota	1.25	.50	.12
□ 597 Jim Magnuson	.85	.34	.08
□ 598 Hal King	.85	.34	.08
□ 599 Billy Champion	.85	.34	.08
□ 600 Al Kaline	12.00	5.00	1.20
□ 601 George Stone	.85	.34	.08
□ 602 Dave Bristol MG	.85	.34	.08
□ 603 Jim Ray	.85	.34	.08
□ 604A Checklist 6	3.50	.40	.08
(copyright on back			
bottom right)			
□ 604B Checklist 6	5.00	.50	.10
(copyright on back			
bottom left)			
□ 605 Nelson Briles	1.00	.40	.10
□ 606 Luis Melendez	.85	.34	.08
□ 607 Frank Duffy	.85	.34	.08
□ 608 Mike Corkins	.85	.34	.08
□ 609 Tom Grieve	1.25	.50	.12
□ 610 Bill Stoneman	.85	.34	.08
□ 611 Rich Reese	.85	.34	.08
□ 612 Joe Decker	.85	.34	.08
□ 613 Mike Ferraro	1.00	.40	.10
□ 614 Ted Uhlaender	.85	.34	.08
□ 615 Steve Hargan	.85	.34	.08
□ 616 Joe Ferguson	1.00	.40	.10
□ 617 Kansas City Royals	1.75	.70	.17
Team Card			
□ 618 Rich Robertson	.85	.34	.08
□ 619 Rich McKinney	.85	.34	.08
□ 620 Phil Niekro	4.00	1.60	.40
□ 621 Commissioners Award	1.00	.40	.10
□ 622 MVP Award	1.00	.40	.10
□ 623 Cy Young Award	1.00	.40	.10
□ 624 Minor League Player	1.00	.40	.10
□ 625 Rookie of the Year	1.00	.40	.10
□ 626 Babe Ruth Award	1.25	.50	.12
□ 627 Moe Drabowsky	.85	.34	.08
□ 628 Terry Crowley	.85	.34	.08
□ 629 Paul Doyle	.85	.34	.08
□ 630 Rich Hebner	1.00	.40	.10
□ 631 John Strohmayer	.85	.34	.08
□ 632 Mike Hegan	.85	.34	.08
□ 633 Jack Hiatt	.85	.34	.08
□ 634 Dick Woodson	.85	.34	.08
□ 635 Don Money	1.00	.40	.10
□ 636 Bill Lee	1.25	.50	.12
□ 637 Preston Gomez MG	.85	.34	.08
□ 638 Ken Wright	.85	.34	.08
□ 639 J.C. Martin	.85	.34	.08
□ 640 Joe Coleman	.85	.34	.08
□ 641 Mike Lum	.85	.34	.08
□ 642 Dennis Riddleberger	.85	.34	.08
□ 643 Russ Gibson	.85	.34	.08
□ 644 Bernie Allen	.85	.34	.08
□ 645 Jim Maloney	1.00	.40	.10
□ 646 Chico Salmon	.85	.34	.08
□ 647 Bob Moose	.85	.34	.08
□ 648 Jim Lyttle	.85	.34	.08
□ 649 Pete Richert	.85	.34	.08
□ 650 Sal Bando	1.00	.40	.10
□ 651 Cincinnati Reds	1.75	.70	.17
Team Card			
□ 652 Marcelino Lopez	.85	.34	.08
□ 653 Jim Fairey	.85	.34	.08
□ 654 Horacio Pina	.85	.34	.08
□ 655 Jerry Grote	.85	.34	.08
□ 656 Rudy May	.85	.34	.08
□ 657 Bobby Wine	2.00	.80	.20
□ 658 Steve Dunning	2.00	.80	.20
□ 659 Bob Aspromonte	2.00	.80	.20
□ 660 Paul Blair	2.50	1.00	.25

□ 661	Bill Virdon	3.00	1.20	.30
□ 662	Stan Bahnsen	2.00	.80	.20
□ 663	Fran Healy	2.00	.80	.20
□ 664	Bobby Knoop	2.00	.80	.20
□ 665	Chris Short	2.00	.80	.20
□ 666	Hector Torres	2.00	.80	.20
□ 667	Ray Newman	2.00	.80	.20
□ 668	Texas Rangers Team Card	4.50	1.80	.45
□ 669	Willie Crawford	2.00	.80	.20
□ 670	Ken Holtzman	2.50	1.00	.25
□ 671	Donn Clendenon	2.50	1.00	.25
□ 672	Archie Reynolds	2.00	.80	.20
□ 673	Dave Marshall	2.00	.80	.20
□ 674	John Kennedy	2.00	.80	.20
□ 675	Pat Jarvis	2.00	.80	.20
□ 676	Danny Cater	2.00	.80	.20
□ 677	Ivan Murrell	2.00	.80	.20
□ 678	Steve Luebber	2.00	.80	.20
□ 679	Astros Rookies Bob Fenwick Bob Stinson	2.00	.80	.20
□ 680	Dave Johnson	3.50	1.40	.35
□ 681	Bobby Pfeil	2.00	.80	.20
□ 682	Mike McCormick	2.50	1.00	.25
□ 683	Steve Hovley	2.00	.80	.20
□ 684	Hal Breeden	2.00	.80	.20
□ 685	Joe Horlen	2.00	.80	.20
□ 686	Steve Garvey	75.00	30.00	7.50
□ 687	Del Unser	2.00	.80	.20
□ 688	St. Louis Cardinals Team Card	4.00	1.60	.40
□ 689	Eddie Fisher	2.00	.80	.20
□ 690	Willie Montanez	2.50	1.00	.25
□ 691	Curt Blefary	2.00	.80	.20
□ 692	Blefary In Action	2.00	.80	.20
□ 693	Alan Gallagher	2.00	.80	.20
□ 694	Gallagher In Action	2.00	.80	.20
□ 695	Rod Carew	60.00	24.00	6.00
□ 696	Carew In Action	20.00	8.00	2.00
□ 697	Jerry Koosman	5.00	2.00	.50
□ 698	Koosman In Action	3.00	1.20	.30
□ 699	Bobby Murcer	5.00	2.00	.50
□ 700	Murcer In Action	3.00	1.20	.30
□ 701	Jose Pagan	2.00	.80	.20
□ 702	Pagan In Action	2.00	.80	.20
□ 703	Doug Griffin	2.00	.80	.20
□ 704	Griffin In Action	2.00	.80	.20
□ 705	Pat Corrales	2.50	1.00	.25
□ 706	Corrales In Action	2.00	.80	.20
□ 707	Tim Foli	2.00	.80	.20
□ 708	Foli In Action	2.00	.80	.20
□ 709	Jim Kaat	6.00	2.40	.60
□ 710	Kaat In Action	3.50	1.40	.35
□ 711	Bobby Bonds	5.00	2.00	.50
□ 712	Bonds In Action	3.00	1.20	.30
□ 713	Gene Michael	2.50	1.00	.25
□ 714	Michael In Action	2.00	.80	.20
□ 715	Mike Epstein	2.00	.80	.20
□ 716	Jesus Alou	2.00	.80	.20
□ 717	Bruce Dal Canton	2.00	.80	.20
□ 718	Del Rice MG	2.00	.80	.20
□ 719	Cesar Geronimo	2.00	.80	.20
□ 720	Sam McDowell	2.50	1.00	.25
□ 721	Eddie Leon	2.00	.80	.20
□ 722	Bill Sudakis	2.00	.80	.20
□ 723	Al Santorini	2.00	.80	.20
□ 724	AL Rookie Pitchers John Curtis Rich Hinton Mickey Scott	2.50	1.00	.25
□ 725	Dick McAuliffe	2.50	1.00	.25
□ 726	Dick Selma	2.00	.80	.20
□ 727	Jose LaBoy	2.00	.80	.20
□ 728	Gail Hopkins	2.00	.80	.20
□ 729	Bob Veale	2.50	1.00	.25
□ 730	Rick Monday	3.00	1.20	.30
□ 731	Baltimore Orioles Team Card	4.00	1.60	.40
□ 732	George Culver	2.00	.80	.20
□ 733	Jim Ray Hart	2.50	1.00	.25
□ 734	Bob Burda	2.00	.80	.20
□ 735	Diego Segui	2.00	.80	.20
□ 736	Bill Russell	3.50	1.40	.35
□ 737	Lenny Randle	2.00	.80	.20
□ 738	Jim Merritt	2.00	.80	.20
□ 739	Don Mason	2.00	.80	.20
□ 740	Rico Carty	3.00	1.20	.30
□ 741	Rookie First Basemen Tom Hutton John Milner Rick Miller	2.50	1.00	.25
□ 742	Jim Rooker	2.00	.80	.20
□ 743	Cesar Gutierrez	2.00	.80	.20
□ 744	Jim Slaton	2.50	1.00	.25
□ 745	Julian Javier	2.50	1.00	.25
□ 746	Lowell Palmer	2.00	.80	.20
□ 747	Jim Stewart	2.00	.80	.20
□ 748	Phil Hennigan	2.00	.80	.20
□ 749	Walter Alston MG	4.50	1.80	.45
□ 750	Willie Horton	2.50	1.00	.25
□ 751	Steve Carlton TR	33.00	12.00	3.00
□ 752	Joe Morgan TR	13.00	5.25	1.30
□ 753	Denny McLain TR	4.50	1.80	.45
□ 754	Frank Robinson TR	13.00	5.25	1.30
□ 755	Jim Fregosi TR	3.50	1.40	.35
□ 756	Rick Wise TR	2.50	1.00	.25
□ 757	Jose Cardenal TR	2.50	1.00	.25
□ 758	Gil Garrido	2.00	.80	.20
□ 759	Chris Cannizzaro	2.00	.80	.20
□ 760	Bill Mazeroski	4.00	1.60	.40
□ 761	Rookie Outfielders Ben Oglivie Ron Cey Bernie Williams	11.00	4.50	1.10
□ 762	Wayne Simpson	2.00	.80	.20
□ 763	Ron Hansen	2.00	.80	.20
□ 764	Dusty Baker	3.50	1.40	.35
□ 765	Ken McMullen	2.00	.80	.20
□ 766	Steve Hamilton	2.00	.80	.20
□ 767	Tom McCraw	2.00	.80	.20
□ 768	Denny Doyle	2.00	.80	.20
□ 769	Jack Aker	2.00	.80	.20
□ 770	Jim Wynn	2.50	1.00	.25
□ 771	San Francisco Giants Team Card	4.00	1.60	.40
□ 772	Ken Tatum	2.00	.80	.20
□ 773	Ron Brand	2.00	.80	.20
□ 774	Luis Alvarado	2.00	.80	.20
□ 775	Jerry Reuss	3.50	1.40	.35
□ 776	Bill Voss	2.00	.80	.20
□ 777	Hoyt Wilhelm	10.00	4.00	1.00
□ 778	Twins Rookies Vic Albury Rick Dempsey Jim Strickland	3.50	1.40	.35
□ 779	Tony Cloninger	2.00	.80	.20
□ 780	Dick Green	2.00	.80	.20
□ 781	Jim McAndrew	2.00	.80	.20
□ 782	Larry Stahl	2.00	.80	.20
□ 783	Les Cain	2.00	.80	.20
□ 784	Ken Aspromonte	2.00	.80	.20
□ 785	Vic Davalillo	2.00	.80	.20
□ 786	Chuck Brinkman	2.00	.80	.20
□ 787	Ron Reed	3.00	1.00	.20

1973 Topps

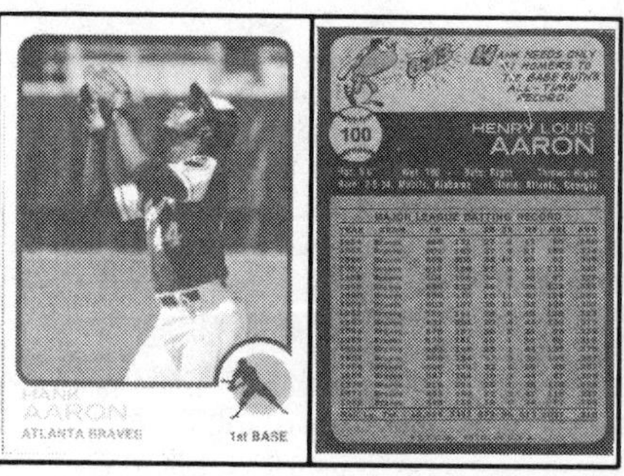

The cards in this 660-card set measure 2 1/2" by 3 1/2". The 1973 Topps set marked the last year in which Topps marketed baseball cards in consecutive series. The last series (529-660) is more difficult to obtain. Beginning in 1974, all Topps cards were printed at the same time, thus eliminating the "high number" factor. The set features team leader cards featuring small individual pictures of the coaching staff members with a larger picture of the manager. The "background" variations below with respect to these leader cards are subtle and are best understood after a side-by-side comparison of the two varieties. An "All-Time Leaders" series (471-

478) appeared for the first time in this set. Kid Pictures appeared again for the second year in a row (341-346). Other topical subsets within the set included League Leaders (61-68), Playoffs cards (201- 202), World Series cards (203-210), and Rookie Prospects (601- 616).

	NRMT	VG-E	GOOD
COMPLETE SET (660)	650.00	250.00	90.00
COMMON PLAYER (1-264)	.25	.10	.02
COMMON PLAYER (265-396)	.25	.10	.02
COMMON PLAYER (397-528)	.50	.20	.05
COMMON PLAYER (529-660)	1.25	.50	.12

	NRMT	VG-E	GOOD
□ 1 All-Time HR Leaders 714 Babe Ruth 673 Hank Aaron 654 Willie Mays	10.00	2.50	.50
□ 2 Rich Hebner	.35	.14	.03
□ 3 Jim Lonborg	.35	.14	.03
□ 4 John Milner	.25	.10	.02
□ 5 Ed Brinkman	.25	.10	.02
□ 6 Mac Scarce	.25	.10	.02
□ 7 Texas Rangers Team	.50	.20	.05
□ 8 Tom Hall	.25	.10	.02
□ 9 Johnny Oates	.25	.10	.02
□ 10 Don Sutton	2.00	.80	.20
□ 11 Chris Chambliss	.50	.20	.05
□ 12A Padres Leaders Don Zimmer MG Dave Garcia CO Johnny Podres CO Bob Skinner CO Whitey Wietelmann CO (Podres no right ear)	.35	.14	.03
□ 12B Padres Leaders (Podres has right ear)	.75	.30	.07
□ 13 George Hendrick	.50	.20	.05
□ 14 Sonny Siebert	.35	.14	.03
□ 15 Ralph Garr	.35	.14	.03
□ 16 Steve Braun	.25	.10	.02
□ 17 Fred Gladding	.25	.10	.02
□ 18 Leroy Stanton	.25	.10	.02
□ 19 Tim Foli	.25	.10	.02
□ 20 Stan Bahnsen	.25	.10	.02
□ 21 Randy Hundley	.35	.14	.03
□ 22 Ted Abernathy	.25	.10	.02
□ 23 Dave Kingman	1.50	.60	.15
□ 24 Al Santorini	.25	.10	.02
□ 25 Roy White	.35	.14	.03
□ 26 Pittsburgh Pirates Team Card	.50	.20	.05
□ 27 Bill Gogolewski	.25	.10	.02
□ 28 Hal McRae	.35	.14	.03
□ 29 Tony Taylor	.25	.10	.02
□ 30 Tug McGraw	.75	.30	.07
□ 31 Buddy Bell	4.00	1.60	.40
□ 32 Fred Norman	.25	.10	.02
□ 33 Jim Breazeale	.25	.10	.02
□ 34 Pat Dobson	.35	.14	.03
□ 35 Willie Davis	.35	.14	.03
□ 36 Steve Barber	.25	.10	.02
□ 37 Bill Robinson	.35	.14	.03
□ 38 Mike Epstein	.25	.10	.02
□ 39 Dave Roberts	.25	.10	.02
□ 40 Reggie Smith	.50	.20	.05
□ 41 Tom Walker	.25	.10	.02
□ 42 Mike Andrews	.25	.10	.02
□ 43 Randy Moffitt	.25	.10	.02
□ 44 Rick Monday	.35	.14	.03
□ 45 Ellie Rodriguez (photo actually John Felske)	.25	.10	.02
□ 46 Lindy McDaniel	.35	.14	.03
□ 47 Luis Melendez	.25	.10	.02
□ 48 Paul Splittorff	.35	.14	.03
□ 49A Twins Leaders Frank Quilici MG Vern Morgan CO Bob Rodgers CO Ralph Rowe CO Al Worthington CO (solid backgrounds)	.35	.14	.03
□ 49B Twins Leaders (natural backgrounds)	.75	.30	.07
□ 50 Roberto Clemente	12.00	5.00	1.20
□ 51 Chuck Seelbach	.25	.10	.02
□ 52 Denis Menke	.25	.10	.02
□ 53 Steve Dunning	.25	.10	.02
□ 54 Checklist 1	1.00	.10	.02
□ 55 Jon Matlack	.35	.14	.03
□ 56 Merv Rettenmund	.25	.10	.02
□ 57 Derrel Thomas	.25	.10	.02
□ 58 Mike Paul	.25	.10	.02
□ 59 Steve Yeager	.50	.20	.05
□ 60 Ken Holtzman	.35	.14	.03
□ 61 Batting Leaders Billy Williams Rod Carew	1.25	.50	.12
□ 62 Home Run Leaders Johnny Bench Dick Allen	1.25	.50	.12
□ 63 RBI Leaders Johnny Bench Dick Allen	1.25	.50	.12
□ 64 Stolen Base Leaders Lou Brock Bert Campaneris	.75	.30	.07
□ 65 ERA Leaders Steve Carlton Luis Tiant	.75	.30	.07
□ 66 Victory Leaders Steve Carlton Gaylord Perry Wilbur Wood	1.00	.40	.10
□ 67 Strikeout Leaders Steve Carlton Nolan Ryan	3.00	1.20	.30
□ 68 Leading Firemen Clay Carroll Sparky Lyle	.50	.20	.05
□ 69 Phil Gagliano	.25	.10	.02
□ 70 Milt Pappas	.35	.14	.03
□ 71 Johnny Briggs	.25	.10	.02
□ 72 Ron Reed	.25	.10	.02
□ 73 Ed Herrmann	.25	.10	.02
□ 74 Billy Champion	.25	.10	.02
□ 75 Vada Pinson	.50	.20	.05
□ 76 Doug Rader	.35	.14	.03
□ 77 Mike Torrez	.35	.14	.03
□ 78 Richie Scheinblum	.25	.10	.02
□ 79 Jim Willoughby	.25	.10	.02
□ 80 Tony Oliva	1.00	.40	.10
□ 81A Cubs Leaders Whitey Lockman MG Hank Aguirre CO Ernie Banks CO Larry Jansen CO Pete Reiser CO (solid backgrounds)	.50	.20	.05
□ 81B Cubs Leaders (natural backgrounds)	.75	.30	.07
□ 82 Fritz Peterson	.25	.10	.02
□ 83 Leron Lee	.25	.10	.02
□ 84 Rollie Fingers	2.00	.80	.20
□ 85 Ted Simmons	1.00	.40	.10
□ 86 Tom McCraw	.25	.10	.02
□ 87 Ken Boswell	.25	.10	.02
□ 88 Mickey Stanley	.35	.14	.03
□ 89 Jack Billingham	.25	.10	.02
□ 90 Brooks Robinson	4.00	1.60	.40
□ 91 Dodgers Team	.75	.30	.07
□ 92 Jerry Bell	.25	.10	.02
□ 93 Jesus Alou	.25	.10	.02
□ 94 Dick Billings	.25	.10	.02
□ 95 Steve Blass	.35	.14	.03
□ 96 Doug Griffin	.25	.10	.02
□ 97 Willie Montanez	.25	.10	.02
□ 98 Dick Woodson	.25	.10	.02
□ 99 Carl Taylor	.25	.10	.02
□ 100 Hank Aaron	13.00	5.25	1.30
□ 101 Ken Henderson	.25	.10	.02
□ 102 Rudy May	.25	.10	.02
□ 103 Celerino Sanchez	.25	.10	.02
□ 104 Reggie Cleveland	.25	.10	.02
□ 105 Carlos May	.25	.10	.02
□ 106 Terry Humphrey	.25	.10	.02
□ 107 Phil Hennigan	.25	.10	.02
□ 108 Bill Russell	.35	.14	.03
□ 109 Doyle Alexander	.75	.30	.07
□ 110 Bob Watson	.35	.14	.03
□ 111 Dave Nelson	.25	.10	.02
□ 112 Gary Ross	.25	.10	.02
□ 113 Jerry Grote	.25	.10	.02
□ 114 Lynn McGlothen	.25	.10	.02
□ 115 Ron Santo	.60	.24	.06
□ 116A Yankees Leaders Ralph Houk MG Jim Hegan CO Elston Howard CO Dick Howser CO Jim Turner CO (solid backgrounds)	.60	.24	.06
□ 116B Yankees Leaders (natural backgrounds)	1.00	.40	.10
□ 117 Ramon Hernandez	.25	.10	.02
□ 118 John Mayberry	.35	.14	.03
□ 119 Larry Bowa	1.00	.40	.10

☐ 120	Joe Coleman	.25	.10	.02
☐ 121	Dave Rader	.25	.10	.02
☐ 122	Jim Strickland	.25	.10	.02
☐ 123	Sandy Alomar	.25	.10	.02
☐ 124	Jim Hardin	.25	.10	.02
☐ 125	Ron Fairly	.35	.14	.03
☐ 126	Jim Brewer	.25	.10	.02
☐ 127	Brewers Team	.50	.20	.05
☐ 128	Ted Sizemore	.25	.10	.02
☐ 129	Terry Forster	.35	.14	.03
☐ 130	Pete Rose	20.00	8.00	2.00
☐ 131A	Red Sox Leaders Eddie Kasko MG Doug Camilli CO Don Lenhardt CO Eddie Popowski CO (no right ear) Lee Stange CO	.35	.14	.03
☐ 131B	Red Sox Leaders (Popowski has right ear showing)	.75	.30	.07
☐ 132	Matty Alou	.35	.14	.03
☐ 133	Dave Roberts	.25	.10	.02
☐ 134	Milt Wilcox	.35	.14	.03
☐ 135	Lee May	.35	.14	.03
☐ 136A	Orioles Leaders Earl Weaver MG George Bamberger CO Jim Frey CO Billy Hunter CO George Staller CO (orange backgrounds)	.75	.30	.07
☐ 136B	Orioles Leaders (dark pale backgrounds)	1.00	.40	.10
☐ 137	Jim Beauchamp	.25	.10	.02
☐ 138	Horacio Pina	.25	.10	.02
☐ 139	Carmen Fanzone	.25	.10	.02
☐ 140	Lou Piniella	.60	.24	.06
☐ 141	Bruce Kison	.35	.14	.03
☐ 142	Thurman Munson	7.00	2.80	.70
☐ 143	John Curtis	.25	.10	.02
☐ 144	Marty Perez	.25	.10	.02
☐ 145	Bobby Bonds	.75	.30	.07
☐ 146	Woodie Fryman	.25	.10	.02
☐ 147	Mike Anderson	.25	.10	.02
☐ 148	Dave Goltz	.25	.10	.02
☐ 149	Ron Hunt	.25	.10	.02
☐ 150	Wilbur Wood	.35	.14	.03
☐ 151	Wes Parker	.35	.14	.03
☐ 152	Dave May	.25	.10	.02
☐ 153	Al Hrabosky	.50	.20	.05
☐ 154	Jeff Torborg	.35	.14	.03
☐ 155	Sal Bando	.35	.14	.03
☐ 156	Cesar Geronimo	.25	.10	.02
☐ 157	Denny Riddleberger	.25	.10	.02
☐ 158	Astros Team	.50	.20	.05
☐ 159	Clarence Gaston	.25	.10	.02
☐ 160	Jim Palmer	4.00	1.60	.40
☐ 161	Ted Martinez	.25	.10	.02
☐ 162	Pete Broberg	.25	.10	.02
☐ 163	Vic Davalillo	.25	.10	.02
☐ 164	Monty Montgomery	.25	.10	.02
☐ 165	Luis Aparicio	2.50	1.00	.25
☐ 166	Terry Harmon	.25	.10	.02
☐ 167	Steve Stone	.35	.14	.03
☐ 168	Jim Northrup	.35	.14	.03
☐ 169	Ron Schueler	.25	.10	.02
☐ 170	Harmon Killebrew	3.50	1.40	.35
☐ 171	Bernie Carbo	.25	.10	.02
☐ 172	Steve Kline	.25	.10	.02
☐ 173	Hal Breeden	.25	.10	.02
☐ 174	Rich Gossage	6.00	2.40	.60
☐ 175	Frank Robinson	3.50	1.40	.35
☐ 176	Chuck Taylor	.25	.10	.02
☐ 177	Bill Plummer	.25	.10	.02
☐ 178	Don Rose	.25	.10	.02
☐ 179A	A's Leaders Dick Williams MG Jerry Adair CO Vern Hoscheit CO Irv Noren CO Wes Stock CO (orange backgrounds)	.35	.14	.03
☐ 179B	A's Leaders (dark pale backgrounds)	.75	.30	.07
☐ 180	Fergie Jenkins	1.25	.50	.12
☐ 181	Jack Brohamer	.25	.10	.02
☐ 182	Mike Caldwell	.50	.20	.05
☐ 183	Don Buford	.35	.14	.03
☐ 184	Jerry Koosman	.60	.24	.06
☐ 185	Jim Wynn	.35	.14	.03
☐ 186	Bill Fahey	.25	.10	.02
☐ 187	Luke Walker	.25	.10	.02
☐ 188	Cookie Rojas	.35	.14	.03
☐ 189	Greg Luzinski	.75	.30	.07
☐ 190	Bob Gibson	3.50	1.40	.35
☐ 191	Tigers Team	.60	.24	.06
☐ 192	Pat Jarvis	.25	.10	.02
☐ 193	Carlton Fisk	4.50	1.80	.45
☐ 194	Jorge Orta	.25	.10	.02
☐ 195	Clay Carroll	.25	.10	.02
☐ 196	Ken McMullen	.25	.10	.02
☐ 197	Ed Goodson	.25	.10	.02
☐ 198	Horace Clarke	.25	.10	.02
☐ 199	Bert Blyleven	1.50	.60	.15
☐ 200	Billy Williams	2.75	1.10	.27
☐ 201	A.L. Playoffs A's over Tigers; Hendrick scores winning run	.75	.30	.07
☐ 202	N.L. Playoffs Reds over Pirates Foster's run decides	.75	.30	.07
☐ 203	World Series Game 1 Tenace the Menace	.75	.30	.07
☐ 204	World Series Game 2 A's two straight	.75	.30	.07
☐ 205	World Series Game 3 Reds win squeeker	.75	.30	.07
☐ 206	World Series Game 4 Tenace singles in ninth	.75	.30	.07
☐ 207	World Series Game 5 Odom out at plate	.75	.30	.07
☐ 208	World Series Game 6 Red's slugging ties series	.75	.30	.07
☐ 209	World Series Game 7 Campy stars winning rally	.75	.30	.07
☐ 210	World Series Summary World champions: A's Win	.75	.30	.07
☐ 211	Balor Moore	.25	.10	.02
☐ 212	Joe Lahoud	.25	.10	.02
☐ 213	Steve Garvey	12.00	5.00	1.20
☐ 214	Steve Hamilton	.25	.10	.02
☐ 215	Dusty Baker	.60	.24	.06
☐ 216	Toby Harrah	.50	.20	.05
☐ 217	Don Wilson	.25	.10	.02
☐ 218	Aurelio Rodriguez	.25	.10	.02
☐ 219	Cardinals Team	.50	.20	.05
☐ 220	Nolan Ryan	10.00	4.00	1.00
☐ 221	Fred Kendall	.25	.10	.02
☐ 222	Rob Gardner	.25	.10	.02
☐ 223	Bud Harrelson	.35	.14	.03
☐ 224	Bill Lee	.35	.14	.03
☐ 225	Al Oliver	1.00	.40	.10
☐ 226	Ray Fosse	.25	.10	.02
☐ 227	Wayne Twitchell	.25	.10	.02
☐ 228	Bobby Darwin	.25	.10	.02
☐ 229	Roric Harrison	.25	.10	.02
☐ 230	Joe Morgan	2.50	1.00	.25
☐ 231	Bill Parsons	.25	.10	.02
☐ 232	Ken Singleton	.35	.14	.03
☐ 233	Ed Kirkpatrick	.25	.10	.02
☐ 234	Bill North	.25	.10	.02
☐ 235	Jim Hunter	2.75	1.10	.27
☐ 236	Tito Fuentes	.25	.10	.02
☐ 237A	Braves Leaders Eddie Mathews MG Lew Burdette CO Jim Busby CO Roy Hartsfield CO Ken Silvestri CO (orange backgrounds)	1.00	.40	.10
☐ 237B	Braves Leaders (dark pale backgrounds)	1.25	.50	.12
☐ 238	Tony Muser	.25	.10	.02
☐ 239	Pete Richert	.25	.10	.02
☐ 240	Bobby Murcer	.60	.24	.06
☐ 241	Dwain Anderson	.25	.10	.02
☐ 242	George Culver	.25	.10	.02
☐ 243	Angels Team	.50	.20	.05
☐ 244	Ed Acosta	.25	.10	.02
☐ 245	Carl Yastrzemski	11.00	4.50	1.10
☐ 246	Ken Sanders	.25	.10	.02
☐ 247	Del Unser	.25	.10	.02
☐ 248	Jerry Johnson	.25	.10	.02
☐ 249	Larry Biittner	.25	.10	.02
☐ 250	Manny Sanguillen	.35	.14	.03
☐ 251	Roger Nelson	.25	.10	.02
☐ 252A	Giants Leaders Charlie Fox MG Joe Amalfitano CO Andy Gilbert CO Don McMahon CO	.35	.14	.03

John McNamara CO
(orange backgrounds)
☐ 252B Giants Leaders .75 .30 .07
(dark pale backgrounds)
☐ 253 Mark Belanger .35 .14 .03
☐ 254 Bill Stoneman .25 .10 .02
☐ 255 Reggie Jackson 14.00 5.75 1.40
☐ 256 Chris Zachary .25 .10 .02
☐ 257A Mets Leaders 1.50 .60 .15
Yogi Berra MG
Roy McMillan CO
Joe Pignatano CO
Rube Walker CO
Eddie Yost CO
(orange backgrounds)
☐ 257B Mets Leaders 2.00 .80 .20
(dark pale backgrounds)
☐ 258 Tommy John 1.50 .60 .15
☐ 259 Jim Holt .25 .10 .02
☐ 260 Gary Nolan .25 .10 .02
☐ 261 Pat Kelly .25 .10 .02
☐ 262 Jack Aker .25 .10 .02
☐ 263 George Scott .35 .14 .03
☐ 264 Checklist 2 1.00 .10 .02
☐ 265 Gene Michael .40 .16 .04
☐ 266 Mike Lum .30 .12 .03
☐ 267 Lloyd Allen .30 .12 .03
☐ 268 Jerry Morales .30 .12 .03
☐ 269 Tim McCarver .60 .24 .06
☐ 270 Luis Tiant .60 .24 .06
☐ 271 Tom Hutton .30 .12 .03
☐ 272 Ed Farmer .30 .12 .03
☐ 273 Chris Speier .40 .16 .04
☐ 274 Darold Knowles .30 .12 .03
☐ 275 Tony Perez 1.25 .50 .12
☐ 276 Joe Lovitto .30 .12 .03
☐ 277 Bob Miller .30 .12 .03
☐ 278 Baltimore Orioles .60 .24 .06
Team Card
☐ 279 Mike Strahler .30 .12 .03
☐ 280 Al Kaline 4.50 1.80 .45
☐ 281 Mike Jorgensen .30 .12 .03
☐ 282 Steve Hovley .30 .12 .03
☐ 283 Ray Sadecki .30 .12 .03
☐ 284 Glenn Borgmann .30 .12 .03
☐ 285 Don Kessinger .40 .16 .04
☐ 286 Frank Linzy .30 .12 .03
☐ 287 Eddie Leon .30 .12 .03
☐ 288 Gary Gentry .30 .12 .03
☐ 289 Bob Oliver .30 .12 .03
☐ 290 Cesar Cedeno .50 .20 .05
☐ 291 Rogelio Moret .30 .12 .03
☐ 292 Jose Cruz .50 .20 .05
☐ 293 Bernie Allen .30 .12 .03
☐ 294 Steve Arlin .30 .12 .03
☐ 295 Bert Campaneris .40 .16 .04
☐ 296 Reds Leaders .50 .20 .05
Sparky Anderson MG
Alex Grammas CO
Ted Kluszewski CO
George Scherger CO
Larry Shepard CO
☐ 297 Walt Williams .30 .12 .03
☐ 298 Ron Bryant .30 .12 .03
☐ 299 Ted Ford .30 .12 .03
☐ 300 Steve Carlton 8.00 3.25 .80
☐ 301 Billy Grabarkewitz .30 .12 .03
☐ 302 Terry Crowley .30 .12 .03
☐ 303 Nelson Briles .40 .16 .04
☐ 304 Duke Sims .30 .12 .03
☐ 305 Willie Mays 13.00 5.25 1.30
☐ 306 Tom Burgmeier .30 .12 .03
☐ 307 Boots Day .30 .12 .03
☐ 308 Skip Lockwood .30 .12 .03
☐ 309 Paul Popovich .30 .12 .03
☐ 310 Dick Allen .60 .24 .06
☐ 311 Joe Decker .30 .12 .03
☐ 312 Oscar Brown .30 .12 .03
☐ 313 Jim Ray .30 .12 .03
☐ 314 Ron Swoboda .40 .16 .04
☐ 315 John Odom .30 .12 .03
☐ 316 San Diego Padres .60 .24 .06
Team Card
☐ 317 Danny Cater .30 .12 .03
☐ 318 Jim McGlothlin .30 .12 .03
☐ 319 Jim Spencer .30 .12 .03
☐ 320 Lou Brock 3.50 1.40 .35
☐ 321 Rich Hinton .30 .12 .03
☐ 322 Garry Maddox .60 .24 .06
☐ 323 Tigers Leaders .75 .30 .07
Billy Martin MG
Art Fowler CO
Charlie Silvera CO
Dick Tracewski CO
☐ 324 Al Downing .40 .16 .04
☐ 325 Boog Powell .75 .30 .07
☐ 326 Darrell Brandon .30 .12 .03
☐ 327 John Lowenstein .30 .12 .03
☐ 328 Bill Bonham .30 .12 .03
☐ 329 Ed Kranepool .40 .16 .04
☐ 330 Rod Carew 7.00 2.80 .70
☐ 331 Carl Morton .30 .12 .03
☐ 332 John Felske .30 .12 .03
☐ 333 Gene Clines .30 .12 .03
☐ 334 Freddie Patek .40 .16 .04
☐ 335 Bob Tolan .40 .16 .04
☐ 336 Tom Bradley .30 .12 .03
☐ 337 Dave Duncan .30 .12 .03
☐ 338 Checklist 3 1.00 .10 .02
☐ 339 Dick Tidrow .30 .12 .03
☐ 340 Nate Colbert .30 .12 .03
☐ 341 KP: Jim Palmer 1.00 .40 .10
☐ 342 KP: Sam McDowell .30 .12 .03
☐ 343 KP: Bobby Murcer .40 .16 .04
☐ 344 KP: Jim Hunter .75 .30 .07
☐ 345 KP: Chris Speier .30 .12 .03
☐ 346 KP: Gaylord Perry .75 .30 .07
☐ 347 Kansas City Royals .60 .24 .06
Team Card
☐ 348 Rennie Stennett .40 .16 .04
☐ 349 Dick McAuliffe .40 .16 .04
☐ 350 Tom Seaver 10.00 4.00 1.00
☐ 351 Jimmy Stewart .30 .12 .03
☐ 352 Don Stanhouse .30 .12 .03
☐ 353 Steve Brye .30 .12 .03
☐ 354 Billy Parker .30 .12 .03
☐ 355 Mike Marshall .40 .16 .04
☐ 356 White Sox Leaders .40 .16 .04
Chuck Tanner MG
Joe Lonnett CO
Jim Mahoney CO
Al Monchak CO
Johnny Sain CO
☐ 357 Ross Grimsley .30 .12 .03
☐ 358 Jim Nettles .30 .12 .03
☐ 359 Cecil Upshaw .30 .12 .03
☐ 360 Joe Rudi .40 .16 .04
(photo actually Gene Tenace)
☐ 361 Fran Healy .30 .12 .03
☐ 362 Eddie Watt .30 .12 .03
☐ 363 Jackie Hernandez .30 .12 .03
☐ 364 Rick Wise .40 .16 .04
☐ 365 Rico Petrocelli .40 .16 .04
☐ 366 Brock Davis .30 .12 .03
☐ 367 Burt Hooton .30 .12 .03
☐ 368 Bill Buckner .75 .30 .07
☐ 369 Lerrin LaGrow .30 .12 .03
☐ 370 Willie Stargell 3.50 1.40 .35
☐ 371 Mike Kekich .30 .12 .03
☐ 372 Oscar Gamble .40 .16 .04
☐ 373 Clyde Wright .30 .12 .03
☐ 374 Darrell Evans .75 .30 .07
☐ 375 Larry Dierker .40 .16 .04
☐ 376 Frank Duffy .30 .12 .03
☐ 377 Expos Leaders .40 .16 .04
Gene Mauch MG
Dave Bristol CO
Larry Doby CO
Cal McLish CO
Jerry Zimmerman CO
☐ 378 Lenny Randle .30 .12 .03
☐ 379 Cy Acosta .30 .12 .03
☐ 380 Johnny Bench 12.00 5.00 1.20
☐ 381 Vicente Romo .30 .12 .03
☐ 382 Mike Hegan .30 .12 .03
☐ 383 Diego Segui .30 .12 .03
☐ 384 Don Baylor 1.00 .40 .10
☐ 385 Jim Perry .50 .20 .05
☐ 386 Don Money .40 .16 .04
☐ 387 Jim Barr .30 .12 .03
☐ 388 Ben Oglivie .50 .20 .05
☐ 389 New York Mets 1.50 .60 .15
Team Card
☐ 390 Mickey Lolich .75 .30 .07
☐ 391 Lee Lacy .50 .20 .05
☐ 392 Dick Drago .30 .12 .03
☐ 393 Jose Cardenal .30 .12 .03
☐ 394 Sparky Lyle .50 .20 .05
☐ 395 Roger Metzger .30 .12 .03
☐ 396 Grant Jackson .30 .12 .03
☐ 397 Dave Cash .50 .20 .05
☐ 398 Rich Hand .50 .20 .05
☐ 399 George Foster 1.50 .60 .15
☐ 400 Gaylord Perry 2.50 1.00 .25
☐ 401 Clyde Mashore .50 .20 .05
☐ 402 Jack Hiatt .50 .20 .05
☐ 403 Sonny Jackson .50 .20 .05

□ 404 Chuck Brinkman .50 .20 .05
□ 405 Cesar Tovar .50 .20 .05
□ 406 Paul Lindblad .50 .20 .05
□ 407 Felix Millan .50 .20 .05
□ 408 Jim Colborn .50 .20 .05
□ 409 Ivan Murrell .50 .20 .05
□ 410 Willie McCovey 3.50 1.40 .35
(Bench behind plate)
□ 411 Ray Corbin .50 .20 .05
□ 412 Manny Mota .75 .30 .07
□ 413 Tom Timmerman .50 .20 .05
□ 414 Ken Rudolph .50 .20 .05
□ 415 Marty Pattin .50 .20 .05
□ 416 Paul Schaal .50 .20 .05
□ 417 Scipio Spinks .50 .20 .05
□ 418 Bobby Grich .75 .30 .07
□ 419 Casey Cox .50 .20 .05
□ 420 Tommie Agee .50 .20 .05
□ 421A Angels Leaders .75 .30 .07
Bobby Winkles MG
Tom Morgan CO
Salty Parker CO
Jimmie Reese CO
John Roseboro CO
(orange backgrounds)
□ 421B Angels Leaders 1.00 .40 .10
(dark pale
backgrounds)
□ 422 Bob Robertson .50 .20 .05
□ 423 Johnny Jeter .50 .20 .05
□ 424 Denny Doyle .50 .20 .05
□ 425 Alex Johnson .50 .20 .05
□ 426 Dave LaRoche .50 .20 .05
□ 427 Rick Auerbach .50 .20 .05
□ 428 Wayne Simpson .50 .20 .05
□ 429 Jim Fairey .50 .20 .05
□ 430 Vida Blue .75 .30 .07
□ 431 Gerry Moses .50 .20 .05
□ 432 Dan Frisella .50 .20 .05
□ 433 Willie Horton .75 .30 .07
□ 434 San Francisco Giants 1.00 .40 .10
Team Card
□ 435 Rico Carty .75 .30 .07
□ 436 Jim McAndrew .50 .20 .05
□ 437 John Kennedy .50 .20 .05
□ 438 Enzo Hernandez .50 .20 .05
□ 439 Eddie Fisher .50 .20 .05
□ 440 Glenn Beckert .75 .30 .07
□ 441 Gail Hopkins .50 .20 .05
□ 442 Dick Dietz .50 .20 .05
□ 443 Danny Thompson .50 .20 .05
□ 444 Ken Brett .50 .20 .05
□ 445 Ken Berry .50 .20 .05
□ 446 Jerry Reuss .75 .30 .07
□ 447 Joe Hague .50 .20 .05
□ 448 John Hiller .75 .30 .07
□ 449A Indians Leaders .75 .30 .07
Ken Aspromonte MG
Rocky Colavito CO
Joe Lutz CO
Warren Spahn CO
(Spahn's right
ear pointed)
□ 449B Indians Leaders 1.00 .40 .10
(Spahn's right
ear round)
□ 450 Joe Torre 1.00 .40 .10
□ 451 John Vuckovich .50 .20 .05
□ 452 Paul Casanova .50 .20 .05
□ 453 Checklist 4 1.25 .15 .03
□ 454 Tom Haller .50 .20 .05
□ 455 Bill Melton .50 .20 .05
□ 456 Dick Green .50 .20 .05
□ 457 John Strohmayer .50 .20 .05
□ 458 Jim Mason .50 .20 .05
□ 459 Jimmy Howarth .50 .20 .05
□ 460 Bill Freehan 1.00 .40 .10
□ 461 Mike Corkins .50 .20 .05
□ 462 Ron Blomberg .50 .20 .05
□ 463 Ken Tatum .50 .20 .05
□ 464 Chicago Cubs 1.00 .40 .10
Team Card
□ 465 Dave Giusti .75 .30 .07
□ 466 Jose Arcia .50 .20 .05
□ 467 Mike Ryan .50 .20 .05
□ 468 Tom Griffin .50 .20 .05
□ 469 Dan Monzon .50 .20 .05
□ 470 Mike Cuellar .75 .30 .07
□ 471 Hits Leaders 3.00 1.20 .30
Ty Cobb 4191
□ 472 Grand Slam Leaders 3.00 1.20 .30
Lou Gehrig 23
□ 473 Total Bases Leaders 3.00 1.20 .30
Hank Aaron 6172
□ 474 RBI Leaders 4.50 1.80 .45
Babe Ruth 2209
□ 475 Batting Leaders 3.00 1.20 .30
Ty Cobb .367
□ 476 Shutout Leaders 1.50 .60 .15
Walter Johnson 113
□ 477 Victory Leaders 1.50 .60 .15
Cy Young 511
□ 478 Strikeout Leaders 1.50 .60 .15
Walter Johnson 3508
□ 479 Hal Lanier .75 .30 .07
□ 480 Juan Marichal 3.50 1.40 .35
□ 481 Chicago White Sox 1.00 .40 .10
Team Card
□ 482 Rick Reuschel 4.00 1.60 .40
□ 483 Dal Maxvill .75 .30 .07
□ 484 Ernie McAnally .50 .20 .05
□ 485 Norm Cash 1.00 .40 .10
□ 486A Phillies Leaders .75 .30 .07
Danny Ozark MG
Carroll Beringer CO
Billy DeMars CO
Ray Rippelmeyer CO
Bobby Wine CO
(orange backgrounds)
□ 486B Phillies Leaders 1.00 .40 .10
(dark pale
backgrounds)
□ 487 Bruce Dal Canton .50 .20 .05
□ 488 Dave Campbell .50 .20 .05
□ 489 Jeff Burroughs .75 .30 .07
□ 490 Claude Osteen .75 .30 .07
□ 491 Bob Montgomery .50 .20 .05
□ 492 Pedro Borbon .50 .20 .05
□ 493 Duffy Dyer .50 .20 .05
□ 494 Rich Morales .50 .20 .05
□ 495 Tommy Helms .75 .30 .07
□ 496 Ray Lamb .50 .20 .05
□ 497A Cardinals Leaders .75 .30 .07
Red Schoendienst MG
Vern Benson CO
George Kissell CO
Barney Schultz CO
(orange backgrounds)
□ 497B Cardinals Leaders 1.00 .40 .10
(dark pale
backgrounds)
□ 498 Graig Nettles 2.25 .90 .22
□ 499 Bob Moose .50 .20 .05
□ 500 Oakland A's Team 1.00 .40 .10
□ 501 Larry Gura .75 .30 .07
□ 502 Bobby Valentine 1.00 .40 .10
□ 503 Phil Niekro 3.50 1.40 .35
□ 504 Earl Williams .50 .20 .05
□ 505 Bob Bailey .50 .20 .05
□ 506 Bart Johnson .50 .20 .05
□ 507 Darrel Chaney .50 .20 .05
□ 508 Gates Brown .75 .30 .07
□ 509 Jim Nash .50 .20 .05
□ 510 Amos Otis .75 .30 .07
□ 511 Sam McDowell .75 .30 .07
□ 512 Dalton Jones .50 .20 .05
□ 513 Dave Marshall .50 .20 .05
□ 514 Jerry Kenney .50 .20 .05
□ 515 Andy Messersmith .75 .30 .07
□ 516 Danny Walton .50 .20 .05
□ 517A Pirates Leaders .75 .30 .07
Bill Virdon MG
Don Leppert CO
Bill Mazeroski CO
Dave Ricketts CO
Mel Wright CO
(Mazeroski has
no right ear)
□ 517B Pirates Leaders 1.00 .40 .10
(Mazeroski has
right ear)
□ 518 Bob Veale .75 .30 .07
□ 519 John Edwards .50 .20 .05
□ 520 Mel Stottlemyre 1.00 .40 .10
□ 521 Atlanta Braves 1.00 .40 .10
Team Card
□ 522 Leo Cardenas .50 .20 .05
□ 523 Wayne Granger .50 .20 .05
□ 524 Gene Tenace .75 .30 .07
□ 525 Jim Fregosi .75 .30 .07
□ 526 Ollie Brown .50 .20 .05
□ 527 Dan McGinn .50 .20 .05
□ 528 Paul Blair .75 .30 .07
□ 529 Milt May 1.25 .50 .12
□ 530 Jim Kaat 3.50 1.40 .35
□ 531 Ron Woods 1.25 .50 .12
□ 532 Steve Mingori 1.25 .50 .12
□ 533 Larry Stahl 1.25 .50 .12
□ 534 Dave Lemonds 1.25 .50 .12
□ 535 John Callison 1.50 .60 .15

□ 536	Philadelphia Phillies Team Card	2.25	.90	.22
□ 537	Bill Slayback	1.25	.50	.12
□ 538	Jim Ray Hart	1.50	.60	.15
□ 539	Tom Murphy	1.25	.50	.12
□ 540	Cleon Jones	1.25	.50	.12
□ 541	Bob Bolin	1.25	.50	.12
□ 542	Pat Corrales	1.50	.60	.15
□ 543	Alan Foster	1.25	.50	.12
□ 544	Von Joshua	1.25	.50	.12
□ 545	Orlando Cepeda	3.00	1.20	.30
□ 546	Jim York	1.25	.50	.12
□ 547	Bobby Heise	1.25	.50	.12
□ 548	Don Durham	1.25	.50	.12
□ 549	Rangers Leaders Whitey Herzog MG Chuck Estrada CO Chuck Hiller CO Jackie Moore CO	2.25	.90	.22
□ 550	Dave Johnson	2.50	1.00	.25
□ 551	Mike Kilkenny	1.25	.50	.12
□ 552	J.C. Martin	1.25	.50	.12
□ 553	Mickey Scott	1.25	.50	.12
□ 554	Dave Concepcion	2.50	1.00	.25
□ 555	Bill Hands	1.25	.50	.12
□ 556	New York Yankees Team Card	3.50	1.40	.35
□ 557	Bernie Williams	1.25	.50	.12
□ 558	Jerry May	1.25	.50	.12
□ 559	Barry Lersch	1.25	.50	.12
□ 560	Frank Howard	2.50	1.00	.25
□ 561	Jim Geddes	1.25	.50	.12
□ 562	Wayne Garrett	1.25	.50	.12
□ 563	Larry Haney	1.25	.50	.12
□ 564	Mike Thompson	1.25	.50	.12
□ 565	Jim Hickman	1.25	.50	.12
□ 566	Lew Krausse	1.25	.50	.12
□ 567	Bob Fenwick	1.25	.50	.12
□ 568	Ray Newman	1.25	.50	.12
□ 569	Dodgers Leaders Walt Alston MG Red Adams CO Monty Basgall CO Jim Gilliam CO Tom Lasorda CO	3.00	1.20	.30
□ 570	Bill Singer	1.25	.50	.12
□ 571	Rusty Torres	1.25	.50	.12
□ 572	Gary Sutherland	1.25	.50	.12
□ 573	Fred Beene	1.25	.50	.12
□ 574	Bob Didier	1.25	.50	.12
□ 575	Dock Ellis	1.25	.50	.12
□ 576	Montreal Expos Team Card	2.25	.90	.22
□ 577	Eric Soderholm	1.25	.50	.12
□ 578	Ken Wright	1.25	.50	.12
□ 579	Tom Grieve	1.75	.70	.17
□ 580	Joe Pepitone	1.50	.60	.15
□ 581	Steve Kealey	1.25	.50	.12
□ 582	Darrell Porter	1.50	.60	.15
□ 583	Bill Grief	1.25	.50	.12
□ 584	Chris Arnold	1.25	.50	.12
□ 585	Joe Niekro	2.50	1.00	.25
□ 586	Bill Sudakis	1.25	.50	.12
□ 587	Rich McKinney	1.25	.50	.12
□ 588	Checklist 5	10.00	1.00	.20
□ 589	Ken Forsch	1.50	.60	.15
□ 590	Deron Johnson	1.25	.50	.12
□ 591	Mike Hedlund	1.25	.50	.12
□ 592	John Boccabella	1.25	.50	.12
□ 593	Royals Leaders Jack McKeon MG Galen Cisco CO Harry Dunlop CO Charlie Lau CO	1.75	.70	.17
□ 594	Vic Harris	1.25	.50	.12
□ 595	Don Gullett	1.50	.60	.15
□ 596	Red Sox Team	2.75	1.10	.27
□ 597	Mickey Rivers	1.75	.70	.17
□ 598	Phil Roof	1.25	.50	.12
□ 599	Ed Crosby	1.25	.50	.12
□ 600	Dave McNally	1.50	.60	.15
□ 601	Rookie Catchers Sergio Robles George Pena Rick Stelmaszek	1.25	.50	.12
□ 602	Rookie Pitchers Mel Behney Ralph Garcia Doug Rau	1.25	.50	.12
□ 603	Rookie 3rd Basemen Terry Hughes Bill McNulty Ken Reitz	1.25	.50	.12
□ 604	Rookie Pitchers Jesse Jefferson Dennis O'Toole Bob Strampe	1.25	.50	.12

□ 605	Rookie 1st Basemen Enos Cabell Pat Bourque Gonzalo Marquez	1.50	.60	.15
□ 606	Rookie Outfielders Gary Matthews Tom Paciorek Jorge Roque	3.00	1.20	.30
□ 607	Rookie Shortstops Pepe Frias Ray Busse Mario Guerrero	1.25	.50	.12
□ 608	Rookie Pitchers Steve Busby Dick Colpaert George Medich	1.50	.60	.15
□ 609	Rookie 2nd Basemen Larvell Blanks Pedro Garcia Dave Lopes	3.00	1.20	.30
□ 610	Rookie Pitchers Jimmy Freeman Charlie Hough Hank Webb	2.00	.80	.20
□ 611	Rookie Outfielders Rich Coggins Jim Wohlford Richie Zisk	1.50	.60	.15
□ 612	Rookie Pitchers Steve Lawson Bob Reynolds Brent Strom	1.25	.50	.12
□ 613	Rookie Catchers Bob Boone Skip Jutze Mike Ivie	8.00	3.25	.80
□ 614	Rookie Outfielders Alonza Bumbry Dwight Evans Charlie Spikes	40.00	16.00	4.00
□ 615	Rookie 3rd Basemen Ron Cey John Hilton Mike Schmidt	200.00	80.00	20.00
□ 616	Rookie Pitchers Norm Angelini Steve Blateric Mike Garman	1.25	.50	.12
□ 617	Rich Chiles	1.25	.50	.12
□ 618	Andy Etchebarren	1.25	.50	.12
□ 619	Billy Wilson	1.25	.50	.12
□ 620	Tommy Harper	1.50	.60	.15
□ 621	Joe Ferguson	1.50	.60	.15
□ 622	Larry Hisle	1.50	.60	.15
□ 623	Steve Renko	1.25	.50	.12
□ 624	Astros Leaders Leo Durocher MG Preston Gomez CO Grady Hatton CO Hub Kittle CO Jim Owens CO	2.25	.90	.22
□ 625	Angel Mangual	1.25	.50	.12
□ 626	Bob Barton	1.25	.50	.12
□ 627	Luis Alvarado	1.25	.50	.12
□ 628	Jim Slaton	1.25	.50	.12
□ 629	Indians Team	2.25	.90	.22
□ 630	Denny McLain	2.75	1.10	.27
□ 631	Tom Matchick	1.25	.50	.12
□ 632	Dick Selma	1.25	.50	.12
□ 633	Ike Brown	1.25	.50	.12
□ 634	Alan Closter	1.25	.50	.12
□ 635	Gene Alley	1.50	.60	.15
□ 636	Rickey Clark	1.25	.50	.12
□ 637	Norm Miller	1.25	.50	.12
□ 638	Ken Reynolds	1.25	.50	.12
□ 639	Willie Crawford	1.25	.50	.12
□ 640	Dick Bosman	1.25	.50	.12
□ 641	Cincinnati Reds Team Card	2.75	1.10	.27
□ 642	Jose LaBoy	1.25	.50	.12
□ 643	Al Fitzmorris	1.25	.50	.12
□ 644	Jack Heidemann	1.25	.50	.12
□ 645	Bob Locker	1.25	.50	.12
□ 646	Brewers Leaders Del Crandall MG Harvey Kuenn CO Joe Nossek CO Bob Shaw CO Jim Walton CO	1.75	.70	.17
□ 647	George Stone	1.25	.50	.12
□ 648	Tom Egan	1.25	.50	.12
□ 649	Rich Folkers	1.25	.50	.12
□ 650	Felipe Alou	1.50	.60	.15

□ 651	Don Carrithers	1.25	.50	.12
□ 652	Ted Kubiak	1.25	.50	.12
□ 653	Joe Hoerner	1.25	.50	.12
□ 654	Twins Team	2.25	.90	.22
□ 655	Clay Kirby	1.25	.50	.12
□ 656	John Ellis	1.25	.50	.12
□ 657	Bob Johnson	1.25	.50	.12
□ 658	Elliott Maddox	1.25	.50	.12
□ 659	Jose Pagan	1.25	.50	.12
□ 660	Fred Scherman	2.50	.65	.10

1974 Topps

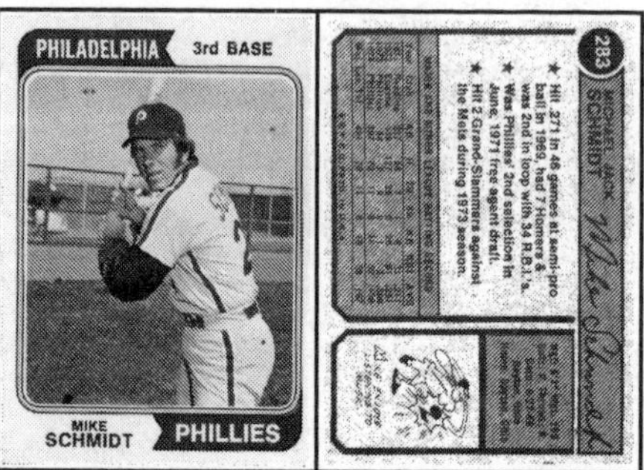

The cards in this 660-card set measure 2 1/2" by 3 1/2". This year marked the first time Topps issued all the cards of its baseball set at the same time rather than in series. Some interesting variations were created by the rumored move of the San Diego Padres to Washington. Fifteen cards (13 players, the team card, and the rookie card #599) of the Padres were printed either as "San Diego" (SD) or "Washington." The latter are the scarcer variety and are denoted in the checklist below by WAS. Each team's manager and his coaches again have a combined card with small pictures of each coach below the larger photo of the team's manager. The first six cards in the set (1-6) feature Hank Aaron and his illustrious career. Other topical subsets included in the set are League Leaders (201-208), All-Star selections (331-339), Playoffs cards (470-471), World Series cards (472-479), and Rookie Prospects (596-608).

No.	Player	NRMT	VG-E	GOOD
	COMPLETE SET (660)	375.00	150.00	45.00
	COMMON PLAYER (1-660)	.25	.10	.02
□ 1	Hank Aaron	15.00	4.00	.80
	Complete ML record			
□ 2	Aaron Special 54-57	3.50	1.40	.35
	Records on back			
□ 3	Aaron Special 58-61	3.50	1.40	.35
	Memorable homers			
□ 4	Aaron Special 62-65	3.50	1.40	.35
	Life in ML's 1954-63			
□ 5	Aaron Special 66-69	3.50	1.40	.35
	Life in ML's 1964-73			
□ 6	Aaron Special 70-73	3.50	1.40	.35
	Milestone homers			
□ 7	Jim Hunter	2.75	1.10	.27
□ 8	George Theodore	.25	.10	.02
□ 9	Mickey Lolich	.60	.24	.06
□ 10	Johnny Bench	8.00	3.25	.80
□ 11	Jim Bibby	.25	.10	.02
□ 12	Dave May	.25	.10	.02
□ 13	Tom Hilgendorf	.25	.10	.02
□ 14	Paul Popovich	.25	.10	.02
□ 15	Joe Torre	.60	.24	.06
□ 16	Baltimore Orioles	.50	.20	.05
	Team Card			
□ 17	Doug Bird	.25	.10	.02
□ 18	Gary Thomasson	.25	.10	.02
□ 19	Gerry Moses	.25	.10	.02
□ 20	Nolan Ryan	7.50	3.00	.75
□ 21	Bob Gallagher	.25	.10	.02
□ 22	Cy Acosta	.25	.10	.02
□ 23	Craig Robinson	.25	.10	.02
□ 24	John Hiller	.35	.14	.03
□ 25	Ken Singleton	.35	.14	.03
□ 26	Bill Campbell	.35	.14	.03
□ 27	George Scott	.35	.14	.03
□ 28	Manny Sanguillen	.35	.14	.03
□ 29	Phil Niekro	2.00	.80	.20
□ 30	Bobby Bonds	.50	.20	.05
□ 31	Astros Leaders	.35	.14	.03
	Preston Gomez MG			
	Roger Craig CO			
	Hub Kittle CO			
	Grady Hatton CO			
	Bob Lillis CO			
□ 32A	Johnny Grubb SD	.35	.14	.03
□ 32B	Johnny Grubb WAS	4.00	1.60	.40
□ 33	Don Newhauser	.25	.10	.02
□ 34	Andy Kosco	.25	.10	.02
□ 35	Gaylord Perry	2.25	.90	.22
□ 36	St. Louis Cardinals	.50	.20	.05
	Team Card			
□ 37	Dave Sells	.25	.10	.02
□ 38	Don Kessinger	.35	.14	.03
□ 39	Ken Suarez	.25	.10	.02
□ 40	Jim Palmer	3.50	1.40	.35
□ 41	Bobby Floyd	.25	.10	.02
□ 42	Claude Osteen	.35	.14	.03
□ 43	Jim Wynn	.35	.14	.03
□ 44	Mel Stottlemyre	.50	.20	.05
□ 45	Dave Johnson	.60	.24	.06
□ 46	Pat Kelly	.25	.10	.02
□ 47	Dick Ruthven	.25	.10	.02
□ 48	Dick Sharon	.25	.10	.02
□ 49	Steve Renko	.25	.10	.02
□ 50	Rod Carew	6.00	2.40	.60
□ 51	Bob Heise	.25	.10	.02
□ 52	Al Oliver	.75	.30	.07
□ 53A	Fred Kendall SD	.35	.14	.03
□ 53B	Fred Kendall WAS	4.00	1.60	.40
□ 54	Elias Sosa	.25	.10	.02
□ 55	Frank Robinson	3.50	1.40	.35
□ 56	New York Mets Team	.75	.30	.07
□ 57	Darold Knowles	.25	.10	.02
□ 58	Charlie Spikes	.25	.10	.02
□ 59	Ross Grimsley	.25	.10	.02
□ 60	Lou Brock	3.50	1.40	.35
□ 61	Luis Aparicio	2.00	.80	.20
□ 62	Bob Locker	.25	.10	.02
□ 63	Bill Sudakis	.25	.10	.02
□ 64	Doug Rau	.25	.10	.02
□ 65	Amos Otis	.35	.14	.03
□ 66	Sparky Lyle	.50	.20	.05
□ 67	Tommy Helms	.35	.14	.03
□ 68	Grant Jackson	.25	.10	.02
□ 69	Del Unser	.25	.10	.02
□ 70	Dick Allen	.60	.24	.06
□ 71	Dan Frisella	.25	.10	.02
□ 72	Aurelio Rodriguez	.25	.10	.02
□ 73	Mike Marshall	.50	.20	.05
□ 74	Twins Team	.50	.20	.05
□ 75	Jim Colborn	.25	.10	.02
□ 76	Mickey Rivers	.35	.14	.03
□ 77A	Rich Troedson SD	.35	.14	.03
□ 77B	Rich Troedson WAS	4.00	1.60	.40
□ 78	Giants Leaders	.35	.14	.03
	Charlie Fox MG			
	John McNamara CO			
	Joe Amalfitano CO			
	Andy Gilbert CO			
	Don McMahon CO			
□ 79	Gene Tenace	.25	.10	.02
□ 80	Tom Seaver	7.00	2.80	.70
□ 81	Frank Duffy	.25	.10	.02
□ 82	Dave Giusti	.25	.10	.02
□ 83	Orlando Cepeda	1.00	.40	.10
□ 84	Rick Wise	.35	.14	.03
□ 85	Joe Morgan	2.50	1.00	.25
□ 86	Joe Ferguson	.25	.10	.02
□ 87	Fergie Jenkins	1.00	.40	.10
□ 88	Fred Patek	.35	.14	.03
□ 89	Jackie Brown	.25	.10	.02
□ 90	Bobby Murcer	.60	.24	.06
□ 91	Ken Forsch	.25	.10	.02
□ 92	Paul Blair	.35	.14	.03
□ 93	Rod Gilbreath	.25	.10	.02
□ 94	Tigers Team	.50	.20	.05
□ 95	Steve Carlton	6.00	2.40	.60
□ 96	Jerry Hairston	.25	.10	.02
□ 97	Bob Bailey	.25	.10	.02
□ 98	Bert Blyleven	.75	.30	.07
□ 99	Brewers Leaders	.35	.14	.03
	Del Crandall MG			
	Harvey Kuenn CO			
	Joe Nossek CO			

Jim Walton CO			
Al Widmar CO			
□ 100 Willie Stargell	3.00	1.20	.30
□ 101 Bobby Valentine	.50	.20	.05
□ 102A Bill Greif SD	.35	.14	.03
□ 102B Bill Greif WAS	4.00	1.60	.40
□ 103 Sal Bando	.35	.14	.03
□ 104 Ron Bryant	.25	.10	.02
□ 105 Carlton Fisk	2.50	1.00	.25
□ 106 Harry Parker	.25	.10	.02
□ 107 Alex Johnson	.25	.10	.02
□ 108 Al Hrabosky	.35	.14	.03
□ 109 Bobby Grich	.35	.14	.03
□ 110 Billy Williams	2.75	1.10	.27
□ 111 Clay Carroll	.25	.10	.02
□ 112 Dave Lopes	.60	.24	.06
□ 113 Dick Drago	.25	.10	.02
□ 114 Angels Team	.50	.20	.05
□ 115 Willie Horton	.35	.14	.03
□ 116 Jerry Reuss	.35	.14	.03
□ 117 Ron Blomberg	.25	.10	.02
□ 118 Bill Lee	.35	.14	.03
□ 119 Phillies Leaders	.35	.14	.03
Danny Ozark MG			
Ray Ripplemeyer CO			
Bobby Wine CO			
Carroll Beringer CO			
Billy DeMars CO			
□ 120 Wilbur Wood	.35	.14	.03
□ 121 Larry Lintz	.25	.10	.02
□ 122 Jim Holt	.25	.10	.02
□ 123 Nellie Briles	.35	.14	.03
□ 124 Bobby Coluccio	.25	.10	.02
□ 125A Nate Colbert SD	.35	.14	.03
□ 125B Nate Colbert WAS	4.00	1.60	.40
□ 126 Checklist 1	1.00	.10	.02
□ 127 Tom Paciorek	.25	.10	.02
□ 128 John Ellis	.25	.10	.02
□ 129 Chris Speier	.35	.14	.03
□ 130 Reggie Jackson	9.00	3.75	.90
□ 131 Bob Boone	1.00	.40	.10
□ 132 Felix Millan	.25	.10	.02
□ 133 David Clyde	.25	.10	.02
□ 134 Denis Menke	.25	.10	.02
□ 135 Roy White	.35	.14	.03
□ 136 Rick Reuschel	.75	.30	.07
□ 137 Al Bumbry	.25	.10	.02
□ 138 Eddie Brinkman	.25	.10	.02
□ 139 Aurelio Monteagudo	.25	.10	.02
□ 140 Darrell Evans	.50	.20	.05
□ 141 Pat Bourque	.25	.10	.02
□ 142 Pedro Garcia	.25	.10	.02
□ 143 Dick Woodson	.25	.10	.02
□ 144 Dodgers Leaders	1.00	.40	.10
Walter Alston MG			
Tom Lasorda CO			
Jim Gilliam CO			
Red Adams CO			
Monty Basgall CO			
□ 145 Dock Ellis	.25	.10	.02
□ 146 Ron Fairly	.35	.14	.03
□ 147 Bart Johnson	.25	.10	.02
□ 148A Dave Hilton SD	.35	.14	.03
□ 148B Dave Hilton WAS	4.00	1.60	.40
□ 149 Mac Scarce	.25	.10	.02
□ 150 John Mayberry	.35	.14	.03
□ 151 Diego Segui	.25	.10	.02
□ 152 Oscar Gamble	.35	.14	.03
□ 153 Jon Matlack	.35	.14	.03
□ 154 Astros Team	.50	.20	.05
□ 155 Bert Campaneris	.35	.14	.03
□ 156 Randy Moffitt	.25	.10	.02
□ 157 Vic Harris	.25	.10	.02
□ 158 Jack Billingham	.25	.10	.02
□ 159 Jim Ray Hart	.35	.14	.03
□ 160 Brooks Robinson	3.50	1.40	.35
□ 161 Ray Burris	.50	.20	.05
□ 162 Bill Freehan	.50	.20	.05
□ 163 Ken Berry	.25	.10	.02
□ 164 Tom House	.35	.14	.03
□ 165 Willie Davis	.50	.20	.05
□ 166 Royals Leaders	.35	.14	.03
Jack McKeon MG			
Charlie Lau CO			
Harry Dunlop CO			
Galen Cisco CO			
□ 167 Luis Tiant	.60	.24	.06
□ 168 Danny Thompson	.25	.10	.02
□ 169 Steve Rogers	.60	.24	.06
□ 170 Bill Melton	.25	.10	.02
□ 171 Eduardo Rodriguez	.25	.10	.02
□ 172 Gene Clines	.25	.10	.02
□ 173A Randy Jones SD	.60	.24	.06
□ 173B Randy Jones WAS	4.00	1.60	.40
□ 174 Bill Robinson	.35	.14	.03
□ 175 Reggie Cleveland	.25	.10	.02
□ 176 John Lowenstein	.25	.10	.02
□ 177 Dave Roberts	.25	.10	.02
□ 178 Garry Maddox	.35	.14	.03
□ 179 Mets Leaders	1.25	.50	.12
Yogi Berra MG			
Rube Walker CO			
Eddie Yost CO			
Roy McMillan CO			
Joe Pignatano CO			
□ 180 Ken Holtzman	.35	.14	.03
□ 181 Cesar Geronimo	.25	.10	.02
□ 182 Lindy McDaniel	.35	.14	.03
□ 183 Johnny Oates	.25	.10	.02
□ 184 Texas Rangers Team Card	.50	.20	.05
□ 185 Jose Cardenal	.25	.10	.02
□ 186 Fred Scherman	.25	.10	.02
□ 187 Don Baylor	1.00	.40	.10
□ 188 Rudy Meoli	.25	.10	.02
□ 189 Jim Brewer	.25	.10	.02
□ 190 Tony Oliva	1.00	.40	.10
□ 191 Al Fitzmorris	.25	.10	.02
□ 192 Mario Guerrero	.25	.10	.02
□ 193 Tom Walker	.25	.10	.02
□ 194 Darrell Porter	.35	.14	.03
□ 195 Carlos May	.25	.10	.02
□ 196 Jim Fregosi	.35	.14	.03
□ 197A Vicente Romo SD	.35	.14	.03
□ 197B Vicente Romo WAS	4.00	1.60	.40
□ 198 Dave Cash	.35	.14	.03
□ 199 Mike Kekich	.25	.10	.02
□ 200 Cesar Cedeno	.35	.14	.03
□ 201 Batting Leaders	3.00	1.20	.30
Rod Carew			
Pete Rose			
□ 202 Home Run Leaders	1.75	.70	.17
Reggie Jackson			
Willie Stargell			
□ 203 RBI Leaders	1.75	.70	.17
Reggie Jackson			
Willie Stargell			
□ 204 Stolen Base Leaders	.60	.24	.06
Tommy Harper			
Lou Brock			
□ 205 Victory Leaders	.50	.20	.05
Wilbur Wood			
Ron Bryant			
□ 206 ERA Leaders	2.25	.90	.22
Jim Palmer			
Tom Seaver			
□ 207 Strikeout Leaders	2.50	1.00	.25
Nolan Ryan			
Tom Seaver			
□ 208 Leading Firemen	.50	.20	.05
John Hiller			
Mike Marshall			
□ 209 Ted Sizemore	.25	.10	.02
□ 210 Bill Singer	.25	.10	.02
□ 211 Chicago Cubs Team	.50	.20	.05
□ 212 Rollie Fingers	1.75	.70	.17
□ 213 Dave Rader	.25	.10	.02
□ 214 Bill Grabarkewitz	.25	.10	.02
□ 215 Al Kaline	4.00	1.60	.40
□ 216 Ray Sadecki	.25	.10	.02
□ 217 Tim Foli	.25	.10	.02
□ 218 John Briggs	.25	.10	.02
□ 219 Doug Griffin	.25	.10	.02
□ 220 Don Sutton	2.00	.80	.20
□ 221 White Sox Leaders	.35	.14	.03
Chuck Tanner MG			
Jim Mahoney CO			
Alex Monchak CO			
Johnny Sain CO			
Joe Lonnett CO			
□ 222 Ramon Hernandez	.25	.10	.02
□ 223 Jeff Burroughs	.50	.20	.05
□ 224 Roger Metzger	.25	.10	.02
□ 225 Paul Splittorff	.35	.14	.03
□ 226A Padres Team SD	1.00	.40	.10
□ 226B Padres Team WAS	5.00	2.00	.50
□ 227 Mike Lum	.25	.10	.02
□ 228 Ted Kubiak	.25	.10	.02
□ 229 Fritz Peterson	.25	.10	.02
□ 230 Tony Perez	1.25	.50	.12
□ 231 Dick Tidrow	.25	.10	.02
□ 232 Steve Brye	.25	.10	.02
□ 233 Jim Barr	.25	.10	.02
□ 234 John Milner	.25	.10	.02
□ 235 Dave McNally	.35	.14	.03
□ 236 Cardinals Leaders	.35	.14	.03
Red Schoendienst MG			
Barney Schultz CO			
George Kissell CO			
Johnny Lewis CO			

Vern Benson CO
☐ 237 Ken Brett .25 .10 .02
☐ 238 Fran Healy HOR .35 .14 .03
(Munson sliding
in background)
☐ 239 Bill Russell .35 .14 .03
☐ 240 Joe Coleman .25 .10 .02
☐ 241A Glenn Beckert SD .35 .14 .03
☐ 241B Glenn Beckert WAS 4.00 1.60 .40
☐ 242 Bill Gogolewski .25 .10 .02
☐ 243 Bob Oliver .25 .10 .02
☐ 244 Carl Morton .25 .10 .02
☐ 245 Cleon Jones .25 .10 .02
☐ 246 Athletics Team .50 .20 .05
☐ 247 Rick Miller .25 .10 .02
☐ 248 Tom Hall .25 .10 .02
☐ 249 George Mitterwald .25 .10 .02
☐ 250A Willie McCovey SD 4.00 1.60 .40
☐ 250B Willie McCovey WAS 21.00 8.50 2.10
☐ 251 Graig Nettles 1.50 .60 .15
☐ 252 Dave Parker 18.00 7.25 1.80
☐ 253 John Boccabella .25 .10 .02
☐ 254 Stan Bahnsen .25 .10 .02
☐ 255 Larry Bowa .60 .24 .06
☐ 256 Tom Griffin .25 .10 .02
☐ 257 Buddy Bell 1.00 .40 .10
☐ 258 Jerry Morales .25 .10 .02
☐ 259 Bob Reynolds .25 .10 .02
☐ 260 Ted Simmons 1.00 .40 .10
☐ 261 Jerry Bell .25 .10 .02
☐ 262 Ed Kirkpatrick .25 .10 .02
☐ 263 Checklist 2 1.00 .10 .02
☐ 264 Joe Rudi .35 .14 .03
☐ 265 Tug McGraw .60 .24 .06
☐ 266 Jim Northrup .35 .14 .03
☐ 267 Andy Messersmith .35 .14 .03
☐ 268 Tom Grieve .35 .14 .03
☐ 269 Bob Johnson .25 .10 .02
☐ 270 Ron Santo .50 .20 .05
☐ 271 Bill Hands .25 .10 .02
☐ 272 Paul Casanova .25 .10 .02
☐ 273 Checklist 3 1.00 .10 .02
☐ 274 Fred Beene .25 .10 .02
☐ 275 Ron Hunt .25 .10 .02
☐ 276 Angels Leaders .35 .14 .03
Bobby Winkles MG
John Roseboro CO
Tom Morgan CO
Jimmie Reese CO
Salty Parker CO
☐ 277 Gary Nolan .25 .10 .02
☐ 278 Cookie Rojas .35 .14 .03
☐ 279 Jim Crawford .25 .10 .02
☐ 280 Carl Yastrzemski 9.00 3.75 .90
☐ 281 Giants Team .50 .20 .05
☐ 282 Doyle Alexander .50 .20 .05
☐ 283 Mike Schmidt 50.00 20.00 5.00
☐ 284 Dave Duncan .25 .10 .02
☐ 285 Reggie Smith .50 .20 .05
☐ 286 Tony Muser .25 .10 .02
☐ 287 Clay Kirby .25 .10 .02
☐ 288 Gorman Thomas 2.00 .80 .20
☐ 289 Rick Auerbach .25 .10 .02
☐ 290 Vida Blue .50 .20 .05
☐ 291 Don Hahn .25 .10 .02
☐ 292 Chuck Seelbach .25 .10 .02
☐ 293 Milt May .25 .10 .02
☐ 294 Steve Foucault .25 .10 .02
☐ 295 Rick Monday .35 .14 .03
☐ 296 Ray Corbin .25 .10 .02
☐ 297 Hal Breeden .25 .10 .02
☐ 298 Roric Harrison .25 .10 .02
☐ 299 Gene Michael .35 .14 .03
☐ 300 Pete Rose 16.00 6.50 1.60
☐ 301 Bob Montgomery .25 .10 .02
☐ 302 Rudy May .25 .10 .02
☐ 303 George Hendrick .35 .14 .03
☐ 304 Don Wilson .25 .10 .02
☐ 305 Tito Fuentes .25 .10 .02
☐ 306 Orioles Leaders .75 .30 .07
Earl Weaver MG
Jim Frey CO
George Bamberger CO
Billy Hunter CO
George Staller CO
☐ 307 Luis Melendez .25 .10 .02
☐ 308 Bruce Dal Canton .25 .10 .02
☐ 309A Dave Roberts SD .35 .14 .03
☐ 309B Dave Roberts WAS 5.00 2.00 .50
☐ 310 Terry Forster .35 .14 .03
☐ 311 Jerry Grote .25 .10 .02
☐ 312 Deron Johnson .25 .10 .02
☐ 313 Barry Lersch .25 .10 .02
☐ 314 Milwaukee Brewers .50 .20 .05
Team Card
☐ 315 Ron Cey 1.00 .40 .10
☐ 316 Jim Perry .35 .14 .03
☐ 317 Richie Zisk .35 .14 .03
☐ 318 Jim Merritt .25 .10 .02
☐ 319 Randy Hundley .35 .14 .03
☐ 320 Dusty Baker .50 .20 .05
☐ 321 Steve Braun .25 .10 .02
☐ 322 Ernie McAnally .25 .10 .02
☐ 323 Richie Scheinblum .25 .10 .02
☐ 324 Steve Kline .25 .10 .02
☐ 325 Tommy Harper .35 .14 .03
☐ 326 Reds Leaders .60 .24 .06
Sparky Anderson MG
Larry Shephard CO
George Scherger CO
Alex Grammas CO
Ted Kluszewski CO
☐ 327 Tom Timmermann .25 .10 .02
☐ 328 Skip Jutze .25 .10 .02
☐ 329 Mark Belanger .35 .14 .03
☐ 330 Juan Marichal 2.50 1.00 .25
☐ 331 All-Star Catchers 1.75 .70 .17
Carlton Fisk
Johnny Bench
☐ 332 All-Star 1B 1.75 .70 .17
Dick Allen
Hank Aaron
☐ 333 All-Star 2B 1.50 .60 .15
Rod Carew
Joe Morgan
☐ 334 All-Star 3B 1.00 .40 .10
Brooks Robinson
Ron Santo
☐ 335 All-Star SS .35 .14 .03
Bert Campaneris
Chris Speier
☐ 336 All-Star LF 2.50 1.00 .25
Bobby Murcer
Pete Rose
☐ 337 All-Star CF .35 .14 .03
Amos Otis
Cesar Cedeno
☐ 338 All-Star RF 2.25 .90 .22
Reggie Jackson
Billy Williams
☐ 339 All-Star Pitchers .50 .20 .05
Jim Hunter
Rick Wise
☐ 340 Thurman Munson 5.00 2.00 .50
☐ 341 Dan Driessen .75 .30 .07
☐ 342 Jim Lonborg .35 .14 .03
☐ 343 Royals Team .50 .20 .05
☐ 344 Mike Caldwell .35 .14 .03
☐ 345 Bill North .25 .10 .02
☐ 346 Ron Reed .25 .10 .02
☐ 347 Sandy Alomar .25 .10 .02
☐ 348 Pete Richert .25 .10 .02
☐ 349 John Vukovich .25 .10 .02
☐ 350 Bob Gibson 3.00 1.20 .30
☐ 351 Dwight Evans 5.50 2.20 .55
☐ 352 Bill Stoneman .25 .10 .02
☐ 353 Rich Coggins .25 .10 .02
☐ 354 Cubs Leaders .35 .14 .03
Whitey Lockman MG
J.C. Martin CO
Hank Aguirre CO
Al Spangler CO
Jim Marshall CO
☐ 355 Dave Nelson .25 .10 .02
☐ 356 Jerry Koosman .50 .20 .05
☐ 357 Buddy Bradford .25 .10 .02
☐ 358 Dal Maxvill .35 .14 .03
☐ 359 Brent Strom .25 .10 .02
☐ 360 Greg Luzinski .75 .30 .07
☐ 361 Don Carrithers .25 .10 .02
☐ 362 Hal King .25 .10 .02
☐ 363 Yankees Team .60 .24 .06
☐ 364A Cito Gaston SD .35 .14 .03
☐ 364B Cito Gaston WAS 5.00 2.00 .50
☐ 365 Steve Busby .35 .14 .03
☐ 366 Larry Hisle .35 .14 .03
☐ 367 Norm Cash .75 .30 .07
☐ 368 Manny Mota .35 .14 .03
☐ 369 Paul Lindblad .25 .10 .02
☐ 370 Bob Watson .35 .14 .03
☐ 371 Jim Slaton .25 .10 .02
☐ 372 Ken Reitz .25 .10 .02
☐ 373 John Curtis .25 .10 .02
☐ 374 Marty Perez .25 .10 .02
☐ 375 Earl Williams .25 .10 .02
☐ 376 Jorge Orta .25 .10 .02
☐ 377 Ron Woods .25 .10 .02
☐ 378 Burt Hooton .25 .10 .02
☐ 379 Rangers Leaders .75 .30 .07
Billy Martin MG

Frank Lucchesi CO
Art Fowler CO
Charlie Silvera CO
Jackie Moore CO
□ 380 Bud Harrelson .35 .14 .03
□ 381 Charlie Sands .25 .10 .02
□ 382 Bob Moose .25 .10 .02
□ 383 Phillies Team .50 .20 .05
□ 384 Chris Chambliss .50 .20 .05
□ 385 Don Gullett .35 .14 .03
□ 386 Gary Matthews .50 .20 .05
□ 387A Rich Morales SD .35 .14 .03
□ 387B Rich Morales WAS 5.00 2.00 .50
□ 388 Phil Roof .25 .10 .02
□ 389 Gates Brown .35 .14 .03
□ 390 Lou Piniella .50 .20 .05
□ 391 Billy Champion .25 .10 .02
□ 392 Dick Green .25 .10 .02
□ 393 Orlando Pena .25 .10 .02
□ 394 Ken Henderson .25 .10 .02
□ 395 Doug Rader .35 .14 .03
□ 396 Tommy Davis .50 .20 .05
□ 397 George Stone .25 .10 .02
□ 398 Duke Sims .25 .10 .02
□ 399 Mike Paul .25 .10 .02
□ 400 Harmon Killebrew 3.00 1.20 .30
□ 401 Elliott Maddox .25 .10 .02
□ 402 Jim Rooker .25 .10 .02
□ 403 Red Sox Leaders .35 .14 .03
Darrell Johnson MG
Eddie Popowski CO
Lee Stange CO
Don Zimmer CO
Don Bryant CO
□ 404 Jim Howarth .25 .10 .02
□ 405 Ellie Rodriguez .25 .10 .02
□ 406 Steve Arlin .25 .10 .02
□ 407 Jim Wohlford .25 .10 .02
□ 408 Charlie Hough .50 .20 .05
□ 409 Ike Brown .25 .10 .02
□ 410 Pedro Borbon .25 .10 .02
□ 411 Frank Baker .25 .10 .02
□ 412 Chuck Taylor .25 .10 .02
□ 413 Don Money .35 .14 .03
□ 414 Checklist 4 1.00 .10 .02
□ 415 Gary Gentry .25 .10 .02
□ 416 White Sox Team .50 .20 .05
□ 417 Rich Folkers .25 .10 .02
□ 418 Walt Williams .25 .10 .02
□ 419 Wayne Twitchell .25 .10 .02
□ 420 Ray Fosse .25 .10 .02
□ 421 Dan Fife .25 .10 .02
□ 422 Gonzalo Marquez .25 .10 .02
□ 423 Fred Stanley .25 .10 .02
□ 424 Jim Beauchamp .25 .10 .02
□ 425 Pete Broberg .25 .10 .02
□ 426 Rennie Stennett .25 .10 .02
□ 427 Bobby Bolin .25 .10 .02
□ 428 Gary Sutherland .25 .10 .02
□ 429 Dick Lange .25 .10 .02
□ 430 Matty Alou .35 .14 .03
□ 431 Gene Garber .35 .14 .03
□ 432 Chris Arnold .25 .10 .02
□ 433 Lerrin LaGrow .25 .10 .02
□ 434 Ken McMullen .25 .10 .02
□ 435 Dave Concepcion .75 .30 .07
□ 436 Don Hood .25 .10 .02
□ 437 Jim Lyttle .25 .10 .02
□ 438 Ed Herrmann .25 .10 .02
□ 439 Norm Miller .25 .10 .02
□ 440 Jim Kaat 1.00 .40 .10
□ 441 Tom Ragland .25 .10 .02
□ 442 Alan Foster .25 .10 .02
□ 443 Tom Hutton .25 .10 .02
□ 444 Vic Davalillo .25 .10 .02
□ 445 George Medich .25 .10 .02
□ 446 Len Randle .25 .10 .02
□ 447 Twins Leaders .35 .14 .03
Frank Quilici MG
Ralph Rowe CO
Bob Rodgers CO
Vern Morgan CO
□ 448 Ron Hodges .25 .10 .02
□ 449 Tom McCraw .25 .10 .02
□ 450 Rich Hebner .35 .14 .03
□ 451 Tommy John 1.50 .60 .15
□ 452 Gene Hiser .25 .10 .02
□ 453 Balor Moore .25 .10 .02
□ 454 Kurt Bevacqua .25 .10 .02
□ 455 Tom Bradley .25 .10 .02
□ 456 Dave Winfield 40.00 16.00 4.00
□ 457 Chuck Goggin .25 .10 .02
□ 458 Jim Ray .25 .10 .02
□ 459 Cincinnati Reds .60 .24 .06
Team Card
□ 460 Boog Powell .60 .24 .06
□ 461 John Odom .25 .10 .02
□ 462 Luis Alvarado .25 .10 .02
□ 463 Pat Dobson .35 .14 .03
□ 464 Jose Cruz .50 .20 .05
□ 465 Dick Bosman .25 .10 .02
□ 466 Dick Billings .25 .10 .02
□ 467 Winston Llenas .25 .10 .02
□ 468 Pepe Frias .25 .10 .02
□ 469 Joe Decker .25 .10 .02
□ 470 AL Playoffs 2.25 .90 .22
A's over Orioles
(Reggie Jackson)
□ 471 NL Playoffs .60 .24 .06
Mets over Reds
(Matlack pitching)
□ 472 World Series Game 1 .60 .24 .06
(Knowles pitching)
□ 473 World Series Game 2 2.25 .90 .22
(Willie Mays batting)
□ 474 World Series Game 3 .60 .24 .06
(Campaneris stealing)
□ 475 World Series Game 4 .60 .24 .06
(Staub batting)
□ 476 World Series Game 5 .60 .24 .06
Cleon Jones scoring)
□ 477 World Series Game 6 2.25 .90 .22
(Reggie Jackson)
□ 478 World Series Game 7 .60 .24 .06
(Campaneris batting)
□ 479 World Series Summary .60 .24 .06
A's celebrate; win
2nd consecutive
championship
□ 480 Willie Crawford .25 .10 .02
□ 481 Jerry Terrell .25 .10 .02
□ 482 Bob Didier .25 .10 .02
□ 483 Atlanta Braves .50 .20 .05
Team Card
□ 484 Carmen Fanzone .25 .10 .02
□ 485 Felipe Alou .35 .14 .03
□ 486 Steve Stone .35 .14 .03
□ 487 Ted Martinez .25 .10 .02
□ 488 Andy Etchebarren .25 .10 .02
□ 489 Pirates Leaders .35 .14 .03
Danny Murtaugh MG
Don Osborn CO
Don Leppert CO
Bill Mazeroski CO
Bob Skinner CO
□ 490 Vada Pinson .60 .24 .06
□ 491 Roger Nelson .25 .10 .02
□ 492 Mike Rogodzinski .25 .10 .02
□ 493 Joe Hoerner .25 .10 .02
□ 494 Ed Goodson .25 .10 .02
□ 495 Dick McAuliffe .35 .14 .03
□ 496 Tom Murphy .25 .10 .02
□ 497 Bobby Mitchell .25 .10 .02
□ 498 Pat Corrales .35 .14 .03
□ 499 Rusty Torres .25 .10 .02
□ 500 Lee May .35 .14 .03
□ 501 Eddie Leon .25 .10 .02
□ 502 Dave LaRoche .25 .10 .02
□ 503 Eric Soderholm .25 .10 .02
□ 504 Joe Niekro .50 .20 .05
□ 505 Bill Buckner .60 .24 .06
□ 506 Ed Farmer .25 .10 .02
□ 507 Larry Stahl .25 .10 .02
□ 508 Expos Team .50 .20 .05
□ 509 Jesse Jefferson .25 .10 .02
□ 510 Wayne Garrett .25 .10 .02
□ 511 Toby Harrah .35 .14 .03
□ 512 Joe Lahoud .25 .10 .02
□ 513 Jim Campanis .25 .10 .02
□ 514 Paul Schaal .25 .10 .02
□ 515 Willie Montanez .25 .10 .02
□ 516 Horacio Pina .25 .10 .02
□ 517 Mike Hegan .25 .10 .02
□ 518 Derrel Thomas .25 .10 .02
□ 519 Bill Sharp .25 .10 .02
□ 520 Tim McCarver .60 .24 .06
□ 521 Indians Leaders .35 .14 .03
Ken Aspromonte MG
Clay Bryant CO
Tony Pacheco CO
□ 522 J.R. Richard .50 .20 .05
□ 523 Cecil Cooper 1.75 .70 .17
□ 524 Bill Plummer .25 .10 .02
□ 525 Clyde Wright .25 .10 .02
□ 526 Frank Tepedino .25 .10 .02
□ 527 Bobby Darwin .25 .10 .02
□ 528 Bill Bonham .25 .10 .02
□ 529 Horace Clarke .25 .10 .02
□ 530 Mickey Stanley .35 .14 .03
□ 531 Expos Leaders .35 .14 .03

	Gene Mauch MG			
	Dave Bristol CO			
	Cal McLish CO			
	Larry Doby CO			
	Jerry Zimmerman CO			
□ 532	Skip Lockwood	.25	.10	.02
□ 533	Mike Phillips	.25	.10	.02
□ 534	Eddie Watt	.25	.10	.02
□ 535	Bob Tolan	.35	.14	.03
□ 536	Duffy Dyer	.25	.10	.02
□ 537	Steve Mingori	.25	.10	.02
□ 538	Cesar Tovar	.25	.10	.02
□ 539	Lloyd Allen	.25	.10	.02
□ 540	Bob Robertson	.25	.10	.02
□ 541	Cleveland Indians Team Card	.50	.20	.05
□ 542	Rich Gossage	1.50	.60	.15
□ 543	Danny Cater	.25	.10	.02
□ 544	Ron Schueler	.25	.10	.02
□ 545	Billy Conigliaro	.35	.14	.03
□ 546	Mike Corkins	.25	.10	.02
□ 547	Glenn Borgmann	.25	.10	.02
□ 548	Sonny Siebert	.35	.14	.03
□ 549	Mike Jorgensen	.25	.10	.02
□ 550	Sam McDowell	.35	.14	.03
□ 551	Von Joshua	.25	.10	.02
□ 552	Denny Doyle	.25	.10	.02
□ 553	Jim Willoughby	.25	.10	.02
□ 554	Tim Johnson	.25	.10	.02
□ 555	Woody Fryman	.25	.10	.02
□ 556	Dave Campbell	.25	.10	.02
□ 557	Jim McGlothlin	.25	.10	.02
□ 558	Bill Fahey	.25	.10	.02
□ 559	Darrell Chaney	.25	.10	.02
□ 560	Mike Cuellar	.35	.14	.03
□ 561	Ed Kranepool	.35	.14	.03
□ 562	Jack Aker	.25	.10	.02
□ 563	Hal McRae	.35	.14	.03
□ 564	Mike Ryan	.25	.10	.02
□ 565	Milt Wilcox	.25	.10	.02
□ 566	Jackie Hernandez	.25	.10	.02
□ 567	Red Sox Team	.50	.20	.05
□ 568	Mike Torrez	.35	.14	.03
□ 569	Rick Dempsey	.35	.14	.03
□ 570	Ralph Garr	.35	.14	.03
□ 571	Rich Hand	.25	.10	.02
□ 572	Enzo Hernandez	.25	.10	.02
□ 573	Mike Adams	.25	.10	.02
□ 574	Bill Parsons	.25	.10	.02
□ 575	Steve Garvey	9.00	3.75	.90
□ 576	Scipio Spinks	.25	.10	.02
□ 577	Mike Sadek	.25	.10	.02
□ 578	Ralph Houk MG	.35	.14	.03
□ 579	Cecil Upshaw	.25	.10	.02
□ 580	Jim Spencer	.25	.10	.02
□ 581	Fred Norman	.25	.10	.02
□ 582	Bucky Dent	1.25	.50	.12
□ 583	Marty Pattin	.25	.10	.02
□ 584	Ken Rudolph	.25	.10	.02
□ 585	Merv Rettenmund	.25	.10	.02
□ 586	Jack Brohamer	.25	.10	.02
□ 587	Larry Christenson	.25	.10	.02
□ 588	Hal Lanier	.35	.14	.03
□ 589	Boots Day	.25	.10	.02
□ 590	Roger Moret	.25	.10	.02
□ 591	Sonny Jackson	.25	.10	.02
□ 592	Ed Bane	.25	.10	.02
□ 593	Steve Yeager	.35	.14	.03
□ 594	Lee Stanton	.25	.10	.02
□ 595	Steve Blass	.35	.14	.03
□ 596	Rookie Pitchers	.35	.14	.03
	Wayne Garland			
	Fred Holdsworth			
	Mark Littell			
	Dick Pole			
□ 597	Rookie Shortstops	.60	.24	.06
	Dave Chalk			
	John Gamble			
	Pete MacKanin			
	Manny Trillo			
□ 598	Rookie Outfielders	2.50	1.00	.25
	Dave Augustine			
	Ken Griffey			
	Steve Ontiveros			
	Jim Tyrone			
□ 599A	Rookie Pitchers WAS	.60	.24	.06
	Ron Diorio			
	Dave Freisleben			
	Frank Riccelli			
	Greg Shanahan			
□ 599B	Rookie Pitchers SD (SD in large print)	3.00	1.20	.30
□ 599C	Rookie Pitchers SD (SD in small print)	4.50	1.80	.45
□ 600	Rookie Infielders	5.00	2.00	.50
	Ron Cash			
	Jim Cox			
	Bill Madlock			
	Reggie Sanders			
□ 601	Rookie Outfielders	2.50	1.00	.25
	Ed Armbrister			
	Rich Bladt			
	Brian Downing			
	Bake McBride			
□ 602	Rookie Pitchers	.50	.20	.05
	Glen Abbott			
	Rick Henninger			
	Craig Swan			
	Dan Vossler			
□ 603	Rookie Catchers	.50	.20	.05
	Barry Foote			
	Tom Lundstedt			
	Charlie Moore			
	Sergio Robles			
□ 604	Rookie Infielders	4.00	1.60	.40
	Terry Hughes			
	John Knox			
	Andy Thornton			
	Frank White			
□ 605	Rookie Pitchers	2.00	.80	.20
	Vic Albury			
	Ken Frailing			
	Kevin Kobel			
	Frank Tanana			
□ 606	Rookie Outfielders	.35	.14	.03
	Jim Fuller			
	Wilbur Howard			
	Tommy Smith			
	Otto Velez			
□ 607	Rookie Shortstops	.35	.14	.03
	Leo Foster			
	Tom Heintzelman			
	Dave Rosello			
	Frank Taveras			
□ 608A	Rookie Pitchers: ERR	2.00	.80	.20
	Bob Apodaco (sic)			
	Dick Baney			
	John D'Acquisto			
	Mike Wallace			
□ 608B	Rookie Pitchers: COR	.35	.14	.03
	Bob Apodaca			
	Dick Baney			
	John D'Acquisto			
	Mike Wallace			
□ 609	Rico Petrocelli	.35	.14	.03
□ 610	Dave Kingman	1.00	.40	.10
□ 611	Rich Stelmaszek	.25	.10	.02
□ 612	Luke Walker	.25	.10	.02
□ 613	Dan Monzon	.25	.10	.02
□ 614	Adrian Devine	.25	.10	.02
□ 615	John Jeter	.25	.10	.02
□ 616	Larry Gura	.35	.14	.03
□ 617	Ted Ford	.25	.10	.02
□ 618	Jim Mason	.25	.10	.02
□ 619	Mike Anderson	.25	.10	.02
□ 620	Al Downing	.35	.14	.03
□ 621	Bernie Carbo	.25	.10	.02
□ 622	Phil Gagliano	.25	.10	.02
□ 623	Celerino Sanchez	.25	.10	.02
□ 624	Bob Miller	.25	.10	.02
□ 625	Ollie Brown	.25	.10	.02
□ 626	Pittsburgh Pirates Team Card	.50	.20	.05
□ 627	Carl Taylor	.25	.10	.02
□ 628	Ivan Murrell	.25	.10	.02
□ 629	Rusty Staub	.60	.24	.06
□ 630	Tommy Agee	.25	.10	.02
□ 631	Steve Barber	.25	.10	.02
□ 632	George Culver	.25	.10	.02
□ 633	Dave Hamilton	.25	.10	.02
□ 634	Braves Leaders	1.00	.40	.10
	Eddie Mathews MG			
	Herm Starrette CO			
	Connie Ryan CO			
	Jim Busby CO			
	Ken Silvestri CO			
□ 635	John Edwards	.25	.10	.02
□ 636	Dave Goltz	.25	.10	.02
□ 637	Checklist 5	1.00	.10	.02
□ 638	Ken Sanders	.25	.10	.02
□ 639	Joe Lovitto	.25	.10	.02
□ 640	Milt Pappas	.35	.14	.03
□ 641	Chuck Brinkman	.25	.10	.02
□ 642	Terry Harmon	.25	.10	.02
□ 643	Dodgers Team	.75	.30	.07
□ 644	Wayne Granger	.25	.10	.02
□ 645	Ken Boswell	.25	.10	.02
□ 646	George Foster	1.25	.50	.12
□ 647	Juan Beniquez	.75	.30	.07
□ 648	Terry Crowley	.35	.14	.03

		NRMT	VG-E	GOOD
	(Munson blocking plate)			
□ 649	Fernando Gonzalez	.25	.10	.02
□ 650	Mike Epstein	.25	.10	.02
□ 651	Leron Lee	.25	.10	.02
□ 652	Gail Hopkins	.25	.10	.02
□ 653	Bob Stinson	.25	.10	.02
□ 654A	Jesus Alou (outfield)	.35	.14	.03
□ 654B	Jesus Alou (no position)	6.00	2.40	.60
□ 655	Mike Tyson	.25	.10	.02
□ 656	Adrian Garrett	.25	.10	.02
□ 657	Jim Shellenback	.25	.10	.02
□ 658	Lee Lacy	.35	.14	.03
□ 659	Joe Lis	.25	.10	.02
□ 660	Larry Dierker	.50	.10	.02

1974 Topps Traded

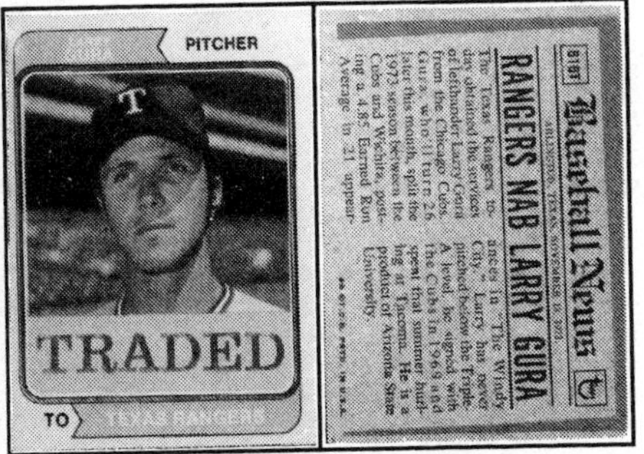

The cards in this 44-card set measure 2 1/2" by 3 1/2". The 1974 Topps Traded set contains 43 player cards and one unnumbered checklist card. The obverses have the word "traded" in block letters and the backs are designed in newspaper style. Card numbers are the same as in the regular set except they are followed by a "T." No known scarcities exist for this set.

		NRMT	VG-E	GOOD
COMPLETE SET (44)		6.50	2.60	.65
COMMON PLAYER		.12	.05	.01
□ 23T	Craig Robinson	.12	.05	.01
□ 42T	Claude Osteen	.20	.08	.02
□ 43T	Jim Wynn	.20	.08	.02
□ 51T	Bobby Heise	.12	.05	.01
□ 59T	Ross Grimsley	.12	.05	.01
□ 62T	Bob Locker	.12	.05	.01
□ 63T	Bill Sudakis	.12	.05	.01
□ 73T	Mike Marshall	.30	.12	.03
□ 123T	Nelson Briles	.20	.08	.02
□ 139T	Aurelio Monteagudo	.12	.05	.01
□ 151T	Diego Segui	.12	.05	.01
□ 165T	Willie Davis	.25	.10	.02
□ 175T	Reggie Cleveland	.12	.05	.01
□ 182T	Lindy McDaniel	.20	.08	.02
□ 186T	Fred Scherman	.12	.05	.01
□ 249T	George Mitterwald	.12	.05	.01
□ 262T	Ed Kirkpatrick	.12	.05	.01
□ 269T	Bob Johnson	.12	.05	.01
□ 270T	Ron Santo	.40	.16	.04
□ 313T	Barry Lersch	.12	.05	.01
□ 319T	Randy Hundley	.20	.08	.02
□ 330T	Juan Marichal	1.50	.60	.15
□ 348T	Pete Richert	.12	.05	.01
□ 373T	John Curtis	.12	.05	.01
□ 390T	Lou Piniella	.35	.14	.03
□ 428T	Gary Sutherland	.12	.05	.01
□ 454T	Kurt Bevacqua	.12	.05	.01
□ 458T	Jim Ray	.12	.05	.01
□ 485T	Felipe Alou	.20	.08	.02
□ 486T	Steve Stone	.20	.08	.02
□ 496T	Tom Murphy	.12	.05	.01
□ 516T	Horacio Pina	.12	.05	.01
□ 534T	Eddie Watt	.12	.05	.01
□ 538T	Cesar Tovar	.12	.05	.01
□ 544T	Ron Schueler	.12	.05	.01
□ 579T	Cecil Upshaw	.12	.05	.01
□ 585T	Merv Rettenmund	.12	.05	.01
□ 612T	Luke Walker	.12	.05	.01
□ 616T	Larry Gura	.20	.08	.02
□ 618T	Jim Mason	.12	.05	.01
□ 630T	Tommie Agee	.15	.06	.01
□ 648T	Terry Crowley	.12	.05	.01
□ 649T	Fernando Gonzalez	.12	.05	.01
□ xxxT	Traded Checklist (unnumbered)	.50	.06	.01

1975 Topps

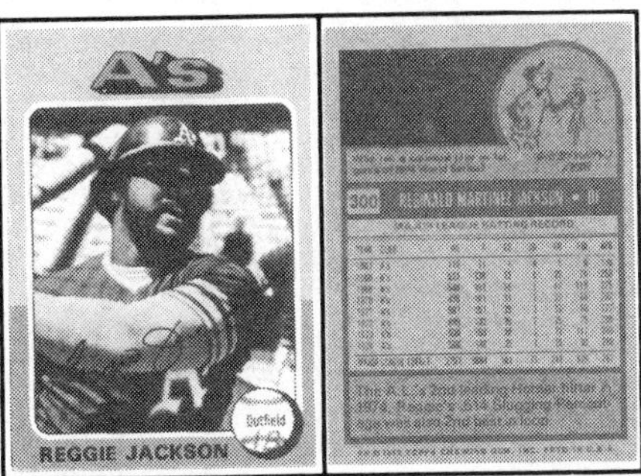

The cards in the 1975 Topps set were issued in two different sizes: a regular standard size (2 1/2" by 3 1/2") and a mini size (2 1/2" by 3 1/8") which was issued as a test in certain areas of the country. The 660-card Topps baseball set for 1975 was radically different in appearance from sets of the preceding years. The most prominent change was the use of a two- color frame surrounding the picture area rather than a single, subdued color. A facsimile autograph appears on the picture, and the backs are printed in red and green on gray. Cards 189-212 depict the MVP's of both leagues from 1951 through 1974. The first seven cards (1-7) feature players breaking records or achieving milestones during the previous season. Cards 306-313 picture league leaders in various statistical categories. Cards 459-466 depict the results of post-season action. Team cards feature a checklist back for players on that team and show a small inset photo of the manager on the front. The Phillies Team card #46 erroneously lists Terry Harmon as #339 instead of #399. This set is quite popular with collectors, at least in part due to the fact that the rookie cards of Robin Yount, George Brett, Jim Rice, Gary Carter, Fred Lynn, and Keith Hernandez are all in the set. Topps minis have the same checklist and are worth approximately double the prices listed below.

		NRMT	VG-E	GOOD
COMPLETE SET (660)		525.00	210.00	50.00
COMMON PLAYER (1-132)		.25	.10	.02
COMMON PLAYER (133-660)		.25	.10	.02
□ 1	RB: Hank Aaron Sets Homer Mark	10.00	2.50	.50
□ 2	RB: Lou Brock 118 Stolen Bases	1.75	.70	.17
□ 3	RB: Bob Gibson 3000th Strikeout	1.75	.70	.17
□ 4	RB: Al Kaline 3000 Hit Club	2.00	.80	.20
□ 5	RB: Nolan Ryan Fans 300 for 3rd Year in a Row	2.25	.90	.22
□ 6	RB: Mike Marshall Hurls 106 Games	.50	.20	.05
□ 7	No Hitters Steve Busby Dick Bosman Nolan Ryan	.60	.24	.06
□ 8	Rogelio Moret	.25	.10	.02

☐	9 Frank Tepedino	.25	.10	.02
☐	10 Willie Davis	.35	.14	.03
☐	11 Bill Melton	.25	.10	.02
☐	12 David Clyde	.25	.10	.02
☐	13 Gene Locklear	.25	.10	.02
☐	14 Milt Wilcox	.25	.10	.02
☐	15 Jose Cardenal	.25	.10	.02
☐	16 Frank Tanana	.60	.24	.06
☐	17 Dave Concepcion	.60	.24	.06
☐	18 Tigers: Team/Mgr. Ralph Houk (checklist back)	.65	.15	.03
☐	19 Jerry Koosman	.50	.20	.05
☐	20 Thurman Munson	4.00	1.60	.40
☐	21 Rollie Fingers	1.50	.60	.15
☐	22 Dave Cash	.25	.10	.02
☐	23 Bill Russell	.35	.14	.03
☐	24 Al Fitzmorris	.25	.10	.02
☐	25 Lee May	.35	.14	.03
☐	26 Dave McNally	.35	.14	.03
☐	27 Ken Reitz	.25	.10	.02
☐	28 Tom Murphy	.25	.10	.02
☐	29 Dave Parker	5.00	2.00	.50
☐	30 Bert Blyleven	.75	.30	.07
☐	31 Dave Rader	.25	.10	.02
☐	32 Reggie Cleveland	.25	.10	.02
☐	33 Dusty Baker	.35	.14	.03
☐	34 Steve Renko	.25	.10	.02
☐	35 Ron Santo	.50	.20	.05
☐	36 Joe Lovitto	.25	.10	.02
☐	37 Dave Freisleben	.25	.10	.02
☐	38 Buddy Bell	.75	.30	.07
☐	39 Andy Thornton	.50	.20	.05
☐	40 Bill Singer	.25	.10	.02
☐	41 Cesar Geronimo	.25	.10	.02
☐	42 Joe Coleman	.25	.10	.02
☐	43 Cleon Jones	.25	.10	.02
☐	44 Pat Dobson	.35	.14	.03
☐	45 Joe Rudi	.35	.14	.03
☐	46 Phillies: Team/Mgr. Danny Ozark (checklist back)	.65	.15	.03
☐	47 Tommy John	1.25	.50	.12
☐	48 Freddie Patek	.35	.14	.03
☐	49 Larry Dierker	.35	.14	.03
☐	50 Brooks Robinson	3.50	1.40	.35
☐	51 Bob Forsch	1.00	.40	.10
☐	52 Darrell Porter	.35	.14	.03
☐	53 Dave Giusti	.25	.10	.02
☐	54 Eric Soderholm	.25	.10	.02
☐	55 Bobby Bonds	.50	.20	.05
☐	56 Rick Wise	.35	.14	.03
☐	57 Dave Johnson	.50	.20	.05
☐	58 Chuck Taylor	.25	.10	.02
☐	59 Ken Henderson	.25	.10	.02
☐	60 Fergie Jenkins	1.00	.40	.10
☐	61 Dave Winfield	11.00	4.50	1.10
☐	62 Fritz Peterson	.25	.10	.02
☐	63 Steve Swisher	.25	.10	.02
☐	64 Dave Chalk	.25	.10	.02
☐	65 Don Gullett	.25	.10	.02
☐	66 Willie Horton	.35	.14	.03
☐	67 Tug McGraw	.50	.20	.05
☐	68 Ron Blomberg	.25	.10	.02
☐	69 John Odom	.25	.10	.02
☐	70 Mike Schmidt	22.00	9.00	2.20
☐	71 Charlie Hough	.50	.20	.05
☐	72 Royals: Team/Mgr. Jack McKeon (checklist back)	.65	.15	.03
☐	73 J.R. Richard	.35	.14	.03
☐	74 Mark Belanger	.35	.14	.03
☐	75 Ted Simmons	.75	.30	.07
☐	76 Ed Sprague	.25	.10	.02
☐	77 Richie Zisk	.35	.14	.03
☐	78 Ray Corbin	.25	.10	.02
☐	79 Gary Matthews	.35	.14	.03
☐	80 Carlton Fisk	2.00	.80	.20
☐	81 Ron Reed	.25	.10	.02
☐	82 Pat Kelly	.25	.10	.02
☐	83 Jim Merritt	.25	.10	.02
☐	84 Enzo Hernandez	.25	.10	.02
☐	85 Bill Bonham	.25	.10	.02
☐	86 Joe Lis	.25	.10	.02
☐	87 George Foster	1.25	.50	.12
☐	88 Tom Egan	.25	.10	.02
☐	89 Jim Ray	.25	.10	.02
☐	90 Rusty Staub	.50	.20	.05
☐	91 Dick Green	.25	.10	.02
☐	92 Cecil Upshaw	.25	.10	.02
☐	93 Dave Lopes	.50	.20	.05
☐	94 Jim Lonborg	.35	.14	.03
☐	95 John Mayberry	.35	.14	.03
☐	96 Mike Cosgrove	.25	.10	.02
☐	97 Earl Williams	.25	.10	.02
☐	98 Rich Folkers	.25	.10	.02
☐	99 Mike Hegan	.25	.10	.02
☐	100 Willie Stargell	3.00	1.20	.30
☐	101 Expos: Team/Mgr. Gene Mauch (checklist back)	.65	.15	.03
☐	102 Joe Decker	.25	.10	.02
☐	103 Rick Miller	.25	.10	.02
☐	104 Bill Madlock	1.25	.50	.12
☐	105 Buzz Capra	.25	.10	.02
☐	106 Mike Hargrove	.50	.20	.05
☐	107 Jim Barr	.25	.10	.02
☐	108 Tom Hall	.25	.10	.02
☐	109 George Hendrick	.35	.14	.03
☐	110 Wilbur Wood	.35	.14	.03
☐	111 Wayne Garrett	.25	.10	.02
☐	112 Larry Hardy	.25	.10	.02
☐	113 Elliott Maddox	.25	.10	.02
☐	114 Dick Lange	.25	.10	.02
☐	115 Joe Ferguson	.25	.10	.02
☐	116 Lerrin LaGrow	.25	.10	.02
☐	117 Orioles: Team/Mgr. Earl Weaver (checklist back)	.65	.15	.03
☐	118 Mike Anderson	.25	.10	.02
☐	119 Tommy Helms	.35	.14	.03
☐	120 Steve Busby (photo actually Fran Healy)	.35	.14	.03
☐	121 Bill North	.25	.10	.02
☐	122 Al Hrabosky	.35	.14	.03
☐	123 Johnny Briggs	.25	.10	.02
☐	124 Jerry Reuss	.35	.14	.03
☐	125 Ken Singleton	.35	.14	.03
☐	126 Checklist 1-132	.90	.10	.02
☐	127 Glenn Borgmann	.25	.10	.02
☐	128 Bill Lee	.35	.14	.03
☐	129 Rick Monday	.35	.14	.03
☐	130 Phil Niekro	2.00	.80	.20
☐	131 Toby Harrah	.35	.14	.03
☐	132 Randy Moffitt	.25	.10	.02
☐	133 Dan Driessen	.35	.14	.03
☐	134 Ron Hodges	.25	.10	.02
☐	135 Charlie Spikes	.25	.10	.02
☐	136 Jim Mason	.25	.10	.02
☐	137 Terry Forster	.35	.14	.03
☐	138 Del Unser	.25	.10	.02
☐	139 Horacio Pina	.25	.10	.02
☐	140 Steve Garvey	6.00	2.40	.60
☐	141 Mickey Stanley	.35	.14	.03
☐	142 Bob Reynolds	.25	.10	.02
☐	143 Cliff Johnson	.25	.10	.02
☐	144 Jim Wohlford	.25	.10	.02
☐	145 Ken Holtzman	.35	.14	.03
☐	146 Padres: Team/Mgr. John McNamara (checklist back)	.65	.15	.03
☐	147 Pedro Garcia	.25	.10	.02
☐	148 Jim Rooker	.25	.10	.02
☐	149 Tim Foli	.25	.10	.02
☐	150 Bob Gibson	2.50	1.00	.25
☐	151 Steve Brye	.25	.10	.02
☐	152 Mario Guerrero	.25	.10	.02
☐	153 Rick Reuschel	.50	.20	.05
☐	154 Mike Lum	.25	.10	.02
☐	155 Jim Bibby	.35	.14	.03
☐	156 Dave Kingman	1.00	.40	.10
☐	157 Pedro Borbon	.25	.10	.02
☐	158 Jerry Grote	.25	.10	.02
☐	159 Steve Arlin	.25	.10	.02
☐	160 Graig Nettles	1.25	.50	.12
☐	161 Stan Bahnsen	.25	.10	.02
☐	162 Willie Montanez	.25	.10	.02
☐	163 Jim Brewer	.25	.10	.02
☐	164 Mickey Rivers	.35	.14	.03
☐	165 Doug Rader	.35	.14	.03
☐	166 Woodie Fryman	.25	.10	.02
☐	167 Rich Coggins	.25	.10	.02
☐	168 Bill Greif	.25	.10	.02
☐	169 Cookie Rojas	.35	.14	.03
☐	170 Bert Campaneris	.35	.14	.03
☐	171 Ed Kirkpatrick	.25	.10	.02
☐	172 Red Sox: Team/Mgr. Darrell Johnson (checklist back)	.65	.15	.03
☐	173 Steve Rogers	.35	.14	.03
☐	174 Bake McBride	.35	.14	.03
☐	175 Don Money	.35	.14	.03
☐	176 Burt Hooton	.35	.14	.03
☐	177 Vic Correll	.25	.10	.02
☐	178 Cesar Tovar	.25	.10	.02
☐	179 Tom Bradley	.25	.10	.02
☐	180 Joe Morgan	3.50	1.40	.35
☐	181 Fred Beene	.25	.10	.02
☐	182 Don Hahn	.25	.10	.02

□ 183 Mel Stottlemyre .... .35 .14 .03
□ 184 Jorge Orta .... .25 .10 .02
□ 185 Steve Carlton .... 5.00 2.00 .50
□ 186 Willie Crawford .... .25 .10 .02
□ 187 Denny Doyle .... .25 .10 .02
□ 188 Tom Griffin .... .25 .10 .02
□ 189 1951 MVP's .... 1.50 .60 .15
Larry (Yogi) Berra
Roy Campanella
(Campy never issued)
□ 190 1952 MVP's .... .50 .20 .05
Bobby Shantz
Hank Bauer
□ 191 1953 MVP's .... .60 .24 .06
Al Rosen
Roy Campanella
□ 192 1954 MVP's .... 1.50 .60 .15
Yogi Berra
Willie Mays
□ 193 1955 MVP's .... 1.50 .60 .15
Yogi Berra
Roy Campanella
(Campy never issued)
□ 194 1956 MVP's .... 3.00 1.20 .30
Mickey Mantle
Don Newcombe
□ 195 1957 MVP's .... 4.50 1.80 .45
Mickey Mantle
Hank Aaron
□ 196 1958 MVP's .... .60 .24 .06
Jackie Jensen
Ernie Banks
□ 197 1959 MVP's .... .60 .24 .06
Nellie Fox
Ernie Banks
□ 198 1960 MVP's .... .75 .30 .07
Roger Maris
Dick Groat
□ 199 1961 MVP's .... 1.00 .40 .10
Roger Maris
Frank Robinson
□ 200 1962 MVP's .... 3.00 1.20 .30
Mickey Mantle
Maury Wills
(Wills never issued)
□ 201 1963 MVP's .... .75 .30 .07
Elston Howard
Sandy Koufax
□ 202 1964 MVP's .... .60 .24 .06
Brooks Robinson
Ken Boyer
□ 203 1965 MVP's .... .75 .30 .07
Zoilo Versalles
Willie Mays
□ 204 1966 MVP's .... .90 .36 .09
Frank Robinson
Bob Clemente
□ 205 1967 MVP's .... .90 .36 .09
Carl Yastrzemski
Orlando Cepeda
□ 206 1968 MVP's .... .60 .24 .06
Denny McLain
Bob Gibson
□ 207 1969 MVP's .... .75 .30 .07
Harmon Killebrew
Willie McCovey
□ 208 1970 MVP's .... .75 .30 .07
Boog Powell
Johnny Bench
□ 209 1971 MVP's .... .50 .20 .05
Vida Blue
Joe Torre
□ 210 1972 MVP's .... .75 .30 .07
Rich Allen
Johnny Bench
□ 211 1973 MVP's .... 3.00 1.20 .30
Reggie Jackson
Pete Rose
□ 212 1974 MVP's .... .60 .24 .06
Jeff Burroughs
Steve Garvey
□ 213 Oscar Gamble .... .35 .14 .03
□ 214 Harry Parker .... .25 .10 .02
□ 215 Bobby Valentine .... .50 .20 .05
□ 216 Giants: Team/Mgr. .... .65 .15 .03
Wes Westrum
(checklist back)
□ 217 Lou Piniella .... .50 .20 .05
□ 218 Jerry Johnson .... .25 .10 .02
□ 219 Ed Herrmann .... .25 .10 .02
□ 220 Don Sutton .... 1.75 .70 .17
□ 221 Aurelio Rodriguez .... .25 .10 .02
□ 222 Dan Spillner .... .35 .14 .03
□ 223 Robin Yount 35.00 14.00 3.50
□ 224 Ramon Hernandez .... .25 .10 .02
□ 225 Bob Grich .... .35 .14 .03
□ 226 Bill Campbell .... .25 .10 .02
□ 227 Bob Watson .... .35 .14 .03
□ 228 George Brett 60.00 24.00 6.00
□ 229 Barry Foote .... .25 .10 .02
□ 230 Jim Hunter .... 2.00 .80 .20
□ 231 Mike Tyson .... .25 .10 .02
□ 232 Diego Segui .... .25 .10 .02
□ 233 Billy Grabarkewitz .... .25 .10 .02
□ 234 Tom Grieve .... .35 .14 .03
□ 235 Jack Billingham .... .25 .10 .02
□ 236 Angels: Team/Mgr. .... .65 .15 .03
Dick Williams
(checklist back)
□ 237 Carl Morton .... .25 .10 .02
□ 238 Dave Duncan .... .25 .10 .02
□ 239 George Stone .... .25 .10 .02
□ 240 Garry Maddox .... .35 .14 .03
□ 241 Dick Tidrow .... .25 .10 .02
□ 242 Jay Johnstone .... .35 .14 .03
□ 243 Jim Kaat .... 1.00 .40 .10
□ 244 Bill Buckner .... .50 .20 .05
□ 245 Mickey Lolich .... .50 .20 .05
□ 246 Cardinals: Team/Mgr. .... .65 .15 .03
Red Schoendienst
(checklist back)
□ 247 Enos Cabell .... .25 .10 .02
□ 248 Randy Jones .... .35 .14 .03
□ 249 Danny Thompson .... .25 .10 .02
□ 250 Ken Brett .... .25 .10 .02
□ 251 Fran Healy .... .25 .10 .02
□ 252 Fred Scherman .... .25 .10 .02
□ 253 Jesus Alou .... .25 .10 .02
□ 254 Mike Torrez .... .35 .14 .03
□ 255 Dwight Evans .... 2.75 1.10 .27
□ 256 Billy Champion .... .25 .10 .02
□ 257 Checklist: 133-264 .... .90 .10 .02
□ 258 Dave LaRoche .... .25 .10 .02
□ 259 Len Randle .... .25 .10 .02
□ 260 Johnny Bench .... 7.50 3.00 .75
□ 261 Andy Hassler .... .25 .10 .02
□ 262 Rowland Office .... .25 .10 .02
□ 263 Jim Perry .... .35 .14 .03
□ 264 John Milner .... .25 .10 .02
□ 265 Ron Bryant .... .25 .10 .02
□ 266 Sandy Alomar .... .25 .10 .02
□ 267 Dick Ruthven .... .25 .10 .02
□ 268 Hal McRae .... .35 .14 .03
□ 269 Doug Rau .... .25 .10 .02
□ 270 Ron Fairly .... .35 .14 .03
□ 271 Jerry Moses .... .25 .10 .02
□ 272 Lynn McGlothen .... .25 .10 .02
□ 273 Steve Braun .... .25 .10 .02
□ 274 Vincente Romo .... .25 .10 .02
□ 275 Paul Blair .... .35 .14 .03
□ 276 White Sox Team/Mgr. .... .65 .15 .03
Chuck Tanner
(checklist back)
□ 277 Frank Taveras .... .25 .10 .02
□ 278 Paul Lindblad .... .25 .10 .02
□ 279 Milt May .... .25 .10 .02
□ 280 Carl Yastrzemski .... 7.50 3.00 .75
□ 281 Jim Slaton .... .25 .10 .02
□ 282 Jerry Morales .... .25 .10 .02
□ 283 Steve Foucault .... .25 .10 .02
□ 284 Ken Griffey .... .60 .24 .06
□ 285 Ellie Rodriguez .... .25 .10 .02
□ 286 Mike Jorgensen .... .25 .10 .02
□ 287 Roric Harrison .... .25 .10 .02
□ 288 Bruce Ellingsen .... .25 .10 .02
□ 289 Ken Rudolph .... .25 .10 .02
□ 290 Jon Matlack .... .35 .14 .03
□ 291 Bill Sudakis .... .25 .10 .02
□ 292 Ron Schueler .... .25 .10 .02
□ 293 Dick Sharon .... .25 .10 .02
□ 294 Geoff Zahn .... .25 .10 .02
□ 295 Vada Pinson .... .60 .24 .06
□ 296 Alan Foster .... .25 .10 .02
□ 297 Craig Kusick .... .25 .10 .02
□ 298 Johnny Grubb .... .25 .10 .02
□ 299 Bucky Dent .... .50 .20 .05
□ 300 Reggie Jackson .... 7.50 3.00 .75
□ 301 Dave Roberts .... .25 .10 .02
□ 302 Rick Burleson .... .50 .20 .05
□ 303 Grant Jackson .... .25 .10 .02
□ 304 Pirates: Team/Mgr. .... .65 .15 .03
Danny Murtaugh
(checklist back)
□ 305 Jim Colborn .... .25 .10 .02
□ 306 Batting Leaders .... .60 .24 .06
Rod Carew
Ralph Garr
□ 307 Home Run Leaders .... .90 .36 .09
Dick Allen
Mike Schmidt

☐ 308 RBI Leaders Jeff Burroughs Johnny Bench	.75	.30	.07
☐ 309 Stolen Base Leaders Bill North Lou Brock	.60	.24	.06
☐ 310 Victory Leaders Jim Hunter Fergie Jenkins Andy Messersmith Phil Niekro	.75	.30	.07
☐ 311 ERA Leaders Jim Hunter Buzz Capra	.60	.24	.06
☐ 312 Strikeout Leaders Nolan Ryan Steve Carlton	2.50	1.00	.25
☐ 313 Leading Firemen Terry Forster Mike Marshall	.50	.20	.05
☐ 314 Buck Martinez	.25	.10	.02
☐ 315 Don Kessinger	.35	.14	.03
☐ 316 Jackie Brown	.25	.10	.02
☐ 317 Joe Lahoud	.25	.10	.02
☐ 318 Ernie McAnally	.25	.10	.02
☐ 319 Johnny Oates	.25	.10	.02
☐ 320 Pete Rose	15.00	6.00	1.50
☐ 321 Rudy May	.25	.10	.02
☐ 322 Ed Goodson	.25	.10	.02
☐ 323 Fred Holdsworth	.25	.10	.02
☐ 324 Ed Kranepool	.35	.14	.03
☐ 325 Tony Oliva	.75	.30	.07
☐ 326 Wayne Twitchell	.25	.10	.02
☐ 327 Jerry Hairston	.25	.10	.02
☐ 328 Sonny Siebert	.35	.14	.03
☐ 329 Ted Kubiak	.25	.10	.02
☐ 330 Mike Marshall	.35	.14	.03
☐ 331 Indians: Team/Mgr. Frank Robinson (checklist back)	.65	.15	.03
☐ 332 Fred Kendall	.25	.10	.02
☐ 333 Dick Drago	.25	.10	.02
☐ 334 Greg Gross	.25	.10	.02
☐ 335 Jim Palmer	3.50	1.40	.35
☐ 336 Rennie Stennett	.25	.10	.02
☐ 337 Kevin Kobel	.25	.10	.02
☐ 338 Rick Stelmaszek	.25	.10	.02
☐ 339 Jim Fregosi	.35	.14	.03
☐ 340 Paul Splittorff	.35	.14	.03
☐ 341 Hal Breeden	.25	.10	.02
☐ 342 Leroy Stanton	.25	.10	.02
☐ 343 Danny Frisella	.25	.10	.02
☐ 344 Ben Oglivie	.35	.14	.03
☐ 345 Clay Carroll	.25	.10	.02
☐ 346 Bobby Darwin	.25	.10	.02
☐ 347 Mike Caldwell	.35	.14	.03
☐ 348 Tony Muser	.25	.10	.02
☐ 349 Ray Sadecki	.25	.10	.02
☐ 350 Bobby Murcer	.50	.20	.05
☐ 351 Bob Boone	.60	.24	.06
☐ 352 Darold Knowles	.25	.10	.02
☐ 353 Luis Melendez	.25	.10	.02
☐ 354 Dick Bosman	.25	.10	.02
☐ 355 Chris Cannizzaro	.25	.10	.02
☐ 356 Rico Petrocelli	.35	.14	.03
☐ 357 Ken Forsch	.25	.10	.02
☐ 358 Al Bumbry	.25	.10	.02
☐ 359 Paul Popovich	.25	.10	.02
☐ 360 George Scott	.35	.14	.03
☐ 361 Dodgers: Team/Mgr. Walter Alston (checklist back)	.75	.25	.04
☐ 362 Steve Hargan	.25	.10	.02
☐ 363 Carmen Fanzone	.25	.10	.02
☐ 364 Doug Bird	.25	.10	.02
☐ 365 Bob Bailey	.25	.10	.02
☐ 366 Ken Sanders	.25	.10	.02
☐ 367 Craig Robinson	.25	.10	.02
☐ 368 Vic Albury	.25	.10	.02
☐ 369 Merv Rettenmund	.25	.10	.02
☐ 370 Tom Seaver	6.50	2.60	.65
☐ 371 Gates Brown	.35	.14	.03
☐ 372 John D'Acquisto	.25	.10	.02
☐ 373 Bill Sharp	.25	.10	.02
☐ 374 Eddie Watt	.25	.10	.02
☐ 375 Roy White	.35	.14	.03
☐ 376 Steve Yeager	.35	.14	.03
☐ 377 Tom Hilgendorf	.25	.10	.02
☐ 378 Derrel Thomas	.25	.10	.02
☐ 379 Bernie Carbo	.25	.10	.02
☐ 380 Sal Bando	.35	.14	.03
☐ 381 John Curtis	.25	.10	.02
☐ 382 Don Baylor	.75	.30	.07
☐ 383 Jim York	.25	.10	.02
☐ 384 Brewers: Team/Mgr. Del Crandall (checklist back)	.65	.15	.03
☐ 385 Dock Ellis	.25	.10	.02
☐ 386 Checklist: 265-396	.90	.10	.02
☐ 387 Jim Spencer	.25	.10	.02
☐ 388 Steve Stone	.35	.14	.03
☐ 389 Tony Solaita	.25	.10	.02
☐ 390 Ron Cey	.60	.24	.06
☐ 391 Don DeMola	.25	.10	.02
☐ 392 Bruce Bochte	.50	.20	.05
☐ 393 Gary Gentry	.25	.10	.02
☐ 394 Larvell Blanks	.25	.10	.02
☐ 395 Bud Harrelson	.35	.14	.03
☐ 396 Fred Norman	.25	.10	.02
☐ 397 Bill Freehan	.50	.20	.05
☐ 398 Elias Sosa	.25	.10	.02
☐ 399 Terry Harmon	.25	.10	.02
☐ 400 Dick Allen	.50	.20	.05
☐ 401 Mike Wallace	.25	.10	.02
☐ 402 Bob Tolan	.35	.14	.03
☐ 403 Tom Buskey	.25	.10	.02
☐ 404 Ted Sizemore	.25	.10	.02
☐ 405 John Montague	.25	.10	.02
☐ 406 Bob Gallagher	.25	.10	.02
☐ 407 Herb Washington	.25	.10	.02
☐ 408 Clyde Wright	.25	.10	.02
☐ 409 Bob Robertson	.25	.10	.02
☐ 410 Mike Cueller (sic, Cuellar)	.35	.14	.03
☐ 411 George Mitterwald	.25	.10	.02
☐ 412 Bill Hands	.25	.10	.02
☐ 413 Marty Pattin	.25	.10	.02
☐ 414 Manny Mota	.35	.14	.03
☐ 415 John Hiller	.35	.14	.03
☐ 416 Larry Lintz	.25	.10	.02
☐ 417 Skip Lockwood	.25	.10	.02
☐ 418 Leo Foster	.25	.10	.02
☐ 419 Dave Goltz	.25	.10	.02
☐ 420 Larry Bowa	.50	.20	.05
☐ 421 Mets: Team/Mgr. Yogi Berra (checklist back)	.75	.25	.04
☐ 422 Brian Downing	.50	.20	.05
☐ 423 Clay Kirby	.25	.10	.02
☐ 424 John Lowenstein	.25	.10	.02
☐ 425 Tito Fuentes	.25	.10	.02
☐ 426 George Medich	.25	.10	.02
☐ 427 Clarence Gaston	.25	.10	.02
☐ 428 Dave Hamilton	.25	.10	.02
☐ 429 Jim Dwyer	.25	.10	.02
☐ 430 Luis Tiant	.50	.20	.05
☐ 431 Rod Gilbreath	.25	.10	.02
☐ 432 Ken Berry	.25	.10	.02
☐ 433 Larry Demery	.25	.10	.02
☐ 434 Bob Locker	.25	.10	.02
☐ 435 Dave Nelson	.25	.10	.02
☐ 436 Ken Frailing	.25	.10	.02
☐ 437 Al Cowens	.35	.14	.03
☐ 438 Don Carrithers	.25	.10	.02
☐ 439 Ed Brinkman	.25	.10	.02
☐ 440 Andy Messersmith	.35	.14	.03
☐ 441 Bobby Heise	.25	.10	.02
☐ 442 Maximino Leon	.25	.10	.02
☐ 443 Twins: Team/Mgr. Frank Quilici (checklist back)	.65	.15	.03
☐ 444 Gene Garber	.25	.10	.02
☐ 445 Felix Millan	.25	.10	.02
☐ 446 Bart Johnson	.25	.10	.02
☐ 447 Terry Crowley	.25	.10	.02
☐ 448 Frank Duffy	.25	.10	.02
☐ 449 Charlie Williams	.25	.10	.02
☐ 450 Willie McCovey	3.00	1.20	.30
☐ 451 Rick Dempsey	.35	.14	.03
☐ 452 Angel Mangual	.25	.10	.02
☐ 453 Claude Osteen	.35	.14	.03
☐ 454 Doug Griffin	.25	.10	.02
☐ 455 Don Wilson	.25	.10	.02
☐ 456 Bob Coluccio	.25	.10	.02
☐ 457 Mario Mendoza	.25	.10	.02
☐ 458 Ross Grimsley	.25	.10	.02
☐ 459 1974 AL Champs A's over Orioles (2B action pictured)	.50	.20	.05
☐ 460 1974 NL Champs Dodgers over Pirates (Taveras/Garvey at 2B)	.75	.30	.07
☐ 461 World Series Game 1 (Reggie Jackson)	1.75	.70	.17
☐ 462 World Series Game 2 (Dodger dugout)	.50	.20	.05
☐ 463 World Series Game 3 (Fingers pitching)	.75	.30	.07
☐ 464 World Series Game 4 (A's batter)	.50	.20	.05

☐ 465 World Series Game 5 ..... .50 .20 .05
(Rudi rounding third)
☐ 466 World Series Summary .. .50 .20 .05
A's do it again;
win third straight
(A's group picture)
☐ 467 Ed Halicki .... .25 .10 .02
☐ 468 Bobby Mitchell .... .25 .10 .02
☐ 469 Tom Dettore .... .25 .10 .02
☐ 470 Jeff Burroughs .... .35 .14 .03
☐ 471 Bob Stinson .... .25 .10 .02
☐ 472 Bruce Dal Canton .... .25 .10 .02
☐ 473 Ken McMullen .... .25 .10 .02
☐ 474 Luke Walker .... .25 .10 .02
☐ 475 Darrell Evans .... .60 .24 .06
☐ 476 Eduardo Figueroa .... .25 .10 .02
☐ 477 Tom Hutton .... .25 .10 .02
☐ 478 Tom Burgmeier .... .25 .10 .02
☐ 479 Ken Boswell .... .25 .10 .02
☐ 480 Carlos May .... .25 .10 .02
☐ 481 Will McEnaney .... .25 .10 .02
☐ 482 Tom McCraw .... .25 .10 .02
☐ 483 Steve Ontiveros .... .25 .10 .02
☐ 484 Glenn Beckert .... .35 .14 .03
☐ 485 Sparky Lyle .... .50 .20 .05
☐ 486 Ray Fosse .... .25 .10 .02
☐ 487 Astros: Team/Mgr. .... .65 .15 .03
Preston Gomez
(checklist back)
☐ 488 Bill Travers .... .25 .10 .02
☐ 489 Cecil Cooper .... 1.00 .40 .10
☐ 490 Reggie Smith .... .50 .20 .05
☐ 491 Doyle Alexander .... .50 .20 .05
☐ 492 Rich Hebner .... .25 .10 .02
☐ 493 Don Stanhouse .... .25 .10 .02
☐ 494 Pete LaCock .... .25 .10 .02
☐ 495 Nelson Briles .... .35 .14 .03
☐ 496 Pepe Frias .... .25 .10 .02
☐ 497 Jim Nettles .... .25 .10 .02
☐ 498 Al Downing .... .35 .14 .03
☐ 499 Marty Perez .... .25 .10 .02
☐ 500 Nolan Ryan .... 6.50 2.60 .65
☐ 501 Bill Robinson .... .35 .14 .03
☐ 502 Pat Bourque .... .25 .10 .02
☐ 503 Fred Stanley .... .25 .10 .02
☐ 504 Buddy Bradford .... .25 .10 .02
☐ 505 Chris Speier .... .35 .14 .03
☐ 506 Leron Lee .... .25 .10 .02
☐ 507 Tom Carroll .... .25 .10 .02
☐ 508 Bob Hansen .... .25 .10 .02
☐ 509 Dave Hilton .... .25 .10 .02
☐ 510 Vida Blue .... .50 .20 .05
☐ 511 Rangers: Team/Mgr. ..... .65 .15 .03
Billy Martin
(checklist back)
☐ 512 Larry Milbourne .... .25 .10 .02
☐ 513 Dick Pole .... .25 .10 .02
☐ 514 Jose Cruz .... .35 .14 .03
☐ 515 Manny Sanguillen .... .35 .14 .03
☐ 516 Don Hood .... .25 .10 .02
☐ 517 Checklist: 397-528 .... .90 .10 .02
☐ 518 Leo Cardenas .... .25 .10 .02
☐ 519 Jim Todd .... .25 .10 .02
☐ 520 Amos Otis .... .50 .20 .05
☐ 521 Dennis Blair .... .25 .10 .02
☐ 522 Gary Sutherland .... .25 .10 .02
☐ 523 Tom Paciorek .... .25 .10 .02
☐ 524 John Doherty .... .25 .10 .02
☐ 525 Tom House .... .35 .14 .03
☐ 526 Larry Hisle .... .35 .14 .03
☐ 527 Mac Scarce .... .25 .10 .02
☐ 528 Eddie Leon .... .25 .10 .02
☐ 529 Gary Thomasson .... .25 .10 .02
☐ 530 Gaylord Perry .... 2.00 .80 .20
☐ 531 Reds: Team/Mgr. .... .75 .25 .04
Sparky Anderson
(checklist back)
☐ 532 Gorman Thomas .... .75 .30 .07
☐ 533 Rudy Meoli .... .25 .10 .02
☐ 534 Alex Johnson .... .25 .10 .02
☐ 535 Gene Tenace .... .35 .14 .03
☐ 536 Bob Moose .... .25 .10 .02
☐ 537 Tommy Harper .... .35 .14 .03
☐ 538 Duffy Dyer .... .25 .10 .02
☐ 539 Jesse Jefferson .... .25 .10 .02
☐ 540 Lou Brock .... 3.00 1.20 .30
☐ 541 Roger Metzger .... .25 .10 .02
☐ 542 Pete Broberg .... .25 .10 .02
☐ 543 Larry Biittner .... .25 .10 .02
☐ 544 Steve Mingori .... .25 .10 .02
☐ 545 Billy Williams .... 2.25 .90 .22
☐ 546 John Knox .... .25 .10 .02
☐ 547 Von Joshua .... .25 .10 .02
☐ 548 Charlie Sands .... .25 .10 .02
☐ 549 Bill Butler .... .25 .10 .02
☐ 550 Ralph Garr .... .25 .10 .02
☐ 551 Larry Christenson .... .25 .10 .02
☐ 552 Jack Brohamer .... .25 .10 .02
☐ 553 John Boccabella .... .25 .10 .02
☐ 554 Rich Gossage .... 1.00 .40 .10
☐ 555 Al Oliver .... .75 .30 .07
☐ 556 Tim Johnson .... .25 .10 .02
☐ 557 Larry Gura .... .35 .14 .03
☐ 558 Dave Roberts .... .25 .10 .02
☐ 559 Bob Montgomery .... .25 .10 .02
☐ 560 Tony Perez .... 1.00 .40 .10
☐ 561 A's: Team/Mgr. .... .65 .15 .03
Alvin Dark
(checklist back)
☐ 562 Gary Nolan .... .25 .10 .02
☐ 563 Wilbur Howard .... .25 .10 .02
☐ 564 Tommy Davis .... .35 .14 .03
☐ 565 Joe Torre .... .60 .24 .06
☐ 566 Ray Burris .... .25 .10 .02
☐ 567 Jim Sundberg .... .60 .24 .06
☐ 568 Dale Murray .... .25 .10 .02
☐ 569 Frank White .... .75 .30 .07
☐ 570 Jim Wynn .... .35 .14 .03
☐ 571 Dave Lemanczyk .... .25 .10 .02
☐ 572 Roger Nelson .... .25 .10 .02
☐ 573 Orlando Pena .... .25 .10 .02
☐ 574 Tony Taylor .... .25 .10 .02
☐ 575 Gene Clines .... .25 .10 .02
☐ 576 Phil Roof .... .25 .10 .02
☐ 577 John Morris .... .25 .10 .02
☐ 578 Dave Tomlin .... .25 .10 .02
☐ 579 Skip Pitlock .... .25 .10 .02
☐ 580 Frank Robinson .... 3.00 1.20 .30
☐ 581 Darrel Chaney .... .25 .10 .02
☐ 582 Eduardo Rodriguez .... .25 .10 .02
☐ 583 Andy Etchebarren .... .25 .10 .02
☐ 584 Mike Garman .... .25 .10 .02
☐ 585 Chris Chambliss .... .50 .20 .05
☐ 586 Tim McCarver .... .50 .20 .05
☐ 587 Chris Ward .... .25 .10 .02
☐ 588 Rick Auerbach .... .25 .10 .02
☐ 589 Braves: Team/Mgr. .... .65 .15 .03
Clyde King
(checklist back)
☐ 590 Cesar Cedeno .... .35 .14 .03
☐ 591 Glenn Abbott .... .25 .10 .02
☐ 592 Balor Moore .... .25 .10 .02
☐ 593 Gene Lamont .... .25 .10 .02
☐ 594 Jim Fuller .... .25 .10 .02
☐ 595 Joe Niekro .... .50 .20 .05
☐ 596 Ollie Brown .... .25 .10 .02
☐ 597 Winston Llenas .... .25 .10 .02
☐ 598 Bruce Kison .... .25 .10 .02
☐ 599 Nate Colbert .... .25 .10 .02
☐ 600 Rod Carew .... 5.00 2.00 .50
☐ 601 Juan Beniquez .... .25 .10 .02
☐ 602 John Vukovich .... .25 .10 .02
☐ 603 Lew Krausse .... .25 .10 .02
☐ 604 Oscar Zamora .... .25 .10 .02
☐ 605 John Ellis .... .25 .10 .02
☐ 606 Bruce Miller .... .25 .10 .02
☐ 607 Jim Holt .... .25 .10 .02
☐ 608 Gene Michael .... .35 .14 .03
☐ 609 Ellie Hendricks .... .25 .10 .02
☐ 610 Ron Hunt .... .25 .10 .02
☐ 611 Yankees: Team/Mgr. ..... .75 .25 .04
Bill Virdon
(checklist back)
☐ 612 Terry Hughes .... .25 .10 .02
☐ 613 Bill Parsons .... .25 .10 .02
☐ 614 Rookie Pitchers .... .35 .14 .03
Jack Kucek
Dyar Miller
Vern Ruhle
Paul Siebert
☐ 615 Rookie Pitchers .... 1.00 .40 .10
Pat Darcy
Dennis Leonard
Tom Underwood
Hank Webb
☐ 616 Rookie Outfielders 30.00 12.00 3.00
Dave Augustine
Pepe Mangual
Jim Rice
John Scott
☐ 617 Rookie Infielders .... 1.75 .70 .17
Mike Cubbage
Doug DeCinces
Reggie Sanders
Manny Trillo
☐ 618 Rookie Pitchers .... 2.75 1.10 .27
Jamie Easterly
Tom Johnson
Scott McGregor
Rick Rhoden

☐ 619	Rookie Outfielders	.35	.14	.03
	Benny Ayala			
	Nyls Nyman			
	Tommy Smith			
	Jerry Turner			
☐ 620	Rookie Catcher/OF	40.00	16.00	4.00
	Gary Carter			
	Marc Hill			
	Danny Meyer			
	Leon Roberts			
☐ 621	Rookie Pitchers	.90	.36	.09
	John Denny			
	Rawly Eastwick			
	Jim Kern			
	Juan Veintidos			
☐ 622	Rookie Outfielders	12.00	5.00	1.20
	Ed Armbrister			
	Fred Lynn			
	Tom Poquette			
	Terry Whitfield			
☐ 623	Rookie Infielders	25.00	10.00	2.50
	Phil Garner			
	Keith Hernandez			
	(sic, bats right)			
	Bob Sheldon			
	Tom Veryzer			
☐ 624	Rookie Pitchers	.35	.14	.03
	Doug Konieczny			
	Gary Lavelle			
	Jim Otten			
	Eddie Solomon			
☐ 625	Boog Powell	.50	.20	.05
☐ 626	Larry Haney	.35	.14	.03
	(photo actually			
	Dave Duncan)			
☐ 627	Tom Walker	.25	.10	.02
☐ 628	Ron LeFlore	.50	.20	.05
☐ 629	Joe Hoerner	.25	.10	.02
☐ 630	Greg Luzinski	.60	.24	.06
☐ 631	Lee Lacy	.35	.14	.03
☐ 632	Morris Nettles	.25	.10	.02
☐ 633	Paul Casanova	.25	.10	.02
☐ 634	Cy Acosta	.25	.10	.02
☐ 635	Chuck Dobson	.25	.10	.02
☐ 636	Charlie Moore	.25	.10	.02
☐ 637	Ted Martinez	.25	.10	.02
☐ 638	Cubs: Team/Mgr.	.65	.15	.03
	Jim Marshall			
	(checklist back)			
☐ 639	Steve Kline	.25	.10	.02
☐ 640	Harmon Killebrew	3.00	1.20	.30
☐ 641	Jim Northrup	.35	.14	.03
☐ 642	Mike Phillips	.25	.10	.02
☐ 643	Brent Strom	.25	.10	.02
☐ 644	Bill Fahey	.25	.10	.02
☐ 645	Danny Cater	.25	.10	.02
☐ 646	Checklist: 529-660	.90	.10	.02
☐ 647	Claudell Washington	2.75	1.10	.27
☐ 648	Dave Pagan	.25	.10	.02
☐ 649	Jack Heidemann	.25	.10	.02
☐ 650	Dave May	.25	.10	.02
☐ 651	John Morlan	.25	.10	.02
☐ 652	Lindy McDaniel	.35	.14	.03
☐ 653	Lee Richard	.25	.10	.02
☐ 654	Jerry Terrell	.25	.10	.02
☐ 655	Rico Carty	.35	.14	.03
☐ 656	Bill Plummer	.25	.10	.02
☐ 657	Bob Oliver	.25	.10	.02
☐ 658	Vic Harris	.25	.10	.02
☐ 659	Bob Apodaca	.25	.10	.02
☐ 660	Hank Aaron	10.00	2.50	.50

1976 Topps

The 1976 Topps set of 660 cards (measuring 2 1/2" by 3 1/2") is known for its sharp color photographs and interesting presentation of subjects. Team cards feature a checklist back for players on that team and show a small inset photo of the manager on the front. A "Father and Son" series (66-70) spotlights five Major Leaguers whose fathers also made the "Big Show." Other subseries include "All Time All Stars" (341-350), "Record Breakers" from the previous season (1-6), League Leaders (191-205), Post-season cards (461-462), and Rookie Prospects (589-599).

		NRMT	VG-E	GOOD
	COMPLETE SET (660)	275.00	110.00	27.00
	COMMON PLAYER (1-660)	.18	.08	.01
☐ 1	RB: Hank Aaron	8.00	2.00	.40
	Most RBI's, 2262			
☐ 2	RB: Bobby Bonds	.35	.14	.03
	Most leadoff HR's 32;			
	plus three seasons			
	30 homers/30 steals			
☐ 3	RB: Mickey Lolich	.35	.14	.03
	Lefthander, Most			
	Strikeouts, 2679			
☐ 4	RB: Dave Lopes	.25	.10	.02
	Most Consecutive			
	SB attempts, 38			
☐ 5	RB: Tom Seaver	1.50	.60	.15
	Most Cons. seasons			
	with 200 SO's, 8			
☐ 6	RB: Rennie Stennett	.25	.10	.02
	Most Hits in a 9			
	inning game, 7			
☐ 7	Jim Umbarger	.18	.08	.01
☐ 8	Tito Fuentes	.18	.08	.01
☐ 9	Paul Lindblad	.18	.08	.01
☐ 10	Lou Brock	2.50	1.00	.25
☐ 11	Jim Hughes	.18	.08	.01
☐ 12	Richie Zisk	.25	.10	.02
☐ 13	John Wockenfuss	.18	.08	.01
☐ 14	Gene Garber	.18	.08	.01
☐ 15	George Scott	.25	.10	.02
☐ 16	Bob Apodaca	.18	.08	.01
☐ 17	New York Yankees	1.00	.25	.04
	Team Card			
	(checklist back)			
☐ 18	Dale Murray	.18	.08	.01
☐ 19	George Brett	16.00	6.50	1.60
☐ 20	Bob Watson	.25	.10	.02
☐ 21	Dave LaRoche	.18	.08	.01
☐ 22	Bill Russell	.25	.10	.02
☐ 23	Brian Downing	.35	.14	.03
☐ 24	Cesar Geronimo	.18	.08	.01
☐ 25	Mike Torrez	.25	.10	.02
☐ 26	Andy Thornton	.25	.10	.02
☐ 27	Ed Figueroa	.18	.08	.01
☐ 28	Dusty Baker	.35	.14	.03
☐ 29	Rick Burleson	.25	.10	.02
☐ 30	John Montefusco	.35	.14	.03
☐ 31	Len Randle	.18	.08	.01
☐ 32	Danny Frisella	.18	.08	.01
☐ 33	Bill North	.18	.08	.01
☐ 34	Mike Garman	.18	.08	.01
☐ 35	Tony Oliva	.75	.30	.07
☐ 36	Frank Taveras	.18	.08	.01
☐ 37	John Hiller	.25	.10	.02
☐ 38	Garry Maddox	.25	.10	.02
☐ 39	Pete Broberg	.18	.08	.01
☐ 40	Dave Kingman	.75	.30	.07
☐ 41	Tippy Martinez	.35	.14	.03
☐ 42	Barry Foote	.18	.08	.01
☐ 43	Paul Splittorff	.25	.10	.02
☐ 44	Doug Rader	.35	.14	.03
☐ 45	Boog Powell	.50	.20	.05
☐ 46	Dodgers Team	.75	.20	.04
	(checklist back)			
☐ 47	Jesse Jefferson	.18	.08	.01
☐ 48	Dave Concepcion	.50	.20	.05
☐ 49	Dave Duncan	.18	.08	.01
☐ 50	Fred Lynn	2.25	.90	.22
☐ 51	Ray Burris	.18	.08	.01
☐ 52	Dave Chalk	.18	.08	.01
☐ 53	Mike Beard	.18	.08	.01

☐ 54	Dave Radar	.18	.08	.01
☐ 55	Gaylord Perry	1.75	.70	.17
☐ 56	Bob Tolan	.18	.08	.01
☐ 57	Phil Garner	.25	.10	.02
☐ 58	Ron Reed	.18	.08	.01
☐ 59	Larry Hisle	.25	.10	.02
☐ 60	Jerry Reuss	.25	.10	.02
☐ 61	Ron LeFlore	.25	.10	.02
☐ 62	Johnny Oates	.18	.08	.01
☐ 63	Bobby Darwin	.18	.08	.01
☐ 64	Jerry Koosman	.50	.20	.05
☐ 65	Chris Chambliss	.35	.14	.03
☐ 66	Father and Son Gus Bell Buddy Bell	.35	.14	.03
☐ 67	Father and Son Ray Boone Bob Boone	.25	.10	.02
☐ 68	Father and Son Joe Coleman Joe Coleman Jr.	.25	.10	.02
☐ 69	Father and Son Jim Hegan Mike Hegan	.25	.10	.02
☐ 70	Father and Son Roy Smalley Roy Smalley Jr.	.25	.10	.02
☐ 71	Steve Rogers	.25	.10	.02
☐ 72	Hal McRae	.35	.14	.03
☐ 73	Baltimore Orioles Team Card (checklist back)	.65	.15	.03
☐ 74	Oscar Gamble	.25	.10	.02
☐ 75	Larry Dierker	.25	.10	.02
☐ 76	Willie Crawford	.18	.08	.01
☐ 77	Pedro Borbon	.18	.08	.01
☐ 78	Cecil Cooper	.90	.36	.09
☐ 79	Jerry Morales	.18	.08	.01
☐ 80	Jim Kaat	.75	.30	.07
☐ 81	Darrell Evans	.60	.24	.06
☐ 82	Von Joshua	.18	.08	.01
☐ 83	Jim Spencer	.18	.08	.01
☐ 84	Brent Strom	.18	.08	.01
☐ 85	Mickey Rivers	.25	.10	.02
☐ 86	Mike Tyson	.18	.08	.01
☐ 87	Tom Burgmeier	.18	.08	.01
☐ 88	Duffy Dyer	.18	.08	.01
☐ 89	Vern Ruhle	.18	.08	.01
☐ 90	Sal Bando	.35	.14	.03
☐ 91	Tom Hutton	.18	.08	.01
☐ 92	Eduardo Rodriguez	.18	.08	.01
☐ 93	Mike Phillips	.18	.08	.01
☐ 94	Jim Dwyer	.18	.08	.01
☐ 95	Brooks Robinson	2.50	1.00	.25
☐ 96	Doug Bird	.18	.08	.01
☐ 97	Wilbur Howard	.18	.08	.01
☐ 98	Dennis Eckersley	4.00	1.60	.40
☐ 99	Lee Lacy	.25	.10	.02
☐ 100	Jim Hunter	2.00	.80	.20
☐ 101	Pete LaCock	.18	.08	.01
☐ 102	Jim Willoughby	.18	.08	.01
☐ 103	Biff Pocoroba	.18	.08	.01
☐ 104	Reds Team (checklist back)	.65	.15	.03
☐ 105	Gary Lavelle	.25	.10	.02
☐ 106	Tom Grieve	.35	.14	.03
☐ 107	Dave Roberts	.18	.08	.01
☐ 108	Don Kirkwood	.18	.08	.01
☐ 109	Larry Lintz	.18	.08	.01
☐ 110	Carlos May	.18	.08	.01
☐ 111	Danny Thompson	.18	.08	.01
☐ 112	Kent Tekulve	1.00	.40	.10
☐ 113	Gary Sutherland	.18	.08	.01
☐ 114	Jay Johnstone	.35	.14	.03
☐ 115	Ken Holtzman	.25	.10	.02
☐ 116	Charlie Moore	.18	.08	.01
☐ 117	Mike Jorgensen	.18	.08	.01
☐ 118	Red Sox Team (checklist back)	.65	.15	.03
☐ 119	Checklist 1-132	.80	.10	.02
☐ 120	Rusty Staub	.50	.20	.05
☐ 121	Tony Solaita	.18	.08	.01
☐ 122	Mike Cosgrove	.18	.08	.01
☐ 123	Walt Williams	.18	.08	.01
☐ 124	Doug Rau	.18	.08	.01
☐ 125	Don Baylor	.60	.24	.06
☐ 126	Tom Dettore	.18	.08	.01
☐ 127	Larvell Blanks	.18	.08	.01
☐ 128	Ken Griffey	.35	.14	.03
☐ 129	Andy Etchebarren	.18	.08	.01
☐ 130	Luis Tiant	.50	.20	.05
☐ 131	Bill Stein	.18	.08	.01
☐ 132	Don Hood	.18	.08	.01
☐ 133	Gary Matthews	.35	.14	.03
☐ 134	Mike Ivie	.18	.08	.01
☐ 135	Bake McBride	.25	.10	.02
☐ 136	Dave Goltz	.18	.08	.01
☐ 137	Bill Robinson	.25	.10	.02
☐ 138	Lerrin LaGrow	.18	.08	.01
☐ 139	Gorman Thomas	.50	.20	.05
☐ 140	Vida Blue	.35	.14	.03
☐ 141	Larry Parrish	1.50	.60	.15
☐ 142	Dick Drago	.18	.08	.01
☐ 143	Jerry Grote	.18	.08	.01
☐ 144	Al Fitzmorris	.18	.08	.01
☐ 145	Larry Bowa	.50	.20	.05
☐ 146	George Medich	.18	.08	.01
☐ 147	Astros Team (checklist back)	.65	.15	.03
☐ 148	Stan Thomas	.18	.08	.01
☐ 149	Tommy Davis	.35	.14	.03
☐ 150	Steve Garvey	4.50	1.80	.45
☐ 151	Bill Bonham	.18	.08	.01
☐ 152	Leroy Stanton	.18	.08	.01
☐ 153	Buzz Capra	.18	.08	.01
☐ 154	Bucky Dent	.35	.14	.03
☐ 155	Jack Billingham	.18	.08	.01
☐ 156	Rico Carty	.25	.10	.02
☐ 157	Mike Caldwell	.25	.10	.02
☐ 158	Ken Reitz	.18	.08	.01
☐ 159	Jerry Terrell	.18	.08	.01
☐ 160	Dave Winfield	6.00	2.40	.60
☐ 161	Bruce Kison	.18	.08	.01
☐ 162	Jack Pierce	.18	.08	.01
☐ 163	Jim Slaton	.18	.08	.01
☐ 164	Pepe Mangual	.18	.08	.01
☐ 165	Gene Tenace	.25	.10	.02
☐ 166	Skip Lockwood	.18	.08	.01
☐ 167	Freddie Patek	.18	.08	.01
☐ 168	Tom Hilgendorf	.18	.08	.01
☐ 169	Graig Nettles	1.00	.40	.10
☐ 170	Rick Wise	.25	.10	.02
☐ 171	Greg Gross	.18	.08	.01
☐ 172	Rangers Team (checklist back)	.65	.15	.03
☐ 173	Steve Swisher	.18	.08	.01
☐ 174	Charlie Hough	.35	.14	.03
☐ 175	Ken Singleton	.35	.14	.03
☐ 176	Dick Lange	.18	.08	.01
☐ 177	Marty Perez	.18	.08	.01
☐ 178	Tom Buskey	.18	.08	.01
☐ 179	George Foster	1.00	.40	.10
☐ 180	Rich Gossage	1.00	.40	.10
☐ 181	Willie Montanez	.18	.08	.01
☐ 182	Harry Rasmussen	.18	.08	.01
☐ 183	Steve Braun	.18	.08	.01
☐ 184	Bill Greif	.18	.08	.01
☐ 185	Dave Parker	3.00	1.20	.30
☐ 186	Tom Walker	.18	.08	.01
☐ 187	Pedro Garcia	.18	.08	.01
☐ 188	Fred Scherman	.18	.08	.01
☐ 189	Claudell Washington	.50	.20	.05
☐ 190	Jon Matlack	.25	.10	.02
☐ 191	NL Batting Leaders Bill Madlock Ted Simmons Manny Sanguillen	.35	.14	.03
☐ 192	AL Batting Leaders Rod Carew Fred Lynn Thurman Munson	1.50	.60	.15
☐ 193	NL Home Run Leaders Mike Schmidt Dave Kingman Greg Luzinski	.75	.30	.07
☐ 194	AL Home Run Leaders Reggie Jackson George Scott John Mayberry	.75	.30	.07
☐ 195	NL RBI Leaders Greg Luzinski Johnny Bench Tony Perez	.60	.24	.06
☐ 196	AL RBI Leaders George Scott John Mayberry Fred Lynn	.35	.14	.03
☐ 197	NL Steals Leaders Dave Lopes Joe Morgan Lou Brock	.75	.30	.07
☐ 198	AL Steals Leaders Mickey Rivers Claudell Washington Amos Otis	.35	.14	.03
☐ 199	NL Victory Leaders Tom Seaver Randy Jones Andy Messersmith	.50	.20	.05
☐ 200	AL Victory Leaders	.75	.30	.07

Jim Hunter			
Jim Palmer			
Vida Blue			
☐ 201 NL ERA Leaders	.50	.20	.05
Randy Jones			
Andy Messersmith			
Tom Seaver			
☐ 202 AL ERA Leaders	1.00	.40	.10
Jim Palmer			
Jim Hunter			
Dennis Eckersley			
☐ 203 NL Strikeout Leaders	.50	.20	.05
Tom Seaver			
John Montefusco			
Andy Messersmith			
☐ 204 AL Strikeout Leaders	.35	.14	.03
Frank Tanana			
Bert Blyleven			
Gaylord Perry			
☐ 205 Leading Firemen	.35	.14	.03
Al Hrabosky			
Rich Gossage			
☐ 206 Manny Trillo	.18	.08	.01
☐ 207 Andy Hassler	.18	.08	.01
☐ 208 Mike Lum	.18	.08	.01
☐ 209 Alan Ashby	.50	.20	.05
☐ 210 Lee May	.25	.10	.02
☐ 211 Clay Carroll	.18	.08	.01
☐ 212 Pat Kelly	.18	.08	.01
☐ 213 Dave Heaverlo	.18	.08	.01
☐ 214 Eric Soderholm	.18	.08	.01
☐ 215 Reggie Smith	.35	.14	.03
☐ 216 Expos Team (checklist back)	.65	.15	.03
☐ 217 Dave Freisleben	.18	.08	.01
☐ 218 John Knox	.18	.08	.01
☐ 219 Tom Murphy	.18	.08	.01
☐ 220 Manny Sanguillen	.25	.10	.02
☐ 221 Jim Todd	.18	.08	.01
☐ 222 Wayne Garrett	.18	.08	.01
☐ 223 Ollie Brown	.18	.08	.01
☐ 224 Jim York	.18	.08	.01
☐ 225 Roy White	.25	.10	.02
☐ 226 Jim Sundberg	.25	.10	.02
☐ 227 Oscar Zamora	.18	.08	.01
☐ 228 John Hale	.18	.08	.01
☐ 229 Jerry Remy	.35	.14	.03
☐ 230 Carl Yastrzemski	6.50	2.60	.65
☐ 231 Tom House	.25	.10	.02
☐ 232 Frank Duffy	.18	.08	.01
☐ 233 Grant Jackson	.18	.08	.01
☐ 234 Mike Sadek	.18	.08	.01
☐ 235 Bert Blyleven	.75	.30	.07
☐ 236 Kansas City Royals Team Card (checklist back)	.65	.15	.03
☐ 237 Dave Hamilton	.18	.08	.01
☐ 238 Larry Biittner	.18	.08	.01
☐ 239 John Curtis	.18	.08	.01
☐ 240 Pete Rose	15.00	6.00	1.50
☐ 241 Hector Torres	.18	.08	.01
☐ 242 Dan Meyer	.18	.08	.01
☐ 243 Jim Rooker	.18	.08	.01
☐ 244 Bill Sharp	.18	.08	.01
☐ 245 Felix Millan	.18	.08	.01
☐ 246 Cesar Tovar	.18	.08	.01
☐ 247 Terry Harmon	.18	.08	.01
☐ 248 Dick Tidrow	.18	.08	.01
☐ 249 Cliff Johnson	.18	.08	.01
☐ 250 Fergie Jenkins	.75	.30	.07
☐ 251 Rick Monday	.25	.10	.02
☐ 252 Tim Nordbrook	.18	.08	.01
☐ 253 Bill Buckner	.35	.14	.03
☐ 254 Rudy Meoli	.18	.08	.01
☐ 255 Fritz Peterson	.18	.08	.01
☐ 256 Rowland Office	.18	.08	.01
☐ 257 Ross Grimsley	.18	.08	.01
☐ 258 Nyls Nyman	.18	.08	.01
☐ 259 Darrel Chaney	.18	.08	.01
☐ 260 Steve Busby	.25	.10	.02
☐ 261 Gary Thomasson	.18	.08	.01
☐ 262 Checklist 133-264	.80	.10	.02
☐ 263 Lyman Bostock	.50	.20	.05
☐ 264 Steve Renko	.18	.08	.01
☐ 265 Willie Davis	.25	.10	.02
☐ 266 Alan Foster	.18	.08	.01
☐ 267 Aurelio Rodriguez	.18	.08	.01
☐ 268 Del Unser	.18	.08	.01
☐ 269 Rick Austin	.18	.08	.01
☐ 270 Willie Stargell	3.00	1.20	.30
☐ 271 Jim Lonborg	.25	.10	.02
☐ 272 Rick Dempsey	.25	.10	.02
☐ 273 Joe Niekro	.35	.14	.03
☐ 274 Tommy Harper	.25	.10	.02
☐ 275 Rick Manning	.25	.10	.02
☐ 276 Mickey Scott	.18	.08	.01
☐ 277 Cubs Team (checklist back)	.65	.15	.03
☐ 278 Bernie Carbo	.18	.08	.01
☐ 279 Roy Howell	.18	.08	.01
☐ 280 Burt Hooton	.18	.08	.01
☐ 281 Dave May	.18	.08	.01
☐ 282 Dan Osborn	.18	.08	.01
☐ 283 Merv Rettenmund	.18	.08	.01
☐ 284 Steve Ontiveros	.18	.08	.01
☐ 285 Mike Cuellar	.25	.10	.02
☐ 286 Jim Wohlford	.18	.08	.01
☐ 287 Pete Mackanin	.18	.08	.01
☐ 288 Bill Campbell	.18	.08	.01
☐ 289 Enzo Hernandez	.18	.08	.01
☐ 290 Ted Simmons	.75	.30	.07
☐ 291 Ken Sanders	.18	.08	.01
☐ 292 Leon Roberts	.18	.08	.01
☐ 293 Bill Castro	.18	.08	.01
☐ 294 Ed Kirkpatrick	.18	.08	.01
☐ 295 Dave Cash	.18	.08	.01
☐ 296 Pat Dobson	.25	.10	.02
☐ 297 Roger Metzger	.18	.08	.01
☐ 298 Dick Bosman	.18	.08	.01
☐ 299 Champ Summers	.18	.08	.01
☐ 300 Johnny Bench	5.50	2.20	.55
☐ 301 Jackie Brown	.18	.08	.01
☐ 302 Rick Miller	.18	.08	.01
☐ 303 Steve Foucault	.18	.08	.01
☐ 304 Angels Team (checklist back)	.65	.15	.03
☐ 305 Andy Messersmith	.25	.10	.02
☐ 306 Rod Gilbreath	.18	.08	.01
☐ 307 Al Bumbry	.18	.08	.01
☐ 308 Jim Barr	.18	.08	.01
☐ 309 Bill Melton	.18	.08	.01
☐ 310 Randy Jones	.25	.10	.02
☐ 311 Cookie Rojas	.25	.10	.02
☐ 312 Don Carrithers	.18	.08	.01
☐ 313 Dan Ford	.25	.10	.02
☐ 314 Ed Kranepool	.25	.10	.02
☐ 315 Al Hrabosky	.25	.10	.02
☐ 316 Robin Yount	7.50	3.00	.75
☐ 317 John Candelaria	3.00	1.20	.30
☐ 318 Bob Boone	.50	.20	.05
☐ 319 Larry Gura	.25	.10	.02
☐ 320 Willie Horton	.25	.10	.02
☐ 321 Jose Cruz	.35	.14	.03
☐ 322 Glenn Abbott	.18	.08	.01
☐ 323 Rob Sperring	.18	.08	.01
☐ 324 Jim Bibby	.25	.10	.02
☐ 325 Tony Perez	.75	.30	.07
☐ 326 Dick Pole	.18	.08	.01
☐ 327 Dave Moates	.18	.08	.01
☐ 328 Carl Morton	.18	.08	.01
☐ 329 Joe Ferguson	.18	.08	.01
☐ 330 Nolan Ryan	5.50	2.20	.55
☐ 331 San Diego Padres Team Card (checklist back)	.65	.15	.03
☐ 332 Charlie Williams	.18	.08	.01
☐ 333 Bob Coluccio	.18	.08	.01
☐ 334 Dennis Leonard	.25	.10	.02
☐ 335 Bob Grich	.35	.14	.03
☐ 336 Vic Albury	.18	.08	.01
☐ 337 Bud Harrelson	.25	.10	.02
☐ 338 Bob Bailey	.18	.08	.01
☐ 339 John Denny	.35	.14	.03
☐ 340 Jim Rice	8.50	3.50	.85
☐ 341 All-Time 1B Lou Gehrig	2.50	1.00	.25
☐ 342 All-Time 2B Rogers Hornsby	1.50	.60	.15
☐ 343 All-Time 3B Pie Traynor	.75	.30	.07
☐ 344 All-Time SS Honus Wagner	1.50	.60	.15
☐ 345 All-Time OF Babe Ruth	4.50	1.80	.45
☐ 346 All-Time OF Ty Cobb	3.00	1.20	.30
☐ 347 All-Time OF Ted Williams	3.00	1.20	.30
☐ 348 All-Time C Mickey Cochrane	.75	.30	.07
☐ 349 All-Time RHP Walter Johnson	1.50	.60	.15
☐ 350 All-Time LHP Lefty Grove	1.25	.50	.12
☐ 351 Randy Hundley	.18	.08	.01
☐ 352 Dave Giusti	.18	.08	.01
☐ 353 Sixto Lezcano	.25	.10	.02
☐ 354 Ron Blomberg	.18	.08	.01
☐ 355 Steve Carlton	4.00	1.60	.40
☐ 356 Ted Martinez	.18	.08	.01

□ 357 Ken Forsch	.25	.10	.02
□ 358 Buddy Bell	.50	.20	.05
□ 359 Rick Reuschel	.50	.20	.05
□ 360 Jeff Burroughs	.25	.10	.02
□ 361 Detroit Tigers Team Card (checklist back)	.65	.15	.03
□ 362 Will McEnaney	.18	.08	.01
□ 363 Dave Collins	.75	.30	.07
□ 364 Elias Sosa	.18	.08	.01
□ 365 Carlton Fisk	1.25	.50	.12
□ 366 Bobby Valentine	.35	.14	.03
□ 367 Bruce Miller	.18	.08	.01
□ 368 Wilbur Wood	.25	.10	.02
□ 369 Frank White	.50	.20	.05
□ 370 Ron Cey	.50	.20	.05
□ 371 Ellie Hendricks	.18	.08	.01
□ 372 Rick Baldwin	.18	.08	.01
□ 373 Johnny Briggs	.18	.08	.01
□ 374 Dan Warthen	.18	.08	.01
□ 375 Ron Fairly	.25	.10	.02
□ 376 Rich Hebner	.25	.10	.02
□ 377 Mike Hegan	.18	.08	.01
□ 378 Steve Stone	.25	.10	.02
□ 379 Ken Boswell	.18	.08	.01
□ 380 Bobby Bonds	.35	.14	.03
□ 381 Denny Doyle	.18	.08	.01
□ 382 Matt Alexander	.18	.08	.01
□ 383 John Ellis	.18	.08	.01
□ 384 Phillies Team (checklist back)	.65	.15	.03
□ 385 Mickey Lolich	.35	.14	.03
□ 386 Ed Goodson	.18	.08	.01
□ 387 Mike Miley	.18	.08	.01
□ 388 Stan Perzanowski	.18	.08	.01
□ 389 Glenn Adams	.18	.08	.01
□ 390 Don Gullett	.25	.10	.02
□ 391 Jerry Hairston	.18	.08	.01
□ 392 Checklist 265-396	.80	.10	.02
□ 393 Paul Mitchell	.18	.08	.01
□ 394 Fran Healy	.18	.08	.01
□ 395 Jim Wynn	.25	.10	.02
□ 396 Bill Lee	.25	.10	.02
□ 397 Tim Foli	.18	.08	.01
□ 398 Dave Tomlin	.18	.08	.01
□ 399 Luis Melendez	.18	.08	.01
□ 400 Rod Carew	4.00	1.60	.40
□ 401 Ken Brett	.18	.08	.01
□ 402 Don Money	.18	.08	.01
□ 403 Geoff Zahn	.18	.08	.01
□ 404 Enos Cabell	.18	.08	.01
□ 405 Rollie Fingers	1.00	.40	.10
□ 406 Ed Herrmann	.18	.08	.01
□ 407 Tom Underwood	.18	.08	.01
□ 408 Charlie Spikes	.18	.08	.01
□ 409 Dave Lemanczyk	.18	.08	.01
□ 410 Ralph Garr	.18	.08	.01
□ 411 Bill Singer	.18	.08	.01
□ 412 Toby Harrah	.25	.10	.02
□ 413 Pete Varney	.18	.08	.01
□ 414 Wayne Garland	.18	.08	.01
□ 415 Vada Pinson	.35	.14	.03
□ 416 Tommy John	1.00	.40	.10
□ 417 Gene Clines	.18	.08	.01
□ 418 Jose Morales	.18	.08	.01
□ 419 Reggie Cleveland	.18	.08	.01
□ 420 Joe Morgan	3.00	1.20	.30
□ 421 A's Team (checklist back)	.65	.15	.03
□ 422 Johnny Grubb	.18	.08	.01
□ 423 Ed Halicki	.18	.08	.01
□ 424 Phil Roof	.18	.08	.01
□ 425 Rennie Stennett	.18	.08	.01
□ 426 Bob Forsch	.25	.10	.02
□ 427 Kurt Bevacqua	.18	.08	.01
□ 428 Jim Crawford	.18	.08	.01
□ 429 Fred Stanley	.18	.08	.01
□ 430 Jose Cardenal	.18	.08	.01
□ 431 Dick Ruthven	.18	.08	.01
□ 432 Tom Veryzer	.18	.08	.01
□ 433 Rick Waits	.18	.08	.01
□ 434 Morris Nettles	.18	.08	.01
□ 435 Phil Niekro	1.75	.70	.17
□ 436 Bill Fahey	.18	.08	.01
□ 437 Terry Forster	.25	.10	.02
□ 438 Doug DeCinces	.50	.20	.05
□ 439 Rick Rhoden	.60	.24	.06
□ 440 John Mayberry	.25	.10	.02
□ 441 Gary Carter	12.00	5.00	1.20
□ 442 Hank Webb	.18	.08	.01
□ 443 Giants Team (checklist back)	.65	.15	.03
□ 444 Gary Nolan	.18	.08	.01
□ 445 Rico Petrocelli	.25	.10	.02
□ 446 Larry Haney	.18	.08	.01
□ 447 Gene Locklear	.18	.08	.01
□ 448 Tom Johnson	.18	.08	.01
□ 449 Bob Robertson	.18	.08	.01
□ 450 Jim Palmer	3.50	1.40	.35
□ 451 Buddy Bradford	.18	.08	.01
□ 452 Tom Hausman	.18	.08	.01
□ 453 Lou Piniella	.35	.14	.03
□ 454 Tom Griffin	.18	.08	.01
□ 455 Dick Allen	.35	.14	.03
□ 456 Joe Coleman	.18	.08	.01
□ 457 Ed Crosby	.18	.08	.01
□ 458 Earl Williams	.18	.08	.01
□ 459 Jim Brewer	.18	.08	.01
□ 460 Cesar Cedeno	.25	.10	.02
□ 461 NL and AL Champs Reds sweep Bucs, Bosox surprise A's	.35	.14	.03
□ 462 '75 World Series Reds Champs	.35	.14	.03
□ 463 Steve Hargan	.18	.08	.01
□ 464 Ken Henderson	.18	.08	.01
□ 465 Mike Marshall	.25	.10	.02
□ 466 Bob Stinson	.18	.08	.01
□ 467 Woodie Fryman	.18	.08	.01
□ 468 Jesus Alou	.18	.08	.01
□ 469 Rawley Eastwick	.18	.08	.01
□ 470 Bobby Murcer	.35	.14	.03
□ 471 Jim Burton	.18	.08	.01
□ 472 Bob Davis	.18	.08	.01
□ 473 Paul Blair	.25	.10	.02
□ 474 Ray Corbin	.18	.08	.01
□ 475 Joe Rudi	.25	.10	.02
□ 476 Bob Moose	.18	.08	.01
□ 477 Indians Team (checklist back)	.65	.15	.03
□ 478 Lynn McGlothen	.18	.08	.01
□ 479 Bobby Mitchell	.18	.08	.01
□ 480 Mike Schmidt	14.00	5.75	1.40
□ 481 Rudy May	.18	.08	.01
□ 482 Tim Hosley	.18	.08	.01
□ 483 Mickey Stanley	.25	.10	.02
□ 484 Eric Raich	.18	.08	.01
□ 485 Mike Hargrove	.25	.10	.02
□ 486 Bruce Dal Canton	.18	.08	.01
□ 487 Leron Lee	.18	.08	.01
□ 488 Claude Osteen	.25	.10	.02
□ 489 Skip Jutze	.18	.08	.01
□ 490 Frank Tanana	.35	.14	.03
□ 491 Terry Crowley	.18	.08	.01
□ 492 Martin Pattin	.18	.08	.01
□ 493 Derrel Thomas	.18	.08	.01
□ 494 Craig Swan	.25	.10	.02
□ 495 Nate Colbert	.18	.08	.01
□ 496 Juan Beniquez	.18	.08	.01
□ 497 Joe McIntosh	.18	.08	.01
□ 498 Glenn Borgmann	.18	.08	.01
□ 499 Mario Guerrero	.18	.08	.01
□ 500 Reggie Jackson	7.00	2.80	.70
□ 501 Billy Champion	.18	.08	.01
□ 502 Tim McCarver	.35	.14	.03
□ 503 Elliott Maddox	.18	.08	.01
□ 504 Pirates Team (checklist back)	.65	.15	.03
□ 505 Mark Belanger	.25	.10	.02
□ 506 George Mitterwald	.18	.08	.01
□ 507 Ray Bare	.18	.08	.01
□ 508 Duane Kuiper	.18	.08	.01
□ 509 Bill Hands	.18	.08	.01
□ 510 Amos Otis	.35	.14	.03
□ 511 Jamie Easterley	.18	.08	.01
□ 512 Ellie Rodriguez	.18	.08	.01
□ 513 Bart Johnson	.18	.08	.01
□ 514 Dan Driessen	.25	.10	.02
□ 515 Steve Yeager	.18	.08	.01
□ 516 Wayne Granger	.18	.08	.01
□ 517 John Milner	.18	.08	.01
□ 518 Doug Flynn	.18	.08	.01
□ 519 Steve Brye	.18	.08	.01
□ 520 Willie McCovey	2.50	1.00	.25
□ 521 Jim Colborn	.18	.08	.01
□ 522 Ted Sizemore	.18	.08	.01
□ 523 Bob Montgomery	.18	.08	.01
□ 524 Pete Falcone	.18	.08	.01
□ 525 Billy Williams	1.75	.70	.17
□ 526 Checklist 397-528	.80	.10	.02
□ 527 Mike Anderson	.18	.08	.01
□ 528 Dock Ellis	.18	.08	.01
□ 529 Deron Johnson	.18	.08	.01
□ 530 Don Sutton	1.50	.60	.15
□ 531 New York Mets Team Card (checklist back)	.75	.20	.04
□ 532 Milt May	.18	.08	.01
□ 533 Lee Richard	.18	.08	.01
□ 534 Stan Bahnsen	.18	.08	.01

□ 535 Dave Nelson	.18	.08	.01
□ 536 Mike Thompson	.18	.08	.01
□ 537 Tony Muser	.18	.08	.01
□ 538 Pat Darcy	.18	.08	.01
□ 539 John Balaz	.18	.08	.01
□ 540 Bill Freehan	.35	.14	.03
□ 541 Steve Mingori	.18	.08	.01
□ 542 Keith Hernandez	7.00	2.80	.70
□ 543 Wayne Twitchell	.18	.08	.01
□ 544 Pepe Frias	.18	.08	.01
□ 545 Sparky Lyle	.35	.14	.03
□ 546 Dave Rosello	.18	.08	.01
□ 547 Roric Harrison	.18	.08	.01
□ 548 Manny Mota	.25	.10	.02
□ 549 Randy Tate	.18	.08	.01
□ 550 Hank Aaron	9.00	3.75	.90
□ 551 Jerry DaVanon	.18	.08	.01
□ 552 Terry Humphrey	.18	.08	.01
□ 553 Randy Moffitt	.18	.08	.01
□ 554 Ray Fosse	.18	.08	.01
□ 555 Dyar Miller	.18	.08	.01
□ 556 Twins Team (checklist back)	.65	.15	.03
□ 557 Dan Spillner	.18	.08	.01
□ 558 Clarence Gaston	.18	.08	.01
□ 559 Clyde Wright	.18	.08	.01
□ 560 Jorge Orta	.18	.08	.01
□ 561 Tom Carroll	.18	.08	.01
□ 562 Adrian Garrett	.18	.08	.01
□ 563 Larry Demery	.18	.08	.01
□ 564 Bubble Gum Champ Kurt Bevacqua	.25	.10	.02
□ 565 Tug McGraw	.35	.14	.03
□ 566 Ken McMullen	.18	.08	.01
□ 567 George Stone	.18	.08	.01
□ 568 Rob Andrews	.18	.08	.01
□ 569 Nelson Briles	.25	.10	.02
□ 570 George Hendrick	.25	.10	.02
□ 571 Don DeMola	.18	.08	.01
□ 572 Rich Coggins	.18	.08	.01
□ 573 Bill Travers	.18	.08	.01
□ 574 Don Kessinger	.25	.10	.02
□ 575 Dwight Evans	1.50	.60	.15
□ 576 Maximino Leon	.18	.08	.01
□ 577 Marc Hill	.18	.08	.01
□ 578 Ted Kubiak	.18	.08	.01
□ 579 Clay Kirby	.18	.08	.01
□ 580 Bert Campaneris	.25	.10	.02
□ 581 Cardinals Team (checklist back)	.65	.15	.03
□ 582 Mike Kekich	.18	.08	.01
□ 583 Tommy Helms	.25	.10	.02
□ 584 Stan Wall	.18	.08	.01
□ 585 Joe Torre	.50	.20	.05
□ 586 Ron Schueler	.18	.08	.01
□ 587 Leo Cardenas	.18	.08	.01
□ 588 Kevin Kobel	.18	.08	.01
□ 589 Rookie Pitchers Santo Alcala Mike Flanagan Joe Pactwa Pablo Torrealba	2.50	1.00	.25
□ 590 Rookie Outfielders Henry Cruz Chet Lemon Ellis Valentine Terry Whitfield	1.25	.50	.12
□ 591 Rookie Pitchers Steve Grilli Craig Mitchell Jose Sosa George Throop	.25	.10	.02
□ 592 Rookie Infielders Willie Randolph Dave McKay Jerry Royster Roy Staiger	5.00	2.00	.50
□ 593 Rookie Pitchers Larry Anderson Ken Crosby Mark Littell Butch Metzger	.35	.14	.03
□ 594 Rookie Catchers/OF Andy Merchant Ed Ott Royle Stillman Jerry White	.35	.14	.03
□ 595 Rookie Pitchers Art DeFillipis Randy Lerch Sid Monge Steve Barr	.35	.14	.03
□ 596 Rookie Infielders Craig Reynolds Lamar Johnson Johnnie LeMaster Jerry Manuel	.50	.20	.05
□ 597 Rookie Pitchers Don Aase Jack Kucek Frank LaCorte Mike Pazik	.75	.30	.07
□ 598 Rookie Outfielders Hector Cruz Jamie Quirk Jerry Turner Joe Wallis	.35	.14	.03
□ 599 Rookie Pitchers Rob Dressler Ron Guidry Bob McClure Pat Zachry	12.00	5.00	1.20
□ 600 Tom Seaver	4.50	1.80	.45
□ 601 Ken Rudolph	.18	.08	.01
□ 602 Doug Konieczny	.18	.08	.01
□ 603 Jim Holt	.18	.08	.01
□ 604 Joe Lovitto	.18	.08	.01
□ 605 Al Downing	.25	.10	.02
□ 606 Milwaukee Brewers Team Card (checklist back)	.65	.15	.03
□ 607 Rich Hinton	.18	.08	.01
□ 608 Vic Correll	.18	.08	.01
□ 609 Fred Norman	.18	.08	.01
□ 610 Greg Luzinski	.50	.20	.05
□ 611 Rich Folkers	.18	.08	.01
□ 612 Joe Lahoud	.18	.08	.01
□ 613 Tim Johnson	.18	.08	.01
□ 614 Fernando Arroyo	.18	.08	.01
□ 615 Mike Cubbage	.18	.08	.01
□ 616 Buck Martinez	.18	.08	.01
□ 617 Darold Knowles	.18	.08	.01
□ 618 Jack Brohamer	.18	.08	.01
□ 619 Bill Butler	.18	.08	.01
□ 620 Al Oliver	.50	.20	.05
□ 621 Tom Hall	.18	.08	.01
□ 622 Rick Auerbach	.18	.08	.01
□ 623 Bob Allietta	.18	.08	.01
□ 624 Tony Taylor	.18	.08	.01
□ 625 J.R. Richard	.25	.10	.02
□ 626 Bob Sheldon	.18	.08	.01
□ 627 Bill Plummer	.18	.08	.01
□ 628 John D'Acquisto	.18	.08	.01
□ 629 Sandy Alomar	.18	.08	.01
□ 630 Chris Speier	.25	.10	.02
□ 631 Braves Team (checklist back)	.65	.15	.03
□ 632 Rogelio Moret	.18	.08	.01
□ 633 John Stearns	.25	.10	.02
□ 634 Larry Christenson	.18	.08	.01
□ 635 Jim Fregosi	.35	.14	.03
□ 636 Joe Decker	.18	.08	.01
□ 637 Bruce Bochte	.25	.10	.02
□ 638 Doyle Alexander	.35	.14	.03
□ 639 Fred Kendall	.18	.08	.01
□ 640 Bill Madlock	.75	.30	.07
□ 641 Tom Paciorek	.18	.08	.01
□ 642 Dennis Blair	.18	.08	.01
□ 643 Checklist 529-660	.80	.10	.02
□ 644 Tom Bradley	.18	.08	.01
□ 645 Darrell Porter	.25	.10	.02
□ 646 John Lowenstein	.18	.08	.01
□ 647 Ramon Hernandez	.18	.08	.01
□ 648 Al Cowens	.25	.10	.02
□ 649 Dave Roberts	.18	.08	.01
□ 650 Thurman Munson	5.00	2.00	.50
□ 651 John Odom	.18	.08	.01
□ 652 Ed Armbrister	.18	.08	.01
□ 653 Mike Norris	.25	.10	.02
□ 654 Doug Griffin	.18	.08	.01
□ 655 Mike Vail	.18	.08	.01
□ 656 Chicago White Sox Team Card (checklist back)	.65	.15	.03
□ 657 Roy Smalley	.60	.24	.06
□ 658 Jerry Johnson	.18	.08	.01
□ 659 Ben Oglivie	.25	.10	.02
□ 660 Dave Lopes	.65	.12	.02

1976 Topps Traded

The cards in this 44-card set measure 2 1/2" by 3 1/2". The 1976 Topps Traded set contains 43 players and one unnumbered checklist card. The

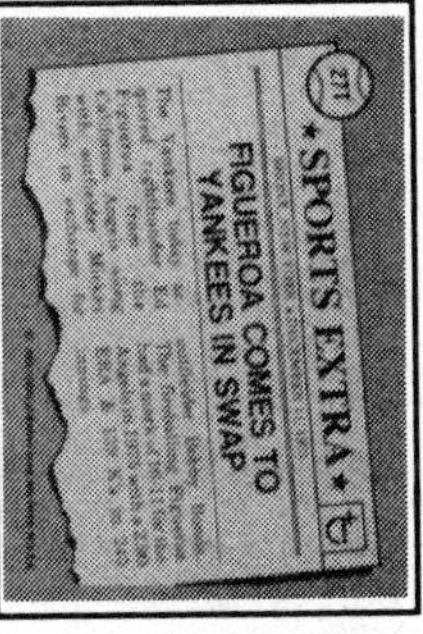

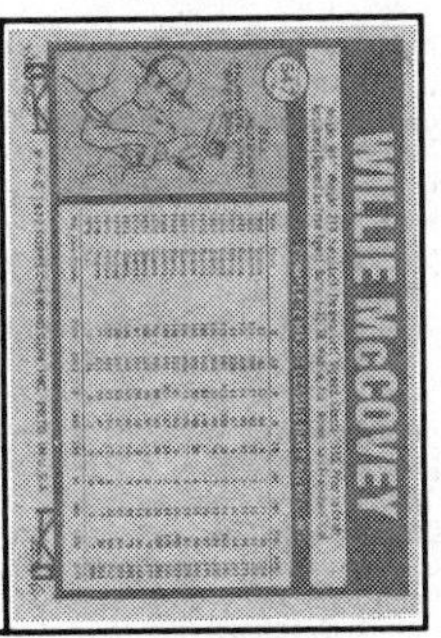

individuals pictured were traded after the Topps regular set was printed. A "Sports Extra" heading design is found on each picture and is also used to introduce the biographical section of the reverse. Each card is numbered according to the player's regular 1976 card with the addition of "T" to indicate his new status.

	NRMT	VG-E	GOOD
COMPLETE SET (44)	6.50	2.60	.65
COMMON PLAYER	.12	.05	.01
☐ 27T Ed Figueroa	.12	.05	.01
☐ 28T Dusty Baker	.30	.12	.03
☐ 44T Doug Rader	.20	.08	.02
☐ 58T Ron Reed	.15	.06	.01
☐ 74T Oscar Gamble	.20	.08	.02
☐ 80T Jim Kaat	.75	.30	.07
☐ 83T Jim Spencer	.12	.05	.01
☐ 85T Mickey Rivers	.15	.06	.01
☐ 99T Lee Lacy	.15	.06	.01
☐ 120T Rusty Staub	.40	.16	.04
☐ 127T Larvell Blanks	.12	.05	.01
☐ 146T George Medich	.12	.05	.01
☐ 158T Ken Reitz	.12	.05	.01
☐ 208T Mike Lum	.12	.05	.01
☐ 211T Clay Carroll	.12	.05	.01
☐ 231T Tom House	.15	.06	.01
☐ 250T Fergie Jenkins	.75	.30	.07
☐ 259T Darrel Chaney	.12	.05	.01
☐ 292T Leon Roberts	.12	.05	.01
☐ 296T Pat Dobson	.15	.06	.01
☐ 309T Bill Melton	.12	.05	.01
☐ 338T Bob Bailey	.12	.05	.01
☐ 380T Bobby Bonds	.30	.12	.03
☐ 383T John Ellis	.12	.05	.01
☐ 385T Mickey Lolich	.30	.12	.03
☐ 401T Ken Brett	.12	.05	.01
☐ 410T Ralph Garr	.15	.06	.01
☐ 411T Bill Singer	.12	.05	.01
☐ 428T Jim Crawford	.12	.05	.01
☐ 434T Morris Nettles	.12	.05	.01
☐ 464T Ken Henderson	.12	.05	.01
☐ 497T Joe McIntosh	.12	.05	.01
☐ 524T Pete Falcone	.12	.05	.01
☐ 527T Mike Anderson	.12	.05	.01
☐ 528T Dock Ellis	.12	.05	.01
☐ 532T Milt May	.12	.05	.01
☐ 554T Ray Fosse	.12	.05	.01
☐ 579T Clay Kirby	.12	.05	.01
☐ 583T Tommy Helms	.15	.06	.01
☐ 592T Willie Randolph	.90	.36	.09
☐ 618T Jack Brohamer	.12	.05	.01
☐ 632T Rogelio Moret	.12	.05	.01
☐ 649T Dave Roberts	.12	.05	.01
☐ xxxT Traded Checklist (unnumbered)	.50	.05	.01

1977 Topps

The cards in this 660-card set measure 2 1/2" by 3 1/2". In 1977 for the fifth consecutive year, Topps produced a 660-card baseball set. The player's name, team affiliation, and his position are compactly arranged over the picture area and a facsimile autograph appears on the photo. Team cards feature a checklist of that team's players in the set and a small picture of the manager on the front of the card. Appearing for the first time are the series "Brothers" (631-634) and "Turn Back The Clock" (433-437). Other subseries in the set are League Leaders (1-8), Record Breakers (231-234), Playoffs cards (276-277), World Series cards (411-413), and Rookie Prospects (472-479 and 487- 494). The key card in the set is the rookie card of Dale Murphy (476). Cards numbered 23 or lower which feature Yankees and do not follow the numbering checklisted below are not necessarily error cards. They are probably Burger King cards, a separate set with its own pricing and mass distribution. Burger King cards are indistinguishable from the corresponding Topps cards except for the card numbering difference and the fact that Burger King cards do not have a printing sheet designation (such as A through F like the regular Topps) anywhere on the card back in very small print.

	NRMT	VG-E	GOOD
COMPLETE SET (660)	275.00	110.00	27.00
COMMON PLAYER (1-660)	.15	.06	.01
☐ 1 Batting Leaders George Brett Bill Madlock	2.00	.00	.00
☐ 2 Home Run Leaders Graig Nettles Mike Schmidt	.75	.30	.07
☐ 3 RBI Leaders Lee May George Foster	.25	.10	.02
☐ 4 Stolen Base Leaders Bill North Dave Lopes	.25	.10	.02
☐ 5 Victory Leaders Jim Palmer Randy Jones	.35	.14	.03
☐ 6 Strikeout Leaders Nolan Ryan Tom Seaver	2.00	.80	.20
☐ 7 ERA Leaders Mark Fidrych John Denny	.25	.10	.02
☐ 8 Leading Firemen Bill Campbell Rawly Eastwick	.25	.10	.02
☐ 9 Doug Rader	.25	.10	.02
☐ 10 Reggie Jackson	7.00	2.80	.70
☐ 11 Rob Dressler	.15	.06	.01
☐ 12 Larry Haney	.15	.06	.01
☐ 13 Luis Gomez	.15	.06	.01
☐ 14 Tommy Smith	.15	.06	.01
☐ 15 Don Gullett	.15	.06	.01
☐ 16 Bob Jones	.15	.06	.01
☐ 17 Steve Stone	.25	.10	.02
☐ 18 Indians Team/Mgr. Frank Robinson (checklist back)	.65	.15	.03
☐ 19 John D'Acquisto	.15	.06	.01
☐ 20 Graig Nettles	.75	.30	.07
☐ 21 Ken Forsch	.15	.06	.01
☐ 22 Bill Freehan	.25	.10	.02
☐ 23 Dan Driessen	.25	.10	.02
☐ 24 Carl Morton	.15	.06	.01

□ 25 Dwight Evans .... 1.50 .60 .15
□ 26 Ray Sadecki .... .15 .06 .01
□ 27 Bill Buckner .... .35 .14 .03
□ 28 Woodie Fryman .... .15 .06 .01
□ 29 Bucky Dent .... .35 .14 .03
□ 30 Greg Luzinski .... .35 .14 .03
□ 31 Jim Todd .... .15 .06 .01
□ 32 Checklist 1 .... .70 .08 .02
□ 33 Wayne Garland .... .15 .06 .01
□ 34 Angels Team/Mgr. .... .65 .15 .03
Norm Sherry
(checklist back)
□ 35 Rennie Stennett .... .15 .06 .01
□ 36 John Ellis .... .15 .06 .01
□ 37 Steve Hargan .... .15 .06 .01
□ 38 Craig Kusick .... .15 .06 .01
□ 39 Tom Griffin .... .15 .06 .01
□ 40 Bobby Murcer .... .35 .14 .03
□ 41 Jim Kern .... .15 .06 .01
□ 42 Jose Cruz .... .25 .10 .02
□ 43 Ray Bare .... .15 .06 .01
□ 44 Bud Harrelson .... .25 .10 .02
□ 45 Rawly Eastwick .... .15 .06 .01
□ 46 Buck Martinez .... .15 .06 .01
□ 47 Lynn McGlothen .... .15 .06 .01
□ 48 Tom Paciorek .... .15 .06 .01
□ 49 Grant Jackson .... .15 .06 .01
□ 50 Ron Cey .... .35 .14 .03
□ 51 Brewers Team/Mgr. .... .65 .15 .03
Alex Grammas
(checklist back)
□ 52 Ellis Valentine .... .15 .06 .01
□ 53 Paul Mitchell .... .15 .06 .01
□ 54 Sandy Alomar .... .15 .06 .01
□ 55 Jeff Burroughs .... .25 .10 .02
□ 56 Rudy May .... .15 .06 .01
□ 57 Marc Hill .... .15 .06 .01
□ 58 Chet Lemon .... .25 .10 .02
□ 59 Larry Christenson .... .15 .06 .01
□ 60 Jim Rice .... 5.00 2.00 .50
□ 61 Manny Sanguillen .... .25 .10 .02
□ 62 Eric Raich .... .15 .06 .01
□ 63 Tito Fuentes .... .15 .06 .01
□ 64 Larry Biittner .... .15 .06 .01
□ 65 Skip Lockwood .... .15 .06 .01
□ 66 Roy Smalley .... .25 .10 .02
□ 67 Joaquin Andujar .... 1.00 .40 .10
□ 68 Bruce Bochte .... .15 .06 .01
□ 69 Jim Crawford .... .15 .06 .01
□ 70 Johnny Bench .... 4.50 1.80 .45
□ 71 Dock Ellis .... .15 .06 .01
□ 72 Mike Anderson .... .15 .06 .01
□ 73 Charles Williams .... .15 .06 .01
□ 74 A's Team/Mgr. .... .65 .15 .03
Jack McKeon
(checklist back)
□ 75 Dennis Leonard .... .25 .10 .02
□ 76 Tim Foli .... .15 .06 .01
□ 77 Dyar Miller .... .15 .06 .01
□ 78 Bob Davis .... .15 .06 .01
□ 79 Don Money .... .15 .06 .01
□ 80 Andy Messersmith .... .25 .10 .02
□ 81 Juan Beniquez .... .15 .06 .01
□ 82 Jim Rooker .... .15 .06 .01
□ 83 Kevin Bell .... .15 .06 .01
□ 84 Ollie Brown .... .15 .06 .01
□ 85 Duane Kuiper .... .15 .06 .01
□ 86 Pat Zachry .... .15 .06 .01
□ 87 Glenn Borgmann .... .15 .06 .01
□ 88 Stan Wall .... .15 .06 .01
□ 89 Butch Hobson .... .15 .06 .01
□ 90 Cesar Cedeno .... .25 .10 .02
□ 91 John Verhoeven .... .15 .06 .01
□ 92 Dave Rosello .... .15 .06 .01
□ 93 Tom Poquette .... .15 .06 .01
□ 94 Craig Swan .... .15 .06 .01
□ 95 Keith Hernandez .... 3.50 1.40 .35
□ 96 Lou Piniella .... .35 .14 .03
□ 97 Dave Heaverlo .... .15 .06 .01
□ 98 Milt May .... .15 .06 .01
□ 99 Tom Hausman .... .15 .06 .01
□ 100 Joe Morgan .... 1.50 .60 .15
□ 101 Dick Bosman .... .15 .06 .01
□ 102 Jose Morales .... .15 .06 .01
□ 103 Mike Bacsik .... .15 .06 .01
□ 104 Omar Moreno .... .25 .10 .02
□ 105 Steve Yeager .... .15 .06 .01
□ 106 Mike Flanagan .... .35 .14 .03
□ 107 Bill Melton .... .15 .06 .01
□ 108 Alan Foster .... .15 .06 .01
□ 109 Jorge Orta .... .15 .06 .01
□ 110 Steve Carlton .... 4.00 1.60 .40
□ 111 Rico Petrocelli .... .25 .10 .02
□ 112 Bill Greif .... .15 .06 .01
□ 113 Blue Jays Leaders .... .50 .10 .02
Roy Hartsfield MG
Don Leppert CO
Bob Miller CO
Jackie Moore CO
Harry Warner CO
(checklist back)
□ 114 Bruce Dal Canton .... .15 .06 .01
□ 115 Rick Manning .... .15 .06 .01
□ 116 Joe Niekro .... .35 .14 .03
□ 117 Frank White .... .35 .14 .03
□ 118 Rick Jones .... .15 .06 .01
□ 119 John Stearns .... .15 .06 .01
□ 120 Rod Carew .... 4.00 1.60 .40
□ 121 Gary Nolan .... .15 .06 .01
□ 122 Ben Oglivie .... .25 .10 .02
□ 123 Fred Stanley .... .15 .06 .01
□ 124 George Mitterwald .... .15 .06 .01
□ 125 Bill Travers .... .15 .06 .01
□ 126 Rod Gilbreath .... .15 .06 .01
□ 127 Ron Fairly .... .15 .06 .01
□ 128 Tommy John .... 1.00 .40 .10
□ 129 Mike Sadek .... .15 .06 .01
□ 130 Al Oliver .... .35 .14 .03
□ 131 Orlando Ramirez .... .15 .06 .01
□ 132 Chip Lang .... .15 .06 .01
□ 133 Ralph Garr .... .15 .06 .01
□ 134 Padres Team/Mgr. .... .65 .15 .03
John McNamara
(checklist back)
□ 135 Mark Belanger .... .25 .10 .02
□ 136 Jerry Mumphrey .... .35 .14 .03
□ 137 Jeff Terpko .... .15 .06 .01
□ 138 Bob Stinson .... .15 .06 .01
□ 139 Fred Norman .... .15 .06 .01
□ 140 Mike Schmidt .... 9.00 3.75 .90
□ 141 Mark Littell .... .15 .06 .01
□ 142 Steve Dillard .... .15 .06 .01
□ 143 Ed Herrmann .... .15 .06 .01
□ 144 Bruce Sutter .... 2.50 1.00 .25
□ 145 Tom Veryzer .... .15 .06 .01
□ 146 Dusty Baker .... .25 .10 .02
□ 147 Jackie Brown .... .15 .06 .01
□ 148 Fran Healy .... .15 .06 .01
□ 149 Mike Cubbage .... .15 .06 .01
□ 150 Tom Seaver .... 4.00 1.60 .40
□ 151 Johnny LeMaster .... .15 .06 .01
□ 152 Gaylord Perry .... 1.75 .70 .17
□ 153 Ron Jackson .... .15 .06 .01
□ 154 Dave Giusti .... .15 .06 .01
□ 155 Joe Rudi .... .25 .10 .02
□ 156 Pete Mackanin .... .15 .06 .01
□ 157 Ken Brett .... .15 .06 .01
□ 158 Ted Kubiak .... .15 .06 .01
□ 159 Bernie Carbo .... .15 .06 .01
□ 160 Will McEnaney .... .15 .06 .01
□ 161 Garry Templeton .... 1.00 .40 .10
□ 162 Mike Cuellar .... .25 .10 .02
□ 163 Dave Hilton .... .15 .06 .01
□ 164 Tug McGraw .... .35 .14 .03
□ 165 Jim Wynn .... .25 .10 .02
□ 166 Bill Campbell .... .15 .06 .01
□ 167 Rich Hebner .... .25 .10 .02
□ 168 Charlie Spikes .... .15 .06 .01
□ 169 Darold Knowles .... .15 .06 .01
□ 170 Thurman Munson .... 4.00 1.60 .40
□ 171 Ken Sanders .... .15 .06 .01
□ 172 John Milner .... .15 .06 .01
□ 173 Chuck Scrivener .... .15 .06 .01
□ 174 Nelson Briles .... .25 .10 .02
□ 175 Butch Wynegar .... .60 .24 .06
□ 176 Bob Robertson .... .15 .06 .01
□ 177 Bart Johnson .... .15 .06 .01
□ 178 Bombo Rivera .... .15 .06 .01
□ 179 Paul Hartzell .... .15 .06 .01
□ 180 Dave Lopes .... .25 .10 .02
□ 181 Ken McMullen .... .15 .06 .01
□ 182 Dan Spillner .... .15 .06 .01
□ 183 Cardinals Team/Mgr. .... .65 .15 .03
Vern Rapp
(checklist back)
□ 184 Bo McLaughlin .... .15 .06 .01
□ 185 Sixto Lezcano .... .15 .06 .01
□ 186 Doug Flynn .... .15 .06 .01
□ 187 Dick Pole .... .15 .06 .01
□ 188 Bob Tolan .... .15 .06 .01
□ 189 Rick Dempsey .... .25 .10 .02
□ 190 Ray Burris .... .15 .06 .01
□ 191 Doug Griffin .... .15 .06 .01
□ 192 Clarence Gaston .... .15 .06 .01
□ 193 Larry Gura .... .25 .10 .02
□ 194 Gary Matthews .... .25 .10 .02
□ 195 Ed Figueroa .... .15 .06 .01
□ 196 Len Randle .... .15 .06 .01
□ 197 Ed Ott .... .15 .06 .01
□ 198 Wilbur Wood .... .25 .10 .02

☐ 199	Pepe Frias	.15	.06	.01
☐ 200	Frank Tanana	.35	.14	.03
☐ 201	Ed Kranepool	.25	.10	.02
☐ 202	Tom Johnson	.15	.06	.01
☐ 203	Ed Armbrister	.15	.06	.01
☐ 204	Jeff Newman	.15	.06	.01
☐ 205	Pete Falcone	.15	.06	.01
☐ 206	Boog Powell	.35	.14	.03
☐ 207	Glenn Abbott	.15	.06	.01
☐ 208	Checklist 2	.70	.08	.01
☐ 209	Rob Andrews	.15	.06	.01
☐ 210	Fred Lynn	1.50	.60	.15
☐ 211	Giants Team/Mgr.	.65	.15	.03
	Joe Altobelli			
	(checklist back)			
☐ 212	Jim Mason	.15	.06	.01
☐ 213	Maximino Leon	.15	.06	.01
☐ 214	Darrell Porter	.15	.06	.01
☐ 215	Butch Metzger	.15	.06	.01
☐ 216	Doug DeCinces	.35	.14	.03
☐ 217	Tom Underwood	.15	.06	.01
☐ 218	John Wathan	1.50	.60	.15
☐ 219	Joe Coleman	.15	.06	.01
☐ 220	Chris Chambliss	.35	.14	.03
☐ 221	Bob Bailey	.15	.06	.01
☐ 222	Francisco Barrios	.15	.06	.01
☐ 223	Earl Williams	.15	.06	.01
☐ 224	Rusty Torres	.15	.06	.01
☐ 225	Bob Apodaca	.15	.06	.01
☐ 226	Leroy Stanton	.15	.06	.01
☐ 227	Joe Sambito	.35	.14	.03
☐ 228	Twins Team/Mgr.	.65	.15	.03
	Gene Mauch			
	(checklist back)			
☐ 229	Don Kessinger	.25	.10	.02
☐ 230	Vida Blue	.35	.14	.03
☐ 231	RB: George Brett	2.00	.80	.20
	Most cons. games			
	with 3 or more hits			
☐ 232	RB: Minnie Minoso	.25	.10	.02
	Oldest to hit safely			
☐ 233	RB: Jose Morales, Most	.25	.10	.02
	pinch-hits, season			
☐ 234	RB: Nolan Ryan	1.75	.70	.17
	Most seasons, 300			
	or more strikeouts			
☐ 235	Cecil Cooper	.50	.20	.05
☐ 236	Tom Buskey	.15	.06	.01
☐ 237	Gene Clines	.15	.06	.01
☐ 238	Tippy Martinez	.25	.10	.02
☐ 239	Bill Plummer	.15	.06	.01
☐ 240	Ron LeFlore	.25	.10	.02
☐ 241	Dave Tomlin	.15	.06	.01
☐ 242	Ken Henderson	.15	.06	.01
☐ 243	Ron Reed	.15	.06	.01
☐ 244	John Mayberry	.35	.14	.03
	(cartoon mentions			
	T206 Wagner)			
☐ 245	Rick Rhoden	.35	.14	.03
☐ 246	Mike Vail	.15	.06	.01
☐ 247	Chris Knapp	.15	.06	.01
☐ 248	Wilbur Howard	.15	.06	.01
☐ 249	Pete Redfern	.15	.06	.01
☐ 250	Bill Madlock	.50	.20	.05
☐ 251	Tony Muser	.15	.06	.01
☐ 252	Dale Murray	.15	.06	.01
☐ 253	John Hale	.15	.06	.01
☐ 254	Doyle Alexander	.35	.14	.03
☐ 255	George Scott	.25	.10	.02
☐ 256	Joe Hoerner	.15	.06	.01
☐ 257	Mike Miley	.15	.06	.01
☐ 258	Luis Tiant	.35	.14	.03
☐ 259	Mets Team/Mgr.	.75	.20	.04
	Joe Frazier			
	(checklist back)			
☐ 260	J.R. Richard	.25	.10	.02
☐ 261	Phil Garner	.25	.10	.02
☐ 262	Al Cowens	.25	.10	.02
☐ 263	Mike Marshall	.25	.10	.02
☐ 264	Tom Hutton	.15	.06	.01
☐ 265	Mark Fidrych	.50	.20	.05
☐ 266	Derrel Thomas	.15	.06	.01
☐ 267	Ray Fosse	.15	.06	.01
☐ 268	Rick Sawyer	.15	.06	.01
☐ 269	Joe Lis	.15	.06	.01
☐ 270	Dave Parker	2.00	.80	.20
☐ 271	Terry Forster	.25	.10	.02
☐ 272	Lee Lacy	.25	.10	.02
☐ 273	Eric Soderholm	.15	.06	.01
☐ 274	Don Stanhouse	.15	.06	.01
☐ 275	Mike Hargrove	.15	.06	.01
☐ 276	AL Champs	.35	.14	.03
	Chambliss' homer			
	decides it			
☐ 277	NL Champs	.35	.14	.03
	Reds sweep Phillies			
☐ 278	Danny Frisella	.15	.06	.01
☐ 279	Joe Wallis	.15	.06	.01
☐ 280	Jim Hunter	1.75	.70	.17
☐ 281	Roy Staiger	.15	.06	.01
☐ 282	Sid Monge	.15	.06	.01
☐ 283	Jerry DaVanon	.15	.06	.01
☐ 284	Mike Norris	.15	.06	.01
☐ 285	Brooks Robinson	2.50	1.00	.25
☐ 286	Johnny Grubb	.15	.06	.01
☐ 287	Reds Team/Mgr.	.75	.20	.04
	Sparky Anderson			
	(checklist back)			
☐ 288	Bob Montgomery	.15	.06	.01
☐ 289	Gene Garber	.15	.06	.01
☐ 290	Amos Otis	.35	.14	.03
☐ 291	Jason Thompson	.35	.14	.03
☐ 292	Rogelio Moret	.15	.06	.01
☐ 293	Jack Brohamer	.15	.06	.01
☐ 294	George Medich	.15	.06	.01
☐ 295	Gary Carter	6.50	2.60	.65
☐ 296	Don Hood	.15	.06	.01
☐ 297	Ken Reitz	.15	.06	.01
☐ 298	Charlie Hough	.25	.10	.02
☐ 299	Otto Velez	.15	.06	.01
☐ 300	Jerry Koosman	.35	.14	.03
☐ 301	Toby Harrah	.25	.10	.02
☐ 302	Mike Garman	.15	.06	.01
☐ 303	Gene Tenace	.25	.10	.02
☐ 304	Jim Hughes	.15	.06	.01
☐ 305	Mickey Rivers	.25	.10	.02
☐ 306	Rick Waits	.15	.06	.01
☐ 307	Gary Sutherland	.15	.06	.01
☐ 308	Gene Pentz	.15	.06	.01
☐ 309	Red Sox Team/Mgr.	.65	.15	.03
	Don Zimmer			
	(checklist back)			
☐ 310	Larry Bowa	.50	.20	.05
☐ 311	Vern Ruhle	.15	.06	.01
☐ 312	Rob Belloir	.15	.06	.01
☐ 313	Paul Blair	.25	.10	.02
☐ 314	Steve Mingori	.15	.06	.01
☐ 315	Dave Chalk	.15	.06	.01
☐ 316	Steve Rogers	.25	.10	.02
☐ 317	Kurt Bevacqua	.15	.06	.01
☐ 318	Duffy Dyer	.15	.06	.01
☐ 319	Rich Gossage	.75	.30	.07
☐ 320	Ken Griffey	.35	.14	.03
☐ 321	Dave Goltz	.15	.06	.01
☐ 322	Bill Russell	.25	.10	.02
☐ 323	Larry Lintz	.15	.06	.01
☐ 324	John Curtis	.15	.06	.01
☐ 325	Mike Ivie	.15	.06	.01
☐ 326	Jesse Jefferson	.15	.06	.01
☐ 327	Astros Team/Mgr.	.65	.15	.03
	Bill Virdon			
	(checklist back)			
☐ 328	Tommy Boggs	.15	.06	.01
☐ 329	Ron Hodges	.15	.06	.01
☐ 330	George Hendrick	.25	.10	.02
☐ 331	Jim Colborn	.15	.06	.01
☐ 332	Elliott Maddox	.15	.06	.01
☐ 333	Paul Reuschel	.15	.06	.01
☐ 334	Bill Stein	.15	.06	.01
☐ 335	Bill Robinson	.25	.10	.02
☐ 336	Denny Doyle	.15	.06	.01
☐ 337	Ron Schueler	.15	.06	.01
☐ 338	Dave Duncan	.15	.06	.01
☐ 339	Adrian Devine	.15	.06	.01
☐ 340	Hal McRae	.25	.10	.02
☐ 341	Joe Kerrigan	.15	.06	.01
☐ 342	Jerry Remy	.15	.06	.01
☐ 343	Ed Halicki	.15	.06	.01
☐ 344	Brian Downing	.25	.10	.02
☐ 345	Reggie Smith	.35	.14	.03
☐ 346	Bill Singer	.15	.06	.01
☐ 347	George Foster	1.25	.50	.12
☐ 348	Brent Strom	.15	.06	.01
☐ 349	Jim Holt	.15	.06	.01
☐ 350	Larry Dierker	.15	.06	.01
☐ 351	Jim Sundberg	.25	.10	.02
☐ 352	Mike Phillips	.15	.06	.01
☐ 353	Stan Thomas	.15	.06	.01
☐ 354	Pirates Team/Mgr.	.65	.15	.03
	Chuck Tanner			
	(checklist back)			
☐ 355	Lou Brock	2.25	.90	.22
☐ 356	Checklist 3	.70	.08	.01
☐ 357	Tim McCarver	.35	.14	.03
☐ 358	Tom House	.25	.10	.02
☐ 359	Willie Randolph	.60	.24	.06
☐ 360	Rick Monday	.25	.10	.02
☐ 361	Ed Rodriguez	.15	.06	.01
☐ 362	Tommy Davis	.25	.10	.02
☐ 363	Dave Roberts	.15	.06	.01

☐ 364	Vic Correll	.15	.06	.01
☐ 365	Mike Torrez	.25	.10	.02
☐ 366	Ted Sizemore	.15	.06	.01
☐ 367	Dave Hamilton	.15	.06	.01
☐ 368	Mike Jorgensen	.15	.06	.01
☐ 369	Terry Humphrey	.15	.06	.01
☐ 370	John Montefusco	.25	.10	.02
☐ 371	Royals Team/Mgr. Whitey Herzog (checklist back)	.65	.15	.03
☐ 372	Rich Folkers	.15	.06	.01
☐ 373	Bert Campaneris	.25	.10	.02
☐ 374	Kent Tekulve	.25	.10	.02
☐ 375	Larry Hisle	.25	.10	.02
☐ 376	Nino Espinosa	.15	.06	.01
☐ 377	Dave McKay	.15	.06	.01
☐ 378	Jim Umbarger	.15	.06	.01
☐ 379	Larry Cox	.15	.06	.01
☐ 380	Lee May	.25	.10	.02
☐ 381	Bob Forsch	.25	.10	.02
☐ 382	Charlie Moore	.15	.06	.01
☐ 383	Stan Bahnsen	.15	.06	.01
☐ 384	Darrel Chaney	.15	.06	.01
☐ 385	Dave LaRoche	.15	.06	.01
☐ 386	Manny Mota	.25	.10	.02
☐ 387	Yankees Team (checklist back)	.75	.20	.04
☐ 388	Terry Harmon	.15	.06	.01
☐ 389	Ken Kravec	.15	.06	.01
☐ 390	Dave Winfield	4.00	1.60	.40
☐ 391	Dan Warthen	.15	.06	.01
☐ 392	Phil Roof	.15	.06	.01
☐ 393	John Lowenstein	.15	.06	.01
☐ 394	Bill Laxton	.15	.06	.01
☐ 395	Manny Trillo	.15	.06	.01
☐ 396	Tom Murphy	.15	.06	.01
☐ 397	Larry Herndon	.35	.14	.03
☐ 398	Tom Burgmeier	.15	.06	.01
☐ 399	Bruce Boisclair	.15	.06	.01
☐ 400	Steve Garvey	3.50	1.40	.35
☐ 401	Mickey Scott	.15	.06	.01
☐ 402	Tommy Helms	.15	.06	.01
☐ 403	Tom Grieve	.25	.10	.02
☐ 404	Eric Rasmussen	.15	.06	.01
☐ 405	Claudell Washington	.25	.10	.02
☐ 406	Tim Johnson	.15	.06	.01
☐ 407	Dave Freisleben	.15	.06	.01
☐ 408	Cesar Tovar	.15	.06	.01
☐ 409	Pete Broberg	.15	.06	.01
☐ 410	Willie Montanez	.15	.06	.01
☐ 411	W.S. Games 1 and 2 Morgan homers opener; Bench stars as Reds take 2nd game	.50	.20	.05
☐ 412	W.S. Games 3 and 4 Reds' stop Yankees; Bench's two homers wrap it up	.50	.20	.05
☐ 413	World Series Summary Cincy wins 2nd straight series	.50	.20	.05
☐ 414	Tommy Harper	.25	.10	.02
☐ 415	Jay Johnstone	.25	.10	.02
☐ 416	Chuck Hartenstein	.15	.06	.01
☐ 417	Wayne Garrett	.15	.06	.01
☐ 418	White Sox Team/Mgr. Bob Lemon (checklist back)	.65	.15	.03
☐ 419	Steve Swisher	.15	.06	.01
☐ 420	Rusty Staub	.35	.14	.03
☐ 421	Doug Rau	.15	.06	.01
☐ 422	Freddie Patek	.15	.06	.01
☐ 423	Gary Lavelle	.15	.06	.01
☐ 424	Steve Brye	.15	.06	.01
☐ 425	Joe Torre	.35	.14	.03
☐ 426	Dick Drago	.15	.06	.01
☐ 427	Dave Rader	.15	.06	.01
☐ 428	Rangers Team/Mgr. Frank Lucchesi (checklist back)	.65	.15	.03
☐ 429	Ken Boswell	.15	.06	.01
☐ 430	Fergie Jenkins	.60	.24	.06
☐ 431	Dave Collins (photo actually Bobby Jones)	.25	.10	.02
☐ 432	Buzz Capra	.15	.06	.01
☐ 433	Turn back clock 1972 Nate Colbert	.25	.10	.02
☐ 434	Turn back clock 1967 Yaz Triple Crown	2.00	.80	.20
☐ 435	Turn back clock 1962 Wills 104 steals	.35	.14	.03
☐ 436	Turn back clock 1957 Keegan hurls Majors' only no-hitter	.25	.10	.02
☐ 437	Turn back clock 1952 Kiner leads NL HR's 7th straight year	.35	.14	.03
☐ 438	Marty Perez	.15	.06	.01
☐ 439	Gorman Thomas	.35	.14	.03
☐ 440	Jon Matlack	.25	.10	.02
☐ 441	Larvell Blanks	.15	.06	.01
☐ 442	Braves Team/Mgr. Dave Bristol (checklist back)	.65	.15	.03
☐ 443	Lamar Johnson	.15	.06	.01
☐ 444	Wayne Twitchell	.15	.06	.01
☐ 445	Ken Singleton	.25	.10	.02
☐ 446	Bill Bonham	.15	.06	.01
☐ 447	Jerry Turner	.15	.06	.01
☐ 448	Ellie Rodriguez	.15	.06	.01
☐ 449	Al Fitzmorris	.15	.06	.01
☐ 450	Pete Rose	9.00	3.75	.90
☐ 451	Checklist 4	.70	.08	.01
☐ 452	Mike Caldwell	.15	.06	.01
☐ 453	Pedro Garcia	.15	.06	.01
☐ 454	Andy Etchebarren	.15	.06	.01
☐ 455	Rick Wise	.15	.06	.01
☐ 456	Leon Roberts	.15	.06	.01
☐ 457	Steve Luebber	.15	.06	.01
☐ 458	Leo Foster	.15	.06	.01
☐ 459	Steve Foucault	.15	.06	.01
☐ 460	Willie Stargell	2.50	1.00	.25
☐ 461	Dick Tidrow	.15	.06	.01
☐ 462	Don Baylor	.60	.24	.06
☐ 463	Jamie Quirk	.15	.06	.01
☐ 464	Randy Moffitt	.15	.06	.01
☐ 465	Rico Carty	.25	.10	.02
☐ 466	Fred Holdsworth	.15	.06	.01
☐ 467	Phillies Team/Mgr. Danny Ozark (checklist back)	.65	.15	.03
☐ 468	Ramon Hernandez	.15	.06	.01
☐ 469	Pat Kelly	.15	.06	.01
☐ 470	Ted Simmons	.50	.20	.05
☐ 471	Del Unser	.15	.06	.01
☐ 472	Rookie Pitchers Don Aase, Bob McClure, Gil Patterson, Dave Wehrmeister	.35	.14	.03
☐ 473	Rookie Outfielders Andre Dawson, Gene Richards, John Scott, Denny Walling	33.00	12.00	3.00
☐ 474	Rookie Shortstops Bob Bailor, Kiko Garcia, Craig Reynolds, Alex Taveras	.25	.10	.02
☐ 475	Rookie Pitchers Chris Batton, Rick Camp, Scott McGregor, Manny Sarmiento	.35	.14	.03
☐ 476	Rookie Catchers Gary Alexander, Rick Cerone, Dale Murphy, Kevin Pasley	65.00	26.00	6.50
☐ 477	Rookie Infielders Doug Ault, Rich Dauer, Orlando Gonzalez, Phil Mankowski	.25	.10	.02
☐ 478	Rookie Pitchers Jim Gideon, Leon Hooten, Dave Johnson, Mark Lemongello	.25	.10	.02
☐ 479	Rookie Outfielders Brian Asselstine, Wayne Gross, Sam Mejias, Alvis Woods	.25	.10	.02
☐ 480	Carl Yastrzemski	5.00	2.00	.50
☐ 481	Roger Metzger	.15	.06	.01
☐ 482	Tony Solaita	.15	.06	.01
☐ 483	Richie Zisk	.15	.06	.01
☐ 484	Burt Hooton	.15	.06	.01
☐ 485	Roy White	.25	.10	.02
☐ 486	Ed Bane	.15	.06	.01
☐ 487	Rookie Pitchers Larry Anderson, Ed Glynn, Joe Henderson, Greg Terlecky	.25	.10	.02
☐ 488	Rookie Outfielders Jack Clark	20.00	8.00	2.00

	Ruppert Jones			
	Lee Mazzilli			
	Dan Thomas			
☐ 489	Rookie Pitchers	.35	.14	.03
	Len Barker			
	Randy Lerch			
	Greg Minton			
	Mike Overy			
☐ 490	Rookie Shortstops	.35	.14	.03
	Billy Almon			
	Mickey Klutts			
	Tommy McMillan			
	Mark Wagner			
☐ 491	Rookie Pitchers	1.00	.40	.10
	Mike Dupree			
	Denny Martinez			
	Craig Mitchell			
	Bob Sykes			
☐ 492	Rookie Outfielders	1.00	.40	.10
	Tony Armas			
	Steve Kemp			
	Carlos Lopez			
	Gary Woods			
☐ 493	Rookie Pitchers	.75	.30	.07
	Mike Krukow			
	Jim Otten			
	Gary Wheelock			
	Mike Willis			
☐ 494	Rookie Infielders	.50	.20	.05
	Juan Bernhardt			
	Mike Champion			
	Jim Gantner			
	Bump Wills			
☐ 495	Al Hrabosky	.25	.10	.02
☐ 496	Gary Thomasson	.15	.06	.01
☐ 497	Clay Carroll	.15	.06	.01
☐ 498	Sal Bando	.25	.10	.02
☐ 499	Pablo Torrealba	.15	.06	.01
☐ 500	Dave Kingman	.50	.20	.05
☐ 501	Jim Bibby	.15	.06	.01
☐ 502	Randy Hundley	.15	.06	.01
☐ 503	Bill Lee	.25	.10	.02
☐ 504	Dodgers Team/Mgr.	.75	.20	.04
	Tom Lasorda			
	(checklist back)			
☐ 505	Oscar Gamble	.25	.10	.02
☐ 506	Steve Grilli	.15	.06	.01
☐ 507	Mike Hegan	.15	.06	.01
☐ 508	Dave Pagan	.15	.06	.01
☐ 509	Cookie Rojas	.25	.10	.02
☐ 510	John Candelaria	.75	.30	.07
☐ 511	Bill Fahey	.15	.06	.01
☐ 512	Jack Billingham	.15	.06	.01
☐ 513	Jerry Terrell	.15	.06	.01
☐ 514	Cliff Johnson	.15	.06	.01
☐ 515	Chris Speier	.15	.06	.01
☐ 516	Bake McBride	.15	.06	.01
☐ 517	Pete Vuckovich	.50	.20	.05
☐ 518	Cubs Team/Mgr.	.65	.15	.03
	Herman Franks			
	(checklist back)			
☐ 519	Don Kirkwood	.15	.06	.01
☐ 520	Garry Maddox	.25	.10	.02
☐ 521	Bob Grich	.25	.10	.02
☐ 522	Enzo Hernandez	.15	.06	.01
☐ 523	Rollie Fingers	1.00	.40	.10
☐ 524	Rowland Office	.15	.06	.01
☐ 525	Dennis Eckersley	1.00	.40	.10
☐ 526	Larry Parrish	.35	.14	.03
☐ 527	Dan Meyer	.15	.06	.01
☐ 528	Bill Castro	.15	.06	.01
☐ 529	Jim Essian	.15	.06	.01
☐ 530	Rick Reuschel	.35	.14	.03
☐ 531	Lyman Bostock	.25	.10	.02
☐ 532	Jim Willoughby	.15	.06	.01
☐ 533	Mickey Stanley	.15	.06	.01
☐ 534	Paul Splittorff	.15	.06	.01
☐ 535	Cesar Geronimo	.15	.06	.01
☐ 536	Vic Albury	.15	.06	.01
☐ 537	Dave Roberts	.15	.06	.01
☐ 538	Frank Taveras	.15	.06	.01
☐ 539	Mike Wallace	.15	.06	.01
☐ 540	Bob Watson	.25	.10	.02
☐ 541	John Denny	.25	.10	.02
☐ 542	Frank Duffy	.15	.06	.01
☐ 543	Ron Blomberg	.15	.06	.01
☐ 544	Gary Ross	.15	.06	.01
☐ 545	Bob Boone	.35	.14	.03
☐ 546	Orioles Team/Mgr.	.75	.20	.04
	Earl Weaver			
	(checklist back)			
☐ 547	Willie McCovey	2.00	.80	.20
☐ 548	Joel Youngblood	.15	.06	.01
☐ 549	Jerry Royster	.15	.06	.01
☐ 550	Randy Jones	.15	.06	.01
☐ 551	Bill North	.15	.06	.01
☐ 552	Pepe Mangual	.15	.06	.01
☐ 553	Jack Heidemann	.15	.06	.01
☐ 554	Bruce Kimm	.15	.06	.01
☐ 555	Dan Ford	.15	.06	.01
☐ 556	Doug Bird	.15	.06	.01
☐ 557	Jerry White	.15	.06	.01
☐ 558	Elias Sosa	.15	.06	.01
☐ 559	Alan Bannister	.15	.06	.01
☐ 560	Dave Concepcion	.35	.14	.03
☐ 561	Pete LaCock	.15	.06	.01
☐ 562	Checklist 5	.70	.08	.01
☐ 563	Bruce Kison	.15	.06	.01
☐ 564	Alan Ashby	.25	.10	.02
☐ 565	Mickey Lolich	.35	.14	.03
☐ 566	Rick Miller	.15	.06	.01
☐ 567	Enos Cabell	.15	.06	.01
☐ 568	Carlos May	.15	.06	.01
☐ 569	Jim Lonborg	.25	.10	.02
☐ 570	Bobby Bonds	.35	.14	.03
☐ 571	Darrell Evans	.50	.20	.05
☐ 572	Ross Grimsley	.15	.06	.01
☐ 573	Joe Ferguson	.15	.06	.01
☐ 574	Aurelio Rodriguez	.15	.06	.01
☐ 575	Dick Ruthven	.15	.06	.01
☐ 576	Fred Kendall	.15	.06	.01
☐ 577	Jerry Augustine	.15	.06	.01
☐ 578	Bob Randall	.15	.06	.01
☐ 579	Don Carrithers	.15	.06	.01
☐ 580	George Brett	8.00	3.25	.80
☐ 581	Pedro Borbon	.15	.06	.01
☐ 582	Ed Kirkpatrick	.15	.06	.01
☐ 583	Paul Lindblad	.15	.06	.01
☐ 584	Ed Goodson	.15	.06	.01
☐ 585	Rick Burleson	.25	.10	.02
☐ 586	Steve Renko	.15	.06	.01
☐ 587	Rick Baldwin	.15	.06	.01
☐ 588	Dave Moates	.15	.06	.01
☐ 589	Mike Cosgrove	.15	.06	.01
☐ 590	Buddy Bell	.35	.14	.03
☐ 591	Chris Arnold	.15	.06	.01
☐ 592	Dan Briggs	.15	.06	.01
☐ 593	Dennis Blair	.15	.06	.01
☐ 594	Biff Pocoroba	.15	.06	.01
☐ 595	John Hiller	.25	.10	.02
☐ 596	Jerry Martin	.15	.06	.01
☐ 597	Mariners Leaders	.50	.10	.02
	Darrell Johnson MG			
	Don Bryant CO			
	Jim Busby CO			
	Vada Pinson CO			
	Wes Stock CO			
	(checklist back)			
☐ 598	Sparky Lyle	.35	.14	.03
☐ 599	Mike Tyson	.15	.06	.01
☐ 600	Jim Palmer	2.00	.80	.20
☐ 601	Mike Lum	.15	.06	.01
☐ 602	Andy Hassler	.15	.06	.01
☐ 603	Willie Davis	.25	.10	.02
☐ 604	Jim Slaton	.15	.06	.01
☐ 605	Felix Millan	.15	.06	.01
☐ 606	Steve Braun	.15	.06	.01
☐ 607	Larry Demery	.15	.06	.01
☐ 608	Roy Howell	.15	.06	.01
☐ 609	Jim Barr	.15	.06	.01
☐ 610	Jose Cardenal	.15	.06	.01
☐ 611	Dave Lemanczyk	.15	.06	.01
☐ 612	Barry Foote	.15	.06	.01
☐ 613	Reggie Cleveland	.15	.06	.01
☐ 614	Greg Gross	.15	.06	.01
☐ 615	Phil Niekro	1.50	.60	.15
☐ 616	Tommy Sandt	.15	.06	.01
☐ 617	Bobby Darwin	.15	.06	.01
☐ 618	Pat Dobson	.25	.10	.02
☐ 619	Johnny Oates	.15	.06	.01
☐ 620	Don Sutton	1.50	.60	.15
☐ 621	Tigers Team/Mgr.	.75	.20	.04
	Ralph Houk			
	(checklist back)			
☐ 622	Jim Wohlford	.15	.06	.01
☐ 623	Jack Kucek	.15	.06	.01
☐ 624	Hector Cruz	.15	.06	.01
☐ 625	Ken Holtzman	.25	.10	.02
☐ 626	Al Bumbry	.15	.06	.01
☐ 627	Bob Myrick	.15	.06	.01
☐ 628	Mario Guerrero	.15	.06	.01
☐ 629	Bob Valentine	.35	.14	.03
☐ 630	Bert Blyleven	.50	.20	.05
☐ 631	Big League Brothers	1.50	.60	.15
	George Brett			
	Ken Brett			
☐ 632	Big League Brothers	.25	.10	.02
	Bob Forsch			
	Ken Forsch			

□ 633 Big League Brothers Lee May Carlos May	.25	.10	.02
□ 634 Big League Brothers Paul Reuschel Rick Reuschel (photos switched)	.25	.10	.02
□ 635 Robin Yount	4.00	1.60	.40
□ 636 Santo Alcala	.15	.06	.01
□ 637 Alex Johnson	.15	.06	.01
□ 638 Jim Kaat	.60	.24	.06
□ 639 Jerry Morales	.15	.06	.01
□ 640 Carlton Fisk	.90	.36	.09
□ 641 Dan Larson	.15	.06	.01
□ 642 Willie Crawford	.15	.06	.01
□ 643 Mike Pazik	.15	.06	.01
□ 644 Matt Alexander	.15	.06	.01
□ 645 Jerry Reuss	.25	.10	.02
□ 646 Andres Mora	.15	.06	.01
□ 647 Expos Team/Mgr. Dick Williams (checklist back)	.65	.15	.03
□ 648 Jim Spencer	.15	.06	.01
□ 649 Dave Cash	.15	.06	.01
□ 650 Nolan Ryan	4.50	1.80	.45
□ 651 Von Joshua	.15	.06	.01
□ 652 Tom Walker	.15	.06	.01
□ 653 Diego Segui	.15	.06	.01
□ 654 Ron Pruitt	.15	.06	.01
□ 655 Tony Perez	.75	.30	.07
□ 656 Ron Guidry	3.00	1.20	.30
□ 657 Mick Kelleher	.15	.06	.01
□ 658 Marty Pattin	.15	.06	.01
□ 659 Merv Rettenmund	.15	.06	.01
□ 660 Willie Horton	.25	.10	.02

1978 Topps

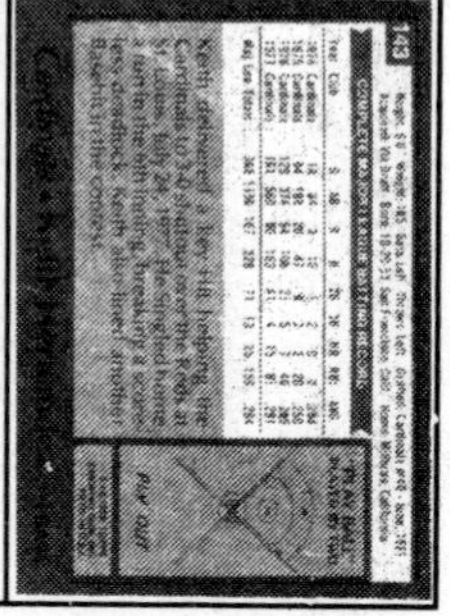

The cards in this 726-card set measure 2 1/2" by 3 1/2". The 1978 Topps set experienced an increase in number of cards from the previous five regular issue sets of 660. Cards 1 through 7 feature Record Breakers (RB) of the 1977 season. Other subsets within this set include League Leaders (201-208), Post-season cards (411-413), and Rookie Prospects (701-711). While no scarcities exist, 66 of the cards are more abundant in supply as they were "double printed." These 66 double-printed cards are noted in the checklist by DP. Team cards again feature a checklist of that team's players in the set on the back. Cards numbered 23 or lower which feature Astros, Rangers, Tigers, or Yankees and do not follow the numbering checklisted below are not necessarily error cards. They are probably Burger King cards, a separate set with its own pricing and mass distribution. Burger King cards are indistinguishable from the corresponding Topps cards except for the card numbering difference and the fact that Burger King cards do not have a printing sheet designation (such as A through F like the regular Topps) anywhere on the card back in very small print.

	NRMT	VG-E	GOOD
COMPLETE SET (726)	200.00	80.00	20.00
COMMON PLAYER (1-726)	.12	.05	.01
COMMON DP's (1-726)	.05	.02	.00
□ 1 RB: Lou Brock Most steals, lifetime	2.00	.40	.08
□ 2 RB: Sparky Lyle Most games, pure relief, lifetime	.20	.08	.02
□ 3 RB: Willie McCovey Most times, 2 HR's in inning, lifetime	.75	.30	.07
□ 4 RB: Brooks Robinson Most consecutive seasons with one club	.90	.36	.09
□ 5 RB: Pete Rose Most hits, switch hitter, lifetime	2.25	.90	.22
□ 6 RB: Nolan Ryan Most games with 10 or more strikeouts, lifetime	1.50	.60	.15
□ 7 RB: Reggie Jackson Most homers, one World Series	2.00	.80	.20
□ 8 Mike Sadek	.12	.05	.01
□ 9 Doug DeCinces	.20	.08	.02
□ 10 Phil Niekro	1.25	.50	.12
□ 11 Rick Manning	.12	.05	.01
□ 12 Don Aase	.12	.05	.01
□ 13 Art Howe	.20	.08	.02
□ 14 Lerrin LaGrow	.12	.05	.01
□ 15 Tony Perez DP	.20	.08	.02
□ 16 Roy White	.20	.08	.02
□ 17 Mike Krukow	.20	.08	.02
□ 18 Bob Grich	.20	.08	.02
□ 19 Darrell Porter	.12	.05	.01
□ 20 Pete Rose DP	4.00	1.60	.40
□ 21 Steve Kemp	.20	.08	.02
□ 22 Charlie Hough	.20	.08	.02
□ 23 Bump Wills	.12	.05	.01
□ 24 Don Money DP	.05	.02	.00
□ 25 Jon Matlack	.20	.08	.02
□ 26 Rich Hebner	.20	.08	.02
□ 27 Geoff Zahn	.12	.05	.01
□ 28 Ed Ott	.12	.05	.01
□ 29 Bob Lacey	.12	.05	.01
□ 30 George Hendrick	.20	.08	.02
□ 31 Glenn Abbott	.12	.05	.01
□ 32 Garry Templeton	.20	.08	.02
□ 33 Dave Lemanczyk	.12	.05	.01
□ 34 Willie McCovey	2.00	.80	.20
□ 35 Sparky Lyle	.30	.12	.03
□ 36 Eddie Murray	35.00	14.00	3.50
□ 37 Rick Waits	.12	.05	.01
□ 38 Willie Montanez	.12	.05	.01
□ 39 Floyd Bannister	1.25	.50	.12
□ 40 Carl Yastrzemski	3.50	1.40	.35
□ 41 Burt Hooton	.12	.05	.01
□ 42 Jorge Orta	.12	.05	.01
□ 43 Bill Atkinson	.12	.05	.01
□ 44 Toby Harrah	.20	.08	.02
□ 45 Mark Fidrych	.30	.12	.03
□ 46 Al Cowens	.12	.05	.01
□ 47 Jack Billingham	.12	.05	.01
□ 48 Don Baylor	.50	.20	.05
□ 49 Ed Kranepool	.12	.05	.01
□ 50 Rick Reuschel	.30	.12	.03
□ 51 Charlie Moore DP	.05	.02	.00
□ 52 Jim Lonborg	.20	.08	.02
□ 53 Phil Garner DP	.05	.02	.00
□ 54 Tom Johnson	.12	.05	.01
□ 55 Mitchell Page	.12	.05	.01
□ 56 Randy Jones	.12	.05	.01
□ 57 Dan Meyer	.12	.05	.01
□ 58 Bob Forsch	.20	.08	.02
□ 59 Otto Velez	.12	.05	.01
□ 60 Thurman Munson	2.25	.90	.22
□ 61 Larvell Blanks	.12	.05	.01
□ 62 Jim Barr	.12	.05	.01
□ 63 Don Zimmer	.20	.08	.02
□ 64 Gene Pentz	.12	.05	.01
□ 65 Ken Singleton	.20	.08	.02
□ 66 White Sox Team (checklist back)	.50	.10	.02
□ 67 Claudell Washington	.20	.08	.02
□ 68 Steve Foucault DP	.05	.02	.00
□ 69 Mike Vail	.12	.05	.01
□ 70 Rich Gossage	.60	.24	.06
□ 71 Terry Humphrey	.12	.05	.01
□ 72 Andre Dawson	6.50	2.60	.65
□ 73 Andy Hassler	.12	.05	.01
□ 74 Checklist 1	.45	.05	.01
□ 75 Dick Ruthven	.12	.05	.01
□ 76 Steve Ontiveros	.12	.05	.01

□ 77 Ed Kirkpatrick .12 .05 .01
□ 78 Pablo Torrealba .12 .05 .01
□ 79 Darrell Johnson DP .05 .02 .00
□ 80 Ken Griffey .20 .08 .02
□ 81 Pete Redfern .12 .05 .01
□ 82 Giants Team .50 .10 .02
(checklist back)
□ 83 Bob Montgomery .12 .05 .01
□ 84 Kent Tekulve .20 .08 .02
□ 85 Ron Fairly .12 .05 .01
□ 86 Dave Tomlin .12 .05 .01
□ 87 John Lowenstein .12 .05 .01
□ 88 Mike Phillips .12 .05 .01
□ 89 Ken Clay .12 .05 .01
□ 90 Larry Bowa .30 .12 .03
□ 91 Oscar Zamora .12 .05 .01
□ 92 Adrian Devine .12 .05 .01
□ 93 Bobby Cox DP .05 .02 .00
□ 94 Chuck Scrivener .12 .05 .01
□ 95 Jamie Quirk .12 .05 .01
□ 96 Orioles Team .50 .10 .02
(checklist back)
□ 97 Stan Bahnsen .12 .05 .01
□ 98 Jim Essian .12 .05 .01
□ 99 Willie Hernandez 1.00 .40 .10
□ 100 George Brett 4.00 1.60 .40
□ 101 Sid Monge .12 .05 .01
□ 102 Matt Alexander .12 .05 .01
□ 103 Tom Murphy .12 .05 .01
□ 104 Lee Lacy .12 .05 .01
□ 105 Reggie Cleveland .12 .05 .01
□ 106 Bill Plummer .12 .05 .01
□ 107 Ed Halicki .12 .05 .01
□ 108 Von Joshua .12 .05 .01
□ 109 Joe Torre .30 .12 .03
□ 110 Richie Zisk .12 .05 .01
□ 111 Mike Tyson .12 .05 .01
□ 112 Astros Team .50 .10 .02
(checklist back)
□ 113 Don Carrithers .12 .05 .01
□ 114 Paul Blair .12 .05 .01
□ 115 Gary Nolan .12 .05 .01
□ 116 Tucker Ashford .12 .05 .01
□ 117 John Montague .12 .05 .01
□ 118 Terry Harmon .12 .05 .01
□ 119 Denny Martinez .20 .08 .02
□ 120 Gary Carter 3.00 1.20 .30
□ 121 Alvis Woods .12 .05 .01
□ 122 Dennis Eckersley .75 .30 .07
□ 123 Manny Trillo .12 .05 .01
□ 124 Dave Rozema .12 .05 .01
□ 125 George Scott .20 .08 .02
□ 126 Paul Moskau .12 .05 .01
□ 127 Chet Lemon .20 .08 .02
□ 128 Bill Russell .20 .08 .02
□ 129 Jim Colborn .12 .05 .01
□ 130 Jeff Burroughs .20 .08 .02
□ 131 Bert Blyleven .50 .20 .05
□ 132 Enos Cabell .12 .05 .01
□ 133 Jerry Augustine .12 .05 .01
□ 134 Steve Henderson .12 .05 .01
□ 135 Ron Guidry DP .60 .24 .06
□ 136 Ted Sizemore .12 .05 .01
□ 137 Craig Kusick .12 .05 .01
□ 138 Larry Demery .12 .05 .01
□ 139 Wayne Gross .12 .05 .01
□ 140 Rollie Fingers .60 .24 .06
□ 141 Ruppert Jones .12 .05 .01
□ 142 John Montefusco .20 .08 .02
□ 143 Keith Hernandez 2.50 1.00 .25
□ 144 Jesse Jefferson .12 .05 .01
□ 145 Rick Monday .12 .05 .01
□ 146 Doyle Alexander .20 .08 .02
□ 147 Lee Mazzilli .12 .05 .01
□ 148 Andre Thornton .20 .08 .02
□ 149 Dale Murray .12 .05 .01
□ 150 Bobby Bonds .30 .12 .03
□ 151 Milt Wilcox .12 .05 .01
□ 152 Ivan DeJesus .12 .05 .01
□ 153 Steve Stone .12 .05 .01
□ 154 Cecil Cooper DP .20 .08 .02
□ 155 Butch Hobson .12 .05 .01
□ 156 Andy Messersmith .20 .08 .02
□ 157 Pete LaCock DP .05 .02 .00
□ 158 Joaquin Andujar .30 .12 .03
□ 159 Lou Piniella .20 .08 .02
□ 160 Jim Palmer 2.00 .80 .20
□ 161 Bob Boone .30 .12 .03
□ 162 Paul Thormodsgard .12 .05 .01
□ 163 Bill North .12 .05 .01
□ 164 Bob Owchinko .12 .05 .01
□ 165 Rennie Stennett .12 .05 .01
□ 166 Carlos Lopez .12 .05 .01
□ 167 Tim Foli .12 .05 .01
□ 168 Reggie Smith .20 .08 .02
□ 169 Jerry Johnson .12 .05 .01
□ 170 Lou Brock 2.00 .80 .20
□ 171 Pat Zachry .12 .05 .01
□ 172 Mike Hargrove .12 .05 .01
□ 173 Robin Yount 2.50 1.00 .25
□ 174 Wayne Garland .12 .05 .01
□ 175 Jerry Morales .12 .05 .01
□ 176 Milt May .12 .05 .01
□ 177 Gene Garber DP .05 .02 .00
□ 178 Dave Chalk .12 .05 .01
□ 179 Dick Tidrow .12 .05 .01
□ 180 Dave Concepcion .30 .12 .03
□ 181 Ken Forsch .12 .05 .01
□ 182 Jim Spencer .12 .05 .01
□ 183 Doug Bird .12 .05 .01
□ 184 Checklist 2 .45 .05 .01
□ 185 Ellis Valentine .12 .05 .01
□ 186 Bob Stanley DP .30 .12 .03
□ 187 Jerry Royster DP .05 .02 .00
□ 188 Al Bumbry .12 .05 .01
□ 189 Tom Lasorda MG .30 .12 .03
□ 190 John Candelaria .30 .12 .03
□ 191 Rodney Scott .12 .05 .01
□ 192 Padres Team .50 .10 .02
(checklist back)
□ 193 Rich Chiles .12 .05 .01
□ 194 Derrel Thomas .12 .05 .01
□ 195 Larry Dierker .12 .05 .01
□ 196 Bob Bailor .12 .05 .01
□ 197 Nino Espinosa .12 .05 .01
□ 198 Ron Pruitt .12 .05 .01
□ 199 Craig Reynolds .12 .05 .01
□ 200 Reggie Jackson 3.50 1.40 .35
□ 201 Batting Leaders .60 .24 .06
Dave Parker
Rod Carew
□ 202 Home Run Leaders DP .12 .05 .01
George Foster
Jim Rice
□ 203 RBI Leaders .20 .08 .02
George Foster
Larry Hisle
□ 204 Steals Leaders DP .12 .05 .01
Frank Taveras
Freddie Patek
□ 205 Victory Leaders .50 .20 .05
Steve Carlton
Dave Goltz
Dennis Leonard
Jim Palmer
□ 206 Strikeout Leaders DP .20 .08 .02
Phil Niekro
Nolan Ryan
□ 207 ERA Leaders DP .12 .05 .01
John Candelaria
Frank Tanana
□ 208 Top Firemen .20 .08 .02
Rollie Fingers
Bill Campbell
□ 209 Dock Ellis .12 .05 .01
□ 210 Jose Cardenal .12 .05 .01
□ 211 Earl Weaver MG DP .12 .05 .01
□ 212 Mike Caldwell .12 .05 .01
□ 213 Alan Bannister .12 .05 .01
□ 214 Angels Team .50 .10 .02
(checklist back)
□ 215 Darrell Evans .40 .16 .04
□ 216 Mike Paxton .12 .05 .01
□ 217 Rod Gilbreath .12 .05 .01
□ 218 Marty Pattin .12 .05 .01
□ 219 Mike Cubbage .12 .05 .01
□ 220 Pedro Borbon .12 .05 .01
□ 221 Chris Speier .12 .05 .01
□ 222 Jerry Martin .12 .05 .01
□ 223 Bruce Kison .12 .05 .01
□ 224 Jerry Tabb .12 .05 .01
□ 225 Don Gullett DP .05 .02 .00
□ 226 Joe Ferguson .12 .05 .01
□ 227 Al Fitzmorris .12 .05 .01
□ 228 Manny Mota DP .12 .05 .01
□ 229 Leo Foster .12 .05 .01
□ 230 Al Hrabosky .12 .05 .01
□ 231 Wayne Nordhagen .12 .05 .01
□ 232 Mickey Stanley .12 .05 .01
□ 233 Dick Pole .12 .05 .01
□ 234 Herman Franks MG .12 .05 .01
□ 235 Tim McCarver .30 .12 .03
□ 236 Terry Whitfield .12 .05 .01
□ 237 Rich Dauer .12 .05 .01
□ 238 Juan Beniquez .12 .05 .01
□ 239 Dyar Miller .12 .05 .01
□ 240 Gene Tenace .20 .08 .02
□ 241 Pete Vuckovich .20 .08 .02
□ 242 Barry Bonnell DP .12 .05 .01
□ 243 Bob McClure .12 .05 .01

☐ 244 Expos Team DP .20 .04 .01
(checklist back)
☐ 245 Rick Burleson .20 .08 .02
☐ 246 Dan Driessen .12 .05 .01
☐ 247 Larry Christenson .12 .05 .01
☐ 248 Frank White DP .12 .05 .01
☐ 249 Dave Goltz DP .05 .02 .00
☐ 250 Graig Nettles DP .12 .05 .01
☐ 251 Don Kirkwood .12 .05 .01
☐ 252 Steve Swisher DP .05 .02 .00
☐ 253 Jim Kern .12 .05 .01
☐ 254 Dave Collins .12 .05 .01
☐ 255 Jerry Reuss .20 .08 .02
☐ 256 Joe Altobelli MG .12 .05 .01
☐ 257 Hector Cruz .12 .05 .01
☐ 258 John Hiller .12 .05 .01
☐ 259 Dodgers Team .50 .10 .02
(checklist back)
☐ 260 Bert Campaneris .20 .08 .02
☐ 261 Tim Hosley .12 .05 .01
☐ 262 Rudy May .12 .05 .01
☐ 263 Danny Walton .12 .05 .01
☐ 264 Jamie Easterly .12 .05 .01
☐ 265 Sal Bando DP .12 .05 .01
☐ 266 Bob Shirley .12 .05 .01
☐ 267 Doug Ault .12 .05 .01
☐ 268 Gil Flores .12 .05 .01
☐ 269 Wayne Twitchell .12 .05 .01
☐ 270 Carlton Fisk .60 .24 .06
☐ 271 Randy Lerch DP .05 .02 .00
☐ 272 Royle Stillman .12 .05 .01
☐ 273 Fred Norman .12 .05 .01
☐ 274 Freddie Patek .12 .05 .01
☐ 275 Dan Ford .12 .05 .01
☐ 276 Bill Bonham DP .05 .02 .00
☐ 277 Bruce Boisclair .12 .05 .01
☐ 278 Enrique Romo .12 .05 .01
☐ 279 Bill Virdon MG .20 .08 .02
☐ 280 Buddy Bell .30 .12 .03
☐ 281 Eric Rasmussen DP .05 .02 .00
☐ 282 Yankees Team .60 .15 .04
(checklist back)
☐ 283 Omar Moreno .12 .05 .01
☐ 284 Randy Moffitt .12 .05 .01
☐ 285 Steve Yeager DP .05 .02 .00
☐ 286 Ben Oglivie .20 .08 .02
☐ 287 Kiko Garcia .12 .05 .01
☐ 288 Dave Hamilton .12 .05 .01
☐ 289 Checklist 3 .45 .05 .01
☐ 290 Willie Horton .20 .08 .02
☐ 291 Gary Ross .12 .05 .01
☐ 292 Gene Richards .12 .05 .01
☐ 293 Mike Willis .12 .05 .01
☐ 294 Larry Parrish .20 .08 .02
☐ 295 Bill Lee .20 .08 .02
☐ 296 Biff Pocoroba .12 .05 .01
☐ 297 Warren Brusstar DP .05 .02 .00
☐ 298 Tony Armas .20 .08 .02
☐ 299 Whitey Herzog MG .20 .08 .02
☐ 300 Joe Morgan 1.50 .60 .15
☐ 301 Buddy Schultz .12 .05 .01
☐ 302 Cubs Team .50 .10 .02
(checklist back)
☐ 303 Sam Hinds .12 .05 .01
☐ 304 John Milner .12 .05 .01
☐ 305 Rico Carty .20 .08 .02
☐ 306 Joe Niekro .30 .12 .03
☐ 307 Glenn Borgmann .12 .05 .01
☐ 308 Jim Rooker .12 .05 .01
☐ 309 Cliff Johnson .12 .05 .01
☐ 310 Don Sutton 1.25 .50 .12
☐ 311 Jose Baez DP .05 .02 .00
☐ 312 Greg Minton .12 .05 .01
☐ 313 Andy Etchebarren .12 .05 .01
☐ 314 Paul Lindblad .12 .05 .01
☐ 315 Mark Belanger .20 .08 .02
☐ 316 Henry Cruz DP .05 .02 .00
☐ 317 Dave Johnson .30 .12 .03
☐ 318 Tom Griffin .12 .05 .01
☐ 319 Alan Ashby .20 .08 .02
☐ 320 Fred Lynn .75 .30 .07
☐ 321 Santo Alcala .12 .05 .01
☐ 322 Tom Paciorek .12 .05 .01
☐ 323 Jim Fregosi DP .12 .05 .01
☐ 324 Vern Rapp MG .12 .05 .01
☐ 325 Bruce Sutter .60 .24 .06
☐ 326 Mike Lum DP .05 .02 .00
☐ 327 Rick Langford DP .05 .02 .00
☐ 328 Milwaukee Brewers .50 .10 .02
Team Card
(checklist back)
☐ 329 John Verhoeven .12 .05 .01
☐ 330 Bob Watson .20 .08 .02
☐ 331 Mark Littell .12 .05 .01
☐ 332 Duane Kuiper .12 .05 .01
☐ 333 Jim Todd .12 .05 .01
☐ 334 John Stearns .12 .05 .01
☐ 335 Bucky Dent .20 .08 .02
☐ 336 Steve Busby .12 .05 .01
☐ 337 Tom Grieve .20 .08 .02
☐ 338 Dave Heaverlo .12 .05 .01
☐ 339 Mario Guerrero .12 .05 .01
☐ 340 Bake McBride .12 .05 .01
☐ 341 Mike Flanagan .20 .08 .02
☐ 342 Aurelio Rodriguez .12 .05 .01
☐ 343 John Wathan DP .12 .05 .01
☐ 344 Sam Ewing .12 .05 .01
☐ 345 Luis Tiant .20 .08 .02
☐ 346 Larry Biittner .12 .05 .01
☐ 347 Terry Forster .20 .08 .02
☐ 348 Del Unser .12 .05 .01
☐ 349 Rick Camp DP .05 .02 .00
☐ 350 Steve Garvey 3.00 1.20 .30
☐ 351 Jeff Torborg .20 .08 .02
☐ 352 Tony Scott .12 .05 .01
☐ 353 Doug Bair .12 .05 .01
☐ 354 Cesar Geronimo .12 .05 .01
☐ 355 Bill Travers .12 .05 .01
☐ 356 New York Mets .50 .10 .02
Team Card
(checklist back)
☐ 357 Tom Poquette .12 .05 .01
☐ 358 Mark Lemongello .12 .05 .01
☐ 359 Marc Hill .12 .05 .01
☐ 360 Mike Schmidt 5.00 2.00 .50
☐ 361 Chris Knapp .12 .05 .01
☐ 362 Dave May .12 .05 .01
☐ 363 Bob Randall .12 .05 .01
☐ 364 Jerry Turner .12 .05 .01
☐ 365 Ed Figueroa .12 .05 .01
☐ 366 Larry Milbourne DP .05 .02 .00
☐ 367 Rick Dempsey .12 .05 .01
☐ 368 Balor Moore .12 .05 .01
☐ 369 Tim Nordbrook .12 .05 .01
☐ 370 Rusty Staub .30 .12 .03
☐ 371 Ray Burris .12 .05 .01
☐ 372 Brian Asselstine .12 .05 .01
☐ 373 Jim Willoughby .12 .05 .01
☐ 374 Jose Morales .12 .05 .01
☐ 375 Tommy John .75 .30 .07
☐ 376 Jim Wohlford .12 .05 .01
☐ 377 Manny Sarmiento .12 .05 .01
☐ 378 Bobby Winkles MG .12 .05 .01
☐ 379 Skip Lockwood .12 .05 .01
☐ 380 Ted Simmons .40 .16 .04
☐ 381 Phillies Team .50 .10 .02
(checklist back)
☐ 382 Joe Lahoud .12 .05 .01
☐ 383 Mario Mendoza .12 .05 .01
☐ 384 Jack Clark 4.00 1.60 .40
☐ 385 Tito Fuentes .12 .05 .01
☐ 386 Bob Gorinski .12 .05 .01
☐ 387 Ken Holtzman .12 .05 .01
☐ 388 Bill Fahey DP .05 .02 .00
☐ 389 Julio Gonzalez .12 .05 .01
☐ 390 Oscar Gamble .12 .05 .01
☐ 391 Larry Haney .12 .05 .01
☐ 392 Billy Almon .12 .05 .01
☐ 393 Tippy Martinez .12 .05 .01
☐ 394 Roy Howell DP .05 .02 .00
☐ 395 Jim Hughes .12 .05 .01
☐ 396 Bob Stinson DP .05 .02 .00
☐ 397 Greg Gross .12 .05 .01
☐ 398 Don Hood .12 .05 .01
☐ 399 Pete Mackanin .12 .05 .01
☐ 400 Nolan Ryan 3.00 1.20 .30
☐ 401 Sparky Anderson MG .20 .08 .02
☐ 402 Dave Campbell .12 .05 .01
☐ 403 Bud Harrelson .12 .05 .01
☐ 404 Tigers Team .50 .10 .02
(checklist back)
☐ 405 Rawly Eastwick .12 .05 .01
☐ 406 Mike Jorgensen .12 .05 .01
☐ 407 Odell Jones .12 .05 .01
☐ 408 Joe Zdeb .12 .05 .01
☐ 409 Ron Schueler .12 .05 .01
☐ 410 Bill Madlock .40 .16 .04
☐ 411 AL Champs .50 .20 .05
Yankees rally to
defeat Royals
☐ 412 NL Champs .50 .20 .05
Dodgers overpower
Phillies in four
☐ 413 World Series 1.25 .50 .12
Reggie and Yankees
reign supreme
☐ 414 Darold Knowles DP .05 .02 .00
☐ 415 Ray Fosse .12 .05 .01
☐ 416 Jack Brohamer .12 .05 .01
☐ 417 Mike Garman DP .05 .02 .00

☐ 418 Tony Muser .12 .05 .01
☐ 419 Jerry Garvin .12 .05 .01
☐ 420 Greg Luzinski .30 .12 .03
☐ 421 Junior Moore .12 .05 .01
☐ 422 Steve Braun .12 .05 .01
☐ 423 Dave Rosello .12 .05 .01
☐ 424 Boston Red Sox .50 .10 .02
Team Card
(checklist back)
☐ 425 Steve Rogers DP .12 .05 .01
☐ 426 Fred Kendall .12 .05 .01
☐ 427 Mario Soto .75 .30 .07
☐ 428 Joel Youngblood .12 .05 .01
☐ 429 Mike Barlow .12 .05 .01
☐ 430 Al Oliver .30 .12 .03
☐ 431 Butch Metzger .12 .05 .01
☐ 432 Terry Bulling .12 .05 .01
☐ 433 Fernando Gonzalez .12 .05 .01
☐ 434 Mike Norris .12 .05 .01
☐ 435 Checklist 4 .45 .05 .01
☐ 436 Vic Harris DP .05 .02 .00
☐ 437 Bo McLaughlin .12 .05 .01
☐ 438 John Ellis .12 .05 .01
☐ 439 Ken Kravec .12 .05 .01
☐ 440 Dave Lopes .20 .08 .02
☐ 441 Larry Gura .12 .05 .01
☐ 442 Elliott Maddox .12 .05 .01
☐ 443 Darrel Chaney .12 .05 .01
☐ 444 Roy Hartsfield MG .12 .05 .01
☐ 445 Mike Ivie .12 .05 .01
☐ 446 Tug McGraw .30 .12 .03
☐ 447 Leroy Stanton .12 .05 .01
☐ 448 Bill Castro .12 .05 .01
☐ 449 Tim Blackwell DP .05 .02 .00
☐ 450 Tom Seaver 2.50 1.00 .25
☐ 451 Minnesota Twins .50 .10 .02
Team Card
(checklist back)
☐ 452 Jerry Mumphrey .12 .05 .01
☐ 453 Doug Flynn .12 .05 .01
☐ 454 Dave LaRoche .12 .05 .01
☐ 455 Bill Robinson .20 .08 .02
☐ 456 Vern Ruhle .12 .05 .01
☐ 457 Bob Bailey .12 .05 .01
☐ 458 Jeff Newman .12 .05 .01
☐ 459 Charlie Spikes .12 .05 .01
☐ 460 Jim Hunter 1.50 .60 .15
☐ 461 Rob Andrews DP .05 .02 .00
☐ 462 Rogelio Moret .12 .05 .01
☐ 463 Kevin Bell .12 .05 .01
☐ 464 Jerry Grote .12 .05 .01
☐ 465 Hal McRae .20 .08 .02
☐ 466 Dennis Blair .12 .05 .01
☐ 467 Alvin Dark MG .12 .05 .01
☐ 468 Warren Cromartie .12 .05 .01
☐ 469 Rick Cerone .12 .05 .01
☐ 470 J.R. Richard .20 .08 .02
☐ 471 Roy Smalley .12 .05 .01
☐ 472 Ron Reed .12 .05 .01
☐ 473 Bill Buckner .30 .12 .03
☐ 474 Jim Slaton .12 .05 .01
☐ 475 Gary Matthews .20 .08 .02
☐ 476 Bill Stein .12 .05 .01
☐ 477 Doug Capilla .12 .05 .01
☐ 478 Jerry Remy .12 .05 .01
☐ 479 Cardinals Team .50 .10 .02
(checklist back)
☐ 480 Ron LeFlore .12 .05 .01
☐ 481 Jackson Todd .12 .05 .01
☐ 482 Rick Miller .12 .05 .01
☐ 483 Ken Macha .12 .05 .01
☐ 484 Jim Norris .12 .05 .01
☐ 485 Chris Chambliss .20 .08 .02
☐ 486 John Curtis .12 .05 .01
☐ 487 Jim Tyrone .12 .05 .01
☐ 488 Dan Spillner .12 .05 .01
☐ 489 Rudy Meoli .12 .05 .01
☐ 490 Amos Otis .20 .08 .02
☐ 491 Scott McGregor .20 .08 .02
☐ 492 Jim Sundberg .12 .05 .01
☐ 493 Steve Renko .12 .05 .01
☐ 494 Chuck Tanner MG .12 .05 .01
☐ 495 Dave Cash .12 .05 .01
☐ 496 Jim Clancy DP .20 .08 .02
☐ 497 Glenn Adams .12 .05 .01
☐ 498 Joe Sambito .12 .05 .01
☐ 499 Seattle Mariners .50 .10 .02
Team Card
(checklist back)
☐ 500 George Foster .60 .24 .06
☐ 501 Dave Roberts .12 .05 .01
☐ 502 Pat Rockett .12 .05 .01
☐ 503 Ike Hampton .12 .05 .01
☐ 504 Roger Freed .12 .05 .01
☐ 505 Felix Millan .12 .05 .01
☐ 506 Ron Blomberg .12 .05 .01
☐ 507 Willie Crawford .12 .05 .01
☐ 508 Johnny Oates .12 .05 .01
☐ 509 Brent Strom .12 .05 .01
☐ 510 Willie Stargell 2.00 .80 .20
☐ 511 Frank Duffy .12 .05 .01
☐ 512 Larry Herndon .12 .05 .01
☐ 513 Barry Foote .12 .05 .01
☐ 514 Rob Sperring .12 .05 .01
☐ 515 Tim Corcoran .12 .05 .01
☐ 516 Gary Beare .12 .05 .01
☐ 517 Andres Mora .12 .05 .01
☐ 518 Tommy Boggs DP .05 .02 .00
☐ 519 Brian Downing .12 .05 .01
☐ 520 Larry Hisle .12 .05 .01
☐ 521 Steve Staggs .12 .05 .01
☐ 522 Dick Williams MG .12 .05 .01
☐ 523 Donnie Moore .30 .12 .03
☐ 524 Bernie Carbo .12 .05 .01
☐ 525 Jerry Terrell .12 .05 .01
☐ 526 Reds Team .50 .10 .02
(checklist back)
☐ 527 Vic Correll .12 .05 .01
☐ 528 Rob Picciolo .12 .05 .01
☐ 529 Paul Hartzell .12 .05 .01
☐ 530 Dave Winfield 2.50 1.00 .25
☐ 531 Tom Underwood .12 .05 .01
☐ 532 Skip Jutze .12 .05 .01
☐ 533 Sandy Alomar .12 .05 .01
☐ 534 Wilbur Howard .12 .05 .01
☐ 535 Checklist 5 .45 .05 .01
☐ 536 Roric Harrison .12 .05 .01
☐ 537 Bruce Bochte .12 .05 .01
☐ 538 Johnny LeMaster .12 .05 .01
☐ 539 Vic Davalillo DP .05 .02 .00
☐ 540 Steve Carlton 2.50 1.00 .25
☐ 541 Larry Cox .12 .05 .01
☐ 542 Tim Johnson .12 .05 .01
☐ 543 Larry Harlow DP .05 .02 .00
☐ 544 Len Randle DP .05 .02 .00
☐ 545 Bill Campbell .12 .05 .01
☐ 546 Ted Martinez .12 .05 .01
☐ 547 John Scott .12 .05 .01
☐ 548 Billy Hunter MG DP .05 .02 .00
☐ 549 Joe Kerrigan .12 .05 .01
☐ 550 John Mayberry .20 .08 .02
☐ 551 Atlanta Braves .50 .10 .02
Team Card
(checklist back)
☐ 552 Francisco Barrios .12 .05 .01
☐ 553 Terry Puhl .40 .16 .04
☐ 554 Joe Coleman .12 .05 .01
☐ 555 Butch Wynegar .12 .05 .01
☐ 556 Ed Armbrister .12 .05 .01
☐ 557 Tony Solaita .12 .05 .01
☐ 558 Paul Mitchell .12 .05 .01
☐ 559 Phil Mankowski .12 .05 .01
☐ 560 Dave Parker 1.75 .70 .17
☐ 561 Charlie Williams .12 .05 .01
☐ 562 Glenn Burke .12 .05 .01
☐ 563 Dave Rader .12 .05 .01
☐ 564 Mick Kelleher .12 .05 .01
☐ 565 Jerry Koosman .20 .08 .02
☐ 566 Merv Rettenmund .12 .05 .01
☐ 567 Dick Drago .12 .05 .01
☐ 568 Tom Hutton .12 .05 .01
☐ 569 Lary Sorensen .12 .05 .01
☐ 570 Dave Kingman .50 .20 .05
☐ 571 Buck Martinez .12 .05 .01
☐ 572 Rick Wise .12 .05 .01
☐ 573 Luis Gomez .12 .05 .01
☐ 574 Bob Lemon MG .30 .12 .03
☐ 575 Pat Dobson .12 .05 .01
☐ 576 Sam Mejias .12 .05 .01
☐ 577 Oakland A's .50 .10 .02
Team Card
(checklist back)
☐ 578 Buzz Capra .12 .05 .01
☐ 579 Rance Mulliniks .20 .08 .02
☐ 580 Rod Carew 2.50 1.00 .25
☐ 581 Lynn McGlothen .12 .05 .01
☐ 582 Fran Healy .12 .05 .01
☐ 583 George Medich .12 .05 .01
☐ 584 John Hale .12 .05 .01
☐ 585 Woodie Fryman DP .05 .02 .00
☐ 586 Ed Goodson .12 .05 .01
☐ 587 John Urrea .12 .05 .01
☐ 588 Jim Mason .12 .05 .01
☐ 589 Bob Knepper 1.75 .70 .17
☐ 590 Bobby Murcer .30 .12 .03
☐ 591 George Zeber .12 .05 .01
☐ 592 Bob Apodaca .12 .05 .01
☐ 593 Dave Skaggs .12 .05 .01
☐ 594 Dave Freisleben .12 .05 .01
☐ 595 Sixto Lezcano .12 .05 .01

□ 596	Gary Wheelock	.12	.05	.01
□ 597	Steve Dillard	.12	.05	.01
□ 598	Eddie Solomon	.12	.05	.01
□ 599	Gary Woods	.12	.05	.01
□ 600	Frank Tanana	.20	.08	.02
□ 601	Gene Mauch MG	.12	.05	.01
□ 602	Eric Soderholm	.12	.05	.01
□ 603	Will McEnaney	.12	.05	.01
□ 604	Earl Williams	.12	.05	.01
□ 605	Rick Rhoden	.30	.12	.03
□ 606	Pirates Team	.50	.10	.02
	(checklist back)			
□ 607	Fernando Arroyo	.12	.05	.01
□ 608	Johnny Grubb	.12	.05	.01
□ 609	John Denny	.20	.08	.02
□ 610	Garry Maddox	.12	.05	.01
□ 611	Pat Scanlon	.12	.05	.01
□ 612	Ken Henderson	.12	.05	.01
□ 613	Marty Perez	.12	.05	.01
□ 614	Joe Wallis	.12	.05	.01
□ 615	Clay Carroll	.12	.05	.01
□ 616	Pat Kelly	.12	.05	.01
□ 617	Joe Nolan	.12	.05	.01
□ 618	Tommy Helms	.12	.05	.01
□ 619	Thad Bosley DP	.12	.05	.01
□ 620	Willie Randolph	.30	.12	.03
□ 621	Craig Swan DP	.12	.05	.01
□ 622	Champ Summers	.12	.05	.01
□ 623	Ed Rodriquez	.12	.05	.01
□ 624	Gary Alexander DP	.05	.02	.00
□ 625	Jose Cruz	.20	.08	.02
□ 626	Blue Jays Team DP	.20	.05	.01
	(checklist back)			
□ 627	David Johnson	.12	.05	.01
□ 628	Ralph Garr	.12	.05	.01
□ 629	Don Stanhouse	.12	.05	.01
□ 630	Ron Cey	.30	.12	.03
□ 631	Danny Ozark MG	.12	.05	.01
□ 632	Rowland Office	.12	.05	.01
□ 633	Tom Veryzer	.12	.05	.01
□ 634	Len Barker	.12	.05	.01
□ 635	Joe Rudi	.20	.08	.02
□ 636	Jim Bibby	.12	.05	.01
□ 637	Duffy Dyer	.12	.05	.01
□ 638	Paul Splittorff	.12	.05	.01
□ 639	Gene Clines	.12	.05	.01
□ 640	Lee May DP	.12	.05	.01
□ 641	Doug Rau	.12	.05	.01
□ 642	Denny Doyle	.12	.05	.01
□ 643	Tom House	.12	.05	.01
□ 644	Jim Dwyer	.12	.05	.01
□ 645	Mike Torrez	.12	.05	.01
□ 646	Rick Auerbach DP	.05	.02	.00
□ 647	Steve Dunning	.12	.05	.01
□ 648	Gary Thomasson	.12	.05	.01
□ 649	Moose Haas	.30	.12	.03
□ 650	Cesar Cedeno	.20	.08	.02
□ 651	Doug Rader	.20	.08	.02
□ 652	Checklist 6	.45	.05	.01
□ 653	Ron Hodges DP	.05	.02	.00
□ 654	Pepe Frias	.12	.05	.01
□ 655	Lyman Bostock	.20	.08	.02
□ 656	Dave Garcia MG	.12	.05	.01
□ 657	Bombo Rivera	.12	.05	.01
□ 658	Manny Sanguillen	.20	.08	.02
□ 659	Rangers Team	.50	.10	.02
	(checklist back)			
□ 660	Jason Thompson	.20	.08	.02
□ 661	Grant Jackson	.12	.05	.01
□ 662	Paul Dade	.12	.05	.01
□ 663	Paul Reuschel	.12	.05	.01
□ 664	Fred Stanley	.12	.05	.01
□ 665	Dennis Leonard	.20	.08	.02
□ 666	Billy Smith	.12	.05	.01
□ 667	Jeff Byrd	.12	.05	.01
□ 668	Dusty Baker	.20	.08	.02
□ 669	Pete Falcone	.12	.05	.01
□ 670	Jim Rice	3.50	1.40	.35
□ 671	Gary Lavelle	.12	.05	.01
□ 672	Don Kessinger	.12	.05	.01
□ 673	Steve Brye	.12	.05	.01
□ 674	Ray Knight	1.25	.50	.12
□ 675	Jay Johnstone	.20	.08	.02
□ 676	Bob Myrick	.12	.05	.01
□ 677	Ed Herrmann	.12	.05	.01
□ 678	Tom Burgmeier	.12	.05	.01
□ 679	Wayne Garrett	.12	.05	.01
□ 680	Vida Blue	.20	.08	.02
□ 681	Rob Belloir	.12	.05	.01
□ 682	Ken Brett	.12	.05	.01
□ 683	Mike Champion	.12	.05	.01
□ 684	Ralph Houk MG	.20	.08	.02
□ 685	Frank Taveras	.12	.05	.01
□ 686	Gaylord Perry	1.75	.70	.17
□ 687	Julio Cruz	.20	.08	.02
□ 688	George Mitterwald	.12	.05	.01
□ 689	Indians Team	.50	.10	.02
	(checklist back)			
□ 690	Mickey Rivers	.20	.08	.02
□ 691	Ross Grimsley	.12	.05	.01
□ 692	Ken Reitz	.12	.05	.01
□ 693	Lamar Johnson	.12	.05	.01
□ 694	Elias Sosa	.12	.05	.01
□ 695	Dwight Evans	1.00	.40	.10
□ 696	Steve Mingori	.12	.05	.01
□ 697	Roger Metzger	.12	.05	.01
□ 698	Juan Bernhardt	.12	.05	.01
□ 699	Jackie Brown	.12	.05	.01
□ 700	Johnny Bench	3.00	1.20	.30
□ 701	Rookie Pitchers	.30	.12	.03
	Tom Hume			
	Larry Landreth			
	Steve McCatty			
	Bruce Taylor			
□ 702	Rookie Catchers	.20	.08	.02
	Bill Nahordony			
	Kevin Pasley			
	Rick Sweet			
	Don Werner			
□ 703	Rookie Pitchers DP	6.50	2.60	.65
	Larry Andersen			
	Tim Jones			
	Mickey Mahler			
	Jack Morris			
□ 704	Rookie 2nd Basemen	7.50	3.00	.75
	Garth Iorg			
	Dave Oliver			
	Sam Perlozzo			
	Lou Whitaker			
□ 705	Rookie Outfielders	.30	.12	.03
	Dave Bergman			
	Miguel Dilone			
	Clint Hurdle			
	Willie Norwood			
□ 706	Rookie 1st Basemen	.20	.08	.02
	Wayne Cage			
	Ted Cox			
	Pat Putnam			
	Dave Revering			
□ 707	Rookie Shortstops	35.00	14.00	3.50
	Mickey Klutts			
	Paul Molitor			
	Alan Trammell			
	U.L. Washington			
□ 708	Rookie Catchers	35.00	14.00	3.50
	Bo Diaz			
	Dale Murphy			
	Lance Parrish			
	Ernie Whitt			
□ 709	Rookie Pitchers	.30	.12	.03
	Steve Burke			
	Matt Keough			
	Lance Rautzhan			
	Dan Schatzeder			
□ 710	Rookie Outfielders	.75	.30	.07
	Dell Alston			
	Rick Bosetti			
	Mike Easler			
	Keith Smith			
□ 711	Rookie Pitchers DP	.12	.05	.01
	Cardell Camper			
	Dennis Lamp			
	Craig Mitchell			
	Roy Thomas			
□ 712	Bobby Valentine	.30	.12	.03
□ 713	Bob Davis	.12	.05	.01
□ 714	Mike Anderson	.12	.05	.01
□ 715	Jim Kaat	.50	.20	.05
□ 716	Clarence Gaston	.12	.05	.01
□ 717	Nelson Briles	.12	.05	.01
□ 718	Ron Jackson	.12	.05	.01
□ 719	Randy Elliott	.12	.05	.01
□ 720	Fergie Jenkins	.40	.16	.04
□ 721	Billy Martin MG	.40	.16	.04
□ 722	Pete Broberg	.12	.05	.01
□ 723	John Wockenfuss	.12	.05	.01
□ 724	Kansas City Royals	.50	.10	.02
	Team Card			
	(checklist back)			
□ 725	Kurt Bevacqua	.12	.05	.01
□ 726	Wilbur Wood	.20	.08	.02

1979 Topps

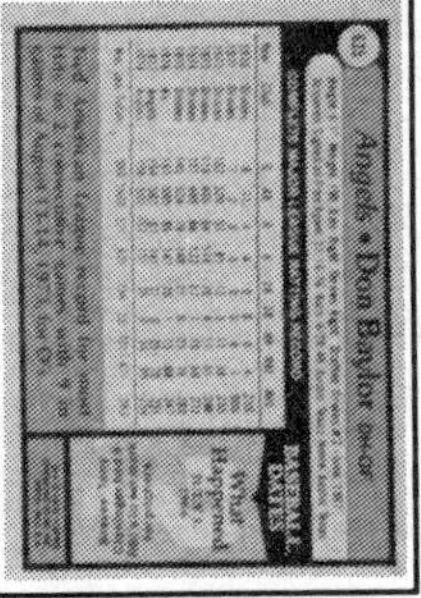

The cards in this 726-card set measure 2 1/2" by 3 1/2". Topps continued with the same number of cards as in 1978. Various series spotlight League Leaders (1-8), "Season and Career Record Holders" (411-418), "Record Breakers of 1978" (201-206) and one "Prospects" card for each team (701-726). Team cards feature a checklist on back of that team's players in the set and a small picture of the manager on the front of the card. There are 66 cards that were double printed and these are noted in the checklist by the abbreviation DP. Bump Wills was initially depicted in a Ranger uniform but with a Blue Jays affiliation; later printings correctly labeled him with Texas. The set price listed does not include the scarcer Wills (Rangers) card. Cards numbered 23 or lower which feature Phillies or Yankees and do not follow the numbering checklisted below are not necessarily error cards. They are probably Burger King cards, a separate set with its own pricing and mass distribution. Burger King cards are indistinguishable from the corresponding Topps cards except for the card numbering difference and the fact that Burger King cards do not have a printing sheet designation (such as A through F like the regular Topps) anywhere on the card back in very small print.

	NRMT	VG-E	GOOD
COMPLETE SET (726)	140.00	56.00	14.00
COMMON PLAYER (1-726)	.10	.04	.01
COMMON DP's (1-726)	.04	.02	.00

	NRMT	VG-E	GOOD
☐ 1 Batting Leaders Rod Carew Dave Parker	1.50	.40	.08
☐ 2 Home Run Leaders Jim Rice George Foster	.30	.12	.03
☐ 3 RBI Leaders Jim Rice George Foster	.30	.12	.03
☐ 4 Stolen Base Leaders Ron LeFlore Omar Moreno	.20	.08	.02
☐ 5 Victory Leaders Ron Guidry Gaylord Perry	.30	.12	.03
☐ 6 Strikeout Leaders Nolan Ryan J.R. Richard	.40	.16	.04
☐ 7 ERA Leaders Ron Guidry Craig Swan	.20	.08	.02
☐ 8 Leading Firemen Rich Gossage Rollie Fingers	.20	.08	.02
☐ 9 Dave Campbell	.10	.04	.01
☐ 10 Lee May	.20	.08	.02
☐ 11 Marc Hill	.10	.04	.01
☐ 12 Dick Drago	.10	.04	.01
☐ 13 Paul Dade	.10	.04	.01
☐ 14 Rafael Landestoy	.10	.04	.01
☐ 15 Ross Grimsley	.10	.04	.01
☐ 16 Fred Stanley	.10	.04	.01
☐ 17 Donnie Moore	.20	.08	.02
☐ 18 Tony Solaita	.10	.04	.01
☐ 19 Larry Gura DP	.10	.04	.01
☐ 20 Joe Morgan DP	.30	.12	.03
☐ 21 Kevin Kobel	.10	.04	.01
☐ 22 Mike Jorgensen	.10	.04	.01
☐ 23 Terry Forster	.20	.08	.02
☐ 24 Paul Molitor	3.50	1.40	.35
☐ 25 Steve Carlton	2.25	.90	.22
☐ 26 Jamie Quirk	.10	.04	.01
☐ 27 Dave Goltz	.10	.04	.01
☐ 28 Steve Brye	.10	.04	.01
☐ 29 Rick Langford	.10	.04	.01
☐ 30 Dave Winfield	2.50	1.00	.25
☐ 31 Tom House DP	.10	.04	.01
☐ 32 Jerry Mumphrey	.10	.04	.01
☐ 33 Dave Rozema	.10	.04	.01
☐ 34 Rob Andrews	.10	.04	.01
☐ 35 Ed Figueroa	.10	.04	.01
☐ 36 Alan Ashby	.10	.04	.01
☐ 37 Joe Kerrigan DP	.04	.02	.00
☐ 38 Bernie Carbo	.10	.04	.01
☐ 39 Dale Murphy	8.50	3.50	.85
☐ 40 Dennis Eckersley	.60	.25	.05
☐ 41 Twins Team/Mgr. Gene Mauch (checklist back)	.40	.10	.02
☐ 42 Ron Blomberg	.10	.04	.01
☐ 43 Wayne Twitchell	.10	.04	.01
☐ 44 Kurt Bevacqua	.10	.04	.01
☐ 45 Al Hrabosky	.10	.04	.01
☐ 46 Ron Hodges	.10	.04	.01
☐ 47 Fred Norman	.10	.04	.01
☐ 48 Merv Rettenmund	.10	.04	.01
☐ 49 Vern Ruhle	.10	.04	.01
☐ 50 Steve Garvey DP	1.25	.50	.12
☐ 51 Ray Fosse DP	.04	.02	.00
☐ 52 Randy Lerch	.10	.04	.01
☐ 53 Mick Kelleher	.10	.04	.01
☐ 54 Dell Alston DP	.04	.02	.00
☐ 55 Willie Stargell	2.00	.80	.20
☐ 56 John Hale	.10	.04	.01
☐ 57 Eric Rasmussen	.10	.04	.01
☐ 58 Bob Randall DP	.04	.02	.00
☐ 59 John Denny DP	.10	.04	.01
☐ 60 Mickey Rivers	.10	.04	.01
☐ 61 Bo Diaz	.20	.08	.02
☐ 62 Randy Moffitt	.10	.04	.01
☐ 63 Jack Brohamer	.10	.04	.01
☐ 64 Tom Underwood	.10	.04	.01
☐ 65 Mark Belanger	.20	.08	.02
☐ 66 Tigers Team/Mgr. Les Moss (checklist back)	.40	.10	.02
☐ 67 Jim Mason DP	.04	.02	.00
☐ 68 Joe Niekro DP	.10	.04	.01
☐ 69 Elliott Maddox	.10	.04	.01
☐ 70 John Candelaria	.20	.08	.02
☐ 71 Brian Downing	.20	.08	.02
☐ 72 Steve Mingori	.10	.04	.01
☐ 73 Ken Henderson	.10	.04	.01
☐ 74 Shane Rawley	1.00	.40	.10
☐ 75 Steve Yeager	.10	.04	.01
☐ 76 Warren Cromartie	.10	.04	.01
☐ 77 Dan Briggs DP	.04	.02	.00
☐ 78 Elias Sosa	.10	.04	.01
☐ 79 Ted Cox	.10	.04	.01
☐ 80 Jason Thompson	.10	.04	.01
☐ 81 Roger Erickson	.10	.04	.01
☐ 82 Mets Team/Mgr. Joe Torre (checklist back)	.40	.10	.02
☐ 83 Fred Kendall	.10	.04	.01
☐ 84 Greg Minton	.10	.04	.01
☐ 85 Gary Matthews	.20	.08	.02
☐ 86 Rodney Scott	.10	.04	.01
☐ 87 Pete Falcone	.10	.04	.01
☐ 88 Bob Molinaro	.10	.04	.01
☐ 89 Dick Tidrow	.10	.04	.01
☐ 90 Bob Boone	.30	.12	.03
☐ 91 Terry Crowley	.10	.04	.01
☐ 92 Jim Bibby	.10	.04	.01
☐ 93 Phil Mankowski	.10	.04	.01
☐ 94 Len Barker	.10	.04	.01
☐ 95 Robin Yount	2.25	.90	.22
☐ 96 Indians Team/Mgr. Jeff Torborg (checklist back)	.40	.10	.02
☐ 97 Sam Mejias	.10	.04	.01
☐ 98 Ray Burris	.10	.04	.01
☐ 99 John Wathan	.30	.12	.03
☐ 100 Tom Seaver DP	1.25	.50	.12
☐ 101 Roy Howell	.10	.04	.01

□ 102 Mike Anderson .... .10 .04 .01
□ 103 Jim Todd .... .10 .04 .01
□ 104 Johnny Oates DP .... .04 .02 .00
□ 105 Rick Camp DP .... .04 .02 .00
□ 106 Frank Duffy .... .10 .04 .01
□ 107 Jesus Alou DP .... .04 .02 .00
□ 108 Eduardo Rodriguez .... .10 .04 .01
□ 109 Joel Youngblood .... .10 .04 .01
□ 110 Vida Blue .... .20 .08 .02
□ 111 Roger Freed .... .10 .04 .01
□ 112 Phillies Team/Mgr. Danny Ozark (checklist back) .... .40 .10 .02
□ 113 Pete Redfern .... .10 .04 .01
□ 114 Cliff Johnson .... .10 .04 .01
□ 115 Nolan Ryan .... 2.25 .90 .22
□ 116 Ozzie Smith 18.00 7.25 1.80
□ 117 Grant Jackson .... .10 .04 .01
□ 118 Bud Harrelson .... .10 .04 .01
□ 119 Don Stanhouse .... .10 .04 .01
□ 120 Jim Sundberg .... .10 .04 .01
□ 121 Checklist 1 DP .... .15 .03 .00
□ 122 Mike Paxton .... .10 .04 .01
□ 123 Lou Whitaker .... 2.00 .80 .20
□ 124 Dan Schatzeder .... .10 .04 .01
□ 125 Rick Burleson .... .20 .08 .02
□ 126 Doug Bair .... .10 .04 .01
□ 127 Thad Bosley .... .10 .04 .01
□ 128 Ted Martinez .... .10 .04 .01
□ 129 Marty Pattin DP .... .04 .02 .00
□ 130 Bob Watson DP .... .10 .04 .01
□ 131 Jim Clancy .... .10 .04 .01
□ 132 Rowland Office .... .10 .04 .01
□ 133 Bill Castro .... .10 .04 .01
□ 134 Alan Bannister .... .10 .04 .01
□ 135 Bobby Murcer .... .20 .08 .02
□ 136 Jim Kaat .... .40 .16 .04
□ 137 Larry Wolfe DP .... .04 .02 .00
□ 138 Mark Lee .... .10 .04 .01
□ 139 Luis Pujols .... .10 .04 .01
□ 140 Don Gullett .... .10 .04 .01
□ 141 Tom Paciorek .... .10 .04 .01
□ 142 Charlie Williams .... .10 .04 .01
□ 143 Tony Scott .... .10 .04 .01
□ 144 Sandy Alomar .... .10 .04 .01
□ 145 Rick Rhoden .... .30 .12 .03
□ 146 Duane Kuiper .... .10 .04 .01
□ 147 Dave Hamilton .... .10 .04 .01
□ 148 Bruce Boisclair .... .10 .04 .01
□ 149 Manny Sarmiento .... .10 .04 .01
□ 150 Wayne Cage .... .10 .04 .01
□ 151 John Hiller .... .10 .04 .01
□ 152 Rick Cerone .... .10 .04 .01
□ 153 Dennis Lamp .... .10 .04 .01
□ 154 Jim Gantner DP .... .10 .04 .01
□ 155 Dwight Evans .... 1.00 .40 .10
□ 156 Buddy Solomon .... .10 .04 .01
□ 157 U.L. Washington .... .10 .04 .01
□ 158 Joe Sambito .... .10 .04 .01
□ 159 Roy White .... .20 .08 .02
□ 160 Mike Flanagan .... .30 .12 .03
□ 161 Barry Foote .... .10 .04 .01
□ 162 Tom Johnson .... .10 .04 .01
□ 163 Glenn Burke .... .10 .04 .01
□ 164 Mickey Lolich .... .30 .12 .03
□ 165 Frank Taveras .... .10 .04 .01
□ 166 Leon Roberts .... .10 .04 .01
□ 167 Roger Metzger DP .... .04 .02 .00
□ 168 Dave Freisleben .... .10 .04 .01
□ 169 Bill Nahorodny .... .10 .04 .01
□ 170 Don Sutton .... 1.25 .50 .12
□ 171 Gene Clines .... .10 .04 .01
□ 172 Mike Bruhert .... .10 .04 .01
□ 173 John Lowenstein .... .10 .04 .01
□ 174 Rick Auerbach .... .10 .04 .01
□ 175 George Hendrick .... .20 .08 .02
□ 176 Aurelio Rodriguez .... .10 .04 .01
□ 177 Ron Reed .... .10 .04 .01
□ 178 Alvis Woods .... .10 .04 .01
□ 179 Jim Beattie DP .... .10 .04 .01
□ 180 Larry Hisle .... .10 .04 .01
□ 181 Mike Garman .... .10 .04 .01
□ 182 Tim Johnson .... .10 .04 .01
□ 183 Paul Splittorff .... .10 .04 .01
□ 184 Darrel Chaney .... .10 .04 .01
□ 185 Mike Torrez .... .10 .04 .01
□ 186 Eric Soderholm .... .10 .04 .01
□ 187 Mark Lemongello .... .10 .04 .01
□ 188 Pat Kelly .... .10 .04 .01
□ 189 Eddie Whitson .... .50 .20 .05
□ 190 Ron Cey .... .30 .12 .03
□ 191 Mike Norris .... .10 .04 .01
□ 192 Cardinals Team/Mgr. Ken Boyer (checklist back) .... .40 .10 .02
□ 193 Glenn Adams .... .10 .04 .01
□ 194 Randy Jones .... .10 .04 .01
□ 195 Bill Madlock .... .30 .12 .03
□ 196 Steve Kemp DP .... .10 .04 .01
□ 197 Bob Apodaca .... .10 .04 .01
□ 198 Johnny Grubb .... .10 .04 .01
□ 199 Larry Milbourne .... .10 .04 .01
□ 200 Johnny Bench DP .... 1.25 .50 .12
□ 201 RB: Mike Edwards Most unassisted DP's, second basemen .... .10 .04 .01
□ 202 RB: Ron Guidry, Most Strikeouts, lefthander, nine inning game .... .30 .12 .03
□ 203 RB: J.R. Richard Most strikeouts, season, righthander .... .20 .08 .02
□ 204 RB: Pete Rose Most consecutive games batting safely .... 1.50 .60 .15
□ 205 RB: John Stearns Most SB's by catcher, season .... .10 .04 .01
□ 206 RB: Sammy Stewart 7 straight SO's, first ML game .... .10 .04 .01
□ 207 Dave Lemanczyk .... .10 .04 .01
□ 208 Clarence Gaston .... .10 .04 .01
□ 209 Reggie Cleveland .... .10 .04 .01
□ 210 Larry Bowa .... .30 .12 .03
□ 211 Denny Martinez .... .20 .08 .02
□ 212 Carney Lansford .... 2.75 1.10 .27
□ 213 Bill Travers .... .10 .04 .01
□ 214 Red Sox Team/Mgr. Don Zimmer (checklist back) .... .40 .10 .02
□ 215 Willie McCovey .... 1.50 .60 .15
□ 216 Wilbur Wood .... .10 .04 .01
□ 217 Steve Dillard .... .10 .04 .01
□ 218 Dennis Leonard .... .20 .08 .02
□ 219 Roy Smalley .... .10 .04 .01
□ 220 Cesar Geronimo .... .10 .04 .01
□ 221 Jesse Jefferson .... .10 .04 .01
□ 222 Bob Beall .... .10 .04 .01
□ 223 Kent Tekulve .... .20 .08 .02
□ 224 Dave Revering .... .10 .04 .01
□ 225 Rich Gossage .... .50 .20 .05
□ 226 Ron Pruitt .... .10 .04 .01
□ 227 Steve Stone .... .10 .04 .01
□ 228 Vic Davalillo .... .10 .04 .01
□ 229 Doug Flynn .... .10 .04 .01
□ 230 Bob Forsch .... .10 .04 .01
□ 231 Johnny Wockenfuss .... .10 .04 .01
□ 232 Jimmy Sexton .... .10 .04 .01
□ 233 Paul Mitchell .... .10 .04 .01
□ 234 Toby Harrah .... .20 .08 .02
□ 235 Steve Rogers .... .10 .04 .01
□ 236 Jim Dwyer .... .10 .04 .01
□ 237 Billy Smith .... .10 .04 .01
□ 238 Balor Moore .... .10 .04 .01
□ 239 Willie Horton .... .20 .08 .02
□ 240 Rick Reuschel .... .30 .12 .03
□ 241 Checklist 2 DP .... .15 .03 .00
□ 242 Pablo Torrealba .... .10 .04 .01
□ 243 Buck Martinez DP .... .04 .02 .00
□ 244 Pirates Team/Mgr. Chuck Tanner (checklist back) .... .40 .10 .02
□ 245 Jeff Burroughs .... .10 .04 .01
□ 246 Darrell Jackson .... .10 .04 .01
□ 247 Tucker Ashford DP .... .04 .02 .00
□ 248 Pete LaCock .... .10 .04 .01
□ 249 Paul Thormodsgard .... .10 .04 .01
□ 250 Willie Randolph .... .30 .12 .03
□ 251 Jack Morris .... 2.75 1.10 .27
□ 252 Bob Stinson .... .10 .04 .01
□ 253 Rick Wise .... .10 .04 .01
□ 254 Luis Gomez .... .10 .04 .01
□ 255 Tommy John .... .60 .24 .06
□ 256 Mike Sadek .... .10 .04 .01
□ 257 Adrian Devine .... .10 .04 .01
□ 258 Mike Phillips .... .10 .04 .01
□ 259 Reds Team/Mgr. Sparky Anderson (checklist back) .... .40 .10 .02
□ 260 Richie Zisk .... .10 .04 .01
□ 261 Mario Guerrero .... .10 .04 .01
□ 262 Nelson Briles .... .10 .04 .01
□ 263 Oscar Gamble .... .10 .04 .01
□ 264 Don Robinson .... .75 .30 .07
□ 265 Don Money .... .10 .04 .01
□ 266 Jim Willoughby .... .10 .04 .01
□ 267 Joe Rudi .... .20 .08 .02
□ 268 Julio Gonzalez .... .10 .04 .01
□ 269 Woodie Fryman .... .10 .04 .01

☐ 270	Butch Hobson	.10	.04	.01
☐ 271	Rawly Eastwick	.10	.04	.01
☐ 272	Tim Corcoran	.10	.04	.01
☐ 273	Jerry Terrell	.10	.04	.01
☐ 274	Willie Norwood	.10	.04	.01
☐ 275	Junior Moore	.10	.04	.01
☐ 276	Jim Colborn	.10	.04	.01
☐ 277	Tom Grieve	.20	.08	.02
☐ 278	Andy Messersmith	.20	.08	.02
☐ 279	Jerry Grote DP	.04	.02	.00
☐ 280	Andre Thornton	.20	.08	.02
☐ 281	Vic Correll DP	.04	.02	.00
☐ 282	Blue Jays Team/Mgr.	.30	.08	.01
	Roy Hartsfield			
	(checklist back)			
☐ 283	Ken Kravec	.10	.04	.01
☐ 284	Johnnie LeMaster	.10	.04	.01
☐ 285	Bobby Bonds	.30	.12	.03
☐ 286	Duffy Dyer	.10	.04	.01
☐ 287	Andres Mora	.10	.04	.01
☐ 288	Milt Wilcox	.10	.04	.01
☐ 289	Jose Cruz	.30	.12	.03
☐ 290	Dave Lopes	.20	.08	.02
☐ 291	Tom Griffin	.10	.04	.01
☐ 292	Don Reynolds	.10	.04	.01
☐ 293	Jerry Garvin	.10	.04	.01
☐ 294	Pepe Frias	.10	.04	.01
☐ 295	Mitchell Page	.10	.04	.01
☐ 296	Preston Hanna	.10	.04	.01
☐ 297	Ted Sizemore	.10	.04	.01
☐ 298	Rich Gale	.10	.04	.01
☐ 299	Steve Ontiveros	.10	.04	.01
☐ 300	Rod Carew	2.25	.90	.22
☐ 301	Tom Hume	.10	.04	.01
☐ 302	Braves Team/Mgr.	.40	.10	.02
	Bobby Cox			
	(checklist back)			
☐ 303	Lary Sorensen	.10	.04	.01
☐ 304	Steve Swisher	.10	.04	.01
☐ 305	Willie Montanez	.10	.04	.01
☐ 306	Floyd Bannister	.20	.08	.02
☐ 307	Larvell Blanks	.10	.04	.01
☐ 308	Bert Blyleven	.40	.16	.04
☐ 309	Ralph Garr	.10	.04	.01
☐ 310	Thurman Munson	2.00	.80	.20
☐ 311	Gary Lavelle	.10	.04	.01
☐ 312	Bob Robertson	.10	.04	.01
☐ 313	Dyar Miller	.10	.04	.01
☐ 314	Larry Harlow	.10	.04	.01
☐ 315	Jon Matlack	.10	.04	.01
☐ 316	Milt May	.10	.04	.01
☐ 317	Jose Cardenal	.10	.04	.01
☐ 318	Bob Welch	2.75	1.10	.27
☐ 319	Wayne Garrett	.10	.04	.01
☐ 320	Carl Yastrzemski	3.00	1.20	.30
☐ 321	Gaylord Perry	1.50	.60	.15
☐ 322	Danny Goodwin	.10	.04	.01
☐ 323	Lynn McGlothen	.10	.04	.01
☐ 324	Mike Tyson	.10	.04	.01
☐ 325	Cecil Cooper	.40	.16	.04
☐ 326	Pedro Borbon	.10	.04	.01
☐ 327	Art Howe	.10	.04	.01
☐ 328	Oakland A's Team/Mgr.	.40	.10	.02
	Jack McKeon			
	(checklist back)			
☐ 329	Joe Coleman	.10	.04	.01
☐ 330	George Brett	3.50	1.40	.35
☐ 331	Mickey Mahler	.10	.04	.01
☐ 332	Gary Alexander	.10	.04	.01
☐ 333	Chet Lemon	.20	.08	.02
☐ 334	Craig Swan	.10	.04	.01
☐ 335	Chris Chambliss	.20	.08	.02
☐ 336	Bobby Thompson	.10	.04	.01
☐ 337	John Montague	.10	.04	.01
☐ 338	Vic Harris	.10	.04	.01
☐ 339	Ron Jackson	.10	.04	.01
☐ 340	Jim Palmer	1.50	.60	.15
☐ 341	Willie Upshaw	.50	.20	.05
☐ 342	Dave Roberts	.10	.04	.01
☐ 343	Ed Glynn	.10	.04	.01
☐ 344	Jerry Royster	.10	.04	.01
☐ 345	Tug McGraw	.30	.12	.03
☐ 346	Bill Buckner	.30	.12	.03
☐ 347	Doug Rau	.10	.04	.01
☐ 348	Andre Dawson	5.00	2.00	.50
☐ 349	Jim Wright	.10	.04	.01
☐ 350	Garry Templeton	.20	.08	.02
☐ 351	Wayne Nordhagen	.10	.04	.01
☐ 352	Steve Renko	.10	.04	.01
☐ 353	Checklist 3	.40	.05	.01
☐ 354	Bill Bonham	.10	.04	.01
☐ 355	Lee Mazzilli	.10	.04	.01
☐ 356	Giants Team/Mgr.	.40	.10	.02
	Joe Altobelli			
	(checklist back)			
☐ 357	Jerry Augustine	.10	.04	.01
☐ 358	Alan Trammell	6.00	2.40	.60
☐ 359	Dan Spillner DP	.04	.02	.00
☐ 360	Amos Otis	.20	.08	.02
☐ 361	Tom Dixon	.10	.04	.01
☐ 362	Mike Cubbage	.10	.04	.01
☐ 363	Craig Skok	.10	.04	.01
☐ 364	Gene Richards	.10	.04	.01
☐ 365	Sparky Lyle	.30	.12	.03
☐ 366	Juan Bernhardt	.10	.04	.01
☐ 367	Dave Skaggs	.10	.04	.01
☐ 368	Don Aase	.10	.04	.01
☐ 369A	Bump Wills ERR	3.00	1.20	.30
	(Blue Jays)			
☐ 369B	Bump Wills COR	4.00	1.60	.40
	(Rangers)			
☐ 370	Dave Kingman	.40	.16	.04
☐ 371	Jeff Holly	.10	.04	.01
☐ 372	Lamar Johnson	.10	.04	.01
☐ 373	Lance Rautzhan	.10	.04	.01
☐ 374	Ed Herrmann	.10	.04	.01
☐ 375	Bill Campbell	.10	.04	.01
☐ 376	Gorman Thomas	.30	.12	.03
☐ 377	Paul Moskau	.10	.04	.01
☐ 378	Rob Picciolo DP	.04	.02	.00
☐ 379	Dale Murray	.10	.04	.01
☐ 380	John Mayberry	.20	.08	.02
☐ 381	Astros Team/Mgr.	.40	.10	.02
	Bill Virdon			
	(checklist back)			
☐ 382	Jerry Martin	.10	.04	.01
☐ 383	Phil Garner	.10	.04	.01
☐ 384	Tommy Boggs	.10	.04	.01
☐ 385	Dan Ford	.10	.04	.01
☐ 386	Francisco Barrios	.10	.04	.01
☐ 387	Gary Thomasson	.10	.04	.01
☐ 388	Jack Billingham	.10	.04	.01
☐ 389	Joe Zdeb	.10	.04	.01
☐ 390	Rollie Fingers	.60	.24	.06
☐ 391	Al Oliver	.30	.12	.03
☐ 392	Doug Ault	.10	.04	.01
☐ 393	Scott McGregor	.20	.08	.02
☐ 394	Randy Stein	.10	.04	.01
☐ 395	Dave Cash	.10	.04	.01
☐ 396	Bill Plummer	.10	.04	.01
☐ 397	Sergio Ferrer	.10	.04	.01
☐ 398	Ivan DeJesus	.10	.04	.01
☐ 399	David Clyde	.10	.04	.01
☐ 400	Jim Rice	2.50	1.00	.25
☐ 401	Ray Knight	.30	.12	.03
☐ 402	Paul Hartzell	.10	.04	.01
☐ 403	Tim Foli	.10	.04	.01
☐ 404	White Sox Team/Mgr	.40	.10	.02
	Don Kessinger			
	(checklist back)			
☐ 405	Butch Wynegar DP	.04	.02	.00
☐ 406	Joe Wallis DP	.04	.02	.00
☐ 407	Pete Vuckovich	.10	.04	.01
☐ 408	Charlie Moore DP	.04	.02	.00
☐ 409	Willie Wilson	1.50	.60	.15
☐ 410	Darrell Evans	.30	.12	.03
☐ 411	Hits Record	.40	.16	.04
	Season: G.Sisler			
	Career: Ty Cobb			
☐ 412	RBI Record	.40	.16	.04
	Season: Hack Wilson			
	Career: Hank Aaron			
☐ 413	Home Run Record	.50	.20	.05
	Season: Roger Maris			
	Career: Hank Aaron			
☐ 414	Batting Record	.40	.16	.04
	Season: R.Hornsby			
	Career: Ty Cobb			
☐ 415	Steals Record	.40	.16	.04
	Season: Lou Brock			
	Career: Lou Brock			
☐ 416	Wins Record	.20	.08	.02
	Season: Jack Chesbro			
	Career: Cy Young			
☐ 417	Strikeout Record DP	.15	.06	.01
	Season: Nolan Ryan			
	Career: W.Johnson			
☐ 418	ERA Record DP	.10	.04	.01
	Season: Dutch Leonard			
	Career: W.Johnson			
☐ 419	Dick Ruthven	.10	.04	.01
☐ 420	Ken Griffey	.20	.08	.02
☐ 421	Doug DeCinces	.20	.08	.02
☐ 422	Ruppert Jones	.10	.04	.01
☐ 423	Bob Montgomery	.10	.04	.01
☐ 424	Angels Team/Mgr.	.40	.10	.02
	Jim Fregosi			
	(checklist back)			
☐ 425	Rick Manning	.10	.04	.01
☐ 426	Chris Speier	.10	.04	.01

□ 427	Andy Replogle	.10	.04	.01
□ 428	Bobby Valentine	.20	.08	.02
□ 429	John Urrea DP	.04	.02	.00
□ 430	Dave Parker	1.25	.50	.12
□ 431	Glenn Borgmann	.10	.04	.01
□ 432	Dave Heaverlo	.10	.04	.01
□ 433	Larry Biittner	.10	.04	.01
□ 434	Ken Clay	.10	.04	.01
□ 435	Gene Tenace	.10	.04	.01
□ 436	Hector Cruz	.10	.04	.01
□ 437	Rick Williams	.10	.04	.01
□ 438	Horace Speed	.10	.04	.01
□ 439	Frank White	.20	.08	.02
□ 440	Rusty Staub	.30	.12	.03
□ 441	Lee Lacy	.10	.04	.01
□ 442	Doyle Alexander	.20	.08	.02
□ 443	Bruce Bochte	.10	.04	.01
□ 444	Aurelio Lopez	.20	.08	.02
□ 445	Steve Henderson	.10	.04	.01
□ 446	Jim Lonborg	.10	.04	.01
□ 447	Manny Sanguillen	.10	.04	.01
□ 448	Moose Haas	.10	.04	.01
□ 449	Bombo Rivera	.10	.04	.01
□ 450	Dave Concepcion	.20	.08	.02
□ 451	Royals Team/Mgr. Whitey Herzog (checklist back)	.40	.10	.02
□ 452	Jerry Morales	.10	.04	.01
□ 453	Chris Knapp	.10	.04	.01
□ 454	Len Randle	.10	.04	.01
□ 455	Bill Lee DP	.10	.04	.01
□ 456	Chuck Baker	.10	.04	.01
□ 457	Bruce Sutter	.60	.24	.06
□ 458	Jim Essian	.10	.04	.01
□ 459	Sid Monge	.10	.04	.01
□ 460	Graig Nettles	.40	.16	.04
□ 461	Jim Barr DP	.04	.02	.00
□ 462	Otto Velez	.10	.04	.01
□ 463	Steve Comer	.10	.04	.01
□ 464	Joe Nolan	.10	.04	.01
□ 465	Reggie Smith	.20	.08	.02
□ 466	Mark Littell	.10	.04	.01
□ 467	Don Kessinger DP	.10	.04	.01
□ 468	Stan Bahnsen DP	.04	.02	.00
□ 469	Lance Parrish	3.00	1.20	.30
□ 470	Garry Maddox DP	.10	.04	.01
□ 471	Joaquin Andujar	.20	.08	.02
□ 472	Craig Kusick	.10	.04	.01
□ 473	Dave Roberts	.10	.04	.01
□ 474	Dick Davis	.10	.04	.01
□ 475	Dan Driessen	.10	.04	.01
□ 476	Tom Poquette	.10	.04	.01
□ 477	Bob Grich	.20	.08	.02
□ 478	Juan Beniquez	.10	.04	.01
□ 479	Padres Team/Mgr. Roger Craig (checklist back)	.40	.10	.02
□ 480	Fred Lynn	.70	.28	.07
□ 481	Skip Lockwood	.10	.04	.01
□ 482	Craig Reynolds	.10	.04	.01
□ 483	Checklist 4 DP	.15	.03	.00
□ 484	Rick Waits	.10	.04	.01
□ 485	Bucky Dent	.20	.08	.02
□ 486	Bob Knepper	.30	.12	.03
□ 487	Miguel Dilone	.10	.04	.01
□ 488	Bob Owchinko	.10	.04	.01
□ 489	Larry Cox (photo actually Dave Rader)	.10	.04	.01
□ 490	Al Cowens	.10	.04	.01
□ 491	Tippy Martinez	.10	.04	.01
□ 492	Bob Bailor	.10	.04	.01
□ 493	Larry Christenson	.10	.04	.01
□ 494	Jerry White	.10	.04	.01
□ 495	Tony Perez	.50	.20	.05
□ 496	Barry Bonnell DP	.04	.02	.00
□ 497	Glenn Abbott	.10	.04	.01
□ 498	Rich Chiles	.10	.04	.01
□ 499	Rangers Team/Mgr. Pat Corrales (checklist back)	.40	.10	.02
□ 500	Ron Guidry	1.00	.40	.10
□ 501	Junior Kennedy	.10	.04	.01
□ 502	Steve Braun	.10	.04	.01
□ 503	Terry Humphrey	.10	.04	.01
□ 504	Larry McWilliams	.30	.12	.03
□ 505	Ed Kranepool	.10	.04	.01
□ 506	John D'Acquisto	.10	.04	.01
□ 507	Tony Armas	.20	.08	.02
□ 508	Charlie Hough	.20	.08	.02
□ 509	Mario Mendoza	.10	.04	.01
□ 510	Ted Simmons	.30	.12	.03
□ 511	Paul Reuschel DP	.04	.02	.00
□ 512	Jack Clark	2.50	1.00	.25
□ 513	Dave Johnson	.20	.08	.02
□ 514	Mike Proly	.10	.04	.01
□ 515	Enos Cabell	.10	.04	.01
□ 516	Champ Summers DP	.04	.02	.00
□ 517	Al Bumbry	.10	.04	.01
□ 518	Jim Umbarger	.10	.04	.01
□ 519	Ben Oglivie	.20	.08	.02
□ 520	Gary Carter	2.50	1.00	.25
□ 521	Sam Ewing	.10	.04	.01
□ 522	Ken Holtzman	.10	.04	.01
□ 523	John Milner	.10	.04	.01
□ 524	Tom Burgmeier	.10	.04	.01
□ 525	Freddie Patek	.10	.04	.01
□ 526	Dodgers Team/Mgr. Tom Lasorda (checklist back)	.50	.12	.02
□ 527	Lerrin LaGrow	.10	.04	.01
□ 528	Wayne Gross DP	.04	.02	.00
□ 529	Brian Asselstine	.10	.04	.01
□ 530	Frank Tanana	.20	.08	.02
□ 531	Fernando Gonzalez	.10	.04	.01
□ 532	Buddy Schultz	.10	.04	.01
□ 533	Leroy Stanton	.10	.04	.01
□ 534	Ken Forsch	.10	.04	.01
□ 535	Ellis Valentine	.10	.04	.01
□ 536	Jerry Reuss	.20	.08	.02
□ 537	Tom Veryzer	.10	.04	.01
□ 538	Mike Ivie DP	.04	.02	.00
□ 539	John Ellis	.10	.04	.01
□ 540	Greg Luzinski	.30	.12	.03
□ 541	Jim Slaton	.10	.04	.01
□ 542	Rick Bosetti	.10	.04	.01
□ 543	Kiko Garcia	.10	.04	.01
□ 544	Fergie Jenkins	.40	.16	.04
□ 545	John Stearns	.10	.04	.01
□ 546	Bill Russell	.10	.04	.01
□ 547	Clint Hurdle	.10	.04	.01
□ 548	Enrique Romo	.10	.04	.01
□ 549	Bob Bailey	.10	.04	.01
□ 550	Sal Bando	.20	.08	.02
□ 551	Cubs Team/Mgr. Herman Franks (checklist back)	.40	.10	.02
□ 552	Jose Morales	.10	.04	.01
□ 553	Denny Walling	.10	.04	.01
□ 554	Matt Keough	.10	.04	.01
□ 555	Biff Pocoroba	.10	.04	.01
□ 556	Mike Lum	.10	.04	.01
□ 557	Ken Brett	.10	.04	.01
□ 558	Jay Johnstone	.20	.08	.02
□ 559	Greg Pryor	.10	.04	.01
□ 560	John Montefusco	.20	.08	.02
□ 561	Ed Ott	.10	.04	.01
□ 562	Dusty Baker	.20	.08	.02
□ 563	Roy Thomas	.10	.04	.01
□ 564	Jerry Turner	.10	.04	.01
□ 565	Rico Carty	.20	.08	.02
□ 566	Nino Espinosa	.10	.04	.01
□ 567	Richie Hebner	.10	.04	.01
□ 568	Carlos Lopez	.10	.04	.01
□ 569	Bob Sykes	.10	.04	.01
□ 570	Cesar Cedeno	.20	.08	.02
□ 571	Darrell Porter	.10	.04	.01
□ 572	Rod Gilbreath	.10	.04	.01
□ 573	Jim Kern	.10	.04	.01
□ 574	Claudell Washington	.20	.08	.02
□ 575	Luis Tiant	.30	.12	.03
□ 576	Mike Parrott	.10	.04	.01
□ 577	Brewers Team/Mgr. George Bamberger (checklist back)	.40	.10	.02
□ 578	Pete Broberg	.10	.04	.01
□ 579	Greg Gross	.10	.04	.01
□ 580	Ron Fairly	.10	.04	.01
□ 581	Darold Knowles	.10	.04	.01
□ 582	Paul Blair	.10	.04	.01
□ 583	Julio Cruz	.10	.04	.01
□ 584	Jim Rooker	.10	.04	.01
□ 585	Hal McRae	.20	.08	.02
□ 586	Bob Horner	2.50	1.00	.25
□ 587	Ken Reitz	.10	.04	.01
□ 588	Tom Murphy	.10	.04	.01
□ 589	Terry Whitfield	.10	.04	.01
□ 590	J.R. Richard	.20	.08	.02
□ 591	Mike Hargrove	.10	.04	.01
□ 592	Mike Krukow	.20	.08	.02
□ 593	Rick Dempsey	.10	.04	.01
□ 594	Bob Shirley	.10	.04	.01
□ 595	Phil Niekro	1.25	.50	.12
□ 596	Jim Wohlford	.10	.04	.01
□ 597	Bob Stanley	.10	.04	.01
□ 598	Mark Wagner	.10	.04	.01
□ 599	Jim Spencer	.10	.04	.01
□ 600	George Foster	.50	.20	.05
□ 601	Dave LaRoche	.10	.04	.01
□ 602	Checklist 5	.45	.05	.01

□ 603 Rudy May	.10	.04	.01
□ 604 Jeff Newman	.10	.04	.01
□ 605 Rick Monday DP	.10	.04	.01
□ 606 Expos Team/Mgr. Dick Williams (checklist back)	.40	.10	.02
□ 607 Omar Moreno	.10	.04	.01
□ 608 Dave McKay	.10	.04	.01
□ 609 Silvio Martinez	.10	.04	.01
□ 610 Mike Schmidt	4.00	1.60	.40
□ 611 Jim Norris	.10	.04	.01
□ 612 Rick Honeycutt	.50	.20	.05
□ 613 Mike Edwards	.10	.04	.01
□ 614 Willie Hernandez	.40	.16	.04
□ 615 Ken Singleton	.20	.08	.02
□ 616 Billy Almon	.10	.04	.01
□ 617 Terry Puhl	.10	.04	.01
□ 618 Jerry Remy	.10	.04	.01
□ 619 Ken Landreaux	.30	.12	.03
□ 620 Bert Campaneris	.10	.04	.01
□ 621 Pat Zachry	.10	.04	.01
□ 622 Dave Collins	.10	.04	.01
□ 623 Bob McClure	.10	.04	.01
□ 624 Larry Herndon	.10	.04	.01
□ 625 Mark Fidrych	.20	.08	.02
□ 626 Yankees Team/Mgr. Bob Lemon (checklist back)	.50	.12	.02
□ 627 Gary Serum	.10	.04	.01
□ 628 Del Unser	.10	.04	.01
□ 629 Gene Garber	.10	.04	.01
□ 630 Bake McBride	.10	.04	.01
□ 631 Jorge Orta	.10	.04	.01
□ 632 Don Kirkwood	.10	.04	.01
□ 633 Rob Wilfong DP	.04	.02	.00
□ 634 Paul Lindblad	.10	.04	.01
□ 635 Don Baylor	.75	.30	.07
□ 636 Wayne Garland	.10	.04	.01
□ 637 Bill Robinson	.20	.08	.02
□ 638 Al Fitzmorris	.10	.04	.01
□ 639 Manny Trillo	.10	.04	.01
□ 640 Eddie Murray	6.00	2.40	.60
□ 641 Bobby Castillo	.10	.04	.01
□ 642 Wilbur Howard DP	.04	.02	.00
□ 643 Tom Hausman	.10	.04	.01
□ 644 Manny Mota	.10	.04	.01
□ 645 George Scott DP	.10	.04	.01
□ 646 Rick Sweet	.10	.04	.01
□ 647 Bob Lacey	.10	.04	.01
□ 648 Lou Piniella	.20	.08	.02
□ 649 John Curtis	.10	.04	.01
□ 650 Pete Rose	4.50	1.80	.45
□ 651 Mike Caldwell	.10	.04	.01
□ 652 Stan Papi	.10	.04	.01
□ 653 Warren Brusstar DP	.04	.02	.00
□ 654 Rick Miller	.10	.04	.01
□ 655 Jerry Koosman	.20	.08	.02
□ 656 Hosken Powell	.10	.04	.01
□ 657 George Medich	.10	.04	.01
□ 658 Taylor Duncan	.10	.04	.01
□ 659 Mariners Team/Mgr. Darrell Johnson (checklist back)	.40	.10	.02
□ 660 Ron LeFlore DP	.10	.04	.01
□ 661 Bruce Kison	.10	.04	.01
□ 662 Kevin Bell	.10	.04	.01
□ 663 Mike Vail	.10	.04	.01
□ 664 Doug Bird	.10	.04	.01
□ 665 Lou Brock	1.50	.60	.15
□ 666 Rich Dauer	.10	.04	.01
□ 667 Don Hood	.10	.04	.01
□ 668 Bill North	.10	.04	.01
□ 669 Checklist 6	.45	.05	.01
□ 670 Jim Hunter DP	.50	.20	.05
□ 671 Joe Ferguson DP	.04	.02	.00
□ 672 Ed Halicki	.10	.04	.01
□ 673 Tom Hutton	.10	.04	.01
□ 674 Dave Tomlin	.10	.04	.01
□ 675 Tim McCarver	.30	.12	.03
□ 676 Johnny Sutton	.10	.04	.01
□ 677 Larry Parrish	.20	.08	.02
□ 678 Geoff Zahn	.10	.04	.01
□ 679 Derrel Thomas	.10	.04	.01
□ 680 Carlton Fisk	.60	.24	.06
□ 681 John Henry Johnson	.10	.04	.01
□ 682 Dave Chalk	.10	.04	.01
□ 683 Dan Meyer DP	.04	.02	.00
□ 684 Jamie Easterly DP	.04	.02	.00
□ 685 Sixto Lezcano	.10	.04	.01
□ 686 Ron Schueler DP	.04	.02	.00
□ 687 Rennie Stennett	.10	.04	.01
□ 688 Mike Willis	.10	.04	.01
□ 689 Orioles Team/Mgr. Earl Weaver (checklist back)	.50	.12	.02
□ 690 Buddy Bell DP	.10	.04	.01
□ 691 Dock Ellis DP	.04	.02	.00
□ 692 Mickey Stanley	.10	.04	.01
□ 693 Dave Rader	.10	.04	.01
□ 694 Burt Hooton	.10	.04	.01
□ 695 Keith Hernandez	2.25	.90	.22
□ 696 Andy Hassler	.10	.04	.01
□ 697 Dave Bergman	.10	.04	.01
□ 698 Bill Stein	.10	.04	.01
□ 699 Hal Dues	.10	.04	.01
□ 700 Reggie Jackson DP	1.50	.60	.15
□ 701 Orioles Prospects Mark Corey, John Flinn, Sammy Stewart	.20	.08	.02
□ 702 Red Sox Prospects Joel Finch, Garry Hancock, Allen Ripley	.20	.08	.02
□ 703 Angels Prospects Jim Anderson, Dave Frost, Bob Slater	.10	.04	.01
□ 704 White Sox Prospects Ross Baumgarten, Mike Colbern, Mike Squires	.10	.04	.01
□ 705 Indians Prospects Alfredo Griffin, Tim Norrid, Dave Oliver	1.00	.40	.10
□ 706 Tigers Prospects Dave Stegman, Dave Tobik, Kip Young	.10	.04	.01
□ 707 Royals Prospects Randy Bass, Jim Gaudet, Randy McGilberry	.20	.08	.02
□ 708 Brewers Prospects Kevin Bass, Eddie Romero, Ned Yost	1.50	.60	.15
□ 709 Twins Prospects Sam Perlozzo, Rick Sofield, Kevin Stanfield	.10	.04	.01
□ 710 Yankees Prospects Brian Doyle, Mike Heath, Dave Rajsich	.30	.12	.03
□ 711 A's Prospects Dwayne Murphy, Bruce Robinson, Alan Wirth	.30	.12	.03
□ 712 Mariners Prospects Bud Anderson, Greg Biercevicz, Byron McLaughlin	.10	.04	.01
□ 713 Rangers Prospects Danny Darwin, Pat Putnam, Billy Sample	.30	.12	.03
□ 714 Blue Jays Prospects Victor Cruz, Pat Kelly, Ernie Whitt	.30	.12	.03
□ 715 Braves Prospects Bruce Benedict, Glenn Hubbard, Larry Whisenton	.30	.12	.03
□ 716 Cubs Prospects Dave Geisel, Karl Pagel, Scot Thompson	.10	.04	.01
□ 717 Reds Prospects Mike LaCoss, Ron Oester, Harry Spilman	.40	.16	.04
□ 718 Astros Prospects Bruce Bochy, Mike Fischlin, Don Pisker	.10	.04	.01
□ 719 Dodgers Prospects Pedro Guerrero, Rudy Law, Joe Simpson	7.00	2.80	.70
□ 720 Expos Prospects Jerry Fry, Jerry Pirtle, Scott Sanderson	.30	.12	.03
□ 721 Mets Prospects Juan Berenguer, Dwight Bernard, Dan Norman	.30	.12	.03

No.	Card	MINT	EXC	G-VG
☐ 722	Phillies Prospects Jim Morrison Lonnie Smith Jim Wright	.30	.12	.03
☐ 723	Pirates Prospects Dale Berra Eugenio Cotes Ben Wiltbank	.30	.12	.03
☐ 724	Cardinals Prospects Tom Bruno George Frazier Terry Kennedy	.30	.12	.03
☐ 725	Padres Prospects Jim Beswick Steve Mura Broderick Perkins	.10	.04	.01
☐ 726	Giants Prospects Greg Johnston Joe Strain John Tamargo	.20	.08	.02

1980 Topps

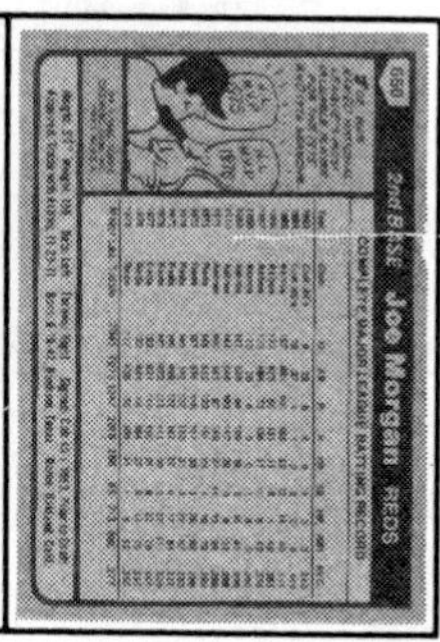

No.	Card	MINT	EXC	G-VG
	COMPLETE SET (726)	140.00	56.00	14.00
	COMMON PLAYER (1-726)	.10	.04	.01
	COMMON DP's (1-726)	.04	.02	.00
☐ 1	HL: Brock and Yaz, Enter 3000 hit circle	1.50	.40	.08
☐ 2	HL: Willie McCovey, 512th homer sets new mark for NL lefties	.65	.26	.06
☐ 3	HL: Manny Mota, All-time pinch-hits, 145	.20	.08	.02
☐ 4	HL: Pete Rose, Career Record 10th season with 200 or more hits	2.00	.80	.20
☐ 5	HL: Garry Templeton, First with 100 hits from each side of plate	.20	.08	.02
☐ 6	HL: Del Unser, 3rd cons. pinch homer sets new ML standard	.10	.04	.01
☐ 7	Mike Lum	.10	.04	.01
☐ 8	Craig Swan	.10	.04	.01
☐ 9	Steve Braun	.10	.04	.01
☐ 10	Denny Martinez	.20	.08	.02
☐ 11	Jimmy Sexton	.10	.04	.01
☐ 12	John Curtis DP	.04	.02	.00
☐ 13	Ron Pruitt	.10	.04	.01
☐ 14	Dave Cash	.10	.04	.01
☐ 15	Bill Campbell	.10	.04	.01
☐ 16	Jerry Narron	.10	.04	.01
☐ 17	Bruce Sutter	.40	.16	.04
☐ 18	Ron Jackson	.10	.04	.01
☐ 19	Balor Moore	.10	.04	.01
☐ 20	Dan Ford	.10	.04	.01
☐ 21	Manny Sarmiento	.10	.04	.01
☐ 22	Pat Putnam	.10	.04	.01
☐ 23	Derrel Thomas	.10	.04	.01
☐ 24	Jim Slaton	.10	.04	.01
☐ 25	Lee Mazzilli	.10	.04	.01
☐ 26	Marty Pattin	.10	.04	.01
☐ 27	Del Unser	.10	.04	.01
☐ 28	Bruce Kison	.10	.04	.01
☐ 29	Mark Wagner	.10	.04	.01
☐ 30	Vida Blue	.20	.08	.02
☐ 31	Jay Johnstone	.20	.08	.02
☐ 32	Julio Cruz DP	.10	.04	.01
☐ 33	Tony Scott	.10	.04	.01
☐ 34	Jeff Newman DP	.04	.02	.00
☐ 35	Luis Tiant	.20	.08	.02
☐ 36	Rusty Torres	.10	.04	.01
☐ 37	Kiko Garcia	.10	.04	.01
☐ 38	Dan Spillner DP	.04	.02	.00
☐ 39	Rowland Office	.10	.04	.01
☐ 40	Carlton Fisk	.50	.20	.05
☐ 41	Rangers Team/Mgr. Pat Corrales (checklist back)	.35	.10	.02
☐ 42	David Palmer	.40	.16	.04
☐ 43	Bombo Rivera	.10	.04	.01
☐ 44	Bill Fahey	.10	.04	.01
☐ 45	Frank White	.30	.12	.03
☐ 46	Rico Carty	.20	.08	.02
☐ 47	Bill Bonham DP	.04	.02	.00
☐ 48	Rick Miller	.10	.04	.01
☐ 49	Mario Guerrero	.10	.04	.01
☐ 50	J.R. Richard	.20	.08	.02
☐ 51	Joe Ferguson DP	.04	.02	.00
☐ 52	Warren Brusstar	.10	.04	.01
☐ 53	Ben Oglivie	.20	.08	.02
☐ 54	Dennis Lamp	.10	.04	.01
☐ 55	Bill Madlock	.30	.12	.03
☐ 56	Bobby Valentine	.20	.08	.02
☐ 57	Pete Vuckovich	.10	.04	.01
☐ 58	Doug Flynn	.10	.04	.01
☐ 59	Eddy Putman	.10	.04	.01
☐ 60	Bucky Dent	.20	.08	.02
☐ 61	Gary Serum	.10	.04	.01
☐ 62	Mike Ivie	.10	.04	.01
☐ 63	Bob Stanley	.10	.04	.01
☐ 64	Joe Nolan	.10	.04	.01
☐ 65	Al Bumbry	.10	.04	.01
☐ 66	Royals Team/Mgr. Jim Frey (checklist back)	.35	.10	.02
☐ 67	Doyle Alexander	.20	.08	.02
☐ 68	Larry Harlow	.10	.04	.01
☐ 69	Rick Williams	.10	.04	.01
☐ 70	Gary Carter	2.00	.80	.20
☐ 71	John Milner DP	.04	.02	.00
☐ 72	Fred Howard DP	.04	.02	.00
☐ 73	Dave Collins	.10	.04	.01
☐ 74	Sid Monge	.10	.04	.01
☐ 75	Bill Russell	.20	.08	.02
☐ 76	John Stearns	.10	.04	.01
☐ 77	Dave Stieb	3.50	1.40	.35
☐ 78	Ruppert Jones	.10	.04	.01
☐ 79	Bob Owchinko	.10	.04	.01
☐ 80	Ron LeFlore	.10	.04	.01
☐ 81	Ted Sizemore	.10	.04	.01
☐ 82	Astros Team/Mgr. Bill Virdon (checklist back)	.35	.10	.02
☐ 83	Steve Trout	.30	.12	.03
☐ 84	Gary Lavelle	.10	.04	.01
☐ 85	Ted Simmons	.40	.16	.04
☐ 86	Dave Hamilton	.10	.04	.01
☐ 87	Pepe Frias	.10	.04	.01
☐ 88	Ken Landreaux	.10	.04	.01
☐ 89	Don Hood	.10	.04	.01
☐ 90	Manny Trillo	.10	.04	.01
☐ 91	Rick Dempsey	.10	.04	.01
☐ 92	Rick Rhoden	.20	.08	.02
☐ 93	Dave Roberts DP	.04	.02	.00
☐ 94	Neil Allen	.40	.16	.04
☐ 95	Cecil Cooper	.30	.12	.03
☐ 96	A's Team/Mgr. Jim Marshall (checklist back)	.35	.10	.02
☐ 97	Bill Lee	.10	.04	.01
☐ 98	Jerry Terrell	.10	.04	.01
☐ 99	Victor Cruz	.10	.04	.01
☐ 100	Johnny Bench	2.50	1.00	.25
☐ 101	Aurelio Lopez	.10	.04	.01
☐ 102	Rich Dauer	.10	.04	.01
☐ 103	Bill Caudill	.30	.12	.03
☐ 104	Manny Mota	.10	.04	.01
☐ 105	Frank Tanana	.20	.08	.02
☐ 106	Jeff Leonard	1.50	.60	.15
☐ 107	Francisco Barrios	.10	.04	.01
☐ 108	Bob Horner	.90	.36	.09
☐ 109	Bill Travers	.10	.04	.01
☐ 110	Fred Lynn DP	.30	.12	.03
☐ 111	Bob Knepper	.20	.08	.02
☐ 112	White Sox Team/Mgr. Tony LaRussa (checklist back)	.35	.10	.02
☐ 113	Geoff Zahn	.10	.04	.01
☐ 114	Juan Beniquez	.10	.04	.01
☐ 115	Sparky Lyle	.20	.08	.02
☐ 116	Larry Cox	.10	.04	.01
☐ 117	Dock Ellis	.10	.04	.01
☐ 118	Phil Garner	.10	.04	.01
☐ 119	Sammy Stewart	.10	.04	.01
☐ 120	Greg Luzinski	.20	.08	.02

☐ 121 Checklist 1	.25	.03	.00
☐ 122 Dave Rosello DP	.04	.02	.00
☐ 123 Lynn Jones	.10	.04	.01
☐ 124 Dave Lemanczyk	.10	.04	.01
☐ 125 Tony Perez	.40	.16	.04
☐ 126 Dave Tomlin	.10	.04	.01
☐ 127 Gary Thomasson	.10	.04	.01
☐ 128 Tom Burgmeier	.10	.04	.01
☐ 129 Craig Reynolds	.10	.04	.01
☐ 130 Amos Otis	.20	.08	.02
☐ 131 Paul Mitchell	.10	.04	.01
☐ 132 Biff Pocoroba	.10	.04	.01
☐ 133 Jerry Turner	.10	.04	.01
☐ 134 Matt Keough	.10	.04	.01
☐ 135 Bill Buckner	.30	.12	.03
☐ 136 Dick Ruthven	.10	.04	.01
☐ 137 John Castino	.10	.04	.01
☐ 138 Ross Baumgarten	.10	.04	.01
☐ 139 Dane Iorg	.20	.08	.02
☐ 140 Rich Gossage	.50	.20	.05
☐ 141 Gary Alexander	.10	.04	.01
☐ 142 Phil Huffman	.10	.04	.01
☐ 143 Bruce Bochte DP	.10	.04	.01
☐ 144 Steve Comer	.10	.04	.01
☐ 145 Darrell Evans	.30	.12	.03
☐ 146 Bob Welch	.50	.20	.05
☐ 147 Terry Puhl	.10	.04	.01
☐ 148 Manny Sanguillen	.20	.08	.02
☐ 149 Tom Hume	.10	.04	.01
☐ 150 Jason Thompson	.10	.04	.01
☐ 151 Tom Hausman DP	.04	.02	.00
☐ 152 John Fulgham	.10	.04	.01
☐ 153 Tim Blackwell	.10	.04	.01
☐ 154 Lary Sorensen	.10	.04	.01
☐ 155 Jerry Remy	.10	.04	.01
☐ 156 Tony Brizzolara	.10	.04	.01
☐ 157 Willie Wilson DP	.20	.08	.02
☐ 158 Rob Picciolo DP	.04	.02	.00
☐ 159 Ken Clay	.10	.04	.01
☐ 160 Eddie Murray	3.50	1.40	.35
☐ 161 Larry Christenson	.10	.04	.01
☐ 162 Bob Randall	.10	.04	.01
☐ 163 Steve Swisher	.10	.04	.01
☐ 164 Greg Pryor	.10	.04	.01
☐ 165 Omar Moreno	.10	.04	.01
☐ 166 Glenn Abbott	.10	.04	.01
☐ 167 Jack Clark	2.00	.80	.20
☐ 168 Rick Waits	.10	.04	.01
☐ 169 Luis Gomez	.10	.04	.01
☐ 170 Burt Hooton	.10	.04	.01
☐ 171 Fernando Gonzalez	.10	.04	.01
☐ 172 Ron Hodges	.10	.04	.01
☐ 173 John Henry Johnson	.10	.04	.01
☐ 174 Ray Knight	.20	.08	.02
☐ 175 Rick Reuschel	.20	.08	.02
☐ 176 Champ Summers	.10	.04	.01
☐ 177 Dave Heaverlo	.10	.04	.01
☐ 178 Tim McCarver	.30	.12	.03
☐ 179 Ron Davis	.20	.08	.02
☐ 180 Warren Cromartie	.10	.04	.01
☐ 181 Moose Haas	.10	.04	.01
☐ 182 Ken Reitz	.10	.04	.01
☐ 183 Jim Anderson DP	.04	.02	.00
☐ 184 Steve Renko DP	.04	.02	.00
☐ 185 Hal McRae	.20	.08	.02
☐ 186 Junior Moore	.10	.04	.01
☐ 187 Alan Ashby	.10	.04	.01
☐ 188 Terry Crowley	.10	.04	.01
☐ 189 Kevin Kobel	.10	.04	.01
☐ 190 Buddy Bell	.30	.12	.03
☐ 191 Ted Martinez	.10	.04	.01
☐ 192 Braves Team/Mgr.	.35	.10	.02
Bobby Cox			
(checklist back)			
☐ 193 Dave Goltz	.10	.04	.01
☐ 194 Mike Easler	.20	.08	.02
☐ 195 John Montefusco	.20	.08	.02
☐ 196 Lance Parrish	1.50	.60	.15
☐ 197 Byron McLaughlin	.10	.04	.01
☐ 198 Dell Alston DP	.04	.02	.00
☐ 199 Mike LaCoss	.20	.08	.02
☐ 200 Jim Rice	1.50	.60	.15
☐ 201 Batting Leaders	.30	.12	.03
Keith Hernandez			
Fred Lynn			
☐ 202 Home Run Leaders	.20	.08	.02
Dave Kingman			
Gorman Thomas			
☐ 203 RBI Leaders	.30	.12	.03
Dave Winfield			
Don Baylor			
☐ 204 Stolen Base Leaders	.20	.08	.02
Omar Moreno			
Willie Wilson			
☐ 205 Victory Leaders	.20	.08	.02
Joe Niekro			
Phil Niekro			
Mike Flanagan			
☐ 206 Strikeout Leaders	.30	.12	.03
J.R. Richard			
Nolan Ryan			
☐ 207 ERA Leaders	.20	.08	.02
J.R. Richard			
Ron Guidry			
☐ 208 Wayne Cage	.10	.04	.01
☐ 209 Von Joshua	.10	.04	.01
☐ 210 Steve Carlton	2.00	.80	.20
☐ 211 Dave Skaggs DP	.04	.02	.00
☐ 212 Dave Roberts	.10	.04	.01
☐ 213 Mike Jorgensen DP	.04	.02	.00
☐ 214 Angels Team/Mgr.	.35	.10	.02
Jim Fregosi			
(checklist back)			
☐ 215 Sixto Lezcano	.10	.04	.01
☐ 216 Phil Mankowski	.10	.04	.01
☐ 217 Ed Halicki	.10	.04	.01
☐ 218 Jose Morales	.10	.04	.01
☐ 219 Steve Mingori	.10	.04	.01
☐ 220 Dave Concepcion	.30	.12	.03
☐ 221 Joe Cannon	.10	.04	.01
☐ 222 Ron Hassey	.30	.12	.03
☐ 223 Bob Sykes	.10	.04	.01
☐ 224 Willie Montanez	.10	.04	.01
☐ 225 Lou Piniella	.20	.08	.02
☐ 226 Bill Stein	.10	.04	.01
☐ 227 Len Barker	.10	.04	.01
☐ 228 Johnny Oates	.10	.04	.01
☐ 229 Jim Bibby	.10	.04	.01
☐ 230 Dave Winfield	2.00	.80	.20
☐ 231 Steve McCatty	.10	.04	.01
☐ 232 Alan Trammell	2.50	1.00	.25
☐ 233 LaRue Washington	.10	.04	.01
☐ 234 Vern Ruhle	.10	.04	.01
☐ 235 Andre Dawson	2.50	1.00	.25
☐ 236 Marc Hill	.10	.04	.01
☐ 237 Scott McGregor	.20	.08	.02
☐ 238 Rob Wilfong	.10	.04	.01
☐ 239 Don Aase	.10	.04	.01
☐ 240 Dave Kingman	.30	.12	.03
☐ 241 Checklist 2	.25	.03	.00
☐ 242 Lamar Johnson	.10	.04	.01
☐ 243 Jerry Augustine	.10	.04	.01
☐ 244 Cardinals Team/Mgr.	.35	.10	.02
Ken Boyer			
(checklist back)			
☐ 245 Phil Niekro	.90	.36	.09
☐ 246 Tim Foli DP	.04	.02	.00
☐ 247 Frank Riccelli	.10	.04	.01
☐ 248 Jamie Quirk	.10	.04	.01
☐ 249 Jim Clancy	.10	.04	.01
☐ 250 Jim Kaat	.40	.16	.04
☐ 251 Kip Young	.10	.04	.01
☐ 252 Ted Cox	.10	.04	.01
☐ 253 John Montague	.10	.04	.01
☐ 254 Paul Dade DP	.04	.02	.00
☐ 255 Dusty Baker DP	.10	.04	.01
☐ 256 Roger Erickson	.10	.04	.01
☐ 257 Larry Herndon	.10	.04	.01
☐ 258 Paul Moskau	.10	.04	.01
☐ 259 Mets Team/Mgr.	.40	.10	.02
Joe Torre			
(checklist back)			
☐ 260 Al Oliver	.30	.12	.03
☐ 261 Dave Chalk	.10	.04	.01
☐ 262 Benny Ayala	.10	.04	.01
☐ 263 Dave LaRoche DP	.04	.02	.00
☐ 264 Bill Robinson	.20	.08	.02
☐ 265 Robin Yount	1.75	.70	.17
☐ 266 Bernie Carbo	.10	.04	.01
☐ 267 Dan Schatzeder	.10	.04	.01
☐ 268 Rafael Landestoy	.10	.04	.01
☐ 269 Dave Tobik	.10	.04	.01
☐ 270 Mike Schmidt DP	1.50	.60	.15
☐ 271 Dick Drago DP	.04	.02	.00
☐ 272 Ralph Garr	.10	.04	.01
☐ 273 Eduardo Rodriguez	.10	.04	.01
☐ 274 Dale Murphy	6.00	2.40	.60
☐ 275 Jerry Koosman	.20	.08	.02
☐ 276 Tom Veryzer	.10	.04	.01
☐ 277 Rick Bosetti	.10	.04	.01
☐ 278 Jim Spencer	.10	.04	.01
☐ 279 Rob Andrews	.10	.04	.01
☐ 280 Gaylord Perry	.90	.36	.09
☐ 281 Paul Blair	.10	.04	.01
☐ 282 Mariners Team/Mgr.	.30	.10	.02
Darrell Johnson			
(checklist back)			
☐ 283 John Ellis	.10	.04	.01
☐ 284 Larry Murray DP	.04	.02	.00
☐ 285 Don Baylor	.40	.16	.04

□ 286	Darold Knowles DP	.04	.02	.00
□ 287	John Lowenstein	.10	.04	.01
□ 288	Dave Rozema	.10	.04	.01
□ 289	Bruce Bochy	.10	.04	.01
□ 290	Steve Garvey	2.00	.80	.20
□ 291	Randy Scarberry	.10	.04	.01
□ 292	Dale Berra	.10	.04	.01
□ 293	Elias Sosa	.10	.04	.01
□ 294	Charlie Spikes	.10	.04	.01
□ 295	Larry Gura	.10	.04	.01
□ 296	Dave Rader	.10	.04	.01
□ 297	Tim Johnson	.10	.04	.01
□ 298	Ken Holtzman	.10	.04	.01
□ 299	Steve Henderson	.10	.04	.01
□ 300	Ron Guidry	.65	.26	.06
□ 301	Mike Edwards	.10	.04	.01
□ 302	Dodgers Team/Mgr. Tom Lasorda (checklist back)	.45	.12	.02
□ 303	Bill Castro	.10	.04	.01
□ 304	Butch Wynegar	.10	.04	.01
□ 305	Randy Jones	.10	.04	.01
□ 306	Denny Walling	.10	.04	.01
□ 307	Rick Honeycutt	.10	.04	.01
□ 308	Mike Hargrove	.10	.04	.01
□ 309	Larry McWilliams	.10	.04	.01
□ 310	Dave Parker	.90	.36	.09
□ 311	Roger Metzger	.10	.04	.01
□ 312	Mike Barlow	.10	.04	.01
□ 313	Johnny Grubb	.10	.04	.01
□ 314	Tim Stoddard	.20	.08	.02
□ 315	Steve Kemp	.20	.08	.02
□ 316	Bob Lacey	.10	.04	.01
□ 317	Mike Anderson DP	.04	.02	.00
□ 318	Jerry Reuss	.20	.08	.02
□ 319	Chris Speier	.10	.04	.01
□ 320	Dennis Eckersley	.50	.20	.05
□ 321	Keith Hernandez	1.50	.60	.15
□ 322	Claudell Washington	.20	.08	.02
□ 323	Mick Kelleher	.10	.04	.01
□ 324	Tom Underwood	.10	.04	.01
□ 325	Dan Driessen	.10	.04	.01
□ 326	Bo McLaughlin	.10	.04	.01
□ 327	Ray Fosse DP	.04	.02	.00
□ 328	Twins Team/Mgr. Gene Mauch (checklist back)	.35	.10	.02
□ 329	Bert Roberge	.10	.04	.01
□ 330	Al Cowens	.10	.04	.01
□ 331	Richie Hebner	.10	.04	.01
□ 332	Enrique Romo	.10	.04	.01
□ 333	Jim Norris DP	.04	.02	.00
□ 334	Jim Beattie	.10	.04	.01
□ 335	Willie McCovey	1.50	.60	.15
□ 336	George Medich	.10	.04	.01
□ 337	Carney Lansford	.60	.24	.06
□ 338	Johnny Wockenfuss	.10	.04	.01
□ 339	John D'Acquisto	.10	.04	.01
□ 340	Ken Singleton	.20	.08	.02
□ 341	Jim Essian	.10	.04	.01
□ 342	Odell Jones	.10	.04	.01
□ 343	Mike Vail	.10	.04	.01
□ 344	Randy Lerch	.10	.04	.01
□ 345	Larry Parrish	.20	.08	.02
□ 346	Buddy Solomon	.10	.04	.01
□ 347	Harry Chappas	.10	.04	.01
□ 348	Checklist 3	.25	.03	.00
□ 349	Jack Brohamer	.10	.04	.01
□ 350	George Hendrick	.20	.08	.02
□ 351	Bob Davis	.10	.04	.01
□ 352	Dan Briggs	.10	.04	.01
□ 353	Andy Hassler	.10	.04	.01
□ 354	Rick Auerbach	.10	.04	.01
□ 355	Gary Matthews	.20	.08	.02
□ 356	Padres Team/Mgr. Jerry Coleman (checklist back)	.35	.10	.02
□ 357	Bob McClure	.10	.04	.01
□ 358	Lou Whitaker	1.00	.40	.10
□ 359	Randy Moffitt	.10	.04	.01
□ 360	Darrell Porter DP	.10	.04	.01
□ 361	Wayne Garland	.10	.04	.01
□ 362	Danny Goodwin	.10	.04	.01
□ 363	Wayne Gross	.10	.04	.01
□ 364	Ray Burris	.10	.04	.01
□ 365	Bobby Murcer	.30	.12	.03
□ 366	Rob Dressler	.10	.04	.01
□ 367	Billy Smith	.10	.04	.01
□ 368	Willie Aikens	.20	.08	.02
□ 369	Jim Kern	.10	.04	.01
□ 370	Cesar Cedeno	.20	.08	.02
□ 371	Jack Morris	1.50	.60	.15
□ 372	Joel Youngblood	.10	.04	.01
□ 373	Dan Petry DP	.60	.24	.06
□ 374	Jim Gantner	.10	.04	.01
□ 375	Ross Grimsley	.10	.04	.01
□ 376	Gary Allenson	.10	.04	.01
□ 377	Junior Kennedy	.10	.04	.01
□ 378	Jerry Mumphrey	.10	.04	.01
□ 379	Kevin Bell	.10	.04	.01
□ 380	Garry Maddox	.10	.04	.01
□ 381	Cubs Team/Mgr. Preston Gomez (checklist back)	.35	.10	.02
□ 382	Dave Freisleben	.10	.04	.01
□ 383	Ed Ott	.10	.04	.01
□ 384	Joey McLaughlin	.10	.04	.01
□ 385	Enos Cabell	.10	.04	.01
□ 386	Darrell Jackson	.10	.04	.01
□ 387A	Fred Stanley (yellow name on front)	1.00	.40	.10
□ 387B	Fred Stanley (red name on front)	.10	.04	.01
□ 388	Mike Paxton	.10	.04	.01
□ 389	Pete LaCock	.10	.04	.01
□ 390	Fergie Jenkins	.40	.16	.04
□ 391	Tony Armas DP	.10	.04	.01
□ 392	Milt Wilcox	.10	.04	.01
□ 393	Ozzie Smith	3.00	1.20	.30
□ 394	Reggie Cleveland	.10	.04	.01
□ 395	Ellis Valentine	.10	.04	.01
□ 396	Dan Meyer	.10	.04	.01
□ 397	Roy Thomas DP	.04	.02	.00
□ 398	Barry Foote	.10	.04	.01
□ 399	Mike Proly DP	.04	.02	.00
□ 400	George Foster	.50	.20	.05
□ 401	Pete Falcone	.10	.04	.01
□ 402	Merv Rettenmund	.10	.04	.01
□ 403	Pete Redfern DP	.04	.02	.00
□ 404	Orioles Team/Mgr. Earl Weaver (checklist back)	.40	.10	.02
□ 405	Dwight Evans	.80	.32	.08
□ 406	Paul Molitor	1.50	.60	.15
□ 407	Tony Solaita	.10	.04	.01
□ 408	Bill North	.10	.04	.01
□ 409	Paul Splittorff	.10	.04	.01
□ 410	Bobby Bonds	.20	.08	.02
□ 411	Frank LaCorte	.10	.04	.01
□ 412	Thad Bosley	.10	.04	.01
□ 413	Allen Ripley	.10	.04	.01
□ 414	George Scott	.10	.04	.01
□ 415	Bill Atkinson	.10	.04	.01
□ 416	Tom Brookens	.10	.04	.01
□ 417	Craig Chamberlain DP	.04	.02	.00
□ 418	Roger Freed DP	.04	.02	.00
□ 419	Vic Correll	.10	.04	.01
□ 420	Butch Hobson	.10	.04	.01
□ 421	Doug Bird	.10	.04	.01
□ 422	Larry Milbourne	.10	.04	.01
□ 423	Dave Frost	.10	.04	.01
□ 424	Yankees Team/Mgr. Dick Howser (checklist back)	.40	.10	.02
□ 425	Mark Belanger	.20	.08	.02
□ 426	Grant Jackson	.10	.04	.01
□ 427	Tom Hutton DP	.04	.02	.00
□ 428	Pat Zachry	.10	.04	.01
□ 429	Duane Kuiper	.10	.04	.01
□ 430	Larry Hisle DP	.10	.04	.01
□ 431	Mike Krukow	.20	.08	.02
□ 432	Willie Norwood	.10	.04	.01
□ 433	Rich Gale	.10	.04	.01
□ 434	Johnnie LeMaster	.10	.04	.01
□ 435	Don Gullett	.10	.04	.01
□ 436	Billy Almon	.10	.04	.01
□ 437	Joe Niekro	.20	.08	.02
□ 438	Dave Revering	.10	.04	.01
□ 439	Mike Phillips	.10	.04	.01
□ 440	Don Sutton	.80	.32	.08
□ 441	Eric Soderholm	.10	.04	.01
□ 442	Jorge Orta	.10	.04	.01
□ 443	Mike Parrott	.10	.04	.01
□ 444	Alvis Woods	.10	.04	.01
□ 445	Mark Fidrych	.20	.08	.02
□ 446	Duffy Dyer	.10	.04	.01
□ 447	Nino Espinosa	.10	.04	.01
□ 448	Jim Wohlford	.10	.04	.01
□ 449	Doug Bair	.10	.04	.01
□ 450	George Brett	3.75	1.50	.37
□ 451	Indians Team/Mgr. Dave Garcia (checklist back)	.35	.10	.02
□ 452	Steve Dillard	.10	.04	.01
□ 453	Mike Bacsik	.10	.04	.01
□ 454	Tom Donohue	.10	.04	.01
□ 455	Mike Torrez	.10	.04	.01
□ 456	Frank Taveras	.10	.04	.01
□ 457	Bert Blyleven	.40	.16	.04
□ 458	Billy Sample	.10	.04	.01

☐ 459 Mickey Lolich DP	.10	.04	.01
☐ 460 Willie Randolph	.30	.12	.03
☐ 461 Dwayne Murphy	.15	.06	.01
☐ 462 Mike Sadek DP	.04	.02	.00
☐ 463 Jerry Royster	.10	.04	.01
☐ 464 John Denny	.10	.04	.01
☐ 465 Rick Monday	.10	.04	.01
☐ 466 Mike Squires	.10	.04	.01
☐ 467 Jesse Jefferson	.10	.04	.01
☐ 468 Aurelio Rodriguez	.10	.04	.01
☐ 469 Randy Niemann DP	.04	.02	.00
☐ 470 Bob Boone	.30	.12	.03
☐ 471 Hosken Powell DP	.04	.02	.00
☐ 472 Willie Hernandez	.30	.12	.03
☐ 473 Bump Wills	.10	.04	.01
☐ 474 Steve Busby	.10	.04	.01
☐ 475 Cesar Geronimo	.10	.04	.01
☐ 476 Bob Shirley	.10	.04	.01
☐ 477 Buck Martinez	.10	.04	.01
☐ 478 Gil Flores	.10	.04	.01
☐ 479 Expos Team/Mgr. Dick Williams (checklist back)	.30	.10	.02
☐ 480 Bob Watson	.20	.08	.02
☐ 481 Tom Paciorek	.10	.04	.01
☐ 482 Rickey Henderson	27.00	11.00	2.70
☐ 483 Bo Diaz	.10	.04	.01
☐ 484 Checklist 4	.25	.03	.00
☐ 485 Mickey Rivers	.20	.08	.02
☐ 486 Mike Tyson DP	.04	.02	.00
☐ 487 Wayne Nordhagen	.10	.04	.01
☐ 488 Roy Howell	.10	.04	.01
☐ 489 Preston Hanna DP	.04	.02	.00
☐ 490 Lee May	.10	.04	.01
☐ 491 Steve Mura DP	.04	.02	.00
☐ 492 Todd Cruz	.10	.04	.01
☐ 493 Jerry Martin	.10	.04	.01
☐ 494 Craig Minetto	.10	.04	.01
☐ 495 Bake McBride	.10	.04	.01
☐ 496 Silvio Martinez	.10	.04	.01
☐ 497 Jim Mason	.10	.04	.01
☐ 498 Danny Darwin	.10	.04	.01
☐ 499 Giants Team/Mgr. Dave Bristol (checklist back)	.35	.10	.02
☐ 500 Tom Seaver	1.75	.70	.17
☐ 501 Rennie Stennett	.10	.04	.01
☐ 502 Rich Wortham DP	.04	.02	.00
☐ 503 Mike Cubbage	.10	.04	.01
☐ 504 Gene Garber	.10	.04	.01
☐ 505 Bert Campaneris	.10	.04	.01
☐ 506 Tom Buskey	.10	.04	.01
☐ 507 Leon Roberts	.10	.04	.01
☐ 508 U.L. Washington	.10	.04	.01
☐ 509 Ed Glynn	.10	.04	.01
☐ 510 Ron Cey	.30	.12	.03
☐ 511 Eric Wilkins	.10	.04	.01
☐ 512 Jose Cardenal	.10	.04	.01
☐ 513 Tom Dixon DP	.04	.02	.00
☐ 514 Steve Ontiveros	.10	.04	.01
☐ 515 Mike Caldwell	.10	.04	.01
☐ 516 Hector Cruz	.10	.04	.01
☐ 517 Don Stanhouse	.10	.04	.01
☐ 518 Nelson Norman	.10	.04	.01
☐ 519 Steve Nicosia	.10	.04	.01
☐ 520 Steve Rogers	.10	.04	.01
☐ 521 Ken Brett	.10	.04	.01
☐ 522 Jim Morrison	.10	.04	.01
☐ 523 Ken Henderson	.10	.04	.01
☐ 524 Jim Wright DP	.04	.02	.00
☐ 525 Clint Hurdle	.10	.04	.01
☐ 526 Phillies Team/Mgr. Dallas Green (checklist back)	.40	.10	.02
☐ 527 Doug Rau DP	.04	.02	.00
☐ 528 Adrian Devine	.10	.04	.01
☐ 529 Jim Barr	.10	.04	.01
☐ 530 Jim Sundberg DP	.10	.04	.01
☐ 531 Eric Rasmussen	.10	.04	.01
☐ 532 Willie Horton	.20	.08	.02
☐ 533 Checklist 5	.25	.03	.00
☐ 534 Andre Thornton	.20	.08	.02
☐ 535 Bob Forsch	.10	.04	.01
☐ 536 Lee Lacy	.10	.04	.01
☐ 537 Alex Trevino	.20	.08	.02
☐ 538 Joe Strain	.10	.04	.01
☐ 539 Rudy May	.10	.04	.01
☐ 540 Pete Rose	4.00	1.60	.40
☐ 541 Miguel Dilone	.10	.04	.01
☐ 542 Joe Coleman	.10	.04	.01
☐ 543 Pat Kelly	.10	.04	.01
☐ 544 Rick Sutcliffe	2.75	1.10	.27
☐ 545 Jeff Burroughs	.10	.04	.01
☐ 546 Rick Langford	.10	.04	.01
☐ 547 John Wathan	.20	.08	.02
☐ 548 Dave Rajsich	.10	.04	.01
☐ 549 Larry Wolfe	.10	.04	.01
☐ 550 Ken Griffey	.20	.08	.02
☐ 551 Pirates Team/Mgr. Chuck Tanner (checklist back)	.35	.10	.02
☐ 552 Bill Nahorodny	.10	.04	.01
☐ 553 Dick Davis	.10	.04	.01
☐ 554 Art Howe	.20	.08	.02
☐ 555 Ed Figueroa	.10	.04	.01
☐ 556 Joe Rudi	.20	.08	.02
☐ 557 Mark Lee	.10	.04	.01
☐ 558 Alfredo Griffin	.30	.12	.03
☐ 559 Dale Murray	.10	.04	.01
☐ 560 Dave Lopes	.20	.08	.02
☐ 561 Eddie Whitson	.20	.08	.02
☐ 562 Joe Wallis	.10	.04	.01
☐ 563 Will McEnaney	.10	.04	.01
☐ 564 Rick Manning	.10	.04	.01
☐ 565 Dennis Leonard	.20	.08	.02
☐ 566 Bud Harrelson	.10	.04	.01
☐ 567 Skip Lockwood	.10	.04	.01
☐ 568 Gary Roenicke	.20	.08	.02
☐ 569 Terry Kennedy	.20	.08	.02
☐ 570 Roy Smalley	.10	.04	.01
☐ 571 Joe Sambito	.10	.04	.01
☐ 572 Jerry Morales DP	.04	.02	.00
☐ 573 Kent Tekulve	.20	.08	.02
☐ 574 Scot Thompson	.10	.04	.01
☐ 575 Ken Kravec	.10	.04	.01
☐ 576 Jim Dwyer	.10	.04	.01
☐ 577 Blue Jays Team/Mgr. Bobby Mattick (checklist back)	.30	.10	.02
☐ 578 Scott Sanderson	.20	.08	.02
☐ 579 Charlie Moore	.10	.04	.01
☐ 580 Nolan Ryan	2.00	.80	.20
☐ 581 Bob Bailor	.10	.04	.01
☐ 582 Brian Doyle	.10	.04	.01
☐ 583 Bob Stinson	.10	.04	.01
☐ 584 Kurt Bevacqua	.10	.04	.01
☐ 585 Al Hrabosky	.10	.04	.01
☐ 586 Mitchell Page	.10	.04	.01
☐ 587 Garry Templeton	.20	.08	.02
☐ 588 Greg Minton	.10	.04	.01
☐ 589 Chet Lemon	.10	.04	.01
☐ 590 Jim Palmer	1.25	.50	.12
☐ 591 Rick Cerone	.10	.04	.01
☐ 592 Jon Matlack	.10	.04	.01
☐ 593 Jesus Alou	.10	.04	.01
☐ 594 Dick Tidrow	.10	.04	.01
☐ 595 Don Money	.10	.04	.01
☐ 596 Rick Matula	.10	.04	.01
☐ 597 Tom Poquette	.10	.04	.01
☐ 598 Fred Kendall DP	.04	.02	.00
☐ 599 Mike Norris	.10	.04	.01
☐ 600 Reggie Jackson	2.50	1.00	.25
☐ 601 Buddy Schultz	.10	.04	.01
☐ 602 Brian Downing	.20	.08	.02
☐ 603 Jack Billingham DP	.04	.02	.00
☐ 604 Glenn Adams	.10	.04	.01
☐ 605 Terry Forster	.20	.08	.02
☐ 606 Reds Team/Mgr. John McNamara (checklist back)	.35	.10	.02
☐ 607 Woodie Fryman	.10	.04	.01
☐ 608 Alan Bannister	.10	.04	.01
☐ 609 Ron Reed	.10	.04	.01
☐ 610 Willie Stargell	1.50	.60	.15
☐ 611 Jerry Garvin DP	.04	.02	.00
☐ 612 Cliff Johnson	.10	.04	.01
☐ 613 Randy Stein	.10	.04	.01
☐ 614 John Hiller	.10	.04	.01
☐ 615 Doug DeCinces	.20	.08	.02
☐ 616 Gene Richards	.10	.04	.01
☐ 617 Joaquin Andujar	.20	.08	.02
☐ 618 Bob Montgomery DP	.04	.02	.00
☐ 619 Sergio Ferrer	.10	.04	.01
☐ 620 Richie Zisk	.10	.04	.01
☐ 621 Bob Grich	.20	.08	.02
☐ 622 Mario Soto	.20	.08	.02
☐ 623 Gorman Thomas	.20	.08	.02
☐ 624 Lerrin LaGrow	.10	.04	.01
☐ 625 Chris Chambliss	.20	.08	.02
☐ 626 Tigers Team/Mgr. Sparky Anderson (checklist back)	.40	.10	.02
☐ 627 Pedro Borbon	.10	.04	.01
☐ 628 Doug Capilla	.10	.04	.01
☐ 629 Jim Todd	.10	.04	.01
☐ 630 Larry Bowa	.30	.12	.03
☐ 631 Mark Littell	.10	.04	.01
☐ 632 Barry Bonnell	.10	.04	.01
☐ 633 Bob Apodaca	.10	.04	.01
☐ 634 Glenn Borgmann DP	.04	.02	.00

□ 635 John Candelaria	.30	.12	.03
□ 636 Toby Harrah	.20	.08	.02
□ 637 Joe Simpson	.10	.04	.01
□ 638 Mark Clear	.20	.08	.02
□ 639 Larry Biittner	.10	.04	.01
□ 640 Mike Flanagan	.20	.08	.02
□ 641 Ed Kranepool	.10	.04	.01
□ 642 Ken Forsch DP	.10	.04	.01
□ 643 John Mayberry	.20	.08	.02
□ 644 Charlie Hough	.20	.08	.02
□ 645 Rick Burleson	.20	.08	.02
□ 646 Checklist 6	.25	.03	.00
□ 647 Milt May	.10	.04	.01
□ 648 Roy White	.20	.08	.02
□ 649 Tom Griffin	.10	.04	.01
□ 650 Joe Morgan	1.00	.40	.10
□ 651 Rollie Fingers	.50	.20	.05
□ 652 Mario Mendoza	.10	.04	.01
□ 653 Stan Bahnsen	.10	.04	.01
□ 654 Bruce Boisclair DP	.04	.02	.00
□ 655 Tug McGraw	.20	.08	.02
□ 656 Larvell Blanks	.10	.04	.01
□ 657 Dave Edwards	.10	.04	.01
□ 658 Chris Knapp	.10	.04	.01
□ 659 Brewers Team/Mgr. George Bamberger (checklist back)	.35	.10	.02
□ 660 Rusty Staub	.30	.12	.03
□ 661 Orioles Rookies Mark Corey Dave Ford Wayne Krenchicki	.15	.06	.01
□ 662 Red Sox Rookies Joel Finch Mike O'Berry Chuck Rainey	.15	.06	.01
□ 663 Angels Rookies Ralph Botting Bob Clark Dickie Thon	.50	.20	.05
□ 664 White Sox Rookies Mike Colbern Guy Hoffman Dewey Robinson	.15	.06	.01
□ 665 Indians Rookies Larry Andersen Bobby Cuellar Sandy Wihtol	.25	.10	.02
□ 666 Tigers Rookies Mike Chris Al Greene Bruce Robbins	.15	.06	.01
□ 667 Royals Rookies Renie Martin Bill Paschall Dan Quisenberry	1.50	.60	.15
□ 668 Brewers Rookies Danny Boitano Willie Mueller Lenn Sakata	.20	.08	.02
□ 669 Twins Rookies Dan Graham Rick Sofield Gary Ward	.50	.20	.05
□ 670 Yankees Rookies Bobby Brown Brad Gulden Darryl Jones	.15	.06	.01
□ 671 A's Rookies Derek Bryant Brian Kingman Mike Morgan	.25	.10	.02
□ 672 Mariners Rookies Charlie Beamon Rodney Craig Rafael Vasquez	.15	.06	.01
□ 673 Rangers Rookies Brian Allard Jerry Don Gleaton Greg Mahlberg	.15	.06	.01
□ 674 Blue Jays Rookies Butch Edge Pat Kelly Ted Wilborn	.15	.06	.01
□ 675 Braves Rookies Bruce Benedict Larry Bradford Eddie Miller	.20	.08	.02
□ 676 Cubs Rookies Dave Geisel Steve Macko Karl Pagel	.15	.06	.01
□ 677 Reds Rookies Art DeFreites Frank Pastore Harry Spilman	.15	.06	.01
□ 678 Astros Rookies Reggie Baldwin Alan Knicely Pete Ladd	.20	.08	.02
□ 679 Dodgers Rookies Joe Beckwith Mickey Hatcher Dave Patterson	.60	.24	.06
□ 680 Expos Rookies Tony Bernazard Randy Miller John Tamargo	.35	.14	.03
□ 681 Mets Rookies Dan Norman Jesse Orosco Mike Scott	7.00	2.80	.70
□ 682 Phillies Rookies Ramon Aviles Dickie Noles Kevin Saucier	.20	.08	.02
□ 683 Pirates Rookies Dorian Boyland Alberto Lois Harry Saferight	.15	.06	.01
□ 684 Cardinals Rookies George Frazier Tom Herr Dan O'Brien	.70	.28	.07
□ 685 Padres Rookies Tim Flannery Brian Greer Jim Wilhelm	.20	.08	.02
□ 686 Giants Rookies Greg Johnston Dennis Littlejohn Phil Nastu	.15	.06	.01
□ 687 Mike Heath DP	.04	.02	.00
□ 688 Steve Stone	.10	.04	.01
□ 689 Red Sox Team/Mgr. Don Zimmer (checklist back)	.35	.10	.02
□ 690 Tommy John	.50	.20	.05
□ 691 Ivan DeJesus	.10	.04	.01
□ 692 Rawly Eastwick DP	.04	.02	.00
□ 693 Craig Kusick	.10	.04	.01
□ 694 Jim Rooker	.10	.04	.01
□ 695 Reggie Smith	.20	.08	.02
□ 696 Julio Gonzalez	.10	.04	.01
□ 697 David Clyde	.10	.04	.01
□ 698 Oscar Gamble	.10	.04	.01
□ 699 Floyd Bannister	.20	.08	.02
□ 700 Rod Carew DP	1.00	.40	.10
□ 701 Ken Oberkfell	.30	.12	.03
□ 702 Ed Farmer	.10	.04	.01
□ 703 Otto Velez	.10	.04	.01
□ 704 Gene Tenace	.10	.04	.01
□ 705 Freddie Patek	.10	.04	.01
□ 706 Tippy Martinez	.10	.04	.01
□ 707 Elliott Maddox	.10	.04	.01
□ 708 Bob Tolan	.10	.04	.01
□ 709 Pat Underwood	.10	.04	.01
□ 710 Graig Nettles	.30	.12	.03
□ 711 Bob Galasso	.10	.04	.01
□ 712 Rodney Scott	.10	.04	.01
□ 713 Terry Whitfield	.10	.04	.01
□ 714 Fred Norman	.10	.04	.01
□ 715 Sal Bando	.15	.06	.01
□ 716 Lynn McGlothen	.10	.04	.01
□ 717 Mickey Klutts DP	.04	.02	.00
□ 718 Greg Gross	.10	.04	.01
□ 719 Don Robinson	.20	.08	.02
□ 720 Carl Yastrzemski DP	1.50	.60	.15
□ 721 Paul Hartzell	.10	.04	.01
□ 722 Jose Cruz	.20	.08	.02
□ 723 Shane Rawley	.20	.08	.02
□ 724 Jerry White	.10	.04	.01
□ 725 Rick Wise	.10	.04	.01
□ 726 Steve Yeager	.20	.08	.02

1981 Topps

The cards in this 726-card set measure 2 1/2" by 3 1/2". League Leaders (1-8), Record Breakers (201-208), and Post-season cards (401-404) are topical subsets found in this set marketed by Topps in 1981. The team cards are all grouped together (661-686) and feature team checklist backs and a very small

photo of the team's manager in the upper right corner of the obverse. The obverses carry the player's position and team in a baseball cap design, and the company name is printed in a small baseball. The backs are red and gray. The 66 double-printed cards are noted in the checklist by DP. The set is quite popular with collectors partly due to the presence of rookie cards of Fernando Valenzuela, Tim Raines, Kirk Gibson, Harold Baines, John Tudor, Lloyd Moseby, Hubie Brooks, Mike Boddicker, and Tony Pena.

	MINT	EXC	G-VG
COMPLETE SET (726)	85.00	34.00	8.50
COMMON PLAYER (1-726)	.07	.03	.01
COMMON DP's (1-726)	.03	.01	.00
□ 1 Batting Leaders	.65	.10	.02
George Brett			
Bill Buckner			
□ 2 Home Run Leaders	.35	.14	.03
Reggie Jackson			
Ben Oglivie			
Mike Schmidt			
□ 3 RBI Leaders	.20	.08	.02
Cecil Cooper			
Mike Schmidt			
□ 4 Stolen Base Leaders	.18	.08	.01
Rickey Henderson			
Ron LeFlore			
□ 5 Victory Leaders	.15	.06	.01
Steve Stone			
Steve Carlton			
□ 6 Strikeout Leaders	.15	.06	.01
Len Barker			
Steve Carlton			
□ 7 ERA Leaders	.10	.04	.01
Rudy May			
Don Sutton			
□ 8 Leading Firemen	.10	.04	.01
Dan Quisenberry			
Rollie Fingers			
Tom Hume			
□ 9 Pete LaCock DP	.03	.01	.00
□ 10 Mike Flanagan	.10	.04	.01
□ 11 Jim Wohlford DP	.03	.01	.00
□ 12 Mark Clear	.07	.03	.01
□ 13 Joe Charboneau	.10	.04	.01
□ 14 John Tudor	1.75	.70	.17
□ 15 Larry Parrish	.10	.04	.01
□ 16 Ron Davis	.07	.03	.01
□ 17 Cliff Johnson	.07	.03	.01
□ 18 Glenn Adams	.07	.03	.01
□ 19 Jim Clancy	.10	.04	.01
□ 20 Jeff Burroughs	.10	.04	.01
□ 21 Ron Oester	.10	.04	.01
□ 22 Danny Darwin	.07	.03	.01
□ 23 Alex Trevino	.07	.03	.01
□ 24 Don Stanhouse	.07	.03	.01
□ 25 Sixto Lezcano	.07	.03	.01
□ 26 U.L. Washington	.07	.03	.01
□ 27 Champ Summers DP	.03	.01	.00
□ 28 Enrique Romo	.07	.03	.01
□ 29 Gene Tenace	.10	.04	.01
□ 30 Jack Clark	.60	.24	.06
□ 31 Checklist 1-121 DP	.07	.01	.00
□ 32 Ken Oberkfell	.07	.03	.01
□ 33 Rick Honeycutt	.07	.03	.01
□ 34 Aurelio Rodriguez	.07	.03	.01
□ 35 Mitchell Page	.07	.03	.01
□ 36 Ed Farmer	.07	.03	.01
□ 37 Gary Roenicke	.07	.03	.01
□ 38 Win Remmerswaal	.07	.03	.01
□ 39 Tom Veryzer	.07	.03	.01
□ 40 Tug McGraw	.15	.06	.01
□ 41 Ranger Rookies	.10	.04	.01
Bob Babcock			
John Butcher			
Jerry Don Gleaton			
□ 42 Jerry White DP	.03	.01	.00
□ 43 Jose Morales	.07	.03	.01
□ 44 Larry McWilliams	.07	.03	.01
□ 45 Enos Cabell	.07	.03	.01
□ 46 Rick Bosetti	.07	.03	.01
□ 47 Ken Brett	.07	.03	.01
□ 48 Dave Skaggs	.07	.03	.01
□ 49 Bob Shirley	.07	.03	.01
□ 50 Dave Lopes	.15	.06	.01
□ 51 Bill Robinson DP	.03	.01	.00
□ 52 Hector Cruz	.07	.03	.01
□ 53 Kevin Saucier	.07	.03	.01
□ 54 Ivan DeJesus	.07	.03	.01
□ 55 Mike Norris	.07	.03	.01
□ 56 Buck Martinez	.07	.03	.01
□ 57 Dave Roberts	.07	.03	.01
□ 58 Joel Youngblood	.07	.03	.01
□ 59 Dan Petry	.10	.04	.01
□ 60 Willie Randolph	.15	.06	.01
□ 61 Butch Wynegar	.07	.03	.01
□ 62 Joe Pettini	.07	.03	.01
□ 63 Steve Renko DP	.03	.01	.00
□ 64 Brian Asselstine	.07	.03	.01
□ 65 Scott McGregor	.10	.04	.01
□ 66 Royals Rookies	.10	.04	.01
Manny Castillo			
Tim Ireland			
Mike Jones			
□ 67 Ken Kravec	.07	.03	.01
□ 68 Matt Alexander DP	.03	.01	.00
□ 69 Ed Halicki	.07	.03	.01
□ 70 Al Oliver DP	.10	.04	.01
□ 71 Hal Dues	.07	.03	.01
□ 72 Barry Evans DP	.03	.01	.00
□ 73 Doug Bair	.07	.03	.01
□ 74 Mike Hargrove	.07	.03	.01
□ 75 Reggie Smith	.15	.06	.01
□ 76 Mario Mendoza	.07	.03	.01
□ 77 Mike Barlow	.07	.03	.01
□ 78 Steve Dillard	.07	.03	.01
□ 79 Bruce Robbins	.07	.03	.01
□ 80 Rusty Staub	.20	.08	.02
□ 81 Dave Stapleton	.10	.04	.01
□ 82 Astros Rookies DP	.10	.04	.01
Danny Heep			
Alan Knicely			
Bobby Sprowl			
□ 83 Mike Proly	.07	.03	.01
□ 84 Johnnie LeMaster	.07	.03	.01
□ 85 Mike Caldwell	.07	.03	.01
□ 86 Wayne Gross	.07	.03	.01
□ 87 Rick Camp	.07	.03	.01
□ 88 Joe Lefebvre	.10	.04	.01
□ 89 Darrell Jackson	.07	.03	.01
□ 90 Bake McBride	.07	.03	.01
□ 91 Tim Stoddard DP	.07	.03	.01
□ 92 Mike Easler	.10	.04	.01
□ 93 Ed Glynn DP	.03	.01	.00
□ 94 Harry Spilman DP	.03	.01	.00
□ 95 Jim Sundberg	.10	.04	.01
□ 96 A's Rookies	.15	.06	.01
Dave Beard			
Ernie Camacho			
Pat Dempsey			
□ 97 Chris Speier	.07	.03	.01
□ 98 Clint Hurdle	.07	.03	.01
□ 99 Eric Wilkins	.07	.03	.01
□ 100 Rod Carew	1.25	.50	.12
□ 101 Benny Ayala	.07	.03	.01
□ 102 Dave Tobik	.07	.03	.01
□ 103 Jerry Martin	.07	.03	.01
□ 104 Terry Forster	.10	.04	.01
□ 105 Jose Cruz	.15	.06	.01
□ 106 Don Money	.07	.03	.01
□ 107 Rich Wortham	.07	.03	.01
□ 108 Bruce Benedict	.07	.03	.01
□ 109 Mike Scott	1.25	.50	.12
□ 110 Carl Yastrzemski	1.75	.70	.17
□ 111 Greg Minton	.07	.03	.01
□ 112 White Sox Rookies	.10	.04	.01
Rusty Kuntz			
Fran Mullin			
Leo Sutherland			
□ 113 Mike Phillips	.07	.03	.01
□ 114 Tom Underwood	.07	.03	.01
□ 115 Roy Smalley	.07	.03	.01
□ 116 Joe Simpson	.07	.03	.01

☐ 117	Pete Falcone	.07	.03	.01
☐ 118	Kurt Bevacqua	.07	.03	.01
☐ 119	Tippy Martinez	.07	.03	.01
☐ 120	Larry Bowa	.15	.06	.01
☐ 121	Larry Harlow	.07	.03	.01
☐ 122	John Denny	.10	.04	.01
☐ 123	Al Cowens	.07	.03	.01
☐ 124	Jerry Garvin	.07	.03	.01
☐ 125	Andre Dawson	1.00	.40	.10
☐ 126	Charlie Leibrandt	.45	.18	.04
☐ 127	Rudy Law	.07	.03	.01
☐ 128	Garry Allenson DP	.03	.01	.00
☐ 129	Art Howe	.15	.06	.01
☐ 130	Larry Gura	.10	.04	.01
☐ 131	Keith Moreland	.40	.16	.04
☐ 132	Tommy Boggs	.07	.03	.01
☐ 133	Jeff Cox	.07	.03	.01
☐ 134	Steve Mura	.07	.03	.01
☐ 135	Gorman Thomas	.20	.08	.02
☐ 136	Doug Capilla	.07	.03	.01
☐ 137	Hosken Powell	.07	.03	.01
☐ 138	Rich Dotson DP	.35	.14	.03
☐ 139	Oscar Gamble	.07	.03	.01
☐ 140	Bob Forsch	.07	.03	.01
☐ 141	Miguel Dilone	.07	.03	.01
☐ 142	Jackson Todd	.07	.03	.01
☐ 143	Dan Meyer	.07	.03	.01
☐ 144	Allen Ripley	.07	.03	.01
☐ 145	Mickey Rivers	.10	.04	.01
☐ 146	Bobby Castillo	.07	.03	.01
☐ 147	Dale Berra	.07	.03	.01
☐ 148	Randy Niemann	.07	.03	.01
☐ 149	Joe Nolan	.07	.03	.01
☐ 150	Mark Fidrych	.15	.06	.01
☐ 151	Claudell Washington	.15	.06	.01
☐ 152	John Urrea	.07	.03	.01
☐ 153	Tom Poquette	.07	.03	.01
☐ 154	Rick Langford	.07	.03	.01
☐ 155	Chris Chambliss	.15	.06	.01
☐ 156	Bob McClure	.07	.03	.01
☐ 157	John Wathan	.15	.06	.01
☐ 158	Fergie Jenkins	.25	.10	.02
☐ 159	Brian Doyle	.07	.03	.01
☐ 160	Garry Maddox	.10	.04	.01
☐ 161	Dan Graham	.07	.03	.01
☐ 162	Doug Corbett	.10	.04	.01
☐ 163	Billy Almon	.07	.03	.01
☐ 164	LaMarr Hoyt	.25	.10	.02
☐ 165	Tony Scott	.07	.03	.01
☐ 166	Floyd Bannister	.10	.04	.01
☐ 167	Terry Whitfield	.07	.03	.01
☐ 168	Don Robinson DP	.03	.01	.00
☐ 169	John Mayberry	.10	.04	.01
☐ 170	Ross Grimsley	.07	.03	.01
☐ 171	Gene Richards	.07	.03	.01
☐ 172	Gary Woods	.07	.03	.01
☐ 173	Bump Wills	.07	.03	.01
☐ 174	Doug Rau	.07	.03	.01
☐ 175	Dave Collins	.07	.03	.01
☐ 176	Mike Krukow	.10	.04	.01
☐ 177	Rick Peters	.07	.03	.01
☐ 178	Jim Essian DP	.03	.01	.00
☐ 179	Rudy May	.07	.03	.01
☐ 180	Pete Rose	3.50	1.40	.35
☐ 181	Elias Sosa	.07	.03	.01
☐ 182	Bob Grich	.15	.06	.01
☐ 183	Dick Davis DP	.03	.01	.00
☐ 184	Jim Dwyer	.07	.03	.01
☐ 185	Dennis Leonard	.10	.04	.01
☐ 186	Wayne Nordhagen	.07	.03	.01
☐ 187	Mike Parrott	.07	.03	.01
☐ 188	Doug DeCinces	.15	.06	.01
☐ 189	Craig Swan	.10	.04	.01
☐ 190	Cesar Cedeno	.15	.06	.01
☐ 191	Rick Sutcliffe	.60	.24	.06
☐ 192	Braves Rookies Terry Harper Ed Miller Rafael Ramirez	.30	.12	.03
☐ 193	Pete Vuckovich	.10	.04	.01
☐ 194	Rod Scurry	.10	.04	.01
☐ 195	Rich Murray	.07	.03	.01
☐ 196	Duffy Dyer	.07	.03	.01
☐ 197	Jim Kern	.07	.03	.01
☐ 198	Jerry Dybzinski	.07	.03	.01
☐ 199	Chuck Rainey	.07	.03	.01
☐ 200	George Foster	.25	.10	.02
☐ 201	RB: Johnny Bench Most homers, lifetime, catcher	.40	.16	.04
☐ 202	RB: Steve Carlton Most strikeouts, lefthander, lifetime	.35	.14	.03
☐ 203	RB: Bill Gullickson Most strikeouts, game, rookie	.10	.04	.01
☐ 204	RB: Ron LeFlore and Rodney Scott Most stolen bases, teammates, season	.10	.04	.01
☐ 205	RB: Pete Rose Most cons. seasons 600 or more at-bats	.75	.30	.07
☐ 206	RB: Mike Schmidt Most homers, third baseman, season	.45	.18	.04
☐ 207	RB: Ozzie Smith Most assists season, shortstop	.15	.06	.01
☐ 208	RB: Willie Wilson Most at-bats, season	.10	.04	.01
☐ 209	Dickie Thon DP	.10	.04	.01
☐ 210	Jim Palmer	.80	.32	.08
☐ 211	Derrel Thomas	.07	.03	.01
☐ 212	Steve Nicosia	.07	.03	.01
☐ 213	Al Holland	.10	.04	.01
☐ 214	Angels Rookies Ralph Botting Jim Dorsey John Harris	.10	.04	.01
☐ 215	Larry Hisle	.10	.04	.01
☐ 216	John Henry Johnson	.07	.03	.01
☐ 217	Rich Hebner	.07	.03	.01
☐ 218	Paul Splittorff	.07	.03	.01
☐ 219	Ken Landreaux	.07	.03	.01
☐ 220	Tom Seaver	1.25	.50	.12
☐ 221	Bob Davis	.07	.03	.01
☐ 222	Jorge Orta	.07	.03	.01
☐ 223	Roy Lee Jackson	.07	.03	.01
☐ 224	Pat Zachry	.07	.03	.01
☐ 225	Ruppert Jones	.07	.03	.01
☐ 226	Manny Sanguillen DP	.07	.03	.01
☐ 227	Fred Martinez	.07	.03	.01
☐ 228	Tom Paciorek	.07	.03	.01
☐ 229	Rollie Fingers	.50	.20	.05
☐ 230	George Hendrick	.10	.04	.01
☐ 231	Joe Beckwith	.07	.03	.01
☐ 232	Mickey Klutts	.07	.03	.01
☐ 233	Skip Lockwood	.07	.03	.01
☐ 234	Lou Whitaker	.40	.16	.04
☐ 235	Scott Sanderson	.10	.04	.01
☐ 236	Mike Ivie	.07	.03	.01
☐ 237	Charlie Moore	.07	.03	.01
☐ 238	Willie Hernandez	.20	.08	.02
☐ 239	Rick Miller DP	.03	.01	.00
☐ 240	Nolan Ryan	1.50	.60	.15
☐ 241	Checklist 122-242 DP	.07	.01	.00
☐ 242	Chet Lemon	.10	.04	.01
☐ 243	Sal Butera	.07	.03	.01
☐ 244	Cardinals Rookies Tito Landrum Al Olmsted Andy Rincon	.15	.06	.01
☐ 245	Ed Figueroa	.07	.03	.01
☐ 246	Ed Ott DP	.03	.01	.00
☐ 247	Glenn Hubbard DP	.03	.01	.00
☐ 248	Joey McLaughlin	.07	.03	.01
☐ 249	Larry Cox	.07	.03	.01
☐ 250	Ron Guidry	.40	.16	.04
☐ 251	Tom Brookens	.07	.03	.01
☐ 252	Victor Cruz	.07	.03	.01
☐ 253	Dave Bergman	.07	.03	.01
☐ 254	Ozzie Smith	1.25	.50	.12
☐ 255	Mark Littell	.07	.03	.01
☐ 256	Bombo Rivera	.07	.03	.01
☐ 257	Rennie Stennett	.07	.03	.01
☐ 258	Joe Price	.10	.04	.01
☐ 259	Mets Rookies Juan Berenguer Hubie Brooks Mookie Wilson	1.75	.70	.17
☐ 260	Ron Cey	.20	.08	.02
☐ 261	Rickey Henderson	4.00	1.60	.40
☐ 262	Sammy Stewart	.07	.03	.01
☐ 263	Brian Downing	.10	.04	.01
☐ 264	Jim Norris	.07	.03	.01
☐ 265	John Candelaria	.15	.06	.01
☐ 266	Tom Herr	.20	.08	.02
☐ 267	Stan Bahnsen	.07	.03	.01
☐ 268	Jerry Royster	.07	.03	.01
☐ 269	Ken Forsch	.07	.03	.01
☐ 270	Greg Luzinski	.20	.08	.02
☐ 271	Bill Castro	.07	.03	.01
☐ 272	Bruce Kimm	.07	.03	.01
☐ 273	Stan Papi	.07	.03	.01
☐ 274	Craig Chamberlain	.07	.03	.01
☐ 275	Dwight Evans	.40	.16	.04
☐ 276	Dan Spillner	.07	.03	.01
☐ 277	Alfredo Griffin	.15	.06	.01
☐ 278	Rick Sofield	.07	.03	.01

☐ 279 Bob Knepper	.15	.06	.01
☐ 280 Ken Griffey	.15	.06	.01
☐ 281 Fred Stanley	.07	.03	.01
☐ 282 Mariners Rookies Rick Anderson Greg Biercevicz Rodney Craig	.10	.04	.01
☐ 283 Billy Sample	.07	.03	.01
☐ 284 Brian Kingman	.07	.03	.01
☐ 285 Jerry Turner	.07	.03	.01
☐ 286 Dave Frost	.07	.03	.01
☐ 287 Lenn Sakata	.07	.03	.01
☐ 288 Bob Clark	.07	.03	.01
☐ 289 Mickey Hatcher	.15	.06	.01
☐ 290 Bob Boone DP	.10	.04	.01
☐ 291 Aurelio Lopez	.07	.03	.01
☐ 292 Mike Squires	.07	.03	.01
☐ 293 Charlie Lea	.20	.08	.02
☐ 294 Mike Tyson DP	.03	.01	.00
☐ 295 Hal McRae	.10	.04	.01
☐ 296 Bill Nahorodny DP	.03	.01	.00
☐ 297 Bob Bailor	.07	.03	.01
☐ 298 Buddy Solomon	.07	.03	.01
☐ 299 Elliott Maddox	.07	.03	.01
☐ 300 Paul Molitor	.45	.18	.04
☐ 301 Matt Keough	.07	.03	.01
☐ 302 Dodgers Rookies Jack Perconte Mike Scioscia Fernando Valenzuela	6.00	2.40	.60
☐ 303 Johnny Oates	.07	.03	.01
☐ 304 John Castino	.07	.03	.01
☐ 305 Ken Clay	.07	.03	.01
☐ 306 Juan Beniquez DP	.03	.01	.00
☐ 307 Gene Garber	.07	.03	.01
☐ 308 Rick Manning	.07	.03	.01
☐ 309 Luis Salazar	.20	.08	.02
☐ 310 Vida Blue DP	.10	.04	.01
☐ 311 Freddie Patek	.07	.03	.01
☐ 312 Rick Rhoden	.15	.06	.01
☐ 313 Luis Pujols	.07	.03	.01
☐ 314 Rich Dauer	.07	.03	.01
☐ 315 Kirk Gibson	6.50	2.60	.65
☐ 316 Craig Minetto	.07	.03	.01
☐ 317 Lonnie Smith	.10	.04	.01
☐ 318 Steve Yeager	.07	.03	.01
☐ 319 Rowland Office	.07	.03	.01
☐ 320 Tom Burgmeier	.07	.03	.01
☐ 321 Leon Durham	.50	.20	.05
☐ 322 Neil Allen	.10	.04	.01
☐ 323 Jim Morrison DP	.07	.03	.01
☐ 324 Mike Willis	.07	.03	.01
☐ 325 Ray Knight	.20	.08	.02
☐ 326 Biff Pocoroba	.07	.03	.01
☐ 327 Moose Haas	.10	.04	.01
☐ 328 Twins Rookies Dave Engle Greg Johnston Gary Ward	.20	.08	.02
☐ 329 Joaquin Andujar	.15	.06	.01
☐ 330 Frank White	.15	.06	.01
☐ 331 Dennis Lamp	.07	.03	.01
☐ 332 Lee Lacy DP	.07	.03	.01
☐ 333 Sid Monge	.07	.03	.01
☐ 334 Dane Iorg	.07	.03	.01
☐ 335 Rick Cerone	.07	.03	.01
☐ 336 Eddie Whitson	.10	.04	.01
☐ 337 Lynn Jones	.07	.03	.01
☐ 338 Checklist 243-363	.15	.02	.00
☐ 339 John Ellis	.07	.03	.01
☐ 340 Bruce Kison	.07	.03	.01
☐ 341 Dwayne Murphy	.07	.03	.01
☐ 342 Eric Rasmussen DP	.03	.01	.00
☐ 343 Frank Taveras	.07	.03	.01
☐ 344 Byron McLaughlin	.07	.03	.01
☐ 345 Warren Cromartie	.07	.03	.01
☐ 346 Larry Christenson DP	.03	.01	.00
☐ 347 Harold Baines	2.50	1.00	.25
☐ 348 Bob Sykes	.07	.03	.01
☐ 349 Glenn Hoffman	.07	.03	.01
☐ 350 J.R. Richard	.15	.06	.01
☐ 351 Otto Velez	.07	.03	.01
☐ 352 Dick Tidrow DP	.03	.01	.00
☐ 353 Terry Kennedy	.10	.04	.01
☐ 354 Mario Soto	.15	.06	.01
☐ 355 Bob Horner	.35	.14	.03
☐ 356 Padres Rookies George Stablein Craig Stimac Tom Tellmann	.10	.04	.01
☐ 357 Jim Slaton	.07	.03	.01
☐ 358 Mark Wagner	.07	.03	.01
☐ 359 Tom Hausman	.07	.03	.01
☐ 360 Willie Wilson	.20	.08	.02
☐ 361 Joe Strain	.07	.03	.01
☐ 362 Bo Diaz	.10	.04	.01
☐ 363 Geoff Zahn	.07	.03	.01
☐ 364 Mike Davis	.45	.18	.04
☐ 365 Graig Nettles DP	.10	.04	.01
☐ 366 Mike Ramsey	.07	.03	.01
☐ 367 Denny Martinez	.10	.04	.01
☐ 368 Leon Roberts	.07	.03	.01
☐ 369 Frank Tanana	.15	.06	.01
☐ 370 Dave Winfield	1.25	.50	.12
☐ 371 Charlie Hough	.15	.06	.01
☐ 372 Jay Johnstone	.15	.06	.01
☐ 373 Pat Underwood	.07	.03	.01
☐ 374 Tom Hutton	.07	.03	.01
☐ 375 Dave Concepcion	.15	.06	.01
☐ 376 Ron Reed	.07	.03	.01
☐ 377 Jerry Morales	.07	.03	.01
☐ 378 Dave Rader	.07	.03	.01
☐ 379 Lary Sorensen	.07	.03	.01
☐ 380 Willie Stargell	1.00	.40	.10
☐ 381 Cubs Rookies Carlos Lezcano Steve Macko Randy Martz	.10	.04	.01
☐ 382 Paul Mirabella	.07	.03	.01
☐ 383 Eric Soderholm DP	.03	.01	.00
☐ 384 Mike Sadek	.07	.03	.01
☐ 385 Joe Sambito	.07	.03	.01
☐ 386 Dave Edwards	.07	.03	.01
☐ 387 Phil Niekro	.70	.28	.07
☐ 388 Andre Thornton	.10	.04	.01
☐ 389 Marty Pattin	.07	.03	.01
☐ 390 Cesar Geronimo	.07	.03	.01
☐ 391 Dave Lemanczyk DP	.03	.01	.00
☐ 392 Lance Parrish	.65	.26	.06
☐ 393 Broderick Perkins	.07	.03	.01
☐ 394 Woodie Fryman	.07	.03	.01
☐ 395 Scot Thompson	.07	.03	.01
☐ 396 Bill Campbell	.07	.03	.01
☐ 397 Julio Cruz	.07	.03	.01
☐ 398 Ross Baumgarten	.07	.03	.01
☐ 399 Orioles Rookies Mike Boddicker Mark Corey Floyd Rayford	1.50	.60	.15
☐ 400 Reggie Jackson	1.50	.60	.15
☐ 401 AL Champs Royals sweep Yanks (Brett swinging)	.50	.20	.05
☐ 402 NL Champs Phillies squeak past Astros	.20	.08	.02
☐ 403 1980 World Series Phillies beat Royals in six	.20	.08	.02
☐ 404 1980 World Series Phillies win first World Series	.20	.08	.02
☐ 405 Nino Espinosa	.07	.03	.01
☐ 406 Dickie Noles	.07	.03	.01
☐ 407 Ernie Whitt	.15	.06	.01
☐ 408 Fernando Arroyo	.07	.03	.01
☐ 409 Larry Herndon	.07	.03	.01
☐ 410 Bert Campaneris	.10	.04	.01
☐ 411 Terry Puhl	.10	.04	.01
☐ 412 Britt Burns	.25	.10	.02
☐ 413 Tony Bernazard	.10	.04	.01
☐ 414 John Pacella DP	.03	.01	.00
☐ 415 Ben Oglivie	.10	.04	.01
☐ 416 Gary Alexander	.07	.03	.01
☐ 417 Dan Schatzeder	.07	.03	.01
☐ 418 Bobby Brown	.07	.03	.01
☐ 419 Tom Hume	.07	.03	.01
☐ 420 Keith Hernandez	.75	.30	.07
☐ 421 Bob Stanley	.07	.03	.01
☐ 422 Dan Ford	.07	.03	.01
☐ 423 Shane Rawley	.15	.06	.01
☐ 424 Yankees Rookies Tim Lollar Bruce Robinson Dennis Werth	.10	.04	.01
☐ 425 Al Bumbry	.07	.03	.01
☐ 426 Warren Brusstar	.07	.03	.01
☐ 427 John D'Acquisto	.07	.03	.01
☐ 428 John Stearns	.07	.03	.01
☐ 429 Mick Kelleher	.07	.03	.01
☐ 430 Jim Bibby	.07	.03	.01
☐ 431 Dave Roberts	.07	.03	.01
☐ 432 Len Barker	.07	.03	.01
☐ 433 Rance Mulliniks	.07	.03	.01
☐ 434 Roger Erickson	.07	.03	.01
☐ 435 Jim Spencer	.07	.03	.01
☐ 436 Gary Lucas	.07	.03	.01
☐ 437 Mike Heath DP	.03	.01	.00
☐ 438 John Montefusco	.10	.04	.01
☐ 439 Denny Walling	.07	.03	.01

☐ 440	Jerry Reuss	.15	.06	.01
☐ 441	Ken Reitz	.07	.03	.01
☐ 442	Ron Pruitt	.07	.03	.01
☐ 443	Jim Beattie DP	.03	.01	.00
☐ 444	Garth Iorg	.07	.03	.01
☐ 445	Ellis Valentine	.07	.03	.01
☐ 446	Checklist 364-484	.15	.02	.00
☐ 447	Junior Kennedy DP	.03	.01	.00
☐ 448	Tim Corcoran	.07	.03	.01
☐ 449	Paul Mitchell	.07	.03	.01
☐ 450	Dave Kingman DP	.10	.04	.01
☐ 451	Indians Rookies	.10	.04	.01
	Chris Bando			
	Tom Brennan			
	Sandy Wihtol			
☐ 452	Renie Martin	.07	.03	.01
☐ 453	Rob Wilfong DP	.03	.01	.00
☐ 454	Andy Hassler	.07	.03	.01
☐ 455	Rick Burleson	.10	.04	.01
☐ 456	Jeff Reardon	.90	.36	.09
☐ 457	Mike Lum	.07	.03	.01
☐ 458	Randy Jones	.07	.03	.01
☐ 459	Greg Gross	.07	.03	.01
☐ 460	Rich Gossage	.30	.12	.03
☐ 461	Dave McKay	.07	.03	.01
☐ 462	Jack Brohamer	.07	.03	.01
☐ 463	Milt May	.07	.03	.01
☐ 464	Adrian Devine	.07	.03	.01
☐ 465	Bill Russell	.10	.04	.01
☐ 466	Bob Molinaro	.07	.03	.01
☐ 467	Dave Stieb	.45	.18	.04
☐ 468	Johnny Wockenfuss	.07	.03	.01
☐ 469	Jeff Leonard	.25	.10	.02
☐ 470	Manny Trillo	.07	.03	.01
☐ 471	Mike Vail	.07	.03	.01
☐ 472	Dyar Miller DP	.03	.01	.00
☐ 473	Jose Cardenal	.07	.03	.01
☐ 474	Mike LaCoss	.07	.03	.01
☐ 475	Buddy Bell	.20	.08	.02
☐ 476	Jerry Koosman	.15	.06	.01
☐ 477	Luis Gomez	.07	.03	.01
☐ 478	Juan Eichelberger	.07	.03	.01
☐ 479	Expos Rookies	8.50	3.50	.85
	Tim Raines			
	Roberto Ramos			
	Bobby Pate			
☐ 480	Carlton Fisk	.35	.14	.03
☐ 481	Bob Lacey DP	.03	.01	.00
☐ 482	Jim Gantner	.07	.03	.01
☐ 483	Mike Griffin	.07	.03	.01
☐ 484	Max Venable DP	.03	.01	.00
☐ 485	Garry Templeton	.15	.06	.01
☐ 486	Marc Hill	.07	.03	.01
☐ 487	Dewey Robinson	.07	.03	.01
☐ 488	Damaso Garcia	.15	.06	.01
☐ 489	John Littlefield	.07	.03	.01
☐ 490	Eddie Murray	1.50	.60	.15
☐ 491	Gordy Pladson	.07	.03	.01
☐ 492	Barry Foote	.07	.03	.01
☐ 493	Dan Quisenberry	.25	.10	.02
☐ 494	Bob Walk	.30	.12	.03
☐ 495	Dusty Baker	.10	.04	.01
☐ 496	Paul Dade	.07	.03	.01
☐ 497	Fred Norman	.07	.03	.01
☐ 498	Pat Putnam	.07	.03	.01
☐ 499	Frank Pastore	.07	.03	.01
☐ 500	Jim Rice	.70	.28	.07
☐ 501	Tim Foli DP	.03	.01	.00
☐ 502	Giants Rookies	.10	.04	.01
	Chris Bourjos			
	Al Hargesheimer			
	Mike Rowland			
☐ 503	Steve McCatty	.07	.03	.01
☐ 504	Dale Murphy	2.50	1.00	.25
☐ 505	Jason Thompson	.07	.03	.01
☐ 506	Phil Huffman	.07	.03	.01
☐ 507	Jamie Quirk	.07	.03	.01
☐ 508	Rob Dressler	.07	.03	.01
☐ 509	Pete Mackanin	.07	.03	.01
☐ 510	Lee Mazzilli	.07	.03	.01
☐ 511	Wayne Garland	.07	.03	.01
☐ 512	Gary Thomasson	.07	.03	.01
☐ 513	Frank LaCorte	.07	.03	.01
☐ 514	George Riley	.07	.03	.01
☐ 515	Robin Yount	1.00	.40	.10
☐ 516	Doug Bird	.07	.03	.01
☐ 517	Richie Zisk	.10	.04	.01
☐ 518	Grant Jackson	.07	.03	.01
☐ 519	John Tamargo DP	.03	.01	.00
☐ 520	Steve Stone	.10	.04	.01
☐ 521	Sam Mejias	.07	.03	.01
☐ 522	Mike Colbern	.07	.03	.01
☐ 523	John Fulgham	.07	.03	.01
☐ 524	Willie Aikens	.07	.03	.01
☐ 525	Mike Torrez	.07	.03	.01
☐ 526	Phillies Rookies	.15	.06	.01
	Marty Bystrom			
	Jay Loviglio			
	Jim Wright			
☐ 527	Danny Goodwin	.07	.03	.01
☐ 528	Gary Matthews	.10	.04	.01
☐ 529	Dave LaRoche	.07	.03	.01
☐ 530	Steve Garvey	1.25	.50	.12
☐ 531	John Curtis	.07	.03	.01
☐ 532	Bill Stein	.07	.03	.01
☐ 533	Jesus Figueroa	.07	.03	.01
☐ 534	Dave Smith	.45	.18	.04
☐ 535	Omar Moreno	.07	.03	.01
☐ 536	Bob Owchinko DP	.03	.01	.00
☐ 537	Ron Hodges	.07	.03	.01
☐ 538	Tom Griffin	.07	.03	.01
☐ 539	Rodney Scott	.07	.03	.01
☐ 540	Mike Schmidt DP	1.00	.40	.10
☐ 541	Steve Swisher	.07	.03	.01
☐ 542	Larry Bradford DP	.03	.01	.00
☐ 543	Terry Crowley	.07	.03	.01
☐ 544	Rich Gale	.07	.03	.01
☐ 545	Johnny Grubb	.07	.03	.01
☐ 546	Paul Moskau	.07	.03	.01
☐ 547	Mario Guerrero	.07	.03	.01
☐ 548	Dave Goltz	.07	.03	.01
☐ 549	Jerry Remy	.07	.03	.01
☐ 550	Tommy John	.35	.14	.03
☐ 551	Pirates Rookies	2.25	.90	.22
	Vance Law			
	Tony Pena			
	Pascual Perez			
☐ 552	Steve Trout	.10	.04	.01
☐ 553	Tim Blackwell	.07	.03	.01
☐ 554	Bert Blyleven	.30	.12	.03
☐ 555	Cecil Cooper	.25	.10	.02
☐ 556	Jerry Mumphrey	.07	.03	.01
☐ 557	Chris Knapp	.07	.03	.01
☐ 558	Barry Bonnell	.07	.03	.01
☐ 559	Willie Montanez	.07	.03	.01
☐ 560	Joe Morgan	.60	.24	.06
☐ 561	Dennis Littlejohn	.07	.03	.01
☐ 562	Checklist 485-605	.15	.02	.00
☐ 563	Jim Kaat	.25	.10	.02
☐ 564	Ron Hassey DP	.07	.03	.01
☐ 565	Burt Hooton	.07	.03	.01
☐ 566	Del Unser	.07	.03	.01
☐ 567	Mark Bomback	.07	.03	.01
☐ 568	Dave Revering	.07	.03	.01
☐ 569	Al Williams DP	.03	.01	.00
☐ 570	Ken Singleton	.15	.06	.01
☐ 571	Todd Cruz	.07	.03	.01
☐ 572	Jack Morris	.60	.24	.06
☐ 573	Phil Garner	.07	.03	.01
☐ 574	Bill Caudill	.07	.03	.01
☐ 575	Tony Perez	.30	.12	.03
☐ 576	Reggie Cleveland	.07	.03	.01
☐ 577	Blue Jays Rookies	.15	.06	.01
	Luis Leal			
	Brian Milner			
	Ken Schrom			
☐ 578	Bill Gullickson	.30	.12	.03
☐ 579	Tim Flannery	.07	.03	.01
☐ 580	Don Baylor	.25	.10	.02
☐ 581	Roy Howell	.07	.03	.01
☐ 582	Gaylord Perry	.50	.20	.05
☐ 583	Larry Milbourne	.07	.03	.01
☐ 584	Randy Lerch	.07	.03	.01
☐ 585	Amos Otis	.15	.06	.01
☐ 586	Silvio Martinez	.07	.03	.01
☐ 587	Jeff Newman	.07	.03	.01
☐ 588	Gary Lavelle	.07	.03	.01
☐ 589	Lamar Johnson	.07	.03	.01
☐ 590	Bruce Sutter	.20	.08	.02
☐ 591	John Lowenstein	.07	.03	.01
☐ 592	Steve Comer	.07	.03	.01
☐ 593	Steve Kemp	.10	.04	.01
☐ 594	Preston Hanna DP	.03	.01	.00
☐ 595	Butch Hobson	.07	.03	.01
☐ 596	Jerry Augustine	.07	.03	.01
☐ 597	Rafael Landestoy	.07	.03	.01
☐ 598	George Vukovich DP	.03	.01	.00
☐ 599	Dennis Kinney	.07	.03	.01
☐ 600	Johnny Bench	1.25	.50	.12
☐ 601	Don Aase	.07	.03	.01
☐ 602	Bobby Murcer	.15	.06	.01
☐ 603	John Verhoeven	.07	.03	.01
☐ 604	Rob Picciolo	.07	.03	.01
☐ 605	Don Sutton	.50	.20	.05
☐ 606	Reds Rookies DP	.07	.03	.01
	Bruce Berenyi			
	Geoff Combe			
	Paul Householder			
☐ 607	Dave Palmer	.10	.04	.01
☐ 608	Greg Pryor	.07	.03	.01

□ 609 Lynn McGlothen	.07	.03	.01
□ 610 Darrell Porter	.07	.03	.01
□ 611 Rick Matula DP	.03	.01	.00
□ 612 Duane Kuiper	.07	.03	.01
□ 613 Jim Anderson	.07	.03	.01
□ 614 Dave Rozema	.07	.03	.01
□ 615 Rick Dempsey	.07	.03	.01
□ 616 Rick Wise	.07	.03	.01
□ 617 Craig Reynolds	.07	.03	.01
□ 618 John Milner	.07	.03	.01
□ 619 Steve Henderson	.07	.03	.01
□ 620 Dennis Eckersley	.30	.12	.03
□ 621 Tom Donohue	.07	.03	.01
□ 622 Randy Moffitt	.07	.03	.01
□ 623 Sal Bando	.10	.04	.01
□ 624 Bob Welch	.20	.08	.02
□ 625 Bill Buckner	.20	.08	.02
□ 626 Tigers Rookies	.10	.04	.01
Dave Steffen			
Jerry Ujdur			
Roger Weaver			
□ 627 Luis Tiant	.15	.06	.01
□ 628 Vic Correll	.07	.03	.01
□ 629 Tony Armas	.15	.06	.01
□ 630 Steve Carlton	1.00	.40	.10
□ 631 Ron Jackson	.07	.03	.01
□ 632 Alan Bannister	.07	.03	.01
□ 633 Bill Lee	.10	.04	.01
□ 634 Doug Flynn	.07	.03	.01
□ 635 Bobby Bonds	.15	.06	.01
□ 636 Al Hrabosky	.10	.04	.01
□ 637 Jerry Narron	.07	.03	.01
□ 638 Checklist 606-726	.15	.02	.00
□ 639 Carney Lansford	.30	.12	.03
□ 640 Dave Parker	.50	.20	.05
□ 641 Mark Belanger	.10	.04	.01
□ 642 Vern Ruhle	.07	.03	.01
□ 643 Lloyd Moseby	1.25	.50	.12
□ 644 Ramon Aviles DP	.03	.01	.00
□ 645 Rick Reuschel	.20	.08	.02
□ 646 Marvis Foley	.07	.03	.01
□ 647 Dick Drago	.07	.03	.01
□ 648 Darrell Evans	.25	.10	.02
□ 649 Manny Sarmiento	.07	.03	.01
□ 650 Bucky Dent	.15	.06	.01
□ 651 Pedro Guerrero	1.50	.60	.15
□ 652 John Montague	.07	.03	.01
□ 653 Bill Fahey	.07	.03	.01
□ 654 Ray Burris	.07	.03	.01
□ 655 Dan Driessen	.07	.03	.01
□ 656 Jon Matlack	.07	.03	.01
□ 657 Mike Cubbage DP	.03	.01	.00
□ 658 Milt Wilcox	.07	.03	.01
□ 659 Brewers Rookies	.10	.04	.01
John Flinn			
Ed Romero			
Ned Yost			
□ 660 Gary Carter	1.50	.60	.15
□ 661 Orioles Team/Mgr.	.25	.05	.01
Earl Weaver			
(checklist back)			
□ 662 Red Sox Team/Mgr.	.20	.05	.01
Ralph Houk			
(checklist back)			
□ 663 Angels Team/Mgr.	.20	.05	.01
Jim Fregosi			
(checklist back)			
□ 664 White Sox Team/Mgr.	.20	.05	.01
Tony LaRussa			
(checklist back)			
□ 665 Indians Team/Mgr.	.20	.05	.01
Dave Garcia			
(checklist back)			
□ 666 Tigers Team/Mgr.	.25	.05	.01
Sparky Anderson			
(checklist back)			
□ 667 Royals Team/Mgr.	.20	.05	.01
Jim Frey			
(checklist back)			
□ 668 Brewers Team/Mgr.	.20	.05	.01
Bob Rodgers			
(checklist back)			
□ 669 Twins Team/Mgr.	.20	.05	.01
John Goryl			
(checklist back)			
□ 670 Yankees Team/Mgr.	.25	.05	.01
Gene Michael			
(checklist back)			
□ 671 A's Team/Mgr.	.25	.05	.01
Billy Martin			
(checklist back)			
□ 672 Mariners Team/Mgr.	.20	.05	.01
Maury Wills			
(checklist back)			
□ 673 Rangers Team/Mgr.	.20	.05	.01
Don Zimmer			
(checklist back)			
□ 674 Blue Jays Team/Mgr.	.20	.05	.01
Bobby Mattick			
(checklist back)			
□ 675 Braves Team/Mgr.	.20	.05	.01
Bobby Cox			
(checklist back)			
□ 676 Cubs Team/Mgr.	.20	.05	.01
Joe Amalfitano			
(checklist back)			
□ 677 Reds Team/Mgr.	.20	.05	.01
John McNamara			
(checklist back)			
□ 678 Astros Team/Mgr.	.20	.05	.01
Bill Virdon			
(checklist back)			
□ 679 Dodgers Team/Mgr.	.25	.05	.01
Tom Lasorda			
(checklist back)			
□ 680 Expos Team/Mgr.	.20	.05	.01
Dick Williams			
(checklist back)			
□ 681 Mets Team/Mgr.	.25	.05	.01
Joe Torre			
(checklist back)			
□ 682 Phillies Team/Mgr.	.20	.05	.01
Dallas Green			
(checklist back)			
□ 683 Pirates Team/Mgr.	.20	.05	.01
Chuck Tanner			
(checklist back)			
□ 684 Cardinals Team/Mgr.	.20	.05	.01
Whitey Herzog			
(checklist back)			
□ 685 Padres Team/Mgr.	.20	.05	.01
Frank Howard			
(checklist back)			
□ 686 Giants Team/Mgr.	.20	.05	.01
Dave Bristol			
(checklist back)			
□ 687 Jeff Jones	.07	.03	.01
□ 688 Kiko Garcia	.07	.03	.01
□ 689 Red Sox Rookies	2.25	.90	.22
Bruce Hurst			
Keith MacWhorter			
Reid Nichols			
□ 690 Bob Watson	.10	.04	.01
□ 691 Dick Ruthven	.07	.03	.01
□ 692 Lenny Randle	.07	.03	.01
□ 693 Steve Howe	.15	.06	.01
□ 694 Bud Harrelson DP	.03	.01	.00
□ 695 Kent Tekulve	.10	.04	.01
□ 696 Alan Ashby	.10	.04	.01
□ 697 Rick Waits	.07	.03	.01
□ 698 Mike Jorgensen	.07	.03	.01
□ 699 Glenn Abbott	.07	.03	.01
□ 700 George Brett	2.00	.80	.20
□ 701 Joe Rudi	.10	.04	.01
□ 702 George Medich	.07	.03	.01
□ 703 Alvis Woods	.07	.03	.01
□ 704 Bill Travers DP	.03	.01	.00
□ 705 Ted Simmons	.20	.08	.02
□ 706 Dave Ford	.07	.03	.01
□ 707 Dave Cash	.07	.03	.01
□ 708 Doyle Alexander	.15	.06	.01
□ 709 Alan Trammell DP	.30	.12	.03
□ 710 Ron LeFlore DP	.07	.03	.01
□ 711 Joe Ferguson	.07	.03	.01
□ 712 Bill Bonham	.07	.03	.01
□ 713 Bill North	.07	.03	.01
□ 714 Pete Redfern	.07	.03	.01
□ 715 Bill Madlock	.15	.06	.01
□ 716 Glenn Borgmann	.07	.03	.01
□ 717 Jim Barr DP	.03	.01	.00
□ 718 Larry Biittner	.07	.03	.01
□ 719 Sparky Lyle	.15	.06	.01
□ 720 Fred Lynn	.25	.10	.02
□ 721 Toby Harrah	.10	.04	.01
□ 722 Joe Niekro	.15	.06	.01
□ 723 Bruce Bochte	.07	.03	.01
□ 724 Lou Piniella	.15	.06	.01
□ 725 Steve Rogers	.10	.04	.01
□ 726 Rick Monday	.20	.08	.02

1981 Topps Traded

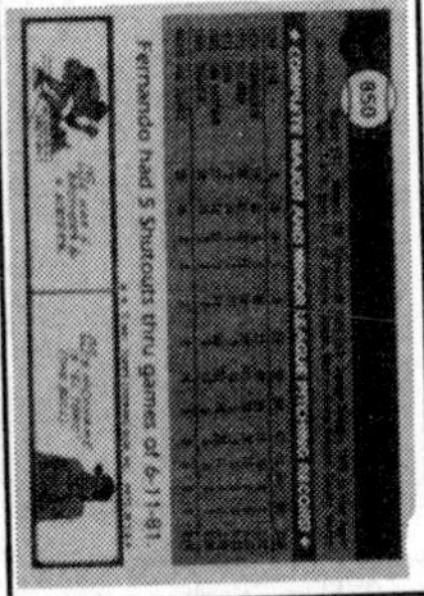

The cards in this 132-card set measure 2 1/2" by 3 1/2". For the first time since 1976, Topps issued a "traded" set in 1981. Unlike the small traded sets of 1974 and 1976, this set contains a larger number of cards and was sequentially numbered, alphabetically, from 727 to 858. Thus, this set gives the impression it is a continuation of their regular issue of this year. The sets were issued only through hobby card dealers and were boxed in complete sets of 132 cards.

	MINT	EXC	G-VG
COMPLETE SET (132)	22.00	9.00	2.20
COMMON PLAYER (727-858)	.08	.03	.01
□ 727 Danny Ainge	.65	.26	.06
□ 728 Doyle Alexander	.20	.08	.02
□ 729 Gary Alexander	.08	.03	.01
□ 730 Billy Almon	.08	.03	.01
□ 731 Joaquin Andujar	.15	.06	.01
□ 732 Bob Bailor	.08	.03	.01
□ 733 Juan Beniquez	.08	.03	.01
□ 734 Dave Bergman	.08	.03	.01
□ 735 Tony Bernazard	.08	.03	.01
□ 736 Larry Biittner	.08	.03	.01
□ 737 Doug Bird	.08	.03	.01
□ 738 Bert Blyleven	.40	.16	.04
□ 739 Mark Bomback	.08	.03	.01
□ 740 Bobby Bonds	.20	.08	.02
□ 741 Rick Bosetti	.08	.03	.01
□ 742 Hubie Brooks	1.25	.50	.12
□ 743 Rick Burleson	.15	.06	.01
□ 744 Ray Burris	.08	.03	.01
□ 745 Jeff Burroughs	.15	.06	.01
□ 746 Enos Cabell	.08	.03	.01
□ 747 Ken Clay	.08	.03	.01
□ 748 Mark Clear	.08	.03	.01
□ 749 Larry Cox	.08	.03	.01
□ 750 Hector Cruz	.08	.03	.01
□ 751 Victor Cruz	.08	.03	.01
□ 752 Mike Cubbage	.08	.03	.01
□ 753 Dick Davis	.08	.03	.01
□ 754 Brian Doyle	.08	.03	.01
□ 755 Dick Drago	.08	.03	.01
□ 756 Leon Durham	.50	.20	.05
□ 757 Jim Dwyer	.08	.03	.01
□ 758 Dave Edwards	.08	.03	.01
□ 759 Jim Essian	.08	.03	.01
□ 760 Bill Fahey	.08	.03	.01
□ 761 Rollie Fingers	.85	.34	.08
□ 762 Carlton Fisk	.70	.28	.07
□ 763 Barry Foote	.08	.03	.01
□ 764 Ken Forsch	.08	.03	.01
□ 765 Kiko Garcia	.08	.03	.01
□ 766 Cesar Geronimo	.08	.03	.01
□ 767 Gary Gray	.08	.03	.01
□ 768 Mickey Hatcher	.20	.08	.02
□ 769 Steve Henderson	.08	.03	.01
□ 770 Marc Hill	.08	.03	.01
□ 771 Butch Hobson	.08	.03	.01
□ 772 Rick Honeycutt	.08	.03	.01
□ 773 Roy Howell	.08	.03	.01
□ 774 Mike Ivie	.08	.03	.01
□ 775 Roy Lee Jackson	.08	.03	.01
□ 776 Cliff Johnson	.08	.03	.01
□ 777 Randy Jones	.15	.06	.01
□ 778 Ruppert Jones	.08	.03	.01
□ 779 Mick Kelleher	.08	.03	.01
□ 780 Terry Kennedy	.15	.06	.01
□ 781 Dave Kingman	.35	.14	.03
□ 782 Bob Knepper	.20	.08	.02
□ 783 Ken Kravec	.08	.03	.01
□ 784 Bob Lacey	.08	.03	.01
□ 785 Dennis Lamp	.08	.03	.01
□ 786 Rafael Landestoy	.08	.03	.01
□ 787 Ken Landreaux	.15	.06	.01
□ 788 Carney Lansford	.35	.14	.03
□ 789 Dave LaRoche	.08	.03	.01
□ 790 Joe Lefebvre	.08	.03	.01
□ 791 Ron LeFlore	.15	.06	.01
□ 792 Randy Lerch	.08	.03	.01
□ 793 Sixto Lezcano	.08	.03	.01
□ 794 John Littlefield	.08	.03	.01
□ 795 Mike Lum	.08	.03	.01
□ 796 Greg Luzinski	.30	.12	.03
□ 797 Fred Lynn	.50	.20	.05
□ 798 Jerry Martin	.08	.03	.01
□ 799 Buck Martinez	.08	.03	.01
□ 800 Gary Matthews	.15	.06	.01
□ 801 Mario Mendoza	.08	.03	.01
□ 802 Larry Milbourne	.08	.03	.01
□ 803 Rick Miller	.08	.03	.01
□ 804 John Montefusco	.15	.06	.01
□ 805 Jerry Morales	.08	.03	.01
□ 806 Jose Morales	.08	.03	.01
□ 807 Joe Morgan	1.25	.50	.12
□ 808 Jerry Mumphrey	.08	.03	.01
□ 809 Gene Nelson	.35	.14	.03
□ 810 Ed Ott	.08	.03	.01
□ 811 Bob Owchinko	.08	.03	.01
□ 812 Gaylord Perry	1.25	.50	.12
□ 813 Mike Phillips	.08	.03	.01
□ 814 Darrell Porter	.15	.06	.01
□ 815 Mike Proly	.08	.03	.01
□ 816 Tim Raines	7.00	2.80	.70
□ 817 Len Randle	.08	.03	.01
□ 818 Doug Rau	.08	.03	.01
□ 819 Jeff Reardon	.60	.24	.06
□ 820 Ken Reitz	.08	.03	.01
□ 821 Steve Renko	.08	.03	.01
□ 822 Rick Reuschel	.25	.10	.02
□ 823 Dave Revering	.08	.03	.01
□ 824 Dave Roberts	.08	.03	.01
□ 825 Leon Roberts	.08	.03	.01
□ 826 Joe Rudi	.15	.06	.01
□ 827 Kevin Saucier	.08	.03	.01
□ 828 Tony Scott	.08	.03	.01
□ 829 Bob Shirley	.08	.03	.01
□ 830 Ted Simmons	.45	.18	.04
□ 831 Lary Sorensen	.08	.03	.01
□ 832 Jim Spencer	.08	.03	.01
□ 833 Harry Spilman	.08	.03	.01
□ 834 Fred Stanley	.08	.03	.01
□ 835 Rusty Staub	.25	.10	.02
□ 836 Bill Stein	.08	.03	.01
□ 837 Joe Strain	.08	.03	.01
□ 838 Bruce Sutter	.40	.16	.04
□ 839 Don Sutton	1.00	.40	.10
□ 840 Steve Swisher	.08	.03	.01
□ 841 Frank Tanana	.20	.08	.02
□ 842 Gene Tenace	.15	.06	.01
□ 843 Jason Thompson	.08	.03	.01
□ 844 Dickie Thon	.20	.08	.02
□ 845 Bill Travers	.08	.03	.01
□ 846 Tom Underwood	.08	.03	.01
□ 847 John Urrea	.08	.03	.01
□ 848 Mike Vail	.08	.03	.01
□ 849 Ellis Valentine	.08	.03	.01
□ 850 Fernando Valenzuela	4.50	1.80	.45
□ 851 Pete Vuckovich	.15	.06	.01
□ 852 Mark Wagner	.08	.03	.01
□ 853 Bob Walk	.25	.10	.02
□ 854 Claudell Washington	.20	.08	.02
□ 855 Dave Winfield	2.00	.80	.20
□ 856 Geoff Zahn	.08	.03	.01
□ 857 Richie Zisk	.15	.06	.01
□ 858 Checklist 727-858	.08	.01	.00

1982 Topps

The cards in this 792-card set measure 2 1/2" by 3 1/2". The 1982 baseball series is the largest set Topps has ever issued at one printing. The 66-card increase from the previous year's total eliminated the "double print" practice which had occurred in

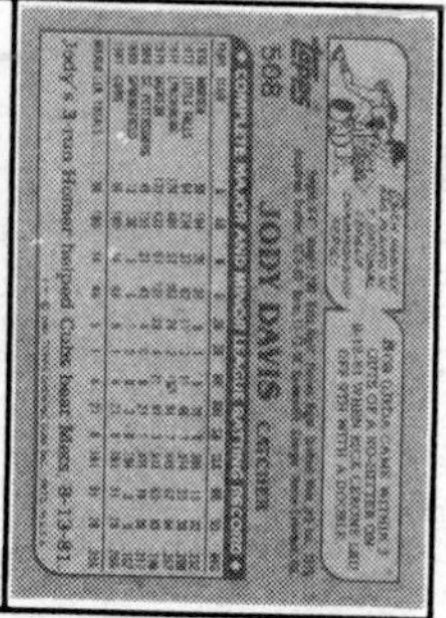

every regular issue since 1978. Cards 1-6 depict Highlights (HL) of the 1981 season, cards 161-168 picture League Leaders, and there are mini-series of AL (547-557) and NL (337-347) All-Stars (AS). The abbreviation "SA" in the checklist is given for the 40 "Super Action" cards introduced in this set. The team cards are actually Team Leader (TL) cards picturing the batting and pitching leader for that team with a checklist back.

		MINT	EXC	G-VG
	COMPLETE SET (792)	85.00	34.00	8.50
	COMMON PLAYER (1-792)	.06	.02	.00
☐ 1	HL: Steve Carlton	.45	.10	.02
	Sets new NL			
	strikeout record			
☐ 2	HL: Ron Davis	.10	.04	.01
	Fans 8 straight			
	in relief			
☐ 3	HL: Tim Raines	.25	.10	.02
	Swipes 71 bases			
	as rookie			
☐ 4	HL: Pete Rose	.75	.30	.07
	Sets NL career			
	hits mark			
☐ 5	HL: Nolan Ryan	.40	.16	.04
	Pitches fifth			
	career no-hitter			
☐ 6	HL: Fern. Valenzuela	.20	.08	.02
	8 shutouts as rookie			
☐ 7	Scott Sanderson	.06	.02	.00
☐ 8	Rich Dauer	.06	.02	.00
☐ 9	Ron Guidry	.30	.12	.03
☐ 10	SA: Ron Guidry	.15	.06	.01
☐ 11	Gary Alexander	.06	.02	.00
☐ 12	Moose Haas	.06	.02	.00
☐ 13	Lamar Johnson	.06	.02	.00
☐ 14	Steve Howe	.06	.02	.00
☐ 15	Ellis Valentine	.06	.02	.00
☐ 16	Steve Comer	.06	.02	.00
☐ 17	Darrell Evans	.15	.06	.01
☐ 18	Fernando Arroyo	.06	.02	.00
☐ 19	Ernie Whitt	.10	.04	.01
☐ 20	Garry Maddox	.10	.04	.01
☐ 21	Orioles Rookies	11.00	4.50	1.10
	Bob Bonner			
	Cal Ripken			
	Jeff Schneider			
☐ 22	Jim Beattie	.06	.02	.00
☐ 23	Willie Hernandez	.20	.08	.02
☐ 24	Dave Frost	.06	.02	.00
☐ 25	Jerry Remy	.06	.02	.00
☐ 26	Jorge Orta	.06	.02	.00
☐ 27	Tom Herr	.15	.06	.01
☐ 28	John Urrea	.06	.02	.00
☐ 29	Dwayne Murphy	.06	.02	.00
☐ 30	Tom Seaver	.65	.26	.06
☐ 31	SA: Tom Seaver	.30	.12	.03
☐ 32	Gene Garber	.06	.02	.00
☐ 33	Jerry Morales	.06	.02	.00
☐ 34	Joe Sambito	.06	.02	.00
☐ 35	Willie Aikens	.06	.02	.00
☐ 36	Rangers TL	.15	.04	.01
	Mgr. Don Zimmer			
	Batting: Al Oliver			
	Pitching: Doc Medich			
☐ 37	Dan Graham	.06	.02	.00
☐ 38	Charlie Lea	.10	.04	.01
☐ 39	Lou Whitaker	.25	.10	.02
☐ 40	Dave Parker	.30	.12	.03
☐ 41	SA: Dave Parker	.15	.06	.01
☐ 42	Rick Sofield	.06	.02	.00
☐ 43	Mike Cubbage	.06	.02	.00
☐ 44	Britt Burns	.06	.02	.00
☐ 45	Rick Cerone	.06	.02	.00
☐ 46	Jerry Augustine	.06	.02	.00
☐ 47	Jeff Leonard	.10	.04	.01
☐ 48	Bobby Castillo	.06	.02	.00
☐ 49	Alvis Woods	.06	.02	.00
☐ 50	Buddy Bell	.15	.06	.01
☐ 51	Cubs Rookies	.35	.14	.03
	Jay Howell			
	Carlos Lezcano			
	Ty Waller			
☐ 52	Larry Andersen	.06	.02	.00
☐ 53	Greg Gross	.06	.02	.00
☐ 54	Ron Hassey	.10	.04	.01
☐ 55	Rick Burleson	.10	.04	.01
☐ 56	Mark Littell	.06	.02	.00
☐ 57	Craig Reynolds	.06	.02	.00
☐ 58	John D'Acquisto	.06	.02	.00
☐ 59	Rich Gedman	.50	.20	.05
☐ 60	Tony Armas	.10	.04	.01
☐ 61	Tommy Boggs	.06	.02	.00
☐ 62	Mike Tyson	.06	.02	.00
☐ 63	Mario Soto	.10	.04	.01
☐ 64	Lynn Jones	.06	.02	.00
☐ 65	Terry Kennedy	.10	.04	.01
☐ 66	Astros TL	.20	.06	.01
	Mgr. Bill Virdon			
	Batting: Art Howe			
	Pitching: Nolan Ryan			
☐ 67	Rich Gale	.06	.02	.00
☐ 68	Roy Howell	.06	.02	.00
☐ 69	Al Williams	.06	.02	.00
☐ 70	Tim Raines	2.00	.80	.20
☐ 71	Roy Lee Jackson	.06	.02	.00
☐ 72	Rick Auerbach	.06	.02	.00
☐ 73	Buddy Solomon	.06	.02	.00
☐ 74	Bob Clark	.06	.02	.00
☐ 75	Tommy John	.25	.10	.02
☐ 76	Greg Pryor	.06	.02	.00
☐ 77	Miguel Dilone	.06	.02	.00
☐ 78	George Medich	.06	.02	.00
☐ 79	Bob Bailor	.06	.02	.00
☐ 80	Jim Palmer	.55	.22	.05
☐ 81	SA: Jim Palmer	.25	.10	.02
☐ 82	Bob Welch	.15	.06	.01
☐ 83	Yankees Rookies	.35	.14	.03
	Steve Balboni			
	Andy McGaffigan			
	Andre Robertson			
☐ 84	Rennie Stennett	.06	.02	.00
☐ 85	Lynn McGlothen	.06	.02	.00
☐ 86	Dane Iorg	.06	.02	.00
☐ 87	Matt Keough	.06	.02	.00
☐ 88	Biff Pocoroba	.06	.02	.00
☐ 89	Steve Henderson	.06	.02	.00
☐ 90	Nolan Ryan	.85	.34	.08
☐ 91	Carney Lansford	.20	.08	.02
☐ 92	Brad Havens	.06	.02	.00
☐ 93	Larry Hisle	.06	.02	.00
☐ 94	Andy Hassler	.06	.02	.00
☐ 95	Ozzie Smith	.45	.18	.04
☐ 96	Royals TL	.20	.06	.01
	Mgr. Jim Frey			
	Batting: George Brett			
	Pitching: Larry Gura			
☐ 97	Paul Moskau	.06	.02	.00
☐ 98	Terry Bulling	.06	.02	.00
☐ 99	Barry Bonnell	.06	.02	.00
☐ 100	Mike Schmidt	1.25	.50	.12
☐ 101	SA: Mike Schmidt	.50	.20	.05
☐ 102	Dan Briggs	.06	.02	.00
☐ 103	Bob Lacey	.06	.02	.00
☐ 104	Rance Mulliniks	.06	.02	.00
☐ 105	Kirk Gibson	1.25	.50	.12
☐ 106	Enrique Romo	.06	.02	.00
☐ 107	Wayne Krenchicki	.06	.02	.00
☐ 108	Bob Sykes	.06	.02	.00
☐ 109	Dave Revering	.06	.02	.00
☐ 110	Carlton Fisk	.30	.12	.03
☐ 111	SA: Carlton Fisk	.15	.06	.01
☐ 112	Billy Sample	.06	.02	.00
☐ 113	Steve McCatty	.06	.02	.00
☐ 114	Ken Landreaux	.06	.02	.00
☐ 115	Gaylord Perry	.35	.14	.03
☐ 116	Jim Wohlford	.06	.02	.00
☐ 117	Rawly Eastwick	.06	.02	.00
☐ 118	Expos Rookies	.35	.14	.03
	Terry Francona			
	Brad Mills			
	Bryn Smith			
☐ 119	Joe Pittman	.06	.02	.00
☐ 120	Gary Lucas	.06	.02	.00
☐ 121	Ed Lynch	.10	.04	.01

□ 122	Jamie Easterly (photo actually Reggie Cleveland)	.06	.02	.00
□ 123	Danny Goodwin	.06	.02	.00
□ 124	Reid Nichols	.06	.02	.00
□ 125	Danny Ainge	.15	.06	.01
□ 126	Braves TL	.15	.04	.01
	Mgr. Bobby Cox			
	Batting: C.Washington			
	Pitching: Rick Mahler			
□ 127	Lonnie Smith	.10	.04	.01
□ 128	Frank Pastore	.06	.02	.00
□ 129	Checklist 1-132	.10	.01	.00
□ 130	Julio Cruz	.06	.02	.00
□ 131	Stan Bahnsen	.06	.02	.00
□ 132	Lee May	.06	.02	.00
□ 133	Pat Underwood	.06	.02	.00
□ 134	Dan Ford	.06	.02	.00
□ 135	Andy Rincon	.06	.02	.00
□ 136	Lenn Sakata	.06	.02	.00
□ 137	George Cappuzzello	.06	.02	.00
□ 138	Tony Pena	.25	.10	.02
□ 139	Jeff Jones	.06	.02	.00
□ 140	Ron LeFlore	.10	.04	.01
□ 141	Indians Rookies	1.25	.50	.12
	Chris Bando			
	Tom Brennan			
	Von Hayes			
□ 142	Dave LaRoche	.06	.02	.00
□ 143	Mookie Wilson	.15	.06	.01
□ 144	Fred Breining	.06	.02	.00
□ 145	Bob Horner	.25	.10	.02
□ 146	Mike Griffin	.06	.02	.00
□ 147	Denny Walling	.06	.02	.00
□ 148	Mickey Klutts	.06	.02	.00
□ 149	Pat Putnam	.06	.02	.00
□ 150	Ted Simmons	.20	.08	.02
□ 151	Dave Edwards	.06	.02	.00
□ 152	Ramon Aviles	.06	.02	.00
□ 153	Roger Erickson	.06	.02	.00
□ 154	Dennis Werth	.06	.02	.00
□ 155	Otto Velez	.06	.02	.00
□ 156	Oakland A's TL	.20	.06	.01
	Mgr. Billy Martin			
	Batting: R.Henderson			
	Pitching: S. McCatty			
□ 157	Steve Crawford	.06	.02	.00
□ 158	Brian Downing	.10	.04	.01
□ 159	Larry Biittner	.06	.02	.00
□ 160	Luis Tiant	.15	.06	.01
□ 161	Batting Leaders	.15	.06	.01
	Bill Madlock			
	Carney Lansford			
□ 162	Home Run Leaders	.20	.08	.02
	Mike Schmidt			
	Tony Armas			
	Dwight Evans			
	Bobby Grich			
	Eddie Murray			
□ 163	RBI Leaders	.30	.12	.03
	Mike Schmidt			
	Eddie Murray			
□ 164	Stolen Base Leaders	.30	.12	.03
	Tim Raines			
	Rickey Henderson			
□ 165	Victory Leaders	.15	.06	.01
	Tom Seaver			
	Denny Martinez			
	Steve McCatty			
	Jack Morris			
	Pete Vuckovich			
□ 166	Strikeout Leaders	.15	.06	.01
	Fernando Valenzuela			
	Len Barker			
□ 167	ERA Leaders	.15	.06	.01
	Nolan Ryan			
	Steve McCatty			
□ 168	Leading Firemen	.15	.06	.01
	Bruce Sutter			
	Rollie Fingers			
□ 169	Charlie Leibrandt	.10	.04	.01
□ 170	Jim Bibby	.06	.02	.00
□ 171	Giants Rookies	1.25	.50	.12
	Bob Brenly			
	Chili Davis			
	Bob Tufts			
□ 172	Bill Gullickson	.10	.04	.01
□ 173	Jamie Quirk	.06	.02	.00
□ 174	Dave Ford	.06	.02	.00
□ 175	Jerry Mumphrey	.06	.02	.00
□ 176	Dewey Robinson	.06	.02	.00
□ 177	John Ellis	.06	.02	.00
□ 178	Dyar Miller	.06	.02	.00
□ 179	Steve Garvey	.85	.34	.08
□ 180	SA: Steve Garvey	.40	.16	.04
□ 181	Silvio Martinez	.06	.02	.00
□ 182	Larry Herndon	.06	.02	.00
□ 183	Mike Proly	.06	.02	.00
□ 184	Mick Kelleher	.06	.02	.00
□ 185	Phil Niekro	.45	.18	.04
□ 186	Cardinals TL	.15	.04	.01
	Mgr. Whitey Herzog			
	Batting K. Hernandez			
	Pitching Bob Forsch			
□ 187	Jeff Newman	.06	.02	.00
□ 188	Randy Martz	.06	.02	.00
□ 189	Glenn Hoffman	.06	.02	.00
□ 190	J.R. Richard	.10	.04	.01
□ 191	Tim Wallach	1.25	.50	.12
□ 192	Broderick Perkins	.06	.02	.00
□ 193	Darrell Jackson	.06	.02	.00
□ 194	Mike Vail	.06	.02	.00
□ 195	Paul Molitor	.35	.14	.03
□ 196	Willie Upshaw	.06	.02	.00
□ 197	Shane Rawley	.10	.04	.01
□ 198	Chris Speier	.06	.02	.00
□ 199	Don Aase	.06	.02	.00
□ 200	George Brett	1.50	.60	.15
□ 201	SA: George Brett	.60	.24	.06
□ 202	Rick Manning	.06	.02	.00
□ 203	Blue Jays Rookies	3.50	1.40	.35
	Jesse Barfield			
	Brian Milner			
	Boomer Wells			
□ 204	Gary Roenicke	.06	.02	.00
□ 205	Neil Allen	.10	.04	.01
□ 206	Tony Bernazard	.06	.02	.00
□ 207	Rod Scurry	.06	.02	.00
□ 208	Bobby Murcer	.15	.06	.01
□ 209	Gary Lavelle	.06	.02	.00
□ 210	Keith Hernandez	.50	.20	.05
□ 211	Dan Petry	.10	.04	.01
□ 212	Mario Mendoza	.06	.02	.00
□ 213	Dave Stewart	1.50	.60	.15
□ 214	Brian Asselstine	.06	.02	.00
□ 215	Mike Krukow	.10	.04	.01
□ 216	White Sox TL	.15	.04	.01
	Mgr. Tony LaRussa			
	Batting: Chet Lemon			
	Pitching: Dennis Lamp			
□ 217	Bo McLaughlin	.06	.02	.00
□ 218	Dave Roberts	.06	.02	.00
□ 219	John Curtis	.06	.02	.00
□ 220	Manny Trillo	.06	.02	.00
□ 221	Jim Slaton	.06	.02	.00
□ 222	Butch Wynegar	.06	.02	.00
□ 223	Lloyd Moseby	.20	.08	.02
□ 224	Bruce Bochte	.06	.02	.00
□ 225	Mike Torrez	.06	.02	.00
□ 226	Checklist 133-264	.10	.01	.00
□ 227	Ray Burris	.06	.02	.00
□ 228	Sam Mejias	.06	.02	.00
□ 229	Geoff Zahn	.06	.02	.00
□ 230	Willie Wilson	.20	.08	.02
□ 231	Phillies Rookies	.40	.16	.04
	Mark Davis			
	Bob Dernier			
	Ozzie Virgil			
□ 232	Terry Crowley	.06	.02	.00
□ 233	Duane Kuiper	.06	.02	.00
□ 234	Ron Hodges	.06	.02	.00
□ 235	Mike Easler	.10	.04	.01
□ 236	John Martin	.06	.02	.00
□ 237	Rusty Kuntz	.06	.02	.00
□ 238	Kevin Saucier	.06	.02	.00
□ 239	Jon Matlack	.06	.02	.00
□ 240	Bucky Dent	.10	.04	.01
□ 241	SA: Bucky Dent	.06	.02	.00
□ 242	Milt May	.06	.02	.00
□ 243	Bob Owchinko	.06	.02	.00
□ 244	Rufino Linares	.06	.02	.00
□ 245	Ken Reitz	.06	.02	.00
□ 246	New York Mets TL	.20	.06	.01
	Mgr. Joe Torre			
	Batting: Hubie Brooks			
	Pitching: Mike Scott			
□ 247	Pedro Guerrero	.75	.30	.07
□ 248	Frank LaCorte	.06	.02	.00
□ 249	Tim Flannery	.06	.02	.00
□ 250	Tug McGraw	.15	.06	.01
□ 251	Fred Lynn	.30	.12	.03
□ 252	SA: Fred Lynn	.15	.06	.01
□ 253	Chuck Baker	.06	.02	.00
□ 254	Jorge Bell	8.00	3.25	.80
□ 255	Tony Perez	.25	.10	.02
□ 256	SA: Tony Perez	.10	.04	.01
□ 257	Larry Harlow	.06	.02	.00
□ 258	Bo Diaz	.10	.04	.01
□ 259	Rodney Scott	.06	.02	.00
□ 260	Bruce Sutter	.20	.08	.02

□ 261 Tigers Rookies .... .10 .04 .01
Howard Bailey
Marty Castillo
Dave Rucker
□ 262 Doug Bair .... .06 .02 .00
□ 263 Victor Cruz .... .06 .02 .00
□ 264 Dan Quisenberry .... .20 .08 .02
□ 265 Al Bumbry .... .06 .02 .00
□ 266 Rick Leach .... .06 .02 .00
□ 267 Kurt Bevacqua .... .06 .02 .00
□ 268 Rickey Keeton .... .06 .02 .00
□ 269 Jim Essian .... .06 .02 .00
□ 270 Rusty Staub .... .15 .06 .01
□ 271 Larry Bradford .... .06 .02 .00
□ 272 Bump Wills .... .06 .02 .00
□ 273 Doug Bird .... .06 .02 .00
□ 274 Bob Ojeda .... .65 .26 .06
□ 275 Bob Watson .... .10 .04 .01
□ 276 Angels TL .... .20 .06 .01
Mgr. Gene Mauch
Batting: Rod Carew
Pitching: Ken Forsch
□ 277 Terry Puhl .... .06 .02 .00
□ 278 John Littlefield .... .06 .02 .00
□ 279 Bill Russell .... .10 .04 .01
□ 280 Ben Oglivie .... .10 .04 .01
□ 281 John Verhoeven .... .06 .02 .00
□ 282 Ken Macha .... .06 .02 .00
□ 283 Brian Allard .... .06 .02 .00
□ 284 Bob Grich .... .10 .04 .01
□ 285 Sparky Lyle .... .15 .06 .01
□ 286 Bill Fahey .... .06 .02 .00
□ 287 Alan Bannister .... .06 .02 .00
□ 288 Garry Templeton .... .10 .04 .01
□ 289 Bob Stanley .... .06 .02 .00
□ 290 Ken Singleton .... .10 .04 .01
□ 291 Pirates Rookies .... 1.25 .50 .12
Vance Law
Bob Long
Johnny Ray
□ 292 David Palmer .... .06 .02 .00
□ 293 Rob Picciolo .... .06 .02 .00
□ 294 Mike LaCoss .... .06 .02 .00
□ 295 Jason Thompson .... .06 .02 .00
□ 296 Bob Walk .... .10 .04 .01
□ 297 Clint Hurdle .... .06 .02 .00
□ 298 Danny Darwin .... .06 .02 .00
□ 299 Steve Trout .... .06 .02 .00
□ 300 Reggie Jackson .... 1.25 .50 .12
□ 301 SA: Reggie Jackson .... .50 .20 .05
□ 302 Doug Flynn .... .06 .02 .00
□ 303 Bill Caudill .... .06 .02 .00
□ 304 Johnnie LeMaster .... .06 .02 .00
□ 305 Don Sutton .... .40 .16 .04
□ 306 SA: Don Sutton .... .20 .08 .02
□ 307 Randy Bass .... .10 .04 .01
□ 308 Charlie Moore .... .06 .02 .00
□ 309 Pete Redfern .... .06 .02 .00
□ 310 Mike Hargrove .... .06 .02 .00
□ 311 Dodgers TL .... .15 .04 .01
Mgr. Tom Lasorda
Batting: Dusty Baker
Pitching: Burt Hooton
□ 312 Lenny Randle .... .06 .02 .00
□ 313 John Harris .... .06 .02 .00
□ 314 Buck Martinez .... .06 .02 .00
□ 315 Burt Hooton .... .06 .02 .00
□ 316 Steve Braun .... .06 .02 .00
□ 317 Dick Ruthven .... .06 .02 .00
□ 318 Mike Heath .... .06 .02 .00
□ 319 Dave Rozema .... .06 .02 .00
□ 320 Chris Chambliss .... .10 .04 .01
□ 321 SA: Chris Chambliss .... .06 .02 .00
□ 322 Garry Hancock .... .06 .02 .00
□ 323 Bill Lee .... .10 .04 .01
□ 324 Steve Dillard .... .06 .02 .00
□ 325 Jose Cruz .... .10 .04 .01
□ 326 Pete Falcone .... .06 .02 .00
□ 327 Joe Nolan .... .06 .02 .00
□ 328 Ed Farmer .... .06 .02 .00
□ 329 U.L. Washington .... .06 .02 .00
□ 330 Rick Wise .... .06 .02 .00
□ 331 Benny Ayala .... .06 .02 .00
□ 332 Don Robinson .... .06 .02 .00
□ 333 Brewers Rookies .... .10 .04 .01
Frank DiPino
Marshall Edwards
Chuck Porter
□ 334 Aurelio Rodriguez .... .06 .02 .00
□ 335 Jim Sundberg .... .10 .04 .01
□ 336 Mariners TL .... .10 .03 .01
Mgr. Rene Lachemann
Batting: Tom Paciorek
Pitching: Glenn Abbott
□ 337 Pete Rose AS .... .75 .30 .07
□ 338 Dave Lopes AS .... .10 .04 .01
□ 339 Mike Schmidt AS .... .40 .16 .04
□ 340 Dave Concepcion AS .... .10 .04 .01
□ 341 Andre Dawson AS .... .20 .08 .02
□ 342A George Foster AS .... .25 .10 .02
(with autograph)
□ 342B George Foster AS .... 1.75 .70 .17
(w/o autograph)
□ 343 Dave Parker AS .... .15 .06 .01
□ 344 Gary Carter AS .... .25 .10 .02
□ 345 Fern. Valenzuela AS .... .15 .06 .01
□ 346 Tom Seaver AS .... .25 .10 .02
□ 347 Bruce Sutter AS .... .10 .04 .01
□ 348 Derrel Thomas .... .06 .02 .00
□ 349 George Frazier .... .06 .02 .00
□ 350 Thad Bosley .... .06 .02 .00
□ 351 Reds Rookies .... .10 .04 .01
Scott Brown
Geoff Coumbe
Paul Householder
□ 352 Dick Davis .... .06 .02 .00
□ 353 Jack O'Connor .... .06 .02 .00
□ 354 Roberto Ramos .... .06 .02 .00
□ 355 Dwight Evans .... .25 .10 .02
□ 356 Denny Lewallyn .... .06 .02 .00
□ 357 Butch Hobson .... .06 .02 .00
□ 358 Mike Parrott .... .06 .02 .00
□ 359 Jim Dwyer .... .06 .02 .00
□ 360 Len Barker .... .06 .02 .00
□ 361 Rafael Landestoy .... .06 .02 .00
□ 362 Jim Wright .... .06 .02 .00
□ 363 Bob Molinaro .... .06 .02 .00
□ 364 Doyle Alexander .... .10 .04 .01
□ 365 Bill Madlock .... .15 .06 .01
□ 366 Padres TL .... .10 .03 .01
Mgr. Frank Howard
Batting: Luis Salazar
Pitching: Eichelberger
□ 367 Jim Kaat .... .15 .06 .01
□ 368 Alex Trevino .... .06 .02 .00
□ 369 Champ Summers .... .06 .02 .00
□ 370 Mike Norris .... .06 .02 .00
□ 371 Jerry Don Gleaton .... .06 .02 .00
□ 372 Luis Gomez .... .06 .02 .00
□ 373 Gene Nelson .... .15 .06 .01
□ 374 Tim Blackwell .... .06 .02 .00
□ 375 Dusty Baker .... .10 .04 .01
□ 376 Chris Welsh .... .06 .02 .00
□ 377 Kiko Garcia .... .06 .02 .00
□ 378 Mike Caldwell .... .06 .02 .00
□ 379 Rob Wilfong .... .06 .02 .00
□ 380 Dave Stieb .... .20 .08 .02
□ 381 Red Sox Rookies .... .50 .20 .05
Bruce Hurst
Dave Schmidt
Julio Valdez
□ 382 Joe Simpson .... .06 .02 .00
□ 383A Pascual Perez ERR 30.00 12.00 3.00
(no position
on front)
□ 383B Pascual Perez COR .... .15 .06 .01
□ 384 Keith Moreland .... .06 .02 .00
□ 385 Ken Forsch .... .06 .02 .00
□ 386 Jerry White .... .06 .02 .00
□ 387 Tom Veryzer .... .06 .02 .00
□ 388 Joe Rudi .... .10 .04 .01
□ 389 George Vukovich .... .06 .02 .00
□ 390 Eddie Murray .... 1.25 .50 .12
□ 391 Dave Tobik .... .06 .02 .00
□ 392 Rick Bosetti .... .06 .02 .00
□ 393 Al Hrabosky .... .10 .04 .01
□ 394 Checklist 265-396 .... .10 .01 .00
□ 395 Omar Moreno .... .06 .02 .00
□ 396 Twins TL .... .10 .03 .01
Mgr. Billy Gardner
Batting: John Castino
Pitching: F. Arroyo
□ 397 Ken Brett .... .06 .02 .00
□ 398 Mike Squires .... .06 .02 .00
□ 399 Pat Zachry .... .06 .02 .00
□ 400 Johnny Bench .... 1.00 .40 .10
□ 401 SA: Johnny Bench .... .40 .16 .04
□ 402 Bill Stein .... .06 .02 .00
□ 403 Jim Tracy .... .06 .02 .00
□ 404 Dickie Thon .... .10 .04 .01
□ 405 Rick Reuschel .... .15 .06 .01
□ 406 Al Holland .... .06 .02 .00
□ 407 Danny Boone .... .06 .02 .00
□ 408 Ed Romero .... .06 .02 .00
□ 409 Don Cooper .... .06 .02 .00
□ 410 Ron Cey .... .15 .06 .01
□ 411 SA: Ron Cey .... .10 .04 .01
□ 412 Luis Leal .... .06 .02 .00
□ 413 Dan Meyer .... .06 .02 .00
□ 414 Elias Sosa .... .06 .02 .00

□ 415 Don Baylor	.15	.06	.01
□ 416 Marty Bystrom	.06	.02	.00
□ 417 Pat Kelly	.06	.02	.00
□ 418 Rangers Rookies John Butcher Bobby Johnson Dave Schmidt	.30	.12	.03
□ 419 Steve Stone	.10	.04	.01
□ 420 George Hendrick	.10	.04	.01
□ 421 Mark Clear	.06	.02	.00
□ 422 Cliff Johnson	.06	.02	.00
□ 423 Stan Papi	.06	.02	.00
□ 424 Bruce Benedict	.06	.02	.00
□ 425 John Candelaria	.10	.04	.01
□ 426 Orioles TL Mgr. Earl Weaver Batting: Eddie Murray Pitching: Sam Stewart	.20	.06	.01
□ 427 Ron Oester	.06	.02	.00
□ 428 LaMarr Hoyt	.10	.04	.01
□ 429 John Wathan	.10	.04	.01
□ 430 Vida Blue	.10	.04	.01
□ 431 SA: Vida Blue	.06	.02	.00
□ 432 Mike Scott	.40	.16	.04
□ 433 Alan Ashby	.06	.02	.00
□ 434 Joe Lefebvre	.06	.02	.00
□ 435 Robin Yount	.75	.30	.07
□ 436 Joe Strain	.06	.02	.00
□ 437 Juan Berenguer	.06	.02	.00
□ 438 Pete Mackanin	.06	.02	.00
□ 439 Dave Righetti	2.25	.90	.22
□ 440 Jeff Burroughs	.10	.04	.01
□ 441 Astros Rookies Danny Heep Billy Smith Bobby Sprowl	.10	.04	.01
□ 442 Bruce Kison	.06	.02	.00
□ 443 Mark Wagner	.06	.02	.00
□ 444 Terry Forster	.10	.04	.01
□ 445 Larry Parrish	.10	.04	.01
□ 446 Wayne Garland	.06	.02	.00
□ 447 Darrell Porter	.06	.02	.00
□ 448 SA: Darrell Porter	.06	.02	.00
□ 449 Luis Aguayo	.06	.02	.00
□ 450 Jack Morris	.45	.18	.04
□ 451 Ed Miller	.06	.02	.00
□ 452 Lee Smith	.80	.32	.08
□ 453 Art Howe	.10	.04	.01
□ 454 Rick Langford	.06	.02	.00
□ 455 Tom Burgmeier	.06	.02	.00
□ 456 Chicago Cubs TL Mgr. Joe Amalfitano Batting: Bill Buckner Pitching: Randy Martz	.10	.03	.01
□ 457 Tim Stoddard	.06	.02	.00
□ 458 Willie Montanez	.06	.02	.00
□ 459 Bruce Berenyi	.06	.02	.00
□ 460 Jack Clark	.40	.16	.04
□ 461 Rich Dotson	.10	.04	.01
□ 462 Dave Chalk	.06	.02	.00
□ 463 Jim Kern	.06	.02	.00
□ 464 Juan Bonilla	.06	.02	.00
□ 465 Lee Mazzilli	.06	.02	.00
□ 466 Randy Lerch	.06	.02	.00
□ 467 Mickey Hatcher	.15	.06	.01
□ 468 Floyd Bannister	.06	.02	.00
□ 469 Ed Ott	.06	.02	.00
□ 470 John Mayberry	.10	.04	.01
□ 471 Royals Rookies Atlee Hammaker Mike Jones Darryl Motley	.20	.08	.02
□ 472 Oscar Gamble	.06	.02	.00
□ 473 Mike Stanton	.06	.02	.00
□ 474 Ken Oberkfell	.06	.02	.00
□ 475 Alan Trammell	.50	.20	.05
□ 476 Brian Kingman	.06	.02	.00
□ 477 Steve Yeager	.06	.02	.00
□ 478 Ray Searage	.06	.02	.00
□ 479 Rowland Office	.06	.02	.00
□ 480 Steve Carlton	.90	.36	.09
□ 481 SA: Steve Carlton	.40	.16	.04
□ 482 Glenn Hubbard	.06	.02	.00
□ 483 Gary Woods	.06	.02	.00
□ 484 Ivan DeJesus	.06	.02	.00
□ 485 Kent Tekulve	.10	.04	.01
□ 486 Yankees TL Mgr. Bob Lemon Batting: J. Mumphrey Pitching: Tommy John	.15	.04	.01
□ 487 Bob McClure	.06	.02	.00
□ 488 Ron Jackson	.06	.02	.00
□ 489 Rick Dempsey	.06	.02	.00
□ 490 Dennis Eckersley	.20	.08	.02
□ 491 Checklist 397-528	.10	.01	.00
□ 492 Joe Price	.06	.02	.00
□ 493 Chet Lemon	.10	.04	.01
□ 494 Hubie Brooks	.20	.08	.02
□ 495 Dennis Leonard	.10	.04	.01
□ 496 Johnny Grubb	.06	.02	.00
□ 497 Jim Anderson	.06	.02	.00
□ 498 Dave Bergman	.06	.02	.00
□ 499 Paul Mirabella	.06	.02	.00
□ 500 Rod Carew	.85	.34	.08
□ 501 SA: Rod Carew	.40	.16	.04
□ 502 Braves Rookies Steve Bedrosian Brett Butler Larry Owen	1.50	.60	.15
□ 503 Julio Gonzalez	.06	.02	.00
□ 504 Rick Peters	.06	.02	.00
□ 505 Graig Nettles	.20	.08	.02
□ 506 SA: Graig Nettles	.10	.04	.01
□ 507 Terry Harper	.06	.02	.00
□ 508 Jody Davis	.60	.24	.06
□ 509 Harry Spilman	.06	.02	.00
□ 510 Fernando Valenzuela	1.00	.40	.10
□ 511 Ruppert Jones	.06	.02	.00
□ 512 Jerry Dybzinski	.06	.02	.00
□ 513 Rick Rhoden	.10	.04	.01
□ 514 Joe Ferguson	.06	.02	.00
□ 515 Larry Bowa	.15	.06	.01
□ 516 SA: Larry Bowa	.06	.02	.00
□ 517 Mark Brouhard	.06	.02	.00
□ 518 Garth Iorg	.06	.02	.00
□ 519 Glenn Adams	.06	.02	.00
□ 520 Mike Flanagan	.10	.04	.01
□ 521 Billy Almon	.06	.02	.00
□ 522 Chuck Rainey	.06	.02	.00
□ 523 Gary Gray	.06	.02	.00
□ 524 Tom Hausman	.06	.02	.00
□ 525 Ray Knight	.10	.04	.01
□ 526 Expos TL Mgr. Jim Fanning Batting: W.Cromartie Pitching: B.Gullickson	.10	.03	.01
□ 527 John Henry Johnson	.06	.02	.00
□ 528 Matt Alexander	.06	.02	.00
□ 529 Allen Ripley	.06	.02	.00
□ 530 Dickie Noles	.06	.02	.00
□ 531 A's Rookies Rich Bordi Mark Budaska Kelvin Moore	.10	.04	.01
□ 532 Toby Harrah	.10	.04	.01
□ 533 Joaquin Andujar	.10	.04	.01
□ 534 Dave McKay	.06	.02	.00
□ 535 Lance Parrish	.30	.12	.03
□ 536 Rafael Ramirez	.06	.02	.00
□ 537 Doug Capilla	.06	.02	.00
□ 538 Lou Piniella	.10	.04	.01
□ 539 Vern Ruhle	.06	.02	.00
□ 540 Andre Dawson	.45	.18	.04
□ 541 Barry Evans	.06	.02	.00
□ 542 Ned Yost	.06	.02	.00
□ 543 Bill Robinson	.10	.04	.01
□ 544 Larry Christenson	.06	.02	.00
□ 545 Reggie Smith	.10	.04	.01
□ 546 SA: Reggie Smith	.06	.02	.00
□ 547 Rod Carew AS	.25	.10	.02
□ 548 Willie Randolph AS	.10	.04	.01
□ 549 George Brett AS	.40	.16	.04
□ 550 Bucky Dent AS	.10	.04	.01
□ 551 Reggie Jackson AS	.40	.16	.04
□ 552 Ken Singleton AS	.10	.04	.01
□ 553 Dave Winfield AS	.30	.12	.03
□ 554 Carlton Fisk AS	.15	.06	.01
□ 555 Scott McGregor AS	.10	.04	.01
□ 556 Jack Morris AS	.15	.06	.01
□ 557 Rich Gossage AS	.10	.04	.01
□ 558 John Tudor	.35	.14	.03
□ 559 Indians TL Mgr. Dave Garcia Batting: Mike Hargrove Pitching: Bert Blyleven	.10	.03	.01
□ 560 Doug Corbett	.06	.02	.00
□ 561 Cardinals Rookies Glenn Brummer Luis DeLeon Gene Roof	.10	.04	.01
□ 562 Mike O'Berry	.06	.02	.00
□ 563 Ross Baumgarten	.06	.02	.00
□ 564 Doug DeCinces	.10	.04	.01
□ 565 Jackson Todd	.06	.02	.00
□ 566 Mike Jorgensen	.06	.02	.00
□ 567 Bob Babcock	.06	.02	.00
□ 568 Joe Pettini	.06	.02	.00
□ 569 Willie Randolph	.10	.04	.01
□ 570 SA: Willie Randolph	.06	.02	.00
□ 571 Glenn Abbott	.06	.02	.00

□ 572 Juan Beniquez .06 .02 .00
□ 573 Rick Waits .06 .02 .00
□ 574 Mike Ramsey .06 .02 .00
□ 575 Al Cowens .06 .02 .00
□ 576 Giants TL .10 .03 .01
Mgr. Frank Robinson
Batting: Milt May
Pitching: Vida Blue
□ 577 Rick Monday .10 .04 .01
□ 578 Shooty Babitt .06 .02 .00
□ 579 Rick Mahler .30 .12 .03
□ 580 Bobby Bonds .15 .06 .01
□ 581 Ron Reed .06 .02 .00
□ 582 Luis Pujols .06 .02 .00
□ 583 Tippy Martinez .06 .02 .00
□ 584 Hosken Powell .06 .02 .00
□ 585 Rollie Fingers .25 .10 .02
□ 586 SA: Rollie Fingers .15 .06 .01
□ 587 Tim Lollar .06 .02 .00
□ 588 Dale Berra .06 .02 .00
□ 589 Dave Stapleton .06 .02 .00
□ 590 Al Oliver .15 .06 .01
□ 591 SA: Al Oliver .06 .02 .00
□ 592 Craig Swan .06 .02 .00
□ 593 Billy Smith .06 .02 .00
□ 594 Renie Martin .06 .02 .00
□ 595 Dave Collins .06 .02 .00
□ 596 Damaso Garcia .10 .04 .01
□ 597 Wayne Nordhagen .06 .02 .00
□ 598 Bob Galasso .06 .02 .00
□ 599 White Sox Rookies .10 .04 .01
Jay Loviglio
Reggie Patterson
Leo Sutherland
□ 600 Dave Winfield .65 .26 .06
□ 601 Sid Monge .06 .02 .00
□ 602 Freddie Patek .06 .02 .00
□ 603 Rich Hebner .06 .02 .00
□ 604 Orlando Sanchez .06 .02 .00
□ 605 Steve Rogers .06 .02 .00
□ 606 Blue Jays TL .10 .03 .01
Mgr. Bobby Mattick
Batting: J.Mayberry
Pitching: Dave Stieb
□ 607 Leon Durham .10 .04 .01
□ 608 Jerry Royster .06 .02 .00
□ 609 Rick Sutcliffe .25 .10 .02
□ 610 Rickey Henderson 1.75 .70 .17
□ 611 Joe Niekro .15 .06 .01
□ 612 Gary Ward .10 .04 .01
□ 613 Jim Gantner .06 .02 .00
□ 614 Juan Eichelberger .06 .02 .00
□ 615 Bob Boone .15 .06 .01
□ 616 SA: Bob Boone .06 .02 .00
□ 617 Scott McGregor .10 .04 .01
□ 618 Tim Foli .06 .02 .00
□ 619 Bill Campbell .06 .02 .00
□ 620 Ken Griffey .10 .04 .01
□ 621 SA: Ken Griffey .06 .02 .00
□ 622 Dennis Lamp .06 .02 .00
□ 623 Mets Rookies 1.25 .50 .12
Ron Gardenhire
Terry Leach
Tim Leary
□ 624 Fergie Jenkins .20 .08 .02
□ 625 Hal McRae .10 .04 .01
□ 626 Randy Jones .06 .02 .00
□ 627 Enos Cabell .06 .02 .00
□ 628 Bill Travers .06 .02 .00
□ 629 Johnny Wockenfuss .06 .02 .00
□ 630 Joe Charboneau .10 .04 .01
□ 631 Gene Tenace .06 .02 .00
□ 632 Bryan Clark .06 .02 .00
□ 633 Mitchell Page .06 .02 .00
□ 634 Checklist 529-660 .10 .01 .00
□ 635 Ron Davis .06 .02 .00
□ 636 Phillies TL .35 .09 .02
Mgr. Dallas Green
Batting: Pete Rose
Pitching: S.Carlton
□ 637 Rick Camp .06 .02 .00
□ 638 John Milner .06 .02 .00
□ 639 Ken Kravec .06 .02 .00
□ 640 Cesar Cedeno .10 .04 .01
□ 641 Steve Mura .06 .02 .00
□ 642 Mike Scioscia .10 .04 .01
□ 643 Pete Vuckovich .10 .04 .01
□ 644 John Castino .06 .02 .00
□ 645 Frank White .10 .04 .01
□ 646 SA: Frank White .06 .02 .00
□ 647 Warren Brusstar .06 .02 .00
□ 648 Jose Morales .06 .02 .00
□ 649 Ken Clay .06 .02 .00
□ 650 Carl Yastrzemski 1.50 .60 .15
□ 651 SA: Carl Yastrzemski .60 .24 .06
□ 652 Steve Nicosia .06 .02 .00
□ 653 Angels Rookies 2.50 1.00 .25
Tom Brunansky
Luis Sanchez
Daryl Sconiers
□ 654 Jim Morrison .06 .02 .00
□ 655 Joel Youngblood .06 .02 .00
□ 656 Eddie Whitson .10 .04 .01
□ 657 Tom Poquette .06 .02 .00
□ 658 Tito Landrum .06 .02 .00
□ 659 Fred Martinez .06 .02 .00
□ 660 Dave Concepcion .15 .06 .01
□ 661 SA: Dave Concepcion .06 .02 .00
□ 662 Luis Salazar .10 .04 .01
□ 663 Hector Cruz .06 .02 .00
□ 664 Dan Spillner .06 .02 .00
□ 665 Jim Clancy .10 .04 .01
□ 666 Tigers TL .10 .03 .01
Mgr. Sparky Anderson
Batting: Steve Kemp
Pitching: Dan Petry
□ 667 Jeff Reardon .25 .10 .02
□ 668 Dale Murphy 2.00 .80 .20
□ 669 Larry Milbourne .06 .02 .00
□ 670 Steve Kemp .10 .04 .01
□ 671 Mike Davis .10 .04 .01
□ 672 Bob Knepper .10 .04 .01
□ 673 Keith Drumright .06 .02 .00
□ 674 Dave Goltz .06 .02 .00
□ 675 Cecil Cooper .20 .08 .02
□ 676 Sal Butera .06 .02 .00
□ 677 Alfredo Griffin .10 .04 .01
□ 678 Tom Paciorek .06 .02 .00
□ 679 Sammy Stewart .06 .02 .00
□ 680 Gary Matthews .10 .04 .01
□ 681 Dodgers Rookies 4.00 1.60 .40
Mike Marshall
Ron Roenicke
Steve Sax
□ 682 Jesse Jefferson .06 .02 .00
□ 683 Phil Garner .06 .02 .00
□ 684 Harold Baines .50 .20 .05
□ 685 Bert Blyleven .20 .08 .02
□ 686 Gary Allenson .06 .02 .00
□ 687 Greg Minton .06 .02 .00
□ 688 Leon Roberts .06 .02 .00
□ 689 Lary Sorensen .06 .02 .00
□ 690 Dave Kingman .20 .08 .02
□ 691 Dan Schatzeder .06 .02 .00
□ 692 Wayne Gross .06 .02 .00
□ 693 Cesar Geronimo .06 .02 .00
□ 694 Dave Wehrmeister .06 .02 .00
□ 695 Warren Cromartie .06 .02 .00
□ 696 Pirates TL .10 .03 .01
Mgr. Chuck Tanner
Batting: Bill Madlock
Pitching:Eddie Solomon
□ 697 John Montefusco .10 .04 .01
□ 698 Tony Scott .06 .02 .00
□ 699 Dick Tidrow .06 .02 .00
□ 700 George Foster .25 .10 .02
□ 701 SA: George Foster .10 .04 .01
□ 702 Steve Renko .06 .02 .00
□ 703 Brewers TL .10 .03 .01
Mgr. Bob Rodgers
Batting: Cecil Cooper
Pitching: P.Vuckovich
□ 704 Mickey Rivers .10 .04 .01
□ 705 SA: Mickey Rivers .06 .02 .00
□ 706 Barry Foote .06 .02 .00
□ 707 Mark Bomback .06 .02 .00
□ 708 Gene Richards .06 .02 .00
□ 709 Don Money .06 .02 .00
□ 710 Jerry Reuss .10 .04 .01
□ 711 Mariners Rookies 1.00 .40 .10
Dave Edler
Dave Henderson
Reggie Walton
□ 712 Denny Martinez .10 .04 .01
□ 713 Del Unser .06 .02 .00
□ 714 Jerry Koosman .15 .06 .01
□ 715 Willie Stargell .60 .24 .06
□ 716 SA: Willie Stargell .25 .10 .02
□ 717 Rick Miller .06 .02 .00
□ 718 Charlie Hough .10 .04 .01
□ 719 Jerry Narron .06 .02 .00
□ 720 Greg Luzinski .15 .06 .01
□ 721 SA: Greg Luzinski .10 .04 .01
□ 722 Jerry Martin .06 .02 .00
□ 723 Junior Kennedy .06 .02 .00
□ 724 Dave Rosello .06 .02 .00
□ 725 Amos Otis .10 .04 .01
□ 726 SA: Amos Otis .06 .02 .00
□ 727 Sixto Lezcano .06 .02 .00
□ 728 Aurelio Lopez .06 .02 .00

□ 729	Jim Spencer	.06	.02	.00
□ 730	Gary Carter	.80	.32	.08
□ 731	Padres Rookies	.10	.04	.01
	Mike Armstrong			
	Doug Gwosdz			
	Fred Kuhaulua			
□ 732	Mike Lum	.06	.02	.00
□ 733	Larry McWilliams	.06	.02	.00
□ 734	Mike Ivie	.06	.02	.00
□ 735	Rudy May	.06	.02	.00
□ 736	Jerry Turner	.06	.02	.00
□ 737	Reggie Cleveland	.06	.02	.00
□ 738	Dave Engle	.06	.02	.00
□ 739	Joey McLaughlin	.06	.02	.00
□ 740	Dave Lopes	.10	.04	.01
□ 741	SA: Dave Lopes	.06	.02	.00
□ 742	Dick Drago	.06	.02	.00
□ 743	John Stearns	.06	.02	.00
□ 744	Mike Witt	1.00	.40	.10
□ 745	Bake McBride	.06	.02	.00
□ 746	Andre Thornton	.10	.04	.01
□ 747	John Lowenstein	.06	.02	.00
□ 748	Marc Hill	.06	.02	.00
□ 749	Bob Shirley	.06	.02	.00
□ 750	Jim Rice	.60	.24	.06
□ 751	Rick Honeycutt	.06	.02	.00
□ 752	Lee Lacy	.06	.02	.00
□ 753	Tom Brookens	.06	.02	.00
□ 754	Joe Morgan	.40	.16	.04
□ 755	SA: Joe Morgan	.15	.06	.01
□ 756	Reds TL	.20	.06	.01
	Mgr. John McNamara			
	Batting: Ken Griffey			
	Pitching: Tom Seaver			
□ 757	Tom Underwood	.06	.02	.00
□ 758	Claudell Washington	.10	.04	.01
□ 759	Paul Splittorff	.06	.02	.00
□ 760	Bill Buckner	.15	.06	.01
□ 761	Dave Smith	.10	.04	.01
□ 762	Mike Phillips	.06	.02	.00
□ 763	Tom Hume	.06	.02	.00
□ 764	Steve Swisher	.06	.02	.00
□ 765	Gorman Thomas	.15	.06	.01
□ 766	Twins Rookies	4.50	1.80	.45
	Lenny Faedo			
	Kent Hrbek			
	Tim Laudner			
□ 767	Roy Smalley	.06	.02	.00
□ 768	Jerry Garvin	.06	.02	.00
□ 769	Richie Zisk	.10	.04	.01
□ 770	Rich Gossage	.25	.10	.02
□ 771	SA: Rich Gossage	.10	.04	.01
□ 772	Bert Campaneris	.10	.04	.01
□ 773	John Denny	.10	.04	.01
□ 774	Jay Johnstone	.10	.04	.01
□ 775	Bob Forsch	.06	.02	.00
□ 776	Mark Belanger	.10	.04	.01
□ 777	Tom Griffin	.06	.02	.00
□ 778	Kevin Hickey	.06	.02	.00
□ 779	Grant Jackson	.06	.02	.00
□ 780	Pete Rose	2.25	.90	.22
□ 781	SA: Pete Rose	.75	.30	.07
□ 782	Frank Taveras	.06	.02	.00
□ 783	Greg Harris	.25	.10	.02
□ 784	Milt Wilcox	.06	.02	.00
□ 785	Dan Driessen	.06	.02	.00
□ 786	Red Sox TL	.10	.03	.01
	Mgr. Ralph Houk			
	Batting: C.Lansford			
	Pitching: Mike Torrez			
□ 787	Fred Stanley	.06	.02	.00
□ 788	Woodie Fryman	.06	.02	.00
□ 789	Checklist 661-792	.10	.01	.00
□ 790	Larry Gura	.06	.02	.00
□ 791	Bobby Brown	.06	.02	.00
□ 792	Frank Tanana	.15	.06	.01

1982 Topps Traded

The cards in this 132-card set measure 2 1/2" by 3 1/2". The 1982 Topps Traded or extended series is distinguished by a "T" printed after the number (located on the reverse). Of the total cards, 70 players represent the American League and 61 represent the National League, with the remaining card a numbered checklist (132T). The Cubs lead the pack with 12 changes, while the Red Sox are the only

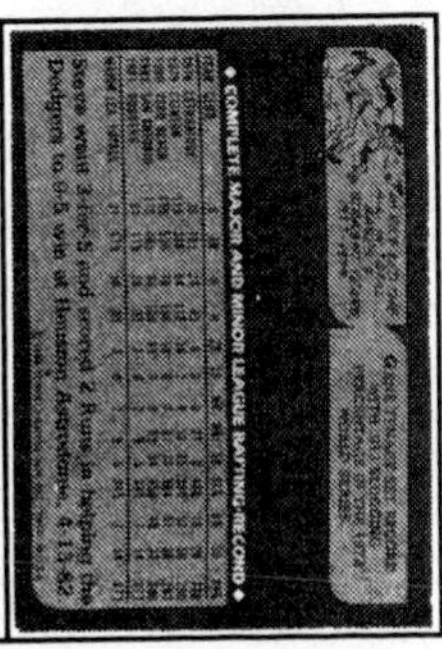

team in either league to have no new additions. All 131 player photos used in the set are completely new. Of this total, 112 individuals are seen in the uniform of their new team, 11 others have been elevated to single card status from "Future Stars" cards, and eight more are entirely new to the 1982 Topps lineup. The backs are almost completely red in color with black print.

		MINT	EXC	G-VG
COMPLETE SET (132)		22.00	9.00	2.20
COMMON PLAYER (1-132)		.08	.03	.01
□ 1T	Doyle Alexander	.20	.08	.02
□ 2T	Jesse Barfield	2.00	.80	.20
□ 3T	Ross Baumgarten	.08	.03	.01
□ 4T	Steve Bedrosian	.85	.34	.08
□ 5T	Mark Belanger	.15	.06	.01
□ 6T	Kurt Bevacqua	.08	.03	.01
□ 7T	Tim Blackwell	.08	.03	.01
□ 8T	Vida Blue	.15	.06	.01
□ 9T	Bob Boone	.20	.08	.02
□ 10T	Larry Bowa	.20	.08	.02
□ 11T	Dan Briggs	.08	.03	.01
□ 12T	Bobby Brown	.08	.03	.01
□ 13T	Tom Brunansky	1.50	.60	.15
□ 14T	Jeff Burroughs	.15	.06	.01
□ 15T	Enos Cabell	.08	.03	.01
□ 16T	Bill Campbell	.08	.03	.01
□ 17T	Bobby Castillo	.08	.03	.01
□ 18T	Bill Caudill	.08	.03	.01
□ 19T	Cesar Cedeno	.20	.08	.02
□ 20T	Dave Collins	.08	.03	.01
□ 21T	Doug Corbett	.08	.03	.01
□ 22T	Al Cowens	.08	.03	.01
□ 23T	Chili Davis	1.50	.60	.15
□ 24T	Dick Davis	.08	.03	.01
□ 25T	Ron Davis	.08	.03	.01
□ 26T	Doug DeCinces	.20	.08	.02
□ 27T	Ivan DeJesus	.08	.03	.01
□ 28T	Bob Dernier	.20	.08	.02
□ 29T	Bo Diaz	.15	.06	.01
□ 30T	Roger Erickson	.08	.03	.01
□ 31T	Jim Essian	.08	.03	.01
□ 32T	Ed Farmer	.08	.03	.01
□ 33T	Doug Flynn	.08	.03	.01
□ 34T	Tim Foli	.08	.03	.01
□ 35T	Dan Ford	.08	.03	.01
□ 36T	George Foster	.40	.16	.04
□ 37T	Dave Frost	.08	.03	.01
□ 38T	Rich Gale	.08	.03	.01
□ 39T	Ron Gardenhire	.15	.06	.01
□ 40T	Ken Griffey	.20	.08	.02
□ 41T	Greg Harris	.15	.06	.01
□ 42T	Von Hayes	1.50	.60	.15
□ 43T	Larry Herndon	.08	.03	.01
□ 44T	Kent Hrbek	4.50	1.80	.45
□ 45T	Mike Ivie	.08	.03	.01
□ 46T	Grant Jackson	.08	.03	.01
□ 47T	Reggie Jackson	2.50	1.00	.25
□ 48T	Ron Jackson	.08	.03	.01
□ 49T	Fergie Jenkins	.40	.16	.04
□ 50T	Lamar Johnson	.08	.03	.01
□ 51T	Randy Johnson	.08	.03	.01
□ 52T	Jay Johnstone	.20	.08	.02
□ 53T	Mick Kelleher	.08	.03	.01
□ 54T	Steve Kemp	.15	.06	.01
□ 55T	Junior Kennedy	.08	.03	.01
□ 56T	Jim Kern	.08	.03	.01
□ 57T	Ray Knight	.25	.10	.02
□ 58T	Wayne Krenchicki	.08	.03	.01
□ 59T	Mike Krukow	.15	.06	.01

□ 60T Duane Kuiper	.08	.03	.01
□ 61T Mike LaCoss	.08	.03	.01
□ 62T Chet Lemon	.15	.06	.01
□ 63T Sixto Lezcano	.08	.03	.01
□ 64T Dave Lopes	.20	.08	.02
□ 65T Jerry Martin	.08	.03	.01
□ 66T Renie Martin	.08	.03	.01
□ 67T John Mayberry	.15	.06	.01
□ 68T Lee Mazzilli	.08	.03	.01
□ 69T Bake McBride	.08	.03	.01
□ 70T Dan Meyer	.08	.03	.01
□ 71T Larry Milbourne	.08	.03	.01
□ 72T Eddie Milner	.15	.06	.01
□ 73T Sid Monge	.08	.03	.01
□ 74T John Montefusco	.15	.06	.01
□ 75T Jose Morales	.08	.03	.01
□ 76T Keith Moreland	.15	.06	.01
□ 77T Jim Morrison	.08	.03	.01
□ 78T Rance Mulliniks	.08	.03	.01
□ 79T Steve Mura	.08	.03	.01
□ 80T Gene Nelson	.15	.06	.01
□ 81T Joe Nolan	.08	.03	.01
□ 82T Dickie Noles	.08	.03	.01
□ 83T Al Oliver	.20	.08	.02
□ 84T Jorge Orta	.08	.03	.01
□ 85T Tom Paciorek	.08	.03	.01
□ 86T Larry Parrish	.15	.06	.01
□ 87T Jack Perconte	.08	.03	.01
□ 88T Gaylord Perry	1.00	.40	.10
□ 89T Rob Picciolo	.08	.03	.01
□ 90T Joe Pittman	.08	.03	.01
□ 91T Hosken Powell	.08	.03	.01
□ 92T Mike Proly	.08	.03	.01
□ 93T Greg Pryor	.08	.03	.01
□ 94T Charlie Puleo	.15	.06	.01
□ 95T Shane Rawley	.15	.06	.01
□ 96T Johnny Ray	.90	.36	.09
□ 97T Dave Revering	.08	.03	.01
□ 98T Cal Ripken	8.50	3.50	.85
□ 99T Allen Ripley	.08	.03	.01
□ 100T Bill Robinson	.15	.06	.01
□ 101T Aurelio Rodriguez	.08	.03	.01
□ 102T Joe Rudi	.15	.06	.01
□ 103T Steve Sax	2.50	1.00	.25
□ 104T Dan Schatzeder	.08	.03	.01
□ 105T Bob Shirley	.08	.03	.01
□ 106T Eric Show	.75	.30	.07
□ 107T Roy Smalley	.15	.06	.01
□ 108T Lonnie Smith	.15	.06	.01
□ 109T Ozzie Smith	2.50	1.00	.25
□ 110T Reggie Smith	.20	.08	.02
□ 111T Lary Sorensen	.08	.03	.01
□ 112T Elias Sosa	.08	.03	.01
□ 113T Mike Stanton	.08	.03	.01
□ 114T Steve Stroughter	.08	.03	.01
□ 115T Champ Summers	.08	.03	.01
□ 116T Rick Sutcliffe	.35	.14	.03
□ 117T Frank Tanana	.15	.06	.01
□ 118T Frank Taveras	.08	.03	.01
□ 119T Garry Templeton	.15	.06	.01
□ 120T Alex Trevino	.08	.03	.01
□ 121T Jerry Turner	.08	.03	.01
□ 122T Ed VandeBerg	.15	.06	.01
□ 123T Tom Veryzer	.08	.03	.01
□ 124T Ron Washington	.08	.03	.01
□ 125T Bob Watson	.15	.06	.01
□ 126T Dennis Werth	.08	.03	.01
□ 127T Eddie Whitson	.15	.06	.01
□ 128T Rob Wilfong	.08	.03	.01
□ 129T Bump Wills	.08	.03	.01
□ 130T Gary Woods	.08	.03	.01
□ 131T Butch Wynegar	.15	.06	.01
□ 132T Checklist: 1-132	.08	.01	.00

1983 Topps

The cards in this 792-card set measure 2 1/2" by 3 1/2". Each regular card of the Topps set for 1983 features a large action shot of a player with a small cameo portrait at bottom right. There are special series for AL and NL All Stars (386-407), League Leaders (701-708) and Record Breakers (1-6). In addition, there are 34 "Super Veteran" (SV) cards and six numbered checklist cards. The Super Veteran cards are oriented horizontally and show two pictures of the featured player, a recent picture and a picture showing the player as a rookie when

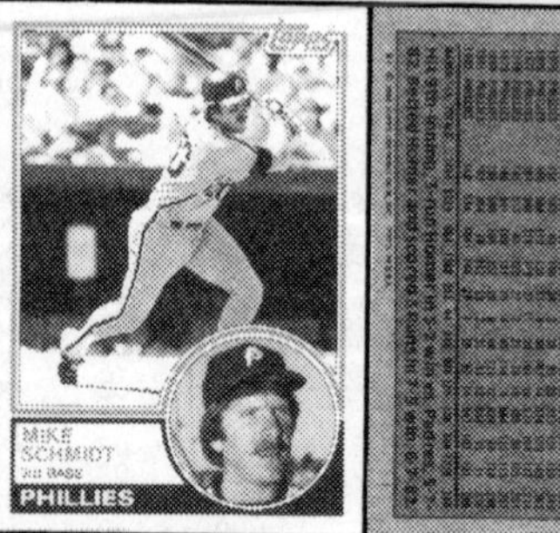

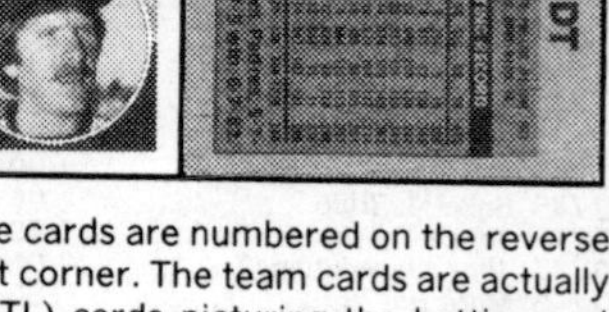

he broke in. The cards are numbered on the reverse at the upper left corner. The team cards are actually Team Leader (TL) cards picturing the batting and pitching leader for that team with a checklist back.

	MINT	EXC	G-VG
COMPLETE SET (792)	90.00	36.00	9.00
COMMON PLAYER (1-792)	.06	.02	.00
□ 1 RB: Tony Armas 11 putouts by rightfielder	.12	.03	.01
□ 2 RB: Rickey Henderson Sets modern record for steals, season	.30	.12	.03
□ 3 RB: Greg Minton 269 1/3 homerless innings streak	.10	.04	.01
□ 4 RB: Lance Parrish Threw out three baserunners in All-Star game	.15	.06	.01
□ 5 RB: Manny Trillo 479 consecutive errorless chances, second baseman	.10	.04	.01
□ 6 RB: John Wathan ML steals record for catchers, 31	.10	.04	.01
□ 7 Gene Richards	.06	.02	.00
□ 8 Steve Balboni	.10	.04	.01
□ 9 Joey McLaughlin	.06	.02	.00
□ 10 Gorman Thomas	.15	.06	.01
□ 11 Billy Gardner MG	.06	.02	.00
□ 12 Paul Mirabella	.06	.02	.00
□ 13 Larry Herndon	.06	.02	.00
□ 14 Frank LaCorte	.06	.02	.00
□ 15 Ron Cey	.15	.06	.01
□ 16 George Vukovich	.06	.02	.00
□ 17 Kent Tekulve	.10	.04	.01
□ 18 SV: Kent Tekulve	.06	.02	.00
□ 19 Oscar Gamble	.06	.02	.00
□ 20 Carlton Fisk	.20	.08	.02
□ 21 Baltimore Orioles TL BA: Eddie Murray ERA: Jim Palmer	.25	.07	.01
□ 22 Randy Martz	.06	.02	.00
□ 23 Mike Heath	.06	.02	.00
□ 24 Steve Mura	.06	.02	.00
□ 25 Hal McRae	.10	.04	.01
□ 26 Jerry Royster	.06	.02	.00
□ 27 Doug Corbett	.06	.02	.00
□ 28 Bruce Bochte	.06	.02	.00
□ 29 Randy Jones	.06	.02	.00
□ 30 Jim Rice	.35	.14	.03
□ 31 Bill Gullickson	.10	.04	.01
□ 32 Dave Bergman	.06	.02	.00
□ 33 Jack O'Connor	.06	.02	.00
□ 34 Paul Householder	.06	.02	.00
□ 35 Rollie Fingers	.25	.10	.02
□ 36 SV: Rollie Fingers	.10	.04	.01
□ 37 Darrell Johnson MG	.06	.02	.00
□ 38 Tim Flannery	.06	.02	.00
□ 39 Terry Puhl	.06	.02	.00
□ 40 Fernando Valenzuela	.40	.16	.04
□ 41 Jerry Turner	.06	.02	.00
□ 42 Dale Murray	.06	.02	.00
□ 43 Bob Dernier	.06	.02	.00
□ 44 Don Robinson	.06	.02	.00
□ 45 John Mayberry	.10	.04	.01
□ 46 Richard Dotson	.10	.04	.01
□ 47 Dave McKay	.06	.02	.00
□ 48 Lary Sorensen	.06	.02	.00

☐ 49	Willie McGee	2.50	1.00	.25
☐ 50	Bob Horner	.25	.10	.02
	('82 RBI total 7)			
☐ 51	Chicago Cubs TL	.15	.04	.01
	BA: Leon Durham			
	ERA: Fergie Jenkins			
☐ 52	Onix Concepcion	.06	.02	.00
☐ 53	Mike Witt	.20	.08	.02
☐ 54	Jim Maler	.06	.02	.00
☐ 55	Mookie Wilson	.10	.04	.01
☐ 56	Chuck Rainey	.06	.02	.00
☐ 57	Tim Blackwell	.06	.02	.00
☐ 58	Al Holland	.06	.02	.00
☐ 59	Benny Ayala	.06	.02	.00
☐ 60	Johnny Bench	.65	.26	.06
☐ 61	SV: Johnny Bench	.25	.10	.02
☐ 62	Bob McClure	.06	.02	.00
☐ 63	Rick Monday	.06	.02	.00
☐ 64	Bill Stein	.06	.02	.00
☐ 65	Jack Morris	.30	.12	.03
☐ 66	Bob Lillis MG	.06	.02	.00
☐ 67	Sal Butera	.06	.02	.00
☐ 68	Eric Show	.40	.16	.04
☐ 69	Lee Lacy	.06	.02	.00
☐ 70	Steve Carlton	.55	.22	.05
☐ 71	SV: Steve Carlton	.25	.10	.02
☐ 72	Tom Paciorek	.06	.02	.00
☐ 73	Allen Ripley	.06	.02	.00
☐ 74	Julio Gonzalez	.06	.02	.00
☐ 75	Amos Otis	.10	.04	.01
☐ 76	Rick Mahler	.10	.04	.01
☐ 77	Hosken Powell	.06	.02	.00
☐ 78	Bill Caudill	.06	.02	.00
☐ 79	Mick Kelleher	.06	.02	.00
☐ 80	George Foster	.20	.08	.02
☐ 81	Yankees TL	.15	.04	.01
	BA: Jerry Mumphrey			
	ERA: Dave Righetti			
☐ 82	Bruce Hurst	.30	.12	.03
☐ 83	Ryne Sandberg	5.50	2.20	.55
☐ 84	Milt May	.06	.02	.00
☐ 85	Ken Singleton	.10	.04	.01
☐ 86	Tom Hume	.06	.02	.00
☐ 87	Joe Rudi	.10	.04	.01
☐ 88	Jim Gantner	.06	.02	.00
☐ 89	Leon Roberts	.06	.02	.00
☐ 90	Jerry Reuss	.10	.04	.01
☐ 91	Larry Milbourne	.06	.02	.00
☐ 92	Mike LaCoss	.06	.02	.00
☐ 93	John Castino	.06	.02	.00
☐ 94	Dave Edwards	.06	.02	.00
☐ 95	Alan Trammell	.40	.16	.04
☐ 96	Dick Howser MG	.10	.04	.01
☐ 97	Ross Baumgarten	.06	.02	.00
☐ 98	Vance Law	.15	.06	.01
☐ 99	Dickie Noles	.06	.02	.00
☐ 100	Pete Rose	2.00	.80	.20
☐ 101	SV: Pete Rose	.75	.30	.07
☐ 102	Dave Beard	.06	.02	.00
☐ 103	Darrell Porter	.06	.02	.00
☐ 104	Bob Walk	.10	.04	.01
☐ 105	Don Baylor	.15	.06	.01
☐ 106	Gene Nelson	.06	.02	.00
☐ 107	Mike Jorgensen	.06	.02	.00
☐ 108	Glenn Hoffman	.06	.02	.00
☐ 109	Luis Leal	.06	.02	.00
☐ 110	Ken Griffey	.10	.04	.01
☐ 111	Montreal Expos TL	.10	.03	.01
	BA: Al Oliver			
	ERA: Steve Rogers			
☐ 112	Bob Shirley	.06	.02	.00
☐ 113	Ron Roenicke	.06	.02	.00
☐ 114	Jim Slaton	.06	.02	.00
☐ 115	Chili Davis	.15	.06	.01
☐ 116	Dave Schmidt	.10	.04	.01
☐ 117	Alan Knicely	.06	.02	.00
☐ 118	Chris Welsh	.06	.02	.00
☐ 119	Tom Brookens	.06	.02	.00
☐ 120	Len Barker	.06	.02	.00
☐ 121	Mickey Hatcher	.15	.06	.01
☐ 122	Jimmy Smith	.06	.02	.00
☐ 123	George Frazier	.06	.02	.00
☐ 124	Marc Hill	.06	.02	.00
☐ 125	Leon Durham	.10	.04	.01
☐ 126	Joe Torre MG	.10	.04	.01
☐ 127	Preston Hanna	.06	.02	.00
☐ 128	Mike Ramsey	.06	.02	.00
☐ 129	Checklist: 1-132	.10	.01	.00
☐ 130	Dave Stieb	.20	.08	.02
☐ 131	Ed Ott	.06	.02	.00
☐ 132	Todd Cruz	.06	.02	.00
☐ 133	Jim Barr	.06	.02	.00
☐ 134	Hubie Brooks	.15	.06	.01
☐ 135	Dwight Evans	.20	.08	.02
☐ 136	Willie Aikens	.06	.02	.00
☐ 137	Woodie Fryman	.06	.02	.00
☐ 138	Rick Dempsey	.06	.02	.00
☐ 139	Bruce Berenyi	.06	.02	.00
☐ 140	Willie Randolph	.10	.04	.01
☐ 141	Indians TL	.10	.03	.01
	BA: Toby Harrah			
	ERA: Rick Sutcliffe			
☐ 142	Mike Caldwell	.06	.02	.00
☐ 143	Joe Pettini	.06	.02	.00
☐ 144	Mark Wagner	.06	.02	.00
☐ 145	Don Sutton	.35	.14	.03
☐ 146	SV: Don Sutton	.15	.06	.01
☐ 147	Rick Leach	.06	.02	.00
☐ 148	Dave Roberts	.06	.02	.00
☐ 149	Johnny Ray	.15	.06	.01
☐ 150	Bruce Sutter	.15	.06	.01
☐ 151	SV: Bruce Sutter	.10	.04	.01
☐ 152	Jay Johnstone	.10	.04	.01
☐ 153	Jerry Koosman	.10	.04	.01
☐ 154	Johnnie LeMaster	.06	.02	.00
☐ 155	Dan Quisenberry	.15	.06	.01
☐ 156	Billy Martin MG	.15	.06	.01
☐ 157	Steve Bedrosian	.15	.06	.01
☐ 158	Rob Wilfong	.06	.02	.00
☐ 159	Mike Stanton	.06	.02	.00
☐ 160	Dave Kingman	.15	.06	.01
☐ 161	SV: Dave Kingman	.10	.04	.01
☐ 162	Mark Clear	.06	.02	.00
☐ 163	Cal Ripken	2.00	.80	.20
☐ 164	David Palmer	.06	.02	.00
☐ 165	Dan Driessen	.06	.02	.00
☐ 166	John Pacella	.06	.02	.00
☐ 167	Mark Brouhard	.06	.02	.00
☐ 168	Juan Eichelberger	.06	.02	.00
☐ 169	Doug Flynn	.06	.02	.00
☐ 170	Steve Howe	.06	.02	.00
☐ 171	Giants TL	.15	.04	.01
	BA: Joe Morgan			
	ERA: Bill Laskey			
☐ 172	Vern Ruhle	.06	.02	.00
☐ 173	Jim Morrison	.06	.02	.00
☐ 174	Jerry Ujdur	.06	.02	.00
☐ 175	Bo Diaz	.06	.02	.00
☐ 176	Dave Righetti	.30	.12	.03
☐ 177	Harold Baines	.25	.10	.02
☐ 178	Luis Tiant	.10	.04	.01
☐ 179	SV: Luis Tiant	.06	.02	.00
☐ 180	Rickey Henderson	.80	.32	.08
☐ 181	Terry Felton	.06	.02	.00
☐ 182	Mike Fischlin	.06	.02	.00
☐ 183	Ed VandeBerg	.10	.04	.01
☐ 184	Bob Clark	.06	.02	.00
☐ 185	Tim Lollar	.06	.02	.00
☐ 186	Whitey Herzog MG	.06	.02	.00
☐ 187	Terry Leach	.20	.08	.02
☐ 188	Rick Miller	.06	.02	.00
☐ 189	Dan Schatzeder	.06	.02	.00
☐ 190	Cecil Cooper	.15	.06	.01
☐ 191	Joe Price	.06	.02	.00
☐ 192	Floyd Rayford	.06	.02	.00
☐ 193	Harry Spilman	.06	.02	.00
☐ 194	Cesar Geronimo	.06	.02	.00
☐ 195	Bob Stoddard	.06	.02	.00
☐ 196	Bill Fahey	.06	.02	.00
☐ 197	Jim Eisenreich	.20	.08	.02
☐ 198	Kiko Garcia	.06	.02	.00
☐ 199	Marty Bystrom	.06	.02	.00
☐ 200	Rod Carew	.65	.26	.06
☐ 201	SV: Rod Carew	.25	.10	.02
☐ 202	Blue Jays TL	.10	.03	.01
	BA: Damaso Garcia			
	ERA: Dave Stieb			
☐ 203	Mike Morgan	.06	.02	.00
☐ 204	Junior Kennedy	.06	.02	.00
☐ 205	Dave Parker	.25	.10	.02
☐ 206	Ken Oberkfell	.06	.02	.00
☐ 207	Rick Camp	.06	.02	.00
☐ 208	Dan Meyer	.06	.02	.00
☐ 209	Mike Moore	.45	.18	.04
☐ 210	Jack Clark	.35	.14	.03
☐ 211	John Denny	.10	.04	.01
☐ 212	John Stearns	.06	.02	.00
☐ 213	Tom Burgmeier	.06	.02	.00
☐ 214	Jerry White	.06	.02	.00
☐ 215	Mario Soto	.10	.04	.01
☐ 216	Tony LaRussa MG	.10	.04	.01
☐ 217	Tim Stoddard	.06	.02	.00
☐ 218	Roy Howell	.06	.02	.00
☐ 219	Mike Armstrong	.06	.02	.00
☐ 220	Dusty Baker	.10	.04	.01
☐ 221	Joe Niekro	.10	.04	.01
☐ 222	Damaso Garcia	.06	.02	.00
☐ 223	John Montefusco	.06	.02	.00
☐ 224	Mickey Rivers	.10	.04	.01
☐ 225	Enos Cabell	.06	.02	.00

☐ 226 Enrique Romo .... .06 .02 .00
☐ 227 Chris Bando .... .06 .02 .00
☐ 228 Joaquin Andujar .... .10 .04 .01
☐ 229 Phillies TL .... .15 .04 .01
BA: Bo Diaz
ERA: Steve Carlton
☐ 230 Fergie Jenkins .... .15 .06 .01
☐ 231 SV: Fergie Jenkins .... .10 .04 .01
☐ 232 Tom Brunansky .... .35 .14 .03
☐ 233 Wayne Gross .... .06 .02 .00
☐ 234 Larry Andersen .... .06 .02 .00
☐ 235 Claudell Washington .... .10 .04 .01
☐ 236 Steve Renko .... .06 .02 .00
☐ 237 Dan Norman .... .06 .02 .00
☐ 238 Bud Black .... .20 .08 .02
☐ 239 Dave Stapleton .... .06 .02 .00
☐ 240 Rich Gossage .... .20 .08 .02
☐ 241 SV: Rich Gossage .... .10 .04 .01
☐ 242 Joe Nolan .... .06 .02 .00
☐ 243 Duane Walker .... .06 .02 .00
☐ 244 Dwight Bernard .... .06 .02 .00
☐ 245 Steve Sax .... .40 .16 .04
☐ 246 George Bamberger MG .. .06 .02 .00
☐ 247 Dave Smith .... .10 .04 .01
☐ 248 Bake McBride .... .06 .02 .00
☐ 249 Checklist: 133-264 .... .10 .01 .00
☐ 250 Bill Buckner .... .15 .06 .01
☐ 251 Alan Wiggins .... .15 .06 .01
☐ 252 Luis Aguayo .... .06 .02 .00
☐ 253 Larry McWilliams .... .06 .02 .00
☐ 254 Rick Cerone .... .06 .02 .00
☐ 255 Gene Garber .... .06 .02 .00
☐ 256 SV: Gene Garber .... .06 .02 .00
☐ 257 Jesse Barfield .... .60 .24 .06
☐ 258 Manny Castillo .... .06 .02 .00
☐ 259 Jeff Jones .... .06 .02 .00
☐ 260 Steve Kemp .... .10 .04 .01
☐ 261 Tigers TL .... .10 .01 .00
BA: Larry Herndon
ERA: Dan Petry
☐ 262 Ron Jackson .... .06 .02 .00
☐ 263 Renie Martin .... .06 .02 .00
☐ 264 Jamie Quirk .... .06 .02 .00
☐ 265 Joel Youngblood .... .06 .02 .00
☐ 266 Paul Boris .... .06 .02 .00
☐ 267 Terry Francona .... .06 .02 .00
☐ 268 Storm Davis .... .75 .30 .07
☐ 269 Ron Oester .... .06 .02 .00
☐ 270 Dennis Eckersley .... .20 .08 .02
☐ 271 Ed Romero .... .06 .02 .00
☐ 272 Frank Tanana .... .10 .04 .01
☐ 273 Mark Belanger .... .10 .04 .01
☐ 274 Terry Kennedy .... .10 .04 .01
☐ 275 Ray Knight .... .10 .04 .01
☐ 276 Gene Mauch MG .... .06 .02 .00
☐ 277 Rance Mulliniks .... .06 .02 .00
☐ 278 Kevin Hickey .... .06 .02 .00
☐ 279 Greg Gross .... .06 .02 .00
☐ 280 Bert Blyleven .... .15 .06 .01
☐ 281 Andre Robertson .... .06 .02 .00
☐ 282 Reggie Smith .... .15 .06 .01
(Ryne Sandberg
ducking back)
☐ 283 SV: Reggie Smith .... .06 .02 .00
☐ 284 Jeff Lahti .... .06 .02 .00
☐ 285 Lance Parrish .... .30 .12 .03
☐ 286 Rick Langford .... .06 .02 .00
☐ 287 Bobby Brown .... .06 .02 .00
☐ 288 Joe Cowley .... .10 .04 .01
☐ 289 Jerry Dybzinski .... .06 .02 .00
☐ 290 Jeff Reardon .... .15 .06 .01
☐ 291 Pirates TL .... .10 .03 .01
BA: Bill Madlock
ERA: John Candelaria
☐ 292 Craig Swan .... .06 .02 .00
☐ 293 Glenn Gulliver .... .06 .02 .00
☐ 294 Dave Engle .... .06 .02 .00
☐ 295 Jerry Remy .... .06 .02 .00
☐ 296 Greg Harris .... .06 .02 .00
☐ 297 Ned Yost .... .06 .02 .00
☐ 298 Floyd Chiffer .... .06 .02 .00
☐ 299 George Wright .... .06 .02 .00
☐ 300 Mike Schmidt .... .90 .36 .09
☐ 301 SV: Mike Schmidt .... .35 .14 .03
☐ 302 Ernie Whitt .... .06 .02 .00
☐ 303 Miguel Dilone .... .06 .02 .00
☐ 304 Dave Rucker .... .06 .02 .00
☐ 305 Larry Bowa .... .10 .04 .01
☐ 306 Tom Lasorda MG .... .10 .04 .01
☐ 307 Lou Piniella .... .10 .04 .01
☐ 308 Jesus Vega .... .06 .02 .00
☐ 309 Jeff Leonard .... .10 .04 .01
☐ 310 Greg Luzinski .... .10 .04 .01
☐ 311 Glenn Brummer .... .06 .02 .00
☐ 312 Brian Kingman .... .06 .02 .00
☐ 313 Gary Gray .... .06 .02 .00
☐ 314 Ken Dayley .... .10 .04 .01
☐ 315 Rick Burleson .... .10 .04 .01
☐ 316 Paul Splittorff .... .06 .02 .00
☐ 317 Gary Rajsich .... .06 .02 .00
☐ 318 John Tudor .... .30 .12 .03
☐ 319 Lenn Sakata .... .06 .02 .00
☐ 320 Steve Rogers .... .06 .02 .00
☐ 321 Brewers TL .... .15 .04 .01
BA: Robin Yount
ERA: Pete Vuckovich
☐ 322 Dave Van Gorder .... .06 .02 .00
☐ 323 Luis DeLeon .... .06 .02 .00
☐ 324 Mike Marshall .... .30 .12 .03
☐ 325 Von Hayes .... .30 .12 .03
☐ 326 Garth Iorg .... .06 .02 .00
☐ 327 Bobby Castillo .... .06 .02 .00
☐ 328 Craig Reynolds .... .06 .02 .00
☐ 329 Randy Niemann .... .06 .02 .00
☐ 330 Buddy Bell .... .15 .06 .01
☐ 331 Mike Krukow .... .10 .04 .01
☐ 332 Glenn Wilson .... .35 .14 .03
☐ 333 Dave LaRoche .... .06 .02 .00
☐ 334 SV: Dave LaRoche .... .06 .02 .00
☐ 335 Steve Henderson .... .06 .02 .00
☐ 336 Rene Lachemann MG ..... .06 .02 .00
☐ 337 Tito Landrum .... .06 .02 .00
☐ 338 Bob Owchinko .... .06 .02 .00
☐ 339 Terry Harper .... .06 .02 .00
☐ 340 Larry Gura .... .06 .02 .00
☐ 341 Doug DeCinces .... .10 .04 .01
☐ 342 Atlee Hammaker .... .10 .04 .01
☐ 343 Bob Bailor .... .06 .02 .00
☐ 344 Roger LaFrancois .... .06 .02 .00
☐ 345 Jim Clancy .... .06 .02 .00
☐ 346 Joe Pittman .... .06 .02 .00
☐ 347 Sammy Stewart .... .06 .02 .00
☐ 348 Alan Bannister .... .06 .02 .00
☐ 349 Checklist: 265-396 .... .10 .01 .00
☐ 350 Robin Yount .... .50 .20 .05
☐ 351 Reds TL .... .10 .03 .01
BA: Cesar Cedeno
ERA: Mario Soto
☐ 352 Mike Scioscia .... .10 .04 .01
☐ 353 Steve Comer .... .06 .02 .00
☐ 354 Randy Johnson .... .06 .02 .00
☐ 355 Jim Bibby .... .06 .02 .00
☐ 356 Gary Woods .... .06 .02 .00
☐ 357 Len Matuszek .... .06 .02 .00
☐ 358 Jerry Garvin .... .06 .02 .00
☐ 359 Dave Collins .... .06 .02 .00
☐ 360 Nolan Ryan .... .60 .24 .06
☐ 361 SV: Nolan Ryan .... .25 .10 .02
☐ 362 Billy Almon .... .06 .02 .00
☐ 363 John Stuper .... .06 .02 .00
☐ 364 Brett Butler .... .10 .04 .01
☐ 365 Dave Lopes .... .10 .04 .01
☐ 366 Dick Williams MG .... .06 .02 .00
☐ 367 Bud Anderson .... .06 .02 .00
☐ 368 Richie Zisk .... .06 .02 .00
☐ 369 Jesse Orosco .... .06 .02 .00
☐ 370 Gary Carter .... .50 .20 .05
☐ 371 Mike Richardt .... .06 .02 .00
☐ 372 Terry Crowley .... .06 .02 .00
☐ 373 Kevin Saucier .... .06 .02 .00
☐ 374 Wayne Krenchicki .... .06 .02 .00
☐ 375 Pete Vuckovich .... .10 .04 .01
☐ 376 Ken Landreaux .... .06 .02 .00
☐ 377 Lee May .... .06 .02 .00
☐ 378 SV: Lee May .... .06 .02 .00
☐ 379 Guy Sularz .... .06 .02 .00
☐ 380 Ron Davis .... .06 .02 .00
☐ 381 Red Sox TL .... .15 .04 .01
BA: Jim Rice
ERA: Bob Stanley
☐ 382 Bob Knepper .... .10 .04 .01
☐ 383 Ozzie Virgil .... .06 .02 .00
☐ 384 Dave Dravecky .... .40 .16 .04
☐ 385 Mike Easler .... .06 .02 .00
☐ 386 Rod Carew AS .... .20 .08 .02
☐ 387 Bob Grich AS .... .10 .04 .01
☐ 388 George Brett AS .... .35 .14 .03
☐ 389 Robin Yount AS .... .20 .08 .02
☐ 390 Reggie Jackson AS .... .30 .12 .03
☐ 391 Rickey Henderson AS ..... .35 .14 .03
☐ 392 Fred Lynn AS .... .10 .04 .01
☐ 393 Carlton Fisk AS .... .10 .04 .01
☐ 394 Pete Vuckovich AS .... .06 .02 .00
☐ 395 Larry Gura AS .... .06 .02 .00
☐ 396 Dan Quisenberry AS .... .10 .04 .01
☐ 397 Pete Rose AS .... .55 .22 .05
☐ 398 Manny Trillo AS .... .06 .02 .00
☐ 399 Mike Schmidt AS .... .30 .12 .03
☐ 400 Dave Concepcion AS ...... .06 .02 .00
☐ 401 Dale Murphy AS .... .45 .18 .04

□ 402	Andre Dawson AS	.20	.08	.02
□ 403	Tim Raines AS	.20	.08	.02
□ 404	Gary Carter AS	.20	.08	.02
□ 405	Steve Rogers AS	.06	.02	.00
□ 406	Steve Carlton AS	.20	.08	.02
□ 407	Bruce Sutter AS	.10	.04	.01
□ 408	Rudy May	.06	.02	.00
□ 409	Marvis Foley	.06	.02	.00
□ 410	Phil Niekro	.35	.14	.03
□ 411	SV: Phil Niekro	.15	.06	.01
□ 412	Rangers TL	.10	.03	.01
	BA: Buddy Bell			
	ERA: Charlie Hough			
□ 413	Matt Keough	.06	.02	.00
□ 414	Julio Cruz	.06	.02	.00
□ 415	Bob Forsch	.06	.02	.00
□ 416	Joe Ferguson	.06	.02	.00
□ 417	Tom Hausman	.06	.02	.00
□ 418	Greg Pryor	.06	.02	.00
□ 419	Steve Crawford	.06	.02	.00
□ 420	Al Oliver	.10	.04	.01
□ 421	SV: Al Oliver	.06	.02	.00
□ 422	George Cappuzello	.06	.02	.00
□ 423	Tom Lawless	.10	.04	.01
□ 424	Jerry Augustine	.06	.02	.00
□ 425	Pedro Guerrero	.45	.18	.04
□ 426	Earl Weaver MG	.06	.02	.00
□ 427	Roy Lee Jackson	.06	.02	.00
□ 428	Champ Summers	.06	.02	.00
□ 429	Eddie Whitson	.06	.02	.00
□ 430	Kirk Gibson	.45	.18	.04
□ 431	Gary Gaetti	4.50	1.80	.45
□ 432	Porfirio Altamirano	.06	.02	.00
□ 433	Dale Berra	.06	.02	.00
□ 434	Dennis Lamp	.06	.02	.00
□ 435	Tony Armas	.10	.04	.01
□ 436	Bill Campbell	.06	.02	.00
□ 437	Rick Sweet	.06	.02	.00
□ 438	Dave LaPoint	.45	.18	.04
□ 439	Rafael Ramirez	.06	.02	.00
□ 440	Ron Guidry	.20	.08	.02
□ 441	Astros TL	.10	.03	.01
	BA: Ray Knight			
	ERA: Joe Niekro			
□ 442	Brian Downing	.10	.04	.01
□ 443	Don Hood	.06	.02	.00
□ 444	Wally Backman	.20	.08	.02
□ 445	Mike Flanagan	.10	.04	.01
□ 446	Reid Nichols	.06	.02	.00
□ 447	Bryn Smith	.10	.04	.01
□ 448	Darrell Evans	.15	.06	.01
□ 449	Eddie Milner	.10	.04	.01
□ 450	Ted Simmons	.15	.06	.01
□ 451	SV: Ted Simmons	.10	.04	.01
□ 452	Lloyd Moseby	.15	.06	.01
□ 453	Lamar Johnson	.06	.02	.00
□ 454	Bob Welch	.10	.04	.01
□ 455	Sixto Lezcano	.06	.02	.00
□ 456	Lee Elia MG	.06	.02	.00
□ 457	Milt Wilcox	.06	.02	.00
□ 458	Ron Washington	.06	.02	.00
□ 459	Ed Farmer	.06	.02	.00
□ 460	Roy Smalley	.06	.02	.00
□ 461	Steve Trout	.06	.02	.00
□ 462	Steve Nicosia	.06	.02	.00
□ 463	Gaylord Perry	.30	.12	.03
□ 464	SV: Gaylord Perry	.15	.06	.01
□ 465	Lonnie Smith	.10	.04	.01
□ 466	Tom Underwood	.06	.02	.00
□ 467	Rufino Linares	.06	.02	.00
□ 468	Dave Goltz	.06	.02	.00
□ 469	Ron Gardenhire	.06	.02	.00
□ 470	Greg Minton	.06	.02	.00
□ 471	K.C. Royals TL	.10	.03	.01
	BA: Willie Wilson			
	ERA: Vida Blue			
□ 472	Gary Allenson	.06	.02	.00
□ 473	John Lowenstein	.06	.02	.00
□ 474	Ray Burris	.06	.02	.00
□ 475	Cesar Cedeno	.10	.04	.01
□ 476	Rob Picciolo	.06	.02	.00
□ 477	Tom Niedenfuer	.10	.04	.01
□ 478	Phil Garner	.06	.02	.00
□ 479	Charlie Hough	.10	.04	.01
□ 480	Toby Harrah	.10	.04	.01
□ 481	Scot Thompson	.06	.02	.00
□ 482	Tony Gwynn	16.00	6.50	1.60
□ 483	Lynn Jones	.06	.02	.00
□ 484	Dick Ruthven	.06	.02	.00
□ 485	Omar Moreno	.06	.02	.00
□ 486	Clyde King MG	.06	.02	.00
□ 487	Jerry Hairston	.06	.02	.00
□ 488	Alfredo Griffin	.10	.04	.01
□ 489	Tom Herr	.10	.04	.01
□ 490	Jim Palmer	.45	.18	.04
□ 491	SV: Jim Palmer	.20	.08	.02
□ 492	Paul Serna	.06	.02	.00
□ 493	Steve McCatty	.06	.02	.00
□ 494	Bob Brenly	.06	.02	.00
□ 495	Warren Cromartie	.06	.02	.00
□ 496	Tom Veryzer	.06	.02	.00
□ 497	Rick Sutcliffe	.15	.06	.01
□ 498	Wade Boggs	32.00	13.00	3.20
□ 499	Jeff Little	.06	.02	.00
□ 500	Reggie Jackson	.85	.34	.08
□ 501	SV: Reggie Jackson	.35	.14	.03
□ 502	Atlanta Braves TL	.25	.07	.01
	BA: Dale Murphy			
	ERA: Phil Niekro			
□ 503	Moose Haas	.06	.02	.00
□ 504	Don Werner	.06	.02	.00
□ 505	Garry Templeton	.10	.04	.01
□ 506	Jim Gott	.40	.16	.04
□ 507	Tony Scott	.06	.02	.00
□ 508	Tom Filer	.15	.06	.01
□ 509	Lou Whitaker	.25	.10	.02
□ 510	Tug McGraw	.10	.04	.01
□ 511	SV: Tug McGraw	.06	.02	.00
□ 512	Doyle Alexander	.10	.04	.01
□ 513	Fred Stanley	.06	.02	.00
□ 514	Rudy Law	.06	.02	.00
□ 515	Gene Tenace	.06	.02	.00
□ 516	Bill Virdon MG	.06	.02	.00
□ 517	Gary Ward	.10	.04	.01
□ 518	Bill Laskey	.06	.02	.00
□ 519	Terry Bulling	.06	.02	.00
□ 520	Fred Lynn	.25	.10	.02
□ 521	Bruce Benedict	.06	.02	.00
□ 522	Pat Zachry	.06	.02	.00
□ 523	Carney Lansford	.15	.06	.01
□ 524	Tom Brennan	.06	.02	.00
□ 525	Frank White	.10	.04	.01
□ 526	Checklist: 397-528	.10	.01	.00
□ 527	Larry Biittner	.06	.02	.00
□ 528	Jamie Easterly	.06	.02	.00
□ 529	Tim Laudner	.10	.04	.01
□ 530	Eddie Murray	.75	.30	.07
□ 531	Oakland A's TL	.15	.04	.01
	BA: Rickey Henderson			
	ERA: Rick Langford			
□ 532	Dave Stewart	.20	.08	.02
□ 533	Luis Salazar	.10	.04	.01
□ 534	John Butcher	.06	.02	.00
□ 535	Manny Trillo	.06	.02	.00
□ 536	Johnny Wockenfuss	.06	.02	.00
□ 537	Rod Scurry	.06	.02	.00
□ 538	Danny Heep	.06	.02	.00
□ 539	Roger Erickson	.06	.02	.00
□ 540	Ozzie Smith	.40	.16	.04
□ 541	Britt Burns	.10	.04	.01
□ 542	Jody Davis	.10	.04	.01
□ 543	Alan Fowlkes	.06	.02	.00
□ 544	Larry Whisenton	.06	.02	.00
□ 545	Floyd Bannister	.06	.02	.00
□ 546	Dave Garcia MG	.06	.02	.00
□ 547	Geoff Zahn	.06	.02	.00
□ 548	Brian Giles	.06	.02	.00
□ 549	Charlie Puleo	.06	.02	.00
□ 550	Carl Yastrzemski	1.00	.40	.10
□ 551	SV: Carl Yastrzemski	.40	.16	.04
□ 552	Tim Wallach	.20	.08	.02
□ 553	Denny Martinez	.10	.04	.01
□ 554	Mike Vail	.06	.02	.00
□ 555	Steve Yeager	.06	.02	.00
□ 556	Willie Upshaw	.10	.04	.01
□ 557	Rick Honeycutt	.06	.02	.00
□ 558	Dickie Thon	.10	.04	.01
□ 559	Pete Redfern	.06	.02	.00
□ 560	Ron LeFlore	.10	.04	.01
□ 561	Cardinals TL	.10	.03	.01
	BA: Lonnie Smith			
	ERA: Joaquin Andujar			
□ 562	Dave Rozema	.06	.02	.00
□ 563	Juan Bonilla	.06	.02	.00
□ 564	Sid Monge	.06	.02	.00
□ 565	Bucky Dent	.10	.04	.01
□ 566	Manny Sarmiento	.06	.02	.00
□ 567	Joe Simpson	.06	.02	.00
□ 568	Willie Hernandez	.10	.04	.01
□ 569	Jack Perconte	.06	.02	.00
□ 570	Vida Blue	.10	.04	.01
□ 571	Mickey Klutts	.06	.02	.00
□ 572	Bob Watson	.10	.04	.01
□ 573	Andy Hassler	.06	.02	.00
□ 574	Glenn Adams	.06	.02	.00
□ 575	Neil Allen	.06	.02	.00
□ 576	Frank Robinson MG	.15	.06	.01
□ 577	Luis Aponte	.06	.02	.00
□ 578	David Green	.06	.02	.00
□ 579	Rich Dauer	.06	.02	.00

☐ 580	Tom Seaver	.60	.24	.06
☐ 581	SV: Tom Seaver	.25	.10	.02
☐ 582	Marshall Edwards	.06	.02	.00
☐ 583	Terry Forster	.10	.04	.01
☐ 584	Dave Hostetler	.06	.02	.00
☐ 585	Jose Cruz	.10	.04	.01
☐ 586	Frank Viola	5.50	2.20	.55
☐ 587	Ivan DeJesus	.06	.02	.00
☐ 588	Pat Underwood	.06	.02	.00
☐ 589	Alvis Woods	.06	.02	.00
☐ 590	Tony Pena	.20	.08	.02
☐ 591	White Sox TL	.10	.03	.01
	BA: Greg Luzinski			
	ERA: LaMarr Hoyt			
☐ 592	Shane Rawley	.10	.04	.01
☐ 593	Broderick Perkins	.06	.02	.00
☐ 594	Eric Rasmussen	.06	.02	.00
☐ 595	Tim Raines	.80	.32	.08
☐ 596	Randy Johnson	.06	.02	.00
☐ 597	Mike Proly	.06	.02	.00
☐ 598	Dwayne Murphy	.06	.02	.00
☐ 599	Don Aase	.06	.02	.00
☐ 600	George Brett	1.00	.40	.10
☐ 601	Ed Lynch	.06	.02	.00
☐ 602	Rich Gedman	.15	.06	.01
☐ 603	Joe Morgan	.35	.14	.03
☐ 604	SV: Joe Morgan	.15	.06	.01
☐ 605	Gary Roenicke	.06	.02	.00
☐ 606	Bobby Cox MG	.06	.02	.00
☐ 607	Charlie Leibrandt	.06	.02	.00
☐ 608	Don Money	.06	.02	.00
☐ 609	Danny Darwin	.06	.02	.00
☐ 610	Steve Garvey	.70	.28	.07
☐ 611	Bert Roberge	.06	.02	.00
☐ 612	Steve Swisher	.06	.02	.00
☐ 613	Mike Ivie	.06	.02	.00
☐ 614	Ed Glynn	.06	.02	.00
☐ 615	Garry Maddox	.10	.04	.01
☐ 616	Bill Nahorodny	.06	.02	.00
☐ 617	Butch Wynegar	.06	.02	.00
☐ 618	LaMarr Hoyt	.10	.04	.01
☐ 619	Keith Moreland	.10	.04	.01
☐ 620	Mike Norris	.06	.02	.00
☐ 621	New York Mets TL	.10	.03	.01
	BA: Mookie Wilson			
	ERA: Craig Swan			
☐ 622	Dave Edler	.06	.02	.00
☐ 623	Luis Sanchez	.06	.02	.00
☐ 624	Glenn Hubbard	.06	.02	.00
☐ 625	Ken Forsch	.06	.02	.00
☐ 626	Jerry Martin	.06	.02	.00
☐ 627	Doug Bair	.06	.02	.00
☐ 628	Julio Valdez	.06	.02	.00
☐ 629	Charlie Lea	.06	.02	.00
☐ 630	Paul Molitor	.25	.10	.02
☐ 631	Tippy Martinez	.06	.02	.00
☐ 632	Alex Trevino	.06	.02	.00
☐ 633	Vicente Romo	.06	.02	.00
☐ 634	Max Venable	.06	.02	.00
☐ 635	Graig Nettles	.15	.06	.01
☐ 636	SV: Graig Nettles	.10	.04	.01
☐ 637	Pat Corrales MG	.06	.02	.00
☐ 638	Dan Petry	.10	.04	.01
☐ 639	Art Howe	.10	.04	.01
☐ 640	Andre Thornton	.10	.04	.01
☐ 641	Billy Sample	.06	.02	.00
☐ 642	Checklist: 529-660	.10	.01	.00
☐ 643	Bump Wills	.06	.02	.00
☐ 644	Joe Lefebvre	.06	.02	.00
☐ 645	Bill Madlock	.15	.06	.01
☐ 646	Jim Essian	.06	.02	.00
☐ 647	Bobby Mitchell	.06	.02	.00
☐ 648	Jeff Burroughs	.10	.04	.01
☐ 649	Tommy Boggs	.06	.02	.00
☐ 650	George Hendrick	.10	.04	.01
☐ 651	Angels TL	.20	.06	.01
	BA: Rod Carew			
	ERA: Mike Witt			
☐ 652	Butch Hobson	.06	.02	.00
☐ 653	Ellis Valentine	.06	.02	.00
☐ 654	Bob Ojeda	.15	.06	.01
☐ 655	Al Bumbry	.06	.02	.00
☐ 656	Dave Frost	.06	.02	.00
☐ 657	Mike Gates	.06	.02	.00
☐ 658	Frank Pastore	.06	.02	.00
☐ 659	Charlie Moore	.06	.02	.00
☐ 660	Mike Hargrove	.06	.02	.00
☐ 661	Bill Russell	.10	.04	.01
☐ 662	Joe Sambito	.06	.02	.00
☐ 663	Tom O'Malley	.06	.02	.00
☐ 664	Bob Molinaro	.06	.02	.00
☐ 665	Jim Sundberg	.06	.02	.00
☐ 666	Sparky Anderson MG	.10	.04	.01
☐ 667	Dick Davis	.06	.02	.00
☐ 668	Larry Christenson	.06	.02	.00
☐ 669	Mike Squires	.06	.02	.00
☐ 670	Jerry Mumphrey	.06	.02	.00
☐ 671	Lenny Faedo	.06	.02	.00
☐ 672	Jim Kaat	.15	.06	.01
☐ 673	SV: Jim Kaat	.10	.04	.01
☐ 674	Kurt Bevacqua	.06	.02	.00
☐ 675	Jim Beattie	.06	.02	.00
☐ 676	Biff Pocoroba	.06	.02	.00
☐ 677	Dave Revering	.06	.02	.00
☐ 678	Juan Beniquez	.06	.02	.00
☐ 679	Mike Scott	.35	.14	.03
☐ 680	Andre Dawson	.45	.18	.04
☐ 681	Dodgers Leaders	.20	.06	.01
	BA: Pedro Guerrero			
	ERA: Fern.Valenzuela			
☐ 682	Bob Stanley	.06	.02	.00
☐ 683	Dan Ford	.06	.02	.00
☐ 684	Rafael Landestoy	.06	.02	.00
☐ 685	Lee Mazzilli	.06	.02	.00
☐ 686	Randy Lerch	.06	.02	.00
☐ 687	U.L. Washington	.06	.02	.00
☐ 688	Jim Wohlford	.06	.02	.00
☐ 689	Ron Hassey	.06	.02	.00
☐ 690	Kent Hrbek	.70	.28	.07
☐ 691	Dave Tobik	.06	.02	.00
☐ 692	Denny Walling	.06	.02	.00
☐ 693	Sparky Lyle	.10	.04	.01
☐ 694	SV: Sparky Lyle	.06	.02	.00
☐ 695	Ruppert Jones	.06	.02	.00
☐ 696	Chuck Tanner MG	.06	.02	.00
☐ 697	Barry Foote	.06	.02	.00
☐ 698	Tony Bernazard	.06	.02	.00
☐ 699	Lee Smith	.15	.06	.01
☐ 700	Keith Hernandez	.45	.18	.04
☐ 701	Batting Leaders	.10	.04	.01
	AL: Willie Wilson			
	NL: Al Oliver			
☐ 702	Home Run Leaders	.15	.06	.01
	AL: Reggie Jackson			
	AL: Gorman Thomas			
	NL: Dave Kingman			
☐ 703	RBI Leaders	.15	.06	.01
	AL: Hal McRae			
	NL: Dale Murphy			
	NL: Al Oliver			
☐ 704	SB Leaders	.25	.10	.02
	AL: Rickey Henderson			
	NL: Tim Raines			
☐ 705	Victory Leaders	.12	.05	.01
	AL: LaMarr Hoyt			
	NL: Steve Carlton			
☐ 706	Strikeout Leaders	.12	.05	.01
	AL: Floyd Bannister			
	NL: Steve Carlton			
☐ 707	ERA Leaders	.10	.04	.01
	AL: Rick Sutcliffe			
	NL: Steve Rogers			
☐ 708	Leading Firemen	.10	.04	.01
	AL: Dan Quisenberry			
	NL: Bruce Sutter			
☐ 709	Jimmy Sexton	.06	.02	.00
☐ 710	Willie Wilson	.15	.06	.01
☐ 711	Mariners TL	.10	.04	.01
	BA: Bruce Bochte			
	ERA: Jim Beattie			
☐ 712	Bruce Kison	.06	.02	.00
☐ 713	Ron Hodges	.06	.02	.00
☐ 714	Wayne Nordhagen	.06	.02	.00
☐ 715	Tony Perez	.20	.08	.02
☐ 716	SV: Tony Perez	.10	.04	.01
☐ 717	Scott Sanderson	.06	.02	.00
☐ 718	Jim Dwyer	.06	.02	.00
☐ 719	Rich Gale	.06	.02	.00
☐ 720	Dave Concepcion	.15	.06	.01
☐ 721	John Martin	.06	.02	.00
☐ 722	Jorge Orta	.06	.02	.00
☐ 723	Randy Moffitt	.06	.02	.00
☐ 724	Johnny Grubb	.06	.02	.00
☐ 725	Dan Spillner	.06	.02	.00
☐ 726	Harvey Kuenn MG	.06	.02	.00
☐ 727	Chet Lemon	.10	.04	.01
☐ 728	Ron Reed	.06	.02	.00
☐ 729	Jerry Morales	.06	.02	.00
☐ 730	Jason Thompson	.06	.02	.00
☐ 731	Al Williams	.06	.02	.00
☐ 732	Dave Henderson	.20	.08	.02
☐ 733	Buck Martinez	.06	.02	.00
☐ 734	Steve Braun	.06	.02	.00
☐ 735	Tommy John	.20	.08	.02
☐ 736	SV: Tommy John	.10	.04	.01
☐ 737	Mitchell Page	.06	.02	.00
☐ 738	Tim Foli	.06	.02	.00
☐ 739	Rick Ownbey	.06	.02	.00
☐ 740	Rusty Staub	.15	.06	.01
☐ 741	SV: Rusty Staub	.10	.04	.01

□ 742 Padres TL BA: Terry Kennedy ERA: Tim Lollar	.10	.03	.01
□ 743 Mike Torrez	.06	.02	.00
□ 744 Brad Mills	.06	.02	.00
□ 745 Scott McGregor	.10	.04	.01
□ 746 John Wathan	.10	.04	.01
□ 747 Fred Breining	.06	.02	.00
□ 748 Derrel Thomas	.06	.02	.00
□ 749 Jon Matlack	.06	.02	.00
□ 750 Ben Oglivie	.10	.04	.01
□ 751 Brad Havens	.06	.02	.00
□ 752 Luis Pujols	.06	.02	.00
□ 753 Elias Sosa	.06	.02	.00
□ 754 Bill Robinson	.10	.04	.01
□ 755 John Candelaria	.10	.04	.01
□ 756 Russ Nixon MG	.06	.02	.00
□ 757 Rick Manning	.06	.02	.00
□ 758 Aurelio Rodriguez	.06	.02	.00
□ 759 Doug Bird	.06	.02	.00
□ 760 Dale Murphy	1.50	.60	.15
□ 761 Gary Lucas	.06	.02	.00
□ 762 Cliff Johnson	.06	.02	.00
□ 763 Al Cowens	.06	.02	.00
□ 764 Pete Falcone	.06	.02	.00
□ 765 Bob Boone	.15	.06	.01
□ 766 Barry Bonnell	.06	.02	.00
□ 767 Duane Kuiper	.06	.02	.00
□ 768 Chris Speier	.06	.02	.00
□ 769 Checklist: 661-792	.10	.01	.00
□ 770 Dave Winfield	.55	.22	.05
□ 771 Twins TL BA: Kent Hrbek ERA: Bobby Castillo	.10	.03	.01
□ 772 Jim Kern	.06	.02	.00
□ 773 Larry Hisle	.06	.02	.00
□ 774 Alan Ashby	.06	.02	.00
□ 775 Burt Hooton	.06	.02	.00
□ 776 Larry Parrish	.10	.04	.01
□ 777 John Curtis	.06	.02	.00
□ 778 Rich Hebner	.06	.02	.00
□ 779 Rick Waits	.06	.02	.00
□ 780 Gary Matthews	.10	.04	.01
□ 781 Rick Rhoden	.10	.04	.01
□ 782 Bobby Murcer	.10	.04	.01
□ 783 SV: Bobby Murcer	.06	.02	.00
□ 784 Jeff Newman	.06	.02	.00
□ 785 Dennis Leonard	.10	.04	.01
□ 786 Ralph Houk MG	.06	.02	.00
□ 787 Dick Tidrow	.06	.02	.00
□ 788 Dane Iorg	.06	.02	.00
□ 789 Bryan Clark	.06	.02	.00
□ 790 Bob Grich	.10	.04	.01
□ 791 Gary Lavelle	.06	.02	.00
□ 792 Chris Chambliss	.15	.05	.01

1983 Topps Traded

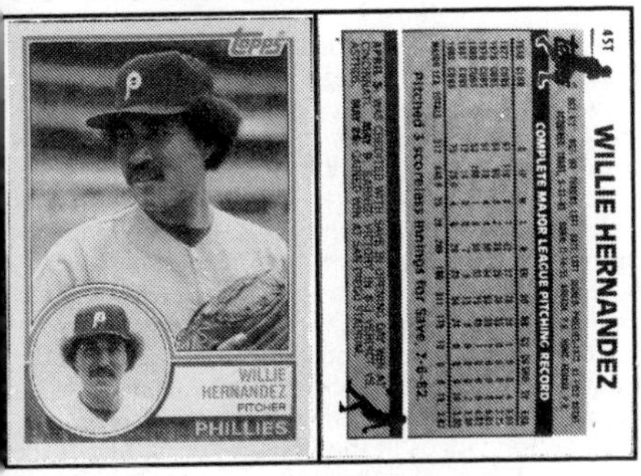

The cards in this 132-card set measure 2 1/2" by 3 1/2". For the third year in a row, Topps issued a 132-card Traded (or extended) set featuring some of the year's top rookies and players who had changed teams during the year, but were featured with their old team in the Topps regular issue of 1983. The cards were available through hobby dealers only and were printed in Ireland by the Topps affiliate in that country. The set is numbered alphabetically by the last name of the player of the card.

	MINT	EXC	G-VG
COMPLETE SET (132)	65.00	26.00	6.50
COMMON PLAYER (1-132)	.07	.03	.01
□ 1T Neil Allen	.15	.06	.01
□ 2T Bill Almon	.07	.03	.01
□ 3T Joe Altobelli MG	.07	.03	.01
□ 4T Tony Armas	.15	.06	.01
□ 5T Doug Bair	.07	.03	.01
□ 6T Steve Baker	.07	.03	.01
□ 7T Floyd Bannister	.15	.06	.01
□ 8T Don Baylor	.25	.10	.02
□ 9T Tony Bernazard	.07	.03	.01
□ 10T Larry Biittner	.07	.03	.01
□ 11T Dann Bilardello	.07	.03	.01
□ 12T Doug Bird	.07	.03	.01
□ 13T Steve Boros MG	.07	.03	.01
□ 14T Greg Brock	.35	.14	.03
□ 15T Mike Brown (Red Sox pitcher)	.15	.06	.01
□ 16T Tom Burgmeier	.07	.03	.01
□ 17T Randy Bush	.40	.16	.04
□ 18T Bert Campaneris	.15	.06	.01
□ 19T Ron Cey	.20	.08	.02
□ 20T Chris Codiroli	.15	.06	.01
□ 21T Dave Collins	.07	.03	.01
□ 22T Terry Crowley	.07	.03	.01
□ 23T Julio Cruz	.07	.03	.01
□ 24T Mike Davis	.15	.06	.01
□ 25T Frank DiPino	.07	.03	.01
□ 26T Bill Doran	1.50	.60	.15
□ 27T Jerry Dybzinski	.07	.03	.01
□ 28T Jamie Easterly	.07	.03	.01
□ 29T Juan Eichelberger	.07	.03	.01
□ 30T Jim Essian	.07	.03	.01
□ 31T Pete Falcone	.07	.03	.01
□ 32T Mike Ferraro MG	.07	.03	.01
□ 33T Terry Forster	.15	.06	.01
□ 34T Julio Franco	1.50	.60	.15
□ 35T Rich Gale	.07	.03	.01
□ 36T Kiko Garcia	.07	.03	.01
□ 37T Steve Garvey	1.50	.60	.15
□ 38T Johnny Grubb	.07	.03	.01
□ 39T Mel Hall	.70	.28	.07
□ 40T Von Hayes	.70	.28	.07
□ 41T Danny Heep	.15	.06	.01
□ 42T Steve Henderson	.07	.03	.01
□ 43T Keith Hernandez	1.00	.40	.10
□ 44T Leo Hernandez	.20	.08	.02
□ 45T Willie Hernandez	.20	.08	.02
□ 46T Al Holland	.07	.03	.01
□ 47T Frank Howard MG	.15	.06	.01
□ 48T Bobby Johnson	.07	.03	.01
□ 49T Cliff Johnson	.07	.03	.01
□ 50T Odell Jones	.07	.03	.01
□ 51T Mike Jorgensen	.07	.03	.01
□ 52T Bob Kearney	.07	.03	.01
□ 53T Steve Kemp	.15	.06	.01
□ 54T Matt Keough	.07	.03	.01
□ 55T Ron Kittle	.60	.24	.06
□ 56T Mickey Klutts	.07	.03	.01
□ 57T Alan Knicely	.07	.03	.01
□ 58T Mike Krukow	.15	.06	.01
□ 59T Rafael Landestoy	.07	.03	.01
□ 60T Carney Lansford	.25	.10	.02
□ 61T Joe Lefebvre	.07	.03	.01
□ 62T Bryan Little	.07	.03	.01
□ 63T Aurelio Lopez	.07	.03	.01
□ 64T Mike Madden	.07	.03	.01
□ 65T Rick Manning	.07	.03	.01
□ 66T Billy Martin MG	.20	.08	.02
□ 67T Lee Mazzilli	.07	.03	.01
□ 68T Andy McGaffigan	.07	.03	.01
□ 69T Craig McMurtry	.15	.06	.01
□ 70T John McNamara MG	.07	.03	.01
□ 71T Orlando Mercado	.15	.06	.01
□ 72T Larry Milbourne	.07	.03	.01
□ 73T Randy Moffitt	.07	.03	.01
□ 74T Sid Monge	.07	.03	.01
□ 75T Jose Morales	.07	.03	.01
□ 76T Omar Moreno	.07	.03	.01
□ 77T Joe Morgan	1.00	.40	.10
□ 78T Mike Morgan	.07	.03	.01
□ 79T Dale Murray	.07	.03	.01
□ 80T Jeff Newman	.07	.03	.01
□ 81T Pete O'Brien	1.75	.70	.17
□ 82T Jorge Orta	.07	.03	.01
□ 83T Alejandro Pena	.65	.26	.06
□ 84T Pascual Perez	.20	.08	.02
□ 85T Tony Perez	.55	.22	.05
□ 86T Broderick Perkins	.07	.03	.01
□ 87T Tony Phillips	.20	.08	.02
□ 88T Charlie Puleo	.07	.03	.01

☐ 89T	Pat Putnam	.07	.03	.01
☐ 90T	Jamie Quirk	.07	.03	.01
☐ 91T	Doug Rader MG	.15	.06	.01
☐ 92T	Chuck Rainey	.07	.03	.01
☐ 93T	Bobby Ramos	.07	.03	.01
☐ 94T	Gary Redus	.45	.18	.04
☐ 95T	Steve Renko	.07	.03	.01
☐ 96T	Leon Roberts	.07	.03	.01
☐ 97T	Aurelio Rodriguez	.07	.03	.01
☐ 98T	Dick Ruthven	.07	.03	.01
☐ 99T	Daryl Sconiers	.07	.03	.01
☐ 100T	Mike Scott	1.00	.40	.10
☐ 101T	Tom Seaver	1.50	.60	.15
☐ 102T	John Shelby	.75	.30	.07
☐ 103T	Bob Shirley	.07	.03	.01
☐ 104T	Joe Simpson	.07	.03	.01
☐ 105T	Doug Sisk	.15	.06	.01
☐ 106T	Mike Smithson	.15	.06	.01
☐ 107T	Elias Sosa	.07	.03	.01
☐ 108T	Darryl Strawberry	50.00	20.00	5.00
☐ 109T	Tom Tellmann	.07	.03	.01
☐ 110T	Gene Tenace	.15	.06	.01
☐ 111T	Gorman Thomas	.20	.08	.02
☐ 112T	Dick Tidrow	.07	.03	.01
☐ 113T	Dave Tobik	.07	.03	.01
☐ 114T	Wayne Tolleson	.15	.06	.01
☐ 115T	Mike Torrez	.07	.03	.01
☐ 116T	Manny Trillo	.07	.03	.01
☐ 117T	Steve Trout	.07	.03	.01
☐ 118T	Lee Tunnell	.20	.08	.02
☐ 119T	Mike Vail	.07	.03	.01
☐ 120T	Ellis Valentine	.07	.03	.01
☐ 121T	Tom Veryzer	.07	.03	.01
☐ 122T	George Vukovich	.07	.03	.01
☐ 123T	Rick Waits	.07	.03	.01
☐ 124T	Greg Walker	.70	.28	.07
☐ 125T	Chris Welsh	.07	.03	.01
☐ 126T	Len Whitehouse	.07	.03	.01
☐ 127T	Eddie Whitson	.07	.03	.01
☐ 128T	Jim Wohlford	.07	.03	.01
☐ 129T	Matt Young	.20	.08	.02
☐ 130T	Joel Youngblood	.07	.03	.01
☐ 131T	Pat Zachry	.07	.03	.01
☐ 132T	Checklist 1T-132T	.07	.01	.00

1983 Topps Glossy 40

The cards in this 40-card set measure 2 1/2" by 3 1/2". The 1983 Topps "Collector's Edition" or "All-Star Set" (popularly known as "Glossies") consists of color ballplayer picture cards with shiny, glazed surfaces. The player's name appears in small print outside the frame line at bottom left. The backs contain no biography or record and list only the set titles, the player's name, team, position, and the card number.

		MINT	EXC	G-VG
COMPLETE SET (40)		12.00	5.00	1.20
COMMON PLAYER (1-40)		.15	.06	.01
☐ 1	Carl Yastrzemski	1.00	.40	.10
☐ 2	Mookie Wilson	.15	.06	.01
☐ 3	Andre Thornton	.15	.06	.01
☐ 4	Keith Hernandez	.40	.16	.04
☐ 5	Robin Yount	.50	.20	.05
☐ 6	Terry Kennedy	.15	.06	.01
☐ 7	Dave Winfield	.50	.20	.05
☐ 8	Mike Schmidt	1.00	.40	.10
☐ 9	Buddy Bell	.20	.08	.02
☐ 10	Fernando Valenzuela	.40	.16	.04
☐ 11	Rich Gossage	.20	.08	.02
☐ 12	Bob Horner	.25	.10	.02
☐ 13	Toby Harrah	.15	.06	.01
☐ 14	Pete Rose	1.25	.50	.12
☐ 15	Cecil Cooper	.20	.08	.02
☐ 16	Dale Murphy	1.00	.40	.10
☐ 17	Carlton Fisk	.25	.10	.02
☐ 18	Ray Knight	.15	.06	.01
☐ 19	Jim Palmer	.45	.18	.04
☐ 20	Gary Carter	.55	.22	.05
☐ 21	Richie Zisk	.15	.06	.01
☐ 22	Dusty Baker	.15	.06	.01
☐ 23	Willie Wilson	.20	.08	.02
☐ 24	Bill Buckner	.15	.06	.01
☐ 25	Dave Stieb	.20	.08	.02
☐ 26	Bill Madlock	.15	.06	.01
☐ 27	Lance Parrish	.25	.10	.02
☐ 28	Nolan Ryan	.65	.26	.06
☐ 29	Rod Carew	.60	.24	.06
☐ 30	Al Oliver	.25	.10	.02
☐ 31	George Brett	1.00	.40	.10
☐ 32	Jack Clark	.35	.14	.03
☐ 33	Ricky Henderson	1.00	.40	.10
☐ 34	Dave Concepcion	.15	.06	.01
☐ 35	Kent Hrbek	.45	.18	.04
☐ 36	Steve Carlton	.60	.24	.06
☐ 37	Eddie Murray	.90	.36	.09
☐ 38	Ruppert Jones	.15	.06	.01
☐ 39	Reggie Jackson	1.00	.40	.10
☐ 40	Bruce Sutter	.20	.08	.02

1984 Topps

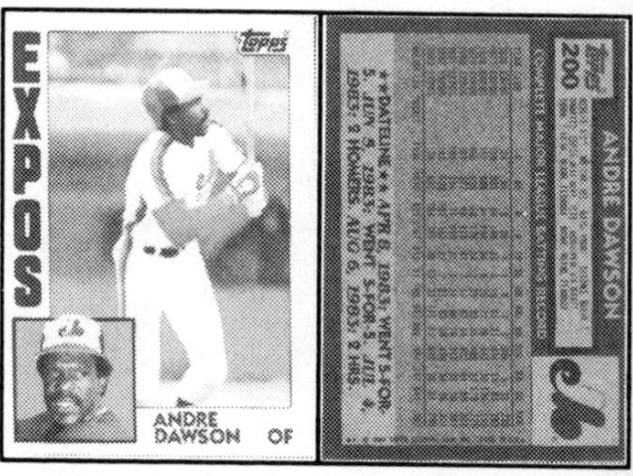

The cards in this 792-card set measure 2 1/2" by 3 1/2". For the second year in a row, Topps utilized a dual picture on the front of the card. A portrait is shown in a square insert and an action shot is featured in the main photo. Card numbers 1-6 feature 1983 Highlights (HL), cards 131-138 depict League Leaders, card numbers 386-407 feature All-Stars and card numbers 701-718 feature active Major League career leaders in various statistical categories. Each team leader (TL) card features the team's leading hitter and pitcher pictured on the front with a team checklist back. There are six numerical checklist cards in the set. The player cards feature team logos in the upper right corner of the reverse. Topps also produced a specially boxed "glossy" edition frequently referred to as the Topps Tiffany set. There were supposedly only 10,000 sets of the Tiffany cards produced; they were marketed to hobby dealers. The checklist of cards (792 regular and 132 Traded) is identical to that of the normal non-glossy cards. There are two primary distinguishing features of the Tiffany cards, white card stock reverses and high gloss obverses. These Tiffany cards are valued at approximately six times the values listed below.

	MINT	EXC	G-VG
COMPLETE SET (792)	100.00	40.00	10.00
COMMON PLAYER (1-792)	.05	.02	.00
□ 1 HL: Steve Carlton	.30	.10	.02
300th win and			
all-time SO king			
□ 2 HL: Rickey Henderson	.25	.10	.02
100 stolen bases,			
three times			
□ 3 HL: Dan Quisenberry	.10	.04	.01
Sets save record			
□ 4 HL: Nolan Ryan,	.25	.10	.02
Steve Carlton, and			
Gaylord Perry			
(All surpass Johnson)			
□ 5 HL: Dave Righetti,	.10	.04	.01
Bob Forsch,			
and Mike Warren			
(All pitch no-hitters)			
□ 6 HL: Johnny Bench	.30	.12	.03
Gaylord Perry, and			
Carl Yastrzemski			
(Superstars retire)			
□ 7 Gary Lucas	.05	.02	.00
□ 8 Don Mattingly	27.00	11.00	2.70
□ 9 Jim Gott	.10	.04	.01
□ 10 Robin Yount	.40	.16	.04
□ 11 Minnesota Twins TL	.10	.03	.01
Kent Hrbek			
Ken Schrom			
□ 12 Billy Sample	.05	.02	.00
□ 13 Scott Holman	.05	.02	.00
□ 14 Tom Brookens	.05	.02	.00
□ 15 Burt Hooton	.05	.02	.00
□ 16 Omar Moreno	.05	.02	.00
□ 17 John Denny	.08	.03	.01
□ 18 Dale Berra	.05	.02	.00
□ 19 Ray Fontenot	.08	.03	.01
□ 20 Greg Luzinski	.10	.04	.01
□ 21 Joe Altobelli MG	.05	.02	.00
□ 22 Bryan Clark	.05	.02	.00
□ 23 Keith Moreland	.05	.02	.00
□ 24 John Martin	.05	.02	.00
□ 25 Glenn Hubbard	.05	.02	.00
□ 26 Bud Black	.05	.02	.00
□ 27 Daryl Sconiers	.05	.02	.00
□ 28 Frank Viola	.80	.32	.08
□ 29 Danny Heep	.05	.02	.00
□ 30 Wade Boggs	7.00	2.80	.70
□ 31 Andy McGaffigan	.05	.02	.00
□ 32 Bobby Ramos	.05	.02	.00
□ 33 Tom Burgmeier	.05	.02	.00
□ 34 Eddie Milner	.05	.02	.00
□ 35 Don Sutton	.30	.12	.03
□ 36 Denny Walling	.05	.02	.00
□ 37 Texas Rangers TL	.10	.03	.01
Buddy Bell			
Rick Honeycutt			
□ 38 Luis DeLeon	.05	.02	.00
□ 39 Garth Iorg	.05	.02	.00
□ 40 Dusty Baker	.08	.03	.01
□ 41 Tony Bernazard	.05	.02	.00
□ 42 Johnny Grubb	.05	.02	.00
□ 43 Ron Reed	.05	.02	.00
□ 44 Jim Morrison	.05	.02	.00
□ 45 Jerry Mumphrey	.05	.02	.00
□ 46 Ray Smith	.05	.02	.00
□ 47 Rudy Law	.05	.02	.00
□ 48 Julio Franco	.45	.18	.04
□ 49 John Stuper	.05	.02	.00
□ 50 Chris Chambliss	.10	.04	.01
□ 51 Jim Frey MG	.05	.02	.00
□ 52 Paul Splittorff	.05	.02	.00
□ 53 Juan Beniquez	.05	.02	.00
□ 54 Jesse Orosco	.05	.02	.00
□ 55 Dave Concepcion	.10	.04	.01
□ 56 Gary Allenson	.05	.02	.00
□ 57 Dan Schatzeder	.05	.02	.00
□ 58 Max Venable	.05	.02	.00
□ 59 Sammy Stewart	.05	.02	.00
□ 60 Paul Molitor	.15	.06	.01
□ 61 Chris Codiroli	.08	.03	.01
□ 62 Dave Hostetler	.05	.02	.00
□ 63 Ed VandeBerg	.05	.02	.00
□ 64 Mike Scioscia	.08	.03	.01
□ 65 Kirk Gibson	.35	.14	.03
□ 66 Houston Astros TL	.15	.04	.01
Jose Cruz			
Nolan Ryan			
□ 67 Gary Ward	.08	.03	.01
□ 68 Luis Salazar	.08	.03	.01
□ 69 Rod Scurry	.05	.02	.00
□ 70 Gary Matthews	.08	.03	.01
□ 71 Leo Hernandez	.08	.03	.01
□ 72 Mike Squires	.05	.02	.00
□ 73 Jody Davis	.08	.03	.01
□ 74 Jerry Martin	.05	.02	.00
□ 75 Bob Forsch	.05	.02	.00
□ 76 Alfredo Griffin	.08	.03	.01
□ 77 Brett Butler	.10	.04	.01
□ 78 Mike Torrez	.05	.02	.00
□ 79 Rob Wilfong	.05	.02	.00
□ 80 Steve Rogers	.05	.02	.00
□ 81 Billy Martin MG	.10	.04	.01
□ 82 Doug Bird	.05	.02	.00
□ 83 Richie Zisk	.05	.02	.00
□ 84 Lenny Faedo	.05	.02	.00
□ 85 Atlee Hammaker	.05	.02	.00
□ 86 John Shelby	.35	.14	.03
□ 87 Frank Pastore	.05	.02	.00
□ 88 Rob Picciolo	.05	.02	.00
□ 89 Mike Smithson	.08	.03	.01
□ 90 Pedro Guerrero	.35	.14	.03
□ 91 Dan Spillner	.05	.02	.00
□ 92 Lloyd Moseby	.15	.06	.01
□ 93 Bob Knepper	.10	.04	.01
□ 94 Mario Ramirez	.05	.02	.00
□ 95 Aurelio Lopez	.05	.02	.00
□ 96 K.C. Royals TL	.10	.03	.01
Hal McRae			
Larry Gura			
□ 97 LaMarr Hoyt	.08	.03	.01
□ 98 Steve Nicosia	.05	.02	.00
□ 99 Craig Lefferts	.15	.06	.01
□ 100 Reggie Jackson	.60	.24	.06
□ 101 Porfirio Altamirano	.05	.02	.00
□ 102 Ken Oberkfell	.05	.02	.00
□ 103 Dwayne Murphy	.05	.02	.00
□ 104 Ken Dayley	.05	.02	.00
□ 105 Tony Armas	.08	.03	.01
□ 106 Tim Stoddard	.05	.02	.00
□ 107 Ned Yost	.05	.02	.00
□ 108 Randy Moffitt	.05	.02	.00
□ 109 Brad Wellman	.05	.02	.00
□ 110 Ron Guidry	.20	.08	.02
□ 111 Bill Virdon MG	.05	.02	.00
□ 112 Tom Niedenfuer	.08	.03	.01
□ 113 Kelly Paris	.08	.03	.01
□ 114 Checklist 1-132	.08	.01	.00
□ 115 Andre Thornton	.08	.03	.01
□ 116 George Bjorkman	.05	.02	.00
□ 117 Tom Veryzer	.05	.02	.00
□ 118 Charlie Hough	.08	.03	.01
□ 119 Johnny Wockenfuss	.05	.02	.00
□ 120 Keith Hernandez	.35	.14	.03
□ 121 Pat Sheridan	.20	.08	.02
□ 122 Cecilio Guante	.08	.03	.01
□ 123 Butch Wynegar	.05	.02	.00
□ 124 Damaso Garcia	.05	.02	.00
□ 125 Britt Burns	.05	.02	.00
□ 126 Atlanta Braves TL	.15	.04	.01
Dale Murphy			
Craig McMurtry			
□ 127 Mike Madden	.05	.02	.00
□ 128 Rick Manning	.05	.02	.00
□ 129 Bill Laskey	.05	.02	.00
□ 130 Ozzie Smith	.30	.12	.03
□ 131 Batting Leaders	.25	.10	.02
Bill Madlock			
Wade Boggs			
□ 132 Home Run Leaders	.25	.10	.02
Mike Schmidt			
Jim Rice			
□ 133 RBI Leaders	.20	.08	.02
Dale Murphy			
Cecil Cooper			
Jim Rice			
□ 134 Stolen Base Leaders	.25	.10	.02
Tim Raines			
Rickey Henderson			
□ 135 Victory Leaders	.08	.03	.01
John Denny			
LaMarr Hoyt			
□ 136 Strikeout Leaders	.15	.06	.01
Steve Carlton			
Jack Morris			
□ 137 ERA Leaders	.08	.03	.01
Atlee Hammaker			
Rick Honeycutt			
□ 138 Leading Firemen	.08	.03	.01
Al Holland			
Dan Quisenberry			
□ 139 Bert Campaneris	.08	.03	.01
□ 140 Storm Davis	.10	.04	.01
□ 141 Pat Corrales MG	.05	.02	.00
□ 142 Rich Gale	.05	.02	.00
□ 143 Jose Morales	.05	.02	.00
□ 144 Brian Harper	.08	.03	.01
□ 145 Gary Lavelle	.05	.02	.00
□ 146 Ed Romero	.05	.02	.00

□ 147	Dan Petry	.08	.03	.01
□ 148	Joe Lefebvre	.05	.02	.00
□ 149	Jon Matlack	.05	.02	.00
□ 150	Dale Murphy	1.00	.40	.10
□ 151	Steve Trout	.05	.02	.00
□ 152	Glenn Brummer	.05	.02	.00
□ 153	Dick Tidrow	.05	.02	.00
□ 154	Dave Henderson	.15	.06	.01
□ 155	Frank White	.10	.04	.01
□ 156	Oakland A's TL	.12	.04	.01
	Rickey Henderson			
	Tim Conroy			
□ 157	Gary Gaetti	.65	.26	.06
□ 158	John Curtis	.05	.02	.00
□ 159	Darryl Cias	.05	.02	.00
□ 160	Mario Soto	.05	.02	.00
□ 161	Junior Ortiz	.05	.02	.00
□ 162	Bob Ojeda	.10	.04	.01
□ 163	Lorenzo Gray	.05	.02	.00
□ 164	Scott Sanderson	.05	.02	.00
□ 165	Ken Singleton	.10	.04	.01
□ 166	Jamie Nelson	.05	.02	.00
□ 167	Marshall Edwards	.05	.02	.00
□ 168	Juan Bonilla	.05	.02	.00
□ 169	Larry Parrish	.08	.03	.01
□ 170	Jerry Reuss	.08	.03	.01
□ 171	Frank Robinson MG	.10	.04	.01
□ 172	Frank DiPino	.05	.02	.00
□ 173	Marvell Wynne	.10	.04	.01
□ 174	Juan Berenguer	.05	.02	.00
□ 175	Graig Nettles	.15	.06	.01
□ 176	Lee Smith	.10	.04	.01
□ 177	Jerry Hairston	.05	.02	.00
□ 178	Bill Krueger	.05	.02	.00
□ 179	Buck Martinez	.05	.02	.00
□ 180	Manny Trillo	.05	.02	.00
□ 181	Roy Thomas	.05	.02	.00
□ 182	Darryl Strawberry	12.00	5.00	1.20
□ 183	Al Williams	.05	.02	.00
□ 184	Mike O'Berry	.05	.02	.00
□ 185	Sixto Lezcano	.05	.02	.00
□ 186	Cardinal TL	.10	.03	.01
	Lonnie Smith			
	John Stuper			
□ 187	Luis Aponte	.05	.02	.00
□ 188	Bryan Little	.05	.02	.00
□ 189	Tim Conroy	.08	.03	.01
□ 190	Ben Oglivie	.08	.03	.01
□ 191	Mike Boddicker	.10	.04	.01
□ 192	Nick Esasky	.35	.14	.03
□ 193	Darrell Brown	.05	.02	.00
□ 194	Domingo Ramos	.05	.02	.00
□ 195	Jack Morris	.20	.08	.02
□ 196	Don Slaught	.15	.06	.01
□ 197	Garry Hancock	.05	.02	.00
□ 198	Bill Doran	.70	.28	.07
□ 199	Willie Hernandez	.20	.08	.02
□ 200	Andre Dawson	.40	.16	.04
□ 201	Bruce Kison	.05	.02	.00
□ 202	Bobby Cox MG	.05	.02	.00
□ 203	Matt Keough	.05	.02	.00
□ 204	Bobby Meacham	.10	.04	.01
□ 205	Greg Minton	.05	.02	.00
□ 206	Andy Van Slyke	2.50	1.00	.25
□ 207	Donnie Moore	.05	.02	.00
□ 208	Jose Oquendo	.35	.14	.03
□ 209	Manny Sarmiento	.05	.02	.00
□ 210	Joe Morgan	.25	.10	.02
□ 211	Rick Sweet	.05	.02	.00
□ 212	Broderick Perkins	.05	.02	.00
□ 213	Bruce Hurst	.15	.06	.01
□ 214	Paul Householder	.05	.02	.00
□ 215	Tippy Martinez	.05	.02	.00
□ 216	White Sox TL	.10	.03	.01
	Carlton Fisk			
	Richard Dotson			
□ 217	Alan Ashby	.05	.02	.00
□ 218	Rick Waits	.05	.02	.00
□ 219	Joe Simpson	.05	.02	.00
□ 220	Fernando Valenzuela	.30	.12	.03
□ 221	Cliff Johnson	.05	.02	.00
□ 222	Rick Honeycutt	.05	.02	.00
□ 223	Wayne Krenchicki	.05	.02	.00
□ 224	Sid Monge	.05	.02	.00
□ 225	Lee Mazzilli	.05	.02	.00
□ 226	Juan Eichelberger	.05	.02	.00
□ 227	Steve Braun	.05	.02	.00
□ 228	John Rabb	.05	.02	.00
□ 229	Paul Owens MG	.05	.02	.00
□ 230	Rickey Henderson	.60	.24	.06
□ 231	Gary Woods	.05	.02	.00
□ 232	Tim Wallach	.15	.06	.01
□ 233	Checklist 133-264	.08	.01	.00
□ 234	Rafael Ramirez	.05	.02	.00
□ 235	Matt Young	.10	.04	.01
□ 236	Ellis Valentine	.05	.02	.00
□ 237	John Castino	.05	.02	.00
□ 238	Reid Nichols	.05	.02	.00
□ 239	Jay Howell	.10	.04	.01
□ 240	Eddie Murray	.55	.22	.05
□ 241	Billy Almon	.05	.02	.00
□ 242	Alex Trevino	.05	.02	.00
□ 243	Pete Ladd	.05	.02	.00
□ 244	Candy Maldonado	.30	.12	.03
□ 245	Rick Sutcliffe	.25	.10	.02
□ 246	New York Mets TL	.12	.04	.01
	Mookie Wilson			
	Tom Seaver			
□ 247	Onix Concepcion	.05	.02	.00
□ 248	Bill Dawley	.10	.04	.01
□ 249	Jay Johnstone	.08	.03	.01
□ 250	Bill Madlock	.10	.04	.01
□ 251	Tony Gwynn	2.50	1.00	.25
□ 252	Larry Christenson	.05	.02	.00
□ 253	Jim Wohlford	.05	.02	.00
□ 254	Shane Rawley	.10	.04	.01
□ 255	Bruce Benedict	.05	.02	.00
□ 256	Dave Geisel	.05	.02	.00
□ 257	Julio Cruz	.05	.02	.00
□ 258	Luis Sanchez	.05	.02	.00
□ 259	Sparky Anderson MG	.05	.02	.00
□ 260	Scott McGregor	.08	.03	.01
□ 261	Bobby Brown	.05	.02	.00
□ 262	Tom Candiotti	.20	.08	.02
□ 263	Jack Fimple	.05	.02	.00
□ 264	Doug Frobel	.05	.02	.00
□ 265	Donnie Hill	.10	.04	.01
□ 266	Steve Lubratich	.05	.02	.00
□ 267	Carmelo Martinez	.25	.10	.02
□ 268	Jack O'Connor	.05	.02	.00
□ 269	Aurelio Rodriguez	.05	.02	.00
□ 270	Jeff Russell	.25	.10	.02
□ 271	Moose Haas	.05	.02	.00
□ 272	Rick Dempsey	.05	.02	.00
□ 273	Charlie Puleo	.05	.02	.00
□ 274	Rick Monday	.08	.03	.01
□ 275	Len Matuszek	.05	.02	.00
□ 276	Angels TL	.12	.04	.01
	Rod Carew			
	Geoff Zahn			
□ 277	Eddie Whitson	.08	.03	.01
□ 278	Jorge Bell	1.25	.50	.12
□ 279	Ivan DeJesus	.05	.02	.00
□ 280	Floyd Bannister	.05	.02	.00
□ 281	Larry Milbourne	.05	.02	.00
□ 282	Jim Barr	.05	.02	.00
□ 283	Larry Biittner	.05	.02	.00
□ 284	Howard Bailey	.05	.02	.00
□ 285	Darrell Porter	.05	.02	.00
□ 286	Lary Sorensen	.05	.02	.00
□ 287	Warren Cromartie	.05	.02	.00
□ 288	Jim Beattie	.05	.02	.00
□ 289	Randy Johnson	.05	.02	.00
□ 290	Dave Dravecky	.08	.03	.01
□ 291	Chuck Tanner MG	.05	.02	.00
□ 292	Tony Scott	.05	.02	.00
□ 293	Ed Lynch	.05	.02	.00
□ 294	U.L. Washington	.05	.02	.00
□ 295	Mike Flanagan	.08	.03	.01
□ 296	Jeff Newman	.05	.02	.00
□ 297	Bruce Berenyi	.05	.02	.00
□ 298	Jim Gantner	.05	.02	.00
□ 299	John Butcher	.05	.02	.00
□ 300	Pete Rose	1.50	.60	.15
□ 301	Frank LaCorte	.05	.02	.00
□ 302	Barry Bonnell	.05	.02	.00
□ 303	Marty Castillo	.05	.02	.00
□ 304	Warren Brusstar	.05	.02	.00
□ 305	Roy Smalley	.05	.02	.00
□ 306	Dodgers TL	.10	.03	.01
	Pedro Guerrero			
	Bob Welch			
□ 307	Bobby Mitchell	.05	.02	.00
□ 308	Ron Hassey	.08	.03	.01
□ 309	Tony Phillips	.08	.03	.01
□ 310	Willie McGee	.35	.14	.03
□ 311	Jerry Koosman	.10	.04	.01
□ 312	Jorge Orta	.05	.02	.00
□ 313	Mike Jorgensen	.05	.02	.00
□ 314	Orlando Mercado	.05	.02	.00
□ 315	Bob Grich	.08	.03	.01
□ 316	Mark Bradley	.05	.02	.00
□ 317	Greg Pryor	.05	.02	.00
□ 318	Bill Gullickson	.05	.02	.00
□ 319	Al Bumbry	.05	.02	.00
□ 320	Bob Stanley	.05	.02	.00
□ 321	Harvey Kuenn MG	.05	.02	.00
□ 322	Ken Schrom	.05	.02	.00
□ 323	Alan Knicely	.05	.02	.00
□ 324	Alejandro Pena	.35	.14	.03

□ 325 Darrell Evans	.10	.04	.01
□ 326 Bob Kearney	.05	.02	.00
□ 327 Ruppert Jones	.05	.02	.00
□ 328 Vern Ruhle	.05	.02	.00
□ 329 Pat Tabler	.25	.10	.02
□ 330 John Candelaria	.10	.04	.01
□ 331 Bucky Dent	.08	.03	.01
□ 332 Kevin Gross	.35	.14	.03
□ 333 Larry Herndon	.05	.02	.00
□ 334 Chuck Rainey	.05	.02	.00
□ 335 Don Baylor	.12	.05	.01
□ 336 Seattle Mariners TL	.10	.03	.01
Pat Putnam			
Matt Young			
□ 337 Kevin Hagen	.05	.02	.00
□ 338 Mike Warren	.10	.04	.01
□ 339 Roy Lee Jackson	.05	.02	.00
□ 340 Hal McRae	.08	.03	.01
□ 341 Dave Tobik	.05	.02	.00
□ 342 Tim Foli	.05	.02	.00
□ 343 Mark Davis	.08	.03	.01
□ 344 Rick Miller	.05	.02	.00
□ 345 Kent Hrbek	.35	.14	.03
□ 346 Kurt Bevacqua	.05	.02	.00
□ 347 Allan Ramirez	.05	.02	.00
□ 348 Toby Harrah	.05	.02	.00
□ 349 Bob L. Gibson	.08	.03	.01
(Brewers Pitcher)			
□ 350 George Foster	.15	.06	.01
□ 351 Russ Nixon MG	.05	.02	.00
□ 352 Dave Stewart	.15	.06	.01
□ 353 Jim Anderson	.05	.02	.00
□ 354 Jeff Burroughs	.05	.02	.00
□ 355 Jason Thompson	.05	.02	.00
□ 356 Glenn Abbott	.05	.02	.00
□ 357 Ron Cey	.10	.04	.01
□ 358 Bob Dernier	.05	.02	.00
□ 359 Jim Acker	.08	.03	.01
□ 360 Willie Randolph	.10	.04	.01
□ 361 Dave Smith	.08	.03	.01
□ 362 David Green	.05	.02	.00
□ 363 Tim Laudner	.08	.03	.01
□ 364 Scott Fletcher	.20	.08	.02
□ 365 Steve Bedrosian	.15	.06	.01
□ 366 Padres TL	.10	.03	.01
Terry Kennedy			
Dave Dravecky			
□ 367 Jamie Easterly	.05	.02	.00
□ 368 Hubie Brooks	.10	.04	.01
□ 369 Steve McCatty	.05	.02	.00
□ 370 Tim Raines	.50	.20	.05
□ 371 Dave Gumpert	.05	.02	.00
□ 372 Gary Roenicke	.05	.02	.00
□ 373 Bill Scherrer	.05	.02	.00
□ 374 Don Money	.05	.02	.00
□ 375 Dennis Leonard	.08	.03	.01
□ 376 Dave Anderson	.15	.06	.01
□ 377 Danny Darwin	.05	.02	.00
□ 378 Bob Brenly	.05	.02	.00
□ 379 Checklist 265-396	.08	.01	.00
□ 380 Steve Garvey	.50	.20	.05
□ 381 Ralph Houk MG	.05	.02	.00
□ 382 Chris Nyman	.05	.02	.00
□ 383 Terry Puhl	.05	.02	.00
□ 384 Lee Tunnell	.10	.04	.01
□ 385 Tony Perez	.15	.06	.01
□ 386 George Hendrick AS	.08	.03	.01
□ 387 Johnny Ray AS	.08	.03	.01
□ 388 Mike Schmidt AS	.30	.12	.03
□ 389 Ozzie Smith AS	.15	.06	.01
□ 390 Tim Raines AS	.15	.06	.01
□ 391 Dale Murphy AS	.35	.14	.03
□ 392 Andre Dawson AS	.15	.06	.01
□ 393 Gary Carter AS	.20	.08	.02
□ 394 Steve Rogers AS	.08	.03	.01
□ 395 Steve Carlton AS	.20	.08	.02
□ 396 Jesse Orosco AS	.08	.03	.01
□ 397 Eddie Murray AS	.15	.06	.01
□ 398 Lou Whitaker AS	.10	.04	.01
□ 399 George Brett AS	.30	.12	.03
□ 400 Cal Ripken AS	.20	.08	.02
□ 401 Jim Rice AS	.15	.06	.01
□ 402 Dave Winfield AS	.15	.06	.01
□ 403 Lloyd Moseby AS	.08	.03	.01
□ 404 Ted Simmons AS	.08	.03	.01
□ 405 LaMarr Hoyt AS	.08	.03	.01
□ 406 Ron Guidry AS	.10	.04	.01
□ 407 Dan Quisenberry AS	.08	.03	.01
□ 408 Lou Piniella	.08	.03	.01
□ 409 Juan Agosto	.15	.06	.01
□ 410 Claudell Washington	.08	.03	.01
□ 411 Houston Jimenez	.08	.03	.01
□ 412 Doug Rader MG	.05	.02	.00
□ 413 Spike Owen	.20	.08	.02
□ 414 Mitchell Page	.05	.02	.00
□ 415 Tommy John	.15	.06	.01
□ 416 Dane Iorg	.05	.02	.00
□ 417 Mike Armstrong	.05	.02	.00
□ 418 Ron Hodges	.05	.02	.00
□ 419 John Henry Johnson	.05	.02	.00
□ 420 Cecil Cooper	.12	.05	.01
□ 421 Charlie Lea	.05	.02	.00
□ 422 Jose Cruz	.10	.04	.01
□ 423 Mike Morgan	.05	.02	.00
□ 424 Dann Bilardello	.05	.02	.00
□ 425 Steve Howe	.05	.02	.00
□ 426 Orioles TL	.15	.04	.01
Cal Ripken			
Mike Boddicker			
□ 427 Rick Leach	.05	.02	.00
□ 428 Fred Breining	.05	.02	.00
□ 429 Randy Bush	.20	.08	.02
□ 430 Rusty Staub	.10	.04	.01
□ 431 Chris Bando	.05	.02	.00
□ 432 Charlie Hudson	.20	.08	.02
□ 433 Rich Hebner	.05	.02	.00
□ 434 Harold Baines	.20	.08	.02
□ 435 Neil Allen	.05	.02	.00
□ 436 Rick Peters	.05	.02	.00
□ 437 Mike Proly	.05	.02	.00
□ 438 Biff Pocoroba	.05	.02	.00
□ 439 Bob Stoddard	.05	.02	.00
□ 440 Steve Kemp	.08	.03	.01
□ 441 Bob Lillis MG	.05	.02	.00
□ 442 Byron McLaughlin	.05	.02	.00
□ 443 Benny Ayala	.05	.02	.00
□ 444 Steve Renko	.05	.02	.00
□ 445 Jerry Remy	.05	.02	.00
□ 446 Luis Pujols	.05	.02	.00
□ 447 Tom Brunansky	.25	.10	.02
□ 448 Ben Hayes	.05	.02	.00
□ 449 Joe Pettini	.05	.02	.00
□ 450 Gary Carter	.40	.16	.04
□ 451 Bob Jones	.05	.02	.00
□ 452 Chuck Porter	.05	.02	.00
□ 453 Willie Upshaw	.05	.02	.00
□ 454 Joe Beckwith	.05	.02	.00
□ 455 Terry Kennedy	.05	.02	.00
□ 456 Chicago Cubs TL	.10	.03	.01
Keith Moreland			
Fergie Jenkins			
□ 457 Dave Rozema	.05	.02	.00
□ 458 Kiko Garcia	.05	.02	.00
□ 459 Kevin Hickey	.05	.02	.00
□ 460 Dave Winfield	.45	.18	.04
□ 461 Jim Maler	.05	.02	.00
□ 462 Lee Lacy	.05	.02	.00
□ 463 Dave Engle	.05	.02	.00
□ 464 Jeff A. Jones	.05	.02	.00
(A's Pitcher)			
□ 465 Mookie Wilson	.08	.03	.01
□ 466 Gene Garber	.05	.02	.00
□ 467 Mike Ramsey	.05	.02	.00
□ 468 Geoff Zahn	.05	.02	.00
□ 469 Tom O'Malley	.05	.02	.00
□ 470 Nolan Ryan	.45	.18	.04
□ 471 Dick Howser MG	.08	.03	.01
□ 472 Mike Brown	.08	.03	.01
(Red Sox Pitcher)			
□ 473 Jim Dwyer	.05	.02	.00
□ 474 Greg Bargar	.05	.02	.00
□ 475 Gary Redus	.25	.10	.02
□ 476 Tom Tellmann	.05	.02	.00
□ 477 Rafael Landestoy	.05	.02	.00
□ 478 Alan Bannister	.05	.02	.00
□ 479 Frank Tanana	.08	.03	.01
□ 480 Ron Kittle	.25	.10	.02
□ 481 Mark Thurmond	.10	.04	.01
□ 482 Enos Cabell	.05	.02	.00
□ 483 Fergie Jenkins	.15	.06	.01
□ 484 Ozzie Virgil	.05	.02	.00
□ 485 Rick Rhoden	.10	.04	.01
□ 486 N.Y. Yankees TL	.10	.03	.01
Don Baylor			
Ron Guidry			
□ 487 Ricky Adams	.05	.02	.00
□ 488 Jesse Barfield	.30	.12	.03
□ 489 Dave Von Ohlen	.05	.02	.00
□ 490 Cal Ripken	.75	.30	.07
□ 491 Bobby Castillo	.05	.02	.00
□ 492 Tucker Ashford	.05	.02	.00
□ 493 Mike Norris	.05	.02	.00
□ 494 Chili Davis	.15	.06	.01
□ 495 Rollie Fingers	.20	.08	.02
□ 496 Terry Francona	.05	.02	.00
□ 497 Bud Anderson	.05	.02	.00
□ 498 Rich Gedman	.10	.04	.01
□ 499 Mike Witt	.12	.05	.01
□ 500 George Brett	.75	.30	.07
□ 501 Steve Henderson	.05	.02	.00

□ 502	Joe Torre MG	.08	.03	.01
□ 503	Elias Sosa	.05	.02	.00
□ 504	Mickey Rivers	.08	.03	.01
□ 505	Pete Vuckovich	.08	.03	.01
□ 506	Ernie Whitt	.05	.02	.00
□ 507	Mike LaCoss	.05	.02	.00
□ 508	Mel Hall	.25	.10	.02
□ 509	Brad Havens	.05	.02	.00
□ 510	Alan Trammell	.35	.14	.03
□ 511	Marty Bystrom	.05	.02	.00
□ 512	Oscar Gamble	.05	.02	.00
□ 513	Dave Beard	.05	.02	.00
□ 514	Floyd Rayford	.05	.02	.00
□ 515	Gorman Thomas	.10	.04	.01
□ 516	Montreal Expos TL Al Oliver Charlie Lea	.10	.03	.01
□ 517	John Moses	.08	.03	.01
□ 518	Greg Walker	.45	.18	.04
□ 519	Ron Davis	.05	.02	.00
□ 520	Bob Boone	.10	.04	.01
□ 521	Pete Falcone	.05	.02	.00
□ 522	Dave Bergman	.05	.02	.00
□ 523	Glenn Hoffman	.05	.02	.00
□ 524	Carlos Diaz	.05	.02	.00
□ 525	Willie Wilson	.12	.05	.01
□ 526	Ron Oester	.05	.02	.00
□ 527	Checklist 397-528	.08	.01	.00
□ 528	Mark Brouhard	.05	.02	.00
□ 529	Keith Atherton	.05	.02	.00
□ 530	Dan Ford	.05	.02	.00
□ 531	Steve Boros MG	.05	.02	.00
□ 532	Eric Show	.08	.03	.01
□ 533	Ken Landreaux	.05	.02	.00
□ 534	Pete O'Brien	1.00	.40	.10
□ 535	Bo Diaz	.05	.02	.00
□ 536	Doug Bair	.05	.02	.00
□ 537	Johnny Ray	.12	.05	.01
□ 538	Kevin Bass	.10	.04	.01
□ 539	George Frazier	.05	.02	.00
□ 540	George Hendrick	.08	.03	.01
□ 541	Dennis Lamp	.05	.02	.00
□ 542	Duane Kuiper	.05	.02	.00
□ 543	Craig McMurtry	.08	.03	.01
□ 544	Cesar Geronimo	.05	.02	.00
□ 545	Bill Buckner	.10	.04	.01
□ 546	Indians TL Mike Hargrove Lary Sorensen	.10	.03	.01
□ 547	Mike Moore	.10	.04	.01
□ 548	Ron Jackson	.05	.02	.00
□ 549	Walt Terrell	.35	.14	.03
□ 550	Jim Rice	.30	.12	.03
□ 551	Scott Ullger	.05	.02	.00
□ 552	Ray Burris	.05	.02	.00
□ 553	Joe Nolan	.05	.02	.00
□ 554	Ted Power	.05	.02	.00
□ 555	Greg Brock	.12	.05	.01
□ 556	Joey McLaughlin	.05	.02	.00
□ 557	Wayne Tolleson	.10	.04	.01
□ 558	Mike Davis	.08	.03	.01
□ 559	Mike Scott	.25	.10	.02
□ 560	Carlton Fisk	.15	.06	.01
□ 561	Whitey Herzog MG	.05	.02	.00
□ 562	Manny Castillo	.05	.02	.00
□ 563	Glenn Wilson	.08	.03	.01
□ 564	Al Holland	.05	.02	.00
□ 565	Leon Durham	.08	.03	.01
□ 566	Jim Bibby	.05	.02	.00
□ 567	Mike Heath	.05	.02	.00
□ 568	Pete Filson	.05	.02	.00
□ 569	Bake McBride	.05	.02	.00
□ 570	Dan Quisenberry	.12	.05	.01
□ 571	Bruce Bochy	.05	.02	.00
□ 572	Jerry Royster	.05	.02	.00
□ 573	Dave Kingman	.15	.06	.01
□ 574	Brian Downing	.08	.03	.01
□ 575	Jim Clancy	.08	.03	.01
□ 576	Giants TL Jeff Leonard Atlee Hammaker	.10	.03	.01
□ 577	Mark Clear	.05	.02	.00
□ 578	Lenn Sakata	.05	.02	.00
□ 579	Bob James	.20	.08	.02
□ 580	Lonnie Smith	.08	.03	.01
□ 581	Jose DeLeon	.25	.10	.02
□ 582	Bob McClure	.05	.02	.00
□ 583	Derrel Thomas	.05	.02	.00
□ 584	Dave Schmidt	.08	.03	.01
□ 585	Dan Driessen	.05	.02	.00
□ 586	Joe Niekro	.10	.04	.01
□ 587	Von Hayes	.18	.08	.01
□ 588	Milt Wilcox	.05	.02	.00
□ 589	Mike Easler	.05	.02	.00
□ 590	Dave Stieb	.15	.06	.01
□ 591	Tony LaRussa MG	.05	.02	.00
□ 592	Andre Robertson	.05	.02	.00
□ 593	Jeff Lahti	.05	.02	.00
□ 594	Gene Richards	.05	.02	.00
□ 595	Jeff Reardon	.10	.04	.01
□ 596	Ryne Sandberg	1.00	.40	.10
□ 597	Rick Camp	.05	.02	.00
□ 598	Rusty Kuntz	.05	.02	.00
□ 599	Doug Sisk	.08	.03	.01
□ 600	Rod Carew	.45	.18	.04
□ 601	John Tudor	.15	.06	.01
□ 602	John Wathan	.05	.02	.00
□ 603	Renie Martin	.05	.02	.00
□ 604	John Lowenstein	.05	.02	.00
□ 605	Mike Caldwell	.05	.02	.00
□ 606	Blue Jays TL Lloyd Moseby Dave Stieb	.10	.03	.01
□ 607	Tom Hume	.05	.02	.00
□ 608	Bobby Johnson	.05	.02	.00
□ 609	Dan Meyer	.05	.02	.00
□ 610	Steve Sax	.25	.10	.02
□ 611	Chet Lemon	.08	.03	.01
□ 612	Harry Spilman	.05	.02	.00
□ 613	Greg Gross	.05	.02	.00
□ 614	Len Barker	.05	.02	.00
□ 615	Garry Templeton	.08	.03	.01
□ 616	Don Robinson	.05	.02	.00
□ 617	Rick Cerone	.05	.02	.00
□ 618	Dickie Noles	.05	.02	.00
□ 619	Jerry Dybzinski	.05	.02	.00
□ 620	Al Oliver	.10	.04	.01
□ 621	Frank Howard MG	.05	.02	.00
□ 622	Al Cowens	.05	.02	.00
□ 623	Ron Washington	.05	.02	.00
□ 624	Terry Harper	.05	.02	.00
□ 625	Larry Gura	.05	.02	.00
□ 626	Bob Clark	.05	.02	.00
□ 627	Dave LaPoint	.08	.03	.01
□ 628	Ed Jurak	.05	.02	.00
□ 629	Rick Langford	.05	.02	.00
□ 630	Ted Simmons	.12	.05	.01
□ 631	Denny Martinez	.08	.03	.01
□ 632	Tom Foley	.05	.02	.00
□ 633	Mike Krukow	.08	.03	.01
□ 634	Mike Marshall	.15	.06	.01
□ 635	Dave Righetti	.18	.08	.01
□ 636	Pat Putnam	.05	.02	.00
□ 637	Phillies TL Gary Matthews John Denny	.10	.03	.01
□ 638	George Vukovich	.05	.02	.00
□ 639	Rick Lysander	.05	.02	.00
□ 640	Lance Parrish	.25	.10	.02
□ 641	Mike Richardt	.05	.02	.00
□ 642	Tom Underwood	.05	.02	.00
□ 643	Mike Brown (Angels OF)	.08	.03	.01
□ 644	Tim Lollar	.05	.02	.00
□ 645	Tony Pena	.12	.05	.01
□ 646	Checklist 529-660	.08	.01	.00
□ 647	Ron Roenicke	.05	.02	.00
□ 648	Len Whitehouse	.05	.02	.00
□ 649	Tom Herr	.08	.03	.01
□ 650	Phil Niekro	.20	.08	.02
□ 651	John McNamara MG	.05	.02	.00
□ 652	Rudy May	.05	.02	.00
□ 653	Dave Stapleton	.05	.02	.00
□ 654	Bob Bailor	.05	.02	.00
□ 655	Amos Otis	.08	.03	.01
□ 656	Bryn Smith	.08	.03	.01
□ 657	Thad Bosley	.05	.02	.00
□ 658	Jerry Augustine	.05	.02	.00
□ 659	Duane Walker	.05	.02	.00
□ 660	Ray Knight	.10	.04	.01
□ 661	Steve Yeager	.05	.02	.00
□ 662	Tom Brennan	.05	.02	.00
□ 663	Johnnie LeMaster	.05	.02	.00
□ 664	Dave Stegman	.05	.02	.00
□ 665	Buddy Bell	.12	.05	.01
□ 666	Detroit Tigers TL Lou Whitaker Jack Morris	.12	.03	.01
□ 667	Vance Law	.08	.03	.01
□ 668	Larry McWilliams	.05	.02	.00
□ 669	Dave Lopes	.08	.03	.01
□ 670	Rich Gossage	.15	.06	.01
□ 671	Jamie Quirk	.05	.02	.00
□ 672	Ricky Nelson	.05	.02	.00
□ 673	Mike Walters	.05	.02	.00
□ 674	Tim Flannery	.05	.02	.00
□ 675	Pascual Perez	.10	.04	.01
□ 676	Brian Giles	.05	.02	.00
□ 677	Doyle Alexander	.08	.03	.01
□ 678	Chris Speier	.05	.02	.00

□ 679 Art Howe .08 .03 .01
□ 680 Fred Lynn .20 .08 .02
□ 681 Tom Lasorda MG .08 .03 .01
□ 682 Dan Morogiello .05 .02 .00
□ 683 Marty Barrett 1.75 .70 .17
□ 684 Bob Shirley .05 .02 .00
□ 685 Willie Aikens .05 .02 .00
□ 686 Joe Price .05 .02 .00
□ 687 Roy Howell .05 .02 .00
□ 688 George Wright .05 .02 .00
□ 689 Mike Fischlin .05 .02 .00
□ 690 Jack Clark .30 .12 .03
□ 691 Steve Lake .05 .02 .00
□ 692 Dickie Thon .05 .02 .00
□ 693 Alan Wiggins .05 .02 .00
□ 694 Mike Stanton .05 .02 .00
□ 695 Lou Whitaker .18 .08 .01
□ 696 Pirates TL .10 .03 .01
Bill Madlock
Rick Rhoden
□ 697 Dale Murray .05 .02 .00
□ 698 Marc Hill .05 .02 .00
□ 699 Dave Rucker .05 .02 .00
□ 700 Mike Schmidt .60 .24 .06
□ 701 NL Active Batting .20 .08 .02
Bill Madlock
Pete Rose
Dave Parker
□ 702 NL Active Hits .20 .08 .02
Pete Rose
Rusty Staub
Tony Perez
□ 703 NL Active Home Run .15 .06 .01
Mike Schmidt
Tony Perez
Dave Kingman
□ 704 NL Active RBI .10 .04 .01
Tony Perez
Rusty Staub
Al Oliver
□ 705 NL Active Steals .10 .04 .01
Joe Morgan
Cesar Cedeno
Larry Bowa
□ 706 NL Active Victory .20 .08 .02
Steve Carlton
Fergie Jenkins
Tom Seaver
□ 707 NL Active Strikeout .20 .08 .02
Steve Carlton
Nolan Ryan
Tom Seaver
□ 708 NL Active ERA .18 .08 .01
Tom Seaver
Steve Carlton
Steve Rogers
□ 709 NL Active Save .10 .04 .01
Bruce Sutter
Tug McGraw
Gene Garber
□ 710 AL Active Batting .20 .08 .02
Rod Carew
George Brett
Cecil Cooper
□ 711 AL Active Hits .18 .08 .01
Rod Carew
Bert Campaneris
Reggie Jackson
□ 712 AL Active Home Run .15 .06 .01
Reggie Jackson
Graig Nettles
Greg Luzinski
□ 713 AL Active RBI .15 .06 .01
Reggie Jackson
Ted Simmons
Graig Nettles
□ 714 AL Active Steals .08 .03 .01
Bert Campaneris
Dave Lopes
Omar Moreno
□ 715 AL Active Victory .18 .08 .01
Jim Palmer
Don Sutton
Tommy John
□ 716 AL Active Strikeout .08 .03 .01
Don Sutton
Bert Blyleven
Jerry Koosman
□ 717 AL Active ERA .15 .06 .01
Jim Palmer
Rollie Fingers
Ron Guidry
□ 718 AL Active Save .12 .05 .01
Rollie Fingers
Rich Gossage
Dan Quisenberry
□ 719 Andy Hassler .05 .02 .00
□ 720 Dwight Evans .15 .06 .01
□ 721 Del Crandall MG .05 .02 .00
□ 722 Bob Welch .08 .03 .01
□ 723 Rich Dauer .05 .02 .00
□ 724 Eric Rasmussen .05 .02 .00
□ 725 Cesar Cedeno .08 .03 .01
□ 726 Brewers TL .10 .03 .01
Ted Simmons
Moose Haas
□ 727 Joel Youngblood .05 .02 .00
□ 728 Tug McGraw .10 .04 .01
□ 729 Gene Tenace .08 .03 .01
□ 730 Bruce Sutter .12 .05 .01
□ 731 Lynn Jones .05 .02 .00
□ 732 Terry Crowley .05 .02 .00
□ 733 Dave Collins .05 .02 .00
□ 734 Odell Jones .05 .02 .00
□ 735 Rick Burleson .08 .03 .01
□ 736 Dick Ruthven .05 .02 .00
□ 737 Jim Essian .05 .02 .00
□ 738 Bill Schroeder .10 .04 .01
□ 739 Bob Watson .08 .03 .01
□ 740 Tom Seaver .40 .16 .04
□ 741 Wayne Gross .05 .02 .00
□ 742 Dick Williams MG .05 .02 .00
□ 743 Don Hood .05 .02 .00
□ 744 Jamie Allen .05 .02 .00
□ 745 Dennis Eckersley .15 .06 .01
□ 746 Mickey Hatcher .05 .02 .00
□ 747 Pat Zachry .05 .02 .00
□ 748 Jeff Leonard .10 .04 .01
□ 749 Doug Flynn .05 .02 .00
□ 750 Jim Palmer .35 .14 .03
□ 751 Charlie Moore .05 .02 .00
□ 752 Phil Garner .05 .02 .00
□ 753 Doug Gwosdz .05 .02 .00
□ 754 Kent Tekulve .08 .03 .01
□ 755 Garry Maddox .08 .03 .01
□ 756 Reds TL .10 .03 .01
Ron Oester
Mario Soto
□ 757 Larry Bowa .10 .04 .01
□ 758 Bill Stein .05 .02 .00
□ 759 Richard Dotson .08 .03 .01
□ 760 Bob Horner .18 .08 .01
□ 761 John Montefusco .05 .02 .00
□ 762 Rance Mulliniks .05 .02 .00
□ 763 Craig Swan .05 .02 .00
□ 764 Mike Hargrove .05 .02 .00
□ 765 Ken Forsch .05 .02 .00
□ 766 Mike Vail .05 .02 .00
□ 767 Carney Lansford .10 .04 .01
□ 768 Champ Summers .05 .02 .00
□ 769 Bill Caudill .05 .02 .00
□ 770 Ken Griffey .08 .03 .01
□ 771 Billy Gardner MG .05 .02 .00
□ 772 Jim Slaton .05 .02 .00
□ 773 Todd Cruz .05 .02 .00
□ 774 Tom Gorman .08 .03 .01
□ 775 Dave Parker .18 .08 .01
□ 776 Craig Reynolds .05 .02 .00
□ 777 Tom Paciorek .05 .02 .00
□ 778 Andy Hawkins .40 .16 .04
□ 779 Jim Sundberg .08 .03 .01
□ 780 Steve Carlton .35 .14 .03
□ 781 Checklist 661-792 .08 .01 .00
□ 782 Steve Balboni .08 .03 .01
□ 783 Luis Leal .05 .02 .00
□ 784 Leon Roberts .05 .02 .00
□ 785 Joaquin Andujar .10 .04 .01
□ 786 Red Sox TL .25 .08 .01
Wade Boggs
Bob Ojeda
□ 787 Bill Campbell .05 .02 .00
□ 788 Milt May .05 .02 .00
□ 789 Bert Blyleven .12 .05 .01
□ 790 Doug DeCinces .08 .03 .01
□ 791 Terry Forster .08 .03 .01
□ 792 Bill Russell .15 .04 .01

1984 Topps Traded

The cards in this 132-card set measure 2 1/2" by 3 1/2". In its now standard procedure, Topps issued its Traded (or extended) set for the fourth year in a row. Because all photos and statistics of its regular set for the year were developed during the fall and

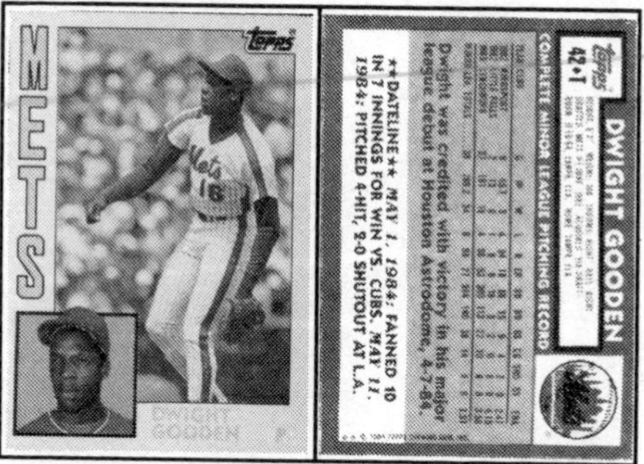

winter months of the preceding year, players who changed teams during the fall, winter and spring months are portrayed with the teams they were with in 1983. The Traded set amends the shortcomings of the regular set by presenting the players with their proper teams for the current year. Rookies not contained in the regular set are also picked up in the Traded set. Again this year, the Topps affiliate in Ireland printed the cards, and the cards were available through hobby channels only.

	MINT	EXC	G-VG
COMPLETE SET (132)	85.00	34.00	8.50
COMMON PLAYER (1-132)	.10	.04	.01

No.	Player	MINT	EXC	G-VG
□ 1T	Willie Aikens	.10	.04	.01
□ 2T	Luis Aponte	.10	.04	.01
□ 3T	Mike Armstrong	.10	.04	.01
□ 4T	Bob Bailor	.10	.04	.01
□ 5T	Dusty Baker	.20	.08	.02
□ 6T	Steve Balboni	.20	.08	.02
□ 7T	Alan Bannister	.10	.04	.01
□ 8T	Dave Beard	.10	.04	.01
□ 9T	Joe Beckwith	.10	.04	.01
□ 10T	Bruce Berenyi	.10	.04	.01
□ 11T	Dave Bergman	.10	.04	.01
□ 12T	Tony Bernazard	.10	.04	.01
□ 13T	Yogi Berra MG	.40	.16	.04
□ 14T	Barry Bonnell	.10	.04	.01
□ 15T	Phil Bradley	1.75	.70	.17
□ 16T	Fred Breining	.10	.04	.01
□ 17T	Bill Buckner	.30	.12	.03
□ 18T	Ray Burris	.10	.04	.01
□ 19T	John Butcher	.10	.04	.01
□ 20T	Brett Butler	.30	.12	.03
□ 21T	Enos Cabell	.10	.04	.01
□ 22T	Bill Campbell	.10	.04	.01
□ 23T	Bill Caudill	.10	.04	.01
□ 24T	Bob Clark	.10	.04	.01
□ 25T	Bryan Clark	.10	.04	.01
□ 26T	Jaime Cocanower	.20	.08	.02
□ 27T	Ron Darling	6.00	2.40	.60
□ 28T	Alvin Davis	4.00	1.60	.40
□ 29T	Ken Dayley	.20	.08	.02
□ 30T	Jeff Dedmon	.20	.08	.02
□ 31T	Bob Dernier	.20	.08	.02
□ 32T	Carlos Diaz	.10	.04	.01
□ 33T	Mike Easler	.10	.04	.01
□ 34T	Dennis Eckersley	.50	.20	.05
□ 35T	Jim Essian	.10	.04	.01
□ 36T	Darrell Evans	.30	.12	.03
□ 37T	Mike Fitzgerald	.20	.08	.02
□ 38T	Tim Foli	.10	.04	.01
□ 39T	George Frazier	.10	.04	.01
□ 40T	Rich Gale	.10	.04	.01
□ 41T	Barbaro Garbey	.20	.08	.02
□ 42T	Dwight Gooden	40.00	16.00	4.00
□ 43T	Rich Gossage	.30	.12	.03
□ 44T	Wayne Gross	.10	.04	.01
□ 45T	Mark Gubicza	2.00	.80	.20
□ 46T	Jackie Gutierrez	.20	.08	.02
□ 47T	Mel Hall	.30	.12	.03
□ 48T	Toby Harrah	.20	.08	.02
□ 49T	Ron Hassey	.20	.08	.02
□ 50T	Rich Hebner	.10	.04	.01
□ 51T	Willie Hernandez	.30	.12	.03
□ 52T	Ricky Horton	.40	.16	.04
□ 53T	Art Howe	.20	.08	.02
□ 54T	Dane Iorg	.10	.04	.01
□ 55T	Brook Jacoby	1.50	.60	.15
□ 56T	Mike Jeffcoat	.20	.08	.02
□ 57T	Dave Johnson MG	.30	.12	.03
□ 58T	Lynn Jones	.10	.04	.01
□ 59T	Ruppert Jones	.10	.04	.01
□ 60T	Mike Jorgensen	.10	.04	.01
□ 61T	Bob Kearney	.10	.04	.01
□ 62T	Jimmy Key	3.00	1.20	.30
□ 63T	Dave Kingman	.30	.12	.03
□ 64T	Jerry Koosman	.20	.08	.02
□ 65T	Wayne Krenchicki	.10	.04	.01
□ 66T	Rusty Kuntz	.10	.04	.01
□ 67T	Rene Lachemann MG	.10	.04	.01
□ 68T	Frank LaCorte	.10	.04	.01
□ 69T	Dennis Lamp	.10	.04	.01
□ 70T	Mark Langston	3.50	1.40	.35
□ 71T	Rick Leach	.10	.04	.01
□ 72T	Craig Lefferts	.10	.04	.01
□ 73T	Gary Lucas	.10	.04	.01
□ 74T	Jerry Martin	.10	.04	.01
□ 75T	Carmelo Martinez	.20	.08	.02
□ 76T	Mike Mason	.20	.08	.02
□ 77T	Gary Matthews	.20	.08	.02
□ 78T	Andy McGaffigan	.10	.04	.01
□ 79T	Larry Milbourne	.10	.04	.01
□ 80T	Sid Monge	.10	.04	.01
□ 81T	Jackie Moore MG	.10	.04	.01
□ 82T	Joe Morgan	1.00	.40	.10
□ 83T	Graig Nettles	.40	.16	.04
□ 84T	Phil Niekro	1.00	.40	.10
□ 85T	Ken Oberkfell	.10	.04	.01
□ 86T	Mike O'Berry	.10	.04	.01
□ 87T	Al Oliver	.20	.08	.02
□ 88T	Jorge Orta	.10	.04	.01
□ 89T	Amos Otis	.20	.08	.02
□ 90T	Dave Parker	.70	.28	.07
□ 91T	Tony Perez	.60	.24	.06
□ 92T	Gerald Perry	1.50	.60	.15
□ 93T	Gary Pettis	.40	.16	.04
□ 94T	Rob Picciolo	.10	.04	.01
□ 95T	Vern Rapp MG	.10	.04	.01
□ 96T	Floyd Rayford	.10	.04	.01
□ 97T	Randy Ready	.35	.14	.03
□ 98T	Ron Reed	.10	.04	.01
□ 99T	Gene Richards	.10	.04	.01
□ 100T	Jose Rijo	1.00	.40	.10
□ 101T	Jeff Robinson (Giants pitcher)	.40	.16	.04
□ 102T	Ron Romanick	.20	.08	.02
□ 103T	Pete Rose	7.00	2.80	.70
□ 104T	Bret Saberhagen	8.00	3.25	.80
□ 105T	Juan Samuel	3.00	1.20	.30
□ 106T	Scott Sanderson	.10	.04	.01
□ 107T	Dick Schofield	.60	.24	.06
□ 108T	Tom Seaver	3.00	1.20	.30
□ 109T	Jim Slaton	.10	.04	.01
□ 110T	Mike Smithson	.10	.04	.01
□ 111T	Lary Sorensen	.10	.04	.01
□ 112T	Tim Stoddard	.10	.04	.01
□ 113T	Champ Summers	.10	.04	.01
□ 114T	Jim Sundberg	.20	.08	.02
□ 115T	Rick Sutcliffe	.45	.18	.04
□ 116T	Craig Swan	.10	.04	.01
□ 117T	Tim Teufel	.35	.14	.03
□ 118T	Derrel Thomas	.10	.04	.01
□ 119T	Gorman Thomas	.30	.12	.03
□ 120T	Alex Trevino	.10	.04	.01
□ 121T	Manny Trillo	.10	.04	.01
□ 122T	John Tudor	.40	.16	.04
□ 123T	Tom Underwood	.10	.04	.01
□ 124T	Mike Vail	.10	.04	.01
□ 125T	Tom Waddell	.20	.08	.02
□ 126T	Gary Ward	.20	.08	.02
□ 127T	Curt Wilkerson	.20	.08	.02
□ 128T	Frank Williams	.30	.12	.03
□ 129T	Glenn Wilson	.20	.08	.02
□ 130T	Johnny Wockenfuss	.10	.04	.01
□ 131T	Ned Yost	.10	.04	.01
□ 132T	Checklist: 1-132	.10	.01	.00

1984 Topps Glossy 22

The cards in this 22-card set measure 2 1/2" by 3 1/2". Unlike the 1983 Topps Glossy set which was not distributed with its regular baseball cards, the 1984 Topps Glossy set was distributed as inserts in Topps Rak-Paks. The set features the nine American and National League All-Stars who started in the 1983 All Star game in Chicago. The managers and team captains (Yastrzemski and Bench) complete

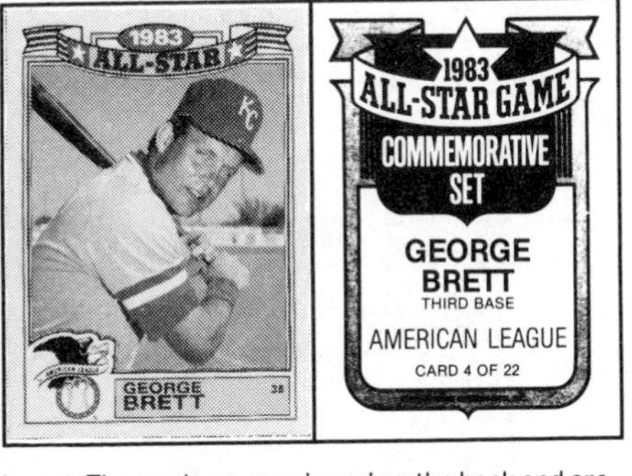

the set. The cards are numbered on the back and are ordered by position within league (AL: 1-11 and NL: 12-22).

	MINT	EXC	G-VG
COMPLETE SET (22)	4.00	1.60	.40
COMMON PLAYER (1-22)	.10	.04	.01

	MINT	EXC	G-VG
□ 1 Harvey Kuenn MG	.10	.04	.01
□ 2 Rod Carew	.40	.16	.04
□ 3 Manny Trillo	.10	.04	.01
□ 4 George Brett	.60	.24	.06
□ 5 Robin Yount	.40	.16	.04
□ 6 Jim Rice	.25	.10	.02
□ 7 Fred Lynn	.20	.08	.02
□ 8 Dave Winfield	.35	.14	.03
□ 9 Ted Simmons	.15	.06	.01
□ 10 Dave Stieb	.15	.06	.01
□ 11 Carl Yastrzemski CAPT	.50	.20	.05
□ 12 Whitey Herzog MG	.10	.04	.01
□ 13 Al Oliver	.15	.06	.01
□ 14 Steve Sax	.25	.10	.02
□ 15 Mike Schmidt	.75	.30	.07
□ 16 Ozzie Smith	.30	.12	.03
□ 17 Tim Raines	.45	.18	.04
□ 18 Andre Dawson	.35	.14	.03
□ 19 Dale Murphy	.70	.28	.07
□ 20 Gary Carter	.35	.14	.03
□ 21 Mario Soto	.10	.04	.01
□ 22 Johnny Bench CAPT	.30	.12	.03

1984 Topps Glossy 40

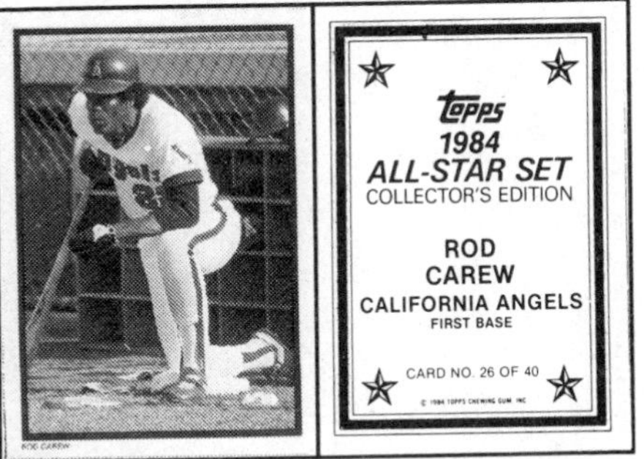

The cards in this 40-card set measure 2 1/2" by 3 1/2". Similar to last year's glossy set, this set was issued as a bonus prize to Topps All-Star Baseball Game cards found in wax packs. Twenty-five bonus runs from the game cards were necessary to obtain a five card subset of the series. There were eight different subsets of five cards. The cards are numbered and contain 20 stars from each league.

	MINT	EXC	G-VG
COMPLETE SET (40)	12.00	5.00	1.20
COMMON PLAYER (1-40)	.15	.06	.01

	MINT	EXC	G-VG
□ 1 Pete Rose	1.25	.50	.12
□ 2 Lance Parrish	.25	.10	.02
□ 3 Steve Rogers	.15	.06	.01
□ 4 Eddie Murray	.85	.34	.08
□ 5 Johnny Ray	.20	.08	.02
□ 6 Rickey Henderson	1.00	.40	.10
□ 7 Atlee Hammaker	.15	.06	.01
□ 8 Wade Boggs	1.75	.70	.17
□ 9 Gary Carter	.45	.18	.04
□ 10 Jack Morris	.25	.10	.02
□ 11 Darrell Evans	.20	.08	.02
□ 12 George Brett	1.00	.40	.10
□ 13 Bob Horner	.25	.10	.02
□ 14 Ron Guidry	.25	.10	.02
□ 15 Nolan Ryan	.65	.26	.06
□ 16 Dave Winfield	.50	.20	.05
□ 17 Ozzie Smith	.30	.12	.03
□ 18 Ted Simmons	.20	.08	.02
□ 19 Bill Madlock	.15	.06	.01
□ 20 Tony Armas	.15	.06	.01
□ 21 Al Oliver	.20	.08	.02
□ 22 Jim Rice	.30	.12	.03
□ 23 George Hendrick	.15	.06	.01
□ 24 Dave Stieb	.15	.06	.01
□ 25 Pedro Guerrero	.35	.14	.03
□ 26 Rod Carew	.45	.18	.04
□ 27 Steve Carlton	.50	.20	.05
□ 28 Dave Righetti	.20	.08	.02
□ 29 Darryl Strawberry	1.75	.70	.17
□ 30 Lou Whitaker	.20	.08	.02
□ 31 Dale Murphy	1.00	.40	.10
□ 32 LaMarr Hoyt	.15	.06	.01
□ 33 Jesse Orosco	.15	.06	.01
□ 34 Cecil Cooper	.20	.08	.02
□ 35 Andre Dawson	.35	.14	.03
□ 36 Robin Yount	.50	.20	.05
□ 37 Tim Raines	.45	.18	.04
□ 38 Dan Quisenberry	.20	.08	.02
□ 39 Mike Schmidt	1.00	.40	.10
□ 40 Carlton Fisk	.25	.10	.02

1984 Topps Cereal

The cards in this 33 card-set measure 2 1/2" by 3 1/2". The cards are numbered both on the front and the back. The 1984 Topps Cereal Series is exactly the same as the Ralston- Purina issue of this year except for a Topps logo and the words "Cereal Series" on the tops of the fronts of the cards in place of the Ralston checkerboard background. The checkerboard background is absent from the reverse, and a Topps logo is on the reverse of the cereal cards. These cards were distributed in unmarked boxes of Ralston-Purina cereal with a pack of four cards (three players and a checklist) being inside random cereal boxes. The back of the checklist details an offer to obtain any twelve cards direct from the issuer for only 1.50.

	MINT	EXC	G-VG
COMPLETE SET (34)	11.00	4.50	1.10
COMMON PLAYER (1-33)	.20	.08	.02

	MINT	EXC	G-VG
□ 1 Eddie Murray	.80	.32	.08
□ 2 Ozzie Smith	.35	.14	.03

☐	3 Ted Simmons	.25	.10	.02
☐	4 Pete Rose	1.25	.50	.12
☐	5 Greg Luzinski	.20	.08	.02
☐	6 Andre Dawson	.35	.14	.03
☐	7 Dave Winfield	.45	.18	.04
☐	8 Tom Seaver	.50	.20	.05
☐	9 Jim Rice	.35	.14	.03
☐	10 Fernando Valenzuela	.35	.14	.03
☐	11 Wade Boggs	1.75	.70	.17
☐	12 Dale Murphy	1.00	.40	.10
☐	13 George Brett	1.00	.40	.10
☐	14 Nolan Ryan	.65	.26	.06
☐	15 Rickey Henderson	1.00	.40	.10
☐	16 Steve Carlton	.50	.20	.05
☐	17 Rod Carew	.45	.18	.04
☐	18 Steve Garvey	.60	.24	.06
☐	19 Reggie Jackson	1.00	.40	.10
☐	20 Dave Concepcion	.20	.08	.02
☐	21 Robin Yount	.50	.20	.05
☐	22 Mike Schmidt	1.00	.40	.10
☐	23 Jim Palmer	.40	.16	.04
☐	24 Bruce Sutter	.25	.10	.02
☐	25 Dan Quisenberry	.25	.10	.02
☐	26 Bill Madlock	.20	.08	.02
☐	27 Cecil Cooper	.20	.08	.02
☐	28 Gary Carter	.55	.22	.05
☐	29 Fred Lynn	.25	.10	.02
☐	30 Pedro Guerrero	.35	.14	.03
☐	31 Ron Guidry	.25	.10	.02
☐	32 Keith Hernandez	.35	.14	.03
☐	33 Carlton Fisk	.25	.10	.02
☐	34 Checklist card (unnumbered)	.25	.05	.01

1985 Topps

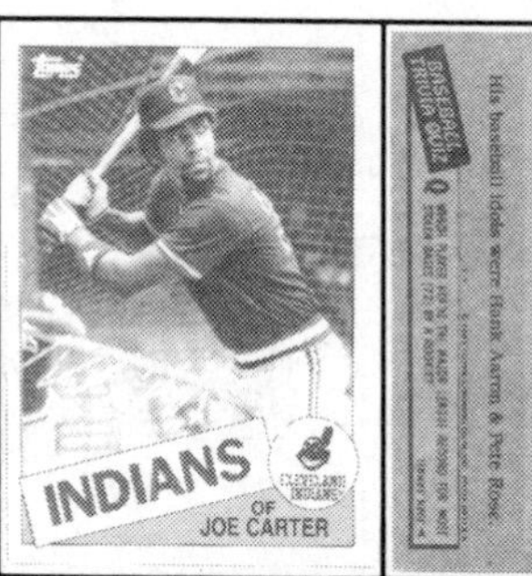

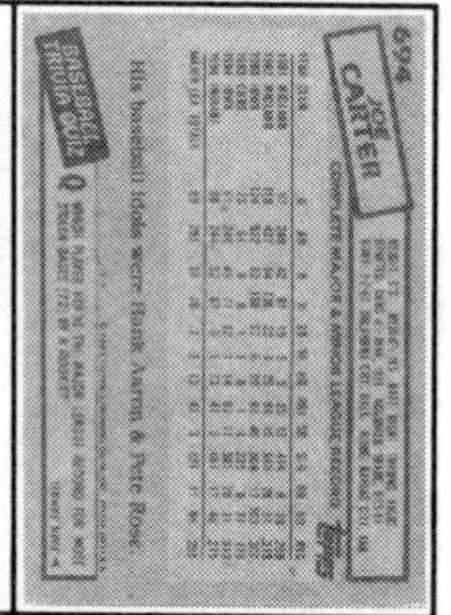

The cards in this 792-card set measure 2 1/2" by 3 1/2". The 1985 Topps set contains full color cards. The fronts feature both the Topps and team logos along with the team name, player's name, and his position. The backs feature player statistics with ink colors of light green and maroon on a gray stock. A trivia quiz is included on the lower portion of the backs. The first ten cards (1-10) are Record Breakers (RB), cards 131-143 are Father and Son (FS) cards, and cards 701 to 722 portray All-Star selections (AS). Cards 271 to 282 represent "First Draft Picks" still active in the Major Leagues and cards 389-404 feature the coach and players on the 1984 U.S. Olympic Baseball Team. The manager cards in the set are important in that they contain the checklist of that team's players on the back. Topps also produced a specially boxed "glossy" edition frequently referred to as the Topps Tiffany set. There were supposedly only 5,000 sets of the Tiffany cards produced; they were marketed to hobby dealers. The checklist of cards (792 regular and 132 Traded) is identical to that of the normal non- glossy cards. There are two primary distinguishing features of the Tiffany cards, white card stock reverses and high gloss obverses. These Tiffany cards are valued at approximately six times the values listed below.

		MINT	EXC	G-VG
	COMPLETE SET (792)	100.00	40.00	10.00
	COMMON PLAYER (1-792)	.04	.02	.00
☐	1 Carlton Fisk RB Longest game by catcher	.15	.04	.01
☐	2 Steve Garvey RB Consecutive error-less games, 1B	.20	.08	.02
☐	3 Dwight Gooden RB Most strikeouts, rookie, season	.75	.30	.07
☐	4 Cliff Johnson RB Most pinch homers, lifetime	.04	.02	.00
☐	5 Joe Morgan RB Most homers, 2B, lifetime	.10	.04	.01
☐	6 Pete Rose RB Most singles, lifetime	.50	.20	.05
☐	7 Nolan Ryan RB Most strikeouts, lifetime	.20	.08	.02
☐	8 Juan Samuel RB Most stolen bases, rookie, season	.15	.06	.01
☐	9 Bruce Sutter RB Most saves, season, NL	.07	.03	.01
☐	10 Don Sutton RB Most seasons, 100 or more K's	.10	.04	.01
☐	11 Ralph Houk MG (checklist back)	.07	.02	.00
☐	12 Dave Lopes	.07	.03	.01
☐	13 Tim Lollar	.04	.02	.00
☐	14 Chris Bando	.04	.02	.00
☐	15 Jerry Koosman	.10	.04	.01
☐	16 Bobby Meacham	.04	.02	.00
☐	17 Mike Scott	.30	.12	.03
☐	18 Mickey Hatcher	.07	.03	.01
☐	19 George Frazier	.04	.02	.00
☐	20 Chet Lemon	.07	.03	.01
☐	21 Lee Tunnell	.04	.02	.00
☐	22 Duane Kuiper	.04	.02	.00
☐	23 Bret Saberhagen	2.50	1.00	.25
☐	24 Jesse Barfield	.25	.10	.02
☐	25 Steve Bedrosian	.12	.05	.01
☐	26 Roy Smalley	.04	.02	.00
☐	27 Bruce Berenyi	.04	.02	.00
☐	28 Dann Bilardello	.04	.02	.00
☐	29 Odell Jones	.04	.02	.00
☐	30 Cal Ripken	.50	.20	.05
☐	31 Terry Whitfield	.04	.02	.00
☐	32 Chuck Porter	.04	.02	.00
☐	33 Tito Landrum	.04	.02	.00
☐	34 Ed Nunez	.07	.03	.01
☐	35 Graig Nettles	.10	.04	.01
☐	36 Fred Breining	.04	.02	.00
☐	37 Reid Nichols	.04	.02	.00
☐	38 Jackie Moore MG (checklist back)	.07	.02	.00
☐	39 John Wockenfuss	.04	.02	.00
☐	40 Phil Niekro	.18	.08	.01
☐	41 Mike Fischlin	.04	.02	.00
☐	42 Luis Sanchez	.04	.02	.00
☐	43 Andre David	.07	.03	.01
☐	44 Dickie Thon	.04	.02	.00
☐	45 Greg Minton	.04	.02	.00
☐	46 Gary Woods	.04	.02	.00
☐	47 Dave Rozema	.04	.02	.00
☐	48 Tony Fernandez	1.25	.50	.12
☐	49 Butch Davis	.07	.03	.01
☐	50 John Candelaria	.07	.03	.01
☐	51 Bob Watson	.07	.03	.01
☐	52 Jerry Dybzinski	.04	.02	.00
☐	53 Tom Gorman	.04	.02	.00
☐	54 Cesar Cedeno	.07	.03	.01
☐	55 Frank Tanana	.07	.03	.01
☐	56 Jim Dwyer	.04	.02	.00
☐	57 Pat Zachry	.04	.02	.00
☐	58 Orlando Mercado	.04	.02	.00
☐	59 Rick Waits	.04	.02	.00
☐	60 George Hendrick	.07	.03	.01
☐	61 Curt Kaufman	.07	.03	.01
☐	62 Mike Ramsey	.04	.02	.00
☐	63 Steve McCatty	.04	.02	.00
☐	64 Mark Bailey	.07	.03	.01
☐	65 Bill Buckner	.10	.04	.01
☐	66 Dick Williams MG (checklist back)	.07	.02	.00

□ 67 Rafael Santana	.25	.10	.02
□ 68 Von Hayes	.15	.06	.01
□ 69 Jim Winn	.07	.03	.01
□ 70 Don Baylor	.10	.04	.01
□ 71 Tim Laudner	.04	.02	.00
□ 72 Rick Sutcliffe	.12	.05	.01
□ 73 Rusty Kuntz	.04	.02	.00
□ 74 Mike Krukow	.04	.02	.00
□ 75 Willie Upshaw	.04	.02	.00
□ 76 Alan Bannister	.04	.02	.00
□ 77 Joe Beckwith	.04	.02	.00
□ 78 Scott Fletcher	.07	.03	.01
□ 79 Rick Mahler	.04	.02	.00
□ 80 Keith Hernandez	.30	.12	.03
□ 81 Lenn Sakata	.04	.02	.00
□ 82 Joe Price	.04	.02	.00
□ 83 Charlie Moore	.04	.02	.00
□ 84 Spike Owen	.04	.02	.00
□ 85 Mike Marshall	.12	.05	.01
□ 86 Don Aase	.04	.02	.00
□ 87 David Green	.04	.02	.00
□ 88 Bryn Smith	.04	.02	.00
□ 89 Jackie Gutierrez	.07	.03	.01
□ 90 Rich Gossage	.12	.05	.01
□ 91 Jeff Burroughs	.04	.02	.00
□ 92 Paul Owens MG (checklist back)	.07	.02	.00
□ 93 Don Schulze	.04	.02	.00
□ 94 Toby Harrah	.04	.02	.00
□ 95 Jose Cruz	.10	.04	.01
□ 96 Johnny Ray	.10	.04	.01
□ 97 Pete Filson	.04	.02	.00
□ 98 Steve Lake	.04	.02	.00
□ 99 Milt Wilcox	.04	.02	.00
□ 100 George Brett	.50	.20	.05
□ 101 Jim Acker	.04	.02	.00
□ 102 Tommy Dunbar	.04	.02	.00
□ 103 Randy Lerch	.04	.02	.00
□ 104 Mike Fitzgerald	.04	.02	.00
□ 105 Ron Kittle	.12	.05	.01
□ 106 Pascual Perez	.04	.02	.00
□ 107 Tom Foley	.04	.02	.00
□ 108 Darnell Coles	.10	.04	.01
□ 109 Gary Roenicke	.04	.02	.00
□ 110 Alejandro Pena	.07	.03	.01
□ 111 Doug DeCinces	.07	.03	.01
□ 112 Tom Tellmann	.04	.02	.00
□ 113 Tom Herr	.07	.03	.01
□ 114 Bob James	.04	.02	.00
□ 115 Rickey Henderson	.45	.18	.04
□ 116 Dennis Boyd	.20	.08	.02
□ 117 Greg Gross	.04	.02	.00
□ 118 Eric Show	.07	.03	.01
□ 119 Pat Corrales MG (checklist back)	.07	.02	.00
□ 120 Steve Kemp	.07	.03	.01
□ 121 Checklist: 1-132	.07	.01	.00
□ 122 Tom Brunansky	.18	.08	.01
□ 123 Dave Smith	.07	.03	.01
□ 124 Rich Hebner	.04	.02	.00
□ 125 Kent Tekulve	.07	.03	.01
□ 126 Ruppert Jones	.04	.02	.00
□ 127 Mark Gubicza	.75	.30	.07
□ 128 Ernie Whitt	.04	.02	.00
□ 129 Gene Garber	.04	.02	.00
□ 130 Al Oliver	.10	.04	.01
□ 131 Buddy/Gus Bell FS	.07	.03	.01
□ 132 Dale/Yogi Berra FS	.12	.05	.01
□ 133 Bob/Ray Boone FS	.07	.03	.01
□ 134 Terry/Tito Francona FS	.07	.03	.01
□ 135 Terry/Bob Kennedy FS	.07	.03	.01
□ 136 Jeff/Jim Kunkel FS	.07	.03	.01
□ 137 Vance/Vern Law FS	.07	.03	.01
□ 138 Dick/Dick Schofield FS	.07	.03	.01
□ 139 Joel/Bob Skinner FS	.07	.03	.01
□ 140 Roy/Roy Smalley FS	.07	.03	.01
□ 141 Mike/D.Stenhouse FS	.07	.03	.01
□ 142 Steve/Dizzy Trout FS	.07	.03	.01
□ 143 Ozzie/Ozzie Virgil FS	.07	.03	.01
□ 144 Ron Gardenhire	.04	.02	.00
□ 145 Alvin Davis	1.50	.60	.15
□ 146 Gary Redus	.04	.02	.00
□ 147 Bill Swaggerty	.04	.02	.00
□ 148 Steve Yeager	.04	.02	.00
□ 149 Dickie Noles	.04	.02	.00
□ 150 Jim Rice	.25	.10	.02
□ 151 Moose Haas	.04	.02	.00
□ 152 Steve Braun	.04	.02	.00
□ 153 Frank LaCorte	.04	.02	.00
□ 154 Argenis Salazar	.04	.02	.00
□ 155 Yogi Berra MG (checklist back)	.12	.04	.01
□ 156 Craig Reynolds	.04	.02	.00
□ 157 Tug McGraw	.10	.04	.01
□ 158 Pat Tabler	.07	.03	.01
□ 159 Carlos Diaz	.04	.02	.00
□ 160 Lance Parrish	.18	.08	.01
□ 161 Ken Schrom	.04	.02	.00
□ 162 Benny Distefano	.10	.04	.01
□ 163 Dennis Eckersley	.15	.06	.01
□ 164 Jorge Orta	.04	.02	.00
□ 165 Dusty Baker	.07	.03	.01
□ 166 Keith Atherton	.04	.02	.00
□ 167 Rufino Linares	.04	.02	.00
□ 168 Garth Iorg	.04	.02	.00
□ 169 Dan Spillner	.04	.02	.00
□ 170 George Foster	.12	.05	.01
□ 171 Bill Stein	.04	.02	.00
□ 172 Jack Perconte	.04	.02	.00
□ 173 Mike Young	.10	.04	.01
□ 174 Rick Honeycutt	.04	.02	.00
□ 175 Dave Parker	.15	.06	.01
□ 176 Bill Schroeder	.04	.02	.00
□ 177 Dave Von Ohlen	.04	.02	.00
□ 178 Miguel Dilone	.04	.02	.00
□ 179 Tommy John	.15	.06	.01
□ 180 Dave Winfield	.35	.14	.03
□ 181 Roger Clemens	10.00	4.00	1.00
□ 182 Tim Flannery	.04	.02	.00
□ 183 Larry McWilliams	.04	.02	.00
□ 184 Carmen Castillo	.04	.02	.00
□ 185 Al Holland	.04	.02	.00
□ 186 Bob Lillis MG (checklist back)	.07	.02	.00
□ 187 Mike Walters	.04	.02	.00
□ 188 Greg Pryor	.04	.02	.00
□ 189 Warren Brusstar	.04	.02	.00
□ 190 Rusty Staub	.10	.04	.01
□ 191 Steve Nicosia	.04	.02	.00
□ 192 Howard Johnson	1.50	.60	.15
□ 193 Jimmy Key	1.25	.50	.12
□ 194 Dave Stegman	.04	.02	.00
□ 195 Glenn Hubbard	.04	.02	.00
□ 196 Pete O'Brien	.10	.04	.01
□ 197 Mike Warren	.04	.02	.00
□ 198 Eddie Milner	.04	.02	.00
□ 199 Denny Martinez	.07	.03	.01
□ 200 Reggie Jackson	.45	.18	.04
□ 201 Burt Hooton	.04	.02	.00
□ 202 Gorman Thomas	.10	.04	.01
□ 203 Bob McClure	.04	.02	.00
□ 204 Art Howe	.07	.03	.01
□ 205 Steve Rogers	.04	.02	.00
□ 206 Phil Garner	.04	.02	.00
□ 207 Mark Clear	.04	.02	.00
□ 208 Champ Summers	.04	.02	.00
□ 209 Bill Campbell	.04	.02	.00
□ 210 Gary Matthews	.07	.03	.01
□ 211 Clay Christiansen	.04	.02	.00
□ 212 George Vukovich	.04	.02	.00
□ 213 Billy Gardner MG (checklist back)	.07	.02	.00
□ 214 John Tudor	.15	.06	.01
□ 215 Bob Brenly	.04	.02	.00
□ 216 Jerry Don Gleaton	.04	.02	.00
□ 217 Leon Roberts	.04	.02	.00
□ 218 Doyle Alexander	.07	.03	.01
□ 219 Gerald Perry	.45	.18	.04
□ 220 Fred Lynn	.15	.06	.01
□ 221 Ron Reed	.04	.02	.00
□ 222 Hubie Brooks	.10	.04	.01
□ 223 Tom Hume	.04	.02	.00
□ 224 Al Cowens	.04	.02	.00
□ 225 Mike Boddicker	.07	.03	.01
□ 226 Juan Beniquez	.04	.02	.00
□ 227 Danny Darwin	.04	.02	.00
□ 228 Dion James	.15	.06	.01
□ 229 Dave LaPoint	.07	.03	.01
□ 230 Gary Carter	.35	.14	.03
□ 231 Dwayne Murphy	.04	.02	.00
□ 232 Dave Beard	.04	.02	.00
□ 233 Ed Jurak	.04	.02	.00
□ 234 Jerry Narron	.04	.02	.00
□ 235 Garry Maddox	.07	.03	.01
□ 236 Mark Thurmond	.04	.02	.00
□ 237 Julio Franco	.12	.05	.01
□ 238 Jose Rijo	.35	.14	.03
□ 239 Tim Teufel	.10	.04	.01
□ 240 Dave Stieb	.12	.05	.01
□ 241 Jim Frey MG (checklist back)	.07	.02	.00
□ 242 Greg Harris	.04	.02	.00
□ 243 Barbaro Garbey	.04	.02	.00
□ 244 Mike Jones	.04	.02	.00
□ 245 Chili Davis	.10	.04	.01
□ 246 Mike Norris	.04	.02	.00
□ 247 Wayne Tolleson	.04	.02	.00
□ 248 Terry Forster	.07	.03	.01
□ 249 Harold Baines	.15	.06	.01
□ 250 Jesse Orosco	.04	.02	.00

□ 251 Brad Gulden .04 .02 .00
□ 252 Dan Ford .04 .02 .00
□ 253 Sid Bream .30 .12 .03
□ 254 Pete Vuckovich .04 .02 .00
□ 255 Lonnie Smith .04 .02 .00
□ 256 Mike Stanton .04 .02 .00
□ 257 Bryan Little .04 .02 .00
□ 258 Mike Brown (Angels OF) .04 .02 .00
□ 259 Gary Allenson .04 .02 .00
□ 260 Dave Righetti .12 .05 .01
□ 261 Checklist: 133-264 .07 .01 .00
□ 262 Greg Booker .04 .02 .00
□ 263 Mel Hall .10 .04 .01
□ 264 Joe Sambito .04 .02 .00
□ 265 Juan Samuel .50 .20 .05
□ 266 Frank Viola .30 .12 .03
□ 267 Henry Cotto .10 .04 .01
□ 268 Chuck Tanner MG (checklist back) .07 .02 .00
□ 269 Doug Baker .04 .02 .00
□ 270 Dan Quisenberry .12 .05 .01
□ 271 Tim Foli FDP68 .04 .02 .00
□ 272 Jeff Burroughs FDP69 .04 .02 .00
□ 273 Bill Almon FDP74 .04 .02 .00
□ 274 Floyd Bannister FDP76 .04 .02 .00
□ 275 Harold Baines FDP77 .10 .04 .01
□ 276 Bob Horner FDP78 .12 .05 .01
□ 277 Al Chambers FDP79 .04 .02 .00
□ 278 D.Strawberry FDP80 .75 .30 .07
□ 279 Mike Moore FDP81 .07 .03 .01
□ 280 Sh.Dunston FDP82 .75 .30 .07
□ 281 Tim Belcher FDP83 .60 .24 .06
□ 282 Shawn Abner FDP84 .45 .18 .04
□ 283 Fran Mullins .04 .02 .00
□ 284 Marty Bystrom .04 .02 .00
□ 285 Dan Driessen .04 .02 .00
□ 286 Rudy Law .04 .02 .00
□ 287 Walt Terrell .04 .02 .00
□ 288 Jeff Kunkel .07 .03 .01
□ 289 Tom Underwood .04 .02 .00
□ 290 Cecil Cooper .10 .04 .01
□ 291 Bob Welch .07 .03 .01
□ 292 Brad Komminsk .04 .02 .00
□ 293 Curt Young .35 .14 .03
□ 294 Tom Nieto .04 .02 .00
□ 295 Joe Niekro .07 .03 .01
□ 296 Ricky Nelson .04 .02 .00
□ 297 Gary Lucas .04 .02 .00
□ 298 Marty Barrett .10 .04 .01
□ 299 Andy Hawkins .07 .03 .01
□ 300 Rod Carew .35 .14 .03
□ 301 John Montefusco .04 .02 .00
□ 302 Tim Corcoran .04 .02 .00
□ 303 Mike Jeffcoat .04 .02 .00
□ 304 Gary Gaetti .30 .12 .03
□ 305 Dale Berra .04 .02 .00
□ 306 Rick Reuschel .10 .04 .01
□ 307 Sparky Anderson MG (checklist back) .07 .03 .01
□ 308 John Wathan .04 .02 .00
□ 309 Mike Witt .10 .04 .01
□ 310 Manny Trillo .04 .02 .00
□ 311 Jim Gott .04 .02 .00
□ 312 Marc Hill .04 .02 .00
□ 313 Dave Schmidt .07 .03 .01
□ 314 Ron Oester .04 .02 .00
□ 315 Doug Sisk .04 .02 .00
□ 316 John Lowenstein .04 .02 .00
□ 317 Jack Lazorko .04 .02 .00
□ 318 Ted Simmons .10 .04 .01
□ 319 Jeff Jones .04 .02 .00
□ 320 Dale Murphy .60 .24 .06
□ 321 Ricky Horton .25 .10 .02
□ 322 Dave Stapleton .04 .02 .00
□ 323 Andy McGaffigan .04 .02 .00
□ 324 Bruce Bochy .04 .02 .00
□ 325 John Denny .07 .03 .01
□ 326 Kevin Bass .10 .04 .01
□ 327 Brook Jacoby .25 .10 .02
□ 328 Bob Shirley .04 .02 .00
□ 329 Ron Washington .04 .02 .00
□ 330 Leon Durham .07 .03 .01
□ 331 Bill Laskey .04 .02 .00
□ 332 Brian Harper .04 .02 .00
□ 333 Willie Hernandez .10 .04 .01
□ 334 Dick Howser MG (checklist back) .07 .02 .00
□ 335 Bruce Benedict .04 .02 .00
□ 336 Rance Mulliniks .04 .02 .00
□ 337 Billy Sample .04 .02 .00
□ 338 Britt Burns .04 .02 .00
□ 339 Danny Heep .04 .02 .00
□ 340 Robin Yount .35 .14 .03
□ 341 Floyd Rayford .04 .02 .00
□ 342 Ted Power .04 .02 .00
□ 343 Bill Russell .07 .03 .01
□ 344 Dave Henderson .10 .04 .01
□ 345 Charlie Lea .04 .02 .00
□ 346 Terry Pendleton .45 .18 .04
□ 347 Rick Langford .04 .02 .00
□ 348 Bob Boone .10 .04 .01
□ 349 Domingo Ramos .04 .02 .00
□ 350 Wade Boggs 3.50 1.40 .35
□ 351 Juan Agosto .04 .02 .00
□ 352 Joe Morgan .18 .08 .01
□ 353 Julio Solano .04 .02 .00
□ 354 Andre Robertson .04 .02 .00
□ 355 Bert Blyleven .10 .04 .01
□ 356 Dave Meier .07 .03 .01
□ 357 Rich Bordi .04 .02 .00
□ 358 Tony Pena .10 .04 .01
□ 359 Pat Sheridan .04 .02 .00
□ 360 Steve Carlton .30 .12 .03
□ 361 Alfredo Griffin .07 .03 .01
□ 362 Craig McMurtry .04 .02 .00
□ 363 Ron Hodges .04 .02 .00
□ 364 Richard Dotson .07 .03 .01
□ 365 Danny Ozark MG (checklist back) .07 .01 .00
□ 366 Todd Cruz .04 .02 .00
□ 367 Keefe Cato .04 .02 .00
□ 368 Dave Bergman .04 .02 .00
□ 369 R.J. Reynolds .20 .08 .02
□ 370 Bruce Sutter .12 .05 .01
□ 371 Mickey Rivers .07 .03 .01
□ 372 Roy Howell .04 .02 .00
□ 373 Mike Moore .07 .03 .01
□ 374 Brian Downing .07 .03 .01
□ 375 Jeff Reardon .10 .04 .01
□ 376 Jeff Newman .04 .02 .00
□ 377 Checklist: 265-396 .07 .01 .00
□ 378 Alan Wiggins .04 .02 .00
□ 379 Charles Hudson .04 .02 .00
□ 380 Ken Griffey .07 .03 .01
□ 381 Roy Smith .04 .02 .00
□ 382 Denny Walling .04 .02 .00
□ 383 Rick Lysander .04 .02 .00
□ 384 Jody Davis .07 .03 .01
□ 385 Jose DeLeon .04 .02 .00
□ 386 Dan Gladden .35 .14 .03
□ 387 Buddy Biancalana .07 .03 .01
□ 388 Bert Roberge .04 .02 .00
□ 389 Rod Dedeaux OLY CO .04 .02 .00
□ 390 Sid Akins OLY .10 .04 .01
□ 391 Flavio Alfaro OLY .07 .03 .01
□ 392 Don August OLY .45 .18 .04
□ 393 Scott Bankhead OLY .30 .12 .03
□ 394 Bob Caffrey OLY .10 .04 .01
□ 395 Mike Dunne OLY .90 .36 .09
□ 396 Gary Green OLY .15 .06 .01
□ 397 John Hoover OLY .15 .06 .01
□ 398 Shane Mack OLY .45 .18 .04
□ 399 John Marzano OLY .35 .14 .03
□ 400 Oddibe McDowell OLY .65 .26 .06
□ 401 Mark McGwire OLY 17.00 7.00 1.70
□ 402 Pat Pacillo OLY .25 .10 .02
□ 403 Cory Snyder OLY 7.00 2.80 .70
□ 404 Billy Swift OLY .20 .08 .02
□ 405 Tom Veryzer .04 .02 .00
□ 406 Len Whitehouse .04 .02 .00
□ 407 Bobby Ramos .04 .02 .00
□ 408 Sid Monge .04 .02 .00
□ 409 Brad Wellman .04 .02 .00
□ 410 Bob Horner .15 .06 .01
□ 411 Bobby Cox MG (checklist back) .07 .01 .00
□ 412 Bud Black .04 .02 .00
□ 413 Vance Law .07 .03 .01
□ 414 Gary Ward .07 .03 .01
□ 415 Ron Darling UER (no trivia answer) 1.00 .40 .10
□ 416 Wayne Gross .04 .02 .00
□ 417 John Franco .85 .34 .08
□ 418 Ken Landreaux .04 .02 .00
□ 419 Mike Caldwell .04 .02 .00
□ 420 Andre Dawson .30 .12 .03
□ 421 Dave Rucker .04 .02 .00
□ 422 Carney Lansford .10 .04 .01
□ 423 Barry Bonnell .04 .02 .00
□ 424 Al Nipper .15 .06 .01
□ 425 Mike Hargrove .04 .02 .00
□ 426 Vern Ruhle .04 .02 .00
□ 427 Mario Ramirez .04 .02 .00
□ 428 Larry Andersen .04 .02 .00
□ 429 Rick Cerone .04 .02 .00
□ 430 Ron Davis .04 .02 .00
□ 431 U.L. Washington .04 .02 .00
□ 432 Thad Bosley .04 .02 .00
□ 433 Jim Morrison .04 .02 .00

□ 434	Gene Richards	.04	.02	.00
□ 435	Dan Petry	.07	.03	.01
□ 436	Willie Aikens	.04	.02	.00
□ 437	Al Jones	.04	.02	.00
□ 438	Joe Torre MG (checklist back)	.07	.01	.00
□ 439	Junior Ortiz	.04	.02	.00
□ 440	Fernando Valenzuela	.25	.10	.02
□ 441	Duane Walker	.04	.02	.00
□ 442	Ken Forsch	.04	.02	.00
□ 443	George Wright	.04	.02	.00
□ 444	Tony Phillips	.04	.02	.00
□ 445	Tippy Martinez	.04	.02	.00
□ 446	Jim Sundberg	.04	.02	.00
□ 447	Jeff Lahti	.04	.02	.00
□ 448	Derrel Thomas	.04	.02	.00
□ 449	Phil Bradley	.65	.26	.06
□ 450	Steve Garvey	.35	.14	.03
□ 451	Bruce Hurst	.15	.06	.01
□ 452	John Castino	.04	.02	.00
□ 453	Tom Waddell	.07	.03	.01
□ 454	Glenn Wilson	.07	.03	.01
□ 455	Bob Knepper	.07	.03	.01
□ 456	Tim Foli	.04	.02	.00
□ 457	Cecilio Guante	.04	.02	.00
□ 458	Randy Johnson	.04	.02	.00
□ 459	Charlie Leibrandt	.04	.02	.00
□ 460	Ryne Sandberg	.40	.16	.04
□ 461	Marty Castillo	.04	.02	.00
□ 462	Gary Lavelle	.04	.02	.00
□ 463	Dave Collins	.04	.02	.00
□ 464	Mike Mason	.07	.03	.01
□ 465	Bob Grich	.07	.03	.01
□ 466	Tony LaRussa MG (checklist back)	.07	.02	.00
□ 467	Ed Lynch	.04	.02	.00
□ 468	Wayne Krenchicki	.04	.02	.00
□ 469	Sammy Stewart	.04	.02	.00
□ 470	Steve Sax	.25	.10	.02
□ 471	Pete Ladd	.04	.02	.00
□ 472	Jim Essian	.04	.02	.00
□ 473	Tim Wallach	.12	.05	.01
□ 474	Kurt Kepshire	.07	.03	.01
□ 475	Andre Thornton	.07	.03	.01
□ 476	Jeff Stone	.15	.06	.01
□ 477	Bob Ojeda	.10	.04	.01
□ 478	Kurt Bevacqua	.04	.02	.00
□ 479	Mike Madden	.04	.02	.00
□ 480	Lou Whitaker	.15	.06	.01
□ 481	Dale Murray	.04	.02	.00
□ 482	Harry Spilman	.04	.02	.00
□ 483	Mike Smithson	.04	.02	.00
□ 484	Larry Bowa	.10	.04	.01
□ 485	Matt Young	.04	.02	.00
□ 486	Steve Balboni	.04	.02	.00
□ 487	Frank Williams	.15	.06	.01
□ 488	Joel Skinner	.07	.03	.01
□ 489	Bryan Clark	.04	.02	.00
□ 490	Jason Thompson	.04	.02	.00
□ 491	Rick Camp	.04	.02	.00
□ 492	Dave Johnson MG (checklist back)	.07	.02	.00
□ 493	Orel Hershiser	6.50	2.60	.65
□ 494	Rich Dauer	.04	.02	.00
□ 495	Mario Soto	.04	.02	.00
□ 496	Donnie Scott	.04	.02	.00
□ 497	Gary Pettis (photo actually Gary's little brother, Lynn)	.25	.10	.02
□ 498	Ed Romero	.04	.02	.00
□ 499	Danny Cox	.20	.08	.02
□ 500	Mike Schmidt	.45	.18	.04
□ 501	Dan Schatzeder	.04	.02	.00
□ 502	Rick Miller	.04	.02	.00
□ 503	Tim Conroy	.04	.02	.00
□ 504	Jerry Willard	.04	.02	.00
□ 505	Jim Beattie	.04	.02	.00
□ 506	Franklin Stubbs	.35	.14	.03
□ 507	Ray Fontenot	.04	.02	.00
□ 508	John Shelby	.04	.02	.00
□ 509	Milt May	.04	.02	.00
□ 510	Kent Hrbek	.25	.10	.02
□ 511	Lee Smith	.07	.03	.01
□ 512	Tom Brookens	.04	.02	.00
□ 513	Lynn Jones	.04	.02	.00
□ 514	Jeff Cornell	.04	.02	.00
□ 515	Dave Concepcion	.07	.03	.01
□ 516	Roy Lee Jackson	.04	.02	.00
□ 517	Jerry Martin	.04	.02	.00
□ 518	Chris Chambliss	.07	.03	.01
□ 519	Doug Rader MG (checklist back)	.07	.02	.00
□ 520	LaMarr Hoyt	.07	.03	.01
□ 521	Rick Dempsey	.04	.02	.00
□ 522	Paul Molitor	.15	.06	.01
□ 523	Candy Maldonado	.10	.04	.01
□ 524	Rob Wilfong	.04	.02	.00
□ 525	Darrell Porter	.04	.02	.00
□ 526	Dave Palmer	.04	.02	.00
□ 527	Checklist: 397-528	.07	.01	.00
□ 528	Bill Krueger	.04	.02	.00
□ 529	Rich Gedman	.10	.04	.01
□ 530	Dave Dravecky	.07	.03	.01
□ 531	Joe Lefebvre	.04	.02	.00
□ 532	Frank DiPino	.04	.02	.00
□ 533	Tony Bernazard	.04	.02	.00
□ 534	Brian Dayett	.04	.02	.00
□ 535	Pat Putnam	.04	.02	.00
□ 536	Kirby Puckett	8.50	3.50	.85
□ 537	Don Robinson	.04	.02	.00
□ 538	Keith Moreland	.04	.02	.00
□ 539	Aurelio Lopez	.04	.02	.00
□ 540	Claudell Washington	.07	.03	.01
□ 541	Mark Davis	.07	.03	.01
□ 542	Don Slaught	.04	.02	.00
□ 543	Mike Squires	.04	.02	.00
□ 544	Bruce Kison	.04	.02	.00
□ 545	Lloyd Moseby	.10	.04	.01
□ 546	Brent Gaff	.04	.02	.00
□ 547	Pete Rose MG (checklist back)	.45	.12	.03
□ 548	Larry Parrish	.04	.02	.00
□ 549	Mike Scioscia	.04	.02	.00
□ 550	Scott McGregor	.04	.02	.00
□ 551	Andy Van Slyke	.35	.14	.03
□ 552	Chris Codiroli	.04	.02	.00
□ 553	Bob Clark	.04	.02	.00
□ 554	Doug Flynn	.04	.02	.00
□ 555	Bob Stanley	.04	.02	.00
□ 556	Sixto Lezcano	.04	.02	.00
□ 557	Len Barker	.04	.02	.00
□ 558	Carmelo Martinez	.04	.02	.00
□ 559	Jay Howell	.04	.02	.00
□ 560	Bill Madlock	.07	.03	.01
□ 561	Darryl Motley	.04	.02	.00
□ 562	Houston Jimenez	.04	.02	.00
□ 563	Dick Ruthven	.04	.02	.00
□ 564	Alan Ashby	.04	.02	.00
□ 565	Kirk Gibson	.30	.12	.03
□ 566	Ed VandeBerg	.04	.02	.00
□ 567	Joel Youngblood	.04	.02	.00
□ 568	Cliff Johnson	.04	.02	.00
□ 569	Ken Oberkfell	.04	.02	.00
□ 570	Darryl Strawberry	2.50	1.00	.25
□ 571	Charlie Hough	.07	.03	.01
□ 572	Tom Paciorek	.04	.02	.00
□ 573	Jay Tibbs	.15	.06	.01
□ 574	Joe Altobelli MG (checklist back)	.07	.02	.00
□ 575	Pedro Guerrero	.25	.10	.02
□ 576	Jaime Cocanower	.04	.02	.00
□ 577	Chris Speier	.04	.02	.00
□ 578	Terry Francona	.04	.02	.00
□ 579	Ron Romanick	.07	.03	.01
□ 580	Dwight Evans	.12	.05	.01
□ 581	Mark Wagner	.04	.02	.00
□ 582	Ken Phelps	.25	.10	.02
□ 583	Bobby Brown	.04	.02	.00
□ 584	Kevin Gross	.04	.02	.00
□ 585	Butch Wynegar	.04	.02	.00
□ 586	Bill Scherrer	.04	.02	.00
□ 587	Doug Frobel	.04	.02	.00
□ 588	Bobby Castillo	.04	.02	.00
□ 589	Bob Dernier	.04	.02	.00
□ 590	Ray Knight	.07	.03	.01
□ 591	Larry Herndon	.04	.02	.00
□ 592	Jeff Robinson (Giants pitcher)	.25	.10	.02
□ 593	Rick Leach	.04	.02	.00
□ 594	Curt Wilkerson	.04	.02	.00
□ 595	Larry Gura	.04	.02	.00
□ 596	Jerry Hairston	.04	.02	.00
□ 597	Brad Lesley	.04	.02	.00
□ 598	Jose Oquendo	.07	.03	.01
□ 599	Storm Davis	.07	.03	.01
□ 600	Pete Rose	1.00	.40	.10
□ 601	Tom Lasorda MG (checklist back)	.07	.02	.00
□ 602	Jeff Dedmon	.04	.02	.00
□ 603	Rick Manning	.04	.02	.00
□ 604	Daryl Sconiers	.04	.02	.00
□ 605	Ozzie Smith	.20	.08	.02
□ 606	Rich Gale	.04	.02	.00
□ 607	Bill Almon	.04	.02	.00
□ 608	Craig Lefferts	.04	.02	.00
□ 609	Broderick Perkins	.04	.02	.00
□ 610	Jack Morris	.15	.06	.01
□ 611	Ozzie Virgil	.04	.02	.00
□ 612	Mike Armstrong	.04	.02	.00

□ 613 Terry Puhl .04 .02 .00
□ 614 Al Williams .04 .02 .00
□ 615 Marvell Wynne .04 .02 .00
□ 616 Scott Sanderson .04 .02 .00
□ 617 Willie Wilson .10 .04 .01
□ 618 Pete Falcone .04 .02 .00
□ 619 Jeff Leonard .07 .03 .01
□ 620 Dwight Gooden 8.50 3.50 .85
□ 621 Marvis Foley .04 .02 .00
□ 622 Luis Leal .04 .02 .00
□ 623 Greg Walker .07 .03 .01
□ 624 Benny Ayala .04 .02 .00
□ 625 Mark Langston 1.25 .50 .12
□ 626 German Rivera .07 .03 .01
□ 627 Eric Davis 13.50 5.00 1.00
□ 628 Rene Lachemann MG (checklist back) .07 .02 .00
□ 629 Dick Schofield .12 .05 .01
□ 630 Tim Raines .35 .14 .03
□ 631 Bob Forsch .04 .02 .00
□ 632 Bruce Bochte .04 .02 .00
□ 633 Glenn Hoffman .04 .02 .00
□ 634 Bill Dawley .04 .02 .00
□ 635 Terry Kennedy .04 .02 .00
□ 636 Shane Rawley .04 .02 .00
□ 637 Brett Butler .07 .03 .01
□ 638 Mike Pagliarulo 1.25 .50 .12
□ 639 Ed Hodge .04 .02 .00
□ 640 Steve Henderson .10 .04 .01
□ 641 Rod Scurry .04 .02 .00
□ 642 Dave Owen .04 .02 .00
□ 643 Johnny Grubb .04 .02 .00
□ 644 Mark Huismann .04 .02 .00
□ 645 Damaso Garcia .04 .02 .00
□ 646 Scot Thompson .04 .02 .00
□ 647 Rafael Ramirez .04 .02 .00
□ 648 Bob Jones .04 .02 .00
□ 649 Sid Fernandez .90 .36 .09
□ 650 Greg Luzinski .10 .04 .01
□ 651 Jeff Russell .04 .02 .00
□ 652 Joe Nolan .04 .02 .00
□ 653 Mark Brouhard .04 .02 .00
□ 654 Dave Anderson .04 .02 .00
□ 655 Joaquin Andujar .10 .04 .01
□ 656 Chuck Cottier MG (checklist back) .07 .02 .00
□ 657 Jim Slaton .04 .02 .00
□ 658 Mike Stenhouse .07 .03 .01
□ 659 Checklist: 529-660 .07 .01 .00
□ 660 Tony Gwynn 1.00 .40 .10
□ 661 Steve Crawford .04 .02 .00
□ 662 Mike Heath .04 .02 .00
□ 663 Luis Aguayo .04 .02 .00
□ 664 Steve Farr .20 .08 .02
□ 665 Don Mattingly 9.00 3.75 .90
□ 666 Mike LaCoss .04 .02 .00
□ 667 Dave Engle .04 .02 .00
□ 668 Steve Trout .04 .02 .00
□ 669 Lee Lacy .04 .02 .00
□ 670 Tom Seaver .30 .12 .03
□ 671 Dane Iorg .04 .02 .00
□ 672 Juan Berenguer .04 .02 .00
□ 673 Buck Martinez .04 .02 .00
□ 674 Atlee Hammaker .04 .02 .00
□ 675 Tony Perez .12 .05 .01
□ 676 Albert Hall .10 .04 .01
□ 677 Wally Backman .07 .03 .01
□ 678 Joe McLaughlin .04 .02 .00
□ 679 Bob Kearney .04 .02 .00
□ 680 Jerry Reuss .07 .03 .01
□ 681 Ben Oglivie .07 .03 .01
□ 682 Doug Corbett .04 .02 .00
□ 683 Whitey Herzog MG (checklist back) .07 .02 .00
□ 684 Bill Doran .10 .04 .01
□ 685 Bill Caudill .04 .02 .00
□ 686 Mike Easler .04 .02 .00
□ 687 Bill Gullickson .04 .02 .00
□ 688 Len Matuszek .04 .02 .00
□ 689 Luis DeLeon .04 .02 .00
□ 690 Alan Trammell .30 .12 .03
□ 691 Dennis Rasmussen .25 .10 .02
□ 692 Randy Bush .07 .03 .01
□ 693 Tim Stoddard .04 .02 .00
□ 694 Joe Carter 1.75 .70 .17
□ 695 Rick Rhoden .07 .03 .01
□ 696 John Rabb .04 .02 .00
□ 697 Onix Concepcion .04 .02 .00
□ 698 Jorge Bell .50 .20 .05
□ 699 Donnie Moore .04 .02 .00
□ 700 Eddie Murray .45 .18 .04
□ 701 Eddie Murray AS .15 .06 .01
□ 702 Damaso Garcia AS .04 .02 .00
□ 703 George Brett AS .25 .10 .02
□ 704 Cal Ripken AS .20 .08 .02
□ 705 Dave Winfield AS .15 .06 .01
□ 706 Rickey Henderson AS .25 .10 .02
□ 707 Tony Armas AS .07 .03 .01
□ 708 Lance Parrish AS .10 .04 .01
□ 709 Mike Boddicker AS .07 .03 .01
□ 710 Frank Viola AS .10 .04 .01
□ 711 Dan Quisenberry AS .10 .04 .01
□ 712 Keith Hernandez AS .15 .06 .01
□ 713 Ryne Sandberg AS .15 .06 .01
□ 714 Mike Schmidt AS .30 .12 .03
□ 715 Ozzie Smith AS .15 .06 .01
□ 716 Dale Murphy AS .35 .14 .03
□ 717 Tony Gwynn AS .30 .12 .03
□ 718 Jeff Leonard AS .07 .03 .01
□ 719 Gary Carter AS .15 .06 .01
□ 720 Rick Sutcliffe AS .10 .04 .01
□ 721 Bob Knepper AS .07 .03 .01
□ 722 Bruce Sutter AS .07 .03 .01
□ 723 Dave Stewart .10 .04 .01
□ 724 Oscar Gamble .04 .02 .00
□ 725 Floyd Bannister .04 .02 .00
□ 726 Al Bumbry .04 .02 .00
□ 727 Frank Pastore .04 .02 .00
□ 728 Bob Bailor .04 .02 .00
□ 729 Don Sutton .25 .10 .02
□ 730 Dave Kingman .10 .04 .01
□ 731 Neil Allen .04 .02 .00
□ 732 John McNamara MG (checklist back) .07 .02 .00
□ 733 Tony Scott .04 .02 .00
□ 734 John Henry Johnson .04 .02 .00
□ 735 Garry Templeton .07 .03 .01
□ 736 Jerry Mumphrey .04 .02 .00
□ 737 Bo Diaz .04 .02 .00
□ 738 Omar Moreno .04 .02 .00
□ 739 Ernie Camacho .04 .02 .00
□ 740 Jack Clark .25 .10 .02
□ 741 John Butcher .04 .02 .00
□ 742 Ron Hassey .04 .02 .00
□ 743 Frank White .07 .03 .01
□ 744 Doug Bair .04 .02 .00
□ 745 Buddy Bell .10 .04 .01
□ 746 Jim Clancy .04 .02 .00
□ 747 Alex Trevino .04 .02 .00
□ 748 Lee Mazzilli .04 .02 .00
□ 749 Julio Cruz .04 .02 .00
□ 750 Rollie Fingers .15 .06 .01
□ 751 Kelvin Chapman .04 .02 .00
□ 752 Bob Owchinko .04 .02 .00
□ 753 Greg Brock .04 .02 .00
□ 754 Larry Milbourne .04 .02 .00
□ 755 Ken Singleton .07 .03 .01
□ 756 Rob Picciolo .04 .02 .00
□ 757 Willie McGee .30 .12 .03
□ 758 Ray Burris .04 .02 .00
□ 759 Jim Fanning MG (checklist back) .07 .02 .00
□ 760 Nolan Ryan .40 .16 .04
□ 761 Jerry Remy .04 .02 .00
□ 762 Eddie Whitson .04 .02 .00
□ 763 Kiko Garcia .04 .02 .00
□ 764 Jamie Easterly .04 .02 .00
□ 765 Willie Randolph .07 .03 .01
□ 766 Paul Mirabella .04 .02 .00
□ 767 Darrell Brown .04 .02 .00
□ 768 Ron Cey .10 .04 .01
□ 769 Joe Cowley .04 .02 .00
□ 770 Carlton Fisk .15 .06 .01
□ 771 Geoff Zahn .04 .02 .00
□ 772 Johnnie LeMaster .04 .02 .00
□ 773 Hal McRae .07 .03 .01
□ 774 Dennis Lamp .04 .02 .00
□ 775 Mookie Wilson .07 .03 .01
□ 776 Jerry Royster .04 .02 .00
□ 777 Ned Yost .04 .02 .00
□ 778 Mike Davis .07 .03 .01
□ 779 Nick Esasky .07 .03 .01
□ 780 Mike Flanagan .07 .03 .01
□ 781 Jim Gantner .04 .02 .00
□ 782 Tom Niedenfuer .04 .02 .00
□ 783 Mike Jorgensen .04 .02 .00
□ 784 Checklist: 661-792 .07 .01 .00
□ 785 Tony Armas .07 .03 .01
□ 786 Enos Cabell .04 .02 .00
□ 787 Jim Wohlford .04 .02 .00
□ 788 Steve Comer .04 .02 .00
□ 789 Luis Salazar .04 .02 .00
□ 790 Ron Guidry .15 .06 .01
□ 791 Ivan DeJesus .04 .02 .00
□ 792 Darrell Evans .15 .06 .01

1985 Topps Glossy 22

The cards in this 22-card set measure 2 1/2" by 3 1/2". Similar in design, both front and back, to last year's Glossy set, this edition features the managers, starting nine players and honorary captains of the National and American League teams in the 1984 All-Star game. The set is numbered on the reverse with plyers essentially ordered by position within league, NL: 1-11 and AL: 12-22.

	MINT	EXC	G-VG
COMPLETE SET (22)	4.00	1.60	.40
COMMON PLAYER (1-22)	.10	.04	.01
☐ 1 Paul Owens MG	.10	.04	.01
☐ 2 Steve Garvey	.40	.16	.04
☐ 3 Ryne Sandberg	.45	.18	.04
☐ 4 Mike Schmidt	.60	.24	.06
☐ 5 Ozzie Smith	.25	.10	.02
☐ 6 Tony Gwynn	.50	.20	.05
☐ 7 Dale Murphy	.60	.24	.06
☐ 8 Darryl Strawberry	.75	.30	.07
☐ 9 Gary Carter	.30	.12	.03
☐ 10 Charlie Lea	.10	.04	.01
☐ 11 Willie McCovey CAPT	.20	.08	.02
☐ 12 Joe Altobelli MG	.10	.04	.01
☐ 13 Rod Carew	.35	.14	.03
☐ 14 Lou Whitaker	.15	.06	.01
☐ 15 George Brett	.60	.24	.06
☐ 16 Cal Ripken	.40	.16	.04
☐ 17 Dave Winfield	.35	.14	.03
☐ 18 Chet Lemon	.10	.04	.01
☐ 19 Reggie Jackson	.60	.24	.06
☐ 20 Lance Parrish	.20	.08	.02
☐ 21 Dave Stieb	.15	.06	.01
☐ 22 Hank Greenberg CAPT	.15	.06	.01

1985 Topps Glossy 40

The cards in this 40-card set measure 2 1/2" by 3 1/2". Similar to last year's glossy set, this set was issued as a bonus prize to Topps All-Star Baseball Game cards found in wax packs. The set could be obtained by sending in the "Bonus Runs" from the "Winning Pitch" game insert cards. For 25 runs and 75 cents, a collector could send in for one of the eight different five card series plus automatically be entered in the Grand Prize Sweepstakes for a chance at a free trip to the All-Star game. The cards are numbered and contain 20 stars from each league.

	MINT	EXC	G-VG
COMPLETE SET (40)	12.00	5.00	1.20
COMMON PLAYER (1-40)	.15	.06	.01
☐ 1 Dale Murphy	1.00	.40	.10
☐ 2 Jesse Orosco	.15	.06	.01
☐ 3 Bob Brenly	.15	.06	.01
☐ 4 Mike Boddicker	.15	.06	.01
☐ 5 Dave Kingman	.20	.08	.02
☐ 6 Jim Rice	.30	.12	.03
☐ 7 Frank Viola	.45	.18	.04
☐ 8 Alvin Davis	.30	.12	.03
☐ 9 Rick Sutcliffe	.25	.10	.02
☐ 10 Pete Rose	1.25	.50	.12
☐ 11 Leon Durham	.15	.06	.01
☐ 12 Joaquin Andujar	.15	.06	.01
☐ 13 Keith Hernandez	.45	.18	.04
☐ 14 Dave Winfield	.50	.20	.05
☐ 15 Reggie Jackson	1.00	.40	.10
☐ 16 Allan Trammell	.35	.14	.03
☐ 17 Bert Blyleven	.20	.08	.02
☐ 18 Tony Armas	.15	.06	.01
☐ 19 Rich Gossage	.20	.08	.02
☐ 20 Jose Cruz	.15	.06	.01
☐ 21 Ryne Sandberg	.45	.18	.04
☐ 22 Bruce Sutter	.20	.08	.02
☐ 23 Mike Schmidt	1.00	.40	.10
☐ 24 Cal Ripken	.85	.34	.08
☐ 25 Dan Petry	.15	.06	.01
☐ 26 Jack Morris	.20	.08	.02
☐ 27 Don Mattingly	2.50	1.00	.25
☐ 28 Eddie Murray	.85	.34	.08
☐ 29 Tony Gwynn	.75	.30	.07
☐ 30 Charlie Lea	.15	.06	.01
☐ 31 Juan Samuel	.25	.10	.02
☐ 32 Phil Niekro	.35	.14	.03
☐ 33 Alejandro Pena	.15	.06	.01
☐ 34 Harold Baines	.20	.08	.02
☐ 35 Dan Quisenberry	.20	.08	.02
☐ 36 Gary Carter	.50	.20	.05
☐ 37 Mario Soto	.15	.06	.01
☐ 38 Dwight Gooden	1.25	.50	.12
☐ 39 Tom Brunansky	.20	.08	.02
☐ 40 Dave Stieb	.20	.08	.02

1985 Topps Traded

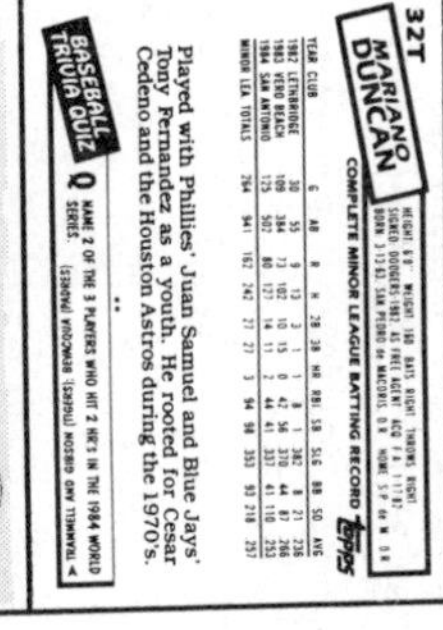

The cards in this 132-card set measure 2 1/2" by 3 1/2". In its now standard procedure, Topps issued its Traded (or extended) set for the fifth year in a row. Because all photos and statistics of its regular set for the year were developed during the fall and winter months of the preceding year, players who changed teams during the fall, winter, and spring months are portrayed in the 1985 regular issue set with the teams they were with in 1984. The Traded set amends the shortcomings of the regular set by presenting the players with their proper teams for the current year. Rookies not contained in the regular set are also picked up in the Traded set. Again this year, the Topps affiliate in Ireland printed the cards, and the cards were available through hobby channels only.

	MINT	EXC	G-VG
COMPLETE SET (132)	14.00	5.75	1.40
COMMON PLAYER (1-132)	.06	.02	.00
☐ 1T Don Aase	.10	.04	.01
☐ 2T Bill Almon	.06	.02	.00
☐ 3T Benny Ayala	.06	.02	.00
☐ 4T Dusty Baker	.10	.04	.01
☐ 5T G.Bamberger MG	.10	.04	.01
☐ 6T Dale Berra	.06	.02	.00
☐ 7T Rich Bordi	.06	.02	.00
☐ 8T Daryl Boston	.10	.04	.01
☐ 9T Hubie Brooks	.20	.08	.02
☐ 10T Chris Brown	.45	.18	.04
☐ 11T Tom Browning	1.25	.50	.12
☐ 12T Al Bumbry	.06	.02	.00
☐ 13T Ray Burris	.06	.02	.00
☐ 14T Jeff Burroughs	.10	.04	.01
☐ 15T Bill Campbell	.06	.02	.00
☐ 16T Don Carman	.30	.12	.03
☐ 17T Gary Carter	.70	.28	.07
☐ 18T Bobby Castillo	.06	.02	.00
☐ 19T Bill Caudill	.06	.02	.00
☐ 20T Rick Cerone	.06	.02	.00
☐ 21T Bryan Clark	.06	.02	.00
☐ 22T Jack Clark	.40	.16	.04
☐ 23T Pat Clements	.15	.06	.01
☐ 24T Vince Coleman	5.00	2.00	.50
☐ 25T Dave Collins	.06	.02	.00
☐ 26T Danny Darwin	.06	.02	.00
☐ 27T Jim Davenport MG	.06	.02	.00
☐ 28T Jerry Davis	.10	.04	.01
☐ 29T Brian Dayett	.06	.02	.00
☐ 30T Ivan DeJesus	.06	.02	.00
☐ 31T Ken Dixon	.15	.06	.01
☐ 32T Mariano Duncan	.20	.08	.02
☐ 33T John Felske MG	.06	.02	.00
☐ 34T Mike Fitzgerald	.06	.02	.00
☐ 35T Ray Fontenot	.06	.02	.00
☐ 36T Greg Gagne	.30	.12	.03
☐ 37T Oscar Gamble	.06	.02	.00
☐ 38T Scott Garrelts	.20	.08	.02
☐ 39T Bob L. Gibson	.06	.02	.00
☐ 40T Jim Gott	.06	.02	.00
☐ 41T David Green	.06	.02	.00
☐ 42T Alfredo Griffin	.15	.06	.01
☐ 43T Ozzie Guillen	.65	.26	.06
☐ 44T Eddie Haas MG	.06	.02	.00
☐ 45T Terry Harper	.06	.02	.00
☐ 46T Toby Harrah	.10	.04	.01
☐ 47T Greg Harris	.06	.02	.00
☐ 48T Ron Hassey	.06	.02	.00
☐ 49T Rickey Henderson	1.00	.40	.10
☐ 50T Steve Henderson	.06	.02	.00
☐ 51T George Hendrick	.10	.04	.01
☐ 52T Joe Hesketh	.20	.08	.02
☐ 53T Teddy Higuera	2.50	1.00	.25
☐ 54T Donnie Hill	.10	.04	.01
☐ 55T Al Holland	.06	.02	.00
☐ 56T Burt Hooton	.06	.02	.00
☐ 57T Jay Howell	.10	.04	.01
☐ 58T Ken Howell	.20	.08	.02
☐ 59T LaMarr Hoyt	.10	.04	.01
☐ 60T Tim Hulett	.15	.06	.01
☐ 61T Bob James	.10	.04	.01
☐ 62T Steve Jeltz	.15	.06	.01
☐ 63T Cliff Johnson	.06	.02	.00
☐ 64T Howard Johnson	1.00	.40	.10
☐ 65T Ruppert Jones	.06	.02	.00
☐ 66T Steve Kemp	.10	.04	.01
☐ 67T Bruce Kison	.06	.02	.00
☐ 68T Alan Knicely	.06	.02	.00
☐ 69T Mike LaCoss	.06	.02	.00
☐ 70T Lee Lacy	.06	.02	.00
☐ 71T Dave LaPoint	.10	.04	.01
☐ 72T Gary Lavelle	.06	.02	.00
☐ 73T Vance Law	.10	.04	.01
☐ 74T Johnnie LeMaster	.06	.02	.00
☐ 75T Sixto Lezcano	.06	.02	.00
☐ 76T Tim Lollar	.06	.02	.00
☐ 77T Fred Lynn	.25	.10	.02
☐ 78T Billy Martin MG	.15	.06	.01
☐ 79T Ron Mathis	.10	.04	.01
☐ 80T Len Matuszek	.06	.02	.00
☐ 81T Gene Mauch MG	.06	.02	.00
☐ 82T Oddibe McDowell	.50	.20	.05
☐ 83T Roger McDowell	.85	.34	.08
☐ 84T John McNamara MG	.06	.02	.00
☐ 85T Donnie Moore	.06	.02	.00
☐ 86T Gene Nelson	.06	.02	.00
☐ 87T Steve Nicosia	.06	.02	.00
☐ 88T Al Oliver	.15	.06	.01
☐ 89T Joe Orsulak	.20	.08	.02
☐ 90T Rob Picciolo	.06	.02	.00
☐ 91T Chris Pittaro	.10	.04	.01
☐ 92T Jim Presley	.75	.30	.07
☐ 93T Rick Reuschel	.15	.06	.01
☐ 94T Bert Roberge	.06	.02	.00
☐ 95T Bob Rodgers MG	.06	.02	.00
☐ 96T Jerry Royster	.06	.02	.00
☐ 97T Dave Rozema	.06	.02	.00
☐ 98T Dave Rucker	.06	.02	.00
☐ 99T Vern Ruhle	.06	.02	.00
☐ 100T Paul Runge	.10	.04	.01
☐ 101T Mark Salas	.15	.06	.01
☐ 102T Luis Salazar	.06	.02	.00
☐ 103T Joe Sambito	.06	.02	.00
☐ 104T Rick Schu	.15	.06	.01
☐ 105T Donnie Scott	.06	.02	.00
☐ 106T Larry Sheets	.45	.18	.04
☐ 107T Don Slaught	.06	.02	.00
☐ 108T Roy Smalley	.06	.02	.00
☐ 109T Lonnie Smith	.10	.04	.01
☐ 110T Nate Snell (headings on back for a batter)	.15	.06	.01
☐ 111T Chris Speier	.06	.02	.00
☐ 112T Mike Stenhouse	.10	.04	.01
☐ 113T Tim Stoddard	.06	.02	.00
☐ 114T Jim Sundberg	.10	.04	.01
☐ 115T Bruce Sutter	.25	.10	.02
☐ 116T Don Sutton	.60	.24	.06
☐ 117T Kent Tekulve	.10	.04	.01
☐ 118T Tom Tellman	.06	.02	.00
☐ 119T Walt Terrell	.10	.04	.01
☐ 120T Mickey Tettleton	.10	.04	.01
☐ 121T Derrel Thomas	.06	.02	.00
☐ 122T Rich Thompson	.10	.04	.01
☐ 123T Alex Trevino	.06	.02	.00
☐ 124T John Tudor	.25	.10	.02
☐ 125T Jose Uribe	.30	.12	.03
☐ 126T Bobby Valentine MG	.10	.04	.01
☐ 127T Dave Von Ohlen	.06	.02	.00
☐ 128T U.L. Washington	.06	.02	.00
☐ 129T Earl Weaver MG	.10	.04	.01
☐ 130T Eddie Whitson	.10	.04	.01
☐ 131T Herm Winningham	.15	.06	.01
☐ 132T Checklist 1-132	.06	.01	.00

1986 Topps

The cards in this 792-card set are standard-size (2 1/2" by 3 1/2"). The first seven cards are a tribute to Pete Rose and his career. Cards 2-7 show small photos of Pete's Topps cards of the given years on the front with biographical information pertaining to those years on the back. The team leader cards were done differently with a simple player action shot on a white background; the player pictured is dubbed the "Dean" of that team, i.e., the player with the longest continuous service with that team. Topps again features a "Turn Back The Clock" series (401-405). Record breakers of the previous year are acknowledged on cards 201 to 207. Cards 701-722 feature All-Star selections from each league. Manager cards feature the team checklist on the reverse. Ryne Sandberg (#690) is the only player card in the set without a Topps logo on the front of the card; this omission was never corrected by Topps. There are two other uncorrected errors involving misnumbered cards; see card numbers 51, 57, 141, and 171 in the checklist below. The backs of all the cards have a distinctive red background. Topps also produced a specially boxed "glossy" edition frequently referred to as the Topps Tiffany set. There were supposedly only 5,000 sets of the Tiffany cards produced; they were marketed to hobby dealers. The checklist of cards (792 regular and 132 Traded) is identical to that of the normal non-glossy cards. There are two primary distinguishing features of the Tiffany cards, white card stock reverses and high gloss obverses. These Tiffany cards are valued at approximately six times the values listed below.

	MINT	EXC	G-VG
COMPLETE SET (792)	28.00	11.50	2.80
COMMON PLAYER (1-792)	.03	.01	.00
□ 1 Pete Rose	1.00	.20	.04
□ 2 Rose Special: '63-'66	.30	.12	.03
□ 3 Rose Special: '67-'70	.30	.12	.03
□ 4 Rose Special: '71-'74	.30	.12	.03
□ 5 Rose Special: '75-'78	.30	.12	.03
□ 6 Rose Special: '79-'82	.30	.12	.03
□ 7 Rose Special: '83-'85	.30	.12	.03
□ 8 Dwayne Murphy	.03	.01	.00
□ 9 Roy Smith	.03	.01	.00
□ 10 Tony Gwynn	.60	.24	.06
□ 11 Bob Ojeda	.10	.04	.01
□ 12 Jose Uribe	.25	.10	.02
□ 13 Bob Kearney	.03	.01	.00
□ 14 Julio Cruz	.03	.01	.00
□ 15 Eddie Whitson	.03	.01	.00
□ 16 Rick Schu	.06	.02	.00
□ 17 Mike Stenhouse	.03	.01	.00
□ 18 Brent Gaff	.03	.01	.00
□ 19 Rich Hebner	.03	.01	.00
□ 20 Lou Whitaker	.10	.04	.01
□ 21 G.Bamberger MG (checklist back)	.06	.01	.00
□ 22 Duane Walker	.03	.01	.00
□ 23 Manny Lee	.10	.04	.01
□ 24 Len Barker	.03	.01	.00
□ 25 Willie Wilson	.10	.04	.01
□ 26 Frank DiPino	.03	.01	.00
□ 27 Ray Knight	.06	.02	.00
□ 28 Eric Davis	2.50	1.00	.25
□ 29 Tony Phillips	.03	.01	.00
□ 30 Eddie Murray	.30	.12	.03
□ 31 Jamie Easterly	.03	.01	.00
□ 32 Steve Yeager	.03	.01	.00
□ 33 Jeff Lahti	.03	.01	.00
□ 34 Ken Phelps	.06	.02	.00
□ 35 Jeff Reardon	.06	.02	.00
□ 36 Tigers Leaders Lance Parrish	.10	.04	.01
□ 37 Mark Thurmond	.03	.01	.00
□ 38 Glenn Hoffman	.03	.01	.00
□ 39 Dave Rucker	.03	.01	.00
□ 40 Ken Griffey	.06	.02	.00
□ 41 Brad Wellman	.03	.01	.00
□ 42 Geoff Zahn	.03	.01	.00
□ 43 Dave Engle	.03	.01	.00
□ 44 Lance McCullers	.30	.12	.03
□ 45 Damaso Garcia	.03	.01	.00
□ 46 Billy Hatcher	.15	.06	.01
□ 47 Juan Berenguer	.03	.01	.00
□ 48 Bill Almon	.03	.01	.00
□ 49 Rick Manning	.03	.01	.00
□ 50 Dan Quisenberry	.10	.04	.01
□ 51 Bobby Wine MG ERR (checklist back) (number of card on back is actually 57)	.10	.03	.01
□ 52 Chris Welsh	.03	.01	.00
□ 53 Len Dykstra	.70	.28	.07
□ 54 John Franco	.10	.04	.01
□ 55 Fred Lynn	.12	.05	.01
□ 56 Tom Niedenfuer	.03	.01	.00
□ 57 Bill Doran (see also 51)	.10	.04	.01
□ 58 Bill Krueger	.03	.01	.00
□ 59 Andre Thornton	.06	.02	.00
□ 60 Dwight Evans	.12	.05	.01
□ 61 Karl Best	.10	.04	.01
□ 62 Bob Boone	.06	.02	.00
□ 63 Ron Roenicke	.03	.01	.00
□ 64 Floyd Bannister	.03	.01	.00
□ 65 Dan Driessen	.03	.01	.00
□ 66 Cardinals Leaders Bob Forsch	.03	.01	.00
□ 67 Carmelo Martinez	.03	.01	.00
□ 68 Ed Lynch	.03	.01	.00
□ 69 Luis Aguayo	.03	.01	.00
□ 70 Dave Winfield	.25	.10	.02
□ 71 Ken Schrom	.03	.01	.00
□ 72 Shawon Dunston	.10	.04	.01
□ 73 Randy O'Neal	.03	.01	.00
□ 74 Rance Mulliniks	.03	.01	.00
□ 75 Jose DeLeon	.03	.01	.00
□ 76 Dion James	.03	.01	.00
□ 77 Charlie Leibrandt	.03	.01	.00
□ 78 Bruce Benedict	.03	.01	.00
□ 79 Dave Schmidt	.03	.01	.00
□ 80 Darryl Strawberry	.75	.30	.07
□ 81 Gene Mauch MG (checklist back)	.06	.01	.00
□ 82 Tippy Martinez	.03	.01	.00
□ 83 Phil Garner	.03	.01	.00
□ 84 Curt Young	.03	.01	.00
□ 85 Tony Perez (Eric Davis also shown on card)	.20	.08	.02
□ 86 Tom Waddell	.03	.01	.00
□ 87 Candy Maldonado	.08	.03	.01
□ 88 Tom Nieto	.03	.01	.00
□ 89 Randy St.Claire	.03	.01	.00
□ 90 Garry Templeton	.06	.02	.00
□ 91 Steve Crawford	.03	.01	.00
□ 92 Al Cowens	.03	.01	.00
□ 93 Scot Thompson	.03	.01	.00
□ 94 Rich Bordi	.03	.01	.00
□ 95 Ozzie Virgil	.03	.01	.00
□ 96 Blue Jays Leaders Jim Clancy	.03	.01	.00
□ 97 Gary Gaetti	.12	.05	.01
□ 98 Dick Ruthven	.03	.01	.00
□ 99 Buddy Biancalana	.03	.01	.00
□ 100 Nolan Ryan	.30	.12	.03
□ 101 Dave Bergman	.03	.01	.00
□ 102 Joe Orsulak	.10	.04	.01
□ 103 Luis Salazar	.03	.01	.00
□ 104 Sid Fernandez	.12	.05	.01
□ 105 Gary Ward	.03	.01	.00
□ 106 Ray Burris	.03	.01	.00
□ 107 Rafael Ramirez	.03	.01	.00
□ 108 Ted Power	.03	.01	.00
□ 109 Len Matuszek	.03	.01	.00
□ 110 Scott McGregor	.03	.01	.00
□ 111 Roger Craig MG (checklist back)	.06	.01	.00
□ 112 Bill Campbell	.03	.01	.00
□ 113 U.L. Washington	.03	.01	.00
□ 114 Mike Brown (Pirates OF)	.03	.01	.00
□ 115 Jay Howell	.03	.01	.00
□ 116 Brook Jacoby	.08	.03	.01
□ 117 Bruce Kison	.03	.01	.00
□ 118 Jerry Royster	.03	.01	.00
□ 119 Barry Bonnell	.03	.01	.00
□ 120 Steve Carlton	.20	.08	.02
□ 121 Nelson Simmons	.08	.03	.01
□ 122 Pete Filson	.03	.01	.00
□ 123 Greg Walker	.08	.03	.01
□ 124 Luis Sanchez	.03	.01	.00
□ 125 Dave Lopes	.06	.02	.00
□ 126 Mets Leaders Mookie Wilson	.03	.01	.00
□ 127 Jack Howell	.30	.12	.03
□ 128 John Wathan	.03	.01	.00
□ 129 Jeff Dedmon	.03	.01	.00
□ 130 Alan Trammell	.20	.08	.02
□ 131 Checklist: 1-132	.06	.01	.00
□ 132 Razor Shines	.06	.02	.00
□ 133 Andy McGaffigan	.03	.01	.00
□ 134 Carney Lansford	.08	.03	.01
□ 135 Joe Niekro	.08	.03	.01
□ 136 Mike Hargrove	.03	.01	.00
□ 137 Charlie Moore	.03	.01	.00
□ 138 Mark Davis	.06	.02	.00
□ 139 Daryl Boston	.06	.02	.00
□ 140 John Candelaria	.06	.02	.00
□ 141 Chuck Cottier MG (checklist back) (see also 171)	.10	.03	.01

□ 142 Bob Jones	.03	.01	.00
□ 143 Dave Van Gorder	.03	.01	.00
□ 144 Doug Sisk	.03	.01	.00
□ 145 Pedro Guerrero	.20	.08	.02
□ 146 Jack Perconte	.03	.01	.00
□ 147 Larry Sheets	.12	.05	.01
□ 148 Mike Heath	.03	.01	.00
□ 149 Brett Butler	.08	.03	.01
□ 150 Joaquin Andujar	.08	.03	.01
□ 151 Dave Stapleton	.03	.01	.00
□ 152 Mike Morgan	.03	.01	.00
□ 153 Ricky Adams	.03	.01	.00
□ 154 Bert Roberge	.03	.01	.00
□ 155 Bob Grich	.06	.02	.00
□ 156 White Sox Leaders Richard Dotson	.03	.01	.00
□ 157 Ron Hassey	.03	.01	.00
□ 158 Derrel Thomas	.03	.01	.00
□ 159 Orel Hershiser	1.25	.50	.12
□ 160 Chet Lemon	.06	.02	.00
□ 161 Lee Tunnell	.03	.01	.00
□ 162 Greg Gagne	.10	.04	.01
□ 163 Pete Ladd	.03	.01	.00
□ 164 Steve Balboni	.03	.01	.00
□ 165 Mike Davis	.03	.01	.00
□ 166 Dickie Thon	.03	.01	.00
□ 167 Zane Smith	.12	.05	.01
□ 168 Jeff Burroughs	.03	.01	.00
□ 169 George Wright	.03	.01	.00
□ 170 Gary Carter	.25	.10	.02
□ 171 Bob Rodgers MG ERR (checklist back) (number of card on back actually 141)	.10	.03	.01
□ 172 Jerry Reed	.03	.01	.00
□ 173 Wayne Gross	.03	.01	.00
□ 174 Brian Snyder	.03	.01	.00
□ 175 Steve Sax	.15	.06	.01
□ 176 Jay Tibbs	.03	.01	.00
□ 177 Joel Youngblood	.03	.01	.00
□ 178 Ivan DeJesus	.03	.01	.00
□ 179 Stu Cliburn	.08	.03	.01
□ 180 Don Mattingly	3.00	1.20	.30
□ 181 Al Nipper	.03	.01	.00
□ 182 Bobby Brown	.03	.01	.00
□ 183 Larry Andersen	.03	.01	.00
□ 184 Tim Laudner	.03	.01	.00
□ 185 Rollie Fingers	.12	.05	.01
□ 186 Astros Leaders Jose Cruz	.03	.01	.00
□ 187 Scott Fletcher	.06	.02	.00
□ 188 Bob Dernier	.03	.01	.00
□ 189 Mike Mason	.03	.01	.00
□ 190 George Hendrick	.06	.02	.00
□ 191 Wally Backman	.06	.02	.00
□ 192 Milt Wilcox	.03	.01	.00
□ 193 Daryl Sconiers	.03	.01	.00
□ 194 Craig McMurtry	.03	.01	.00
□ 195 Dave Concepcion	.06	.02	.00
□ 196 Doyle Alexander	.06	.02	.00
□ 197 Enos Cabell	.03	.01	.00
□ 198 Ken Dixon	.06	.02	.00
□ 199 Dick Howser MG (checklist back)	.06	.01	.00
□ 200 Mike Schmidt	.40	.16	.04
□ 201 RB: Vince Coleman Most stolen bases, season, rookie	.20	.08	.02
□ 202 RB: Dwight Gooden Youngest 20 game winner	.30	.12	.03
□ 203 RB: Keith Hernandez Most game-winning RBI's	.15	.06	.01
□ 204 RB: Phil Niekro Oldest shutout pitcher	.10	.04	.01
□ 205 RB: Tony Perez Oldest grand slammer	.10	.04	.01
□ 206 RB: Pete Rose Most hits, lifetime	.35	.14	.03
□ 207 RB: Fern.Valenzuela Most cons. innings, start of season, no earned runs	.12	.05	.01
□ 208 Ramon Romero	.03	.01	.00
□ 209 Randy Ready	.06	.02	.00
□ 210 Calvin Schiraldi	.08	.03	.01
□ 211 Ed Wojna	.08	.03	.01
□ 212 Chris Speier	.03	.01	.00
□ 213 Bob Shirley	.03	.01	.00
□ 214 Randy Bush	.03	.01	.00
□ 215 Frank White	.06	.02	.00
□ 216 A's Leaders Dwayne Murphy	.03	.01	.00
□ 217 Bill Scherrer	.03	.01	.00
□ 218 Randy Hunt	.03	.01	.00
□ 219 Dennis Lamp	.03	.01	.00
□ 220 Bob Horner	.10	.04	.01
□ 221 Dave Henderson	.03	.01	.00
□ 222 Craig Gerber	.03	.01	.00
□ 223 Atlee Hammaker	.03	.01	.00
□ 224 Cesar Cedeno	.06	.02	.00
□ 225 Ron Darling	.20	.08	.02
□ 226 Lee Lacy	.03	.01	.00
□ 227 Al Jones	.03	.01	.00
□ 228 Tom Lawless	.03	.01	.00
□ 229 Bill Gullickson	.03	.01	.00
□ 230 Terry Kennedy	.03	.01	.00
□ 231 Jim Frey MG (checklist back)	.06	.01	.00
□ 232 Rick Rhoden	.06	.02	.00
□ 233 Steve Lyons	.03	.01	.00
□ 234 Doug Corbett	.03	.01	.00
□ 235 Butch Wynegar	.03	.01	.00
□ 236 Frank Eufemia	.03	.01	.00
□ 237 Ted Simmons	.08	.03	.01
□ 238 Larry Parrish	.03	.01	.00
□ 239 Joel Skinner	.03	.01	.00
□ 240 Tommy John	.10	.04	.01
□ 241 Tony Fernandez	.20	.08	.02
□ 242 Rich Thompson	.03	.01	.00
□ 243 Johnny Grubb	.03	.01	.00
□ 244 Craig Lefferts	.03	.01	.00
□ 245 Jim Sundberg	.03	.01	.00
□ 246 Phillies Leaders Steve Carlton	.12	.05	.01
□ 247 Terry Harper	.03	.01	.00
□ 248 Spike Owen	.03	.01	.00
□ 249 Rob Deer	.20	.08	.02
□ 250 Dwight Gooden	1.50	.60	.15
□ 251 Rich Dauer	.03	.01	.00
□ 252 Bobby Castillo	.03	.01	.00
□ 253 Dann Bilardello	.03	.01	.00
□ 254 Ozzie Guillen	.30	.12	.03
□ 255 Tony Armas	.06	.02	.00
□ 256 Kurt Kepshire	.03	.01	.00
□ 257 Doug DeCinces	.06	.02	.00
□ 258 Tim Burke	.25	.10	.02
□ 259 Dan Pasqua	.15	.06	.01
□ 260 Tony Pena	.08	.03	.01
□ 261 Bobby Valentine MG (checklist back)	.06	.01	.00
□ 262 Mario Ramirez	.03	.01	.00
□ 263 Checklist: 133-264	.06	.01	.00
□ 264 Darren Daulton	.10	.04	.01
□ 265 Ron Davis	.03	.01	.00
□ 266 Keith Moreland	.03	.01	.00
□ 267 Paul Molitor	.12	.05	.01
□ 268 Mike Scott	.25	.10	.02
□ 269 Dane Iorg	.03	.01	.00
□ 270 Jack Morris	.12	.05	.01
□ 271 Dave Collins	.03	.01	.00
□ 272 Tim Tolman	.03	.01	.00
□ 273 Jerry Willard	.03	.01	.00
□ 274 Ron Gardenhire	.03	.01	.00
□ 275 Charlie Hough	.06	.02	.00
□ 276 Yankees Leaders Willie Randolph	.03	.01	.00
□ 277 Jaime Cocanower	.03	.01	.00
□ 278 Sixto Lezcano	.03	.01	.00
□ 279 Al Pardo	.03	.01	.00
□ 280 Tim Raines	.25	.10	.02
□ 281 Steve Mura	.03	.01	.00
□ 282 Jerry Mumphrey	.03	.01	.00
□ 283 Mike Fischlin	.03	.01	.00
□ 284 Brian Dayett	.03	.01	.00
□ 285 Buddy Bell	.08	.03	.01
□ 286 Luis DeLeon	.03	.01	.00
□ 287 John Christensen	.03	.01	.00
□ 288 Don Aase	.03	.01	.00
□ 289 Johnnie LeMaster	.03	.01	.00
□ 290 Carlton Fisk	.12	.05	.01
□ 291 Tom Lasorda MG (checklist back)	.10	.03	.01
□ 292 Chuck Porter	.03	.01	.00
□ 293 Chris Chambliss	.06	.02	.00
□ 294 Danny Cox	.08	.03	.01
□ 295 Kirk Gibson	.25	.10	.02
□ 296 Geno Petralli	.03	.01	.00
□ 297 Tim Lollar	.03	.01	.00
□ 298 Craig Reynolds	.03	.01	.00
□ 299 Bryn Smith	.03	.01	.00
□ 300 George Brett	.40	.16	.04
□ 301 Dennis Rasmussen	.06	.02	.00
□ 302 Greg Gross	.03	.01	.00
□ 303 Curt Wardle	.03	.01	.00
□ 304 Mike Gallego	.03	.01	.00
□ 305 Phil Bradley	.08	.03	.01
□ 306 Padres Leaders	.03	.01	.00

	Terry Kennedy			
□ 307	Dave Sax	.03	.01	.00
□ 308	Ray Fontenot	.03	.01	.00
□ 309	John Shelby	.03	.01	.00
□ 310	Greg Minton	.03	.01	.00
□ 311	Dick Schofield	.03	.01	.00
□ 312	Tom Filer	.03	.01	.00
□ 313	Joe DeSa	.03	.01	.00
□ 314	Frank Pastore	.03	.01	.00
□ 315	Mookie Wilson	.06	.02	.00
□ 316	Sammy Khalifa	.08	.03	.01
□ 317	Ed Romero	.03	.01	.00
□ 318	Terry Whitfield	.03	.01	.00
□ 319	Rick Camp	.03	.01	.00
□ 320	Jim Rice	.20	.08	.02
□ 321	Earl Weaver MG	.06	.01	.00
	(checklist back)			
□ 322	Bob Forsch	.03	.01	.00
□ 323	Jerry Davis	.03	.01	.00
□ 324	Dan Schatzeder	.03	.01	.00
□ 325	Juan Beniquez	.03	.01	.00
□ 326	Kent Tekulve	.03	.01	.00
□ 327	Mike Pagliarulo	.10	.04	.01
□ 328	Pete O'Brien	.08	.03	.01
□ 329	Kirby Puckett	1.25	.50	.12
□ 330	Rick Sutcliffe	.10	.04	.01
□ 331	Alan Ashby	.03	.01	.00
□ 332	Darryl Motley	.03	.01	.00
□ 333	Tom Henke	.10	.04	.01
□ 334	Ken Oberkfell	.03	.01	.00
□ 335	Don Sutton	.15	.06	.01
□ 336	Indians Leaders	.03	.01	.00
	Andre Thornton			
□ 337	Darnell Coles	.03	.01	.00
□ 338	Jorge Bell	.20	.08	.02
□ 339	Bruce Berenyi	.03	.01	.00
□ 340	Cal Ripken	.30	.12	.03
□ 341	Frank Williams	.03	.01	.00
□ 342	Gary Redus	.03	.01	.00
□ 343	Carlos Diaz	.03	.01	.00
□ 344	Jim Wohlford	.03	.01	.00
□ 345	Donnie Moore	.03	.01	.00
□ 346	Bryan Little	.03	.01	.00
□ 347	Teddy Higuera	.90	.36	.09
□ 348	Cliff Johnson	.03	.01	.00
□ 349	Mark Clear	.03	.01	.00
□ 350	Jack Clark	.20	.08	.02
□ 351	Chuck Tanner MG	.06	.01	.00
	(checklist back)			
□ 352	Harry Spilman	.03	.01	.00
□ 353	Keith Atherton	.03	.01	.00
□ 354	Tony Bernazard	.03	.01	.00
□ 355	Lee Smith	.06	.02	.00
□ 356	Mickey Hatcher	.06	.02	.00
□ 357	Ed VandeBerg	.03	.01	.00
□ 358	Rick Dempsey	.03	.01	.00
□ 359	Mike LaCoss	.03	.01	.00
□ 360	Lloyd Moseby	.08	.03	.01
□ 361	Shane Rawley	.06	.02	.00
□ 362	Tom Paciorek	.03	.01	.00
□ 363	Terry Forster	.06	.02	.00
□ 364	Reid Nichols	.03	.01	.00
□ 365	Mike Flanagan	.06	.02	.00
□ 366	Reds Leaders	.03	.01	.00
	Dave Concepcion			
□ 367	Aurelio Lopez	.03	.01	.00
□ 368	Greg Brock	.03	.01	.00
□ 369	Al Holland	.03	.01	.00
□ 370	Vince Coleman	1.50	.60	.15
□ 371	Bill Stein	.03	.01	.00
□ 372	Ben Oglivie	.06	.02	.00
□ 373	Urbano Lugo	.03	.01	.00
□ 374	Terry Francona	.03	.01	.00
□ 375	Rich Gedman	.06	.02	.00
□ 376	Bill Dawley	.03	.01	.00
□ 377	Joe Carter	.30	.12	.03
□ 378	Bruce Bochte	.03	.01	.00
□ 379	Bobby Meacham	.03	.01	.00
□ 380	LaMarr Hoyt	.06	.02	.00
□ 381	Ray Miller MG	.06	.01	.00
	(checklist back)			
□ 382	Ivan Calderon	.60	.24	.06
□ 383	Chris Brown	.35	.14	.03
□ 384	Steve Trout	.03	.01	.00
□ 385	Cecil Cooper	.08	.03	.01
□ 386	Cecil Fielder	.15	.06	.01
□ 387	Steve Kemp	.03	.01	.00
□ 388	Dickie Noles	.03	.01	.00
□ 389	Glenn Davis	1.25	.50	.12
□ 390	Tom Seaver	.30	.12	.03
□ 391	Julio Franco	.10	.04	.01
□ 392	John Russell	.03	.01	.00
□ 393	Chris Pittaro	.03	.01	.00
□ 394	Checklist: 265-396	.06	.01	.00
□ 395	Scott Garrelts	.06	.02	.00
□ 396	Red Sox Leaders	.08	.03	.01
	Dwight Evans			
□ 397	Steve Buechele	.20	.08	.02
□ 398	Earnie Riles	.20	.08	.02
□ 399	Bill Swift	.06	.02	.00
□ 400	Rod Carew	.30	.12	.03
□ 401	Turn Back 5 Years	.10	.04	.01
	Fern.Valenzuela '81			
□ 402	Turn Back 10 Years	.15	.06	.01
	Tom Seaver '76			
□ 403	Turn Back 15 Years	.15	.06	.01
	Willie Mays '71			
□ 404	Turn Back 20 Years	.10	.04	.01
	Frank Robinson '66			
□ 405	Turn Back 25 Years	.15	.06	.01
	Roger Maris '61			
□ 406	Scott Sanderson	.03	.01	.00
□ 407	Sal Butera	.03	.01	.00
□ 408	Dave Smith	.06	.02	.00
□ 409	Paul Runge	.03	.01	.00
□ 410	Dave Kingman	.08	.03	.01
□ 411	Sparky Anderson MG	.06	.01	.00
	(checklist back)			
□ 412	Jim Clancy	.03	.01	.00
□ 413	Tim Flannery	.03	.01	.00
□ 414	Tom Gorman	.03	.01	.00
□ 415	Hal McRae	.06	.02	.00
□ 416	Denny Martinez	.06	.02	.00
□ 417	R.J. Reynolds	.03	.01	.00
□ 418	Alan Knicely	.03	.01	.00
□ 419	Frank Wills	.03	.01	.00
□ 420	Von Hayes	.08	.03	.01
□ 421	Dave Palmer	.03	.01	.00
□ 422	Mike Jorgensen	.03	.01	.00
□ 423	Dan Spillner	.03	.01	.00
□ 424	Rick Miller	.03	.01	.00
□ 425	Larry McWilliams	.03	.01	.00
□ 426	Brewers Leaders	.03	.01	.00
	Charlie Moore			
□ 427	Joe Cowley	.03	.01	.00
□ 428	Max Venable	.03	.01	.00
□ 429	Greg Booker	.03	.01	.00
□ 430	Kent Hrbek	.15	.06	.01
□ 431	George Frazier	.03	.01	.00
□ 432	Mark Bailey	.03	.01	.00
□ 433	Chris Codiroli	.03	.01	.00
□ 434	Curt Wilkerson	.03	.01	.00
□ 435	Bill Caudill	.03	.01	.00
□ 436	Doug Flynn	.03	.01	.00
□ 437	Rick Mahler	.03	.01	.00
□ 438	Clint Hurdle	.03	.01	.00
□ 439	Rick Honeycutt	.03	.01	.00
□ 440	Alvin Davis	.15	.06	.01
□ 441	Whitey Herzog MG	.06	.01	.00
	(checklist back)			
□ 442	Ron Robinson	.08	.03	.01
□ 443	Bill Buckner	.06	.02	.00
□ 444	Alex Trevino	.03	.01	.00
□ 445	Bert Blyleven	.08	.03	.01
□ 446	Lenn Sakata	.03	.01	.00
□ 447	Jerry Don Gleaton	.03	.01	.00
□ 448	Herm Winningham	.10	.04	.01
□ 449	Rod Scurry	.03	.01	.00
□ 450	Graig Nettles	.10	.04	.01
□ 451	Mark Brown	.06	.02	.00
□ 452	Bob Clark	.03	.01	.00
□ 453	Steve Jeltz	.03	.01	.00
□ 454	Burt Hooton	.03	.01	.00
□ 455	Willie Randolph	.06	.02	.00
□ 456	Braves Leaders	.15	.06	.01
	Dale Murphy			
□ 457	Mickey Tettleton	.08	.03	.01
□ 458	Kevin Bass	.08	.03	.01
□ 459	Luis Leal	.03	.01	.00
□ 460	Leon Durham	.06	.02	.00
□ 461	Walt Terrell	.03	.01	.00
□ 462	Domingo Ramos	.03	.01	.00
□ 463	Jim Gott	.03	.01	.00
□ 464	Ruppert Jones	.03	.01	.00
□ 465	Jesse Orosco	.03	.01	.00
□ 466	Tom Foley	.03	.01	.00
□ 467	Bob James	.03	.01	.00
□ 468	Mike Scioscia	.03	.01	.00
□ 469	Storm Davis	.06	.02	.00
□ 470	Bill Madlock	.08	.03	.01
□ 471	Bobby Cox MG	.06	.01	.00
	(checklist back)			
□ 472	Joe Hesketh	.06	.02	.00
□ 473	Mark Brouhard	.03	.01	.00
□ 474	John Tudor	.10	.04	.01
□ 475	Juan Samuel	.12	.05	.01
□ 476	Ron Mathis	.08	.03	.01
□ 477	Mike Easler	.03	.01	.00
□ 478	Andy Hawkins	.06	.02	.00
□ 479	Bob Melvin	.10	.04	.01

☐ 480	Oddibe McDowell	.15	.06	.01
☐ 481	Scott Bradley	.10	.04	.01
☐ 482	Rick Lysander	.03	.01	.00
☐ 483	George Vukovich	.03	.01	.00
☐ 484	Donnie Hill	.03	.01	.00
☐ 485	Gary Matthews	.06	.02	.00
☐ 486	Angels Leaders Bobby Grich	.03	.01	.00
☐ 487	Bret Saberhagen	.30	.12	.03
☐ 488	Lou Thornton	.08	.03	.01
☐ 489	Jim Winn	.03	.01	.00
☐ 490	Jeff Leonard	.08	.03	.01
☐ 491	Pascual Perez	.06	.02	.00
☐ 492	Kelvin Chapman	.03	.01	.00
☐ 493	Gene Nelson	.03	.01	.00
☐ 494	Gary Roenicke	.03	.01	.00
☐ 495	Mark Langston	.10	.04	.01
☐ 496	Jay Johnstone	.06	.02	.00
☐ 497	John Stuper	.03	.01	.00
☐ 498	Tito Landrum	.03	.01	.00
☐ 499	Bob L. Gibson	.03	.01	.00
☐ 500	Rickey Henderson	.35	.14	.03
☐ 501	Dave Johnson MG (checklist back)	.06	.01	.00
☐ 502	Glen Cook	.08	.03	.01
☐ 503	Mike Fitzgerald	.03	.01	.00
☐ 504	Denny Walling	.03	.01	.00
☐ 505	Jerry Koosman	.06	.02	.00
☐ 506	Bill Russell	.03	.01	.00
☐ 507	Steve Ontiveros	.08	.03	.01
☐ 508	Alan Wiggins	.03	.01	.00
☐ 509	Ernie Camacho	.03	.01	.00
☐ 510	Wade Boggs	2.00	.80	.20
☐ 511	Ed Nunez	.03	.01	.00
☐ 512	Thad Bosley	.03	.01	.00
☐ 513	Ron Washington	.03	.01	.00
☐ 514	Mike Jones	.03	.01	.00
☐ 515	Darrell Evans	.08	.03	.01
☐ 516	Giants Leaders Greg Minton	.03	.01	.00
☐ 517	Milt Thompson	.25	.10	.02
☐ 518	Buck Martinez	.03	.01	.00
☐ 519	Danny Darwin	.03	.01	.00
☐ 520	Keith Hernandez	.25	.10	.02
☐ 521	Nate Snell	.08	.03	.01
☐ 522	Bob Bailor	.03	.01	.00
☐ 523	Joe Price	.03	.01	.00
☐ 524	Darrell Miller	.08	.03	.01
☐ 525	Marvell Wynne	.03	.01	.00
☐ 526	Charlie Lea	.03	.01	.00
☐ 527	Checklist: 397-528	.06	.01	.00
☐ 528	Terry Pendleton	.06	.02	.00
☐ 529	Marc Sullivan	.03	.01	.00
☐ 530	Rich Gossage	.10	.04	.01
☐ 531	Tony LaRussa MG (checklist back)	.06	.01	.00
☐ 532	Don Carman	.20	.08	.02
☐ 533	Billy Sample	.03	.01	.00
☐ 534	Jeff Calhoun	.03	.01	.00
☐ 535	Toby Harrah	.03	.01	.00
☐ 536	Jose Rijo	.06	.02	.00
☐ 537	Mark Salas	.03	.01	.00
☐ 538	Dennis Eckersley	.10	.04	.01
☐ 539	Glenn Hubbard	.03	.01	.00
☐ 540	Dan Petry	.06	.02	.00
☐ 541	Jorge Orta	.03	.01	.00
☐ 542	Don Schulze	.03	.01	.00
☐ 543	Jerry Narron	.03	.01	.00
☐ 544	Eddie Milner	.03	.01	.00
☐ 545	Jimmy Key	.10	.04	.01
☐ 546	Mariners Leaders Dave Henderson	.03	.01	.00
☐ 547	Roger McDowell	.45	.18	.04
☐ 548	Mike Young	.08	.03	.01
☐ 549	Bob Welch	.06	.02	.00
☐ 550	Tom Herr	.06	.02	.00
☐ 551	Dave LaPoint	.06	.02	.00
☐ 552	Marc Hill	.03	.01	.00
☐ 553	Jim Morrison	.03	.01	.00
☐ 554	Paul Householder	.03	.01	.00
☐ 555	Hubie Brooks	.08	.03	.01
☐ 556	John Denny	.06	.02	.00
☐ 557	Gerald Perry	.12	.05	.01
☐ 558	Tim Stoddard	.03	.01	.00
☐ 559	Tommy Dunbar	.03	.01	.00
☐ 560	Dave Righetti	.10	.04	.01
☐ 561	Bob Lillis MG (checklist back)	.06	.01	.00
☐ 562	Joe Beckwith	.03	.01	.00
☐ 563	Alejandro Sanchez	.03	.01	.00
☐ 564	Warren Brusstar	.03	.01	.00
☐ 565	Tom Brunansky	.12	.05	.01
☐ 566	Alfredo Griffin	.06	.02	.00
☐ 567	Jeff Barkley	.03	.01	.00
☐ 568	Donnie Scott	.03	.01	.00
☐ 569	Jim Acker	.03	.01	.00
☐ 570	Rusty Staub	.08	.03	.01
☐ 571	Mike Jeffcoat	.03	.01	.00
☐ 572	Paul Zuvella	.03	.01	.00
☐ 573	Tom Hume	.03	.01	.00
☐ 574	Ron Kittle	.10	.04	.01
☐ 575	Mike Boddicker	.08	.03	.01
☐ 576	Expos Leaders Andre Dawson	.12	.05	.01
☐ 577	Jerry Reuss	.06	.02	.00
☐ 578	Lee Mazzilli	.03	.01	.00
☐ 579	Jim Slaton	.03	.01	.00
☐ 580	Willie McGee	.15	.06	.01
☐ 581	Bruce Hurst	.12	.05	.01
☐ 582	Jim Gantner	.03	.01	.00
☐ 583	Al Bumbry	.03	.01	.00
☐ 584	Brian Fisher	.25	.10	.02
☐ 585	Garry Maddox	.06	.02	.00
☐ 586	Greg Harris	.03	.01	.00
☐ 587	Rafael Santana	.03	.01	.00
☐ 588	Steve Lake	.03	.01	.00
☐ 589	Sid Bream	.03	.01	.00
☐ 590	Bob Knepper	.06	.02	.00
☐ 591	Jackie Moore MG (checklist back)	.06	.01	.00
☐ 592	Frank Tanana	.06	.02	.00
☐ 593	Jesse Barfield	.20	.08	.02
☐ 594	Chris Bando	.03	.01	.00
☐ 595	Dave Parker	.15	.06	.01
☐ 596	Onix Concepcion	.03	.01	.00
☐ 597	Sammy Stewart	.03	.01	.00
☐ 598	Jim Presley	.20	.08	.02
☐ 599	Rick Aguilera	.25	.10	.02
☐ 600	Dale Murphy	.40	.16	.04
☐ 601	Gary Lucas	.03	.01	.00
☐ 602	Mariano Duncan	.15	.06	.01
☐ 603	Bill Laskey	.03	.01	.00
☐ 604	Gary Pettis	.06	.02	.00
☐ 605	Dennis Boyd	.08	.03	.01
☐ 606	Royals Leaders Hal McRae	.03	.01	.00
☐ 607	Ken Dayley	.03	.01	.00
☐ 608	Bruce Bochy	.03	.01	.00
☐ 609	Barbaro Garbey	.03	.01	.00
☐ 610	Ron Guidry	.10	.04	.01
☐ 611	Gary Woods	.03	.01	.00
☐ 612	Richard Dotson	.06	.02	.00
☐ 613	Roy Smalley	.03	.01	.00
☐ 614	Rick Waits	.03	.01	.00
☐ 615	Johnny Ray	.08	.03	.01
☐ 616	Glenn Brummer	.03	.01	.00
☐ 617	Lonnie Smith	.03	.01	.00
☐ 618	Jim Pankovits	.03	.01	.00
☐ 619	Danny Heep	.03	.01	.00
☐ 620	Bruce Sutter	.10	.04	.01
☐ 621	John Felske MG (checklist back)	.06	.01	.00
☐ 622	Gary Lavelle	.03	.01	.00
☐ 623	Floyd Rayford	.03	.01	.00
☐ 624	Steve McCatty	.03	.01	.00
☐ 625	Bob Brenly	.03	.01	.00
☐ 626	Roy Thomas	.03	.01	.00
☐ 627	Ron Oester	.03	.01	.00
☐ 628	Kirk McCaskill	.30	.12	.03
☐ 629	Mitch Webster	.25	.10	.02
☐ 630	Fernando Valenzuela	.20	.08	.02
☐ 631	Steve Braun	.03	.01	.00
☐ 632	Dave Von Ohlen	.03	.01	.00
☐ 633	Jackie Gutierrez	.03	.01	.00
☐ 634	Roy Lee Jackson	.03	.01	.00
☐ 635	Jason Thompson	.03	.01	.00
☐ 636	Cubs Leaders Lee Smith	.03	.01	.00
☐ 637	Rudy Law	.03	.01	.00
☐ 638	John Butcher	.03	.01	.00
☐ 639	Bo Diaz	.03	.01	.00
☐ 640	Jose Cruz	.08	.03	.01
☐ 641	Wayne Tolleson	.03	.01	.00
☐ 642	Ray Searage	.03	.01	.00
☐ 643	Tom Brookens	.03	.01	.00
☐ 644	Mark Gubicza	.08	.03	.01
☐ 645	Dusty Baker	.06	.02	.00
☐ 646	Mike Moore	.06	.02	.00
☐ 647	Mel Hall	.06	.02	.00
☐ 648	Steve Bedrosian	.10	.04	.01
☐ 649	Ronn Reynolds	.03	.01	.00
☐ 650	Dave Stieb	.10	.04	.01
☐ 651	Billy Martin MG (checklist back)	.10	.03	.01
☐ 652	Tom Browning	.15	.06	.01
☐ 653	Jim Dwyer	.03	.01	.00
☐ 654	Ken Howell	.03	.01	.00
☐ 655	Manny Trillo	.03	.01	.00
☐ 656	Brian Harper	.03	.01	.00
☐ 657	Juan Agosto	.03	.01	.00

☐ 658	Rob Wilfong	.03	.01	.00
☐ 659	Checklist: 529-660	.06	.01	.00
☐ 660	Steve Garvey	.35	.14	.03
☐ 661	Roger Clemens	2.00	.80	.20
☐ 662	Bill Schroeder	.03	.01	.00
☐ 663	Neil Allen	.03	.01	.00
☐ 664	Tim Corcoran	.03	.01	.00
☐ 665	Alejandro Pena	.03	.01	.00
☐ 666	Rangers Leaders Charlie Hough	.03	.01	.00
☐ 667	Tim Teufel	.03	.01	.00
☐ 668	Cecilio Guante	.03	.01	.00
☐ 669	Ron Cey	.06	.02	.00
☐ 670	Willie Hernandez	.08	.03	.01
☐ 671	Lynn Jones	.03	.01	.00
☐ 672	Rob Picciolo	.03	.01	.00
☐ 673	Ernie Whitt	.03	.01	.00
☐ 674	Pat Tabler	.08	.03	.01
☐ 675	Claudell Washington	.06	.02	.00
☐ 676	Matt Young	.03	.01	.00
☐ 677	Nick Esasky	.03	.01	.00
☐ 678	Dan Gladden	.06	.02	.00
☐ 679	Britt Burns	.03	.01	.00
☐ 680	George Foster	.10	.04	.01
☐ 681	Dick Williams MG (checklist back)	.06	.01	.00
☐ 682	Junior Ortiz	.03	.01	.00
☐ 683	Andy Van Slyke	.20	.08	.02
☐ 684	Bob McClure	.03	.01	.00
☐ 685	Tim Wallach	.08	.03	.01
☐ 686	Jeff Stone	.03	.01	.00
☐ 687	Mike Trujillo	.03	.01	.00
☐ 688	Larry Herndon	.03	.01	.00
☐ 689	Dave Stewart	.10	.04	.01
☐ 690	Ryne Sandberg (no Topps logo on front)	.25	.10	.02
☐ 691	Mike Madden	.03	.01	.00
☐ 692	Dale Berra	.03	.01	.00
☐ 693	Tom Tellmann	.03	.01	.00
☐ 694	Garth Iorg	.03	.01	.00
☐ 695	Mike Smithson	.03	.01	.00
☐ 696	Dodgers Leaders Bill Russell	.03	.01	.00
☐ 697	Bud Black	.03	.01	.00
☐ 698	Brad Komminsk	.03	.01	.00
☐ 699	Pat Corrales MG (checklist back)	.06	.01	.00
☐ 700	Reggie Jackson	.35	.14	.03
☐ 701	Keith Hernandez AS	.15	.06	.01
☐ 702	Tom Herr AS	.06	.02	.00
☐ 703	Tim Wallach AS	.06	.02	.00
☐ 704	Ozzie Smith AS	.12	.05	.01
☐ 705	Dale Murphy AS	.30	.12	.03
☐ 706	Pedro Guerrero AS	.12	.05	.01
☐ 707	Willie McGee AS	.10	.04	.01
☐ 708	Gary Carter AS	.15	.06	.01
☐ 709	Dwight Gooden AS	.30	.12	.03
☐ 710	John Tudor AS	.06	.02	.00
☐ 711	Jeff Reardon AS	.06	.02	.00
☐ 712	Don Mattingly AS	.80	.32	.08
☐ 713	Damaso Garcia AS	.06	.02	.00
☐ 714	George Brett AS	.25	.10	.02
☐ 715	Cal Ripken AS	.20	.08	.02
☐ 716	Rickey Henderson AS	.25	.10	.02
☐ 717	Dave Winfield AS	.15	.06	.01
☐ 718	Jorge Bell AS	.12	.05	.01
☐ 719	Carlton Fisk AS	.10	.04	.01
☐ 720	Bret Saberhagen AS	.10	.04	.01
☐ 721	Ron Guidry AS	.10	.04	.01
☐ 722	Dan Quisenberry AS	.06	.02	.00
☐ 723	Marty Bystrom	.03	.01	.00
☐ 724	Tim Hulett	.03	.01	.00
☐ 725	Mario Soto	.03	.01	.00
☐ 726	Orioles Leaders Rick Dempsey	.03	.01	.00
☐ 727	David Green	.03	.01	.00
☐ 728	Mike Marshall	.08	.03	.01
☐ 729	Jim Beattie	.03	.01	.00
☐ 730	Ozzie Smith	.15	.06	.01
☐ 731	Don Robinson	.03	.01	.00
☐ 732	Floyd Youmans	.30	.12	.03
☐ 733	Ron Romanick	.03	.01	.00
☐ 734	Marty Barrett	.08	.03	.01
☐ 735	Dave Dravecky	.03	.01	.00
☐ 736	Glenn Wilson	.03	.01	.00
☐ 737	Pete Vuckovich	.03	.01	.00
☐ 738	Andre Robertson	.03	.01	.00
☐ 739	Dave Rozema	.03	.01	.00
☐ 740	Lance Parrish	.12	.05	.01
☐ 741	Pete Rose MG (checklist back)	.35	.12	.02
☐ 742	Frank Viola	.25	.10	.02
☐ 743	Pat Sheridan	.03	.01	.00
☐ 744	Lary Sorensen	.03	.01	.00
☐ 745	Willie Upshaw	.03	.01	.00
☐ 746	Denny Gonzalez	.03	.01	.00
☐ 747	Rick Cerone	.03	.01	.00
☐ 748	Steve Henderson	.03	.01	.00
☐ 749	Ed Jurak	.03	.01	.00
☐ 750	Gorman Thomas	.06	.02	.00
☐ 751	Howard Johnson	.20	.08	.02
☐ 752	Mike Krukow	.03	.01	.00
☐ 753	Dan Ford	.03	.01	.00
☐ 754	Pat Clements	.10	.04	.01
☐ 755	Harold Baines	.10	.04	.01
☐ 756	Pirates Leaders Rick Rhoden	.03	.01	.00
☐ 757	Darrell Porter	.03	.01	.00
☐ 758	Dave Anderson	.03	.01	.00
☐ 759	Moose Haas	.03	.01	.00
☐ 760	Andre Dawson	.25	.10	.02
☐ 761	Don Slaught	.03	.01	.00
☐ 762	Eric Show	.06	.02	.00
☐ 763	Terry Puhl	.03	.01	.00
☐ 764	Kevin Gross	.03	.01	.00
☐ 765	Don Baylor	.10	.04	.01
☐ 766	Rick Langford	.03	.01	.00
☐ 767	Jody Davis	.08	.03	.01
☐ 768	Vern Ruhle	.03	.01	.00
☐ 769	Harold Reynolds	.35	.14	.03
☐ 770	Vida Blue	.06	.02	.00
☐ 771	John McNamara MG (checklist back)	.06	.01	.00
☐ 772	Brian Downing	.06	.02	.00
☐ 773	Greg Pryor	.03	.01	.00
☐ 774	Terry Leach	.08	.03	.01
☐ 775	Al Oliver	.08	.03	.01
☐ 776	Gene Garber	.03	.01	.00
☐ 777	Wayne Krenchicki	.03	.01	.00
☐ 778	Jerry Hairston	.03	.01	.00
☐ 779	Rick Reuschel	.06	.02	.00
☐ 780	Robin Yount	.25	.10	.02
☐ 781	Joe Nolan	.03	.01	.00
☐ 782	Ken Landreaux	.03	.01	.00
☐ 783	Ricky Horton	.03	.01	.00
☐ 784	Alan Bannister	.03	.01	.00
☐ 785	Bob Stanley	.03	.01	.00
☐ 786	Twins Leaders Mickey Hatcher	.03	.01	.00
☐ 787	Vance Law	.06	.02	.00
☐ 788	Marty Castillo	.03	.01	.00
☐ 789	Kurt Bevacqua	.03	.01	.00
☐ 790	Phil Niekro	.15	.06	.01
☐ 791	Checklist: 661-792	.06	.01	.00
☐ 792	Charles Hudson	.06	.02	.00

1986 Topps Wax Box Cards

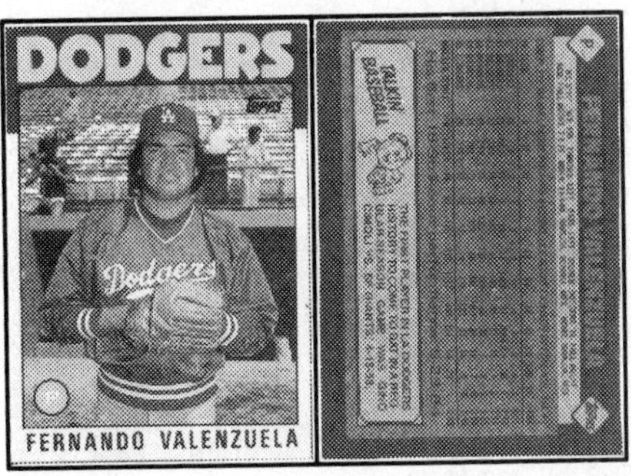

Topps printed cards (each measuring the standard 2 1/2" by 3 1/2") on the bottoms of their wax pack boxes for their regular issue cards; there are four different boxes, each with four cards. These sixteen cards ("numbered" A through P) are listed below; they are not considered an integral part of the regular set but are considered a separate set. They are styled almost exactly like the 1986 Topps regular issue cards.

	MINT	EXC	G-VG
COMPLETE SET (16)	6.00	2.40	.60
COMMON PLAYER (A-P)	.10	.04	.01

☐ A Jorge Bell	.25	.10	.02
☐ B Wade Boggs	1.00	.40	.10
☐ C George Brett	.50	.20	.05
☐ D Vince Coleman	1.00	.40	.10
☐ E Carlton Fisk	.10	.04	.01
☐ F Dwight Gooden	.75	.30	.07
☐ G Pedro Guerrero	.20	.08	.02
☐ H Ron Guidry	.15	.06	.01
☐ I Reggie Jackson	.50	.20	.05
☐ J Don Mattingly	1.50	.60	.15
☐ K Oddibe McDowell	.15	.06	.01
☐ L Willie McGee	.20	.08	.02
☐ M Dale Murphy	.65	.26	.06
☐ N Pete Rose	1.00	.40	.10
☐ O Bret Saberhagen	.20	.08	.02
☐ P Fernando Valenzuela	.15	.06	.01

1986 Topps Glossy 22

This 22-card set was distributed as an insert, one card per rak pack. The players featured are the starting lineups of the 1985 All-Star Game played in Minnesota. Cards are very colorful with a high gloss finish and are standard-size, 2 1/2" by 3 1/2". Cards are numbered on the back.

	MINT	EXC	G-VG
COMPLETE SET (22)	4.00	1.60	.40
COMMON PLAYER (1-22)	.10	.04	.01
☐ 1 Sparky Anderson MG	.10	.04	.01
☐ 2 Eddie Murray	.30	.12	.03
☐ 3 Lou Whitaker	.15	.06	.01
☐ 4 George Brett	.40	.16	.04
☐ 5 Cal Ripken	.30	.12	.03
☐ 6 Jim Rice	.25	.10	.02
☐ 7 Rickey Henderson	.40	.16	.04
☐ 8 Dave Winfield	.30	.12	.03
☐ 9 Carlton Fisk	.20	.08	.02
☐ 10 Jack Morris	.20	.08	.02
☐ 11 AL Team Photo	.10	.04	.01
☐ 12 Dick Williams MG	.10	.04	.01
☐ 13 Steve Garvey	.30	.12	.03
☐ 14 Tom Herr	.10	.04	.01
☐ 15 Graig Nettles	.15	.06	.01
☐ 16 Ozzie Smith	.20	.08	.02
☐ 17 Tony Gwynn	.40	.16	.04
☐ 18 Dale Murphy	.50	.20	.05
☐ 19 Darryl Strawberry	.50	.20	.05
☐ 20 Terry Kennedy	.10	.04	.01
☐ 21 LaMarr Hoyt	.10	.04	.01
☐ 22 NL Team Photo	.10	.04	.01

1986 Topps Glossy 60

This 60-card glossy set was produced by Topps and distributed ten cards at a time based on the offer found on the wax packs. Cards measure the standard 2 1/2" by 3 1/2". Each series of ten cards was available by sending in 1.00 plus six "special offer" cards inserted one per wax pack. The card backs are printed in red and blue on white card stock. The card

fronts feature a white border and a green frame surrounding a full-color photo of the player.

	MINT	EXC	G-VG
COMPLETE SET (60)	12.00	5.00	1.20
COMMON PLAYER (1-60)	.10	.04	.01
☐ 1 Oddibe McDowell	.15	.06	.01
☐ 2 Reggie Jackson	.50	.20	.05
☐ 3 Fernando Valenzuela	.25	.10	.02
☐ 4 Jack Clark	.25	.10	.02
☐ 5 Rickey Henderson	.50	.20	.05
☐ 6 Steve Balboni	.10	.04	.01
☐ 7 Keith Hernandez	.25	.10	.02
☐ 8 Lance Parrish	.20	.08	.02
☐ 9 Willie McGee	.20	.08	.02
☐ 10 Chris Brown	.15	.06	.01
☐ 11 Darryl Strawberry	.75	.30	.07
☐ 12 Ron Guidry	.20	.08	.02
☐ 13 Dave Parker	.20	.08	.02
☐ 14 Cal Ripken	.30	.12	.03
☐ 15 Tim Raines	.30	.12	.03
☐ 16 Rod Carew	.35	.14	.03
☐ 17 Mike Schmidt	.60	.24	.06
☐ 18 George Brett	.60	.24	.06
☐ 19 Joe Hesketh	.10	.04	.01
☐ 20 Dan Pasqua	.15	.06	.01
☐ 21 Vince Coleman	.60	.24	.06
☐ 22 Tom Seaver	.35	.14	.03
☐ 23 Gary Carter	.35	.14	.03
☐ 24 Orel Hershiser	.75	.30	.07
☐ 25 Pedro Guerrero	.25	.10	.02
☐ 26 Wade Boggs	1.00	.40	.10
☐ 27 Bret Saberhagen	.20	.08	.02
☐ 28 Carlton Fisk	.20	.08	.02
☐ 29 Kirk Gibson	.35	.14	.03
☐ 30 Brian Fisher	.10	.04	.01
☐ 31 Don Mattingly	2.00	.80	.20
☐ 32 Tom Herr	.10	.04	.01
☐ 33 Eddie Murray	.40	.16	.04
☐ 34 Ryne Sandberg	.30	.12	.03
☐ 35 Dan Quisenberry	.15	.06	.01
☐ 36 Jim Rice	.25	.10	.02
☐ 37 Dale Murphy	.60	.24	.06
☐ 38 Steve Garvey	.40	.16	.04
☐ 39 Roger McDowell	.15	.06	.01
☐ 40 Earnie Riles	.10	.04	.01
☐ 41 Dwight Gooden	.90	.36	.09
☐ 42 Dave Winfield	.35	.14	.03
☐ 43 Dave Stieb	.15	.06	.01
☐ 44 Bob Horner	.15	.06	.01
☐ 45 Nolan Ryan	.45	.18	.04
☐ 46 Ozzie Smith	.25	.10	.02
☐ 47 Jorge Bell	.20	.08	.02
☐ 48 Gorman Thomas	.15	.06	.01
☐ 49 Tom Browning	.20	.08	.02
☐ 50 Larry Sheets	.15	.06	.01
☐ 51 Pete Rose	1.00	.40	.10
☐ 52 Brett Butler	.15	.06	.01
☐ 53 John Tudor	.15	.06	.01
☐ 54 Phil Bradley	.15	.06	.01
☐ 55 Jeff Reardon	.15	.06	.01
☐ 56 Rich Gossage	.15	.06	.01
☐ 57 Tony Gwynn	.50	.20	.05
☐ 58 Ozzie Guillen	.15	.06	.01
☐ 59 Glenn Davis	.30	.12	.03
☐ 60 Darrell Evans	.15	.06	.01

1986 Topps Mini Leaders

The 1986 Topps Mini set of Major League Leaders features 66 cards of leaders of the various statistical categories for the 1985 season. The cards are numbered on the back and measure 2 1/8" by 2 15/16". They are very similar in design to the Team Leader "Dean" cards in the 1986 Topps regular issue.

	MINT	EXC	G-VG
COMPLETE SET (66)	6.50	2.60	.65
COMMON PLAYER (1-66)	.05	.02	.00
□ 1 Eddie Murray	.25	.10	.02
□ 2 Cal Ripken	.25	.10	.02
□ 3 Wade Boggs	.60	.24	.06
□ 4 Dennis Boyd	.05	.02	.00
□ 5 Dwight Evans	.15	.06	.01
□ 6 Bruce Hurst	.10	.04	.01
□ 7 Gary Pettis	.05	.02	.00
□ 8 Harold Baines	.10	.04	.01
□ 9 Floyd Bannister	.05	.02	.00
□ 10 Britt Burns	.05	.02	.00
□ 11 Carlton Fisk	.10	.04	.01
□ 12 Brett Butler	.10	.04	.01
□ 13 Darrell Evans	.10	.04	.01
□ 14 Jack Morris	.15	.06	.01
□ 15 Lance Parrish	.15	.06	.01
□ 16 Walt Terrell	.05	.02	.00
□ 17 Steve Balboni	.05	.02	.00
□ 18 George Brett	.25	.10	.02
□ 19 Charlie Leibrandt	.05	.02	.00
□ 20 Bret Saberhagen	.15	.06	.01
□ 21 Lonnie Smith	.05	.02	.00
□ 22 Willie Wilson	.10	.04	.01
□ 23 Bert Blyleven	.10	.04	.01
□ 24 Mike Smithson	.05	.02	.00
□ 25 Frank Viola	.20	.08	.02
□ 26 Ron Guidry	.10	.04	.01
□ 27 Rickey Henderson	.25	.10	.02
□ 28 Don Mattingly	1.00	.40	.10
□ 29 Dave Winfield	.25	.10	.02
□ 30 Mike Moore	.05	.02	.00
□ 31 Gorman Thomas	.10	.04	.01
□ 32 Toby Harrah	.05	.02	.00
□ 33 Charlie Hough	.05	.02	.00
□ 34 Doyle Alexander	.10	.04	.01
□ 35 Jimmy Key	.10	.04	.01
□ 36 Dave Stieb	.10	.04	.01
□ 37 Dale Murphy	.30	.12	.03
□ 38 Keith Moreland	.05	.02	.00
□ 39 Ryne Sandberg	.20	.08	.02
□ 40 Tom Browning	.05	.02	.00
□ 41 Dave Parker	.15	.06	.01
□ 42 Mario Soto	.05	.02	.00
□ 43 Nolan Ryan	.25	.10	.02
□ 44 Pedro Guerrero	.15	.06	.01
□ 45 Orel Hershiser	.45	.18	.04
□ 46 Mike Scioscia	.05	.02	.00
□ 47 Fernando Valenzuela	.20	.08	.02
□ 48 Bob Welch	.10	.04	.01
□ 49 Tim Raines	.25	.10	.02
□ 50 Gary Carter	.25	.10	.02
□ 51 Sid Fernandez	.15	.06	.01
□ 52 Dwight Gooden	.50	.20	.05
□ 53 Keith Hernandez	.20	.08	.02
□ 54 Juan Samuel	.15	.06	.01
□ 55 Mike Schmidt	.35	.14	.03
□ 56 Glenn Wilson	.05	.02	.00
□ 57 Rick Reuschel	.10	.04	.01
□ 58 Joaquin Andujar	.05	.02	.00
□ 59 Jack Clark	.20	.08	.02
□ 60 Vince Coleman	.35	.14	.03
□ 61 Danny Cox	.05	.02	.00
□ 62 Tom Herr	.05	.02	.00
□ 63 Willie McGee	.15	.06	.01
□ 64 John Tudor	.10	.04	.01
□ 65 Tony Gwynn	.35	.14	.03
□ 66 Checklist card	.05	.01	.00

1986 Topps Traded

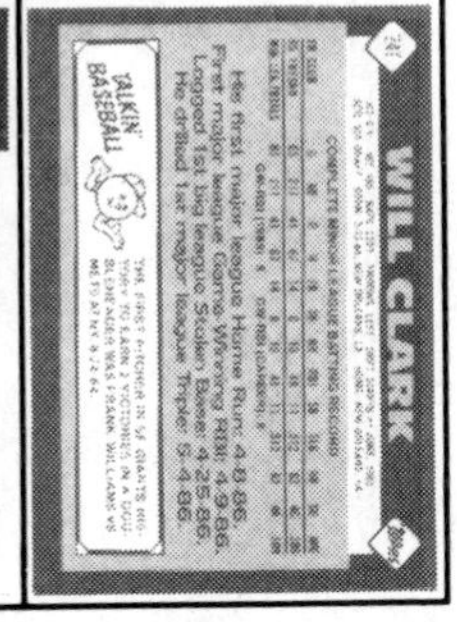

This 132-card Traded or extended set was distributed by Topps to dealers in a special red and white box as a complete set. The card fronts are identical in style to the Topps regular issue and are also 2 1/2" by 3 1/2". The backs are printed in red and black on white card stock. Cards are numbered (with a T suffix) alphabetically according to the name of the player.

	MINT	EXC	G-VG
COMPLETE SET (132)	17.00	7.00	1.70
COMMON PLAYER (1-132)	.05	.02	.00
□ 1T Andy Allanson	.15	.06	.01
□ 2T Neil Allen	.05	.02	.00
□ 3T Joaquin Andujar	.10	.04	.01
□ 4T Paul Assenmacher	.15	.06	.01
□ 5T Scott Bailes	.15	.06	.01
□ 6T Don Baylor	.15	.06	.01
□ 7T Steve Bedrosian	.15	.06	.01
□ 8T Juan Beniquez	.05	.02	.00
□ 9T Juan Berenguer	.05	.02	.00
□ 10T Mike Bielecki	.10	.04	.01
□ 11T Barry Bonds	1.00	.40	.10
□ 12T Bobby Bonilla	1.00	.40	.10
□ 13T Juan Bonilla	.05	.02	.00
□ 14T Rich Bordi	.05	.02	.00
□ 15T Steve Boros MG	.05	.02	.00
□ 16T Rick Burleson	.10	.04	.01
□ 17T Bill Campbell	.05	.02	.00
□ 18T Tom Candiotti	.10	.04	.01
□ 19T John Cangelosi	.20	.08	.02
□ 20T Jose Canseco	8.00	3.25	.80
□ 21T Carmen Castillo	.05	.02	.00
□ 22T Rick Cerone	.05	.02	.00
□ 23T John Cerutti	.15	.06	.01
□ 24T Will Clark	3.50	1.40	.35
□ 25T Mark Clear	.05	.02	.00
□ 26T Darnell Coles	.10	.04	.01
□ 27T Dave Collins	.05	.02	.00
□ 28T Tim Conroy	.05	.02	.00
□ 29T Joe Cowley	.05	.02	.00
□ 30T Joel Davis	.15	.06	.01
□ 31T Rob Deer	.15	.06	.01
□ 32T John Denny	.10	.04	.01
□ 33T Mike Easler	.05	.02	.00
□ 34T Mark Eichhorn	.15	.06	.01
□ 35T Steve Farr	.05	.02	.00
□ 36T Scott Fletcher	.15	.06	.01
□ 37T Terry Forster	.10	.04	.01
□ 38T Terry Francona	.05	.02	.00
□ 39T Jim Fregosi MG	.05	.02	.00
□ 40T Andres Galarraga	1.25	.50	.12
□ 41T Ken Griffey	.10	.04	.01
□ 42T Bill Gullickson	.05	.02	.00
□ 43T Jose Guzman	.20	.08	.02
□ 44T Moose Haas	.05	.02	.00

☐ 45T	Billy Hatcher	.15	.06	.01
☐ 46T	Mike Heath	.05	.02	.00
☐ 47T	Tom Hume	.05	.02	.00
☐ 48T	Pete Incaviglia	.70	.28	.07
☐ 49T	Dane Iorg	.05	.02	.00
☐ 50T	Bo Jackson	1.75	.70	.17
☐ 51T	Wally Joyner	2.00	.80	.20
☐ 52T	Charlie Kerfeld	.15	.06	.01
☐ 53T	Eric King	.15	.06	.01
☐ 54T	Bob Kipper	.05	.02	.00
☐ 55T	Wayne Krenchicki	.05	.02	.00
☐ 56T	John Kruk	.35	.14	.03
☐ 57T	Mike LaCoss	.05	.02	.00
☐ 58T	Pete Ladd	.05	.02	.00
☐ 59T	Mike Laga	.10	.04	.01
☐ 60T	Hal Lanier MG	.05	.02	.00
☐ 61T	Dave LaPoint	.10	.04	.01
☐ 62T	Rudy Law	.05	.02	.00
☐ 63T	Rick Leach	.05	.02	.00
☐ 64T	Tim Leary	.20	.08	.02
☐ 65T	Dennis Leonard	.10	.04	.01
☐ 66T	Jim Leyland MG	.05	.02	.00
☐ 67T	Steve Lyons	.05	.02	.00
☐ 68T	Mickey Mahler	.05	.02	.00
☐ 69T	Candy Maldonado	.15	.06	.01
☐ 70T	Roger Mason	.10	.04	.01
☐ 71T	Bob McClure	.05	.02	.00
☐ 72T	Andy McGaffigan	.05	.02	.00
☐ 73T	Gene Michael MG	.05	.02	.00
☐ 74T	Kevin Mitchell	.30	.12	.03
☐ 75T	Omar Moreno	.05	.02	.00
☐ 76T	Jerry Mumphrey	.05	.02	.00
☐ 77T	Phil Niekro	.30	.12	.03
☐ 78T	Randy Niemann	.05	.02	.00
☐ 79T	Juan Nieves	.15	.06	.01
☐ 80T	Otis Nixon	.15	.06	.01
☐ 81T	Bob Ojeda	.15	.06	.01
☐ 82T	Jose Oquendo	.10	.04	.01
☐ 83T	Tom Paciorek	.05	.02	.00
☐ 84T	Dave Palmer	.05	.02	.00
☐ 85T	Frank Pastore	.05	.02	.00
☐ 86T	Lou Piniella MG	.10	.04	.01
☐ 87T	Dan Plesac	.30	.12	.03
☐ 88T	Darrell Porter	.05	.02	.00
☐ 89T	Rey Quinones	.20	.08	.02
☐ 90T	Gary Redus	.05	.02	.00
☐ 91T	Bip Roberts	.10	.04	.01
☐ 92T	Billy Jo Robidoux	.10	.04	.01
☐ 93T	Jeff Robinson (Giants pitcher)	.15	.06	.01
☐ 94T	Gary Roenicke	.05	.02	.00
☐ 95T	Ed Romero	.05	.02	.00
☐ 96T	Argenis Salazar	.05	.02	.00
☐ 97T	Joe Sambito	.05	.02	.00
☐ 98T	Billy Sample	.05	.02	.00
☐ 99T	Dave Schmidt	.10	.04	.01
☐ 100T	Ken Schrom	.05	.02	.00
☐ 101T	Tom Seaver	.40	.16	.04
☐ 102T	Ted Simmons	.15	.06	.01
☐ 103T	Sammy Stewart	.05	.02	.00
☐ 104T	Kurt Stillwell	.30	.12	.03
☐ 105T	Franklin Stubbs	.05	.02	.00
☐ 106T	Dale Sveum	.30	.12	.03
☐ 107T	Chuck Tanner MG	.05	.02	.00
☐ 108T	Danny Tartabull	.75	.30	.07
☐ 109T	Tim Teufel	.05	.02	.00
☐ 110T	Bob Tewksbury	.15	.06	.01
☐ 111T	Andres Thomas	.20	.08	.02
☐ 112T	Milt Thompson	.15	.06	.01
☐ 113T	Robby Thompson	.30	.12	.03
☐ 114T	Jay Tibbs	.05	.02	.00
☐ 115T	Wayne Tolleson	.05	.02	.00
☐ 116T	Alex Trevino	.05	.02	.00
☐ 117T	Manny Trillo	.05	.02	.00
☐ 118T	Ed VandeBerg	.05	.02	.00
☐ 119T	Ozzie Virgil	.05	.02	.00
☐ 120T	Bob Walk	.10	.04	.01
☐ 121T	Gene Walter	.10	.04	.01
☐ 122T	Claudell Washington	.10	.04	.01
☐ 123T	Bill Wegman	.15	.06	.01
☐ 124T	Dick Williams MG	.05	.02	.00
☐ 125T	Mitch Williams	.20	.08	.02
☐ 126T	Bobby Witt	.40	.16	.04
☐ 127T	Todd Worrell	.50	.20	.05
☐ 128T	George Wright	.05	.02	.00
☐ 129T	Ricky Wright	.05	.02	.00
☐ 130T	Steve Yeager	.05	.02	.00
☐ 131T	Paul Zuvella	.05	.02	.00
☐ 132T	Checklist 1-132	.05	.01	.00

1987 Topps

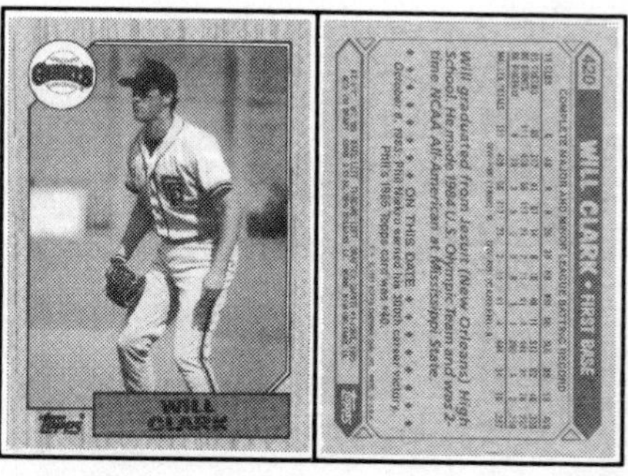

This 792-card set is reminiscent of the 1962 Topps baseball cards with their simulated wood grain borders. The backs are printed in yellow and blue on gray card stock. The manager cards contain a checklist of the respective team's players on the back. Subsets in the set include Record Breakers (1-7), Turn Back The Clock (311-315), and All-Star selections (595-616). The Team Leader cards typically show players conferring on the mound inside a white cloud. The wax pack wrapper gives details of "Spring Fever Baseball" where a lucky collector can win a trip for four to Spring Training. Topps also produced a specially boxed "glossy" edition frequently referred to as the Topps Tiffany set. This year Topps did not disclose the number of sets they produced or sold; it is apparent from the availability that there were many more sets produced this year compared to the 1984-86 Tiffany sets. The checklist of cards (792 regular and 132 Traded) is identical to that of the normal non- glossy cards. There are two primary distinguishing features of the Tiffany cards, white card stock reverses and high gloss obverses. These Tiffany cards are valued at approximately four times the values listed below.

		MINT	EXC	G-VG
	COMPLETE SET (792)	27.00	11.00	2.70
	COMMON PLAYER (1-792)	.03	.01	.00
☐ 1	RB: Roger Clemens Most strikeouts, nine inning game	.40	.10	.02
☐ 2	RB: Jim Deshaies Most cons. K's, start of game	.06	.02	.00
☐ 3	RB: Dwight Evans Earliest home run, season	.08	.03	.01
☐ 4	RB: Davey Lopes Most steals, season, 40-year-old	.06	.02	.00
☐ 5	RB: Dave Righetti Most saves, season	.08	.03	.01
☐ 6	RB: Ruben Sierra Youngest player to switch hit homers in game	.12	.05	.01
☐ 7	RB: Todd Worrell Most saves, season, rookie	.10	.04	.01
☐ 8	Terry Pendleton	.06	.02	.00
☐ 9	Jay Tibbs	.03	.01	.00
☐ 10	Cecil Cooper	.08	.03	.01
☐ 11	Indians Team (mound conference)	.03	.01	.00
☐ 12	Jeff Sellers	.12	.05	.01
☐ 13	Nick Esasky	.03	.01	.00
☐ 14	Dave Stewart	.08	.03	.01
☐ 15	Claudell Washington	.06	.02	.00
☐ 16	Pat Clements	.03	.01	.00
☐ 17	Pete O'Brien	.08	.03	.01
☐ 18	Dick Howser MG (checklist back)	.06	.01	.00

□ 19 Matt Young .03 .01 .00
□ 20 Gary Carter .20 .08 .02
□ 21 Mark Davis .03 .01 .00
□ 22 Doug DeCinces .06 .02 .00
□ 23 Lee Smith .06 .02 .00
□ 24 Tony Walker .08 .03 .01
□ 25 Bert Blyleven .08 .03 .01
□ 26 Greg Brock .03 .01 .00
□ 27 Joe Cowley .03 .01 .00
□ 28 Rick Dempsey .03 .01 .00
□ 29 Jimmy Key .08 .03 .01
□ 30 Tim Raines .20 .08 .02
□ 31 Braves Team .03 .01 .00
(Hubbard/Ramirez)
□ 32 Tim Leary .06 .02 .00
□ 33 Andy Van Slyke .15 .06 .01
□ 34 Jose Rijo .06 .02 .00
□ 35 Sid Bream .03 .01 .00
□ 36 Eric King .10 .04 .01
□ 37 Marvell Wynne .03 .01 .00
□ 38 Dennis Leonard .06 .02 .00
□ 39 Marty Barrett .08 .03 .01
□ 40 Dave Righetti .10 .04 .01
□ 41 Bo Diaz .03 .01 .00
□ 42 Gary Redus .03 .01 .00
□ 43 Gene Michael MG .06 .01 .00
(checklist back)
□ 44 Greg Harris .03 .01 .00
□ 45 Jim Presley .08 .03 .01
□ 46 Dan Gladden .06 .02 .00
□ 47 Dennis Powell .03 .01 .00
□ 48 Wally Backman .06 .02 .00
□ 49 Terry Harper .03 .01 .00
□ 50 Dave Smith .03 .01 .00
□ 51 Mel Hall .06 .02 .00
□ 52 Keith Atherton .03 .01 .00
□ 53 Ruppert Jones .03 .01 .00
□ 54 Bill Dawley .03 .01 .00
□ 55 Tim Wallach .08 .03 .01
□ 56 Brewers Team .03 .01 .00
(mound conference)
□ 57 Scott Nielsen .10 .04 .01
□ 58 Thad Bosley .03 .01 .00
□ 59 Ken Dayley .03 .01 .00
□ 60 Tony Pena .08 .03 .01
□ 61 Bobby Thigpen .25 .10 .02
□ 62 Bobby Meacham .03 .01 .00
□ 63 Fred Toliver .03 .01 .00
□ 64 Harry Spilman .03 .01 .00
□ 65 Tom Browning .12 .05 .01
□ 66 Marc Sullivan .03 .01 .00
□ 67 Bill Swift .03 .01 .00
□ 68 Tony LaRussa MG .06 .01 .00
(checklist back)
□ 69 Lonnie Smith .03 .01 .00
□ 70 Charlie Hough .06 .02 .00
□ 71 Mike Aldrete .20 .08 .02
□ 72 Walt Terrell .03 .01 .00
□ 73 Dave Anderson .03 .01 .00
□ 74 Dan Pasqua .06 .02 .00
□ 75 Ron Darling .15 .06 .01
□ 76 Rafael Ramirez .03 .01 .00
□ 77 Bryan Oelkers .03 .01 .00
□ 78 Tom Foley .03 .01 .00
□ 79 Juan Nieves .10 .04 .01
□ 80 Wally Joyner 1.25 .50 .12
□ 81 Padres Team .03 .01 .00
(Hawkins/Kennedy)
□ 82 Rob Murphy .20 .08 .02
□ 83 Mike Davis .03 .01 .00
□ 84 Steve Lake .03 .01 .00
□ 85 Kevin Bass .06 .02 .00
□ 86 Nate Snell .03 .01 .00
□ 87 Mark Salas .03 .01 .00
□ 88 Ed Wojna .03 .01 .00
□ 89 Ozzie Guillen .06 .02 .00
□ 90 Dave Stieb .10 .04 .01
□ 91 Harold Reynolds .06 .02 .00
□ 92A Urbano Lugo .25 .10 .02
ERR (no trademark)
□ 92B Urbano Lugo COR .06 .02 .00
□ 93 Jim Leyland MG .06 .01 .00
(checklist back)
□ 94 Calvin Schiraldi .06 .02 .00
□ 95 Oddibe McDowell .08 .03 .01
□ 96 Frank Williams .03 .01 .00
□ 97 Glenn Wilson .06 .02 .00
□ 98 Bill Scherrer .03 .01 .00
□ 99 Darryl Motley .03 .01 .00
□ 100 Steve Garvey .25 .10 .02
□ 101 Carl Willis .06 .02 .00
□ 102 Paul Zuvella .03 .01 .00
□ 103 Rick Aguilera .03 .01 .00
□ 104 Billy Sample .03 .01 .00
□ 105 Floyd Youmans .06 .02 .00
□ 106 Blue Jays Team .12 .05 .01
(Bell/Barfield)
□ 107 John Butcher .03 .01 .00
□ 108 Jim Gantner .06 .02 .00
(Brewers logo
reversed) ERR
□ 109 R.J. Reynolds .03 .01 .00
□ 110 John Tudor .10 .04 .01
□ 111 Alfredo Griffin .06 .02 .00
□ 112 Alan Ashby .03 .01 .00
□ 113 Neil Allen .03 .01 .00
□ 114 Billy Beane .06 .02 .00
□ 115 Donnie Moore .03 .01 .00
□ 116 Bill Russell .03 .01 .00
□ 117 Jim Beattie .03 .01 .00
□ 118 Bobby Valentine MG .06 .01 .00
(checklist back)
□ 119 Ron Robinson .03 .01 .00
□ 120 Eddie Murray .20 .08 .02
□ 121 Kevin Romine .10 .04 .01
□ 122 Jim Clancy .03 .01 .00
□ 123 John Kruk .30 .12 .03
□ 124 Ray Fontenot .03 .01 .00
□ 125 Bob Brenly .03 .01 .00
□ 126 Mike Loynd .08 .03 .01
□ 127 Vance Law .03 .01 .00
□ 128 Checklist 1-132 .06 .01 .00
□ 129 Rick Cerone .03 .01 .00
□ 130 Dwight Gooden .70 .28 .07
□ 131 Pirates Team .03 .01 .00
(Bream/Pena)
□ 132 Paul Assenmacher .08 .03 .01
□ 133 Jose Oquendo .03 .01 .00
□ 134 Rich Yett .03 .01 .00
□ 135 Mike Easler .03 .01 .00
□ 136 Ron Romanick .03 .01 .00
□ 137 Jerry Willard .03 .01 .00
□ 138 Roy Lee Jackson .03 .01 .00
□ 139 Devon White .70 .28 .07
□ 140 Bret Saberhagen .18 .08 .01
□ 141 Herm Winningham .03 .01 .00
□ 142 Rick Sutcliffe .10 .04 .01
□ 143 Steve Boros MG .06 .01 .00
(checklist back)
□ 144 Mike Scioscia .03 .01 .00
□ 145 Charlie Kerfeld .03 .01 .00
□ 146 Tracy Jones .30 .12 .03
□ 147 Randy Niemann .03 .01 .00
□ 148 Dave Collins .03 .01 .00
□ 149 Ray Searage .03 .01 .00
□ 150 Wade Boggs 1.00 .40 .10
□ 151 Mike LaCoss .03 .01 .00
□ 152 Toby Harrah .03 .01 .00
□ 153 Duane Ward .08 .03 .01
□ 154 Tom O'Malley .03 .01 .00
□ 155 Eddie Whitson .03 .01 .00
□ 156 Mariners Team .03 .01 .00
(mound conference)
□ 157 Danny Darwin .03 .01 .00
□ 158 Tim Teufel .03 .01 .00
□ 159 Ed Olwine .08 .03 .01
□ 160 Julio Franco .08 .03 .01
□ 161 Steve Ontiveros .03 .01 .00
□ 162 Mike LaValliere .12 .05 .01
□ 163 Kevin Gross .03 .01 .00
□ 164 Sammy Khalifa .03 .01 .00
□ 165 Jeff Reardon .08 .03 .01
□ 166 Bob Boone .06 .02 .00
□ 167 Jim Deshaies .15 .06 .01
□ 168 Lou Piniella MG .08 .02 .00
(checklist back)
□ 169 Ron Washington .03 .01 .00
□ 170 Bo Jackson .90 .36 .09
□ 171 Chuck Cary .10 .04 .01
□ 172 Ron Oester .03 .01 .00
□ 173 Alex Trevino .03 .01 .00
□ 174 Henry Cotto .03 .01 .00
□ 175 Bob Stanley .03 .01 .00
□ 176 Steve Buechele .03 .01 .00
□ 177 Keith Moreland .03 .01 .00
□ 178 Cecil Fielder .06 .02 .00
□ 179 Bill Wegman .06 .02 .00
□ 180 Chris Brown .08 .03 .01
□ 181 Cardinals Team .03 .01 .00
(mound conference)
□ 182 Lee Lacy .03 .01 .00
□ 183 Andy Hawkins .06 .02 .00
□ 184 Bobby Bonilla .70 .28 .07
□ 185 Roger McDowell .08 .03 .01
□ 186 Bruce Benedict .03 .01 .00
□ 187 Mark Huismann .03 .01 .00
□ 188 Tony Phillips .03 .01 .00
□ 189 Joe Hesketh .03 .01 .00
□ 190 Jim Sundberg .03 .01 .00
□ 191 Charles Hudson .03 .01 .00

☐ 192 Cory Snyder	.60	.24	.06
☐ 193 Roger Craig MG (checklist back)	.06	.01	.00
☐ 194 Kirk McCaskill	.03	.01	.00
☐ 195 Mike Pagliarulo	.08	.03	.01
☐ 196 Randy O'Neal (wrong ML career W-L totals)	.03	.01	.00
☐ 197 Mark Bailey	.03	.01	.00
☐ 198 Lee Mazzilli	.03	.01	.00
☐ 199 Mariano Duncan	.03	.01	.00
☐ 200 Pete Rose	.40	.16	.04
☐ 201 John Cangelosi	.08	.03	.01
☐ 202 Ricky Wright	.03	.01	.00
☐ 203 Mike Kingery	.08	.03	.01
☐ 204 Sammy Stewart	.03	.01	.00
☐ 205 Graig Nettles	.08	.03	.01
☐ 206 Twins Team (Frank Viola and Tim Laudner)	.06	.02	.00
☐ 207 George Frazier	.03	.01	.00
☐ 208 John Shelby	.03	.01	.00
☐ 209 Rick Schu	.03	.01	.00
☐ 210 Lloyd Moseby	.08	.03	.01
☐ 211 John Morris	.03	.01	.00
☐ 212 Mike Fitzgerald	.03	.01	.00
☐ 213 Randy Myers	.40	.16	.04
☐ 214 Omar Moreno	.03	.01	.00
☐ 215 Mark Langston	.10	.04	.01
☐ 216 B.J. Surhoff	.35	.14	.03
☐ 217 Chris Codiroli	.03	.01	.00
☐ 218 Sparky Anderson MG (checklist back)	.06	.01	.00
☐ 219 Cecilio Guante	.03	.01	.00
☐ 220 Joe Carter	.18	.08	.01
☐ 221 Vern Ruhle	.03	.01	.00
☐ 222 Denny Walling	.03	.01	.00
☐ 223 Charlie Leibrandt	.03	.01	.00
☐ 224 Wayne Tolleson	.03	.01	.00
☐ 225 Mike Smithson	.03	.01	.00
☐ 226 Max Venable	.03	.01	.00
☐ 227 Jamie Moyer	.15	.06	.01
☐ 228 Curt Wilkerson	.03	.01	.00
☐ 229 Mike Birkbeck	.10	.04	.01
☐ 230 Don Baylor	.08	.03	.01
☐ 231 Giants Team (Bob Brenly and Jim Gott)	.03	.01	.00
☐ 232 Reggie Williams	.08	.03	.01
☐ 233 Russ Morman	.10	.04	.01
☐ 234 Pat Sheridan	.03	.01	.00
☐ 235 Alvin Davis	.10	.04	.01
☐ 236 Tommy John	.10	.04	.01
☐ 237 Jim Morrison	.03	.01	.00
☐ 238 Bill Krueger	.03	.01	.00
☐ 239 Juan Espino	.03	.01	.00
☐ 240 Steve Balboni	.03	.01	.00
☐ 241 Danny Heep	.03	.01	.00
☐ 242 Rick Mahler	.03	.01	.00
☐ 243 Whitey Herzog MG (checklist back)	.06	.01	.00
☐ 244 Dickie Noles	.03	.01	.00
☐ 245 Willie Upshaw	.03	.01	.00
☐ 246 Jim Dwyer	.03	.01	.00
☐ 247 Jeff Reed	.03	.01	.00
☐ 248 Gene Walter	.03	.01	.00
☐ 249 Jim Pankovits	.03	.01	.00
☐ 250 Teddy Higuera	.15	.06	.01
☐ 251 Rob Wilfong	.03	.01	.00
☐ 252 Denny Martinez	.06	.02	.00
☐ 253 Eddie Milner	.03	.01	.00
☐ 254 Bob Tewksbury	.10	.04	.01
☐ 255 Juan Samuel	.12	.05	.01
☐ 256 Royals Team (Brett/F.White)	.10	.04	.01
☐ 257 Bob Forsch	.03	.01	.00
☐ 258 Steve Yeager	.03	.01	.00
☐ 259 Mike Greenwell	4.00	1.60	.40
☐ 260 Vida Blue	.06	.02	.00
☐ 261 Ruben Sierra	.90	.36	.09
☐ 262 Jim Winn	.03	.01	.00
☐ 263 Stan Javier	.03	.01	.00
☐ 264 Checklist 133-264	.06	.01	.00
☐ 265 Darrell Evans	.08	.03	.01
☐ 266 Jeff Hamilton	.15	.06	.01
☐ 267 Howard Johnson	.10	.04	.01
☐ 268 Pat Corrales MG (checklist back)	.06	.01	.00
☐ 269 Cliff Speck	.06	.02	.00
☐ 270 Jody Davis	.06	.02	.00
☐ 271 Mike Brown (Mariners pitcher)	.03	.01	.00
☐ 272 Andres Galarraga	.90	.36	.09
☐ 273 Gene Nelson	.03	.01	.00
☐ 274 Jeff Hearron	.10	.04	.01

(duplicate 1986 stat line on back)

☐ 275 LaMarr Hoyt	.03	.01	.00
☐ 276 Jackie Gutierrez	.03	.01	.00
☐ 277 Juan Agosto	.03	.01	.00
☐ 278 Gary Pettis	.03	.01	.00
☐ 279 Dan Plesac	.20	.08	.02
☐ 280 Jeff Leonard	.06	.02	.00
☐ 281 Reds Team (Pete Rose, Bo Diaz, and Bill Gullickson)	.10	.04	.01
☐ 282 Jeff Calhoun	.03	.01	.00
☐ 283 Doug Drabek	.20	.08	.02
☐ 284 John Moses	.03	.01	.00
☐ 285 Dennis Boyd	.06	.02	.00
☐ 286 Mike Woodard	.03	.01	.00
☐ 287 Dave Von Ohlen	.03	.01	.00
☐ 288 Tito Landrum	.03	.01	.00
☐ 289 Bob Kipper	.03	.01	.00
☐ 290 Leon Durham	.06	.02	.00
☐ 291 Mitch Williams	.20	.08	.02
☐ 292 Franklin Stubbs	.03	.01	.00
☐ 293 Bob Rodgers MG (checklist back)	.06	.01	.00
☐ 294 Steve Jeltz	.03	.01	.00
☐ 295 Len Dykstra	.08	.03	.01
☐ 296 Andres Thomas	.12	.05	.01
☐ 297 Don Schulze	.03	.01	.00
☐ 298 Larry Herndon	.03	.01	.00
☐ 299 Joel Davis	.03	.01	.00
☐ 300 Reggie Jackson	.30	.12	.03
☐ 301 Luis Aquino UER (no trademark, never corrected)	.06	.02	.00
☐ 302 Bill Schroeder	.03	.01	.00
☐ 303 Juan Berenguer	.03	.01	.00
☐ 304 Phil Garner	.03	.01	.00
☐ 305 John Franco	.08	.03	.01
☐ 306 Red Sox Team (Tom Seaver, John McNamara, and Rich Gedman)	.06	.02	.00
☐ 307 Lee Guetterman	.12	.05	.01
☐ 308 Don Slaught	.03	.01	.00
☐ 309 Mike Young	.03	.01	.00
☐ 310 Frank Viola	.15	.06	.01
☐ 311 Turn Back 1982 Rickey Henderson	.12	.05	.01
☐ 312 Turn Back 1977 Reggie Jackson	.12	.05	.01
☐ 313 Turn Back 1972 Roberto Clemente	.12	.05	.01
☐ 314 Turn Back 1967 UER Carl Yastrzemski (sic, 112 RBI's on back)	.12	.05	.01
☐ 315 Turn Back 1962 Maury Wills	.06	.02	.00
☐ 316 Brian Fisher	.03	.01	.00
☐ 317 Clint Hurdle	.03	.01	.00
☐ 318 Jim Fregosi MG (checklist back)	.06	.01	.00
☐ 319 Greg Swindell	.45	.18	.04
☐ 320 Barry Bonds	.70	.28	.07
☐ 321 Mike Laga	.03	.01	.00
☐ 322 Chris Bando	.03	.01	.00
☐ 323 Al Newman	.06	.02	.00
☐ 324 Dave Palmer	.03	.01	.00
☐ 325 Garry Templeton	.06	.02	.00
☐ 326 Mark Gubicza	.08	.03	.01
☐ 327 Dale Sveum	.20	.08	.02
☐ 328 Bob Welch	.06	.02	.00
☐ 329 Ron Roenicke	.03	.01	.00
☐ 330 Mike Scott	.20	.08	.02
☐ 331 Mets Team (Gary Carter and Darryl Strawberry)	.15	.06	.01
☐ 332 Joe Price	.03	.01	.00
☐ 333 Ken Phelps	.06	.02	.00
☐ 334 Ed Correa	.15	.06	.01
☐ 335 Candy Maldonado	.06	.02	.00
☐ 336 Allan Anderson	.25	.10	.02
☐ 337 Darrell Miller	.03	.01	.00
☐ 338 Tim Conroy	.03	.01	.00
☐ 339 Donnie Hill	.03	.01	.00
☐ 340 Roger Clemens	.90	.36	.09
☐ 341 Mike Brown (Pirates OF)	.03	.01	.00
☐ 342 Bob James	.03	.01	.00
☐ 343 Hal Lanier MG (checklist back)	.06	.01	.00
☐ 344A Joe Niekro (copyright inside righthand border)	.10	.04	.01
☐ 344B Joe Niekro (copyright outside	.30	.12	.03

righthand border)
☐ 345 Andre Dawson .25 .10 .02
☐ 346 Shawon Dunston .08 .03 .01
☐ 347 Mickey Brantley .10 .04 .01
☐ 348 Carmelo Martinez .03 .01 .00
☐ 349 Storm Davis .06 .02 .00
☐ 350 Keith Hernandez .20 .08 .02
☐ 351 Gene Garber .03 .01 .00
☐ 352 Mike Felder .06 .02 .00
☐ 353 Ernie Camacho .03 .01 .00
☐ 354 Jamie Quirk .03 .01 .00
☐ 355 Don Carman .03 .01 .00
☐ 356 White Sox Team .03 .01 .00
(mound conference)
☐ 357 Steve Fireovid .06 .02 .00
☐ 358 Sal Butera .03 .01 .00
☐ 359 Doug Corbett .03 .01 .00
☐ 360 Pedro Guerrero .15 .06 .01
☐ 361 Mark Thurmond .03 .01 .00
☐ 362 Luis Quinones .08 .03 .01
☐ 363 Jose Guzman .08 .03 .01
☐ 364 Randy Bush .03 .01 .00
☐ 365 Rick Rhoden .06 .02 .00
☐ 366 Mark McGwire 2.50 1.00 .25
☐ 367 Jeff Lahti .03 .01 .00
☐ 368 John McNamara MG .06 .01 .00
(checklist back)
☐ 369 Brian Dayett .03 .01 .00
☐ 370 Fred Lynn .10 .04 .01
☐ 371 Mark Eichhorn .08 .03 .01
☐ 372 Jerry Mumphrey .03 .01 .00
☐ 373 Jeff Dedmon .03 .01 .00
☐ 374 Glenn Hoffman .03 .01 .00
☐ 375 Ron Guidry .10 .04 .01
☐ 376 Scott Bradley .03 .01 .00
☐ 377 John Henry Johnson .03 .01 .00
☐ 378 Rafael Santana .03 .01 .00
☐ 379 John Russell .03 .01 .00
☐ 380 Rich Gossage .08 .03 .01
☐ 381 Expos Team .03 .01 .00
(mound conference)
☐ 382 Rudy Law .03 .01 .00
☐ 383 Ron Davis .03 .01 .00
☐ 384 Johnny Grubb .03 .01 .00
☐ 385 Orel Hershiser .30 .12 .03
☐ 386 Dickie Thon .03 .01 .00
☐ 387 T.R. Bryden .06 .02 .00
☐ 388 Geno Petralli .03 .01 .00
☐ 389 Jeff Robinson .06 .02 .00
(Giants pitcher)
☐ 390 Gary Matthews .06 .02 .00
☐ 391 Jay Howell .03 .01 .00
☐ 392 Checklist 265-396 .06 .01 .00
☐ 393 Pete Rose MG .35 .14 .03
(checklist back)
☐ 394 Mike Bielecki .03 .01 .00
☐ 395 Damaso Garcia .03 .01 .00
☐ 396 Tim Lollar .03 .01 .00
☐ 397 Greg Walker .06 .02 .00
☐ 398 Brad Havens .03 .01 .00
☐ 399 Curt Ford .08 .03 .01
☐ 400 George Brett .30 .12 .03
☐ 401 Billy Jo Robidoux .06 .02 .00
☐ 402 Mike Trujillo .03 .01 .00
☐ 403 Jerry Royster .03 .01 .00
☐ 404 Doug Sisk .03 .01 .00
☐ 405 Brook Jacoby .08 .03 .01
☐ 406 Yankees Team .25 .10 .02
(Henderson/Mattingly)
☐ 407 Jim Acker .03 .01 .00
☐ 408 John Mizerock .03 .01 .00
☐ 409 Milt Thompson .06 .02 .00
☐ 410 Fernando Valenzuela .18 .08 .01
☐ 411 Darnell Coles .03 .01 .00
☐ 412 Eric Davis .90 .36 .09
☐ 413 Moose Haas .03 .01 .00
☐ 414 Joe Orsulak .03 .01 .00
☐ 415 Bobby Witt .25 .10 .02
☐ 416 Tom Nieto .03 .01 .00
☐ 417 Pat Perry .03 .01 .00
☐ 418 Dick Williams MG .06 .01 .00
(checklist back)
☐ 419 Mark Portugal .06 .02 .00
☐ 420 Will Clark 1.75 .70 .17
☐ 421 Jose DeLeon .03 .01 .00
☐ 422 Jack Howell .03 .01 .00
☐ 423 Jaime Cocanower .03 .01 .00
☐ 424 Chris Speier .03 .01 .00
☐ 425 Tom Seaver .25 .10 .02
☐ 426 Floyd Rayford .03 .01 .00
☐ 427 Edwin Nunez .03 .01 .00
☐ 428 Bruce Bochy .03 .01 .00
☐ 429 Tim Pyznarski .10 .04 .01
☐ 430 Mike Schmidt .35 .14 .03
☐ 431 Dodgers Team .03 .01 .00
(mound conference)
☐ 432 Jim Slaton .03 .01 .00
☐ 433 Ed Hearn .06 .02 .00
☐ 434 Mike Fischlin .03 .01 .00
☐ 435 Bruce Sutter .08 .03 .01
☐ 436 Andy Allanson .08 .03 .01
☐ 437 Ted Power .03 .01 .00
☐ 438 Kelly Downs .25 .10 .02
☐ 439 Karl Best .03 .01 .00
☐ 440 Willie McGee .12 .05 .01
☐ 441 Dave Leiper .06 .02 .00
☐ 442 Mitch Webster .03 .01 .00
☐ 443 John Felske MG .06 .01 .00
(checklist back)
☐ 444 Jeff Russell .03 .01 .00
☐ 445 Dave Lopes .06 .02 .00
☐ 446 Chuck Finley .08 .03 .01
☐ 447 Bill Almon .03 .01 .00
☐ 448 Chris Bosio .10 .04 .01
☐ 449 Pat Dodson .10 .04 .01
☐ 450 Kirby Puckett .45 .18 .04
☐ 451 Joe Sambito .03 .01 .00
☐ 452 Dave Henderson .06 .02 .00
☐ 453 Scott Terry .10 .04 .01
☐ 454 Luis Salazar .03 .01 .00
☐ 455 Mike Boddicker .06 .02 .00
☐ 456 A's Team .03 .01 .00
(mound conference)
☐ 457 Len Matuszek .03 .01 .00
☐ 458 Kelly Gruber .03 .01 .00
☐ 459 Dennis Eckersley .10 .04 .01
☐ 460 Darryl Strawberry .45 .18 .04
☐ 461 Craig McMurtry .03 .01 .00
☐ 462 Scott Fletcher .06 .02 .00
☐ 463 Tom Candiotti .03 .01 .00
☐ 464 Butch Wynegar .03 .01 .00
☐ 465 Todd Worrell .18 .08 .01
☐ 466 Kal Daniels .90 .36 .09
☐ 467 Randy St.Claire .03 .01 .00
☐ 468 George Bamberger MG .06 .01 .00
(checklist back)
☐ 469 Mike Diaz .10 .04 .01
☐ 470 Dave Dravecky .03 .01 .00
☐ 471 Ronn Reynolds .03 .01 .00
☐ 472 Bill Doran .08 .03 .01
☐ 473 Steve Farr .03 .01 .00
☐ 474 Jerry Narron .03 .01 .00
☐ 475 Scott Garrelts .03 .01 .00
☐ 476 Danny Tartabull .75 .30 .07
☐ 477 Ken Howell .03 .01 .00
☐ 478 Tim Laudner .03 .01 .00
☐ 479 Bob Sebra .10 .04 .01
☐ 480 Jim Rice .15 .06 .01
☐ 481 Phillies Team .06 .02 .00
(Glenn Wilson,
Juan Samuel, and
Von Hayes)
☐ 482 Daryl Boston .03 .01 .00
☐ 483 Dwight Lowry .08 .03 .01
☐ 484 Jim Traber .08 .03 .01
☐ 485 Tony Fernandez .10 .04 .01
☐ 486 Otis Nixon .08 .03 .01
☐ 487 Dave Gumpert .03 .01 .00
☐ 488 Ray Knight .06 .02 .00
☐ 489 Bill Gullickson .03 .01 .00
☐ 490 Dale Murphy .40 .16 .04
☐ 491 Ron Karkovice .06 .02 .00
☐ 492 Mike Heath .03 .01 .00
☐ 493 Tom Lasorda MG .08 .02 .00
(checklist back)
☐ 494 Barry Jones .10 .04 .01
☐ 495 Gorman Thomas .08 .03 .01
☐ 496 Bruce Bochte .03 .01 .00
☐ 497 Dale Mohorcic .15 .06 .01
☐ 498 Bob Kearney .03 .01 .00
☐ 499 Bruce Ruffin .15 .06 .01
☐ 500 Don Mattingly 1.50 .60 .15
☐ 501 Craig Lefferts .03 .01 .00
☐ 502 Dick Schofield .03 .01 .00
☐ 503 Larry Andersen .03 .01 .00
☐ 504 Mickey Hatcher .06 .02 .00
☐ 505 Bryn Smith .03 .01 .00
☐ 506 Orioles Team .03 .01 .00
(mound conference)
☐ 507 Dave Stapleton .03 .01 .00
(infielder)
☐ 508 Scott Bankhead .06 .02 .00
☐ 509 Enos Cabell .03 .01 .00
☐ 510 Tom Henke .06 .02 .00
☐ 511 Steve Lyons .03 .01 .00
☐ 512 Dave Magadan .40 .16 .04
☐ 513 Carmen Castillo .03 .01 .00
☐ 514 Orlando Mercado .03 .01 .00
☐ 515 Willie Hernandez .08 .03 .01
☐ 516 Ted Simmons .08 .03 .01

☐ 517 Mario Soto .... .03 .01 .00
☐ 518 Gene Mauch MG .... .06 .01 .00
(checklist back)
☐ 519 Curt Young .... .03 .01 .00
☐ 520 Jack Clark .... .18 .08 .01
☐ 521 Rick Reuschel .... .06 .02 .00
☐ 522 Checklist 397-528 .... .06 .01 .00
☐ 523 Earnie Riles .... .03 .01 .00
☐ 524 Bob Shirley .... .03 .01 .00
☐ 525 Phil Bradley .... .08 .03 .01
☐ 526 Roger Mason .... .03 .01 .00
☐ 527 Jim Wohlford .... .03 .01 .00
☐ 528 Ken Dixon .... .03 .01 .00
☐ 529 Alvaro Espinoza .... .03 .01 .00
☐ 530 Tony Gwynn .... .35 .14 .03
☐ 531 Astros Team .... .08 .03 .01
(Y.Berra conference)
☐ 532 Jeff Stone .... .03 .01 .00
☐ 533 Argenis Salazar .... .03 .01 .00
☐ 534 Scott Sanderson .... .03 .01 .00
☐ 535 Tony Armas .... .06 .02 .00
☐ 536 Terry Mulholland .... .10 .04 .01
☐ 537 Rance Mulliniks .... .03 .01 .00
☐ 538 Tom Niedenfuer .... .03 .01 .00
☐ 539 Reid Nichols .... .03 .01 .00
☐ 540 Terry Kennedy .... .03 .01 .00
☐ 541 Rafael Belliard .... .08 .03 .01
☐ 542 Ricky Horton .... .03 .01 .00
☐ 543 Dave Johnson MG .... .08 .02 .00
(checklist back)
☐ 544 Zane Smith .... .08 .03 .01
☐ 545 Buddy Bell .... .08 .03 .01
☐ 546 Mike Morgan .... .03 .01 .00
☐ 547 Rob Deer .... .12 .05 .01
☐ 548 Bill Mooneyham .... .08 .03 .01
☐ 549 Bob Melvin .... .03 .01 .00
☐ 550 Pete Incaviglia .... .65 .26 .06
☐ 551 Frank Wills .... .03 .01 .00
☐ 552 Larry Sheets .... .08 .03 .01
☐ 553 Mike Maddux .... .15 .06 .01
☐ 554 Buddy Biancalana .... .03 .01 .00
☐ 555 Dennis Rasmussen .... .08 .03 .01
☐ 556 Angels Team .... .06 .02 .00
(Lachemann/Witt/Boone)
☐ 557 John Cerutti .... .12 .05 .01
☐ 558 Greg Gagne .... .03 .01 .00
☐ 559 Lance McCullers .... .06 .02 .00
☐ 560 Glenn Davis .... .25 .10 .02
☐ 561 Rey Quinones .... .15 .06 .01
☐ 562 Bryan Clutterbuck .... .06 .02 .00
☐ 563 John Stefero .... .03 .01 .00
☐ 564 Larry McWilliams .... .03 .01 .00
☐ 565 Dusty Baker .... .06 .02 .00
☐ 566 Tim Hulett .... .03 .01 .00
☐ 567 Greg Mathews .... .20 .08 .02
☐ 568 Earl Weaver MG .... .08 .02 .00
(checklist back)
☐ 569 Wade Rowdon .... .06 .02 .00
☐ 570 Sid Fernandez .... .10 .04 .01
☐ 571 Ozzie Virgil .... .03 .01 .00
☐ 572 Pete Ladd .... .03 .01 .00
☐ 573 Hal McRae .... .06 .02 .00
☐ 574 Manny Lee .... .03 .01 .00
☐ 575 Pat Tabler .... .06 .02 .00
☐ 576 Frank Pastore .... .03 .01 .00
☐ 577 Dann Bilardello .... .03 .01 .00
☐ 578 Billy Hatcher .... .08 .03 .01
☐ 579 Rick Burleson .... .06 .02 .00
☐ 580 Mike Krukow .... .03 .01 .00
☐ 581 Cubs Team .... .03 .01 .00
(Cey/Trout)
☐ 582 Bruce Berenyi .... .03 .01 .00
☐ 583 Junior Ortiz .... .03 .01 .00
☐ 584 Ron Kittle .... .08 .03 .01
☐ 585 Scott Bailes .... .10 .04 .01
☐ 586 Ben Oglivie .... .06 .02 .00
☐ 587 Eric Plunk .... .06 .02 .00
☐ 588 Wallace Johnson .... .06 .02 .00
☐ 589 Steve Crawford .... .03 .01 .00
☐ 590 Vince Coleman .... .25 .10 .02
☐ 591 Spike Owen .... .03 .01 .00
☐ 592 Chris Welsh .... .03 .01 .00
☐ 593 Chuck Tanner MG .... .06 .01 .00
(checklist back)
☐ 594 Rick Anderson .... .08 .03 .01
☐ 595 Keith Hernandez AS .... .10 .04 .01
☐ 596 Steve Sax AS .... .08 .03 .01
☐ 597 Mike Schmidt AS .... .20 .08 .02
☐ 598 Ozzie Smith AS .... .10 .04 .01
☐ 599 Tony Gwynn AS .... .20 .08 .02
☐ 600 Dave Parker AS .... .10 .04 .01
☐ 601 Darryl Strawberry AS ..... .20 .08 .02
☐ 602 Gary Carter AS .... .12 .05 .01
☐ 603A Dwight Gooden AS .... .75 .30 .07
ERR (no trademark)
☐ 603B Dwight Gooden AS COR .30 .12 .03
☐ 604 Fern. Valenzuela AS ...... .12 .05 .01
☐ 605 Todd Worrell AS .... .08 .03 .01
☐ 606A Don Mattingly AS .... 1.50 .60 .15
ERR (no trademark)
☐ 606B Don Mattingly AS COR . .60 .24 .06
☐ 607 Tony Bernazard AS .... .06 .02 .00
☐ 608 Wade Boggs AS .... .35 .14 .03
☐ 609 Cal Ripken AS .... .15 .06 .01
☐ 610 Jim Rice AS .... .12 .05 .01
☐ 611 Kirby Puckett AS .... .20 .08 .02
☐ 612 George Bell AS .... .12 .05 .01
☐ 613 Lance Parrish AS .... .08 .03 .01
☐ 614 Roger Clemens AS .... .25 .10 .02
☐ 615 Teddy Higuera AS .... .08 .03 .01
☐ 616 Dave Righetti AS .... .08 .03 .01
☐ 617 Al Nipper .... .03 .01 .00
☐ 618 Tom Kelly MG .... .08 .02 .00
(checklist back)
☐ 619 Jerry Reed .... .03 .01 .00
☐ 620 Jose Canseco .... 4.50 1.80 .45
☐ 621 Danny Cox .... .06 .02 .00
☐ 622 Glenn Braggs .... .25 .10 .02
☐ 623 Kurt Stillwell .... .20 .08 .02
☐ 624 Tim Burke .... .03 .01 .00
☐ 625 Mookie Wilson .... .06 .02 .00
☐ 626 Joel Skinner .... .03 .01 .00
☐ 627 Ken Oberkfell .... .03 .01 .00
☐ 628 Bob Walk .... .03 .01 .00
☐ 629 Larry Parrish .... .03 .01 .00
☐ 630 John Candelaria .... .06 .02 .00
☐ 631 Tigers Team .... .03 .01 .00
(mound conference)
☐ 632 Rob Woodward .... .06 .02 .00
☐ 633 Jose Uribe .... .03 .01 .00
☐ 634 Rafael Palmeiro .... .90 .36 .09
☐ 635 Ken Schrom .... .03 .01 .00
☐ 636 Darren Daulton .... .03 .01 .00
☐ 637 Bip Roberts .... .06 .02 .00
☐ 638 Rich Bordi .... .03 .01 .00
☐ 639 Gerald Perry .... .08 .03 .01
☐ 640 Mark Clear .... .03 .01 .00
☐ 641 Domingo Ramos .... .03 .01 .00
☐ 642 Al Pulido .... .06 .02 .00
☐ 643 Ron Shepherd .... .06 .02 .00
☐ 644 John Denny .... .03 .01 .00
☐ 645 Dwight Evans .... .10 .04 .01
☐ 646 Mike Mason .... .03 .01 .00
☐ 647 Tom Lawless .... .03 .01 .00
☐ 648 Barry Larkin .... .90 .36 .09
☐ 649 Mickey Tettleton .... .03 .01 .00
☐ 650 Hubie Brooks .... .08 .03 .01
☐ 651 Benny Distefano .... .06 .02 .00
☐ 652 Terry Forster .... .06 .02 .00
☐ 653 Kevin Mitchell .... .25 .10 .02
☐ 654 Checklist 529-660 .... .06 .01 .00
☐ 655 Jesse Barfield .... .15 .06 .01
☐ 656 Rangers Team .... .03 .01 .00
(Valentine/R.Wright)
☐ 657 Tom Waddell .... .03 .01 .00
☐ 658 Robby Thompson .... .20 .08 .02
☐ 659 Aurelio Lopez .... .03 .01 .00
☐ 660 Bob Horner .... .10 .04 .01
☐ 661 Lou Whitaker .... .10 .04 .01
☐ 662 Frank DiPino .... .03 .01 .00
☐ 663 Cliff Johnson .... .03 .01 .00
☐ 664 Mike Marshall .... .10 .04 .01
☐ 665 Rod Scurry .... .03 .01 .00
☐ 666 Von Hayes .... .08 .03 .01
☐ 667 Ron Hassey .... .03 .01 .00
☐ 668 Juan Bonilla .... .03 .01 .00
☐ 669 Bud Black .... .03 .01 .00
☐ 670 Jose Cruz .... .06 .02 .00
☐ 671A Ray Soff ERR .... .08 .03 .01
(no D* before
copyright line)
☐ 671B Ray Soff COR .... .08 .03 .01
(D* before
copyright line)
☐ 672 Chili Davis .... .08 .03 .01
☐ 673 Don Sutton .... .12 .05 .01
☐ 674 Bill Campbell .... .03 .01 .00
☐ 675 Ed Romero .... .03 .01 .00
☐ 676 Charlie Moore .... .03 .01 .00
☐ 677 Bob Grich .... .06 .02 .00
☐ 678 Carney Lansford .... .08 .03 .01
☐ 679 Kent Hrbek .... .15 .06 .01
☐ 680 Ryne Sandberg .... .20 .08 .02
☐ 681 George Bell .... .20 .08 .02
☐ 682 Jerry Reuss .... .03 .01 .00
☐ 683 Gary Roenicke .... .03 .01 .00
☐ 684 Kent Tekulve .... .03 .01 .00
☐ 685 Jerry Hairston .... .03 .01 .00
☐ 686 Doyle Alexander .... .03 .01 .00
☐ 687 Alan Trammell .... .15 .06 .01

□ 688 Juan Beniquez .03 .01 .00
□ 689 Darrell Porter .03 .01 .00
□ 690 Dane Iorg .03 .01 .00
□ 691 Dave Parker .12 .05 .01
□ 692 Frank White .06 .02 .00
□ 693 Terry Puhl .03 .01 .00
□ 694 Phil Niekro .12 .05 .01
□ 695 Chico Walker .08 .03 .01
□ 696 Gary Lucas .03 .01 .00
□ 697 Ed Lynch .03 .01 .00
□ 698 Ernie Whitt .03 .01 .00
□ 699 Ken Landreaux .03 .01 .00
□ 700 Dave Bergman .03 .01 .00
□ 701 Willie Randolph .06 .02 .00
□ 702 Greg Gross .03 .01 .00
□ 703 Dave Schmidt .06 .02 .00
□ 704 Jesse Orosco .03 .01 .00
□ 705 Bruce Hurst .10 .04 .01
□ 706 Rick Manning .03 .01 .00
□ 707 Bob McClure .03 .01 .00
□ 708 Scott McGregor .03 .01 .00
□ 709 Dave Kingman .08 .03 .01
□ 710 Gary Gaetti .10 .04 .01
□ 711 Ken Griffey .06 .02 .00
□ 712 Don Robinson .03 .01 .00
□ 713 Tom Brookens .03 .01 .00
□ 714 Dan Quisenberry .08 .03 .01
□ 715 Bob Dernier .03 .01 .00
□ 716 Rick Leach .03 .01 .00
□ 717 Ed VandeBerg .03 .01 .00
□ 718 Sfeve Carlton .20 .08 .02
□ 719 Tom Hume .03 .01 .00
□ 720 Richard Dotson .06 .02 .00
□ 721 Tom Herr .06 .02 .00
□ 722 Bob Knepper .06 .02 .00
□ 723 Brett Butler .08 .03 .01
□ 724 Greg Minton .03 .01 .00
□ 725 George Hendrick .06 .02 .00
□ 726 Frank Tanana .06 .02 .00
□ 727 Mike Moore .06 .02 .00
□ 728 Tippy Martinez .03 .01 .00
□ 729 Tom Paciorek .03 .01 .00
□ 730 Eric Show .06 .02 .00
□ 731 Dave Concepcion .06 .02 .00
□ 732 Manny Trillo .03 .01 .00
□ 733 Bill Caudill .03 .01 .00
□ 734 Bill Madlock .08 .03 .01
□ 735 Rickey Henderson .25 .10 .02
□ 736 Steve Bedrosian .10 .04 .01
□ 737 Floyd Bannister .03 .01 .00
□ 738 Jorge Orta .03 .01 .00
□ 739 Chet Lemon .06 .02 .00
□ 740 Rich Gedman .06 .02 .00
□ 741 Paul Molitor .10 .04 .01
□ 742 Andy McGaffigan .03 .01 .00
□ 743 Dwayne Murphy .03 .01 .00
□ 744 Roy Smalley .03 .01 .00
□ 745 Glenn Hubbard .03 .01 .00
□ 746 Bob Ojeda .08 .03 .01
□ 747 Johnny Ray .08 .03 .01
□ 748 Mike Flanagan .06 .02 .00
□ 749 Ozzie Smith .15 .06 .01
□ 750 Steve Trout .03 .01 .00
□ 751 Garth Iorg .03 .01 .00
□ 752 Dan Petry .06 .02 .00
□ 753 Rick Honeycutt .03 .01 .00
□ 754 Dave LaPoint .06 .02 .00
□ 755 Luis Aguayo .03 .01 .00
□ 756 Carlton Fisk .10 .04 .01
□ 757 Nolan Ryan .25 .10 .02
□ 758 Tony Bernazard .03 .01 .00
□ 759 Joel Youngblood .03 .01 .00
□ 760 Mike Witt .08 .03 .01
□ 761 Greg Pryor .03 .01 .00
□ 762 Gary Ward .03 .01 .00
□ 763 Tim Flannery .03 .01 .00
□ 764 Bill Buckner .06 .02 .00
□ 765 Kirk Gibson .15 .06 .01
□ 766 Don Aase .03 .01 .00
□ 767 Ron Cey .06 .02 .00
□ 768 Dennis Lamp .03 .01 .00
□ 769 Steve Sax .12 .05 .01
□ 770 Dave Winfield .25 .10 .02
□ 771 Shane Rawley .06 .02 .00
□ 772 Harold Baines .10 .04 .01
□ 773 Robin Yount .25 .10 .02
□ 774 Wayne Krenchicki .03 .01 .00
□ 775 Joaquin Andujar .06 .02 .00
□ 776 Tom Brunansky .10 .04 .01
□ 777 Chris Chambliss .06 .02 .00
□ 778 Jack Morris .12 .05 .01
□ 779 Craig Reynolds .03 .01 .00
□ 780 Andre Thornton .06 .02 .00
□ 781 Atlee Hammaker .03 .01 .00
□ 782 Brian Downing .06 .02 .00
□ 783 Willie Wilson .08 .03 .01
□ 784 Cal Ripken .20 .08 .02
□ 785 Terry Francona .03 .01 .00
□ 786 Jimy Williams MG .06 .01 .00
(checklist back)
□ 787 Alejandro Pena .03 .01 .00
□ 788 Tim Stoddard .03 .01 .00
□ 789 Dan Schatzeder .03 .01 .00
□ 790 Julio Cruz .03 .01 .00
□ 791 Lance Parrish .15 .06 .01
UER (no trademark, never corrected)
□ 792 Checklist 661-792 .06 .01 .00

1987 Topps Wax Box Cards

This set of 8 cards is really four different sets of two smaller (2 1/8" by 3") cards which were printed on the side of the wax pack box; these eight cards are lettered A through H and are very similar in design to the Topps regular issue cards. The card backs are done in a newspaper headline style describing something about that player that happened the previous season. The card backs feature blue and yellow ink on gray card stock.

	MINT	EXC	G-VG
COMPLETE SET (8)	1.25	.50	.12
COMMON PLAYER (A-H)	.10	.04	.01
□ A Don Baylor	.15	.06	.01
□ B Steve Carlton	.25	.10	.02
□ C Ron Cey	.10	.04	.01
□ D Cecil Cooper	.10	.04	.01
□ E Rickey Henderson	.50	.20	.05
□ F Jim Rice	.20	.08	.02
□ G Don Sutton	.20	.08	.02
□ H Dave Winfield	.30	.12	.03

1987 Topps Glossy All-Stars 22

This set of 22 glossy cards was inserted one per rack pack. Players selected for the set are the starting players (plus manager and two pitchers) in the 1986

All-Star Game in Houston. Cards measure standard size, 2 1/2" by 3 1/2" and the backs feature red and blue printing on a white card stock.

	MINT	EXC	G-VG
COMPLETE SET (22)	4.00	1.60	.40
COMMON PLAYER (1-22)	.10	.04	.01
□ 1 Whitey Herzog MG	.10	.04	.01
□ 2 Keith Hernandez	.20	.08	.02
□ 3 Ryne Sandberg	.25	.10	.02
□ 4 Mike Schmidt	.40	.16	.04
□ 5 Ozzie Smith	.20	.08	.02
□ 6 Tony Gwynn	.35	.14	.03
□ 7 Dale Murphy	.50	.20	.05
□ 8 Darryl Strawberry	.50	.20	.05
□ 9 Gary Carter	.30	.12	.03
□ 10 Dwight Gooden	.50	.20	.05
□ 11 Fernando Valenzuela	.25	.10	.02
□ 12 Dick Howser MG	.10	.04	.01
□ 13 Wally Joyner	.60	.24	.06
□ 14 Lou Whitaker	.15	.06	.01
□ 15 Wade Boggs	.75	.30	.07
□ 16 Cal Ripken	.25	.10	.02
□ 17 Dave Winfield	.30	.12	.03
□ 18 Rickey Henderson	.40	.16	.04
□ 19 Kirby Puckett	.45	.18	.04
□ 20 Lance Parrish	.20	.08	.02
□ 21 Roger Clemens	.50	.20	.05
□ 22 Teddy Higuera	.20	.08	.02

1987 Topps Jumbo Glossy Rookies

Inserted in each supermarket jumbo pack is a card from this series of 22 of 1986's best rookies as determined by Topps. Jumbo packs consisted of 100 (regular issue 1987 Topps baseball) cards with a stick of gum plus the insert "Rookie" card. The card fronts are in full color and measure 2 1/2" by 3 1/2". The card backs are printed in red and blue on white card stock and are numbered at the bottom essentially by alphabetical order.

	MINT	EXC	G-VG
COMPLETE SET (22)	10.00	4.00	1.00
COMMON PLAYER (1-22)	.20	.08	.02
□ 1 Andy Allanson	.20	.08	.02
□ 2 John Cangelosi	.20	.08	.02
□ 3 Jose Canseco	2.50	1.00	.25
□ 4 Will Clark	1.50	.60	.15
□ 5 Mark Eichhorn	.20	.08	.02
□ 6 Pete Incaviglia	.60	.24	.06
□ 7 Wally Joyner	1.25	.50	.12
□ 8 Eric King	.20	.08	.02
□ 9 Dave Magadan	.40	.16	.04
□ 10 John Morris	.20	.08	.02
□ 11 Juan Nieves	.20	.08	.02
□ 12 Rafael Palmeiro	.50	.20	.05
□ 13 Billy Jo Robidoux	.20	.08	.02
□ 14 Bruce Ruffin	.20	.08	.02
□ 15 Ruben Sierra	.90	.36	.09
□ 16 Cory Snyder	.90	.36	.09
□ 17 Kurt Stillwell	.30	.12	.03
□ 18 Dale Sveum	.30	.12	.03
□ 19 Danny Tartabull	.90	.36	.09
□ 20 Andres Thomas	.30	.12	.03
□ 21 Robby Thompson	.30	.12	.03
□ 22 Todd Worrell	.60	.24	.06

1987 Topps Glossy 60

Topps issued this set through a mail-in offer explained and advertised on the wax packs. This 60-card set features glossy fronts with each card measuring 2 1/2" by 3 1/2". The offer provided your choice of any one of the six 10-card subsets (1-10, 11-20, etc.) for 1.00 plus six of the Special Offer ("Spring Fever Baseball") insert cards, which were found one per wax pack. The last two players (numerically) in each ten- card subset are actually "Hot Prospects."

	MINT	EXC	G-VG
COMPLETE SET (60)	12.00	5.00	1.20
COMMON PLAYER (1-60)	.10	.04	.01
□ 1 Don Mattingly	1.50	.60	.15
□ 2 Tony Gwynn	.60	.24	.06
□ 3 Gary Gaetti	.30	.12	.03
□ 4 Glenn Davis	.25	.10	.02
□ 5 Roger Clemens	.90	.36	.09
□ 6 Dale Murphy	.60	.24	.06
□ 7 Lou Whitaker	.15	.06	.01
□ 8 Roger McDowell	.15	.06	.01
□ 9 Cory Snyder	.50	.20	.05
□ 10 Todd Worrell	.25	.10	.02
□ 11 Gary Carter	.30	.12	.03
□ 12 Eddie Murray	.35	.14	.03
□ 13 Bob Knepper	.10	.04	.01
□ 14 Harold Baines	.15	.06	.01
□ 15 Jeff Reardon	.10	.04	.01
□ 16 Joe Carter	.25	.10	.02
□ 17 Dave Parker	.20	.08	.02
□ 18 Wade Boggs	1.25	.50	.12
□ 19 Danny Tartabull	.45	.18	.04
□ 20 Jim Deshaies	.15	.06	.01
□ 21 Rickey Henderson	.50	.20	.05
□ 22 Rob Deer	.15	.06	.01
□ 23 Ozzie Smith	.25	.10	.02
□ 24 Dave Righetti	.20	.08	.02
□ 25 Kent Hrbek	.25	.10	.02
□ 26 Keith Hernandez	.25	.10	.02
□ 27 Don Baylor	.15	.06	.01
□ 28 Mike Schmidt	.60	.24	.06
□ 29 Pete Incaviglia	.45	.18	.04
□ 30 Barry Bonds	.45	.18	.04
□ 31 George Brett	.60	.24	.06
□ 32 Darryl Strawberry	.90	.36	.09
□ 33 Mike Witt	.10	.04	.01
□ 34 Kevin Bass	.10	.04	.01
□ 35 Jesse Barfield	.20	.08	.02
□ 36 Bob Ojeda	.10	.04	.01
□ 37 Cal Ripken	.30	.12	.03
□ 38 Vince Coleman	.30	.12	.03
□ 39 Wally Joyner	.90	.36	.09
□ 40 Robby Thompson	.20	.08	.02
□ 41 Pete Rose	.75	.30	.07
□ 42 Jim Rice	.25	.10	.02
□ 43 Tony Bernazard	.10	.04	.01
□ 44 Eric Davis	1.00	.40	.10
□ 45 George Bell	.25	.10	.02
□ 46 Hubie Brooks	.15	.06	.01
□ 47 Jack Morris	.20	.08	.02
□ 48 Tim Raines	.30	.12	.03

☐ 49 Mark Eichhorn	.10	.04	.01
☐ 50 Kevin Mitchell	.15	.06	.01
☐ 51 Dwight Gooden	.70	.28	.07
☐ 52 Doug DeCinces	.10	.04	.01
☐ 53 Fernando Valenzuela	.25	.10	.02
☐ 54 Reggie Jackson	.50	.20	.05
☐ 55 Johnny Ray	.15	.06	.01
☐ 56 Mike Pagliarulo	.15	.06	.01
☐ 57 Kirby Puckett	.60	.24	.06
☐ 58 Lance Parrish	.20	.08	.02
☐ 59 Jose Canseco	2.00	.80	.20
☐ 60 Greg Mathews	.20	.08	.02

1987 Topps Mini Leaders

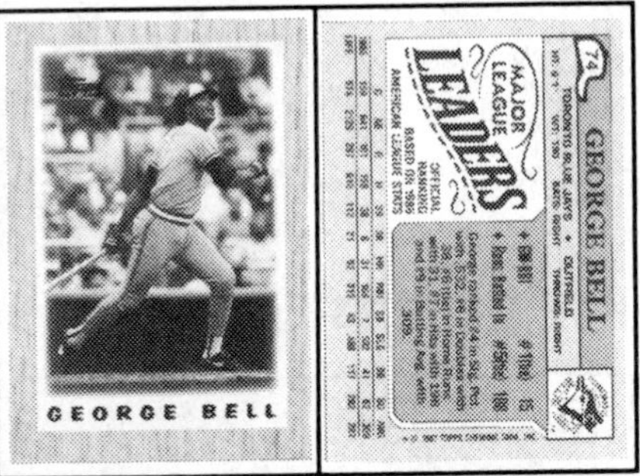

The 1987 Topps Mini set of Major League Leaders features 77 cards of leaders of the various statistical categories for the 1986 season. The cards are numbered on the back and measure 2 5/32" by 3". The card backs are printed in orange and brown on white card stock. They are very similar in design to the Team Leader cards in the 1987 Topps regular issue. The cards were distributed as a separate issue in wax packs of seven for 30 cents. Eleven of the cards were double printed and are hence more plentiful; they are marked DP in the checklist below.

	MINT	EXC	G-VG
COMPLETE SET (77)	7.00	2.80	.70
COMMON PLAYER (1-77)	.06	.02	.00
COMMON PLAYER DP	.03	.01	.00
☐ 1 Bob Horner DP	.06	.02	.00
☐ 2 Dale Murphy	.35	.14	.03
☐ 3 Lee Smith	.06	.02	.00
☐ 4 Eric Davis	.65	.26	.06
☐ 5 John Franco	.06	.02	.00
☐ 6 Dave Parker	.10	.04	.01
☐ 7 Kevin Bass	.06	.02	.00
☐ 8 Glenn Davis DP	.10	.04	.01
☐ 9 Bill Doran DP	.06	.02	.00
☐ 10 Bob Knepper DP	.03	.01	.00
☐ 11 Mike Scott	.15	.06	.01
☐ 12 Dave Smith	.06	.02	.00
☐ 13 Mariano Duncan	.06	.02	.00
☐ 14 Orel Hershiser	.45	.18	.04
☐ 15 Steve Sax DP	.10	.04	.01
☐ 16 Fernando Valenzuela	.20	.08	.02
☐ 17 Tim Raines	.25	.10	.02
☐ 18 Jeff Reardon	.06	.02	.00
☐ 19 Floyd Youmans	.06	.02	.00
☐ 20 Gary Carter DP	.15	.06	.01
☐ 21 Ron Darling	.15	.06	.01
☐ 22 Sid Fernandez	.10	.04	.01
☐ 23 Dwight Gooden	.50	.20	.05
☐ 24 Keith Hernandez	.25	.10	.02
☐ 25 Bob Ojeda	.10	.04	.01
☐ 26 Darryl Strawberry	.60	.24	.06
☐ 27 Steve Bedrosian	.10	.04	.01
☐ 28 Von Hayes DP	.06	.02	.00
☐ 29 Juan Samuel	.10	.04	.01
☐ 30 Mike Schmidt	.45	.18	.04
☐ 31 Rick Rhoden	.06	.02	.00
☐ 32 Vince Coleman	.20	.08	.02
☐ 33 Danny Cox	.06	.02	.00
☐ 34 Todd Worrell	.20	.08	.02
☐ 35 Tony Gwynn	.45	.18	.04
☐ 36 Mike Krukow	.06	.02	.00
☐ 37 Candy Maldonado	.06	.02	.00
☐ 38 Don Aase	.06	.02	.00
☐ 39 Eddie Murray	.35	.14	.03
☐ 40 Cal Ripken	.35	.14	.03
☐ 41 Wade Boggs	.75	.30	.07
☐ 42 Roger Clemens	.50	.20	.05
☐ 43 Bruce Hurst	.10	.04	.01
☐ 44 Jim Rice	.20	.08	.02
☐ 45 Wally Joyner	.40	.16	.04
☐ 46 Donnie Moore	.06	.02	.00
☐ 47 Gary Pettis	.06	.02	.00
☐ 48 Mike Witt	.06	.02	.00
☐ 49 John Cangelosi	.06	.02	.00
☐ 50 Tom Candiotti	.06	.02	.00
☐ 51 Joe Carter	.15	.06	.01
☐ 52 Pat Tabler	.06	.02	.00
☐ 53 Kirk Gibson DP	.10	.04	.01
☐ 54 Willie Hernandez	.10	.04	.01
☐ 55 Jack Morris	.15	.06	.01
☐ 56 Alan Trammell DP	.10	.04	.01
☐ 57 George Brett	.45	.18	.04
☐ 58 Willie Wilson	.10	.04	.01
☐ 59 Rob Deer	.10	.04	.01
☐ 60 Teddy Higuera	.15	.06	.01
☐ 61 Bert Blyleven DP	.06	.02	.00
☐ 62 Gary Gaetti DP	.06	.02	.00
☐ 63 Kirby Puckett	.45	.18	.04
☐ 64 Rickey Henderson	.40	.16	.04
☐ 65 Don Mattingly	1.00	.40	.10
☐ 66 Dennis Rasmussen	.10	.04	.01
☐ 67 Dave Righetti	.10	.04	.01
☐ 68 Jose Canseco	1.25	.50	.12
☐ 69 Dave Kingman	.10	.04	.01
☐ 70 Phil Bradley	.10	.04	.01
☐ 71 Mark Langston	.10	.04	.01
☐ 72 Pete O'Brien	.10	.04	.01
☐ 73 Jesse Barfield	.15	.06	.01
☐ 74 George Bell	.20	.08	.02
☐ 75 Tony Fernandez	.15	.06	.01
☐ 76 Tom Henke	.10	.04	.01
☐ 77 Checklist Card	.06	.01	.00

1987 Topps Traded

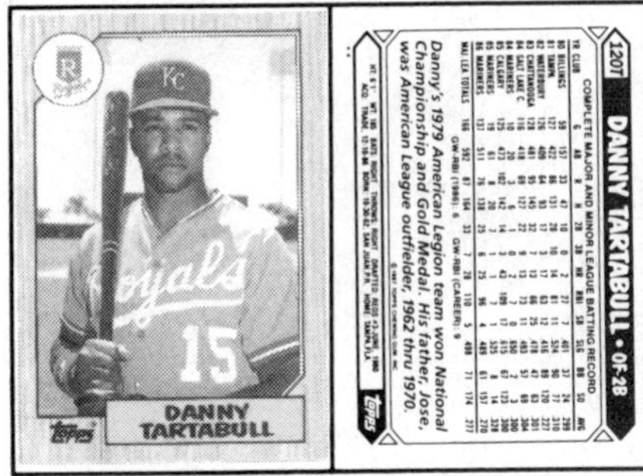

This 132-card Traded or extended set was distributed by Topps to dealers in a special green and white box as a complete set. The card fronts are identical in style to the Topps regular issue and are also 2 1/2" by 3 1/2". The backs are printed in yellow and blue on white card stock. Cards are numbered (with a T suffix) alphabetically according to the name of the player.

	MINT	EXC	G-VG
COMPLETE SET (132)	12.00	5.00	1.20
COMMON PLAYER (1-132)	.05	.02	.00
☐ 1T Bill Almon	.05	.02	.00
☐ 2T Scott Bankhead	.10	.04	.01
☐ 3T Eric Bell	.10	.04	.01
☐ 4T Juan Beniquez	.05	.02	.00
☐ 5T Juan Berenguer	.05	.02	.00
☐ 6T Greg Booker	.05	.02	.00
☐ 7T Thad Bosley	.05	.02	.00
☐ 8T Larry Bowa MG	.10	.04	.01
☐ 9T Greg Brock	.10	.04	.01
☐ 10T Bob Brower	.15	.06	.01
☐ 11T Jerry Browne	.10	.04	.01

□ 12T	Ralph Bryant	.10	.04	.01
□ 13T	DeWayne Buice	.10	.04	.01
□ 14T	Ellis Burks	1.75	.70	.17
□ 15T	Ivan Calderon	.20	.08	.02
□ 16T	Jeff Calhoun	.05	.02	.00
□ 17T	Casey Candaele	.10	.04	.01
□ 18T	John Cangelosi	.10	.04	.01
□ 19T	Steve Carlton	.20	.08	.02
□ 20T	Juan Castillo	.10	.04	.01
□ 21T	Rick Cerone	.05	.02	.00
□ 22T	Ron Cey	.10	.04	.01
□ 23T	John Christensen	.05	.02	.00
□ 24T	Dave Cone	2.00	.80	.20
□ 25T	Chuck Crim	.10	.04	.01
□ 26T	Storm Davis	.10	.04	.01
□ 27T	Andre Dawson	.35	.14	.03
□ 28T	Rick Dempsey	.10	.04	.01
□ 29T	Doug Drabek	.10	.04	.01
□ 30T	Mike Dunne	.20	.08	.02
□ 31T	Dennis Eckersley	.20	.08	.02
□ 32T	Lee Elia MG	.05	.02	.00
□ 33T	Brian Fisher	.10	.04	.01
□ 34T	Terry Francona	.05	.02	.00
□ 35T	Willie Fraser	.10	.04	.01
□ 36T	Billy Gardner MG	.05	.02	.00
□ 37T	Ken Gerhart	.15	.06	.01
□ 38T	Danny Gladden	.10	.04	.01
□ 39T	Jim Gott	.10	.04	.01
□ 40T	Cecilio Guante	.05	.02	.00
□ 41T	Albert Hall	.10	.04	.01
□ 42T	Terry Harper	.05	.02	.00
□ 43T	Mickey Hatcher	.10	.04	.01
□ 44T	Brad Havens	.05	.02	.00
□ 45T	Neal Heaton	.05	.02	.00
□ 46T	Mike Henneman	.30	.12	.03
□ 47T	Donnie Hill	.05	.02	.00
□ 48T	Guy Hoffman	.05	.02	.00
□ 49T	Brian Holton	.15	.06	.01
□ 50T	Charles Hudson	.05	.02	.00
□ 51T	Danny Jackson	.25	.10	.02
□ 52T	Reggie Jackson	.45	.18	.04
□ 53T	Chris James	.45	.18	.04
□ 54T	Dion James	.10	.04	.01
□ 55T	Stan Jefferson	.25	.10	.02
□ 56T	Joe Johnson	.10	.04	.01
□ 57T	Terry Kennedy	.10	.04	.01
□ 58T	Mike Kingery	.10	.04	.01
□ 59T	Ray Knight	.10	.04	.01
□ 60T	Gene Larkin	.30	.12	.03
□ 61T	Mike LaValliere	.10	.04	.01
□ 62T	Jack Lazorko	.05	.02	.00
□ 63T	Terry Leach	.15	.06	.01
□ 64T	Tim Leary	.20	.08	.02
□ 65T	Jim Lindeman	.20	.08	.02
□ 66T	Steve Lombardozzi	.10	.04	.01
□ 67T	Bill Long	.15	.06	.01
□ 68T	Barry Lyons	.15	.06	.01
□ 69T	Shane Mack	.20	.08	.02
□ 70T	Greg Maddux	.60	.24	.06
□ 71T	Bill Madlock	.10	.04	.01
□ 72T	Joe Magrane	.50	.20	.05
□ 73T	Dave Martinez	.20	.08	.02
□ 74T	Fred McGriff	1.50	.60	.15
□ 75T	Mark McLemore	.05	.02	.00
□ 76T	Kevin McReynolds	.25	.10	.02
□ 77T	Dave Meads	.10	.04	.01
□ 78T	Eddie Milner	.05	.02	.00
□ 79T	Greg Minton	.05	.02	.00
□ 80T	John Mitchell	.15	.06	.01
□ 81T	Kevin Mitchell	.15	.06	.01
□ 82T	Charlie Moore	.05	.02	.00
□ 83T	Jeff Musselman	.15	.06	.01
□ 84T	Gene Nelson	.05	.02	.00
□ 85T	Graig Nettles	.15	.06	.01
□ 86T	Al Newman	.05	.02	.00
□ 87T	Reid Nichols	.05	.02	.00
□ 88T	Tom Niedenfuer	.05	.02	.00
□ 89T	Joe Niekro	.10	.04	.01
□ 90T	Tom Nieto	.05	.02	.00
□ 91T	Matt Nokes	.65	.26	.06
□ 92T	Dickie Noles	.05	.02	.00
□ 93T	Pat Pacillo	.15	.06	.01
□ 94T	Lance Parrish	.15	.06	.01
□ 95T	Tony Pena	.15	.06	.01
□ 96T	Luis Polonia	.25	.10	.02
□ 97T	Randy Ready	.10	.04	.01
□ 98T	Jeff Reardon	.15	.06	.01
□ 99T	Gary Redus	.05	.02	.00
□ 100T	Jeff Reed	.05	.02	.00
□ 101T	Rick Rhoden	.10	.04	.01
□ 102T	Cal Ripken Sr. MG	.05	.02	.00
□ 103T	Wally Ritchie	.10	.04	.01
□ 104T	Jeff Robinson (Tigers pitcher)	.45	.18	.04
□ 105T	Gary Roenicke	.05	.02	.00
□ 106T	Jerry Royster	.05	.02	.00
□ 107T	Mark Salas	.05	.02	.00
□ 108T	Luis Salazar	.05	.02	.00
□ 109T	Benny Santiago	1.00	.40	.10
□ 110T	Dave Schmidt	.10	.04	.01
□ 111T	Kevin Seitzer	1.50	.60	.15
□ 112T	John Shelby	.05	.02	.00
□ 113T	Steve Shields	.15	.06	.01
□ 114T	John Smiley	.35	.14	.03
□ 115T	Chris Speier	.05	.02	.00
□ 116T	Mike Stanley	.20	.08	.02
□ 117T	Terry Steinbach	.40	.16	.04
□ 118T	Les Straker	.15	.06	.01
□ 119T	Jim Sundberg	.10	.04	.01
□ 120T	Danny Tartabull	.30	.12	.03
□ 121T	Tom Trebelhorn MG	.05	.02	.00
□ 122T	Dave Valle	.05	.02	.00
□ 123T	Ed VandeBerg	.05	.02	.00
□ 124T	Andy Van Slyke	.25	.10	.02
□ 125T	Gary Ward	.10	.04	.01
□ 126T	Alan Wiggins	.05	.02	.00
□ 127T	Bill Wilkinson	.15	.06	.01
□ 128T	Frank Williams	.05	.02	.00
□ 129T	Matt Williams	.45	.18	.04
□ 130T	Jim Winn	.05	.02	.00
□ 131T	Matt Young	.05	.02	.00
□ 132T	Checklist	.05	.01	.00

1988 Topps

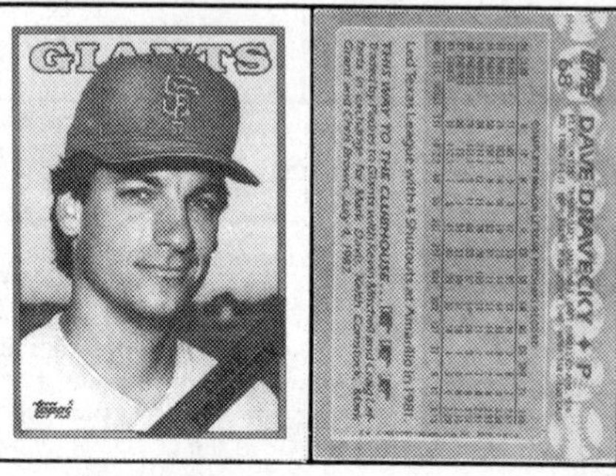

This 792-card set features backs which are printed in orange and black on white card stock. The manager cards contain a checklist of the respective team's players on the back. Subsets in the set include Record Breakers (1-7), Turn Back The Clock (661-665), and All-Star selections (386-407). The Team Leader cards typically show two players together inside a white cloud. Topps also produced a specially boxed "glossy" edition frequently referred to as the Topps Tiffany set. This year again Topps did not disclose the number of sets they produced or sold; it is apparent from the availability that there were many more sets produced this year compared to the 1984-86 Tiffany sets. The checklist of cards (792 regular and 132 Traded) is identical to that of the normal non-glossy cards. There are two primary distinguishing features of the Tiffany cards, white card stock reverses and high gloss obverses. These Tiffany cards are valued at approximately four times the values listed below.

		MINT	EXC	G-VG
COMPLETE SET (792)		24.00	10.00	2.40
COMMON PLAYER (1-792)		.03	.01	.00
□ 1	Vince Coleman RB 100 Steals for Third Cons. Season	.25	.07	.01
□ 2	Don Mattingly RB Six Grand Slams	.40	.16	.04
□ 3A	Mark McGwire RB ERR Rookie Homer Record (white spot behind left foot)	1.00	.40	.10

□	3B	Mark McGwire RB COR Rookie Homer Record (no white spot)	.40	.16	.04
□	4A	Eddie Murray RB ERR .. Switch Home Runs, Two Straight Games (caption in box on card front)	2.00	.80	.20
□	4B	Eddie Murray RB COR . Switch Home Runs, Two Straight Games (no caption on front)	.25	.10	.02
□	5	Phil/Joe Niekro RB .... Brothers Win Record	.06	.02	.00
□	6	Nolan Ryan RB .... 11th Season with 200 Strikeouts	.15	.06	.01
□	7	Benito Santiago RB .... 34-Game Hitting Streak, Rookie Record	.20	.08	.02
□	8	Kevin Elster	.20	.08	.02
□	9	Andy Hawkins	.06	.02	.00
□	10	Ryne Sandberg	.15	.06	.01
□	11	Mike Young	.03	.01	.00
□	12	Bill Schroeder	.03	.01	.00
□	13	Andres Thomas	.03	.01	.00
□	14	Sparky Anderson MG ..... (checklist back)	.06	.01	.00
□	15	Chili Davis	.06	.02	.00
□	16	Kirk McCaskill	.03	.01	.00
□	17	Ron Oester	.03	.01	.00
□	18A	Al Leiter ERR .... (photo actually Jeff George, right ear visible)	1.25	.50	.12
□	18B	Al Leiter COR .... (left ear visible)	1.00	.40	.10
□	19	Mark Davidson	.12	.05	.01
□	20	Kevin Gross	.03	.01	.00
□	21	Red Sox TL .... Wade Boggs and Spike Owen	.12	.05	.01
□	22	Greg Swindell	.10	.04	.01
□	23	Ken Landreaux	.03	.01	.00
□	24	Jim Deshaies	.03	.01	.00
□	25	Andres Galarraga	.20	.08	.02
□	26	Mitch Williams	.03	.01	.00
□	27	R.J. Reynolds	.03	.01	.00
□	28	Jose Nunez	.10	.04	.01
□	29	Argenis Salazar	.03	.01	.00
□	30	Sid Fernandez	.08	.03	.01
□	31	Bruce Bochy	.03	.01	.00
□	32	Mike Morgan	.03	.01	.00
□	33	Rob Deer	.08	.03	.01
□	34	Ricky Horton	.03	.01	.00
□	35	Harold Baines	.08	.03	.01
□	36	Jamie Moyer	.03	.01	.00
□	37	Ed Romero	.03	.01	.00
□	38	Jeff Calhoun	.03	.01	.00
□	39	Gerald Perry	.08	.03	.01
□	40	Orel Hershiser	.20	.08	.02
□	41	Bob Melvin	.03	.01	.00
□	42	Bill Landrum	.10	.04	.01
□	43	Dick Schofield	.03	.01	.00
□	44	Lou Piniella MG .... (checklist back)	.06	.01	.00
□	45	Kent Hrbek	.12	.05	.01
□	46	Darnell Coles	.03	.01	.00
□	47	Joaquin Andujar	.06	.02	.00
□	48	Alan Ashby	.03	.01	.00
□	49	Dave Clark	.08	.03	.01
□	50	Hubie Brooks	.06	.02	.00
□	51	Orioles TL .... Eddie Murray and Cal Ripken	.15	.06	.01
□	52	Don Robinson	.03	.01	.00
□	53	Curt Wilkerson	.03	.01	.00
□	54	Jim Clancy	.03	.01	.00
□	55	Phil Bradley	.08	.03	.01
□	56	Ed Hearn	.03	.01	.00
□	57	Tim Crews	.10	.04	.01
□	58	Dave Magadan	.08	.03	.01
□	59	Danny Cox	.06	.02	.00
□	60	Rickey Henderson	.25	.10	.02
□	61	Mark Knudson	.10	.04	.01
□	62	Jeff Hamilton	.06	.02	.00
□	63	Jimmy Jones	.10	.04	.01
□	64	Ken Caminiti	.18	.08	.01
□	65	Leon Durham	.03	.01	.00
□	66	Shane Rawley	.03	.01	.00
□	67	Ken Oberkfell	.03	.01	.00
□	68	Dave Dravecky	.03	.01	.00
□	69	Mike Hart	.08	.03	.01
□	70	Roger Clemens	.50	.20	.05
□	71	Gary Pettis	.03	.01	.00
□	72	Dennis Eckersley	.10	.04	.01
□	73	Randy Bush	.03	.01	.00
□	74	Tom Lasorda MG .... (checklist back)	.08	.02	.00
□	75	Joe Carter	.12	.05	.01
□	76	Denny Martinez	.03	.01	.00
□	77	Tom O'Malley	.03	.01	.00
□	78	Dan Petry	.03	.01	.00
□	79	Ernie Whitt	.03	.01	.00
□	80	Mark Langston	.08	.03	.01
□	81	Reds TL .... Ron Robinson and John Franco	.03	.01	.00
□	82	Darrel Akerfelds	.10	.04	.01
□	83	Jose Oquendo	.03	.01	.00
□	84	Cecilio Guante	.03	.01	.00
□	85	Howard Johnson	.08	.03	.01
□	86	Ron Karkovice	.03	.01	.00
□	87	Mike Mason	.03	.01	.00
□	88	Earnie Riles	.03	.01	.00
□	89	Gary Thurman	.20	.08	.02
□	90	Dale Murphy	.25	.10	.02
□	91	Joey Cora	.10	.04	.01
□	92	Len Matuszek	.03	.01	.00
□	93	Bob Sebra	.03	.01	.00
□	94	Chuck Jackson	.10	.04	.01
□	95	Lance Parrish	.08	.03	.01
□	96	Todd Benzinger	.25	.10	.02
□	97	Scott Garrelts	.03	.01	.00
□	98	Rene Gonzales	.12	.05	.01
□	99	Chuck Finley	.03	.01	.00
□	100	Jack Clark	.15	.06	.01
□	101	Allan Anderson	.06	.02	.00
□	102	Barry Larkin	.12	.05	.01
□	103	Curt Young	.03	.01	.00
□	104	Dick Williams MG .... (checklist back)	.06	.01	.00
□	105	Jesse Orosco	.03	.01	.00
□	106	Jim Walewander	.15	.06	.01
□	107	Scott Bailes	.03	.01	.00
□	108	Steve Lyons	.03	.01	.00
□	109	Joel Skinner	.03	.01	.00
□	110	Teddy Higuera	.08	.03	.01
□	111	Expos TL .... Hubie Brooks and Vance Law	.03	.01	.00
□	112	Les Lancaster	.10	.04	.01
□	113	Kelly Gruber	.03	.01	.00
□	114	Jeff Russell	.03	.01	.00
□	115	Johnny Ray	.08	.03	.01
□	116	Jerry Don Gleaton	.03	.01	.00
□	117	James Steels	.08	.03	.01
□	118	Bob Welch	.06	.02	.00
□	119	Robbie Wine	.12	.05	.01
□	120	Kirby Puckett	.30	.12	.03
□	121	Checklist 1-132	.06	.01	.00
□	122	Tony Bernazard	.03	.01	.00
□	123	Tom Candiotti	.03	.01	.00
□	124	Ray Knight	.06	.02	.00
□	125	Bruce Hurst	.10	.04	.01
□	126	Steve Jeltz	.03	.01	.00
□	127	Jim Gott	.03	.01	.00
□	128	Johnny Grubb	.03	.01	.00
□	129	Greg Minton	.03	.01	.00
□	130	Buddy Bell	.08	.03	.01
□	131	Don Schulze	.03	.01	.00
□	132	Donnie Hill	.03	.01	.00
□	133	Greg Mathews	.03	.01	.00
□	134	Chuck Tanner MG .... (checklist back)	.06	.01	.00
□	135	Dennis Rasmussen	.06	.02	.00
□	136	Brian Dayett	.03	.01	.00
□	137	Chris Bosio	.03	.01	.00
□	138	Mitch Webster	.03	.01	.00
□	139	Jerry Browne	.03	.01	.00
□	140	Jesse Barfield	.12	.05	.01
□	141	Royals TL .... George Brett and Bret Saberhagen	.15	.06	.01
□	142	Andy Van Slyke	.15	.06	.01
□	143	Mickey Tettleton	.03	.01	.00
□	144	Don Gordon	.10	.04	.01
□	145	Bill Madlock	.06	.02	.00
□	146	Donnell Nixon	.10	.04	.01
□	147	Bill Buckner	.06	.02	.00
□	148	Carmelo Martinez	.03	.01	.00
□	149	Ken Howell	.03	.01	.00
□	150	Eric Davis	.60	.24	.06
□	151	Bob Knepper	.03	.01	.00
□	152	Jody Reed	.35	.14	.03
□	153	John Habyan	.03	.01	.00
□	154	Jeff Stone	.03	.01	.00
□	155	Bruce Sutter	.08	.03	.01
□	156	Gary Matthews	.03	.01	.00
□	157	Atlee Hammaker	.03	.01	.00

☐ 158	Tim Hulett	.03	.01	.00
☐ 159	Brad Arnsberg	.10	.04	.01
☐ 160	Willie McGee	.10	.04	.01
☐ 161	Bryn Smith	.03	.01	.00
☐ 162	Mark McLemore	.03	.01	.00
☐ 163	Dale Mohorcic	.03	.01	.00
☐ 164	Dave Johnson MG (checklist back)	.06	.01	.00
☐ 165	Robin Yount	.20	.08	.02
☐ 166	Rick Rodriquez	.10	.04	.01
☐ 167	Rance Mulliniks	.03	.01	.00
☐ 168	Barry Jones	.03	.01	.00
☐ 169	Ross Jones	.10	.04	.01
☐ 170	Rich Gossage	.08	.03	.01
☐ 171	Cubs TL Shawon Dunston and Manny Trillo	.03	.01	.00
☐ 172	Lloyd McClendon	.10	.04	.01
☐ 173	Eric Plunk	.03	.01	.00
☐ 174	Phil Garner	.03	.01	.00
☐ 175	Kevin Bass	.06	.02	.00
☐ 176	Jeff Reed	.03	.01	.00
☐ 177	Frank Tanana	.06	.02	.00
☐ 178	Dwayne Henry	.06	.02	.00
☐ 179	Charlie Puleo	.03	.01	.00
☐ 180	Terry Kennedy	.03	.01	.00
☐ 181	Dave Cone	1.00	.40	.10
☐ 182	Ken Phelps	.06	.02	.00
☐ 183	Tom Lawless	.03	.01	.00
☐ 184	Ivan Calderon	.08	.03	.01
☐ 185	Rick Rhoden	.03	.01	.00
☐ 186	Rafael Palmeiro	.25	.10	.02
☐ 187	Steve Kiefer	.06	.02	.00
☐ 188	John Russell	.03	.01	.00
☐ 189	Wes Gardner	.20	.08	.02
☐ 190	Candy Maldonado	.06	.02	.00
☐ 191	John Cerutti	.03	.01	.00
☐ 192	Devon White	.12	.05	.01
☐ 193	Brian Fisher	.03	.01	.00
☐ 194	Tom Kelly MG (checklist back)	.06	.01	.00
☐ 195	Dan Quisenberry	.08	.03	.01
☐ 196	Dave Engle	.03	.01	.00
☐ 197	Lance McCullers	.06	.02	.00
☐ 198	Franklin Stubbs	.03	.01	.00
☐ 199	Dave Meads	.10	.04	.01
☐ 200	Wade Boggs	.70	.28	.07
☐ 201	Rangers TL Bobby Valentine, Pete O'Brien, Pete Incaviglia, and Steve Buechele	.06	.02	.00
☐ 202	Glenn Hoffman	.03	.01	.00
☐ 203	Fred Toliver	.03	.01	.00
☐ 204	Paul O'Neill	.08	.03	.01
☐ 205	Nelson Liriano	.12	.05	.01
☐ 206	Domingo Ramos	.03	.01	.00
☐ 207	John Mitchell	.12	.05	.01
☐ 208	Steve Lake	.03	.01	.00
☐ 209	Richard Dotson	.03	.01	.00
☐ 210	Willie Randolph	.06	.02	.00
☐ 211	Frank DiPino	.03	.01	.00
☐ 212	Greg Brock	.03	.01	.00
☐ 213	Albert Hall	.03	.01	.00
☐ 214	Dave Schmidt	.03	.01	.00
☐ 215	Von Hayes	.08	.03	.01
☐ 216	Jerry Reuss	.03	.01	.00
☐ 217	Harry Spilman	.03	.01	.00
☐ 218	Dan Schatzeder	.03	.01	.00
☐ 219	Mike Stanley	.06	.02	.00
☐ 220	Tom Henke	.06	.02	.00
☐ 221	Rafael Belliard	.03	.01	.00
☐ 222	Steve Farr	.03	.01	.00
☐ 223	Stan Jefferson	.10	.04	.01
☐ 224	Tom Trebelhorn MG (checklist back)	.06	.01	.00
☐ 225	Mike Scioscia	.03	.01	.00
☐ 226	Dave Lopes	.06	.02	.00
☐ 227	Ed Correa	.03	.01	.00
☐ 228	Wallace Johnson	.03	.01	.00
☐ 229	Jeff Musselman	.08	.03	.01
☐ 230	Pat Tabler	.06	.02	.00
☐ 231	Pirates TL Barry Bonds and Bobby Bonilla	.10	.04	.01
☐ 232	Bob James	.03	.01	.00
☐ 233	Rafael Santana	.03	.01	.00
☐ 234	Ken Dayley	.03	.01	.00
☐ 235	Gary Ward	.03	.01	.00
☐ 236	Ted Power	.03	.01	.00
☐ 237	Mike Heath	.03	.01	.00
☐ 238	Luis Polonia	.20	.08	.02
☐ 239	Roy Smalley	.03	.01	.00
☐ 240	Lee Smith	.06	.02	.00
☐ 241	Damaso Garcia	.03	.01	.00
☐ 242	Tom Niedenfuer	.03	.01	.00
☐ 243	Mark Ryal	.08	.03	.01
☐ 244	Jeff D. Robinson (Pirates pitcher)	.03	.01	.00
☐ 245	Rich Gedman	.03	.01	.00
☐ 246	Mike Campbell	.15	.06	.01
☐ 247	Thad Bosley	.03	.01	.00
☐ 248	Storm Davis	.06	.02	.00
☐ 249	Mike Marshall	.08	.03	.01
☐ 250	Nolan Ryan	.25	.10	.02
☐ 251	Tom Foley	.03	.01	.00
☐ 252	Bob Brower	.10	.04	.01
☐ 253	Checklist 133-264	.06	.01	.00
☐ 254	Lee Elia MG (checklist back)	.06	.01	.00
☐ 255	Mookie Wilson	.06	.02	.00
☐ 256	Ken Schrom	.03	.01	.00
☐ 257	Jerry Royster	.03	.01	.00
☐ 258	Ed Nunez	.03	.01	.00
☐ 259	Ron Kittle	.08	.03	.01
☐ 260	Vince Coleman	.18	.08	.01
☐ 261	Giants TL (five players)	.03	.01	.00
☐ 262	Drew Hall	.10	.04	.01
☐ 263	Glenn Braggs	.06	.02	.00
☐ 264	Les Straker	.10	.04	.01
☐ 265	Bo Diaz	.03	.01	.00
☐ 266	Paul Assenmacher	.03	.01	.00
☐ 267	Billy Bean	.15	.06	.01
☐ 268	Bruce Ruffin	.03	.01	.00
☐ 269	Ellis Burks	1.00	.40	.10
☐ 270	Mike Witt	.08	.03	.01
☐ 271	Ken Gerhart	.08	.03	.01
☐ 272	Steve Ontiveros	.03	.01	.00
☐ 273	Garth Iorg	.03	.01	.00
☐ 274	Junior Ortiz	.03	.01	.00
☐ 275	Kevin Seitzer	.90	.36	.09
☐ 276	Luis Salazar	.03	.01	.00
☐ 277	Alejandro Pena	.03	.01	.00
☐ 278	Jose Cruz	.06	.02	.00
☐ 279	Randy St.Claire	.03	.01	.00
☐ 280	Pete Incaviglia	.18	.08	.01
☐ 281	Jerry Hairston	.03	.01	.00
☐ 282	Pat Perry	.03	.01	.00
☐ 283	Phil Lombardi	.08	.03	.01
☐ 284	Larry Bowa MG (checklist back)	.06	.01	.00
☐ 285	Jim Presley	.08	.03	.01
☐ 286	Chuck Crim	.10	.04	.01
☐ 287	Manny Trillo	.03	.01	.00
☐ 288	Pat Pacillo	.06	.02	.00
☐ 289	Dave Bergman	.03	.01	.00
☐ 290	Tony Fernandez	.10	.04	.01
☐ 291	Astros TL Billy Hatcher and Kevin Bass	.06	.02	.00
☐ 292	Carney Lansford	.08	.03	.01
☐ 293	Doug Jones	.25	.10	.02
☐ 294	Al Pedrique	.10	.04	.01
☐ 295	Bert Blyleven	.08	.03	.01
☐ 296	Floyd Rayford	.03	.01	.00
☐ 297	Zane Smith	.06	.02	.00
☐ 298	Milt Thompson	.03	.01	.00
☐ 299	Steve Crawford	.03	.01	.00
☐ 300	Don Mattingly	1.25	.50	.12
☐ 301	Bud Black	.03	.01	.00
☐ 302	Jose Uribe	.03	.01	.00
☐ 303	Eric Show	.06	.02	.00
☐ 304	George Hendrick	.06	.02	.00
☐ 305	Steve Sax	.10	.04	.01
☐ 306	Billy Hatcher	.06	.02	.00
☐ 307	Mike Trujillo	.03	.01	.00
☐ 308	Lee Mazzilli	.03	.01	.00
☐ 309	Bill Long	.10	.04	.01
☐ 310	Tom Herr	.06	.02	.00
☐ 311	Scott Sanderson	.03	.01	.00
☐ 312	Joey Meyer	.20	.08	.02
☐ 313	Bob McClure	.03	.01	.00
☐ 314	Jimy Williams MG (checklist back)	.06	.01	.00
☐ 315	Dave Parker	.10	.04	.01
☐ 316	Jose Rijo	.06	.02	.00
☐ 317	Tom Nieto	.03	.01	.00
☐ 318	Mel Hall	.03	.01	.00
☐ 319	Mike Loynd	.03	.01	.00
☐ 320	Alan Trammell	.15	.06	.01
☐ 321	White Sox TL Harold Baines and Carlton Fisk	.08	.03	.01
☐ 322	Vicente Palacios	.12	.05	.01
☐ 323	Rick Leach	.03	.01	.00
☐ 324	Danny Jackson	.15	.06	.01
☐ 325	Glenn Hubbard	.03	.01	.00
☐ 326	Al Nipper	.03	.01	.00
☐ 327	Larry Sheets	.08	.03	.01

☐ 328 Greg Cadaret .12 .05 .01
☐ 329 Chris Speier .03 .01 .00
☐ 330 Eddie Whitson .03 .01 .00
☐ 331 Brian Downing .03 .01 .00
☐ 332 Jerry Reed .03 .01 .00
☐ 333 Wally Backman .03 .01 .00
☐ 334 Dave LaPoint .03 .01 .00
☐ 335 Claudell Washington .06 .02 .00
☐ 336 Ed Lynch .03 .01 .00
☐ 337 Jim Gantner .03 .01 .00
☐ 338 Brian Holton .08 .03 .01
☐ 339 Kurt Stillwell .03 .01 .00
☐ 340 Jack Morris .12 .05 .01
☐ 341 Carmen Castillo .03 .01 .00
☐ 342 Larry Andersen .03 .01 .00
☐ 343 Greg Gagne .03 .01 .00
☐ 344 Tony LaRussa MG .06 .01 .00
(checklist back)
☐ 345 Scott Fletcher .03 .01 .00
☐ 346 Vance Law .03 .01 .00
☐ 347 Joe Johnson .03 .01 .00
☐ 348 Jim Eisenreich .03 .01 .00
☐ 349 Bob Walk .03 .01 .00
☐ 350 Will Clark .60 .24 .06
☐ 351 Cardinals TL .03 .01 .00
Red Schoendienst
and Tony Pena
☐ 352 Billy Ripken .15 .06 .01
☐ 353 Ed Olwine .03 .01 .00
☐ 354 Marc Sullivan .03 .01 .00
☐ 355 Roger McDowell .06 .02 .00
☐ 356 Luis Aguayo .03 .01 .00
☐ 357 Floyd Bannister .03 .01 .00
☐ 358 Rey Quinones .03 .01 .00
☐ 359 Tim Stoddard .03 .01 .00
☐ 360 Tony Gwynn .30 .12 .03
☐ 361 Greg Maddux .35 .14 .03
☐ 362 Juan Castillo .08 .03 .01
☐ 363 Willie Fraser .03 .01 .00
☐ 364 Nick Esasky .03 .01 .00
☐ 365 Floyd Youmans .03 .01 .00
☐ 366 Chet Lemon .03 .01 .00
☐ 367 Tim Leary .08 .03 .01
☐ 368 Gerald Young .25 .10 .02
☐ 369 Greg Harris .03 .01 .00
☐ 370 Jose Canseco 1.50 .60 .15
☐ 371 Joe Hesketh .03 .01 .00
☐ 372 Matt Williams .30 .12 .03
☐ 373 Checklist 265-396 .06 .01 .00
☐ 374 Doc Edwards MG .06 .01 .00
(checklist back)
☐ 375 Tom Brunansky .08 .03 .01
☐ 376 Bill Wilkinson .10 .04 .01
☐ 377 Sam Horn .30 .12 .03
☐ 378 Todd Frohwirth .10 .04 .01
☐ 379 Rafael Ramirez .03 .01 .00
☐ 380 Joe Magrane .25 .10 .02
☐ 381 Angels TL .12 .05 .01
Wally Joyner and
Jack Howell
☐ 382 Keith Miller .20 .08 .02
(New York Mets)
☐ 383 Eric Bell .03 .01 .00
☐ 384 Neil Allen .03 .01 .00
☐ 385 Carlton Fisk .08 .03 .01
☐ 386 Don Mattingly AS .40 .16 .04
☐ 387 Willie Randolph AS .06 .02 .00
☐ 388 Wade Boggs AS .30 .12 .03
☐ 389 Alan Trammell AS .08 .03 .01
☐ 390 George Bell AS .10 .04 .01
☐ 391 Kirby Puckett AS .15 .06 .01
☐ 392 Dave Winfield AS .12 .05 .01
☐ 393 Matt Nokes AS .15 .06 .01
☐ 394 Roger Clemens AS .20 .08 .02
☐ 395 Jimmy Key AS .06 .02 .00
☐ 396 Tom Henke AS .06 .02 .00
☐ 397 Jack Clark AS .10 .04 .01
☐ 398 Juan Samuel AS .06 .02 .00
☐ 399 Tim Wallach AS .06 .02 .00
☐ 400 Ozzie Smith AS .10 .04 .01
☐ 401 Andre Dawson AS .12 .05 .01
☐ 402 Tony Gwynn AS .15 .06 .01
☐ 403 Tim Raines AS .12 .05 .01
☐ 404 Benny Santiago AS .15 .06 .01
☐ 405 Dwight Gooden AS .20 .08 .02
☐ 406 Shane Rawley AS .06 .02 .00
☐ 407 Steve Bedrosian AS .06 .02 .00
☐ 408 Dion James .03 .01 .00
☐ 409 Joel McKeon .03 .01 .00
☐ 410 Tony Pena .06 .02 .00
☐ 411 Wayne Tolleson .03 .01 .00
☐ 412 Randy Myers .08 .03 .01
☐ 413 John Christensen .03 .01 .00
☐ 414 John McNamara MG .06 .01 .00
(checklist back)
☐ 415 Don Carman .03 .01 .00
☐ 416 Keith Moreland .03 .01 .00
☐ 417 Mark Ciardi .08 .03 .01
☐ 418 Joel Youngblood .03 .01 .00
☐ 419 Scott McGregor .03 .01 .00
☐ 420 Wally Joyner .35 .14 .03
☐ 421 Ed VandeBerg .03 .01 .00
☐ 422 Dave Concepcion .06 .02 .00
☐ 423 John Smiley .20 .08 .02
☐ 424 Dwayne Murphy .03 .01 .00
☐ 425 Jeff Reardon .06 .02 .00
☐ 426 Randy Ready .03 .01 .00
☐ 427 Paul Kilgus .12 .05 .01
☐ 428 John Shelby .03 .01 .00
☐ 429 Tigers TL .15 .06 .01
Alan Trammell and
Kirk Gibson
☐ 430 Glenn Davis .12 .05 .01
☐ 431 Casey Candaele .03 .01 .00
☐ 432 Mike Moore .03 .01 .00
☐ 433 Bill Pecota .10 .04 .01
☐ 434 Rick Aguilera .03 .01 .00
☐ 435 Mike Pagliarulo .08 .03 .01
☐ 436 Mike Bielecki .03 .01 .00
☐ 437 Fred Manrique .10 .04 .01
☐ 438 Rob Ducey .15 .06 .01
☐ 439 Dave Martinez .08 .03 .01
☐ 440 Steve Bedrosian .08 .03 .01
☐ 441 Rick Manning .03 .01 .00
☐ 442 Tom Bolton .10 .04 .01
☐ 443 Ken Griffey .06 .02 .00
☐ 444 Cal Ripken, Sr. MG .06 .01 .00
(checklist back)
UER (two copyrights)
☐ 445 Mike Krukow .03 .01 .00
☐ 446 Doug DeCinces .03 .01 .00
☐ 447 Jeff Montgomery .15 .06 .01
☐ 448 Mike Davis .03 .01 .00
☐ 449 Jeff M. Robinson .30 .12 .03
(Tigers pitcher)
☐ 450 Barry Bonds .15 .06 .01
☐ 451 Keith Atherton .03 .01 .00
☐ 452 Willie Wilson .08 .03 .01
☐ 453 Dennis Powell .03 .01 .00
☐ 454 Marvell Wynne .03 .01 .00
☐ 455 Shawn Hillegas .15 .06 .01
☐ 456 Dave Anderson .03 .01 .00
☐ 457 Terry Leach .06 .02 .00
☐ 458 Ron Hassey .03 .01 .00
☐ 459 Yankees TL .08 .03 .01
Dave Winfield and
Willie Randolph
☐ 460 Ozzie Smith .12 .05 .01
☐ 461 Danny Darwin .03 .01 .00
☐ 462 Don Slaught .03 .01 .00
☐ 463 Fred McGriff .40 .16 .04
☐ 464 Jay Tibbs .03 .01 .00
☐ 465 Paul Molitor .10 .04 .01
☐ 466 Jerry Mumphrey .03 .01 .00
☐ 467 Don Aase .03 .01 .00
☐ 468 Darren Daulton .03 .01 .00
☐ 469 Jeff Dedmon .03 .01 .00
☐ 470 Dwight Evans .10 .04 .01
☐ 471 Donnie Moore .03 .01 .00
☐ 472 Robby Thompson .03 .01 .00
☐ 473 Joe Niekro .06 .02 .00
☐ 474 Tom Brookens .03 .01 .00
☐ 475 Pete Rose MG .30 .10 .02
(checklist back)
☐ 476 Dave Stewart .08 .03 .01
☐ 477 Jamie Quirk .03 .01 .00
☐ 478 Sid Bream .03 .01 .00
☐ 479 Brett Butler .06 .02 .00
☐ 480 Dwight Gooden .35 .14 .03
☐ 481 Mariano Duncan .03 .01 .00
☐ 482 Mark Davis .06 .02 .00
☐ 483 Rod Booker .10 .04 .01
☐ 484 Pat Clements .03 .01 .00
☐ 485 Harold Reynolds .03 .01 .00
☐ 486 Pat Keedy .10 .04 .01
☐ 487 Jim Pankovits .03 .01 .00
☐ 488 Andy McGaffigan .03 .01 .00
☐ 489 Dodgers TL .12 .05 .01
Pedro Guerrero and
Fernando Valenzuela
☐ 490 Larry Parrish .03 .01 .00
☐ 491 B.J. Surhoff .08 .03 .01
☐ 492 Doyle Alexander .03 .01 .00
☐ 493 Mike Greenwell 1.25 .50 .12
☐ 494 Wally Ritchie .10 .04 .01
☐ 495 Eddie Murray .20 .08 .02
☐ 496 Guy Hoffman .03 .01 .00
☐ 497 Kevin Mitchell .06 .02 .00
☐ 498 Bob Boone .06 .02 .00
☐ 499 Eric King .03 .01 .00

□ 500	Andre Dawson	.20	.08	.02
□ 501	Tim Birtsas	.03	.01	.00
□ 502	Danny Gladden	.06	.02	.00
□ 503	Junior Noboa	.08	.03	.01
□ 504	Bob Rodgers MG	.06	.01	.00
	(checklist back)			
□ 505	Willie Upshaw	.03	.01	.00
□ 506	John Cangelosi	.03	.01	.00
□ 507	Mark Gubicza	.08	.03	.01
□ 508	Tim Teufel	.03	.01	.00
□ 509	Bill Dawley	.03	.01	.00
□ 510	Dave Winfield	.20	.08	.02
□ 511	Joel Davis	.03	.01	.00
□ 512	Alex Trevino	.03	.01	.00
□ 513	Tim Flannery	.03	.01	.00
□ 514	Pat Sheridan	.03	.01	.00
□ 515	Juan Nieves	.03	.01	.00
□ 516	Jim Sundberg	.03	.01	.00
□ 517	Ron Robinson	.03	.01	.00
□ 518	Greg Gross	.03	.01	.00
□ 519	Mariners TL	.03	.01	.00
	Harold Reynolds and			
	Phil Bradley			
□ 520	Dave Smith	.03	.01	.00
□ 521	Jim Dwyer	.03	.01	.00
□ 522	Bob Patterson	.10	.04	.01
□ 523	Gary Roenicke	.03	.01	.00
□ 524	Gary Lucas	.03	.01	.00
□ 525	Marty Barrett	.06	.02	.00
□ 526	Juan Berenguer	.03	.01	.00
□ 527	Steve Henderson	.03	.01	.00
□ 528A	Checklist 397-528	.50	.10	.02
	ERR (455 S. Carlton)			
□ 528B	Checklist 397-528	.06	.01	.00
	COR (455 S. Hillegas)			
□ 529	Tim Burke	.03	.01	.00
□ 530	Gary Carter	.20	.08	.02
□ 531	Rich Yett	.03	.01	.00
□ 532	Mike Kingery	.03	.01	.00
□ 533	John Farrell	.20	.08	.02
□ 534	John Wathan MG	.06	.01	.00
	(checklist back)			
□ 535	Ron Guidry	.08	.03	.01
□ 536	John Morris	.03	.01	.00
□ 537	Steve Buechele	.03	.01	.00
□ 538	Bill Wegman	.03	.01	.00
□ 539	Mike LaValliere	.03	.01	.00
□ 540	Bret Saberhagen	.10	.04	.01
□ 541	Juan Beniquez	.03	.01	.00
□ 542	Paul Noce	.10	.04	.01
□ 543	Kent Tekulve	.03	.01	.00
□ 544	Jim Traber	.03	.01	.00
□ 545	Don Baylor	.08	.03	.01
□ 546	John Candelaria	.06	.02	.00
□ 547	Felix Fermin	.10	.04	.01
□ 548	Shane Mack	.10	.04	.01
□ 549	Braves TL	.06	.02	.00
	Albert Hall,			
	Dale Murphy,			
	Ken Griffey,			
	and Dion James			
□ 550	Pedro Guerrero	.15	.06	.01
□ 551	Terry Steinbach	.15	.06	.01
□ 552	Mark Thurmond	.03	.01	.00
□ 553	Tracy Jones	.08	.03	.01
□ 554	Mike Smithson	.03	.01	.00
□ 555	Brook Jacoby	.08	.03	.01
□ 556	Stan Clarke	.08	.03	.01
□ 557	Craig Reynolds	.03	.01	.00
□ 558	Bob Ojeda	.06	.02	.00
□ 559	Ken Williams	.20	.08	.02
□ 560	Tim Wallach	.08	.03	.01
□ 561	Rick Cerone	.03	.01	.00
□ 562	Jim Lindeman	.08	.03	.01
□ 563	Jose Guzman	.03	.01	.00
□ 564	Frank Lucchesi MG	.06	.01	.00
	(checklist back)			
□ 565	Lloyd Moseby	.08	.03	.01
□ 566	Charlie O'Brien	.10	.04	.01
□ 567	Mike Diaz	.03	.01	.00
□ 568	Chris Brown	.06	.02	.00
□ 569	Charlie Leibrandt	.03	.01	.00
□ 570	Jeffrey Leonard	.06	.02	.00
□ 571	Mark Williamson	.10	.04	.01
□ 572	Chris James	.18	.08	.01
□ 573	Bob Stanley	.03	.01	.00
□ 574	Graig Nettles	.08	.03	.01
□ 575	Don Sutton	.10	.04	.01
□ 576	Tommy Hinzo	.10	.04	.01
□ 577	Tom Browning	.08	.03	.01
□ 578	Gary Gaetti	.12	.05	.01
□ 579	Mets TL	.15	.06	.01
	Gary Carter and			
	Kevin McReynolds			
□ 580	Mark McGwire	1.00	.40	.10
□ 581	Tito Landrum	.03	.01	.00
□ 582	Mike Henneman	.20	.08	.02
□ 583	Dave Valle	.06	.02	.00
□ 584	Steve Trout	.03	.01	.00
□ 585	Ozzie Guillen	.06	.02	.00
□ 586	Bob Forsch	.03	.01	.00
□ 587	Terry Puhl	.03	.01	.00
□ 588	Jeff Parrett	.15	.06	.01
□ 589	Geno Petralli	.03	.01	.00
□ 590	George Bell	.15	.06	.01
□ 591	Doug Drabek	.03	.01	.00
□ 592	Dale Sveum	.03	.01	.00
□ 593	Bob Tewksbury	.03	.01	.00
□ 594	Bobby Valentine MG	.06	.01	.00
	(checklist back)			
□ 595	Frank White	.06	.02	.00
□ 596	John Kruk	.08	.03	.01
□ 597	Gene Garber	.03	.01	.00
□ 598	Lee Lacy	.03	.01	.00
□ 599	Calvin Schiraldi	.03	.01	.00
□ 600	Mike Schmidt	.25	.10	.02
□ 601	Jack Lazorko	.03	.01	.00
□ 602	Mike Aldrete	.06	.02	.00
□ 603	Rob Murphy	.03	.01	.00
□ 604	Chris Bando	.03	.01	.00
□ 605	Kirk Gibson	.15	.06	.01
□ 606	Moose Haas	.03	.01	.00
□ 607	Mickey Hatcher	.06	.02	.00
□ 608	Charlie Kerfeld	.03	.01	.00
□ 609	Twins TL	.10	.04	.01
	Gary Gaetti and			
	Kent Hrbek			
□ 610	Keith Hernandez	.15	.06	.01
□ 611	Tommy John	.10	.04	.01
□ 612	Curt Ford	.03	.01	.00
□ 613	Bobby Thigpen	.06	.02	.00
□ 614	Herm Winningham	.03	.01	.00
□ 615	Jody Davis	.06	.02	.00
□ 616	Jay Aldrich	.10	.04	.01
□ 617	Oddibe McDowell	.08	.03	.01
□ 618	Cecil Fielder	.03	.01	.00
□ 619	Mike Dunne	.12	.05	.01
	(inconsistent design,			
	black name on front)			
□ 620	Cory Snyder	.18	.08	.01
□ 621	Gene Nelson	.03	.01	.00
□ 622	Kal Daniels	.18	.08	.01
□ 623	Mike Flanagan	.03	.01	.00
□ 624	Jim Leyland MG	.06	.01	.00
	(checklist back)			
□ 625	Frank Viola	.15	.06	.01
□ 626	Glenn Wilson	.03	.01	.00
□ 627	Joe Boever	.10	.04	.01
□ 628	Dave Henderson	.03	.01	.00
□ 629	Kelly Downs	.03	.01	.00
□ 630	Darrell Evans	.06	.02	.00
□ 631	Jack Howell	.03	.01	.00
□ 632	Steve Shields	.03	.01	.00
□ 633	Barry Lyons	.10	.04	.01
□ 634	Jose DeLeon	.03	.01	.00
□ 635	Terry Pendleton	.03	.01	.00
□ 636	Charles Hudson	.03	.01	.00
□ 637	Jay Bell	.15	.06	.01
□ 638	Steve Balboni	.03	.01	.00
□ 639	Brewers TL	.03	.01	.00
	Glenn Braggs			
	and Tony Muser CO			
□ 640	Garry Templeton	.06	.02	.00
	(inconsistent design,			
	green border)			
□ 641	Rick Honeycutt	.03	.01	.00
□ 642	Bob Dernier	.03	.01	.00
□ 643	Rocky Childress	.08	.03	.01
□ 644	Terry McGriff	.08	.03	.01
□ 645	Matt Nokes	.45	.18	.04
□ 646	Checklist 529-660	.06	.01	.00
□ 647	Pascual Perez	.06	.02	.00
□ 648	Al Newman	.03	.01	.00
□ 649	DeWayne Buice	.10	.04	.01
□ 650	Cal Ripken	.18	.08	.01
□ 651	Mike Jackson	.15	.06	.01
□ 652	Bruce Benedict	.03	.01	.00
□ 653	Jeff Sellers	.03	.01	.00
□ 654	Roger Craig MG	.06	.01	.00
	(checklist back)			
□ 655	Len Dykstra	.08	.03	.01
□ 656	Lee Guetterman	.03	.01	.00
□ 657	Gary Redus	.03	.01	.00
□ 658	Tim Conroy	.03	.01	.00
	(inconsistent design,			
	name in white)			
□ 659	Bobby Meacham	.03	.01	.00
□ 660	Rick Reuschel	.06	.02	.00
□ 661	Turn Back Clock 1983	.15	.06	.01
	Nolan Ryan			

☐ 662 Turn Back Clock 1978 ... .08 .03 .01
Jim Rice
☐ 663 Turn Back Clock 1973 ... .03 .01 .00
Ron Blomberg
☐ 664 Turn Back Clock 1968 ... .10 .04 .01
Bob Gibson
☐ 665 Turn Back Clock 1963 ... .15 .06 .01
Stan Musial
☐ 666 Mario Soto ... .03 .01 .00
☐ 667 Luis Quinones ... .03 .01 .00
☐ 668 Walt Terrell ... .03 .01 .00
☐ 669 Phillies TL ... .06 .02 .00
Lance Parrish
and Mike Ryan CO
☐ 670 Dan Plesac ... .06 .02 .00
☐ 671 Tim Laudner ... .03 .01 .00
☐ 672 John Davis ... .12 .05 .01
☐ 673 Tony Phillips ... .03 .01 .00
☐ 674 Mike Fitzgerald ... .03 .01 .00
☐ 675 Jim Rice ... .15 .06 .01
☐ 676 Ken Dixon ... .03 .01 .00
☐ 677 Eddie Milner ... .03 .01 .00
☐ 678 Jim Acker ... .03 .01 .00
☐ 679 Darrell Miller ... .03 .01 .00
☐ 680 Charlie Hough ... .03 .01 .00
☐ 681 Bobby Bonilla ... .15 .06 .01
☐ 682 Jimmy Key ... .08 .03 .01
☐ 683 Julio Franco ... .08 .03 .01
☐ 684 Hal Lanier MG ... .06 .01 .00
(checklist back)
☐ 685 Ron Darling ... .10 .04 .01
☐ 686 Terry Francona ... .03 .01 .00
☐ 687 Mickey Brantley ... .08 .03 .01
☐ 688 Jim Winn ... .03 .01 .00
☐ 689 Tom Pagnozzi ... .12 .05 .01
☐ 690 Jay Howell ... .03 .01 .00
☐ 691 Dan Pasqua ... .06 .02 .00
☐ 692 Mike Birkbeck ... .03 .01 .00
☐ 693 Benny Santiago ... .60 .24 .06
☐ 694 Eric Nolte ... .12 .05 .01
☐ 695 Shawon Dunston ... .06 .02 .00
☐ 696 Duane Ward ... .03 .01 .00
☐ 697 Steve Lombardozzi ... .03 .01 .00
☐ 698 Brad Havens ... .03 .01 .00
☐ 699 Padres TL ... .20 .08 .02
Benito Santiago
and Tony Gwynn
☐ 700 George Brett ... .25 .10 .02
☐ 701 Sammy Stewart ... .03 .01 .00
☐ 702 Mike Gallego ... .03 .01 .00
☐ 703 Bob Brenly ... .03 .01 .00
☐ 704 Dennis Boyd ... .06 .02 .00
☐ 705 Juan Samuel ... .08 .03 .01
☐ 706 Rick Mahler ... .03 .01 .00
☐ 707 Fred Lynn ... .10 .04 .01
☐ 708 Gus Polidor ... .06 .02 .00
☐ 709 George Frazier ... .03 .01 .00
☐ 710 Darryl Strawberry ... .35 .14 .03
☐ 711 Bill Gullickson ... .03 .01 .00
☐ 712 John Moses ... .03 .01 .00
☐ 713 Willie Hernandez ... .06 .02 .00
☐ 714 Jim Fregosi MG ... .06 .01 .00
(checklist back)
☐ 715 Todd Worrell ... .10 .04 .01
☐ 716 Lenn Sakata ... .03 .01 .00
☐ 717 Jay Baller ... .03 .01 .00
☐ 718 Mike Felder ... .03 .01 .00
☐ 719 Denny Walling ... .03 .01 .00
☐ 720 Tim Raines ... .18 .08 .01
☐ 721 Pete O'Brien ... .06 .02 .00
☐ 722 Manny Lee ... .03 .01 .00
☐ 723 Bob Kipper ... .03 .01 .00
☐ 724 Danny Tartabull ... .20 .08 .02
☐ 725 Mike Boddicker ... .06 .02 .00
☐ 726 Alfredo Griffin ... .06 .02 .00
☐ 727 Greg Booker ... .03 .01 .00
☐ 728 Andy Allanson ... .03 .01 .00
☐ 729 Blue Jays TL ... .10 .04 .01
George Bell and
Fred McGriff
☐ 730 John Franco ... .06 .02 .00
☐ 731 Rick Schu ... .03 .01 .00
☐ 732 Dave Palmer ... .03 .01 .00
☐ 733 Spike Owen ... .03 .01 .00
☐ 734 Craig Lefferts ... .03 .01 .00
☐ 735 Kevin McReynolds ... .20 .08 .02
☐ 736 Matt Young ... .03 .01 .00
☐ 737 Butch Wynegar ... .03 .01 .00
☐ 738 Scott Bankhead ... .03 .01 .00
☐ 739 Daryl Boston ... .03 .01 .00
☐ 740 Rick Sutcliffe ... .08 .03 .01
☐ 741 Mike Easler ... .03 .01 .00
☐ 742 Mark Clear ... .03 .01 .00
☐ 743 Larry Herndon ... .03 .01 .00
☐ 744 Whitey Herzog MG ... .06 .01 .00
(checklist back)
☐ 745 Bill Doran ... .06 .02 .00
☐ 746 Gene Larkin ... .20 .08 .02
☐ 747 Bobby Witt ... .06 .02 .00
☐ 748 Reid Nichols ... .03 .01 .00
☐ 749 Mark Eichhorn ... .03 .01 .00
☐ 750 Bo Jackson ... .30 .12 .03
☐ 751 Jim Morrison ... .03 .01 .00
☐ 752 Mark Grant ... .03 .01 .00
☐ 753 Danny Heep ... .03 .01 .00
☐ 754 Mike LaCoss ... .03 .01 .00
☐ 755 Ozzie Virgil ... .03 .01 .00
☐ 756 Mike Maddux ... .03 .01 .00
☐ 757 John Marzano ... .08 .03 .01
☐ 758 Eddie Williams ... .12 .05 .01
☐ 759 A's TL ... .35 .14 .03
Mark McGwire
and Jose Canseco
☐ 760 Mike Scott ... .12 .05 .01
☐ 761 Tony Armas ... .06 .02 .00
☐ 762 Scott Bradley ... .03 .01 .00
☐ 763 Doug Sisk ... .03 .01 .00
☐ 764 Greg Walker ... .06 .02 .00
☐ 765 Neal Heaton ... .03 .01 .00
☐ 766 Henry Cotto ... .03 .01 .00
☐ 767 Jose Lind ... .18 .08 .01
☐ 768 Dickie Noles ... .03 .01 .00
☐ 769 Cecil Cooper ... .08 .03 .01
☐ 770 Lou Whitaker ... .10 .04 .01
☐ 771 Ruben Sierra ... .18 .08 .01
☐ 772 Sal Butera ... .03 .01 .00
☐ 773 Frank Williams ... .03 .01 .00
☐ 774 Gene Mauch MG ... .06 .01 .00
(checklist back)
☐ 775 Dave Stieb ... .08 .03 .01
☐ 776 Checklist 661-792 ... .06 .01 .00
☐ 777 Lonnie Smith ... .03 .01 .00
☐ 778A Keith Comstock ERR ... 6.00 2.40 .60
(white "Padres")
☐ 778B Keith Comstock COR ... .15 .06 .01
(blue "Padres")
☐ 779 Tom Glavine ... .15 .06 .01
☐ 780 Fernando Valenzuela ... .12 .05 .01
☐ 781 Keith Hughes ... .18 .08 .01
☐ 782 Jeff Ballard ... .12 .05 .01
☐ 783 Ron Roenicke ... .03 .01 .00
☐ 784 Joe Sambito ... .03 .01 .00
☐ 785 Alvin Davis ... .08 .03 .01
☐ 786 Joe Price ... .03 .01 .00
(inconsistent design,
orange team name)
☐ 787 Bill Almon ... .03 .01 .00
☐ 788 Ray Searage ... .03 .01 .00
☐ 789 Indians' TL ... .10 .04 .01
Joe Carter and
Cory Snyder
☐ 790 Dave Righetti ... .08 .03 .01
☐ 791 Ted Simmons ... .08 .03 .01
☐ 792 John Tudor ... .10 .04 .01

1988 Topps Wax Box Cards

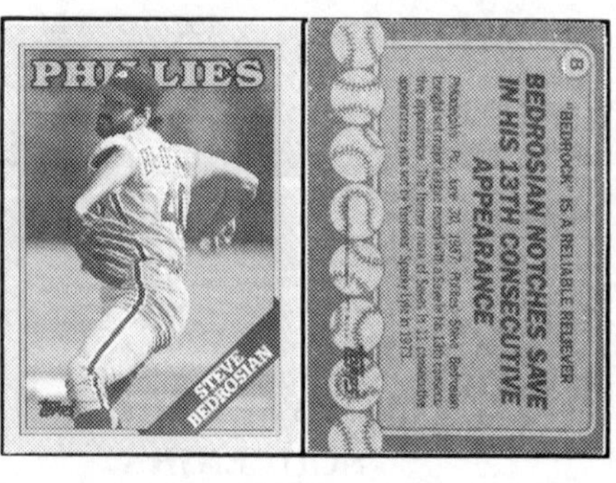

The cards in this 16-card set measure the standard 2 1/2" by 3 1/2". Cards have essentially the same design as the 1988 Topps regular issue set. The cards were printed on the bottoms of the regular issue wax pack boxes. These 16 cards, "lettered" A through P, are considered a separate set in their own right and are not typically included in a complete set of the

CENTER FIELD

BUY & SELL

BASEBALL AND FOOTBALL CARDS

- Over 500,000 in stock!
- 1952 - Topps to present, Bowman Football
- SUPER STARS: 1952 - present

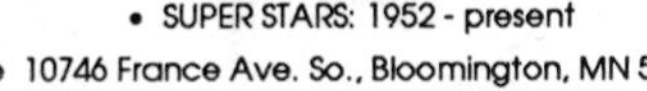

Store 10746 France Ave. So., Bloomington, MN 55431

Rick & Jo Ann Hamilton
612-884-0355

P.O. Box 20143
Bloomington, MN 55420

SASE requested

BASEBALL
JIM

WE

SELL - BUY - TRADE

BOB

Locker Room

SPORTS CARDS
(617) 770-0362
557 HANCOCK ST.
QUINCY, MA 02170

FOOTBALL

HOCKEY
JOE

BASKETBALL

Roanoke Coin Exchange
Towers Mall
Roanoke, VA 24015
703-982-8587

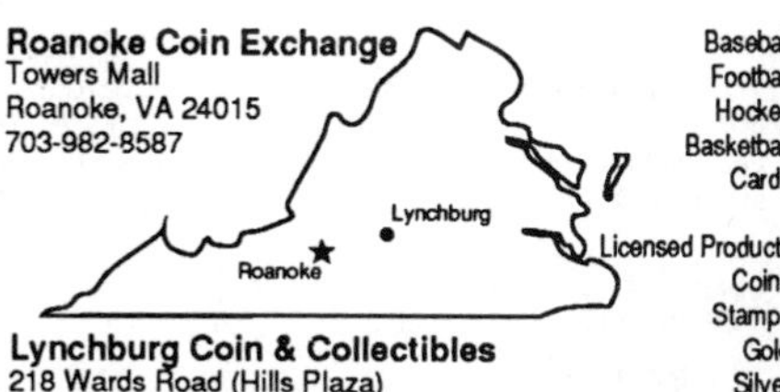

Baseball
Football
Hockey
Basketball
Cards

Licensed Products
Coins
Stamps
Gold
Silver
Bought & Sold Daily
Selection of all related hobby supplies

Lynchburg Coin & Collectibles
218 Wards Road (Hills Plaza)
Lynchburg, VA 24502
804-237-2741

RICK MALONEY
314-894-8069

TUES. - FRI. (11-9)
SAT. (9-5) SUN. (12-4)

WORLD OF BASEBALL CARDS II

Buying - Selling - Trading
We Also Have
Large Selection of Sports Memorabilia
Check Our Non Sport Cards & Packs

3187 LEMAY FERRY RD.
ST. LOUIS, MISSOURI 63125
Across the road from Mehlville High School
NO MAIL ORDER

A AND M BASEBALL CARDS

ROOKIES • ALLSTARS • OLDTIMERS
Anthony and Max Fabrizio

818-846-2903

415 East Magnolia Blvd. Burbank, CA 91501

---

(415) 680-8395

The Card Connection

Baseball Card Shop
Baseball Cards, Hats and Jerseys

12 Gregory Lane, Suite 6
Pleasant Hill, CA 94523

Steve Walton
Owner

MASTERCARD
VISA

AM. EXPRESS
DISCOVER

SPORTS

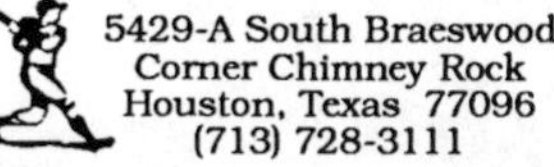

5429-A South Braeswood
Corner Chimney Rock
Houston, Texas 77096
(713) 728-3111

ONLY THE VERY BEST IN SPORTS COLLECTIBLES

BASEBALL, FOOTBALL, BASKETBALL & HOCKEY CARDS,
PRO CAPS, JERSEYS & SATIN JACKETS - SPORT VIDEOS

SECOND DECK

Baseball Card Shop

1319 Galindo Street, Concord, CA 94520

(415) 825-1610

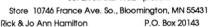

regular issue 1988 Topps cards. The value of the panels uncut is slightly greater, perhaps by 25% greater, than the value of the individual cards cut up carefully.

	MINT	EXC	G-VG
COMPLETE SET (16)	2.50	1.00	.25
COMMON PLAYER (A-P)	.05	.02	.00
☐ A Don Baylor	.10	.04	.01
☐ B Steve Bedrosian	.10	.04	.01
☐ C Juan Beniquez	.05	.02	.00
☐ D Bob Boone	.10	.04	.01
☐ E Darrell Evans	.10	.04	.01
☐ F Tony Gwynn	.35	.14	.03
☐ G John Kruk	.15	.06	.01
☐ H Marvell Wynne	.05	.02	.00
☐ I Joe Carter	.20	.08	.02
☐ J Eric Davis	.50	.20	.05
☐ K Howard Johnson	.15	.06	.01
☐ L Darryl Strawberry	.50	.20	.05
☐ M Rickey Henderson	.35	.14	.03
☐ N Nolan Ryan	.35	.14	.03
☐ O Mike Schmidt	.35	.14	.03
☐ P Kent Tekulve	.05	.02	.00

1988 Topps Glossy All-Stars 22

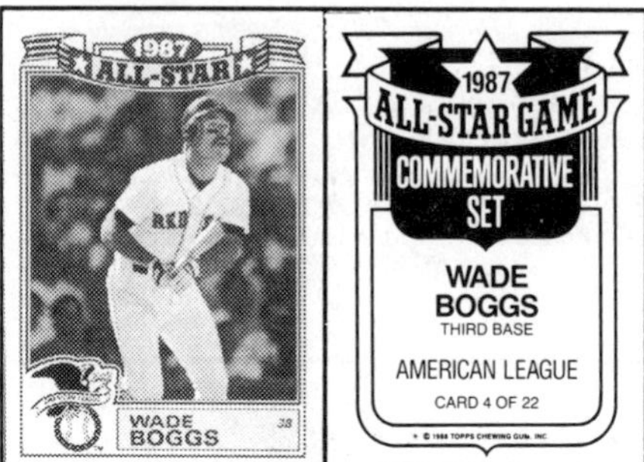

This set of 22 glossy cards was inserted one per rack pack. Players selected for the set are the starting players (plus manager and honorary captain) in the 1987 All-Star Game in Oakland. Cards measure standard size, 2 1/2" by 3 1/2" and the backs feature red and blue printing on a white card stock.

	MINT	EXC	G-VG
COMPLETE SET (22)	4.00	1.60	.40
COMMON PLAYER (1-22)	.10	.04	.01
☐ 1 John McNamara MG	.10	.04	.01
☐ 2 Don Mattingly	.65	.26	.06
☐ 3 Willie Randolph	.10	.04	.01
☐ 4 Wade Boggs	.50	.20	.05
☐ 5 Cal Ripken	.25	.10	.02
☐ 6 George Bell	.20	.08	.02
☐ 7 Rickey Henderson	.30	.12	.03
☐ 8 Dave Winfield	.25	.10	.02
☐ 9 Terry Kennedy	.10	.04	.01
☐ 10 Bret Saberhagen	.15	.06	.01
☐ 11 Jim Hunter CAPT	.15	.06	.01
☐ 12 Dave Johnson MG	.10	.04	.01
☐ 13 Jack Clark	.20	.08	.02
☐ 14 Ryne Sandberg	.20	.08	.02
☐ 15 Mike Schmidt	.35	.14	.03
☐ 16 Ozzie Smith	.20	.08	.02
☐ 17 Eric Davis	.45	.18	.04
☐ 18 Andre Dawson	.25	.10	.02
☐ 19 Darryl Strawberry	.45	.18	.04
☐ 20 Gary Carter	.25	.10	.02
☐ 21 Mike Scott	.15	.06	.01
☐ 22 Billy Williams CAPT	.15	.06	.01

1988 Topps Jumbo Rookies

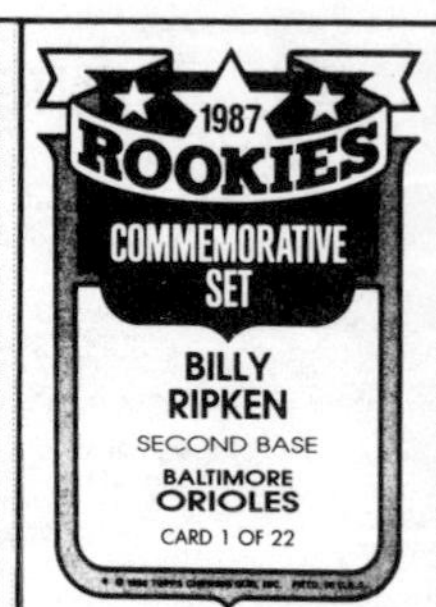

Inserted in each supermarket jumbo pack is a card from this series of 22 of 1987's best rookies as determined by Topps. Jumbo packs consisted of 100 (regular issue 1988 Topps baseball) cards with a stick of gum plus the insert "Rookie" card. The card fronts are in full color and measure 2 1/2" by 3 1/2". The card backs are printed in red and blue on white card stock and are numbered at the bottom.

	MINT	EXC	G-VG
COMPLETE SET (22)	10.00	4.00	1.00
COMMON PLAYER (1-22)	.20	.08	.02
☐ 1 Billy Ripken	.30	.12	.03
☐ 2 Ellis Burks	1.25	.50	.12
☐ 3 Mike Greenwell	1.75	.70	.17
☐ 4 DeWayne Buice	.20	.08	.02
☐ 5 Devon White	.50	.20	.05
☐ 6 Fred Manrique	.20	.08	.02
☐ 7 Mike Henneman	.30	.12	.03
☐ 8 Matt Nokes	.60	.24	.06
☐ 9 Kevin Seitzer	1.00	.40	.10
☐ 10 B.J. Surhoff	.40	.16	.04
☐ 11 Casey Candaele	.20	.08	.02
☐ 12 Randy Myers	.40	.16	.04
☐ 13 Mark McGwire	1.50	.60	.15
☐ 14 Luis Polonia	.30	.12	.03
☐ 15 Terry Steinbach	.40	.16	.04
☐ 16 Mike Dunne	.40	.16	.04
☐ 17 Al Pedrique	.20	.08	.02
☐ 18 Benny Santiago	.90	.36	.09
☐ 19 Kelly Downs	.30	.12	.03
☐ 20 Joe Magrane	.40	.16	.04
☐ 21 Jerry Browne	.20	.08	.02
☐ 22 Jeff Musselman	.20	.08	.02

1988 Topps Revco League Leaders

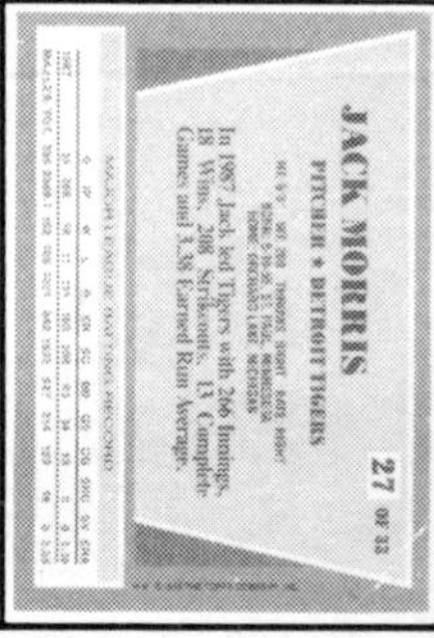

Topps produced this 33-card boxed set for Revco stores subtitled "League Leaders". The cards measure 2 1/2" by 3 inside a white border. The card backs are printed in red and black on white card

stock. The cards are numbered on the back. The statistics provided on the card backs cover only two lines, last season and Major League totals.

	MINT	EXC	G-VG
COMPLETE SET (33)	4.50	1.80	.45
COMMON PLAYER (1-33)	.10	.04	.01
□ 1 Tony Gwynn	.30	.12	.03
□ 2 Andre Dawson	.20	.08	.02
□ 3 Vince Coleman	.20	.08	.02
□ 4 Jack Clark	.20	.08	.02
□ 5 Tim Raines	.20	.08	.02
□ 6 Tim Wallach	.10	.04	.01
□ 7 Juan Samuel	.15	.06	.01
□ 8 Nolan Ryan	.30	.12	.03
□ 9 Rick Sutcliffe	.15	.06	.01
□ 10 Kent Tekulve	.10	.04	.01
□ 11 Steve Bedrosian	.15	.06	.01
□ 12 Orel Hershiser	.40	.16	.04
□ 13 Rick Reuschel	.10	.04	.01
□ 14 Fernando Valenzuela	.20	.08	.02
□ 15 Bob Welch	.10	.04	.01
□ 16 Wade Boggs	.50	.20	.05
□ 17 Mark McGwire	.40	.16	.04
□ 18 George Bell	.20	.08	.02
□ 19 Harold Reynolds	.10	.04	.01
□ 20 Paul Molitor	.20	.08	.02
□ 21 Kirby Puckett	.40	.16	.04
□ 22 Kevin Seitzer	.30	.12	.03
□ 23 Brian Downing	.10	.04	.01
□ 24 Dwight Evans	.15	.06	.01
□ 25 Willie Wilson	.10	.04	.01
□ 26 Danny Tartabull	.25	.10	.02
□ 27 Jimmy Key	.10	.04	.01
□ 28 Roger Clemens	.40	.16	.04
□ 29 Dave Stewart	.15	.06	.01
□ 30 Mark Eichhorn	.10	.04	.01
□ 31 Tom Henke	.10	.04	.01
□ 32 Charlie Hough	.10	.04	.01
□ 33 Mark Langston	.15	.06	.01

1988 Topps Rite-Aid Team MVP's

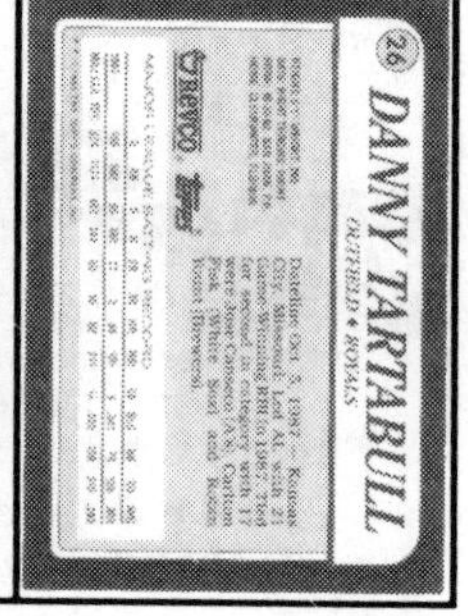

Topps produced this 33-card boxed set for Rite Aid Drug and Discount Stores subtitled "Team MVP's". The Rite Aid logo is at the top of every obverse. The cards measure 2 1/2" by 3 1/2" and feature a high-gloss, full-color photo of the player inside a red, white, and blue border. The card backs are printed in blue and black on white card stock. The cards are numbered on the back and the checklist for the set is found on the back panel of the small collector box. The statistics provided on the card backs cover only two lines, last season and Major League totals.

	MINT	EXC	G-VG
COMPLETE SET (33)	4.50	1.80	.45
COMMON PLAYER (1-33)	.10	.04	.01
□ 1 Dale Murphy	.35	.14	.03
□ 2 Andre Dawson	.20	.08	.02
□ 3 Eric Davis	.40	.16	.04
□ 4 Mike Scott	.15	.06	.01
□ 5 Pedro Guerrero	.20	.08	.02
□ 6 Tim Raines	.25	.10	.02
□ 7 Darryl Strawberry	.50	.20	.05
□ 8 Mike Schmidt	.35	.14	.03
□ 9 Mike Dunne	.15	.06	.01
□ 10 Jack Clark	.20	.08	.02
□ 11 Tony Gwynn	.30	.12	.03
□ 12 Will Clark	.45	.18	.04
□ 13 Cal Ripken	.25	.10	.02
□ 14 Wade Boggs	.50	.20	.05
□ 15 Wally Joyner	.30	.12	.03
□ 16 Harold Baines	.15	.06	.01
□ 17 Joe Carter	.20	.08	.02
□ 18 Alan Trammell	.20	.08	.02
□ 19 Kevin Seitzer	.25	.10	.02
□ 20 Paul Molitor	.20	.08	.02
□ 21 Kirby Puckett	.40	.16	.04
□ 22 Don Mattingly	.60	.24	.06
□ 23 Mark McGwire	.40	.16	.04
□ 24 Alvin Davis	.15	.06	.01
□ 25 Ruben Sierra	.25	.10	.02
□ 26 George Bell	.20	.08	.02
□ 27 Jack Morris	.15	.06	.01
□ 28 Jeff Reardon	.10	.04	.01
□ 29 John Tudor	.15	.06	.01
□ 30 Rick Reuschel	.10	.04	.01
□ 31 Gary Gaetti	.20	.08	.02
□ 32 Jeffrey Leonard	.10	.04	.01
□ 33 Frank Viola	.25	.10	.02

1988 Topps UK Minis

The 1988 Topps UK (United Kingdom) Mini set of "American Baseball" features 88 cards. The cards are numbered on the back and measure approximately 2 1/8" by 3". The card backs are printed in blue, red, and yellow on white card stock. The cards were distributed as a separate issue in packs. A custom black and yellow small set box was also available for holding a complete set; the box has a complete checklist on the back panel. The set player numbering is accoring to alphabetical order.

	MINT	EXC	G-VG
COMPLETE SET (88)	7.50	3.00	.75
COMMON PLAYER (1-88)	.05	.02	.00
□ 1 Harold Baines	.10	.04	.01
□ 2 Steve Bedrosian	.10	.04	.01
□ 3 Goerge Bell	.15	.06	.01
□ 4 Wade Boggs	.65	.26	.06
□ 5 Barry Bonds	.15	.06	.01
□ 6 Bob Boone	.10	.04	.01
□ 7 George Brett	.35	.14	.03
□ 8 Hubie Brooks	.10	.04	.01
□ 9 Ivan Calderon	.10	.04	.01
□ 10 Jose Canseco	1.25	.50	.12
□ 11 Gary Carter	.25	.10	.02
□ 12 Joe Carter	.20	.08	.02
□ 13 Jack Clark	.20	.08	.02
□ 14 Will Clark	.50	.20	.05
□ 15 Roger Clemens	.50	.20	.05
□ 16 Vince Coleman	.20	.08	.02
□ 17 Alvin Davis	.10	.04	.01
□ 18 Eric Davis	.50	.20	.05
□ 19 Glenn Davis	.20	.08	.02
□ 20 Andre Dawson	.25	.10	.02
□ 21 Mike Dunne	.10	.04	.01
□ 22 Dwight Evans	.15	.06	.01
□ 23 Tony Fernandez	.15	.06	.01
□ 24 John Franco	.10	.04	.01

☐ 25 Gary Gaetti	.15	.06	.01
☐ 26 Kirk Gibson	.25	.10	.02
☐ 27 Dwight Gooden	.45	.18	.04
☐ 28 Pedro Guerrero	.15	.06	.01
☐ 29 Tony Gwynn	.35	.14	.03
☐ 30 Billy Hatcher	.05	.02	.00
☐ 31 Rickey Henderson	.35	.14	.03
☐ 32 Tom Henke	.05	.02	.00
☐ 33 Keith Hernandez	.25	.10	.02
☐ 34 Orel Hershiser	.50	.20	.05
☐ 35 Teddy Higuera	.10	.04	.01
☐ 36 Charlie Hough	.05	.02	.00
☐ 37 Kent Hrbek	.15	.06	.01
☐ 38 Brook Jacoby	.10	.04	.01
☐ 39 Dion James	.05	.02	.00
☐ 40 Wally Joyner	.35	.14	.03
☐ 41 John Kruk	.10	.04	.01
☐ 42 Mark Langston	.10	.04	.01
☐ 43 Jeffrey Leonard	.05	.02	.00
☐ 44 Candy Maldonado	.05	.02	.00
☐ 45 Don Mattingly	1.00	.40	.10
☐ 46 Willie McGee	.10	.04	.01
☐ 47 Mark McGwire	.50	.20	.05
☐ 48 Kevin Mitchell	.10	.04	.01
☐ 49 Paul Molitor	.15	.06	.01
☐ 50 Jack Morris	.15	.06	.01
☐ 51 Lloyd Moseby	.10	.04	.01
☐ 52 Dale Murphy	.40	.16	.04
☐ 53 Eddie Murray	.30	.12	.03
☐ 54 Matt Nokes	.25	.10	.02
☐ 55 Dave Parker	.15	.06	.01
☐ 56 Larry Parrish	.05	.02	.00
☐ 57 Kirby Puckett	.45	.18	.04
☐ 58 Tim Raines	.25	.10	.02
☐ 59 Willie Randolph	.10	.04	.01
☐ 60 Harold Reynolds	.10	.04	.01
☐ 61 Cal Ripken	.30	.12	.03
☐ 62 Nolan Ryan	.35	.14	.03
☐ 63 Bret Saberhagen	.15	.06	.01
☐ 64 Juan Samuel	.10	.04	.01
☐ 65 Ryne Sandberg	.25	.10	.02
☐ 66 Benny Santiago	.30	.12	.03
☐ 67 Mike Schmidt	.35	.14	.03
☐ 68 Mike Scott	.15	.06	.01
☐ 69 Kevin Seitzer	.25	.10	.02
☐ 70 Larry Sheets	.10	.04	.01
☐ 71 Ruben Sierra	.20	.08	.02
☐ 72 Ozzie Smith	.20	.08	.02
☐ 73 Zane Smith	.10	.04	.01
☐ 74 Cory Snyder	.25	.10	.02
☐ 75 Dave Stewart	.10	.04	.01
☐ 76 Darryl Strawberry	.50	.20	.05
☐ 77 Rick Sutcliffe	.10	.04	.01
☐ 78 Danny Tartabull	.25	.10	.02
☐ 79 Alan Trammell	.20	.08	.02
☐ 80 Fernando Valenzuela	.15	.06	.01
☐ 81 Andy Van Slyke	.20	.08	.02
☐ 82 Frank Viola	.20	.08	.02
☐ 83 Greg Walker	.10	.04	.01
☐ 84 Tim Wallach	.10	.04	.01
☐ 85 Dave Winfield	.30	.12	.03
☐ 86 Mike Witt	.10	.04	.01
☐ 87 Robin Yount	.30	.12	.03
☐ 88 Checklist	.05	.01	.00

1988 Topps Send-In Glossy 60

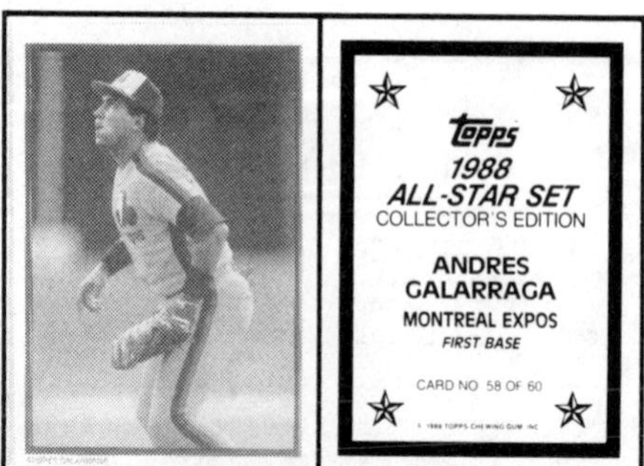

Topps issued this set through a mail-in offer explained and advertised on the wax packs. This 60-card set features glossy fronts with each card measuring 2 1/2" by 3 1/2". The offer provided your choice of any one of the six 10-card subsets (1-10, 11-20, etc.) for 1.25 plus six of the Special Offer ("Spring Fever Baseball") insert cards, which were found one per wax pack. The last two players (numerically) in each ten- card subset are actually "Hot Prospects."

	MINT	EXC	G-VG
COMPLETE SET (60)	12.00	5.00	1.20
COMMON PLAYER (1-60)	.10	.04	.01
☐ 1 Andre Dawson	.25	.10	.02
☐ 2 Jesse Barfield	.20	.08	.02
☐ 3 Mike Schmidt	.35	.14	.03
☐ 4 Ruben Sierra	.20	.08	.02
☐ 5 Mike Scott	.15	.06	.01
☐ 6 Cal Ripken	.25	.10	.02
☐ 7 Gary Carter	.30	.12	.03
☐ 8 Kent Hrbek	.20	.08	.02
☐ 9 Kevin Seitzer	.35	.14	.03
☐ 10 Mike Henneman	.15	.06	.01
☐ 11 Don Mattingly	1.25	.50	.12
☐ 12 Tim Raines	.30	.12	.03
☐ 13 Roger Clemens	.75	.30	.07
☐ 14 Ryne Sandberg	.25	.10	.02
☐ 15 Tony Fernandez	.15	.06	.01
☐ 16 Eric Davis	.60	.24	.06
☐ 17 Jack Morris	.20	.08	.02
☐ 18 Tim Wallach	.15	.06	.01
☐ 19 Mike Dunne	.15	.06	.01
☐ 20 Mike Greenwell	1.25	.50	.12
☐ 21 Dwight Evans	.15	.06	.01
☐ 22 Darryl Strawberry	.75	.30	.07
☐ 23 Cory Snyder	.25	.10	.02
☐ 24 Pedro Guerrero	.20	.08	.02
☐ 25 Rickey Henderson	.40	.16	.04
☐ 26 Dale Murphy	.45	.18	.04
☐ 27 Kirby Puckett	.45	.18	.04
☐ 28 Steve Bedrosian	.15	.06	.01
☐ 29 Devon White	.20	.08	.02
☐ 30 Benny Santiago	.30	.12	.03
☐ 31 George Bell	.20	.08	.02
☐ 32 Keith Hernandez	.25	.10	.02
☐ 33 Dave Stewart	.15	.06	.01
☐ 34 Dave Parker	.20	.08	.02
☐ 35 Tom Henke	.10	.04	.01
☐ 36 Willie McGee	.15	.06	.01
☐ 37 Alan Trammell	.20	.08	.02
☐ 38 Tony Gwynn	.35	.14	.03
☐ 39 Mark McGwire	.50	.20	.05
☐ 40 Joe Magrane	.15	.06	.01
☐ 41 Jack Clark	.20	.08	.02
☐ 42 Willie Randolph	.15	.06	.01
☐ 43 Juan Samuel	.15	.06	.01
☐ 44 Joe Carter	.20	.08	.02
☐ 45 Shane Rawley	.10	.04	.01
☐ 46 Dave Winfield	.35	.14	.03
☐ 47 Ozzie Smith	.20	.08	.02
☐ 48 Wally Joyner	.30	.12	.03
☐ 49 B.J. Surhoff	.15	.06	.01
☐ 50 Ellis Burks	.75	.30	.07
☐ 51 Wade Boggs	.75	.30	.07
☐ 52 Howard Johnson	.15	.06	.01
☐ 53 George Brett	.40	.16	.04
☐ 54 Dwight Gooden	.50	.20	.05
☐ 55 Jose Canseco	1.50	.60	.15
☐ 56 Lee Smith	.10	.04	.01
☐ 57 Paul Molitor	.20	.08	.02
☐ 58 Andres Galarraga	.30	.12	.03
☐ 59 Matt Nokes	.30	.12	.03
☐ 60 Casey Candaele	.10	.04	.01

1988 Topps Big Cards

This set of 264 cards was issued as three separately distributed series of 88 cards each. Cards were distributed in wax packs with seven cards for a suggested retail of 40 cents. These cards are very reminiscent in style of the 1956 Topps card set and are popular with collectors perhaps for that reason. The cards measure approximately 2 5/8" by 3 3/4" and are oriented horizontally.

	MINT	EXC	G-VG
COMPLETE SET (264)	27.00	11.00	2.70
COMMON PLAYER (1-88)	.05	.02	.00

BOSTON & NEW ENGLAND COLLECTORS
visit SPORTS NOSTALGIA

We Stock Complete Sets of Bowman, Topps, Fleer & Donruss Baseball, FB, Bask. & Hock. Cards, Singles & Star cards, Yearbooks, Programs, Pennants, Posters, Guides, Souvenirs, etc...

SEND $1.00 & A Self Addressed Stamped Envelope for our Illustrated Price List!

77A Beach St., Revere, MA 02151
Tel: (617) 284-9597 or 284-9268
Hours: 6PM to 8PM Mon. thru Fri., 10AM to 5PM Saturdays

PIN CITY USA
SPORTS & CARTOON CHARACTER COLLECTIBLES

- Disney, Olympics
- MLB, NFL, NBA
- Coca Cola, McDonalds
- Space Shuttle
- Frames
- Baseball Cards & Supplies

Mail Order Only
PIN CITY USA
6312 E. Santa Ana Cyn Rd. #308
Anaheim Hills, CA 92807

Joe & Toni Ballestero
(714) 491-0622

BUY/SELL

BEVERLY HILLS BASEBALL CARD SHOP

Specializing in:
- Baseball Cards
- Sports Memorabilia
- Sport Novelties

109 N. Robertson
Beverly Hills, CA 90211
(1/2 block north of Wilshire)
(213) 652-CARD

Tues. thru Sun. 11:00-5:00

BUY • SELL • TRADE

WORLD SERIES CARDS, INC.

Baseball, football, basketball, hockey, non-sport cards and sports memorabilia

Neil Armstrong • Carol Armstrong

Mon.-Fri. 10:30-6:00 Sat. & Sun. 10:00-6:00
17638 Sherman Way, Van Nuys, CA 91406 • Tel 818/708-0480

- BASEBALL CARDS
- FOOTBALL CARDS
- HOBBY SUPPLIES
- LICENSED PRODUCTS

Two Locations!

3114 N.W. 23rd
Oklahoma City, OK 73107
(405) 949-2255

1523 E. 2nd
Edmond, OK 73034
(405) 348-8667

SPORTS NOSTALGIA FROM YESTERDAY, OF TODAY AND FOR TOMORROW

"Mail orders Welcome"

Plan-O Sportscards

101 Suite A West Parker
Plano, Texas 75023

BUYING AND SELLING
Baseball Cards, Football Cards and Memorabilia

Fred Barfitt
(214) 578-9046

Monday thru Saturday 9:30 - 6:00

COTTONE SPORTS CARDS

9 Wheeler
Irvine, CA 92720
(714) 651-9060

Buy - Sell - Trade

803-268-9306
3228-A Wade Hampton Blvd. #1
Taylors, S.C. 29687

SAM & CHRIS STAGGS
Owners

	COMMON PLAYER (89-176)	.05	.02	.00
	COMMON PLAYER (177-264)	.05	.02	.00
☐ 1	Paul Molitor	.12	.04	.01
☐ 2	Milt Thompson	.05	.02	.00
☐ 3	Billy Hatcher	.05	.02	.00
☐ 4	Mike Witt	.05	.02	.00
☐ 5	Vince Coleman	.12	.05	.01
☐ 6	Dwight Evans	.12	.05	.01
☐ 7	Tim Wallach	.08	.03	.01
☐ 8	Alan Trammell	.15	.06	.01
☐ 9	Will Clark	.75	.30	.07
☐ 10	Jeff Reardon	.08	.03	.01
☐ 11	Dwight Gooden	.50	.20	.05
☐ 12	Benny Santiago	.15	.06	.01
☐ 13	Jose Canseco	1.75	.70	.17
☐ 14	Dale Murphy	.40	.16	.04
☐ 15	George Bell	.20	.08	.02
☐ 16	Ryne Sandberg	.20	.08	.02
☐ 17	Brook Jacoby	.08	.03	.01
☐ 18	Fernando Valenzuela	.12	.05	.01
☐ 19	Scott Fletcher	.05	.02	.00
☐ 20	Eric Davis	.75	.30	.07
☐ 21	Willie Wilson	.10	.04	.01
☐ 22	B.J. Surhoff	.10	.04	.01
☐ 23	Steve Bedrosian	.10	.04	.01
☐ 24	Dave Winfield	.35	.14	.03
☐ 25	Bobby Bonilla	.15	.06	.01
☐ 26	Larry Sheets	.08	.03	.01
☐ 27	Ozzie Guillen	.08	.03	.01
☐ 28	Checklist 1-88	.05	.01	.00
☐ 29	Nolan Ryan	.35	.14	.03
☐ 30	Bob Boone	.08	.03	.01
☐ 31	Tom Herr	.08	.03	.01
☐ 32	Wade Boggs	1.00	.40	.10
☐ 33	Neal Heaton	.05	.02	.00
☐ 34	Doyle Alexander	.05	.02	.00
☐ 35	Candy Maldonado	.05	.02	.00
☐ 36	Kirby Puckett	.50	.20	.05
☐ 37	Gary Carter	.25	.10	.02
☐ 38	Lance McCullers	.08	.03	.01
☐ 39	Terry Steinbach	.12	.05	.01
☐ 40	Gerald Perry	.10	.04	.01
☐ 41	Tom Henke	.05	.02	.00
☐ 42	Leon Durham	.05	.02	.00
☐ 43	Cory Snyder	.15	.06	.01
☐ 44	Dale Sveum	.05	.02	.00
☐ 45	Lance Parrish	.12	.05	.01
☐ 46	Steve Sax	.15	.06	.01
☐ 47	Charlie Hough	.05	.02	.00
☐ 48	Kal Daniels	.20	.08	.02
☐ 49	Bo Jackson	.35	.14	.03
☐ 50	Ron Guidry	.12	.05	.01
☐ 51	Bill Doran	.08	.03	.01
☐ 52	Wally Joyner	.50	.20	.05
☐ 53	Terry Pendleton	.08	.03	.01
☐ 54	Marty Barrett	.08	.03	.01
☐ 55	Andres Galarraga	.20	.08	.02
☐ 56	Larry Herndon	.05	.02	.00
☐ 57	Kevin Mitchell	.08	.03	.01
☐ 58	Greg Gagne	.05	.02	.00
☐ 59	Keith Hernandez	.25	.10	.02
☐ 60	John Kruk	.10	.04	.01
☐ 61	Mike LaValliere	.05	.02	.00
☐ 62	Cal Ripken	.30	.12	.03
☐ 63	Ivan Calderon	.10	.04	.01
☐ 64	Alvin Davis	.10	.04	.01
☐ 65	Luis Polonia	.08	.03	.01
☐ 66	Robin Yount	.25	.10	.02
☐ 67	Juan Samuel	.10	.04	.01
☐ 68	Andres Thomas	.08	.03	.01
☐ 69	Jeff Musselman	.05	.02	.00
☐ 70	Jerry Mumphrey	.05	.02	.00
☐ 71	Joe Carter	.15	.06	.01
☐ 72	Mike Scioscia	.05	.02	.00
☐ 73	Pete Incaviglia	.20	.08	.02
☐ 74	Barry Larkin	.15	.06	.01
☐ 75	Frank White	.08	.03	.01
☐ 76	Willie Randolph	.08	.03	.01
☐ 77	Kevin Bass	.08	.03	.01
☐ 78	Brian Downing	.08	.03	.01
☐ 79	Willie McGee	.12	.05	.01
☐ 80	Ellis Burks	.50	.20	.05
☐ 81	Hubie Brooks	.08	.03	.01
☐ 82	Darrell Evans	.08	.03	.01
☐ 83	Robby Thompson	.08	.03	.01
☐ 84	Kent Hrbek	.15	.06	.01
☐ 85	Ron Darling	.12	.05	.01
☐ 86	Stan Jefferson	.10	.04	.01
☐ 87	Teddy Higuera	.10	.04	.01
☐ 88	Mike Schmidt	.40	.16	.04
☐ 89	Barry Bonds	.15	.06	.01
☐ 90	Jim Presley	.10	.04	.01
☐ 91	Orel Hershiser	.75	.30	.07
☐ 92	Jesse Barfield	.20	.08	.02
☐ 93	Tom Candiotti	.05	.02	.00
☐ 94	Bret Saberhagen	.15	.06	.01
☐ 95	Jose Uribe	.08	.03	.01
☐ 96	Tom Browning	.12	.05	.01
☐ 97	Johnny Ray	.08	.03	.01
☐ 98	Mike Morgan	.05	.02	.00
☐ 99	Lou Whitaker	.10	.04	.01
☐ 100	Jim Sundberg	.05	.02	.00
☐ 101	Roger McDowell	.08	.03	.01
☐ 102	Randy Ready	.05	.02	.00
☐ 103	Mike Gallego	.05	.02	.00
☐ 104	Steve Buechele	.05	.02	.00
☐ 105	Greg Walker	.08	.03	.01
☐ 106	Jose Lind	.10	.04	.01
☐ 107	Steve Trout	.05	.02	.00
☐ 108	Rick Rhoden	.08	.03	.01
☐ 109	Jim Pankovits	.05	.02	.00
☐ 110	Ken Griffey	.08	.03	.01
☐ 111	Danny Cox	.08	.03	.01
☐ 112	Franklin Stubbs	.05	.02	.00
☐ 113	Lloyd Moseby	.08	.03	.01
☐ 114	Mel Hall	.08	.03	.01
☐ 115	Kevin Seitzer	.30	.12	.03
☐ 116	Tim Raines	.25	.10	.02
☐ 117	Juan Castillo	.05	.02	.00
☐ 118	Roger Clemens	.75	.30	.07
☐ 119	Mike Aldrete	.08	.03	.01
☐ 120	Mario Soto	.05	.02	.00
☐ 121	Jack Howell	.08	.03	.01
☐ 122	Rick Schu	.05	.02	.00
☐ 123	Jeff Robinson	.08	.03	.01
☐ 124	Doug Drabek	.05	.02	.00
☐ 125	Henry Cotto	.05	.02	.00
☐ 126	Checklist 89-176	.05	.01	.00
☐ 127	Gary Gaetti	.15	.06	.01
☐ 128	Rick Sutcliffe	.10	.04	.01
☐ 129	Howard Johnson	.12	.05	.01
☐ 130	Chris Brown	.08	.03	.01
☐ 131	Dave Henderson	.08	.03	.01
☐ 132	Curt Wilkerson	.05	.02	.00
☐ 133	Mike Marshall	.10	.04	.01
☐ 134	Kelly Gruber	.05	.02	.00
☐ 135	Julio Franco	.08	.03	.01
☐ 136	Kurt Stillwell	.08	.03	.01
☐ 137	Donnie Hill	.05	.02	.00
☐ 138	Mike Pagliarulo	.10	.04	.01
☐ 139	Von Hayes	.10	.04	.01
☐ 140	Mike Scott	.12	.05	.01
☐ 141	Bob Kipper	.05	.02	.00
☐ 142	Harold Reynolds	.08	.03	.01
☐ 143	Bob Brenley	.05	.02	.00
☐ 144	Dave Concepcion	.10	.04	.01
☐ 145	Devon White	.10	.04	.01
☐ 146	Jeff Stone	.05	.02	.00
☐ 147	Chet Lemon	.08	.03	.01
☐ 148	Ozzie Virgil	.05	.02	.00
☐ 149	Todd Worrell	.12	.05	.01
☐ 150	Mitch Webster	.05	.02	.00
☐ 151	Rob Deer	.08	.03	.01
☐ 152	Rich Gedman	.08	.03	.01
☐ 153	Andre Dawson	.20	.08	.02
☐ 154	Mike Davis	.05	.02	.00
☐ 155	Nelson Liriano	.05	.02	.00
☐ 156	Greg Swindell	.12	.05	.01
☐ 157	George Brett	.35	.14	.03
☐ 158	Kevin McReynolds	.25	.10	.02
☐ 159	Brian Fisher	.08	.03	.01
☐ 160	Mike Kingery	.05	.02	.00
☐ 161	Tony Gwynn	.35	.14	.03
☐ 162	Don Baylor	.10	.04	.01
☐ 163	Jerry Browne	.05	.02	.00
☐ 164	Dan Pasqua	.08	.03	.01

□ 165 Rickey Henderson	.40	.16	.04
□ 166 Brett Butler	.10	.04	.01
□ 167 Nick Esasky	.08	.03	.01
□ 168 Kirk McCaskill	.08	.03	.01
□ 169 Fred Lynn	.12	.05	.01
□ 170 Jack Morris	.12	.05	.01
□ 171 Pedro Guerrero	.15	.06	.01
□ 172 Dave Stieb	.10	.04	.01
□ 173 Pat Tabler	.08	.03	.01
□ 174 Floyd Bannister	.05	.02	.00
□ 175 Rafael Belliard	.05	.02	.00
□ 176 Mark Langston	.10	.04	.01
□ 177 Greg Mathews	.08	.03	.01
□ 178 Claudell Washington	.08	.03	.01
□ 179 Mark McGwire	1.00	.40	.10
□ 180 Bert Blyleven	.08	.03	.01
□ 181 Jim Rice	.15	.06	.01
□ 182 Mookie Wilson	.08	.03	.01
□ 183 Willie Fraser	.05	.02	.00
□ 184 Andy Van Slyke	.15	.06	.01
□ 185 Matt Nokes	.20	.08	.02
□ 186 Eddie Whitson	.05	.02	.00
□ 187 Tony Fernandez	.10	.04	.01
□ 188 Rick Reuschel	.08	.03	.01
□ 189 Ken Phelps	.08	.03	.01
□ 190 Juan Nieves	.05	.02	.00
□ 191 Kirk Gibson	.25	.10	.02
□ 192 Glenn Davis	.20	.08	.02
□ 193 Zane Smith	.08	.03	.01
□ 194 Jose DeLeon	.05	.02	.00
□ 195 Gary Ward	.05	.02	.00
□ 196 Pascual Perez	.08	.03	.01
□ 197 Carlton Fisk	.12	.05	.01
□ 198 Oddibe McDowell	.08	.03	.01
□ 199 Mark Gubicza	.10	.04	.01
□ 200 Glenn Hubbard	.05	.02	.00
□ 201 Frank Viola	.20	.08	.02
□ 202 Jody Reed	.10	.04	.01
□ 203 Len Dykstra	.08	.03	.01
□ 204 Dick Schofield	.05	.02	.00
□ 205 Sid Bream	.05	.02	.00
□ 206 Guillermo Hernandez	.08	.03	.01
□ 207 Keith Moreland	.05	.02	.00
□ 208 Mark Eichhorn	.05	.02	.00
□ 209 Rene Gonzalez	.08	.03	.01
□ 210 Dave Valle	.05	.02	.00
□ 211 Tom Brunansky	.10	.04	.01
□ 212 Charles Hudson	.05	.02	.00
□ 213 John Farrell	.08	.03	.01
□ 214 Jeff Treadway	.10	.04	.01
□ 215 Eddie Murray	.30	.12	.03
□ 216 Checklist 177-264	.05	.01	.00
□ 217 Greg Brock	.05	.02	.00
□ 218 John Shelby	.05	.02	.00
□ 219 Craig Reynolds	.05	.02	.00
□ 220 Dion James	.05	.02	.00
□ 221 Carney Lansford	.08	.03	.01
□ 222 Juan Berenguer	.05	.02	.00
□ 223 Luis Rivera	.05	.02	.00
□ 224 Harold Baines	.10	.04	.01
□ 225 Shawon Dunston	.10	.04	.01
□ 226 Luis Aguayo	.05	.02	.00
□ 227 Pete O'Brien	.08	.03	.01
□ 228 Ozzie Smith	.15	.06	.01
□ 229 Don Mattingly	1.50	.60	.15
□ 230 Danny Tartabull	.35	.14	.03
□ 231 Andy Allanson	.05	.02	.00
□ 232 John Franco	.08	.03	.01
□ 233 Mike Greenwell	1.25	.50	.12
□ 234 Bob Ojeda	.08	.03	.01
□ 235 Chili Davis	.08	.03	.01
□ 236 Mike Dunne	.10	.04	.01
□ 237 Jim Morrison	.05	.02	.00
□ 238 Carmelo Martinez	.05	.02	.00
□ 239 Ernie Whitt	.05	.02	.00
□ 240 Scott Garrelts	.05	.02	.00
□ 241 Mike Moore	.08	.03	.01
□ 242 Dave Parker	.12	.05	.01
□ 243 Tim Laudner	.05	.02	.00
□ 244 Bill Wegman	.05	.02	.00
□ 245 Bob Horner	.10	.04	.01
□ 246 Rafael Santana	.08	.03	.01
□ 247 Alfredo Griffin	.08	.03	.01
□ 248 Mark Bailey	.05	.02	.00
□ 249 Ron Gant	.25	.10	.02
□ 250 Bryn Smith	.05	.02	.00
□ 251 Lance Johnson	.08	.03	.01
□ 252 Sam Horn	.15	.06	.01
□ 253 Darryl Strawberry	.75	.30	.07
□ 254 Chuck Finley	.05	.02	.00
□ 255 Darnell Coles	.05	.02	.00
□ 256 Mike Henneman	.10	.04	.01
□ 257 Andy Hawkins	.08	.03	.01
□ 258 Jim Clancy	.05	.02	.00
□ 259 Atlee Hammaker	.05	.02	.00
□ 260 Glenn Wilson	.05	.02	.00
□ 261 Larry McWilliams	.05	.02	.00
□ 262 Jack Clark	.15	.06	.01
□ 263 Walt Weiss	.50	.20	.05
□ 264 Gene Larkin	.15	.06	.01

1988 Topps Mini Leaders

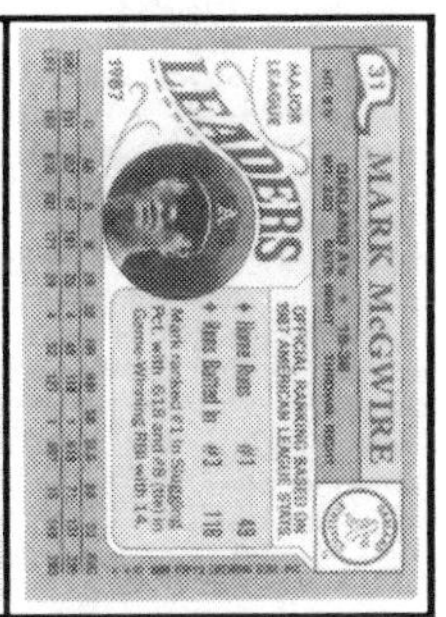

The 1988 Topps Mini set of Major League Leaders features 77 cards of leaders of the various statistical categories for the 1987 season. The cards are numbered on the back and measure approximately 2 1/8" by 3". The card backs are printed in blue, red, and yellow on white card stock. The cards were distributed as a separate issue in wax packs.

	MINT	EXC	G-VG
COMPLETE SET (77)	7.00	2.80	.70
COMMON PLAYER (1-77)	.05	.02	.00
□ 1 Wade Boggs	.60	.24	.06
□ 2 Roger Clemens	.45	.18	.04
□ 3 Dwight Evans	.10	.04	.01
□ 4 DeWayne Buice	.05	.02	.00
□ 5 Brian Downing	.05	.02	.00
□ 6 Wally Joyner	.35	.14	.03
□ 7 Ivan Calderon	.10	.04	.01
□ 8 Carlton Fisk	.12	.05	.01
□ 9 Gary Redus	.05	.02	.00
□ 10 Darrell Evans	.10	.04	.01
□ 11 Jack Morris	.12	.05	.01
□ 12 Alan Trammell	.15	.06	.01
□ 13 Lou Whitaker	.10	.04	.01
□ 14 Bret Saberhagen	.12	.05	.01
□ 15 Kevin Seitzer	.25	.10	.02
□ 16 Danny Tartabull	.20	.08	.02
□ 17 Willie Wilson	.10	.04	.01
□ 18 Teddy Higuera	.10	.04	.01
□ 19 Paul Molitor	.12	.05	.01
□ 20 Dan Plesac	.10	.04	.01
□ 21 Robin Yount	.25	.10	.02
□ 22 Kent Hrbek	.15	.06	.01
□ 23 Kirby Puckett	.35	.14	.03
□ 24 Jeff Reardon	.08	.03	.01
□ 25 Frank Viola	.15	.06	.01
□ 26 Rickey Henderson	.35	.14	.03
□ 27 Don Mattingly	1.00	.40	.10
□ 28 Willie Randolph	.08	.03	.01
□ 29 Dave Righetti	.10	.04	.01
□ 30 Jose Canseco	1.25	.50	.12
□ 31 Mark McGwire	.75	.30	.07
□ 32 Dave Stewart	.08	.03	.01
□ 33 Phil Bradley	.08	.03	.01
□ 34 Mark Langston	.08	.03	.01
□ 35 Harold Reynolds	.08	.03	.01
□ 36 Charlie Hough	.05	.02	.00
□ 37 George Bell	.15	.06	.01
□ 38 Tom Henke	.05	.02	.00
□ 39 Jimmy Key	.08	.03	.01
□ 40 Dion James	.05	.02	.00
□ 41 Dale Murphy	.35	.14	.03
□ 42 Zane Smith	.08	.03	.01
□ 43 Andre Dawson	.20	.08	.02
□ 44 Lee Smith	.08	.03	.01
□ 45 Rick Sutcliffe	.10	.04	.01
□ 46 Eric Davis	.45	.18	.04
□ 47 John Franco	.08	.03	.01
□ 48 Dave Parker	.12	.05	.01
□ 49 Billy Hatcher	.08	.03	.01
□ 50 Nolan Ryan	.30	.12	.03

☐ 51	Mike Scott	.15	.06	.01
☐ 52	Pedro Guerrero	.15	.06	.01
☐ 53	Orel Hershiser	.45	.18	.04
☐ 54	Fernando Valenzuela	.15	.06	.01
☐ 55	Bob Welch	.08	.03	.01
☐ 56	Andres Galarraga	.20	.08	.02
☐ 57	Tim Raines	.20	.08	.02
☐ 58	Tim Wallach	.08	.03	.01
☐ 59	Len Dykstra	.08	.03	.01
☐ 60	Dwight Gooden	.45	.18	.04
☐ 61	Howard Johnson	.10	.04	.01
☐ 62	Roger McDowell	.08	.03	.01
☐ 63	Darryl Strawberry	.50	.20	.05
☐ 64	Steve Bedrosian	.08	.03	.01
☐ 65	Shane Rawley	.08	.03	.01
☐ 66	Juan Samuel	.08	.03	.01
☐ 67	Mike Schmidt	.35	.14	.03
☐ 68	Mike Dunne	.10	.04	.01
☐ 69	Jack Clark	.15	.06	.01
☐ 70	Vince Coleman	.20	.08	.02
☐ 71	Willie McGee	.12	.05	.01
☐ 72	Ozzie Smith	.15	.06	.01
☐ 73	Todd Worrell	.12	.05	.01
☐ 74	Tony Gwynn	.35	.14	.03
☐ 75	John Kruk	.10	.04	.01
☐ 76	Rick Reuschel	.08	.03	.01
☐ 77	Checklist	.05	.01	.00

1988 Topps Traded

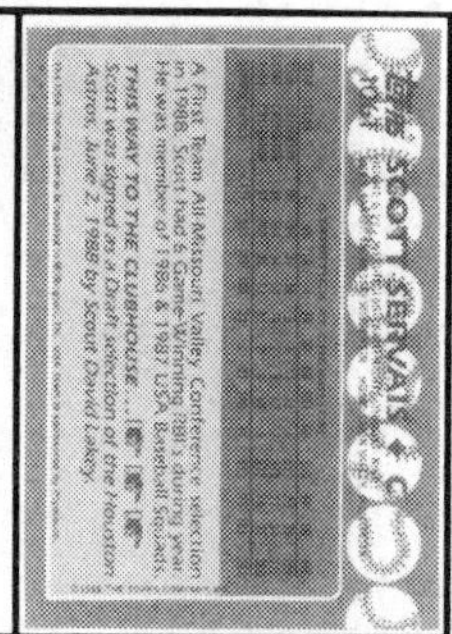

This 132-card Traded or extended set was distributed by Topps to dealers in a special blue and white box as a complete set. The card fronts are identical in style to the Topps regular issue and are also 2 1/2" by 3 1/2". The backs are printed in orange and black on white card stock. Cards are numbered (with a T suffix) alphabetically according to the name of the player. This set has generated additional interest due to the inclusion of the 1988 U.S. Olympic Baseball team members. These Olympians are indicated in the checklist below by OLY.

		MINT	EXC	G-VG
COMPLETE SET (132)		14.00	5.75	1.40
COMMON PLAYER (1-132)		.05	.02	.00
☐ 1T	Jim Abbott OLY	1.00	.40	.10
☐ 2T	Juan Agosto	.05	.02	.00
☐ 3T	Luis Alicea	.15	.06	.01
☐ 4T	Roberto Alomar	.35	.14	.03
☐ 5T	Brady Anderson	.35	.14	.03
☐ 6T	Jack Armstrong	.25	.10	.02
☐ 7T	Don August	.15	.06	.01
☐ 8T	Floyd Bannister	.05	.02	.00
☐ 9T	Bret Barberie OLY	.20	.08	.02
☐ 10T	Jose Bautista	.15	.06	.01
☐ 11T	Don Baylor	.10	.04	.01
☐ 12T	Tim Belcher	.15	.06	.01
☐ 13T	Buddy Bell	.10	.04	.01
☐ 14T	Andy Benes OLY	.65	.26	.06
☐ 15T	Damon Berryhill	.35	.14	.03
☐ 16T	Bud Black	.05	.02	.00
☐ 17T	Pat Borders	.15	.06	.01
☐ 18T	Phil Bradley	.10	.04	.01
☐ 19T	Jeff Branson OLY	.20	.08	.02
☐ 20T	Tom Brunansky	.10	.04	.01
☐ 21T	Jay Buhner	.35	.14	.03
☐ 22T	Brett Butler	.10	.04	.01
☐ 23T	Jim Campanis OLY	.20	.08	.02
☐ 24T	Sil Campusano	.25	.10	.02
☐ 25T	John Candelaria	.10	.04	.01
☐ 26T	Jose Cecena	.15	.06	.01
☐ 27T	Rick Cerone	.05	.02	.00
☐ 28T	Jack Clark	.15	.06	.01
☐ 29T	Kevin Coffman	.10	.04	.01
☐ 30T	Pat Combs OLY	.20	.08	.02
☐ 31T	Henry Cotto	.05	.02	.00
☐ 32T	Chili Davis	.10	.04	.01
☐ 33T	Mike Davis	.05	.02	.00
☐ 34T	Jose DeLeon	.05	.02	.00
☐ 35T	Richard Dotson	.10	.04	.01
☐ 36T	Cecil Espy	.15	.06	.01
☐ 37T	Tom Filer	.05	.02	.00
☐ 38T	Mike Fiore OLY	.30	.12	.03
☐ 39T	Ron Gant	.45	.18	.04
☐ 40T	Kirk Gibson	.20	.08	.02
☐ 41T	Rich Gossage	.10	.04	.01
☐ 42T	Mark Grace	1.50	.60	.15
☐ 43T	Alfredo Griffin	.10	.04	.01
☐ 44T	Ty Griffin OLY	1.00	.40	.10
☐ 45T	Bryan Harvey	.30	.12	.03
☐ 46T	Ron Hassey	.05	.02	.00
☐ 47T	Ray Hayward	.10	.04	.01
☐ 48T	Dave Henderson	.10	.04	.01
☐ 49T	Tom Herr	.10	.04	.01
☐ 50T	Bob Horner	.15	.06	.01
☐ 51T	Ricky Horton	.05	.02	.00
☐ 52T	Jay Howell	.05	.02	.00
☐ 53T	Glenn Hubbard	.05	.02	.00
☐ 54T	Jeff Innis	.20	.08	.02
☐ 55T	Danny Jackson	.15	.06	.01
☐ 56T	Darrin Jackson	.20	.08	.02
☐ 57T	Roberto Kelly	.35	.14	.03
☐ 58T	Ron Kittle	.10	.04	.01
☐ 59T	Ray Knight	.10	.04	.01
☐ 60T	Vance Law	.10	.04	.01
☐ 61T	Jeffrey Leonard	.10	.04	.01
☐ 62T	Mike Macfarlane	.20	.08	.02
☐ 63T	Scotti Madison	.15	.06	.01
☐ 64T	Kirt Manwaring	.15	.06	.01
☐ 65T	Mark Marquess OLY	.05	.02	.00
☐ 66T	Tino Martinez OLY	1.00	.40	.10
☐ 67T	Billy Masse OLY	.25	.10	.02
☐ 68T	Jack McDowell	.15	.06	.01
☐ 69T	Jack McKeon MG	.05	.02	.00
☐ 70T	Larry McWilliams	.05	.02	.00
☐ 71T	Mickey Morandini OLY	.25	.10	.02
☐ 72T	Keith Moreland	.05	.02	.00
☐ 73T	Mike Morgan	.05	.02	.00
☐ 74T	Charles Nagy OLY	.25	.10	.02
☐ 75T	Al Nipper	.05	.02	.00
☐ 76T	Russ Nixon MG	.05	.02	.00
☐ 77T	Jesse Orosco	.05	.02	.00
☐ 78T	Joe Orsulak	.05	.02	.00
☐ 79T	Dave Palmer	.05	.02	.00
☐ 80T	Mark Parent	.15	.06	.01
☐ 81T	Dave Parker	.10	.04	.01
☐ 82T	Dan Pasqua	.10	.04	.01
☐ 83T	Melido Perez	.25	.10	.02
☐ 84T	Steve Peters	.15	.06	.01
☐ 85T	Dan Petry	.05	.02	.00
☐ 86T	Gary Pettis	.05	.02	.00
☐ 87T	Jeff Pico	.15	.06	.01
☐ 88T	Jim Poole OLY	.20	.08	.02
☐ 89T	Ted Power	.05	.02	.00
☐ 90T	Rafael Ramirez	.05	.02	.00
☐ 91T	Dennis Rasmussen	.10	.04	.01
☐ 92T	Jose Rijo	.10	.04	.01
☐ 93T	Ernie Riles	.05	.02	.00
☐ 94T	Luis Rivera	.15	.06	.01
☐ 95T	Doug Robbins OLY	.20	.08	.02
☐ 96T	Frank Robinson MG	.10	.04	.01
☐ 97T	Cookie Rojas MG	.05	.02	.00
☐ 98T	Chris Sabo	1.75	.70	.17
☐ 99T	Mark Salas	.05	.02	.00
☐ 100T	Luis Salazar	.05	.02	.00
☐ 101T	Rafael Santana	.05	.02	.00
☐ 102T	Nelson Santovenia	.15	.06	.01
☐ 103T	Mackey Sasser	.25	.10	.02
☐ 104T	Calvin Schiraldi	.05	.02	.00
☐ 105T	Mike Schooler	.15	.06	.01
☐ 106T	Scott Servais OLY	.20	.08	.02
☐ 107T	Dave Silvestri OLY	.20	.08	.02
☐ 108T	Don Slaught	.05	.02	.00
☐ 109T	Joe Slusarski OLY	.20	.08	.02
☐ 110T	Lee Smith	.10	.04	.01
☐ 111T	Pete Smith	.15	.06	.01
☐ 112T	Jim Snyder MG	.05	.02	.00
☐ 113T	Ed Sprague OLY	.30	.12	.03
☐ 114T	Pete Stanicek	.15	.06	.01
☐ 115T	Kurt Stillwell	.10	.04	.01

		MINT	EXC	G-VG
□ 116T	Todd Stottlemyre	.15	.06	.01
□ 117T	Bill Swift	.10	.04	.01
□ 118T	Pat Tabler	.05	.02	.00
□ 119T	Scott Terry	.05	.02	.00
□ 120T	Mickey Tettleton	.05	.02	.00
□ 121T	Dickie Thon	.05	.02	.00
□ 122T	Jeff Treadway	.20	.08	.02
□ 123T	Willie Upshaw	.05	.02	.00
□ 124T	Robin Ventura OLY	1.25	.50	.12
□ 125T	Ron Washington	.05	.02	.00
□ 126T	Walt Weiss	1.25	.50	.12
□ 127T	Bob Welch	.10	.04	.01
□ 128T	David Wells	.15	.06	.01
□ 129T	Glenn Wilson	.05	.02	.00
□ 130T	Ted Wood OLY	.35	.14	.03
□ 131T	Don Zimmer MG	.05	.02	.00
□ 132T	Checklist 1T-132T	.05	.01	.00

1989 Topps

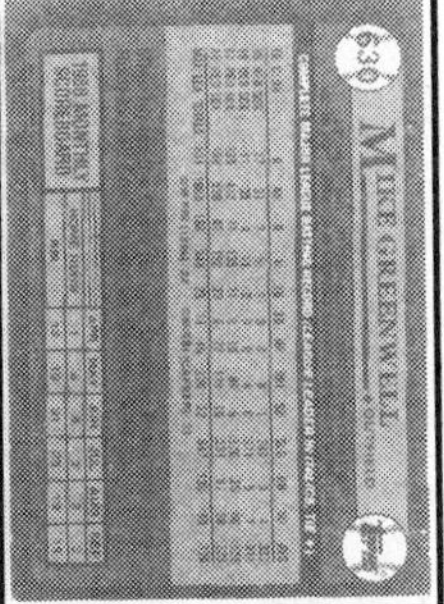

This 792-card set features backs which are printed in pink and black on gray card stock. The manager cards contain a checklist of the respective team's players on the back. Subsets in the set include Record Breakers (1-7), Turn Back the Clock (661-665), and All-Star selections (386-407). The bonus cards distributed throughout the set are indicated on the Topps checklist cards are actually Team Leader (TL) cards. Also sprinkled throughout the set are Future Stars (FS) and First Draft Picks (FDP).

		MINT	EXC	G-VG
	COMPLETE SET (792)	24.00	10.00	2.40
	COMMON PLAYER (1-792)	.03	.01	.00
□ 1	George Bell RB Slams 3 HR on Opening Day	.12	.03	.01
□ 2	Wade Boggs RB Gets 200 Hits 6th Straight Season	.15	.06	.01
□ 3	Gary Carter RB Sets Record for Career Putouts	.10	.04	.01
□ 4	Andre Dawson RB Logs Double Figures in HR and SB	.10	.04	.01
□ 5	Orel Hershiser RB Pitches 59 Scoreless Innings	.12	.05	.01
□ 6	Doug Jones RB Earns His 15th Straight Save	.06	.02	.00
□ 7	Kevin McReynolds RB Steals 21 Without Being Caught	.08	.03	.01
□ 8	Dave Eiland	.12	.05	.01
□ 9	Tim Teufel	.03	.01	.00
□ 10	Andre Dawson	.10	.04	.01
□ 11	Bruce Sutter	.08	.03	.01
□ 12	Dale Sveum	.03	.01	.00
□ 13	Doug Sisk	.03	.01	.00
□ 14	Tom Kelly MG (team checklist back)	.06	.01	.00
□ 15	Robby Thompson	.03	.01	.00
□ 16	Ron Robinson	.03	.01	.00
□ 17	Brian Downing	.03	.01	.00
□ 18	Rick Rhoden	.03	.01	.00
□ 19	Greg Gagne	.03	.01	.00
□ 20	Steve Bedrosian	.08	.03	.01
□ 21	Chicago White Sox TL Greg Walker	.03	.01	.00
□ 22	Tim Crews	.03	.01	.00
□ 23	Mike Fitzgerald Montreal Expos	.03	.01	.00
□ 24	Larry Andersen	.03	.01	.00
□ 25	Frank White	.06	.02	.00
□ 26	Dale Mohorcic	.03	.01	.00
□ 27	Orestes Destrade	.20	.08	.02
□ 28	Mike Moore	.03	.01	.00
□ 29	Kelly Gruber	.03	.01	.00
□ 30	Doc Gooden	.30	.12	.03
□ 31	Terry Francona	.03	.01	.00
□ 32	Dennis Rasmussen	.06	.02	.00
□ 33	B.J. Surhoff	.06	.02	.00
□ 34	Ken Williams	.03	.01	.00
□ 35	John Tudor	.08	.03	.01
□ 36	Mitch Webster	.03	.01	.00
□ 37	Bob Stanley	.03	.01	.00
□ 38	Paul Runge	.03	.01	.00
□ 39	Mike Maddux	.03	.01	.00
□ 40	Steve Sax	.10	.04	.01
□ 41	Terry Mulholland	.03	.01	.00
□ 42	Jim Eppard	.08	.03	.01
□ 43	Guillermo Hernandez	.06	.02	.00
□ 44	Jim Snyder MG (team checklist back)	.06	.01	.00
□ 45	Kal Daniels	.10	.04	.01
□ 46	Mark Portugal	.03	.01	.00
□ 47	Carney Lansford	.06	.02	.00
□ 48	Tim Burke	.03	.01	.00
□ 49	Craig Biggio	.12	.05	.01
□ 50	George Bell	.10	.04	.01
□ 51	California Angels TL Mark McLemore	.03	.01	.00
□ 52	Bob Brenly	.03	.01	.00
□ 53	Ruben Sierra	.10	.04	.01
□ 54	Steve Trout	.03	.01	.00
□ 55	Julio Franco	.06	.02	.00
□ 56	Pat Tabler	.06	.02	.00
□ 57	Alejandro Pena	.03	.01	.00
□ 58	Lee Mazzilli	.03	.01	.00
□ 59	Mark Davis	.06	.02	.00
□ 60	Tom Brunansky	.08	.03	.01
□ 61	Neil Allen	.03	.01	.00
□ 62	Alfredo Griffin	.06	.02	.00
□ 63	Mark Clear	.03	.01	.00
□ 64	Alex Trevino	.03	.01	.00
□ 65	Rick Reuschel	.06	.02	.00
□ 66	Manny Trillo	.03	.01	.00
□ 67	Dave Palmer	.03	.01	.00
□ 68	Darrell Miller	.03	.01	.00
□ 69	Jeff Ballard	.03	.01	.00
□ 70	Mark McGwire	.40	.16	.04
□ 71	Mike Boddicker	.06	.02	.00
□ 72	John Moses	.03	.01	.00
□ 73	Pascual Perez	.06	.02	.00
□ 74	Nick Leyva MG (team checklist back)	.06	.01	.00
□ 75	Tom Henke	.03	.01	.00
□ 76	Terry Blocker	.12	.05	.01
□ 77	Doyle Alexander	.03	.01	.00
□ 78	Jim Sundberg	.03	.01	.00
□ 79	Scott Bankhead	.03	.01	.00
□ 80	Cory Snyder	.12	.05	.01
□ 81	Montreal Expos TL Tim Raines	.08	.03	.01
□ 82	Dave Leiper	.03	.01	.00
□ 83	Jeff Blauser	.10	.04	.01
□ 84	Bill Bene FDP	.25	.10	.02
□ 85	Kevin McReynolds	.12	.05	.01
□ 86	Al Nipper	.03	.01	.00
□ 87	Larry Owen	.03	.01	.00
□ 88	Darryl Hamilton	.20	.08	.02
□ 89	Dave LaPoint	.03	.01	.00
□ 90	Vince Coleman	.12	.05	.01
□ 91	Floyd Youmans	.03	.01	.00
□ 92	Jeff Kunkel	.03	.01	.00
□ 93	Ken Howell	.03	.01	.00
□ 94	Chris Speier	.03	.01	.00
□ 95	Gerald Young	.06	.02	.00
□ 96	Rick Cerone	.03	.01	.00
□ 97	Greg Mathews	.03	.01	.00
□ 98	Larry Sheets	.06	.02	.00
□ 99	Sherman Corbett	.10	.04	.01
□ 100	Mike Schmidt	.20	.08	.02
□ 101	Les Straker	.03	.01	.00
□ 102	Mike Gallego	.03	.01	.00
□ 103	Tim Birtsas	.03	.01	.00
□ 104	Dallas Green MG (team checklist back)	.06	.01	.00
□ 105	Ron Darling	.08	.03	.01
□ 106	Willie Upshaw	.03	.01	.00

□ 107 Jose DeLeon	.03	.01	.00
□ 108 Fred Manrique	.03	.01	.00
□ 109 Hipolito Pena	.12	.05	.01
□ 110 Paul Molitor	.10	.04	.01
□ 111 Cincinnati Reds TL	.10	.04	.01
Eric Davis			
(swinging bat)			
□ 112 Jim Presley	.06	.02	.00
□ 113 Lloyd Moseby	.06	.02	.00
□ 114 Bob Kipper	.03	.01	.00
□ 115 Jody Davis	.06	.02	.00
□ 116 Jeff Montgomery	.03	.01	.00
□ 117 Dave Anderson	.03	.01	.00
□ 118 Checklist 1-132	.06	.01	.00
□ 119 Terry Puhl	.03	.01	.00
□ 120 Frank Viola	.12	.05	.01
□ 121 Garry Templeton	.06	.02	.00
□ 122 Lance Johnson	.10	.04	.01
□ 123 Spike Owen	.03	.01	.00
□ 124 Jim Traber	.03	.01	.00
□ 125 Mike Krukow	.03	.01	.00
□ 126 Sid Bream	.03	.01	.00
□ 127 Walt Terrell	.03	.01	.00
□ 128 Milt Thompson	.03	.01	.00
□ 129 Terry Clark	.15	.06	.01
□ 130 Gerald Perry	.08	.03	.01
□ 131 Dave Otto	.10	.04	.01
□ 132 Curt Ford	.03	.01	.00
□ 133 Bill Long	.03	.01	.00
□ 134 Don Zimmer MG	.06	.01	.00
(team checklist back)			
□ 135 Jose Rijo	.03	.01	.00
□ 136 Joey Meyer	.10	.04	.01
□ 137 Geno Petralli	.03	.01	.00
□ 138 Wallace Johnson	.03	.01	.00
□ 139 Mike Flanagan	.06	.02	.00
□ 140 Shawon Dunston	.06	.02	.00
□ 141 Cleveland Indians TL	.06	.02	.00
Brook Jacoby			
□ 142 Mike Diaz	.03	.01	.00
□ 143 Mike Campbell	.03	.01	.00
□ 144 Jay Bell	.03	.01	.00
□ 145 Dave Stewart	.06	.02	.00
□ 146 Gary Pettis	.03	.01	.00
□ 147 DeWayne Buice	.03	.01	.00
□ 148 Bill Pecota	.03	.01	.00
□ 149 Doug Dascenzo	.15	.06	.01
□ 150 Fernando Valenzuela	.10	.04	.01
□ 151 Terry McGriff	.03	.01	.00
□ 152 Mark Thurmond	.03	.01	.00
□ 153 Jim Pankovits	.03	.01	.00
□ 154 Don Carman	.03	.01	.00
□ 155 Marty Barrett	.06	.02	.00
□ 156 Dave Gallagher	.15	.06	.01
□ 157 Tom Glavine	.03	.01	.00
□ 158 Mike Aldrete	.03	.01	.00
□ 159 Pat Clements	.03	.01	.00
□ 160 Jeffrey Leonard	.06	.02	.00
□ 161 Gregg Olson FDP	.30	.12	.03
□ 162 John Davis	.03	.01	.00
□ 163 Bob Forsch	.03	.01	.00
□ 164 Hal Lanier MG	.06	.01	.00
(team checklist back)			
□ 165 Mike Dunne	.06	.02	.00
□ 166 Doug Jennings	.20	.08	.02
□ 167 Steve Searcy FS	.25	.10	.02
□ 168 Willie Wilson	.08	.03	.01
□ 169 Mike Jackson	.03	.01	.00
□ 170 Tony Fernandez	.10	.04	.01
□ 171 Atlanta Braves TL	.03	.01	.00
Andres Thomas			
□ 172 Frank Williams	.03	.01	.00
□ 173 Mel Hall	.06	.02	.00
□ 174 Todd Burns	.20	.08	.02
□ 175 John Shelby	.03	.01	.00
□ 176 Jeff Parrett	.03	.01	.00
□ 177 Monty Fariss FDP	.30	.12	.03
□ 178 Mark Grant	.03	.01	.00
□ 179 Ozzie Virgil	.03	.01	.00
□ 180 Mike Scott	.10	.04	.01
□ 181 Craig Worthington	.20	.08	.02
□ 182 Bob McClure	.03	.01	.00
□ 183 Oddibe McDowell	.06	.02	.00
□ 184 John Costello	.10	.04	.01
□ 185 Claudell Washington	.06	.02	.00
□ 186 Pat Perry	.03	.01	.00
□ 187 Darren Daulton	.03	.01	.00
□ 188 Dennis Lamp	.03	.01	.00
□ 189 Kevin Mitchell	.06	.02	.00
□ 190 Mike Witt	.08	.03	.01
□ 191 Sil Campusano	.20	.08	.02
□ 192 Paul Mirabella	.03	.01	.00
□ 193 Sparky Anderson MG	.06	.01	.00
(team checklist back)			
□ 194 Greg W. Harris	.20	.08	.02
San Diego Padres			
□ 195 Ozzie Guillen	.06	.02	.00
□ 196 Denny Walling	.03	.01	.00
□ 197 Neal Heaton	.03	.01	.00
□ 198 Danny Heep	.03	.01	.00
□ 199 Mike Schooler	.12	.05	.01
□ 200 George Brett	.20	.08	.02
□ 201 Blue Jays TL	.03	.01	.00
Kelly Gruber			
□ 202 Brad Moore	.15	.06	.01
□ 203 Rob Ducey	.06	.02	.00
□ 204 Brad Havens	.03	.01	.00
□ 205 Dwight Evans	.08	.03	.01
□ 206 Roberto Alomar	.20	.08	.02
□ 207 Terry Leach	.06	.02	.00
□ 208 Tom Pagnozzi	.03	.01	.00
□ 209 Jeff Bittiger	.12	.05	.01
□ 210 Dale Murphy	.20	.08	.02
□ 211 Mike Pagliarulo	.06	.02	.00
□ 212 Scott Sanderson	.03	.01	.00
□ 213 Rene Gonzales	.03	.01	.00
□ 214 Charlie O'Brien	.03	.01	.00
□ 215 Kevin Gross	.03	.01	.00
□ 216 Jack Howell	.03	.01	.00
□ 217 Joe Price	.03	.01	.00
□ 218 Mike LaValliere	.03	.01	.00
□ 219 Jim Clancy	.03	.01	.00
□ 220 Gary Gaetti	.10	.04	.01
□ 221 Cecil Espy	.10	.04	.01
□ 222 Mark Lewis FDP	.30	.12	.03
□ 223 Jay Buhner	.15	.06	.01
□ 224 Tony LaRussa MG	.06	.01	.00
(team checklist back)			
□ 225 Ramon Martinez	.25	.10	.02
□ 226 Bill Doran	.06	.02	.00
□ 227 John Farrell	.03	.01	.00
□ 228 Nelson Santovenia	.10	.04	.01
□ 229 Jimmy Key	.06	.02	.00
□ 230 Ozzie Smith	.10	.04	.01
□ 231 San Diego Padres TL	.10	.04	.01
Roberto Alomar			
(G.Carter at plate)			
□ 232 Ricky Horton	.03	.01	.00
□ 233 Gregg Jefferies FS	2.50	1.00	.25
□ 234 Tom Browning	.08	.03	.01
□ 235 John Kruk	.06	.02	.00
□ 236 Charles Hudson	.03	.01	.00
□ 237 Glenn Hubbard	.03	.01	.00
□ 238 Eric King	.03	.01	.00
□ 239 Tim Laudner	.03	.01	.00
□ 240 Greg Maddux	.10	.04	.01
□ 241 Brett Butler	.06	.02	.00
□ 242 Ed Vandeberg	.03	.01	.00
□ 243 Bob Boone	.06	.02	.00
□ 244 Jim Acker	.03	.01	.00
□ 245 Jim Rice	.10	.04	.01
□ 246 Rey Quinones	.03	.01	.00
□ 247 Shawn Hillegas	.03	.01	.00
□ 248 Tony Phillips	.03	.01	.00
□ 249 Tim Leary	.06	.02	.00
□ 250 Cal Ripken	.15	.06	.01
□ 251 John Dopson	.12	.05	.01
□ 252 Billy Hatcher	.06	.02	.00
□ 253 Jose Alvarez	.10	.04	.01
□ 254 Tom Lasorda MG	.06	.01	.00
(team checklist back)			
□ 255 Ron Guidry	.08	.03	.01
□ 256 Benny Santiago	.12	.05	.01
□ 257 Rick Aguilera	.03	.01	.00
□ 258 Checklist 133-264	.06	.01	.00
□ 259 Larry McWilliams	.03	.01	.00
□ 260 Dave Winfield	.15	.06	.01
□ 261 St.Louis Cardinals TL	.06	.02	.00
Tom Brunansky			
(with Luis Alicea)			
□ 262 Jeff Pico	.10	.04	.01
□ 263 Mike Felder	.03	.01	.00
□ 264 Rob Dibble	.12	.05	.01
□ 265 Kent Hrbek	.10	.04	.01
□ 266 Luis Aquino	.03	.01	.00
□ 267 Jeff Robinson	.08	.03	.01
Detroit Tigers			
□ 268 Keith Miller	.15	.06	.01
Philadelphia Phillies			
□ 269 Tom Bolton	.03	.01	.00
□ 270 Wally Joyner	.15	.06	.01
□ 271 Jay Tibbs	.03	.01	.00
□ 272 Ron Hassey	.03	.01	.00
□ 273 Jose Lind	.03	.01	.00
□ 274 Mark Eichhorn	.03	.01	.00
□ 275 Danny Tartabull	.12	.05	.01
□ 276 Paul Kilgus	.03	.01	.00
□ 277 Mike Davis	.03	.01	.00
□ 278 Andy McGaffigan	.03	.01	.00
□ 279 Scott Bradley	.03	.01	.00

Always Actively Buying Quality Collections

GEORGIA MUSIC & SPORTS
Dick DeCourcy
1867 Flat Shoals Rd.
Riverdale, GA 30296
404-996-3385

A PERSONAL MESSAGE TO THE DEALERS OF THE HOBBY

Baseball Cards have been good to us.

Georgia Music & Sports has been a regular advertiser in hobby publications since 1983. We have set up at over 40 shows per year. Both through our ads and the shows we have met many regular customers—for this we are very thankful.

Most of our customers and dealers order from four to six times a month. We try to cultivate repeat business. It is far more important for us to obtain a customer for the long term than ever to think of a quick buck on one deal.

It is not possible to intentory every item in the hobby, but we always try to have on hand Mint sets from the last 10 years as well as unopened, unsearched products from the last 10 years.

We have at present over 300 dealers that order from us every month. We work on the average of 15% profit on most items. Some of our prices may be high and some may be low, but we do try and have the major products always on hand at all times. By having the product, we can save you hours of searching.

We pride ourselves on service . . . we spell service S-P-E-E-D. If you are a regular account and you call in an order today before 2 p.m., we ship it today. Also, 99% of our accounts pay us just as quickly as we ship, the same day they get their product. The rest pay interest.

We will soon be entering our 13th year of business. To those customers who have kept us going for all these years, we give thanks and trust that this union will continue for many years to come. To those new and honorable dealers and store owners who are entering this fast-paced, exciting and growing baseball card hobby, we welcome your business. We have a staff of 11 people to help serve your needs.

Please write or call for our current price list.

Sincerely,
Dick

Dick DeCourcy, President
Georgia Music and Sports

MEMBER

Atlanta Area Chamber of Commerce
Atlanta Area Better Business Bureau
Atlanta Area Sports Collectors Association
National Association of Music Merchants

☐ 280 Bob Knepper	.03	.01	.00
☐ 281 Gary Redus	.03	.01	.00
☐ 282 Cris Carpenter	.20	.08	.02
☐ 283 Andy Allanson	.03	.01	.00
☐ 284 Jim Leyland MG (team checklist back)	.06	.01	.00
☐ 285 John Candelaria	.06	.02	.00
☐ 286 Darrin Jackson	.15	.06	.01
☐ 287 Juan Nieves	.03	.01	.00
☐ 288 Pat Sheridan	.03	.01	.00
☐ 289 Ernie Whitt	.03	.01	.00
☐ 290 John Franco	.06	.02	.00
☐ 291 New York Mets TL Darryl Strawberry (with K.Hernandez and K.McReynolds)	.12	.05	.01
☐ 292 Jim Corsi	.15	.06	.01
☐ 293 Glenn Wilson	.03	.01	.00
☐ 294 Juan Berenguer	.03	.01	.00
☐ 295 Scott Fletcher	.03	.01	.00
☐ 296 Ron Gant	.25	.10	.02
☐ 297 Oswald Peraza	.12	.05	.01
☐ 298 Chris James	.08	.03	.01
☐ 299 Steve Ellsworth	.12	.05	.01
☐ 300 Darryl Strawberry	.30	.12	.03
☐ 301 Charlie Leibrandt	.03	.01	.00
☐ 302 Gary Ward	.03	.01	.00
☐ 303 Felix Fermin	.03	.01	.00
☐ 304 Joel Youngblood	.03	.01	.00
☐ 305 Dave Smith	.03	.01	.00
☐ 306 Tracy Woodson	.10	.04	.01
☐ 307 Lance McCullers	.06	.02	.00
☐ 308 Ron Karkovice	.03	.01	.00
☐ 309 Mario Diaz	.08	.03	.01
☐ 310 Rafael Palmeiro	.10	.04	.01
☐ 311 Chris Bosio	.03	.01	.00
☐ 312 Tom Lawless	.03	.01	.00
☐ 313 Dennis Martinez	.03	.01	.00
☐ 314 Bobby Valentine MG (team checklist back)	.06	.01	.00
☐ 315 Greg Swindell	.08	.03	.01
☐ 316 Walt Weiss	.40	.16	.04
☐ 317 Jack Armstrong	.20	.08	.02
☐ 318 Gene Larkin	.06	.02	.00
☐ 319 Greg Booker	.03	.01	.00
☐ 320 Lou Whitaker	.08	.03	.01
☐ 321 Boston Red Sox TL Jody Reed	.08	.03	.01
☐ 322 John Smiley	.03	.01	.00
☐ 323 Gary Thurman	.03	.01	.00
☐ 324 Bob Milacki	.20	.08	.02
☐ 325 Jesse Barfield	.10	.04	.01
☐ 326 Dennis Boyd	.06	.02	.00
☐ 327 Mark Lemke	.20	.08	.02
☐ 328 Rick Honeycutt	.03	.01	.00
☐ 329 Bob Melvin	.03	.01	.00
☐ 330 Eric Davis	.25	.10	.02
☐ 331 Curt Wilkerson	.03	.01	.00
☐ 332 Tony Armas	.06	.02	.00
☐ 333 Bob Ojeda	.06	.02	.00
☐ 334 Steve Lyons	.03	.01	.00
☐ 335 Dave Righetti	.08	.03	.01
☐ 336 Steve Balboni	.03	.01	.00
☐ 337 Calvin Schiraldi	.03	.01	.00
☐ 338 Jim Adduci	.03	.01	.00
☐ 339 Scott Bailes	.03	.01	.00
☐ 340 Kirk Gibson	.15	.06	.01
☐ 341 Jim Deshaies	.03	.01	.00
☐ 342 Tom Brookens	.03	.01	.00
☐ 343 Gary Sheffield FS	1.50	.60	.15
☐ 344 Tom Trebelhorn MG (team checklist back)	.06	.01	.00
☐ 345 Charlie Hough	.03	.01	.00
☐ 346 Rex Hudler	.03	.01	.00
☐ 347 John Cerutti	.03	.01	.00
☐ 348 Ed Hearn	.03	.01	.00
☐ 349 Ron Jones	.30	.12	.03
☐ 350 Andy Van Slyke	.10	.04	.01
☐ 351 San Fran. Giants TL Bob Melvin (with Bill Fahey CO)	.03	.01	.00
☐ 352 Rick Schu	.03	.01	.00
☐ 353 Marvell Wynne	.03	.01	.00
☐ 354 Larry Parrish	.03	.01	.00
☐ 355 Mark Langston	.08	.03	.01
☐ 356 Kevin Elster	.06	.02	.00
☐ 357 Jerry Reuss	.03	.01	.00
☐ 358 Ricky Jordan	1.25	.50	.12
☐ 359 Tommy John	.08	.03	.01
☐ 360 Ryne Sandberg	.15	.06	.01
☐ 361 Kelly Downs	.03	.01	.00
☐ 362 Jack Lazorko	.03	.01	.00
☐ 363 Rich Yett	.03	.01	.00
☐ 364 Rob Deer	.06	.02	.00
☐ 365 Mike Henneman	.03	.01	.00
☐ 366 Herm Winningham	.03	.01	.00
☐ 367 Johnny Paredes	.10	.04	.01
☐ 368 Brian Holton	.03	.01	.00
☐ 369 Ken Caminiti	.03	.01	.00
☐ 370 Dennis Eckersley	.08	.03	.01
☐ 371 Manny Lee	.03	.01	.00
☐ 372 Craig Lefferts	.03	.01	.00
☐ 373 Tracy Jones	.06	.02	.00
☐ 374 John Wathan MG (team checklist back)	.06	.01	.00
☐ 375 Terry Pendleton	.03	.01	.00
☐ 376 Steve Lombardozzi	.03	.01	.00
☐ 377 Mike Smithson	.03	.01	.00
☐ 378 Checklist 265-396	.06	.01	.00
☐ 379 Tim Flannery	.03	.01	.00
☐ 380 Rickey Henderson	.20	.08	.02
☐ 381 Baltimore Orioles TL Larry Sheets	.03	.01	.00
☐ 382 John Smoltz	.20	.08	.02
☐ 383 Howard Johnson	.08	.03	.01
☐ 384 Mark Salas	.03	.01	.00
☐ 385 Von Hayes	.08	.03	.01
☐ 386 Andres Galarraga AS	.10	.04	.01
☐ 387 Ryne Sandberg AS	.10	.04	.01
☐ 388 Bobby Bonilla AS	.08	.03	.01
☐ 389 Ozzie Smith AS	.10	.04	.01
☐ 390 Darryl Strawberry AS	.15	.06	.01
☐ 391 Andre Dawson AS	.10	.04	.01
☐ 392 Andy Van Slyke AS	.10	.04	.01
☐ 393 Gary Carter AS	.12	.05	.01
☐ 394 Orel Hershiser AS	.12	.05	.01
☐ 395 Danny Jackson AS	.08	.03	.01
☐ 396 Kirk Gibson AS	.10	.04	.01
☐ 397 Don Mattingly AS	.25	.10	.02
☐ 398 Julio Franco AS	.08	.03	.01
☐ 399 Wade Boggs AS	.20	.08	.02
☐ 400 Alan Trammell AS	.10	.04	.01
☐ 401 Jose Canseco AS	.30	.12	.03
☐ 402 Mike Greenwell AS	.20	.08	.02
☐ 403 Kirby Puckett AS	.15	.06	.01
☐ 404 Bob Boone AS	.08	.03	.01
☐ 405 Roger Clemens AS	.15	.06	.01
☐ 406 Frank Viola AS	.08	.03	.01
☐ 407 Dave Winfield AS	.12	.05	.01
☐ 408 Greg Walker	.06	.02	.00
☐ 409 Ken Dayley	.03	.01	.00
☐ 410 Jack Clark	.10	.04	.01
☐ 411 Mitch Williams	.03	.01	.00
☐ 412 Barry Lyons	.03	.01	.00
☐ 413 Mike Kingery	.03	.01	.00
☐ 414 Jim Fregosi MG (team checklist back)	.06	.01	.00
☐ 415 Rich Gossage	.08	.03	.01
☐ 416 Fred Lynn	.08	.03	.01
☐ 417 Mike LaCoss	.03	.01	.00
☐ 418 Bob Dernier	.03	.01	.00
☐ 419 Tom Filer	.03	.01	.00
☐ 420 Joe Carter	.10	.04	.01
☐ 421 Kirk McCaskill	.03	.01	.00
☐ 422 Bo Diaz	.03	.01	.00
☐ 423 Brian Fisher	.03	.01	.00
☐ 424 Luis Polonia	.03	.01	.00
☐ 425 Jay Howell	.03	.01	.00
☐ 426 Danny Gladden	.03	.01	.00
☐ 427 Eric Show	.03	.01	.00
☐ 428 Craig Reynolds	.03	.01	.00
☐ 429 Minnesota Twins TL Greg Gagne (taking throw at 2nd)	.03	.01	.00
☐ 430 Mark Gubicza	.06	.02	.00
☐ 431 Luis Rivera	.03	.01	.00
☐ 432 Chad Kreuter	.20	.08	.02
☐ 433 Albert Hall	.03	.01	.00
☐ 434 Ken Patterson	.10	.04	.01
☐ 435 Len Dykstra	.08	.03	.01
☐ 436 Bobby Meacham	.03	.01	.00
☐ 437 Andy Benes FDP	.35	.14	.03
☐ 438 Greg Gross	.03	.01	.00
☐ 439 Frank DiPino	.03	.01	.00
☐ 440 Bobby Bonilla	.10	.04	.01
☐ 441 Jerry Reed	.03	.01	.00
☐ 442 Jose Oquendo	.03	.01	.00
☐ 443 Rod Nichols	.10	.04	.01
☐ 444 Moose Stubing MG (team checklist back)	.06	.01	.00
☐ 445 Matt Nokes	.10	.04	.01
☐ 446 Rob Murphy	.03	.01	.00
☐ 447 Donell Nixon	.03	.01	.00
☐ 448 Eric Plunk	.03	.01	.00
☐ 449 Carmelo Martinez	.03	.01	.00
☐ 450 Roger Clemens	.25	.10	.02
☐ 451 Mark Davidson	.03	.01	.00
☐ 452 Israel Sanchez	.10	.04	.01
☐ 453 Tom Prince	.10	.04	.01
☐ 454 Paul Assenmacher	.03	.01	.00

□ 455 Johnny Ray .06 .02 .00
□ 456 Tim Belcher .06 .02 .00
□ 457 Mackey Sasser .08 .03 .01
□ 458 Donn Pall .10 .04 .01
□ 459 Seattle Mariners TL .03 .01 .00
Dave Valle
□ 460 Dave Stieb .08 .03 .01
□ 461 Buddy Bell .08 .03 .01
□ 462 Jose Guzman .03 .01 .00
□ 463 Steve Lake .03 .01 .00
□ 464 Bryn Smith .03 .01 .00
□ 465 Mark Grace .85 .34 .08
□ 466 Chuck Crim .03 .01 .00
□ 467 Jim Walewander .03 .01 .00
□ 468 Henry Cotto .03 .01 .00
□ 469 Jose Bautista .10 .04 .01
□ 470 Lance Parrish .08 .03 .01
□ 471 Steve Curry .12 .05 .01
□ 472 Brian Harper .03 .01 .00
□ 473 Don Robinson .03 .01 .00
□ 474 Bob Rodgers MG .06 .01 .00
(team checklist back)
□ 475 Dave Parker .08 .03 .01
□ 476 Jon Perlman .08 .03 .01
□ 477 Dick Schofield .03 .01 .00
□ 478 Doug Drabek .03 .01 .00
□ 479 Mike Macfarlane .12 .05 .01
□ 480 Keith Hernandez .12 .05 .01
□ 481 Chris Brown .06 .02 .00
□ 482 Steve Peters .12 .05 .01
□ 483 Mickey Hatcher .06 .02 .00
□ 484 Steve Shields .03 .01 .00
□ 485 Hubie Brooks .06 .02 .00
□ 486 Jack McDowell .15 .06 .01
□ 487 Scott Lusader .10 .04 .01
□ 488 Kevin Coffman .10 .04 .01
□ 489 Phila. Phillies TL .12 .05 .01
Mike Schmidt
□ 490 Chris Sabo .85 .34 .08
□ 491 Mike Birkbeck .03 .01 .00
□ 492 Alan Ashby .03 .01 .00
□ 493 Todd Benzinger .06 .02 .00
□ 494 Shane Rawley .03 .01 .00
□ 495 Candy Maldonado .06 .02 .00
□ 496 Dwayne Henry .03 .01 .00
□ 497 Pete Stanicek .10 .04 .01
□ 498 Dave Valle .03 .01 .00
□ 499 Don Heinkel .10 .04 .01
□ 500 Jose Canseco 1.00 .40 .10
□ 501 Vance Law .03 .01 .00
□ 502 Duane Ward .03 .01 .00
□ 503 Al Newman .03 .01 .00
□ 504 Bob Walk .06 .02 .00
□ 505 Pete Rose MG .25 .07 .01
(team checklist back)
□ 506 Kirt Manwaring .10 .04 .01
□ 507 Steve Farr .03 .01 .00
□ 508 Wally Backman .03 .01 .00
□ 509 Bud Black .03 .01 .00
□ 510 Bob Horner .08 .03 .01
□ 511 Richard Dotson .06 .02 .00
□ 512 Donnie Hill .03 .01 .00
□ 513 Jesse Orosco .03 .01 .00
□ 514 Chet Lemon .03 .01 .00
□ 515 Barry Larkin .08 .03 .01
□ 516 Eddie Whitson .03 .01 .00
□ 517 Greg Brock .03 .01 .00
□ 518 Bruce Ruffin .03 .01 .00
□ 519 New York Yankees TL .03 .01 .00
Willie Randolph
□ 520 Rick Sutcliffe .08 .03 .01
□ 521 Mickey Tettleton .03 .01 .00
□ 522 Randy Kramer .10 .04 .01
□ 523 Andres Thomas .03 .01 .00
□ 524 Checklist 397-528 .06 .01 .00
□ 525 Chili Davis .06 .02 .00
□ 526 Wes Gardner .03 .01 .00
□ 527 Dave Henderson .06 .02 .00
□ 528 Luis Medina .35 .14 .03
□ 529 Tom Foley .03 .01 .00
□ 530 Nolan Ryan .15 .06 .01
□ 531 Dave Hengel .10 .04 .01
□ 532 Jerry Browne .03 .01 .00
□ 533 Andy Hawkins .03 .01 .00
□ 534 Doc Edwards MG .06 .01 .00
(team checklist back)
□ 535 Todd Worrell .08 .03 .01
□ 536 Joel Skinner .03 .01 .00
□ 537 Pete Smith .10 .04 .01
□ 538 Juan Castillo .03 .01 .00
□ 539 Barry Jones .03 .01 .00
□ 540 Bo Jackson .15 .06 .01
□ 541 Cecil Fielder .03 .01 .00
□ 542 Todd Frohwirth .03 .01 .00
□ 543 Damon Berryhill .15 .06 .01
□ 544 Jeff Sellers .03 .01 .00
□ 545 Mookie Wilson .06 .02 .00
□ 546 Mark Williamson .03 .01 .00
□ 547 Mark McLemore .03 .01 .00
□ 548 Bobby Witt .06 .02 .00
□ 549 Chicago Cubs TL .03 .01 .00
Jamie Moyer
(pitching)
□ 550 Orel Hershiser .20 .08 .02
□ 551 Randy Ready .03 .01 .00
□ 552 Greg Cadaret .03 .01 .00
□ 553 Luis Salazar .03 .01 .00
□ 554 Nick Esasky .03 .01 .00
□ 555 Bert Blyleven .08 .03 .01
□ 556 Bruce Fields .03 .01 .00
□ 557 Keith Miller .03 .01 .00
New York Mets
□ 558 Dan Pasqua .06 .02 .00
□ 559 Juan Agosto .03 .01 .00
□ 560 Tim Raines .12 .05 .01
□ 561 Luis Aguayo .03 .01 .00
□ 562 Danny Cox .06 .02 .00
□ 563 Bill Schroeder .03 .01 .00
□ 564 Russ Nixon MG .06 .01 .00
(team checklist back)
□ 565 Jeff Russell .03 .01 .00
□ 566 Al Pedrique .03 .01 .00
□ 567 David Wells .08 .03 .01
□ 568 Mickey Brantley .06 .02 .00
□ 569 German Jimenez .10 .04 .01
□ 570 Tony Gwynn .15 .06 .01
□ 571 Billy Ripken .03 .01 .00
□ 572 Atlee Hammaker .03 .01 .00
□ 573 Jim Abbott FDP .75 .30 .07
□ 574 Dave Clark .06 .02 .00
□ 575 Juan Samuel .08 .03 .01
□ 576 Greg Minton .03 .01 .00
□ 577 Randy Bush .03 .01 .00
□ 578 John Morris .03 .01 .00
□ 579 Houston Astros TL .06 .02 .00
Glenn Davis
(batting stance)
□ 580 Harold Reynolds .03 .01 .00
□ 581 Gene Nelson .03 .01 .00
□ 582 Mike Marshall .08 .03 .01
□ 583 Paul Gibson .10 .04 .01
□ 584 Randy Velarde .08 .03 .01
□ 585 Harold Baines .08 .03 .01
□ 586 Joe Boever .03 .01 .00
□ 587 Mike Stanley .03 .01 .00
□ 588 Luis Alicea .10 .04 .01
□ 589 Dave Meads .03 .01 .00
□ 590 Andres Galarraga .12 .05 .01
□ 591 Jeff Musselman .03 .01 .00
□ 592 John Cangelosi .03 .01 .00
□ 593 Drew Hall .03 .01 .00
□ 594 Jimy Williams MG .06 .01 .00
(team checklist back)
□ 595 Teddy Higuera .08 .03 .01
□ 596 Kurt Stillwell .03 .01 .00
□ 597 Terry Taylor .15 .06 .01
□ 598 Ken Gerhart .03 .01 .00
□ 599 Tom Candiotti .03 .01 .00
□ 600 Wade Boggs .40 .16 .04
□ 601 Dave Dravecky .03 .01 .00
□ 602 Devon White .08 .03 .01
□ 603 Frank Tanana .03 .01 .00
□ 604 Paul O'Neill .03 .01 .00
□ 605 Bob Welch .06 .02 .00
□ 606 Rick Dempsey .03 .01 .00
□ 607 Willie Ansley FDP .30 .12 .03
□ 608 Phil Bradley .06 .02 .00
□ 609 Detroit Tigers TL .06 .02 .00
Frank Tanana
(with Alan Trammell
and Mike Heath)
□ 610 Randy Myers .06 .02 .00
□ 611 Don Slaught .03 .01 .00
□ 612 Dan Quisenberry .08 .03 .01
□ 613 Gary Varsho .15 .06 .01
□ 614 Joe Hesketh .03 .01 .00
□ 615 Robin Yount .12 .05 .01
□ 616 Steve Rosenberg .10 .04 .01
□ 617 Mark Parent .10 .04 .01
□ 618 Rance Mulliniks .03 .01 .00
□ 619 Checklist 529-660 .06 .01 .00
□ 620 Barry Bonds .10 .04 .01
□ 621 Rick Mahler .03 .01 .00
□ 622 Stan Javier .03 .01 .00
□ 623 Fred Toliver .03 .01 .00
□ 624 Jack McKeon MG .06 .01 .00
(team checklist back)
□ 625 Eddie Murray .15 .06 .01
□ 626 Jeff Reed .03 .01 .00
□ 627 Greg Harris .03 .01 .00

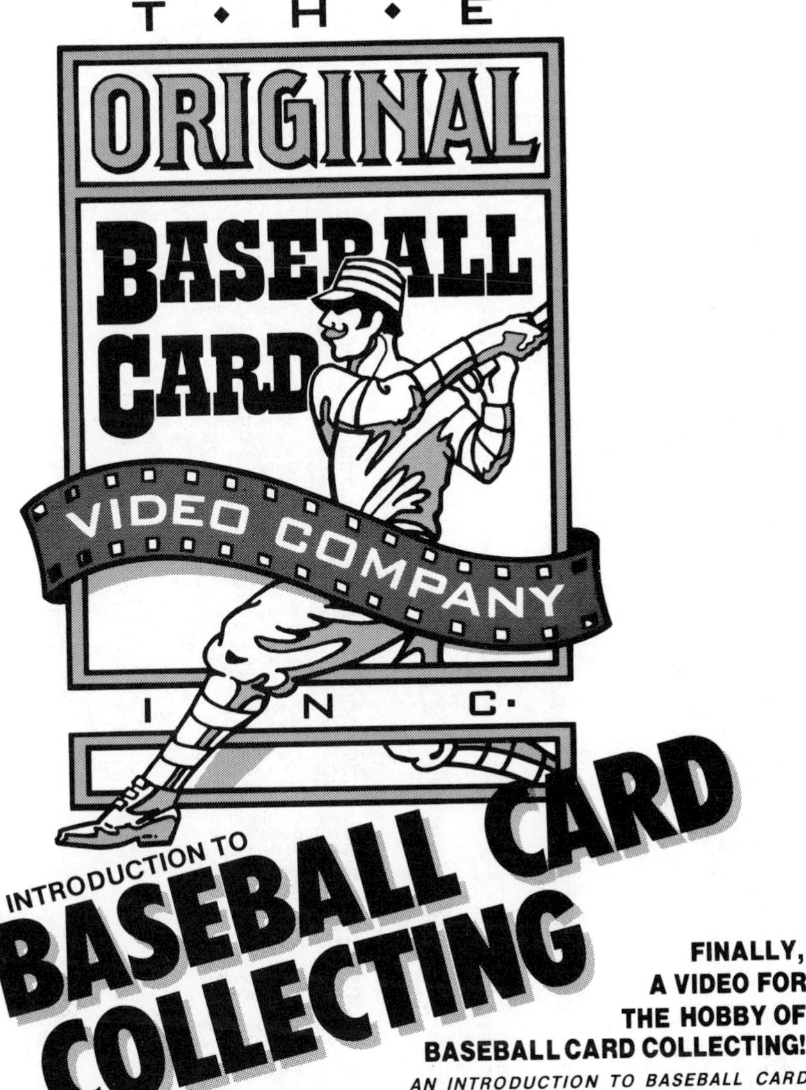
T • H • E
ORIGINAL
BASEBALL
CARD
VIDEO COMPANY
I N C.
AN INTRODUCTION TO
BASEBALL CARD
COLLECTING

	Philadelphia Phillies			
☐ 628	Matt Williams	.08	.03	.01
☐ 629	Pete O'Brien	.06	.02	.00
☐ 630	Mike Greenwell	.50	.20	.05
☐ 631	Dave Bergman	.03	.01	.00
☐ 632	Bryan Harvey	.25	.10	.02
☐ 633	Daryl Boston	.03	.01	.00
☐ 634	Marvin Freeman	.03	.01	.00
☐ 635	Willie Randolph	.06	.02	.00
☐ 636	Bill Wilkinson	.03	.01	.00
☐ 637	Carmen Castillo	.03	.01	.00
☐ 638	Floyd Bannister	.03	.01	.00
☐ 639	Oakland A's TL Walt Weiss	.12	.05	.01
☐ 640	Willie McGee	.08	.03	.01
☐ 641	Curt Young	.03	.01	.00
☐ 642	Argenis Salazar	.03	.01	.00
☐ 643	Louie Meadows	.10	.04	.01
☐ 644	Lloyd McClendon	.03	.01	.00
☐ 645	Jack Morris	.10	.04	.01
☐ 646	Kevin Bass	.06	.02	.00
☐ 647	Randy Johnson	.20	.08	.02
☐ 648	Sandy Alomar FS	.90	.36	.09
☐ 649	Stewart Cliburn	.03	.01	.00
☐ 650	Kirby Puckett	.20	.08	.02
☐ 651	Tom Niedenfuer	.03	.01	.00
☐ 652	Rich Gedman	.06	.02	.00
☐ 653	Tommy Barrett	.12	.05	.01
☐ 654	Whitey Herzog MG (team checklist back)	.06	.01	.00
☐ 655	Dave Magadan	.06	.02	.00
☐ 656	Ivan Calderon	.06	.02	.00
☐ 657	Joe Magrane	.06	.02	.00
☐ 658	R.J. Reynolds	.03	.01	.00
☐ 659	Al Leiter	.15	.06	.01
☐ 660	Will Clark	.25	.10	.02
☐ 661	Dwight Gooden TBC84	.12	.05	.01
☐ 662	Lou Brock TBC79	.08	.03	.01
☐ 663	Hank Aaron TBC74	.10	.04	.01
☐ 664	Gil Hodges TBC69	.08	.03	.01
☐ 665	Tony Oliva TBC64 (fabricated card)	.08	.03	.01
☐ 666	Randy St.Claire	.03	.01	.00
☐ 667	Dwayne Murphy	.03	.01	.00
☐ 668	Mike Bielecki	.03	.01	.00
☐ 669	L.A. Dodgers TL Orel Hershiser (mound conference with Mike Scioscia)	.15	.06	.01
☐ 670	Kevin Seitzer	.15	.06	.01
☐ 671	Jim Gantner	.03	.01	.00
☐ 672	Allan Anderson	.06	.02	.00
☐ 673	Don Baylor	.06	.02	.00
☐ 674	Otis Nixon	.03	.01	.00
☐ 675	Bruce Hurst	.08	.03	.01
☐ 676	Ernie Riles	.03	.01	.00
☐ 677	Dave Schmidt	.03	.01	.00
☐ 678	Dion James	.03	.01	.00
☐ 679	Willie Fraser	.03	.01	.00
☐ 680	Gary Carter	.15	.06	.01
☐ 681	Jeff Robinson Pittsburgh Pirates	.03	.01	.00
☐ 682	Rick Leach	.03	.01	.00
☐ 683	Jose Cecena	.10	.04	.01
☐ 684	Dave Johnson MG (team checklist back)	.06	.01	.00
☐ 685	Jeff Treadway	.10	.04	.01
☐ 686	Scott Terry	.03	.01	.00
☐ 687	Alvin Davis	.08	.03	.01
☐ 688	Zane Smith	.06	.02	.00
☐ 689	Stan Jefferson	.06	.02	.00
☐ 690	Doug Jones	.06	.02	.00
☐ 691	Roberto Kelly	.15	.06	.01
☐ 692	Steve Ontiveros	.03	.01	.00
☐ 693	Pat Borders	.15	.06	.01
☐ 694	Les Lancaster	.03	.01	.00
☐ 695	Carlton Fisk	.08	.03	.01
☐ 696	Don August	.06	.02	.00
☐ 697	Franklin Stubbs	.03	.01	.00
☐ 698	Keith Atherton	.03	.01	.00
☐ 699	Pittsburgh Pirates TL Al Pedrique (Tony Gwynn sliding)	.06	.02	.00
☐ 700	Don Mattingly	.75	.30	.07
☐ 701	Storm Davis	.06	.02	.00
☐ 702	Jamie Quirk	.03	.01	.00
☐ 703	Scott Garrelts	.03	.01	.00
☐ 704	Carlos Quintana	.30	.12	.03
☐ 705	Terry Kennedy	.03	.01	.00
☐ 706	Pete Incaviglia	.10	.04	.01
☐ 707	Steve Jeltz	.03	.01	.00
☐ 708	Chuck Finley	.03	.01	.00
☐ 709	Tom Herr	.06	.02	.00
☐ 710	Dave Cone	.20	.08	.02
☐ 711	Candy Sierra	.12	.05	.01
☐ 712	Bill Swift	.03	.01	.00
☐ 713	Ty Griffin FDP	.50	.20	.05
☐ 714	Joe Morgan MG (team checklist back)	.06	.02	.00
☐ 715	Tony Pena	.06	.02	.00
☐ 716	Wayne Tolleson	.03	.01	.00
☐ 717	Jamie Moyer	.03	.01	.00
☐ 718	Glenn Braggs	.03	.01	.00
☐ 719	Danny Darwin	.03	.01	.00
☐ 720	Tim Wallach	.06	.02	.00
☐ 721	Ron Tingley	.10	.04	.01
☐ 722	Todd Stottlemyre	.15	.06	.01
☐ 723	Rafael Belliard	.03	.01	.00
☐ 724	Jerry Don Gleaton	.03	.01	.00
☐ 725	Terry Steinbach	.08	.03	.01
☐ 726	Dickie Thon	.03	.01	.00
☐ 727	Joe Orsulak	.03	.01	.00
☐ 728	Charlie Puleo	.03	.01	.00
☐ 729	Texas Rangers TL Steve Buechele	.03	.01	.00
☐ 730	Danny Jackson	.10	.04	.01
☐ 731	Mike Young	.03	.01	.00
☐ 732	Steve Buechele	.03	.01	.00
☐ 733	Randy Bockus	.10	.04	.01
☐ 734	Jody Reed	.08	.03	.01
☐ 735	Roger McDowell	.06	.02	.00
☐ 736	Jeff Hamilton	.03	.01	.00
☐ 737	Norm Charlton	.12	.05	.01
☐ 738	Darnell Coles	.03	.01	.00
☐ 739	Brook Jacoby	.06	.02	.00
☐ 740	Dan Plesac	.06	.02	.00
☐ 741	Ken Phelps	.06	.02	.00
☐ 742	Mike Harkey FS	.45	.18	.04
☐ 743	Mike Heath	.03	.01	.00
☐ 744	Roger Craig MG (team checklist back)	.06	.01	.00
☐ 745	Fred McGriff	.15	.06	.01
☐ 746	German Gonzalez	.10	.04	.01
☐ 747	Will Tejada	.03	.01	.00
☐ 748	Jimmy Jones	.06	.02	.00
☐ 749	Rafael Ramirez	.03	.01	.00
☐ 750	Bret Saberhagen	.10	.04	.01
☐ 751	Ken Oberkfell	.03	.01	.00
☐ 752	Jim Gott	.03	.01	.00
☐ 753	Jose Uribe	.03	.01	.00
☐ 754	Bob Brower	.03	.01	.00
☐ 755	Mike Scioscia	.03	.01	.00
☐ 756	Scott Medvin	.10	.04	.01
☐ 757	Brady Anderson	.20	.08	.02
☐ 758	Gene Walter	.03	.01	.00
☐ 759	Milwaukee Brewers TL Rob Deer	.06	.02	.00
☐ 760	Lee Smith	.06	.02	.00
☐ 761	Dante Bichette	.20	.08	.02
☐ 762	Bobby Thigpen	.06	.02	.00
☐ 763	Dave Martinez	.03	.01	.00
☐ 764	Robin Ventura FDP	.85	.34	.08
☐ 765	Glenn Davis	.10	.04	.01
☐ 766	Cecilio Guante	.03	.01	.00
☐ 767	Mike Capel	.12	.05	.01
☐ 768	Bill Wegman	.03	.01	.00
☐ 769	Junior Ortiz	.03	.01	.00
☐ 770	Alan Trammell	.12	.05	.01
☐ 771	Ron Kittle	.06	.02	.00
☐ 772	Ron Oester	.03	.01	.00
☐ 773	Keith Moreland	.03	.01	.00
☐ 774	Frank Robinson MG (team checklist back)	.08	.02	.00
☐ 775	Jeff Reardon	.06	.02	.00
☐ 776	Nelson Liriano	.03	.01	.00
☐ 777	Ted Power	.03	.01	.00
☐ 778	Bruce Benedict	.03	.01	.00
☐ 779	Craig McMurtry	.03	.01	.00
☐ 780	Pedro Guerrero	.10	.04	.01
☐ 781	Greg Briley	.12	.05	.01
☐ 782	Checklist 661-792	.06	.01	.00
☐ 783	Trevor Wilson	.15	.06	.01
☐ 784	Steve Avery FDP	.25	.10	.02
☐ 785	Ellis Burks	.20	.08	.02
☐ 786	Melido Perez	.15	.06	.01
☐ 787	Dave West	.45	.18	.04
☐ 788	Mike Morgan	.03	.01	.00
☐ 789	Kansas City Royals TL Bo Jackson (throwing)	.10	.04	.01
☐ 790	Sid Fernandez	.08	.03	.01
☐ 791	Jim Lindeman	.03	.01	.00
☐ 792	Rafael Santana	.06	.02	.00

1989 Topps Wax Box Cards

The cards in this 16-card set measure the standard 2 1/2" by 3 1/2". Cards have essentially the same design as the 1989 Topps regular issue set. The cards were printed on the bottoms of the regular issue wax pack boxes. These 16 cards, "lettered" A through P, are considered a separate set in their own right and are not typically included in a complete set of the regular issue 1989 Topps cards. The value of the panels uncut is slightly greater, perhaps by 25% greater, than the value of the individual cards cut up carefully. The sixteen cards in this set honor players (and one manager) who reached career milestones during the 1988 season.

	MINT	EXC	G-VG
COMPLETE SET (16)	3.00	1.20	.30
COMMON PLAYER (A-P)	.05	.02	.00
☐ A George Brett 475th Double	.35	.14	.03
☐ B Bill Buckner 2600th Hit	.10	.04	.01
☐ C Darrell Evans 400th Home Run	.10	.04	.01
☐ D Rich Gossage 300th Save	.10	.04	.01
☐ E Greg Gross 125th Pinch Hit	.05	.02	.00
☐ F Rickey Henderson 775th Stolen Base	.40	.16	.04
☐ G Keith Hernandez 125th Game-Winning RBI	.20	.08	.02
☐ H Tom Lasorda 1000th Managerial Win	.10	.04	.01
☐ I Jim Rice 1400th Run Batted In	.20	.08	.02
☐ J Cal Ripken 1000th Cons. Game	.30	.12	.03
☐ K Nolan Ryan 4700th Strikeout	.35	.14	.03
☐ L Mike Schmidt 1000th Long Hit	.40	.16	.04
☐ M Bruce Sutter 300th Save	.10	.04	.01
☐ N Don Sutton 750th Game Started	.20	.08	.02
☐ O Kent Tekulve 1000th Appearance	.05	.02	.00
☐ P Dave Winfield 1400th Run Batted In	.30	.12	.03

1989 Topps Glossy All-Stars 22

These glossy cards were inserted with Topps rack packs and honor the starting line-ups, managers, and honorary captains of the 1988 National and American League All-Star teams. The cards are standard size, 2 1/2" by 3 1/2" and very similar to the design Topps has used since 1984. The backs are printed in red and blue on white card stock.

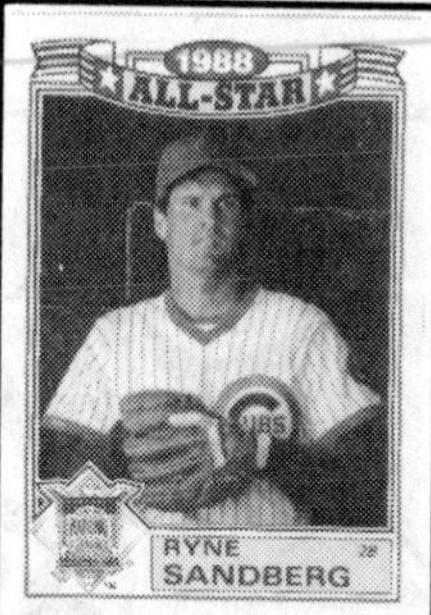

	MINT	EXC	G-VG
COMPLETE SET (22)	4.00	1.60	.40
COMMON PLAYER (1-22)	.10	.04	.01
☐ 1 Tom Kelly MG	.10	.04	.01
☐ 2 Mark McGwire	.40	.16	.04
☐ 3 Paul Molitor	.20	.08	.02
☐ 4 Wade Boggs	.50	.20	.05
☐ 5 Cal Ripken	.25	.10	.02
☐ 6 Jose Canseco	.75	.30	.07
☐ 7 Rickey Henderson	.30	.12	.03
☐ 8 Dave Winfield	.30	.12	.03
☐ 9 Terry Steinbach	.15	.06	.01
☐ 10 Frank Viola	.20	.08	.02
☐ 11 Bobby Doerr CAPT	.15	.06	.01
☐ 12 Whitey Herzog MG	.10	.04	.01
☐ 13 Will Clark	.40	.16	.04
☐ 14 Ryne Sandberg	.20	.08	.02
☐ 15 Bobby Bonilla	.20	.08	.02
☐ 16 Ozzie Smith	.20	.08	.02
☐ 17 Vince Coleman	.20	.08	.02
☐ 18 Andre Dawson	.20	.08	.02
☐ 19 Darryl Strawberry	.40	.16	.04
☐ 20 Gary Carter	.30	.12	.03
☐ 21 Doc Gooden	.35	.14	.03
☐ 22 Willie Stargell CAPT	.20	.08	.02

1989 Topps Jumbo Rookies

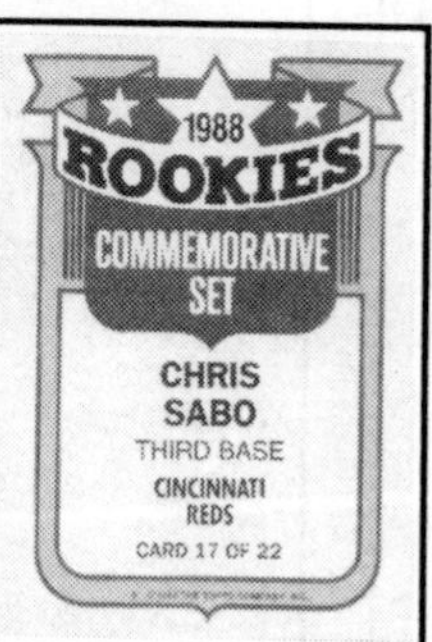

Inserted in each supermarket jumbo pack is a card from this series of 22 of 1988's best rookies as determined by Topps. Jumbo packs consisted of 100 (regular issue 1989 Topps baseball) cards with a stick of gum plus the insert "Rookie" card. The card fronts are in full color and measure 2 1/2" by 3 1/2". The card backs are printed in red and blue on white card stock and are numbered at the bottom.

	MINT	EXC	G-VG
COMPLETE SET (22)	10.00	4.00	1.00
COMMON PLAYER (1-22)	.20	.08	.02
☐ 1 Roberto Alomar	.50	.20	.05
☐ 2 Brady Anderson	.45	.18	.04

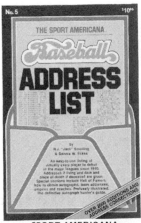

		MINT	EXC	G-VG
□ 3	Tim Belcher	.35	.14	.03
□ 4	Damon Berryhill	.40	.16	.04
□ 5	Jay Buhner	.50	.20	.05
□ 6	Kevin Elster	.35	.14	.03
□ 7	Cecil Espy	.30	.12	.03
□ 8	Dave Gallagher	.40	.16	.04
□ 9	Ron Gant	.75	.30	.07
□ 10	Paul Gibson	.20	.08	.02
□ 11	Mark Grace	1.00	.40	.10
□ 12	Darrin Jackson	.30	.12	.03
□ 13	Gregg Jefferies	2.00	.80	.20
□ 14	Ricky Jordan	1.00	.40	.10
□ 15	Al Leiter	.50	.20	.05
□ 16	Melido Perez	.40	.16	.04
□ 17	Chris Sabo	1.00	.40	.10
□ 18	Nelson Santovenia	.30	.12	.03
□ 19	Mackey Sasser	.35	.14	.03
□ 20	Gary Sheffield	1.00	.40	.10
□ 21	Walt Weiss	.75	.30	.07
□ 22	David Wells	.25	.10	.02

1987 Toys'R'Us Rookies

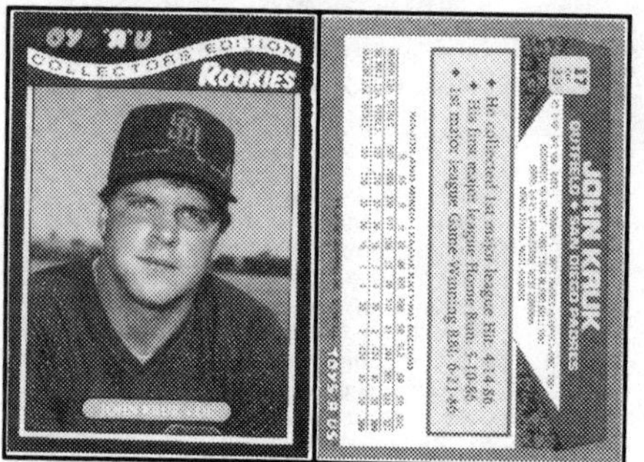

Topps produced this 33-card boxed set for Toys 'R' Us stores. The set is subtitled "Baseball Rookies" and features predominantly younger players. The cards measure 2 1/2" by 3 1/2" and feature a high-gloss, full-color photo of the player inside a black border. The card backs are printed in orange and blue on white card stock.

		MINT	EXC	G-VG
COMPLETE SET (33)		5.00	2.00	.50
COMMON PLAYER (1-33)		.10	.04	.01
□ 1	Andy Allanson	.10	.04	.01
□ 2	Paul Assenmacher	.10	.04	.01
□ 3	Scott Bailes	.10	.04	.01
□ 4	Barry Bonds	.35	.14	.03
□ 5	Jose Canseco	1.25	.50	.12
□ 6	John Cerutti	.10	.04	.01
□ 7	Will Clark	.75	.30	.07
□ 8	Kal Daniels	.60	.24	.06
□ 9	Jim Deshaies	.15	.06	.01
□ 10	Mark Eichhorn	.10	.04	.01
□ 11	Ed Hearn	.10	.04	.01
□ 12	Pete Incaviglia	.25	.10	.02
□ 13	Bo Jackson	.50	.20	.05
□ 14	Wally Joyner	.65	.26	.06
□ 15	Charlie Kerfeld	.10	.04	.01
□ 16	Eric King	.15	.06	.01
□ 17	John Kruk	.20	.08	.02
□ 18	Barry Larkin	.40	.16	.04
□ 19	Mike LaValliere	.15	.06	.01
□ 20	Greg Mathews	.15	.06	.01
□ 21	Kevin Mitchell	.20	.08	.02
□ 22	Dan Plesac	.20	.08	.02
□ 23	Bruce Ruffin	.15	.06	.01
□ 24	Ruben Sierra	.50	.20	.05
□ 25	Cory Snyder	.40	.16	.04
□ 26	Kurt Stillwell	.20	.08	.02
□ 27	Dale Sveum	.20	.08	.02
□ 28	Danny Tartabull	.40	.16	.04
□ 29	Andres Thomas	.15	.06	.01
□ 30	Robby Thompson	.15	.06	.01
□ 31	Jim Traber	.15	.06	.01
□ 32	Mitch Williams	.15	.06	.01
□ 33	Todd Worrell	.20	.08	.02

1988 Toys'r'Us Rookies

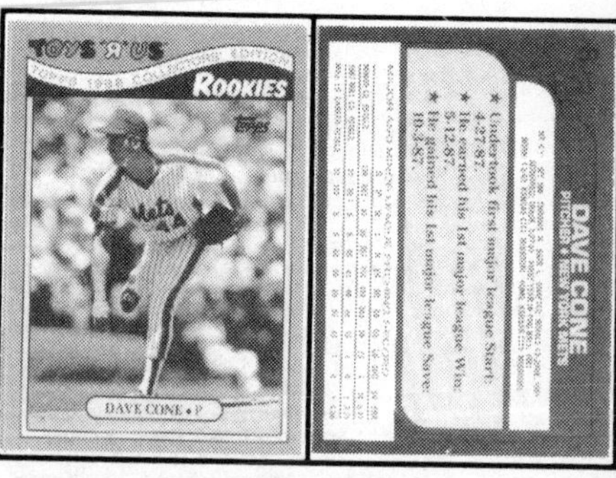

Topps produced this 33-card boxed set for Toys 'R' Us stores. The set is subtitled "Baseball Rookies" and features predominantly younger players. The cards measure 2 1/2" by 3 1/2" and feature a high-gloss, full-color photo of the player inside a blue border. The card backs are printed in pink and blue on white card stock. The cards are numbered on the back and the checklist for the set is found on the back panel of the small collector box. The statistics provided on the card backs cover only three lines, Minor League totals, last season, and Major League totals.

		MINT	EXC	G-VG
COMPLETE SET (33)		5.00	2.00	.50
COMMON PLAYER (1-33)		.10	.04	.01
□ 1	Todd Benzinger	.30	.12	.03
□ 2	Bob Brower	.20	.08	.02
□ 3	Jerry Browne	.10	.04	.01
□ 4	DeWayne Buice	.10	.04	.01
□ 5	Ellis Burks	1.00	.40	.10
□ 6	Ken Caminiti	.20	.08	.02
□ 7	Casey Candaele	.10	.04	.01
□ 8	Dave Cone	1.00	.40	.10
□ 9	Kelly Downs	.20	.08	.02
□ 10	Mike Dunne	.20	.08	.02
□ 11	Ken Gerhart	.15	.06	.01
□ 12	Mike Greenwell	1.25	.50	.12
□ 13	Mike Henneman	.20	.08	.02
□ 14	Sam Horn	.20	.08	.02
□ 15	Joe Magrane	.20	.08	.02
□ 16	Fred Manrique	.10	.04	.01
□ 17	John Marzano	.15	.06	.01
□ 18	Fred McGriff	1.00	.40	.10
□ 19	Mark McGwire	1.00	.40	.10
□ 20	Jeff Musselman	.10	.04	.01
□ 21	Randy Myers	.30	.12	.03
□ 22	Matt Nokes	.30	.12	.03
□ 23	Al Pedrique	.10	.04	.01
□ 24	Luis Polonia	.20	.08	.02
□ 25	Billy Ripken	.20	.08	.02
□ 26	Benny Santiago	.50	.20	.05
□ 27	Kevin Seitzer	.75	.30	.07
□ 28	John Smiley	.20	.08	.02
□ 29	Mike Stanley	.15	.06	.01
□ 30	Terry Steinbach	.30	.12	.03
□ 31	B.J. Surhoff	.20	.08	.02
□ 32	Bobby Thigpen	.20	.08	.02
□ 33	Devon White	.25	.10	.02

1983 True Value White Sox

This 23-card set was sponsored by True Value Hardware Stores and features full-color (2 5/8" by 4 1/4") cards of the Chicago White Sox. Most of the set was intended for distribution two cards per game at selected White Sox Tuesday night home games. The cards are unnumbered except for uniform number given in the lower right corner of the obverse. The card backs contain statistical

information in basic black and white. The cards of Harold Baines, Salome Barojas, and Marc Hill were not issued at the park; hence they are more difficult to obtain than the other 20 cards and are marked SP in the checklist below.

	MINT	EXC	G-VG
COMPLETE SET (23)	28.00	11.50	2.80
COMMON PLAYER (1-23)	.35	.14	.03
□ 1 Scott Fletcher	.90	.36	.09
□ 3 Harold Baines SP	6.00	2.40	.60
□ 5 Vance Law	.60	.24	.06
□ 7 Marc Hill SP	3.00	1.20	.30
□ 10 Tony LaRussa MG	.75	.30	.07
□ 11 Rudy Law	.35	.14	.03
□ 14 Tony Bernazard	.35	.14	.03
□ 17 Jerry Hairston	.35	.14	.03
□ 19 Greg Luzinski	.75	.30	.07
□ 24 Floyd Bannister	.60	.24	.06
□ 25 Mike Squires	.35	.14	.03
□ 30 Salome Barojas SP	3.00	1.20	.30
□ 31 LaMarr Hoyt	.50	.20	.05
□ 34 Richard Dotson	.50	.20	.05
□ 36 Jerry Koosman	.50	.20	.05
□ 40 Britt Burns	.35	.14	.03
□ 41 Dick Tidrow	.35	.14	.03
□ 42 Ron Kittle	1.00	.40	.10
□ 44 Tom Paciorek	.35	.14	.03
□ 45 Kevin Hickey	.35	.14	.03
□ 53 Dennis Lamp	.35	.14	.03
□ 67 Jim Kern	.35	.14	.03
□ 72 Carlton Fisk	.90	.36	.09

1984 True Value White Sox

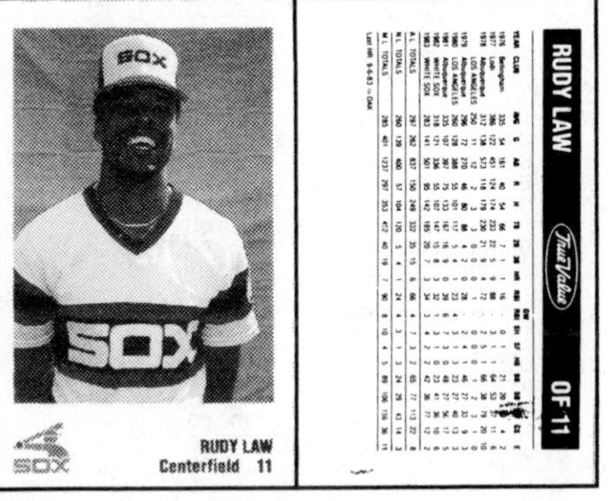

This 30-card set features full color (2 1/2" by 4") cards of the Chicago White Sox. Most of the set was distributed two cards per game at selected White Sox Tuesday home games. Faust and Minoso were not given out although their cards were available through direct (promotional) contact with them. Brennan and Hulett were not released directly since they were sent down to the minors. The cards are unnumbered except for uniform number given in the lower right corner of the obverse. The card backs contain statistical information in basic black and white.

	MINT	EXC	G-VG
COMPLETE SET (30)	22.00	9.00	2.20
COMMON PLAYER (1-30)	.30	.12	.03
□ 1 Juan Agosto	.30	.12	.03
□ 2 Luis Aparicio	2.00	.80	.20
□ 3 Harold Baines	1.50	.60	.15
□ 4 Floyd Bannister	.50	.20	.05
□ 5 Salome Barojas	.30	.12	.03
□ 6 Tom Brennan	1.50	.60	.15
□ 7 Britt Burns	.40	.16	.04
□ 8 Coaching Staff (blank back)	.30	.12	.03
□ 9 Julio Cruz	.30	.12	.03
□ 10 Richard Dotson	.60	.24	.06
□ 11 Jerry Dybzinski	.30	.12	.03
□ 12 Nancy Faust (organist) (blank back)	1.50	.60	.15
□ 13 Carlton Fisk	.75	.30	.07
□ 14 Scott Fletcher	.50	.20	.05
□ 15 Jerry Hairston	.30	.12	.03
□ 16 Marc Hill	.30	.12	.03
□ 17 LaMarr Hoyt	.40	.16	.04
□ 18 Tim Hulett	1.50	.60	.15
□ 19 Ron Kittle	.75	.30	.07
□ 20 Tony LaRussa MG	.50	.20	.05
□ 21 Rudy Law	.30	.12	.03
□ 22 Vance Law	.40	.16	.04
□ 23 Greg Luzinski	.60	.24	.06
□ 24 Minnie Minoso	2.00	.80	.20
□ 25 Tom Paciorek	.30	.12	.03
□ 26 Ron Reed	.30	.12	.03
□ 27 Tom Seaver	2.00	.80	.20
□ 28 Dave Stegman	.30	.12	.03
□ 29 Mike Squires	.30	.12	.03
□ 30 Greg Walker	.60	.24	.06

1986 True Value

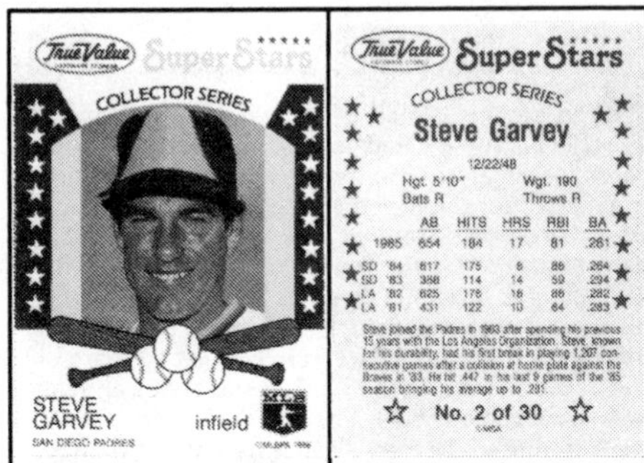

The 1986 True Value set consists of 30 cards each 2 1/2" by 3 1/2" which were printed as panels of four although one of the cards in the panel only pictures a featured product. The complete panel measures 10 3/8" by 3 1/2". The True Value logo is in the upper left corner of the obverse of each card. Supposedly the cards were distributed to customers purchasing 5.00 or more at the store. Cards are frequently found with perforations intact and still in the closed form where only the top card in the folded panel is visible. The card number appears at the bottom of the reverse. Team logos have been surgically removed (airbrushed) from the photos.

	MINT	EXC	G-VG
COMPLETE SET (30)	6.50	2.60	.65
COMMON PLAYER (1-30)	.10	.04	.01
□ 1 Pedro Guerrero	.20	.08	.02
□ 2 Steve Garvey	.30	.12	.03
□ 3 Eddie Murray	.30	.12	.03
□ 4 Pete Rose	.50	.20	.05
□ 5 Don Mattingly	.80	.32	.08
□ 6 Fernando Valenzuela	.25	.10	.02
□ 7 Jim Rice	.25	.10	.02
□ 8 Kirk Gibson	.25	.10	.02
□ 9 Ozzie Smith	.20	.08	.02
□ 10 Dale Murphy	.40	.16	.04
□ 11 Robin Yount	.30	.12	.03
□ 12 Tom Seaver	.30	.12	.03
□ 13 Reggie Jackson	.40	.16	.04
□ 14 Ryne Sandberg	.25	.10	.02
□ 15 Bruce Sutter	.15	.06	.01
□ 16 Gary Carter	.25	.10	.02
□ 17 George Brett	.40	.16	.04
□ 18 Rick Sutcliffe	.10	.04	.01
□ 19 Dave Stieb	.10	.04	.01
□ 20 Buddy Bell	.10	.04	.01
□ 21 Alvin Davis	.15	.06	.01
□ 22 Cal Ripken	.25	.10	.02
□ 23 Bill Madlock	.10	.04	.01
□ 24 Kent Hrbek	.15	.06	.01
□ 25 Lou Whitaker	.15	.06	.01
□ 26 Nolan Ryan	.30	.12	.03
□ 27 Dwayne Murphy	.10	.04	.01
□ 28 Mike Schmidt	.50	.20	.05
□ 29 Andre Dawson	.30	.12	.03
□ 30 Wade Boggs	.65	.26	.06

1911 T3 Turkey Red

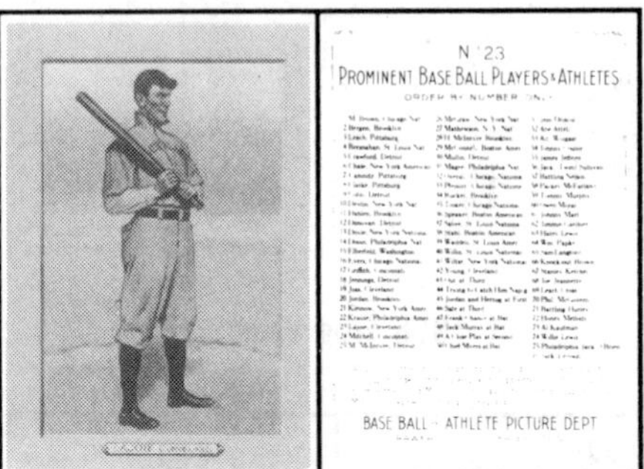

The cards in this 126-card set measure 5 3/4" by 8". The 1911 "Turkey Red" set of color cabinet style cards, designated T3 in the American Card Catalog, is named after the brand of cigarettes with which it was offered as a premium. Cards 1-50 and 77-126 depict baseball players while the middle series (51-76) portrays boxers. The cards themselves are not numbered but were assigned numbers for ordering purposes by the manufacturer. This list appears on the backs of cards in the 77- 126 sub-series and has been used in the checklist below. The boxers (51-76) were formerly assigned a separate catalog number (T9) but have now been returned to the classification to which they properly belong and are indicated in the checklist below by BOX.

	NRMT	VG-E	GOOD
COMPLETE SET (126)	27500.	11000.	3000.
COMMON BASEBALL (1-50)	165.00	70.00	15.00
COMMON BOXERS (51-76)	80.00	32.00	8.00
COMMON BASEBALL (77-126)	200.00	80.00	20.00
□ 1 M. Brown: Chicago NL	350.00	140.00	35.00
□ 2 Bergen: Brooklyn	165.00	70.00	15.00
□ 3 Leach: Pittsburgh	165.00	70.00	15.00
□ 4 Bresnahan: St.L. NL	275.00	110.00	27.00
□ 5 Crawford: Detroit	300.00	120.00	30.00
□ 6 Chase: New York AL	225.00	90.00	22.00
□ 7 Camnitz: Pittsburgh	165.00	70.00	15.00
□ 8 Clarke: Pittsburgh	300.00	120.00	30.00
□ 9 Cobb: Detroit	3250.00	1250.00	250.00
□ 10 Devlin: New York NL	165.00	70.00	15.00
□ 11 Dahlen: Brooklyn	200.00	80.00	20.00
□ 12 Donovan: Detroit	165.00	70.00	15.00
□ 13 Doyle: New York NL	165.00	70.00	15.00
□ 14 Dooin: Phila. NL	165.00	70.00	15.00
□ 15 Elberfeld: Wash	165.00	70.00	15.00
□ 16 Evers: Chicago NL	350.00	140.00	35.00
□ 17 Griffith: Cinc.	300.00	120.00	30.00
□ 18 Jennings: Detroit	300.00	120.00	30.00
□ 19 Joss: Cleveland	350.00	140.00	35.00
□ 20 Jordan: Brooklyn	165.00	70.00	15.00
□ 21 Kleinow: New York NL	165.00	70.00	15.00
□ 22 Krause: Phila. AL	165.00	70.00	15.00
□ 23 Lajoie: Cleveland	600.00	240.00	60.00
□ 24 Mitchell: Cincinnati	165.00	70.00	15.00
□ 25 M. McIntyre: Detroit	165.00	70.00	15.00
□ 26 McGraw: New York NL	400.00	160.00	40.00
□ 27 Mathewson: N.Y. NL	900.00	360.00	90.00
□ 28 H. McIntyre: Brk	165.00	70.00	15.00
□ 29 McConnell: Boston AL	165.00	70.00	15.00
□ 30 Mullin: Detroit	165.00	70.00	15.00
□ 31 Magee: Phila. NL	165.00	70.00	15.00
□ 32 Overall: Chicago NL	165.00	70.00	15.00
□ 33 Pfeister: Chicago NL	165.00	70.00	15.00
□ 34 Rucker: Brooklyn	165.00	70.00	15.00
□ 35 Tinker: Chicago NL	300.00	120.00	30.00
□ 36 Speaker: Boston AL	650.00	260.00	65.00
□ 37 Sallee: St. Louis NL	165.00	70.00	15.00
□ 38 Stahl: Boston AL	165.00	70.00	15.00
□ 39 Waddell: St.Louis AL	350.00	140.00	35.00
□ 40 Willis: St.Louis NL	225.00	90.00	22.00
□ 41 Wiltse: New York NL	165.00	70.00	15.00
□ 42 Young: Cleveland	700.00	280.00	70.00
□ 43 Out At Third	165.00	70.00	15.00
□ 44 Trying to Catch Him Napping	165.00	70.00	15.00
□ 45 Jordan and Herzog at First	165.00	70.00	15.00
□ 46 Safe At Third	165.00	70.00	15.00
□ 47 Frank Chance At Bat	300.00	120.00	30.00
□ 48 Jack Murray At Bat	165.00	70.00	15.00
□ 49 Close Play At Second	165.00	70.00	15.00
□ 50 Chief Myers At Bat	165.00	70.00	15.00
□ 51 Jim Driscoll BOX	80.00	32.00	8.00
□ 52 Abe Attell BOX	80.00	32.00	8.00
□ 53 Ad. Walgast BOX	80.00	32.00	8.00
□ 54 Johnny Coulon BOX	80.00	32.00	8.00
□ 55 James Jeffries BOX	150.00	60.00	15.00
□ 56 Jack Sullivan BOX (Twin)	100.00	40.00	10.00
□ 57 Battling Nelson BOX	100.00	40.00	10.00
□ 58 Packey McFarland BOX	80.00	32.00	8.00
□ 59 Tommy Murphy BOX	80.00	32.00	8.00
□ 60 Owen Moran BOX	80.00	32.00	8.00
□ 61 Johnny Marto BOX	80.00	32.00	8.00
□ 62 Jimmie Gardner BOX	80.00	32.00	8.00
□ 63 Harry Lewis BOX	80.00	32.00	8.00
□ 64 Wm. Papke BOX	80.00	32.00	8.00
□ 65 Sam Langford BOX	80.00	32.00	8.00
□ 66 Knock-out Brown BOX	80.00	32.00	8.00
□ 67 Stanley Ketchel BOX	125.00	50.00	12.50
□ 68 Joe Jeannette BOX	80.00	32.00	8.00
□ 69 Leach Cross BOX	80.00	32.00	8.00
□ 70 Phil. McGovern BOX	80.00	32.00	8.00
□ 71 Battling Hurley BOX	80.00	32.00	8.00
□ 72 Honey Mellody BOX	80.00	32.00	8.00
□ 73 Al Kaufman BOX	80.00	32.00	8.00
□ 74 Willie Lewis BOX	80.00	32.00	8.00
□ 75 Jack O'Brien BOX "Philadelphia"	100.00	40.00	10.00
□ 76 Jack Johnson BOX	175.00	70.00	18.00
□ 77 Ames: New York NL	200.00	80.00	20.00
□ 78 Baker: Phila. AL	350.00	140.00	35.00
□ 79 Bell: Brooklyn	200.00	80.00	20.00
□ 80 Bender: Phila. AL	350.00	140.00	35.00
□ 81 Bescher: Cincinnati	200.00	80.00	20.00
□ 82 Bransfield: Phila. NL	200.00	80.00	20.00
□ 83 Bridwell: Phila. NL	200.00	80.00	20.00
□ 84 Browne: Wash. and Chicago	200.00	80.00	20.00
□ 85 Burns: Chi. and Cin.	200.00	80.00	20.00
□ 86 Carrigan: Boston AL	200.00	80.00	20.00
□ 87 Collins: Phila. AL	400.00	160.00	40.00
□ 88 Coveleski: Cinc.	200.00	80.00	20.00
□ 89 Criger: New York AL	200.00	80.00	20.00
□ 90 Doolan: Phila. NL	200.00	80.00	20.00
□ 91 Downey: Cincinnati	200.00	80.00	20.00
□ 92 Dygert: Phila. AL	200.00	80.00	20.00
□ 93 Fromme: Cincinnati	200.00	80.00	20.00
□ 94 Gibson: Pittsburgh	200.00	80.00	20.00
□ 95 Graham: Boston NL	200.00	80.00	20.00
□ 96 Groom: Washington	200.00	80.00	20.00
□ 97 Hoblitzell: Cinc.	200.00	80.00	20.00
□ 98 Hofman: Chicago NL	200.00	80.00	20.00
□ 99 Johnson: Washington	1000.00	400.00	90.00

□ 100 D. Jones: Detroit	200.00	80.00	20.00
□ 101 Keeler: New York NL	450.00	180.00	45.00
□ 102 Kling: Chicago NL	200.00	80.00	20.00
□ 103 Konetchy: St.Louis NL	200.00	80.00	20.00
□ 104 Lennox: Brooklyn	200.00	80.00	20.00
□ 105 Lobert: Cincinnati	200.00	80.00	20.00
□ 106 Lord: Bos. and Chi.	200.00	80.00	20.00
□ 107 Manning: N.Y. AL	200.00	80.00	20.00
□ 108 Merkle: New York NL	200.00	80.00	20.00
□ 109 Moran: Chi. and Phila.	200.00	80.00	20.00
□ 110 McBride: Washington	200.00	80.00	20.00
□ 111 Niles: Bos. and Cleve.	200.00	80.00	20.00
□ 112 Paskert: Cincinnati	200.00	80.00	20.00
□ 113 Raymond: N.Y. NL	200.00	80.00	20.00
□ 114 Rhoades: Cleveland	250.00	100.00	25.00
□ 115 Schlei: New York NL	200.00	80.00	20.00
□ 116 Schmidt: Detroit	200.00	80.00	20.00
□ 117 Schulte: Chicago NL	200.00	80.00	20.00
□ 118 Smith: Chi. and Bos.	200.00	80.00	20.00
□ 119 Stone: St.L. AL	200.00	80.00	20.00
□ 120 Street: Washington	200.00	80.00	20.00
□ 121 Sullivan: Chi. AL	200.00	80.00	20.00
□ 122 Tenney: New York NL	200.00	80.00	20.00
□ 123 Thomas: Phila. AL	200.00	80.00	20.00
□ 124 Wallace: St.Louis AL	325.00	130.00	32.00
□ 125 Walsh: Chicago AL	350.00	140.00	35.00
□ 126 Wilson: Pittsburgh	200.00	80.00	20.00

1913 T200 Fatima

The cards in this 16-card set measure 2 5/8" by 5 13/16". The 1913 Fatima Cigarettes issue contains unnumbered glossy surface team cards. Both St. Louis team cards are considered difficult to obtain. A large 13" by 21" unnumbered, heavy cardboard premium issue is also known to exist and is quite scarce. These unnumbered team cards are ordered below by team alphabetical order within league.

	NRMT	VG-E	GOOD
COMPLETE SET (16)	2500.00	1000.00	300.00
COMMON TEAM (1-16)	125.00	50.00	12.50
□ 1 Boston AL	175.00	70.00	18.00
□ 2 Chicago AL	125.00	50.00	12.50
□ 3 Cleveland AL	125.00	50.00	12.50
□ 4 Detroit AL	225.00	90.00	22.00
□ 5 New York AL	425.00	170.00	42.00
□ 6 Philadelphia AL	125.00	50.00	12.50
□ 7 St. Louis AL	325.00	130.00	32.00
□ 8 Washington AL	125.00	50.00	12.50
□ 9 Boston NL	225.00	90.00	22.00
□ 10 Brooklyn NL	125.00	50.00	12.50
□ 11 Chicago NL	125.00	50.00	12.50
□ 12 Cincinnati NL	125.00	50.00	12.50
□ 13 New York NL	125.00	50.00	12.50
□ 14 Philadelphia NL	125.00	50.00	12.50
□ 15 Pittsburg NL	125.00	50.00	12.50
□ 16 St. Louis NL	225.00	90.00	22.00

1911 T201 Mecca

The cards in this 50-card set measure 2 1/4" by 4 11/16". The 1911 Mecca Double Folder issue contains unnumbered cards. This issue was one of the first to list statistics of players portrayed on the cards. Each card portrays two players, one when the card is folded, another when the card is unfolded. The card of Dougherty and Lord is considered scarce.

	NRMT	VG-E	GOOD
COMPLETE SET (50)	2700.00	1200.00	350.00
COMMON PAIR (1-50)	28.00	11.50	2.80
□ 1 F.Baker and Collins	100.00	40.00	10.00
□ 2 Barry and Lapp	28.00	11.50	2.80
□ 3 Bergen and Z.Wheat	45.00	18.00	4.50
□ 4 Blair and Hartzell	28.00	11.50	2.80
□ 5 Bresnahan and Huggins	90.00	36.00	9.00
□ 6 Bridwell and Mathewson	200.00	80.00	20.00
□ 7 Butler and Abstein	28.00	11.50	2.80
□ 8 Byrne and F.Clarke	45.00	18.00	4.50
□ 9 Chance and Evers	100.00	40.00	10.00
□ 10 Clark and Gaspar	28.00	11.50	2.80
□ 11 Cobb and S.Crawford	500.00	200.00	50.00
□ 12 Cole and Kling	28.00	11.50	2.80
□ 13 Coombs and Thomas	28.00	11.50	2.80
□ 14 Daubert and Rucker	28.00	11.50	2.80
□ 15 Dougherty and Lord	250.00	100.00	25.00
□ 16 Dooin and Titus	28.00	11.50	2.80
□ 17 Downie and Baker	28.00	11.50	2.80
□ 18 Dygert and Seymour	28.00	11.50	2.80
□ 19 Elberfeld and McBride	28.00	11.50	2.80
□ 20 Falkenberg and Lajoie	90.00	36.00	9.00
□ 21 Fitzpatrick , Killian	28.00	11.50	2.80
□ 22 Gardner and Speaker	90.00	36.00	9.00
□ 23 Gibson and Leach	28.00	11.50	2.80
□ 24 Graham and Mattern	28.00	11.50	2.80
□ 25 Hauser and Lush	28.00	11.50	2.80
□ 26 Herzog and Miller	28.00	11.50	2.80
□ 27 Hinchman and Hickman	28.00	11.50	2.80
□ 28 Hofman and M.Brown	45.00	18.00	4.50
□ 29 Jennings and Summers	45.00	18.00	4.50
□ 30 Johnson and Ford	28.00	11.50	2.80
□ 31 McCarty and McGinnity	45.00	18.00	4.50
□ 32 McGlyn and Barrett	28.00	11.50	2.80
□ 33 McLean and Grant	28.00	11.50	2.80
□ 34 Merkle and Wiltse	28.00	11.50	2.80
□ 35 Meyers and Doyle	28.00	11.50	2.80
□ 36 Moore and Lobert	28.00	11.50	2.80
□ 37 Odwell and Downs	28.00	11.50	2.80
□ 38 Oldring and Bender	45.00	18.00	4.50
□ 39 Payne and Walsh	45.00	18.00	4.50
□ 40 Simon and Leifield	28.00	11.50	2.80
□ 41 Starr and McCabe	28.00	11.50	2.80
□ 42 Stephens and LaPorte	28.00	11.50	2.80
□ 43 Stovall and Turner	28.00	11.50	2.80
□ 44 Street and W.Johnson	200.00	80.00	20.00
□ 45 Stroud and Donovan	28.00	11.50	2.80
□ 46 Sweeney and Chase	28.00	11.50	2.80
□ 47 Thoney and Cicotte	28.00	11.50	2.80
□ 48 Wallace and Lake	45.00	18.00	4.50
□ 49 Ward and Foster	28.00	11.50	2.80
□ 50 Williams and Woodruff	28.00	11.50	2.80

1912 T202 Triple Folders

The cards in this 134-card set measure 2 1/4" by 5 1/4". The 1912 T202 Hassan Triple Folder issue is perhaps the most ingenious baseball card ever issued. The two end cards of each panel are full color, T205-like individual cards whereas the black and white center panel pictures an action photo or portrait. The end cards can be folded across the center panel and stored in this manner. Seventy-six different center panels are known to exist; however, many of the center panels contain more than one combination of end cards. The center panel titles are listed below in alphabetical order while the different combinations of end cards are listed below each center panel as they appear left to right on the front of the card. A total of 132 different card fronts exist. The set price below includes all panel and player combinations listed in the checklist. Back color variations (red or black) also exist. The Birmingham's Home Run card is difficult to obtain as are other cards whose center panel exists with but one combination of end cards. The Devlin with Mathewson end panels on numbers 29A and 74C picture Devlin as a Giant. Devlin is pictured as a Rustler on 29B and 74D.

	NRMT	VG-E	GOOD
COMPLETE SET (134)	19000.00	8000.00	2500.00
COMMON PANEL (1-76)	80.00	32.00	8.00
□ 1A A Close Play at Home: Wallace-LaPorte	120.00	50.00	12.00
□ 1B A Close Play at Home: Wallace-Pelty	120.00	50.00	12.00

□ 2 A Desperate Slide: O'Leary-Cobb	800.00	320.00	80.00
□ 3A A Great Batsman: Barger-Bergen	80.00	32.00	8.00
□ 3B A Great Batsman: Rucker-Bergen	80.00	32.00	8.00
□ 4 Ambrose McConnell at Bat: Blair-Quinn	90.00	36.00	9.00
□ 5 A Wide Throw Saves Crawford: Mullin-Stanage	120.00	50.00	12.00
□ 6 Baker Gets His Man: Collins-Baker	175.00	70.00	18.00
□ 7 Birmingham Gets to Third: Johnson-Street	250.00	100.00	25.00
□ 8 Birmingham's Home Run Birmingham-Turner	250.00	100.00	25.00
□ 9 Bush Just Misses Austin: Moran-Magee	90.00	36.00	9.00
□ 10A Carrigan Blocks His Man: Gaspar-McLean	80.00	32.00	8.00
□ 10B Carrigan Blocks His Man: Wagner-Carrigan	80.00	32.00	8.00
□ 11 Catching Him Napping: Oakes-Bresnahan	120.00	50.00	12.00
□ 12 Caught Asleep Off First: Bresnahan-Harmon	120.00	50.00	12.00
□ 13A Chance Beats Out a Hit: Chance-Foxen	150.00	60.00	15.00
□ 13B Chance Beats Out a Hit: McIntire-Archer	120.00	50.00	12.00
□ 13C Chance Beats Out a Hit: Overall-Archer	120.00	50.00	12.00
□ 13D Chance Beats Out a Hit: Rowan-Archer	120.00	50.00	12.00
□ 13E Chance Beats Out a Hit: Shean-Chance	150.00	60.00	15.00
□ 14A Chase Dives into Third: Chase-Wolter	90.00	36.00	9.00
□ 14B Chase Dives into Third: Gibson-Clarke	120.00	50.00	12.00
□ 14C Chase Dives into Third: Phillippe-Gibson	90.00	36.00	9.00
□ 15A Chase Gets Ball Too Late: Egan-Mitchell	90.00	36.00	9.00
□ 15B Chase Gets Ball Too Late: Wolter-Chase	90.00	36.00	9.00
□ 16A Chase Guarding First: Chase-Wolter	90.00	36.00	9.00
□ 16B Chase Guarding First: Gibson-Clarke	120.00	50.00	12.00
□ 16C Chase Guarding First: Leifield-Gibson	90.00	36.00	9.00
□ 17 Chase Ready Squeeze Play: Paskert-Magee	90.00	36.00	9.00
□ 18 Chase Safe at Third: Barry-Baker	120.00	50.00	12.00
□ 19 Chief Bender Waiting: Bender-Thomas	150.00	60.00	15.00
□ 20 Clarke Hikes for Home: Bridwell-Kling	120.00	50.00	12.00
□ 21 Close at First: Ball-Stovall	90.00	36.00	9.00
□ 22A Close at the Plate: Walsh-Payne	120.00	50.00	12.00
□ 22B Close at the Plate: White-Payne	80.00	32.00	8.00
□ 23 Close at Third (Speaker): Wood-Speaker	200.00	80.00	20.00
□ 24 Close at Third (Wagner): Wagner-Carrigan	90.00	36.00	9.00
□ 25A Collins Easily Safe: Byrne-Clarke	120.00	50.00	12.00
□ 25B Collins Easily Safe: Collins-Baker	200.00	80.00	20.00
□ 25C Collins Easily Safe: Collins-Murphy	150.00	60.00	15.00
□ 26 Crawford About to Smash: Stanage-Summers	120.00	50.00	12.00
□ 27 Cree Rolls Home: Daubert-Hummell	90.00	36.00	9.00
□ 28 Davy Jones' Great Slide: Delahanty-Jones	90.00	36.00	9.00
□ 29A Devlin Gets His Man: Devlin (Giants)-Mathewson	600.00	240.00	60.00
□ 29B Devlin Gets His Man: Devlin (Rustlers)-Mathewson	200.00	80.00	20.00
□ 29C Devlin Gets His Man: Fletcher-Mathewson	200.00	80.00	20.00
□ 29D Devlin Gets His Man: Meyers-Mathewson	200.00	80.00	20.00
□ 30A Donlin Out at First: Camnitz-Gibson	80.00	32.00	8.00
□ 30B Donlin Out at First: Doyle-Merkle	80.00	32.00	8.00
□ 30C Donlin Out at First: Leach-Wilson	80.00	32.00	8.00
□ 30D Donlin Out at First: Magee-Dooin	80.00	32.00	8.00
□ 30E Donlin Out at First: Phillippe-Gibson	80.00	32.00	8.00
□ 31A Dooin Gets His Man: Dooin-Doolan	80.00	32.00	8.00
□ 31B Dooin Gets His Man: Lobert-Dooin	80.00	32.00	8.00
□ 31C Dooin Gets His Man: Titus-Dooin	80.00	32.00	8.00
□ 32 Easy for Larry: Doyle-Merkle	80.00	32.00	8.00
□ 33 Elberfeld Beats: Milan-Elberfeld	80.00	32.00	8.00
□ 34 Elberfeld Gets His Man: Milan-Elberfeld	80.00	32.00	8.00
□ 35 Engle in a Close Play: Speaker-Engle	150.00	60.00	15.00
□ 36A Evers Makes Safe Slide: Archer-Evers	150.00	60.00	15.00
□ 36B Evers Makes Safe Slide: Evers-Chance	175.00	70.00	18.00
□ 36C Evers Makes Safe Slide: Overall-Archer	120.00	50.00	12.00
□ 36D Evers Makes Safe Slide: Reulbach-Archer	120.00	50.00	12.00
□ 36E Evers Makes Safe Slide: Tinker-Chance	350.00	140.00	35.00
□ 37 Fast Work at Third: O'Leary-Cobb	800.00	320.00	80.00
□ 38A Ford Putting Over Spitter: Ford-Vaughn	80.00	32.00	8.00
□ 38B Ford Putting Over Spitter: Sweeney-Ford	80.00	32.00	8.00
□ 39 Good Play at Third: Moriarty-Cobb	800.00	320.00	80.00
□ 40 Grant Gets His Man: Hoblitzel-Grant	80.00	32.00	8.00
□ 41A Hal Chase Too Late: McIntyre-McConnell	90.00	36.00	9.00
□ 41B Hal Chase Too Late: Suggs-McLean	90.00	36.00	9.00
□ 42 Harry Lord at Third: Lennox-Tinker	120.00	50.00	12.00
□ 43 Hartzell Covering: Scanlon-Dahlen	90.00	36.00	9.00
□ 44 Hartzell Strikes Out: Groom-Gray	90.00	36.00	9.00
□ 45 Held at Third: Tannehill-Lord	90.00	36.00	9.00
□ 46 Jake Stahl Guarding: Cicotte-Stahl	90.00	36.00	9.00
□ 47 Jim Delahanty at Bat: Delahanty-Jones	90.00	36.00	9.00
□ 48A Just Before the Battle: Ames-Meyers	80.00	32.00	8.00
□ 48B Just Before the Battle: Bresnahan-McGraw	175.00	70.00	18.00
□ 48C Just Before the Battle: Crandall-Meyers	80.00	32.00	8.00
□ 48D Just Before the Battle: Devore-Becker	80.00	32.00	8.00
□ 48E Just Before the Battle: Fletcher-Mathewson	200.00	80.00	20.00
□ 48F Just Before the Battle: Marquard-Meyers	120.00	50.00	12.00
□ 48G Just Before the Battle: McGraw-Jennings	175.00	70.00	18.00
□ 48H Just Before the Battle: Meyers-Mathewson	200.00	80.00	20.00

☐ 48I	Just Before the Battle: Snodgrass-Murray	80.00	32.00	8.00
☐ 48J	Just Before the Battle: Wiltse-Meyers	80.00	32.00	8.00
☐ 49	Knight Catches Runner: Knight-Johnson	250.00	100.00	25.00
☐ 50A	Lobert Almost Caught: Bridwell-Kling	80.00	32.00	8.00
☐ 50B	Lobert Almost Caught: Kling-Young	150.00	60.00	15.00
☐ 50C	Lobert Almost Caught: Mattern-Kling	80.00	32.00	8.00
☐ 50D	Lobert Almost Caught: Steinfeldt-Kling	80.00	32.00	8.00
☐ 51	Lobert Gets Tenney: Lobert-Dooin	90.00	36.00	9.00
☐ 52	Lord Catches His Man: Tannehill-Lord	90.00	36.00	9.00
☐ 53	McConnell Caught: Richie-Needham	90.00	36.00	9.00
☐ 54	McIntyre at Bat: McIntrye-McConnell	90.00	36.00	9.00
☐ 55	Moriarty Spiked: Willett-Stanage	90.00	36.00	9.00
☐ 56	Nearly Caught: Bates-Bescher	120.00	50.00	12.00
☐ 57	Oldring Almost Home: Lord-Oldring	80.00	32.00	8.00
☐ 58	Schaefer on First: McBride-Milan	80.00	32.00	8.00
☐ 59	Schaefer Steals Second: McBride-Griffith	120.00	50.00	12.00
☐ 60	Scoring from Second: Lord-Oldring	90.00	36.00	9.00
☐ 61A	Scrambling Back: Barger-Bergen	80.00	32.00	8.00
☐ 61B	Scrambling Back: Wolter-Chase	80.00	32.00	8.00
☐ 62	Speaker Almost Caught: Miller-Clarke	200.00	80.00	20.00
☐ 63	Speaker Rounding Third: Wood-Speaker	300.00	120.00	30.00
☐ 64	Speaker Scores: Speaker-Engle	225.00	90.00	22.00
☐ 65	Stahl Safe: Stovall-Austin	90.00	36.00	9.00
☐ 66	Stone About to Swing: Sheckard-Schulte	90.00	36.00	9.00
☐ 67A	Sullivan Puts Up High One: Evans-Huggins	120.00	50.00	12.00
☐ 67B	Sullivan Puts Up High One: Sweeney-Ford	80.00	32.00	8.00
☐ 68A	Sweeney Gets Stahl: Ford-Vaughn	80.00	32.00	8.00
☐ 68B	Sweeney Gets Stahl: Sweeney-Ford	80.00	32.00	8.00
☐ 69	Tenney Lands Safely: Raymond-Latham	90.00	36.00	9.00
☐ 70A	The Athletic Infield: Barry-Baker	120.00	50.00	12.00
☐ 70B	The Athletic Infield: Brown-Graham	80.00	32.00	8.00
☐ 70C	The Athletic Infield: Hauser-Konetchy	80.00	32.00	8.00
☐ 70D	The Athletic Infield: Krause-Thomas	80.00	32.00	8.00
☐ 71	The Pinch Hitter: Hoblitzel-Egan	90.00	36.00	9.00
☐ 72	The Scissors Slide: Birmingham-Turner	90.00	36.00	9.00
☐ 73A	Tom Jones at Bat: Fromme-McLean	80.00	32.00	8.00
☐ 73B	Tom Jones at Bat: Gaspar-McLean	80.00	32.00	8.00
☐ 74A	Too Late for Devlin: Ames-Meyers	80.00	32.00	8.00
☐ 74B	Too Late for Devlin: Crandall-Meyers	80.00	32.00	8.00
☐ 74C	Too Late for Devlin: Devlin (Giants)-Mathewson	600.00	240.00	60.00
☐ 74D	Too Late for Devlin: Devlin (Rustlers)-Mathewson	200.00	80.00	20.00
☐ 74E	Too Late for Devlin: Marquard-Meyers	120.00	50.00	12.00
☐ 74F	Too Late for Devlin: Wiltse-Meyers	80.00	32.00	8.00
☐ 75A	Ty Cobb Steals Third: Jennings-Cobb	1200.00	450.00	90.00
☐ 75B	Ty Cobb Steals Third: Moriarty-Cobb	1000.00	400.00	90.00
☐ 75C	Ty Cobb Steals Third: Stovall-Austin	1000.00	400.00	90.00
☐ 76	Wheat Strikes Out: Dahlen-Wheat	150.00	60.00	15.00

T204 Ramly

The cards in this 121-card set measure 2" by 2 1/2". The Ramly baseball series, designated T204 in the ACC, contains unnumbered cards. This set is one of the most distinguished ever produced, containing ornate gold borders around a black and white portrait of each player. There are spelling errors, and two distinct backs, "Ramly" and "TT", are known. Much of the obverse card detail is actually embossed. The players have been alphabetized and numbered for reference in the checklist below.

		NRMT	VG-E	GOOD
	COMPLETE SET (121)	16500.00	7000.00	2300.00
	COMMON PLAYER (1-121)	125.00	50.00	12.50
☐ 1	Whitey Alperman	125.00	50.00	12.50
☐ 2	John J. Anderson	125.00	50.00	12.50
☐ 3	Jimmy Archer	125.00	50.00	12.50
☐ 4	Frank Arellanes	125.00	50.00	12.50
☐ 5	Jim Ball (Boston NL)	125.00	50.00	12.50
☐ 6	Neal Ball (N.Y. AL)	125.00	50.00	12.50
☐ 7	Dave Bancroft	250.00	100.00	25.00
☐ 8	Johnny Bates	125.00	50.00	12.50
☐ 9	Fred Beebe	125.00	50.00	12.50
☐ 10	George Bell	125.00	50.00	12.50
☐ 11	Chief Bender	250.00	100.00	25.00
☐ 12	Walter Blair	125.00	50.00	12.50
☐ 13	Cliff Blankenship	125.00	50.00	12.50
☐ 14	Frank Bowerman	125.00	50.00	12.50
☐ 15	Kitty Bransfield	125.00	50.00	12.50
☐ 16	Roger Bresnahan	250.00	100.00	25.00
☐ 17	Al Bridwell	125.00	50.00	12.50
☐ 18	Mordecai Brown	250.00	100.00	25.00
☐ 19	Fred Burchell	125.00	50.00	12.50
☐ 20	Jesse Burkett	350.00	140.00	35.00
☐ 21	Robert Byrne	125.00	50.00	12.50
☐ 22	Bill Carrigan	125.00	50.00	12.50
☐ 23	Frank Chance	300.00	120.00	30.00
☐ 24	Charles Chech	125.00	50.00	12.50
☐ 25	Eddie Cicotte	150.00	60.00	15.00
☐ 26	Otis Clymer	125.00	50.00	12.50
☐ 27	Andrew Coakley	125.00	50.00	12.50
☐ 28	Eddie Collins	350.00	140.00	35.00
☐ 29	Jimmy Collins	350.00	140.00	35.00
☐ 30	Wid Conroy	125.00	50.00	12.50
☐ 31	Jack Coombs	175.00	70.00	18.00
☐ 32	Doc Crandall	125.00	50.00	12.50
☐ 33	Lou Criger	125.00	50.00	12.50
☐ 34	Harry(Jasper) Davis	125.00	50.00	12.50
☐ 35	Art Devlin	125.00	50.00	12.50
☐ 36	Bill Dineen	125.00	50.00	12.50
☐ 37	Pat Donahue	125.00	50.00	12.50
☐ 38	Mike Donlin	125.00	50.00	12.50
☐ 39	Wild Bill Donovan	125.00	50.00	12.50
☐ 40	Gus Dorner	125.00	50.00	12.50
☐ 41	Joe Dunn	125.00	50.00	12.50
☐ 42	Norman Elberfield (sic) Elberfeld	125.00	50.00	12.50

☐ 43	Johnny Evers	300.00	120.00	30.00
☐ 44	George L. Ewing	125.00	50.00	12.50
☐ 45	George Ferguson	125.00	50.00	12.50
☐ 46	Hobe Ferris	125.00	50.00	12.50
☐ 47	James J. Freeman	125.00	50.00	12.50
☐ 48	Art Fromme	125.00	50.00	12.50
☐ 49	Bob Ganley	125.00	50.00	12.50
☐ 50	Harry (Doc) Gessler	125.00	50.00	12.50
☐ 51	George Graham	125.00	50.00	12.50
☐ 52	Clark Griffith	250.00	100.00	25.00
☐ 53	Roy Hartzell	125.00	50.00	12.50
☐ 54	Charlie Hemphill	125.00	50.00	12.50
☐ 55	Dick Hoblitzell	125.00	50.00	12.50
☐ 56	George (Del) Howard	125.00	50.00	12.50
☐ 57	Harry Howell	125.00	50.00	12.50
☐ 58	Miller Huggins	300.00	120.00	30.00
☐ 59	John Hummel	125.00	50.00	12.50
☐ 60	Walter Johnson	1000.00	400.00	90.00
☐ 61	Charles Jones	125.00	50.00	12.50
☐ 62	Michael Kahoe	125.00	50.00	12.50
☐ 63	Ed Karger	125.00	50.00	12.50
☐ 64	Willie Keeler	350.00	140.00	35.00
☐ 65	Ed Kenotchey (sic) Konetchy	125.00	50.00	12.50
☐ 66	John (Red) Kleinow	125.00	50.00	12.50
☐ 67	John Knight	125.00	50.00	12.50
☐ 68	Vive Lindeman	125.00	50.00	12.50
☐ 69	Hans Loebert (sic) Lobert	125.00	50.00	12.50
☐ 70	Harry Lord	125.00	50.00	12.50
☐ 71	Harry Lumley	125.00	50.00	12.50
☐ 72	Ernie Lush	125.00	50.00	12.50
☐ 73	Rube Manning	125.00	50.00	12.50
☐ 74	James McAleer	125.00	50.00	12.50
☐ 75	Amby McConnell	125.00	50.00	12.50
☐ 76	Moose McCormick	125.00	50.00	12.50
☐ 77	Matthew McIntyre	125.00	50.00	12.50
☐ 78	Larry McLean	125.00	50.00	12.50
☐ 79	Fred Merkle	150.00	60.00	15.00
☐ 80	Clyde Milan	125.00	50.00	12.50
☐ 81	Michael Mitchell	125.00	50.00	12.50
☐ 82	Pat Moran	125.00	50.00	12.50
☐ 83	Harry (Cy) Morgan	125.00	50.00	12.50
☐ 84	Tim Murnane	125.00	50.00	12.50
☐ 85	Danny Murphy	125.00	50.00	12.50
☐ 86	Red Murray	125.00	50.00	12.50
☐ 87	Eustace(Doc) Newton	125.00	50.00	12.50
☐ 88	Simon Nichols (sic) Nicholls	125.00	50.00	12.50
☐ 89	Harry Niles	125.00	50.00	12.50
☐ 90	Bill O'Hara	125.00	50.00	12.50
☐ 91	Charley O'Leary	125.00	50.00	12.50
☐ 92	Dode Paskert	125.00	50.00	12.50
☐ 93	Barney Pelty	125.00	50.00	12.50
☐ 94	Jack Pfeister	125.00	50.00	12.50
☐ 95	Eddie Plank	400.00	160.00	40.00
☐ 96	Jack Powell	125.00	50.00	12.50
☐ 97	Bugs Raymond	125.00	50.00	12.50
☐ 98	Thomas Reilly	125.00	50.00	12.50
☐ 99	Lewis Ritchie (sic) Richie	125.00	50.00	12.50
☐ 100	Nap Rucker	125.00	50.00	12.50
☐ 101	Ed Ruelbach (sic) Reulbach	125.00	50.00	12.50
☐ 102	Slim Sallee	125.00	50.00	12.50
☐ 103	Germany Schaefer	125.00	50.00	12.50
☐ 104	Jimmy Schekard (sic) Sheckard	125.00	50.00	12.50
☐ 105	Admiral Schlei	125.00	50.00	12.50
☐ 106	Frank Schulte	125.00	50.00	12.50
☐ 107	James Sebring	125.00	50.00	12.50
☐ 108	Bill Shipke	125.00	50.00	12.50
☐ 109	Anthony Smith	125.00	50.00	12.50
☐ 110	Tubby Spencer	125.00	50.00	12.50
☐ 111	Jake Stahl	150.00	60.00	15.00
☐ 112	Harry Steinfeldt	125.00	50.00	12.50
☐ 113	Jim Stephens	125.00	50.00	12.50
☐ 114	Gabby Street	125.00	50.00	12.50
☐ 115	William Sweeney	125.00	50.00	12.50
☐ 116	Fred Tenney	125.00	50.00	12.50
☐ 117	Ira Thomas	125.00	50.00	12.50
☐ 118	Joe Tinker	250.00	100.00	25.00
☐ 119	Bob Unglaub	125.00	50.00	12.50
☐ 120	Heine Wagner	125.00	50.00	12.50
☐ 121	Bobby Wallace	250.00	100.00	25.00

T205 Gold Border

The cards in this 208-card set measure 1 1/2" by 2 5/8". The T205 set (ACC designation), also known as the "Gold Border" set, was issued in 1911 in packages of the following cigarette brands: American Beauty, Broadleaf, Cycle, Drum, Hassan, Honest Long Cut, Piedmont, Polar Bear, Sovereign and Sweet Caporal. All the above were products of the American Tobacco Company, and the ads for the various brands appear below the biographical section on the back of each card. There are pose variations noted in the checklist (which is alphabetized and numbered for reference) and there are 12 minor league cards of a more ornate design which are somewhat scarce. The numbers below correspond to alphabetical order within each team by team nickname, i.e., Philadelphia Athletics AL (1-13), St. Louis Browns (14-20), St. Louis Cardinals (21-32), Chicago Cubs (33- 51), New York Giants (52-72), Cleveland Naps (73-78), Philadelphia Phillies (79-90), Pittsburgh Pirates (91-103), Cincinnati Reds (104-114), Boston Red Sox (115-122), Boston Rustlers (123-131), Washington Senators (132-139), Brooklyn Superbas (140-153), Detroit Tigers (154-167), Chicago White Sox (168-182), New York Yankees (183-196), and Minor Leaguers (197- 208). The gold borders of T205 cards chip easily and they are hard to find in "Mint" condition.

		NRMT	VG-E	GOOD
	COMPLETE SET (208)	19000.00	8000.00	2500.00
	COMMON PLAYERS (1-208)	50.00	20.00	5.00
☐ 1	Frank Baker	150.00	60.00	15.00
☐ 2	John J. Barry	50.00	20.00	5.00
☐ 3	Charles A. Bender	150.00	60.00	15.00
☐ 4	Edward T. Collins (mouth closed)	150.00	60.00	15.00
☐ 5	Edward T. Collins (mouth open)	300.00	120.00	30.00
☐ 6	James H. Dygert	50.00	20.00	5.00
☐ 7	Frederick T. Hartsel	50.00	20.00	5.00
☐ 8	Harry Krause	50.00	20.00	5.00
☐ 9	Pat'k J. Livingston	50.00	20.00	5.00

☐ 10	Briscoe Lord	50.00	20.00	5.00
☐ 11	Daniel Murphy	50.00	20.00	5.00
☐ 12	Reuben N. Oldring	50.00	20.00	5.00
☐ 13	Ira Thomas	50.00	20.00	5.00
☐ 14	William Bailey	50.00	20.00	5.00
☐ 15	Daniel J. Hoffman	50.00	20.00	5.00
☐ 16	Frank LaPorte	50.00	20.00	5.00
☐ 17	B. Pelty	50.00	20.00	5.00
☐ 18	George Stone	50.00	20.00	5.00
☐ 19	Roderick J. Wallace (with cap)	150.00	60.00	15.00
☐ 20	Roderick J. Wallace (without cap)	300.00	120.00	30.00
☐ 21	Roger Bresnahan (mouth closed)	150.00	60.00	15.00
☐ 22	Roger Bresnahan (mouth open)	300.00	120.00	30.00
☐ 23	Frank J. Corridon	50.00	20.00	5.00
☐ 24	Louis Evans	50.00	20.00	5.00
☐ 25	Robert Harmon (both ears)	50.00	20.00	5.00
☐ 26	Robert Harmon (left ear only)	175.00	70.00	18.00
☐ 27	Arnold J. Hauser	50.00	20.00	5.00
☐ 28	Miller Huggins	150.00	60.00	15.00
☐ 29	Edward Konetchy	50.00	20.00	5.00
☐ 30	John Lush	50.00	20.00	5.00
☐ 31	Rebel Oakes	50.00	20.00	5.00
☐ 32	Edward Phelps	50.00	20.00	5.00
☐ 33	James P. Archer	50.00	20.00	5.00
☐ 34	Mordecai Brown	150.00	60.00	15.00
☐ 35	Frank L. Chance	150.00	60.00	15.00
☐ 36	John J. Evers	150.00	60.00	15.00
☐ 37	William A. Foxen	50.00	20.00	5.00
☐ 38	George F. Graham	350.00	140.00	35.00
☐ 39	John Kling	50.00	20.00	5.00
☐ 40	Floyd M. Kroh	50.00	20.00	5.00
☐ 41	Harry McIntire	50.00	20.00	5.00
☐ 42	Thomas J. Needham	50.00	20.00	5.00
☐ 43	Orval Overall	50.00	20.00	5.00
☐ 44	John A. Pfiester	50.00	20.00	5.00
☐ 45	Edward M. Reulbach	50.00	20.00	5.00
☐ 46	Lewis Richie	50.00	20.00	5.00
☐ 47	Frank M. Schulte	50.00	20.00	5.00
☐ 48	David Shean (Cubs)	350.00	140.00	35.00
☐ 49	James T. Sheckard	50.00	20.00	5.00
☐ 50	Harry Steinfeldt	50.00	20.00	5.00
☐ 51	Joseph B. Tinker	150.00	60.00	15.00
☐ 52	Leon Ames	50.00	20.00	5.00
☐ 53	Beals Becker	50.00	20.00	5.00
☐ 54	Albert Bridwell	50.00	20.00	5.00
☐ 55	Otis Crandall	50.00	20.00	5.00
☐ 56	Arthur Devlin	50.00	20.00	5.00
☐ 57	Joshua Devore	50.00	20.00	5.00
☐ 58	W.R. Dickson	50.00	20.00	5.00
☐ 59	Lawrence Doyle	50.00	20.00	5.00
☐ 60	Arthur Fletcher	50.00	20.00	5.00
☐ 61	W.A. Latham	50.00	20.00	5.00
☐ 62	Richard Marquard	150.00	60.00	15.00
☐ 63	Christy Mathewson	400.00	160.00	40.00
☐ 64	John J. McGraw	200.00	80.00	20.00
☐ 65	Fred Merkle	65.00	26.00	6.50
☐ 66	John T. Meyers	50.00	20.00	5.00
☐ 67	John J. Murray	50.00	20.00	5.00
☐ 68	Arthur L. Raymond	175.00	70.00	18.00
☐ 69	George H. Schlei	50.00	20.00	5.00
☐ 70	Fred C. Snodgrass	50.00	20.00	5.00
☐ 71	George Wiltse (both ears)	50.00	20.00	5.00
☐ 72	George Wiltse (right ear only)	175.00	70.00	18.00
☐ 73	Neal Ball	50.00	20.00	5.00
☐ 74	Joseph Birmingham	50.00	20.00	5.00
☐ 75	Addie Joss	350.00	140.00	35.00
☐ 76	George T. Stovall	50.00	20.00	5.00
☐ 77	Terence Turner	175.00	70.00	18.00
☐ 78	Denton T. Young	350.00	140.00	35.00
☐ 79	John W. Bates	50.00	20.00	5.00
☐ 80	Wm. E. Bransfield	50.00	20.00	5.00
☐ 81	Charles S. Dooin	50.00	20.00	5.00
☐ 82	Michael Doolan	50.00	20.00	5.00
☐ 83	Robert Ewing	50.00	20.00	5.00
☐ 84	Fred Jacklitsch	50.00	20.00	5.00
☐ 85	John Lobert	50.00	20.00	5.00
☐ 86	Sherwood R. Magee	50.00	20.00	5.00
☐ 87	Patrick J. Moran	50.00	20.00	5.00
☐ 88	George Paskert	50.00	20.00	5.00
☐ 89	John A. Rowan	175.00	70.00	18.00
☐ 90	John Titus	50.00	20.00	5.00
☐ 91	Robert Byrne	50.00	20.00	5.00
☐ 92	Howard Camnitz	50.00	20.00	5.00
☐ 93	Fred Clarke	150.00	60.00	15.00
☐ 94	John Flynn	50.00	20.00	5.00
☐ 95	George Gibson	50.00	20.00	5.00
☐ 96	Thomas W. Leach	50.00	20.00	5.00
☐ 97	Sam Leever	50.00	20.00	5.00
☐ 98	Albert P. Leifield	50.00	20.00	5.00
☐ 99	Nicholas Maddox	50.00	20.00	5.00
☐ 100	John D. Miller	50.00	20.00	5.00
☐ 101	Charles Phillippe	65.00	26.00	6.50
☐ 102	Kirb White	175.00	70.00	18.00
☐ 103	J. Owen Wilson	50.00	20.00	5.00
☐ 104	Robert H. Bescher	50.00	20.00	5.00
☐ 105	Thomas W. Downey	50.00	20.00	5.00
☐ 106	Richard J. Egan	50.00	20.00	5.00
☐ 107	Arthur Fromme	50.00	20.00	5.00
☐ 108	Harry L. Gaspar	50.00	20.00	5.00
☐ 109	Edward L. Grant	175.00	70.00	18.00
☐ 110	Clark Griffith	150.00	60.00	15.00
☐ 111	Richard Hoblitzell	50.00	20.00	5.00
☐ 112	John B. McLean	50.00	20.00	5.00
☐ 113	Michael Mitchell	50.00	20.00	5.00
☐ 114	George Suggs	175.00	70.00	18.00
☐ 115	William Carrigan	50.00	20.00	5.00
☐ 116	Edward V. Cicotte	65.00	26.00	6.50
☐ 117	Clyde Engle	50.00	20.00	5.00
☐ 118	Edward Karger	175.00	70.00	18.00
☐ 119	John Kleinow	175.00	70.00	18.00
☐ 120	Tris Speaker	300.00	120.00	30.00
☐ 121	Jacob G. Stahl	65.00	26.00	6.50
☐ 122	Charles Wagner	175.00	70.00	18.00
☐ 123	Edward J. Abbaticchio	50.00	20.00	5.00
☐ 124	Frederick T. Beck	50.00	20.00	5.00
☐ 125	G.C. Ferguson	50.00	20.00	5.00
☐ 126	Wilbur Good	50.00	20.00	5.00
☐ 127	George F. Graham	50.00	20.00	5.00
☐ 128	Charles L. Herzog	50.00	20.00	5.00
☐ 129	A.A. Mattern	50.00	20.00	5.00
☐ 130	Bayard H. Sharpe	50.00	20.00	5.00
☐ 131	David Shean (Boston)	50.00	20.00	5.00
☐ 132	Norman Elberfeld	50.00	20.00	5.00
☐ 133	Gray	50.00	20.00	5.00
☐ 134	Robert Groom	50.00	20.00	5.00
☐ 135	Walter Johnson	650.00	260.00	65.00
☐ 136	George F. McBride	50.00	20.00	5.00
☐ 137	J. Clyde Milan	50.00	20.00	5.00
☐ 138	Herman Schaefer	50.00	20.00	5.00
☐ 139	Charles E. Street	50.00	20.00	5.00
☐ 140	Edward B. Barger (full B)	50.00	20.00	5.00
☐ 141	Edward B. Barger (part B)	175.00	70.00	18.00
☐ 142	George G. Bell	50.00	20.00	5.00
☐ 143	William Bergen	50.00	20.00	5.00
☐ 144	William Dahlen	175.00	70.00	18.00
☐ 145	Jacob Daubert	65.00	26.00	6.50
☐ 146	John E. Hummell	50.00	20.00	5.00
☐ 147	Edgar Lennox	50.00	20.00	5.00
☐ 148	Pryor McElveen	50.00	20.00	5.00
☐ 149	G.N. Rucker	50.00	20.00	5.00
☐ 150	W.D. Scanlan	175.00	70.00	18.00
☐ 151	Tony Smith	50.00	20.00	5.00
☐ 152	Zach D. Wheat	150.00	60.00	15.00
☐ 153	Irvin K. Wilhelm	175.00	70.00	18.00
☐ 154	Tyrus Raymond Cobb	1350.00	500.00	125.00
☐ 155	James Delahanty	50.00	20.00	5.00
☐ 156	Hugh Jennings	150.00	60.00	15.00
☐ 157	David Jones	50.00	20.00	5.00
☐ 158	Thomas Jones	50.00	20.00	5.00
☐ 159	Edward Killian	50.00	20.00	5.00
☐ 160	George Moriarity	50.00	20.00	5.00
☐ 161	George J. Mullin	50.00	20.00	5.00
☐ 162	Charles O'Leary	50.00	20.00	5.00
☐ 163	Charles Schmidt	50.00	20.00	5.00
☐ 164	George Simmons	50.00	20.00	5.00
☐ 165	Oscar Stanage	50.00	20.00	5.00
☐ 166	Edgar Summers	50.00	20.00	5.00
☐ 167	Edgar Willett	50.00	20.00	5.00
☐ 168	Russell Blackburne	50.00	20.00	5.00
☐ 169	J. Donohue	125.00	50.00	12.50
☐ 170A	Patsy Dougherty (white stocking)	100.00	40.00	10.00
☐ 170B	Patsy Dougherty (red stocking)	75.00	30.00	7.50
☐ 171	Hugh Duffy	200.00	80.00	20.00
☐ 172	Frank Lang	50.00	20.00	5.00
☐ 173	Harry D. Lord	50.00	20.00	5.00
☐ 174	Ambrose McConnell	50.00	20.00	5.00
☐ 175	Matthew McIntyre	50.00	20.00	5.00
☐ 176	Frederick Olmstead	50.00	20.00	5.00
☐ 177	F. Parent	50.00	20.00	5.00
☐ 178	Fred Payne	50.00	20.00	5.00
☐ 179	James Scott	50.00	20.00	5.00
☐ 180	Lee Ford Tannehill	50.00	20.00	5.00
☐ 181	Edward Walsh	250.00	100.00	25.00
☐ 182	G.H. White	50.00	20.00	5.00
☐ 183	James Austin	50.00	20.00	5.00
☐ 184	Harold W. Chase (Chase only)	250.00	100.00	25.00
☐ 185	Harold W. Chase (Hal Chase)	65.00	26.00	6.50

☐ 186	Louis Criger	50.00	20.00	5.00
☐ 187	Ray Fisher	175.00	70.00	18.00
☐ 188	Russell Ford (dark cap)	50.00	20.00	5.00
☐ 189	Russell Ford (light cap)	175.00	70.00	18.00
☐ 190	Earl Gardner	50.00	20.00	5.00
☐ 191	Charles Hemphill	50.00	20.00	5.00
☐ 192	Jack Knight	50.00	20.00	5.00
☐ 193	John Quinn	50.00	20.00	5.00
☐ 194	Edward Sweeney	175.00	70.00	18.00
☐ 195	James Vaughn	175.00	70.00	18.00
☐ 196	Harry Wolter	50.00	20.00	5.00
☐ 197	Dr.Merle T. Adkins: Baltimore	150.00	60.00	15.00
☐ 198	John Dunn: Baltimore	175.00	70.00	18.00
☐ 199	George Merritt: Buffalo	150.00	60.00	15.00
☐ 200	Charles Hanford: Jersey City	150.00	60.00	15.00
☐ 201	Forrest D. Cady: Newark	150.00	60.00	15.00
☐ 202	James Frick: Newark	150.00	60.00	15.00
☐ 203	Wyatt Lee: Newark	150.00	60.00	15.00
☐ 204	Lewis McAllister: Newark	150.00	60.00	15.00
☐ 205	John Nee: Newark	150.00	60.00	15.00
☐ 206	James Collins: Providence	300.00	120.00	30.00
☐ 207	James Phelan: Providence	150.00	60.00	15.00
☐ 208	Henry Batch: Rochester	150.00	60.00	15.00

T206 White Border

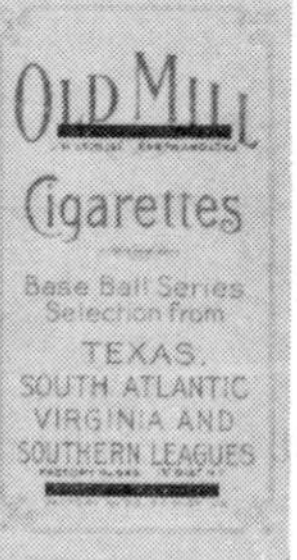

The cards in this 523-card set measure 1 1/2" by 2 5/8". The T206 set was and is the most popular of all the tobacco issues. The set was issued from 1909 to 1911 with sixteen different brands of cigarettes: American Beauty, Broadleaf, Cycle, Carolina Brights, Drum, El Principe de Gales, Hindu, Lenox, Old Mill, Piedmont, Polar Bear, Sovereign, Sweet Caporal, Tolstoi, Ty Cobb and Uzit. The Ty Cobb brand back is very scarce. The minor league cards are supposedly slightly more difficult to obtain than the cards of the major leaguers, with the Southern League player cards being the most difficult. Minor League players were obtained from the American Association and the Eastern league. Southern League players were obtained from a variety of leagues including the following: South Atlantic League, Southern League, Texas League, and Virginia League. The set price below does not include ultra-expensive Wagner, Plank, Magie error, or Doyle variation.

	NRMT	VG-E	GOOD
COMPLETE SET (520)	37000.	13000.	4000.
COMMON MAJORS (1-389)	35.00	14.00	3.50
COMMON MINORS (390-475)	27.00	11.00	2.70
COMMON SOUTHERN(476-523)	100.00	40.00	10.00

No.	Player	NRMT	VG-E	GOOD
☐ 1	Abbaticchio: Pitt. Batting follow thru	35.00	14.00	3.50
☐ 2	Abbaticchio: Pitt. Batting waiting pitch	40.00	16.00	4.00
☐ 3	Abstein: Pitt.	35.00	14.00	3.50
☐ 4	Alperman: Brooklyn	40.00	16.00	4.00
☐ 5	Ames: Giants, Port.	40.00	16.00	4.00
☐ 6	Ames: Giants, Hands over head	35.00	14.00	3.50
☐ 7	Ames: Giants, Hands in front of chest	40.00	16.00	4.00
☐ 8	Arellanes: Boston AL	35.00	14.00	3.50
☐ 9	Atz: Chicago AL	35.00	14.00	3.50
☐ 10	Baker: Phila. AL	125.00	50.00	12.50
☐ 11	Ball: Cleveland	35.00	14.00	3.50
☐ 12	Ball: N.Y. AL	40.00	16.00	4.00
☐ 13	Barbeau: St.L. NL	35.00	14.00	3.50
☐ 14	Barry: Phila. AL	35.00	14.00	3.50
☐ 15	Bates: Boston NL	40.00	16.00	4.00
☐ 16	Beaumont: Boston NL	40.00	16.00	4.00
☐ 17	Beck: Boston NL	35.00	14.00	3.50
☐ 18	Becker: Boston NL	35.00	14.00	3.50
☐ 19	Bell: Brooklyn pitching, follow thru)	35.00	14.00	3.50
☐ 20	Bell: Brooklyn, Hands over head	40.00	16.00	4.00
☐ 21	Bender: Phila. AL Portrait	150.00	60.00	15.00
☐ 22	Bender: Phila. AL (pitching) trees	125.00	50.00	12.50
☐ 23	Bender: Phila. AL (pitching) no trees	125.00	50.00	12.50
☐ 24	Bergen: Brooklyn, Catching	35.00	14.00	3.50
☐ 25	Bergen: Brooklyn, Batting	40.00	16.00	4.00
☐ 26	Berger: Cleveland	35.00	14.00	3.50
☐ 27	Bescher: Cinc., Catching fly ball	35.00	14.00	3.50
☐ 28	Bescher: Cinc. Portrait	35.00	14.00	3.50
☐ 29	Birmingham: Cleve.	40.00	16.00	4.00
☐ 30	Bliss: St.L. NL	35.00	14.00	3.50
☐ 31	Bowerman: Bost. NL	40.00	16.00	4.00
☐ 32	Bradley: Cleveland, Portrait	40.00	16.00	4.00
☐ 33	Bradley: Cleveland, Batting	35.00	14.00	3.50
☐ 34	Bransfield: Phila. NL	40.00	16.00	4.00
☐ 35	Bresnahan: St.L. NL, Portrait	150.00	60.00	15.00
☐ 36	Bresnahan: St.L. NL, Batting	125.00	50.00	12.50
☐ 37	Bridwell: N.Y. NL, Portrait	40.00	16.00	4.00
☐ 38	Bridwell: N.Y. NL, Wearing sweater	35.00	14.00	3.50
☐ 39	G. Brown (sic): Chicago NL	100.00	40.00	10.00
☐ 40	G. Brown (sic): Washington	350.00	140.00	35.00
☐ 41	M. Brown: Chicago NL Portrait	150.00	60.00	15.00
☐ 42	M. Brown: Chicago NL Chicago down front of shirt	125.00	50.00	12.50
☐ 43	M. Brown: Chicago NL, Cubs across chest	200.00	80.00	20.00
☐ 44	Burch: Brooklyn, Fielding	35.00	14.00	3.50
☐ 45	Burch: Brooklyn, Batting	100.00	40.00	10.00
☐ 46	Burns: Chicago AL	35.00	14.00	3.50
☐ 47	Bush: Detroit	35.00	14.00	3.50
☐ 48	Byrne: St.L. NL	35.00	14.00	3.50

☐ 49	Camnitz: Pitt., Arms folded over chest	40.00	16.00	4.00
☐ 50	Camnitz: Pitt., Hands over head	35.00	14.00	3.50
☐ 51	Camnitz: Pitt., Throwing	35.00	14.00	3.50
☐ 52	Campbell: Cinc.	35.00	14.00	3.50
☐ 53	Carrigan: Boston AL	35.00	14.00	3.50
☐ 54	Chance: Chicago NL, Cubs across chest	150.00	60.00	15.00
☐ 55	Chance: Chicago NL, Chicago down front of shirt	125.00	50.00	12.50
☐ 56	Chance: Chicago NL, Batting	125.00	50.00	12.50
☐ 57	Charles: St.L. NL	35.00	14.00	3.50
☐ 58	Chase: N.Y. AL, Port. blue bkgd.	60.00	24.00	6.00
☐ 59	Chase: N.Y. AL, Port., pink bkgd.	125.00	50.00	12.50
☐ 60	Chase: N.Y. AL, Holding cup	60.00	24.00	6.00
☐ 61	Chase: N.Y. AL, Throwing, dark cap	60.00	24.00	6.00
☐ 62	Chase: N.Y. AL, Throwing, white cap	125.00	50.00	12.50
☐ 63	Chesbro: N.Y. AL	200.00	80.00	20.00
☐ 64	Cicotte: Boston AL	60.00	24.00	6.00
☐ 65	Clarke: Pitt., Portrait	150.00	60.00	15.00
☐ 66	F. Clarke: Pitt.	125.00	50.00	12.50
☐ 67	J.J. Clarke: Cleve.	40.00	16.00	4.00
☐ 68	Cobb: Detroit, Port., red bkgd.	850.00	340.00	85.00
☐ 69	Cobb: Detroit, Port. green background	1500.00	550.00	125.00
☐ 70	Cobb: Detroit, Bat on shoulder	900.00	360.00	90.00
☐ 71	Cobb: Detroit, Bat away from shoulder	850.00	340.00	85.00
☐ 72	Collins: Phila. AL	125.00	50.00	12.50
☐ 73	Conroy: Washington, Fielding	40.00	16.00	4.00
☐ 74	Conroy: Wash., Bat on shoulder	35.00	14.00	3.50
☐ 75	Covaleski: Phil. NL (Harry)	40.00	16.00	4.00
☐ 76	Crandall: N.Y. NL, without cap	40.00	16.00	4.00
☐ 77	Crandall: N.Y. NL, sweater and cap	35.00	14.00	3.50
☐ 78	Crawford: Detroit, Batting	125.00	50.00	12.50
☐ 79	Crawford: Detroit, Throwing	150.00	60.00	15.00
☐ 80	Cree: N.Y. AL	35.00	14.00	3.50
☐ 81	Criger: St.L. AL	40.00	16.00	4.00
☐ 82	Criss: St.L. AL	40.00	16.00	4.00
☐ 83	Dahlen: Brooklyn	175.00	70.00	18.00
☐ 84	Dahlen: Bost. NL	60.00	24.00	6.00
☐ 85	Davis: Phila. AL	35.00	14.00	3.50
☐ 86	G. Davis: Chicago AL	40.00	16.00	4.00
☐ 87	H. Davis: Phila. AL	40.00	16.00	4.00
☐ 88	Delehanty: Wash.	40.00	16.00	4.00
☐ 89	Demmitt: St.L. AL	2250.00	750.00	200.00
☐ 90	Demmitt: N.Y. AL	35.00	14.00	3.50
☐ 91	Devlin: N.Y. NL	40.00	16.00	4.00
☐ 92	Devore: N.Y. NL	35.00	14.00	3.50
☐ 93	Dineen: St.L. AL	35.00	14.00	3.50
☐ 94	Donlin: N.Y. NL, Fielding	75.00	30.00	7.50
☐ 95	Donlin: N.Y. NL, Sitting	40.00	16.00	4.00
☐ 96	Donlin: N.Y. NL, Batting	35.00	14.00	3.50
☐ 97	Donohue: Chicago AL	40.00	16.00	4.00
☐ 98	Donovan: Detroit, Portrait	40.00	16.00	4.00
☐ 99	Donovan: Detroit, Throwing	35.00	14.00	3.50
☐ 100	Dooin: Phila. NL	40.00	16.00	4.00
☐ 101	Doolan: Phila. NL, Fielding	35.00	14.00	3.50
☐ 102	Doolan: Phila. NL, Batting	35.00	14.00	3.50
☐ 103	Doolin (sic, Doolan): Phila. NL,	40.00	16.00	4.00
☐ 104	Dougherty: Chic. AL, Portrait	40.00	16.00	4.00
☐ 105	Dougherty: Chic. AL, Fielding	35.00	14.00	3.50
☐ 106	Downey: Cinc., Batting	35.00	14.00	3.50
☐ 107	Downey: Cinc., Fielding	35.00	14.00	3.50
☐ 108A	Doyle: N.Y. (hands over head)	40.00	16.00	4.00
☐ 108B	Doyle: N.Y. NAT'L (hands over head)	15000.00	6500.00	1250.00
☐ 109	Doyle: N.Y. NL, Sweater	35.00	14.00	3.50
☐ 110	Doyle: N.Y. NL, Throwing	40.00	16.00	4.00
☐ 111	Doyle: N.Y. NL, Bat on shoulder	35.00	14.00	3.50
☐ 112	Dubuc: Cin.	35.00	14.00	3.50
☐ 113	Duffy: Chicago AL	125.00	50.00	12.50
☐ 114	Dunn: Brooklyn	35.00	14.00	3.50
☐ 115	Durham: N.Y. NL	40.00	16.00	4.00
☐ 116	Dygert: Phila. AL	35.00	14.00	3.50
☐ 117	Easterly: Cleveland	35.00	14.00	3.50
☐ 118	Egan: Cinc.	35.00	14.00	3.50
☐ 119	Elberfeld: Wash., Fielding	35.00	14.00	3.50
☐ 120	Elberfeld: Wash., Portrait	750.00	300.00	75.00
☐ 121	Elberfeld: N.Y. AL, Portrait	40.00	16.00	4.00
☐ 122	Engle: N.Y. AL	35.00	14.00	3.50
☐ 123	Evans: St.L. NL	35.00	14.00	3.50
☐ 124	Evers: Chicago NL, Portrait	150.00	60.00	15.00
☐ 125	Evers: Chicago NL, Cubs across chest	200.00	80.00	20.00
☐ 126	Evers: Chicago NL, Chicago down front of shirt	125.00	50.00	12.50
☐ 127	Ewing: Cinc.	40.00	16.00	4.00
☐ 128	Ferguson: Boston NL	35.00	14.00	3.50
☐ 129	Ferris: St.L. AL	40.00	16.00	4.00
☐ 130	Fiene: Chicago AL, Portrait	35.00	14.00	3.50
☐ 131	Fiene: Chicago AL, Throwing	35.00	14.00	3.50
☐ 132	Fletcher: N.Y. NL	35.00	14.00	3.50
☐ 133	Flick: Cleveland	175.00	70.00	18.00
☐ 134	Ford: N.Y. AL	35.00	14.00	3.50
☐ 135	Frill: N.Y. AL	35.00	14.00	3.50
☐ 136	Fromme: Cinc.	35.00	14.00	3.50
☐ 137	Gandil: Chicago AL	60.00	24.00	6.00
☐ 138	Ganley: Washington	40.00	16.00	4.00
☐ 139	Gasper: Cinc.	35.00	14.00	3.50
☐ 140	Geyer: St.L. NL	35.00	14.00	3.50
☐ 141	Gibson: Pitt.	40.00	16.00	4.00
☐ 142	Gilbert: St.L. NL	40.00	16.00	4.00
☐ 143	Goode (sic): Cleve.	40.00	16.00	4.00
☐ 144	Graham: Boston NL	35.00	14.00	3.50
☐ 145	Graham: St.L. AL	35.00	14.00	3.50
☐ 146	Gray: Washington	35.00	14.00	3.50
☐ 147	Griffith: Cinc., Portrait	150.00	60.00	15.00
☐ 148	Griffith: Cinc., Batting	125.00	50.00	12.50
☐ 149	Groom: Washington	35.00	14.00	3.50
☐ 150	Hahn: Chicago AL	40.00	16.00	4.00
☐ 151	Hartsel: Phila. AL	35.00	14.00	3.50
☐ 152	Hemphill: N.Y. AL	40.00	16.00	4.00
☐ 153	Herzog : N.Y. NL	40.00	16.00	4.00
☐ 154	Herzog: Boston NL	35.00	14.00	3.50
☐ 155	Hinchman: Cleveland	40.00	16.00	4.00
☐ 156	Hoblitzell: Cinc.	35.00	14.00	3.50
☐ 157	Hoffman: St.L. AL	35.00	14.00	3.50
☐ 158	Hofman: Chicago NL	35.00	14.00	3.50
☐ 159	Howard: Chicago NL	35.00	14.00	3.50
☐ 160	Howell: St.L. AL, Portrait	35.00	14.00	3.50
☐ 161	Howell: St.L. AL, Left hand on hip	35.00	14.00	3.50
☐ 162	Huggins: Cinc., Portrait	150.00	60.00	15.00
☐ 163	Huggins: Cinc., Hands to mouth	125.00	50.00	12.50
☐ 164	Hulswitt: St.L. NL	35.00	14.00	3.50
☐ 165	Hummel: Brooklyn	35.00	14.00	3.50
☐ 166	Hunter: Brooklyn	35.00	14.00	3.50
☐ 167	Isbell: Chicago AL	40.00	16.00	4.00
☐ 168	Jacklitsch: Phila.NL	40.00	16.00	4.00
☐ 169	Jennings: Detroit, Portrait	150.00	60.00	15.00
☐ 170	Jennings: Detroit, Yelling	125.00	50.00	12.50
☐ 171	Jennings: Detroit, Dancing for joy	125.00	50.00	12.50
☐ 172	Johnson: Washington, Portrait	450.00	180.00	45.00
☐ 173	Johnson: Washington, Ready to pitch	400.00	160.00	40.00
☐ 174	Jones: St.L. AL	40.00	16.00	4.00
☐ 175	Jones: Detroit	35.00	14.00	3.50
☐ 176	F. Jones: Chic. AL,	40.00	16.00	4.00

	Portrait			
☐ 177	F. Jones: Chic. AL, Hands on hips	40.00	16.00	4.00
☐ 178	Jordan: Brooklyn, Portrait	40.00	16.00	4.00
☐ 179	Jordan: Brooklyn, Batting	35.00	14.00	3.50
☐ 180	Joss: Cleveland, Portrait	200.00	80.00	20.00
☐ 181	Joss: Cleveland, Ready to pitch	150.00	60.00	15.00
☐ 182	Karger: Cinc.	40.00	16.00	4.00
☐ 183	Keeler: N.Y. AL, Portrait	200.00	80.00	20.00
☐ 184	Keeler: N.Y. AL, Batting	175.00	70.00	18.00
☐ 185	Killian: Detroit, Portrait	40.00	16.00	4.00
☐ 186	Killian: Detroit, Pitching	35.00	14.00	3.50
☐ 187	Kleinow: N.Y. AL, Batting	40.00	16.00	4.00
☐ 188	Kleinow: N.Y. AL, Catching	35.00	14.00	3.50
☐ 189	Kleinow: Bost. AL, Catching	200.00	80.00	20.00
☐ 190	Kling: Chicago NL	40.00	16.00	4.00
☐ 191	Knabe: Phila. NL	35.00	14.00	3.50
☐ 192	Knight: N.Y. AL, Portrait	35.00	14.00	3.50
☐ 193	Knight: N.Y. AL, Batting	35.00	14.00	3.50
☐ 194	Konetchy: St.L. NL, Awaiting low ball	35.00	14.00	3.50
☐ 195	Konetchy: St.L. NL, Glove above head	40.00	16.00	4.00
☐ 196	Krause: Phila. AL, Portrait	35.00	14.00	3.50
☐ 197	Krause: Phila. AL, Pitching	35.00	14.00	3.50
☐ 198	Kroh: Chicago NL	35.00	14.00	3.50
☐ 199	Lajoie: Cleveland, Portrait	225.00	90.00	22.00
☐ 200	Lajoie: Cleveland, Batting	175.00	70.00	18.00
☐ 201	Lajoie: Cleveland, Throwing	225.00	90.00	22.00
☐ 202	Lake: N.Y. AL	40.00	16.00	4.00
☐ 203	Lake: St.L. AL, Hands over head	35.00	14.00	3.50
☐ 204	Lake: St.L. AL, Throwing	35.00	14.00	3.50
☐ 205	LaPorte: N.Y. AL	35.00	14.00	3.50
☐ 206	Latham: N.Y. NL	35.00	14.00	3.50
☐ 207	Leach: Pitt., Portrait	40.00	16.00	4.00
☐ 208	Leach: Pitt., In fielding position	35.00	14.00	3.50
☐ 209	Leifield: Pitt., Batting	35.00	14.00	3.50
☐ 210	Leifield: Pitt., Hands behind head	40.00	16.00	4.00
☐ 211	Lennox: Brooklyn	35.00	14.00	3.50
☐ 212	Liebhardt: Cleve.	40.00	16.00	4.00
☐ 213	Lindaman: Boston NL	60.00	24.00	6.00
☐ 214	Livingstone: Phila.AL	35.00	14.00	3.50
☐ 215	Lobert: Cinc.	40.00	16.00	4.00
☐ 216	Lord: Bost. AL	35.00	14.00	3.50
☐ 217	Lumley: Brooklyn	40.00	16.00	4.00
☐ 218	Lundgren: Chicago NL	250.00	100.00	25.00
☐ 219	Maddox: Pitt.	35.00	14.00	3.50
☐ 220	Magee: Phila. NL, Portrait	40.00	16.00	4.00
☐ 221	Magee: Phila. NL, Batting	35.00	14.00	3.50
☐ 222	Magie: Phila. NL (sic) Portrait, name misspelled	7000.00	3000.00	800.00
☐ 223	Manning: N.Y. AL, Batting	40.00	16.00	4.00
☐ 224	Manning: N.Y. AL, Hands over head	35.00	14.00	3.50
☐ 225	Marquard: N.Y. NL, Portrait	150.00	60.00	15.00
☐ 226	Marquard: N.Y. NL, Pitching	125.00	50.00	12.50
☐ 227	Marquard: N.Y. NL, Standing	150.00	60.00	15.00
☐ 228	Marshall: Brooklyn	35.00	14.00	3.50
☐ 229	Mathewson: N.Y. NL, Portrait	400.00	160.00	40.00
☐ 230	Mathewson: N.Y. NL, Pitching, white cap	400.00	160.00	40.00
☐ 231	Mathewson: N.Y. NL, Pitching, dark cap	350.00	140.00	35.00
☐ 232	Mattern: Boston NL	35.00	14.00	3.50
☐ 233	McAleese: St.L. AL	35.00	14.00	3.50
☐ 234	McBride: Washington	35.00	14.00	3.50
☐ 235	McCormick: N.Y. NL	35.00	14.00	3.50
☐ 236	McElveen: Brooklyn	35.00	14.00	3.50
☐ 237	McGraw: N.Y. NL, Portrait, no cap	225.00	90.00	22.00
☐ 238	McGraw: N.Y. NL, Wearing sweater	150.00	60.00	15.00
☐ 239	McGraw: N.Y. NL, pointing	175.00	70.00	18.00
☐ 240	McGraw: N.Y. NL, Glove on hip	175.00	70.00	18.00
☐ 241	McIntyre: Detroit	35.00	14.00	3.50
☐ 242	McIntyre: Brooklyn	40.00	16.00	4.00
☐ 243	McIntyre: Brooklyn and Chicago NL	35.00	14.00	3.50
☐ 244	McLean: Cinc.	35.00	14.00	3.50
☐ 245	McQuillan: Phila. NL, Throwing	40.00	16.00	4.00
☐ 246	McQuillan: Phila. NL, Batting	35.00	14.00	3.50
☐ 247	Merkle: N.Y. NL, Portrait	50.00	20.00	5.00
☐ 248	Merkle: N.Y. NL, Throwing	40.00	16.00	4.00
☐ 249	Meyers: N.Y. NL	35.00	14.00	3.50
☐ 250	Milan: Washington	35.00	14.00	3.50
☐ 251	Miller: Pitt.	35.00	14.00	3.50
☐ 252	Mitchell: Cinc.	35.00	14.00	3.50
☐ 253	Moran: Chicago NL	35.00	14.00	3.50
☐ 254	Moriarty: Detroit	35.00	14.00	3.50
☐ 255	Mowrey: Cinc.	35.00	14.00	3.50
☐ 256	Mullen: Detroit	35.00	14.00	3.50
☐ 257	Mullin: Detroit, Throwing	40.00	16.00	4.00
☐ 258	Mullin: Detroit, Batting	35.00	14.00	3.50
☐ 259	Murphy: Phila. AL, Throwing	40.00	16.00	4.00
☐ 260	Murphy: Phila. AL, Bat on shoulder	35.00	14.00	3.50
☐ 261	Murray: N.Y. NL, Sweater	35.00	14.00	3.50
☐ 262	Murray: N.Y. NL, Bat on shoulder	35.00	14.00	3.50
☐ 263	Myers (sic): N.Y. NL, Fielding	35.00	14.00	3.50
☐ 264	Myers (sic): N.Y. NL, Batting	35.00	14.00	3.50
☐ 265	Needham: Chicago NL	35.00	14.00	3.50
☐ 266	Nicholls: Phila. AL	40.00	16.00	4.00
☐ 267	Nichols(sic): Phila. AL	35.00	14.00	3.50
☐ 268	Niles: Boston AL	40.00	16.00	4.00
☐ 269	Oakes: Cinc.	35.00	14.00	3.50
☐ 270	O'Hara: St.L. NL	2250.00	750.00	250.00
☐ 271	O'Hara: N.Y. NL	35.00	14.00	3.50
☐ 272	Oldring: Phila. AL, Fielding	40.00	16.00	4.00
☐ 273	Oldring: Phila. AL, Bat on shoulder	35.00	14.00	3.50
☐ 274	O'Leary: Detroit, Portrait	40.00	16.00	4.00
☐ 275	O'Leary: Detroit, Hands on knees	35.00	14.00	3.50
☐ 276	Overall: Chicago NL, Portrait	40.00	16.00	4.00
☐ 277	Overall: Chicago NL, Pitching, follow thru	35.00	14.00	3.50
☐ 278	Overall: Chicago NL, Pitching hiding ball in glove	35.00	14.00	3.50
☐ 279	Owen: Chicago AL	40.00	16.00	4.00
☐ 280	Parent: Chicago AL	40.00	16.00	4.00
☐ 281	Paskert: Cinc.	35.00	14.00	3.50
☐ 282	Pastorius: Brooklyn	40.00	16.00	4.00
☐ 283	Pattee: Brooklyn	75.00	30.00	7.50
☐ 284	Payne: Chicago AL	35.00	14.00	3.50
☐ 285	Pelty: St.L. AL, HOR	75.00	30.00	7.50
☐ 286	Pelty: St.L. AL, VERT	35.00	14.00	3.50
☐ 287	Perring: Cleveland	35.00	14.00	3.50
☐ 288	Pfeffer: Chicago NL	35.00	14.00	3.50
☐ 289	Pfeister: Chic. NL, Sitting	35.00	14.00	3.50
☐ 290	Pfeister: Chic. NL, Pitching	35.00	14.00	3.50
☐ 291	Phelps: St.L. NL	35.00	14.00	3.50
☐ 292	Phillippe: Pitt.	40.00	16.00	4.00
☐ 293	Plank: Phila. AL	9000.00	3750.00	1000.00
☐ 294	Powell: St.L. AL	40.00	16.00	4.00
☐ 295	Powers: Phil. AL	75.00	30.00	7.50
☐ 296	Purtell: Chicago AL	35.00	14.00	3.50
☐ 297	Quinn: N.Y. AL	35.00	14.00	3.50
☐ 298	Raymond: N.Y. NL	35.00	14.00	3.50

□ 299	Reulbach: Chicago NL, ... Pitching	35.00	14.00	3.50
□ 300	Reulbach: Chicago NL, ... Hands at side	75.00	30.00	7.50
□ 301	Rhoades: Cleveland, ... Hand in air	35.00	14.00	3.50
□ 302	Rhoades: Cleveland, ... Ready to pitch	35.00	14.00	3.50
□ 303	Rhodes: St.L. NL	35.00	14.00	3.50
□ 304	Ritchey: Boston NL	40.00	16.00	4.00
□ 305	Rossman: Detroit	35.00	14.00	3.50
□ 306	Rucker: Brooklyn, ... Portrait	40.00	16.00	4.00
□ 307	Rucker: Brooklyn, ... Pitching	35.00	14.00	3.50
□ 308	Schaefer: Washington	35.00	14.00	3.50
□ 309	Schaefer: Detroit	40.00	16.00	4.00
□ 310	Schlei: N.Y. NL, ... Sweater	35.00	14.00	3.50
□ 311	Schlei: N.Y. NL, ... Batting	35.00	14.00	3.50
□ 312	Schlei: N.Y. NL, ... Fielding	40.00	16.00	4.00
□ 313	Schmidt: Detroit, ... Portrait	35.00	14.00	3.50
□ 314	Schmidt: Detroit, ... Throwing	40.00	16.00	4.00
□ 315	Schulte: Chicago NL, ... Batting, back turned	35.00	14.00	3.50
□ 316	Schulte: Chicago NL, ... Batting, front pose	40.00	16.00	4.00
□ 317	Scott: Chicago AL	35.00	14.00	3.50
□ 318	Seymour: N.Y. NL, ... Portrait	35.00	14.00	3.50
□ 319	Seymour: N.Y. NL, ... Throwing	35.00	14.00	3.50
□ 320	Seymour: N.Y. NL, ... Batting	40.00	16.00	4.00
□ 321	Shaw: St.L. NL	40.00	16.00	4.00
□ 322	Sheckard: Chic. NL, ... Throwing	35.00	14.00	3.50
□ 323	Sheckard: Chic. NL, ... Side view	40.00	16.00	4.00
□ 324	Shipke: Washington	40.00	16.00	4.00
□ 325	Smith: Chicago AL	35.00	14.00	3.50
□ 326	Smith: Chicago and .... Boston AL	300.00	120.00	30.00
□ 327	F. Smith: Chicago AL	40.00	16.00	4.00
□ 328	Happy Smith: Brk.	35.00	14.00	3.50
□ 329	Snodgrass: N.Y. NL, ... Batting	35.00	14.00	3.50
□ 330	Snodgrass: N.Y. NL, ... Catching	35.00	14.00	3.50
□ 331	Spade: Cinc.	40.00	16.00	4.00
□ 332	Speaker: Boston AL	225.00	90.00	22.00
□ 333	Spencer: Boston AL	40.00	16.00	4.00
□ 334	Stahl: Boston AL, ... Catching fly ball	35.00	14.00	3.50
□ 335	Stahl: Boston AL, ... Standing, arms down	50.00	20.00	5.00
□ 336	Stanage: Detroit	35.00	14.00	3.50
□ 337	Starr: Boston NL	35.00	14.00	3.50
□ 338	Steinfeldt: Chic. NL, ... Portrait	40.00	16.00	4.00
□ 339	Steinfeldt: Chic. NL, ... Batting	35.00	14.00	3.50
□ 340	Stephens: St.L. AL	35.00	14.00	3.50
□ 341	Stone: St.L. AL	40.00	16.00	4.00
□ 342	Stovall: Cleveland, ... Portrait	40.00	16.00	4.00
□ 343	Stovall: Cleveland, ... Batting	35.00	14.00	3.50
□ 344	Street: Washington, ... Portrait	35.00	14.00	3.50
□ 345	Street: Washington, ... Catching	35.00	14.00	3.50
□ 346	Sullivan: Chicago AL	40.00	16.00	4.00
□ 347	Summers: Detroit	35.00	14.00	3.50
□ 348	Sweeney: N.Y. AL	35.00	14.00	3.50
□ 349	Sweeney: Bost. NL	35.00	14.00	3.50
□ 350	L. Tannehill: Chic.AL	40.00	16.00	4.00
□ 351	Tannehill: Chicago AL	35.00	14.00	3.50
□ 352	Tannehill: Wash.	35.00	14.00	3.50
□ 353	Tenney: N.Y. NL	40.00	16.00	4.00
□ 354	Thomas: Phila. AL	35.00	14.00	3.50
□ 355	Tinker: Chicago NL, ... Ready to hit	125.00	50.00	12.50
□ 356	Tinker: Chicago NL, ... Bat on shoulder	125.00	50.00	12.50
□ 357	Tinker: Chicago NL, ... Portrait	150.00	60.00	15.00
□ 358	Tinker: Chicago NL, ... Hands on knees	150.00	60.00	15.00
□ 359	Titus: Phila. NL	35.00	14.00	3.50
□ 360	Turner: Cleveland	40.00	16.00	4.00
□ 361	Unglaub: Washington	35.00	14.00	3.50
□ 362	Waddell: St.L. AL, ... Portrait	150.00	60.00	15.00
□ 363	Waddell: St.L. AL, ... Pitching	150.00	60.00	15.00
□ 364	Wagner: Boston AL, ... Bat on left shoulder	75.00	30.00	7.50
□ 365	Wagner: Boston AL, ... Bat on right shoulder	50.00	20.00	5.00
□ 366	Wagner: Pitt.	90000.	40000.	10000.
□ 367	Wallace: St.L. AL	150.00	60.00	15.00
□ 368	Walsh: Chicago AL	150.00	60.00	15.00
□ 369	Warhop: N.Y. AL	35.00	14.00	3.50
□ 370	Weimer: N.Y. NL	40.00	16.00	4.00
□ 371	Wheat: Brooklyn	125.00	50.00	12.50
□ 372	White: Chicago AL, ... Portrait	40.00	16.00	4.00
□ 373	White: Chicago AL, ... Pitching	35.00	14.00	3.50
□ 374	Wilhelm: Brooklyn, ... Batting	35.00	14.00	3.50
□ 375	Wilhelm: Brooklyn, ... Hands to chest	40.00	16.00	4.00
□ 376	Willett: Detroit, ... Batting	35.00	14.00	3.50
□ 377	Willetts (sic): .... Detroit, Pitching	35.00	14.00	3.50
□ 378	Williams: St.L. AL	40.00	16.00	4.00
□ 379	Willis: Pitt.	75.00	30.00	7.50
□ 380	Willis: St.L. NL, ... Pitching	60.00	24.00	6.00
□ 381	Willis: St.L. NL, ... Batting	60.00	24.00	6.00
□ 382	Wilson: Pitt.	35.00	14.00	3.50
□ 383	Wiltse: N.Y. NL, ... Portrait	40.00	16.00	4.00
□ 384	Wiltse: N.Y. NL, ... Sweater	35.00	14.00	3.50
□ 385	Wiltse: N.Y. NL, ... Pitching	35.00	14.00	3.50
□ 386	Young: Cleveland, ... Portrait	275.00	110.00	27.00
□ 387	Young: Cleveland, ... Pitch, front view	200.00	80.00	20.00
□ 388	Young: Cleveland, ... Pitch, side view	200.00	80.00	20.00
□ 389	Zimmerman: .... Chicago NL	35.00	14.00	3.50
□ 390	Fred Abbott: Toledo	27.00	11.00	2.70
□ 391	Merle (Doc) Adkins: .... Baltimore	27.00	11.00	2.70
□ 392	John Anderson: Prov.	27.00	11.00	2.70
□ 393	Herman Armbruster: ...... St. Paul	27.00	11.00	2.70
□ 394	Harry Arndt: Prov.	27.00	11.00	2.70
□ 395	Cy Barger: Rochester	27.00	11.00	2.70
□ 396	John Barry: .... Milwaukee	27.00	11.00	2.70
□ 397	Emil H. Batch: Roch.	27.00	11.00	2.70
□ 398	Jake Beckley: K.C.	125.00	50.00	12.50
□ 399	Russell Blackburne .... (Lena): Providence	27.00	11.00	2.70
□ 400	David Brain: Buffalo	27.00	11.00	2.70
□ 401	Roy Brashear: K.C.	27.00	11.00	2.70
□ 402	Fred Burchell: .... Buffalo	27.00	11.00	2.70
□ 403	Jimmy Burke: Ind.	27.00	11.00	2.70
□ 404	John Butler: Roch.	27.00	11.00	2.70
□ 405	Charles Carr: Ind.	27.00	11.00	2.70
□ 406	James Peter Casey .... (Doc): Montreal	27.00	11.00	2.70
□ 407	Peter Cassidy: Balt.	27.00	11.00	2.70
□ 408	Wm. Chappelle: Roch.	27.00	11.00	2.70
□ 409	Wm. Clancy: Buffalo	27.00	11.00	2.70
□ 410	Joshua Clark: Col.	27.00	11.00	2.70
□ 411	William Clymer: Col.	27.00	11.00	2.70
□ 412	Jimmy Collins: Minn.	150.00	60.00	15.00
□ 413	Bunk Congalton: .... Columbus	27.00	11.00	2.70
□ 414	Gavvy Cravath: Minn.	50.00	20.00	5.00
□ 415	Monte Cross: Ind.	27.00	11.00	2.70
□ 416	Paul Davidson: Ind.	27.00	11.00	2.70
□ 417	Frank Delehanty: .... Louisville	27.00	11.00	2.70
□ 418	Rube Dessau: Balt.	27.00	11.00	2.70
□ 419	Gus Dorner: K.C.	27.00	11.00	2.70
□ 420	Jerome Downs: Minn.	27.00	11.00	2.70
□ 421	Jack Dunn: Baltimore	27.00	11.00	2.70
□ 422	James Flanagan: .... Buffalo	27.00	11.00	2.70
□ 423	James Freeman: Tol.	27.00	11.00	2.70
□ 424	John Ganzel: Roch.	27.00	11.00	2.70
□ 425	Myron Grimshaw: Tor. ...	27.00	11.00	2.70
□ 426	Robert Hall: Balt.	27.00	11.00	2.70
□ 427	William Hallman: .... Kansas City	27.00	11.00	2.70

☐ 428	John Hannifan: J.C.	27.00	11.00	2.70
☐ 429	Jack Hayden: Ind.	27.00	11.00	2.70
☐ 430	Harry Hinchman: Tol.	27.00	11.00	2.70
☐ 431	Harry C. Hoffman (Izzy): Providence	27.00	11.00	2.70
☐ 432	James B. Jackson: Baltimore	27.00	11.00	2.70
☐ 433	Joe Kelley: Tor.	150.00	60.00	15.00
☐ 434	Rube Kisinger: Buff. (sic) Kissinger	27.00	11.00	2.70
☐ 435	Otto Kruger: Col. (sic) Krueger	27.00	11.00	2.70
☐ 436	Wm. Lattimore: Tol.	27.00	11.00	2.70
☐ 437	James Lavender: Providence	27.00	11.00	2.70
☐ 438	Carl Lundgren: K.C.	27.00	11.00	2.70
☐ 439	Wm. Malarkey: Buff.	27.00	11.00	2.70
☐ 440	Wm. Maloney: Roch.	27.00	11.00	2.70
☐ 441	Dennis McGann: Milwaukee	27.00	11.00	2.70
☐ 442	James McGinley: Tor.	27.00	11.00	2.70
☐ 443	Joe McGinnity: New.	125.00	50.00	12.50
☐ 444	Ulysses McGlynn: Milwaukee	27.00	11.00	2.70
☐ 445	George Merritt: J.C.	27.00	11.00	2.70
☐ 446	Wm. Milligan: J.C.	27.00	11.00	2.70
☐ 447	Fred Mitchell: Tor.	27.00	11.00	2.70
☐ 448	Dan Moeller: J.C.	27.00	11.00	2.70
☐ 449	Joseph Herbert Moran: Providence	27.00	11.00	2.70
☐ 450	Wm. Nattress: Buffalo	27.00	11.00	2.70
☐ 451	Frank Oberlin: Minn.	27.00	11.00	2.70
☐ 452	Peter O'Brien: St. Paul	27.00	11.00	2.70
☐ 453	Wm. O'Neil: Minn.	27.00	11.00	2.70
☐ 454	James Phelan: Prov.	27.00	11.00	2.70
☐ 455	Oliver Pickering: Minneapolis.	27.00	11.00	2.70
☐ 456	Philip Poland: Balt.	27.00	11.00	2.70
☐ 457	Ambrose Puttman: Louisville	27.00	11.00	2.70
☐ 458	Lee Quillen: Minn.	27.00	11.00	2.70
☐ 459	Newton Randall: Milwaukee	27.00	11.00	2.70
☐ 460	Louis Ritter: K.C.	27.00	11.00	2.70
☐ 461	Dick Rudolph: Tor.	27.00	11.00	2.70
☐ 462	George Schirm: Buffalo	27.00	11.00	2.70
☐ 463	Larry Schlafly: Newark	27.00	11.00	2.70
☐ 464	Ossie Schreck: Col. (sic) Schreckengost	27.00	11.00	2.70
☐ 465	William Shannon: Kansas City	27.00	11.00	2.70
☐ 466	Bayard Sharpe: Newark	27.00	11.00	2.70
☐ 467	Royal Shaw: Prov.	27.00	11.00	2.70
☐ 468	James Slagle: Balt.	27.00	11.00	2.70
☐ 469	George Henry Smith: Buffalo	27.00	11.00	2.70
☐ 470	Samuel Strang: Balt.	27.00	11.00	2.70
☐ 471	Luther(Dummy) Taylor: Buffalo	27.00	11.00	2.70
☐ 472	John Thielman: Louisville	27.00	11.00	2.70
☐ 473	John F. White: Buff.	27.00	11.00	2.70
☐ 474	William Wright: Tol.	27.00	11.00	2.70
☐ 475	Irving M. Young: Minneapolis	27.00	11.00	2.70
☐ 476	Jack Bastian: San Antonio	100.00	40.00	10.00
☐ 477	Harry Bay: Nashv.	100.00	40.00	10.00
☐ 478	Wm. Bernhard: Nashville	100.00	40.00	10.00
☐ 479	Ted Breitenstein: New Orleans	100.00	40.00	10.00
☐ 480	George(Scoops)Carey: Memphis	100.00	40.00	10.00
☐ 481	Cad Coles: Augusta	100.00	40.00	10.00
☐ 482	Wm. Cranston: Memph.	100.00	40.00	10.00
☐ 483	Roy Ellam: Nashville	100.00	40.00	10.00
☐ 484	Edward Foster: Charleston	100.00	40.00	10.00
☐ 485	Charles Fritz: N.O.	100.00	40.00	10.00
☐ 486	Ed Greminger: Montg.	100.00	40.00	10.00
☐ 487	Guiheen: Portsmouth	100.00	40.00	10.00
☐ 488	William F. Hart Little Rock	100.00	40.00	10.00
☐ 489	James Henry Hart: Montgomery	100.00	40.00	10.00
☐ 490	J.R. Helm: Columbus (Georgia)	100.00	40.00	10.00
☐ 491	Gordon Hickman: Mobile	100.00	40.00	10.00
☐ 492	Buck Hooker: Lynchburg	100.00	40.00	10.00
☐ 493	Ernie Howard: Sav.	100.00	40.00	10.00
☐ 494	A.O. Jordan: Atlanta	100.00	40.00	10.00
☐ 495	J.F. Kiernan: Columbia	100.00	40.00	10.00
☐ 496	Frank King: Danville	100.00	40.00	10.00
☐ 497	James LaFitte: Macon	100.00	40.00	10.00
☐ 498	Harry Lentz: Little Rock (sic) Sentz	100.00	40.00	10.00
☐ 499	Perry Lipe: Richmond	100.00	40.00	10.00
☐ 500	George Manion: Columbia	100.00	40.00	10.00
☐ 501	McCauley: Portsmouth	100.00	40.00	10.00
☐ 502	Charles B. Miller: Dallas	100.00	40.00	10.00
☐ 503	Carlton Molesworth: Birmingham	100.00	40.00	10.00
☐ 504	Dominic Mullaney: Jacksonville	100.00	40.00	10.00
☐ 505	Albert Orth: Lynchb.	100.00	40.00	10.00
☐ 506	William Otey: Norf.	100.00	40.00	10.00
☐ 507	George Paige: Charleston	100.00	40.00	10.00
☐ 508	Hub Perdue: Nashv.	100.00	40.00	10.00
☐ 509	Archie Persons: Montgomery	100.00	40.00	10.00
☐ 510	Edward Reagan: N.O.	100.00	40.00	10.00
☐ 511	R.H. Revelle: Richm.	100.00	40.00	10.00
☐ 512	Isaac Rockenfeld: Montgomery	100.00	40.00	10.00
☐ 513	Ray Ryan: Roanoke	100.00	40.00	10.00
☐ 514	Charles Seitz: Norf.	100.00	40.00	10.00
☐ 515	Frank(Shag) Shaughnessy: Roanoke	100.00	40.00	10.00
☐ 516	Carlos Smith: Shreveport	100.00	40.00	10.00
☐ 517	Sid Smith: Atlanta	100.00	40.00	10.00
☐ 518	M.R. (Dolly) Stark: San Antonio	100.00	40.00	10.00
☐ 519	Tony Thebo: Waco	100.00	40.00	10.00
☐ 520	Woodie Thornton: Mobile	100.00	40.00	10.00
☐ 521	Juan Violat: Jacksonville: (sic) Viola	100.00	40.00	10.00
☐ 522	James Westlake: Danville	100.00	40.00	10.00
☐ 523	Foley White: Houston	100.00	40.00	10.00

T207 Brown Background

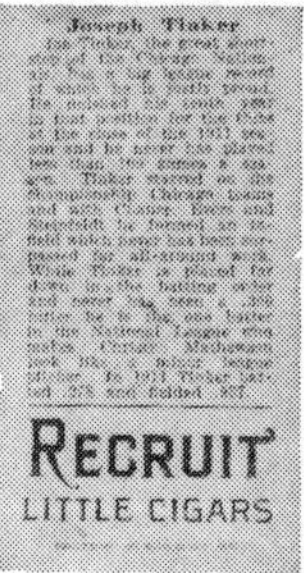

The cards in this 207-card set measure 1 1/2" by 2 5/8". The T207 set, also known as the "Brown Background" set was issued with Broadleaf, Cycle, Napoleon, Recruit and anonymous (Factories no. 2, 3 or 25) backs in 1912. Broadleaf, Cycle and anonymous backs are difficult to obtain. Although many scarcities and cards with varying degrees of difficulty to obtain exist (see prices below), the Loudermilk, Lewis (Boston NL) and Miller (Chicago NL) cards are the rarest, followed by Saier and Tyler. The cards are numbered below for reference in alphabetical order by player's name. The complete set price below does not include the Lewis variation missing the Braves patch on the sleeve.

		NRMT	VG-E	GOOD
COMPLETE SET (207)		19000.00	8100.00	2400.00
COMMON PLAYER (1-207)		40.00	16.00	4.00
□ 1	Adams: Cleve AL	75.00	30.00	7.50
□ 2	Ainsmith: Wash AL	40.00	16.00	4.00
□ 3	Almeida: Cinc AL	75.00	30.00	7.50
□ 4	Austin: StL AL with StL on shirt	40.00	16.00	4.00
□ 5	Austin: StL AL without StL on shirt	100.00	40.00	10.00
□ 6	Ball: Cleve AL	40.00	16.00	4.00
□ 7	Barger: Brk NL	40.00	16.00	4.00
□ 8	Barry: Phil AL	40.00	16.00	4.00
□ 9	Bauman: Det AL	100.00	40.00	10.00
□ 10	Becker: NY NL	40.00	16.00	4.00
□ 11	Bender: Phil AL	125.00	50.00	12.50
□ 12	Benz: Chi AL	75.00	30.00	7.50
□ 13	Bescher: Cinc NL	40.00	16.00	4.00
□ 14	Birmingham: Cleve AL	75.00	30.00	7.50
□ 15	Blackburne: Chi AL	75.00	30.00	7.50
□ 16	Blanding: Cleve AL	75.00	30.00	7.50
□ 17	Block: Chi AL	40.00	16.00	4.00
□ 18	Bodie: Chi AL	40.00	16.00	4.00
□ 19	Bradley: Bos AL	40.00	16.00	4.00
□ 20	Bresnahan: StL NL	100.00	40.00	10.00
□ 21	Bushelman: Bos AL	75.00	30.00	7.50
□ 22	Butcher: Cleve AL	75.00	30.00	7.50
□ 23	Byrne: Pitt NL	40.00	16.00	4.00
□ 24	Callahan: Chi AL	40.00	16.00	4.00
□ 25	Camnitz: Pitt NL	40.00	16.00	4.00
□ 26	Carey: Pitt NL	125.00	50.00	12.50
□ 27	Carrigan: Bos AL correct back	40.00	16.00	4.00
□ 28	Carrigan: Bos AL Wagner back	150.00	60.00	15.00
□ 29	Chalmers: Phil NL	40.00	16.00	4.00
□ 30	Chance: Chi NL	150.00	60.00	15.00
□ 31	Cicotte: Bos AL	60.00	24.00	6.00
□ 32	Clarke: Cinc NL	40.00	16.00	4.00
□ 33	Cole: Chi NL	40.00	16.00	4.00
□ 34	Collins: Chi AL	200.00	80.00	20.00
□ 35	Coulson: Brk NL	40.00	16.00	4.00
□ 36	Covington: Det AL	40.00	16.00	4.00
□ 37	Crandall: NY NL	40.00	16.00	4.00
□ 38	Cunningham: Wash AL	60.00	24.00	6.00
□ 39	Danforth: Phil AL	40.00	16.00	4.00
□ 40	Daniels: NY AL	40.00	16.00	4.00
□ 41	Daubert: Brk NL	60.00	24.00	6.00
□ 42	Davis: Cleve AL	40.00	16.00	4.00
□ 43	Delahanty: Det AL	40.00	16.00	4.00
□ 44	Derrick: Phil AL	40.00	16.00	4.00
□ 45	Devlin: Bos NL	40.00	16.00	4.00
□ 46	Devore: NY NL	40.00	16.00	4.00
□ 47	Donlin: Pitt NL	75.00	30.00	7.50
□ 48	Donnelly: Bos NL	75.00	30.00	7.50
□ 49	Dooin: Phil NL	40.00	16.00	4.00
□ 50	Downey: Phil NL	75.00	30.00	7.50
□ 51	Doyle: NY NL	40.00	16.00	4.00
□ 52	Drake: Det AL	40.00	16.00	4.00
□ 53	Easterly: Cleve AL	40.00	16.00	4.00
□ 54	Ellis: StL NL	40.00	16.00	4.00
□ 55	Engle: Bos AL	40.00	16.00	4.00
□ 56	Erwin: Brk NL	40.00	16.00	4.00
□ 57	Evans: StL NL	40.00	16.00	4.00
□ 58	Ferry: Pitt NL	40.00	16.00	4.00
□ 59	Fisher: NY AL white cap	100.00	40.00	10.00
□ 60	Fisher: NY AL blue cap	60.00	24.00	6.00
□ 61	Fletcher: NY NL	40.00	16.00	4.00
□ 62	Fournier: Chi AL	75.00	30.00	7.50
□ 63	Fromme: Cinc NL	40.00	16.00	4.00
□ 64	Gainor: Det AL	40.00	16.00	4.00
□ 65	Gardner: Bos AL	40.00	16.00	4.00
□ 66	George: Cleve AL	40.00	16.00	4.00
□ 67	Golden: StL NL	40.00	16.00	4.00
□ 68	Gowdy: Bos NL	40.00	16.00	4.00
□ 69	Graham: Phil NL	75.00	30.00	7.50
□ 70	Graney: Cleve AL	40.00	16.00	4.00
□ 71	Gregg: Cleve AL	75.00	30.00	7.50
□ 72	Hageman: Bos AL	40.00	16.00	4.00
□ 73	Hall: Bos AL	40.00	16.00	4.00
□ 74	Hallinan: St.L. AL	40.00	16.00	4.00
□ 75	E. Hamilton: St.L. AL	40.00	16.00	4.00
□ 76	Harmon: St.L. NL	40.00	16.00	4.00
□ 77	Hartley: NY NL	75.00	30.00	7.50
□ 78	Henriksen, Bos AL	40.00	16.00	4.00
□ 79	Henry: Wash AL	60.00	24.00	6.00
□ 80	Herzog: NY NL	75.00	30.00	7.50
□ 81	Higgins: Brk NL	40.00	16.00	4.00
□ 82	Hoff: NY AL	75.00	30.00	7.50
□ 83	Hogan: StL AL	40.00	16.00	4.00
□ 84	Hooper: Bos AL	300.00	120.00	30.00
□ 85	Houser: Bos NL	75.00	30.00	7.50
□ 86	Hyatt: Pitt NL	75.00	30.00	7.50
□ 87	Johnson: Wash AL	500.00	200.00	50.00
□ 88	Kaler: Cleve AL	40.00	16.00	4.00
□ 89	Kelly: Pitt NL	75.00	30.00	7.50
□ 90	Kirke: Bos NL	75.00	30.00	7.50
□ 91	Kling: Bos NL	40.00	16.00	4.00
□ 92	Knabe: Phil NL	40.00	16.00	4.00
□ 93	Knetzer: Brk NL	40.00	16.00	4.00
□ 94	Konetchy: StL NL	40.00	16.00	4.00
□ 95	Krause: Phil AL	40.00	16.00	4.00
□ 96	Kuhn: Chi AL	75.00	30.00	7.50
□ 97	Kutina: StL AL	75.00	30.00	7.50
□ 98	Lange: Chi AL	75.00	30.00	7.50
□ 99	Lapp: Phil AL	40.00	16.00	4.00
□ 100	Latham: NY NL	40.00	16.00	4.00
□ 101	Leach: Pitt NL	40.00	16.00	4.00
□ 102	Leifield: Pitt NL	40.00	16.00	4.00
□ 103	Lennox: Chi NL	40.00	16.00	4.00
□ 104	Lewis: Bos AL	40.00	16.00	4.00
□ 105A	Lewis: Bos NL (Braves patch on sleeve)	2000.00	800.00	250.00
□ 105B	Lewis: Bos NL (nothing on sleeve)	2250.00	900.00	250.00
□ 106	Lively: Det AL	40.00	16.00	4.00
□ 107	Livingston: Cleve AL "A" shirt	150.00	60.00	15.00
□ 108	Livingston: Cleve AL "C" shirt	150.00	60.00	15.00
□ 109	Livingston: Cleve AL "c" shirt	60.00	24.00	6.00
□ 110	Lord: Phil AL	40.00	16.00	4.00
□ 111	Lord: Chi AL	40.00	16.00	4.00
□ 112	Loudermilk: StL NL	2000.00	800.00	250.00
□ 113	Marquard: NY NL	125.00	50.00	12.50
□ 114	Marsans: Cinc NL	40.00	16.00	4.00
□ 115	McBride: Wash AL	40.00	16.00	4.00
□ 116	McCarthy: Pitt NL	150.00	60.00	15.00
□ 117	McDonald: Bos NL	40.00	16.00	4.00
□ 118	McGraw: NY NL	175.00	70.00	18.00
□ 119	McIntire: Chi NL	40.00	16.00	4.00
□ 120	McIntyre: Chi AL	40.00	16.00	4.00
□ 121	McKechnie: Pitt NL	250.00	100.00	25.00
□ 122	McLean: Cinc NL	40.00	16.00	4.00
□ 123	Milan: Wash AL	40.00	16.00	4.00
□ 124	Miller: Pitt NL	40.00	16.00	4.00
□ 125	Miller: Chi NL	1800.00	800.00	225.00
□ 126	Miller: Brk NL	75.00	30.00	7.50
□ 127	Miller: Bos NL	75.00	30.00	7.50
□ 128	Mitchell: Cinc NL	40.00	16.00	4.00
□ 129	Mitchell: Cleve AL	60.00	24.00	6.00
□ 130	Mogridge: Chi AL	75.00	30.00	7.50
□ 131	Moore: Phil NL	75.00	30.00	7.50
□ 132	Moran: Phil NL	40.00	16.00	4.00
□ 133	Morgan: Phil AL	40.00	16.00	4.00
□ 134	Morgan: Wash AL	40.00	16.00	4.00
□ 135	Moriarity: Det AL	75.00	30.00	7.50
□ 136	Mullin: Det AL with "D" on cap	60.00	24.00	6.00
□ 137	Mullin: Det AL without "D" on cap	150.00	60.00	15.00
□ 138	Needham: Chi NL	40.00	16.00	4.00
□ 139	Nelson: StL AL	75.00	30.00	7.50
□ 140	Northen: Brk NL	40.00	16.00	4.00
□ 141	Nunamaker: Bos AL	40.00	16.00	4.00
□ 142	Oakes: StL NL	40.00	16.00	4.00
□ 143	O'Brien: Bos AL	40.00	16.00	4.00
□ 144	Oldring: Phil AL	40.00	16.00	4.00
□ 145	Olson: Cleve AL	40.00	16.00	4.00
□ 146	O'Toole: Pitt NL	40.00	16.00	4.00
□ 147	Paskert: Phil NL	40.00	16.00	4.00
□ 148	Pelty: StL AL	75.00	30.00	7.50
□ 149	Perdue: Bos NL	40.00	16.00	4.00
□ 150	Peters: Chi AL	75.00	30.00	7.50
□ 151	Phelan: Cinc NL	75.00	30.00	7.50
□ 152	Quinn: NY AL	40.00	16.00	4.00
□ 153	Ragan: Brk NL	400.00	160.00	40.00
□ 154	Rasmussen: Phil NL	300.00	120.00	30.00
□ 155	Rath: Chi AL	75.00	30.00	7.50
□ 156	Reulbach: Chi NL	40.00	16.00	4.00
□ 157	Rucker: Brk NL	40.00	16.00	4.00
□ 158	Ryan: Cleve AL	75.00	30.00	7.50
□ 159	Saier: Chi NL	600.00	240.00	60.00
□ 160	Scanlon: Phil NL	40.00	16.00	4.00
□ 161	Schaefer: Wash AL	40.00	16.00	4.00
□ 162	Schardt: Brk NL	40.00	16.00	4.00
□ 163	Schulte: Chi NL	40.00	16.00	4.00
□ 164	Scott: Chi AL	40.00	16.00	4.00
□ 165	Severeid: Cinc NL	40.00	16.00	4.00
□ 166	Simon: Pitt NL	40.00	16.00	4.00
□ 167	Smith: StL NL	40.00	16.00	4.00
□ 168	Smith: Cinc NL	40.00	16.00	4.00
□ 169	Snodgrass: NY NL	40.00	16.00	4.00

□ 170 Speaker: Bos AL	600.00	240.00	60.00
□ 171 Spratt: Bos NL	40.00	16.00	4.00
□ 172 Stack: Brk NL	40.00	16.00	4.00
□ 173 Stanage: Det AL	40.00	16.00	4.00
□ 174 Steele: StL NL	40.00	16.00	4.00
□ 175 Steinfeldt: StL NL	40.00	16.00	4.00
□ 176 Stovall: StL AL	40.00	16.00	4.00
□ 177 Street: NY AL	40.00	16.00	4.00
□ 178 Strunk: Phil AL	40.00	16.00	4.00
□ 179 Sullivan: Chi AL	40.00	16.00	4.00
□ 180 Sweeney: Bos NL	100.00	40.00	10.00
□ 181 Tannehill: Chi AL	40.00	16.00	4.00
□ 182 Thomas: Bos AL	40.00	16.00	4.00
□ 183 Tinker: Chi NL	125.00	50.00	12.50
□ 184 Tooley: Brk NL	40.00	16.00	4.00
□ 185 Turner: Cleve AL	40.00	16.00	4.00
□ 186 Tyler: Bos NL	600.00	240.00	60.00
□ 187 Vaughn: NY AL	40.00	16.00	4.00
□ 188 Wagner: Bos AL correct back	60.00	24.00	6.00
□ 189 Wagner: Bos AL Carrigan back	150.00	60.00	15.00
□ 190 Walker: Wash AL	40.00	16.00	4.00
□ 191 Wallace: St.L. AL	125.00	50.00	12.50
□ 192 Warhop: NY AL	40.00	16.00	4.00
□ 193 Weaver: Chi AL	100.00	40.00	10.00
□ 194 Wheat: Brk NL	125.00	50.00	12.50
□ 195 White: Chi AL	75.00	30.00	7.50
□ 196 Wilie: St.L. NL	60.00	24.00	6.00
□ 197 Williams: NY AL	40.00	16.00	4.00
□ 198 Wilson: NY NL	75.00	30.00	7.50
□ 199 Wilson: Pitt NL	40.00	16.00	4.00
□ 200 Wiltse: NY NL	40.00	16.00	4.00
□ 201 Wingo: StL NL	40.00	16.00	4.00
□ 202 Wolverton: NY AL	40.00	16.00	4.00
□ 203 Wood: Bos AL	100.00	40.00	10.00
□ 204 Woodburn: StL NL	75.00	30.00	7.50
□ 205 Works: Det AL	200.00	80.00	20.00
□ 206 Yerkes: Bos AL	40.00	16.00	4.00
□ 207 Zeider: Chi AL	75.00	30.00	7.50

1988 Umpire Cards

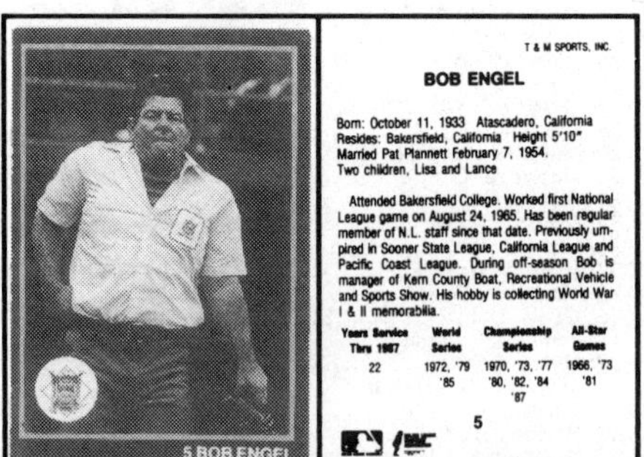

This set of 64 cards was distributed as a small boxed set featuring Major League umpires exclusively. The box itself is blank, white, and silver. The set was produced by T and M Sports under licenses from Major League Baseball and the Major League Umpires Association. The cards are in color and are standard size, 2 1/2" by 3 1/2". Card backs are printed in black on light blue. All the cards are black bordered, but the American Leaguers have a red thin inner border, whereas the National Leaguers have a green thin inner border. A short biographical sketch is given on the back for each umpire. The cards are numbered on the back; the number on the front of each card refers to the umpire's uniform number.

	MINT	EXC	G-VG
COMPLETE SET (64)	12.00	5.00	1.20
COMMON PLAYER (1-64)	.25	.10	.02
□ 1 Doug Harvey	.35	.14	.03
□ 2 Lee Weyer	.25	.10	.02
□ 3 Billy Williams	.25	.10	.02
□ 4 John Kibler	.25	.10	.02
□ 5 Bob Engel	.25	.10	.02
□ 6 Harry Wendelstedt	.35	.14	.03
□ 7 Larry Barnett	.25	.10	.02
□ 8 Don Denkinger	.35	.14	.03
□ 9 Dave Phillips	.35	.14	.03
□ 10 Larry McCoy	.25	.10	.02
□ 11 Bruce Froemming	.35	.14	.03
□ 12 John McSherry	.35	.14	.03
□ 13 Jim Evans	.25	.10	.02
□ 14 Frank Pulli	.25	.10	.02
□ 15 Joe Brinkman	.25	.10	.02
□ 16 Terry Tata	.25	.10	.02
□ 17 Paul Runge	.25	.10	.02
□ 18 Dutch Rennert	.25	.10	.02
□ 19 Nick Bremigan	.25	.10	.02
□ 20 Jim McKean	.25	.10	.02
□ 21 Terry Cooney	.25	.10	.02
□ 22 Rich Garcia	.25	.10	.02
□ 23 Dale Ford	.25	.10	.02
□ 24 Al Clark	.25	.10	.02
□ 25 Greg Kose	.25	.10	.02
□ 26 Jim Quick	.25	.10	.02
□ 27 Ed Montague	.25	.10	.02
□ 28 Jerry Crawford	.25	.10	.02
□ 29 Steve Palermo	.25	.10	.02
□ 30 Durwood Merrill	.25	.10	.02
□ 31 Ken Kaiser	.35	.14	.03
□ 32 Vic Voltaggio	.25	.10	.02
□ 33 Mike Reilly	.25	.10	.02
□ 34 Eric Gregg	.35	.14	.03
□ 35 Ted Hendry	.25	.10	.02
□ 36 Joe West	.25	.10	.02
□ 37 Dave Pallone	.25	.10	.02
□ 38 Fred Brocklander	.25	.10	.02
□ 39 John Shulock	.25	.10	.02
□ 40 Derryl Cousins	.25	.10	.02
□ 41 Charlie Williams	.25	.10	.02
□ 42 Rocky Roe	.25	.10	.02
□ 43 Randy Marsh	.25	.10	.02
□ 44 Bob Davidson	.25	.10	.02
□ 45 Drew Coble	.25	.10	.02
□ 46 Tim McClelland	.25	.10	.02
□ 47 Dan Morrison	.25	.10	.02
□ 48 Rick Reed	.25	.10	.02
□ 49 Steve Rippley	.25	.10	.02
□ 50 John Hirshbeck	.25	.10	.02
□ 51 Mark Johnson	.25	.10	.02
□ 52 Gerry Davis	.25	.10	.02
□ 53 Dana DeMuth	.25	.10	.02
□ 54 Larry Young	.25	.10	.02
□ 55 Tim Welke	.25	.10	.02
□ 56 Greg Bonin	.25	.10	.02
□ 57 Tom Hallion	.25	.10	.02
□ 58 Dale Scott	.25	.10	.02
□ 59 Tim Tschida	.25	.10	.02
□ 60 Dick Stello	.25	.10	.02
□ 61 All-Star	.25	.10	.02
□ 62 World Series	.25	.10	.02
□ 63 Jocko Conlan	.50	.20	.05
□ 64 Checklist	.25	.03	.01

1989 Upper Deck

This attractive set was introduced in 1989 as an additional major card set. The cards feature full color on both the front and the back. The cards are distinguished by the fact that each card has a hologram on the reverse, thus making the cards essentially copy proof. Cards 668-693 feature a

"Collector's Choice" (CC) colorful drawing of a player (by artist Vernon Wells) on the card front and a checklist of that team on the card back. The cards apppear to be on thick card stock.

	MINT	EXC	G-VG
COMPLETE SET (700)	38.00	15.00	3.00
COMMON PLAYER (1-700)	.05	.02	.00

	MINT	EXC	G-VG
□ 1 Ken Griffey Jr.	1.25	.50	.12
□ 2 Luis Medina	.50	.20	.05
□ 3 Tony Chance	.30	.12	.03
□ 4 Dave Otto	.20	.08	.02
□ 5 Sandy Alomar Jr.	1.00	.40	.10
□ 6 Rolando Roomes	.20	.08	.02
□ 7 Dave West	.60	.24	.06
□ 8 Cris Carpenter	.25	.10	.02
□ 9 Gregg Jefferies	2.00	.80	.20
□ 10 Doug Dascenzo	.20	.08	.02
□ 11 Ron Jones	.35	.14	.03
□ 12 Luis De Los Santos	.30	.12	.03
□ 13 Gary Sheffield	1.50	.60	.15
□ 14 Mike Harkey	.60	.24	.06
□ 15 Lance Blankenship	.20	.08	.02
□ 16 William Brennan	.20	.08	.02
□ 17 John Smoltz	.25	.10	.02
□ 18 Ramon Martinez	.35	.14	.03
□ 19 Mark Lemke	.20	.08	.02
□ 20 Juan Bell	.30	.12	.03
□ 21 Rey Palacios	.20	.08	.02
□ 22 Felix Jose	.25	.10	.02
□ 23 Van Snider	.25	.10	.02
□ 24 Dante Bichette	.25	.10	.02
□ 25 Randy Johnson	.25	.10	.02
□ 26 Carlos Quintana	.40	.16	.04
□ 27 Star Rookie Checklist	.05	.01	.00
□ 28 Mike Schooler	.20	.08	.02
□ 29 Randy St.Claire	.05	.02	.00
□ 30 Jerald Clark	.25	.10	.02
□ 31 Kevin Gross	.05	.02	.00
□ 32 Dan Firova	.20	.08	.02
□ 33 Jeff Calhoun	.05	.02	.00
□ 34 Tommy Hinzo	.05	.02	.00
□ 35 Ricky Jordan	1.25	.50	.12
□ 36 Larry Parrish	.05	.02	.00
□ 37 Bret Saberhagen	.15	.06	.01
□ 38 Mike Smithson	.05	.02	.00
□ 39 Dave Dravecky	.05	.02	.00
□ 40 Ed Romero	.05	.02	.00
□ 41 Jeff Musselman	.05	.02	.00
□ 42 Ed Hearn	.05	.02	.00
□ 43 Rance Mulliniks	.05	.02	.00
□ 44 Jim Eisenreich	.05	.02	.00
□ 45 Sil Campusano	.25	.10	.02
□ 46 Mike Krukow	.05	.02	.00
□ 47 Paul Gibson	.15	.06	.01
□ 48 Mike LaCoss	.05	.02	.00
□ 49 Larry Herndon	.05	.02	.00
□ 50 Scott Garrelts	.05	.02	.00
□ 51 Dwayne Henry	.05	.02	.00
□ 52 Jim Acker	.05	.02	.00
□ 53 Steve Sax	.15	.06	.01
□ 54 Pete O'Brien	.08	.03	.01
□ 55 Paul Runge	.05	.02	.00
□ 56 Rick Rhoden	.08	.03	.01
□ 57 John Dopson	.15	.06	.01
□ 58 Casey Candaele	.05	.02	.00
□ 59 Dave Righetti	.10	.04	.01
□ 60 Joe Hesketh	.05	.02	.00
□ 61 Frank DiPino	.05	.02	.00
□ 62 Tim Laudner	.05	.02	.00
□ 63 Jamie Moyer	.05	.02	.00
□ 64 Fred Toliver	.05	.02	.00
□ 65 Mitch Webster	.05	.02	.00
□ 66 John Tudor	.10	.04	.01
□ 67 John Cangelosi	.05	.02	.00
□ 68 Mike Devereaux	.12	.05	.01
□ 69 Brian Fisher	.05	.02	.00
□ 70 Mike Marshall	.10	.04	.01
□ 71 Zane Smith	.08	.03	.01
□ 72 Brian Holton	.05	.02	.00
□ 73 Jose Guzman	.05	.02	.00
□ 74 Rick Mahler	.05	.02	.00
□ 75 John Shelby	.05	.02	.00
□ 76 Jim Deshaies	.05	.02	.00
□ 77 Bobby Meacham	.05	.02	.00
□ 78 Bryn Smith	.05	.02	.00
□ 79 Joaquin Andujar	.08	.03	.01
□ 80 Richard Dotson	.08	.03	.01
□ 81 Charlie Lea	.05	.02	.00
□ 82 Calvin Schiraldi	.05	.02	.00
□ 83 Les Straker	.05	.02	.00
□ 84 Les Lancaster	.05	.02	.00
□ 85 Allan Anderson	.10	.04	.01
□ 86 Junior Ortiz	.05	.02	.00
□ 87 Jesse Orosco	.05	.02	.00
□ 88 Felix Fermin	.10	.04	.01
□ 89 Dave Anderson	.05	.02	.00
□ 90 Rafael Belliard	.05	.02	.00
□ 91 Franklin Stubbs	.05	.02	.00
□ 92 Cecil Espy	.12	.05	.01
□ 93 Albert Hall	.05	.02	.00
□ 94 Tim Leary	.10	.04	.01
□ 95 Mitch Williams	.05	.02	.00
□ 96 Tracy Jones	.10	.04	.01
□ 97 Danny Darwin	.05	.02	.00
□ 98 Gary Ward	.05	.02	.00
□ 99 Neal Heaton	.05	.02	.00
□ 100 Jim Pankovits	.05	.02	.00
□ 101 Bill Doran	.08	.03	.01
□ 102 Tim Wallach	.08	.03	.01
□ 103 Joe Magrane	.08	.03	.01
□ 104 Ozzie Virgil	.05	.02	.00
□ 105 Alvin Davis	.08	.03	.01
□ 106 Tom Brookens	.05	.02	.00
□ 107 Shawon Dunston	.08	.03	.01
□ 108 Tracy Woodson	.10	.04	.01
□ 109 Nelson Liriano	.05	.02	.00
□ 110 Devon White	.10	.04	.01
□ 111 Steve Balboni	.05	.02	.00
□ 112 Buddy Bell	.10	.04	.01
□ 113 German Jimenez	.12	.05	.01
□ 114 Ken Dayley	.05	.02	.00
□ 115 Andres Galarraga	.12	.05	.01
□ 116 Mike Scioscia	.05	.02	.00
□ 117 Gary Pettis	.05	.02	.00
□ 118 Ernie Whitt	.05	.02	.00
□ 119 Bob Boone	.08	.03	.01
□ 120 Ryno Sandberg	.15	.06	.01
□ 121 Bruce Benedict	.05	.02	.00
□ 122 Hubie Brooks	.08	.03	.01
□ 123 Mike Moore	.08	.03	.01
□ 124 Wallace Johnson	.05	.02	.00
□ 125 Bob Horner	.10	.04	.01
□ 126 Chili Davis	.08	.03	.01
□ 127 Manny Trillo	.05	.02	.00
□ 128 Chet Lemon	.08	.03	.01
□ 129 John Cerutti	.05	.02	.00
□ 130 Orel Hershiser	.25	.10	.02
□ 131 Terry Pendleton	.08	.03	.01
□ 132 Jeff Blauser	.12	.05	.01
□ 133 Mike Fitzgerald	.05	.02	.00
□ 134 Henry Cotto	.05	.02	.00
□ 135 Gerald Young	.08	.03	.01
□ 136 Luis Salazar	.05	.02	.00
□ 137 Alejandro Pena	.05	.02	.00
□ 138 Jack Howell	.05	.02	.00
□ 139 Tony Fernandez	.10	.04	.01
□ 140 Mark Grace	.85	.34	.08
□ 141 Ken Caminiti	.08	.03	.01
□ 142 Mike Jackson	.05	.02	.00
□ 143 Larry McWilliams	.05	.02	.00
□ 144 Andres Thomas	.05	.02	.00
□ 145 Nolan Ryan	.20	.08	.02
□ 146 Mike Davis	.05	.02	.00
□ 147 DeWayne Buice	.05	.02	.00
□ 148 Jody Davis	.08	.03	.01
□ 149 Jesse Barfield	.10	.04	.01
□ 150 Matt Nokes	.12	.05	.01
□ 151 Jerry Reuss	.05	.02	.00
□ 152 Rick Cerone	.05	.02	.00
□ 153 Storm Davis	.08	.03	.01
□ 154 Marvell Wynne	.05	.02	.00
□ 155 Will Clark	.35	.14	.03
□ 156 Luis Aguayo	.05	.02	.00
□ 157 Willie Upshaw	.05	.02	.00
□ 158 Randy Bush	.05	.02	.00
□ 159 Ron Darling	.10	.04	.01
□ 160 Kal Daniels	.12	.05	.01
□ 161 Spike Owen	.05	.02	.00
□ 162 Luis Polonia	.05	.02	.00
□ 163 Kevin Mitchell	.08	.03	.01
□ 164 Dave Gallagher	.20	.08	.02
□ 165 Benito Santiago	.20	.08	.02
□ 166 Greg Gagne	.05	.02	.00
□ 167 Ken Phelps	.08	.03	.01
□ 168 Sid Fernandez	.08	.03	.01
□ 169 Bo Diaz	.05	.02	.00
□ 170 Cory Snyder	.15	.06	.01
□ 171 Eric Show	.05	.02	.00
□ 172 Rob Thompson	.05	.02	.00
□ 173 Marty Barrett	.08	.03	.01
□ 174 Dave Henderson	.08	.03	.01
□ 175 Ozzie Guillen	.08	.03	.01
□ 176 Barry Lyons	.05	.02	.00
□ 177 Kelvin Torve	.15	.06	.01
□ 178 Don Slaught	.05	.02	.00
□ 179 Steve Lombardozzi	.05	.02	.00
□ 180 Chris Sabo	1.00	.40	.10

□ 181	Jose Uribe	.05	.02	.00
□ 182	Shane Mack	.10	.04	.01
□ 183	Ron Karkovice	.05	.02	.00
□ 184	Todd Benzinger	.08	.03	.01
□ 185	Dave Stewart	.08	.03	.01
□ 186	Julio Franco	.08	.03	.01
□ 187	Ron Robinson	.05	.02	.00
□ 188	Wally Backman	.05	.02	.00
□ 189	Randy Velarde	.10	.04	.01
□ 190	Joe Carter	.12	.05	.01
□ 191	Bob Welch	.08	.03	.01
□ 192	Kelly Paris	.05	.02	.00
□ 193	Chris Brown	.08	.03	.01
□ 194	Rick Reuschel	.08	.03	.01
□ 195	Roger Clemens	.40	.16	.04
□ 196	Dave Concepcion	.08	.03	.01
□ 197	Al Newman	.05	.02	.00
□ 198	Brook Jacoby	.08	.03	.01
□ 199	Mookie Wilson	.08	.03	.01
□ 200	Don Mattingly	1.00	.40	.10
□ 201	Dick Schofield	.05	.02	.00
□ 202	Mark Gubicza	.08	.03	.01
□ 203	Gary Gaetti	.10	.04	.01
□ 204	Dan Pasqua	.08	.03	.01
□ 205	Andre Dawson	.12	.05	.01
□ 206	Chris Speier	.05	.02	.00
□ 207	Kent Tekulve	.05	.02	.00
□ 208	Rod Scurry	.05	.02	.00
□ 209	Scott Bailes	.05	.02	.00
□ 210	Rickey Henderson	.20	.08	.02
□ 211	Harold Baines	.08	.03	.01
□ 212	Tony Armas	.08	.03	.01
□ 213	Kent Hrbek	.12	.05	.01
□ 214	Darrin Jackson	.20	.08	.02
□ 215	George Brett	.20	.08	.02
□ 216	Rafael Santana	.05	.02	.00
□ 217	Andy Allanson	.05	.02	.00
□ 218	Brett Butler	.08	.03	.01
□ 219	Steve Jeltz	.05	.02	.00
□ 220	Jay Buhner	.20	.08	.02
□ 221	Bo Jackson	.20	.08	.02
□ 222	Angel Salazar	.05	.02	.00
□ 223	Kirk McCaskill	.05	.02	.00
□ 224	Steve Lyons	.05	.02	.00
□ 225	Bert Blyleven	.08	.03	.01
□ 226	Scott Bradley	.05	.02	.00
□ 227	Bob Melvin	.05	.02	.00
□ 228	Ron Kittle	.08	.03	.01
□ 229	Phil Bradley	.08	.03	.01
□ 230	Tommy John	.10	.04	.01
□ 231	Greg Walker	.08	.03	.01
□ 232	Juan Berenguer	.05	.02	.00
□ 233	Pat Tabler	.08	.03	.01
□ 234	Terry Clark	.20	.08	.02
□ 235	Rafael Palmeiro	.15	.06	.01
□ 236	Paul Zuvella	.05	.02	.00
□ 237	Willie Randolph	.08	.03	.01
□ 238	Bruce Fields	.05	.02	.00
□ 239	Mike Aldrete	.08	.03	.01
□ 240	Lance Parrish	.10	.04	.01
□ 241	Greg Maddux	.15	.06	.01
□ 242	John Moses	.05	.02	.00
□ 243	Melido Perez	.15	.06	.01
□ 244	Willie Wilson	.08	.03	.01
□ 245	Mark McLemore	.05	.02	.00
□ 246	Von Hayes	.08	.03	.01
□ 247	Matt Williams	.10	.04	.01
□ 248	John Candelaria	.08	.03	.01
□ 249	Harold Reynolds	.05	.02	.00
□ 250	Greg Swindell	.10	.04	.01
□ 251	Juan Agosto	.05	.02	.00
□ 252	Mike Felder	.05	.02	.00
□ 253	Vince Coleman	.15	.06	.01
□ 254	Larry Sheets	.08	.03	.01
□ 255	George Bell	.12	.05	.01
□ 256	Terry Steinbach	.10	.04	.01
□ 257	Jack Armstrong	.25	.10	.02
□ 258	Dickie Thon	.05	.02	.00
□ 259	Ray Knight	.08	.03	.01
□ 260	Darryl Strawberry	.50	.20	.05
□ 261	Doug Sisk	.05	.02	.00
□ 262	Alex Trevino	.05	.02	.00
□ 263	Jeffrey Leonard	.08	.03	.01
□ 264	Tom Henke	.08	.03	.01
□ 265	Ozzie Smith	.12	.05	.01
□ 266	Dave Bergman	.05	.02	.00
□ 267	Tony Phillips	.05	.02	.00
□ 268	Mark Davis	.08	.03	.01
□ 269	Kevin Elster	.08	.03	.01
□ 270	Barry Larkin	.12	.05	.01
□ 271	Manny Lee	.05	.02	.00
□ 272	Tom Brunansky	.10	.04	.01
□ 273	Craig Biggio	.20	.08	.02
□ 274	Jim Gantner	.05	.02	.00
□ 275	Eddie Murray	.15	.06	.01
□ 276	Jeff Reed	.05	.02	.00
□ 277	Tim Teufel	.05	.02	.00
□ 278	Rick Honeycutt	.05	.02	.00
□ 279	Guillermo Hernandez	.08	.03	.01
□ 280	John Kruk	.08	.03	.01
□ 281	Luis Alicea	.15	.06	.01
□ 282	Jim Clancy	.05	.02	.00
□ 283	Billy Ripken	.08	.03	.01
□ 284	Craig Reynolds	.05	.02	.00
□ 285	Robin Yount	.15	.06	.01
□ 286	Jimmy Jones	.08	.03	.01
□ 287	Ron Oester	.05	.02	.00
□ 288	Terry Leach	.08	.03	.01
□ 289	Dennis Eckersley	.12	.05	.01
□ 290	Alan Trammell	.15	.06	.01
□ 291	Jimmy Key	.08	.03	.01
□ 292	Chris Bosio	.05	.02	.00
□ 293	Jose DeLeon	.05	.02	.00
□ 294	Jim Traber	.05	.02	.00
□ 295	Mike Scott	.10	.04	.01
□ 296	Roger McDowell	.08	.03	.01
□ 297	Garry Templeton	.08	.03	.01
□ 298	Doyle Alexander	.08	.03	.01
□ 299	Nick Esasky	.05	.02	.00
□ 300	Mark McGwire	.50	.20	.05
□ 301	Darryl Hamilton	.25	.10	.02
□ 302	Dave Smith	.05	.02	.00
□ 303	Rick Sutcliffe	.10	.04	.01
□ 304	Dave Stapleton	.10	.04	.01
□ 305	Alan Ashby	.05	.02	.00
□ 306	Pedro Guerrero	.10	.04	.01
□ 307	Ron Guidry	.10	.04	.01
□ 308	Steve Farr	.05	.02	.00
□ 309	Curt Ford	.05	.02	.00
□ 310	Claudell Washington	.08	.03	.01
□ 311	Tom Prince	.10	.04	.01
□ 312	Chad Kreuter	.25	.10	.02
□ 313	Ken Oberkfell	.05	.02	.00
□ 314	Jerry Browne	.05	.02	.00
□ 315	R.J. Reynolds	.05	.02	.00
□ 316	Scott Bankhead	.05	.02	.00
□ 317	Milt Thompson	.05	.02	.00
□ 318	Mario Diaz	.10	.04	.01
□ 319	Bruce Ruffin	.05	.02	.00
□ 320	Dave Valle	.05	.02	.00
□ 321	Gary Varsho	.20	.08	.02
□ 322	Paul Mirabella	.05	.02	.00
□ 323	Chuck Jackson	.10	.04	.01
□ 324	Drew Hall	.05	.02	.00
□ 325	Don August	.08	.03	.01
□ 326	Israel Sanchez	.12	.05	.01
□ 327	Denny Walling	.05	.02	.00
□ 328	Joel Skinner	.05	.02	.00
□ 329	Danny Tartabull	.15	.06	.01
□ 330	Tony Pena	.08	.03	.01
□ 331	Jim Sundberg	.05	.02	.00
□ 332	Jeff Robinson Pittsburgh Pirates	.05	.02	.00
□ 333	Oddibe McDowell	.08	.03	.01
□ 334	Jose Lind	.05	.02	.00
□ 335	Paul Kilgus	.05	.02	.00
□ 336	Juan Samuel	.08	.03	.01
□ 337	Mike Campbell	.15	.06	.01
□ 338	Mike Maddux	.05	.02	.00
□ 339	Darnell Coles	.05	.02	.00
□ 340	Bob Dernier	.05	.02	.00
□ 341	Rafael Ramirez	.05	.02	.00
□ 342	Scott Sanderson	.05	.02	.00
□ 343	B.J. Surhoff	.08	.03	.01
□ 344	Billy Hatcher	.08	.03	.01
□ 345	Pat Perry	.05	.02	.00
□ 346	Jack Clark	.12	.05	.01
□ 347	Gary Thurman	.08	.03	.01
□ 348	Timmy Jones	.20	.08	.02
□ 349	Dave Winfield	.20	.08	.02
□ 350	Frank White	.08	.03	.01
□ 351	Dave Collins	.05	.02	.00
□ 352	Jack Morris	.10	.04	.01
□ 353	Eric Plunk	.05	.02	.00
□ 354	Leon Durham	.05	.02	.00
□ 355	Jose DeJesus	.12	.05	.01
□ 356	Brian Holman	.12	.05	.01
□ 357	Dale Murphy	.25	.10	.02
□ 358	Mark Portugal	.05	.02	.00
□ 359	Andy McGaffigan	.05	.02	.00
□ 360	Tom Glavine	.05	.02	.00
□ 361	Keith Moreland	.05	.02	.00
□ 362	Todd Stottlemyre	.15	.06	.01
□ 363	Dave Leiper	.05	.02	.00
□ 364	Cecil Fielder	.05	.02	.00
□ 365	Carmelo Martinez	.05	.02	.00
□ 366	Dwight Evans	.10	.04	.01
□ 367	Kevin McReynolds	.15	.06	.01
□ 368	Rich Gedman	.08	.03	.01
□ 369	Len Dykstra	.08	.03	.01

□ 370 Jody Reed .08 .03 .01
□ 371 Jose Canseco 1.00 .40 .10
□ 372 Rob Murphy .05 .02 .00
□ 373 Mike Henneman .05 .02 .00
□ 374 Walt Weiss .60 .24 .06
□ 375 Rob Dibble .15 .06 .01
□ 376 Kirby Puckett .35 .14 .03
□ 377 Dennis Martinez .08 .03 .01
□ 378 Ron Gant .30 .12 .03
□ 379 Brian Harper .05 .02 .00
□ 380 Nelson Santovenia .15 .06 .01
□ 381 Lloyd Moseby .08 .03 .01
□ 382 Lance McCullers .08 .03 .01
□ 383 Dave Stieb .08 .03 .01
□ 384 Tony Gwynn .25 .10 .02
□ 385 Mike Flanagan .08 .03 .01
□ 386 Bob Ojeda .08 .03 .01
□ 387 Bruce Hurst .10 .04 .01
□ 388 Dave Magadan .08 .03 .01
□ 389 Wade Boggs .60 .24 .06
□ 390 Gary Carter .15 .06 .01
□ 391 Frank Tanana .08 .03 .01
□ 392 Curt Young .05 .02 .00
□ 393 Jeff Treadway .12 .05 .01
□ 394 Darrell Evans .08 .03 .01
□ 395 Glenn Hubbard .05 .02 .00
□ 396 Chuck Cary .05 .02 .00
□ 397 Frank Viola .15 .06 .01
□ 398 Jeff Parrett .12 .05 .01
□ 399 Terry Blocker .15 .06 .01
□ 400 Dan Gladden .08 .03 .01
□ 401 Louie Meadows .12 .05 .01
□ 402 Tim Raines .15 .06 .01
□ 403 Joey Meyer .15 .06 .01
□ 404 Larry Andersen .05 .02 .00
□ 405 Rex Hudler .05 .02 .00
□ 406 Mike Schmidt .25 .10 .02
□ 407 John Franco .08 .03 .01
□ 408 Brady Anderson .20 .08 .02
□ 409 Don Carman .05 .02 .00
□ 410 Eric Davis .35 .14 .03
□ 411 Bob Stanley .05 .02 .00
□ 412 Pete Smith .12 .05 .01
□ 413 Jim Rice .12 .05 .01
□ 414 Bruce Sutter .08 .03 .01
□ 415 Oil Can Boyd .08 .03 .01
□ 416 Ruben Sierra .12 .05 .01
□ 417 Mike LaValliere .05 .02 .00
□ 418 Steve Buechele .05 .02 .00
□ 419 Gary Redus .05 .02 .00
□ 420 Scott Fletcher .05 .02 .00
□ 421 Dale Sveum .05 .02 .00
□ 422 Bob Knepper .05 .02 .00
□ 423 Luis Rivera .05 .02 .00
□ 424 Ted Higuera .08 .03 .01
□ 425 Kevin Bass .08 .03 .01
□ 426 Ken Gerhart .05 .02 .00
□ 427 Shane Rawley .05 .02 .00
□ 428 Paul O'Neill .05 .02 .00
□ 429 Joe Orsulak .05 .02 .00
□ 430 Jackie Gutierrez .05 .02 .00
□ 431 Gerald Perry .08 .03 .01
□ 432 Mike Greenwell .75 .30 .07
□ 433 Jerry Royster .05 .02 .00
□ 434 Ellis Burks .30 .12 .03
□ 435 Ed Olwine .05 .02 .00
□ 436 Dave Rucker .05 .02 .00
□ 437 Charlie Hough .05 .02 .00
□ 438 Bob Walk .05 .02 .00
□ 439 Bob Brower .05 .02 .00
□ 440 Barry Bonds .10 .04 .01
□ 441 Tom Foley .05 .02 .00
□ 442 Rob Deer .08 .03 .01
□ 443 Glenn Davis .12 .05 .01
□ 444 Dave Martinez .05 .02 .00
□ 445 Bill Wegman .05 .02 .00
□ 446 Lloyd McClendon .10 .04 .01
□ 447 Dave Schmidt .05 .02 .00
□ 448 Darren Daulton .05 .02 .00
□ 449 Frank Williams .05 .02 .00
□ 450 Don Aase .05 .02 .00
□ 451 Lou Whitaker .08 .03 .01
□ 452 Goose Gossage .08 .03 .01
□ 453 Ed Whitson .05 .02 .00
□ 454 Jim Walewander .10 .04 .01
□ 455 Damon Berryhill .20 .08 .02
□ 456 Tim Burke .05 .02 .00
□ 457 Barry Jones .05 .02 .00
□ 458 Joel Youngblood .05 .02 .00
□ 459 Floyd Youmans .05 .02 .00
□ 460 Mark Salas .05 .02 .00
□ 461 Jeff Russell .05 .02 .00
□ 462 Darrell Miller .05 .02 .00
□ 463 Jeff Kunkel .05 .02 .00
□ 464 Sherman Corbett .15 .06 .01
□ 465 Curtis Wilkerson .05 .02 .00
□ 466 Bud Black .05 .02 .00
□ 467 Cal Ripken Jr. .15 .06 .01
□ 468 John Farrell .05 .02 .00
□ 469 Terry Kennedy .05 .02 .00
□ 470 Tom Candiotti .05 .02 .00
□ 471 Roberto Alomar .20 .08 .02
□ 472 Jeff Robinson .10 .04 .01
Detroit Tigers
□ 473 Vance Law .05 .02 .00
□ 474 Randy Ready .05 .02 .00
□ 475 Walt Terrell .05 .02 .00
□ 476 Kelly Downs .05 .02 .00
□ 477 Johnny Paredes .12 .05 .01
□ 478 Shawn Hillegas .05 .02 .00
□ 479 Bob Brenly .05 .02 .00
□ 480 Otis Nixon .05 .02 .00
□ 481 Johnny Ray .08 .03 .01
□ 482 Geno Petralli .05 .02 .00
□ 483 Stu Cliburn .05 .02 .00
□ 484 Pete Incaviglia .12 .05 .01
□ 485 Brian Downing .05 .02 .00
□ 486 Jeff Stone .05 .02 .00
□ 487 Carmen Castillo .05 .02 .00
□ 488 Tom Niedenfuer .05 .02 .00
□ 489 Jay Bell .12 .05 .01
□ 490 Rick Schu .05 .02 .00
□ 491 Jeff Pico .12 .05 .01
□ 492 Mark Parent .12 .05 .01
□ 493 Eric King .05 .02 .00
□ 494 Al Nipper .05 .02 .00
□ 495 Andy Hawkins .08 .03 .01
□ 496 Daryl Boston .05 .02 .00
□ 497 Ernie Riles .05 .02 .00
□ 498 Pascual Perez .08 .03 .01
□ 499 Bill Long .05 .02 .00
□ 500 Kirt Manwaring .12 .05 .01
□ 501 Chuck Crim .05 .02 .00
□ 502 Candy Maldonado .08 .03 .01
□ 503 Dennis Lamp .05 .02 .00
□ 504 Glenn Braggs .08 .03 .01
□ 505 Joe Price .05 .02 .00
□ 506 Ken Williams .08 .03 .01
□ 507 Bill Pecota .05 .02 .00
□ 508 Rey Quinones .05 .02 .00
□ 509 Jeff Bittiger .15 .06 .01
□ 510 Kevin Seitzer .20 .08 .02
□ 511 Steve Bedrosian .08 .03 .01
□ 512 Todd Worrell .10 .04 .01
□ 513 Chris James .08 .03 .01
□ 514 Jose Oquendo .05 .02 .00
□ 515 David Palmer .05 .02 .00
□ 516 John Smiley .05 .02 .00
□ 517 Dave Clark .05 .02 .00
□ 518 Mike Dunne .08 .03 .01
□ 519 Ron Washington .05 .02 .00
□ 520 Bob Kipper .05 .02 .00
□ 521 Lee Smith .08 .03 .01
□ 522 Juan Castillo .05 .02 .00
□ 523 Don Robinson .05 .02 .00
□ 524 Kevin Romine .05 .02 .00
□ 525 Paul Molitor .10 .04 .01
□ 526 Mark Langston .08 .03 .01
□ 527 Donnie Hill .05 .02 .00
□ 528 Larry Owen .05 .02 .00
□ 529 Jerry Reed .05 .02 .00
□ 530 Jack McDowell .15 .06 .01
□ 531 Greg Mathews .05 .02 .00
□ 532 John Russell .05 .02 .00
□ 533 Dan Quisenberry .08 .03 .01
□ 534 Greg Gross .05 .02 .00
□ 535 Danny Cox .08 .03 .01
□ 536 Terry Francona .05 .02 .00
□ 537 Andy Van Slyke .12 .05 .01
□ 538 Mel Hall .05 .02 .00
□ 539 Jim Gott .05 .02 .00
□ 540 Doug Jones .08 .03 .01
□ 541 Craig Lefferts .05 .02 .00
□ 542 Mike Boddicker .08 .03 .01
□ 543 Greg Brock .05 .02 .00
□ 544 Atlee Hammaker .05 .02 .00
□ 545 Tom Bolton .10 .04 .01
□ 546 Mike Macfarlane .15 .06 .01
□ 547 Rich Renteria .15 .06 .01
□ 548 John Davis .05 .02 .00
□ 549 Floyd Bannister .05 .02 .00
□ 550 Mickey Brantley .08 .03 .01
□ 551 Duane Ward .05 .02 .00
□ 552 Dan Petry .05 .02 .00
□ 553 Mickey Tettleton .05 .02 .00
□ 554 Rick Leach .05 .02 .00
□ 555 Mike Witt .08 .03 .01
□ 556 Sid Bream .05 .02 .00
□ 557 Bobby Witt .08 .03 .01
□ 558 Tommy Herr .08 .03 .01

☐ 559 Randy Milligan .15 .06 .01
☐ 560 Jose Cecena .12 .05 .01
☐ 561 Mackey Sasser .15 .06 .01
☐ 562 Carney Lansford .08 .03 .01
☐ 563 Rick Aguilera .05 .02 .00
☐ 564 Ron Hassey .05 .02 .00
☐ 565 Dwight Gooden .40 .16 .04
☐ 566 Paul Assenmacher .05 .02 .00
☐ 567 Neil Allen .05 .02 .00
☐ 568 Jim Morrison .05 .02 .00
☐ 569 Mike Pagliarulo .08 .03 .01
☐ 570 Ted Simmons .10 .04 .01
☐ 571 Mark Thurmond .05 .02 .00
☐ 572 Fred McGriff .25 .10 .02
☐ 573 Wally Joyner .25 .10 .02
☐ 574 Jose Bautista .12 .05 .01
☐ 575 Kelly Gruber .05 .02 .00
☐ 576 Cecilio Guante .05 .02 .00
☐ 577 Mark Davidson .05 .02 .00
☐ 578 Bobby Bonilla .12 .05 .01
☐ 579 Mike Stanley .05 .02 .00
☐ 580 Gene Larkin .08 .03 .01
☐ 581 Stan Javier .05 .02 .00
☐ 582 Howard Johnson .08 .03 .01
☐ 583 Mike Gallego .05 .02 .00
☐ 584 David Cone .30 .12 .03
☐ 585 Doug Jennings .25 .10 .02
☐ 586 Charlie Hudson .05 .02 .00
☐ 587 Dion James .05 .02 .00
☐ 588 Al Leiter .25 .10 .02
☐ 589 Charlie Puleo .05 .02 .00
☐ 590 Roberto Kelly .20 .08 .02
☐ 591 Thad Bosley .05 .02 .00
☐ 592 Pete Stanicek .15 .06 .01
☐ 593 Pat Borders .15 .06 .01
☐ 594 Bryan Harvey .30 .12 .03
☐ 595 Jeff Ballard .12 .05 .01
☐ 596 Jeff Reardon .08 .03 .01
☐ 597 Doug Drabek .05 .02 .00
☐ 598 Edwin Correa .05 .02 .00
☐ 599 Keith Atherton .05 .02 .00
☐ 600 Dave LaPoint .05 .02 .00
☐ 601 Don Baylor .08 .03 .01
☐ 602 Tom Pagnozzi .12 .05 .01
☐ 603 Tim Flannery .05 .02 .00
☐ 604 Gene Walter .05 .02 .00
☐ 605 Dave Parker .10 .04 .01
☐ 606 Mike Diaz .05 .02 .00
☐ 607 Chris Gwynn .15 .06 .01
☐ 608 Odell Jones .05 .02 .00
☐ 609 Carlton Fisk .10 .04 .01
☐ 610 Jay Howell .05 .02 .00
☐ 611 Tim Crews .05 .02 .00
☐ 612 Keith Hernandez .12 .05 .01
☐ 613 Willie Fraser .05 .02 .00
☐ 614 Jim Eppard .10 .04 .01
☐ 615 Jeff Hamilton .05 .02 .00
☐ 616 Kurt Stillwell .05 .02 .00
☐ 617 Tom Browning .10 .04 .01
☐ 618 Jeff Montgomery .12 .05 .01
☐ 619 Jose Rijo .08 .03 .01
☐ 620 Jamie Quirk .05 .02 .00
☐ 621 Willie McGee .10 .04 .01
☐ 622 Mark Grant .05 .02 .00
☐ 623 Bill Swift .05 .02 .00
☐ 624 Orlando Mercado .05 .02 .00
☐ 625 John Costello .15 .06 .01
☐ 626 Jose Gonzalez .08 .03 .01
☐ 627 Bill Schroeder .05 .02 .00
☐ 628 Fred Manrique .05 .02 .00
☐ 629 Ricky Horton .05 .02 .00
☐ 630 Dan Plesac .08 .03 .01
☐ 631 Alfredo Griffin .08 .03 .01
☐ 632 Chuck Finley .05 .02 .00
☐ 633 Kirk Gibson .15 .06 .01
☐ 634 Randy Myers .08 .03 .01
☐ 635 Greg Minton .05 .02 .00
☐ 636 Herm Winningham .05 .02 .00
☐ 637 Charlie Leibrandt .08 .03 .01
☐ 638 Tim Birtsas .05 .02 .00
☐ 639 Bill Buckner .08 .03 .01
☐ 640 Danny Jackson .12 .05 .01
☐ 641 Greg Booker .05 .02 .00
☐ 642 Jim Presley .08 .03 .01
☐ 643 Gene Nelson .05 .02 .00
☐ 644 Rod Booker .12 .05 .01
☐ 645 Dennis Rasmussen .08 .03 .01
☐ 646 Juan Nieves .05 .02 .00
☐ 647 Bobby Thigpen .08 .03 .01
☐ 648 Tim Belcher .12 .05 .01
☐ 649 Mike Young .05 .02 .00
☐ 650 Ivan Calderon .08 .03 .01
☐ 651 Oswaldo Peraza .12 .05 .01
☐ 652 Pat Sheridan .05 .02 .00
☐ 653 Mike Morgan .05 .02 .00
☐ 654 Mike Heath .05 .02 .00
☐ 655 Jay Tibbs .05 .02 .00
☐ 656 Fernando Valenzuela .12 .05 .01
☐ 657 Lee Mazzilli .05 .02 .00
☐ 658 AL CY: Frank Viola .10 .04 .01
☐ 659 AL MVP: Jose Canseco .35 .14 .03
☐ 660 AL ROY: Walt Weiss .15 .06 .01
☐ 661 NL CY: Orel Hershiser .20 .08 .02
☐ 662 NL MVP: Kirk Gibson .12 .05 .01
☐ 663 NL ROY: Chris Sabo .15 .06 .01
☐ 664 ALCS MVP: J.Canseco .35 .14 .03
☐ 665 NLCS MVP: O.Hershiser .20 .08 .02
☐ 666 Great WS Moment .10 .04 .01
☐ 667 WS MVP: O.Hershiser .20 .08 .02
☐ 668 Angels Checklist .20 .08 .02
Wally Joyner
☐ 669 Astros Checklist .20 .08 .02
Nolan Ryan
☐ 670 Athletics Checklist .60 .24 .06
Jose Canseco
☐ 671 Blue Jays Checklist .20 .08 .02
Fred McGriff
☐ 672 Braves Checklist .20 .08 .02
Dale Murphy
☐ 673 Brewers Checklist .15 .06 .01
Paul Molitor
☐ 674 Cardinals Checklist .15 .06 .01
Ozzie Smith
☐ 675 Cubs Checklist .15 .06 .01
Ryne Sandberg
☐ 676 Dodgers Checklist .15 .06 .01
Kirk Gibson
☐ 677 Expos Checklist .15 .06 .01
Andres Galaragga
☐ 678 Giants Checklist .25 .10 .02
Will Clark
☐ 679 Indians Checklist .15 .06 .01
Cory Snyder
☐ 680 Mariners Checklist .15 .06 .01
Alvin Davis
☐ 681 Mets Checklist .35 .14 .03
Darryl Strawberry
☐ 682 Orioles Checklist .20 .08 .02
Cal Ripken
☐ 683 Padres Checklist .20 .08 .02
Tony Gwynn
☐ 684 Phillies Checklist .20 .08 .02
Mike Schmidt
☐ 685 Pirates Checklist .15 .06 .01
Andy Van Slyke
☐ 686 Rangers Checklist .15 .06 .01
Ruben Sierra
☐ 687 Red Sox Checklist .35 .14 .03
Wade Boggs
☐ 688 Reds Checklist .25 .10 .02
Eric Davis
☐ 689 Royals Checklist .15 .06 .01
George Brett
☐ 690 Tigers Checklist .15 .06 .01
Alan Trammell
☐ 691 Twins Checklist .15 .06 .01
Frank Viola
☐ 692 White Sox Checklist .15 .06 .01
Harold Baines
☐ 693 Yankees Checklist .50 .20 .05
Don Mattingly
☐ 694 Checklist 1-100 .05 .01 .00
☐ 695 Checklist 101-200 .05 .01 .00
☐ 696 Checklist 201-300 .05 .01 .00
☐ 697 Checklist 301-400 .05 .01 .00
☐ 698 Checklist 401-500 .05 .01 .00
☐ 699 Checklist 501-600 .05 .01 .00
☐ 700 Checklist 601-700 .05 .01 .00

1985 Wendy's Tigers

This 22-card set features Detroit Tigers; cards measure 2 1/2" by 3 1/2". The set was co-sponsored by Wendy's and Coca-Cola and was distributed in the Detroit metropolitian area. Coca-Cola purchasers were given a pack which contained three Tiger cards plus a header card. The orange-bordered player photos are different from those used by Topps in their regular set. The cards were produced by Topps as evidenced by the similarity of the card backs with the Topps regular set backs. The set is numbered on the back; the order corresponds to the alphabetical order of the player's names.

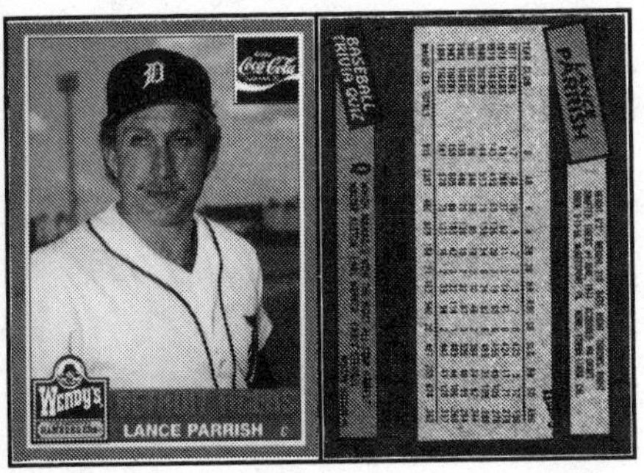

	MINT	EXC	G-VG
COMPLETE SET (22)	8.00	3.25	.80
COMMON PLAYER (1-22)	.20	.08	.02
☐ 1 Sparky Anderson MG (checklist back)	.35	.10	.02
☐ 2 Doug Bair	.20	.08	.02
☐ 3 Juan Berenguer	.25	.10	.02
☐ 4 Dave Bergman	.20	.08	.02
☐ 5 Tom Brookens	.20	.08	.02
☐ 6 Marty Castillo	.20	.08	.02
☐ 7 Darrell Evans	.40	.16	.04
☐ 8 Barbaro Garbey	.20	.08	.02
☐ 9 Kirk Gibson	1.25	.50	.12
☐ 10 Johnny Grubb	.20	.08	.02
☐ 11 Willie Hernandez	.35	.14	.03
☐ 12 Larry Herndon	.25	.10	.02
☐ 13 Rusty Kuntz	.20	.08	.02
☐ 14 Chet Lemon	.30	.12	.03
☐ 15 Aurelio Lopez	.20	.08	.02
☐ 16 Jack Morris	1.00	.40	.10
☐ 17 Lance Parrish	1.00	.40	.10
☐ 18 Dan Petry	.30	.12	.03
☐ 19 Bill Scherrer	.20	.08	.02
☐ 20 Alan Trammell	1.25	.50	.12
☐ 21 Lou Whitaker	.75	.30	.07
☐ 22 Milt Wilcox	.20	.08	.02

1982 Wheaties Indians

The cards in this 30-card set measure 2 13/16" by 4 1/8". This set of Cleveland Indians baseball players was co- produced by the Indians baseball club and Wheaties, whose respective logos appear on the front of every card. The cards were given away in groups of 10 as a promotion during games on May 30 (1-10), June 19 (11-20) and July 16, 1982 (21-30). The manager (MG), four coaches (CO), and 25 players are featured in a simple format of a color picture, player name and position. The cards are not numbered and the backs contain a Wheaties ad. The set was later sold at the Cleveland Indians gift shop. The cards are ordered below alphabetically within groups of ten as they were issued.

	MINT	EXC	G-VG
COMPLETE SET (30)	9.00	3.50	.70
COMMON PLAYER (1-30)	.25	.08	.02
☐ 1 Bert Blyleven	.65	.24	.06
☐ 2 Joe Charboneau	.30	.10	.02
☐ 3 Jerry Dybzinski	.25	.08	.02
☐ 4 Dave Garcia MG	.25	.08	.02
☐ 5 Toby Harrah	.35	.12	.03
☐ 6 Ron Hassey	.30	.10	.02
☐ 7 Dennis Lewallyn	.25	.08	.02
☐ 8 Rick Manning	.25	.08	.02
☐ 9 Tommy McCraw CO	.25	.08	.02
☐ 10 Rick Waits	.25	.08	.02
☐ 11 Chris Bando	.25	.08	.02
☐ 12 Len Barker	.30	.10	.02
☐ 13 Tom Brennan	.25	.08	.02
☐ 14 Rodney Craig	.25	.08	.02
☐ 15 Mike Fischlin	.25	.08	.02
☐ 16 Johnny Goryl CO	.25	.08	.02
☐ 17 Mel Queen CO	.25	.08	.02
☐ 18 Lary Sorensen	.25	.08	.02
☐ 19 Andre Thornton	.50	.18	.04
☐ 20 Eddie Whitson	.35	.12	.03
☐ 21 Alan Bannister	.25	.08	.02
☐ 22 John Denny	.35	.14	.03
☐ 23 Miguel Dilone	.25	.08	.02
☐ 24 Mike Hargrove	.30	.10	.02
☐ 25 Von Hayes	.90	.36	.09
☐ 26 Bake McBride	.25	.08	.02
☐ 27 Jack Perconte	.25	.08	.02
☐ 28 Dennis Sommers CO	.25	.08	.02
☐ 29 Dan Spillner	.25	.08	.02
☐ 30 Rick Sutcliffe	.75	.28	.07

1983 Wheaties Indians

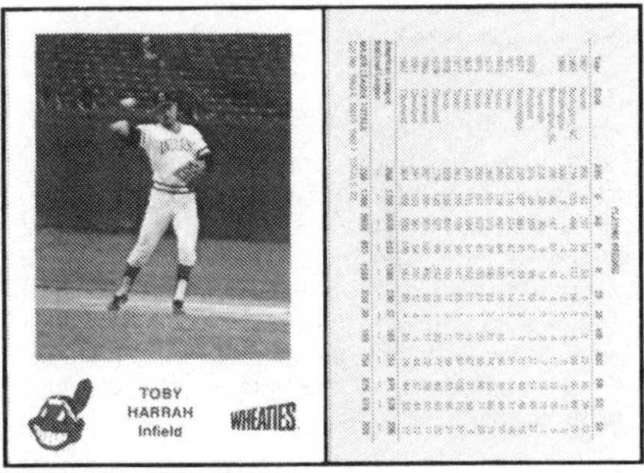

The cards in this 32-card set measure 2 13/16" by 4 1/8". The full color set of 1983 Wheaties Indians is quite similar to the Wheaties set of 1982. The backs, however, are significantly different. They contain complete career playing records of the players. The complete sets were given away at the ball park on May 15, 1983. The set was later made available at the Indians Gift Shop. The manager (MG) and several coaches (CO) are included in the set. The cards below are ordered alphabetically by the subject's name.

	MINT	EXC	G-VG
COMPLETE SET (32)	7.00	2.80	.70
COMMON PLAYER (1-32)	.20	.08	.02
☐ 1 Bud Anderson	.20	.08	.02
☐ 2 Jay Baller	.20	.08	.02
☐ 3 Chris Bando	.20	.08	.02
☐ 4 Alan Bannister	.20	.08	.02

□ 5 Len Barker	.25	.10	.02
□ 6 Bert Blyleven	.50	.20	.05
□ 7 Wil Culmer	.20	.08	.02
□ 8 Miguel Dilone	.20	.08	.02
□ 9 Juan Eichelberger	.20	.08	.02
□ 10 Jim Essian	.20	.08	.02
□ 11 Mike Ferraro MG	.20	.08	.02
□ 12 Mike Fischlin	.20	.08	.02
□ 13 Julio Franco	.75	.30	.07
□ 14 Ed Glynn	.20	.08	.02
□ 15 Johnny Goryl CO	.20	.08	.02
□ 16 Mike Hargrove	.25	.10	.02
□ 17 Toby Harrah	.30	.12	.03
□ 18 Ron Hassey	.20	.08	.02
□ 19 Neal Heaton	.20	.08	.02
□ 20 Rick Manning	.20	.08	.02
□ 21 Bake McBride	.25	.10	.02
□ 22 Don McMahon CO	.20	.08	.02
□ 23 Ed Napoleon CO	.20	.08	.02
□ 24 Broderick Perkins	.20	.08	.02
□ 25 Dennis Sommers CO	.20	.08	.02
□ 26 Lary Sorensen	.20	.08	.02
□ 27 Dan Spillner	.20	.08	.02
□ 28 Rick Sutcliffe	.70	.28	.07
□ 29 Andre Thornton	.45	.18	.04
□ 30 Manny Trillo	.20	.08	.02
□ 31 George Vukovich	.20	.08	.02
□ 32 Rick Waits	.20	.08	.02
□ 37 Don Schulze	.20	.08	.02
□ 38 Luis Aponte	.20	.08	.02
□ 44 Neal Heaton	.20	.08	.02
□ 46 Mike Jeffcoat	.20	.08	.02
□ 54 Tom Waddell	.20	.08	.02
□ xx Indians Coaches: (unnumbered) John Goryl, Dennis Sommers, Ed Napoleon, Bobby Bonds, Don McMahon	.20	.08	.02
□ xx Tom-E-Hawk (Mascot) (unnumbered)	.20	.08	.02

1984 Wheaties Indians

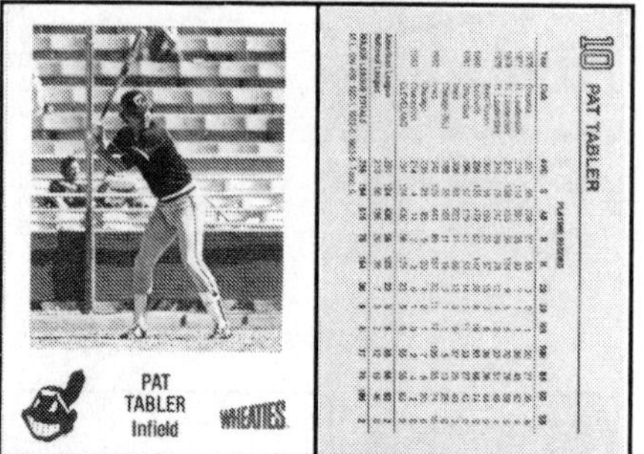

The cards in this 29-card set measure 2 13/16" by 4 1/8". For the third straight year, Wheaties distributed a set of Cleveland Indians baseball cards. These over-sized cards were passed out at a Baseball Card Day at the Cleveland Stadium. Similar in appearance to the cards of the past two years, both the Indians and the Wheaties logos appear on the obverse, along with the name, team and position. Cards are numbered on the back by the player's uniform number.

	MINT	EXC	G-VG
COMPLETE SET (29)	7.00	2.80	.70
COMMON PLAYER	.20	.08	.02
□ 2 Brett Butler	.50	.20	.05
□ 4 Tony Bernazard	.25	.10	.02
□ 8 Carmelo Castillo	.20	.08	.02
□ 10 Pat Tabler	.45	.18	.04
□ 13 Ernie Camacho	.25	.10	.02
□ 14 Julio Franco	.60	.24	.06
□ 15 Broderick Perkins	.20	.08	.02
□ 16 Jerry Willard	.20	.08	.02
□ 18 Pat Corrales MG	.20	.08	.02
□ 21 Mike Hargrove	.25	.10	.02
□ 22 Mike Fischlin	.20	.08	.02
□ 23 Chris Bando	.20	.08	.02
□ 24 George Vukovich	.20	.08	.02
□ 26 Brook Jacoby	.50	.20	.05
□ 27 Steve Farr	.20	.08	.02
□ 28 Bert Blyleven	.45	.18	.04
□ 29 Andre Thornton	.35	.14	.03
□ 30 Joe Carter	1.00	.40	.10
□ 31 Steve Comer	.20	.08	.02
□ 33 Roy Smith	.20	.08	.02
□ 34 Mel Hall	.40	.16	.04
□ 36 Jamie Easterly	.20	.08	.02

1954 Wilson

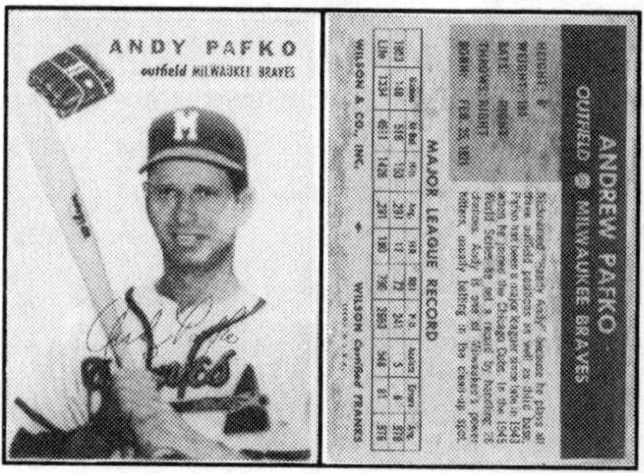

The cards in this 20-card set measure 2 5/8" by 3 3/4". The 1954 "Wilson Weiners" set contains 20 full color, unnumbered cards. The obverse design of a package of hot dogs appearing to fly through the air is a distinctive feature of this set. Uncut sheets have been seen. Cards are numbered below alphabetically by player's name.

	NRMT	VG-E	GOOD
COMPLETE SET (20)	5500.00	2350.00	600.00
COMMON PLAYER (1-20)	125.00	50.00	12.50
□ 1 Roy Campanella	600.00	240.00	60.00
□ 2 Del Ennis	125.00	50.00	12.50
□ 3 Carl Erskine	175.00	70.00	18.00
□ 4 Ferris Fain	125.00	50.00	12.50
□ 5 Bob Feller	500.00	200.00	50.00
□ 6 Nelson Fox	225.00	90.00	22.00
□ 7 Johnny Groth	125.00	50.00	12.50
□ 8 Stan Hack	125.00	50.00	12.50
□ 9 Gil Hodges	350.00	140.00	35.00
□ 10 Ray Jablonski	125.00	50.00	12.50
□ 11 Harvey Kuenn	200.00	80.00	20.00
□ 12 Roy McMillan	125.00	50.00	12.50
□ 13 Andy Pafko	125.00	50.00	12.50
□ 14 Paul Richards MG	125.00	50.00	12.50
□ 15 Hank Sauer	125.00	50.00	12.50
□ 16 Red Schoendienst	175.00	70.00	18.00
□ 17 Enos Slaughter	350.00	140.00	35.00
□ 18 Vern Stephens	125.00	50.00	12.50
□ 19 Sammy White	125.00	50.00	12.50
□ 20 Ted Williams	2000.00	750.00	200.00

1985 Woolworth's

This 44-card set features color as well as black and white cards of All Time Record Holders. The cards are standard size (2 1/2" by 3 1/2") and are printed with blue ink on an orange and white back. The set was produced for Woolworth's by Topps and was packaged in a colorful box which contained a checklist of the cards in the set on the back panel. The numerical order of the cards coincides alphabetically with player's name.

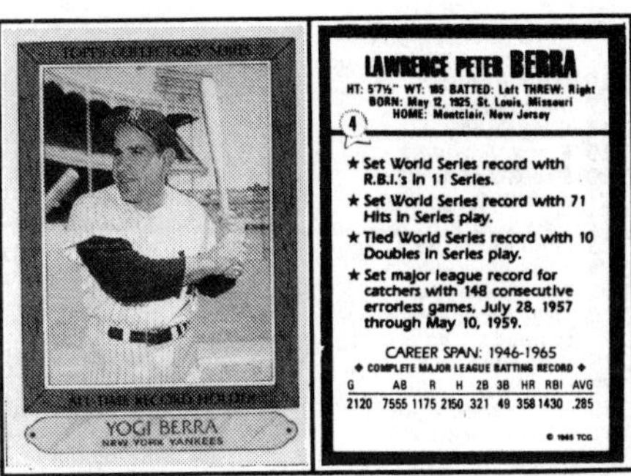

	MINT	EXC	G-VG
COMPLETE SET (44)	4.00	1.60	.40
COMMON PLAYER (1-44)	.05	.02	.00
□ 1 Hank Aaron	.20	.08	.02
□ 2 Grover C. Alexander	.05	.02	.00
□ 3 Ernie Banks	.15	.06	.01
□ 4 Yogi Berra	.15	.06	.01
□ 5 Lou Brock	.10	.04	.01
□ 6 Steve Carlton	.10	.04	.01
□ 7 Jack Chesbro	.05	.02	.00
□ 8 Ty Cobb	.30	.12	.03
□ 9 Sam Crawford	.05	.02	.00
□ 10 Rollie Fingers	.05	.02	.00
□ 11 Whitey Ford	.10	.04	.01
□ 12 John Frederick	.05	.02	.00
□ 13 Frankie Frisch	.05	.02	.00
□ 14 Lou Gehrig	.30	.12	.03
□ 15 Jim Gentile	.05	.02	.00
□ 16 Dwight Gooden	.30	.12	.03
□ 17 Rickey Henderson	.20	.08	.02
□ 18 Rogers Hornsby	.10	.04	.01
□ 19 Frank Howard	.05	.02	.00
□ 20 Cliff Johnson	.05	.02	.00
□ 21 Walter Johnson	.15	.06	.01
□ 22 Hub Leonard	.05	.02	.00
□ 23 Mickey Mantle	.50	.20	.05
□ 24 Roger Maris	.15	.06	.01
□ 25 Christy Mathewson	.10	.04	.01
□ 26 Willie Mays	.20	.08	.02
□ 27 Stan Musial	.15	.06	.01
□ 28 Don Quisenberry	.05	.02	.00
□ 29 Frank Robinson	.07	.03	.01
□ 30 Pete Rose	.35	.14	.03
□ 31 Babe Ruth	.50	.20	.05
□ 32 Nolan Ryan	.15	.06	.01
□ 33 George Sisler	.05	.02	.00
□ 34 Tris Speaker	.10	.04	.01
□ 35 Ed Walsh	.05	.02	.00
□ 36 Lloyd Waner	.05	.02	.00
□ 37 Earl Webb	.05	.02	.00
□ 38 Ted Williams	.20	.08	.02
□ 39 Maury Wills	.05	.02	.00
□ 40 Hack Wilson	.07	.03	.01
□ 41 Owen Wilson	.05	.02	.00
□ 42 Willie Wilson	.05	.02	.00
□ 43 Rudy York	.05	.02	.00
□ 44 Cy Young	.10	.04	.01

1986 Woolworth's

This boxed set of 33 cards was produced by Topps for Woolworth's variety stores. The set features players who hold or have held hitting, home run or RBI titles. Cards are the standard 2 1/2" by 3 1/2" and have a glossy finish. The card fronts are bordered in yellow with the subtitle "Topps Collectors' Series" across the top. The card backs are printed in green and blue ink on white card stock. The custom box gives the set checklist on the back.

	MINT	EXC	G-VG
COMPLETE SET (33)	4.00	1.60	.40
COMMON PLAYER (1-33)	.06	.02	.00

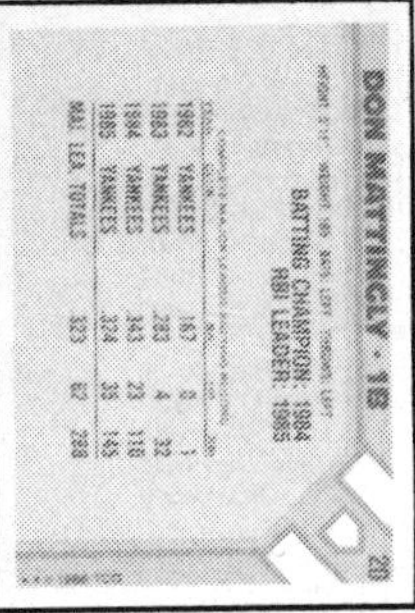

	MINT	EXC	G-VG
□ 1 Tony Armas	.06	.02	.00
□ 2 Don Baylor	.10	.04	.01
□ 3 Wade Boggs	.65	.26	.06
□ 4 George Brett	.40	.16	.04
□ 5 Bill Buckner	.06	.02	.00
□ 6 Rod Carew	.25	.10	.02
□ 7 Gary Carter	.25	.10	.02
□ 8 Cecil Cooper	.10	.04	.01
□ 9 Darrell Evans	.10	.04	.01
□ 10 Dwight Evans	.10	.04	.01
□ 11 George Foster	.10	.04	.01
□ 12 Bob Grich	.06	.02	.00
□ 13 Tony Gwynn	.40	.16	.04
□ 14 Keith Hernandez	.20	.08	.02
□ 15 Reggie Jackson	.40	.16	.04
□ 16 Dave Kingman	.10	.04	.01
□ 17 Carney Lansford	.10	.04	.01
□ 18 Fred Lynn	.10	.04	.01
□ 19 Bill Madlock	.06	.02	.00
□ 20 Don Mattingly	.85	.34	.08
□ 21 Willie McGee	.15	.06	.01
□ 22 Hal McRae	.06	.02	.00
□ 23 Dale Murphy	.45	.18	.04
□ 24 Eddie Murray	.25	.10	.02
□ 25 Ben Oglivie	.06	.02	.00
□ 26 Al Oliver	.06	.02	.00
□ 27 Dave Parker	.10	.04	.01
□ 28 Jim Rice	.20	.08	.02
□ 29 Pete Rose	.50	.20	.05
□ 30 Mike Schmidt	.40	.16	.04
□ 31 Gorman Thomas	.10	.04	.01
□ 32 Willie Wilson	.10	.04	.01
□ 33 Dave Winfield	.25	.10	.02

1987 Woolworth's Highlights

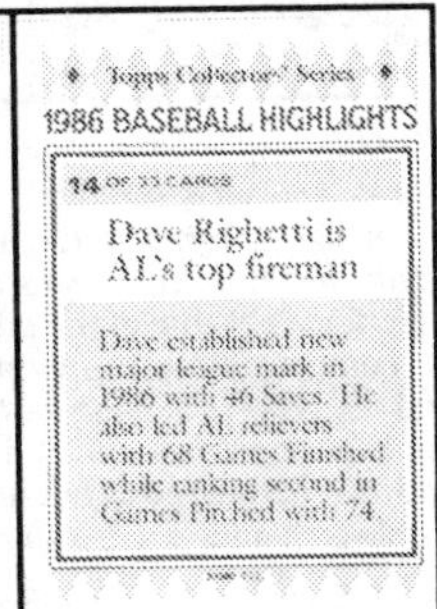

Topps produced this 33-card set for Woolworth's stores. The set is subtitled "Topps Collectors' Series Baseball Highlights" and consists of high gloss card fronts with full- color photos. The cards show and describe highlights of the previous season. The card backs are printed in gold and purple and are numbered. The set was sold nationally in Woolworth's for a 1.99 suggested retail price.

	MINT	EXC	G-VG
COMPLETE SET (33)	4.00	1.60	.40
COMMON PLAYER (1-33)	.07	.03	.01

□ 1	Steve Carlton	.25	.10	.02
□ 2	Cecil Cooper	.10	.04	.01
□ 3	Rickey Henderson	.35	.14	.03
□ 4	Reggie Jackson	.35	.14	.03
□ 5	Jim Rice	.20	.08	.02
□ 6	Don Sutton	.20	.08	.02
□ 7	Roger Clemens	.45	.18	.04
□ 8	Mike Schmidt	.35	.14	.03
□ 9	Jesse Barfield	.15	.06	.01
□ 10	Wade Boggs	.60	.24	.06
□ 11	Tim Raines	.30	.12	.03
□ 12	Jose Canseco	1.00	.40	.10
□ 13	Todd Worrell	.15	.06	.01
□ 14	Dave Righetti	.15	.06	.01
□ 15	Don Mattingly	.85	.34	.08
□ 16	Tony Gwynn	.35	.14	.03
□ 17	Marty Barrett	.07	.03	.01
□ 18	Mike Scott	.15	.06	.01
□ 19	Bruce Hurst	.10	.04	.01
□ 20	Calvin Schiraldi	.07	.03	.01
□ 21	Dwight Evans	.15	.06	.01
□ 22	Dave Henderson	.07	.03	.01
□ 23	Len Dykstra	.10	.04	.01
□ 24	Bob Ojeda	.07	.03	.01
□ 25	Gary Carter	.25	.10	.02
□ 26	Ron Darling	.15	.06	.01
□ 27	Jim Rice	.20	.08	.02
□ 28	Bruce Hurst	.10	.04	.01
□ 29	Darryl Strawberry	.60	.24	.06
□ 30	Ray Knight	.07	.03	.01
□ 31	Keith Hernandez	.25	.10	.02
□ 32	Mets Celebration	.07	.03	.01
□ 33	Ray Knight	.07	.03	.01

1988 Woolworth's Highlights

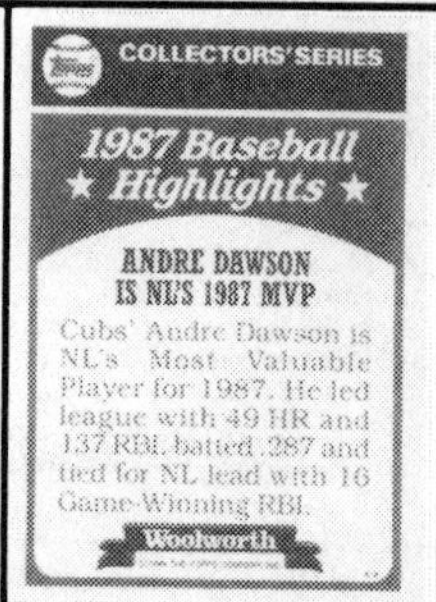

Topps produced this 33-card set for Woolworth's stores. The set is subtitled "Topps Collectors' Series Baseball Highlights" and consists of high gloss card fronts with full- color photos. The cards show and describe highlights of the previous season. Cards 19-33 commemorate the World Series with highlights and key players of each game in the series. The card backs are printed in red and blue on white card stock and are numbered. The set was sold nationally in Woolworth's for a 1.99 suggested retail price.

		MINT	EXC	G-VG
COMPLETE SET (33)		4.00	1.60	.40
COMMON PLAYER (1-33)		.05	.02	.00
□ 1	Don Baylor	.08	.03	.01
□ 2	Vince Coleman	.12	.05	.01
□ 3	Darrell Evans	.08	.03	.01
□ 4	Don Mattingly	.75	.30	.07
□ 5	Eddie Murray	.20	.08	.02
□ 6	Nolan Ryan	.20	.08	.02
□ 7	Mike Schmidt	.25	.10	.02
□ 8	Andre Dawson	.15	.06	.01
□ 9	George Bell	.12	.05	.01
□ 10	Steve Bedrosian	.08	.03	.01
□ 11	Roger Clemens	.40	.16	.04
□ 12	Tony Gwynn	.30	.12	.03
□ 13	Wade Boggs	.50	.20	.05
□ 14	Benny Santiago	.20	.08	.02
□ 15	Mark McGwire UER (referenced on card back as NL ROY, sic)	.50	.20	.05
□ 16	Dave Righetti	.08	.03	.01
□ 17	Jeffrey Leonard	.05	.02	.00
□ 18	Gary Gaetti	.08	.03	.01
□ 19	Frank Viola WS1	.10	.04	.01
□ 20	Dan Gladden WS1	.05	.02	.00
□ 21	Bert Blyleven WS2	.08	.03	.01
□ 22	Gary Gaetti WS2	.10	.04	.01
□ 23	John Tudor WS3	.08	.03	.01
□ 24	Todd Worrell WS3	.10	.04	.01
□ 25	Tom Lawless WS4	.05	.02	.00
□ 26	Willie McGee WS4	.10	.04	.01
□ 27	Danny Cox WS5	.08	.03	.01
□ 28	Curt Ford WS5	.05	.02	.00
□ 29	Don Baylor WS6	.08	.03	.01
□ 30	Kent Hrbek WS6	.10	.04	.01
□ 31	Kirby Puckett WS7	.20	.08	.02
□ 32	Greg Gagne WS7	.05	.02	.00
□ 33	Frank Viola WS-MVP	.12	.05	.01

1931 W517

The cards in this 54-card set measure 3" by 4". This 1931 set of numbered, blank backed cards was placed in the "W" category in the ACC because (1) its producer was unknown and (2) it was issued in strips of three. The photo is black and white but the entire obverse of each card is generally found tinted in tones of sepia, blue, green, yellow, rose, black or gray. The cards are numbered in a small circle on the front. A solid dark line at one end of a card entitled the purchaser to another piece of candy as a prize. There are two different cards of both Babe Ruth and Mickey Cochrane.

		NRMT	VG-E	GOOD
COMPLETE SET (54)		4400.00	1850.00	550.00
COMMON PLAYER (1-54)		30.00	12.00	3.00
□ 1	Earl Combs	60.00	24.00	6.00
□ 2	Pie Traynor	75.00	30.00	7.50
□ 3	Eddie Rousch	75.00	30.00	7.50
□ 4	Babe Ruth	750.00	300.00	75.00
□ 5	Chalmer Cissell	30.00	12.00	3.00
□ 6	Bill Sherdel	30.00	12.00	3.00
□ 7	Bill Shore	30.00	12.00	3.00
□ 8	George Earnshaw	30.00	12.00	3.00
□ 9	Bucky Harris	60.00	24.00	6.00
□ 10	Charlie Klein	75.00	30.00	7.50
□ 11	George Kelly	60.00	24.00	6.00
□ 12	Travis Jackson	60.00	24.00	6.00
□ 13	Willie Kamm	30.00	12.00	3.00
□ 14	Harry Heilman	75.00	30.00	7.50
□ 15	Grover Alexander	100.00	40.00	10.00
□ 16	Frank Frisch	75.00	30.00	7.50
□ 17	Jack Quinn	30.00	12.00	3.00
□ 18	Cy Williams	30.00	12.00	3.00
□ 19	Kiki Cuyler	60.00	24.00	6.00
□ 20	Babe Ruth	900.00	360.00	90.00

□ 21 Jimmy Foxx	150.00	60.00	15.00
□ 22 Jimmy Dykes	35.00	14.00	3.50
□ 23 Bill Terry	75.00	30.00	7.50
□ 24 Freddy Lindstrom	60.00	24.00	6.00
□ 25 Hugh Critz	30.00	12.00	3.00
□ 26 Pete Donahue	30.00	12.00	3.00
□ 27 Tony Lazzeri	50.00	20.00	5.00
□ 28 Heine Manush	60.00	24.00	6.00
□ 29 Chick Hafey	60.00	24.00	6.00
□ 30 Melvin Ott	100.00	40.00	10.00
□ 31 Bing Miller	30.00	12.00	3.00
□ 32 George Haas	30.00	12.00	3.00
□ 33 Lefty O'Doul	50.00	20.00	5.00
□ 34 Paul Waner	60.00	24.00	6.00
□ 35 Lou Gehrig	500.00	200.00	50.00
□ 36 Dazzy Vance	60.00	24.00	6.00
□ 37 Mickey Cochrane	90.00	36.00	9.00
□ 38 Rogers Hornsby	150.00	60.00	15.00
□ 39 Lefty Grove	125.00	50.00	12.50
□ 40 Al Simmons	75.00	30.00	7.50
□ 41 Rube Walberg	30.00	12.00	3.00
□ 42 Hack Wilson	100.00	40.00	10.00
□ 43 Art Shires	30.00	12.00	3.00
□ 44 Sammy Hale	30.00	12.00	3.00
□ 45 Ted Lyons	60.00	24.00	6.00
□ 46 Joe Sewell	60.00	24.00	6.00
□ 47 Goose Goslin	60.00	24.00	6.00
□ 48 Lou Fonseca	30.00	12.00	3.00
□ 49 Bob Meusel	40.00	16.00	4.00
□ 50 Lu Blue	30.00	12.00	3.00
□ 51 Earl Averill	60.00	24.00	6.00
□ 52 Eddy Collins	75.00	30.00	7.50
□ 53 Joe Judge	30.00	12.00	3.00
□ 54 Mickey Cochrane	90.00	36.00	9.00

W576 1950-56 Callahan HOF

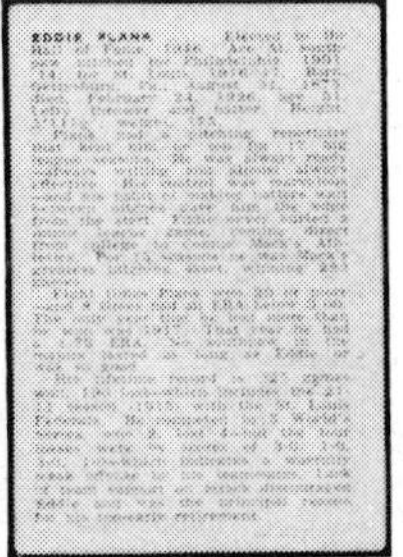

The cards in this 82-card set measure 1 3/4" by 2 1/2". The 1950-56 Callahan Hall of Fame set was issued over a number of years at the Baseball Hall of Fame museum in Cooperstown, New York. New cards were added to the set each year when new members were inducted into the Hall of Fame. The cards with (2) in the checklist exist with two different biographies. The year of each card's first inclusion in the set is also given in parentheses; those not listed parenthetically below were issued in 1950 as well as in all the succeeding years and are hence the most common. Naturally the supply of cards is directly related to how many years a player was included in the set; cards that were not issued until 1955 are much scarcer than those printed all the years between 1950 and 1956. The ACC designation is W576. One frequently finds "complete" sets in the original box; take care to investigate the year of issue, the set may be complete in the sense of all the cards issued up to a certain year, but not all 82 cards below. For example, a "complete" 1950 set would obviously not include any of the cards marked below with ('52), ('54), or ('55) as none of those cards existed in 1950 since those respective players had not yet been inducted. The complete set price below refers to a set including all 82 cards below with variations. Since the cards are unnumbered, they are numbered below for reference alphabetically by player's name.

	NRMT	VG-E	GOOD
COMPLETE SET (82)	325.00	135.00	40.00
COMMON PLAYER ('50)	1.25	.50	.12
COMMON PLAYER ('52)	2.50	1.00	.25
COMMON PLAYER ('54)	3.50	1.40	.35
COMMON PLAYER ('55)	5.00	2.00	.50
□ 1 Grover Alexander	2.50	1.00	.25
□ 2 Cap Anson	1.50	.60	.15
□ 3 Frank Baker ('55)	5.00	2.00	.50
□ 4 Edward Barrow ('54)	3.50	1.40	.35
□ 5 Chief Bender(2)('54)	3.50	1.40	.35
□ 6 Roger Bresnahan	1.25	.50	.12
□ 7 Dan Brouthers	1.25	.50	.12
□ 8 Mordecai Brown	1.25	.50	.12
□ 9 Morgan Bulkeley	1.25	.50	.12
□ 10 Jesse Burkett	1.25	.50	.12
□ 11 Alexander Cartwright	1.25	.50	.12
□ 12 Henry Chadwick	1.25	.50	.12
□ 13 Frank Chance	1.25	.50	.12
□ 14 Happy Chandler ('52)	20.00	8.00	2.00
□ 15 Jack Chesbro	1.25	.50	.12
□ 16 Fred Clarke	1.25	.50	.12
□ 17 Ty Cobb	25.00	10.00	2.50
□ 18A Mickey Cochran ERR (sic, Cochrane)	6.00	2.40	.60
□ 18B Mickey Cochrane COR	6.00	2.40	.60
□ 19 Eddie Collins (2)	1.50	.60	.15
□ 20 Jimmie Collins	1.25	.50	.12
□ 21 Charles Comiskey	1.25	.50	.12
□ 22 Tom Connolly ('54)	3.50	1.40	.35
□ 23 Candy Cummings	1.25	.50	.12
□ 24 Dizzy Dean ('54)	12.50	5.00	1.25
□ 25 Ed Delahanty	1.25	.50	.12
□ 26 Bill Dickey ('54)(2)	7.50	3.00	.75
□ 27 Joe DiMaggio ('55)	60.00	24.00	6.00
□ 28 Hugh Duffy	1.25	.50	.12
□ 29 Johnny Evers	1.25	.50	.12
□ 30 Buck Ewing	1.25	.50	.12
□ 31 Jimmie Foxx	5.00	2.00	.50
□ 32 Frank Frisch	1.50	.60	.15
□ 33 Lou Gehrig	25.00	10.00	2.50
□ 34 Charles Gehringer	2.50	1.00	.25
□ 35 Clark Griffith	1.25	.50	.12
□ 36 Lefty Grove	3.50	1.40	.35
□ 37 Gabby Hartnett ('55)	5.00	2.00	.50
□ 38 Harry Heilmann ('52)	2.50	1.00	.25
□ 39 Rogers Hornsby	5.00	2.00	.50
□ 40 Carl Hubbell	1.50	.60	.15
□ 41 Hughey Jennings	1.25	.50	.12
□ 42 Ban Johnson	1.25	.50	.12
□ 43 Walter Johnson	6.00	2.40	.60
□ 44 Willie Keeler	1.25	.50	.12
□ 45 Mike Kelly	1.50	.60	.15
□ 46 Bill Klem ('54)	3.50	1.40	.35
□ 47 Napoleon Lajoie	2.50	1.00	.25
□ 48 Kenesaw Landis	1.25	.50	.12
□ 49 Ted Lyons ('55)	5.00	2.00	.50
□ 50 Connie Mack	1.50	.60	.15
□ 51 Walter Maranville('54)	3.50	1.40	.35
□ 52 Christy Mathewson	6.00	2.40	.60
□ 53 Tommy McCarthy	1.25	.50	.12
□ 54 Joe McGinnity	1.25	.50	.12
□ 55 John McGraw	1.25	.50	.12
□ 56 Charles Nicholls	1.25	.50	.12
□ 57 Jim O'Rourke	1.25	.50	.12
□ 58 Mel Ott	2.50	1.00	.25
□ 59 Herb Pennock	1.25	.50	.12
□ 60 Eddie Plank	1.50	.60	.15
□ 61 Charles Radbourne	1.25	.50	.12
□ 62 Wilbert Robinson	1.25	.50	.12
□ 63 Babe Ruth	60.00	24.00	6.00
□ 64 Ray Schalk ('55)	5.00	2.00	.50
□ 65 Al Simmons ('54)	3.50	1.40	.35
□ 66 George Sisler (2)	1.50	.60	.15
□ 67 A.G. Spalding	1.25	.50	.12
□ 68 Tris Speaker	3.50	1.40	.35
□ 69 Bill Terry ('54)	5.00	2.00	.50
□ 70 Joe Tinker	1.25	.50	.12
□ 71 Pie Traynor	1.50	.60	.15
□ 72 Dazzy Vance ('55)	5.00	2.00	.50
□ 73 Rube Waddell	1.25	.50	.12
□ 74 Hans Wagner	6.00	2.40	.60
□ 75 Bobby Wallace ('54)	5.00	2.00	.50
□ 76 Ed Walsh	1.25	.50	.12
□ 77 Paul Waner ('52)	4.00	1.60	.40
□ 78 George Wright	1.25	.50	.12
□ 79 Harry Wright ('54)	3.50	1.40	.35
□ 80 Cy Young	3.50	1.40	.35
□ 81 Museum Interior ('54) (2)	3.50	1.40	.35

☐ 82 Museum Exterior ('54) (2)	3.50	1.40	.35

W605 1955 Robert Gould

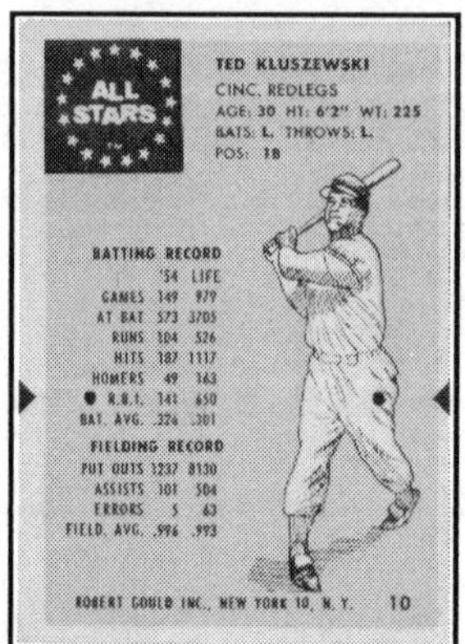

The cards in this 28-card set measure 2 1/2" by 3 1/2". The 1955 Robert F. Gould set of black and white on green cards were toy store cardboard holders for small plastic statues. The statues were attached to the card by a rubber band through two holes on the side of the card. The ACC designation is W605. The cards are numbered in the bottom right corner of the obverse and are blank-backed.

	NRMT	VG-E	GOOD
COMPLETE SET (28)	1000.00	450.00	125.00
COMMON PLAYER (1-28)	20.00	8.00	2.00
☐ 1 Willie Mays	250.00	100.00	25.00
☐ 2 Gus Zernial	20.00	8.00	2.00
☐ 3 Red Schoendienst	30.00	12.00	3.00
☐ 4 Chico Carrasquel	20.00	8.00	2.00
☐ 5 Jim Hegan	20.00	8.00	2.00
☐ 6 Curt Simmons	25.00	10.00	2.50
☐ 7 Bob Porterfield	20.00	8.00	2.00
☐ 8 Jim Busby	20.00	8.00	2.00
☐ 9 Don Mueller	25.00	10.00	2.50
☐ 10 Ted Kluszewski	40.00	16.00	4.00
☐ 11 Ray Boone	20.00	8.00	2.00
☐ 12 Smokey Burgess	25.00	10.00	2.50
☐ 13 Bob Rush	20.00	8.00	2.00
☐ 14 Early Wynn	65.00	26.00	6.50
☐ 15 Bill Bruton	20.00	8.00	2.00
☐ 16 Gus Bell	20.00	8.00	2.00
☐ 17 Jim Finigan	20.00	8.00	2.00
☐ 18 Granny Hamner	20.00	8.00	2.00
☐ 19 Hank Thompson	20.00	8.00	2.00
☐ 20 Joe Coleman	20.00	8.00	2.00
☐ 21 Don Newcombe	35.00	14.00	3.50
☐ 22 Richie Ashburn	50.00	20.00	5.00
☐ 23 Bobby Thomson	35.00	14.00	3.50
☐ 24 Sid Gordon	20.00	8.00	2.00
☐ 25 Gerry Coleman	25.00	10.00	2.50
☐ 26 Ernie Banks	125.00	50.00	12.50
☐ 27 Billy Pierce	30.00	12.00	3.00
☐ 28 Mel Parnell	25.00	10.00	2.50

1938-39 W711-1

The cards in this 32-card set measure 2" by 3". The 1938-39 Cincinnati Reds Baseball player set was printed in orange and gray tones. Many back variations exist and there are two poses of Vander Meer, portrait (PORT) and an action (ACT) poses. The set was sold at the ballpark and was printed on thin cardboard stock. The cards are unnumbered but

have been alphabetized and numbered in the checklist below.

	NRMT	VG-E	GOOD
COMPLETE SET (32)	375.00	160.00	45.00
COMMON PLAYER (1-32)	8.00	3.25	.80
☐ 1 Wally Berger (2)	10.00	4.00	1.00
☐ 2 Nino Bongiovanni (39)	30.00	12.00	3.00
☐ 3 Stanley Bordagaray Frenchy (39)	30.00	12.00	3.00
☐ 4 Joe Cascarella (38)	8.00	3.25	.80
☐ 5 Allen Dusty Cooke (38)	8.00	3.25	.80
☐ 6 Harry Craft	8.00	3.25	.80
☐ 7 Ray (Peaches) Davis	8.00	3.25	.80
☐ 8 Paul Derringer (2)	12.00	5.00	1.20
☐ 9 Linus Frey (2)	8.00	3.25	.80
☐ 10 Lee Gamble (2)	8.00	3.25	.80
☐ 11 Ival Goodman (2)	8.00	3.25	.80
☐ 12 Hank Gowdy	8.00	3.25	.80
☐ 13 Lee Grissom (2)	8.00	3.25	.80
☐ 14 Willard Hershberger (2)	8.00	3.25	.80
☐ 15 Eddie Joost (39)	8.00	3.25	.80
☐ 16 Wes Livengood (39)	75.00	30.00	7.50
☐ 17 Ernie Lombardi (2)	30.00	12.00	3.00
☐ 18 Frank McCormick	10.00	4.00	1.00
☐ 19 Bill McKechnie (2)	21.00	8.50	2.10
☐ 20 Lloyd Whitey Moore (2)	8.00	3.25	.80
☐ 21 Billy Myers (2)	8.00	3.25	.80
☐ 22 Lew Riggs (2)	8.00	3.25	.80
☐ 23 Eddie Roush COA (38)	25.00	10.00	2.50
☐ 24 Les Scarsella (39)	8.00	3.25	.80
☐ 25 Gene Schott (38)	8.00	3.25	.80
☐ 26 Eugene Thompson	8.00	3.25	.80
☐ 27 Johnny VanderMeer PORT	21.00	8.50	2.10
☐ 28 Johnny VanderMeer ACT	21.00	8.50	2.10
☐ 29 Wm.(Bucky) Walters (2)	10.00	4.00	1.00
☐ 30 Jim Weaver	8.00	3.25	.80
☐ 31 Bill Werber (39)	8.00	3.25	.80
☐ 32 Jimmy Wilson (39)	8.00	3.25	.80

1941 W711-2

The cards in this 34-card set measure 2 1/8" by 2 5/8". The W711-2 Cincinnati Reds set contains unnumbered, black and white cards. This issue is sometimes called the "Harry Hartman" set. The cards are numbered below in alphabetical order by player's name with non-player cards listed at the end.

	NRMT	VG-E	GOOD
COMPLETE SET (34)	300.00	120.00	30.00
COMMON PLAYER (1-28)	9.00	3.75	.90
COMMON CARD (29-34)	6.00	2.40	.60
□ 1 Morris Arnovich	9.00	3.75	.90
□ 2 William (Bill) Baker	9.00	3.75	.90
□ 3 Joseph Beggs	9.00	3.75	.90
□ 4 Harry Craft	9.00	3.75	.90
□ 5 Paul Derringer	13.50	5.00	1.00
□ 6 Linus Frey	9.00	3.75	.90
□ 7 Ival Goodman	9.00	3.75	.90
□ 8 Hank Gowdy	10.00	4.00	1.00
□ 9 Witt Guise	9.00	3.75	.90
□ 10 Willard Hershberger	9.00	3.75	.90
□ 11 John Hutchings	9.00	3.75	.90
□ 12 Edwin Joost	9.00	3.75	.90
□ 13 Ernie Lombardi	30.00	12.00	3.00
□ 14 Frank McCormick	12.00	5.00	1.20
□ 15 Myron McCormick	9.00	3.75	.90
□ 16 William McKechnie	20.00	8.00	2.00
□ 17 Whitey Moore	9.00	3.75	.90
□ 18 William (Bill) Myers	9.00	3.75	.90
□ 19 Elmer Riddle	9.00	3.75	.90
□ 20 Lewis Riggs	9.00	3.75	.90
□ 21 James A. Ripple	9.00	3.75	.90
□ 22 Milburn Shoffner	9.00	3.75	.90
□ 23 Eugene Thompson	9.00	3.75	.90
□ 24 James Turner	10.00	4.00	1.00
□ 25 John VanderMeer	18.00	7.25	1.80
□ 26 Bucky Walters	12.00	5.00	1.20
□ 27 Bill Werber	9.00	3.75	.90
□ 28 James Wilson	9.00	3.75	.90
□ 29 Results 1940 World Series	6.00	2.40	.60
□ 30 The Cincinati Reds (Title Card)	6.00	2.40	.60
□ 31 The Cincinnati Reds World's Champions (Title Card)	6.00	2.40	.60
□ 32 Debt of Gratitude to Wm. Koehl Co.	6.00	2.40	.60
□ 33 Tell the World About Our Reds	6.00	2.40	.60
□ 34 Harry Hartman	6.00	2.40	.60

1941 W753 Browns

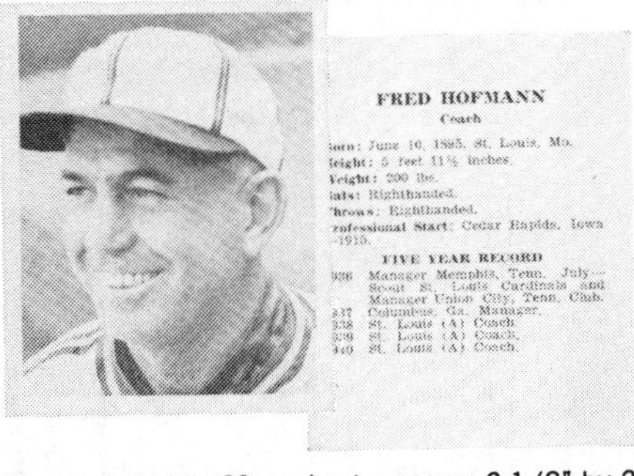

The cards in this 29-card set measure 2 1/8" by 2 5/8". The 1941 W753 set features unnumbered cards of the St. Louis Browns. The cards are numbered below alphabetically by player's name.

	NRMT	VG-E	GOOD
COMPLETE SET (29)	325.00	130.00	32.00
COMMON PLAYER (1-29)	10.00	4.00	1.00
□ 1 Johnny Allen	10.00	4.00	1.00
□ 2 Elden Auker	10.00	4.00	1.00
□ 3 Donald L. Barnes	10.00	4.00	1.00
□ 4 Johnny Beradino	12.50	5.00	1.25
□ 5 George Caster	10.00	4.00	1.00
□ 6 Harland Clift	10.00	4.00	1.00
□ 7 Roy J. Cullenbine	10.00	4.00	1.00
□ 8 William O. DeWitt	10.00	4.00	1.00
□ 9 Robert Estalella	10.00	4.00	1.00
□ 10 Rick Ferrell	35.00	14.00	3.50
□ 11 Dennis W. Galehouse	10.00	4.00	1.00
□ 12 Joseph L. Grace	10.00	4.00	1.00
□ 13 Frank Grube	10.00	4.00	1.00
□ 14 Robert A. Harris	10.00	4.00	1.00
□ 15 Donald Heffner	10.00	4.00	1.00
□ 16 Fred Hofmann	10.00	4.00	1.00
□ 17 Walter F. Judnich	10.00	4.00	1.00
□ 18 Jack Kramer	10.00	4.00	1.00
□ 19 Chester (Chet) Laabs	10.00	4.00	1.00
□ 20 John Lucadello	10.00	4.00	1.00
□ 21 George H. McQuinn	10.00	4.00	1.00
□ 22 Robert Muncrief Jr.	10.00	4.00	1.00
□ 23 John Niggeling	10.00	4.00	1.00
□ 24 Fritz Ostermueller	10.00	4.00	1.00
□ 25 James (Luke) Sewell	12.50	5.00	1.25
□ 26 Alan C. Strange	10.00	4.00	1.00
□ 27 Bob Swift	10.00	4.00	1.00
□ 28 James (Zack) Taylor	10.00	4.00	1.00
□ 29 Bill Trotter	10.00	4.00	1.00

1941 W754 Cardinals

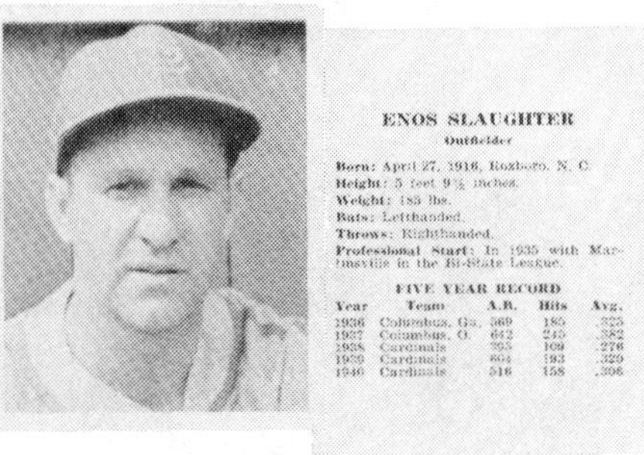

The cards in this 29-card set measure 2 1/8" by 2 5/8". The 1941 W754 set of unnumbered cards features St. Louis Cardinals. The cards are numbered below alphabetically by player's name.

	NRMT	VG-E	GOOD
COMPLETE SET (29)	350.00	140.00	35.00
COMMON PLAYER (1-29)	10.00	4.00	1.00
□ 1 Sam Breadon	10.00	4.00	1.00
□ 2 Jimmy Brown	10.00	4.00	1.00
□ 3 Mort Cooper	12.50	5.00	1.25
□ 4 Walker Cooper	10.00	4.00	1.00
□ 5 Estel Crabtree	10.00	4.00	1.00
□ 6 Frank Crespi	10.00	4.00	1.00
□ 7 Bill Crouch	10.00	4.00	1.00
□ 8 Mike Gonzalez	10.00	4.00	1.00
□ 9 Harry Gumpert	10.00	4.00	1.00
□ 10 John Hopp	12.50	5.00	1.25
□ 11 Ira Hutchinson	10.00	4.00	1.00
□ 12 Howie Krist	10.00	4.00	1.00
□ 13 Eddie Lake	10.00	4.00	1.00
□ 14 Max Lanier	12.50	5.00	1.25
□ 15 Gus Mancuso	10.00	4.00	1.00
□ 16 Marty Marion	20.00	8.00	2.00
□ 17 Steve Mesner	10.00	4.00	1.00
□ 18 John Mize	35.00	14.00	3.50
□ 19 Terry Moore	16.00	6.50	1.60
□ 20 Sam Nahem	10.00	4.00	1.00
□ 21 Don Padgett	10.00	4.00	1.00
□ 22 Branch Rickey	30.00	12.00	3.00
□ 23 Clyde Shoun	10.00	4.00	1.00
□ 24 Enos Slaughter	35.00	14.00	3.50
□ 25 Billy Southworth	10.00	4.00	1.00
□ 26 Coaker Triplett	10.00	4.00	1.00
□ 27 Buzzy Wares	10.00	4.00	1.00
□ 28 Lon Warneke	12.50	5.00	1.25
□ 29 Ernie White	10.00	4.00	1.00

ROY CAMPANELLA
Catcher LOS ANGELES DODGERS

Height: 5'10" Weight: 218
Home: Glen Cove, New York
Throws: Right Bats: Right
Born: November 19, 1921

Roy Campanella has been named The Most Valuable Player in the National League on 3 occasions! His finest season was in 1953 when he hit 41 home runs and piled up 142 runs batted in—an all-time high in Dodger history. In his ten campaigns with the Dodgers, Roy has hit 242 homers and only twice has dropped below 20.

MAJOR LEAGUE RECORD

YEAR	CLUB	GAMES	HITS	HR	RBI	AVG.
1948	Dodgers	83	72	9	45	.258
1949	"	130	125	22	82	.287
1950	"	126	123	31	89	.281
1951	"	143	164	33	108	.325
1952	"	128	126	22	97	.269
1953	"	144	162	41	142	.312
1954	"	111	82	19	51	.207
1955	"	123	142	32	107	.318
1956	"	124	85	20	73	.219
1957	"	103	80	13	62	.242

1958 Bell Brand

1959 Morrell

1960 Morrell

1961 Morrell

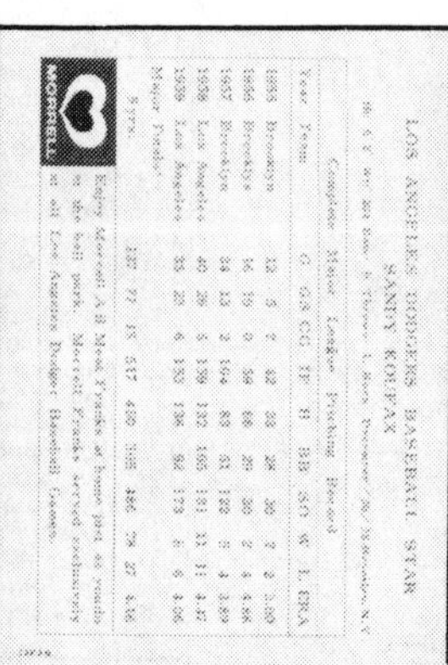

MORRELL
LOS ANGELES DODGERS BASEBALL STAR
DON DRYSDALE

MICKEY MANTLE

OUTFIELDER — NEW YORK YANKEES

Tagged as the greatest potential baseball player in the game today, the straw haired kid from Commerce, Oklahoma, swings equally well from both sides of the plate. A long ball hitter, Mickey is destined to be one of the Yankee "all-time greats." Not only is Mantle's big bat a potent factor in the "Bomber's" attack but his flashing speed and great arm makes him a respected outfielder and headache on the bases.

MAJOR LEAGUE BATTING RECORD

MAJOR LEAGUE FIELDING RECORD

HEY KIDS!

WIN FREE TICKETS TO

YANKEE · GIANT · DODGER GAMES

HURRY! Deadline for entries, August 21, 1953

1953 Stahl Meyer

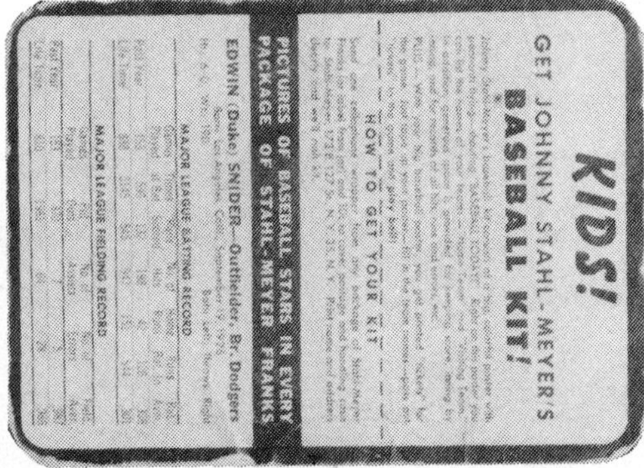

1954 Stahl Meyer

1955 Stahl Meyer

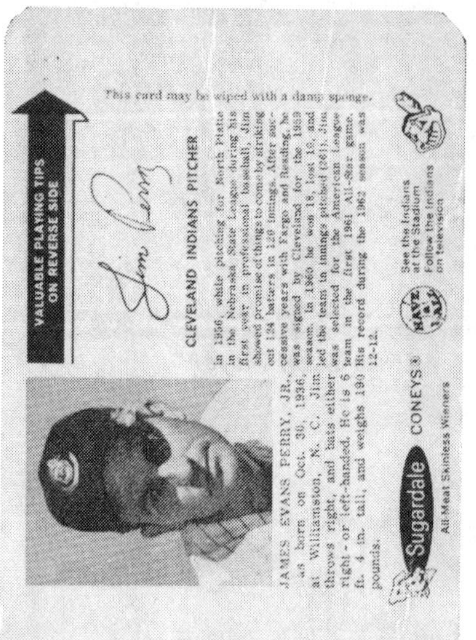

1962 Sugardale

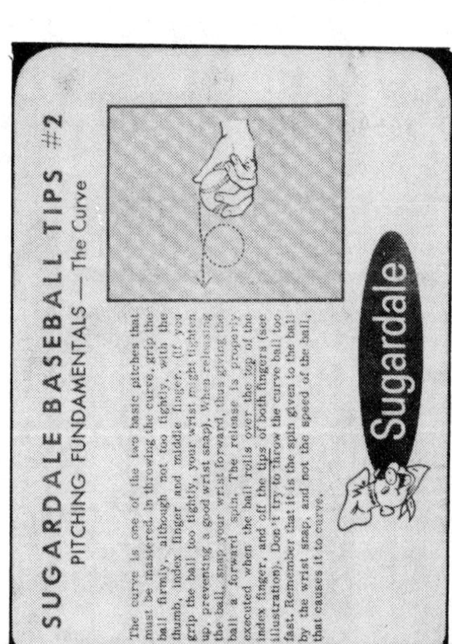

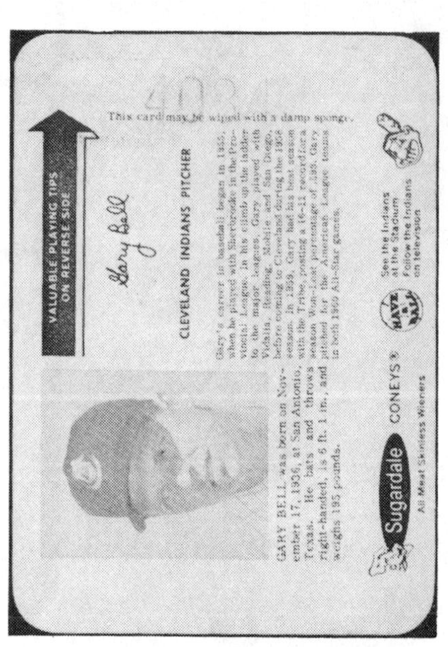

1963 Sugardale

BROOKLYN DODGERS

TOP ROW (left to right): Billy Cox, Bobby Morgan, Carl Erskine, Erv Palica, Tommy Brown, Preacher Roe, Joe Hatten, Steve Lembo, Carl Furillo, Eddie Miksis, Rex Barney.

THIRD ROW (left to right): Traveling Secretary Harold Parrott, Trainer Harold E .Wendler, Dan Bankhead, Gil Hodges, Chris Van Cuyk, Don Newcombe, Mal Mallette, Billy Loes, Duke Snider, Pee Wee Reese, Bruce Edwards, Clubhouse Custodian John Griffin, Jackie Robinson.

SECOND ROW (left to right): Roy Campanella, Jim Russell, Ralph Branca, Coach Clyde Sukeforth, Coach Jake Pitler, Manager B. E. Shotton, Coach Milt Stock, Bullpen Catcher Sam Narron, Cal Abrams, Gene Hermanski, Wayne Belardi.

BOTTOM ROW (left to right): Ball Boy Marvin Parshall, Bat Boy Stanley Strull.

1951 Topps Teams

CINCINNATI REDS

FRONT ROW (left to right): Ed Erautt, Sammy Meeks, Hobie Landrith, Coach Gus Mancuso, Ass't to President Gabriel Paul, Manager Luke Sewell, Coach Tony Cuccinello, Coach Phil Page, Bobby Adams, Kent Peterson, Danny Litwhiler.

SECOND ROW: Equipment Manager Larry McManus ,Ken Raffensberger, Bud Byerly, John Hetki, Bobby Usher, Lloyd Merriman, Joe Adcock, Herman Wehmeier, John Pramesa, Harry Perkowski, Howard Fox, Ewell Blackwell, Trainer Wilbur Bohm.

TOP ROW: Grady Hatton, Homer Howell, Willard Ramsdell, Connie Ryan, John Wyrostek, Ted Kluszewski, Virgil Stallcup, Edgar Bailey, Ted Tappe, Frank Smith.

1951 Topps Current All-Stars

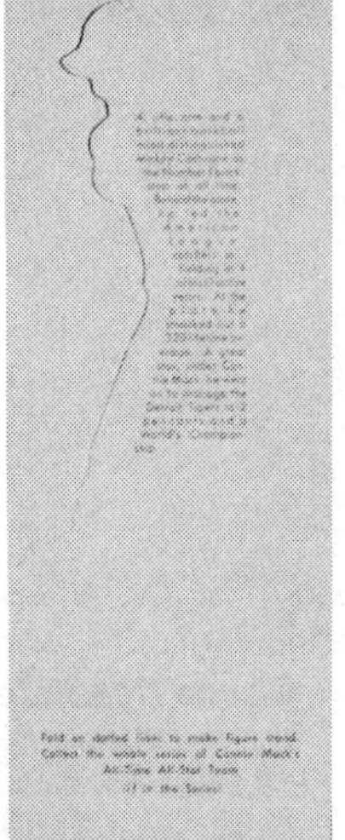

1951 Topps Connie Mack All-Stars

T200 Fatima Teams

Special Offer

On receipt of 40 "FATIMA" Cigarette coupons, we will send you an enlarged copy (size 13 x 21) of this picture (without advertising) or of any other picture in this series (National League and American League teams). This picture is mounted, and ready for framing. Write plainly your name and address, stating picture desired.

PREMIUM DEPARTMENT
Liggett & Myers Tob. Co.
7th Ave. & 16th St., New York City, N.Y.

FACTORY NO.

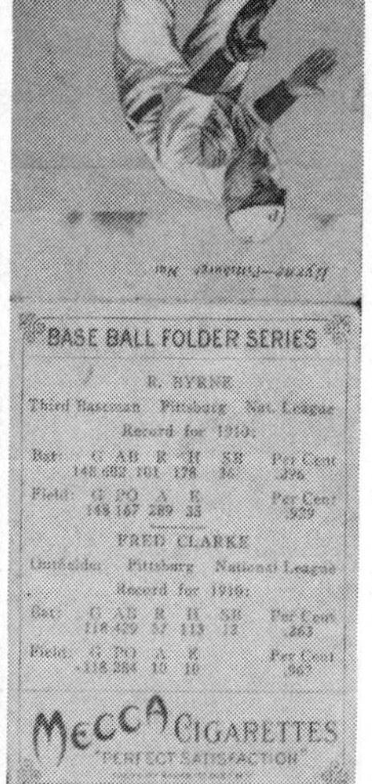

BASE BALL FOLDER SERIES

R. BYRNE
Third Baseman Pittsburg Nat. League
Record for 1910:

	G	AB	R	H	SB	Per Cent
Bat:	148	602	101	178	36	.296

	G	PO	A	E	Per Cent
Field:	148	167	289	33	.929

FRED CLARKE
Outfielder Pittsburg National League
Record for 1910:

	G	AB	R	H	SB	Per Cent
Bat:	118	429	57	113	12	.263

	G	PO	A	E	Per Cent
Field:	118	284	10	10	.967

MECCA CIGARETTES
"PERFECT SATISFACTION"

T201 Mecca Doublefolders

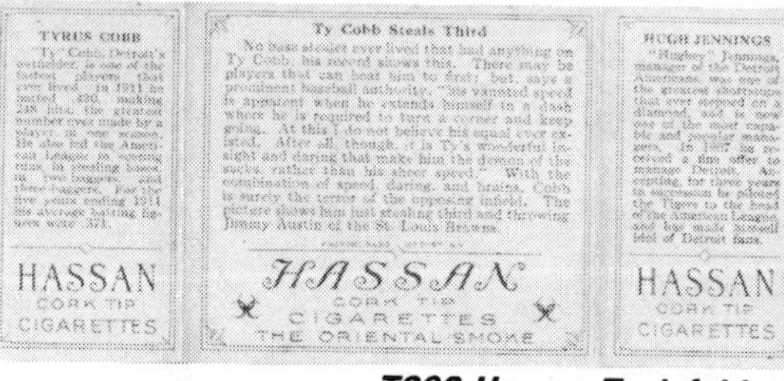

TYRUS COBB

HASSAN
CORK TIP
CIGARETTES

Ty Cobb Steals Third

HASSAN
CORK TIP
CIGARETTES
THE ORIENTAL SMOKE

HUGH JENNINGS

HASSAN
CORK TIP
CIGARETTES

T202 Hassan Trplefolders

CLASSIFIED ADVERTISING

BE SURE TO LET our advertisers know that you saw their ad in this publication.

LOUISVILLE, KENTUCKY'S Biggest, Best, and Most Comprehensive Card Hobby Store. Baseball Cards-N-More in Saint Matthews Station. (502) 893-0818.

BASEBALL CARDS, pins, statues, books wanted (1886-1972) from gum, candy, cigarettes, etc. Top prices paid. Gerhardt's World, 6442 Albermarle Road, Charlotte, NC 28212.

SEND FOR OUR FREE baseball card pricelist. Include first-class stamp for postage. B&F Sports Cards, Dept. 54, 78 Sixth Avenue, Woonsocket, RI 02895.

BUYING TICKET STUBS, programs, pennants from World Series, All-Star, Super Bowls, championship fights, hockey, basketball playoffs. Any sports happening (602-996-3393). Ron Adelson, 13447 N. 59th Place, Scottsdale, AZ 85254.

1952-55 REDMANS WANTED. Paying the highest prices for all cards with tabs in EX to NrMint condition. Also interested in purchasing premium caps and unopened packs of Redman tobacco. Dick Cianciotto, 196 Mulberry Drive, Macedon, NY 14502 (315) 986-3111.

1989 ROOKIES PRICE GUIDE - Send $3.00 for a Sample Copy of Doug Ingram's R.I.G., P.O. Box 281, E. Rock, NY 11518.

QUARTERLY FLYER full of Super Specials. Single Cards, Wax Packs, Group Lots, Complete Sets, Rookies, Stars, and Limited Edition Sets. Prices never higher than Guide. Send just $2.00 for a full year. East Texas Sports Cards, P.O. Box 1334, Jacksonville, Texas, 75766. Want Lists Welcome. Send SASE.

DOUBLE YOUR PLEASURE. If hot stars, great rookies, and legendary players are your bag. Double your sports cards and memorabilia pleasure with a subscription to the hobby leader: *Beckett Baseball Card Monthly*.

FREE! BASEBALL CARD CATALOG. Singles, Sets, 1/4, 1/2 and Full Cases. Unsearched Boxes and Lots. Collector Supplies and more. Send your Name and Address to The Baseball Collector, P.O. Box 141, Baltimore, MD 21136.

HOME PLATE CARDS: Buy-Sell. Send lists of what you have and what you want, many stars, rookies, and commons. Send SASE to Home Plate, 956 Connor Drive, Eastlake, Ohio 44094.

WANTED Baseball All-Star, World Series, playoff programs, yearbooks (1940s-1970s), ticket stubs, pennants, souvenirs, Super Bowls, basketball, hockey, football, boxing, all paper material (602-996-3393). Ron Adelson, 13447 N. 59th Place, Scottsdale, AZ 85254.

1953 - 1989. Specializing in Near Mint or better material. Stars, commons, sets. Buy, sell, trade. Bill Wise, Box 614, Chicago, IL 60690.

WHEN IN CLEVELAND, visit L.A. Comics & Collectibles, 6672 Pearl Rd., Parma Hts., Ohio 44130. Specialties include Baseball, Comics, and Movie Posters. Send SASE for list.

WANT LISTS APPRECIATED! *Use Guide ** Indicate Condition ** Enclose check/SASE. Money refunded if unavailable or price change. Postage $1.50, minimum order $20.00. Thanks! San Francisco Card Exchange, 1316-C 18th Ave., San Francisco, CA 94122. Phone (415) 665-TEAM.

STORE OPENING? Convention Selling? We provide a complete inventory. Your start up costs $500-$100,000. *Sport *Non-Sport *Comics. Suddenly it's happened! Call today or write with specifics. SASE appreciated. San Francisco Card Exchange, 1316-X 18th Ave., San Francisco, CA 94122. Phone (415) 665-TEAM.

CONSIGNMENT DEALERS WANTED. *Beckett Baseball Card Monthly* is the best seller in the hobby. Stock *Beckett*, increase your sales and walk-in trade. Call (214) 991-6657.

MILLIONS OF NON-SPORTS cards for sale. Sample copy $2.00. Write: The Wrapper, Dept. BK, 1903 Ronzheimer, St. Charles, IL 60174. (312) 377-7921.

FREE! Baseball Card Investment Advisory Newsletter. Rookies, Stars, Commons are all here. Send SASE to Investment Advisory, P.O. Box 141, Baltimore, MD 21117.

POLICE/SAFETY SETS: My speciality. Buying, Selling, Trading. Write. Murvin Sterling, 227 Emporia Lane, Duncanville, TX 75116.

CLASSIFIED ADVERTISING

20% OFF!!! Most cards (*Beckett Monthly* and *Beckett #11* are used for prices). Send want lists, with self-addressed, stamped envelope to Pat's Coins & Cards, 3229 West 24th Street, Erie, PA 16506.

ADVERTISING PAYS. Your classified ad here would be read by thousands of avid collectors.

THOUSANDS OF PUBLICATIONS for sale. World Series, All-Star, yearbooks, programs, all sports. Also ticket stubs, pennants, memorabilia. Send want list with SASE (602-996-3393). Ron Adelson, 13447 N. 59th Place, Scottsdale, AZ 85254.

SEND S.A.S.E. Gene Funkhouser, 1307 John Carroll Dr., Pensacola, FL 32504.

BARGAINS GALORE! Rookies, superstars, lots and more, 1957-1989, all conditions. Send SASE and 25¢ for 400+ card monthly auction list. Speedy service. Rick Krikorian, 531 Main St. #512, El Segundo, CA 90245.

WE MUST LIQUIDATE up to 20% of our current inventory to complete our upcoming move. Send SASE for wholesale prices and/or $2.00 for our current price list of merchandise. Northern Virginia Sports Card Exchange, P.O. Box 610, Dept. B11, Haymarket, VA 22069.

GROUP LOTS: Very Good or better condition. 1960-1969: (250) $110; (500) $200; (1000) $390. 1970-1979: (250) $35; (500) $65; (1000) $120. 1980-1987: (250) $15; (500) $28; (1000) $50. All Postpaid. Bill Henderson's Cards-CL, 2320 Ruger Ave., Janesville, WI 53545.

TOPPS SETS 1988 or 1989: $18.95 ea. + $2.50 P/H, 6 for $18.75 ea. + $9 P/H, 18 for $18.25 ea. + $20 P/H, 54 for $17.75 ea. + $60 P/H. Bill Henderson's Cards-CL, 2320 Ruger Ave., Janesville, WI 53545.

WANTED: Commons, stars, superstars, HOF-ers, sets. Pre-1973 EX or better condition. Fair offers made, good prices paid. Call/write: Jeff Baker, 8872 NW 114 Terrace, Hialeah Gardens, FL 33016. (305) 823-1171.

BASEBALL CARDS & SUPPLIES - Topps, Score, Fleer, Donruss, unopened wax boxes, cases, factory sets. Albums $4.50, vinyl pages as low as 9 cents, etc. Quantity discounts on supplies and cards. Especially need old cards, memorabilia. Ask for sale list! (509) 943-6547, (509) 946-9192. Coin House, 777 Stevens, Richland, WA 99352.

BASEBALL CARDS MADE! Highest quality, full color, custom-made cards. Create your own design. Fantastic business card, promotional item or gift. Millions made. Featured in "Washington Post," "Chicago Tribune," "Detroit News" and other major papers. Minimum order 3,000 (of the same card). Priced from $250. Quantity discounts available. For further information, contact Concept Cards®, 1722 Republic Road Silver Spring, MD 20902. (301) 649-7118.

WHOLESALE SUPPLIES - Lin Terry. National distributor of all Enor products. Major League Licensed 8 X 10 photos. Binders, pages, corrugated, Lucites, individual holders, ball holders, price guides, all baseball books. Call Lin Terry, (201) 385-4706, 59 E. Madison Ave. Dept. B, Dumont, NJ 07628.

WHEN IN CHICAGO, visit YESTERDAY, 1143 Addison near Wrigley Field. Specializing in Baseball, Movie Memorabilia. Extravagant Selections. Unbelievably Reasonable Prices!

DON'T DELAY!! Send for your subscription to *Beckett Baseball Card Monthly* today. Only $19.95 for a full year's worth of up-to-the-minute card values and pleasurable reading. Address: Beckett Publications, Subscriptions, 3410 MidCourt, Suite 110, Carrollton, TX 75006.

BECKETT
May 1988
$2.50

The Perfect Pair

Ruth and Gehrig. Mantle and Maris. DiMaggio and Monroe. Canseco and McGwire. And now, a match made in collectors' heaven . . . the **Sport Americana Baseball Card Price Guide #11** and **The Sport Americana Price Guide to Baseball Collectibles #2**.

The only suitable companion to **Beckett #11** is **The Baseball Collectibles #2**. With virtually no overlap to **Beckett #11**, **Collectibles #2** is the ONLY place to find many sets of cards (like Centennial, Tom Barker, Walter Mails, Sommer & Kaufman, Sunbeam, Fud's, Cloverleaf, Bee-Hive, Papa Gino's, and Challenge the Yankees).

In other words, if you can't find what you're looking for in **Beckett #11**, you'll find it in **Collectibles #2**!

You'll also find definitive sections on Press Pins, PM10 Stadium Pins, and most other baseball-related player pins and stamps in more than 400 pages of accurate values and photos.

Call it the "Collectors' Combo." "The Perfect Pair." Undoubtedly the "Twin Towers" of the hobby.

BECKETT PRICE GUIDES

Go to your nearest bookstore!